Harvard Guide to American History   Volume I

VOLUME I

Harvard Guide to American History

REVISED EDITION

Frank Freidel, Editor
With the assistance of Richard K. Showman

The Belknap Press of Harvard University Press

Cambridge, Massachusetts
and London, England

Preface

The changes in this new edition of the *Harvard Guide to American History* reflect the shifting interests and the spectacular growth in the literature of American history during the past two decades. About a third of the titles are new, the arrangement of a substantial part of them is topical, and the *Guide* has expanded into two volumes. The opening chapters, for the most part finding aids, are now essentially for reference use. The syllabi at the beginning of bibliographical chapters, a key component of the original manual, no longer appear; neither do the extensive sections on historical sources. Few readers now use them.

Nevertheless, this voluminous new edition continues the fundamental purpose of its predecessors, to serve as a basic reference work. In a small book, which appeared in 1896, Albert Bushnell Hart and Edward Channing presented an outline and key bibliography for a course in American history to 1865. It was an indication of the growing interest in the methods and literature of scientific history. So successful was this first handbook that in 1912 Hart and Channing, joined by Frederick Jackson Turner, who had recently arrived from the University of Wisconsin, revised it as the *Guide to the Study and Reading of American History* (1912), carrying the subject down to 1910. In 1953, the American historians at Harvard, Oscar Handlin, Arthur Meier Schlesinger, Samuel Eliot Morison, Frederick Merk, Arthur Meier Schlesinger, Jr., and Paul Herman Buck, under the sponsorship of the Department of History, brought out an essentially new volume in response to the transformation forty years had wrought. Some of their essays in the forepart of the book have been standard discussions by no means superseded in the new edition.

Through its several editions some of the purposes of the *Guide* have remained constant. Hart and Channing declared in the preface to the first edition:

"The immense mass of rich material on American history cannot be condensed into a single volume; and doubtless much has been omitted that ought to go in, or inserted that might well be left out . . . However, the plan of the work does not admit of complete bibliographical information on any topic. It has been our endeavor to select out of the available material that likely to be most immediately useful to the searcher into political, social, constitutional, and economic history. For the antiquarian and genealogist we have not been able to provide. We have, however, noted as many as possible of the more elaborate bibliographies, to serve as guides to more complete information."

And we would echo the words of Oscar Handlin and the editors of the 1953 edition:

"This volume is addressed to the intelligent general reader, to the student, and to the scholar. For the first named, it will supply a thorough guide to the great body of literature of our country's past, and, for the student, a manual unlocking the methods and resources of American history. We hope also it may speed the scholar on his way. It will not, of course, take the place of the scholar's own investigations, but as a reference tool it may simplify his problems. Its selectivity, in this sense, will be an asset rather than a liability."

A further word is necessary on the methods of bibliographical selection for the present edition. Inclusion of a bibliographical citation is not an accolade, nor omission a censure. Much of scholarly merit does not appear because it is redundant or too highly specialized. This is especially true of articles; more than 6,000 concerning American history now appear each year. Much of lesser merit appears on significant topics where literature is scarce. The criterion for inclusion was potential usefulness to those consulting the *Guide*. Thus in the biographical section, along with the most modern interpretations, many of the old "life and letters" biographies are still listed since they often contain source material not readily available elsewhere. On the other hand, the frequent specific references to the great classic multivolumed American histories no longer appear throughout the chronological chapters since, while these works are still monuments of scholarship, more recent monographs have largely superseded them. They are seldom consulted, except perhaps as literature.

As was true in earlier editions, there is no absolute uniformity of concept and style. Certain periods and topics have interested historical writers more than others, and therefore coverage is not even. Nor in this edition is there any separation between primary and secondary materials. Writings covering recent years are not easily separable, and often editors' introductions to sources are valuable secondary studies.

The purpose of the new arrangement of bibliographical materials is to make them more readily usable to present-day readers and scholars. A large part of the bibliography in Volume I appears under topical headings, and is heavily economic, social, and cultural. Volume I also contains the listing of biographies and personal accounts. In volume II the arrangement (with a single major exception) is chronological, with an emphasis upon political and diplomatic history. The exception in volume two is the large number of citations, topically arranged, to works in economic, social, and cultural history falling entirely or largely within the Colonial period. These are within the chapters on the Colonial period.

The terminal date of publication for books and articles cited is June 30, 1970. There are occasional exceptions.

The present edition of the *Guide* is under the sponsorship of the Charles Warren Center for Studies in American History. The revision has been the responsibility solely of the editors and their staff.

While the editors alone are responsible for any shortcomings, only through assistance from many sources has the new edition been possible. We have profited from the suggestions and cooperation of Donald Fleming, Director of the Charles Warren Center, and its Administrative Committee, including Bernard Bailyn, Franklin L. Ford, Oscar Handlin, and Ernest R. May. Numerous Research Fellows of the Center and scholars at Harvard University and elsewhere have been helpful. We particularly acknowledge the contributions of Francis Paul Prucha. We are indebted to Frank O. Spinney of the Cooperstown Graduate Program.

The resources of the Harvard University Library and the response of its staff to innumerable inquiries have been indispensable. Other librarians and several archivists also have been generous with their time and information. We especially thank Sheila Hart, Reference Librarian, Harvard University Library, and Y. T. Feng, Reference Librarian, Boston Public Library.

Throughout this lengthy undertaking, Sheila Madden has shared much of the burdens and supervisory responsibilities of the editorial processes at the Charles Warren Center. Susan Coleman Clark and Marylyn Lentine have provided services. Among student assistants, Christopher Bensick, Roger Kindler, Robert Silberman, and David Westfall deserve special mention. Aiding in the organization of bibliographies were: Robert McCarthy, Helen Rakove, Jack Rakove, Robert Rosen, Glenn Shealey, George D. Smith, and James Turner. Others providing editorial aid include: Celia Betsky, John Driscoll, David Jost, Winston Kendall, David Knudson, Barbara Niemczyk, Samuel Price, Lee Rousell, Angel Rabasa, Kenneth Reeves, Larry Wilson, Edwin Randall, and Patricia Young. For secretarial help, the editors wish to thank Alicia Zintl, Administrative Assistant at the Charles Warren Center, and Yvonne Chang, Sonia Harris, and Violette St. Justin.

In the final editorial preparation of the manuscript, Mary L. Fisher of the Harvard University Press has contributed resourcefully, well beyond the call of duty.

As did the editors of the previous edition, we conclude: "The *Guide* will best have served its purpose if it is quickly outdated by the writings of those who use it." We have no doubt it will be.

Frank Freidel
Richard K. Showman

January, 1973

Contents

Part Three   Comprehensive and Area Histories

Part Four   Histories of Special Subjects

Serial Abbreviations

AAUP *Bull.*	American Association of University Professors, *Bulletin*
Aerospace Hist.	*Aerospace History*
Agric. Hist.	*Agricultural History*
AHA Newsletter	*American Historical Association Newsletter*
AHR	*American Historical Review*
Ala. Rev.	*Alabama Review*
Am. Acad. Pol. Soc. Sci., *Annals*	American Academy of Political and Social Science, *Annals*
Am. Anthropol.	*American Anthropologist*
Am. Antiq. Soc., *Proc.*	American Antiquarian Society, *Proceedings*
Am. Archivist	*American Archivist*
Am. Assoc. State Local Hist., *Bull.*	American Association for State and Local History, *Bulletins*
Am. Bar Assoc. *Jour.*	*American Bar Association Journal*
Am. Cath. Hist. Soc., *Records*	American Catholic Historical Society, *Records*
Am. Eccles. Rev.	*American Ecclesiastical Review*
Am. Econ. Assoc., *Publ.*	American Economic Association, *Publications*
Am. Econ. Rev.	*American Economic Review*
Am. For. Serv. *Jour.*	*American Foreign Service Journal*
Am. Geneal.	*American Genealogist*
Am. Geog. Soc. *Jour.*	*American Geographical Society Journal*
Am. Heritage	*American Heritage*
Am. Hist. Assoc., *Papers*	American Historical Association, *Papers*
Am. Hist. Assoc., *Report*	American Historical Association, *Report*
Am. Instit. Crim. Law and Criminol., *Jour.*	American Institute of Criminal Law and Criminology, *Journal*
Am. Jew. Archives	American Jewish Archives

Am. Jew. Hist. Quar.	*American Jewish Historical Quarterly*
Am. Jew. Hist. Soc., *Publ.*	American Jewish Historical Society, *Publications*
Am. Jew. Yr. Bk.	*American Jewish Yearbook*
Am. Jour. Econ. Sociol.	*American Journal of Economics and Sociology*
Am. Jour. Internatl. Law	*American Journal of International Law*
Am. Jour. Legal Hist.	*American Journal of Legal History*
Am. Jour. Phys. Anthropol.	*American Journal of Physical Anthropology*
Am. Jour. Psychiatry	*American Journal of Psychiatry*
Am. Jour. Sociol.	*American Journal of Sociology*
Am. Lit.	*American Literature*
Am. Mag. Art	*American Magazine of Art*
Am. Neptune	*American Neptune*
Am. Philos. Soc., *Lib. Bull.*	American Philosophical Society, *Library Bulletin*
Am. Philos. Soc., *Proc.*	American Philosophical Society, *Proceedings*
Am. Philos. Soc., *Yearbook*	American Philosophical Society, *Yearbook*
Am. Pol. Sci. Rev.	*American Political Science Review*
Am. Quar.	*American Quarterly*
Am. Rev.	*American Review*
Am. Scholar	*American Scholar*
Am. Soc. Church Hist., *Papers*	American Society of Church History, *Papers*
Am. Soc. Civil Engineers, *Trans.*	American Society of Civil Engineers, *Transactions*
Am. Sociol. Rev.	*American Sociological Review*
Am. Speech	*American Speech*
Am. Stat. Assoc., *Jour.*	American Statistical Association, *Journal*
Am. Stat. Assoc., *Quar. Publ.*	American Statistical Association, *Quarterly Publications*
Am. Studies	*American Studies*
Am. Univ. Law Rev.	*American University Law Review*
Am. West	*American West*
Anchor Rev.	*Anchor Review*
Ann. Iowa	*Annals of Iowa*
Ann. Med. Hist.	*Annals of Medical History*
Antioch Rev.	*Antioch Review*
Ariz. and West	*Arizona and the West*
Ariz. Hist. Rev.	*Arizona Historical Review*

Arizona Law Rev.	*Arizona Law Review*
Ariz. Quar.	*Arizona Quarterly*
Ark. Hist. Assoc., *Publ.*	Arkansas Historical Association, *Publications*
Ark. Hist. Quar.	*Arkansas Historical Quarterly*
Art Bull.	*Art Bulletin*
Art in Am.	*Art in America*
Art Jour.	*Art Journal*
Arts Mag.	*Arts Magazine*
Asiatic Soc. Japan, *Trans.*	Asiatic Society of Japan, *Transactions*
Assoc. Am. Geographers, *Annals*	Association of American Geographers, *Annals*
Atl. Community Quar.	*Atlantic Community Quarterly*
Atlantic	*Atlantic Magazine*
Bapt. Hist. and Heritage	*Baptist History and Heritage*
Baylor Law Rev.	*Baylor Law Review*
Bibliog. Soc. Am., *Papers*	Bibliographical Society of America, *Papers*
Birmingham Univ. Hist. Jour.	*Birmingham University Historical Journal*
Boston Pub. Lib., *Quar.*	Boston Public Library, *Quarterly*
Boston Univ. Law Rev.	*Boston University Law Review*
Brit. Assoc. Am. Studies, *Bull.*	British Association for American Studies, *Bulletin*
Brit. Jour. Sociol.	*British Journal of Sociology*
Buffalo Hist. Soc., *Publ.*	Buffalo Historical Society, *Publications*
Buffalo Law Rev.	*Buffalo Law Review*
Bull. Atomic Scientists	*Bulletin of Atomic Scientists*
Bull. Hist. Med.	*Bulletin of the History of Medicine*
Bur. Am. Ethnol., *Annual Report*	Bureau of American Ethnology, *Annual Report*
Bur. Amer. Ethnol., *Bull.*	Bureau of American Ethnology, *Bulletin*
Bus. Hist. Rev.	*Business History Review*
Bus. Hist. Soc., *Bull.*	Business Historical Society, *Bulletin*
CAAS, *Bull.*	Canadian Association for American Studies, *Bulletin*
Calif. Hist. Soc., *Quar.*	California Historical Society, *Quarterly*
Calif. Law Rev.	*California Law Review*
Can. Hist. Assoc., *Ann. Rep.*	Canadian Historical Association, *Annual Report*

Can. Hist. Rev.	*Canadian Historical Review*
Can. Jour. Hist.	*Canadian Journal of History*
Cath. Hist. Rev.	*Catholic Historical Review*
Cath. Univ. Law Rev.	*Catholic University of America Law Review*
Centennial Rev.	*Centennial Review of Arts and Science*
Chicago Hist.	*Chicago History*
Chicago Rev.	*Chicago Review*
Chronicles Okla.	*Chronicles of Oklahoma*
Church Hist.	*Church History*
Civil War Hist.	*Civil War History*
Classical Jour.	*Classical Journal*
Col. Hist. Soc., Rec.	Columbia Historical Society, *Records*
Col. Soc. Mass., Publ.	Colonial Society of Massachusetts, *Publications*
Col. Soc. Mass., Trans.	Colonial Society of Massachusetts, *Transactions*
Colo. Mag.	*Colorado Magazine*
Colo. Quar.	*Colorado Quarterly*
Columbia Law Rev.	*Columbia Law Review*
Columbia Univ. Forum	*Columbia University Forum*
Comp. Studies in Society and Hist.	*Comparative Studies in Society and History*
Conn. Acad. Arts & Sci., Trans.	Connecticut Academy of Arts and Sciences, *Transactions*
Conn. Hist. Soc., Bull.	Connecticut Historical Society, *Bulletin*
Conn. Hist. Soc., Coll.	Connecticut Historical Society, *Collections*
Cornell Law Rev.	*Cornell Law Review*
Dakota Law Rev.	*Dakota Law Review*
Dalhousie Rev.	*Dalhousie Review*
Del. Hist.	*Delaware History*
Del . Notes	*Delaware Notes*
Delaware Hist. Soc., *Papers*	Delaware Historical Society, *Papers*
Duke Univ., Trinity Coll. Hist. Soc., *Papers*	Duke University, Trinity College Historical Society, *Historical Papers*
Duquesne Hisp. Rev.	*Duquesne Hispanic Review*
Duquesne Rev.	*Duquesne Review*
Early Am. Lit.	*Early American Literature*
East Tenn. Hist. Soc., *Publ.*	East Tennessee Historical Society, *Publications*
Econ. Hist. Rev.	*Economic History Review*
Econ. Jour.	*Economic Journal*

Educ. Forum	*Educational Forum*
Educ. Rev.	*Education Review*
Eng. Hist. Rev.	*English Historical Review*
Essex Inst., *Hist. Coll.*	Essex Institute, *Historical Collections*
Explorations in Entrepren. Hist.	*Explorations in Entrepreneurial History*
Filson Club Hist. Quar.	*Filson Club History Quarterly*
Fla. Hist. Quar.	*Florida Historical Quarterly*
For. Affairs	*Foreign Affairs*
Forest Hist.	*Forest History*
Franklin Inst., *Jour.*	Franklin Institute, *Journal*
French Am. Rev.	*French American Review*
Friends' Hist. Assoc., *Bull.*	Friends' Historical Association, *Bulletin*
Ga. Bar Jour.	*Georgia Bar Journal*
Ga. Hist. Quar.	*Georgia Historical Quarterly*
Ga. Hist. Soc., *Coll.*	Georgia Historical Society, *Collections*
Geog. Rev.	*Geographical Review*
George Washington Law Rev.	*George Washington Law Review*
Georgetown Law Jour.	*Georgetown Law Journal*
Gt. Plains Jour.	*Great Plains Journal*
Harpers Mag.	*Harper's Magazine*
Harv. Bus. Rev.	*Harvard Business Review*
Harv. Educ. Rev.	*Harvard Educational Review*
Harv. Law Rev.	*Harvard Law Review*
Harv. Lib. Bull.	*Harvard Library Bulletin*
Harv. Theol. Rev.	*Harvard Theological Review*
Hastings Law Jour.	*Hastings Law Journal*
Hisp. Am. Hist. Rev.	*Hispanic-American Historical Review*
Hist. and Phil. Soc. of Ohio, *Trans.*	Historical and Philosophical Society of Ohio, *Transactions*
Hist. and Theory	*History and Theory*
Hist. Educ. Jour.	*History of Education Journal*
Hist. Educ. Quar.	*History of Education Quarterly*
Hist. Jour.	*Historical Journal*
Hist. Mag. Prot. Episc. Church	*Historical Magazine of the Protestant Episcopal Church*
Hist. Mexicana	*Historical Mexicana*
Hist. N.H.	*Historical New Hampshire*
Hist. Soc. of Montana, *Contributions*	Historical Society of Montana, *Contributions*

Hist. Soc. Penn, Publ.	Historical Society of Pennsylvania, *Publications*
Hist. Today	*History Today*
Howard Law Jour.	*Howard Law Journal*
Huntington Lib. Quar.	Henry E. Huntington Library, *Quarterly*
Ill. Hist. Coll.	Illinois State Historical Library, *Collections*
Ill. Law Rev.	*Illinois Law Review*
Ill. State Hist. Soc., Jour.	*Journal of the Illinois State Historical Society*
Ill. State Univ. Jour.	*Illinois State University Journal*
Ind. Hist. Soc., Publ.	Indiana Historical Society, *Publications*
Ind. Law Jour.	*Indiana Law Journal*
Ind. Mag. Hist.	*Indiana Magazine of History*
Ind. Univ. Extension Division, Bull.	Indiana University Extension Division, *Bulletin*
India Quar.	*India Quarterly*
Indust. and Labor Rel. Rev.	*Industrial and Labor Relations Review*
Infantry Jour.	*Infantry Journal*
Internatl. Affairs	*International Affairs*
Internatl. Cong. Hist. Sci., Proc.	International Congress of Historical Sciences, *Proceedings*
Internatl. Jour.	*International Journal*
Internatl. Organ.	*International Organization*
Internatl. Studies	*International Studies; Quarterly Journal of the Indian School of International Studies*
Iowa Jour. Hist.	*Iowa Journal of History*
Iowa Jour. Hist. and Pol.	*Iowa Journal of History and Politics*
JAH	*Journal of American History*
James Sprunt Hist. Publ.	*James Sprunt Historical Publications*
Jew. Quar. Rev.	*Jewish Quarterly Review*
Jour. Aesthetics and Art Crit.	*Journal of Aesthetics and Art Criticism*
Jour. Am. Folklore	*Journal of American Folklore*
Jour. Am. Inst. Archit.	*Journal of the American Institute of Architecture*
Jour. Am. Studies	*Journal of American Studies*
Jour. Brit. Studies	*Journal of British Studies*
Jour. Church and State	*Journal of Church and State*
Jour. Conflict Resolution	*Journal of Conflict Resolution*
Jour. Contemp. Hist.	*Journal of Contemporary History*

Jour. Crim. Law	Journal of Criminal Law, Criminology and Police Science
Jour. Devel. Areas	Journal of Developmental Areas
Jour. Eccl. Hist.	Journal of Ecclesiastical History
Jour. Econ. and Bus. Hist.	Journal of Economic and Business History
Jour. Econ. Hist.	Journal of Economic History
Jour. Farm Hist.	Journal of Farm History
Jour. Folklore Inst.	Journal of the Folklore Institute
Jour. Hist. Behavioral Sci.	Journal of the History of the Behavioral Sciences
Jour. Hist. Ideas	Journal of the History of Ideas
Jour. Hist. Med.	Journal of the History of Medicine
Jour. Hist. Phil.	Journal of the History of Philosophy
Jour. Human Rel.	Journal of Human Relations
Jour. Inter-Am. Studies	Journal of Inter-American Studies and World Affairs
Jour. Land Public Utility Econ.	Journal of Land and Public Utility Economics
Jour. Law and Econ.	Journal of Law and Economic Development
Jour. Legal Ed.	Journal of Legal Education
Jour. Lib. Hist.	Journal of Library History
Jour. Miss. Hist.	Journal of Mississippi History
Jour. Mod. Hist.	Journal of Modern History
Jour. Negro Educ.	Journal of Negro Education
Jour. Negro Hist.	Journal of Negro History
Jour. of Abnormal and Soc. Psych.	Journal of Abnormal and Social Psychology
Jour. of Business	Journal of Business
Jour. of Folklore Inst.	Folklore Institute Journal
Jour. of Int. Affairs	Journal of International Affairs
Jour. of Relig.	Journal of Religion
Jour. of Soc. Issues	Journal of Social Issues
Jour. of West	Journal of the West
Jour. of World Hist.	Journal of World History
Jour. Pac. Hist.	Journal of Pacific History
Jour. Philos.	Journal of Philosophy
Jour. Pol. Econ.	Journal of Political Economy
Jour. Politics	Journal of Politics
Jour. Presby. Hist.	Journal of Presbyterian History
Jour. Pub. Law	Journal of Public Law
Jour. Relig. Hist.	Journal of Religious History
Jour. Research in Music Educ.	Journal of Research in Music Education
Jour. Soc. Hist.	Journal of Social History
Jour. Soc. Philos.	Journal of Social Philosophy

Jour. Soc. Sci.	*Journal of Social Sciences*
Jour. Society Archit. Historians	*Journal of the Society of Architectural Historians*
Jour. Urban Law	*Journal of Urban Law*
Journalism Quar.	*Journalism Quarterly*
JSH	*Journal of Southern History*
Kan. Acad. Sci., Trans.	*Transactions of the Kansas Academy of Science*
Kan. Hist. Quar.	*Kansas Historical Quarterly*
Kan. Law Rev.	*Kansas Law Review*
Kan. State Hist. Soc., *Coll.*	Kansas State Historical Society, *Collections*
Kenyon Rev.	*Kenyon Review*
Ky. Hist. Soc., *Reg.*	Kentucky Historical Society, *Register*
Ky. Law Jour.	*Kentucky Law Journal*
L.I. Hist. Soc., *Memoirs*	Long Island Historical Society, *Memoirs*
La. Hist.	*Louisiana History*
La. Hist. Quar.	*Louisiana Historical Quarterly*
La. Law Rev.	*Louisiana Law Review*
Labor Hist.	*Labor History*
Lancaster County Hist. Soc., *Papers*	Lancaster County Historical Society, *Papers*
Law and Contemp. Problems	*Law and Contemporary Problems*
Law Lib. Jour.	*Law Library Journal*
Law Quar. Rev.	*Law Quarterly Review*
Lib. Quar.	*Library Quarterly*
Lib. Trends	*Library Trends*
Mag. of Art	*Magazine of Art*
Mag. of Hist.	*Magazine of History*
Maine Hist. Soc., *Coll.*	Maine Historical Society, *Collections*
Marquette Law Rev.	*Marquette Law Review*
Marxist Quar.	*Marxist Quarterly*
Mass. Hist. Soc., *Coll.*	Massachusetts Historical Society, *Collections*
Mass. Hist. Soc., *Proc.*	Massachusetts Historical Society, *Proceedings*
Md. Hist. Mag.	*Maryland Historical Magazine*
Md. Hist. Soc., *Fund-Publ.*	Maryland Historical Society, *Fund-Publications*
Md. Law Rev.	*Maryland Law Review*
Mennonite Quar. Rev.	*Mennonite Quarterly Review*
Mich. Acad. Sci., *Papers*	Michigan Academy of, Arts, and Letters, *Papers*
Mich. Alumni Quar. Rev.	*Michigan Alumni Quarterly Review*

Mich. Hist.	*Michigan History*
Mich. Law Rev.	*Michigan Law Review*
Midcontinent Am Studies Jour.	*Midcontinent American Studies Journal*
Midw. Jour. Pol. Sci.	*Midwest Journal of Political Science*
Midw. Quar.	*Midwest Quarterly*
Mil. Affairs	*Military Affairs*
Mil. Rev.	*Military Review*
Minn. Hist.	*Minnesota History*
Minn. Hist. Bull.	*Minnesota History Bulletin*
Minn. Law Rev.	*Minnesota Law Review*
Miss. Hist. Soc., Publ.	Mississippi Historical Society, *Publications*
Miss. Law Jour.	*Mississippi Law Journal*
Miss. Quar.	*Mississippi Quarterly*
Miss. Valley Hist. Assoc., Proc.	Mississippi Valley Historical Association, *Proceedings*
Mo. Hist. Rev.	*Missouri Historical Review*
Mo. Hist. Soc., Bull.	Missouri Historical Society, *Bulletin*
Mont. Mag. Hist.	*Montana, the Magazine of Western History*
Monthly Lab. Rev.	*Monthly Labor Review*
MVHR	*Mississippi Valley Historical Review*
Narragansett Club, *Publ.*	Narragansett Club, *Publications*
Natl. Acad. of Sciences, Proc.	National Academy of Sciences, *Proceedings*
Natl. Geographic	*National Geographic Magazine*
Navy Rec. Soc., *Publ.*	Navy Records Society, *Publications*
Neb. Hist.	*Nebraska History*
Negro Hist. Bull.	*Negro History Bulletin*
NEQ	*New England Quarterly*
New Eng. Hist. Geneal. Reg.	*New England Historical and Genealogical Register*
New Engl. Mag.	*New England Magazine*
New Haven Colony Hist. Soc., *Papers*	New Haven Colony Historical Society, *Papers*
New Mex. Hist. Rev.	*New Mexico Historical Review*
New Princeton Rev.	*New Princeton Review*
Newcomen Soc., *Trans.*	Newcomen Society, *Transactions*
N.J. Hist.	*New Jersey History*
N.J. Hist. Soc., Proc.	New Jersey Historical Society, *Proceedings*
No. Am. Rev.	*North American Review*
No. Car. Hist. Rev.	*North Carolina Historical Review*

No. Car. Law Rev.	North Carolina Law Review
No. Dak. Hist.	North Dakota History
No. Dak. Hist. Quar.	North Dakota Historical Quarterly
No. Dak. Quar.	North Dakota Quarterly
Northw. Ohio Quar.	Northwest Ohio Quarterly
Northw. Univ. Law Rev.	Northwestern University Law Review
Norwegian-Am. Stud. and Rec.	Norwegian-American Studies and Records
N.Y. Hist.	New York History
N.Y. Hist. Soc., Coll.	New York Historical Society, Collections
N.Y. Hist. Soc. Quar.	New York Historical Society Quarterly
N.Y. Law Forum	New York Law Forum
N.Y. Law Rev.	New York Law Review
N.Y. Pub. Lib., Bull.	New York Public Library, Bulletin
N.Y. State Hist. Assoc., Quar. Jour.	New York State Historical Association, Quarterly Journal
N.Y. Times Bk. Rev.	New York Times Book Review
N.Y.U. Law Rev.	New York University Law Review
Ohio Hist.	Ohio History
Ohio Hist. Quar.	Ohio Historical Quarterly
Ohio State Archaeol. and Hist. Quar.	Ohio State Archaeological and Historical Quarterly
Ontario Hist.	Ontario History
Ontario Hist. Soc., Papers	Ontario Historical Society, Papers and Records
Ore. Hist. Quar.	Oregon Historical Quarterly
Ore. Hist. Soc., Quar.	Oregon Historical Society, Quarterly
Ore. Law Rev.	Oregon Law Review
Pac. Affairs	Pacific Affairs
Pac. Hist. Rev.	Pacific Historical Review
Pac. Northw. Quar.	Pacific Northwest Quarterly
Pac. Northwesterner	Pacific Northwesterner
Partisan Rev.	Partisan Review
Patent Off. Soc., Jour.	Journal of the Patent Office Society
Penn. German Soc., Proc.	Pennsylvania German Society, Proceedings
Penn. Hist.	Pennsylvania History
Penn. Mag. Hist. Biog.	Pennsylvania Magazine of History and Biography

Perspectives in Am. Hist.	Perspectives in American History
Philos. of Science	Philosophy of Science
Pol. Quar.	Political Quarterly
Pol. Sci. Quar.	Political Science Quarterly
Princeton Rev.	Princeton Review
Psych. Bull.	Psychological Bulletin
Pub. Archives Can., Report	Public Archives of Canada, Report
Pub. Admin. Rev.	Public Administration Review
Pub. Opinion Quar.	Public Opinion Quarterly
Pub. Policy	Public Policy
Quaker Hist.	Quaker History
Quar. Jour. Econ.	Quarterly Journal of Economics
Quar. Jour. Lib. of Congress	Quarterly Journal of the Library of Congress
Quar. Jour. of Current Acquisitions	Quarterly Journal of Current Acquisitions
Quar. Jour. Speech	Quarterly Journal of Speech
Quar. Rev.	Quarterly Review
Quartermaster Rev.	Quartermaster Review
Queen's Quar.	Queen's Quarterly
Queen's Univ., Bull	Queen's University, Department of History and of Political and Economic Science, Bulletin
Register of Kentucky Hist. Soc.	Register of the Kentucky Historical Society
Relig. Educ.	Religious Education Association, Proc.
Rev. and Expositor	Review and Expositor
Rev. Econ. Stat.	Review of Economic Statistics
Rev. Hist. Am. Fr.	Revue d'histoire de l'Amérique française
Rev. Politics	Review of Politics
R.I. Hist.	Rhode Island History
R.I. Hist. Soc., Coll.	Rhode Island Historical Society, Collections
R.I. Jewish Historical Notes	Rhode Island Jewish Historical Notes
Rochester Hist. Soc., Publ. Fund Ser.	Rochester Historical Society, Publication Fund Series
Rochester Hist.	Rochester History
Rocky Mtn. Law Rev.	Rocky Mountain Law Review
Rocky Mtn. Soc. Sci. Jour.	Rocky Mountain Social Science Journal
Royal Hist. Soc., Trans.	Royal Historical Society, Transactions

Royal Soc. Canada, *Proc.*	Royal Society of Canada, *Proceedings*
Rural Sociol.	*Rural Sociology*
Scandinavian Econ. Hist. Rev.	*Scandinavian Economic and Historical Review*
School Rev.	*School Review*
Scient. Am.	*Scientific American*
Scient. Monthly	*Scientific Monthly*
Slavonic & East Eur. Rev.	*Slavonic and East European Review*
Smithsonian Jour. Hist.	*Smithsonian Journal of History*
So. Atl. Quar.	*South Atlantic Quarterly*
So. Calif. Quar.	*Southern California Quarterly*
So. Car. Hist. Assoc., *Proc.*	South Carolina Historical Association, *Proceedings*
So. Car. Hist. Geneal. Mag.	*South Carolina Historical and Genealogical Magazine*
So. Car. Hist. Mag.	*South Carolina Historical and Genealogical Magazine*
So. Dak. Hist.	*South Dakota History*
So. Dak. Hist. Coll.	*South Dakota Historical Collections*
Soc. Army Hist. Research, *Jour.*	Society for Army Historical Research, *Journal*
Soc. Sci. Res. Council, *Bull.*	Social Science Research Council, *Bulletin*
Social Sci. Quar.	*Social Science Quarterly*
South. Econ. Jour.	*Southern Economic Journal*
South. Folklore Quar.	*Southern Folklore Quarterly*
South. Hist. Assoc., *Publ.*	Southern Historical Association, *Publications*
South. Hist. Soc., *Papers*	Southern Historical Society, *Papers*
South. Quar.	*Southern Quarterly Review*
Southw. Hist. Quar.	*Southwestern Historical Quarterly*
Southw. Pol. Sci. Quar.	*Southwest Political Science Quarterly*
Southw. Rev.	*Southwest Review*
Southw. Soc. Sci. Quar.	*Southwestern Social Science Quarterly*
Soviet Rev.	*Soviet Review*
Stanford Law Rev.	*Stanford Law Review*
State Dept. of Archives and Hist., *Report*	State Department of Archives and History, *Report* [West Virginia]
Supreme Ct. Rev.	*Supreme Court Review*
Swedish Hist. Soc., *Yearbook*	Swedish Historical Society, *Yearbook*

Teachers College Rec.	*Teachers College Record*
Tech. and Cult.	*Technology and Culture*
Tenn. Hist. Mag.	*Tennessee Magazine of History*
Tenn. Hist. Quar.	*Tennessee Historical Quarterly*
Tex. Law Rev.	*Texas Law Review*
Tex. Quar.	*Texas Quarterly*
Tex. State Hist. Assoc., Quar.	Texas State Historical Association, *Quarterly*
Tri-Quar.	*Tri-Quarterly*
Tulane Law Rev.	*Tulane Law Review*
Tyler's Quar.	*Tyler's Quarterly*
UCLA Law Rev.	*University of California, Los Angeles, Law Review*
Univ. of Chi. Law Rev.	*University of Chicago Law Review*
Univ. of Cinc. Law Rev.	*University of Cincinnati Law Review*
Univ. of Colo., Studies	University of Colorado, *Studies*
Univ. Kan. City Rev.	*University of Kansas City Review*
Univ. of Maine, Studies	University of Maine, *Studies*
Univ. of Mo., Studies	University of Missouri, *Studies*
Univ. Penn. Law Rev.	*University of Pennsylvania Law Review*
Univ. of Wyoming Publ.	*University of Wyoming Publications*
U.S. Natl. Museum, Bull.	*United States National Museum, Bulletin*
U.S. Naval Inst., Proc.	United States Naval Institute, *Proceedings*
U.S. News & World Rep.	*U.S. News & World Report*
Utah Hist. Quar.	*Utah Historical Quarterly*
Va. Hist. Soc., Coll.	Virginia Historical Society, *Collections*
Va. Law Rev.	*Virginia Law Review*
Va. Mag. Hist. Biog.	*Virginia Magazine of History and Biography*
Va. Quar. Rev.	*Virginia Quarterly Review*
Va. State Lib. Bull.	Virginia State Library *Bulletin*
Vanderbilt Law Rev.	Vanderbilt Law Review
Vt. Hist.	*Vermont History*
W. Va. Hist.	*West Virginia History*
Wash. and Lee Law Rev.	*Washington and Lee Law Review*
Wash. Hist. Quar.	*Washington Historical Quarterly*

Wash. Law Rev.	*Washington Law Review*
Wash. Univ. Law Rev.	*Washington University Law Review*
West. Econ. Jour.	*Western Economic Journal*
West. Humanities Rev.	*Western Humanities Review*
West. Penn. Hist. Mag.	*Western Pennsylvania History Magazine*
West. Pol. Quar.	*Western Political Quarterly*
West. Reserve Law Rev.	*Western Reserve Law Review*
Westchester Co. Hist. Soc., *Publ.*	Westchester County Historical Society, *Publications*
Western Reserve Hist. Soc., *Tracts*	Western Reserve Historical Society, *Tracts*
Wis. Acad. Sciences, Trans.	Wisconsin Academy of Sciences, Arts and Letters, *Transactions*
Wis. Hist. Soc., Proc.	State Historical Society of Wisconsin, *Proceedings*
Wis. Law Rev.	*Wisconsin Law Review*
Wis. Mag. Hist.	*Wisconsin Magazine of History*
WMQ	*William and Mary Quarterly*
Women's Bur., *Bull.*	Women's Bureau, *Bulletin*
Yale Law Jour.	*Yale Law Journal*
Yale Jour. Biol. and Med.	*Yale Journal of Biology and Medicine*
Yale Rev.	*Yale Review*
YIVO	*YIVO Annual of Jewish Social Science*

He must ever remember that while the worst offense of which he can be guilty is to write vividly and inaccurately, yet that unless he writes vividly he cannot write truthfully; for no amount of dull, painstaking detail will sum up the whole truth unless the genius is there to paint the truth.

Theodore Roosevelt's trumpet call fell largely on deaf ears, at least in the academic historical profession. A whole generation has passed without producing more than a very few great works on American history. Plenty of good books, valuable books, and new interpretations and explorations of the past; but none with fire in the eye, none to make a young man want to fight for his country in war or live to make it a better country in peace. There has been a sort of chain reaction of dullness. Professors who have risen to positions of eminence by writing dull, solid, valuable monographs that nobody reads outside the profession, teach graduate students to write dull, solid, valuable monographs like theirs; the road to academic security is that of writing dull, solid, valuable monographs. And so the young men who have a gift for good writing either leave the historical field for something more exciting, or write more dull, solid, valuable monographs. The few professional historians who have had a popular following or appeal during the last thirty years either started their careers as journalists or broke loose young from academic trammels.

The tremendous plowing of the past by well-trained scholars is all to the good. Scholars know more about America's past than ever; they are opening new furrows and finding new artifacts, from aboriginal arrowheads to early twentieth-century hub caps. But they are heaping up pay dirt for others. Journalists, novelists, and free-lance writers are the ones that extract the gold; and they deserve every ounce they get because they write histories that people care to read. What we wish to see is a few more Ph.D.'s in history winning book-of-the-month adoptions and reaping a harvest of dividends.

There are no special rules for writing history; any good manual of rhetoric or teacher of composition will supply the rules for writing English. But what terrible stuff passes for English in Ph.D. dissertations, monographs, and articles in the historical reviews! Long, involved sentences that one has to read two or three times in order to grasp the meaning; poverty in vocabulary, ineptness of expression, weakness in paragraph structure, constant misuse of words and, of late, the introduction of pseudoscientific and psychological jargon. There is no fundamental cure for this except better teaching of English in our schools and by all teachers, *whatever their other subjects.* If historical writing is infinitely better in France than in America, and far better in the British Isles than in America, it is because every French and British teacher of history drills his pupils in their mother tongue, requiring a constant stream of essays and reports and criticizing written work not only as history but as literature. The American university teacher who gives honor grades to students who have not yet learned to write English, for industrious compilations of facts or feats of memory, is wanting in professional pride or competency.

Of course what we should all like to attain in writing history is style, "the last acquirement of the educated mind; . . . the ultimate morality of mind." Unfortunately, there is no royal road to style. It cannot be attained by mere industry; it can never be achieved through imitation, although it may be promoted by example. Reading the greatest literary artists among historians will help, but what was acceptable style in 1850 might seem

Part One   Research Methods and Materials

1 Research, Writing, and Publication

1.1 HISTORY AS A LITERARY ART

Historical writing at its best is art as well as science. To be fully effec
the historian must be precise, accurate, and judicious. Even techn
monographs should meet basic literary standards.

Samuel Eliot Morison's classic plea for literary merit is of continu
relevance. Itself a landmark, it appears here unchanged from the 1
edition of the *Harvard Guide to American History*:

Exploring American history has been a very absorbing and exci
business now for three quarters of a century. Thousands of gradu
students have produced thousands of monographs on every aspect of
history of the Americas. But the American reading public for the most
is blissfully ignorant of this vast output. When John Citizen feels the
to read history, he goes to the novels of Kenneth Roberts or Marg
Mitchell, not the histories of Professor this or Doctor that. Why?

Because American historians, in their eagerness to present facts
their laudable anxiety to tell the truth, have neglected the literary asp
of their craft. They have forgotten that there is an art of writing hist

Even the earliest colonial historians like Bradford and Beverley k
that; they put conscious art into their narratives. And the historians of
classical period, Prescott and Motley, Irving and Bancroft, Parkman
Fiske, were great literary craftsmen. Their many-volumed works sol
sufficient quantities to give them handsome returns; even today they
widely read. But the first generation of seminar-trained historians,
cated in Germany or by teachers trained there, imagined that his
would tell itself, provided one were honest, thorough, and painstak
Some of them went so far as to regard history as pure science and to as
that writers thereof had no more business trying to be "literary" than
writers of statistical reports or performers of scientific experiments.
fessors warned their pupils against "fine writing." And in this fligh
history from literature, the public got left behind. American his
became a bore to the reader and a drug on the market; even histor
with something to say and the talent for saying it (Henry Adams,
instance) could not sell their books. The most popular American histo
of the period 1890–1905 were those of John Fiske, a philosopher who
no historical training but wrote with life and movement.

Theodore Roosevelt in his presidential address before the Amer
Historical Association in 1912 made a ringing plea to the young histo
to do better:

turgid today. We can still read Macaulay with admiration and pleasure, we can still learn paragraph structure and other things from Macaulay, but anyone who tried to imitate Macaulay today would be a pompous ass. The writer of history had better not work consciously to develop a style but concentrate on day-by-day improvement in craftsmanship. Then perhaps he may find some day that his industry, which left readers cold, is carried to a large popular audience by something that the critics call style.

A few hints as to literary craftsmanship may be useful to budding historians. First and foremost, *get writing*! Young scholars generally wish to secure the last fact before writing anything, just as General McClellan refused to advance until the last mule was shod. But there is the "indispensablest beauty in knowing how to get done," said Carlyle. In every research there comes a point, which you should recognize like a call of conscience, when you must get down to writing. And when you once are writing, go on writing as long as you can; there will be plenty of time later to add footnotes or return to the library for extra information. Above all, *start* writing. Nothing is more pathetic than the historian who from graduate school on is promising to write a magnum opus but never completes his research and dies without anything to show for a lifetime's work.

Dictation is usually fatal to good historical writing. Write out your first draft in longhand or, if you compose easily on the typewriter, type it out yourself, revise with pencil or pen, and have it retyped clean. Don't stop to consult notes for every clause or sentence; it is better to get what you have to say in your mind and dash it off, then return to your notes and compose your next few pages or paragraphs. After a little experience you may find that you think best with your fingers on the typewriter keys or your pen poised over the paper. For some, the mere writing of a few words seems to point up vague thoughts and make jumbled facts array themselves in neat order. Whichever method you choose, composing before you write or as you write, do not return to your raw material or verify facts and quotations or insert footnotes until you have written a substantial amount, an amount that will increase with practice. It is significant that two of our greatest American historians, Prescott and Parkman, were nearly blind during a good part of their active careers. They had to have the sources read to them and turn the matter over and over in their minds before they could give anything out.

The purpose of this quick, warm synthesis of research, thinking, and writing is to attain the three prime qualities of historical composition—clarity, vigor, and objectivity. You must think about your facts, analyze your material, and decide exactly what you mean before you can write it so that the average reader will understand. Do not slip into the fallacy of supposing that "facts speak for themselves." Most of the facts that you excavate from the archives, like all relics of past human activity, are dumb things; it is for you to make them speak by proper selection, arrangement, and emphasis. Dump your entire collection of facts on paper, and the result will be unreadable if not incomprehensible.

So, too, with vigor. If your whole paragraph or chapter is but a hypothesis, say so at the beginning, but do not bore and confuse the reader with numerous "buts," "excepts," "perhaps," "howevers" and "possiblys." Use direct rather than indirect statements, the active rather than the passive voice, and make every sentence and paragraph an organic whole. Above all, if you are writing historical narrative, make it move. Do not take time out in the middle of a political or military campaign to introduce special developments or literary trends as McMaster did to the confusion of his readers. Place those admittedly important matters in a chapter or chapters by themselves so that your reader's attention will not be lost by constant interruption.

That brings us to the third essential quality—objectivity. Keep the reader constantly in mind. You are not writing history for yourself or for the professors who (you may imagine) know more about it than you do. Assume that you are writing for intelligent people who know nothing about your particular subject but whom you wish to convince of its interest and significance. The late Senator Beveridge was once asked why his *Life of John Marshall,* despite its great length and scholarly apparatus, was so popular. He replied, "The trouble with you professors of history is that you write for each other. I write for people almost completely ignorant of American history, as I was when I began my research."

Social history puts a greater strain on literary expression and the sense of balance than any other kind. Hitherto the novelists have been very much better at writing it than the historians. The latter need to improve their human perception as well as their literary style if they expect to be the teachers of social history that, for instance, Marcel Proust was and Conrad Richter is. Historians notably lack the talent at description which novelists have developed to a high degree; Prescott had it, of course, and Parkman; but few American historians now living can describe a scene, an event, or a natural setting in such a way that the reader can see it. The reason is largely that the writer cannot see it himself; he sits in a library and writes instead of going about by whatever means of transportation is available, and finding out for himself what historic sites look like today. Then, too, some social historians forget that history is a *story* that moves; they divorce their subject altogether from the main stream of history, giving it no context and no time. The American historian of architecture, education, labor, medicine, or any other social subject, should have a sense of chronology and make history move.

Now for a few practical details. Even if the work you are writing does not call for footnotes, keep them in your copy until the last draft, for they will enable you to check up on your facts, statements, and quotations. And since accuracy is a prime virtue of the historian, this checking must be done, either by the author or by someone else. You will be surprised by the mistakes that creep in between a first rough draft and a final typed copy. And, the better you write, the more critics will enjoy finding misquotations and inaccuracies.

The matter of handling quotations seems to be a difficult one for young historians. There is nothing that adds so much to the charm and effectiveness of a history as good quotations from the sources, especially if the period be somewhat remote. Note how effectively this was done in Professor McIlwain's presidential address before the American Historical Association (*Am. Hist. Rev.,* 42 [1937], 207). There is nothing so disgusting to the reader as long, tedious, broken quotations in small print, especially those in which, to make sense, the author has to interpolate words in square brackets. Young writers are prone to use quotations in places where their own words would be better, and to incorporate in the text source excerpts that belong in footnotes or appendices. Avoid ending chapters with quotations, and never close your book with one. Above all, do not be afraid to revise and rewrite. Reading aloud is a good test—historians' wives have to stand a lot of that!

Undoubtedly the writer of history can enrich his mind and broaden his literary experience as well as better his craftsmanship by his choice of leisure reading. If he is so fortunate as to have had a classical education, no time will be better spent in making him an effective historian than in reading Latin and Greek authors. Both these ancient languages are such superb instruments of thought that a knowledge of them cures slipshod English and helps one to attain a clear, muscular style. All our greatest historical stylists—notably Prescott, Parkman, Fiske and Frederick J. Turner—had a classical education and read the ancient historians in the original before they approached American history.

If you have little Latin and less Greek and feel unable to spare the time and effort to add them to your stock of tools, read the ancient classics in the best literary translations, such as North's Plutarch, Rawlinson's Herodotus, John J. Chapman's Sophocles, Gilbert Murray's Euripides and, above all, Jowett's or Livingstone's Thucydides. Through them you will gain the content and spirit of the ancient classics which will break down your provincialism, refresh your spirit, and give you a better philosophical insight into the ways of mankind than most of such works as the new science of psychology has brought forth. Moreover, you will be acquiring the same background as many of the great Americans of past generations, thus aiding your understanding of them.

The reading of English classics will tend in the same direction and will also be a painless and unconscious means of improving your literary style. Almost every English or American writer of distinction is indebted to Shakespeare and the English Bible. The Authorized Version is not only the great source book of spiritual experience of English-speaking peoples, it is a treasury of plain, pungent words and muscular phrases, beautiful in themselves and with long associations, that we are apt to replace by smooth words lacking in punch, or by hackneyed or involved phrases. Of course much of the biblical phraseology is obsolete, and there are other literary quarries for historians. You can find many appropriate words, phrases, similies, and epigrams in American authors such as Mark Twain, Emerson, and Thoreau.

What of imagination in history? A historian or biographer has restrictions unknown to a novelist. He has no right to override facts by his own imagination. If he is writing on a remote or obscure subject on which very few facts are available, his imagination may legitimately weave them into a pattern. But to be honest, he must make clear what is fact and what is hypothesis. The quality of imagination, if properly restrained by the conditions of historical discipline, is of great assistance in enabling one to discover problems to be solved, to grasp the significance of facts, to form hypotheses, to discern causes in their first beginnings and, above all, to relate the past creatively to the present. There are many opportunities in historical narrative for bold, imaginative expressions. "A complete statement in the imaginative form of an important truth arrests attention," wrote Emerson, "and is repeated and remembered." Imagination used in this way invests an otherwise pedestrian narrative with vivid and exciting qualities.

Finally, the historian should have frequent recourse to the book of life. The richer his personal experience, the wider his human contacts, the more likely he is to effect a living contact with his audience. In writing, similes drawn from the current experience of this mechanical age rather than those rifled from the literary baggage of past eras are the ones that will go home to his reader. The great historians, with few exceptions, are those who have not merely studied but lived, and whose studies have ranged over a much wider field than the period or subject of which they write. Veterans of the wars, who have seen man at his best and his worst, can read man's doings in the past with far greater understanding than if they had spent these years in sheltered academic shades.

To young men especially, we say (as the poet Chapman said to the young Elizabethan), "Be free, all worthy spirits, and stretch yourselves!" Bring all your knowledge of life to bear on everything that you write. Never let yourself bog down in pedantry and detail. Bring History, the most humane and noble form of letters, back to the proud position she once held, knowing that your words, if they be read and remembered, will enter into the stream of life, and perhaps move men to thought and action centuries hence, as do those of Thucydides after more than two thousand years.

For a fuller version, see Samuel Eliot Morison's pamphlet, *History as a Literary Art* published by the Old South Association, Old South Meeting House, Boston, Mass., reprinted in Samuel Eliot Morison, *By Land and by Sea* (1953).

1.2 TOPICS FOR RESEARCH

At the outset, the historian must choose an original, feasible, and significant topic for research. Often this search for a topic is a perplexing and time-consuming task, but unless the topic is appropriate, the ensuing task of research and writing may be wasted time. Surveys suggesting research subjects appear occasionally, but they are soon outdated. Various surveys and historiographical essays which may indicate gaps or deficiencies in existing writings appear at the appropriate locations in the *Guide.*

No matter how significant the topic, the historian cannot successfully write upon it unless adequate materials are available to him. Essential documents are sometimes scattered, fragmentary, or lost. Manuscript and archival collections are sometimes closed to research until some future date.

The historian must make sure no one else is well advanced in research upon the same topic. Ph.D. candidates in history can avoid conflict with other candidates by registering their theses topics with the American Historical Association. It is more difficult to find out whether a scholar beyond his Ph.D. is working on a subject. Sometimes archivists and manuscript librarians can informally help by providing information.

The American Historical Association annually publishes a *List of Doctoral Dissertations in History Now in Progress or Completed at Universities in the United States, 1909– *. Originally issued by the Carnegie Institution, it has been published by the American Historical Association since 1947.

Other lists of research in progress (or recently completed) appear in:

The American Quarterly.
Institute of Early American History and Culture, *Newsletter.*
*Index to American Doctoral Dissertations, 1955/56– *. A broad subject index to dissertations accepted in the United States and Canada during the academic year covered, as well as those available on microfilm from University Microfilm. Appears annually as no. 13 of *Dissertation Abstracts.*

Kuehl, Warren F., *Dissertations in History: Index to Dissertations Completed in History Departments of United States and Canadian Universities, 1873–1960* (1965).

1.3 METHODS OF NOTE-TAKING

Historians in the past have used a wide variety of methods for accumulating and arranging the data that will be the basis of their narrative accounts. The essential requisite of a successful system of note-taking is that it permit the organization of the factual material in forms in which it may readily be used, ordered, and reordered in accord with the writer's needs. Any system is suitable to the degree that it relieves the historian of dependence upon his memory and enables him to draw, when he wishes, upon a store of verifiable facts.

The nineteenth-century historians were rather limited in this respect. Often the difficulty of rearranging their information compelled them to write from a single body of records—diplomatic or governmental documents, correspondence, or newspapers—and frequently the internal organization of their narrative reflected the organization, often arbitrary, of the sources from which they worked. Some scholars, like George Bancroft, first filled their notebooks with abstracts or transcriptions, then drew upon those as best they could while they wrote. Even the most careful could not guard against errors of quotation and citation. Others worked directly from books with notes only to guide them to the relevant pages; they were therefore restricted to what they possessed or could borrow. At least one historian, in a period of lower publishing costs, made a practice of tearing what he needed out of his journals and books as a preliminary to the task of composition.

More recently the development of filing devices has eased the labors of the historian. Each research worker before long discovers the type of equipment most appropriate to his needs. Index cards of various sizes (3×5, 4×6, 5×8) are available. Where the magnitude of a task makes these bulky, paper slips may be substituted. In any case the actual process of note-taking is one of isolating references to facts, principles, or ideas which can then be arranged along the line of the writer's own argument. Success depends upon the ability to discern the significant information, to abstract it as concisely and economically as possible, and to transcribe it accurately and in such form as will allow easy checking.

There are occasional conditions under which the usual methods of note-taking are not feasible. If the sources are out of reach or are contained in libraries difficult of access, it may be profitable to make use of the mechanical devices that aid note-taking. Manuscripts no longer need be copied by hand; and historians are not now, as Prescott and Parkman were, dependent upon the slow, laborious, and uncertain services of copyists. Mechanical developments have cheapened the process, speeded it, and eliminated the possibility of error in transcription.

When the source consists of a large number of items in sequence, the most useful device is microfilming, by which a photographic copy is made on 35-mm. film, generally one page or one sheet to a frame. This process is inexpensive, expeditious, and produces a compact copy. On the other hand it calls for the use of a special reading device. When material to be copied is scattered or is small in quantity, it is better to depend upon xeroxing. Most libraries and archives in the United States, and some abroad, provide inexpensive xeroxing service. Some libraries do not permit extensive microfilm or xerox copying of manuscript materials. It is illegal to xerox in entirety books that are covered by copyright. Some scholars prefer to use their own portable copying devices. Libraries usually will not allow the use of this equipment if it contains liquid chemicals.

None of these devices absolves the historian from the necessity of digesting and assimilating the material he uses, but, properly applied, they can relieve him from some of the drudgery of his task.

See:

Barzun, Jacques, and Henry F. Graff, *The Modern Researcher* (1970).
Cantor, Norman F., and Richard I. Schneider, *How to Study History* (1967).
Gottschalk, Louis, *Understanding History* (1960).
Gray, Wood, et al., *Historian's Handbook* (1964).

1.4 QUANTITATIVE AND SOCIAL SCIENCE TECHNIQUES

Historians are utilizing a number of techniques of empirical conceptualization developed in the social sciences. In addition to statistical analysis, for example, they are experimenting with the building and testing of models. They are borrowing specific methods and models from other social science disciplines, especially economics, demography, and psychology, and applying them to historical problems.

Computer data processing in particular has broadened the dimensions of historical as well as social research. Through use of computers, the quantitative historian can run complex analyses of data. Great stores of data exist, and new collections are becoming available. Computers are serving as data banks, as well as analytical tools. See Elizabeth I. Wood, *Report on Project History Retrieval: Optic-Coincidence System for Historical Materials* (1966).

1.4.1 History, Quantification, and the Social Sciences

Andreano, Ralph L., ed., *The New Economic History* (1970).
Aydelotte, William O., "Quantification in History," *AHR,* 71 (1966), 803.
Benson, Lee, "Research Problems in American Political Historiography," in Mirra Komarovsky, ed., *Common Frontiers of the Social Sciences* (1957), 113.
Berkhofer, Robert F., Jr., *A Behavioral Approach to Historical Analysis* (1969). Best general introduction available.
Cahnman, Werner J., and Alvin Boskoff, eds., *Sociology and History* (1964).
Clubb, Jerome M., and Howard Allen, "Computers and Historical Studies," *JAH,* 54 (1967), 599.
Hartz, Louis, "American Historiography and Comparative Analysis: Further Reflections," *Comparative Studies in Soc. and Hist.,* 5 (1963), 365.
Hauser, Philip M., "Demography and Ecology," Am. Acad. Pol. Soc. Sci., *Annals,* 362 (1965), 129.
Hays, Samuel P., "Quantification in History," *AHR,* 71 (1966), 803.
Higham, John, "The Schism in American Scholarship," *AHR,* 72 (1966), 1.
Hofstadter, Richard, "History and the Social Sciences," in Fritz Stern, ed., *Varieties of History* (1956).
Hughes, H. Stuart, "Historian and Social Scientist," *AHR,* 66 (1960), 20.
———— *History as Art and as Science: Twin Vistas on the Past* (1964).
Komarovsky, Mirra, ed., *Common Frontiers of the Social Sciences* (1957).
Mazlish, Bruce, ed., *Psychoanalysis and History* (1963).
Mead, Margaret, "Anthropologist and Historian," *Am. Quar.* 3 (1951), 3.

Rothstein, Morton, et al., "Quantification and American History," in Herbert J. Bass, ed., *State of American History* (1970).
Saveth, Edward N., *American History and the Social Sciences* (1964).
Social Science Research Council, *Social Sciences in Historical Study: A Report of the Committee on Historiography* (1954).
Woolf, Harry, ed., *Quantification: History of the Meaning of Measurement* (1961).
Wrigley, E. A., *Population and History* (1969).
Wyatt, Frederick, "A Psychologist Looks at History," *Jour. of Social Issues,* 17 (1961), 66.

Journals

Historical Methods Newsletter: Quantitative Analyses of Social, Economic and Political Development 1967–
Journal of Interdisciplinary History 1970–

1.4.2 Social Science Technique

There follow some general collections which contain examples of the application to history of social science techniques. Other examples of the treatment of specific subjects will be found under the appropriate topical headings.

Anderson, Lee, et al., *Legislative Roll-Call Analysis* (1966).
Andreano, Ralph L., ed., *New Views on American Economic Development* (1965).
Blalock, Hubert M., Jr., *Causal Inferences in Nonexperimental Research* (1964).
———and Ann B. Blalock, eds., *Methodology in Social Research* (1968).
Blalock, Hubert M., Jr., *Theory Construction* (1969).
Davis, Lance E., et al., "Aspects of Quantitative Research in Economic History," *Jour. Econ. Hist.,* 20 (1960), 639.
Glass, D. V., and D. E. C. Eversley, *Population in History* (1965).
Goldstein, Sidney, et al., *The Norristown Study: An Experiment in Interdisciplinary Research Training* (1961).
Hammarberg, Melvyn A., "Designing a Sample from Incomplete Historical Lists," *Am. Quar.,* 23 (1971), 542.
Lipset, Seymour M., and Richard Hofstadter, eds., *Sociology and History: Methods* (1968).
Rowney, Don K., and James Q. Graham, Jr., *Quantitative History: Selected Readings* (1969).
Saveth, Edward N., ed., *American History and the Social Sciences* (1964).
Selltiz, Claire, et al., *Research Methods in Social Relations* (1959).
Swierenga, Robert D., ed., *Quantification in American History* (1970).
Thernstrom, Stephan, and Richard Sennett, eds., *Nineteenth Century Cities: Essays in New Urban History* (1969).
Wrigley, E. A., ed., *Introduction to English Historical Demography* (1966).

1.4.3 Statistical Analysis:

Blalock, Hubert M., *Social Statistics* (1960).
Buckland, William R., and Ronald A. Fox, *Bibliography of Basic Texts and Monographs on Statistical Methods, 1945–1960* (1963).
Fisz, Marek, *Probability Theory and Mathematical Statistics* (1963).
Hays, William L., *Statistics for Psychologists* (1963).
——— *Basic Statistics* (1967).
Kendall, Maurice G., and Alison G. Doig, *Bibliography of Statistical Literature,* 3 vols. (1962–68).
Key, V. O., Jr., *Primer of Statistics for Political Scientists* (1954).
Lancaster, H. O., *Bibliography of Statistical Bibliographies* (1968).
McArthur, Norma, *Introducing Population Statistics* (1961).

MacRae, Duncan, Jr., *Issues and Parties in Legislative Voting: Methods of Statistical Analysis* (1970).
Mueller, J. H., and K. F. Schuessler, *Statistical Reasoning in Sociology* (1961).
Stuart, Alan, *Basic Ideas of Scientific Sampling* (1962).

1.4.4 Computer Application:

Borko, Harold, ed., *Computer Applications in the Behavioral Sciences* (1962).
Clubb, Jerome M., and Howard Allen, "Computers and Historical Studies," *JAH*, 54 (1967), 599.
Dollar, Charles, "Innovation in Historical Research: A Computer Approach," *Computers and the Humanities*, 3 (1969), 139.
Hays, Samuel P., "Computers and Historical Research," in Edmund A. Bowles, ed., *Computers in Humanistic Research* (1967), 62.
Thernstrom, Stephan, "The Historian and the Computer," in Edmund A. Bowles, ed., *Computers in Humanistic Research* (1967), 73.
Computers and the Humanities 1966–

1.5 WRITING FOR PUBLICATION

Publishers of historical journals and books vary in their recommendations for preparation of copy and their stylistic usages. If a manuscript is being prepared for a given journal or press, its specific house style should serve as a guide. Most important are scholarly standards, which require that the style be consistent throughout a manuscript, and that the citations, whatever their form, supply the essential information in a manner readily intelligible. It is the reader's convenience, not the author's, that should be the criterion.

Many publishers, learned-society editors, graduate schools, and departments of history have their own specifications, one of the most comprehensive compilations being *A Manual of Style*, of the University of Chicago Press. *The MLA Style Sheet*, 2nd ed. (1970) is available from the Modern Language Association of America. It governs the usage of many journals, including the *American Historical Review* and the *Journal of the History of Ideas*. Legal citations often pose special problems. The style preferred by scholars in that field is set forth in *A Uniform System of Citation*, (12th ed., 1972), sponsored by the *Law Reviews* of Columbia, Harvard, the University of Pennsylvania, and Yale.

The following instructions are drawn from *Mostly for Authors: A Handbook*, published by Harvard University Press (1970) and *A Handbook of Style*, prepared by the Charles Warren Center for Studies in American History.

Preparation of Manuscript

The ribbon copy of the manuscript should be submitted, with a second copy if possible. You will want to retain a third copy for your own reference. A Xerox copy may be used in lieu of a carbon for the second copy. Use a good grade of 8½ × 11-inch bond paper; do not use paper that has been treated to make erasing easy.

Use one side of the paper only. Leave margins at least one inch wide all around, preferably wider at the left and top. It is not necessary to fill every sheet with typing. Number front-matter pages, starting with one. Number the rest of the manuscript separately, starting with one for the first page after the front matter.

Double-space *all* material, including quotations, notes, bibliographies, and legends for illustrations; it is helpful to triple-space between notes and between entries in a bibliography. *Do not single-space anything.* Long quoted passages should be set off from the text by indenting five spaces from the left-hand margin. If there is more than one level of subhead in the text, differentiate clearly between major and subordinate ones. Hyphenating at ends of lines is to be avoided, particularly in foreign words; we do not mind uneven margins.

If changes must be made after the manuscript has been typed, they should be made sparingly and in place, not in the margins. Inserts should be made by cutting and pasting in such a way that the text continues to read consecutively. Do not use staples or shiny tape.

Notes should be numbered consecutively, chapter by chapter. They should be indicated in the text by arabic numerals, unmarked in any way, raised slightly above the line, and outside the punctuation. In the notes themselves the numbers should be placed on the line, with a period, and each note should begin with a paragraph indention. Do not type the notes on the text pages; type them on separate pages, beginning a new page for each chapter, and put them all together at the end of the manuscript.

Preliminary material (front matter) should be included in the following order: title page; dedication, if any; preface; table of contents; and lists of tables, maps, and illustrations, if any. If the preface is long, it should follow the table of contents.

Tables should be typed on pages separate from the text. Notes to tables should be indicated by letters a, b, c, etc., raised slightly above the line; the notes should be typed on the same page as the table to which they refer. The captions to tables should be typed in upper and lower case, not all in capitals.

Style Guidelines

Spelling should follow consistently some recognized standard such as *Webster's Third New International Dictionary.* When there are variant spellings, the first listed is preferred. Possessives are normally formed by adding 's. Exceptions are words of more than one syllable ending in a sibilant, which take only the apostrophe (Curtis').

Abbreviations are to be avoided within the text but they are preferred in the citations.

The usual rules of punctuation are followed, but questions often come up concerning:

(1) Quotations. Use no quotation marks around long quotations set off as extracts. Short quotations are enclosed in double quotation marks; quotations within quotations take single quotation marks. Commas and periods appear inside end quotations, colons and semicolons outside; other punctuation marks appear either inside or outside end quotations depending on the context. Omissions within quotations are indicated by ellipsis marks—three dots with a space before and after.

(2) Dates. The 1780's or the eighties; 1780–1790 for a span of years; January 23, 1935; January 1935.

(3) Numerals. Round numbers and numbers below one hundred are

spelled out except in mathematical discussions or within a series of numbers. Except in indexes, page reference numbers are repeated in full: 444-445; 444-446. Be as specific in citing pages as possible; 76-81 is preferred to 76ff.

(4) Capitalization. When in doubt use lower case. Titles that directly precede the specific person's names are capitalized (Secretary Dillon); usually all others with the exception of President of the United States are lower cased (the secretary of the treasury). In manuscript, small caps (A.D., B.C., A.M., P.M.) are indicated by two underlines.

Titles of books, journals, articles, poems, etc., in English, are capitalized except prepositions, conjunctions, and articles. In French, Italian, and Spanish the first substantive and proper nouns are capitalized. In German all nouns and, in proper names, all adjectives as well are capitalized. Classical Latin titles are lower-cased throughout, except for the first word, proper nouns, and proper adjectives. Transliterated Greek titles may follow the English system. In every case, the first word following a colon in a title is capitalized.

Notes

First references should be complete, subsequent references shortened. If there is no bibliography, it is advisable to repeat the full citation at the first reference in each chapter. Citations should be to a cloth edition, not to a paperback reprint.

Ibid. may be used when it refers to the immediately preceding citation. *Op. cit.* and *loc. cit.* are not acceptable.

When adhered to consistently throughout the manuscript, some definite scheme of abbreviations may be used in the notes for sources repeatedly cited (such as *DNB* for *Dictionary of National Biography*, MA for Massachusetts Archives). In this case a list of abbreviations should be provided.

Sample notes follow.

Books

[1]Margaret Nicholson, *A Manual of Copyright Practice for Writers, Publishers, and Agents*, 2nd ed. (New York Oxford University Press: 1956), pp. 154–157.

[2]*Ibid.*, p. 156.

[3][Matthew Bacon], *A New Abridgment of the Law* (London, 1736–1766), IV, 166.

[4]Nicholson, *Copyright Practice*, p. 145.

[5]François Gilbert de Coston, *Biographie des premières années de Napoléon Bonaparte* (Paris, 1840-1841), II, 347–350.

[6]*Geoffrey Chaucer, The Complete Works,* Fred N. Robinson, ed. (Boston: Houghton Mifflin, 1933). (Hereafter cited as *Works.)*

[7]*Encyclopedia Americana* (New York, 1923), XXV, 187.

[8]Montesquieu, *Spirit of the Laws*, chap. xx.

Articles

[9]George M. Dutcher, "The Rise of Republican Government in the United States," *Political Science Quarterly, 55* (1940), 199–216.

[10]Dutcher, "Republican Government," p. 215.

[11]Kenneth Colegrove, "New England Town Mandates," *Publications of the Colonial Society of Massachusetts,* XXI *(Transactions,* 1919), 411–449.

Documents

[12]U.S. Congress. House, *Certain Illegal Tonnage Duties,* 46th Cong., 2nd sess., H.R. 467 (March 10, 1880), 1–16.

[13]*U.S. Statutes at Large,* XVIII, pt. 1 (1873–1874), 336–337.

[14]*Civil Rights Cases,* 109 U.S. 3 (1883).

[15]*Laws of the State of New York . . . 96th Session* (1873), p. 303.

[16]*Cong. Globe,* 42d Cong., 2nd sess. (1872), 429–434.

[17]*Journal of the Senate,* 43d Cong., 1st sess. (1873), 33.

[18]U.S. Congress. Senate, *Hearings before a Special Committee to Investigate Lobbying Activities,* 74th Cong., 3d sess., pt. 7 (1938), 2139–2148. (Hereafter cited as Lobby Committee, *Hearings.)*

[19]Gerrit Smith, *Equal Rights for Blacks and Whites* (letter to George Downing, March 6, 1874, published as broadside, Peterboro, N.H., 1874).

[20]Sugar Act (4 George III c. 15), sec. 29, in *Statutes at Large,* XXVI, 33 (1764).

Newspaper

[21]*Boston Globe,* March 1–30, 1932.

Manuscripts

[22]Amos Stoddard to W. C. C. Claiborne and J. Wilkinson, March 26, 1804, Stoddard MSS (Missouri Historical Society).

[23]Sheldon Nietz, "The Socio-Economic Advantages of Harvard Square" (Ph.D. diss., Harvard, 1966), p. 1262.

[24]Morgan Library MS. 819, fol. 17.

[25]"Opinions as to Bill before its Introduction" in Pamphlet Box, 1890, George Frisbie Hoar Papers (Massachusetts Historical Society).

[26]Transcript of interview with John Spargo, Oral History Collection, Columbia Univ., pp. 247–249. (Consulted by permission of John Spargo.)

[27]George Otis Smith to Senator Walter E. Edge, May 20, 1921, United States Coal Commission Records, Record Group 68, Drawer 16 (National Archives). (Hereafter cited as USCCR.)

Bibliography

A bibliography is not always necessary. If there is to be a formal list rather than a bibliographical essay, the list should be arranged alphabetically by name of author, unless there is special reason for arranging it chronologically or (rarely) in some other way. The author's name should be given last name first, but if there is more than one author the names after the first should be given in normal order. Anonymous works and public documents should be inserted in the alphabetical list according to the first word of the title other than *A, An,* or *The* or their foreign equivalents, but when one of these words is a part of the title it should not be omitted. The bibliography should be typed with hanging indention, as in the examples given below. Often a bibliographical note on sources is useful.

Book references should include facts of publication in the usual form— place (comma or colon): publisher (comma), date (period). Place names and such terms as "edited," "revised," and "translated"—almost always abbreviated to "ed.," "rev.," and "trans."—should be given in English: "edited," not "herausgegeben," "Turin," not "Torino." It is especially important to include the names of publishers when citing twentieth-century books. It is assumed that, unless there are valid reasons to the contrary, our authors will cite the best scholarly text of the works of a writer discussed, the latest revised edition of a scholarly study, and the standard edition of any work rather than a paperback reprint, which is likely to be unavailable in libraries.

Periodical references should be given by volume number if the journal is paginated consecutively throughout the volume, or by date of issue if it is not. Citation by date alone is especially appropriate for newspapers and periodicals paginated separately by issue. In either case the date—at least the year—must be given. If there is another periodical of the same name, or if the periodical is not widely known, the place of publication should be given: *Nature* (Paris).

A few sample citations follow.

Adams, Henry. *Letters of Henry Adams, 1858–1891,* W. C. Ford, ed. Boston: Houghton Mifflin, 1930.

Copleston, Frederick. *A History of Philosophy.* Vol. II: *Medieval Philosophy: Augustine to Scotus.* Westminster, Md., Newman Press, 1962.

Garraty, John A. "The United States Steel Corporation versus Labor: The Early Years," *Labor History* (New York), I (1960), 3–38.

Haskins, C. H. *Studies in the History of Medieval Science,* 2nd ed. Cambridge, Mass.: Harvard University Press, 1927.

—— and R. H. Lord. *Some Problems of the Peace Conference.* Cambridge, Mass.: Harvard University Press, 1920.

Shackelford, George G. "William Short: Jefferson's Adoptive Son," Ph.D. University of Virginia, 1955.

White, Lynn. "The Byzantinization of Sicily," *American Historical Review,* 42 (1936–1937), 1–21.

Williams, J. C. "Some New Sketches by Rubens," *American Art Bulletin,* October 1937, pp. 45–72.

Permissions and Copyright

Permission must be obtained to quote published material that is still protected by copyright and to quote any unpublished material.

Published material is controlled by the holder of the copyright. Copyright in the United States runs for twenty-eight years from the date of the copyright and may be renewed for another twenty-eight; after fifty-six years, published material copyrighted in the United States is in the public domain. In most other countries, copyright runs for fifty years after the death of the writer.

Permission to quote published material in copyright must be obtained from the holder of the right to publish, who is usually either the publisher or, less frequently, the author. Even when a book is copyrighted in the name of the author, the publisher, by contractual agreement, usually retains the rights to subsequent publication.

Unpublished material is controlled, under common-law copyright, by the writer or his heirs or assigns—that is, people to whom control has passed by the writer's will or by a contract or by common law. Quoting anything from unpublished letters or other writings requires permission from the writer or other holder of the right of publication. It is incumbent on the author to make a reasonable search for the holder of such rights if he is not immediately known or available.

Even when an author is not quoting unpublished material but is merely paraphrasing, or incorporating facts, he should be certain that his use of the material cannot be objected to. Permission to publish the content of manuscripts can be secured at the same time as permission to read them.

Requests for permission to quote copyrighted material are usually addressed to the publisher. Published poetry requires permission if more than one line is quoted. We consider it fair to quote 300 words from any one book without asking permission, so long as full acknowledgment (of author, title, and publisher) is made. Most university presses permit the quotation of up to 1,000 words.

The total number of words quoted from each copyrighted work is not the total of the longest quotation but the total of all quotations from the copyrighted work, even though these quotations are taken from many parts of the work and are scattered throughout one's own book.

In requesting permission to quote, give the title (or tentative title) of your book, state the prospective publisher and date of publication, specify the pages, the approximate number of words or lines, and the opening and closing words of each passage in the book you wish to quote from.

Permissions for illustrations, whether original paintings, drawings, or photographs are also required. Permission must be sought from the holder of publication rights.

Proof Procedure

The publisher will deliver to the author two sets of galley proof along with the original manuscript. The marked proof is the master proof, which when corrected, should be returned with the manuscript by the date specified. The duplicate set is for the author's file. All corrections should be copied onto the duplicate set, in case the master proof is lost in the mail.

A similar procedure is followed with page proof.

Proof—including capitals, italics, and all punctuation—should be read very carefully.

Make corrections clearly in sharp black pencil on the proof only; make no marks on the manuscript. If one letter, or one word, is to be substituted for another, simply draw a line through the letter or word to be removed, and write in the adjacent margin the letter or word that is to replace it—without carets or delete signs. Use a caret within the text only when something is to be inserted at a point where nothing is deleted; use a delete sign in the margin only when nothing is inserted at a point where something is deleted. When several corrections are to be made in one line, put them in sequence from left to right, using both margins if necessary, and separate them with diagonal slashes. If a complicated correction requires a word or two of explanation or clarification, draw a circle around the explanation; do not circle anything that is to be set in type—to the printer the circle means "Do not set this." Be sure all printer's queries are answered. Print your corrections; do not write them in longhand. Clean proof and clear, legible corrections reduce chances of error and, by saving the typesetter's and proofreader's time, help keep down the charges for author's alterations. Label each error that the printer has made and not marked for correction by writing PE (for "printer's error") beside your correction; do not label PE any printer's error resulting from unclear copy.

All changes in proof that are not corrections of printer's errors are classified by the printer as author's alterations. One cannot say precisely how many changes may be made without incurring an author's alterations bill, except that from experience, an average of more than one one-line change per galley usually results in such a bill. Polishing style in proof can cost hundreds of dollars.

Corrections should be made as economically as possible. If you add a word, delete in the same or an adjacent line another word of about the same length. If you delete a word, add another to take its place; otherwise all the rest of the paragraph will probably have to be reset.

Common Proofreader's Marks

To indicate that an addition is to be made within the text, inset a caret (⋏) where the addition is to appear and write the addition in the margin of the same line of type.

⌁	delete	⅋	superior figure[2]
⋏	insert	⅌	inferior figure[3]
x	broken type	⊡	1 em
‖	align vertically	⊞	2 ems
=	align horizontally	/⊢/	1 en dash
[	move to left	/⊥/	1 em dash
]	move to right	/2/	2 em dash
⊓	move up	⊱#	equal space
⊔	move down	wf	wrong font
#	space	.....	let it stand
⁋	paragraph	stet	let it stand
tr	transpose	lc	lower case
⌒	close up	Cap	capital (or CAPS)
⊙	period	sc	small capitals
⁏/	comma	Ital	italics
;/	semicolon	Rom	roman
⊙	colon	bf	bold face
⌄	apostrophe	Sp	spell out
=/	hyphen	Pe	printer's error
❝❞	quotation marks	!	exclamation mark
(/)	parentheses	?	question mark
9	invert	⑦	printer: please verify
⌁	push down		

Indexing

Every historical monograph or larger work when printed should have an index. Most often, it should include subjects as well as names. If a given item is referred to repeatedly and in some detail, sufficient explanatory comment should be inserted to enable the reader to find readily the particular reference he desires. Usually the most satisfactory way to prepare an index is to write each item and page number on an individual slip of paper or card. The index may be begun by working from the duplicate set of galleys, then transferring the galley numbers to page numbers when page proofs are received. The slips may then be alphabetized, edited, and the manuscript of the index typed from them with double-spacing. See B. E. Josephson, "Indexing," *Am. Archivist,* 10 (1947), 133.

1.6 BOOK REVIEWING

The day when he is first asked to write a formal book review marks an epoch in the young scholar's life. If the invitation comes from the *American Historical Review* or from one of the regional historical quarterlies, he regards it as an accolade hardly less important than the Ph.D. How is he to go about it? The following suggestions to reviewers, written by J. Franklin Jameson for the *American Historical Review,* are excellent.

1. Reviews of books are addressed to an audience more special than that of the body-articles, consisting, in the case of each book, of those particularly interested in its special subject. While reviews consisting of minute criticisms are to be deprecated, it is hoped that reviewers will not hesitate to write for the special student rather than for the general reader, with a scientific rather than a literary intention, and with definiteness and precision in both praise and dispraise.

2. It is desired that the review of a book shall be such as will convey to the reader a clear and comprehensive notion of its nature, of its contents, of its merits, of its place in the literature of the subject, and of the amount of its positive contribution to knowledge. The Editors do not favor that type of review which deals with only a part of a book, or makes the book merely a text for a digressive essay. The interests of readers require that the pages headed "Reviews of Books" be filled with reviews in the literal sense; for original contributions, however brief, another place is reserved.

3. It is hoped that the reviewer will take pains, first of all, to apprehend the author's conception of the nature and intent of his book and to criticize it with a due regard to its species and purpose. It should, however, be remembered that the review is intended for the information and assistance of readers, and not for the satisfaction of the author of the book. Sympathy, courtesy, a sense of attachment, readiness to make allowance for a different point of view, should not therefore withhold the reviewer from the straightforward expression of adverse judgment sincerely entertained; otherwise, the *Review* cannot fulfill the important function of upholding a high standard of historical writing.

4. Reviewers are asked to take great pains to be exact in their quotations.

In the third section, the editor places his finger on the chief vice of historical reviewers—softness. Young men fear to pull to pieces the work of an old hand that deserves it, lest they make enemies or be considered too uppish; older men are too kind to deprecate a young historian's maiden effort; colleagues hesitate to speak ill of one another. In consequence, far too many reviews are weakly amiable.

The wise editor will not give a book for review to the author's colleague, teacher, pupil, close friend, or bitter rival. It should always be possible to find an expert in the special field outside these relationships; and anyone so related should decline to review the book. The professional audience wants of a book review a critical appraisal by a man who knows the subject as well as, or better than, the author, and whose opinion will not be distorted by prejudice. Very few professional journals pay reviewers. The copy of the book itself and the consciousness of having performed a service for fellow historians are the reviewer's only rewards.

In order to test an author's accuracy, the reviewer should check some of his references and quotations. Symptomatic inaccuracies or misquotations revealing prejudice should be noticed, and a few examples may be quoted; but a review is no place for a list of errata.

The general scope of the work should be indicated; but no attempt ought to be made to reproduce the table of contents. Quotations may be made as examples of the author's approach or style. The sources that he used should be indicated, important omissions noted, and the conclusions summarized. If a textbook is under review, the amount of space allotted to different periods or branches may well be noted as an indication of the author's set of values. The quality of the maps and index, if any (or absence of them if, as is often the case, they are wanting), should be noted. Remarks about paper, presswork, format, and binding are out of place unless there is something extraordinary about them.

Reviewing in nonprofessional periodicals is a different matter. Every young historian would do well to establish relations with a newspaper in his vicinity that has a book column, and to try his hand with some of the histories and historical biographies that are sent to the editor for review. After filling several columns of newspaper type with his reviews, he may send some of the best of them to the literary editor of a weekly such as *The Saturday Review* or the *New York Times Book Review*. An historian can perform a real service by reviewing for these publications, or for newspapers that are widely read, and he should be paid for doing it.

In reviewing for newspapers, general periodicals, and literary weeklies, many of the *American Historical Review* suggestions do not apply. The main questions that the reader of these journals wants answered are: What is the book about? Can I read it with pleasure or profit? Is it the truth? and Does it upset any of the accepted theories taught us in school or college? Occasionally a new work may give the the reviewer an opportunity to expose a fresh trend or development among professional historians with which the public is not yet acquainted, and thus pave the way for a favorable reception of other works of the new school.

Professional reviewers in general periodicals should expose dishonest, inaccurate, and slipshod work, especially if so charmingly presented as to conceal its shortcomings from the public. But the test of honesty, accuracy, and neatness should be the book itself, and not the author's methods. Young men trained in seminars are apt to overvalue method and underrate achievement; to assume that any book without copious footnotes and a thick bibliography is superficial and, conversely, that any book which makes the right methodological gestures is thorough and sound. A literary artist can sometimes write better and truer history without conventional methods or manuscript sources than historians can do with the most laborious and scientific methods. Praise should be given where praise is due, but puff and gush are out of place in a general, as in a historical, periodical. The reviewer should not hesitate to say, "This is an exceedingly erudite and important work, but addressed to the specialist rather than the general reader"; or, "This biography of so-and-so is inferior to the two earlier books on him, and there was no real reason for publishing it." If the enormous potential market for history among the intelligent American public is to be developed, historians must serve as discriminating guides.

The revised instructions that the *American Historical Review* sends to reviewers include the following remarks: "Keep within the assigned wordage . . . Do not take up valuable space in listing minor errors in substance or typography, unless the quality of the work is materially affected by them; even then, illustrate sparingly. . . The editors of the *AHR* welcome candor and genuine debate, subject to the usual scholarly expectations of clarity, pertinence, and courtesy."

2 Care and Editing of Manuscripts

2.1 HANDLING AND PRESERVATION

A brief résumé of the methods of handling manuscripts may be of use to historical students. Not infrequently, a historical researcher is admitted to some untouched private or public archive, or as secretary of a historical society is presented with a collection which has never been disturbed and which requires a certain amount of processing before historical data can be extracted from it.

Down to the middle of the nineteenth century, letters and other documents were generally preserved in dockets; that is, they were folded up and tied or wrapped in bundles of more or less uniform size. Gradually the modern system of vertical filing evolved, and most private and public archives of recent years will be found in filing cases in the exact order that they were left by a filing clerk. However, the investigator may discover manuscripts all jumbled together in trunks, chests, and bundles, torn, eaten by mice and insects, damaged by mold, dust, or heat. Collections, on the other hand, are generally left in good order by the collector, who paid good money for them.

In the classification and arrangement of archives, two leading principles—one negative and the other positive—should almost invariably be followed. The negative one is: never catalogue or arrange manuscripts as if they were books, that is, alphabetically by author or signer and subject. The positive one is what professional archivists call *respect des fonds,* "the method of classifying archives according to which each document is placed in the collection, and in the series of that collection to which it belonged when that collection was a living organism" (V. H. Paltsits, quoting Dr. S. Muller, Fz. of Utrecht, Am. Hist. Assoc., *Report,* 1912, 260).

In most cases, *respect des fonds* will require that the documents be left in the order in which they were found, just as they were filed by the department, firm, family, or individual to whom they belonged. But if the documents have been hopelessly jumbled, or if the task is to reassemble a dispersed, scattered, and imperfect archive from various sources, it will probably be better to arrange the manuscripts in chronological order. Common sense must determine the decision, of course. A continuous diary, for instance, should not be broken up and filed with letters of the same date; account books and loose accounts may profitably be placed in a separate file from letters.

Manuscripts found in folded dockets should first be opened and laid out flat, and all pins, clips, and rubber bands should be removed. In almost every docket or collection of manuscripts, some will be more or less damaged. Amateur attempts at repair by transparent mending tape or other means should be entered on with great caution. It will be better not to mend a document that is legible. Safe library tapes with gum arabic or neutral glues and transparent gummed muslin may be obtained at library supply houses, but plastic tape sometimes contains chemicals that rot paper. Thousands of manuscripts in the Massachusetts Archives were ruined by members of a WPA project covering them with cellophane tape.

Crumbling or torn manuscripts should be processed either by *silking* or *lamination*. The former, covering documents with a fine gauze called crepeline or Japanese tissue, is practiced in most important libraries and public archives, where advice may be sought for the names of private firms who can do it for individuals. Lamination means covering both sides of the document with a sheet of transparent cellulose acetate foil, or cellulose acetate-butyrate sheeting, and subjecting it to heat and pressure in a hydraulic press. This is the process used at the National Archives. For preservation by lamination, see:

Wilson, W. K., and B. W. Forshee, *Preservation of Documents by Lamination* (1959).
"Symposium on Lamination," *Am. Archivist*, 28 (1965), 285.
Barrow, William J., *Barrow Method of Restoring Deteriorated Documents* (1965).

After the manuscripts have been assembled, they may be filed or preserved in a number of ways. The simplest is merely to lay them in manila folders and to place the folders in cardboard, buckram, or steel filing boxes, properly labeled. Both boxes and documents should be numbered to facilitate reference. But documents that are likely to have much handling, or that are written on modern wood-pulp paper, or that will be used in places where readers cannot be watched by the librarian, may be mounted with transparent linen hinges on sheets of rag paper of uniform size, and numbered. These sheets should then be bound into books. The loose-filing system is used at the New York Public Library, the more expensive bound system at the Library of Congress.

For care and administration of manuscripts, see:

Bahmer, Robert H., *Recent American Developments in Archival Repairs, Preservation, and Photography* (1960).
Barrow, William J., *Manuscripts and Documents: Their Deterioration and Restoration* (1955).
Burnette, O. Lawrence, Jr., *Beneath the Footnote: A Guide to the Use and Preservation of American Historical Sources* (1969).
Kane, Lucille M., *A Guide to the Care and Administration of Manuscripts* (1960).
Langwell, W. H., *The Conservation of Books and Documents* (1957).

The annual bibliography in the *American Archivist* includes articles on manuscript preservation.

2.2 CALENDARING AND INDEXING

A calendar, in diplomatics, is a list of documents in *chronological* order. If the list is in any other order, it is not a calendar but an index or catalogue. The individual researcher, or librarian of a historical society, as he opens up and arranges manuscripts, should make at least a brief calendar of them. As each document is opened, list a few particulars about it on a slip or standard 3″ × 5″ library card, one to each document; the cards can then be arranged in chronological order. Write on the top line of the card, a heading and the date, followed by a brief digest of the contents. You may add a "code" abbreviation such as ALS (autograph letter signed), DS (document signed). For ready reference the card entries, after being arranged chronologically, should be typewritten on 8½″ × 11″ or larger paper, and those sheets bound. It saves researchers time and spares the manuscripts from unnecessary handling to have such a calendar ready for consultation. Any printed volume of documents should have a calendar at the beginning, like a table of contents. Good examples are the Boyd edition of the *Papers of Thomas Jefferson,* and the *Winthrop Papers* published by the Massachusetts Historical Society.

A more extended sort of calendar is common to British and Canadian official publications, such as the *Calendar of State Papers, Colonial and West Indies,* the *Reports* of the Historical Manuscripts Commission, and the *Reports* of the Canadian Archives. In this form of calendar, a digest of each document is printed and the more important and interesting parts are quoted. Thus a large part of the expense of printing the documents in full is saved, yet the meat of them is rendered available to students. As Americans are such inveterate indexers, arrangers, and bibliographers, it seems strange that they have seldom used this cheap but excellent method of presenting the heart of a manuscript collection or archive to the public. Of course the preparation of this sort of calendar requires much more intelligence than the other sort, or even than printing *in extenso.* See:

Gordon, Robert S., "Suggestions for Organization and Description of Archival Holdings of Local Historical Societies," *Am. Archivist,* 26 (1963), 19.
Holmes, Oliver W., "Archival Arrangement—Five Different Operations at Five Different Levels," *Am. Archivist,* 27 (1964), 21.
National Archives, *Control of Records at Record Group Level* (1950).
National Archives, *Principles of Arrangement* (1951).
Radoff, Morris L., "Guide to Practical Calendaring," *Am. Archivist,* 11 (1948), 123.
Wilson, William Jerome, "Manuscript Cataloging," *Tradito,* 12 (1956), 458.

2.3 DATING OF MANUSCRIPTS

In studying, arranging, and calendaring documents, you will find many that are undated. Endeavor to date these either from their position in the collection (provided the order has been undisturbed) or from internal evidence, such as the events and persons that are mentioned or the persons who sign the document. Even an approximate date is better than none. The best book on problems of dating, including tables for regnal years and law terms, is J. J. Bond, *Handy-Book of Rules and Tables for Verifying Dates* (London, 1889).

Unfortunately, the date written on a document is not always conclusive. Letter writers are apt to write the date of the old year by mistake after the first of January. And there is the problem of Old Style and New Style, and of numbered months.

Old Style (commonly abbreviated O.S.) means the Julian Calendar. Pope Gregory XIII decreed New Style (N.S.) or the Gregorian Calendar, by a bull of February 24, 1582. It went into effect in Spain and parts of Italy in the fall of that year, the calendar jumping from October 4 to October 15. France and the Dutch provinces of Holland and Zeeland adopted it before the end of 1582, Catholic Germany in 1584; but there were no more adoptions in countries that are important for early American history until the last decade of the seventeenth century, when Protestant Germany, Switzerland, and the Scandinavian countries went New Style.

England held out until 1752. By act of 24 George II, c. 23, the next day after September 2, 1752, was September 14 in Great Britain and all British colonies. The Russian branch of the Orthodox or Greek Church has not changed to this day; and those countries where the Orthodox was the established church adopted New Style for civil purposes comparatively recently. Bulgaria went New Style on April 1/14, 1916; Russia on February 1/14, 1918; Yugoslavia and Rumania in 1919; Greece on October 1/14, 1923.

A further complication is the date of the New Year. In England from the twelfth century to 1752, and in most other countries using the Julian Calendar, the New Year began on March 25. All dates between January 1 and March 24 inclusive belonged to the old year. About 1670 it began to be customary to hyphenate the old and new years between January 1 and March 24 in some such manner as this:

March 14, 1732/33

3 February 1689–90

January 26, $17\frac{03}{04}$.

March was reckoned the first month of the year, which made February the twelfth. This must be kept in mind, since Puritan and Quaker prejudice against using "pagan" names for months impelled members of those sects to number them, placing the month number second. Here are a few examples:

12. 12. 12 means 12 February 1612/13

7. 1 m° 1654 means 7 March 1654/55

21 iv 72 means 21 June 1672

In American history one often has to translate one calendar into another. Down to 1582 *everyone* was using the Julian Calendar; but in tracing the course of discoverers one often has to know the date by the Gregorian Calendar in order to calculate a phase of the moon or to check data in sea journals. When dealing with international events, or using French, Spanish, or Dutch sources for English colonial history, one must remember that two different calendars are in force to September 3/14, 1752, when the English colonies went New Style, and the Julian Calendar has to be reckoned with in Alaskan history, and in Russo-American and Hellenic-American relations almost to the present day.

When dating documents or events, historians should use the current style of the country or colony with which they are dealing. If they are concerned with two countries (as in an Anglo-Spanish war) they may either reduce all their dates to one style or give double dates consistently. The first method is more difficult, but it is easier for the reader to comprehend.

CONVERSION TABLE

Dates from Julian Calendar (O.S.) into Gregorian Calendar (N.S.)

(All dates are inclusive)

From 1 March $\frac{1399}{1400}$ to 29 February $\frac{1499}{1500}$ add 9 days.

" 1 March $\frac{1499}{1500}$ to 18 February $\frac{1699}{1700}$ add 10 days.

" 19 February $\frac{1699}{1700}$ to 17 February 1800 add 11 days.

" 18 February 1800 to 16 February 1900 add 12 days.

" 17 February 1900 to 28 February 2100 add 13 days.

In the early nineteenth century it was customary for antiquarians to translate all Old Style dates into New Style dates. This made trouble because the pedants were not always bright enough to add the right factor. Thus, although the "Landing of the Pilgrims" at Plymouth took place December 11, 1620, Old Style, when the day began to be celebrated in the eighteenth century, the date December 22 was chosen. It should have been December 21 if changed, but why not celebrate December 11? Persons whose lives spanned the change of style generally added eleven days to their birthdays. Thus Washington, born February 11, 1732, celebrated his birthday on February 22 after 1752.

The rule now is that, unless you have to deal with dates in both styles, leave them as you find them. An exception may be made of the number of the year, before 1752. Either state the year as if January 1 were New Year's Day; or, better, give both years to avoid misunderstanding. Thus, the Charter of Massachusetts Bay is dated "the Fourth Day of March, in the Fourth yeare of Charles I." A contemporary would have called this 4 March 1628. The historian should either call it 4 March 1629; or, if he wishes to leave no room for doubt, 4 March 1628/29. Toward the close of the seventeenth century, English writers began to consider the new year as beginning January 1. Hence, the historian must be careful not to step up the date when it has already been done.

In printing or transcribing a manuscript, *never* step up, alter, or translate a date. Print it exactly as written, explaining it if necessary, in square brackets or a footnote. Thus, if the date is between January 1 and March 24, and the manuscript gives only the old year, the double date or the new year may be added in square brackets thus:

> James Town, 22 February 1618 [1619]
> Salem, 18. 1. 1652 [18 March 1652/53]
> Philadelphia, January 1, 1699 [1700]
> 15 Jany. 1671 [1672]

If the month is numbered the whole date may be repeated in square brackets.

2.4 COPYING OF MANUSCRIPTS

Most repositories of manuscripts provide facilities both for photoduplication and microfilming, and some, for a fee, will make copies for the researcher. Xeroxing is usually best for copying scattered items, while microfilming is often preferable for numbers of documents in sequence.

Microfilm is usually cheaper and has the advantage of taking up very little space, but it necessitates the subsequent use of a reading machine. Sometimes librarians and archivists object to the copying of large, complete collections. Other collections, such as the manuscripts of many presidents, may be obtained in total on microfilm. For problems of photocopying manuscripts and archival holdings, see Walter Rundell, Jr., "To Serve Scholarship," *Am. Archivist,* 30 (1967), 547. For reports on the rapid advances in microfilm technique, see current issues of the *American Archivist.*

The average student using a manuscript collection, and finding only here and there a sentence or passage of interest to him, will prefer to copy what he wants in longhand or on his typewriter, using the same sorts of cards or slips that he employs for all his notes. In copying he should take care to place a heading of his own on each card or slip, and to give an exact reference to the source, together with the date if it does not appear in the matter copied. The transcript should be made literally and exactly, with all abbreviations, contractions, misspellings, and the like, just as in the original. Whatever system may be used in printing manuscripts (and the decision may not rest with the copyist), an exact copy in one's notes is indispensable.

The making of transcripts on a typewriter for another person, or for an institution that is collecting transcripts, presents special problems which have been well stated by G. L. Nute in *Copying Manuscripts: Rules Worked Out by the Minnesota Historical Society* (n.d.). These may be condensed as follows:

In the first place, the standard keyboard of a typewriter owned by anyone who does much copying of manuscripts should be altered by replacing some of the symbols and fractions infrequently used with [ ], §, £, and the straight tilde –. For French, the three accents and the cedilla; for German, the umlaut; and for Spanish, the curved tilde ~ and the reversed question mark are also desirable.

The transcriber should supply for each document:

1. A descriptive heading, such as:
   John C. Calhoun to Henry Clay
   Minutes of Discussions, National Security Board
   Ledger of Jones, Peters & Co.
   Deed of Pecos Ranch from Martin Rodriguez to John Doe

2. The date, if it does not appear at the head of the document.

3. The "code," which includes a reference to the source, and a conventional abbreviation indicating the sort of document it is. The abbreviations most commonly used are:

A.L.S. Autograph Letter Signed (a letter in the writer's own hand, with his signature)

C. Copy (with addition of At. if attested; S. if signed, and Cb. if a carbon copy)

Df. Draft (rough copy of a letter, kept by the writer)

D.S. Document Signed (for any sort of document not a letter that has one or more signatures)

L.P.C. Letterpress Copy (copy on thin paper made in one of the oldfashioned letterpresses)

L.S. Letter Signed (a letter not in the writer's hand, but with his signature)

After the heading and the code, proceed with the body of the document according to the directions for the literal method of printing, as in 2.5.

2.4.1 Deciphering: Elementary Paleography

The first requisite for deciphering manuscripts is a knowledge of the language in which they are written. Unless a student is willing to undergo the preliminary discipline of learning to read a foreign language—or, for that matter, Elizabethan English—he had better keep clear of manuscript sources save those in his own language of the last three centuries.

Once the language is mastered, deciphering is comparatively easy; for there are handbooks of paleography from which one may learn the forms of letters, contractions, and abbreviations used in all the western languages. Once these forms are learned, only practice is needed to make the reading of all but the most illegible manuscripts as easy as print. The following manuals will be useful to students of American history:

Wright, Andrew, *Court-Hand Restored, or The Student's Assistant in Reading Old Deeds, Charters, Records,* 10th ed. Corrected by C. T. Martin. (London, 1912.) Excellent for Latin and English medieval documents, with numerous examples, tables of contractions and diacritical marks, Latin glossary, and alphabets, sufficient to carry the student through the seventeenth century.

Jenkinson, Hilary, *The Later Court Hands in England, from the Fifteenth to the Seventeenth Century* (Cambridge, Eng., 1927). Accompanied by a portfolio of 44 plates. The various alphabets and examples in this comprehensive work supply all forms of letters found in English manuscripts relating to, or emanating from, the colonies in the sixteenth and seventeenth centuries.

Bolton, C. K., "Colonial Handwriting," *Essex Antiquarian,* I (1897), 175. Reproduces the alphabets used in early New England, Virginia, and Maryland. Most of the letters are given in the facsimiles in 2.5.

Prou, Maurice, *Manuel de paléographie latine et française,* 4th ed. (Paris, 1924). Accompanied by a portfolio of 24 plates, and the best for French and Papal documents.

Muñoz y Rivero, Jesús, *Manual de paleografía diplomática española de los siglos xvi al xvii,* 2nd ed. (Madrid, 1917). Agustín Millares Carlo, *Tratado de paleografía española,* 2nd ed. (Madrid, 1932). These volumes are the best for Spanish and Portuguese documents.

For the identification of handwriting, see Mary A. Benjamin, *Autographs* (1963).

2.5 EDITING AND PRINTING

Many historical students will confront the problem of preparing manuscripts for printing. An older guide that is still valuable is R. L. Poole et al., "Report on Editing Historical Documents," University of London, Institute of Hist. Research, *Bull.,* 1 (1923), 6. For a more modern discussion of the problem see the following articles and book by four eminent historical editors:

Butterfield, Lyman H., and Julian P. Boyd, "Historical Editing in the United States," Amer. Antiq. Soc. *Proc.,* 72 (1962), 283.

Butterfield, Lyman H., "Editing American Historical Documents," Mass. Hist. Soc. *Proc.,* 78 (1966), 81.

Cappon, Lester J., "The Historian as Editor," in William B. Hesseltine and Donald H. McNeil, eds., *In Support of Clio* (1958).

——— "Rationale for Historical Editing, Past and Present," *WMQ,* 23 (1966), 56.

Carter, Clarence E., *Historical Editing* (1952).

The following pages are an attempt to set forth general principles of editing American documents. But no set of rules can cover every case, and each editor will have to use a certain flexibility and much common sense. The one rule always to be observed is that of consistency. State a method in the preface or preliminary note, and abide by it.

Difficulties arise from the fact that a longhand manuscript cannot be reproduced exactly by a printing process. Before the invention of printing and for three centuries thereafter, writers used a large number of abbreviations, signs, and contractions. Renaissance printers cast type to represent these characters in the attempt to make their books resemble manuscripts. *Bibliotheca Americana: Catalogue of the John Carter Brown Library* employs over a hundred specially cast characters and diacritical signs in order to reproduce early book titles exactly, and the editors of the *Rolls Series* of English medieval documents were almost as lavish.

Earlier American editors such as Peter Force and Jared Sparks took excessive liberties in printing manuscripts. They cared little for consistency and even attempted to improve the text. As a reaction from these practices, later editors resorted to meticulous accuracy. In official publications for which expense was no object, such as Shurtleff, *Records of the Governor and Company of the Massachusetts Bay,* the manuscript text was followed as closely as type allowed, and some thirty characters were cast to represent seventeenth-century forms of the ampersand, crossed *b's, d's, h's, l's,* three differently tailed *p's,* tailed *c's, m's, n's,* and *q's. U's* and *v's* were printed as written, and canceled type was used for erased words. This sort of reproduction is proper for very important documents such as charters, or drafts of the Declaration of Independence. It is very well for de luxe printing, but far too expensive for the ordinary publication.

The methods by which manuscripts of American history are usually printed today may be reduced to three: the *literal,* the *expanded,* and the *modernized.* In addition there is one that we might call the *garbled* or *bowdlerized,* which should be avoided.

Directions That Apply To All Three Methods

1. Supply a heading (2.4) and print it in a different type from the text. State the source of every document unless it is one of a collection in the same repository, which may be explained in the preface. The provenance should be printed right under the heading, or given as a footnote to the heading, together with a reference to any earlier printing of the document. Code letters such as A.L.S. are generally of no interest to readers, and may be omitted when printing.

2. The address of a letter should be printed either in *italics* under the heading, or at the end. The date line, even if found at the end in the original, may be printed at the head, so long as the practice is consistent. Anything significant in the endorsements—and they often are the only clue to the identity of the writer—may be printed at the end with the word [*Endorsed*] preceding them. The salutation ("MY DEAR SMITH," or "WORSHIPFUL SIR") should be in SMALL CAPITALS.

3. All matter interpolated in the text by the editor should be printed in *italics* and enclosed in square brackets. Thus [*torn*], [*blotted*], [*illeg.*] take the places of a word or words lost by mutilation, defacement, or illegibility. Another means of dealing with illegibility is to insert within square brackets approximately as many asterisks or short dashes as there are illegible letters. If a lost word can be inferred with reasonable certainty

from the context, it should be printed in Roman type within square brackets; the same should be done with part of a long word, but if only one to four letters are missing, brackets are unnecessary and pedantic. A mere conjecture, as distinct from a certain inference, can be followed by the question mark and placed within square brackets. Thus, if the edge of a Civil War letter is torn, leaving at the end two words "Stonewall Jack", the editor should print "Stonewall Jackson" because it could be nothing else. But, if a letter of 1788 says, "I do not share your opinion of the Con [*blotted*]," the editor had better print "Con[stitution ?]" because it might be "Congress" or "Convention." If the greater part of any edge or a large corner is torn off, print what exists, line for line, leaving the torn part blank. Very doubtful or alternate readings had better be placed in a footnote.

4. Every omission made by the editor within a sentence should be indicated by suspension points, thus, . . . , preserving the punctuation, if any, that occurs before the omission. If a whole paragraph or a line or more of poetry is omitted, insert a line of points or of asterisks.

5. Place in square brackets the number of each new page of a long manuscript at the point where it begins, in order to facilitate comparison with the original. Place [*sic*] after a very strange spelling or mistake of the original writer, which the reader might suppose to be a printer's error; but use *sic* sparingly; it is a tiresome interpolation. One may correct, without notice, obvious slips of the writer's pen such as "an an hour ago."

6. Blank spaces in the manuscript, where the writer intended to insert a word and did not, should be represented by a blank space in the printed text, or by "[*blank*]."

7. Interlineations are to be brought down into the line of text at the place indicated by the writer; canceled passages are omitted unless they contain something of particular interest, when they may be inserted in a footnote. In court and similar records, where marginal glosses have been written in by the clerk for his convenience in reference, these may either be omitted, or used as subheadings to save expense.

8. All words underlined should be printed in *italics;* words underlined twice in SMALL CAPITALS. Words strongly emphasized by being written in larger letters than the rest may be printed in LARGE CAPITALS or boldface type. Signatures may be printed in LARGE AND SMALL CAPITALS, if desired. The initial *ff,* which is only an old form of the capital F, should be printed F. The long-tailed *s* (ſ) should be represented by the modern lower-case *s,* never by *f.*

9. In reprinting a document it is better to prepare a fresh text from the manuscript or photostat; for if an earlier printed edition is used as the basis, one is apt to repeat some of the former editor's errors, or maybe add others of one's own.

Special Directions for the Literal Method

1. Follow the manuscript absolutely in spelling, capitalization, and punctuation. Exceptions: in very illiterate manuscripts, where little or no punctuation is used, a minimum necessary to understand the text may be supplied; and in documents where the writer begins practically every word with a capital, the editor may use his discretion. In either case, the practice followed should be stated in a preliminary note.

2. Superior letters are printed as such, in smaller point; for instance, y^e, Capt, Co^{r}t. But the period or colon usually found under superior letters may be omitted.

3. The tilde should be reproduced either as a straight or curved line, according to the text, over the letter or letters where it occurs.

4. All contractions and abbreviations should be printed exactly as written *within the limitations of available type.* If a supply of differently tailed *p's* is to be had, they should be used; but it is better to expand tailed *p's* into *per-, pro-,* and *pre-,* than to use a single type of tailed *p* to represent two or three different ones.

5. Remember that every diacritical mark (commonly called "wiggle") represented, in the scribe's mind, one or more letters. If the limitations of type forbid the use of these marks, the omitted letters *must* be supplied by the editor. For instance:

> *acs* should be printed *acres*, not *acs*;
> *lre* should be printed *lettre*, not *lre* or *letter*;
> *mann* should be printed *manner*, not *mann*

Manuscript abbreviations for *-es, -us, -que* and the like should be spelled out. There is no need for special type to represent obsolete forms of the ampersand or of individual letters.

On the other hand, the writer's use of *u* and *v, i* and *j* should be followed through all vagaries. In the seventeenth century it was usual to begin a word with a *v,* but to place *u* in the middle, no matter whether *u* or *v* was meant. Thus: *vse, riuer.* The same character was commonly used for capital I and capital J. Small *i* was often used for *j* ("whom God hath ioyned"). Follow all this exactly. A long-tailed *i,* which may be represented in print by *j,* is often used for the final *i* on a Roman numeral ending with 7 or 8, such as xxviij. Follow this usage if you wish; but as this apparent *j* is really an *i,* it may, consistent with this method, be printed *i.* Some scribes used the long-tailed *i* almost exclusively; in that case, print it *i,* just as you represent the long-tailed *s* (ſ) by *s.*

Special Directions for the Expanded Method

A very good set of directions for this method is set forth by Boyd, in his edition of *The Papers of Thomas Jefferson,* I, xxv. These differ in certain particulars, noted below, from the practice preferred by the editors of the *Harvard Guide.*

1. Follow the spelling, capitalization, and punctuation as in 1; but always capitalize the first word and put a period at the end of the sentence no matter what the writer does.

2. In general, spell out all abbreviations except those still used today (like *Mr., U.S., H.M.S.*), and those of months, proper names, and titles (*Dec., Tho:, Jno:, Fr., H.E.,* for examples). A reason for *not* expanding such abbreviations is the doubt of their meaning. *Fr.* may mean Francis or Frances; *Jno.,* John or Jonathan; *H.E.,* may stand for His Excellency or His Eminence. Almost every other type of manuscript abbreviation should be expanded as follows:

a. Expand all *th* abbreviations such as *y^e, y^t, y^m, y^n,* to *the, that, them,* *then.* For this apparent *y* is really a debased form of the early English letter *þ* (thorn).

b. Bring superior letters down to the line of text. In so doing, supply the letter or letters omitted in the manuscript, *provided they are in the middle of the word,* but not otherwise. Thus, *w^{ch}, Co^{r}t, Mo^{th}* are printed: which, Court, Month; but *Capt, m^{o}, s^{h}* are printed: *Capt., mo., sh.* If the abbreviation is still obscure after superior letters are brought down and a point added, the additional letters may be supplied in square brackets; e.g., *m^{o}* might be rendered *mo[nth]* if desired; *y^{r} w^{or}* as *Your wor[ship].* Note that *y^{r}* may mean either your or their; *y^{ow}* is an eccentric form for *you* and may be so printed.

c. The tilde, except in Spanish words, is replaced by the letter or letters it represents. *Ham̃ond,* print *Hammond; ac̃con,* print *accion* or action; it is often uncertain whether *c̃* means *ci* or *ti.*

d. Tailed *p's* are expanded and all diacritical marks rendered by the corresponding letters, as under the Literal Method. Boyd, however, retains the contraction *ⱹ* for *per-, pre-,* and *pro-.*

e. The ampersand in all its forms is printed *and;* and *&c* becomes *etc.* whether the writer uses the full stop or not. Exception: preserve the ampersand in names of firms and companies, as Texas & Pacific R. R., A. Brown & Co.

3. Standardize monetary and weight and measure abbreviations. Thus, "25^{li} 7^{s} 3^{d}" may be rendered "25*li* 7*s* 3*d*" or "£25 7*s* 3*d*." Points after monetary abbreviations are superfluous. Odd crossed capital L's should all be printed £; odd dollar signs in the early days of the republic should all be printed $, but need not necessarily be placed before the sum. The sign ⧣ in French documents, which means *livres tournois,* should be printed *l.t.* Similarly, decide what abbreviations you will use for pounds, grams, millimeters, and yards, and be consistent. But Boyd retains all monetary, weight, and measure designations as written.

4. As regards *u* and *v, i* and *j,* there are two schools of thought. The first, which is preferable, points out that the *v* in *vp,* for instance, is not really a *v,* but an optional form of *u;* and the *u* in *liue* is really a kind of *v.* Consequently modern forms should be used if the expanded method is to be followed. The other school insists that these letters should be printed exactly as they are, on the principle of respecting spelling.

5. Certain editors always begin a proper name with a capital, and even standardize the spelling of them to help identification. This practice is undesirable. An apparently erratic spelling of a proper name may be a clue to its pronunciation; and "Roger cook" in an early document may mean a cook whose given name is *Roger,* not Roger Cook.

6. Some editors begin every new sentence with a capital letter, even if the writer does not. This is unobjectionable if it is clear where the writer intended a new sentence to begin; but often it is not clear. Punctuation in all manuscripts before the nineteenth century is highly irregular; and if you once start replacing dashes by commas, semicolons, or periods, as the sense may seem to warrant, you are asking for trouble. Note the example from one of Washington's letters, below.

The Modernized Method

This method may properly be used in an English translation from another language, or to make an early document, chronicle, or narrative intelligible to the average reader who is put off by obsolete spelling and erratic punctuation. The texts of recent editions of Shakespeare, Dryden, and the King James Bible have been established by this method.

1. Modernize the spelling, capitalization, and punctuation, but pay scrupulous respect to the language; do not attempt to improve the writer's grammar, syntax, or choice of words, or you will be called a bowdlerizer. Where the original writer has obviously omitted a word like *not*, or, for instance, has written *east* when you know he means *west*, the editor may add or correct a word; but he should place it within square brackets. Paragraphs and sentences that are too long may be broken up.

2. Expand all abbreviations as in the Expanded Method above, excepting only such as are in common use today.

3. In translations, the translator should endeavor to use such words and phrases as will best convey the meaning of the original, and not aim at literary elegance.

Illustrations

We shall now give facsimiles of a few examples of the different methods and comment upon them.

A Passage from William Bradford, *Plimmoth Plantation*

1. Part of fol. 53 of the original manuscript.

2. Same passage as printed in the Commonwealth of Massachusetts edition (Boston, 1897), 107, supposedly by the Literal Method but not altogether consistent. Note following:

a. Line 1: The paragraphing is correct, as the previous line stopped before the margin. Writers did not commonly indent paragraphs until the eighteenth century. The centered periods around "15" and other arabic numerals should have been printed as written, as in (3). The italics are unnecessary for the underlined words because inspection of the manuscript shows that the underlining was not done by Bradford but by a later reader. The colon after *Desem*[r] is unnecessary, and misplaced.

b. Lines 2 and 3: *u* and *v* are modernized, while superior letters are retained.

c. Line 8: the tilde is over the wrong letter, and the comma after *them* is omitted.

3. Same passage as printed in Massachusetts Historical Society edition (Boston, 1912), I, 177, ed. by W. C. Ford. A modified but not consistent Expanded Method.

Line 1: The square brackets in the month might have been, and the colon should have been, omitted. Use of italics more consistent than in 1 but unnecessary, as explained above.

4. Same passage as printed in Morison edition (N.Y., 1952), 72. Modernized Method. All spellings are corrected, and abbreviations spelled out.

a. Line 1: *th* added to *15*.

b. Line 4: *afterwards* made one word.

c. Line 6: position of comma altered.

5. The following is a sample of the garbled or bowdlerized method, the same quotation "Rendered into Modern English" by Harold Paget (1920), 73:

". . . came within two leagues of it, but had to bear up again. On the 16th day the wind came fair, and they arrived safe in the harbour. Afterwards they took a better view of the place, . . ."

William Bradford, Plimmoth Plantation

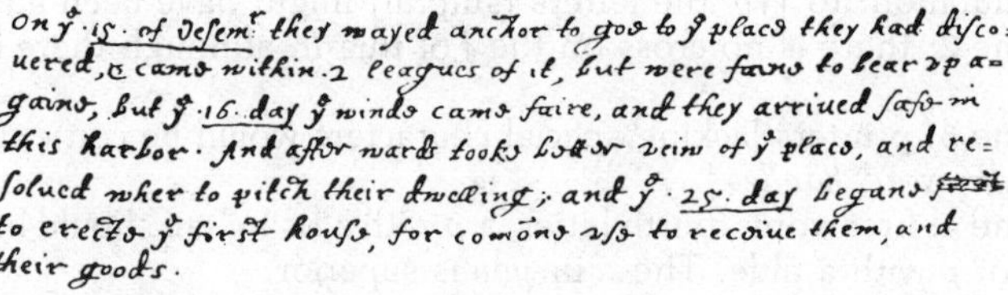

[handwritten manuscript facsimile]

Bradford Ms., p. 53

On yᵉ 15. *of Desem*ʳ*:* they wayed anchor to goe to yᵉ place they had discovered, & came within 2. leagues of it, but were faine to bear up againe; but yᵉ 16. *day* yᵉ winde came faire, and they arrived safe in this harbor. And after wards tooke better view of yᵉ place, and resolved wher to pitch their dwelling; and yᵉ 25. *day* begane to erecte yᵉ first house for com͞one use to receive them and their goods.

Bradford, Commonwealth ed., p. 107

On the ·*15*· *of Desem[be]r:*[3] they wayed anchor to goe to the place they had discovered, and came within ·*2*· leagues of it, but were faine to bear up againe; but the ·*16*· *day* the winde came faire, and they arrived safe in this harbor.[4] And after wards tooke better view of the place, and resolved wher to pitch their dwelling; and the ·*25*· *day*[5] begane to erecte the first house for commone use to receive them and their goods.[6]

Bradford, Ford ed., I, 177

On the 15th of December they weighed anchor to go to the place they had discovered, and came within two leagues of it, but were fain to bear up again; but the 16th day, the wind came fair, and they arrived safe in this harbor. And afterwards took better view of the place, and resolved where to pitch their dwelling; and the 25th day began to erect the first house for common use to receive them and their goods.

Bradford, S. E. Morison ed., p. 72

Abraham Piersey to Sir Edwin Sandys, May 24, 1621
1. The original, in the Ferrar Mss., Magdalene College, Cambridge.

2. A very fine example of the Literal Method, with special type, as printed in S. M. Kingsbury, ed., *Records of the Virginia Company* (§ 46), III, 454. But note following:

a. Salutation: to *Wo*ʳ the letters [shipful] might have been added.

b. Line 2: there is no cross on the *l* of this *lr*, although there is on the next.

c. Line 3: printers lacking special characters would be content to print the fourth word *handes*.

d. Line 4: first word, fourth letter, a *p* with a rising tail should have been used, not *p* with a tilde. The *u* in *you* is superior.

3. A good example of garbling, from *Va. Mag. of Hist*, X (1902–03), 418. The editor uses a long dash for words he cannot decipher, misreads others, spells some in the modern way but leaves others as is.

Abraham Peirsey to Sir Edwin Sandys, May 24, 1621

Ferrar Papers, Magdalene College, Cambridge—List of Recs., No. 248

Right Woʳ
my last was by the Tryall of London not doubting my lr is saffly Come to yoʳ handɛ, & haue nowe sent In the Generall lr to the Compᵽ A Coppye of the Accompt of the bussnes wᶜʰ you desyred of mee wᵗʰ A Retorne of the fishing voyag by the George to new found land, Invested In good Tobacco. & for othʳ bussnes I haue there in Refferrd my selfe to the Generall lr beeing sorrye the Country is not pvyded of any

Records of Virginia Company, III, 454

Right Woʳ :
My last was by the Tryall of London not doubting my lʳᵉ is saffly come to yoʳ hands, & have yours but in the General lʳᵉ to the Compˢ a coppye of the Accompᵗ of the business—which you desired of me wᵗʰ a —— of the fishing voyage by the George to new foundland —— in good Tobaccoe for the business I have therein proffered my self to the Generall lʳᵉ beeing sorry the

Virginia Magazine of History and Biography, X (1902–03), 418

George Washington to Joseph Reed, Middlebrook, March 28, 1779

An autograph draft of a letter by George Washington, a more modern example, is the sort of document with which American historians generally deal, and offers few difficulties.

1. Original, in Library of Congress.
2. Printed version in W. C. Ford, *Writings of Washington* (N.Y., 1890), VII, 386, which follows no particular method. Note following:
   a. Lines 1 and 6: No good reason for replacing the dashes by commas and a period.
   b. Line 2: the spelling of *enterprize* has been corrected.
   c. Line 3: since this editor always prints *&* as *and*, it would be consistent to expand *wch* to *which*; and the semicolon after *up* has been replaced by a comma. *People* should have a capital *P*.
   d. Line 4: *may*, underlined by Washington, should have been printed in italics.
   e. Line 5: a comma has been omitted.
3. Printed version in J. C. Fitzpatrick, *Writings of George Washington*, XIV, 307 (§ 55). Good example of Expanded Method.
   a. Lines 1 and 2: the same inconsistency between treatment of *&* and *wch* as in 2c.
   b. Line 5: Washington's dash has been replaced by a semicolon, as this editor thinks he did not intend to end a sentence there.

Jared Sparks, the first to print this letter, in his *Writings of George Washington* (Boston, 1834), VI, 209, improved the General's English by expanding "for wch" to "concerning which," and changing "the fears . . . are up" to "the fears . . . are awake." He doubtless thought "for" was the wrong preposition and that "up" was vulgar.

George Washington to Joseph Reed, Middlebrook, 28 March 1779

George Washington Mss., Library of Congress

preparations have been too long making, too formidable, and too open, for any enterprise against New London, for wch. place the fears of the people are up, and, as we cannot tell where it may fall, we should, as far as human prudence and the means in our hands will enable us, be guarded at all points.   The

Writings of George Washington (W. C. Ford, ed., 1890), VII (1778–79), 386

long making, too formidable, and too open for any enterprize against New London for wch place the fears of the People are up; and as we cannot tell where it *may* fall, we should, as far as human prudence, and the means in our hands will enable us, be guarded at all points; the sole purpose therefore of this

Writings of Washington (Fitzpatrick, ed., 1936), 307

Choice of Method

Whether the Literal, Expanded, or Modernized Method should be used depends partly on the kind of document in question, but mainly on practical considerations, especially on the purpose of the publication. In printing English, Spanish, or French documents of the sixteenth and seventeenth centuries that are full of contractions or abbreviations, and where expense is no object, the Literal Method is preferable in a publication destined for scholarly readers only. The Expanded Method is much easier to read and cheaper to print, since monotype and linotype operators find it difficult to deal with superior letters, diacritical marks, or special symbols. The young student will be put off by texts such as A2, B2, and B3 above, but he can read A3 and A4 readily enough. For the student A3 is better than A4 because the wording, spelling, and punctuation of the original give it a certain flavor. For a translation, or for a new edition of some classic such as the Virginia "Lament for Mr. Nathaniel Bacon," or the poetry of Edward Taylor, the Modernized Method is best. It is particularly unfortunate to print y^e as ye since the general reader will imagine that it is to be read and pronounced as ye instead of as *the*.

For extracts and quotations from documents incorporated in a secondary work, the Expanded Method is far preferable to the literal, since the latter clashes unnecessarily with a modern text and makes readers pause to puzzle over odd spellings and abbreviations. Historians are apt to be careless and inconsistent about this. Nor is it good style to interpolate an explanation within a quotation as in the following example, where the abbreviation for *Christian* should either have been spelled out or explained in a footnote:

. . . and peculiarly need the Candour of my Xtn. [= Christian] friends (W. C. Bronson, *History of Brown University* [Providence, 1914], 92).

Every printed document or quotation from a document should be compared word for word with the original, or with a microfilm or photographic copy. And whoever prints historical documents might well make his motto:

Accuracy without Pedantry.
Consistency first, last, and always.

3 Materials of History

3.1 HISTORICAL COLLECTIONS

Not until the last quarter of the nineteenth century did libraries accept as a part of their responsibilities the task of assembling the books and manuscripts essential to historical research. Then the example of the English universities and, even more, of such German universities as Göttingen stirred up a feverish activity in the United States that produced an impressive array of great storehouses of learning. Progress since the 1870's has been rapid; numerous libraries now devote themselves to furnishing students with the services necessary for study and research.

History—and particularly American history—has always been a prominent interest of libraries in this country. The largest ones are also the richest in their holdings of works on American history. Furthermore, scores of smaller ones contain valuable collections in many special fields.

The Library of Congress is the greatest research library in the United States. Established in 1800, it suffered from fires in 1814, in 1825, and in 1851, and did not play an important role until the end of the century. In 1870 it acquired the right to copies of every book copyrighted in the United States. Its period of great growth began in 1899 when Herbert Putnam became librarian. It contains approximately fifteen million books as well as pamphlets, bound newspapers, microfilms, manuscripts, motion picture reels, and phonograph records. Among its notable collections are over three million maps and atlases, files of state and federal documents, photographs, plans of early American buildings, and the manuscripts of many of the Presidents and other public figures. It also has extensive series of reproductions of materials on American history in European libraries and archives. See chapter 6.

The Harvard College Library, second in size of its research collection, was established in 1638, two years after the founding of the university. It is thus the oldest library in the United States and only a little younger than the Bodleian in England. All but about four hundred of the five thousand volumes in the old Harvard library were destroyed by fire in 1764. Reestablished, the library grew slowly thereafter. It now possesses over 8,000,000 books and pamphlets and is especially rich in the general literature of American history. Its collection of maps, charts, and newspapers started with the acquisition of the library of the German scholar Ebeling, who died in 1817, and it has been added to steadily since. Its manuscript resources include the papers of prominent alumni such as Charles Sumner and materials gathered by scholars including Jared

Sparks. In addition to the main collection there are important special libraries, including the unparalleled Langdell Library of the Law School with over 1,000,000 volumes, and the Baker Library of business and economics with 450,000 volumes. The Jordan collection on the English-speaking theater is one of the world's largest. At Radcliffe College is The Arthur and Elizabeth Schlesinger Library on the History of Women in America, outstanding in its manuscript holdings.

The New York Public Library, organized in 1895, quickly assembled a splendid collection strong in American history. The library has a reference catalogue outstanding in the extent to which subjects are indexed. Among its more important holdings of books and manuscripts dealing with American history are the Lenox, Bancroft, Ford, Emmett, and Myers collections. It has some 124,000 prints, many relevant to American history, and large newspaper, map, and music sections strong in Americana. Among other notable holdings are the Robinson genealogy collection, the business records of many New York City firms, the Gompers labor collection, the Henry George collection, the Berg collection of American literature, the Arents collection on tobacco, and the Schomburg collection of Negro literature and history. The total number of volumes in the library is approaching 8,000,000.

Total size of holdings, of course, is not the sole determinant in a library's usefulness to the historian. Many smaller libraries have large holdings in general American history or in some aspects of it.

Historical societies have always regarded the maintenance of libraries as their most important function. Many now possess outstanding accumulations of material for American history. See American Association for State and Local History, *Directory of Historical Societies and Agencies in the United States and Canada* (1956–   ) and Walter Muir Whitehill, *Independent Historical Societies* (1962).

The Massachusetts Historical Society, founded in Boston in 1791, specializes in the history of Massachusetts and early New England and houses the most important collection of American manuscripts outside the Library of Congress. It holds the Dowse and Waterston libraries, many colonial newspapers, Civil War materials, valuable American portraits, coins, and maps, as well as important groups of manuscripts, including the Adams, Winthrop, Pickering, and Parkman collections, and Jefferson's private papers. The New York Historical Society has an excellent collection of Americana. The Historical Society of Pennsylvania in Philadelphia has over 4,000,000 items of Americana, including collections of colonial laws, Pennsylvania newspapers, of French Americana, and of pamphlets and manuscripts on the formation and adoption of the American Constitution. The American Antiquarian Society at Worcester, Massachusetts, has the largest collection of American newspapers printed before 1820 and the best collection of American state, county, and local histories. The American Philosophical Society in Philadelphia holds significant collections on the history of science in America as well as on the American Revolution. The State Historical Society of Wisconsin includes a collection on socialism and the labor movement, together with the Thwaites and Draper collection of Americana. Many other societies have more specialized collections. The Essex Institute at Salem has concentrated on the records of New England settlement and seafaring, the McCormick Historical Association (Chi.) on agriculture, the American Geographical Society (N.Y.) on maps and atlases, the Minnesota Historical Society (St. Paul) on the Scandinavians in the United States, the New England Historic Genealogical Society (Boston) on family records and printed genealogies, and the others generally on the districts in which they are situated.

All the great universities possess collections on American history for research purposes. Many have focused on special fields. The William L. Clements Library of the University of Michigan holds a striking collection of materials on colonial and Revolutionary history. Yale University has the magnificent W. R. Coe collection of western Americana, as well as notable sections on the history of religion and on the World War and the peace conference (1914–19). The Columbia University Library is strong in law, politics, government, and the history of education, and thanks to the oral-history project, possesses a series of recorded interviews with prominent Americans. Among the important research holdings of the Princeton University Library are the Grenville Kane Early Americana, the Rollins Western Americana, the Pierson Civil War, and the Woodrow Wilson, collections. The University of Pennsylvania Library holds the Curtis collection of Franklin imprints, the Carey collection on early economic history, and the Biddle Law library. The University of Chicago Library owns large collections on the Civil War. The University of North Carolina and the University of Virginia are rich in Southern History. Duke University Library has a noteworthy accumulation of material on the history of the South and also the archives of the Socialist Party of America. Stanford University possesses good files of colonial and early American newspapers as well as the Hoover Library on War, Revolution, and Peace. At the University of California is the Hubert Howe Bancroft Collection of original Western materials. Other university libraries, such as those of Cornell, California, Texas, and Louisiana, emphasize the history of their own regions. The Catholic University of America, Georgetown University, and the University of Notre Dame are the best on the history of Catholicism, while Haverford College has a fine collection on the history of the Quakers. Other special holdings include those of Brown University on Lincoln and of The Johns Hopkins on slavery, trade unions, and medicine.

The Center for Research Libraries is an organization operated and maintained by its member institutions, including a number of universities throughout the United States, for the purpose of increasing the library materials available to their readers for research. Any material owned by the Center can be borrowed by a member library for research use by its readers on the same basis as if it were the library's own material. The Center has over sixty members and associate members and a collection of nearly three million volumes of material. It is strong in microprints and microfilms of early American books, pamphlets and broadsides, American fiction, and a selection of American popular magazines and comic books published since 1952. Its newspaper holdings comprise two thousand titles, including about one hundred American papers of general circulation, three hundred foreign language papers, and twenty published primarily for blacks.

Some of the private libraries still serve a significant function. The Boston Athenaeum (1807) is strong in the entire field of Americana, has the bulk of George Washington's private library and a remarkable collection of Confederate imprints. The John Carter Brown Library (Providence) has the best collection of European imprints on the discovery and exploration of the Western Hemisphere. The Library Company of Philadelphia is strong in materials on the Revolutionary period, on internal improvements, and on the westward movement. The John Crerar Library in Chicago owns collections on American labor, on social and economic subjects, and on science and technology. The Newberry Library in Chicago has books, maps, and manuscripts emphasizing the era of discovery, American Revolution, slavery, the Civil War, Indians, the cultural history of the Middle West, and railroad developments. The Henry E. Huntington Library at San Marino, California, has a splendid collection on the history of literature, on the seventeenth and eighteenth century in England and America, and on California.

Though the public libraries have focused their energies on serving the general public rather than scholars, many of the larger ones have valuable historical collections. The Boston Public Library, for example, has a fine statistical collection, a strong section on patent history, the John Adams and Prince libraries, and an extensive holding of general Americana. The Detroit Public Library possesses the Burton collections on the history of the old Northwest and the westward movement. Other public and state libraries have holdings equally valuable for the historian, but they are too numerous to list here. Information on these is included in the biennial *American Library Directory*, arranged geographically, giving for each library number of volumes, microfilming facilities, and subject strengths. Directories of local and state libraries such as *Directory of Libraries and Informational Services in Philadelphia and Vicinity* (11th ed., 1964) and *Library and Reference Facilities in the Area of the District of Columbia* (7th ed., 1966) provide supplemental data.

Many specialized libraries possess unique collections, such as the National Library of Medicine in Bethesda, Maryland, which has the greatest store of books in the world on the history of medicine and public health. The most comprehensive guide to these distinctive collections, limited by subject and function, is Anthony T. Kruzas, ed., *Directory of Special Libraries and Information Centers* (2nd ed., 1968). It provides a subject index to the alphabetical listings of libraries ranging from departmental collections and professional libraries of universities to government libraries and those of industrial firms. There are also guides to the resources of individual states and regions, such as Robert B. Downs, ed., *Resources of Missouri Libraries* (1966), and his *Resources of Southern Libraries* (1938). See also the directories of the regional Special Libraries Association.

The research student should not forget the materials in the great libraries of other countries; guides to their resources are listed in chapter six. In addition, the Farmington Plan has made many foreign research materials available in American libraries by the allocation of acquisition responsibility. Information and listings are in Edwin E. Williams, *Farmington Plan Handbook* (1961), supplemented by the *Farmington Plan Newsletter*.

Lee Ash and Denis Lorenz's *Subject Collections* (3d ed., 1967) is a guide to special book collections with subject emphasis as reported by university, college, public, and special libraries. A guide to the library resources of individual states and regions is Robert B. Downs, *American Library Resources: A Bibliographical Guide* (1951), *Supplement 1950–1961* (1962). Printed catalogs of many important library collections are available, as are individual library histories which include discussions of their holdings.

Through the volumes of the *National Union Catalog, Pre-1956 Imprints* (Mansell) and the *National Union Catalog, 1958–* , a research student may locate copies of books not available in his own library. He can often borrow them on interlibrary loan or obtain micro-reproductions of them. The scholar should check these alternatives before traveling long distances. See also Jesse H. Shera, *Historians, Books, and Libraries* (1953) and Clifford L. Lord, ed., *Keepers of the Past* (1965).

3.2 STATISTICAL SOURCES

The accumulation and the analysis of statistics developed in the early modern period out of the desire of legislators and administrators for information to help them deal with the concrete problems of state. American historians can draw upon a wide variety of statistics in their research and writing, but they must examine with care the validity and reliability of these data. The source is of paramount importance. For writings on the use of statistics see 1.4.

These considerations are particularly important in the early periods of American history, before the organization of the present state and federal governments. A substantial fund of quantitative data for the colonial era is scattered through the reports of officials, through the administrative records of English and provincial authorities, through tax lists, parish records, and the like. Such material, uncertain as to origin, must be treated with discrimination. Nevertheless, used with care it may yield a wide variety of significant information. See for example, E. B. Greene and V. D. Harrington, *American Population before the Federal Census of 1790* (1932) and S. H. Sutherland, *Population Distribution in Colonial America* (1936).

Fortunately the fund of statistical data has grown rapidly, particularly in the last century. As earlier, much of the accumulation has been by agencies of government, and the development of techniques of collection and analysis has reflected the expansion of the role of government in society. This is particularly true of the federal government, the publications of which have a general importance, are best classified, and are most readily available. A number of general guides will introduce the student to these sources. See chapter 5.

The earliest statistical work of the federal government sprang out of the customs and census services. Duties on foreign imports were long the main source of federal revenue, and reports on them were compiled by the Treasury Department. Figures on foreign commerce and navigation became increasingly detailed and broader in scope, particularly after the creation of the Bureau of Foreign and Domestic Commerce. These materials are supplemented, especially after 1875, by records of internal commerce and finance.

The census was originally taken by United States marshals under the direction of the State Department, for purposes of fixing Congressional representation. It listed white males over and under age sixteen, white females, other free persons, and slaves. To population figures were added, in 1810, manufactures; in 1820, occupations; in 1840, mines, agriculture, commerce, illiteracy, insanity, and pensioners; in 1850, libraries, newspapers and periodicals, and criminals. The machinery and techniques of enumeration were not equal to these ambitious programs, and the results were correspondingly open to error. Not until 1830 were uniform printed schedules introduced. The census of 1850 was the first to aspire to scientific accuracy. The raw data then were compiled and classified in a central office in the new Interior Department. But not until 1880 was there centralized control of supervisors and enumerators; the census for that year was tabulated in twenty-four volumes, five times as many as in any previous census. Machine tabulation was introduced in 1890, and in 1902 a permanent Census Bureau with its own staff was created. The Bureau broke up the decennial census by enumerations at more frequent intervals, such as the biennial census of manufactures. In 1906 a religious census was added, and in 1940 sampling techniques made their appearance in the census.

Regulatory bureaus established to deal with specific problems—agriculture, immigration, labor, conservation, public health, to name a few—include statistical information in their reports. Independent commissions, like the Interstate Commerce Commission, release statistics gathered in the course of investigation and regulation. The Federal Reserve Board and Banks similarly collect data on finance.

Apart from such official statistics accumulated in the routine administration of government, there is also a useful body of data gathered as the result of special *ad hoc* inquiries. Congress, through its committees; administrative agencies; and the courts have all conducted such inquiries from time to time. The results of these investigations are valuable because they probe topical and controversial questions; on the other hand, they are correspondingly subject to bias.

Beginning in 1878, *The Statistical Abstract of the United States*, issued annually, has contained general statistics on practically every subject for which data are collected by governmental (and certain other) agencies. Besides annual figures, it includes the most recent statistics collected at longer intervals. In 1965 the Bureau of the Census issued a supplement, *Historical Statistics of the United States, Colonial times to 1962*, a convenient compendium and collation of statistical materials, together with valuable notes on sources and their use.

Published compilations of election statistics are:

Burnham, Walter Dean, *Presidential Ballots, 1836–1892* (1955).
Robinson, Edgar E., *Presidential Vote, 1896–1932* (1934).
——*They Voted for Roosevelt* (1947);
Scammon, Richard M., ed., *America at the Polls: A Handbook of American Presidential Election Statistics, 1920–1964* (1965).
——*America Votes: A Handbook of Contemporary American Election Statistics* (6 vols., 1956–1964).

State and municipal materials vary considerably in nomenclature, quantity, and quality. Early in the nineteenth century most states had registration laws that supplied them with information on births, marriages, and deaths. Local, like federal, governments faced problems of taxation and representation that called for statistical data. The city and state agencies were the first to feel pressure for information as the changing currents of political thought stressed their police and reform functions; they needed data on public carriers, public health, education, industry, and the conditions of labor. The earliest statistics in these fields must be sought in state rather than in national sources. In addition, Massachusetts, New York, and Michigan for a time had more comprehensive censuses than the federal one. State agencies also served as the training ground for many statisticians who later commanded the federal government's expanding statistical apparatus. Thus the Massachusetts Bureau of Labor Statistics, organized in 1869, earliest of many similar state bureaus, provided Carroll D. Wright with the experience he used in organizing the national department. The general bibliographies of state documents are helpful in locating and assessing material. See especially 5.6, 5.7.

Privately collected statistics must meet only private standards, and vary accordingly. Most useful are special and continuing inquiries of industrial and commercial organizations into production and exchange. The American Iron and Steel Institute has long gathered such information. Stock-exchange records begin early and are reliable. Such material may be available in periodic reports or in trade journals, like *Iron Age* or the *Publishers' Weekly*, or through the business sections of newspapers. Chambers of commerce and boards of trade often gather and publish data. Private manuals, like Moody's and Standard and Poor, and periodicals of general business interest, like *Barron's*, conveniently draw together statistical information gathered elsewhere. Farmer, labor, and professional organizations compile and publish data; the American Medical Association, for example, keeps track of the number, distribution, and education of its members. Occasional advertising agencies like J. Walter Thompson have compiled studies that touch on the problems of population and marketing. Insurance companies are often useful sources for data on fires, floods, and theft, as well as on mortality, health, and population. Early and late, reformers gathered the "facts" to prove their case, argued in behalf of abolition, prohibition, suffrage, education, or eugenics. Handled with care, their work may be useful.

Of a different order are fact-books or almanacs, often associated with newspapers. The *New York Times Encyclopedic Almanac*, the *World Almanac*, and the *Information Please Almanac* are the modern versions of the compilations of Tench Coxe, Pelatiah Webster, and Adam Seybert, as well as of registers like Niles and Hazard. In addition many early gazetteers were repositories of miscellaneous information (3.4).

In a special class is the American Statistical Association. Founded in emulation of the English society in 1838–1839 by a group of Boston professional men led by Lemuel Shattuck, it early focused its interest on technical problems. Particularly useful was its criticism of the census of 1840. After 1880, it attracted a national constituency in the universities and in government service. Its *Journal* (1888–   ) and other publications include miscellaneous statistics and discussions of high quality which are themselves of considerable historical interest. A selective cumulative index covers its publications through 1939 only.

More specialized statistical research organizations have entered the field. The National Bureau of Economic Research, the National Industrial Conference Board, and the Brookings Institution have sponsored investigations into areas the government was slow to consider: for instance, the determination of national income, of employment, of the labor force, and of productivity.

The number and holdings of data archives in the United States are rapidly growing. There are two of special interest to American historians. The Inter-University Consortium for Political Research, P. O. Box 1248, Ann Arbor, Mich. 48106, contains political statistics extending back to the early 1800's. The Roper Public Opinion Research Center, Williams College, Williamstown, Mass. 01267, has public opinion surveys from the United States and forty-three other nations on politics, economics and business, education, health and welfare, occupations and professions, mass communications, public opinion, and numerous other topics. For a more complete listing, see *Social Science Data Archives in the United States*, published by the Council of Social Science Data Archives, 605 W. 115th St., New York, N.Y. 10025.

For the history of statistics see:

Baldwin, F. S., "Statistics in the Service of the Municipality," Am. Stat. Assoc., *Quar. Publ.*, 14 (1914), 103.
Hill, J. A., "Historical Value of the Census Records," Am. Hist. Assoc., *Report* (1908), 197.
Holt, W. S., *The Bureau of the Census* (1929).
Hull, C. H., "Service of Statistics to History," in John Koren, ed., *The History of Statistics, Their Development and Progress in Many Countries* (1918).
Leiby, James, *Carrol Wright: Origin of Labor Statistics* (1960).
Stephan, F. F., "The History of the Uses of Modern Sampling Procedures," Am. Stat. Assoc., *Journal*, 43 (1948), 12.
Wright, C. D., and W. C. Hunt, *The History and Growth of the United States Census* (1900).

Guides to statistical sources include, in addition to those in chapter five:

Andriot, John L., *Guide to U.S. Government Statistics* (3d ed., 1961.)
Dubester, Henry J., ed., *Catalog of United States Census Publications, 1790–1945* (1950).
———*State Censuses: Annotated Bibliography of Censuses of Population Taken after the Year 1790* (1948).
Eldredge, Hope T., *The Materials of Demography: Bibliography* (1959).
Hauser, Philip M., and William R. Leonard, *Government Statistics for Business Use* (2nd ed., 1956).
Texas University, Population Research Center, *International Population Census Bibliography*. Vol. IV: *North America* (1966).
U.S. Bureau of the Budget, *Statistical Services of the United States Government* (rev. ed., 1963).
U.S. Bureau of the Census, *Catalog, 1946– .*
Vital Statistics of the United States 1937– . Prepared by the U. S. Public Health Service, Vital Statistics Division.
Wasserman, Paul, et al., eds., *Statistical Sources* (2nd ed., 1965).

See also the chapter on microform material for National Archives, *Federal Population Censuses, 1840–1880: Microfilm copies of the Original Schedules* (1955), and other Census Bureau data.

3.3 MAPS

To the historian maps are eloquent documents. They constitute the common language used by men of different races and tongues to express the relationship of their society—its needs, ideas, and growth—to a geographic environment. As sources for the study of the history of the western world in modern times maps are well-nigh indispensable.

Their impact is especially clear in the field of geographic exploration. Explorers from the time of the discovery of the New World to our own day have relied upon maps to guide their journeys. Christopher Columbus formed his concepts of the unknown sea he proposed to sail from a series of charts which the ancient geographer Ptolemy was believed to have drawn and which Cardinal d'Ailly reinterpreted. After Columbus, maps and atlases, flowing in a steady stream from the printing presses of

Europe, served to guide explorers and to illustrate to present-day students of history the gradual growth of geographic knowledge. Some information appearing on these maps was the work of sheer fancy; it was not for that reason less important in producing historical results. The mythical Strait of Anian, a supposed passage to the Orient through the newly discovered continent of America, persisted on maps in one form or another for centuries, teasing the imagination of governments and explorers, and influencing successive exploring expeditions and measures of state policy. The great survey by Captain George Vancouver of the Northwest Coast of North America at the end of the eighteenth century was motivated still by the hope of finding such a strait.

In the field of diplomacy, maps have had a similar importance. They have furnished to diplomats basic information for boundary and other settlements. The foreign offices of modern governments have found maps of such usefulness that they have created libraries of them for current use, often of considerable size, and have kept in close touch, as special need has arisen, with the larger map collections. Not only correct, but incorrect, information on early maps of North America, has shaped American history. The charting of a vast wilderness led almost inevitably to errors, and these, in diplomacy, to boundary disputes. Thus the inaccuracies of the John Mitchell map of North America of 1775, the map relied on by the negotiators of the peace of 1782, produced such results as the Northwest boundary gap, the Maine boundary controversy, and the "Battle of the Maps." In the Oregon negotiation of 1818, American diplomats, relying on British maps which exhibited a mythical "Caledonia River," set the stage for later difficulties of boundary settlement.

In the field of economic development, maps have had a like significance. They have been instruments shaping development and, in the process, have been themselves reshaped. In the fur trade, which was an early economic interest of Europeans in North America, maps guided traders, traders redrew maps. The Hudson's Bay Company provided the information which gave distinction to the North American maps of the great London cartographer, Aaron Arrowsmith. The North West Company maintained on its payroll, as geographer, David Thompson, one of the greatest of American explorers and surveyors. In the field of transportation the surveys made of railroad routes to the Pacific in the 1850's were formative of policy and are now the materials of the historian. The nautical charts issued by the Coast and Geodetic Survey, the aeronautical charts issued by the several agencies of the federal government, the soil maps and the climate maps of bureaus of the Department of Agriculture, the topographic maps of the Geological Survey, the maps of river systems executed by the Corps of Engineers, these, and scores of other varieties of maps put forth by the federal government have been the basis of economic planning and action, and have become prime documents to later students.

An ever widening range of data of social nature has appeared on maps, such as vital statistics, ethnic groupings, local option regarding alcoholic beverages, the incidence of disease, church affiliation, illiteracy, education, woman suffrage, tenancy prevalence, and distribution of wealth. Such maps are often the tools of social planning, whether urban, regional, or national, and are of corresponding value to the historian.

In warfare, maps and charts have been traditionally important. They have been relied on by military headquarters and by armies and navies for fighting battles and for planning the logistics of campaigns. With the advent of the airplane and the development of air reconnaissance and strategic bombing, the range and variety of military mapping has been vastly expanded. Among the major mapping agencies of the federal government are at present the several branches of the military service. Among the more important depositories of the map collections in the United States and Canada are the following:

Library of Congress, Washington, D. C., 20540
National Archives, Washington, D. C., 20408
Army Map Service, Washington, D. C., 20315
American Geographical Society, New York, N. Y., 10017
New York Public Library, New York, N. Y., 10017
Hispanic Society of America, New York, N. Y., 10017
Yale University Library, New Haven, Conn., 06520
John Carter Brown Library, Providence, R. I., 02912
Harvard University Library, Cambridge, Mass., 02138
William L. Clements Library, Ann Arbor, Mich., 48104
Newberry Library, Chicago, Ill., 60610
State Historical Society of Wisconsin Library, Madison, Wisc., 53706
University of California Library, Berkeley, Calif., 94720
Henry E. Huntington Library, San Marino, Calif., 91108
University of North Carolina Library, Chapel Hill, N. C., 27514
Canadian Archives, Ottawa, Canada

See also the following works:

Special Libraries Association, *Map Collections in the United States and Canada* (1954). A state-by-state directory of collections, including size and subject. Appended is a listing of U.S. Army Map Service depository libraries.
Thiele, Walter, *Official Map Publications* (1938). Chapters seven and eight summarize the mapping of the North American continent from the sixteenth to the nineteenth centuries as associated with discovery and surveying, with helpful bibliographical footnotes.

Of the special guides and aids relating to American cartography the following are of particular value:

Lunny, Robert M., *Early Maps of North America* (1961). Tells the story of American cartography up to 1810.
U.S. Library of Congress, Map Division, *A Guide to Historical Cartography: Selected, Annotated List of References on the History of Maps and Map Making*, Walter W. Ristow and Clara E. LeGear, comps., (2nd ed., 1960).
Wheat, Carl I., *Mapping the Transmississippi West, 1540–1861* (5 vols., 1957–1963).

For lists of maps see the following:

American Geographical Society of New York, *Index to Maps in Books and Periodicals* (10 vols., 1968).
British Museum Catalogue of Printed Maps, Charts, and Plans (15 vols., 1967). Extensive American material throughout, arranged alphabetically by place name.
Ladd, Richard S., comp., *Maps Showing Explorers' Routes, Trails and Early Roads in the United States: An Annotated List* (1962).
Logan, Marguerite, *Geographical Bibliography for All the Major Nations of the World: Selected Books and Magazine Articles* (1959), especially Part 2, "Readings on Geography of Anglo-America," with thorough regional coverage of America.

Stephenson, Richard W., comp., *Land Ownership Maps: A Checklist of Nine-teenth Century County Maps in the Library of Congress* (1967).
Thiele, Walter, *Official Map Publications* (1938). Contains useful bibliographic references.
U.S. Library of Congress, Map Division, *A List of Geographical Atlases in the Library of Congress, with Bibliographical Notes* (6 vols., 1909–).
———*A List of Maps of America in the Library of Congress*, Philip L. Phillips, comp. (1901). Still a useful guide to many old state and county maps and city plans.
———*United States Atlases: A List of National, State, County, City, and Regional Atlases in the Library of Congress*, Clara E. LeGear, comp., (2 vols., 1950–1953).
Wheat, James C., and Christian F. Brun, *Maps and Charts Published in America before 1800: A Bibliography* (1969).

Atlases of the United States, include:

Historical

Adams, James T., *Atlas of American History* (1943).
The American Heritage Pictorial Atlas of United States History (1966).
Lord, Clifford, and Elizabeth H. Lord, *Historical Atlas of the United States* (rev. ed., 1953). A useful supplement to Paullin or Adams.
Miller, Theodore R., *Graphic History of the Americas* (1969). Atlases from 1660 to 1965.
Paullin, Charles O., *Atlas of the Historical Geography of the United States*, John K. Wright, ed. (1932). Still the most comprehensive work of its kind; contains a useful bibliographical discussion of special topics and map sources and reproductions of early maps.
U.S. Military Academy, West Point, *The West Point Atlas of American Wars, 1689–1953*, V. J. Esposito, ed. (2 vols., 1959).

Current

U. S. Geological Survey, *National Atlas of the United States of America* (1970).

3.4 GAZETTEERS

Gazetteers are compilations of the names of localities in a given state, nation, or wider area, arranged in alphabetical order. They provide for each locality listed the location and population, and, for the more im-portant places, descriptive matter such as transportation facilities, trade, industry, building developments, and intellectual or educational facilities. A well-known work of this character, which has been in circulation in the United States in various editions since 1855, is Lippincott's, reissued in revised form as *Columbia Lippincott Gazetteer of the World* (1962).

Gazetteers of past periods are of value to historians for information as to names that have disappeared from the map, local populations that have dwindled or grown, transportation facilities that were once of importance, or industries that have decayed or flourished. Sometimes they give details of routes of travel or rates of fare or fugitive information of other sorts difficult to find elsewhere.

There is no geographical dictionary devoted exclusively to the United States, although *Webster's Geographical Dictionary* (1962) gives priority to American place names and historical information. N. W. Ayer, *American Newspaper Annual*, 1880– , gives brief, up-to-date descriptive, and economic information about each city or town for which a newspaper is listed. Gazetteers for selected states and localities are listed in the *Bulletin* of the United States Geological Survey.

Some useful, older gazetteers are:

Amphlett, William, *The Emigrant's Directory to the Western States of North America* (1819).

Appletons' Companion Hand-Book of Travel to the United States and British Provinces (1861).

Blowe, Daniel, *Geographical, Historical, Commercial, and Agricultural View of the United States* (1820).

Brown, S. R., *The Western Gazetteer, or Emigrant's Directory* (1817).

Browne, J. R., *Resources of the Pacific Slope* (1869).

Cobbett, William, *The Emigrant's Guide; in Ten Letters, Addressed to the Tax-Payers of England* (1829).

Coolidge, A. J., and J. B. Mansfield, *History and Description of New England, General and Local.* Vol. I: *Maine, New Hampshire, and Vermont* (1859). No more published.

Cumings, Samuel, *The Western Pilot, Containing Charts of the Ohio River, and of the Mississippi* (1825). Rev. eds., 1829–54.

Curley, E. A., *Nebraska, Its Advantages, Resources and Drawbacks* (1875).

Dakota: Department of Immigration, *Resources of Dakota* (1887). Other editions.

Dana, Edmund, *Description of the Bounty Lands in the State of Illinois* (1819). Contains also the principal roads and routes, by land and water, in the United States, from New Brunswick to the Pacific.

———*Geographical Sketches on the Western Country: Designed for Emigrants and Settlers* (1819). Contains also a list of the public roads from Eastport to the Missouri River.

Darby, William, *The Emigrants' Guide to the Western and Southwestern States and Territories* (1818).

———*Geographical Description of the State of Louisiana* (1816).

Davison, G. M., *The Traveller's Guide through the Middle and Northern States and the Provinces of Canada* (8th ed., 1840). Early eds. (1825–1830) were called *The Fashionable Tour.*

Disturnell, John, *A Trip through the Lakes of North America. . . . A Complete Guide for the Pleasure Traveler and Emigrant* (1857).

——— *The Western Traveller; Embracing the Canal and Railroad Routes, from Albany to Troy, to Buffalo and Niagara Falls* (1844).

Dwight, Theodore, *The Northern Traveller and Northern Tour* (1825). 5th ed. (1834).

The Emigrants' Guide; or, Pocket Geography of the Western States and Territories (1818).

Fisher, R. S., *A New and Complete Statistical Gazetteer of the United States of America* (1853).

Flint, Timothy, *History and Geography of the Mississippi Valley* (1828). 3d ed., 1833.

Hayward, John, *Gazetteer of the United States of America* (1853). Hayward also compiled *The New England Gazetteer* (1839) and gazetteers of Massachusetts, New Hampshire, and Vermont.

Hazard, Samuel, ed., *Hazard's United States Commercial and Statistical Register* (6 vols. 1840–42).

Hewett, Daniel, *The American Traveller* (1825).

Hittell, J. S., *Resources of California* (6th ed. 1874).

Hutchinson, C. C., *Resources of Kansas* (1871).

Indiana Gazetteer, or Topographical Dictionary (1833, 1849).

Jones, A. D., *Illinois and the West* (1838). Especially good on pioneer conditions.

Melish, John, *Geographical Description of the United States* (1826). Earlier eds., 1816–1822. Some of the material was published in 1815 as Pt. 1 of *The Traveller's Directory* (below).

———*Information and Advice to Emigrants to the United States* (1819).

———*The Traveller's Directory through the United States* (5th ed., 1819). Earlier eds., 1815–18; enlarged ed. called *A Statistical View of the United States,* 1825. The second part of the work is *A Description of the Roads in the United States* (1814).

Mitchell, S. A., *An Accompaniment to Mitchell's Reference and Distance Map of the United States* (1834).

———*Illinois in 1837* (1837).

Montana, Bureau of Agriculture, *The Treasure State: Montana and Its Magnificent Resources* (1899).

Morse, Jedidiah, *The American Gazetteer* (1797). 2nd and 3rd eds., rev. and enlarged, 1804, 1810.

———*The American Geography* (1789).

New Empires in the Northwest. ("Library of Tribune Extras," I, No. 8), (1889).

Oregon, Immigration Board, *Pacific Northwest: Information for Settlers and Others* (1883). Various later eds.

Peck, J. M., *A Guide for Emigrants, Containing Sketches of Illinois, Missouri.* (1831).

———*A New Guide for Emigrants to the West.* (1837).

Scott, Joseph, *Geographical Dictionary of the United States of North America* (1805).

———*United States Gazetteer* (1795).

Seyd, Ernest, *California and Its Resources* (1858).

Shaw, Joshua, *United States Directory for the Use of Travellers and Merchants, Giving an Account of the Principal Establishments, of Business and Pleasure, Throughout the Union* (1822).

Smith, J. C., *Western Tourist and Emigrant's Guide.* (1840).

Spafford, H. G., *Pocket Guide for the Tourist and Traveller along the Line of the Canals and the Interior Commerce of the State of New York.* (1824).

Steele, O. G., *Steele's Western Guide Book and Emigrant's Directory* (1832). 11th ed., 1839.

Tanner, H. S., *The American Traveller; or Guide through the United States* (8th ed., 1842).

———*The Central Traveller, or Tourist's Guide through the States of Pennsylvania, New Jersey, Delaware, Maryland* (2nd ed., 1844).

———*Geographical, Historical, and Statistical View of the Central or Middle United States* (1841).

Temple, George, *The American Tourist's Pocket Companion; or a Guide to the Springs, and Trip to the Lakes* (1812).

Warden, D. B., *Statistical, Political, and Historical Account of the United States of North America* (3 vols., 1819).

Winser, H. J., *The Great Northwest; a Guide Book and Itinerary* (1883).

3.5 PLACE NAMES

Place names are sometimes sources of historical information. They may commemorate Indian tribes that once occupied the land, the preoccupations and nationalist aspirations of explorers and fur traders, the location of forts, the activities of land speculators, the sectional or foreign origins of early settlers, the impression made by the landscape on first comers, the national moods and fashions of different eras, and much else of national and local interest. The most comprehensive bibliography of books and articles is Richard B. Sealock and Pauline A. Seely, *Bibliography of Place-Name Literature, United States and Canada* (2nd ed., 1967).

See also:

Stewart, George R., *American Place-Names: A Concise and Selective Dictionary for the Continental United States of America* (1970).

———*Names on Land: A Historical Account of Place-Naming in the United States* (3d ed., 1967).

3.6 PICTORIAL RECORDS

Pictorial materials are vivid supplements to the written records in recapturing the past, and sometimes they are the only record we have. Imaginative delineations are least trustworthy historically because of the possibility that the artist, however unintentionally, may have distorted the truth. A classic example is John Trumbull's painting, "The Signing of the Declaration of Independence" (1794), which, though faithfully reproducing the likenesses of the individual participants, misrepresents them as having all attached their signatures at one time. In any event, it is better to consult the originals of paintings or drawings than the engravings, which may have been executed with considerable license. Portraits, photographs, and other graphic representations often provide data in regard to dress, artifacts, and everyday living—the retail traffic of life—that escaped the written records and may even have eluded museum collectors.

Caricatures and cartoons are of value not only for the light they cast upon shifting conceptions of humor, but also because they may incidentally tell much about social customs and political conditions. Such sketches, moreover, besides registering feelings and attitudes of the time, sometimes helped to create them. A notable example is Thomas Nast's pictorial crusade in *Harper's Weekly*, 1869–1872, against the infamous Tweed Ring in New York City.

Among periodicals valuable for illustrations of the nineteenth century are *Gleason's Pictorial Drawing-Room Companion, Harper's Weekly* and *Frank Leslie's Illustrated Newspaper*, and beginning in the 1930's, *Life* and *Look*. News distributing agencies such as the Associated Press and the United Press maintain picture files and will provide prints for a fee. In the 1930's the Works Progress Administration compiled checklists of American portraits in New Jersey, Connecticut, Rhode Island, Massachusetts, Maine, and New Hampshire. Copies are available in the Library of Congress and in regional archives branches. The National Portrait Gallery of the Smithsonian Institution, F Street at 8th, N.W., Washington, is preparing a catalog of 200,000 portraits of Americans. The Gallery contains a portrait collection and prepares exhibits.

Most state and city public libraries and some museums maintain circulating collections of pictures available to the public, in some instances through interlibrary loan. Most collections provide reference pictures for users. The largest is the New York Public Library picture collection, Fifth Ave. and 42d St., New York, N. Y., 10018, which serves more professional users than any other picture collection in the world.

The largest comprehensive collection of American pictures is at the Library of Congress, Print and Photography Division, Washington, D.C., 20540. It specializes in American life and scenes, Civil War, early American architecture, and political cartoons. A catalog to this collection is Paul Vanderbilt, comp., *Guide to Special Collections of Prints and Photographs in the Library of Congress* (1955).

The Still Picture Branch, Audio-visual Records Division, National Archives, 9th and Constitution Ave., N.W., Washington D.C., 20408, houses the largest collection bearing on all phases of federal government activities and some other areas as well. It contains the Brady collection of Civil War pictures.

The Index of American Design, National Gallery of Art, Smithsonian Institution, Washington D.C., 20565, specializes in early American crafts and folk art through 1900. The Library Photo and Slide Collections & Services, Museum of Modern Art, 11 W. 53rd St., New York, N.Y., 10019, has retrospective American and primitive art. The Audio-Visual Library, Colonial Williamsburg, Goodwin Building, Williamsburg, Va., 23185, collects items of eighteenth century Americana. The American History Division, Room 315A, New York Public Library, Fifth Ave. and 42d St., New York, N.Y., 10018, has American Indian and American life items. The International Museum of Photography, Rochester, N.Y., 14607, specializes in the history of photography, and the Wells Fargo Bank, 30 Montgomery St., San Francisco, Calif., 94104, has pictures of the express business. State and local historical societies often maintain collections of pictures illustrating the history of their areas.

Picture-finding tools include:

Ellis, Jessie C., *Index to Illustrations* (1966).
Kaplan, Milton, comp., *Pictorial America* (1955), a select catalog from which prints may be ordered, of photographic negatives in the Prints and Photographic Division of the Library of Congress.
Picturescope (1953–   ). Newsletter to the Picture Division of the Special Libraries Association.
Special Libraries Association, *Picture Sources*, Celestine G. Frankenberg, ed., (1964) lists historical society collections. It also provides a key to commercial firms and a few publishing houses which provide pictures for a fee.

The following are the more important published illustrated collections, examples of pictorial surveys, and books unusually rich in pictures. For specific topics, see the appropriate sections of the *Guide*.

Adams, James T., ed., *Album of American History* (rev. ed., 5 vols., 1961).
Andrews, Wayne, *Architecture in America: Photographic History* (1960).
Butterfield, Roger P., *The American Past: A History of the United States from Concord to the Nuclear Age* (1957).
Cahill, Holger, ed., *American Folk Art: The Art of the Common Man, 1750–1900* (1932).
Cirker, Hayward, et al., eds., *Dictionary of American Portraits* (1967).
Davidson, Marshall B., ed., *Life in America* (2 vols., 1951).
Dreppard, C. W., *Early American Prints* (1930). From colonial times to the Civil War.
Dunbar, Seymour, *History of Travel in America* (4 vols., 1915).
Eliot, Alexander, *Three Hundred Years of American Painting* (1957).
Faulkner, Harold V. U., and Herbert C. Rosenthal, *Visual History of the United States* (2nd ed., 1961).
Gabriel, R. H., ed., *The Pageant of America* (15 vols., 1926–29). Colonial times.
Green, Samuel M., *American Art* (1966).
Gurney, Gene, *A Pictorial History of the United States Army* (1966).
Horning, C. P., ed., *Handbook of Early American Advertising Art* (1947). Through the 1890's.
Hughes, Langston, and Milton Meltzer, *A Pictorial History of the Negro in America* (3d ed., 1968).
Kane, Harnett T., *Gone Are the Days: Illustrated History of the Old South* (1960).
Kouwenhoven, John A., *Made in America* (1948).
Kredel, Fritz, and F. P. Todd, *Soldiers of the American Army, 1775–1954* (1954).
Larkin, Oliver W., *Art and Life in America* (rev. ed., 1960).
Lehner, Ernst, comp., *American Symbols* (1957).
Lorant, Stefan, *Pittsburgh* (1964).
Mendelowitz, Daniel M., *History of American Art* (1960).
Montgomery, Charles F., ed., *America's Arts and Skills* (1957).

Murrell, William, *A History of American Graphic Humor* (2 vols., 1933–1938). From colonial times.
National Geographic, *America's Historylands* (1967).
Nevins, Allan, ed., *A Century of Political Cartoons* (1944).
Pierson, William H., Jr., and Martha Davidson, eds., *Arts of the United States: Pictorial Survey* (1960).
Richardson, Edgar P., *Painting in America: From 1502 to Present* (1965).
Robinson, John, and G. F. Dow, eds., *The Sailing Ships of New England, 1607–1907* (3 vols., 1922–28).
Rogers, Agnes, and F. L. Allen, eds., *The American Procession: American Life since 1860 in Photographs* (1933).
Roscoe, Theodore, and Fred Freeman, *Picture History of U.S. Navy, 1776–1897* (1956).
Stokes, I. N. P., and D. C. Haskell, comps., *American Historical Prints, Early Views of American Cities, Etc.* (1932). Through 1849.
U.S. Library of Congress, *An Album of American Battle Art, 1755–1918* (1947).
Wilson, Mitchell, *American Science and Invention* (1954).

3.7 MOTION PICTURES AND VIDEO TAPES

Two varieties of motion pictures and video tapes of television possess a particular importance for the historian. One consists of films and tapes of events and people. In the Library of Congress collection, documentary films go back as far as 1894. Such films may supply irrefutable historical evidence. Thus, when Japanese air bombers sank the neutral United States gunboat *Panay* on December 12, 1937, during the Sino-Japanese war, a Universal newsreel proved that, contrary to Tokyo's allegations, American flags were plainly exhibited on the vessel. Fictional films and tapes, on the other hand, are of varying worth as social and intellectual history.

Major cinema collections are found in the Library of Congress, the National Archives in Washington, and the Museum of Modern Art in New York. The Museum maintains a card index of important films produced since 1889. Many universities maintain substantial collections of films, of which many are cataloged.

Guides include:

Niver, Kemp R., *Motion Pictures from the Library of Congress Paper Print Collection, 1894–1912*, Bebe Bergsten, ed. (1967).
U.S. Copyright Office, *Motion Pictures, 1894–1959* (4 vols., 1953–1960).
U.S. Library of Congress, *The Civil War in Motion Pictures: A Bibliography of Films Produced in the United States since 1897* (1961).
————*Guide to United States Government Motion Pictures* (1947–   ).
————*Motion Pictures and Filmstrips 1953/57–   *. With quarterly, annual, and quinquennial cumulations. Motion pictures and film strips for which cards were printed by the Library of Congress were first listed in the *Library of Congress Author Catalog . . .* , the 1951 annual volume and the 1948–1952 quinquennial compilation.

For film loan libraries see:

Reid, Seerley, and Anita Carpenter, eds., *A Directory of 3600 16mm Film Libraries* [U.S. Office of Education, *Bulletin*, 4] (1959) Lists companies, institutions, and organizations which lend or rent films; arranged by state and city.
Reid, Seerley, *Loan and Rental Sources of U.S. Government Films* (1954).
U.S. Dept. of Army, *Index of Army Motion Pictures, Film Strips, Slides and Phono Recordings* (1962).

3.8 SOUND RECORDINGS

Sound recordings add a further dimension to the historian's knowledge of the past and provide a means of making history live in the classroom. There are records and tapes of historic events, invoking or recording the voices of those involved, and there are numerous recordings of our musical heritage. The standard catalog of commercially produced records is the *Schwann Long Playing Record Catalog: Monthly Guide to Mono and Stereo Records.* The *Schwann Supplementary Catalog,* published twice yearly, includes plays and famous addresses.

Many libraries have fine record collections. The Archive of American Folk Song in the Library of Congress is outstanding. A selective list of the best of more than 16,000 recordings in this collection is *Folk Music: Catalog of Folk Songs, Ballads, Dances, Instrumental Pieces, and Folk Tales of the United States and Latin America on Phonograph Records* (1964). These records may be purchased from the Library of Congress. See also:

U.S. Library of Congress, *Music and Phonorecords,* 1953– . With semi-annual, annual, and quinquennial cumulations. Music and phonorecords for which cards were printed by the Library of Congress were first listed in the *Library of Congress Author Catalog . . . ,* 1948–1952.

3.9 NON-DOCUMENTARY SOURCES

In addition to the written sources of history, there exists a variety of non-documentary sources of information and understanding in the form of three-dimensional survivals from the past—both man-made and natural. To view Ford's Theater or drive through the Donner Pass, to examine a flintlock musket or the Spirit of St. Louis, to observe the tools and processes related to spinning and weaving yields a wealth of facts and impressions, available in no other way, about the events, people, and ideas of the past. The evidence is especially rich and revealing in the fields of architecture, technology, and the decorative arts, but in every area of human endeavor many non-documentary sources have survived to fill the gaps in the written record, or to corroborate and flesh out that record.

The natural environment constitutes the most extensive physical survival from the past. Despite the alterations brought about by men, large areas—especially mountainous and forested regions—remain essentially unchanged, many of them protected by law. Even where agriculture, lumbering, industrialization, and urbanization have disfigured the face of the land, the general physiography is relatively unaffected.

The historian's chief concern, of course, is with the man-made environment. Notwithstanding the depredations upon it in the name of progress or as the result of neglect and catastrophe, an enormous variety of physical survivals from every stage of our history has come down to us. These include roads, canals, bridges, earthworks, dams, battlefields, buildings of all descriptions, and the myriad artifacts with which Americans have surrounded themselves. The selective process of survival has been an extremely haphazard one during most of our history—far more so than with written documents. In the case of buildings, durability has been a factor, but more often than not, it has been sheer chance that has determined a structure's survival.

In recent years, continued survival of a building has depended less on chance and more on the preservation movement. This originated more than a century ago with the efforts of the Mount Vernon Ladies' Association to save Washington's home. Their ultimate success stimulated other voluntary associations, such as the Association for the Preservation of Virginia Antiquities and the Society for the Preservation of New England Antiquities, and these in turn inspired many state and local historical societies or special preservation groups to save their most historic buildings. The first major study of the movement down to 1926 is Charles B. Hosmer, Jr., *Presence of the Past* (1965).

The resources of most volunteer preservation groups were exhausted with the purchase and restoration of a few buildings. Their more important role proved to be creating an awareness of the need for preservation and encouraging individuals and other volunteer groups to undertake preservation projects. They also proved to be effective lobbyists with federal, state, and local governments. They were instrumental in getting various levels of government to designate historic sites, allocate funds for preservation and restoration, and pass enabling legislation for historic zoning. One government agency, the National Park Service, became a leader in the preservation movement.

Another important role played by the preservation movement has been the gradual accumulation of scholarly knowledge on the subject and the development of techniques. Today, a nation-wide group of professional preservationists apply the same rigorous standards to their work as do the professional historians. Since 1949 the National Trust for Historic Preservation, a voluntary association established by act of Congress, has served as a clearing house for information and as a coordinating agency for the many projects being undertaken throughout the nation.

The preservation movement has enlarged its objectives over the years. Early efforts, growing out of filio-pietism or patriotism, centered on saving landmarks associated with important events or persons, or, less often, on saving structures that were venerated simply for their antiquity and rarity. In the latter part of the nineteenth century, an increasing emphasis was placed on preserving early examples of architecture. The tendency was to preserve architectural gems, especially the more elegant and elaborate among them. Not until the past fifty years has there been great concern in preserving vernacular architecture or the more mundane examples of every-day life and work.

The scope of preservation also has changed. It has been extended to include restoration. The simplest kind of preservation requires some restoration—if only renewal of weakened timbers and replacement of elements exposed to weather. In the twentieth century, restoration has become more extensive. Buildings are restored to an earlier condition, after thorough study, by removal of later additions and anachronisms. This type of restoration may be limited to the exterior of the building, or, as in the case of most of the 1800 historic buildings open to the public, may include a faithful restoration of all interior features. Preservationists are not always in accord on the desirability of destroying later additions to a building.

The extent of preservation has also been enlarged to include extensive areas. The most ambitious example is the restoration of Williamsburg, Virginia to its eighteenth-century appearance, a work that was begun in 1926 and is only now nearing completion. This involved preservation, restoration, and in many cases the reconstruction of buildings and gardens that had disappeared. Such outdoor museums re-equip buildings and landscape with the artifacts of the era they represent, and as nearly as possible recreate the life of the time by a great variety of authentic activities.

Another type of outdoor museum consists of antique buildings which have been moved or reassembled in the pattern of a village that would be typical of the time and area. Old Sturbridge Village in Massachusetts, Mystic Seaport in Connecticut, and the Farmers Museum at Cooperstown, New York are fine examples. All are the result of intensive scholarship and verification. Scores of other outdoor museums have sprung up over America, not all of them as authentically done. Of great use to historians will be the results of a survey being conducted by the American Association of Museums. Museums will be rated on the thoroughness of the scholarship behind them as well as the care with which they have carried out their findings. Obvious commercial ventures will not be rated.

Area preservation or restoration sometimes involves historic sections of a city, such as the area around Independence Hall in Philadelphia or Old Salem in Winston Salem, North Carolina. Many cities have preserved smaller core areas. The Providence Preservation Society has encouraged the restoration of scores of eighteenth and nineteenth-century buildings which stand alongside buildings of more recent vintage.

Study of non-documentary materials is hampered by the fact that information about them is not always published, exhibited, or registered. There are no systematic state or national surveys of museum holdings. Thus the individual wishing to locate and use artifacts will be obliged to search out and find them on a museum-by-museum basis. Most historians trained in the use of documentary materials will find that the "language" of objects is new and puzzling.

There are guides to the location of such materials that will give the seeker of artifacts help in getting started.

The Official Museum Directory, United States and Canada, (1971) published by the American Association of Museums and Crowell-Collier Educational Corporation, Washington, D.C., briefly indicates the holdings of nearly 6000 museums.

The Directory: Historical Societies and Agencies in the United States and Canada is issued periodically by the American Association for State and Local History. It is limited to historic houses, historical societies, and history museums. This organization also publishes the monthly *History News,* which contains information about work in this field.

The Chronicle is the publication of the Early American Industries Association. It contains materials about tools and processes.

Historical Archaeology, published by the Society for Historical Archaeology, deals with post-settlement archaeological work, especially non-domestic structures such as canals, bridges, mines, and factories.

The National Register of Historic Places is published bienially by The National Park Service.

Historic Preservation, published by the National Trust for Historic Preservation, deals with architectural preservation on a national scale.

Many museums and historical societies publish newsletters and journals that contain information about their collections. There are numerous handbooks listing the historic buildings of America which can be visited. The latest handbook published by American Heritage describes some 1800 buildings, their location, hours of visitation, and cost of admission. The

National Park Service has extensive materials about its properties, which include buildings, battlefields, and other historically important sites. An indispensable guide is Frederick L. Rath, Jr. and Merrilyn Rogers O'Connell, *Guide to Historic Preservation, Historical Agencies, and Museum Practices: A Selective Bibliography* (rev. ed., 1970). A highly selective list of works on the subject follows:

Alexander, Edward P., "Historical Restorations," in William B. Hesseltine and Don McNeil, eds., *In Support of Clio* (1958).
American Heritage, *American Heritage Book of Great Historic Places* (1957).
Bailey, Worth, *Safeguarding a Heritage: Historic American Survey* (1963).
Bell, Whitfield J., Jr., et al., *Cabinet of Curiosities: Five Episodes in Evolution of American Museums* (1967).
Cartwright, Aubrey W., *Guide to Art Museums in the United States* (1958).
Christensen, Erwin O., *Guide to Art Museums in the United States* (1968).
Coleman, Laurence Vail, *College and University Museums* (1942).
———*Company Museums* (1943).
———*Historic House Museums* (1933).
———*Museum Buildings* (1950).
———*Museum in America* (3 vols., 1939).
Directory: U.S. Army Museums. Office of Chief of Military History (1968).
Directory of Historical Societies and Agencies in the United States and Canada, 1969–1970. Biennial.
Finley, David E., *History of the National Trust for Historic Preservation, 1947–1963* (1965).
Haas, Irwin, *America's Historic Houses and Restorations* (1966).
Hosmer, Charles B., Jr., *Presence of the Past: History of the Preservation Movement in the United States before Williamsburg* (1965). This is the first major study of the movement.
Katz, Herbert and Marjorie Katz, *Museum Adventures: An Introduction to Discovery* (1969).
———*Museums, U.S.A., History and Guide* (1965)
Lee, Ronald F., *United States: Historical and Architectural Monuments* (1951).
Lord, Clifford L., *Keepers of the Past* (1965).
National Geographic Society, *America's Historylands* (1967).
Hume, Ivor Noel, *Here Lies Virginia: An Archaeologist's View of Colonial Life and History* (1963).
———*Historical Archaeology: Comprehensive Guide for Both Amateurs and Professionals to the Techniques and Methods of Excavating Historical Sites* (1969).
Sarles, Frank B., Jr., and Charles E. Shedd, *Colonials and Patriots: Historic Places Commemorating our Forebears, 1700–1783.* Volume 6 of *National Survey of Historic Sites and Buildings* (1964).
Schlebecker, John T., *Living Historical Farms: A Walk into the Past* (1969).
Borhegyi, Stephan F., and Elba A. Dodson, *Bibliography of Museums and Museum Work, 1900–1960* (1960).
Borhegyi, Stephan F., and Irene A. Hanson, *A Bibliography: Supplementary Volume 1960–1961* (1960).
Clifford, William, comp., *Bibliography of Museums and Museology* (1923).
Smith, Ralph C. A., *A Bibliography of Museums and Museum Work* (1928).
Rath, Frederick L., Jr., and Merrilyn Rogers O'Connell, comps., *Guide to Historic Preservation, Historical Agencies, and Museum Practices: A Selective Bibliography* (rev. ed., 1970). An indispensable guide to the field.

3.10 TEACHING OF HISTORY

A continuing concern of historians is the teaching of history at the secondary level. It was one of the principal reasons for the publication in 1896 of the first *Harvard Guide*, which contained a syllabus for the guidance of those preparing American history courses. Later editions also feature the syllabus form, but in recent years the proliferation of first-rate textbooks and a wide variety of study materials has minimized the usefulness of the syllabus format.

The American Historical Association, 400 A Street, S.E., Washington, D.C., 20003, publishes two series of relevant pamphlets. *AHA Pamphlets* summarize recent topical or period interpretations and contain brief critical bibliographies. *Discussions on Teaching,* devoted to problems of interest to teachers, cover interpretation, method, and classroom approaches.

The American Association for State and Local History, founded in 1940, has done much to encourage both research and teaching of local history through its regular publication of *History News* and its technical leaflets and bulletin series. It has been a principal sponsor of the junior history movement, which is represented in more than a dozen states by formal organizations. *History News* devotes a regular column to the movement.

Specific books and articles which are useful to the history teacher include:

Alexander, Carter, and Arvid J. Burke, *How to Locate Educational Information and Data* (4th ed., 1958). A guide to educational references as well as a handbook on methods of research.

Cartwright, William H., and Richard L. Watson, Jr., eds., *Interpreting and Teaching American History* (1961). The 31st yearbook of the National Council for the Social Studies covers the more important sources in all areas of American history. Each chapter was prepared by a specialist.

Faissler, Margareta, *Key to the Past: Some History Books for Pre-College Readers* (2nd ed., 1959).

Kenworthy, Leonard S., *Guide to Social Studies Teaching* (2nd ed., 1966). A practical guide to supplementary materials.

Klein, Bernard, *Guide to Educational Directories* (1963).

Logasa, Hannah, ed., *Historical Fiction* (8th ed., 1964). A collection of titles for school use at various age levels.

Lord, Clifford L., *Teaching History with Community Resources: Localized History Series* (1965).

Montgomery, Robert W., "History for Young People: Organizing a Junior Society," *History News,* 22 (1967), 9.

National Council for the Social Studies, *Social Studies Curriculum Improvement: A Guide for Local Committees.* Bulletin no. 36 (1965).

Wiltz, John E., *Books in American History: A Basic List for High Schools* (1964).

4　Aids to Historical Research

4.1 FINDING AIDS

The printed materials of American history comprise all the extant works of American presses, from the earliest to the latest, together with a portion of the works published in other countries. This is an embarrassment of riches, a vast body of books, pamphlets, documents, broadsheets, maps, periodicals, and newspapers. Fortunately for the researcher there is a great variety of guides into the labyrinth of the research library's holdings. Also the reference librarian is able and willing to help the beginning scholar, but he would do well to become acquainted with the following two invaluable guides to reference books:

Walford, A. J., ed., *Guide to Reference Material* (2nd ed., 3 vols., 1968). Volume 2, covering philosophy, psychology, religion, social sciences, geography, biography and history, has 3330 items and subsumed entries for a further 1500. It has more of a British slant than Winchell's *Guide to Reference Books*.

Winchell, Constance M., ed., *Guide to Reference Books* (8th ed., 1967); *First Supplement, 1965–1966* (1968); *Second Supplement, 1967–1968* (1970). This standard work contains almost 4000 entries in all fields of knowledge and provides an evaluation of each item. It is arranged topically and has an excellent index.

Two bibliographies of bibliographies are recommended for examination early in any research program. They are:

Besterman, Theodore, ed., *World Bibliography of Bibliographies* (4th ed., 5 vols., 1965–1966). This edition records bibliographies in all fields published through 1963, with some later additions. There are some 117,000 items arranged alphabetically by subject.

Bibliographic Index: A Cumulative Bibliography of Bibliographies (1937–   ). Issued semiannually, with annual and additional cumulations, this is a guide to current bibliographies. Entries are arranged topically, and consist of separately published bibliographies, those included in more than 1000 periodicals, and a limited number of bibliographies taken from books.

4.2 GENERAL HISTORY BIBLIOGRAPHIES

American Historical Association, *Guide to Historical Literature* (1961). Successor to the 1931 guide edited by George M. Dutchet et al., it is a selective,

annotated bibliography arranged by large subject and country groups; each
group is selected and described by experts.
Boehm, Eric H., and Lalit Adolphus, *Historical Periodicals* (1961). An annotated
world list of historical and related serial publications. Supersedes the *World List
of Historical Periodicals* by P. Caron and M. Jaryc (1939), although the latter is
still useful for early discontinued titles.
Coulter, E. M., and Melanie Gerstenfeld, eds., *Historical Bibliographies* (1935).
UNESCO, *World List of Social Science Periodicals,* (3d ed., 1966). Includes periodicals published to the end of 1963.
White, Carl M. et al., *Sources of Information in the Social Sciences: Guides to the
Literature* (1964). Each of the eight chapters, including one on history, consists
of a bibliographical essay, written by a specialist, and annotated lists of references. Includes information not in Winchell's *Guide to Reference Books*.

4.3 AMERICAN HISTORY BIBLIOGRAPHIES

Beers, H. P., ed., *Bibliographies in American History* (2nd ed., 1942). Although
dated, this is still useful for retrospective searching. There are subject bibliographies for economic, constitutional, diplomatic, social, cultural, and scientific history, and bibliographies for each of the states. The scope of each work
is stated without critical comment.
Griffin, A. P. C., ed., *Bibliography of American Historical Societies* (2nd ed.,
1907). An analysis and index of each volume of the publications of American
and Canadian historical societies to 1905.
Mugridge, Donald H., and Blanche P. McCrum, *A Guide to the Study of United
States of America* (1960). A compilation of works on various aspects of American civilization. Includes about 6500 annotated entries published prior to 1958.
Writings on American History, 1902/1959–   (1904/1959–   ). Each volume
contains an exhaustive list of books and articles on American history published
during the year. Entries are arranged topically and have brief annotations.
Until 1940 it covered British North America, and until 1936, Latin America.
Indexed annually. A cumulative index covers the years 1902–1940. Volumes for
1904–1905 and 1941–1947 have never been issued. Although the *Writings* are
now more than a decade behind, the National Historical Publications Commission is taking steps to make them more current.

The card catalogs of major research libraries are especially useful
bibliographical aids. An increasing number of these are available in print.
The published shelf lists of these collections, such as the American history
volumes of the Widener Library Shelflist at Harvard University, although
essentially locating aids for particular books or pamphlets, also serve as
bibliographies. The printed catalog of special library collections may well
be the most complete bibliography on a particular subject. (See 4.4).
Bibliographies of articles and lists of books appear regularly in the *American Historical Review, Journal of American History, Journal of Southern
History, American Quarterly,* and other journals covering national and
state history. The student should also keep in mind that footnotes in
scholarly articles and monographs will often lead him to secondary works
and sources which might otherwise elude him.

4.4 SUBJECT BIBLIOGRAPHIES

Several of the important bibliographies of special topics will be found
scattered throughout this guide under their appropriate heading. For

example, Everett E. Edwards, *Bibliography of the History of Agriculture in the United States* (1930), is cited under Agriculture. There are so many bibliographies of special topics, and new ones so frequently appear, that the *Harvard Guide* does not contain a complete listing.

Specialized professional journals usually include lists of current publications in their fields in addition to the books reviewed. The lists are often cumulative, such as the annual bibliography of the history of science in *Isis*. More selective, though less current, are the bibliographies in special monographs.

The card catalogs of major research libraries are as useful in preparing bibliographies of special topics as they are in the general field of American history. Printed catalogs of special libraries or of special collections, such as New York Public Library's *Schomburg Collection of Negro Literature and History: Dictionary Catalog* (9 vols., 1962), constitute indispensable bibliographies of their subject. Many special collections are cited in Lee Ash, *Subject Collections* (3d ed., 1967).

4.5 PERIOD BIBLIOGRAPHIES

Not until the advent of the publishers' trade lists in the mid-nineteenth century was there any systematic attempt to keep up with the yearly output of books and pamphlets published in America, and it was the end of the century before the listings began to be fairly complete. Any comprehensive American catalog which lists books published before 1850, whether printed in America or about America, was compiled retrospectively. The monumental task of catching up with this backlog began in the 1870's and only now is being completed.

The following catalogs and checklists of imprints are arranged as nearly as possible by date of publication of the works cited. Included are both retrospective and contemporary listings, and books about America published elsewhere as well as those published in the United States. As noted beside each entry they vary greatly in their usefulness to the historian. Some are mere checklists, but they are valuable for verification. Others have subject indexes and annotations, and some give locations of one or more copies.

It is as a finding aid that such works can be most helpful—especially to a student who is not near one of the great research libraries. A book traced to a distant library can sometimes be borrowed through an interlibrary loan. If this is not possible, a locating aid can help him plan a research trip more effectively. Many rare books have been duplicated in microform. All of the works cited in the Evans bibliography below, for example, have been reproduced on Readex cards and are available in many libraries across the country. Chapter seven lists guides to microform reproduction.

Sabin, Joseph, et al., *Bibliotheca Americana: A Dictionary of Books Relating to America, from Its Discovery to the Present Time* (29 vols., 1868–1936). Begun by Joseph Sabin, continued by Wilberforce Eames, and completed by R. W. G. Vail. It includes a great range of books, periodicals, and pamphlets printed in America and works published about America in several countries and languages from 1492 to the 1870's, and up to the 1890's for the western states. Arrangement is by author, up to date of publication; therefore coverage varies. Title and subject indexes are lacking.

Evans, Charles, *American Bibliography: A Chronological Dictionary of All Books, Pamphlets and Periodical Publications Printed in the United States of America, 1639–1800* (14 vols., 1903–1959). The most important general list of early American publications, arranged by year of publication. Each volume has three indexes: author, subject, and printers and publishers. Volume 13, compiled by Clifford K. Shipton, carries this work through 1800. Volume 14, edited by Roger P. Bristol, is a cumulative author-title index to the whole work. A supplement including titles not found in Evans has been issued in parts since 1952 as Evans' *American Bibliography*, edited by Roger P. Bristol.

Shipton, Clifford K., and James E. Mooney, eds., *National Index of American Imprints Through 1800: The Short-Title Evans* (2 vols., 1969). A short-title list of works in Evans and additional items since Evans (2 vols., 1969). The sub-title is misleading. Entries are arranged by author, giving for each item the short title, edition, place and publisher, date, collation, and location of a copy. It includes in one alphabetical sequence works mentioned in Evans and those uncovered since, incorporating all corrections found necessary by the American Antiquarian Society in its works on American imprints.

Shaw, Ralph R., and Richard H. Shoemaker, *American Bibliography: A Preliminary Checklist* (19 vols., 1958–1965). Designed as a first step in filling the gap in American national bibliography between 1800 when Evans stops, and 1820 when Roorbach starts. Each volume covers one year. Arrangement within is by author.

Shoemaker, Richard H., *Checklist of American Imprints, 1820–   . (1964–   ).* Planned as a continuation of Shaw to emend the early period of Roorbach and to list more than eight times as many titles. Coverage does not include periodicals and newspapers.

Roorbach, Orville A., *Bibliotheca Americana, 1820–1861* (4 vols., 1852–1861; repr. 1939). The first significant American trade bibliography. Includes periodicals and reprints. Volume one, covering the period 1820–1852, was compiled retrospectively. Arrangement is by author and title. Serves also as a subject bibliography for biography during the period.

Kelly, James, *American Catalogue of Books Published in the United States from 1861 to 1871* (2 vols., 1866–1871; repr. 1938). A publishers' trade catalog following the scope and format of Roorbach. Although incomplete and sometimes inaccurate, it is the most general list available for the period.

Publishers' Weekly, 1872–1876. A trade list weekly arranged by author and title. *Publishers' Weekly* continues to the present (see below), but the four years cited here fill the gap between Kelly and the *American Catalogue of Books.*

American Catalogue of Books, 1876–1910 (9 vols., 1876–1910; repr. 13 vols., 1941). A fairly complete author, title, and subject list of books published in the United States during the thirty-five years.

United States Catalog: Books in Print January 1, 1928 (1899; 4th ed., 1928). Earlier editions issued with supplements entitled *Cumulative Book Index.* A comprehensive listing of all books published in the United States and many published in the English language in other countries; entries under author, title, subject, and series.

Cumulative Book Index: A World List of Books in the English Language, 1928/ 32–   . A Wilson publication now appearing ten times yearly, with periodic cumulations. A remarkably accurate dictionary catalog (i.e., with author, title, subject, and series entries), this is a most valuable listing of contemporaneously published books in English.

Publishers' Weekly, (1872–   ). A weekly trade list of books published in the United States, arranged alphabetically by author or main entry. Also included are forecasts of books to be published, and in several special issues each year a more extensive listing of publishers' announcements.

American Book Publishing Record, 1960–   . A monthly cumulation of *Publishers' Weekly* listings, rearranged by subject, and cumulated annually.

Books in Print, 1948–   . An annual author and title index to *Publishers' Trade List Annual* (a multi-volume collection of publishers' catalogs), listing books currently available from U.S. publishers. Since 1957 it has been supplemented by *Subject Guide to Books in Print.*

4.6 LIBRARY OF CONGRESS CATALOGS AND THE *NATIONAL UNION CATALOG*

U.S. Library of Congress, *A Catalog of Books Represented by Library of Congress Printed Cards Issued to July 31, 1942* (167 vols., 1942–1946). A catalog of author cards for each book for which Library of Congress cards were printed.

————,————*Supplement; Cards Issued August 1942–December 31, 1947* (42 vols., 1948).

————*Library of Congress Author Catalog: A Cumulative List of Works Represented by Library of Congress Printed Cards, 1948–1952* (24 vols., 1953).

————*National Union Catalog: A Cumulative Author List Representing Library of Congress Printed Cards and Titles Reported by Other American Libraries, 1953–1957* (28 vols., 1958).

————,————*1958/1962–*

————*1952–1955 Imprints: Author List Representing Library of Congress Printed Cards and Titles Reported by Other American Libraries* (30 vols., 1961). Additional locations for titles previously included.

The great innovation in 1956 was the inclusion in the National Union catalog of monographs not represented by Library of Congress printed cards, but reported by over 750 North American libraries, together with the indication of location of titles by symbols of libraries. The current catalog is printed in nine monthly issues, with quarterly, annual and quinquennial cumulations. Included in the 1963–1967 edition of the *National Union Catalog . . .* there is a volume, *Register of Additional Locations*, which notes locations reported after annual or quinquennial cumulations. Reporting is presently on a current basis.

The National Union Catalog: Pre-1956 Imprints (1968–   ) is expected to exceed 600 volumes. This project, sponsored by the Library of Congress (and often referred to as Mansell), is the combined bibliographic record of publications prior to 1956. It contains both the holdings represented by Library of Congress printed cards and those reported by other public and private participating libraries.

The most valuable subject guide for books published since World War II is the *Library of Congress Subject Catalog* of which the initial set of volumes appeared in 1948. As of 1950 it became a quinquennial cumulation, *Library of Congress Catalog: A Cumulative List of Works Represented by Library of Congress Printed Cards. Books: Subjects, 1950/1954–* This catalog arranges alphabetically by subject all the publications since 1945 for which Library of Congress cards were printed. It is continued by quarterly and annual supplements.

4.7 BRITISH BOOK CATALOGS

Retrospective British catalogs are especially useful to the student of colonial history.

Pollard, A. W., and G. R. Redgrave, eds., *Short-Title Catalogue of Books Printed in England, Scotland and Ireland, and of English Books Printed Abroad 1475–1640* (1926). Most comprehensive record for this period.

Bishop, William W., *A Checklist of American Copies of "Short-Title Catalogue" Books* (2nd ed., 1950). A guide to location of titles in selected American libraries.

Wing, D. G., *Short-Title Catalogue of Books Printed in England, Scotland, Ireland, Wales, and British North, and of English Books Printed in Other Countries,*

1641–1700 (3 vols., 1945–1951). Published as a continuation of Pollard and Redgrave with revised location symbols. Includes books printed in the American colonies during this period. Each entry carries one or more library location, where copies may be found.

For a complete catalog of printed books from the fifteenth century held by the British Museum, see:

British Museum, *General Catalogue of Printed Books.* Photolithographic Edition to 1955 (263 vols., 1959–1966).
———*Ten Year Supplement, 1956–1965* (50 vols., 1968).

For a subject approach to the British Museum *Catalogue,* see:

Peddie, Robert A., *Subject Index of Books Published before 1880* (4 vols., 1933–1948).
British Museum, *Subject Index of the Modern Works Added to the Library, 1880–1900,* G. K. Fortescue, ed. (3 vols., 1902–1903).
———*Supplement 1901/05–*

4.8 BOOK REVIEW MEDIA

Reviews of some of the recently published books will be found in *New York Review of Books, The New York Times Book Review,* the book sections and supplements of other newspapers, and special sections of weekly and monthly magazines. Less current, although usually more comprehensive and critical reviews appear in the professional journals of history, political science, economics, law, and other fields. Particularly helpful is the *United States Quarterly Book Review* (1945–   ), published by the Library of Congress.

The *Book Review Digest (1905–   )* reproduces abbreviated reviews from more than eighty English and American periodicals. *Book Review Index* (1965–   ), a monthly, with quarterly cumulations, lists reviews in more than 200 periodicals. The *Index to Book Reviews in the Humanities* (1906–   ), an annual index to book reviews from some 700 periodicals published in English, includes review in the social sciences as well as the humanities.

4.9 INDEXES TO PERIODICALS

Poole's Index to Periodical Literature, 1802–1881, (rev. ed., 1891). With supplements through 1906. This pioneer index is by subject only and is limited to selective American and English periodicals.
Nineteenth Century Readers' Guide to Periodical Literature, 1890–1899. An author-subject index to some fifty periodicals, most of them general in nature.
Readers' Guide to Periodical Literature (1900–   ). Issued monthly and cumulated in an annual volume and permanent two-year volumes. The number of periodicals has steadily increased and varies volume to volume. In 1903 it absorbed the *Cumulative Index* and in 1911 the field of the *Annual Library Index.* Entries are by author and subject, and by title as necessary.
Social Science and Humanities Index (1916–   ). Formerly *International Index to Periodicals* (1916-1965). Similar in format to *Readers' Guide,* but covers the more scholarly journals. Restricted to American and English periodicals, it is issued quarterly and cumulated in annual and permanent volumes.
Annual Magazine Subject Index (43 vols., 1908–1952). Covers by subject, Ameri-

can and British periodicals, largely historical, and includes state historical
society journals. A large number of periodicals have been indexed from their
first issue, the oldest going back to 1876. Ceased publication in 1949. In 1964,
Cumulated Magazine Subject Index, 1907–1949 appeared in two volumes. This
arranges all the entries in the forty-three volumes into one alphabetical sequence.
Canadian Periodical Index (1928–   ). Title varies. A monthly, subject index.
Cumulations are by author and subject.

An unpublished index to early American periodical literature covering
351 periodicals of the years 1728–1870—a W.P.A. project of the 1930's—is
housed at New York University. A mimeographed list of the periodicals
covered was issued in 1940.

Indexes to periodicals of special interest are so numerous that they can
be listed only by some examples in the more important fields.

Agriculture

Biological and Agricultural Index 1964–   . A monthly, subject index to agricultural periodicals and bulletins. Supersedes *Agricultural Index* (1916–1964).
U.S. Office of Experiment Stations, *General Index to Experiment Station Record,
1889–1939* (1903–1949). Served as an index to agricultural periodical literature.

Applied Science

Applied Science and Technology Index 1913–   . Formerly *Industrial Arts Index.*
A monthly subject index with annual cumulations.

Art

Art Index 1929–   . A subject and author index, issued quarterly and in permanent cumulations.

Biography

Biography Index 1946–   . A quarterly index, with annual and three-year cumulations, of biographical material in magazines and books in the English language.

Business

Business Periodicals Index 1958–   . Formerly a part of *Industrial Arts Index.* A
monthly subject index with annual cumulations.

Education

Education Index 1929–   . A subject index to some 200 periodicals. Before 1961,
it included books and pamphlets and an author index.

Economics

American Economic Association, *Index of Economic Journals 1886–1959.* Lists
articles in English from eighty-nine journals in various languages.

Labor

Index to Labor Union Periodicals 1960–   . An annotated subject index to fifty labor union periodicals. A monthly, cumulating annually.

Law

An Index to Legal Periodical Literature 1791–1937. This is a subject index (and a brief author index) to American, English, Canadian, and British colonial legal periodicals. Volumes 4–5 are practically a consolidation of Volumes 1–25 of *Index to Legal Periodicals.*
Index to Legal Periodicals 1908–   . A quarterly, with an annual and later, permanent cumulation.

Medical Science

Index Medicus 1960–   . A comprehensive index to several thousand periodicals compiled as a partial printout of MEDLARS (Medical Literature Analysis and Retrieval System). It cumulates annually into *Cumulated Index Medicus* 1960–   . Supersedes *Current List of Medical Literature,* 1950–1959 which was a continuation of *Quarterly Cumulative Index Medicus* 1927–1956, a practically complete index to the journal literature of the field. Issued quarterly and cumulated semiannually. Preceded by *Index Medicus; A Classified Index of Current Medical Literature of the World* 1879-1927, an index of periodicals and books. Suspended 1899–1900 during which time its place was taken by the French *Bibliographica Medica* (Paris, 1899–1900).

Music

Music Index 1949–   . Indexes by author and subject articles in some 180 periodicals. Includes obituaries. A monthly, cumulating annually.

Performing Arts

Guide to the Performing Arts 1957–   . An annual index to articles and illustrations in more than three dozen periodicals, primarily in English. From 1953 to 1956 it was a supplement to Sara Y. Belknap's *Guide to the Musical Arts* (1957).

Population

Population Index 1935–   . Title varies. An annotated bibliography of books and periodical articles. Quarterly with annual cumulations.

Religion

American Theological Library Association, *Index to Religious Periodical Literature* 1949/52–
Catholic Periodical Index 1930–   . A quarterly author and subject index, with biennial cumulations.
Religious Periodicals Index 1970–   . Quarterly.

A useful, although dated, guide to cumulative indexes to individual periodicals is D. C. Haskell, *Checklist of Cumulative Indexes to Periodicals in the New York Public Library* (1942). Jean S. Kujoth, *Subject Guide to Periodical Indexes and Review Indexes* (1969) will lead the student to lists of indexing sources in various fields.

Files of older periodicals and those of restricted interest are often obtainable only in the larger libraries and in special collections. It is important to know, therefore, where some of the more nearly complete sets may be consulted. This information is given in *Union List of Serials in Libraries of the United States and Canada*, (3d ed., 5 vols., 1965). Titles published before 1950 are located in 956 cooperating libraries in the United States and Canada. Information includes date of first issue and extent of libraries' holdings. It is an indispensable aid to researchers.

For periodicals commencing after December 31, 1949 or for those pre-1950 periodicals not in the *Union List,* consult *New Serial Titles, 1950/1960–* . It notes locations in some 700 libraries; it is continued by monthly issues with annual cumulations. These are self-cumulative through periods of at least five years. Both include foreign serials, but government serials are excluded.

These union lists necessarily can cover only the holdings of larger libraries. *Union Lists of Serials: A Bibliography*, compiled by Ruth S. Freitag, (1964), provides more than 1200 union lists and updates an earlier bibliography, compiled by D. C. Haskell and Karl Brown, included in the 2nd edition of the *Union List of Serials in Libraries of the United States and Canada*, (1943). See your nearest research library for the availability of a local or regional list.

4.10 ABSTRACTS

America: History and Life, 1964– . Appears three times annually. Lengthy abstracts drawn from a broad range of periodicals. Cumulative indexes.

Economic Abstracts 1953– . Semimonthly. Covering economics, finance, trade and industry, management, and labor. Includes a detailed subject index.

Historical Abstracts, 1775–1945 (1955–). Quarterly. Covers the world's periodical literature with signed abstracts contributed by scholars, mainly from the United States. Classified arrangement with annual indexes cumulating every five years.

Poverty and Human Resources Abstracts 1966– . A bi-monthly service researching published and mimeographed materials. Arrangement is by broad subject groupings. A detailed subject index is appended. There is also a cumulative author and subject index to the volume. Each essay is introduced with an essay on a relevant topic.

Psychological Abstracts 1927– . A monthly. Signed abstracts of books, articles, and dissertations—in classified arrangement. Cumulative subject, and annual author index.

Sociological Abstracts 1952– . Issued 9 times a year. Classified abstract journal covering a broad range of sociological articles in periodicals.

5   Printed Public Documents

5.1 NATURE OF PUBLIC DOCUMENTS

Public documents are among the most abundant and most useful sources of information available to the historian. Material of this nature exists for the discovery and earliest settlement of the Americas, and both the quantity and the scope of it increase through the centuries.

In general, the reliability of these documents springs from the fact that they are public and are used in the regular course of official business. Often they are published promptly and even those that remain in manuscript form are open to scholars and other citizens. There is therefore little likelihood of falsification or forgery. The precautions the historian must take in using these materials are of another order: he must examine them in their context, determine if they are what they purport to be, and use them for what they are.

The largest fund of public records consists of those which arise from the normal administrative procedures of various government agencies. These records have a high degree of reliability since they are kept for the information of the officials who use them in the usual processes of their work. Nevertheless, even such records must be scrutinized with care. Sometimes the responsible officials may lack the technical means of assuring accuracy. The colonial governors who sent home statistics of population were only passing on informed guesses. Furthermore, the data may not always be what it is labeled: there are times when an estimate of imports is only an estimate of imports on which a duty was paid or when the volume of immigration is only the volume of immigration by sea through certain ports. The scholar would have to take account of what goods were smuggled or of what newcomers entered by land. Nevertheless, these administrative documents ordinarily bear on their face clear indications of their origins and purposes and the historian can use them with confidence.

Official records also contain a variety of texts, including the correspondence of executives, the statutes of legislatures, and the decisions of courts. In the modern period these are almost always edited and printed with care and need little in the way of verification. But the accuracy of the text is, of course, no guarantee of the accuracy of the facts cited in it or of the logic of the arguments it contains.

This is even more true of the records of the deliberations of various legislative and executive bodies. The *Congressional Record* will reveal what a senator said, or would like to have said, but the historian must himself determine how much weight to give the utterance. Representatives and senators have the right to revise their remarks. Speeches inserted in the rear of the *Congressional Record* were not delivered on the floor of the House or Senate. In some cases, moreover, the official record is less informative than other sources. Letters are frequently written "for the record." Not only may they give the historian no clue as to how decisions were arrived at, but they may actually mislead him, providing an inaccurate indication of actions. For instance, an historian would have difficulty learning from the records of the Civil Service Commission that most federal manpower in World War II was recruited through other agencies. The most useful sources of information as to what happens in cabinet meetings are the diaries of members.

In the last half century, official records have come to include still another category of material. Both the administrative agencies and the legislative arms of the government depend increasingly upon fact-finding inquiries to pursue their work. The result is a large number of investigations into every branch of life with which the government is concerned. These investigations have as their prime objective the accumulation of data on the bases of which action may be taken. Such data have also substantial historical value, yet the very purposes for which these inquiries are undertaken may distort their factual findings as well as their conclusions. Being closely related to specific political proposals, these investigations often suffer from the bias of the investigators as well as from inaccuracies of technique and from faults of procedure. They must, therefore, be used with caution, but so used, they contain exceedingly valuable information.

Public documents are generally arranged for the convenience of the officials who use them. The historian will find his way through them more easily if he has a knowledge of the general administrative organization of the government—whether it be federal, state, or local. The *United States Government Organization Manual*, 1940–   , is an annual handbook of the federal government. It is particularly useful in understanding the overall organization and in determining the official names of departments, bureaus, agencies, and commissions. It includes a selected list of the most important publications of each.

See also:

Boyd, A. M., ed., *United States Government Publications: Sources of Information for Librarians*, R. E. Rips, rev. ed. (1949). Although somewhat dated, this is still useful for its organization of material. Documents are listed according to the agency of the federal government which issues them rather than by subject. The index serves the latter purpose.
Schmeckebier, Laurence F., and Roy B. Eastin, eds., *Government Publications and Their Use* (4th ed., 1969). Includes the uses of indexes, catalogs, and bibliographies of government publications as they relate to the fields of government operation. Describes also the approach to a great variety of executive, legislative, and judicial documents—including state constitutions and laws. Explanation is provided for the classification system of federal documents by the Superintendent of Documents office and for the ordering of important government serials.
Powell, John H., *The Books of a New Nation: United States Government Publications, 1774–1814* (1957). An informative bibliographical essay on the history and problems of tracing government documents.
Price, Miles O., and Harry Bitner, *Effective Legal Research: A Practical Manual of*

Law Books and Their Use (1953; rev. ed. for students, 1969).

Shaw, Thomas S., ed., "Federal, State and Local Government Publications," *Library Trends*, 15 (1966). Entire issue.

U.S. Library of Congress, *Popular Names of U. S. Government Reports: A Catalog*, Bernard A. Bernier, Jr. and Charlotte M. David, comps. (1970).

5.2 BIBLIOGRAPHY OF BIBLIOGRAPHIES

Body, Alexander C., *Annotated Bibliography of Bibliographies on Selected Government Publications* (1967). *Supplement* (1968). Covers period 1960 to 1968; includes classified list of government authors (departments and agencies).

Brown, Everett S., *Manual of Government Publications, United States and Foreign* (1950). Primarily a bibliography of selected materials, divided by subject area; still useful as a retrospective bibliography and for the history of government printing activities.

Childs, James B., *Government Document Bibliography in the United States and Elsewhere* (3d ed., 1942). Somewhat dated but still useful for information on lesser-known works, especially in the area of state and Confederate government documents.

Wilcox, Jerome K., *Bibliography of New Guides and Aids to Public Documents Use, 1953–1956* (1957). Includes general, federal, state, municipal, and foreign guides; a supplement to two earlier bibliographies for the years 1945–1948 *Special Libraries*, 90 (1949), 406; and for 1949–1952, ibid., 45 (1954), 32.

5.3 CATALOGS, CHECKLISTS, AND INDEXES

Access to the federal documents is gained through checklists, catalogs, and indexes which together cover government publications from 1774 to date. In quality those prepared since 1895 are much superior to those prepared earlier. The most important comprehensive works are:

Greely, A. W., ed., *Public Documents of the First Fourteen Congresses, 1789–1817* (56th Cong., 1 sess., *S. Doc.* no. 428). A good descriptive list. A supplement to it is published in Am. Hist. Assoc., *Report*, I (1903), 343.

Poore, B. P., ed., *Descriptive Catalogue of the Government Publications of the United States, 1774–1881* (1885). Gives brief abstracts of the documents it lists. Must be used with care as its listings are incomplete, especially for departmental publications. The index is defective.

Ames, J. G., ed., *Comprehensive Index to the Publications of the United States Government, 1881–1893* (1905). A good index covering both congressional and departmental series for its period. As an index to items in the congressional set, it is complete. Its listing of departmental documents is limited.

U.S. Superintendent of Documents, *Checklist of United States Public Documents, 1789–1970* (4th ed., 1971). This work is an approximately complete checklist of all public documents of the period. Provides bibliographic data on more than 1,500,000 United States government publications. Especially useful are its lists of publications of departments and bureaus. Gives serial numbers for congressional documents.

————*Catalog of the Public Documents . . . 1893–1940* (25 vols., 1896–1945). Commonly cited as the *Document Catalog*. A complete bibliographical guide in the form of a dictionary catalog. Covers congressional and departmental publications. It is a continuation of Ames *Comprehensive Index*. Each Congress is covered by one volume except the 54th Congress which has two. Prior to the 70th Congress, the *Document Catalog* listed only the printed government publications, thereafter it included the more important processed works as well.

————*Monthly Catalog of United States Government Publications*, 1895–

Title varies; current bibliography of publications issued by all branches of the government. Includes both the congressional and the department and bureau publications. An annual index appears in the December issue. There are decennial indexes for the years beginning 1941–1950. The February issue of the *Monthly Catalog of U.S. Government Publications* contains a list of new serial publications issued by the Government Printing Office.

————*Price List, Government Periodicals and Subscription Services,* 1967– Revised annually, this is a listing by title of all periodicals available for sale from the Superintendent of Documents. Since it is confined to GPO publications, it is considerably more limited in scope than Andriot's guide.

Wood, Jennings, *United States Government Publications: A Partial List of Non-GPO Imprints* (1964). A listing of the most frequently used periodicals and publications printed for government bodies outside the GPO; identifies titles not in *Monthly Catalog of U.S. Government Publications.* This has been supplemented by *Non-GPO Imprints.*

U.S. Library of Congress, Exchange and Gifts Division, *Non-GPO Imprints Received in the Library of Congress, July 1967 through December 1969: A Selective Checklist* (1970).

Andriot, John L., ed., *Guide to United States Government Serials and Periodicals* (7th ed., 3 vols., 1971). Provides full bibliographical description of items with annotations, and a short history of the publishing agency. It includes information on deceased government agencies and publications. There is a title index.

U.S. Superintendent of Documents, *Numerical Lists and Schedule of Volumes of the Reports and Documents . . . 1934– .* Because the *Monthly Catalog* does not contain serial numbers, these lists must be used to gain access to Congressional Reports and Documents in the Congressional Set, beginning with 77th Congress, 1st session, 1941. One volume is published for each session.

Congressional hearings on bills of public interest or on issues of public policy before committees of either House or Senate are an important source of historical materials. Citations to printed hearings are included in the *Catalog of Public Documents* and the *Monthly Catalog.* For early hearings, the *Checklist of United States Public Documents 1789–1970* should be consulted under the name of the committee. Since 1938 all printed hearings are available in depositories.

The following are also useful indexes to congressional hearings:

Thomen, Harold O., *Checklist of Hearings before Congressional Committees through the Sixty-Seventh Congress* [1921/23] (1957–1959). Records over 5,000 titles, many of which were previously unrecorded entirely or inadequately described.

U.S. Congress. House Library, *Index of Congressional Committee Hearings in the Library of the U.S. House of Representatives Prior to Jan. 1, 1951* (1954). *Supplemental Index to 1955* (1956).

U.S. Congress. Senate Library, *Index of Congressional Committee Hearings (Not Confidential in Character) Prior to January 3, 1935 in the Senate Library* (1935). Updated by a cumulative index to January 3, 1959 and a quadrennial supplement thereafter.

Congressional Information Service/Index 1970– . A two-volume monthly loose-leaf service, with quarterly and annual cumulations. Volume two includes an index to current hearings, abstracted in volume one.

There is no single comprehensive index to all the federal statutes from beginning to date. The *Index Analysis of the Federal Statutes, 1789–1873,* compiled by Middleton G. Beaman and A. K. McNamara, and the *Index to the Federal Statutes, 1874–1931,* compiled by Walter H. McClenon and Wilfred C. Gilbert, are invaluable for a retrospective subject search of public general laws through 1931. For a thorough search in the period following, indexes of the annual volumes of the *Statutes at Large* must be used. The subject index volumes of the *United States Code* will suffice for search of federal public laws of a permanent nature *now in force*.

Presidential executive orders are indexed by the Historical Records Survey, *List and Index of Presidential Executive Orders, 1789–1941* (1942). This is supplemented by *Table of Executive Orders Appearing in the Federal Register and the Code of Federal Regulations* (1955), covering the years, 1936–1954, and by the annual supplements to Title 3 of the *Code of Federal Regulations*. Current executive agreements can be traced through the indexes of each issue of the *United States Code Congressional and Administrative News*, also through its annual index.

5.4 SUBJECT GUIDES

Hirshberg, H. S., and C. H. Melinat, eds., *Subject Guide to United States Government Publications* (1947). Arrangement is by subject. Primarily limited to documents from 1927 to 1947, it is nevertheless still a useful guide for subject indexing in depth of the period. It is updated by:

Jackson, Ellen, *Subject Guide to Major United States Government Publications* (1968). Emphasis, as in Hirshberg, is on government documents of major and lasting interest.

Leidy, William P., *A Popular Guide to Government Publications* (3d ed., 1965). List of items issued between 1950 and 1965 that are of general appeal

5.5 IMPORTANT COLLECTIONS OF FEDERAL DOCUMENTS

Beginning with the organization of the federal government in 1789, Congress was required to keep a journal of its actions and to record its receipts and expenditures. For a long time congressional publications were the most important federal documents. Subsequently each of the executive departments and the judiciary established series of their own. As the federal government expanded, so did the number of printed documents.

In recent years the government has been liberal in making these documents available in depositories in every state. A list of current depository libraries is published each year in the September issue of the *Monthly Catalog*.

The list of documents which follows includes only the most important and frequently cited collections of federal documents, many of which are now available in microform. For the period up to 1789 records were not differentiated by departments; since then material has been organized according to the branches of the government within which the documents originate.

5.5.1 Records of the Federal Government Before 1789

Elliot, Jonathan, ed., *Debates in the Several State Conventions on the Adoption of the Federal Constitution . . . Together with the Journal of the Federal Convention* [and other papers]. (2nd ed., 5 vols., 1861).

Farrand, Max, ed., *Records of the Federal Convention of 1787* (4 vols., 1911–1937).

Force, Peter, ed., *American Archives . . . A Documentary History of . . . the North American Colonies.* 4 ser., 6 vols. (March 7, 1774–Aug. 21, 1776); 5 ser., 3 vols. (May 3, 1776–December 31, 1776). (1837–1853). No more published.

Ford, W.C. et al., ed., *Journals of the Continental Congress, 1774–1789* (34 vols., 1904–1937).
Tansill, C. C., ed., *Documents Illustrative of the Formation of the Union of the American States* (69th Cong., 1st sess., H. Doc. no. 398).
U.S. Department of State. Bureau of Rolls and Library, *Documentary History of the Constitution of the United States* (5 vols., 1894–1905).
Wharton, Francis, ed., *Revolutionary Diplomatic Correspondence* (6 vols., 1889).

5.5.2 Federal Statutes

The laws passed by Congress comprise the federal statutes. For the period 1789–1873 they were published privately, thereafter by the federal government. Title and content vary somewhat.

Statutes at Large of the United States of America, 1789–1873 (17 vols., 1850–1873).
United States Statutes at Large Containing the Laws and Concurrent Resolutions Enacted during the . . . Session of the . . . Congress . . . , and Proclamations, Treaties, and International Agreements other than Treaties, 1874– . Since 1951 each volume includes public and private laws, concurrent resolutions, and proclamations. There is a name and subject index for each session; the indexes are not cumulative. There is a useful table of the legislative history of the public laws enacted.
United States Code (13 vols, 1970). First edition published in 1926, revised every six years. New ed. contains the general and permanent laws of the United States in force on January 6, 1970. The arrangement is by subject; there are cumulative supplements.

Recently enacted legislation is available as printed slip laws; they are listed in the *Monthly Catalog* under the heading, "*Congress.*"

5.5.3 Congressional Documents

Congressional publications include bills and resolutions, hearings, *Journals*, giving an account of the actions of each house, *Annals* and its successors, supplying a record of debates, and reports and documents containing materials supplied to Congress by its own committees and by the executive branch. A more detailed account of the contents of these documents may be found in Schmeckebier and Eastin, *Government Publications.*

The proceedings of Congress prior to 1874 were printed by private publishing houses. There was no systematic contemporaneous reporting of the debates of the first seventeen Congresses or of the first session of the eighteenth, but the *Annals* provide a kind of record, "compiled from authentic materials," of congressional debates from 1789 to 1824. From 1824 to 1837 the debates were reported and published as *Register of Debates in Congress.* The *Congressional Globe,* began in 1833; until the end of the first session of the twenty-fifth Congress, both the *Register* and the *Globe* reported the proceedings. From 1837 to 1873 the *Globe* provided the only continuous report. The *Congressional Record,* thereafter published by the government is distributed to depository libraries. As noted earlier in this chapter, speeches delivered in Congress are often edited and rewritten before incorporation in the *Record,* and sometimes speeches are printed therein which were never delivered on the floor. In certain cases, thus, newspapers furnish a more exact version of the actual proceedings than does the *Record.*

Journal of the House of Representatives of the United States. Annual. 1789–   .

Journal of the Senate of the United States. Annual. 1789–   .
Journal of the Executive Proceedings of the Senate of the United States, 1789–1905.
    (90 vols. 1828–1848). Contains nominations to office and treaties omitted from
    the public journals.

*   *   *   *   *   *   *

[Annals of Congress.] *Debates and Proceedings in the Congress of the United
    States, 1789–1824* (42 vols., 1834–1856.)
[Congressional Debates.] *Register of Debates in Congress, 1825–1837* (29 vols.
    1825–1837.)
Congressional Globe, Containing the Debates and Proceedings, 1833–1873. (109
    vols., 1834–1873.)
*Congressional Record, Containing the Proceedings and Debates, 1873–   .
    (1873–   ).

*   *   *   *   *   *   *

American State Papers: Documents, Legislative and Executive (38 vols., 1832–
    1861). Covers the first through the twenty-fifth Congresses, 1789–1838.
Senate Documents, 1817–1849.
State Papers, 1817–1830. Made up of House documents.
Executive Documents, 1830–1847. Made up largely of House documents.
Senate Executive Documents, 1847–1895.
Senate Miscellaneous Documents, 1847–1876.
*Senate Reports, 1847–   .
House Executive Documents, 1847–1895.
House Miscellaneous Documents, 1847–1876.
*House Reports, 1819–   .
*Senate Documents, 1876–   .
*House Documents, 1876–   .

The documents of the 1st–14th Congress are collated as the *American
State Papers.* From the 15th to the 82d Congress, the Congressional Set
contains Reports (of full committees), Documents (excluding Executive
Documents), and Journals. Commencing with the 83d Congress, the set
excludes Journals. Each volume of the Congressional Set (beginning with
volume one, the 15th Congress, 1817) carries a continuous number
regardless of Congress and session. The serial number alone is not
sufficient when referring to a component of one of the volumes of the Set,
because a serial volume may contain many Documents and Reports, or
alternatively, one Report may run over to more than one serial numbered
volume.

5.5.4 Reports of Judicial Decisions

The most important judicial documents are the decisions of the various
courts. Until 1874 Supreme Court reports were issued under the name of
the official court reporter. Beginning in 1875 they bear the title *United
States Reports,* and are usually cited that way.

Dallas, A. J., *Reports of Cases in the Courts of the United States, and Penn-
    sylvania, 1790–1800.* 3 vols. Numerous editions.
Cranch, William, *Reports of Cases Argued and Adjudged in the Supreme Court of
    the United States, 1801–1815.* (9 vols., 1804–1817).
Wheaton, Henry, *Reports of Cases Argued and Adjudged in the Supreme Court,
    1816–1827* (12 vols. 1816–1827).
Peters, Richard, Jr., *Reports of Cases Argued and Adjudged in the Supreme Court,
    1828–1842* (17 vols., 1828–1843).

Howard, B. C., *Reports of Cases Argued and Adjudged in the Supreme Court, 1843–1861.* (24 vols., 1843–1861).
Black, J. S., *Reports of Cases Argued and Determined in the Supreme Court, 1861–1862.* (2 vols., [1862–1863]).
Wallace, J. W., *Cases Argued and Adjudged in the Supreme Court, 1863–1874.* (23 vols., 1864–1876).
United States Reports, Supreme Court, 1875–   . W. T. Otto, J. C. B. Davis, C. H. Butler, Ernest Knaebel, and Walter Wyatt, reporters. 1876–   . These volumes are numbered 91–   , continuously with the earlier series.

These reports have often been digested and abridged. The best such compilation, *United States Supreme Court Digest 1754–*   (1944–   ), is kept current by cumulative supplements.

The decisions of the lower (circuit and district) courts may be found in the following sources:

Federal Cases, 1789–1879. 31 vols.
Federal Reporter, 1880–1924. 300 vols.
Federal Reporter, 1924–   . 2d ser.
Federal Supplement, 1932–   .
Court of Claims Reports, 1855–   .
American Law Reports–Federal, 1969–   .

On occasion the historian may wish to consult the other documents in a particular case. These are preserved in the libraries and in the clerks' offices of the various courts. However, in recent years, appeal papers have generally been printed and deposited also in the Library of Congress.

5.5.5 General Executive Documents

Documents emanating from executive departments and commissions and bureaus responsible to them have grown steadily in bulk and importance. Below are listed the more significant series.

Code of Federal Regulations. A multi-volumed codification by subject. First published in 1938, revised in 1949, now completely revised each year to include texts and amended administrative rules and regulations in effect on January 1 of each year. For a thorough search of the most current applicable regulation issued during the year, consult the *Federal Register,* "Lists of Sections Affected."
Federal Register, March 14, 1936–   . Published four times weekly. Includes rules, regulations, and decisions of all administrative units of the federal government, as well as presidential proclamations and executive orders. Indexed monthly, quarterly, and annually.
U.S. Congress. Senate Library, *Presidential Vetoes* (1969). List of bill vetoes from the 1st through the 90th Congress, 1789–1968.
U.S. President, *Compilation of the Messages and Papers of the Presidents* (20 vols. to 1929). The first ten volumes, published under the editorship of J. D. Richardson, cover the period 1789–1897. The second ten volumes, commercially published, bring the record to 1929. Presidents Herbert Hoover and Franklin D. Roosevelt published the papers of their administrations. For a listing of the latter see 10.3.

The compilation of presidential papers is officially continued by:

Public Papers of the Presidents of the United States, 1958–   , an annual, beginning with the Tru..-n administration, 1945, and designed to include the public messages and papers of each president.

————*Weekly Compilation of Presidential Documents*, 1965–   . An official publication of presidential speeches, statements, news conferences, messages to Congress, and other material. Indexed annually.

5.5.6   Federal Records Relating to Foreign Affairs

Hackworth, G. H., ed., *Digest of International Law* (8 vols. 1940–1944). Covers the period, 1906–1940.

Hudson, M. O., ed., *International Legislation, a Collection of the Texts of Multipartite International Instruments of General Interest* (4 vols., 1931). Deals particularly with the period, 1919–1929.

Malloy, W. M., C. F. Redmond, and E. J. Treworth, eds., *Treaties, Conventions, International Acts, Protocols, and Agreements between the United States and Other Powers. 1776–1937* (4 vols., 1910–1938).

Manning, W. R., ed., *Diplomatic Correspondence of the United States. Canadian Relations 1784–1860* (4 vols., 1940–1945).

————*Diplomatic Correspondence of the United States Concerning the Independence of the Latin-American Nations* (3 vols., 1925).

————*Diplomatic Correspondence of the United States Inter-American Affairs 1831–1860* (12 vols., 1932–1939).

Marraro, H. R., ed., *Diplomatic Relations between the United States and the Kingdom of the Two Sicilies* (2 vols., 1951–1952).

Miller, Hunter, ed., *Treaties and Other International Acts of the United States of America, 1776–1863* (8 vols., 1931–1948).

Moore, J. B., ed., *Digest of International Law, as Embodied in Diplomatic Discussions, Treaties, and Other International Agreements, International Awards, the Decisions of Municipal Courts, and the Writings of Jurists, and Especially in Documents, Published and Unpublished, Issued by Presidents and Secretaries of State of the United States, the Opinions of the Attorneys General, and the Decisions of Courts, Federal, and State* (8 vols., 1906).

————*History and Digest of the International Arbitrations to Which the United States Has Been a Party* (6 vols., 1898).

————*International Adjudications, Ancient and Modern: History and Documents* (8 vols., 1929–1936).

Scott, J. B., ed., *Diplomatic Correspondence between the United States and Germany August 1, 1914–April 6, 1917* (1918).

————*Treaties for the Advancement of Peace between the United States and Other Powers Negotiated by the Honorable William J. Bryan, Secretary of State of the United States.* (1920).

Stock, L. F., *Consular Relations between the United States and the Papal States* (1945).

————*United States Ministers to the Papal States . . . 1848–1868* (1933).

Whiteman, Marjorie M., *Digest of International Law* (1963–   ). Successor to the Hackworth work, but does not incorporate it.

The above compilations contain diplomatic material systematically arranged. The documents published directly by the U.S. Department of State include the following series:

American Foreign Policy, Current Documents 1956–   . An annual, one-volume compilation of the principal published official papers, selected to indicate the scope, goals, and implementation of the foreign policy of the United States. *A Decade of American Foreign Policy Documents, 1941–49* (1950), and *American Foreign Policy, 1950–55: Basic Documents* (2 vols., 1957) cover the earlier periods.

Foreign Relations of the United States: Diplomatic Papers, 1861–   . An annual collection (excepting in 1869) of official papers relating to foreign relations of the United States. There is a considerable time lag between the period covered and the date of publication. In 1970 the series had reached the volumes for 1946. There are indexes for the years 1861–1899 (1902) and 1900–1918 (1941).

The following special supplements have been issued:

The Lansing Papers, 1914–1920 (2 vols., 1939–1940).
The World War, 1916–1918 (6 vols., 1929–1933).
The Paris Peace Conference, 1919 (13 vols., 1929–1933).
Russia, 1919 (1937).
Japan, 1931–1941 (2 vols., 1943).
Soviet Union, 1933–1939 (1952).
China, 1942 (1956).
Conference at Cairo and Teheran, 1943 (1961).
Conference of Berlin (Potsdam Conference), 1945 (1960–1961).
Africa Series, 1960–   .
Arbitration Series, 1929–   .
Commercial Policy Series, 1934–   .
Conference Series, 1929–47. 105 nos. 1929–47.
Department and Foreign Service Series, 1948–   .
East Asian and Pacific Series, 1954–   . Formerly Far Eastern Series.
Economic Cooperation Series, 1948–   .
European and British Commonwealth Series, 1948–   .
European Series, 1930–47. 29 nos. 1930–47.
Far Eastern Series, 1932–   .
General Foreign Policy Series, 1948–   .
Immigration Series, 1936–?. Ceased publication.
Inter-American Series, 1929–   .
International Information and Cultural Series, 1948–   .
International Organization and Conference Series, 1948–   .
Latin American Series, 1929–1937. 15 nos. 1929–1937.
Map Series, 1932–?. Ceased publication.
Near and Middle Eastern Series, 1948–   . Formerly Near Eastern Series.
Passport Series, 1929–?. Ceased publication.
Russian Series, 1919. 1919.
Treaties and Other International Acts, December 1945–   . Combines Treaty
  Series and Executive Agreement Series. Each text is published separately in
  pamphlet form.
List of Treaties Submitted to the Senate, 1789–1934 (1935) and 1935–1944 (1945).
United States Treaties and Other International Agreements, 1950–   . Prior to
  this, treaties were included in Statutes at Large. This collation is now the
  annual bound form of Treaties and Other International Acts. Each volume is
  indexed by both country and subject.
United States Treaty Developments, 1947–   . Loose-leaf volume kept up to date
  which combines List of Treaties in Force, Submitted to the Senate and Treaty
  Developments.

In addition there are miscellaneous collections of related public documents published both officially and unofficially. An example of the former
is U.S. Department of State, Territorial Papers of the United States,
Clarence E. Carter and John Porter Bloom, eds. (27 vols., 1934–1969).

Documents on American Foreign Relations (1938/39–   , is an unofficial
publication of the Council on Foreign Relations, who took over the project
from the World Peace Foundation with volume 14 in 1952. It is an annual
which presents in reference form the principal documents relating to
foreign policy, with five year cumulative indexing beginning 1961/65.

5.6 STATE DOCUMENTS

The published documents of the American states are rich and relatively
unused sources of data for students of American history. Their value grew
with the expansion of state activity. Almost all the state legislatures and

executive departments put forth bulletins and reports comparable to their federal counterparts. Some states lack, however, full sets of their own printed documents, an indication of the confusion that has attended the printing and housing of state publications. The best collections are those in the Library of Congress, the University of North Carolina Library, the Massachusetts State Library, the New York State Library, the New York Public Library, and the Library of the State Historical Society of Wisconsin.

There is no complete bibliography of official state publications. Partial bibliographical records can be traced through the publications of state agencies, societies, and libraries, but most readily through the guides listed below. Covering the states collectively are:

Bowker, R. R., ed., *State Publications: A Provisional List of the Official Publications of the Several States of the United States from Their Organization* (4 pts., 1899–1908). This is a checklist of state publications to 1900. It is incomplete, although painstakingly compiled, owing to lack of cooperation from some states. Moreover it lists the documents of the states only from the date of their organization as states.
Jenkins, William S., *Collected Public Documents of the States: A Check List* (1947). Covers colonial, territorial, and state periods.
U.S. Library of Congress, *Monthly Checklist of State Publications*, 1910– . A current bibliography, arranged alphabetically by state, of the publications of the states. Though limited to the publications received by the Library of Congress, it has been increasingly possible to elicit cooperation through a movement toward at least a minimum depository system. This list is not cumulative. Beginning in 1963, lists of periodical publications appear in June and December, the latter being cumulative.
Wilcox, J. K., *Manual on the Use of State Publications* (1940). Useful for description of state materials. Contains a pared bibliography of state publications.

There is wide variation among the states in the character and quality of their publications; few follow any consistent format. Exemplifying bibliographical control of a single state's publications is: New York State Library, *Current Checklist of State Publications* (1962).

Unlike the federal government, the states have given frequent review of their constitutions at conventions. See:

Shearer, A. H., ed., *List of Documentary Material Relating to State Constitutional Conventions 1776–1912* (1915).
University of Chicago Libraries, *Official Publications Relating to American State Constitutional Conventions* (1936). Materials, grouped by state, are ordered colonial, provincial, and territorial, followed by those for the period of statehood.
Halévy, Balfour, *A Select Bibliography on State Constitutional Revision* (2nd ed., 1967).

For a compilation of state constitutions, see *Constitutions of the United States: National and State* (2 vols., 1962). Its companion volume, *Index-Digest of State Constitutions* (2nd ed., 1959) provides subject access to the constitutions.

Many states have published the journals of their legislatures. Published records of legislative debates are less usual. For many periods and places, the historian, to know what happened in the legislatures, must consult the newspapers or records at the state capitol. A more consistent record of printing has been maintained with regard to the statutes; all states publish the laws enacted at each session, and they prepare also occasional compilations of codes. There are now commercially published editions of the statutory code for every state with annotations to relevant judicial decisions. Most states publish the decisions of their highest court of appeals; there are unofficial court reports covering every state. The following works provide a list of the legislative records and the laws of the states in their colonial, territorial, and state periods.

National Association of State Libraries, *Check-list of Legislative Journals of the States of the United States of America*, comp. by Grace E. Macdonald (1938). Continued by:
Jenkins, William S., ed., *Supplement Check-list of Legislative Journals Issued since 1937* (1943). Continued by:
Pullen, William R., *A Check-list of Legislative Journals Issued since 1937 by the States of the United States* (1955).

Macdonald, Grace E., ed., *Check-list of Session Laws* (1936). *Supplement* by F. H. Pollack (1941).
———*Check-list of Statutes* (1937). Includes revisions, compilations, digests, codes, and indexes of state statutes to date of publication.
Pimsleur, Meira G., *Checklists of Basic American Legal Publications*, 1962– .
A loose-leaf compilation divided into three sections: statutes, session laws, and attorneys' general actions.

Index to statutes of the states follow in order of their coverage.

New York State Library, *Bulletin: Legislation*, nos. 1–39 (1891–1908). An annual index to the legislation of the states.
State Law Index (12 vols., 1929–1949). Index of state legislation enacted between 1925–1948.
American Bar Association, *Computerized Law Index*, 1963– . Appeared earlier under variant titles, *Current State Legislation* and *Automated Statutory Reporter*.

Subject access to state statutes may also be attained through the annual indexes in the session law volumes.

For the standard bibliography of state and federal court reports, see C. C. Soule, *Lawyer's Reference Manual of Law Books and Citations* (1883). This is updated by Miles O. Price and Harry Bitner, *Effective Legal Research*, the 1953 edition only, and by Carlton B. Putnam, *How to Find the Law* (4th ed., 1949), 522. Later editions of the first mentioned guide omit bibliographical appendices. For further retrospective study, see also Lawrence Keitt, *Annotated Bibliography of Bibliographies of Statutory Materials* (1934).

Deserving special mention is A. R. Hasse, *Index of Economic Material in Documents of the States of the United States* (Carnegie Institution, Publ. no. 85, 13 vols. in 16, 1907–1922) covering the period to 1904 and the states: California, Delaware, Illinois, Kentucky, Maine, Massachusetts, New Hampshire, New Jersey, New York, Ohio, Pennsylvania, Rhode Island, and Vermont. A broad interpretation is given in them to the term "economic material."

5.7 LOCAL GOVERNMENT DOCUMENTS

There are few guides to records and publications of American towns and municipalities, although there exists abundant documentary material in published and manuscript form. See:

Hodgson, J. G., ed., *Official Publications of American Counties: A Union List* (1937). A checklist that indicates the holdings of 184 American libraries.
Manvel, A. D., ed., *Checklist of Basic Municipal Documents* (U.S. Bureau of the Census, State and Local Government Special Studies, no. 27, 1948).

5.8 COLONIAL AND CONFEDERATION RECORDS

Connecticut

Acts and Laws of His Majesty's Colony of Connecticut in New England (1715; 1769). Supplements to 1779.
Acts and Laws of the State of Connecticut, in America (1784). Supplements to 1779.
Dexter, Franklin B., *New Haven Town Records* [to 1769] (3 vols., 1917).
The General Laws and Liberties of Connecticut Colonie (1673; repr. 1865).
Hoadly, C. J., ed., *New Haven Colonial Records* [1638–1665] (2 vols., 1857–1858).
———and Leonard W. Labaree, eds., *Public Records of the State of Connecticut* [1776–1803] (11 vols., 1894–   ).
Proprietors' Records of the Town of Waterbury, Connecticut, 1677–1761 (1911).
Trumbull, J. H., and C. J. Hoadly, eds., *Public Records of the Colony of Connecticut* [1636–1776] (15 vols., 1850–1890).

Delaware

American Historical Association, *Court Records of Kent County, Delaware, 1680–1705*, Leon deValinger, Jr., ed. (1959).
Delaware Archives (5 vols., 1911). Military records through 1815.
Johnson, Amandus, ed., *The Instruction of Johan Printz for Governor of New Sweden* (1930).
Laws of the State of Delaware [1700–1797] (1797).
"Minutes of the Council of the Delaware State, from 1776 to 1792," Delaware Hist. Soc., *Papers*, 6 (1887).
O'Callaghan, E. B., and Berthold Fernow, eds., *Documents Relative to the Colonial History of the State of New York*. Vol. XII: *Documents Relating to the History of the Dutch and Swedish Settlements on the Delaware River*. (15 vols., 1856–1887).
Records of the Court of New Castle on Delaware, 1676–1681 (1904).
Reed, Henry C. et al., eds., *Minutes of House of Representatives of the Government of the Counties of New Castle, Kent and Sussex upon Delaware* [1765–1770] (1879).
George Staughten, et al., eds., *Charter to William Penn and Laws of the Province of Pennsylvania* [1672–1700] (1879).

Florida

Connor, J. T., ed., *Colonial Records of Spanish Florida, 1570–1580* (2 vols., 1925–1930).
Sanz, Manuel Serrano y, ed., *Documents historicos de la Florida y la Luisiana* (1912).

Georgia

Chandler, A. D., ed., *Colonial Records of the State of Georgia* [1732–1782] (26 vols., 1904–1916).
———*Revolutionary Records of Georgia* [1769–1784] (3 vols., 1908).
Davidson, G. G., ed., *Early Records of Georgia, Wilkes County* (2 vols., 1932).
Hawes, Lilla M., ed., *Proceedings and Minutes of the Governor and Council of Georgia, October 4, 1774 through November 7, 1775 and September 6, 1779 through September 20, 1780* Ga. Hist. Soc. *Coll.*, 10 (1952).

Jones, Charles C., ed., *Acts Passed by the General Assembly of the Colony of Georgia, 1755 to 1774* (1881).
"Proceedings of the First Provincial Congress of Georgia, 1775," Ga. Hist. Soc. *Coll.*, 5 (1901), 1.
"Proceedings of the Georgia Council of Safety 1775 to 1777," Ga. Hist. Soc. *Coll.*, 5 (1901), 15.
Saye, Albert B., ed., *Georgia's Charter of 1732* (1942).

Louisiana

O'Reilly, D. A., *Ordonnances* (1769). Published in French in Appendix to C. E. A. Gayarré, *Histoire de la Louisiane* (2 vols., 1846), in English in B. F. French, *Historical Collections of Louisiana* (1846–1853), V, 254–258, and in *American State Papers*, folio edition, *Miscellaneous*, I, 363. O'Reilly's *Regulations* of 1770 and in regard to land grants are also printed in English in the two sources last named, and in *American State Papers, Public Lands*, V, 729.
[Smith, Buckingham, ed.] *Coleccion de varios documentos para la historia de la Florida y tierras adyacentes* (1857).

Maryland

An Abridgement of the Laws in Force and Use in Her Majesty's Plantation, viz: of Virginia, New England, Jamaica, New York, Barbadoes, Carolina, and Maryland (1704).
Acts of Assembly, Passed in the Province of Maryland from 1692 to 1715. (1723).
Alexander, Julian J., *British Statutes in Force in Maryland* (1912).
American Historical Association, *Court Records of Prince George's County, Maryland, 1696–1699,* Joseph H. Smith and Philip A. Crowl, eds. (1964).
——*Proceedings of the Maryland Court of Appeals, 1695–1729,* Carroll T. Bond, ed. (1922).
Bacon, Thomas, *Laws of Maryland at Large* (1765).
Bisett, James, *Abridgement and Collection of the Acts of Assembly of the Province of Maryland at Present in Force* (1759).
Brumbaugh, G. M., *Maryland Records: Colonial, Revolutionary, County and Church* (2 vols., 1915–1928).
Convention of Maryland. *Proceedings of the Conventions of the Province of Maryland, held at the City of Annapolis in 1774, 1775 and 1776* (1836).
Dorsey, Clement, ed., *The General Public Statutory Law and Public Local Law of the State of Maryland, from the Year 1692 to 1839 inclusive* (1840).
Hall, Clayton C., *Narratives of Early Maryland 1633–1684* (1910).
Hanson, A. C., *Laws of Maryland Made since 1763* (1787).
Harris, Thomas and John McHenry, eds., *Maryland Reports: Being a Series of the Most Important Law Cases Argued and Determined in the Provincial Court and Court of Appeals of the then Province of Maryland from the Year 1700 down to the American Revolution* (4 vols., 1809–1840).
Hartsook, Elizabeth and Gust Skordas, *Land Office and Prerogative Court Records of Colonial Maryland* (1946).
Herty, Thomas, *Digest of the Laws of Maryland, 1637–1797* (1799–1804).
Jones, Evan, ed., *Laws of the Province of Maryland, 1692–1718* (1718).
Kilty, John, *The Land-Holder's Assistant, and Land Office Guide* (1808).
Kilty, William, ed., *Laws of Maryland 1692–1799, with Charter, Bill of Rights, and Constitution* (1799–1800).
——*A Report of all Such English Statutes . . .* (1811).
Maryland Historical Society, *Archives of Maryland,* William Hand et al., eds. (1833–   ). 71 volumes to date. Partial contents include:

Correspondence of Governor Horatio Sharpe, 1753–1765. 4. vols.
County Court Proceedings, 1648–1674. 3 vols. *Journal and Correspondence of Council of Safety, 1775–1777.* 3 vols.
Journal and Correspondence of the State Council, 1777–1789. 7 vols.

Journal of the Maryland Convention, July 26–August 14, 1775. 1 vol.
Proceedings and Acts of the General Assembly, 1637/38–March-April, 1774.
  32 vols.
Proceedings of the Court of Chancery, 1669–1679, 1 vol.
Proceedings of the Provincial Council, 1636–1770. 11 vols.
Proceedings of the Provincial Court, 1637–1683. 11 vols.
Revolutionary War Muster Rolls, 1 vol.
Maryland Historical Society, *The Calvert Papers* (Fund publications 28, 34, 35,
  1889–1899).
Maxcy, Virgil, *Laws of Maryland with Charter, etc., 1692–1809* (1811).
Parks, William, *A Compleat Collection of the Laws of Maryland* [1692–1727]
  (1727).

Massachusetts

Acts and Laws of the Commonwealth of Massachusetts [*1780–1797*] (1781–1796;
  repr., 9 vols., 1890–1896). *Supplement,* 1780–1784, E. M. Bacon ed. (1896).
Acts and Resolves, Public and Private, of the Province of the Massachusetts Bay
  [*1692–1786*] (21 vols., 1869–1922).
*Book of the General Lawes and Libertyes Concerning the Inhabitants of the Mas-
  sachusets* (1660). Reprinted in facsimile, with supplements to 1672, in W. H.
  Whitmore, *Colonial Laws of Massachusetts.* (1889).
Bradford, Alden, ed., *Speeches of the Governors of Massachusetts from 1765 to
  1775; and the Answers of the House of Representatives, with Their Resolutions*
  (1818).
*The General Laws and Liberties of the Massachusetts Colony; Revised and Re-
  printed.* By Order of the General Court Holden at Boston, May 15th, 1672.
  Edward Rawson, Secr. Cambridge (1672). Reprinted in facsimile, with supplements through 1686, in W. H. Whitmore, *Colonial Laws of Massachusetts*
  (1889).
Hutchinson, Thomas, ed., *Collection of Original Papers Relative to the History of
  the Colony of Massachusetts-Bay.* (1769. repr. 2 vols., 1865).
Journals of the House of Representatives of Massachusetts, 1715–1760 (36 vols.,
  1919–1964).
Lincoln, William, ed., *Journals of Each Provincial Congress of Massachusetts in
  1774 and 1775 . . . and Other Documents* (1838).
Records of the Court of Assistants of the Colony of Massachusetts Bay, 1630–1692
  (3 vols., 1901–1928).
Shurtleff, Nathaniel B., et al., eds., *Records of the Colony of New Plymouth in
  New England* [*1620–1692*] (12 vols., 1855–1861).
Shurtleff, Nathaniel B., ed., *Records of the Governor and Company of the Mas-
  sachusetts Bay in New England* [*1628–1686*] (5 vols., 1853–1854).
Whitmore, W. H., ed., *Bibliographical Sketch of the Laws of the Massachusetts
  Colony from 1630 to 1686* (1890).

Local records include:

Abstract and Index of the Records of the Inferiour Court of Pleas [*Suffolk County
  Court*] *Held at Boston 1680–1698* (1940).
Bates, S. A., ed., *Records of the Town of Braintree, 1640 to 1793* (1886). *Cata-
  logue of Records and Files in the Office of the Clerk of the Supreme Judicial
  Court for the County of Suffolk* (1890).
Davis, W. A., ed., *The Old Records of the Town of Fitchburgh, Massachusetts* (8
  vols., 1898–1913).
Hill, D. G., ed., *Dedham Records, 1635–1845* (5 vols., 1886–1899).
Hough, F. B., ed., *Papers Relating to the Island of Nantucket* (1856).
Muddy River and Brookline Records, 1634–1838. "By the Inhabitants of Brookline
  in Town Meeting," (1875).
Nourse, H. S., ed., *Early Records of Lancaster, 1643–1725* (1884). Supplement
  (1900).
———*Military Annals of Lancaster, 1740–1865* (1889). Supplement (1900).
Pierce, M. F., *Town of Weston, Records* [*1746–1826*] (2 vols., 1893–1894).

The Probate Records of Essex County, 1635–1681 (3 vols., 1916–1920).
The Proprietors' Records of the Town of Mendon (1899).
Records and Files of the Quarterly Courts of Essex County, Massachusetts. 1656–1683 (8 vols., 1912–1921).
"Records of the Suffolk County Court 1671–1680," Colonial Society of Massachusetts, *Coll.*, XXIX, XXX (1933).
Records of the Town of Plymouth [1636–1783] (3 vols., 1889–1903).
The Register Book of the Lands and Houses in the "New Towne" and the Town of Cambridge (1896).
Reports of the Record Commissioners of the City of Boston (39 vols. 1876–1909).
Rice, F. P., ed., *Worcester Town Records . . . [1722–1848]* (7 vols. 1879–1895).
Suffolk Deeds. Libri I-XIV (1629–1697). 1880–1906.
Upham, W. P., "Town Records of Salem, 1634–1659," Essex Inst., *Hist. Coll.*, 2 ser., I (1869).
Watertown Historical Society, *Watertown Records [1634–1829]*. (8 vols. 1894–1939).

Mississippi

Rowland, Dunbar, and A. G. Sanders, eds., *Mississippi Provincial Archives: French Dominion. 1729–1740* (3 vols., 1927–1932).
Rowland, Dunbar, ed., *Mississippi Provincial Archives: English Dominion. 1763–1766.* (1911).

Missouri

Houck, Louis, ed., *Spanish Regime in Missouri: a Collection of Papers and Documents* (2 vols. 1909).
Leopard, Buel, and F. C. Shoemaker, eds., *Messages and Proclamations of the Governors of the State of Missouri* (16 vols. 1922–1951).

New Hampshire

Bouton, Nathaniel, et al., eds., *Documents and Records Relating to the Province [1623–1800]* (40 vols. 1867–1943). Commonly cited as *New Hampshire Provincial (or State) Papers.*
Concord Town Records, 1732–1820 (1894).
Hackett, F. W., ed., *Portsmouth Records, 1645–1656* (1886).

New Jersey

Allinson, Samuel, ed., *Acts of the General Assembly of the Province of New Jersey, 1702–1776* (1776).
Calendar of the State Library Manuscript Collection (1939).
Edsall, P. W., ed., *Journal of the Courts of Common Right and Chancery of East New Jersey, 1683–1702* (1937).
Hood, John, ed., *Index . . . of Laws of New Jersey between . . . 1663 and 1903* (1905).
Journal and Votes of the House of Representatives of the Province of Nova Cesarea of New Jersey (1872).
Journal of the Procedure of the Governor and Council of the Province of East New Jersey from and after the First Day of December Anno Domini 1682 (1872).
Leaming, Aaron, and Jacob Spicer, *Grants, Concessions, and Original Constitutions of the Province of New Jersey [1664–1682]* (1752; repr. 1881).
Minutes of the Board of Proprietors of the Eastern Division of New Jersey from 1685 to 1705 (1949).
Minutes of the Council of Safety of the State of New Jersey, 1777–1778 (1872).
Minutes of the Provincial Congress and the Council of Safety of the State of New Jersey, 1774–1776 (1879).

Paterson, William, ed., *Laws of the State of New Jersey* [1703–1798] (1800).
Reed, H. C., and G. J. Miller, eds., *Burlington Court Book, a Record of Quaker Jurisprudence in West New Jersey, 1680–1709* (1944).
Scot, George, *Model of the Government of the Province of East New Jersey.* (1685; repr. in W. A. Whitehead, *East Jersey under the Proprietary Governments,* 1846).
Whitehead, W. A., et al., eds., *Archives of the State of New Jersey 1631–1800* (30 vols. 1880–1906).
Wilson, Peter, comp., *Acts of the General Assembly of the State of New Jersey* [*1776–1783*] (1784).

New York

Acts of Assembly Passed in the Province of New York from 1691 to 1718 (1719).
Colonial Laws of New York from the Year 1664 to the Revolution (5 vols., 1894–1896).
Corwin, E. T., ed., *Ecclesiastical Records of the State of New York* (7 vols., 1901–1916).
Hastings, Hugh, ed., *Military Minutes of the Council of Appointment of the State of New York, 1783–1821* (4 vols. 1901).
Journal of the Legislative Council of the Colony of New York [*1691–1775*] (2 vols., 1861).
Journal of the Votes and Proceedings of the General Assembly of the Colony of New York [*1691–1765*] (2 vols. 1746–1766).
Journals of the Provincial Congress, Provincial Convention, etc., of the State of New York [*1775–1777*] (2 vols., 1842. The journals are also printed, in part, in O'Callaghan and Fernow, *Documents* (below) v. 15).
Laws of New York from 1691 to 1773 (1774).
Laws of the State of New York [*1777–1801*] (5 vols., 1886–1887).
Lincoln, C. Z., ed., *Messages from the Governors . . . 1863 . . . 1906* (11 vols., 1909).
N. Y. State Library, Calendar of Council Minutes 1668–1783 (1902).
O'Callaghan, E. B., ed., *Documentary History of the State of New York* (4 vols., 1849–1851).
———and Berthold Fernow, eds., *Documents Relative to the Colonial History of the State of New York* Vol. XI: *General Index.* Vol. XV: *State Archives.* (15 vols., 1856–1887).
O'Callaghan, E. B., *Laws and Ordinances of New Netherland, 1638–1674* (1868).
Paltsits, V. H., ed., *Minutes of the Executive Council of the Province of New York,* [with] *Collateral and Illustrative Documents, 1668–1673* (2 vols., 1910).
Revised Statutes of the State of New York (3 vols., 1829).
Second Annual Report of the State Historian of the State of New York (2 vols., 1896–1897).
Van Ness, W. P., and John Woodworth, eds., *Laws of the State of New York* [*1784–1813*] (2 vols., 1813).

Local records include:

Case, J. W., ed., *Southold (L.I.) Town Records* (2 vols., 1882–1884).
Fernow, Berthold, ed., *Minutes of the Orphanmasters of New Amsterdam 1655–1663* (1902).
———*Records of New Amsterdam* (1653–1674) (7 vols., 1897).
Frost, J. C., ed., *Records of the Town of Jamaica, Long Island, New York* (3 vols. 1914).
Minutes of the Common Council of the City of New York 1675–1776 (8 vols., 1905).
Minutes of the Common Council of the City of New York, 1784–1831 (21 vols., 1917–1930).
Morris, R. B., ed., *Select Cases of the Mayor's Court of New York City, 1674–1784* (1935).

Munsell, Joel, *Annals of Albany (1609–1858)* (10 vols., 1850–1859).
Oyster Bay Town Records, 1653–1763 (6 vols., 1916–1931).
Pearson, Jonathan, comp., *Early Records of the City and County of Albany and Colony of Rensselaerswyck* (4 vols., 1916).
Records of the Town of Brookhaven, New York, 1798–1886 (2 vols., 1888–1893).
Records of the Town of East-Hampton, Long Island (5 vols., 1887–1905).
Records of the Towns of North and South Hempstead, Long Island, New York (8 vols., 1896–1904).
Street, C. R., ed., *Huntington Town Records including Babylon, Long Island, New York, 1653–1873* (3 vols., 1887–1889).
Transcriptions of Early Town Records of New York: Minutes of the Town Courts of Newtown, 1656–1734 (3 vols., 1940–1941).
Van Laer, A. J. F., ed., *Minutes of the Court of Albany, Rensselaerswyck and Schenectady, 1668–1685* (3 vols., 1926–1932).
———*Van Rensselaer Bowier Manuscripts* (1908).

North Carolina

Clark, Walter, ed., *State Records of North Carolina, 1777–1790* (16 vols., 1895–1905).
Crittenden, C. C., and Dan Lacy, eds., *Historical Records of North Carolina: The County Records* (3 vols., 1938–1939).
North Carolina Charters and Constitutions, 1578–1698, Mattie E. E. Parker, ed. (1963).
North Carolina Higher Court Records, 1670–1696, Mattie E. E. Parker, ed. (1968).
Powell, William S., ed., *Countie of Albermarle in Carolina: A Collection of Documents, 1664–1675* (1958).
Saunders, William L., ed., *Colonial Records of North Carolina* [1662–1776] (10 vols., 1886–1890).
Weeks, Stephen B., ed., *Index to the Colonial and State Records of North Carolina* (3 vols., 1909).

Pennsylvania

[*Colonial Records of Pennsylvania, 1683–1790.*] (16 vols., 1852–1853). *General Index* (1860).
George, Staughton, et al., eds., *Charter to William Penn and Laws of the Province of Pennsylvania Passed between 1682 and 1700 Preceded by Duke of Yorke's Book of Laws* [1676–1682] (1879).
Hazard, Samuel, et al., eds., *Pennsylvania Archives, 1664–* (1852–1949). Published in 9 series, 138 vols.; Index by H. E. Eddy (1949).
Mitchell, J. T., and Henry Flanders, eds., *Statutes at Large of Pennsylvania from 1682 to 1801* (1896–1908).
Votes and Proceedings of the House of Representatives of the Province of Pennsylvania (1682–1776). (6 vols., 1752–1756).

Rhode Island

Acts and Laws of His Majesty's Colony of Rhode-Island and Providence-Plantations in New England (1745, 1764, and 1767). All editions are imperfect.
Bartlett, J. R., ed., *Records of the Colony of Rhode Island and Providence Plantations in New England* [1636–1792] (10 vols., 1856–1865).
Kimball, G. S., ed., *Correspondence of the Colonial Governors of Rhode Island, 1723–1775* (2 vols., 1902–1903).
Rhode Island Court Records, 1647–1670 (2 vols., 1920–1922).
Rhode Island Land Evidences, 1648–1696 (1921).
Smith, J. J., ed., *Civil and Military List of Rhode Island (1647–1850)* (3 vols., 1900–1907).
Towle, D. S., ed., *Records of the Vice-Admiralty Court of Rhode Island 1716–1752* (1936).

Local records include:

Bowen, R. L., ed., *Index to the Early Records of the Town of Providence* (1949).
Early Records of the Town of Portsmouth [1639–1697] (1901).
Early Records of the Town of Warwick (1926).
Pelkly, W. C., ed., *Early Records of the Town of Providence* (21 vols., 1892–1915).
Records of the Town of Plymouth, 1636–1783 (3 vols., 1889–1903).

South Carolina

Brevard, Joseph, ed., *Alphabetical Digest of the Public Statute Law of South Carolina* (3 vols., 1814).
Cooper, Thomas, and D. J. McCord, eds., *Statutes at Large of South Carolina* (10 vols., 1836–1841).
Easterby, J. H., and Ruth S. Green, eds., *Colonial Records of South Carolina: Journals of the Commons House of Assembly* [*1736/1750–*   ] (9 vols., 1951/ 62–   ).
Gregorie, A. K., and J. N. Frierson, eds., *Records of the Court of Chancery of South Carolina, 1671–1779* (1950).
Grimké, J. F., ed., *Public Laws of the State of South Carolina* [1694–1790] (1790).
Hemphill, W. Edwin, Wylma A. Wates, and R. Nicholas Olsberg, *Journal of General Assembly and House of Representatives, 1776–1780* (1970).
McDowell, W. L., ed., *Documents Relating to Indian Affairs, 1750–1765* (2 vols., 1958–1970).
———*Journals of the Commissioners of the Indian Trade, September 20, 1710– August 29, 1718* (1955).
Salley, A. S., ed., *Commissions and Instructions from the Lords Proprietors of Carolina to Public Officials of South Carolina, 1685–1715* (1916).
———*Documents Relating to the History of South Carolina during the Revolutionary War* (1908).
———*Journal of His Majesty's Council for South Carolina May 29, 1721–June 10, 1721* (1930).
———*Journal of the Commissioners of the Navy 1776–1780* (2 vols., 1912–1913).
———*Journal of the Commons House of Assembly of South Carolina* [1692–1735, Jan.–Aug. 1765] (25 vols., 1907–1949). For continuation of the *Journal, see* J. H. Easterby above.
———*Journal of the Convention of South Carolina Which Ratified the Constitution of the United States May 23, 1788* (1928).
———*Journal of the Grand Council of South Carolina* (1907).
———*Records in the British Public Record Office Relating to South Carolina 1663–1710* (5 vols., 1928–1947).
———*Records of the Secretary of the Province and the Register of the Province of South Carolina, 1671–1675* (1944).
———*South Carolina Treasury: Accounts Audited of Revolutionary Claims against South Carolina* (3 vols., 1935–1943).
———and Wylma A. Wates, eds., *Stub Entries to Indents Issued in Payment of Claims against South Carolina* (12 vols., 1910–1957).
Salley, A. S., ed., *Warrants for Lands in South Carolina, 1672–1711* (3 vols., 1910–1915).
Trott, Nicholas, ed., *Laws of the Province of South Carolina before 1734* (2 vols., 1736).
Weston, P. C. J., ed., *Documents Connected with the History of South Carolina* (1856).

Local records include:

Digest of the Ordinance of the City Council of Charleston . . . 1783–1818 (1818).
Salley, A. S., ed., *Minutes of the Vestry of St. Helena's Parish, South Carolina, 1726–1812* (1919).
———*Minutes of the Vestry of St. Matthew's Parish, South Carolina, 1767–1838* (1939).
———*Register of St. Philip's Parish, Charles Town, South Carolina, 1720–1810* (2 vols., 1904–1927).

Vermont

Hoyt, Edward A., ed., *State Papers of Vermont. General Petitions, 1778–1799* (1952–1962).
Slade, William, ed., *Vermont State Papers: Being a Collection of Records and Documents* (1823).
Walton, E. P., ed., *Records of the Council of Safety and Governor and Council of the State of Vermont, 1775–1836* (8 vols., 1873–1880).

Virginia

Barton, R. T., ed., *Virginia Colonial Decisions . . . Reports by Sir John Randolph and by Edward Barradall of Decisions of the General Court of Virginia, 1728–1741* (2 vols., 1909).
Eckenrode, H. J., ed., *Fifth Annual Report of the Library Board, Calendar of Legislative Petitions Arranged by Counties Accomac-Bedford* (1908).
Hening, W. W., ed., *The Statutes at Large Being a Collection of All the Laws of Virginia (1619–1792)* (13 vols., 1809–1823).
Journals of the Council of the State of Virginia, 1776–1781, (4 vols., 1967).
Kingsbury, S. M., ed., *Records of the Virginia Company of London: The Court Book, from the Manuscript in the Library of Congress* (4 vols., 1906–1935).
McIlwaine, H. R., and W. L. Hall, eds., *Executive Journals of the Council of Colonial Virginia, 1680–1754* (5 vols., 1925–1945).
McIlwaine, H. R., and J. P. Kennedy, eds., *Journals of the House of Burgesses of Virginia* [1619–1776] (13 vols., 1905–1915).
McIlwaine, H. R., *Minutes of the Council and General Court of Colonial Virginia, 1622–1632, 1670–1676* (1924).
————ed., *Official Letters of the Governors of the State of Virginia* (3 vols., 1926–1929).
Palmer, W. P., et al., eds., *Calendar of Virginia State Papers and Other Manuscripts . . . Preserved . . . at Richmond* [1652–1869] (11 vols., 1875–1893).
Report of the Committee of Revisors Appointed by the General Assembly of Virginia in 1776 (1784).
Virginia Colonial Abstracts, 1652–1820 (40 vols., 1937–1949, 1952–1961).
Winfree, Waverly K., comp., *The Laws of Virginia; Being a Supplement to Hening's, The Statutes at Large* (1969).
Wynne, T. H., and W. S. Gilman, eds., *Colonial Records of Virginia* [1619–1680] (1874).

Local records include:

Bell, Landon C., ed., *Charles Parish, York County, Virginia, History and Registers, Births 1648–1789, Deaths, 1665–1787* (1932).
————*Cumberland Parish, Lunenburg County, Virginia, 1746–1816, Vestry Book, 1746–1816* (1912).
Chalkley, Lyman, ed., *Chronicles of the Scotch-Irish Settlement in Virginia Extracted from the Original Court Records of Augusta County 1745–1800* (3 vols., 1912).
Chamberlayne, C. G., ed., *Vestry Book of Blisland (Blissland) Parish, New Kent and James City Counties, Virginia, 1721–1786* (1935).
————*Vestry Book of Petsworth Parish, Gloucester County, Virginia, 1677–1793* (1933).
————*Vestry Book of St. Paul's Parish, Hanover County, Virginia, 1706–86* (1940).
————*Vestry Book and Register of St. Peter's Parish, New Kent and James City Counties, Virginia, 1684–1786* (1937).
————*Vestry Book of Stratton Major Parish, King and Queen County, Virginia, 1729–1783* (1931).
Cocke, Charles F., ed., *Parish Lines, Diocese of Southern Virginia* (1964).
————*Parish Lines, Diocese of Southwestern Virginia* (1960).
————*Parish Lines, Diocese of Virginia* (1967).
Crozier, W. A., ed., *Virginia County Records* (11 vols., 1905–1913).

Hall, W. L., ed., *Vestry Book of the Upper Parish, Nansemond County, Virginia, 1743–1793* (1949).

5.9 FOREIGN GOVERNMENT PUBLICATIONS

Like the American federal and state governments, the governments of foreign countries have issued series of published documents, which are important sources for the American historian. These vary in thoroughness, regularity of appearance, and relevance to American history. In most American libraries they are found in broken sets only. Information as to what holdings individual libraries have is, therefore, essential to the researcher. See Winifred Gregory, *List of Serial Publications of Foreign Governments, 1815–1931* (1932).

The following are the more important documentary publications of governments and published collections of interest to American historians. See also UNESCO, *A Study of Current Bibliographies of National Official Publications* (1958).

5.9.1 Great Britain and Ireland

British documentary publications are voluminous, and as might be expected, they center about the operations of Parliament. For a general introduction to the materials, see:

Ford, Percy and Grace Ford, *A Guide to Parliamentary Papers* (1955).
Great Britain. H. M. Stationery Office, *Published by HMSO: A Brief Guide to Official Publications* (1960).
Horrocks, Sidney, *The State as Publisher* (1952).

Parliamentary debates were not officially recorded until the nineteenth century. For earlier years the most satisfactory compilation is William Cobbett's *Parliamentary History of England from the Earliest Period to the Year 1803* (36 vols., 1806–1820). After 1803 reports are continuously given in *Hansard's Parliamentary Debates*. Both houses also publish journals which are indexed periodically. Especially useful to students of American history is L. F. Stock, *Proceedings and Debates of the British Parliaments Respecting North America 1452–1727* (3 vols., 1924–1930). For a selective guide to Parliamentary papers see:

Ford, Percy, and Grace Ford, *A Breviate of Parliamentary Papers, 1900–1916* (1957); ———*1917–1939* (1952; and ———*1940–1954* (1961). This is a continuation of:
Ford, Percy, and Grace Ford, *Select List of British Parliamentary Papers, 1833–1899* (1953). Includes annotations and is a supplement to:
Great Britain. H. M. Stationery Office, *General Index to Parliamentary Papers, 1900–1949* (1960).
Great Britain. Parliament. House of Commons, *Catalogue of Parliamentary Reports and a Breviate of Their Contents: Arranged Under Heads According to the Subjects, 1696–1837* (2 vols., 1834–1837).

Statutes for the period 1235-1948 may be found in *The Statutes (1235-1948)* (3d rev. ed., 32 vols., 1950) with the exception of legislation for the years between 1642 and 1660 which is given in C. H. Firth and R. S. Rait, eds., *Acts and Ordinances of the Interregnum, 1642–1660* (3 vols., 1911). The laws of more recent years are in annual *Public General Acts* (1921–   ), as well as in unofficial compilations such as Butterworth's, Chitty's, and Halsbury's.

Since the heads of the executive departments are ministers responsible to Parliament, much of the work of those departments is reported in sessional papers presented to the House of Commons and the House of Lords. There are good files of those papers in American libraries either in microprint or in regular format. These and other parliamentary materials may be traced through the following:

General Alphabetical Index to the Bills, Reports, Estimates, Accounts, Printed by Order of the House of Commons and to the Papers Presented by Command, 1801–1948/49 (4 vols., 1853–1960).
List of the Bills, Reports, Estimates and Accounts and Papers Printed by Order of the House of Commons and of the Papers Presented by Command with a General Alphabetical Index Thereto (1920–   ). Published annually as the last volume of the sessional papers.
General Index to Sessional Papers Printed by Order of the House of Lords or Presented by Special Command (3 vols., 1860–   ). An annual.

Between 1915 and 1921 H. M. Stationery Office published two monthly lists of publications, one for those materials emanating from Parliament, the other for additional categories of official publications. Since that date, it has published a monthly *Catalogue of Government Publications*, the December issue of which is an annual cumulation of all the public documents of the year. These are consolidated in the quinquennial publication *Consolidated List of Government Publications*, (1936–   ).

All the publications of the Public Records Office are listed in *Government Publications, Sectional List* of H. M. Stationery Office. Many lists are not published and are only available in typescript in the reading rooms of the Public Records Office, but smaller handbooks on specific subjects are available. Examples of those of value to an American historian are:

Pugh, R. B., ed., *The Records of the Colonial and Dominions Offices* (1964).
———*List of Cabinet Papers 1880–1914* (1964).

Important publications of Great Britain's Foreign Office include:

British and Foreign State Papers, 1812/14–   (1841–   ).
Gooch, G. P., and Harold Temperley, eds., *British Documents on the Origins of the War 1898–1914* (11 vols., 1926–1938).
Great Britain, Parliament. House of Lords, *Manuscripts of the House of Lords,* new series, (1514–   ).
Temperley, Harold, and L. M. Penson, eds., *A Century of Diplomatic Blue Books, 1814–1914* (1938).
Vogel, Robert, *A Breviate of British Diplomatic Blue Books, 1919–1939* (1963).
Woodward, E. L., and Rohan Butler, eds., *Documents on British Foreign Policy, 1919–*   (1946–   ).

Ireland, since the recognition of its separate status, has published its own documentary series, including the debates in the Dáil (1922–   ). That is also true of the Parliament of Northern Ireland (1921–   ). In general, the series of these states follow the British in form. Further aids for research are:

ASLIB Directory: A Guide to Sources of Information in Great Britain and Ireland, Miriam Alman, ed. (2 vols., 1957).
Burkett, Jack, *Special Library and Information Services in the United Kingdom* (1961).

Clark, G. Kitson, and G. R. Elton, *Guide to Research Facilities in History* (1963).
Hewitt, Arthur R., *Guide to Resources for Commonwealth Studies* (1957).
Irwin, Raymond, *The Libraries of London* (2nd ed., 1961).
Mullins, E. L. C., *Texts and Calendars: An Analytical Guide to Serial Publications* (1958).
Munby, A. N. L., *Cambridge College Libraries: Aids for Research Students* (2nd ed., 1962).

5.9.2 France

The published French documents fall into no consistent series. Before 1789 the most important are the royal decrees, for which see: Jourdan et al., eds., *Recueil général des anciennes lois françaises* (29 vols., 1829–1833). Indexed. After that date fluctuations in legislative forms are reflected in frequent changes in the nature of the documents. The changes in form of government and in the constitution and powers of the legislature naturally altered the character of their publications. The *Bulletin des lois* regularly printed the laws and was indexed annually. *Précis verbaux* were accounts of proceedings, and the *Annales* of the various legislative bodies were counterparts of American *Journals*. The *Moniteur* or *Gazette nationale* (1789–1810) carried a variety of governmental decrees; it was continued as the *Moniteur universel* (1811–1870) and as *Le journal officiel de la république française* 1870–   . For the period 1839 the best edition of the debates is in a later compilation: M. J. Mavidal et al., eds., *Archives parlementaires de 1787 à 1860* (209 vols., 1879–1913). After 1870 *Le journal officiel de la république française* is the most reliable source. It is in ten parts, carries its own index and is supplemented by a number of *Annexes* of a documentary nature. In addition, there is a large body of administrative publications, including the reports of departments and bureaus, those on trade and colonies being particularly valuable for American historians.

Jacques de Dampierre, *Les publications officielles des pouvoirs publics: Étude critique et administrative* (1942) contains a detailed historical description of the official publications of France. Supplement F of *Bibliographie de la France* entitled *Publications officielles* (1950–   ) includes national, local, and overseas government publications; it has an annual index. Supplement F also serves as a partial index to the *Journal officiel*.
Collections that may be useful to American historians include:

Archives diplomatiques (193 vols., 1861–1914). Semi-official, published monthly.
Documents diplomatiques français [1871–1914] (33 vols., 1929–   ).
Recueil des instructions données aux ambassadeurs et ministres de France depuis les traités de Westphalie jusqu'à la révolution française (26 vols., 1884–1929).
Wroth, Lyman C., and G. L. Annan, eds., *Acts of French Royal Administration Concerning Canada, Guiana, the West Indies, and Louisiana, prior to 1791* (1930).

5.9.3 Germany

Nineteenth-century German records are unusually confusing because Germany was not unified until the latter part of the century. Each of the governmental entities issued publications of laws and decrees, legislative proceedings, and reports of the ministries. An index to the Reichstag proceedings, *Generalregister* was published sessionally for the period 1867–1933. For the period since 1870, the *Reichsgesetzblatt* is a compendious record of items passed by the Reichstag including laws and regulations. The *Monatliches Verzeichnis der reichsdeutschen amtlichen Druckschriften* (17 vols., 1928–1944), and thereafter *Deutsche Bibliographie: Verzeichnis Amtlicher Druckscriften, 1957/58–* (1962) a biennial, lists official publications of the German Federal Republic, as well as of the states of the Republic and West Berlin. Other guides to governmental publications include Otto Neuberger, *Official Publications of Present Day Germany* (1942), and for a later period James B. Childs, *German Federal Republic Official Publications, 1949–1957, with Inclusion of preceding Zonal Official Publications* (1958). Publications of the member states are omitted here.

5.9.4 Spain and Portugal

Spanish materials are relevant primarily for the colonial era and particularly for the sections that were at one time under the control of Spain. The archives are extensive. In the list of guides, the Chapman *Catalogue* is particularly useful; but see also above under California, Florida, Texas; below under Latin America; and the Hill and Shepherd guides above.

Anais das bibliotecas, arquivo e museus municipais. Lisbon, 1931–   .
Anais das bibliotecas e arquivos de Portugal. Coimbra, 1914–
Azevedo, Pedro A. de, and Antonio Baião, *O Archivo da Torre do Tombo.* Lisbon, 1905.
Boletim de bibliographia portugueza e revista dos arquivos nacionaes. Coimbra, 1879–   .
Mesquita de Figueiredo, António, *Arquivo nacional da Torre do Tombo.* Lisbon, 1922.
Revista de archivos, bibliotecas y museos. Madrid, 1871–   .
Revista de la biblioteca, archivo y museo. Madrid, 1924–   .
Rodríguez Marín, Francisco, *Guia histórica y descriptiva de los archivos, bibliotecas y museos arqueologicos de Espana.* 2 vols. Madrid, 1916–1925.
Torre Revello, José, "El Archivo General de Indias de Sevilla," Instituto de Investigaciones Historicas (Buenos Aires), *Publ.,* L (1929).

The most important published Spanish documents are the records of the Cortes (1810–   ). Some departmental collections are also useful. See, thus: *Boletin de la Dirección General de emigración* (Madrid, 1925–   ).

5.9.5 Other European Countries

The documentary resources of other European countries are less likely to prove rewarding to American historians. The contact with the United States has been less direct and, while all have extensive archives and published series, useful material in them is scattered and difficult to locate. A first approach can be made through Winifred Gregory, *List of Serial Publications of Foreign Governments, 1815–1931* (1932). For Denmark see *Bibliografi over Denmarks Offentlige Publikationer* (1948–   ), and for Norway, *Bibliografi over Norges Offentlige Publikasjoner* (1956–   ). Official Italian and Swedish reports relating to immigration have an obvious importance to the student of American history. Diplomatic historians will find useful such collections as Ludwig Bittner et al., eds. *Oesterreich-Ungarns Aussenpolitik von der bosnischen Krise, 1908, bis zum Kriegsausbruch* (9 vols., 1930). Students may also consult with profit collections of purely internal concern such as *Le Assemblee del Risorgimento* (15 vols., 1911).

5.9.6 Latin America and the West Indies

Much of the material for the years when these areas were colonial dependencies of the European powers will be found in the archives and publications of Spain, Portugal, Holland, France, and Great Britain. But each of the governmental entities in South and Central America has, in addition, developed collections and publication series of its own. Among the more important current documentary series are the legislative journals for each country and for most of the colonies, the *Memoria* of each presidential administration and the reports of colonial governors as well as a wide variety of departmental publications. Among the more helpful guides are the Gregory *List* and the Library of Congress, *Guide to the Official Publications of the Other American Republics* (19 vols., 1945–1949). See also:

Childs, J. B., ed., *Colombian Government Publications* (1941).
————*Memorias of the Republics of Central America and the Antilles* (1932).

General information about the Organization of American States documents including the treaty series and conference proceedings will be found in *Guide to the Use of the OAS Official Records Series*. Items are indexed in the annual *Documentos oficiales de la Organizacion de los Estados Americanos, indice y lista general* (1960–   ). These publications are available from the Publications Department, Pan American Union, Washington, D. C. 20006.

5.9.7 Canada

Many Canadian historical documents of interest to students of the history of the United States have been published as monographs or in collections. The more important include:

Akins, T. B., ed., *Selections from the Public Documents of the Province of Nova Scotia* (1869).
Egerton, H. E., and W. P. Grant, eds., *Canadian Constitutional Development Shown by Selected Speeches and Dispatches* [1763–1865] (1907).
Houston, William, ed., *Documents Illustrative of the Canadian Constitution* (1891).
Kingsford, William, ed., *History of Canada* [1608–1841] (10 vols., 1888–1898).
Roy, P. G., ed., *Inventaire des concessions en fief et seigneurie . . . conservés aux archives de la province de Québec* (4 vols., 1927–1928).
Shortt, Adam, and A. G. Doughty, eds., *Documents Relating to the Constitutional History of Canada, 1759–1791* (1907).

Official Canadian publications, both parliamentary and departmental, are included in *Canadian Government Publications: Catalogue 1953–   *, an annual cumulation of the *Monthly Catalogue*. It succeeds the *Catalogue of Official Publications of the Parliament and Government of Canada, 1928–1948*. Useful for its period is Marion V. Higgins, *Canadian Government Publications* (1935), which lists Canadian government publications from 1608 to 1935, including an historical summary of the issuing bodies.

The Dominion and the provinces also publish extensive documents, generally modeled after those of Great Britain. Since the provinces antedate the Dominion, their papers go back farther. The Dominion publishes a *Gazette*, journals and debates of the Senate and of the House of

Commons, sessional papers, the reports of special commissions and of the heads of departments. The *Canada Statistical Yearbook* (1885–   ) is helpful. Quebec, Ontario, Manitoba, British Columbia, Alberta, Saskatchewan, Newfoundland, Nova Scotia, Prince Edward's Island, and New Brunswick each issue their own legislative documents and departmental papers.
See:

Bishop, Olga B., *Publications of the Province of Canada, 1841–1867* (1963).
———*Publications of the Governments of Nova Scotia, Prince Edward Island, New Brunswick, 1758–1952* (1957).
Holmes, Marjorie C., *Publications of the Government of British Columbia, 1871–1947* (1950).
MacDonald, Christine, *Publications of the Governments of the Northwest Territories, 1876–1905 and of the Province of Saskatchewan, 1905–1952* (1952).

See also:

Bowles, W. C., et al., eds., *General Index to the Journals of the House of Commons of the Dominion of Canada and of the Sessional Papers of Parliament from 1867 to [1930]* (5 vols., 1880–1932).
Cole, A. H., ed., *Finding-List of Royal Commission Reports in the British Dominions* (1939).
Henderson, George F., *Federal Royal Commissions in Canada 1867–1966: A Checklist* (1967).
Sydère, A. H. et al., eds., *General Index to the Journals and Sessessional Papers of the Legislative Assembly of the Province of Ontario (1867–1927)* (6 vols., 1888–1927).
Todd, Alfred, ed., *General Index to the Journals of the House of Assembly of . . . Upper Canada . . . 1825 . . . –1839/40* (1848).
———*General Index to the Journals of the Legislative Assembly of Canada 1841–1866* (2 vols., 1855–1867).

5.10 INTERNATIONAL AGENCY PUBLICATIONS

Most international acts are still the acts of sovereign states, recorded in the documents of the contracting powers. But in the twentieth century, the appearance of several international bodies has produced a corpus of documentary sources emanating from the agencies themselves. Such agencies vary widely, ranging from permanent official bodies such as the Hague Tribunal and the Red Cross, to temporary official organizations like the International Military Tribunal and UNRRA, and to unofficial associations such as the Olympic Organization and the International Institute of Agriculture.

The League of Nations established with headquarters in Geneva after the First World War included, at one time or another, every important country except for the United States. The documents it published contain a good deal of material relevant to American history including its *Official Journal* (with supplements, 1920–1940), and a *Monthly Summary* (1921–1940), as well as regular records of the sessions of its deliberative agencies. In addition, it issued thirteen series of publications and a variety of special reports, together with a subject list of its documents. All these may be traced through:

Aufricht, Hans, *Guide to League of Nations Publications . . . 1920–1947* (1951).

von Breycha-Vauthier, A. C., *Sources of Information: A Handbook of the Publications of the League of Nations* (1939).
Carroll, M. J., *Key to League of Nations Documents, 1920–* [1936] (5 vols., 1930–1938). *Supplement, 1937–1947* (1953), prepared in the Law Library of Columbia University.

The International Labor Office antedated the League of Nations, some of its activities going back to 1902. Although the I.L.O. became a constituent body within the League, it survived the dissolution of the parent organization. Through its lifetime the I.L.O. has published an impressive list of reports, studies, conferences, statistical series, and yearbooks. See:

Rounds, J. B., *Research Facilities of the International Labour Office Available to American Libraries* (1939).
Bibliography of the International Labour Organization . . . 1919–1938 (1938).
International Labor Office, *Bibliography on the International Labour Organization* (1959).

The United Nations was the outgrowth of the alliance that won the Second World War. The documentary record of its formation may be found in *United Nations Documents, 1941–1945* (1946). The U.N. and its constituent bodies—among them the General Assembly, the Security Council, the World Health Organization, the Economic and Social Council, and the Educational, Scientific, and Cultural Organization (UNESCO)—publish extensive series of official records, conference reports, and documents. A *Journal* (1946–   ), issued daily during Assembly sessions, contains important reports and documents. Among the more useful regular U.N. publications are its *Treaty Series* (1946/47–   ), a *Handbook* (1946–   ), and *Yearbook* (1946/47–   ).
The Department of Public Information has published a cumulative sales catalog, *Ten Years of United Nations Publications 1945 to 1955: A Complete Catalogue* (1955), continued by *United Nations Publications 1955–1958*, and annual volumes thereafter. The Office of Conference Services issues a complete listing of official records by year, *United Nations Official Records, 1948–1962* (1963), kept up to date by annual issues. The *Checklist of United Nations Documents, 1946–1949* (1949–52) is a helpful guide published by the Dag Hammarskjold Library, continued in part by the monthly *United Nations Documents Index, 1950–   *. Beginning in 1963 these issues are superseded by two separate annual cumulations. The U.N. also publishes *U.N. Books in Print* (1960) with supplements, which lists publications available for sale, but omits official records. See also Brenda Brimmer et al., *A Guide to the Use of United Nations Documents* (1962), and C. C. Moor and Waldo Chamberlain, *How to Use United Nations Documents* (1952).

6 Unpublished Primary Sources

6.1 INTRODUCTION

A large part of the existing materials of American history is still in manuscript form. Despite the winnowing and destruction that eliminates some of these materials, the bulk continues to grow rapidly. These unpublished primary sources may be divided into two categories, archives and manuscript collections. (Archivists would prefer to refer to the division as one between archives and private papers). In general, an archive is organic and a collection is inorganic and fortuitous—but the differences between the two are not always easy to delineate.

A prominent archivist, Ernst Posner, has defined archives as "records of a government agency or other organization or institution having enduring values because of the information they contain. The term is also applied to the records of families and individuals, especially if consciously organized for preservation." [*American State Archives* (University of Chicago Press, 1964), p. 368]. Records include more than manuscripts and unpublished primary sources. Another archivist, Theodore R. Schellenberg, has revised the official definition of records to read,

"All books, papers, maps, photographs, or other documentary materials, regardless of physical form or characteristics, made or received by any public or private institution in pursuance of its legal obligations or in connection with the transaction of its proper business and preserved or appropriated for preservation by that institution or its legitimate successor as evidence of its functions, policies, procedures, operations, or other activities or because of the informational value of the data contained therein." [*Modern Archives: Principles and Techniques* (University of Chicago Press, 1956), p. 16].

Historical manuscripts, or private papers, according to Lester J. Cappon, may cover "(1) bodies or groups of papers with organic unity, in the nature of archives, personal or institutional; (2) artificial collections of manuscripts acquired by a private collector from various sources, usually according to plan but without regard for *respect des fonds*; (3) individual manuscripts acquired by the repository for their special importance to research and comprising a collection of what, for want of a better term, are sometimes called 'miscellaneous manuscripts.' " ["Historical Manuscripts as Archives," *Am. Archivist*, 19 (1956), 104–105].

American Historical Association, "Report of the Ad Hoc Committee on Manuscripts," *Proceedings of the American Historical Association* (1950).

Brooks, Philip C., *Research in Archives: The Use of Unpublished Primary Sources* (1969).
Cappon, Lester J., "Historical Manuscripts as Archives: Some Definitions and Their Application," *Am. Archivist,* 19 (1956), 101.
Hesseltine, William B., and Donald R. McNeil, eds., *In Support of Clio* (1958).
Posner, Ernst, *American State Archives* (1964).
———*Archives and the Public Interest* (1967).
Schellenberg, Theodore R., *Modern Archives: Principles and Techniques* (1956).
———*The Management of Archives* (1965).

6.2 NATIONAL ARCHIVES

The National Archives is custodian of federal public records. Each federal department kept its own records, which were often difficult to find and use, until in 1934 Congress established the National Archives, charging it with responsibility for accumulating, appraising, destroying or preserving, and storing all archives or records belonging to the government of the United States. In 1949 the renamed National Archives and Records Service became part of the General Services Administration. Within twenty years the Archives had accumulated 918,000 cubic feet of permanently valuable federal records, including documents, correspondence files, oral history tapes, phonograph records, maps, photographs, and motion picture films. These records are usually deposited with the Archives by government agencies after twenty years. Only records of lasting value or historical interest are transferred. The Archives also accepts some private papers and audiovisual materials relating to federal activities.

While most materials are available for research, some have restrictions upon their use or publication. Defense-classified records in the National Archives, such as some State Department and Department of Defense materials, are available only to United States citizens, complying with procedures akin to security clearance. An applicant wishing to use defense-classified records should write far in advance to the Archivist of the United States. An applicant for research in unrestricted material need only furnish proper identification, or in some instances a letter of reference or introduction. If one writes in advance, one can usually learn whether sufficient materials are available to warrant a visit. These application procedures apply to the Federal Records Centers and the presidential libraries as well as to the National Archives in Washington.

Information about material in the National Archives can be found in the *Comprehensive Guide to the National Archives* (1972), supplemented by accession notices in *Prologue,* the journal of the National Archives, published three times yearly since 1969. In addition, the Archives has prepared several hundred *Preliminary Inventories . . .* of the holdings of departments or agencies. Too numerous to cite here, they are listed in the annual bibliography of *American Archivist* and in the *Publications of the National Archives and Records Service,* frequently revised. Since the inventories must be exhaustive, they are not as useful to the individual researcher as are the special lists that describe small parts of the holdings, such as Forrest R. Holdcamper, comp., *List of American Flag Merchant Vessels that Received Certificates of Enrollment or Registry at the Port of New York, 1789–1867* (2 vols., 1968). The National Archives also issues reference information papers analyzing records in the Archives, such as *Age and Citizenship Records in the National Archives* (1966) or *Materials in* the *National Archives of the United States Relating to the Independence of Latin American Nations* (1968). These special lists and reference information papers are available without charge to scholars and are listed in *Publications of the National Archives and Records Service.*

The Archives also issues a number of comprehensive guides such as the two-volume *Federal Records of World War II* (1950–1951).

Useful, non-official guides to materials in the National Archives include:

Beers, Henry P., *Guide to the Archives of the Government of the Confederate States of America* (1968).
Fishbein, Meyer H., "Business History Resources in the National Archives," *Bus. Hist. Rev.*, 38 (1964), 232.
Lee, G. A., "General Records of the United States Department of Agriculture in the National Archives," *Agric. Hist.*, 19 (1945), 242.
Lewinson, Paul, *Guide to Documents in the National Archives for Negro Studies* (1947).
Munden, Kenneth W., and Henry P. Beers, *Guide to Federal Archives Relating to the Civil War* (1962).

6.2.1 Regional Archival Centers

Regional archives branches in Federal Records Centers contain materials of historical interest, for the most part regional in nature. These include U.S. District and Circuit Court records, customs records, materials relating to federal land sales and Indian affairs, and to the waterways and harbor projects of the Army Engineers. Each center contains the volumes of the valuable U.S. Works Projects Administration, *Survey of Federal Archives in the States*, published in series under topics (such as series 2, Federal Courts; series 4, Department of War). Each volume deals with a given region. Gradually all the relevant records are being transferred from the agencies to the centers. The regional archives branches also contain sets of National Archives microfilm publications.

For further information, address the Federal Records Center Manager at the following locations:

Atlanta: 1557 St. Joseph Avenue, East Point, Ga. 30044
Boston: 380 Trapelo Road, Waltham, Mass. 02154
Chicago: 7201 South Leamington Avenue, Chicago, Ill. 60638
Denver: Building 48, Denver Federal Center, Denver Colo. 80225
Fort Worth: 4900 Hemphill Street, Fort Worth, Tex. 76115
Kansas City: 2306 East Bannister Road, Kansas City, Mo. 64131
Los Angeles: 4747 Eastern Avenue, Bell, Calif. 90201
New York: 641 Washington Street, New York, N.Y. 10014
Philadelphia: 5000 Wissahickon Avenue, Philadelphia, Pa. 19144
San Francisco: 100 Harrison Street, San Francisco, Calif. 94105
Seattle: 6125 Sand Point Way, Seattle, Wash. 98115
Washington: Washington, D. C. 20409

6.2.2 Presidential Libraries

A growing number of Presidential Libraries, operating as part of the National Archives system, contain important collections of presidential records and private papers. They include not only the papers of each President, but also the papers of many of his associates. Thus the Harry Hopkins papers and Henry Morgenthau, Jr. diaries are at the Roosevelt Library, and the Clark M. Clifford papers are at the Truman Library. For the most part the manuscripts, books, and other materials focus on the president and his administration, but some collections are further afield, representing a president's interests. There are manuscripts at the Roosevelt Library on the early history of Dutchess County, New York. President Roosevelt himself oversaw the planning and construction of the Roosevelt Library; it has served as a model for subsequent libraries. The Presidential Libraries Act of 1955 provides for the maintenance of existing libraries and the establishment of future ones. The Archives has adopted two procedures which aid researchers in the Presidential Libraries: (1) visiting scholars will be given an annotated list of groups of records in the particular library; and (2) any new editing projects undertaken by the staff of a Presidential Library will be announced in an appropriate journal and in the announcements distributed to visitors. Accessions and the opening of previously closed papers are announced in *Prologue* and usually in the *AHA Newsletter*. Researchers will find that the same regulations are in effect at Presidential Libraries as at the National Archives. The general policy is that papers open to one researcher are open to all.

The Truman Library Institute offers a limited number of research grants and fellowships. Other presidential library institutes are being formed. Address inquiries to the Director:

Herbert Hoover Library, West Branch, Iowa 52358
Franklin D. Roosevelt Library, Hyde Park, N.Y. 12538
Harry S. Truman Library, Independence, Mo. 64050
Dwight D. Eisenhower Library, Abilene, Kans. 67410
John F. Kennedy Library, 380 Trapelo Rd., Waltham, Mass. 02154
Lyndon B. Johnson Library, Austin, Tex. 78712

6.3 STATE AND LOCAL ARCHIVES

State and local records parallel those of the federal government.

Up to the Revolution the records of the colonies were divided among the colonial capitals, the local county seats, and the center of imperial government in London. By and large the documents have remained where they were originally lodged, although many of the records in English depositories have been transcribed or printed and are available in the United States.

After the Revolution each state government, in its own fashion, accumulated its own fund of documents. Most were slow to take adequate precautions to preserve materials. By the Civil War the increase in interest in historical studies led to the formation of central archival establishments in some of the states. But throughout the nineteenth century all such efforts were haphazard. Many records did not survive the occasional transfer of the capital from city to city; others were victims of fire; and still others fell into private hands or into the possession of libraries or historical societies. Most state archives remain in relative disarray. Only recently have some state administrators begun housing these documents properly and making them readily available to scholars.

In 1964 Ernst Posner published *American State Archives*, the first state-by-state study of archival agencies and their programs. It is not a guide to the holdings of these agencies. Rather, it highlights the need for guides as well as other major improvements before the archives will be fully useful to the scholar. It contains an excellent bibliography.

There is no single, overall guide to American state and local government archives. The last bibliography of official state publications was published in 1947. However the contents of state and local archives can be traced in various ways, and guides do exist. Philip M. Hamer, ed., *Guide to Archives and Manuscripts in the United States* (1961) is of some assistance. Reports and publications of various state commissions, archivists, state historians, and historical societies include accessions lists of new publications, checklists, and guides to manuscript collections. The *American Archivist* contains the most useful annual bibliography.

The Historical Records Survey of the Works Progress Administration, prepared in the 1930's, still provides the basic guide to many archives. Of its numerous projects, the 628 volumes of county archival inventories published in 1942 were the most successful. In addition, the Survey prepared inventories of collections in every state. It often listed private collections and church archives, early American imprints and portraits, as well as public archives. The best evaluation of the work of the survey is found in David L. Smiley, "The W. P. A. Historical Records Survey," in W. B. Hesseltine and D. R. McNeil, eds., *In Support of Clio* (1958). See also:

Catholic University of America, *American Imprints Inventory* (1964).
Child, S. B., and D. P. Holmes, *Bibliography of Research Project Reports: Checklist of Historical Records Survey Publications* (1943).
Colby, M. E., *Final Report on Disposition of Unpublished Materials of the W. P. A. Writers Program* (1943).

The most accurate source of information on archival collections is the state archive itself. Address inquiries to:

Alabama: Director, Alabama State Department of Archives and History Library, War Memorial Bldg., Washington St., Montgomery, Alabama 36104
Alaska: Librarian, Alaska Historical Library, Box 2051, Juneau, Alaska 99801. This is not an official state archive; many records are in the Federal Records Center, GSA, Bldg. 5-D, U.S. Naval Air Station, Seattle, Washington 98502
Arizona: Director, Arizona State Dept. of Library and Archives, Capitol Bldg., 3rd floor, Phoenix, Arizona 85007
Arkansas: Librarian, Arkansas History Commission Library, Old State House, West Wing, 300 W. Markham St., Little Rock Arkansas 72201. Has only a few records.
California: State Archivist, State Archives and Central Records Depository, Office of the Secretary of State, 1020 O St., Sacramento, California 95814
Colorado: State Archivist, Division of State Archives and Public Records, 1530 Sherman St., Denver, Colorado 80203
Connecticut: Archivist, Connecticut State Library, 231 Capitol Ave., Hartford, Connecticut 06115
Delaware: State Archivist, Delaware Public Archives Commission, Hall of Records, Dover, Delaware 19901
Florida: Librarian, Florida State Library, Supreme Court Bldg., Tallahassee, Florida 32304
Georgia: Directory, Department of Archives and History, c/o Office of the Secretary of State, Atlanta, Georgia 30334
Hawaii: State Archivist, Public Archives Library, Iolani Palace Grounds, Honolulu, Hawaii 96813
Idaho: Historian and Archivist, Idaho State Historical Society, His-

	torical and Geneological Library, 610 N. Julia Davis Drive, Boise, Idaho 83706
Illinois:	Assistant State Archivist, Illinois State Library, Centennial Bldg., Springfield, Illinois 62706
Indiana:	State Archivist, Indiana State Library, 140 N. Senate Ave., Indianapolis, Indiana 46204
Iowa:	Curator, Iowa State Department of History and Archives, Historical Bldg., Des Moines, Iowa 50319
Kansas:	State Archivist, Kansas State Historical Society, Division of Archives Library, Memorial Bldg., Tenth St. and Jackson, Topeka, Kansas 66612
Kentucky:	Librarian, Kentucky State Historical Society Library, Old Capitol, Box 104, Frankfort, Kentucky 40601. No real state archival program; write also Archivist, Margaret I. King Library, University of Kentucky Library, Lexington, Kentucky 40506
Louisiana:	Archivist, Department of Archives, Louisiana State University Library, Baton Rouge, Louisiana 70803. There is no state-run archival agency.
Maine:	No central archive; write individual bureaus and departments.
Maryland:	Archivist Hall of Records Commission Library, College Ave and St. John's St., Box 828, Annapolis, Maryland 21404
Massachusetts:	Archivist for Commonwealth of Massachusetts, Office of the Secretary, State House, Boston, Massachusetts 02133
Michigan:	Chief of Archives Division, Michigan Historical Commission, Lewis Cass Bldg., Lansing, Michigan 48913
Minnesota:	State Archivist, Minnesota State Archives Commission, 117 University Ave., St. Paul, Minnesota 55103
Mississippi:	Director, Mississippi Department of Archives and History, War Memorial Bldg., Box 571, Jackson, Mississippi 39205
Missouri:	Librarian, Missouri Historical Society Library, Jefferson Memorial Bldg., St. Louis, Missouri 63112. No official status; state has no agency.
Montana:	Librarian, Montana Historical Society Library, Corner Sixth Ave. and Robert Sts., Helena, Montana 59601. Not an official agency.
Nebraska:	Archivist, Nebraska State Historical Society Library, 1500 R. St., Lincoln, Nebraska 68508
Nevada:	Director, Nevada State Historical Society, State Bldg., Reno, Nevada 89501
New Hampshire:	Director and Curator, New Hampshire Historical Society Library, 30 Park St., Concord, New Hampshire 03301. Not an official agency.
New Jersey:	State Librarian, New Jersey State Library, Department of Education, 185 W. State St., Trenton, New Jersey 08625
New Mexico:	Senior Archivist, State Records Center and Archives, Santa Fe., New Mexico 87501
New York:	Director, New York State Library, 12224, Albany, New York. New York mostly relies on exceptional local records programs.
North Carolina:	State Archivist, Department of Archives and History, P.O. Box 1881, Raleigh, North Carolina 27602
North Dakota:	Librarian, North Dakota State Historical Library, Liberty Memorial Bldg., State Capitol Grounds, Bismarck, North Dakota 58501. Quasi-official.
Ohio:	State Archivist, Ohio State Historical Society, 1813 North High St., Columbus, Ohio 43201
Oklahoma:	Director, Oklahoma Department of Libraries, 109 State Capitol, Box 53344,Z, Oklahoma City, 73105
Oregon:	Chief Librarian, Oregon Historical Society Library, 1230 S. W. Park Ave, Portland, Oregon 97205

Pennsylvania:	Executive Director, Pennsylvania Historical and Museum Commission, William Penn Memorial Bldg., 327 Market St., Harrisburg, Pennsylvania 17101
Puerto Rico:	Director, Puerto Rico General Archives, 305 San Francisco Ave., San Juan, Puerto Rico 00927
Rhode Island:	Assistant for Archives, Rhode Island State Archives, Department of State, 314 State House, Providence, Rhode Island 02903
South Carolina:	Director, South Carolina Archives Department, 1430 Senate St., Columbia, South Carolina 29201
South Dakota:	Secretary, South Dakota State Historical Society, Soldiers' Memorial Bldg., Capitol Ave., Pierre, South Dakota 57501. No official program.
Tennessee:	Director of Archives, Tennessee State Library and Archives, Seventh Ave N., Nashville, Tennessee 37219
Texas:	Archivist, Texas State Library, Texas Archives and Library Bldg., 1201 Brazos St., Austin, Texas 78711
Utah:	State Archivist, Utah State Archives, 603 East South Temple, Salt Lake City, Utah 84102
Vermont:	State Historian, Secretary of State's Office, State Office Bldg., Montpelier, Vermont 05602
Virginia:	Archivist, Virginia State Library, Capitol St., Richmond, Virginia 23219
Washington:	State Archivist, Washington State Archives, Department of General Administration, Olympia, Washington 98502
West Virginia:	Director, Department of Archives and History, State Capitol Bldg., Room E-400, Charleston, West Virginia, 25305
Wisconsin:	State Archivist, Division of Archives and Manuscripts, State Historical Society, 816 State St., Madison, Wisconsin 53706
Wyoming:	Director, Wyoming State Archives and Historical Department, State Office Bldg., Cheyenne, Wyoming 82001

6.4 FOREIGN ARCHIVES OF INTEREST TO AMERICAN HISTORIANS

The historian of the United States often has occasion to research the records of foreign governments. Scholars planning to make use of foreign archives would do well to check availability of materials and archival regulations in advance of their visits.

A list of guides to archival records printed in Europe from 1934 to 1950 and outside Europe from 1900 to 1950 is in Robert-Henri Bautier, *Bibliographie selective des guides d'archives* (1953), a supplement to *Guide international des archives* (1934).

See also:

Hill, Roscoe R., *American Missions in European Archives* (1951).
Thomas, Daniel H., and Lynn M. Case, *Guide to the Diplomatic Archives of Western Europe* (1959).
Matteson, David M., *List of Manuscripts Concerning American History in European Libraries* (1925). Useful especially for manuscript collections: Richard C. Lewanski, *European Library Directory* (1968), a companion to his *Subject Collections in European Libraries* (1965). The annual bibliography in *American Archivist* includes guides to foreign archives. *See also chapter 7 on microforms.*

These guides and lists give the student no more than leads; there is no substitute for visiting the repository, for using its shelf lists, and for enlisting the aid of a librarian or archivist to help find what may be relevant.

6.4.1 Great Britain and Ireland

The archives of Great Britain and Ireland contain the largest stores of material relevant to American history and have been most frequently used by American historians. Established in 1838, the Public Record Office, Chancery Lane, London, W.C.2, has since become the central depository for all records of the British government. The statutory period governing access to records was reduced from fifty to thirty years in 1968. Calendars, lists, and indexes are available for many of these holdings. A great deal of this material is now available in microform and extensive abstracts exist. Archives exist also in Dublin, Belfast, and Edinburgh. These holdings can be traced in *Archives*, the journal of the British Records Association.

The Royal Commission of Historical Manuscripts (also known as the Historical Manuscripts Commission) was established in 1869 to locate and report on private manuscript collections in the United Kingdom. Since then the Commission has issued more than 200 volumes of *Reports* with indexes. It maintains the National Register of Archives, whose *Bulletin* gives accounts of important collections throughout the Commonwealth. Inquiries should be sent to the Secretary, Historical Manuscripts Commission, Quality House, Quality Court, Chancery Lane, London W.C. 2.

The following guides are helpful:

Andrews, C. M., *Guide to the Materials for American History, to 1783, in the Public Record Office of Great Britain* (2 vols., 1912–1914).
———and F. G. Davenport, *Guide to the Manuscript Materials for the History of the United States to 1783, in the British Museum, in Minor London Archives, and in the Libraries of Oxford and Cambridge* (1908).
Crick, Bernard R., and Miriam Alman, *A Guide to Manuscripts Relating to America in Great Britain and Ireland* (1961).
Emmitson, F. G., and Irvine Gray, *County Records* (1948).
Galbraith, Vivian H., *Introduction to the Use of the Public Records* (1934). Corrected edition published in 1952.
———*Studies in the Public Records* (1949).
Giuseppi, M. S., *Guide to the Manuscripts Preserved in the Public Record Office* (2 vols., 1923–24). Updated by Public Record Office: *Guide to the Contents of the Public Record Office* (2 vols., 1963).
Hayes, Richard J., ed., *Manuscript Sources for History of Irish Civilization* (11 vols., 1965).
Hepworth, Philip, *Archives and Manuscripts in Libraries* (2nd ed. 1964).
Jones, P. E., ed., *Guide to the Records in the Corporation of London Records Office* (1951).
Livingstone, Matthew, ed., *Guide to the Public Records of Scotland* (1905).
Scotland Record Office, *Source List of Manuscripts Relating to the U.S.A. and Canada in the Scottish Record Office* (1964).
Virginia Colonial Records Project, *The British Public Record Office: Materials for American History* (1960).
West, John, *Village Records* (1962).
Wood, Herbert, ed., *Guide to the Records in the Public Record Office of Ireland* (1919).

6.4.2 France

The connections between the United States and France have been long and intimate, yet the American student will find some difficulty in using the materials in French archives outside the orbit marked out in W. G. Leland and J. J. Meng, *Guide to the Materials for American History in the Libraries and Archives of Paris* (2 vols., 1932–1943). The archives have many branches (such as the annex at Aix-en-Provence, which is the repository of archives from French overseas territories) and are consequently rather unwieldy. There are some guides and inventories available. Written inquiries can be addressed to Monsieur Le Directeur Général des Archives de France, 60 rue des Francs-Bourgeois, 75 Paris IIIe.

The French Ministry of Foreign Affairs and the French Army and Navy have their own historical sections and have retained control of their archives. The foreign affairs records, "les archives diplomatiques," are in a wing of the ministry itself. Inquiries and requests to use these archives may be addressed to Monsieur Le Ministre Plénipotentiaire, Directeur des Archives Diplomatiques, Ministère des Affaires Etrangères, 75 Paris VIIe. The more important guides follow:

Annales d'histoire économique et sociale. (1929).
Annuaire des bibliothèques et des archives. (1886–   ).
Archives et bibliothèques. (1935–   ).
Bordier, H. L., ed., Les Archives de France. (1855).
[Henri Courteault] État des inventaires des archives nationales, départmentales, communales, et hospitalières. (1938).
Etat sommaire par series des documents conservées aux archives nationales. (1891–   ).
Leroy, Emile, Guide practique des bibliothèques de Paris. (1937).
Posner, Ernst, Archival Repositories in France. (1943).
Revue des bibliothèques. (1891–   ).
Repertoire des bibliothèques d'étude et organismes de documentation. (1963).

Perhaps more readily useful will be:

Beers, Henry P., The French in North America: Bibliographical Guide to French Archives (1957).
———French and British in the Old Northwest: Bibliographical Guide to Archive and Manuscript Sources (1964).
Nasatir, A. P., ed., French Activities in California: An Archival Calendar-Guide (1945).
Surrey, N. M. M., Calendar of Manuscripts in Paris Archives and Libraries Relating to the History of the Mississippi Valley to 1803 (2 vols., 1926–1928).

6.4.3 Spain and Portugal

Spanish materials are relevant primarily for the colonial era and particularly for the sections that were at one time under the control of Spain. The archives are extensive, and the following guides are useful: C. E. Chapman, Catalogue of Materials in the Archivo General de Indias for the History of the Pacific Coast and the American Southwest (1919); R. R. Hill, Descriptive Catalogue of the Documents Relating to the History of the United States in the Papeles Procedentes de Cuba. Deposited in . . . Seville (1916); W. R. Shepherd, Guide to the Materials for the History of the United States in Spanish Archives (1907). See also the following:

Anais das bibliotecas, arquivo e museus municipals (1931–   ).
Anais das bibliotecas e arquivos de Portugal (1914–   ).
Azevedo, Pedro A. de, and Antonio Baião, O Archivo da Torre do Tombo (1905).
Boletim de bibliographia portugueza e revista dos arquivos nacionaes (1879).
Guía de los archivos de Madrid (1952).
Guía de las bibliotecas de Madrid (1953).
Gomez del Campillo, Miguel, Relaciones diplomáticas entre España y los Estados Unidos segun los documentes del Archivo Histórico Nacional (2 vols., 1944–1946).

Mesquita de Figueiredo, Antonio, *Arquivo nacional da Torre do Tombo* (1922).
Revista de archivos, bibliotecas y museos (1871–   ).
Revista de la biblioteca, archivo y museo (1924–   ).
Rodríguez Marín, Francisco, *Guía historica y descriptiva de los archivos, bibliotecas y museos arqueológicos de España* (2 vols., 1916–1925).
Torre Revello, José, "El Archivo General de Indias de Sevilla," Instituto de Investigaciones Históricas (Buenos Aires), *Publicaciones,* 50 (1929).
Torres y Lanzas, Pedro, *Independencia de América fuentes para su estudio Catalogo de documentes conservados en el Archivo General de Indias de Seville* (6 vols., 1912).
Tudela De La Orden, José, *Los manuscritos de America en las bibliotecas de España* (1954).
Paz, Julian, *Catálogo de manuscritos de América existentes en la Biblioteca Nacional* (1933).

6.4.4 Germany

German materials are often useful for the student of American history, particularly for the nineteenth and the twentieth centuries. But they are complex and difficult to use, partly because the United States was not large in the consciousness of central Europeans until recently and partly because German governmental forms have passed through numerous transformations in the last century and a half. Those who wish to use the archives and the public documents must take account not only of those of the separate states—Prussia, Bavaria, Baden, and the like—but also of those of free cities like Frankfort and Hamburg, as well as of the central confederations. Furthermore, such states as Prussia were themselves divided into provinces. Each of these entities possessed its own archives and issued its own series of publications.

The Archives of the Federal Republic of Germany were established in March 1950 and house materials of all federal ministers and government organizations except the Ministry of Foreign Affairs. Its major job has been the restitution of the materials in archives that were confiscated and dispersed during and after World War II. In 1961 a guide was published, *Das Bundesarchiv und seine Bestaende,* and since then additional material has been acquired from federal ministries, through restitution from the United States, and through donation and purchase of personal collections. Inquiries should be sent to the President of the Federal Archives, Am Woellershof 12, Koblenz, Federal Republic of Germany.

Important sources on these archives are: *Minerva: Jahrbuch der Gelehrten Welt* (4 vols., 1966–1970), and for East Germany *Archive und Dokumentationsstellen der Deutschen Democratischen Republik, 1959–* (1961–   ); United States National Archives, *Archival Repositories in Germany* (1944). Such journals as *Der Archivar 1947–* and the older *Archivalische Zeitschrift* (1876–1950) will also be helpful.

A vital source in American history is the monumental *Americana in Deutschen Sammlungen* (11 vols., 1967), which is ten times larger than M. D. Learned, *Guide to the Manuscript Materials Relating to American History in the German State Archives* (1912). The former is a guide to archival and similar records pertaining specifically to American history in West German collections. Another significant project is *Documents on German Foreign Policy, 1918–1945, from the Archives of the German Foreign Ministry* (1949–   ), for which scholars representing the United States, British, and French governments have selected documents for microfilming. A complete collection of microfilms of German records confiscated during World War II is available on loan from the Center for Research Libraries, 5721 Cottage Grove Ave., Chicago, Ill., 60637.

6.4.5 Other European Countries

The documentary resources of other European countries are less likely to prove rewarding to American historians. The contact with the United States has been less direct and, while all have extensive archives and published series, useful material in them is scattered and difficult to locate. The archives are best approached through the guides listed below and through the periodicals published in the various countries. The annual bibliography in *Am. Archivist* includes these countries.

Annuario delle Bibliotheche Italiane (2nd ed., 3 vols., 1956–1959).
Archive, Bibliotheken und Dokumentationsstellen der Schweiz (3d ed., 1958).
Bibliotheek-en Documentatiegids voor Nederland (1957).
Einersen, Henning, and Mogens Iversen, *Dansk Biblioteksfører* (1955).
Faust, Albert B., *Guide to the Materials for American History in Swiss and Austrian Archives* (1916).
Fish, C. R., *Guide to the Materials for American History in Roman and Other Italian Archives* (1911).
Golder, F. A., *Guide to Materials for American History in Russian Archives* (2 vols., 1917–1937).
Handbuch Österreichhischer Bibliotheken (2nd ed., 3 vols., 1961–63).
Jenkinson, Hilary, and H. E. Bell, *Italian Archives during the War and at Its Close* (1947).
Linvald, Axel, *Dansk Arkivvaesen* (1933).
Manigaulte, John W., "Sources for American History in Three Italian Archives," *Am. Archivist*, 27 (1964), 57.
Nivanka, Eino, *Guide to the Research Libraries of Finland* (3d ed., 1962).
Ottervik, Gosta et al., *Libraries and Archives in Sweden* (1954).

6.4.6 Latin America and the West Indies

Much of the material for the years when these areas were colonial dependencies of the European powers will be found in the archives and publications of Spain, Portugal, Holland, France, and Great Britain. But each of the governmental entities in South and Central America has, in addition, developed collections and published series of its own.

Bell, H. C. et al., *Guide to British West Indian Archive Materials in London and in the Islands, for the History of the United States* (1926).
Bolton, Herbert E., *Guide to Materials for the History of the United States in the Principal Archives of Mexico* (1913).
Canedo, Lino Gomez, *Los Archivos de la historia de America* (1961).
Perez, L. M., *Guide to the Materials for American History* in Cuban Archives (1907).

The following works will be helpful in approaching the archives and resources of these countries:

Bibliotecas Especializadas Brasileiras (1962).
Baker, E. C., *A Guide to the Records in the Leeward Islands* (1965).
Burdon, J. A., ed., *Archives of British Honduras* (3 vols., 1931–1935).
Castañeda, C. E., and J. A. Dabbs, eds., *Guide to the Latin American Materials in the University of Texas Library* (1939).
Castelo de Zavala, Maria, "El Archivo Nacional del Peru," *Revista de historia de America*, no. 20 (1945), 371.

Chandler, M. J., *A Guide to Records in Barbados* (1965).
Donoso, Ricardo, "El Archivo Nacional de Chile," *Revista de historia de America*, no. 11 (1941), 47.
Gomez Cañedo, Lino, *Los archivos historicos de Puerto Rico* (1964).
Gropp, A. E., ed., *Guide to Libraries and Archives in Central America and the West Indies, Panama, Bermuda, and British Guiana* (1940).
Hill, R. R., ed., *National Archives of Latin America* (1945).
Llaverias, Joaquin, *Historia de los archivos de Cuba* (2nd ed., 1949).
Pattee, Richard, "Libraries and Archives for Historical Research in Ecuador," *Hisp. Am. Hist. Rev.*, 17 (1937), 231.
Rubio Mañe, J. I., "El Archivo General de la Nación, México," *Revista de historia de America*, no. 9 (1940), 63.
Revello, José Torre, "El Archivo General de la Nación Argentina," *Revista de historia de America*, no. 1 (1938), 41.
Savage, E. A., *The Libraries of Bermuda, the Bahamas, the British West Indies, British Guiana, British Honduras, Puerto Rico, and the American Virgin Islands* (1934).

6.4.7 Canada

The history of Canada has been closely related to that of the United States. The public documents of the Dominion, of its predecessors, and of its provinces are therefore of the highest value to the student of American history. The Dominion itself and each of the provinces have well-arranged archives, adequate guides to which are available. The annual reports of the archivist of Canada (1872–   ) are useful, as are those of the Province of Quebec. The more important works are listed below:

Brown, G. W., "Problem of Records in Canada," *Can. Hist. Rev.*, 25 (1944), 1.
Ells, Margaret, ed., *Calendar of the White Collection of Manuscripts in the Public Archives of Nova Scotia* (1940).
Harvey, D. C., "Archives in the Maritimes," *Dalhousie Rev.*, 23 (1943), 193.
McClung, H. A., "Department of Public Records and Archives of Ontario," *Am. Archivist*, 10 (1947), 184.
Parker, David W., ed., *Guide to the Documents in the Manuscript Room at the Public Archives, Ottawa* (1914).
———*Guide to the Materials for United States History in Canadian Archives* (1913).
Roy, P. G., ed., *Les archives de la province et nos inventaires* (1926), Quebec.
Union List of Manuscripts in Canadian Repositories (1968).

6.5 GUIDES TO MANUSCRIPT COLLECTIONS

Until recently general guides to manuscript collections were lacking. The Library of Congress has made a beginning toward systematic bibliographic control in its *National Union Catalog of Manuscript Collections* (1961–   ), commonly known as NUCMC. It describes manuscript collections reported by repositories, permanently housed and regularly open to researchers. An index giving subject access to these volumes first appeared in 1964. Additional volumes and cumulative indexes have since been published, with slight organizational changes.

Philip Hamer's *Guide to Archives and Manuscripts in the United States* (1961) is a single volume survey compiled for the National Historical Publications Commission. It covers the holdings of thirteen hundred repositories and twenty thousand collections, both official and private, in all fifty states. It is arranged by cities and towns within state groupings and has a subject index so that one may find all the repositories that reported holding papers of one individual or organization. It includes a fairly detailed analysis of the holdings of the Library of Congress Manuscript Division.

While far from perfect, the coverage given by these two projects has greatly aided the researcher.

See also:

Binkley, William C., "A Historian Looks at the National Union Catalog of Manuscript Collections," *Am. Archivist*, 28 (1965), 399.
Burke, Frank G., "Manuscripts and Archives," *Lib. Trends*, 15 (1967), 430.
"A Preliminary Listing of Published Materials Relating to Foreign Manuscript Collections in the United States," *Appendix to the Library of Congress Information Bulletin*, Feb. 16, 1967 and Oct. 26, 1967.

In addition to these guides, there are also lists of specialized, topical guides to non-government archives and manuscript collections. These are listed in the annual volumes of *Writings in American History*, in accounts of accessions in historical journals and in the publications of individual libraries and societies. Especially useful is an annual bibliography published since 1943 in the American Archivist entitled "Writings on Archives, Current Records and Historical Manuscripts." It discusses the development of various archives and offers guides to collections, both governmental and non-governmental. Examples of guides are the following:

Allison, W. H., comp., *Inventory of Unpublished Material for American Religious History in Protestant Church Archives and Other Repositories* (1910).
Bell, Whitfield J., Jr., and Murphy D. Smith, *Guide to Archives and Manuscripts of American Philosophical Society* (1966).
Billington, Ray A., comp., *Guides to American History Manuscript Collections in Libraries of the United States* (1952).
Deutrich, Mabel E., "American Church Archives," *Am.Archivist*, 24 (1961), 387.
Finneran, Helen T., "Records of the National Grange in Its Washington Office," *Am. Archivist*, 27 (1964), 103.
Freeman, J. F., and M. D. Smith, *Guide to Manuscripts Relating to the American Indian in the Library of the American Philosophical Society* (1966).
Jeffreys, A., "Manuscript Sources for History of Science," *Archives*, 7 (1965), 75.

The collections of the Manuscript Division of the Library of Congress consist largely of the personal papers of important persons and organizations or of particular events that have been important in American history. The greater portions of the collections have been acquired since 1897 as gifts from benefactors. They comprise the personal papers of presidents from Washington to Coolidge, ministers, cabinet members, members of Congress and the federal judiciary, scientists, novelists, and societies. Included also are extensive transcriptions and photographic copies of documents in foreign archives that relate to United States history. See also chapter 7. There are close to 20,000,000 pieces of personal information available to serious researchers.

These collections may be traced through the following guides, in addition to Hamer mentioned above:

Garrison, Curtis W., *List of Manuscript Collections in the Library of Congress to July 1931* (1932).
Handbook of Manuscripts in the Library of Congress (1918).
Powell, C. Percy, *List of Manuscript Collections Received in the Library of Congress, July 1931 to July 1938* (1939).

See also the *Annual Report of the Library of Congress* (1938–1942), the *Quarterly Journal of Current Acquisitions,* 1943–   for lists of accessions and descriptions of particular manuscript groups, and the calendars, indexes, and registers listed in *Library of Congress Publications in Print.*

6.6 ORAL HISTORY

A relatively new development which supplements conventional source materials is oral history. As a conscious creation of additional source material, it is a kind of historical document and a form of archive. Most commonly scholars use written and corrected transcripts taken from the original taped interview. Allan Nevins developed the first major oral history program at Columbia University in 1948. Oral history projects are now numerous and widespread, although their value and uses are still controversial and their growth uneven. Gradually techniques are becoming standardized, and oral history is being used more effectively to fill gaps in the more usual historical source material. For example, oral interviews augment documentary holdings of the Truman, Kennedy, and Johnson libraries.

Oral History in the United States (1971), compiled by Gary L. Shumway, brings to attention 230 projects active in the United States. The scope and activity of each is described concisely. A subject index is provided as well as a list of institutions whose projects are not widely available to scholars. The *National Union Catalog of Manuscript Collections* contains a list of approximately seventy-five collections of oral history in nineteen repositories. The Cornell program in Oral History issues a semi-annual *Bulletin* 1966– , which makes known its institutional collection.

In 1967 Elizabeth I. Dixon began writing a column on oral history for the *Journal of Library History.* For a thorough discussion of the subject see:

Dixon, Elizabeth I., and James V. Mink, eds., *Oral History at Arrowhead: Proceedings of the First National Colloquium* (1967).
Starr, Louis M., ed., *The Second National Colloquium on Oral History* (1968). The Oral History Association was established at the second colloquium.

See also Donald J. Schippers and Adelaide G. Tusler, *A Bibliography of Oral History* (1967), which includes suggestions for those interested in developing the oral history technique; and Willa K. Baum, *Oral History for the Local Historical Society* (1969), an interesting "how-to-do-it" manual.

6.7 AUTOMATED FINDING AIDS AND DATA RETRIEVAL

Automation is providing new keys to information in archives. An entire issue of *American Archivist* is devoted to automation in archives and manuscript collections. See particularly:

Fisher, Barbara, and Frank B. Evans, "Automation Information and the Administration of Archives and Manuscript Collections: A Bibliographic Review," *Am. Archivist,* 30 (1967), 255.

Both the Library of Congress and the National Archives are developing automated methods to apply, for example, to the Presidential Papers program. For a discussion of this and other applications see:

Rhoads, J. B., "Historian and New Technology," *Am. Archivist,* 32 (1969), 209.
Shelley, Fred, "The Presidential Papers Program in the Library of Congress," *Am. Archivist,* 25 (1962), 429.
Smith, Russell M., "Item Indexing [of the Presidential Papers] by Automated Processes," *Am. Archivist,* 30 (1967), 295.
Wood, Elizabeth I., *Report on Project History Retrieval* (1966).

7 Microform Materials

The photocopying of historical documents is almost as old as photography itself, but only with the development of microphotography did the mass duplication of historical materials become practicable. Since its inception with 35 mm transparent microfilm, microphotography has developed a bewildering array of forms. Microform is the term which has come to be applied to all varieties of microreproduction. Microfilm now comes in 16 mm. and 8 mm. size, and reels have given way to cartridges and cassettes. Roll film, in turn, has been supplemented by microcard, microprint, microfiche, and ultra-microfiche in several sizes.

Microphotography grew out of the need to conserve storage space and not the user's convenience. Most researchers prefer "hard copy" to a projected image, but they console themselves that the alternative might well be to do without the document, for few libraries would have the unique or rare books and documents that are now in microform or have the space and money for those that are not so rare.

The amount of historical material in microform is already so voluminous that it is impossible to predict what will be available within a few years. In 1970, seventy six research libraries reported average holdings of 450,000 microform units. Many units comprise more than one title; ten volumes, for example, are being reproduced on one 4 x 6 card in ultra-microfiche. Syracuse University Library, with the largest holdings, reported over one million units. In this chapter it is possible only to point out the principal guides to microforms and to give a sampling of the more important projects that have been completed or are under way.

Two annuals are available, both edited by Albert J. Diaz: *Guide to Microforms in Print* (1961–   ) and *Subject Guide to Microforms in Print* (1962–   ). *Guide to Microforms in Print* is periodically updated and published by NCR-Microcard Editions. The latest edition contains approximately 18,000 titles, many individual titles representing collections of hundreds of books and documents. These guides identify the publisher of each title; for more complete information the researcher can turn to the publishers' catalogs.

7.1 PRINTED GOVERNMENT DOCUMENTS

Many federal documents are available in microform. One third of the entries in the Diaz *Guide*, in fact, refer to United States government documents. Since 1953 all non-depository items in the *Monthly Catalog* have been reproduced by Readex Microprints, and since 1956 all depository items have been added. They are listed by *Monthly Catalog* number in the Readex catalog.

For documents printed before 1953 and microprinted before 1963, see Helen McReynolds, *Microforms of the United States Government Publications* (1963) and the chapter on "Microfacsimile Editions of Government Publications" in Laurence F. Schmeckebier and Roy B. Eastman, *Government Publications* (rev. ed., 1969). Peter Scott, "The Present and Future of Government Documents in Microform," *Library Trends*, 15 (1966), 72, contains some interesting speculations on the future.

The United States Historical Documents Institute has just published the *Proceedings of the U. S. Congress, 1789–1964* (1971) on 479 reels of microfilm, and have reprinted in full-size volumes the *Indexes* to go with them. Greenwood Corporation has contracted to film over one thousand volumes of House and Senate hearings from the 41st to the 73d Congress. Additional projects completed or in process include the *United States Congressional Serial Set* (15th to 47th Congress), *American State Papers* (1789–1838), *Supreme Court Records and Briefs,* and papers relating to the foreign relations of the United States.

Relatively few state government documents have been reproduced in microform. Those that are available are recorded in the *Legislative Research Checklist,* issued by the Council of State Governments. Commercial publishers have filmed certain types of state documents on a selective basis. Greenwood Corporation, for example, has put various state Labor Reports and records of the state constitutional conventions on microfiche. Most of the state documents on microform have been reproduced since 1961, and thus are to be found in the Diaz *Guide.*

Most foreign governments are beginning to film their records. The British are reproducing *Hansards Parliamentary Debates* and the *Debates of the House of Commons, 1667–1694.* The French are filming their *Journal officiel* and *Debats parlementaires, Chambres des Deputes, 1881–1940* as well as *Documents diplomatiques français, 1871–1914.*

Both the United Nations and the Organization of American States have launched extensive reproduction programs. Research Publications, Inc. has begun microfilming both the published and unpublished documents of the League of Nations.

7.2 BOOKS, MAGAZINES, AND NEWSPAPERS

The number of books now in microform or planned would constitute a large library of primary and secondary sources. Most of them are out of print; many of them are extremely rare. The vast majority are chosen on the basis of a common theme or a well known bibliographical collection.

One of the most notable sets is Charles Evans, *American Bibliography,* published by Readex on microcards in association with the American Antiquarian Society. Lost Cause Press has published the volumes in Joseph Sabin's *Dictionary of Books Relating to America from Its Discovery to the Present Time* on both microcard and microfiche. Encyclopaedia Britannica has just issued its Library of American Civilization, consisting of several thousand printed works. Other large collections center on travel literature, black history, agricultural history, and similar themes running through American history or aspects of American life. They will be found in the Diaz *Guide*.

Magazines in microform not only make it possible for new and expanding libraries to acquire important source material; they permit established libraries with only partial runs of periodicals to complete their files. Examples are Greenwood's publication of *Radical Periodicals in the United States, 1890–1960,* and Negro Periodicals and Research Publications' projected release of learned periodicals of the 17th and 18th centuries. Scores of other periodicals are in the process of being filmed, and the end is not in sight. University Microfilms has issued a catalog, *An Annotated Bibliography of Periodicals on Microfilm Recommended for Public Libraries,* compiled by Bill Katz (1971).

Most current newspapers are being microfilmed, and many back issues of important papers are in microform as noted in chapter 8. The State Historical Society of Wisconsin is in process of microfilming its huge collection of American newspapers.

7.3 UNPUBLISHED SOURCES

Researchers now have available to them through microform large quantities of materials previously available only in archival or manuscript collections. Through use of microform, they are often able to shorten or eliminate costly research trips. A wide range of archival materials from local records to German diplomatic correspondence may be obtained.

Richard W. Hale, *Guide to Photocopied Historical Materials in the United States and Canada* (1961) lists by geographical area personal papers, government, and church records. The National Archives will supply scholars with microfilm copies of particular documents or series. By 1970 over 150,000 rolls of microfilm were available. See the National Archives annual *List of National Archives Microfilm Publications.* The National Historical Publications Commission, *Catalog of Microfilm Publications* (4th ed., 1970) lists 85 microfilm publications. Inquiries should be sent to Executive Director, National Historical Publications Commission, National Archives Bldg., Washington, D. C., 20408.

The Library of Congress has published on microfilm most of the presidential series. Non-governmental institutions are issuing the private papers of several presidents, such as the Adams papers by the Massachusetts Historical Society.

A Microcard edition of the Historical Records Survey [of state and county archives], *American Imprints Inventory,* has been published in total. It includes several check lists which had not been published when the work of the Survey ceased in 1942. Several states have begun filming essential records, but progress is uneven.

The most important general collection of early state and local records has been microfilmed by the Library of Congress and the University of North Carolina. The reels contain the surviving records of legislative proceedings, statutes, constitutional data, and administrative documents, together with some court records and county records. *A Guide to the Microfilm Collection of Early State Records,* Lillian A. Hamrick, ed., and William S. Jenkins, comp. (1950) indexes more than 2,500,000 pages of records. The *Supplement,* William S. Jenkins, ed. (1951) is a guide to an additional 170 reels of microfilm.

The Church of Jesus Christ of Latter Day Saints in Salt Lake City, Utah has a massive microfilm collection of town and county records dating from the early colonial period. Much of the collection is available for the use of scholars.

Since 1905 the Library of Congress has carried on a systematic program of copying foreign documents and manuscripts pertaining to American History, especially those of England and France. Such guides as G. G. Griffin, *A Guide to Manuscripts Relating to American History in British Depositories Reproduced for the Division of Manuscripts* (1946) and James E. O'Neill, "Copies of French Manuscripts for American History in the Library of Congress," *JAH*, 51 (1965), 674 reveal the extent of the program and the types of documents copied. Reproductions of documents and manuscripts from other foreign depositories bring the total to some two million, most of them on 35 mm. positive film. Current acquisitions are listed in *Library of Congress Information Bulletin* and its *Quarterly Journal.* Two additional guides to British records in microform are L. K. Born, comp., *British Manuscripts Project: Checklist of Microfilms Prepared for the American Council of Learned Societies, 1941–1945* (1955) and Micro Methods Ltd., *British Records Relating to America in Microform* (1966).

In 1965 the Center for the Coordination of Foreign Manuscript Copying was established in the Library of Congress to identify extensive photo-copying projects completed, planned, or under way, record the location of copies in this country, and avoid duplication of effort. A description of these projects, not all of which relate to American history, appears twice yearly in a special appendix to the *Library of Congress Information Bulletin.* The appendices discuss such projects as the Virginia Colonial Records Project started in 1955 to film British records. They also list guides to many other collections and additions such as John Young, comp., *Checklist of Microfilm Reproductions of Selected Archives of the Japanese Army, Navy and Other Government Agencies, 1868–1945* (1959).

The most unusual microfilm collection of foreign archival records is that made from captured German documents at the end of World War II, located in the National Archives. Guides to this huge collection include the following:

American Historical Association. Committee for the Study of War Documents, *A Catalogue of Files and Microfilms of the German Foreign Ministry Archives, 1867–1920* (Oxford, 1959).
———*Guides to German Records Microfilmed at Alexandria, Va.* (1958–   ). Each part described the filmed records of one of the Reich ministries or other records groups.
———*Index of Microfilmed Records of the German Foreign Ministry and the Reich's Chancellery Covering the Weimar Period* (1958). Covers 1919–1933.
———*A List of Archival References and Data of Documents from the Archives of the German Foreign Ministry, 1867–1920* (1957).
Kent, George O., comp., *Catalog of Files and Microfilm of the German Foreign Ministry Archives, 1920–1945* (vols. ¹/₄–   , 1962–   ).
U.S. Department of State, *A Catalog of Files and Microfilms of the German Foreign Ministry Archives, 1920–1945* (1962–   ).
Weinberg, Gerhard L., *Guide to Captured German Documents* (1952); Supplement (1959).

8   Printed Historical Works

8.1 REFERENCE WORKS

The more important American dictionaries, chronologies, and encyclopedias covering American history are listed below following an enumeration of almanacs and yearbooks. See 1.4 for statistical compilations, and 10.2 for biographical dictionaries. Specialized dictionaries and encyclopedias appear under appropriate headings.

A good general reference work which includes American history is William L. Langer, ed., *An Encyclopedia of World History* (4th ed., 1968).

Adams, James T., ed., *Dictionary of American History* (5 vols., 1940); Joseph G. E. Hopkins and Wayne Andrews, eds. (vol. 6, 1961).
Carruth, Gorton, et al., eds., *Encyclopedia of American Facts and dates* (4th ed., 1966).
Cochran, Thomas C., and Wayne Andrews, eds., *Concise Dictionary of American History* (1962). A one-volume condensation of Adams' five-volume work listed above.
Encyclopedia Americana.
Encyclopaedia Britannica.
Gould, Julius, and William L. Kolb, eds., *Dictionary of the Social Sciences* (1964).
International Encyclopedia of the Social Sciences (17 vols., 1968). Includes index.
Johnson, Thomas H., *Oxford Companion to American History* (1966). In dictionary form; forty percent of the entries are biographical.
Kull, Irving S., and Nell M. Kull, *Short Chronology of American History, 1492–1950* (1952).
Martin, Michael, and Leonard Gelber, *Dictionary of American History* (1965).
Morris, Richard B., ed., *Encyclopedia of American History* (rev. ed., 1965).
Seligman, E. R. A., ed., *Encyclopedia of the Social Sciences* (15 vols., 1930–1935).
Webster's Guide to American History (1971).

8.2 ALMANACS, ANNUALS, AND BIENNIALS

These compilations supply summary information, generally with a high degree of reliability. The usefulness of one important category of this material is discussed by C. S. Brigham, "An Account of American Almanacs and Their Value for Historical Study," Am. Antiq. Soc., *Proc.* new ser., 35 (1925), 195 and Esther Jerabek, "Almanacs as Historical Sources," *Minn. Hist.,* 15 (1934), 444. A bibliography of almanacs is to be found in Milton Drake, comp., *Almanacs of the United States* (2 vols., 1962).

In the select list below, the titles are given first, as is usual in citing them. All are issued annually unless otherwise noted.

America Votes, A Handbook of Contemporary American Election Statistics 1954/ 55–   . Biennial.
The American Almanac and Repository of Useful Knowledge, 1830–1861.
American Almanac and Treasury of Facts, Statistical, Financial, and Political, 1878–1889.
The American Annual of Photography and Photographic Times Almanac, 1887– 1952.
The American Annual Register for the Years 1825/26–1832/33.
The American Jewish Year Book. 1899–   .
American Art Annual, 1898–1948. Frequency varied.
The American Labor Year Book, 1916–1932.
The American Year Book: A Record of Events and Progress, 1910–1919; 1926–1950.
Annual Record of Science and Industry, 1871–1878.
Annual Register of World Events, 1758–   . London. General indexes for 1758– 1780, 1781–1792, and 1758–1819; annual indexes thereafter.
Annual of Scientific Discovery: or, Year-Book of Facts in Science and Art. 1850– 1871.
An Astronomical Diary, or Almanack, 1726–1827. Nathaniel Ames, ed. until 1764, followed by his son Nathaniel Low until 1827. Title varied.
Book of the States, 1935–   . Biennial.
Canadian Almanac and Directory, 1847–   .
Economic Almanac, 1940–1965. Biennial.
A Hand-Book of Politics. 1868–1894. Edward McPherson, ed. Biennial.
Information Please Almanac, Atlas and Yearbook, 1947–   .
Labor Fact Book, 1931–   . Biennial.
Major Problems of United States Foreign Policy. 1947–1952. Brookings Institution, ed.
Municipal Year Book: The Authoritative Resume of Activities and Statistical Data of American Cities, 1934–   .
The Musical Year Book of the United States, 1886–1893.
The National Calendar, 1820–1833. 11 vols.
The Negro Almanac, 2nd, 1971. Harry A. Ploski and Ernest Kaiser, eds.
Negro Year Book, 1912–1952.
Newsweek's History of Our Times, 1950–   .
New York Times Encyclopedic Almanac, 1970–   .
The Political Almanac, 1946; 1952.
Political Handbook of the World, 1927–   . Title varies.
Poor Richard, an Almanack, 1732–1767. Title varied. Benjamin Franklin, ed.
    Continued thereafter under various editors and titles and with many imitators.
Reader's Digest Almanac, 1966–   .
The Statesman's Year Book, 1864–   . Although oriented toward the Commonwealth, beginning with 1906, a special section has been devoted to the United States and to separate countries and dependencies.
The Theatre Book of the Year, 1942/43–   .
The Tribune Almanac, 1856–1914. Title varied: *The Whig Almanac,* 1843–1855; *The Politician's Register,* 1839–1841; *The Whig Almanac and Politician's Register,* 1838.
U.S. Bureau of the Census. *Statistical Abstract of the United States,* 1878–   .
U.S. Bureau of the Census, *Vital Statistics of the United States,* 1937–   . Supersedes *Mortality Statistics,* 1906–1938, and *Birth, Stillbirth and Infant Mortality Statistics,* 1915–1936.
U.S. Camera, N.Y., 1935–   .
U.S. Congress. House. *Statistics of the Presidential and Congressional Election,* 1920–1962. Biennial.
The United States in World Affairs, 1931–   . Supersedes *Survey of American Foreign Relations,* 1928–1931.
Whitaker's Almanack, 1869–   . London.

The World Almanac and Book of Facts, 1868–
Yearbook of the United Nations, 1946/47–

8.3 SCHOLARLY JOURNALS CURRENTLY PUBLISHED

The following scholarly journals are primarily regional or national in scope. A few, such as the *American Historical Review* and *Isis* are international journals. Most are issued quarterly, a few appear as often as six times a year or as annuals. If the sponsoring organization also publishes other series they will be found under the name of the organization in 8.6. State journals of history appear in 8.7.

Agricultural History, Agricultural History Cumulative Society. 1927–   . Index through 1950.
American Anthropologist, American Anthropological Association. 1888–   . Periodic Cumulative indexes.
American Archivist, Society of American Archivists. 1938–   . Periodic cumulative indexes.
American Economic Review, American Economic Association. 1911–   .
American–German Review, Carl Schurz Memorial Foundation. 1934–   .
American Historical Review, American Historical Association. 1895–   . Periodic cumulative indexes.
American Jewish Archives, Jewish Institute of Religion, Hebrew Union College. 1949–   .
American Jewish Historical Quarterly, American Jewish Historical Society. 1960–   .
American Journal of Economics and Sociology, 1941–   .
American Journal of International Law, American Society of International Law. 1907–   . Cumulative index through 1940.
American Journal of Legal History, American Society for Legal History. 1957–   . Periodic cumulative indexes.
American Journal of Sociology, University of Chicago. 1895–   .
American Literature. 1929–   . Analytical index, 1929–1959.
American Neptune. 1941–   .
American Political Science Review, American Political Science Association. 1906–   . Periodic cumulative indexes.
American Quarterly, University of Pennsylvania with cooperation of American Studies Association. 1949–   .
American Scandinavian Review, American-Scandinavian Foundation. 1913–   .
American Sociological Review, American Sociological Society. 1936–   . Cumulative index through 1955.
American Sociologist, American Sociological Association. 1965–   .
American Speech, 1925–   .
American West, Western History Association. 1964–   .
The Americas, Academy of American Franciscan History. 1944–   . Cumulative index through 1964.
Art Bulletin, College Art Association, 1913–   . Cumulative index through 1948.
Aztlan: Chicano Journal of the Social Sciences and the Arts, Mexican American Cultural Center. 1970–   .
Baptist History and Heritage, Southern Baptist Historical Society and the Historical Commission of the Southern Baptist Convention. 1966–   .
Behavioral Science, Mental Health Research Institute. 1956–   .
Bulletin of the History of Medicine, American Association of the History of Medicine and the Johns Hopkins Institute of the History of Medicine. 1933–   . Periodic cumulative indexes.
Business History Review, Business Historical Society. 1954–   . Supersedes *Bulletin,* 1926–1954.
Catholic Historical Review, American Catholic Historical Association. 1915–   . Cumulative index through 1935.

Centennial Review of Arts and Sciences. College of Arts and Letters, Michigan State University, 1957– .

Church History, American Society of Church History, 1932– .

Civil Rights Digest, U.S. Commission on Civil Rights. 1968– .

Civil War History: A Journal of the Middle Period. 1955– .

Comparative Politics, City University of New York. 1968– .

Comparative Studies in Society and History. 1958– .

Daedalus: Journal of the American Academy of Arts and Sciences. 1846– .

Economic Geography, Clark University. 1925– .

Ethnohistory. American Indian Ethnohistoric Conference (supersedes Ohio Valley Historical Indian Conference). 1954– .

Explorations in Economic History. Supersedes *Explorations in Entrepreneurial History.* 1949–1958. Second series, 1964– .

Foreign Affairs, Council on Foreign Relations. Cumulative 1922– . Index through 1931.

Forest History, Forest History Foundation. 1957– .

Geographical Review, American Geographical Society. 1916– . Periodic cumulative indexes.

Government and Opposition: Journal of Comparative Politics, London School of Economics and Political Science. 1966– .

Great Plains Journal. Great Plains Historical Association. 1961– .

Harvard Business Review, Harvard Business School. 1922– . Periodic cumulative indexes.

Harvard Library Bulletin, Harvard University Library. 1947–1960; 1967– . Cumulative index through 1960.

Hispanic-American Historical Review, 1918–1921; 1927– .

Historian, Phi Alpha Theta. 1938– . Indexed quinquenially.

Historic Preservation, National Trust for Historic Preservation. 1948– .

Historical Magazine (Dawson's). 1857–1875.

Historical Magazine of the Protestant Episcopal Church, Joint Commission of the General Convention. 1932– .

History and Theory: Studies in the Philosophy of History, Wesleyan University Press. 1962– .

History News, American Association for State and Local History. 1944– .

History of Education Quarterly, History of Education Society. 1961– .

Huntington Library Quarterly, Huntington Library. 1937– .

The Indian Historian, American Indian Historical Society. 1968– .

Industrial and Labor Relations Review, Cornell University, New York State School of Industrial and Labor Relations. 1947– .

Infantry Journal, United States Infantry Association. 1904– .

Inland Seas, Great Lakes Historical Society. 1945– .

Inter-American Economic Affairs, Institute of Inter-American Studies. 1947– .

Isis: International Review Devoted to the History of Science and Civilization, History of Science Society. 1913– .

Jewish Journal of Sociology. 1959– .

Jewish Social Studies, Conference on Jewish Relations. 1939– .

Journal, American Bar Association. 1915– . Cumulative index through 1937.

Journal, American Statistical Association. Cumulative 1922– . Index through 1939.

Journal, Confederate Historical Society. 1962– .

Journal, Indiana University, Folklore Institute. 1964– .

Journal of American Folk-Lore, American Folk-Lore Society. 1888– .

Journal of American History, Organization of American Historians. April 1964– . Supersedes *Mississippi Valley Historical Review* (1914–January 1964). New title follows consecutive numbering of earlier title.

Journal of Applied Behavioral Science, National Training Laboratories. 1965– .

Journal of Church and State, Baylor University, J. M. Dawson Studies in Church and State. 1959– .

Journal of Conflict Resolution, University of Michigan. 1957– .

Journal of Contemporary History, Institute of Contemporary History. 1966– .

Journal of Economic History, Economic History Association. 1941– .

Journal of Human Relations, Central State University. 1953–   .
Journal of Human Resources: Education, Manpower, and Welfare Policies, Indus-
   trial Relations Research Institute, Center for Studies in Vocational and Techni-
   cal Education, Institute for Research on Poverty, and University of Wisconsin
   Press. 1964–   .
Journal of Inter-American Studies, Florida University School of Inter-American
   Studies. 1959–   .
Journal of International Affairs, Columbia University School of International
   Affairs. 1947–   .
Journal of Law and Economics, University of Chicago Law School. 1958–   .
Journal of Library History, Florida State University Library School. 1966–   .
Journal of Mexican American History, University of California, Santa Barbara.
   1970–   .
Journal of Modern History. 1929–   .
Journal of Negro History, Association for the Study of Negro Life and History.
   1916–   .
Journal of Political Economy, University of Chicago. 1892–   .
Journal of Politics, Southern Political Science Association. 1939–   .
Journal of Popular Culture, Modern Language Associaiton of America and the
   Folklore Section of the Midwest Modern Language Association. 1967–   .
Journal of Presbyterian History, Presbyterian Historical Society. 1901–   . Title
   varies.
Journal of Religion, Divinity Faculty and Conference of the University of Chicago.
   1921   .
Journal of Social History, University of California. 1968–   .
Journal of Southern History, Southern Historical Association. 1935–   . Cumula-
   tive index through 1954.
Journal of the History of Behavioral Science, 1965–   .
Journal of the History of Biology, Harvard University. 1967–   .
Journal of the History of Ideas. 1940–   .
Journal of the History of Medicine and Allied Science, Yale University Dept. of
   History of Science. 1946–   .
Journal of the West. 1962–   .
Journal for Scientific Study of Religion. 1962–   .
Journalism Quarterly, American Association of Schools and Departments of
   Journalism and the American Association of Teachers of Journalism. Cumula-
   tive 1924–   . Index through 1948.
Labor History. 1960–   .
Land Economics, University of Wisconsin, Institute for Research in Land Eco-
   nomics and Public Utilities. 1925–   .
Latin American Research Review, Latin American Studies Association. 1965–   .
Library of Congress Quarterly Journal, 1943–   .
Library Quarterly, Chicago University Graduate Library School. 1931–   .
Magazine of American History. 1877–1893; 1901–1917.
Magazine of History. 1905–1922. *Extra Numbers.* 1908–1935.
Mennonite Historical Bulletin, Historical and Research Committee of Mennonite
   General Conference. 1940–   .
Methodist History, Association of Methodist Historical Societies and World
   Methodist Council. 1962–   .
Mid-America, Loyola University, Institute of Jesuit History. 1918–   .
Midcontinent American Studies Journal, Midcontinent American Studies Associa-
   tion and University of Kansas. 1960–   .
Midwest Journal of Political Science, Midwest Political Science Association.
   1957–   .
Midwest Quarterly: A Journal of Contemporary Thought, Kansas State College of
   Pittsburg. 1959–   . Supersedes *Educational Leader*, 1937–1959.
Military Affairs, American Military Institute. Supersedes *Journal of the American
   Military Historical Society*, 1937–
Military Collector and Historian, Company of Military Collectors and Historians.
   1949–   .
National Genealogical Society Review, National Genealogical Society. 1912–   .

New England Quarterly. 1928– . Cumulative index through 1937.
Orbis: A Quarterly Journal of World Affairs, Foreign Policy Research Institute of University of Pennsylvania. 1957– .
Pacific Historian, California History Foundation and the Jedediah Smith Society. 1957– . Periodic cumulative indexes.
Pacific Historical Review, Pacific Coast Branch, American Historical Association. 1932– . Cumulative index through 1943.
Perspectives in American History, Charles Warren Center for Studies in American History. 1966– . Annual.
Political Science Quarterly, Academy of Political Science. *1886–* . Periodic cumulative indexes.
Prologue: Journal of the National Archives, National Archives and Records Service of the General Services Administration. 1969– .
Public Opinion Quarterly, Princeton University. 1937– .
Public Policy, John F. Kennedy School of Government at Harvard. 1940– .
Quaker History, Friends Historical Association. 1912– .
Quarterly Journal of Economics, Harvard University. 1886– . Cumulative index through 1935.
Recorder, American-Irish Historical Society. 1901–1902. Suspended 1903–1922. 1923– .
Review of Politics, University of Notre Dame. 1938– .
SAIS Review, School of Advanced International Studies at Johns Hopkins University. 1956– .
Science and Society: A Marxian Quarterly. 1936– .
Smithsonian Journal of History, Smithsonian Institution. 1966– .
Social Education, National Council for Social Studies. 1937– .
Social Forces, University of North Carolina. 1922– . Title varies.
Social Problems, Society for the Study of Social Problems. 1953– .
Social Studies, 1934– . Cumulative index through 1935. Supersedes *History Teacher's Magazine,* 1909–1918, and *Historical Outlook,* 1918–1933.
Sociological Quarterly, Midwest Sociological Society. 1960– .
Soundings: Journal of Interdisciplinary Studies. 1966– . Supersedes *Christian Scholar,* 1918–1966.
Southern Quarterly, University of Southern Mississippi. 1962– .
Southwestern Studies, Texas Western College. 1962– .
Studies in History and Philosophy of Science, London. 1970– .
Swedish Pioneer Historical Quarterly, Swedish Pioneer Historical Society. 1950– .
Technology and Culture, Society for the History of Technology. 1959– .
Theological Education. 1965– .
Transaction: Social Science and the Community, Community Leadership Project, Washington University. 1963– .
Transactions, Moravian Historical Society. 1876– .
Western Historical Quarterly, Western History Association and Utah State University. 1970– .
Western Politica, Stanford University. 1966– .
Western Political Quarterly, University of Utah, Institute of Government. 1948– .
William and Mary Quarterly, Institute of Early American History and Culture. Third series, 1944– . First and second series (1892–1944) sponsored by College of William and Mary.

8.4 JOURNALS PUBLISHED OUTSIDE OF THE UNITED STATES

Although scholarly journals in many languages contain articles that are pertinent to American history, the following list is limited to those published in English. Some are entirely devoted to American subjects, others contain occasional articles of interest to American historians.

American Studies in Scandinavia, Uppsala, Sweden. 1967– .
Canadian Historical Review. 1920– . Periodic cumulative indexes.

Canadian Journal of History, University of Saskatchewan. 1966–   .
Canadian Review of American Studies, Canadian Association for American
    Studies. 1970–   .
Economic History Review, Economic History Society, London. 1948–   .
English Historical Review, London. 1886–   . Cumulative index through 1955.
History, Historical Association, London. 1912–   .
History Today. London. 1951–   .
Indian Journal of American Studies, American Studies Research Center, Hyder-
    abad, India. 1969–   .
Journal of American Studies, British Association for American Studies. 1967–   .
Journal of Ecclesiastical History, London. 1950–   .
Journal of Religious History, University of Sydney, Australia. 1960–   .
Law Quarterly Review, London. 1885–   .
Studies in History and Philosophy of Science, London. 1970–   .

8.5 LAW REVIEWS AND JOURNALS

The following legal journals have been selected because they frequently
contain articles of historic interest.

American Journal of Comparative Law, 1952–   . Periodic cumulative indexes.
American Journal of International Law, 1907–   . Periodic cumulative indexes.
American Journal of Jurisprudence, 1969–   . Supersedes *Natural Law Forum*.
American University Law Review, 1952–   . Supersedes *Intramural Law Review*,
    1952–1956. Index, 1952–1956.
American Journal of Legal History, 1957–   . Periodic cumulative indexes.
Arizona Law Review, 1959–   . Cumulative index through 1962.
Baylor Law Review, 1948–   . Periodic cumulative indexes.
Boston University Law Review, 1921–   . Cumulative index, through 1946.
California Law Review, 1912–   . Periodic cumulative indexes
Catholic University Law Review, 1950–   .
Columbia Law Review, 1901–   . Periodic cumulative indexes.
Cornell Law Review, 1966–   . Supersedes *Cornell Law Quarterly*, 1915–66.
    Periodic cumulative indexes.
George Washington Law Review, 1932–   .
Harvard Civil Rights–Civil Liberties Law Review, 1966–   .
Harvard Law Review, 1887–   . Periodic cumulative indexes.
Hastings Law Journal, 1950–   . Supersedes *The Hastings Journal*, 1949–1950.
Howard Law Journal, 1955–   .
Indiana Law Journal, 1925–   . Cumulative index through 1952.
Journal of Criminal Law, Criminology and Police Science, 1910–   . Title varies.
    Cumulative index through 1934.
Journal of Law and Economics, 1958–   . Periodic cumulative indexes.
Journal of Public Law, 1952–   .
Journal of Urban Law, 1966–   . Supersedes *University of Detroit Law Journal*.
    Volumes are numbered consecutively.
Kentucky Law Journal. 1913–   . Periodic indexes.
Law Quarterly Review, London. 1885–   . Cumulative index through 1964.
Maryland Law Review, 1936–   . Periodic cumulative indexes.
Michigan Law Review, 1902–   . Cumulative index, through 1937.
Minnesota Law Review: Journal of the State Bar Association, 1917–   . Formerly
    Minnesota Law Review, 1917–1922. Periodic cumulative indexes.
Mississippi Law Journal, 1928–   . Periodic cumulative indexes.
Notre Dame Lawyer, 1925–   . Periodic cumulative indexes.
Northwestern University Law Review, 1906–   . Title varies. Cumulative index
    through 1931.
Stanford Law Review, 1948–   . Cumulative index through 1948–1963.
Supreme Court Review, 1960–   .
Tulane Law Review, 1929–   . Supersedes *Southern Law Quarterly*, 1916–1918.
    Cumulative index through 1951.
University of Chicago Law Review, 1933–   .

University of Cincinnati Law Review, 1927–1943; 1947– .
University of Pennsylvania Law Review, 1852– . Supersedes *The American Law
Register*, 1852–1891; *The American Law Register and Review*, 1892–1897; *The
American Law Register*, 1898–1907; *University of Pennsylvania Law Review and
American Law Register*, 1908–1944. Cumulative index through 1934.
UCLA Law Review, 1953– . Title varies. Cumulative index through 1953–1958.
Vanderbilt Law Review, 1947– . Cumulative index through 1957.
Virginia Law Review, 1913– . Periodic cumulative indexes.
Villanova Law Review, 1956– .
William and Mary Law Review, 1957– . Supersedes *William and Mary Review
of Virginia Law*. Cumulative index through 1957–1966.
Wisconsin Law Review, 1920– . Periodic cumulative indexes.
Yale Law Journal, 1891– . Cumulative index, through 1929–1934.

8.6 SOCIETY PUBLICATIONS

Abraham Lincoln Association, *Papers*, 1924–1939. *Bulletin*, 1923–1939. *Abraham
Lincoln Quarterly*, 1940–1952.
Academy of Political Science, *Proceedings*, 1910– . *Political Science Quarterly*,
1886– .
Agricultural History Society, *Papers*, 1921–1925. *Agricultural History*, 1927– .
American Academy of Political and Social Science, *Annals*, 1890– .
American Anthropological Association, *Memoirs*, 1905– . *American Anthro-
pologist*, 1888– .
American Antiquarian Society, *Archaeologia Americana: Transactions and Collec-
tions*, 1820–1922. *Proceedings*, 1843– .
American Association for Labor Legislation, *American Labor Legislation Review*,
1911–1942.
American Association for State and Local History, *Bulletin*, 1941– . *American
Heritage*, 1947–1952. *History News*, 1945– .
American Bar Association, *Report*, 1878– . *Journal*, 1915– .
American Catholic Historical Association, *Catholic Historical Review. Papers*,
1926– . *Documents*, 1933– .
American Catholic Historical Society, *American Catholic Historical Researches*,
1884–1912. *Records*, 1884– .
American Economic Association, *Publications*, 1886–1910. Title varied. Continued
as *American Economic Review*, 1911– .
American Folk-Lore Society, *Memoirs*, 1894– . *Journal of American Folk-Lore*,
1888– .
American Geographical Society, *Journal*, 1859–1900. Continued as *Bulletin*,
1901–1915; as *Geographical Review*, 1916– . *Focus*, 1950– .
American Historical Association, *Papers*, 1885–1891. *Annual Report*, 1890– .
American Historical Review, 1895– . *AHA Newsletter*, 1962– .
American-Irish Historical Society, *Journal*, 1898–1932. *Recorder*, 1923– .
American Jewish Historical Society, *Publications*, 1893–1960. Continued as *Amer-
ican Jewish Historical Quarterly*, 1960– .
American Philosophical Society, *Transactions*, 1771– . *Proceedings*, 1838– .
American Political Science Association, *Proceedings*, 1904–1914. *American Politi-
cal Science Review*, 1906– .
American Social Science Association, *Journal of Social Science*, 1869–1909.
American Society of International Law, *Proceedings*, 1907– . *American Journal
of International Law*, 1907– .
American Society of Medical History, *Medical Life*, 1894–1938. Title varied.
American Sociological Society, *Papers and Proceedings*, 1906–1935. *American
Sociological Review*, 1965– .
American Statistical Association, *Publications*, 1888–1921. *Journal*, 1922– .
Annals of Medical History, 1917–1942.
Association of History Teachers of the Middle States and Maryland, *Proceedings*,
1903– .

Association of Methodist Historical Societies and World Methodist Council, *Methodist History*, 1962– . Supersedes *World Parish*, 1948–1962.
Business Historical Society, *Business Historical Studies*, 1928. *Bulletin*, 1926–1954, continued as *Business History Review*, 1954– . *Journal of Economic and Business History* with Harvard Graduate School of Business Administration, 1928–1932.
Canadian Historical Association, *Reports*, 1915– . Title varies.
Friends' Historical Association, *Bulletin*, 1906– . *Quaker History*, 1912– .
German American Historical Society, *Americana Germanica*, 1897–1902. Continued as *German American Annals*, 1903–1919.
Mississippi Valley Historical Association, *Proceedings*, 1907–1924. *Mississippi Valley Historical Review*, 1914–1964. Continued as *Journal of American History*, 1964– . Clarence Walworth Alvord Memorial Commission, *Publications*, 1942– .
Naval History Society, *Publications*. 1911–1932.
New England Historic Genealogical Society, *New England Historical and Genealogical Register*. 1847– .
Norwegian-American Historical Association, *Studies and Records*. 1926– . *Travel and Description Series*, 1926–1929.
Pacific Coast Branch, American Historical Association, *Proceedings*, 1904–1930. *Pacific Historical Review*, 1932– .
Railway and Locomotive Historical Society, *Bulletin*, 1921– .
Scotch-Irish Society of America, *The Scotch-Irish in America: Proceedings of the Scotch-Irish Congress*, 1889–1901.
Southern Historical Society, *Papers*, 1876– .
Southern History Association, *Publications*, 1897–1907.
Southern Political Science Association, *Proceedings*, 1833–1938. *Journal of Politics*, 1939– .
Swedish Historical Society of America, *Yearbook*, 1905–1926. *Swedish-American Historical Bulletin*, 1928–1932.
Unitarian Historical Society, *Proceedings*, 1925– .
United States Catholic Historical Society, *U.S. Catholic Historical Magazine*, 1887–1890. *Historical Records and Studies*, 1900– . *Monograph Series*, 1902– .
Western History Association, *Western Historical Quarterly*, 1970– . *American West*, 1964– .

8.7 STATE HISTORICAL PUBLICATIONS

Alabama

Alabama Historical Society, *Transactions*. 1825, 1855, 1898–1906.
State Department of Archives and History, *Alabama Historical Quarterly*. 1930–1931; 1940– . Periodic cumulative indexes.
University of Alabama, *Alabama Review: A Journal of Alabama History*, 1948– . Periodic cumulative indexes.

Arizona

Arizona Pioneers Historical Society, *Journal of Arizona History*, 1960– .
State Historian of Arizona, *Arizona Historical Review*, 1928–1936.
University of Arizona, *Arizona and the West*, 1959– . Cumulative index through 1963.

Arkansas

Arkansas Historical Association, *Publications*, 1906–1917. *Arkansas Historical Quarterly*, 1942– .

California

California History Foundation and Jedediah Smith Society, *Pacific Historian,* 1957–   . Cumulative index through 1961.
California Historical Society, *Quarterly,* 1922–   . Cumulative index through 1961.
Historical Society of Southern California, *Annual Publication,* 1884–1934. Continued as *Quarterly Publication,* 1935–   . Title varies. Cumulative index through 1957.
Society of California Pioneers, *Quarterly,* 1924–   . *Publications,* 1941–   .

Colorado

Colorado Quarterly, University of Colorado, 1953–   .
State Historical Society of Colorado, *Colorado Magazine,* 1923–   . Cumulative index through 1960.

Connecticut

Connecticut Historical Society, *Collections,* 1860–1932. *Bulletin,* 1934–   . Indexed quinquennially.
New Haven Colony Historical Society, *Papers,* 1865–1918. *Journal,* 1952–   .

Delaware

Historical Society of Delaware, *Papers,* 1879–   . *Delaware History,* 1946–   .

Florida

Florida Historical Society, *Quarterly,* 1908–   . Cumulative index through 1957.
Florida State Historical Society, *Publications,* 1922–   .

Georgia

Georgia Historical Society, *Collections,* 1840–1916. *Georgia Historical Quarterly,* 1917–   . Cumulative indexes to *Quarterly* through 1943.

Hawaii

Hawaiian Historical Society, *Annual Report,* 1892–   . *Papers,* 1892–1940.

Idaho

Idaho State Historical Society, *Biennial Report,* 1907–   . *Idaho Yesterdays,* 1957–   .

Illinois

Chicago Historical Society, *Collections,* 1882–1928. *Bulletin,* 1922–1926; 1934–1940. *Chicago History,* 1945–   .
Illinois State Historical Library, *Publications,* 1899–1937. Continued as *Papers in Illinois History and Transactions,* 1937–   . *Collections,* 1903–   . Cumulative indexes to both through 1947.
Illinois State Historical Society, *Transactions,* 1900–1936. Continued as *Papers in Illinois History and Transactions,* 1937–   . *Journal,* 1908–   . Cumulative indexes to *Journal* through 1953.

Indiana

Historical Bureau of the Indiana Library and Historical Department, *Indiana Historical Collections*, 1916–   . *Indiana History Bulletin*, 1923–   .
Indiana Historical Society, *Publications*, 1895–   .
Indiana Magazine of History, Indiana University, 1905–   . Cumulative indexes through 1929.

Iowa

Historical, Memorial, and Art Department of Iowa, *Annals of Iowa*, 1882–   . Cumulative indexes through 1929.
State Historical Society of Iowa, *Annals*, 1863–1874. *Iowa Historical Record*, 1885–1902. Continued as *Iowa Journal of History and Politics*, 1903–1961; cumulative index, 1903–1942. *Studies in Iowa History 1969–   . Iowa Applied History Series*, 1912–   . *Iowa Biographical Series*, 1907–   . *Iowa Economic History Series*, 1910–   . *Iowa Social History Series*, 1915–   . *Palimpsest*, *1920–   *; indexed decennially through 1940.

Kansas

Kansas State Historical Society, *Transactions*, 1881–1908. Continued as *Collections*, 1910–1928. Replaced by *Kansas Historical Quarterly*, 1931–   .

Kentucky

Filson Club, *Publications*, 1884–   . *History Quarterly*, 1926–   . Cumulative indexes to both through 1937.
Kentucky State Historical Society, *Register*, 1903–   . Cumulative indexes through 1945.

Louisiana

Louisiana History Association, *Louisiana History*, 1960–   .
Louisiana Historical Society, *Publications*, 1896–1917. Continued as *Louisiana Historical Quarterly*, 1917–   . Cumulative index to *Publications;* to *Quarterly* through 1950.
Louisiana Studies Institute, *Louisiana Studies*, 1962–   .

Maine

Maine Historical Society, *Collections*, 1831–1906. Title varied. *Proceedings*, 1902–1914. *Province and Court Records*, 1928–1947. Cumulative index to *Collections* through 1891.

Maryland

Maryland Historical Society, *Fund Publications*, 1867–1901. *Archives of Maryland*, 1883–   . *Maryland Historical Magazine*, 1906–   . *Studies in Maryland History*, 1953–   .

Massachusetts

Colonial Society of Massachusetts, *Publications*, 1895–   . Cumulative index through 1924.
Essex Institute, *Historical Collections*, 1859–   . Cumulative indexes through 1949.

Massachusetts Historical Society, *Collections*, 1792– . *Proceedings*, 1859– .
Collections and *Proceedings* are self-indexed every 20 vols. *Photostat Americana*, 1919–1930. *Winthrop Papers*, 1929– . *Journals of the House of Representatives of Massachusetts* [1715–], 1919– . *Sibley's Harvard Graduates*, 1933– . *MHS Miscellany*, 1954– . *Massachusetts Historical Society Picture Books*, 1954– .
Prince Society, *Publications*. 1865–1920.

Michigan

Michigan Historical Commission (Pioneer Society of the State of Michigan, 1874–1886; Pioneer and Historical Society of the State of Michigan, 1887–1912), *Historical Collections*. Title varies. Lansing, 1874–1929. *Michigan History Magazine*, 1917– . Cumulative index to *Historical Collections*, 1874–1915.

Minnesota

Minnesota Historical Society, *Collections*, 1850–1920. *Minnesota History*, 1915– . *Narratives and Documents*, 1932– . Cumulative index to *Collections* through 1904; to *History*, through 1929.

Mississippi

Mississippi Historical Society, *Publications*, 1898–1914. Continued as *Centenary Series*, 1916– . *Journal of Mississippi History*, 1939– .

Missouri

Missouri Historical Society, *Collections*, 1880–1931. *Glimpses of the Past*, 1933–1942. *Bulletin*, 1944– .
State Historical Society of Missouri, *Documentary Publications*, 1920– . *Missouri Historical Review*, 1906– . Cumulative index to *Review* through 1951.

Montana

Historical Society of Montana, *Contributions*, 1876– . *Montana: The Magazine of Western History*, 1951– . Cumulative index to Montana through 1960.

Nebraska

Nebraska State Historical Society, *Transactions and Reports*, 1885–1893. Continued as *Proceedings and Collections*, 1894–1902; then as *Publications*, 1906– . *Nebraska History Magazine*, 1918– . Title varies. Index to both through 1958.

Nevada

Nevada Historical Society, *Report*, 1909– . *Papers*, 1913– . *Applied History Series*, 1918– . *Nevada Historical Society Quarterly*, 1957– .

New Hampshire

New Hampshire Historical Society, *Collections*, 1824–1939. *Proceedings*, 1874–1917. *Historical New Hampshire*, 1946– .

New Jersey

New Jersey Historical Society, *Collections*, 1846– . *Proceedings*, 1847– .
New Jersey Archives, 1880– . General index to *Proceedings* through 1919,
1920–1931. *New Jersey History*, 1846– .

New Mexico

Historical Society of New Mexico, *Publications*, 1881– . *Publications in History*, 1926– . *New Mexico Historical Review*, 1926– . Cumulative index
to *Review* through 1940, 1941–1956.
University of New Mexico, *New Mexico Quarterly*, 1931–1969.

New York

Buffalo Historical Society, *Publications*, 1879– . *Niagara Frontier*, 1953– .
New York Historical Society, *Collections*, 1811–1859. *John Watts de Peyster Publication Fund Series*, 1868– . *John Divine Jones Fund Series*, 1879– . *Quarterly*, 1917– .
New York State Historical Association, *Proceedings*. 1901–1919. *Series*. N.Y.,
1932– . *Quarterly Journal*. Albany, 1919–1931. Continued as *New York
History*, 1932– . Cumulative index to *Proceedings*, to *Journal* through 1931,
and to *History* through 1965.
Rochester Historical Society, *Publication Fund Series*, 1922–1949. *Scrapbook*,
1950– . Cumulative index to *Fund Series* through 1936.
Rochester Public Library *Rochester History*, 1940– .

North Carolina

North Carolina Historical Commission (Since 1943, State Department of
Archives and History), *Bulletin*, 1907– . *North Carolina Historical Review*,
1924– . Cumulative index to *Review* through 1963.

North Dakota

State Historical Society of North Dakota, *Collections*, 1906–1926. Continued as
North Dakota Historical Quarterly, 1926–1944; as *North Dakota History*,
1945– .
University of North Dakota, *North Dakota Quarterly*, 1933– .

Ohio

Historical and Philosophical Society of Ohio, *Publications*, 1906–1943. Title
varied.
Historical Society of Northwestern Ohio, *Northwest Ohio Quarterly*, 1929– .
Ohio State Archaeological and Historical Society, *Ohio Archaeological and Historical Quarterly*, 1887–1954. Title varied. *Ohio Historical Collections*, 1931–1944.
Cumulative index to *Quarterly* through 1902; cumulative table of contents,
1887–1953.
Ohio Historical Society (formerly Ohio State Archaeological and Historical Society), *Ohio Historical Quarterly*, 1955–1961. Continued as *Ohio History*,
1962– .

Oklahoma

Oklahoma Historical Society, *Historia*, 1909–1922. Continued as *Chronicles of
Oklahoma*, 1921– . Cumulative index to *Chronicles* through 1959.

Oregon

Oregon Historical Quarterly, 1926–   . Supersedes Oregon Historical Society, *Quarterly,* 1900–1926. Index through 1939.

Pennsylvania

Historical Society of Pennsylvania, *Memoirs,* 1826–1895. *Pennsylvania Magazine of History and Biography,* 1877–   . Cumulative index to *Magazine* through 1950.
Historical Society of Western Pennsylvania, *Western Pennsylvania Historical Magazine,* 1918–   . Cumulative index through 1960.
Pennsylvania-German Society, *Proceedings and Addresses,* 1891–   . Cumulative index through 1923.
Pennsylvania Historical Association, *Pennsylvania History,* 1934–   . *Pennsylvania Historical Studies.* 1947–   .
Pennsylvania Historical Commission, *Bulletin,* 1932–   . *Publications,* 1930–   .

Rhode Island

Rhode Island Historical Society, *Collections,* 1827–1941. *Proceedings,* 1872–92; 1900–1914. *Publications,* 1893–1900. *Rhode Island History,* 1941–   . Cumulative index to *History* through 1956.

South Carolina

South Carolina Historical Society, *Collections,* 1857–97. *South Carolina Historical Magazine,* 1900–   . Formerly *South Carolina Historical and Genealogical Magazine.* Subject index to the magazine through 1960.

South Dakota

State Historical Society of South Dakota, *South Dakota Historical Collections,* 1902–   . *South Dakota Historical Review,* 1935–   . Cumulative index to *Collections* through 1935.

Tennessee

East Tennessee Historical Society, *Publications,* 1929–   . Cumulative index through 1963.
Tennessee Historical Society, *Tennessee Historical Magazine,* 1915–1937. *Tennessee Historical Quarterly* (in cooperation with the Tennessee Historical Commission), 1942–   . Cumulative index to *Magazine* through 1926.

Texas

Texas State Historical Association, *Quarterly,* 1897–1912. Continued as *Southwestern Historical Quarterly,* 1912–   . Cumulative index through 1937.
West Texas Historical Association, *Year Book,* 1925–   .

Utah

Utah State Historical Society, *Utah Historical Quarterly,* 1928–   . Indexed triennially.

Vermont

Vermont Historical Society, *Proceedings*, 1860–1952. Continued as *Vermont History*, 1953–   . Cumulative index through 1953.

Virginia

Virginia Historical Society, *Virginia Historical Register*. 1843–1853. *Virginia Historical Reporter*, 1854–1860. *Collections*, 1882–1892. *Virginia Magazine of History and Biography*, 1893–   . General index to the *Register* and *Magazine* through 1930 in E. G. Swem, comp., *Virginia Historical Index* (2 vols., 1934–1936).
Virginia State Library, *Virginia Cavalcade*, 1951–   .

Washington

Washington State Historical Society, *Publications*, 1906–1914.
Washington University State Historical Society, *Washington Historical Quarterly*, 1906–1935. Continued as *Pacific Northwest Quarterly*, 1936–   . Cumulative index, 1906–1962.

West Virginia

State Department of Archives and History, *West Virginia History*, 1939–   .

Wisconsin

State Historical Society of Wisconsin, *Reports and Collections*, 1855–1888. Continued as *Collections*, 1888–   . *Proceedings*, 1875–   . *Calendar Series*, 1915–1929. *Wisconsin Domesday Book*, 1922–1937. *History Series*, 1925–   . *Wisconsin Biography Series*, 1930–1940. *Wisconsin Magazine of History*, 1917–   . Cumulative index to first 20 vols. of *Collections*, to *Proceedings* through 1901, to *Magazine* through 1946.
Wisconsin Academy of Sciences, Arts, and Letters, *Transactions*, 1870–   . Cumulative index through 1932.

Wyoming

State Department of History, *Annals of Wyoming*, 1923–   . Title varies. Cumulative indexes through 1959.

8.8 GENERAL PERIODICALS

Aside from specialized journals in history and allied fields, there is considerable material of importance to historians in magazines addressed primarily to other audiences. These periodicals, dating from feeble beginnings in 1741, include popular, professional, commercial, scientific, literary, religious, propagandist, and recreational types. General indexes make subject matter available, but they do not cover the advertising sections, which often document American social and economic development. For a description of union lists used in locating files of general magazines and a discussion of microreproductions, see sections 4.9 and 7.2 respectively.

A classic study of American magazines is Frank L. Mott, *A History of American Magazines* (5 vols., 1930–1968). Related works, including histories of individual magazines, will be found in 27.3.

Advocate of Peace. See *World Affairs.*
American Agriculturalist, 1842– . Title varies.
American History Illustrated, 1966– .
American Mercury, 1924– .
American Museum, 1787–1792.
American Quarterly Review, 1827–1837.
American Scholar, 1932– .
American Whig Review, 1845–1852. Title varied.
The Annalist, 1913–1940. Merged with *Business Week.*
Antiques, 1922– .
Appletons' Journal, 1869–1881.
Arena, 1889–1909.
Art in America, 1913– . Title varies.
Art Forum, 1962– .
Atlantic Monthly, 1857– .
Business Week, 1929– . Superseded *Magazine of Business,* 1900–1929.
Catholic World, 1865– .
Century Magazine, 1881–1930. Superseded *Scribner's Monthly,* 1870–1881.
   Merged with *Forum.*
Charities. See *Survey.*
Charities Review, 1891–1901.
Chautauquan, 1880–1914. Merged with *Independent.*
Christian Century, 1884– .
Christian Disciple and Theological Review [Unitarian]. See *Christian Examiner.*
Christian Examiner, 1824–1869. Superseded *Christian Disciple and Theological
   Review,* 1813–1822.
Christian Leader [Unitarian], 1819–1897. Title varied.
Christian Register. See *Unitarian Register.*
Christian Union, 1870–1893. Continued as *Outlook,* 1893–1935.
Collier's, 1888–1957.
Commentary, 1945– .
Commercial and Financial Chronicle, 1865– .
Commonweal, 1924– .
Current History, 1914– . Title varies.
Current Literature, See *Current Opinion.*
Current Opinion, 1913–1925. Superseded *Current Literature,* 1888–1912. Merged
   with *Literary Digest.*
Cyclopedic Review of Current History, 1893–1902. Superseded *Quarterly Register
   of Current History,* 1891–1893. Merged with *Current Literature.*
De Bow's Review, 1846–1864; 1866–1870; 1879–1880; Title varied.
Democratic Review, 1837–1859. Title varied.
Dial, 1881–1929.
Dial: A Magazine for Literature, Philosophy, and Religion, 1840–1844.
Dissent, 1954– .
Eclectic Magazine of Foreign Literature, Science and Art, 1844–1907.
Encounter, London. 1953– .
Esquire, 1933– .
Events, 1937–1941. Merged with *Current History.*
Everybody's Magazine, 1899–1929.
Forbes, 1917– .
Fortune, 1930– .
Forum, 1886–1940. Merged with *Current History.*
Frank Leslie's Illustrated Newspaper, 1855–1922. Title varied.
Friend of Peace, 1816–1828.
Frontier and Midland, 1933–1939. Superseded *Frontier, A Magazine of the North-
   west,* 1920–1933.
Galaxy, 1866–1878. Merged with *Atlantic Monthly.*
Gleason's [from 1855, *Ballou's*] *Pictorial Drawing-Room Companion,* 1851–1859.
Godey's Lady's Book, 1830–1898. Title varied.
Graham's Magazine, 1826–1858. Title varied.
Harper's (formerly *Harper's Monthly Magazine,* 1850– .
Harper's Bazaar, 1867– .

Harper's Weekly, 1857–1916. Merged with *Independent*.
Human Events, 1944– .
Hunt's Merchants' Magazine and Commercial Review, 1839–1870. Title varied.
  Merged with the *Commercial and Financial Chronicle*.
I. F. Stone's Bi-Weekly, 1953–1972. Title varied.
Independent, 1848–1928. Merged with *Outlook*.
International Review, 1874–1883.
Judge, 1881–1939.
Knickerbocker Magazine, 1833–1865.
Lend-a-Hand, 1886–1897. Merged with *Charities Review*.
The Liberator, 1918–1924. Superseded *The Masses*, 1911–1917.
Life, 1883– . Changed from a humorous to a pictorial magazine in 1936.
Lippinott's Magazine, 1868–1916. Merged with *Scribner's Magazine*.
Literary Digest, 1890–1938. Merged with *Time*.
Literary World, 1847–1853.
Littell's Living Age, 1844–1941. Title varied.
Look, 1937–1971.
Lowell Offering, 1840–1845.
McClure's Magazine, 1893–1929.
Magazine of Business, See *Business Week*.
Manufacturer's Record, 1882– .
Massachusetts Magazine, 1789–1796.
The Masses. See *The Liberator*.
Methodist Review, 1818–1931. Title varied.
Munsey's Magazine, 1889–1929.
Nation, 1865– .
National Geographic, 1888– .
National Review, 1948– .
Nation's Business, 1912– .
New England Farmer (Fessenden's), 1822–1913.
New Englander. See *Yale-Review*.
New Republic, 1914– .
New York Magazine, 1790–1797.
New York Magazine, 1968– .
New York Mirror, 1823–1847. Title varied.
New York Review of Books, 1963– .
New Yorker, 1925– .
Newsweek, 1933– .
Niles' Weekly Register, 1811–1849. Title varied.
North American Review, 1815–1940.
Outing, 1882–1923.
Outlook, 1893–1935. See *Christian Union*.
Overland Monthly, 1868–1875; 1883–1935. Title varied.
Panoplist, 1805–1851. Title varies.
Partisan Review, 1934– .
Peterson's Ladies' National Magazine, 1842–1898.
Popular Science Monthly, 1872– .
Port Folio (Dennie's), 1801–1827.
Princeton Review, 1825–1888. Title varied.
The Public Interest, 1965– .
Public Opinion, 1886–1906. Merged with *Literary Digest*.
Publisher's Weekly, 1872– .
Puck, 1877–1918.
Quarterly Register of Current History. See *Cyclopedic Review of Current History*.
Ramparts, 1962– .
Reader's Digest, 1922– .
Reporter, 1949–1968.
Review of Reviews, 1890–1937. Title varied.
Saturday Evening Post, 1821–1969; 1971– .
Saturday Review, 1924– . Formerly *Saturday Review of Literature*.
Science, 1883– .
Scientific American, 1845– .

Scientific Monthly, 1915–1957. Merged with *Science.*
Scribner's Magazine, 1887–1939.
Scribner's Monthly. See *Century Magazine.*
Sewanee Review, 1892–   .
Smart Set, 1900–1930.
South Atlantic Quarterly, 1902–   .
Southern Literary Messenger, 1834–1864; 1939–1945.
Southern Quarterly Review, 1842–1857.
Southern Review, 1935–1943. New series 1965–   .
Street's Pandex to the News and Cumulative Index to Current History, 1903–1917.
Survey, 1909–1952. Supersedes *Charities,* 1897–1909.
Survey Graphic, 1921–1949. Merged with *Survey.*
Time, 1923–   .
Unitarian Register, 1960–   . Title varies. Superseded *Christian Register,* 1821–
    1960.
U.N. Monthly Chronicle, 1964–   . Superseded *United Nations Review,* 1954–
    1964; *United Nations Weekly Bulletin,* 1946–1954.
U.S. News and World Report, 1933–   . Title varies.
Vanity Fair, 1913–1936.
Virginia Quarterly Review, 1925–   .
Vogue, 1892–   .
Washington Monthly, 1969–   .
Western Messenger, 1835–1841.
Western Monthly Magazine, 1830–1837. Title varied.
World Affairs, 1932–   . Superseded *Advocate of Peace.* 1837–1932.
Yale Review, 1892–   . Superseded *New Englander,* 1843–1892.

8.9 NEWSPAPERS

8.9.1 Introduction

Newspapers are indispensable to the historian for both the direct and indirect information they afford. Compiled in haste and often edited with bias, they must be used with critical caution. They constitute a voluminous source, for in no other respect has America been so articulate as in her daily and weekly press.

Because of their ephemeral nature, newspapers have often been preserved in a haphazard fashion, especially the early ones. Some of our great historical repositories nevertheless have succeeded in gathering and preserving a remarkably large number of early papers. An indispensable guide for locating these is C. S. Brigham, *History and Bibliography of American Newspapers, 1690–1820* (2 vols., 1947; additions and corrections, 1961). See also U.S. Library of Congress. Periodicals Division, *Check List of American 18th-Century Newspapers in the Library of Congress* (rev. ed., 1936). For locating files of later papers see Winifred Gregory, *American Newspapers, 1821–1936: A Union List of Files Available in the United States and Canada* (1937). Its arrangement is similar to that of Brigham; however it lacks a title index.

In addition to these national lists there are numerous state guides such as Donald E. Oehlerts's *Guide to Wisconsin Newspapers, 1833–1957* (1958). Many libraries have also published lists of their newspaper holdings. Guides to specialized newspapers include Karl J. R. Arndt and May E. Olson, *German-American Newspapers and Periodicals, 1732–1955* (1961) and Warren Brown, *Check List of Negro Newspapers in the United States, 1827–1946* (1946).

In the last two decades many repositories have been microfilming back files of their newspaper collections as well as current acquisitions in order to save space, and at the same time they are making many of these available on positive microfilm to libraries and individuals. If a positive copy is not available in a particular library it may often be obtained on inter-library loan or by purchase from the original holder. To locate files of both negative and positive microfilms consult Library of Congress, Union Catalog Division, *Newspapers on Microfilm* (6th ed., 1967). Some 15,000 entries are of American newspapers.

The student interested in a particular state or region would do well to obtain up-to-date state or regional lists of newspapers from the appropriate institutions. Some contemporary newspapers, such as the *New York Times,* are issued on microfilm by the publisher. Many repositories are putting their collections of newspapers on microfilm or microcards. The Jewish Institute of Religion at Hebrew Union College, for example, is attempting to microfilm all Jewish newspapers published in the United States before 1925 as well as a selective group of papers published since that date. The American Antiquarian Society is in the process of putting its outstanding collection of newspapers published before 1820 on microcards.

Few American newspapers have been indexed. The historian is fortunate if an index exists for the papers in which he is interested. An index to a national or regional paper, however, can be a valuable guide to many papers by citing events (with dates) that may be reported more fully in a paper that is not indexed. Herbert Brayer has compiled a "Preliminary Guide to Indexed Newspapers in the United States, 1850–1900, *MVHR,* 33 (1946), 237. Perhaps the most widely useful indexes are Lester J. Cappon and Stella M. Duff, *Virginia Gazette* (2 vols., 1950), bridging the years 1736–1780 and covering advertisements as well as editorial items; the *New York Tribune,* 1841–1907; the *Brooklyn Daily Eagle,* 1891–1902; the *United States Daily,* 1926–1933; and the *New York Times,* 1851–1858, 1860, 1863–1905 and 1913–   . Of the current indexes, the *New York Times* is the most useful, but see also the *Christian Science Monitor,* 1960–   , and the *Wall Street Journal,* 1958–   . For the outstanding English journal, *The Times,* see *Palmer's Index to "The Times" Newspaper, 1790–June 1941,* continued by *Index to the Times,* 1906–   .

During the 1930's the WPA indexed some newspapers of regional significance on 3 × 5 cards, but they were never published. The Milwaukee Public Library, for example, has index cards for the *Milwaukee Sentinel,* 1837–1880. The student working in local or regional newspapers would do well to inquire about such indexes with state or local agencies.

General works on journalism in the United States and histories of individual newspapers will be found under COMMUNICATION- Newspapers.

The following is a selective list of newspapers, although the colonial period is more comprehensive than the later periods. If a paper spans two or more periods it is repeated. Inclusion of a paper does not imply that it is a "better" paper than some that are omitted. Rather it reflects an attempt to cover the various regions of the United States by listing important city dailies with regional coverage. For papers in smaller cities and towns, see Ayer's *Annual Directory of Newspapers and Periodicals,* 1880–   .

8.9.2 1704–1788

Annapolis *Maryland Gazette,* 1745–1777; 1779–1839.
Boston *Essex Gazette,* 1768–1775; *Independent Chronicle,* 1776–1840; *Semi-Weekly Advertiser,* 1840–1876.

Boston *Evening-Post,* 1735–1775.
Boston *Gazette,* 1719–1798.
Boston *Massachusetts Centinel,* 1784–1790; *Columbian Centinel,* 1791–1840.
Boston *Massachusetts Spy,* 1770–1775. Moved to Worcester in 1775.
Boston *News-Letter,* 1704–1776. Title varied.
Charleston *South-Carolina Gazette,* 1732–1775.
Hartford *Courant,* 1764–   . Title varies.
Lexington, *Kentucky Gazette,* 1787–1848.
Newport [R.I.] *Mercury,* 1758–1775, 1780–1928; *Mercury and Weekly News,* 1928–
New York *Gazette,* 1725–1744.
New York *Gazette or Weekly Post-Boy,* 1747–1773.
New York *Journal,* 1766–1776.
New York *Weekly Journal* [Zenger], 1733–1751.
Philadelphia *Pennsylvania Gazette,* 1728–1815.
Philadelphia *Pennsylvania Journal,* 1742–1793.
Pittsburgh *Gazette,* 1786–1877; *Commercial Gazette,* 1877–1901; *Gazette,* 1901–1906; *Gazette-Times,* 1906–1927; *Post-Gazette,* 1927–   .
Williamsburg *Virginia Gazette,* 1736–1780.
Worcester *Massachusetts Spy,* Worcester, 1775–1904; Printed in Boston, 1770–1775.

8.9.3 1789 to the Present

Albany *Argus,* 1813–1921.
Albany *Knickerbocker News,* 1842–   .
Albany *Times-Union,* 1856–   .
Albuquerque *Tribune,* 1922–   .
Albuquerque *Journal,* 1880–   .
Annapolis *Maryland Gazette,* 1779–1839
Atlanta *Constitution,* 1868–   .
Baltimore *Sun,* 1837–   .
Bismark, N.D. *Tribune,*
Boise, Idaho *Idaho Statesman,* 1864–   .
Boston *Christian Science Monitor,* 1908–   .
Boston *Gazette,* 1719–1798.
Boston *Globe,* 1872–
Boston *Herald Traveler,* 1825–1972; Herald Traveler-Record American 1972–   .
Boston *Independent Chronicle,* 1776–1840.
Boston *Liberator,* 1831–1865.
Boston *Massachusetts Centinel,* 1784–1790.
Boston *New-England Palladium,* 1803–1840; *Mercury and New-England Palladium,* 1801–1803; *Massachusetts Mercury,* 1793–1800.
Boston *Semi-Weekly Advertiser,* 1840–1876.
Boston *Transcript,* 1830–1941.
Brooklyn *Daily Eagle,* 1841–1955.
Buffalo *Evening News,* 1880–   .
Burlington [Iowa] *Hawk-Eye,* 1839–1933.
Charleston [S.C.] *News and Courier,* 1873–   ; *Courier,* 1803–1873.
Charleston, [S.C.] *Mercury,* 1822–1868.
Chicago *Daily News,* 1876–   .
Chicago *Inter Ocean,* 1872–1914.
Chicago *Sun-Times,* 1947–   .
Chicago *Times,* 1854–1895.
Chicago *Tribune,* 1847–   .
Cincinnati *Enquirer,* 1841–   .
Cincinnati *Post & Times Star,* 1881–   .
Cleveland *Plain Dealer,* 1842–   .
Columbus [Ohio] *Citizen-Journal,* 1899–   .
Columbus [Ohio] *Dispatch,* 1871–   .
Dallas *Morning News,* 1885–   .

Dallas *Times Herald,* 1876– .
Denver *Post,* 1892– .
Denver *Republican,* 1876–1913.
Des Moines *Register,* 1849– .
Des Moines *Tribune,* 1881– .
Detroit *Free Press,* 1831– .
Detroit *News,* 1873– .
Emporia [Kan.] *Gazette,* 1890– .
Galveston *Daily News,* 1842– .
Garden City [N.Y.] *Newsday,* 1940– .
Greenville [Miss.] *Delta Democrat-Times,* 1888– .
Hartford *Courant,* 1764– .
Houston *Chronicle,* 1901– .
Houston *Post,* 1885– .
Indianapolis *Journal,* 1823–1904.
Indianapolis *News,* 1869– .
Indianapolis *Star,* 1903– .
Jackson [Miss.] *Clarion-Ledger-News,* 1837– .
Kansas City *Star,* 1880– .
Lincoln [Neb.] *Journal,* 1867– .
Lincoln [Neb.] *Star,* 1902– .
Little Rock *Arkansas Gazette,* 1819– .
Los Angeles *Herald-Examiner,* 1871– .
Los Angeles *Times,* 1881– .
Louisville *Courier-Journal,* 1868–   ; *Journal,* 1830–1868.
Miami *Herald,* 1910– .
Milwaukee *Herold,* 1861–1932.
Milwaukee *Journal,* 1882– .
Milwaukee *Sentinel,* 1837– .
Minneapolis *Star,* 1878– .
Minneapolis *Tribune,* 1867– .
Montgomery, Ala. *Advertiser,* 1828– .
Nashville *Banner,* 1876– .
Nashville *Tennessean,* 1812– .
Newark *Star-Ledger,* 1917– .
New Orleans *LeCourier de la Louisiana,* 1807–1860.
New Orleans *Times-Picayune,* 1914–   ; *Picayune,* 1837–1914.
New York *Daily News,* 1919– .
New York *Evening Post,* 1801–   . Title varies.
New York *Herald,* 1835–1924. Merged with *Tribune.*
New York *Herald Tribune,* 1924–1966.
New York *Journal,* 1882– .
New York *Journal of Commerce and Commercial,* 1927–   ; *Journal of Commerce and Commercial Bulletin,* 1893–1926; *Journal of Commerce,* 1827–1893.
New York *Morning Courier and Enquirer,* 1829–1861; *Morning Courier,* 1827–1829.
New York *National Anti-Slavery Standard,* 1840–1864.
New York *Staats-Zeitung,* 1834– .
New York *Sun,* 1833–1950; Incorporated with New York *World Telegram.*
New York *Times,* 1851– .
New York *Tribune,* 1841–1924. Merged with *Herald.*
New York *Wall Street Journal,* 1889– .
New York *World Telegram,* 1931–1966; *World,* 1860–1931.
Newport [R.I.] *Mercury,* 1780–1928.
Norfolk [Va.] *Ledger-Star,* 1876– .
Norfolk *Virginian-Pilot,* 1865– .
Oakland [Calif.] *Tribune,* 1874– .
Oklahoma City *Daily Oklahoman,* 1894– .
Oklahoma City *Times,* 1889– .
Omaha [Neb.] *Bee,* 1871–1938.
Omaha [Neb.] *World-Herald,* 1885– .
Philadelphia *Aurora,* 1794–1829, 1834–1835; *General Advertiser,* 1790–1794.
Philadelphia *Bulletin,* 1847– .

Philadelphia *Inquirer*, 1829– .
Philadelphia *Pennsylvania Gazette*, 1728–1815.
Philadelphia *Pennsylvania Journal*, 1742–1793.
Philadelphia *Press*, 1857–1920. Merged with *Public Ledger*.
Philadelphia *Public Ledger*, 1836–1934. Merged with *Inquirer*.
Phoenix *Arizona Gazette*, 1880– .
Phoenix *Arizona Republic*, 1890– .
Pittsburgh *Post-Gazette*, 1927– ; *Gazette-Times*, 1906–1927; *Gazette*, 1901–
1906; *Commercial Gazette*, 1877–1901; *Gazette*, 1786–1877.
Pittsburgh *Press*, 1884– .
Portland [Maine] *Press-Herald*, 1862– .
Portland *Oregonian*, 1850– .
Providence *Evening Bulletin*, 1863– .
Providence *Journal*, 1829– .
Raleigh *News and Observer*, 1880– ; *News*, 1872–1880.
Richmond *Enquirer*, 1804–1877.
Richmond *Times-Dispatch*, 1903– ; *Dispatch*, 1850–1903.
Sacramento [Calif.] *Bee*, 1857– .
St. Louis *Globe-Democrat*, 1852– .
St. Louis *Post-Dispatch*, 1878– .
St. Louis *Republic*, 1888–1919; *Missouri Gazette*, 1808–1822; *Missouri Republican*,
1822–1888; Merged with *Globe-Democrat*.
St. Louis *Westliche Post*, 1857–1939.
St. Paul *Minnesota Pioneer*, 1849–1875.
St. Paul *Pioneer Press*, 1857– .
St. Petersburg *Independent*, 1907– .
St. Petersburg *Times*, 1884– .
Salt Lake City *Deseret News*, 1850– .
Salt Lake City *Tribune*, 1871– .
San Francisco *Alta California*, 1849–1891.
San Francisco *Chronicle*, 1865– .
San Francisco *Examiner*, 1855– .
Seattle *Post-Intelligencer*, 1881– ; *Intelligencer*, 1867–1881.
Seattle *Times*, 1886– .
Sioux Falls [So. Dak.] *Argus-Leader*, 1885– .
South Bend [Ind.] *Tribune*, 1872– .
Spokane [Wash.] *Chronicle*, 1886– .
Spokane [Wash.] *Spokesman-Review*, 1883– .
Springfield [Mass.] *Republican*, 1824– .
Tampa *Times*, 1892– .
Tampa *Tribune*, 1893– .
Toledo *Blade*, 1835– .
Toronto *Globe and Mail*, 1844– .
Trenton [N.J.] *Times*, 1882– .
Tulsa [Okla.] *Tribune*, 1904– .
Tulsa [Okla.] *World*, 1906– .
Washington *Globe*, 1830–1845.
Washington *National Era*, 1847–1860.
Washington *National Intelligencer*, 1800–1870.
Washington *National Observer*, 1882– .
Washington *Post*, 1877– .
Washington *Star*, 1852– .
Washington *United States Daily*, 1926–1933.
Washington *United States Telegraph*, 1826–1837.
Wichita *Eagle and Beacon*, 1872– .
Worcester *Gazette*, 1866– .
Worcester *Massachusetts Spy*, 1775–1904.
Worcester *Telegram*, 1884– .

Part Two Biographies and Personal Records

9 Travels and Description

Travelers' accounts constitute an important source of information about the American past. They deal, in some cases, with the geographic and physiographic features of the country, in others, with its people. By making explicit and vivid what local residents take for granted, travelers' accounts provide a kind of color, detail, and human interest available in no other historical source. In addition, the occasional penetrating analysis by a first-rate mind may give the historian suggestive and far-reaching insights. Such accounts, of course, must be used with caution. Every student will, soon enough, become aware of the gullibility of travelers in strange lands, of their capacity for getting things wrong, of their instinct for automatic praise or automatic censure.

It is often difficult to decide whether a given book is a "travel account" or an "autobiography;" hence it would be well to see also the following chapter, Biographies and Selected Writings.

9.1 COLLECTIONS AND SYNTHESES

Angle, Paul M., *Prairie State: Impressions of Illinois 1673–1967 by Travelers* (1968).

Athearn, Robert G., *Westward the Briton* (1953). Synthesis of his travels to the West after Civil War.

Beck, Earl R., *Germany Rediscovers America* (1968). Weimar period.

Blegen, T. C., and P. D. Jordan, eds., *With Various Voices: Recordings of North Star Life* (1949).

Brauer, Jerald C., *Images of Religion in America* (1967).

Brooks, John G., *As Others See Us: A Study of Progress in the United States* (1908).

Carson, Jane, ed., *Travelers in Tidewater Virginia, 1700–1800: A Bibliography* (1965).

Chester, Edward W., *Europe Views America* (1962).

French, Joseph L., ed., *The Pioneer West: Narratives* (1923).

Hafen, LeRoy R., and Ann W. Hafen, *Handcarts to Zion, 1856–1860* (1960) [Mormons from Europe]

Hafen, LeRoy R., and Ann W. Hafen, eds., *Journals of Forty-Niners, Salt Lake to Los Angeles* (1954).

—— *Reports from Colorado: Wildman Letters and Other Reports, 1859* (1961).

—— *To Rockies and Oregon, 1839–1842: Diaries and Accounts* (1955).

Handlin, Oscar, ed., *This Was America* (1949).

Hulbert, A. B., ed., *Forty-Niners: The Chronicle of the California Trail* (1931).

Hoskins, Janina W., "The Image of America in Accounts of Polish Travelers of the 18th and 19th Centuries," *Quar. Jour. of the Library of Congress*, 22 (1965), 226.

Joseph, Franz M., ed., *As Others See Us: United States through Foreign Eyes* (1959).

Lang, W. B., ed., *The First Overland Mail: Butterfield Trail, San Francisco to Memphis, 1858–1861* (1940).

McMaster, J. B., ed., *The Trail Makers* (17 vols., 1903–1905). The series includes among its volumes the following travel accounts: *Journey of Cabeca de Vaca and His Companions*, A. F. Bandelier, ed.; *Narratives of De Soto*, E. G. Bourne, ed. (2 vols.); *Voyages of Champlain*, E. G. Bourne, ed. (2 vols.); *Journey of Coronado*, G. P. Winship, ed.; *Journey of La Salle and His Companions*, I. J. Cox, ed. (2 vols.); *Lewis and Clark Expedition*, J. B. McMaster, ed. (3 vols.); D. W. Harmon, *Journal of Voyages and Travels*; Alexander Mackenzie, *Voyages through North America* [1789, 1793] (2 vols.); W. F. Butler, *The Wild Northland* [1872–1873].

Mesick, J. L., *The English Traveller in America, 1785–1835* (1922).

Mirsky, Jeanette, *Westward Crossings* (1946).

Morgan, Dale, ed., *Overland in 1846: Diaries and Letters* (2 vols., 1963).

Nevins, Allan, ed., *America through British Eyes* (1948).

Pierce, Bessie L., ed., *As Others See Chicago: Impressions of Visitors, 1673–1933* (1933).

Pomfret, John E., ed., *California Gold Rush Voyages, 1848–1849* (1954).

Rémond, René, *Les Etats-Unis devant L'opinion francaise 1815–1852* (2 vols., 1962).

Sherrill, C. H., *French Memories of Eighteenth-Century America* [1775–1800] (1915).

Studley, Miriam V., *Historic New Jersey through Visitors' Eyes* (1964).

Thwaites, Reuben G., ed., *Early Western Travels, 1748–1846* (32 vols., 1904–1907).

———— *Jesuit Relations and Allied Documents, 1610–1791* (73 vols., 1896–1901).

Tryon, Warren S., ed., *Mirror for Americans: Life and Manners in United States, 1790–1870, as Recorded by American Travelers* (3 vols., 1952).

Williams, Samuel C., ed., *Early Travels in the Tennessee Country, 1540–1800* (1928).

9.2 BIBLIOGRAPHY AND HISTORIOGRAPHY

Adams, Percy G., *Travelers and Travel Liars, 1660–1800.* (1962).

Clark, Thomas D., "Great Visitation to American Democracy," *MVHR*, 44 (1957), 3.

———— ed., *Travels in the Old South: A Bibliography* (3 vols., 1956–1960). Covers the period, 1527–1860.

———— *Travels in New South: A Bibliography, 1865–1955* (2 vols., 1962).

Coulter, E. Merton, ed., *Travels in the Confederate States: A Bibliography* (1947).

Cox, Edward G., *A Reference Guide to the Literature of Travel* (1938).

Hubach, Robert R., *Early Midwestern Travel Narratives: Bibliography, 1634–1850* (1961).

———— "Unpublished Travel Narratives on Early Midwest, 1720–1850: Preliminary Bibliography," *MVHR*, 42 (1955), 525.

Larson, Esther E., *Swedish Commentators on America, 1638–1865: Annotated List* (1963).

McDermott, John F., ed., *Travelers on Western Frontier* (1970).

———— "Travelers on the Western Waters," *Proc. of Am. Antiquarian Soc.*, 77 (1967), 255.

Monaghan, Frank, *French Travellers in the United States, 1765–1932* (1932). *Supplement* by Samuel J. Marino, (1961).

Severin, Timothy, *Explorers of Mississippi* (1968).

Sibley, Marilyn M., *Travelers in Texas, 1761–1860* (1967).

de Smet, Antoine, *Voyageurs Belges aux Etats-Unis du XVII Siècle à 1900: Notices bio-bibliographiques* (1959).

Thompson, Lawrence S., *Foreign Travellers in the South, 1900–1950* (1954).
Tuckerman, H. T., *America and Her Commentators* (1864).
Wagner, Henry R., *Plains and Rockies: A Bibliography of Original Narratives of Travel and Adventure, 1800–1865,* 3d ed. rev. by Charles L. Camp (1937).

9.3 FROM THE BEGINNING OF SETTLEMENT TO 1789

Anbury, Thomas [British officer], *Travels through the Interior Parts of America* [1776–1781] (2 vols., 1789; repr., 1923).
J. C. B., *Travels in New France* [1751–1761], S. S. Stevens et al., eds. (1941).
Bartram, William [naturalist], *Travels through North & South Carolina, Georgia, East & West Florida* [1773–1778] (1791; repr. 1940; new ed., 1958).
Beattie, Charles, *Journal of a Two Months' Tour among the Frontier Inhabitants of Pennsylvania* (1768).
Birket, James, *Some Cursory Remarks* [Portsmouth, N.H. to Philadelphia, 1750–1751] (1916).
Bonnet, J. E. [French émigré], *Réponse aux principales questions . . . sur les Etats-Unis* (2 vols., 1788).
Bossu, Jean B., *Travels in Interior of North America, 1751–1762,* Seymour Feiler, ed. and trans. (1962).
de Bougainville, Louis Antoine, *American Journals, 1756–1760,* Edward P. Hamilton, ed. and trans. (1964).
Brissot de Warville, Jacques P., *New Travels in United States, 1788,* Durand Echeverria, ed. and trans., Mara S. Vamos, trans. (1964).
Buettner, J. C., *Büttner der Amerikaner: Eine Selbstbiographie* (1828). *Narrative . . . in the American Revolution,* William H. Royce, ed., C. F. Heartman, trans. (1915).
Burnaby, Andrew, *Travels through the Middle Settlements in North America* [1759–1760] (1775).
Carver, Jonathan, *Travels through the Interior Parts of North America, 1766–68* (1778).
Castiglioni, Luigi [Italian naturalist], *Viaggio negli Stati Uniti dell' America, 1785–87* (2 vols., 1790).
Céleron de Blainville, Pierre Joseph, "Journal," A. A. Lambing, ed., *Ohio State Archaeol. Hist. Quar.,* 29 (1920), 335.
de Chastellux, F. J. Marquis, *Voyages . . . dans l'Amérique septentrionale* [1780–1782] (2 vols., 1786).
Cresswell, Nicholas, *Journal, 1774–1777* [Virginia, Ohio, New York] (1924).
de Crèvecoeur, M. G. St. Jean, *Letters from an American Farmer* [1770–1781] (1782).
Croghan, George, *Journal of His Trip to Detroit in 1767,* H. H. Peckham, ed., (1939).
Danckaerts, Jasper [Labadist], *Journal* [New Netherland, Maryland, Boston, 1679–1680]. (1867).
Davies, Samuel, *Diary of Journey to England and Scotland 1753–55,* George W. Pilcher, ed. (1967).
Durand, of Dauphine, *Un Français en Virginie* (1687). *Frenchman in Virginia Being the Memoirs of a Huguenot Refugee in 1686,* Fairfax Harrison, trans. and ed., (1923).
Du Roi, August Wilhelm [Burgoyne prisoner], *Journal, 1776–78,* Charlotte S. J. Epping, trans. (1911). from a German manuscript.
Eddis, William [Maryland loyalist], *Letters from America,* [1769–1777] (1792); Aubrey C. Land, ed. (1969).
[Farmer, John], "First American Journey, 1711–1714," H. J. Cadbury, ed., Am. Antiquarian Soc., *Proc.,* new ser., 53 (1943), 79.
de Fersen, Axel [staff officer with Rochambeau], *Lettres à son père* [1780–1783] (1929).
Gage, Thomas, *Thomas Gage's Travels in New World,* J. Eric S. Thompson, ed. (1958).
Garcés, Francisco [missionary priest], *Travels through Sonora, Arizona, and California, 1775–1776.* (2 vols., 1900).

Gist, Christopher, *Journals* [Ohio and Kentucky 1750–1753], W. M. Darlington, ed. (1893).

Grant, Anne [loyalist], *Memoirs of an American Lady; with Sketches of Manners and Scenery in America, . . . Previous to the Revolution* [chiefly upper New York] (2 vols., 1808; later ed., 1876).

Hadfield, Joseph, *An Englishman in America, 1785* [Northern states and Canada] (1933).

Hamilton, Alexander [Maryland physician], *Itinerarium* [New York and New England, 1744] Carl Bridenbaugh, ed., under title, *Gentleman's Progress* (1948).

Hazard, Ebenezer, "Travels through Maryland in 1777," Fred Shelley, ed., *Md. Hist. Mag.*, 46 (1951), 44.

Honyman, Robert, *Colonial Panorama, 1775*, Philip Padelford, ed. (1939).

Hunter, Robert, Jr., *Quebec to Carolina in 1785–1786; Being the Travel Diary and Observations of . . . a Young Merchant of London*, L. B. Wright and Marion Tinling, eds. (1943).

Josselyn, John, *An Account of Two Voyages to New England* [1638, 1663] (1674–1675; repr. 1865). Also published in Mass. Hist. Soc., *Coll.*, 3 ser., 3 (1833).

"Journal of a French Traveller in the Colonies, 1765," *AHR*, 26 (1921), 726; 27 (1922), 70.

Kalm, Pehr [Swedish naturalist], *En Resa til Norra Amerika* [1748–1751] (1753–1761); A. B. Benson, trans. and ed. (2 vols., 1937).

Kenny, James, "Journal to Ye Westward, 1758–59," John W. Jordan, ed., *Penn. Mag. Hist. Biog.*, 37 (1913), 395.

Knight, Sarah, *Journal* [Boston to New York, 1704] (1825).

Knox, John, *An Historical Journal of the Campaigns in North America, 1757–60*, 2 vols., 1769.

Ledyard, John, *Journal of Captain Cook's Last Voyage to the Pacific Ocean, and in Quest of a North-West Passage* (1783; repr. 1963).

Mackenzie, Alexander, *Journal, 1789*, T. H. McDonald, ed. (1966).

M'Roberts, Patrick, *A Tour through Part of the North Provinces of America, 1774–75* (1776). Repr. in *Penn. Mag. of Hist. and Biog.*, 59 (1935), 134.

Mason, G. C., "An Atlantic Crossing of the Seventeenth Century," *Am. Neptune*, 11 (1951), 35.

May, John, *Journal and Letters, Relative to Two Journeys to the Ohio Country* [1788–1789]. Hist. and Phil. Soc. of Ohio, *Trans.*, new ser., (1839); supplement in *Penn. Mag. Hist. Biog.*, 45 (1921), 101.

de Miranda, Francisco, *New Democracy in America: Travels, 1783–84*, John S. Ezell, ed. and Judson P. Wood, trans. (1963).

Mittelberger, Gottlieb, *Journey to Pennsylvania* (1756); Oscar Handlin and John Clive, eds. and trans. (1960).

Moore, Francis, *Voyage to Georgia, Begun in the Year 1735.* (1744). Also published in Georgia Hist. Soc., *Coll.*, 1 (1840), 79.

Moravian Journals Relating to Central New York [1745–1766] (1916).

Owen, William, "Narrative of American Voyages and Travels [1766–1771]," N. Y. Pub. Lib., *Bull.*, 35 (1931). Entire issue.

Pénicaut, André, *Fleur de Lys and Calumet: Narrative Adventure in Louisiana*, Richebourg G. McWilliams, ed. and trans. (1953).

Quincy, Josiah, Jr., "Journals" [New York, Pennsylvania and South Carolina, 1773] Mass. Hist. Soc., *Proc.*, 40 (1916), 424.

Robertson, Archibald [royal engineer], *Diaries and Sketches in America* [1762–1780] (1930).

Robin, Abbé, [chaplain with Rochambeau], *Nouveau voyage dans l'Amérique Septentrionale* [1781] (1782); Philip Freneau, trans. (1783).

Schöpf, J. D., *Reise durch einige der mittlern und südlichen vereinigten nordamerikanischen Staaten* [1783–1784] (1788). Trans. (1911).

Seeber, Edward D., trans., *On Threshold of Liberty: Journal of a Frenchman's Tour of American Colonies in 1777* (1959).

Smith, James, "Tours into Kentucky and the Northwest Territory [1783–1797]," *Ohio State Archaeol. and Hist. Quar.*, (1907), 348.

Smith, John, *True Travels, Adventures, and Observations* (1630); John G. Fletcher, ed., (1930).

Smith, Richard [New Jersey lawyer], *A Tour of Four Great Rivers, the Hudson, Mohawk, Susquehanna, and Delaware, in 1769* (1906).
Smyth, J. F. D., *A Tour in the United States of America* [1784] (2 vols., 1784).
Spöri, Felix-Christian [Swiss surgeon], *Americanische Reisebeschreibung nach den Caribes Insslen und Neu Engelland* [West Indies and Rhode Island, 1661] (1677, 1915). Translated in part in *NEQ*, 10 (1937), 535.
Tennent, William, "Writings, 1740–1777," Newton B. Jones, ed., *So. Car. Hist. Mag.*, 61 (1960), 129.

9.4 1790–1865

Abdy, E. S., *Journal of a Residence and Tour in the United States, 1833–34* (3 vols., 1835).
Acton, Lord [historian], "American Diaries" [1853], *Fortnightly Review*, 110 (1921), 727; 111 (1922), 63.
Addington, Henry U., *Residence in United States of America, 1822–25: Selections*, Bradford Perkins, ed. (1960).
Alexander, J. E., *Transatlantic Sketches* (2 vols., 1833).
Allardice, R. B., *Agricultural Tour in the United States and Upper Canada* (1842).
Ampère, J. J. [scientist], *Promenade en Amérique* [Northwestern states, 1851–1852] (2 vols., 1855).
Anderson, William M., *Journals . . . 1834*, Dale L. Morgan and Eleanor T. Harris, eds. (1967).
Arese, Francesco, "Notes du Voyage" [1837–1838], in Romualdo Bonfadini, *Vita di Francesco Arese* (1894), 451. Translated under title *A Trip to the Prairies* (1934).
Arfwedson, C. D., *The United States and Canada* [1832–1834] (2 vols., 1834).
Ashe, Thomas, *Travels in America in 1806* [Ohio and Mississippi valleys] (1808).
Audubon, J. J., [artist and naturalist], *Journals* [Labrador, 1833; Missouri River, 1843; "episodes" from Labrador to Florida, 1808–1834], Elliott Coues, ed. (2 vols., 1897).
Audubon, J. J., *Journal of John James Audubon Made During His Trip to New Orleans in 1820–1821*, Howard Corning, ed. (1929).
Audubon, J. J., *Journal of John James Audubon Made While Obtaining Subscriptions to His "Birds of America", 1840–1843*, Howard Corning, ed. (1929).
Audubon, J. W., [son of J. J. Audubon], *Western Journal, 1849–50* [New York, Texas, Mexico, California] (1852). Also published in *Mag. of Hist.*, Extra no. 41 (1915).
de Bacourt, A. F., *Souvenirs d'un diplomate: lettres intimes sur l'Amérique* [1840–1842].
Baily, Francis, *Journal of a Tour in the Unsettled Parts of North America, 1796–1797* (1856).
François, Marquis de Barbè-Marbois, *Our Revolutionary Forefathers* (1929). Diary and letters during residence in the United States, 1779–1785, translated from the French.
Barnard, Henry, "The South Atlantic States in 1833, as Seen by a New Englander," *Md. Hist. Mag.*, 13 (1918), 267.
Bartlett, J. R., *Personal Narrative of Explorations and Incidents in Texas, New Mexico, California, Sonora, and Chihuahua* [Boundary Commission, 1850–1853] (2 vols., 1854).
Baxter, W. E., *America and the Americans* (1855).
de Beaujour, Félix, *Aperçu des Etats-Unis, 1800–10* (1814).
Bell, John R., *Journal . . . Official Journalist for the Stephen H. Long Expedition to Rocky Mountains, 1850*, Harlin M. Fuller and LeRoy R. Hafen, eds. (1957).
—— *Journal of Captain John R. Bell, 1820* [Rocky Mountains] LeRoy R. and Ann W. Hafen, eds., (1957).
Bell, M. V. H. Dwight [Connecticut gentlewoman], *A Journey to Ohio in 1810*, Max Farrand, ed. (1912).
Bell, William A. [railroad surveyor], *New Tracks in North America* [1867–1868] (2 vols., 1869).

Benjamin, I. J., *Three Years in America, 1859–1862*, Charles Reznikoff, trans. (2 vols., 1956).

Benton, Colbee C., *Visitor to Chicago in Indian Days*, Paul M. Angle and James R. Getz, eds. (1957).

Berger, Max, *The British Traveller in America, 1836–1860* (1943).

Bernard, John [actor-manager], *Retrospections of America, 1797–1811* (1887).

Bernhard, Duke of Saxe-Weimar-Eisenach, *Reise . . . durch Nord-Amerika . . . 1825 und 1826.* (1828). Trans., (2 vols., 1828).

Beste, J. R., *The Wabash; or Adventures of an English Gentleman's Family in the Interior of America* (2 vols., 1855).

Bierce, Lucius V., *Travels in the Southland, 1822–1823: Journal*, George W. Knepper, ed. (1966).

Billigmeier, Robert H., and Fred A. Picard, eds. and trans., *Old Land and New: Journals of Two Swiss Families in America in the 1820's* (1965).

Birkbeck, Morris, *Letters from Illinois* (1818).

—— *Notes on a Journey in America, from Virginia to Illinois* (1817).

Bishop, I. [B.], *The Englishwoman in America* (1856).

Blane, W. N., *An Excursion through the United States and Canada, 1822–1823* (1824).

Boardman, James, *America and the Americans* [Canada also] (1833).

Bollaert, William, *Texas*, W. Eugene Hollon and Ruth L. Butler, eds. (1956).

Boudinot, Elias, *Journey to Boston in 1809*, Milton H. Thomas, ed. (1955).

Brackenridge, Henry M., *Views of Louisiana, Together with a Journal of a Voyage up the Missouri River in 1811* (1814).

Bradbury, John [naturalist], *Travels in the Interior of America* [1809–1811] (1817). Also published in Reuben G. Thwaites, *Early Western Travels* (vol. 5., 1904).

Brandon, Edgar E., ed., *Lafayette, Guest of the Nation, 1824–1825* (3 vols., 1950–1957).

Bremer, Fredrika [Swedish novelist], *Hemmen i den nya Verlden* [1849–1851], Mary Howett, trans. (3 vols., 1853). Selections also published in *America of the Fifties* (1924).

Brewer, W. H., *Up and Down California in 1860–1864* (1930); 3d ed. (1966).

Brewerton, G. D., *Overland with Kit Carson: A Narrative of the Old Spanish Trail in '48* (1930).

Bridel, Louis, *Le Pour et le contre* [Kentucky and Western New York, 1803] (1803); repr. in Buffalo Hist. Soc., *Publ.*, 18 (1914), 257.

Bromme, Traugott, *Reisen durch die Vereinigten Staaten und Ober-Canada* (3 vols., 1834–1835).

Brothers, Thomas, *The United States as They Are; Being a Cure for Radicalism* (1840).

Bryant, Edwin, *What I Saw in California: Being the Journal of a Tour, 1846–47* (1848).

Buckingham, J. S. [British lecturer and M.P.], *America, Historical, Statistic, and Descriptive* [1837–1838] (2 vols., 1841).

—— *The Eastern and Western States of America* [1839–1840]. (3 vols, 1842).

—— *The Slave States of America* [1939] (2 vols., 1842)

Burlend, Rebecca, *A True Picture of Emigration* [Illinois] (1848).

Burn, J. D., *Three Years among the Working-Classes in the U.S. during the War* (1865).

Burton, Richard F., *City of Saints and Across Rocky Mountains* (1861); Fawn M. Brodie, ed. (1963).

Butler, A. E. R., ed., "Mrs. Butler's 1853 Diary of Rogue River Valley," *Ore. Hist. Quar.*, 41 (1940), 337.

Carter, W. A., "Diary" [1857 Kansas to Wyoming], *Annals of Wyo.*, 11 (1939), 75.

Carvalho, Solomon N., *Incidents of Travel in Far West*, Bertram W. Korn, ed. (1954).

Catlin, George, *Episodes from Life among Indians*, Marvin C. Ross, ed. (1959).

Cazenove, Théophile [Dutch banker], "Journal" [New Jersey and Pennsylvania in 1794] Trans. from the French, R. W. Kelsey, ed., Haverford College, *Studies*, no. 13 (1922).

de Chateaubriand, François, Vicomte, *Voyages en Amérique, en France, et en Italie* [1791–1793] (2 vols., 1828–1829).

Chevalier, Michel, *Lettres sur l'Amérique du Nord* [1833–1835] (2 vols., 1836). Translated under title, *Society, Manners and Politics in the United States* (1839).
Clark, Charles M., *Trip to Pike's Peak* (1861); Robert Greenwood, ed. (1958).
Clark, William, *Field Notes, 1803–1805*, Ernest S. Osgood, ed. (1964).
——— "A Trip Across the Plains in 1857," *Iowa Jour. of Hist. and Pol.* 20 (1922), 163.
[Clemens, Samuel L.] *Life on the Mississippi* [1850's] (1883).
Clyman, James, "Diaries and Reminiscences" [Gold Rush], Calif. Hist. Soc., *Quar.*, 4–6 (1925–1927).
Cobbett, William [English radical], *A Year's Residence in the United States of America* (3 vols., 1818).
Cobden, Richard, *American Diaries* [1835 and 1859], Elizabeth H. Cawley, ed. (1952).
Coke, E. T., *A Subaltern's Furlough* [1832] (2 vols., 1833).
Colbert, E. C. V., Comte de Maulevrier, *Voyage dans l'intérieur des Etats-Unis et au Canada* [1798] (1935).
Collot, Victor, *A Journey in North America* [1796] (1826).
Combe, George, *Notes on the United States during a Phrenological Visit in 1838–40* (2 vols., 1841).
Cooper, Thomas, *Some Information Respecting America* (1794).
Corrêa da Serra, José Francesco, *Abbé Corrêa in America, 1812–1820*, Richard B. Davis, ed. (1955).
Cox, Ross, *Adventures on the Columbia River* (1831). Published under the variant title, *Columbia River*, Edgar I. and Jane R. Stewart, eds. (1957). Covers the period 1811–1817.
Cowell, E. M., *The Cowells in America* (1934). Diary of Sam Cowell's concert tour, 1860–1861, illustrated by his wife.
Craig, Alexander, *America and the Americans* (1810).
de Crèvecoeur, M. G. St. Jean, *Travels in Pennsylvania and New York*, Percy G. Adams, trans. and ed. (1961).
Damon, S. C., *A Journey to Lower Oregon and Upper California, 1848–49* (1927).
Darby, William, *Tour from New York to Detroit in 1818* (1819).
Davis, John [novelist], *Travels . . . in the United States* [1798–1802] (1803).
Dawson, Nicholas, *California in '41; Texas in '51. Memoirs* (1901?).
Dean, Thomas, "Journal of . . . a Voyage to Indiana in 1817," Ind. Hist. Soc., *Publ.*, no. 2, (1918).
Decker, Peter, *Diaries: Overland to California in 1849*, Helen S. Giffen, ed. (1966).
Delano, Alonzo, *Life on the Plains and among the Diggings* (1854).
Derbec, Etienne, *French Journalist in California Gold Rush: Letters*, Abraham P. Nasatir, ed. (1964).
Dicey, Edward, *Six Months in the Federal States* (2 vols., 1863).
Dickens, Charles, *American Notes* (1842).
Douglas, David [botanist], *Journal during His Travels in North America, 1823–27* (1914).
Dresel, Gustav, *Houston Journal, 1837–1841*, Max Freund, ed. and trans. (1954).
Duden, Gottfried, *Bericht über eine Reise nach den westlichen Staaten Nordamerikas* [1824–1827] (1829).
Duncan, J. M., *Travels through Part of the United States and Canada, 1818–19* (2 vols., 1823).
Duvergier de Hauranne, Ernest, *Huit Mois en Amérique 1864–65* (2 vols., 1866).
——— *Les Etats-Unis pendant la guerre de sécession: Vus par un journaliste français* (1966).
Dwight, Timothy [Yale president] *Travels in New England and New York* [1796–1815], Barbara M. Solomon, ed. (4 vols., 1969).
Eastland, T. B., and J. G. Eastland, "To California through Texas and Mexico" [1849], Calif. Hist. Soc., *Quar.*, 18 (1939), 99.
Eder, Joseph, "A Bavarian's Journey to New Orleans and Nacogdoches in 1853–1864," K. J. R. Arndt, Trans. and ed. in *La. Hist. Quar.*, 23 (1940), 485.
Ellicott, Andrew, *Journal* (1803; repr., 1962).
Eno, Henry, *Letters from California and Nevada, 1848–1871*, W. Turrentine Jackson, ed. (1965).

Evarts, Jeremiah, *Through the South and West in 1826*, J. Orin Oliphant, ed. (1956).

Farnham, T. J. [Vermont lawyer], *Travels in the Great Western Prairies . . . and . . . Oregon Territory* [1839] (2 vols., 1843). Also published in Reuben G. Thwaites, *Early Western Travels*, vols. 28, 29 (1906–1907).

Faux, William [English Farmer], *Memorable Days in America* [1818–1829] (1823). Also published in Reuben G. Thwaites, *Early Western Travels*, vols. 11, 12 (1904–1905).

Fearon, H. B. [advance agent for immigrants], *Sketches of America: A Narrative of a Journey of Five Thousand Miles through the Eastern and Western States* (1818).

Featherstonhaugh, G. W., *Excursion through the Slave States* (2 vols., 1844).

Ferguson, Robert, *America during and after the War* (1866).

Ferguson, William, *America by River and Rail* (1856).

Fidler, Isaac [English teacher], *Observations in the United States and Canada* (1833).

Field, Matthew C., *Matt Field on the Santa Fe Trail*, John E. Sunder, ed. (1960).

F[lagg], E[dmund], *The Far West: or, A Tour beyond the Mountains* (2 vols., 1838).

Fletcher, Robert S., *Eureka: Cleveland by Ship to California, 1849–1850* (1959).

Flint, James [Scot], *Letters from America* [1818–1820] (1822). Also published in Reuben G. Thwaites, *Early Western Travels*, vol. 11 (1905).

Fordham, E. P. [English engineer], *Personal Narrative of Travels in Virginia, Maryland, Pennsylvania, Ohio, Indiana, Kentucky, and Illinois: 1817–1818* (1906).

Forman, Samuel S., *Narrative of a Journey in 1789–90* (1888).

Foster, Augustus John, *Jeffersonian America: Notes, 1805–12*, Richard B. Davis, ed. (1954).

Fowler, Jacob, *Journal from Arkansas to . . .* [Arizona], 1821–22 (1898).

Franchère, Gabriel, *Adventure at Astoria, 1810–1814*, Hoyt C. Franchère, trans. and ed. (1967).

—— *Voyage to the Northwest Coast of America* (1820); J. V. Huntington, trans. (1854); Milo M. Quaife, ed. (1968).

Fraser, Simon, *Letters and Journals, 1806–1808*, W. Kaye Lamb, ed. (1960).

Fremantle, A. J. L., *Three Months in the Southern States, April–June 1863* (1863).

Frémont, John C., *Expeditions of John Charles Frémont*. Vol. I: *Travels from 1838 to 1844*, Donald Jackson and Mary Lee Spence, eds. (1970).

—— *Geographical Memoir upon Upper California, in Illustration of His Map of Oregon and California* (1848); Allan Nevins and Dale L. Morgan, eds. (1964).

—— *Fourth Expedition, 1848–1849*, LeRoy R. and Ann W. Hafen, eds. (1960).

—— *Report of the Exploring Expedition to the Rocky Mountains . . . Oregon, and North California* [1842–1844] (1845).

Froebel, Julius, *Aus Amerika. Erfahrungen, Reisen und Studien* [especially New York and the Southwest] (2 vols., 1857–1858). An abridged translation, *Seven Years' Travel in the Far West* (1859).

Gaillardet, Frédéric, *Sketches of Early Texas and Louisiana*, James Shepherd III, trans. and ed. (1966).

Gardini, Carlo, *Gli Stati Uniti* (2 vols., 1887).

Garnier, Pierre, *Medical Journey in California* [1851–1852], Doyce B. Nunis, Jr., ed., L. Jay Oliva, trans. (1967).

Gass, Patrick, *Journal of Voyages and Travels under Lewis and Clark* (1958).

Gates, Charles M., ed., *Five Fur Traders of Northwest: Narrative and Diaries* (1933).

Girard, Charles, *Visit to Confederate States in 1863: Memoir Addressed to Napoleon III*, William S. Hoole, trans. and ed. (1962).

Gladstone, T. H. [London *Times* correspondent], *The Englishman in Kansas* (1857).

Grassi, Giovanni, *Notizie varie sullo stato presente della repubblica degli Stati Uniti . . . 1818* (1819).

Grattan, T. C. [British consul at Boston], *Civilized America* (2 vols. 1859).

Gray, William F., *From Virginia to Texas, 1835: Diary* (1840).

Greeley, Horace, *Overland Journey from New York to San Francisco in Summer of 1859*, Charles T. Duncan, ed. (1964).

Green, Robert B., *On Arkansas Route to California in 1849: Journal of Robert B. Green of Pennsylvania*, J. Orin Oliphant, ed. (1955).
Greenough, Horatio, *Travels, Observations, and Experience of a Yankee Stonecutter* (1852).
Gregg, Josiah, *Commerce of the Prairies: or, The Journal of a Santa Fé Trader* [1831–1839] (2 vols., 1844). Also published in Reuben G. Thwaites, vols. 19, 20 (1905). *Early Western Travels*, and M. M. Quaife, ed. (2 vols., 1941).
Griesinger, Theodor, *Lebende Bilder aus Amerika* (1858).
Grund, F. J., *The Americans in Their Moral, Social, and Political Relations* (2 vols., 1837).
—— *Aristocracy in America* (2 vols., 1839).
Gustorf, Frederick J., *Journal and Letters* [Mississippi Valley, 1830's], Fred and Gisela Gustorf, trans. (1969).
Hall, Basil, *Travels in North America* [1827–28] (3 vols., 1828).
Hall, Margaret, *The Aristocratic Journey*, Una Pope-Hennessy, ed. (1931).
Hamilton, Thomas, *Men and Manners in America* (2 vols., 1833).
Hancock, Samuel, *The Narrative . . . 1845–60* [Oregon Trail], A. D. H. Smith, ed. (1927).
Harris, Benjamin B., *Gila Trail: Texas Argonauts and California Gold Rush*, Richard H. Dillon, ed. (1960).
Hastings, L. W., *Emigrants' Guide to Oregon and California* (1845).
Hay, Henry, "Journal from Detroit to the Miami River" [1789–1790], M. M. Quaife, ed., Wisc. Hist. Soc., *Proc.* (1914), 208.
Heap, Gwinn H., *Central Route to Pacific* [1850's], LeRoy and Ann W. Hafen, eds. (1957).
Heckewelder, John, *Thirty Thousand Miles* [Ohio Valley and Great Lakes, 1780's–1810], Paul A. W. Wallace, ed. (1958).
Herz, Henri [musician], *Mes Voyages en Amérique* [1846] (1866).
Hodgson, Adam, *Remarks during a Journey through North America, 1819–1821* (2 vols., 1823).
Hoffman, C. F., *A Winter in the Far West* [Chicago] (2 vols., 1835).
Hollon, W. Eugene, *Beyond the Cross Timbers: Travels of Randolph B. Marcy* [the West, mid-nineteenth century] (1955).
Holmes, Isaac, *Account of the United States of America, Derived from Actual Observation during a Residence of Four Years* (1823).
Hughes, Richard B., *Pioneer Years in the Black Hills* [1870's], Agnes W. Spring, ed. (1957).
Hunter, George, *Western Journals, 1796–1805*, John F. McDermott, ed. (1963).
Irving, Washington, *Adventures of Captain Bonneville* [Rocky Mountains and Far West] (1843); Edgeley W. Todd, ed. (1961).
—— *Tour on the Prairies* (1835).
Janson, C. W., *The Stranger in America* [1793–1806] (1807).
Janssens, Agustin, *Adventures in California, 1834–1856*, William H. Ellison and Francis Price, eds. (1953).
Kemble, Frances A. [Butler, actress], *Journal* [1823–1833] (2 vols., 1835).
—— *Journal of a Residence on a Georgian Plantation in 1838–39* (1863).
Kendall, E. A., *Travels through the Northern Parts of the United States* (3 vols., 1809).
Kingsley, Charles, *Letters from a Lecture Tour, 1874*, Robert B. Martin, ed. (1958).
Kirkland, C. M. S., *A New Home—Who'll Follow? or, Glimpses of Western Life* (1839).
Klinkowström, Baron, *America, 1818–1820*, Franklin D. Scott, trans. and ed. (1952).
Kroeber, Clifton B., ed., "James O. Pattie on the Colorado in 1826," *Ariz. and West*, 6 (1964), 119.
Lambert, John, *Travels through Canada and the United States* [1806–1808] (3 vols., 1810).
Landerholm, Carl, ed., *Notices and Voyages of Famed Quebec Mission to Pacific Northwest* (1956).
von Langsdorff, G. H., *Narrative of the Rezanov Voyage to Nueva California in 1806* (1927).

Langworthy, Franklin, *Scenery of the Plains, Mountains and Mines* [1850–1853] (1855).

duc de La Rochefoucauld-Liancourt, François, *Voyage dans les Etats-Unis* [1795–1797] (8 vols., 1799).

Larpenteur, Charles, *Forty Years a Fur Trader on the Upper Missouri* [1833–1872] (2 vols., 1898).

de La Tour du Pin, Marquise, *Journal d'une femme de cinquante ans* [Boston and upper New York, 1794–1795] (2 vols., 1913). Translated under title *Recollections of the Revolution and the Empire* (1920).

Latrobe, B. H. [architect], *Journal* [Pennsylvania, Virginia, Louisiana, Washington, 1796–1820] (1905).

Latrobe, C. J., *The Rambler in North America, 1832–33* [chiefly the West] (2 vols., 1835).

Lesueur, C. A., *Artiste et savant français en Amérique de 1816 à 1839* [sketches and watercolors], Adrien Loir, ed. (1920).

Lewis, Henry, *Das Illustrirte Mississippithal* [1847–1849]. Colored sketches with descriptive text by G. B. Douglas (1857; repr., 1923).

Lewis, Meriwether, and William Clark, *History of the Expedition to the Sources of the Missouri, across the Rocky Mountains and down the Columbia to the Pacific* [1804–1806] Biddle ed. (2 vols., 1814). Published under variant title, *Original Journals of the Lewis and Clark Expedition, 1804–06*, Reuben G. Thwaites, ed. (8 vols., 1904–1905. Bernard De Voto, ed., abr. ed. (1953).

Lewis, Meriwether, and John Ordway, *Journals, 1803–1806*, Milo M. Quaife, ed. (1916; repr. 1965).

Lewis, Meriwether, and William Clark, *Letters of the Expedition with Related Documents*, Donald Jackson, ed. (1962).

Lieber, Francis, *The Stranger in America* (1835).

Lienhard, Heinrich, *From St. Louis to Sutter's Fort, 1846*, Erwin G. and Elisabeth K. Gudde, trans. and eds. (1961).

Long, S. H. [army engineer], Edwin James [botanist], et al., *Account of an Expedition from Pittsburgh to the Rocky Mountains* [1819–1820] (2 vols., 1823). Also published in Reuben G. Thwaites, *Early Western Travels*, vols. 14–16 (1905).

Long, S. H., W. H. Keating, et al., *Narrative of an Expedition to the Lake of the Woods* [1823] (2 vols., 1824).

Loomis, Noel M., and Abraham P. Nasatir, *Pedro Vial and Roads to Santa Fe* (1967).

Lowe, Percival G., *Five Years a Dragoon*, Don Russell, ed. (1965).

Lyell, Charles [geologist], *Travels in North America* [1841–1842] (2 vols., 1845).

——— *A Second Visit to the United States* [1845–1846] (2 vols., 1849).

Lyman, C. S. [scientist], *Around the Horn to the Sandwich Islands and California* [1845–1850] (1924).

McClure, Alexander K., *Three Thousand Miles through Rocky Mountains* (1869).

McCollum, William, *California as I Saw It* [1850], Dale L. Morgan, ed. (1960).

McDermott, John F., ed., *Audubon in the West* [up the Missouri River, 1843] (1965).

Mackay, Alexander, *The Western World; or, Travels in the United States in 1846–47* (2 vols., 1849).

Mackay, Charles, *Life and Liberty in America; or, Sketches of a Tour in the United States and Canada in 1857–58* (2 vols., 1859).

Magoffin, S. S., *Down the Santa Fé Trail and into Mexico* [diary, 1846–1847], S. M. Drumm, ed. (1926).

Marcy, R. B., *Marcy & the Gold Seekers: The Journal*, Grant Foreman, ed. (1939).

Marryat, Frederick, *A Diary in America, with Remarks on Its Institutions* (2 pts, 3 vols. each, 1839); S. W. Jackson, ed. (1962).

Marti, Werner H., *Messenger of Destiny: California Adventures, 1846–1847, of Archibald H. Gillespie* (1960).

Martineau, Harriet, *Retrospect of Western Travel* [travelogue, 1834–1836] (3 vols., 1838; repr. 1938).

——— *Society in America* [analysis, 1834–1836] (3 vols., 1837). Seymour M. Lipset, ed. (1 vol. abr., 1962; repr., 1968).

Mason, Charles, and Jeremiah Dixon, *Journal* [1763–1768], A. Hughlett Mason, ed. (1969).

Mason, R. L. [Maryland gentleman], *Narrative in the Pioneer West, 1819* (1915).

de Massey, Ernest, "A Frenchman in the Gold Rush," Calif. Hist. Soc., *Quar.*, 5 (1926), 3; 6 (1927), 37.

Massie, J. W., *America: the Origin of Her Present Conflict, Illustrated by Incidents of Travel in 1863*, (1864).

May, John, *Western Journals of John May, Ohio Company Agent* (1961).

Mayer, F. B., *With Pen and Pencil on the Frontier in 1851* [diary and sketches] (1872).

Meline, James F., *Two Thousand Miles on Horseback, Santa Fe and Back, 1866* (1867).

Melish, John [cartographer], *Travels in the United States* [1806–1807; 1809–1811] (2 vols., 1812).

Michaux, André [botanist], "Journal" [1793–1796], Am. Phil. Soc., *Proc.* 26 (1889). Translated in Reuben G. Thwaites, *Early Western Travels*, vol. 3 (1904).

Michaux, F. A. [naturalist, son of André Michaux], *Voyage à l'ouest des Monts Alléghanys* [1802] (1804). Also published in Reuben G. Thwaites, *Early Western Travels*, vol. 3 (1904).

de Montlezun, Baron, *Voyage de New Yorck à la Nouvelle Orléans* [1816–1817] (2 vols., 1818).

de Montulé, Edouard, *Travels in America, 1816–1817*, Edward Seeber, trans. (1951).

Méry, M. L. E. Moreau de Saint [Haitian émigré and bookseller], *Voyage aux Etats-Unis de l'Amérique* [1793–1798] (1913). Translated by Kenneth and A. M. Roberts, (1947).

Mumey, Nolie, *John Williams Gunnison: Last of the Western Explorers* (1955).

Murat, Achille [Napoleonic prince], *Lettres sur les Etats-Unis* [1826–1827] (1820). Translated and greatly extended under title, *America and the Americans* (1849).

Murray, A. M. [maid of honor to the Queen], *Letters from The United States, Cuba, and Canada* (2 vols., 1856).

Murray, C. A. [master of household to the Queen], *Travels in North America, Including a Summer Residence with the Pawnees* [1834–1836] (1839).

Neilson, Peter, *Recollections of Six Years in the United States* (1830).

Newell, Robert, *Memoranda: Travels in Missourie*, Dorothy O. Johansen, ed. (1959).

Niemcewicz, Julian U., *Under Vine and Fig Tree: Travels through America in 1797–1799*, (1805); Metchie J. E. Budka, trans. and ed. (1965).

Nuttall, Thomas [ornithologist], *Journal of Travels into the Arkansas Territory* [1819] (1821). Also published in Reuben G. Thwaites, *Early Western Travels*, vol. 13 (1905).

Ogden, Peter S., *Snake Country Journal, 1826–1827*, K. G. Davies, ed. (1961).

Oliver, William, *Eight Months in Illinois* (1843).

Olliffe, Charles, *American Scenes*, Ernest Falbo and Lawrence A. Wilson, trans. (1964).

Olmstead, Frederick L., *Cotton Kingdom: Traveller's Observations* (1861); Arthur M. Schlesinger, ed. (1953).

—— *Journey in the Back Country* [1853–1854] (1860).

—— *Journey in the Seaboard Slave States* [1853] (1856).

—— *Journey through Texas* [1853–1854] (1857).

Osbun, Albert G., *To California and the South Seas: Diary, 1849–1851*, John H. Kemble, ed. (1966).

Owen, John, *Journals and Letters* [1850–1871, far Northwest] (2 vols., 1927).

Owen, Robert D., *Holland and New Harmony: Travel Journal, 1825–26*, Josephine M. Elliott, ed. (1969).

Parker, A. A. [of New Hampshire], *Trip to the West and Texas* (1835).

Pattie, J. O. [of Kentucky], *Personal Narrative* [St. Louis to California, Mexico, 1824–1830] (1831). Also published in Reuben G. Thwaites, *Early Western Travels*, vol. 18 (1905).

Parker, Samuel, *Journal of an Exploring Tour beyond the Rocky Mountains* (1838).

Parkinson, Richard, [English agriculturist], *Tour in America* [1798–1800, mostly Virginia and Maryland] (1805; rev. ed., 1807).

Parkman, Francis, *The Oregon Trail* (1849).
Parsons, John, [Virginia lawyer], *A Tour through Indiana in 1840* (1920).
Pavie, Théodore, *Souvenirs atlantiques: Voyage aux Etats-Unis et au Canada* (2 vols., 1833).
Pease, Seth, "Journals to and from New Connecticutt, 1796–98," Western Reserve Hist. Soc., *Tracts*, no. 94, pt. 2 (1914).
Perkins, Elisha D., *Gold Rush Diary, 1849*, Thomas D. Clark, ed. (1967).
Péron, François, *Mémoires . . . sur ses voyages* [includes New England, 1797–1799] (2 vols., 1824).
Perrin du Lac, F. M., *Voyage dans les deux Louisianes* [Ohio and Mississippi Valleys, 1801–1803] (1805). Translated in *Collection of Modern Voyages*, Richard Phillips, ed. Vol. 7, (1807).
Piercy, Frederick H., *Route from Liverpool to Great Salt Lake Valley* (1885); Fawn M. Brodie, ed. (1962).
Pike, Albert, "Narrative of a Journey in the Prairie" [1831], Arkansas Hist. Assoc., *Publ.*, 4 (1917), 66.
Pike, Zebulon M., *An Account of Expeditions to the Sources of the Mississippi* [1805–1807] (4 vols., 1810); Elliott Coues, ed. (1895).
——— *Journals, with Letters and Related Documents*, Donald Jackson, ed. (2 vols., 1966).
Point, Nicholas, *Wilderness Kingdom, 1840–1847: Journals and Paintings* (1868); Joseph P. Donnelly, ed. (1967).
Pope, John, "Report of Exploration of a Route for the Pacific Railroad . . . from the Red River to the Rio Grande," 33d Cong., 1st sess., 1854, *H. Exec. Doc.*, 129 (Serial Set 737).
——— *A Tour through the Southern and Western Territories of the United States* (1792).
von Pourtalès, Albert G., *On Western Tour with Washington Irving: Journal and Letters*, George F. Spaulding, ed., and Seymour Feiler, trans. (1968).
Power, Tyrone, [actor], *Impressions of America* [1833–1835] (1836).
Preuss, Charles, *Exploring with Frémont: Diaries*, Erwin G. and Elisabeth K. Gudde, eds. and trans. (1958).
Priest, William, *Travels* (1802).
Pritchard, James A., *Overland Diary, 1849*, Dale L. Morgan, ed. (1959).
Pulszky, Francis, and Theresa Pulszky, with Louis Kossuth, *White, Red, Black: Sketches of American Society* (2 vols., 1853).
Raeder, O. M., *America in the Forties* (1929) Translated from Norwegian.
Read, G. W., *A Pioneer of 1850* [Missouri to California, 1850; New York to California via Panama, 1862] (1927).
Reid, J. C., *Reid's Tramp* [Texas to California] (1858).
Robin, C. C. [naturalist], *Voyages dans l'intérieur de la Louisiane, de la Floride Occidentale, et dans les Isles* [1802–1806] (3 vols., 1807).
Rooth, Signe A., *Seeress of Northland: Frederika Bremer's American Journey, 1849–1851* (1955).
de Rothschild, Salomon, *Letters, 1859–1861*, Sigmund Diamond, trans. and ed. (1961).
Royall, Anne [Washington journalist], *The Black Book; Or A Continuation of Travels* (3 vols., 1828–1829).
——— *Letters from Alabama* [1817–1822] (1830).
——— *Mrs. Royall's Pennsylvania* (2 vols., 1829).
——— *Mrs. Royall's Southern Tour* (2 vols., 1830).
——— *Sketches of History, Life, and Manners in the United States* (1826).
Rude, Fernand, ed., *Voyage en Icarie en 1855* [Illinois] (1952).
Russell, Osborne, *Journal of a Trapper, or Nine Years in the Rocky Mountains* [1834–1843] (1914).
Russell, W. H., *American Letters to the London Times, 1861–62*. n.d.
Sala, G. A., *My Diary in America in the Midst of War* (2 vols., 1865).
Schallenberger, Moses, *Opening of the California Trail* (1855); George R. Stewart, ed. (1953).
Schiel, Jacob H., *Journey through the Rocky Mountains and Humbolt Mountains to Pacific Ocean*, Thomas N. Bonner, trans. and ed. (1959).
Schoolcraft, Henry R., *Expedition to Lake Itasca*, (1834); Philip P. Mason, ed. (1958).

—— *Journal of Tour into Interior of Missouri and Arkansas in 1818 and 1819,* Hugh Park, ed. (1955).
—— *Literary Voyager,* Philip P. Mason, ed. (1962).
—— *Narrative Journal through Northwestern Regions of the United States in 1820,* Mentor L. Williams, ed. (1953).
—— *Scenes and Adventures in the Ozark Mountains* (1853). Journal of a tour in 1818.
Shirreff, Patrick [Scots farmer], *Tour through North America* (1835).
Sibley, George Chaplin et al., *Road to Santa Fe: Journal and Diaries, 1825–27,* Kate L. Gregg, ed. (1952).
Simonin, Louis L., *Rocky Mountain West in 1867,* Wilson O. Clough, trans. (1966).
Simpson, James H., *Navaho Expedition: Journal of 1849,* Frank McNitt, ed. (1964).
De Smet, Pierre J., *Letters and Sketches: With a Narrative of a Year's Residence among the Indian Tribes of the Rocky Mountains* (1843). Also published in Reuben G. Thwaites, *Early Western Travels,* vol. 27 (1906).
De Smet, Pierre-Jean, *Life, Letters and Travels* (4 vols, 1905).
—— *Oregon Missions and Travels . . . in 1845–46* (1847). Also published in Reuben G. Thwaites, *Early Western Travels,* vol. 29 (1906).
Smith, Alson J., *Men against the Mountains: Jedediah Smith and South West Expedition of 1826–1829* (1965).
Smith, Jedediah S., "Journals," [1822–1829] in M. S. Sullivan, ed., *The Travels of Jedediah Smith* (1934); H. C. Dale, ed., *The Ashley-Smith Explorations* (rev. ed., 1941).
Smith, W. L., "Journal, 1790–91" [New York, New England, and Philadelphia to Charleston], Mass. Hist. Soc., *Proc.,* 51 (1917), 35.
Spence, James, *American Union* (1862).
Steele, John, *Across the Plains in 1850* (1930).
Stirling, James [of Glasgow], *Letters from the Slave States* (1857).
Stuart, James, *Three Years in North America* [1828–1831] (2 vols., 1833).
Stuart, Robert, *The Discovery of the Oregon Trail; Robert Stuart's Narratives* [1811–1813], P. A. Rollins, ed. (1935).
—— *On the Oregon Trail: Journal,* Kenneth A. Spaulding, ed. (1953).
Sturge, Joseph [British abolitionist, 1793–1859], *A Visit to the United States in 1841* (1842).
Sutcliff, Robert, *Travels in Some Parts of North America* [1804–1806] (1811).
Tabeau, P. A., *Tabeau's Narrative of Loisel's Expedition to the Upper Missouri* [1803–1805], A. H. Abel, ed. (1939).
Tallack, William [Quaker], *Friendly Sketches in America* (1861).
Tanner, John, *Narrative of Captivity* (1830); Edwin James, ed. (1956).
Thompson, David, *Narrative, 1784–1812,* Richard Glover, ed. (1962).
Thorne, Samuel, *The Journal of a Boy's Trip on Horseback* [Charleston, S. C., to New York, 1848] (1936).
Thornton, Walter, *Criss-Cross Journeys* [U.S. on eve of Civil War] (2 vols., 1873).
de Tocqueville, Alexis, *Democracy in America* (1835), J. P. Mayer and Max Lerner, eds., George Lawrence, trans. (2 vols., 1966).
—— *Journey to America,* J. P. Mayer ed., George Lawrence, trans. (1960).
Tolmie, William F. [Scottish doctor and fur trader in Pacific Northwest, 1832–1835], *Journals* (1963).
Trollope, Anthony, *North America.* (2 vols., 1862); rev. ed. Donald Smalley and B. A. Booth, eds. (1951).
Trollope, F. M. (British, 1780–1863), *Domestic Manners of the Americans* (2 vols., 1832; repr., 1960).
Tudor, William, *Letters on the Eastern States* (1820).
Turner, Henry S., *Original Journals with Stephen Watts Kearny to New Mexico and California, 1846–1847,* Dwight L. Clarke, ed. (1966).
Twining, Thomas, *Travels in America 100 Years Ago* [1795–1796] (1894).
Unonius, Gustaf, *Pioneer in Northwest America, 1841–1858: Memoirs,* Nils W. Olsson, ed., and Jonas O. Backlund, trans. (2 vols., 1950–1960).
de Volney, C. F. C., comte, *Tableau du climat et du sol des Etats-Unis* [1783, 1795–1798] (2 vols., 1803).

Webb, J. J., *Adventures in the Santa Fé Trade, 1844–1847* (1931).
Weld, Isaac, Jr., *Travels through North America and Canada* [1795–1797] (2 vols., 1799).
Wilkins, James F., *1849 Diary and Sketches*, John F. McDermott, ed. (1968).
Wislizenus, F. A., *Ein Ausflug nach den Felsen-gebirgen im Jahre 1839* (1840).
Word, Samuel, "Diary across the Plains, 1863," Hist. Soc. of Montana, *Contributions*, 8 (1917).
Wortley, E. S., *Travels in the United States* [Mexico and South America also] (1851).
Wright, Frances [1795–1852; British philanthropist], *Views of Society and Manners in America* [1818–1820] (1821); Paul R. Baker, ed. (1963).
Wyeth, N. J., *Correspondence and Journals, 1831–36*, in Oregon Hist. Soc., *Sources of the History of Oregon*, (1899).
Yount, George C., *Chronicles of West*, Charles L. Camp, ed. (1966).
de Zavala, Lorenzo [Mexican], *Viaje a los Estados-Unidos* (1834).

9.5 1866–1900

Archer, William, *America To-day: Observations and Reflections* (1899).
Arnold, Matthew, *Civilization in the United States* (1888).
Bandelier, Adolph F., *Southwestern Journals, 1880–1882*, Charles H. Lange and Carroll L. Riley, eds. (1966).
Barneby, W. H., *Life and Labour in the Far, Far West* (1884).
Beadle, J. H., *Western Wilds, and the Men Who Redeem Them* [1868–1874]. (1878).
Boddam-Whetham, J. W., *Western Wanderings* (1874).
Boissevain, Charles, *Van 't Noorden naar 't Zuiden* (2 vols., 1881–1882).
Bourget, Paul, *Outre-Mer: Impressions of America* (1895).
Bowles, Samuel, *Across the Continent* (1866).
Bridge, J. H., *Uncle Sam at Home* (1888).
Bryan, Jerry, *Illinois Gold Hunter in the Black Hills: Diary Mar. 13 to Aug. 20, 1876*, Clyde C. Walton, ed. (1960).
Bryce, James, *The American Commonwealth* (2 vols., 1888). Abr. ed. (1959).
Campbell, George, *White and Black, the Outcome of a Visit to the United States* (1879).
Carego di Muricce, Francesco, *In America: Stati Uniti, Avana, Portorico, Cuba, Messico* (2 vols., 1875).
Clemenceau, Georges, *American Reconstruction, 1865–1870* [Letters to the Paris *Temps*] Fernand Baldensperger, ed., Margaret MacVeagh, trans. (1928).
[Clemens, Samuel L.] *Roughing It* [Far West in 1860's] (1871).
Clyman, James, *Reminiscences and Diaries* (1928); Charles L. Camp, ed. (1960).
Conant, Roger, *Journal* [trip to Seattle by ship in 1866] Lenna A. Deutsch, ed. (1960).
Duvergier de Hauranne, Ernest, *Les Etats-Unis en 1867* (1867).
Faithfull, Emily [English feminist], *Three Visits to America* [1872, 1882, 1884] (1884).
Freeman, E. A. [historian], *Some Impressions of the United States* (1883).
Giacosa, Giuseppe, *Impressioni d'America* [dramatist's visit in 1898] (1908).
Griffin, L. H. [Tory], *The Great Republic* (1884).
Hamsun, Knut, *Fra det moderne Amerikas aandsliv* (1889).
Hardy, Lady Duffus, *Through Cities and Prairie Lands* (1881).
Herz, Henri [musician], *My Travels in America* [Boston to New Orleans, 1846], Henry B. Hill, trans. (1963).
Hole, Samuel R., *Tour in America* (1895).
Hopp, E. O., *Transatlantisches Skizzenbuch, Federzeich-ungen aus den amerikanischen Leben* (1876).
Hübner, J. A. von [Austrian diplomat], *Promenade autour du monde, 1871* [Most of vol. I deals with the United States] (2 vols., 1873; trans. 1874).
Hudson, T. S., *Scamper through America* (1882).
Hughes, Richard B., *Pioneer Years in the Black Hills*, Agnes W. Spring, ed. (1957).

Jannet, Claudio, *Les Etats-Unis contemporaines* (1875).
Kipling, Rudyard, *American Notes* (1891).
Leng, John, *America in 1876* (1877).
MacMillan, Alexander, *A Night with the Yankees* [lecture in Cambridge, England, dealing chiefly with Massachusetts] (1868).
Macrae, David, *The Americans at Home* (2 vols., 1870).
Marshall, W. G., *Through America; or, Nine Months in the United States* (1881).
Marti, José, *En los Estados Unidos* [1880's] (2 vols., 1902–1905).
Maycock, A. M., *With Mr. Chamberlain in the United States and Canada, 1887–88* (1914).
Mayor des Planches, Edmondo, *Attraverso gli Stati Uniti per l'emigrazione italiana* (1913).
Meline, James F., *Two Thousand Miles on Horseback, Santa Fe and Back, 1866* (1867).
Muir, John, *My First Summer in the Sierras* [1869] (1911).
Muir, John, *Travels in Alaska* [1879–1880, 1890] (1915).
Muirhead, J. F. [Baedeker compiler], *The Land of Contrasts: A Briton's View of His American Kin* (1898).
Murphy, J. M., *Rambles in North-western America, from the Pacific Ocean to the Rocky Mountains* (1879).
Powell, John Wesley, *Exploration of the Colorado River* [1869–1872] (1875; repr., 1961).
Reed, E. B., ed., *The Commonwealth Fund Fellows' Impressions of America* [1925–1931] (1932).
Reid, Whitelaw, *After the War: A Tour of the Southern States, 1865–1866,* C. Vann Woodward, ed. (1866; repr., 1965).
Richardson, A. D., *Beyond the Mississippi* [1857–1867] (1867).
Rose, Richard, *The Great Country* (1868).
Rosebery, A. P. P., *North American Journal, 1873,* A. R. C. Grant, ed. (1967).
Rossi, Adolfo, *Un Italiano in America* [New York City and Far West] (2nd ed., 1894).
Russell, W. H., *Hesperothen: Notes from the West* (2 vols., 1882).
Sala, G. A. [British editor], *America Revisited* (2 vols., 1880).
Saunders, William, *Through the Light Continent; or, the United States in 1877–8* (1879).
Schiel, Jacob H., *Journey through the Rocky Mountains and Humbolt Mountains to Pacific Ocean,* Thomas N. Bonner, trans. and ed. (1959).
Sealsfield, Charles, *America: Glorious and Chaotic Land,* Emil L. Jordan, trans. and ed. (1969).
Simonin, Louis L., *Rocky Mountain West in 1867,* Wilson O. Clough, trans. (1966).
Somers, Robert, *The Southern States since the War* [1870–1871] (1871).
Steevens, G. W., *The Land of the Dollar* (1897).
Stewart, George R., ed., *Opening of California Trail: Reminiscences of Moses Schallenberger as Set Down for H. H. Bancroft about 1885* (1953).
Stoddard, C. W., *Diary of a Visit to Molokai in 1884* (1933).
Townshend, Richard B., *Tenderfoot in Colorado* (1923).
Tverskoy, P. A. [pseud. of P. A. Demens], *Ocherki Sievero-Amerikanskikh Soedinenykh Shtatov* (1895).
Vivian, A. P., [sporting M.P.], *Wanderings in the Western Land* (1879).
Vivian, H. H., *Notes of a Tour in America* [1877] (1878).
A Visit to the States [repr. from London *Times*] (2 vols., 1887–1888).
Warner, C. D., *Studies in the South and West, with Comments on Canada* (1889).
Webb, Beatrice, *American Diary, 1898,* David A. Shannon, ed. (1963).
Yelverton, M. T., viscountess Avomore, *Teresina in America* (2 vols., 1875).
Youngman, W. E., *Gleanings from Western Prairies* [Kansas] (1882).
Zagoskin, Lieutenant, *Travels in Russian America, 1842–1844,* Henry N. Michael, ed. (1967).
Zannini, Alessandro, *De l'Atlantique au Mississippi: souvenirs d'un diplomate* (1884).
Zinke, F. B., *Last Winter in the United States* [chiefly the South] (1868).

9.6 1901 TO THE PRESENT

Alphandéry, Claude, *L'Amérique est-elle trop riche?* (1960).
Anderson, A. A., *Experiences and Impressions* (1933).
Armer, L. A., *Southwest* (1935).
de Beauvoir, Simone, *L'Amérique au jour le jour* (1948).
Belloc, Hilaire, *The Contrast* (1923).
Bennett, Arnold, *Your United States* (1912).
Birkenhead, Lord, *My American Visit* (1918).
Birmingham, G. A. [pseud. of J. A. Hannay, Irish wit and clergyman], *Dublin to Chicago* (1914).
Bose, Sudhindra, [Indian scholar], *Fifteen Years in America* (1920).
Bretherton, C. H., *Midas, or the United States and the Future* (1926).
Brogan, D. W., *The American Character* (1944; rev. ed. 1950).
Brown, Elijah [Alan Raleigh], *The Real America* (1913).
Camba, Julio, *Un año en el otro mondo* [1916] 3d ed. (1927).
Carpenter, F. G., *Alaska, Our Northern Wonderland* (1928).
Carpenter, W. M., *So Long, Ohio* (1935).
Chapman, Frank M., *Journal and Letters*, Elizabeth S. Austin, ed. (1967).
Chesterton, G. K., *What I Saw in America* (1921).
Cooke, Alistair, *One Man's America* (1952).
Daniels, Jonathan, *A Southerner Discovers New England* (1940).
—— *A Southerner Discovers the South* (1938).
Dekobra, Maurice, *Sept ans chez les hommes libres* (1946).
Duhamel, Georges, *Scènes de la vie future* (1930). Translated under title, *America: the Menace* (1931).
Duteil, H. J., *Great American Parade* (1953).
Enock, C. R., *Farthest West: Life and Travel in the United States* (1910).
Estournelles de Constant, Paul de, *America and Her Problems* (1915).
Ewing, A. M., *Seeing America First* (1922).
Fay, Bernard, *The American Experiment* (1929).
Feiler, Arthur, ed., *Amerika-Europa* (1926). Translated under title, *America Seen through German Eyes* (1928).
Fitzgerald, W. G. [Ignatius Phayre], *Can America Last?* (1933).
Foldes, Lili, *Two on a Continent* (1947).
Gibbs, Philip, *Land of Destiny* (1920).
Graham, Stephen, *With Poor Immigrants to America* (1914).
Gunther, John, *Inside U.S.A.* (1951).
Hauser, Henri [historian], *L'Amérique vivante* (1924).
Hedin, A. I. S., *Arbetsglädje; Lärdomar från Amerika* (1920).
Heren, Louis [English journalist], *New American Commonwealth* [1960's] (1968).
Ilf, Ilya, and Eugene Petrov, *Little Golden America* (1937).
James, Henry, *The American Scene* (1907); Leon Edel, ed. (1968).
Kerr, Lennox, *Back Door Guest* (1930).
Keun, Odette, *I Think Aloud in America* (1939).
Egon Erwin Kisch beehrt sich darzubieten: Paradies Amerika (1930).
Klein, Félix [Catholic priest], *Au pays de "la vie intense"* (1905).
Longstreet, Stephen, *The Last Man Comes Home: American Travel Journals, 1941–1942* (1942).
Low, A. M., *America at Home* (1905).
—— *The American People* (2 vols., 1909–1911).
Macrae, David, *America Revisited* (1908).
Maurois, André, *Etats-Unis 39 journal d'un voyage en Amérique* (1939).
Mitchell, R. E., *America: A Practical Handbook* (1935).
Morehouse, Ward, *American Reveille* (1942).
Morris, James, *As I Saw the U.S.A.* (1956).
—— *The Great Port: Passage Through New York* [Welsh visitor, 1960's] (1969).
Muir, Ramsay, *America the Golden* (1927).
Münsterberg, Hugo [German-American psychologist], *American Traits from the Point of View of a German* (1901).
—— *Die Amerikaner*, E. B. Holt, trans. (2 vols., 1904).

Myrdal, Alva, and Gunnar Myrdal, *Kontakt med Amerika* [1941].
Newman, Bernard, *American Journey* (1943).
Peck, A. M., and Enid Johnson, *Roundabout America* (2 vols., 1933).
Price, W. E., and M. P. Price [British parliamentarians], *America after Sixty Years* [1869, 1878, and 1934] (1936).
Rainier, P. W., *American Hazard* [1942].
Santayana, George, *Character and Opinion in the United States* (1920).
Siegfried, André, *America at Mid-Century*, Margaret Ledesert, trans. (1955).
—— *Les Etats-Unis d'aujourd'hui* (1927). Translated under title, *America Comes of Age* (1927).
Sienkiewicz, Henry, *Letters*, Charles Morley, trans. and ed. (1959).
Sleeswijk, J. G., *Van Menschen en Dingen in Amerika* (1933).
Teeling, William, *American Stew* (1933).
Toller, Ernst, *Quer Durch. Reisebilder und Reden* (1930).
Vasiliev, N., *Amerika's Chernogo Khoda* [Moscow] (1949).
Vay de Vaya und Luskod, Count [Hungarian], *The Inner Life of the United States* (1908).
Vernon, P. E., *Coast to Coast by Motor* (1930).
di Visconti-Venosta, Enrico, marchese, *Impressions of America* (1933).
Wagner, Charles [author], *My Impressions of America*, Mary Louise Hendee, trans. (1906).
Wells, H. G., *The Future in America* (1906).
Wilson, Edmund, *Travels in Two Democracies* [U.S.A. and U.S.S.R., 1932–1935] (1936).

10 Biographies and Writings

10.1 INTRODUCTION

American historical literature is particularly rich in biographies. They are indispensable because they frequently contain the fullest and most perceptive accounts of specific phases of American history. The autobiographies, diaries, and collected writings of historic figures are among the most important sources on many subjects.

The following list is selective. Privately printed, or very scarce works, brief sketches in composite works, memoirs in the publications of learned and professional societies, obituaries, and campaign biographies are usually omitted. Few popular biographies appear, except where scholarly works do not exist. Many older titles (a number of them available in reprint) are cited because they were written in the "life and letters" style and contain excerpts from correspondence.

Some specialized biographies, diaries and journals, and occasional collective biographies not appearing in this section are noted elsewhere in the *Guide* in connection with relevant subject matter. Some biographies of important persons will be found wanting, because no adequate life of them exists. Biographies or writings of some less important persons appear because they contain material useful to the student of American civilization.

10.2 REFERENCE SOURCES

The most important biographical cyclopedias are the *Dictionary of American Biography*, which cover notable personages deceased as of December 1940, and Edward T. James, Janet Wilson James, and Paul S. Boyer, eds., *Notable American Women, 1607–1950* (see below). Some of their sketches are superior to longer biographies published separately. The bibliographies offer more complete information than the limits of the *Guide* permit.

Biographical information about living, or recently deceased persons is to be found in *Who's Who in America* (see below) or regional, occupational and ethnic directories. Registers supply information on government officials, officers of the armed forces, the alumni of many colleges, and members of learned societies. County and other local histories (see 12.3) often contain extensive biographical sections. Manuscript census data and geneaological records provide basic information. Newspaper obituaries and clippings in libraries that newspapers maintain are sometimes useful sources.

Other biographical reference sources include:

Biographical Directory of the American Congress, 1774–1961 (1961).
Concise Dictionary of American Biography (1964). Based on the multi-volumed *Dictionary of American Biography.*
Current Biography, 1940– . Monthly with annual cumulations.
Dexter, Franklin B., *Biographical Sketches of Graduates of Yale College* (6 vols., 1885–1912).
Dictionary of American Biography, Allen Johnson and Dumes Malone, eds. (20 vols. and index, 1928–1937. Supplements 1-2, 1944–1958).
Dictionary of Canadian Biography (1966–). Projected as a twenty-volume work.
Friedman, Leon, and Fred L. Israel, eds., *Justices of the United States Supreme Court, 1789–1969: Their Lives and Major Opinions* (4 vols., 1969).
Hamersly, T. H. S., *Complete Army and Navy Register* (1888).
Historical Register and Dictionary of the United States Army from Its Organization, September 29, 1789 to March 2, 1903 (2 vols., 1903).
Longacre, J. B., and James Herring, comps., *The National Portrait Gallery of Distinguished Americans* (4 vols., 1834–1839).
Mosher, R. B., *Executive Register of the United States, 1789–1902* (1903).
New York Times Obituary Index, 1858–1968 (1970).
Notable American Women, 1607–1950, Edward T. James, Janet Wilson James, and Paul S. Boyer, eds. (3 vols., 1971).
Sibley, John L., *Biographical Sketches of Those Who Attended Harvard College* (14 vols., 1873–1968). Vols. IV-XIV edited by Clifford K. Shipton.
U.S. Bureau of Naval Personnel, *Register of Commissioned and Warrant Officers of the United States Navy and Marine Corps and Reserve Officers on Active Duty* (1814–).
Webster's Biographical Dictionary (rev. ed., 1966).
Who Was Who in America, a five-volume dictionary of deceased persons. Except for the historical volume, the entries are taken from *Who's Who in America* and assigned to the period in which the person died. Volumes I-IV cover the periods 1897–1942, 1943–1950, 1951–1960, and 1961–1968 respectively.
Who's Who in America: Biographical Dictionary of Notable Living Men and Women. 1899– . Biennial.
Who's Who in the East, 1943– .
Who's Who in the Midwest, 1949– .
Who's Who in the South and Southwest, 1950– .
Who's Who in the West, 1949– .
Biography Index: A Cumulative Index to Biographical Material in Books and Magazines, 1947– . Quarterly.
Dargan, Marion, *Guide to American Biography* (2 vols., 1949–1952). Chronological arrangement, further subdivided by geographical regions.
Forbes, Harriett M., *New England Diaries, 1602–1800: Descriptive Catalogue of Diaries, Orderly Books, and Sea Journals* (1923).
Index to Obituary Notices in the Boston Transcript (5 vols., n.d.). Covers the period, 1875–1930.
Kaplan, Louis et al., *A Bibliography of American Autobiographies* (1961).
Lillard, Richard G., *American Life in Autobiography: A Comparative Guide* (1956). Of some 400 persons since 1900.
Mathews, William, *American Diaries: An Annotated Bibliography of American Diaries Written Prior to the Year 1861* (1945).
O'Neill, E. H., ed., *Biography by Americans, 1685–1936: A Subject Bibliography* (1939).
Slocum, Robert B., *Biographical Dictionaries and Related Works: An International Bibliography of Collective Biographies* (1967).

10.3 INDIVIDUAL BIOGRAPHY AND SELECTED WRITINGS

ABBEY, EDWIN AUSTIN 1852–1911, illustrator
Lucas, Edward V., *Edwin Austin Abbey* (2 vols., 1921).

ABBOTT, LYMAN 1835–1922, Congregational clergyman, magazine editor
Abbott, Lyman, *Reminiscences* (1915).
Brown, Ira V., *Lyman Abbott, Christian Evolutionist* (1953).

ABBOTT, ROBERT SENGSTACKE 1868–1940, newspaper editor
Ottley, Roi, *Lonely Warrior: Robert S. Abbott* (1955).

ACHESON, DEAN GOODERHAM 1893–1971, secretary of state
Acheson, Dean G., *Morning and Noon* (1965).
——— *Pattern of Responsibility*, McGeorge Bundy, ed. (1952).
Acheson, Dean, *Present at the Creation* (1969).
——— *Sketches from Life of Men I Have Known* (1961).

ADAMIC, LOUIS 1899–1951, writer
Adamic, Louis, *Laughing in the Jungle* (1932).

ADAMS, ABIGAIL 1744–1818, wife of John Adams
Adams, Abigail, *Letters*, Charles Francis Adams, ed. (1848).
——— *New Letters*, Stewart Mitchell, ed. (1947).
——— John Adams, and Thomas Jefferson, *Correspondence*, Lester J. Cappon, ed. (2 vols., 1959).
Adams, John and Abigail Adams, *Familiar Letters*, Charles Francis Adams, ed. (1875).
Oliver, Andrew, *Portraits of John and Abigail Adams* (1967).
Whitney, Janet, *Abigail Adams* (1947).

ADAMS, BROOKS 1848–1927, grandson of John Quincy Adams, writer
Beringause, Arthur F., *Brooks Adams* (1955).

ADAMS, CHARLES FRANCIS 1807–1886, son of John Quincy Adams, diplomat
Adams, Charles Francis and Henry Adams, *A Cycle of Adams Letters, 1861–65*, W. C. Ford, ed. (2 vols., 1920).
Adams, Charles F., *Diary*, Aïda DiPace Donald, David Donald, Marc Friedlaender, and Lyman H. Butterfield, eds. (4 vols., 1964–1968).
Adams, Charles Francis, Jr., *Charles Francis Adams* (1900).
Duberman, Martin B., *Charles Francis Adams* (1961).

ADAMS, CHARLES FRANCIS, JR. 1835–1915, railroad expert, civic leader, grandson of John Quincy Adams
Adams, Charles Francis, Jr., *Autobiography*, W. C. Ford, ed. (1916).
Kirkland, Edward C., *Charles F. Adams, Jr.* (1965).

ADAMS, HENRY BROOKS 1838–1918, historian, grandson of John Quincy Adams
Adams, Charles Francis, and Henry Adams, *A Cycle of Adams Letters 1861–65*, W. C. Ford, ed. (2 vols., 1920).
Adams, Henry, *Education of Henry Adams* (1918).
——— *Henry Adams and Friends: Letters*, Harold D. Cater, ed. (1947).
——— *Henry Adams Reader*, Elizabeth Stevenson, ed. (1958).
——— *Letters*, W. C. Ford, ed. (1930).
——— "Letters to Henry Vignaud and Charles Scribner, 1879–1913," C. Waller Barrett, ed., Mass. Hist. Soc., *Proc.*, 72 (1959), 204.
Jordy, William H., *Henry Adams: Scientific Historian* (1952).
Levenson, J. C., *Mind and Art of Henry Adams* (1957).
Samuels, Ernest, *Henry Adams* (3 vols., 1948–1964).
Stevenson, Elizabeth, *Henry Adams* (1956).

ADAMS, HENRY CARTER 1851–1921, economist, statistician
Coats, A. W., "Henry Carter Adams: A Case Study in Social Sciences, 1850–1900," *Jour. Am. Studies*, 2 (1968), 177.

ADAMS, HERBERT BAXTER 1850–1901, historian
Adams, Herbert B., *Historical Scholarship in the United States, 1876–1901*, W. Stull Holt, ed. (1938).

ADAMS, JAMES TRUSLOW 1878–1949, historian
Nevins, Allan, *James Truslow Adams* (1968).

ADAMS, JOHN 1735–1826, president
Adams, Abigail, John Adams, and Thomas Jefferson, *Correspondence,* Lester J. Cappon, ed. (2 vols., 1959).
Adams, Charles F., *Life of John Adams* (2 vols., 1874).
Adams, John, *Diary and Autobiography,* Lyman H. Butterfield et al., eds. (4 vols., 1961). *Supplement* (1966).
—— *Legal Papers,* L. Kinvin Wroth and Hiller B. Zobel, eds. (3 vols., 1965).
—— and Abigail Adams, *Familiar Letters,* Charles Francis Adams, ed. (1875).
—— and Benjamin Rush, *Dialogues, 1805–1813,* John A. Schutz and Douglass Adair, eds. (1966).
—— and John Quincy Adams, *Selected Writings,* Adrienne Koch and William Peden, eds. (1946).
Bailyn, Bernard, "Butterfield's Adams," *WMQ,* 3 ser., 19 (1962), 238.
Bowen, Catherine D., *John Adams and the American Revolution* (1950).
Chinard, Gilbert, *Honest John Adams* (1933).
Handler, Edward, *America and Europe in Political Thought of John Adams* (1964).
Haraszti, Zoltán, *John Adams and Prophets of Progress* (1952).
Howe, John R., Jr., *Changing Political Thought of John Adams* (1966).
Kurtz, Stephen G., "Political Science of John Adams," *WMQ,* 3 ser., 25 (1968), 605.
Oliver, Andrew, *Portraits of John and Abigail Adams* (1967).
Smith, Page, *John Adams* (2 vols., 1962).

ADAMS, JOHN QUINCY 1767–1848, president
Adams, John, and John Quincy Adams, *Selected Writings,* Adrienne Koch and William Peden, eds. (1946).
Adams, John Q., *Letters, Papers and Speeches,* Walter LaFeber, ed. (1965).
—— *Memoirs,* Charles Francis Adams, ed. (12 vols., 1874–1877). Allan Nevins has edited selections published under title, *Diary* (1929).
—— *Writings* [1779–1823] W. C. Ford, ed. (7 vols., 1913–1917).
Bemis, Samuel F., *John Quincy Adams* (2 vols., 1949–1956).
East, Robert A., *John Quincy Adams, 1785–1794* (1962).

ADAMS, SAMUEL 1722–1803, Revolutionary leader
Adams, Samuel, *Writings,* H. A. Cushing, ed. (4 vols., 1904–1908).
Harlow, Ralph V., *Samuel Adams: Promoter of American Revolution* (1923).
Miller, John C., *Sam Adams* (1936).

ADAMS FAMILY
Adams Family, *Correspondence,* Lyman H. Butterfield, ed. (2 vols., 1963).
Adams, James T., *Adams Family* (1930).

ADDAMS, JANE 1860–1935, social reformer
Addams, Jane, *Centennial Reader* (1960).
—— *Forty Years at Hull House* (1935). Incorporates two volumes published earlier.
—— *Social Thought,* Christopher Lasch, ed. (1965).
Conway, Jill, "Jane Addams," *Daedalus,* 93 (1964), 761.
Curti, Merle, "Jane Addams," *Jour. Hist. Ideas,* 22 (1961), 240.
Farrell, John C., *Beloved Lady: Jane Addams' Ideas* (1967).
Linn, James W., *Jane Addams* (1935).
Wise, W. E., *Jane Addams* (1935).

ADE, GEORGE 1866–1944, playwright, humorist
Coyle, Lee, *George Ade* (1964).

AGASSIZ, ALEXANDER 1835–1910, zoologist, mine operator
Agassiz, Alexander, *Letters and Recollections,* George Agassiz, ed. (1913).

AGASSIZ, ELIZABETH CARY 1822–1907, educator, wife of Louis Agassiz
Patton, L. A., *Elizabeth Cary Agassiz* (1919).

AGASSIZ, JEAN LOUIS RUDOLPHE 1807–1873, naturalist
Agassiz, Elizabeth C., *Louis Agassiz, His Life and Correspondence* (2 vols., 1885).

Agassiz, Louis, *Intelligence of Agassiz: Scientific Writings*, Guy Davenport, ed. (1963).
Baird, Spencer F., and Louis Agassiz, *Correspondence*, Elmer C. Herber, ed. (1963).
Lurie, Edward, *Louis Agassiz* (1960).
Marcou, Jules, *Life, Letters and Works of Louis Agassiz* (2 vols., 1896).

AGASSIZ FAMILY
Tharp, Louise H., *Adventurous Alliance: Agassiz Family* (1959).

AIKEN, CONRAD 1889– , poet
Hoffman, Frederick J., *Conrad Aiken* (1962).

AINSLIE, THOMAS fl. 1774, army officer
Ainslie, Thomas, *Journal*, Sheldon S. Cohen, ed. (1969).

ALBEE, EDWARD 1928– , playwright
Amacher, Richard E., *Edward Albee* (1968).

ALBRIGHT, HORACE MARSDEN 1890–1962, conservationist, director of National Park Service
Swain, Donald C., *Wilderness Defender: Albright and Conservation* (1970).

ALCORN, JAMES LUSK 1816–1894, governor of Mississippi, senator
Pereyra, Lillian A., *James Lusk Alcorn: Persistent Whig* (1966).

ALCOTT, AMOS BRONSON 1799–1888, transcendentalist, educator
Alcott, Amos Bronson, *Essays on Education*, Walter Harding, ed. (1960).
——— *Journals*, Odell Shepard, ed. (1938).
——— *Letters*, Richard L. Herrnstadt, ed. (1969).
McCuskey, Dorothy, *Bronson Alcott, Teacher* (1940).
Sanborn, Franklin B., and W. T. Harris, *A. Bronson Alcott: His Life and Philosophy* (2 vols., 1893).
Shepard, Odell, *Pedlar's Progress* (1937).

ALCOTT, LOUISA MAY 1832–1888, author
Anthony, Katharine, *Louisa May Alcott* (1938).
Cheney, Ednah D., *Louisa May Alcott: Her Life, Letters, and Journals* (1889).

ALDERMAN, EDWIN ANDERSON 1861–1931; president of University of Virginia
Malone, Dumas, *Edwin A. Alderman* (1940).

ALDRICH, NELSON WILMARTH 1841–1915, Rhode Island senator
Stephenson, N. W., *Nelson W. Aldrich, a Leader in American Politics* (1930).

ALDRICH, THOMAS BAILEY 1836–1907, author
Greenslet, Ferris, *Life of Thomas Bailey Aldrich* (1908).
Samuels, Charles E., *Thomas Bailey Aldrich* (1965).

ALDRIDGE, IRA FREDERICK 1805–1867, actor
Marshall, Herbert, and Mildred Stock, *Ira Aldridge: Negro Tragedian* (1958).

ALEXANDER, JAMES 1691–1756, lawyer
MacCracken, Henry N., *Prologue to Independence: Trials of James Alexander* (1964).

ALEXANDER, WILL 1884–1956, southern reformer
Dykeman, Wilma, and James Stokely, *Seeds of Southern Change: Will Alexander* (1962).

ALGER, HORATIO 1834–1899, writer
Tebbel, John W., *From Rags to Riches* (1963).

ALLEN, ETHAN 1737/8–1789, Revolutionary soldier
Jellison, Charles A., *Ethan Allen* (1969).
Pell, John, *Ethan Allen* (1929).

ALLEN, FLORENCE ELLINWOOD 1884–1966, judge
Allen, Florence E., *To Do Justly* (1965).

ALLEN, HENRY WATKINS 1820–1866, lawyer, planter
Cassidy, Vincent H., and Amos E. Simpson, *Henry Watkins Allen of Louisiana* (1964).

ALLEN, IRA 1751–1814, Vermont political leader
Wilbur, J. B., *Ira Allen* (1928).

ALLEN, JAMES LANE 1849–1925, novelist
Bottorff, William K., *James Lane Allen* (1964).

ALLEN, RICHARD 1760–1831, founder of African Methodist Church
Wesley, C. H., *Richard Allen* (1935).

ALLEN, WILLIAM 1803–1879, Ohio political leader
McGrane, R. C., *William Allen* (1925).

ALLISON, WILLIAM BOYD 1829–1908, Iowa senator
Sage, Leland L., *William Boyd Allison* (1956).

ALLSTON, WASHINGTON 1779–1843, painter
Flagg, Jared B., *Life and Letters of Washington Allston* (1892).
Richardson, Edgar P., *Washington Allston: Romantic Artist* (1948).

ALSOP, RICHARD 1761–1815, satirist
Harrington, Karl P., *Richard Alsop, "Hartford Wit"* (1969).

ALTGELD, JOHN PETER 1847–1902, Illinois governor
Altgeld, John P., *Writings and Addresses*, Henry M. Christman, ed. (1960).
Barnard, Harry, *"Eagle Forgotten:" John Peter Altgeld* (1938).

AMES, ADELBERT 1847–1939, Reconstruction senator and governor of Mississippi
Butler, Blanche, and Adelbert Ames, *Family Letters,* Blanche B. Ames, ed.
(2 vols., 1957).
Current, Richard N., *Three Carpetbag Governors* (1968).

AMES, EDWARD SCRIBNER 1870–1958, theologian
Ames, Edward S., *Beyond Theology: Autobiography*, V. M. Ames, ed.
(1959).

AMES, EZRA 1768–1836, painter
Bolton, Theodore, and Irwin F. Cortelyou, *Ezra Ames of Albany: Portrait Painter, Craftsman, Banker* (1955).

AMES, FISHER 1758–1808, Federalist leader
Ames, Fisher, *Speeches in Congress* (1871).
———— *Works*, Seth Ames, ed. (2 vols., 1854).
Bernhard, Winfred E. A., *Fisher Ames, Federalist and Statesman, 1758–1808* (1965).

AMES, NATHANIEL, JR. fl. 1758–1822, Jeffersonian Republican
Warren, Charles, *Jacobin and Junto: Or, Early American Politics as Viewed in the Diary of Dr. Nathaniel Ames, 1758–1822* (1931).

ANDERSON, LARZ 1866–1937, diplomat
Anderson, Larz, *Letters and Journals* (1940).

ANDERSON, MARIAN 1902–   , singer
Anderson, Marian, *My Lord, What a Morning: Autobiography* (1956).

ANDERSON, RICHARD CLOUGH, JR. 1788–1826, diplomat, Kentucky congressman
Anderson, Richard C., Jr., *Diary and Journal, 1814–1826*, Alfred Tischendorf and E. Taylor Parks, eds. (1964).

ANDERSON, ROBERT 1805–1871, army officer
Anderson, Robert, *An Artillery Officer in the Mexican War . . . Letters*, E. A. Lawton, ed. (1911).

ANDERSON, SHERWOOD 1876–1941, writer
Anderson, Sherwood, *Letters*, Howard Mumford Jones and Walter B. Rideout, eds. (1953).
———— *Memoirs*, Ray L. White, ed. (1969).
Howe, Irving, *Sherwood Anderson* (1966).

ANDREW, JOHN ALBION 1818–1867, Massachusetts governor, abolitionist
Pearson, Henry G., *Life of John A. Andrew* (2 vols., 1904).

ANDREWS, CHARLES MCLEAN 1863–1943, historian
Eisenstadt, Abraham S., *Charles McLean Andrews* (1956).

ANGELL, JAMES BURRILL 1829–1916, president of University of Michigan
Angell, J. B., *Reminiscences* (1912).

ANTHONY, SUSAN BROWNELL 1820–1906, reformer
Anthony, Katharine S., *Susan B. Anthony* (1954).
Dorr, R. C., *Susan B. Anthony* (1928).

Harper, Ida H., *Life and Work of Susan B. Anthony* (3 vols., 1898–1908).
Lutz, Alma, *Susan B. Anthony* (1959).

ANTIN, MARY 1881–1949; writer
Antin, Mary, *The Promised Land.* (1912).

APPLESEED, JOHNNY, See JOHN CHAPMAN

ARMSTRONG, SAMUEL CHAPMAN 1839–1893, educator
Talbot, E. A., *Samuel Chapman Armstrong* (1904).

ARNOLD, BENEDICT 1741–1801, army officer
Sellers, Charles C., *Benedict Arnold* (1930).
Wallace, Willard M., *Traitorous Hero: Benedict Arnold* (1954).

ARNOLD, THURMAN WESLEY 1891–1970, lawyer
Arnold, Thurman W., *Fair Fights and Foul: Dissenting Lawyer's Life* (1965).
Kearny, Edwin N., *Thurman Arnold* (1970).

ARP, BILL. See CHARLES HENRY SMITH

ARTHUR, CHESTER ALAN 1830–1886, president
Howe, George F., *Chester A. Arthur* (1934).

ASBURY, FRANCIS 1745–1816, Methodist clergyman
Asbury, Francis, *Journal and Letters*, Elmer T. Clark et al., eds. (3 vols., 1958).
Rudolph, L. C., *Francis Asbury* (1966).

ASHURST, HENRY FOUNTAIN 1874–1962, Arizona senator
Ashurst, Henry F., *A Many-colored Toga: Diary*, George F. Sparks, ed. (1962).

ASTOR, JOHN JACOB 1763–1848, fur trader, capitalist
Parton, James, *Life of John Jacob Astor* (1865).
Porter, Kenneth W., *John Jacob Astor, Business Man* (2 vols., 1931).

ASTOR FAMILY
O'Connor, Harvey, *Astors* (1941).

ATCHISON, DAVID RICE 1807–1886, Missouri senator
Parrish, William E., *David Rice Atchison of Missouri* (1961).

ATKINSON, EDWARD 1827–1905, businessman, economist
Williamson, Harold F., *Edward Atkinson* (1934).

ATKINSON, HENRY 1782–1842, army officer
Nichols, Roger L., *General Henry Atkinson* (1965).

AUDUBON, JOHN JAMES 1785–1851, naturalist
Audubon, John J., *Audubon, by Himself*, Alice Ford, ed. (1969).
——— *Wildlife: Selections from Writings*, Edwin W. Teale, ed. (1964).
Audubon, M. R., *Audubon and His Journals*, Elliott Coues, ed. (2 vols., 1897–1900).
Burroughs, John, *John James Audubon* (1902).
Ford, Alice, *John James Audubon* (1964).
Herrick, Francis W., *Audubon the Naturalist* (2 vols., 1917).

AUSTIN, MARY 1868–1934, novelist, essayist
Pearce, T. M., *Mary Austin* (1965).

AUSTIN, STEPHEN FULLER 1793–1836, land promoter
Austin, Stephen F., *Papers*, E. C. Barker, ed. (4 vols., 1924–1928).
Barker, Eugene C., *Life of Stephen F. Austin, Founder of Texas* (1926).

AYCOCK, CHARLES BRANTLEY 1859–1912, North Carolina governor
Orr, Oliver H., Jr., *Charles Brantley Aycock* (1961).

AYDELOTTE, FRANK 1880–1956, historian, president of Swarthmore College
Blanshard, Frances, *Frank Aydelotte* (1970).

BACHE, ALEXANDER DALLAS 1806–1867, physicist
Odgers, Merle M., *Alexander Dallas Bache: Scientist and Educator* (1947).

BACKUS, ISAAC 1724–1806, Baptist preacher
Backus, Isaac, *On Church, State and Calvinism: Pamphlets, 1754–1789*, William G. McLoughlin, ed. (1968).
McLoughlin, William G., *Isaac Backus* (1967).

BACON, DELIA SALTER 1811–1859, author
Hopkins, Vivian C., *Prodigal Puritan: Delia Bacon* (1959).

BACON, LEONARD 1802–1881, antislavery Congregational clergyman
Bacon, T. D., *Leonard Bacon* (1931).

BACON, NATHANIEL 1647–1676, Virginia leader
Washburn, Wilcomb E., *Governor and Rebel: Bacon's Rebellion in Virginia* (1957).
Wertenbaker, Thomas J., *Torchbearer of Revolution* (1940).

BAILEY, JOE 1863–1929, Texas senator
Acheson, S. H., *Joe Bailey* (1932).

BAILEY, JOSIAH WILLIAM 1873–1946, North Carolina senator
Moore, John R., *Senator Josiah William Bailey of North Carolina* (1968).

BAILEY, LIBERTY HYDE 1858–1954, agriculturist
Dorf, Philip, *Liberty Hyde Bailey* (1956).
Rodgers, Andrew D., *Liberty Hyde Bailey* (1949).

BAINBRIDGE, WILLIAM 1774–1833, naval officer
Dearborn, Henry A. S., *Life of William Bainbridge* (1931).

BAIRD, SPENCER FULLERTON 1823–1887, zoologist
Baird, Spencer F., and Louis Agassiz, *Correspondence*, Elmer C. Herber, ed. (1963).
Dall, W. H., *Spencer Fullerton Baird* (1915).

BAKER, GEORGE PIERCE 1866–1935, playwriting instructor
Kinne, Wisner P., *George Pierce Baker and the American Theatre* (1954).

BAKER, NEWTON DIEHL 1871–1937, secretary of war
Cramer, Clarence H., *Newton D. Baker,* (1961).

BAKER, RAY STANNARD 1870–1946, journalist
Bannister, Robert C., Jr., *Ray Stannard Baker: A Progressive* (1966).
Semonche, John E., *Ray Stannard Baker* (1969).

BALDWIN, LOAMMI, JR. 1780–1838, civil engineer, lawyer, author
Vose, G. L., *Sketch of Loammi Baldwin* (1885).

BALDWIN, SIMEON EBEN 1840–1927, Connecticut jurist, legal reformer
Jackson, Frederick H., *Simeon Eben Baldwin* (1955).

BALL, WILLIAM WATTS 1868–1952, Charleston editor
Ball, William W., *The Editor and the Republic: Papers,* Anthony Harrigan, ed. (1954).
Stark, John D., *Damned Upcountryman: William Watts Ball* (1968).

BALLOU, HOSEA 1771–1852, Universalist clergyman, reformer
Cassara, Ernest, *Hosea Ballou: Challenge to Orthodoxy* (1961).

BANCROFT, FREDERIC 1860–1945, historian
Cooke, Jacob E., *Frederic Bancroft* (1957).

BANCROFT, GEORGE 1800–1891, historian
Howe, Mark A. DeW., *Life and Letters of George Bancroft* (2 vols., 1908).
Nye, Russel B., *George Bancroft* (1944).

BANCROFT, HUBERT HOWE 1832–1918, historian
Caughey, John W., *H. H. Bancroft* (1946).

BANISTER, JOHN, 1650–1692, clergyman, botanist
Ewan, Joseph, and Nesta Ewan, *John Bannister and His Natural History of Virginia, 1678–1692* (1970).

BANGS, SAMUEL ca. 1794–ca. 1853, pioneer printer
Spell, Lota M., *Pioneer Printer: Samuel Bangs in Mexico and Texas* (1963).

BANKS, NATHANIEL PRENTISS 1816–1894, Civil War general; Massachusetts politician
Harrington, Fred H., *Fighting Politician: Major General N. P. Banks* (1948).

BARBER, SAMUEL 1910–   , composer
Broder, Nathan, *Samuel Barber* (1954).

BARBOUR, THOMAS 1884–1946, zoologist
Barbour, Thomas, *Naturalist at Large* (1943).

BARD, THOMAS ROBERT 1841–1915, California oilman
Hutchinson, William H., *Oil, Land and Politics: Thomas Robert Bard* (2 vols., 1965).

BARKLEY, ALBEN W., 1877–1956, vice president
Barkley, Alben W., *That Reminds Me* (1954).

BARLOW, JOEL 1754–1812, poet, statesman
Todd, C. B., *Life and Letters of Joel Barlow* (1886).
Woodress, James, *A Yankee's Odyssey: Joel Barlow* (1958).
Zunder, T. A., *Early Days of Joel Barlow* (1934).

BARNARD, FREDERICK AUGUSTUS PORTER 1809–1889, president of Columbia University
Fulton, John, *Memoirs of Frederick A. P. Barnard* (1896).

BARNARD, HENRY 1811–1900; educator, editor
Barnard, Henry, *On Education*, John S. Brubacher, ed. (1931).
Blair, Anna L., *Henry Barnard: School Administrator* (1938).
Monroe, Will S., *Educational Labors of Henry Barnard* (1893).

BARNEY, JOSHUA 1759–1818, naval officer in Revolution and War of 1812
Footner, Hulbert, *Sailor of Fortune: Commodore Barney* (1940).

BARNUM, PHINEAS TAYLOR 1810–1891, showman
Barnum, P. T., *Struggles and Triumphs* (1927).
Werner, M. R., *Barnum* (1923).

BARRON, CLARENCE WALKER 1855–1928, financial editor
Barron, C. W., *They Told Barron* (1930).
——— *More They Told Barron*, Arthur Pound and S. T. Moore, eds. (1931).

BARRY, JOHN 1745–1803; naval officer
Clark, William B., *Gallant John Barry, 1745–1803: Naval Hero of Two Wars* (1938).
Gurn, Joseph, *Commodore John Barry* (1933).

BARRYMORE, JOHN 1882–1942, actor
Barrymore, John, *Confessions of an Actor* (1926).
Fowler, Gene, *Good Night, Sweet Prince* (1944).

BARRYMORE FAMILY
Alpert, Hollis, *The Barrymores* (1964).

BARTON, CLARA 1821–1912; organizer of American Red Cross
Barton, Clara, *Story of My Childhood* (1907).
Barton, William E., *Life of Clara Barton* (2 vols., 1922).
Ross, Ishbel, *Angel of the Battlefield: Clara Barton* (1956).

BARTRAM, JOHN 1699–1777, naturalist
Bartram, John, and William Bartram, *Selections from Writings*, Helen G. Cruickshank, ed. (1957).
Earnest, Ernest, *John and William Bartram* (1940).

BARTRAM, WILLIAM 1739–1823, son of John Bartram, naturalist
Bartram, John and William, *Selections from Writings*, Helen G. Cruickshank, ed. (1957).
Bartram, William, *Travels: Naturalist's Edition*, Francis Harper, ed. (1958).
Earnest, Ernest, *John and William Bartram* (1940).

BARUCH, BERNARD MANNES 1870–1965, financier
Baruch, Bernard M., *Baruch* (2 vols., 1957–1960).
Coit, Margaret L., *Mr. Baruch* (1957).

BASCOM, JOHN 1827–1911, president of University of Wisconsin
Bascom, John, *Things Learned by Living* (1913).

BATES, EDWARD 1793–1869, attorney general
Bates, Edward, "Diary," Howard K. Beale, ed., Am. Hist. Assoc., *Report*, (1930), IV.
Cain, Marvin R., *Lincoln's Attorney General: Edward Bates* (1965).

BATES, FREDERICK 1777–1825, governor of Missouri
Marshall, Thomas M., *Life and Papers of Frederick Bates* (1926).

BAYARD, JAMES ASH(E)TON 1767–1815; Delaware senator, diplomat
Borden, Morton, *Federalism of James A. Bayard* (1955).

BAYARD, THOMAS FRANCIS 1828–1898, congressman, statesman
Tansill, C. C., *Congressional Career of Thomas F. Bayard* (1946).
——— *Foreign Policy of Thomas F. Bayard* (1940).

BEAL, WILLIAM JAMES 1833–1924, botanist
Baker, Ray S., and J. B. Baker, *An American in Science* (1925).

BEARD, CHARLES AUSTIN 1874–1948, historian
Beale, Howard K., ed., *Charles A. Beard* (1954).
Beard, Mary R., *The Making of Charles A. Beard* (1955).
Hofstadter, Richard, *Progressive Historians: Turner, Beard, Parrington* (1968).

BEAUMONT, WILLIAM 1785–1853, surgeon, medical researcher
Myer, J. S., *Life and Letters of Dr. William Beaumont* (1912).
Rosen, George, *Reception of William Beaumont's Discovery in Europe* (1942).

BEAUREGARD, PIERRE GUSTAVE TOUTANT 1818–1893, Confederate general
Williams, T. Harry, *P. G. T. Beauregard* (1955).

BECK, JAMES MONTGOMERY 1861–1936, Pennsylvania congressman
Keller, Morton, *In Defense of Yesterday: James M. Beck* (1958).

BECKER, CARL 1873–1945, historian
Becker, Carl L., *Detachment and Writing of History: Essays and Letters*, Phil L.
Snyder, ed. (1958).
Wilkins, Burleigh T., *Carl Becker: Biographical Study in American Intellectual
History* (1961).

BEECHER, CATHERINE ESTHER 1800–1878, abolitionist, educator
Grimké, Angelina E., *Letters to Catherine E. Beecher* (1838).
Harveson, Mae E., *Catherine Esther Beecher* (1969).

BEECHER, EDWARD 1803–1895, abolitionist, Congregational clergyman
Meredith, Robert, *Politics of the Universe: Edward Beecher, Abolition and
Orthodoxy* (1968).

BEECHER, HENRY WARD 1813–1887, abolitionist, Congregational clergyman
Hibben, Paxton, *Henry Ward Beecher: An American Portrait (1927)*.
McLoughlin, William G., *The Meaning of Henry Ward Beecher: An Essay on
Shifting Values of Mid-Victorian America, 1840–1870* (1970).
Shaplen, Robert, *Free Love and Heavenly Sinners: Henry Ward Beecher Scandal*
(1954).

BEECHER, LYMAN 1775–1863, Presbyterian clergyman
Beecher, Lyman, *Autobiography and Correspondence*, Barbara Cross, ed.
(1961).

BEEKMAN FAMILY
Beekman, Gerard G., and James Beekman, *Mercantile Papers, 1746–1799*,
Philip L. White, ed. (3 vols., 1956).
White, Philip L., *Beekmans of New York, 1647–1877* (1956).

BEISSEL, JOHANN CONRAD 1690–1768, Seventh Day Baptist leader
Klein, Walter C., *Johann Conrad Beissel, 1690–1786* (1942).

BELASCO, DAVID 1854–1931, producer, actor, dramatist
Timberlake, Craig, *David Belasco, Bishop of Broadway* (1954).

BELK, WILLIAM HENRY 1862–1952, southern businessman
Blythe, LeGette, *William Henry Belk: Merchant of the South* (rev. ed., 1958).

BELL, ALEXANDER GRAHAM 1847–1922, inventor
Mackenzie, Catherine, *Alexander Graham Bell* (1928).

BELL, JOHN 1797–1869; Tennessee senator
Parks, Joseph H., *John Bell of Tennessee* (1930).

BELLAMY, EDWARD 1850–1898, utopian socialist, author
Bowman, Sylvia E., *The Year 2000: Edward Bellamy* (1958).
Morgan, Arthur E., *Edward Bellamy* (1944).
Thomas, John L., "Introduction," in Edward Bellamy, *Looking Backward*
(1967).

BELLOW, SAUL 1915–   , author
Clayton, John J., *Saul Bellow* (1968).

BELLOWS, GEORGE WESLEY 1882–1925, artist
Eggers, George W., *George Bellows* (1931).
Morgan, Charles H., *George Bellows: Painter* (1965).

BELMONT, AUGUST 1816–1890, businessman, Democratic leader
Katz, Irving, *August Belmont* (1968).

BENCHLEY, ROBERT 1889–1945, humorist
Yates, Norris W., *Robert Benchley* (1968).

BENEDICT, RUTH FULTON 1887–1948, anthropologist
Benedict, Ruth, *An Anthropologist at Work*, Margaret Mead, ed. (1959).

BENÉT, STEPHEN VINCENT 1898–1943, poet
Fenton, Charles A., *Stephen Vincent Benét* (1958).
Stroud, Parry E., *Stephen Vincent Benét* (1962).

BENEZET, ANTHONY 1713–1784, Quaker philanthropist, teacher
Brooks, George S., *Friend Anthony Benezet* (1937).

BENJAMIN, JUDAH PHILIP 1811–1884, Confederate cabinet member
Meade, Robert D., *Judah P. Benjamin* (1943).
Osterweis, R. G., *Judah P. Benjamin, Statesman of the Lost Cause* (1933).

BENNET, HUGH HAMMOND 1881–1960, soil scientist and conservationist
Brink, Wellington, *Big Hugh* (1951).

BENNETT, JONATHAN M. 1814–1887, Virginia and West Virginia political and
business leader
Rice, Harvey M., *Life of Jonathan M. Bennett* (1943).

BENNETT, JAMES GORDON 1795–1872, publisher
Carlson, Oliver, *Man Who Made News: James Gordon Bennett* (1942).

BENNETT FAMILY
Seitz, D. C., *The James Gordon Bennetts, Father and Son* (1928).

BENT, GEORGE 1843–1917, Indian-white Cheyenne warrior
Hyde, George E., *Life of George Bent*, Savoie Lottinville, ed. (1967).

BENTLEY, WILLIAM 1759–1819, Unitarian clergyman
Bentley, William, *Diary* (4 vols., 1905–1914) Covers period on Salem, 1784–
1819.

BENTON, THOMAS HART 1782–1858, Missouri senator
Benton, Thomas Hart, *Thirty Years View* (2 vols., 1854–1856).
Chambers, William N., *Old Bullion Benton* (1956).
Roosevelt, Theodore, *Thomas H. Benton* (1887).
Smith, Elbert B., *Magnificent Missourian: Thomas Hart Benton* (1957).

BENTON, THOMAS HART 1889–   , artist
Benton, Thomas Hart, *An American in Art: Professional and Technical Autobi-
ography* (1969).
Benton, Thomas H., *An Artist in America* (3d ed., 1968).

BERLIN, IRVING 1888–   , composer
Ewen, David, *Irving Berlin* (1950).

BERNAYS, EDWARD L. 1891–   , public relations counsel
Bernays, Edward L., *Biography of an Idea: Memoirs of Public Relations Counsel*
(1963).

BETHUNE, MARY MCLEOD 1875–1955, educator
Holt, Rackham, *Mary McLeod Bethune* (1964).
Peare, C. O., *Mary McLeod Bethune* (1951).
Sterne, Emma G., *Mary McLeod Bethune* (1957).

BEVERIDGE, ALBERT JEREMIAH 1862–1927, Indiana senator
Bowers, Claude G., *Beveridge and the Progressive Era* (1932).

BIDDLE, FRANCIS 1886–1968, attorney general
Biddle, Francis, *A Casual Past* (1961).
———— *In Brief Authority* (1962).

BIDDLE, GEORGE 1885–   , painter
Biddle, George, *American Artist's Story* (1939).

BIDDLE, NICHOLAS 1750–1778, Revolutionary naval officer
Clark, William B., *Captain Dauntless: Nicholas Biddle* (1949).

BIDDLE, NICHOLAS 1786–1844, financier
Biddle, Nicholas, *Correspondence*, R. C. McGrane, ed. (1919).
Govan, Thomas P., *Nicholas Biddle* (1959).

BIENVILLE, JEAN BAPTISTE LE MOYNE, SIEUR de 1680–1767, explorer
King, Grace, *Jean Baptiste le Moyne, Sieur de Bienville* (1892).

BIERCE, AMBROSE 1842–1914, author
McWilliams, Carey, *Ambrose Bierce* (1929).

BIGELOW, JOHN 1817–1911, editor, diplomat
Bigelow, John, *Retrospections of an Active Life* (5 vols., 1909–1913).
Clapp, Margaret A., *Forgotten First Citizen: John Bigelow* (1947).

BIGELOW, POULTNEY 1855–1954, author
Bigelow, Poultney, *Seventy Summers* (2 vols., 1925).

BIGGS, HERMANN MICHAEL 1859–1923, pioneer in preventive medicine
Winslow, Charles-Edward A., *Hermann M. Biggs* (1929).

BILBO, THEODORE GILMORE 1877–1947, Mississippi senator
Green, A. Wigfall, *The Man Bilbo* (1963).

BILLINGS, JOHN SHAW 1838–1913, librarian, surgeon
Billings, John S., *Selected Papers*, Frank B. Rogers, ed. (1965).
Garrison, Fielding H., *John Shaw Billings* (1916).
Lydenberg, H. M., *J. S. Billings* (1924).

BILLINGS, WILLIAM 1764–1800, composer
Lindstrom, C. E., "William Billings and His Times," *Musical Quarterly*, October 1939.

BINGHAM, GEORGE CALEB 1811–1879; artist
Bloch, Maurice, *George Caleb Bingham* (2 vols., 1967).
Christ-Janer, Albert, *George Caleb Bingham of Missouri* (1940).
McDermott, John F., *George Caleb Bingham: River Portraitist* (1959).

BINGHAM, WILLIAM 1752–1804, Philadelphia banker, Federalist
Alberts, Robert C., *Life and Times of William Bingham, 1752–1804* (1970),

BINNEY, HORACE 1780–1875, Philadelphia lawyer
Binney, C. C., *Life of Horace Binney, with Selections from His Letters* (1903).

BIRNEY, JAMES GILLESPIE 1792–1857, abolitionist
Birney, William, *James G. Birney and His Times* (1890).
Fladeland, Betty L., *James G. Birney: Slaveholder to Abolitionist* (1955).

BISNO, ABRAHAM fl. late 19th century; union leader
Bisno, Abraham, *Autobiographical Account of Early Life and Unionism in Women's Garment Industry* (1967).

BLACK, HUGO 1886–1971, Supreme Court justice
Black, Hugo, *One Man's Stand for Freedom: Supreme Court Opinions*, Irving Dilliard, ed (1963).
Frank, John P., *Mr. Justice Black* (1949).
Mendelson, Wallace, *Justices Black and Frankfurter: Conflict in the Court* (2nd ed., 1966).
Strickland, Stephen P., ed., *Hugo Black and the Supreme Court: A Symposium* (1967).
Williams, Charlotte, *Hugo L. Black* (1950).

BLACK, JEREMIAH SULLIVAN 1810–1883, Attorney-general
Black, Jeremiah S., *Essays and Speeches*, Chauncey F. Black, ed. (1885).
Brigance, W. N., *Jeremiah Sullivan Black* (1934).

BLACK HAWK 1767–1838, Sauk war chief
Cole, Cyrenus, *I am a Man: The Indian Black Hawk* (1938).
Hawk, Black, *An Autobiography* (1833) Donald Jackson, ed. (1955).

BLACKFORD, MARY BERKELEY MINOR 1802–1896, Virginia Unionist
Blackford, Launcelot M., *Mine Eyes Have Seen the Glory: Story of Mary Berkeley Minor Blackford, 1802–1896* (1954).

BLACKWELL, ELIZABETH 1821–1910, first woman doctor
Ross, Ishbel, *Child of Destiny: First Woman Doctor* (1949).

BLAINE, JAMES GILLESPIE 1830–1893, Maine senator, secretary of state
Blaine, James G., *Twenty Years of Congress: From Lincoln to Garfield* (2 vols., 1884–1886).
Harrison, Benjamin, and James G. Blaine, *Correspondence, 1882–1893*, Albert T. Volwiler, ed. (1940).
Muzzey, David S., *James G. Blaine* (1943).

BLAIR, JAMES 1655–1743, founder of William and Mary College
Motley, Daniel E., *Life of Commissary James Blair, Founder of William and Mary College* (1901).

BLANCHARD, JONATHAN 1811–1892, reformer
Kilby, Clyde S., *Minority of One: Jonathan Blanchard* (1959).

BLAND, RICHARD PARKS 1835–1899, Free Silver leader
Byars, W. V., *An American Commoner* (1900).

BLAVATSKY, HELENA 1831–1891, founder of Theosophists
Bechofer-Roberts, C. E., *Mysterious Madame* (1913).

BLENNERHASSETT, HARMAN 1756–1831, associate of Aaron Burr
Safford, W. H., *Harman Blennerhassett* (1850).

BLISS, TASKER HOWARD 1853–1930, Chief of Staff, World War I
Trask, David F., *General Tasker Howard Bliss and "Sessions of the World,"* *1919* (1966).

BLIVEN, BRUCE 1889–   , journalist, author
Bliven, Bruce, *Five Million Words Later: An Autobiography* (1970).

BLOOM, SOL 1870–1949, New York Congressman
Bloom, Sol, *Autobiography* (1948).

BLOOMER, AMELIA 1818–1894, reformer
Bloomer, Dexter C., *Life and Writings of Amelia Bloomer* (1895).

BLOUNT, JOHN GRAY 1752–1833, North Carolina political leader
Blount, John G., *Papers, 1764–1802*, Alice B. Keith and William H. Masterson, eds. (3 vols., 1952–1965).

BLOUNT, WILLIAM 1749–1800, North Carolina, Tennessee political leader
Masterson, William H., *William Blount* (1954).

BOAS, FRANZ 1858–1942, anthropologist
Kroeber, Alfred L., *Franz Boaz* (1943).

BODENHEIM, MAXWELL 1893–1954, poet
Moore, Jack B., *Maxwell Bodenheim* (1970).

BOHR, NIELS HENDRIK DAVID 1885–1962, physicist
Moore, Ruth E., *Niels Bohr* (1966).
Pauli, Wolfgang, ed., *Niels Bohr and the Development of Physics* (1965).
Rozental, Stefan, *Niels Bohr* (1967).

BOK, EDWARD WILLIAM 1863–1930, editor
Bok, Edward, *Americanization of Edward Bok* (1920).

BOKER, GEORGE HENRY 1823–1890, Philadelphia writer
Bradley, Edward S., *George Henry Boker, Poet and Patriot* (1927).

BONAPARTE, CHARLES JOSEPH 1851–1921, Cabinet officer, reformer
Goldman, Eric F., *Charles J. Bonaparte* (1943).

BOONE, DANIEL 1734–1820; frontiersman
Bakeless, John, *Daniel Boone* (1939).
Bruce, Henry A., *Daniel Boone and the Wilderness Road* (1910).
Thwaites, Reuben G., *Daniel Boone* (1902).

BORAH, WILLIAM EDGAR 1865–1940, Idaho senator
Johnson, Claudius O., *Borah of Idaho* (1936).
McKenna, Marian C., *Borah* (1961).
Maddox, Robert J., *William E. Borah and American Foreign Policy* (1970).
Vinson, John Chalmers, *William E. Borah and Outlawry of War* (1957).

BORING, EDWIN GARRIGUES 1886–1969, psychologist
Boring, Edwin G., *Psychologist at Large: Autobiography and Selected Essays* (1961).

BOUCICAULT, DION 1820–1890, playwright, actor
Hogan, Robert, *Dion Boucicault* (1970).

BOUDINOT, ELIAS 1740–1821, Revolutionary statesman
Boyd, George A., *Elias Boudinot: Patriot and Statesman* (1952).
Gabriel, Ralph H., *Elias Boudinot* (1941).

BOURNE, GEORGE 1780–1845, clergyman, abolitionist
Christie, John W., and Dwight L. Dumond, *George Bourne* (1969).

BOURNE, RANDOLPH SILLIMAN 1886–1918, pacifist
Moreau, John A., *Randolph Bourne* (1966).

BOWDITCH, HENRY INGERSOLL 1808–1892, physician
Bowditch, V. Y., *Life and Correspondence of Henry Ingersoll Bowditch* (2 vols., 1902).

BOWDITCH, NATHANIEL 1773–1838, astronomer, mathematician
Wylie, Paul E., "Nathaniel Bowditch and His Work," *Navigation,* 3 (1952), 160.
Young, Alexander, *Discourse on Nathaniel Bowditch* (1838).

BOWLES, CHESTER 1901–   , World War II administrator, diplomat
Bowles, Chester, *Promises to Keep, 1941–1969* (1971).
—— *Selected Writings and Speeches* (1962).

BOWLES, WILLIAM AUGUSTUS 1763–1805, white leader of Creek Indians
Wright, J. Leitch, Jr., *William Augustus Bowles: Director General of Creek Nation* (1967).

BRACKENRIDGE, HENRY MARIE 1786–1871, lawyer, author
Keller, William F., *Nation's Advocate: Henry Marie Brackenridge* (1956).

BRACKENRIDGE, HUGH HENRY 1748–1816, jurist, author
Marder, Daniel, *Hugh Henry Brackenridge* (1967).
Newlin, Claude M., *Life and Writings of Hugh Henry Brackenridge* (1932).

BRADFORD, ANDREW 1686–1742, Philadelphia printer, son of William Bradford, printer
DeArmond, Anna J., *Andrew Bradford, Colonial Journalist* (1949).

BRADFORD, WILLIAM 1589/90–1657, governor of Plymouth
Bradford, William, *Of Plymouth Plantation,* Samuel E. Morison, ed. (1952).

BRADFORD, WILLIAM 1663–1752, early printer of the middle colonies
Wall, Alexander J., Jr., "William Bradford: Colonial Printer," Am. Antiq. Soc., *Proc.,* 73 (1963), 361.

BRADLEY, JOSEPH P. 1813–1892, lawyer, Supreme Court justice
Bradley, Joseph P., *Miscellaneous Writings* (1902).

BRADLEY, OMAR NELSON 1893–   , World War II general
Bradley, Omar N., *Soldier's Story* (1951).

BRADSTREET, ANNE 1612 (?)–1672, poet
Bradstreet, Anne, *Works,* J. H. Ellis, ed. (1887).
Piercy, Josephine K., *Anne Bradstreet* (1964).

BRADY, MATHEW B. ca. 1823–1896, Civil War photographer
Horan, James D., *Mathew Brady: Historian with a Camera* (1955).

BRAGG, BRAXTON 1817–1876, Confederate general
McWhiney, Grady, *Braxton Bragg and Confederate Defeat* (1969).

BRAINERD, DAVID 1718–1747, missionary to Indians
Brainerd, David, *Account of Life,* Jonathan Edwards, ed. (1749; repr. 1970).

BRANDEIS, LOUIS DEMBITZ 1856–1941, Supreme Court justice
Brandeis, Louis D., *Letters,* Vol. I: *1870–1907: Urban Reformer,* Melvin Urofsky and David W. Levy, eds. (1971).
—— *Social and Economic Views,* Alfred Lief, ed. (1930).
—— *Unpublished Opinions of Justice Brandeis,* Alexander M. Bickel, ed. (1957).
Mason, Alpheus T., *Brandeis* (2nd ed., 1956).
Rabinowitz, Ezekiel, *Justice Louis D. Brandeis: Zionist Chapter of His Life* (1968).
Todd, Alden L., *Justice on Trial: Brandeis* (1964).

BRANT, JOSEPH, 1742–1807, Mohawk Chief
Chalmers, Harvey, and Ethel B. Monture, *Joseph Brant: Mohawk* (1955).

BRASHEAR, JOHN ALFRED 1840–1920, maker of astronomical lenses
Gaul, Harriet A., and Ruby Eiseman, *John Alfred Brashear, Scientist and Humanitarian* (1940).

BRAY, THOMAS 1656–1729/30, Anglican clergyman, founder of libraries
Thompson, H. P., *Thomas Bray* (1954).

BRECKINRIDGE, JOHN 1760–1806, Kentucky senator
Harrison, Lowell H., *John Breckinridge, Jeffersonian Republican* (1969).

BRICE, FANNY, 1891–1951, actress
Katkov, Norman, *Fabulous Fanny* (1953).

BRIDGER, JAMES 1804–1881, frontiersman
Alter, Cecil, *James Bridger, Frontiersman* (1925).
Vestal, Stanley, *Jim Bridger, Mountain Man* (1970).

BRIDGMAN, PERCY WILLIAMS 1882–1961, physicist
Bridgman, Percy W., *The Way Things Are* (1959).

BRINKERHOFF, ROELIFF 1828–1911, lawyer, penologist
Brinkerhoff, Roeliff, *Recollections* (1900).

BRISTOW, JOSEPH LITTLE 1861–1944, Kansas senator
Sageser, A. Bower, *Joseph L. Bristow: Kansas Progressive* (1968).

BRODERICK, DAVID COLBRETH 1820–1859, New York politician
Williams, David A., *David C. Broderick* (1969).

BROMFIELD, LOUIS 1896–1956, novelist
Anderson, David D., *Louis Bromfield* (1963).

BROOKS, EUGENE CLYDE 1871–1947, North Carolina educator
Gatewood, Willard B., *Eugene C. Brooks: Educator and Public Servant* (1960).

BROOKS, PHILLIPS 1835–1893, Episcopal clergyman
Albright, Raymond W., *Focus on Infinity: Life of Phillips Brooks* (1961).
Allen, Alexander V. G., *Life and Letters of Phillips Brooks* (2 vols., 1900).

BROOKS, VAN WYCK 1886–1963, critic
Vitelli, J. R., *Van Wyck Brooks* (1968).

BROPHY, JOHN 1883– , United Mine Worker's president
Brophy, John, *A Miner's Life: Autobiography*, John O. P. Hall, ed. (1964).

BROWN, BENJAMIN GRATZ 1826–1885, Missouri senator
Peterson, Norma L., *Freedom and Franchise: B. Gratz Brown* (1965).

BROWN, CHARLES BROCKDEN 1771–1810, novelist, journalist
Clark, David L., *Charles Brockden Brown: Pioneer Voice of America* (1952).
Ringe, Donald A., *Charles Brockden Brown* (1966).

BROWN, CLAUDE 1937– , Negro author
Brown, Claude, *Manchild in the Promised Land* (1965).

BROWN, JOHN 1800–1859, abolitionist
DuBois, W. E. B., *John Brown* (1909).
Oates, Stephen B., *To Purge This Land with Blood: John Brown* (1970).
Ruchames, Louis, ed., *John Brown Reader* (1959).
Sanborn, Franklin B., *Life and Letters of John Brown* (1891).
Villard, Oswald G., *John Brown* (1943).
Warren, Robert P., *John Brown* (1929).

BROWN, JOSEPH EMERSON 1821–1894, Georgia governor
Fielder, Herbert, *J. E. Brown* (1883).
Hill, Louise B., *Joseph E. Brown and the Confederacy* (1939).
Roberts, Derrell C., *Joseph E. Brown and Reconstruction* (1970).

BROWN, MOSES 1738–1836, Rhode Island reformer
Thompson, Mack, *Moses Brown: Reluctant Reformer* (1962).

BROWN, WILLIAM WELLS ca. 1816–1884, Negro reformer
Farrison, William E., *William Wells Brown: Author and Reformer* (1969).

BROWN FAMILY
Hedges, James B., *Browns of Providence Plantations* (2 vols., 1952, 1968).

BROWNE, CHARLES FARRAR 1834–1867, humorist; Artemus Ward, pseud.
Austin, James C., *Artemus Ward* (1963).
Seitz, D. C., *Artemus Ward* (1919).

BROWNE, JOHN ROSS 1821–1875, author

Browne, J. Ross, *Letters, Journals and Writings*, Lina F. Browne, ed. (1969).
Dillon, Richard H., *J. Ross Browne: Confidential Agent in Old California* (1965).

BROWNE, WILLIAM MONTAGUE 1823–1883, Confederate colonel
Coulter, Ellis M., *William Montague Browne, Anglo-Irish American* (1968).

BROWNING, JOHN MOSES 1855–1926, inventor
Browning, John, and Curt Gentry, *John M. Browning, American Gunmaker* (1964).

BROWNING, ORVILLE HICKMAN 1806–1881, Illinois senator
Baxter, Maurice G., *Orville H. Browning: Lincoln's Friend and Critic* (1957).
Browning, Orville H., *Diary, 1850–1881*, T. C. Pease, and J. G. Randall, eds. (2 vols., 1925–1931).

BROWNLOW, LOUIS 1879–1963, journalist, municipal reformer
Brownlow, Louis, *Autobiography* (2 vols., 1955–1958).

BROWNLOW, WILLIAM G. 1805–1877, Methodist clergyman, politician
Coulter, E. Merton, *William G. Brownlow* (1937).

BROWNSON, ORESTES AUGUSTUS 1803–1876, philosopher, author
Brownson, Henry F., *Orestes A. Brownson* (3 vols., 1898–1900).
Brownson, Orestes A., *Works*, Henry F. Brownson, ed. (20 vols., 1882–1907).
Lapati, Americo D., *Orestes Brownson* (1965).
Schlesinger, Arthur M., Jr., *Orestes A. Brownson* (1939).

BRYAN, WILLIAM JENNINGS 1860–1925, political leader
Bryan, William Jennings, *Memoirs* (1925).
—— *Selections*, Ray Ginger, ed. (1967).
Coletta, Paolo E., *William Jennings Bryan* (3 vols., 1964–1969).
Curti, Merle, *Bryan and World Peace* (1931).
Glad, Paul W., *The Trumpet Soundeth: William Jennings Bryan, 1896–1912* (1960).
Koenig, Louis W., *Bryan: A Political Biography* (1971).
Levine, Lawrence W., *Defender of the Faith: William Jennings Bryan, 1915–1925* (1965).

BRYANT, WILLIAM CULLEN 1794–1878, editor, poet
Godwin, Parke, *A Biography of William Cullen Bryant, with Extracts from His Private Correspondence* (2 vols., 1883).
McLean, Albert F., Jr., *William Cullen Bryant* (1964).

BUCHANAN, JAMES 1791–1868, President
Buchanan, James, *Mr. Buchanan's Administration on the Eve of the Rebellion* (1866).
Buchanan, James, *Works*, J. B. Moore, ed. (12 vols., 1908–1911).
Curtis, George T., *Life of James Buchanan* (2 vols., 1883).
Klein, Philip S., *President James Buchanan* (1962).

BUCK, PEARL 1892–   , novelist
Doyle, Paul A., *Pearl Buck* (1965).

BUCKLAND, WILLIAM 1734–1774, architect
Beirne, Rosamond R., and John H. Scarff, *William Buckland: Architect of Virginia and Maryland* (1958).

BUCKNER, EMORY 1877–1941, trial lawyer
Mayer, Martin, *Emory Buckner* (1968).

BUCKNER, SIMON BOLÍVAR 1823–1914, Confederate general
Stickles, Arndt M., *Simon Bolívar Buckner* (1940).

BUEL, JESSE 1778–1839, agriculturist
Carman, H. J., *Jesse Buel* (1947).

BUELL, ABEL 1741/42–1822, silversmith, engraver
Wroth, Lawrence C., *Abel Buell: Silversmith, Type Founder & Engraver* (1926).

BULFINCH, CHARLES 1763–1844, architect
Bulfinch, Ellen S., ed., *Life and Letters of Charles Bulfinch* (1896).
Kirker, Harold, *Architecture of Charles Bulfinch* (1969).

Place, Charles A., *Charles Bulfinch, Architect* (1925).

BULLITT, WILLIAM CHRISTIAN 1891–1967, diplomat
Farnsworth, Beatrice, *William C. Bullitt and the Soviet Union* (1967).

BUNTLINE, NED. See EDWARD ZANE CARROLL JUDSON.

BURBANK, LUTHER 1849–1926, plant breeder
Burbank, Luther, and Wilbur Hall, *Harvest of the Years.* (1927).
Howard, Walter L., *Luther Burbank, Victim of Hero Worship* (1945).
Williams, Henry Smith, *Luther Burbank, His Life and Work* (1915).

BURD, JAMES 1726–1793, Pennsylvania frontiersman
Nixon, Lilly L., *James Burd: Frontier Defender, 1726–1793* (1941).

BURGESS, JOHN WILLIAM 1844–1931, political scientist
Brown, Bernard E., *American Conservatives: Francis Lieber and John W. Burgess* (1951).
Burgess, John W., *Reminiscences of an American Scholar: Beginnings of Columbia University* (1934).

BURK, JOHN DALY, 1775–1808, Jeffersonian Republican
Shulim, Joseph I., *John Daly Burk: Irish Revolutionist* (1964).

BURKE, THOMAS 1849–1925, Seattle judge, entrepreneur
Nesbit, Robert C., *"He Built Seattle": Judge Thomas Burke* (1961).

BURNET, DAVID GOUVERNEUR 1788–1870, first president of Texas
Clarke, Mary W., *David G. Burnet* (1969).

BURNETT, PETER HARDEMAN 1807–1895, pioneer, California governor
Burnett, Peter H., *Recollections* (1880).

BURNHAM, DANIEL H. 1846–1912, architect, city planner
Moore, Charles, *Daniel H. Burnham: Architect, Planner of Cities* (2 vols., 1921).

BURNSIDE, AMBROSE EVERETT 1824–1881, Union general
Poore, Ben P., *Life of Ambrose E. Burnside* (1882).

BURR, AARON 1756–1836, vice-president
Abernethy, Thomas P., *Burr Conspiracy* (1954).
Burr, Aaron, *Memoirs, with Miscellaneous Selections from Correspondence,* (Mary Lee Davis, ed. 1836–37).
——— *Private Journal in Europe, with Selections from Correspondence,* Mary Lee Davis, ed. (2 vols., 1838).
——— *"Some Papers,"* W. C. Ford, ed., Am. Antiq. Soc., *Proc., 29* (1919), 43.
Carpenter, T., *Trial of Aaron Burr,* (4 vols., 1807).
Parmet, Herbert S., and Marie B. Hecht, *Aaron Burr* (1967).
Parton, James, *The Life and Times of Aaron Burr* (1858).
Schachner, Nathan, *Aaron Burr,* (1937).

BURRITT, ELIHU 1810–1879, linguist, reformer
Curti, Merle E., *The Learned Blacksmith* (1937).
Tolis, Peter, *Elihu Burritt* (1968).

BURROUGHS, JOHN 1837–1921, naturalist
Barrus, Clara, *Life and Letters of John Burroughs* (2 vols., 1925).
Wiley, Farida A., ed., *John Burroughs' America* (1951).

BUSHNELL, HORACE 1802–1876, Congregational clergyman
Cheney, Mary B., *Life and Letters of Horace Bushnell* (1880).
Cross, Barbara M., *Horace Bushnell* (1958).
Smith, H. Shelton, ed., *Horace Bushnell* (1965).

BUTLER, BENJAMIN FRANKLIN 1818–1893, Union general, Massachusetts politician
Butler, Benjamin F., *Autobiography and Personal Reminiscences* (1892).
Butler, Benjamin F., *Correspondence during Civil War* (5 vols., 1917).
Holzman, Robert S., *Stormy Ben Butler* (1954).
Trefousse, Hans L., *Ben Butler* (1957).
West, Richard S., Jr., *Lincoln's Scapegoat General: Benjamin F. Butler, 1818–1893* (1965).

BUTLER, BURRIDGE DAVENAL 1868–1948, publisher, Chicago radio broadcaster
Evans, James F., *Prairie Farmer and WLS: The Burridge D. Butler Years* (1969).

BYLES, MATHER 1706/07–1788, Congregational clergyman
Eaton, Arthur W. H., *The Famous Mather Byles* (1914).

BYRD, HARRY FLOOD 1887–1966, Virginia senator
Wilkinson, J. Harvie III, *Harry Byrd and Virginia Politics, 1945–1966* (1968).

BYRD, WILLIAM 1674–1744, Virginia planter
Beatty, R. C., *William Byrd of Westover* (1932).
Byrd, William, *London Diary (1717–1721) and Other Writings*, Louis B. Wright and Marion Tinling, eds. (1958).
―――― *Prose Works*, Louis B. Wright, ed., (1966).
―――― *The Secret Diary of William Byrd of Westover, 1709–1712*, Louis B. Wright and Marion Tinling, eds. (1941).
―――― *Writings*, J. S. Bassett, ed., (1901).
Marambaud, Pierre, "William Byrd of Westover: Cavalier, Diarist, and Chronicler," *Va. Mag. Hist. Biog.*, 78 (1970), 144.

BYRD FAMILY
Hatch, Alden, *Byrds of Virginia* (1969).

BYRNES, JAMES FRANCIS 1879–1972; Supreme Court justice, secretary of state
Byrnes, James F., *All in One Lifetime* (1958).
―――― *Speaking Frankly* (1947).
Curry, George, *James F. Byrnes* (1965).

CABELL, JAMES BRANCH 1879–1958, author
Cabell, James Branch, *As I Remember It* (1955).
―――― *Letters*, Padraic Colum and Margaret Freeman Cabell, eds. (1962).
―――― *Quiet Please* (1952).
Davis, Joe Lee, *James Branch Cabell* (1962).
Tarrant, Desmond, *James Branch Cabell* (1967).

CABLE, GEORGE WASHINGTON 1844–1925, author
Biklé, Lucy L. C., *George W. Cable: His Life and Letters* (1928).
Butcher, Philip, *George Washington Cable* (1962).
Rubin, Louis D., *George W. Cable: A Southern Heretic* (1969).
Turner, Arlin, *George W. Cable* (1956).

CABOT, GEORGE 1752–1823, merchant, politician
Lodge, Henry C., *Life and Letters of George Cabot* (1877).

CABOT, GODFREY LOWELL 1861–1962, manufacturer, inventor
Harris, Leon A., *Only to God: Godfrey Lowell Cabot* (1967).

CAIN, JAMES M. 1892– , novelist
Madden, David, *James M. Cain* (1970).

CALDER, ALEXANDER, 1898– , sculptor
Arnason, H. Harvard, *Calder* (1966).
Calder, Alexander, *Autobiography* (1966).
Sweeney, James J., *Alexander Calder* (1951).

CALDWELL, CHARLES 1772–1853, southern medical educator
Caldwell, Charles, *Autobiography*, H. W. Warner, ed. (1855).

CALDWELL, ERSKINE 1903– , southern writer
Caldwell, Erskine, *Call It Experience* (1951)

CALHOUN, JOHN CALDWELL 1782–1850; South Carolina political leader
Boucher, Chauncy S., and R. P. Brooks, ed., *Correspondence Addressed to Calhoun, 1837–1849* (1930).
Calhoun, John C., *Basic Documents*, John M. Anderson, ed. (1952).
―――― *Papers*, Robert L. Meriwether and W. Edwin Hemphill, eds., vols. 1/5– , 1959/71– .
―――― *Works*, R. K. Crallé, ed. (6 vols., 1853–1855; repr. 1968).
Capers, Gerald M., *John C. Calhoun—Opportunist* (1960).
Coit, Margaret L., *John C. Calhoun* (1950).
Current, Richard N., ed., *John C. Calhoun* (1963).
Spain, August O., *Political Theory of Calhoun* (1951).
Thomas, John L., ed., *John C. Calhoun* (1968).
Wiltse, Charles M., *John C. Calhoun* (3 vols., 1944–1951).

CALL, RICHARD KEITH 1791–1862, lawyer, politician
Doherty, Herbert J., Jr., *Richard K. Call: Southern Unionist* (1961).

CALVERT, GEORGE 1580–1632; Maryland proprietor
Browne, William H., *George Calvert and Cecilius Calvert, Barons of Baltimore* (1890).

CAMERON, SIMON 1799–1889, Lincoln's secretary of war
Bradley, Erwin S., *Simon Cameron, Lincoln's Secretary of War* (1966).

CAMPBELL, ALEXANDER 1788–1866, founder of Disciples of Christ
Campbell, Alexander, *Memoirs*, Robert Richardson, ed. (2 vols., 1868–1870).
Eames, S. Morris, *Philosophy of Alexander Campbell* (1966).

CAMPBELL, GEORGE WASHINGTON 1769–1848, Tennessee political leader
Jordan, Weymouth T., *George Washington Campbell of Tennessee* (1955).

CAMPBELL, JOHN ARCHIBALD 1811–1889, Supreme Court justice
Connor, Henry G., *John Archibald Campbell* (1920).

CANBY, EDWARD RICHARD SPRIGG 1817–1873, Union soldier
Heyman, Max L., Jr., *Prudent Soldier: Major General E. R. S. Canby* (1959).

CANDLER, ASA GRIGGS 1851–1929, Georgia manufacturer, philanthropist
Candler, Charles H., *Asa Griggs Candler* (1950).

CANDLER, WARREN AKIN 1857–1941, Methodist bishop
Pierce, Alfred M., *Giant against the Sky: Bishop Warren Akin Candler* (1948).

CANNON, JAMES, JR. 1864–1944, Methodist bishop, prohibitionist
Cannon, James, Jr., *Bishop Cannon's Own Story*, Richard L. Watson, Jr., ed. (1955).
Dabney, Virginius, *Dry Messiah: The Life of Bishop Cannon* (1949).

CANNON, JOSEPH GURNEY 1836–1926, Speaker of the House
Busbey, L. W., *Uncle Joe Cannon* (1927).
Gwinn, William R., *Uncle Joe Cannon* (1957).

CANNON, WALTER BRADFORD 1871–1945, physiologist
Cannon, Walter B., *Way of an Investigator: A Scientist's Experiences in Medical Research* (1945).

CAPPER, ARTHUR 1865–1951, publisher, Kansas senator
Socolofsky, Homer E., *Arthur Capper: Publisher, Politician, and Philanthropist* (1962).

CARDOZO, BENJAMIN NATHAN 1870–1938, Supreme Court justice
Cardozo, Benjamin N., *Selected Writings*, Margaret E. Hall, ed. (1947).
Hellman, George S., *Benjamin N. Cardozo* (1940).
Levy, Beryl H., *Cardozo and Frontiers of Legal Thinking* (rev. ed., 1969).
Pollard, Joseph P., *Mr. Justice Cardozo* (1935).

CARDOZO, JACOB NEWTON 1786–1873, southern free-trader
Leiman, Melvin M., *Jacob N. Cardozo: Economic Thought in Antebellum South* (1966).

CAREY, HENRY CHARLES 1793–1879, economist
Elder, William, *Memoir of Henry C. Carey* (1880).
Green, Arnold W., *Henry Charles Carey, Nineteenth Century Sociologist* (1951).
Smith, George W., *Henry C. Carey and American Sectional Conflict* (1951).

CAREY, MATHEW 1760–1839, publisher, economist
Bradsher, E. L., *Mathew Carey* (1912).
Rowe, K. W., *Mathew Carey, a Study in American Economic Development* (1933).

CARLISLE, JOHN GRIFFIN 1835–1910, Kentucky senator, Secretary of Treasury
Barnes, J. A., *Carlisle* (1931).

CARNEGIE, ANDREW 1835–1919, manufacturer, philanthropist
Carnegie, Andrew, *Autobiography*, J. C. Van Dyke, ed. (1920).
—— *Gospel of Wealth and Other Essays* (1890). Edward C. Kirkland, ed. (1962).
Hacker, Louis M., *World of Andrew Carnegie, 1865–1901* (1968).
Hendrick, B. J., *The Life of Andrew Carnegie* (2 vols., 1932).
Wall, Joseph Frazier, *Andrew Carnegie* (1970).

CARPENTER, MATTHEW HALE 1824–1881, Wisconsin senator
Thompson, E. Bruce, *Matthew Hale Carpenter* (1954).

CARR, EUGENE ASA 1830–1910, frontier general
  King, James T., *War Eagle: General Eugene A. Carr* (1963).
CARR, WILBUR JOHN 1870–1942, Assistant Secretary of State
  Crane, Katherine, *Mr. Carr of State* (1960).
CARROLL, CHARLES 1737–1832; Revolutionary leader
  Carroll, Charles, *Unpublished Letters*, Thomas M. Field, ed. (1902).
  Rowland, K. M., *Life of Charles Carroll of Carrollton, 1737–1832, with His
    Correspondence and Public Papers* (2 vols., 1898).
  Smith, Ellen H., *Charles Carroll of Carrollton* (1942).
CARROLL, JOHN 1735–1815, Roman Catholic bishop
  Guilday, P. K., *Life and Times of John Carroll* (2 vols., 1922).
  Melville, Annabelle M., *John Carroll of Baltimore: Founder of American Catho-
    lic Hierarchy* (1955).
CARSON, CHRISTOPHER "KIT" 1809–1868, Western trapper, guide
  Blackwelder, Bernice, *Great Westerner: The Story of Kit Carson* (1962).
  Carson, Christopher, *Autobiography*, Milo M. Quaife, ed. (1966).
  Carter, Harvey L., *"Dear Old Kit:" The Historical Christopher Carson* (1968).
  Estergreen, M. Morgan, *Kit Carson* (1962).
  Sabin, E. L., *Kit Carson Days* (rev. ed., 2 vols., 1922).
CARSON, RACHEL L. 1907–1964, biologist
  Sterling, Philip, *Sea and Earth: Rachel Carson* (1970).
CARTER, LANDON 1710–1778, Virginia planter and leader
  Carter, Landon, *Diary*, Jack P. Greene, ed. (2 vols., 1965).
  Wineman, Walter R., *Landon Carter Papers: Calendar and Biographical Sketch*
    (1962).
CARTER, ROBERT 1663–1732, Virginia official, planter
  Carter, Robert, *Letters, 1720–1727,* Louis B. Wright, ed. (1940).
  Dowdey, Clifford, *Virginia Dynasties: "King" Carter and Golden Age* (1969).
CARTWRIGHT, PETER 1785–1872, Methodist clergyman
  Cartwright, Peter, *Autobiography* (1929).
CARVER, GEORGE WASHINGTON, 1864–1943, Negro scientist
  Elliott, Lawrence, *George Washington Carver* (1966).
  Holt, Rackham, *George Washington Carver* (1943).
CARVER, W. F. 1840–1927, originator of Wild West show
  Thorp, Raymond W., *Spirit Gun of the West: Doc W. F. Carver* (1957).
CASH, WILBUR JOSEPH 1901–1941, newspaperman
  Morrison, Joseph L., *W. J. Cash: Southern Prophet* (1967).
CASS, LEWIS 1782–1866, Michigan political leader, secretary of war
  McLaughlin, Andrew C., *Lewis Cass* (1899).
  Woodford, Frank B., *Lewis Cass: Last Jeffersonian* (1950).
CASSATT, MARY 1845–1926, artist
  Sweet, Frederick A., *Miss Mary Cassatt: Impressionist from Pennsylvania*
    (1966).
CATESBY, MARK 1679–1749, naturalist
  Frick, George F., and Raymond P. Stearns, *Mark Catesby: Colonial Audubon*
    (1961).
CATHER, WILLA 1873–1947, author
  Bennett, Mildred R., *World of Willa Cather* (rev. ed., 1961).
  Brown, Edward K., and Leon Edel, *Willa Cather* (1953).
  Lewis, Edith, *Willa Cather Living* (1953).
CATLIN, GEORGE 1796–1872, artist
  Catlin, George, *Episodes from Life among Indians*, Marvin C. Ross, ed. (1959).
  Catlin, George, *Letters*, Marjorie Catlin Roehm, ed. (1966). Includes diary of
    Francis Catlin.
  McCracken, Harold, *George Catlin and the Old Frontier* (1959).
CATT, CARRIE CHAPMAN 1859–1947, suffragette, reformer
  Peck, M. G., *Carrie C. Catt* (1944).
CAYTON, HORACE ROSCOE 1903–   , sociologist

Cayton, Horace R., *Long Old Road: An Autobiography* (1965).
CERMAK, ANTON JOSEPH 1873–1933, Chicago mayor
  Gottfried, Alex, *Boss Cermak of Chicago* (1962).
CHAMBERLAIN, JOSHUA LAWRENCE 1828–1914, general, Maine governor, Florida
  promoter
  Wallace, Willard M., *Soul of the Lion: General Joshua L. Chamberlain* (1960).
CHANDLER, WILLIAM EATON 1835–1917, New Hampshire senator
  Richardson, Leon B., *Chandler* (1940).
CHANDLER, ZACHARIAH 1813–1879, Michigan senator
  George, Mary K., *Zachariah Chandler: Political Biography* (1969).
  Harris, W. C., *Public Life of Zachariah Chandler, 1851–1875* (1917).
CHANNING, WILLIAM ELLERY 1780–1842, Unitarian clergyman
  Brown, Arthur W., *William Ellery Channing* (1961).
  Channing, William E., *Works* (one vol. ed., 1875).
  Edgell, David P., *William Ellery Channing* (1955).
  Rice, Madeleine H., *Federal Street Pastor: William Ellery Channing* (1961).
CHANNING, WILLIAM ELLERY II 1818–1901; transcendentalist nephew of William
  Ellery Channing
  McGill, Frederick T., Jr., *Channing of Concord: William Ellery Channing II*
  (1967).
CHAPIN, CHARLES VALUE 1856–1941, public health officer
  Cassedy, James H., *Charles V. Chapin and Public Health Movement* (1962).
CHAPLIN, CHARLES 1889–   , actor
  Chaplin, Charles, *My Autobiography* (1964).
  Huff, Theodore, *Charlie Chaplin* (1951).
CHAPMAN, FRANK M. 1864–1945, ornithologist
  Chapman, Frank M., *Journal and Letters*, Elizabeth S. Austin, ed. (1967).
CHAPMAN, JOHN 1775–1847, frontier character
  Price, Robert, *Johnny Appleseed* (1954).
CHAPMAN, JOHN JAY 1862–1933; essayist, poet
  Bernstein, Melvin H., *John Jay Chapman* (1964).
  Chapman, John J., *Memories and Milestones* (1915).
  ——— *Selected Writings* (1968).
  Hovey, Richard B., *John Jay Chapman* (1959).
  Howe, Mark A. De W., *John Jay Chapman and His Letters* (1937).
CHAPMAN, JOHN WILBUR 1859–1918; Presbyterian evangelist
  Ramsay, John C., *John Wilbur Chapman: The Man, His Methods and His
  Message* (1962).
CHARLESS, JOSEPH 1772–1834, editor, publisher
  Kaser, David, *Joseph Charless: Printer in Western Country* (1963).
CHASE, MARY ELLEN 1887–   , scholar and author
  Westbrook, Perry D., *Mary Ellen Chase* (1965).
CHASE, SALMON PORTLAND 1808–1873, Ohio politician, secretary of treasury
  Belden, Thomas G., and Marva R. Belden, *So Fell the Angels* (1956).
  Chase, Salmon P., *Inside Lincoln's Cabinet: Civil War Diaries*, David Donald,
  ed. (1954).
  Hart, Albert B., *Salmon P. Chase* (1899).
  Schuckers, J. W., *Life and Public Services of Salmon P. Chase* (1874).
CHAUNCY, CHARLES 1705–1787, Congregational clergyman
  Bernhard, Harold E., *Charles Chauncy: Colonial Liberal* (1948).
CHESNUTT, CHARLES WADDELL 1858–1932, writer
  Chesnutt, Helen M., *Charles Waddell Chesnutt: Pioneer of the Color Line*
  (1952).
CHEW, BENJAMIN 1722–1810, Pennsylvania jurist
  Konkle, Burton A., *Benjamin Chew, 1722–1810* (1932).
CHILD, LYDIA MARIA 1802–1880, abolitionist, writer
  Baer, Helene G., *Heart is Like Heaven: Lydia Maria Child* (1964).
  Child, Lydia M., *Letters*, H. W. Sewall, ed. (1883).

CHILDS, RICHARD SPENCER 1882–   ; city management reformer
  East, John P., *Council-Manager Government: Political Thought of Its Founder, Richard S. Childs* (1965).

CHOATE, JOSEPH HODGES 1832–1917, lawyer, diplomat
  Martin, Edward S., *Life of Joseph Hodges Choate* (2 vols., 1920).

CHOATE, RUFUS 1799–1859, lawyer, statesman
  Choate, Rufus, *Works: With a Memoir of His Life*, S. G. Brown, ed. (2 vols., 1862).
  Fuess, Claude M., *Rufus Choate: The Wizard of the Law* (1928).

CHOUART, MÉDARD ca. 1621–ca. 1698, fur trader, explorer
  Nute, G. L., *Caesars of the Wilderness: Médard Chouart and Pierre Esprit Radisson, 1618–1710* (1943).

CHRYSLER, WALTER PERCY 1875–1940, automobile manufacturer
  Chrysler, Walter P., and Boyden Sparkes, *Life of an American Workman* (1938).

CHURCH, WILLIAM CONANT 1836–1917, editor
  Bigelow, Donald N., *William Conant Church and the Army and Navy Journal* (1952).

CHURCHILL, WINSTON 1871–1947, American author
  Titus, Warren I., *Winston Churchill* (1963).

CLAIBORNE, WILLIAM CHARLES COLES 1775–1817, lawyer, governor of Louisiana Territory
  Claiborne, W. C. C., *Official Letter Books . . . 1801–1816,* Dunbar Rowland, ed. (6 vols., 1917).

CLAP, THOMAS 1703–1767, president of Yale University
  Tucker, Louis L., *Puritan Protagonist: President Thomas Clap of Yale College* (1962).

CLARK, CHAMP 1850–1921, Speaker of the House
  Clark, Champ, *My Quarter Century of American Politics* (2 vols., 1920).

CLARK, GEORGE ROGERS 1752–1818, frontier Revolutionary general
  Bakeless, John E., *Background to Glory: George Rogers Clark* (1957).
  Barnhart, J. D., *Henry Hamilton and George Rogers Clark* (1951).
  Clark, George R., "Papers, 1771–81," James A. James, ed., *Ill. Hist. Coll.,* 8 (1912); 19 (1926).
  James, James A., *Life of George Rogers Clark* (1928).

CLARK, WALTER 1846–1924, North Carolina jurist
  Brooks, Aubrey L., *Walter Clark: Fighting Judge* (1944).

CLARK, WILLIAM 1770–1838, explorer
  Clark, William, *Original Journals of the Lewis and Clark Expedition, 1804–06,* Reuben G. Thwaites, ed. (8 vols., 1904–1905).
  Cutright, Paul R., *Lewis and Clark* (1969).

CLARKE, JAMES FREEMAN 1810–1888, Unitarian clergyman
  Bolster, Arthur S., Jr., *James Freeman Clarke* (1954).
  Clarke, James F., *Autobiography, Diary and Correspondence*, E. E. Hale, ed. (1891).

CLARKE, JOHN HESSIN 1857–1945, Supreme Court justice
  Warner, Hoyt L., *Mr. Justice Clarke* (1959).

CLAY, CASSIUS MARCELLUS 1810–1903, Kentucky abolitionist
  Clay, Cassius M., *Life, Written and Compiled by Himself* (1886).
  Smiley, David L., *Lion of White Hall: Cassius M. Clay* (1962).

CLAY, HENRY 1777–1852, Kentucky senator
  Clay, Henry, *Papers, 1797–1824,* James F. Hopkins and Mary W. M. Hargreaves, eds. (3 vols., 1959–1963).
  ———— *Private Correspondence*, Calvin Colton, ed. (1855).
  Eaton, Clement, *Henry Clay and the Art of American Politics* (1957).
  Mayo, Bernard, *Henry Clay* (1937). Covers period to 1812.
  Poage, George R., *Clay and Whig Party* (1936).
  Van Deusen, Glyndon G., *The Life of Henry Clay* (1937).

CLAY, JOHN RANDOLPH 1808–1885, diplomat
  Oeste, George I., *John Randolph Clay: First Career Diplomat* (1966).
CLAY, LAURA 1849–1941, suffragette
  Goodman, Clavia, *Bitter Harvest: Laura Clay's Suffrage Work* (1946).
CLAY FAMILY
  Nuremberger, Ruth K., *The Clays of Alabama* (1958).
CLAYTON, JOHN 1685–1733, botanist
  Berkeley, Edmund, and Dorothy Berkeley, *John Clayton: Pioneer of American Botany* (1963).
  Clayton, John, *Scientific Writings and Related Papers*, Edmund and Dorothy Berkeley, eds. (1965).
CLAYTON, WILLIAM LOCKHART 1880–1966; state department official, businessman
  Garwood, Ellen Clayton, *Will Clayton: A Short Biography* (1958).
CLEAGE, ALBERT B., JR. 1911–   , black minister
  Ward, Hiley H., *Prophet of the Black Nation: Rev. Albert B. Cleage* (1969).
CLEMENS, SAMUEL LANGHORNE 1835–1910, author; Mark Twain, pseud.
  Brooks, Van Wyck, *Ordeal of Mark Twain* (2nd. ed., 1933).
  Budd, Louis J., *Mark Twain* (1962).
  DeVoto, Bernard, ed., *Mark Twain in Eruption* (1940).
  —— *Mark Twain's America* (1932).
  —— *Mark Twain at Work* (1942).
  Kaplan, Justin, *Mr. Clemens and Mark Twain* (1966).
  Lorch, Fred W., *Trouble Begins at Eight: Twain's Lecture Tours* (1968).
  Paine, Albert B., *Mark Twain* (3 vols., 1912; abridged, 1920).
  Smith, Henry Nash, *Mark Twain* (1962).
  Twain, Mark, *Autobiography*, Albert B. Paine, ed. (2 vols., 1924).
  —— *Letters*, Albert B. Paine, ed. (2 vols., 1917).
  —— and William D. Howells, *Correspondence, 1872–1910*, Henry Nash Smith and William M. Gibson, eds., (2 vols., 1960).
  —— *Selected Mark Twain-Howells Letters*, Frederick Anderson, William M. Gibson, and Henry Nash Smith, eds. (1967).
  Wecter, Dixon, *Sam Clemens of Hannibal* (1952).
CLEVELAND, GROVER 1837–1908, President
  Cleveland, Grover, *Letters* (1933).
  —— *Writings and Speeches* (1892).
  Merrill, Horace S., *Bourbon Leader: Grover Cleveland* (1957).
  Nevins, Allan, *Grover Cleveland: A Study in Courage* (1932).
  Tugwell, Rexford G., *Grover Cleveland* (1968).
CLINCH, DUNCAN LAMONT 1787–1849, Florida leader
  Patrick, Rembert W., *Aristocrat in Uniform: General Duncan L. Clinch* (1963).
CLINTON, DE WITT 1769–1828, New York politician, canal promoter
  Bobbé, Dorothie, *De Witt Clinton* (1933).
  Campbell, W. W., *Life and Writings of De Witt Clinton* (1933).
CLINTON, GEORGE 1739–1812, New York political leader
  Clinton, George, *Public Papers*, Hugh Hastings and J. A. Holden, eds. (10 vols., 1899–1914).
  Spaulding, Ernest W., *His Excellency George Clinton* (2nd ed., 1964).
COBB, HOWELL 1815–1868, Georgia lawyer, politician
  Johnson, Zachary T., *Political Policies of Howell Cobb* (1929).
  Montgomery, Horace, *Howell Cobb's Confederate Career* (1959).
COCKRAN, (WILLIAM) BOURKE 1854–1923, Tammany politician
  McGurrin, James, *Bourke Cockran* (1948).
CODDINGTON, WILLIAM 1601–1678, founder of Newport
  Turner, Henry E., *William Coddington* (1878).
CODY, WILLIAM FREDERICK "BUFFALO BILL" 1846–1917, scout, showman
  Cody, William F., *Adventures of Buffalo Bill* (1904) and *Story of Wild West* (1902).
  Russell, Don, *Lives and Legends of Buffalo Bill* (1960).
  Walsh, Richard J., *Making of Buffalo Bill* (1928).

COFFIN, HENRY SLOANE 1877–1954, clergyman
Noyes, Morgan P., *Henry Sloane Coffin* (1964).

COFFIN, LEVI 1789–1877, Indiana abolitionist
Coffin, Levi, *Reminiscences* (1876).

COFFIN, ROBERT PETER TRISTRAM 1892–1955, poet
Swain, Raymond C., *Breath of Maine: Robert P. Tristram Coffin* (1967).

COHAN, GEORGE MICHAEL 1878–1942, theatrical figure, song writer
Cohan, George M., *Twenty Years on Broadway* (1925).
Morehouse, Ward, *George M. Cohan* (1943).

COHEN, MORRIS RAPHAEL 1880–1947, philosopher
Cohen, Morris R., *American Thought*, Felix S. Cohen, ed. (1954).

COIT, JOSHUA 1758–1798, federalist
Destler, Chester M., *Joshua Coit: American Federalist, 1758–1798* (1962).

COKER FAMILY
Simpson, George L., *Cokers of Carolina* (1956).

COLDEN, CADWALLADER 1688–1776, Loyalist
Colden, Cadwallader, "Letters and Papers, 1711–1775," N. Y. Hist. Soc., *Coll.*, 50–56, vols. 67–68 (1936–1937).
Keys, Alice M., *Cadwallader Colden: Eighteenth Century Official* (1906).

COLE, THOMAS 1801–1848, artist
Noble, Louis L., *Life and Works of Thomas Cole* (1856). Elliot S. Vessel, ed., (1964).

COLFAX, SCHUYLER 1823–1885, vice-president
Smith, Willard H., *Schuyler Colfax* (1952).

COLLIER, JOHN 1884–1968, head of Indian Bureau
Collier, John, *From Every Zenith: A Memoir and Some Essays on Life and Thought* (1963).

COLLINS, ISAAC 1746–1817, newspaperman, publisher, bookseller
Hixson, Richard F., *Isaac Collins: Quaker Printer in 18th Century America* (1968).

COLMAN, BENJAMIN 1673–1747, Baptist clergyman
Colman, Benjamin, "Unpublished Letters, 1717–1725," Niel Caplan, ed., Mass. Hist. Soc., *Proc.*, 77 (1965), 101.

COLMAN, NORMAN JAY 1827–1911, the first secretary of agriculture
Lemmer, George F., *Norman J. Colman and Colman's Rural World* (1953).

COLT, SAMUEL 1814–1862, inventor, manufacturer
Edwards, William B., *Col. Samuel Colt* (1953).

COMMONS, JOHN R. 1862–1945, economist
Harter, Lafayette G., Jr., *John R. Commons* (1962).

COMSTOCK, ANTHONY 1844–1915, reformer
Broun, Heywood, and Margaret Leech, *Anthony Comstock, Roundsman of the Lord* (1927).
Comstock, Anthony, *Traps for the Young* (1883). Robert Bremner, ed. (1967).

CONANT, JAMES BRYANT 1893–   , president of Harvard University
Conant, James B. *My Several Lives* (1970).

CONANT, ROGER 1592–1679, Massachusetts settler
Shipton, C. K., *Roger Conant* (1944).

CONKLING, ROSCOE 1829–1888, New York senator
Chidsey, D. B., *The Gentleman from New York: A Life of Roscoe Conkling* (1935).
Conkling, A. R., *Life and Letters of Roscoe Conkling* (1889).
Jordan, David M., *Roscoe Conkling of New York* (1971).

CONNALLY, THOMAS TERRY 1877–1963, Texas senator
Connally, Thomas T., *My Name is Tom Connally* (1954). As told to Alfred Steinberg

CONRIED, HEINRICH 1855–1909, manager of Metropolitan Opera
Moses, M. J., *Life of Heinrich Conried* (1916).

CONWAY, MONCURE 1832–1907, author, clergyman
  Burtis, Mary E., *Moncure Conway* (1952).
  Conway, Moncure D., *Autobiography* (2 vols., 1904).
COOKE, JAY 1821–1905, financier
  Larson, Henrietta M., *Jay Cooke, Private Banker* (1936).
  Oberholtzer, E. P., *Jay Cooke, Financier of the Civil War* (2 vols., 1907).
COOKE, MORRIS LLEWELLYN 1872–1960, director of Rural Electrification Administration
  Trombley, Kenneth E., *Life and Times of a Happy Liberal: Morris Llewellyn Cooke* (1954).
COOKE, PHILIP ST. GEORGE 1809–1895, frontier army officer
  Young, Otis E., *The West of Philip St. George Cooke* (1955).
COOLIDGE, CALVIN 1872–1933, president
  Coolidge, Calvin, *Autobiography* (1929).
  ——— *Talkative President: Press Conferences*, Robert H. Ferrell and Howard H. Quint, eds.
  Fuess, Claude M., *Calvin Coolidge* (1940).
  Lathem, Edward C., *Meet Calvin Coolidge* (1960).
  McCoy, Donald R., *Calvin Coolidge* (1967).
  White, William A., *Puritan in Babylon: Calvin Coolidge* (1938).
COOLIDGE, WILLIAM DAVID 1873–   , physical chemist, developer of radiology
  Miller, John A., *Yankee Scientist—William David Coolidge* (1963).
COOPER, JAMES FENIMORE 1789–1851, author
  Cooper, James Fenimore, *Letters and Journals*, James F. Beard, ed. (6 vols., 1960–1968).
  ——— *Correspondence*, J. F. Cooper, ed. (2 vols., 1922).
  Ringe, Donald A., *James Fenimore Cooper* (1962).
  Spiller, Robert E., *Fenimore Cooper* (1931).
  Waples, Dorothy, *Whig Myth of James Fenimore Cooper* (1938).
COOPER, PETER 1791–1883, manufacturer, inventor, philanthropist
  Mack, Edward C., *Peter Cooper of New York* (1949).
  Nevins, Allan, *Abram S. Hewitt: With Some Account of Peter Cooper* (1935).
COOPER, THOMAS 1759–1839, scientist, educator
  Bell, Whitfield J., Jr., "Thomas Cooper as Professor of Chemistry at Dickinson College, 1811–1815," *J. Hist. Med.*, 8 (1953), 70.
  Malone, Dumas, *Public Life of Thomas Cooper, 1783–1839* (1926).
COPE, EDWARD DRINKER 1840–1897, zoologist, paleontologist
  Osborn, Henry F., *Cope, Master Naturalist* (1931).
  Plate, Robert, *Dinosaur Hunters: Marsh and Cope* (1964).
COPLAND, AARON 1900–   , composer
  Berger, Arthur V., *Aaron Copland* (1953).
  Smith, Julia, *Aaron Copland* (1955).
COPLEY, JOHN SINGLETON 1738–1815, artist
  Copley, John Singleton, and Henry Pelham, "Letters and Papers," Mass. Hist. Soc., *Coll.*, 71 (1914).
  Flexner, James T., *John Singleton Copley* (1948).
  Parker, Barbara N., and Anne B. Wheeler, *John Singleton Copley: American Portraits with Biographical Sketches* (1938).
  Plate, Robert, *John Singleton Copley: Artist* (1969).
  Prown, Jules D., *John Singleton Copley* (2 vols., 1966).
CORBETT, JAMES J. "Gentleman Jim" 1866–1933, pugilist
  Corbett, James J., *Roar of the Crowd* (1925).
CORBIN, DANIEL CHASE 1837–1918, railroad promoter in Northwest
  Fahey, John, *Inland Empire: D. C. Corbin and Spokane* (1965).
CORNELL, EZRA 1807–1874, capitalist, founder of Cornell University
  Dorf, Philip, *The Builder: Ezra Cornell* (1952).
CORNELL, KATHARINE 1898–   ; actress
  Cornell, Katharine, *I Wanted to Be an Actress* (1939).

CORNER, GEORGE WASHINGTON 1889–   , anatomist
Corner, George W., *Anatomist at Large: Autobiography and Essays* (1958).

CORNING, ERASTUS 1794–1872, merchant, financier
Neu, Irene D., *Erastus Corning: Merchant and Financier* (1960).

COTTON, JOHN 1584–1652, Puritan theologian
Emerson, Everett H., *John Cotton* (1965).
Ziff, Larzer, *The Career of John Cotton* (1962).

COTTRELL, FREDERICK GARDNER 1877–1948, chemist
Cameron, Frank, *Cottrell: Samaritan of Science* (1952).

COUDERT, FREDERICK RENÉ, 1871–1955, expert in international law
Coudert, Frederic R., *Half Century of International Problems: A Lawyer's Views*, Allan Nevins, ed. (1954).

COUGHLIN, CHARLES 1891–   ; Catholic priest, political leader
Tull, Charles J., *Father Coughlin and New Deal* (1965).

COUSINS, NORMAN 1912–   , editor
Cousins, Norman, *Present Tense: Editor's Odyssey* (1967).

COUZENS, JAMES 1872–1936, Michigan senator
Barnard, Harry, *Independent Man: Senator James Couzens* (1958).

COX, JAMES MIDDLETON 1870–1957, publisher, Ohio governor
Cox, James M., *Journey through My Years* (1946).

COX, SAMUEL SULLIVAN "SUNSET" 1824–1889, Ohio political leader
Lindsey, David, *"Sunset" Cox: Irrepressible Democrat* (1959).

COXE, TENCH 1755–1824, political economist
Hutcheson, Harold, *Tench Coxe* (1938).

CRABTREE, LOTTA 1847–1924, actress
Dempsey, David K., *Triumphs and Trials of Lotta Crabtree* (1968).

CRADDOCK, CHARLES E., See MARY N. MURFREE

CRAM, RALPH ADAMS 1863–1942, architect
Cram, Ralph A., *My Life in Architecture* (1936).

CRANE, HAROLD HART 1899–1932, poet
Horton, Philip, *Hart Crane* (1937).
Quinn, Vincent, *Hart Crane* (1963).
Unterecker, John, *Voyager: Hart Crane* (1969).
Weber, Brom, *Hart Crane* (1948).

CRANE, STEPHEN 1871–1900, author
Berryman, John, *Stephen Crane* (1950).
Cady, Edwin, *Stephen Crane* (1962).
Crane, Stephen, *Letters*, R. W. Stallman and Lillian Gilkes, eds. (1960).
Stallman, Robert W., *Stephen Crane* (1968).

CRANE, WINTHROP MURRAY 1853–1920, Massachusetts senator
Johnson, Carolyn W., *Winthrop Murray Crane: Republican Leadership, 1892–1920* (1967).

CRAPO, HENRY H. fl. 1855–1869, lumberman
Lewis, Martin D., *Lumberman from Flint: Henry H. Crapo, 1855–1869* (1958).

CRAWFORD, FRANCIS MARION 1854–1909, author
Elliott, Maud H., *My Cousin, F. Marion Crawford* (1934).
Pilkington, John, Jr., *F. Marion Crawford* (1964).

CRAWFORD, THOMAS 1813–1857, sculptor
Gale, Robert L., *Thomas Crawford* (1964).
Hicks, Thomas, *Thomas Crawford: Career, Character, and Works* (1858).

CRAWFORD, WILLIAM HARRIS 1772–1834, Georgia political leader, secretary of treasury
Green, Philip J., *William H. Crawford* (1965).

CRAZY HORSE ca. 1849–1877, Oglala chief
Sandoz, Mari, *Crazy Horse of the Oglalas* (1942).

CREEL, GEORGE 1876–1953, journalist, author
Creel, George, *Rebel at Large* (1947).

CRESAP, THOMAS ca. 1702–1790, Maryland frontiersman
Bailey, Kenneth P., *Thomas Cresap: Maryland Frontiersman* (1944).

CRÈVECOEUR, MICHAEL GUILLAUME JEAN DE 1735–1813, French-American writer
Philbrick, Thomas, *St. John De Crèvecoeur* (1970).

CRILE, GEORGE WASHINGTON 1864–1943, surgeon
Crile, George W., *Autobiography* (2 vols., 1947).

CRITTENDEN, JOHN JORDAN 1787–1863, Kentucky senator
Coleman, Ann M. B., *Life of John J. Crittenden* (2 vols., 1871).
Kirwan, Albert D., *John J. Crittenden* (1962).

CROCKETT, DAVID 1786–1836, frontiersman
Crockett, David, *A Narrative . . . Written by Himself* (1834).
Shackford, James A., *David Crockett,* John B. Shackford, ed. (1956).

CROGHAN, GEORGE ? –1782, Indian trader, land speculator
Croghan, George, "Journal, 1759–1763," Nicholas B. Wainwright, ed., *Penn. Mag. Hist. Biog.,* 71 (1947), 303.
Volwiler, A. T., *George Croghan and the Westward Movement, 1741–82* (1926).
Wainwright, Nicholas B., *George Croghan: Wilderness Diplomat* (1959).

CROKER, RICHARD 1841–1922, Tammany boss
Stoddard, Theodore L., *Master of Manhattan* (1931).

CROLY, HERBERT DAVID 1869–1930, political philosopher
Forcey, Charles, *Crossroads of Liberalism: Croly Weyl, Lippman* (1961).

CROOK, GEORGE 1829–1890, frontier general
Crook, George, *Autobiography,* Martin F. Schmitt, ed. (new ed., 1960).

CROZET, CLAUDIUS 1790–1864, soldier, engineer
Couper, William, *Claudius Crozet* (1936).

CRUMP, EDWARD HULL ? –1954, Memphis boss
Miller, William D., *Mr. Crump of Memphis* (1964).

CUBBERLEY, ELLWOOD PATTERSON 1868–1941, professor of education
Sears, Jesse B., and Adin D. Henderson, *Cubberley of Stanford and American Education* (1957).

CULLEN, COUNTEE 1903–1946, Negro teacher, author
Ferguson, Blanche E., *Countee Cullen and the Negro Renaissance* (1966).

CULLEN, THOMAS STEPHEN 1868–1953, surgeon
Robinson, Judith, *Tom Cullen of Baltimore* (1949).

CULLINAN, JOSEPH STEPHEN 1860–1937, Texas oilman
King, John O., *Joseph Stephen Cullinan: A Study of Leadership in the Texas Petroleum Industry, 1897–1937* (1970).

CULLOM, SHELBY MOORE 1829–1914, Illinois senator
Cullom, S. M., *Fifty Years of Public Service: Personal Recollections* (1911).
Neilson, James W., *Shelby M. Cullom: Prairie State Republican* (1962).

CUMMINGS, EDWARD ESTLIN 1894–1962, poet
Marks, Barry A., *E. E. Cummings* (1963).

CURLEY, JAMES MICHAEL 1874–1958, Boston mayor, Massachusetts governor
Dinneen, J. F., *Purple Shamrock: Curley of Boston* (1949).

CURRIER, NATHANIEL 1813–1888, lithographic printer, publisher
Peters, Harry T., *Currier and Ives, Printmakers to the American People* (2 vols., 1925–1931).

CURRY, JABEZ LAMAR MONROE 1825–1903, educator in New South
Alderman, E. A., and A. C. Gordon, *J. L. M. Curry* (1911).

CURRY, JOHN STEUART 1897–1946, painter
Schmeckebier, Laurence F., *John Steuart Curry's Pageant* (1943).

CURTIS, BENJAMIN ROBBINS 1809–1874, Supreme Court justice
Curtis, Benjamin R. [son], *Memoir of Benjamin Robbins Curtis, with Writings* (2 vols., 1879).

CURTIS, CHARLES 1860–1936, vice-president
Ewy, Marvin, *Charles Curtis of Kansas: Vice-President of the United States, 1929–1933* (1961).

CURTIS, GEORGE WILLIAM 1824–1892, author, reformer
Cary, Edward, *George William Curtis* (1894).
Milne, Gordon, *George William Curtis and Genteel Tradition* (1956).

CURWEN, SAMUEL 1715–1802, Loyalist
Curwen, Samuel, *Journal and Letters*, G. A. Ward, ed. (1842).
———— *Journal of Samuel Curwin, Loyalist*, Andrew Oliver, ed. (1972).

CUSHING, CALEB 1800–1879, Massachusetts political leader
Fuess, Claude M., *Life of Caleb Cushing* (2 vols., 1923).
Hodgson, Sister Michael C., *Caleb Cushing: Attorney General, 1853–1857* (1955).

CUSHING, HARVEY 1869–1939, neurological surgeon
Thomson, Elizabeth H., *Harvey Cushing* (1950).
Fulton, John F., *Harvey Cushing* (1946).

CUSHMAN, CHARLOTTE SAUNDERS 1816–1876, actress
Stebbins, Emma, *Charlotte Cushman: Her Letters and Memories of Her Life* (1878).

CUSTER, GEORGE ARMSTRONG 1839–1876, frontier officer
Custer, George A., *My Life on the Plains* (1874).
———— and Elizabeth Custer, *Letters*, Marguerite A. Merington, ed. (1950).
Monaghan, Jay, *General George Armstrong Custer* (1959).

CUTLER, MANASSEH 1742–1823, Ohio land promoter
Cutler, William P., and Julia P. Cutler, *Life, Journals, and Correspondence of Rev. Manasseh Cutler* (2 vols., 1888).

CUTLER, ROBERT 1895– , banker, federal official
Cutler, Robert, *No Time for Rest* (1966).

DABNEY, THOMAS SMITH GREGORY 1798–1885, planter
Smedes, Susan D., *Memorials of a Southern Planter* (1887); Fletcher M. Green, ed. (1965).

DAGGETT, ROLLIN MALLORY 1831–1901, journalist
Weisenburger, Francis P., *Idol of the West: Rollin Mallory Daggett* (1965).

DALEY, RICHARD J. 1902– , Chicago mayor
Royko, Mike, *Boss: Richard J. Daley of Chicago* (1971).

DALLAS, ALEXANDER JAMES 1759–1817, secretary of treasury
Dallas, G. M., *Life and Writings of Alexander James Dallas* (1871).
Walters, Raymond, Jr., *Alexander James Dallas: Lawyer–Politician–Financier* (1943).

DALY, JOHN AUGUSTIN 1838–1899, playwright
Daly, J. F., *Life of Augustin Daly* (1917).
Felheim, Marvin, *Theatre of Augustin Daly: Late Nineteenth Century American Stage* (1956).

DAMROSCH, WALTER 1862–1950, conductor
Damrosch, Walter, *My Musical Life* (1923).

DANA, CHARLES ANDERSON 1819–1897, editor
Rosebault, C. J., *When Dana Was the Sun* (1931).
Stone, Candace, *Dana and the Sun* (1938).

DANA, JAMES DWIGHT 1813–1895, geologist, scientific explorer
Gilman, Daniel C., *The Life of James Dwight Dana, Scientific Explorer, Mineralogist, Geologist, Zoologist* (1899).

DANA, RICHARD HENRY, JR. 1815–1882, author, lawyer
Adams, Charles F., Jr., *Richard Henry Dana* (2 vols., 1890–1891).
Dana, Richard H., Jr., *Journal*, Robert F. Lucid, ed. (3 vols., 1968).
Gale, Robert L., *Richard Henry Dana* (1969).
Shapiro, Samuel, *Richard Henry Dana, Jr.* (1961).

DANCY, JOHN C. 1888– , leader of Detroit Urban League
Dancy, John C., *Sand against the Wind* (1966).

DANIEL, PETER VIVIAN 1784–1860, Supreme Court justice
Frank, John P., *Justice Daniel Dissenting: Peter V. Daniel* (1964).

DANIELS, JOSEPHUS 1862–1948, editor, secretary of navy

Cronon, E. David, *Josephus Daniels in Mexico* (1960).
Daniels, Josephus, *Cabinet Diaries, 1913–1921,* E. David Cronon, ed. (1963).
——— *Editor in Politics* (1941).
——— *Shirt-Sleeve Diplomat* (1947).
——— *Tar Heel Editor* (1939).
——— *Wilson Era* (2 vols., 1944–1946).
Kilpatrick, Carroll, *Roosevelt and Daniels: A Friendship in Politics* (1952).
Morrison, Joseph L., *Josephus Daniels* (1966).
DARROW, CLARENCE SEWARD 1857–1938, lawyer
Darrow, Clarence S., *My Life* (1932).
Ravitz, Abe C., *Clarence Darrow and American Literary Tradition* (1962).
DAVIDSON, GEORGE 1825–1911, geodist, geographer, astronomer
Lewis, Oscar, *George Davidson, Pioneer West Coast Scientist* (1954).
DAVIE, WILLIAM RICHARDSON 1756–1820, North Carolina governor
Robinson, Blackwell P., *William R. Davie* (1957).
DAVIES, SAMUEL 1723–1761, Presbyterian clergyman, president of the College of
New Jersey
Davies, Samuel, *Diary of Journey to England and Scotland, 1753–55,* George W.
Pilcher, ed. (1967).
DAVIS, CHARLES HENRY 1807–1877, Naval officer, scientist
Davis, Charles H., Jr., *Life of Charles Henry Davis* (1899).
DAVIS, DAVID 1815–1886, Illinois politician, Supreme Court justice
King, Willard L., *Lincoln's Manager: David Davis* (1960).
DAVIS, ELMER HOLMES 1890–1958, newspaperman
Burlingame, Roger, *Don't Let Them Scare You: Life of Elmer Davis* (1961).
DAVIS, HENRY WINTER 1817–1865, Maryland congressman
Steiner, B. C., *Life of Henry Winter Davis* (1916).
DAVIS, JAMES JOHN 1873–1947, secretary of labor, Pennsylvania senator
Davis, James John, *The Iron Puddler: My Life in the Rolling Mills and What
Came of It* (1922).
DAVIS, JEFFERSON 1808–1889, Confederate president
Davis, Jefferson, *Constitutionalist, His Letters, Papers, and Speeches,* Dunbar
Rowland, ed. (10 vols., 1923).
——— *Messages and Papers, 1861–1865,* James D. Richardson, ed. (2nd ed., 2
vols., 1966).
——— *Private Letters, 1823–1889,* Hudson Strode, ed. (1966).
Davis, Varina H., *Jefferson Davis* (2 vols., 1890).
McElroy, Robert M., *Jefferson Davis, the Unreal and The Real* (2 vols., 1937).
Patrick, Rembert W., *Jefferson Davis and His Cabinet* (1944).
Strode, Hudson, *Jefferson Davis* (3 vols., 1955–1964).
DAVIS, JOHN WILLIAM 1873–1955, lawyer, presidential candidate, diplomat
Huntley, Theodore A., *John W. Davis* (1924).
DAVIS, RICHARD HARDING 1864–1915, journalist
Davis, Richard Harding, *Adventures and Letters,* C. B. Davis, ed. (1917).
Langford, Gerald, *Richard Harding Davis Years* (1961).
DAVIS, WESTMORELAND 1859–1942, Virginia governor
Kirby, Jack T., *Westmoreland Davis: Virginia Planter-Politician* (1968).
DAVIS, WILLIAM HEATH 1822–1909, California pioneer
Rolle, Andrew F., *American in California: William Heath Davis* (1956).
DAVISON, HENRY P. 1867–1922, financier
Lamont, Thomas William, *Henry P. Davison* (1933).
DAWES, CHARLES GATES 1865–1951, vice-president
Dawes, Charles G., *Journal* (1950).
Timmons, Bascom N., *Charles G. Dawes* (1953).
DAY, WILLIAM RUFUS 1849–1923, Supreme Court justice
McLean, Joseph E., *William Rufus Day: Supreme Court Justice from Ohio*
(1946).
DEANE, SILAS 1737–1789, member of Continental Congress, diplomat
Clark, George L., *Silas Deane* (1913).

DE BOW, JAMES DUNWOODY BROWNSON 1820–1867, editor
Skipper, Ottis C., *J. D. B. De Bow: Magazinist of Old South* (1958).

DEBS, EUGENE VICTOR 1855–1926, socialist leader
Debs, Eugene V., *Writings and Speeches*, Arthur M. Schlesinger, Jr., ed. (1948).
Ginger, Ray, *The Bending Cross: Debs* (1949).
Karsner, Davis, *Debs: His Authorized Life and Letters* (1919).
Morgan, H. Wayne, *Eugene V. Debs: Socialist for President* (1962).

DE CHEVERUS, JEAN LEFÉBVRE 1768–1836, Catholic priest
Melville, Annabelle M., *Jean Lefébvre De Cheverus* (1958).

DE FOREST, JOHN WILLIAM 1826–1906, Union officer, novelist
De Forest, John W., *Union Officer in Reconstruction*, James H. Croushore and David M. Potter, eds. (1948).
Light, James F., *John William De Forest* (1965).

DE FOREST, LEE 1873–1961, pioneer radio inventor
Carneal, Georgette, *Conqueror of Space: DeForest* (1930).
De Forest, Lee, *Father of Radio: Autobiography* (1950).

DE KOONING, WILLEM 1904–   , artist
Hess, Thomas B., *Willem de Kooning* (1969).

DE LEON, DANIEL 1852–1914, socialist leader
Daniel De Leon, The Man and His Work: A Symposium (1920).

DENNIE, JOSEPH 1768–1812, Federalist essayist
Dennie, Joseph, "Letters . . . 1768–1812," L. G. Pedder, ed., Univ. of Maine, *Studies*, 37 (1936).
Ellis, Harold M., *Joseph Dennie and His Circle* (1915).

DEPEW, CHAUNCEY MITCHELL 1834–1928, railway president, New York senator
Depew, Chauncey M., *My Memories of Eighty Years* (1922).
——— *Orations, Addresses, and Speeches*, J. D. Champlin, ed. (8 vols., 1910).

DERBY, GEORGE HORATIO 1823–1861, humorist; John Phoenix, pseud.
Stewart, George R., *John Phoenix, Esq.* (1937).

DERBY, RICHARD 1712–1783, Salem merchant
Phillips, James Duncan, *Life and Times of Richard Derby, Merchant of Salem, 1712 to 1783* (1929).

DE SMET, PIERRE-JEAN 1801–1873, missionary, explorer, pioneer
De Smet, Pierre-Jean, *Life, Letters and Travels* (4 vols., 1905).
Terrell, John U., *Black Robe: Pierre-Jean De Smet—Missionary* (1964).

DEVOTO, BERNARD AUGUSTINE 1897–1955, magazine editor, historian, author
Bowen, Catherine D. et al., *Four Portraits and One Subject: Bernard DeVoto* (1963).
Sawey, Orlan, *Bernard DeVoto* (1969).

DEWEY, GEORGE 1837–1917, admiral in Spanish-American War
Dewey, George, *Autobiography* (1913).

DEWEY, JOHN 1859–1952, philosopher
Edman, Irwin, *John Dewey: Contributions to American Tradition* (1955).
Geiger, George R., *John Dewey in Perspective* (1958).

DEWEY, THOMAS EDMUND 1902–1971, New York governor
Walker, Stanley, *Dewey* (1944).

DICKINSON, ANNA ELIZABETH 1842–1932, actress, abolitionist orator
Chester, Giraud, *Embattled Maiden: Anna Dickinson* (1951).

DICKINSON, EMILY 1830–1886, poet
Dickinson, Emily, *Letters*, Thomas H. Johnson, ed. (3 vols., 1958).
——— *Selected Letters*, Thomas H. Johnson, ed. (one vol. ed., 1971).
Dickinson, Emily, *Letters*, M. L. Todd, ed. (1937).
Higgins, David J., *Portrait of Emily Dickinson* (1967).
Johnson, Thomas H., *Emily Dickinson* (1955).
Whicher, G. F., *This Was a Poet* (1938).

DICKINSON, JOHN 1732–1808, Revolutionary leader
Colburn, H. Trevor, "John Dickinson," *Penn. Mag. Hist. Biog.*, (1959), 271.

Dickinson, John, *Writings*, Paul L. Ford, ed. (1895).
Jacobson, David L., *John Dickinson and Revolution in Pennsylvania* (1965).
Stillé, C. J., *Life and Times of John Dickinson* (1891).

DIRKSEN, EVERETT MC KINLEY 1896–1969, Illinois senator
McNeil, Neil, *Dirksen: Portrait of a Public Man* (1971).

DISNEY, WALTER ELIA 1901–1968, motion picture producer
Schickel, Richard, *Disney Version: Life, Times, Art and Commerce of Walt Disney* (1968).

DIVINE, FRANK H. 1865–1941, clergyman
Harris, Sara, *Father Divine, Holy Husband* (1953).

DIX, DOROTHEA 1802–1887, humanitarian
Marshall, Helen E., *Dorothea Dix: Forgotten Samaritan* (1937).

DIX, JOHN ADAMS 1798–1879, New York political leader
Dix, Morgan, *Memoirs of John Adams Dix* (2 vols., 1883).

DIXON, THOMAS 1864–1946, author, clergyman
Cook, Raymond A., *Fire from Flint: Thomas Dixon* (1968).

DOBBS, ARTHUR 1689–1765, North Carolina governor
Clarke, Desmond, *Arthur Dobbs, Governor of North Carolina* (1957).

DOCK, CHRISTOPHER ca. 1698–1771, Mennonite schoolmaster
Brumbaugh, Martin G., *Life and Works of Christopher Dock* (1908).

DODD, WILLIAM EDWARD 1869–1940, scholar, diplomat
Dallek, Robert, *Democrat and Diplomat: William E. Dodd* (1968).
Dodd, William E., *Ambassador Dodd's Diary, 1933–1938*, William E. Dodd, Jr. and Martha Dodd, eds. (1941).

DODGE, GRENVILLE MELLEN 1831–1916, railroad promoter
Farnham, Wallace D., "Grenville Dodge and Union Pacific: Study of Historical Legends," *JAH*, 51 (1965), 632.
Hirshson, Stanley P., *Grenville M. Dodge: Soldier, Politician, Railroad Pioneer* (1967).

DODGE, WILLIAM EARL 1805–1883, merchant, philanthropist
Lowitt, Richard, *Merchant Prince of Nineteenth Century: William E. Dodge* (1954).

DOE, CHARLES 1830–1896; New Hampshire jurist
Reid, John P., *Chief Justice: Charles Doe* (1967).

DOLE, SANFORD B. 1844–1926, Hawaii jurist, political leader
Damon, Ethel M., *Sanford B. Dole and His Hawaii* (1957).
Dole, Sanford B., *Memoirs of Hawaiian Revolution* (1936).

DOLLIVER, JONATHAN PRENTISS 1858–1910, Iowa senator
Ross, Thomas R., *Jonathan Prentiss Dolliver* (1958).

DONNELLY, IGNATIUS 1831–1901, Populist leader
Ridge, Martin, *Ignatius Donnelly: Politician* (1962).

DONOVAN, JAMES B. 1916–1970, lawyer
Donovan, James B., *Challenges: Reflections of a Lawyer-at-large* (1967).

DONOVAN, WILLIAM JOSEPH "WILD BILL" 1883–1959, director of Office of Strategic Services
Ford, Corey, *Donovan of O.S.S.* (1970).

DORR, THOMAS WILSON 1805–1854, politician, reformer
King, Dan, *Life and Times of Thomas Wilson Dorr* (1859).

DOS PASSOS, JOHN 1896–1970, writer
Wrenn, John H., *John Dos Passos* (1961).

DOSTER, FRANK 1847–1933, Kansas judge
Brodhead, Michael J., *Persevering Populist: Frank Doster* (1969).

DOUGLAS, STEPHEN ARNOLD 1813–1861, Illinois senator
Capers, Gerald M., *Stephen A. Douglas: Defender of the Union* (1959).
Douglas, Stephen A., *Letters*, Robert W. Johannsen, ed. (1961).
Milton, George F., *The Eve of Conflict: Stephen A. Douglas and the Needless War* (1934).

DOUGLASS, FREDERICK 1817–1895, Negro abolitionist
Douglass, Frederick, *Life and Writings*, Philip S. Foner, ed. (4 vols., 1950–1955).
—— *Narrative of the Life of an American Slave* (1845). Benjamin Quarles, ed. (1960).
Foner, Philip S., *Frederick Douglass* (1964).
Graham, Shirley, *There Was Once a Slave: Frederick Douglass* (1947).
Quarles, Benjamin, *Frederick Douglass* (1948).
Washington, Booker T., *Frederick Douglass* (1907).

DOW, HERBERT HENRY 1866–1930, chemical manufacturer
Campbell, Murray, and Harrison Hatton, *Herbert H. Dow: Pioneer in Creative Chemistry* (1951).

DOW, LORENZO 1777–1834, evangelist
Sellers, Charles C., *Lorenzo Dow* (1928).

DOW, NEAL 1804–1897, prohibition leader
Byrne, Frank L., *Prophet of Prohibition: Neal Dow* (1961).
Dow, Neal, *Reminiscences* (1898).

DRAKE, DANIEL 1785–1852, medical educator
Drake, Daniel, *Physician to the West: Selected Writings on Science and Society*, Henry D. Shapiro and Zane L. Miller, eds. (1970).
—— *Pioneer Life in Kentucky: Letters*, C. M. Drake, ed. (1870).
Horine, Emmet F., *Daniel Drake: Pioneer Physician* (1961).
Mansfield, Edward D., *Memoirs of the Life and Services of Daniel Drake, M.D.* (1855).

DRAPER, JOHN WILLIAM 1811–1882, scientist, philosopher of science, historian
Fleming, Donald, *John William Draper and the Religion of Science* (1950).

DRAPER, LYMAN COPELAND 1815–1891, historian
Hesseltine, William B., *Pioneer's Mission: Lyman Copeland Draper* (1954).

DRAYTON, WILLIAM 1742–1779, Revolutionary leader
Dabney, William M., and Marion Dargan, *William Drayton and American Revolution* (1962).

DREISER, THEODORE 1871–1945, novelist
Dreiser, Helen, *My Life with Dreiser* (1951).
Dreiser, Theodore, *A Book about Myself* (1922).
—— *Letters*, Robert H. Elias, ed. (3 vols., 1959).
—— *A Traveler at Forty* (1913).
Elias, Robert H., *Theodore Dreiser, Apostle of Nature* (1949).
Gerber, Philip L., *Theodore Dreiser* (1963).
Lehan, Richard D., *Theodore Dreiser: His World and His Novels* (1969).
Matthiessen, F. O., *Theodore Dreiser* (1951).

DREW, JOHN 1853–1927, actor
Drew, John, *My Years on the Stage* (1922).

DUANE, JAMES 1733–1797, Revolutionary jurist
Alexander, Edward P., *Revolutionary Conservative: James Duane of New York* (1938).

DUBOIS, WILLIAM EDWARD BURGHARDT 1868–1963, Negro leader, historian
Broderick, Francis L., *W. E. B. Dubois* (1959).
Du Bois, W. E. B., *Autobiography*, Herbert Aptheker, ed. (1968).
Rudwick, Elliott M., *W. E. B. DuBois: Propagandist of the Negro Protest* (2nd ed., 1969).

DUCHESNE, ROSE PHILIPPINE 1769–1852, pioneer missionary
Callan, Louise, *Philippine Duchesne: Frontier Missionary* (1957; abridged ed., 1965).

DUDLEY, JOSEPH 1647–1720, Massachusetts governor
Kimball, Everett, *The Public Life of Joseph Dudley* (1911).

DUKE, JAMES BUCHANAN 1856–1925, tobacco manufacturer
Jenkins, John W., *James B. Duke, Master Builder* (1927).
Winkler, John K., *Tobacco Tycoon: James Buchanan Duke* (1942).

DULANY FAMILY
Land, Aubrey C., *The Dulanys of Maryland: Daniel Dulany the Elder (1685–1753) and Daniel Dulany the Younger (1722–1797)* (1955).

DULLES, JOHN FOSTER 1888–1959, Secretary of State
Beal, John R., *John Foster Dulles* (1957).
Gerson, Louis L., *John Foster Dulles* (1968).

DUNBAR, PAUL LAURENCE 1872–1906, Negro poet
Brawley, Benjamin G., *Paul Laurence Dunbar* (1936).

DUNCAN, ISADORA 1878–1927, dancer
Schneider, Ilya I., *Isadora Duncan: Russian Years*, David Magarshack, trans. (1969).
Duncan, Isadora, *My Life* (1927).
Terry, Walter, *Isadora Duncan* (1964).

DUNGLISON, ROBLEY 1798–1869, medical educator
Dunglison, Robley, *Autobiography*, Samuel X. Radbill, ed. (1963).

DUNLAP, WILLIAM 1766–1839, playwright
Canary, Robert H., *William Dunlap* (1970).

DUNNE, FINLEY PETER 1867–1936, humorist
Ellis, Elmer, *Mr. Dooley's America: Finley Peter Dunne* (1941).

DU PONT, ALFRED IRÉNÉE 1864–1935, banker
James, Marquis, *Alfred I. Du Pont* (1941).

DU PONT, ELEUTHÈRE IRÉNÉE 1771–1834, manufacturer
Du Pont, B. D., *Life of Eleuthere Irénée Du Pont* (12 vols., 1923–1926).

DU PONT [DE NEMOURS], PIERRE SAMUEL 1739–1817, French publisher and physiocrat, first of the American Du Ponts

Jefferson, Thomas, and Pierre S. Du Pont de Nemours, *Correspondence*, Gilbert Chinard, ed. (1931). A less complete collection, but with the French letters translated into English, Dumas Malone, ed. (1930).
Saricks, Ambrose, *Pierre Samuel Du Pont de Nemours* (1965).

DU PONT, SAMUEL FRANCIS 1803–1865, naval officer
Du Pont, Henry A., *Rear-Admiral Samuel Francis Du Pont* (1926).
Du Pont, Samuel F., *Civil War Letters*, John D. Hayes, ed. (3 vols., 1969).

DU PONT FAMILY
Carr, William, *Du Ponts of Delaware* (1964).
Dorian, Max, *Du Ponts* (1962).
Winkler, John K., *Du Pont Dynasty* (1935).

DUPORTAIL, LOUIS LEBEQUE 1743–1802, Revolutionary officer
Kite, Elizabeth S., *Brigadier General Louis L. Duportail* (1933).

DURAND, ASHER BROWN 1796–1886, engraver, painter
Durand, John, *Life and Times of A. B. Durand* (1894).

DURANG, JOHN fl. 1785–1816, actor
Durang, John, *Memoir*, Alan S. Downer, ed. (1966).

DUUS, OLAUS F. fl. 1855–1858, Norwegian clergyman
Duus, Olaus F., *Letters, 1855–1858*, Theodore C. Blegen, ed. (1947).

DUVENECK, FRANK 1848–1919, painter, etcher, teacher
Heermann, Norman, *Frank Duveneck* (1918).

DWIGHT, TIMOTHY 1752–1817, president of Yale University
Cunningham, Charles E., *Timothy Dwight, 1752–1817* (1942).
Dwight, Timothy, *Travels in New England and New York* [1796–1815], Barbara M. Solomon, ed. (4 vols., 1969).
Silverman, Kenneth, *Timothy Dwight* (1969).

EADS, JAMES BUCHANAN 1820–1887, bridge builder
How, Louis, *James B. Eads* (1900).

EAKINS, THOMAS 1844–1916, artist
Goodrich, Lloyd, *Thomas Eakins* (1933).
Schendler, Sylvan, *Eakins* (1967).

EARL(E), RALPH 1751–1801, painter
Goodrich, Lawrence B., *Ralph Earl: Recorder for an Era* (1967).

EARLY, JUBAL ANDERSON 1816–1894, Confederate general
Early, Jubal A., *Autobiographical Sketch* (1912).

EASTMAN, GEORGE 1854–1932, inventor and manufacturer of photographic equipment
Ackerman, C. W., *George Eastman* (1930).

EASTMAN, JOSEPH BARTLETT 1882–1944, public official, railroad expert
Eastman, Joseph B., *Selected Papers and Addresses, 1942–44* (1948).
Fuess, Claude M., *Joseph B. Eastman* (1952).

EASTMAN, MAX 1883–   , writer
Cantor, Milton, *Max Eastman* (1970).
Eastman, Max, *Love and Revolution: My Journey Through an Epoch* (1965).

EASTMAN, SETH 1808–1875, western painter
McDermott, John F., *Seth Eastman: Pictorial Historian of the Indian* (1961).

EATON, AMOS 1776–1842, geologist, founder of Rennselaer Polytechnic Institute
McAllister, Ethel M., *Amos Eaton, Scientist and Educator* (1941).
Rezneck, Samuel, "Amos Eaton, 'Old Schoolmaster'," *N.Y. Hist.*, 39 (1958), 165.

EATON, MARGARET L. O'NEALE 1796–1879, wife of William Eaton
Eaton, Margaret L., *Autobiography of Peggy Eaton* (1932).
Pollack, Queena, *Peggy Eaton* (1931).

EATON, WILLIAM 1764–1811, diplomat, general
Edwards, S., *Barbary General: The Life of William Eaton* (1967).

ECCLES, MARRINER STODDARD 1890–   , banker, public official, economist
Eccles, Marriner S., *Beckoning Frontiers* (1951).

EDDY, MARY BAKER 1821–1910, founder of the Church of Christ, Scientist
Dakin, Edwin F., *Mrs. Eddy* (rev. ed., 1930).
Eddy, Mary Baker, *Retrospection* (1891).
Peel, Robert, *Mary Baker Eddy* (1966).

EDISON, THOMAS ALVA 1847–1931, inventor
Josephson, Matthew, *Edison* (1959).
Silverberg, Robert, *Light for the World: Edison and the Power Industry* (1967).

EDSALL, DAVID LINN 1869–1945
Aub, Joseph C., and Ruth K. Hapgood, *Pioneer in Modern Medicine: David Linn Edsall of Harvard* (1970).

EDWARDS, JONATHAN 1703–1758, Congregational theologian
Davidson, Edward H., *Jonathan Edwards* (1968).
Edwards, Jonathan, *Collected Writings*, Vergilius Ferm, ed. (1953).
——— *Freedom of the Will*, Paul Ramsey, ed. (1957).
——— *Works* (8 vols., 1806–1811).
Faust, C. H., and T. H. Johnson, eds., *Jonathan Edwards* (1935).
Miller, Perry, *Jonathan Edwards* (1949).
Winslow, Ola E., *Jonathan Edwards* (1940).

EDWARDS, NINIAN 1775–1833; Illinois Territory governor
Edwards, Ninian W., *Life and Times of Ninian Edwards* (1870).

EGGLESTON, EDWARD 1837–1902, writer
Eggleston, George C., *TheFirst of the Hoosiers: Reminiscences of Edward Eggleston* (1903).
Randel, William P., *Edward Eggleston* (1946).

EINSTEIN, ALBERT 1879–1955, mathematician, physicist
Clark, Ronald W., *Einstein: Life and Times* (1971).
Einstein, Albert, *Out of My Later Years* (1967).
Forsee, Aylesa, *Albert Einstein* (1963).
Frank, Philipp, *Einstein* (1953).

EINSTEIN, LEWIS 1877–1949, diplomat
Einstein, Lewis, *Diplomat Looks Back*, Lawrence E. Gelfand, ed. (1968).
Holmes, Oliver W., and Lewis Einstein, *Correspondence, 1903–1935*, James B. Peabody, ed. (1964).

EISENHOWER, DWIGHT DAVID 1890–1969, World War II commander, president
Ambrose, Stephen E., *Supreme Commander: War Years of Eisenhower* (1970).

Childs, Marquis W., *Eisenhower: Captive Hero* (1958).
Eisenhower, Dwight D., *Crusade in Europe* (1948).
—— *Papers: War Years*, Alfred D. Chandler, Jr. et al., eds. (5 vols., 1970).
—— *Peace with Justice: Selected Addresses* (1961).
—— *Public Papers* (8 vols., 1958–1961).
—— *White House Years* (2 vols., 1963–1965).
Hughes, Emmet J., *Ordeal of Power: Eisenhower Years* (1963).
Larson, Arthur, *Eisenhower* (1968).
Summersby, Kathleen, *Eisenhower* (1948).

ELIOT, CHARLES 1859–1897, architect
Eliot, Charles W., *Charles Eliot, Landscape Architect* (1902).

ELIOT, CHARLES WILLIAM 1834–1926, president of Harvard University
Hawkins, Hugh, "Charles W. Eliot, 1869–1909," *JAH*, 51 (1964), 191.
James, Henry, *Charles W. Eliot* (2 vols., 1930).
Neilson, W. A., *Charles W. Eliot: The Man and His Beliefs* (2 vols., 1926).

ELIOT, JARED 1685–1763, Congregational minister, developer of iron ore
Thoms, Herbert, *Jared Eliot, Minister, Doctor, Scientist, and His Connecticut* (1967).

ELIOT, JOHN 1604–1690, missionary to Indians
Winslow, Ola E., *John Eliot, Apostle to Indians* (1968).

ELIOT, THOMAS STEARNS 1888–1965, poet, essayist, playwright
Headings, Philip R., *T. S. Eliot* (1964).
Matthiessen, F. O., *Achievement of T. S. Eliot* (2nd ed., 1947).

ELKINS, STEPHEN BENTON 1841–1911, West Virginia senator
Lambert, Oscar D., *Stephen Benton Elkins* (1955).

ELLET, CHARLES JR. 1810–1862, civil engineer
Lewis, Gene D., *Charles Ellet, Jr., Engineer, 1810–1862* (1968).

ELLICOTT, ANDREW 1754–1820, surveyor, mathematician
Mathews, Catharine V. C., *Andrew Ellicott, His Life and Letters* (1908).

ELLINGTON, EDWARD KENNEDY "DUKE" 1899– , musician
Ulanov, Barry, *Duke Ellington* (1946).

ELLIOTT, MATTHEW fl. 1776–1812, British Indian agent
Horsman, Reginald, *Matthew Elliott, British Indian Agent* (1964).

ELLIS, JOHN WILLIS fl. 1841–1861, North Carolina governor
Ellis, John W., *Papers*, Noble J. Tolbert, ed. (2 vols., 1964).

ELLSWORTH, ELMER EPHRAIM 1837–1861, Civil War colonel
Randall, Ruth P., *Colonel Elmer Ellsworth: Lincoln's Friend* (1960).

ELLSWORTH, OLIVER 1745–1807, Connecticut senator
Brown, William G., *The Life of Oliver Ellsworth* (1905).

ELY, RICHARD T. 1854–1943, economist
Ely, Richard T., *Ground under Our Feet* (1938).
Rader, Benjamin G., *Academic Mind and Reform: Richard T. Ely* (1966).

EMERSON, RALPH WALDO 1803–1882, transcendentalist, essayist, poet
Cabot, James E., *Memoir of Ralph Waldo Emerson* (2 vols., 1887).
Emerson, Ralph Waldo, *Journals*, E. W. Emerson and W. E. Gorbes, eds. (10 vols, 1909–1914).
—— *Journals and Miscellaneous Notebooks*, William H. Gilman et al., eds., (vols. 1/9– , 1960/72–).
Porte, Joel, *Emerson and Thoreau: Transcendentalists in Conflict* (1966).
Rusk, Ralph L., *The Life of Ralph Waldo Emerson* (1949).
Whicher, Stephen E., *Freedom and Fate: Ralph Waldo Emerson* (1953).

EMMET, THOMAS ADDIS 1764–1827, Irish patriot, New York attorney general
Emmet, Thomas Addis, *Memoir of Thomas Addis and Robert Emmet* (2 vols., 1915).

ENDECOTT, JOHN 1589–1665, Massachusetts governor
Mayo, Lawrence S., *John Endecott: A Biography* (1936).

ENGLAND, JOHN 1786–1842, Catholic bishop of Charleston
Guilday, Peter K., *Life and Times of John England* (2 vols., 1927).

ERICSSON, JOHN 1803–1889, engineer, inventor
Church, W. C., *Life of John Ericsson* (2 vols., 1890).
White, Ruth, *Yankee from Sweden: Days of John Ericsson* (1960).

ERIKSON, ERIC H. 1902–   , psychoanalyst
Coles, Robert, *Achievement of Erik Erikson* (1970).

ERSKINE, ROBERT 1735–1780, geographer, hydraulic engineer
Heusser, Albert H., *The Forgotten General: Robert Erskine, Geographer* (1928).

EVANS, CHARLES 1850–1935, librarian, bibliographer
Holley, Edward G., *Charles Evans: Bibliographer* (1963).

EVANS, LEWIS 1700–1756, geographer
Gipson, Lawrence H., *Lewis Evans* (1939).

EVANS, OLIVER 1755–1819, steam engine builder
Bathe, Greville, and Dorothy Bathe, *Oliver Evans* (1935).

EVANS, ROBLEY DUNGLISON 1846–1912, naval officer
Falk, E. A., *"Fighting Bob" Evans* (1931).

EVANS, WILLIAM GRAY 1855–1924, Denver street railway executive
Breck, Allen D., *William Gray Evans, 1855–1924: Western Executive* (1964).

EVARTS, WILLIAM MAXWELL 1818–1901, lawyer, secretary of state
Barrow, Charles L., *William M. Evarts* (1941).
Dyer, Brainerd, *The Public Career of William M. Evarts* (1933).
Evarts, William M., *Arguments and Speeches*, Sherman Evarts, ed. (3 vols., 1919).

EVERETT, EDWARD 1794–1865, Massachusetts political leader, diplomat
Frothingham, Paul R., *Edward Everett, Orator and Statesman* (1925).

FAIRBANKS, DOUGLAS 1883–1939, motion picture actor
Hancock, Ralph, and Letitia Fairbanks, *Douglas Fairbanks* (1953).

FAIRCHILD, LUCIUS 1831–1896, Wisconsin governor, diplomat
Ross, Sam, *Empty Sleeve: Lucius Fairchild* (1964).

FAIRFAX, THOMAS, LORD 1693–1781, Virginia landholder
Brown, Stuart E., Jr., *Virginia Baron:Thomas 6th Lord Fairfax* (1965).

FARLEY, JAMES ALOYSIUS 1888–   , Democratic political leader
Farley, James A., *Behind the Ballots* (1938).
——— *Jim Farley's Story* (1948).

FARRAGUT, DAVID GLASGOW 1801–1870, Civil War admiral
Lewis, Charles L., *David Glasgow Farragut* (2 vols., 1941–1943).

FAULKNER, WILLIAM 1897–1962, novelist
Hoffman, Frederick J., *William Faulkner* (1960).
——— and O. W. Vickery, eds., *William Faulkner* (1951).
Howe, Irving, *William Faulkner* (1952).

FEKE, ROBERT ca. 1705–ca. 1750, portrait painter
Foote, Henry W., *Robert Feke* (1936).

FELTON, REBECCA (LATIMER) 1835–1930, Georgia feminist
Talmadge, John E., *Rebecca Latimer Felton* (1960).

FENWICK, EDWARD DOMINIC 1768–1832, Catholic bishop of Boston
O'Daniel, V. F., *The Right Rev. Edward Dominic Fenwick* (1920).

FENWICK, JOHN 1618–1683, founder of first Quaker settlement in New Jersey
Johnson, R. G., "John Fenwicke," N. J. Hist. Soc., *Proc.*, 4 (1849), 53.

FERMI, ENRICO 1901–1954, nuclear physicist
Fermi, Enrico, *Collected Papers* (2 vols., 1962, 1965).
Fermi, Laura, *Atoms in the Family: My Life with Enrico Fermi* (1954).
Segre, Emilio, *Enrico Fermi* (1970).

FERNOW, BERNHARD EDUARD 1851–1923, forester
Rogers, Andrew D. III, *Bernhard Eduard Fernow: Story of North American Forestry* (1951).

FESSENDEN, THOMAS GREEN 1771–1837, poet, journalist
Perrin, R. F., *Life and Works of Thomas Green Fessenden* (1925).

FESSENDEN, WILLIAM PITT 1806–1869, Maine senator

Fessenden, Francis, *Life and Public Services of William Pitt Fessenden* (2 vols., 1907).

Jellison, Charles A., *Fessenden of Maine: Civil War Senator* (1962).

FIEDLER, ARTHUR 1894– , conductor
Moore, Robin, *Fiedler: Colorful Mr. Pops* (1968).

FIELD, CYRUS WEST 1819–1892, promoter of transatlantic cable
Carter, Samuel, *Cyrus Field* (1968).
Judson, Isabella F., *Cyrus W. Field, His Life and Work* (1896).

FIELD, DAVID DUDLEY 1781–1867, Connecticut Congregational clergyman, historian
Field, Emilia A., *Record of the Life of David Dudley Field, His Ancestors and Descendants* (1931).

FIELD, EUGENE 1850–1895, writer
Thompson, Slason, *Life of Eugene Field* (1927).

FIELD, MARSHALL 1834–1906, merchant
Tebbel, John W., *Marshall Field* (1947).

FIELD, STEPHEN JOHNSON 1816–1899, Supreme Court justice
Swisher, Carl B., *Stephen J. Field, Craftsman of the Law* (1930).

FIELDS, JAMES THOMAS 1817–1881, publisher
Austin, James C., *Fields of the Atlantic Monthly: Letters to an Editor, 1861–1870* (1953).
Fields, Annie Adams, *James T. Fields: Biographical Notes and Personal Sketches* (1881).
Tryon, Warren S., *Parnassus Corner: James T. Fields, Publisher to the Victorians* (1963).

FIELDS, W. C. (DUKENFIELD) 1880–1946, motion picture comedian
Taylor, Robert L., *W.C. Fields* (1949).

FIESER, LOUIS FREDERICK 1899– , chemist
Fieser, Louis F., *Scientific Method: Personal Account* (1964).

FILLMORE, MILLARD 1800–1874, president
Fillmore, Millard, "Papers," F. H. Severance, ed., Buffalo Hist. Soc., *Publ.*, 10–11 (1907).
Rayback, Robert J., *Millard Fillmore* (1959).

FINNEY, CHARLES GRANDISON 1792–1875, revivalist, president of Oberlin College
Finney, Charles G., *Memoirs . . . Written by Himself* (1876).

FIRESTONE, HARVEY 1868–1938, rubber manufacturer
Firestone, H. S., and Samuel Crowther, *Men and Rubber* (1926).
Lief, Alfred, *Harvey Firestone* (1951).

FISH, HAMILTON 1808–1893, secretary of state
Nevins, Allan, *Hamilton Fish: The Inner History of the Grant Administration* (1936).

FISH, JOSEPH, 1840–1926, Mormon diarist
Fish, Joseph, *Life and Times of Mormon Pioneer*, John H. Krenkel, ed. (1970).

FISHER, JONATHAN 1768–1847, portrait painter
Chase, Mary E., *Jonathan Fisher* (1948).

FISHER, SIDNEY GEORGE 1809–1871, lawyer, author
Fisher, Sidney G., *Philadelphia Perspective: Diary 1834–1871*, Nicholas B. Wainwright, ed. (1967).

FISK, JAMES 1834–1872, capitalist, speculator
Swanberg, William A., *Jim Fisk* (1959).

FISKE, DANIEL WILLARD 1831–1904, scholar, librarian
White, Horatio S., *Willard Fiske, Life and Correspondence* (1925).

FISKE, JOHN 1744–1797, naval commander, merchant
Perry, Thomas S., *John Fiske* (1906).

FISKE, JOHN 1842–1901, philosopher, historian
Berman, Milton, *John Fiske* (1961).
Clark, John S., *The Life and Letters of John Fiske* (2 vols., 1917).
Commager, Henry S., "John Fiske," Mass. Hist. Soc., *Proc.*, 66 (1942), 332.

Fiske, John, *Letters,* E. F. Fiske, ed., (1940).

FITCH, JOHN 1743–1798, metal craftsman, inventor
Boyd, Thomas A., *Poor John Fitch* (1935).

FITCH, WILLIAM CLYDE 1865–1909, playwright
Moses, M. J., and Virginia Gerson, *Clyde Fitch and His Letters* (1924).

FITZGERALD, FRANCIS SCOTT KEY 1896–1940, novelist
Eble, Kenneth, *F. Scott Fitzgerald* (1963).
Fitzgerald, F. Scott, *Letters,* Andrew Turnbull, ed. (1963).
Hindus, Milton, *F. Scott Fitzgerald* (1968).
Mizener, Arthur, *The Far Side of Paradise: A Biography of F. Scott Fitzgerald* (1951).

FITZHUGH, GEORGE 1806–1881, sociologist, defender of slavery
Fitzhugh, George, *Cannibals All! Or, Slaves without Masters* (1857). C. Vann Woodward, ed. (1960).
Wish, Harvey, *George Fitzhugh* (1943).

FITZHUGH, WILLIAM 1651–1701, lawyer, merchant
Fitzhugh, William, *Letters and Other Documents, 1676–1701,* Richard B. Davis, ed. (1963).
Fitzhugh, William, *William Fitzhugh and His Chesapeake World, 1676–1701,* Richard B. Davis, ed. (1963).

FITZPATRICK, THOMAS 1799–1854, fur trapper, guide
Hafen, Leroy R., and William J. Ghent, *Broken Hand: Thomas Fitzpatrick* (1931).

FLETCHER, JOHN GOULD 1886–1950, writer
Stephens, Edna B., *John Gould Fletcher* (1968).

FLEXNER, ABRAHAM 1866–1959, educator
Flexner, Abraham, *Autobiography* (1960).

FLINT, TIMOTHY 1780–1840, missionary, writer
Flint, Timothy, *Recollections of the Last Ten Years* (1826; repr. 1968).
Folsom, James K., *Timothy Flint* (1965).

FLOYD, JOHN 1783–1837, surgeon, Virginia governor
Ambler, Charles H., *Life and Diary of John Floyd* (1918).

FLYNN, EDWARD JOSEPH 1891–1953, New York political leader, lawyer
Flynn, Edward J., *You're the Boss* (1947).

FLYNN, ELIZABETH GURLEY 1890–   , radical leader
Flynn, Elizabeth Gurley, *I Speak My Own Piece* (1955).

FOLK, JOSEPH WINGATE 1869–1923, Missouri reformer
Geiger, Louis G., *Joseph W. Folk of Missouri* (1953).

FOLKS, HOMER 1867–1963, social work leader
Trattner, Walter I., *Homer Folks: Pioneer in Social Welfare* (1968).

FOLLEN, CHARLES 1796–1840, scholar, abolitionist
Follen, Charles, *Works,* E. L. Follen, ed. (5 vols., 1841).

FORAKER, JOSEPH BENSON 1846–1917, Ohio Senator
Foraker, Joseph B., *Notes of a Busy Life* (2 vols., 1916).
Foraker, Julia B., *I Would Live It Again* (1932).
Walters, Everett, *Joseph Benson Foraker* (1948).

FORBES, JOHN MURRAY 1813–1898, merchant, capitalist, railroad builder
Forbes, John M., *Letters and Recollections,* S. F. Hughes, ed. (2 vols., 1899).
Pearson, Henry G., *An American Railroad Builder* (1911).

FORD, HENRY 1863–1947, automobile manufacturer
Bennett, Harry, and Paul Marcus, *We Never Called Him Henry* (1951).
Ford, Henry and Samuel Crowther, *My Life and Work* (1922).
Herndon, Booton, *Ford: An Unconventional Biography of the Men and Their Times* (1969).
Nevins, Allan, and Frank E. Hill, *Ford* (3 vols., 1954–1962).
Sward, Keith T., *Legend of Henry Ford* (1948).

FORD, HENRY II 1917–   , automobile manufacturer
Herndon, Booton, *Ford* (1969).

FORD, JOHN SALMON "RIP" fl. 1836–1896, Texas pioneer politician, military commander
Ford, John S., *Rip Ford's Texas*, Stephen B. Oates, ed. (1963).
Hughes, W. J., *Rebellious Ranger: Rip Ford* (1964).

FORREST, EDWIN 1806–1872, actor
Alger, W. R., *Life of Edwin Forrest* (2 vols., 1877).
Moody, Richard, *Edwin Forrest: First Star of American Stage* (1960).

FORREST, NATHAN BEDFORD 1821–1877, Confederate general
Henry, Robert S., ed., *As They Saw Forrest: Recollections of Contemporaries* (1956).
Henry, Robert S., *"First with the Most" Forrest* (1944).
Lytle, Andrew N., *Bedford Forrest and His Critter Company* (1931; rev. ed., 1960).

FORRESTAL, JAMES 1892–1949, secretary of defense
Albion, Robert G., and Robert H. Connery, *Forrestal and Navy* (1962).
Forrestal, James, *The Forrestal Diaries*, Walter Millis and E. S. Duffield, eds. (1951).
Rogow, Arnold A., *James Forrestal* (1963).

FORSYTH, JOHN 1780–1841, Georgia senator, secretary of state
Duckett, Alvin L., *John Forsyth* (1962).

FOSDICK, RAYMOND BLAINE 1883– , lawyer, president of General Education Board
Fosdick, Raymond B., *Chronicle of a Generation: An Autobiography* (1958).
—— *Letters on League of Nations* (1966).

FOSTER, JOHN WATSON 1836–1917, secretary of state, diplomat
Foster, J. W., *Diplomatic Memoirs* (2 vols., 1909).

FOSTER, STEPHEN COLLINS 1826–1864, composer
Howard, John T., *Stephen Foster* (1934; rev. ed., 1953).
Walters, Raymond, *Stephen Foster* (1937).

FOX, GEORGE 1624–1691, founder of Society of Friends
Fox, George, *Journal* (1952).
Noble, Vernon, *Man in Leather Breeches: George Fox* (1953).

FOX, GUSTAVUS VASA 1821–1883, assistant secretary of navy
Fox, Gustavus V., *Confidential Correspondence, 1861–65,* R. M. Thompson and Richard Wainwright, eds. (2 vols., 1918–1919).

FRANK, JEROME N. 1889–1957, jurist
Paul, Julius, *Legal Realism of Jerome N. Frank* (1959).

FRANK, WALDO DAVID 1889–1967, author
Carter, Paul J., *Waldo Frank* (1967).

FRANKFURTER, FELIX 1882–1965, Supreme Court justice
Baker, Liva, *Felix Frankfurter* (1969).
Frankfurter, Felix, *Felix Frankfurter Reminisces: Recorded in Talks with Harlan B. Phillips* (1960).
—— *Of Law and Life: Papers and Addresses, 1956–1963,* Philip B. Kurland, ed. (1965).
Mendelson, Wallace, *Justices Black and Frankfurter* (2nd ed., 1966).
Roosevelt, Franklin D., and Felix Frankfurter, *Correspondence, 1928–1945,* Max Freedman, ed. (1967).
Thomas, Helen S., *Felix Frankfurter* (1960).

FRANKLIN, BENJAMIN 1706–1790, printer, scientist, inventor, diplomat, writer
Aldridge, Alfred O., *Benjamin Franklin and Nature's God* (1967).
—— *Franklin and French Contemporaries* (1957).
Becker, Carl, *Benjamin Franklin* (1946).
Best, John H., ed., *Benjamin Franklin on Education* (1962).
Cohen, I. Bernard, ed., *Benjamin Franklin's Experiments* (1941).
Cohen, I. Bernard, *Franklin and Newton* (1956).
Conner, Paul W., *Poor Richard's Politicks: Benjamin Franklin* (1965).
Crane, Verner W., *Benjamin Franklin and a Rising People* (1954).
Fay, Bernard, *Franklin: Apostle of Modern Times* (1929).

Franklin, Benjamin, *Autobiography*, Leonard W. Labaree et al., eds. (1964).
———— *Benjamin Franklin and Catherine Ray Greene: Their Correspondence* (1949).
———— *Letters of Benjamin Franklin and Jane Mecom* (1950).
———— *Letters of Franklin and Richard Jackson*, Carl Van Doren, ed. (1947).
———— *Letters to the Press, 1758–1775* (1950).
———— *Memoirs*, Max Farrand, ed. (1949). Parallel text edition
———— *"New-England Courant": Selection of Writings of Benjamin Franklin* (1956).
———— *Papers*, Leonard W. Labaree et al., eds. (14 vols., 1959–1970).
———— *Political Thought of Franklin*, Ralph L. Ketcham, ed. (1965).
———— *Some Account of the Pennsylvania Hospital*, I. Bernard Cohen, ed. (1954).
———— *Writings* (1905–1907).
Hall, Max, *Benjamin Franklin and Polly Baker* (1960).
Lopez, Claude-Anne, *Mon Cher Papa: Franklin and Ladies of Paris* (1966).
Pace, Antonio, *Benjamin Franklin and Italy* (1959).
Parton, James, *Life of Benjamin Franklin* (2 vols., 1864).
Sellers, Charles C., *Benjamin Franklin in Portraiture* (1962).
Stourzh, Gerald, *Benjamin Franklin and American Foreign Policy* (2nd ed., 1969).
Van Doren, Carl, *Benjamin Franklin* (1938).
———— et al., *Meet Dr. Franklin* (1943).
Woody, Thomas, ed., *Educational Views of Benjamin Franklin* (1931).
Wright, Esmond, *Benjamin Franklin and American Independence* (1966).
FRANKS FAMILY fl. 1733–1748
Hershkowitz, Leo, and Isidore S. Meyer, eds., *Lee Max Friedman Collection: Letters of the Franks Family* (1968). Covers the period 1733–1748.
FREDERIC, HAROLD 1856–1898, novelist, journalist
Franchere, Hoyt C., and Thomas F. O'Donnell, *Harold Frederic* (1960).
FREEMAN, MARY WILKINS 1852–1930, writer
Westbrook, Perry D., *Mary Wilkins Freeman* (1968).
FRELINGHUYSEN, THEODORUS JACOBUS 1691–ca. 1748, Dutch Reformed clergyman
Tanis, James, *Theodorus J. Frelinghuysen* (1967).
FRÉMONT, JOHN CHARLES 1813–1890, explorer, army officer
Bartlett, Ruhl J., *John C. Frémont and Republican Party* (1930).
Frémont, John C., *Memoirs of My Life* (1887).
Nevins, Allan, *Frémont: Pathmaker of West* under title, *The West's Greatest Adventurer* (2 vols., 1928). Reissued (1955).
FRENCH, DANIEL CHESTER 1850–1931, sculptor
Adams, Adeline, *Daniel Chester French, Sculptor* (1932).
Cresson, Margaret, *Journey into Fame* (1947).
FRENEAU, PHILIP MORIN 1752–1832, poet, editor
Axelrad, Jacob, *Philip Freneau* (1967).
Freneau, Philip, *Poems*, F. L. Pattee, ed. (3 vols., 1902–1907).
Marsh, Philip M., *Philip Freneau, Poet and Journalist* (1968).
FRICK, HENRY CLAY 1849–1919, steel manufacturer
Harvey, George, *Henry Clay Frick* (1928).
FROHMAN, CHARLES 1860–1915, theatrical producer
Marcosson, I. F., and Daniel Frohman, *Charles Frohman* (1916).
FROST, ROBERT 1874–1963, poet
Gerber, Philip L., *Robert Frost* (1966).
Thompson, Lawrance, *Robert Frost, 1874–1938* (2 vols., 1966–1970).
FROTHINGHAM, OCTAVIUS BROOKS 1822–1895, Unitarian clergyman
Frothingham, O. B., *Recollections and Impressions, 1822–90.* (1891).
FRY, WILLIAM HENRY 1815–1864, composer
Upton, William T., *William Henry Fry, American Journalist and Composer Critic* (1954).
FUESS, CLAUDE MOORE 1885–1963, historian, headmaster

Fuess, Claude M., *Independent Schoolmaster* (1952).

FULBRIGHT, JAMES WILLIAM 1905–   ; Arkansas senator
Coffin, Tristram, *Senator Fulbright* (1966).
Johnson, Haynes B., and Bernard M. Gwertzman, *Fulbright: The Dissenter* (1968).
Meyer, Karl E., ed., *Fulbright of Arkansas* (1963).

FULLER, RICHARD BUCKMINSTER 1895–   , architect
Fuller, Buckminster, *Ideas and Integrities* (1963).
Marks, Robert W., *Dymaxion World of Buckminster Fuller* (1960).
McHale, John, *R. Buckminster Fuller* (1962).

FULLER [OSSOLI], SARAH MARGARET 1810–1850, transcendentalist writer
Anthony, Katharine, *Margaret Fuller* (1920).
Brown, Arthur W., *Margaret Fuller* (1963).
Deiss, Joseph J., *Margaret Fuller* (1969).
Fuller, Margaret, *Memoirs*, Ralph W. Emerson et al., eds. (2 vols., 1852).
———— *Writings*, Mason Wade, ed. (1941). Perry Miller, ed. (1963).
Stern, Madeleine B., *Margaret Fuller* (1942).
Wade, Mason, *Margaret Fuller* (1940).

FULLER, MELVILLE WESTON 1833–1910, Supreme Court justice
King, Willard L., *Melville Weston Fuller* (1950).

FULTON, ROBERT 1765–1815, inventor, engineer
Dickinson, Henry W., *Robert Fulton, Engineer and Artist: His Life and Works* (1913).

FURUSETH, ANDREW 1854–1938, head of seamen's union
Weintraub, Hyman, *Andrew Furuseth* (1959).

GADSDEN, CHRISTOPHER 1724–1805, merchant, South Carolina leader
Gadsden, Christopher, *Writings, 1746–1805*, Richard Walsh, ed. (1966).

GAINE, HUGH 1726/27–1807, printer, bookseller
Gaine, Hugh, *Journals of Hugh Gaine*, Paul L. Ford, ed. (2 vols., 1902).

GAINES, EDMUND PENDLETON 1777–1849, frontier general
Silver, James W., *Edmund Pendleton Gaines* (1949).

GALE, ZONA 1874–1938, novelist
Simonson, Harold P., *Zona Gale* (1962).

GALLATIN, ABRAHAM ALBERT 1761–1849, secretary of treasury
Adams, Henry, *Life of Albert Gallatin* (1879).
Badollet, John, and Albert Gallatin, *Correspondence, 1804–1836*, Gayle Thornbrough, ed. (1963).
Balinky, Alexander, *Albert Gallatin: Fiscal Theories* (1958).
Gallatin, Albert, *Selected Writings*, E. James Ferguson, ed. (1967).
———— *Writings*, Henry Adams, ed. (3 vols., 1879).
Walters, Raymond, Jr., *Albert Gallatin: Jeffersonian Financier and Diplomat* (1957).

GALLAUDET, EDWARD MINER 1837–1917, educator of deaf
Boatner, Maxine T., *Voice of the Deaf: Edward Miner Gallaudet* (1959).

GANSEVOORT FAMILY
Kenney, Alice P., *The Gansevoorts of Albany: Dutch Patricians in the Upper Hudson Valley* (1969).

GARDEN, ALEXANDER 1730–1791, South Carolina naturalist, physician
Berkeley, Edmund, and Dorothy S. Berkeley, *Dr. Alexander Garden of Charles Town* (1969).

GARFIELD, JAMES ABRAM 1831–1881, president
Caldwell, Robert G., *James A. Garfield, Party Chieftain* (1931).
Garfield, James A., *Diary, 1848–1874* Harry J. Brown and Frederick D. Williams, ed. (2 vols., 1967).
———— and Burke A. Hinsdale, *Letters*, Mary L. Hinsdale, ed. (1949).
———— *Wild Life of Army: Civil War Letters*, Frederick D. Williams, ed. (1964).
Hoyt, Edwin P., *James A. Garfield* (1964).
Smith, Theodore C., *Life and Letters of James Abram Garfield* (2 vols., 1925).

GARLAND, HAMLIN 1860–1940, author

Garland, Hamlin, *Boy Life on Prairie* (1899).
—— *Diaries*, Donald Pizer, ed. (1968).
—— *Son of the Middle Border* (1917).
—— *Trail-Makers of the Middle Border* (1926).
Holloway, Jean, *Hamlin Garland* (1960).

GARNER, JOHN NANCE 1868–1967, vice-president
Timmons, Bascom N., *Garner of Texas* (1948).

GARRISON, JAMES HARVEY 1842–1931, Disciples of Christ clergyman
Tucker, William E., *J. H. Garrison and Disciples of Christ* (1964).

GARRISON, WILLIAM LLOYD 1805–1879, abolitionist
Garrison, Francis J., and W. P. Garrison, *William Lloyd Garrison, 1805–1879* (4 vols., 1885–1889).
Garrison, William Lloyd, *The Garrison Letters.* Vol. I: *I Will Be Heard, 1822–1835,* Walter M. Merrill, ed.; Vol. II: *A House Dividing against Itself, 1836–1840,* Louis Ruchames, ed. (1971–   ).
Korngold, Ralph, *Two Friends of Man . . . William Lloyd Garrison and Wendell Phillips* (1950).
Merrill, Walter M., *Against Wind and Tide: William Lloyd Garrison* (1963).
Nye, Russel B., *William Lloyd Garrison and Humanitarian Reformers* (1955).
Ruchames, Louis, "William Lloyd Garrison and the Negro Franchise," *Jour. Negro Hist.,* 50 (1965), 37.
Thomas, John L., *Liberator, William Lloyd Garrison* (1963).
Wyatt-Brown, Bertram, "William Lloyd Garrison and Antislavery Unity," *Civil War Hist.,* 13 (1967), 5.

GARVEY, MARCUS 1887–1940, Negro leader
Cronon, E. David, *Black Moses: Marcus Garvey and the Universal Negro Improvement Association* (1955).
Garvey, Marcus, *Philosophy and Opinions, or Africa for the Africans,* Amy Jacques Garvey, ed. (2nd ed. 1967).

GARY, ELBERT HENRY 1846–1927, lawyer, financier, chairman of board of U.S. Steel Corp.
Tarbell, Ida M., *Life of Elbert H. Gary* (1925).

GATES, HORATIO 1728/29–1806, Revolutionary general
Patterson, Samuel W., *Horatio Gates* (1941).

GAY, EDWIN F. 1867–1946, economist
Heaton, Herbert, *Scholar in Action: Edwin F. Gay* (1952).

GAYNOR, WILLIAM JAY 1849–1913, mayor of New York City
Smith, Mortimer, *William Jay Gaynor* (1950).
Thomas, Lately, *Mayor Who Mastered New York: Life and Opinions of William J. Gaynor* (1969).

GEARY, JOHN WHITE 1819–1873, engineer, soldier, Pennsylvania political leader
Tinkcom, Harry M., *John White Geary, Soldier-Statesman* (1940).

GENÊT, EDMOND CHARLES 1763–1834, diplomat
Bathe, Greville, *Citizen Genêt: Diplomat & Inventor* (1946).

GEORGE, HENRY 1839–1897, economist, reformer
Barker, Charles A., *Henry George* (2 vols., 1955).
Cord, Steven B., *Henry George* (1965).
DeMille, Anna A. G., *Henry George* (1950).
George, Henry, *Complete Works* (10 vols., 1906–1911).
George, Henry, Jr., *Life of Henry George* (1900).
Rose, Edward J., *Henry George* (1968).

GERRY, ELBRIDGE 1744–1814, diplomat, Massachusetts governor
Austin, James T., *Life of Elbridge Gerry* (2 vols., 1827–1829).
Gerry, Elbridge, *Letterbook: Paris, 1797–1798,* Russell W. Knight, ed. (1966).
Morison, Samuel E., "Elbridge Gerry, Gentleman-Democrat," in *By Land and By Sea* (1953).
Warren, James, and Elbridge Gerry, *Correspondence,* C. Harvey Gardiner, ed. (1968).

GERSHWIN, GEORGE 1898–1937, composer

Ewen, David, *Journey to Greatness: George Gershwin* (1956).

GIBBONS, JAMES 1834–1921, cardinal of Baltimore
Boucher, Arline, and John Tehan, *James Cardinal Gibbons* (1962).
Ellis, John T., *Life of Cardinal Gibbons* (2 vols., 1953).
Gibbons, James, *A Retrospect of Fifty Years* (1916).

GIBBS, JOSIAH WILLARD 1790–1861, mathematician, physicist
Wheeler, Lynde P., *Josiah Willard Gibbs* (1951).

GIDDINGS, JOSHUA REED 1795–1864, abolitionist, Ohio political leader
Julian, George W., *Life of Joshua R. Giddings* (1892).
Stewart, James B., *Joshua R. Giddings and Tactics of Radical Politics* (1970).

GILDER, RICHARD WATSON 1844–1909, poet
Gilder, Richard W., *Letters* (1916).
Smith, Herbert F., *Richard Watson Gilder* (1970).

GILES, WILLIAM BRANCH 1762–1830, Virginia political leader
Anderson, Dice R., *William Branch Giles* (1914).

GILMAN, DANIEL COIT 1831–1908; president of University of California and Johns
Hopkins University
Flexner, Abraham, *Gilman* (1946).
Franklin, Fabian, *The Life of Daniel Coit Gilman* (1910).

GINSBERG, ALLEN 1926–   , poet
Merrill, Thomas F., *Allen Ginsberg* (1970).

GIRARD, STEPHEN 1750–1831, merchant, financier, philanthropist
Brown, Kenneth L., "Stephen Girard, Promoter of Second Bank of United
States," *Jour. Econ. Hist.* 1-2 (1941–1942), 125.
McMaster, John B., *Stephen Girard* (2 vols., 1918).

GLACKENS, WILLIAM 1870–1938, artist
Glackens, Ira, *William Glackens and the Ashcan Group* (1957).

GLADDEN, WASHINGTON 1836–1918, Congregational clergyman, social gospel pro-
ponent
Dorn, Jacob H., *Washington Gladden: Prophet of Social Gospel* (1967).
Gladden, Washington, *Recollections* (1909).
Knudten, Richard D., *Systematic Thought of Washington Gladden* (1968).

GLASGOW, ELLEN 1874–1945, author
Glasgow, Ellen, *Letters*, Blair Rouse, ed. (1958).
McDowell, Frederick P., *Ellen Glasgow and the Ironic Art of Fiction* (1960).
Rouse, Blair, *Ellen Glasgow* (1962).

GLASPELL, SUSAN 1882–1948, playwright
Waterman, Arthur E., *Susan Glaspell* (1966).

GLASS, CARTER 1858–1946, Virginia senator, secretary of Treasury
Smith, Rixey, and Norman Beasley, *Carter Glass* (1939).

GLOVER, JOHN 1732–1797, Revolutionary general
Billias, George A., *General John Glover and His Marblehead Mariners* (1960).

GODDARD, ROBERT HUTCHINGS 1882–1945, physicist, developer of rocketry
Goddard, Robert H., *Papers*, Esther C. Goddard and G. Edward Pendray, eds.
(3 vols., 1970).
Lehman, Milton, *This High Man: Robert H. Goddard* (1963).

GODDARD, WILLIAM 1740–1817, newspaperman
Miner, Ward L., *William Goddard, Newspaperman* (1962).

GODKIN, EDWIN LAWRENCE 1831–1902, journalist
Armstrong, William M., *E. L. Godkin and American Foreign Policy, 1865–1900*
(1957).
Ogden, Rollo, *Life and Letters of Edwin Lawrence Godkin* (2 vols., 1907).

GOETHALS, GEORGE WASHINGTON 1858–1928, engineer, soldier, builder of Panama
Canal
Bishop, Joseph B., and Farnham Bishop, *Goethals: Genius of the Panama Canal*
(1930).

GOFF, NATHAN, JR. 1843–1920, West Virginia senator, secretary of navy
Smith, Gerald W., *Nathan Goff, Jr.* (1959).

GOLDBERG, ARTHUR JOSEPH 1908–   ; secretary of labor, Supreme Court justice
Goldberg, Arthur J., *Public Papers*, Daniel P. Moynihan, ed. (1966).

GOLDBERGER, JOSEPH 1874–1929, directed pellagra research
Parsons, Robert P., *Trail to Light: Joseph Goldberger* (1943).

GOLDMAN, EMMA 1869–1940, anarchist
Drinnon, Richard, *Rebel in Paradise: Emma Goldman* (1961).
Goldman, Emma, *Living My Life* (2 vols., 1936).

GOLDSCHMIDT, RICHARD BENEDICT 1878–1958, geneticist
Goldschmidt, Richard B., *Autobiography* (1960).

GOLDWATER, BARRY 1909–   , Arizona senator
Bell, Jack L., *Mr. Conservative: Barry Goldwater* (1962).

GOMPERS, SAMUEL 1850–1924, president of American Federation of Labor
Gompers, Samuel, *Seventy Years of Life and Labor.* (2 vols., 1925).
Greenbaum, Fred, "The Social Ideas of Samuel Gompers," *Labor Hist.* 7 (1966), 35.
Harvey, Rowland H., *Samuel Gompers, Champion of the Toiling Masses* (1935).
Mandel, Bernard, *Samuel Gompers* (1963).
Reed, Louis S., *Labor Philosophy of Gompers* (1930).

GOODHUE, BERTRAM GROSVENOR 1869–1924, architect
Whitaker, Charles H., *Bertram Grosvenor Goodhue, Architect and Master of Many Arts* (1925).

GOODRICH, SAMUEL GRISWOLD 1793–1860, author of children's books
Goodrich, S. G., *Recollections of a Lifetime* (1856).
Roselle, Daniel, *Samuel Griswold Goodrich: Creator of Peter Parley* (1968).

GOODYEAR, CHARLES 1800–1860, inventor
Wolf, Ralph F., *India Rubber Man: The Story of Charles Goodyear* (1939).

GOOKIN, DANIEL 1612–1686/87, Massachusetts soldier and magistrate
Gookin, F. W., *Daniel Gookin* (1912).

GORDON, JOHN BROWN 1832–1904, Confederate general, Georgia political leader
Tankersley, Allen P., *John B. Gordon* (1955).

GORE, THOMAS P. 1870–1949, Oklahoma senator
Billington, Monroe L., *Thomas P. Gore: Blind Senator from Oklahoma* (1967).

GORGAS, WILLIAM CRAWFORD 1854–1920, sanitarian
Dolan, Edward F., Jr., and H. T. Silver, *William Crawford Gorgas* (1968).
Gibson, John M., *Physician to the World* (1950).
Gorgas, Marie D., and B. J. Hendrick, *William Crawford Gorgas: His Life and Work* (1924).

GORMAN, ARTHUR PUE 1839–1906, Maryland senator
Lambert, John R., *Arthur Pue Gorman* (1953).

GORTON, SAMUEL ca. 1592–1677, Rhode Island colonist, theologian
Janes, L. G., *Samuel Gorton* (1896).

GOSNOLD, BARTHOLOMEW 1572–1607, explorer
Gookin, Warner F., *Bartholomew Gosnold, Discoverer and Planter* (1963).

GOUGH, JOHN BARTHOLOMEW 1817–1886, temperance lecturer
Gough, J. B., *Autobiography and Personal Recollections* (1869).
Morrow, Honoré W., *Tiger! Tiger! The Life Story of John B. Gough* (1930).

GOULD, JAY 1836–1892, financier
Grodinsky, Julius, *Jay Gould: Business Career, 1867–1892* (1957).

GOWEN, FRANKLIN BENJAMIN 1836–1889, railroad president
Schlegel, Marvin W., *Ruler of the Reading: Franklin B. Gowen* (1947).

GRADY, HENRY WOODFIN 1851–1889, editor
Nixon, R. B., *Henry W. Grady* (1943).

GRAHAM, MARTHA 1895–   , dancer
Leatherman, LeRoy, *Martha Graham* (1966).

GRAHAM, WILLIAM ALEXANDER 1804–1875, secretary of navy, North Carolina political leader
Graham, William A., *Papers*, J. G. de Roulhac Hamilton, ed. (4 vols., 1957–1961).

GRAHAM, WILLIAM FRANKLIN 1918–   , evangelist
McLoughlin, William G., *Billy Graham* (1960).

GRANT, JULIA T. DENT 1826–1902, first lady
Ross, Ishbel, *General's Wife: Mrs. Ulysses S. Grant* (1959).

GRANT, ULYSSES SIMPSON 1822–1885, president, Civil War general
Badeau, Adam, *Military History of U. S. Grant* (3 vols., 1868–1881).
Catton, Bruce, *Grant Moves South* (1960).
—— *Grant Takes Command* (1969).
—— *U. S. Grant and the American Military Tradition* (1954).
Grant, Ulysses S., *Letters to Father and Youngest Sister, 1857–1878* J. G.
Cramer, ed. (1912).
—— *Mr. Lincoln's General: Illustrated Autobiography*, Roy Meredith, ed.
(1959).
—— *Papers*, John Y. Simon, ed. (4 vols., 1967–   ).
—— *Personal Memoirs* (2 vols., 1885–1886).
Hesseltine, William B., *U. S. Grant, Politician* (1935).
Lewis, Lloyd, *Captain Sam Grant* (1950).

GRAY, ASA 1810–1888, botanist
Dupree, A. Hunter, *Asa Gray* (1959).
Gray, Asa, *Letters*, J. L. Gray, ed. (2 vols., 1893).

GRAYDON, ALEXANDER 1752–1818, Revolutionary soldier
Graydon, Alexander, *Memoirs of a Life, Chiefly Passed in Pennsylvania, within
the Last Sixty Years* (1811). (Later ed. 1846).

GREELEY, HORACE 1811–1872, editor
Greeley, Horace, *Recollections of a Busy Life* (1868).
Hale, William H., *Horace Greeley* (1950).
Isely, J. A., *Horace Greeley and Republican Party, 1853–1861* (1947).
Van Deusen, Glyndon G., *Horace Greeley: Nineteenth-Century Crusader*
(1953).

GREELEY, WILLIAM B. 1879–1955; forester
Morgan, George T., Jr., *William B. Greeley: Forester* (1961).

GREEN, ANDREW HASWELL 1820–1903; lawyer, New York City official
Foord, John, *A. H. Green* (1913).

GREEN, THEODORE FRANCIS 1867–1966, Rhode Island governor, senator
Levine, Erwin L., *Theodore F. Green* (1963).

GREENE, NATHANAEL 1742–1786, Revolutionary general
Greene, George W., *The Life of Nathanael Greene* (3 vols., 1867–1871).
Thayer, Theodore, *Nathanael Greene* (1960).

GREENOUGH, HORATIO 1805–1852, sculptor
Greenough, Horatio, *Letters to His Brother Henry*, F. B. Greenough, ed. (1887).
Wright, Nathalia, *Horatio Greenough, First American Sculptor* (1963).

GREGG, ALAN 1890–1957, physician
Wilde, Penfield, *Difficult Art of Giving: Epic of Alan Gregg* (1967).

GREGG, JOSIAH 1806–1850, Santa Fé trader
Gregg, Josiah, *Diary and Letters*, M. G. Fulton, ed. (2 vols., 1941–1944).

GREGG, WILLIAM 1800–1867, cotton manufacturer
Mitchell, Broadus, *William Gregg* (1928).

GREGORY, DICK 1932–   ; entertainer
Gregory, Dick, *Nigger: Autobiography* (1964).

GREGORY, JOHN MILTON 1822–1898, president of University of Illinois
Kersey, Harry A., Jr., *John Milton Gregory and the University of Illinois* (1968).

GRESHAM, WALTER QUINTIN 1832–1895, Indiana political leader, secretary of state
Gresham, Matilda, *Life of W. Q. Gresham* (1919).

GREW, JOSEPH CLARK 1880–1965, diplomat
Grew, Joseph C., *Ten Years in Japan* (1944).
Heinrichs, Waldo H., Jr., *American Ambassador: Joseph C. Grew* (1966).

GRIERSON, FRANCIS 1848–1927, essayist
Simonson, Harold P., *Francis Grierson* (1966).

GRIMES, JAMES WILSON 1816–1872, Iowa senator, governor
Salter, William, *James W. Grimes* (1876).

GRIMKÉ SISTERS, abolitionists
Birney, C. H., *The Grimké Sisters* (1885).
Grimké, Angelina E., *Letters to Catherine E. Beecher* (1838).
Lerner, Gerda, *The Grimké Sisters* (1967).
Weld, T. D., Angelina G. Weld, and Sarah Grimké, *Letters, 1822–1844*, G. H.
Barnes and D. L. Dumond, eds. (2 vols., 1934).

GRINNELL, JOSIAH BUSHNELL 1821–1891, railway promoter, founder of Grinnell
College
Grinnell, J. B., *Men and Events of Forty Years* (1891).
Payne, C. E., *Josiah Bushnell Grinnell* (1938).

GROPIUS, WALTER 1883–1969, architect
Fitch, James M., *Walter Gropius* (1960).
Giedion, Sigfried, *Walter Gropius* (1954).

GROUARD, FRANK 1850–1905, Indian scout
DeBarthe, Joseph, *Life and Adventures of Frank Grouard* (1894); Edgar I.
Stewart, ed. (1958).

GROW, GALUSHA AARON 1822–1907, Speaker of the House, advocate of Homestead
Act
DuBois, James T., and G. S. Mathews, *Galusha A. Grow* (1917).

GRUBBE, EMIL H. 1875–1960, doctor
Hodges, Paul C., *Life and Times of Emil H. Grubbe* (1964).

GRUNDY, FELIX 1777–1840, criminal lawyer, jurist, politician
Parks, Joseph H., *Felix Grundy* (1940).

GUIGNARD FAMILY
Childs, Arney R., ed., *Planters and Business Men: Guignard Family of South
Carolina, 1795–1930* (1957).

GUNNISON, JOHN WILLIAMS 1812–1853, explorer
Mumey, Nolie, *John Williams Gunnison: Last of the Western Explorers* (1955).

GUROWSKI, ADAM 1805–1866, journalist
Fischer, LeRoy H., *Lincoln's Gadfly, Adam Gurowski* (1964).
Gurowski, Adam, *Diary* (3 vols., 1862–1866).

GUTHRIE, WOODROW W. 1912–1967, folk singer, composer
Guthrie, Woodie, *Bound for Glory* (1943).

HALE, EDWARD EVERETT 1822–1909, author, Unitarian clergyman
Hale, Edward E., *Memories of a Hundred Years* (2 vols., 1902–1904).
——— *A New England Boyhood and Other Bits of Autobiography* (1900).
Hale, Edward E., Jr., *The Life and Letters of Edward Everett Hale* (2 vols.,
1917).
Holloway, Jean, *Edward Everett Hale* (1956).

HALE, GEORGE ELLERY 1868–1938, astronomer
Wright, Helen, *Explorer of Universe: George Ellery Hale* (1966).

HALE, JOHN PARKER 1806–1873, New Hampshire senator, abolitionist
Sewell, Richard H., *John P. Hale* (1965).

HALE, NATHAN 1775–1776, Revolutionary spy
Johnston, Henry P., *Nathan Hale* (rev. ed., 1914).

HALE, SARAH JOSEPHA 1788–1879, editor
Finley, Ruth E., *Lady of Godey's, Sarah Josepha Hale* (1931).

HALL, ABRAHAM OAKEY 1826–1898, politician, journalist
Bowen, Croswell, *Elegant Oakey* (1956).

HALL, GRANVILLE STANLEY 1846–1924, psychologist, president of Clark University
Hall, Granville S., *Life and Confessions of a Psychologist* (1923).
Pruette, Lorine, *G. S. Hall* (1926).

HALL, JAMES 1793–1868, author, jurist, banker
Randall, Randolph C., *James Hall* (1964).

HALL, JAMES 1811–1898, geologist, paleontologist
Clarke, John M., *James Hall: Geologist and Paleontologist* (1921).

HALLECK, HENRY WAGER 1815–1872, Union general
Ambrose, Stephen E., *Halleck: Lincoln's Chief of Staff* (1962).

HALSTED, WILLIAM STEWART 1852–1922, surgeon
Crowe, Samuel J., *Halsted of Johns Hopkins: The Man and His Men* (1957).
Halsted, William S., *Surgical Papers* (2 vols., 1924).
MacCallum, William G., *William Stewart Halsted* (1930).

HAMILTON, ALEXANDER 1755–1804, secretary of treasury
Cooke, Jacob E., ed., *Alexander Hamilton* (1967).
Hacker, Louis M., *Alexander Hamilton in the American Tradition* (1957).
Hamilton, Alexander, *Industrial and Commercial Correspondence*, A. H. Cole, ed. (1928).
———— *Law Practice*, Julius Goebel, Jr. et. al., eds. (2 vols., 1964–1969).
———— *Papers*, Harold C. Syrett and Jacob E. Cooke, eds. (15 vols., 1961–   ).
———— *Pay Book*, E. P. Panagopoulos, ed. (1961).
———— *Works*, J. C. Hamilton, ed. (7 vols., 1850–1851).
———— *Writings*, Richard B. Morris, ed., (1957).
Hamilton, John C., *Alexander Hamilton* (1834–1840).
Lycan, Gilbert L., *Alexander Hamilton and American Foreign Policy: A Design for Greatness* (1970).
Miller, John C., *Alexander Hamilton: Portrait in Paradox* (1959).
Mitchell, Broadus, *Alexander Hamilton* (2 vols., 1957–1962).
———— *Heritage from Hamilton* (1957).
Schachner, Nathan, *Alexander Hamilton* (2nd ed., 1957).
Stourzh, Gerald, *Alexander Hamilton and Idea of Republican Government* (1970).

HAMILTON, ALICE 1869–1970, physician
Hamilton, Alice, *Autobiography* (1943).

HAMILTON, ANDREW 1676–1741, attorney general of Pennsylvania, defender of Peter Zenger
Konkle, Burton A., *The Life of Andrew Hamilton, 1676–1741* (1941).

HAMILTON, ANDREW JACKSON 1815–1875, Texas governor
Waller, John L., *Colossal Hamilton of Texas: Biography of Andrew Jackson Hamilton* (1968).

HAMILTON, JAMES ALEXANDER 1788–1878, lawyer, politician
Hamilton, James A., *Reminiscences during Three Quarters of a Century* (1869).

HAMLIN, HANNIBAL 1809–1891, vice-president, Maine senator
Hamlin, Charles E., *Life and Times of Hannibal Hamlin* (1899).
Hunt, H. Draper, *Hannibal Hamlin: Lincoln's First Vice-President* (1969).

HAMMERSTEIN, OSCAR 1895–1960, librettist
Taylor, Deems, *Some Enchanted Evenings: Rodgers and Hammerstein* (1953).

HAMMOND, JAMES H. 1807–1864, South Carolina governor, senator
Merritt, Elizabeth, *James Henry Hammond* (1923).

HAMMOND, JOHN HAYS 1855–1936, mining engineer
Hammond, John H., *Autobiography* (2 vols., 1935).

HAMPTON, WADE III 1818–1902, Confederate officer, South Carolina governor
Jarrell, Hampton M., *Wade Hampton and the Negro: The Road Not Taken* (1949).
Wellman, Manly W., *Giant in Gray: Wade Hampton* (1949).

HAMPTON FAMILY - fl. 1752–1902, South Carolina
Hampton, Wade, *Family Letters of Three Wade Hamptons, 1782–1901*, Charles E. Cauthen, ed. (1953).

HANCOCK, JOHN 1736–1793, merchant, politician
Allan, Herbert S., *John Hancock* (1948).

HANCOCK, WINFIELD SCOTT 1824–1886, Union general
Tucker, Glenn, *Hancock the Superb* (1960).
Walker, Francis A., *General Hancock* (1894).

HANNA, MARCUS ALONZO 1837–1904, Ohio senator, industrialist
Beer, Thomas, *Hanna* (1929).

Croly, Herbert D., *Marcus Alonzo Hanna* (1912).

HARDING, SETH 1734–1814, Revolutionary naval officer
Howard, James L., *Seth Harding, Mariner: A Naval Picture of the Revolution* (1930).

HARDING, WARREN GAMALIEL 1865–1923, president
Downes, Randolph C., *Rise of Warren Gamaliel Harding, 1865–1920* (1971).
Murray, Robert K., *Harding Era* (1969).
Russell, Francis, *Shadow of Blooming Grove: Warren G. Harding* (1968).
Sinclair, Andrew, *Available Man: Warren G. Harding* (1965).

HARE, GEORGE EMLEN 1808–1892, Episcopal clergyman
Howe, Mark A. DeW., *Bishop George E. Hare* (1911).

HARE, ROBERT 1781–1858, chemist
Smith, Edgar F., *Life of Robert Hare* (1917).

HARLAN, JAMES 1820–1899, Iowa senator, secretary of interior
Brigham, Johnson, *James Harlan*, (1913).

HARLAN, JOHN MARSHALL 1833–1911, Supreme Court justice
Abraham, Henry J., "John M. Harlan," *Va.Law Rev.*, 41 (1955), 871.
Westin, Alan F., "John Marshall Harlan and Constitutional Rights of Negroes," *Yale Law Jour.*, 66 (1957), 637.

HARLAN, JOHN MARSHALL 1899–1971, Supreme Court justice
Harlan, John M., *Selected Opinions and Papers*, David L. Shapiro, ed. (1969).

HARNETT, CORNELIUS 1723?–1781, North Carolina Revolutionary leader
Connor, R. D. W., *Cornelius Harnett* (1909).

HARPER, WILLIAM RAINEY 1856–1906, president of University of Chicago
Goodspeed, Thomas W., *William Rainey Harper* (1928).

HARRIMAN, EDWARD HENRY 1848–1909, railroad executive
Kennan, George, *E. H. Harriman* (2 vols., 1922).

HARRIMAN, W. AVERELL 1891– , diplomat, New York governor
Harriman, Averell, *America and Russia in a Changing World: A Half Century of Personal Observations* (1971).

HARRIS, GEORGE WASHINGTON 1814–1869, humorist
Rickels, Milton, *George Washington Harris* (1965).

HARRIS, JOEL CHANDLER 1848–1908, author
Brookes, Stella B., *Joel Chandler Harris: Folklorist* (1950).
Cousins, Paul M., *Joel Chandler Harris* (1968).
Harris, Julia C., *The Life and Letters of Joel Chandler Harris* (1918).

HARRIS, TOWNSEND 1804–1878, diplomat
Crow, Carl, *He Opened the Door* (1939).
Harris, Townsend, *Complete Journal*, M. E. Cosenza, ed. (1930), 2nd rev. ed., intro. by Douglas MacArthur II, (1959).

HARRIS, WILLIAM TORREY 1835–1909, philosopher
Leidecker, K. F., *Yankee Teacher* (1946).
Roberts, John S., *William T. Harris* (1924).

HARRISON, BENJAMIN 1833–1901, president
Harrison, Benjamin, and James G. Blaine, *Correspondence, 1882–1893*, Albert T. Volewiler, ed. (1940).
Sievers, Harry J., *Benjamin Harrison* (3 vols., 1960–1966).

HARRISON, CARTER HENRY 1825–1893, mayor of Chicago
Harrison, Carter H., *Stormy Years* (1935).
Johnson, Claudius O., *Carter H. Harrison* (1928).

HARRISON, CONSTANCE CARY 1843–1920, novelist
Harrison, Constance C., *Recollections Grave and Gay* (1911).

HARRISON, PETER 1716–1775, architect
Bridenbaugh, Carl, *Peter Harrison, First American Architect* (1949).

HARRISON, WILLIAM HENRY 1773–1841, president
Cleaves, Freeman, *Old Tippecanoe; William Henry Harrison* (1939).
Goebel, D. B., *William Henry Harrison* (1926).
Green, J. A., *William Henry Harrison* (1941).

Hoffnagle, Warren M., *Road to Fame: William H. Harrison and the Northwest* (1959).

HARROD, JAMES 1742–1793, frontiersman
Mason, Kathryn H., *James Harrod of Kentucky* (1951).

HART, MOSS 1904–1961, playwright
Hart, Moss, *Act One: Autobiography* (1959).

HART, WILLIAM S. 1872–1946, motion picture actor
Hart, William S., *My Life* (1929).

HARTE, FRANCIS BRETT 1836–1902, author; Bret Harte, pseud.
Harte, Bret, *Letters*, G. B. Harte, ed. (1926).
O'Connor, Richard, *Bret Harte: A Biography* (1966).
Stewart, George R., Jr., *Bret Harte* (1931).

HASSLER, FERDINAND RUDOLPH 1770–1843, geodesist, superintendent of Coast Survey
Cajori, Florian, *The Chequered Career of Ferdinand Rudolph Hassler* (1929).
Hassler, F. R., *Memoirs*, Emil Zschokke, ed. (1877; trans. 1882).

HATFIELD, HENRY DRURY 1871–1962, West Virginia governor
Karr, Carolyn, "Political Biography of Henry Hatfield," *W. Va. Hist.*, 28 (1966), 35.

HAWKINS, BENJAMIN 1754–1816, Indian agent
Hawkins, Benjamin, *Letters* (1916).
Pound, Merritt B., *Benjamin Hawkins, Indian Agent* (1951).

HAWLEY, JOSEPH 1723–1788, lawyer, Revolutionary leader
Brown, Ernest F., *Joseph Hawley, Colonial Radical* (1931).

HAWTHORNE, NATHANIEL 1804–1864, author, transcendentalist
Arvin, Newton, *Hawthorne* (1929).
Hawthorne, Nathaniel, *The American Notebooks*, Randall Stewart, ed. (1932).
——— *The English Notebooks*, Randall Stewart, ed. (1941).
Martin, Terence, *Nathaniel Hawthorne* (1964).
Stewart, Randall, *Nathaniel Hawthorne* (1948).
Van Doren, Mark, *Nathaniel Hawthorne* (1949).
Wagenknecht, Edward Charles, *Nathaniel Hawthorne* (1961)
Waggoner, Hyatt H., *Hawthorne* (rev. ed., 1963).

HAY, JOHN M. 1838–1905, journalist, statesman, diplomat
Dennett, Tyler, *John Hay* (1933).
Hay, John, *Letters and Extracts from Diary*, Henry Adams, ed. (3 vols., 1908).
Thayer, William R., *Life and Letters of John Hay* (2 vols., 1915).

HAYES, RUTHERFORD BIRCHARD 1822–1893, president
Barnard, Harry, *Rutherford B. Hayes* (1954).
Eckenrode, H. J., *Rutherford B. Hayes, Statesman of Reunion* (1930).
Hayes, Rutherford B., *Correspondence: Slater Fund for Negro Education, 1881–1893*, Louis D. Rubin, Jr., ed. (2 vols., 1959).
——— *Diary 1875–1881*, T. Harry Williams, ed. (1964).
——— *Diary and Letters*, Charles R. Williams, ed. (5 vols., 1922–1926).
Williams, Charles R., *Life of Rutherford Birchard Hayes* (2 vols., 1914).
Williams, T. Harry, *Hayes of the Twenty-Third, Civil War Volunteer Officer* (1965).

HAYNE, ROBERT YOUNG 1791–1839, South Carolina governor, senator
Jervy, Theodore D., *Robert Y. Hayne and His Times* (1909).

HAYWOOD, WILLIAM DUDLEY 1869–1928, radical leader
Conlin, Joseph R., *Big Bill Haywood and the Radical Union Movement* (1969).
Haywood, William D., *Bill Haywood's Book* (1929).

HEALY, GEORGE PETER ALEXANDER 1813–1894, painter
Healy, George P. A., *Reminiscences of a Portrait Painter* (1894).
de Mare, Marie, *G. P. A. Healy, American Artist* (1954).

HEARN, LAFCADIO 1850–1904, author, newspaperman
Bisland, Elizabeth, *Life and Letters of Lafcadio Hearn* (2 vols., 1906).
Kunst, Arthur E., *Lafcadio Hearn* (1969).
McWilliams, Vera, *Lafcadio Hearn* (1946).

HEARST, WILLIAM RANDOLPH 1863–1951, publisher
  Carlson, Oliver, and Ernest S. Bates, *Hearst, Lord of San Simeon* (1936).
  Hearst, William R., *William Randolph Hearst: A Portrait in His Own Words*,
    Edmond D. Coblentz, ed. (1952).
  Swanberg, William A., *Citizen Hearst* (1961).

HECKER, ISAAC THOMAS 1819–1888, founder of Paulist Fathers
  Elliott, William, *Life of Father Hecker* (1891).

HECKEWELDER, JOHN 1743–1823, Moravian missionary
  Heckewelder, John, *Thirty Thousand Miles*, Paul A. W. Wallace, ed. (1958).

HEINZE, FREDERICK AUGUSTUS 1869–1914, copper magnate
  McNelis, Sarah, *Copper King at War: Biography of F. Augustus Heinze* (1968).

HEINZEN, KARL 1809–1880, German revolutionist
  Wittke, Carl, *Against the Current: The Life of Karl Heinzen* (1945).

HELLMAN, LILLIAN 1905–   , playwright
  Hellman, Lillian, *Unfinished Woman: Memoir* (1969).

HELPER, HINTON ROWAN 1829–1909, journalist
  Bailey, Hugh C., *Hinton Rowan Helper: Abolitionist-Racist* (1965).

HEMINGWAY, ERNEST 1899–1961, author
  Baker, Carlos H., *Ernest Hemingway* (1969).
  Hemingway, Leicester, *My Brother, Ernest Hemingway* (1962).
  Hotchner, A. E., *Papa Hemingway* (1966).
  Ross, Lillian, *Portrait of Hemingway* (1961).
  Rovit, Earl H., *Ernest Hemingway* (1963).
  Young, Philip, *Ernest Hemingway* (1952).

HENNI, JOHN MARTIN 1805–1881, Catholic archbishop of Milwaukee
  Johnson, Peter L., *Crosier on the Frontier: John Martin Henni* (1959).

HENNINGS, THOMAS 1903–1960, Missouri senator
  Kemper, Donald J., *Decade of Fear: Senator Hennings and Civil Liberties*
    (1965).

HENRI, ROBERT 1865–1929, painter
  Homer, William I., *Robert Henri and His Circle* (1969).
  Yarrow, William, and Louis Bouche, *Robert Henri: His Life and Works* (1921).

HENRY, JOSEPH 1797–1878, physicist, secretary of Smithsonian Institution.
  Coulson, Thomas, *Joseph Henry* (1950).

HENRY, O. See PORTER, WILLIAM SYDNEY

HENRY, PATRICK 1736–1799, Revolutionary leader
  Henry, William W., *Patrick Henry: Life, Correspondence and Speeches* (3 vols.,
    1891).
  Meade, Robert D., *Patrick Henry* (2 vols., 1957–1969).

HERBERT, VICTOR 1859–1924, composer, conductor
  Waters, Edward N., *Victor Herbert: Life in Music* (1955).

HERNDON, WILLIAM HENRY 1818–1891, lawyer
  Donald, David, *Lincoln's Herndon* (1948).

HERRICK, MYRON TIMOTHY 1854–1929, diplomat
  Mott, Thomas B., *Myron T. Herrick, Friend of France* (1929).

HERRICK, ROBERT WELCH 1868–1938, novelist
  Herrick, Robert, *Memoirs* (1905); Daniel Aaron, ed., (1963).

HERSEY, JOHN 1914–   , novelist
  Sanders, David, *John Hersey* (1967).

HEWITT, ABRAM STEVENS 1822–1903, iron manufacturer, mayor of New York City,
  philanthropist
  Nevins, Allan, *Abram S. Hewitt; With Some Account of Peter Cooper* (1935).

HEWITT, PETER COOPER 1861–1921, scientist, inventor, son of Abram S. Hewitt
  Pupin, Michael I., *In Memoriam of Peter Cooper Hewitt* (1921).

HEYWARD, DUBOSE 1885–1940, writer
  Durham, Frank, *Du Bose Heyward* (1954).

HICKOCK, JAMES BUTLER "WILD BILL" 1837–1876, United States marshall

Rosa, Joseph G., *They Called Him Wild Bill: James Butler Hickok* (1964).

HICKS, EDWARD 1780–1849, artist
Ford, Alice, *Edward Hicks: Painter* (1952).

HICKS, ELIAS 1748–1830, Quaker leader
Forbush, Bliss, *Elias Hicks, Quaker Liberal* (1956).

HICKS, ISAAC 1767–1820, New York merchant
Davison, Robert A., *Isaac Hicks: New York Merchant and Quaker, 1767–1820* (1964).

HICKS, JOHN DONALD 1890– , historian
Hicks, John D., *My Life with History: Autobiography* (1968).

HIGGINSON, HENRY LEE 1834–1919, banker, philanthropist
Perry, Bliss, *Life and Letters of Henry Lee Higginson* (1921).

HIGGINSON, THOMAS WENTWORTH 1823–1911, Unitarian minister, Union officer
Edelstein, Tilden G., *Strange Enthusiasm: Thomas Wentworth Higginson* (1968).
Higginson, Mary T., *T. W. Higginson* (1914).
Higginson, Thomas W., *Cheerful Yesterdays* (1898).
——— *Letters and Journals*, M. T. Higginson, ed. (1921).
Meyer, Howard N., *Colonel of the Black Regiment: Thomas W. Higginson* (1967).
Wells, Anna Mary, *Dear Preceptor: Thomas Wentworth Higginson* (1963).

HILL, AMBROSE POWELL 1825–1865, Confederate general
Hassler, William W., *A. P. Hill, Lee's Forgotten General* (1957).

HILL, DANIEL HARVEY 1821–1889, Confederate general
Bridges, Hal, *Lee's Maverick General: Daniel Harvey Hill* (1961).

HILL, DAVID BENNETT 1843–1910, New York senator
Bass, Herbert J., *"I Am a Democrat": David Bennett Hill* (1961).

HILL, JAMES JEROME 1838–1916, railroad promoter
Pyle, J. G., *The Life of James J. Hill* (2 vols., 1917).

HILLMAN, SIDNEY 1887–1946, labor leader
Josephson, Matthew, *Sidney Hillman* (1953).

HITCHCOCK, ETHAN ALLEN 1798–1870, Union general, scientist
Cohen, I. Bernard, *Ethan Allen Hitchcock* (1952).
Hitchcock, Ethan A., *Diary*, W. A. Croffut, ed. (1909).

HOAR, EBENEZER ROCKWOOD 1816–1895, Attorney General
Storey, Moorfield, and Edward W. Emerson, *E. R. Hoar* (1911).

HOAR, GEORGE FRISBIE 1826–1904, Massachusetts senator
Hoar, George F., *Autobiography of Seventy Years* (2 vols., 1903).
Welch, Richard E., Jr., *George F. Hoar and the Half-Breed Republicans* (1971).

HOCKING, WILLIAM ERNEST 1873–1966, philosopher
Robinson, Daniel S., *Royce and Hocking: American Idealists* (1968).
Rouner, Leroy S., *Within Human Experience: The Philosophy of William Ernest Hocking* (1969).

HOGG, JAMES STEPHEN 1851–1906, Texas governor
Cotner, Robert C., *James Stephen Hogg* (1959).

HOLDEN, WILLIAM WOODS 1818–1892, North Carolina governor
Holden, William W., *Memoirs*, W. K. Boyd, ed. (1911).

HOLLADAY, BEN 1819–1887, western railroad and steamship entrepreneur
Lucia, Ellis, *Saga of Ben Holladay* (1959).

HOLLAND, JOHN PHILIP 1840–1914, inventor of submarine
Morris, Richard K., *John P. Holland: Inventor of the Modern Submarine* (1966).

HOLLAND, JOSIAH GILBERT 1819–1881, newspaper and magazine editor
Peckham, Howard H., *Josiah G. Holland* (1940).

HOLMES, EZEKIEL 1801–1865, agriculturist
Day, Clarence, *Ezekiel Holmes* (1968).

HOLMES, JOHN HAYNES 1879–1964, clergyman, reformer
Holmes, John H., *I Speak for Myself: Autobiography* (1959).

HOLMES, OLIVER WENDELL 1809–1894, physician, writer
Holmes, Oliver Wendell, *Writings* (13 vols., 1891).
Howe, Mark A. DeW., *Autocrat of the Breakfast Table* (1939).
Morse, John T. Jr., *Life and Letters of Oliver Wendell Holmes* (2 vols., 1896).
Small, Miriam R., *Oliver Wendell Holmes* (1962).
Tilton, Eleanor M., *Amiable Autocrat: Oliver Wendell Holmes* (1947).

HOLMES, OLIVER WENDELL, JR. 1841–1935, Supreme Court justice
Biddle, Francis, *Mr. Justice Holmes* (1942).
Frankfurter, Felix, *Mr. Justice Holmes* (2nd ed., 1961).
Holmes, Oliver W., Jr., and Lewis Einstein, *Correspondence, 1903–1935,* James
B. Peabody, ed. (1964).
────── and Harold J. Laski, *Holmes-Laski Letters: Correspondence, 1916–1935,*
Mark DeW. Howe, ed. (2 vols., 1953).
────── and Frederick Pollock, *Holmes-Pollock Letters: Correspondence,
1874–1932,* Mark DeW. Howe, ed. (2nd ed., 1961).
────── *Dissenting Opinions,* Alfred Lief, ed. (1929).
Holmes, Oliver W., Jr., *Speeches,* Mark DeW. Howe, comp. (1962).
────── *Touched with Fire: Civil War Letters and Diary, 1861–1864,* Mark DeW.
Howe, ed. (1946)
Howe, Mark DeW., *Justice Oliver W. Holmes* (2 vols., 1957–1963).
Hurst, James Willard, *Justice Holmes on Legal History* (1964).
Lerner, Max, ed., *Mind and Faith of Justice Holmes* (new ed., 1954).

HOLT, HAMILTON 1872–1951, president of Rollins College, journalist
Kuehl, Warren F., *Hamilton Holt: Journalist* (1960).

HOLT, HENRY 1840–1926, publisher
Holt, Henry, *Garrulities of an Octogenarian Elder* (1923).

HOMER, WINSLOW 1836–1910, painter
Downes, W. H., *The Life and Works of Winslow Homer* (1911).
Goodrich, Lloyd, *Winslow Homer* (1944).

HONE, PHILIP 1780–1851, auctioneer, mayor of New York City
Hone, Philip, *Diary, 1828–1851,* Allan Nevins, ed. (1927).

HOOD, JOHN BELL 1831–1879, Confederate general
Dyer, John P., *The Gallant Hood* (1950).

HOOKER, JOSEPH 1814–1879, Union general
Hebert, Walter H., *Fighting Joe Hooker* (1944).

HOOKER, THOMAS 1586–1647, founder of Connecticut
Archibald, Warren S., *Thomas Hooker* (1933).
Walker, George L., *Thomas Hooker* (1891).

HOOPER, BEN W. 1870–1957, Tennessee governor
Hooper, Ben W., *Autobiography,* Everett R. Boyce, ed. (1963).

HOOVER, HERBERT 1874–1964, president
Blainey, Geoffrey, "Herbert Hoover's Forgotten Years," *Business Archives and
Hist.* [Australia] 3 (1963), 53.
Brandes, Joseph, *Herbert Hoover and Economic Diplomacy: Department of
Commerce Policy* 1921–1928 (1962).
Hoover, Herbert, *Memoirs* (3 vols., 1951–1952).
────── *State Papers,* William S. Myers, ed. (2 vols., 1934).
Lyons, Eugene, *Herbert Hoover* (1964).

HOPE, JOHN 1868–1936, president of Morehouse College
Torrence, Ridgely, *Story of John Hope* (1948).

HOPKINS, HARRY LLOYD 1890–1946, New Deal administrator
Charles, Searle F., *Minister of Relief: Harry Hopkins and the Depression*
(1963).
Sherwood, Robert E., *Roosevelt and Hopkins: An Intimate History* (1950).

HOPKINS, JOHNS 1795–1873, merchant, philanthropist
Thom, H. H., *Johns Hopkins: A Silhouette* (1929).

HOPKINS, MARK 1802–1887, philosopher, president of Williams College
Denison, J. H., *Mark Hopkins: A Biography* (1935).
Rudolph, Frederick, *Mark Hopkins and the Log: Williams College, 1836–1872*
(1956).

HOPKINS, STEPHEN 1707–1785, merchant, journalist, Rhode Island Revolutionary leader
Foster, William E., *Stephen Hopkins* (1884).

HOPKINSON, FRANCIS 1737–1791, Revolutionary leader, musician
Hastings, George E., *Life and Works of Francis Hopkinson* (1926).
Sonneck, Oscar T., *Francis Hopkinson and James Lyon* (1905).

HOPKINSON, JOSEPH 1770–1842, lawyer, composer
Konkle, Burton A., *Joseph Hopkinson, 1770–1842* (1931).

HOPPER, DE WOLFE 1858–1935, actor, light-opera singer
Hopper, DeWolfe, *Once a Clown Always a Clown* (1927).

HOPPER, EDWARD 1882–1967, artist
Goodrich, Lloyd, *Edward Hopper* (1950).
O'Doherty, Brian, "Edward Hopper," *Art. in Am.* 52 (1964), 68.

HOSACK, DAVID 1769–1835, medical educator
Robbins, Christine C., *David Hosack* (1964).

HOUGHTON, DOUGLASS 1809–1845, geologist
Rintala, Edsel K., *Douglass Houghton: Michigan's Pioneer Geologist* (1954).

HOUSE, EDWARD MANDELL 1858–1938, Wilson's advisor
George, Alexander L., and Juliett L. George, *Woodrow Wilson and Colonel House: A Personality Study* (1956).
House, Edward M., *Intimate Papers,* Charles Seymour, ed. (4 vols., 1926–1928).
Richardson, Rupert N., *Colonel Edward M. House: Texas Years, 1858–1912* (1964).

HOUSTON, DAVID FRANKLIN 1866–1940, Texas educator, secretary of agriculture, secretary of treasury
Houston, David F., *Eight Years with Wilson's Cabinet* (2 vols., 1926).

HOUSTON, SAMUEL 1793–1863, president of Texas
Friend, Llerena B., *Sam Houston: Great Designer* (1954).
Gregory, Jack, and Rennard Strickland, *Sam Houston with the Cherokees, 1829–1833* (1967).
Houston, Sam, *Autobiography*, Donald Day and Harry H. Ullom, eds. (1954).
James, Marquis, *The Raven, a Biography of Sam Houston* (1929).
Wisehart, M. K., *Sam Houston* (1962).

HOWARD, OLIVER OTIS 1830–1909, Union soldier, Commissioner of the Freedmen's Bureau, president of Howard University
Carpenter, John A., *Sword and Olive Branch: O. O. Howard* (1964).
Howard, Oliver O., *Autobiography* (2 vols., 1903).
McFeely, William S., *Yankee Stepfather: General O. O. Howard and Freedman* (1968).

HOWE, EDGAR WATSON 1853–1937, newspaper editor, author
Pickett, Calder M., *Ed Howe: Country Town Philosopher* (1968).

HOWE, JULIA WARD 1819–1910, suffrage leader, writer
Howe, Julia W., *Reminiscences* (1899).
Richards, Laura E., and M. H. Elliott, *Julia Ward Howe* (2 vols., 1916).
Tharp, Louise H., *Three Saints and a Sinner, Julia Ward Howe, Louisa, Annie, and Sam Ward* (1956).

HOWE, LOUIS MCHENRY 1871–1936, advisor to F. D. Roosevelt
Rollins, Alfred B., Jr., *Roosevelt and Howe* (1962).
Stiles, Lela, *Man Behind Roosevelt: Louis McHenry Howe* (1954).

HOWE, SAMUEL GRIDLEY 1801–1876, physician, educator of the blind
Howe Samuel G., *Letters and Journals,* Laura E. Rich.ards, ed. (2 vols., 1906–1909).
Richards, Laura E., *Samuel Gridley Howe* (1935).
Schwartz, Harold, *Samuel Gridley Howe, Social Reformer* (1956).

HOWELLS, WILLIAM DEAN 1837–1920, author, critic, editor
Brooks, Van Wyck, *Howells: His Life and World* (1959).
Carter, Everett, *Howells and Age of Realism* (1954).
Cooke, Delmar G., *William Dean Howells* (1922).

Hough, Robert L., *Quiet Rebel: William Dean Howells* (1959).
Howells, William Dean, *Life in Letters*, Mildred Howells, ed. (2 vols., 1928).
—— *Literary Friends and Acquaintances* (1900).
—— *Recollections* (1895).
—— *Years of My Youth* (1916).
Kirk, Rudolf, and Clara Kirk, *William Dean Howells* (1962).
Lynn, Kenneth S., *William Dean Howells* (1971).
Vanderbilt, Kermit, *Achievement of William Dean Howells: A Reinterpretation* (1968).
Wagenknecht, Edward, *William Dean Howells: The Friendly Eye* (1969).

HUBBARD, ELBERT GREEN 1856–1915, author
Champney, Freeman, *Art and Glory: Elbert Hubbard* (1968).

HUDSON, WILLIAM CADWALADER 1843–1915, journalist
Hudson, William C., *Random Recollections of an Old Political Reporter* (1911).

HUGHES, CHARLES EVANS 1889–1950, Supreme Court Chief Justice, Secretary of State
Freund, Paul A., "Charles Evans Hughes as Chief Justice," *Harv. Law Rev.*, 81 (1967), 4.
Glad, Betty, *Charles Evans Hughes and the Illusions of Innocence* (1966).
Hendel, Samuel, *Charles Evans Hughes and Supreme Court* (1951).
Perkins, Dexter, *Charles Evans Hughes* (1956).
Pusey, Merlo J., *Charles Evans Hughes* (2 vols., 1951).
Wesser, Robert F., *Charles Evans Hughes: Politics and Reform in New York, 1905–1910* (1967).

HUGHES, JOHN JOSEPH 1797–1864, Catholic archbishop of New York City
Brann, H. A., *Most Rev. John Hughes* (1892).

HUGHES, (JAMES) LANGSTON 1902–1967, poet
Hughes, Langston, *The Big Sea* (1940).
—— *I Wonder as I Wander: Autobiographical Journey* (1956).
Meltzer, Milton, *Langston Hughes* (1968).

HULL, CORDELL 1871–1955, secretary of state
Hinton, H. B., *Cordell Hull* (1942).
Hull, Cordell, *Memoirs* (2 vols., 1948).
Pratt, Julius W., *Cordell Hull, 1933–44* (1964).

HULL, ISAAC 1773–1843, naval officer
Grant, Bruce, *Isaac Hull, Captain of Old Ironsides* (1947).
Hull, Isaac, *Papers*, Gardner W. Allen, ed. (1929).

HULL, JOHN 1624–1683, merchant, mint-master
Clarke, Hermann F., *John Hull* (1940).

HULL, JOSEPHINE 1886–1957, actress
Carson, William G. B., *Dear Josephine: Theatrical Career of Josephine Hull* (1963).

HUME, ROBERT DENISTON 1845–1908, salmon canner
Dodds, Gordon B., *Salmon King of Oregon: R. D. Hume* (1963).

HUMPHREY, GEORGE MAGOFFIN 1890–1970, Secretary of Treasury
Humphrey, George M., *Basic Papers as Secretary of Treasury, 1953–1957*, Nathaniel R. Howard, ed. (1965).

HUMPHREY, HUBERT HORATIO 1911– , Minnesota senator, Vice-President
Ryskind, Allan H., *Hubert: Unauthorized Biography of the Vice-President* (1968).

HUMPHREYS, DAVID 1752–1818, soldier, statesman, poet
Humphreys, F. L., *Life and Times of David Humphreys* (1917).

HUNEKER, JAMES GIBBONS 1860–1921, musician, critic
Huneker, James G., *Intimate Letters*, Josephine Huneker, ed. (1924).
—— *Letters*, Josephine Huneker, ed. (2 vols. 1922).
Schwab, Arnold T., *James Gibbons Huneker* (1963).

HUNT, WILLIAM MORRIS 1824–1879, painter
Knowlton, Helen M., *Art-Life of William Morris Hunt* (1899).

HUNTER, ROBERT MERCER TALIAFERRO 1809–1887, Virginia senator

Simms, H. H., *Life of Robert M. T. Hunter: A Study in Sectionalism and Secession* (1935).

HUNTINGTON, HENRY EDWARDS 1850–1927, railroad magnate, founder of Huntington Library and Art Gallery
Marcosson, I. F., *A Little Known Master of Millions* (1914).

HURSTON, ZORA NEAL 1901–1960, Negro writer
Hurston, Zora N., *Dust Tracks on a Road: Autobiography* (1942).

HUSSEY, OBED 1792–1860, farm machinery inventor
Greeno, Follett L., *Obed Hussey* (1912).

HUTCHINSON, ANNE 1591–1643, pioneer, religious liberal
Curtis, Edith R., *Anne Hutchinson* (1930).
Rugg, W. K., *Unafraid: A Life of Anne Hutchinson* (1930).

HUTCHINSON, THOMAS 1711–1780, merchant, Massachusetts governor
Freiberg, Malcolm, "Thomas Hutchinson: First Fifty Years," *WMQ*, 3 ser., 15 (1958), 35.
Hosmer, James K., *The Life of Thomas Hutchinson* (1896).
Hutchinson, Thomas, *Diary and Letters*, P. O. Hutchinson, ed. (2 vols., 1883–1886).

HYDE, WILLIAM DE WITT 1858–1917, president of Bowdoin College
Burnett, C. T., *Hyde of Bowdoin: William DeWitt Hyde* (1931).

IBERVILLE, PIERRE LE MOYNE, SIEUR DE 1661–1706, explorer
Reed, Charles B., *The First Great Canadian* (1910).

ICKES, HAROLD LE CLAIR 1874–1952, Secretary of Interior
Ickes, Harold L., *The Autobiography of a Curmudgeon* (1943).
—— *Secret Diary*, (3 vols., 1953–1954).

INGALLS, JOHN JAMES 1833–1900, Kansas senator
Connelley, William E., *Ingalls of Kansas* (1909).
Ingalls, John J., *Collection of Writings*, William E. Connelley, ed. (1902).

INGE, WILLIAM 1913– , playwright
Shuman, R. Baird, *William Inge* (1965).

INGERSOLL, CHARLES JARED 1782–1862, Pennsylvania Democrat
Meigs, William M., *Life of Charles J. Ingersoll* (1897).

INGERSOLL, JARED 1722–1781, lawyer, Loyalist
Gipson, Lawrence H., *Jared Ingersoll: A Study of American Loyalism* (1920).

INGERSOLL, ROBERT GREEN 1833–1899, lecturer, agnostic
Cramer, Clarence H., *Royal Bob: Robert G. Ingersoll* (1952).
Ingersoll, Robert G., *Letters*, E. I. Wakefield, ed. (1951).
Smith, Edward G., *Ingersoll* (1904).

INNESS, GEORGE 1825–1894, painter
Inness, George, Jr., *Life, Art, and Letters of George Inness* (1917).
Ireland, LeRoy, *Works of George Inness* (1965).
McCausland, Elizabeth, *George Inness, American Landscape Painter* (1946).

INSULL, SAMUEL 1859–1938, utilities magnate
McDonald, Forrest, *Insull* (1962).

IREDELL, JAMES 1751–1799, jurist, Revolutionary leader
McRee, Griffith J., *Life and Correspondence of James Iredell* (2 vols., 1857–1858).

IRELAND, JOHN 1838–1918, Catholic Archbishop of St. Paul, co-founder of Catholic University
Moynihan, James H., *Archibishop Ireland* (1953).

IRVING, WASHINGTON 1783–1859, author
Hedges, William L., *Washington Irving, 1802–1832* (1965).
Irving, Washington, *Journal, 1823–1824*, Stanley T. Williams, ed. (1931).
—— *Life and Letters* Pierre M. Irving, ed. (4 vols., 1863–1864; repr. 1967).
Wagenknecht, Edward, *Washington Irving* (1962).
Williams, Stanley T., *Life of Washington Irving* (2 vols., 1935).

ISHERWOOD, BENJAMIN FRANKLIN 1822–1915, naval engineer
Sloan, Edward W., III, *Benjamin Franklin Isherwood, Naval Engineer, 1861–1869* (1966).

IVES, CHARLES 1874–1954, composer
Cowell, Henry, and Sidney, *Charles Ives* (1955).

IVES, JAMES MERRITT 1824–1895, lithographer
Peters, Harry T., *Currier and Ives: Printmakers to the American People* (2 vols., 1925–1931).

IZARD, RALPH 1741/42–1804, diplomat, South Carolina senator
Izard, Ralph, *Correspondence*, A. I. Deas, ed. (1844).

JACKSON, ANDREW 1767–1845, president
Bassett, J. S., *Life of Andrew Jackson* (2 vols., 1925).
Jackson, Andrew, *Correspondence*, J. S. Bassett and J. F. Jameson, eds. (7 vols., 1926–1935).
James, Marquis, *Andrew Jackson* (2 vols., 1933–1937).
Parton, James, *Life of Andrew Jackson* (3 vols., 1860).
Remini, Robert V., *Andrew Jackson* (1966).
Syrett, Harold C., *Andrew Jackson* (1953).
Ward, John W., *Andrew Jackson* (1955).

JACKSON, HELEN MARIA FISKE HUNT 1830–1885, author
Odell, Ruth, *Helen Hunt Jackson* (1939).

JACKSON, JAMES 1757–1806, Georgia senator
Foster, William O., *James Jackson: Duelist and Militant Statesman* (1960).

JACKSON, JAMES 1777–1867, founder of Massachusetts General Hospital
Putnam, James J., *Memoir of Dr. James Jackson* (1905).

JACKSON, JOHN BAPTIST 1701–1780?, artist, wood engraver
Kainen, Jacob, *John Baptist Jackson: Master of Color Woodcut* (1962).

JACKSON, ROBERT HOUGHWOUT 1892–1954, Supreme Court justice
Gerhart, Eugene C., *America's Advocate: Robert H. Jackson* (1958).

JACKSON, THOMAS JONATHAN "STONEWALL" 1824–1863, Confederate general
Davis, Burke, *They Called Him Stonewall* (1954).
Henderson, George F. R., *Stonewall Jackson and the American Civil War* (2 vols., 1898).
Tate, Allen, *Stonewall Jackson* (2nd ed., 1957).
Vandiver, Frank E., *Mighty Stonewall* (1957).

JACKSON, WILLIAM HENRY 1843–1942, western photographer
Jackson, Clarence S., *Picture Maker of the Old West: William H. Jackson* (1947).
Jackson, William H., *Diaries*, LeRoy and Ann W. Hafen, eds. (1959).

JACOBI, MARY PUTNAM 1842–1906, physician
Putnam, Ruth, *Life and Letters of Mary Putnam Jacobi* (1925).

JAMES, HENRY 1843–1916, novelist
Bell, Millicent, *Edith Wharton and Henry James* (1965).
Edel, Leon, *Henry James* (4 vols., 1953–1969).
James, Henry, *Letters*, Percy Lubbock, ed. (2 vols., 1920).
———— *The Middle Years* (1917).
———— *Notes of a Son and Brother* (1914).
———— *A Small Boy and Others* (1913).
Kelley, Cornelia P., *Early Development of Henry James* (rev. ed., 1965).
McElderry, Brice R., Jr., *Henry James* (1965).
Matthiessen, F. O., *Henry James, Major Phase* (1946).

JAMES, JESSE 1847–1882, outlaw
Settle, William A., Jr., *Jesse James Was His Name* (1966).

JAMES, JOHN HOUGH 1800–1881, lawyer, banker, railroad builder
Smith, William E., and Ophia D., *Buckeye Titan* (1953).

JAMES, WILLIAM 1842–1910, philosopher, psychologist
Allen, Gay W., *William James* (1967).
Brennan, Bernard P., *William James* (1968).
James, William, *Letters*, Henry James, ed. (2 vols., 1920).
Moore, Edward C., *William James* (1966).
Perry, Ralph Barton, *The Thought and Character of William James* (2 vols., 1935).

JAMES FAMILY
Matthiessen, Francis O., *The James Family* (1947).

JAMES, HENRY 1811–1882, author, philosopher
Warren, Austin, *The Elder Henry James* (1934).

JAMESON, JOHN FRANKLIN 1859–1937, historian
Jameson, John Franklin, *Correspondence*, Elizabeth Donnan and Leo F. Stock, eds. (1956).

JARRELL, RANDALL 1914–1965, poet
Lowell, Robert, Peter Taylor, and Robert Penn Warren, eds., *Randall Jarrell* (1967).

JARVES, JAMES JACKSON 1818–1888, merchant, art critic
Steegmuller, Francis, *Two Lives of James Jackson Jarves* (1951).

JARVIS, JOHN WESLEY 1781–1839, painter
Dickson, Harold E., *John Wesley Jarvis, Painter* (1949).

JARVIS, THOMAS JORDAN 1836–1915, North Carolina political leader, governor
Jarvis, Thomas J., *Papers, 1869–1882*, Wilfred B. Yearns, ed. (vol. 1, 1969–).

JAY, JOHN 1745–1829, Revolutionary leader, diplomat, Chief justice
Jay, John, *Correspondence and Public Papers*, H. P. Johnston, ed. (4 vols., 1890–1893).
—— *Diary, during Peace Negotiations of 1782* Frank Monaghan, ed. (1934).
Monaghan, Frank, *John Jay* (1935).
Morris, Richard B., *John Jay, the Nation, and the Court* (1967).

JAY, WILLIAM 1789–1858, anti-slavery leader
Tuckerman, Bayard, *William Jay and the Constitutional Movement for the Abolition of Slavery* (1893).

JEFFERS, ROBINSON 1887–1962, poet
Bennett, Melba B., *Robinson Jeffers* (1966).
Carpenter, Frederic I., *Robinson Jeffers* (1962).
Powell, Lawrence C., *Robinson Jeffers* (1934).

JEFFERSON, JOSEPH 1829–1905, actor
Jefferson, Joseph, *Autobiography* (1897). Alan S. Downer, ed. (1964).
Winter, William, *Life and Art of Joseph Jefferson* (1894).

JEFFERSON, MARK 1863–1949, geographer
Martin, Geoffrey J., *Mark Jefferson: Geographer* (1968).

JEFFERSON, THOMAS 1743–1826, president
Berman, Eleanor D., *Jefferson among the Arts* (1947).
Brown, Stuart G., *Thomas Jefferson* (1966).
Conant, James B., *Thomas Jefferson and Public Education* (1962).
Dumbauld, Edward, *Jefferson, American Tourist* (1946).
Fleming, Thomas J., *Man from Monticello: Jefferson* (1969).
Jefferson, Thomas, *Adams-Jefferson Letters*, Lester J. Cappon, ed. (2 vols., 1959).
—— *Autobiography*, Dumas Malone, ed. (1959).
—— and P. S. Du Pont de Nemours, *Correspondence*, Gilbert Chinard, ed. (1931). A less complete collection but with the French letters translated into English, Dumas Malone, ed., (1930).
—— *Family Letters*, Edwin M. Betts and James A. Bear, Jr., eds. (1966).
—— *Farm Book*, Edwin M. Betts, ed. (1953).
—— and Robley Dunglison, *Letters*, John M. Dorsey, ed. (1960).
—— *Notes on the State of Virginia 1781* William Peden, ed. (1955).
—— *On Education*, Gordon C. Lee, ed. (1961).
—— *Papers*, Julian P. Boyd et al., eds. (vols. 1/18– , 1950/71–).
—— *Some Correspondence*, W. C. Ford, ed. (1902).
—— *Writings*, Paul L. Ford, ed. (10 vols., 1892–1899).
—— *Writings*, A. A. Lipscomb and A. E. Bergh, eds. (20 vols., 1903).
Kimball, Fiske, *Thomas Jefferson, Architect* (1916).
Kimball, Marie, *Jefferson* (3 vols., 1943–1950).
Koch, Adrienne, *Jefferson and Madison* (1950).

Malone, Dumas, *Jefferson and His Time* (4 vols., 1948–1970).
—— *Thomas Jefferson as Political Leader* (1963).
Martin, Edwin T., *Thomas Jefferson: Scientist* (1952).
Patterson, Caleb P., *Constitutional Principles of Thomas Jefferson* (1953).
Peterson, Merrill D., *Thomas Jefferson* (1970).
Randall, H. S., *Life of Thomas Jefferson* (3 vols., 1858).
Randolph, Sarah N., *Domestic Life of Thomas Jefferson* (1939).
Schachner, Nathan, *Thomas Jefferson* (2 vols., 1951).

JENNYS, RICHARD fl. 1760–1790, painter
Sherman, Frederick F., *Richard Jennys, New England Portrait Painter* (1941).

JENSEN, JENS 1860–1951, landscape architect
Eaton, Leonard K., *Landscape Artist in America, Jens Jensen* (1964).

JEWETT, SARAH ORNE 1849–1909, writer
Cary, Richard, *Sarah Orne Jewett* (1962).

JOGUES, ISAAC 1607–1646, Jesuit missionary
Birch, J. J., *Saint of the Wilderness: Isaac Joques* (1936).
Scott, Martin J., *Isaac Joques, Missioner and Martyr* (1927).

JOHNSON, ANDREW 1808–1875, president
Johnson, Andrew, *Papers, 1822–1857*, LeRoy P. Graf and Ralph W. Haskins, eds. (Vols. 1/2– , 1967/70–
Johnson, Andrew, *Speeches*, Frank Moore, ed. (1865).
Lomask, Milton, *Andrew Johnson* (1960).
McKitrick, Eric L., *Andrew Johnson and Reconstruction* (1960).
Notaro, Carmen A., "Biographic Treatment of Andrew Johnson in Twentieth Century," *Tenn. Hist. Quar.*, 24 (1965), 143.
Stryker, Lloyd P., *Andrew Johnson: A Study in Courage* (1936).
Thomas, Lately, *First President Johnson* (1968).

JOHNSON, CLAUDIA ALTA "LADY BIRD", 1912– , first lady
Johnson, Claudia A., *White House Diary* (1970).

JOHNSON, EASTMAN 1824–1906, artist
Bauer, John I. H., *American Genre Painter, Eastman Johnson* (1940).

JOHNSON, HERSCHEL VESPASIAN 1812–1880, Georgia governor, jurist
Flippin, Percy S., *Herschel V. Johnson* (1931).

JOHNSON, HIRAM WARREN 1866–1945, California governor, senator
Olin, Spencer C., Jr., *California's Prodigal Sons: Hiram Johnson and Progressives, 1911–1917* (1968).

JOHNSON, JAMES WELDON 1871–1938, author, secretary of NAACP
Johnson, James Weldon, *Along My Way* (1933).

JOHNSON, JOHN ALBERT 1861–1909, Minnesota governor
Helmes, W. G., *John A. Johnson* (1949).

JOHNSON, LYNDON BAINES 1908– , president
Baker, Leonard, *The Johnson Eclipse* (1966).
Davie, Michael, *LBJ: A Foreign Observer's Viewpoint* (1966).
Evans, Rowland, and Robert Novak, *Lyndon B. Johnson* (1966).
Geyelin, Philip, *Lyndon B. Johnson and the World* (1966).
Goldman, Eric F., *Tragedy of Lyndon Johnson* (1969).
Johnson, Lyndon B., *No Retreat from Tomorrow: 1967 Messages to 90th Congress* (1968).
—— *Public Papers* (10 vols., 1964–1969).
—— *To Heal and To Build,* James M. Burns, ed. (1968).
—— *The Vantage Point: Perspectives on the Presidency, 1963–1969* (1971)
Johnson, Sam Houston, *My Brother Lyndon* (1970).
Sidey, Hugh, *Lyndon Johnson* (1968).
Wicker, Tom, *JFK and LBJ* (1968).

JOHNSON, PHILIP CORTELYOU 1906– ; architect
Jacobus, John M., Jr., *Philip Johnson* (1962).

JOHNSON, REVERDY 1796–1876, Maryland senator, diplomat
Steiner, Bernard C., *Reverdy Johnson* (1914).

JOHNSON, RICHARD MENTOR 1780–1850, Vice-President
Meyer, Leland W., *Life and Times of Col. Richard M. Johnson of Kentucky* (1932).

JOHNSON, ROBERT 1676–1735, South Carolina governor
Sherman, Richard P., *Robert Johnson: Royal Governor of South Carolina* (1966).

JOHNSON, ROBERT UNDERWOOD 1853–1937, editor and poet
Johnson, Robert U., *Remembered Yesterdays* (1923).

JOHNSON, SAMUEL 1696–1772, Anglican clergyman, president of King's College
Beardsley, E. E., *Life and Correspondence of Samuel Johnson, D.D.* (2nd ed., 1874).
Johnson, Samuel, *Samuel Johnson, President of King's College: His Career and Writings* Herbert and Carol Schneider, eds. (4 vols., 1929).

JOHNSON, THOMAS 1732–1819, Maryland governor, Supreme Court justice
Delaplaine, E. S., *Life of Thomas Johnson* (1927).

JOHNSON, TOM LOFTIN 1854–1911, mayor of Cleveland
Johnson, Tom L., *My Story* (1911).

JOHNSON, SIR WILLIAM 1715–1774, Colonial superintendant of Indian affairs
Flexner, James T., *Mohawk Baronet: Sir William Johnson* (1959).
Johnson, William, *Papers*, J. Sullivan, A. C. Flick, and M. W. Hamilton, eds. (13 vols., 1921–1962).
Pound, Arthur, *Johnson of the Mohawks* (1930).
Seymour, Flora W., *Lords of the Valley: Sir William Johnson* (1930).
Stone, William L., *Life and Times of Sir William Johnson, Bart* (2 vols., 1865).

JOHNSON, WILLIAM 1771–1834, Supreme Court justice
Morgan, Donald G., *Justice William Johnson the First Dissenter* (1954).

JOHNSON, WILLIAM 1809–1851, free Negro barber
Davis, Edwin A., and William R. Hogan, *Barber of Natchez* (1954).
Johnson, William, *Ante-Bellum Diary*, William R. Hogan and Edwin A. Davis, eds. (1951).

JOHNSON, WILLIAM SAMUEL 1727–1819, Revolutionary leader, Constitutional Convention delegate, Supreme Court justice
Beardsley, E. E., *Life and Times of William Samuel Johnson* (2nd ed., 1886).
Groce, G. C., Jr., *William Samuel Johnson: A Maker of the Constitution* (1937).
Johnson, William Samuel, *Superior Court Diary, 1772–1773 of Colony of Connecticut*, John T. Farrell, ed. (1942).

JOHNSTON, ALBERT SIDNEY 1803–1862, Confederate general
Johnston, William P., *Life of General Albert Sidney Johnston* (1878).
Roland, Charles P., *Albert S. Johnston* (1964).

JOHNSTON, HENRIETTA fl. 1720, painter
Middleton, Margaret S., *Henrietta Johnston of Charles Town: America's First Pastellist* (1966).

JOHNSTON, JOSEPH EGGLESTON 1807–1891, Confederate general
Govan, Gilbert E., and James W. Livingood, *Different Valor: General Joseph E. Johnston* (1956).
Johnston, Joseph E., *Narrative of Military Operations* (1874).

JOHNSTON, OLIN DEWITT 1896–   ; South Carolina senator
Huss, John E., *Senator for the South: Olin D. Johnston* (1961).

JONES, CHARLES JESSE 1844–1919, experimenter in animal breeding
Easton, Robert, and Mackenzie Brown, *Lord of Beasts: Buffalo Jones* (1961).

JONES, JESSE HOLMAN 1874–1956, financier, chairman of Reconstruction Finance Corporation
Jones, Jesse, *Fifty Billion Dollars: My Thirteen Years with the R.F.C., 1932–1945* (1951).
Timmons, Bascom N., *Jesse H. Jones* (1956).

JONES, JOHN PAUL 1747–1792, Revolutionary naval officer
De Koven, Anna, *Life and Letters of John Paul Jones* (2 vols., 1913).
Morison, Samuel E., *John Paul Jones* (1959).

JONES, MARY HARRIS "MOTHER" 1830–1930, labor leader
  Jones, Mother, *Autobiography*, M. F. Parton, ed. (1925).
JORDAN, DAVID STARR 1851–1931, biologist, president of Stanford University
  Burns, Edward M., *David Starr Jordan* (1953).
  Jordan, David S., *The Days of a Man; Being Memories of a Naturalist, Teacher, and Minor Prophet of Democracy* (2 vols., 1922).
JOSEPH, CHIEF 1840–1904, Nez Percé chief
  Beal, Merrill D., *"I Will Fight No More Forever": Chief Joseph and Nez Percé War* (1963).
JUDD, GERRIT PARMELE 1803–1873, advisor to Hawaiian king
  Judd, Gerrit P. IV, *Dr. Judd, Hawaii's Friend* (1960).
JUDSON, ADONIRAM 1788–1850, Baptist missionary
  Wayland, Francis, *Memoir of the Life and Labors of the Rev. Adoniram Judson* (2 vols., 1853).
JUDSON, EDWARD ZANE CARROLL 1823–1886, author; Ned Buntline, pseud.
  Monaghan, Jay, *Great Rascal: Ned Buntline* (1952).
JULIAN, GEORGE WASHINGTON 1817–1899, abolitionist politician
  Julian, George W., *Political Recollections* (1884).
  Riddleberger, Patrick W., *George Washington Julian, Radical Republican* (1966).
KAHN, LOUIS I. 1901–   , architect
  Scully, Vincent J., Jr., *Louis I. Kahn* (1962).
KALB, JOHANN 1721–1780, Revolutionary general
  Kapp, Friedrich, *The Life of Johann Kalb* (1884).
KANE, ELISHA KENT 1820–1857, explorer
  Mirsky, Jeannette, *Elisha Kent Kane and Seafaring Frontier* (1954).
KASSON, JOHN ADAM 1822–1910, Iowa congressman, diplomat
  Younger, Edward, *John A. Kasson: Politics and Diplomacy from Lincoln to McKinley* (1955).
KEANE, JOHN JOSEPH 1839–1918, Catholic archbishop of Dubuque
  Ahern, Patrick H., *Life of John J. Keane: Educator and Archbishop* (2nd., 1955).
KEARNY, LAWRENCE 1789–1868, naval commander in Far East
  Alden, Carroll S., *Lawrence Kearny* (1936).
KEARNY, PHILIP 1814–1862, Union general
  Kearny, Thomas, *General Philip Kearny* (1937).
  de Peyster, J. W., *Personal and Military History of Philip Kearny, Major-General* (1869).
KEARNY, STEPHEN WATTS 1794–1848, frontier general
  Clarke, Dwight L., *Stephen Watts Kearny: Soldier of the West* (1961).
KEATON, BUSTER 1896–1966, comedian
  Blesh, Rudi, *Keaton* (1966).
KEFAUVER, ESTES 1903–1963, Tennessee senator
  Gorman, Joseph Bruce, *Kefauver: A Political Biography* (1971).
KEITH, GEORGE 1638–1716, founder of "Christian Quakers"
  Kirby, Ethyn W., *George Keith, 1638–1716* (1942).
KEITH, WILLIAM 1839–1911, landscape painter
  Cornelius, Fidelis, *Keith, Old Master of California* (1942).
  Neuhaus, Eugen, *William Keith, Artist* (1938).
KELLER, HELEN 1880–1968, blind deaf-mute
  Brooks, Van Wyck, *Helen Keller* (1956).
  Keller, Helen, *Story of My Life* (1903).
KELLEY, FLORENCE 1859–1932, reformer
  Blumberg, Dorothy R., *Florence Kelley: Social Pioneer* (1966).
  Goldmark, Josephine, *Impatient Crusader: Florence Kelley* (1953).
KELLOGG, FRANK BILLINGS 1856–1937, secretary of state, diplomat
  Bryn-Jones, David, *Frank B. Kellogg* (1937).
  Ellis, L. Ethan, *Frank B. Kellogg and American Foreign Relations, 1925–1929* (1961).

Ferrell, Robert H., *Kellogg and Stimson* (1961).
KELLY, HOWARD ATWOOD 1858–1943, surgeon
Davis, Audrey W., *Dr. Kelly of Hopkins* (1959).
KEMBLE, FRANCES ANNE "FANNY" 1809–1893, actress
Driver, L. S., *Fanny Kemble* (1933).
KENDALL, AMOS 1789–1869, politician, journalist
Kendall, Amos, *Autobiography*, William Stickney, ed. (1872).
KENDALL, GEORGE WILKINS 1809–1867, editor
Copeland, Fayette, *Kendall of the Picayune* (1943).
KENNAN, GEORGE FROST 1904– , diplomat
Kennan, George F., *Memoirs, 1925–1950* (1967).
KENNEDY, JOHN FITZGERALD 1917–1963, president
Burns, James M., *John Kennedy* (1960).
Heath, Jim F., *John F. Kennedy and Business Community* (1969).
Kennedy, John F., *Public Papers* (3 vols., 1963–1964).
——— *Strategy of Peace*, Allan Nevins, ed. (1960).
——— *To Turn the Tide*, John W. Gardner, ed. (1962).
Kennedy, Rose and Joseph P. et al., *John Fitzgerald Kennedy As We Remember Him*, Joan B. Meyers, ed. (1965).
Sable, Martin H., *A Bio-Bibliography of the Kennedy Family* (1969).
Salinger, Pierre, *With Kennedy* (1966).
Schlesinger, Arthur M., Jr., *A Thousand Days: John F. Kennedy*, (1965).
Sidey, Hugh, *John F. Kennedy* (1963).
Sorensen, Theodore C., *Kennedy* (1965).
U. S. Library of Congress, *John Fitzgerald Kennedy; Chronological List of References* (1964).
Wicker, Tom, *JFK and LBJ* (1968).
KENNEDY, JOHN PENDLETON 1795–1870, novelist
Ridgely, J. V., *John Pendleton Kennedy* (1966).
KENNEDY, JOSEPH PATRICK 1888–1969, businessman, diplomat
Whalen, Richard J., *Founding Father: Joseph P. Kennedy* (1964).
KENNEDY, ROBERT FRANCIS 1925–1968, attorney general, New York senator
Halberstam, David, *Unfinished Odyssey of Robert Kennedy* (1969).
Newfield, Jack, *Robert Kennedy: Memoir* (1969).
Ross, Douglas, *Robert F. Kennedy* (1968).
Shannon, William V., *Heir Apparent: Robert Kennedy* (1967).
Witcover, Jules, *85 Days: Robert Kennedy* (1969).
KENNEDY FAMILY
Sable, Martin H., *A Bio-Bibliography of the Kennedy Family* (1969).
Sorensen, Theodore C., *The Kennedy Legacy* (1969).
KENT, JAMES 1763–1847, jurist, legal commentator
Horton, John T., *James Kent* (1939).
KENTON, SIMON 1755–1836, frontiersman, Indian fighter
Kenton, Edna, *Simon Kenton* (1930).
KERFOOT, JOHN BARRETT 1816–1881, Episcopal bishop
Harrison, Hall, *Life of the Right Rev. John Barrett Kerfoot* (2 vols., 1886).
KERN, EDWARD MEYER 1823–1863, explorer, illustrator
Hine, Robert W., *Edward Kern and American Expansion* (1962).
KERN, JEROME 1885–1945, composer
Ewen, David, *World of Jerome Kern* (1960).
KEY, DAVID MCKENDREE 1824–1900, Tennessee senator, postmaster general
Abshire, David M., *South Rejects a Prophet: Senator D. M. Key* (1967).
KEYES, ERASMUS D. 1810–1895, soldier, businessman
Keyes, E. D., *Fifty Years' Observation* (1884).
KILMER, ALFRED JOYCE 1886–1918, poet
Kilmer, Joyce, *Poems, Essays and Letters*, R. C. Holliday, ed. (2 vols., 1918).
KILPATRICK, WILLIAM HEARD 1871–1965, educator
Tenenbaum, Samuel, *William Heard Kilpatrick* (1951).

KIMMEL, HUSBAND EDWARD 1882–1968, admiral
Kimmel, Husband E., *Admiral Kimmel's Story* (1955).

KING, CLARENCE 1842–1901, director of U.S. Geological Survey
Wilkins, Thurman, *Clarence King* (1958).

KING, GRACE ELIZABETH 1852–1932, author
King, Grace E., *Memories of a Southern Woman of Letters* (1932).

KING, JUDSON 1872–1958, public power advocate
King, Judson, *The Conservation Fight* (1959).

KING, MARTIN LUTHER, JR. 1929–1968, Negro leader
Bennett, Lerone, Jr., *What Manner of Man: Martin Luther King, Jr.* (3d ed., 1968).
King, Coretta Scott, *My Life with Martin Luther King, Jr.* (1969).
Lewis, David L., *King: A Critical Biography* (1970).
Lincoln, C. Eric, ed., *Martin Luther King, Jr.* (1970).

KING, RUFUS 1755–1827; New York senator, Federalist
Ernst, Robert, *Rufus King: American Federalist* (1968).
King, Charles R., *Life and Correspondence of Rufus King* (6 vols., 1894–1900).

KING, THOMAS BUTLER 1800–1864, Georgia Congressman
Steel, Edward M., Jr., *T. Butler King of Georgia* (1964).

KINNERSLEY, EBENEZER 1711–1778, experimenter with electricity, Baptist clergyman
Lemay, J. A. Leo, *Ebenezer Kinnersley: Franklin's Friend* (1964).

KINO, EUSEBIO FRANCISCO 1645–1711, Jesuit missionary, explorer
Bolton, Herbert E., *Rim of Christendom: A Biography of Eusebio Francisco Kino* (1936).
Kino, Eusebio F., *Historical Memoir*, Herbert E. Bolton, ed. (2 vols., 1919).

KIRBY-SMITH, EDMUND 1824–1893, Confederate general
Parks, Joseph H., *General Edmund Kirby Smith, C.S.A.* (1954).

KIRKWOOD, SAMUEL JORDAN 1813–1894, Iowa governor
Clark, Dan E., *Samuel Jordan Kirkwood* (1917).

KITCHIN, CLAUDE 1869–1923, North Carolina congressman
Arnett, A. M., *Claude Kitchin* (1937).

KNAPLUND, PAUL 1885–1964, historian
Knaplund, Paul, *Moorings Old and New: Entries in an Immigrant's Log* (1963).

KNAPP, SEAMAN ASAHEL 1833–1911, agricultural educator
Bailey, Joseph C., *Seaman A. Knapp* (1945).

KNOX, HENRY 1750–1806, Revolutionary general
Brooks, Noah, *Henry Knox, A Soldier of the Revolution* (1900).
Callahan, North, *Henry Knox: Washington's General* (1958).
Drake, Francis S., *Life and Correspondence of Henry Knox* (1873).

KORNBERG, ARTHUR 1918– , biochemist
Kornberg, Arthur, *Enzymatic Synthesis of DNA* (1962).

KÖRNER, GUSTAV PHILIPP 1809–1896, jurist, diplomat
Körner, G. P., *Memoirs, 1809–1896*, T. J. McCormack, ed. (1909).

KOUSSEVITZKY, SERGEI 1874–1951, conductor
Lourie, Arthur, *Sergei Koussevitzky* (1931).
Smith, Moses, *Koussevitzky* (1947).

LADD, GEORGE TRUMBULL 1842–1921, psychologist
Mills, Eugene S., *George Trumbull Ladd* (1969).

LADD, WILLIAM 1778–1841, founder of American Peace Society
Hemmenway, John, *The Apostle of Peace: Memoir of William Ladd* (1872).

LAEMMLE, CARL 1867–1939, motion picture producer
Drinkwater, John, *Life of Carl Laemmle* (1931).

LA FARGE, JOHN 1835–1910, painter
Cortissoz, Royal, *John La Farge* (1911).

LA FARGE, JOHN, JR. 1880–1963, Jesuit, editor of *America*
La Farge, John, Jr., *The Manner is Ordinary* (1957).

LAFITTE, JEAN 1780–1821, merchant, outlaw
Charnley, M. V., *Jean Lafitte, Gentleman Smuggler* (1934).

LA FOLLETTE, PHILIP 1897–1965, Wisconsin governor
La Follette, Philip, *Adventure in Politics: Memoirs*, Donald Young, ed. (1970).

LA FOLLETTE, ROBERT MARION 1855–1925, Wisconsin governor, senator
La Follette, Belle C., and Fola La Follette, *Robert M. La Follette* (2 vols., 1953).
La Follette, Robert M., *Autobiography* (1913, rev. ed., 1919).
Maxwell, Robert S., *La Follette and Rise of Progressives in Wisconsin* (1956).
Stirn, E. W., *Annotated Bibliography of Robert M. LaFollette* (1937).

LA FOLLETTE, ROBERT MARION, JR. 1895–1953, Wisconsin senator
Johnson, Roger T., *Robert M. La Follette, Jr. and the Decline of the Progressive Party in Wisconsin* (1964).

LA GUARDIA, FIORELLO H. 1882–1947, mayor of New York City
Carter, John F., *La Guardia* (1937).
Garrett, Charles, *La Guardia Years* (1961).
La Guardia, Fiorello H., *The Making of an Insurgent* (1948).
Mann, Arthur, *La Guardia* (2 vols., 1959–1965).
Zinn, Howard, *La Guardia in Congress* (1959).

LAHR, BERT 1895–1967; comedian
Lahr, John, *Notes on a Cowardly Lion* (1969).

LAMAR, LUCIUS QUINTUS CINCINNATUS 1825–1893, Mississippi senator, Supreme Court justice
Cate, W. A., *Lucius Q. C. Lamar; Secession and Reunion* (1935).
Mayes, Edward, *Lucius Q. C. Lamar: His Life, Times, and Speeches* (1896).

LAMAR, MIRABEAU BUONAPARTE 1798–1859, president of Texas
Gambrell, Herbert P., *Mirabeau Buonaparte Lamar: Troubadour and Crusader* (1934).
Lamar, Mirabeau B., *Papers*, C. A. Gulick et al., eds. (6 vols., 1921–1927).

LANDON, ALFRED MOSSMAN 1887–   , Kansas governor
McCoy, Donald R., *Landon of Kansas* (1966).

LANE, FITZ HUGH 1804–1865, painter
Wilmerding, John, *Fitz Hugh Lane* (1964).

LANE, FRANKLIN KNIGHT 1864–1921, secretary of interior
Lane, Franklin K., *Letters*, A. W. Lane and L. H. Hall, eds. (1922).

LANE, JOSEPH 1801–1881, Oregon senator
Hendrickson, James E., *Joe Lane of Oregon* (1967).

LANGLEY, SAMUEL PIERPONT 1834–1906, aviation experimenter
Vaeth, Joseph G., *Langley, Man of Science and Flight* (1966).

LANGMUIR, IRVING 1881–1957, physicist
Rosenfeld, Albert, *Men of Physics: Irving Langmuir* (1966).

LANGSTON, JOHN MERCER 1829–1897, lawyer, educator, diplomat
Langston, John M., *From Virginia Plantation to the Capitol: An Autobiography* (1894).

LANIER, SIDNEY 1842–1881, poet
Parks, Edd W., *Sidney Lanier* (1968).
Starke, Aubrey H., *Sidney Lanier* (1933).

LANSING, ROBERT 1864–1928, secretary of state
Beers, Burton F., *Vain Endeavor: Robert Lansing's Attempts to End American-Japanese Rivalry* (1962).
Lansing, Robert, *War Memoirs* (1935).
Smith, Daniel M., *Robert Lansing and American Neutrality* (1958).

LARCOM, LUCY 1824–1893, author
Addison, D. D., *Lucy Larcom: Life, Letters, and Diary* (1894).
Larcom, Lucy, *A New England Girlhood* (1889).

LARDNER, RINGGOLD WILMER 1885–1933, author
Lardner, Ringgold W., *Round Up* (929).
Walton, Patrick R., *Ring Lardner* (1963).

LARISON, CORNELIUS WILSON 1837–1910, physician, educator, publisher

Weiss, Harry B., *Country Doctor: Cornelius W. Larison* (1953).

LARKIN, THOMAS OLIVER 1802–1858, merchant, consul
Larkin, Thomas O., *Papers*, George P. Hammond, ed. (11 vols., 1951–1968).
—— *Selection of Letters*, John A. Hawgood, ed. (1962).

LA SALLE, ROBERT CAVELIER Sieur de 1643–1687, explorer
Constantin-Weyer, Maurice, *The French Adventurer: The Life and Exploits of La Salle* (1931).
Parkman, Francis, *La Salle and the Discovery of the Great West* (1879).

LATROBE, BENJAMIN HENRY 1764–1820, architect, engineer
Hamlin, Talbot F., *Benjamin Henry Latrobe* (1955).
Latrobe Benjamin H., *Impressions Respecting New Orleans, 1818–1820,* Samuel Wilson, Jr., ed. (1951).
Latrobe Benjamin H., *Journal* (1905).

LATROBE, JOHN HAZLEHURST BONEVAL 1803–1891, lawyer, inventor
Semmes, John E., *John H. B. Latrobe and His Times* (1917).

LAURENS, HENRY 1724–1792, Revolutionary leader
Hamer, Philip M., "Henry Laurens of South Carolina," Mass. Hist. Soc., *Proc.*, 77 (1965), 3.
Laurens, Henry, *Papers,* Philip M. Hamer and George C. Rogers, Jr., eds. (vols. 1/2–   , 1968/71–   ).
Wallace, David D., *Life of Henry Laurens* (1915).

LA VÉRENDRYE, PIERRE 1685–1749, explorer, soldier
Champagne, Antoine, *Les La Vérendrye et le Poste de l'Ouest* (1968).
Crouse, Nellis M., *La Vérendrye: Fur Trader and Explorer* (1956).

LAW, ANDREW 1749–1821, psalmodist
Crawford, Richard A., *Andrew Law, American Psalmodist* (1968).

LAWRENCE, AMOS ADAMS 1814–1886, merchant, textile, manufacturer
Lawrence, Amos, *Extracts from the Diary and Correspondence*, W. R. Lawrence, ed. (1855).
Lawrence, William, *Life of Amos A. Lawrence with Extracts from His Diary and Correspondence* (1888).

LAWRENCE, ERNEST ORLANDO 1901–1958, physicist
Childs, Herbert, *American Genius: Ernest Orlando Lawrence* (1968).
Davis, Nuel P., *Lawrence & Oppenheimer* (1968).

LEA, HENRY CHARLES 1825–1909, publisher, historian
Bradley, Edward S., *Henry Charles Lea* (1931).

LEAHY, WILLIAM D. 1875–1959, World War II admiral
Leahy, William D., *I Was There* (1950).

LE CONTE, JOSEPH 1823–1901, geologist
LeConte, Joseph, *Autobiography*, W. D. Armes, ed. (1903).
—— *Journal of Ramblings through High Sierra* (1930).

LEDERER, JOHN fl. 1668–1671, explorer
Lederer, John, *Discoveries with Unpublished Letters*, Douglas L. Rights and William P. Cumming, eds. (1958).

LEE, ARTHUR 1740–1792, diplomat
Lee, Charles H., *Vindication of Arthur Lee* (1894).
Lee, Richard H., *Life of Arthur Lee, LL.D. . . . With His Correspondence and Papers* (2 vols., 1829).

LEE, CHARLES 1731–1782, Revolutionary general
Alden, John R., *General Charles Lee* (1951).
Lee, Charles, "Papers," N.Y. Hist. Soc., *Coll.*, 4-7 (1871–1874).

LEE, HENRY "LIGHT-HORSE HARRY" 1756–1818, Revolutionary general
Boyd, Thomas H., *Light-Horse Harry Lee* (1931).
Gerson, Noel B., *Light-Horse Harry: Washington's Great Cavalryman* (1966).

LEE, IVY LEDBETTER 1871–1934, public relations counsel
Hiebert, Ray E., *Courtier to the Crowd* (1966).

LEE, JASON 1803–1845, Methodist missionary, Oregon pioneer

Brosnan, Cornelius J., *Jason Lee* (1932).
Gay, Theressa, *Life and Letters of Mrs. Jason Lee* (1936).

LEE, JOHN DOYLE 1812–1877, Mormon elder
Brooks, Juanita, *John Doyle Lee* (1961).
Lee, John D., *Diaries, 1848–1876,* Robert G. Cleland and Juanita Brooks, eds. (2 vols., 1955).

LEE, RICHARD HENRY 1732–1794, Revolutionary leader
Chitwood, Oliver P., *Richard H. Lee, Statesman of the Revolution* (1968).
Lee, Richard Henry, *Letters,* J. C. Ballagh, ed. (2 vols., 1911–1914).

LEE, ROBERT EDWARD 1807–1870, Confederate general
Davis, Burke, *Gray Fox: Robert E. Lee and Civil War* (1956).
Dowdey, Clifford, *Lee* (1965).
Fishwick, Marshall W., *Lee after the War* (1963).
Freeman, Douglas S., *R. E. Lee: A Biography* (4 vols., 1934–1935).
Lee, Robert E., *Letters to Jefferson Davis and the War Department of the Confederate States of America, 1862–65,* Grady McWhiney, ed. (1957).
———— *Recollections and Letters* (1904).
———— *Wartime Papers,* Clifford Dowdey and Louis H. Manarin, eds. (1961).
Maurice, Frederick B., *Robert E. Lee, the Soldier* (1925).
Miers, Earl S., *Robert E. Lee* (1956).
Rister, Carl C., *Robert E. Lee in Texas* (1946).

LEE, WILLIAM 1739–1795, merchant diplomat
Lee, William, *Letters,* W. C. Ford, ed. (3 vols., 1891).

LEE, WILLIAM fl. 1796–1840, consul in France 1801–1816
Lee, William, *Diary and Letters Written from 1796 to 1840,* Mary L. Mann, ed. (1958).

LEGARÉ, HUGH SWINTON 1797–1843, South Carolina leader
Rhea, Linda, *Hugh Swinton Legaré, a Charleston Intellectural* (1934).

LEGGE, ALEXANDER 1866–1933, manufacturer
Crissey, Forrest, *Alexander Legge* (1936).

LEHMAN, HERBERT HENRY 1878–1963, New York senator, governor, financier
Nevins, Allan, *Herbert H. Lehman* (1963).

LEISERSON, WILLIAM MORRIS 1883–1957, economist, labor arbitor
Eisner, J. Michael, *William Morris Leiserson* (1967).

LELAND, CHARLES GODFREY 1824–1903, writer
Leland, Charles G., *Memoirs* (1893).
Pennell, Elizabeth R., *Charles Godfrey Leland: a Biography* (1906).

LELAND, HENRY MARTYN 1843–1932, auto manufacturer
Leland, Mrs. Wilfred C. [Ottilie M.], and Minnie D. Millbrook, *Henry M. Leland* (1966).

LELAND, JOHN 1754–1841, Baptist minister, advocate of disestablishment
Butterfield, Lyman H., "Elder John Leland, Jeffersonian Itinerant," Am. Antiq. Soc., *Proc.,* 62 (1952), 155.

LEMAY, CURTIS E. 1906–   , air force general
LeMay, Curtis E., and Mackinlay Kantor, *Mission with LeMay* (1965).

LEMKE, WILLIAM 1878–1950, agrarian leader, North Dakota congressman
Blackorby, Edward C., *Prairie Rebel: William Lemke* (1963).

L'ENFANT, PIERRE CHARLES 1754–1825, engineer, city planner
Caemmerer, Hans Paul, *Life of Pierre Charles L'Enfant* (1950).

LESLIE, MIRIAM FLORENCE (FOLLINE) ca. 1836–1914, publisher
Stern, Madeleine B., *Purple Passage: Mrs. Frank Leslie* (1953).

LETCHER, JOHN 1813–1884, Virginia governor
Boney, F. N., *John Letcher of Virginia: Civil War Governor* (1966).

LEVINE, JACK 1915–   , artist
Levine, Jack, *Jack Levine,* Frank Getlein, ed. (1966).

LEWIS, HENRY CLAY 1825–1850, physician
Lewis, Henry C., *Louisiana Swamp Doctor,* John Q. Anderson, ed. (1962).

LEWIS, JOHN LLEWELLYN 1880–1969, labor leader

Alinsky, Saul D., *John L. Lewis* (1949).
Wechsler, James A., *Labor Baron: John L. Lewis* (1944).

LEWIS, MERIWETHER 1774–1809, explorer
Clark, William, *Original Journals of the Lewis and Clark Expedition, 1804–06,* Reuben G. Thwaites, ed. (8 vols., 1904–1905).
Cutright, Paul R., *Lewis and Clark* (1969).
Dillon, Richard H., *Meriwether Lewis* (1965).
Quaife, Milo Milton, ed., *Journals of Lewis and Ordway* (1916).

LEWIS, SINCLAIR 1885–1951, novelist
Lewis, Sinclair, *From Main Street to Stockholm: Letters, 1919–1930,* Harrison Smith, ed. (1952).
Schorer, Mark, *Sinclair Lewis* (1961).
Sheean, Vincent, ed., *Dorothy and Red: A Literary Biography* (1963).

LEWISOHN, LUDWIG 1883–1955, author
Lewisohn, Ludwig, *Expression in America* (1932).
—— *Mid-Channel* (1929).
—— *Upstream* (1922).

LIEBER, FRANCIS 1798–1872, political scientist
Brown, Bernard E., *American Conservatives; the Political Thought of Lieber and Burgess* (1951).
Freidel, Frank, *Francis Lieber* (1947).
Lieber, Francis, *Miscellaneous Writings* (2 vols., 1881).
Perry, Thomas S., *Life and Letters of Francis Lieber* (1882).

LIGGETT, HUNTER 1857–1935, World War I general
Liggett, Hunter, *Commanding an American Army* (1925).

LILIENTHAL, DAVID ELI 1899–   , director of Tennessee Valley Authority
Lilienthal, David E., *Journals* (4 vols., 1964–1966).
Whitman, Willson, *David Lilienthal* (1948).

LILLIE, GORDON WILLIAM 1860–?   , ranchman, showman
Shirley, Glenn, *Pawnee Bill: Major Gordon W. Lillie* (1958).

LINCECUM, GIDEON 1793–1874, frontier physician
Burkhalter, Lois W., *Gideon Lincecum* (1965).

LINCOLN, ABRAHAM 1809–1865, president
Anderson, David D., *Abraham Lincoln* (1970).
Angle, Paul M., and Earl S. Miers, eds., *The Living Lincoln* (1955).
Baringer, William E., C. Percy Powell, and Earl S. Miers, eds., *Lincoln Day by Day* (3 vols., 1960).
Basler, Roy P., *Lincoln* (1962).
Beveridge, Albert J., *Abraham Lincoln, 1809–1858* (2 vols., 1928).
Carpenter, Francis B., *Inner Life of Abraham Lincoln: Six Months at the White House* (1867).
Current, Richard N., *The Lincoln Nobody Knows* (1958).
Donald, David, *Lincoln Reconsidered* (1962).
Duff, John J., *A. Lincoln: Prairie Lawyer* (1960).
Fehrenbacher, Don E., *Prelude to Greatness: Lincoln in the 1850's* (1962).
Frank, John P., *Lincoln as a Lawyer* (1961).
Graebner, Norman A., ed., *Enduring Lincoln* (1959).
Grierson, Francis, *Valley of Shadows* (1909).
Hamilton, Charles, and Lloyd Ostendorf, eds., *Lincoln in Photographs* (1963).
Herndon, W. H., and J. W. Weik, *Herndon's Lincoln* (3 vols., 1889).
Lincoln, Abraham, *Collected Works,* Roy P. Basler, ed. (9 vols., 1953–1955).
—— *Complete Works,* John G. Nicolay, John Hay, and F. D. Tandy, eds. (12 vols., 1905).
—— and Stephen Douglas, *Debates of 1858,* Robert W. Johannsen, ed. (1965).
Lincoln, Abraham, *Political Thought,* Richard N. Current, ed. (1967).
—— and Stephen Douglas, *Speeches and Writings in the Ohio Campaign of 1859,* Harry V. Jaffa and Robert W. Johannsen, eds. (1959).
Lorant, Stefan, *The Life of Abraham Lincoln* (1954).
Luthin, Reinhard H., *The First Lincoln Campaign* (1944).

———— *The Real Abraham Lincoln* (1960).
Mearns, David C., *Largely Lincoln* (1961).
Mitgang, Herbert, ed., *Lincoln as They Saw Him* (1956).
Nevins, Allan, *Emergence of Lincoln* (1950).
Nicolay, John G., and John Hay, *Abraham Lincoln, A History* (10 vols., 1890).
Quarles, Benjamin, *Lincoln and the Negro* (1962).
Randall, James G., *Lincoln the Liberal Statesman* (1947).
———— *Lincoln the President* (4 vols., 1945–1955). Vol. IV completed by Richard N. Current.
Randall, Ruth P., *Courtship of Mr. Lincoln* (1957).
———— *Lincoln's Sons* (1955).
Riddle, Donald W., *Congressman Abraham Lincoln* (1957).
———— *Lincoln Runs for Congress* (1948).
Sandburg, Carl, *Abraham Lincoln* (6 vols., 1926–1939).
Segal, Charles M., ed., *Conversations with Lincoln* (1961).
Shaw, Archer, ed., *Lincoln Encyclopedia* (1950).
Thomas, Benjamin P., *Abraham Lincoln* (1952).
Warren, Louis A., *Lincoln's Youth: Indiana Years, 1816–1630* (1959).

LINCOLN, MARY TODD 1818–1882, first lady
Randall, Ruth P., *Courtship of Mr. Lincoln* (1957).
———— *Mary Lincoln* (1953).

LIND, JOHN 1854–1930, Minnesota governor
Stephenson, George M., *John Lind* (1935).

LINDBERGH, CHARLES AUGUSTUS 1902–   , aviator
Davis, Kenneth S., *The Hero: Charles A. Lindbergh* (1959).
Lindbergh, Charles A., *Spirit of St. Louis* (1953).
———— *Wartime Journals* (1970).
Ross, Walter S., *Last Hero: Charles A. Lindbergh* (1968).

LINDEMAN, EDUARD CHRISTIAN 1885–1953, sociologist, social work leader
Konopka, Gisela, *Lindeman and Social Work Philosophy* (1958).

LINDERMAN, FRANK 1869–1938, author, Montana leader
Linderman, Frank B., *Montana Adventure: Recollections*, Harold G. Merriam, ed. (1968).

LINDSAY, NICHOLAS VACHEL 1879–1931, poet
Masters, Edgar Lee, *Vachel Lindsay* (1935).
Ruggles, Eleanor, *West-going Heart: Vachel Lindsay* (1959).

LIPMAN, JACOB 1874–1939, agricultural scientist
Waksman, Selman A., *Jacob G. Lipman* (1966).

LIPPMANN, WALTER 1889–   , philosopher, publicist
Forcey, Charles, *Crossroads of Liberalism* (1961).
Syed, Anwar H., *Walter Lippmann's Philosophy of International Politics* (1963).
Wellborn, Charles, *Twentieth Century Pilgrimage: Lippmann and the Public Philosophy* (1969).

LIST, GEORG FRIEDRICH 1789–1846, economist, journalist
Hirst, M. E., *Life of Friedrich List, and Selections from His Writings* (1909).

LITTLE, MALCOLM 1925–1965, Black Muslim
Breitman, George, *The Last Year of Malcolm X* (1968).
Clarke, John H., ed., *Malcolm X: The Man and His Time* (1969).
Malcolm X, *Autobiography*, (1965).
———— *Speeches at Harvard*, Archie Epps, ed. (1968).

LITTLEFIELD, MILTON S. 1830–1899, carpetbagger
Daniels, Jonathan, *Prince of Carpetbaggers* (1958).

LIVERMORE, MARY ASHTON 1820–1905, reformer, women's rights advocate
Livermore, Mary A., *Story of My Life* (1897).

LIVERMORE, ROBERT 1876–1959, mining engineer and executive
Livermore, Robert, *Journal, 1892–1915*, Gene M. Gressley, ed. (1968).

LIVINGSTON, EDWARD 1764–1836, lawyer, secretary of state
Hatcher, William B., *Edward Livingston* (1940).

LIVINGSTON, ROBERT 1654–1728, landowner, trader

Leder, Lawrence H., *Robert Livingston and the Politics of Colonial New York* (1961).

—— and Vincent P. Carosso, "Robert Livingston (1654–1728): Businessman of Colonial New York," *Bus. Hist. Rev.*, 30 (1956), 18.

LIVINGSTON, ROBERT R. 1746–1813, Revolutionary leader, diplomat
Dangerfield, George, *Chancellor Robert R. Livingston, 1746–1813* (1960).

LIVINGSTON, WILLIAM 1723–1790, lawyer, Revolutionary leader, New Jersey governor
Dillon, Dorothy R., *New York Triumvirate: William Livingston, John Morin Scott and William Smith Jr.* (1949).
Klein, Milton, "Rise of the New York Bar: Legal Career of William Livingston," *WMQ*, 3 ser., 15 (1958), 334.

LLOYD, DAVID 1656–1731, Pennsylvania leader
Lokken, Roy N., *David Lloyd, Colonial Lawmaker* (1959).

LLOYD, HENRY DEMAREST 1847–1903, reformer
Destler, Chester M., *Henry Demarest Lloyd* (1963).
Lloyd, Curtis Gates, *Henry Demarest Lloyd, 1847–1903* (2 vols., 1912).

LOCKE, DAVID ROSS 1833–1888, satirist; Petroleum V. Nasby, pseud.
Austin, James C., *Petroleum V. Nasby* (1965).
Harrison, John M., *The Man Who Made Nasby: David Ross Locke* (1969).

LODGE, GEORGE CABOT 1873–1909, poet
Adams, Henry, *Life of George Cabot Lodge* (1911).

LODGE, HENRY CABOT 1850–1924, Massachusetts senator
Garraty, John A., *Henry Cabot Lodge* (1953).
Lodge, Henry C., *Early Memories* (1913).
—— and Theodore Roosevelt, *Selections from the Correspondence* (2 vols., 1925).

LODGE, HENRY CABOT, II 1902–   , Massachusetts senator, diplomat
Miller, William J., *Henry Cabot Lodge* (1967).

LOEB, JACQUES 1859–1924, biologist
Loeb, Jacques, *Mechanistic Conception of Life*, Donald Fleming, ed., (1964).

LOEB, MORRIS 1863–1912, physical chemist
Richards, T. W., *The Scientific Work of Morris Loeb* (1913).

LOEWI, OTTO 1873–1961, physiologist
Loewi, Otto, *From the Workshop of Discoveries* (1953).

LOGAN, BENJAMIN 1743–1802, frontiersman
Talbert, Charles G., *Benjamin Logan: Kentucky Frontiersman* (1962).

LOGAN, GEORGE 1753–1821, Pennsylvania senator
Tolles, Frederick B., *George Logan of Philadelphia* (1953).

LOGAN, JAMES 1674–1751, secretary to William Penn
Lokken, Roy N., "Social Thought of James Logan," *WMQ*, ser., 27 (1970), 68.
Tolles, Frederick B., *James Logan and Culture of Provincial America* (1957).

LOGAN, JOHN ALEXANDER 1826–1886, Union general
Dawson, George F., *Life and Services of General John A. Logan* (1887).

LOMAX, JOHN AVERY 1867–1948, musicologist
Lomax, John A., *Adventures of a Ballad Hunter* (1947).

LONDON, JACK 1876–1916, author
London, Charmian K., *The Book of Jack London* (2 vols., 1921).
O'Connor, Richard, *Jack London* (1964).
Walker, Franklin, *Jack London and the Klondike* (1966).

LONDON, MEYER 1871–1926, socialist, labor leader
Rogoff, Harry, *An East Side Epic: The Life of Meyer London* (1930).

LONG, CRAWFORD WILLIAMSON 1815–1878, surgeon, pioneer anaesthetist
Boland, Frank K., *First Anesthetic: Story of Crawford W. Long* (1950).
Taylor, Frances, *Crawford W. Long* (1928).

LONG, HUEY PIERCE 1893–1935, Louisiana governor and senator
Graham, Hugh D., ed., *Huey Long* (1970).
Sindler, Allan P., *Huey Long's Louisiana, 1920–1952* (1956).

Williams, T. Harry, *Huey Long* (1969).

LONG, JOHN DAVIS 1838–1915, Massachusetts governor, secretary of navy
Long, John D., *America of Yesterday, as Reflected in the Journal of John Davis Long*, L. S. Mayo, ed. (1923).

LONG, STEPHEN HARRIMAN 1784–1864, explorer
Long, Stephen H., and Edwin James et al., *Account of Expedition from Pittsburgh to Rocky Mountains* [1819–20] (2 vols., 1823).
Wood, Richard G., *Stephen Harriman Long: Army Engineer, Explorer, Inventor* (1966).

LONGFELLOW, HENRY WADSWORTH 1807–1882, poet
Arvin, Newton, *Longfellow* (1963).
Longfellow, Henry W., *Letters*, Andrew R. Hilen, ed., (2 vols., 1967).
Longfellow, Samuel, *Life of Henry Wadsworth Longfellow with Extracts from His Journals and Correspondence* (3 vols., 1891).
Thompson, Lawrance, *Young Longfellow, 1807–1843* (1938).
Wagenknecht, Edward C., *Longfellow* (1955).
Williams, Cecil B., *Henry Wadsworth Longfellow* (1964).

LONGSTREET, AUGUSTUS BALDWIN 1790–1870; lawyer, humorist
Wade, J. D., *Augustus Baldwin Longstreet* (1924); M. Thomas Inge, ed. (1969).

LONGSTREET, JAMES 1821–1904, Confederate general
Sanger, Donald B., and Thomas R. Hay, *James Longstreet* (1952).

LONGWORTH, NICHOLAS 1869–1931, Speaker of the House
De Chambrun, C. L., *Nicholas Longworth* (1933).

LOPEZ, AARON 1731–1782, merchant
Chyet, Stanley F., *Lopez of Newport: Colonial American Merchant Prince* (1970)

LOUIS, MORRIS 1912–1962, painter
Fried, Michael, *Morris Louis* (1970).

LOUCHHEIM, KATIE SCOFIELD 1903–   ; vice-chairman of Democratic National committee
Louchheim, Katie, *By the Political Sea* (1970).

LOVEJOY, ELIJAH PARISH 1802–1837, abolitionist, editor
Dillon, Merton L., *Elijah P. Lovejoy, Abolitionist Editor* (1961).
Gill, John, *Tide without Turning: Elijah P. Lovejoy and Freedom of the Press* (1958).

LOVEJOY, OWEN 1811–1864, Illinois congressman, abolitionist
Magdol, Edward, *Owen Lovejoy: Abolitionist* (1967).

LOVETT, ROBERT MORSS 1870–1956, educator
Lovett, Robert M., *All Our Years, Autobiography* (1948).

LOW, SETH 1850–1916, merchant, mayor of New York City
Low, Benjamin R. C., *Seth Low* (1925).

LOWDEN, FRANK ORREN 1861–1943, Illinois governor
Hutchinson, William T., *Frank O. Lowden* (2 vols., 1957).

LOWE, THADDEUS S. C. 1832–1913, balloonist, inventor
Block, Eugene B., *Above the Civil War: Thaddeus Lowe* (1966).

LOWELL, ABBOTT LAWRENCE 1856–1943, president of Harvard University
Yeomans, H. A., *Abbott Lawrence Lowell* (1948).

LOWELL, AMY 1874–1925, poet
Damon, S. Foster, *Amy Lowell* (1935).

LOWELL, JAMES RUSSELL 1819–1891, poet, educator
Child, Francis J., and James Russell Lowell, *Scholar Friends: Letters*, Mark A. DeW. Howe and G. W. Cottrell, Jr., eds. (1952).
Duberman, Martin H., *James Russell Lowell* (1966).
Greenslet, Ferris, *James Russell Lowell* (1905).
Lowell, James Russell, *New Letters*, Mark DeW. Howe, ed. (1932).
McGlinchee, Claire, *James Russell Lowell* (1967).
Scudder, Horace E., *James Russell Lowell* (2 vols., 1901).
Wagenknecht, Edward, *Lowell: Portrait of a Many-sided Man* (1971).

LOWELL, JOSEPHINE SHAW 1843–1905, reformer
Stewart, William R., *The Philanthropic Work of Josephine Shaw Lowell* (1905).

LOWELL, PERCIVAL 1855–1916, astronomer
Lowell, Abbott L., *Biography of Percival Lowell* (1935).

LOWELL FAMILY
Greenslet, Ferris, *The Lowells and Their Seven Worlds* (1946).
Weeks, Edward, *The Lowells and Their Institute* (1966).

LOWIE, ROBERT HARRY 1883–1957, ethnologist
Lowie, Robert H., *Ethnologist: A Personal Record* (1959).

LOWNDES, WILLIAM 1782–1822, planter, South Carolina congressman
Ravenel, H. H., *Life and Times of William Lowndes of South Carolina* (1901).

LUCE, CLARE BOOTHE 1903– , playwright, congresswoman, ambassador
Shadegg, Stephen, *Clare Boothe Luce* (1971).

LUCE, HENRY ROBINSON 1898–1967, publisher
Kobler, John, *Luce: His Time, Life and Fortune* (1968).

LUCE, STEPHEN BLEECKER 1827–1917, admiral
Gleaves, Albert, *Life and Letters of Admiral Stephen B. Luce: Founder of Naval War College* (1925).

LUKS, GEORGE 1867–1933, painter
Carey, Elisabeth, *George Luks* (1931).

LUNDY, BENJAMIN 1789–1839, abolitionist
Dillon, Merton L., *Benjamin Lundy and the Struggle for Negro Freedom* (1966).
Lundy, Benjamin, *The Life, Travels and Opinions*, Thomas Earle, ed. (1847).

LYON, JAMES. See HOPKINSON, FRANCIS

LYON, MARY 1797–1849, educator
Gilchrist, Beth B., *Life of Mary Lyon* (1910).
Lansing, M. F., ed., *Mary Lyon* (1937).

LYNCH, JOHN ROY 1847–1939, southern black leader
Lynch, John Roy, *Reminiscences of an Active Life,* John Hope Franklin, ed. (1970).

MCADOO, WILLIAM GIBBS 1863–1941, secretary of treasury
McAdoo, William G., *Crowded Years* (1931).

MACARTHUR, DOUGLAS 1880–1964, World War II general
Gunther, John, *Riddle of MacArthur* (1951).
James, D. Clayton, *Years of MacArthur, 1880–1941* (1970).
MacArthur, Douglas, *Public Papers and Speeches*, Vorin E. Whan, Jr., ed. (1965).
—— *Reminiscences* (1964).
Whitney, Courtney, *MacArthur: Rendezvous with History* (1956).

MCAULEY, JEREMIAH 1839–1884, operated mission house
Bonner, Arthur, *Jerry McAuley and His Mission* (1967).

MCCARTHY, JOSEPH RAYMOND 1908–1957, Wisconsin senator
Buckley, William F., Jr., *McCarthy and His Enemies* (rev. ed., 1961).
Griffith, Robert, *Politics of Fear: Joseph R. McCarthy and Senate* (1970).
McCarthy, Joseph, *Major Speeches and Debates* (1953).
Matusow, Allen J., ed., *Joseph R. McCarthy* (1970).
Rovere, Richard H., *Senator Joe McCarthy* (1959).

MCCARTHY, MARY 1912– , author
McCarthy, Mary, *Memories of a Catholic Girlhood* (1957).
McKenzie, Barbara, *Mary McCarthy* (1966).

MCCLELLAN, GEORGE BRINTON 1826–1885, Union general
Eckenrode, Hamilton J., and Bryan Conrad, *George B. McClellan* (1941).
Hassler, Warren W., Jr., *General George B. McClellan* (1957).
McClellan, George B., *McClellan's Own Story* (1887).
Myers, W. S., *A Study in Personality: General George Brinton McClellan* (1934).

MCCLELLAN, GEORGE BRINTON, JR. 1865–1940, mayor of New York City
McClellan, George B., Jr., *Gentleman and the Tiger: Autobiography* (1956).

MCCLOSKEY, JOHN 1810–1885, cardinal
Farley, John M., *The Life of John Cardinal McCloskey* (1918).

MCCLURE, ALEXANDER KELLY 1828–1909, newspaper editor, Pennsylvania Republican leader
McClure, A. K., *Recollections* (1902).

MCCLURE, SAMUEL SIDNEY 1857–1949, publisher
Lyon, Peter, *Success Story: Life and Times of S. S. McClure* (2nd ed., 1967).
McClure, Samuel S., *My Autobiography* (1914).

MCCOLLUM, ELMER VERNER 1879–1967, nutritionist
McCollum, Elmer V., *Autobiography* (1964).

MCCONNELL, FRANCIS JOHN 1871–1953, Ohio Methodist bishop
McConnell, Francis J., *By the Way: An Autobiography* (1952).

MCCORMICK, CYRUS HALL 1809–1884, manufacturer, farm machinery inventor
Hutchinson, William T., *Cyrus Hall McCormick* (2 vols., 1930–35)

MCCORMICK, NETTIE FOWLER 1835–1923, philanthropist
Burgess, Charles O., *Nettie Fowler McCormick: Philanthropist* (1962).

MCCOSH, JAMES 1811–1894, president of College of New Jersey
McCosh, James, *Life*, W. M. Sloane, ed. (1896).

MCCULLERS, CARSON SMITH 1917–1967, author
Evans, Oliver W., *Carson McCullers* (1965).

MCCULLOCH, HUGH 1808–1895, banker, secretary of treasury
McCulloch, Hugh, *Men and Measures of Half a Century* (1888).

MACDOWELL, EDWARD 1861–1908, composer
Gilman, Lawrence, *Edward MacDowell* (1909).
Porte, J. F., *Edward MacDowell* (1922).

MCDOWELL, MARY 1854–1936, settlement house founder
Wilson, Howard E., *Mary McDowell* (1928).

MACFADDEN, BERNARR 1868–1955, publisher and health faddist
MacFadden, Mary, and Emile Gauvreau, *Dumbbells and Carrot Strips: Bernarr MacFadden* (1953).

MCGAVOCK, RANDAL W. 1826–1863, Nashville figure
McGavock, Randal W., *Journals*, Herschel Gower and Jack Allen, eds. (1959).

MCGLYNN, EDWARD 1837–1900, Catholic clergyman, reformer
Bell, Stephen, *Rebel, Priest and Prophet* (1937).

MCGRAW, JOHN J. 1873–1934, baseball manager
Durso, Joseph, *Days of Mr. McGraw* (1969).
McGraw, John J., *My Thirty Years in Baseball* (1923).

MCGUFFEY, WILLIAM HOLMES 1800–1873, textbook writer
Crawford, Benjamin F., *William Holmes McGuffey: Schoolmaster of the Nation* (1963).
Minnich, Harvey C., *William Holmes McGuffey and His Readers* (1936).
Tope, Melancthon, *A Biography of William Holmes McGuffey* (1929).

MCHENRY, JAMES 1753–1816, Revolutionary surgeon, novelist
Steiner, B. C., *Life and Correspondence of James McHenry* (1907).

MCINTIRE, SAMUEL 1757–1811, architect, woodcarver
Cousins, Frank, and P. M. Riley, *Samuel McIntire, the Wood-Carver of Salem* (1916).
Kimball, Fiske, *Mr. Samuel McIntire, Carver: Architect of Salem* (1940).
Labaree, Benjamin W., ed., *Samuel McIntire* (1957).

MCINTYRE, OSCAR ODD 1884–1938, journalist
Driscoll, C. B., *Life of O.O. McIntyre* (1938).

MCIVER, CHARLES DUNCAN 1861–1906, president of North Carolina Women's College
Holder, Rose H., *McIver of North Carolina* (1957).

MCKAY, DONALD 1810–1880, shipbuilder
McKay, Richard C., *Some Famous Sailing Ships and Their Builder, Donald McKay* (1928).

MACKAYE, JAMES MORRISON STEELE, 1842–1894, playwright
MacKaye, Percy, *Epoch, the Life of Steele MacKaye* (2 vols. 1927).

MACKENZIE, RANALD SLIDELL 1840–1889, Union general
   Wallace, Ernest, *Ranald MacKenzie on Texas Frontier* (1964).
MCKIM, CHARLES FOLLEN 1847–1909, architect
   Moore, Charles, *The Life and Times of Charles Follen McKim* (1929).
   Granger, Alfred H., *Charles F. McKim: Life and Work* (1913).
MCKINLEY, WILLIAM 1843–1901, president
   Leech, Margaret, *In the Days of McKinley* (1959).
   Morgan, H. Wayne, *William McKinley* (1963).
   Olcott, C. S., *Life of William McKinley* (2 vols., 1916).
MACLAY, WILLIAM 1734–1804, Pennsylvania senator
   Maclay, William, *Journal, 1789–1791*, E. S. Maclay, ed. (1890).
MCLEAN, JOHN 1785–1861, politician, Supreme Court justice
   Weisenburger, F. P., *John McLean* (1937).
MACLEISH, ARCHIBALD 1892–   , poet
   Falk, Signi, *Archibald MacLeish* (1965).
MCLOUGHLIN, JOHN 1784–1857, fur trader
   Johnson, Robert C., *John McLoughlin, Patriarch of the Northwest* (1935).
   McLoughlin, John, *Letters*, Burt B. Barker, ed. (1948).
   Montgomery, Richard G., *The White-Headed Eagle, John McLoughlin* (1935).
MCMASTER, JOHN BACH 1852–1932, historian
   Goldman, Eric F., *McMaster* (1943).
MCMILLAN, JOHN 1752–1833, Presbyterian clergyman
   Guthrie, Dwight R., *John McMillan: Presbyterianism in the West, 1752–1833*
      (1952).
MCMURTRY, JOHN 1812–1890, Kentucky architect
   Lancaster, Clay, *Back Streets and Pine Trees: John McMurtry, Nineteenth
      Century Architect-Builder of Kentucky* (1956).
MCNUTT, PAUL VORIES 1891–1955, Indiana governor, political leader
   Blake, I. George, *Paul V. McNutt: Hoosier Statesman* (1966).
MACON, NATHANIEL 1758–1837, North Carolina senator
   Dodd, William E., *Life of Nathaniel Macon* (1903).
   Macon, Nathaniel, "Correspondence," W. E. Dodd, ed., *John P. Branch Hist.
      Papers*, 3 (1909), 27.
   —— *Letters of Nathaniel Macon, John Steele and William Barry Grove*, K. P.
      Battle, ed. (1902).
MCPHERSON, JAMES BIRDSEYE 1828–1864, Union general
   Whaley, Elizabeth J., *Forgotten Hero: General James B. McPherson* (1955).
MCQUAID, BERNARD JOHN 1823–1909, Catholic bishop of Rochester
   Zwierlein, F. J., *Life and Letters of Bishop McQuaid* (3 vols., 1925–1927).
MCRAE, MILTON A. 1858–1930, founder of newspaper chain
   McRae, Milton A., *Forty Years in Newspaperdom* (1924).
MCVICKAR, JOHN 1787–1868, political economist
   Langstaff, John B., *Enterprising Life: John McVickar* (1961).
MADISON, DOLLY 1768–1849, first lady
   Cutts, L. B., *Memoirs and Letters of Dolly Madison* (1886).
MADISON, JAMES 1750/51–1836, president
   Brant, Irving, *James Madison* (6 vols., 1941–1961). Abridged (1970).
   Burns, Edward M., *James Madison: Philosopher of the Constitution* (rev. ed.,
      1968).
   Hunt, Gaillard, *Life of James Madison* (1920).
   Koch, Adrienne, *Jefferson and Madison* (1950).
   Madison, James, "Autobiography," Douglass Adair, ed., *WMQ* 3 ser., 2
      (1945), 191.
   —— *Notes of Debates in the Federal Convention of 1787*, Adrienne Koch, ed.
      (1966).
   —— *Papers*, William T. Hutchinson and William M. Rachal, eds. (6 vols.,
      1962–1969).
   —— *Writings*, Gaillard Hunt, ed. (9 vols., 1900–1910).
   Smith, Abbot E., *James Madison, Builder* (1937).

MAHAN, ALFRED THAYER 1840–1914, naval theorist
Mahan, Alfred T., *From Sail to Steam: Recollections of a Naval Life* (1907).
Puleston, William D., *Mahan* (1939).
Taylor, Charles C., *The Life of Admiral Mahan* (1920).

MAHONE, WILLIAM 1826–1895, Virginia senator
Blake, Nelson Morehouse, *William Mahone of Virginia* (1935).

MALAMUD, BERNARD 1914–   , novelist
Richman, Sidney, *Bernard Malamud* (1966).

MALBONE, EDWARD GREENE 1777–1807, miniature painter
Tolman, Ruel P., *Edward Greene Malbone* (1958).

MALCOLM X. See LITTLE, MALCOLM

MALL, FRANKLIN PAINE 1862–1917, anatomist, embryologist
Sabin, Florence R., *Franklin Paine Mall* (1934).

MALLORY, STEPHEN RUSSELL 1813–1873, Confederate secretary of navy
Durkin, Joseph T., *Stephen R. Mallory: Confederate Navy Chief* (1954).

MALVIN, JOHN 1795–1880, free Negro
Malvin, John, *North into Freedom: Autobiography*, Allan Peskin, ed. (1966).

MANGUM, WILLIE PERSON 1792–1861, North Carolina senator
Mangum, Willie P., *Papers*, Henry T. Shanks, ed. (5 vols. 1950–1956).

MANN, HORACE 1796–1859, educator
Hinsdale, B. A., *Horace Mann* (1898).
Mann, Horace, *Crisis in Education*, Louis Filler, ed. (1965).
Mann, Mary, *Life and Works of Horace Mann* (rev. ed.; 5 vols., 1891).
Tharp, Louise H., *Until Victory: Horace Mann and Mary Peabody* (1953).

MANSFIELD, EDWARD D. 1801–1880, author and editor
Mansfield, Edward D., *Personal Memories* (1879).

MANSFIELD, RICHARD 1854–1907, actor
Winter, William, *Life and Art of Richard Mansfield* (2 vols., 1910).

MARBLE, MANTON MALONE 1834–1917, editor
Phelan, Mary C., *Manton Marble of the New York "World"* (1957).

MARCANTONIO, VITO 1902–1954, New York congressman
Schaffer, Alan, *Vito Marcantonio, Radical in Congress* (1966).

MARCH, PEYTON CONWAY 1864–1955, World War I general
Coffman, Edward M., *Hilt of the Sword: Peyton C. March* (1966).

MARCY, RANDOLPH B. 1812–1887, Civil War general, western explorer
Hollon, W. Eugene, *Beyond the Cross Timbers: Randolph B. Marcy* (1955).

MARCY, WILLIAM LEARNED 1786–1857, secretary of war, secretary of state
Spencer, Ivor D., *Victor and Spoils: William L. Marcy* (1959).

MARIN, JOHN 1872–1953, painter
Benson, Emanuel M., *John Marin* (1935).
McBride, Henry et al., *John Marin* (1966).
Williams, William Carlos, Duncan Phillips, and Dorothy Norman, *John Marin* (1956).

MARION, FRANCIS 1732–1795, Revolutionary general
Bass, Robert D., *Swamp Fox: General Francis Marion* (1959).

MARLAND, ERNEST WHITWORTH 1874–1941, oil producer, Oklahoma governor
Mathews, John J., *Life and Death of An Oilman: E. W. Marland* (1951).

MARQUAND, JOHN PHILIP 1893–1960, author
Gross, John J., *John P. Marquand* (1963).

MARQUETTE, JACQUES 1637–1675, explorer
Donnelly, Joseph P., *Jacques Marquette, 1637–1675* (1968).
Thwaites, Reuben G., *Father Marquette* (1902).

MARSH, GEORGE PERKINS 1801–1882, diplomat, conservationist
Lowenthal, David, *George Perkins Marsh: Versatile Vermonter* (1958).

MARSH, OTHNIEL CHARLES 1831–1899, paleontologist
Plate, Robert, *Dinosaur Hunters: Marsh and Cope* (1964).
Schubert, Charles, and C. M. LeVene, *O. C. Marsh, Pioneer in Paleontology* (1940).

MARSHALL, GEORGE CATLETT 1880–1959, chief of staff World War II, secretary of state
Ferrell, Robert H., *George C. Marshall* (1966).
Pogue, Forrest C., *George C. Marshall* (2 vols., 1963–1966).
Wilson, Rose P., *General Marshall Remembered* (1968).

MARSHALL, JOHN 1755–1835, Supreme Court Chief Justice
Beveridge, Albert J., *Life of John Marshall* (4 vols., 1916–1919).
Corwin, Edward S., *John Marshall and the Constitution* (1919).
Faulkner, Robert K., *The Jurisprudence of John Marshall* (1968).
Jones, William M., ed., *Chief Justice John Marshall* (1956).
Rhodes, Irwin S., *Papers of John Marshall: A Descriptive Calendar* (2 vols., 1969).
Marshall, John, *My Dearest Polly: Letters to His Wife, 1779–1831*, Frances N. Mason, ed. (1961).
———— *Reader*, Erwin C. Surrency, ed., (1955).
———— *Writings* (1839).

MARSHALL, LOUIS 1856–1929, lawyer, Jewish leader
Adler, Cyrus, *Louis Marshall* (1931).
Marshall, Louis, *Papers and Addresses*, Charles Reznikoff, ed. (2 vols., 1957).
Rosenstock, Morton, *Louis Marshall, Defender of Jewish Rights* (1965).

MARTIN, JOSEPH WILLIAM 1884–1968, Mass. Congressman, Speaker of the House
Martin, Joseph, *My First Fifty Years in Politics* (1960).

MARTIN, LUTHER 1748–1826, attorney general of Maryland
Clarkson, Paul S., and R. Samuel Jett, *Luther Martin of Maryland* (1970).

MARX BROTHERS 20th-century comedians
Crichton, K.S., *Marx Brothers* (1950).
Goldblatt, Burt, and Paul Zimmerman, *Marx Brothers* (1968).
Marx, Harpo with Rowland Barber, *Harpo Speaks* (1961).

MASON, GEORGE 1725–1792, Revolutionary leader
Hill, Helen D., *George Mason: Constitutionalist* (1938).
Mason, George, *Papers, 1725–1792*, Robert A. Rutland, ed. (3 vols., 1970).
Rowland, K. M., *Life of George Mason, 1725–1792* (2 vols., 1892).
Rutland, Robert A., *George Mason* (1961).

MASON, JAMES MURRAY 1798–1871, diplomat
Mason, Virginia, *Public Life and Diplomatic Correspondence of James M. Mason* (1903).

MASON, LOWELL 1792–1872, musical educator
Rich, Arthur L., *Lowell Mason* (1946).

MASON, STEVENS THOMSON 1811–1843, Michigan governor
Hemans, L. T., *Life and Times of Stevens Thomson Mason, the Boy Governor of Michigan* (1920).
Sagendorph, Kent, *Stevens Thomson Mason* (1947).

MASON, WILLIAM 1829–1908, musician
Mason, William, *Memories of a Musical Life* (1901).

MATHER, COTTON 1662/3–1727/28, Congregational clergyman, scholar
Beall, Otho T., Jr., and Richard H. Shryock, *Cotton Mather: First Significant Figure in American Medicine* (1954).
Boas, Ralph P., and Louise Boas, *Cotton Mather* (1928).
Mather, Cotton, *Diary of Cotton Mather, D.D., F.R.S., for the Year 1712*, William R. Manierre II, ed. (1964).
———— "Diary," Worthington C. Ford, ed., Mass. Hist. Soc. *Coll.*, 7 ser., 7-8 (1911–1912).
———— *Selections from Cotton Mather*, Kenneth B. Murdock, ed. (1926).
Wendell, Barrett, *Cotton Mather* (1891).

MATHER, INCREASE 1639–1723, Congregational clergyman, author
Mather, Increase, "Autobiography," Michael G. Hall, ed., Am. Antiq. Soc., *Proc.*, 71 (1961), 271.
Murdock, Kenneth B., *Increase Mather* (1925).

MATHER, STEPHEN TYNG 1867–1930, organizer and director of National Park Service
Shankland, Robert, *Steve Mather of the National Parks* (1954).

MATTHEWS, JAMES BRANDER 1852–1929, critic
Matthews, James Brander, *These Many Years* (1917).

MATTSON, HANS 1832–1893, Minnesota pioneer, emigration agent
Mattson, Hans, *Reminiscences* (1891).

MAURY, MATTHEW FONTAINE 1806–1873, oceanographer, naval officer
Lewis, Charles L., *Matthew Fontaine Maury* (1927).
Williams, Frances L., *Matthew F. Maury: Scientist of the Seas* (1963).

MAVERICK, MAURY 1895– , Texas congressman
Henderson, Richard, *Maury Maverick* (1970).

MAXIM, HIRAM STEVENS 1840–1916, inventor
Maxim, Hiram S., *My Life* (1915).

MAY, SAMUEL JOSEPH 1797–1871, Unitarian clergyman, abolitionist
May, Samuel J., *Recollections of Our Anti-Slavery Conflict* (1869).

MAYHEW, JONATHAN 1720–1766, Congregational clergyman
Akers, Charles W., *Called unto Liberty: Jonathan Mayhew* (1964).
Bradford, Alden, *Memoir of the Life and Writings of Rev. Jonathan Mayhew* (1838).
Bailyn, Bernard, "Religion and Revolution: Three Biographical Studies . . . Jonathan Mayhew," *Perspectives in Am. Hist.*, 4 (1970), 85.

MAYO, CHARLES WILLIAM 1898–1968, surgeon
Mayo, Charles W., *Mayo: My Career* (1968).

MAYO FAMILY
Clapesattle, Helen, *Doctors Mayo* (1941).

MAYS, BENJAMIN ELIJAH 1895– , president of Morehouse College
Mays, Benjamin E., *Born to Rebel: An Autobiography* (1971).

MAZZEI, PHILIP 1730–1816, physician, horticulturist, foreign agent
Marraro, H. R., *Philip Mazzei: Virginia's Agent in France* (1935).
Mazzei, Philip, *Memoirs*, H. R. Marraro, trans. (1942).

MEADE, GEORGE GORDON 1815–1872, Union general
Cleaves, Freeman, *Meade of Gettysburg* (1960).
Meade, George G., *The Life and Letters of George Gordon Meade* (2 vols., 1913).

MEANS, JAMES 1853–1920, aeronautical experimenter
Means, James H., *James Means and Problem of Man-Flight, 1882–1920* (1964).

MEIGS, MONTGOMERY CUNNINGHAM 1816–1892, Union quarter-master general
Weigley, Russell F., *Quartermaster General of Union Army: M. C. Meigs* (1959).

MELLON, ANDREW 1855–1937, financier, secretary of treasury
Love, Philip H., *Andrew Mellon* (1929).
O'Connor, Harvey, *Mellon's Millions* (1933).

MELVILLE, HERMAN 1819–1891, writer
Anderson, Charles R., *Melville in the South Seas* (1939).
Arvin, Newton, *Herman Melville*, (1950).
Berthoff, Warner, *Example of Melville* (1963).
Hillway, Tyrus, *Herman Melville* (1963).
Leyda, Jay, *The Melville Log: A Documentary Life* (2 vols., 1951).
Mumford, Lewis, *Herman Melville* (rev. ed., 1962).
Sedgwick, William E., *Herman Melville* (1944).

MEMMINGER, CHRISTOPHER GUSTAVUS 1803–1888, Confederate secretary of treasury
Capers, H. D., *Life and Times of C. G. Memminger* (1893).

MENCKEN, HENRY LOUIS 1880–1956, journalist, critic
Bode, Carl, *Henry L. Mencken* (1969).
Manchester, William R., *Disturber of the Peace: H. L. Mencken* (1951).
Mencken, Henry L., *Happy Days* (1940).
——— *Heathen Days* (1943).
——— *Letters*, Guy J. Forgue, ed. (1961).
Nolte, William H., *H. L. Mencken, Literary Critic* (1967).

MENDELSOHN, ERIC 1887–1953, architect
Whittick, Arnold, *Eric Mendelsohn* (2nd ed., 1956).

MENNINGER, KARL 1893–   , psychiatrist
Menninger, Karl, *Psychiatrist's World: Selected Papers*, Bernard H. Hall, ed. (1959).

MENNINGER, WILLIAM CLAIRE 1899–1966, psychiatrist
Menninger, William C., *Psychiatrist for Troubled World* (2 vols., 1967).

MERCER, GEORGE 1733–1784, land speculator
James, Alfred P., *George Mercer of the Ohio Company* (1963).
Mercer, George, *Papers Relating to Ohio Company of Virginia*, Lois Mulkearn, ed. (1954).

MERIWETHER, DAVID 1800–1892, Kentucky senator, Indian trader, New Mexico Territory governor
Meriwether, David, *My Life in the Mountains and on the Plains*, Robert A. Griffen, ed. (1965).

MEUSEBACH, JOHN fl. mid-nineteenth century; German immigrant leader
King, Irene M., *John O. Meusebach: German Colonizer in Texas* (1967).

MEYER, ADOLF 1866–1950, psychiatrist
Meyer, Adolf, *Fifty-Two Selected Papers*, Alfred Lief, ed. (1948).

MEYER, GEORGE VON LENGERKE 1858–1918, diplomat, Secretary of Navy
Howe, Mark A. DeW., *George von Lengerke Meyer* (1919).

MICHENER, JAMES A. 1907–   , novelist
Day, A. Grove, *James A. Michener* (1964).

MIES VAN DER ROHE, LUDWIG 1886–1969, architect
Blake, Peter, *Mies van der Rohe* (1964).
Blaser, Werner, *Mies Van Der Rohe: Art of Structure* (1966).
Drexler, Arthur, *Ludwig Mies van der Rohe* (1960).

MIFFLIN, THOMAS 1744–1800, Revolutionary leader
Rossman, Kenneth R., *Thomas Mifflin and Politics of American Revolution* (1952).

MILES, NELSON APPLETON 1839–1925, frontier general
Johnson, Virginia W., *Unregimented General: Nelson A. Miles* (1962).
Miles, Nelson A., *Serving the Republic; Memoirs of Civil and Military Life* (1911).

MILLAY, EDNA ST. VINCENT 1892–1950, poet
Brittin, Norman A., *Edna St. Vincent Millay* (1967).
Millay, Edna St. Vincent, *Letters*, A. R. MacDougall, ed. (1952).

MILLER, ARTHUR 1915–   , playwright
Moss, Leonard, *Arthur Miller* (1967).

MILLER, CINCINNATUS HINER (JOAQUIN) 1839–1913, poet
Frost, O. W., *Joaquin Miller* (1967).

MILLER, HENRY 1891–   , author
Gordon, William A., *Mind and Art of Henry Miller* (1967).
Widmer, Kingley, *Henry Miller* (1963).

MILLER, JOAQUIN. See CINCINNATUS HINER MILLER

MILLER, LEWIS 1829–1899, farm implement inventor, founder of Chautauqua
Hendrick, Ellwood, *Lewis Miller* (1925).

MILLER, SAMUEL FREEMAN 1816–1890, Supreme Court justice
Fairman, Charles, *Mr. Justice Miller and the Supreme Court, 1862–1890* (1939).

MILLES, CARL 1875–1955, Swedish-American sculptor
Rogers, Meyric R., *Carl Milles* (1940).

MILLS, ROBERT 1781–1855, architect
Gallagher, Helen M., *Robert Mills, Architect of the Washington Monument* (1935).
Wilson, Charles C., *Robert Mills, Architect* (1919).

MINOT, GEORGE RICHARDS 1885–1950, physician
Rackemann, Francis M., *Inquisitive Physician: George Richards Minot* (1956).

MITCHEL, JOHN PURROY 1879–1918, Mayor of New York
Lewinson, Edwin R., *John Purroy Mitchel, the Boy Mayor of New York* (1965)

MITCHELL, EDWARD PAGE 1852–1927, editor

Mitchell, Edward P., *Memoirs of an Editor: Fifty Years of American Journalism* (1924).

MITCHELL, JOHN 1870–1919, mine union leader
Glück, Elsie, *John Mitchell, Miner* (1929).

MITCHELL, MARIA 1818–1889, astronomer
Mitchell, Maria, *Life, Letters, and Journals*, P. M. Kendall, comp. (1896).

MITCHELL, SILAS WEIR 1829–1914, physician, neurologist, author
Burr, Anna R., *Weir Mitchell: His Life and Letters* (1929).
Walter, Richard D., *S. Weir Mitchell* (1970).

MITCHELL, WESLEY CLAIR 1874–1948, economist
Burns, Arthur F., ed., *Wesley Clair Mitchell* (1952).

MITCHELL, WILLIAM 1879–1936, Air Corps general
Burlingame, Roger, *General Billy Mitchell* (1952).
Davis, Burke, *Billy Mitchell Affair* (1967).
Hurley, Alfred F., *Billy Mitchell: Crusader for Air Power* (1964).

MITCHILL, SAMUEL LATHAM 1764–1831, physician, scientist
Hall, Courtney R., *Scientist in Early Republic: Samuel Latham Mitchill* (1934).

MIZNER FAMILY Florida promoters
Johnston, Alva, *Legendary Mizners* (1953).

MOFFETT, WILLIAM ADGER 1869–1933, naval aviation pioneer
Arpee, Edward, *From Frigates to Flat-Tops: Rear Admiral William Adger Moffett, U.S.N.* (1953).

MOLEY, RAYMOND 1886–   ; advisor to F. D. Roosevelt, journalist
Moley, Raymond, *After Seven Years* (1939).
Moley, Raymond, *First New Deal* (1966).

MONROE, HARRIET 1860–1936; editor and poet
Monroe, Harriet, *Poet's Life* (1938)

MONROE, JAMES 1758–1831, president
Ammon, Harry, *James Monroe: Quest for National Identity* (1971).
Cresson, W. P., *James Monroe* (1946).
Monroe, James, *Autobiography*, Stuart G. Brown, ed. (1959).
——— *Writings*, S. M. Hamilton, ed. (7 vols., 1898–1903).
Wilmerding, Lucius, Jr., *James Monroe: Public Claimant* (1960).

MONTAGUE, ANDREW JACKSON 1862–1937, Virginia governor
Larsen, William E., *Andrew Jackson Montague of Virginia* (1965).

MONTGOMERY, JOHN BERRIEN 1794–1873, naval officer
Rogers, Fred B., *Montgomery and the Portsmouth* (1958).

MOODY, DWIGHT LYMAN 1837–1899, evangelist
Findlay, James F., Jr., *Dwight L. Moody: American Evangelist, 1837–1899* (1969).
Moody, William R., *Dwight L. Moody* (1930).

MOODY, WILLIAM VAUGHN 1869–1910, poet, playwright
Halpern, Martin, *William Vaughn Moody* (1964).
Henry, David D., *William Vaughn Moody* (1934).
Moody, William V., *Some Letters*, D. G. Mason, ed. (1913).

MOONEY, FRED 1888–1952, mine union officer
Mooney, Fred, *Struggle in Coal Fields: Autobiography*, J. W. Hess, ed. (1967).

MOORE, EDWIN WARD 1810–1865, commander of Texas navy
Wells, Tom H., *Commodore Moore and Texas Navy* (1960).

MOORE, JOHN BASSETT 1860–1947, scholar, international jurist
Moore, John B., *Collected Papers* (1944).

MOORE, MARIANNE 1887–1972, poet
Engel, Bernard F., *Marianne Moore* (1963).

MORAN, THOMAS 1837–1926, artist
Fryxell, Fritiof M., ed., *Thomas Moran, Explorer in Search of Beauty* (1958).
Wilkins, Thurman, *Thomas Moran: Artist* (1966).

MORE, PAUL ELMER 1864–1937, writer, critic
Dakin, Arthur H., *Paul Elmer More* (1960).

Davies, Robert M., *Humanism of Paul Elmer More* (1958).
Duggan, Francis X., *Paul Elmer More* (1966).

MORGAN, CHARLES 1795–1878, steamship, railroad magnate
Baughman, James P., *Charles Morgan and the Development of Southern Transportation* (1968).

MORGAN, DANIEL 1736–1802, Revolutionary general
Callahan, North, *Daniel Morgan: Ranger of Revolution* (1961).
Higginbotham, Don, *Daniel Morgan: Revolutionary Rifleman* (1961).

MORGAN, DANIEL EDGAR 1877–1949, judge, city manager of Cleveland
Campbell, Thomas F., *Daniel E. Morgan* (1966).

MORGAN, EDWIN DENISON 1811–1883, New York governor
Rawley, James A., *Edwin D. Morgan, 1811–1883* (1955).

MORGAN, GEORGE 1743–1810, land speculator
Savelle, Max, *George Morgan* (1932).

MORGAN, JOHN 1735–1789, medical educator
Bell, Whitfield J., Jr., *John Morgan: Continental Doctor* (1965).

MORGAN, JOHN PIERPONT 1837–1913, financier
Allen, Frederick L., *The Great Pierpont Morgan* (1949).
Corey, Lewis, *The House of Morgan* (1930).
Satterlee, H. L., *The Life of J. Pierpont Morgan* (1937).

MORGAN, LEWIS HENRY 1818–1881, anthropologist
McIlvaine, Joshua H., *The Life and Works of Lewis H. Morgan* (1882).
Resek, Carl, *Lewis Henry Morgan: Scholar* (1960).
Stern, Bernhard J., *Lewis Henry Morgan, Social Evolutionist* (1931).

MORGENTHAU, HENRY 1856–1946, diplomat
Morgenthau, Henry, *All in a Life-Time* (1922).

MORGENTHAU, HENRY, JR., 1891–1967, secretary of treasury
Morgenthau, Henry, Jr., *From the Diaries*, John M. Blum, ed. (3 vols., 1959–1967).
———— *Roosevelt and Morgenthau*, John M. Blum ed. (1970).

MORRILL, JUSTIN SMITH 1810–1898, Vermont senator
Parker, William B., *The Life and Public Services of Justin Smith Morrill, 1810–1898* (1924).

MORRIS, GOUVERNEUR 1752–1816, Revolutionary leader
Mintz, Max M., *Gouverneur Morris and the American Revolution* (1970).
Morris, Gouverneur, *A Diary of the French Revolution*, B. C. Davenport, ed. (2 vols., 1939).
———— *Diary and Letters*, A. C. Morris, ed. (2 vols., 1888).
Swiggett, Howard, *Extraordinary Mr. Morris* (1952).
Walther, Daniel, *Gouverneur Morris, Witness of Two Revolutions* (1934).

MORRIS, ROBERT 1734–1806, Revolutionary financier
Oberholtzer, Ellis P., *Robert Morris, Patriot and Financier* (1903).
Ver Steeg, Clarence L., *Robert Morris, Revolutionary Financier* (1954).

MORRIS, WRIGHT 1910–   , novelist
Madden, David, *Wright Morris* (1964).

MORROW, DWIGHT 1873–1931, financier, diplomat
Nicolson, Harold, *Dwight Morrow* (1935).

MORROW, JOHN HOWARD 1910–   , diplomat
Morrow, John H., *First American Ambassador to Guinea* (1968).

MORSE, JEDIDIAH 1761–1826, Congregational clergyman, geographer
Morse, James K., *Jedidiah Morse* (1939).

MORSE, SAMUEL FINLEY BREESE 1791–1872, inventor, artist
Larkin, Oliver W., *Samuel F. B. Morse and American Democratic Art* (1954).
Mabie, Carleton, *The American Leonardo: A Life of Samuel F. B. Morse* (1943).
Morse, Samuel F. B., *Letters and Journals*, E. L. Morse, ed. (2 vols., 1914).

MORSE, WAYNE LYMAN 1900–   , Oregon senator
Smith, Arthur R., *Tiger in the Senate: Wayne Morse* (1962).

MORTON, FERDINAND JOSEPH "JELLY ROLL" 1885–1941, jazz musician

Lomax, Alan, *Mister Jelly Roll* (1950).

MORTON, J. STERLING 1832–1902, secretary of agriculture
Olson, J. C., *J. S. Morton* (1942).

MORTON, LEVI PARSONS 1824–1920, banker, diplomat, vice-president
McElroy, R. M., *Levi Parsons Morton: Banker, Diplomat and Statesman* (1930).

MORTON, OLIVER PERRY 1823–1877, Indiana governor, senator
Foulke, W. D., *Life of Oliver P. Morton* (2 vols., 1899).

MORTON, THOMAS ca.1590–ca.1647, satirist
Connors, Donald F., *Thomas Morton* (1969).

MOSBY, JOHN SINGLETON 1833–1916, Confederate raider
Jones, Virgil C., *Ranger Mosby* (1944).
Mosby, John S., *Memoirs* (1917).

MOST, JOHANN 1846–1906, anarchist
Most, Johann J., *Memorien, Erlebtes, Erforschtes und Erdachtes* (2 vols., 1903).
Rocker, Rudolph, *Johann Most* (1924).

MOTLEY, JOHN LOTHROP 1814–1877, historian, diplomat
Holmes, Oliver W., *John Lothrop Motley* (1879).
Motley, John L., *Correspondence*, G. W. Curtis, ed. (2 vols., 1889).
—— *Writings*, G. W. Curtis, ed. (17 vols., 1900).

MOTON, ROBERT RUSSA 1867–1940, principal of Tuskegee Institute
Hughes, William H., and Frederick D. Patterson, eds., *Robert Russa Moton of Hampton and Tuskegee* (1956).
Moton, Robert R., *Finding a Way Out* (1920).

MOTT, LUCRETIA 1793–1880, abolitionist
Cromwell, Otelia, *Lucretia Mott* (1958).
Hallowell, A. D., *James and Lucretia Mott: Life and Letters* (1884).

MOUNT, WILLIAM SIDNEY 1807–1868, painter
Cowdrey, Bartlett, and Herman W. Williams, Jr., *William Sidney Mount, American Painter* (1944).

MOWATT, ANNA CORA OGDEN 1819–1870, actress, writer
Barnes, Eric W., *Lady of Fashion: Life and Theatre of Anna Cora Mowatt* (1954).

MUHLENBERG, HENRY MELCHIOR 1711–1787, founder of Lutheran church in America
Mann, W. J., *Life and Times of Henry Melchior Mühlenberg* (1887).
Muhlenberg, Henry M., *Journals*, Theodore G. Tappert and John W. Doberstein, eds. (3 vols., 1942–1958).
—— *Notebook of a Colonial Clergyman*, Theodore G. Tappert and John W. Doberstein, eds. (1959).

MUHLENBERG, JOHN PETER GABRIEL 1746–1807, Lutheran pastor, Revolutionary general
Hocker, E. W., *The Fighting Parson of the American Revolution: Biography of General Peter Muhlenberg* (1936).

MUHLENBERG, WILLIAM AUGUSTUS 1796–1877, Episcopal clergyman
Newton, William W., *Dr. Muhlenberg* (1890).

MUHLENBURG FAMILY
Wallace, Paul A. W., *The Muhlenbergs of Pennsylvania* (1950).

MUIR, JOHN 1838–1914, naturalist, conservationist
Jones, Holway R., *John Muir and the Sierra Club* (1964).
Muir, John, *The Story of My Boyhood and Youth* (1913).
—— *Writings*, W. F. Badè, ed. (10 vols., 1916–1924).
Smith, Herbert F., *John Muir* (1964).
Wolfe, L. M., *Son of the Wilderness: John Muir* (1945).

MUNFORD, ROBERT ca.1730–1784, playwright
Baine, Rodney M., *Robert Munford: First Comic Dramatist* (1967).

MUNSEY, FRANK ANDREW 1854–1925, publisher
Britt, George, *Forty Years—Forty Millions* (1935).

MURFREE, MARY NOAILLES 1850–1922, novelist; Charles Egbert Craddock, pseud.
Parks, E. W., *Craddock* (1941).

MURPHY, CHARLES FRANCIS 1858–1924, New York City boss
  Weiss, Nancy J., *Charles Francis Murphy, 1858–1924: Tammany Politics* (1968).
MURPHY, EDGAR GARDNER 1869–1913, Episcopal clergyman, Southern reformer
  Bailey, Hugh C., *Edgar Gardner Murphy* (1968).
MURPHY, FRANK 1890–1949, Michigan governor, Supreme Court justice
  Howard, J. Woodford, Jr., *Mr. Justice Murphy: A Political Biography* (1968).
  Lunt, Richard D., *High Ministry of Government: Frank Murphy* (1965).
MURRAY, JOHN 1741–1815, founder of Universalism in America
  Murray, John, and J. S. Murray, *Life of Rev. John Murray* (1870).
MURRAY, WILLIAM "ALFALFA BILL" 1869–1956, Oklahoma governor
  Bryant, Keith L., Jr., *Alfalfa Bill Murray* (1968).
MURROW, EDWARD ROSCOE 1908–1965, journalist, television commentator
  Kendrick, Alexander, *Prime Time: Life of Edward R. Murrow* (1969).
MYERS, MYER 1723–1795, goldsmith
  Rosenbaum, Jeanette W., *Myer Myers: Goldsmith* (1954).
NASBY, PETROLEUM V. See DAVID ROSS LOCKE
NAST, THOMAS 1840–1902, cartoonist
  Keller, Morton, *Art and Politics of Thomas Nast* (1968).
  Paine, Albert B., *Thomas Nast, His Period and Pictures* (1904).
NAST, WILLIAM 1807–1899, Methodist clergyman
  Wittke, Carl, *William Nast: Patriarch of German Methodism* (1959).
NATHAN, ROBERT 1894–   , writer
  Sandelin, Clarence K., *Robert Nathan* (1969).
NEILSON, JAMES 1784–1862, business man
  Thompson, Robert T., *Colonel James Neilson* (1940).
NELSON, KNUTE 1843–1923, Minnesota senator
  Odland, M. W., *The Life of Knute Nelson* (1926).
NELSON, THOMAS AMOS ROGERS 1812–1873, Tennessee unionist leader
  Alexander, Thomas B., *Thomas A. R. Nelson of East Tennessee* (1956).
NEUTRA, RICHARD 1892–1970, architect
  Boesiger, Willy, ed., *Richard Neutra* (3 vols., 1966).
  McCoy, Esther, *Richard Neutra* (1960).
  Neutra, Richard, *Life and Shape* (1962).
NEVIN, ETHELBERT 1862–1901, composer
  Thompson, Vance, *Life of Ethelbert Nevin* (1913).
NEVIN, JOHN WILLIAMSON 1803–1886, Reformed church theologian
  Appel, Theodore, *John Williamson Nevin* (1889).
NEWCOMB, SIMON 1835–1909, astronomer
  Newcomb, Simon, *Reminiscences of an Astronomer* (1903).
NEWLANDS, FRANCIS GRIFFITH 1848–1917, Nevada senator
  Newlands, Francis G., *Public Papers*, A. B. Darling, ed. (2 vols., 1932).
NEWMAN, HENRY 1670–1743, colonial agent
  Cowie, Leonard W., *Henry Newman: An American in London, 1708–43* (1956).
NICHOLS, GEORGE 1778–1865, Salem shipmaster and merchant
  Nichols, George, *Salem Shipmaster: Autobiography*, Martha Nichols, ed.
  (1913).
NICHOLS, ROY FRANKLIN 1896–   , historian
  Nichols, Roy F., *Historian's Progress* (1968).
NICHOLS, THOMAS LOW 1815–1901, hydrotherapist, dietician
  Nichols, T. L., *Fifty Years of American Life* (2 vols., 1864; repr. 1937).
NICOLAY, JOHN GEORGE 1832–1901, journalist, Lincoln's secretary, consul
  Nicolay, Helen, *Lincoln's Secretary* (1949).
NIEBUHR, REINHOLD 1892–1971, theologian, editor
  Kegley, Charles W., and R. W. Bretall, eds., *Reinhold Niebuhr* (1956).
  Niebuhr, Reinhold, *Leaves from the Notebook of a Tamed Cynic* (1929).
NIMITZ, CHESTER WILLIAM 1885–1966, World War II admiral
  Potter, E. B., "Chester William Nimitz, 1885–1966," U.S. Naval Inst. *Proc.* 92
  (1966), 30.

NIXON, RICHARD MILHOUS 1913–   , president
   Mazo, Earl, and Stephen Hess, *Nixon: A Political Portrait* (rev. ed., 1969).
   Nixon, Richard M., *Public Papers* (vol. 1–   , 1970–   ).
   ———— *Six Crises* (1962).

NOAH, MORDECAI MANUEL 1785–1851, journalist, editor, playwright
   Goldberg, Isaac, *Major Noah: American Jewish Pioneer* (1936).

NOCK, ALBERT JAY 1872–1945, author, educator
   Crunden, Robert M., *Mind and Art of Albert Jay Nock* (1964).

NOGUCHI, HIDEYO 1876–1928, bacteriologist
   Eckstein, Gustav, *Noguchi* (1931).

NOGUCHI, ISAMU 1904–   ; sculptor
   Gordon, John, *Isamu Noguchi* (1968).

NORDICA, LILLIAN 1859–1914, opera singer
   Glackens, Ira, *Yankee Diva: Lillian Nordica and the Golden Days of Opera*
   (1963).

NORRIS, FRANK 1870–1902, novelist
   Dillingham, William B., *Frank Norris: Instinct and Art* (1969).
   French, Warren, *Frank Norris* (1962).
   Marchand, Ernest, *Frank Norris* (1942).
   Walker, Franklin, *Frank Norris* (1932).

NORRIS, GEORGE WILLIAM 1861–1944, Nebraska senator
   Lief, Alfred, *Democracy's Norris* (1939).
   Lowitt, Richard, *George W. Norris: Making of a Progressive, 1861–1912* (1963).
   ———— *George W. Norris: Persistence of a Progressive, 1913–1933* (1971).
   Norris, George W., *Fighting Liberal* (1945).
   Zucker, Norman L., *George W. Norris* (1966).

NORTH, FRANK JOSHUA 1840–1885, frontiersman
   Grinnell, G. B., *Two Great Scouts and Their Pawnee Battalion: Frank J. North
   and Luther H. North* (1928).

NORTH, JOHN WELSEY 1815–1890, western politician, entrepreneur
   Stonehouse, Merlin, *John Wesley North* (1965).

NORTH, LUTHER fl. 1856–1882, frontiersman
   Grinnell, G. B., *Two Great Scouts and Their Pawnee Battalion: Frank J. North
   and Luther H. North* (1928).
   North, Luther, *Recollections, 1856–1882*, Donald F. Danker, ed. (1961).

NORTHROP, CYRUS 1834–1922, president of University of Minnesota
   Firkins, O. W., *Cyrus Northrop* (1925).

NORTON, CHARLES ELIOT 1827–1908, author, educator
   Norton, Charles E., *Letters*, Sarah Norton and M.A. De W. Howe, eds.
   (2 vols., 1913).
   Vanderbilt, Kermit, *Charles Eliot Norton* (1959).

NOTT, ELIPHALET 1773–1866, president of Union College, Presbyterian clergyman,
   inventor
   Van Santvoord, Cornelius, *Eliphalet Nott* (1876).

NOYES, JOHN HUMPHREY 1811–1886, founder of Oneida community
   Noyes, G. W., ed., *John Humphrey Noyes* (1931).
   Noyes, John Humphrey, *Religious Experience*, G. W. Noyes, ed. (1923).
   ———— *The Putney Community*, G. W. Noyes, ed. (1931).
   Noyes, Pierrepont B., *My Father's House* (1937).
   Parker, Robert A., *A Yankee Saint: John Humphrey Noyes and the Oneida
   Community* (1935).

NUTTALL, THOMAS 1786–1859, naturalist
   Graustein, Jeannette E., *Thomas Nuttall, Naturalist* (1967).

NYE, EDGAR WILSON "BILL" 1850–1896, humorist
   Nye, Bill, *His Own Life Story*, F. W. Nye, comp. (1926).

NYE, GERALD PRENTICE 1892–   , North Dakota senator
   Cole, Wayne S., *Senator Gerald P. Nye and Foreign Relations* (1962).

O'CONNELL, WILLIAM HENRY 1859–1944, Boston Cardinal

O'Connell, William Cardinal, *Recollections of Seventy Years* (1934).
Wayman, Dorothy G., *Cardinal O'Connell of Boston* (1955).

ODETS, CLIFFORD 1906–   , playwright
Mendelsohn, Michael, *Clifford Odets: Humane Dramatist* (1969).
Shuman, R. Baird, *Clifford Odets* (1962).

OGLETHORPE, JAMES EDWARD 1696–1785, founder of the colony of Georgia
Church, L. F., *Oglethorpe: A Study of Philanthropy in England and Georgia* (1932).
Ettinger, Amos A., *James Edward Oglethorpe, Imperialist Idealist* (1936).

O'HARA, JOHN 1905–1971, novelist
Grebstein, Sheldon N., *John O'Hara* (1966).

O'HARA, JOHN FRANCIS 1888–1960, educator
McAvoy, Thomas T., *Father O'Hara of Notre Dame* (1966).

O'KELLY, JAMES ca. 1735–1826; Methodist clergyman
Kilgore, Charles F., *James O'Kelly: Schism in Methodist Episcopal Church* (1963).

OLDER, FREMONT 1856–1935, western editor, penal reformer
Older, Fremont, *My Own Story* (1919).

OLDS, RANSOM ELI 1864–1950, automobile manufacturer
Niemeyer, Glenn A., *Automotive Career of Ransom E. Olds* (1963).

OLIVER, ROBERT ca. 1757–1819, merchant
Bruchey, Stuart W., *Robert Oliver, Merchant of Baltimore, 1783–1819* (1956).

OLMSTED, FREDERICK LAW 1822–1903, landscape architect
Fabos, Julius G. et al., *Frederick Law Olmsted* (1968).
Mitchell, Broadus, *Frederick Law Olmsted* (1924).
Olmsted, Frederick L., *Forty Years of Landscape Architecture: Professional Papers*, Frederick L. Olmsted, Jr., and Theodora Kimball, eds. (1928).

OLNEY, RICHARD 1835–1917, secretary of state
James, Henry, *Richard Olney* (1923).

OLSON, FLOYD B. 1891–1936, Minnesota governor
Mayer, G. H., *Political Career of Floyd B. Olson* (1951).

O'NEILL, EUGENE 1888–1953, playwright
Carpenter, Frederic I., *Eugene O'Neill* (1964).
Clark, Barrett H., *Eugene O'Neill* (1947).
Gelb, Barbara, and Arthur Gelb, *O'Neill* (1962).
Shaeffer, Louis, *O'Neill, Son and Playwright* (1968).

OPPENHEIMER, JULIUS ROBERT 1904–1967, physicist
Davis, Nuel P., *Lawrence and Oppenheimer* (1968).
Oppenheimer, J. Robert, *Open Mind* (1955).
Rouzé, Michel, *Robert Oppenheimer*, Patrick Evans, trans. (1965).
Stern, Philip M., *Security on Trial: J. Robert Oppenheimer* (1969).
Strout, Cushing, ed., *Conscience, Science and Security: Dr. J. Robert Oppenheimer* (1963).

O'REILLY, JOHN BOYLE 1844–1890, poet, editor
McManamin, F. G., *American Years of John Boyle O'Reilly, 1870–1890* (1959).
Roche, J. J., *Life of John Boyle O'Reilly* (1891).

OSBORNE, THOMAS MOTT 1859–1926, prison reformer
Chamberlain, Rudolph W., *There is No Truce: A Life of Thomas Mott Osborne* (1935).

OSGOOD, HERBERT LEVI 1855–1918, historian
Fox, Dixon R., *Herbert Levi Osgood: An American Scholar* (1924).

OSLER, WILLIAM 1849–1919, medical researcher, head of Johns Hopkins Medical School
Cushing, Harvey, *Life of Sir William Osler* (2 vols., 1925).
McGovern, John P., and Charles G. Roland, *William Osler: The Continuing Education* (1969).
Osler, William, *Continual Remembrance: Letters to Ned Milburn, 1865–1919*, Howard L. Holley, ed. (1968).

White, William, *Sir William Osler: Historian and Literary Essayist* (1951).

OSSOLI, SARAH MARGARET FULLER. See MARGARET FULLER

OTIS, HARRISON GRAY 1765–1848, Federalist
  Morison, Samuel E., *Harrison Gray Otis: Urbane Federalist* (1969).

OTIS, JAMES 1725–1783, colonial political leader
  Otis, James, "Some Political Writings," C. F. Mullett, ed., Univ. of Mo.,
    Studies, 4 nos. 3, 4, (1929).
  Tudor, William, *Life of James Otis* (1823).

OTIS FAMILY
  Waters, John J., *Otis Family in Massachusetts* (1968).

OWEN, ROBERT DALE 1801–1877, reformer
  Leopold, Richard W., *Robert Dale Owen* (1940).

PAGE, THOMAS NELSON 1853–1922, diplomat, author
  Gross, Theodore L., *Thomas Nelson Page* (1968).
  Page, Rosewell, *Thomas Nelson Page* (1923).

PAGE, WALTER HINES 1855–1918, editor, diplomat
  Gregory, Ross, *Walter Hines Page: Ambassador to Court of St. James* (1970).
  Hendrick, Burton J., *Life and Letters of Walter Hines Page* (3 vols., 1922–1925).
  ———— *The Training of an American* (1928).

PAGE, WILLIAM 1811–1885, painter
  Taylor, Joshua C., *William Page* (1957).

PAINE, THOMAS 1737–1809, pamphleteer
  Aldridge, Alfred O., *Man of Reason: Thomas Paine* (1959).
  Conway, Moncure D., *Life of Thomas Paine* (2 vols., 1892).
  Paine, Thomas, *Complete Writings*, Phillip S. Foner, ed. (2 vols., 1945).
  ———— *Representative Selections*, Harry H. Clark, ed. (1944).
  ———— *Writings*, Moncure D. Conway, ed. (4 vols., 1894–1896).
  Pearson, Hesketh, *Tom Paine, Friend of Mankind* (1937).

PALFREY, JOHN GORHAM 1796–1881, Unitarian clergyman, abolitionist
  Gatell, Frank O., *John Gorham Palfrey and the New England Conscience* (1963).

PALMER, ALEXANDER MITCHELL 1872–1936, Attorney General
  Coben, Stanley, *A. Mitchell Palmer* (1963).

PALMER, ALICE ELVIRA FREEMAN 1855–1902, president of Wellesley College
  Palmer, George H., *The Life of Alice Freeman Palmer* (1908).

PALMER, EDWARD 1831–1911, botanist
  McVaugh, Rogers, *Edward Palmer: Plant Explorer* (1956).

PALMER, GEORGE HERBERT 1842–1933, philosopher
  Palmer, George H., *Autobiography of a Philosopher* (1930).

PARK, EDWARD AMASA 1808–1900, Congregational clergyman, theologian
  Foster, Frank H., *Life of Edward Amasa Park* (1935).

PARK, WILLIAM HALLOCK 1863–1939, doctor
  Oliver, Wade W., *William Hallock Park, M.D.* (1941).

PARKER, CARLETON HUBBELL 1878–1918, economist, labor conciliator
  Parker, Carleton S., *An American Idyll: The Life of Carleton H. Parker* (1919).

PARKER, FRANCIS WAYLAND 1837–1902, progressive educator
  Campbell, Jack K., *Colonel Francis W. Parker: Childrens Crusader* (1967).

PARKER, HORATIO 1863–1919, composer
  Chadwick, G. W., *Horatio Parker* (1921).

PARKER, ISAAC CHARLES 1838–1896, Missouri congressman, Arkansas jurist
  Harrington, Fred H., *Hanging Judge* (1951).

PARKER, THEODORE 1810–1860, Unitarian clergyman
  Commager, Henry S., *Theodore Parker* (1936).
  Parker, Theodore, *An Anthology*, Henry S. Commager, ed. (1960).
  Weiss, John, *Life and Correspondence of Theodore Parker* (2 vols., 1864).

PARKMAN, FRANCIS 1823–1893, historian
  Doughty, Howard, *Francis Parkman* (1962).
  Parkman, Francis, *Journals*, Mason Wade, ed. (2 vols., 1947).
  ———— *Letters*, Wilbur R. Jacobs, ed. (2 vols., 1960).

Wade, Mason, *Francis Parkman* (1942).

PARKS, WILLIAM 1698–1750, printer, newspaper publisher
Wroth, Lawrence C., *William Parks, Printer and Journalist* (1926).

PARRINGTON, VERNON LOUIS 1871–1929, historian
Hofstadter, Richard, *Progressive Historians: Turner, Beard, Parrington* (1968).

PARSONS, THEOPHILUS 1750–1813, jurist
Parsons, Theophilus, Jr., *Memoir of Theophilus Parsons* (1859).

PASTORIUS, FRANCIS DANIEL 1651–1719/20, Pennsylvania lawyer, school master
Learned, M. D., *The Life of Francis Daniel Pastorius* (1908).

PATRICK, ROBERT 1835–1866, Confederate soldier
Patrick, Robert, *Diary, 1861–1865,* F. Jay Taylor, ed. (1959).

PATTEN, GILBERT 1866–1945, popular writer; Burt L. Standish, pseud.
Patten, Gilbert, *Frank Merriwell's "Father": Autobiography,* Harriet Hinsdale and Tony London, eds. (1964).

PATTEN, SIMON NELSON 1852–1922, economist
Fox, Daniel M., *Discovery of Abundance: Simon N. Patten and Transformation of Social Theory* (1967).

PATTERSON, JOHN HENRY 1844–1922, cash register manufacturer
Crowther, Samuel, *John H. Patterson: Pioneer in Industrial Welfare* (1923).

PATTON, GEORGE SMITH 1885–1945, U.S. Army general
Patton, George S., *Patton Papers, 1885–1940,* Martin Blumenson, ed. (1971).

PAULDING, JAMES KIRKE 1778–1860, author, naval official
Herold, Amos L., *James Kirke Paulding* (1926).
Paulding, James K., *Letters,* Ralph M. Aderman, ed. (1962).
Paulding, W. I., *Literary Life of James K. Paulding* (1867).

PAYNE, DANIEL ALEXANDER 1811–1893, president of Wilberforce University
Payne, Daniel A., *Recollections of Seventy Years* (1888; repr. 1968).

PAYNE, JOHN HOWARD 1791–1852, actor, dramatist
Chiles, R. P., *John Howard Payne* (1930).

PEABODY, ELIZABETH PALMER 1804–1894, kindergarten pioneer
Baylor, Ruth M., *Elizabeth Palmer Peabody* (1965).

PEABODY, ENDICOTT 1857–1944, schoolmaster
Ashburn, Frank D., *Peabody of Groton* (2nd. ed., 1967).

PEABODY, GEORGE 1795–1869, merchant, financier, philanthropist
Curry, J. L. M., *Sketch of George Peabody and a History of the Peabody Education Fund* (1898).

PEABODY, GEORGE FOSTER 1852–1938, banker, philanthropist
Ware, Louise, *George Foster Peabody: Banker, Philanthropist, Publicist* (1951).

PEABODY, JOSEPH 1757–1844, East India merchant
Endicott, William C., and Walter M. Whitehill, eds., *Captain Joseph Peabody, East India Merchant of Salem* (1962).

PEABODY, JOSEPHINE PRESTON 1874–1922, poet, dramatist
Peabody, Josephine P., *Diary and Letters,* C. H. Baker, ed. (1925).

PEABODY FAMILY
Tharp, Louise H., *Peabody Sisters of Salem* (1950).

PEALE, CHARLES WILLSON 1741–1827, artist
Briggs, Berta N., *Charles Willson Peale, Artist & Patriot* (1952).
Sellers, Charles C., *Charles Willson Peale* (1969).

PEALE, TITIAN RAMSAY 1799–1885, artist-naturalist
Poesch, Jessie, *Titian Ramsay Peale and His Journals of the Wilkes Expedition* (1961).

PEALE FAMILY
Elam, Charles H., ed., *Peale Family: Three Generations of Artists* (1967).

PEARSON, DREW 1897–1969, columnist
Klurfeld, Herman, *Behind the Lines: The World of Drew Pearson* (1968).

PEARY, ROBERT EDWIN 1856–1920, explorer
Hobbs, W. H., *Peary* (1936).

Weems, John E., *Peary: Explorer* (1967).

PECK, JOHN MASON 1789–1858, Baptist clergyman, missionary in West
Peck, John M., *Forty Years of Pioneer Life: Memoir,* Rufus Babcock, ed. (1965).

PEIRCE, BENJAMIN 1809–1880, mathematician, astronomer
Archibald, R. C., *Benjamin Peirce, 1809–1880* (1925).
Lenzen, V. F., *Benjamin Peirce and the U.S. Coast Survey* (1968).

PEIRCE, CHARLES SANTIAGO SANDERS 1839–1914, mathematician, philosopher,
founder of pragmatism
Bernstein, Richard J., ed., *Perspectives on Peirce* (1965).
Boler, John F., *Charles Peirce and Scholastic Realism* (1968).
Murphey, Murray G., *Development of Peirce's Philosophy* (1961).
Peirce, Charles S., *Collected Papers,* Charles S. Hartshorne and Paul Weiss,
eds. (8 vols., 1931–1958).

PEMBERTON, ISRAEL 1715–1779, merchant, philanthropist
Thayer, Theodore, *Israel Pemberton, King of the Quakers* (1943).

PEMBERTON, JOHN CLIFFORD 1814–1881, Confederate general
Pemberton, John C., Jr., *Pemberton: Defender of Vicksburg* (1942).

PENDLETON, EDMUND 1721–1803, Revolutionary leader
Mays, David J., *Edmund Pendleton* (2 vols., 1952).
Pendleton, Edmund, *Letters and Papers,* David J. Mays, ed. (2 vols., 1967).

PENN, HANNAH 1671–1726, wife of William Penn
Drinker, Sophie H., *Hannah Penn and Proprietorship of Pennsylvania* (1958).

PENN, WILLIAM 1644–1718, founder of Pennsylvania
Beatty, E. C. O., *William Penn as Social Philosopher* (1939).
Buranelli, Vincent, *King and Quaker: William Penn and James II* (1962).
Dunn, Mary M., *William Penn* (1967).
Illick, Joseph E., *William Penn the Politician* (1965).
Peare, Catherine O., *William Penn* (1957).
Penn, William, *Collection of His Works,* Joseph Besse, ed. (2 vols., 1726).
——— and James Logan, "Correspondence," Deborah Logan and Edward
Armstrong, eds., Hist. Soc. of Penn., *Publ.,* 9-10 (1870–1872).
——— *Witness of William Penn,* Frederick B. Tolles and E. Gordon Alderfer,
eds. (1957).

PENNELL, JOSEPH 1857–1926, etcher, lithographer
Pennell, Joseph, *Adventures of an Illustrator* (1925).

PENNEY, JAMES CASH 1875–1971, chain store magnate
Penney, J. C., *Man with a Thousand Partners* (1931).

PENNYPACKER, SAMUEL WHITAKER 1843–1916, Pennsylvania governor
Pennypacker, Samuel W., *Autobiography of a Pennsylvanian* (1918).

PENROSE, BOIES 1860–1921, Pennsylvania senator
Bowden, R. D., *Boies Penrose* (1937).
Davenport, Walter, *Power and Glory: Boies Penrose* (1931).

PEPPERRELL FAMILY
Fairchild, Byron, *Messrs. William Pepperrell: Merchants* (1954).

PERKINS, DEXTER 1889–   , historian
Perkins, Dexter, *Autobiography* (1969).

PERKINS, FRANCES 1882–1965, secretary of labor
Perkins, Frances, *The Roosevelt I Knew* (1946).

PERKINS, GEORGE WALBRIDGE 1862–1920, financier, life insurance manager
Garraty, John A., *Right-Hand Man: George W. Perkins* (1960).

PERKINS, JACOB 1766–1849, inventor
Bathe, Greville, and Dorothy Bathe, *Jacob Perkins* (1943).

PERRY, MATTHEW CALBRAITH 1794–1858, naval officer
Barrows, Edward M., *The Great Commodore: The Exploits of Matthew Cal-
braith Perry* (1935).
Morison, Samuel E., *"Old Bruin": Commodore Matthew G. Perry* (1967).

PERRY, OLIVER HAZARD 1785–1819, naval officer
Dutton, Charles J., *Oliver Hazard Perry* (1935).

PERSHING, JOHN JOSEPH 1860–1948, World War I general
Palmer, Frederick, *John J. Pershing, General of the Armies* (1948).
Pershing, John J., *My Experiences* (2 vols., 1931).

PETER, HUGH 1598–1660, Congregational clergyman
Stearns, Raymond P., *Strenuous Puritan: Hugh Peter* (1954).

PETIGRU, JAMES LOUIS 1789–1863, South Carolina Unionist
Carson, James P., *Life, Letters and Speeches of James Louis Petigru, the Union Man of South Carolina* (1920).

PHILIPP, EMANUEL LORENZ 1861–1925, Wisconsin governor
Maxwell, Robert S., *Emanuel L. Philipp: Wisconsin Stalwart* (1959).

PHILLIPS, DAVID GRAHAM 1867–1911, novelist, journalist
McGovern, James R., "David Graham Phillips and Virility Impulse of Progressives," *NEQ*, 39 (1966), 334.
Ravitz, Abe C., *David Graham Phillips* (1966).

PHILLIPS, ULRICH BONNELL 1877–1934, historian
Genovese, Eugene D., "Appraisal of Work of Ulrich B. Phillips," *Agric. Hist.*, 41 (1967), 345.

PHILLIPS, WENDELL 1811–1884, abolitionist
Bartlett, Irving H., *Wendell Phillips: Brahmin Radical* (1961).
Korngold, Ralph, *Two Friends of Man . . . William Lloyd Garrison and Wendell Phillips* (1950).
Phillips, Wendell, *Speeches, Lectures, and Letters.* (1863).
Sherwin, Oscar, *Prophet of Liberty: Wendell Phillips* (1958).

PHILLIPS, WILLIAM 1878–1968, under secretary of state, diplomat
Phillips, William, *Ventures in Diplomacy* (1953).

PHOENIX, JOHN. See GEORGE HORATIO DERBY

PICKENS, ANDREW 1739–1817, Revolutionary general
Waring, Alice N., *Fighting Elder: Andrew Pickens* (1962).

PICKERING, TIMOTHY 1745–1829, Federalist leader
Pickering, Octavius, and C. W. Upham, *The Life of Timothy Pickering* (4 vols., 1867–1873).
Prentiss, H. P., *Timothy Pickering as the Leader of New England Federalism, 1800–1815* (1934).

PICKETT, GEORGE EDWARD 1825–1875, Confederate general
Pickett, G. E., *Soldier of the South: Letters to His Wife*, A. C. Inman, ed. (1928).

PIERCE, FRANKLIN 1804–1869, president
Nichols, Roy F., *Franklin Pierce* (2nd ed., 1958).

PIKE, ALBERT 1809–1891, Confederate general
Duncan, Robert L., *Reluctant General: Albert Pike* (1961).

PIKE, JAMES SHEPHERD 1811–1882, journalist
Durden, Robert F., *James Shepherd Pike: Republicanism and the American Negro, 1850–1882* (1957).

PIKE, ZEBULON MONTGOMERY 1779–1813, explorer
Hollon, W. Eugene, *Lost Pathfinder: Zebulon Pike* (1949).
Pike, Zebulon M., *An Account of Expeditions to the Sources of the Mississippi* [*1805–07*], Elliott Coues, ed. (4 vols., 1810).
—— *Arkansaw Journal*, S. H. Hart and A. B. Hulbert, eds. (1932).
—— *Journals, with Letters and Related Documents*, Donald Jackson, ed. (2 vols., 1966).
Terrell, John U., *Zebulon Pike* (1968).

PILCHER, JOSHUA 1790–1840, fur trader
Sunder, John E., *Joshua Pilcher: Fur Trader and Indian Agent* (1968).

PINCHOT, GIFFORD 1865–1946, conservationist, Pennsylvania governor
Fausold, Martin L., *Gifford Pinchot* (1961).
McGeary, M. Nelson, *Gifford Pinchot* (1960).
Pinchot, Gifford, *Breaking New Ground* (1947).
Pinkett, Harold T., *Gifford Pinchot: Private and Public Forester* (1970).

PINCKNEY, CHARLES COTESWORTH 1746–1825, Revolutionary leader, diplomat
Zahniser, Marvin R., *Charles Cotesworth Pinckney* (1967).

PINCKNEY, ELIZA (ELIZABETH LUCAS) 1722–1793, planter
Ravenel, H. H., *Eliza Pinckney* (1896).

PINCKNEY, THOMAS 1750–1828, Revolutionary leader, South Carolina governor
Pinckney, Charles C., *Life of General Thomas Pinckney* (1895).

PINGREE, HAZEN STUART 1840–1901, manufacturer, Michigan politician
Holli, Melvin G., *Reform in Detroit: Hazen S. Pingree and Urban Politics*
(1969).

PINKERTON, ALLAN 1819–1884, detective
Horan, James D., *Pinkertons* (1968).
Pinkerton, Allan, *Criminal Reminiscenses and Detective Sketches* (1879).
Pinkerton, Allan, *Thirty Years a Detective* (1884).

PINKHAM, LYDIA ESTES 1819–1883; manufacturer of patent medicine
Washburn, Robert C., *The Life and Times of Lydia E. Pinkham* (1931).

PINKNEY, EDWARD COOTE 1802–1828, poet, lawyer
Mabbott, T. O., and F. L. Pleadwell, *The Life and Works of Edward Coote Pinkney* (1926).

PINKNEY, WILLIAM 1764–1822, lawyer, diplomat
Pinkney, William, Jr., *Life of William Pinkney* (1853; repr. 1969).

PITTMAN, KEY 1872–1940, Nevada senator
Israel, Fred L., *Nevada's Key Pittman* (1963).

PLATT, ORVILLE HITCHCOCK 1827–1905; Connecticut senator
Coolidge, Louis A., *An Old-Fashioned Senator: Orville H. Platt* (1910).

PLATT, THOMAS COLLIER 1833–1910, New York senator
Gosnell, Harold F., *Boss Platt* (1924).
Platt, Thomas C., *Autobiography*, L. J. Lang, ed. (1910).

PLUMER, WILLIAM 1759–1850, New Hampshire senator
Plumer, William, Jr., *Life of William Plumer* (1856).
Turner, Lynn W., *William Plumer of New Hampshire, 1759–1850* (1962).

POCAHONTAS 1595–1617, daughter of Chief Powhatan
Barbour, Philip L., *Pocahontas and Her World* (1970).
Woodward, Grace S., *Pocahontas* (1969).

POE, CLARENCE HAMILTON 1881–1964, Southern editor
Poe, Clarence H., *My First 80 Years* (1963).

POE, EDGAR ALLAN 1809–1849, writer
Allen, Hervey, *Israfel* [Edgar Allen Poe] (1926).
Buranelli, Vincent, *Edgar Allan Poe* (1961).
Fagin, Nathan B., *Histrionic Mr. Poe* (1949).
Pope-Hennessy, Una B., *Edgar Allen Poe* (1934).
Wagenknecht, Edward C., *Edgar Allan Poe* (1963).
Woodberry, G. E., *The Life of Edgar Allan Poe*, (rev. ed., 2 vols., 1909).

POINSETT, JOEL ROBERTS 1779–1851; diplomat, secretary of war
Putnam, Herbert E., *Joel Roberts Poinsett* (1935).
Rippy, James F., *Joel R. Poinsett* (1935).

POLK, JAMES KNOX 1795–1849, president
McCormac, Eugene I., *James K. Polk* (1922).
Polk, James K., *Correspondence, 1817–1832,* Herbert Weaver and Paul H.
Bergeron, eds. (1969).
—— *Diary*, Milo M. Quaife, ed. (4 vols., 1910). Extracts edited by Allan
Nevins (1929).
Sellers, Charles G., Jr., *James K. Polk* (2 vols., 1957–1966).

POLK, LEONIDAS 1806–1864, Episcopal bishop, Confederate general
Parks, Joseph H., *General Leonidas Polk, C. S. A.: Fighting Bishop* (1962).
Polk, W. M., *Leonidas Polk* (rev. ed., 2 vols., 1915).

POLLOCK, JACKSON 1912–1956, artist
O'Connor, Francis V., *Jackson Pollock* (1967).

POLLOCK, OLIVER 1737–1823, Louisiana planter, financier of Revolutionary War in West
James, James A., *Oliver Pollock* (1937).

PONTIAC ?–1769; Ottawa chief
Peckham, Howard H., *Pontiac and the Indian Uprising* (1947).

POOLE, WILLIAM FREDERICK 1821–1894, librarian
Williamson, William L., *William Frederick Poole and the Modern Library Movement* (1963).

POOR, HENRY VARNUM 1812–1905, business editor
Chandler, Alfred D., Jr., *Henry Varnum Poor: Business Editor, Analyst, and Reformer* (1956).

POORE, BENJAMIN PERLEY 1820–1887, journalist
Poore, Benjamin P., *Perley's Reminiscences* (2 vols., 1886).

PORTER, DAVID 1780–1843, naval officer
Long, David F., *Nothing Too Daring: Commodore David Porter* (1970).
Porter, David Dixon, *Memoir of Commodore David Porter* (1875).
Soley, J. R., *Admiral Porter* (1903).

PORTER, DAVID DIXON 1813–1891, Union naval officer
West, Richard S., Jr., *Second Admiral: David Dixon Porter* (1937).

PORTER, KATHERINE ANNE 1894–   , writer
Hartley, Lodwick, and George Core, eds., *Katherine Anne Porter: Symposium* (1969).
Hendrick, George, *Katherine Anne Porter* (1965).
Nance, William L., *Katherine Anne Porter* (1967).

PORTER, RUFUS 1792–1884, inventor, itinerant mural painter
Lipman, Jean, *Rufus Porter: Yankee Pioneer* (1968).

PORTER, WILLIAM SYDNEY 1862–1910, author; O. Henry, pseud.
Current-Garcia, Eugene, *O. Henry* (1965).
Smith, Charles A., *O. Henry* (1916).

PORTER, WILLIAM TROTTER 1809–1858, humorist
Yates, Norris W., *William T. Porter and "Spirit of Times": Big Bear School of Humor* (1957).

POWDERLY, TERENCE VINCENT 1849–1924, labor leader
Powderly, Terence V., *The Path I Trod*, H. J. Carman, Henry David, and P. N. Guthrie, eds. (1940).
———— *Thirty Years of Labor* (1889).

POWELL, JOHN WESLEY 1834–1902, geologist, explorer
Darrah, William C., *Powell of the Colorado* (1951).
Stegner, Wallace E., *Beyond the Hundredth Meridian: John Wesley Powell* (1954).
Terrell, John U., *The Man Who Re-Discovered America: The Life of John Wesley Powell* (1969).

POWNALL, THOMAS 1722–1805, Massachusetts governor
Pownall, C. A. W., *Thomas Pownall, M.P., F.R.S., Governor of Massachusetts Bay* (1908).
Schutz, John A., *Thomas Pownall, British Defender of American Liberty* (1951).

PRATT, RICHARD HENRY 1840–1924, soldier, Indian educator
Eastman, Elaine G., *Pratt: the Red Man's Moses* (1935).

PRESCOTT, WILLIAM HICKLING 1796–1859, historian
Gardiner, C. Harvey, *William Hickling Prescott* (1969).
Prescott, William H., *Correspondence 1833–1847*, Roger Wolcott, ed. (1925).
———— *Papers*, C. Harvey Gardiner, ed. (1964).
———— *Unpublished Letters*, C. L. Penney, ed. (1927).
Ticknor, George, *Life of William Hickling Prescott* (1864).

PRIESTLEY, JOSEPH 1733–1804, scientist, theologian
Gibbs, Frederick W., *Joseph Priestley* (1965).
Holt, Anne, *Life of Joseph Priestley* (1931).

Robbins, Caroline, "Joseph Priestley in America, 1794–1804," Am. Phil. Soc. *Proc.*, 106 (1962), 60.

Smith, Edgar F., *Priestley in America, 1794–1804* [1920].

PULITZER, JOSEPH 1847–1911, publisher
Seitz, Don C., *Joseph Pulitzer, His Life and Letters* (1924).
Swanberg, William A., *Pulitzer* (1967).

PUMPELLY, RAPHAEL 1837–1923, geologist, explorer
Pumpelly, Raphael, *My Reminiscences* (2 vols., 1918).
—— *Travels and Adventures of Raphael Pumpelly, Mining Engineer, Geologist, and Explorer*, O. S. Rice, ed. (1920).
Willis, Bailey, *Biographical Memoir of Raphael Pumpelly, 1837–1923* (1934).

PUPIN, MICHAEL IDVORSKY 1858–1935, physicist
Pupin, Michael I., *From Immigrant to Inventor* (1933).

PUTNAM, GEORGE HAVEN 1844–1930, publisher, son of George Palmer Putnam
Putnam, George H., *Memories of a Publisher* (1915).

PUTNAM, GEORGE PALMER 1814–1872, publisher
Putnam, George H., *A Memoir of George Palmer Putnam* (1903).

PUTNAM, RUFUS 1738–1824, soldier and pioneer
Buell, Rowena, *Memoirs of Rufus Putnam* (1903).

PYLE, HOWARD 1853–1911, illustrator
Abbott, Charles D., *Howard Pyle* (1925).

PYNCHON, WILLIAM 1590–1662, merchant
McIntyre, Ruth A., *William Pynchon* (1961).

QUANTRILL, WILLIAM CLARKE 1837–1865, guerilla leader
Castel, Albert E., *William Clarke Quantrill* (1962).

QUICK, (JOHN) HERBERT 1861–1925, author, mayor of Sioux City
Quick, Herbert, *One Man's Life* (1925).

QUINCY, JOSIAH, JR. 1744–1775, Revolutionary leader
Quincy, Josiah, *Memoir of the Life of Josiah Quincy, Jun.* (1825).

QUINCY, JOSIAH III 1772–1864, president of Harvard University, mayor of Boston
Quincy, Edmund, *Life of Josiah Quincy* (1867).
Quincy, Josiah, IV, *Figures of the Past, from the Leaves of Old Journals*, 1833; Mark A. De Wolfe Howe, ed. (1926).

QUINN, JOHN 1870–1924, art collector
Reid, Benjamin L., *Man from New York: John Quinn* (1968).

QUITMAN, JOHN ANTHONY 1798–1858, Mississippi leader, soldier
Claiborne, J. F. H., *Life and Correspondence of John A. Quitman* (1860).

RADISSON, PIERRE ESPRIT 1636–1710, fur trader
Nute, Grace L., *Caesars of the Wilderness: Chouart and Radisson, 1618–1710* (1943).
Vestal, Stanley, *King of the Fur Traders: Pierre Esprit Radisson* (1940).

RAFINESQUE, CONSTANTINE SAMUEL 1783–1840, naturalist
Fitzpatrick, T. J., *Rafinesque: A Sketch of His Life with Bibliography* (1911).
Rafinesque, C. S., *A Life of Travels and Researches in North America and South Europe* (1836).

RAINSFORD, WILLIAM S. 1850–1933, clergyman, free thinker
Rainsford, William S., *Story of a Varied Life* (1924).

RAMSAY, DAVID 1749–1815, Revolutionary leader, South Carolina legislator, historian
Brunhouse, Robert L., "David Ramsay, 1749–1815: Selections," Am. Philos. Soc., *Trans.*, 55 pt. 4 (1965).

RAMSEY, JAMES GETTYS MCCREADY 1797–1884, Confederate treasury agent
Ramsey, James G. M., *Autobiography and Letters*, William B. Hesseltine, ed. (1954).

RANDALL, DAVID ANTON 1905– , bookseller, librarian
Randall, David A., *Dukedom Large Enough* (1969).

RANDOLPH, EDMUND 1753–1813, Revolutionary leader

Conway, Moncure D., *Omitted Chapters of History: Life and Papers of Edmund Randolph* (1888).

RANDOLPH, EDWARD 1632–1703, British agent, official
Toppan, R. N., and A. T. S. Goodrick, *Edward Randolph; Including His Letters and Official Papers . . . 1676–1703* (7 vols., 1898–1909).

RANDOLPH, JOHN 1773–1833, Virginia senator
Adams, Henry, *John Randolph* (1882).
Bruce, William C., *John Randolph of Roanoke* (2 vols., 1922).
Garland, H. A., *Life of John Randolph* (2 vols., 1856).
Kirk, Russell, *John Randolph of Roanoke* (rev. ed., 1964).

RANDOLPH FAMILY
Eckenrode, Hamilton J., *The Randolphs: Story of a Virginia Family* (1946).

RANSOM, JOHN CROWE 1888–   , poet, essayist
Parsons, Thornton H., *John Crowe Ransom* (1969).

RAPP, GEORGE 1757–1847, religious leader
Arndt, Karl J., *George Rapp's Harmony Society, 1785–1847* (1965).

RASCOE, BURTON 1892–1957, writer
Hensley, Donald M., *Burton Rascoe* (1970).

RAUSCHENBUSCH, WALTER 1861–1918, Baptist theologian
Niebuhr, Reinhold, "Walter Rauschenbusch in Historical Perspective," *Religion in Life*, 27 (Autumn 1958), 527.
Sharpe, W. R., *Rauschenbusch* (1942).

RAVENEL, HENRY WILLIAM 1814–1887, planter, botanist
Ravenel, Henry W., *Private Journal, 1859–1887*, Arney R. Childs, ed. (1947).

RAWLINGS, MARJORIE KINNAN 1896–1953, writer
Bigelow, Gordon E., *Frontier Eden: Literary Career of Marjorie Kinnan Rawlings* (1966).

RAWLINS, JOHN AARON 1831–1869, Union general, secretary of war
Wilson, James H., *John A. Rawlins, Lawyer* (1916).

RAY, CHARLES HENRY 1821–1870, Illinois editor
Monaghan, Jay, *The Man Who Elected Lincoln* (1956).

RAYBURN, SAMUEL 1882–1961, Speaker of the House
Dorough, C. Dwight, *Mr. Sam* (1962).

RAYMOND, HENRY JARVIS 1820–1869, editor, politician
Brown, Ernest F., *Raymond of the Times* (1951).

READ, CHARLES 1713–1774, ironmaster, agricultural experimenter
Woodward, Carl R., *Ploughs and Politics: Charles Read of New Jersey* (1941).

READ, GEORGE 1733–1798, Revolutionary leader, Delaware senator
Read, William T., *Life and Correspondence of George Read* (1870).

READ, OPIE PERCIVAL 1852–1939, humorist
Morris, Robert L., *Opie Read, American Humorist* (1965).

REAGAN, JOHN HENNINGER 1818–1905, Confederate postmaster general, Texas senator
Procter, Ben H., *Not without Honor: John H. Reagan* (1962).

RED JACKET ca. 1758–1830, Seneca chief
Stone, William L., *Life and Times of Red-Jacket, or Sa-go-ye-wat-ha* (1841).

REDPATH, JAMES 1833–1891; lecture manager
Horner, Charles F., *Life of James Redpath and the Development of the Modern Lyceum* (1926).

REED, JOHN 1887–1920, radical journalist
Hicks, Granville, *John Reed; The Making of a Revolutionary* (1936).
O'Connor, Richard, and Dale L. Walker, *Lost Revolutionary: John Reed* (1967).

REED, JOSEPH 1741–1785, Revolutionary soldier, lawyer
Reed, William Bradford, *Life and Correspondence of Joseph Reed* (2 vols., 1847).
Roche, John F., *Joseph Reed: Moderate in the American Revolution* (1957).

REED, THOMAS BRACKETT 1869–1902, Maine congressman, Speaker of the House
McCall, Samuel W., *The Life of Thomas Brackett Reed* (1914).

Robinson, William Alexander, *Thomas B. Reed* (1930).

REED, WALTER 1851–1902, physician
Kelly, Howard A., *Walter Reed and Yellow Fever* (rev. ed., 1923).

REID, WHITELAW 1837–1912, journalist, diplomat
Cortissoz, Royal, *The Life of Whitelaw Reid* (2 vols., 1921).
Reid, Whitelaw, *Diary, 1898*, H. Wayne Morgan, ed. (1965).

REMINGTON, FREDERICK 1861–1909, artist
McCracken, Harold, *Frederick Remington, Artist of the Old West* (1947).
Vail, R. W. G., *Frederic Remington, Chronicler of the Vanished West* (1929).

REVERE, PAUL 1735–1818, Revolutionary leader, metalsmith, engraver
Buhler, Kathryn C., *Paul Revere, Goldsmith* (1956).
Forbes, Esther, *Paul Revere and the World He Lived In* (1942).
Goss, Elbridge H., *The Life of Colonel Paul Revere* (2 vols., 1891).

RHETT, ROBERT BARNWELL 1800–1876, secessionist leader
White, Laura A., *Robert Barnwell Rhett, Father of Secession* (1931).

RHODES, JAMES FORD 1848–1927, historian
Cruden, Robert, *James Ford Rhodes* (1961).
Howe, Mark A. DeW., *James Ford Rhodes, American Historian* (1929).

RICE, ELMER 1892–1967, playwright
Durham, Frank, *Elmer Rice* (1970).

RICHARD, GABRIEL 1767–1832, Catholic clergyman, Detroit pioneer
Dionne, N. E., *Gabriel Richard, Sulpicien, Curé et Second Fondateur de la Ville de Détroit* (1911).
Woodford, Frank B., and Albert Hyma, *Gabriel Richard: Frontier Ambassador* (1958).

RICHARDSON, HENRY HOBSON 1838–1886, architect
Hitchcock, Henry R., *The Architecture of H. H. Richardson and His Times* (1936).
Van Rennselaer, Marina G., *Henry H. Richardson and His Works* (1888).

RICHTER, CONRAD 1890–1971, novelist
Gaston, Edwin W., *Conrad Richter* (1965).

RICKENBACKER, EDWARD VERNON 1890– , World War I aviator
Rickenbacker, Edward V., *Rickenbacker* (1967).

RIDGWAY, MATTHEW BUNKER 1895– , general
Ridgway, Matthew B., *Memoirs* (1956). As told to Harold H. Martin.

RIEDESEL, BARONESS FREDRIKA VON 1746–1808
von Riedesel, Fredrika, *Journal and Correspondence, 1776–1783*, Marvin L. Brown, Jr., ed. and trans. (1965).
Tharp, Louise H., *Baroness and General* (1962).

RIIS, JACOB AUGUST 1849–1914, reform journalist
Riis, Jacob A., *Making of an American* (1901) Roy Lubove, ed., (1966).
Ware, Louise, *Jacob A. Riis* (1939).

RILEY, JAMES WHITCOMB 1849–1916, author
Crowder, Richard, *Those Innocent Years: James Whitcomb Riley* (1957).
Dickey, Marcus, *James Whitcomb Riley* (2 vols., 1919–1922).
Revell, Peter, *James Whitcomb Riley* (1970).
Riley, James W., *Letters*, W. L. Phelps, ed. (1930).

RINEHART, WILLIAM HENRY 1825–1874, sculptor
Rusk, William S., *William Henry Rinehart, Sculptor* (1939).

RINGLING FAMILY
North, Henry R., and A. Hatch, *Circus Kings: Our Ringling Family Story* (1960).

RIPLEY, GEORGE 1802–1880, Unitarian clergyman, transcendentalist
Crowe, Charles, *George Ripley: Transcendentalist and Utopian Socialist* Frothingham, O. B., *George Ripley* (1882).
(1967).

RITCHIE, THOMAS 1778–1854, journalist
Ambler, Charles H., *Thomas Ritchie: A Study in Virginia Politics* (1913).

RITTENHOUSE, DAVID 1732–1796, astronomer, instrument-maker
Barton, William, *Memoirs of Life of David Rittenhouse* (1813).
Ford, Edward, *David Rittenhouse* (1946).
Hindle, Brooke, *David Rittenhouse* (1964).

RIVERS, THOMAS MILTON 1888–1962, virologist
Rivers, Thomas M., *Reflections: Oral Memoir Prepared by Saul Benison* (1967).

ROACH, JOHN 1813–1887, shipbuilder
Swann, Leonard A., Jr., *John Roach: Naval Contractor, 1862–1886* (1965).

ROBERTS, ELIZABETH MADOX 1886–1941, writer
McDowell, Frederick P., *Elizabeth Madox Roberts* (1963).

ROBERTS, SAMUEL JUDSON 1858–1913, Welsh colonizer
Shepperson, Wilbur S., *Samuel Roberts: Welsh Colonizer in Civil War Tennessee* (1961).

ROBESON, PAUL 1898–   , singer
Hoyt, Edwin B., *Paul Robeson, American Othello* (1967).
Robeson, Paul, *Here I Stand* (1958).

ROBINS, MARGARET DREIER 1869–1945, reformer
Dreier, Mary, *Margaret Dreier Robins* (1950).

ROBINSON, CHARLES 1818–1894, pioneer, Kansas governor
Blackmar, F. W., *Charles Robinson* (1902).

ROBINSON, EDWIN ARLINGTON 1869–1935, poet
Coxe, Louis O., *Edwin Arlington Robinson* (1969).
Franchere, Hoyt C., *Edwin Arlington Robinson* (1968).
Neff, Emery, *Edwin A. Robinson* (1948).
Robinson, Edwin A., *Letters to Edith Brewer*, Richard Cary, ed. (1968).
—— *Selected Letters*, Ridgely Torrence, ed. (1940).
Robinson, Edwin A., *Untriangulated Stars: Letters of Edwin Arlington Robinson to Harry de Forest Smith, 1890–1905* (1947).
Smith, Chard P., *Where the Light Fails: A Portrait of Edwin Arlington Robinson* (1965).

ROBINSON, JAMES HARVEY 1863–1936, historian
Hendricks, L. V., *James Harvey Robinson* (1946).

ROBINSON, JOHN ROOSEVELT "JACKIE" 1919–1972; baseball player
Robinson, Jackie, *My Own Story* (1948).

ROBINSON, SOLON 1803–1880, agriculturist, writer
Kellar, H. A., ed., *Solon Robinson* (1936).
Robinson, Solon, *Selected Writings*, Herbert A. Kellar, ed. (1936).

ROBINSON, WILLIAM STEVENS 1818–1876, journalist, abolitionist
Robinson, William S., *"Warrington" Pen-Portraits* (1877).

ROCKEFELLER, JOHN DAVISON 1839–1937, industrialist, philanthropist
Latham, Earl, *John D. Rockefeller* (1949).
Nevins, Allan, *Study in Power: John D. Rockefeller* (2 vols., 1953).

ROCKEFELLER, JOHN DAVISON, JR. 1874–1960, philanthropist
Fosdick, Raymond B., *John D. Rockefeller, Jr.* (1956).

ROCKHILL, WILLIAM WOODVILLE 1854–1914, diplomat
Varg, Paul A., *Open Door Diplomat: W.W. Rockhill* (1952).

ROCKNE, KNUTE KENNETH 1888–1931, football coach
Rockne, Knute K., *Autobiography* (1931).

RODGERS, JOHN 1812–1882, naval officer
Johnson, Robert E., *Rear Admiral John Rodgers* (1967).
Paullin, C. O., *John Rodgers* (1909).

RODGERS, RICHARD 1902–   , composer
Green, Stanley, *Rodgers and Hammerstein Story* (1963).
Taylor, Deems, *Some Enchanted Evenings: Rodgers and Hammerstein* (1953).

RODNEY, CAESAR 1728–1784, Revolutionary leader
Rodney, Caesar, *Letters, 1756–1784*, G. H. Ryden, ed. (1933).

ROEBLING, JOHN AUGUSTUS, 1806–1869 and WASHINGTON AUGUSTUS ROEBLING, 1837–1926, engineers, bridge builders

Schuyler, Hamilton, *The Roeblings: A Century of Engineers, Bridge-Builders and Industrialists* (1931).
Steinman, D. B., *Builders of the Bridge* (1945).

ROETHKE, THEODORE 1908–1963, poet
Mills, Ralph J., Jr., *Theodore Roethke* (1963).
Roethke, Theodore, *Selected Letters*, Ralph J. Mills, Jr., ed. (1968).
Seager, Allan, *Glass House: Theodore Roethke* (1968).

ROGERS, JOHN 1829–1904, popular sculptor
Wallace, David H., *John Rogers; People's Sculptor* (1967).

ROGERS, ROBERT 1731–1795, officer in French and Indian War
Cuneo, John R., *Robert Rogers of the Rangers* (1959).
Rogers, Robert, *Journals*, (1795); F. B. Hough, ed. (1883).

ROMANS, BERNARD 1720–1784, civil engineer, naturalist
Phillips, Philip L., *Notes on Life and Works of Bernard Romans* (1924).

ROOSEVELT, ANNA ELEANOR 1884–1962, first lady
Hareven, Tamara K., *Eleanor Roosevelt* (1968).
Kearney, James R., *Anna Eleanor Roosevelt* (1968).
Lash, Joseph P., *Eleanor and Franklin* (1971).
Roosevelt, Eleanor, *Autobiography* (3 vols., 1937–1958).
—— *This I Remember* (1949).
—— *This is My Story* (1937).

ROOSEVELT, FRANKLIN DELANO 1882–1945, president
Bellush, Bernard, *Franklin D. Roosevelt as Governor of New York* (1955).
Burns, James M., *Roosevelt* (2 vols., 1956–1970).
Freidel, Frank, *Franklin D. Roosevelt* (Vols. 1/3–   , 1952–   ).
—— *F.D.R. and the South* (1965).
Fusfeld, Daniel R., *Economic Thought of Franklin D. Roosevelt* (1956).
Greer, Thomas H., *What Roosevelt Thought: Franklin D. Roosevelt* (1958).
Gunther, John, *Roosevelt in Retrospect* (1950).
Hassett, William D., *Off the Record with F.D.R. 1942–1945* (1958).
Kilpatrick, Carroll, *Roosevelt and Daniels: A Friendship in Politics* (1952).
Lindley, E. K., *Franklin D. Roosevelt* (1931).
Morgenthau, Henry, Jr., *Roosevelt and Morgenthau*, John M. Blum ed. (1970).
Nash, Gerald D., ed., *Franklin Delano Roosevelt* (1967).
Perkins, Frances, *The Roosevelt I Knew* (1946).
Range, Willard, *Franklin D. Roosevelt's World Order* (1959).
Rollins, Alfred B., Jr., *Roosevelt and Howe* (1962).
Roosevelt, Franklin D., *Conservation, 1911–1945*, Edgar B. Nixon, ed. (2 vols., 1957).
—— and Felix Frankfurter, *Correspondence, 1928–1945*, Max Freedman, ed. (1967).
—— *Franklin D. Roosevelt and Foreign Affairs*, Edgar B. Nixon, ed. (3 vols., 1969).
—— *F.D.R.: His Personal Letters*, Elliott Roosevelt, ed. (4 vols., 1947–1950).
Roosevelt, James, and Sidney Shalett, *Affectionately, F.D.R.: Son's Story* (1959).
Roosevelt, Sarah D., *My Boy Franklin* (1933).
Rosenman, S. I., *Working with Roosevelt* (1952).
Sherwood, Robert E., *Roosevelt and Hopkins: An Intimate History* (1950).
Stettinius, Edward, *Roosevelt and the Russians* (1949).
Stewart, William J., comp., *Era of Franklin D. Roosevelt: Bibliography of Periodical and Dissertation Literature, 1945–1966* (1967).
Tugwell, Rexford G., *Democratic Roosevelt* (1957).
Wann, A. J., *President as Chief Administrator: Franklin D. Roosevelt* (1968).

ROOSEVELT, THEODORE 1858–1919, president
Beale, Howard K., *Theodore Roosevelt and the Rise of America to World Power* (1956).
Blum, John M., *Republican Roosevelt* (1954).
Burton, David H., *Theodore Roosevelt: Confident Imperialist* (1969).
Chessman, G. Wallace, *Governor Theodore Roosevelt* (1965).
—— *Theodore Roosevelt and Politics of Power* (1969).

Grantham, Dewey W., Jr., "Theodore Roosevelt in Historical Writings, 1945–1960," *Mid-America,* 43 (1961), 3.

Harbaugh, William H., *Power and Responsibility: Life and Times of Theodore Roosevelt* (1961).

Lodge, Henry Cabot, and Theodore Roosevelt, *Selections from the Correspondence* (2 vols., 1925).

Lorant, Stefan, *Life and Times of Theodore Roosevelt* (1959).

Mowry, George E., *Theodore Roosevelt and the Progressive Movement* (1946).

Pringle, H. F., *Theodore Roosevelt* (1931).

Putnam, Carleton, *Theodore Roosevelt* (1958).

Roosevelt, Nicholas, *Theodore Roosevelt* (1967).

Roosevelt, Theodore, *Autobiography* (1913) 2nd ed., Wayne Andrews, ed., (1958).

——— *Letters,* Elting E. Morison et al., eds. (8 vols., 1951–1954).

——— *Works* (24 vols., 1923–1926).

Wagenknecht, Edward C., *Seven Worlds of Theodore Roosevelt* (1958).

ROOSEVELT FAMILY
Hagedorn, Hermann, *Roosevelt Family of Sagamore Hill* (1954).
Schriftgiesser, Karl, *Amazing Roosevelt Family* (1942).

ROOT, ELIHU 1845–1937, Secretary of War, Secretary of State
Jessup, P. C., *Elihu Root* (2 vols., 1938; repr. 1964).
Leopold, Richard W., *Elihu Root and Conservative Tradition* (1954).
Root, Elihu, *Addresses,* Robert Bacon and James B. Scott, eds. (1925).

ROOT, JOHN WELLBORN 1850–1891, architect
Monroe, Harriet, *John Wellborn Root* (1896).

ROSECRANS, WILLIAM STARKE 1819–1898, Union general
Lamers, William M., *Edge of Glory: General William S. Rosecrans* (1961).

ROSENWALD, JULIUS 1862–1932, merchant, philanthropist
Werner, Morris R., *Julius Rosenwald* (1939).

ROSS, CHARLES BENJAMIN 1876–1946, Idaho governor
Malone, Michael P., *C. Ben Ross and the New Deal in Idaho* (1970).

ROSS, EDWARD A. 1866–1951, social scientist
Ross, Edward A., *Seventy Years of It* (1936).

ROSS, HAROLD WALLACE 1892–1951, founder of *New Yorker* magazine
Grant, Jane, *Ross, the New Yorker and Me* (1968).
Thurber, James, *The Years With Ross* (1957).

ROWSON, SUSANNA HASWELL 1762–1824, novelist
Vail, R. W. G., *Susanna Haswell Rowson, the Author of Charlotte Temple* (1933).

ROYCE, JOSIAH 1855–1916, philosopher
Buranelli, Vincent, *Josiah Royce* (1963).
Robinson, Daniel S., *Royce and Hocking: American Idealists* (1968).

ROYCE, SARAH fl. 1849, California gold rush pioneer
Royce, Sarah B., *A Frontier Lady,* R. H. Gabriel, ed. (1932).

RUFFIN, EDMUND 1794–1865, agricultural experimenter
Craven, Avery O., *Edmund Ruffin* (1932).
Sitterson, J. Carlyle, "Introduction" in Edmund Ruffin, *Essay on Calcareous Manures* (1961).

RUFFIN, THOMAS 1787–1870, jurist
Ruffin, Thomas *Papers,* J. G. deR. Hamilton, ed. (4 vols., 1918–1920).

RUMFORD, COUNT. See THOMPSON, BENJAMIN

RUSH, BENJAMIN 1745–1813, physician
Adams, John, and Benjamin Rush, *Dialogues, 1805–1813,* John A. Schutz and Douglass Adair, eds. (1966).
Binger, Carl, *Revolutionary Doctor: Benjamin Rush* (1966).
Goodman, Nathan G., *Benjamin Rush, Physician and Citizen, 1746–1813* (1934).
Hawke, David F., *Benjamin Rush: Revolutionary Gadfly* (1971).
Rush, Benjamin, *Autobiography, Together with His Commonplace Book for 1789–1813,* G. W. Corner, ed. (1948).

—— *Letters*, Lyman H. Butterfield, ed. (2 vols., 1951).
—— "Further Letters," Lyman H. Butterfield, ed., *Penn. Mag. Hist. Biog.*, 68 (1954), 244.

RUSH, RICHARD 1780–1859, lawyer, diplomat
Powell, John H., *Richard Rush* (1942).
Rush, Richard, *Memoranda of a Residence at the Court of London* (1883). Covers the period 1817–January 1819.
—— *Memoranda of a Residence* (1845).
—— *Memoranda of A Residence at the Court of London, 1819–1825* (2 vols., 1845).
—— *Narrative of a Residence at the Court of London* (1833).

RUTH, GEORGE HERMAN "BABE" 1894–1948, baseball player
Meany, Tom, *Babe Ruth* (1947).

RUTHENBERG, CHARLES EMIL 1882–1927, editor of the *Daily Worker*
Ruthenberg, C. E., *Speeches and Writings*, Jay Lovestone, ed. (1928).

RUTLEDGE, JOHN 1739–1800, Revolutionary leader, South Carolina governor
Barry, R. H., *Mr. Rutledge of South Carolina* (1942).

RUTLEDGE, WILEY 1894–1949, Supreme Court justice
Harper, Fowler V., *Justice Rutledge* (1965).

RYAN, EDWARD GEORGE 1810–1880, Wisconsin jurist
Beitzinger, Alfons J., *Edward G. Ryan* (1960).

RYAN, JOHN AUGUSTINE 1869–1945, Catholic reformer
Broderick, Francis L., *Right Reverend New Dealer: John A. Ryan* (1963).

RYDER, ALBERT PINKHAM 1847–1917, artist
Goodrich, Lloyd, *Albert P. Ryder* (1959).
Price, Frederic N., *Ryder* (1932).

SAARINEN, EERO 1910–1961, architect
Temko, Allan, *Eero Saarinen* (1962).

SAARINEN, ELIEL 1873–1950, architect
Christ-Janer, Albert, *Eliel Saarinen* (1948).

SACAJAWEA ca. 1787–1812, interpreter for Lewis and Clark
Hebard, Grace R., *Sacajawea* (1967).

SAGE, HENRY WILLIAMS 1814–1897, lumberman
Goodstein, Anita S., *Biography of a Businessman: Henry W. Sage* (1962).

ST. DENIS (DENYS) LOUIS JUCHEREAU DE 1676–1744, explorer
Phares, Ross, *Cavalier in the Wilderness: Louis Juchereau de St. Denis* (1952).

SAINT-GAUDENS, AUGUSTUS 1848–1907, sculptor
Saint-Gaudens, Augustus, *Reminiscences*, Homer Saint-Gaudens, ed. (2 vols., 1913).
Saint-Gaudens, Homer, *The American Artist and His Times* (1941).
Tharp, Louise Hall, *Saint-Gaudens and the Gilded Era* (1969).

SALINGER, JEROME DAVID 1919–   , writer
French, Warren, *J. D. Salinger* (1963).

SALOMON, HAYM 1740–1785, Revolutionary leader, merchant
Russell, Charles E., *Haym Salomon and the Revolution* (1930).

SALTUS, EDGAR 1855–1920, essayist
Sprague, Claire, *Edgar Saltus* (1968).

SANBORN, FRANKLIN BENJAMIN 1831–1917, author, abolitionist
Sanborn, F. B., *Recollections of Seventy Years* (2 vols., (1909).

SANDBURG, CARL 1878–1967, poet, biographer
Callahan, North, *Carl Sandburg: A Biography* (1969).
Crowder, Richard, *Carl Sandburg* (1963).
Sandburg, Carl, *Always the Young Strangers* (1952).
—— *Letters*, Herbert Mitgang, ed. (1968).

SANDOZ, JULES AMI 1857?–1928, Nebraska pioneer
Sandoz, Mari, *Old Jules* (1935).

SANDYS, GEORGE 1577/78–1643/44, author

Davis, Richard B., *George Sandys, Poet-Adventurer: Anglo-American Culture in Seventeenth Century* (1955).

SANGER, MARGARET 1883–1966, birth control advocate
Coigney, Virginia, *Margaret Sanger* (1969).
Douglas, Emily T., *Margaret Sanger* (1969).
Kennedy, David M., *Birth Control in America: Career of Margaret Sanger* (1970).

SANTAYANA, GEORGE 1863–1952, philosopher
Arnett, Williard E., *George Santayana* (1968).
Santayana, George, *Persons and Places: The Background of My Life* (1944).

SARGENT, JOHN SINGER 1856–1925, artist
Charteris, Evan, *John Sargent* (1927).
Downes, W. H., *John S. Sargent, His Life and Works* (1925).
Mount, Charles M., *John Singer Sargent* (1955).

SAROYAN, WILLIAM 1908–   , writer
Floan, Howard R., *William Saroyan* (1966).
Saroyan, William, *Here Comes, There Goes, You Know Who* (1961).

SARTAIN, JOHN 1808–1897, engraver
Sartain, John, *Reminiscences, 1808–1897* (1899).

SAWYER, CHARLES 1887–   , Secretary of Commerce, lawyer
Sawyer, Charles, *Concerns of a Conservative Democrat* (1968).

SAWYER, PHILETUS 1816–1900, lumberman, Wisconsin senator
Current, Richard N., *Pine Logs and Politics: Philetus Sawyer* (1950).

SAYRE, FRANCIS BOWES 1885–1972, State Department official, diplomat
Sayre, Francis, *Glad Adventure* (1957).

SCHAFF, PHILIP 1819–1893, German Reformed minister, church historian
Schaff, D. S., *Philip Schaff* (1897).

SCHIFF, JACOB HENRY 1847–1920, financier, philanthropist
Adler, Cyrus, *Jacob H. Schiff: His Life and Letters* (2 vols., 1928).

SCHLESINGER, ARTHUR MEIER 1888–1965, historian
Schlesinger, Arthur, *In Retrospect: History of a Historian* (1963).

SCHLEY, WINFIELD SCOTT 1839–1909, admiral
Schley, Winfield S., *Forty-five Years Under the Flag* (1904).

SCHUMAN, WILLIAM HOWARD 1910–   , composer
Schreiber, Flora R., and Vincent Persichetti, *William Schuman* (1954).

SCHUMPETER, JOSEPH ALOIS 1883–1950, economist
Harris, Seymour E., ed., *Schumpeter, Social Scientist* (1951).

SCHURZ, CARL 1829–1906, German-American political leader
Easum, Chester V., *Americanization of Carl Schurz* (1929).
Fuess, Claude M., *Carl Schurz, Reformer* (1932).
Schurz, Carl, *Reminiscences* (3 vols., 1907–1908).
Schurz, Carl, *Speeches, Correspondence and Political Papers*, Frederic Bancroft, ed. (6 vols., 1913).

SCHUYLER, PHILIP JOHN 1733–1804, Revolutionary general, New York Senator
Bush, Martin H., *Revolutionary Enigma: Re-Appraisal of General Philip Schuyler* (1969)
Gerlach, Don R., *Philip Schuyler and the American Revolution in New York, 1733–1777* (1964).
Tuckerman, Bayard, *Life of General Philip Schuyler* (1903).

SCOTT, WILLIAM ANDERSON 1813–1885, Presbyterian clergyman
Drury, Clifford M., *William Anderson Scott* (1967).

SCOTT, WINFIELD 1786–1866, Mexican War general
Elliott, Charles W., *Winfield Scott* (1937).
Scott, Winfield, *Memoirs* (2 vols., 1864).
Smith, Arthur D. H., *Old Fuss and Feathers; The Life of Winfield Scott* (1937).

SCRIPPS, EDWARD WYLLIS 1854–1926, newspaper publisher
Cochran, N. D., *E. W. Scripps* (1933).

Gardner, Gilson, *Lusty Scripps: The Life of E. W. Scripps* (1932).
Scripps, Edward W., *Damned Old Crank*, C. R. McCabe, ed. (1951).
—— *I Protest*, Oliver Knight, ed. (1966).

SEABURY, SAMUEL 1729–1796, Episcopal clergyman, Loyalist
Beardsley, E. E., *Life and Correspondence of the Right Rev. Samuel Seabury* (1881).
Thoms, Herbert, *Samuel Seabury: Priest and Physician, Bishop of Connecticut* (1962).

SEABURY, SAMUEL 1873–1949, jurist, reformer
Mitgang, Herbert, *Man Who Rode the Tiger: The Life and Times of Judge Samuel Seabury* (1963).

SEDGWICK, THEODORE 1746–1813, Massachusetts senator
Welch, Richard E., Jr., *Theodore Sedgwick, Federalist* (1965).

SEMMES, RAPHAEL 1809–1877, commander of C.S.S. Alabama
Meriwether, Colyer, *Raphael Semmes* (1913).
Semmes, Raphael, *Memoirs of Service Afloat, during the War between the States* (1869).

SEQUOYAH ca. 1770–1843, invented Cherokee syllabary
Foreman, Grant, *Sequoyah* (1938).
Foster, George E., *Sequoyah, the American Cadmus and Modern Moses: A Complete Biography of the Greatest of Redmen* (1885).

SERRA, JUNIPERO 1713–1784, California missionary
Geiger, Maynard J., *Life and Times of Fray Junípero Serra (1713–1784)* (2 vols., 1959)
Palou, Francisco, *Life of Fray Junípero Serra* (1787); Maynard J. Geiger, trans. and ed. (1955).

SETON, ELIZABETH ANN, MOTHER 1774–1821, founder of religious order
Dirvin, Joseph J., *Mrs. Seton* (1962).

SEVIER, JOHN 1745–1815, Tennessee pioneer
Driver, C. S., *John Sevier, Pioneer of the Old Southwest* (1932).

SEWALL, SAMUEL 1652–1730, merchant, magistrate
Sewall, Samuel, "Diary," Mark Van Doren, ed., Mass. Hist. Soc., *Coll.*, 5 ser., 5-7 (1878–1882).
Strandness, Theodore B., *Samuel Sewall* (1967).
Winslow, Ola E., *Samuel Sewall of Boston* (1964).

SEWARD, FREDERICK WILLIAM 1830–1915, journalist, diplomat
Seward, Frederick W., *Reminiscences, 1830–1915* (1916).

SEWARD, WILLIAM HENRY 1801–1872, New York senator, Secretary of State
Bancroft, Frederic, *Life of W. H. Seward* (2 vols., 1900).
Seward, William H., *Autobiography, from 1801 to 1834*, F. W. Seward, ed. (3 vols., 1877–1891).
—— *Works*, G. E. Baker, ed. (5 vols., 1853–1854).
Van Deusen, Glyndon G., *William Henry Seward* (1967).

SEYMOUR, HORATIO 1810–1886, lawyer, New York governor
Mitchell, Stewart, *Horatio Seymour* (1938).

SHAHN, BEN 1898–1969; artist
Rodman, Selden, *Portrait of the Artist as an American: Ben Shahn* (1951).

SHALER, NATHANIEL SOUTHGATE 1841–1906, geologist
Shaler, Nathaniel S., *Autobiography, with a Supplementary Memoir by His Wife* (1909).

SHAW, ANNA HOWARD 1847–1919, physician
Shaw, Anna H., *The Story of a Pioneer* (1915).

SHAW, LEMUEL 1781–1861, jurist
Chase, Frederic H., *Lemuel Shaw, Chief Justice of the Supreme Judicial Court of Massachusetts* (1918).
Levy, Leonard W., *Law of the Commonwealth and Chief Justice Shaw* (1957).

SHEELER, CHARLES 1883– , artist
Rourke, Constance, *Charles Sheeler, Artist* (1938).

SHEPPARD, MOSES 1775?–1857, Baltimore merchant, philanthropist
Forbush, Bliss, *Moses Sheppard: Quaker Philanthropist of Baltimore* (1968).

SHERIDAN, PHILIP HENRY 1831–1888, Union general
O'Connor, Richard, *Sheridan* (1953).
Sheridan, Philip H., *Personal Memoirs* (2 vols., 1888).

SHERMAN, JOHN 1823–1900, Ohio senator
Burton, Theodore E., *John Sherman* (1906).
Sherman, John, *Recollections of Forty Years in the House, Senate and Cabinet* (2 vols., 1895).

SHERMAN, ROGER 1721–1793, Revolutionary leader
Boardman, Roger S., *Roger Sherman, Signer and Statesman* (1938).

SHERMAN, STUART PRATT 1881–1926, critic
Sherman, Stuart P., *Americans* (1922).
Zeitlin, Jacob, and Homer Woodbridge, *Life and Letters of Stuart P. Sherman* (2 vols., 1929).

SHERMAN, WILLIAM TECUMSEH 1820–1891, Union general
Athearn, Robert G., *William Tecumseh Sherman and Settlement of West* (1956).
Hart, B. H. Liddell, *Sherman: Soldier, Realist, American* (1929).
Lewis, Lloyd, *Sherman, Fighting Prophet* (1958).
Miers, Earl S., *The General Who Marched to Hell: William Tecumseh Sherman* (1951).
Sherman, William T., *Home Letters*, M. A. DeW. Howe, ed. (1909).
—— *Memoirs*, B. H. Liddell Hart, ed., (2 vols., 1957).

SHERWOOD, ROBERT EMMET 1896–1955, playwright
Brown, John Mason, *The Ordeal of a Playwright: Robert E. Sherwood and the Challenge of War* (1970).
Shuman, R. Baird, *Robert E. Sherwood* (1963).

SHIPPEN, WILLIAM 1736–1808, physician, medical educator
Corner, Betsy C., William Shippen, Jr., *Pioneer in American Medical Education* (1951).

SHIRER, WILLIAM LAWRENCE 1904–   , foreign correspondent
Shirer, William L., *Berlin Diary, 1934–1941* (1941).

SHIRLEY, WILLIAM 1694–1771, Massachusetts governor
Schutz, John A., *William Shirley: King's Governor of Massachusetts* (1961).
Shirley, William, *Correspondence, 1731–1760*, C. H. Lincoln, ed. (2 vols., 1912).
Wood, George A., *William Shirley, Governor of Massachusetts* (1920).

SICKLES, DANIEL EDGAR 1825–1914, Union general, diplomat
Swanberg, William A., *Sickles the Incredible* (1956).

SIEBER, AL 1844–1907, Indian scout
Thrapp, Daniel L., *Al Sieber: Chief of Scouts* (1964).

SIGOURNEY, LYDIA HOWARD 1791–1865, poet
Haight, G. S., *Mrs. Sigourney, the Sweet Singer of Hartford* (1930).

SIHLER, WILHELM 1801–1885, Lutheran clergyman
Spitz, Lewis W., *Life in Two Worlds: William Sihler* (1968).

SILL, EDWARD ROWLAND 1841–1887, poet
Parker, William B., *Edward Rowland Sill: His Life and Work* (1915).

SILLIMAN, BENJAMIN 1779–1864, chemist, geologist, naturalist
Fisher, George P., *Life of Benjamin Silliman* (2 vols., 1866).
Fulton, John F., and E. H. Thomson, *Benjamin Silliman, 1779–1864* (1947).

SIMMS, WILLIAM GILMORE 1806–1870, novelist
Ridgely, Joseph V., *William Gilmore Simms* (1962).
Simms, William G., *Letters*, Mary C. Simms Oliphant et al., ed. (5 vols., 1952–1956).
—— *Views and Reviews in American Literature, History, and Fiction* (1845). C. Hugh Holman, ed. (1962).
Trent, William P., *William Gilmore Simms* (1892).

SIMONS, ALGIE MARTIN 1870–1950, social reformer
Kreuter, Kent, and Gretchen Kreuter, *An American Dissenter: The Life of Algie Martin Simons, 1870–1950* (1969).

SIMPSON, JERRY 1842–1905, Populist leader
Bicha, Karel D., "Jerry Simpson; Populist," *JAH*, 54 (1967), 291.

SIMPSON, MATTHEW 1811–1884, Methodist bishop
Clark, Robert D., *Life of Matthew Simpson* (1956).

SIMS, JAMES MARION 1813–1883, gynecologist
Harris, Seale, and Frances W. Browin, *Woman's Surgeon: J. Marion Sims* (1950).
Sims, James M., *Story of My Life* (1884).

SIMS, WILLIAM SOWDEN 1858–1936, World War I admiral
Morison, Elting E., *Admiral Sims and the Modern American Navy* (1942).

SINCLAIR, UPTON 1878–1971, writer, reformer
Dell, Floyd, *Upton Sinclair* (1927).
Sinclair, Upton, *Autobiography* (1962).

SITTING BULL 1834?–1890, Sioux chief
Vestal, Stanley, *Sitting Bull* (1932; rev. ed., 1957).

SKINNER, OTIS 1858–1942, actor
Skinner, Otis, *Footlights and Spotlights* (1924).

SLATER, SAMUEL 1768–1835, textile innovator
Cameron, Edward H., *Samuel Slater, Father of American Manufactures* (1960).
White, George Savage, *Memoir of Samuel Slater, the Father of American Manufactures* (1836).

SLIDELL, JOHN 1793–1871, Louisiana senator, Confederate diplomat
Sears, Louis M., *John Slidell* (1925).
Willson, Beckles, *Slidell in Paris* (1932).

SLOAN, JOHN 1871–1951, artist
Brooks, Van Wyck, *John Sloan: A Painter's Life* (1955).
Goodrich, Lloyd, *John Sloan* (1952).
Sloan, John, *Diaries, Notes and Correspondence 1906–1913*, Bruce St. John, ed. (1965).

SMIBERT, JOHN 1688–1751, painter
Foote, Henry W., *John Smibert, Painter* (1950).
Smibert, John, *Notebook; with Essays* by Sir David Evans, John Kerslake, and Andrew Oliver and With Notes Relating to Smibert's American Portraits, by Andrew Oliver (1969).

SMITH, ALFRED EMMANUEL 1873–1944, New York governor
Handlin, Oscar, *Al Smith and His America* (1958).
Josephson, Matthew and Hannah Josephson, *Al Smith: A Political Portrait* (1970).
O'Connor, Richard, *First Hurrah: Alfred E. Smith* (1970).

SMITH, CHARLES HENRY 1826–1903, satirist; Bill Arp, pseud.
Austin, James C., *Bill Arp* (1970).

SMITH, CHARLES PERRIN 1819–1883, New Jersey politician
Smith, Charles P., *New Jersey Political Reminiscences, 1828–1882*, Hermann K. Platt, ed. (1965).

SMITH, EDMUND KIRBY. See EDMUND KIRBY-SMITH

SMITH, FRANK ELLIS 1918–   , Mississippi congressman
Smith, Frank E., *Congressman from Mississippi* (1964).

SMITH, GERRIT 1797–1874, reformer, abolitionist
Harlow, R. V., *Gerrit Smith* (1939).

SMITH, HOKE 1855–1931, Georgia governor, senator
Grantham, Dewey W., Jr., *Hoke Smith and the Politics of the New South* (1958).

SMITH, HOMER WILLIAM 1895–1962, marine biologist
Smith, Homer W., *Scientific and Literary Achievements*, Herbert Chasis and William Goldring, eds. (1965).

SMITH, JAMES MONROE 1839–1915, planter
Coulter, E. Merton, *James Monroe Smith* (1961).

SMITH, JEDEDIAH 1789–1831, trapper, explorer
Morgan, Dale L., *Jedediah Smith and the Opening of the West* (1953).

SMITH, JEREMIAH 1759–1842, New Hampshire governor, jurist
  Morison, John H., *Life of Hon. Jeremiah Smith, LL.D.* (1845).
SMITH, JOHN 1579/80–1631, founder of Virginia
  Barbour, Philip L., *Three Worlds of Captain John Smith* (1964).
  Chatterton, Edward K., *Captain John Smith* (1927).
  Smith, Bradford, *Captain John Smith* (1953).
  Smith, John, *Works*, Edward Arber and A. G. Bradley, eds. (2 vols., 1910).
  Wharton, Henry, *John Smith, English Soldier* (1957).
SMITH, JOSEPH 1805–1844, founder of Mormon church
  Brodie, Fawn M., *No Man Knows My History: The Life of Joseph Smith* (1945).
  Evans, John H., *Joseph Smith: An American Prophet* (1933).
SMITH, JOSEPH RUSSELL 1874–1966, geographer, conservationist
  Rowley, Virginia M., *J. Russell Smith* (1964).
SMITH, JUNIUS 1780–1853, organizer of steamship company
  Pond, E. L., *Junius Smith: A Biography of the Father of the Atlantic Liner* (1927).
SMITH, MARGARET BAYARD 1778–1844, society leader, author
  Smith, Margaret B., *First Forty Years of Washington Society*, Gaillard Hunt, ed. (1906) .
SMITH, RICHARD 1596–1666, Rhode Island settler
  Updike, Daniel B., *Richard Smith: First English Settler of Narragansett Country* (1937).
SMITH, WILLIAM 1727–1803, Episcopal clergyman, founder of Washington College
  Gegenheimer, A. F., *William Smith, Educator and Churchman* (1943).
  Smith, Horace W., *Life and Correspondence of the Rev. William Smith, D.D.* (2 vols., 1880).
SMITH, WILLIAM 1728–1793, New York jurist, Loyalist
  Dillon, Dorothy R., *New York Triumvirate: William Livingston, John Morin Scott and William Smith, Jr.* (1949).
  Smith, William, *Historical Memoirs from 1763–1776*, William H. W. Sabine, ed. (1956).
  Smith, William, *Diary and Selected Papers, 1784–1793*, Leslie F. S. Upton, ed. (2 vols., 1963–1965).
  Upton, Leslie F. S., *Loyal Whig: William Smith of New York and Quebec* (1969).
SMITH, WILLIAM LOUGHTON 1758–1812, South Carolina lawyer, Federalist
  Rogers, George C., Jr., *Evolution of a Federalist: William Loughton Smith of Charleston* (1962).
  Smith, William Loughton, "Journal, 1790–1791," Mass. Hist. Soc., *Proc.*, 51, (1917), 35
SMITH FAMILY political satirists, writers
  Wyman, M. A., *Two American Pioneers, Seba Smith* [Major Jack Downing] *and Elizabeth Oakes Smith* (1927).
SMITHSON, JAMES 1765–1829, philanthropist
  Carmichael, Leonard, and J. C. Long, *James Smithson and Smithsonian Story* (1965).
  Rhees, W. J., *An Account of Smithsonian Institution, Its Founder* (1857).
SPALDING, HENRY HARMON 1803–1874, poet and writer
  Drury, C. M., *Henry Harmon Spalding* (1936).
SPALDING, JOHN LANCASTER 1840–1916, Catholic bishop, writer
  Ellis, John T., *John Lancaster Spalding, First Bishop of Peoria* (1962).
  Sweeney, David F., *Life of John Lancaster Spalding: First Bishop of Peoria, 1840–1916* (1965).
SPARKS, JARED 1789–1866, historian, president of Harvard University
  Adams, Herbert B., *Life and Writings of Jared Sparks* (2 vols., 1893).
SPENCER, CORNELIA PHILLIPS 1825–1908, author, educator
  Spencer, Cornelia P., *Selected Papers*, Louis R. Wilson, ed. (1953).
SPOONER, JOHN COIT 1843–1919, Wisconsin senator
  Fowler, Dorothy G., *John Coit Spooner: Defender of Presidents* (1961).

SPOTSWOOD, ALEXANDER 1676–1740, Lieutenant governor of Virginia
  Havighurst, Walter, *Alexander Spotswood: Governor* (1968).
  Spotswood, Alexander, *The Official Letters, 1710–1722*, R. A. Brock, ed.
    (2 vols., 1882–1885).

SPRAGUE, KATE CHASE 1840–1899, Washington hostess
  Belden, Thomas G., and Marva R. Belden, *So Fell the Angels* (1956).
  Ross, Ishbel, *Proud Kate* (1953).

SPRECKELS, CLAUS 1828–1908, Hawaiian sugar producer
  Adler, Jacob, *Claus Spreckels* (1966).

SPRUANCE, RAYMOND AMES 1886–   , World War II admiral
  Forrestel, E. P., *Admiral Raymond A. Spruance, USN* (1966).

SQUIBB, EDWARD ROBINSON 1819–1900, pharmaceutical manufacturer
  Blochman, Lawrence G., *Doctor Squibb* (1958).

STANDISH, BURT L. See PATTEN, GILBERT

STANDLEY, WILLIAM HARRISON 1872–1963, admiral, diplomat
  Standley, William H., and Arthur A. Ageton, *Admiral Ambassador to Russia*
    (1955).

STANLEY, HENRY MORTON 1841–1904, journalist
  Stanley, H. M., *Autobiography*, Dorothy Stanley, ed. (1909).

STANTON, EDWIN MC MASTERS 1814–1869, Secretary of War
  Gorham, George C., *Life and Public Services of Edwin M. Stanton* (2 vols.,
    1899).
  Thomas, Benjamin P., and H. M. Hyman, *Stanton* (1962).

STANTON, ELIZABETH CADY 1815–1902, suffrage leader
  Stanton, Elizabeth, *Eighty Years and More: Reminiscences* (1898).
  —— *Elizabeth Cady Stanton, as Revealed in Her Letters, Diary and Reminiscences*, Theodore Stanton and H. S. Blatch, eds. (2 vols., 1922).

STARRETT, PAUL 1866–1957, architect
  Starrett, Paul, *Changing the Skyline: Autobiography* (1938).

STEDMAN, EDMUND CLARENCE 1833–1908, poet, critic
  Stedman, Laura, and G. M. Gould, *Life and Letters of Edmund Clarence
    Stedman* (2 vols., 1910).

STEFFENS, LINCOLN 1866–1935, journalist
  Steffens, Lincoln, *Autobiography* (1931).
  —— *Letters*, Ella Winter and Granville Hicks, eds. (2 vols., 1938).

STEICHEN, EDWARD 1879–   , photographer
  Steichen, Edward, *Life in Photography* (1968).

STEIN, GERTRUDE 1874–1946, writer
  Stein, Gertrude, *My Mother and I* (1917).
  Stewart, Allegra, *Gertrude Stein and the Present* (1967).

STEINBECK, JOHN ERNST 1902–1968, author
  French, Warren, *John Steinbeck* (1961).

STEINER, EDWARD ALFRED 1866–1956, sociologist
  Steiner, Edward A., *From Alien to Citizen* (1914).

STELLA, FRANK 1936–   , artist
  Rubin, William S., *Frank Stella* (1970).

STELLA, JOSEPH 1880–1946, artist
  Jaffe, Irma B., *Joseph Stella* (1970).

STEPHENS, ALEXANDER HAMILTON 1812–1883, vice-president of Confederacy
  Johnston, Robert M., and William H. Browne, *A. H. Stephens* (1878).
  Stephens, A. H., *Recollections [and] Diary Kept when a Prisoner, 1865*,
    M. L. Avary, ed. (1910).
  Abele, Rudolph Von, *Alexander H. Stephens* (1946).

STEPHENS, JOHN LLOYD 1805–1852, archaeologist
  Hagen, Victor W. Von, *Maya Explorer: John Lloyd Stephens* (1947).

STERNBERG, GEORGE MILLER 1838–1915, bacteriologist, epidemiologist
  Gibson, John M., *Soldier in White: General George Miller Sternberg* (1958).

STETTINIUS, EDWARD RILEY, JR. 1900–1949, secretary of state
  Walker, Richard L., *Edward R. Stettinius, Jr. 1944–45* (1965).
STEVENS, JOHN 1749–1838, engineer, inventor
  Turnbull, A. D., *John Stevens: An American Record* (1928).
STEVENS, THADDEUS 1792–1868, lawyer, political leader
  Brodie, Fawn M., *Thaddeus Stevens* (1959).
  Current, Richard N., *Old Thad Stevens* (1942).
STEVENS, WALLACE 1879–1955, poet
  Burney, William, *Wallace Stevens* (1968).
STEVENSON, ADLAI EWING 1900–1965, Illinois governor
  Brown, Stuart G., *Conscience in Politics: Adlai E. Stevenson* (1961).
  Cochran, Bert, *Adlai Stevenson: Patrician among the Politicians* (1969).
  Davis, Kenneth S., *Politics of Honor: Adlai E. Stevenson* (1967).
  Muller, Herbert J., *Adlai Stevenson* (1967).
  Stevenson, Adlai E., *Major Campaign Speeches, 1952* (1953).
  —————— *New America*, S. E. Harris et al., eds. (1957).
  —————— *What I Think* (1956).
  Walton, Richard J., *Remnants of Power: Last Years of Adlai Stevenson* (1968).
STIEGLITZ, ALFRED 1864–1946, photographer
  Bry, Doris, *Alfred Stieglitz* (1965).
STILES, EZRA 1727–1795, Congregational clergyman, president of Yale University
  Morgan, Edmund S., *Gentle Puritan: Ezra Stiles* (1962).
  Stiles, Ezra, *Extracts from Itineraries, with Selections from His Correspondence,*
    F. B. Dexter, ed. (1916).
  —————— *Literary Diary*, F. B. Dexter, ed. (3 vols., 1910).
STILLMAN, JAMES 1850–1918, banker, capitalist
  Burr, A. R., *Portrait of a Banker* (1927).
STILWELL, JOSEPH WARREN 1883–1946, World War II general
  Stilwell, Joseph, *Stilwell Papers*, Theodore H. White, ed. (1948).
  Tuchman, Barbara, *Stilwell and the American Experience in China, 1911–45*
    (1971).
STIMSON, HENRY LEWIS 1867–1950, secretary of state, secretary of war
  Current, Richard N., *Secretary Stimson* (1954).
  Ferrell, Robert H., *Kellogg and Stimson* (1961).
  Morison, Elting E., *Turmoil and Tradition: Henry L. Stimson* (1960).
  Rappaport, Armin, *Henry L. Stimson and Japan: 1931–1933* (1963).
  Stimson, Henry L., *On Active Service in Peace and War* (1948).
STOCKTON, FRANCIS RICHARD 1834–1902, author
  Griffin, Martin I. J., *F. R. Stockton* (1939).
STODDARD, RICHARD HENRY 1825–1903, poet, critic
  Stoddard, Richard H., *Recollections, Personal and Literary* (1903).
STOKES, THOMAS LUNSFORD, JR. 1898–1958, journalist
  Stokes, Thomas L., *Chip Off My Shoulder* (1940).
STONE, BARTON WARREN 1772–1844, Disciples of Christ evangelist
  West, William G., *Barton Warren Stone: Early American Advocate of Christian
    Unity* (1954).
STONE, HARLAN FISKE 1872–1946, Supreme Court Chief justice
  Konefsky, Samuel J., *Chief Justice Stone and the Supreme Court* (1945).
  Mason, Alpheus T., *Harlan Fiske Stone* (1956).
STONE, LUCY 1818–1893, reformer
  Blackwell, A. S., *Lucy Stone, Pioneer of Woman's Rights* (1930).
  Hays, Elinor R., *Morning Star: Lucy Stone* (1961).
STONE, MELVILLE E. 1848–1929, editor, head of Associated Press
  Stone, Melville E., *Fifty Years a Journalist* (1921).
STOREY, MOORFIELD 1845–1929, lawyer, reformer
  Howe, Mark A. DeW., *Portrait of an Independent; Moorfield Storey* (1932).
STOREY, WILBUR FISK 1819–1884, Chicago editor
  Walsh, Justin E., *A Biography of Wilbur F. Storey* (1968).

STORY, JOSEPH 1779–1845, Supreme Court justice
Dunne, Gerald T., *Justice Joseph Story and the Rise of the Supreme Court* (1971).
Schwartz, Mortimer D., and John G. Hogan, eds., *Joseph Story: Eminent Jurist* (1959).
Story, W. W., *Life and Letters of Joseph Story* (2 vols., 1851).

STORY, WILLIAM WETMORE 1819–1895, sculptor, author
James, Henry, *William Wetmore Story and His Friends* (2 vols., 1903).

STOWE, HARRIET BEECHER 1811–1896, abolitionist author
Adams, John R., *Harriet Beecher Stowe* (1963).
Foster, Charles H., *Rungless Ladder: Harriet Beecher Stowe* (1954).
Gilbertson, Catherine, *Harriet Beecher Stowe* (1937).
Stowe, Harriet B., *Letters and Journals,* Charles E. Stowe, comp. (1889).
Wagenknecht, Edward C., *Harriet Beecher Stowe* (1965).
Wilson, Forrest, *Crusader in Crinoline: The Life of Harriet Beecher Stowe* (1941).

STRACHEY, WILLIAM 1572–1621, Secretary of Virginia colony
Culliford, S. G., *William Strachey* (1965).

STRAIGHT, WILLARD DICKERMAN 1880–1918, financier, diplomat, magazine publisher
Croly, Herbert D., *Willard Straight* (1924).

STRANG, JAMES JESSE 1813–1856, leader of Mormon schism
Strang, James J., *Diary,* Mark A. Strang, ed. (1961).

STRAUS, OSCAR SOLOMON 1850–1926, secretary of commerce, diplomat
Cohen, Naomi, *A Dual Heritage: Public Career of Oscar S. Straus* (1969).
Straus, Oscar S., *Under Four Administrations: From Cleveland to Taft* (1922).

STRICKLAND, WILLIAM 1787–1854, architect
Gilchrist, Agnes A., *William Strickland, Architect and Engineer* (1950).
——— "William Strickland, Architect and Engineer, 1788–1854," *Jour. Society Archit. Historians,* 13 (1954), 1.

STRONG, BENJAMIN 1872–1928, banker, Federal Reserve governor
Chandler, Lester V., *Benjamin Strong, Central Banker* (1958).

STRONG, GEORGE T. 1820–1875, New York lawyer
Strong, George T., *Diary,* Allan Nevins and M. H. Thomas, eds. (4 vols., 1952).

STRONG, MOSES MC CURE 1810–1894, Wisconsin promoter
Duckett, Kenneth W., *Frontiersman of Fortune: Moses M. Strong of Mineral Point* (1955).

STROTHER, DAVID HUNTER 1816–1888, writer, painter
Eby, Cecil D., Jr., *"Porte Crayon": David Hunter Strother* (1960).
Strother, David H., *Virginia Yankee in the Civil War: Diaries,* Cecil D. Eby, Jr., ed. (1961).

STUART, GILBERT 1755–1828, painter
Flexner, James T., *Gilbert Stuart* (1955).
Morgan, John H., *Gibert Stuart* (4 vols., 1926).
Mount, Charles M., *Gilbert Stuart* (1964).
Park, Lawrence, *Gilbert Stuart: Illustrated Descriptive List of His Works* (4 vols., 1926).

STUART, JAMES EWELL BROWN 1833–1864, Confederate general
Davis, Burke, *Jeb Stuart, Last Cavalier* (1957).
McClellan, H. B., *I Rode with Jeb Stuart,* Burke Davis, ed. (1958).
Thomason, J. W., Jr., *Jeb Stuart* (1930).

STUART, JESSE 1907– , author
Blair, Everetta L., *Jesse Stuart: His Life and Works* (1967).
Foster, Ruel E., *Jesse Stuart* (1968).
Stuart, Jesse, *Beyond Dark Hills: Personal Story* (1938).

STUART, JOHN 1700–1779, colonial Indian agent
Alden, John R., *John Stuart and the Southern Colonial Frontier* (1944).

STUYVESANT, PETER "PETRUS" 1592–1672, Director-General of New Netherlands
 Kessler, Henry H., and Eugene Rachlis, *Peter Stuyvesant and His New York* (1959).
 Tuckerman, Bayard, *Peter Stuyvesant, Director-General for West India Company in New Netherland* (1893).

SUBLETTE, ANDREW 1808–1853, fur trader
 Nunis, Doyce B., Jr., *Andrew Sublette: Rocky Mountain Prince, 1808–1853* (1960).

SUBLETTE, WILLIAM LEWIS ca. 1799–1845, fur trader
 Sunder, John E., *Bill Sublette* (1959).

SUCKOW, RUTH 1892–1960, writer
 Kissane, Leedice M., *Ruth Suckow* (1969).

SULLIVAN, JAMES 1744–1808, Revolutionary leader
 Amory, T. C., *Life of James Sullivan* (2 vols., 1859).

SULLIVAN, JOHN 1740–1795, Revolutionary general
 Sullivan, John, *Letters and Papers*, O. G. Hammond, ed. (2 vols., 1930–1931).
 Whittemore, Charles P., *General of Revolution: John Sullivan of New Hampshire* (1961).

SULLIVAN, JOHN LAWRENCE 1858–1918, pugilist
 Dibble, R. F., *John L. Sullivan* (1925).

SULLIVAN, LOUIS HENRI 1856–1924, architect
 Bush-Brown, Albert, *Louis Sullivan* (1960).
 Connely, Willard, *Louis Sullivan* (1960).
 Morrison, Hugh, *Louis Sullivan: Prophet of Modern Architecture* (1935).
 Paul, Sherman, *Louis Sullivan: Architect in American Thought* (1962).
 Sullivan, Louis H., *Autobiography of an Idea* (1924).
 ——— *Testament of Stone: Writings*, Maurice English, ed. (1963).
 Szarkowski, John, *Idea of Louis Sullivan* (1956).

SULLIVAN, WILLIAM 1774–1839, lawyer, author
 Sullivan, William, *Familiar Letters on Public Characters and Public Events* (1834). Covers the period 1783–1815.

SULLY, THOMAS 1783–1872, painter
 Biddle, Edward, and Mantle Fielding, *The Life and Works of Thomas Sully* (1921).

SULZBERGER, CYRUS LEO 1912–   , journalist
 Sulzberger, C. L., *Long Row of Candles: Memoirs and Diaries, 1934–1954* (1969).

SUMNER, CHARLES 1811–1874, Massachusetts senator
 Donald, David H., *Charles Sumner* (2 vols., 1960–1970).
 Pierce, Edward L., *Memoir and Letters of Charles Sumner* (4 vols., 1877–1893).
 Sumner, Charles, *Works* (15 vols., 1870–1883).

SUMNER, WILLIAM GRAHAM 1840–1910, sociologist
 Davie, Maurice R., *William Graham Sumner* (1963).
 Starr, H. E., *William G. Sumner* (1925).

SUMTER, THOMAS 1734–1832, Revolutionary general
 Bass, Robert D., *Gamecock: General Thomas Sumter* (1961).

SUNDAY, WILLIAM ASHLEY, "BILLY" 1862–1935, evangelist
 McLoughlin, William G., *Billy Sunday* (1955).

SUTHERLAND, GEORGE 1862–1942, Supreme Court justice
 Paschal, J. F., *Mr. Justice George Sutherland* (1951).

SUTTER, JOHN AUGUSTUS 1803–1880, California colonizer
 Sutter, J. A., *Sutter's Own Story* (1936).
 Zollinger, J. P., *Sutter: the Man and His Empire* (1939).

SUTRO, ADOLPH 1830–1898, mining promoter
 Stewart, Robert E., Jr., and Mary F. Stewart, *Adolph Sutro* (1962).

SWAIN, CLARA A. 1834–1910, missionary doctor
 Wilson, Dorothy C., *Palace of Healing: Dr. Clara Swain, First Woman Missionary Doctor* (1968).

SWIFT, GUSTAVUS FRANKLIN 1839–1903, meatpacker

Swift, L. F., and Arthur Van Vlissingen, Jr., *Yankee of the Yards: The Biography of Gustavus F. Swift* (1927).

SWIFT, LUCIUS BURRIE 1844–1929, civil service reformer
Foulke, W. D., *Lucius B. Swift* (1930).

SYLVIS, WILLIAM H. 1828–1869, labor leader
Grossman, J. P., *William H. Sylvis* (1945).
Todes, Charlotte, *William H. Sylvis and National Labor Union* (1942).

SYMMES, JOHN CLEVES 1742–1814, Ohio pioneer
Symmes, John C., *Correspondence*, B. W. Bond, Jr., ed. (1926).
——— *Letters, Including Those of His Daughter, Mrs. William Henry Harrison* (1956).

TAFT, JESSIE 1882–1960, social work educator
Robinson, Virginia P., ed., *Jessie Taft, Therapist and Social Work Educator* (1962).

TAFT, LORADO ZADOC 1860–1936, sculptor
Taft, Ada B., *Lorado Taft* (1946).

TAFT, ROBERT ALPHONSO 1889–1953, Ohio senator
White, William S., *Taft Story* (1954).

TAFT, WILLIAM HOWARD 1857–1930, President, Supreme Court chief justice
Mason, Alpheus T., *William Howard Taft: Chief Justice* (1965).
Pringle, Henry F., *The Life and Times of William Howard Taft* (2 vols., 1939).

TALBOT, JOHN 1645–1727, Anglican clergyman
Pennington, Edgar, *Apostle of New Jersey: John Talbot, 1645–1727* (1938).

TALCOTT, JAMES FREDERICK, 1866–1944, merchant
Hillyer, W. H., *James Talcott* (1937).

TALLMADGE, BENJAMIN 1754–1835, Connecticut Federalist, congressman
Hall, Charles S., *Benjamin Tallmadge* (1943).

TANEY, ROGER BROOKE 1777–1864, Supreme Court chief justice
Harris, Robert J., "Chief Justice Taney," *Vanderbilt Law Rev.*, 10 (1957), 227.
Lewis, Walker, *Without Fear or Favor: Chief Justice Roger Brooke Taney* (1965).
Swisher, Carl B., *Roger B. Taney* (1935).

TANNER, HENRY OSSAWA 1859–1937, Negro painter
Mathews, Marcia M., *Henry Ossawa Tanner* (1969).

TAPPAN, ARTHUR 1786–1865, merchant, reformer
Tappan, Lewis, *The Life of Arthur Tappan* (1870).

TAPPAN, LEWIS 1788–1873, merchant, abolitionist
Wyatt-Brown, Bertram, *Lewis Tappan and the Evangelical War against Slavery* (1969).

TATE, ALLEN 1899– , poet, critic
Bishop, Ferman, *Allen Tate* (1968).

TAYLOR, BAYARD 1825–1878, traveler, author, diplomat
Beatty, R. C., *Bayard Taylor, Laureate of the Gilded Age* (1936).

TAYLOR, EDWARD 1645–1729, poet
Grabo, Norman S., *Edward Taylor* (1961).

TAYLOR, FREDERICK WINSLOW 1856–1915, industrial engineer
Copley, F. B., *Frederick W. Taylor, Father of Scientific Management* (2 vols., 1923).
Haber, Samuel, *Efficiency and Uplift: Scientific Management in Progressive Era* (1964).

TAYLOR, GRAHAM 1851–1938, theologian, social work educator
Wade, Louise C., *Graham Taylor* (1964).

TAYLOR, JOHN 1753–1824, political theorist
Mudge, E. T., *The Social Philosophy of John Taylor of Caroline* (1939).

TAYLOR, NATHANIEL WILLIAM 1786–1858, liberal theologian
Mead, Sidney E., *Nathaniel William Taylor, 1786–1858: Connecticut Liberal* (1942).

TAYLOR, ZACHARY 1784–1850, president
Dyer, Brainerd, *Zachary Taylor* (1946).

Hamilton, Holman, *Zachary Taylor* (2 vols., 1941–1951).
Taylor, Zachary, *Letters from the Battlefields of Mexican War*, W. H. Samson, ed. (1908).
TECUMSEH 1768–1813, Shawnee chief
Raymond, E. T., *Tecumseh* (1915).
Tucker, Glenn, *Tecumseh* (1956).
TEEDYUSCUNG ca. 1700–1763, Delaware chief
Wallace, Anthony F. C., *King of the Delawares: Teedyuscung, 1700–1763* (1949).
TELLER, HENRY MOORE 1830–1914, Colorado senator
Ellis, Elmer, *Henry M. Teller* (1941).
TERRY, DAVID SMITH 1823–1889, California jurist
Buchanan, A. Russell, *David S. Terry of California* (1956).
THALBERG, IRVING 1889–1936, motion picture producer
Thomas, Bob, *Thalberg* (1969).
THAXTER, CELIA 1835–1894, poet
Thaxter, Rosamund, *Sandpiper: The Life and Letters of Celia Thaxter* (rev. ed., 1963).
THAYER, ABBOTT HANDERSON 1849–1921, painter
White, Nelson C., *Abbott H. Thayer, Painter and Naturalist* (1951).
THEUS, JEREMIAH 1719–1774, painter
Middleton, Margaret S., *Jeremiah Theus: Colonial Artist of Charles Town* (1953).
THOMAS, GEORGE HENRY 1816–1870, Union general
Cleaves, Freeman, *Rock of Chickamauga: The Life of General George H. Thomas* (1948).
McKinney, Francis F., *Education in Violence: George H. Thomas* (1961).
THOMAS, ISAIAH 1750–1831, printer
Shipton, Clifford K., *Isaiah Thomas: Printer, Patriot and Philanthropist, 1749–1831* (1948).
THOMAS, NORMAN 1884–1969, Socialist leader
Fleischman, Harry, *Norman Thomas: A Biography* (1964).
Seidler, Murray B., *Norman Thomas* (1961).
THOMAS, (CHRISTIAN FRIEDRICH) THEODORE 1835–1905, conductor
Russell, Charles E., *The American Orchestra and Theodore Thomas* (1927).
Thomas, Rose F., *Memoirs of Theodore Thomas* (1911).
Thomas, Theodore, *A Musical Autobiography*, G. P. Upton, ed. (2 vols., 1905).
THOMPSON, BENJAMIN (COUNT RUMFORD) 1753–1814, scientist, philanthropist
Brown, Sanborn C., *Count Rumford* (1964).
Ellis, George E., *Memoir of Sir Benjamin Thompson, Count Rumford, with Notices of His Daughter* (1871).
Larsen, Egon, *American in Europe: Benjamin Thompson, Count Rumford* (1953).
Sparrow, W. J., *Knight of the White Eagle: Sir Benjamin Thompson, Count Rumford of Woburn, Mass.* (1966).
Thompson, Benjamin, *Collected Works of Count Rumford*, Sanborn C. Brown, ed. (5 vols., 1968–1970).
Thompson, James Alden, *Count Rumford of Massachusetts* (1935).
THOMPSON, DAVID 1770–1857, fur trader, map maker
Thompson, David, *David Thompson's Narrative* (1962).
THOMPSON, RICHARD WIGGINTON 1809–1900, Indiana Whig, Republican, secretary of navy
Roll, Charles, *Colonel Dick Thompson: Persistent Whig* (1948).
THOMPSON, VIRGIL 1896–   , composer
Hoover, Kathleen, and John Cage, *Virgil Thompson: Life and Music* (1959).
THOMPSON, WILLIAM BOYCE 1869–1930, mine operator
Hagedorn, Hermann, *The Magnate: William Boyce Thompson* (1935).
THOMSON, ELIHU 1853–1937, scientist, inventor, electrical manufacturer
Woodbury, David O., *Elihu Thomson: Beloved Scientist* (1960).

THOREAU, HENRY DAVID 1817–1862, essayist, transcendentalist
Canby, Henry S., *Thoreau* (1939).
Christie, John A., *Thoreau as World Traveler* (1965).
Glick, Wendell, *Recognition of Henry D. Thoreau* (1969).
Harding, Walter, *Days of Henry Thoreau* (1965).
Harding, Walter, ed., *Thoreau: Man of Concord* (1960).
Hough, Henry B., *Thoreau of Walden* (1956).
Murray, James G., *Henry David Thoreau* (1968).
Porte, Joel, *Emerson and Thoreau* (1966).
Sanborn, Franklin B., *Life of Henry D. Thoreau* (1917).
Thoreau, Henry D., *Correspondence*, Walter Harding and Carl Bode, eds.
(1958).
Van Doren, Mark, *Henry David Thoreau* (1916).

THORNDIKE, EDWARD LEE 1874–1949, psychologist
Jonçich, Geraldine, *The Sane Positivist: Edward L. Thorndike* (1968).

THORNDIKE, ISRAEL 1755–1832, merchant, Far Eastern trader
Forbes, John D., *Israel Thorndike, Federalist Financier* (1953).

THORNWELL, JAMES HENLEY 1812–1862, Presbyterian theologian
Palmer, Benjamin M., *Life and Letters of James Henry Thornwell* (1969).

THORPE, THOMAS BANGS 1815–1878, artist, humorist
Rickels, Milton, *Thomas Bangs Thorpe: Humorist of the Old
Southwest* (1962).

THURBER, JAMES 1894–1961, humorist
Morsberger, Robert E., *James Thurber* (1964).
Thurber, James, *The Years With Ross* (1957).
Tobias, Richard C., *Art of James Thurber* (1969).

TICKNOR, GEORGE 1791–1871, scholar, author
Ticknor, George, *Life, Letters and Journals*, G. S. Hillard, ed. (2 vols., 1876).
Tyack, David B., *George Ticknor and Boston Brahmins* (1967).

TIFFANY, LOUIS COMFORT 1848–1933, painter, glassmaker
Koch, Robert C., *Louis C. Tiffany* (1964).

TILDEN, SAMUEL JONES 1814–1886, New York governor
Bigelow, John, *The Life of Samuel J. Tilden* (2 vols., 1895).
Flick, A. C., and G. S. Lobrano, *Samuel Jones Tilden* (1939).
Kelley, Robert L., "Samuel J. Tilden," *Historian,* 26 (1964), 176.

TILLICH, PAUL 1886–1965, theologian
Hopper, David H., *Tillich: A Theological Portrait* (1968).

TILLMAN, BENJAMIN 1847–1918, South Carolina senator, Populist
Simkins, F. B., *"Pitchfork" Benjamin Tillman* (1944).

TIMROD, HENRY 1828–1867, confederate poet
Parks, Edd Winfield, *Henry Timrod* (1963).

TINSLEY, WILLIAM 1804–1885, architect
Forbes, John D., *Victorian Architect: William Tinsley* (1953).

TIPTON, JOHN 1786–1839, Indiana senator
Tipton, John, *Papers*, N. A. Robertson et al., eds. (3 vols., 1942).

TOMPKINS, DANIEL AUGUSTUS 1851–1914, textile manufacturer
Winston, G. T., *Builder of the New South, Daniel Augustus Tompkins* (1920).

TOMPKINS, DANIEL D. 1774–1825, New York governor, vice-president
Irwin, Ray W., *Daniel D. Tompkins* (1968).
Tompkins, Daniel D., *Public Papers*, Hugh Hastings, ed. (3 vols., 1898–1902).

TOMPSON, BENJAMIN 1642–1714, poet
Hall, H. J., *Benjamin Tompson, 1642–1714, First Native-Born Poet of America*
(1924).

TOOKER, LEWIS FRANK 1855–1925, editor
Tooker, Lewis Frank, *The Joys and Tribulations of an Editor* (1924).

TOOMBS, ROBERT 1810–1885, Georgia senator
Phillips, Ulrich B., *Life of Robert Toombs* (1913).
Thompson, William Y., *Robert Toombs of Georgia* (1966).

TOSCANINI, ARTURO 1867–1957, conductor
Antek, Samuel, and Robert Hupka, *Toscanini* (1963).

TOURGÉE, ALBION WINEGAR 1838–1905, North Carolina carpetbag jurist, author
Franklin, John Hope, "Introduction," in Albion W. Tourgée, *A Fool's Errand* (1961).
Gross, Theodore L., *Albion W. Tourgée* (1963).
Olsen, Otto H., *Carpetbagger's Crusade: Albion Winegar Tourgée* (1965).

TOWER, CHARLEMAGNE 1848–1923, developer of iron deposits, diplomat
Bridges, Hal, *Iron Millionaire: Charlemagne Tower* (1952).

TRAIN, GEORGE FRANCIS 1829–1904, merchant, reformer, shipowner
Thornton, Willis, *Nine Lives of Citizen Train* (1948).
Train, G. F., *My Life in Many States and Foreign Lands* (1902).
Turnbull, Clive, *Bonanza: George Francis Train* (1946).

TRENT, WILLIAM 1715–1787, fur trader, land speculator
Slick, Sewell E., *William Trent and the West* (1947).

TROTTER, NATHAN 1787–1853, merchant
Tooker, Elva, *Nathan Trotter: Philadelphia Merchant* (1955).

TROTTER, WILLIAM MONROE 1872–1934, Negro editor
Fox, Stephen R., *Guardian of Boston: William Monroe Trotter* (1970).

TRUDEAU, EDWARD LIVINGSTON 1848–1915, physician, tuberculosis researcher
Harrod, Kathryn E., *Man of Courage: Dr. Edward L. Trudeau* (1959).
Trudeau, E. L., *An Autobiography* (1916).

TRUMAN, HARRY S. 1884–   , president
Daniels, Jonathan, *Man of Independence* (1950).
Phillips, Cabell, *Truman Presidency* (1966).
Steinberg, Alfred, *Man from Missouri: Harry S. Truman* (1962).
Truman, Harry S., *Memoirs* (2 vols., 1955–1956).
——— *Mr. President*, William Hillman, ed. (1952).
——— *Public Papers* (4 vols., 1961–1964).

TRUMBULL, JOHN 1750–1831, poet
Cowie, Alexander, *John Trumbull: Connecticut Wit* (1936).

TRUMBULL, JOHN "COLONEL" 1756–1843, artist
Sizer, Theodore, *Works of John Trumbull: Artist of the Revolution* (rev. ed., 1967).
Trumbull, John, *Autobiography* (1841), Theodore Sizer, ed. (1953).
Weir, J. F., *John Trumbull* (1901).

TRUMBULL, JONATHAN 1710–1785, Connecticut governor
Trumbull, Jonathan, *Jonathan Trumbull, Governor of Connecticut* (1919).
Weaver, Glenn, *Jonathan Trumbull: Connecticut's Merchant Magistrate* (1956).

TRUMBULL, LYMAN 1813–1896, Illinois senator
White, Horace, *Life of Lyman Trumbull* (1913).

TRUXTUN, THOMAS 1755–1822, naval officer
Ferguson, Eugene S., *Commodore Thomas Truxtun, U.S. Navy, 1755–1822* (1956).

TRYON, WILLIAM 1729–1788, North Carolina governor
Dill, Alonzo T., *Governor Tryon and His Palace* (1955).

TUCKER, GEORGE 1775–1861, political economist
McLean, Robert C., *George Tucker: Moral Philosopher* (1961).

TUCKERMAN, JOSEPH 1778–1840, clergyman
McColgan, D. T., *Joseph Tuckerman* (1940).

TUMULTY, JOSEPH PATRICK 1879–1954, secretary to President Wilson
Blum, John M., *Joe Tumulty and the Wilson Era* (1951).

TURNER, FREDERICK JACKSON 1861–1932, historian
Hofstadter, Richard, *Progressive Historians* (1968).
Lawrence, Burnette O., Jr., comp., *Wisconsin Witness to Frederick Jackson Turner* (1961).
Turner, Frederick Jackson, and Alice F. P. Hooper, *"Dear Lady": Letters of*

Frederick Jackson Turner and Alice Forbes Perkins Hooper, 1910–1932, Ray A. Billington, and Walter Muir Whitehill, eds., (1970).

Turner, Frederick J., *Selections from His Correspondence*, Wilbur R. Jacobs, ed. (1968).

TURNER, JONATHAN BALDWIN 1805–1899, agriculturist, educator, urged establishment of University of Illinois.
Carriel, Mary T., *Life of Jonathan B. Turner* (1911).

TWAIN, MARK. See SAMUEL L. CLEMENS

TWEED, WILLIAM 1823–1878, New York political boss
Callow, Alexander B., Jr., *Tweed Ring* (1966).
Lynch, D. T., *Tweed* (1927).
Mandelbaum, Seymour, *Boss Tweed's New York* (1965).

TYLER, JOHN 1790–1862, president
Chitwood, Oliver P., *John Tyler* (1939).
Seeger, Robert II, *John and Julia Tyler* (1963).
Tyler, Lyon G., *Letters and Times of the Tylers* (3 vols., 1884–1896).

TYLER, MOSES COIT 1835–1900, historian
Jones, Howard M., *The Life of Moses Coit Tyler* (1933).

TYLER, PRISCILLA COOPER 1816–1889, actress, hostess of White House
Coleman, Elizabeth T., *Priscilla Cooper Tyler and the American Scene, 1816–1889* (1955).

TYLER, ROBERT 1816–1877, lawyer, Alabama editor
Auchampaugh, P. G., *Robert Tyler* (1934).

TYLER, ROYALL 1757–1826, playwright, novelist, jurist
Tanselle, G. Thomas, *Royall Tyler* (1967).

UNDERWOOD, OSCAR WILDER 1862–1929, Alabama senator
Underwood, O. W., *Drifting Sands of Party Politics* (1928). A 2nd ed. (1931) included a biographical sketch by C. G. Bowers.

UNONIUS, GUSTAF fl. 1841–1858, Swedish immigrant
Unonius, Gustaf, *Pioneer in Northwest America, 1841–1858: Memoirs*, Nils W. Olsson, ed., Jonas O. Backlund, trans. (2 vols., 1950–1960).

UNWIN, RAYMOND 1867–1940, town planner
Unwin, Raymond, *Legacy: Human Pattern for Planning*, Walter L. Creese, ed. (1967).

UPJOHN, RICHARD 1802–1878, architect
Upjohn, Everard M., *Richard Upjohn, Architect and Churchman* (1939).

UPSHUR, ABEL PARKER 1791–1844, secretary of navy
Hall, Claude H., *Abel Parker Upshur: Conservative Virginian* (1963).

UPTON, EMORY 1839–1881, Union General, tactics expert
Ambrose, Stephen E., *Upton and the Army* (1964).

USHER, JOHN PALMER 1816–1889, secretary of interior
Richardson, Elmo R., and Alan W. Farley, *John Palmer Usher: Lincoln's Secretary of Interior* (1960).

VAIL, THEODORE NEWTON 1845–1920, telephone executive
Paine, Albert B., *Theodore N. Vail* (1929).

VALLANDIGHAM, CLEMENT LAIRD 1820–1871, copperhead leader
Vallandigham, James L., *Clement L. Vallandigham* (1872).
Klement, Frank, *Limits of Dissent: Vallandigham and the Civil War* (1970).

VAN BRUNT, HENRY 1832–1903, architect
Coles, William A., "Henry Van Brunt–Life and Career," in Henry Van Brunt, *Architecture and Society: Selected Essays*, William A. Coles, ed. (1969).

VAN BUREN, MARTIN 1782–1862, president
Alexander, Holmes, *The American Talleyrand: Martin Van Buren* (1935).
Curtis, James C., *The Fox at Bay: Martin Van Buren and the Presidency, 1837–1841* (1970).
Remini, Robert V., *Van Buren and Democratic Party* (1959).
Van Buren, Martin, "Autobiography," J. C. Fitzpatrick, ed., Am. Hist. Assoc., *Report*, (1918), 2.

VANCE, ZEBULON BAIRD 1830–1894; Confederate governor of North Carolina
Tucker, Glenn, *Zeb Vance* (1966).
Vance, Zebulon B., *Papers, 1843–1862*, W. Johnston, ed. (1963).
Yates, Richard E., *Confederacy and Zeb Vance* (1958).

VANCOUVER, GEORGE 1758–1798, explorer of Puget Sound
Anderson, Bern, *Surveyor of the Sea: Captain George Vancouver* (1960).

VANDEGRIFT, ALEXANDER ARCHER 1887–   , Marine general, World War II
Vandegrift, A. A., *Once a Marine: Memoirs as Told to Robert B. Asprey* (1964).

VANDENBERG, ARTHUR HENDRICK 1884–1951, Michigan senator
Vandenberg, A. H., *Private Papers*, A. H. Vandenberg, Jr. and J. H. Morris,
eds. (1952).

VANDERBILT, CORNELIUS 1794–1877, steamship, railroad promoter
Smith, Arthur D. H., *Commodore Vanderbilt* (1927).

VAN DER KEMP, FRANCIS ADRIAN 1752–1829, clergyman, scholar
Jackson, Harry F., *Francis Adrian Van der Kemp* (1963).

VANDERLYN, JOHN 1775–1852, painter
Mondello, Salvatore, "John Vanderlyn," *N. Y. Hist. Soc. Quar.*, 52 (1968), 161.

VAN DORN, EARL 1820–1863, Confederate general
Hartje, Robert G., *Van Dorn: Confederate General* (1967).

VAN HISE, CHARLES RICHARD 1857–1918, geologist, president of University of Wisconsin, conservationist
Vance, Maurice M., *Charles Richard Van Hise: Scientist Progressive* (1960).

VAN VECHTEN, CARL 1880–1964, author
Kellner, Bruce, *Carl Van Vechten and the Irreverent Decades* (1968).
Lueders, Edward, *Carl Van Vechten* (1964).

VARDAMAN, JAMES KIMBLE 1861–1930, Mississippi agrarian politician
Holmes, William F., *The White Chief: James Kimble Vardaman* (1970).

VASSAR, MATTHEW 1792–1868, brewer, founder of Vassar College
Vassar, Matthew, *Autobiography and Letters*, E. H. Haight, ed. (1916).

VAUX, ROBERTS 1786–1835, philanthropist, reformer
McCadden, Joseph J., *Education in Pennsylvania: Roberts Vaux* (1937).

VEBLEN, THORSTEIN 1857–1929, economist
Dorfman, Joseph, *Thorstein Veblen and His America* (1934).
Riesman, David, *Thorstein Veblen* (1953).

VERY, JONES 1813–1880, poet, transcendentalist
Bartlett, William I., *Jones Very* (1942).
Gittleman, Edwin, *Jones Very, 1833–1840* (1967).

VETCH, SAMUEL 1668–1732, trader, soldier
Waller, G. M., *Samuel Vetch, Colonial Enterpriser* (1960).

VILAS, WILLIAM FREEMAN 1840–1908, postmaster general, Wisconsin senator
Merrill, Horace S., *William Freeman Vilas* (1954).

VIERECK, PETER 1916–   , poet
Henault, Marie, *Peter Viereck* (1968).

VILLARD, HENRY 1835–1900, journalist, railroad promoter
Hedges, James B., *Henry Villard and the Railways of the Northwest* (1967).
Villard, Henry, *Memoirs* (2 vols., 1904).

VILLARD, OSWALD GARRISON 1872–1949, reform editor
Humes, D. Joy, *Villard, Liberal of the 1920's* (1960).
Villard, Oswald G., *Fighting Years* (1939).
Wreszin, Michael, *Oswald G. Villard: Pacifist* (1965).

VINCENT, JOHN HEYL 1832–1920, Methodist bishop, leader of Chautauqua movement
Vincent, L. H., *John H. Vincent* (1925).

VOLLMER, AUGUST 1876–1955, criminologist
Parker, Alfred E., *Crime Fighter: August Vollmer* (1961).

VON KARMAN, THEODORE 1881–1963, aeronautical engineer
von Karman, Theodore, and Lee Edson, *The Wind and Beyond* (1967).

VON STEUBEN, FREDERICK WILLIAM 1730–1794, Revolutionary general
  Kapp, Friedrich, *Major General Frederick William Von Steuben* (1859).
  Palmer, John M., *General von Steuben* (1937).

VOORHEES, DANIEL WOLSEY 1827–1897, Indiana senator
  Kenworthy, Leonard S., *Tall Sycamore of the Wabash: Daniel Wolsey Voorhees*
  (1936).

VROOMAN FAMILY
  Paulson, Ross E., *Radicalism and Reform: Vrooman Family and American
  Social Thought, 1837–1937* (1968).

WADE, BENJAMIN FRANKLIN 1800–1878, Ohio senator
  Riddle, Albert G., *Life of Benjamin F. Wade* (1886).
  Trefousse, Hans L., *Benjamin Franklin Wade* (1963).

WAGNER, ROBERT FERDINAND 1877–1953, New York senator
  Huthmacher, J. Joseph, *Senator Robert F. Wagner and Urban Liberalism* (1968).

WAINWRIGHT, RICHARD 1849–1926, admiral
  Cummings, Damon E., *Admiral Richard Wainwright* (1962).

WAITE, MORRISON REMICK 1816–1888, Supreme Court chief justice
  Magrath, C. Peter, *Morrison R. Waite* (1963).
  Trimble, Bruce B., *Chief Justice Waite* (1970).

WAKSMAN, SELMAN ABRAHAM 1888–   , microbiologist
  Waksman, Selman A., *Scientific Contributions*, H. Boyd Woodruff, ed. (1968).

WALKER, FRANCIS AMASA 1840–1897, statistician, economist, president of Massachusetts Institute of Technology
  Munroe, J. P., *Life of Francis Amasa Walker* (1923).

WALKER, JOHN WILLIAMS 1783–1823, Alabama pioneer
  Bailey, Hugh C., *John Williams Walker: Life of the Old Southwest* (1964).

WALKER, LEROY POPE 1817–1884, Confederate secretary of war
  Harris, William C., *Leroy Pope Walker: Confederate Secretary of War* (1962).

WALKER, MARY EDWARDS 1832–1919, physician
  Snyder, Charles M., *Dr. Mary Walker* (1962).

WALKER, ROBERT JOHN 1801–1869, secretary of treasury, Kansas Territory
  governor
  Dodd, William E., *Robert J. Walker, Imperialist* (1914).
  Shenton, James P., *Robert John Walker: Politician from Jackson to Lincoln*
  (1961).

WALKER, WILLIAM 1824–1860, adventurer
  Greene, Laurence, *The Filibuster: The Career of William Walker* (1937).

WALLACE, GEORGE CORLEY 1919–   , Alabama governor
  Frady, Marshall, *Wallace* (1968).

WALLACE, HENRY 1836–1916, Presbyterian clergyman, agricultural editor
  Wallace, Henry, *Uncle Henry's Own Story of His Life* (3 vols., 1917–1919).

WALLACE, HENRY AGARD 1888–1965, editor, secretary of agriculture, vice-president
  Macdonald, Dwight, *Henry Wallace* (1948).
  Schapsmeier, Edward L., and Frederick H., *Henry A. Wallace of Iowa, 1910–
  1965* (2 vols., 1968–1970).

WALLACE, HENRY CANTWELL 1866–1924, editor, secretary of agriculture
  Winters, Donald L., *Henry Cantwell Wallace as Secretary of Agriculture, 1921–
  1924* (1970).

WALLACE, LEW 1827–1905, author, soldier, official, diplomat
  Wallace, Lew, *An Autobiography* (2 vols., 1906).

WALLACE FAMILY
  Lord, Russell, *Wallaces of Iowa* (1947).

WALLACK, LESTER 1820–1888, actor, dramatist
  Wallack, Lester, *Memories of Fifty Years* (1889).

WALSH, DAVID IGNATIUS 1872–1947, Massachusetts senator
  Wayman, Dorothy G., *David I. Walsh: Citizen-Patriot* (1952).

WALSH, THOMAS JAMES 1859–1933, Montana senator

O'Keane, Josephine, *Thomas J. Walsh* (1959).

WALTER, BRUNO 1876–1962, conductor
Walter, Bruno, *Theme and Variations: An Autobiography* (1946).

WANAMAKER, JOHN 1838–1922, retailer, Postmaster General
Gibbons, Herbert A., *John Wanamaker* (2 vols., 1926)

WARD, ARTEMUS. See BROWNE, CHARLES FARRAR

WARD, LESTER FRANK 1841–1913, sociologist
Chugerman, Samuel, *Lester Frank Ward: American Aristotle* (1965).

WARD, SAMUEL 1814–1884, lobbyist
Elliott, Maud H., *Uncle Sam Ward* (1938).
Thomas, Lately, *Sam Ward, "King of the Lobby"* (1965).

WARD, SAMUEL 1725–1776, Rhode Island governor, Revolutionary leader
Ward, Samuel, *Correspondence*, Bernhard Knollenberg, ed. (1952).

WARD, SAMUEL RINGGOLD 1817–1866, Negro abolitionist
Ward, Samuel R., *Autobiography of a Fugitive Negro* (1855).

WARMOTH, HENRY CLAY 1842–1931, carpetbag Louisiana governor
Current, Richard N., *Three Carpetbag Governors* (1967).

WARNER, CHARLES DUDLEY 1829–1900, journalist, essayist
Lounsbury, Thomas R., *Biographical Sketch of Charles Dudley Warner* (1905).

WARREN, EARL 1891–   , California governor, Supreme Court Chief Justice
Harvey, Richard B., *Earl Warren: Governor of California* (1969).
Katcher, Leo, *Earl Warren: A Political Biography* (1967).
Warren, Earl, *Public Papers*, Henry M. Christman, ed. (1959).
Weaver, John D., *Warren: The Man, the Court, the Era* (1967).

WARREN, GOUVERNEUR KEMBLE 1830–1882, Union general, railroad surveyor
Taylor, Emerson G., *Gouverneur Kemble Warren* (1932).

WARREN, JAMES 1726–1808, Revolutionary leader
Warren, James, and Elbridge Gerry, *Correspondence*, C. Harvey Gardiner, ed. (1968).
Warren, James, and Mercy [Otis] Warren, "Warren-Adams Letters," W. C. Ford, ed., Mass. Hist. Soc. *Coll.*, 72-73 (1917–1925).

WARREN, JOHN COLLINS 1778–1856, surgeon
Arnold, Howard P., *Memoir of John Collins Warren* (1882).
Warren, Edward, *Life of John Warren, M.D.* (1874).
Warren, J. Collins, *To Work in the Vineyard of Surgery: Reminiscences* (1958).

WARREN, JOSEPH 1741–1775, physician, Revolutionary leader
Cary, John, *Joseph Warren: Physician, Politician, Patriot* (1961).
Frothingham, Richard, *Life and Times of Joseph Warren* (1965).

WARREN, JOSIAH 1798–1874, musician, inventor, anarchist
Bailie, William, *Josiah Warren: The First American Anarchist* (1906).

WARREN, MERCY OTIS 1728–1814, author, dramatist, historian, wife of James Warren
Brown, Alice, *Mercy Warren* (1896).
Warren, James, and Mercy [Otis] Warren, "Warren-Adams Letters," W. C. Ford, ed., Mass. Hist. Soc., *Coll.*, 72–73 (1917–1925).

WARREN, ROBERT PENN 1905–   , poet, novelist
Bohner, Charles H., *Robert Penn Warren* (1964).

WARREN, WILLIAM 1812–1888, actor
Warren, William, *Life and Memoirs* (1889).

WARREN FAMILY
Truax, Rhoda, *Doctors Warren of Boston* (1968).

WASHBURN FAMILY
Hunt,Gaillard, *Israel, Elihu, and Cadwallader Washburn* (1925).

WASHINGTON, BOOKER TALIAFERRO 1856–1915, Negro educational leader
Harlan, Louis R., "Booker T. Washington in Biographical Perspective," *AHR*, 75 (1970), 1581.
Mathews, Basil J., *Booker T. Washington* (1948).

Scott, Emmett J., and L. B. Stowe, *B. T. Washington* (1916).
Spencer, Samuel R., Jr., *Booker T. Washington and Negro's Place in American Life* (1955).
Washington, Booker T., *My Larger Education* (1911).
────── *Story of My Life* (1900).
────── *Up From Slavery* (1901).

WASHINGTON, GEORGE 1732–1799, president
Ambler, Charles H., *George Washington and the West* (1936).
Boller, Paul F., *George Washington and Religion* (1963).
Cunliffe, Marcus, *George Washington: Man and Monument* (1958).
Flexner, James T., *George Washington* (3 vols., 1965–1970).
Freeman, Douglas S., *George Washington* (7 vols., 1948–1957). The last volume by John C. Alexander and Mary W. Ashworth. One-vol. abridged by Richard Harwell (1968).
Kinnaird, Clark, *George Washington: A Pictorial Biography* (1967).
Knollenberg, Bernhard, *George Washington: Virginia Period* (1964).
────── *Washington and the Revolution* (1940).
Nettels, Curtis P., *George Washington and American Independence* (1951).
Prussing, Eugene E., *The Estate of George Washington* (1927).
Stephenson, Nathaniel W., and W. H. Dunn, *George Washington* (2 vols., 1940).
Washington, George, *Basic Selections from Public and Private Writings,* Saul K. Padover, ed. (1955).
────── *Diaries, 1748–1799,* J. C. Fitzpatrick, ed. (4 vols., 1925).
────── *Writing,* J. C. Fitzpatrick, ed. (39 vols. 1931–1944).
Weems, Mason L., *Life of Washington* (1809); Marcus Cunliffe, ed. (1962).
Wright, Esmond, *Washington and the American Revolution* (1957).

WATSON, ELKANAH 1758–1842, merchant, agriculturist
Watson, Elkanah, *Men and Times of the Revolution; or, Memoirs* (1856).

WATSON, THOMAS EDWARD 1856–1922, Georgia senator
Woodward, C. Vann, *Tom Watson: Agrarian Rebel* (rev. ed., 1955).

WATSON, THOMAS JOHN 1874–1956, chairman of IBM
Belden, Thomas G., and Marva R. Belden, *Lengthening Shadow: Thomas J. Watson* (1962).

WATTERSON, HENRY 1840–1921, journalist, statesman
Wall, Joseph F., *Henry Watterson, Reconstructed Rebel* (1956).
Watterson, Henry, *"Marse Henry": An Autobiography* (2 vols., 1919).

WAUGH, FREDERICK J. 1861–1940, painter
Havens, George R., *Frederick J. Waugh, Marine Painter* (1969).

WAYLAND, FRANCIS 1796–1865, educator, president of Brown University
Crone, Theodore R., *Francis Wayland: Political Economist as Educator* (1962).
Roelker, William G., *Francis Wayland, Neglected Pioneer of Higher Education* (1944).
Wayland, Francis, *Memoir of the Late President of Brown University* (2 vols., 1867).

WAYNE, ANTHONY 1745–1796, Revolutionary general
Knopf, Richard C., ed., *Anthony Wayne, A Name in Arms* (1960).
Wildes, H. E., *Anthony Wayne* (1941).

WEATHERFORD, WILLIS DUKE 1875–   , educator
Dykeman, William, *Prophet of Plenty: W.D. Weatherford* (1966).

WEBSTER, DANIEL 1782–1852, Massachusetts senator
Baxter, Maurice G., *Daniel Webster and the Supreme Court* (1966).
Brown, Norman D., *Daniel Webster and the Politics of Availability* (1969).
Current, Richard N., *Daniel Webster* (1955).
Curtis, George T., *Life of Daniel Webster* (1870).
Fuess, Claude M., *Daniel Webster* (2 vols., 1930).
Parish, Peter J., "Daniel Webster, New England, and the West," *JAH,* 54 (1967), 524.
Webster, Daniel, *Letters,* C. H. Van Tyne, ed. (1902).
────── *Writings and Speeches,* J. W. McIntyre, ed. (18 vols., 1903).

WEBSTER, NOAH 1758–1843, lexicographer
Shoemaker, Ervin C., *Noah Webster, Pioneer of Learning* (1936).
Warfel, Henry R., *Noah Webster: Schoolmaster to America* (1936).
Webster, Noah, *Letters*, Harry R. Warfel, ed. (1953).
——— *On Being American: Selected Writings, 1783–1828*, Homer D. Babbidge, Jr., ed. (1967).

WEED, THURLOW 1797–1882, journalist, New York politician
Barnes, T. W., *Life of Thurlow Weed* (2 vols., 1884).
Van Deusen, Glyndon G., *Thurlow Weed* (1947).

WEIR, JULIAN ALDEN 1852–1919, painter
Young, Dorothy W., *Life and Letters of J. Alden Weir* (1960).

WEISER, (JOHANN) CONRAD 1696–1760, Indian agent
Wallace, P. A. W., *Conrad Weiser, 1696–1760* (1945).

WEITLING, WILHELM CHRISTIAN 1808–1871, reformer
Wittke, Carl, *Utopian Communist: Wilhelm Weitling* (1950).

WELCH, WILLIAM HENRY 1850–1934, pathologist, medical educator
Fleming, Donald, *William H. Welch and the Rise of Modern Medicine* (1954).
Flexner, Simon, and James T. Flexner, *William Henry Welch and American Medicine* (rev. ed., 1968).
Welch, William H., *Papers and Addresses,* Walter C. Burket, ed. (3 vols., 1920).

WELD, THEODORE 1803–1895, abolitionist
Thomas, Benjamin P., *Theodore Weld* (1950).
Weld, T. D., Angelina G. Weld, and Sarah Grimké, *Letters, 1822–1844*, G. H. Barnes and D. L. Dumond, eds. (2 vols., 1934).

WELLES, GIDEON 1802–1878, secretary of navy
Welles, Gideon, *Diary,* Howard K. Beale and Alan W. Brownsword, eds. (3 vols., 1960).
West, Richard S., Jr., *Gideon Welles: Lincoln's Navy Department* (1943).

WELLS, HORACE 1815–1848, dentist
Wells, Horace, *Life and Letters: Discoverer of Anesthesia*, William H. Archer, ed. (1945).

WELLS [BARNETT], IDA B., 1862–1931, Negro journalist, reformer
Wells, Ida B., *Crusade for Justice*, Alfreda M. Duster, ed. (1970).

WELTY, EUDORA 1909–   , writer
Kieft, Ruth M. Vande, *Eudora Welty* (1962).

WENDELL, BARRETT 1855–1921, educator, literary scholar
Howe, Mark A. DeW, *Barrett Wendell* (1924).

WENTWORTH, JOHN 1815–1888, mayor of Chicago, congressman, editor, real estate magnate
Fehrenbacher, Don E., *Chicago Giant: "Long John" Wentworth* (1957).

WESCOTT, GLENWAY 1901–   , writer
Rueckert, William H., *Glenway Wescott* (1965).

WEST, BENJAMIN 1738–1820, painter
Evans, Grose, *Benjamin West and the Taste of His Times* (2 vols., 1959).
Galt, John, *Life of Benjamin West* (1820, repr. 1960).

WEST, NATHANAEL 1902–1940, author
Comerchero, Victor, *Nathanael West: The Ironic Prophet* (1964).
Light, James F., *Nathanael West* (1961).

WESTINGHOUSE, GEORGE 1846–1914, inventor, electrical manufacturer
Leupp, F. E., *George Westinghouse* (1918).
Prout, H. G., *Life of George Westinghouse* (1921).

WEYL, WALTER EDWARD 1873–1919, political economist
Forcey, Charles, *Crossroads of Liberalism: Croly, Weyl, Lippmann* (1961).

WHARTON, EDITH 1862–1937, author
Bell, Millicent, *Edith Wharton and Henry James* (1965).
Lubbock, Percy, *Portrait of Edith Wharton* (1947).

WHEAT, ROBERDEAU 1826–1862, Tennessee adventurer, Confederate soldier
Dufour, Charles L., *Gentle Tiger: Roberdeau Wheat* (1957).

WHEELER, BURTON KENDALL 1882–   , Montana senator
Wheeler, Burton K., *Yankee from the West* (1962).

WHEELER, JOSEPH 1836–1906, Confederate general
Dyer, John P., *"Fightin' Joe" Wheeler* (1941).

WHEELOCK, ELEAZAR 1711–1779, Congregational clergyman, founder of Dartmouth College
McCallum, James D., *Eleazar Wheelock: Founder of Dartmouth College* (1939).
Wheeler, Eleazar, *Memoirs*, David McClure and Elijah Parish, eds. (1811).

WHIPPLE, HENRY BENJAMIN 1822–1901, Episcopal bishop, reformer of Indian policies
Whipple, Henry B., *Bishop Whipple's Southern Diary, 1843–44*, Lester B. Shippee, ed. (1937).

WHISTLER, JAMES MCNEILL 1834–1903, painter
Pennell, E. R., and Joseph Pennell, *Life of James McNeill Whistler* (rev. ed., 1919).
Sutton, Denys, *Nocturne: Art of James McNeil Whistler* (1964).

WHITE, ANDREW DICKSON 1832–1918, president of Cornell University
White, Andrew D., *Autobiography* (2 vols., 1905).

WHITE, EDWARD DOUGLAS 1845–1921, Supreme Court chief justice
Hagemann, Gerard, *Man on the Bench* (1962).
Klinkhamer, Marie C., *Edward Douglas White* (1943).

WHITE, HENRY 1850–1927, diplomat
Nevins, Allan, *Henry White: Thirty Years of American Diplomacy* (1930).

WHITE, JOHN 1575–1648, Massachusetts settler
Rose-Troup, Frances, *John White, Founder of Massachusetts* (1930).

WHITE, STANFORD 1853–1906, architect
Baldwin, Charles Crittenton, *Stanford White* (1931).

WHITE, STEPHEN MALLORY 1853–1901, California senator
Dobie, Edith, *Political Career of Stephen Mallory White* (1927).

WHITE, WALTER FRANCIS, 1893–1955, Negro leader, author
White, Walter Francis, *How Far the Promised Land?* (1955).
——— *A Man Called White* (1948).

WHITE, WILLIAM ALANSON 1870–1937, psychiatrist
White, William Alanson, *Autobiography of a Purpose* (1938).

WHITE, WILLIAM ALLEN 1868–1944, editor
Johnson, Walter, *William Allen White's America* (1947).
White, William A., *Autobiography* (1946).
——— *Selected Letters*, Walter Johnson, ed. (1947).

WHITEFIELD, GEORGE 1714–1770, Methodist evangelist
Henry, Stuart C., *George Whitefield: Wayfaring Witness* (1957).
Tyerman, Luke, *The Life of the Rev. George Whitefield* (2 vols., 1930).

WHITEHEAD, ALFRED NORTH 1861–1947, philosopher
Lowe, Victor, *Understanding Whitehead* (1962).

WHITLOCK, BRAND 1869–1934, author, mayor of Toledo, diplomat
Anderson, David D., *Brand Whitlock* (1968).
Crunden, Robert M., *Hero in Spite of Himself: Brand Whitlock* (1969).
Tager, Jack, *The Intellectual as Urban Reformer: Brand Whitlock* (1968).
Whitlock, Brand, *Forty Years of It* (1925).
——— *Letters and Journal*, Allan Nevins, ed. (1936).

WHITMAN, MARCUS 1802–1847, physician, Presbyterian missionary in Northwest
Drury, C. M., *Marcus Whitman* (1937).
Jones, Nard, *The Great Command: Marcus and Narcissa Whitman and Oregon Country Pioneers* (1960).

WHITMAN, NARCISSA 1808–1847, missionary in Northwest
Allen, Opal S., *Narcissa Whitman* (1959).

WHITMAN, WALT 1819–1892, poet
Allen, Gay W., *Solitary Singer: Walt Whitman* (rev. ed., 1967).
Arvin, Newton, *Whitman* (1938).
Canby, Henry S., *Walt Whitman* (1943).

Miller, James E., *Walt Whitman* (1962).
Perry, Bliss, *Walt Whitman: His Life and Work* (1906).
Traubel, H. L., *With Walt Whitman in Camden* (3 vols., 1906–1914).

WHITNEY, ELI 1765–1825, inventor
Green, Constance M., *Eli Whitney and the Birth of American Technology* (1956).
Mirsky, Jeanette, and Alan Nevins, *World of Eli Whitney* (1962).
Whitney, Eli, "Correspondence," *AHR* 3 (1897), 90.

WHITNEY, JOSIAH DWIGHT 1819–1896, geologist, chemist
Brewster, E. T., *Life and Letters of Josiah Dwight Whitney* (1909).

WHITNEY, WILLIAM C. 1841–1904, financier, sportsman, political leader
Hirsch, Mark D., *William C. Whitney* (1948).

WHITTIER, JOHN GREENLEAF 1807–1892, poet
Leary, Lewis, *John Greenleaf Whittier* (1961).
Mordell, Albert, *Quaker Militant, John Greenleaf Whittier* (1933).
Pickard, Samuel T., *Life and Letters of John Greenleaf Whittier* (rev. ed., 2 vols., 1907).
Pollard, John A., *John Greenleaf Whittier* (1969).
Wagenknecht, Edward C., *John Greenleaf Whittier* (1967).

WICKARD, CLAUDE RAYMOND 1893–1967, secretary of agriculture
Albertson, Dean, *Roosevelt's Farmer: Claude R. Wickard in the New Deal* (1961).

WICKES, LAMBERT 1735?–1777, sea raider
Clark, William B., *Lambert Wickes* (1933).

WIENER, NORBERT 1894–1964, mathematician
Wiener, Norbert, *My Childhood and Youth* (1953).
———— *I Am a Mathematician: The Later Life of a Prodigy* (1956).

WIGGLESWORTH, MICHAEL 1631–1705, Congregational clergyman, author
Crowder, Richard, *No Featherbed to Heaven: Michael Wigglesworth* (1962).
Wigglesworth, Michael, *Diary, 1653–1657*, Edmund S. Morgan, ed. (1965).

WILBUR, RAY LYMAN 1875–1949, physician, secretary of interior, president of Stanford University
Wilbur, Ray L., *Memoirs*, Edgar E. Robinson and Paul C. Edwards, eds. (1960).

WILDER, THORNTON 1897–   , novelist, playwright
Burbank, Rex, *Thornton Wilder* (1961).

WILEY, HARVEY W. 1844–1930, chemist, pure food reformer
Anderson, Oscar E., *Health of a Nation: Harvey W. Wiley's Fight for Pure Food* (1958).
Wiley, Harvey W., *Autobiography* (1930).

WILKES, CHARLES 1798–1877, explorer
Henderson, Daniel, *Hidden Coasts: Admiral Charles Wilkes* (1953).

WILKINSON, JAMES 1757–1825, general
Cox, I. J., "General Wilkinson and His Later Intrigues," *AHR*, 19 (1914), 794.
Hay, Thomas R., and M. R. Werner, *The Admirable Trumpeter, General James Wilkinson* (1941).
Jacobs, James R., *Tarnished Warrior* (1938).
Wilkinson, James, *Memoirs of My Own Times* (3 vols., 1816).

WILKINSON, JEMIMA 1752–1819, religious leader
Wisbey, Herbert A., Jr., *Pioneer Prophetess: Jemima Wilkinson* (1964).

WILLARD, EMMA H. 1787–1870, educator
Lutz, Alma, *Emma Willard* (1929).

WILLARD, FRANCES E., 1839–1898, suffragist, temperance reformer
Earhart, Mary, *Frances Willard* (1944).
Strachey, R. C., *Frances Willard* (1912).
Willard, Frances E., *Glimpses of Fifty Years* (1889).

WILLETT, MARINUS 1740–1830, merchant, Revolutionary soldier
Thomas, Howard, *Marinus Willett: Soldier-Patriot* (1954).

WILLIAMS, DANIEL HALE 1858–1931, Negro surgeon

Buckler, Helen, *Daniel Hale Williams, Negro Surgeon* (1968).

WILLIAMS, JOHN SHARP 1854–1923, Mississippi senator
Osborn, George C., *John Sharp Williams: Planter-Statesman of Deep South* (1943).

WILLIAMS, ROBERT LEE 1868–1948, Oklahoma jurist
Dale, Edward E., and James D. Morrison, *Pioneer Judge: Robert Lee Williams* (1958).

WILLIAMS, ROGER 1603–1682/83, Baptist leader
Brockunier, S. H., *The Irrepressible Democrat: Roger Williams* (1940).
Chupack, Henry, *Roger Williams* (1970).
Ernst, James E., *Political Thought of Roger Williams* (1929).
—— *Roger Williams* (1932).
Garrett, John, *Roger Williams: Witness Beyond Christendom, 1603–1683* (1970).
Miller, Perry, *Roger Williams* (1953).
Moore, LeRoy, Jr., "Roger Williams and Historians," *Church Hist.*, 32 (1963), 432.
Morgan, Edmund S., *Roger Williams* (1967).
Simpson, Alan, "How Democratic was Roger Williams?" *WMQ*, 3 ser., 13 (1956), 53.
Williams, Roger, *Complete Writings*, Perry Miller, ed. (7 vols., 1963).
Winslow, Ola E., *Master Roger Williams* (1957).

WILLIAMS, TENNESSEE 1914–   , playwright
Falk, Signi, *Tennessee Williams* (1961).
Jackson, Esther M., *Broken World of Tennessee Williams* (1965).

WILLIAMS, WILLIAM CARLOS 1883–1963, poet
Whitaker, Thomas R., *William Carlos Williams* (1968).

WILLIAMSON, CHARLES S. 1872–1933, physician
Cowan, H. I., *Charles Williamson* (1941).

WILLING, THOMAS 1731–1821, president of first bank of United States
Konkle, B. A., *Thomas Willing* (1937).
Willing, Thomas, *Letters and Papers*, Thomas W. Balch, ed. (1922).

WILLIS, NATHANIEL PARKER 1806–1867, journalist, author
Auser, Cortland P., *Nathaniel P. Willis* (1968).
Beers, Henry A., *Nathaniel Parker Willis* (1885).

WILLKIE, WENDELL 1892–1944, utility executive, presidential candidate
Barnard, Ellsworth, *Wendell Willkie* (1966).
Barnes, Joseph, *Willkie* (1952).
Dillon, Mary E., *Wendell L. Willkie* (1952).
Johnson, Donald B., *Republican Party and Willkie* (1960).
Moscow, Warren, *Roosevelt and Willkie* (1968).

WILMOT, DAVID 1814–1868, Pennsylvania congressman
Going, Charles B., *David Wilmot, Free-Soiler* (1924).

WILSON, ALEXANDER 1766–1813, naturalist
Cantwell, Robert, *Alexander Wilson: Naturalist and Pioneer* (1961).
Wilson, James S., *Alexander Wilson: Poet-Naturalist* (1906).

WILSON, EDMUND 1895–1972, critic
Frank, Charles P., *Edmund Wilson* (1969).
Paul, Sherman, *Edmund Wilson* (1965).

WILSON, HENRY LANE 1857–1932, lawyer, diplomat
Wilson, Henry L., *Diplomatic Episodes in Mexico, Belgium and Chile* (1927).

WILSON, JAMES 1742–1798, Revolutionary leader
Smith, C. Page, *James Wilson, Founding Father, 1742–1798* (1956).
Wilson, James, *Works*, (1896), Robert G. McCloskey, ed. (2 vols., 1967).

WILSON, WILLIAM LYNE 1843–1900, postmaster general
Summers, Festus P., *William L. Wilson and Tariff Reform* (1953).
Wilson, William L., *Cabinet Diary, 1896–1897*, Festus P. Summers, ed. (1957).

WILSON, WOODROW 1856–1924, President
Baker, Ray S., *Woodrow Wilson: Life and Letters* (6 vols., 1927–1937).
—— *Woodrow Wilson and World Settlement* (3 vols., 1922).

Blum, John M., *Woodrow Wilson and Politics of Morality* (1956).
Bragdon, Henry W., *Woodrow Wilson: The Academic Years* (1967).
Craig, Hardin, *Woodrow Wilson at Princeton* (1960).
Cronon, E. David, ed., *Political Thought of Woodrow Wilson* (1965).
Garraty, John A., *Woodrow Wilson* (1956).
George, Alexander L., and Juliett L. George, *Woodrow Wilson and Colonel House: A Personality Study* (1956).
Grayson, Cary T., *Woodrow Wilson: Intimate Memoir* (1960).
Hoover, Herbert, *Ordeal of Woodrow Wilson* (1958).
Latham, Earl, ed., *Philosophy and Policies of Woodrow Wilson* (1958).
Link, Arthur S., *Wilson* (vols. 1/5–   , 1947–   ).
——— *Woodrow Wilson: A Brief Biography* (1963).
Osborn, George C., *Woodrow Wilson* (1968).
Tumulty, Joseph P., *Woodrow Wilson* (1921).
Walworth, Arthur C., *Woodrow Wilson* (2 vols., 1958).
Wilson, Woodrow, *Papers*, Arthur S. Link et al., eds. (vols. 1/–   1966/72–   ).
——— *Politics of Woodrow Wilson: Selections from Speeches and Writings*, August Heckscher, ed. (1956).
——— *Public Papers*, R. S. Baker and W. E. Dodd, eds. (6 vols., 1925–1927).
——— *Selected Literary and Political Papers* (3 vols., 1925–1927).
——— *Writings and Speeches*, Albert Fried, ed. (1965).

WINANT, JOHN GILBERT 1889–1947, New Hampshire governor, diplomat
Bellush, Bernard, *He Walked Alone: John Gilbert Winant* (1968).

WINSLOW, JOHN ANCRUM 1811–1873, Union naval officer
Ellicott, John M., *Life of John Ancrum Winslow, Rear Admiral United States Navy* (1902).

WINTER, WILLIAM 1836–1917, dramatic critic, historian of the stage
Winter, William, *Old Friends: Being Literary Recollections of Other Days* (1909).
——— *Other Days: Being Chronicles and Memories of the Stage* (1908).
——— *The Wallet of Time* (2 vols., 1913).

WINTHROP, JOHN 1587/88 o.s.–1649; Massachusetts governor
Morgan, Edmund, *Puritan Dilemma: John Winthrop* (1958).
Winthrop, John, *Journal, History of New England, 1630–1649*, James K. Hosmer, ed. (2 vols., 1908).
Winthrop, John, *Winthrop Papers* (vols. 1/5–   , 1929–   ).

WINTHROP, JOHN 1605/6–1676, Connecticut governor
Black, Robert C., III, *Younger John Winthrop* (1966).

WINTHROP, ROBERT C. 1809–1894, Massachusetts congressman
Winthrop, Robert C., Jr., *Memoir of Robert C. Winthrop* (1897).

WINTHROP FAMILY
Dunn, Richard S., *Puritans and Yankees: Winthrop Dynasty, 1630–1717* (1962).

WIRT, WILLIAM 1772–1834, attorney general
Kennedy, John Pendleton, *Memoirs of the Life of William Wirt, Attorney-General of the United States* (2 vols., 1849).

WISE, HENRY ALEXANDER 1806–1876, Virginia governor
Wise, B. H., *Life of Henry A. Wise* (1899).

WISE, ISAAC MAYER 1819–1900, rabbi
Heller, James G., *Isaac M. Wise* (1965).
Knox, Israel, *Rabbi in America: Isaac M. Wise* (1957).

WISE, JOHN 1652–1725, Congregational clergyman
Cook, George A., *John Wise* (1952).

WISE, JOHN SERGEANT 1846–1913, counsel for street railways, author
Wise, John S., *The End of the Era* (1899; repr. 1965).

WISTER, OWEN 1860–1938, author
Wister, Owen, *Journals and Letters*, Fanny K. Wister, ed. (1958).

WITHERSPOON, JOHN 1723–1794, Presbyterian clergyman, president of College of New Jersey

Butterfield, Lyman H., *John Witherspoon Comes to America* (1953).
Collins, Varnum L., *President Witherspoon* (2 vols., 1925).
Witherspoon, John, *Works* (3 vols., 1800).

WITTE, EDWIN EMIL 1887–1960, economist, social security advocate
Schlabach, Theron F., *Edwin E. Witte* (1969).

WOLFE, THOMAS CLAYTON 1900–1938, author
McElderry, Bruce R., Jr., *Thomas Wolfe* (1963).
Nowell, Elizabeth, *Thomas Wolfe* (1960).
Turnbull, Andrew, *Thomas Wolfe* (1967).
Walser, Richard, ed., *Enigma of Thomas Wolfe* (1953).
Wolfe, Thomas, *Letters*, Elizabeth Nowell, ed. (1956).
—— *Letters to His Mother*, John S. Terry, ed. (1943).

WOLFSKILL, WILLIAM 1798–1866, fur trapper
Wilson, Iris H., *William Wolfskill* (1965).

WOOD, FERNANDO 1812–1881, New York City political leader
Pleasants, Samuel A., *Fernando Wood* (1948).

WOOD, GRANT 1892–1942, artist
Garwood, Darrell, *Artist in Iowa: Grant Wood* (1944).

WOOD, LEONARD 1860–1927, military surgeon, army officer, administrator
Hagedorn, Hermann, *Leonard Wood* (2 vols., 1931).

WOODBURY, LEVI 1789–1851, statesman, jurist
Woodbury, Levi, *Writings* (3 vols., 1852).

WOODHOUSE, JAMES 1770–1809, physician
Smith, Edgar F., *James Woodhouse* (1918).

WOODHULL, VICTORIA CLAFLIN 1838–1927, women's rights advocate, adventuress
Johnston, Johanna, *Mrs. Satan: Victoria C. Woodhull* (1967).

WOODMAN, CYRUS 1814–1889, Wisconsin promoter
Gara, Larry, *Westernized Yankee: Cyrus Woodman* (1956).

WOODS, ROBERT ARCHEY 1865–1925, founder of settlement house, sociologist, reformer
Woods, Eleanor H., *Robert A. Woods, Champion of Democracy* (1929).

WOODWARD, AUGUSTUS BREVOORT 1774–1827, Michigan jurist
Woodford, Frank B., *Mr. Jefferson's Disciple: Justice Woodward* (1953).

WOODWARD, WALTER CARLETON 1878–1942, Quaker frontiersman
Emerson, Elizabeth H., *Walter C. Woodward* (1952).

WOOLLEY, MARY EMMA 1863–1947, president of Mount Holyoke College
Marks, Jeannette, *Life and Letters of Mary Emma Woolley* (1955).

WOOLMAN, JOHN 1720–1772, Quaker leader
Cady, Edwin H., *John Woolman* (1965).
Rosenblatt, Paul, *John Woolman* (1969).
Whitney, Janet, *John Woolman* (1942).
Woolman, John, *Journal, 1774*, A. M. Gummere, ed. (1922); Janet Whitney, ed. (1950).

WOOLSON, CONSTANCE FENIMORE 1840–1894, novelist
Moore, Rayburn S., *Constance F. Woolson* (1962).

WOOLWORTH, FRANK 1852–1919, retailer
Winkler, J. K., *Five and Ten: Life of Frank W. Woolworth* (1940).

WORMSLOE FAMILY
Coulter, E. Merton, *Wormsloe: A Georgia Family* (1955).

WORTH, JONATHAN 1802–1869, North Carolina governor
Zuber, Richard L., *Jonathan Worth* (1965).

WORTH, WILLIAM JENKINS 1794–1849, Mexican War general
Wallace, Edward S., *General William Jenkins Worth: Monterey's Forgotten Hero* (1953).

WORTHINGTON, THOMAS 1773–1827, Ohio governor, senator
Sears, Alfred B., *Thomas Worthington: Father of Ohio Statehood* (1958).

WRIGHT, CARROLL DAVIDSON 1840–1909, statistician
  Leiby, James, *Carroll Wright: Origin of Labor Statistics* (1960).
WRIGHT, CHAUNCEY 1830–1875, mathematician, philosopher
  Madden, Edward H., *Chauncey Wright and the Foundations of Pragmatism* (1963).
  Wright, Chauncey, *Letters*, J. B. Thayer, ed. (1878).
WRIGHT, FRANCES 1795–1852, reformer
  Waterman, W. R., *Frances Wright* (1924).
WRIGHT, FRANK LLOYD 1869–1959, architect
  Manson, Grant H., *Frank Lloyd Wright: The First Golden Age* (1958).
  Scully, Vincent, Jr., *Frank Lloyd Wright* (1960).
  Wright, Frank Lloyd, *Autobiography* (1932).
  Wright, Olgivanna L., *Frank Lloyd Wright* (1966).
WRIGHT BROTHERS, inventors of airplane
  Wright, Wilbur, and Orville Wright, *Papers*, Marvin W. McFarland, ed. (2 vols., 1953).
  Kelly, F. C., *The Wright Brothers: Fathers of Flight* (1943).
WRIGHT, RICHARD 1908–1960, Negro author
  Webb, Constance, *Richard Wright* (1968).
WRIGHT, SILAS 1795–1847, New York senator, lawyer
  Garraty, John A., *Silas Wright* (1949).
WYETH, ANDREW 1917–   , artist
  Meryman, Richard, *Andrew Wyeth* (1968).
WYLIE, ELINOR 1885–1928, poet, novelist
  Gray, Thomas A., *Elinor Wylie* (1970).
WYZANSKI, CHARLES EDWARD, JR. 1906–   , jurist
  Wyzanski, Charles E., Jr., *Whereas: A Judge's Premises* (1965).
YANCEY, WILLIAM LOWNDES 1814–1863, secession leader
  DuBose, J. W., *Life and Times of William Lowndes Yancey* (1892).
  McMillan, Malcolm C., "William L. Yancey and the Historians: One Hundred Years," *Ala. Rev.* 20 (1967), 163.
YATES, RICHARD 1860–1936, Illinois governor
  Yates, Richard, *An Autobiography* (1968).
YOUMANS, EDWARD LIVINGSTON 1821–1887, scientific editor
  Fiske, John, *Edward L. Youmans* (1894).
YOUNG, ART 1866–1943, cartoonist, author
  Young, Art, *His Life and Times*, J. N. Beffel, ed. (1939).
YOUNG, BRIGHAM 1801–1877, Mormon leader
  Cannon, Frank L., and George L. Knapp, *Brigham Young and His Mormon Empire* (1913).
  Gates, Susa Y., and L. D. Widtsoe, *The Life Story of Brigham Young* (1930).
  Hirshson, Stanley P., *Lion of the Lord: Biography of Brigham Young* (1969).
  Werner, M. R., *Brigham Young* (1925).
  Young, Brigham et al., *Journal of Discourses* (26 vols., 1854–1886).
YOUNG, ELLA FLAGG 1845–1918, educational administrator, president of National Education Association
  McManis, John T., *Ella Flagg Young and a Half-Century of the Chicago Public Schools* (1916).
YOUNG, OWEN D. 1874–1962, lawyer, chairman of board of General Electric
  Tarbell, Ida M., *Owen D. Young* (1932).
YOUNG, PIERCE MANNING BUTLER 1836–1896, Confederate general, diplomat
  Holland, Lynwood M., *Pierce M.B. Young* (1964).
YOUNG, ROBERT RALPH 1897–1958, financier
  Borkin, Joseph, *Robert R. Young, Populist of Wall Street* (1969).
ZENGER, JOHN PETER 1697–1746, printer
  Cheslaw, Irving G., *John Peter Zenger* (1952).
  Rutherfurd, Livingston, *John Peter Zenger* (1904).

ZINZENDORF, NICOLAUS LUDWIG, count Von 1700–1760, Moravian leader and
  bishop
  Spangenberg, A. G., *Life of Nicolas Lewis, Count Zinzendorf*, Samuel Jackson,
  trans. (1838).
ZOLLICOFFER, FELIX K. 1812–1862, Tennessee editor and politician
  Myers, Raymond E., *Zollie Tree* (1964).

Part Three Comprehensive and Area Histories

11 Introduction to American History

11.1 INTERPRETATIVE SURVEYS

Allen, Harry C., *The United States: A Concise History* (1964).
Beard, Charles A., and Mary R. Beard, *Beards' New Basic History of the United States*, William Beard, ed. (rev. ed., 1960).
Boorstin, Daniel J., *The Americans: The National Experience* (1965).
Degler, Carl N., *Out of Our Past* (2nd ed., 1970).
Handlin, Oscar, *The Americans* (1963).
Miller, William, *A New History of the United States* (3d ed., 1969).
Morison, Samuel E., *Oxford History of the American People* (1965).
Nevins, Allan, and Henry S. Commager, *Pocket History of the United States* (rev. ed., 1956).
Parkes, Henry B., *The American Experience* (rev. ed., 1955).
Thistlethwaite, Frank, *Great Experiment* (1955).

11.2 COMPREHENSIVE HISTORIES

Adams, Henry, *History of the United States: During the Administrations of Jefferson and Madison* (9 vols., 1889–1891; 4 vol. ed., 1930).
Andrews, Charles M., *The Colonial Period of American History* (4 vols., 1934–1938).
Bancroft, George, *History of the United States* (10 vols., 1834–1874; 6 vol. ed. carrying the work to 1789, 1883–1885).
Bancroft, Hubert H., *History of the Pacific States of North America* (34 vols., 1882–1890).
—————— *Native Races of the Pacific States of North America* (5 vols., 1874–1876).
Channing, Edward, *A History of the United States* (6 vols., 1905–1925).
Gipson, Lawrence H., *The British Empire before the American Revolution* (15 vols., 1936–1970).
Hildreth, Richard, *The History of the United States* (6 vols., 1849–1856; rev. ed., 1880–1882).
von Holst, H. E., *The Constitutional and Political History of the United States,* J. J. Lalor et al., trans. (7 vols., 1876–1892).
McMaster, J. B., *A History of the People of the United States from the Revolution to the Civil War* (8 vols., 1883–1913). *A History of the People of the United States during Lincoln's Administration* (1927) continues the narrative through 1865.
Oberholtzer, Ellis P., *A History of the United States since the Civil War* (5 vols., 1917–1937).
Osgood, Herbert L., *The American Colonies in the Seventeenth Century* (3 vols., 1904–1907). *The American Colonies in the Eighteenth Century* (4 vols., 1924–1925).
Parkman, Francis, *France and England in North America* (9 vols., 1865–1892).

Supplemented by *The Conspiracy of Pontiac* (2 vols., 1851). Reprinted in his
Works (12 vols., 1926).
Rhodes, J. F., *History of the United States from the Compromise of 1850* (7 vols.,
1893–1906). Two supplementary works continue the account to 1909: *History
of the United States from Hayes to McKinley* (1919), and *The McKinley and
Roosevelt Administrations* (1922). These were later added to the original set as
vols. 8 and 9.
Schouler, James, *History of the United States under the Constitution* (6 vols.,
1880–1899; rev. ed. with added vol. carrying the work to 1877, 7 vols., 1894–
1913).
Tucker, George, *The History of the United States* (4 vols., 1856–1857).
Winsor, Justin, ed., *Narrative and Critical History of America* (8 vols., 1884–
1889).

11.3 HISTORIES IN SERIES

American Foreign Policy Library, Sumner Welles et al., eds. (1945–   ).
American Nation: A History, Albert B. Hart, ed. (1904–1917).
American Secretaries of State and Their Diplomacy, Samuel F. Bemis, ed. (1927).
Chicago History of American Civilization, Daniel J. Boorstin, ed. (1956–   ).
Chronicles of America, Allen Johnson and Allan Nevins, eds. (1918–1951).
Economic History of the United States, Henry David et al., eds. (1945–   ).
History of American Life, Arthur M. Schlesinger and D. R. Fox, eds. (1927–
1948).
History of the South, Wendell H. Stephenson and E. Merton Coulter, eds.
(1947–1967).
New American Nation, Henry Steele Commager and Richard B. Morris, eds.
(1954–   ).

11.4 COLLECTIONS OF ORIGINAL SOURCES

Bartlett, Ruhl J., ed., *The Record of American Diplomacy* (4th ed., 1964).
Beston, Henry, ed., *American Memory: Being a Mirror of the Stirring and Pic-
turesque Past of Americans and the American Nation* (1937).
Boorstin, Daniel J., ed., *An American Primer* (2 vols., 1966).
Burnett, Edmund C., ed., *Letters of Members of the Continental Congress* (8 vols.,
1921–1938).
Casgrain, H. R., ed., *Collection de documents inédits sur le Canada et l'Amérique,
publiés par le Canada-français* (3 vols., 1888–1890).
Champlain Society, *Publications* (31 vols., 1907–1952).
Commager, Henry S., ed., *Documents of American History* (8th ed., 1968).
Commons, John R. et al., eds., *Documentary History of American Industrial
Society* (10 vols., 1910–1911).
Force, Peter, ed., *Tracts and Other Papers Relating Principally to the Colonies in
North America* (4 vols., 1836–1846).
Hakluyt Society, *Works Issued by the Hakluyt Society* (196 vols., 1847–1951).
Hart, Albert B., ed., *American History Told by Contemporaries* (5 vols., 1897–
1929).
Hofstadter, Richard, ed., *Great Issues in American History: A Documentary
Record, 1765–1969* (2 vols., 1969).
Jameson, John F., ed., *Original Narratives of Early American History* (19 vols.,
1906–1917).
MacDonald, William, ed., *Select Charters and Other Documents Illustrative of
American History, 1606–1775* (1899).
Richardson, James D., ed., *Compilation of the Messages and Papers of the
Confederacy, Including the Diplomatic Correspondence* (2 vols., 1905).
——— *Compilation of the Messages and Papers of the Presidents, 1789–1897* (10
vols., 1969).

Thwaites, Reuben G., ed., *Early Western Travels, 1748–1846* (32 vols., 1904–1907).
────── *Jesuit Relations and Allied Documents, 1610–1791* (73 vols., 1896–1901).
Ver Steeg, Clarence L., and Richard Hofstadter, eds., *Great Issues in American History: From Settlement to Revolution, 1584–1776* (1969).

11.5 TEXTBOOKS

Bailey, Thomas A., *American Pageant* (4th ed., 1970).
Baldwin, Leland D., *Stream of American History* (4th ed., 2 vols., 1969).
Barck, Oscar T., Jr., and Hugh T. Lefler, *A History of the United States* (2 vols., 1968).
Beard, Charles A., and Mary R. Beard, *Rise of American Civilization* (4 vols., 1927–1942).
Billington, Ray A., et al. *Making of American Democracy* (3 vols. in one, 1950).
Blum, John M. et al. *The National Experience: A History of the United States* (2nd ed., 1968).
Carman, Harry J., et al., *A History of the American People* (3d ed., 2 vols., 1967).
Caughey, John W., and Ernest R. May, *A History of the United States* (1964).
Chitwood, Oliver P., et al., *American People* (3d ed., 2 vols., 1962).
Craven, Avery O., and Walter Johnson, *American History* (1961).
Craven, Avery O., and Walter Johnson, *The United States: An Experiment in Democracy* (2nd ed., 1962).
Crow, H. L., and W. L. Turnbull, *American History: Problems Approach* (1971).
Current, Richard N., T. Harry Williams, and Frank Freidel, *American History* (3d ed., 1971).
Curti, Merle, et al., *History of American Civilization* (1953).
Fielding, R. Kent, and Eugene E. Campbell, *The United States: An Interpretive History* (1964).
Garraty, John A., *The American Nation* (2nd ed., 1971).
Gelormino, Alphonse G., and Margaret R. Gotti, *Challenge of Our Heritage: A Social, Political and Economic History of the United States* (1970).
Graebner, Norman A., Gilbert C. Fite and Philip L. White, *A History of the American People* (1970).
Graebner, Norman A., et al., *A History of the United States* (2 vols., 1970).
Handlin, Oscar, *America: A History* (1968).
────── *History of the United States* (2 vols., 1967–1968).
Hicks, John D., et al., *American Nation, from 1865* (4th ed., 1963).
────── *History of American Democracy* (3d ed., 1966).
Hofstadter, Richard, et al., *The United States* (3d ed., 2 vols., 1970).
Link, Arthur S., and Stanley Coben, *The Democratic Heritage: A History of the United States* (1971).
Malone, Dumas, and Basil Rauch, *Empire for Liberty: Growth of the United States* (2 vols., 1960).
Morison, Samuel E., Henry S. Commager, and William E. Leuchtenburg, *Growth of the American Republic* (6th ed., 2 vols., 1969).
Morris, Richard B., William Greenleaf, and Robert Ferrell, *America: A History of the People* (1971).
Morris, Richard B., and William Greenleaf, *U.S.A.: A History of a Nation* (2 vols., 1969).
Ostrander, Gilman M., *A Profile History of the United States* (1964).
Parkes, Henry B., *United States of America* (3d ed., 1968).
Perkins, Dexter, and Glyndon G. Van Deusen, *American Democracy* (2nd ed., 2 vols., 1968).
Sanders, Jennings B., *A College History of the United States* (1962).
Savelle, Max, and Tremaine McDowell, *Short History of American Civilization* (1957).
Sellers, Charles G., and Henry May, *A Synopsis of American History* (2nd ed., 1969).

Williams, T. Harry, Richard N. Current, and Frank Freidel, *A History of the United States* (3d ed., 2 vols., 1969).
Wright, Louis B. et al., *Democratic Experience: Short History* (1968).

11.6 INTERPRETATIVE ESSAYS

Baldwin, Leland D., *Meaning of America: Essays* (1955).
Bernstein, Barton J., ed., *Towards a New Past* (1968).
Curti, Merle B., *American Paradox: Conflict of Thought and Action* (1956).
O'Gorman, Edmundo, *Invention of America* (1961).
Perkins, Dexter, *American Way* (1957).
Schlesinger, Arthur M., *New Viewpoints in American History* (1922).
—— *Paths to the Present* (rev. ed., 1964).

11.7 INTERPRETATIONS OF AMERICAN CHARACTERISTICS

Berthoff, Rowland, "American Social Order," *AHR*, 65 (1960), 495.
Blum, John M., *Promise of America* (1965).
Boorstin, Daniel J., *The Americans: The National Experience* (1965).
—— *The Image: Or What Happened to the American Dream* (1962).
Brock, William R., *Character of American History* (2nd ed., 1965).
Cawelti, John G., *Apostles of the Self-Made Man* (1965).
Degler, Carl N., *Out of Our Past* (rev. ed., 1970).
Dudden, Arthur P., "Nostalgia and the American," *Jour. Hist. Ideas,* 22 (1961), 515.
Fishwick, Marshall, *The Hero, American Style* (1969).
Handlin, Oscar, ed., *American Principles and Issues* (1961).
—— *The Americans* (1963).
——— *Chance or Destiny: Turning Points in American History* (1955).
Lipset, Seymour M., *First New Nation: United States in Perspective* (1963).
Miller, Perry, "American Character," *NEQ,* 28(1955), 435.
Nef, John U., *United States and Civilization* (2nd ed., 1967).
Pierson, George W., "M-Factor in American History," *Am. Quar.,* 14 (1962), 275.
—— "A Restless Temper," *AHR,* 69 (1964), 969.
Potter, David M., *People of Plenty: Economic Abundance and American Character* (1954).
Smith, Henry Nash, *Virgin Land: The American West as Symbol and Myth* (1950).
Wecter, Dixon, *The Hero in America* (1941).
Williams, William A., *Contours of American History* (1961).
Wyllie, Irvin G., *Self-Made Man in America* (1954).

Topical and period bibliographies are cited throughout the *Guide.* An excellent, fully annotated bibliography covering all of American history is Donald H. Mugridge and Blanche P. McCrum, *A Guide to the Study of the United States: Representative Books* (1960). It contains over 6000 citations, arranged topically.

11.8 POLITICAL INTERPRETATIONS

Auerbach, M. Morton, *The Conservative Illusion* (1959).
Boorstin, Daniel J., *Genius of American Politics* (1953).
Brogan, Denis W., *Politics in America* (2nd. ed., 1960).
Ekirch, Arthur A., Jr., *The American Democratic Tradition: A History* (1963).
—— *Decline of American Liberalism* (1955).

Guttmann, Allen, *Conservative Tradition in America* (1967).
Handlin, Oscar, and Mary Handlin, *Dimensions of Liberty* (1961).
Hartz, Louis, *Liberal Tradition in America* (1955).
Hofstadter, Richard, *The American Political Tradition and the Men Who Made It* (1948).
―――― *Paranoid Style in American Politics* (1965).
Koch, Adrienne, "Values and Democratic Political Theory," *Ethics,* 68 (1958), 166.
Labaree, Leonard W., *Conservatism in Early American History* (1948).
Mason, Alpheus T., and Richard H. Leach, *In Quest of Freedom: American Political Thought and Practice* (1959).
Ostrander, Gilman M., *Rights of Man in America, 1606–1861* (1960).

11.9 HISTORIOGRAPHY

11.9.1 General

Adams, Herbert B., *Historical Scholarship in the United States, 1876–1901: Correspondence,* W. Stull Holt, ed. (1938).
Bass, Herbert J., ed., *State of American History* (1970).
Bassett, John S., *Middle Group of American Historians* (1917).
Billias, George A., and Gerald N. Grob, eds., *American History: Retrospect and Prospect* (1971).
Brock, William R., *Character of American History* (2nd ed., 1965).
Callcott, George H., *History of United States, 1800–1860: Its Practice and Purpose* (1970).
Commager, Henry S., *Search for Usable Past and Other Essays in Historiography* (1967).
Cunliffe, Marcus, and Robin W. Winks, eds., *Pastmasters: Essays on American Historians* (1969).
Donald, David, "Radical Historians on Move," *N.Y. Times Bk. Rev.* (July 19, 1970), 1.
Eisenstadt, Abraham S., "Redefining American Experience," *Am. Rev.,* 3 (1963), 134.
Gatell, Frank O., and Allen Weinstein, eds., *American Themes: Essays in Historiography* (1968).
Herbst, Jurgen, *German Historical School in American Scholarship* (1965).
Herrick, Francis H., "The Profession of History," *Pac. Hist. Rev.,* 31 (1962), 1.
Higham, John, et al., *History* (1965).
Higham, John, ed., *Reconstruction of American History* (1962).
Holt, W. Stull, et al., "American Historical Writing, 1900–1950: A Symposium," *MVHR,* 40 (1954).
Holt, W. Stull, "Scientific History," *Jour. Hist. Ideas,* 1 (1940), 352.
Hoover, Dwight W., "Recent United States Historiography," *Am. Quar.,* 17 (1965), 299.
Iggers, Georg G., "The Image of Ranke in American and German Historical Thought," *Hist. and Theory,* 2 (1962), 17.
Katz, Stanley N., and Stanley L. Kutler, eds., *New Perspectives on American Past* (2 vols., 1969).
Kraus, Michael, *Writing of American History* (rev. ed., 1953).
Sanders, Jennings B., *Historical Interpretations and American Historianship* (1966).
Shafer, Boyd C., "Historical Study in the United States," in Boyd C. Shafer, ed., *Historical Study in the West* (1968), 173.
Sheehan, Donald, and Harold C. Syrett, eds., *Essays in American Historiography: In Honor of Allan Nevins* (1960).
Sorenson, Lloyd R., "Historical Currents in America," *Am. Quar.,* 7 (1955), 234.
Stephenson, Wendell H., "Quarter Century of American Historiography," *MVHR,* 45 (1958), 3.

Unger, Irwin, "The 'New Left' and American History: Recent Trends in Historiography," *AHR,* 72 (1967), 1237.
Van Tassel, David D., *Recording America's Past: Historical Studies, 1607–1884*
(1960).
Wish, Harvey, *The American Historian* (1960).

11.9.2 Special Topics

Billington, Ray A. et al., *Historian's Contribution to Anglo-American Misunder-
standing: Report on National Bias in History Textbooks* (1966).
Bremner, Robert H., ed., *Essays on History and Literature* (1966).
"Comparative Study in American History," *Comp. Studies in Society and Hist.,* 5
(1962/63). Entire issue.
Curti, Merle E., "Democratic Theme in Historical Literature," *MVHR,* 39
(1952), 3.
––––––– *Human Nature in American Historical Thought* (1968).
––––––– *Probing Our Past* (1955).
Dorson, Richard M., "Oral Tradition and Written History: The Case for the
United States," *Jour. Folklore Inst.* 1 (1965), 220.
Duberman, Martin B., *The Uncompleted Past* (1969).
Hacker, Louis M., "The Anticapitalist Bias of American Historians," in F. A.
Hayek, ed., *Capitalism and the Historians* (1954).
Hartz, Louis, "American Historiography and Comparative Analysis: Further Re-
flections," *Comp. Studies in Society and Hist.,* 5 (1963), 365.
Higham, John, "Cult of American Consensus," *Commentary,* 27 (1959), 93.
––––––– "Historian as Moral Critic," *AHR,* 67 (1962), 609.
"The Historian and the World of the Twentieth Century," *Daedalus,* 100 (1971).
Entire issue.
Hollingsworth, J. Rogers, "Consensus and Continuity in Historical Writing," *So.
Atl. Quar.,* 61 (1962), 40.
Lankford, John E., and David Reimers, eds., *Essays on American Social History*
(1970).
Levin, David, *In Defense of Historical Literature: Essays on American History,
Autobiography, Drama and Fiction* (1967).
Lewis, Archibald R., and Thomas F. McGann, *The New World Looks at Its
History* (1963).
Malin, James C., *Contriving Brain and Skillful Hand in the United States* (1955).
––––––– *On Nature of History: Essays* (1954).
"Middle States Tradition in American Historiography," Am. Philos. Soc., *Proc.,*
108 (1964). Entire issue.
Morison, Samuel E., *By Land and By Sea: Essays* (1953).
––––––– *Vistas of History* (1964).
Pole, J. R., "American Past," *Jour. Am. Studies,* 1 (April 1967), 63.
Potter, David M., "Historians' Use of Nationalism and Vice Versa, *AHR,* 67
(1962), 924.
Van Zandt, Roland, *Metaphysical Foundations of American History* (1959).
Wiebe, Robert H., "Confinements of Consensus," *Tri-Quar.,* 6 (1966), 155.
Wish, Harvey, "American Historian and New Conservatism," *So. Atl. Quar.,* 65
(1966), 178.
Woodward, C. Vann, "Age of Reinterpretation," *AHR,* 66 (1960), 1.
––––––– ed., *Comparative Approach to American History* (1968).

11.9.3 History Profession in the United States

Beale, Howard K., "The Professional Historian," *Pac. Hist. Rev.,* 22 (1953), 227.
Perkins, Dexter, et al., *Education of Historians in United States* (1962).
Perman, Dagmar H., ed., *Bibliography and the Historian* (1968).
Shafer, Boyd C., "Study of History in United States," AAUP *Bull.,* 50 (1964),
232.
Shera, Jesse H., *Historians, Books, and Libraries* (1953).

11.9.4 Writing of Biography

Bowen, Catherine D., *Writing of Biography* (1952).
Frantz, Joe B., "Adventuring in Biography," *Historian* 16 (1953), 45.
Garraty, John A., *Nature of Biography* (1957).
Handlin, Oscar, "History in Men's Lives," *Va. Quar. Rev.,* 30 (1954), 534.
Merrill, D. K., *Development of American Biography* (1932).
O'Neill, Edward H., *History of American Biography: 1800–1935* (1935).
Tolles, Frederick B., "Biographer's Craft," *So. Atl. Quar.,* 53 (1954), 508.

11.9.5 Philosophy of History

Bloch, Marc, *The Historian's Craft* (1953).
Butterfield, Herbert, *Man on His Past: History of Historical Scholarship* (1955).
Carr, Edward H., *What Is History?* (1962).
Fischer, David H., *Historians' Fallacies: Toward a Logic of Historical Thought* (1970).
Gottschalk, Louis, ed., *Generalization in the Writing of History* (1963).
Hockett, Homer C., *Critical Method in Historical Research and Writing* (1955).
Kahler, Erich, *Meaning of History* (1964).
Meyerhoff, Hans, "History and Philosophy: An Introductory Survey," *The Philosophy of History In Our Time,* (1959).
Shafer, Robert J., et al., eds., *Guide to Historical Method* (1969).
Smith, Page, *The Historian and History* (1964).
Social Science Research Council, *Theory and Practice in Historical Study* (1946).
Weiss, Paul, *History: Written and Lived* (1962).
White, Morton G., *Foundations of Historical Knowledge* (1965).

11.9.6 The Progressive Historians

Benson, Lee, *Turner and Beard: Reconsidered* (1960).
Blackwood, George D., "Frederick J. Turner and John R. Commons," *MVHR,* 41 (1954), 471.
Coleman, Peter J., "Beard, McDonald, and Economic Determinism in American Historiography," *Bus. Hist. Rev.,* 34 (1960), 113.
Crowe, Charles, "Progressive History," *Jour. Hist. Ideas,* 27 (1966), 109.
Cunliffe, Marcus, and Robin W. Winks, eds., *Pastmasters: Essays on American Historians* (1969).
Hofstadter, Richard, *Progressive Historians: Turner, Beard, Parrington* (1968).
Jacobs, Wilbur R., et al., *Turner, Bolton, and Webb* (1965).
Skotheim, Robert A., "Environmental Interpretations of Ideas by Beard, Parrington and Curti," *Pac. Hist. Rev.,* 33 (1964), 35.
Strout, Cushing, *Pragmatic Revolt in American History: Carl Becker and Charles Beard* (1958).

11.9.7 Individual Historians

ADAMS, BROOKS
Beisner, Robert L., "Brooks Adams and Charles Francis Adams, Jr.," *NEQ,* 35 (1962), 48.
Donovan, Timothy P., *Henry Adams and Brooks Adams: Education of Two American Historians* (1961).
Hirschfeld, Charles, "Brooks Adams and American Nationalism," *AHR,* 69 (1964), 371.

ADAMS, CHARLES FRANCIS, JR.
Beisner, Robert L., "Brooks Adams and Charles Francis Adams, Jr.," *NEQ,* 35 (1962), 48.

ADAMS, HENRY
Cairns, John C., "Successful Quest of Henry Adams," *So. Atl. Quar.,* 57 (1958), 168.

Donovan, Timothy P., *Henry Adams and Brooks Adams: Education of Two American Historians* (1961).

Jordy, William H., *Henry Adams: Scientific Historian* (1952).

Lindsay, Barbara, "Henry Adams' History: A Study in Limitations," *West. Humanities Rev.*, 8 (1954), 99.

Mindel, Joseph, "Henry Adams and Symbols of Science," *Jour. Hist. Ideas*, 26 (1965), 89.

Peterson, Merrill D., "Henry Adams on Jefferson the President," *Va. Quar. Rev.*, 39 (1963), 187.

Rozwenc, Edwin C., "Henry Adams and the Federalists," in H. Stuart Hughes, ed., *Teachers of History* (1954).

Shaw, Peter, "Henry Adams' History," *NEQ*, 40 (1967), 163.

Vitzthum, Richard C., "Henry Adams' Paraphrase of Sources in the History of the United States," *Am. Quar.*, 17 (1965), 81.

ANDREWS, CHARLES MCLEAN

Eisenstadt, Abraham S., *Charles McLean Andrews* (1956).

BANCROFT, GEORGE

Nye, Russel B., *George Bancroft* (1944).

Rathbun, J. W., "George Bancroft on Man and History," Wis. Acad. Sciences, *Trans.*, 43 (1954), 51.

Vitzthum, Richard C., "Theme and Method in Bancroft's History of the United States," *NEQ*, 51 (1968), 362.

BEARD, CHARLES A.

Beale, Howard K., ed., *Charles A. Beard: An Appraisal* (1954).

Deininger, Whitaker T., "The Skepticism and Historical Faith of Charles A. Beard," *Jour. Hist. Ideas* 15 (1954), 573.

Hofstadter, Richard, *Progressive Historians: Turner, Beard, Parrington* (1968).

Kennedy, Thomas C., "Charles A. Beard," *Historian*, 25 (1963), 439.

Marks, Harry J., "Beard's Relativism," *Jour. Hist. Ideas*, 14 (1953), 628.

Morison, Samuel E., "History Through a Beard," in *By Land and By Sea* (1953).

Nash, Gerald D., "Self-Education in Historiography: Charles A. Beard," *Pac. Northw. Quar.*, 52 (1961), 108.

Phillips, Harlan B., "Charles Beard: The English Lectures, 1899–1901," *Jour. Hist. Ideas*, 14 (1953), 451.

Skotheim, Robert A., "Environmental Interpretations of Ideas by Beard, Parrington and Curti," *Pac. Hist. Rev.*, 33 (1964), 35.

Sorenson, Lloyd R., "Charles Beard and German Historiographical Thought," *MVHR*, 42 (1955), 274.

Strout, Cushing, *Pragmatic Revolt in American History: Carl Becker and Charles Beard* (1958).

Williams, William A., "Note on Charles A. Beard's Search for General Theory of Causation," *AHR*, 62 (1956), 59.

BECKER, CARL

Cairns, John C., "Carl Becker: American Liberal," *Jour. Politics*, 16 (1954), 623.

Noble, David W., "Carl Becker," *Ethics*, 67 (1957), 233.

Smith, Charlotte W., *Carl Becker: On History* (1956).

Strout, Cushing, *Pragmatic Revolt in American History: Carl Becker and Charles Beard* (1958).

Wilkins, Burleigh T., *Carl Becker: Intellectual History* (1961).

Zagorin, Perez, and Leo Gershoy, "Carl Becker on History," *AHR*, 62 (1956), 1.

BOLTON, HERBERT E.

Ives, Ronald L., "Herbert E. Bolton, 1870–1953," Am. Cath. Hist. Soc., *Records*, 65 (1954), 40.

de Onis, José, "Americas of Herbert E. Bolton," *The Americas*, 12 (1955), 157.

BURGESS, JOHN WILLIAM

Loewenberg, Bert J., "John William Burgess, the Scientific Method, and the Hegelian Philosophy of History," *MVHR*, 42 (1955), 490.

CHANNING, EDWARD

Weaver, Glenn, "Edward Channing," *Social Studies*, 54 (1963), 83.

COMMAGER, HENRY S.

Nevins, Allan, "Henry S. Commager as Historian: An Appreciation," in Harold

M. Hyman and Leonard W. Levy, eds., *Freedom and Reform: Essays in Honor of Henry Steele Commager* (1967).

DUNNING, WILLIAM A.
Harper, Alan D., "William A. Dunning: The Historian as Nemesis," *Civil War History,* 10 (1964), 54.

EGGLESTON, EDWARD
Wolford, Thorp L., "Edward Eggleston: Historian," *Ind. Mag. Hist.,* 63 (1967), 17.

GREEN, FLETCHER MELVIN
Copeland, J. Isaac, "Fletcher Melvin Green: A Bibliography," *Writing Southern History: Essays in Historiography in honor of Fletcher M. Green* (1965).

LEA, HENRY C.
Armstrong, William M., "Henry C. Lea," *Penn. Mag. Hist. and Biog.,* 80 (1956), 465.

MYERS, GEORGE A.
Myers, George A., and James F. Rhodes, *Correspondence, 1910–1923,* John A. Garraty, ed. (1956).

NEVINS, ALLAN
Walsh, Lyle S., and Michael Lamanna, "Biographies of Allan Nevins," *Social Science,* 28 (1953), 34.

OSGOOD, HERBERT LEVI
Fox, Dixon Ryan, *Herbert Levi Osgood, American Scholar* (1924).

PARKMAN, FRANCIS
Jacobs, Wilbur R., "Some Social Ideas of Francis Parkman," *Am. Quar.,* 9 (1957), 387.
Morison, Samuel E., "Introduction," in *The Parkman Reader* (1955).
Pease, Otis A., *Parkman's History: The Historian as Literary Artist* (1953).

PARRINGTON, VERNON L.
Colwell, James L., "Populist Image of Vernon L. Parrington," *MVHR,* 49 (1962), 52.
Hofstadter, Richard, "Parrington and Jeffersonian Tradition," *Jour. Hist. Ideas,* 2 (1941), 391.
Peterson, Merrill D., "Parrington and American Liberalism," *Va. Quar. Rev.,* 30 (1954), 35.
Skotheim, Robert A., and Kermit Vanderbilt, "Vernon L. Parrington: Mind and Art of a Historian of Ideas," *Pac. Northw. Quar.,* 53 (1962), 100.

PAXSON, FREDERIC L.
Pomeroy, Earl S., "Frederic L. Paxson and His Approach to History," *MVHR,* 39 (1953), 673.

PHILLIPS, ULRICH B.
Genovese, Eugene D., "Race and Class in Southern History: Appraisal of Work of Ulrich B. Phillips," *Agric. Hist.,* 41 (1967), 345.
Kugler, Ruben F., "U. B. Phillips' Use of Sources," *Jour. Negro Hist.,* 47 (1962), 153.
Salem, Sam E., "U. B. Phillips and Scientific Tradition," *Ga. Hist. Quar.,* 44 (1960), 172.

PRESCOTT, WILLIAM HICKLING
Cline, Howard F., C. Harvey Gardiner, and Charles Gibson, eds., *William Hickling Prescott* (1959).
Prescott, William H., *Literary Memoranda,* C. Harvey Gardiner, ed. (2 vols., 1961).
Humphreys, Robert A., "William Hickling Prescott: The Man and the Historian," *Hispanic Am. Hist. Rev.,* 39 (1959), 1.

RAMSAY, DAVID
Brunhouse, Robert L., "David Ramsay, 1749–1815: Selections," Am. Philos. Soc., *Trans.,* 55, pt. 4 (1965).

RANDALL, JAMES GARFIELD
Pratt, Harry E., "James Garfield Randall, 1881–1953," Ill. State Hist. Soc., *Jour.,* 46 (1953), 119.

RHODES, JAMES FORD

Myers, George A., and James F. Rhodes, *Correspondence, 1910–1923,* John A. Garraty, ed. (1956).

ROBINSON, JAMES HARVEY

Wish, Harvey, "James Harvey Robinson and the New History," *The New History* (1965).

ROOSEVELT, THEODORE

Sellen, Robert W., "Theodore Roosevelt: Historian with a Moral," *Mid-America,* 41 (1959), 223.

SCHLESINGER, ARTHUR M.

Schlesinger, Arthur M., *In Retrospect: History of a Historian* (1963).

SIMONS, A. M.

Kreuter, Kent, and Gretchen Kreuter, "The Vernacular History of A. M. Simons," *Jour. Am. Studies,* 2 (1968), 65.

TURNER, FREDERICK JACKSON

Billington, Ray A., "Why Some Historians Rarely Write History: A Case Study of Frederick Jackson Turner," *MVHR,* 50 (1963), 3.

Bolton, Herbert E., "Turner," *Mid-America,* 36 (1954), 541.

See also 13.7.2, Westward Expansion and the Frontier–Turner Thesis.

12 Regional, State, and Local Histories

12.1 REGIONALISM

A considerable part of American history focuses upon specific regions and regional themes, especially concerning the South and the West. The nature of regionalism or sectionalism has been a subject of sustained inquiry and debate among historians. The following are some of the more general or basic books on these topics.

Jensen, Merrill, ed., *Regionalism in America* (1951).
National Resources Committee, *Thirteen Regional Planning Reports* (1936–1943).
Odum, Howard W., and H. E. Moore, *American Regionalism: Cultural-Historical Approach to National Integration* (1938).
Odum, Howard W., *Folk, Region and Society: Selected Papers,* Katharine Jocher et al., eds. (1964).
Odum, Howard W., and Katherine Jocher, eds., *In Search of Regional Balance* (1945).
Peate, Iowerth C., ed., *Studies in Regional Consciousness and Environment* (1930).
Sharkansky, Ira, *Regionalism in American Politics* (1969).
Turner, Frederick Jackson, *The Significance of Sections in American History* (Introduction by Max Farrand, 1950).
Veysey, Laurence R., "Myth and Reality in Approaching American Regionalism," *Am. Quar.,* 12 (1960), 31.
White, C. Langdon, and Edwin J. Foscue, *Regional Geography of North America* (1943).

12.2 REGIONAL HISTORIES

The titles listed below are but a sampling of regional histories. The majority of references to New England in the colonial period will be found in volume two. Section 13.3, Westward Expansion and the Frontier– Regional Studies, in this volume, should also be examined for supplementary titles. Chapter 9, Travels and Description, contains references to important supplementary source materials on the states and localities; the materials are often applicable collectively to the various regions.

12.2.1 New England

Adams, James T., *New England in the Republic, 1776–1850* (1926).
Black, John D., *The Rural Economy of New England: A Regional Study* (1950).
Kirkland, Edward C., *Men, Cities and Transportation; A Study in New England History, 1820–1900* (2 vols., 1948).

Weeden, W. B., *Economic and Social History of New England, 1620–1789* (2 vols., 1890).

12.2.2 Middle Atlantic States

Bell, Whitfield J., Jr., "Middle States Tradition in American Historiography," Am. Philos. Soc., *Proc.*, 108 (1964), 145.
Bowen, Ezra, *Middle Atlantic States* (1968).
Ellis, David M., "New York and Middle Atlantic Regionalism," *N.Y. Hist.*, 35 (1954), 3.
Thompson, D. G. Brinton, *Gateway to a Nation: Middle Atlantic States* (1956).

12.2.3 Middle West

Atherton, Lewis, *Main Street on the Middle Border* (1966).
Clark, Dan E., *The Middle West* (1966).
Dondore, Dorothy, *Prairie and Making of Middle America* (2nd ed., 1961).
Fenton, John H., *Midwest Politics* (1966).
Fox, Dixon R., ed., *Sources of Culture in the Middle West* (1934).
Glazer, Sidney, *The Middle West* (1962).
Henderson, James M., and Anne O. Krueger, *National Growth and Economic Change in the Upper Midwest* (1965).
Hutton, Graham, *Midwest at Noon* (1946).
Jensen, Richard, *The Winning of the Midwest: Social and Political Comflict, 1888–1896* (1971).
Kraenzel, Carl F., *Great Plains in Transition* (1955).
Merrill, Horace S., *Bourbon Democracy of Middle West, 1865–1896* (1953).
Murray, John J., ed., *Heritage of Middle West* (1958).
Nute, Grace L., *Lake Superior* (1944).
Ottoson, Howard W. et al., *Land and People in Northern Plains Transition Area* (1966).

12.2.4 South

Cash, Wilbur J., *Mind of the South* (1941).
Clark, Thomas D., *Emerging South* (2nd ed., 1968).
———— "Modern South in Changing America," Am. Philos. Soc. *Proc.*, 107 (1963), 121.
———— and Albert D. Kirwan, *South since Appomattox* (1967).
———— *Three Paths to Modern South: Education, Agriculture and Conservation* (1965).
Cunningham, Horace H., "Southern Mind since the Civil War," in Arthur S. Link, ed., *Writing Southern History: Essays in Historiography in Honor of Fletcher M. Green* (1965).
Davis, Allison et al., *Deep South: A Social Anthropological Study of Caste and Class* (1965).
Doherty, Herbert J., Jr., "Mind of the Antebellum South," in Arthur S. Link, ed., *Writing Southern History: Essays in Historiography in Honor of Fletcher M. Green* (1965).
Durisch, Lawrence L., "Southern Regional Planning and Development," *Jour. Politics*, 26 (1964), 41.
Eaton, Clement, *Growth of Southern Civilization, 1790–1860* (1961).
Ezell, John S., *The South since 1865* (1963).
Gaston, Paul M., *New South Creed: A Study in Southern Mythmaking* (1970).
Grantham, Dewey W., Jr., *Democratic South* (1963).
———— "South and Reconstruction of American Politics," *JAH*, 53 (1966), 227.
———— ed., *South and the Sectional Image* (1967).

Greenhut, Melvin L., and W. Tate Whitman, eds., *Essays in Southern Economic Development* (1964).
Hawk, E. Q., *Economic History of South* (1934).
Hesseltine, William B., and David L. Smiley, *South in American History* (2nd ed., 1960).
Key, V. O., Jr., *Southern Politics in State and Nation* (1949).
Maclachlan, John M., and J. S. Floyd, *This Changing South* (1956).
McGill, Ralph E., *The South and the Southerner* (1963).
McKinney, John C., and Edgar T. Thompson, eds., *South in Continuity and Change* (1965).
Morris, Willie, ed., *The South Today* (1965).
Nicholls, William H., *Southern Tradition and Regional Progress* (1960).
Potter, David M., *South and Sectional Conflict* (1968).
Rubin, Louis D., Jr., *Faraway Country: Writers of Modern South* (1963).
―――― and James J. Kilpatrick, *Lasting South* (1957).
Rubin, Louis D., Jr., and Robert D. Jacobs, eds., *South: Modern Literature* (1961).
Sellers, Charles G., ed., *The Southerner as American* (1960).
Simkins, Francis B., *History of the South* (3d ed., 1963).
Sitterson, J. Carlyle, ed., *Studies in Southern History in Memory of Albert Ray Newsome* (1957).
Stephenson, W. H., and E. M. Coulter, eds., *History of the South* (10 vols., 1948–1967).
Tindall, George B., *Emergence of New South, 1913–1945* (1967).
Van Noppen, Ina W., *The South: A Documentary History* (1958).
Williams, T. Harry, *Romance and Realism in Southern Politics* (1960).
Woodward, C. Vann, *The Burden of Southern History* (rev. ed., 1968).
―――― "Irony of Southern History," *JSH,* 19 (1953), 3.
―――― *Origins of the New South, 1877–1913* (1951).
―――― "Search for Southern Identity," *Va. Quar. Rev.,* 34 (1958), 321.
―――― "Southern Ethic in a Puritan World," *WMQ,* 3 ser., 25 (1968), 343.

See also volume two for additional references to the anti-bellum South and the South during the Civil War Period.

* * * * * * *

Cave, Alfred A., "Main Themes in Recent Southern History," *West. Humanities Rev.,* 20 (1966), 97.
Craven, Avery, "The 'Turner Theories' and the South," *JSH,* 5 (1939), 291.
Eaton, Clement, "Recent Trends in Writing Southern History," *La. Hist. Quar.,* 38 (1955), 26.
Grantham, Dewey W., Jr., "The Regional Imagination: Social Scientists and the American South," *JSH,* 34 (1968), 3.
Link, Arthur S., and Rembert W. Patrick, eds., *Writing Southern History: Essays in Historiography in Honor of Fletcher M. Green* (1965).
Mathews, Joseph J., "Study of History in the South," *JSH,* 31 (1965), 3.
Noggle, Burl, "Variety and Ambiguity: Recent Approach to Southern History," *Miss. Quar.,* 17 (1963), 21.
Phillips, Ulrich B., "The Central Theme of Southern History," *AHR,* 33 (1928), 30.
Potter, David M., "Historians' Use of Nationalism and Vice Versa, *AHR,* 67 (1962), 924.
Rundell, Walter, Jr., "Southern History from Local Sources: A Survey of Graduate History Training," *JSH,* 34 (1968), 214.
Stephenson, Wendell H., *South Lives in History: Southern Historians* (1955).
―――― *Southern History in the Making: Pioneer Historians* (1964).
Tindall, George B., ed., *Pursuit of Southern History: Presidential Addresses of Southern Historical Association, 1935–1963* (1964).

See also 13.3.2, Southern Frontier.

12.2.5 West

American Heritage History of the Great West (1965).

Athearn, Robert G., *High Country Empire: High Plains and Rockies* (1960).

Bancroft, Hubert H., *New Pacific* (1913).

Bartlett, Richard A., *Great Surveys of the American West* (1962).

Billington, Ray A., *America's Frontier Heritage* (1966).

——— *Far Western Frontier, 1830–1860* (1956).

Bogue, Allan G. et al., eds., *The West of the American People* (1970).

Briggs, Harold E., *Frontiers of Northwest* (1940).

Caughey, John W., *American West: Frontier and Region,* Norris Hundley, Jr. and John A. Schutz, eds. (1969).

——— *History of the Pacific Coast* (1933).

Clark, John G., ed., *Frontier Challenge* (1971).

Coman, Katherine, *Economic Beginnings of Far West* (2 vols., 1925).

Drache, Hiram M., *Day of the Bonanza: Bonanza Farming in Red River Valley* (1964).

Drago, Harry S., *Roads to Empire: American West* (1968).

Ellis, David M., ed., *The Frontier in American Development: Essays in Honor of Paul Wallace Gates* (1969).

Farquhar, Francis P., *History of the Sierra Nevada* (1965).

Faulk, Odie B., *Land of Many Frontiers: History of American Southwest* (1968).

Fenneman, Nevin M., *Physiography of Western United States* (1931).

Fite, Gilbert C., *The Farmers' Frontier, 1865–1900* (1966).

Goetzmann, William H., *Exploration and Empire: Explorer and Scientist in Winning of West* (1966).

Greever, William S., *Bonanza West: Western Mining Rushes, 1848–1900* (1963).

Hafen, LeRoy R., and Ann W. Hafen, eds., *The Far West and Rockies Series* (15 vols., 1954–1961).

Hafen, Leroy R. et al., *Western America* (3d. ed., 1970).

Hollon, W. Eugene, *Great American Desert: Then and Now* (1966).

Johansen, Dorothy O., and Charles M. Gates, *Empire of the Columbia* (2nd ed., 1967). Pacific Northwest.

Lavender, David S., *Land of Giants: Drive to the Pacific Northwest 1750–1950* (1958).

Moore, R. Laurence, "Continuing Search for a Southwest: A Study in Regional Interpretation," *Ariz. and West,* 6 (1964), 275.

Murray, Stanley N., *Valley Comes of Age: Agriculture in the Valley of the Red River, 1812–1920* (1967).

Ottoson, Howard W., et al., *Land and People in Northern Plains Transition Area* (1966).

Paul, Rodman W., *Mining Frontiers of the Far West: 1848–1880* (1963).

Pomeroy, Earl S., *The Pacific Slope* (1965).

Powell, John W., *Report on the Lands of the Arid Region of the United States* (1878); Wallace Stegner, ed. (1962).

Pritchett, John P., *Red River Valley, 1811–1849* (1942).

Richmond, Robert W., and Robert W. Mardock, eds., *Nation Moving West: Readings* (1966).

Ridge, Martin, and Ray A. Billington, eds., *America's Frontier Story: A Documentary History* (1969).

Smith, Henry Nash, *Virgin Land: The American West as Symbol and Myth* (1950).

Spence, Clark C., ed., *The American West: A Source Book* (1966).

Toole, K. Ross, et al., *Probing the American West* (1962).

Turner, Frederick Jackson, *Rise of the New West, 1819–1829* (1906).

Warren, Sidney, *Farthest Frontier: The Pacific Northwest* (1949).

Webb, Walter, *The Great Plains* (1931).

Winther, Oscar O., *Great Northwest* (1947).

——— *Old Oregon Country: Frontier Trade, Transportation and Travel* (1949).

See also chapter 13, Westward Expansion and the Frontier.

12.3 STATE AND LOCAL HISTORY

For too long professional historians left the writing of local history to antiquarians and amateurs. Within recent years, inspired by French and English scholars and American colleagues in the social sciences, they have begun to explore the records of communities in order to ask new questions and test familiar generalizations about the American people. For a landmark team approach to local history which stresses quantitative analysis, see Merle E. Curti et al., *Making of an American Community: Democracy in a Frontier County.* For a modern approach by individual authors see especially the books on Plymouth, Andover, and Dedham, Massachusetts by John Demos, Phillip Greven, and Kenneth Lockridge respectively; and on Kent, Connecticut by Charles S. Grant.

Local histories written in the early periods continue to be valuable sources of information and data for analytic scholars. Most of the local histories cited in this chapter fall into this category.

State history, on the other hand, has long been the domain of the scholar. Many state histories are applicable to still broader studies. They are also useful for the econmic, social, or intellectual history of a given state. The reader who is seeking references to these topics in chapters 13 through 29 should bear this in mind, for there are no cross references in those chapters to general state histories.

Chapter 9, Travels and Description, contains a wealth of primary source material on all states and many localities—especially related to the early stages of their development.

In a somewhat special category are a large number of state, county, and urban histories, commonly known as "mug books." The production of these volumes began in the last quarter of the nineteenth century and continued into the 1930's. Turned out by publishing firms that specialized in this work, they are generally multivolumed, large, well-printed, and expensive. Their reason for being is the long section in each devoted to the biographies of the locally prominent persons who doubtless subscribed for the sake of seeing themselves photographed and extolled in print. Nevertheless, these books occasionally have historical sections of considerable value, and even the biographical volumes may provide information not elsewhere available.

Guides and Bibliographies

Bradford, T. L., and S. V. Henkels, *Bibliographer's Manual of American History, Containing an Account of All State, Territory, Town and County Histories* (5 vols., 1907–1910).

Griffin, A. P. C., *Index of Articles upon American Local History in Historical Collections* (1889).

—— *Index of the Literature of American Local History, in Collections Published in 1890–1895* (1896).

Perkins, F. B., *Check List for American Local History* (1876).

Peterson, C. S., *Bibliography of County Histories of the 3111 Counties in the 48 States* (1946).

Rader, J. L., ed., *South of Forty from the Mississippi to the Rio Grande: A Bibliography* (1947).

Stocker, C. L., "Genealogical Material and Local Histories in the St. Louis Public Library," *St. Louis Public Library Monthly Bull.*, 25 (1927), 193.

The journals of the state historical societies contain many articles of value, traceable through their indexes. The Writers' Project of the WPA undertook a large number of studies in this field, few of which have been published. Some such material was also included in the various state guide books issued by the WPA. For the remainder, see: M. E. Colby, *Final Report on Disposition of Unpublished Materials of the WPA Writers' Program.*

The list which follows is selective and illustrative. Within the section for each state and territory, general state histories are mentioned first, then followed by local histories, and finally guides and bibliographies.

Alabama

Brown, Virginia P., and H. M. Akens, *Alabama Heritage: A Picture History* (1966).
Elliott, Carl, ed., *Annals of Northwest Alabama* (3 vols., 1958–1965).
Haagen, Victor B., *Alabama* (1968).
Jordan, Weymouth T., *Ante-Bellum Alabama* (1957).
McMillan, Malcolm C., *Constitutional Development in Alabama, 1798–1901* (1955).
Moore, A. B., *History of Alabama* (1935).
Owen, M. B., *Our State, Alabama* (1927).
Owen, T. M., *History of Alabama and Dictionary of Alabama Biography* (4 vols., 1921).
Pickett, Albert J., *History of Alabama and Georgia and Mississippi* (1851; repr. 1962).

Hamilton, P. J., *Colonial Mobile* (1910).
Henley, John C., Jr., *This is Birmingham* (1960).
Jefferson County and Birmingham, Alabama (1887).
Leftwich, Nina, *Two Hundred Years of Muscle Shoals* (1935).
Little, J. B., *The History of Butler County, Alabama* (1885).
Memorial Record of Alabama (2 vols., 1893).
Moss, F. H. W., *Building Birmingham and Jefferson County* (1947).
Summersell, Charles G., *Mobile: History of Seaport Town* (1949).

Alaska

Adams, Ben, *Last Frontier: Alaska* (1961).
Andrews, C. L., *The Story of Alaska* (1938).
Bancroft, Hubert H., *Alaska* (1886).
Chevigny, Hector, *Russian America: Alaskan Venture, 1741–1867* (1965).
Farrar, Victor, *Annexation of Russian America to the United States* (1937).
Gruening, Ernest, *State of Alaska* (1954).
Jensen, Billie B., "Alaska's Pre-Klondike Mining: Men, Methods and Minerals," *Jour. of West,* 6 (1967), 417.
Johnson, Hugh A., and Harold T. Jorgenson, *Land Resources of Alaska* (1963).
Krasheninnikov, S. P., *History of Kamtschatka, and the Kurilski Islands, with Countries Adjacent,* James Grieve, trans. (2nd ed., 1764).
Nichols, Jeannette P., *Alaska* (1924).
Rogers, George W., *Future of Alaska* (1962).
Sherwood, Morgan B., *Exploration of Alaska, 1865–1900* (1965).

*   *   *   *   *   *   *

Allen, Robert V., "Alaska before 1867 in Soviet Literature," *Quar. Jour. Lib. of Congress,* 23 (1966), 243.

Lada-Mocarski, Valerian, ed., *Bibliography of Books on Alaska Published before 1868* (1969).
Wickersham, James, *Bibliography of Alaskan Literature* (1927).

Arizona

Bancroft, Hubert H., *Arizona and New Mexico* (1888).
Farish, T. E., *History of Arizona* (8 vols., 1915).
Hallenbeck, Cleve, *Land of the Conquistadores* (1950).
Lockwood, Frank C., *Pioneer Days in Arizona from the Spanish Occupation to Statehood* (1932).
Lutrell, Estelle, *Newspapers and Periodicals of Arizona, 1859–1911* (1949).
Miller, Joseph, *Arizona* (1956).
Peek, Ann M., *March of Arizona History* (1962).
Peplow, Edward H., *History of Arizona* (3 vols., 1958).
Sloan, R. E., and W. R. Adams, *History of Arizona* (4 vols., 1930).
Spring, John, *Arizona*, A. M. Gustafson, ed. (1966).
Wagoner, Jay J., *Arizona Territory, 1863–1912: Political History* (1970).
Wyllys, R. K., *Arizona: The History of a Frontier State* (1950).

Burns, Walter N., *Tombstone* (1917).
Fuchs, James R., *History of Williams, Arizona, 1876–1951* (1955).
Schultz, Vernon B., *Southwestern Town: Willcox, Arizona* (1964).
Stevens, Robert C., *History of Chandler, Arizona* (1954).

*   *   *   *   *   *   *

Wallace, Andrew, *Sources and Readings in Arizona's History: Checklist* (1965).

Arkansas

Fletcher, John G., *Arkansas* (1947).
Hallum, John, *Biographical and Pictorial History of Arkansas* (1887).
Herndon, D. T., *Arkansas History Catalog* (1923).
McNutt, W. S., O. E. McKnight and G. A. Hubbell, *A History of Arkansas* (1933).
Thomas, D. Y., *Arkansas and Its People, 1541–1930* (1930).
White, Lonnie J., *Politics on Southwestern Frontier: Arkansas Territory, 1819–1836* (1964).

Richards, Ira D., *Story of a Rivertown: Little Rock in Nineteenth Century* (1969).

California

Bancroft, Hubert H., *California* (7 vols., 1884–1890).
Bean, Walton, *California* (1968).
Caughey, John W., *California* (1940).
—— ed., *California Heritage: An Anthology of History and Literature* (1962).
Chapman, Charles E., *The Founding of Spanish California, 1687–1783* (1916).
—— *A History of California: The Spanish Period* (1921).
Cleland, Robert G., *California in Our Time* (1947).
—— *From Wilderness to Empire: California*, Glenn S. Dumke, ed. (rev. ed., 1959).
—— *A History of California, the American Period* (1922).

Cook, Sherburne F., *Conflict between California Indian and White Civilization* (1943).
Ellison, Joseph, *California and the Nation, 1850–1869: A Study of the Relations of a Frontier Community with the Federal Government* (1927).
Fehrenbacher, Don E., *Basic History of California* (1964).
────── and Norman E. Tutorow, *California: Illustrated History* (1968).
Gates, Paul W., ed., *California Ranchos and Farms, 1846–1862* (1967).
Hutchinson, C. Alan, *Frontier Settlement in Mexican California* (1969).
Hutchinson, William H., *California* (1969).
Kirsch, Robert R., and William S. Murphy, *West of the West: California Experience, 1542–1906* (1967).
Melendy, H. Brett, and Benjamin F. Gilbert, *Governors of California: Peter H. Burnett to Edmund G. Brown* (1965).
Nash, Gerald D., *State Government and Economic Development: Administrative Policies in California 1849–1933* (1964).
Richman, I. B., *California under Spain and Mexico, 1535–1847 . . .* (1911).
Robinson, Alfred, *Life in California before the Conquest* (2nd ed., 1968).
Rolle, Andrew F., *California* (2nd ed., 1969).
Roske, Ralph J., *Everyman's Eden: California* (1968).

Bean, Walton, *Boss Ruef's San Francisco* (1952).
Cox, Isaac, *The Annals of Trinity County* (1858; new ed., 1940).
Coy, Owen C., *Humboldt Bay Region, 1850–1875* (1929).
Ferrier, W. W., *Berkeley, California* (1933).
Fogelson, Robert M., *Fragmented Metropolis: Los Angeles, 1850–1930* (1967).
Kinnaird, Lawrence, *History of Greater San Francisco Bay Region* (3 vols., 1966).
McGowan, Joseph A., *History of Sacramento Valley* (3 vols., 1961).
Merritt, F. C., *History of Alameda County, California* (2 vols., 1928).
Pleasants, J. E., *History of Orange County, California* (3 vols., 1931).
Scott, Mellier G., *San Francisco Bay Area* (1959).
Soulé, Frank, J. H. Gihon, and James Nisbet, *The Annals of San Francisco* (1855). *Index*, C. F. Griffin, comp. (1935).
Winther, Oscar O., "Rise of Metropolitan Los Angeles," *Huntington Library Quar.*, 10 (1947), 391.
Young, J. P., *San Francisco, a History of the Pacific Coast Metropolis* (2 vols., [1913]).

*   *   *   *   *   *   *

Cowan, Robert E., *A Bibliography of the History of California, 1510–1930* (4 vols., 1933–1964).
────── *A Bibliography of the History of California and the Pacific Coast* (1952).
Coy, Owen C., *Guide to County Archives of California* (1919).
Hager, Anna Maria, and Everett G. Hager, comps., *Historical Society of Southern California Bibliography of Published Works, 1884–1957*.
Rocq, Margaret M., ed., *California Local History: Bibliography and Union List of Library Holdings* (2nd ed., 1970).
Stoughton, Gertrude K., *Books of California* (1968).

Colorado

Bancroft, Hubert H., *Nevada, Colorado, and Wyoming* (1890).
Fritz, P. S., *Colorado, the Centennial State* (1941).
Hafen, LeRoy R., ed., *Colorado and Its People: Narrative and Topical History* (4 vols., 1948).
────── *Colorado: Story of a Western Commonwealth* (1933).
Hall, Frank, *History of Colorado* (4 vols., 1889–1895).
Stone, Wilbur F., *History of Colorado* (3 vols., 1918).
Ubbelohde, Carl W., *A Colorado History* (1965).

Willard, James F., and Colin B. Goodykoontz, eds., *Experiments in Colorado Colonization, 1869–1872* (1926).
Wolle, M. S., *Stampede to Timberline* (1949).

Bancroft, Caroline, *Gulch of Gold: History of Central City* (1958).
Black, Robert C., III, *Island in the Rockies: Grand County, Colorado* (1969).
Smiley, J. C., *History of Denver* (1903).
Willard, James F., ed., *Union Colony at Greeley, Colorado, 1869–1871* (1918).

*   *   *   *   *   *   *

Oehlerts, Donald, *Guide to Colorado Newspapers, 1859–1963* (1964).
Ubbelohde, Carl W., *Colorado: Student's Guide* (1965).
Wilcox, Virginia L., ed., *Colorado: Selected Bibliography of Its Literature, 1858–1952* (1954).

Connecticut

Bingham, Harold J., *History of Connecticut* (4 vols., 1962).
Burpee, C. W., *The Story of Connecticut* (4 vols., 1939).
Bushman, Richard L., *From Puritan to Yankee: Character and Social Order in Connecticut, 1690–1765* (1967).
Jones, Mary J. A., *Congregational Commonwealth: Connecticut, 1636–1662* (1968).
Morgan, Forrest, *Connecticut as a Colony and as a State, or One of the Original Thirteen* (4 vols., 1904).
Morse, J. M., *A Neglected Period of Connecticut's History, 1818–1850* (1933).
Niven, John, *Connecticut: Role in Civil War* (1965).
Osborn, N. G., *History of Connecticut in Monographic Form* (5 vols., 1925).
Purcell, Richard J., *Connecticut in Transition, 1775–1818* (1918).
Trumbull, Benjamin, *A Complete History of Connecticut* (1818; repr. 2 vols., 1898).
Van Dusen, Albert, *Connecticut: An Illustrated History of the State from the Seventeenth Century* (1961).

Allen, Francis O., *History of Enfield* (3 vols., 1900).
Anderson, Joseph, *The Town and City of Waterbury, Connecticut, from the Aboriginal Period to the Year Eighteen Hundred and Ninety-Five* (3 vols., 1896).
Atwater, E. E., *History of the Colony of New Haven to Its Absorption into Connecticut* (1881).
Bailey, J. M., *History of Danbury, Connecticut 1684–1896* (1896).
Banks, Elizabeth, *This is Fairfield, 1639–1940* (1960).
Bedini, Silva, *Ridgefield in Review* (1958).
Bowen, C. W., *The History of Woodstock, Connecticut* (4 vols., 1926–1932).
Castle, Henry Allen, *History of Plainville, Connecticut, 1640–1918* (1967).
Caulkins, F. M., *History of New London, from the First Survey of the Coast in 1612* (1852).
——— *History of Norwich, from Its Possession by the Indians to 1873* (1874).
Fowler, Herbert E., *History of New Britain* (1960).
Grant, Charles S., *Democracy in the Connecticut Frontier Town of Kent* (1961).
Green, Constance M., *History of Naugatuck* (1948).
Hartley, Rachel M., *History of Hamden* (1959).
Hawley, Emily C., *Annals of Brookfield, Connecticut* (1929).
Litchfield, Norman, and Sabina C. Hoyt, *History of Oxford* (1960).
Love, William De Loss, *Colonial History of Hartford* (2nd ed., 1935).
Orcutt, Samuel, *The History of the Old Town of Derby, Connecticut, 1642–1880* (1880).

———— *A History of the Old Town of Stratford and the City of Bridgeport, Connecticut* (2 vols., 1886).

Osterweis, Rollin G., *Three Centuries of New Haven, 1638–1938* (1953).

Peck, Epaphroditus, *A History of Bristol, Connecticut* (1932).

Schenck, E. H., *The History of Fairfield, Connecticut 1639–1818* (2 vols., 1889).

Spiess, Mathias, *History of Manchester* (1924).

Starr, Edward C., *History of Cornwall* (1926).

Steiner, B. C., *History of the Plantation of Menunkatuck and of the Original Town of Guilford, Connecticut, Comprising the Present Towns of Guilford and Madison* (1897).

Stiles, H. R., *History and Genealogies of Ancient Windsor 1635–1891* (2 vols., 1891–1892).

White, Alain, *History of the Town of Litchfield, 1720–1920* (1920).

*　　*　　*　　*　　*　　*　　*

Crofut, Florence S. M., *Guide to History and Historic Sites of Connecticut* (2 vols., 1937).

Flagg, C. A., "Reference List of Connecticut Local History," New York State Library, *Bull.*, no. 53 (1900).

Delaware

Conrad, H. C., *History of the State of Delaware* (3 vols., 1908).

Eckman, Jeannette et al., eds., *Delaware: A Guide to the First State* (1955).

Johnson, Amandus, *Swedish Settlements on the Delaware, 1638–1664* (2 vols., 1911).

Reed, H. C. Roy, ed., *Delaware: History of the First State* (3 vols., 1947).

Scharf, J. T., *History of Delaware, 1609–1888* (2 vols., 1888).

———————————

Cooch, F. A., *Little Known History of Newark, Delaware, and Its Environs* (1936).

Eckman, Jeannette, ed., *New Castle on the Delaware* (1950).

History of Wilmington (1894).

Lincoln, A. T., *Wilmington, Delaware, 1609–1937* (1937).

Wooten, Mrs. Bayard, and Anthony Higgins, *New Castle, Delaware 1651–1939* (1939).

*　　*　　*　　*　　*　　*　　*

Munroe, John A., *Delaware: Students' Guide* (1965).

Reed, H. Clay, and Marion B. Reed, *A Bibliography of Delaware through 1960* (1966).

District of Columbia

Brooks, Noah, *Washington in Lincoln's Time* (1895); Herbert Mitgang, ed. (1958).

Bryan, Wilhelmus B., *History of National Capital* (2 vols., 1914–1916).

Green, Constance M., *Washington, 1800–1950* (2 vols., 1962–1963).

Leech, Margaret, *Reveille in Washington, 1860–1865* (1941).

Tindall, William, *Standard History of the City of Washington* (1914).

Webb, W. B., and John Wooldridge, *Centennial History of the City of Washington, D.C.* (1892).

Whyte, James H., *Uncivil War: Washington During Reconstruction, 1865–1878* (1958).

Florida

Bennett, Charles E., *Settlement of Florida* (1968).

Brevard, C. M., and J. A. Robertson, *A History of Florida, from the Treaty of 1763 to Our Own Times* (2 vols., 1924).

Cash, W. T., and Dorothy Dodd, *Florida Becomes a State* (1945).
Chambers, Henry E., *West Florida* (1898).
Cox, Isaac J., *West Florida Controversy* (1918).
Dovell, Junius E., *Florida* (4 vols., 1952).
Gaffarel, Paul, *Histoire de la Floride française* (1875).
Hanna, Alfred J., and Kathryn A. Hanna, *Florida's Golden Sands* (1950).
Hanna, Kathryn A., *Florida, Land of Change* (1948).
Martin, S. W., *Florida during the Territorial Days* (1944).
Patrick, Rembert W., and Allen Morris, *Florida under Five Flags* (4th ed., 1967).
Thompson, Arthur W., *Jacksonian Democracy on the Florida Frontier* (1961).
Williams, John L., *The Territory of Florida* (1837); Herbert J. Doherty, ed. (1962).

Browne, Jefferson B., *Key West* (1912).
Cohen, Isidor, *Historical Sketches and Sidelights of Miami, Florida* (1925).
Davis, Thomas F., *History of Jacksonville* (1925).
Dewhurst, W. W., *History of Saint Augustine, Florida* (1881).
McDuffee, Lillie B., *Lures of Manatee* (1961).
Paisley, Clifton, *From Cotton to Quail: Agricultural Chronicle of Leon County, Florida, 1860–1967* (1968).
Panagopoulos, E. P., *New Smyrna: Eighteenth Century Greek Odyssey* (1966).
Rawlings, Marjorie K., *Cross Creek* (1942).
Tebeau, Charlton W., *Florida's Last Frontier: Collier County* (1966).
Weidling, Philip J., and August Burghard, *Checkered Sunshine: Fort Lauderdale, 1793–1955.*

Georgia

Abbott, William W., *Royal Governors of Georgia* (1959).
Bonner, James C., *History of Georgia Agriculture, 1732–1860* (1964).
——— and L. E. Roberts, *Georgia History and Government* (1940).
Coulter, E. Merton, *Georgia* (1947).
Griffin, Louis T., and John E. Talmadge, *Georgia Journalism, 1763–1950* (1951).
Heath, Milton S., *Constructive Liberalism: Role of State in Economic Development of Georgia to 1860* (1954).
Johnson, Amanda, *Georgia, as Colony and State* (1938).
Jones, Charles C., *History of Georgia* (2 vols., 1883).
King, Spencer B., Jr., *Georgia Voices: Documentary History to 1872* (1966).
Montgomery, Horace, *Cracker Parties* (1950).
——— ed., *Georgians in Profile: Essays in Honor of Ellis Merton Coulter* (1958).
Murray, Paul, *Whig Party in Georgia, 1825–1853* (1948).
Range, Willard, *Century of Agriculture in Georgia, 1850–1950* (1954).
Saye, Albert B., *Constitutional History of Georgia, 1732–1945* (1948).
——— *New Viewpoints in Georgia History* (1943).
Ware, Ethel K., *Constitutional History of Georgia* (1947).

Battey, G. M., *A History of Rome and Floyd County, 1540–1922* (1922).
Cain, Andrew W., *History of Lumpkin County, 1832–1932* (1932).
Cooper, Walter G., *Official History of Fulton County* (1934).
Coulter, E. Merton, *Old Petersburg and Broad River Valley* (1965).
Elrod, Frary, *Historical Notes on Jackson County* (1967).
Garrett, Franklin M., *Atlanta and Environs* (1954).
Harris, Virginia S., *History of Pulaski and Blackley County* (1957).
Hays, Louise F., *History of Macon County Georgia* (1933).
Huxford, Folks, *The History of Brooks County, Georgia* (1948).
Rice, Theddeus B., and Carolyn Williams, *History of Greene County, Georgia* (1961).
Ritchie, Andrew J., *Sketches of Rabun County History* (1948).
Rogers, William, *Ante-Bellum Thomas County, 1825–1861* (1963).

—— *Thomas County during the Civil War* (1964).
Sams, Anita B., *Wayfarers in Walton* [County] (1967).
Temple, S. B. G., *The First Hundred Years: A Short History of Cobb County in Georgia* (1935).

*   *   *   *   *   *   *

Bonner, James C., *Georgia: Students' Guide* (1965).
Bonner, John W., Jr., *Bibliography of Georgia Authors, 1949–1965* (1966).
Flanders, Bertrand H., *Early Georgia Magazines* (1949).
Rowland, Arthur R., *Bibliography of Writings on Georgia History* (1966).

Hawaii

Alexander, M. C., *Story of Hawaii* (1912).
Allen, Gwenfread E., *Hawaii's War Years, 1941–1945* (1950).
Anthony, Joseph G., *Hawaii under Army Rule* (1955).
Bradley, Harold W., *American Frontier in Hawaii, 1789–1843* (1942).
Burrows, Edwin G., *Hawaiian Americans: Account of Mingling of Japanese, Chinese, Polynesian and American Cultures* (1947).
Conroy, Francis H., *Japanese Frontier in Hawaii, 1868–1898* (1953).
Daws, Gavan, *Shoal of Time: Hawaiian Islands* (1968).
Day, A. Grove, *Hawaii and Its People* (1955).
Johannessen, Edward, *Hawaiian Labor Movement* (1956).
Judd, Gerrit Parmele, *Hawaii: An Informal History* (1961).
Kuykendall, Ralph S. *Hawaiian Kingdom* (3 vols., 1938–1967).
—— and Arthur G. Day, *Hawaii* (rev. ed., 1961).
Lind, Andrew W., *Hawaii's People* (1967).
Morgan, Theodore, *Hawaii, Century of Economic Change, 1778–1876* (1948).
Russ, William A., Jr., *Hawaiian Revolution, 1893–94* (1959).
Schmitt, Robert C., *Demographic Statistics of Hawaii, 1778–1965* (1968).
Smith, Bradford, *Americans from Japan* (1948).
—— *Yankees in Paradise: New England Impact on Hawaii* (1956).
Stevens, S. K., *American Expansion in Hawaii, 1842–1898* (1945).
Tate, Merze, *Hawaii: Reciprocity or Annexation* (1968).

*   *   *   *   *   *   *

Judd, Gerrit P., *Hawaii: Students' Guide* (1966).
Murdoch, Clare G., and Masae Gotanda, *Basic Hawaiiana* (1969).
U. S. Library of Congress. Division of Bibliography, *The Hawaiian Islands: A Bibliographical List* (1931).

Idaho

Barber, Floyd R., and Dan W. Martin, *Idaho in the Pacific Northwest* (1956).
Beal, M. D., *History of Idaho* (1959).
—— *A History of Southeastern Idaho* (1942).
Donaldson, Thomas, *Idaho of Yesterday* (1941).
Elsensohn, M. A., *Pioneer Days in Idaho County* (1947).
Fisher, Vardis, ed., *Idaho Encyclopedia* (1938).
Hailey, John, *History of Idaho* (1910).
Hawley, J. H., *History of Idaho, The Gem of the Mountains* (4 vols., 1920).
Livingston-Little, Dallas E., *Economic History of North Idaho* (1965).

———————————

Bancroft, Hubert H., *History of Washington, Idaho, and Montana* (1890).
Bird, A. L., *Boise, the Peace Valley* (1934).
Brown, J. B., *Fort Hall, on the Oregon Trail* (1932).
McConnell, W. J., *Early History of Idaho* (1913).

*   *   *   *   *   *   *

Wells, Merle, *Idaho: Students' Guide to Localized History* (1965).

Illinois

Alvord, Clarence W., ed., *Centennial History of Illinois* (5 vols., 1918–1920).
—— *Illinois Country, 1673–1818* (1920).
Angle, Paul M., *Prairie State: Impressions of Illinois 1673–1967 by Travelers* (1968).
—— *Bloody Williamson: American Lawlessness* (1952).
—— and R. L. Beyer, *Handbook of Illinois History* (1943).
Boggess, A. C., *Settlement of Illinois, 1778–1830* (1908).
Bogue, Allan G., *From Prairie to Corn Belt: Farming on Illinois and Iowa Prairies in the Nineteenth Century* (1963).
Calkins, Earnest E., *They Broke the Prairie* (1937).
Monaghan, Jay, *This is Illinois: Pictorial History* (1949).
Pease, Theodore C., *The Frontier State, 1818–1848* (1918).
—— *Story of Illinois* (1925); 3d ed. rev. by Marguerita J. Pease (1965).
Pooley, W. V., *Settlement of Illinois* (1908).
Steiner, Gilbert Y., and Samuel K. Gove, *Legislative Politics in Illinois* (1960).
Tingley, Donald F., ed., *Essays in Illinois History in Honor of Glenn Huron Seymour* (1968).

Andreas, A. T., *History of Chicago* (3 vols., 1885).
Angle, Paul M., *Here I Have Lived* (1950). Springfield.
Boewe, Charles, *Prairie Albion: An English Settlement in Pioneer Illinois* (1962).
Burtschi, Mary, *Vandalia: Capital of Lincoln's Land* (1963).
Lewis, Lloyd, and H. J. Smith, *Chicago* (1929).
Pierce, Bessie L., *As Others See Chicago: Impressions of Visitors, 1673–1933* (1933).
—— *History of Chicago* (3 vols., 1937–1957).
Spencer, J. W., and J. M. D. Burrows, *The Early Days of Rock Island and Davenport* (1942).
Wagenknecht, Edward C., *Chicago* (1964).

*   *   *   *   *   *   *

Angle, Paul M., *Suggested Readings in Illinois History with Selected List of Historical Fiction* (1935).
Foster, Olive S., *Illinois: Students' Guide* (1968).
Kaige, Richard H., and Evelyn L. Vaughan, comps., "Illinois County Histories," *Illinois Libraries,* 50 (1968), 694.
Shipton, Dorothy, "Illinois: Bibliography," *Ill. State Univ. Jour.,* 31 (1968), 15.

Indiana

Barnhart, John D., and Donald Carmony, *Indiana from Frontier to Industrial Commonwealth* (4 vols., 1954).
Cockrum, W. M., *Pioneer History of Indiana* (1907).
Dillon, J. B., *A History of Indiana from Its Earliest Exploration by Europeans to the Close of the Territorial Government in 1816* (1859).
Dunn, J. P., *Indiana and Indianans* (5 vols., 1919).
Esarey, Logan, *A History of Indiana* (2 vols., 1915–1918).
—— *Indiana Home* (1953).
Levering, J. H., *Historic Indiana* (1910).
Phillips, Clifton J., *Indiana in Transition: Emergence of Industrial Commonwealth, 1880–1920* (1968).

Thornbrough, Gayle, and Dorothy Riker, comps., *Readings in Indiana History* (1956).
Wilson, William E., *Indiana* (1966).

Brice, W. A., *History of Fort Wayne* (1868).
Dunn, Jacob P., *Greater Indianapolis* (2 vols., 1910).
Wilson, William E., *Angel and Serpent: New Harmony* (1964).

*   *   *   *   *   *   *

Esarey, Logan, "Indiana Local History: A Guide," Ind. Univ. Extension Division, *Bull.*, 1, no. 7 (1916).

Iowa

Bogue, Allan G., *From Prairie to Corn Belt: Farming on Illinois and Iowa Prairies in the Nineteenth Century* (1963).
Brigham, Johnson, *Iowa: History and Its Foremost Citizens* (3 vols., 1916).
Briggs, J. E., *Iowa, Old and New* (1939).
Cole, Cyrenus, *A History of the People of Iowa* (1921).
——— *Iowa through the Years* (1940).
Gue, B. F., *History of Iowa from the Earliest Times* (4 vols., [1903]).
Hake, Herbert V., *Iowa Inside Out* (1967).
Harlan, Edgar Rubey, *A Narrative History of the People of Iowa* (4 vols., 1931).
Lokken, Roscoe L., *Iowa Public Land Disposal* (1942).
McFarland, Julian E., *The Pioneer Era on the Iowa Prairies* (1970).
Parker, G. F., *Iowa Pioneer Foundations* (2 vols., 1940).
Petersen, William J., *Iowa History Reference Guide* (1952).
Richman, Irving, *Ioway to Iowa* (1931).
Sabin, Henry, and E. L. Sabin, *The Making of Iowa* (1900).
Salter, William, *Iowa, the First Free State in the Louisiana Purchase* (1905).
Shambaugh, B. F., *The Constitutions of Iowa* (1934).
Todd, John, *Early Settlement and Growth of Western Iowa* (1906).

Brigham, Johnson, *Des Moines Together with the History of Polk County, Iowa* (3 vols., 1911).
Moe, E. W., and C. C. Taylor, *Irwin, Iowa* (1942).
Nichols, I. A., *Pioneer Days in Iowa Falls* (1944).
——— *History of Iowa Falls, 1900–1950* (1956).
Parker, Leonard F., *History of Poweshiek County, Iowa* (2 vols., 1911).
Reed, Benjamin F., *History of Kossuth County, Iowa* (2 vols., 1913).
Shambaugh, Bertha M., *Amana That Was and Amana That Is* (1932).
White, Edward S., *Past and Present of Shelby County, Iowa* (1915).
Yambura, Barbara S., and Eunice W. Bodine, *Change and Parting: Amana* (1960).

*   *   *   *   *   *   *

Hurst, Frances, *Teacher's Curriculum Guide to Teaching Iowa History* (1969).

Kansas

Baughman, Robert W., *Kansas in Maps* (1961).
Blackmar, F. W., ed., *Kansas: A Cyclopedia of State History . . .* (2 vols., 1912).
Bright, John D., ed. *Kansas: The First Century* (4 vols., 1956).
Connelley, W. E., *History of Kansas* (5 vols., 1928).
Dykstra, Robert R., *Cattle Towns* (1968).

Gates, Paul W., *Fifty Million Acres: Kansas Land Policy, 1854–1890* (1954).
Kansas, University of, *Territorial Kansas: Studies Commemorating the Centennial* (1954).
Mechem, Kirke, and Jennie Small Owen, eds., *The Annals of Kansas, 1886–1925* (2 vols., 1954–1956).
Miller, Nyle H. et al., *Kansas: A Pictorial History* (1961).
——— *Kansas in Newspapers* (1963).
Zornow, William F., *Kansas: Jayhawk State* (1957).

———

Bell, E. H., *Sublette, Kansas* (1942).
Brown, Andrew T., *Frontier Community: Kansas City to 1870* (1963).
Giles, F. W., *Thirty Years in Topeka: A Historical Sketch* (1886).
Harrington, G. W., *Annals of Brown County, Kansas* (1903).
Jones, Horace, *Up From the Sod* (1968). Rice County, Kansas.
Long, Richard M., *Wichita Century* (1970).
Lowther, C. C., *Dodge City, Kansas* (1940).
Millbrook, Minnie Dubbs, *Ness County, Kansas* (1955).
Slagg, Winifred S., *Riley County, Kansas* (1968).

*   *   *   *   *   *   *

Anderson, Lorene, and Alan W. Farley, comps., "Bibliography of Town and County Histories of Kansas," *Kans. Hist. Quar.*, 24 (1955), 513.
Miller, Nyle H., *Kansas: Students' Guide* (1965).

Kentucky

Clark, Thomas D., *History of Kentucky* (1960).
——— *Kentucky: Land of Contrast* (1968).
Collins, Lewis, *Collins' Historical Sketches of Kentucky* (1966).
Connelley, William E., and E. Merton Coulter, *History of Kentucky* (5 vols., 1922).
Cotterill, Robert S., *History of Pioneer Kentucky* (1917).
Davenport, F. G., *Ante-bellum Kentucky* (1943).
McElroy, R. M., *Kentucky in the Nation's History* (1909).
Moore, Arthur K., *Frontier Mind: Kentucky* (1957).
Smith, Z. F., *History of Kentucky* (1886).
Sonne, Niels H., *Liberal Kentucky, 1780–1828* (1968).
Wallis, F. A., and Hambleton Tapp, *A Sesqui-Centennial History of Kentucky* (1945).

———

Johnson, A. P., *A Century of Wayne County, Kentucky, 1800–1900* (1939).
McMeekin, I. M., *Louisville, the Gateway City* (1946).
Ranck, G. W., *History of Lexington, Kentucky* (1872).
Rothert, O. A., *A History of Muhlenberg County* (1913).
Willis, G. L., *History of Shelby County, Kentucky* (1929).

*   *   *   *   *   *   *

Coleman, J. W., Jr., *A Bibliography of Kentucky History* (1949).
Harrison, Annie, comp., *Kentucky History: Secondary Sources for Secondary Schools* (1966).

Louisiana

Arsenault, Bona, *History of Acadians* (1966).
Chambers, Henry E., *History of Louisiana* (3 vols., 1925).

Davis, Edwin A., *Louisiana, a Narrative History* (3d ed., 1970).
—— *Story of Louisiana* (4 vols., 1960–1963).
Dufour, Charles L., *Ten Flags in the Wind: Louisiana* (1967).
Fortier, Alcée, *Louisiana* (3 vols., 1909).
Gayarré, Charles, *History of Louisiana* (rev. ed., 4 vols., 1903).
Guénin, Eugène, *La Louisiane* (1904).
Hair, William I., *Bourbonism and Agrarian Protest: Louisiana Politics, 1877–1900* (1969).
Hardin, J. Fair, *Northwestern Louisiana: Watershed of Red River, 1714–1937* (3 vols., 1937).
Heinrich, Pierre, *La Louisiane sous la Compagnie des Indes, 1717–1732* (1908).
Kane, Harnett, *Louisiana Hayride* (1941).
McGinty, Garnie W., *History of Louisiana* (3d ed., 1951).
Robertson, J. A., ed., *Louisiana under the Rule of Spain, France and the United States, 1785–1807* (2 vols., 1911). Contemporary accounts by Paul Alliot and others.
Rodriguez, Vicente, *Primeros años de dominación española en la Luisiana* (1942).
Sindler, Allan P., *Huey Long's Louisiana, 1920–1952* (1956).
Terrage, Marc de Villiers du, *Les dernières années de la Louisiane française* (1904).
Williamson, Frederick W., and Lillian H. Williamson, *Northeast Louisiana, 1840–1875* (1939).

Carter, Hodding et al., eds., *Past as Prelude: New Orleans, 1718–1968* (1968).
Clark, John G., *New Orleans 1718–1812: An Economic History* (1970).
Kendall, John S., *History of New Orleans* (3 vols., 1922).
King, Grace, *New Orleans: The Place and the People* (1895).
O'Pry, M. G., *Chronicles of Shreveport* (1928).
Rightor, Henry, *Standard History of New Orleans, Louisiana* (1900).
Saxon, Lyle, *Fabulous New Orleans* (1939).

Maine

Abbott, J. S. C., and E. H. Elwell, *History of Maine* (1892).
Hatch, L. C., *Maine: A History* (3 vols., 1919).
Jewett, Fred E., *Financial History of Maine* (1937).
Rowe, W. H., *The Maritime History of Maine* (1948).
Smith, Marion J., *History of Maine, 1497–1820* (1949).
Sullivan, James, *History of the District of Maine* (1795).
Sylvester, H. M., *Maine Pioneer Settlements* (1909).
Williamson, W. D., *History of the State of Maine* (2 vols., 1832).

Allen, C. E., *History of Dresden, Maine* (1931).
Chase, F. S., *Wiscasset in Pownalborough* (1941).
Coffin, R. P. T., *Kennebec: Cradle of Americans* (1937).
Eaton, Cyrus, *Annals of Town of Warren, with the Early History of St. George's, Broad Bay and Neighboring Settlements* (2nd ed., 1877).
—— *History of Thomaston, Rockland, and South Thomaston, Maine from 1605* (2 vols., 1865).
Greene, F. B., *History of Boothbay, Southport and Boothbay Harbor, Maine* (1906).
Hale, R. W., *The Story of Bar Harbor* (1949).
Hanson, J. W., *History of Old Towns: Norridgewock and Canaan* (1849).
Hatch, W. C., *A History of the Town of Industry: Franklin County, Maine* (1893).
Locke, John L., *Sketches of History of Camden* (1859).
North, James W., *History of Augusta from Earliest Settlement to Present* (1870).
Owen, Henry W., *The Edward Clarence Plummer History of Bath, Maine* (1936).
—— *History of Bath* (1936).

Remich, Daniel, *History of Kennbunk to 1890* (1911).
Rowe, W. H., *Ancient North Yarmouth and Yarmouth, Maine* (1937).
Stahl, Jasper J., *History of Old Broad Bay and Waldoboro* (2 vols., 1956).
Wheeler, George A., *History of Castine, Penobscot and Brooksville, Maine* (1875).
—— and Henry W. Wheeler, *History of Brunswick, Topsham, and Harpswell, Maine* (1878).
Williamson, Joseph, and Alfred Johnson, *History of the City of Belfast* (2 vols., 1913).
Willis, William, *The History of Portland, from 1632 to 1864* (1865).

*   *   *   *   *   *   *

Hall, D. B., "Reference List on Maine Local History," New York State Library, *Bull.,* no. 63 (1910).
Huston, A. J., *A Check List of Maine Local Histories* (1915).

Maryland

Andrews, M. P., *The Founding of Maryland* (1933).
—— *History of Maryland: Province and State* (1929).
Baer, Elizabeth, *Seventeenth Century Maryland* (1949).
Cunz, Dieter, *The Maryland Germans* (1948).
Mereness, N. D., *Maryland as a Proprietary Province* (1901).
Richardson, H. D., *Side-lights on Maryland History* (2 vols., 1903).
Riley, Elihu S., *History of General Assembly of Maryland, 1635–1904* (1905).
Scharf, J. T., *History of Maryland from the Earliest Period to the Present Day* (3 vols., 1879).
Steiner, B. C., *Maryland during the English Civil Wars* (2 vols., 1906–1907).
—— *Maryland under the Commonwealth 1649–1658* (1911).

Beirne, Francis F., *Baltimore: Picture History 1858–1958* (1957).
Hirschfeld, Charles, *Baltimore, 1870–1900: Studies in Social History* (1941).
Johnston, George, *History of Cecil County, Maryland* (1881).
Jones, Elias, *Revised History of Dorchester County, Maryland* (1925).
Klapthor, Margaret B., and Paul D. Brown, *History of Charles County, Maryland* (1958).
Owens, Hamilton, *Baltimore on the Chesapeake* (1941).
Scharf, J. T., *Chronicles of Baltimore* (1874).
Semmes, Raphael, ed., *Baltimore as Seen by Visitors, 1783–1860* (1953).
Tilghman, Oswald, *History of Talbot County, Maryland, 1661–1861* (2 vols., 1915).

*   *   *   *   *   *   *

Manakee, Harold R., *Maryland: Students' Guide to Localized History* (1968).

Massachusetts

Adams, Brooks, *The Emancipation of Massachusetts* (1887).
Adams, Charles F., *Massachusetts, Its Historians and Its History* (1893).
—— *Three Episodes of Massachusetts History* (2 vols., 1892).
Barber, J. W., *Massachusetts Towns: An 1840 View,* Ivan Sandrof, ed. (1963).
Bradford, William, *Of Plymouth Plantation, 1620–1647,* W. C. Ford, ed. (2 vols., 1912); Samuel E. Morison, ed. (1952).
Chickering, Jesse, *Statistical View of Population of Massachusetts, 1765 to 1840* (1946).
Hart, Albert B., *Commonwealth History of Massachusetts* (5 vols., 1927–1930).
Holland, Josiah G., *History of Western Massachusetts* (2 vols., 1855).

Hutchinson, Thomas, *The History of the Colony and Province of Massachusetts Bay* (1760–1768). New ed. (3 vols., 1936).

Litt, Edgar, *Political Cultures of Massachusetts* (1965).

Marsh, D. L., and W. H. Clark, *The Story of Massachusetts* (4 vols., 1938).

Minot, George R., *Continuation of History of the Province of Massachusetts Bay, from the Year 1748 to 1765* (2 vols., 1798–1803).

Morison, Samuel E., *Maritime History of Massachusetts 1783–1860* (1921).

Sly, J. F., *Town Government in Massachusetts, 1620–1930* (1930).

Winthrop, John, *History of New England 1630–1649,* James Savage, ed. (2 vols., 1853). Identical with his *Journal,* J. K. Hosmer, ed. (2 vols., 1908).

Adams, Charles F., *History of Braintree, the North Precinct of Braintree, and the Town of Quincy* (1891).

Banks, C. E., *The History of Martha's Vineyard* (3 vols., 1911–1925).

Birdsall, Richard D., *Berkshire County* (1959).

Bolton, Charles K., *Brookline* (1897).

Boston Looks Seaward (1941).

Brown, Richard D., *Urbanization in Springfield Massachusetts, 1790–1830* (1962).

Chamberlain, Mellen, *A Documentary History of Chelsea* (2 vols., 1908).

Chase, George W., *History of Haverhill* (1861).

Clarke, George K., *History of Needham, Massachusetts, 1711–1911* (1912).

Cook, Edward M., Jr., "Social Behavior and Changing Values in Dedham, Massachusetts, 1700 to 1775," *WMQ,* 3 ser., 27 (1970), 546.

Crawford, Mary C., *Romantic Days in Old Boston* (1910).

Currier, J. J., *History of Newbury, Massachusetts* (1902).

—— *History of Newburyport, Massachusetts* (2 vols., 1909).

Curtis, John W., *History of Town of Brookline, Massachusetts* (1933).

Daggett, John, *Sketch of the History of Attleborough* (1834).

Darling, A. B., *Political Changes in Massachusetts* (1925).

Davis, William T., *Ancient Landmarks of Plymouth* (1883).

Demos, John, *Little Commonwealth: Family Life in Plymouth Colony* (1970).

Drake, Samuel G., *History of Middlesex County* (2 vols., 1880).

Earl, Henry H., *History of Fall River, 1656 to 1857* (1877).

Felt, Joseph B., *History of Ipswich, Essex, and Hamilton* (1834).

Freeman, Frederick, *History of Cape Cod* (2 vols., 1860–1862).

Frisch, Michael H., *Town into City: Springfield Massachusetts, and the Meaning of Community, 1840–1880* (1972).

Green, Constance M., *Holyoke* (1933).

Green, Mason A., *Springfield, 1636–1886* (1888).

Green, Samuel A., *Groton Historical Series* (4 vols., 1887–1899).

Greven, Philip J., Jr., *Four Generations: Population, Land, and Family in Colonial Andover, Massachusetts* (1970).

Handlin, Oscar, *Boston's Immigrants* (1941).

Herlihy, E. M. et al., *Fifty Years of Boston* (1932).

History of the Town of Hingham (3 vols., 1893).

Hudson, Alfred S., *History of Concord* (1904).

Hudson, Charles, *History of the Town of Lexington* (2 vols., 1913).

Hunnewell, James F., *Century of Town Life: Charlestown, Massachusetts, 1775–1887* (2 vols., 1888).

Huntoon, Daniel T. V., *History of Town of Canton* (1893).

Jewett, Amos E., and Emily M. A. Jewett, *Rowley, Massachusetts, 1639–1850* (1946).

Judd, Sylvester, *History of Hadley* (1963); George Sheldon, ed. (1905).

Kellogg, Lucy C., *History of Greenfield, 1900–1929* (3 vols., 1931).

Labaree, Benjamin W., *Patriots and Partisans: Merchants of Newburyport, 1764–1815* (1962).

Lane, Roger, *Policing the City: Boston 1822–1885* (1967).

Langdon, George D., Jr., *Pilgrim Colony* (1966).

Lincoln, William, *History of Worcester to September 1836* (2nd ed., 1862).

Lockridge, Kenneth A., *New England Town, First Hundred Years: Dedham, Massachusetts, 1636–1736* (1970).

Lockwood, John H., *Westfield* (2 vols., 1922).
—— et al., *Western Massachusetts: 1636–1925* (4 vols., 1926).
Lord, Robert H., et al., *History of Archdiocese of Boston* (3 vols., 1944).
Merrill, Joseph, *History of Amesbury and Merrimac* (1880).
Paige, L. R., *History of Cambridge, 1630–1877* (1877).
Parsons, Herbert C., *Puritan Outpost* (1937). Northfield.
Partridge, George F., *History of Bellingham, Massachusetts, 1719–1919* (1919).
Perley, Sidney, *The History of Salem* (2 vols., 1924–1926).
Phillips, James D., *Salem and the Indies* (1947).
—— *Salem in Seventeenth Century* (1933).
—— *Salem in Eighteenth Century* (1937).
Powell, Sumner C., *Puritan Village* (1963). Sudbury.
Rand, Christopher, *Cambridge U.S.A.* (1964).
Rowe, Henry K., *Tercentenary History of Newton, 1630–1930* (1930).
Rutman, Darrett, *Winthrop's Boston* (1965).
Scudder, Townsend, *Concord* (1947).
Shattuck, Lemuel, *History of Town of Concord to 1832* (1835).
Sheldon, George, *History of Deerfield* (2 vols., 1895–1896).
Smith, Edward C., and P. M. Smith, *History of Town of Middlefield, Massachusetts* (1924).
Smith, Frank, *A History of Dedham, Massachusetts* (1936).
Smith, Joseph E. A., *History of Pittsfield, 1734–1876* (1869–1876).
Stone, Edward M., *History of Beverly, 1630 to 1842* (1843).
Taylor, Charles J., *History of Great Barrington* (1928).
Thernstrom, Stephan, *Poverty and Progress: Social Mobility in a Nineteenth Century City* (1964). Newburyport.
Thompson, F. M., *History of Greenfield* (3 vols., 1904).
Warden, Gerald B., *Boston, 1689–1776* (1970).
Waters, Thomas F., *Ipswich in Massachusetts Bay Colony* (2 vols., 1905–1917).
Weston, Thomas, *History of the Town of Middleboro, Massachusetts* (1906).
Whitehill, Walter M., *Boston: A Topographical History* (2nd ed., 1968).
Winsor, Justin, *Memorial History of Boston, 1630–1880* (4 vols., 1880–1881).
Wood, David H., *Lenox: Massachusetts Shire Town* (1969).

*   *   *   *   *   *   *

Boston Public Library. Tercentenary Celebration, 1630–1930, *The Massachusetts Bay Colony and Boston: A Selected List of Works* (1930).
Colburn, Jeremiah, *Bibliography of the Local History of Massachusetts* (1871).
Flagg, Charles A., *Guide to Massachusetts Local History* (1907).

Michigan

Bald, F. Clever, *Michigan in Four Centuries* (rev. ed., 1961).
Campbell, J. V., *Outlines of the Political History of Michigan* (1876).
Cooley, T. M., *Michigan* (1905).
Dunbar, Willis F., *Michigan* (1965).
Fuller, G. N., *Economic and Social Beginnings of Michigan* (1916).
—— *Michigan: A Centennial History of the State and Its People* (2 vols., 1939).
Goodrich, Calvin, *The First Michigan Frontier* (1940).
Russell, N. V., *The British Regime in Michigan and the Old Northwest 1760–1796* (1939).
Sarasohn, Stephen B., and Vera H. Sarasohn, *Political Party Patterns in Michigan* (1957).
Streeter, F. B., *Political Parties in Michigan, 1837–1860* (1918).

———————————

Burroughs, Raymond D., *Peninsular Country* (1965).
Crow, Carl, *City of Flint* (1945).
Dain, Floyd R., *Every House a Frontier* (1956). Detroit after 1815.
Darling, Birt, *City of the Forest: Lansing* (1950).

Dunbar, Willis F., *Kalamazoo and How It Grew* (1959).
Glazer, Sidney, *Detroit* (1966).
Goss, Dwight, *History of Grand Rapids and Its Industry* (2 vols., 1906).
Gross, Stuart D., *Indians, Jacks, and Pines: Saginaw* (1962).
Hesslink, George K., *Black Neighbors: Negroes in Northern Rural Community* (1968).
Lydens, Z. Z., *The Story of Grand Rapids* (1966).
Reber, J. Benjamin, *History of St. Joseph* (1924).
Stark, George, *City of Destiny* (1943). Detroit.
Stephenson, O. W., *Ann Arbor* (1927).
White, Arthur S., *Old Grand Rapids* (1925).
Williams, Oliver P., and Charles R. Adrian, *Four Cities: Comparative Policy Making* (1963).
Wood, Arthur, *Hamtramck* (1955).
Woodford, Frank B., and Arthur M., *All Our Yesterdays: A History of Detroit* (1969).

*   *   *   *   *   *   *

Greenly, Albert H., *Selective Bibliography of Important Books, Pamphlets, and Broadsides Relating to Michigan History* (1958).
Streeter, F. B., *Michigan Bibliography* (2 vols., 1921).

Minnesota

Blegen, Theodore C., *Minnesota* (1963).
Brings, L. M., *Minnesota Heritage: A Panoramic Narrative* (1960).
Folwell, William W., *History of Minnesota* (4 vols., 1921–1930).
Gilman, R. R., and J. D. Holmquist, eds., *Minnesota History: Selections* (1965).
Gluek, Alvin C., Jr., *Minnesota and Canadian Northwest* (1965).
Heilbron, Bertha L., *Thirty-second State: Pictorial History of Minnesota* (2nd ed., 1966).
Hubbard, L. F., et al., *Minnesota in Three Centuries, 1655–1908* (4 vols., 1908).
Jones, Evan, *Citadel in the Wilderness: Fort Snelling and Old Northwest Frontier* (1966).
Kunz, V. B., *Muskets to Missiles: Military History of Minnesota* (1958).
Le Sueur, Meridel, *North Star Country* (1945).
Nelson, Lowry, *Minnesota Community* (1960).
Nute, Grace L., *Rainy River Country* (1950).
────── *Voyageur's Highway: Minnesota's Border Lake Land* (1941).

Atwater, Isaac, *History of the City of Minneapolis* (2 vols., 1893).
Castle, H. A., *History of St. Paul and Vicinity* (3 vols., 1912).
Easton, A. B., *History of the Saint Croix Valley* (2 vols., 1909).
Kane, Lucille M., *Waterfall That Built a City: Falls of St. Anthony in Minneapolis* (1966).
Walker, Charles R., *American City* (1937). Minneapolis.

*   *   *   *   *   *   *

Blegen, Theodore C., and Theodore L. Nydahl, *Minnesota History: A Guide to Reading* (1960).
Fridley, Russell W., *Minnesota: Student's Guide to Localized History* (1966).

Mississippi

Bettersworth, John K., *Mississippi* (1959).
Carter, Hodding, *Lower Mississippi* (1942).
Claiborne, J. F. H., *Mississippi as a Province, Territory, and State* (1880).

Kane, Harnett T., *Natchez on the Mississippi* (1947).
Kirwan, Albert D., *Revolt of the Rednecks* (1951).
Lowry, Robert, and W. H. McCardle, *History of Mississippi* (1891).
Rowland, Dunbar, *Encyclopedia of Mississippi History* (1907).
—— *History of Mississippi, the Heart of the South* (2 vols., 1925).
Silver, James W., *Mississippi: Closed Society* (rev. ed., 1966).

Bailey, Earl L., *Economic Patterns in Pontotoc County* (1954).
—— *A Look at Natchez: Its Economic Resources* (1953).
Bryan, Gordon K., *Mississippi County: An Historical Sketch* (1952).
Lipscomb, W. L., *A History of Columbus, Mississippi, during the Nineteenth Century* (1909).
McCain, W. D., *Story of Jackson* (1953).
Smith, Frank Ellis, *Yazoo River* (1954).

＊   ＊   ＊   ＊   ＊   ＊   ＊

Moore, John J., *Mississippi: Students' Guide to Localized History* (1968).
Owen, T. M., "Bibliography of Mississippi," Am. Hist. Assoc., *Report,* I (1899), 633.

Missouri

Conard, H. L., *Encyclopedia of the History of Missouri* (6 vols., 1901).
Culmer, F. A., *A New History of Missouri* (1938).
Ellis, James F., *The Influence of Environment on the Settlement of Missouri* (1929).
Houck, Louis, *History of Missouri, from the Earliest Explorations . . . until the Admission of the State into the Union* (3 vols., 1908).
—— *Spanish Regime in Missouri.*
McReynolds, Edwin C., *Missouri* (1962).
March, David D., *History of Missouri* (4 vols., 1967).
Meyer, Duane G., *Heritage of Missouri* (1963).
Nasatir, Abraham P., ed., *Before Lewis and Clark: Documents Illustrating the History of the Missouri, 1785–1804* (2 vols., 1952).
Shoemaker, Floyd C., *Missouri's Struggle for Statehood, 1804–1821* (1916).
Stevens, W. B., *Centennial History of Missouri: One Hundred Years in the Union, 1820–1921* (6 vols., 1921).
Violette, Eugene M., and Forrest Wolverton Jr., *History of Missouri* (rev. ed., 1955).

Brown, A. Theodore, *Frontier Community: Kansas City to 1870* (1963).
—— *Politics of Reform: Kansas City's Municipal Government, 1925–1950* (1958).
Ford, James Everett, *A History of Jefferson City and of Cole County* (1938).
Glaab, Charles N., *Kansas City and the Railroads* (1962).
McDermott, John F., ed., *Early Histories of St. Louis* (1952).
Scharf, J. T., *History of Saint Louis, City and County, from the Earliest Periods to the Present Day* (2 vols., 1883).
Stevens, Walter B., *St. Louis, 1764–1909* (3 vols., 1909).
Whitney, C. W., *Kansas City, Missouri: Its History and Its People 1808–1908* (3 vols., 1908).

Montana

Abbott, Newton C., *Montana in the Making* (10th ed., 1951).
Bancroft, Hubert H., *Washington, Idaho and Montana* (1890).
Burlingame, Merrill G., and K. Ross Toole, *History of Montana* (3 vols., 1957).

Burlingame, Merrill G., *The Montana Frontier* (1942).
Connolly, C. P., *The Devil Learns to Vote: The Story of Montana* (1938).
Coon, S. J., "Gold Camps and Development of Western Montana," *Jour. Pol. Econ.*, 38 (1930), 580.
Gilbert, Frank T., *Resources, Business, and Business Men of Montana* (1888).
Glasscock, C. B., *The War of the Copper Kings* [1935].
Hamilton, James M., *From Wilderness to Statehood: Montana, 1805–1900,* Merrill G. Burlingame, ed. (1957).
Howard, J. K., *Montana, High, Wide and Handsome* (1943).
Leeson, M. A., *History of Montana, 1739–1885* (1885).
Peters, William S., and Maxine C. Johnson, *Public Lands in Montana: Their History and Current Significance* (1959).
Raymer, R. G., *Montana, the Land of the People* (3 vols., 1930).
Renne, Roland R., *Government and Administration of Montana* (1958).
Sanders, H. F., *A History of Montana* (3 vols., 1913).
Sharp, Paul F., *Whoop-Up Country: The Canadian-American West, 1865–1885* (1955).
Stout, Tom, *Montana: Its Story and Biography* (3 vols., 1921).
Toole, K. Ross, *Montana* (1959).

Nebraska

Andreas, A. T., *History of the State of Nebraska* (1882).
Breckenridge, Adam C., *One House for Two: Nebraska's Unicameral Legislature* (1957).
Faulkner, Virginia, ed., *Roundup: A Nebraska Reader* (1957).
Johnson, John R., *Representative Nebraskans* (1954).
Morton, Julius S., et al., *Illustrated History of Nebraska* (3 vols., 1905–1906).
Nicoll, Bruce M., *Nebraska: Pictorial History* (1967).
Olson, James C., *History of Nebraska* (2nd ed., 1966).
Sheldon, A. E., *Nebraska: Its Land and People* (3 vols., 1931).

Hayes, Arthur B., and S. D. Cox, *History of City of Lincoln* (1889).
Sorenson, Alfred, *The Story of Omaha* (1923).
Stough, D. P., *History of Hamilton and Clay Counties, Nebraska* (2 vols., 1921).

Nevada

Angel, Myron, ed., *History of Nevada* (1881).
Davis, Sam P., *History of Nevada* (2 vols., 1913).
Elliott, Russell R., *Nevada's Twentieth-Century Mining Boom* (1966).
Hulse, James W., *Nevada Adventure* (1965).
Lillard, R. G., *Desert Challenge, an Interpretation of Nevada* (1942).
Mack, E. M., *Nevada: A History of the State from the Earliest Times through the Civil War* (1936).
Ostrander, Gilman M., *Nevada: The Great Rotten Borough, 1859–1964* (1966).

Miller, Max, *Reno* (1941).

* * * * * * *

Elliott, Russell R., and Helen J. Poulton, *Writings on Nevada: Selected Bibliography* (1963).

New Hampshire

Belknap, Jeremy, *History of New Hampshire* (3 vols., 1791–1792; 2nd ed., 1813).
Fry, W. H., *New Hampshire as a Royal Province* (1908).

Guyol, Philip, *Democracy Fights* (1951).
Hill, Ralph N., *Yankee Kingdom: Vermont and New Hampshire* (1960).
Kinney, Charles B., Jr., *Church & State: Separation in New Hampshire, 1630–1900* (1955).
McClintock, J. N., *History of New Hampshire* (1888).
Page, Elwin L., *Judicial Beginnings in New Hampshire, 1640–1700* (1959).
Pillsbury, Hobart, *New Hampshire* (4 vols., 1927).
Sanborn, F. B., *The History of New Hampshire* (1904).
Squires, James D., *Granite State* (4 vols., 1956).
Stackpole, E. S., *History of New Hampshire* (4 vols., [1916]).
Upton, R. F., *Revolutionary New Hampshire* (1936).

Armstrong, John B., *Factory under the Elms: Harrisville, New Hampshire, 1774–1969* (1969).
Bell, C. H., *History of the Town of Exeter* (1888).
Brown, Warren, *History of Hampton Falls, 1640–1900* (2 vols., 1900–1918).
Chase, Benjamin, *History of Old Chester* (1869).
Concord, N. H. City History Commission, *History of Concord, New Hamshire* (1903).
Dow, Joseph, *History of Hampton* (2 vols., 1893).
Eastman, J. R., *History of the Town of Andover, N.H.* (1910).
Frizzell, Martha McD., *History of Charlestown* (1955).
—— *History of Walpole* (2 vols., 1963).
Johnson, Frances Ann, *History of Monroe, 1761–1954* (1955).
Leonard, L. W., and J. L. Seward, *The History of Dublin, New Hampshire* (1920).
Lyford, J. O., *History of the Town of Canterbury* (2 vols., 1912).
Macleish, Kenneth, and Kimball Young, *Landaff, New Hampshire* (1942).
May, Ralph, *Early Portsmouth History* (1926).
Musgrove, R. W., *History of the Town of Bristol* (1904).
Nelson, Walter R., *History of Goshen* (1957).
Rawson, M. N., *New Hampshire Borns a Town* (1942). Alstead.
Runnels, M. T., *History of Sanbornton* (2 vols., 1882).
Saltonstall, W. G., *Ports of Piscataqua* (1941).
Saunderson, H. H., *History of Charlestown* (1876).
Squires, James D., *Mirror to America: History of New London* (1952).
Stearns, Ezra, *History of Rindge, 1736–1874* (1875).
Wallace, W. A., *The History of Canaan, New Hampshire* (1910).

*   *   *   *   *   *   *

Hammond, O. G., *Checklist of New Hampshire Local History* (1925). *Supplements* (1941, 1954).

New Jersey

Bebout, John E., and Ronald J. Grele, *Where Cities Meet: Urbanization of New Jersey* (1964).
Boyd, Julian P., ed., *Fundamental Laws and Constitutions of New Jersey, 1664–1964* (1964).
Burr, Nelson R., *The Anglican Church in New Jersey* (1954).
Cadman, J. W., *The Corporation in New Jersey* (1949).
Chambers, Theodore F., *Early Germans of New Jersey* (1895).
Cowen, David L., *Medicine and Health in New Jersey: History* (1964).
Cunningham, John T., *Garden State: Agriculture in New Jersey* (1955).
—— *Made in New Jersey: Industrial Story* (1954).
—— *New Jersey, America's Main Road* (1966).
Faden, William, *Province of New Jersey* (1777; repr. 1960).
Fee, W. R., *The Transition from Aristocracy to Democracy in New Jersey, 1789–1829* (1933).
Fisher, Edgar J., *New Jersey as Royal Province, 1738 to 1776* (1911).

French, Bruce H., *Banking and Insurance in New Jersey* (1965).
Gerdts, William H., *Painting and Sculpture in New Jersey* (1964).
Gowans, Alan, *Architecture in New Jersey* (1964).
Heston, A. M., *South Jersey, a History, 1664–1924* (4 vols., 1924).
Kemmerer, Donald L., *Path to Freedom, the Struggle for Self-Government in Colonial New Jersey, 1703–1776* (1940).
Kull, Irving S., ed., *New Jersey* (6 vols., 1930–1932).
Lee, Francis B., *New Jersey as a Colony and a State* (4 vols., 1902).
Leiby, James, *Charity and Correction in New Jersey: History of State Welfare Institutions* (1967).
Lockard, Duane, *New Jersey Governor, Study in Political Power* (1964).
McCormick, Richard P., *History of Voting in New Jersey: 1664–1911* (1953).
——— *Experiment in Independence, New Jersey in Critical Period, 1781–1789* (1950).
——— *New Jersey from Colony to State, 1609–1789* (1964).
Maring, Norman H., *Baptists in New Jersey* (1964).
Myers, William S., ed., *Story of New Jersey* (5 vols., 1945).
Pierce, Arthur D., *Iron in the Pines: New Jersey's Ghost Towns and Bog Iron* (1957).
Pomfret, John E., *New Jersey Proprietors and their Lands, 1664–1776* (1964).
——— *Province of East New Jersey, 1609–1702* (1962).
——— *Province of West New Jersey, 1609–1702* (1956).
Schonbach, Morris, *Radicals and Visionaries: History of Dissent in New Jersey* (1964).
Smith, Samuel, *History of the Colony of Nova-Caesaria, or New Jersey* (1765).
Snyder, John P., *Story of New Jersey's Civil Boundaries, 1606–1968* (1968).
Studley, Mariam V., *Historic New Jersey through Visitors' Eyes* (1964).
Wilson, Harold F., et al., *Outline History of New Jersey* (1950).
Tanner, Edwin P., *Province of New Jersey 1664–1738* (1908).
Troy, Leo, *Organized Labor in New Jersey* (1965).
Vecoli, Rudolph J., *People of New Jersey* (1965).
West, Roscoe L., *History of Elementary Education in New Jersey* (1964).
Wilson, Harold F., *The Jersey Shore* (3 vols., 1953).

Atkinson, Joseph, *History of Newark* (1878).
De Cou, George, *Burlington: A Provincial Capital* [1945].
Hageman, J. F., *History of Princeton* (2 vols., 1879).
Hatfield, E. F., *History of Elizabeth* (1868).
Heston, A. M., *Absegami: Annals of Eyren Haven and Atlantic City, 1609–1904* (2 vols., 1904).
A History of the City of Newark, New Jersey (3 vols., 1913).
Mellick, A. D., Jr., *The Story of an Old Farm* (1889).
Monnette, O. E., *First Settlers of Ye Plantations of Piscataway and Woodbridge Olde East New Jersey, 1664–1714* (4 vols., 1930–1935).
Sickler, J. S., *The History of Salem County, New Jersey* (1937).
Walker, Edwin R., et al., *History of Trenton, 1679–1929* (2 vols., 1929).
Westervelt, F. A., *History of Bergen County, New Jersey, 1630–1923* (3 vols., 1923).

*　　*　　*　　*　　*　　*　　*

Burr, Nelson R., *Narrative and Descriptive Bibliography of New Jersey* (1964).
New Jersey Library Association, *New Jersey and the Negro: A Bibliography* (1967).

New Mexico

Bancroft, Hubert H., *Arizona and New Mexico* (1889).
Bandelier, A. F., and F. R. Bandelier, *Historical Documents Relating to New Mexico, Nueva Vizcaya, and Approaches Thereto, to 1773* (3 vols., 1923).

Beck, Warren A., and Ynez D. Haase, *Historical Atlas of New Mexico* (1969).
Beck, Warren A., *New Mexico: History of Four Centuries* (1962).
Fergusson, Erna, *New Mexico, a Pageant of Three Peoples* (1951).
Gregg, Andrew K., *New Mexico in Nineteenth Century: Pictorial Archive* (1968).
Larson, Robert W., *New Mexico's Quest for Statehood, 1846–1912* (1968).
Twitchell, R. E., *The Leading Facts of New Mexican History* (5 vols., 1911).
Westphall, Victor, *Public Domain in New Mexico, 1854–1891* (1965).

Keleher, William A., *Violence in Lincoln County, 1869–1881* (1957).
La Farge, Oliver, and Arthur N. Morgan, *Santa Fe: Autobiography of a Southwestern Town* (1959).

New York

Alexander, De Alva S., *Political History of the State of New York, 1774–1882*
(3 vols., 1906–1909).
Brodhead, J. R., *History of the State of New York* (2 vols., 1853–1891).
Ellis, David M., et al., *Short History of New York State* (rev. ed., 1967).
Flick, Alexander C., ed., *History of State of New York* (10 vols., 1933–1937).
Fox, Dixon R., *Yankees and Yorkers* (1940).
Halsey, Francis W., *Old New York Frontier, 1614–1800* (1901).
Hammond, Jabez D., *History of Political Parties in State of New York* (2 vols.,
1846).
Horton, John T., *History of Northwestern New York* (3 vols., 1947).
Raesly, E. L., *Portrait of New Netherland* (1945).
Schuyler, G. W., *Colonial New York: Phillip Schuyler and His Family* (2 vols.,
1885).
Smith, William, Jr., *The History of the Province of New York*. Vol. I: *From the
Discovery to the Year 1732.* Vol. II: *A Continuation, 1732–1762,* Michael Kam-
men, ed. (1972).
Van Balen, W. J., *Holland aan de Hudson, Amsterdam* (1943).

Albion, Robert G., *Rise of New York Port, 1815–1860* (1939).
Atkins, Gordon, *Health, Housing and Poverty in New York City: 1865–1898*
(1947).
Baird, Charles W., *History of Rye, New York* (1871).
Bingham, R. W., *The Cradle of the Queen City: A History of Buffalo to the
Incorporation of the City* (1931).
Booth, Mary L., *History of City of New York* (1880).
Bradley, Hugh, *Such Was Saratoga* (1940).
Brown, Henry C., *In the Golden Nineties* (1928).
—— *Last Fifty Years in New York* (1926).
—— *New York in the Elegant Eighties* (1926).
Chapin, Anna A., *Greenwich Village* (1917).
Dix, John A., *History of Parish of Trinity Church in City of New York* (5 vols.,
1898–1950).
Ernst, Robert, *Immigrant Life in New York City, 1825–1863* (1949).
Foreman, Edward R., *Centennial History of Rochester, New York* (4 vols., 1931–
1934).
Frost, James A., *Life on Upper Susquehanna, 1783–1860* (1951).
Hasbrouck, Frank, *The History of Dutchess County, New York* (1909).
Howell, George R., and Jonathan Tenney, eds., *Bicentennial History of Albany.
History of the County of Albany N. Y. from 1609 to 1886* (1886).
Howell, George R., *Early History of Southampton, L. I.* (2nd ed., 1887).
Kuwenhoven, John A., *Columbia Historical Portrait of New York* (1953).
Lamb, Martha J., *History of City of New York* (2 vols., 1877–1880).
Lancaster, Clay, *Old Brooklyn Heights* (1961).
MacCracken, Henry N., *Blithe Dutchess: Flowering of an American County from
1812* (1958).

McKelvey, Blake, *Rochester, 1812–1961* (4 vols., 1945–1961).
Mandelbaum, Seymour J., *Boss Tweed's New York* (1965).
Monaghan, Frank, and Marvin Lowenthal, *This Was New York: the Nation's Capital in 1789* (1943).
Monroe, Joel H., *Schenectady, Ancient and Modern, 1661–1914* (1914).
Olmsted, Frederick L., *Landscape into Cityscape: Plans for Greater New York City*, Albert Fein, ed. (1968).
Overton, Jacqueline, *Long Island's Story* [1929].
Pomerantz, Sidney I., *New York 1783–1803* (1938).
Reed, John, *Hudson River Valley* (1960).
Riker, James, *Revised History of Harlem* (1904).
Ruttenber, E. M., *History of the County of Orange . . . with a History of the Town and City of Newburgh* (1875).
Scharf, John T., *History of Westchester County, New York* (2 vols., 1886).
Schoonmaker, Marius, *History of Kingston, New York, from Its Early Settlement to the Year 1820* (1888).
Shepherd, W. R., *The Story of New Amsterdam* (1926).
Simpson, Elizabeth M., *Mexico: Mother of Towns* (1949).
Singleton, Esther, *Social New York under the Georges 1714–1776* (1902).
Snyder, Charles M., *Oswego* (1968).
Stiles, H. R., *The Civil, Political, Professional and Ecclesiastical History and Commercial and Industrial Record of the City of Brooklyn, New York, 1683–1884* [1884].
——— *History of the City of Brooklyn* (3 vols., 1867–1870).
Still, Bayrd, *Mirror for Gotham: New York as Seen by Contemporaries from Dutch Days to Present* (1956).
Stokes, I. N. P., *Iconography of Manhattan Island* (6 vols., 1895–1928).
Syrett, Harold C., *City of Brooklyn, 1865–1898* (1944).
Thompson, Benjamin F., *History of Long Island* (3 vols., 1918).
Turner, Orsamus, *History of the Pioneer Settlement of Phelps and Gorham's Purchase* (1870).
——— *Pioneer History of the Holland Purchase* (1849).
Van Rensselaer, M. G., *History of the City of New York in the Seventeenth Century* (2 vols., 1909).
Whitaker, Epher, *History of Southold, L. I.: Its First Century* (1881). Rev. ed., C. E. Craven (1931).
Wilson, James G., ed., *Memorial History of City of New York* (4 vols., 1892–1893).

*　*　*　*　*　*　*

Breuer, Ernest H., *Constitutional Developments in New York, 1777–1958: A Bibliography* (1958). *Supplement* (1969).
Cone, Gertrude, comp., *Selective Bibliography of Publications on the Champlain Valley* (1959).
Flagg, C. A., and J. T. Jennings, "Bibliography of New York Colonial History," N.Y. State Library, *Bull.*, no. 56, "Bibliography, 24" (1901).
Nestler, Harold, *Bibliography of New York State Communities, Counties, Towns, Villages* (1968).

North Carolina

Arthur, John P., *Western North Carolina* (1914). Covers the period, 1730 to 1913.
Ashe, Samuel A., Stephen B. Weeks, and Charles L. Van Noppen, eds., *Biographical History of North Carolina from Colonial Times to the Present* (8 vols., 1905–1917).
Ashe, Samuel A., *History of North Carolina* (2 vols., 1908).
Boyd, William K., *History of North Carolina, 1783–1860* (2 vols., 1919).
Corbitt, David L., *Formation of the North Carolina Counties, 1663–1943* (1969).
Henderson, Archibald, *North Carolina: The Old North State and the New* (5 vols., 1941).

Hunter, C. L., *Sketches of Western North Carolina* (1877).
Johnson, Guion G., *Ante-Bellum North Carolina: Social History* (1937).
Jones, Houston Gwynne, *For History's Sake: The Preservation and Publication of North Carolina History, 1663–1903* (1966).
Lefler, Hugh T., and Albert R. Newsome, *North Carolina* (rev. ed., 1963).
Lefler, Hugh T., *North Carolina History Told by Contemporaries* (1934).
Matthews, Donald R., comp., *North Carolina Votes: General Election Returns by County 1868–1960* (1962).
Merrens, Harry R., *Colonial North Carolina in the Eighteenth Century: Study in Historical Geography* (1964).
Parker, Mattie E. E., ed., *North Carolina Charters and Constitutions, 1578–1698* (1963).
Raper, C. L., *North Carolina: A Study in English Colonial Government* (1904).
Williamson, Hugh, *History of North Carolina* (2 vols., 1812).

Allen, W. C., *The Annals of Haywood County North Carolina* (n.p., 1935).
Boyd, William K., *The Story of Durham, City of the South* (1925).
Leonard, J. C., *Centennial History of Davidson County, North Carolina* (2 vols., 1927).
O'Neall, J. B., and J. A. Chapman, *The Annals of Newberry* (1892).
Paschal, Herbert R., *History of Colonial Bath* (1955).
Robinson, Blackwell P., *History of Moore County, 1747–1847* (1956).
Rumple, Jethro, *A History of Rowan County, North Carolina* (1881).
Sherrill, W. L., *Annals of Lincoln County, North Carolina* (1937).
Sondley, F. A., *A History of Buncombe County, North Carolina* (1930).
Sprunt, James, *Chronicles of the Cape Fear River, 1660–1916* (1916).
Tompkins, D. A., *History of Mecklenburg County and the City of Charlotte, 1740–1903* (1903).
Wellman, Manly W., *County of Moore, 1847–1947* (1962).
—— *County of Warren, North Carolina, 1586–1917* (1959).

*   *   *   *   *   *   *

Lefler, Hugh T., *Guide to Study and Reading of North Carolina History* (3d ed., 1969).
Powell, William S., *North Carolina: A Student's Guide to Localized History* (1965).
—— *North Carolina County Histories: A Bibliography* (1958).
Thornton, Mary L., comp., *Bibliography of North Carolina, 1589–1956* (1958).

North Dakota

Armstrong, M. K., *The Early Empire Builders of the Great West* (1901).
Compendium of History and Biography of North Dakota (1900).
Kazeck, Melvin E., *North Dakota: Human and Economic Geography* (1956).
Lounsberry, C. A., *Early History of North Dakota* (1919).
Omdahl, Lloyd, *Insurgents: History of North Dakota Politics 1947–1960* (1961).
Robinson, Elwyn B., *History of North Dakota* (1966).
Williams, Mary Ann Barnes, *Origins of North Dakota Place Names* (1966).

Ohio

Allbeck, Willard D., *Century of Lutherans in Ohio* (1966). Covers the period, 1803–1917.
Barnhart, John D., *Valley of Democracy: Frontier in the Ohio Valley, 1775–1818* (1953).
Bond, B. W., *Foundations of Ohio* (1941).
Collins, W. R., *Ohio* (4th ed., 1968).
Hatcher, Harlan, *Western Reserve: Story of New Connecticut in Ohio* (1966).
Jordan, Philip D., *Ohio Comes of Age, 1873–1900* (1943).

Lindsey, David, *Ohio's Western Reserve: Story of its Place Names* (1955).
Randall, E. O., and D. J. Ryan, *History of Ohio, the Rise and Progress of an American State* (5 vols., 1912).
Roseboom, E. H., and Francis P. Weisenburger, *History of Ohio* (1953).
Winter, N. O., *A History of Northwest Ohio* (3 vols., 1917).
Wittke, Carl, ed., *The History of the State of Ohio* (6 vols., 1941–1944).

Bushnell, Henry, *History of Granville, Licking County, Ohio* (1889).
de Chambrun, C. L., *Cincinnati, Story of the Queen City* (1939).
Chapman, Edmund H., *Cleveland: Village to Metropolis: A Case Study of Problems of Urban Development in Nineteenth Century America* (1965).
Crew, H. W., ed., *History of Dayton* (1889).
Ford, H. A., and K. B. Ford, *History of Cincinnati* (1881).
Greve, C. T., *Centennial History of Cincinnati* (2 vols., 1904).
Hatcher, Harlan, *Western Reserve: Story of New Connecticut in Ohio* (1966).
Heald, E. T., and Edward Thornton, *The Stark County Story* (1949).
Heiser, A. H., *Hamilton in the Making* (1941).
Hover, J. C., et al., *Memoirs of the Miami Valley* (3 vols. 1919).
Miller, Zane L., *Boss Cox's Cincinnati: Urban Politics in the Progressive Era* (1968).
Orth, S. P., *A History of Cleveland, Ohio* (3 vols., 1910).
Reighard, F. H., *A Standard History of Fulton County, Ohio* (2 vols., 1920).
Rose, W. G., *Cleveland, the Making of a City* (1950).
Santmyer, Helen H., *Ohio Town* (1962). Xenia.
Summers, T. J., *History of Marietta* (1903).
[The Samuel Bissell Memorial Library Association], *Twinsburg, Ohio, 1817–1917* (1917).
Taylor, William A., *Centennial History of Columbus and Franklin County, Ohio* (2 vols., 1909).
Upton, H. T., *History of the Western Reserve* (3 vols., 1910).

* * * * * * *

Thomson, P. G., *A Bibliography of the State of Ohio; Being a Catalogue of the Books and Pamphlets Relating to the History of the State, with Collations and Bibliographical and Critical Notes* (1880).
——— *Catalogue of Books Relating to the State of Ohio, the West and Northwest* (1890).
Weisenburger, Francis P., *Ohio: Students' Guide to Localized History* (1965).

Oklahoma

Ally, John, *City Beginnings in Oklahoma Territory* (1939).
Buck, Solon J., *Settlement of Oklahoma* (1907).
Dale, Edward E., and M. L. Wardell, *History of Oklahoma* (1948).
Dale, Edward E., and J. L. Rader, *Readings in Oklahoma History* (1930).
Foreman, Grant, *A History of Oklahoma* (1942).
Gibson, Arrell, *Oklahoma, History of Five Centuries* (1965).
Gittinger, Roy, *Formation of the State of Oklahoma* (1939).
Hurst, Irvin, *The 46th Star: History of Oklahoma's Constitutional Convention and Early Statehood* (1957).
McReynolds, Edwin C., et al., *Oklahoma: Past and Present* (rev. ed., 1967).
Stewart, D. A., *Government and Development of Oklahoma Territory* (1933).
Thoburn, J. B., and Muriel H. Wright, *Oklahoma* (4 vols., 1929).
Wright, Muriel H., *A Guide to the Indian Tribes of Oklahoma* (1951).
——— *Story of Oklahoma* (1949).

Benedict, John D., *Muskogee and Northeastern Oklahoma* (3 vols., 1922).

Biles, J. Hugh, *Early History of Ada* (1954).
Chapman, Berlin B., *The Founding of Stillwater* (1948).
Debo, Angie, *Prairie City* (1969).
——— *Tulsa: From Creek Town to Oil Capital* (1943).
Rainey, George, *Cherokee Strip* (1933).
Scott, Angelo, *The Story of Oklahoma City* (1939).
Shirk, Lucyl, *Oklahoma City* (1957).

*   *   *   *   *   *   *

Dale, Edward E., and M. L. Wardell, *Outline and References for Oklahoma
    History* (1924).
Gibson, Arrell M., *Oklahoma: Student's Guide to Localized History* (1965).

Oregon

Bancroft, Hubert H., *Oregon* (2 vols., 1886–1888).
Carey, C. H., *A General History of Oregon prior to 1861* (2 vols., 1935–1936).
——— *History of Oregon* (1922).
Corning, Howard M., *Dictionary of Oregon History* (1956).
Gaston, Joseph, *The Centennial History of Oregon, 1811–1912* (1912).
Jacobs, Melvin C., *Winning Oregon* (1938).
Lyman, H. S., *History of Oregon* (4 vols., 1903).
McArthur, L. A., *Oregon Geographic Names* (3d ed., 1952).
McMurtrie, D. C., *Oregon Imprints, 1847–1870* (1950). *Supplement* by G. N.
    Belknap (1966).
Scott, H. W., *History of the Oregon Country* (6 vols., 1924).
Winther, Oscar O., *Old Oregon Country: Frontier Trade, Transportation and
    Travel* (1949).

Clark, R. C., *History of the Willamette Valley, Oregon* (1927).
French, Giles L., *Golden Land: History of Sherman County* (1958).
Irving, Washington, *Astoria* (2 vols., 1839).
Moore, L. W., et al., *The Story of Eugene* (1949).

Pennsylvania

Bolles, A. S., *Pennsylvania, Province and State, 1609–1790* (2 vols., 1899).
Bradley, Erwin S., *Triumph of Militant Republicanism: Pennsylvania, 1860–1872*
    (1964).
Buck, Solon J., and E. H. Buck, *Planting of Civilization in Western Pennsylvania*
    (1939).
Donehoo, George P., ed., *Pennsylvania* (7 vols., 1926).
Dunaway, Wayland F., *History of Pennsylvania* (2nd ed., 1948).
Evans, Frank B., *Pennsylvania Politics, 1872–1877* (1966).
Hartz, Louis, *Economic Policy and Democratic Thought: Pennsylvania, 1776–1860*
    (1948).
Higginbotham, Sanford W., *Keystone in the Democratic Arch: Pennsylvania Poli-
    tics, 1800–1816* (1952).
Jenkins, H. M., *Pennsylvania; Colonial and Federal; a History, 1608–1903* (3 vols.,
    1903).
Klein, P. S., *Pennsylvania Politics, 1817–1832: A Game without Rules* (1940).
McKnight, W. J., *A Pioneer Outline History of Northwestern Pennsylvania* (1905).
Proud, Robert, *History of Pennsylvania, from . . . 1681, till after the Year 1742*
    (2 vols., 1797–1798).
Sharpless, Isaac, *History of Quaker Government in Pennsylvania* (2 vols., 1898–
    1899).
Shepherd, W. R., *History of Proprietary Government in Pennsylvania* (1896).
Snyder, Charles M., *Jacksonian Heritage: Pennsylvania Politics, 1833–1848* (1958).

Stevens, Sylvester K., Ralph W. Cordier, and Florence O. Benjamin, *Exploring Pennsylvania* (3d ed., 1968).
Stevens, Sylvester K., *Pennsylvania* (1964).
—— *Pennsylvania: Keystone State* (2 vols., 1956).
Wallace, Paul A. W., *Pennsylvania: Seed of a Nation* (1962).

Albright, Raymond W., *Two Centuries of Reading, Pennsylvania, 1748–1948* (1948).
American Philosophical Society, *Historic Philadelphia from Founding to Early Nineteenth Century* (1953).
Baldwin, Leland D., *Pittsburgh, Story of a City* (1937).
Bausman, J. H., *History of Beaver County, Pennsylvania and Its Centennial Celebration* (2 vols., 1904).
Bethlehem of Pennsylvania: 1741–1841 (1968).
Burt, Struthers, *Philadelphia, Holy Experiment* (1945).
Collins, Herman L., *Philadelphia, Story of Progress* (4 vols., 1941).
Davis, William W. H., *History of Bucks County, Pennsylvania* (1876).
Fleming, George T., *History of Pittsburgh and Environs* (4 vols., 1922).
Hadden, James, *A History of Uniontown* (1913).
Heverly, Clement F., *History of the Towandas, 1770–1886* (1886).
Keyser, N. H., et al., *History of Old Germantown* (1907).
Klein, H. M. J., *Lancaster County, Pennsylvania, a History* (4 vols., 1924).
Lorant, Stefan, *Pittsburgh* (1964).
Lubove, Roy, *Twentieth-Century Pittsburgh* (1969).
Mombert, J. I., *Authentic History of Lancaster County* (1869).
Nolan, James B., *Foundation of Town of Reading Pennsylvania* (1929).
Oberholtzer, E. P., *Philadelphia, a History of the City and Its People* (4 vols., 1912).
Repplier, Agnes, *Philadelphia, the Place and the People* (1898).
Riddle, William, *The Story of Lancaster: Old and New* (1917).
Scharf, John T., and Thompson Westcott, *History of Philadelphia, 1609–1884* (3 vols., 1884).
Tinkcom, Harry M., Margaret Tinkcom, and Grant M. Simon, *Historic Germantown, to Early Part of Nineteenth Century* (1955).
Walker, Joseph E., *Hopewell: History of an Iron-Making Community* (1966).
Warner, Sam B., Jr., *Private City: Philadelphia* (1968).
Watson, John F., *Annals of Philadelphia and Pennsylvania in the Olden Time* (2 vols., 1857).
Wright, H. B., *Historical Sketches of Plymouth* (1873).
Young, John R., *Memorial History of City of Philadelphia* (2 vols., 1895–1898).

* * * * * * *

Bausman, L. M., *A Bibliography of Lancaster County, Pennsylvania, 1745–1912* (1917).
Long, Wesley H., and Robert C. Posatko, *Annotated Bibliography of County Economic Information for Pennsylvania* (1967).
Nelson, Daniel, *Checklist of Writings on Economic History of Greater Philadelphia-Wilmington Region* (1968).
Pennsylvania State Library, *Year's Work in Pennsylvania Studies, 1965–1968* (4 vols., 1966–1969).
Wilkinson, Norman B., et al., comps., *Bibliography of Pennsylvania* (2nd ed., 1957).

Puerto Rico

Bourne, Dorothy D., and James R., *Thirty Years of Change in Puerto Rico* (1966).
Friedlander, Stanley L., *Labor Migration and Economic Growth* (1960).
Goodsell, Charles T., Jr., *Administration of a Revolution: Executive Reform in Puerto Rico under Governor Tugwell, 1941–1946* (1965).

Hanson, Earl P., *Transformation: Modern Puerto Rico* [1898–1954] (1955).
Tugwell, Rexford G., *Stricken Land* (1947).
Wells, Henry, *Modernization of Puerto Rico: A Political Study of Changing Values and Institutions* (1969).

Rhode Island

Arnold, Samuel G., *History of Rhode Island* (2 vols., 1859).
Bates, Frank G., *Rhode Island and Formation of the Union* (1898).
Bicknell, T. W., *The History of the State of Rhode Island and Providence Plantations* (4 vols., 1920).
Carroll, Charles, *Rhode Island: Three Centuries of Democracy* (4 vols., 1932).
Chapin, Howard M., *Documentary History of Rhode Island* (2 vols., 1916–1919).
Coleman, Peter J., *Transformation of Rhode Island, 1790–1860* (1963).
Field, Edward, *State of Rhode Island and Providence Plantations at the End of the Century: A History* (3 vols., 1902).
Lovejoy, David S., *Rhode Island Politics and American Revolution, 1760–1776* (1958).
Polishook, Irwin H., *Rhode Island and Union, 1774–1795* (1969).
Richman, I. B., *Rhode Island: Its Making and Its Meaning* (2 vols., 1902).
Tanner, Earl C., *Rhode Island* (1954).
Weeden, W. B., *Early Rhode Island: A Social History of the People* (1910).

Howe, Mark A. DeW., *Bristol* (1930).
Kimball, Gertrude S., *Providence in Colonial Times* (1912).
Staples, William R., *Annals of Town of Providence* (1843).
Stokes, Howard K., *Finances and Administration of Providence, 1636–1901* (1903).

*   *   *   *   *   *   *

Bartlett, John R., *Bibliography of Rhode Island* (1864).
Brigham, Clarence S., *Bibliography of Rhode Island History* (1902).
——— "List of Books upon Rhode Island History," *Rhode Island Educational Circulars,* Hist. Ser. I (1908).
Monahon, Clifford P., *Rhode Island: Students' Guide to Localized History* (1965).

South Carolina

Cooper, William J., *Conservative Regime: South Carolina, 1877–1890* (1968).
Lander, Ernest M., *History of South Carolina, 1865–1960* (2nd ed., 1970).
McCrady, Edward, *The History of South Carolina 1670–1783* (4 vols., 1897–1902).
Meriwether, R. L., *The Expansion of South Carolina, 1729–65* (1940).
Sirmans, M. Eugene, *Colonial South Carolina: Political History, 1663–1763* (1966).
Smith, William Roy, *South Carolina as a Royal Province, 1719–1776* (1903).
Taylor, Rosser H., *Ante-Bellum South Carolina* (1942).
Wallace, David D., *South Carolina, Short History, 1520–1948* (1951).

Green, Edwin L., *History of Richland County, 1732–1805* (1932).
Gregorie, A. K., *History of Sumter County* (1954).
Hennig, H. K., *Columbia, 1786–1936* (1936). *Supplement, 1936–1966* by Charles E. Lee (1966).
Kirkland, T. J., and R. M. Kennedy, *Historic Camden* (2 vols., 1905–1925).
Ravenel, H. H., *Charleston, the Place and the People* (1906).
Rogers, George C., *Charleston in the Age of the Pinckneys* (1969).
——— *History of Georgetown County* (1970).
Salley, A. S., *The History of Orangeburg County, South Carolina* (1898).
Stoney, Samuel G., *Plantations of Carolina Low Country,* Albert Simons and Samuel Lapham, Jr., eds. (4th ed., 1955).

*   *   *   *   *   *   *

Easterby, J. H., *Guide to the Study and Reading of South Carolina History* (1950).
Moore, J. H., *Research Materials in South Carolina* (1967).
Turnbull, R. J., *Bibliography of South Carolina, 1563–1950* (6 vols., 1956).

South Dakota

Coursey, O. W., *Literature of South Dakota* (4th ed., 1925).
Lamar, Howard R., *Dakota Territory, 1861–1889* (1956).
Robinson, Doane, *History of South Dakota* (2 vols. n.p., 1904).
Schell, Herbert S., *Dakota Territory during the Eighteen Sixties* (1954).
——— *History of South Dakota* (1961).
Smith, G. M., *South Dakota, Its History and Its People* (5 vols., 1915).

Bingham, John N., and Nora V. Peters, *Short History of Brule County* (1947).
Fite, Gilbert C., *Mount Rushmore* (1952).

Tennessee

Abernethy, Thomas P., *From Frontier to Plantation in Tennessee* (1932).
Caldwell, Joshua W., *Studies in Constitutional History of Tennessee* (1907).
Combs, W. H., and W. E. Cole, *Tennessee, a Political Study* (1940).
Folmsbee, Stanley J., Robert E. Corlew, and Enoch L. Mitchell, *History of
  Tennessee* (4 vols., 1960).
Folmsbee, Stanley J., et al., *Tennessee: A Short History* (1969).
Hale, William T., and D. L. Merritt, *History of Tennessee and Tennesseeans*
  (8 vols., 1913).
Hamer, Philip M., ed., *Tennessee: A History, 1673–1932* (4 vols., 1933).
Isaac, Paul E., *Prohibition and Politics: Turbulent Decades of Tennessee* (1965).
Moore, John T., and A. P. Foster, *Tennessee: The Volunteer State, 1769–1923*
  (4 vols., 1923).

Arnow, Harriette L. S., *Flowering of the Cumberland* (1963).
Capers, Gerald M., *Biography of a River Town: Memphis, Its Heroic Age* (1939).
Durham, Walter T., *Great Leap Westward: History of Sumner County, from Its
  Beginning to 1805* (1969).
Govan, Gilbert, *Chattanooga Country, 1540–1951* (1952).
East Tennessee Historical Society, *History of Knoxville* (1945).
McIlwaine, Shields, *Memphis, Down in Dixie* (1948).
McRaven, Henry, Nashville, *Athens of the South* (1949).
Ramsey, J. G. M., *Annals of Tennessee History* (1853).
Williams, Emma I., *Historic Madison, the Story of Jackson and Madison County,
  Tennessee* (1946).
Wooldridge, John, ed., *History of Nashville, Tennessee* (1890).

*   *   *   *   *   *   *

Alderson, William T., and Robert H. White, *Guide to Study and Reading of
  Tennessee History* (1959).
Alderson, William T., *Tennessee: Students' Guide to Localized History* (1965).
Tennessee State Library and Archives, *Writings on Tennessee Counties* (1967).
  Includes local history.

Texas

Bancroft, Hubert H., *North Mexican States and Texas* (1883–1889).
Bolton, Herbert E., *Texas in the Middle Eighteenth Century* (1915).

Faulk, Odie B., *The Last Years of Spanish Texas, 1778–1821* (1964).
Fehrenbach, T. R., *Lone Star: Texas* (1968).
Ferguson, Walter K., *Geology and Politics in Frontier Texas, 1845–1909* (1969).
Hatcher, Mattie A., *The Opening of Texas to Foreign Settlements, 1801–1821* (1927).
Hogan, William R., *The Texas Republic: A Social and Economic History* (1946).
Horgan, Paul, *Great River: Rio Grande in North American History* (2 vols., 1954).
Jaques, M. J., *Texan Ranch Life* (1894).
Johnson, Francis W., *History of Texas and Texans* (5 vols., 1914).
Lathrop, Barnes F., *Migration into East Texas, 1835–1860* (1949).
McKay, Seth S., *Texas Politics, 1906–1944* (1952).
Richardson, Rupert N., *Frontier of Northwest Texas, 1846 to 1876* (1963).
—— et al., *Texas, the Lone Star State* (3d ed., 1970).
Siegel, Stanley, *Political History of Texas Republic, 1836–1845* (1956).
Smith, Justin H., *Annexation of Texas* (1911).
Soukup, James R., Clifton McCleskey, and Harry Holloway, *Party and Factional Division in Texas* (1964).
Wallace, Ernest, ed., *Documents of Texas History* (1963).
Webb, Walter P. et al., eds., *Handbook of Texas* (2 vols., 1952).
Wooten, Dudley G., ed., *Comprehensive History of Texas* (2 vols., 1898).

Howard, James K., *Big D Is for Dallas* (1957).
Knight, Oliver, *Fort Worth* (1953).
Sonnichsen, C. L., *Pass of the North: Four Centuries on the Rio Grande* (1968). El Paso.
Taylor, Ira T., and N. A. Taylor, *Cavalcade of Jackson County* (1938).
White, Owen, *Out of the Desert, the Historical Romance of El Paso* (1923).

*   *   *   *   *   *   *

Barr, Alwyn, "Texas Civil War Historiography," *Texas Libraries* (Winter 1964), 160.
Carroll, H. Bailey, *Texas County Histories: A Bibliography* (1943).
Dobie, J. Frank, *Guide to Life and Literature of Southwest* (rev. ed., 1952).
Jenkins, John H., *Cracker Barrel Chronicles: Bibliography of Texas Town and Country Chronicles* (1965).
Nesmith, Frances, "Bibliography of Texas Bibliographies," *Texas Libraries* (Fall 1965), 133.
Oates, Stephen B., "Guide to the Literature of Texas," *Texas Libraries* (Fall 1963), 109.
Raines, C. W., *A Bibliography of Texas, being a Descriptive List of Books, Pamphlets, and Documents Relating to Texas in Print and Manuscript since 1536* (1896).
Streeter, Thomas W., ed., *Bibliography of Texas, 1795–1845* (5 vols., 1955–1960).
Winkler, E. W., *Check List of Texas Imprints 1846–1860* (1949).

Utah

Alter, J. C., *Utah, the Storied Domain* (3 vols., 1932).
Anderson, Nels, *Desert Saints: The Mormon Frontier in Utah* (1942).
Arrington, Leonard J., *Great Basin Kingdom: An Economic History of the Latter-Day Saints, 1830–1900* (1958).
Bancroft, Hubert H., *Utah* (1889).
Creer, Leland H., *Founding of an Empire: Exploration and Colonization of Utah, 1776–1856* (1942).
—— *Utah and Nation* (1929).
Hunter, Milton R., *Utah in Her Western Setting* (1943).
—— *Utah: The Story of Her People, 1540–1947* (1946).
Neff, Andrew L., *History of Utah 1847 to 1869* (1940).
Warrum, Noble, ed., *Utah since Statehood* (4 vols., 1919).

Whitney, O. F., *History of Utah* (4 vols., 1892–1904).
Young, L. E., *The Founding of Utah* (1923).

* * * * * * *

Cooley, Everett L., *Utah: Students' Guide to Localized History* (1968).

Vermont

Allen, Ira, *Natural and Political History of the State of Vermont* (1798).
Crockett, W. H., *Vermont, the Green Mountain State* (4 vols., 1921).
Hall, Benjamin H., *History of Eastern Vermont, from Its Earliest Settlement to the Close of the Eighteenth Century* (1858).
Hall, Hiland, *History of Vermont, from Its Discovery to Its Admission into the Union in 1791* (1868).
Hemenway, A. M., *Vermont Historical Gazetteer* (5 vols., 1867–1891).
Hill, R. N., *Contrary Country, a Chronicle of Vermont* (1950).
Lee, John P., *Uncommon Vermont* (1926).
Ludlum, D. M., *Social Ferment in Vermont, 1791–1850* (1939).
Newton, E. W., *The Vermont Story* (1949).
Thompson, Charles M., *Independent Vermont* (1942).
[Vermont Historical Society] *Essays in the Early History of Vermont* (1943).
―――― *Essays in the Social and Economic History of Vermont* (1943).
Williamson, Chilton, *Vermont in Quandary: 1763–1825* (1949).
Wilson, Harold F., *Hill Country of Northern New England* (1947).

Bigelow, Edwin L., *Manchester, Vermont, 1761–1961* (1961).
Bogart, E. L., *Peacham* (1948).
Cabot, Mary R., *Annals of Brattleboro, 1681–1895* (2 vols., 1921).
Cudworth, A. E., *The History with Genealogical Sketches of Londonderry* (1935).
Kull, N. M., *History of Dover, Vermont: Two Hundred Years* (1961).
Newton, William M., *History of Barnard, Vermont* (2 vols., 1928).
Vail, H. H., *Pomfret* (2 vols., 1930).
[Vermont Historical Society] *The Upper Connecticut* (1943).

* * * * * * *

Gilman, Marcus D., *Bibliography of Vermont* (1897).
Jones, Matt B., *List of Additions to Gilman's Bibliography of Vermont* (1926).

Virginia

Andrews, Matthew P., *Soul of a Nation* (1943).
―――― *Virginia the Old Dominion* (1937).
Bell, Landon C., *The Old Free State* (2 vols., 1927).
Beverley, Robert, *History of Virginia, in Four Parts 1584–1720* (2nd ed., 1722); Louis B. Wright, ed., 1947).
Brown, Alexander, *The First Republic in America* (1898).
Bruce, P. A., *Economic History of Virginia in the Seventeenth Century* (2 vols., 1896).
―――― *Institutional History of Virginia in the Seventeenth Century* (2 vols., 1910).
Fishwick, Marshall W., *Virginia: New Look at Old Dominion* (1959).
―――― *Virginia Tradition* (1956).
Hemphill, William E., Marvin W. Schlegel, and Sadie E. Engelberg, *Cavalier Commonwealth: History and Government of Virginia* (1957).
Langhorne, Orra, *Southern Sketches from Virginia, 1881–1901*, Charles E. Wynes, ed. (1964).
Moger, Allen W., *Virginia: Bourbonism to Byrd, 1870–1925* (1968).
Randolph, Edmund, *History of Virginia* (1970).

Ryland, Garnett, *Baptists of Virginia, 1699–1926* (1955).
Sams, C. W., *The Conquest of Virginia* (4 vols., 1916–1939).
Stith, William, *History of the First Discovery and Settlement of Virginia* (1747).
Sweet, William W., *Virginia Methodism* (1955).
Wust, Klaus, *Virginia Germans* (1969).

Ames, Susie M., *Studies of the Virginia Eastern Shore in the Seventeenth Century* (1940).
Bagby, Alfred, *King and Queen County, Virginia* (1908).
Bell, Landon C., *The Old Free State: A Contribution to the History of Lunenburg County and Southside Virginia* (2 vols., 1927).
Boddie, J. B., *Seventeenth Century Isle of Wight County, Virginia* (1938).
Bradshaw, Herbert C., *History of Prince Edward County, Virginia* (1955).
Campbell, Thomas E., *Colonial Caroline: History of Caroline County, Virginia* (1954).
Christian, W. A., *Richmond, Her Past and Present* (1912).
Clement, M. C., *The History of Pittsylvania County, Virginia* (1929).
Couper, William, *History of the Shenandoah Valley* (3 vols., 1952).
Eckenrode, Hamilton J., ed., *Richmond, Capital of Virginia* (1938).
Forman, Henry C., *Jamestown and St. Mary's Buried Cities of Romance* (1938).
Greene, Katherine G., *Winchester, Virginia and Its Beginnings, 1743–1814* (1926).
Gwathmey, J. H., *Twelve Virginia Counties* (1937).
Hanson, Raus M., *Virginia Place Names, Derivations, Historical Uses* (1969).
Harman, J. N., *Annals of Tazewell County, Virginia 1800–1922* (2 vols., 1922).
Johnston, David E., *History of Middle New River Settlements* (1906).
Kegley, F. B., *Kegley's Virginia Frontier: The Beginnings of the Southwest* (1938).
Kercheval, Samuel, *History of the Valley of Virginia* (1833); 4th ed., 1925.
Lutz, Francis E., *Chesterfield: Old Virginia County* (1954).
Moore, Gay M., *Seaport in Virginia* (1949).
Moore, Virginia, *Scottsville on the James* (1969).
Niederer, Frances J., *Town of Fincastle, Virginia* (1965).
Pendleton, William C., *History of Tazewell County and Southeast Virginia, 1748–1920* (1920).
Porter, Albert O., *County Government in Virginia: Legislative History, 1607–1904* (1947).
Ryland, Elizabeth H., *King William County, Virginia* (1955).
Schlegel, Marvin W., *Conscripted City: Norfolk in World War II* (1951).
Waddell, J. A., *Annals of Augusta County, Virginia* (1886).
Wertenbaker, Thomas J., *Norfolk* (1931). 2nd ed. rev. by Marvin W. Schlegel (1962).
—— *Norfolk, Historic Southern Port* (rev. ed., 1962).
Whitaker, R. T., *Virginia's Eastern Shore* (2 vols., 1951).
Wingfield, Marshall, *A History of Caroline County, Virginia* (1924).
Wise, Jennings C., *Ye Kingdome of Accawmacke or the Eastern Shore of Virginia in the Seventeenth Century* (1911).

*   *   *   *   *   *   *

Cappon, Lester J., *Bibliography of Virginia History since 1865* (1930).
Swem, Earl G., *Virginia Historical Index* (2 vols., 1934–1936).

Washington

Avery, Mary W., *Washington* (1965).
Bancroft, Hubert H., *History of Washington, Idaho, and Montana* (1890; repr. 1967).
Barko, H. E., and Catherine Bullard, *History of the State of Washington* (1947).
Beckett, Paul L., *From Wilderness to Enabling Act: Evolution of State of Washington* (1968).

Hunt, Herbert, and F. C. Kaylor, *Washington West of the Cascades* (1917).
Meany, E. S., *History of the State of Washington* (1929).
Meinig, Donald W., *Great Columbia Plain: Historical Geography, 1805–1910* (1968).
Ogden, Daniel M., Jr., and Hugh A. Bone, *Washington Politics* (1960).
Pollard, Lancaster, *History of the State of Washington* (4 vols., 1937).
Snowden, C. A., *History of Washington* (4 vols., 1909).

Fahey, John, *Inland Empire: D. C. Corbin and Spokane* (1965).
Hanford, C. H., *Seattle and Environs 1852–1924* (1924).
Steinbrueck, Victor, *Seattle Cityscape* (1962).

West Virginia

Ambler, Charles H., and Festus P. Summers, *West Virginia, the Mountain State* (rev. ed., 1958).
Callahan, James M., *History of West Virginia, Old and New* (3 vols., 1923).
Cometti, Elizabeth, and Festus B. Summers, *Thirty-fifth State: Documentary History of West Virginia* (1966).
Conley, Phil, *West Virginia: Brief History of the Mountain State* (1963).
—— and Boyd B. Stutler, *West Virginia, Yesterday and Today* (4th ed., 1966).
Lambert, Oscar D., *West Virginia: Its People and Its Progress* (1958).
Miller, T. C., *West Virginia and Its People* (3 vols., 1913).
Moore, George E., *Banner in the Hills: West Virginia's Statehood* (1963).
Myers, Sylvester, *History of West Virginia* (2 vols., 1915).
Rice, Otis K., *Allegheny Frontier: West Virginia Beginnings, 1730–1830* (1970).
Shawkey, M. P., *West Virginia in History, Life, Literature and Industry* (5 vols., 1928).
Tams, W. P., *The Smokeless Coal Fields of West Virginia* (1963).

Bushong, M. K., *A History of Jefferson County, West Virginia* (1941).
Peters, J. T., and J. B. Carden, *History of Fayette County, West Virginia* (1926).
Reed, Louis, *Warning in Appalachia: Wirt County, West Virginia* (1967).
Smith, E. C., *A History of Lewis County, West Virginia* (1920).

* * * * * * *

"Bibliography of West Virginia," State Dept. of Archives and Hist., *Report*, (1938).
Ham, F. Gerald, ed., *Guide to Manuscripts and Archives in West Virginia Collection, 1958–62* (1965).
Munn, Robert F., *Index to West Virginiana* (1960).
Shetler, Charles, *West Virginia Civil War Literature* (1963).

Wisconsin

Austin, H. Russell, *The Wisconsin Story* (rev. ed., 1957).
Campbell, H. C., ed., *Wisconsin in Three Centuries, 1634–1905* (4 vols., 1906).
Carstensen, Vernon R., *Farms or Forests: Land Policy for Northern Wisconsin, 1850–1932* (1958).
Dictionary of Wisconsin Biography (1960).
Epstein, Leon D., *Politics in Wisconsin* (1958).
Gara, Larry, *Short History of Wisconsin* (1962).
Helgeson, Arlan, *Farms in Cutover: Northern Wisconsin* (1962).
Hunt, Robert S., *Law and Locomotives: Wisconsin in the Nineteenth Century* (1958).
Jorgenson, Lloyd P., *Founding of Public Education in Wisconsin* (1956).

Kellogg, Louise P., *British Regime in Wisconsin and the Northwest* (1935).
―――― *French Regime in Wisconsin and the Northwest* (1925).
Kuehnl, George J., *The Wisconsin Business Corporation* (1959).
Lampard, Eric E., *Rise of the Dairy Industry in Wisconsin, 1820–1920* (1963).
McDonald, Forrest, *Let There Be Light: Electric Utility Industry in Wisconsin, 1881–1955* (1957).
McDonald, M. Justille, *History of Irish in Wisconsin in Nineteenth Century* (1954).
Merk, Frederick, *Economic History of Wisconsin during the Civil War Decade* (1916).
Raney, William F., *Wisconsin, a Story of Progress* (1940).
Thwaites, Reuben G., *Wisconsin: The Americanization of a French Settlement* (1908).

Curti, Merle E., et al., *Making of an American Community: Democracy in a Frontier County* (1959). Trempeleau.
Durrie, D. S., *History of Madison* (1874).
Glaab, Charles N., and Lawrence H. Larsen, *Factories in the Valley: Neenah Menasha, 1870–1915* (1969).
Neville, E. H., S. G. Martin, and D. B. Martin, *Historic Green Bay, 1634–1840* (1893).
Roemer, Theodore, *St. Joseph in Appleton* (1943).
Sanford, A. H., and H. J. Hirshheimer, *A History of La Crosse, Wisconsin, 1841–1900* (1951).
Schafer, Joseph, *Four Wisconsin Counties, Prairie and Forest* (1927).
Smith, Alice E., *Millstone and Saw: Origins of Neenah-Menasha* (1966).
Still, Bayrd, *Milwaukee* (rev. ed., 1965).

*　　*　　*　　*　　*　　*　　*

Schlinkert, Leroy, comp., *Subject Bibliography of Wisconsin History* (1947).

Wyoming

Bancroft, Hubert H., *Nevada, Colorado, and Wyoming* (1890).
Coutant, C. G., *History of Wyoming* (1899; repr. with index, 1966).
Gould, Lewis L., *Wyoming, 1868–1896* (1968).
Larson, Taft A., *History of Wyoming* (1965).
Linford, Velma, *Wyoming, Frontier State* (1947).

Brown, Mark Herbert, *Plainsmen of Yellowstone: History of Yellowstone Basin* (1960).
Mokler, A. J., *History of Natrona County, Wyoming, 1888–1922* (1923).
Mumey, Nolie, *The Teton Mountains: Their History and Tradition* (1947).

*　　*　　*　　*　　*　　*　　*

Homsher, Lola M., *Wyoming: Students' Guide to Localized History* (1966).

13   Westward Expansion and the Frontier

The frontier, a stage in the early settlement of every region of America, began at the Atlantic seaboard in the early seventeenth century, and moved across the continent during the following three centuries. The advance of settlement was sporadic, and although its general direction was westward, it often extended in long lobes along land or water routes, and then turned north or south, or even back eastward. Sometimes it leap-frogged into the unsettled back-country, forming islands of settlement which expanded until they met the main advance.

Works on the older colonial frontier, which was largely confined to the area east of the Appalachians, will be found in volume II. Most of this chapter is taken up with Transmississippi-West because historians have cultivated this last frontier more assiduously.

Many of the secondary works cited in chapter 12, Regional, State and Local Histories, are relevant to the frontier period of a particular locality, while vast amounts of source material will be found in chapter 9, Travels and Description.

13.1 GENERAL

Alden, John R., *Pioneer America* (1966).
American Heritage History of the Great West (1965).
Baur, John E., *Health Seekers of Southern California, 1870–1900* (1959).
Billington, Ray A., *America's Frontier Heritage* (1966).
—— *Far Western Frontier, 1830–1860* (1956).
—— and James B. Hodges, *Westward Expansion, a History of the American Frontier* (3d ed., 1967).
Bogue, Allan G. et al., eds., *The West of American People* (1970).
Branch, E. Douglas, *Westward* (1930).
Clark, John G., ed., *Frontier Challenge* (1971).
Clark, Thomas D., *Frontier America: the Westward Movement* (2nd ed., 1969).
Coman, Katherine, *Economic Beginnings of Far West* (2 vols., 1925).
Drago, Harry S., *Roads to Empire: American West* (1968).
Ellis, David M., ed., *The Frontier in American Development: Essays in Honor of Paul Wallace Gates* (1969).
Ghent, W. J., *The Early Far West* (1931).
Graebner, Norman A., *Empire on the Pacific* (1955).
Hafen, Leroy R. et al., *Western America* (3d ed., 1970).
Hawgood, John A., *America's Western Frontiers: Exploration and Settlement of the Trans-Mississippi West* (1967).
Jones, Billy M., *Health-Seekers in the Southwest, 1817–1900* (1967).
McCaleb, Walter F., *The Conquest of the West* (1947).

Paul, Rodman W., *The Frontier and the American West* (1971).

Paxson, Frederick L., *History of the American Frontier* (1924).

Richmond, Robert W., and Robert W. Mardock, eds., *Nation Moving West: Readings* (1966).

Ridge, Martin, and Ray A. Billington, eds., *America's Frontier Story: Documentary History of Westward Expansion* (1969).

Smith, Henry Nash, *Virgin Land: American West as Symbol and Myth* (1950).

────── "The West as an Image of the American Past," *Univ. Kan. City Rev.,* 18 (1951), 29.

Spence, Clark C., ed., *The American West: A Source Book* (1966).

Toole, K. Ross et al., *Probing the American West* (1962).

U.S. Department of State, *Territorial Papers of the United States,* Clarence C. Carter and John Porter Bloom, eds. (27 vols., 1934–1969).

Van Every, Dale, *Frontier People of America, 1754–1845* (4 vols., 1961–1964).

Wright, Louis B., *Culture on Moving Frontier* (1955).

*   *   *   *   *   *   *

Adams, Ramon F., *Burs under the Saddle: Books and Histories of the West* (1964).

Billington, Ray A., *Westward Expansion* (3d ed., 1967). Pp. 765–893.

Carter, Harvey L., *The Far West in American History* (1960).

Clark, Thomas D., *Frontier America: The Westward Movement* (2nd ed., 1969). Pp. 769–803.

Denver Public Library, *Catalog of the Western History Department* (7 vols., 1970).

Dobie, J. Frank, *Guide to Life and Literature of the Southwest* (rev. ed., 1952).

Green, Lola Beth, and Dahlia Terrell, comps., *Bold Land: A Bibliography* (1970).

Hafen, Leroy R., and Ann W. Hafen, *Their Writings and Their Notable Collection of Americana Given to Brigham Young University Library* (1962).

Newberry Library, *A Catalog of the Everett D. Graff Collection of Western Americana* (1968).

────── *Dictionary Catalog of Edward E. Ayer Collection of Americana and American Indians* (16 vols., 1961).

Turner, Frederick J., and Frederick Merk, *References on History of the West* (rev. ed., 1942).

Wallace, William S., *Bibliography of Published Bibliographies on the History of the Eleven Western States, 1941–1947* (1954).

Winther, Oscar O., *Classified Bibliography of Periodical Literature of the Trans-Mississippi West, 1811–1957.* (1961).

────── and R. A. Van Orman, *Classified Bibliography of Periodical Literature of the Trans-Mississippi West, 1957–1967* (1970).

See 13.7 for Historiography.

See also 12.2.5, Regional–West; 25.7 Nationalism and Mission; 25.8, Nature and the West.

13.2 EXPLORATION

Andreev, Aleksandr I., ed., *Russian Discoveries in the Pacific and in North America in the Eighteenth and Nineteenth Centuries: A Collection of Materials* (1952).

Bartlett, Richard A., *Great Surveys of the American West* (1962).

Bell, John R., *Journal . . . Official Journalist for the Stephen H. Long Expedition to Rocky Mountains, 1850,* Harlin M. Fuller and Le Roy R. Hafen, eds. (1957).

Beltrami, Giacomo C., *Pilgrimage in America, Leading to the Discovery of the Sources of the Mississippi and Bloody River* (1824).

Brebner, J. Bartlett, *The Explorers of North America, 1492–1806* (1933).

Cline, Gloria G., *Exploring the Great Basin* (1963).

Dale, Harrison C., *Ashley-Smith Explorations* (rev. ed., 1941).

DeVoto, Bernard, *The Course of Empire* (1952).

────── *Year of Decision, 1846* (1943).

Dillon, Richard H., "Stephen Long and the Great American Desert," *Mont. Mag. Hist.*, 18, no. 3 (1968), 58.
Dodge, Ernest S., *Northwest by Sea* (1961).
Farquhar, Francis P., *History of the Sierra Nevada* (1965).
Ghent, W. J., *The Early Far West* (1931).
Gilbert, Edmund W., *Exploration of Western America, 1800–1850* (1933).
Goetzmann, William H., *Army Exploration in American West, 1803–1863* (1959).
—— *Exploration and Empire: Explorer and Scientist in American West* (1966).
Harris, Edward, *Up the Missouri with Audubon*, John F. McDermott, ed. (1951).
Hasse, A. R., *Reports of Explorations Printed in Documents of Government* (1899).
Hebard, Grace R., *Pathbreakers* (1933).
Irving, Washington, *Captain Bonneville*, and *Astoria* (2 vols., 1895).
Lavender, David S., *Land of Giants: Drive to Pacific Northwest 1750–1950* (1958).
Morris, R. C., "Notion of Great American Desert," *MVHR*, 13 (1926), 190.
Nasatir, Abraham P., ed., *Before Lewis and Clark: Documents Illustrating the History of the Missouri, 1785–1804* (2 vols., 1952).
Powell, John Wesley, *Exploration of the Colorado River of the West and Its Tributaries* (1875). Covers the period, 1869–1872.
Quaife, Milo M., ed., *Southwestern Expedition of Zebulon M. Pike* (1925).
Rawling, Gerald, *The Pathfinders: America's First Westerners* (1964).
Smith, Alson J., *Men against the Mountains: Jedediah Smith and South West Expedition of 1826–1829* (1965).
Thwaites, Reuben G., *Early Western Travels, 1748–1846* (32 vols., 1904–1907).
Wheat, Carl I., *Mapping the Transmississippi-West, 1540–1861* (5 vols., 1957–1963).
Wilkes, Charles, *Narrative of United States Exploring Expedition* (5 vols., 1845).

See also 10.3 for biographies/writings of:

Bridger, James, 1804–1881
Carson, Christopher "Kit", 1809–1868
Clark, William, 1770–1838
De Smet, Pierre-Jean, 1801–1873
Frémont, John C., 1813–1890
Gunnison, John W., 1812–1853
Kern, Edward M., 1823–1863
Lewis, Meriwether, 1774–1809
Long, Stephen H., 1784–1864
Marcy, Randolph B., 1812–1887
Nuttall, Thomas, 1786–1859
Pike, Zebulon M., 1779–1813
Powell, John W., 1834–1902
Sacajawea, ca. 1787–1812
Smith, Jedediah, 1789–1831

See also chapter 9, Travels and Description.

13.3 REGIONAL STUDIES

13.3.1 Middle West

Allbeck, Willard D., *Century of Lutherans in Ohio* (1966). Covers the period, 1803–1917.
Alvord, Clarence W., *Illinois Country, 1673–1818* (1920).
Angle, Paul M., "Morris Birkbeck: Illustrious Illinoisan," *Chicago Hist.*, 8 (1967), 144.
—— *Prairie State: Impressions of Illinois 1673–1967 by Travelers* (1968).
Barnhart, John D., *Valley of Democracy: Frontier in the Ohio Valley, 1775–1818* (1953).

Benton, Elbert J., *Wabash Trade Route in Old Northwest* (1903).

Blegen, Theodore C., *Grass Roots History* (1947).

Blume, William W., "Civil Procedure on American Frontier, 1796–1805," *Mich. Law Rev.*, 56 (1957), 161.

—— "Legislation on American Frontier," *Mich. Law Rev.*, 60 (1962), 317.

Boewe, Charles, *Prairie Albion: An English Settlement in Pioneer Illinois* (1962).

Boggess, A. C., *Settlement of Illinois, 1778–1830* (1908).

Bogue, Allan G., *From Prairie to Corn Belt: Farming on Illinois and Iowa Prairies in the Nineteenth Century* (1963).

—— "Iowa Claim Clubs," *MVHR*, 45 (1958), 231.

Bond, Beverley W., *Civilization of Old Northwest* (1934).

Brown, Andrew T., *Frontier Community: Kansas City to 1870* (1963).

Buck, Solon J., *Illinois in 1818* (1917).

Buley, R. Carlyle, *The Old Northwest: Pioneer Period, 1815–1840* (2 vols., 1950).

Caruso, John A., *Appalachian Frontier* (1961).

—— *Great Lakes Frontier* (1961).

—— *Mississippi Valley Frontier* (1966).

Cockrum, W. M., *Pioneer History of Indiana* (1907).

Cooley, T. M., *Michigan* (1905).

Dillon, J. B., *A History of Indiana from Its Earliest Exploration by Europeans to the Close of the Territorial Government in 1816* (1859).

Downes, Randolph C., *Frontier Ohio, 1788–1803* (1935).

Ellis, James F., *The Influence of Environment on the Settlement of Missouri* (1929).

Fuller, George N., *Economic and Social Beginnings of Michigan* (1916).

Gue, B. F., *History of Iowa from the Earliest Times* (4 vols., [1903]).

Hatcher, Harlan, *Western Reserve: Story of New Connecticut in Ohio* (1966).

Havighurst, Walter, *Wilderness for Sale: The First Western Land Rush* (1956).

Hinsdale, B. A., *Old Northwest* (1891).

Horsman, Reginald, *The Frontier in Formative Years, 1783–1815* (1970).

Houck, Louis, *History of Missouri, from the Earliest Explorations . . . until the Admission of the State into the Union* (3 vols., 1908).

Hubbard, L. F. et al., *Minnesota in Three Centuries, 1655–1908* (4 vols., 1908).

Hulbert, A. B., ed., *Records of the Ohio Company* (2 vols., 1917).

Kellogg, L. P., *British Regime in Wisconsin and the Northwest* (1935).

Kohlmeier, A. L., *Old Northwest* (1938).

Kommers, Donald P., "Law and Justice in Pre-Territorial Wisconsin," *Am. Jour. Legal Hist.*, 8 (1964), 20.

McFarland, Julian E., *The Pioneer Era on the Iowa Prairies* (1970).

Mathews [Rosenberry], Lois K., *Expansion of New England* (1909).

Miller, James M., *The Genesis of Western Culture: The Upper Ohio Valley, 1800–1825* (1938).

Miyakawa, T. Scott, *Protestants and Pioneers* (1964).

Newhall, John B., *Glimpse of Iowa in 1846* (2nd ed., 1846).

Nicholson, Meredith, *Hoosiers* (1915).

Ogg, Frederick A., *The Old Northwest: A Chronicle of the Ohio Valley and Beyond* (1919).

Parker, G. F., *Iowa Pioneer Foundations* (2 vols., 1940).

Patterson, A. W., *History of the Backwoods or the Region of Ohio from the Earliest Accounts* (1943).

Pease, Theodore C., *The Frontier State 1818–1848* (1918). Illinois.

Peckham, Howard H., "Books and Reading on Ohio Valley Frontier," *MVHR*, 44 (1958), 649.

Philbrick, Francis S., *Rise of the West, 1754–1830* (1965).

Pooley, W. V., *Settlement of Illinois* (1908).

Power, Richard L., *Planting Corn Belt Culture: The Impress of the Upland Southerner and Yankee in the Old Northwest* (1953).

Prescott, Philander, *Recollections of Frontiersman of the Old Northwest,* Donald D. Parker, ed. (1966).

Randall, E. O., and D. J. Ryan, *History of Ohio, the Rise and Progress of an American State* (5 vols., 1912).

Scheiber, Harry N., ed., *Old Northwest: Regional History, 1787–1910* (1969).

Smith, Alice E., *James Doty* (1954).

Stilwell, Lewis D., *Migration from Vermont* (1937). Covers the period, 1776–1860.
The Susquehanna Company Papers (11 vols., 1930–1971). Vols. 1–4 ed. Julian Boyd, vols. 5–11 ed. Robert J. Taylor.
Tohill, L. A., *Robert Dickson* (1927).
Viles, Jonas, "Missouri before 1804," *Mo. Hist. Rev.,* 5 (1911), 189.
Wade, Richard C., *The Urban Frontier: The Rise of Western Cities, 1790–1830* (1959).
Wish, Harvey, "French of Old Missouri," *Mid America,* 23 (1941), 167.

See also 10.3 for biographies/writings of:

Boone, Daniel, 1734–1820
Cass, Lewis, 1782–1866
Chapman, John "Johnny Appleseed", 1775–1847
Crockett, David, 1786–1836
Cutler, Manasseh, 1742–1823
Drake, Daniel, 1785–1852
Hall, James, 1793–1868
Harrod, James, 1742–1793
Henni, John M., 1805–1881
Kenton, Simon, 1755–1836
Logan, Benjamin, 1743–1802
Mercer, George, 1733–1784
Peck, John Mason, 1789–1858
Putnam, Rufus, 1738–1824
Richard, Gabriel, 1767–1832
Sevier, John, 1745–1815
Strong, Moses M., 1810–1894
Symmes, John C., 1742–1814
Woodman, Cyrus, 1814–1889
Woodward, Augustus B., 1774–1827

See also 18.11.2.3, Agriculture–Midwest: 12.3, State and Local Histories, for individual state histories.

13.3.2 Southern Frontier

Abernethy, Thomas P., *Formative Period in Alabama* (1922).
—— *Frontier to Plantation in Tennessee* (1932).
Arnow, Harriett L. S., *Flowering of the Cumberland* (1963).
—— *Seedtime on the Cumberland* (1960).
Bailey, Kenneth P., *Thomas Cresap: Maryland Frontiersman* (1944).
Bennett, Charles E., *Settlement of Florida* (1968).
Campbell, John C., *Southern Highlanders* (1921).
Caruso, John A., *Mississippi Valley Frontier* (1966).
—— *Southern Frontier* (1963).
Chambers, Henry E., *West Florida* (1898).
Clark, Thomas D., *Kentucky* (1937).
—— *The Rampaging Frontier: Manners and Humors of Pioneer Days in South and Middle West* (1939). Covers the period, 1775–1850.
Connelley, William E., and E. Merton Coulter, *History of Kentucky* (5 vols., 1922).
Cox, Isaac J., *West Florida Controversy* (1918).
Dewhurst, W. W., *History of Saint Augustine, Florida* (1881).
Dick, Everett, *Dixie Frontier* (1948).
Gaffarel, Paul, *Histoire de la Floride Française* (1875).
Hamer, Philip M., ed., *Tennessee: A History, 1673–1932* (4 vols., 1933).
Henderson, Archibald, *Conquest of the Old Southwest, 1740–1790* (1920).
Lewis, Henry, *The Valley of the Mississippi Illustrated,* A. Hermina Poatgieter, trans., and Bertha L. Heilbron, ed. (1967).
Lowery, Charles D., "Great Migration to the Mississippi Territory, 1798–1819," *Jour. Miss. Hist.,* 30 (1968), 173.

Mathews, Lois K., "Some Activities of the Congregational Church West of the Mississippi," in Guy Stanton Ford, ed., *Essays in American History Dedicated to Frederick Jackson Turner* (1910).

Moore, Arthur K., *Frontier Mind: Kentucky* (1957).

Nasatir, Abraham P., ed., *Before Lewis and Clark: Missouri, 1785–1804* (2 vols., 1952).

Odum, Howard W., *Southern Regions* (1936).

Owsley, Frank L., "Pattern of Migration and Settlement on Southern Frontier," *JSH*, 11 (1945), 147.

Patrick, Rembert W., and Allen Morris, *Florida Under Five Flags* (4th ed., 1967).

Pickett, Albert J., *History of Alabama and Georgia and Mississippi* (1851).

Posey, Walter B., *Religious Strife on the Southern Frontier* (1965).

Thompson, Arthur W., *Jacksonian Democracy on the Florida Frontier* (1961).

Toulmin, Harry, *Western Country in 1793: Kentucky and Virginia*, Marion Tinling and Godfrey Davies, eds. (1948).

Williams, John L., *The Territory of Florida* (1837); Herbert J. Doherty, ed. (1962).

*   *   *   *   *   *   *

Edwards, Everett E., *References on Mountaineers of Southern Appalachians* (1935).

See also 10.3 for biographies/writings of:

Bates, Frederick, 1777–1825
Duchesne, Rose P., 1769–1852
Flint, Timothy, 1780–1840
Hawkins, Benjamin, 1754–1816
Lincecum, Gideon, 1793–1874
Morgan, George, 1743–1810
Walker, John W., 1783–1823

See also 12.3, State and Local Histories, for individual state histories.

13.3.3 Great Plains

Athearn, Robert G., *High Country Empire: High Plains and Rockies* (1960).

Barnard, Evan G., *Rider of Cherokee Strip* (1936).

Dodge, Richard I., *Plains of the Great West* (1877).

Drache, Hiram M., *Day of the Bonanza: Bonanza Farming in Red River Valley* (1964).

Foreman, Grant, *Advancing the Frontier, 1830–1860* (1933).

Kansas, University of, *Territorial Kansas: Studies Commemorating the Centennial* (1954).

Murray, Stanley N., *Valley Comes of Age: Agriculture in Valley of Red River, 1812–1920* (1967).

Ottoson, Howard W. et al., *Land and People in Northern Plains Transition Area* (1966).

Pritchett, John P., *Red River Valley, 1811–1849* (1942).

Sanford, Mollie D., *Journal in Nebraska and Colorado Territories, 1857–1866*, Donald F. Danker, ed. (1959).

Sutley, Z. T., *Last Frontier* (1930).

Webb, Walter P., *The Great Plains* (1931).

*   *   *   *   *   *   *

Wagner, Henry R., ed., *The Plains and the Rockies: A Bibliography of Original Narratives of Travel and Adventure, 1800–1865*, Charles L. Camp, ed. (3d ed., 1953).

See also 10.3 for biographies/writings of:

Cody, William F., 1846–1917
Gregg, Josiah, 1806–1850
Keane, John J., 1839–1918
North, Frank J., 1840–1885
North, Luther, fl. 1856–1882
Robinson, Charles, 1818–1894
Sandoz, Jules A., 1857?–1928
Walker, Robert J., 1801–1869
Williams, Robert Lee, 1868–1948

See also 12.3, State and Local Histories, for individual state histories.

13.3.4 Mountain West

Anderson, Nels, *Desert Saints: The Mormon Frontier in Utah* (1942).
Arrington, Leonard J., *Great Basin Kingdom: An Economic History of the Latter-Day Saints, 1830–1900* (1958).
Athearn, Robert G., *High Country Empire: High Plains and Rockies* (1960).
Bancroft, Hubert H., *History of Washington, Idaho, and Montana* (1890).
—— *Nevada, Colorado, and Wyoming* (1890).
Briggs, Harold E., *Frontiers of the Northwest* (1940).
Brooks, Juanita, *Mountain Meadows Massacre* (1950).
Burlingame, Merrill G., *Montana Frontier* (1942).
Brough, C. H., *Irrigation in Utah* (1898).
Cannon, M. H., "Migration of English Mormons," *AHR*, 52 (1947), 436.
Creer, Leland H., *Founding of an Empire: Utah, 1776–1856* (1947).
—— *Utah and Nation* (1929).
Elsensohn, M. A., *Pioneer Days in Idaho County* (1947).
Hafen, Leroy R., and Ann W. Hafen, ed., *The Far West and Rockies Historical Series* (15 vols., 1954–1961).
Hakola, John W., *Frontier Omnibus* (1962).
Hall, Frank, *History of Colorado* (4 vols., 1889–1895).
Hunter, Milton R., *Utah, the Story of Her People, 1540–1947* (1946).
Larson, Gustive O., *Prelude to Kingdom: Mormon Desert Conquest* (1947).
Linn, William A., *The Story of the Mormons* (1902).
McNiff, William J., *Heaven on Earth* (1940).
Marshall, Thomas M., *Western Boundary of Louisiana Purchase* (1914).
Mulder, William, *Homeward to Zion: Mormon Migration from Scandinavia* (1957).
Nelson, Lowry, *Mormon Village* (1952).
Roberts, Brigham H., *Church of Latter Day Saints* (6 vols., 1930).
Stegner, Wallace E., *Gathering of Zion: The Mormon Trail* (1964).
Stone, Wilbur F., *History of Colorado* (3 vols., 1918).
Taylor, Philip A. M., *Expectations Westward: Mormons and Emigration of Their British Converts in the Nineteenth Century* (1966).
Willard, James F., ed., *Union Colony at Greeley, Colorado, 1869–1871* (1918).
—— and Colin B. Goodykoontz, eds., *Experiments in Colorado Colonization, 1869–1872* (1926).

*　　*　　*　　*　　*　　*　　*

Wagner, Henry R., ed., *The Plains and the Rockies: A Bibliography of Original Narratives of Travel and Adventure, 1800–1865*, Charles L. Camp, ed. (3d. ed., 1953).

See also 10.3 for biographies/writings of:

Bridger, James, 1804–1881
De Smet, Pierre-Jean, 1801–1873
Grouard, Frank, 1850–1905
Young, Brigham, 1801–1877

See also 24.7.10, Religion–Mormonism; 12.3, State and Local Histories, for individual state histories.

13.3.5 Spanish Borderlands

Bannon, John F., ed., *Bolton and the Spanish Borderlands* (1964).
—— *Spanish Borderlands Frontier* (1970).
Beck, Warren A., *New Mexico: History of Four Centuries* (1962).
Bieber, R. P., and L. R. Hafen, eds., *Southwest Historical Series* (12 vols., 1931–1943).
Bean, Lowell J., and William M. Mason, eds., *The Romero Expeditions, 1823–1826* (1963).
Bolton, Herbert E., *Outpost of Empire* (1931).
—— *Pageant in the Wilderness* (1951).
—— *The Spanish Borderlands* (1921).
—— *Texas in the Middle Eighteenth Century* (1915).
Brinckerhoff, Sidney B., "Last Years of Spanish Arizona," *Ariz. and West*, 9 (1967), 5.
Connor, Seymour V., *The Peters Colony of Texas: A History and Biographical Sketches of the Early Settler* (1959).
Cox, Isaac J., "Louisiana-Texas Frontier," Texas State Hist. Assoc., *Quar.*, 10 (1907), 1.
Dobie, J. Frank, *Guide to Life and Literature of Southwest* (rev. ed., 1952).
Dominguez, Francisco A., *Missions of New Mexico, 1776*, Eleanor B. Adams and Fray Angelico Chavez, trans. and ed. (1956).
Faulk, Odie B., *Land of Many Frontiers: American Southwest* (1968).
—— *Last Years of Spanish Texas, 1778–1821* (1964).
Forbes, Jack D., *Apache, Navaho and Spaniard* (1960).
—— "The Development of the Yuma Route before 1826," *Calif. Hist. Soc. Quar.*, 43 (1964), 99.
Foreman, Grant, *Indians and Pioneers: American Southwest before 1830* (1937).
Garcés, Francisco, *Diary and Itinerary . . . Travels through Sonora, Arizona and California, 1775–1776*, Elliott Coues, ed. (2 vols., 1900).
Hatcher, Mattie A., *The Opening of Texas to Foreign Settlements, 1801–1821* (1927).
Hollon, W. Eugene, *Great American Desert: Then and Now* (1966).
—— *The Southwest: Old and New* (1961).
Horgan, Paul, *Great River: Rio Grande in North American History* (2 vols., 1954).
Lathrop, Barnes F., *Migration into East Texas, 1835–1860* (1949).
Lavender, David, *The American Heritage History of the Great West*, Alvin M. Josephy, ed. (1965).
Lockwood, Frank C., *Pioneer Days in Arizona from the Spanish Occupation to Statehood* (1932).
Martinez, Antonio, *Letters: Spanish Governor of Texas, 1817–1822*, Virginia H. Taylor, ed. (1957).
Noggle, Burl, "Anglo Observers of Southwest Borderlands, 1825–1890," *Ariz. and West*, 1 (1959), 105.
Posey, Walter B., *Frontier Mission: Religion West of the Southern Appalachians to 1861* (1966) .
Richardson, Rupert N., *Frontier of Northwest Texas, 1846–1876* (1963).
—— and Carl C. Rister, *The Greater Southwest* (1934).
Rister, Carl C., *Southwestern Frontier* (1928).
Ross, Calvin, *River of the Sun: Stories of the Storied Gila* (1946).
Sedelmayr, Jacobo, *Explorer in Arizona: Narratives, 1744–1751*, Peter M. Dunne, trans. and ed. (1955).
Smith, Justin H., *Annexation of Texas* (1911).
Spicer, Edward H., *Cycles of Conquest: Impact on the Indians of the Southwest, 1533–1960* (1962).
Thomas, Alfred B., ed., *The Plains Indians and New Mexico, 1751–1778* (1940).
Tunstall, John H., *Letters and Diaries*, Frederick W. Nolan, ed. (1965).
Warner, Ted J., "Frontier Defense," *New Mex. Hist. Rev.*, 41 (1966), 5.

Weddle, Robert S., *San Juan Bautista: Gateway to Spanish Texas* (1968).
———— *The San Sabô Mission: Spanish Pivot in Texas* (1964).
Wellman, Paul I., *Glory, God and Gold* (1954).
Wooten, Dudley G., ed., *Comprehensive History of Texas* (2 vols., 1898).
Wyllys, R. K., *Arizona: The History of a Frontier State* (1950).

*   *   *   *   *   *   *

Kurtz, S. Kenneth, *Literature of the Southwest: Selected Bibliography* (1956).
Wallace, Andrew, *Sources and Readings in Arizona's History: Checklist* (1965).

See also 10.3 for biographies/writings of:

Austin, Stephen F., 1793–1836
Bangs, Samuel, ca.1794–ca.1853
Burnet, David G., 1788–1870
Ford, John S. "Rip", fl. 1836–1896
Houston, Samuel, 1793–1863
Meriwether, David, 1800–1892
Meusebach, John O., fl. mid-nineteenth century

See also 12.3, State and Local Histories, for individual state histories.

13.3.6 California

Berger, John A., *Franciscan Missions of California* (1941).
Bolton, Herbert E., ed., *Anza's California Expeditions* (5 vols., 1930).
Bolton, Herbert E., *Font's Complete Diary: A Chronicle of the Founding of San Francisco* (1933).
———— *Fray Juan Crespi* (1927).
———— *Pacific Ocean in History* (1915).
Caughey, John W., *California* (1940).
Caughey, John W., and LaRee Caughey, eds., *California Heritage: An Anthology of History and Literature* (1962).
Caughey, John W., *History of the Pacific Coast* (1933).
Chapman, Charles E., *The Founding of Spanish California, 1687–1783* (1916).
———— *History of California: The Spanish Period* (1921).
Chevigny, Hector, *Lost Empire: Life of Rezánov* (1937).
Cleland, Robert G., *California* (1922).
———— *From Wilderness to Empire: California*, Glenn S. Dumke, ed. (rev. ed., 1959).
Coughlin, Magdalen, "California Ports, 1820–1845," *Jour. of West*, 5 (1966), 153.
Dillon, Richard H., *J. Ross Browne: Confidential Agent in Old California* (1965).
Dunne, Peter M., *Black Robes in Lower California* (1952).
Engelhardt, Zephyrin, *Missions and Missionaries of California* (4 vols., 1908–1915).
Garnier, Pierre, *Medical Journey in California*, Doyce B. Nunis, Jr., ed., L. Jay Oliva, trans. (1967). Covers the period, 1851–1852.
Geiger, Maynard J., *Franciscan Missionaries in Hispanic California, 1769–1848: A Biographical Dictionary* (1969).
Hutchinson, C. Alan, *Frontier Settlement in Mexican California* (1969).
Kirsch, Robert R., and William S. Murphy, *West of the West: California Experience, 1542–1906* (1967).
Lyman, George D., *John Marsh: Pioneer on Six Frontiers* (1930).
MacMullen, Jerry, *Paddle Wheel Days in California* (1944).
Palóu, Francisco, *Noticias de la Nueva California*, Herbert E. Bolton, ed. (4 vols., 1926).
Richman, I. B., *California under Spain and Mexico, 1535–1847* . . . (1911).
Robinson, Alfred, *Life in California before the Conquest* (2nd ed., 1968).

Rolle, Andrew F., *California* (2nd ed., 1969).
Rydell, R. A., *Cape Horn to Pacific* (1952).
Thompson, Alpheus B., *China Trade Days in California: Selected Letters from the Thompson Papers, 1832–1863*, Donald M. Brown, ed. (1947).
Underhill, R. L., *From Cowhides to Golden Fleece* (1946).

*   *   *   *   *   *   *

Cowan, Robert E., *A Bibliography of the History of California, 1510–1930* (4 vols., 1933–1964).

See also 10.3 for biographies/writings of:

Burnett, Peter H., 1807–1895
Davis, William Heath, 1822–1909
Kino, Eusebio Francisco, 1645–1711
Larkin, Thomas O., 1802–1858
Schallenberger, Moses, 1826–1909
Señan, Jose, O.F.M., fl. 1796–1823
Serra, Fray Junípero, 1713–1784
Terry, Davis S., 1823–1889

See also 13.4.10.2, California Gold Rush.

13.3.7 Pacific Northwest

Bancroft, Hubert H., *New Pacific* (1913).
Bancroft, Hubert H., *Oregon* (2 vols., 1886–1888).
Briggs, Harold E., *Frontiers of Northwest* (1940).
Carey, C. H., *A General History of Oregon prior to 1861* (2 vols., 1935–1936).
Caughey, John W., *History of the Pacific Coast* (1933).
Cox, Ross, *Adventures on the Columbia River* (1831). Published under variant title, *Columbia River*, Edgar I. and Jane R. Stewart, eds. (1957). Covers the period 1811–1817.
Drury, C. M., *Elkanah and Mary Walker* (1940).
———— *Henry Harmon Spaulding* (1936).
Gay, Theressa, *Life and Letters of Mrs. Jason Lee* (1936).
Gilbert, James H., *Trade and Currency in Early Oregon* (1907).
Hafen, LeRoy R., and Ann W. Hafen, eds., *The Far West and Rockies Series* (15 vols., 1954–1961).
Holman, Frederick V., *Dr. John McLoughlin, Father of Oregon* (1907).
Jacobs, Melvin C., *Winning Oregon* (1938).
Johansen, Dorothy O., and Charles M. Gates, *Empire of Columbia: A History of the Pacific Northwest* (1957).
Lavender, David S., *Land of Giants: Drive to the Pacific Northwest 1750–1950* (1958).
Pomeroy, Earl S., *The Pacific Slope* (1965).
Warren, Sidney, *Farthest Frontier: The Pacific Northwest* (1949).
Winser, H. J., *The Great Northwest: A Guidebook and Itinerary* (1883).
Winther, Oscar O., *Great Northwest* (1947).
———— *Old Oregon Country: Frontier Trade, Transportation and Travel* (1949).

*   *   *   *   *   *   *

Cowan, Robert E., *A Bibliography of the History of California and the Pacific Coast* (1952).
Nute, G. L., *Documents Relating to Northwest Missions, 1815–27* (1942).
Oregon Historical Society, *A Bibliography of Pacific Northwest History* (1958).
Smith, Charles Wesley, *Pacific Northwest Americana: A Checklist of Books and Pamphlets*, Isabel Mayhew, ed. (3d ed., 1950).

Vaughan, Thomas, and Priscilla Knuth, *A Bibliography of Pacific Northwest History* (1958).

See also 10.3 for biographies/writings of:

Corbin, Daniel Chase, 1837–1918
Lane, Joseph, 1801–1881
Lee, Jason, 1803–1845
McLoughlin, John, 1784–1857
Villard, Henry, 1835–1900
Whitman, Marcus, 1802–1847
Whitman, Narcissa, 1808–1847

See also 12.3, State and Local Histories, for individual state histories.

13.3.8 Alaska

Adams, Ben, *The Last Frontier: Alaska* (1961).
Andrews, C. L., *The Story of Alaska* (1938)
Bancroft, Hubert H., *Alaska* (1886).
Chevigny, Hector, *Russian America: Alaskan Venture, 1741–1867* (1965).
Sherwood, Morgan B., *Exploration of Alaska, 1865–1900* (1965).

* * * * * * *

Lada-Mocarski, Valerian, ed., *Bibliography of Books on Alaska Published before 1868* (1969).
Wickersham, James, *Bibliography of Alaskan Literature* (1927).

13.4 TOPICAL STUDIES

13.4.1 Military Frontier

Athearn, Robert G., *Forts of the Upper Missouri* (1967).
Bearss, Edwin C., and A. M. Gibson, *Fort Smith* (1969).
Beers, H. P., *Western Military Frontier* (1935).
Bender, Averam B., *March of Empire: Frontier Defense in the Southwest, 1848–1860* (1952).
Brown, Dee, *Fort Phil Kearny* (1962).
Carriker, Robert C., *Fort Supply, Indian Territory: Frontier Outpost on the Plains* (1970).
Emmett, Chris, *Fort Union and the Winning of the Southwest* (1965).
Flipper, Henry O., *Negro Frontiersman: Western Memoirs*, Theodore D. Harris, ed. (1963).
Foreman, Grant, *Fort Gibson* (1936).
Frazer, Robert W., *Forts of the West: Military Forts and Presidios and Posts Commonly Called Forts West of the Mississippi* (1965).
Goetzmann, William H., *Army Exploration in the American West, 1803–1863* (1959).
Hafen, Leroy R., *Fort Laramie* (1938).
Hansen, Marcus L., *Old Fort Snelling, 1819–1858* (1918).
Havighurst, Walter, *Three Flags at the Straits: Forts of Mackinac* (1966).
Howard, Robert W., *Thundergate: The Forts of Niagara* (1968).
Hussey, John A., *The History of Fort Vancouver and Its Physical Structures* (1957).
Jones, Evan, *Citadel in the Wilderness: Fort Snelling and Old Northwest Frontier* (1966).
Lavender, David, *Bent's Fort* (1954).

Mahan, Bruce T., *Old Fort Crawford and the Frontier* (1926).
Mansfield, Joseph K., *On the Condition of Western Forts, 1853–54*, Robert W. Frazer, ed. (1963).
Mapes, Ruth B., *Old Fort Smith: Cultural Center on Southwestern Frontier* (1965).
Morrison, William B., *Military Posts and Camps in Oklahoma* (1936).
Murray, Robert A., *Military Posts in Powder River Country of Wyoming, 1865–1894* (1969).
Nye, Wilbur S., *Carbine and Lance: Old Fort Sill* (1937).
Oliva, Leo E., *Soldiers on the Santa Fe Trail* (1967).
Prucha, Francis P., *Broadax and Bayonet: Army in the Northwest, 1815–1860* (1953).
——— *Guide to the Military Posts of the United States, 1789–1895* (1964).
——— *Sword of the Republic: Army on Frontier, 1783–1846* (1964).
Thornbrough, Gayle, ed., *Outpost on the Wabash, 1787–1791: Letters and Documents Selected from Harmar Papers in William L. Clements Library* (1957).
Wesley, E. B., *Guarding the Frontier* (1935).

See also 10.3 for biographies/writings of:

Atkinson, Henry, Gen., 1782–1842
Carr, Eugene A., 1830–1910
Cooke, Philip St. George, 1809–1895
Crook, George 1829–1890
Custer, George A., 1839–1876
Gaines, Edmund P., 1777–1849
Humphreys, David, 1752–1818
Kearny, Stephen W., 1794–1848
Miles, Nelson A., 1839–1925
Moore, Edwin W., 1810–1865
Pratt, Richard H., 1840–1924

See also 20.11.14, Indian Wars after 1865.

13.4.2 Fur Trade

Belden, Albert L., *The Fur Trade of America and Some of the Men Who Maintain It . . .* (1917).
Bryce, George, *Remarkable History of Hudson's Bay Company* (1900).
Chittenden, Hiram M., *American Fur Trade of the Far West* (rev. ed., 3 vols., 1935).
Clayton, James L., "Growth and Economic Significance of the American Fur Trade," *Minn. Hist.*, 40 (1966), 210.
Cleland, Robert G., *This Reckless Breed: Trappers of the Southwest* (1950).
De Voto, Bernard, *Across the Wide Missouri* (1947).
Dick, Everett, *Vanguards of Frontier* (1941).
Dillon, Richard, *Legend of Grizzly Adams: California's Greatest Mountain Man* (1966).
Galbraith, John S., *The Hudson's Bay Company as an Imperial Factor, 1821–1869* (1957).
Goetzmann, William H., "Mountain Man as Jacksonian Man," *Am. Quar.*, 15 (1963), 402.
Hafen, LeRoy R., ed., *Mountain Men and the Fur Trade of the Far West: Biographical Sketches* (6 vols., 1965–1968).
Irving, Washington, *Astoria* (1860); Edgeley W. Todd, ed. (1964).
Johnson, Ida A., *Michigan Fur Trade* (1919).
Kelly, Charles, and M. L. Howe, *Miles Goodyear, First Citizen of Utah* (1937).
——— *Old Greenwood: The Story of Caleb Greenwood* (1965).
Lavender, David S., *Fist in the Wilderness* (1964).
Lent, D. Geneva, *West of the Mountains: James Sinclair and Hudson's Bay Company* (1963).

Leonard, Zenas, *Adventures of Fur Trader* (1839); John C. Ewers, ed. (1959).

Lippincott, Isaac, *Century and a Half of Fur Trade at St. Louis* (1916).

MacKay, Douglas, *Honourable Company* (1936).

Morgan, Dale L., *Jedediah Smith and Opening of West* (1953).

—— ed., *The West of William H. Ashley: Struggle for the Fur Trade, 1822–1838* (1964).

Nunis, Doyce B., Jr., "The Enigma of the Sublette Overland Party, 1845," *Pac. Hist. Rev.*, 28 (1959), 331.

—— "The Fur Men: Key to Westward Expansion, 1822–1830," *Historian*, 23 (1961), 167.

Nute, Grace L., "The Papers of the American Fur Company," Am. Hist. Assoc., *Report*, 1944. Covers the period, 1834–1847.

Ogden, Adele, *California Sea Otter Trade* (1941).

Ogden, Peter S., *Snake Country Journal, 1826–1827*, K. G. Davies, ed. (1961).

Oglesby, Richard E., *Manuel Lisa and Opening of Missouri Fur Trade* (1963).

Parkhill, Forbes, *The Blazed Trail of Antoine Leroux* (1966).

Phillips, Paul C., *Fur Trade* (2 vols., 1961).

Pratt, Julius W., "Fur Trade Strategy," *AHR*, 40 (1935), 246.

Rich, Edwin E., *Hudson's Bay Company, 1670–1870* (3 vols., 1961).

Ross, Alexander, *Fur Hunters of Far West* (1855); Kenneth A. Spaulding, ed. (1956).

Russell, Carl P., *Firearms, Traps and Tools of Mountain Men* (1967).

—— *Guns on Early Frontiers* (1957).

Sage, Rufus B., *Letters and Papers, 1836–1847*, LeRoy R. and Ann W. Hafen, eds. (2 vols., 1956).

Saum, Lewis O., *The Fur Trader and the Indian* (1965).

Simpson, George, *Fur Trade and Empire*, Frederick Merk, ed. (rev. ed., 1968). New York, 1824–1825.

Skinner, Constance L., *Adventures of Oregon: Fur Trade* (1920).

Stevens, Wayne E., *Northwest Fur Trade, 1763–1800* (1928).

Stuart, Robert, *The Discovery of the Oregon Trail: Robert Stuart's Narratives*, P. A. Rollins, ed. (1935). Covers the period, 1811–1813.

Sunder, John E., *The Fur Trade on Upper Missouri, 1840–1865* (1965).

Templeton, Sardis, *The Lame Captain: The Life and Adventures of Pegleg Smith* (1965).

Thompson, David, *Narrative*, Richard Glover, ed. (new ed., 1962).

Tohill, L. A., *Robert Dickson* (1927).

Tolmie, William F., *Journals of Physician and Fur Trader* (1963). Covers the period, 1830–1842.

Vandiveer, Clarence A., *Fur Trade and Early Western Exploration* (1929).

Washburn, Wilcomb E., "Symbol, Utility and Aesthetics in Indian Fur Trade," *Minn. Hist.*, 40 (1966), 198.

Way, R. B., "Factory System for Trading," *MVHR*, 6 (1920), 220.

Wilson, Iris H., *William Wolfskill* (1965).

Yount, George C., *Chronicles of West*, Charles L. Camp, ed. (1966). Early California.

*   *   *   *   *   *   *

Morgan, Dale L., "Fur Trade and Its Historians," *Am. West*, 3 (1966), 28.

See also 10.3 for biographies/writings of:

Astor, John Jacob, 1763–1848
Carson, Christopher, 1809–1868
Fitzpatrick, Thomas, 1799–1854
McLoughlin, John, 1784–1857
Pilcher, Joshua, 1790–1840
Smith, Jedediah, 1789–1831
Sublette, Andrew, 1808–1853
Sublette, William L., ca. 1799–1845
Thompson, David, 1770–1857

Trent, William, 1715–1787

See also 32.2.2, Exploration and Fur Trade.

13.4.3 Law Enforcement

Gard, Wayne, *Frontier Justice* (1949).
Garnett, Porter, and Mary F. Williams, eds., *Papers of San Francisco Committee of Vigilance* (3 vols., 1910–1919).
Langford, Nathaniel P., *Vigilante Days and Ways* (1890).
Mercer, Asa S., *Banditti of the Plains* (1894).
Raine, W. M., *Famous Sheriffs and Western Outlaws* (1929).
───── *Guns of Frontier* (1940).
Rister, Carl C., "Outlaws and Vigilantes of Southern Plains," *MVHR*, 19 (1933), 537.
Shirley, Glenn, *Law West of Fort Smith: A History of Frontier Justice in the Indian Territory* (1957).
Webb, Walter P., *Texas Rangers* (1935).

See also 10.3 for biographies/writings of:

Hickock, James B. "Wild Bill", 1837–1876
James, Jesse, 1847–1882
Parker, Isaac C., 1838–1896

13.4.4 Pioneer Life

Brandt, R. O., "Prairie Pioneering," *Norwegian-Am Stud. and Rec.,* 7 (1933), 1.
Brown, Dee A., *Gentle Tamers: Women of the Old West* (1958).
Clark, Thomas D., *Pills, Petticoats and Plows: The Southern Country Store* (1944).
Cruikshank, E. A., *Political Adventures of John Henry* (1936).
Dale, Edward E., *Frontier Ways* (1959).
Dick, Everett, *Sod-House Frontier* (new ed., 1954).
Drury, Clifford M., ed., *First White Women over the Rockies: Diaries, Letters, and Biographical Sketches* (1966).
Egleston, N. H., *Village and Village Life* (1878).
Eno, Henry, *Letters from California and Nevada, 1848–1871*, W. Turrentine Jackson, ed. (1965).
Esarey, Logan, *Indiana Home* (1953).
Hilleary, William M., *Diary, 1864–1866*, Herbert B. Nelson and Preston E. Onstad, eds. (1965).
Ise, John, *Sod and Stubble* (1936).
Miller, James M., *Genesis of Western Culture* (1938).
Nicholson, Meredith, *Hoosiers* (1915).
Otero, M. A., *My Life on the Frontier* (2 vols., 1935–1939).
Pritchard, James A., *Overland Diary, 1849*, Dale L. Morgan, ed. (1959).
Reinhart, Herman F., *Recollections*, Doyce B. Nunis, Jr., ed. (1962).
Ross, Nancy W., *Westward the Women* (1945).
Ruede, Howard, *Sod-House Days* (1937).
Ruxton, George F., *Life in the Far West* (1849); LeRoy R. Hafen, ed. (1951).
Sanford, Mollie D., *Journal in Nebraska and Colorado Territories, 1857–1866*, Donald F. Danker, ed. (1959).
Smith, Helena Huntington, "Pioneers in Petticoats," *Am. Heritage*, 10, no. 2 (1959) 36.
Stewart, George R., ed., *Opening of California Trail: Reminiscences of Moses Schallenberger as Set Down for H. H. Bancroft about 1885* (1953).
Still, Bayrd, *West: A Contemporary Account of Westward Expansion* (1961).
Tunstall, John H., *Letters and Diaries*, Frederick W. Nolan, ed. (1965).
Wallace, Allie B., *Frontier Life in Oklahoma* (1964).
Ward, Harriet S., *Prairie Schooner Lady: Journal, 1853*, Ward G. and Florence S. DeWitt, eds. (1959).
Wright, John E., and Doris S. Corbett, *Pioneer Life* (1940).

13.4.5 Trails

Frey, Howard C., *Conestoga Wagon, 1750–1850* (1964).
Garrard, Lewis H., *Wah-to-yah and Taos Trail* (1850); LeRoy R. Hafen, ed., (1955).
Geiger, Vincent, and Wakeman Bryarly, *Trail to California: Journal*, David M. Potter, ed. (1962).
Ghent, W. J., *Road to Oregon* (1929).
Gregg, Josiah, *Commerce of the Prairies: Or, the Journal of a Santa Fè Trader* (2 vols., 1844). Covers the period, 1831–1839.
—— *Diary and Letters* (2 vols., 1941–1944).
Hafen, LeRoy R., *Overland Routes to Gold Fields, 1859* (1942).
Hulbert, A. B., *Overland to Pacific* (8 vols., 1933–1941).
—— *Transcontinental Trails* (6 vols., 1925–1928).
Ide, L. A., "In a Prairie Schooner," *Wash. Hist. Quar.*, 18 (1927), 122.
Kelly, Charles, *Salt Desert Trail* (1930).
Lavender, David S., *Westward Vision: Oregon Trail* (1963).
Magoffin, Susan S., *Down the Santa Fe Trail and into Mexico*, Stella M. Drumm, ed. (1926).
Moorhead, Max L., *New Mexico's Royal Road: Chihuahua Trail* (1958).
Nunis, Doyce B., Jr., "Sublette Overland Party, 1845," *Pac. Hist. Rev.*, 28 (1959), 331.
Paden, Irene D., *Wake of Prairie Schooner* (1943).
Parkman, Francis, *Oregon Trail* (1849).
Stewart, George R., *The California Trail* (1962).
—— *Ordeal by Hunger: Donner Party* (rev. ed., 1960).
White, Helen M., ed., *Ho! For the Gold Fields: Wagon Trains of 1860's* (1966).

See also 18.16.2, Early Roads and Turnpikes; 18.16.3, Stagecoaches and Express Business; 9.4 and 9.5, Travels and Description.

13.4.6 The Western Hero

Davis, David B., "Ten-Gallon Hero," *Am. Quar.*, 6 (1954), 111.
Lyon, Peter, "Wild, Wild West," *Am. Heritage*, 11 (1960), 33.
Sollid, Roberta B., *Calamity Jane: Study in Historical Criticism* (1958).
Steckmesser, K. L., *Western Hero in History and Legend* (1965).

See also 13.4.7, Cowboys and Cattle Raising.

13.4.7 Cowboys and Cattle Raising

Abbott, Edward C., and Helene H. Smith, *We Pointed Them North* (1939).
Adams, Andy, *Log of Cowboy* (1903).
Atherton, Lewis E., *Cattle Kings* (1961).
Branch, E. Douglas, *Cowboy and His Interpreters* (1926).
Burroughs, John R., *Where the Old West Stayed Young* (1962).
Cauley, T. J., "Early Business Methods in Texas Cattle Industry," *Jour. Econ. and Bus. Hist.*, 4 (1932), 461.
Cleland, Robert G., *Cattle on a Thousand Hills* (1941).
Coe, Wilbur, *Ranch on Ruidoso: Pioneer Family in New Mexico, 1871–1968* (1968).
Dale, E. E., *Cow Country* (rev. ed., 1965).
—— *Range Cattle Industry* (2nd ed., 1960).
Dick, Everett, "Long Drive," Kan State Hist. Soc., *Coll.*, 17 (1926), 27.
Dobie, J. F., *Longhorns* (1941).
Drago, Harry S., *Great American Cattle Trails* (1965).
Durham, Philip, and Everett L. Jones, *The Negro Cowboys* (1965).
Dykstra, Robert R., *Cattle Towns* (1968).
Fletcher, Robert H., *Free Grass to Fences: Montana Cattle Range* (1960).
Foss, Philip O., *Politics and Grass: Grazing on Public Domain* (1960).

Frantz, Joe B., and Julian E. Choate, Jr., *American Cowboy: Myth and Reality* (1955).

French, William, *Recollections of Western Ranchman* (1928).

Frink, Maurice, W. Turrentine Jackson, and Agnes W. Spring, *When Grass Was King: Range Cattle Industry* (1956).

Gard, Wayne, *Chisholm Trail* (1954).

Gates, Paul W., "Cattle Kings in the Prairies," *MVHR*, 35 (1948), 379.

Gressley, Gene M., *Bankers and Cattlemen* (1966).

Haskett, Bert, "Early Cattle Industry in Arizona," *Ariz. Hist. Rev.*, 6, no. 4 (1935), 3.

Henderson, J. C., "Reminiscences of Range Rider," *Chronicles Okla.*, 3 (1925), 253.

Henlein, Paul C., *Cattle Kingdom in the Ohio Valley, 1783–1860* (1959).

Hunter, John M., ed., *Trail Drivers of Texas* (1925).

Jaques, M. J., *Texan Ranch Life* (1894).

Morrisey, R. J., "Early Range Cattle Industry in Arizona," *Agric. Hist.*, 24 (1950), 151.

Oliphant, J. Orin, *Cattle Ranges of Oregon Country* (1968).

Osgood, E. S., *Day of the Cattlemen* (1929).

Peake, Ora B., *Colorado Range Cattle Industry* (1937).

Pelzer, Louis, *The Cattlemen's Frontier* (1936).

Phillips, Rufus, "Cowboy Life in Arkansas Valley," *Colo. Mag.*, 7 (1930), 165.

Ridings, S. P., *Chisholm Trail* (1936).

Rister, Carl C., *Southern Plainsmen* (1938).

Rollins, P. A., *Cowboy* (1936).

Sandoz, Mari, *The Cattlemen* (1958).

Schlebecker, John T., *Cattle Raising on the Plains, 1900–1961* (1963).

Stephens, Alva R., *Taft Ranch: Texas* (1964).

Tanberg, Frank, "Cowboy Life in Colorado," *Colo. Mag.*, 12 (1935), 23.

Taylor, Thomas U., *Chisholm Trail and Other Routes* (1936).

Towne, Charles W., and Edward N. Wentworth, *Cattle and Men* (1955).

Wellman, P. I., *Trampling Herd* (1939).

Westermeier, Clifford P., ed., *Trailing the Cowboy: Frontier Journalists* (1955).

Wilson, James A., "Arizona Cattle Industry," *Ariz. and West*, 8 (1966), 339.

*   *   *   *   *   *   *

Adams Ramon F., *Rampaging Herd: Bibliography of the Cattle Industry* (1959).

Kahn, Herman, "Records in National Archives Relating to Range Cattle Industry," *Agric. Hist.*, 20 (1946), 187.

13.4.8 Buffalo

Branch, E. Douglas, *Hunting of Buffalo* (1929).

Burlingame, M. G., "Buffalo in Trade and Commerce," *No. Dak. Hist.*, 3 (1929), 262.

Gard, Wayne, *Great Buffalo Hunt* (1959).

Garretson, Martin S., *American Bison* (1938).

Mayer, Frank H., and Charles B. Roth, *Buffalo Harvest* (1958).

Rister, Carl C., "Destruction of Buffalo in Southwest," *Southw. Hist. Quar.*, 33 (1929), 34.

Sandoz, Mari, *Buffalo Hunters* (1954).

Trexler, H. A., "Buffalo Range of Northwest," *MVHR*, 7 (1920), 348.

13.4.9 Government Policy and the Territories

Albright, R. E., "Western Statehood Movement," *Pacific Hist. Rev.*, 3 (1934), 296.

Colgrove, K. W., "Attitude of Congress toward Pioneers," *Iowa Jour. Hist. and Pol.*, 8 (1910), 3.

Eblen, Jack E., *First and Second United States Empires: Governors and Territorial Government, 1784–1912* (1968).

Ellison, Joseph, *California and the Nation, 1850–1869: A Study of the Relations of a Frontier Community with the Federal Government* (1927).

Hicks, John D., *Constitutions of Northwest States* (1923).

Hockett, Homer C., "Federalism and West," in Guy Stanton Ford, ed., *Essays in American History Dedicated to Frederick Jackson Turner* (1910).

Lamar, Howard R., *Dakota Territory, 1861–1889* (1956).

Neil, William M., "American Territorial System since Civil War," *Ind. Mag. Hist.*, 60 (1964), 219.

Paxson, Frederick L., "Admission of Omnibus States," *Wisc. Hist. Soc., Proc.*, 59 (1911), 77.

Pomeroy, Earl S., *The Territories and the United States 1861–1890* (1949).

Still, Bayrd, "Statehood Process, 1800 to 1850," *MVHR*, 23 (1936), 189.

See also 25.7, Nationalism and Mission.

13.4.10 Frontier Mining

13.4.10.1 General

Fisher, Vardis, and Opal L. Holmes, *Gold Rushes and Mining Camps of Early American West* (1968).

Greever, William S., *Bonanza West: Western Mining Rushes, 1848–1900* (1963).

Hill, Jim D., "Early Mining Camp," *Pac. Hist. Rev.*, 1 (1932), 295.

Lewis, Marvin, ed., *Mining Frontier: Contemporary Accounts from Nineteenth Century* (1967).

Paul, Rodman W., *Mining Frontiers of Far West, 1848–1880* (1963).

Quiett, G. C., *Pay Dirt* (1936).

Shinn, Charles H., *Mining Camps: American Frontier Government* (1885).

Smith, Duane A., *Rocky Mountain Mining Camps* (1967).

Spence, Clark C., *British Investments and American Mining Frontier, 1860–1901* (1958).

——— *Mining Engineers and the West: Lace-Boot Brigade, 1849–1933* (1970).

Thompson, Thomas G., "Far Western Mining Frontier," *Colo. Mag.*, 41 (1964), 105.

See also 18.15.11, Industry–Mining

13.4.10.2 California Gold Rush

Bateson, Charles, *Gold Fleet for California: Forty-Niners from Australia and New Zealand* (1964).

Bieber, Ralph P., "California Gold Mania," *MVHR*, 35 (1948), 3.

Bruff, J. Goldsborough, *Gold Rush: Journals,* George W. Read and Ruth Gaines, eds. (2 vols., 1944).

Caughey, John W., *Gold is Cornerstone* (1948).

Clappe, Louise A. K. S., *Shirley Letters from California Mines, 1851–1852,* Carl I. Wheat, ed. (1961).

Davis, Stephen C., *California Gold Rush Merchant: Journal,* Benjamin B. Richards, ed. (1956).

Foreman, Grant, ed., *Marcy and the Gold Seekers* (2 vols., 1939).

McCollum, William, *California as I Saw It,* Dale L. Morgan, ed. (1960).

Monaghan, Jay, *Australians and Gold Rush, 1849–1854* (1966).

Moorman, Madison B., *Diary, 1850–1851,* Irene D. Paden, ed. (1948).

Osbun, Albert G., *To California and the South Seas: Diary, 1848–1851,* John H. Kemble, ed. (1966).

Paul, Rodman W., *California Gold* (1947).

——— ed., *California Gold Discovery: Sources* (1966).

Quaife, Milo M., ed., *Pictures of Gold Rush California* (1949).

Roske, Ralph J., "World Impact of California Gold Rush, 1849–1857," *Ariz. and West*, 5 (1963), 187.

Royce, Sarah B., *A Frontier Lady*, R. H. Gabriel, ed. (1932).
Wyman, Walker D., ed., *California Emigrant Letters* (1952).

*   *   *   *   *   *   *

Wheat, Carl I., *Books of the California Gold Rush* (1949).

See also 10.3 for biographies/writings of:

Bancroft, Hubert H., 1832–1918
Clemens [Mark Twain], Samuel L., 1835–1910
Field, Stephen J., 1816–1899
Harte, Francis Brett, 1836–1902
Miller, [Joaquin], Cincinnatus H., 1839–1910
Sutter, John A., 1803–1880
Whitney, Josiah D., 1819–1896

13.4.10.3 Other Gold Rushes

Bancroft, Caroline, *Gulch of Gold: History of Central City* (1958). Colorado.
Briggs, Harold E., "Black Hills Gold Rush," *No. Dak. Hist.*, 5 (1930), 71.
Coon, S. J., "Gold Camps and Development of Western Montana," *Jour. Pol. Econ.*, 38 (1930), 580.
Coulter, E. Merton, *Auraria: The Story of a Georgia Gold-Mining Town* (1956).
Fisher, Vardis, and Opal L. Holmes, *Gold Rushes and Mining Camps of Early American West* (1968).
Hafen, LeRoy R., *Colorado Gold Rush* (1941).
Jackson, Donald D., *Custer's Gold: Cavalry Expedition of 1874* (1966).
Stokes, George W., and H. R. Briggs, *Deadwood Gold* (1926).
Trexler, H. A., *Flour and Wheat in Montana Gold Camps* (1918).
Willison, G. F., *Here They Dug Gold* (1932).

13.4.10.4 Silver Lodes

Brown, Robert L., *An Empire of Silver: A History of the San Juan Silver Rush* (1965).
Burns, Walter N., *Tombstone* (1933).
Elliott, Russell R., *Nevada's Twentieth-Century Mining Boom* (1966).
Jackson, W. Turrentine, *Treasure Hill: Silver Mining Camp* (1963).
Jensen, Billie B., "Alaska's Pre-Klondike Mining: Men, Methods and Minerals," *Jour. of West*, 6 (1967), 417.
Lewis, Oscar, *Silver Kings* (1947).
Livermore, Robert, *Journal, 1892–1915*, Gene M. Gressley, ed. (1968).
Lord, Eliot, *Comstock Mining and Miners*, (1880); David Myrick, ed. (1959).
Lyman, George D., *Ralston's Ring: California Plunders Comstock Lode* (1934).
——— *Saga of Comstock Lode* (1934).
Smith, George Horace, *History of Comstock Lode* (1943).
Wilson, Neill C., *Silver Stampede* (1937).

See also 10.3 for biographies/writings of:

Clemens [Mark Twain], Samuel L., 1835–1910
Sutro, Adolph, 1830–1898

13.5 PHOTOGRAPHY AND ART

Brown, Mark H., and W. R. Felton, *The Frontier Years: L. A. Huffman, Photographer of the Plains* (1955).
Ewers, John C., *Artists of the Old West* (1965).
Hine, Robert V., *Bartlett's West: Mexican Boundary* (1968).

Lewis, Henry, *Valley of the Mississippi Illustrated* (1854); A. Hermina Poatgieter, trans., Bertha L. Heilbron, ed. (1967).

Miller, Alfred J., *The West of Alfred Jacob Miller* [1837] *from the Notes and Water Colors in the Walters Art Gallery*, Marvin C. Ross, ed. (rev. ed., 1967).

Tilden, Freeman, *Following the Frontier with F. Jay Haynes, Pioneer Photographer of Old West* (1964).

See also 10.3 for biographies/writings of:

Bingham, George Caleb, 1811–1879
Catlin, George, 1796–1872
Eastman, Seth, 1808–1875
Keith, William, 1839–1911
Remington, Frederick, 1861–1909

See also 20.11.2, Indian Life in Paintings and Photographs.

13.6 GUIDEBOOKS–BIBLIOGRAPHY

Billington, Ray A., "Books That Won the West: Guidebooks of the Forty-Niners and Fifty-Niners," *Am. West*, 4 (1967), 25.

Hafen, Leroy R., ed., *Pike's Peak Guide Books of 1859* (1941).

Kroll, Helen B., "The Books that Enlightened the Emigrants," *Ore. Hist. Quar.*, 45 (1944), 103. Oregon.

Savage, James P., "Do-It-Yourself Books for Illinois Immigrants," Ill. State Hist. Soc., *Jour.*, 57 (1964), 30.

13.7 HISTORIOGRAPHY

13.7.1 General

Bourne, E. G., *Essays in Historical Criticism* (1901).

Carroll, John A., and James R. Kluger, ed., *Reflections of Western Historians* (1969).

Caughey, John W., "Toward an Understanding of West," *Utah Hist. Quar.*, 27 (1959), 7.

Davis, W. N., Jr., "Will West Survive as Field in American History," *MVHR*, 50 (1964), 672.

Ferris, Robert G., ed., *The American West: An Appraisal* (1963).

Fite, Gilbert C., "History and Historians of Great Plains," *No. Dak. Quar.*, 34 (1966), 89.

Gressley, Gene M., ed., *American West* (1966).

Haynes, Robert V., "Historians and Mississippi Territory," *Jour. Miss. Hist.* 29 (1967), 409.

Lewis, Archibald R., and Thomas F. McGann, *The New World Looks at Its History* (1963).

Pomeroy, Earl S., "Rediscovering the West," *Am. Quar.*, 12 (1960), 20.

———— "Toward Reorientation of Western History" *MVHR*, 41 (1955), 579.

———— "What Remains of the West," *Utah Hist. Quar.*, 35 (1967), 37.

Webb, Walter P., "American West," *Harpers Mag.*, 214 (May 1957), 25.

———— "Reflections on Age of Frontier," *Harpers Mag.*, 203 (Oct. 1951) 25.

Wyman, Walker D., and Clifton B. Kroeber, eds., *Frontier in Perspective* (1957).

13.7.2 Turner Thesis

Allen, Harry C., "F. J. Turner and the Frontier in American History," in H. C. Allen and C. P. Hill, eds., *British Essays in American History* (1957).

Becker, Carl, "Frederick Jackson Turner," in Howard W. Odum, ed., *American Masters of Social Science* (1927).

Benson, Lee, *Turner and Beard: American Historical Writing Reconsidered* (1960).

Berkhofer, Robert F., Jr., "Space, Time, Culture and the New Frontier," *Agric. Hist.*, 38 (1964), 21.

Billington, Ray A., "Frederick J. Turner," *MVHR*, 50 (1963), 3.

——— *Frontier Thesis: Valid Interpretation of American History?* (1966).

Blackwood, George D., "Frederick J. Turner and John R. Commons," *MVHR*, 41 (1954), 471.

Bolkhovitinov, N. N., "Role of 'Frontier' in the History of the U.S.A.," *Soviet Rev.*, 5 (1964), 22.

Burnette, O. Lawrence, Jr., comp., *Wisconsin Witness to Frederick Jackson Turner* (1961).

Coleman, William "Science and Symbol in Turner Frontier Hypothesis," *AHR*, 72 (1966), 22.

Craven, Avery, "Frederick Jackson Turner," in William T. Hutchinson, ed., *Marcus W. Jernegan Essays in American Historiography* (1937).

Edwards, Everett E., "Bibliography," in Frederick J. Turner, *Early Writings* (1938), 231.

Elkins, Stanley M., and Eric McKitrick, "A Meaning for Turner's Frontier," *Pol. Sci. Quar.*, 69 (1954), 321.

Evanoff, Alexander, "Turner Thesis and Mormon Beginnings," *Utah Hist. Quar.*, 33 (1965), 155.

Gressley, Gene M., "Turner Thesis," *Agric. Hist.*, 32 (1958), 227.

Hayes, Carlton J. H., "The American Frontier—Frontier of What?" *AHR*, 51 (1946), 199.

Hofstadter, Richard, *Progressive Historians: Turner, Beard, Parrington* (1968).

——— "Turner and the Frontier Myth," *Am. Scholar*, 18 (1949), 433.

——— and Seymour M. Lipset, ed., *Turner and the Sociology of the Frontier* (1968).

Jacobs, Wilbur R. et al., *Turner, Bolton and Webb* (1965).

Kesselman, Steven, "Frontier Thesis and Great Depression," *Jour. Hist. Ideas*, 29 (1968), 253.

Lewis, Archibald R., and Thomas F. McGann, *The New World Looks at Its History* (1963).

Malin, James C., *Essays in Historiography* (1946).

Murphy, George G. S., and Arnold Zellner, "Sequential Growth, the Labor-Safety-Valve Doctrine and the Development of American Unionism," *Jour. Econ. Hist.* 19 (1959), 402.

Noble, David W., *Historians against History: Frontier Thesis and the National Covenant* (1965).

Ostrander, Gilman, "Turner and the Germ Theory," *Agric. Hist.* 32 (1958), 258.

Pierson, George W., "The Frontier and American Institutions," *NEQ*, 15 (1942), 224.

——— "The Frontier and Frontiersmen of Turner's Essays," *Penn. Mag. Hist. Biog.*, 64 (1940), 449.

Pomeroy, Earl S., "Toward a Reorientation of Western History: Continuity and Environment," *MVHR*, 41 (1955), 579.

Riegel, Robert E., "American Frontier Theory," *Jour. of World Hist.*, 3 (1956), 356.

Rundell, Walter, Jr., "Concepts of the 'Frontier' and the 'West'," *Ariz. and West*, 1 (1959), 13.

Shannon, Fred A., "Homestead Act and Labor Surplus," *AHR*, 41 (1936), 637.

——— "A Post Mortem on the Labor-Safety-Valve Theory," *Agric. Hist.*, 19 (1945), 31.

Simler, Norman J., "The Safety-Valve Doctrine Re-evaluated," *Agric. Hist.*, 32 (1958), 250.

Smith, Henry Nash, *Virgin Land: The American West as Symbol and Myth* (1950).

Turner, Frederick J., *Early Writings* (1938).

——— *Frontier and Section: Selected Essays*, Ray A. Billington, ed. (1961).

——— *The Frontier in American History* (1950).

—— *Rise of the New West* (1906).
—— *The Significance of Sections in American History* (1950).
—— *Unpublished Writings in American History*, Wilbur R. Jacobs, ed. (1965).
Tuttle, William M., Jr., "Forerunners of Frederick Jackson Turner," *Agric. Hist.* 41 (1967), 219.
Von Nardroff, Ellen, "American Frontier as Safety-Valve," *Agric. Hist.*, 36 (1962), 123.
Wade, Richard C., *The Urban Frontier: The Rise of Western Cities, 1790–1830* (1959).
Woolfolk, George R., "Turner's Safety-Valve and Free Negro Westward Migration," *Jour. Negro Hist.*, 50 (1965), 185.
Wright, Benjamin F., "American Democracy and the Frontier," *Yale Rev.*, 20 (1930), 349.
—— "Political Institutions and the Frontier," in Dixon R. Fox, ed., *Sources of Culture in the Middle West* (1934), 15.

See also 10.3 for biographies/writings of:

Turner, Frederick J., 1861–1932

13.7.3 Comparative Frontiers

Allen, Harry C., *Bush and Backwoods: Frontiers in Australia and United States* (1959).
Gerhard, Dietrich, "The Frontier in Comparative View," *Comp. Studies in Society and Hist.*, 1 (1959), 205.
Hartz, Louis et al., *Founding of New Societies* (1964).
Lewis, Archibald R., and Thomas F. McGann, eds., *The New World Looks at Its History* (1963).
Moog, Vianna, *Bandeirantes and Pioneers*, L. L. Barrett, trans. (1964). Brazil compared with the United States.
Mikesell, Marvin, "Comparative Studies in Frontier History," Assoc. Am. Geographers, *Annals*, 50 (1960), 62.
Paullada, Stephen, *Rawhide and Song: A Comparative Study of the Cattle Cultures of the Argentine Pampa and the North American Plains* (1963).
Price, Archibald G., *Western Invasions of the Pacific and Its Continents, 1513–1958* (1963).
Sharp, Paul F., "Comparative Studies of Canadian, American, and Australian Settlement," *Pac. Hist. Rev.*, 24 (1955), 369.
—— "Northern Great Plains: Canadian-American Regionalism," *MVHR*, 39 (1952), 61.
—— *Whoop-Up Country: Canadian-American West, 1865–1885* (1955).
Webb, Walter P., *Great Frontier* (1952).
Wyman, Walker D., and Clifton B. Kroeber, eds., *Frontier in Perspective* (1957).

Part Four Histories of Special Subjects

14 Physical Environment

14.1 PHYSIOGRAPHY

Atwood, Wallace W., *Physiographic Provinces of North America* (1940).
Callison, Charles, ed., *America's Natural Resources* (rev. ed., 1967).
Eardley, Armand J., *Structural Geology of North America* (2nd ed., 1962).
Fenneman, Nevin, *Physiography of the Eastern United States* (1948).
———— *Physiography of the Western United States* (1931).
Hulbert, Archer B., *Soil: Its Influence on the History of the United States* (1930).
Hunt, Charles B., *Physiography of the United States* (1967).
Kellogg, Charles E., *The Soils that Support Us* (1941).
Martin, Lawrence, *Physical Geography of Wisconsin* (3d ed., 1965),
Whitaker, J. R., and Edward Ackerman, *American Resources* (1951).

14.2 HISTORICAL GEOGRAPHY

Brown, Ralph H., *Historical Geography of the United States* (1948).
———— *Mirror for Americans: Likeness of the Eastern Seaboard, 1810* (1943).
Dunbar, Gary S., *Historical Geography of the North Carolina Outer Banks,* Fred Kniffen, ed. (1958).
Meinig, Donald W., *Great Columbia Plain: Historical Geography, 1805–1910* (1968).
Merrens, H. Roy, *Colonial North Carolina in Eighteenth Century: Historical Geography* (1964).
Paterson, John H., *North America: A Regional Geography* (2nd ed., 1962).
Powell, John W., *Report on the Lands of the Arid Region of the United States* (1878); Wallace Stegner, ed. (1962).
Semple, Ellen C., *American History and its Geographic Conditions* (1933); Clarence F. Jones, ed., (1968).
White, C. Langdon et al., *Regional Geography of Anglo-America* (3d ed., 1964).
White, C. Langdon, and Edwin J. Foscue, *Regional Geography of North America* (1943).
Wright, A. J., *United States and Canada: An Economic Geography* (1948).

*   *   *   *   *   *   *

Ackerman, Edward A., *Geography as a Fundamental Research Discipline* (1958).
Hartshorne, Richard, *Perspective on the Nature of Geography* (1959).
Merrens, H. Roy, "Historical Geography and Early American History," *WMQ,* 22 (Oct. 1965), 529.

Two popular publishers' series, of uneven quality, are the Rivers of America and the American Lakes series.

14.3 CLIMATE

Flora, Snowden D., *Hailstorms of the United States* (1956).
—— *Tornadoes of the United States* (rev. ed., 1954).
Holden, William C., "West Texas Drouths," *Southwestern Hist. Quar.*, 32 (1928), 103.
Hoyt, William G., and Walter B. Langbein, *Floods* (1955).
Kimble, George H., *Our American Weather* (1955).
Ludlum, David M., *Early American Hurricanes, 1492–1870* (1963).
—— *Early American Winters, 1604–1820* (1966).
Malin, James C., *Dust Storms* (1946).
Schell, Herbert S., "Drought in Eastern Dakota," *Ag. Hist.*, 5 (1931), 162.
Sears, Paul B., *Deserts on the March* (3d ed., 1959).
U.S. Department of Agriculture, *Climate and Man* (1941).
Visher, Stephen S., *Climatic Atlas of the United States* (1954).
Ward, Robert De C., *Climates of the United States* (1925).

14.4 FLORA AND FAUNA

Caras, Roger, *North American Mammals: Fur-bearing Animals of the U.S. and Canada* (1967).
Hall, E. Raymond, and Keith R. Kelson, *Mammals of North America* (2 vols., 1959).
Livingston, Burton E., and Forrest Shreve, *The Distribution of Vegetation in the United States* (1921).
Malin, James C., *Grassland of North America* (1956).
Platt, Rutherford H., *Great American Forest* (1965).
Weaver, John E., and Frederick W. Albertson, *Grasslands of the Great Plains* (1956).
Weaver, John E., *North American Prairie* (1954).

14.5 CONSERVATION

Bates, J. Leonard, "Conservation Movement, 1907 to 1921," *MVHR*, 44 (1957), 29.
Blackorby, Edward C., "T. Roosevelt's Conservation Policies," *No. Dak. Quar.*, 25 (1958), 107.
Carstensen, Vernon R., *Farms or Forests: Land Policy for Northern Wisconsin, 1850–1932* (1958).
Clepper, Henry E., ed., *Origins of American Conservation* (1966).
Coyle, David C., *Conservation: Story of Conflict and Accomplishment* (1957).
Durisch, L. L., and H. L. Macon, *Upon Its Own Resources: Conservation and State Administration* (1951).
Graham, Frank, Jr., *History of Conservation in America* (1970).
Gustafson, Axel F. et al., *Conservation in the United States* (3d ed., 1949).
Hays, Samuel P., *Conservation and the Gospel of Efficiency: The Progressive Conservation Movement, 1890–1920* (1959).
Highsmith, Richard M. et al., *Conservation in the United States* (2nd ed., 1969).
Ise, John, *Oil Policy* (1926).
Jarrett, Henry, ed., *Perspectives on Conservation: Essay on Natural Resources* (1959).
King, Judson, *The Conservation Fight: From Theodore Roosevelt to the Tennessee Valley Authority* (1959).
Leopold, Aldo, *Sand County Almanac* (1949).
Lively, Charles E., and Jack J. Preiss, *Conservation Education in American Colleges* (1957).
Nash, Roderick, comp., *American Environment: Readings in the History of Conservation* (1968).

Penick, James L., *Progressive Politics and Conservation: Ballinger-Pinchot Affair* (1968).
Pinchot, Gifford, *Breaking New Ground* (1947).
—— *Fight for Conservation* (1910).
—— "How Conservation Began," *Ag. Hist.*, 11 (1937), 255.
Richardson, Elmo R., *The Politics of Conservation, 1897–1913* (1962).
Salmond, John A., *Civilian Conservation Corps, 1933–1942* (1967).
Smith, Frank E., *Politics of Conservation* (1966).
Smith, Guy H., ed., *Conservation of Natural Resources* (3d ed., 1965).
Swain, Donald C., *Federal Conservation Policy, 1921–1933* (1963).
Udall, Stewart L., *Quiet Crisis* (1963).
U.S. Department of Interior, *Years of Progress, 1945–52* (1953).
U.S. President's Materials Policy Commission, *Resources for Freedom* (5 vols., 1952).
Van Hise, C. R., *The Conservation of Natural Resources in the United States* (1924).

*   *   *   *   *   *   *

Dodds, Gordon B., "The Historiography of American Conservation," *Pac. Northw. Quar.*, 56 (1965), 75.
Le Duc, Thomas, "Historiography of Conservation," *Forest Hist.*, 9, no. 3 (1965), 23.
Nash, Roderick, "State of Environmental History," in Herbert J. Bass, ed., *State of American History* (1970).

See also 10.3 for biographies/writings of:

Bennett, Hugh H., 1881–1960
Fernow, Bernhard E., 1851–1923
Greeley, William B., 1879–1955
Ickes, Harold L., 1874–1952
Marsh, George P., 1801–1882
Mather, Stephen T., 1867–1930
Muir, John, 1838–1914
Pinchot, Gifford, 1865–1946
Roosevelt, Franklin D., 1882–1945
Roosevelt, Theodore, 1858–1919
Smith, Joseph Russell, 1874–
Van Hise, Charles R., 1857–1918

14.6 PARKS AND FORESTS

Brockman, Christian F., *Recreational Use of Wild Lands* (1959).
Dana, Samuel T., *Forest and Range Policy: Its Development* (1956).
Freeman, Orville, et al., *National Forests of America* (1968).
Greeley, William B., *Forest Policy, 1878–1953* (1953).
Hamilton, Lawrence S., "Federal Forest Regulation Issue," *Forest Hist.*, 9, no. 1, (1965), 2.
Hansbrough, Thomas, ed., *Southern Forests and Southern People* (1964).
Ise, John, *Forest Policy* (1920).
—— *Our National Park Policy: A Critical History* (1961).
Kaufman, Herbert, *Forest Ranger: A Study in Administrative Behavior* (1960).
Lillard, R. G., *Great Forest* (1947).
Platt, Rutherford H., *Great American Forest* (1965).
Raney, W. F., "Timber Culture Acts," *Miss. Valley Hist. Assoc., Proc.*, 10 (1921), 219.
Schenck, Carl A., *Biltmore Story: Beginning of Forestry* (1955).
Smith, H. A., "Early Forestry Movement in the United States," *Agric. Hist.*, 12 (1938), 326.

Tilden, Freeman, *National Parks* (1968).
Wessel, Thomas R., "Prologue to the Shelterbelt, 1870–1934," *Jour. of West,* 6 (1967), 119.

*   *   *   *   *   *   *

Shideler, James H., "Opportunities and Hazards in Forest History Research," *Forest Hist.,* 7, no. 1/2 (1963), 10.

14.7 WATER RESOURCES AND FLOOD CONTROL

Cleary, Edward J., *ORSANCO Story: Water Quality Mangement in the Ohio Valley* (1967).
DeRoos, R. W., *Thirsty Land: Central Valley Project* (1948).
Fesler, J. W., ed., "Government and Water Resources," *Am. Pol. Sci. Rev.,* 44 (1950), 575.
Frank, Arthur D., *Development of Federal Flood Control on the Mississippi River* (1930).
Hoyt, William G., and W. B. Langbein, *Floods* (1955).
Kerwin, J. K., *Federal Water-Power Legislation* (1926).
Maass, Arthur, *Muddy Waters: The Army Engineers and the Nation's Rivers* (1951).
U.S. President's Water Resources Policy Commission, *Report* (3 vols., 1950).

14.8 RECLAMATION

Ganoe, John T., "Desert Land Act in Operation," *Agric. Hist.* 11 (1937), 142.
——— "Desert Land Act Since 1891," *Agric. Hist.,* 11 (1937), 266.
——— "Origin of a National Reclamation Policy," *MVHR,* 18 (1931), 34.
Golzé, A. R., *Reclamation in the United States* (1952).
Gressley, Gene M., "Arthur Powell Davis, Reclamation and the West," *Agric. Hist.,* 42 (1968) 241.
Hollon, W. Eugene, *Great American Desert: Then and Now* (1966).
Kleinsorge, P. L., *Boulder Canyon Project* (1941).
Lampen, Dorothy, *Economic and Social Aspects of Federal Reclamation* (1930).
Smythe, W. E., *Conquest of Arid America* (1907).
Wessel, Thomas R., "Prologue to the Shelterbelt, 1870–1934," *Jour. of West,* 6 (1967), 119.

14.9 POLLUTION

Carson, Rachel, *Silent Spring* (1962).
Davies, J. Clarence, III, *Politics of Pollution* (1970).
Goldman, M., ed., *The Economics of a Cleaner America* (1967).
Graham, Frank, *Disaster by Default: Politics and Water Pollution* (1966).
——— *Since Silent Spring* (1970).
Linton, Ron, *Terracide: America's Destruction of Her Living Environment* (1970).
Murphy, Earl F., *Water Purity: Legal Control of Natural Resources* (1961).
Rudd, Robert L., *Pesticides and Living Landscape* (1964).
Stewart, George R., *Not So Rich As You Think* (1967).

15 Government

15.1 GENERAL

Eliot, Thomas H., et al., *American Government* (2nd ed., 1965).
Fiser, Webb S., et al., *Government in the United States* (1967).
Lees, John D., *The Political System of the United States* (1970).
McLaughlin, A. C., and Albert B. Hart, eds., *Cyclopedia of American Government* (3 vols., 1914).
Nichols, Roy F., *Blueprints for Leviathan: American Style* (1963).
Odegard, Peter, et al., *American Republic: Its Government and Politics* (2nd ed., 1969).
Wheare, Kenneth C., *Federal Government* (1953).

15.2 THE CONSTITUTION AND CONSTITUTIONAL DEVELOPMENT

15.2.1 General

Beth, Loren P., *Politics, the Constitution, and the Supreme Court* (1962).
Dumbauld, Edward, *Constitution of the United States* (1964).
Corwin, Edward S., *American Constitutional History: Essays by Edward S. Corwin,* Alpheus T. Mason and Gerald Garvey, eds. (1964).
Hockett, H. C., *The Constitutional History of the United States, 1776–1876* (2 vols., 1939).
Kelly, A. H., and W. A. Harbison, *The American Constitution* (1948; 4th ed., 1970).
Levy, Leonard W., *American Constitutional Law: Essays* (1966).
Maggs, Douglas B., et al., eds., *Selected Essays on Constitutional Law* (5 vols., 1938).
Martin, Philip L., "Convention Ratification of Federal Constitutional Amendments," *Pol. Sci. Quar.,* 82 (1967), 61.
Miller, Charles A., "Constitutional Law and the Rhetoric of Race," *Perspectives in Am. Hist.,* 5 (1971), 147.
Mitchell, Broadus, and Louise P. Mitchell, *Biography of the Constitution* (1964).
Pritchett, Charles H., *American Constitution* (2nd ed., 1968).
Schwartz, Bernard, *Commentary on the Constitution of the United States* (2 vols., 1963).
—— *Reins of Power: A Constitutional History of United States* (1963).
Small, Norman J., ed., *Constitution of the United States: Analysis and Interpretation* (rev. ed., 1964).
Smith, James Morton, and Paul L. Murphy, eds., *Liberty and Justice; Forging the Federal Union: American Constitutional Development to 1869* (1965).
—— *Liberty and Justice; The Modern Constitution: American Constitutional Development since 1865* (rev. ed., 1968).
Sutherland, Arthur E., *Constitutionalism in America* (1965).

Swisher, Carl B., *American Constitutional Development* (2nd ed., 1954).

* * * * * * *

Bellot, H. Hale, "The Literature of the Last Half-Century on the Constitutional History of United States," Royal Hist. Soc., *Trans.*, 5 ser., 7 (1957), 159.
Murphy, Paul L., "Challenge of American Constitutional History," *AHR,* 69 (1963), 64.

See also volume two for references to Constitutional Convention and Ratification.

15.2.2 Civil Rights

15.2.2.1 General

Abernathy, Mabra G., *Civil Liberties under the Constitution* (1968).
Beaney, William M., "Civil Liberties and Statutory Construction," *Jour. Pub. Law,* 8 (1959), 66.
Brant, Irving, *Bill of Rights* (1966).
Caldwell, Wallace F., "Fair Housing Laws and Fundamental Liberties," *Jour. Human Rel.,* 14 (1966), 230.
Carmen, Ira H., "One Civil Libertarian Among the Many: The Case of Mr. Justice Goldberg," *Mich. Law Rev.,* 65 (1966), 301.
Carr, R. K., *Federal Protection of Civil Rights* (1947).
Caughey, John W., *In Clear and Present Danger* (1958).
Congressional Quarterly Service, *Revolution in Civil Rights* (4th ed., 1968).
Cox, Archibald, Mark DeW. Howe, and J. R. Wiggins, *Civil Rights, The Constitution and the Courts* (1967).
Dorsen, Norman, Thomas I. Emerson and David Haber, *Political and Civil Rights in United States* (3d ed., 1967).
Elliff, John T., "Aspects of Federal Civil Rights Enforcement: The Justice Department and the FBI, 1939–1964," Perspectives in Am. Hist., 5 (1971), 605.
Fraenkel, Osmund S., *Supreme Court and Civil Liberties* (rev. ed., 1952).
Freund, Paul A., "Civil Rights and Limits of Law," *Buffalo Law Rev.,* 14 (1964), 199.
—— "Supreme Court and Civil Liberties," *Vanderbilt Law Rev.,* 4 (1951), 533.
Gellhorn, Walter, *American Rights: Constitution in Action* (1960).
—— *Individual Freedom and Governmental Restraints* (1956).
Green, John R., "Supreme Court, the Bill of Rights and the States," *Univ. Penn. Law Rev.,* 97 (1949), 608.
Greenberg, Jack, "The Supreme Court, Civil Rights, and Civil Dissonance," *Yale Law Jour.,* 77 (1968), 1520.
Gross, Hyman, *Privacy: Its Legal Protection* (1964).
Hand, Learned, *The Bill of Rights* (1958).
—— *Spirit of Liberty* (3d ed., 1960).
Holcombe, Arthur N., *Securing the Blessings of Liberty: Constitutional System* (rev. ed., 1969).
Howe, Mark DeW., "Federalism and Civil Rights," Mass. Hist. Soc., *Proc.,* 77 (1965), 15.
Jensen, Joan M., *Price of Vigilance* (1968).
Johnson, Donald D., *Challenge to American Freedoms: Civil Liberties Union* (1963).
Kelly, Alfred H., *Foundations of Freedom in the American Constitution* (1958).
Konvitz, Milton R., and Clinton Rossiter, eds., *Aspects of Liberty: Essays to Robert E. Cushman* (1958).
Konvitz, Milton R., and Theodore Leskes, *A Century of Civil Rights, with a Study of State Law against Discrimination* (1961).
Konvitz, Milton R., *The Constitution and Civil Rights* (1947).
—— *Expanding Liberties: Postwar America* (1966).
Krislov, Samuel, *Supreme Court and Political Freedom* (1968).

Long, Edward V., *The Intruders: Invasion of Privacy* (1967).

Lowi, Theodore, ed., *Private Life and Public Order* (1968).

Mason, Alpheus T., "Warren Court and Bill of Rights," *Yale Rev.,* 56 (1967), 197.

Murphy, Walter F., "Civil Liberties in 1963 Term," *Am. Pol. Sci. Rev.,* 59 (1965), 64.

Norris, Harold, *Mr. Justice Murphy and the Bill of Rights* (1965).

O'Brian, John L., "Changing Attitudes Toward Freedom," *Washington and Lee Law Rev.,* 9 (1952), 157.

—— "New Encroachments on Individual Freedom," *Harvard Law Rev.,* 66 (1952), 1.

Packard, Vance, *The Naked Society* (1964).

Pfeffer, Leo, *Liberties of an American: The Supreme Court Speaks* (2nd ed., 1963).

Pound, Roscoe, *Development of Constitutional Guarantees of Liberty* (1957).

Preston, William, Jr., *Aliens and Dissenters: Federal Suppression of Radicals, 1903–1933* (1963).

Pritchett, Charles H., *Civil Liberties and the Vinson Court* (1954).

—— *Political Offender and the Warren Court* (1958).

Roche, John P., *Quest for the Dream: Civil Rights* (1963).

U.S. President's Committee on Civil Rights, *To Secure These Rights* (1947).

Vile, M. J. C., *Constitutionalism and Separation of Powers* (1967).

Wiener, Frederick B., "Courts-Martial and Bill of Rights," *Harv. Law Rev.,* 72 (1958), 1.

Wilcox, Clair, ed., *Civil Liberties under Attack* (1951).

Zelermyer, William, *Invasion of Privacy* (1959).

See also 20.11.8, Contemporary Indian Problems; 20.12.7.2, Negro Protest–Civil Rights.

15.2.2.2 Rights Guaranteed by Specific Amendments

Abernathy, Glenn, *Right of Assembly and Association* (1961).

Antieau, Chester J., "First Amendment Freedoms," *Marquette Law Rev.,* 34 (1950), 57.

Auerbach, Jerold S., "Zechariah Chafee, Jr., and Freedom of Speech," *NEQ,* 42 (1969), 511.

Boudin, Louis B., "Fourteenth Amendment," *N.Y.U. Law Rev.,* 16 (1938), 19.

Brennan, William J., Jr., "Supreme Court and Meiklejohn Interpretation of First Amendment," *Harv. Law Rev.,* 79 (1965), 1.

Claude, Richard, "Constitutional Voting Rights and Early U.S. Supreme Court Doctrine," *Jour. Negro Hist.,* 51 (1966), 114.

Emerson, Thomas I., "Freedom of Association and Freedom of Expression," *Yale Law Jour.,* 74 (1964), 1.

—— "Toward General Theory of First Amendment," *Yale Law Jour.,* 72 (1963), 877.

Fairman, Charles, "Does Fourteenth Amendment Incorporate Bill of Rights?" *Stanford Law Rev.,* 2 (1949), 5.

Frank, John P., and Robert F. Munro, "Original Understanding of 'Equal Protection of the Laws'," *Columbia Law Rev.,* 50 (1950), 131.

Gillette, William, *The Right to Vote: Politics and the Passage of the Fifteenth Amendment* (1969).

Graham, Howard J., *Everyman's Constitution: Historical Essays on the Fourteenth Amendment, the "Conspiracy Theory," and American Constitutionalism* (1968).

—— "Our 'Declaratory' Fourteenth Amendment," *Stanford Law Rev.,* 7 (1954), 3.

Green, John R., "Liberty under Fourteenth Amendment," *Wash. Univ. Law Quar.,* 27 (1942), 497.

Griswold, Erwin N., *5th Amendment Today* (1955).

Harris, Robert J., *The Quest for Equality: The Constitution, Congress and the Supreme Court* (1960).

Howe, Mark DeW., *The Garden and the Wilderness: Religion and Government* (1967).

Hudon, Edward G., *Freedom of Speech and Press in America* (1963).

Kelly, John, "Criminal Libel and Free Speech," *Kan. Law Rev.,* 6 (1958), 295.

Konvitz, Milton R., *First Amendment Freedoms* (1963).
—— *Fundamental Liberties of a Free People* (1957).
—— *Religious Liberty and Conscience: A Constitutional Inquiry* (1968).
Landynski, Jacob W., *Search and Seizure and the Supreme Court* (1966).
Lasson, Nelson, *History and Development of the Fourth Amendment* (1937).
Levy, Leonard W., *Origins of Fifth Amendment* (1968).
Mayers, Lewis, "Federal Witness' Privilege against Self-Incrimination," *Am. Jour. Legal Hist.*, 4 (1960), 107.
Meiklejohn, Alexander, *Free Speech and Its Relation to Self-Government* (1948).
—— "What Does First Amendment Mean?" *Univ. of Chi. Law Rev.*, 20 (1953), 461.
Morgan, E. M., "Privilege Against Self-Incrimination," *Minn. Law Rev.*, 34 (1949), 1.
Morrison, Stanley, "Does the Fourteenth Amendment Incorporate the Bill of Rights? The Judicial Interpretation," *Stanford Law Rev.*, 2 (1949), 140.
Murphy, Walter F., "Mr. Justice Jackson, Free Speech, and Judicial Function," *Vanderbilt Law Rev.*, 12 (1959), 1019.
Murthy, N. V. K., "Freedom of Press and Fair Trial in U.S.A.," *Journalism Quar.*, 36 (1959), 307.
Patterson, Giles J., *Free Speech and Free Press* (1939).
"The Privilege against Self Incrimination Under American Law," *Jour. Crim. Law*, 51 (1960), 131.
Rogge, O. John, "'Congress Shall Make No Law . . . '," *Mich. Law Rev.*, 56 (1958), 331, 579.
Shapiro, Martin, *Freedom of Speech: The Supreme Court and Judicial Review* (1966).
Sutherland, Arthur E., "Crime and Confession," *Harv. Law Rev.*, 79 (1965), 21.
Tussman, Joseph, and Jacobus tenBroek, "Equal Protection of the Laws," *Calif. Law Rev.*, 37 (1949), 341.

See also 19.7.2, Feminism (Nineteenth Amendment).

15.2.2.3 Censorship

Blanshard, Paul, *Right to Read* (1955).
Boyer, Paul S., *Purity in Print: The Vice-Society Movement and Book Censorship in America* (1968).
Ernst, Morris L., and Alan U. Schwartz, *Censorship, The Search for the Obscene* (1964).
Gardiner, Harold C., [S.J.] *Catholic Viewpoint on Censorship* (1958).
Haney, Robert W., *Comstockery in America: Censorship and Control* (1960).
Kilpatrick, James J., *Smut Peddlers* (1960).
Kuh, Richard H., *Foolish Figleaves? Pornography* (1967).
Larrabee, Eric, "Cultural Context of Sex Censorship," *Law and Contemp. Problems*, 20 (1955), 672.
Legman, Gershon, *Love & Death, a Study in Censorship* (1949).
Lippmann, Walter, *American Inquisitors* (1928).
Paul, James C. N., and Murray L. Schwartz, *Federal Censorship: Obscenity in the Mail* (1961).
Rembar, Charles, *The End of Obscenity: The Trials of Lady Chatterly, Tropic of Cancer and Fanny Hill* (1968).

See also 10.3 for biographies/writings of:

Cabot, Godfrey L., 1861–1962
Comstock, Anthony, 1844–1915

15.3 FEDERAL–STATE RELATIONS

Anderson, William, *The Nation and the States* (1955).
Bassett, John S., *Federalist System* (1906).

Clark, J. P., *Rise of New Federalism* (1938).

Cohen, Jacob, and Morton Grodzins, "Economic Sharing in American Federalism," *Am. Pol. Sci. Rev.,* 57 (1963), 5.

Cooley, Thomas M., *Treatise on Constitutional Limitations of States* (1868); V. H. Lane, ed. (8th ed., 1927).

Corwin, Edward S., "Dual Federalism," *Va. Law Rev.* 36 (1950), 1.

Elazar, Daniel J., *American Federalism: A View from the States* (1966).

—— *American Partnership: Intergovernmental Co-operation in the Nineteenth Century* (1962).

Graves, W. Brooke, *American Intergovernmental Relations* (1964).

Maxwell, James A., *Fiscal Impact of Federalism in the United States* (1946).

Nagel, Paul C., *One Nation Indivisible: The Union in American Thought, 1776–1861* (1964).

Pound, Roscoe, et al., *Federalism as a Democratic Process* (1942).

Roettinger, Ruth L., *Supreme Court and State Police Power: Federalism* (1957).

Schmidhauser, John R., *Supreme Court as Final Arbiter in Federal-State Relations, 1789–1957* (1958).

Sprague, John D., *Voting Patterns of the United States Supreme Court: Cases in Federalism, 1889–1959* (1967).

Vile, M. J. C., *Structure of American Federalism* (1961).

Wildavsky, Aaron B., *American Federalism in Perspective* (1967).

See also 46.4, Secession Crisis.

15.4 STATE, TERRITORIAL, AND LOCAL GOVERNMENTS

Adrian, Charles R., *State and Local Governments* (2nd ed., 1967).

Agger, Robert E., et al., *Rulers and the Ruled: Political Power and Impotence in American Communities* (1964).

Anderson, William, et al., *Government in the Fifty States* (rev. ed., 1960).

Blair, George S., *American Legislatures* (1967).

—— *American Local Government* (1964).

Buechner, John C., *State Government in the Twentieth Century* (1967).

Cooley, Thomas M., *Treatise on Constitutional Limitations of States* (1868); V. H. Lane, ed., 8th ed. (1927).

Crane, Wilder, and M. Watts, *State Legislative System* (1968).

Dealey, J. Q., *Growth of American State Constitutions* (1915).

Dodd, Walter F., *Revision and Amendment of State Constitutions* (1910).

Eblen, Jack E., *First and Second Empires: Governors and Territorial Government, 1784–1912* (1968).

Fairlie, J. A., *Local Government in Counties, Towns and Villages* (1906).

Fordham, Jefferson B., *State Legislative Institutions* (1959).

Lockard, Duane, *Governing the States and Localities* (1969).

McGrane, R. C., *Foreign Bondholders and State Debts* (1935).

Neil, William M., "American Territorial System since Civil War," *Ind. Mag. Hist.,* 60 (1964), 219.

Nevins, Allan, *American States during and after the Revolution, 1775–1798* (1924).

Pomeroy, Earl S., *Territories and the United States, 1861–1890* (1947).

Ratchford, B. U., *American State Debts* (1941).

Snider, Clyde F., *Local Government in Rural America* (1957).

Still, Bayrd, "Statehood Process, 1800 to 1850," *MVHR,* 23 (1936), 189.

Thomas, Dana L., *Story of American Statehood* (1961).

*   *   *   *   *   *   *

Graves, W. Brooke, et al., *American State Government and Administration: Bibliography* (1949).

See also 13.4.9, Government Policy and the Territories; 19.3.3, Municipal Administration.

15.5 FISCAL POLICY

Babilot, George, and Joan Anderson, "Personal Income Taxes, 1951–1962," *South Econ. Jour.*, 33 (1967), 518.

Benson, George C. S. et al., *American Property Tax* (1965).

Blakey, Roy G., and Gladys C. Blakey, *Federal Income Tax* (1940).

Buchanan, James M., *Public Finance in Democratic Process* (1967).

Butters, J. Keith, et al., *Effects of Taxation: Investments by Individuals* (1953).

Ellis, Elmer, "Public Opinion and Income Tax, 1860–1900," *MVHR*, 27 (1940), 225.

Ezell, John S., *Fortune's Merry Wheel: The Lottery in America* (1960).

Heilbroner, Robert L., and Peter L. Bernstein, *Primer on Government Spending* (1963).

Kahn, C. Harry, *Business and Professional Income under the Personal Income Tax* (1964).

Kimmel, Lewis H., *Federal Budget and Fiscal Policy, 1789–1958* (1959).

Mosher, Frederick C., and Orville F. Poland, *The Costs of American Government* (1964).

National Bureau of Economic Research and Brookings Institution, *Role of Direct and Indirect Taxes in the Federal Revenue System* (1964).

Paul, Randolph E., *Taxation in the United States* (1954).

Powell, Fred W., comp., *Control of Federal Expenditures: A Documentary History, 1775–1894* (1939).

Ratner, Sidney, *Taxation and Democracy in America* (1967).

Robinson, Marshall A., "Federal Debt Management," *Am. Econ. Rev.*, 45 (1955), 388.

Smithies, Arthur, *Budgetary Process in the United States* (1955).

Surrey, Stanley S., "Congress and Tax Lobbyist," *Harv. Law Rev.*, 70 (1957), 1145.

Wildavsky, Aaron B., *Politics of Budgetary Process* (1964).

Wilmerding, Lucius, Jr., *Spending Power: Efforts of Congress to Control Expenditures* (1943).

Yearley, C. K., *The Money Machines: The Breakdown and Reform of Governmental and Party Finance in the North, 1860–1920* (1970).

See also 18.14.5, Monetary History.

15.6 LEGISLATIVE BRANCH

15.6.1 General

Burns, James M., *Congress on Trial: The Legislative Process and the Administrative State* (1949).

Congressional Quarterly Service, *Legislators and Lobbyists* (2nd ed., 1968).

Cummings, Milton C., *Congressmen and the Electorate* (1966).

Goodwin, George, Jr., "Seniority System in Congress," *Am. Pol. Sci. Rev.*, 53 (1959), 412.

Horn, Stephen, *The Cabinet and Congress* (1960).

Kofmehl, Kenneth, *Professional Staffs of Congress* (1962).

Lees, John D., *Committee System of the United States Congress* (1968).

Morgan, Donald G., *Congress and the Constitution: A Study of Responsibility* (1966).

Polsby, Nelson W., *Congress and the Presidency* (1965).

Pusey, Merlo J., *The Way We Go To War* (1969).

Robinson, James A., *Congress and Foreign Policy-making* (rev. ed., 1967).

Ripley, Randall B., *Majority Party Leadership in Congress* (1969).

U.S. Congress, *Biographical Directory of the American Congress, 1774–1961* (1961).

Wallace, Robert A., *Congressional Control of Federal Spending* (1960).

*   *   *   *   *   *   *

Jones, Charles, and Randall B. Ripley, *Role of Political Parties in Congress: A Bibliography and Guide* (1966).

15.6.2 Senate

Burdette, F. L., *Filibustering in the Senate* (1940).
Clark, Joseph S., et al., *Senate Establishment* (1963).
Harris, Joseph P., *Advice and Consent of the Senate* (1953).
Haynes, George H., *The Senate: History and Practice* (2 vols., 1938).
Holt, W. Stull, *Treaties Defeated by the Senate* (1933).
Matthews, Donald, *United States Senators and Their World* (1960).
Pettit, Lawrence K., and Edward Keynes, eds., *Legislative Process in the United States Senate* (1969).
Preston, Nathaniel S., *Senate Institution* (1969).
Rothman, David J., *Politics and Power: Senate, 1869–1901* (1966).
White, William S., *Citadel: U.S. Senate* (1957).

15.6.3 House of Representatives

Alexander, De Alva S., *History and Procedure of House of Representatives* (1916).
Carroll, Holbert N., *House of Representatives and Foreign Affairs* (rev. ed., 1966).
Galloway, George B., *History of House of Representatives* (1961).
Hacker, Andrew, *Congressional Districting* (rev. ed., 1964).
MacNeil, Neil, *Forge of Democracy: House of Representatives* (1963).
Ripley, Randall B., *Party Leaders in House of Representatives* (1967).
Shannon, W. Wayne, *Party, Constituency and Congressional Voting: House of Representatives* (1968).
Smith, William H., *Speakers of the House of Representatives* (1928).
White, William S., *Home Place: U.S. House of Representatives* (1965).

15.7 EXECUTIVE BRANCH

15.7.1 Presidency

Bailey, Thomas A., *Presidential Greatness* (1966).
Bassett, Margaret, *Profiles and Portraits of American Presidents and their Wives* (1969).
Binkley, Wilfred E., *Man in the White House: His Powers and Duties* (1958).
—— *President and Congress* (3d rev. ed., 1962).
Brown, Stuart G., *The American Presidency* (1966).
Burns, James M., *Presidential Government* (1966).
Cornwell, Elmer E., Jr., *Presidential Leadership of Public Opinion* (1965).
Corwin, Edward S., *The President—Office and Powers, 1787–1957* (4th rev. ed., 1957).
Coyle, David C., *Ordeal of the Presidency* (1960).
Cronin, Thomas E., and Sanford D. Greenberg, eds., *The Presidential Advisory System* (1969).
Cunliffe, Marcus, *American Heritage History of the Presidency* (1968).
Fersh, Seymour H., *View from the White House: State of Union Messages* (1961).
Freidel, Frank, *Our Country's Presidents* (3d ed. 1970).
Grundstein, Nathan D., *Presidential Delegation of Authority in Wartime* (1961).
Henry, Laurin L., *Presidential Transitions* (1960).
Herring, Edward P., *Presidential Leadership: Congress and the Chief Executive* (1940).
"The Office of the American Presidency," Sidney Hyman, ed., Am. Acad. Pol. Soc. Sci., *Annals,* 307 (1956), 1.

Israel, Fred L., ed., *State of the Union Messages of the Presidents, 1790–1966* (3 vols., 1966).
Jackson, Carlton, *Presidential Vetoes, 1792–1945* (1967).
Koenig, Louis E., *Chief Executive* (1964).
Longaker, Richard P., *Presidency and Individual Liberties* (1961).
Lorant, Stefan, *Glorious Burden: The American Presidency* (1968). Pictorial.
Lott, Davis N., ed., *Inaugural Addresses of American Presidents* (1961).
May, Ernest R., ed., *Ultimate Decision: President as Commander in Chief* (1960).
Morris, Richard B., *Great Presidential Decisions* (rev. ed., 1967).
Neustadt, Richard E., *Presidential Power* (1960).
Paolucci, Henry, *War, Peace and Presidency* (1968).
Patterson, C. Perry, *Presidential Government in the United States* (1947).
Pollard, J. E., *The Presidents and the Press* (1947).
Rich, Bennett M., *The Presidents and Civil Disorder* (1941).
Rossiter, Clinton, *The American Presidency* (rev. ed., 1966).
————— *Supreme Court and the Commander in Chief* (1951).
Schubert, Glendon A., Jr., *Presidency in the Courts* (1957).
Schwartz, Bernard, *Commentary on the Constitution of the United States.* Vol. II: *Powers of Government: Powers of the President.* (1963).
Smith, John Malcolm, and Cornelius P. Cotter, *Powers of the President during Crises* (1960).
Stanwood, Edward, *History of the Presidency* (rev. ed., 2 vols., 1921).
Tourtellot, Arthur B., *Presidents on the Presidency* (1964).

*   *   *   *   *   *   *

Mugridge, Donald H., *Presidents of United States 1789–1962: A Selected List of References* (1963).

See also 17.4, Presidential Conventions and Elections.

15.7.2 Vice-Presidency

Hatch, Louis C., *History of the Vice-Presidency* (1934).
Williams, Irving G., *Rise of the Vice-Presidency* (1956).
Young, K. H., and Lamar Middleton, *Heirs Apparent* (1948).

15.7.3 Departments and Administrative Agencies

For State Department see 15.8 Foreign Relations, for War Department, Navy Department, and Defense Department see 15.9.

Altshuler, Alan A., *Politics of the Federal Bureaucracy* (1968).
Aronson, Sidney H., *Status and Kinship in the Higher Civil Service: Standards of Selection in the Administrations of John Adams, Thomas Jefferson and Andrew Jackson* (1964).
Chamberlain, Joseph P., et al., *Judicial Function in Federal Administrative Agencies* (1942).
Chamberlain, Lawrence H., *The President, Congress, and Legislation* (1946).
Cullinan, Gerald, *The Post Office Department* (1968).
Cummings, Homer, and Carl McFarland, *Federal Justice* (1937).
Cushman, R. E., *Independent Regulatory Commissions* (1941).
Fenno, Richard F., Jr., *The President's Cabinet: An Analysis in the Period from Wilson to Eisenhower* (1959).
Fish, Carl R., *The Civil Service and the Patronage* (1905).
Fowler, Dorothy G., *Cabinet Politician: The Postmasters General, 1829–1909* (1943).
Gellhorn, Walter, *Federal Administrative Proceedings* (1941).
Haines, C. G., "Adaptation of Administrative Law to Constitutional Theories," *Am. Pol. Sci. Rev.,* 34 (1940), 1.

Herring, E. Pendleton, *Federal Commissioners* (1936).
—— *Public Administration and Public Interest* (1936).
Hobbs, Edward H., *Behind the President: Study of Executive Office Agencies* (1954).
Huston, Luther A., *Department of Justice* (1967).
Landis, J. M., *Administrative Process* (1938).
Learned, Henry B., *President's Cabinet* (1912).
Leiserson, Avery, *Administrative Regulation* (1942).
Neal, Harry E., *Protectors: Food and Drug Administration* (1968).
Nicholls, W. H., "Federal Regulatory Agencies and Courts," *Am. Econ. Rev.,* 34 (1944), 56.
Parris, Addison W., *Small Business Administration* (1968).
Perros, George P., et al., comps., *Papers of Senate Relating to Presidential Nominations, 1789–1901* (1964).
Pound, Roscoe, *Administrative Law* (1942).
Schmeckebier, Lawrence F., *Customs Service* (1924).
Short, Lloyd M., *Development of National Administrative Organization* (1923).
Stein, Harold, ed., *Public Administration and Policy Development* (1952).
U.S. Civil Service Commission, *Biography of an Ideal: The Diamond Anniversary History of the Federal Civil Service* (1959).
U.S. Department of Agriculture, Economic Research Service, *A Century of Service: The First One Hundred Years of the Department of Agriculture* (1963).
Van Riper, Paul P., *History of the United States Civil Service* (1958).
Warner, William Lloyd, Jr., et. al., *The American Federal Executive: Social and Personal Characteristics of the Civilian and Military Leaders of the United States Federal Government* (1963).
White, Leonard D., *Federalists: A Study in Administrative History, 1789–1801* (1948).
—— *Jacksonians: A Study in Administrative History, 1829–1861* (1954).
—— *Jeffersonians: A Study in Administrative History, 1801–1829* (1951).
—— *Republican Era, 1869–1901: A Study in Administrative History* (1958).
Whitnah, Donald R., *History of United States Weather Bureau* (1961).
Willmann, John B., *Department of Housing and Urban Development* (1967).

*   *   *   *   *   *   *

Graves, W. Brooke, *Intergovernmental Relations in United States: Bibliography* (1955).

15.8 FOREIGN RELATIONS

15.8.1 General

Bailey, Thomas A., *A Diplomatic History of the American People* (8th ed., 1969).
Bemis, Samuel F., *American Foreign Policy and the Blessings of Liberty and Other Essays* (1962).
—— *A Diplomatic History of the United States* (5th ed., 1965).
—— *A Short History of American Foreign Policy and Diplomacy* (1959).
Curti, Merle, and Kendall Birr, *Prelude to Point Four: Technical Missions Overseas, 1838–1938* (1954).
De Conde, Alexander, *History of Foreign Policy* (1963).
Dulles, Foster R., *Prelude to World Power: Diplomatic History, 1860–1900* (1965).
Ellis, L. Ethan, *A Short History of American Diplomacy* (1951).
Eubank, Keith, *Summit Conferences, 1919–1960* (1966).
Ferrell, Robert H., *American Diplomacy* (1959).
Goetzmann, William H., *When the Eagle Screamed: American Diplomacy, 1800–1860* (1966).
Kelly, Alfred H., ed., *American Foreign Policy and American Democracy* (1954).
Kuehl, Warren F., *Seeking World Order: United States and International Organization to 1920* (1969).

Lerche, Charles O., *Foreign Policy of American People* (3d ed., 1967).
Perkins, Dexter, *Foreign Policy and American Spirit,* Glyndon G. Van Deusen and Richard C. Wade, eds. (1957).
Pratt, Julius W., *History of United States Foreign Policy* (2nd ed., 1965).
U.S. Department of State, *Secretaries of State* (1956).

*   *   *   *   *   *   *

Bemis, Samuel F., and Grace G. Griffin, eds., *Guide to the Diplomatic History of the United States, 1775–1921* (1935).
Plischke, Elmer, *American Foreign Relations: A Bibliography* (1955).

See also volume two for references to foreign relations within the chronological periods.

15.8.2 Interpretations

Bailey, Thomas A., *Art of Diplomacy: American Experience* (1968).
Baldwin, David A., *Economic Development and American Foreign Policy* (1966).
Bartlett, Ruhl J., *Policy and Power: American Foreign Relations* (1963).
Cole, Wayne S., *Interpretive History of American Foreign Relations* (1968).
Ekirch, Arthur A., Jr., *Ideas, Ideals, and American Diplomacy* (1966).
Feis, Herbert, et al., *Historian and Diplomat: Historians in American Foreign Policy,* Francis L. Loewenheim, ed. (1967).
Graber, Doris A., *Crisis Diplomacy: U.S. Intervention Policies* (1959).
Graebner, Norman A., ed., *Ideas and Diplomacy* (1964).
Holt, Robert T., and Robert W. van de Velde, *Strategic Psychological Operations and American Foreign Policy* (1960).
Kolko, Gabriel, *The Roots of American Foreign Policy: An Analysis of Power and Purpose* (1969).
LaFeber, Walter, *New Empire: American Expansion, 1860–1898* (1963).
May, Ernest R., *American Imperialism* (1968).
Perkins, Dexter, *American Approach to Foreign Policy* (rev. ed., 1962).
——— *America's Quest for Peace* (1962).
——— "The Department of State and American Public Opinion," in Gordon Craig and Felix Gilbert, eds., *The Diplomats, 1919–1939* (1953).
Perkins, Whitney T., *Denial of Empire: The United States and Its Dependencies* (1962).
Plischke, Elmer, *Summit Diplomacy: Personal Diplomacy of the President* (1958).
Radosh, Ronald, *American Labor and Foreign Policy* (1970).
Tannenbaum, Frank, *American Tradition in Foreign Policy* (1955).
Thompson, Kenneth W., *American Diplomacy and Emergent Patterns* (1962).
Tompkins, E. Berkeley, *Anti-Imperialism in the United States: The Great Debate, 1890–1920* (1970).
Van Alstyne, Richard W., *American Diplomacy in Action* (2nd ed., 1947).
——— *The Rising American Empire* (1960).
Van Hoogstrate, Dorothy J., *American Foreign Policy: Catholic Interpretation* (1960).
Vevier, Charles, "American Continentalism: An Idea of Expansion, 1845–1910," *AHR,* 65 (1960), 323.
Warburg, James P., *United States in a Changing World: Foreign Policy* (1954).
Williams, William A., "Frontier Thesis and American Foreign Policy," *Pac. Hist. Rev.,* 24 (1955), 379.
——— *Tragedy of American Diplomacy* (rev. ed., 1962).
Wriston, Henry M., *Diplomacy in a Democracy* (1956).

15.8.3 State Department

Barnes, William, and John H. Morgan, *Foreign Service of the United States* (1961).
Bemis, Samuel F., et al., eds., *American Secretaries of State and Their Diplomacy* (17 vols., 1927–1967).

De Conde, Alexander, *The American Secretary of State* (1962).
Elder, Robert E., *The Policy Machine:Department of State and American Foreign Policy* (1959).
Ilchman, Warren F., *Professional Diplomacy in the United States, 1779–1939* (1961).
McKenna, Joseph C., *Diplomatic Protest in Foreign Policy* (1962).
Moffat, Jay P., *Selections from Diplomatic Journals, 1919–1943,* Nancy H. Hooker, ed. (1956).
Paullin, Charles O., *Diplomatic Negotiations of American Naval Officers* (1912).
Price, Don K., ed., *Secretary of State* (1960).
Simpson, Smith, *Anatomy of the State Department* (1967).
Spaulding, E. Wilder, *Ambassadors Ordinary and Extraordinary* (1961).
Stuart, Graham H., *Department of State: History of Its Organization, Procedure and Personnel* (1949).
Villard, Henry S., *Affairs at State* (1965).
Wriston, H. M., *Executive Agents in American Foreign Relations* (1929).

15.8.4 Relations with Regions and Individual Nations

15.8.4.1 Canada

Callahan, J. M., *American Foreign Policy in Canadian Relations* (1937).
Clark, Gerald, *Canada: Uneasy Neighbor* (1965).
Corbett, Percy E., *Settlement of Canadian-American Disputes* (1937).
Craig, Gerald M., *The United States and Canada* (1968).
Deener, David R., ed., *Canada-United States Treaty Relations* (1963).
Gluek, Alvin C., Jr., *Minnesota and Canadian Northwest* (1965).
Hitsman, J. Mackay, *Safeguarding Canada, 1763–1871* (1968).
Keenleyside, H. L., and G. S. Brown, *Canada and United States* (1952).
Mitchell, J. R., *United States and Canada* (1968).
Piper, Don C., "Intergovernmental Machinery in Canadian-American Relations," *So. Atl. Quar.,* 62 (1963), 551.
Roussin, Marcel, *Le Canada et le système Interaméricain* (1959).
Tansill, C. C., *Canadian-American Relations* (1943).
Willoughby, William R., *St. Lawrence Waterway: Politics and Diplomacy* (1961).
Wilson, Robert R., et al., *Canada-United States Treaty Relations,* David R. Deener, ed. (1963).
Wise, Sydney F., and Robert C. Brown, *Canada Views United States: Nineteenth-Century Attitudes* (1967).

15.8.4.2 Inter-American Relations

GENERAL

Bemis, Samuel F., *The Latin American Policy of the United States* (1943).
Bernstein, Harry, *Making an Inter-American Mind* (1961).
Burr, Robert N., and Roland D. Hussey, *Documents on Inter-American Cooperation* (2 vols., 1955).
Callcott, Wilfrid H., *Western Hemisphere: Influence on United States Policies to End of World War II.*
Connell-Smith, Gordon, *Inter-American System* (1966).
Dozer, Donald M., *Are We Good Neighbors? Inter-American Relations, 1930–1960* (1959).
Duggan, Laurence, *Americas: Search for Hemispheric Security* (1949).
Inman, Samuel G., *Inter-American Conferences 1826–1954* (1965).
Lieuwen, Edwin, *Arms and Politics in Latin America* (rev. ed., 1961).
—— *U.S. Policy in Latin America* (1965).
Mecham, John L., *United States and Inter-American Security, 1889–1960* (1961).
Palmer, Thomas W., *Search for a Latin American Policy* (1957).
Perkins, Dexter, *A History of the Monroe Doctrine* (1955).
—— *The United States and Latin America* (1961).
Thomas, Ann V., and A. J. Thomas, Jr., *Non-Intervention* (1956).
Whitaker, Arthur P., *Western Hemisphere Idea* (1954).

* * * * * * *

Bayitch, Stojan A., *Latin America and the Caribbean: A Bibliographical Guide to Works in English* (1967).
Trask, David F., et al., eds., *Bibliography of United States-Latin American Relations since 1810* (1968).

CENTRAL AMERICA AND THE CARIBBEAN

Brenner, Anita, *Wind That Swept Mexico: Mexican Revolution, 1910–1942* (1943).
Callahan, J. M., *American Foreign Policy in Mexican Relations* (1932).
Callcott, Wilfrid H., *Caribbean Policy of the United States, 1890–1920* (1942).
Cline, Howard F., *The United States and Mexico* (rev. ed., 1963).
Fagg, John E., *Cuba, Haiti, and the Dominican Republic* (1965).
Foner, Philip S., *History of Cuba and Relations with the United States* (2 vols., 1963).
Hundley, Norris, Jr., *Dividing the Waters: United States and Mexico* (1966).
Jones, Chester L., et al., *United States and the Caribbean* (1929).
Langley, Lester D., *Cuban Policy of the United States* (1968).
Proudfoot, Mary, *Britain and the United States in the Caribbean* (1953).
Rippy, J. Fred, *United States and Mexico* (1931).
Smith, Robert F., *United States and Cuba, 1917–1960* (1960).

SOUTH AMERICA

Carey, James C., *Peru and United States, 1900–1962* (1964).
Evans, H. C., *Chile and the United States* (1927).
Haring, Clarence H., *Argentina and the United States* (1941).
Hill, L. F., *United States and Brazil* (1932).
Marsh, M. A., *Bankers in Bolivia* (1928).
McGann, Thomas F., *Argentina, The United States and the Inter-American System, 1880–1914* (1957).
Parks, E. T., *Colombia and United States* (1935).
Peterson, Harold F., *Argentina and the United States, 1810–1960* (1964).
Pike, Frederick B., *Chile and the U.S., 1880–1962* (1963).
Rippy, J. Fred, *Capitalists and Colombia* (1931).
Sherman, W. R., *Diplomatic Relations of United States and Chile* (1926).
Smith, Oscar Edmund, Jr., *Yankee Diplomacy in Argentina* (1953).
Whitaker, Arthur P., *The United States and Argentina* (1954).
———— *The United States and South America* (1948).

15.8.4.3 Great Britain and Dominions

See 15.8.4.1, for references to Canada.

Allen, Harry C., *Great Britain and the United States: Relations, 1783–1952* (1955).
Bourne, Kenneth, *Britain and the Balance of Power in North America, 1815–1908* (1967).
Brinton, Crane, *The United States and Britain* (1948).
Clark, William, *Less than Kin: Anglo-American Relations* (1957).
Mowat, Robert B., *Diplomatic Relations of Great Britain and the United States* (1925).
Nicholas, Herbert G., *Britain and U.S.A.* (1963).
Pelling, Henry, *America and British Left: Bright to Bevan* (1957).
Perkins, Bradford, *Castlereagh and Adams: England and the United States, 1812–1823* (1964).
———— *First Rapprochement:England and United States, 1795–1805* (1955).
———— *Prologue to War: England and United States, 1805–1812* (1961).
Russett, Bruce M., *Community and Contention: Britain and America in Twentieth Century* (1963).
Ward, Alan J., *Ireland and Anglo-American Relations, 1899–1921* (1969).

15.8.4.4 Europe

Adams, Henry M., *Prussian-American Relations, 1775–1871* (1960).
Beloff, Max, *The United States and the Unity of Europe* (1963).
Beutin, Ludwig, *Bremen und Amerika* (1953).
Blumenthal, Henry, *France and United States, 1789–1914* (1970).
—— *Reappraisal of Franco-American Relations, 1830–1871* (1959).
Brinton, Crane, *The Americans and the French* (1968).
Erdman, Paul E., *Swiss-American Economic Relations* (1959).
Field, James A., Jr., *America and the Mediterranean World, 1776–1882* (1969).
Larrabee, Stephen A., *Hellas Observed: American Experience of Greece, 1775–1865* (1957).
McKay, Donald C., *The United States and France* (1951).
Marraro, Howard R., ed., *Diplomatic Relations between the United States and the Kingdom of Two Sicilies, 1816–1861* (2 vols., 1951).
Meier, Heinz K., *The United States and Switzerland in the Nineteenth Century* (1963).
Scott, Franklin D., *The United States and Scandinavia* (1950).
Villard, Léonie, *La France et les États-Unis: Échanges et recontres, 1524–1800* (1952).

*   *   *   *   *   *   *

de Courten, Régis, and Wanda Rokicka, *Die Schweiz und die Vereinigten Staaten von Amerika . . . Bibliographie* (1964).

15.8.4.5 Russia

Adler, Cyrus, and A. M. Margalith, *With Firmness in Right* (1946).
Andreev, Aleksandr I., ed., *Russian Discoveries in the Pacific and North America in the Eighteenth and Nineteenth Centuries,* C. Ginsburg, trans. (1952).
Bailey, Thomas A., *America Faces Russia* (1950).
Bolkhovitinov, Nikolai N., *Stanovlenie Russko-Amerikanshkikh Otnoshenii, 1775–1815* (1966).
Chevigny, Hector, *Russian America: Alaskan Venture, 1741–1867* (1965).
Dean, Vera Micheles, *The United States and Russia* (1948).
Donnelly, Desmond, *Struggle for the World: Cold War, 1917–1965* (1965).
Dulles, Foster R., *The Road to Teheran: The Story of Russia and America, 1781–1943* (1946).
Farrar, Victor, *Annexation of Russian America to the United States* (1937).
Fleming, Denna F., *Cold War and Its Origins, 1917–1960* (2 vols., 1961).
Hoelzle, Erwin, *Russland und Amerika* (1953).
Kennan, George F., *Russia and the West under Lenin and Stalin* (1961).
Shaw, Malcolm, *Anglo-American Democracy* (1968).
Thomas, B. P., *Russo-American Relations 1815–1867* (1930).
Tompkins, Pauline, *American-Russian Relations in the Far East* (1949).
Williams, William A., *American-Russian Relations, 1781–1947* (1952).

15.8.4.6 Middle and Near East

Brown, Norman, *The United States and India and Pakistan* (rev. ed., 1963).
Daniel, Robert L., "American Influences in Near East before 1861," *Am. Quar.,* 16 (1964), 72.
De Novo, John A., *American Interests and Policies in the Middle East, 1900–1939* (1963).
Finnie, David H., *Pioneers East: The Early American Experience in the Middle East* (1967).
Fisher, Sydney N., "Two Centuries of American Interest in Turkey," in David H. Pinkney and Theodore Ropp, eds., *Festschrift for Frederick Artz* (1964).
Gordon, Leland J., *American Relations with Turkey* (1932).
Manuel, F. E., *Realities of American-Palestine Relations* (1949).
Polk, William R., *The United States and the Arab World* (rev. ed., 1969).
Speiser, Ephraim A., *The United States and Near East* (rev. ed., 1949).
Taylor, Arnold H., *American Diplomacy and Narcotics Traffic, 1900–1939* (1970).

Thornburg, Max W., *People and Policy in the Middle East* (1964).
Tibawi, Abdul L., *American Interests in Syria, 1800–1901: Educational, Literary and Religious Work* (1966).
Safran, Nadav, *The United States and Israel* (1963).
Thomas, Lewis V., and R. N. Frye, *The United States and Turkey and Iran* (1951).
Yeselson, Abraham, *United States-Persian Diplomatic Relations, 1883–1921* (1956).

15.8.4.7 East Asia and Southwest Pacific

Battistini, Lawrence H., *Rise of American Influence in Asia and the Pacific* (1960).
——— *The United States and Asia* (1956).
Borg, Dorothy, ed., *Historians and American Far Eastern Policy* (1966).
Dennett, Tyler, *Americans in Eastern Asia* (1922).
Gould, James W., *Americans in Sumatra* (1961).
——— *The United States and Malaysia* (1969).
Grattan, C. Hartley, *The United States and the Southwest Pacific* (1961).
Griffin, Eldon, *Clippers and Consuls: American Consular and Commercial Relations with Eastern Asia, 1845–1860* (1938).
Griswold, A. W., *The Far Eastern Policy of the United States* (1938).
Iriye, Akira, *Across the Pacific: American-East Asian Relations* (1967).
Livermore, Seward W., "American Naval-Base Policy in the Far East, 1850–1914," *Pac. Hist. Rev.*, 13 (1944), 113.
O'Connor, Richard, *Pacific Destiny: U.S. in the Far East, 1776–1968* (1969).
Price, Archibald G., *Western Invasions of the Pacific and Its Continents, 1513–1958* (1963).
Quigley, Harold S., and George H. Blakeslee, *Far East* (1938).
Rostow, Walt W., *American Policy in Asia* (1955).
Strauss, Wallace P., *Americans in Polynesia, 1783–1842* (1963).
Tuleja, Thaddeus V., *Statesmen and Admirals: Far Eastern Naval Policy* (1963).

CHINA

Ch'ing, Ju-chi, *Mei-kuo ch'in Hua shih* (Peking, Vols. 1/2–   , 1952–   ). History of American aggression against China.
Clyde, P. H., ed., *United States Policy toward China, 1838–1939* (1940).
Curti, Merle, and John Stalker, "American Image in China, 1840–1900," *Am. Philos. Soc., Proc.*, 96 (1952), 663.
Danton, George H., *Culture Contacts of United States and China, 1784–1844* (1931).
Dulles, Foster R., *China and America: Relations since 1784* (1946).
——— *Old China Trade* (1930).
Fairbank, John K., *The United States and China* (3d ed., 1971).
Holden, Reuben A., *Yale in China, 1901–1951* (1964).
Huang, Chia-mu, *Meikuo yu T'ai-wan, 1784–1895* (1966) United States and Taiwan.
Latourette, Kenneth Scott, *History of Christian Missions in China* (1929).
Liu, Kwang-Ching, *American Missionaries in China* (1966).
Morse, H. B., *International Relations of Chinese Empire* (3 vols., 1910–1918). Abr. by H. F. McNair under title, *Far Eastern International Relations* (1931).
Ting-i, Li, *Chung-Mei wai-chiao shih, 1784–1860* (Taipei, 1960). History of Chinese-American diplomatic relations.
Pao, Ming-ch'ien, *Open Door Policy in Relation to China* (1923).
Swisher, Earl, *China's Management of the American Barbarians: A Study of Sino-American Relations, 1841–1861, with Documents* (1953).
Tong, Te-kong, *United States Diplomacy in China, 1844–60* (1964).
Varg, Paul A., *Making of a Myth: The United States and China, 1879–1912* (1968).
——— *Missionaries, Chinese, and Diplomats: American Protestant Missionary Movement in China, 1890–1952* (1958).
Wang, Yi Chu, *Chinese Intellectuals and the West, 1872–1949* (1966).

*   *   *   *   *   *   *

Irick, Robert L. et al., *American-Chinese Relations, 1784–1941: Chinese Language Materials at Harvard* (1960).
Liu, Kwang-ching, *Americans and Chinese: A Historical Essay and a Bibliography* (1963).

JAPAN

Battistini, Lawrence H., *Japan and America* (1954).
Bennett, John W., Herbert Passin, and Robert K. McKnight, *In Search of Identity: Japanese Overseas Scholar in America and Japan* (1958).
Clinard, O. J., *Japan's Influence on Naval Power* (1947).
Dulles, Foster R., *Yankees and Samurai, 1791–1900* (1965).
———— *Forty Years of American-Japanese Relations* (1937).
Falk, E. A., *From Perry to Pearl Harbor* (1943).
Iglehart, Charles W., *Century of Protestant Christianity in Japan* (1959).
Ikado, Fujio, and James R. McGovern, comps., *Bibliography of Christianity in Japan: Protestantism in English Sources 1859-1959* (Tokyo, 1966).
Kamikawa, Hikomatsu, ed., *Japan-American Diplomatic Relations in the Meiji-Taisho Era* (Tokyo, 1958).
Neumann, William L., *America Encounters Japan* (1963).
Ohara, Keishi, ed., *Japanese Trade and Industry in Meiji-Taisho Era* (1957).
Reischauer, Edwin O., *The United States and Japan* (3d ed., 1965).
Schwantes, Robert S., *Japanese and Americans: Cultural Relations* (1955).
Sakamaki, Shunzo, "Japan and United States, 1790–1853," *Asiatic Soc. Japan, 218, Trans.*, ser. (1939).
Thomas, Winburn T., *Protestant Beginnings in Japan, 1859–1889* (1959).
Treat, P. J., *Diplomatic Relations between the United States and Japan, 1853–1905* (3 vols., 1932–1938).
Tupper, Eleanor, and G. E. McReynolds, *Japan in American Opinion* (1937).
Watanabe, Masao, "Meiji shoki no Nihon ni okeru Beikoku kagaku no eikyo," [Influence of American science in Japan of early Meiji era] in Masao Watanabe, *Science in the History of Modern Culture* (1963).
Wildes, Harry Emerson, *Aliens in the East; A New History of Japan's Foreign Intercourse* (1937).

KOREA

Conroy, Hilary, *Japanese Seizure of Korea, 1868–1910* (1961).
Harrington, Fred H., *God, Mammon and the Japanese* (1944).
Henderson, Gregory, *Korea: The Politics of the Vortex* (1968).
Kim, C. I. Eugene, and Han-kyo-Kim, *Korea and the Politics of Imperialism, 1876–1910* (1967).
McCune, George M., John A. Harrison, and Spencer Palmer, eds., *Korean-American Relations: Documents, 1883–1895* (2 vols., 1951–1963).
U.S. Department of State, *Historical Summary of United States-Korean Relations, 1834–1962* (1962).

PHILIPPINES

Agoncillo, Teodoro A., *Short History of the Philippines* (1969).
Bowditch, Nathaniel, *Early American-Philippine Trade: Journal in Manila, 1796,* Thomas R. and Mary C. McHale, eds. (1962).
Corpuz, Onofre D., *The Philippines* (1965).
Grunder, Garel A., and William E. Livezey, *Philippines and the United States* (1951).
Zaide, Gregorio F., *Philippine Political and Cultural History* (1949).

15.8.5 Treaties

Byrd, Elbert M., Jr., *Treaties and Executive Agreements,* (1960).
Holt, W. S., *Treaties Defeated by the Senate* (1933).

Reiff, Henry, *United States and Treaty Law of the Sea* (1959).
Wilson, Robert R., *International Law Standard in Treaties of United States* (1953).

See also 5.5.6, Federal Records Relating to Foreign Affairs.

15.9 THE MILITARY

15.9.1 General

Bernardo, C. Joseph, and Eugene H. Bacon, *American Military Policy since 1775* (2nd ed., 1961).
Dupuy, R. E., and William H. Baumer, *Little Wars of the United States* (1968).
Dupuy, R. E., and T. N. Dupuy, *Military Heritage of Americans* (1956).
Greene, Fred, "Military View of American National Policy, 1904–1940," *AHR*, 66 (1961), 354.
Hammond, Paul Y., *Organizing for Defense: Military Establishment in the Twentieth Century* (1961).
Hittle, J. D., *The Military Staff* (1949).
Janowitz, Morris, *The Professional Soldier* (1960).
Matloff, Maurice, ed., *American Military History* (1969).
Millis, Walter, *American Military Thought* (1966).
—— *Arms and Men: Military History* (1956).
Mugridge, Donald H., comp., *Album of American Battle Art, 1755–1918* (1947).
O'Connor, Raymond G., ed., *American Defense Policy in Perspective* (1965).
Ransom, Harry Howe, *The Intelligence Establishment* (1970). A revision of *Central Intelligence and National Security* (1958).
Reinhardt, George C., and William R. Kintner, *Haphazard Years: How America Has Gone to War* (1960).
Rutkowski, Edwin H., *Politics of Military Aviation Procurement, 1926–1934* (1966).
Schelling, Thomas C., *Arms and Influence* (1966).
Weigley, Russell F., *Towards an American Army: Military Thought from Washington to Marshall* (1962).
Williams, T. Harry, *Americans at War: Military System* (1960).

*　　*　　*　　*　　*　　*　　*

Conn, Stetson, "The Pursuit of Military History," *Mil. Affairs*, 30 (1966), 1.
Eisenstadt, Abraham S., "Redefining American Experience," *Am. Rev.*, 3 (1963), 134.
Millett, Allan R., "American Military History," in Herbert J. Bass, ed., *State of American History* (1970), 157.
Morton, Louis, "Historian and War," *MVHR*, 48 (1962), 599.

See also 13.4.1, Military Frontier; 20.11.13, Indian Wars before 1865; 20.11.14, Indian Wars after 1865; 29.1.10, Atomic Energy and Atomic Weapons; 29.2.7, Aeronautics and Astronautics.

15.9.2 Army

Ambrose, Stephen E., *Duty, Honor, Country: West Point* (1966).
Brophy, Leo P. et al., *The Chemical Warfare Service* (3 vols., 1959).
Esposito, Vincent J., ed., *West Point Atlas* (2 vols., 1959).
Fleming, Thomas J., *West Point* (1969).
Foner, Jack D., *The United States Soldier Between the Two Wars: Army Life and Reforms, 1865–1898* (1970).
Forman, Sidney, *West Point: A History* (1950).
—— "Why the United States Military Academy Was Established in 1802," *Mil. Affairs*, 29 (1965), 16.

Glines, Carroll V., *Compact History of the United States Air Force* (1963).
Goldberg, Alfred, ed., *History of the United States Air Force, 1907–1957* (1957).
Gurney, Gene, *Pictorial History of the United States Army* (1966).
Heitman, Francis B., *Historical Register and Dictionary of United States Army, Sept. 29, 1789, to Mar. 2, 1903* (2 vols., 1903).
Herr, John K., and Edward S. Wallace, *Story of the U.S. Cavalry, 1775–1942* (1953).
Hill, Forest G., *Roads, Rails, and Waterways; The Army Engineers and Early Transportation* (1957).
Holt, W. Stull, *The Office of Chief of Engineers of the Army: Its Non-Military History* (1923).
Huston, James A., *Sinews of War: Army Logistics, 1775–1953* (1966).
Janowitz, Morris, *Professional Soldier* (1960).
Kredel, Fritz, and F. P. Todd, *Soldiers of the American Army, 1775–1954* (1954).
Lyons, Gene M., and John W. Masland, *Education and Military Leadership: R.O.T.C.* (1959).
Masland, John W., and Laurence I. Radway, *Soldiers and Scholars: Military Education and National Policy* (1957).
Merrill, James M., *Spurs to Glory: United States Cavalry* (1966).
Risch, Erna, *A History of the* [Quartermaster] *Corps, 1775–1939* (1962).
Weigley, Russell F., *History of the United States Army* (1967).

*   *   *   *   *   *   *

Greenfield, Kent R., *Historian and the Army* (1954).

15.9.3 Navy

Alden, Carroll S., *United States Navy: A History* (rev. ed., 1945).
Bauer, K. Jack, "Naval Shipbuilding, 1794–1860," *Mil. Affairs*, 29 (1965), 29.
Chapelle, Howard I., *History of American Sailing Navy* (1949).
Davis, George T., *Navy Second to None: Modern American Naval Policy* (1940).
Davis, Vincent, *Admirals Lobby* (1967).
Hailey, Foster B., and Milton Lancelot, *Clear for Action: Photographic Story of Modern Naval Combat, 1898–1964* (1964).
Harris, Brayton, *Age of the Battleship, 1890–1922* (1965).
Heinl, Robert D., Jr., *Soldiers of the Sea: Marine Corps, 1775–1962* (1962).
Herrick, Walter R., Jr., *American Naval Revolution* (1966).
Howeth, L. S., *History of Communications: Electronics in the Navy* (1963).
Knox, Dudley W., *History of United States Navy* (rev. ed., 1948).
Langley, Harold D., *Social Reform in the United States Navy, 1789–1862* (1967).
MacDonald, Scot, *Evolution of Aircraft Carriers* (1964).
Metcalf, C. H., *A History of the United States Marine Corps* (1939).
Mitchell, Donald W., *History of the Modern Navy, from 1883 through Pearl Harbor* (1946).
Paullin, Charles O., "Naval Administration in America, 1861–1911." U. S. Naval Inst., *Proc.*, 38 (1912), 1309; 39 (1913), 165.
Potter, Elmer B., ed., *United States and World Sea Power* (1955).
"Recollections of the Early History of Naval Aviation: A Session in Oral History," *Tech. and Cult.*, 4 (1963).
Roscoe, Theodore, and Fred Freeman, *Picture History of the U.S. Navy, 1776–1897* (1956).
Smith, Richard K., *Airships "Akron" and "Macon": Flying Aircraft Carriers of the United States Navy* (1965).
Sprout, Harold, and Margaret Sprout, *Rise of American Naval Power, 1776–1918* (1943).
Stambler, Irwin, *Battle for Inner Space—Undersea Warfare* (1962).
Tuleja, Thaddeus V., *Statesmen and Admirals: Far Eastern Naval Policy* (1963).
Turnbull, Archibald D., and Clifford L. Lord, *History of United States Naval Aviation* (1949).
U.S. Department of Navy, *United States Naval Aviation, 1910–1960* (1960).

van Deurs, George, *Wings for the Fleet: Naval Aviation's Early Development, 1910–1916* (1966).

*   *   *   *   *   *   *

Albion, Robert G., *Naval and Maritime History: An Annotated Bibliography* (3d ed., 1963).
Merrill, James M., "Writings on American Naval History, 1914–60," *MVHR*, 50 (1963), 79.

15.9.4 Civil-Military Relations

Blum, Albert A., *Drafted or Deferred: Practices Past and Present* (1967).
Cunliffe, Marcus, *Soldiers and Civilians: Martial Spirit in America, 1775–1865* (1968).
Derthick, Martha A., *The National Guard in Politics* (1965).
Ekirch, Arthur A., Jr., *Civilian and Military* (1956).
Fulbright, J. William, *Arrogance of Power* (1967).
Gerhardt, James M., *The Draft and Public Policy: Issues in Military Manpower Procurement, 1945–1970* (1970).
Huntington, Samuel P., *The Soldier and the State: The Theory and Politics of Civil-Military Relations* (1957).
Israel, Fred L., "New York's Citizen Soldiers: Militia and Their Armories," *N.Y. Hist.*, 42 (1961), 145.
Leach, Jack F., *Conscription in the United States* (1952).
Riker, William H., *Soldiers of the States: National Guard* (1957).
Sax, Joseph L., "Conscience and Anarchy: The Prosecution of War Resisters," *Yale Rev.*, 67 (1968), 481.
Schlissel, Lillian, *Conscience in America: Conscientious Objection, 1757–1967* (1968).
Stein, Harold, ed., *American Civil-Military Decisions: Case Studies* (1963).
Yarmolinsky, Adam, *The Military Establishment: Impact on American Society* (1971).

*   *   *   *   *   *   *

Larson, Arthur D., *Civil-Military Relations and Militarism: A Classified Bibliography Covering the United States and other Nations of the World, with Introductions* (1871).

15.10 JUDICIAL BRANCH

15.10.1 General

Bruce, Andrew A., *American Judge* (1924).
Callender, Clarence N., *American Courts: Organization and Procedure* (1927).
Carpenter, W. S., *Judicial Tenure in the United States* (1918).
Dolbeare, Kenneth M., *Trial Courts in Urban Politics* (1967).
Grossman, Joel B., *Lawyers and Judges: ABA and Judicial Selection* (1965).
Heller, Louis B., *Do You Solemnly Swear?* (1968).
Jacob, Herbert, *Justice in America* (1965).
Jahnige, T. P., and S. Goldman, eds., *The Federal Judicial System* (1968).
James, Howard, *Crisis in the Courts* (1968).
Laurent, Francis W., *Business of a Trial Court: Circuit Court for Chippewa County, Wisconsin* (1959).
Peltason, Jack W., *Federal Courts in the Political Process* (1955).
Roche, John, *Courts and Rights: American Judiciary in Action* (rev. ed., 1966).
Spiegel, Frederick C., *Illinois Court of Claims: Liability* (1962).

U.S. Library of Congress, *Creation of Federal Judiciary: Review of Debates*, G. J. Schultz, ed. (1938).
Virtue, Maxine B., *Survey of Metropolitan Courts* (1962).
Wendell, Mitchell, *Relations between Federal and State Courts* (1949).
Wyzanski, Charles E., Jr., *Whereas: A Judge's Premises* (1965).

See also 10.3 for biographies/writings of:

Allen, Florence E., 1884–
Baldwin, Simeon E., 1840–1927
Burke, Thomas, 1849–1925
Clark, Walter, 1846–1924
Doe, Charles, 1830–1896
Dole, Sanford B., 1844–1926
Doster, Frank, 1847–1933
Grundy, Felix, 1777–1840
Hall, James, 1793–1868
Kent, James, 1763–1847
Korner, Gustav P., 1809–1896
Morgan, Daniel E., 1877–1949
Parsons, Theophilus, 1750–1813
Ruffin, Thomas, 1787–1870
Ryan, Edward G., 1810–1880
Shaw, Lemuel, 1781–1861
Smith, Jeremiah, 1759–1842
Terry, David S., 1823–1889
Williams, Robert L., 1868–1948
Woodward, Augustus B., 1774–1827

See also 21.12.4, Law Enforcement.

15.10.2 Supreme Court

15.10.2.1 General

Bartholomew, Paul C., *Leading Cases on the Constitution* (1965).
Becker, Theodore L., ed., *Impact of Supreme Court Decisions: Empirical Studies* (1969).
Boudin, Louis, *Government by Judiciary* (2 vols., 1932).
Cahn, Edmond N., ed., *Supreme Court and Supreme Law* (1954).
Frank, John P., *Marble Palace: Supreme Court in American Life* (1958).
Frankfurter, Felix, "Supreme Court in Mirror of Justices," *Univ. Penn. Law Rev.*, 105 (1957), 781.
Freund, Paul, *The Supreme Court of the United States. Its Business, Purposes and Performance* (1961).
Harrell, Mary Ann, and Stuart E. Jones, *Equal Justice Under Law: Supreme Court in American Life* (1965). Pictorial.
Hughes, Charles E., *Supreme Court* (1936).
Jackson, Robert H., *The Supreme Court in the American System of Government* (1955).
Johnson, Marion M., et al., comps., *Index to the Manuscript and Revised Printed Opinions of the Supreme Court in the National Archives, 1808–73* (1965).
Kutler, Stanley, *The Supreme Court and the Constitution* (1969).
McCloskey, Robert G., *The American Supreme Court* (1960).
Mason, Alpheus T., and William M. Beaney, *Supreme Court in a Free Society* (1959).
Pfeffer, Leo, *This Honorable Court: A History of the Supreme Court* (1965).
Rodell, Fred, *Nine Men: Supreme Court from 1790 to 1955* (1955).
Steamer, Robert J., *The Supreme Court in Crisis: A History of Conflict* (1971).
Stern, Robert L., and Eugene Gressman, *Supreme Court Practice* (1969).

Swisher, Carl B., *Historic Decisions of the Supreme Court* (2nd ed., 1969).

Twiss, Benjamin, *Lawyers and the Constitution: How Laissez-Faire Came to the Supreme Court* (1942).

Warren, Charles, *The Supreme Court in United States History* (rev. ed., 2 vols., 1937).

Westin, Alan F., "Out-of-Court Commentary by Supreme Court Justices, 1790–1962," *Columbia Law Rev.*, 62 (1962), 633.

——— ed., *Supreme Court: Views from the Inside* (1961).

15.10.2.2 Nineteenth Century

Crosskey, William W., "John Marshall," *Univ. of Chi. Law Rev.*, 23 (1956), 377.

Dowd, Morgan D., "Justice Joseph Story: Jeffersonian Judge," *Vanderbilt Law Rev.*, 18 (1965), 643.

Fairman, Charles, *Mr. Justice Miller and the Supreme Court, 1862–1890* (1939).

Faulkner, Robert Kenneth, *The Jurisprudence of John Marshall* (1968).

Frankfurter, Felix, "John Marshall and the Judicial Function," *Harv. Law Rev.*, 69 (1955) 217.

Harris, Robert J., "Chief Justice Taney," *Vanderbilt Law Rev.*, 10 (1957), 227.

Hatcher, William H., "John Marshall and States' Rights," *South. Quar.*, 3 (1965), 207.

Jones, William M., ed., *Chief Justice John Marshall* (1956).

Lerner, Max, "John Marshall and the Campaign of History," in Leonard W. Levy, ed., *American Constitutional Law: Historical Essays* (1966).

Loth, David G., *Chief Justice John Marshall and the Growth of the Republic* (1949).

Morgan, Donald G., *Justice William Johnson the First Dissenter* (1954).

Palmer, Benjamin W., *Marshall and Taney: Statesmen of the Law* (1939).

Roper, Donald M., "Judicial Unanimity and Marshall Court," *Am. Jour. Legal Hist.*, 9 (1965), 118.

Silver, David, *Lincoln's Supreme Court* (1956).

Smith, William R., "John Marshall's Historical Method," *Historian*, 26 (1963), 19.

Thayer, James B., et al., *James Bradley Thayer, Oliver Wendell Holmes, and Felix Frankfurter on John Marshall* (1967).

15.10.2.3 Twentieth Century

Barnett, V. M., Jr., "Mr. Justice Jackson and Supreme Court," *Western Pol. Quar.*, 1 (1948), 223.

Biddle, Francis, *Justice Holmes, Natural Law, and the Supreme Court* (1961).

Brandeis, Louis D., *The Unpublished Opinions of Mr. Justice Brandeis: The Supreme Court at Work*, Alexander M. Bickel, ed. (1957).

Clark, F. B., *Constitutional Doctrines of Justice Harlan* (1915).

Daly, John J., *Use of History in Decisions of Supreme Court, 1900–1930* (1954).

Danelski, David J., *A Supreme Court Justice is Appointed* (1964). Justice Butler.

Desmond, Charles S., et al., *Mr. Justice Jackson: Four Lectures in His Honor* (1969).

Doro, Marion E., "The Brandeis Brief," *Vanderbilt Law Rev.*, 11 (1958), 783.

Douglas, William O., "Right of Association," *Columbia Law Rev.*, 63 (1963), 1361.

Fine, Sidney, "Mr. Justice Murphy in World War II," *JAH*, 53 (1966), 90.

Frank, John P., "Fred Vinson and Chief Justiceship," *Univ. of Chi. Law Rev.*, 21 (1954), 212.

Freund, Paul A., "Charles Evans Hughes as Chief Justice," *Harv. Law Rev.*, 81 (1967), 4.

——— "Mr. Justice Brandeis," *Harv. Law Rev.*, 70 (1957), 769.

Grey, David L., *Supreme Court and News Media* (1968).

Hand, Learned, "Justice Louis D. Brandeis," *Jour. Soc. Philos.*, 4 (1939), 144.

Harper, Fowler V., *Justice [Wiley] Rutledge* (1965).

Hurst, J. Willard, *Justice Holmes on Legal History* (1964).

Jaffe, Louis L., "Was Brandeis an Activist?" *Harv. Law Rev.* 80 (1967), 986.

Konefsky, Samuel J., *Constitutional World of Frankfurter* (1949).
——— *Legacy of Holmes and Brandeis* (1956).
Levy, Beryl H., *Cardozo and the Frontiers of Legal Thinking* (rev. ed., 1969).
McCloskey, Robert G., *The Modern Supreme Court* (1972).
Mason, Alpheus T., "Chief Justice Taft at Helm," *Vanderbilt Law Rev.*, 18 (1965), 367.
——— *The Supreme Court from Taft to Warren* (rev. ed., 1968).
Mendelson, Wallace, *Justices Black and Frankfurter: Conflict in the Court* (1961).
Miller, Charles A., *The Supreme Court and the Uses of History* (1970). Justice Harlan.
Murphy, Walter F., *Elements of Judicial Strategy* (1964).
Rumble, Wilfrid E., Jr., "Sociological Jurisprudence and Mr. Justice Holmes," *Jour. Hist. Ideas,* 26 (1965), 547.
Shapiro, Marvin, *The Modern Supreme Court* (1972).
Shick, Marvin, *Learned Hand's Court* (1970).
Swindler, William F., *Court and Constitution in the 20th Century: The Old Legality, 1889–1932* (1969).
Thomas, Helen S., "Justice William O. Douglas and Concept of 'Fair Trial'," *Vanderbilt Law Rev.,* 18 (1965), 701.
Woodford, Howard, "Justice Murphy: Freshman Years," *Vanderbilt Law Rev.,* 18 (1965), 473.

WARREN COURT

Bartholomew, Paul C., "Supreme Court, 1964–1965," *West. Pol. Quar.,* 18 (1965), 741.
Bickel, Alexander M., *Politics and the Warren Court* (1965).
Brennan, William J., Jr., *Affair with Freedom: Opinions and Speeches,* Stephen J. Friedman, ed. (1967).
Cox, Archibald, *The Warren Court: Constitutional Decision as an Instrument of Reform* (1968).
Frank, John P., and Yousuf Kársh, *The Warren Court* (1964).
Johnson, Richard M., *Dynamics of Compliance: Supreme Court Decision-Making* (1967).
Lewis, Anthony, *Warren Court: A Critical Evaluation* (1969).
Lytle, Clifford M., *Warren Court and Its Critics* (1968).
Mason, Alpheus T., "Understanding the Warren Court," *Pol. Sci. Quar.,* 81 (1966), 523.
Mitau, G. Theodore, *Decade of Decision: Supreme Court, 1954–1964* (1967).
Sayler, Richard H., Barry B. Boyer, and Robert E. Gooding, Jr., eds., *Warren Court: A Critical Analysis* (1969).
Swisher, Carl B., *Supreme Court in Modern Role* (1958).
Wechsler, Herbert, "Toward Neutral Principles of Constitutional Law," *Harv. Law Rev.,* 73 (1959). 1.

15.10.2.4 Judicial Review

Carr, R. K., *The Supreme Court and Judicial Review* (1942).
Commager, Henry S., *Majority Rule and Minority Rights* (1943).
Corwin, Edward S., *Doctrine of Judicial Review and Other Essays* (1914).
Givens, Richard A., "Chief Justice Stone and Judicial Review," *Va. Law Rev.,* 47 (1961), 1321.
Haines, Charles G., *American Doctrine of Judicial Supremacy* (2nd. ed., 1932).
——— "Judicial Review of Legislation in United States," *Tex. Law Rev.,* 2 (1924), 257; 3 (1924), 1.
Hurst, J. Willard, "Judicial Review and the Distribution of National Powers," in Edmond Cahn, ed., *Supreme Court and Supreme Law* (1954).
Mendelson, Wallace, "Jefferson on Judicial Review," *Univ. of Chi. Law Rev.,* 29 (1962), 327.
Rostow, Eugene V., "Democratic Character of Judicial Review," *Harv. Law Rev.,* 66 (1952), 193.

15.10.2.5 Supreme Court and Politics

Bickel, Alexander M., *Least Dangerous Branch: Supreme Court at Bar of Politics* (1962).

—— *Politics and the Warren Court* (1965).

Cahill, F. V., Jr., *Judicial Legislation* (1952).

Claude, Richard, *Supreme Court and Electoral Process* (1970).

Curtis, Charles P., Jr., *Lions under the Throne* (1947).

"Congressional Reversal of Supreme Court Decisions, 1945–1957," *Harv. Law Rev.*, 71 (1958), 1324.

Dahl, Robert A., "Supreme Court as Policy-Maker," *Jour. Pub. Law*, 6 (1957), 279.

Haines, Charles G., and Foster H. Sherwood, *Role of the Supreme Court in Government and Politics, 1835–1864* (1957).

Kutler, Stanley, *Judicial Power and Reconstruction Politics* (1968).

McLaughlin, A. C., *Courts, Constitution and Parties* (1912).

Mendelson, Wallace, "Judicial Review and Party Politics," *Vanderbilt Law Rev.*, 12 (1959), 447.

Murphy, Walter F., *Congress and the Court* (1962).

Nagel, Stuart S., "Court-Curbing Periods in American History," *Vanderbilt Law Rev.*, 18 (1965), 925.

Post, Charles G., *The Supreme Court and Political Questions* (1936).

Pritchett, Charles H., *Congress versus the Supreme Court, 1957–1960* (1961).

Ratner, Leonard G., "Congressional Power over Appellate Jurisdiction of Supreme Court," *Univ. Penn. Law Rev.*, 109 (1960), 157.

Rostow, Eugene V., "Supreme Court and People's Will," *Notre Dame Lawyer*, 33 (1958), 573.

Shapiro, Martin M., *Law and Politics in the Supreme Court* (1964).

—— *The Supreme Court and Administrative Agencies* (1968).

15.10.2.6 Collective Biographies

Dunham, Allison, and Philip B. Kurland, eds., *Mr. Justice* (rev. ed., 1964).

Ewing, C. A. M., *Judges of Supreme Court* (1938).

Friedman, Leon, and Fred L. Israel, eds., *Justices of Supreme Court, 1789–1969* (4 vols., 1969).

McCune, Wesley, *Nine Young Men* (1947).

See also 10.3 for biographies/writings of:

Black, Hugo, 1886–1971
Bradley, Joseph P., 1813–1892
Brandeis, Louis D., 1856–1941
Byrnes, James F., 1879–1972
Campbell, John Archibald, 1811–1889
Cardozo, Benjamin N., 1870–1938
Clarke, John H., 1857–1945
Curtis, Benjamin R., 1809–1874
Daniel, Peter V., 1784–1860
Davis, David, 1815–1886
Day, William R., 1849–1923
Field, Stephen J., 1816–1899
Frankfurter, Felix, 1882–1965
Fuller, Melville W., 1833–1910
Harlan, John Marshall, 1833–1911
Harlan, John Marshall, 1899–1971
Holmes, Oliver Wendell, Jr., 1841–1935
Hughes, Charles Evans, 1889–1950
Jackson, Robert H., 1892–1954
Jay, John, 1745–1829
Johnson, Thomas, 1732–1819
Johnson, William, 1771–1834
Johnson, William S., 1727–1819

Lamar, Lucius Q., 1825–1893
McLean, John, 1785–1861
Marshall, John, 1755–1835
Miller, Samuel Freeman, 1816–1890
Murphy, Frank, 1890–1949
Rutledge, Wiley, 1894–1949
Stone, Harlan F., 1872–1946
Story, Joseph, 1779–1845
Sutherland, George, 1862–1942
Taft, William Howard, 1857–1930
Taney, Roger B., 1777–1864
Waite, Morrison R., 1816–1888
Warren, Earl, 1891–
White, Edward D., 1845–1921

16 Law

16.1 GENERAL

Aumann, F. R., *Changing American Legal System* (1940).
Brown, Elizabeth G., in consultation with W. W. Blume, *British Statutes in American Law* (1964).
Brownell, Emery A., *Legal Aid in the United States* (1951).
Cohen, Julius, et al., *Parental Authority: The Community and the Law* (1958).
Flaherty, David H., ed., *Essays in the History of Early American Law* (1969).
Forkosch, Morris D., ed., *Essays in Legal History in Honor of Felix Frankfurter* (1966).
Grant, James A. C., *Our Common Law Constitution* (1960).
Gray, Charles M., *Copyhold, Equity, and the Common Law* (1963).
Haar, Charles M., ed., *Golden Age of American Law* (1965).
Hall, Ford W., "Common Law: Its Reception in the United States," *Vanderbilt Law Rev.*, 4 (1951), 791.
Hogue, Arthur R., *Origins of Common Law* (1966).
Holmes, Oliver W., *The Common Law* (1881); Mark DeW. Howe, ed. (1963).
Horwitz, Morton J., "The Emergence of an Instrumental Conception of American Law, 1780–1820," *Perspectives in Am. Hist.*, 5 (1971), 287.
Howe, Mark DeW., *Readings in American Legal History* (1949).
Hurst, J. Willard, *The Growth of American Law: The Lawmakers* (1950).
―――― *Law and the Conditions of Freedom in Nineteenth Century United States* (1956).
―――― *Law and Social Process in United States History* (1960).
―――― "Legal Elements in United States History," *Perspectives in Am. Hist.*, 5 (1971), 3.
Morris, Richard B., *Studies in History of American Law* (2nd ed., 1959).
Mott, Rodney L., *Due Process of Law: Historical and Analytical Treatise* (1926).
Paul, Arnold M., *Conservative Crisis: Attitudes of Bar and Bench, 1887–1895* (1960).
Pound, Roscoe, *Formative Era of American Law* (1938).
―――― *Spirit of the Common Law* (1921).
Stein, Peter, "Attraction of Civil Law in Post-Revolutionary America," *Va. Law Rev.*, 52 (1966), 403.

*   *   *   *   *   *   *

Friedman, Lawrence M., "Problems and Possibilities of American Legal History," in Herbert J. Bass, ed., *State of American History* (1970).
Hamlin, Paul M., "A History of American Law: Possibilities, Progress, and Resources and Initial Requirements," *N.Y. Law Forum*, 2 (1956), 76.

Mason, Malcolm S., "On Teaching Legal History Backwards," *Jour. Legal Ed.*, 18 (1966), 155.

Nunis, Doyce B., Jr., "Historical Studies in United States Legal History, 1950–59: Bibliography of Articles Published in Scholarly Non-Law Journals," *Am. Jour. Legal Hist.*, 7 (1963), 1.

Stone, Julius, *Social Dimensions of Law and Justice* (1966).

Woodard, Calvin, "History, Legal History, and Legal Education," *Va. Law Rev.*, 53 (1967), 89.

See also 13.4.3, Westward Expansion and the Frontier–Law Enforcement; 15.10, Judicial Branch; 18.12.2, Law and Business; 18.12.3, Development of the Corporation; 21.12, Crime.

16.2 LEGAL THOUGHT

Bodenheimer, Edgar, *Jurisprudence: Philosophy and Method of Law* (1962).

Cohen, Felix S., *Legal Conscience: Selected Papers,* Lucy Kramer Cohen, ed. (1960).

Cohen, Morris R., *Law and the Social Order: Essays In Legal Philosophy* (1933).

——— "Legal Philosophy in America," *Law: A Century of Progress* (1937), II, 266.

Frank, Jerome, *Law and Modern Mind* (1930).

Freund, Paul A., *On Law and Justice* (1968).

Hand, Learned, *Decisions,* Hershel Shanks, ed. (1968).

Jacobs, Clyde E., *Law Writers and the Courts* (1954).

Levy, Leonard W., *Law of the Commonwealth and Chief Justice Shaw* (1957).

Llewellyn, K. N., "Realistic Jurisprudence," *Columbia Law Rev.*, 30 (1930), 431.

——— "Some Realism about Realism," *Harv. Law Rev.*, 44 (1931), 1222.

Pound, Roscoe, "Call for Realist Jurisprudence," *Harv. Law Rev.*, 44 (1931), 697.

——— *Introduction to the Philosophy of Law* (rev. ed., 1954).

Rumble, Wilfred E., Jr., *American Legal Realism: Skepticism, Reform, and the Judicial Process* (1968).

Sutherland, Arthur E., *Law and One Man among Many* (1956).

Williston, Samuel, *Some Modern Tendencies in Law* (1929).

Wright, Benjamin F., *American Interpretations of Natural Law* (1931).

16.3 LEGAL PROFESSION

Auerbach, Jerold S., "Enmity and Amity: Law Teachers and Practitioners, 1900–1922," *Perspectives in Am. Hist.*, 5 (1971), 551.

Blaustein, Albert P., and Charles O. Porter, *The American Lawyer* (1954).

Boyden, Albert, *Ropes-Gray* (1942).

Brown, Elizabeth G., and William W. Blume, *Legal Education at Michigan, 1859–1959* (new ed., 1959).

Carlin, Jerome, *Lawyers on Their Own: A Study of Individual Practitioners in Chicago* (1962).

Chroust, Anton-Hermann, *Rise of the Legal Profession* (2 vols., 1965).

Goebel, Julius, Jr., ed., *History of the School of Law, Columbia University* (1955).

Griswold, Erwin N., *Law and Lawyers in the United States: Common Law* (1964).

Handler, Joel F., *Lawyer and His Community: Practicing Bar in a Middle-Sized City* (1967).

Lewis, W. D., ed., *Great American Lawyers* (8 vols., 1907–1909).

McKean, Dayton D., *Integrated Bar* (1963).

Martin, George, *Causes and Conflicts: The Centennial History of the Association of the Bar of the City of New York, 1870–1970* (1970).

Nash, Gary B., "Philadelphia Bench and Bar, 1800–1861," *Comp. Studies in Soc.. and Hist.*, 7 (1965), 203.

Smigel, Erwin O., *The Wall Street Lawyer* (1964).

Stevens, Robert, "Two Cheers for 1870: The American Law School," *Perspectives in Am. Hist.*, 5 (1971), 405.
Sutherland, Arthur E., *The Law at Harvard, 1817–1967* (1967).
Swaine, R. T., *Cravath Firm* (2 vols., 1946).
Warren, Charles, *A History of the American Bar* (1911).

*　　*　　*　　*　　*　　*　　*

Brockman, Norbert C., "History of American Bar Association: Bibliographic Essay," *Amer. Jour. Legal Hist.*, 6 (1962), 269.

See also 10.3 for biographies/writings of:

Allen, Henry W., 1820–1866
Arnold, Thurman W., 1891–1970
Baldwin, Jr., Loammi., 1780–1838
Binney, Horace, 1780–1875
Brackenridge, Henry M., 1786–1871
Buckner, Emory, 1877–1941
Call, Richard K., 1791–1862
Choate, Joseph H., 1832–1917
Claiborne, William C. C., 1775–1817
Cobb, Howell, 1815–1868
Dana, Richard Henry, 1815–1882
Darrow, Clarence S., 1857–1938
Davis, John W., 1873–1955
Donovan, James B., 1916–1970
Evarts, William M., 1818–1901
Fisher, Sidney G., 1809–1871
Flynn, Edward J., 1891–1953
Frank, Jerome N., 1889–1957
Goldberg, Arthur J., 1908–
Green, Andrew H., 1820–1903
Grundy, Felix, 1777–1840
Hamilton, James A., 1788–1878
Hopkinson, Joseph, 1770–1842
James, John H., 1800–1881
Langston, John M., 1829–1897
Latrobe, John H. B., 1803–1891
Longstreet, Augustus B., 1790–1870
Marshall, Louis, 1856–1929
Rush, Richard, 1780–1859
Seymour, Horatio, 1810–1886
Smith, William L., 1758–1812
Stevens, Thaddeus, 1792–1868
Sullivan, William, 1774–1839
Tyler, Robert, 1816–1877
Wilson, Henry L., 1857–1932
Wright, Silas, 1795–1847

See also 13.4.3, Westward Expansion and the Frontier—Law Enforcement; 15.10, Judicial Branch; 18.12.2, Law and Business; 21.12, Crime.

17 Politics

This chapter is limited to general surveys and institutional histories. Reference to most works on politics will be found in volume two, within the chronological periods.

17.1 GENERAL

Bogue, Allan G., "United States: the 'New' Political History," *Jour. Cont. Hist.*, 3 (1968), 5.

Boorstin, Daniel, *The Genius of American Politics* (1953).

Bunzel, John H., *Anti-politics in America* (1967).

Dahl, Robert A., *Pluralist Democracy in the United States: Conflict and Consent* (1967).

Hess, Stephen, *America's Political Dynasties from Adams to Kennedy* (1966).

—— and Milton Kaplan, *Ungentlemanly Art* (1968). Political cartoons.

Hofstadter, Richard, *American Political Tradition* (1948).

Kelley, Stanley, Jr., *Professional Public Relations and Political Power* (1956).

Key, V. O., Jr., *Politics, Parties and Pressure Groups* (3d ed., 1952).

—— *Primer of Statistics for Political Scientists* (1962).

Lipset, Seymour M., *Political Man: Social Bases of Politics* (1960).

Madison, Charles A., *Leaders and Liberals in 20th Century America* (1961).

Marsh, Benjamin C., *Lobbyist for the People* (1953).

Mayer, George, *Evaluation of the American Political System and Ideology* (1970).

Morgenthau, Hans J., *Politics in Twentieth Century* (3 vols., 1962).

—— *Purpose of American Politics* (1960).

Nevins, Allan, and Frank Weitenkampf, *Century of Political Cartoons, 1800–1900* (1944).

Odegard, Peter H., and Elva A. Helms, *American Politics: A Study in Political Dynamics* (2nd ed., 1947).

Sharkansky, Ira, *Regionalism in American Politics* (1969).

Smith, Edward C., and Arnold J. Zurcher, *Dictionary of American Politics* (2nd ed., 1968).

Sperber, Hans, and Travis Trittschuh, *American Political Terms: A Historical Dictionary* (1962).

See also 15.10.2.5, Supreme Court and Politics; 19.3.8, Urban Politics; 20.12.6, Negroes–Politics; 25.5, Political Thought.

17.2 SUFFRAGE AND VOTING BEHAVIOR

Baker, Gordon E., *The Reapportionment Revolution: Representation, Political Power and the Supreme Court* (1966).

Beisner, Edward N., "A Comparative Analysis of State and Federal Judicial
  Behavior: The Reapportionment Cases," *Am. Pol. Sci. Rev.,* 62 (1968), 788.
Bickel, Alexander M., "Reapportionment and Liberal Myths," *Commentary,* 35
  (1963), 483.
Burdick, Eugene, and Arthur J. Brodbeck, eds. *American Voting Behavior* (1959).
Campbell, Angus, et al., *The American Voter: An Abridgement* (1964).
——— et al., *Elections and Political Order* (1966).
Chandler, Julian A., *History of Suffrage in Virginia* (1901).
Chute, Marchette G., *First Liberty: Right to Vote in America, 1619–1850* (1969).
de Grazia, Alfred, *Apportionment and Representative Government* (1963).
Fenton, John H., *The Catholic Vote* (1960).
Fredman, L. E., *Australian Ballot* (1968).
Jewell, Malcolm E., ed., *Politics of Reapportionment* (1962).
Lee, Calvin B. T., *One Man, One Vote; WMCA and the Struggle for Equal
  Representation* (1967).
McCormick, Richard P., *History of Voting in New Jersey: 1664–1911* (1953).
——— "Suffrage Classes and Party Alignments: Voter Behavior," *MVHR,* 46
  (1959), 397. To mid-nineteenth century.
McKay, Robert B., *Reapportionment: The Law and Politics of Equal Representa-
  tion* (1965).
Matthews, Donald R., ed., *North Carolina Votes: General Election Returns, by
  County, 1868–1960* (1962).
Pole, J. R., "Election Statistics in Pennsylvania, 1790–1840," *Penn. Mag. Hist.
  Biog.,* 82 (1958), 217.
Porter, K. H., *A History of Suffrage in the United States* (1918).
Riker, Dorothy, and Gayle Thornbrough, comps., *Indiana Election Returns,
  1816–1851* (1960).
Williamson, Chilton, *American Suffrage from Property to Democracy, 1760–1860*
  (1960).

17.3 POLITICAL PARTIES

Works on minor and short-lived parties will be found in volume two.

Bailey, Thomas A., *Democrats vs. Republicans* (1968).
Binkley, Wilfred E., *American Political Parties* (4th ed., 1963).
Bone, Hugh, *Party Committees and National Politics* (1958).
Chambers, William N., and Walter Dean Burnham, eds., *American Party Sys-
  tems* (1967).
Chambers, William N., *The Democrats, 1789–1964* (1964).
——— *Political Parties in a New Nation, 1776–1809* (1963).
Cotter, Cornelius P., and Bernard C. Hennessy, *Politics Without Power: National
  Party Committees* (1964).
Goldman, R. M., *Democratic Party in American Politics* (1966).
Goodman, William, *Two-Party System in the United States* (3d ed., 1964).
Haynes, Frederick E., *Third Party Movements since the Civil War* (1916).
Hofstadter, Richard, *Idea of a Party System: 1780–1840* (1969).
Howe, Irving, and Lewis Coser, *American Communist Party, 1919–1957* (1957).
Kent, Frank R., *Democratic Party: A History* (1928).
Kuhn, Henry, and O. M. Johnson, *Socialist Labor Party* (1931).
Mayer, George H., *Republican Party, 1854–1966* (2nd ed., 1967).
Moos, Malcolm C., *Republicans: A History of Their Party* (1956).
Myers, William S., *Republican Party: A History* (1928).
Nash, Howard P., Jr., *Third Parties in American Politics* (1958).
Nichols, Roy F., *Invention of the American Political Parties* (1967). Covers the
  period 1800–1850.
Ostrogorski, Moisei, *Democracy and Organization of Political Parties* (1902);
  Seymour M. Lipset, ed. (2 vols., 1964).
Rossiter, Clinton, *Parties and Politics in America* (1960).
Sellers, Charles G., Jr., "Equilibrium Cycle in Two-Party Politics," *Pub. Opinion
  Quar.,* 29 (1965), 16.

Shannon, David A., *Socialist Party of America* (1955).
Stedman, Murray S., Jr., and Susan W. Stedman, *Discontent at the Polls: Farmer and Labor Parties, 1827–1948* (1950).

17.4 PRESIDENTIAL CONVENTIONS AND ELECTIONS

Agar, Herbert, *People's Choice, from Washington to Harding* (1933).
Bain, Richard C., *Convention Decisions and Voting Records* (1960).
Brown, William B., *People's Choice: Presidential Image in Campaign Biography* (1960).
Burnham, Walter Dean, *Presidential Ballots, 1836–1892* (1955).
Cummings, Milton C., Jr., *Congressmen and the Electorate: Elections for the U. S. House and the President, 1920–1964* (1966).
David, Paul T., Ralph M. Goldman, and Richard C. Bain, *Politics of National Party Conventions* (1960).
Davis, James W., *Presidential Primaries: Road to the White House* (1967).
Eaton, Herbert, *Presidential Timber: Nominating Conventions, 1868–1960* (1964).
Key, V. O., Jr., *The Responsible Electorate: Rationality in Presidential Voting, 1936–1960* (1966).
Miller, Warren E., "Presidential Coattails: Study in Political Myth and Methodology," *Pub. Opinion Quar.*, 19 (1956), 353.
Peirce, Neal R., *People's President: Electoral College and Direct-Vote* (1968).
Polsby, Nelson W., and Aaron B. Wildavsky, *Presidential Elections* (2nd ed., 1968).
Pomper, Gerald, *Nominating the President* (1963).
Porter, Kirk H., and Donald B. Johnson, comps., *National Party Platforms, 1840–1964* (3d ed., 1966).
Roseboom, Eugene H., *History of Presidential Elections* (2nd ed., 1964).
———— *Short History of Presidential Elections* (1967).
Scammon, Richard M., ed., *America at the Polls: Handbook of Presidential Election Statistics* (1965).
Schlesinger, Arthur M., Jr., and Fred I Israel, eds., *History of American Presidential Elections, 1789–1968* (4 vols., 1971).
Sproul, Kathleen, ed., *Politics of National Party Conventions* (1960).
Tillett, Paul, ed., *Inside Politics: National Conventions, 1960* (1962).
Tugwell, Rexford G., *How They Became President* (1964).
Warren, Sidney, *Battle for the Presidency* (1968).
Wilmerding, Lucius, Jr., *Electoral College* (1958).

17.5 STATE AND REGIONAL POLITICS

Buchanan, William, *Legislative Partisanship: Case of California* (1963).
Casdorph, Paul D., *History of the Republican Party in Texas, 1865–1965* (1965).
Chandler, Julian A., *History of Suffrage in Virginia* (1901).
Delmatier, Royce D., et al., eds, *The Rumble of California Politics: 1848–1970* (1970).
Epstein, Leon D., *Politics in Wisconsin* (1958).
Ewing, Cortez A. M., *Primary Elections in the South: Uniparty Politics* (1953). Covers the period 1911–1948.
Fenton, John H., *Politics in the Border States* (1957).
Ferguson, Walter K., *Geology and Politics in Frontier Texas, 1845–1909* (1969).
Grantham, Dewey W., Jr., *Democratic South* (1963).
Griffith, Elmer C., *Gerrymander* (1907).
Havard, William C., and Loren P. Beth, *Politics of Mis-Representation: Rural-Urban Conflict in the Florida Legislature* (1962).
Holmes, Jack E., *Politics in New Mexico* (1967).
Howard, Perry H., *Political Tendencies in Louisiana, 1812–1952* (1957).
Jacob, Herbert, and K. N. Vines, *Politics in the American States* (1965).

Jensen, Richard, *The Winning of the Midwest: Social and Political Conflict, 1888–1896* (1971).

Jewell, Malcolm E., and Everett W. Cunningham, *Kentucky Politics* (1968).

Kaufman, Herbert, *Politics and Policies in State and Local Governments* (1963).

Key, V. O., Jr., *American State Politics* (1956).

Kleppner, Paul, *The Cross of Culture: A Social Analysis of Midwestern Politics* (1970).

Lockard, Duane, *New England State Politics* (1959).

—— *New Jersey Governor: A Study in Political Power* (1964).

Maass, Arthur, ed., *Area and Power: A Theory of Local Government* (1959).

McCormick, Richard P., *History of Voting in New Jersey: 1664–1911* (1953).

Matthews, Donald R., ed., *North Carolina Votes: General Election Returns, by County, 1868–1960* (1962).

Merrill, Horace S., *Bourbon Democracy of Middle West 1865–1896* (1953).

Moger, Allen W., *Virginia: Bourbonism to Byrd, 1870–1925* (1968).

Montgomery, Horace, *Cracker Parties* (1950).

Morlan, Robert L., and Leroy C. Hardy, *Politics in California* (1968).

Moscow, Warren, *Politics in the Empire State* (1948).

Nye, Russel B., *Midwestern Progressive Politics, 1870–1958* (rev. ed., 1959).

Pole, J. R., "Election Statistics in Pennsylvania, 1790–1840," *Penn. Mag. Hist. Biog.*, 82 (1958), 217.

Pulley, Raymond H., *Old Virginia Restored: An Interpretation of the Progressive Impulse, 1870–1930* (1968).

Reichley, James, *States in Crisis: Politics in Ten American States, 1950–1962* (1964).

Riker, Dorothy, and Gayle Thornbrough, comps., *Indiana Election Returns, 1816–1851* (1960).

Sarasohn, Stephen B., and Vera H. Sarasohn, *Political Party Patterns in Michigan* (1957). Covers the period, 1900–1956.

Schlesinger, Joseph A., *How They Became Governor: Comparative State Politics, 1870–1950* (1957).

Smith, Charles P., *New Jersey Political Reminiscences, 1828–1882,* Hermann K. Platt, ed. (1965).

Sorauf, Frank J., *Party and Representation, Legislative Politics in Pennsylvania* (1963).

Soukup, James R., Clifton McCleskey, and Harry Holloway, *Party and Factional Division in Texas* (1964).

Steiner, Gilbert Y., and Samuel K. Gove, *Legislative Politics in Illinois* (1960).

Wachman, Marvin, *History of Social Democratic Party of Milwaukee* (1945).

Williams, T. Harry, *Romance and Realism in Southern Politics* (1960).

* * * * * * *

Press, Charles, *Main Street Politics: Policy-Making at the Local Level: A Survey of the Periodical Literature since 1950* (1962).

See also 19.3.8, Urban Politics.

18 Economic History

18.1 GENERAL

Bining, Arthur C., and Thomas C. Cochran, *Rise of American Economic Life* (4th ed., 1964).

Bolino, August C., *Development of the American Economy* (2nd ed., 1966).

Clough, Shepard B., and Theodore F. Marburg, *Economic Basis of American Civilization* (1968).

David, Henry, et al., *Economic History of United States* (10 vols. projected, 1945–   ). Individual volumes are cited in appropriate sections.

Davis, Lance E., Jonathan R. T. Hughes, and Duncan M. McDougall, *American Economic History* (3d ed., 1969).

Dewey, David R., *Financial History of the United States* (12th ed., 1934).

Faulkner, Harold U., *American Economic History* (8th ed., 1960).

Fite, Gilbert C., and Jim E. Reese, *Economic History of United States* (2nd ed., 1965).

Hacker, Louis M., *The Course of American Growth and Development* (1970).

Harris, Seymour E., ed., *American Economic History* (1961).

Hession, Charles H., and Hyman Sardy, *Ascent to Affluence: History of American Economic Development* (1969).

Johnson, Edgar A. J., and Herman E. Krooss, *American Economy* (1960).

Jones, Peter d'A., *America's Wealth: Economic History* (1963).

———— *The Consumer Society: History of American Capitalism* (1965).

Kemmerer, Donald L., and C. Clyde Jones, *American Economic History* (1959).

Kirkland, Edward C., *History of American Economic Life* (4th ed., 1969).

Krooss, Herman E., *American Economic Development* (2nd ed., 1966).

Leontief, Wassily W., et al., *Studies in the Structure of the American Economy* (1953).

Levy, Lester S., and Roy J. Sampson, *American Economic Development* (1962).

North, Douglass C., *Growth and Welfare in the American Past* (1966).

Perloff, Harvey S., et al., *Regions, Resources, and Economic Growth* (1960).

Robertson, Ross M., *History of the American Economy* (2nd ed., 1964).

Russel, Robert R., *History of the American Economic System* (1964).

Scheiber, Harry N., ed., *United States Economic History: Selected Readings* (1964).

Schultz, W. J., and M. R. Caine, *Financial Development of the United States* (1937).

Soule, George, and Vincent P. Carosso, *American Economic History* (1957).

Spence, Clark C., *Sinews of American Capitalism* (1964).

Studenski, Paul, and Herman E. Krooss, *Financial History of the United States* (2nd ed., 1963).

Williamson, Harold F., ed., *The Growth of the American Economy* (2nd ed., 1965).

*   *   *   *   *   *   *

Andreano, Ralph L., ed., *New Economic History: Recent Papers on Methodology* (1970).

Cole, Arthur H., "Economic History in the United States: Formative Years of a Discipline," *Jour. Econ. Hist.* 28 (1968), 556.

—— Historical Development of Economic and Business Literature (1957).

Dowd, Douglas F., "Economic History of United States in the Twentieth Century," in Herbert J. Bass, ed., *State of American History* (1970).

Fogel, Robert W., "Reappraisals in American Economic History," *Am. Econ. Rev.,* 54 (1964), 377.

Harper, L. A., et al., "Recent Contributions to Economic History," *Jour. Econ. Hist.,* 19 (1959).

Harvard University. Graduate School of Business Administration, *Library Catalogue, Kress Library* (3 vols., 1956–1964).

Krooss, Herman E., "Economic History and New Business History," *Jour. Econ. Hist.,* 18 (1958), 467.

Lovett, Robert W., ed., *American Economic and Business History, A Guide to Information Sources* (1971).

Nash, Gerald D., ed., *Issues in American Economic History* (1964).

North, Douglass C., "Quantitative Research in American Economic History," *Am. Econ. Rev.,* 53 (1963), 128.

Schleiffer, Hedwig, and Ruth Crandall, *Index to Economic History Essays in Festschriften, 1900–1950* (1953).

18.2 NINETEENTH CENTURY

Bruchey, Stuart, *Roots of American Economic Growth 1607–1861* (1965).

Bursk, Edward C., ed., *Business and Religion: A New Depth Dimension in Management* (1959).

Cochran, Thomas C., and William Miller, *Age of Enterprise, Social History of Industrial America* (2nd ed., 1961).

Goodrich, Carter, "Recent Contributions to Economic History, 1789–1860," *Jour. Econ. Rev.,* 19 (1959), 25.

Hendrick, Burton J., *Age of Big Business* (1919).

Kirkland, Edward C., *Industry Comes of Age, 1860–1897* (1961).

National Bureau of Economic Research, *Trends in the American Economy in the Nineteenth Century* (1960).

Nettels, Curtis P., *Emergence of a National Economy, 1775–1815* (1962).

North, Douglass C., and Robert P. Thomas, eds., *Growth of the American Economy to 1860* (1968).

Shannon, Fred A., *Centennial Years: America from the Late 1870's to the Early 1890's,* Robert H. Jones, ed. (1967).

Taylor, George R., *Transportation Revolution, Industry 1815–1860* (1951).

18.3 TWENTIETH CENTURY

Cochran, Thomas C., *American Business in the Twentieth Century* (2nd ed., 1972).

Dewhurst, James Frederic et al., *America's Needs and Resources* (1955).

Faulkner, Harold U., *Decline of Laissez-Faire, 1897–1917* (1951).

Goldsmith, Raymond W., *National Wealth in the Post-War Period* (1962).

Hansen, Alvin H., *Postwar American Economy* (1964).

Hendrick, Burton J., *Age of Big Business* (1919).

Hickman, Bert G., *Growth and Stability of the Postwar Economy* (1960).

Mitchell, Broadus, *Depression Decade* (1947).

Soule, George, *Prosperity Decade, 1917–1929* (1947).

Vatter, Harold G., *The U.S. Economy in the 1950's* (1963).

18.4 REGIONAL AND LOCAL HISTORIES

18.4.1 North

Black, John D., *Rural Economy of New England* (1950).
Cadman, John W., Jr., *The Corporation in New Jersey: Business and Politics, 1791–1875* (1949).
Eisenmenger, Robert W., *The Dynamics of Growth in New England's Economy, 1870–1964* (1967).
Estall, Robert C., *New England: Industrial Adjustment* (1966).
Green, Constance M., *Holyoke, Massachusetts: A Case History of the Industrial Revolution in America* (1939).
Harris, Seymour E., *Economics of New England* (1952).
Kirkland, Edward C., *Men, Cities and Transportation: A Study in New England History, 1820–1900* (1948).
Mayer, Kurt B., *Economic Development and Population Growth in Rhode Island* (1953).
Shlakman, Vera, *Economic History of a Factory Town: Chicopee, Massachusetts* (1935).
Stevens, Sylvester K., *Pennsylvania: Titan of Industry* (3 vols., 1948).
U.S. Council of Economic Advisers, *New England Economy* (1951).

18.4.2 South

Carson, William Joseph, ed., *Coming of Industry to the South* (1931).
Greene, Lee S. et al., *Rescued Earth: Public Administration of Natural Resources in Tennessee* (1948).
Hoover, Calvin B., and B. U. Ratchford, *Economic Resources and Policies of the South* (1951).
———— *Impact of Federal Policies on Economy of South* (1949).
Lander, Ernest M., Jr., "Charleston," *JSH,* 26 (1960), 330.
Lepawsky, Albert, *State Planning and the Economic Development in the South* (1949).
McLaughlin, G. E., and Stefan Robock, *Why Industry Moves South* (1949).
Mezerik, A. G., *Revolt of the South and the West* (1946).
Mitchell, G. S., and Broadus Mitchell, *Industrial Revolution in South* (1930).
Tang, Anthony M., *Economic Development in Southern Piedmont, 1860–1950* (1958).

*   *   *   *   *   *   *

Nash, Gerald D., "Research Opportunities in Economic History of the South after 1800," *JSH,* 32 (1966), 308.

18.4.3 Midwest

Hunker, Henry L., *Industrial Evolution of Columbus, Ohio* (1958).
Hunter, Louis C., *Studies in Economic History of the Ohio Valley* (1934).
Lippincott, Isaac, *History of Manufacturing in the Ohio Valley* (1914).
Merk, Frederick, *Economic History of Wisconsin during the Civil War Decade* (1916).
Sheridan, Richard, *Economic Development in South Central Kansas* (1956).

*   *   *   *   *   *   *

Stevens, Harry R., "Recent Writings on Midwestern Economic History," *Ohio Hist. Quar.* 69 (1960), 1.

18.4.4 West

Arrington, Leonard J., "The Changing Economic Structure of the Mountain West, 1850–1950," *Utah Monograph Series,* 10, no. 3 (1963). Entire issue.
—— *Great Basin Kingdom: An Economic History of the Latter-Day Saints, 1830–1900* (1958).
Berge, Wendell, *Economic Freedom for the West* (1946).
Coman, Katherine, *Economic Beginnings of the Far West* (2 vols., 1912).
Gilbert, Benjamin F., "Economic Developments in Alaska, 1867–1910," *Jour. of West,* 4 (1965), 504.
McDonald, Stephen L., "Recent Economic Development of the Southwest," *Southw. Soc. Sci. Quar.,* 45 (1965), 329.
Morgan, Theodore, *Hawaii, Century of Economic Change, 1778–1876* (1948).
Spratt, John S., *Road to Spindletop: Economic Change in Texas, 1875–1901* (1955).
Winther, Oscar, *The Old Oregon Country: History of Trade, Transportation, and Travel* (1950).
Wolman, William, *Development of Manufacturing Industry in State of Washington* (1958).

* * * * * * *

Nash, Gerald D., "Western Economic History as a Field for Research," *West. Econ. Jour.,* 3 (1964), 86.

18.5 ECONOMIC THOUGHT

See 25.17, Social Sciences, for references to economics as a field of study and for a biographical list of economists.

Berle, Adolf A., *American Economic Republic* (1963).
Dorfman, Joseph, *Economic Mind in American Civilization* (5 vols., 1946–1959).
Fusfield, Daniel R., *Age of the Economists: Development of Modern Economic Thought* (1966).
Gruchy, Allan G., *Modern Economic Thought: The American Contribution* (1947).
Leiman, Melvin M., *Jacob N. Cardozo: Economic Thought in the Antebellum South* (1966).
Spiegel, Henry W., ed., *Rise of American Economic Thought* (1960). Nineteenth century.
Ward, Alfred D., *American Economy* (1955).

18.6 NATIONAL INCOME AND GROWTH

Andreano, Ralph L., ed., *New Views on American Economic Development* (1965).
Berry, Thomas S., *Estimated Annual Variations in Gross National Product, 1789–1909* (1968).
Cochran, Thomas C., and Thomas B. Brewer, eds., *Views of American Economic Growth* (2 vols., 1966).
David, Paul A., "The Growth of Real Product in the United States before 1840: New Evidence, Controlled Conjectures" *Jour. Econ. Hist.* 27 (1967), 151.
Denison, Edward F., *Sources of Economic Growth* (1962).
Felix, David, "Profit, Inflation and Industrial Growth," *Quar. Jour. Econ.,* 70 (1956), 441.
Frickey, Edwin, *Production in United States, 1860–1914* (1947).
Hacker, Louis M., *The Course of American Growth and Development* (1970).
Hamilton, Earl J., "Prices as Factor in Business Growth," *Jour. Econ. Hist.,* 12 (1952), 325.
Hickman, Bert G., "The Postwar Retardation: Another Long Swing in the Rate of Growth?" *Am. Econ. Rev.,* 53 (1963), 490.
Janeway, Eliot, *Economics of Crisis: War, Politics, and the Dollar* (1968).

Kendrick, John W., and Ryuzo Sato, "Factor, Prices, Productivity, and Economic Growth," *Am. Econ. Rev.*, 53 (1963), 974.

Kuznets, Simon, and Raymond W. Goldsmith, *Income and Wealth of United States: Trends and Structure* (1952).

Kuznets, Simon, *National Income* (1946).

—— et al., *Population Redistribution and Economic Growth, United States, 1870–1950* (3 vols., 1957–1964).

—— *Postwar Economic Growth* (1964).

Lebergott, Stanley, *Manpower in Economic Growth* (1964).

Martin, Robert F., *National Income, 1799–1938* (1938).

National Bureau of Economic Research, *Output, Employment, and Productivity after 1800* (1966).

—— *Trends in the American Economy in the Nineteenth Century* (1960).

North, Douglass C., "Early National Income Estimates of the U.S.," *Economic Development and Cultural Change, 9* (1961), 387.

—— *Economic Growth of the United States, 1790–1860* (1961).

Peterson, Wallace C., "Recent Growth Record of the American Economy," *Am. Jour. Econ. Sociol.*, 23 (1964), 1.

Potter, Neal, and F. T. Christy, Jr., *Trends in Natural Resource Commodities, 1870–1957* (1962).

Scoville, James G., *Job Content of the U.S. Economy, 1940–1970* (1969).

Shaw, William H., *Value of Commodity Output since 1869* (1947).

Slichter, Sumner H., *Economic Growth in the United States* (1961).

Taylor, George R., "American Economic Growth before 1840," *Jour. Econ. Hist.*, 24 (1964), 427.

U.S. Department of Commerce, *National Income and Product Accounts of the United States, 1925–1965* (1966).

Valavanis-Vail, S., "An Econometric Model of Growth: U.S.A. 1869–1953," *Am. Econ. Rev.*, 45 (1955), 208.

Woytinsky, Emma S., *Profile of the U.S. Economy* (1967).

See also 18.16.6.6, Railroads and Economic Growth.

18.7 BUSINESS CYCLES

Abramovitz, Moses, *Evidences of Long Swings in Construction since Civil War* (1964).

Barnett, Paul, *Business Cycle Theory in United States, 1860–1900* (1941).

Collman, C. A., *Our Mysterious Panics, 1830–1930: Events and Men Involved* (1931).

Copeland, Morris A., *Trends in Government Financing* (1961).

Duesenberry, James S., *Business Cycles and Economic Growth* (1958).

Fabricant, Solomon, and Robert F. Lipsey, *Trend of Government Activity since 1900* (1952).

Fels, Rendigs, *American Business Cycles, 1865–1897* (1959).

Hansen, Alvin H., *Business Cycles and National Income* (rev. ed., 1964).

Hughes, J. R. T., and Nathan Rosenberg, "Business Cycle before 1860: Some Problems of Interpretation," *Econ. Hist. Rev.*, 15 (1963), 476.

Johnson, Arthur M., *Government-Business Relations: Pragmatic Approach to the American Experience* (1965).

Klein, Lawrence R., *Economic Fluctuations in the United States, 1921–1941* (1950).

Lightner, Otto C., *History of Business Depressions* (1922).

Manning, Thomas G., and David M. Potter, *Government and the American Economy, 1870 to the Present* (1950).

Nash, Gerald D., *State Government and Economic Development, 1849–1933* (1964).

Rezneck, Samuel, *Business Depressions and Financial Panics: Essays in American Business and Economic History* (1968).

Schluter, W. C., *Pre-War Business Cycle 1907–1914* (1923).

Schumpeter, Joseph A., *Business Cycles* (rev. ed., 1964).

Smith, Walter B., and Arthur H. Coleman, *Fluctuations in American Business, 1790–1860* (1935).
Sobel, Robert, *Panic on Wall Street: America's Financial Disasters* (1968).

18.8 INTERPRETATIVE STUDIES

Berle, Adolf A., *Power without Property* (1959).
—— *20th Century Capitalist Revolution* (1954).
Galbraith, John K., *Affluent Society* (2nd ed., 1969).
—— *American Capitalism: Countervailing Power* (1956).
—— *New Industrial State* (1967).
Hacker, Louis M., *Triumph of American Capitalism* (1940).
Heilbroner, Robert L., *Limits of American Capitalism* (1966).
Means, Gardiner C., *Corporate Revolution in America* (1962).
Monsen, R. Joseph, Jr., *Modern American Capitalism* (1963).
Myrdal, Gunnar, *Challenge to Affluence* (rev. ed., 1965).

See also 25.5.2, Political Thought–Radicalism.

18.9 GOVERNMENT AND THE ECONOMY

18.9.1 General

Adams, Walter, and Horace M. Gray, *Monopoly in America: Government as Promoter* (1955).
Barrett, Paul, *An Analysis of State Industrial Development Programs* (1944).
Copeland, Morris A., *Trends in Government Financing* (1961).
Dacy, Douglas C., and Howard Kunreuther, *Economics of Natural Disasters: Federal Policy* (1969).
Davis, Lance E., and John Legler, "Government in American Economy, 1815–1902," *Jour. Econ. Hist.*, 26 (1966), 514.
Durisch, Lawrence L., "Southern Regional Planning and Development," *Jour. Politics*, 26 (1964), 41.
Fabricant, Solomon, and R. E. Lipsey, *Trend of Government Activity since 1900* (1952).
Fainsod, Merle, and Lincoln Gordon, *Government and American Economy* (3d ed., 1959).
Farnham, Wallace D., "'Weakened Spring of Government': Study in Nineteenth Century American History," *AHR* 68 (1963), 662.
Goodrich, Carter, *Government Promotion of Canals and Railroads, 1800–1890* (1960).
Handlin, Oscar, and Mary F. Handlin, *Commonwealth: A Study of the Role of Government in the American Economy: Massachusetts, 1774–1861* (rev. ed., 1969).
Hartz, Louis, *Economic Policy and Democratic Thought: Pennsylvania, 1776–1860* (1948).
Heath, Milton S., *Constructive Liberalism: Role of the State in Economic Development in Georgia to 1860* (1954).
Ise, John, *United States Oil Policy* (1926).
Johnson, Arthur M., *Government-Business Relations: Pragmatic Approach to the American Experience* (1965).
Krenkel, John H., *Illinois Internal Improvements, 1818–1848* (1958).
Lyon, Leverett S., Myron W. Watkins, and Victor Abramson, *Government and Economic Life* (2 vols., 1939–1940).
Manning, Thomas G., and David M. Potter, *Government and the American Economy, 1870 to the Present* (1950).
Meeker, Royal, *History of Shipping Subsidies* (1905).
Miller, Nathan, *Enterprise of a Free People: Economic Development in New York State, 1792–1838* (1962).

Nash, Gerald D., *State Government and Economic Development, 1849–1933* (1964).
—— *United States Oil Policy, 1890–1964* (1969).
Primm, James N., *Economic Policy in Development of a Western State: Missouri, 1820–1860* (1954).
Scheiber, Harry N., "The Road to Munn: Eminent Domain and the Concept of Public Purpose in the State Courts," *Perspectives in Am. Hist.,* 5 (1971), 329.
Schriftgiesser, Karl, *Business Comes of Age: Committee for Economic Development, 1942–1960* (1960).

See also 15.5, Fiscal Policy; 18.11.5, Government and Agriculture; 18.12.3, Development of the Corporation; 18.14.4, Federal Reserve System; 18.14.5, Monetary History; 18.16.6.5, Railroads–Land Grants; 27.8.2, Radio and Television–Government Regulation.

18.9.2 Tariff

Abelarde, Pedro E., *American Tariff Policy towards the Philippines, 1898–1946* (1947).
Berglund, Abraham, and P. G. Wright, *Tariff on Iron and Steel* (1929).
Bidwell, P. W., *Tariff Policy of United States* (1933).
Edminster, L. R., *Cattle Industry and Tariff* (1926).
Jones, Joseph M., Jr., *Tariff Retaliation* (1934).
Koontz, Harold, and Richard W. Gable, *Public Control of Economic Enterprise* (1956).
Miller, Clarence L., *Old Northwest and Tariff* (1929).
Schattschneider, E. E., *Politics, Pressures and Tariff* (1935).
Smith, Mark A., *Tariff on Wool* (1926).
Stanwood, Edward, *American Tariff Controversies* (1903).
Tarbell, Ida M., *Tariff in Our Times* (1911).
Taussig, Frank W., *The Tariff History of the United States* (7th ed., 1923).
—— "United States Tariff Commission," *Am. Econ. Rev.,* 26 (1926), 171.
Wright, Philip G., *American Tariff and Oriental Trade* (1931).
—— *Sugar in Relation to the Tariff* (1924).
—— *Tariff on Animal and Vegetable Oils* (1928).

18.9.3 Public Domain and Land Disposal

Anderson, J. H., "Jurisdiction over Federal Lands within the States," *No. Car. Law Rev.,* 7 (1929), 299.
Carlson, Theodore L., *Illinois Military Tract* (1951).
Carstensen, Vernon R., *Farms or Forests: Land Policy for Northern Wisconsin, 1850–1932* (1958).
—— *The Public Lands* (1963).
Cherry, P. P., *Western Reserve and Early Ohio* (1921).
Clawson, Marion, "Administration of Federal Range Lands," *Quar. Jour. Econ.,* 53 (1939), 435.
—— and Burnell Held, *Federal Lands* (1957). *Supplement* (1967).
Cole, Arthur C., "Variations in Sale of Public Lands," *Rev. Econ. Stat.,* 9 (1927), 41.
Dick, Everett, *The Lure of the Land: A Social History of the Public Lands from the Articles of Confederation to the New Deal* (1970).
Donaldson, Thomas, *Public Domain* (1884).
Dunham, H. H., "Crucial Years of General Land Office," *Agric. Hist.,* 11 (1937), 117.
—— *Government Handout: A Study in the Administration of the Public Lands, 1875–1891* (1941).
Ellis, David M., ed., *The Frontier in American Development: Essays in Honor of Paul Wallace Gates* (1969).
—— *Land Lords and Farmers in the Hudson-Mohawk Region, 1790–1850* (1946).

Gates, Paul W., "Disposal of Public Domain in Illinois 1848–1856," *Jour. Econ. and Bus Hist.,* 3 (1931), 216.
—— and Robert W. Swenson, *History of Public Land Law Development* (1968).
Gates, Paul W., "Homestead Law in an Incongruous Land System," *AHR,* 41 (1936), 652.
—— "Homestead Law in Iowa," *Agric. Hist.* 38 (1964), 67.
Hibbard, Benjamin H., *A History of Public Land Policies* (1924).
James, Edmund J., *Origins of Land Grant Act of 1862* (1910).
Lokken, R. L., *Iowa Public Land Disposal* (1942).
Miller, Thomas L., *Bounty and Donation Land Grants of Texas, 1835–1888* (1967).
Peffer, E. Louise, *Closing of Public Domain, 1900–1950* (1951).
Pomeroy, K. B., and J. G. Yoho, *North Carolina Lands* (1965).
Robbins, Roy M., *Our Landed Heritage: the Public Domain 1776–1936* (1942).
Rohrbough, Malcolm J., *Land Office Business: Public Lands, 1789–1837* (1968).
Scheiber, Harry N., "State Policy and Public Domain: Ohio Canal Lands," *Jour. Econ. Hist.,* 25 (1965), 86.
Sheldon, A. E., *Land Systems and Land Policies in Nebraska* (1936).
Socolofsky, Homer E., "Land Disposal in Nebraska, 1854–1906." *Neb. Hist.,* 48 (1967), 225.
Stephenson, George M., *Political History of Public Lands, 1840–1862* (1917).
Stewart, Lowell O., *Public Land Surveys* (1935).
Treat, P. J., *National Land System* (1910).
Wellington, R. G., *Political and National Influence of Public Lands, 1826–1842* (1914).
Zahler, H. S., *Eastern Workingmen and Land Policy, 1829–1862* (1941).

*   *   *   *   *   *   *

Bercaw, L. O., *Bibliography on Land Settlement* (1934).
Conover, Milton, *General Land Office* (1923).

See also 14.5, Conservation; 14.8, Reclamation; 18.16.6.5, Railroads–Land Grants.

18.10 LAND USE AND SPECULATION

Allis, Frederick S., ed., *William Bingham's Maine Lands, 1790–1820* (1954).
Bogue, Allan G., and Margaret B. Bogue, "Frontier Land Speculator," *Jour. Econ. Hist.,* 17 (1957), 1.
Bogue, Margaret B., *Patterns from the Sod: Land Use and Tenure in Grand Prairie, 1850–1900* (1959).
Clawson, Marion, *Man and Land in the United States* (1964).
Evans, P. D., *Holland Land Company* (1924).
Fox, Edith M., *Land Speculation in Mohawk Country* (1949).
Galbraith, John S., "The Early History of the Puget's Sound Agricultural Company, 1838–43," *Ore. Hist. Quar.,* 55 (1954), 234.
Gates, Paul W., "Land Policy and Tenancy," *Jour. Econ. Hist.,* 1 (1941), 60.
—— "Role of Land Speculator in Western Development," *Penn. Mag. Hist. Biog.,* 66 (1942), 314.
Haskins, C. H., "Yazoo Land Companies," *Am. Hist. Assoc., Papers,* 5 (1891), 393.
Johnson, Hildegard B., "Rational and Ecological Aspects of the Quarter Section: Minnesota," *Geog. Rev.,* 47 (1957), 330.
LeDuc, Thomas, "Land Use in American Agriculture," *Agric. Hist.,* 37 (1963), 3.
Livermore, Shaw, *Early American Land Companies: Their Influence on Corporate Development* (1939).
Magrath, C. Peter, *Yazoo: Law and Politics in the New Republic, the Case of Fletcher V. Peck* (1966).
Mark, Irving, "Homestead Ideas and Public Domain," *Am. Jour. Econ. Sociol.,* 22 (1963), 263.

Ottoson, Howard W., et al., *Land and People in the Northern Plains Transition Area* (1966).
Ottoson, Howard W., ed., *Land Use Policy and Problems in the United States* (1963).
Sakolski, Aaron M., *The Great American Land Bubble* (1932).
────── *Land Tenure and Taxation in America* (1957).
Saloutos, Theodore, "Land Policy and Its Relation to Agricultural Production and Distribution, 1862 to 1933," *Jour. Econ. Hist.,* 22 (1962), 445.
Sayers, Wilson B., , "Changing Land Ownership Pattern in United States," *Forest Hist.,* 9, no. 2 (1965), 2.
Severson, Robert F., Jr., et al., "Mortgage Borrowing as a Frontier Developed: Champaign County, Illinois, 1836–1895," *Jour. Econ. Hist.,* 26 (1966), 147.
Stewart, W. J., "Speculation and Nebraska's Public Domain, 1863–1872," *Neb. Hist.,* 45 (1964), 265.
Swierenga, Robert P., *Pioneers and Profits: Land Speculation on the Iowa Frontier* (1968).
Thrower, Norman J. W., *Original Survey and Land Subdivision* (1967).

18.11 AGRICULTURE

18.11.1 General

Barger, Harold, and H. H. Landsberg, *American Agriculture, 1899–1939* (1942).
Bogart, E. L., *Economic History of American Agriculture* (1923).
Carrier, Lyman, *Beginnings of Agriculture in America* (1923).
Fite, Gilbert C., *Farmer's Frontier, 1865–1900* (1966).
Gates, Paul W., *Farmer's Age: Agriculture, 1815–1860* (1960).
Gras, N. S. B., *History of Agriculture in Europe and America* (2nd ed., 1940).
Griswold, A. Whitney, *Farming and Democracy* (2nd ed., 1952).
Haystead, Ladd, and Gilbert C. Fite, *The Agricultural Regions of the United States* (1955).
Hedrick, Ulysses P., *History of Horticulture in America to 1860* (1950).
Hough, Emerson, *Passing of Frontier* (1921).
Schafer, Joseph, *Social History of American Agriculture* (1936).
Shannon, Fred A., *The Farmers' Last Frontier: Agriculture, 1860–1897* (1945).
Wilcox, Walter W., *The Farmer in the Second World War* (1947).

*   *   *   *   *   *   *

Adams, Ramon F., *Rampaging Herd: Bibliography of the Cattle Industry* (1959).
Brown, D. A., "Historical Prices of Farm Products by States: A Bibliography," *Agric. Hist.* 36 (1962), 169.
Douglas, Louis H., ed., *Agrarianism in American History* (1969).
Edwards, Everett E., *Bibliography of the History of Agriculture* (1930).
────── *Selected References on the History of Agriculture in the United States* (1939).
Fite, Gilbert, "Expanded Frontiers in Agricultural History," *Agric. Hist.,* 35 (1961), 175.
Kahn, Herman, "Records in National Archives Relating to Range Cattle Industry," *Agric. Hist.,* 20 (1946), 187.
Kellar, Herbert A., ed., *Pioneer and Agriculturist: Selected Writings* (1936).
Landis, B. Y., *Guide to Literature of Rural Life* (1932).
Nordin, Dennis, *Preliminary List of References for History of Granger Movement* (1967).
Rasmussen, Wayne D., "Forty Years of Agricultural History," *Agric. Hist.,* 33 (1959), 177.
Schlebecker, John T., ed., *Bibliography of Books and Pamphlets on History of Agriculture in the United States, 1706–1967* (1968).
Schlebecker, John T., "Research in Agricultural History at the Smithsonian Institution," *Agric. Hist.,* 40 (1966), 207.

U.S. National Agricultural Library, *Dictionary Catalog of the National Agricultural Library, 1862–1965* (73 vols., 1965–1970).

Woodman, Harold, D., "The State of Agricultural History," in Herbert J. Bass, ed., *State of American History* (1970).

See also 18.9.3, Public Domain and Land Disposal; 18.10, Land Use and Speculation.

18.11.2 Regional Histories

18.11.2.1 North

Bidwell, P. W., and J. I, Falconer, *History of Agriculture in the Northern United States, 1620–1860* (1925).

Black, John D., *The Rural Economy of New England* (1950).

Danhoff, Clarence H., *Change in Agriculture: The Northern United States, 1820–1870* (1969).

Day, Clarence A., *History of Maine Agriculture, 1604–1860* (1954).

Ellis, David M., *Landlords and Farmers in Hudson-Mohawk Region* (1946).

Fletcher, Stevenson W., *Pennsylvania Agriculture and Country Life* (2 vols., 1950–1955).

Hedrick, Ulysses P., *History of Agriculture in the State of New York* (1933; 2nd ed. 1966).

McNall, Neal A., *Agricultural History of the Genesee Valley, 1790–1860* (1952).

McNall, N. A., *First Half Century of Wadsworth Tenancy* (1945).

Mighell, Ronald L., and John D. Black, *Interregional Competition in Agriculture: With Reference to Dairy Farming in the Lake States and New England* (1951).

Pabst, M. R., "Agricultural Trends in Connecticut Valley," *Smith College Studies in History,* 26 (1941).

Purcell, R. J., *Connecticut in Transition, 1775–1818* (1918).

Wilson, Harold F., *Hill Country of Northern New England* (1936).

Woodward, Carl R., *Development of Agriculture in New Jersey* (1927).

18.11.2.2 South

Bennett, Hugh H., *Soils of Southern States* (1921).

Bonner, James C., *History of Georgia Agriculture, 1732–1860* (1964).

Brandfon, Robert L., *Cotton Kingdom of the New South: A History of the Yazoo Mississippi Delta from Reconstruction to the Twentieth Century* (1967).

Cathey, Cornelius O., *Agricultural Developments in North Carolina, 1783–1860* (1956).

Davis, Charles S., *Cotton Kingdom in Alabama* (1939).

Fulmer, J. L., *Agricultural Progress in Cotton Belt* (1950).

Gray, Lewis C., *History of Agriculture in Southern United States to 1860* (2 vols., 1933).

Haley, J. Evetts, *XIT Ranch of Texas and Early Days of the Llano Estacado* (new ed., 1953).

Karanikas, Alexander, *Tillers of a Myth: Southern Agrarians as Social and Literary Critics* (1966).

Laird, William E., and James R. Rinehart, "Deflation, Agriculture, and Southern Development," *Agric. Hist.,* 42 (1968), 115.

McGinty, Garnie W., "Changes in Louisiana Agriculture," *La. Hist. Quar.,* 18 (1935), 407.

Moore, John H., *Agriculture in Ante-Bellum Mississippi* (1958).

Paisley, Clifton, *From Cotton to Quail: Agricultural Chronicle of Leon County, Florida, 1860–1967* (1968).

Range, Willard, *Century of Georgia Agriculture, 1850–1950* (1954).

Richardson, Rupert N., *Frontier of Northwest Texas, 1846 to 1876* (1963).

Stephens, Alva R., *Taft Ranch: Texas* (1964).

Tang, Anthony M., *Economic Development in Southern Piedmont, 1860–1950: Its Impact on Agriculture* (1958).

Wiley, Bell I., "Farming in Lower Mississippi Valley," *JSH*, 3 (1937), 441.
——— "Southern Agriculture since Civil War," *Agric. Hist.*, 13 (1939), 65.

*   *   *   *   *   *   *

Thompson, Edgar T., *The Plantation: A Bibliography* (1957).

See also volume two for additional references to southern agriculture before the Civil War.

18.11.2.3 Midwest

Bardolph, Richard, *Agricultural Literature and the Early Illinois Farmer* (1948).
Bogue, Allan G., *From Prairie to Corn Belt: Farming on Illinois and Iowa Prairies in Nineteenth Century* (1963).
Carter, Hodding L., "Rural Indiana in Transition," *Agric. Hist.*, 20 (1946), 107.
Helgeson, Arlan, *Farms in Cutover: Northern Wisconsin* (1962).
Hibbard, B. H., *History of Agriculture in Dane County* (1904).
Iowa State College of Agriculture, *A Century of Farming in Iowa, 1846–1946* (1946).
Jarchow, Merrill E., *The Earth Brought Forth: Minnesota Agriculture to 1885* (1949).
Lampard, Eric, *Rise of Dairy Industry in Wisconsin, 1820–1920* (1963).
Ross, Earle D., *Iowa Agriculture* (1951).
Schafer, Joseph, *History of Agriculture in Wisconsin* (1922).
Taylor, Henry C., *Tarpleywick: A Century of Iowa Farming* (1970).

18.11.2.4 West

Drache, Hiram M., *Day of the Bonanza: Farming in the Red River Valley of the North* (1964).
Fite, Gilbert C., "Daydreams and Nightmares: Late Nineteenth-Century Agricultural Frontiers." *Agric. Hist.*, 40 (1966), 285.
Hargreaves, Mary W. M., *Dry Farming in Northern Great Plains, 1900–1925* (1957).
Hutchison, Claude B., ed., *California Agriculture* (1946).
McCallum, Henry D., and Frances T. McCallum, *The Wire that Fenced the West* (1965).
Murray, Stanley N., *Valley Comes of Age: A History of Agriculture in the Valley of the Red River of the North, 1812–1920* (1967).
Schlebecker, John T., "Agriculture in Western Nebraska," *Neb. Hist.*, 48 (1967), 249.
Steinel, A. T., and D. W. Working, *Agriculture in Colorado* (1926).
Taylor, Fred R., "North Dakota Agriculture since World War II," *No. Dak. Hist.*, 34 (1967), 47.
Warren, John Q. A., *California Ranchos and Farms, 1846–1862, Letters of 1861*, Paul W. Gates, ed. (1967).

*   *   *   *   *   *   *

Olsen, Michael L., *Preliminary List of References for the History of Agriculture in the Pacific Northwest and Alaska* (1967).

18.11.3 Rural Life

Agee, James, *Let Us Now Praise Famous Men* (1941).
Bell, Earl, *Culture of a Contemporary Rural Community; Sublette, Kansas* (1942).
Britt, Albert, *An America That Was: An Illinois Farm Seventy Years Ago* (1964).
Brunner, E. de S., *Immigrant Farmers and Children* (1929).
Conrad, David E., *The Forgotten Farmer: Story of Sharecroppers in the New Deal* (1965).
Davis, John H., and Kenneth Hinshaw, *Farmer in a Business Suit* (1957).

Dykstra, Robert R., *Cattle Towns* (1968).
Fuller, Wayne E., *RFD: Changing Face of Rural America* (1964).
Hagood, Margaret, *Mothers of the South: White Tenant Farm Women* (1939).
Higbee, Edward, *Farms and Farmers in an Urban Age* (1963).
Johnstone, Paul, "In Praise of Husbandry," *Agric. Hist.,* 11 (1937), 80.
——— "Turnips and Romanticism," *Agric. Hist.,* 12 (1938), 224.
Kirkpatrick, Ellis L., et al., *Family Living in Farm Homes* (1924).
Kirkpatrick, Ellis L. with J. T. Sanders, *Relation between Ability to Pay and Standard of Living among Farmers* (1926).
Moe, E. O., and C. C. Taylor, *Culture of a Contemporary Rural Community: Irwin, Iowa* (1942).
Nelson, Lowry, *American Farm Life* (1954).
——— *Rural Sociology: Origin and Growth* (1969).
Shannon, Fred A., "Culture and Agriculture," *MVHR,* 41 (1954), 3.
Taylor, Carl C., et al., *Rural Life in the United States* (1949).
U.S. President's National Advisory Commission on Rural Poverty, *Report* (1968).
Williams, James M., *Expansion of Rural Life* (1926).

*   *   *   *   *   *   *

Landis, B. Y., *Guide to Literature of Rural Life* (1932).

See also 13.4.4, Pioneer Life.

18.11.4 Agricultural Economics

Bogue, Allan G., *Money at Interest: Farm Mortgage on Middle Border* (1955).
Brannen, C. O., *Relation of Land Tenure to Plantation Organization* (1924).
Breimyer, Harold F., *Individual Freedom and Economic Organization of Agriculture* (1965).
Ciriacy-Wantrup, Siegfried V., *Major Economic Forces Affecting Agriculture with Particular Reference to California* (1947).
Conrad, David E., *The Forgotten Farmer: Story of Sharecroppers in the New Deal* (1965).
Duggan, I. W., and R. U. Battles, *Financing Farm Business* (1950).
Finley, Robert M., "A Budgeting Approach to the Question of Homestead Size on the Plains," *Agric. Hist.,* 42 (1968), 109.
Galambos, Louis, "The Agrarian Image of the Large Corporation, 1879–1920: A Study in Social Accommodation," *Jour. Econ. Hist.,* 28 (1968), 341.
Gates, Paul W., "Frontier Landlords and Pioneer Tenants," Illinois State Historical Society, *Journal,* 38 (1945), 143.
Goldenweiser, E. A., and L. E. Truesdell, *Farm Tenancy* (1924).
Hayter, Earl W., *Troubled Farmer, 1850–1900: Adjustment to Industrialism* (1968).
Heady, Earl O., et al., eds., *Agricultural Adjustment Problems in a Growing Economy* (1958).
Hibbard, Benjamin H., *Marketing Agricultural Products* (1921).
National Farm Institute, *Corporate Farming and Family Farm* (1970).
Nourse, E. G., *American Agriculture and the European Market* (1924).
Peterson, A. G., *Historical Study of Prices Received by Producers of Farm products in Virginia* (1929).
Pressly, Thomas J., and William H. Scofield, eds., *Farm Real Estate Values in United States by Counties, 1850–1959* (1965).
Saloutos, Theodore, "The Agricultural Problem and Nineteenth-Century Industrialism," in Joseph H. Lambie and Richard V. Clemence, eds., *Economic Change in America: Readings in the Economic History of the United States* (1954).
Schultz, Theodore W., *Agriculture in an Unstable Economy* (1945).
Soth, Lauren K., *Farm Trouble* (1957).
Sparks, E. S., *History and Theory of Agricultural Credit* (1932).
Taylor, Henry C., and A. D. Taylor, *Story of Agricultural Economics* (1952).
Tostlebe, Alvin S., *Capital in Agriculture: Its Formation and Financing Since 1870* (1957).

Woofter, Thomas J., *Landlord and Tenant on the Cotton Plantation* (1936).
Wright, Ivan, *Bank Credit and Agriculture* (1922).

*   *   *   *   *   *   *

Brown, D. A., "Historical Prices of Farm Products by States: A Bibliography,"
Agric. Hist., 36 (1962), 169.

See also 18.13.4, Pricing.

18.11.5 Government and Agriculture

Baker, Gladys L., et al., *Century of Service: First Hundred Years of Department of Agriculture* (1963).
Benedict, Murray R., and Oscar C. Stine, *The Agricultural Commodity Program: Two Decades of Experience* (1956).
Benedict, Murray R., *Farm Policies of the United States, 1790–1950* (1953).
Fite, Gilbert, and George N. Peek, *Fight for Farm Parity* (1954).
Halcrow, Harold C., *Agricultural Policy of the United States* (1953).
Hathaway, Dale E., *Government and Agriculture* (1963).
Kirkendall, Richard S., *Social Scientists and Farm Politics in the Age of Roosevelt* (1966).
Klose, Nelson, *America's Crop Heritage: The History of Foreign Plant Introduction by the Federal Government* (1950).
Moore, Ernest G., *The Agricultural Research Service* (1967).
Pinkett, Harold T., "A Century of Federal Assistance to Agriculture," *AHR*, 69 (1964), 689.
Rau, Allan, *Agriculture Policy and Trade Liberalization 1934–1956* (1957).

See also 14.7, Water Resources and Flood Control; 14.8, Reclamation; 18.11.11, Irrigation.

18.11.6 Farm Labor

Bishop, Charles E., ed., *Farm Labor in the United States* (1967).
Burford, Roger L., "Federal Cotton Programs and Farm Labor Force Adjustments," *South. Econ. Jour.*, 33 (1966), 223.
Cox, L. F., "Agricultural Wage Earner, 1865–1900," *Agric. Hist.*, 22 (1948), 95.
Ducoff, L. J., *Wages of Agricultural Labor* (1944).
Fine, Nathan, *Labor and Farmer Parties* (1928).
Gilmore, N. Ray, and Gladys W. Gilmore, "Bracero in California," *Pac. Hist. Rev.*, 32 (1963), 265.
Hawley, Ellis W., "Politics of Mexican Labor Issue," *Agric. Hist.*, 40 (1966), 157.
Jamieson, Stuart M., *Labor Unionism in American Agriculture* (1945).
McWilliams, Carey, *Factories in the Field* (1939).
Padfield, Harland, and W. E. Martin, *Farmers, Workers and Machines: Technological and Social Change in Farm Industries of Arizona* (1965).
Pitrone, Jean M., *Chavez: Man of the Migrants* (1971).
Primack, Martin L., "Farm Construction as Use of Farm Labor, 1850–1910," *Jour. Econ. Hist.*, 25 (1965), 114.
"Twentieth Century Farm Strikes," *Agric. Hist.*, 39 (1965), 196.
U.S. President's Commission on Migratory Labor, *Migratory Labor in American Agriculture* (1951).
Wright, Dale, *They Harvest Despair: Migrant Farm Worker* (1965).

18.11.7 Agrarianism and Farmers' Associations

Arnold, Carl R., *Farmers Build Their Own Production Credit System, 1933–1958* (1958).
Barns, William D., "Oliver H. Kelley and the Grange," *Agric. Hist.*, 41 (1967), 229.

Chambers, Clarke A., "Cooperative League, 1916–1961," *Agric. Hist.,* 36, (1962), 59.
Fite, Gilbert C., *Farm to Factory: Consumers Cooperative Association* (1965).
Gardner, Charles M., *The Grange: Friend of the Farmer* (1949).
Hopkins, James T., *Fifty Years of Citrus: Florida Citrus Exchange, 1909–1959* (1960).
Jackson, W. Turrentine, "Wyoming Stock Growers' Association," *MVHR,* 33 (1947), 571.
Knapp, Joseph G., *Rise of Cooperative Enterprise, 1620–1920* (1969).
Kramer, Dale, *Wild Jackasses: American Farmer in Revolt* (1956).
Noblin, Stuart L., *Grange in North Carolina, 1929–1954* (1954).
Parker, Florence E., *First 125 Years: Distributive and Service Cooperation, 1829–1954* (1956).
Saloutos, Theodore and John D. Hicks, *Agricultural Discontent in the Middle West, 1900–1939* (1951).
Saloutos, Theodore, *Farmer Movements in the South, 1865–1933* (1960).
Schmidt, Louis B., "Agrarian Pressure Groups," *Agric. Hist.,* 30 (1956), 49.
Shannon, Fred A., *American Farmers' Movements* (1957).
Taylor, Carl C., *Farmers' Movement, 1620–1920* (1953).
Tontz, Robert L., "Memberships of General Farmers' Organizations, United States, 1874–1960," *Agric. Hist.,* 38 (1964), 143.
Wiest, Edward, *Agricultural Organization in the United States* (1923).
Wysor, William G., *History and Philosophy of Southern States Cooperative* (1940).

*   *   *   *   *   *

Douglas, Louis H., ed., *Agrarianism in American History* (1969).
Morrison, Denton E., ed., *Farmers' Organization and Movements: Research Needs and a Bibliography of United States and Canada* (1970).
Nordin, Dennis, *Preliminary List of References for the History of the Granger Movement* (1967).

18.11.8 Scientific Agriculture

Ashton, J., and R. F. Lord, ed., *Research, Education and Extension in Agriculture* (1969).
Beardsley, Harry H., *Harry L. Russell and Agricultural Science in Wisconsin* (1969).
Benjamin, Harold R. W., "Agricultural Education in Different Stages of National Development" *Jour. Econ. Hist.,* 22 (1962), 547.
Feller, Irwin, "Inventive Activity in Agriculture, 1837–1890," *Jour. Econ. Hist.,* 22 (1962), 560.
Harding, T. Swan, *Two Blades of Grass* (1947).
Hayes, Herbert K., *Professor's Story of Hybrid Corn* (1963).
Kellogg, Charles E., and David C. Knapp, *College of Agriculture* (1966).
Kniffen, Fred, "The American Agricultural Fair: Time and Place," Assoc. of Am. Geographers, *Annals,* 41 (1951), 42.
Neely, Wayne C., *Agriculture Fair* (1935).
Reck, Franklin M., *4–H Club Story* (1951).
Rozwenc, Edwin C., "Agricultural Education and Politics in Vermont," *Vt. Hist.,* 26 (1958), 69.
Smith, Clarence B., and M. C. Wilson, *Agricultural Extension System* (1930).
True, Alfred C., *History of Agricultural Education* (1937).
—— *History of Agricultural Experimentation* (1937).
—— *History of Agricultural Extension Work* (1928).
Wells, George S., *Science in Agriculture* (1969).

*   *   *   *   *   *

Pursell, Carrol W., Jr., and Earl M. Rogers, *Preliminary List of References for the History of Agricultural Science and Technology* (1966).

See also 10.3 for biographies/writings of:

Bailey, Liberty Hyde, 1858–1954
Bennett, Hugh, 1881–1960
Buel, Jesse, 1778–1839
Holmes, Ezekiel, 1801–1865
Knapp, Seaman A., 1833–1911
Lipman, Jacob, 1874–1939
Robinson, Solon, 1803–1880
Ruffin, Edmund, 1794–1865
Turner, Jonathan B., 1805–1899
Watson, Elkanah, 1758–1842

See also 23.13.2, Land Grant System and the State University.

18.11.9 Agricultural Press

Abbott, Richard H., "The Agricultural Press Views the Yeoman: 1819–1859,"
Agric. Hist., 42 (1968), 35.
Bardolph, Richard, *Agricultural Literature and the Early Illinois Farmer* (1948).
Demaree, A. L., *American Agricultural Press* (1941).
Kirschner, Don S., "Henry A. Wallace as Farm Editor," *Am. Quar.,* 17 (1965),
187.
Ogilvie, William E., *Pioneer Agricultural Journalists* (1927).
Schapsmeier, Edward L., and Frederick H. Schapsmeier, "The Wallaces and
Their Farm Paper: A Story of Agrarian Leadership," *Journalism Quar.,* 44
(1967), 289.
Schlebecker, John T., and Andrew W. Hopkins, *History of Dairy Journalism in
United States, 1810–1950* (1957).
Tucker, Gilbert M., *American Agricultural Periodicals* (1909).
Wallace, Wesley H., "North Carolina's Agricultural Journals, 1838–1861," *No.
Car. Hist. Rev.,* 36 (1959), 275.

See also 10.3 for biographies/writings of:

Wallace, Henry, 1836–1916
Wallace, Henry A., 1888–1965
Wallace, Henry C., 1866–1924

18.11.10 Technology

Cathey, Cornelius O., "Agricultural Implements in North Carolina, 1783–1860,"
Agric. Hist., 25 (1951), 128.
Day, Richard H., "Technological Change and Demise of Sharecropper," *Am.
Econ. Rev.,* 57 (1967), 427.
Downs, Eldon W., and George F. Lemmer, "Origins of Aerial Crop Dusting,"
Agric. Hist., 39 (1965), 123.
Fussell, G. E., *Farmer's Tools, 1500–1900* (1952).
Johnson, Sherman E., *Changes in American Farming* (1949).
Kendall, Edward C., *John Deere's Steel Plow* (1959).
Kohlmeyer, Fred W., and Floyd L. Herum, "Science and Engineering in Agricul-
ture," *Tech. and Cult.,* 2 (1961), 368.
Lamb, Robert B., *Mule in Southern Agriculture* (1963).
Peterson, Gale E., "Discovery and Development of 2, 4-D," *Agric. Hist.,* 41
(1967), 243.
Rasmussen, Wayne D., "Impact of Technological Change on American Agricul-
ture, 1862–1962," *Jour. Econ. Hist.,* 22 (1962), 578.
Rogin, Leo, *Introduction of Farm Machinery in Relation to Productivity of Labor*
(1931).
Street, James H., *New Revolution in Cotton Economy* (1957).
Swingle, F. B., "Invention of Twine Binder," *Wis. Mag. Hist.* 10 (1926), 35.

U.S. Department of Agriculture, *Technology of the Farm* (1940).
Wik, Reynold M., *Steam Power on American Farm* (1953).

* * * * * * *

Pursell, Carroll W., Jr., and Earl M. Rogers, eds., *Preliminary List of References for the History of Agricultural Sciences and Technology in the United States* (1966).

See also 10.3 for biography/writings of:

McCormick, Cyrus H., 1809–1884

18.11.11 Irrigation

Boening, R. M., "History of Irrigation in Washington," *Wash. Hist. Quar.,* 9 (1918), 259; 10 (1919), 21.
Brough, C. H., *Irrigation in Utah* (1898).
Ganoe, John T., "Beginnings of Irrigation," *MVHR,* 25 (1938), 59.
Lilley, William, III, and Lewis L. Gould, "The Western Irrigation Movement, 1878–1902: A Reappraisal," *Univ. of Wyoming Publ.,* 32 (1966), 57.
Sageser, A. Bower, "Windmill and Pump Irrigation on Great Plains," *Neb. Hist.,* 48 (1967), 107.
Shelton, F. H., "Windmills: Motors of the Past," Franklin Inst., *Jour.,* 187 (1919), 171.
Sterling, Everett W., "Powell Irrigation Survey, 1888–1893," *MVHR,* 27 (1940), 421.

See also 14.7, Water Resources and Flood Control; 14.8, Reclamation.

18.11.12 Cotton and Tobacco

Brooks, Jerome E., *Mighty Leaf: Tobacco Through the Centuries* (1952).
Davis, Charles S., *Cotton Kingdom in Alabama* (1939).
Herndon, G. Melvin, *William Tatham and Culture of Tobacco* (1969).
Nixon, Herman C., "The New South and the Old Crop," in Avery Craven, ed., *Essays in Honor of William E. Dodd* (1935).
Robert, Joseph C., *Tobacco Kingdom* (1938).
Tilley, Nannie M., *Bright-Tobacco Industry, 1860–1929* (1948).
Waller, J. L., "Overland Movement of Cotton," *Southwestern Hist. Quar.,* 35 (1931), 137.
Woodman, Harold D., *King Cotton and His Retainers, 1800–1925* (1968).

18.11.13 Grains

Ball, C. R., "History of Wheat Improvement," *Agric. Hist.,* 4 (1930), 48.
Boyle, J. E., *Chicago Wheat Prices* (1922).
Clark, John G., *Grain Trade in Old Northwest* (1966).
Crabb, Alexander R., *Hybrid Corn Makers* (1947).
Hayes, Herbert K., *Professor's Story of Hybrid Corn* (1963).
Johnson, David G., and Robert L. Gustafson, *Grain Yields and American Food Supply* (1962).
Larson, Henrietta M., *Wheat Market and Farmer in Minnesota* (1926).
Kemmerer, Donald L., "The Pre-Civil War South's Leading Crop, Corn," *Agric. Hist.,* 23 (1949), 236.
Malin, James C., *Winter Wheat in Kansas* (1944).
Saloutos, Theodore, "The Spring-Wheat Farmer in a Maturing Economy, 1870–1920," *Jour. Econ. Hist.,* 6 (1946), 173.
Thompson, John G., *Rise and Decline of Wheat Growing in Wisconsin* (1909).
Walden, Howard T., *Native Inheritance: Story of Corn in America* (1966).
Wallace, Henry A., and William L. Brown, *Corn and Its Early Fathers* (1956).

18.11.14 Livestock

Bateman, Fred, "Improvement in American Dairy Farming, 1850–1910; A Quantitative Analysis," *Jour. Econ. Hist.* 28 (1968), 255.
Clemen, R. A., *The American Livestock Industry* (1923).
Gilfillan, Archer B., *Sheep: Life on South Dakota Range* (1957).
Hayter, E. W., "Barbed Wire Fencing," *Agric. Hist.* 13 (1939), 189.
Henlein, Paul C., *Cattle Kingdom in the Ohio Valley, 1783–1860* (1959).
Howard, Robert W., *Horse in America* (1965).
Jones, Robert L., "Horse and Mule Industry in Ohio to 1865," *MVHR* 33 (1946), 61.
Kerr, Homer L., "Introduction of Forage Plants into Ante-Bellum United States," *Agric. Hist.*, 38 (1964), 87.
Lampard, Eric E., *Rise of the Dairy Industry in Wisconsin, 1820–1920* (1963).
Leavitt, Charles T., "Cattle Breeds in United States, 1790–1860," *Agric. Hist.*, 7 (1933), 51.
Oliphant, J. O., "Livestock Industry in the Pacific Northwest," *Ore. Hist. Quar.*, 41 (1948), 3.
Pirtle, T. R., *Dairy Industry* (1926).
Prentice, Ezra P., *American Dairy Cattle* (1942).
Thompson, James W., "History of Livestock Raising in the United States, 1607–1860," *Agricultural History Series*, 5 (1942).
Topel, David G., ed., *Pork Industry* (1969).
Towne, C. W., and Edward N. Wentworth, *Shepherd's Empire* (1945).
Wentworth, Edward N., *America's Sheep Trails* (1948).
Wiest, Edward, *Butter Industry* (1916).

See also 13.4.7, Cowboys and Cattle Raising.

18.11.15 Other Crops

Arrington, Leonard J., *Beet Sugar in the West: Utah-Idaho Sugar Company, 1891–1966* (1966).
Carosso, Vincent P., *California Wine Industry, 1830–1895* (1951).
Glazer, Sidney, "Early Silk Industry in Michigan," *Agric. Hist.*, 18 (1944), 92.
Hopkins, James F., *History of the Hemp Industry in Kentucky* (1951).
Johnson, F. Roy, *The Peanut Story* (1964).
Loeffler, M. John, "Beet-Sugar Production on the Colorado Piedmont," *Assoc. Am. Geographers, Annals*, 53 (1963), 364.
Sitterson, J. Carlyle, *Sugar Country: Cane Sugar Industry in the South, 1753–1950* (1953).

18.12 BUSINESS

18.12.1 General

Aitken, Hugh J. G., ed., *Explorations in Enterprise* (1965).
Beard, Miriam, *History of Business* (2 vols., 1962–1963).
Bendix, R., and Frank W. Hawton, "Social Mobility and Business Elite," *Brit. Jour. Sociol.*, 8 (1957), 357; 9 (1958), 1.
Brooks, John, *Business Adventures* (1968).
Chamberlain, John, *Enterprising Americans: Business History* (1963).
Chandler, Alfred D., Jr., *Strategy and Structure: Chapters in the History of Industrial Enterprise* (1962).
Cheit, Earl F., ed., *The Business Establishment* (1964).
Cochran, Thomas C., *American Business in the Twentieth Century* (1972).
—— *Basic History of American Business* (2nd ed., 1968).
—— "Organization Men in Historical Perspective," *Penn. Hist.*, 25 (1958), 9.
—— *The Puerto Rican Businessman: A Study in Cultural Change* (1959).
Cole, Arthur H., *Business Enterprise in Its Social Setting* (1959).

Diamond, Sigmund, *The Reputation of American Businessman* (1955).

Fuller, Justin, "Alabama Business Leaders, 1865–1900," *Ala. Rev.,* 16 (1963), 279; 17 (1964), 63.

Gras, Norman S. B., *Business and Capitalism: Introduction to Business History* (1939).

Hendrick, Burton J., *Age of Big Business* (1919).

McClelland, David C., *The Achieving Society* (1961).

Michelman, Irving S., *Business at Bay: Critics and Heretics of American Business* (1969).

Miller, William, ed., *Men in Business: Essays on the Historical Role of the Entrepreneur* (rev. ed., 1962).

Newcomer, Mabel, *The Big Business Executive: The Factors That Made Him, 1900–1950* (1955).

Phillips, Joseph D., *Little Business in the American Economy* (1958).

Redlich, Fritz L., *History of American Business Leaders* (2 vols., 1940–1951).

Taussig, Frank W., and C. S. Joslyn, *American Business Leaders: A Study in Social Origin and Social Stratification* (1932).

Walton, Clarence C., ed., *Business and Social Progress: Views of Two Generations of Executives* (1970).

Warner, W. Lloyd, and James C. Abegglen, *Occupational Mobility in American Business and Industry, 1928–1952* (1955).

Whyte, William H., Jr., *The Organization Man* (1956).

*   *   *   *   *   *   *

Cole, Arthur H., *Historical Development of Economic and Business Literature* (1957).

Daniells, Lorna M., *Business Literature: Annotated List* (rev. ed., 1968).

—— *Studies in Enterprise: Selected Bibliography of American and Canadian Company Histories and Biographies of Businessmen* (1957).

Harvard University. Graduate School of Business Administration, *Library Catalogue, Kress Library* (3 vols., 1956–1964).

Hutchins, John G. B., "Recent Contributions to Business History," *Jour. Econ. Hist.,* 19 (1959), 103.

Kolko, Gabriel, "Premises of Business Revisionism, *Bus. Hist. Rev.,* 33 (1959), 330.

Kroos, Herman E., "Economic History and New Business History," *Jour. Econ. Hist.,* 18 (1958), 467.

Larson, Henrietta M., *Guide to Business History* (1948).

Lovett, Robert W., ed., *American Economic and Business History, A Guide to Information Sources* (1971).

Lovett, Robert W., "The Case for Business History," *Vt. Hist.,* 32 (1964), 29.

Miller, William, "American Historians and Business Elite," *Jour. Econ. Hist.,* 9 (1949), 184.

Sawyer, John E., "Entrepreneurial Studies, 1948–1958, *Bus. Hist. Rev.,* 32 (1958), 434.

Woodruff, W., "History and the Businessman," *Bus. Hist. Rev.,* 30 (1956), 241.

18.12.2 Law and Business

Dorfman, Joseph, "Chancellor Kent and American Economy," *Columbia Law Rev.,* 61 (1961), 1290.

Frankfurter, Felix, *Commerce Clause* (1937).

Friedman, Lawrence M., *Contract Law in America* (1965).

Hunt, Robert S., *Law and Locomotives: Impact of the Railroad on Wisconsin Law in the Nineteenth Century* (1958).

Hunting, W. B., *Obligation of Contracts Clause* (1919).

Hurst, J. Willard, *Law and Economic Growth: Lumber Industry in Wisconsin, 1836–1915* (1964).

—— *Legitimacy of the Business Corporation in the Law of the United States* (1970).

Le Duc, Thomas, "Carriers, Courts, and Commodities Clause," *Bus. Hist. Rev.,* 39 (1965), 57.
McCloskey, Robert G., "Economic Due Process and the Supreme Court: An Exhumation and Reburial," in Leonard W. Levy, ed., *American Constitutional Law: Historical Essays* (1966).
Miller, Arthur S., *Supreme Court and American Capitalism* (1968).
Pound, Roscoe, "Liberty of Contract," *Yale Law Jour.,* 18 (1909), 454.
Roche, John P., "Entrepreneurial Liberty and Commerce Power," *Univ. of Chi. Law Rev.,* 30 (1963), 680.
———— "Entrepreneurial Liberty and the Fourteenth Amendment," *Labor Hist.,* 4 (1963), 3.
Rostow, Eugene V., *Planning for Freedom: Public Law of Capitalism* (1959).
Rottschaefer, Henry, "Constitution and a 'Planned Economy'," *Mich. Law Rev.,* 38 (1940), 1133.
Stern, Robert L., "The Problems of Yesteryear—Commerce and Due Process," in Leonard W. Levy, ed., *American Constitutional Law: Historical Essays* (1966).
Wright, Benjamin F., *Contract Clause* (1938).
Ziegler, Benjamin M., ed., *Supreme Court and American Economic Life* (1962).

18.12.3 Development of the Corporation

Abbott, C. C., *The Rise of the Business Corporation* (1936).
Berle, Adolf A., and Gardiner C. Means, *Modern Corporation and Private Property* (rev. ed., 1969).
Bronson, Leisa, comp., *Cartels and International Patent Agreements* (1943).
Cadman, John W., Jr., *The Corporation in New Jersey: Business and Politics, 1791–1875* (1949).
Dewing, Arthur S., *Financial Policy of Corporations* (2 vols., 5th ed. 1953).
Dodd, Edwin M., *American Business Corporations until 1860, with Special Reference to Massachusetts* (1954).
Drucker, Peter F., *Concept of the Corporation* (1946).
Eells, Richard, *The Government of Corporations* (1962).
Evans, George H., *Business Incorporations in the United States, 1800–1845* (1948).
Handlin, Oscar, and Mary F. Handlin, "Origins of American Business Corporation," *Jour. Econ. Hist.,* 5 (1945), 1.
Hawkins, David F., "Financial Reporting Practices among Manufacturing Corporations," *Bus. Hist. Rev.,* 37 (1963), 135.
Hurst, J. Willard, *Legitimacy of the Business Corporation* (1970).
Kuehnl, George J., *The Wisconsin Business Corporation* (1959).
Larner, Robert J., "Ownership and Control in 200 Largest Non-Financial Corporations 1929 and 1963," *Am. Econ. Rev.,* 56 (1966), 777.
Mason, Edward S., ed., *The Corporation in Modern Society* (1960).
Means, Gardiner C., *The Corporate Revolution in America* (1962).
Warner, William Lloyd, *The Corporation in Emergent American Society* (1962).
Wilson, George W., "Democracy and the Modern Corporation," *West. Pol. Quar.,* 13 (1960), 45.

18.12.4 Government Regulation of Business

Adelman, M. A., "Effective Competition and Anti-Trust Laws," *Harv. Law Rev.,* 61 (1948), 1289.
Arnold, Thurman W., "Free Enterprise," *Am. Heritage,* 11 (1960), 52.
Bernstein, Marver H., *Regulating Business by Independent Commission* (1955).
Blaisdell, T. C., *Federal Trade Commission* (1932).
Burns, Arthur R., and Walter E. Caine, *Electric Power and Government Policy* (1948).
Clark, John D., *Federal Trust Policy* (1931).
Conant, Michael, *Anti-Trust in Motion Picture Industry* (1960).
Cox, Edward F., Robert C. Fellmeth, and John E. Schultz, *'The Nader Report' on the Federal Trade Commission* (1969).

Cushman, Robert E., *The Independent Regulatory Commissions* (1941).
Dean, Arthur H., "Federal Securities Regulation," *Columbia Law Rev.*, 59 (1959), 697.
Firth, Robert E., *Public Power in Nebraska: Report on State Ownership* (1962).
Handler, Milton, *Antitrust in Perspective* (1957).
Henderson, Gerard C., *Federal Trade Commission* (1925).
Hetherington, John A. C., "State Economic Regulation and Substantive Due Process of Law," *Northw. Univ. Law Rev.*, 53 (1958), 13.
Hilton, George W., "Interstate Commerce Act," *Jour. Laws and Econ.*, 9 (1966), 87.
Hofstadter, Richard, "Antitrust in America," *Commentary*, 38 (1964), 47.
Kauper, Thomas E., "Cease and Desist: The History, Effect, and Scope of Clayton Act Orders of the Federal Trade Commission" *Mich. Law Rev.*, 66 (1968), 1095.
Kohlmeier, Louis M., Jr., *The Regulators* (1969).
Kramer, Victor H., "Antitrust Division and the Supreme Court, 1890–1953," *Va. Law Rev.*, 40 (1954), 433.
Lane, Robert E., *Regulation of Businessmen* (1954).
McConnell, Grant, *Private Power and American Democracy* (1966).
Martin, David D., *Mergers and the Clayton Act* (1959).
Taylor, George W., *Government Regulation of Industrial Relations* (1948).
Thorelli, Hans B., *Federal Antitrust Policy* (1955).
U.S. Federal Trade Commission, *Merger Movement* (1948).
Watkins, M. W., *Public Regulation of Competitive Practices* (1940).
Whitney, Simon N., *Antitrust Policies: American Experience in Twenty Industries* (1958).
Williams, Ernest W., Jr., *Regulation of Rail-Motor Rate Competition* (1958).

* * * * * * *

McDermott, Beatrice S., and Freada A. Coleman, *Government Regulation of Business Including Antitrust: Annotated Bibliography* (1967).

See also 18.15.13, Public Utilities; 18.16.6.4, Railroads–Government Regulation; 27.8.2, Radio and Television–Government Regulation.

18.12.5 Economic Concentration and Monopoly

Bernheim, A. L., ed., *Big Business* (1937).
Bonbright, James C., and Gardiner C. Means, *Holding Company: Its Public Significance and Its Regulation* (1932).
Burns, Arthur R., *Decline of Competition* (1932).
Chamberlin, Edward H., *Theory of Monopolistic Competition: A Re-orientation of the Theory of Value* (8th ed., 1962).
Chandler, Alfred D., Jr., "'Big Business' in American Industry," *Bus. Hist. Rev.*, 33 (1959), 1.
Cox, Reavis, *Competition in the Tobacco Industry, 1911–1932* (1933).
Dell, S., "Economic Integration," *Econ. Jour.*, 69 (1959), 39.
Edwards, Corwin D., *Maintaining Competition: Requisites of a Governmental Policy* (1949).
Fabricant, Solomon, "Is Monopoly Increasing?" *Jour. of Econ. Hist.*, 13 (1953), 89.
Glover, John D., *The Attack on Big Business* (1954).
Hendrick, B. J., *The Age of Big Business* (1920).
Hexner, Ervin, and Adelaide Walters, *International Cartels* (1945).
Holbrook, Stewart H., *The Age of the Moguls* (1953).
Huettig, Mae D., *Economic Control of the Motion Picture Industry: A Study in Industrial Organization* (1944).
Josephson, Matthew, *The Robber Barons: The Great American Capitalists, 1861–1901* (1934).
Kirkland, Edward C., "Divide and Ruin," *MVHR*, 43 (1956), 3.

Laidler, H. W., *Concentration of Control in American Industry* (1931).
Lilienthal, David E., *Big Business: A New Era* (1953).
Lloyd, Henry D., *Wealth against Commonwealth* (1894).
McCloskey, Robert G., *American Conservatism in an Age of Enterprise* (1951).
Mason, Edward S., *Economic Concentration and the Monopoly Problem* (1957).
Moody, John, *Masters of Capital* (1919).
Mueller, Willard F., *The Celler-Kefauver Act: Sixteen Years of Enforcement: Staff Report to the Antitrust Subcommittee of the Committee on the Judiciary of the House of Representatives* (90 Cong., 1st sess., H. R. Comm. Print, 1967).
Myers, Gustavus, *History of the Great American Fortunes* (rev. ed., 3 vols., 1936).
Nelson, Ralph L., *Merger Movements in American Industry, 1895–1956* (1959).
Nutter, Gilbert Warren, and Henry A. Einhorn, *Enterprise Monopoly in the United States, 1899–1958* (1969).
Phillips, Almarin, ed., *Perspectives on Antitrust Policy* (1965).
Ripley, William Z., ed., *Trusts, Pools and Corporations* (1916).
Seager, H. R., and C. A. Gulick, *Trust and Corporation Problems* (1929).
Stocking, George W., and Myron W. Watkins, *Monopoly and Free Enterprise* (1951).
Vatter, Harold G., *Small Enterprise and Oligopoly:* (1955).
Watkins, Myron W., *Industrial Combinations and Public Policy* (1927).
Worcester, Dean A., Jr., *Monopoly, Big Business, and Welfare in the Postwar United States* (1967).

18.12.5.1 "Robber Barons"

Bornet, Vaughn D., "Those 'Robber Barons'," *West. Pol. Quar.,* 6 (1953), 342.
Bridges, Hal, "Robber Baron Concept," *Bus. Hist. Rev.,* 32 (1958), 1.
Clark, John W., *Religion and the Moral Standards of American Businessmen* (1966).
Cochran, Thomas C., "Legend of Robber Barons," *Penn. Mag. Hist. Biog.,* 74 (1950), 307.
Jones, Peter D., comp., *Robber Barons Revisited* (1968).
Josephson, Matthew, *Robber Barons: Great American Capitalists, 1860–1901* (1934).
Kirkland, Edward C., "Robber Barons," *AHR,* 66 (1960), 68.
Solganick, Allen, "Robber Baron Concept and Its Revisionists," *Science and Society,* 29 (1965), 257.

18.12.6 Ideology

Bernstein, Marver H., "Political Ideas of Business Journals," *Pub. Opinion Quar.,* 17 (1953), 258.
Bunzel, John H., "Ideology of Small Business," Pol. Sci. Quar. (1955), 87.
Chapman, Charles C., *Development of Business and Banking Thought, 1913–1936* (1936).
Cheit, Earl F., ed., *Business Establishment* (1965).
Cochran, Thomas C., "Business Society," *JAH,* 54 (1967), 5.
Cole, Arthur H., *Historical Development of Economic and Business Literature* (1957).
Curti, Merle E., and Karsten, Peter, "Men and Businessmen: Changing Concepts of Human Nature as Reflected in the Writing of American Business History," *Jour. Hist. Behavioral Sci.,* 4 (1968), 3.
Destler, Chester M., "Opposition of Businessmen to Social Control during the 'Gilded Age'," *MVHR,* 39 (1953), 641.
Fine, Sidney, *Laissez Faire and General-Welfare State: A Study of Conflict in American Thought, 1865–1901* (1956).
Forsyth, David P., *Business Press, 1750–1865* (1964).
Heald, Morrell, "Business Thought in the Twenties," *Am. Quar.,* 13 (1961), 126
——— *The Social Responsibilities of Business; Company and Community. 1900–1960* (1970).
Hines, Thomas S., Jr., "Reactions of Businessmen to 'Babbitt'," *Bus. Hist. Rev.,* 41 (1967), 123
Hofstadter, Richard, *Social Darwinism in American Thought* (rev. ed., 1955).

Kirkland, Edward C., *Business in the Gilded Age* (1952).
—— *Dream and Thought in the Business Community, 1860–1900* (1956).
Michelman, Irving S., *Business at Bay: Critics and Heretics of American Business* (1955).
Prothro, James W., "Business Ideas and the American Tradition," *Jour. of Pol.*, 15 (1953), 67.
—— *Dollar Decade: Business Ideas in the 1920's* (1954).
Sutton, Francis X., et al., *The American Business Creed* (1956).
Wyllie, Irvin G., "Social Darwinism and Businessman," Am. Philos. Soc., *Proc.*, 103 (1959), 629.

See also 18.13.3, Advertising and Public Relations.

18.12.7 Associations

Donald, W. J. A., *Trade Associations* (1933).
Galambos, Louis, *Competition & Cooperation: Emergence of a National Trade Association* (1966). The Cotton Textile Institute.
Nelson, Milton N., *Open Price Associations* (1922).
Steigerwalt, Albert K., *National Association of Manufacturers, 1895–1914* (1964).

18.12.8 Management and Training

Aitken, Hugh G. J., *Taylorism at the Watertown Arsenal, 1908–1915* (1960).
The American Association of Collegiate Schools of Business, 1916–1966 (1966).
Baritz, Loren, *Servants of Power: Social Science in American Industry* (1960).
Baughman, James P., ed., *History of American Management* (1969).
Bendix, Reinhard, *Work and Authority in Industry: Management in Industrialization* (1956).
Brown, James Alexander Campbell, *Social Psychology of Industry* (1954).
Carey, John L., *Rise of the Accounting Profession* (2 vols., 1969–1970).
Chandler, Alfred D. Jr., "Management Decentralization," *Bus. Hist. Rev.*, 21 (1956), 111.
Edwards, James D., *History of Public Accounting in the United States* (1960).
Haber, Samuel, *Efficiency and Uplift: Scientific Management in the Progressive Era, 1890–1920* (1964).
Hall, Courtney R., *History of American Industrial Science* (1954).
Haynes, Benjamin R., and Harry P. Jackson, *History of Business Education in the United States* (1935).
Kakar, Sudhir, *Frederick Taylor: A Study in Personality and Innovation* (1970).
Levinson, Harry, *The Exceptional Executive: A Psychological Conception* (1968).
Miller, Jay W., and William J. Hamilton, *The Independent Business School in American Education* (1964).
Strauss, George, and Leonard R. Sayles, *Personnel: Human Problems of Management* (1960).
Taylor, Frederick W., *Principles of Scientific Management* (1911).
—— *Shop Management* (1911).
Wilkinson, Norman B., "In Anticipation of Frederick W. Taylor: A Study of Work by Lammot du Pont, 1872," *Tech. and Cult.*, 6 (1965), 208.

18.13 COMMERCE

18.13.1 General

Barger, Harold, *Distribution's Place in American Economy since 1869* (1955).
Day, Clive, *A History of Commerce of the United States* (rev. ed., 1922).
Fishlow, Albert, "Antebellum Interregional Trade," *Am. Econ. Rev.*, 54 (1964), 352.

Frederick, John H., *The Development of American Commerce* (1932).

Johnson, Emery R. et al., *History of Domestic and Foreign Commerce of the United States* (2 vols., 1915).

Livingood, J. W., *Philadelphia-Baltimore Trade Rivalry* (1947).

Martin, Margaret E., *Merchants and Trade of the Connecticut River Valley, 1750–1820* (1939).

Romaine, Lawrence B., *Guide to American Trade Catalogs, 1744–1900* (1960).

Schmidt, Louis R., "Internal Commerce and National Economy before 1860," *Jour. Pol. Econ.,* 47 (1939), 798.

Vose, E. N. *Seventy-five Years of R. G. Dun & Co.* (1916).

Wyatt-Brown, Bertram, . . . "God and Dun & Bradstreet, 1841–1851," *Bus. Hist. Rev.,* 40 (1966), 432.

18.13.2 Merchandising and the Consumer

Atherton, Lewis E., "Itinerant Merchandising," Bus. Hist. Soc., *Bull.,* 19 (1945), 53.

—— *Pioneer Merchant* (1939).

—— *Southern Country Store, 1800–1860* (1949).

Carson, Gerald, *Old Country Store* (1954).

Cassady, Ralph Jr., and Wylie L. Jones, *Wholesale Grocery Trade, Los Angeles, 1920–1946* (1949).

Clark, Thomas D., *Pills, Petticoats and Plows: Southern Country Store* (1944).

Cross, Jennifer, *The Supermarket Trap: The Consumer and the Food Industry* (1970).

De Voe, Thomas F., *The Market Book* (2 vols., 1862).

Emmet, Boris, and John E. Jeuck, *Catalogues and Counters: History of Sears Roebuck* (1950).

Houthakker, Hendrik S., and Lester D. Taylor, *Consumer Demand in United States: Analipes and Projections* (2nd ed., 1970).

Hower, Ralph M., *History of Macy's of New York, 1858–1919* (1943).

Hymans, Saul H., "Cyclical Behavior of Consumers' Income and Spending, 1921–1961," *South. Econ. Jour.,* 32 (1965), 23.

Johnson, Laurence A., *Over the Counter and on the Shelf: Country Storekeeping in America, 1620–1920* (1961).

Jones, Fred Mitchell, *Middlemen in Domestic Trade of United States 1800–1860* (1937).

Jones, Peter d'A., *The Consumer Society: History of American Capitalism* (1965).

Kaplan, Abraham D. H., et al., *Pricing in Big Business* (1958).

Katona, George, and Eva Mueller, *Consumer Attitudes and Demand, 1950–52* (1953).

Lebhar, Godfrey M., *Chain Stores in America, 1859–1959* (1959).

Lynn, Robert A., "Installment Credit before 1870," *Bus. Hist. Rev.,* 31 (1957), 414.

Martin, Edgar W., *The Standard of Living in 1860* (1942).

Mueller, Willard F., and Leon Garoian, *Changes in Market Structure of Grocery Retailing* (1961).

Parish, William J., *The Charles Ilfeld Company: A Study of the Rise and Decline of Mercantile Capitalism in New Mexico* (1961).

Polak, J. J., "Fluctuations in Consumption, 1919–1932," *Rev. Econ. Stat.,* 21 (1939), 1.

Resseguie, Harry E., "A. T. Stewart's Marble Palace: Department Store," *N.Y. Hist. Soc. Quar.,* 48 (1964), 131.

—— "Alexander T. Stewart and the Development of the Department Store, 1823–1876," *Bus. Hist. Rev.,* 39 (1965), 301.

Robinson, Dwight E., "Importance of Fashions in Taste to Business History," *Bus. Hist. Rev.,* 37 (1963), 5.

Seligman, E. R. A., *Economics of Installment Selling* (1927).

Silk, Alvin J., and Louis W. Stern, "Innovation in Marketing: Study of Selected Business Leaders, 1852–1958," *Bus. Hist. Rev.,* 37 (1963), 182.

Smith, Paul F., *Consumer Credit Costs, 1949–1959* (1964).

Throckmorton, Arthur L., *Oregon Argonauts: Merchant Adventurers on the Western Frontier* (1961).

Twyman, Robert W., *History of Marshall Field & Co., 1852–1906* (1954).

U.S. Department of Labor, *How American Buying Habits Change* (1959).

Wendt, Lloyd, and Herman Kogan, *Give the Lady What She Wants! Marshall Field & Company* (1952).

Wingate, J. W., and Arnold Corbin, *Changing Patterns in Retailing* (1956).

See also 10.3 for biographies/writings of:

Cabot, George, 1752–1823
Field, Marshall, 1834–1906
Forbes, John M., 1813–1898
Girard, Stephen, 1750–1831
Hicks, Isaac, 1767–1820
Hopkins, Johns, 1795–1873
Jarves, James J., 1818–1888
Larkin, Thomas O., 1802–1858
Lawrence, Amos A., 1814–1886
Low, Seth, 1850–1916
Nichols, George, 1778–1865
Oliver, Robert, ca. 1757–1819
Peabody, George, 1795–1869
Penney, James C., 1875–1971
Pepperell Family
Rosenwald, Julius, 1862–1932
Sheppard, Moses, 1775?–1857
Talcott, James Frederick, 1866–1944
Tappan, Arthur, 1786–1865
Tappan, Lewis, 1788–1873
Thorndike, Israel, 1755–1832
Train, George F., 1829–1904
Trotter, Nathan, 1787–1853
Wanamaker, John, 1838–1922
Watson, Elkanah, 1758–1842
Willett, Marinus, 1740–1830
Woolworth, Frank, 1852–1919

18.13.3 Advertising and Public Relations

Bauer, Raymond A., and S. A. Greyser, *Advertising in America: The Consumer View* (1968).

Burt, F. A., *American Advertising Agencies* (1940).

Curti, Merle E., "Changing Concept of 'Human Nature' in American Advertising," *Bus. Hist. Rev.*, 41 (1967), 335.

Disbrow, M. E., *Criticism of Newspaper Advertising since 1915* (1931).

Golden, L. L. L., *Only by Public Consent: American Corporations Search for Favorable Opinion* (1968).

Goldman, Eric F., *Two-Way Street: Emergence of Public Relations Counsel* (1948).

Hiebert, Ray E., *Courtier to the Crowd: Story of Ivy Lee and the Development of Public Relations* (1966).

Houck, John W., ed., *Outdoor Advertising: History and Regulation* (1969).

Hower, Ralph M., *History of an Advertising Agency: N. W. Ayer & Son, 1869–1949* (rev. ed., 1949).

Packard, Vance O., *Hidden Persuaders* (1957).

Pease, Otis, *Responsibilities of American Advertising: Private Control and Public Influence, 1920–1940* (1958).

Presbrey, Frank S., *History and Development of Advertising* (1929).

Raucher, Alan R., *Public Relations and Business, 1900–1929* (1968).

Simon, Raymond, ed., *Perspectives in Public Relations* (1966).

Wood, James P., *Story of Advertising* (1958).

See also 10.3 for biographies/writings of:

Bernays, Edward L., 1891–
Lee, Ivy L., 1877–1934

18.13.4 Pricing

Berry, Thomas S., *Western Prices before 1861: A Study of the Cincinnati Market* (1943).
Bezanson, Anne, *Wholesale Prices in Philadelphia, 1784–1861* (1936).
Brady, Dorothy S., "Prices in Nineteenth Century," *Jour. Econ. Hist.,* 24 (1964), 145.
Cole, Arthur H., *Wholesale Commodity Prices in the United States, 1700–1861* (1938).
Edwards, Corwin D., *Price Discrimination Law* (1959).
Machlup, Fritz, *The Basing-Point System* (1949).
Means, Gardiner C., *Pricing Power and the Public Interest: A Study Based on Steel* (1962).
Mills, Frederick C., *Economic Tendencies and Behavior of Prices* (1927).
Nicholls, William H., *Price Policies in Cigarette Industry, 1911–1950* (1951).
Sage, G. H., *Basing-Point Pricing Systems* (1951).
Stocking, George W., *Basing Point Pricing and Regional Development: Iron and Steel Industry* (1954).
Warren, George F., Frank A. Pearson and H. Stoker, *Wholesale Prices, 1720–1932* (1932).

18.13.5 Foreign Trade

Adler, J. H., et al., *Pattern of Import Trade since 1923* (1952).
Bennett, Norman R., and George E. Brooks, Jr., eds., *New England Merchants in Africa: 1802–1865* (1966).
Benns, F. L., *American Struggle for British West India Carrying Trade* (1923).
Booth, Alan, "American Trade with South Africa, 1784–1832," *Essex Inst. Hist. Coll.,* 101 (1965), 83.
Bruchey, Stuart, "American Merchants in Foreign Trade in the Eighteenth and Early Nineteenth Centuries," *Bus. Hist. Rev.,* 32 (1958), 272.
Buck, Norman S., *Development of Anglo-American Trade* (1925).
Coatsworth, John H., "American Trade with European Colonies in Caribbean and South America, 1790–1812," *WMQ,* 3 ser., 24 (1967), 243.
Crosby, Alfred W., Jr., *America, Russia, Hemp, and Napoleon: American Trade with Russia and the Baltic, 1783–1812* (1965).
Dennett, Tyler, *Americans in Eastern Asia* (1941).
Duetsch, Karl W., and Alexander Eckstein, "National Industrialization and the Declining Share of the International Economic Sector, 1890–1959," *World Politics,* 13 (1961), 267.
Dulles, Foster R., *Old China Trade* (1930).
Helmers, Henrik O., *United States-Canadian Automobile Agreement* (1967).
Kolko, Gabriel, "American Business and Germany, 1930–1941," *West. Pol. Quar.,* 15 (1962), 713.
Krause, Lawrence B., *European Economic Integration and the United States* (1968).
Lipsey, Robert E., *Price and Quantity Trends in Foreign Trade* (1963).
McCreary, Edward A., *Americanization of Europe* (1964).
Mazur, Paul M., *America Looks Abroad* (1930).
Mintz, Ilse, *American Exports during Business Cycles, 1879–1958* (1961).
—— *Trade Balances during Business Cycles: U.S. and Britain since 1880* (1959).
National Industrial Conference Board, *Trends in Foreign Trade of United States* (1930).
Rothstein, Morton, "Antebellum Wheat and Cotton Exports," *Agric. Hist.,* 40 (1966), 91.
Rasch, Aage, "American Trade in Baltic, 1783–1807," *Scandinavian Econ. Hist. Rev.,* 13 (1965), 31.

Rowe, John W. F., *Primary Commodities in International Trade* (1965).
U.S. Department of Commerce; *The United States in the World Economy* (1943).
Williams, William A., "Mercantilism: American Political Economy, 1763 to 1828," *WMQ*, 3 ser., 15 (1958), 419.

* * * * * * *

Novack, David E. and Matthew Simon, "Commercial Responses to the American Export Invasion, 1871–1914: An Essay in Attitudinal History," *Explorations in Entrepreneurial Hist.*, 2 ser., 3 (1966), 121.

See also 18.14.5, Monetary History, for foreign exchange.

18.14 FINANCE

18.14.1 General

Brown, John C., *Hundred Years of Merchant Banking* (1909).
Carosso, Vincent P., et al., *Investment Banking in America: A History* (1970).
Chapman, John Martin, *Concentration of Banking* (1934).
Conant, C. A., and Marcus Nadler, *A History of Modern Banks of Issue* (6th ed., 1927).
Dewey, Davis R., *Financial History of the United States* (12th ed., 1934).
Fischer, Gerald C., *American Banking Structure* (1960).
Hammond, Bray, *Banks and Politics in America from the Revolution to the Civil War* (1957).
Helderman, Leonard C., *National and State Banks* (1931).
Knox, John J., *History of Banking in the United States* (1900).
Miller, Henry Edward, *Banking Theories before 1860* (1927).
Mints, Lloyd W., *History of Banking Theory in Great Britain and United States* (1945).
Myers, Margaret G., *A Financial History of the United States* (1970).
Redlich, Fritz, *Molding of American Banking* (2 vols., 1947–1951).
Schneider, Wilbert M., *American Bankers Association* (1956).
Schultz, W. J., and M. R. Caine, *Financial Development of the United States* (1937).
Secrist, Horace, *National Bank Failures and Non-Failures* (1938).
Stern, Siegfried, *United States in International Banking* (1951).
Trescott, Paul B., *Financing American Enterprise: The Story of Commercial Banking* (1963).
U.S. Congress. Senate. Committee on Banking and Currency, *Federal Banking Laws and Reports, 1780–1912* (1963).
Van Fenstermaker, Joseph, *Development of American Commercial Banking, 1782–1837* (1965).
———— *Statistical Summary of Commercial Banks Incorporated in the U.S. Prior to 1819* (1965).
Warburton, Clark, "Economic Growth and Banking Developments in United States from 1835 to 1885," *Jour. Econ. Hist.*, 18 (1958), 283.

See also 10.3 for biographies/writings of:

BANKERS AND FINANCIERS

Astor, John Jacob, 1763–1848
Baruch, Bernard M., 1870–1965
Belmont, August, 1816–1890
Biddle, Nicholas, 1786–1844
Bingham, William, 1752–1804
Cooke, Jay, 1821–1905
Corning, Erastus, 1794–1872

Cutler, Robert, 1895–
Davison, Henry P., 1867–1922
Du Pont, Alfred I., 1864–1935
Eccles, Marriner S., 1890–
Fisk, James, 1834–1872
Forbes, John M., 1813–1898
Girard, Stephen, 1750–1831
Gould, Jay, 1836–1892
Hall, James, 1793–1868
Higginson, Henry Lee, 1834–1919
James, John H., 1800–1881
Jones, Jesse H., 1874–1956
Kennedy, Joseph P., 1888–1969
Lehman, Herbert H., 1878–1963
McCullock, Hugh, 1808–1895
Mellon, Andrew, 1855–1937
Morgan, John Pierpont, 1837–1913
Morrow, Dwight, 1873–1931
Morton, Levi P., 1824–1920
Peabody, George F., 1852–1938
Perkins, George W., 1862–1920
Schiff, Jacob H., 1847–1920
Stillman, James, 1850–1918
Straight, Willard D., 1880–1918
Whitney, William C., 1841–1904
Willing, Thomas, 1731–1821
Young, Robert R., 1897–1958

18.14.2 State Banking

Andersen, Theodore A., *Century of Banking in Wisconsin* (1954).
Cable, J. Ray, *Bank of State of Missouri* (1923).
Caldwell, Stephen A., *Banking History of Louisiana* (1935).
Campbell, Claude A., *Development of Banking in Tennessee* (1932).
Chaddock, Robert E., *Safety Fund Banking System in New York, 1829–1866*
    (1910).
Cole, David M., *Development of Banking in District of Columbia* (1959).
Cross, I. B., *Financing an Empire: Banking in California* (4 vols., 1927).
Dewey, Davis R., *State Banking before the Civil War* (1910).
Dowrie, George W., *Development of Banking in Illinois, 1817–1863* (1913).
French, Bruce H., *Banking and Insurance in New Jersey* (1965).
Huntington, Charles C., "Banking and Currency in Ohio," *Ohio State Archaeol.
    and Hist. Quar.,* 24 (1915), 235.
James, Frank C., *Growth of Chicago Banks, 1816–1938* (2 vols., 1938).
Kuhn, William E., *History of Nebraska Banking* (1968).
Parsons, Francis, *History of Banking in Connecticut* (1935).
Stucki, Roland, *Commercial Banking in Utah, 1847–1966* (1967).

18.14.3 Specific Banks and Banking Houses

Berle, Adolf A., *The Bank that Banks Built: Savings Banks Trust Company,
    1933–1958* (1959).
Corey, Lewis, *House of Morgan* (1930).
Davis, Lance E., and Peter L. Payne, "Two Savings Banks," *Bus. Hist. Rev.,* 32
    (1958), 386.
Gras, Norman S. B., *Massachusetts First National Bank* (1937).
James, Marquis, and Bessie R. James, *Biography of a Bank: Bank of America* (1954).
McFerrin, John B., *Caldwell and Company: Southern Financial Empire* (1967).
Wainwright, Nicholas B., *History of the Philadelphia-National Bank, 1893–1953*
    (1953).

Wiebe, Robert H., "House of Morgan and the Executive, 1905–1913," *AHR*, 65 (1959), 49.

18.14.4 Federal Reserve System

Ahearn, Daniel S., *Federal Reserve Policy, 1951–1959* (1963).
Chandler, Lester V., "Federal Reserve Policy and Federal Debt," *Am. Econ. Rev.*, 39 (1949), 405.
Clark, Lawrence E., *Central Banking Under Federal Reserve System* (1935).
Clarke, Stephen V. O., *Central Bank Cooperation, 1924–1931* (1967).
Fforde, J. S., *Federal Reserve System, 1945–1949* (1954).
Groseclose, Elgin, *Fifty Years of Managed Money: The Federal Reserve, 1913–1963* (1965).
Harris, Seymour E., *Twenty Years of Federal Reserve Policy* (2 vols., 1933).
Knipe, James L., *Federal Reserve and the American Dollar, 1946–1964* (1965).
Laughlin, James L., *Federal Reserve Act* (1933).
Miller, A. C., "Responsibility for Federal Reserve Policies," *Am. Econ. Rev.*, 25 (1935), 442.
Warburg, Paul M., *Federal Reserve System* (2 vols., 1930).
Wicker, Elmus R., *Federal Reserve Monetary Policy, 1917–1933* (1966).

18.14.5 Monetary History

Barger, Harold, *Management of Money: American Experience* (1964).
Bloomfield, Arthur I., *Monetary Policy under International Gold Standard, 1880–1914* (1959).
Cagan, Phillip, *Determinants and Effects of Changes in Stock of Money, 1875–1960* (1965).
Davis, Lance E., and J. R. T. Hughes, "Dollar-Sterling Exchange, 1803–1895," *Econ. Hist. Rev.*, 13 (1960), 52.
Douglas, Paul H., *America in the Market Place: Trade, Tariffs, and the Balance of Payments* (1966).
Dunne, Gerald T., *Monetary Decisions of the Supreme Court* (1960).
Einzig, Paul, *Foreign Exchange Crises* (1968).
Friedman, Milton, and Anna J. Schwartz, *Monetary History of the United States, 1867–1960* (1963).
Goldenweiser, Emanuel A., *American Monetary Policy* (1951).
Harrod, Roy F., *The Dollar* (2nd ed., 1963).
Hepburn, Alonzo B., *History of Currency in the United States* (rev. ed., 1924).
Heilbroner, Robert L., *All Kinds of Money: Explanation of Our Country's Credit System* (1953).
Jackendoff, Nathaniel, *Money, Flow of Funds and Economic Policy* (1968).
Knipe, James L., *Federal Reserve and the American Dollar, 1946–1964* (1965).
Laughlin, James L., *History of Bimetalism* (1900).
Mayer, Thomas, *Monetary Policy in United States* (1968).
Nugent, Walter T. K., *Money and American Society, 1865–1880* (1968).
Nussbaum, Arthur, *Money in the Law* (rev. ed., 1950).
Tobin, James, "Monetary Interpretation of History," *Am. Econ. Rev.*, 55 (1965), 464.
Williamson, Jeffrey C., *American Growth and Balance of Payments* (1964).

See also 15.5, Government–Fiscal Policy.

18.14.6 Capital Formation and Investment

Abbott, Charles C., *New York Bond Market, 1920–1930* (1937).
Abramovitz, Moses, ed., *Capital Formation and Economic Growth* (1955).
Beckhart, B. H., ed., *New York Money Market* (4 vols., 1931–1932).
Bishop, George W. Jr., "Stock Prices," *Bus. Hist. Rev.*, 39 (1965), 403.
Carosso, Vincent P., et al., *Investment Banking in America: A History* (1970).

Copeland, Morris A., *Trends in Government Financing* (1961).
Cottle, Charles S., and Tate Whitman, *Corporate Earning Power and Market Valuation, 1935–1955* (1959).
Cowing, Cedric B., *Populists, Plungers and Progressives: History of Speculation, 1890–1936* (1965).
Creamer, Daniel B., et al., *Capital in Manufacturing and Mining* (1960).
Davis, Lance, "The Capital Markets and Industrial Concentration; The US and The UK, A Comparative Study," *Econ. Hist. Rev.* (1966), 255.
—— "New England Textile Mills and Capital Markets, 1840–1860," *Jour. Econ. Hist.*, 20 (1960), 1.
Edwards, George W., *Evolution of Finance Capitalism* (1938).
Goldsmith, Raymond W., *Financial Intermediaries in the American Economy since 1900* (1958).
—— *Flow of Capital Funds in Postwar Economy* (1965).
—— et al., *Study of Saving* (3 vols., 1955–1956).
Goodhart, C. A. E., *The New York Money Market and the Finance of Trade, 1900–1913* (1969).
Hickman, W. Braddock, *Corporate Bond Quality and Investor Experience* (1958). 1900–1943.
Homer, Sidney, and Richard I. Johannesen, *Price of Money, 1946–1969: United States and Foreign Interest Rates* (1969).
Juster, Francis T., *Household Capital Formation and Financing, 1867–1962* (1966).
Koch, Albert R., *Financing of Large Corporations, 1920–1939* (1943).
Kuznets, Simon, and Elizabeth Jenks, *Capital in the American Economy* (1961).
Myers, Margaret G., *New York Money Market* (1931).
Noyes, Alexander D., *Market Place* (1938).
Ripley, W. Z., *Main Street and Wall Street* (1927).
Smith, Alice E., *George Smith's Money: Scottish Investor* (1966).
Sobel, Robert, *Big Board: History of New York Stock Market* (1965).
—— *Great Bull Market: Wall Street in 1920's* (1968).
Ulmer, Melville J., *Capital in Transportation, Communications, and Public Utilities* (1960).

*　　*　　*　　*　　*　　*　　*

Cam, Gilbert A., *Survey of Literature on Investment Companies, 1864–1957* (1958).

18.14.6.1 American Investment Abroad

Aitken, Hugh G. J., *American Capital and Canadian Resources* (1961).
Brash, Donald T., *American Investment in Australian Industry* (1966).
Dakin, A. W., "Foreign Securities in the American Money Market," *Harv. Bus. Rev.*, 10 (1932), 227.
Hellmann, Rainer, *Amerika auf dem Europamarkt* (1966).
Johnstone, Allan W., *United States Direct Investment in France* (1965).
Kepner, C. D., and J. H. Soothill, *Banana Empire* (1935).
Kindleberger, Charles P., *American Business Abroad: Six Lectures on Direct Investment* (1969).
Kuczynski, R. R., *American Loans to Germany* (1927).
—— *Bankers' Profits from German Loans* (1927).
Lewis, Cleona, *America's Stake in International Investments* (1938).
Madden, John T., et al., *America's Experience as Creditor* (1937).
Marsh, Margaret A., *Bankers in Boliva* (1928).
Marshall, Herbert, et al., *Canadian-American Industry* (1936).
Mikesell, Raymond F., *U.S. Private and Government Investment Abroad* (1962).
Phelps, Clyde W., *Foreign Expansion of American Banks* (1927).
Pletcher, David M., *Rails, Mines and Progress: Seven American Promoters in Mexico, 1867–1911* (1958).
Remer, Charles F., *Foreign Investments In China* (1933).
Rippy, J. Fred *Capitalists and Columbia* (1931).
Southard, F. A., *American Industry in Europe* (1931).
U.S. Department of Commerce, *Handbook of American Underwriting of Foreign Securities, 1914–1929* (1930).

Vernon, Raymond, ed., *How Latin America Views the U.S. Investor* (1966).
Whitman, Marina V., *Government Risk-Sharing in Foreign Investment* (1965).
Winkler, Max, *Foreign Bonds* (1933).
———— *Investments of United States Capital in Latin America* (1929).

18.14.6.2 Foreign Investment in the United States

Clements, Roger V., "British Investment in the Trans-Mississippi West, 1870–1914," *Pac. Hist. Rev.*, 29 (1960), 35.
Hidy, Ralph W., *The House of Baring in American Trade and Finance: English Merchant Bankers at Work, 1763–1861* (1949).
Jackson, W. Turrentine, "British Impact on the Utah Mining Industry," *Utah Hist. Quar.*, 31 (1963), 347.
Jenks, Leland H., *Migration of British Capital* (1927).
McGrane, Reginald C., *Foreign Bondholders and American State Debts* (1935).
North, Douglass C., "International Capital and Development of American West," *Jour. Econ. Hist.*, 16 (1956), 493.
Spence, Clark C., *British Investments and American Mining Frontier, 1860–1901* (1958).
Taylor, Virginia H., *Franco-Texan Land Company* (1969).
Thomas, Brinley, *Migration and Economic Growth: Great Britain and Atlantic Economy* (1954).

18.14.7 Insurance

Buley, R. Carlyle, *American Life Convention: History of Life Insurance, 1906–1952* (2 vols., 1953).
———— *Equitable Life Assurance Society* (2 vols., 1967).
Clough, Shepard B., *Century of American Life Insurance: Mutual Life Insurance Company* (1946).
Considine, Robert, *Man against Fire: Fire Insurance* (1955).
James, Marquis, *Metropolitan Life* (1947).
Keller, Morton, *The Life Insurance Enterprise, 1885–1910: A Study in the Limits of Corporate Power* (1963).
Kimball, Spencer L., *Insurance and Public Policy* (1960).
Knight, Charles K., *Life Insurance in United States to 1870* (1920).
Stalson, J. Owen, *Marketing Life Insurance: Its History in America* (1942).
Todd, Alden L., *A Spark Lighted in Portland: Record of National Board of Fire Underwriters* (1966).
White, Gerald T., *History of Massachusetts Hospital Life Insurance Company* (1955).
Williamson, Harold F., and Orange A. Smalley, *Northwestern Mutual Life: A Century of Trusteeship* (1957).

18.15 INDUSTRY

18.15.1 General

Adams, Walter, ed., *Structure of American Industry: Some Case Studies* (rev. ed., 1954).
Bishop, James L., *History of American Manufactures from 1608 to 1860* (3 vols., rev. ed. 1868).
Bliss, C. A., *Structure of Manufacturing Production* (1939).
Bowden, Witt, *Industrial History of the United States* (1930).
Burns, Arthur F., *Production Trends since 1870* (1934).
Chandler, Alfred D., Jr., *Strategy and Structure: The Industrial Enterprise* (1962).
Clark, Victor S., *History of Manufactures in United States* (rev. ed., 3 vols., 1929).
Day, E. E., and Woodlief Thomas, *Growth of Manufactures 1899–1923* (1928).
Fabricant, Solomon, *Output of Manufacturing 1899–1937* (1940).
Fisher, Marvin M., *Workship in the Wilderness: European Response to American Industrialization, 1830–1860* (1967).

Frickey, Edwin, *Production in the United States, 1860–1914* (1947).

Fuchs, Victor R., *Changes in Location of Manufacturing since 1929* (1962).

Glover, John G., and William B. Cornell, eds., *Development of American Industries* (3d ed., 1951).

Green, Constance M., *Holyoke, Massachusetts: A Case History of the Industrial Revolution in America* (1939).

Harris, Chauncy D., "The Market as a Factor in the Localization of Industry in the United States," Assoc. of Am. Geographers, *Annals,* (1954), 315.

Kirkland, Edward C., *Industry Comes of Age, 1860–1897* (1961).

Shlakman, Vera, *Economic History of a Factory Town: Chicopee, Massachusetts* (1935).

Tryon, Rolla M., *Household Manufactures in the United States, 1640–1860: A Study in Industrial History* (1917).

Vance, Stanley, *American Industries* (1955).

See also 29.1.4, Science in Industry; 29.2, Technology.

18.15.2 Aircraft and Automobiles

Beasley, Norman, and G. W. Stark, *Made in Detroit* (1957).

Chandler, Alfred D., Jr., *Giant Enterprise: Ford, General Motors, and the Automobile Industry* (1964).

Denison, Merrill, *The Power to Go: Story of the Automotive Industry* (1956).

Edwards, Charles E., *Dynamics of the United States Automobile Industry* (1965).

Flink, James J., *America Adopts the Automobile, 1895–1910* (1970).

Greenleaf, William, *Monopoly on Wheels: Henry Ford and the Selden Automobile Patent* (1961).

Helmers, Henrik O., *United States-Canadian Automobile Agreement* (1967).

Nader, Ralph, *Unsafe at Any Speed* (1965).

Nevins, Allan, and Frank E. Hill, *Ford* (3 vols., 1954–1962).

Rae, John B., *American Automobile* (1965).

––––––– *American Automobile Manufacturers* (1959).

––––––– *Climb to Greatness: Aircraft Industry, 1920–1960* (1968).

Wilkins, Mira, and Frank E. Hill, *American Business Abroad: Ford* (1964).

See also 10.3 for biographies/writings of:

Chrysler, Walter, P., 1875–1940
Ford, Henry, 1863–1947
Ford, Henry, II, 1917–
Olds, Ransom E., 1864–1950

18.15.3 Chemicals

Dorian, Max, *Du Ponts: From Gunpowder to Nylon* (1962).

Dutton, W. S., *Du Pont* (1942).

Haber, Ludwig F., *Chemical Industry during the Nineteenth Century* (1958).

Haynes, Williams, *American Chemical Industries* (6 vols., 1945–1954).

Hollander, Samuel, *The Sources of Increased Efficiency: Dupont Rayon Plants* (1965).

Van Gelder, A. P., and Hugo Schlatter, *Explosives Industry* (1927).

18.15.4 Construction

Ambromovitz, Moses, *Evidences of Long Swings in Aggregate Construction since the Civil War* (1964).

Condit, Carl W., *American Building Art* (2 vols., 1960–1961).

Maxwell, W. F., "The Building Industry since the War," *Rev. Econ. Stat.,* 13 (1931), 68.

Meyerson, Martin, et al., *Housing, People, and Cities* (1962).

Randall, Frank A., *History of Development of Building Construction in Chicago* (1949).

See also 28.8.7, Architecture–Construction.

18.15.5 Electrical Manufacturing

Bennett, Howard F., *Precision Power: Bodine Electric Company* (1959).
Bright, Arthur A., *Electric-Lamp Industry: Technological Change and Economic Development from 1800 to 1947* (1949).
Hammond, John W., *Men and Volts: Story of General Electric* (1941).
Loth, David G., *Swope of G.E.: Gerard Swope and General Electric in American Business* (1958).
MacLaren, Malcolm, *Rise of the Electrical Industry during the Nineteenth Century* (1943).
Passer, Harold C., *The Electrical Manufacturers, 1875–1900: A Study in Competition, Entrepreneurship, Technical Change, and Economic Growth* (1953).

18.15.6 Fisheries and Whaling

Ackerman, Edward Augustus, *New England's Fishing Industry* (1941).
Hohman, E. P., *The American Whaleman* (1928).
Innis, H. A., *The Cod Fisheries* (rev. ed., 1954).
McFarland, Raymond, *A History of the New England Fisheries* (1911).
Moment, David, "Business of Whaling in America in 1850's" *Bus. Hist. Rev.*, 31 (1957), 261.
Stackpole, Edouard A., *Sea-Hunters: New England Whalemen, 1635–1835* (1953).
Tower, W. S., *A History of the American Whale Fishery* (1907).

18.15.7 Food and Beverages

Arnold, John P., and Frank Penman, *Brewing Industry* (1933).
Arrington, Leonard J., *Beet Sugar in West: Utah–Idaho Sugar Company, 1891–1966* (1966).
———— "Western Beet Sugar Industry," *Agric. Hist.*, 41 (1967), 1.
Baron, Stanley, *Brewed in America: A History of Beer and Ale in the United States* (1962).
Blakey, R. G., *United States Beet Sugar Industry* (1912).
Carosso, Vincent P., *California Wine Industry, 1830–1895* (1951).
Carson, Gerald, *Cornflake Crusade* (1957).
Cochran, Thomas C., *Pabst Brewing Company: History of an American Business* (1948).
Collins, James H., *Canned Foods* (1924).
Corey, Lewis, *Meat and Man: Monopoly, Unionism and Food Policy* (1949).
Eichner, Alfred S., *Emergence of Oligopoly: Sugar Refining as a Case Study* (1969).
Frantz, Joe B., *Gail Borden: Dairyman to a Nation* (1951).
Hampe, Edward C., Jr., and Merle Wittenberg, *Lifeline of America: Food Industry* (1964).
Kuhlmann, C. B., *Development of the Flour Milling Industry in the United States* (1929).
Nixon, H. C., "Rise of Cottonseed Oil Industry," *Jour. Pol. Econ.*, 38 (1930), 73.
Panschar, William G., and Charles C. Slater, *Baking in America* (2 vols., 1956).
Sitterson, J. Carlyle, *Sugar Country: Cane Sugar Industry in the South, 1753–1950* (1953).
Slater, Charles C., *Economic Changes in the Baking Industry* (1958).
Steen, Herman, *Flour Milling in America* (1963).
Storck, John, and Walter D. Teague, *Flour for Man's Bread: History of Milling* (1952).
Thornton, H. J., *Quaker Oats Company* (1933).

Weber, G. M., and C. L. Alsberg, *American Vegetable-Shortening Industry* (1934).

18.15.8 Iron and Steel

Bridge, J. H., *Carnegie Steel Company* (1903).
Broude, Henry W., *Steel Decisions and National Economy* (1963).
Bruce, Kathleen, *Virginia Iron Manufacture in Slave Era* (1930).
Burn, Duncan L., *Economic History of Steelmaking* (1940).
Butler, Joseph G., Jr., *Fifty Years of Iron and Steel* (1923).
Cappon, Lester J., "Southern Iron Industry," *Jour. Econ. and Bus. Hist.,* 2 (1930), 353.
Chapman, Herman H., et al., *Iron and Steel Industries of South* (1953).
Cotter, Arundel, *Authentic History of United States Steel Corporation* (1916).
Fuller, Justin, "From Iron to Steel; Alabama's Industrial Revolution," *Ala. Rev.,* 17 (1964), 137.
Hunter, Louis C., "Influence of Market upon Technique in the Iron Industry," *Jour. Econ. and Bus. Hist.,* 1 (1929), 241.
Lander, Ernest M., Jr., "The Iron Industry in Ante-Bellum South Carolina," *JSH,* 20 (1954), 337.
Norris, James D., *Frontier Iron: Maramec Iron Works, 1826–1876* (1964).
Pierce, Arthur D., *Family Empire in Jersey Iron: Richards Enterprises* (1964).
Ransom, James M., *Vanishing Ironworks of New Jersey-New York Border* (1966).
Rodgers, Allan, "Industrial Inertia—Major Factor in the Location of Steel Industry in United States," *Geog. Rev.,* 42 (1952), 56.
Rowe, Frank H., *History of Iron and Steel Industry in Scioto County* (1938).
Schroeder, Gertrude G., *Growth of Major Steel Companies, 1900–1950* (1953).
Temin, Peter, *Iron and Steel in Nineteenth Century America* (1964).
Wertime, Theodore A., *Coming of Age of Steel* (1962).
Walker, Joseph E., *Hopewell Village: A Social and Economic History of an Iron-making Community* (1966).

See also 29.2.6, Metallurgy.

18.15.9 Leather and Shoes

Allen, Frederick J., *Shoe Industry* (1922).
Hazard, B. E., *Organization of Boot and Shoe Industry* (1921).
Hoover, Edgar M., Jr., *Location Theory and the Shoe and Leather Industries* (1937).
McDermott, Charles H., ed., *A History of the Shoe and Leather Industries* (2 vols., 1920).
Welsh, Peter C., *Tanning in United States to 1850* (1964).

18.15.10 Lumbering

Defebaugh, J. E., *History of the Lumber Industry of America* (2 vols., 1906–1907).
Fries, Robert F., *Empire in Pine: Lumbering in Wisconsin, 1830–1900* (1951).
Hempstead, A. G., *Penobscot Boom* (1931).
Hickman, Nollie, *Mississippi Harvest: Lumbering, 1840–1915* (1962).
Hidy, Ralph W., et al., *Timber and Men: Weyerhauser Story* (1963).
Hurst, J. Willard, *Law and Economic Growth: History of Lumber Industry in Wisconsin, 1836–1915* (1964).
Larson, Agnes M., *History of the White Pine Industry* (1949).
Lewis, Martin D., *Lumberman from Flint: Henry H. Crapo, 1855–1869* (1958).
Moore, John H., *Andrew Brown and Cypress Lumbering in Old Southwest* (1967).
Rector, William G., *Log Transportation in Lake States Lumber Industry, 1840–1918* (1953).
Reynolds, Arthur R., *Daniel Shaw Lumber Company: Wisconsin* (1957).
Schenck, Carl A., *Biltmore Story: Beginning of Forestry* (1955).

Steer, Henry B., *Lumber Production in United States, 1799–1946* (1948).
Wood, Richard G., *History of Lumbering in Maine* (1935).

*   *   *   *   *   *   *

Miller, Joseph A., *Pulp and Paper History: Selected List of Publications in the History of the Industry in North America* (1966).

18.15.11 Mining

Armes, Ethel, *Story of Coal and Iron in Alabama* (1910).
Arrington, Leonard J., "Commercial Mining," *Utah Hist. Quar.,* 31 (1963), 192.
Barger, Harold, and S. H. Schurr, *Mining Industries, 1899–1939* (1944).
Christenson, C. L., *Economic Redevelopment in Bituminous Coal, 1930–1960* (1962).
Davis, Edward W., *Pioneering with Taconite* (1964).
Eavenson, Howard N., *First Century and a Quarter of American Coal Industry* (1942).
Fisher, Waldo E., and Charles M. James, *Minimum Price Fixing in Bituminous Coal* (1955).
Gates, William B., Jr., *Michigan Copper and Boston Dollars* (1951).
Hansen, Gary B., "Copper in Utah," *Utah Hist. Quar.,* 31 (1963), 262.
Henderson, James M., *Efficiency of the Coal Industry* (1958).
Ingalls, W. R., *Lead and Zinc* (1908).
Kelley, Robert L., *Gold vs. Grain: Hydraulic Mining Controversy in California's Sacramento Valley: A Chapter in the Decline of the Concept of Laissez Faire* (1959).
Lambie, Joseph T., *From Mine to Market: Coal Transportation on the Norfolk and Western Railway* (1954).
Maddala, G. S., "Productivity and Technological Change in the Bituminous Coal Industry, 1919–1954," *Jour. Pol. Econ.,* 73 (1965), 352.
Moyer, Reed, *Competition in Midwestern Coal Industry* (1964).
Norris, James D., *American Zinc Company* (1968).
Parker, Watson, *Gold in the Black Hills* (1966).
Rickard, Thomas A., *The History of American Mining* (1932).
Sprague, Marshall, *Money Mountain: Cripple Creek Gold* (1953).
Spencer, Vivian E., *Production, Employment and Productivity in the Mineral Extractive Industries* (1940).
Tams, W. P., *The Smokeless Coal Fields of West Virginia* (1963).
Weiss, Harry B., and Grace M. Weiss, *Old Copper Mines of New Jersey* (1963).
Wirth, F. P., *Minnesota Iron Lands* (1937).
Wright, James E., *Galena Lead District: Federal Policy and Practice, 1824–1847* (1967).
Yearley, Clifton K., Jr., *Enterprise and Anthracite: Schuylkill County, 1820–1875* (1961).

*   *   *   *   *   *   *

McCarty, J., "Suggestions for Economic History of North American Mining in the Nineteenth Century," in Norman Harper, ed., *Pacific Circle* (1968).
Munn, Robert F., *The Coal Industry in America: A Bibliography and Guide to Studies* (1965).

See also 10.3 for biographies/writings of:

Agassiz, Alexander, 1835–1910
Sutro, Adolph, 1830–1898
Thompson, William B., 1869–1930
Tower, Charlemagne, 1848–1923

See also 13.4.10, Frontier Mining.

18.15.12 Petroleum

Beaton, Kendall, *Enterprise in Oil: Shell* (1957).

Chalmers, David M., "Standard Oil and Business Historian," *Am. Jour. Econ. and Sociol.,* 20 (1960), 47.

Clark, J. Stanley, *The Oil Century* (1958).

Destler, Chester M., *Roger Sherman and the Independent Oil Men* (1967). Standard Oil.

Engler, Robert, *Politics of Oil* (1961).

Enos, John L., *Petroleum Progress and Profits* (1962).

Fanning, Leonard M., *American Oil Operations* (1947).

────── *Rise of American Oil* (1936).

Gibb, George S., and Evelyn H. Knowlton, *History of Standard Oil Company, 1911–1927* (1956).

Giddens, Paul H., *Birth of Oil Industry* (1938).

────── *Early Days of Oil* (1948).

────── *Standard Oil Company (Indiana)* (1956).

Hamilton, Daniel C., *Competition in Oil: Gulf Coast Refinery Market, 1925–1950* (1958).

Hidy, Ralph W., "Implications of Recent Literature on Petroleum Industry," *Bus. Hist. Rev.,* 30 (1956), 329.

────── and Muriel E. Hidy, *Pioneering in Big Business, 1882–1911: Standard Oil Company* (1955).

Ise, John, *United States Oil Policy* (1926).

Johnson, Arthur M., *The Development of American Petroleum Pipelines: A Study in Private Enterprise and Public Policy, 1862–1959* (2 vols., 1956–1967).

Larson, Henrietta M., and Kenneth W. Porter, *History of Humble Oil and Refining Company* (1959).

Leeston, Alfred M., et. al., *The Dynamic Natural Gas Industry* (1963).

Loos, John L., *Oil on Stream! Interstate Oil Pipe Line Company, 1909–1959* (1959).

Nash, Gerald D., *United States Oil Policy, 1890–1964* (1969).

Neuner, Edward J., *Natural Gas Industry: Monopoly and Competition in the Field Market* (1960).

Rister, Carl C., *Oil! Titan of Southwest* (1949).

Stocking, G. W., *Oil Industry and Competitive System* (1925).

Tarbell, Ida M., *Standard Oil Company* (1904); David Chalmers, ed. (abr., ed. 1966).

White, Gerald T., *Formative Years in the Far West: Standard Oil Company of California through 1919* (1962).

Williamson, Harold F., and Arnold R. Daum, *American Petroleum Industry, 1859–1959* (2 vols., 1959–1963).

18.15.13 Public Utilities

Bauer, John, and Nathaniel Gold, *Electric Power Industry* (1939).

Buchanan, N. S., "Origin and Development of Public Utility Holding Company," *Jour. Pol. Econ.,* 44 (1936), 31.

Burns, Arthur R., and Walter E. Caine, *Electric Power and Government Policy* (1948).

Coon, Horace, *American Tel. & Tel.* (1939).

Danielian, N. R., *A. T. & T.* (1939).

Firth, Robert E., *Public Power in Nebraska: Report on State Ownership* (1962).

Glaeser, Martin G., *Public Utilities in American Capitalism* (1957).

Gould, Jacob M., *Output and Productivity in Electric and Gas Utilities, 1899–1942* (1946).

McDonald, Forrest, *Let There Be Light: Electric Utility Industry in Wisconsin, 1881–1955* (1957).

Martin, Thomas W., *Forty Years of Alabama Power Company, 1911–1951* (1952).

Miller, Raymond C., *Kilowatts at Work: Detroit Edison Company* (1957).

Silverberg, Robert, *Light for the World: Edison and the Power Industry* (1967).

Thompson, Robert L., *Wiring a Continent: History of the Telegraph Industry, 1832–1866* (1947).

Walsh, Joseph L., *Connecticut Pioneers in Telephony: Origin and Growth of the Telephone Industry* (1950).
Waterman, M. H., *Financial Policies of Public Utility Holding Companies* (1932).

18.15.14 Textiles

Armstrong, John B., *Factory under the Elms: History of Harrisville, New Hampshire, 1774–1969* (1969).
Bendure, Zelma, and Gladys Pfeiffer, *America's Fabrics* (1946).
Blicksilver, Jack, *Cotton Manufacturing in Southeast: Historical Analysis* (1959).
Bruchey, Stuart, ed., *Cotton and the Growth of the American Industry, 1790–1860: Sources and Readings* (1967).
Cohn, David L., *Life and Times of King Cotton* (1956).
Cole, Arthur H., and W. F. Williamson, *The American Carpet Manufacture* (1941).
Cole, Arthur H., *The American Wool Manufacture* (2 vols., 1926).
Coleman, Peter J., "Rhode Island Cotton Manufacturing," *R.I. Hist.*, 23 (1964), 65.
Copeland, M. T., *The Cotton Manufacturing Industry in the United States* (1913).
Crockett, Norman L., *The Woolen Industry of the Midwest* (1970).
Ewing, John S., and Nancy P. Norton, *Broadlooms and Businessmen: Bigelow-Sanford Carpet Company* (1955).
Gibo, George S., *The Saco-Lowell Shops: Textile Machinery Building in New England, 1813–1949* (1950).
Griffin, Richard W., "Industrial Revolution in Maryland: Textile Industry, 1789–1826," *Md. Hist. Mag.*, 61 (1966), 24.
Jewkes, John and Sylvia, "Hundred Years of Change in Cotton Industry," *Jour. Law and Econ.*, 9 (1966), 115.
Josephson, Hannah, *Golden Threads: New England Mill Girls and Magnates* (1949).
Knowlton, Evelyn H., *Pepperell's Progress: Cotton Textile Company, 1844–1945* (1948).
Lander, Ernest M., *Textile Industry in Antebellum South Carolina* (1969).
Lemert, Benjamin F., *Cotton Textile Industry of Southern Appalachian Piedmont* (1933).
McGouldrick, Paul F., *New England Textiles in the Nineteenth Century: Profits and Investment* (1968).
Matsui, Shichiro, *History of the Silk Industry in the United States* (1930).
Mitchell, Broadus, *Rise of Cotton Mills in South* (1921).
Moore, John H., "Mississippi's Ante-Bellum Textile Industry," *Jour. Miss. Hist.*, 16 (1954), 81.
Morris, James A., *Woolen and Worsted Manufacturing in Southern Piedmont* (1952).
Smith, Robert S., *Mill on the Dan: Dan River Mills, 1882–1950* (1960).
Smith, Thomas R., *Cotton Textile Industry of Fall River, Massachusetts* (1944).
Ware, Caroline F., *Early New England Cotton Manufacture* (1931).

18.15.15 Miscellaneous Industries

Baer, W. N., *Cigar Industry* (1933).
Brayley, Arthur W., *History of the Granite Industry of New England* (2 vols., 1913).
Cowles, Alfred, *True Story of Aluminum* (1958).
Coyne, Franklin E., *Development of the Cooperage Industry, 1620–1940* (1940).
Cummings, Richard O., *American Ice Harvests* (1949).
Davis, Pearce, *Development of American Glass Industry* (1949).
Deyrup, Felicia J., *Arms Makers of Connecticut Valley, 1798–1870* (1948).
Eastman, Whitney, *History of Linseed Oil Industry in the United States* (1968).
Gibb, George S., *Whitesmiths of Taunton: A History of Reed & Barton, Silversmiths, 1824–1943* (1943).
Goyne, Nancy A., "Britannia in America: The Introduction of a New Alloy and a New Industry," *Winterthur Portfolio*, 2 (1965), 160.

Howard, Frank A., and Ralph Wolf, *Rubber* (1936).
Hussey, Miriam, *From Merchants to "Colour Men": Samuel Wetherill's White Lead Business* (1956).
Lathrop, William G., *Brass Industry* (1926).
Moore, Charles W., *Timing a Century: Waltham Watch Company* (1945).
Morison, Samuel E., *Ropemakers of Plymouth* (1950).
Rainwater, Dorothy T., *American Silver Manufacturers* (1966).
Rodgers, William H., *Think: Biography of the Watsons and IBM* (1969).
Scoville, Warren C., *Revolution in Glass-Making:Entrepreneurship and Technological Change in the American Industry, 1880–1920* (1948).
Taber, Martha V., *History of the Cutlery Industry in Connecticut Valley* (1955).
Tennant, Richard B., *American Cigarette Industry: Economic Analysis and Public Policy* (1950).
Tilley, Nannie M., *Bright-Tobacco Industry, 1860–1929* (1948).
Tyler, David B., *American Clyde: Iron and Steel Shipbuilding on the Delaware from 1840 to World War I* (1958).
Weeks, L. H., *A History of Paper Manufacturing in the United States 1690–1916* (1916).
Woodruff, R. J., "American Hosiery Industry," *Jour. Econ. and Bus. Hist.*, 4 (1931), 18.

* * * * * * *

Miller, Joseph A., *Pulp and Paper History: Selected List of Publications in the History of the Industry in North America* (1966).

See also 27.4, Book Publishing; 29.3.8, Pharmacy and the Drug Industry.

18.16 TRANSPORTATION

18.16.1 General

Ambler, Charles H., *History of Transportation in the Ohio Valley* (1932).
Barger, Harold, *Transportation Industries, 1899–1946* (1951).
Chinitz, Benjamin, *Freight and the Metropolis: The Impact of America's Transport Revolutions on the New York Region* (1960).
Dunbar, Seymour, *History of Travel in America* (4 vols., 1915).
Gebhard, W. F., *Transportation and Industrial Development in the Middle West* (1900).
Goodrich, Carter, *Government Promotion of American Canals and Railroads, 1800–1890* (1960).
Haefele, Edwin T., ed., *Transport and National Goals* (1969).
Hill, Forest G., *Roads, Rails and Waterways: Army Engineers and Transportation* (1957).
Kirkland, Edward C., *Men, Cities and Transportation: A Study in New England History, 1820–1900* (2 vols., 1948).
Lebergott, Stanley, "United States Transport Advance," *Jour. Econ. Hist.*, 26 (1966), 437.
Meyer, Balthasar H., et al., *History of Transportation Before 1860* (1917).
Meyer, John R., et al., *The Economics of Competition in the Transportation Industries* (1959).
Phillips, Ulrich B., *History of Transportation in Eastern Cotton Belt* (1908).
Rubin, Julius, *Canal or Railroad? Response to Erie Canal* (1961).
Taylor, George R., *Transportation Revolution, 1815–1860* (1951).
Winther, Oscar O., *Transportation: Trans-Mississippi West 1865–1890* (1964).

18.16.2 Early Roads and Turnpikes

Colles, Christopher, *Survey of Roads of America, 1789,* Walter W. Ristow, ed. (1961).
Durrenberger, J. A., *Turnpikes* (1931).
Hulbert, A. B., *Historic Highways of America* (16 vols., 1902–1905).

——— *Paths of Inland Commerce* (1920).

Hunter, Robert F., "Turnpike Construction in Antebellum Virginia," *Tech. and Cult.*, 4 (1963), 177.

Jackson, W. Turrentine, *Wagon Roads West: A Study of Federal Road Surveys and Construction in the Trans-Mississippi West, 1846–1869* (1952).

Moorhead, Max L., *New Mexico's Royal Road: Chihuahua Trail* (1958).

Prucha, Francis Paul, *Broadax and Bayonet: Army in the Northwest, 1815–1860* (1953).

Pusey, W. A., *Wilderness Road* (1921).

Searight, T. B., *Old Pike, History of National Road* (1894).

Wood, Frederick J., *Turnpikes of New England* (1919).

See also 13.4.5, Westward Expansion and the Frontier–Trails.

18.16.3 Stagecoaches and Express Business

Berkebile, Don H., *Conestoga Wagons in Braddock's Campaign, 1755* (1959).

Boot, Frank A., and W. B. Connelley, *Overland Stage to California* (1901).

Bradley, Glenn D., *Story of the Pony Express* (1913).

Coleman, John W., *Stage Coach Days in Blue Grass* (1935).

Conkling, Roscoe P., and Margaret B. Conkling, *Butterfield Overland Mail, 1857–1869* (3 vols., 1947).

Hafen, Leroy R., *Overland Mail* (1926).

Hungerford, Edward, *Wells Fargo* (1947).

Jackson, W. Turrentine, "Wells Fargo, Stagecoaches, and Pony Express," *Calif. Hist. Soc. Quar.*, 45 (1966), 291.

Moody, Ralph, *Stagecoach West* (1967).

Settle, Raymond W., and Mary L. Settle, *War Drums and Wagon Wheels: Russell, Majors and Waddell* (1966).

Shumway, George, Edward Durell, and Howard C. Frey, *Conestoga Wagon 1750–1850* (2nd ed., 1966).

Strahorn, C. A., *Fifteen Thousand Miles by Stage* (1911).

Walker, Henry P., *Wagonmasters: High Plains Freighting to 1880* (1966).

Wallace, Paul A., *Indian Paths of Pennsylvania* (1965).

Wiltsee, E. A., *Pioneer Miner and the Pack Mule Express* (1931).

18.16.4 Modern Highways and Motor Transport

Cleveland, Reginald M., and S. T. Williamson, *Road is Yours* (1951).

Dearing, C. L., *American Highway Policy* (1941).

Friedlaender, Ann F., *Interstate Highway System: A Study in Public Investment* (1966).

Halprin, Lawrence, *Freeways* (1966).

Harper, Donald V., *Economic Regulation of the Trucking Industry by States* (1959).

Karolevitz, Robert F., *This Was Trucking* (1966).

Kendrick, Bayard H., *Florida Trails to Turnpikes, 1914–1964* (1964).

Labatut, Jean, and Wheaton J. Lane, eds., *Highways in Our National Life: A Symposium* (1950).

Mowbray, A. Q., *Road to Ruin* (1969).

Oliver, Smith H., and D. H. Berkebile, *Smithsonian Collection of Automobiles and Motorcycles* (1968).

Taft, Charles A., *Commercial Motor Transportation* (rev. ed., 1955).

18.16.5 Water Transport

18.16.5.1 Maritime History

Albion, Robert G., *National Shipping Authority: Origin and Early Development* (1953).

——— *Rise of New York Port, 1815–60* (1939).

———— *Seaports South of Sahara: Achievements of an American Steamship Service* (1959).

Baker, William A., *History of Boston Marine Society* (1968).

Bowen, Frank C., *Century of Atlantic Travel* (1930).

Bryant, Samuel W., *Sea and States: Maritime History* (1967).

Bunting, William H., *Portrait of a Port: Boston, 1852–1914* (1971).

Colby, Charles C., *North Atlantic Arena: Water Transport* (1966).

Cutler, Carl C., *Queens of the Western Ocean: Mail and Passenger Sailing Lines* (1961).

Gorter, Wytze, and George H. Hildebrand, Jr., *Pacific Coast Maritime Shipping Industry, 1930–1948* (2 vols., 1952–1954).

Hutchins, J. G. B., *The American Maritime Industries and Public Policy, 1789–1914: An Economic History* (1941).

Liu, Kwang-ching, *Anglo-American Steamship Rivalry in China* (1962).

Matthews, Frederick C., *American Merchant Ships* (1930–1931).

Meeker, Royal, *History of Shipping Subsidies* (1905).

Morison, Samuel E., *Maritime History of Massachusetts, 1783–1860* (1921).

Nichols, Roy F., *Advance Agents of American Destiny* (1956).

Rowe, William H., *Maritime History of Maine* (1948).

Tyler, David B., *Steam Conquers Atlantic* (1939).

*   *   *   *   *   *   *

Marine History Association, *Untapped Sources and Research Opportunities in Field of American Maritime History: A Symposium at G. W. Blunt White Library* (1966).

See also 10.3 for biographies/writings of:

SHIPBUILDERS

McKay, Donald, 1810–1880

Roach, John, 1813–1887

18.16.5.2 Sailing Ships and Steam Vessels

Albion, Robert G., *Square Riggers on Schedule* (1938).

Bathe, Greville, *Rise and Decline of the Paddle Wheel* (1962).

Burgess, Robert H., and H. Graham Wood, *Steamboats Out of Baltimore* (1968).

Bruke, J. G., "Bursting Boilers and Federal Power," [1816–1852] *Tech. and Cult.*, 7 (1966), 1.

Chapelle, Howard I., *The Baltimore Clipper* (1930).

———— *The History of American Sailing Ships* (1935).

Cutler, Carl C., *Greyhound of the Sea: The Story of the American Clipper Ship* (1930).

Fairburn, William A., *Merchant Sail* (6 vols, 1945–1955).

Flexner, James T., *Steamboats Come True* (1944).

Hunter, Louis C., *Steamboats on the Western Rivers: An Economic and Technological History* (1949).

Laing, A. K., *Clipper Ship Men* (1944).

Lass, William E., *History of Steamboating on the Upper Missouri* (1962).

Lowrey, Walter M., "The Engineers and The Mississippi," *Louisiana Hist.*, 5 (1964), 233.

Morrison, John H., *History of American Steam Navigation* (1903).

Petersen, William J., *Steamboating on the Upper Mississippi* (1937).

Ridgely-Nevitt, Cedric, "'Steam Boat,' 1807–1814," *Am. Neptune*, 27 (1967), 5.

Robinson, John, and George F. Dow, *Sailing Ships of New England, 1607–1907* (1953).

18.16.5.3 Inland Waterways

Baldwin, Leland D., *Keelboat Age on Western Waters* (1941).

Bishop, Auard L., *State Works of Pennsylvania* (1907).

Dunaway, W. F., *History of James River and Kanawha Company* (1922).

Goodrich, Carter, ed., *Canals and American Economic Development* (1961).

Gray, Ralph D., *National Waterway: Chesapeake and Delaware Canal, 1769–1965* (1967).

Harlow, Alvin F., *Old Towpaths* (1926).

Hartsough, Mildred L., *From Canoe to Steel Barge on Upper Mississippi* (1934).

Jones, Chester L., *Economic History of Anthracite-Tidewater Canals* (1908).

Mills, James C., *Our Inland Seas, Their Shipping and Commerce for Three Centuries* (1910).

Putnam, James W., *Illinois and Michigan Canal* (1918).

Quick, Herbert, *American Inland Waterways* (1909).

Rae, J. B., "Federal Land Grants in Aid of Canals," *Jour. Econ. Hist.,* 4 (1944), 167.

Ransom, Roger L., "Canals and Development," *Am. Econ. Rev.,* 54 (1964), 365.

Roberts, Christopher, *Middlesex Canal* (1938).

Sanderlin, Walter S., *Great National Project: Chesapeake and Ohio Canal* (1946).

Scheiber, Harry N., *Ohio Canal Era: A Case Study of Government and the Economy, 1820–1861* (1969).

Shaw, Ronald E., *Erie Water West: Erie Canal, 1792–1854* (1966).

Still, John S., "Ethan Allen Brown and Ohio's Canal System," *Ohio Hist. Quar.,* 66 (1957), 22.

Waggoner, Madeline S., *Long Haul West: Canal Era, 1817–1850* (1958).

Whitford, N. E., *History of Barge Canal of New York State* (1922).

See also 10.3 for biography/writings of:

Clinton, De Witt, 1769–1828

18.16.5.4 Panama Canal

DuVal, Miles P., Jr., *And the Mountains Will Move: The Panama Canal* (1947).

Padelford, Norman J., *Panama Canal in Peace and War* (1942).

Smith, Darrell H., *Panama Canal: Its History, Activities and Organization* (1927).

See also 10.3 for biographies/writings of:

Goethals, George W., 1858–1928
Roosevelt, Theodore, 1858–1919

18.16.6 Railroads

18.16.6.1 General

Bruce, Alfred W., *The Steam Locomotive in America, Its Development in the Twentieth Century* (1952).

Chandler, Alfred D., Jr., ed., *The Railroads: Sources and Readings* (1965).

Haney, L. H., *Congressional History of Railways* (2 vols., 1908–1910). Covers the period to 1887.

Hultgren, Thor, *American Transportation in Prosperity and Depression* (1948).

Lyon, Peter, *To Hell in a Day Coach: American Railroads* (1968).

Stover, John F., *American Railroads* (1961).

—— *Life and Decline of the American Railroad* (1970).

Taylor, George R., and Irene D. Neu, *The American Railroad Network, 1861–1890* (1956).

Thompson, Slason, *American Railways* (1925).

Ullman, Edward L., "Railroad Pattern of the United States," *Geog. Rev.,* 39 (1949), 242.

White, John H., Jr., *American Locomotives: An Engineering History, 1830–1880* (1968).

See also 10.3 for biographies/writings of:

Adams, Charles Francis, Jr., 1835–1915
Cooke, Jay, 1821–1905

Corbin, Daniel C., 1837–1918
Depew, Chauncey M., 1834–1928
Dodge, Grenville M., 1831–1916
Forbes, John M., 1813–1898
Gowen, Franklin B., 1836–1889
Grinnell, Josiah B., 1821–1891
Harriman, Edward H., 1848–1909
Hill, James J., 1838–1916
Holladay, Ben, 1819–1887
Huntington, Henry E., 1850–1927
James, John H., 1800–1881
Morgan, Charles, 1795–1878
Poor, Henry Varnum, 1812–1905
Vanderbilt, Cornelius, 1794–1877
Villard, Henry, 1835–1900

18.16.6.2 Regional Railroads

Anderson, George L., *Kansas West* (1963).
Athearn, Robert G., *Rebel of the Rockies: Denver and Rio Grande Western Railroad* (1962).
Baker, George P., *The Formation of New England Railroad System: A Study of Railroad Combination in the Nineteenth Century* (1968).
Bogen, J. I., *Anthracite Railroads* (1927).
Bradley, Glenn D., *Story of the Santa Fé* (1920).
Brayer, H. O., *William Blackmore, Early Financing of the Denver and Rio Grande Railway and Ancillary Land Companies, 1871–1878* (1949).
Burgess, George H., and M. C. Kennedy, *Centennial History of the Pennsylvania Railroad Company* (1949).
Clark, Ira G., *Then Came Railroads: From Steam to Diesel in the Southwest* (1958).
Corliss, C. J., *Main Line of Mid-America: The Story of the Illinois Central* (1950).
Curry, Leonard P., *Rail Routes South: Louisville's Fight for the Southern Market, 1865–1872* (1969).
Daggett, Stuart, *Chapters on Southern Pacific* (1922).
Derrick, S. M., *Centennial History of the South Carolina Railroad* (1930).
Dodge, G. M., *How We Built the Union Pacific Railway* (1910).
Doster, James F., *Railroads in Alabama Politics, 1875–1914* (1957).
Dozier, H. D., *History of Atlantic Coast Line Railroad* (1920).
Eilson, Neil C., and F. J. Taylor, *Southern Pacific* (1952).
Ellis, D. M., "New York Central and Erie Canal," *N.Y. Hist.,* 29 (1948), 268.
Fish, Carl R., *Restoration of Southern Railroads* (1919).
Fogel, Robert W., *Union Pacific Railroad: A Case of Premature Enterprise* (1960).
Galloway, J. D., *First Transcontinental Railroad* (1950).
Griswold, Wesley S., *Work of Giants: Transcontinental Railroad* (1962).
Harlow, Alvin F., *Steelways of New England* (1946).
Hedges, James B., *Villard and Railways of Northwest* (1930).
Hilton, George W., *Great Lakes Car Ferries* (1962).
Hungerford, Edward, *Baltimore and Ohio Railroad* (2 vols., 1928).
―― *Men and Iron: The New York Central* (1938).
Irwin, Leonard B., *Pacific Railways and Nationalism in Canadian-American Northwest, 1845–1873* (1939).
Kistler, Thelma M., *Rise of Railroads in the Connecticut River Valley* (1938).
Klein, Maury, *Great Richmond Terminal* (1970).
―― and Kozo Yamamura, "Southern Railroads, 1865–1893," *Bus. Hist. Rev.,* 41 (1967), 358.
Lesley, L. B., "Transcontinental Railroad into California," *Pacific Hist. Rev.,* 5 (1936), 52.
McAllister, S. B., "Building the Texas and Pacific West of Fort Worth," *West Texas Hist. Assoc.,* Yearbook, 4 (1928), 50.
McCague, James, *Moguls and Iron Men: First Transcontinental Railroad* (1964).
McGuire, P. S., "Railroads of Georgia," *Ga. Hist. Quar.,* 16 (1932), 179.

Masterson, Vincent V., *Katy Railroad and Last Frontier* (1952).
Mott, E. H., *Between the Ocean and the Lakes: The Story of Erie* (1901).
Overton, Richard C., *Burlington Route* (1965).
—— *Burlington West: A Colonization History of the Burlington Railroad* (1941).
—— *Gulf to Rockies: Heritage of Fort Worth and Denver-Colorado and Southern Railways, 1861–1898* (1953).
Peterson, H. F., "Projects of Northern Pacific," *Minn. Hist.* 10 (1929), 127.
Pierce, Harry H., *Railroads of New York: Government Aid, 1826–1875* (1953).
Reed, Merl E., *New Orleans and the Railroads, 1830–1860* (1966).
Riegel, R. E., *The Story of the Western Railroads* (1926).
Russel, Robert R., *Improvement of Communication with Pacific Coast as Issue in American Politics, 1783–1864* (1948).
Stevens, Frank W., *Beginnings of the New York Central Railroad* (1926).
Turner, Charles W., *Chessie's Road* (1956). The Chesapeake and Ohio.
Waters, L. L., *Steel Rails to Santa Fé* (1950).
Zobrist, Benedict K., "Steamboat Men versus Railroad Men; The First Bridging of the Mississippi." *Mo. Hist. Rev.* 59 (1965), 159.

18.16.6.3 Financing and Organization

Baughman, James P., *Charles Morgan and Development of Southern Transportation* (1968).
Bonbright, J. C., *Railroad Capitalization* (1920).
Campbell, Edward G., *Reorganization of Railroad System, 1893–1900* (1938).
Chandler, Alfred D., Jr., "Railroads," *Bus. Hist. Rev.,* 39 (1965), 16.
Cleveland, Frederick A., and F. W. Powell, *Railroad Promotion and Capitalization in the United States* (1909).
Cochran, Thomas C., *Railroad Leaders, 1845–1890: The Business Mind in Action* (1953).
Conant, Michael, *Railroad Mergers and Abandonments* (1965).
Daggett, Stuart, *Railroad Reorganization* (1908).
Gagan, David P., "Railroads and Public, 1870–1881: Charles E. Perkins' Business Ethics," *Bus. Hist. Rev.,* 39 (1965), 41.
Grodinsky, Julius, *Iowa Pool: A Study in Railroad Competition, 1870–1884* (1950).
—— *Transcontinental Railway Strategy, 1869–1893: A Study of Businessmen* (1962).
Johnson, Arthur M., and Barry E. Supple, *Boston Capitalists and Western Railroads: A Study in the Nineteenth-Century Railroad Investment Process* (1967).
Klein, Maury, "Southern Railroad Leaders, 1865–1893: Identities and Ideologies," *Bus. Hist. Rev.,* 43 (1968), 288.
—— "The Strategy of Southern Railroads," *AHR,* 73 (1968), 1052.
Leonard, William N., *Railroad Consolidation under Transportation Act of 1920* (1946).
Lewis, Oscar, *Big Four: Huntington, Stanford, Hopkins, and Crocker and the Building of the Central Pacific* (1938).
Moody, John, *Railroad Builders* (1919).
O'Neil, John T., *Policy Formation in Railroad Finance: Refinancing the Burlington, 1936–1945* (1956).
Ripley, W. Z., *Railroads: Finance and Organization* (1915).
Salsbury, Stephen M., *The State, the Investor, and the Railroad: Boston & Albany, 1825–1867* (1967).
Staples, H. L., and A. T. Mason, *Fall of a Railroad Empire: Brandeis and New Haven Merger Battle* (1947).
Stover, John F., *Railroads of the South, 1865–1900: Finance and Control* (1955).

18.16.6.4 Government Regulation

Benson, Lee, *Merchants, Farmers and Railroads: Railroad Regulation and New York Politics, 1850–1887* (1955).
Dixon, F. H., *Railroads and Government* (1922).
Doster, James F., *Alabama's First Railroad Commission, 1881–1885* (1949).
Ferguson, Maxwell, *State Regulation of Railroads in the South* (1916).
Harbeson, Robert W., "Railroads and Regulation, 1877–1916: Conspiracy or Public Interest?" *Jour. Econ. Hist.,* 27 (1967), 230.

Hellerich, Mahlon H., "Railroad Regulation in Consitutional Convention of 1873," *Penn. Hist.*, 26 (1959), 35.

Hillman, Jordan J., *Competition and Railroad Price Discrimination* (1968).

Hunt, Robert S., *Law and Locomotives: The Impact of the Railroad on Wisconsin Law in the Nineteenth Century* (1958).

Joubert, William H., *Southern Freight Rates in Transition* (1949).

Kerr, K. Austin, *American Railroad Politics, 1914–1920* (1968).

Kolko, Gabriel, *Railroads and Regulation, 1877–1916* (1965).

Lively, Robert A., *The South in Action: Crusade Against Freight Rate Discrimination* (1949).

MacAvoy, Paul W., *Economic Effects of Regulation: Trunk-Line Railroad Cartels and Interstate Commerce Commission before 1900* (1965).

Nelson, James C., *Railroad Transportation and Public Policy* (1959).

18.16.6.5 Land Grants

Decker, Leslie E., *Railroads, Lands, and Politics: Taxation of Land Grants, 1864–1897* (1964).

Ellis, David M., "Forfeiture of Railroad Land Grants," *MVHR,* 33 (1946), 27.

Farnham, Wallace D., "'Weakened Spring of Government': Study in Nineteenth Century American History," *AHR,* 68 (1963), 662.

Gates, Paul W., *The Illinois Central Railroad and Its Colonization Work* (1934).

Greever, William S., *Arid Domain: Sante Fe Railway: Its Western Land Grant* (1954).

Overton, Richard C., *Burlington West: A Colonization History of the Burlington Railroad* (1941).

Parker, E. M., "Southern Pacific Railroad and Settlement in Southern California," *Pac. Hist. Rev.,* 6 (1937), 103.

Peterson, H. F., "Early Minnesota Railroads and Quest for Settlers," *Minn. Hist.,* 13 (1932), 25.

Rae, J. B., "Commissioner Sparks and Railroad Land Grants, *MVHR,* 25 (1938), 211.

Ralston, Leonard F., "Iowa Railroads and Land Grant of 1846," *Iowa Jour. Hist.,* 56 (1958), 97.

Sanborn, John B., *Congressional Grants of Land in Aid of Railways* (1899).

Scott, Roy V., "American Railroads and Agricultural Extension, 1900–1914," *Bus. Hist. Rev.,* 39 (1965), 74.

Sutton, Robert M., "The Origins of American Land-Grant Railroad Rates," *Bus. Hist. Rev.,* 40 (1966), 66.

18.16.6.6 Railroads and Economic Growth

Cootner, Paul H., "Railroads in Economic Growth," *Jour. Econ. Hist.,* 23 (1963), 477.

Fishlow, Albert, *American Railroads and the Transformation of the Ante-Bellum Economy* (1965).

Fogel, Robert W., *Railroads and Economic Growth* (1964).

Jenks, Leland H., "Railroads as Economic Force in American Development," *Jour. Econ. Hist.,* 4 (1944), 1.

McClelland, Peter D., "Railroads, American Growth, & the New Economics History: A Critique," *Jour. Econ. Hist.,* 28 (1968), 102.

Nerlove, Marc, "Railroads and American Economic Growth," *Jour. Econ. Hist.,* 26 (1966), 107.

18.16.7 Air Transport

Caves, Richard E., *Air Transport and Its Regulators: An Industry Study* (1962).

Collinge, George, and John W. Underwood, *Transport Aircraft of the United States since 1919* (1969).

Morris, Lloyd, and Kendall Smith, *Ceiling Unlimited: American Aviation* (1953).

Munson, Kenneth, *Civil Aircraft of Yesteryear* (1968).

Richmond, Samuel B., *Regulation and Competition in Air Transportation* (1961).

Smith, Henry Ladd, *Airways: History of Commercial Aviation in United States* (1942).
—— *Airways Abroad: The Story of American World Air Routes* (1950).
Straszheim, Mahlon R., *International Airline Industry* (1969).
Taylor, Frank J., *High Horizons* (rev. ed., 1962). United Airlines.
Whitnah, Donald R., *Safer Skyways: Federal Control of Aviation, 1926–1966* (1966).

18.17 EMPLOYMENT AND OCCUPATIONS

18.17.1 General

Anderson, Hudson D., and P. E. Davidson, *Occupational Trends in American Labor* (1945).
Bancroft, Gertrude, *American Labor Force* (1958).
Barger, Harold, *Outlay and Income, 1921–1938* (1942).
Durand, J. D., *Labor Force, 1890–1960* (1948).
Fabricant, Solomon, *Employment in Manufacturing 1899–1939* (1942).
Lansing, John B., et al., *Geographic Mobility of Labor* (1967).
Lebergott, Stanley, *Manpower in Economic Growth* (1964).
Long, Clarence D., *Labor Force under Changing Income and Employment* (1958).
McEntire, Davis, *Labor Force in California, 1900–1950* (1952).
Montgomery, David, "Working Classes of Pre-Industrial American City, 1780–1830," *Labor Hist.*, 9 (1968), 3.
Reed, Anna Y., *Occupational Placement: Its History* (1946).
Schwartzman, David, "The Contribution of Education to the Quality of Labor, 1929–1963," *Am. Econ. Rev.* 58 (1968), 508.
Scoville, James G., *Job Content of the U.S. Economy, 1940–1970* (1969).
Stigler, G. J., *Domestic Servants in United States, 1900–1940* (1946).
—— *Trends in Output and Employment* (1947).
Walker, Charles R., *The Man on the Assembly Line* (1952).

See also 18.11.6, Farm Labor; 20.1.5, Immigrant and the Economy; 20.12.5, Negroes–Economic Conditions and Status.

18.17.2 Working Conditions

Cahill, Marion C., *Shorter Hours: A Study of the Movement Since the Civil War* (1932).
Downey, E. H., *Workmen's Compensation* (1924).
Kornhauser, Arthur, *Mental Health of Industrial Worker: Detroit* (1965).
Lee, R. Alton, "Phossy Jaw: Federal Police Power," *Historian*, 29 (1966), 1.
Michelbacker, Gustav F., and T. M. Niel, *Workmen's Compensation Insurance* (1925).
Teper, Lazare, *Hours of Labor* (1932).
Weinstein, James, "Big Business and the Origins of Workmen's Compensation," *Labor Hist.*, 8 (1967), 156.
Woodbury, R. M., *Workers' Health and Safety* (1927).

18.17.3 Wages

Ahearn, Daniel J., Jr., *Wages of Farm and Factory Laborers, 1914–1924* (1945).
Beney, M. A., *Wages, Hours and Employment, 1914–1936* (1936).
Brissenden, P. F., *Earnings of Factory Workers, 1899–1927* (1929).
Douglas, Paul H., *Real Wages* (1930).
Layer, Robert G., *Earnings of Cotton Mill Operatives, 1825–1914* (1955).
Lewis, H. Gregg, *Unionism and Relative Wages in the United States* (1963).
Long, Clarence D., *Wages and Earnings in the United States, 1860–1890* (1960).
Mitchell, Wesley C., *Gold, Prices and Wages under Greenback Standard* (1908).

National Industrial Conference Board, *Wages in the United States, 1914–1930* (1931).
—— *Cost of Living, 1914–1930* (1931).
Ozanne, Robert, *Wages in Practice and Theory: McCormick and International Harvester, 1860–1960* (1968).
Patterson, James T., "Mary Dewson and Minimum Wage Movement," *Labor Hist.,* 5 (1964), 134.
Rees, Albert, *Real Wages in Manufacturing, 1890–1914* (1961).
Smith, Walter B., "Wage Rates on Erie Canal, 1828–1881," *Jour. Econ. Hist.,* 23 (1963), 298.
U.S. Bureau of Labor Statistics, "History of Wages," *Bull.,* no. 604 (1934).
Wilson, Thomas, *Fluctuations in Income and Employment* (1948).
Woytinksy, W. S., et al., *Employment and Wages in United States* (1953).

18.17.4 Occupational Mobility

Adams, Leonard P., and Robert L. Aronson, *Workers and Industrial Change* (1957).
Anderson, Hudson D., and P. E. Davidson, *Occupational Mobility in an American Community* (1937).
Duncan, Otis D., "Trend of Occupational Mobility," *Am. Sociol. Rev.,* 30 (1965), 491.
Gallaway, Lowell E., "Labor Mobility, Resource Allocation, and Structural Unemployment," *Am. Econ. Rev.,* 53 (1963), 694.
Ladinsky, Jak, "Occupational Determinants of Geographic Mobility among Professional Workers," *Am. Sociol. Rev.,* 32 (1967), 253.
Rogoff, Natalie, *Recent Trends in Occupational Mobility* (1953).

18.17.5 Unemployment

Gilpatric, Eleanor G., *Structural Unemployment and Aggregate Demand* (1966).
Gordon, Robert A., and Margaret S. Gordon, eds., *Prosperity and Unemployment: A Conference* (1966).
Hart, Hornell N., *Fluctuations in Unemployment 1902–1917* (1918).
Larson, Arthur G., and Merrill G. Murray, "The Development of Unemployment Insurance in the United States," *Vanderbilt Law Rev.,* 8 (1955), 181.
Lebergott, Stanley, *Manpower in Economic Growth* (1964).
Nelson, Daniel, *Unemployment Insurance, 1915–1935* (1969).
Okun, Arthur, ed., *Battle against Unemployment* (1965).
Thompson, Laura A., *Unemployment Insurance and Reserves* (1935).

18.17.6 Apprenticeship

Douglas, Paul H., *American Apprenticeship and Industrial Education* (1921).
Kursh, Harry, *Apprenticeships in America* (rev. ed., 1965).
Marshall, F. Ray, and V. M. Briggs, Jr., *The Negro and Apprenticeship* (1967).
U.S. Department of Labor. Bureau of Apprenticeship, *Apprenticeship Training since Colonial Days* (1950).

See also 23.10, Vocational Education.

18.17.7 Child Labor

Davidson, Elizabeth H., *Child Labor Legislation in Southern Textile States* (1939).
Felt, Jeremy P., *Hostages of Fortune: Child Labor Reform in New York State* (1965).
Field, A. S., *The Child Labor Policy of New Jersey* (1909).
Sumner, H. L., and E. A. Merritt, *Child Labor Legislation in the United States* (1915).
Tobey, J. A., *Children's Bureau* (1925).

Trattner, Walter I., *Crusade for the Children: A History of the National Child Labor Committee and Child Labor Reform in America* (1970).
Wood, Stephen B., *Constitutional Politics in Progressive Era: Child Labor* (1968).

18.17.8 Employment of Women

Abbott, Edith, *Women in Industry* (1910).
Anderson, Mary, and M. N. Winslow, *Woman at Work* (1952).
Baker, Elizabeth F., *Technology and Woman's Work, 1800–1960* (1964).
Beyer, C. M., "History of Labor Legislation for Women," Women's Bur., *Bull.*, no. 66 (1929).
Boone, Gladys, *Women's Trade Union Leagues in Great Britain and United States* (1942).
Clark, Sue Ainslie, and Edith Wyatt, *Making Both Ends Meet: Income and Outlay of New York Working Girls* (1911).
Clymer, Eleanor Lowenston, and Lillian Erlich, *Modern American Career Women* (1959).
Cussler, Margaret, *The Woman Executive* (1958).
Davis, Allen F., "Women's Trade Union League," *Labor Hist.*, 5 (1964), 3.
Gildersleeve, Genevieve, *Women in Banking* (1959).
Harrison, Evelyn, "The Working Woman: Barriers in Employment," *Public Admin. Rev.*, 24 (1964), 78.
Herron, Belva M., *Labor Organization among Women* (1905).
Hill, Joseph A., *Women in Gainful Occupations, 1870–1920* (1929).
Hourwich, Andria T., and Gladys L. Palmer, eds., *I Am a Woman Worker: Scrapbook of Autobiographies* (1936).
Josephson, Hannah, *Golden Threads: New England's Mill Girls and Magnates* (1949).
Kelley, Florence, *Some Ethical Gains through Legislation* (1910).
Mattfeld, Jacquelyn A., and Carol G. Van Aken, eds., *Women and the Scientific Professions* (1965).
Matthews, Lillian Ruth, *Women in Trade Unions in San Francisco* (1913).
Pennington, Patience, *Woman Rice Planter* (1913); Cornelius O. Cathey, ed. (1961).
Shields, Emma L., *Negro Women in Industry* (1922).
Smuts, Robert W., *Women and Work in America* (1959).
Stein, Leon, *Triangle Fire* (1962).
U.S. Bureau of the Census, *Women in Gainful Occupations, 1870–1920* (1929).
U.S. Department of Labor, *Negro Women . . . in the Population and the Labor Force* (1967).
Wolfson, Theresa, *Woman Worker and Trade Unions* (1926).

18.17.9 Professions

Adams, Walter, ed., *Brain Drain* (1968).
Calhoun, Daniel H., *Professional Lives in America, 1750–1850* (1965).
Etzioni, Amitai, *Semi-Professionals and their Organization* (1969).
Gilb, Corinne L., *Hidden Hierarchies: Professions and Government* (1966).
Gould, Jay M., *Technical Elite* (1966).
Ladinsky, Jak, "Occupational Determinants of Geographic Mobility among Professional Workers," *Am. Sociol. Rev.*, 32 (1967), 253.
Lynn, Kenneth S. et al., eds., *Professions in America* (1965).
Moore, Wilbert E., *Professions: Roles and Rules* (1970).
Natural Research Council, *Careers of Ph. D's* (1968).
Parsons, Talcott, "The Professions and Social Structure," *Social Forces*, 17 (1939), 457.
Quattlebaum, Charles A., "Development of Scientific, Engineering, and other Professional Manpower," *The Legislative Reference Service of the Library of Congress* (1957), II.
Vollmer, Howard M., and D. L. Mills, eds., *Professionalization* (1966).
Whyte, William H., Jr., *The Organization Man* (1956).

18.18 ORGANIZED LABOR

18.18.1 General

Beard, Mary, *Short History of American Labor Movement* (1924).
Blum, Albert A., "Why Unions Grow," *Labor Hist.*, 9 (1968), 39.
Brooks, Thomas R., *Toil and Trouble: A History of American Labor* (1964).
Commons, John R. et al., *Documentary History of American Industrial Society* (10 vols., 1910–1911).
———— *History of Labour in the United States* (4 vols., 1918–1935).
Derber, Milton, *The American Idea of Industrial Democracy, 1865–1965* (1970).
Douty, H. M., ed., *Labor in the South* (1946).
Dulles, Foster R., *Labor in America* (3d. ed., 1966).
Faulkner, Harold U., and Mark Starr, *Labor in America,* new rev. ed. (1957).
Foner, Philip S., *History of the Labor Movement in the United States* (3 vols., 1947–1964).
Hutchinson, John, *The Imperfect Union: History of Corruption in American Trade Unions* (1970).
Litwack, Leon, *The American Labor Movement* (1962).
Pelling, Henry, *American Labor* (1960).
Perlman, Mark, *Labor Union Theories in America: Background and Development* (1958).
Perlman, Selig, *A History of Trade Unionism in the United States* (1922).
———— *A Theory of the Labor Movement* (1928).
Rayback, Joseph G., *History of American Labor,* Expanded and updated (1966).
Stimson, Grace H., *Rise of the Labor Movement in Los Angeles* (1955).
Taft, Philip, *Organized Labor in American History* (1964).
———— *The Structure and Government of Labor Unions* (1954).
Troy, Leo, *Organized Labor in New Jersey* (1965).
Wolman, Leo, *Boycott in American Trade Unions* (1916).

*   *   *   *   *   *   *

Neufeld, Maurice F., *Representative Bibliography of American Labor History* (1964).
Reynolds, L. G., and C. C. Killingsworth, *Trade Unions Publications* (3 vols., 1945).

See also 10.3 for biographies/writings of:

LABOR LEADERS

Brophy, John, 1883–
Furuseth, Andrew, 1854–1938
Gompers, Samuel, 1850–1924
Haywood, William D., 1869–1928
Hillman, Sidney, 1887–1946
Jones, Mother Mary, 1830–1930
Lewis, John L., 1880–1969
London, Meyer, 1871–1926
Mitchell, John, 1870–1919
Mooney, Fred, 1888–1952
Powderly, Terence V., 1849–1924
Sylvis, William H., 1828–1869

LABOR MEDIATORS

Leiserson, William M., 1883–1957
Parker, Carleton H., 1878–1918

See also 20.12.5.1, Negroes–Labor Unions.

18.18.2 Nineteenth Century

Browne, Henry J., *The Catholic Church and the Knights of Labor* (1949).

Grob, Gerald N., "Reform Unionism: The National Labor Union," *Jour. Econ. Hist.*, 14 (1954), 126.

—— "Knights of Labor and Trade Unions, 1878–1886," *Jour. Econ. Hist.*, 18 (1958), 176.

—— *Workers and Utopia: A Study of the Ideological Conflicts in the American Labor Movement, 1865–1900* (1961).

Gutman, Herbert G., "Protestantism and the American Labor Movement: The Christian Spirit in the Gilded Age," *AHR*, 72 (1966), 74.

Hugins, Walter E., *Jacksonian Democracy and the Working Class: A Study of the New York Workingmen's Movement, 1829–1837* (1960).

Mayer, Thomas, "Some Characteristics of Union Members in 1880's and 1890's" *Labor Hist.*, 5 (1964), 57.

Meltzer, Milton, *Bread and Roses: The Struggle of American Labor, 1865–1915* (1967).

Pessen, Edward, *Most Uncommon Jacksonians: The Radical Leaders of Early Labor Movement* (1967).

Sullivan, William A., *The Industrial Worker in Pennsylvania, 1800–1840* (1955).

Todes, Charlotte, *William H. Sylvis and the National Labor Union* (1942).

Ulman, Lloyd, *The Rise of the National Trade Union: The Development and Significance of Its Structure, Governing Institutions, and Economic Policies* (2nd ed., 1966).

Ware, Norman J., *The Industrial Worker, 1840–1860 The Reaction of American Industrial Society to the Advance of the Industrial Revolution* (1924).

—— *The Labor Movement in the United States: A Study in Democracy, 1860–1895* (1929).

18.18.3 Twentieth Century

Allen, Ruth A., *Chapters in the History of Organized Labor in Texas* (1941).

American Academy of Political and Social Science. *Crisis in American Trade-Union Movement* (1963).

Bernstein, Irving, "The Growth of American Unions, 1945–60," *Labor Hist.*, 2 (1961) 131.

—— *The Lean Years: A History of the American Worker, 1920–1933* (1960).

—— *Turbulent Years: A History of the American Worker, 1933–1941* (1970).

—— *History of American Worker, 1920–1941* (2 vols., 1960–1969).

Cross, I. B., *Labor Movement in California* (1935).

Dubofsky, Melvyn, *When Workers Organize: New York City in the Progressive Era* (1968).

"Fifty Years of Progress in American Labor," *Monthly Labor Rev.*, 71 (1950), 1.

Greenstone, J. David, *Labor in American Politics* (1969).

Harris, Evelyn L. K., and Frank J. Krebs, *From Humble Beginnings: West Virginia Federation of Labor, 1903–1957* (1960).

Jacobs, Paul, *The State of the Unions* (1963).

Klein, Lawrence, ed., "Labor in the South," *Monthly Labor Rev.*, 91 (1968), 1.

Knight, Robert E. L., *Industrial Relations in the San Francisco Bay Area, 1900–1918* (1960).

McGinley, James J., *Labor Relations in New York Rapid Transit Systems, 1904–1944* (1949).

Marshall, F. Ray, *Labor in the South* (1967).

Newell, Barbara W., *Chicago and Labor Movement: Unionism in the 1930's* (1961).

Perry, Louis B., and Richard S. Perry, *History of the Los Angeles Labor Movement, 1911–1941* (1963).

Schweppe, Emma, *Firemen's and Patrolmen's Unions in the City of New York* (1948).

Taft, Philip, *Labor Politics American Style: California State Federation of Labor* (1968).

Tyler, Gus, *The Labor Revolution: Trade Unionism in a New America* (1967).

Yellowitz, Irwin, *Labor and the Progressive Movement in New York* (1965).

18.18.4 AFL and CIO

AFL–CIO, *A.F. of L.: History, Encyclopedia, and Reference Book, 1881–1955* (3 vols., 1960).
Galenson, Walter, *The CIO Challenge to the AFL, 1935–1941* (1960).
—— *Rival Unionism* (1940).
Goldberg, Arthur J., *AFL–CIO: Labor United* (1956).
Harris, Herbert, *Labor's Civil War* (1940).
Lorwin, Lewis L., *The American Federation of Labor: History, Policies and Prospects* (1933).
McKelvey, Jean T., *AFL Attitudes toward Production, 1900–1932* (1952).
Morris, James O., *Conflict Within the AFL: A Study of Craft vs. Industrialism, 1901–1938* (1958).
Preis, Art, *Labor's Giant Step: Twenty Years of the CIO* (1964).
Seidman, Joel, "Efforts toward Merger, 1935–1955," *Indust. and Labor Rel. Rev.,* 9 (1956), 353.
Stolberg, Benjamin, *The Story of the CIO* (1938).
Taft, Philip, *The AF of L* (2 vols., 1957–1959).

18.18.5 IWW and Left-Wing Unionism

Bedford, Henry F., *Socialism and the Workers in Massachusetts, 1886–1912* (1966).
Chaplin, Ralph, *Wobbly: The Rough and Tumble Story of an American Radical* (1948).
Conlin, Joseph R., *Big Bill Haywood and the Radical Union Movement* (1969).
Dubofsky, Melvyn, *We Shall Be All: Industrial Workers of the World* (1969).
Frost, Richard H., *The Mooney Case* (1968).
Gambs, John S., *The Decline of the I.W.W.* (1932).
Grover, David H., *Debaters and Dynamiters: The Story of the Haywood Trial* (1964).
Kampelman, Max M., *The Communist Party vs. the C.I.O.: A Study in Power Politics* (1957).
Kornbluh, Joyce L., ed., *Rebel Voices: An I.W.W. Anthology* (1964).
Laslett, John H. M., *Labor and the Left: A Study of Socialist and Radical Influences in the American Labor Movement, 1881–1924* (1970).
Lindblom, C. E., *Unions and Capitalism* (1949).
O'Brien, F. S., "The 'Communist-Dominated' Unions in the United States since 1950," *Labor Hist.* 9 (1968), 184.
Saposs, David J., *Left Wing Unionism: A Study of Radical Policies and Tactics* (1926).
Schneider, David M., *Workers' (Communist) Party and American Trade Unions* (1928).
Taft, Philip, "Federal Trials of I.W.W.," *Labor Hist.,* 3 (1962), 57.
—— "I.W.W. in the Grain Belt," *Labor Hist.,* 1 (1960), 53.
Tyler, Robert L., *Rebels of the Woods: The I.W.W. in the Pacific Northwest* (1967).

18.18.6 Collective Bargaining

Chernish, William N., *Coalition Bargaining: A Study of Trade Union Tactics and Public Policy* (1969).
Derber, Milton, "The Idea of Industrial Democracy in America, 1898–1915; 1915–1935," *Labor Hist.,* 7 (1966), 259.
Dunlop, John T., and James J. Healy, *Collective Bargaining,* rev. ed. (1953).
Levy, B. H., "Collective Bargaining," *Harvard Bus. Rev.,* 26 (1948), 468.
Twentieth Century Fund, *Trends in Collective Bargaining,* prepared by Samuel T. Williamson and Herbert Harris.
U.S. Congress. Senate. Labor Committee, *Factors in Successful Collective Bargaining* (1951).
Warne, Colston E., ed., *Industry-wide Collective Bargaining: Promise or Menace?* (1950).

* * * * * * *

Kessler, S. P., comp., *Industry-wide Collective Bargaining: An Annotated Bibliography* (1948).

18.18.7 Labor Strife

Adamic, Louis, *Dynamite: The Story of Class Violence in America* (1931).

Adams, Graham, Jr., *Age of Industrial Violence, 1910–15: The Activities and Findings of the Commission on Industrial Relations* (1966).

Allen, Ruth A., *Great Southwest Strike* (1942).

Angle, Paul M., *Bloody Williamson: A Chapter in American Lawlessness* (1952).

Broehl, Wayne G., Jr., *The Molly Maguires* (1964).

Bruce, Robert V., *1877: Year of Violence* (1959).

Buder, Stanley, *Pullman: Experiment in Industrial Order, 1880–1930* (1967).

David, Henry, *A History of the Haymarket Affair: A Study in the American Social-Revolutionary and Labor Movements* (2d ed., 1958).

Friedheim, Robert L., *Seattle General Strike* (1964).

Fuchs, Estelle, *Pickets at the Gates: A Problem in Administration* (1965).

Kogan, Bernard R., ed., *The Chicago Haymarket Riot: Anarchy on Trial* (1959).

Laidler, Harry W., *Boycotts and the Labor Struggle* (1914).

Langdon, Emma F., *Cripple Creek Strike: History of Industrial Wars in Colorado, 1903–1905* (1905).

Peterson, Florence, *Strikes in United States* (1938).

Sofchalk, Donald G., "The Chicago Memorial Day Incident," *Labor Hist., 6* (1965), 3.

Ward, Robert D., and William W. Rogers, *Labor Revolt in Alabama: The Great Strike of 1894* (1965).

West, George P., *Report on the Colorado Strike* (1915).

Wolff, Leon, *Lockout: The Homestead Strike of 1892; A Study of Violence, Unionism, and the Carnegie Steel Empire* (1965).

Yellen, Samuel, *American Labor Struggles* (1936).

18.18.8 Employers' Resistance to Labor Organization

Berthoff, Rowland, "The Freedom to Control in American Business History," in *A Festschrift for Frederick B. Artz* (1964).

Bonnett, C. E., *Employers' Associations* (1922).

Calkins, Clinch, *Spy Overhead* (1937).

Dunn, Robert W., *Americanization of Labor: Employers' Offensive Against Trade Unions* (1927).

Horan, James D., *Pinkertons: The Detective Dynasty* (1968).

Howard, Sidney, *Labor Spy* (1924).

Huberman, Leo, *Labor Spy Racket* (1937).

Levinson, Edward, *I Break Strikes* (1935).

Seidman, Joel I., *Yellow Dog Contract* (1932).

Taylor, Albion G., *Labor Policies of the National Association of Manufacturers* (1927).

Zimand, Savel, *Open Shop Drive* (1921).

18.18.9 Government and Labor

Berman, Edward, *Labor and Sherman Act* (1930).

——— "Supreme Court Interprets Railway Labor Act," *Am. Econ. Rev., 20* (1930), 619.

Boudin, Louis B., "Sherman Act," *Columbia Law Rev., 39* (1939), 1283; 40 (1940), 14.

Frankfurter, Felix, and Nathan Greene, *The Labor Injunction* (1930).

Groat, G. G., *Attitude of American Courts on Labor Cases,* (1911).

Hays, Arthur G., *Trial by Prejudice* (1933).

Kutler, Stanley I., "Labor, Clayton Act, and Supreme Court," *Labor Hist.,* 3 (1962), 19.

Levy, Leonard W., *Law of the Commonwealth and Chief Justice Shaw* (1957).

Lieberman, Elias, *Unions before the Bar* (1950).

Murray, Robert K., "Public Opinion, Labor, and Clayton Act," *Historian,* 21 (1959), 255.

Nelles, Walter, "Commonwealth *v.* Hunt," *Columbia Law Rev.,* 32 (1932), 1128.

Spaeth, Harold J., "Judicial Attitudes in Labor Relations Decisions of Warren Court," *Jour. Politics,* 25 (1963), 290.

Tarrow, Sidney G., "Lochner vs. N.Y.," *Labor Hist.,* 5 (1964), 277.

Taylor, George W., *Government Regulation of Industrial Relations* (1948).

Turner, Marjorie B. S., *Early American Labor Conspiracy Cases* (1967).

18.18.10 State Labor Legislation

Barnard, J. L., *Factory Legislation in Pennsylvania: Its History and Administration* (1907).

Beckner, E. R., *A History of Labor Legislation in Illinois* (1929).

Brown, Virginia H., *Development of Labor Legislation in Tennessee* (1945).

Doan, M. C., "State Labor Relations Acts," *Quar. Jour. Econ.,* 56 (1942), 507.

Eaves, Lucile, *California Labor Legislation* (1910).

Edwards, A. M., *The Labor Legislation of Connecticut* (1907).

Fairchild, F. R., *The Factory Legislation of the State of New York* (1905).

Haferbecker, Gordon M., *Wisconsin Labor Laws* (1958).

Killingsworth, C. C., *State Labor Relations Acts* (1948).

Morris, Victor P., *Oregon's Experience with Minimum Wage Legislation* (1930).

Towles, J. K., *Factory Legislation of Rhode Island* (1908).

18.18.11 Unions by Industry

18.18.11.1 Automobile

Bernstein, Barton J., "Walter Reuther and General Motors Strike of 1945–1946," *Mich. Hist.,* 40.

Fine, Sidney, *Automobile Under Blue Eagle* (1963).

——— "Origins of United Automobile Workers," *Jour. Econ. Hist.,* 18 (1958), 249.

——— *Sit-Down: The General Motors Strike of 1936–1937* (1969).

——— "Toledo Chevrolet Strike of 1935," *Ohio Hist. Quar.,* 67 (1958), 326.

——— "Tool and Die Makers Strike of 1933," *Mich. Hist.,* 42 (1958), 297.

Hoffman, Claude E., *Sit-Down in Anderson: UAW Local 663, Anderson, Indiana* (1968).

Howe, Irving, and B. J. Widick, *U.A.W. and Walter Reuther* (1949).

MacDonald, Robert M., *Collective Bargaining in the Automobile Industry* (1963).

18.18.11.2 Clothing

Braun, Kurt, *Union-Management Co-operation: Clothing Industry* (1947).

Budish, J. M., and George Soule, *New Unionism in Clothing Industry* (1920).

Epstein, Melech, *Jewish Labor in U.S.A.* (1950).

——— *Jewish Labor in U.S.A., 1914–1952* (1953).

Levine, Louis, *Women's Garment Workers* (1924).

Seidman, Joel, *Needle Trades* (1942).

Stein, Leon, *Triangle Fire* (1962).

Stolberg, Benjamin, *Tailors Progress* (1944).

18.18.11.3 Construction

Bates, Harry, *Bricklayers' Century of Craftsmanship* (1955).

Christie, Robert A., *Empire in Wood: the Carpenters' Union* (1956).

Haber, William, *Industrial Relations in Building* (1930).

Hilton, William S., *Industrial Relations in Construction* (1968).
Horowitz, Morris A., *Structure and Government of Carpenters' Union* (1962).

18.18.11.4 Iron and Steel

Brody, David, *Labor in Crisis: The Steel Strike of 1919* (1965).
——— *Steelworkers in America: The Nonunion Era* (1960).
Harbison, Frederick H., and Robert C. Spencer, "Collective Bargaining: Postwar Record in Steel," *Am. Pol. Sci. Rev.*, 48 (1954), 705.
Interchurch World Movement, Commission of Inquiry, *Report on Steel Strike of 1919* (1920).
Rees, Albert, "Wage-Price Relations in Basic Steel Industry, 1945–1948," *Indust. and Labor Rel. Rev.*, 6 (1953), 195.
Robinson, Jesse S., *Amalgamated Association of Iron, Steel and Tin Workers* (1920).
Sofchalk, Donald G., "The Chicago Memorial Day Incident," *Labor Hist.*, 6 (1965), 3.
Stockton, F. T., *International Molders Union* (1921).
Wolff, Leon, *Lockout: Homestead Strike of 1892* (1965).

18.18.11.5 Leather and Shoe

Galster, Augusta E., *Labor Movement in Shoe Industry* (1924).
Lescohier, Don D., *Knights of St. Crispin* (1910). Shoemakers.
Norton, Thomas L., *Trade-Union Policies in Massachusetts Shoe Industry, 1919–29* (1932).

18.18.11.6 Lumbering

Allen, Ruth A., *East Texas Lumber Workers, 1870–1950* (1961).
Hyman, Harold M., *Soldiers and Spruce: Loyal Legion of Loggers and Lumbermen* (1963).
Jensen, Vernon H., *Lumber and Labor* (1945).

18.18.11.7 Maritime

Albrecht, A. E., *International Seamen's Union* (1923).
Goldberg, Joseph P., *Maritime Story: Labor-Management Relations* (1958).
Healey, James C., *Foc'sle and Glory Hole: Merchant Seaman* (1936).
Hohman, Elmo P., *History of American Merchant Seamen* (1956).

18.18.11.8 Mining

Angle, Paul M., *Bloody Williamson: American Lawlessness* (1952).
Baratz, Morton S., *Union and Coal Industry* (1955).
Broehl, Wayne G., Jr., *The Molly Maguires* (1964).
Coleman, John W., *Molly Maguire Riots* (1936).
Coleman, McAlister, *Men and Coal* (1943).
Cornell, Robert J., *Anthracite Coal Strike of 1902* (1957).
Elliott, Russell R., *Radical Labor in Nevada Mining Booms, 1900–1920* (1961).
Ertl, Tell, and T. T. Read, *Labor Standards and Metal Mining* (1947).
Evans, Chris, *History of the United Mine Workers* (2 vols., 1918–1920).
Fisher, Waldo E., and Anne Bezanson, *Wage Rates in Bituminous Coal* (1932).
Greene, Victor R., *Slavic Community on Strike: Immigrant Labor in Pennsylvania Anthracite* (1968).
Harvey, Katherine A., *Best Dressed Miners; Life and Labor in the Maryland Coal Region, 1845–1910* (1969).
Hinrichs, Albert F., *United Mine Workers and Non-Union Coal Fields* (1923).
Langdon, Emma F., *Cripple Creek Strike: History of Industrial Wars in Colorado, 1903–1905* (1905).
Nelson, James, *Mine Workers' District 50: Growth into a National Union* (1955).
Suffern, A. E., *Coal Miners' Struggle* (1926).
Walsh, William J., *United Mine Workers* (1931).
Wiebe, Robert H., "Anthracite Strike of 1902," *MVHR*, 48 (1961), 229.

18.18.11.9 Printing

Lipset, Seymour M., "Democracy in Private Government: A Case Study of the International Typographical Union," *Brit. Jour. Sociol.,* 3 (1952), 47.

Loft, Jacob, *Printing Trades* (1944).

Munson, Fred C., *Labor Relations in the Lithographic Industry* (1963).

Seybold, John W., *Philadelphia Printing Industry* (1949).

Stewart, Ethelbert, *Documentary History of Early Organizations of Printers* (1907).

18.18.11.10 Railroad

Brazeal, B. R., *Brotherhood of Sleeping Car Porters* (1946).

Cottrell, W. F., *Railroader* (1940).

Eggert, Gerald G., *Railroad Labor Disputes: Beginnings of Federal Strike Policy* (1967).

McMurry, Donald L., *The Great Burlington Strike of 1888* (1956).

Northrup, H. R., "Railway Labor Act and Railway Labor Disputes," *Am. Econ. Rev.,* 36 (1946), 324.

Richardson, Reed C., *Locomotive Engineer, 1863–1963* (1963).

Robbins, Edwin C., *Railway Conductors* (1914).

Troy, Leo, "Labor Representation on American Railways," *Labor Hist.,* 2 (1961), 295.

Wolf, Harry D., *Railway Labor Board* (1927).

Wood, Louis A., *Union-Management Cooperation on Railroads* (1931).

Zieger, Robert H., "Railroad Labor Policy in the 1920's," *Labor Hist.,* 9 (1968), 23.

18.18.11.11 Textile

Herring, H. L., *Welfare Work in Mill Villages: The Story of Extra-Mill Activities in North Carolina* (1929).

Josephson, Hannah, *The Golden Threads, New England's Mill Girls and Magnates* (1949).

Lahne, H. J., *Cotton Mill Worker* (1944).

MacDonald, Lois, *Southern Mill Hands* (1928).

Mitchell, G. S., *Textile Unionism and South* (1931).

Pope, Liston, *Millhands and Preachers: Gastonia* (1942).

Potwin, Marjorie A., *Cotton Mill People of Piedmont* (1927).

Senate Labor Committee, *Labor-Management Relations in Southern Textile Industry* (1952).

Vorse, M. H., *Passaic Textile Strike, 1926–1927* (1927).

Weisbord, Albert, *Passaic* (1926).

18.18.11.12 Miscellaneous Industries

American Federation of Teachers, Commission on Educational Reconstruction, *Organizing Teaching Profession* (1955).

Barbash, Jack, *Unions and Telephones* (1952).

Brody, David, *The Butcher Workmen: A Study of Unionization* (1964).

Corey, Lewis, *Meat and Man: Monopoly, Unionism and Food Policy* (1949).

Deibler, F. S., *Amalgamated Wood Workers' International Union* (1912).

Feis, Herbert, *Labor Relations in Procter and Gamble* (1928).

Foltman, Felicia F., *White-and-Blue Collars in a Mill Shutdown: Case Study* (1968).

Gouldner, Alvin W., *Wildcat Strike: Worker-Management* Relationships (1954). General Gypsum Company.

Green, Charles H., *Headwear Workers* (1944).

Horowitz, Morris A., *The New York Hotel Industry: A Labor Relations Study* (1960).

James, Ralph C., and Estelle D. James, *Hoffa and the Teamsters* (1965).

Jensen, Vernon H., *Heritage of Conflict: Labor Relations in Nonferrous Metals Industry Up to 1930* (1950).

Kramer, Leo, *Labor's Paradox; American Federation of State, County, and Municipal Employees AFL-CIO* (1962).

Leiter, Robert D., *Teamsters Union* (1957).

Mangum, Garth L., *The Operating Engineers: Economic History of a Trade Union* (1964).

"The Mechanics," *Labor Hist.*, 5 (1964), 215.

O'Connor, Harvey, *History of Oil Workers Intl. Union (CIO)* (1950).

Ozanne, Robert, *Century of Labor-Management Relations at McCormick and International Harvester* (1967).

Perlman, Mark, *The Machinists: A New Study in American Trade Unionism* (1961).

Roberts, Harold S., *Rubber Workers* (1944).

19   Demography and Social Structure

19.1 DEMOGRAPHY

19.1.1 General

Bogue, Donald J., *Population of United States* (1959).
Cassedy, James H., *Demography in Early America: Beginnings of the Statistical Mind, 1600–1800* (1969).
Chickering, Jesse., *Statistical View of Population of Massachusetts, 1765 to 1840* (1846).
Coale, Ansley J., and Melvin Zelnik, *New Estimates of Fertility and Population in the United States* (1963).
Day, Lincoln H., and Alice T. Day, *Too Many Americans* (1965).
Easterlin, Richard A., "Economic-Demographic Interactions," *Am. Econ. Rev.,* 56 (1966), 1063.
Grabill, Wilson H. et al., *Fertility of American Women* (1958).
Hawley, Amos H., *The Changing Shape of Metropolitan America: Deconcentration Since 1920* (1956).
Kiser, Clyde V., *Group Differences in Urban Fertility: A Study Derived from the National Health Survey* (1942).
Kiser, Clyde V., et al., *Trends and Variations in Fertility in the United States* (1968).
Monahan, Thomas P., *Pattern of Age at Marriage in United States* (2 vols., 1951).
National Academy of Sciences, *Growth of United States Population* (1965).
Okun, Bernard, *Trends in Birth Rates since 1870* (1958).
Potter, J., "The Growth of Population in American, 1700–1860," in David Glass and D. Eversley, eds., *Population in History,* (1965).
Price, Daniel O., *Ninety-ninth Hour: The Population Crisis in the United States* (1967).
Rossiter, W. S., *Century of Population Growth* (1909).
Shapiro, Sam, et al., *Infant, Perinatal, Maternal, and Childhood Mortality in the United States* (1968).
Sheldon, Henry D., *Older Population of United States* (1958).
Silver, Morris, "Births, Marriages, and Business Cycles," *Jour. Pol. Econ.,* 73 (1965), 237.
Stockwell, Edward G., "Notes on the Changing Age Composition of the Population of the United States." *Rural Sociol.,* 29 (1964), 67.
—————— *Population and People* (1968).
Taeuber, Conrad, and Irene Taeuber, *Changing Population of the United States* (1958).
Taeuber, Irene B., "Demographic Transitions and Population Problems in the United States," Am Acad. Pol. Soc. Sci., *Annals,* 269 (1967), 131.
Thompson, Warren S., and Pascal K. Whelpton, *Population Trends* (1933).
Truesdell, L. E., *Farm Population* (1926).
U.S. Bureau of the Census, *Century of Population Growth, 1790–1900* (1909).
—————— *Historical Statistics of United States, Colonial Times to 1957* (1960).

———— Statistical Abstract of the United States, 1878–   . Annual.
Wattenberg, Ben J., and Richard M. Scammon, This U.S.A.: Family Portrait of 194,067,296 Americans Drawn from the Census (1965).
Willcox, Walter F., Studies in American Demography (1940).
Yasuba, Yasukichi, Birth Rates of White Population in United States, 1800–1860 (1962).

19.1.2 Migration

Baker, Oliver E., "Rural-Urban Migration," Assoc. Am. Geographers, Annals, 23 (1933), 59.
Bogue, Donald J. et al., Subregional Migration in the United States, 1935–40 (2 vols., 1957).
Carver, T. N., "Rural Depopulation," Jour. Farm. Econ., 9 (1927), 1.
Davis, Joseph S., "Our Changed Population Outlook," Am. Econ. Rev., 42 (1952), 304.
Gee, Wilson, "Qualitative Study of Rural Depopulation" Am. Jour. Sociol., 39 (1933), 210.
Gillette, J. M., and G. R. Davies, "Measure of Rural Migration," Am. Stat. Assoc., Quar. Publ., 14 (1915), 642.
Hicks, John D., "Western Middle West," Agric. Hist, 20 (1946), 65.
Perlman, Jacob, "Recent Recession of Farm Population," Jour. Land Public Utility Econ., 4 (1928), 45.
Taylor, Carl C., "Our Rural Population Debacle," Am. Econ Rev, 16 (1926), 156.
Thornthwaite, C. W., Internal Migration (1934).

*   *   *   *   *   *   *

George Washington University, Report on World Population as Related to the United States: Survey of Past Studies and Recent Researches (1956).
Hauser, Philip M., "Demography and Ecology," Am. Acad. Pol. Soc. Sci., Annals, 362 (1965), 129.

See also 20.1.1, Immigration and Immigrants–General.

19.2 Social and Economic Classes

Amory, Cleveland, Who Killed Society? (1960).
Baltzell, E. Digby, Philadelphia Gentlemen (1958). Originially published as American Business Aristocracy.
———— Protestant Establishment: Aristocracy and Caste in America (1964).
Bendix, Reinhard, and Seymour M. Lipset, eds., Class, Status and Power: A Reader in Social Stratification (rev. ed., 1966).
Berthoff, Rowland, "Social Order of Anthracite Region, 1825–1902," Penn. Mag. Hist. Biog., 89 (1965), 261.
Birmingham, Stephen, Right People: American Social Establishment (1968).
Centers, Richard, Psychology of Social Classes (1949).
Champlin, J. D., Jr., "Manufacture of Ancestors," Forum, 10 (1891), 565.
Crockett, A. S., Peacocks on Parade (1931).
Cuber, John F., and William F. Kenkel, Social Stratification in the United States (1954).
Curti, Merle, Judith Green, and Roderick Nash, "Millionaires in Late Nineteenth Century," Am. Quar., 15 (1963), 416.
Domhoff, William, and Hoyt Ballard, C. Wright Mills and the Power Elite (1968).
Fishwick, Marshall W., "FFV's," Am. Quar., 11 (1959), 147.
Gettleman, Marvin E., "Charity and Social Classes in the United States, 1874–1900," Am. Jour. Econ. Sociol., 22 (1963), 313.
Goodman, Paul, "Ethics and Enterprise: The Values of a Boston Elite, 1800–1860," Am. Quar., 18 (1966), 437.

Hall, Richard H., *Occupations and the Social Structure* (1969).

Harris, P. M. G., "The Social Origins of American Leaders: The Demographic Foundations," *Perspectives in Am. Hist.*, 3 (1969), 159.

Hodges, Harold, *Social Stratification* (1964).

Jaher, Frederic C., ed., *Age of Industrialism: Essays in Social Structure and Cultural Values* (1968).

Kahl, Joseph, *The American Class Structure* (1957).

Kolko, Gabriel, *Wealth and Power in America: An Analysis of Social Class and Income Distribution* (1962).

Kuznets, Simon, and Elizabeth Jenks, *Shares of Upper Income Groups in Income and Savings* (1953).

Lampman, Robert J., *Share of the Top Wealth-Holders in National Wealth, 1922–56* (1962).

McAllister, Ward, *Society as I Found It* (1890).

Mayer, Kurt B., "The Changing Shape of the American Class Structure," *Social Research*, 30 (1963), 458.

——— "Class and Status in United States," *Quar. Rev.*, 303 (1965), 450.

Miller, S. M., "American Lower Class," *Social Research*, 31 (1964), 1.

Mills, C. Wright, *Power Elite* (1956).

——— *White Collar: American Middle Classes* (1951).

Myers, Gustavus, *History of Great American Fortunes* (3 vols., 1910).

Parsons, Talcott, "Distribution of Power in American Society," *World Politics*, 10 (1957), 123.

Presthus, Robert, *Men at the Top: A Study in Community Power* (1964).

Reiss, Albert J., Jr., et. al., *Occupations and Social Status* (1962).

Reissman, Leonard, *Class in American Society* (1959).

Riesman, David, *Faces in the Crowd* (1952).

Roach, Jack L., et al., *Social Stratification in the United States* (1969).

Rose, Arnold, *Power Structure: Political Process in American Society* (1967).

Rovere, Richard, *The American Establishment* (1964).

Smith, Daniel S., "Cyclical, Secular, and Structural Change in American Elite Composition," *Perspectives in Am. Hist.*, 4 (1970), 351.

Van Rensselaer, M. K., and Frederic Van de Water, *Social Ladder* (1924).

Veblen, Thorstein, *The Theory of the Leisure Class* (1899).

Warner, William Lloyd, et al., *Social Class in America* (rev. ed., 1960).

Warner, William Lloyd, and P. S. Lunt, *Status System of a Modern Community* (1942).

Wecter, Dixon, *The Saga of American Society* (1937). High society.

Welch, Maryon, "Ranking of Occupations on the Basis of Social Status," *Occupations*, 27 (1949), 237.

*   *   *   *   *   *   *

Glenn, Norval, et al., *Social Stratification: Bibliography* (1969).

See also 19.6, Community Sociological Studies; 20.1.6, Acculturation.

19.2.1 Social Mobility

Bell, Colin R., *Middle Class Families: Social and Geographical Mobility* (1968).

Bendix, R., and Frank W. Hawton, "Social Mobility and Business Elite," *Brit. Jour. Sociol.*, 8 (1957), 357; 9 (1958), 1.

Chinoy, Ely, "Social Mobility Trends in the United States," *Am. Social Rev.*, 20 (1955), 180.

Deeg, M. E., and D. G. Paterson, "Changes in Social Status of Occupations," *Occupations*, 25 (1947), 205.

Fish, Carl R., *Rise of the Common Man* (1937).

Lipset, Seymour M., and Reinhard Bendix, *Social Mobility in Industrial Society* (1959).

Lopreato, Joseph, "Upward Social Mobility and Political Orientation," *Am. Sociol. Rev.,* 32 (1967), 586.

Petersen, William, "Is America Still the Land of Opportunity? What Recent Studies Show About Social Mobility," *Commentary,* 16 (1953), 477.

Sjoberg, Gideon, "Are Social Classes in America Becoming More Rigid?" *Am. Sociol. Rev.,* 16 (1951), 775.

Thernstrom, Stephan, *Poverty and Progress: Social Mobility in a Nineteenth Century City* (1964).

19.3 URBAN HISTORY

19.3.1 General

See Chapter 12 for histories of particular cities. Noteworthy among the few scholarly histories of cities are those of Rochester, Washington, D.C., Chicago, Milwaukee, and Kansas City.

Alexandersson, Gunnar, *Industrial Structure of American Cities* (1956).

Bartholomew, Harland, *Land Uses in American Cities* (1955).

Callow, Alexander B., Jr., ed., *American Urban History: An Interpretive Reader with Commentaries* (1969).

Duhl, Leonard, ed., *The Urban Condition: People and Policy in the Metropolis* (1963).

Glaab, Charles N., *The American City: Documentary History* (1963).

—— and A. Theodore Brown, *History of Urban America* (1967).

Goodall, Leonard E., *American Metropolis* (1968).

Green, Constance M., *American Cities in Growth of the Nation* (1957).

—— *Rise of Urban America* (1965).

Green, Lee S., et al., *States and the Metropolis* (1968).

Hauser, Philip M., and Leo F. Schnore, eds., *Study of Urbanization* (1965).

Hawley, Amos H., *Changing Shape of Metropolitan America: Decentralization since 1920* (1956).

Jacobs, Jane, *Death and Life of Great American Cities* (1961).

—— *Economy of Cities* (1969).

Kirschner, Don S., *City and Country: Rural Responses to Urbanization in the 1920's* (1970).

Lynch, Kevin, *The Image of the City* (1960).

McKelvey, Blake, *Emergence of Metropolitan America, 1915–1966* (1968).

—— *Urbanization of America, 1860–1915* (1963).

Madden, Carl H., "On Some Indications of Stability in the Growth of Cities in the United States," *Economic Development and Cultural Change,* 4 (1955–56), 236.

—— "Some Spatial Aspects of Urban Growth in the United States," *Economic Development and Cultural Change,* 4 (1955–56), 371.

Morrissett, Irving, "The Economic Structure of American Cities," *Papers and Proceedings of the Regional Science Association* (1958), 239.

Northam, Ray M., "Declining Urban Centers: 1940–1960," Assoc. Am. Geographers, *Annals,* 53 (1963), 50.

Pred, Allan, *Spatial Dynamics of U.S. Urban Growth 1800–1914* (1970).

Schlesinger, Arthur M., *Rise of the City* (1933).

Schmitt, Peter J., *Back to Nature: The Arcadian Myth in Urban America* (1969).

Taylor, George R., "American Urban Growth Preceding the Railway Age," *Jour. Econ. Hist.* 27 (1967), 309.

Thompson, Warren S., *Population, The Growth of Metropolitan Districts in the United States, 1900–1940* (1947).

Weber, Adna F., *Growth of Cities* (1899).

* * * * * * *

Daland, R. T., "Political Science and the Study of Urbanism: A Bibliographical Essay," *Am. Pol. Sci. Rev.,* 51 (1957), 491.

Davis, Allen F., "American Historian vs. City," *Social Studies,* 56 (1965), 91.

Glaab, Charles N., "Historian and American Urban Tradition," *Wis. Mag. Hist.,* 47 (1963), 12.

———— "Historian and the American City: Bibliographic Survey," in Philip M. Hauser and Leo F. Schnore, eds., *The Study of Urbanization* (1965).

Goldman, Eric F., *Historiography and Urbanization* (1941).

Handlin, Oscar, and John Burchard, eds., *Historian and the City* (1963).

Lampard, Eric E., "Aspects of Urbanization," in Philip M. Hauser and Leo F. Schnore, Eds., *Study of Urbanization* (1965).

———— "Historians and Urbanization," *AHR,* 67 (1961), 49.

Thernstrom, Stephan, "Reflections on the New Urban History," *Daedalus,* 100 (1971), 359.

Wade, Richard C., "Agenda for Urban History," in Herbert J. Bass, ed., *State of American History* (1970), 43.

Warner, Sam B., Jr., "If All the World Were Philadelphia: Scaffolding for Urban History, 1774–1930," *AHR,* 74 (1968), 26.

Wohl, R. Richard, and A. Theodore Brown, "The Usable Past: A Study of Historical Traditions in Kansas City," *Huntington Lib. Quar.,* 23 (1960), 237.

19.3.2 Regional Studies

Bebout, John E., and Ronald J. Grele, *Where Cities Meet: Urbanization of New Jersey* (1964).

Gilchrist, David T., ed., *Growth of Seaport Cities, 1790–1825* (1967).

Gottmann, Jean, *Megalopolis: Urbanized Northeastern Seaboard of United States* (1961).

Kulski, Julian E., *Land of Urban Promise: A Search for Significant Urban Space in the Urbanized Northeast* (1967).

Nelson, Howard J., "Artificial Landscape over Southern California," Assoc. Am. Geographers, *Annals,* 49 (1959), 80.

Vance, Rupert B., and Nicholas J. Demerath, eds., *Urban South* (1954).

Wade, Richard C., *Urban Frontier: Rise of Western Cities, 1790–1830* (1959).

Wheeler, Kenneth W., *To Wear a City's Crown: Urban Growth in Texas, 1836–1865* (1968).

Wohl, R. Richard, and A. Theodore Brown, "Usable Past: Historical Traditions in Kansas City," *Huntington Lib. Quar.,* 23 (1960), 237.

19.3.3 Municipal Administration

Bradford, E. S., *Commission Government in American Cities* (1911).

Chang, Tao-Shuen, *History and Analysis of Commission and City Manager Plans* (1918).

East, John P., *Council-Manager Government: Political Thought of Its Founder, Richard S. Childs* (1965).

Griffith, Ernest S., *History of American City Government* (1938).

———— *Modern Development of City Government in United Kingdom and United States* (2 vols., 1927).

Herson, Lawrence J. R., "Municipal Government," *Am. Pol. Sci. Rev.,* 51 (1957), 330.

MacGregor, F. H., *City Government by Commission* (1911).

Maass, Arthur ed., *Area and Power: A Theory of Local Government* (1959).

Mosher, Frederick C., et al., *City Manager Government in Seven Cities* (1940).

Patton, Clifford W., *Battle for Municipal Reform 1875–1900* (1940).

Stewart, Frank M., *Half-Century of Municipal Reform: National Municipal League* (1950).

Stone, Harold A., et. al., *City Manager Government: Review after Twenty-five Years* (1940).

Weinstein, James, "Organized Business and City Commission and Manager Movements," *JSH,* 28 (1962), 166.

Williams, Oliver P., and Charles R. Adrian, *Four Cities: Comparative Policy Making* (1963).

19.3.4 Municipal Services

Baker, Moses N., *Municipal Engineering and Sanitation* (1906).
Blake, Nelson Manfred, *Water for the Cities* (1956).
Brieger, Gert H., "Sanitary Reform in New York City," *Bull. Hist. Med.*, 40 (1966), 407.
Eddy, H. P., et al., "Development of Sanitary Engineering," Am. Soc. Civil Engineers, *Trans.*, 92 (1928), 1207.
Fosdick, Raymond B., *American Police Systems* (1920).
Gorman, Mel, "Charles F. Brush and First Public Electric Street Lighting System in America," *Ohio Hist. Quar.*, 70 (1961) 128.
King, Clyde L., *Regulation of Municipal Utilities* (1912).
Lane, Roger, *Policing the City: Boston 1822–1885* (1967).
Morse, William F., *Municipal Waste* (1908).
Rafter, G. W., and M. N. Baker, *Sewage Disposal* (1894).
Richardson, James F., *New York Police, Colonial Times to 1901* (1970).
Schroeder, Henry, *Electric Light* (1923).
Waring, George E., Jr., *Modern Methods of Sewage Disposal* (1894).
—— *Sanitary Drainage* (1876).
—— *Street-Cleaning* (1897).
Wilcox, D. F., *Municipal Franchises* (2 vols., 1910).

19.3.5 Urban Transportation

Gilmore, Harlan W., *Transportation and Growth of Cities* (1953).
Hilton, George W., and John F. Due, *Electric Interurban Railways in America* (1960).
Meyer, John R., et al., *The Urban Transportation Problem* (1965).
Miller, John A., *Fares, Please!* (1941).
Mumford, Lewis, *Highway and City* (1963).
Owen, Wilfred, *Metropolitan Transportation Problem* (rev. ed., 1966).
Pell, Claiborne, *Megalopolis Unbound: Transportation of Tomorrow* (1966).
Reeves, W. F., "Elevated Lines in New York," *N.Y. Hist. Soc. Quar.*, 18 (1935), 59.
Taylor, George R., "Beginnings of Mass Transportation in Urban America," *Smithsonian Jour. Hist.*, 1, no. 2 (1966), 35; no. 3, 31.
Walker, James B., *Fifty Years of Rapid Transit* (1918).

19.3.6 City Planning

Lubove, Roy, *Community Planning in the 1920's: Regional Planning Association* (1963).
Olmsted, Frederick L., *Landscape into Cityscape: Plans for Greater New York City,* Albert Fein, ed. (1968).
Perloff, Harvey S., ed., *Planning and the Urban Community* (1961).
Reps, John W., *Making of Urban America: City Planning* (1965).
—— *Monumental Washington: Planning and Development* (1967).
Scott, Mel, *American City Planning* (1969).
Tunnard, Christopher, and Henry H. Reed, *American Skyline* (1955).
Tunnard, Christopher, *City of Man* (1953).
Walker, Robert, *Planning Function in Urban Government* (1950).

*   *   *   *   *   *   *

Bestor, George C., *City Planning: Basic Bibliography of Sources and Trends* (1966).

Branch, Melville, *Comprehensive Urban Planning: Selective Annotated Bibliography* (1970).
Council of Planning Librarians, *Exchange Bibliography* no. 1 (1958).

19.3.7 Housing and Renewal

Abbott, Edith, *Tenements of Chicago. 1908–1935* (1936).
Anderson, Martin, *Federal Bulldozer: Urban Renewal, 1949–1962* (1965).
Aronovici, Carol, *Housing the Masses* (1939).
Bremner, Robert H., "New York Tenement House," *AHR,* 64 (1958), 54.
Fisher, Robert M., *20 Years of Public Housing* (1959).
Ford, James, et al., *Slums and Housing* (1936).
Friedman, Lawrence M., *Government and Slum Housing: A Century of Frustration* (1968).
—— and Michael J. Spector, "Tenement House Legislation in Wisconsin," *Am. Jour. Legal Hist.,* 9 (1965), 41.
Hoyt, Homer, *Structure and Growth of Residential Neighborhoods in American Cities* (1939).
Lubove, Roy, "Phelps Stokes: Tenement Architect, Economist, Planner," *Jour. Society Archit. Historians,* 23 (1964), 75.
—— *Progressives and the Slums: Tenement House Reform in New York City, 1890–1917* (1962).
McDonnell, Timothy L., *Wagner Housing Act* (1957).
McKelvey, Blake, "Housing and Urban Renewal: Rochester," *Rochester Hist.,* 27 (1965), 1.
Moore, Joan, et al., *Residential Segregation in the Urban Southwest* (1966).
Rodwin, Lloyd, *Housing and Economic Progress: Boston's Middle-Income Families* (1961).
Wilson, James Q., ed., *Urban Renewal: The Record and Controversy* (1967).
Wood, Edith E., *Housing the Unskilled Wage Earner* (1919).
Wright, Henry, *Rehousing Urban America* (1935).

19.3.8 Urban Politics

19.3.8.1 General

Banfield, Edward C., *Big City Politics: Political Systems of Nine American Cities* (1965).
Banfield, Edward C., and James Q. Wilson, *City Politics* (1963).
Banfield, Edward C., *Political Influence: New Theory of Urban Politics* (1961).
—— *Unheavenly City: Nature and Future of Our Urban Crisis* (1969).
Degler, Carl N., "American Political Parties and Rise of the City," *JAH,* 51 (1964), 41.
Gold, David, and John R. Schmidhauser, "Urbanization and Party Competition: Iowa," *Midw. Jour. Pol. Sci.,* 4 (1960), 62.
Greer, Scott A., *Emerging City* (1962).
Hunter, Floyd, *Community Power Structure* (1953).
Huthmacher, J. Joseph, "Urban Liberalism and Age of Reform," *MVHR,* 49 (1962), 231.
Mann, Arthur, *Yankee Reformers in the Urban Age* (1954).
Orth, S. P., *Boss and Machine* (1919).
Patton, Clifford W., *Battle for Municipal Reform* (1940).
Polsby, Nelson W., *Community Power and Political Theory* (1963).
Ruchelman, Leonard I., ed., *Big City Mayors: Crisis in Urban Politics* (1970).
Steffens, Lincoln, *Shame of the Cities* (1904).
—— *Struggle for Self-Government* (1906).
Stewart, Frank M., *Half-Century of Municipal Reform: National Municipal League* (1950).
Tolman, W. H., *Municipal Reform Movements* (1895).
Wilson, James Q., *The Amateur Democrat: Club Politics in Three Cities* (1962).
Zink, Harold, *City Bosses in the United States* (1930).

19.3.8.2 Local Studies

Bean, Walter, *Boss Ruef's San Francisco* (1952).

Brown, A. Theodore, *Politics of Reform: Kansas City's Municipal Government, 1925–1950* (1958).

Callow, Alexander, Jr., *The Tweed Ring* (1966). New York.

Crooks, James B., *Politics & Progress: Urban Progressivism in Baltimore 1895 to 1911* (1968).

Dahl, Robert A., *Who Governs? Democracy and Power in an American City* (1961). New Haven.

Derthick, Martha A., *City Politics in Washington, D.C.* (1962).

Dorsett, Lyle W., *Pendergast Machine* (1968). Kansas City.

Eisenstein, Louis, and Elliot Rosenberg, *Stripe of Tammany's Tiger* (1966).

Gosnell, Harold F., *Machine Politics: Chicago* (2nd ed., 1968).

Holli, Melvin G., *Reform in Detroit: Hazen S. Pingree and Urban Politics* (1969).

Holt, Michael F., *Forging a Majority: Republican Party in Pittsburgh, 1848–1860* (1969).

Lowi, Theodore J., *At the Pleasure of the Mayor: Patronage in New York City, 1898–1958* (1964).

Lubove, Roy, *Twentieth-Century Pittsburgh: Government, Business, and Environmental Change* (1969).

Mandelbaum, Seymour, *Boss Tweed's New York* (1965).

Miller, William D., *Memphis during Progressive Era* (1957).

Miller, Zane L., *Boss Cox's Cincinnati* (1968).

Milligan, Maurice M., *Missouri Waltz: Pendergast Machine* (1948).

Moscow, Warren, *What Have You Done for Me Lately? New York City Politics* (1967).

Pratt, John W., "Boss Tweed's Public Welfare Program," *N.Y. Hist. Soc. Quar.*, 45 (1961), 396.

Reynolds, George M., *Machine Politics in New Orleans, 1897–1926* (1936).

Straetz, Ralph A., *PR Politics in Cincinnati* (1958).

Thernstrom, Stephan, *Poverty and Politics in Boston: Origins of ABCD* (1969).

Wendt, Lloyd, and Herman Kogan, *Bosses in Lusty Chicago: Bath-House John and Hinky Dink* (1967). Issued in 1943 under the title, *Lords of the Levee*.

See also 10.3 for biographies/writings of the following mayors:

BOSTON

Curley, James M., 1874–1958

CHICAGO

Cermak, Anton J., 1873–1933
Daley, Richard J., 1902–
Harrison, Carter H., 1825–1893
Wentworth, John, 1815–1888

CLEVELAND

Johnson, Tom L., 1854–1911

NEW YORK CITY

Gaynor, William J., 1849–1913
Hewitt, Abram S., 1822–1903
Hone, Philip, 1780–1851
La Guardia, Fiorello H., 1882–1947
Low, Seth, 1850–1916
McClellan, George B., Jr., 1865–1940
Mitchel, John P., 1879–1918

TOLEDO

Whitlock, Brand, 1869–1934

19.3.9 Contemporary Urban Problems

Abrams, Charles, *The City is the Frontier* (1965).
Canty, Donald, *A Single Society: Alternatives to Urban Apartheid* (1969).
Eldredge, H. Wentworth, ed., *Taming Megalopolis* (2 vols., 1967).
Hadden, Jeffrey K. et al., eds., *Metropolis in Crisis, Social and Political Perspectives* (1967).
Lowe, Jeanne R., *Cities in a Race with Time* (1967).
Lyford, Joseph, *The Airtight Cage: A Study of New York's West Side* (1966).
Warner, Sam B., Jr., ed., *Planning for a Nation of Cities* (1966).
Wilson, James Q., ed., *The Metropolitan Enigma: Inquiries into the Nature and Dimensions of America's Urban Crisis* (rev. ed., 1968).

19.4 SUBURBIA

Berger, Bennett M., *Working-Class Suburb: A Study of Auto Workers in Suburbia* (1960).
Brush, John E., and Howard L. Gauthier, Jr., *Service Centers and Consumer Trips: Studies on Philadelphia Metropolitan Fringe* (1968).
Donaldson, Scott, *The Suburban Myth* (1969).
Gans, Herbert, *Levittowners: Ways of Life and Politics in New Suburban Community* (1967).
Gilbert, Charles E., *Governing the Suburbs* (1967).
Lancaster, Clay, *Old Brooklyn Heights: New York's First Suburb* (1961).
Seeley, J. R., et al., *Crestwood Heights: A Study of the Culture of Suburban Life* (1956).
Spectorsky, Auguste C., *Exurbanites* (1955).
Tunnard, Christopher, "Romantic Suburb in America," *Mag. of Art.* 40 (1947), 184.
Ward, David, "Comparative Historical Geography of Streetcar Suburbs in Boston, Massachusetts and Leeds, England, 1850–1920," Assoc. Am. Geographers, *Annals,* 54 (1964), 477.
Warner, Sam B., Jr., *Streetcar Suburbs: The Process of Growth in Boston, 1870–1900* (1962).
Wissink, G. A., *American Cities in Perspective, with Special Reference to Development of Fringe Areas* (1962).
Wood, Robert C., *Suburbia: People and Politics* (1959).

19.5 TOWNS

Allen, James B., *Company Town in the West* (1966).
Atherton, Lewis E., *Main Street on the Middle Border* (1954).
Black, John D., and Ayers Brinser, *Planning One Town: Petersham—A Hill Town in Massachusetts* (1952).
Dykstra, Robert R., *The Cattle Towns* (1968).
——— "Town-Country Conflict," *Agric. Hist.,* 38 (1964), 195.
Reps, John W., *Town Planning in Frontier America* (1969).
Smith, Page, *As a City Upon a Hill: Town in American History* (1966).
Vidich, Arthur J., and Joseph Bensman, *Small Town in Mass Society* (1958).

See also 18.11.3, Rural Life.

19.6 COMMUNITY SOCIOLOGICAL STUDIES

Bell, Earl Hoyt, *Sublette, Kansas* (1942)
Blumenthal, Albert, *Small Town Stuff* (1932).
Cohen, Irwin B., et al., *Economic and Social Survey of Botetourt County* (1942).

Dollard, John, *Caste and Class in a Southern Town* (1937).

Drake, St. Clair, and Horace R. Cayton, *Black Metropolis: A Study of Negro Life in a Northern City* (rev. ed., 1963).

Frazier, Edward F., *The Negro Family in Chicago* (1932).

Galpin, C. J., *Social Anatomy of an Agricultural Community* (1915).

Handlin, Oscar, "Yankee City Series," *New Eng. Quar.*, 15 (1942), 554.

Kohler, Lucille T., *Neosho, Missouri under the Impact of Army Camp Construction* (1944).

Kollmorgan, W. M., *The Old Order Amish of Lancaster County, Pennsylvania* (1942).

Leonard , Olen, and C. P. Loomis, *El Cerrito, New Mexico* (1941).

Lynd, Robert S., and Helen M. Lynd, *Middletown* (1929).

—— *Middletown in Transition* (1937).

McKenzie, Roderick D., *The Neighborhood: A Study of Local Life in the City of Columbus, Ohio* (1923).

Macleish, Kenneth, and Kimball Young, *Landaff, New Hampshire* (1942).

Moe, E. O., and Carl C. Taylor, *Irwin, Iowa* (1942).

Sims, N. L., *A Hoosier Village* (1912).

Voss, J. E., *Summer Resort: An Ecological Analysis of a Satellite Community* (1941).

Walker, Charles R., *Steeltown* (1950).

Ware, Caroline F., *Greenwich Village* (1935).

Warner, W. Lloyd, and Paul S. Lunt, *The Social Life of a Modern Community* (1941). Yankee City series.

—— and Leo Srole, *The Social Systems of American Ethnic Groups* (1945). Yankee City series.

—— and J. O. Low, *The Social System of the Modern Factory: The Strike: A Social Analysis* (1947), Yankee City series.

—— *The Living and the Dead: A Study of the Symbolic Life of Americans* (1959). Yankee City series.

—— et al., *Yankee City* (1963). One-volume abridgement of the above-mentioned titles in series.

West, James, *Plainville, U.S.A.* (1945).

Whyte, W. F., *Street Corner Society* (1943).

Williams, James M., *An American Town* (1906).

Wilson, Warren H., *Quaker Hill* (1907).

Wirth, Louis, *The Ghetto* (1928).

Wynne, Waller, *Harmony, Georgia* (1943).

Zorbaugh, H. W., *The Gold Coast and the Slum* (1929).

19.7 WOMEN

19.7.1 General

Benson, Mary S., *Women in Eighteenth Century America* (1935).

Breckinridge, Sophonisba P., *Women in the Twentieth Century* (1933).

Cassara, Beverly B., ed., *American Women* (1962).

Gruenberg, S. M., and H. S. Krech, *Many Lives of Modern Woman* (1952).

Irwin, Inez H., *Angels and Amazons* (1933).

Notable American Women, 1607–1950, Edward T. James, Janet Wilson James, and Paul S. Boyer, eds. (3 vols., 1971).

Lifton, Robert Jay, ed., *Woman in America* (1964). Reprinted from *Daedalus, 93,* no. 2 (1964).

Lundberg, Ferdinand, and M. F. Farnham, *Modern Woman* (1947).

McGovern, James R., *The American Woman's Pre-World War I Freedom in Manners and Morals* (1968).

Mead, Margaret, and Frances B. Kaplan, eds., *American Women* (1966).

Melder, Keith, "Ladies Bountiful: Organized Women's Benevolence in Early 19th Century America" *N.Y. Hist.*, 48 (1967), 231.

Nebraska Governor's Commission, *Nebraska Women, 1867–1967* (1967).

Ossoli, Margaret Fuller, *Woman in the Nineteenth Century* (1855).
Rogers, Agnes, ed., *Women Are Here to Stay.* (1949). Pictorial.
Scott, Anne Firor, *The Southern Lady: From Pedestal to Politics, 1830–1930* (1970).
U.S. President's Commission on Status of Women, *Report* (1963).
Welter, Barbara, "Anti-Intellectualism and American Woman," *Mid-America,* 48 (1966), 258.
———— "Cult of True Womanhood, 1820–1860," *Am. Quar.,* 18 (1966), 151.
Wittenmyer, A. T., *Woman's Temperance Crusade* (1877).
Wood, Mary I., *General Federation of Women's Clubs* (1912).
Wylie, Philip, *Generation of Vipers* (1942).

See also 18.17.8, Employment of Women.

19.7.2 Feminism

Blumberg, Dorothy R., "Unpublished Letters, 1884–1894, of Florence Kelley to Friedrich Engels," *Labor Hist.,* 5 (1964), 103.
Board, John C., "Jeannette Rankin: Lady from Montana," *Mont. Mag. Hist.,* 17 (1967), 2.
Brown, Ira V., "Woman's Rights Movement in Pennsylvania, 1848–1873," *Penn. Hist.,* 32 (1965), 153.
Catt, Carrie C., and N. R. Shuler, *Woman Suffrage and Politics* (1923).
Degler, Carl N., "Charlotte Perkins Gilman on Feminism," *Am. Quar.,* 8 (1956), 21.
Flexner, Eleanor, *Century of Struggle: The Woman's Rights Movement in the United States* (1959).
Friedan, Betty, *Feminine Mystique* (1963).
Gattey, Charles N., *Bloomer Girls* (1968).
Grimes, Alan P., *Puritan Ethic and Woman Suffrage* (1967).
Irwin, Inez H., *Story of Woman's Party* (1921).
Jensen, Oliver, *Revolt of American Woman* (1952).
Kenneally, James J., "Catholicism and Woman Suffrage in Massachusetts," *Cath. Hist. Rev.,* 53 (1967), 43.
Kraditor, Aileen S., *Ideas of the Woman Suffrage Movement, 1890–1920* (1965).
Lamson, Peggy, *Few Are Chosen: American Women in Political Life Today* (1968).
Millett, Kate, *Sexual Politics* (1970).
Neu, Charles E., "Olympia Brown and Woman's Suffrage Movement," *Wis. Mag. Hist.,* 43, (1960), 277.
Noun, Louise R., *Strong-Minded Women: Woman-Suffrage in Iowa* (1970).
O'Connor, Lillian, *Pioneer Women Orators: Ante-Bellum Reform Movement* (1954).
O'Neill, William L., *Everyone Was Brave: Feminism in America* (1969).
———— *The Woman Movement: Feminism in the United States and England* (1969).
Riegel, Robert E., *American Feminists* (1963).
———— "Women's Clothes and Women's Rights," *Am. Quar.,* 15 (1963), 390.
Root, G. C., *Women and Repeal* (1934).
Schaffer, Ronald, "The Montana Woman Suffrage Campaign, 1863–1872," *Neg. Hist.* 45 (1964).
Scott, Anne F., "After Suffrage: Southern Women in the Twenties," *JSH,* 30 (1964), 298.
Sinclair, Andrew, *The Better Half: Emancipation of American Woman* (1965).
Stanton, Elizabeth, Susan B. Anthony, and M. J. Gage, eds., *History of Woman Suffrage* (6 vols., 1881–1922).
Taylor, Elizabeth A., "The Women Suffrage Movement in Mississippi, 1890–1920," *Jour. Miss. Hist.,* 30 (1968), 1.
Taylor, Antoinette E., *Woman Suffrage Movement in Tennessee* (1957).
Thorp, Margaret F., *Female Persuasion: Six Strong-Minded Women* (1949). Nineteenth Century.
Violette, A. G., *Economic Feminism* (1925).
Werner, Emmy E., "Women in Congress, 1917–1964." *West. Pol. Quar.,* 19 (1966), 16.

See also 10.3 for biographies/writings of:

Anthony, Susan B., 1820–1906
Bloomer, Amelia, 1818–1894
Catt, Carrie Chapman, 1859–1947
Clay, Laura, 1849–1941
Felton, Rebecca L., 1835–1930
Fuller, Margaret, 1810–1850
Howe, Julia Ward, 1819–1910
Livermore, Mary A., 1820–1905
Sanger, Margaret, 1883–1966
Stanton, Elizabeth Cady, 1815–1902
Stone, Lucy, 1818–1893
Willard, Frances, 1839–1898
Woodhull, Victoria C., 1838–1927

19.8 MARRIAGE AND THE FAMILY

Baber, R. E., and E. A. Ross, *Changes in Size of American Families* (1924).
Bayles, G. J., *Woman and the Law* (1901).
Bridges, William E., "Family Patterns and Social Values in America, 1825–1875," *Am. Quar.,* 17 (1965), 3.
Calhoun, A. W., *A Social History of the American Family* (3 vols., 1917–1919).
Carson, W. E., *Marriage Revolt* (1915).
Cavan, Ruth Shonle, *The American Family* (1953).
Dennett, M. W., *Birth Control Laws* (1926).
Ditzion, Sidney H., *Marriage, Morals, and Sex in America: A History of Ideas* (1953).
Goodsell, Willystine, *History of the Family as a Social and Educational Institution* (1915).
Gordon, Albert I., *Intermarriage: Interfaith, Interracial, Interethnic* (1964).
Grabill, Wilson H., et al., *Fertility of American Women* (1958).
Hall, F. S., and E. W. Brooke, *American Marriage Laws* (1919).
Howard, George E., *History of Matrimonial Institutions, Chiefly in England and United States* (3 vols., 1904).
Kinsey, A. C., *Sexual Behavior in the Human Female* (1953).
———— et al., *Sexual Behavior in the Human Male* (1948).
Komarovsky, Mirra, *Blue-Collar Marriage* (1964).
Kuhn, Anne L., *Mother's Role in Childhood Education: New England Concepts, 1830–1860* (1947).
Kyrk, Hazel, *The Family in the American Economy* (1953).
Lindquist, Ruth, *Family in Present Social Order* (1931).
Masters, William H., and Virginia E. Johnson, *Human Sexual Inadequacy* (1970).
———— *Human Sexual Response* (1966).
Monahan, Thomas P., *Pattern of Age at Marriage in United States* (2 vols., 1951).
National Conference on Family Life, *American Family* (1949).
Parsons, Talcott and Robert F. Bales, *Family, Socialization and Interaction Process* (1955).
Partridge, Bellamy, and Otto Bettmann, *As We Were, Family Life in America, 1850-1900* (1946). Pictorial.
Rainwater, Lee, and Karol K. Weinstein, *And the Poor Get Children: Sex, Contraception and Family Planning in the Working Class* (1960).
Rainwater, Lee, *Behind Ghetto Walls: Black Family Life in a Federal Slum* (1970).
———— et al., *Workingman's Wife* (1959).
Rovit, Earl H., "American Concept of Home," *Am. Scholar,* 29 (1960), 521.
Sirjamaki, John, *The American Family in the Twentieth Century* (1953).
Stern, Bernard J., *The Family, Past and Present* (1938).
Truxal, Andrew G., and Francis E. Merrill, *Marriage, and the Family in American Culture* (1953).

Vernier, Chester G., *American Family Laws: A Comparative Study* (5 vols., 1931–1938).

Westoff, Charles, et al., *Family Growth in Metropolitan America* (1961).

Young, Kimball, *Isn't One Wife Enough?* (1954). Mormonism.

*   *   *   *   *   *   *

Aldous, Joan, and Reuben Hill, eds., *International Bibliography of Research in Marriage and the Family, 1900–1964* (1967).

Saveth, Edward N., "The Problem of American Family History," *Am. Quar.,* 21 (1969), 311.

19.8.1 Divorce

Blake, Nelson Manfred, *Road to Reno: A History of Divorce in the United States* (1962).

Cohen, Alfred, *Statistical Analysis of American Divorce* (1932).

Covers, Duncan, *Marriage and Divorce* (1889).

Keezer, F., *Marriage and Divorce* (3d ed., 1946); *Supplement* (1959).

Lichtenberger, J. P., *Divorce* (1909).

Mayer, Michael F., *Divorce and Annulment* (1966).

O'Neill, William L., *Divorce in Progressive Era* (1967).

Schouler, James, *Law of Domestic Relations* (1889).

Willcox, Walter F., *Divorce Problem* (1897).

Woolsey, T. D., *Divorce and Divorce Legislation* (1869).

19.9 YOUTH

19.9.1 General

Bell, Howard, *Youth Tell Their Story* (1938).

Bremner, Robert H., et al., eds., *Children and Youth in America: A Documentary History, 1600–1932* (2 vols., 1970).

Bronfenbrenner, Urie, *Two Worlds of Childhood: U.S. and USSR* (1970).

Coleman, James S., *The Adolescent Society: The Social Life of the Teenager and Its Impact on Education* (1961).

Coles, Robert, *Children of Crisis* (3 vols., 1968–1971).

Davis, Maxine, *Lost Generation* (1936).

Eisenstadt, S. N., *From Generation to Generation: Age Groups and Social Structure* (1964).

Erikson, Erik H., *Identity: Youth and Crisis* (1968).

——— ed., *Youth: Change and Challenge* (1963).

Ferguson, Thomas, and A. W. Kerr, *Handicapped Youth* (1959).

Friedenberg, Edgar Z., *Coming of Age In America* (1965).

Glazer, Nathan, "Student Politics in Democratic Society," *Am. Scholar,* 36 (1967), 202.

Goodman, Paul, *Growing Up Absurd* (1960).

Handlin, Oscar, and Mary F. Handlin, *Facing Life: Youth and the Family in American History* (1971).

Hollingshead, A. deB., *Elmtown's Youth* (1949).

Keniston, Kenneth, *Uncommitted: Alienated Youth* (1965).

——— "Youth, Change and Violence," *Am.Scholar,* 37 (1968), 227.

Kiefer, Monica M., *American Children through Their Books, 1700–1835* (1948).

Kuhn, Anne L., *Mother's Role in Childhood Education: New England Concepts, 1830–1860* (1947).

Lindsey, B. B., *Revolt of Modern Youth* (1925).

Rapson, Richard C., "American Children as Seen by British Travelers, 1845–1935," *Am. Quar.,* 17 (1965), 520.

Riessman, Frank, *The Culturally Deprived Child* (1962).

Roszak, Theodore, *The Making of a Counter Culture* (1969).
Stendler, C. B., *Children of Brasstown* (1949).
Strecker, E. A., *Their Mothers' Sons* (1951).
White House Conference on Children, *Children in a Democracy* (1940).
Winslow, Thacher, and F. P. Davidson, eds., *American Youth* (1940).
Wishy, Bernard, *Child and Republic: The Dawn of Modern Child Nurture* (1967).

See also 18.17.7, Child Labor.

19.9.2 Neglected and Delinquent Youth

Asbury, Herbert, *Gangs of New York* (1928).
Braeman, John, "Albert J. Beveridge and Child Labor Bill," *Ind. Mag. Hist.*, 60 (1964), 1.
Cicourel, Aaron V., *Social Organization of Juvenile Justice* (1967).
Cohen, Albert, *Delinquent Boys: The Culture of the Gang* (1955).
Deutsch, Albert, *Our Rejected Children* (1950).
Folks, Homer, *Care of Destitute, Neglected and Delinquent Children* (1902).
Glueck, Sheldon, "Juvenile Delinquency," *Jour. Crim. Law*, 51 (1960), 283.
────── and Eleanor Glueck, *Unraveling Juvenile Delinquency* (1950).
Hart, H. H., ed., *Preventive Treatment of Neglected Children* (1915).
Liebow, Elliot, *Tally's Corner: A Study of Negro Streetcorner Men* (1967).
Lou, H. H., *Juvenile Courts* (1927).
Mangold, J. B., *Problems of Child Welfare* (1914).
Matza, David, *Delinquency and Drift* (1964).
Scott, Marvin B., *The Racing Game* (1968).
Spergel, Irving, *Racketville, Slumtown, Haulburg* (1964).
Stevens, A. P., et al., "Child Slavery," *Arena*, 10 (1894), 117.
Thrasher, Frederic M., *Study of 1313 Gangs in Chicago*, James F. Short, Jr., ed. (rev. and abridged ed., 1963).
U.S. President's Commission on Law Enforcement and Administration of Justice. *Task Force Report: Juvenile Delinquency and Crime* (1967).
Yablonsky, Lewis, *The Hippie Trip* (1963).

*　　*　　*　　*　　*　　*　　*

U.S. Attorney General's Advisory Committee on Crime, *Bibliography on Juvenile Delinquency* (1936).

19.9.3 Reform Movements

Coleman, Sydney H., *Humane Society Leaders* (1924).
Eddy, Sherwood, *A Century with Youth: YMCA* (1944).
Hopkins, Charles H., *History of the Y.M.C.A. in North America* (1951).
Latourette, Kenneth S., *World Service: YMCA* (1957).
Lee, Joseph, *Constructive and Preventive Philanthropy* (1902).
McCrea, Roswell C., *Humane Movement* (1910).
Pence, Owen E., *Y.M.C.A. and Social Need* (1939).
Pickett, Robert S., *House of Refuge: Origins of Juvenile Reform in New York State, 1815–1857* (1969).
Rainwater, C. E., *Play Movement* (1921).
Tobey, J. A., *Children's Bureau* (1925).
Ufford, W. S., *Fresh Air Charity* (1897).

19.10 FRATERNAL AND SERVICE ORGANIZATIONS

Basye, Walter, *History and Operation of Fraternal Insurance* (1919).
Daraul, Akron, *History of Secret Societies* (1968).

Ferguson, Charles W., *Fifty Million Brothers* (1937).

Gist, N. P., *Secret Societies* (1940).

Hausknecht, Murray, *Joiners: A Study of Voluntary Associations in the United States* (1962).

Hill, Frank E., *Man-made Culture: Educational Activities of Men's Clubs* (1938).

Hill, W. B., "Great American Safety-Valve," *Century,* 44 (1892), 383.

Marden, Charles F., *Rotary and Its Brothers* (1935).

Meyer, Balthasar H., "Beneficiary Societies," *Am. Jour Sociol.* 6 (1901), 646.

Preuss, Arthur, *Dictionary of Secret and Other Societies* (1924).

Schlesinger, Arthur M., "Biography of a Nation of Joiners," in *Paths to the Present* (1949).

Smith, Constance, and Anne Freedman, *Voluntary Associations: Perspectives in the Literature* (1972).

20 Immigration and Ethnicity

20.1 IMMIGRATION

20.1.1 General

Abbott, Edith, *Historical Aspects of Immigration Problems: Select Documents* (1926).
Adamic, Louis, *From Many Lands* (1940).
———— *Nation of Nations* (1945).
Ander, O. Fritiof, ed., *In the Trek of the Immigrants: Essay to Carl Wittke* (1964).
Brown, Lawrence G., *Immigration* (1933).
Commager, Henry S., ed., *Immigration and American History: Essays in Honor of Theodore C. Blegen* (1961).
Davie, Maurice R., *World Immigration with Special Reference to the United States* (1936).
Fairchild, Henry P., *Immigration* (1925).
Ferenczi, Imre, *International Migrations.* Vol. I: *Statistics* (1929).
George Washington University, *Report on World Population Migrations as Related to the United States* (1956).
Guillet, Edwin C., *Great Migration: Atlantic Crossing by Sailing-ship since 1770* (2nd ed., 1963).
Handlin, Oscar, ed., *Immigration as a Factor in American History* (1959).
———— *Race and Nationality in American Life* (1957).
Hansen, Marcus L., *The Immigrant in American History,* Arthur M. Schlesinger, ed. (1940).
Huthmacher, J. Joseph, *Nation of Newcomers: Ethnic Minorities* (1967).
Jones, Maldwyn A., *American Immigration* (1960).
Stephenson, George M., *History of American Immigration* (1926).

* * * * * * *

George Washington University, *Report on World Population Migrations as Related to the United States* (1956). See bibliographies in its introductory essays.
Handlin, Oscar, and Mary F. Handlin, "New History and the Ethnic Factor in American Life," *Perspectives in Am. Hist.,* 4 (1970), 5.
Janeway, W. R., *Bibliography of Immigration 1900–1930* (1934).
Saveth, Edward N., *American Historians and European Immigrants* (1948).
Spear, Allan H., "Marcus Lee Hansen and Historiography of Immigration," *Wis. Mag. Hist.,* 44 (1961), 258.
U.S. Library of Congress, *Immigration* (1930).
———— *Immigration* (1943).
———— *List on the "National Origins" Provision* (1926).
Vecoli, Rudolph J., "Ethnicity: Neglected Dimension of American History," in Herbert J. Bass, ed., *State of American History* (1970), 70.

See also 21.11, Nativism and Bigotry.

20.1.2 Federal Policies

Bennett, Marion T., *American Immigration Policies* (1963).
Bernard, William S., *American Immigration Policy* (1950).
———— "Arms and the Alien: Post-war Hysteria," *Rocky Mtn. Law Rev.*, 11 (1939), 243.
Carey, Jane P., *Deportation of Aliens from United States to Europe* (1931).
Clyde, P. H., *United States Policy toward China, 1838–1939* (1940).
Divine, Robert A., *American Immigration Policy, 1924–1952* (1957).
Franklin, Frank G., *Legislative History of Naturalization* (1906).
Garis, Roy L., *Immigration Restriction* (1927).
Higham, John, *Strangers in the Land* (1967).
Kansas, Sidney, *United States Immigration, Exclusion and Deportation* (1940).
MacGeorge, A. E., "Restriction of Immigration, 1920 to 1925," *Monthly Lab. Rev.*, 22 (1926), 510.
Mann, Arthur, "Immigration," Am. Jew. Hist. Soc., *Publ.*, 46 (1957), 289.
Paul, Rodman W., *Abrogation of Gentlemen's Agreement* (1936).
Post, Louis F., *Deportations Delirium* (1923).
Preston, William, *Aliens and Dissenters: Federal Suppression of Radicals, 1903–1933* (1963).
Shaloo, J. P., "United States Immigration Policy, 1882–1948," in Dwight E. Lee and G. E. McReynolds, eds., *Essays in Honor of George H. Blakeslee* (1949).
Smith, Darrell H., and H. G. Herring, *Bureau of Immigration* (1924).
Tsiang, I-mien, *Question of Expatriation in America Prior to 1907* (1942).
U.S. President's Commission on Immigration and Naturalization, *Whom We Shall Welcome* (1953).

*   *   *   *   *   *   *

U.S. Library of Congress, *Deportation of Aliens* (1931).

20.1.3 Immigrants and the City

Cole, Donald B., *Immigrant City: Lawrence, Massachusetts, 1845–1921* (1963).
Ernst, Robert, *Immigrant Life in New York City, 1825–1863* (1949).
Gans, Herbert, *The Urban Villagers: Group and Class in the Life of Italian-Americans* (1962).
Glazer, Nathan, and Daniel P. Moynihan, *Beyond the Melting Pot: New York City* (rev. ed., 1970).
Gordon, Daniel N., "Immigrants and Urban Governmental Form in American Cities, 1933–1960," *Am. Jour. Sociology*, 74 (1968), 158.
Handlin, Oscar, *The Newcomers: Negroes and Puerto Ricans in a Changing Metropolis* (1959).
Hapgood, Hutchins, *Spirit of the Ghetto* (1902). Moses Rischin, ed. (1967).
Korman, Gerd, *Industrialization, Immigrants and Americanizers: Milwaukee, 1866–1921* (1967).
Lieberson, Stanley, *Ethnic Patterns in American Cities* (1963).
Samora, Julian, and Richard Lamanna, *Mexican-Americans in a Midwest Metropolis: East Chicago* (1967).
Suttles, Gerald, *Social Order of the Slum: Ethnicity and Territory in the Inner City* (1968).
Ward, David, "Emergence of Central Immigrant Ghettoes in American Cities, 1840–1920," Assoc. Am. Geographers, *Annals*, 58 (1968), 343.
Williams, Robin M., *Strangers Next Door: Ethnic Relations in American Communities* (1964).

20.1.4 Refugees and Immigrants Since 1930

Carey, Jane, "Admission and Integration of Refugees," *Jour. of Int. Affairs*, 7 (1953), 66.

"Characteristics of New Immigration," American Academy of Political and Social Science, *Annals, 367* (1966), 4.

Committee for the Study of Recent Immigration from Europe, *Refugees in America*. Report by Maurice R. Davie et al. (1947).

Displaced Persons Commission, *Memo to America: Final Report* (1952).

Feingold, Henry L., *The Politics of Rescue: The Roosevelt Administration and the Holocaust, 1938–1945* (1970).

Fermi, Laura, *Illustrious Immigrants: Intellectual Migration from Europe, 1930–41* (1968).

Fleming, Donald, and Bernard Bailyn, eds., *Intellectual Migration: Europe and America, 1930–1960* (1969).

Heberle, Rudolph, and Dudley S. Hall, *New Americans: Displaced Persons in Louisiana and Mississippi* (1951).

Kent, Donald P., *Refugee Intellectual, 1933–1941* (1953).

Wyman, David S., *Paper Walls: Refugee Crisis, 1938–1941* (1968).

20.1.5 Immigrants and the Economy

Barbash, Jack, "Ethnic Factors in the Development of the American Labor Movement," in Industrial Relations Research Association, *Interpreting the Labor Movement* (1952).

Erickson, Charlotte, *American Industry and the European Immigrant, 1860–1885* (1957).

Feldman, Herman, *Racial Factors in American Industry* (1931).

Gates, Paul W., *The Illinois Central Railroad and Its Colonization Work* (1934).

Heald, Morrell, "Business Attitudes toward European Immigration, 1800–1900," *Jour. Econ. Hist.* 13 (1953), 291.

Heaton, Herbert, "Industrial Immigrant in United States, 1783–1812," *Am. Philos. Soc. Proc.,* 45 (1951), 519.

Hedges, James B., "Promotion of Immigration to Pacific Northwest by Railroads," *MVHR,* 15 (1928), 183.

Hiestand, Dale L., *Economic Growth and Employment Opportunities for Minorities* (1964).

Hourwich, I. S., *Immigration and Labor* (1912).

Jerome, Harry V., *Migration and Business Cycles* (1926).

Leiserson, William M., *Adjusting Immigrant and Industry* (1924).

Overton, Richard C., *Burlington West: A Colonization History of the Burlington Railroad* (1941).

Taylor, Paul S., *Mexican Labor in the United States* (3 vols., 1930–1933).

Thomas, Brinley, *Migration and Economic Growth* (1954).

Warne, Frank J., *The Slav Invasion and the Mine Workers* (1904).

Yearley, Clifton K., Jr., *Britons in American Labor* (1957).

20.1.6 Acculturation

Borrie, Wilfred D., et al., *Cultural Integration of Immigrants* (1959).

Brown, Francis J., and Joseph S. Roucek, eds., *One America: History, Contributions and Present Problems of Our Racial and National Minorities* (3d ed., 1952).

Carter, Edward C. II, "Naturalization in Philadelphia, 1789–1806," *Penn. Mag. Hist. Biog.,* 94 (1970), 331.

Fishman, Joshua A., et al., *Language Loyalty: Maintenance of Non-English Mother Tongues* (1966).

Glazer, Nathan, and Daniel P. Moynihan, *Beyond the Melting Pot: New York City* (rev. ed., 1970).

Gleason, Philip, "Immigrant Group's Interest in Progressive Reform: German-American Catholics," *AHR,* 73 (1967), 367.

—— "Melting Pot: Symbol of Fusion or Confusion?" *Am. Quar.,* 16 (1964), 20.

Gordon, Milton M., *Assimilation in American Life: The Role of Race, Religion and National Origins* (1964).

Handlin, Oscar, *The American People in the Twentieth Century* (1954).

—— *Boston's Immigrants: A Study in Acculturation* (rev. ed., 1959).

—— ed., *Children of Uprooted* (1966).

———— *The Uprooted* (1950).

Hartmann, Edward G., *Movement to Americanize the Immigrant* (1948).

Hutchinson, Edward P., *Immigrants and Their Children, 1850–1950* (1956).

Kariel, Henry S., *Decline of American Pluralism* (1961).

Kelly, Mary G., *Catholic Immigrant Colonization Projects in the United States, 1815–1860* (1939).

Marden, Charles F., and Gladys Meyer, *Minorities in American Society* (3d ed., 1968).

Nam, Charles B., "Nationality Groups and Social Stratification in America," *Social Forces,* 37 (1959), 328.

Neidle, Cecyle S., ed., *New Americans* (1967).

Park, Robert E., *Immigrant Press and Its Control* (1922).

Rose, Arnold, and Caroline Rose, *America Divided: Minority Group Relations* (1948).

Shannon, James P., *Catholic Colonization on the Western Frontier* (1957).

Smith, William C., *Americans in the Making* (1939).

Solomon, Barbara M., *Ancestors and Immigrants: A Changing New England Tradition* (1956).

Warner, W. Lloyd, and Leo Srole, *Social Systems of American Ethnic Groups* (1945).

Wolfinger, Raymond E., "Ethnic Voting," *Am. Pol. Sci. Rev.,* 59 (1965), 896.

Young, Donald R., *Minority Peoples in the Depression* (1937).

* * * * * * *

Handlin, Oscar and Mary F. Handlin, "New History and the Ethnic Factor in American Life," *Perspectives in Am. Hist.,* 4 (1970), 5.

20.2 FRENCH CANADIANS

Hamon, E., *Canadiens-Français de la Nouvelle Angleterre* (1891).

Hansen, Marcus L., *Mingling of the Canadian and American Peoples* (1940).

Lower, A. R. M., "New France in New England," *NEQ,* 2 (1929), 278.

20.3 SPANISH-SPEAKING PEOPLE

Álvarez, José Hernández, "Mexican Immigration, 1910–1950," *Jour. Inter-Am. Studies,* 8 (1966), 471.

Fitzpatrick, Joseph P., *Puerto Rican Americans: The Meaning of Migration to the Mainland.* (1971).

Fogel, Walter A., *Education and Income of Mexican-Americans in Southwest* (1965).

———— *Mexican Americans in Southwest Labor Markets* (1967).

Gamio, Manuel, *Mexican Immigration to United States* (1930).

Gonzalez, Nancie L., *Spanish Americans of New Mexico* (1969).

Griffith, Beatrice, *American Me* (1948).

Handlin, Oscar, *The Newcomers: Negroes and Puerto Ricans in a Changing Metropolis* (1959).

McWilliams, Carey, *North from Mexico: Spanish-Speaking People of United States* (1948).

Matthiessen, Peter, *Salsipuedes: Cesar Chavez and the New American Revolution* (1970).

Mittelbach, Frank G., and Grace Marshall, *Burden of Poverty* (1966). Mexicans in the Southwest.

Pitt, Leonard, *Decline of Californios: Spanish-Speaking Californians, 1846–1890* (1966).

Robinson, Cecil, "Mexican Presence in American Southwest," *Am. West,* 3 (1966), 6.

———— *With the Ears of Strangers: The Mexican in American Literature* (1963).

Rubel, Arthur J., *Across the Tracks: Mexican-Americans in a Texas City* (1966).

Samora, Julian, and Richard Lamanna, *Mexican-Americans in a Midwest Metropolis: East Chicago* (1967).

Sanchez, George I., *Forgotten People: New Mexicans* (1940).

Scruggs, Otey M., "Texas and the Bracero Program, 1942–1947," *Pac. Hist. Rev.,* 32 (1963), 251.

Servin, Manuel P., "Pre-World War II Mexican-American: An Interpretation," *Calif. Hist. Soc. Quar.,* 45 (1966), 325.

Taylor, Paul S., *An American-Mexican Frontier: Nueces County, Texas* (1934).

────── *Mexican Labor in United States* (2 vols., 1930–32).

Tuck, Ruth D., *Not with the Fist: Mexican-Americans in a Southwest City* (1946).

*   *   *   *   *   *   *

Johnson, John J., et al., eds., *The Mexican American: Selected and Annotated Bibliography* (1969).

20.4 ENGLISH, SCOTS, AND WELSH

Berthoff, Rowland T., *British Immigrants in Industrial America, 1790–1950* (1953).

Buchanan, Frederick S., "Scots Among the Mormons," *Utah Hist. Quar.,* 36 (1968), 328.

Conway, Alan, ed., *Welsh in America: Letters from Immigrants* (1961).

Dodd, Arthur H., *Character of Early Welsh Emigration* (1953).

Dunaway, Wayland F., *Scotch Irish of Colonial Pennsylvania* (1944).

Erickson, Charlotte, "Agrarian Myths of English Immigrants," in *In the Trek of the Immigrants: Essays Presented to Carl Wittke* (1964).

Ford, Henry J., *The Scotch-Irish in America* (1914).

Glasgow, Maude, *Scotch-Irish in Northern Ireland and American Colonies* (1936).

Graham, Ian C. C., *Colonists from Scotland: Emigration to North America, 1707–1783* (1856).

Green, Edward R. R., ed., *Essays in Scotch-Irish History* (1969).

Hartman, Edward G., *Americans from Wales* (1967).

Johnson, Stanley C., *History of Emigration from United Kingdom to North America, 1763–1912* (1913).

Klett, Guy S., *Scotch-Irish in Pennsylvania* (1948).

Leyburn, James G., *The Scotch-Irish* (1962).

Rowse, Alfred L., *Cousin Jacks: Cornish in America* (1969).

Shepperson, Wilbur S., *British Emigration to North America: Early Victorian Period* (1957).

────── *Promotion of British Emigration by Agents for American Lands, 1840–1860* (1954).

Winther, Oscar O., "English Migration to American West, 1865–1900," *Huntington Lib. Quar.,* 27 (1964), 159.

Yearley, Clifton K., Jr., *Britons in American Labor, 1820–1914* (1957).

20.5 IRISH

Adams, William Forbes, *Ireland and Irish Emigration* (1932).

Brown, Thomas N., *Irish-American Nationalism, 1870–1890* (1966).

D'Arcy, William, *Fenian Movement in United States, 1858–1886* (1947).

Glanz, Rudolph, *Jew and Irish* (1966).

Handlin, Oscar, *Boston's Immigrants: A Study in Acculturation* (1959).

Levine, Edward M., *The Irish and Irish Politicians* (1966).

McDonald, Sister Justille, *History of the Irish in Wisconsin in the Nineteenth Century* (1954).

Niehaus, Earl F., *Irish in New Orleans, 1800–1860* (1965).

Potter, George, *To the Golden Door: Irish in Ireland and America* (1960).

Shannon, William V., *American Irish* (rev. ed., 1966).

Wittke, Carl, *Irish in America* (1956).

20.6 SCANDINAVIANS

Ander, O. Fritiof, "Americanization of Swedish Immigrant," Ill. State Hist. Soc.,
    Jour., 26 (1933–34), 136.
Anderson, Arlow W., *Emigrant Takes His Stand: Norwegian-American Press,
    1847–1872* (1953).
Babcock, Kendric C., *Scandinavian Element* (1914).
Benson, A. B., and Naboth Hedin, *Americans from Sweden* (1950).
Bjork, Kenneth, *Saga in Steel and Concrete: Norwegian Engineers* (1947).
——— *West of the Great Divide: Norwegian Migration to Pacific Coast, 1847–1893*
    (1958).
Blegen, Theodore C., *Grass Roots History* (1947).
——— ed., *Land of Their Choice: Immigrants* (1955).
——— *Norwegian Migration to America* (2 vols., 1931–40).
Capps, Finis H., *From Isolationism to Involvement: Swedish Immigrant Press,
    1914–1945* (1966).
Christensen, Thomas P., *History of Danes in Iowa* (1952).
Dowie, James Iverne, *Prairie Grass Dividing* (1959). Swedish immigrants in
    Nebraska.
Haugen, Einar I., *Norwegian Language in America: Bilingual Behavior* (2nd ed.,
    2 vols., 1969).
Hoglund, A. William, *Finnish Immigrants in America, 1880–1920* (1960).
Jalkanen, Ralph J., ed., *Finns in North America: A Symposium* (1969).
Janson, Florence E., *Background of Swedish Immigration* (1931).
Kolehmainen, John I., and George W. Hill, *Haven in the Woods: Finns in
    Wisconsin* (1965).
Lindberg, J. S., *Background of Swedish Emigration* (1930).
Lindquist, Emory K., "The Swedish Immigrant and Life in Kansas" *Kans. Hist.
    Quar.* 29 (1963), 1.
Mulder, William, *Homeward to Zion: Mormon Migration from Scandinavia* (1957).
Nelson, Olaf N., ed., *Scandinavians* (1899).
Norwegian-American Historical Association, *Records* (21 vols., 1926–1962).
Qualey, C. C., *Norwegian Settlement in the United States* (1938).
Scott, Franklin D., "Sweden's Constructive Opposition to Emigration," *Jour.
    Mod. Hist.,* 37 (1965), 307.
Stephenson, George M., *Religious Aspects of Swedish Immigration* (1932).
——— ed., "Typical 'America Letters,'" Swedish Hist. Soc., *Year-Book,* 7
    (1921), 52.
Walters, Thorstina J., *Modern Sagas: Icelanders in North America* (1953).
Westin, Gunnar, "Background of Swedish Immigration, 1840–1850," in *Swedish
    Immigrant Community in Transition: Essays in Honor of Dr. Conrad Bergendoff*
    (1963).

*   *   *   *   *   *   *

Ander, O. Fritiof, *Cultural Heritage of Swedish Immigrant: Selected References*
    (1956).
Kolehmainen, John I., *Finns in America: Bibliographical Guide* (1947).

20.7 OTHER WEST EUROPEANS

Barry, Coleman J., *Catholic Church and German Americans* (1953).
Childs, Frances S., *French Refugee Life in the United States, 1790–1800* (1940).
Davis-DuBois, Rachel, and Emma Schweppe, *Germans in American Life* (1936).
Dobert, Eitel W., *Deutsche Demokraten in Amerika: die Achtundvierziger und ihre
    Schriften* (1958).
Easum, Chester V., *Americanization of Carl Schurz* (1929).
Faust, A. B., *German Element in the United States* (rev. ed., 2 vols., 1927).
Foerster, R. F., *Italian Immigration* (1919).
Gilkey, George R., "United States and Italy: Migration and Repatriation," *Jour.
    Devel. Areas,* 2 (1967), 23.

Gleason, Philip, *Conservative Reformers. German-American Catholics and Social Order* (1968).
Hawgood, J. A., *Tragedy of German-America* (1940).
Huizinga, G. F., *What the Dutch Have Done in the West* (1909).
Jordan, Terry G., *German Seed in Texas Soil* (1966).
Klees, Frederic, *The Pennsylvania Dutch* (1950). Germans.
Leibbrandt, Georg, "Emigration of German Mennonites from Russia," *Mennonite Quar. Rev.*, 6 (1932), 205; 7 (1933), 5.
Lucas, Henry S., ed., *Dutch Immigrant Memoirs and Related Writings* (2 vols., 1955).
―――― *Netherlanders in America* (1955).
Magnan, D. M. A., *Histoire de la race française aux Etats-Unis* (1912).
Meier, Heinz K., *United States and Switzerland in the Nineteenth Century* (1963).
Mulder, Arnold, *Americans from Holland* (1947).
Nelli, Humbert S., *Italians in Chicago, 1880–1930* (1970).
O'Connor, Richard, *German-Americans* (1968).
Pochmann, Henry A., et al., *German Culture in America, 1600–1900* (1957).
Reimer, Gustav E., and G. R. Gaeddert, *Exiled by the Czar: Cornelius Jansen and Mennonite Migration, 1874* (1956).
Rolle, Andrew F., *Immigrant Upraised: Italian Adventurers and Colonists* (1968).
Schafer, Joseph, "Yankee and Teuton in Wisconsin," *Wis. Mag. Hist.* 6 (1922), 125.
Schlarman, Joseph H., *From Quebec to New Orleans: French in America* (1929).
Vagts, Alfred, *Deutsch-Amerikanische Rückwanderung* (1960).
Wabeke, Bertus H., *Dutch Emigration, 1624–1860* (1944).
Williams, Phyllis H., *South Italian Folkways in Europe and America* (1938).
Wittke, Carl, *German-Language Press in America* (1957).
―――― *Refugees of Revolution: German Forty-Eighters in America* (1952).
Wust, Klaus, *The Virginia Germans* (1969).
Zucker, Adolph E., ed., *Forty-eighters* (1950).

*   *   *   *   *   *   *

Pochmann, Henry A., *Bibliography of German Culture in America to 1840* (1953).

See also 24.7.6, German Sects.

20.8 EAST EUROPEANS

Balch, Emily G., *Our Slavic Fellow Citizens* (1910).
Çada, Joseph, *Czech-American Catholics, 1850–1920* (1964).
Čapek, Thomas, *Čechs in America* (1920).
Fairchild, Henry P., *Greek Immigration to the United States* (1911).
Govorchin, Gerald G., *Americans from Yugoslavia* (1961).
Konnyu, Leslie, *Hungarians in the United States* (1967).
Lengyel, Emil, *Americans from Hungary* (1948).
Lerski, Jerzy J., *A Polish Chapter in Jacksonian America* (1958).
Miller, Kenneth D., *Czecho-Slovaks in America* (1922).
Saloutos, Theodore, *Greeks in the United States* (1964).
―――― *They Remember America: Repatriated Greek-Americans* (1956).
Simirenko, Alex, *Pilgrims, Colonists, and Frontiersmen* (1964). Russians in Minneapolis.
Smith, Charles H., *Coming of Russian Mennonities* (1927).
Souders, David A., *Magyars in America* (1922).
Thomas, William I., and Florian Znaniecki, *The Polish Peasant in Europe and America* (1918).
Wytrwal, Joseph A., *America's Polish Heritage* (1961).

*   *   *   *   *   *   *

Wepsiec, Jan, *Polish American Serial Publications, 1842–1966: Annotated Bibliography* (1968).

See also 24.7.11, Denominational Histories–Orthodox for Greeks and Ukranians.

20.9 EAST ASIANS

Barth, Gunther, *Bitter Strength: A History of the Chinese in the United States, 1850–1870* (1964).
Chiu, Ping, *Chinese Labor in California, 1850–1880* (1963).
Clyde, P. H., *United States Policy toward China, 1838–1939* (1940).
Coletta, Paolo E., "Bryan and the California Alien Lien Legislation," *Pac. Hist. Rev.*, 36 (1967), 163.
Daniels, Roger, *Politics of Prejudice: Anti-Japanese Movement in California* (1962).
Dillon, Richard H., *Hatchet Men: Tong Wars in San Francisco's Chinatown* (1962).
Gordon, Donald C., "Roosevelt's 'Smart Yankee' Trick," *Pac. Hist. Rev.*, 30 (1961), 351.
Hosokawa, Bill, *Nisei: Quiet Americans* (1969).
Ichihashi, Yamato, *Japanese in United States* (1932).
Iwata, Masakazu, "Japanese Immigrants in California Agriculture," *Agric. Hist.*, 36 (1962), 25.
Karlin, Jules, "Anti-Chinese Outbreaks in Seattle, 1885-1886," *Pac. Northw. Quar.*, 39 (1948), 103.
Karlin, Jules, "The Anti-Chinese Outbreak in Tacoma, 1885," *Pac. Hist. Rev.*, 23 (1954), 271.
Konvitz, Milton R., *Alien and the Asiatic in American Law* (1946).
Kung, S. W., *Chinese in American Life* (1962).
Lancaster, Clay, *Japanese Influence in America* (1963).
Lee, Rose H., *Chinese in the United States* (1960).
Lind, A. W., *Hawaii's Japanese* (1946).
Loewen, James W., *The Mississippi Chinese: Between Black and White* (1971). From Reconstruction to the present.
McWilliams, Carey, *Prejudice* (1944).
Mearns, Eliot G., *Resident Orientals on the American Pacific Coast* (1927).
Miller, Stuart C., *Unwelcome Immigrant: American Image of Chinese, 1785–1882* (1969).
Miyamoto, S. Frank, "Japanese Minority in Pacific Northwest," *Pac. Northw. Quar.*, 54 (1963), 143.
Pursinger, Marvin G., "Japanese Settle in Oregon, 1880–1920," *Jour. of West,* 5 (1966), 251.
Riggs, F. W., *Pressures on Congress: Repeal of Chinese Exclusion* (1950).
Sandmeyer, E. C., *Anti-Chinese Movement in California* (1939).
Seager, Robert II, "Denominational Reactions to Chinese Immigration to California, 1856–1892," *Pac. Hist. Rev.,* 28 (1959), 49.
Smith, Bradford, *Americans from Japan* (1948).
Sung, Betty L., *Mountain of Gold: Chinese in America* (1967).
Tupper, Eleanor, and G. E. McReynolds, *Japan in American Public Opinion* (1937).
Williams, Frederick W., *Anson Burlingame and First Chinese Mission* (1912).

*   *   *   *   *   *   *

Jones, Helen G. D., *Japanese in United States: Selected List of References* (1946).
Cowan, R. E., and Boutwell Dunlap, *Bibliography of Chinese Question* (1909).
Liu, Kwang-ching, *Americans and Chinese: A Historical Essay and a Bibliography* (1963).
U.S. Library of Congress, *Select List on Chinese Immigration* (1929).

20.10 JEWS

20.10.1 General

American Jewish Archives, *Essays in American Jewish History* (1959).
American Jewish Year Book 1899–   . Annual.
Berman, Hyman, "Jewish Labor Movement," *Am. Jew. Hist. Quar.*, 52 (1962), 79.
Blau, Joseph L., and Salo W. Baron, eds., *Jews of the United States, 1790–1840: Documentary History* (3 vols., 1963).
Cohen, Henry, "Crisis and Reaction" *Am. Jewish Archives*, 5 (1953), 71.
Dinnerstein, Leonard, *Leo Frank Case* (1966).
Edidin, Ben M., *Jewish Community Life in America* (1947).
Foner, Philip S., *Jews in American History, 1654–1865* (1946).
Friedman, Lee M., *Pilgrims in a New Land* (1948).
Fuchs, Lawrence H., *Political Behavior of American Jews* (1956).
Glanz, Rudolf, *Jew and Irish* (1966).
——— *Jew in Old American Folklore* (1961).
——— "Jewish Social Conditions as Seen by the Muckrakers," *YIVO* Annual of Jewish Social Science, 9 (1954), 308.
Gordon, Albert I., *Jews in Transition* (1949).
Guttmann, Allen, "Jewish Radicals, Jewish Writers," *Am. Scholar*, 32 (1963), 563.
Halperin, Samuel, *Political World of American Zionism* (1961).
Handlin, Oscar, *Adventure in Freedom: Three Hundred Years of Jewish Life in America* (1954).
Higham, John, "Anti-Semitism in Gilded Age," *MVHR*, 43 (1957), 559.
Isaacs, Harold R., *American Jews in Israel* (1967).
Karpf, M. J., *Jewish Community Organization* (1938).
Korn, Bertram W., *Eventful Years and Experiences: Nineteenth Century American Jewish History* (1954).
Kramer, Judith R., and Seymour Leventman, *Children of the Gilded Ghetto: American Jews* (1961).
Lebeson, Anita L., *Jewish Pioneers in America, 1492–1848* (1931).
——— *Pilgrim People* (1950).
McWilliams, Carey, *Mask for Privilege: Anti-Semitism* (1948).
Marcus, Jacob R., ed., *Memoirs of American Jews, 1775–1865* (3 vols., 1955–1956).
Meyer, Isidore S., ed., *Early History of Zionism in America* (1958).
Panitz, Esther L., "In Defense of the Jewish Immigrant (1891–1924)," *Am. Jew. Hist. Quar.*, 55 (1965), 57.
——— "Jewish Immigration, 1891–1924," *Am. Jewish Hist. Quar.*, 53 (1963), 99; 55 (1965), 57.
——— "Polarity of Jewish Attitudes to Immigration," *Am. Jew. Hist. Quar.*, 53 (1963), 99.
Pollack, Norman, "Myth of Populist Anti-Semitism," *AHR*, 68 (1962), 76.
Rosenbloom, Joseph R., *Biographical Dictionary of Early American Jews through 1800* (1960).
Rosenswaike, Ira, "Jewish Population of United States 1820," *Am. Jew. Hist. Quar.*, 53 (1963), 131.
Selznick, Gertrude J., and Stephen Steinberg, *Tenacity of Prejudice: Anti-Semitism in Contemporary America* (1969).
Sherman, Charles B., *The Jew within American Society: Ethnic Individuality* (1961).
Sklare, Marshall, ed., *Jews: Social Patterns* (1958).
Stembler, Charles H., et al., *Jews in the Mind of America*, George Salomon, ed. (1966).
Strong, Donald S., *Organized Anti-Semitism in America 1930–40* (1941).
Szajkowski, Zosa, "Private and Organized Jewish Overseas Relief, 1914–1938," *Am. Jew. Hist. Quar.*, 57 (1967), 52.
Teller, Judd L., *Strangers and Natives: Evolution of American Jew from 1921 to Present* (1968).
Wiernik, Peter, *Jews in America* (1931).

*   *   *   *   *   *   *

Berg, Harry, Mrs., and Jacob R. Marcus, eds., *Jewish Americana* (1954).
Davis, Moshe, and Isadore S. Meyer, eds., *Writing of American Jewish History* (1957).
Kaganoff, Nathan M., "Judaica America," *Am. Jew. Hist. Quar.*, 55 (1965), 235.
Rischin, Moses, *Inventory of American Jewish History* (1954).
Rosenbach, A. S. W., *An American Jewish Bibliography until 1850* (1926).
Tumin, Melvin M., *An Inventory and Appraisal of Research on American Anti-Semitism* (1961).

See also 21.11, Nativism and Bigotry; 24.77, Judaism; 25.14 Racial Thought.

20.10.2 Group Histories

Adler, Selig, and Thomas E. Connolly, *From Ararat to Suburbia: Jewish Community of Buffalo* (1960).
Breck, Allen duP., *Centennial History of Jews of Colorado, 1859–1959* (1960).
Broches, Samuel, *Jews in New England* (2 vols., 1942).
Gartner, Lloyd P., "Jews of New York's East Side, 1890–1893," *Am. Jew. Hist. Quar.*, 53 (1964), 264.
Glanz, Rudolph, *Jews of California: From Discovery of Gold until 1880* (1960).
Goren, Arthur A., *New York Jews and Quest for Community: Kehillah Experiment, 1908–1922* (1970).
Grinstein, Hyman B., *Rise of Jewish Community of New York, 1654–1860* (1945).
Kohn, S. Joshua, *Jewish Community of Utica, New York, 1847–1948* (1949).
Korn, Bertram W., *Early Jews of New Orleans* (1969).
Plaut, W. Gunther, *Jews in Minnesota: The First Seventy-Five Years* (1959).
Pool, David de S., *Portraits in Stone: Jewish Settlers, 1682–1831* (1952). New York.
Rischin, Moses, *The Promised City: New York's Jews, 1870–1914* (1962).
Rosenberg, Stuart E., *Jewish Community in Rochester, 1843–1925* (1954).
Rudolph, Bernard G., *From a Minyan to a Community: A History of the Jews of Syracuse* (1970).
Solomon, Barbara M., *Pioneers in Service: Associated Jewish Philanthropies of Boston* (1956).
Swichkow, Louis J., and Lloyd P. Gartner, *History of Jews of Milwaukee* (1963).
Vorspan, Max, and Lloyd P. Gartner, *History of Jews of Los Angeles* (1970).
Wolf II, Edwin, and Maxwell Whiteman, *History of Jews of Philadelphia from Colonial Times to the Age of Jackson* (1957).

*   *   *   *   *   *   *

Stern, Norton B., ed., *California Jewish History. Bibliography: Gold Rush to Post-World War I* (1967).

20.11 INDIANS

20.11.1 General

American Heritage, Book of Indians (1961).
"American Indians and American Life," Am. Acad. Pol. and Soc. Sci., *Annals*, (May 1957). Entire issue.
Collier, John, *Indians of the Americas* (1947).
Debo, Angie, *History of Indians of the United States* (1971).
Ellis, George E., *Red Man and White Man in North America from Its Discovery to Present Time* (1882).
Fey, Harold E., and D'Arcy McNickle, *Indians and Other Americans: Two Ways of Life Meet* (1959).
Forbes, Jack D., ed., *Indian in America's Past* (1964).

Hagan, William T., *American Indians* (1961).
Hodge, Frederick W., *Handbook of American Indians North of Mexico* (2 vols:, 1907–1910).
Josephy, Alvin M., Jr., *Patriot Chiefs: American Indian Leadership* (1961).
Leupp, Francis E., *In Red Man's Land* (1914).
McLeod, William C., *American Indian Frontier* (1928).
McNickle, D'Arcy, *They Came Here First: Epic of the American Indian* (1949).
Matthew, Stirling, et al., *Indians of the Americas* (1963).
Moorehead, Warren K., *The American Indian in the United States, 1850–1914* (1914).
Spicer, Edward H., *Short History of Indians of the United States* (1969).
U.S. Department of Interior, *Biographical and Historical Index of American Indians and Persons Involved in Indian Affairs* (8 vols., 1966). A subject catalog.
Washburn, Wilcomb E., ed., *Indian and White Man* (1964).

*   *   *   *   *   *   *

Dockstader, Frederick J., *The American Indian in Graduate Studies: Bibliography of Theses and Dissertations* (1957).
Freeman, John F., comp., *Guide to Manuscripts Relating to the American Indian in Library of American Philosophical Society* (1965).
Newberry Library, *Dictionary Catalog of Ayer Collection of Americana and American Indians* (16 vols., 1961).
U.S. Bureau of American Ethnology, *List of Publications of the Bureau of American Ethnology with Index to Authors and Titles* (rev. ed., 1962).

See also 10.3 for biographies/writings of:

Black Hawk, 1767–1838
Brant, Joseph, 1742–1807
Chief Joseph 1840–1904
Crazy Horse, ca. 1849–1877
Red Jacket, ca. 1758–1830
Sitting Bull, 1834–1890
Tecumseh, 1768–1813

20.11.2 Indian Life in Paintings and Photographs

Catlin, George, *Episodes from Life among the Indians,* Marvin C. Ross, ed. (1959).
Harper, J. Russell, ed., *Paul Kane's Frontier* (1971).
Kinietz, W. Vernon, *John Mix Stanley and His Indian Painting* (1942).
La Farge, Oliver, *Pictorial History of the American Indian* (1956).
McCracken, Harold, *George Catlin and the Old Frontier* (1959).
McDermott, John F., *Seth Eastman: Pictorial Historian of the Indian* (1961).
McKenny, Thomas L., and James Hall, *History of Indian Tribes of North America* (3 vols., 1836–1844).
Point, Nicholas, *Wilderness Kingdom, 1840–1847: Journals and Paintings* (1868), Joseph P. Donnelly, ed. (1967).
Prettyman, William S., *Indian Territory: Photographic Record,* Robert E. Cunningham, ed. (1957).
Remington, Frederic, *Drawings* (1897).
——— *Remington's Frontier Sketches* (1898).

20.11.3 Pre-Columbian Studies

Alexander, Hartly B., *World's Rim: North American Indians* (1953).
Armillas, Pedro, *Native Period in History of the New World* (1962).
Brennan, Louis A, *No Stone Unturned* (1959).
Bryan, Alan L., *Paleo-American Prehistory* (1965).
Bushnell, Geoffrey H. S., *First Americans: Pre-Columbian Civilizations* (1968).

Gladwin, Harold S., *History of Ancient Southwest* (1957).

Griffen, James B., ed., *Archaeology of Eastern United States* (1952).

Hopkins, David M., ed., *Bering Land Bridge* (1967).

Hyde, George E., *Indians of the High Plains from Prehistoric Period to Coming of Europeans* (1959).

Jennings, Jesse D., and Edward Norbeck, eds., *Prehistoric Man in the New World* (1964).

Jennings, Jesse D., *Prehistory of North America* (1968).

Kroeber, A. L., *Cultural and Natural Areas of Native North America* (1939).

Macgowan, Kenneth, and Joseph A. Hester, Jr., *Early Man in the New World* (rev. ed., 1962).

McGregor, John C., *Southwestern Archaeology* (2nd ed., 1965).

Martin, Paul S., George I. Quimby, and Donald Collier, *Indians before Columbus* (1947).

Quimby, George I., *Indian Life in Upper Great Lakes: 11,000 B.C. to A.D. 1800* (1966).

Wauchope, Robert, *Lost Tribes and Sunken Continents* (1962).

Wedel, Waldo R., *Prehistoric Man on Great Plains* (1961).

Willey, Gordon R., *Introduction to American Archaeology*. Vol. I: *North and Middle America* (1966).

20.11.4 Ethnology

Bancroft, Hubert H., *Native Races of the Pacific States* (5 vols., 1882).

Catlin, George, *Letters and Notes on the North American Indians Written during Eight Years' Travel, 1832–1839* (2 vols., 1841).

Curtis, Edwin S., *The North American Indian: Volumes Picturing and Describing the Indians of United States and Alaska* (20 vols., 1907–30).

Dellenbaugh, Frederick S., *North Americans of Yesterday: A Comparative Study of Indian Life* (1900).

Driver, Harold E., *Indians of North America* (1961).

Embree, Edwin R., *Indians of the Americas* (1939).

Ewers, John C., *The Horse in Blackfoot Indian Culture* (1955).

Farb, Peter, *Man's Rise to Civilization as Shown by Indians of North America* (1968).

Farrand, Livingston, *Basis of American History, 1500–1900* (1904).

Grinnell, George B., *Story of the Indian* (1895).

Huntington, Ellsworth, *Red Man's Continent* (1919).

Josephy, Alvin M., Jr., *Indian Heritage of America* (1968).

Kroeber, Alfred L., *Cultural and Natural Areas of Native North America* (1939).

Morgan, Lewis H., *Indian Journals, 1859–62,* Leslie A. White, ed. (1959).

Oswalt, Wendell H., *This Land Was Theirs: The North American Indian* (1966).

Owen, Roger, C., et al., *North American Indians* (1967).

Radin, Paul, *Story of the American Indian* (rev. ed., 1934).

Roe, Frank G., *The Indians and the Horse* (1955).

Schoolcraft, Henry R., *Historical and Statistical Information, Respecting the History, Condition and Prospects of Indian Tribes of United States* (6 vols., 1851–1857). Index compiled by Frances S. Nichols in Bur. Am. Ethnol., *Bull.* 152 (1954). Entire issue.

Swanton, John R., *Indian Tribes of North America* (1952).

——— *Indians of Southeastern United States* (1946).

Underhill, Ruth M., *Red Man's America* (1953).

Verrill, A. Hyatt, *The Real Americans* (1954).

Wissler, Clark, *American Indian: Four Centuries of History and Culture* (3d ed., 1938).

——— *Indians of the United States* (1940); Lucy W. Kluckhohn, ed. (rev. ed., 1968).

*   *   *   *   *   *   *

Murdock, George P., *Ethnographic Bibliography of North America* (3d ed., 1960).

20.11.5 Regional Tribal Histories

Andrist, Ralph K., *Long Death: Last Days of Plains Indians* (1964).
Berlandier, Jean L., *Indians of Texas in 1830,* John C. Ewers, ed., and Patricia R. Leclercq. trans. (1969).
Chapman, Berlin B., *The Otoes and Missourias: Indian Removal and Legal Aftermath* (1965).
Cotterill, Robert S., *Southern Indians: The Civilized Tribes before Removal* (1954).
Cushman, Horatio B., *History of the Choctaw, Chickasaw, and Natchez Indians* (1962).
Dale, Edgar E., *Indians of the Southwest* (1949).
Debo, Angie, *And Still the Waters Run* (1940). Five Civilized Tribes.
De Forest, John W., *History of Indians of Connecticut* (1851).
Ewers, John C., *Indian Life on Upper Missouri* (1968).
Forbes, Jack D., *Apache, Navaho and Spaniard* (1960).
Foreman, Grant, *Five Civilized Tribes* (1934).
Grinnell, George B., *Pawnee, Blackfoot and Cheyenne* (1961).
Hagan, William T., *The Sac and Fox Indians* (1958).
Spicer, Edward H., *Cycles of Conquest: Impact on the Indians of the Southwest, 1533–1960* (1962).
Wallace, Paul A. W., *Indians in Pennsylvania* (1961).
Winfrey, Dorman H., ed., *Texas Indian Papers, 1825–1916* (4 vols., 1959–1961).
Wissler, Clark, *North American Indians of Plains* (1920).
Wright, Muriel H., *Guide to Indian Tribes of Oklahoma* (1951).

20.11.6 Individual Tribal Histories

Apaches

Lockwood, Francis C., *Apache Indians* (1938).
Ogle, R. H., *Federal Control of Western Apaches* (1940).
Sonnichsen, C. L., *Mescalero Apaches* (1958).

Bannocks

Madsen, Brigham D., *The Bannock of Idaho* (1958).

Blackfeet

Ewers, John C., *The Blackfeet* (1958).

Catawbas

Brown, Douglas S., *The Catawba Indians: People of the River* (1966).

Cherokees

Brown, John P., *Old Frontiers: The Story of the Cherokee Indians from Earliest Times to the Date of Their Removal to the West, 1838* (1938).
Dale, Edward E., and Gaston Litton, *Cherokee Cavaliers: Forty Years of Cherokee History as Told by Correspondence of the Ridge-Watie-Boudinot Family* (1939).
Foreman, Grant, *Sequoyah* (1938).
Kilpatrick, Jack F. and Anna G. Kilpatrick, *Shadow of Sequoia: Social Documents of Cherokees, 1862–1964* (1965).
Malone, Henry T., *Cherokees of Old South* (1956).
Royce, Charles C., "The Cherokee Nation of Indians," U.S. Bureau Am. Ethnology, *Annual Report, 1883–1884* (1887), 121.
Starkey, Marion L., *Cherokee Nation* (1946).
Woodward, Grace S., *The Cherokees* (1963).

Cheyennes

Berthrong, Donald J., *Southern Cheyennes* (1963).
Cohoe, *A Cheyenne Sketchbbok* (1964).
Grinnell, George B., *The Fighting Cheyennes* (1915).

Sandoz, Mari, *Cheyenne Autumn* (1953).
Stands in Timber, John, and Margot Liberty, *Cheyenne Memories* (1967).

Chippewas. See Ojibways

Choctaws
    Debo, Angie, *Rise and Fall of Choctaw Republic* (2nd ed., 1961).

Comanches
    Wallace, Ernest, and E. Adamson Hoebel, *Comanches* (1952).

Creeks
    Caughey, John W., *McGillivray of Creeks* (1938).
    Debo, Angie, *The Road to Disappearance: History of the Creek Indians* (1941).

Crows
    Lowie, Robert H., *Crow Indians* (1935).

Hopis
    O'Kane, Walter C., *The Hopis* (1953).
    Thompson, Laura, *Culture in Crisis: A Study of the Hopi* (1950).

Iroquois
    Beauchamp, William M., *A History of the New York Iroquois, Now Commonly Called the Six Nations,* N.Y. State Mus., *Bull.* 78 (1905).
    Wallace, Anthony F. C., et al., *The Death and Rebirth of the Seneca: History and Culture of the Great Iroquois Nation* (1970).
    Wallace, Paul A. W., "Iroquois," *Penn. Hist.* 23 (1956), 15.

Kansas
    Unrau, William E., *The Kansas Indians* (1971).

Kickapoos
    Gibson, Arrell Morgan, *The Kickapoos* (1963).

Kiowas
    Mayhall, Mildred P., *The Kiowas* (1962).
    Nye, Wilbur S., *Bad Medicine and Good: Tales of Kiowas* (1962).

Klamaths
    Stern, Theodore, *Klamath Tribe* (1966).

Miamis
    Anson, Bert, *Miami Indians* (1970).

Navajos
    Coolidge, Dane, and Mary R. Coolidge, *Navajo Indians* (1930).
    Kluckhohn, Clyde, and Dorothea Leighton. *The Navaho* (rev. ed., 1972).
    Kluckhohn, Clyde, W. W. Hill, and Lucy Walls Kluckhohn, *Navaho Material Culture* (1971).
    McCombe, Leonard, et al., *Navaho Means People* (1951).
    Underhill, Ruth M., *The Navajos* (1956).

Nez Perces
    Haines, Francis, *Nez Perces* (1955).
    Josephy, Alvin M., Jr., *Nez Perce Indians and Opening of Northwest* (1965).

See also 20.11.14.4, Nez Perce War.

Ojibways

    Warren, William W., *History of Ojibway Nation* (1885).

Osages

    Mathews, John J., *The Osages* (1961).

Pawnees

    Hyde, George E., *Pawnee Indians* (1951).
    Weltfish, Gene, *Lost Universe* (1965).

Seminoles

    Covington, James W., "Migration of Seminoles into Florida, 1700–1820," *Fla. Hist. Quar.*, 46 (1968), 340.
    McReynolds, Edwin C., *Seminoles* (1957).

Shawnees

    Harvey, Henry, *History of the Shawnee Indians, from the Year 1681 to 1854* (1855).

Shoshonis

    Trenholm, Virginia C., and Maurine Carley, *The Shoshonis* (1964).

Sioux

    Bad Heart Bull, Amos, and Helen H. Blish, *A Pictographic History of Oglala Sioux* (1967).
    Hyde, George E., *Red Cloud's Folk* (1937).
    ——— *Sioux Chronicle* (1956).
    ——— *Spotted Tail's Folk: Brulé Sioux* (1961).
    Meyer, Roy W., *History of Santee Sioux: United States Indian Policy on Trial* (1967).
    Olson, James C., *Red Cloud and Sioux Problem* (1965).
    Robinson, Doane, *History of the Dakota or Sioux Indians* (1904).
    Standing Bear, Luther, *My People the Sioux* (1928).
    Utley, Robert M., *Last Days of the Sioux Nation* (1963).

Spokanes

    Ruby, Robert H., and John A. Brown, *Spokane Indians: Children of the Sun* (1970).

Utes

    Emmitt, Robert, *Last War Trail: Utes and Settlement of Colorado* (1954).

Yumas

    Forbes, Jack O., *Warriors of Colorado: Yumas* (1965).

20.11.7 Indian-White Relations

    Beaver, R. Pierce, *Church, State and the American Indians* (1966).
    Brown, L. N., "Dawes Commission," *Chronicles Okla.*, 9 (1931), 71.
    Brown, Roger H., *Struggle for the Indian Stream Territory* (1955).
    Clark, Stanley, "Ponca Publicity," *MVHR*, 29 (1943), 495.
    Collier, John, *From Every Zenith: A Memoir and Some Essays on Life and Thought* (1963).
    Cotterill, Robert S., "Federal Indian Management in the South, 1789–1825," *MVHR*, 20 (1933), 333.

De Rosier, Arthur H., Jr., *The Removal of the Choctaw Indians* (1970).

Downes, Randolph C., "A Crusade for Indian Reform, 1922–1934," *MVHR,* 32 (1945), 331.

Ellis, Richard N., *General Pope and U.S. Indian Policy* (1970).

Foreman, Grant, *Indian Removal: The Emigration of the Five Civilized Tribes of Indians* (1956).

—— *Last Trek of Indians* (1946).

Fritz, Henry E., *Movement for Indian Assimilation, 1860–1890* (1963).

Gabriel, Ralph Henry, *The Lure of the Frontier: A Story of Race Conflict* (1929).

Hagan, William T., *Indian Police and Judges* (1966).

Harmon, George D., *Sixty Years of Indian Affairs* (1941).

Hayter, E. W., "Ponca Removal," *No. Dak. Hist. Quar.,* 6 (1932), 262.

Hoopes, A. W., *Indian Affairs* (1932).

Horsman, Reginald, *Expansion and American Indian Policy, 1783–1812* (1967).

Jackson, Helen Hunt, *Century of Dishonor* (1881).

Kelly, Lawrence C., *Navajo Indians and Federal Indian Policy, 1900–1935* (1968).

Kenner, Charles L., *History of New Mexican-Plains Indian Relations* (1969).

Kinney, J. P., *A Continent Lost—A Civilization Won* (1937).

Le Duc, Thomas, "The Work of Indian Claims Commission under Act of 1946," *Pac. Hist. Rev.,* 26 (1957), 1.

Leupp, F. E., *The Indian and His Problem* (1910).

Lumpkin, Wilson, *Removal of Cherokee* (1907).

McKenzie, F. A., *The Indian in Relation to the White Population* (1908).

McNitt, Frank, *The Indian Traders* (1962).

Macleod, W. C., *American Indian Frontier* (1928).

Mardock, Robert W., *Reformers and the American Indian* (1970).

Meriam, Lewis, *The Problem of Indian Administration* (1928).

Peake, Ora B., *History of United States Indian Factory System, 1795–1822* (1954).

Priest, Loring B., *Uncle Sam's Stepchildren* (1942).

Prucha, Francis P., *American Indian Policy in the Formative Years: The Indian Trade and Intercourse Acts, 1790–1834* (1962).

—— "Indian Removal and Great American Desert," *Ind. Mag. Hist.,* 69 (1963), 299.

—— "Jackson's Indian Policy: A Reassessment," *JAH,* 56 (1969), 527.

Turner, Katherine, *Red Men Calling on Great White Father* (1951).

Tyler, S. Lyman, *Indian Affairs: A Study of Changes in Policy of the United States* (1964).

Van Every, Dale, *The Disinherited: The Lost Birthright of the American Indian* (1966).

Vestal, Stanley, ed., *New Sources of Indian History* (1934).

Young, Mary E., "Indian Removal and Land Allotment: Jacksonian Justice," *AHR,* 64 (1958), 31.

—— *Redskins, Ruffleshirts, and Rednecks: Indian Allotments in Alabama and Mississippi, 1830–1860* (1961).

*   *   *   *   *   *   *

Fenton, William N., Lyman H. Butterfield, and Wilcomb E. Washburn, *American Indian and White Relations to 1830: Needs and Opportunities for Study* (1957).

Sheehan, Bernard W., "Indian-White Relations in Early America: A Review Essay," *WMQ,* 3 ser., 26 (1969), 267.

Washburn, Wilcomb E., "Moral History of Indian-White Relations: Needs and Opportunities for Study," *Ethnohistory,* 4 (1957), 55.

See also 25.14, Racial Thought.

20.11.8 Contemporary Indian Problems

"American Indians and American Life," Am. Acad. Pol. and Soc. Sci., *Annals,* (May 1957). Entire issue.

Baerreis, David A., ed., *The Indian in Modern America: A Symposium* (1956).

Brophy, William A., and Sophie D. Aberle, comps., *The Indian: America's Unfinished Business* (1966).
Deloria, Vine, Jr., *Custer Died For Your Sins* (1969).
────── *We Talk, You Listen* (1970).
La Farge, Oliver, ed., *The Changing Indian* (1942).
La Farge, Oliver, "Enduring Indian," *Scient. Am.*, 202, no. 2 (1960), 37.
Levine, Stuart, and Nancy O. Lurie, eds., *The American Indian Today* (rev. ed., 1968).
Steiner, Stan, *The New Indians* (1968).
Wilson, Edmund, *Apologies to the Iroquois* (1959).

20.11.9 Laws and Treaties

Cohen, Felix S., *Handbook of Federal Indian Law* (1942).
Johnston, Charles M., ed., *Valley of the Six Nations: Documents on the Indian Lands of the Grand River* (1964).
Kapler, C. J., ed., *Indian Affairs: Laws and Treaties* (2 vols., 1904).
U.S. Department of Interior. Office of the Solicitor, *Federal Indian Law.* (1958). Continuation of Cohen's *Handbook.*

* * * * * * *

DuPuy, H. F., ed., Bibliography of the English *Colonial Treaties with the American Indians, Including a Synopsis of each Treaty* (1917).
Hargrett, Lester, *Bibliography of the Constitutions and Laws of American Indians* (1947).

20.11.10 Indian Bureau

Clum, Woodworth, *Apache Agent* (1936).
Collier, John, *From Every Zenith: A Memoir and Some Essays on Life and Thought* (1963).
Galliher, Ruth A., "The Indian Agent in the United States Before 1850," *Iowa Jour. Hist. and Pol.,* 14 (1916), 3.
────── "The Indian Agent in the United States Since 1850," *Iowa Jour. Hist. and Pol.,* 14 (1916), 173.
Jackson, Donald, "William Ewing, Agricultural Agent to the Indians," *Agric. Hist.* 31 (1957), 3.
McGillycuddy, Julia B., *McGillycuddy Agent: A Biography of Dr. Valentine T. McGillycuddy* (1941).
McLaughlin, James, *My Friend the Indian* (1910).
Mathews, John J., *Wah Kon-Tah [Maj. Laban J. Miles]: The Osage and the White Man's Road* (1932).
Schmeckebier, Laurence F., *Office of Indian Affairs* (1927).
Seymour, Flora W., *Indian Agents* (1941).
Thornbrough, Gayle, ed., *Letter Book of the Indian Agency at Fort Wayne, 1809–1815* (1961).

See also 10.3 for biographies/writings of:

Hawkins, Benjamin, 1754–1816

20.11.11 Missions and Schools

Adams, Evelyn C., *American Indian Education: Government Schools and Economic Progress* (1946).
Bass, Althea, *Cherokee Messenger* (1936). Samuel Austin Worcester.
Beaver, R. Pierce, *Church, State and the American Indians* (1966).
Berkhofer, Robert F., Jr., "Model Zions for the American Indian," *Am. Quar.,* 15 (1963), 176.

———— "Protestants, Pagans and Sequences among the North American Indians, 1760–1860," *Ethnohistory*, 10 (1963), 201.

———— *Salvation and the Savage: Protestant Missions and Indian Response, 1787–1862* (1965).

Eastman, Elaine G., *Pratt: Red Man's Moses* (1935).

Edwards, Martha L., "Problem of Church and State in 1870's," *MVHR*, 11 (1924), 37.

Kelsey, Raynor W., *Friends and the Indians, 1655–1917* (1917).

Lewit, Robert T., "Indian Missions and Antislavery Sentiment: Conflict of Evangelical and Humanitarian Ideals," *MVHR*, 50 (1963), 39.

Lindquist, Gustavus E. E., *Red Man in the United States* (1923).

McCoy, Isaac, *History of Baptist Indian Missions* (1840).

Pratt, Richard H., *Battlefield and Classroom: Four Decades with the American Indian, 1867–1904* (1964). Author was founder of Carlisle Institute.

Rahill, Peter J., *Catholic Indian Missions and Grant's Peace Policy, 1870–1884* (1953).

Shea, John D. G., *History of Catholic Missions among Indian Tribes, 1529–1854* (1855).

Smith, Glenn, "Education for the Natives of Alaska: The Work of the United States Bureau of Education, 1884–1931," *Jour. of West*, 6 (1967), 440.

Whipple, Henry B., *Lights and Shadows of a Long Episcopate* (1899).

See also 10.3 for biographies/writings of:

Hare, George Emlen, 1808–1892
Pratt, Richard H., 1840–1924

20.11.12 Impact on the White Man

Barry, J. Neilson, "Indian Words in Our Language," *Ore. Hist. Soc., Quar.*, 16 (1915), 338.

Cohen, Felix S., "Americanizing the White Man," *Am. Scholar*, 21 (1952), 177.

Edwards, Everett E., "American Indian Contributions to Civilization," *Minn. Hist.*, 15 (1934), 255.

Haas, Theodore H., "Impact of American Indian on American Life," *Midw. Jour. Pol. Sci.*, 3 (1950–51), 115.

Hallowell, Alfred I., "Impact of American Indian on American Culture," *Am. Anthropol.*, 59 (1957), 201.

Herndon, G. Melvin, "Indian Agriculture in Southern Colonies," *No. Car. Hist. Rev.*, 44 (1967), 283.

Keiser, Albert, *Indian in American Literature* (1933).

Verrill, A. Hyatt, *Foods America Gave the World* (1937).

*   *   *   *   *   *   *

Edwards, Everett E., and W. D. Rasmussen, *Bibliography on Agriculture of Indians* (1942).

20.11.13 Wars before 1865

Boyd, Mark F., "Seminole War: Background and Onset," *Fla. Hist. Quar.*, 30 (1951), 3.

Burns, Robert I., *Jesuits and Indian Wars of Northwest* (1966).

Cole, Cyrenus, *I Am a Man: The Indian Black Hawk* (1938).

Downey, Fairfax D., *Indian Wars of the Army, 1776–1865* (1963).

Hafen, LeRoy R., and Ann W. Hafen, eds., *Relations with Indians of the Plains, 1857–1861: A Documentary Account* (1959).

Halbert, Henry S., and T. H. Ball, *The Creek War of 1813 and 1814* (1895).

Horsman, Reginald, "British Indian Policy in Northwest, 1807–1812," *MVHR*, 45 (1958), 51.

—— "Role of the Indian in the War," in Philip P. Mason, ed., *After Tippeca-noe: Some Aspects of War of 1812* (1963).

Jacobs, James R., *Beginnings of the United States Army, 1783–1812* (1947).

Laumer, Frank, *Massacre* (1968).

Mahon, John K., *History of the Second Seminole War, 1835–1842* (1967).

Prucha, Francis P., *Sword of Republic: Army on the Frontier, 1783–1846* (1969).

Sprague, John T., *Origin, Progress and Conclusion of the Florida War* (1848).

Stanley, George F. G., "Indians in War of 1812," *Can. Hist. Rev.,* 31 (1950), 145.

Stevens, Frank E., *Black Hawk War, Including Review of Black Hawks' Life* (1903).

Thwaites, Reuben G., "Story of Black Hawk War," Wis. Hist. *Coll.,* 12 (1892), 217.

Utley, Robert M., *Frontiersmen in Blue: United States Army and Indian, 1848–1865* (1967).

Wakefield, John A., *History of War between United States and Sac and Fox Nations* (1834); Reissued as *Wakefield's History of the Black Hawk War,* Frank E. Stevens, ed. (1908).

See also 10.3 for biographies/writings of:

Gaines, General Edmund P., 1777–1849

See also 13.4.1, Military Frontier.

20.11.14 Wars After 1865

20.11.14.1 General

Brown, Dee A., *Galvanized Yankees* (1963).

Coffman, Edward M., "Army Life on Frontier, 1865–1898," *Mil. Affairs,* 20 (1956), 193.

Downey, Fairfax D., *Indian-Fighting Army* (1941).

Dunn, Jacob P., *Massacres of Mountains* (1886).

Glassley, Ray H., *Pacific Northwest Indian Wars* (1953).

Knight, Oliver, *Following the Indian Wars: Newspaper Correspondents among the Indian Campaigners* (1960).

Leckie, William H., *Buffalo Soldiers: Negro Cavalry in the West* (1967).

—— *Military Conquest of the Southern Plains* (1963).

National Park Service, comp., *Soldier and Brave: Indian and Military Affairs in Trans-Mississippi West* (1963).

Nye, Wilbur S., *Carbine and Lance: Old Fort Sill* (1937).

—— *Plains Indian Raiders* (1968).

Richardson, Rupert N., *Comanche Barrier to South Plains Settlement* (1933).

Rickey, Don, Jr., "Enlisted Men of the Indian Wars," *Affairs,* 23 (1959), 91.

—— *Forty Miles a Day on Beans and Hay: Enlisted Soldier Fighting Indian Wars* (1963).

Tebbel, John, and Keith Jennison, *American Indian Wars* (1960).

Vestal, Stanley, *Warpath and Council Fire: Plains Indians, 1851–1891* (1948).

Wellman, Paul I., *Indian Wars of West* (1954).

See also 10.3 for biographies/writings of:

Canby, Edward R. S., 1817–1873
Carr, Eugene A., 1830–1910
Crook, George, 1829–1890
Grouard, Frank, 1850–1905
Sherman, William Tecumseh, 1820–1891
Sieber, Al, 1844–1907

See also 13.4.1, Military Frontier.

20.11.14.2 Regional Wars

Carley, Kenneth, *Sioux Uprising of 1862* (1961).
Faulk, Odie B., *Geronimo Campaign* (1969).
Jones, Robert H., *Civil War in the Northwest* (1960).
Oehler, Charles M., *Great Sioux Uprising* (1959).
Roddis, Louis H., *Indian Wars of Minnesota* (1956).

20.11.14.3 Battle of Little Big Horn

Dustin, Fred, *Custer Tragedy* (1939).
Graham, William A., *Story of Little Big Horn* (1926).
Stewart, Edgar I., *Custer's Luck* (1955).
Utley, Robert M., *Custer Battlefield National Monument, Montana* (1969).

*   *   *   *   *   *   *

Stewart, Edgar, I., "The Literature of the Custer Fight," *Pac. Northwesterner,* 1 (1956–57), 1.

See also 10.3 for biographies/writings of:

Custer, George A., 1839–1876

20.11.14.4 Nez Perce War

Beal, Merrill D., *"I Will Fight No More Forever": Nez Perce War* (1963).
Brown, Mark H., *Flight of the Nez Perce* (1967).
Fee, Chester A., *Chief Joseph* (1936).

20.11.14.5 Southwest Wars

Betzinez, Jason, *I Fought with Geronimo* (1959).
Bourke, John G., *Apache Campaign in the Sierra Madre, 1883* (1886).
Davis, Britton, *Truth about Geronimo* (1929).
Faulk, Odie B., *Geronimo Campaign* (1969).
Thrapp, Daniel L., *Conquest of Apacheria* (1967).

20.11.14.6 Other Wars

Arnold, Royal R., *Indian Wars of Idaho* (1932).
Brimlow, G. F., *Bannock Indian War of 1878* (1938).
Hoig, Stanley, *Sand Creek Massacre* (1961).
Murray, Keith A., *Modocs and Their War* (1959).
Shields, G. O., *Battle of Big Hole* (1889).
Smith, Helena H., *War on Powder River* (1966).
Sprague, Marshall, *Massacre: Tragedy at White River* (1957).
Vaughn, Jesse W., *Battle of Platte Bridge* (1963).
––––– *Indian Fights: New Facts on Seven Encounters* (1966).
––––– *Reynolds Campaign on Powder River* (1961).
Ware, Eugene F., *Indian War of 1864* (1911); Clyde C. Walton, ed., (1960).

20.11.14.7 Military Accounts

Bourke, J. G., *On Border With Crook* (1891).
Browne, John R., *Adventures in Apache Country* (1869).
Carrington, Frances C., Mrs., *My Army Life* (1910).
Cook, James H., *Fifty Years on the Old Frontier* (1891).
Drannan, W. F., *Thirty-One Years on the Plains* (1908).
Finerty, John F., *War Path and Bivouac: Conquest of the Sioux* (1890).
Forsyth, George A., *Story of the Soldier* (1900).
Howard, Oliver O., *My Life and Experiences among Hostile Indians* (1907).
Johnson, Richard W., *Soldier's Reminiscences* (1886).
King, Charles, *Campaigning with Crook* (1880).

Marcy, Randolph B., *Thirty Years of Army Life* (1866).
Miles, Nelson A., *Personal Recollections and Observations* (1896).
Rister, Carl C., *Border Command: General Phil Sheridan* (1944).

20.11.15 Indian-Negro Relations

Andrews, Thomas F., "Freedmen in Indian Territory: A Post-Civil War Dilemma," *Jour. of West,* 4 (1965), 367.
Johnston, James H., "Documentary Evidence of Relations of Negroes and Indians," *Jour. Negro Hist.,* 14 (1929), 21.
Porter, Kenneth W., "Negroes and Indians on the Texas Frontier, 1831–1876," *Jour. Negro Hist.,* 41 (1956), 185.
——— "Notes Supplementary to 'Relations between Negroes and Indians'," *Jour. Negro Hist.,* 18 (1933), 282.
——— "Relations between Negroes and Indians within the Present Limits of the United States," *Jour. Negro Hist.,* 18 (1932), 282.
Willis, William S., "Red, White, and Black in the Southeast," *Jour. Negro Hist.,* 48 (1963), 157.
Woodson, Carter G., "Relations of Negroes and Indians in Massachusetts," *Jour. Negro Hist.,* (1920), 45.

20.11.16 Indian Captivities

Pearce, Roy H., "Significances of the Captivity Narrative," *Am. Lit.* 19 (1947), 1.
Peckham, Howard H., *Captured by Indians: True Tales of Pioneer Survivors* (1954).

*   *   *   *   *   *   *

Newberry Library, *Narratives of Captivity among the Indians: Ayer Collection of Newberry Library* (1912). Supplement (1928).

20.12 NEGROES

20.12.1 General

Aptheker, Herbert, *To Be Free* (1948).
Aptheker, Herbert, ed., *Documentary History of Negro People in United States, 1661–1910* (2 vols., 1959).
Banton, Michael, *Race Relations* (1967).
Bennett, Lerone, Jr., *Before the Mayflower: A History of the Negro in America, 1619–1964* (4th ed., 1969).
Broom, Leonard, and Norval D. Glenn, *Transformation of the Negro American* (1965).
Brown, Ina C., *The Story of the American Negro* (2d rev. ed., 1957).
Clark, Kenneth B., and Talcott Parsons, eds., *The Negro American* (1966).
Curtis, James C., and Lewis L. Gould, eds., *Black Experience in America: Selected Essays* (1970).
Davis, Allison, and John Dollard, *Children of Bondage* (1940).
Embree, E. R., *Brown Americans* (1943).
Fishel, Leslie H., Jr., and Benjamin Quarles, eds., *The Black American: A Documentary History* (rev. ed., 1970). Originally issued under the title, *The Negro American.*
Franklin, John Hope, *From Slavery to Freedom* (3d ed., 1967).
Frazier, E. Franklin, *Black Bourgeoisie: Rise of New Middle Class* (1957).
——— *The Negro in the United States* (rev. ed., 1957).
Fullinwider, S. P., *Mind and Mood of Black America: 20th Century Thought* (1969).
Goldston, Robert C., *The Negro Revolution* (1968).

Green, Constance M., *The Secret City: A History of Race Relations in the Nation's Capital* (1967).
Grier, William H., and Price M. Cobbs, *Black Rage* (1968).
Harris, Marvin, *Patterns of Race in the Americas* (1964).
Herskovits, Melville J., *American Negro* (1928).
—— *Myth of the Negro Past* (1941).
—— *New World Negro: Selected Papers in Afro-American Studies,* Frances S. Herskovits, ed. (1966).
Hughes, Langston, and Milton Meltzer, *A Pictorial History of the Negro in America* (3d ed., 1968).
Isaacs, Harold R., *The New World of Negro Americans* (1963).
Katz, William L., *Eyewitness: The Negro in American History* (1967).
Locke, Alain, *The New Negro: An Interpretation* (1925).
Logan, Rayford W., *The Betrayal of the Negro, from Rutherford B. Hayes to Woodrow Wilson* (new enl. ed., 1965). Originally issued under the title, *The Negro in American Life and Thought: The Nadir, 1877–1901.*
—— *The Negro in the United States: A Brief Review* (1957).
—— ed., *What the Negro Wants* (1944).
Meier, August, and Elliott M. Rudwick, *From Plantation to Ghetto: An Interpretative History of American Negroes* (1966).
Meier, August, *Negro Thought in America, 1880–1915* (1963).
Miller, Charles A., "Constitutional Law and the Rhetoric of Race," *Perspectives in Am. Hist.,* 5 (1971), 147.
Myrdal, Gunnar, *An American Dilemma* (rev. ed., 2 vols., 1964).
The Negro Handbook (1966).
Negro Year Book (1912–1952).
Osofsky, Gilbert, ed., *Burden of Race: Documentary of Negro-White Relations* (1967).
Ottley, Roi, *No Green Pastures* (1951).
Parsons, Talcott, and Kenneth B. Clark, eds. *(Daedalus) The Negro American* (1966).
Pettigrew, Thomas F., *A Profile of the Negro American* (1964).
Ploski, Harry A., and Ernest Kaiser, eds., *The Negro Almanac,* 2nd ed. (1971).
Quarles, Benjamin, *The Negro in the Making of America* (1964).
Rose, Arnold M., *Negro in Postwar America* (1950).
—— *The Negro in America* (1948), Condensation of Myrdal's *An American Dilemma.*
Schoell, Franck L., *Histoire de la race noire aux Etats-Unis du XVII*^e *siecle à nos jours* (1959).
Thorpe, Earl E., *The Mind of the Negro: An Intellectual History of Afro Americans* (1961).
Weatherford, Willis D., and Charles S. Johnson, *Race Relations: Adjustment of Whites and Negroes* (1934).
Woodson, Carter G., and Charles H. Wesley, *The Negro in Our History* (1922); 10th rev. ed. (1962).

*   *   *   *   *   *   *

Aptheker, Herbert, *The Negro People in America: A Critique of Gunnar Myrdal's "An American Dilemma"* (1946).
Black History Viewpoints: A Selected Bibliographical Guide to Resources for Afro-American and African History (1969).
Brown, Warren, comp., *Check List of Negro Newspapers in the United States, 1827–1946* (1946).
Drimmer, Melvin, ed., *Black History: A Reappraisal* (1968).
Handy, Robert T., "Negro History and American Church Historiography," in Jerald C. Brauner, *Reinterpretation in American Church History* (1968).
Kaiser, Ernest, "Racial Dialectics: Aptheker-Myrdal School Controversy," *Phylon,* 9 (1948), 295.
McPherson, James, et al., *Blacks in America: Bibliographical Essays* (1971).
Miller, Elizabeth W., comp., *The Negro in America: A Bibliography* (1966); 2nd rev. ed. by Mary L. Fisher (1970).

Porter, Dorothy B., comp., *The Negro in the United States: A Selected Bibliography* (1970).

Price, Armistead S., ed., *Negro Newspapers on Microfilm* (1953).

Redding, Saunders, "Black Revolution in American Studies," *Am. Studies, 9* (1970), 3.

Salk, Edwin A., ed., *A Layman's Guide to Negro History* (1967).

Starobin, Robert, "The Negro: A Central Theme in American History," *Jour. Contemp. Hist.* 3 (1968), 37.

Thompson, Edgar T., and Alma M. Thompson, *Race and Religion: Descriptive Bibliography Compiled with Reference to Relations between Whites and Negroes in United States* (1949).

Thorpe, Earl E., *Central Theme of Black History* (1969).

—— *Negro Historians in the United States* (1958).

Welsch, Erwin K., *The Negro in United States: A Research Guide* (1965).

Wesley, Charles H., "Creating and Maintaining an Historical Tradition," *Jour. Negro Hist.,* 49 (1964), 13.

—— "W.E.B. DuBois—the Historian," *Jour. Negro Hist.,* 50 (1965), 147.

See also 20.11.15, Indian–Negro Relations; 21.12.3.2, Interracial Violence; 25.14, Racial Thought; 47.11.2, Era of Reconstruction–Negroes–State Studies.

20.12.1.1 Negroes in the South Since 1865

Baker, Ray S., *Following the Color Line* (1908). Reissued with an introduction by Dewey W. Grantham (1964).

Barnwell, William H., *In Richard's World: Battle of Charleston, 1966* (1968).

Carter, Hodding, *First Person Plural* (1963).

—— *So the Heffners Left McComb* (1965).

—— *Southern Legacy* (1950).

Dollard, John, *Caste and Class in a Southern Town* (3d ed., 1957).

Folmsbee, S. J., "Origin of First 'Jim Crow' Law," *JSH,* 15 (1949), 235.

Harris, William C., "Formulation of the First Mississippi Plan: The Black Code of 1865," *Jour. Miss. Hist.,* 29 (1967), 181.

Hyman, Jacob D., "Segregation and the Fourteenth Amendment," *Vanderbilt Law Rev.,* 4 (1951), 555.

Johnson, Charles S., *Growing Up in the Black Belt* (1941).

—— et al., *Into the Main Stream: A Survey of Best Practices in Race Relations in the South* (1947).

Johnson, Charles S., *Patterns of Negro Segregation* (1943).

Johnson, Guion G., "Ideology of White Supremacy, 1876–1910," in Fletcher Green, ed., *Essays in Southern History* (1949).

Kaplan, Sidney, "Albion W. Tourgee: Attorney for the Segregated," *Jour. Negro Hist.,* 49 (1964), 128.

Logan, Frenise A., *The Negro in North Carolina, 1876–1894* (1964).

Moore, John Hammond, "Jim Crow in Georgia," *So. Atl. Quar.,* 66 (1967), 554.

Newby, Idus A., *Jim Crow's Defense: Anti-Negro Thought, 1900–1930* (1965).

Nolen, Claude H., *The Negro's Image in the South: The Anatomy of White Supremacy* (1967).

Norris, Marjorie M., "Nonviolence: Louisville Demonstrations of 1870–71," *JSH,* 32 (1965), 488.

Powdermaker, Hortense, *After Freedom* (1939).

Quint, Howard H., *Profile in Black and White: South Carolina* (1958).

Redding, J. Saunders, *No Day of Triumph* (1942).

Reed, Germaine A., "Race Legislation in Louisiana, 1864–1920," *La. Hist.,* 6 (1965), 379.

Rice, Roger L., "Residential Segregation by Law 1910–1917," *JSH,* 34 (1968), 179.

Rohrer, John H., and M. S. Edmonson, *The Eighth Generation: Cultures and Personalities of New Orleans Negroes* (1960).

Rowan, Carl T., *South of Freedom* (1952).

Sanders, Albert N., "Jim Crow Comes to South Carolina," *So. Car. Hist. Assoc., Proc.,* 35 (1966), 27.

Schnore, Leo F., and Philip C. Evenson, "Segregation in Southern Cities," *Am. Jour. Soc.,* 72 (1966), 58.

Smith, Lillian E., *Killers of the Dream* (rev. ed., 1961).

Tindall, George B., *South Carolina Negroes, 1877–1900* (1952).

—— "Southern Negroes since Reconstruction: Dissolving the Static Image," in Arthur S. Link and Rembert W. Patrick, eds., *Writing Southern History: Essays in Historiography in Honor of Fletcher M. Green* (1965).

Warren, Robert Penn, *Who Speaks for the Negro?* (1965).

Williamson, Joel, ed., *The Origins of Segregation* (1968).

Woodward, C. Vann, *The Strange Career of Jim Crow* (2nd rev. ed., 1966).

Wynes, Charles E., "Jim Crow Laws in Twentieth Century Virginia," *Phylon,* 28 (1967), 416.

—— *The Negro in the South since 1865* (1965).

—— *Race Relations in Virginia, 1870–1902* (1961).

20.12.1.2 Negroes in the North Since 1865

Ashmore, Harry S., *The Other Side of Jordan* (1960).

Bartlett, Irving H., *From Slave to Citizen: Negro in Rhode Island* (1954).

Bloch, Herman D., *Circle of Discrimination: Economic and Social Study of the Black Man in New York* (1969).

Clark, Kenneth B., *Dark Ghetto* (1965).

Cuban, Larry, "Negro Leadership in Cleveland, 1900–1919," *Phylon,* 28 (1967), 299.

Drake, St. Clair, and Horace R. Clayton, *Black Metropolis: A Study of Negro Life in a Northern City* (rev. ed., 1963).

DuBois, W. E. B., *Philadelphia Negro* (1899).

Grodzins, Morton, *The Metropolitan Area as a Racial Problem* (1958). Pittsburgh.

Handlin, Oscar, *The Newcomers: Negroes and Puerto Ricans in a Changing Metropolis* (1959).

Johnson, James W., *Black Manhattan* (1930).

Katz, Schlomo, ed., *Negro and Jew: An Encounter in America* (1967).

McKay, Claude, *Harlem* (1940).

The Negro and the City (1968).

Osofsky, Gilbert, "The Enduring Ghetto," *JAH,* 55 (1968), 243.

—— *Harlem: The Making of a Ghetto, 1890–1930* (1966).

Ottley, Roi, and William J. Weatherby, eds., *The Negro in New York: An Informal Social History, 1626–1939* (rev. ed., 1969).

Ovington, Mary White, *Half a Man: Status of the Negro in New York* (1911).

Parks, Gordon, *The Learning Tree* (1963).

Scheiner, Seth M., *Negro Mecca: A History of the Negro in New York City, 1865–1920* (1965).

Spear, Allan H., *Black Chicago: The Making of a Negro Ghetto, 1890–1920* (1967).

Thornbrough, Emma Lou, *The Negro in Indiana* (1957).

Weaver, Robert C., *The Negro Ghetto* (1948).

20.12.2 Collective Biographies

Bardolph, Richard, *The Negro Vanguard* (1959).

Bontemps, Arna, *One Hundred Years of Negro Freedom* (1961).

Cherry, Gwendolyn, et al., *Portraits in Color: Lives of Colorful Negro Women* (1962).

Metcalf, George R., *Black Profiles* (rev. ed., 1970).

Redding, J. Saunders, *The Lonesome Road: The Negro's Part in America* (1958).

Robinson, Wilhelmina A., *Historical Negro Biographies* (2nd ed., 1968).

Who's Who in Colored America. Ceased publication with 7th ed., in 1950.

Williams, Ethel L., *Biographical Directory of Negro Ministers* (2nd ed., 1970).

20.12.3 Demography

Hart, John F., "Changing Distribution of American Negro," Assoc. Am. Geographers, *Annals,* 50 (1960), 242.

Kennedy, Louise V., *Negro Peasant Turns Cityward* (1930).

Lewis, Edward E., *Mobility of the Negro* (1931).

Mayo, Selz C., and C. Horace Hamilton, "The Rural Negro Population of the South in Transition," *Phylon*, 24 (1963), 160.

Smith, T. Lynn, "Redistribution of the Negro Population of the United States, 1910–1960," *Jour. Negro Hist.*, 51 (1966), 155.

Taeuber, Karl E., and Alma F. Taeuber, "Changing Character of Negro Migration," *Am. Jour. Sociol.*, 70 (1965), 429.

————— *Negroes in Cities: Residential Segregation and Neighborhood Change* (1965).

U.S. Bureau of the Census, *Estimates of the Population of the United States by Age, Race, and Sex: July 1, 1969* (1969).

————— *Negro Population, by County: 1960 and 1950* (1966).

————— *Negro Population in the United States, 1790–1915* (1918).

————— *Negro Population of Selected Areas of the United States in Which Special Censuses Have Been Taken: January 1, 1965 to June 30, 1968* (1968).

Valien, Preston, "General Demographic Characteristics of Negro Population in United States," *Jour. Negro Educ.*, 32 (1963), 329.

Van Deusen, J. G., "Exodus of 1879," *Jour. Negro Hist.*, 21 (1936), 111.

Woodson, Carter G., *Negro Migration* (1918).

*　　*　　*　　*　　*　　*　　*

Aptheker, Herbert, "Central Theme of Southern History—A Re-examination," in *Toward Negro Freedom* (1956).

Ross, Frank A., and L. V. Kennedy, *Bibliography of Negro Migration* (1934).

Woolfolk, George R., "Turner's Safety-Valve and Free Negro Westward Migration," *Jour. Negro Hist.*, 50 (1965), 185.

20.12.4 Family

Baughman, Earl, and W. Grant Dahlstrom, *Negro and White Children: A Psychological Study in the Rural South* (1968).

Billingsley, Andrew, and Amy T. Billingsley, *Black Families in White America* (1968).

Frazier, E. Franklin, *Free Negro Family* (1932).

————— *The Negro Family in the United States* (1939).

————— *Negro Youth* (1940).

Glick, Paul C., *American Families* (1957).

Moynihan, Daniel P., *The Negro Family: The Case for National Action* (1965).

Rainwater, Lee, and William L. Yancey, *The Moynihan Report and the Politics of Controversy* (1967).

20.12.5 Economic Conditions and Status

Allen, Robert L., *Black Awakening in Capitalist America* (1969).

Becker, Gary S., *The Economics of Discrimination* (1957).

Campbell, Joel T., and Leon Belcher, "Changes in Non-White Employment, 1960–1966," *Phylon*, 28 (1967), 325.

Carnegie, Mary Elizabeth, "The Impact of Integration on the Nursing Profession: An Historical Sketch," *Negro Hist. Bull.* 28 (1965), 154.

Durham, Philip, and Everett L., Jones, *The Negro Cowboys* (1965).

Eatherly, Billy J., "Occupational Progress of Mississippi Negros, 1940–1960," *Miss. Quar.*, 21 (1968), 48.

Edwards, G. Franklin, *The Negro Professional Class* (1959).

Edwards, Harry, *The Revolt of the Black Athlete* (1969).

Ferman, Lous A., *Negro and Equal Employment Opportunities: Twenty Companies* (1968).

Glenn, Norval D., "Some Changes in the Relative Status of American Non-whites, 1940–1960," *Phylon*, 24 (1963), 109.

Harmon, J. H., Arnett G. Lindsay and Carter G. Woodson, *The Negro as Businessman* (1929).

Harris, Abram L., *The Negro as Capitalist: A Study of Banking and Business among American Negroes* (1936).

Kain, John F., ed., *Race and Poverty: The Economics of Discrimination* (1969).

Krislov, Samuel, *The Negro in Federal Employment: The Quest for Equal Opportunity* (1967).

Lewis, Edward E., "Southern Negro and Labor Supply," *Pol. Sci. Quar.,* 48 (1933), 172.

Marshall, F. Ray, *The Negro Worker* (1967).

Norgren, Paul H., and Samuel Hill, *Toward Fair Employment* (1964).

Peterson, Robert W., *Only the Ball Was White* (1970).

Reitzes, Dietrich C., *Negroes and Medicine* (1958).

Ross, Arthur M., and Herbert Hill, eds., *Employment, Race and Poverty: Disadvantaged Status of Negro Workers from 1865 to 1965* (1967).

Ruchames, Louis, *Race, Jobs, and Politics: FEPC* (1953).

Shields, Emma L., *Negro Women in Industry* (1922).

Staupers, Mabel K., *No Time for Prejudice: Integration of Negroes in Nursing in United States* (1961).

Sterner, Richard M. E., *The Negro's Share: Income, Consumption, Housing and Public Assistance* (2nd ed., 1943).

Weaver, Robert C., *Negro Labor* (1946).

Wolters, Raymond, *Negroes and the Great Depression: The Problem of Economic Recovery* (1970).

Woodson, Carter G., *The Negro Professional Man and the Community* (1934).

Zeichner, Oscar, "Transition from Slave to Free Labor," *Agric. Hist.,* 13 (1939), 65.

20.12.5.1 Labor Unions

Bloch, Herman D., "Craft Unions and the Negro," *Jour. Negro Hist.,* 43 (1958), 10.

—— "Labor and the Negro, 1866–1910," *Jour. Negro Hist.,* 50 (1965), 163.

Brooks, Tom, "Negro Militants, Jewish Liberals, and Unions," *Commentary,* 32 (1961), 209.

Cayton, Horace R., and George S. Mitchell, *Black Workers and the New Unions* (1939).

Franklin, Charles L., *Negro Unionist* (1936).

Green, Lorenzo J., and Carter G. Woodson, *The Negro Wage Earner* (1930).

Grob, Gerald N., "Organized Labor and the Negro Worker, 1865–1900," *Labor Hist.,* 1 (1960), 164.

Hill, Herbert, "Organized Labor and the Negro Wage Earner," *New Politics,* 1 (1962), 8.

Jacobson, Julius, ed., *The Negro and the American Labor Movement* (1968).

Kessler, Sidney H., "Organization of Negroes in Knights of Labor," *Jour. Negro Hist.,* 37 (1952), 248.

Mandel, Bernard, "Samuel Gompers and Negro Workers, 1886–1914," *Jour. Negro Hist.,* 40 (1955), 34.

Marshall, F. Ray, *The Negro and Organized Labor* (1965).

"The Negro and American Labor Movement: Some Selected Chapters," *Labor Hist.,* 10 (1969). Entire issue.

Northrup, Herbert R., *Organized Labor and the Negro* (1944).

Spero, S. D., and Abram L. Harris, *Black Worker* (1931).

U.S. Commission on Civil Rights, *Reports on Apprenticeship* (1964).

Wesley, C. H., *Negro Labor* (1927).

20.12.5.2 Negroes in the Armed Forces Since 1865

Billington, Monroe, "Freedom to Serve: The President's Committee on Equality of Treatment and Opportunity in the Armed Forces, 1949–1950," *Jour. Negro Hist.,* 51 (1966), 262.

Dalfiume, Richard M., *Desegregation of U.S. Armed Forces: Fighting on Two Fronts, 1939–1953* (1969).

Gianakos, Perry E., "Spanish American War and Double Paradox of Negro American," *Phylon,* 26 (1965), 34.

Leckie, William H., *Buffalo Soldiers: Negro Cavalry in the West* (1967).

Lee, Ulysses, *The Employment of Negro Troops: United States Army in World War II* (1966).

Paszek, Lawrence J., "Negroes and the Air Force, 1939–1949, *Mil. Affairs,* 31 (1967), 1.

Silvera, John D., ed., *The Negro in World War II* (1968).

Stillman, Richard J. II, *Integration of Negro in the U.S. Armed Forces* (1968).

* * * * * * *

Slonaker, John, *U.S. Army and the Negro: A Military History Bibliography* (1971).

U.S. Army Military History Research Collection, *U.S. Army and Domestic Disturbances* (1971).

20.12.6 Politics

20.12.6.1 General

Brooks, Maxwell R., *The Negro Press Re-examined: Political Content of Leading Negro Newspapers* (1959).

Brotz, Howard, ed., *Negro Social and Political Thought, 1850–1920: Representative Texts* (1966).

Fishel, Leslie H., Jr., "Negro in the New Deal Era," *Wis. Mag. Hist.,* 48 (1964), 111.

Gosnell, Harold F., *Negro Politicans* (1935).

Harrell, James A., "Negro Leadership in Election Year 1936," *JSH,* 34 (1968), 546.

Hirshson, Stanley P., *Farewell to Bloody Shirt: Northern Republicans and the Southern Negro, 1877–1893* (1953).

Marvick, Dwaine, "Political Socialization of American Negro," Am. Acad. Pol. Soc. Sci., *Annals,* 361 (1965), 112.

Nowlin, William F., *The Negro in American National Politics* (1931).

Sherman, Richard B., "Harding Administration and the Negro," *Jour. Negro Hist.,* 49 (1964), 151.

———— "Republicans and Negroes: Lessons of Normalcy," *Phylon,* 27 (1966), 63.

Smith, Samuel D., *The Negro in Congress, 1870–1901* (1940).

Stone, Chuck, *Black Political Power in America* (1968).

Tatum, E. L., *Changed Political Thought of the Negro, 1915–1940* (1951).

Weiss, Nancy J., "Fighting Wilsonian Segregation," *Pol. Sci. Quar.,* 84 (1969), 61.

Wilson, James Q., *Negro Politics: Search for Leadership* (1960).

Wolgemuth, Kathleen L., "Woodrow Wilson and Federal Segregation," *Jour. Negro Hist.,* 44 (1959), 158.

20.12.6.2 Southern Politics Since 1865

Buni, Andrew, *The Negro in Virginia Politics, 1902–1965* (1967).

Callcott, Margaret L., *The Negro in Maryland Politics, 1870–1912* (1969).

Cheek, William B., "A Negro Runs for Congress: John Mercer Langston and the Virginia Campaign of 1888," *Jour. Negro Hist.,* 52 (1967), 14.

Graves, John W., "Negro Disfranchisement in Arkansas," *Ark. Hist. Quar.,* 26 (1967), 199.

Ladd, Everett Carel, Jr., *Negro Political Leadership in the South* (1966).

Lewinson, Paul, *Race, Class, and Party: A History of Negro Suffrage and White Politics in the South* (1932).

Lewis, Elsie M., "Political Mind of the Negro, 1865–1900," *JSH,* 21 (1955), 189.

Mabry, William A., *The Negro in North Carolina Politics since Reconstruction* (1940).

Matthews, Donald R., and James W. Prothro, *Negroes and New Southern Politics* (1966).

Price, Hugh D., *Negro and Southern Politics: A Chapter in Florida History* (1957).

Strong, Donald S., *Negroes, Ballots, and Judges: National Voting Rights Legislation in the Federal Courts* (1968).

Watters, Pat, and Reese Cleghorn, *Climbing Jacob's Ladder: Negroes in Southern Politics* (1967).

20.12.6.3 Northern Politics Since 1865

Allswang, John M., "Chicago Negro Vote, 1918–1936," Ill. State Hist. Soc., Jour., 60 (1967), 145.

Blair, John L., "A Time for Parting: The Negro during the Coolidge Years," Jour. Am. Studies, 3 (1969), 177.

Chafe, William H., "The Negro and Populism: A Kansas Case Study," JSH, 34 (1968), 402.

Fishel, Leslie H. Jr., "The Negro in Northern Politics, 1870–1900," MVHR, 42 (1955), 466.

Glantz, Oscar, "Negro Voter in Northern Industrial Cities," West. Pol. Quar., 13 (1960), 999. Since World War II.

Gutman, Herbert G., "Peter H. Clark: Negro Socialist, 1877," Jour. Negro Educ., 34 (1965), 413. A Cincinnati educator.

Hadden, Jeffrey K. et al., "The Making of the Negro Mayors, 1967," Transaction, 5 (1968), 21. Cleveland and Gary.

Hickey, Neil, and Ed Edwin, Adam Clayton Powell and the Politics of Race (1965).

McKenna, William J., "Negro Vote in Philadelphia Elections," Penn. Hist., 32 (1965), 406. Covers the period, 1963–1965.

Osofsky, Gilbert, "Progressivism and the Negro: New York, 1900–1915," Am. Quar., 16 (1964), 153.

Robinson, G. F., Jr., "Negro in Politics in Chicago," Jour. Negro Hist., 17 (1932), 180.

Southern, David, Malignant Heritage: Yankee Progressives and the Negro Question, 1901–1914 (1968).

20.12.7 Negro Protest

Aptheker, Herbert, Toward Negro Freedom (1956).

Baldwin, James, The Fire Next Time (1963).

—— Notes of a Native Son (1955).

Brink, William, and Louis Harris, The Negro Revolution in America (1964).

Brisbane, Robert H., The Black Vanguard: Origins of the Negro Social Revolution, 1900–1960 (1970).

Commager, Henry S., ed., Struggle for Racial Equality: A Documentary Record (1967).

Dalfiume, Richard M., "'The Forgotten Years' of the Negro Revolution," JAH, 55 (1968), 90. Covers the period, 1939–1945.

Killian, Lewis M., and Charles Grigg, Racial Crisis in America: Leadership in Conflict (1964).

Lomax, Louis E., The Negro Revolt (1962).

McKissick, Floyd, Three-Fifths of a Man (1969).

Rose, Arnold, and Caroline Rose, America Divided (1948).

Saunders, Doris E., The Day They Marched (1963).

Silberman, Charles E., Crisis in Black and White (1964).

White, Walter F., How Far the Promised Land? (1955).

Wright, Richard, Twelve Million Black Voices (1943).

20.12.7.1 Organizations

Adelman, Lynn, "James Weldon Johnson," Jour. Negro Hist., 52 (1967), 128.

Bell, Inge P., CORE and the Strategy of Nonviolence (1968).

Burns, William H., The Voices of Negro Protest in America (1963).

DuBois, W. E. B., Souls of Black Folk: Essays and Sketches (1903).

Hughes, Langston, Fight for Freedom: The Story of the NAACP (1962).

Jack, Robert L., History of the National Association for the Advancement of Colored People (1943).

Kellogg, Charles F., NAACP: A History of the National Association for the Advancement of Colored People. Vol. I: 1909–1920 (1967).

Levy, Charles J., Voluntary Servitude: Whites in the Negro Movement (1968).

National Association for Advancement of Colored People, Annual Report, 1911–

Ovington, Mary W., The Walls Came Tumbling Down (1947).

Record, Wilson, "Negro Intellectuals and Negro Movements," Am. Quar., 8 (1956), 3.

———— *Race and Radicalism: The NAACP and the Communist Party in Conflict* (1964).

Rudwick, Elliott M., "The Niagara Movement," *Jour. Negro Hist.*, 42 (1957), 177.

Strickland, Arvarh E., *History of the Chicago Urban League* (1966).

Thornbrough, Emma L., "Booker T. Washington as Seen by His White Contemporaries," *Jour. Negro Hist.*, 53 (1968), 161.

Toppin, Edgar A., "Walter White and the Atlanta NAACP's Fight for Equal Schools 1916–1971," *Hist. Educ. Quar.*, 7 (1967), 3.

White, Walter F., *How Far the Promised Land?* (1955).

Zinn, Howard, *SNCC: The New Abolitionists* (1964).

See 10.3 for biographies/writings of:

DuBois, W. E. B., 1868–1963
Garvey, Marcus, 1887–1940
King, Martin Luther, Jr., 1929–1968
White, Walter F., 1893–1955

20.12.7.2 Civil Rights

Bartley, Numan V., *The Rise of Massive Resistance: Race and Politics in the South During the 1950's* (1969).

Berger, Morroe, *Equality by Statute: The Revolution in Civil Rights* (rev. ed., 1967).

Blaustein, Albert P., and Robert L. Zangrando, eds., *Civil Rights and the American Negro: A Documentary History* (1968).

Brown, Ira V., "Pennsylvania and Rights of Negro, 1865–1887," *Penn. Hist.*, 28 (1961), 45.

Carr, Robert K., *Federal Protection of Civil Rights* (1947).

Congressional Quarterly Service, *The Revolution in Civil Rights* (4th ed., 1968).

Elliff, John T., "Aspects of Federal Civil Rights Enforcement: The Justice Department and the FBI, 1939–1964," *Perspectives in Am. Hist.*, 5 (1971), 605.

Franklin, John Hope, and Isidore Starr, eds., *The Negro in Twentieth-Century America: A Reader on the Struggle for Civil Rights* (1967).

Handlin, Oscar, *Fire-Bell in the Night: The Crisis in Civil Rights* (1964).

Harris, Robert J., *The Quest for Equality: The Constitution, Congress and the Supreme Court* (1960).

Ianello, Lynne, ed., *Milestones along the March: Twelve Historic Civil Rights Documents from World War II to Selma* (1965).

Konvitz, Milton R., and Theodore Leskes, *A Century of Civil Rights, with a Study of State Law against Discrimination* (1961).

Konvitz, Milton R., *The Constitution and Civil Rights* (1947).

Lewis, Anthony, *Portrait of a Decade: The Second American Revolution* (1964).

Lytle, Clifford M., "Civil Rights Bill of 1964," *Jour. Negro Hist.*, 51 (1966), 275.

Mangum, Charles S., Jr., *The Legal Status of Negro* (1940).

Marshall, Burke, *Federalism and Civil Rights* (1964).

Miller, Loren, *Petitioners: Supreme Court and the Negro* (1966).

Murray, Pauli, ed., *States' Laws on Race and Color* (1951).

Nelson, Bernard H., *The Fourteenth Amendment and the Negro since 1920* (1946).

Reppy, Alison, *Civil Rights* (1951).

Roche, John P., *The Quest for the Dream: The Development of Civil Rights and Human Relations in Modern America* (1963).

Sobel, Lester A., ed., *Civil Rights, 1960–66* (1967).

Tussman, Joseph, ed., *The Supreme Court on Racial Discrimination* (1963).

Vose, Clement E., "NAACP Strategy in Covenant Cases," *West. Reserve Law Rev.*, 6 (1955), 101.

Westin, Alan F., "John Marshall Harlan and Constitutional Rights of Negroes," *Yale Law Jour.*, 66 (1957), 637.

*   *   *   *   *   *   *

Cable, George W., *The Negro Question: A Selection of Writings on Civil Rights in the South*, Arlin Turner, ed. (1958).

20.12.7.3 Black Nationalism and Black Power

Barbour, Floyd B., ed., *The Black Power Revolt: A Collection of Essays* (1968).

Bennett, Lerone, Jr., *Confrontation: Black and White* (1965).

Berger, Morroe, "The Black Muslims," *Horizon,* 6 (1964), 49.

Bracey, John H., Jr., et al., eds., *Black Nationalism in America* (1970).

Breitman, George, *The Last Year of Malcolm X* (1967).

Brisbane, R. G., Jr., "Some New Light on Garvey," *Jour. Negro Hist.,* 36 (1951), 53.

Carmichael, Stokely, and Charles V. Hamilton, *Black Power* (1967).

Clarke, John Henrik, ed., *Malcolm X: The Man and His Times* (1969).

Cleage, Albert B., Jr., *The Black Messiah* (1968).

Cleaver, Eldridge, *Soul on Ice* (1968).

Delany, M. R., and Robert Campbell, *Search for a Place: Black Separatism and Africa, 1860* (1861). Reissued with a new introduction by Howard H. Bell (1969). Official report of Niger Valley exploring party.

Essien-Udom, E. U., *Black Nationalism: A Search for an Identity in America* (1962).

Graham, Hugh D., "The Storm over Black Power," *Va. Quar. Rev.,* 43 (1967), 545.

Lincoln, C. Eric, *The Black Muslims in America* (1961).

McEvoy, James, and Abraham Miller, *Black Power and Student Rebellion* (1969).

Marx, Gary T., *Protest and Prejudice: A Study of Belief in the Black Community* (1967).

Muse, Benjamin, *The American Negro Revolution: From Non-Violence to Black Power, 1963–1967* (1968).

Redkey, Edwin S., *Black Exodus: Black Nationalists and the Back-to-Africa Movements, 1890–1910* (1969).

Shepperson, George, "American Negro and Africa," Brit. Assoc. Am. Studies, *Bull.,* 8 (1964), 3.

Woodson, Carter G., *African Background Outlined* (1936).

Wright, Nathan, Jr., *Black Power and Urban Unrest: Creative Possibilities* (1967).

*   *   *   *   *   *   *

Williams, Daniel T., and Carolyn L. Redden, *Black Muslims in the United States: selected Bibliography* (1964).

See also 10.3 for biographies/writings of:

DuBois, W. E. B., 1868–1963
Garvey, Marcus, 1887–1940
King, Martin Luther, Jr., 1929–1968
Malcolm X, 1925–1965
White, Walter F., 1893–1955

20.12.7.4 White Response

Culver, Dwight W., *Negro Segregation in the Methodist Church* (1953).

Grimes, Alan P., *Equality in America: Religion, Race and the Urban Majority* (1964).

Hough, Joseph C., Jr., *Black Power and White Protestants: A Christian Response to the New Negro Pluralism* (1968).

Loescher, Frank S., *The Protestant Church and Negro* (1948).

Miller, Robert M., "Attitudes of American Protestantism toward the Negro, 1919–1939," *Jour. Negro Hist.,* 41 (1956), 215.

Osborne, William A., *Segregated Covenant: Race Relations and American Catholics* (1967).

Reimers, David M., *White Protestants and the Negro* (1965).

20.12.8 Education

Barrett, Russell H., *Integration at Ole Miss* (1965).

Bates, Daisy, *The Long Shadow of Little Rock: A Memoir* (1962).

Bernstein, Barton J., "Plessy V. Ferguson: Conservative Sociological Jurisprudence," *Jour. of Negro Hist.,* 48 (1963), 196.

Bickel, Alexander M., "The Decade of School Desegregation: Progress and Prospects" *Columbia Law Rev.,* 64 (1964), 193.

—— "The Original Understanding and the Segregation Decision," *Harv. Law Rev.,* 69 (1955), 1.

Billington, Monroe, "Public School Integration in Missouri, 1954–1964," *Jour. Negro Educ.,* 35 (1966), 252.

Blaustein, Albert P., and Clarence C. Ferguson, Jr., *Desegregation and the Law: The Meaning and Effect of the School Segregation Cases* (2nd ed. rev., 1962).

Blossom, Virgil T., *It Has Happened Here* (1959). Little Rock.

Bond, Horace M., *The Education of the Negro in the American Social Order* (1934). Reissued with a new preface and chapter (1966).

Brazziel, William F., "Federal Aid and Negro Colleges," *Teachers College Rec.,* 68 (1967), 300.

Bullock, Henry A., *A History of Negro Education in the South: From 1619 to the Present* (1967).

Clement, Rufus E., "Historical Development of Higher Education for Negro Americans," *Jour. Negro Hist.* 35 (1966), 299.

Clift, Virgil A., et al., *Negro Education in America* (1962).

Coles, Robert, *Children of Crisis* (3 vols., 1967–1971).

Damerell, Reginald G., *Triumph in a White Suburb: The Dramatic Story of Teaneck, N.J., the First Town in the Nation to Vote for Integrated Schools* (1968).

Ehle, John, *The Free Men* (1965). Chapel Hill, N.C.

Franklin, John Hope, "Genesis of Legal Segregation in Southern Schools," *So. Atl. Quar.,* 58 (1959), 225.

Gates, Robbins L., *Making of Massive Resistance: Virginia's Politics of Public School Desegregation, 1954–1956* (1964).

Graham, Hugh D., *Crisis in Print: Desegregation and the Press in Tennessee* (1967).

Graham, Howard J., "Fourteenth Amendment and School Segregation," *Buffalo Law Rev.,* 3 (1953), 1.

Grunbaum, Werner F., "Desegregation in Texas," *Pub. Opinion Quar.,* 28 (1964), 604.

Harlan, Louis R., *Separate and Unequal: School Campaigns and Racism in Southern Seaboard States, 1901–1915* (1958).

Hayes, Rutherford B., *Teach the Freeman: Slater Fund for Negro Education, 1881–1893,* Louis D. Rubin, Jr., ed. (2 vols., 1959).

Herndon, James, *The Way It Spozed to Be* (1968).

"Higher Education of Negro Americans," *Jour. Negro Educ.,* 36 (1967), 187.

Holmes, Dwight O. W., *The Evolution of the Negro College* (1934).

Inger, Morton, *Politics and Reality in an American City: New Orleans School Crisis of 1960* (1969).

Jencks, Christopher, and David Riesman, "The American Negro College," *Harv. Educ. Rev.,* 37 (1967), 3. Response by Stephen J. Wright et. al., ibid., 451.

Kelly, Alfred H., "Congressional Controversy over School Segregation, 1867–1875," *AHR,* 64 (1959), 537.

Leflar, Robert A., and Wylie H. Davis, "Segregation in Public Schools—1953," *Harv. Law Rev.,* 67 (1953), 377.

McGrath, Earl J., *The Predominantly Negro Colleges and Universities in Transition* (1965).

Mack, Raymond W., ed., *Our Children's Burden: Studies of Desegregation in Nine American Communities* (1968).

Muse, Benjamin, *Ten Years of Prelude: The Story of Integration Since the Supreme Court's 1954 Decision* (1964).

"Negro Education in United States," *Harv. Educ. Rev.,* 30 (1960), 177.

"The Negro Private and Church-Related College," *Jour. Negro Educ.,* 29 (1960), 211.

Orfield, Gary, *The Reconstruction of Southern Education: The Schools and the 1964 Civil Rights Act* (1969).

Puryear, Paul L., "Equity Power and School Desegregation Cases," *Harv. Educ. Rev.*, 33 (1963), 421.

Range, Willard, *Rise and Progress of Negro Colleges in Georgia, 1865–1949* (1951).

Record, Wilson, and Jane C. Record, eds., *Little Rock, U.S.A.* (1960).

Sarratt, Reed, *The Ordeal of Desegregation: The First Decade* (1966).

Sekora, John, "The Emergence of Negro Higher Education in America, a Review," *Race,* 10 (1968), 79.

Silver, James W., *Mississippi: The Closed Society* (rev. ed., 1966).

Smith, Robert C., *They Closed Their Schools: Prince Edward County, Virginia, 1951–1964* (1965).

Smith, Samuel L., *Builders of Goodwill: State Agents of Negro Education in the South, 1910 to 1950* (1950).

Sullivan, Neil V., *Bound for Freedom: An Educator's Adventures in Prince Edward County, Virginia* (1965).

—— and Evelyn S. Stewart, *Now Is the Time: Integration in the Berkeley Schools* (1970).

Thompson, Charles H., ed., "Desegregation and the Negro College," *Jour. Negro Educ.,* 27 (1958), 209.

Weinberg, Meyer, *Race and Place: A Legal History of the Neighborhood School* (1967).

West, Earle H., "Peabody Education Fund and Negro Education, 1867–1880," *Hist. Educ. Quar.,* 6 (1966), 3.

Wish, Harvey, "Negro Education and the Progressive Movement," *Jour. Negro Hist.,* 49 (1964), 184.

*   *   *   *   *   *   *

Weinberg, Meyer, ed., *School Integration: A Comprehensive Bibliography* (1967).

20.12.9 Religion

DuBois, W. E. B., ed., *The Negro Church* (1903).

Fauset, Arthur H., *Black Gods of the Metropolis: Negro Religious Cults of the Urban North* (1944).

Frazier, E. Franklin, *The Negro Church in America* (1963).

Haynes, Leonard L., *Negro Community within American Protestantism, 1619–1844* (1953).

Johnston, Ruby F., *The Religion of Negro Protestants, Changing Religious Attitudes and Practices* (1956).

Mays, Benjamin E., and Joseph W. Nicholson, *Negro's Church* (1933).

Murray, Andrew E., *Presbyterians and the Negro* (1966).

Pipes, William H., *Say Amen, Brother! Old-Time Preaching: A Study in American Frustration* (1951).

Richardson, Harry V. B., *Dark Glory, A Picture of the Church among Negroes in the Rural South* (1947).

Washington, Joseph R., Jr., *Black Religion: The Negro and Christianity in the United States* (1964).

—— *The Politics of God: The Future of the Black Churches* (1967).

Weatherford, Willis D., *American Churches and the Negro: An Historical Study from Early Slave Days to the Present* (1957).

Woodson, Carter G., *The History of the Negro Church* (1921).

*   *   *   *   *   *   *

20.12.10 Art, Literature, and Theater

Abramson, Doris E., *Negro Playwrights in the American Theatre, 1925–1959* (1969).

Bond, Frederick W., *The Negro and the Drama* (1940).

Bone, Robert A., *The Negro Novel in America* (rev. ed., 1965).

Brown, Sterling A., Arthur P. Davis and Ulysses G. Lee, eds., *The Negro Caravan: Writings by American Negroes* (1941).

Cook, Mercer, and Stephen E. Henderson, *The Militant Black Writer in Africa and The United States* (1969).

Cruse, Harold, *The Crisis of the Negro Intellectual* (1967).

Dover, Cedric, *American Negro Art* (3d ed., 1965).

Gloster, Hugh M., *Negro Voices in American Fiction* (1948).

Hill, Herbert, ed., *Anger and Beyond: The Negro Writer in the United States* (1966).

Hughes, Carl M., *The Negro Novelist: A Discussion of the Writings of American Negnovelists, 1940–1950* (1953). A sequel to Gloster's work.

Hughes, Langston, and Milton Meltzer, *Black Magic: A Pictorial History of the Negro in American Entertainment* (1967).

Lewis, Samella S., and Ruth G. Waddy, eds., *Black Artists on Art* (1969).

Littlejohn, David, *Black on White: A Critical Survey of Writing by American Negroes* (1966).

Locke, Alain L., *Negro Art Past and Present* (1936).

Loggins, Vernon, *The Negro Author: His Development in America to 1900* (1931).

Margolies, Edward, *Native Sons: A Critical Study of Twentieth-Century Negro American Authors* (1968).

Mathews, Marcia M., *Henry Ossawa Tanner, American Artist,* John Hope Franklin, ed. (1969).

Ottley, Roi, *New World A-Coming* (1943).

Patterson, Lindsay, ed., *The Negro in Music and Art* (2nd ed., 1967).

Porter, James A., *Modern Negro Art* (1943).

*　　*　　*　　*　　*　　*　　*

Whiteman, Maxwell, *A Century of Fiction by American Negroes, 1853–1952: Descriptive Bibliography* (1955).

20.12.11 Music

Courlander, Harold, *Negro Folk Music, U.S.A.* (1963).

Deft, R. N., *Religious Folk Songs of the Negro* (1927).

Fisher, Miles M., *Negro Slave Songs in the United States* (1953).

Garrett, Romeo B., "African Survivals in American Culture," *Jour. Negro Hist.,* 51 (1966), 239.

Jackson, George Pullen, *White and Negro Spirituals, Their Life Span and Kinship, Tracing 200 Years of Untrammeled Song and Singing among our Country Folk* (1944).

Johnson, James W., *The Book of American Negro Spirituals* (1925).

——— *The Second Book of Negro Spirituals* (1926).

Jones, LeRoi, *Black Music* (1967).

——— *Blues People: Negro Music in White America* (1963).

Krehbiel, Henry E., *Afro-American Folksongs* (1914).

Locke, Alain L., *The Negro and His Music* (1936).

Nathan, Hans, *Dan Emmett and the Rise of Early Negro Minstrelsy* (1962).

Odum, Howard W., and Guy B. Johnson, *The Negro and His Songs* (1925).

Scarborough, Dorothy, *On the Trail of Negro Folk-Songs* (1925).

See also 28.9.6, Jazz and Blues.

Social Ills and Reform

21.1 GENERAL

21.1.1 1789–1865

Blau, Jospeh L., ed., *Social Theories of Jacksonian Democracy* (1954).
Commager, Henry S., *Era of Reform, 1830–1860* (1960).
Davis, David B., comp., *Ante-Bellum Reform* (1967).
Griffen, Clifford S., *Ferment of Reform, 1830–1860* (1967).
——— *Their Brothers' Keepers: Moral Stewardship in United States, 1800–1865* (1960).
Ludlum, D. M., *Social Ferment in Vermont 1791–1850* (1939).
Ratner, Lorman, *Pre-Civil War Reform* (1967).
Schlesinger, Arthur M., *The American as Reformer* (1950).
Smith, Timothy L., *Revivalism and Social Reform in Mid-Nineteenth-Century America* (1957).
Thomas, John L., "Romantic Reform in America, 1815–1865," *Am. Quar.*, 17 (1965), 656.
Tyler, Alice F., *Freedom's Ferment: Phases of American Social History to 1860* (1944).

See also 10.3 for biographies/writings of:

Ballou, Hosea, 1771–1852
Brown, Moses, 1738–1836
Burritt, Elihu, 1810–1879
Dix, Dorothea, 1802–1887
Dorr, Thomas W., 1805–1854
Smith, Gerrit, 1797–1874
Tappan, Arthur, 1786–1865
Vaux, Roberts, 1786–1836
Weitling, Wilhelm C., 1808–1871
Wright, Frances (Fanny), 1795–1852

See also 19.9.3 Youth–Reform Movements; 23.7, Education–Reform and Ideology; 44.8 Abolitionist Movement, 1789–1850.

21.1.2 1866 to the Present

Aaron, Daniel, *Men of Good Hope: A Story of American Progressives* (1951).
Addams, Jane, *Democracy and Social Ethics* (1907); Anne Firor Scott, ed. (1964).
Becker, Dorothy, "Social Welfare Leaders as Spokesmen for the Poor," *Social Casework*, 49 (1968), 82. Covers the period 1880–1914.
Bellamy, Edward, *Looking Backward* (1888); John L. Thomas, ed. (1967).

Croly, Herbert D., *The Promise of American Life* (1909); Arthur M. Schlesinger, Jr., ed. (1965).

Curti, Merle, "Jane Addams," *Jour. Hist. Ideas,* 22 (1961), 240.

Farrell, John C., *Beloved Lady: Jane Addams' Ideas* (1967).

Faulkner, Harold U., *Quest for Social Justice, 1898–1914* (1931).

Filler, Louis, *Dictionary of American Social Reform* (1963).

Fine, Sidney, *Laissez-Faire and the General Welfare State* (1964).

Forcey, Charles, *Crossroads of Liberalism* (1961).

Fox, Daniel M., *Discovery of Abundance: Simon N. Patten and the Transformation of Social Theory* (1967).

Geiger, G. R., *Philosophy of Henry George* (1931).

George, Henry, *Progress and Poverty* (1879).

Greer, Thomas H., *American Social Reform Movements since 1865* (1949).

Gronlund, Laurence, *Cooperative Commonwealth* (1884); Stow Persons, ed. (1965).

Hayes, Samuel P., *Response to Industrialism, 1885–1914* (1957).

Henderson, Charles R., *Social Spirit in America* (1897).

Jaher, Frederic C., *Doubters and Dissenters: Cataclysmic Thought in America, 1885–1918* (1964).

Kirkland, Edward C., "Rhetoric and Rage over the Division of Wealth in the Eighteen Nineties," Am. Antiq. Soc. *Proc.,* 79 (1969), 227.

Lasch, Christopher, *New Radicalism in America: The Intellectual as Social Type* (1965). 1889–1963.

Levine, Daniel, *Varieties of Reform Thought* (1964).

Lippmann, Walter, *Drift and Mastery* (1914).

Lloyd, Henry D., *Wealth against Commonwealth* (1894); Thomas Cochrane, ed. (1963).

Madison, Charles A., *Critics and Crusaders: A Century of American Protest* (2nd ed., 1959).

Mallan, John P., "Roosevelt, Brooks Adams and Lea: Warrior Critique of Business Civilization," *Am. Quar.,* 8 (1956), 216.

Mann, Arthur, "British Social Thought and American Reformers of the Progressive Era," *MVHR,* 42 (1956), 672.

—— *Yankee Reformers in the Urban Age* (1954).

Morgan, Arthur E., *Philosophy of Bellamy* (1945).

Noble, David W., *Paradox of Progressive Thought* (1958).

—— "Veblen and Progress," *Ethics,* 65 (1955), 271.

Pickens, Donald K., *Eugenics and Progressives* (1968).

Riesman, David, *Thorstein Veblen* (1953).

Saxton, Alexander, "'Caesar's Column': Utopia and Catastrophe," *Am. Quar.,* 19 (1967), 224.

Scott, Anne F., "Jane Addams and the City," *Va. Quar. Rev.,* 43 (1967), 53.

Smith, James A., *Spirit of American Government* (1907); Cushing Strout, ed. (1965).

Sproat, John G., *Best Men: Liberal Reformers in the Gilded Age* (1968).

Strong, Josiah, *Our Country* (1891); Jurgen Herbst, ed. (1963).

Veblen, Thorstein, *Theory of Business Enterprise* (1904).

—— *Theory of the Leisure Class* (1899).

Vecoli, Rudolph J., "Sterilization: A Progressive Measure?" *Wis. Mag. Hist.,* 43 (1960), 190.

Ward, Lester, *Welfare State,* Henry S. Commager, ed. (1967).

Wellborn, Charles, *Twentieth-Century Pilgrimage: Walter Lippman and Public Philosophy* (1969).

Weyl, W. E., *New Democracy* (1912).

White, Morton G., *Social Thought in America: Revolt against Formalism* (rev. ed., 1957).

Wilensky, Harold L., and Charles N. Lebeaux, *Industrial Society and Social Welfare* (1965).

Young, Arthur N., *Single Tax Movement* (1916).

*   *   *   *   *   *   *

Bremner, Robert H., "State of Social Welfare History," in Herbert J. Bass, ed., *State of American History* (1970).

See also 10.3 for biographies/writings of:

Addams, Jane, 1860–1935
Bellamy, Edward, 1850–1898
Bourne, Randolph S., 1886–1918
Croly, Herbert D., 1869–1930
Curtis, George W., 1824–1892
Folks, Homer, 1867–1963
George, Henry, 1839–1897
Holmes, John Haynes, 1879–1964
Kelley, Florence, 1859–1932
Lippmann, Walter, 1889–
Lloyd, Henry Demarest, 1847–1903
Lowell, Josephine S., 1843–1905
McGlynn, Edward, 1837–1900
Murphy, Edgar G., 1869–1913
Robins, Margaret D., 1869–1945
Ryan, John A., 1869–1945
Simons, Algie M., 1870–1950
Train, George F., 1829–1904
Veblen, Thorstein, 1857–1929
Vrooman family, 1837–1937
Whitlock, Brand, 1869–1934
Woods, Robert A., 1865–1925

See also 18.18.5, IWW and Left-Wing Unionism; 21.4, Social Service; 24.3, Church and Social Issues; 25.5.2, Political Thought–Radicalism.

21.2 PUBLIC WELFARE

Boies, H. M., *Prisoners and Paupers* (1893).
Breckinridge, Sophonisba P., comp., *Public Welfare Administration* (1927).
Capen, Edward W., *Historical Development of the Poor Law in Connecticut* (1905).
Coll, Blanche D., *Perspectives on Public Welfare* (1969).
Creech, Margaret, *Three Centuries of Poor Law Administration: Legislation in Rhode Island* (1936).
Donovan, John, *Politics of Poverty* (1970).
Farnam, H. W., *Chapters in the History of Social Legislation in the United States to 1860* (1938).
Kelso, Robert W., *History of Poor Relief in Massachusetts* (1922).
Leiby, James, *Charity and Correction in New Jersey: State Welfare* (1967).
Lutzker, Michael A., "Abolition of Imprisonment for Debt in New Jersey [1842]," N. J. Hist. Soc., *Proc.,* 84 (1966), 1.
Mencher, Samuel, *Poor Law to Poverty Program: Economic Security Policy in Britain and United States* (1967).
Moynihan, Daniel P., *Maximum Feasible Misunderstanding: Community Action in War on Poverty* (1969).
Riesenfeld, Stefan A., "American Public Assistance Law," *Calif. Law Rev.,* 43 (1955), 175
Schneider, David M., *History of Public Welfare in New York State* (1938).
Smith, Reginald H., *Justice and the Poor* (1919).
Steiner, Gilbert Y., *The State of Welfare* (1971).
U.S. Department of Health, Education and Welfare, *Services for People, Report of the Task Force on Organization of Social Services* (1968).
Worcester, Dean A., Jr., *Monopoly, Big Business, and Welfare in Postwar United States* (1967).

Wyllie, Irvin G., "Search for American Law of Charity, 1776–1844," *MVHR*, 46 (1959), 203.

21.3 PRIVATE CHARITIES AND PHILANTHROPY

American Philosophical Society, *History and Role of Philanthropy in American Society* (1961).
Andrews, F. Emerson, *Corporation Giving* (1952).
────── *Legal Instruments of Foundations* (1958).
────── *Philanthropic Giving* (1950).
Bremner, Robert H., *American Philanthropy* (1960).
Brownell, Emery A., *Legal Aid in the United States* (1951).
Curti, Merle E., "American Philanthropy," *Am. Quar.*, 10 (1958), 420.
────── *American Philanthropy Abroad* (1963).
────── and Roderick Nash, *Philanthropy in the Shaping of American Higher Education* (1965).
────── "Tradition and Innovation in American Philanthropy" *Am. Philos. Soc., Proc.*, 105 (1961), 146.
Cutlip, Scott M., *Fund Raising Role in Philanthropy* (1965).
Dulles, Foster R., *The American Red Cross: A History* (1950).
Embree, Edwin R., and Julia Waxman, *Investment in People: Julius Rosenwald Fund* (1949).
Flexner, Abraham, *Funds and Foundations* (1952).
Fosdick, Raymond B., *Adventure in Giving: General Education Board* (1962).
────── *Story of Rockefeller Foundation* (1952).
Fox, Daniel M., *Engines of Culture: Philanthropy and Art Museums* (1963).
Fremont-Smith, Marion R., *Foundations and Government* (1965).
Glenn, John M., et al., *Russell Sage Foundation, 1907–1946* (1947).
Gracia, Alfred de, ed., *Grass Roots Private Welfare* (1958).
Greenleaf, William, *From These Beginnings: The Early Philanthropies of Henry and Edsel Ford, 1911–1936* (1964).
Huggins, Nathan I., *Protestants against Poverty: Boston's Charities, 1870–1900* (1970).
Joseph, Samuel, *History of Baron de Hirsch Fund* (1935).
Lankford, John, *Congress and the Foundations in the Twentieth Century* (1964).
Lester, Robert M., *Forty Years of Carnegie Giving* (1941).
Miller, Howard S., *Legal Foundations of American Philanthropy, 1776–1844* (1961).
Rusk, Dean, *Role of the Foundation in American Life* (1961).
Russell Sage Foundation, *Report of Princeton Conference on Philanthropy* (1956).
Savage, Howard J., *Fruit of an Impulse: Carnegie Foundation, 1905–1950* (1953).
Sills, David U., *Volunteers: Means and Ends in a National Organization* (1957). In terms of National Foundation for Infantile Paralysis.
Watson, Frank D., *The Charity Organization Movement in the United States* (1922).
Weaver, Warren, et al., *U.S. Philanthropic Foundations* (1967).
Wisbey, Herbert A., Jr., *Soldiers without Swords: Salvation Army* (1955).

* * * * * * *

Curti, Merle E., "The History of American Philanthropy as a Field of Research," *A.H.R.*, 62 (1957), 352.

See also 10.3 for biographies/writings of:

Cooper, Peter, 1791–1883
Dodge, William E., 1805–1883
Girard, Stephen, 1750–1831
Hewitt, Abram S., 1822–1903
Higginson, Henry Lee, 1834–1919
Hopkins, Johns, 1795–1873
McCormick, Nettie Fowler, 1835–1923
Peabody, George, 1795–1869
Peabody, George F., 1852–1938.
Pemberton, Israel, 1715–1779
Rockefeller, John D., 1839–1937
Rockefeller, John D., Jr., 1874–1960
Rosenwald, Julius, 1862–1932
Schiff, Jacob H., 1847–1920
Sheppard, Moses, 1775?–1875
Smithson, James, 1765–1829
Vaux, Roberts, 1786–1836

See also 23.13.4, Higher Education–Financial Support.

21.4 SOCIAL SERVICE

Abbott, Edith, ed., *Pioneers in Social Welfare* (1937).
Addams, Jane, *Democracy and Social Ethics* (1907); Anne Firor Scott, ed. (1964).
——— et al., *Philanthropy and Social Progress* (1893).
Bonner, Arthur, *Jerry McAuley and His Mission* (1967).
Bruno, Frank J., *Trends in Social Work, 1874–1956* (2nd ed., 1957).
Campbell, Thomas F., *SASS: Fifty Years of Social Work Education* (1967).
Chambers, Clarke A., *Seedtime of Reform: American Social Service and Social Action, 1918–1933* (1963).
Davis, Allen F., *Spearheads for Reform: Social Settlements and Progressive Movement, 1890–1914* (1967).
Dunstan, John L., *A Light to the City: 150 Years of the City Missionary Society of Boston, 1816–1966* (1966).
Gans, Herbert J., "Redefining the Settlement's Function for War on Poverty," *Social Work,* 9 (1964), 3.
Henderson, Charles R., *Social Settlements* (1899).
Kennedy, Albert J., et al., *Social Settlements in New York City* (1935).
Lubove, Roy, *The Professional Altruist: The Emergence of Social Work as a Career, 1880–1930* (1965).
Miller, Kenneth D., *Man and God in the City* (1954).
——— and Ethel Prince, *The People Are the City: 150 Years of Social and Religious Concern in New York City* (1962).
National Association of Social Workers, *So All May Live in Decency and Dignity* (1967).
Pumphrey, Ralph E., and Muriel W. Pumphrey, eds., *Heritage of American Social Work: Readings* (1961).
Wade, Louise C., *Graham Taylor: Pioneer for Social Justice, 1851–1938* (1964). Founder of Chicago Commons.
——— "Heritage from Chicago's Early Settlement Houses," Ill. State Hist. Soc., *Jour.,* 60 (1967), 411.
Warner, Amos G., et al., *American Charities and Social Work* (1930).
Woods, Robert A., ed., *Americans in Process: Settlement Study by Residents and Associates of South End House* (1902).
——— *The City Wilderness: Settlement Study* (1898).
——— and A. J. Kennedy, *Settlement Horizon* (1922).

See also 10.3 for biographies/writings of:

Addams, Jane, 1860–1935

Taft, Jessie, 1882–1960
Taylor, Graham, 1851–1938

21.4.1 Care of the Handicapped

Best, Harry, *Blindness and the Blind in the United States* (1934).
––––– *Deafness and the Deaf in the United States* (1943).
Cohen, Julius S., et al., *Vocational Rehabilitation and the Socially Disabled* (1966).
Ferguson, Thomas, and A. W. Kerr, *Handicapped Youth* (1959).
Irwin, Robert B., *As I Saw It*, (1955). An account of helping the blind.
Kessler, Henry H., *Rehabilitation of the Physically Handicapped* (rev. ed., 1953).
McCrea, R. C., *Humane Movement* (1910).
Rooff, Madeline, *Volunteer Societies and Social Policy* (1957).
Ten Broek, Jacobus, and Floyd W. Matson, *Hope Deferred: Public Welfare and the Blind* (1959).
U.S. Bureau of Labor Statistics, *Care of Aged Persons* (1930).
Watson, Thomas J., *Education of Hearing-handicapped Children* (1967).

See also 10.3 for biographies/writings of:

Gallaudet, Edward Miner, 1837–1917
Howe, Samuel Gridley, 1801–1876
Keller, Helen, 1880–1968

21.5 COLLECTIVIST AND UTOPIAN COMMUNITIES

Anderson, Russell H., "Agriculture among the Shakers," *Agric. Hist.*, 24 (1950), 113.
Andrews, Edward D., *People Called Shakers* (1953).
Armytage, W. H. G., *Yesterday's Tomorrows: Historical Survey of Future Societies* (1968).
Arndt, Karl J. R., *George Rapp's Harmony Society, 1785–1847* (1965).
Arrington, Leonard J., *Great Basin Kingdom: Economic History of Latter-Day Saints, 1830–1900* (1958).
Bestor, Arthur E., Jr., *Backwoods Utopias: Sectarian and Owenite Phases of Communitarian Socialism in America, 1663–1829* (1950).
––––– "Education and Reform at New Harmony," Ind. Hist. Soc., *Publ.*, 15 (1948), 283.
Conkin, Paul K., *Two Paths to Utopia: Hutterites and Llano Colony* (1964).
Dohrman, H. T., *California Cult: "Mankind United"* (1958).
Geddes, Joseph A., *United Order among Mormons* (1924).
Gollin, Gillian L., *Moravians in Two Worlds* (1967).
Greenwalt, Emmett A., *Point Loma Community in California, 1897–1942* (1955).
Harrison, J. F. C., *Quest for New Moral World: Robert Owen and Owenites in Britain and America* (1969).
Hinds, William A., *American Communities and Co-operative Colonies* (1908).
Hine, Robert W., *California's Utopian Colonies* (1953).
Holloway, Mark, *Heavens on Earth: Utopian Communities in America, 1680–1880* (1951).
Hostetler, John A., *Amish Society* (rev. ed., 1968).
Kanter, Rosabeth M., *Commitment and Community: Utopians and Communes in Perspective* (1972).
McBee, A. H., *Utopia to Florence* (1947).
Maclure, William, and Marie D. Fretageot, *Correspondence, 1820–1833*, Arthur Bestor, Jr., ed. (1948) New Harmony.
Nordhoff, Charles, *Communistic Societies of the United States* (1875).
Noyes, John H., *American Socialism* (1870).
Parrington, Vernon L., Jr., *American Dreams: Utopias* (1947).
Pease, William H., and Jane H. Pease, *Black Utopia: Negro Communal Experiments in America* (1963). Includes Canada.

Russell, C. Allyn, "Rise and Decline of Shakers," *N.Y. Hist.*, 49 (1968), 29.
Sears, Clara E., *Bronson Alcott's Fruitlands* (1915).
Shambaugh, Bertha M., *Amana That Was and Amana That Is* (1932).
Shaw, Albert, *Icaria* (1884).
Swift, Lindsay, *Brook Farm* (1900).
Syracuse University Library, *Oneida Community Collections*, Nelson M. Blake and Lester G. Wells, eds. (1961).
Webber, Everett, *Escape to Utopia: Communal Movement* (1959).
Yambura, Barbara S., and Eunice W. Bodine, *Change and Parting: Amana* (1960).

21.6 SOCIAL SECURITY AND UNEMPLOYMENT INSURANCE

Altmeyer, Arthur J., *The Formative Years of Social Security* (1966).
Feder, Leah H., *Unemployment Relief* (1936).
Gagliardo, Domenico, *American Social Insurance* (1955).
Larson, Arthur G., and Merrill G. Murray, "Unemployment Insurance in the United States," *Vanderbilt Law Rev.*, 8 (1955), 181.
Lubove, Roy, *The Struggle for Social Security, 1900–1935* (1968).
Nelson, Daniel, *Unemployment Insurance, 1915–1935* (1969).
Neuberger, Richard L., and Kelly Loe, *Army of the Aged* (1936).
Somers, Gerald G., ed., *Retraining the Unemployed* (1968).
Turnbull, John G., *The Changing Faces of Economic Insecurity* (1966).
Witte, Edwin E., *Development of the Social Security Act* (1962).
——— *Social Security Perspectives: Essays*, Robert J. Lampman, ed. (1962).

See also 10.3 for biographies/writings of:

Witte, Edwin E., 1887–1960

21.7 POVERTY IN THE POST-WAR PERIOD

Bagdikian, Ben H., *In the Midst of Plenty: The Poor in America* (1966).
Bond, Floyd A., et al., *Our Needy Aged: A California Study of a National Problem* (1954).
Caudill, Harry M., *Night Comes to the Cumberlands: Biography of a Depressed Area* (1963).
Coles, Robert, and Al Clayton, *Still Hungry in America* (1969).
Ferman, Louis A., et al., eds., *Poverty in America* (rev. ed., 1968).
Fishman, Leo, ed., *Poverty Amid Affluence* (1966).
Gallaway, Lowell E., "Aged and the Extent of Poverty in the United States," *South. Econ. Jour.*, 33 (1966), 212.
Gallaway, Lowell E., "Foundations of 'War on Poverty'," *Am. Econ. Rev.*, 55 (1965), 122. Concerns the period 1947–1963.
Gladwin, Thomas, *Poverty U.S.A.* (1967).
Hamilton, David, "Not So Affluent Society," *Colo. Quar.*, 9 (1960), 183.
Harrington, Michael, *The Other America: Poverty in the United States* (1962).
Hunger and Malnutrition in the United States, *Hunger, U.S.A.* (1968). Citizens' Board of Inquiry.
Kosa, John, Aaron Antonovsky, and Irving Kenneth Lola, eds., *Poverty and Health: A Sociological Analysis* (1969).
Larner, Jeremy, and Irving Howe, eds., *Poverty: Views from the Left* (1969).
Lens, Sidney, *Poverty: America's Enduring Paradox* (1969).
MacIver, R. M., ed., *The Assault on Poverty and Individual Responsibility* (1965).
Miller, Herman P., *Rich Man, Poor Man* (2nd ed., 1971).
Moynihan, Daniel P., *On Understanding Poverty: Perspectives from the Social Sciences* (1969).
Seligman, Ben B., *Permanent Poverty: American Syndrome* (1965).

U.S. President's National Advisory Commission on Rural Poverty, *Report* (1968).
Vatter, Harold G., and Robert E. Will, "Technology and New Philosophy of Poverty," *South. Econ. Jour.*, 33 (1967), 559.

* * * * * * *

Schlesinger, Benjamin, *Poverty in Canada and the United States: Overview and Annotated Bibliography* (1966).

21.8 TEMPERANCE AND PROHIBITION

Asbury, Herbert, *Great Illusion: Prohibition* (1950).
Burnham, J. C., "New Perspectives on the Prohibition 'Experiment' in the 1920's," *Jour. Soc. Hist.*, 2 (1968), 51.
Cherington, E. H., *Evolution of Prohibition* (1920).
Clark, Norman H., *Dry Years: Prohibition in Washington* [state] (1965).
Clubb, H. S., *Maine Liquor Law* (1856).
Gusfield, Joseph R., *Symbolic Crusade: Status Politics and the American Temperance Movement* (1963).
Hendricks, E. A., "South Carolina Dispensary System," *No. Car. Hist. Rev.*, 22 (1945), 176.
Isaac, Paul E., *Prohibition and Politics: Tennessee, 1885–1920* (1965).
Johnsen, Julia E., *Problem of Liquor Control* (1934).
Krout, John A., *The Origins of Prohibition* (1925).
Lee, Henry W., *How Dry We Were: Prohibition* (1963).
Odegard, P. H., *Pressure Politics* (1928).
Ostrander, Gilman M., *Prohibition Movement in California, 1848–1933* (1957).
Pearson, C. C., and J. Edwin Hendricks, *Liquor and Anti-Liquor in Virginia, 1619–1919* (1967).
Schmeckebier, Lawrence F., *Bureau of Prohibition* (1929).
Sellers, James B., *Prohibition Movement in Alabama, 1702–1943* (1943).
Sinclair, Andrew, *Prohibition: Era of Excess* (1962).
Slosson, P. W., *Great Crusade and After* (1930).
Stone, Melville E., *American Liquor Control* (1943).
Tillitt, M. H., *Price of Prohibition* (1932).
Timberlake, James H., *Prohibition and the Progressive Movement, 1900–1920* (1963).
Warburton, Clark, *Economic Results of Prohibition* (1932).
Whitener, Daniel J., *Prohibition in North Carolina, 1715–1945* (1945).

* * * * * * *

Nicholson, Dorothy C., and R. P. Graves, *Selective Bibliography on the Eighteenth Amendment* (1931).

See also 10.3 for biographies/writings of:

Cannon, James, Jr., 1864–1944
Dow, Neal, 1804–1897
Gough, John B., 1817–1886
Willard, Frances E., 1839–1898

21.9 PACIFISM AND ANTI-MILITARISM

Allen, Devere, *Fight for Peace* (1930).
Beales, A. C. F., *History of Peace* (1931).
Brock, Peter, *Pacifism in the United States: Colonial Era to the First World War* (1968).
Curti, Merle E., *American Peace Crusade* (1929).

—— Peace or War: The American Struggle, 1636–1936 (1936).
Galpin, William F., Pioneering for Peace (1933).
Hawkes, James H., "Antimilitarism at State Universities: Campaign against Compulsory ROTC, 1920–1940," Wis. Mag. Hist., 49 (1965), 41.
Horst, Samuel, Mennonites in the Confederacy: Civil War Pacifism (1967).
Lynd, Staughton, ed., Nonviolence in America: A Documentary History (1966).
Martin, David A., Pacifism: A Historical and Sociological Study (1966).
Moellering, Ralph L., Modern War and the American Churches (1956).
Nelson, John K., Peace Prophets: Pacifist Thought, 1919–1941 (1967).
Peterson, Horace C., and Gilbert C. Fite, Opponents of War, 1917–1918 (1957).
Phelps, C. G., Anglo-American Peace Movement (1930).
Schlissel, Lillian, Conscience in America: Conscientious Objection, 1757–1967 (1968).
Sibley, Mulford Q., Conscription of Conscience: The American State and the Conscientious Objector, 1940–1947 (1952).
Whitney, Edson, American Peace Society (1928).
Wittner, Lawrence S., Rebels against War: American Peace Movement, 1941–1960 (1969).

See also 10.3 for biographies/writings of:

Burritt, Elihu, 1810–1879

21.10 PATRIOTISM AND DISLOYALTY

Agar, William, and Aaron Levenstein, Freedom's Advocate (1965).
Bonteccu, Eleanor, Federal Loyalty-Security Program (1953).
Brown, Ralph S., Jr., Loyalty and Security: Employment Tests (1960).
Chapin, Bradley, American Law of Treason: Revolutionary and Early National Origins (1964).
Curti, Merle E., Roots of Loyalty (1946).
Davies, Wallace E., Patriotism on Parade: The Story of Veterans' and Hereditary Organizations in America, 1783–1900 (1955).
Dearing, Mary R., Veterans in Politics: G.A.R. (1952).
Hurst, J. Willard, "Treason in the United States," Harv. Law Rev., 58 (1944–45), 226.
Hyman, Harold M., To Try Men's Souls: Loyalty Tests (1959).
Manwaring, David R., Render unto Caesar: Flag-Salute Controversy (1962).
Minott, Rodney G., Peerless Patriots: Organized Veterans (1962).
Quaife, Milo M., et al., History of the United States Flag (1961).
Rappaport, Armin, The Navy League of the United States (1962).
Ross, Davis R. B., Preparing for Ulysses: Politics and Veterans during World War II (1969).
Schaar, John H., Loyalty in America (1957).
Strayer, Martha, D.A.R. (1958).
Tyler, Robert L., "American Veterans Committee," Am. Quar., 18 (1966), 419.
Wecter, Dixon, When Johnny Comes Marching Home (1944).
Westin, Alan F., "Loyalty Controversy," Commentary, 28 (1959), 528.
Weyl, Nathaniel, The Battle Against Disloyalty (1951).
—— Treason: The Story of Disloyalty and Betrayal in American History (1950).

See also 25.7, Nationalism and Mission.

21.11 NATIVISM AND BIGOTRY

Allport, Gordon, Nature of Prejudice (1954).
Barry, Colman J., "Some Roots of American Nativism," Cath. Hist. Rev., 44 (1958), 137.

Billington, Ray A., *Protestant Crusade, 1800–1860* (1938).
Davis, David B., "Anti-Masonic, Anti-Catholic, and Anti-Mormon Literature," *MVHR,* 47 (1960), 205.
Handlin, Oscar, *Boston's Immigrants: A Study in Acculturation* (rev. ed., 1959).
––––––– *Race and Nationality in American Life* (1957).
Higham, John, *Strangers in the Land: American Nativism, 1860–1925* (rev. ed., 1963).
Kinzer, Donald L., *An Episode in Anti-Catholicism: the American Protective Association* (1964).
Lowenthal, Leo, and Norbert Guterman, *Prophets of Deceit* (1949).
McGann, A. G., *Nativism in Kentucky* (1944).
Marcus, Lloyd, *Treatment of Minorities in Secondary School Textbooks* (1961).
Murphy, Paul L., "Intolerance in the 1920's" *JAH,* 51 (1964), 60.
––––––– "Normalcy, Intolerance, and American Character," *Va. Quar. Rev.,* 40 (1964), 445.
Myers, Gustavus, *History of Bigotry in the United States* (1943).
Nugent, Walter T. K., *Tolerant Populists: Kansas Populism and Nativism.* (1963).
Overdyke, W. D., *Know-Nothing Party in the South* (1950).
Scisco, Louis D., *Political Nativism in New York* (1901).
Solomon, Barbara M., *Ancestors and Immigrants: A Changing New England Tradition* (1956).
Stauffer, Vernon, *New England and the Bavarian Iluminati* (1918).
Weinberg, Julius, "E. A. Ross: Progressive as Nativist," *Wis. Mag. Hist.,* 50 (1967), 242.

See also 21.12.3, Violence, Mobs, and Vigilantism; 25.14, Racial Thought.

21.12 CRIME

21.12.1 General

Allen, Francis A., *Borderland of Criminal Justice* (1964).
Barnes, H. E., and N. K. Teeters, *New Horizons in Criminology* (1947).
Becker, Harold K., et al., *New Dimensions in Criminal Justice* (1968).
Bell, Daniel, "Crime as an American Way of Life," *Antioch Rev.,* 13 (1953), 131.
Blumberg, Abraham S., *Criminal Justice* (1967).
Bruce, Andrew A., *Administration of Criminal Justice in Illinois* (1929).
Clark, Ramsey, *Crime in America: Observations on its Nature, Causes, Prevention, and Control* (1970).
Eldridge, William B., *Narcotics and the Law* (2nd ed., 1967).
Gardiner, John A., "Public Attitudes toward Gambling and Corruption," *Am. Acad. Pol. Soc. Sci., Annals,* 374 (1967), 123.
Glueck, Sheldon, *Crime and Justice* (1945).
Henriques, Fernando, *Prostitution and Society.* Vol II: *Prostitution in Europe and the New World* (1963).
Irey, E. L., and W. J. Slocum, *Tax Dodgers* (1948).
Karlen, Delmar, et al., *Anglo-American Criminal Justice* (1968).
Kefauver, Estes, *Crime in America* (1951).
Lubove, Roy, "Progressives and the Prostitute," *Historian,* 24 (1962), 308.
Millspaugh, A. C., *Crime Control by National Government* (1937).
Pye, A. Kenneth, "Administration of Criminal Justice," *Columbia Law Rev.,* 66 (1966), 286.
Rosenberg, Charles E., *Trial of Assassin Guiteau: Psychiatry and Law in Gilded Age* (1968).
Sellin, Thorsten, *Crime in Depression* (1937).
Sutherland, Arthur E., "Crime and Confession," *Harv. Law Rev.,* 79 (1965), 21.
U.S. President's Commission on Law Enforcement and Administration of Justice, *Challenge of Crime in a Free Society* (1967).
Washburn, Charles, *Come into My Parlor: Biography of the Aristocratic Everleigh Sisters of Chicago* (1936).

Waterman, Willoughby C., *Prostitution and Its Repression in New York City, 1900–1931* (1932).
Williams, Jack K., *Vogues in Villainy: Crime and Retribution in Ante-Bellum South Carolina* (1959).
Woolston, H. B., *Prostitution in the United States* (1921).

*   *   *   *   *   *   *

Culver, D. C., *Bibliography of Crime and Criminal Justice, 1927–1931* (1934).
Cumming, John, *Contribution Towards a Bibliography Dealing with Crime and Cognate Subjects* (3d ed., 1970).
Kuhlman, A. F., *Guide to Material on Crime and Criminal Justice* (1929).
U.S. Attorney General's Advisory Committee on Crime, *Bibliography on Housing and Crime* (1936).
U.S. Library of Congress, *Crime and Criminal Justice* (1930). Supplement (1935).

See also 19.9.2, Neglected and Delinquent Youth.

21.12.2 Organized Crime

American Bar Association. Commission on Organized Crime, *Organized Crime and Law Enforcement,* Morris Ploscowe, ed. (2 vols., 1952–1953).
Clarke, Donald H., *In Reign of Rothstein* (1929).
Cook, Fred J., *Secret Rulers: Criminal Syndicates and How They Control the United States Underworld* (1966).
Cressey, Donald R., *Theft of the Nation: Organized Crime in America* (1969).
Glueck, Sheldon, and Eleanor T. Glueck, *Later Criminal Careers* (1937).
Hostetter, G. L., and T. Q. Beesley, *It's a Racket* (1929).
Kavanaugh, M. A., *The Criminal and His Allies* (1928).
King, Rufus, *Gambling and Organized Crime* (1969).
Kobler, John, *Capone: The Life and World of Al Capone* (1971).
Landesco, John, *Organized Crime in Chicago* (2nd ed., 1968).
Lewis, Norman, *Honored Society* (1964). The Mafia.
Maas, Peter, *Valachi Papers* (1968).
Pantaleone, Michele, *Mafia and Politics* (1966).
Reid, Ed, *Grim Reapers: The Anatomy of Organized Crime in America* (1969).
Schiavo, Giovanni, *The Truth About the Mafia* (1962).
Thompson, Craig, and Allen Raymond, *Gang Rule in New York* (1940).
Tyler, Gus, ed., "Combating Organized Crime," Am. Acad. Pol. Soc. Sci., *Annals,* 347 (1963), 1.
—— *Organized Crime in America* (1962).

21.12.3 Violence, Mobs, and Vigilantism

21.12.3.1.General

Adamic, Louis, *Dynamite: The Story of Class Violence in America* (1931).
Adams, Graham, Jr., *Age of Industrial Violence: The Activities and Findings of the Commission on Industrial Relations* (1966).
Angle, Paul M., *Bloody Williamson: American Lawlessness* (1952). Illinois County.
Billington, Ray A., "The Burning of the Charlestown [Massachusetts] Convent," *NEQ,* 10 (1937), 4.
Broehl, Wayne G., Jr., *The Molly Maguires* (1964).
Brown, Richard Maxwell, "Legal and Behavioral Perspectives on American Vigilantism," *Perspectives in Am. Hist.,* 5 (1971), 95.
Bruce, Robert V., *1877: Year of Violence* (1959).
Caughey, John W., *Their Majesties the Mob* (1960).
Cooke, Jacob E., "Whiskey Insurrection," *Penn. Hist.,* 30 (1963), 316.
David, Henry, *A History of the Haymarket Affair: A Study in the American Social Revolutionary and Labor Movements* (2nd ed. 1958).
Donovan, H. D. A., *Barnburners* (1925).

Gard, Wayne, *Frontier Justice* (1949).

Graham, Hugh D., and Ted R. Gurr, eds., *Violence in America: Historical and Comparative Perspectives: A Report to the National Commission on the Causes and Prevention of Violence* (1969).

Grover, David H., *Debaters and Dynamiters: The Story of the Haywood Trial* (1964).

Headley, Joel T., *Great Riots of New York, 1712–1873* (1970).

Heaps, Willard A., *Riots, U.S.A., 1765–1970* (rev. ed., 1970).

Higham, Robin, ed., *Bayonets in the Streets: The Use of Troops in Civil Disturbances* (1969).

Hofstadter, Richard, and Michael Wallace, eds., *American Violence: A Documentary History* (1970).

Kogan, Bernard R., ed., *The Chicago Haymarket Riot: Anarchy on Trial* (1959).

Laidler, Harry W., *Boycotts and the Labor Struggle* (1914).

Langdon, Emma F., *Cripple Creek Strike: History of Industrial Wars in Colorado, 1903–1905* (1905).

Langford, N. P., *Vigilante Days and Ways* (1890).

Nall, James O., *The Tobacco Night Riders of Kentucky and Tennessee, 1905–1909* (1939).

Raper, Arthur F., *The Tragedy of Lynching* (1938).

Rich, Bennett M., *The Presidents and Civil Disorder* (1941).

Rubenstein, Richard E., *Rebels in Eden: Mass Political Violence in the United States* (1970).

Smith, Robert W., *Coeur d'Alene Mining War of 1892* (1961).

Sofchalk, Donald G., "The Chicago Memorial Day Incident," *Labor Hist.*, 6 (1965), 3.

Stevens, Alden, *Arms and the People* (1942).

U.S. National Advisory Commission on Civil Disorders, *Report* (1968). The Kerner Report.

U.S. National Commission on the Causes and Prevention of Violence, *Rights in Conflict* (1968).

Vanderwood, Paul J., *Night Riders of Reelfoot Lake* (1969). Tennessee, 1908.

West, George P., *Report on the Colorado Strike,* (1915).

Wolff, Leon, *Lockout: The Homestead Strike of 1892: A Study of Violence, Unionism, and the Carnegie Steel Empire* (1965).

Wolfgang, Marvin E., ed., "Patterns of Violence," Am. Acad. Pol. Soc. Sci., *Annals*, 364 (1966), 1.

See also Military History–Recruiting, Conscription, Draft Riots, and Desertion.

21.12.3.2 Ku Klux Klan

Alexander, Charles C., *Ku Klux Klan in the Southwest* (1965).

Chalmers, David M., *Hooded Americanism: Ku Klux Klan, 1865–1965* (1965).

——— "Ku Klux Klan in the Sunshine State: 1920's," *Fla. Hist. Quar.*, 42 (1964), 209.

Davis, James H., "Colorado under the Klan," *Colo. Mag.*, 42 (1965), 93.

Degler, Carl N., "Century of the Klans," *JSH*, 31 (1965), 435.

Horn, Stanley F., *Invisible Empire: The Story of the Ku Klux Klan, 1866–1871* (1939).

Jackson, Charles O., "William J. Simmons: A Career in Ku Kluxism," *Ga. Hist. Quar.*, 50 (1966), 351.

Jackson, Kenneth T., *Ku Klux Klan in the City, 1915–1930* (1967).

Randel, William P., *Ku Klux Klan* (1965).

Rice, Arnold S., *The Ku Klux Klan in American Politics* (1962).

See also volume two for references to Reconstruction.

21.12.3.3 Inter-Racial Violence

Abernethy, Lloyd M., "Washington Race War of July, 1919," *Md. Hist. Mag.*, 52 (1963), 309.

Boskin, Joseph, and Fred Krinsky, *Urban Racial Violence in the Twentieth Century* (1969).

Brown, Earl L., *Why Race Riots? Lessons from Detroit* (1944). The riot of 1943.

Carter, Dan T., *Scottsboro: A Tragedy of the American South* (1969).

Chalmers, Allan K., *They Shall Be Free* (1951). Scottsboro trial.

Chicago Commission on Race Relations, *The Negro in Chicago: Race Riot in 1919* (1922).

Conot, Robert E., *Rivers of Blood, Years of Darkness: The Unforgettable Classic Account of the Watts Riot* (1967).

Fogelson, Robert M., "White on Black: A Critique of the McCone Commission Report on The Los Angeles Riots," *Pol. Sci. Quar.*, 82 (1967), 337.

———— comp., *The Los Angeles Riots* (1969).

Gilbert, Ben W., *Ten Blocks from the White House: Anatomy of the Washington Race Riots of 1968* (1968).

Grimshaw, Allen D., ed., *Racial Violence in the United States* (1969).

Hayden, Thomas, *Rebellion in Newark: Official Violence and Ghetto Response* (1967).

Lieberson, Stanley, and Arnold R. Silverman, "The Precipitants and Underlying Conditions of Race Riots," *Am. Sociol. Rev.*, 30 (1965), 887. Covers the period 1913–1963.

Lincoln, James H., *Anatomy of a Riot: A Detroit Judge's Report* (1968).

McMillan, George, *Racial Violence and Law Enforcement* (1960).

Osofsky, Gilbert, "Race Riot, 1900: A Study of Ethnic Violence," *Jour. Negro Educ.*, 32 (1963), 16.

Patterson, Haywood, and Earl Conrad, *Scottsboro Boy* (1950).

Raper, Arthur F., *The Tragedy of Lynching* (1933).

Rudwick, Elliott M., *Race Riot at East St. Louis, July 2, 1917* (1964).

Shogan, Robert, and Tom Craig, *The Detroit Race Riot: A Study in Violence* (1964).

U.S. National Advisory Commission on Civil Disorders, *Report* (1968). The Kerner Report.

Waskow, Arthur I., *From Race Riot to Sit-In, 1919 and the 1960s* (1966).

Zangrando, Robert L., "The NAACP and a Federal Antilynching Bill, 1934–1940," *Jour. Negro Hist.*, 50 (1965), 106.

*   *   *   *   *   *   *

U.S. Library of Congress, *List on Lynching* (1940).

21.12.4 Law Enforcement

Becker, Harold K., *Issues in Police Administration* (1970).

Chevigny, Paul G., *Police Power: Police Abuses in New York City* (1969).

Cook, Fred J., *The F.B.I. Nobody Knows* (1964).

Deutsch, Albert, *The Trouble with Cops* (1955).

Fosdick, Raymond B., *American Police Systems* (1920).

Horan, James D., *The Pinkertons: The Detective Dynasty That Made History* (1967).

La Fave, Wayne, *Arrest: The Decision to Take a Suspect into Custody* (1965).

Lane, Roger, *Policing the City: Boston 1822–1885* (1967).

Overstreet, Harry A., and Bonaro Overstreet, *F.B.I. in Our Open Society* (1969).

Pound, Roscoe, *Criminal Justice in America* (1930).

Radano, Gene, *Walking the Beat: A New York Policeman Tells What It's Like on His Side of the Law* (1968).

Richardson, James F., *New York Police, Colonial Times to 1901* (1970).

Skolnick, Jerome, *Justice Without Trial: Law Enforcement in a Democratic Society* (1966).

Smith, Bruce, *Police Systems in the United States* (rev. ed., 1949).

———— *State Police* (1925).

Turner, William W., *Invisible Witness: New Technology of Crime Investigation* (1968).

———— *Police Establishment* (1968).

Whittemore, L. H., *Cop! Closeup of Violence and Tragedy* (1969).
Wilson, James Q., *Varieties of Police Behavior* (1968).
Wilson, Orlando W., *Police Administration* (1950).

* * * * * * *

Becker, Harold K., and George T. Law, *Law Enforcement: A Selected Bibliography* (1968).
Hewitt, William H., *Bibliography of Police Administration, Public Safety, and Criminology* (1967).

21.12.5 Punishment

Barnes, Harry E., *Evolution of Penology in Pennsylvania* (1927).
Beckman, Gail M., "Penal Codes," *Am. Jour. Legal Hist.*, 10 (1966), 148.
Clemmer, Donald, *The Prison Community* (rev. ed., 1958).
Cressey, Donald R., ed., *The Prison: Studies in Institutional Organization and Change* (1961).
Davis, David B., "The Movement to Abolish Capital Punishment in America, 1787–1861, *AHR*, 63 (1957), 23.
De Puy, LeRoy B., "'Pennsylvania System' at Penitentiaries," *Penn. Hist.*, 21 (1954), 128.
Dix, Dorothea L., *Remarks on Prisons* (2nd ed., 1845); Leonard D. Savitz, ed. (1967).
Goffman, Erving, *Asylums* (1961).
Hazelrigg, Lawrence, ed., *Prison Within Society: A Reader in Penology* (1968).
Klein, Philip, *Prison Methods in New York State* (1920).
Lawes, Lewis E., *Twenty Thousand Years in Sing Sing* (1932).
Leiby, James, *Charity and Correction in New Jersey: A History of State Welfare Institutions* (1967).
Lewis, Orlando F., *The Development of American Prisons and Prison Customs, 1776–1845* (1922).
Lewis, W. David, *Prom Newgate to Dannemora: The Rise of the Penitentiary in New York, 1796–1848* (1965).
McKelvey, Blake, *American Prisons Prior to 1915* (1936).
Minton, Robert J., Jr., ed., *Inside: Prison American Style* (1971).
Powell, J. C., *American Siberia* (1891).
Semmes, Raphael, *Crime and Punishment in Early Maryland* (1938).
Tannenbaum, Frank, *Osborne of Sing Sing* (1933).
Teeters, Negley K., and John D. Shearer, *The Prison at Philadelphia: Cherry Hill* (1957).
Wines, F. H., *Punishment and Reformation* (1895).

* * * * * * *

U.S. Attorney General's Advisory Committee on Crime, *Bibliography on Jails* (1937).

22 Social Manners and Customs

22.1 GENERAL

American Heritage, *American Album,* Oliver O. Jensen, ed. (1968).
—— *American Manners and Morals: Picture History,* Mary Cable, ed. (1969).
Barnett, James H., *The American Christmas* (1954).
Carson, Gerald, *Polite Americans* (1966).
Earle, Alice M., *Customs and Fashions in Old New England* (1893).
Lynes, Russell, *Domesticated Americans* (1963).
Mitford, Jessica, *The American Way of Death* (1963).
Morris, Wright, *The Inhabitants* (1946). Photographs.
Mussey, Jane Barrows, ed., *Yankee Life as Told by Those Who Lived It* (rev. ed., 1947).
Power, Richard L., *Planting Corn Belt Culture: Impress of Upland Southerner and Yankee in the Old Northwest* (1953).
Robinson, Dwight E., "Importance of Fashions in Taste to Business History," *Bus. Hist. Rev.,* 37 (1963), 5.
Ross, Ishbel, *Taste in America: An Illustrated History* (1967).
Schlesinger, Arthur M., *Learning How to Behave* (1946).
Tyler, Alice F., *Freedom's Ferment: Social History from Colonial Period to the Civil War* (1944).
Walker, Robert W., *Everyday Life in the Age of Enterprise, 1865–1900* (1968).
Warner, W. L., and P. S. Lunt, *Social Life of Modern Community* (1941).
Wright, Frances, *Views of Society and Manners in America* (1821); Paul R. Baker, ed. (1963).
Yoder, Paton, "Private Hospitality in the South, 1775–1850," *MVHR,* 47 (1960), 419.
Zelomek, A. Wilbert, *Changing America: At Work and Play* (1959).

*   *   *   *   *   *   *

Bobbitt, Mary R., comp., *Bibliography of Etiquette Books published in America before 1900* (1947).

See also 13.4.4, Pioneer Life; 18.11.3, Rural Life; 19.6, Community Sociological Studies; 28.7, Popular Culture.

22.2 FOOD AND COSTUME

American Heritage, *American Heritage Cookbook and Illustrated History of American Eating and Drinking,* Cleveland Amory, ed. (1964).
Brown, John Hull, *Early American Beverages* (1966).
Carson, Jane, *Colonial Virginia Cookery* (1968).
Cummings, R. O., *The American and His Food* (1940).

Earle, Alice M., *Two Centuries of Costume in America* (2 vols., 1903).
Huenefeld, Irene P., *International Directory of Historical Clothing* (1967).
Levin, Phyllis Lee, *The Wheels of Fashion* (1965).
McClellan, Elisabeth, *History of American Costume, 1607–1870* (1937).
Monro, Isabel S., and Dorothy E. Cook, eds., *Costume Index* (1937). Supplement (1957).
Nystrom, P. H., *Economics of Fashion* (1928).
Riegel, Robert E., "Women's Clothes and Women's Rights," *Am. Quar.*, 15 (1963), 390.
Simmons, Amelia, *American Cookery* (1796); Mary T. Wilson, ed. (1958).
Stoehr, Ruth M., "Favorite American Foods and the Role they Played in History," *West. Penn. Hist. Mag.*, 40 (1957), 89.
Thomas, Gertrude I., *Foods of Our Forefathers* (1941).
Thomas, Lately, *Delmonico's* (1967).
Wilcox, Ruth T., *Five Centuries of American Costume* (1963).
Wilson, Mary T., "Amelia Simmons Fills a Need: American Cookery, 1796," *WMQ*, 3 ser., 14 (1957), 16.

*   *   *   *   *   *   *

Hiler, Hilaire, and Meyer Hiler, *Bibliography of Costume,* Helen G. Cushing, ed. (1939).

22.3 RECREATION AND LEISURE

22.3.1 General

Chafetz, Henry, *Play the Devil: History of Gambling in the United States* (1960).
Denney, Reuel, *The Astonished Muse* (1957).
Doell, Charles E., *Brief History of Parks and Recreation in the United States* (1954).
Dulles, Foster R., *History of Recreation: America Learns to Play* (1966).
Ezell, John S., *Fortune's Merry Wheel: The Lottery in America* (1960).
Green, Arnold W., *Recreation, Leisure, and Politics* (1964).
Kaplan, Max, *Leisure in America—Social Inquiry* (1960).
Larrabee, Eric, and Rolf Meyersohn, eds., *Mass Leisure* (1960).
Madow, Pauline, ed., *Recreation in America* (1965).
May, Earl C., *Circus from Rome to Ringling* (1932).
Nash, Jay B., *Philosophy of Leisure and Recreation* (1953).
Neumeyer, Martin H., and Esther S. Neumeyer, *Leisure and Recreation* (1958).
Steiner, J. F., *Americans at Play* (1933).
——— *Recreation in Depression* (1937).
U.S. President's Commission on Outdoor Recreation Resources, *Outdoor Recreation for America: Report* (1962).
Weinberger, Julius, "Economic Aspects of Recreation," *Harv. Bus. Rev.*, 15 (1937), 448.
Winthrop, Henry, "Developmental Leisure Time Activity in the United States in Relation to Cultural Ideals," *Jour. Human Rel.*, 14 (1966), 267.

22.3.2 Tourism

Amory, Cleveland, *The Last Resorts* (1952).
Baker, Paul R., *Fortunate Pilgrims: Americans in Italy, 1800–1860* (1964).
Barrett, Richmond, *Good Old Summer Days: Newport, Narragansett Pier, Saratoga, Long Branch, Bar Harbor* (1952).
Dallas, Sandra, *No More than Five in a Bed* (1967).
Dulles, Foster R., *Americans Abroad* (1964).
Earle, Alice M., *Stage Coach and Tavern Days* (1900).
Ise, John, *Our National Park Policy: A Critical History* (1961).

King, Doris E., "First-Class Hotel and the Age of the Common Man," *JSH*, 23 (1957), 172.
Pomeroy, Earl S., *In Search of the Golden West: Tourist in Western America* (1957).
Spiller, Robert E., *American in England during the First Half Century of Independence* (1926).
Tilden, Freeman, *National Parks* (1968).
Van Orman, Richard A., *Room for the Night: Hotels of the Old West* (1966).
Williamson, Jefferson, *American Hotel* (1930).
Yoder, Paton, *Taverns and Travelers: Inns of the Early Midwest* (1969).

22.3.3 Sports

22.3.3.1 General

Betts, John R., "Mind and Body in Early American Thought," *JAH*, 54 (1968), 787.
——— "Technological Revolution and the Rise of Sport, 1850–1900," *MVHR*, 40 (1953), 231.
Boyle, Robert H., *Sport—Mirror of American Life* (1963).
Cole, Arthur C., "Our Sporting Grandfathers," *Atlantic Monthly*, 150 (July 1932), 88.
Cozens, Frederick W., and Florence S. Stumpf, *Sports in American Life* (1953).
Danzig, Allison, and Peter Brandwein, *Sport's Golden Age* (1948).
Durant, John, and Otto Bettman, *Pictorial History of American Sports* (1952).
Frost, A. B., *Sports and Games in the Open* (1899).
Gallico, Paul, *Farewell to Sport* (1938).
Holliman, Jennie, *American Sports (1785–1835)* (1931).
Janssen, F. W., comp., *American Amateur Athletic and Aquatic History* (1893).
Krout, John A., *Annals of American Sport* (1929).
Leonard, Fred E., *Physical Education* (1923).
Manchester, Herbert, *Four Centuries of Sport* (1931).
Menke, Frank G., *Encyclopedia of Sports*, Roger Treat, ed. (rev. ed., 1969).
Moreland, G. L., *Balldom* (1914).
Rice, Grantland, *The Tumult and the Shouting* (1954).
Sports Illustrated, *Yesterday in Sport* (1968).
Stone, Gregory P., "American Sports," *Chicago Rev.*, 9 (1955), 83.
Tunis, John R., *The American Way in Sport* (1958).
——— *Democracy in Sport* (1941).
Weaver, Robert B., *Amusements and Sports* (1939).
Wind, Herbert W., *Gilded Age of Sport* (1961).

*   *   *   *   *   *   *

Henderson, Robert W., *Early American Sport: A Checklist of Books by American and Foreign Authors Published in America Prior to 1860* (2nd ed., 1953).

22.3.3.2 Baseball

Bealle, Morris A., *Softball Story* (1957).
Bouton, Jim, *Ball Four* (1970).
Evers, J. J., and H. S. Fullerton, *Touching Second* (1910).
Peterson, Robert W., *Only the Ball Was White* (1970).
Seymour, Harold, *Baseball: Early Years* (1960).
Smith, Robert M., *Baseball* (rev. ed., 1970).
Voigt, David, *American Baseball* (2 vols., 1966–1970).

22.3.3.3 Football

Claassen, Harold, *History of Professional Football* (1963).
Danzig, Allison, *History of American Football* (1956).
Kramer, Jerry, *Instant Replay* (1968).
Meggyesy, Dave, *Out of Their League* (1970).

Plimpton, George, *Paper Lion* (1966).
Stagg, A. A., and W. W. Stout, *Touchdown* (1927).
Weyand, A. M., *American Football: Its History and Development* (1926).

22.3.3.4 Other

Akers, Dwight, *Drivers Up: Story of American Harness Racing* (2nd ed., 1947).
Damon, S. Foster, "History of Square-Dancing," Am. Antiq. Soc., *Proc.,* 62 (1953), 63.
Danzig, Allison, *The Racquet Game* (1930).
Elmer, R. P., *Archery* (1933).
Farnol, Jeffery, *Famous Prize Fights* (1928).
Fleischer, Nathaniel S., *Heavyweight Championship: Informal History from 1719 to Present Day* (1949).
Hervey, John, *Racing in America, 1665–1865* (2 vols., 1944). Horse racing.
——— *Racing in America, 1922–1936* (1937).
Johnston, Alexander, *Ten—and Out! Story of the Prize Ring in America* (3d ed., 1947).
Kelley, Robert F., *Rowing* (1932).
Landis, D. B., "Evolution of the Bicycle," Lancaster County Hist. Soc., *Papers,* 35 (1931), 277.
Laney, Al, *Covering the Court: Game of Tennis* (1968).
Lindsay, Nigel, *The America's Cup* (1930).
Padwe, Sandy, *Basketball* (1970).
Paret, J. P., *Lawn Tennis* (1912).
Riggs, Robert L., *Tennis is my Racket* (1949).
Sarazen, Gene, and H. W. Wind, *Thirty Years of Golf* (1950).
Stephens, William P., *Yachting* (1904).
Vosburgh, Walter S., *Racing in America, 1866–1921* (1922). Horse Racing.
Wind, H. W., *Story of American Golf* (1948).

23 Education

23.1 GENERAL

Bailyn, Bernard, *Education in the Forming of American Society: Needs and Opportunities for Study* (1960).
Butts, R. Freeman, and Lawrence A. Cremin, *History of Education* (1953).
Callahan, Raymond E., *Introduction to Education in American Society* (2nd ed., 1960).
Cremin, Lawrence A., *American Common School* (1951).
Cubberley, Ellwood P., *Public Education in the United States* (rev. ed., 1934).
———— comp., *Readings in Public Education in the United States* (1934).
Edwards, Newton, and Herman G. Richey, *School in the American Social Order* (2nd ed., 1963).
Good, Harry G., *History of American Education* (2nd ed., 1962).
Goodsell, Willystine, ed., *Pioneers of Women's Education in the United States* (1931).
Jackson, Sidney L., *America's Struggle for Free Schools* (1941).
Knight, Edgar W., *Education in United States* (3d ed., 1951).
———— and Clifton L. Hall, eds., *Readings in American Educational History* (1951).
Krug, Edward A., *Shaping of American High School* (1964).
McLachlan, James, *American Boarding Schools: A Historical Study* (1970).
Masters, Nicholas A., Robert H. Salisbury, and Thomas H. Eliot, *State Politics and Public Schools* (1964).
Meyer, Adolphe E., *Educational History of the American People* (1957).
Noble, Stuart G., *History of American Education* (rev. ed., 1954).
Pounds, Ralph L., and James R. Bryner, *School in American Society* (1959).
Reisner, E. H., *Evolution of Common School* (1930).
Rippa, S. Alexander, *Education in Free Society* (1967).
———— *Role of the School in American Society* (2nd ed., 1966).
Welter, Rush, *Popular Education and Democratic Thought in America* (1962).
Woody, Thomas, *Women's Education in the United States* (2 vols., 1929).

* * * * * * *

Anderson, Archibald W., "History of Education," *Hist. Educ. Jour.,* 7 (1956), 37.
Bailyn, Bernard, *Education in the Forming of American Society: Needs and Opportunities for Study* (1960).
Brickman, William W., *Guide to Research in Educational History* (1949).
Butts, R. Freeman, "Civilization-Building and Modernization Process: History of Education," *Hist. Educ. Quar.,* 7 (1967), 147.
Committee on Role of Education in American History, *Education and American History* (1965).
Cremin, Lawrence A., "History of Education as a Field of Study," *Hist. Educ. Quar.,* 7 (1955) 1.

————— E. P. Cubberley: Historiography of American Education (1965).
Monroe, Walter S., and Louis Shores, Bibliographies and Summaries in Education to July 1935 (1936).
Park, Joe, ed., Rise of American Education: Annotated Bibliography (1965).
Thomas M. H., and H. W. Schneider, Bibliography of John Dewey (1939).
Tyack, David B., "New Perspectives on History of Education," in Herbert J. Bass, ed., State of American History (1970).

See also 20.11.11, Indians–Missions and Schools; 20.12.8 Negroes–Education.

23.2 NINETEENTH CENTURY

Aborn, C. D., et al., eds., Pioneers of Kindergarten (1924).
Carlton, Frank T., Economic Influences upon Educational Progress, 1820–1850 (1966).
Grizzell, Emit D., Origin and Development of the High School in New England before 1865 (1923).
Monroe, Paul, Founding of American Public School System (1940).
Sizer, Theodore R., Secondary Schools at the Turn of the Century (1964).

23.3 TWENTIETH CENTURY

Coleman, James S., Adolescent Society: Impact on Education (1961).
Conant, James B., The American High School Today (1959).
————— Comprehensive High School: Second Report (1967).
————— Education in a Divided World (1948).
————— Slums and Suburbs: Schools in Metropolitan Areas (1961).
Flexner, Abraham, Do Americans Really Value Education? (1927).
Ginzberg, Eli, and D. W. Bray, Uneducated (1953).
Goodlad, John I., and Robert H. Anderson, The Nongraded Elementary School (rev. ed., 1963).
Gross, Neal, Who Runs Our Schools? (1958). [Massachusetts].
Kandel, Isaac L., American Education in the Twentieth Century (1957).
————— End of An Era (1941).
————— Impact of War upon American Education (1948).
Koos, Leonard V., Junior High School Trends (1955).
Lee, Gordon C., Introduction to Education in Modern America (rev. ed., 1957).
Meiklejohn, Alexander, Education between Two Worlds (1942).
Nelson, Jack, and Gene Roberts, Jr., Censors and Schools (1963).
Raywid, Mary Anne, Ax-Grinders: Critics of Our Public Schools (1962).
Silberman, Charles, Crisis in the Classroom (1970).
Ulich, Robert, Crisis in American Education (1951).

23.4 REGIONAL AND STATE STUDIES

23.4.1 North

Bole, Robert D., and Laurence B. Johnson, New Jersey High School (1964).
Burr, Nelson R., Education in New Jersey, 1630–1871 (1942).
Hansen, Allen O., Early Educational Leadership in the Ohio Valley (1923).
Jorgenson, Lloyd P., Founding of Public Education in Wisconsin (1956).
Lazerson, Marvin, Origins of the Urban School: Public Education in Massachusetts, 1870–1915 (1971).
Lottich, Kenneth V., New England Transplanted (1964).

McCadden, Joseph J., *Education in Pennsylvania: Roberts Vaux* (1937).
Marr, Harriet W., *Old New England Academies Founded before 1826* (1959).
Miller, Edward A., *History of Educational Legislation in Ohio, 1803–1850* (1918).
Miller, George F., *Academy System of New York* (1922).
West, Roscoe L., *History of Elementary Education in New Jersey* (1964).
Wickersham, J. P., *History of Education in Pennsylvania* (1886).

23.4.2 South

Dabney, Charles W., *Universal Education in South* (2 vols., 1936).
Knight, Edgar W., ed., *Documentary History of Education in the South before 1860* (5 vols., 1952–1953).
Knight, Edgar W., *Public Education in South* (1922).
McVey, Frank L., *Gates Open Slowly: Education in Kentucky* (1949).
Noble, Marcus C. S., *History of Public Schools of North Carolina* (1930).
Orr, Dorothy B., *History of Education in Georgia* (1950).

23.4.3 West

Bolton, Frederick E., *History of Education in Washington* (1935).
Cloud, Ray W., *Education in California: Leaders, Organization and Accomplishments of the First Hundred Years* (1952).
Moffitt, John C., *History of Public Education in Utah* (1946).
Swett, John, *History of the Public School System in California* (1876).
U.S. Department of Interior, U.S. Office of Education, *Survey of Public Higher Education in Oregon* (1931).

23.5 RELIGION AND PUBLIC SCHOOLS

Beggs, David W., and R. Bruce McQuigg, III, eds., *America's Schools and Churches, Partners in Conflict* (1965).
Bell, Sadie, *Church, State and Education in Virginia* (1930).
Boles, Donald E., *The Bible, Religion and Public Schools* (1965).
Brickman, William W., and Stanley Lehrer, eds., *Religion, Government, and Education* (1961).
Braiterman, Marvin, *Religion and the Public Schools* (1958).
Brown, Nicholas C., ed., *Study of Religion in Public Schools* (1958).
Butts, R. Freeman, *American Tradition in Religion and Education* (1950).
Culver, Raymond B., *Horace Mann and Religion in Massachusetts Public Schools* (1929).
Curran, Francis X., *The Churches and the Schools: Protestantism and Elementary Education* (1954).
Dierenfield, R. B., "Impact of Supreme Court Decisions on Religion in Public Schools," *Relig. Educ.*, 62 (1967), 445.
—— *Religion in American Public Schools* (1962).
Dunn, William K., *What Happened to Religious Education? Decline of Religious Teaching in Elementary Schools, 1776–1861* (1958).
Griffiths, William E., *Religion, the Courts, and the Public Schools: A Century of Litigation* (1966).
Healey, Robert M., *Jefferson on Religion in Public Education* (1962).
Helmreich, Ernst C., *Religion and the Maine Schools* (1960).
Kauper, Paul G., "Prayer, Public Schools and Supreme Court," *Mich. Law Rev.*, 61 (1963), 1031.
Lannie, Vincent P., *Public Money and Parochial Education: New York* (1968). Covers the period, 1840–1842.
—— "William Seward and New York School Controversy, 1840–1842," *Hist. Educ. Quar.*, 6, (1966), 52.
Muir, William K., Jr., *Prayer in the Public Schools* (1967).

Pratt, John W., "Governor Seward and New York City School Controversy, 1840–1842," *N.Y. Hist.*, 42 (1961), 351.

——— "Religious Conflict in Development of the New York City Public School System," *Hist. Educ. Quar.*, 5 (1965), 110.

Sky, Theodore, "The Establishment Clause, Congress and the Schools," *Va. Law Rev.*, 52 (1966), 1395.

Smith, Seymour A., *Religious Cooperation in State Universities* (1957).

Smith, Timothy L., "Protestant Schooling and American Nationality, 1800–1850," *JAH*, 53 (1967), 679.

Stokes, Anson P., *Church and State in the United States* (1950).

Sutherland, Arthur E., "Establishment of Religion—1968," *Case Western Reserve Law Rev.*, 19 (1968), 3.

Thayer, Vivian T., *Attack upon American Secular School* (1951).

Van Deusen, Glyndon G., "Seward and School Question Reconsidered," *JAH*, 52 (1965), 313.

Walter, Erich A., ed., *Religion and State University* (1958).

* * * * * * *

Library of Jewish Information, *Church, State and Education* (1949).

Little, Lawrence C., *Religion and Public Education: A Bibliography* (1966).

See also 24.2, Church and State.

23.6 FEDERAL GOVERNMENT AND EDUCATION

Buehler, E. E., *Federal Aid for Education* (1934).

Fellman, David, ed., *Supreme Court and Education* (1960).

Going, Allen J., "South and Blair Education Bill," *MVHR*, 44 (1957), 267.

Hales, Dawson W., *Federal Control of Public Education: A Critical Appraisal* (1954).

Kursh, Harry, *United States Office of Education* (1965).

Lee, Gordon C., *Struggle for Federal Aid* (1949). Covers the period, 1870–1890.

See also 23.13.4.1, Higher Education–Federal Aid.

23.7 REFORM AND IDEOLOGY

"American Intellectuals and the Schools," *Harv., Educ. Rev.*, 36 (1966), 391.

Baker, Melvin, *Foundations of John Dewey's Educational Theory* (1955).

Beck, Robert H., "Caroline Pratt," *Teachers College Rec.*, 60 (1958), 129.

——— "Progressive Education: Felix Adler," *Teachers College Rec.*, 60 (1958), 77.

Bowers, C. A., "Progressive Education," *Hist. Educ. Quar.*, 7 (1967), 452.

——— *Progressive Educator and Depression: Radical Years* (1969).

Burgess, Charles, "William Maclure and Education, *Hist. Educ. Quar.*, 3 (1963), 58.

Chambliss, Joseph J., *Boyd H. Bode's Philosophy of Education* (1963).

Cohen, Sol, *Progressives and Urban School Reform: Public Education Assocation of New York City, 1895–1954* (1964).

Conant, James B., *Thomas Jefferson and Public Education* (1962).

Coons, John E., William H. Clune, and Stephen D. Sugarman, *Private Wealth and Public Education* (1970).

Cremin, Lawrence A., "Origins of Progressive Education," *Educ. Forum*, 24 (1960), 133.

——— *Transformation of the School: Progressivism, 1876–1957* (1961).

Cubberley, Ellwood P., *Changing Conceptions of Education* (1909).

Curti, Merle, *Social Ideas of American Educators* (2nd ed., 1959).

Dykhuizen, George, "John Dewey in Chicago: Some Biographical Notes," *Jour. Hist. Phil.,* 3 (1965), 217.

Filler, Louis, "Progressivist American Education," *Hist. Educ. Jour.,* 8 (1957), 33.

Graham, Patricia A., *Progressive Education Association, 1919–1955* (1967).

Handlin, Oscar, *John Dewey's Challenge to Education* (1959).

Honeywell, Roy J., *Educational Work of Thomas Jefferson* (1931).

Hook, Sidney, *John Dewey* (1939).

Karier, Clarence J., *Man, Society and Education: American Educational Ideas* (1967).

Katz, Michael B., *The Irony of Early School Reform: Educational Innovation in Mid-Nineteenth Century Massachusetts* (1968).

Kolesnik, Walter B., *Mental Discipline in Modern Education* (1958).

McCluskey, Neil G., *Public Schools and Moral Education: Influence of Horace Mann, William Torrey Harris and John Dewey* (1958).

Mann, Horace, *Republic and the School,* Lawrence A. Cremin, ed., (1957).

Messerli, Jonathan C., "Common School Reform," *Teachers College Rec.,* 66 (1965), 749.

——— "James G. Carter's Liabilities as Common School Reformer," *Hist. Educ. Quar.,* 5 (1965), 14.

——— "Localism and State Control in Horace Mann's Reform of Common Schools," *Am. Quar.,* 17 (1965), 104.

Miller, Thomas W., "Influence of Progressivism on Music Education, 1917–1947," *Jour. Research in Music Educ.,* 14 (1966), 3.

Monroe, Will S., *History of the Pestalozzian Movement in the United States* (1907).

Perkinson, Henry J., *Imperfect Panacea: American Faith in Education, 1865–1965* (1968).

Rudolph, Frederick, ed., *Essays on Education in the Early Republic* (1965).

Smith, Timothy L., "Progressivism in American Education, 1880–1900," *Harv. Educ. Rev.,* 31 (1961), 168.

Strickland, Charles E., "Uses of Cultural History in Elementary School Experiments of Eighteen-Nineties," *Hist. Educ. Quar.,* 7 (1967), 474.

Thayer, Vivian T., *Formative Ideas in American Education* (1965).

Tyack, David B., "Education and Social Unrest, 1873–1878," *Harv. Educ. Rev.,* 31 (1961), 194.

Wirth, Arthur G., *John Dewey as Educator, 1894–1904* (1966).

See also 10.3 for biographies/writings of:

Alcott, Amos Bronson, 1799–1888
Barnard, Henry, 1811–1900
Dewey, John, 1859–1952
Gallaudet, Edward Miner, 1837–1917
Howe, Samuel Gridley, 1801–1876
Mann, Horace, 1796–1859
Parker, Francis W., 1837–1902
Peabody, Elizabeth P., 1804–1894
Washington, Booker T., 1856–1915
Willard, Emma H., 1787–1870

23.8 TEACHERS AND ADMINISTRATORS

American Federation of Teachers. Commission on Educational Reconstruction, *Organizing Teaching Profession* (1955).

Andress, J. Mace, "Education in Normal School," *Education,* 32 (1912), 614.

Borrowman, Merle L., *The Liberal and Technical in Teacher Education* (1956).

——— ed., *Teacher Education in America: A Documentary History* (1965).

Callahan, Raymond E., *Education and Cult of Efficiency: Social Forces that Shaped Administration of Public Schools* (1962).

Conant, James B., *Education of American Teachers* (1963).
Cremin, Lawrence A., David A. Shannon, and Mary E. Townsend, *History of Teachers College, Columbia University* (1954).
Edwards, Newton, *Courts and Public Schools: Legal Basis of School Organization and Administration* (1955).
Elsbree, Willard S., *American Teacher* (1939).
Mangun, V. L., *American Normal School: Its Rise and Development in Massachusetts* (1928).
Pangburn, J. M., *Evolution of American Teachers College* (1932).
Peirce, Cyrus, and Mary Swift, *First State Normal School in America: Journals of Cyrus Peirce and Mary Swift,* Albert O. Norton, ed. (1926).
Shils, Edward B., and C. Taylor Whittier, *Teachers, Administrators, and Collective Bargaining* (1968).
Stigler, G. J., *Employment and Compensation in Education* (1950).
Thursfield, R. E., *Henry Barnard's "American Journal of Education"* (1945).
Wesley, Edgar B., *NEA: First Hundred Years* (1957).
Whittemore, Richard, "Nicholas Murray Butler and the Teaching Profession," *Hist. Educ. Quar.,* 1 (1961), 22.

See also 10.3 for biographies/writings of:

Beecher, Catherine E., 1800–1878
Brooks, Eugene Clyde, 1871–1947
Cubberley, Ellwood P., 1868–1941
Fuess, Claude M., 1885–1963
Kilpatrick, William H., 1871–1965
Lyon, Mary, 1797–1849
Peabody, Endicott, 1857–1944
Young, Ella F., 1845–1918

23.9 TEXTBOOKS AND CURRICULUM

Bagley, William C., and Thomas Alexander, *Teacher of the Social Studies* (1937).
Callcott, George H., "History Enters Schools," *Am. Quar.,* 11 (1959), 470.
Carpenter, Charles, *History of American Schoolbooks* (1963).
Degler, Carl N., "The South in Southern History Textbooks," *JSH,* 30 (1964), 48.
Elson, Ruth M., *Guardians of Tradition: American Schoolbooks of the Nineteenth Century* (1964).
England, J. Merton, "Democratic Faith in Schoolbooks, 1783–1860," *Am. Quar.,* 15 (1963), 191.
Leonard, John P., *Developing the Secondary School Curriculum* (rev. ed., 1953).
Mosier, R. D., *Making the American Mind: McGuffey Readers* (1947).
Nietz, John A., *Evolution of American Secondary School Textbooks* (1967).
―――― *Old Textbooks, from Colonial Days to 1900* (1961).
Pierce, Bessie L., *Public Opinion and the Teaching of History* (1926).
Rice, Emmett A., *Brief History of Physical Education* (1924).
Vail, Henry H., *History of McGuffey Readers* (1910).

See also 10.3 for biography/writings of:

McGuffey, William H., 1800–1873

23.10 VOCATIONAL EDUCATION

Anderson, Lewis F., *History of Manual and Industrial School Education* (1926).
Bawden, William T., *Leaders in Industrial Education* (1950).
Bennett, Charles A., *Manual and Industrial Education up to 1870* (1926).
Fisher, Berenice M., *Industrial Education* (1967).

Hawkins, Layton S., Charles S. Prosser and John C. Wright, *Development of Vocational Education* (1951).

Haynes, Benjamin R., and Harry P. Jackson, *History of Business Education in the United States* (1935).

Smith, Harriette, *Lowell Institute* (1898).

Stombaugh, Ray, *Survey of Movements Culminating in Industrial Arts Education in Secondary Schools* (1936).

Struck, F. Theodore, *Foundations of Industrial Education* (1930).

23.11 ADULT EDUCATION

Beals, R. A., and Leon Brody, comps., *Literature of Adult Education* (1941).

Bode, Carl, *American Lyceum* (1956).

Gould, Joseph E., *Chautauqua Movement* (1961).

Grattan, C. Hartley, ed., *American Ideas about Adult Education, 1710–1951* (1959).

Harrison, Harry P., and Karl Detzer, *Culture under Canvas: Tent Chautauqua* (1958).

Hayes, Cecil B., *American Lyceum* (1932).

Horner, Charles F., *Strike the Tents: Chautauqua* (1954).

Knowles, Malcolm, *Adult Education Movement in United States* (1968).

Liveright, Alexander A., *Study of Adult Education in the United States* (1968).

Richmond, R. L., *Chautauqua* (1943).

Thornton, H. J., "Chautauqua and Midwest." *Wis. Mag. Hist.,* 33 (1949–50), 152.

Thornton, H. J., "Critics and Reformers at Chautauqua," *N.Y. Hist.,* 26 (1945), 307.

Wagner, Vern, "Lecture Lyceum and Problem of Controversy," *Jour. Hist. Ideas,* 15 (1954), 119.

Weeks, Edward, *Lowells and Their Institute* (1966).

23.12 CATHOLIC AND LUTHERAN EDUCATION

Burns, James A., *Growth and Development of Catholic School System* (1912). [After 1840].

———— et al., *History of Catholic Education* (1937).

Buetow, Harold A., *Of Singular Benefit: Story of U.S. Catholic Education* (1970).

Jahsmann, Allan H., *What's Lutheran in Education* (1960).

McAvoy, Thomas T., "Public Schools vs. Catholic Schools and James McMaster," *Rev. Politics,* 28 (1966), 19.

McCluskey, Neil G., *Catholic Education in America: A Documentary History* (1964).

———— *Catholic Viewpoint on Education* (1959).

Power, Edward J., *History of Catholic Higher Education* (1958).

Reinert, Paul C., *The Urban Catholic University* (1970).

Rossi, Peter H., and Alice S., "Parochial School Education," *Harv. Educ. Rev.,* 27 (1957), 168.

Shuster, George N., *Catholic Education in a Changing World* (1967).

23.13 HIGHER EDUCATION

23.13.1 General

Barnes, Sherman B., "Entry of Science and History in College Curriculum, 1865–1914," *Hist. Educ. Quar.,* 4 (1964), 44.

Barzun, Jacques, *The Teacher in America* (1945).

Braubacher, John S., and Willis Rudy, *Higher Education, 1636–1956* (1958).

Brickman, William W., and Stanley Lehrer, *Century of Higher Education* (1962).

Butler, Richard, *God on the Secular Campus* (1963).
De Vane, William C., *Higher Education in the Twentieth Century* (1965).
Dober, Richard P., *Campus Planning* (1964).
Earnest, Ernest, *Academic Procession: The American College, 1936 to 1953* (1953).
Flexner, Abraham, *Universities: American, English, German* (1930).
Gossman, Charles S., et al., *Migration of College and University Students in United States* (1968).
Harvard University. Committee on Objectives of a General Education in a Free Society, *General Education in a Free Society* (1945).
Hillway, Tyrus, *American Two-Year College* (1958).
Hintz, Howard W., *Religion and Public Higher Education* (1955).
Hofstadter, Richard, and Wilson Smith, eds., *American Higher Education: Documentary* (2 vols., 1961).
Jencks, Christopher, and David Riesman, *The Academic Revolution* (1968).
Kiger, Joseph C., *American Learned Societies* (1963).
Koos, L. V., *Junior College* (2 vols., 1924).
Madsen, David, *The National University: Enduring Dream* (1966).
Michaelsen, Robert, *The Study of Religion in American Universities* (1965).
Peterson, George E., *New England College in Age of the University* (1964).
Power, Edward J., *History of Catholic Higher Education* (1958).
Pusey, Nathan M., *The Age of the Scholar: Observation on Education in a Troubled Decade* (1963).
Reinert, Paul C., *The Urban Catholic University* (1970).
Rudolph, Frederick, *The American College and University* (1962).
Sack, Saul, *History of Higher Education in Pennsylvania* (2 vols., 1963).
Sanford, Nevitt, ed., *The American College* (1962).
Schmidt, George P., *Liberal Arts College* (1957).
Selden, William K., *Accreditation: Struggle over Standards in Higher Education* (1960).
Shedd, Clarence P., *Two Centuries of Student Christian Movements: Their Origin and Intercollegiate Life* (1934).
Tewksbury, D. G., *The Founding of American Colleges and Universities before the Civil War* (1932).
Thomas, Russell, *Search for Common Learning: General Education, 1800–1960* (1962).
Underwood, Kenneth W., *The Church, the University, and Social Policy* (2 vols., 1969).
Van Doren, Mark, *Liberal Education* (1943).
Veysey, Laurence R., *Emergence of the American University* (1965).
Walter, Erich A., ed., *Religion and the State University* (1958).

*   *   *   *   *   *   *

Rarig, Emory W., Jr., ed., *The Community Junior College: An Annotated Bibliography* (1966).

See also 10.3 for biographies/writings of:

FOUNDERS OF COLLEGES AND UNIVERSITIES

Blair, James, 1655–1743
Cornell, Ezra, 1807–1874
Eaton, Amos, 1776–1842
Grinnell, Josiah B., 1821–1891
Peck, John M., 1789–1858
Smith, William, 1727–1803
Vassar, Matthew, 1792–1868
Wheelock, Eleazar, 1711–1779

COLLEGE PRESIDENTS

Alderman, Edwin A., 1861–1931
Angell, James B., 1829–1916
Aydelotte, Frank, 1880–1956

Barnard, Frederick A. P., 1809–1889
Bascom, John, 1827–1911
Conant, James B., 1893–
Dwight, Timothy, 1752–1817
Eliot, Charles W., 1834–1926
Finney, Charles G., 1792–1875
Gilman, Daniel C., 1831–1908
Gregory, John M., 1822–1898
Hall, Granville Stanley, 1846–1924
Harper, William Rainey, 1856–1906
Holt, Hamilton, 1872–1951
Hope, John, 1868–1936
Hopkins, Mark, 1802–1887
Hyde, William DeW., 1858–1917
Jordan, David Starr, 1851–1931
Lowell, Abbott Lawrence, 1856–1943
McCosh, James, 1811–1894
McIver, Charles D., 1861–1906
Mays, Benjamin E., 1895–
Moton, Robert R., 1867–1940
Northrop, Cyrus, 1834–1922
Nott, Eliphalet, 1773–1866
Palmer, Alice E., 1855–1902
Payne, Daniel A., 1811–1893
Quincy, Josiah, III, 1772–1864
Sparks, Jared, 1789–1866
Van Hise, Charles R., 1857–1918
Walker, Francis A., 1840–1897
Wayland, Francis, 1796–1865
White, Andrew D., 1832–1918
Wilbur, Ray Lyman, 1875–1949
Witherspoon, John, 1723–1794
Woolley, Mary E., 1863–1947

23.13.2 Land Grant System and the State University

Allen, Herman R., *Open Door to Learning: Land-Grant System* (1963).
Andrews, Benjamin F., *Land Grant Act of 1862 and Land Grant Colleges* (1918).
Borrowman, Merle L., "The False Dawn of the State University," *Hist. Educ. Quar.*, 1 (1961), 6.
Dunbar, Willis F., *Michigan Record in Higher Education* (1963).
Eddy, Edward D., *Colleges for Our Land and Times: Land Grant Idea* (1957).
Foerster, Norman, *American State University* (1937).
Gates, Paul W., "Western Opposition to the Agricultural College Act," *Indiana Mag. Hist.*, 37 (1941), 103.
Glenny, Lyman A., *Autonomy of Public Colleges* (1959).
McGiffert, Michael, *Higher Learning in Colorado, 1860–1940* (1964).
Nevins, Allan, *State Universities and Democracy* (1962).
Ross, Earle D., "Contributions of Land-Grant Education to History," *Agric. Hist.*, 34 (1960). 51.
—— *Democracy's College: The Land-Grant Movement in the Formative Stage* (1942).
Simon, John Y., "Politics of Morrill Act," *Agric. Hist.* 37 (1963), 103.
Smith, Seymour A., *Religious Cooperation in State Universities* (1957).
University of Illinois, *Early View of Land-Grant Colleges, 1871* (1967).

23.13.3 Individual Colleges and Universities

Histories of individual colleges and universities are far too numerous to list here comprehensively. In quality they range from Curti and Carstensen's scholarly history of the University of Wisconsin to filio-pietistic works intended for alumni or public relations volumes used in fund raising. The following list is a sampling of better histories of a variety of institutions. For a comprehensive bibliography see Frederick Rudolph's *The American College and University* (1962).

Barnard, John, *From Evangelicalism to Progressivism at Oberlin College, 1866–1917* (1969).
Bishop, Morris, *History of Cornell* (1962).
Bruce, Philip A., *History of the University of Virginia* (1920–1922).
Callcott, George H., *History of University of Maryland* (1966).
Clark, Thomas D., *Indiana University: Midwestern Pioneer* (1970).
Cole, Arthur C., *Hundred Years of Mount Holyoke College* (1940).
Crenshaw, Ollinger, *General Lee's College: Washington and Lee University* (1969).
Curti, Merle, and Vernon R. Carstensen, *University of Wisconsin, 1848–1925* (2 vols., 1949).
Demarest, William H. S., *History of Rutgers, 1766–1924* (1924).
Eschenbacher, Herman F., *University of Rhode Island* (1967).
Gabriel, Ralph H., *Religion and Learning at Yale, 1757–1957* (1958).
Gray, James, *University of Minnesota, 1851–1951* (1951).
Hamilton, Raphael N., *Story of Marquette University* (1953).
Hawkins, Hugh, *Pioneer: Johns Hopkins University, 1874–1889* (1960).
LeDuc, Thomas, *Piety and Intellect at Amherst College, 1865–1912* (1946).
Miner, Dwight C., *History of Columbia College on Morningside* (1954).
Morison, Samuel E., *Three Centuries of Harvard, 1636–1936* (1936).
Peck, Elisabeth S., *Berea's First Century, 1855–1955* (1955).
Pierson, George W., *Yale: College and University* (2 vols., 1952–1955).
Pollard, James E., *History of Ohio State University, 1873–1948* (1952).
Porter, Earl W., *Trinity and Duke, 1892–1924: Duke University* (1964).
Prescott, Samuel C., *When M.I.T. was "Boston Tech," 1861–1916* (1954).
Ross, Earle D., *Land-Grant Idea at Iowa State College, 1858–68* (1958).
Rudolph, Frederick, *Mark Hopkins and the Log: Williams College, 1836–1872* (1956).
Solberg, Winton U., *University of Illinois, 1867–1894* (1968).
Stadtman, Verne A., *University of California, 1868–1968* (1970).
Storr, Richard J., *Harper's University: Beginnings of the University of Chicago* (1966).
Wilson, Louis R., *University of North Carolina, 1900–1930* (1957).

23.13.4 Financial Support

Commission on Financing Higher Education, *Nature and Needs of Higher Education* (1952).
Curti, Merle, and Roderick Nash, *Philanthropy and American Higher Education* (1965).
Fishlow, Albert, "Nineteenth-Century American Investment in Education," *Jour. Econ. Hist.,* 26 (1966), 418.
Flexner, Abraham, *Funds and Foundations* (1952).
Fosdick, Raymond B., *Adventure in Giving: General Education Board* (1962).
Harris, Seymour E., *How Shall We Pay for Education?* (1948).
Hollis, Ernest V., *Philanthropic Foundations and Higher Education* (1938).
Kaysen, Carl, *The Higher Learning: The Universities and the Public* (1969).
Millett, John D., *Financing Higher Education* (1952).
Parker, Franklin, "George Peabody's Influence on Southern Educational Philanthropy," *Tenn. Hist. Quar.,* 20 (1961), 65.
Sears, Jesse B., *Philanthropy in Higher Education* (1922).
Swint, Henry L., "Rutherford B. Hayes, Educator," *MVHR,* 39 (1952), 45.

See also 10.3 for biographies/writings of:

Flexner, Abraham, 1866–1959
Fosdick, Raymond B., 1883–

23.13.4.1 Federal Aid

Babbidge, Homer D., Jr., and Robert M. Rosenzweig, *Federal Interest in Higher Education* (1962).
Barber, Richard J., *Politics of Research* (1966).
Brazziel, William F., "Federal Aid and Negro Colleges," *Teachers College Rec.,* 68 (1967), 300.
Dupree, A. Hunter, "Structure of the Government-University Partnership after World War II," *Bull. Hist. Med.,* 39 (1965), 245.
Kidd, Charles V., *American Universities and Federal Research* (1959).
National Academy of Sciences. Committee on Science and Public Policy. *Federal Support of Basic Research in Institutions of Higher Learning* (1964).
Piel, Gerard, "Treason of the Clerks," *Am. Philos. Soc., Proc.,* 109 (1965), 259.

23.13.5 Academic Freedom

Beale, Howard K., *Are American Teachers Free?* (1936).
—— *History of Freedom of Teaching* (1941).
Byse, Clark M., and Louis Joughlin, *Tenure in American Higher Education* (1959).
Conant, James B., *Education and Liberty* (1953).
Gardner, David P., *California Oath Controversy* (1967).
Hofstadter, Richard, and Walter P. Metzger, *Development of Academic Freedom* (1955).
MacIver, Robert M., *Academic Freedom in Our Times* (1955).
Metzger, Walter P., et al., *Dimensions of Academic Freedom* (1969).
Schlabach, Theron F., "Richard T. Ely," *Wis. Mag. Hist.,* 47 (1963), 146.
Scimecca, Joseph, and Roland Damiano, *Crisis at St. John's: Strike and Revolution on Catholic Campus* (1967).

23.13.6 Graduate Education

Berelson, Bernard, *Graduate Education in the U.S.* (1960).
Cordasco, Francesco, *Daniel Coit Gilman and Protean PhD: Graduate Education* (1960).
Curti, Merle E., *American Scholarship in the Twentieth Century* (1953).
Herbst, Jurgen, *German Historical School in American Scholarship* (1965).
McGrath, Earl J., *The Graduate School and the Decline of Liberal Education* (1959).
Pierson, Mary B., *Graduate Work in the South* (1947).
Radcliffe College. Committee on Graduate Education of Women, *Graduate Education for Women: The Radcliff Ph.D.* (1956).
Ryan, Will C., *Early Graduate Education* (1939).
Storr, Richard J., *Beginnings of Graduate Education in America* (1953).

See also 11.9.3, History Profession in the United States; 18.11.8, Scientific Agriculture; 25.16, Behavioral Sciences; 25.17, Social Sciences; 29.12, Scientific Profession; 29.3.3, Medical Education and Research.

24 Religion

24.1 GENERAL

Abell, Aaron I., "America: Religious Aspect," *Rev. Politics*, 21 (1959), 24.

Bates, Ernest S., *American Faith: Its Religious, Political, and Economic Foundations* (1957).

Brauer, Jerald C., "Rule of Saints in American Politics," *Church Hist.*, 27 (1958), 240.

Cairns, Earle E., *Christianity in the United States* (1964).

Clebsch, William A., *From Sacred to Profane America: Religion in American History* (1968).

Clinchy, Everett R., *Growth of Good Will: Sketch of Protestant-Catholic-Jewish Relations* (1953).

Cogley, John, ed., *Religion in America* (1958).

Drucker, Peter F., "Organized Religion and American Creed," *Rev. Politics,* 18 (1956), 296.

Eddy, George S., *The Kingdom of God and the American Dream: The Religious and Secular Ideals of American History* (1941).

Gaustad, Edwin S., *Historical Atlas of Religion* (1962).

—— *Religious History of America* (1966).

Hall, Thomas C., *Religious Background of American Culture* (1930).

Henry, Stuart C., ed., *Miscellany of American Christianity: Essays in Honor of H. Shelton Smith* (1963).

Herberg, Will, *Protestant, Catholic, Jew: American Religious Sociology* (2nd ed., 1960).

Hudson, Winthrop S., *Great Tradition of American Churches* (1953).

—— *Religion in America* (1965).

Latourette, Kenneth S., *Christianity in a Revolutionary Age*. Vol. V: *Twentieth Century Outside Europe* (1962).

McGiffert, Michael, ed., *Puritanism and American Experience* (1969).

McLoughlin, William G., and Robert N. Bellah, eds., *Religion in America* (1968).

Marty, Martin E., Stuart E. Rosenberg, and Andrew M. Greeley, *What Do We Believe? Stance of Religion in America* (1968).

Mayer, Frederick E., *The Religious Bodies of America* (1956).

Mead, Frank S., *Handbook of Denominations in the United States* (4th ed., 1965).

Mead, Sidney, *Lively Experiment: Christianity in America* (1963).

Munro, William F., *A Brief Dictionary of the Denominations* (1964).

Nichols, Roy F., *Religion and American Democracy* (1959).

Niebuhr, H. Richard, *Kingdom of God in America* (1937).

Olmstead, Clifton E., *History of Religion in the United States* (1960).

Raab, Earl, ed., *Religious Conflict in America: Studies of the Problems Beyond Bigotry* (1964).

"Religion in America," *Daedalus*, 96 (1967). Entire issue covers period, 1952–1966.

Salisbury, W. Seward, *Religion in American Culture, a Sociological Interpretation* (1964).

Schaff, Philip, H. C. Potter, and S. M. Jackson, eds., *The American Church History Series* (13 vols., 1893–1898).
Silcox, Clarence E., *Catholics, Jews and Protestants: A Study of Relationships in the United States and Canada* (1934).
Smith, Hilrie S., Robert T. Handy and Lefferts A. Loetscher, *American Christianity, 1607–1820* (1960).
Smith, James W., and A. Leland Jameson, eds., *Religion in American Life* (4 vols., 1961).
Sperry, Willard L., *Religion in America* (1946).
Sweet, William W., *Religion in Development of American Culture* (1952).
———— *The Story of Religion in America* (rev. ed., 1950).
Vogt, Von O., *Cult and Culture: A Study of Religion and American Culture* (1951).
Weigle, Luther A., *American Idealism* (1928).
Weisenburger, Francis P., *Ordeal of Faith: Crisis of Church-Going America, 1865–1900* (1959).
Yearbook of American Churches, 1916–   . Annual.

*   *   *   *   *   *   *

Ahlstrom, Sydney E., "The Moral and Theological Revolution of the Sixties and Its Implications for American Religious Historiography," in Herbert Bass, ed., *The State of American History* (1970).
Barrow, John G., *Bibliography of Bibliographies in Religion* (1955).
Bowden, Henry W., "Science and Church History," *Church Hist.,* 36 (1967), 308.
Brauer, Jerald C., ed., *Reinterpretation in American Church History* (1968).
Burr, Nelson R., "The Church's Librarians, the Historians and the Layman," *Hist. Mag. Prot. Episc. Church,* 37 (1968), 311.
Burr, Nelson R., *A Critical Bibliography of Religion in America.* Vol. IV of James W. Smith and A. Leland Jameson, eds., *Religion in American Life* (1961).
Carter, Paul A., "Recent Historiography of Protestant Churches," *Church Hist.,* 37 (1968), 95.
Case, Shirley J., et al., *Bibliographical Guide to History of Christianity* (1931).
Clebsch, William, "New Historiography of American Religion," *Hist. Mag. Prot. Episc. Church,* 32 (1963), 225.
Cunliffe, Marcus, "American Religious History," *Jour. Am. Studies,* 1 (1967), 105.
Gaustad, Edwin S., *American Religious History* (1966).
May, Henry F., "American Religious History," *AHR,* 70 (1964), 79.
Mead, Sidney E., "Church History Explained," *Church Hist.,* 32 (1963), 17.

See also 20.12.9, Negroes–Religion.

24.2 CHURCH AND STATE

Antieau, Chester J., Phillip M. Carroll and Thomas C. Burke, *Religion under the State Constitutions* (1965).
Beth, Loren P., *American Theory of Church and State* (1958).
Blau, Joseph L., *Cornerstones of Religious Freedom in America* (rev. ed., 1964).
Blanshard, Paul, *American Freedom and Catholic Power* (1949).
Carroll, William A., "Constitution, Supreme Court, and Religion," *Am. Pol. Sci. Rev.,* 61 (1967), 657.
Cushing, John D., "Disestablishment in Massachusetts 1780–1833," *WMQ,* 3 ser., 26 (1969), 169.
Drinan, Robert F., *Religion, the Courts, and Public Policy* (1963).
Eckenrode, H. J., *Separation of Church and State in Virginia* (1910).
Fellman, David, *Religion in American Public Law* (1965).
Greene, Evarts B., *Religion and the State* (1941).
Greene, Maria L., *Development of Religious Liberty in Connecticut* (1905).

Guttmann, Allen, "From Brownson to Eliot: Conservative Theory of Church and State," *Am. Quar.,* 17 (1965), 483.

Howe, Mark DeW., *Cases on Church and State* (1952).

——— *The Garden and the Wilderness: Religion and Government in American Constitutional History* (1965).

Johnson, Alvin W., and F. H. Yost, *Separation of Church and State in the U.S.* (1948).

Katz, Wilbur G., *Religion and American Constitutions* (1964).

Ketcham, Ralph L., "James Madison and Religion—A New Hypothesis," *Jour. Presby. Hist. Soc.,* 38 (1960), 65.

Kinney, Charles B., Jr., *Church and State: Separation in New Hampshire, 1630–1900* (1955).

Kurland, Philip B., *Religion and the Law of Church and State and the Supreme Court* (1962).

McLoughlin, William G., *New England Dissent, 1630–1833: The Baptists and the Separation of Church and State* (1971).

Manwaring, David R., *Render unto Caesar: Flag-Salute Controversy* (1962). Jehovah's Witnesses.

Marnell, William H., *The First Amendment; The History of Religious Freedom in America* (1964).

Meyer, Jacob C., *Church and State in Massachusetts* (1930).

Moehlman, Conrad H., comp., *The American Constitutions and Religion . . . A Sourcebook on Church and State in the United States* (1938).

Moehlman, Conrad H., *Wall of Separation* (1951).

Norman, Edward R., *Conscience of the State in North America* (1968).

Oaks, Dallin H., ed., *The Wall Between Church and State* (1963).

O'Neill, J. M., *Catholicism and American Freedom* (1952).

Pfeffer, Leo, *Church, State, and Freedom* (rev. ed., 1967).

Pratt, John W., *Religion, Politics, and Diversity: Church-State Theme in New York History* (1967).

Roy, R. L., *Apostles of Discord* (1953).

Shields, Currin V., *Democracy and Catholicism in America* (1958).

Stokes, Anson P., and Leo Pfeffer, *Church and State in the United States* (rev. ed., 1964).

Strickland, Reba C., *Religion and State in Georgia* (1939).

Sutherland, Arthur E., "Establishment of Religion—1968," *Case Western Reserve Law Rev.,* 19 (1968), 3.

Thorning, Francis J., *Religious Liberty in Transition: A Study of the Removal of Constitutional Limitations* (1931).

Tussman, Joseph, *Supreme Court on Church and State* (1962).

Wilson, John F., ed., *Church and State in American History* (1965).

Zabel, Orville H., *God and Caesar in Nebraska: Church and State, 1854–1954* (1955).

See also 23.5, Religion and Public Schools.

24.3 CHURCH AND SOCIAL ISSUES

Abell, Aaron I., comp., *American Catholic Thought on Social Questions* (1968).

Abell, Aaron I., *American Catholicism and Social Action, 1865–1950* (1960).

——— "Reception of Leo XIII's Labor Encyclical," *Rev. Politics,* 7 (1945), 464.

——— *Urban Impact on American Protestantism* (1943).

Aiken, John R., "Walter Rauschenbusch," *Church Hist.,* 36 (1967), 456.

Barnes, Roswell P., *Under Orders: The Churches and Public Affairs* (1961).

Bodo, John R., *Protestant Clergy and Public Issues, 1812–1848* (1954).

Brill, Earl H., *The Creative Edge of American Protestantism* (1966).

Browne, Henry J., *Catholic Church and Knights of Labor* (1947).

Carter, Paul A., *Decline and Revival of Social Gospel: Social and Political Liberalism in American Protestant Churches, 1920–1940* (1956).

Cole, Charles C., Jr., *The Social Ideas of the Northern Evangelists, 1826–1860* (1966).
Commons, John R., *Social Reform and Church* (1894).
Cox, Harvey G., *The Secular City: Secularization and Urbanization in Theological Perspective* (1965).
Cross, Robert D., ed., *Church and City, 1865–1910* (1967).
—— *Walter Rauschenbusch: Christianity and the Social Crisis* (1964).
Daniel, John, *Labor, Industry, and the Church: A Study of the Interrelationships Involving the Church, Labor, and Management (1957).*
Dirks, Lee E., *Religion in Action: How America's Faiths are Meeting New Challenges* (1965).
Dombrowski, James, *Early Days of Christian Socialism* (1936).
Everett, John R., *Religion in Economics: A Study of John Bates Clark, Richard T. Ely [and] Simon N. Patten* (1946).
Farnham, Henry M., *Protestant Churches and Industrial America* (1949).
Gladden, Washington, *Applied Christianity* (1886).
Griffen, Clyde C., "Rich Laymen and Early Social Christianity," *Church Hist.,* 36 (1967), 45. Covers the period, 1880–1900.
Handy, Robert T., ed., *Social Gospel, 1870–1920* (1966).
High, Stanley, *The Church in Politics* (1930).
Hopkins, Charles H., *Rise of the Social Gospel in American Protestantism* (1940).
Hutchison, James A., ed., *Christian Faith and Social Action* (1953).
Johnson, R. H., "Baptists in Age of Big Business," *Jour. of Relig.,* 11 (1931), 63.
Kennedy, Gail, ed., *Democracy and the Gospel of Wealth* (1949).
Laubenstein, Paul F., *A History of Christian Socialism in America* (1925).
Lee, Robert, and Martin E. Marty, eds., *Religion and Social Conflict* (1964).
McGiffert, Arthur C., Jr., *The Rise of Modern Religious Ideas* (1929).
McGowan, Chester C., *The Genesis of the Social Gospel* (1929).
Macintosh, Douglas C., *Social Religion* (1939).
McQuade, Vincent A., *The American Catholic Attitude on Child Labor Since 1891* (1938).
May, Henry F., *Protestant Churches and Industrial America* (1949).
Meyer, Donald B., *The Protestant Search for Political Realism, 1919–1941* (1960).
Miller, Haskell M., *Compassion and Community: An Appraisal of the Church's Changing Role in Social Welfare* (1961).
Miller, Robert M., *American Protestantism and Social Issues, 1919–1939* (1958).
Morrison, Charles C., *The Social Gospel and the Christian Cults* (1933).
Niebuhr, H. Richard, *The Kingdom of God in America* (1937).
—— *Social Sources of Denominationalism* (1940).
Niebuhr, Reinhold, *Faith and Politics* (1968).
—— "Walter Rauschenbusch in Historical Perspective" *Religion in Life,* 27 (1958), 527.
O'Brien, David J., *American Catholics and Social Reform: New Deal* (1968).
Odegard, Peter H., *Pressure Politics: Story of the Anti-Saloon League* (1967).
Rader, Benjamin G., "Richard T. Ely: Lay Spokesman for Social Gospel," *JAH,* 53 (1966), 61.
Rapson, Richard L., "The Religious Feelings of the American People, 1845–1935: A British View," *Church Hist.,* 35 (1966), 311.
Rauschenbusch, Walter, *Christianity and the Social Crisis* (1907).
—— *A Rauschenbusch Reader: The Kingdom of God and the Social Gospel,* Benson Y. Landis, comp. (1957).
Riegler, Gordon A., *Socialization of the New England Clergy, 1800 to 1860* (1945).
Roberts, Robert R., "Social Gospel and Trust Busters," *Church Hist.,* 25 (1956), 239.
Schulze, Andrew, *Fire from the Throne: Race Relations in the Church* (1968).
Smith, Timothy L., *Revivalism and Social Reform in Mid-Nineteenth Century America* (1957).
Starkey, Lycurgus M., Jr., *Money, Mania and Morals: Churches and Gambling* (1964).
Stedman, Murray S., Jr., *Religion and Politics in America* (1964).
Strong, Josiah, *Religious Movements for Social Betterment* (1900).

Thompson, Ernest T., *Plenty and Want: The Responsibility of the Church* (1966).
Winter, Gibson, *The Suburban Captivity of the Churches: An Analysis of Protestant Responsibility in the Expanding Metropolis* (1961).

See also 20.12.7.4, Negro Protest–White Response; 21.5, Collectivist and Utopian Communities.

24.4 DARWINISM AND RELIGION

Betts, John R., "Darwinism, Evolution and American Catholic Thought, 1860–1900," *Cath. Hist. Rev.,* 45 (1959), 161.
Cole, Stewart G., *The History of Fundamentalism* (1931).
de Camp, Lyon S., *Great Monkey Trial* (1968).
Furniss, Norman F., *Fundamentalist Controversy, 1918–1931* (1954).
Gatewood, Willard B., Jr., ed., *Controversy in the Twenties: Fundamentalism, Modernism, and Evolution* (1969).
Gatewood, Willard B., Jr., *Preachers, Pedagogues, & Politicians: Evolution Controversy in North Carolina, 1920–1927* (1966).
Ginger, Ray, *Six Days or Forever? Tennessee* v. *John Thomas Scopes* (1958).
Hofstadter, Richard, *Social Darwinism in American Thought* (rev. ed., 1959).
Kennedy, Gail, ed., *Evolution and Religion. The Conflict Between Science and Theology in Modern America* (1957).
Loewenberg, Bert J., "Controversy over Evolution in New England," *NEQ,* 8 (1935), 232.
——— "Darwinism Comes to America, 1859–1900," *MVHR,* 28 (1941), 339.
Morrison, John L., "William Seton—a Catholic Darwinist," *Rev. Politics,* 21 (1959), 566.
Osborn, Henry F., *Evolution and Religion in Education: Polemics of the Fundamentalist Controversy of 1922 to 1926* (1926).
Roberts, Winsor H., *The Reaction of American Protestant Churches to the Darwinian Philosophy, 1860–1900* (1938).
Sandeen, Ernest R., *The Origins of Fundamentalism: Toward a Historical Understanding* (1968).
Scopes, John T., and James Presley, *Center of the Storm: Memoirs of John T. Scopes* (1967).
Thompkins, Jerry T., ed., *D-Days at Dayton: Scopes Trial* (1965).
White, Edward A., *Science and Religion in American Thought: The Impact of Naturalism* (1952).

See also 10.3 for biographies/writings of:

Beecher, Henry Ward, 1813–1887
Bryan, William Jennings, 1860–1925
Darrow, Clarence, 1857–1938
Draper, John W., 1811–1882
Fiske, John, 1842–1901

24.5 HOME MISSIONS AND FRONTIER CHURCHES

Berkhofer, Robert F., Jr., *Salvation and the Savage: Protestant Missions and Indian Response, 1787–1862* (1965).
Brunger, Ronald A., "Methodist Circuit Riders," *Mich. Hist.,* 51 (1967), 252.
Callan, Louise, *Philippine Duchesne: Frontier Missionary of Sacred Heart, 1769–1852* (1957).
Elsbree, Oliver W., *Rise of Missionary Spirit in America* (1928).
Farish, H. D., *Circuit Rider Dismounts* (1938).
Goodykoontz, Colin B., *Home Missions on the American Frontier* (1939).
Gunther, Peter F., ed., *The Fields at Home: Studies in Home Missions* (1963).

Hooker, Elizabeth R., *Religion in the Highlands: Native Churches and Missionary Enterprises in the Southern Appalachian Area* (1933).
Kuhns, Frederick, "Religious Rivalries in Old Northwest," *Jour. Presby. Hist.,* 36 (1958), 19.
McAvoy, Thomas T., "Americanism and Frontier Catholicism," *Rev. Politics,* 5 (1943), 275.
McGuire, Frederick A., ed., *Mission to Mankind* (1963). Catholic missions.
Miyakawa, Tetsuo S., *Protestants and Pioneers* (1964).
Mode, Peter G., *Frontier Spirit in American Christianity* (1923).
Moore, John M., *The Challenge of Change, What is Happening to Home Missions* (1931).
Phares, Ross, *Bible in Pocket, Gun In Hand; The Story of Frontier Religion* (1964).
Posey, Walter B., *Frontier Mission: Religion West of Southern Appalachians to 1861* (1966).
———— *Religious Strife on Southern Frontier* (1965). [To 1845].
Shannon, James P., *Catholic Colonization on Western Frontier* (1957).
Sweet, William W., *Religion on American Frontier* (4 vols., 1931–1939).

See also 20.11.11, Indians–Missions and Schools.

24.6 PROTESTANTISM

24.6.1 General

Bailey, Kenneth K., *Southern White Protestantism in Twentieth Century* (1964).
Baltzell, E. Digby, *Protestant Establishment: Aristocracy & Caste in America* (1964).
Brauer, Jerald C., *Protestantism in America* (rev. ed., 1965).
Cole, Stewart G., *History of Fundamentalism* (1931).
Davies, Alfred M., *Foundation of American Freedom* (1955). Calvinism.
Demerath, Nicholas J., III, *Social Class in American Protestantism* (1965).
Douglass, H. P., and E. deS. Brunner, *The Protestant Church as a Social Institution* (1935).
Drummond, A. L., *American Protestantism* (1949).
Ferm, Vergilius T. A., ed., *The American Church of the Protestant Heritage* (1953).
Foster, Charles I., *Errand of Mercy: Evangelical United Front, 1790–1837* (1960).
Handy, Robert T., *The Protestant Quest for a Christian America, 1830–1930* (1967).
Hardon, John A., *The Protestant Churches of America* (rev. ed., 1958).
Hudson, Winthrop S., *American Protestantism* (1961).
Littell, Franklin H., *From State Church to Pluralism: Protestant Interpretation of Religion in American History* (1962).
McCavert, Samuel, *American Churches in the Ecumenical Movement, 1900–1968* (1968).
McLoughlin, William G., "Pietism and American Character," *Am. Quar.,* 17 (1965), 163.
Marty, Martin E., *Righteous Empire: The Protestant Experience in America* (1970).
Mead, Sidney, "Denominationalism: Protestantism in America," *Church Hist.,* 23 (1954), 291.
Means, Richard, "Auxiliary Theories to Weber's Protestant Ethic," *Social Forces,* 44 (1966), 372.
Niebuhr, H. Richard, *Social Sources of Denominationalism* (1929).
Osborn, Ronald E., *The Spirit of American Christianity* (1958).
Sandeen, Ernest R., "Historical Interpretation of Origins of Fundamentalism," *Church Hist.,* 36 (1967), 66.
———— *Roots of Fundamentalism: British and American Millenarianism, 1800–1930* (1970).

Sanderson, Ross W., *Church Cooperation in the U.S.: The Nationwide Backgrounds and Ecumenical Significance of State and Local Councils of Churches in Their Historical Perspectives* (1961).

Sanford, E. B., *Origin and History of Federal Council* (1916).

Shewmaker, William O., "Training Protestant Ministry before Establishment of Theological Seminaries," *Papers of American Society of Church History*, 2 ser., 6 (1921), 71.

Shippey, Frederick A., *Protestantism in Suburban Life* (1964).

Stephenson, George M., *Puritan Heritage* (1952). [Democratic Protestantism to 1850].

* * * * * * *

Carter, Paul Allen, "Recent Historiography of the Protestant Churches in America," *Church History*, 37 (1968), 95.

24.6.2 Religious Thought and Theology

Adams, James L., *Paul Tillich's Philosophy of Culture, Science and Religion* (1965).

Ahlstrom, Sydney E., "Continental Influence on American Christian Thought since World War I," *Church Hist.*, 27 (1958), 256.

―――― ed., *Theology in America: Major Protestant Voices* (1967).

Allison, Christopher F., *Rise of Moralism: From Hooker to Baxter* (1966).

Altizer, Thomas J. J., and William Hamilton, *Radical Theology and the Death of God* (1966).

Averill, Lloyd J., *American Theology in the Liberal Tradition* (1967).

Bent, Charles N., *The Death-of-God Movement: A Study of Gabriel Vahanian, William Hamilton, Paul Van Buren, and Thomas J. J. Altizer* (1967).

Braden, Charles S., *Spirits in Rebellion: Development of New Thought* (1963).

Brown, Ira V., "Higher Criticism Comes to America, 1880–1900," *Jour. Presby. Hist.*, 38 (1960), 193.

Brown, Jerry W., *The Rise of Biblical Criticism in America 1800–1870: The New England Scholars* (1969).

Buckham, John W., *Progressive Religious Thought in America: A Survey of the Enlarging Pilgrim Faith* (1919).

Carnell, Edward J., *The Theology of Reinhold Niebuhr* (1951).

Carter, Paul A., "Idea of Progress in American Protestant Thought, 1930–1960," *Church Hist.*, 32 (1963), 75.

Cauthen, Kenneth, *Impact of American Religious Liberalism* (1962). Covers the period from 1900 to World War II.

Coffin, Henry S., *Religion Yesterday and Today* (1940).

Comstock, W. Richard, "Santayana and Tillich," *Harv. Theol. Rev.*, 60 (1967), 39.

Dirks, John E., *The Critical Theology of Theodore Parker* (1948).

Ferm, Vergilius T. A., ed., *Contemporary American Theology: Theological Autobiographies* (2 vols., 1932–1933).

Gibson, Raymond E., *God, Man and Time: Human Destiny in American Theology* (1966).

Gillespie, Neal C., "George Frederick Holmes: Religious Conservatism in Old South," *JSH*, 32 (1966), 291.

Hammar, George, *Christian Realism in Contemporary American Theology* (1940).

Harland, Gordon, *The Thought of Reinhold Niebuhr* (1960).

Harlow, Victor E., *Bibliography and Genetic Study of Realism* (1931).

Hofmann, Hans, *The Theology of Reinhold Niebuhr* (1956).

Hutchison, William R., ed., *American Protestant Thought: The Liberal Era* (1968).

Kegley, Charles W., and Robert W. Bretall, eds., *Reinhold Niebuhr, His Religious, Social and Political Thought* (1956).

―――― eds., *Theology of Paul Tillich* (1953).

Loetscher, Lefferts A., *The Broadening Church: A Study of Theological Issues in the Presbyterian Church Since 1869* (1954).

Martin, James A., *Empirical Philosophies of Religion, with Special Reference to Boodin, Brightman, Hocking, Macintosh and Wieman* (1947).

Mead, Sidney E., "American Protestantism since the Civil War," 36 (1956), 1.

Meyer, Donald, *Positive Thinkers: American Quest for Health, Wealth and Personal Power from Mary Baker Eddy to Norman Vincent Peale* (1965).

Nichols, James H., *Romanticism in American Theology: Nevin and Schaff at Mercersberg* (1961).

Niebuhr, H. Richard, and Daniel D. Williams, eds., *The Ministry in Historical Perspectives* (1956).

Niebuhr, Reinhold, *Children of Light and Children of Darkness* (1960).

———— *Faith and History* (1949).

———— *Irony of American History* (1952).

———— *Moral Man and Immoral Society* (1932).

———— and Alan Heimert, *Nation So Conceived* (1963).

Niebuhr, Reinhold, *Nature and Destiny of Man* (2 vols., 1941–1943).

Post, Albert, *Popular Free Thought in America* (1943).

Ramsey, Paul, ed., *Faith and Ethics: The Theology of H. Richard Niebuhr* (1957).

Roth, Robert J., *American Religious Philosophy* (1967).

Schneider, Herbert W., *Religion in 20th Century America* (1952).

Schneider, Louis, and Sanford M. Dornbusch, *Popular Religion: Inspirational Books in America* (1958).

Smith, Gerald B., ed., *Religious Thought in the Last Quarter Century* (1927).

Smith, H. Shelton, *Changing Conceptions of Original Sin: American Theology since 1750* (1955).

Soper, David W., *Major Voices in American Theology* (2 vols., 1953–1955).

Thelen, Mary F., *Man as Sinner in Contemporary American Realistic Theology* (1946).

Tillich, Paul, *The Courage to Be* (1952).

———— *Theology of Culture*, Robert C. Kimball, ed. (1959).

Warren, Sidney, *American Freethought, 1860–1914* (1943).

West, Robert F., *Alexander Campbell and Natural Religion* (1948).

Wieman, Henry N., and Bernard E. Meland, *American Philosophies of Religion* (1936).

Williams, Daniel D., *What Present-Day Theologians Are Thinking* (1959).

*   *   *   *   *   *   *

Harlow, Victor E., *Bibliography and Genetic Study of Realism* (1931).

O'Brien, Elmer, ed., *Theology in Transition: A Bibliographical Evaluation of the "Decisive Decade," 1954–1964* (1965).

See also 10.3 for biographies/writings of:

Ames, Edward S., 1870–1958
Bushnell, Horace, 1802–1876
Niebuhr, Reinhold, 1892–1971
Taylor, Graham, 1851–1938
Taylor, Nathaniel W., 1786–1858
Tillich, Paul, 1886–1965

24.6.3 Revivalism and Evangelism

Beardsley, Frank G., *American Revivals* (1912).

———— *Religious Progress through Religious Revivals* (1943).

Cleveland, Catherine C., *Great Revival in the West* (1916).

Cole, Charles C., Jr., *The Social Ideas of the Northern Evangelists, 1826–1860* (1966).

Cross, Whitney R., *Burned-Over District* (1950).

Finney, Charles G., *Lectures on Revivals of Religion* (1835), William G. McLoughlin, ed. (1960).

Fox, Dixon R., "Protestant Counter-Reformation," *N.Y. Hist.,* 16 (1935), 19.

Greene, Evarts B., "Puritan Counter-Reformation," Am. Antiq. Soc., *Proc.*, 42 (1932), 17.

Hall, Gordon L., *The Sawdust Trail: The Story of American Evangelism* (1964).

Johnson, Charles A., *Frontier Camp Meeting* (1955).

Keller, Charles R., *Second Great Awakening in Connecticut* (1942).

Loetscher, Lefferts A., *Presbyterianism and Revivals in Philadelphia since 1875* (1944).

Loud, Grover C., *Evangelized America* (1928).

McLoughlin, William G., *Modern Revivalism: Charles Grandison Finney to Billy Graham* (1959).

Muncy, William L., *A History of Evangelism in the United States* (1945).

Scharpff, Paulus, *History of Evangelism: Three Hundred Years of Evangelism in Germany, Great Britain, and the United States of America* (1966).

Shelley, Bruce L., *Evangelicalism in America* (1967).

Smith, Timothy L., *Revivalism and Social Reform in Mid-Nineteenth Century America* (1957).

Sweet, William W., *Revivalism in America* (1944).

Weber, Herman C., *Evangelism* (1928).

Weisberger, Bernard A., *They Gathered at the River: Great Revivalists* (1958).

See also 10.3 for biographies/writings of:

Chapman, John W., 1859–1918
Dow, Lorenzo, 1777–1834
Finney, Charles G., 1792–1875
Graham, Billy F., 1918–
Moody, Dwight L., 1837–1899
Beecher, Lyman, 1775–1863
Sunday, William A. "Billy", 1862–1935

24.6.4 Foreign Missions

American Board of Commissioners for Foreign Missions, *Annual Reports*, 1810– .

Drury, Clifford M., *Presbyterian Panorama: One Hundred and Fifty Years of National Missions History* (1952).

Latourette, Kenneth S., *History of Christian Missions in China* (1929).

——— *World Service: YMCA* (1957).

Liu, Kwang-ching, ed., *American Missionaries in China: Papers from Harvard Seminars* (1966).

Lord, Donald C., "The King and the Apostle: Mongkut, Bradley and American Missionaries," *So. Atl. Quar.*, 66 (1967), 326. [Thailand].

McCutcheon, James M., "Missionary and Diplomat in China," *Jour. Presby, Hist.*, 41 (1963), 224.

Phillips, Clifton J., *Protestant America and Pagan World: American Board of Commissioners for Foreign Missions, 1810–1860* (1969).

Pier, Arthur S., *American Apostles to Philippines* (1950).

Strong, William E., *American Board of Missions* (1910).

Tibawi, Abdul L., *American Interests in Syria, 1800–1901: Educational, Literary and Religious Work* (1966).

Torbet, Robert G., *Venture of Faith: American Baptist Foreign Mission Society, 1814–1954* (1955).

Varg, Paul A., *Missionaries, Chinese, and Diplomats: American Protestant Missionary Movement in China, 1890–1952* (1958).

24.6.5 Religious Education

Brown, Marianna C., *Sunday-School Movements in America* (1901).

Eavey, Charles B., *History of Christian Education* (1964).

Fergusson, E. Morris, *Historic Chapters in Christian Education in America, A Brief History of the American Sunday School Movement and the Rise of the Modern Church School* (1935).

Lankard, Frank G., *A History of the American Sunday School Curriculum* (1927).

Myers, A. J. W., *Horace Bushnell and Religious Education* (1937).

Rice, Edwin W., *The Sunday-School Movement, 1780–1917, and the American Sunday-School Union, 1817–1917* (1917).

24.7 CHURCHES AND RELIGIOUS GROUPS

24.7.1 Baptist

Armstrong, O. K., and Marjorie M. Armstrong, *The Indomitable Baptists: A Narrative of Their Role in Shaping American History* (1967).

Bailey, Kenneth K., "Southern Baptists, 1940–1963, As Viewed by a Secular Historian," *Bapt. Hist. and Heritage,* 3 (1968) 17.

Barnes, William W., *History of the Southern Baptist Convention, 1845–1953* (1954).

Baxter, Norman A., *History of the Freewill Baptists: A Study in New England Separatism* (1957).

Maring, Norman H., *Baptists in New Jersey* (1964).

Paschal, George W., *History of North Carolina Baptists, 1663–1805* (1930).

Posey, Walter B., *The Baptist Church in Lower Mississippi Valley, 1776–1845* (1957).

Ryland, Garnett, *Baptists of Virginia, 1699–1926* (1955).

Spain, Rufus B., *At Ease in Zion: Southern Baptists, 1865–1900* (1967).

Torbet, Robert G., *History of the Baptists* (rev. ed., 1963).

*　*　*　*　*　*　*

Starr, Edward C., *A Baptist Bibliography* (6 vols., 1947–1958).

See also 10.3 for biographies/writings of:

Backus, Isaac, 1724–1806
Judson, Adoniram, 1788–1850
Leland, John, 1754–1841
Peck, John M., 1789–1858
Rauschenbusch, Walter, 1861–1918

24.7.2 Christian Science

Beasley, Norman, *The Continuing Spirit* (1956) Covers the period since 1910.
—— *The Cross and the Crown: History of Christian Science* (1952).

Braden, Charles S., *Christian Science Today: Power, Policy, Practice* (1958).

Cunningham, Raymond J., "Impact of Christian Science on American Churches, 1880–1910," *AHR,* 72 (1967), 885.

Peel, Robert, *Christian Science: Its Encounter With American Culture* (1958).

See also 10.3 for biographies/writings of:

Eddy, Mary Baker, 1821–1910

24.7.3 Congregationalism and United Church of Christ

Atkins, Gaius Glenn, and Frederick L. Fagley, *History of American Congregationalism* (1942).

Fagley, Frederick L., *Story of the Congregational Christian Churches* (1941).
Horton, Douglas, *United Church of Christ* (1962).
Starkey, Marion L., *Congregational Way* (1966).
Sweet, William W., *Religion on the American Frontier*. Vol. III: *Congregational-ists, 1783–1850*. (1946).

See also 10.3 for biographies/writings of:

Abbott, Lyman, 1835–1922
Bacon, Leonard, 1802–1881
Beecher, Henry Ward, 1813–1887
Bushnell, Horace, 1802–1876
Field, David D., 1781–1867
Gladden, Washington, 1836–1918
Morse, Jedidiah, 1761–1826
Park, Edward A., 1808–1900

24.7.4 Disciples of Christ

Abbott, Byrdine A., *The Disciples: An Interpretation* (1964).
Boren, Carter E., *Religion on the Texas Frontier* (1968).
Garrison, Winfred E., and Alfred T. DeGroot, *Disciples of Christ* (1948).
Harrell, David E., Jr., *Social History of the Disciples of Christ*. Vol I: *Quest for a Christian America* (1966). Covers the period to 1866.
Short, Howard E., *Doctrine and Thought of the Disciples of Christ* (1951).

*   *   *   *   *   *   *

Pierson, Roscoe M., "The Literature of the Disciples of Christ and Closely Related Groups," *Religion in Life,* 26 (1957), 274.

See also 10.3 for biographies/writings of:

Campbell, Alexander, 1788–1866
Garrison, James H., 1842–1931
Stone, Barton W., 1772–1844

24.7.5 Episcopalianism

Albright, Raymond W., *History of the Protestant Episcopal Church* (1964).
Beardsley, E. Edward, *The History of the Episcopal Church in Connecticut* (2 vols., 1869).
Breck, Allen, *Episcopal Church in Colorado, 1860–1963* (1963).
Cushman, Joseph D., Jr., *Goodly Heritage: Episcopal Church in Florida, 1821–1892* (1965).
Dawley, Powel M., *The Episcopal Church and Its Work* (1955).
DeMille, George E., *The Catholic Movement in the American Episcopal Church* (2nd ed., 1950).
Lankford, John, "The Contemporary Revolution in Historiography and the History of the Episcopal Church," *Hist. Mag. of the Prot. Episc. Church,* 36 (1967), 11.
Manross, William W., *Episcopal Church in the United States, 1800–1840* (1938).
────── *History of the American Episcopal Church* (2nd ed., 1950).
Posey, Walter B., "Protestant Episcopal Church: American Adaptation," *JSH,* 25 (1959), 3.
Rayner, K., "American Episcopal Church and Anglican Communion, 1865–1900," *Jour. Relig. Hist.,* 3 (1964), 158.
Woolverton, John F., "Histories of Episcopal Church in America," *Hist. Mag. Prot. Episc. Church,* 34 (1965), 59.

*   *   *   *   *   *   *

Boscher, Robert S., comp., "The Episcopal Church and American Christianity: A Bibliography," *Hist. Mag. Prot. Episc. Church,* 19 (1950), 369.

See also 10.3 for biographies/writings of:

Brooks, Phillips, 1835–1893
Hare, George E., 1808–1892
Kerfoot, John B., 1816–1881
Muhlenberg, William A., 1796–1877
Murphy, Edgar G., 1869–1913
Polk, Leonidas, 1806–1864
Seabury, Samuel, 1729–1796
Smith, William, 1727–1803
Whipple, Henry B., 1822–1901

24.7.6 German Sects

Brumbaugh, Martin G., *A History of the German Baptist Brethren in Europe and America* (1961).
Eisenbach, George J., *Pietism and the Russian Germans in the United States* (1948).
Gollin, Gillian L., *Moravians in Two Worlds: A Study of Changing Communities* (1967).
Gross, Paul S., *The Hutterite Way: The Inside Story of the Life, Customs, Religion, and Traditions of the Hutterites* (1965).
Hamilton, John T., and Kenneth G. Hamilton, *History of the Moravian Church: The Renewed Unitas Fratrum, 1722–1957* (1967).
Hostetler, John A., *Amish Society* (rev. ed., 1968).
——— and Gertrude E. Huntington, *The Hutterites in North America* (1967).
Rice, Charles S., and Rollin C. Steinmetz, *The Amish Year* (1956).
Schreiber, William I., *Our Amish Neighbors* (1962).
Smith, Charles H., *The Story of the Mennonites* (4th ed., 1957).
Wenger, John C., *The Mennonite Church in America* (1966).

*   *   *   *   *   *   *

Durnbaugh, Donald F., and L. W. Schultz, *A Brethren Bibliography, 1713–1963: Two Hundred and Fifty Years of Brethren Literature* (1964).
Hostetler, John A., *Annotated Bibliography on the Amish . . .* (1951).

24.7.7 Judaism

Davis, Moshe, *Emergence of Conservative Judaism: 19th Century* (1963).
Glazer, Nathan, *American Judaism* (1957).
Kaplan, Mordecai M., *The Greater Judaism in the Making: A Study of the Modern Evolution of Judaism* (1960).
Leiser, Joseph, *American Judaism* (1925).
Leventman, Seymour, and Judith R. Kramer, *Children of the Gilded Ghetto: Conflict Resolutions of Three Generations of American Jews* (1961).
Lurie, Harry L., *A Heritage Affirmed: Jewish Federation Movement in America* (1961).
Philipson, David, *Reform Movement in Judaism* (1931).
Pool, Tamar, and David De S. Pool, *An Old Faith in New World: Sherith Israel, 1654–1954* (1955).
Sklare, Marshall, *Conservative Judaism* (1955).
Teller, Judd L., "Critique of New Jewish Theology," *Commentary,* 15 (1958), 243.
Waxman, Meyer, *American Judaism in the Light of History: Three Hundred Years* (1955).
Waxman, Mordecai, ed., *Tradition and Change: The Development of Conservative Judaism* (1958).

24.7.8 Lutheranism

Allbeck, Willard D., *Century of Lutherans in Ohio* (1966). Covers the period 1803–1917.

Anderson, Hugh G., *Lutheranism in Southeastern States, 1860–1886* (1969).

Arden, Gothard E., *Augustana Heritage: The Augustana Lutheran Church* (1963).

Forster, Walter O., *Zion on the Mississippi: Saxon Lutherans in Missouri, 1839–1841* (1953).

Jensen, John M., *United Evangelical Lutheran Church* (1964).

Klein, Harry H. J., *History of the Eastern Synod of the Reformed Church in the U.S.* (1943).

Marty, Myron A., *Lutherans and Roman Catholicism: The Changing Conflict, 1917–1963* (1968).

Meuser, Fred W., *The Formation of the American Lutheran Church: A Case Study in Lutheran Unity* (1958).

Mortensen, Enok, *The Danish Lutheran Church in America: The History and Heritage of the American Evangelical Lutheran Church* (1967).

Nelson, E. Clifford, and Eugene L. Fevold, *The Lutheran Church among Norwegian Americans: History of the Evangelical Lutheran Church* (2 vols., 1960).

Neve, Herbert T., and Benjamin A. Johnson, eds., *Maturing of American Lutheranism* (1958).

Nyholm, Paul C., *The Americanization of the Danish Lutheran Churches in America: A Study in Immigrant History* (1963).

Spaude, Paul W., *The Lutheran Church under American Influence: Its Relation to Various Modifying Forces in the United States* (1943).

Wentz, Abdel R., *Basic History of Lutheranism* (rev. ed., 1964).

Wentz, Frederick K., *Lutherans in Concert: Story of the National Lutheran Council, 1918–1955* (1968).

*   *   *   *   *   *   *

Schmidt, Herbert H., "The Literature of the Lutherans in America," *Religion in Life,* 27 (1958), 583.

See also 10.3 for biographies/writings of:

Duus, Olaus, fl. 1855–1858
Muhlenberg, John P., 1746–1807
Sihler, Wilhelm, 1801–1885

24.7.9 Methodism

Anderson, Arlow W., *Salt of the Earth: Norwegian-Danish Methodism* (1962).

Baker, George C., *Introduction to History of Early New England Methodism 1789–1839* (1941).

Barclay, Wade C., *Early American Methodism, 1769–1844* (1949).

—— *Methodist Episcopal Church, 1845–1939* (1957).

Farish, Hunter D., *The Circuit Rider Dismounts: A Social History of Southern Methodism, 1865–1900* (1938).

Morrow, Ralph E., *Northern Methodism and Reconstruction* (1956).

Norwood, John M., *Schism in Methodist Church, 1844* (1923).

Peters, John L., *Christian Perfection and American Methodism* (1956).

Posey, Walter B., *Development of Methodism in the Old Southwest* (1933).

Sweet, William W., *Methodism in American History* (1933).

—— *Virginia Methodism* (1955).

*   *   *   *   *   *   *

Fortney, Edward L., "The Literature of the History of Methodism," *Religion in Life,* 24 (1955), 443.

See also 10.3 for biographies/writings of:

Asbury, Francis, 1745–1816
Brownlow, William G., 1805–1877
Candler, Warren A., 1857–1941
Cannon, James Jr., 1864–1944
Cartwright, Peter, 1785–1872
Dow, Lorenzo, 1777–1834
Lee, Jason, 1803–1845
McConnell, Francis J., 1871–1953
Nast, William, 1807–1899
O'Kelly, James, ca. 1735–1826
Simpson, Matthew, 1811–1884
Vincent, John H., 1832–1920
Whitefield, George, 1714–1770

24.7.10 Mormonism

Anderson, Nels, *Desert Saints: The Mormon Frontier in Utah* (1966).
Arrington, Leonard J., *Great Basin Kingdom: An Economic History of Latter-day Saints, 1830–1900* (1958).
Backman, Milton V., *American Religions and the Rise of Mormonism* (1965).
Burton, Richard F., *City of Saints and Across Rocky Mountains,* Fawn M. Brodie, ed. (1963).
Flanders, Robert B., *Nauvoo: Kingdom on Mississippi* (1965).
Furniss, Norman F., *Mormon Conflict, 1850–1859* (1960).
Hansen, Klaus J., *Quest for Empire: Kingdom of God and Council of Fifty in Mormon History* (1967).
Ivins, Stanley S., "Notes on Mormon Polygamy," *Utah Hist. Quar.,* 35 (1967), 309.
Lyon, T. Edgar, "Religious Activities and Development in Utah, 1847–1910," *Utah Hist. Quar.,* 35 (1967), 292.
Mulder, William, and A. Russell Mortensen, eds., *Among Mormons* (1958).
Mulder, William, *Homeward to Zion: Mormon Migration from Scandinavia* (1957).
O'Dea, Thomas F., *Mormons* (1957).
Quaife, Milo M., *Kingdom of St. James: A Narrative of the Mormons* (1930).
Roberts, Brigham H., *Comprehensive History of Church of Jesus Christ of Latter-Day Saints* (6 vols., 1930).
Stegner, Wallace E., *Gathering of Zion: The Mormon Trail* (1964).
Stout, Hosea, *On the Mormon Frontier: Diary, 1844–1861,* Juanita Brooks, ed. (2 vols., 1964).
Taylor, Philip A. M., *Expectations Westward: Mormons and Emigration of Their British Converts in Nineteenth Century* (1966).
Turner, Wallace, *Mormon Establishment* (1966).
Vetterli, Richard, *Mormonism, Americanism and Politics* (1961).
West, Ray B., Jr., *Kingdom of the Saints: Brigham Young and the Mormons* (1957).
Whalen, William J., *The Latter-Day Saints in the Modern Day World: An Account of Contemporary Mormonism* (1964).
Young, Kimball, *Isn't One Wife Enough?* (1954).

*   *   *   *   *   *   *

Alexander, Thomas G., and James B. Allen, eds., "The Mormons In The Mountain West: A Selected Bibliography," *Ariz. and West.,* 9 (1967), 365.
Arrington, Leonard J., "Scholarly Studies of Mormonism in the Twentieth Century" *Dialogue,* 1 (Spring 1966), 24.
Evanoff, Alexander, "Turner Thesis and Mormon Beginnings," *Utah Hist. Quar.,* 33 (1965), 155.
Hill, Marvin S., "Historiography of Mormonism," *Church Hist.,* 28 (1959), 418.

Paul, Rodman W., "Mormons as Theme in Western Historical Writing," *JAH*, 54 (1967), 511.
Taylor, Philip, A. M., "Recent Writing on Utah and Mormons," *Ariz. and West*, 4 (1962), 249.

See also 10.3 for biographies/writings of:

Lee, John D., 1812–1877
Smith, Joseph, 1805–1844
Strang, James J., 1813–1856
Young, Brigham, 1801–1877

24.7.11 Orthodox Churches

Bensin, Basil M., *History of the Russian Orthodox Greek Catholic Church of North America* (1941).
Bilon, Peter, *Ukrainians and Their Church* (1953).
Bogolepov, Alexander A., *Toward an American Orthodox Church* (1964).
Emhardt, William C., *The Eastern Church in the Western World* (1928).
Shaw, Plato E., *American Contacts with the Eastern Churches, 1820–1870* (1937).
Stylianopoulos, Theodore G., "The Orthodox Church in America," *Am. Acad. Pol. Sci., Annals*, 387 (1970), 41.

24.7.12 Pentecostal Churches

Brumback, Carl, *Suddenly . . . From Heaven: A History of the Assemblies of God* (1961).
Conn, Charles W., *Like A Mighty Army Moves the Church of God* (1955).
Horton, Wade H., ed., *The Glossolalia Phenomenon* (1966).
Kelsey, Morton T., *Tongue Speaking: An Experiment in Spiritual Experience* (1964).
Winehouse, Irwin, *The Assemblies of God, A Popular Survey* (1959).
Wood, William W., *Culture and Personality: Aspects of the Pentecostal Holiness Religion* (1965).

24.7.13 Presbyterianism

Anderson, Charles A., *The Presbyterian Enterprise; Sources of American Presbyterian History* (1956).
Loetscher, Lefferts A., *Brief History of the Presbyterians* (rev. ed., 1958).
——— *The Broadening Church: Presbyterian Church since 1869* (1954).
Melton, Julius *Presbyterian Worship since 1787* (1967).
Posey, Walter B., *Presbyterian Church in Old Southwest, 1778–1838* (1952).
Rudolph, L. C., *Hoosier Zion: Presbyterians in Early Indiana* (1963).
Smith, Elwyn A., *The Presbyterian Ministry in American Culture: A Study in Changing Concepts, 1700–1900* (1962).
Sweet, William W., *Religion on the American Frontier*. Vol. II: *Presbyterians, 1783–1840* (1946).
Thompson, Ernest T., *Presbyterians in the South, 1607–1861* (1963).
——— "Presbyterians North and South—Reunion," *Jour. Presby. Hist.*, 43 (1965).

* * * * * * *

Spence, Thomas H., Jr., "A Brief Bibliography of Presbyterian History," *Religion in Life*, 25 (1956), 603.

See also 10.3 for biographies/writings of:

Beecher, Lyman, 1775–1863
McMillan, John, 1752–1833

Nott, Eliphalet, 1773–1866
Scott, William A., 1813–1885
Thornwell, James H., 1812–1862
Wallace, Henry, 1836–1916
Whitman, Marcus, 1802–1847

Quaker. See Society of Friends

24.7.14 Roman Catholicism

24.7.14.1 General

Cada, Joseph, *Czech-American Catholics, 1850–1920* (1964).
Casper, Henry W., *History of Catholic Church in Nebraska* (3 vols., 1960–1966).
Cross, Robert D., *The Emergence of Liberal Catholicism in America* (1958).
Eberhardt, Newman C., *A Survey of American Church History* (1964).
Ellis, John T., *American Catholicism* (1956).
—— ed., *Documents of American Catholic History* (rev. ed., 1962).
Ellis, John T., *Perspectives in American Catholicism* (1963).
Gannon, Michael V., *Cross in the Sand: Catholic Church in Florida, 1513–1870* (1965).
Garraghan, Gilbert, *Jesuits of Middle United States* (3 vols., 1938).
Greeley, Andrew M., *Catholic Experience* (1967).
Herr, Dan, and Joel Wells, eds., *Through Other Eyes: Some Impressions of American Catholicism by Foreign Visitors from 1777 to the Present* (1965).
Kane, John J., *Catholic-Protestant Conflicts in America* (1955).
Kelly, Mary G., *Catholic Immigrant Colonization Projects in the United States, 1815–1860* (1939).
Landis, Benson Y., *The Roman Catholic Church in the United States; A Guide to Recent Developments* (1966).
McAvoy, Thomas T., *Americanist Heresy in Roman Catholicism, 1895–1900.*
—— *Catholic Church in Indiana* (1940).
—— *History of the Catholic Church in the United States* (1969).
MacDonald, Fergus, *Catholic Church and Secret Societies* (1946).
Marty, Myron A., *Lutherans and Roman Catholicism: The Changing Conflict, 1917–1963* (1968).
Maynard, Theodore, *American Catholicism* (1941).
Shea, John G., *History of Catholic Church in United States* (4 vols., 1886–1892).
Wakin, Edward, and Joseph F. Scheuer, *The De-Romanization of the American Catholic Church* (1966).

*   *   *   *   *   *   *

Ellis, John Tracy, *Guide to American Catholic History* (1959).
Geiger, Maynard, *Franciscan Missionaries in Hispanic California, 1769–1848: Biographical Dictionary* (1969).
O'Brien, David J., "American Catholic Historiography: A Post-Conciliar Evaluation," *Church Hist., 37* (1968), 80.
Vollmar, Edward R., *Catholic Church in America: An Historical Bibliography* (2nd ed., 1964).

See also 10.3 for biographies/writings of:

CATHOLIC PRELATES

Carroll, John, 1735–1815
England, John, 1786–1842
Fenwick, Edward D., 1768–1832
Gibbons, James, 1834–1921
Henni, John M., 1805–1881
Hughes, John J., 1797–1864
Ireland, John, 1838–1918

Keane, John J., 1839–1918
McCloskey, John, 1810–1885
McQuaid, Bernard J., 1823–1909
Spalding, John L., 1840–1916

PRIESTS AND MISSIONARIES

Coughlin, Charles 1891–
De Cheverus, Jean L., 1768–1836
De Smet, Pierre-Jean, 1801–1873
Duchesne, Rose Philippine, 1769–1852
La Farge, John, Jr., 1888–
McGlynn, Edward, 1837–1900
Richard, Gabriel, 1767–1832
Senan, José, fl. 1796–1823
Serra, Junipero, 1713–1784
Seton, Elizabeth A. [Mother], 1774–1821

See also 21.11, Nativism and Bigotry, for anti-Catholicism; 23.12, Catholic and
Lutheran Education.

24.7.14.2 Twentieth Century

Colaianni, James, *Catholic Left: Radicalism* (1968).
Cronon, E. David, "American Catholics and Mexican Anticlericalism,
1933–1936," *MVHR*. 45 (1958), 201.
Dawson, Christopher, "Catholic Culture in America," *Critic,* 17 (1959), 7.
DeSantis, Vincent P., "American Catholics & McCarthyism," *Cath. Hist. Rev.,*
51 (1965), 1.
Flynn, George Q., *American Catholics & Roosevelt Presidency, 1932–1936* (1968).
Gardiner, Harold C., *Catholic Viewpoint on Censorship* (1958).
Greeley, Andrew M., *The Church and The Suburbs* (1959).
Hennesey, James, *First Council of the Vatican: American Experience* (1963).
Lally, Francis J., *The Catholic Church in Changing America* (1962).
McAvoy, Thomas T., "Catholic Church between Two Wars," *Rev. Politics,* 4
(1942), 409.
——— "Catholic Minority after Americanist Controversy, 1899–1917," *Rev. Politics,* 21 (1959), 53.
——— *The Great Crisis in American Catholic History, 1895–1900* (1957).
O'Grady, John, *Catholic Charities* (1931).
Valaik, J. David, "American Catholic Dissenters and the Spanish Civil War,"
Cath. Hist. Rev., 53 (1968), 537.
——— "Catholics, Neutrality, and the Spanish Embargo, 1937–1939," *JAH,* 54
(1967), 73.
Yzermans, Vincent A., ed., *American Participation in the Second Vatican Council*
(1967).

24.7.15 Society of Friends

Bacon, Margaret H., *Quiet Rebels: Story of the Quakers in America* (1969).
Brinton, Howard H., *Friends for 300 Years* (1952).
Bronner, Edwin B., ed., *American Quakers Today* (1966).
Doherty, Robert W., *Hicksite Separation: Sociological Analysis of Schism in the
Early Nineteenth Century* (1967).
Jones, Rufus M., *Faith and Practice of the Quakers* (1927).
——— *Later Periods of Quakerism* (1921).
Kershner, Howard E., *Quaker Service in Modern War* (1950).
Tolles, Frederick B., *Quakers and Atlantic Culture* (1960).
Trueblood, David E., *The People Called Quakers* (1966).
Williams, Walter R., *The Rich Heritage of Quakerism* (1962).

See also 10.3 for biographies/writings of:

Hicks, Elias, 1748–1830

24.7.16 Unitarian-Universalism

Cheetham, Henry H., *Unitarianism and Universalism: An Illustrated History* (1962).
Cole, Alfred S., *Our Liberal Heritage* (1951).
Crompton, Arnold, *Unitarianism on the Pacific Coast: The First Sixty Years* (1957).
Eddy, Richard, *Universalism in America, A History* (2 vols., 1884–1886).
Lyttle, Charles H., *Freedom Moves West: A History of the Western Unitarian Conference, 1852–1952* (1952).
Scott, Clinton L., *These Live Tomorrow: Twenty Unitarian Universalist Biographies* (1964).
Wilbur, Earl M., *History of Unitarianism* (2 vols., 1945–1952).
Wright, Conrad, *The Beginnings of Unitarianism in America* (1955).

See also 10.3 for biographies/writings of:

Ballou, Hosea, 1771–1852
Bentley, William, 1759–1819
Channing, William Ellery, 1780–1842
Clarke, James F., 1810–1888
Frothingham, Octavious B., 1822–1895
Hale, Edward Everett, 1822–1909
Higginson, Thomas Wentworth, 1823–1911
May, Samuel J., 1797–1871
Palfrey, John Gorham, 1796–1881
Parker, Theodore, 1810–1860
Ripley, George, 1802–1880

24.7.17 Other Religious Groups and Cults

Albright, Raymond W., *History of Evangelical Church* (1942).
Andrews, Edward D., *People Called Shakers* (1953).
Bechofer-Roberts, C. E., *Mysterious Madame* (1913). Helena Blavatsky, founder of Theosophists.
Braden, Charles S., *These Also Believe: Modern Cults and Movements* (1949).
Chesham, Sallie, *Born to Battle: The Salvation Army in America* (1965).
Clark, Elmer T., *Small Sects in America* (rev. ed., 1949).
Clark, Walter H., *The Oxford Group, Its History and Significance* (1951).
Cohn, Werner, "Jehovah's Witnesses as Proletarian Movement," *Am. Scholar*, 24 (1955), 281.
Cole, Marley, *Triumphant Kingdom* (1957).
Davies, Horton, *Christian Deviations: The Challenge of the New Spiritual Movements* (1965).
Dillett, James, *The Story of Unity* (1954).
Dohrman, Henry T., *California Cult: "Mankind United"* (1958).
Fornell, Earl W., *Unhappy Medium: Margaret Fox* (1964). On Spiritualism.
Henderson, Alice, *Brothers of Light; The Penitentes of the Southwest* (1962).
Jones, Rufus M., *New Studies in Mystical Religion* (1927).
Kellett, Arnold, *Isms and Ologies; A Guide to Unorthodox and Non-Christian Beliefs* (1965).
Kuhn, A. B., *Theosophy* (1930).
LaBarre, Weston, *They Shall Take Up Serpents: Psychology of the Southern Snake-Handling Cult* (1961).
Mathison, Richard R., *Faiths, Cults, and Sects of America from Atheism to Zen* (1960).

Melcher, Marguerite F., *The Shaker Adventure* (1941).

Seventh-Day Adventist Encyclopedia (1966).

Smith, David E., "Millenarian Scholarship in America," *Am. Quar.*, 17 (1965), 535.

Smith, Timothy L., *Called unto Holiness: Nazarenes* (1962).

Stroup, Herbert H., *Jehovah's Witnesses* (1945).

Whalen, William J., *Armageddon Around the Corner; A Report on Jehovah's Witnesses* (1962).

—————— *Faiths for the Few: A Study of Minority Religions* (1963).

White, Timothy, *A People for His Name: A History of Jehovah's Witnesses and an Evaluation* (1968).

Williamson, Geoffrey, *Inside Buchmanism* (1954). The Oxford group.

Wisbey, Herbert A., Jr., *Pioneer Prophetess: Jemima Wilkinson* (1964).

25 Intellectual History

25.1 GENERAL

Boller, Paul F., Jr., *American Thought in Transition* (1959).
Boorstin, Daniel J., "Place of Thought in American Life," *Am. Scholar*, 25 (1956), 137.
Cohen, Morris R., *American Thought*, Felix S. Cohen, ed. (1954).
Commager, Henry S., *The American Mind* (1950).
Curti, Merle E., *The Growth of American Thought* (3d ed., 1964).
Dudden, Arthur P., "Nostalgia and the American," *Jour. Hist. Ideas*, 22 (1961), 515.
Gabriel, Ralph H., *The Course of American Democratic Thought* (rev. ed., 1956).
Hofstadter, Richard, *Anti-intellectualism in American Life* (1963).
Hollingsworth, J. Rogers, "American Anti-Intellectualism," *So. Atl. Quar.*, 63 (1964), 267.
Jones, Howard M., *Pursuit of Happiness* (1953).
Miller, Perry, "The Shaping of the American Character," *NEQ*, 28 (1955), 435.
Nye, Russel B., *This Almost Chosen People: Essays in History of American Ideas* (1966).
Ostrander, Gilman M., *Rights of Man in America, 1606–1861* (2nd ed., 1969).
Parrington, Vernon L., *Main Currents in American Thought: An Interpretation of American Literature from the Beginnings to 1920* (3 vols., 1927–1930).
Perry, Bliss, *The American Mind* (1912).
Persons, Stow, *American Minds: History of Ideas* (1958).
Peterson, Merrill D., *Jefferson Image in the American Mind* (1960).
Schlesinger, Arthur M., Jr., and Morton M. White, *Paths of American Thought* (1963).
Williams, Raymond, *Culture and Society, 1780–1950* (1958).
Wish, Harvey, *Society and Thought in America* (2 vols., 1950–1962).

* * * * * * *

Greene, John C., "Objectives and Methods in Intellectual History," *MVHR*, 44 (1957), 58.
Higham, John, "American Intellectual History," *Am. Quar.*, 13 (1961), 219.
———— "Intellectual History and Its Neighbors," *Jour. Hist. Ideas*, 15 (1954), 339.
———— "The Rise of American Intellectual History," *AHR*, 56 (1951), 453.
Lovejoy, Arthur O., "Reflections on History of Ideas," *Jour. Hist. Ideas*, 1 (1940), 3.
Skotheim, Robert A., *American Intellectual Histories and Historians* (1966).
———— "Writing of American Histories of Ideas," *Jour. Hist. Ideas*, 25 (1964), 257.

25.2 1789–1860

Bertelson, David, *Lazy South* (1967).
Blau, Joseph L., ed., *Social Theories of Jacksonian Democracy* (1955).
Boas, George, ed., *Romanticism in America* (1940).
Davis, Richard B., *Intellectual Life in Virginia, 1790–1830* (1964).
Doherty, Herbert J., Jr., "Mind of the Antebellum South," in Arthur S. Link, ed., *Writing Southern History Essays in Historiography in Honor of Fletcher M. Green* (1965).
Eaton, Clement, *Freedom-of-Thought Struggle in the Old South* (rev. ed., 1964).
Goodman, Paul, "Ethics and Enterprise: The Values of a Boston Elite, 1800–1860," *Am. Quar.*, 18 (1966), 437.
Hazen, Charles D., *Contemporary American Opinion of French Revolution* (1897).
Houghton, Walter E., *Victorian Frame of Mind, 1830–1870* (1959).
Kerber, Linda K., *Federalists in Dissent: Imagery and Ideology in Jeffersonian America* (1970).
Mansfield, Stephen, "Thomas Roderick Dew at William and Mary," *Va. Mag. Hist. Biog.*, 75 (1967), 429.
Miller, Perry, *Life of the Mind: From the Revolution to the Civil War* (1965).
Moore, Arthur K., *Frontier Mind: Kentucky* (1957).
Mudge, Eugene T., *Social Philosophy of John Taylor of Carolina* (1939).
Taylor, William, *Cavalier and Yankee: Old South and American National Character* (1961).

25.3 1861–1918

Adams, Henry, *The Education of Henry Adams* (1918).
——— *The Degradation of the Democratic Dogma*, Brooks Adams, ed. (1919).
Bloomfield, Maxwell H., *Alarms and Diversions: American Mind through American Magazines, 1900–1914* (1967).
Carnegie, Andrew, *The Gospel of Wealth and Other Essays* (1890); Edward C. Kirkland, ed., (1962).
Cunningham, Horace H., "Southern Mind since the Civil War," in Arthur S. Link, ed., *Writing Southern History: Essays in Historiography in Honor of Fletcher M. Green* (1965).
Fine, Sidney, *Laissez Faire and General-Welfare State, 1865–1901* (1956).
Fredrickson, George, *The Inner Civil War: Northern Intellectuals* (1965).
Jaher, Frederick C., *Doubters and Dissenters, 1885–1918* (1964).
Kennedy, Gail, *Democracy and the Gospel of Wealth* (1949).
McCloskey, Robert G., *American Conservatism in Age of Enterprise* (1951).
May, Henry F., *End of American Innocence, 1912–1917* (1959).
White, G. Edward, *Eastern Establishment and Western Experience: Frederic Remington, Theodore Roosevelt and Owen Wister* (1968).

25.4 1919 TO THE PRESENT

Arnold, Thurmond W., *Folklore of Capitalism* (1937).
——— *Symbols of Government* (1935).
Burns, Arthur F., "Brookings Inquiry," *Quar. Jour. Econ.*, 50 (1936), 476.
De Mott, Benjamin , *Supergrow: Imagination in America* (1969).
Diggins, John P., "American Pragmatic Liberals and Mussolini's Italy," *AHR*, 71 (1966), 487.
Ekirch, Arthur A., Jr., *Ideologies and Utopias: Impact of the New Deal on American Thought* (1969).
Erikson, Erik H., ed., *Youth* (1963).
Frisch, Morton J., and Martin Diamond, eds., *The Thirties* (1968).
Hartshorne, Thomas L., *Distorted Image: Changing Conceptions of American Character since Turner* (1968).

Kemler, Edgar, *Deflation of American Ideals* (1941).
Keniston, Kenneth, "Alienation and Decline of Utopia," *Am. Scholar*, 29 (1960), 161.
Ladd, Everett C., Jr., *Ideology in America: Change and Response in a City, a Suburb, and a Samll Town* (1969).
Lerner, Max, *America as a Civilization* (1957).
—— *Ideas Are Weapons* (1939).
Lippmann, Walter, *The Good Society* (1937).
—— *Method of Freedom* (1934).
Lipset, Seymour M., and Leo Lowenthal, eds., *Culture and Social Character: The Work of David Riesman Reviewed* (1961).
Spiller, Robert E., and Eric Larrabee, eds., *American Perspectives: The National Self-Image in the Twentieth Century* (1961).
Spitz, David, *Patterns of Anti-Democratic Thought* (1949).
Warren, Frank A., III, *Liberals and Communism: "Red Decade"* (1966).
Wilson, R. Jackson, "The Reassessment of Liberalism," *Jour. Contemp. Hist.*, 2 (1967) 93.
Young, James P., *Politics of Affluence: Ideology in United States since World War II* (1968).
Zinn, Howard, ed., *New Deal Thought* (1966).

25.5 POLITICAL THOUGHT

25.5.1 General

Bell, Daniel, *End of Ideology: On Exhaustion of Political Ideas in the Fifties* (1960).
Boller, Paul F., "Calhoun on Liberty," *So. Atl. Quar.*, 66 (1967), 395.
Cronon, E. David, ed., *Political Thought of Woodrow Wilson* (1965).
Current, Richard N., "John C. Calhoun, Philosopher of Reaction," *Antioch Review*, 3 (1943), 223.
Ekirch, Arthur A., *The American Democratic Tradition* (1963).
Freehling, William W., "Spoilsmen and Interests in Thought and Career of John C. Calhoun," *JAH*, 52 (1965), 25.
Grimes, Alan P., *American Political Thought* (2nd ed., 1960).
Guttmann, Allen, *The Conservative Tradition in America* (1967).
Hartz, Louis, *Liberal Tradition in America* (1955).
Hofstadter, Richard, *Age of Reform: Bryan to F.D.R.* (1955).
—— *American Political Tradition and the Men Who Made It* (1948).
Kirk, Russel, *The Conservative Mind: Burke to Santayana* (1953).
—— *John Randolph of Roanoke* (rev. ed., 1964).
Lewis, Edward R., *History of American Political Thought from the Civil War to the World War* (1937).
Merriam, Charles E., *History of American Political Theories* (1920).
Rhodes, Harold V., *Utopia in American Political Thought* (1967).
Rossiter, Clinton, *Conservatism in America* (2nd ed., 1962).
Spain, August O., *Political Theory of John C. Calhoun* (1951).
Wiltse, Charles M., *The Jeffersonian Tradition in American Democracy* (2nd ed., 1960).

25.5.2 Radicalism

Aaron, Daniel, *Writers on the Left* (1961).
Bell, Daniel, *Marxian Socialism in the United States* (1967).
Bottomore, T. B., *Critics of Society: Radical Thought in North America* (1968).
Cole, George D. H., *Socialist Thought: Marxism and Anarchism, 1850–1890* (1954).
Egbert, Donald D., and Stow Persons, eds., *Socialism and American Life* (2 vols., 1952).

Gettleman, Marvin E., and David Mermelstein, eds., *Great Society Reader: Failure of American Liberalism* (1967).
Goldberg, Harvey, ed., *American Radicals* (1957).
Harris, David J., *Socialist Origins in the United States, 1817–1832* (1966).
Herreshoff, David, *American Disciples of Marx to the Progressive Era* (1967).
Hillquit, Morris, *History of Socialism in the United States* (rev. ed., 1910).
Jacobs, Paul, and Saul Landau, *New Radicals* (1966).
Kaufman, Arnold S., *Radical Liberal* (1968).
Kipnis, Ira, *American Socialist Movement* (1952).
Lasch, Christopher, *Agony of the American Left* (1969).
———— *The New Radicalism in America, 1889–1963: The Intellectual as a Social Type* (1965).
Lens, Sidney, *Radicalism in America* (1966).
Lynd, Staughton, *Intellectual Origins of American Radicalism* (1968).
Martin, James J., *Men Against the State: Individualist Anarchism, 1827–1908* (1953).
Moore, R. Laurence, *European Socialists and the American Promised Land* (1970).
O'Neal, James, and G. A. Werner, *American Communism* (1947).
Paulson, Ross E., *Radicalism and Reform: Vrooman Family and American Social Thought, 1837–1937* (1968).
Quint, Howard H., *Forging of American Socialism* (1953). The 1870's to 1900.
Reichert, William O., "Philosophical Anarchism of Adin Ballou," *Huntington Lib. Quar.,* 27 (1964) 357.
Schuster, E. M., *Native American Anarchism* (1932).
Weinstein, James, *Decline of Socialism in America, 1912–1925* (1967).
Williams, William A., *Great Evasion: Contemporary Relevance of Karl Marx* (1964).
Young, Alfred F., ed., *Dissent: American Radicalism* (1968).

* * * * * * *

Friedberg, Gerald, "Sources for Study of Socialism, 1901–1919," *Labor Hist.,* 6 (1965), 159.
Seidman, Joel I., et al., eds., *Communism in United States: A Bibliography* (1969).

See also 10.3 for biographies/writings of:

Debs, Eugene V., 1855–1926
De Leon, Daniel, 1852–1914
Goldman, Emma, 1869–1940
Most, Johann, 1846–1906

25.6 TRANSCENDENTALISM

Christy, Arthur, *The Orient in American Transcendentalism* (1932).
Crowe, Charles, "Phalansteries and Transcendentalists," *Jour. Hist. Ideas,* 20 (1959), 495.
Frothingham, O. B., *Transcendentalism in New England* (1876).
Goddard, Harold C., *Studies in New England Transcendentalism* (1908).
Gohdes, Clarence L. F., *Periodicals of American Transcendentalism* (1931).
Harding, Walter, ed., *Thoreau: Century of Criticism* (1954).
Hutchison, William R., *Transcendentalist Ministers* (1959).
Miller, Perry, ed., *The American Transcendentalists* (1950).
Patterson, Robert Leet, *The Philosophy of William Ellery Channing* (1952).
Pochmann, Henry A., *New England Transcendentalism and St. Louis Hegelianism* (1948).
Porte, Joel M., *Emerson and Thoreau: Transcendentalists in Conflict* (1966).
Spence, Robert, "D. A. Wasson, Forgotten Transcendentalist," *Am. Lit.,* 27 (1955), 31.

Thomas, John Wesley, *James Freeman Clarke: Apostle of German Culture to America* (1949).
Vogel, Stanley M., *German Literary Influences on American Transcendentalists* (1955).
Warren, Austin, "Concord School of Philosophy," *NEQ,* 2 (1929), 199.
Wellek, René, "Emerson and German Philosophy," *NEQ,* 16 (1943), 41.
—— "Minor Transcendentalists and German Philosophy," *NEQ,* 15 (1942), 652.
Wells, Ronald V., *Three Christian Transcendentalists: James Marsh, Caleb Sprague Henry, and Frederick Henry Hedge* (1943).
Whicher, George F., ed., *Transcendentalist Revolt against Materialism* (1949).
Whicher, Stephen E., *Freedom and Fate: Ralph Waldo Emerson* (1953).

See also 10.3 for biographies/writings of:

Alcott, Amos Bronson, 1799–1888
Brownson, Orestes A., 1803–1876
Channing, William Ellery, II, 1818–1901
Clarke, James Freeman, 1810–1888
Emerson, Ralph Waldo, 1803–1882
Fuller, Sara Margaret (Ossoli) 1810–1850
Ripley, George, 1802–1880
Thoreau, Henry D., 1817–1862
Very, Jones, 1813–1880

25.7 NATIONALISM AND MISSION

Alexander, Charles C., *Nationalism in American Thought, 1930–1945* (1969).
Arieli, Yehoshua, *Individualism and Nationalism* (1964).
Burns, Edward M., *American Idea of Mission* (1957).
Curti, Merle, *The Roots of American Loyalty* (1946).
Hirschfeld, Charles, "Brooks Adams and American Nationalism," *AHR,* 69 (1964), 371.
Kohn, Hans, *American Nationalism* (1957).
Merk, Frederick, *Manifest Destiny and Mission in American History* (1963).
Muller, Dorothea R., "Josiah Strong and American Nationalism: A Re-evaluation," *JAH,* 53 (1966), 487.
Nagel, Paul C., *One Nation Indivisible: The Union in American Thought, 1776–1861* (1964).
Somkin, Fred, *Unquiet Eagle: Memory and Desire in American Freedom, 1815–1860* (1967).
Spencer, Benjamin T., *Quest for Nationality: American Literary Campaign* (1957).
Strong, Josiah, *Our Country* (1891); Jurgen Herbst, ed. (1963).
Tuveson, Ernest L., *Redeemer Nation: America's Millennial Role* (1968).
Van Alstyne, Richard W., "American Nationalism and Its Mythology," *Queen's Quar.,* 65 (1958), 423.
Webster, Noah, *On Being American: Selected Writings, 1783–1828,* Homer D. Babbidge, Jr., ed. (1967).
Weinberg, Albert K., *Manifest Destiny* (1958).

*   *   *   *   *   *   *

Deutsch, Karl W., *Interdisciplinary Bibliography on Nationalism, 1935–53* (1956).

See also 10.3 for biographies/writings of:

Lieber, Francis, 1800–1872
Webster, Noah, 1758–1843

See also 21.10, Patriotism and Disloyalty; 21.11, Nativism and Bigotry.

25.8 NATURE AND THE WEST

Allen, Walter, *Urgent West: American Dream and Modern Man* (1969).
Ekirch, Arthur A., Jr., *Man and Nature in America* (1963).
Huth, Hans, *Nature and the American* (1957).
Marx, Leo, *Technology and the Pastoral Ideal* (1964).
Nash, Roderick, *Wilderness and the American Mind* (1967).
Sheehan, Bernard W., "Paradise and Noble Savage in Jeffersonian Thought,"
   WMQ, 3 ser., 26 (1969), 327.
Smith, Henry Nash, *Virgin Land: The American West as Symbol and Myth*
   (1950).
Walker, Robert H., "Poets Interpret the Western Frontier," *MVHR*, 47 (1961),
   619.

25.9 IDEA OF PROGRESS

Chambers, Clarke A., "Belief in Progress in Twentieth-Century America," *Jour.
   Hist. Ideas*, 19 (1958), 197.
Chinard, Gilbert, "Progress and Perfectibility in Samuel Miller's Intellectual
   History," in *Studies in Intellectual History* (1953).
Ekirch, Arthur A., Jr., *Idea of Progress in America, 1815–1860* (1944).

25.10 INDIVIDUALISM AND THE SELF-MADE MAN

Arieli, Yehoshua, *Individualism and Nationalism* (1964).
Cawelti, John G., *Apostles of the Self-Made Man* (1965).
Greene, Theodore P., *America's Heroes: The Changing Models of Success in
   American Magazines* (1970).
Hartz, Louis, "Individualism in Modern America," *Tex. Quar.*, 6 (1963), 100.
Lynn, Kenneth S., *Dream of Success: The Modern American Imagination* (1955).
Rischin, Moses, ed., *The American Gospel of Success: Individualism* (1965).
Tebbel, John W., *From Rags to Riches* (1963).
Weiss, Richard, *American Myth of Success from Horatio Alger to Norman Vincent
   Peale* (1969).
Wyllie, Irvin G., *Self-Made Man in America* (1954).

25.11 THE CITY IN AMERICAN THOUGHT

Bailey, Liberty H., *Country-Life Movement* (1911).
Donaldson, Scott, *The Suburban Myth* (1969).
Mumford, Lewis, *The Culture of Cities* (1938).
Schmitt, Peter J., *Back to Nature: The Arcadian Myth in Urban America* (1969).
Strauss, Anselm L., *Images of American City* (1961).
——— ed., *American City: Sourcebook of Urban Imagery* (1968).
White, Morton, and Lucia White, *The Intellectual Versus the City* (1962).
Wright, Frank Lloyd, *Living City* (1958).

25.12 SCIENTIFIC MANAGEMENT

Aitken, H. G. J., *Taylorism at Watertown Arsenal, 1908–1915* (1960).
Baritz, Loren, *Servants of Power: Use of Social Science in American Industry*
   (1960).

Haber, Samuel, *Efficiency and Uplift: Scientific Management in the Progressive Era, 1890–1920* (1964).
Kakar, Sudhir, *Frederick Taylor: A Study in Personality and Innovation* (1970).
Nadworny, Milton J., *Scientific Management and the Unions, 1900–1932* (1955).
Taylor, Frederick W., *Principles of Scientific Management* (1911).

See also 10.3 for biographies/writings of:

Taylor, Frederick W., 1856–1915
Veblen, Thorstein B., 1857–1929

25.13 IMPACT OF SCIENCE AND TECHNOLOGY

American Studies Association, *Impact of Darwinian Thought* (1959).
Dewey, John, *The Influence of Darwin on Philosophy* (1910).
Fleming, Donald, "Attitude: History of a Concept," *Perspectives in Am. Hist.,* 1 (1967), 287.
Greene, John C., *Death of Adam: Evolution and Its Impact on Western Thought* (1959).
Haller, Mark H., *Eugenics: Hereditarian Attitudes in American Thought* (1963).
Handlin, Oscar, "First Encounters with the Machine," *Am. Scholar,* 33 (1964), 408.
Hofstadter, Richard, *Social Darwinism* (2nd ed., 1959).
Marx, Leo, *Machine in the Garden: Technology and the Pastoral Ideal in America* (1964).
Persons, Stow, ed., *Evolutionary Thought in America* (1950).
Randall, John H., Jr., "Changing Impact of Darwin on Philosophy," *Jour. Hist. Ideas,* 22 (1961), 435.
Russett, Cynthia E., *Concept of Equilibrium in Social Thought* (1966).
Wiener, Philip P., *Evolution and Founders of Pragmatism* (1949).
Wyllie, Irvin G., "Social Darwinism and the Businessman," *Am. Phil. Soc., Proc.,* 103 (1959), 629.

See also 10.3 for biographies/writings of:

Adams, Henry Brooks, 1838–1918
Carnegie, Andrew, 1835–1919
Draper, John W., 1811–1882
Fiske, John, 1842–1901
Sumner, William Graham, 1840–1910

See also 24.4, Darwinism and Religion; 29.1.7, Darwinism and American Science.

25.14 RACIAL THOUGHT

Baudet, Ernest H. P., *Paradise on Earth: European Images of Non-European Man,* Elizabeth Wentholt, trans. (1965).
Bettelheim, Bruno, and Morris Janowitz, *Dynamics of Prejudice* (1950).
Bidney, David, "Idea of the Savage in North American Ethnohistory," *Jour. Hist. Ideas,* 15 (1954), 322.
Binder, Frederick M., *Color Problem in Early America as Viewed by John Adams, Jefferson and Jackson* (1968).
Blair, Lewis H., *Southern Prophecy* (1899); C. Vann Woodward, ed. (1964).
Carpenter, Marie E., *Treatment of the Negro in American History School Textbooks* (1941).
Cripps, Thomas R., "Death of Rastus: Negroes in American Films since 1945," *Phylon,* 28 (1967), 267.

Degler, Carl N., "Slavery and the Genesis of American Race Prejudice," *Comparative Studies in Society and History*, 2 (1959), 49.

Fredrickson, George, *Black Image in the White Mind, 1817–1914* (1971).

Gossett, Thomas F., *Race: History of an Idea in America* (1963).

Greenberg, Jack, *Race Relations and American Law* (1959).

Greene, John C., "Negro's Place in Nature, 1780–1815," *Jour. Hist. Ideas*, 15 (1954), 384.

Gross, Seymour L., and John E. Hardy, eds., *Images of the Negro in American Literature* (1966).

Handlin, Oscar, "Prejudice and Capitalist Exploitation: Does Economics Explain Racism?" *Commentary*, 6 (1948), 79.

———— *Race and Nationality in American Life* (1957).

Jordan, Winthrop D., *White over Black: American Attitudes toward the Negro, 1550–1812* (1968).

Mardock, Robert W., "Strange Concepts of the American Indian since Civil War," *Montana*, 7 (1957), 36.

Newby, I. A., *Jim Crow's Defense: Anti-Negro Thought in America, 1900–1930* (1965).

Pearce, Roy H., *Savagism and Civilization: The Indian and the American Mind* (1967). Replaces *Savages of America* (1953).

Price, A. Grenfell, *White Settlers and Native People: Racial Contacts between English-Speaking White and Aboriginal Peoples in the United States, Canada, Australia and New Zealand* (1949).

Puzzo, Dante A., "Racism and Western Tradition," *Jour. Hist. Ideas*, 25 (1964), 579.

Rose, Arnold M., *Race Prejudice and Discrimination* (1951).

Rose, Peter I., *The Subject Is Race: Traditional Ideologies and the Teaching of Race Relations* (1968).

Saum, Lewis O., *Fur Trader and Indian* (1965).

Schwartz, Mildred A., *Trends in White Attitudes toward Negroes* (1967).

Seabrook, Isaac D., *Before and After: Or the Relations of the Races at the South*, John H. Moore, ed. (1967). The period about 1875.

Smith, Samuel S., *An Essay on the Causes of the Variety of Complexion and Figure in the Human Species* (1787); Winthrop Jordan, ed. (1965).

Stanton, William, *The Leopard's Spots: Scientific Attitudes toward Race in America, 1815–59* (1960).

Thompson, Edgar T., and Everett C. Hughes, eds., *Race: Individual and Collective Behavior* (1958).

Warner, William Lloyd, et al., *Color and Human Nature* (1941).

See also 20.11.7, Indian–White Relations; 20.11.15, Indian–Negro Relations; 21.11, Nativism and Bigotry.

25.15 PHILOSOPHY

Ahlstrom, Sydney E., "Scottish Philosophy and American Theology," *Church Hist.*, 24 (1955), 257.

Anderson, Paul R., and M. H. Fisch, *Philosophy in America* (1939).

Blau, Joseph L., ed., *American Philosophic Addresses, 1700–1900* (1946).

Blau, Joseph L., *Men and Movements in American Philosophy* (1952).

Bernstein, Richard J., ed., *Perspectives on Peirce* (1965).

Cohen, Morris, "Santayana," in *Cambridge History of American Literature*, vol. 3, (1921).

Conkin, Paul K., *Puritans & Pragmatists* (1968).

Cotton, James Harry, *Royce on the Human Self* (1954).

Curti, Merle, "The Great Mr. Locke: America's Philosopher, 1783–1861," *Huntington Lib. Quar.*, 11 (1937) 107.

Dewey, John, "James Marsh and American Philosophy," *Jour. Hist. Ideas*, 2 (1941), 131.

Feldman, William T., *Philosophy of John Dewey* (1934).

Forbes, Cleon, "St. Louis School of Thought," *Mo. Hist. Rev.,* 25 (1930), 83, 26 (1931), 68.
Harmon, Frances A., *The Social Philosophy of the St. Louis Hegelians* (1943).
Howe, Daniel Walker, *The Unitarian Conscience: Harvard Moral Philosophy, 1805–1861* (1970).
Kennedy, Gail, *Pragmatism and American Culture* (1950).
Madden, Edward H., *Chauncey Wright and the Foundations of Pragmatism* (1963).
—— *Civil Disobedience and Moral Law in Nineteenth-Century American Philosophy* (1968).
Moore, Edward C., *American Pragmatism* (1961).
Murphey, Murray G., *Development of Peirce's Philosophy* (1961).
Nash, Gary B., "American Clergy and French Revolution," *WMQ,* 3 ser., 22 (1965) 392.
Passmore, John, *Hundred Years of Philosophy* (3d ed., 1966).
Pochmann, Henry A., *New England Transcendentalism and St. Louis Hegelianism* (1948).
Randall, John H., Jr., "Josiah Royce and American Idealism," *Jour. Philos.,* 63 (1966), 57.
Riley, Isaac W., *American Thought from Puritanism to Pragmatism and Beyond* (1923).
Rucker, Darnell, *Chicago Pragmatists* (1969).
Schilpp, P. A., ed., *Philosophy of John Dewey* (1939).
Schneider, Herbert W., *History of American Philosophy* (2nd ed., 1963).
Smith, John E., *Spirit of American Philosophy* (1963).
Smith, Wilson, *Professors and Public Ethics: Northern Moral Philosophers before the Civil War* (1956).
Thayer, Horace S., *Meaning and Action: Critical History of Pragmatism* (1968).
Townsend, H. G., *Philosophical Ideas in United States* (1934).
Werkmeister, W. H., *A History of Philosophical Ideas in America* (1949).
White, Edward A., *Science and Religion in American Thought* (1952).
White, Morton G., *Origins of Dewey's Instrumentalism* (1964).
—— *Social Thought in America* (3d ed., 1957).
Wiener, Philip P., *Evolution and Founders of Pragmatism* (1949).
Wilson, R. Jackson, *In Quest of Community: Social Philosophy in the United States, 1860–1920* (1968).

See also 10.3 for biographies/writings of:

See also 23.7, Education–Reform and Ideology; 25.6, Transcendentalism; 25.13, Impact of Science and Technology.

25.16 BEHAVIORAL SCIENCES

Ben-David, Joseph, "Social Factors in the Origins of a New Science: The Case of Psychology," *Am. Sociol. Rev.,* 31 (1966), 451.
Boring, Edwin G., et al., eds., *History of Psychology in Autobiography* (vol. IV, 1952).
Broadbent, Donald, *Behavior* (1961).

Brown, James A. C., *Freud and the Post-Freudians* (1961).
——— *Social Psychology of Industry* (1954).
Burnham, John C., "Psychiatry, Psychology and the Progressive Movement,"
 Am. Quar., 12 (1960), 457.
Curti, Merle E., "Dreams and Dreamers," *Jour. Hist. Ideas,* 27 (1966), 391.
Erikson, Erik H., *Identity: Youth and Crisis* (1968).
Fay, John W., *American Psychology before William James* (1939).
Fernberger, S. W., "American Psychological Association," *Psych. Bull.,* 29
 (1932), 1.
Helm, June, ed., *Pioneers of American Anthropology* (1966).
James, William, *Principles of Psychology* (2 vols., 1890).
Karpf, Fay Berger, *American Social Psychology, Its Origins, Development and
 European Background* (1932).
Matthews, F. H., "Americanization of Sigmund Freud: Adaptations of Psycho-
 analysis before 1917," *Jour. Am. Studies,* 1 (1967), 39.
Mitra, Panchanana, *History of American Anthropology* (1933).
Murchison, C., ed., *History of Psychology in Autobiography* (3 vols., 1930).
Roback, Abraham A., *History of American Psychology* (rev. ed., 1964).
Shakow, David, and David Rapaport, *Influence of Freud on American Psychology*
 (1964).
Stanton, William, "Scientific Approach to the Study of Man in America," *Cahiers
 d'Histoire Mondiale,* 8 (1965), 768.
Stocking, George W., Jr., *Race, Culture, and Evolution: Essays in History of
 Anthropology* (1968).
Watson, John B., *Behaviorism* (1930).
Watson, Robert I., "Historical Background for National Trends in Psychology,"
 Jour. Hist. Behavioral Sci., 1 (1965), 130.
Woodworth, Robert S., and Mary R. Sheehan, *Contemporary Schools of Psy-
 chology* (3d ed., 1964).

See also 10.3 for biographies/writings of:

PSYCHOLOGISTS

Boring, Edwin Garrigues, 1886–1969
Erikson, Eric H., 1902–
Hall, Granville Stanley, 1846–1924
James, William, 1842–1910
Ladd, George T., 1842–1921
Thorndike, Edward L., 1874–1949

ANTHROPOLOGISTS

Benedict, Ruth F., 1887–1948
Boaz, Franz, 1858–1942
Lowie, Robert H., 1883–1957
Morgan, Lewis Henry, 1818–1881

25.17 SOCIAL SCIENCES

Baritz, Loren, *Servants of Power: Social Science in American Industry* (1960).
Bernard, Luther L., and Jessie Bernard, *Origins of American Sociology* (1943).
Coats, A. W., "Henry Carter Adams: Case Study in Emergence of Social Sci-
 ences in United States, 1850–1900," *Jour. Am. Studies,* 2 (1968), 177.
Cooley, Charles H., *Human Nature and Social Order* (1902).
——— *Social Organization* (1909).
Haddow, Anna, *Political Science in American Colleges and Universities, 1636–1900*
 (1939).
Hinkle, Roscoe C., Jr., and Gisela J. Hinkle, *Development of Modern Sociology in
 United States* (1954).
Landes, David S., and Charles W. Tilley, *History as Social Science* (1971).

Madge, John, *Origins of Scientific Sociology* (1962).
Merton, Robert K., *Social Theory and Social Structure* (3d ed., 1968).
Nelson, Lowry, *Rural Sociology: Origin and Growth* (1969).
O'Conner, Michael J. L., *Origins of Academic Economics in United States* (1944).
Odum, Howard W., *American Masters of Social Science* (1927).
Page, Charles H., *Class and American Sociology: From Ward to Ross* (1940).
Parrish, John B., "Rise of Economics as an Academic Discipline: Formative Years to 1900," *South Econ. Jour.,* 34 (1967), 1.
Small, A. W., *Origins of Sociology* (1924).
Stocking, George W., Jr., *Race, Culture, and Evolution: Essays in History of Anthropology* (1968).
Stone, Richard, *Mathematics in the Social Sciences and Other Essays* (1966).
Ward, Lester, *Welfare State,* Henry S. Commager, ed. (1967).

See also 10.3 for biographies/writings of:

ECONOMISTS

Adams, Henry Carter, 1851–1921
Atkinson, Edward, 1837–1905
Carey, Henry C., 1793–1879
Carey, Mathew, 1760–1839
Commons, John R., 1862–1944
Coxe, Tench, 1755–1824
Eccles, Marriner S., 1890–
Ely, Richard T., 1854–1943
Gay, Edwin F., 1867–1946
Leiserson, William M., 1883–1957
List, George F., 1789–1846
McVickar, John, 1787–1868
Mitchell, Wesley C., 1874–1948
Parker, Carleton H., 1878–1918
Patten, Simon N., 1852–1922
Schumpeter, Joseph A., 1883–1950
Tucker, George, 1775–1861
Veblen, Thorstein B., 1857–1929
Walker, Francis A., 1840–1897
Weyl, Walter E., 1873–1919
Witte, Edwin E., 1887–1960
Wright, Carroll D., 1840–1909

See also 18.5, Economic Thought.

SOCIOLOGISTS

Cayton, Horace R., 1903–
Lindeman, Eduard C., 1885–1953
Ross, Edward A., 1866–1951
Steiner, Edward A., 1866–1956
Sumner, William Graham, 1840–1910
Ward, Lester, 1841–1913
Woods, Robert A., 1865–1925

25.18 TRANSATLANTIC THOUGHT AND IMAGE

Baumer, Franklin L., "Intellectual History," *Jour. Mod. Hist.,* 21 (1949), 191.
Bernstein, Harry, *Making an Inter-American Mind* (1961).
Boorstin, Daniel J., *America and the Image of Europe* (1960).
Bowers, David F., ed., *Foreign Influences in American Life: Essays and Critical Bibliographies* (1944).
Cargill, Oscar, *Intellectual America* (1941).

Denny, Margaret, and William H. Gilman, eds., *American Writer and European Tradition* (1950).

Dowie, J. Iverne, and J. Thomas Tredway, eds., *Immigration of Ideas: North Atlantic Community* (1968).

Echeverria, Durand, *Mirage in the West: French Image of American Society to 1815* (1957).

Fermi, Laura, *Illustrious Immigrants: Intellectual Migration from Europe, 1930–41* (1968).

Fleming, Donald, and Bernard Bailyn, eds., *The Intellectual Migration: Europe and America, 1930–1960* (1969).

Friedrich, Carl J., *Impact of American Constitutionalism Abroad* (1967).

Jones, Howard M., *American and French Culture* (1927).

Kelley, Robert, *Transatlantic Persuasion: The Liberal-Democratic Mind in Age of Gladstone* (1969).

Kent, Donald P., *Refugee Intellectual* (1953).

Lillibridge, George D., "American Impact Abroad: Past and Present," *Am. Scholar,* 35 (1965), 39.

—— *Beacon of Freedom: Impact of American Democracy upon Great Britain, 1830–1870* (1954).

Long, Orie W., *Literary Pioneers* (1935).

Mann, Arthur, "British Social Thought and American Reformers of Progressive Era," *MVHR,* 42 (1956), 672.

Martin, Terence, *Instructed Vision: Scottish Common Sense Philosophy and American Fiction* (1961).

Mead, Robert O., *Atlantic Legacy: Essays in American-European Cultural History* (1969).

Merton, Robert K., "Sociology of Knowledge," *Isis,* 27 (1937), 493.

Read, Allen W., "Spread of German Linguistic Learning in New England during the Lifetime of Noah Webster," *Am. Speech,* 41 (1966), 163.

Salomone, William A., "Nineteenth-Century Discovery of Italy: An Essay in American Cultural History. Prolegomena to a Historiographical Problem," *AHR,* 73 (1968), 1359.

Samuelson, Paul A., "Economists and History of Ideas," *Am. Econ. Rev.,* 52 (1962), 1.

Sanford, Charles L., *Quest for Paradise* (1961).

Servan-Schreiber, Jean J., *American Challenge,* Ronald Steel, trans. (1968).

Skard, Sigmund, *American Studies in Europe* (2 vols., 1958).

Strout, Cushing, *American Image of Old World* (1963).

Wellek, Rene, *Confrontations: Intellectual and Literary Relations between Germany, England and United States during the Nineteenth Century* (1965).

Welter, Rush, "History of Ideas in America," *JAH,* 51 (1965), 599.

Williams, Stanley T., *Spanish Background of American Literature* (2 vols., 1955).

See also 25.6, Transcendentalism.

26 Literature

26.1 GENERAL

Angoff, Charles, *Literary History of American People* (1935).
Berthoff, Warner, *Ferment of Realism: American Literature, 1884–1919* (1965).
Brooks, Van Wyck, *Makers and Finders: History of the Writer in America, 1800–1915* (5 vols., 1936–1952).
Cowie, Alexander, *Rise of the American Novel* (1951).
Geismar, Maxwell D., *The Last of the Provincials: The American Novel 1915–1925* (1947).
——— *Rebels and Ancestors: The American Novel 1890–1915* (1953).
——— *Writers in Crisis: The American Novel between Two Wars* (1942).
Hicks, Granville, *Great Tradition* (rev. ed., 1935).
Hubbell, Jay B., *South in American Literature, 1607–1900* (1954).
Parrington, Vernon L., *Main Currents in American Thought* (3 vols., 1927–1930).
Quinn, Arthur H., ed., *Literature of American People* (1951).
Spiller, Robert E., et al., *Literary History of the United States* (2 vols., 3d ed., 1963).
Stegner, Wallace E., ed., *The American Novel: James Fenimore Cooper to William Faulkner* (1965).
Trent, W. P., et al., *Cambridge History of American Literature* (4 vols., 1917–1921).
Van Doren, Carl, *American Novel* (1940).
Wagenknecht, Edward C., *Cavalcade of American Novel* (1952).
Wells, Henry W., *American Way of Poetry* (1943).
Wilson, Edmund, *Shock of Recognition: Literature in the United States Recorded by Men Who Made It* (2nd ed., 1955).
Winterich, John T., *Writers in America, 1842–1967* (1968).

*   *   *   *   *   *   *

Agnew, J. M., *Southern Bibliography: Fiction, 1929–1938* (1939).
Blanck, Jacob, comp., *Bibliography of American Literature* (5 vols., 1955–1969).
Coan, Otis W., and Richard G. Lillard, *America in Fiction: Annotated List of Novels* (4th ed., 1956).
Dickinson, Arthur T., *American Historical Fiction* (2nd ed., 1963).
Gohdes, Clarence L. F., comp., *Bibliographical Guide to the Study of the Literature of the U.S.A.* 3d rev. annual. (1970).
Jones, Howard M., and Richard M. Ludwig, *Guide to American Literature and Its Backgrounds since 1890* (4th ed., 1972).
Jones, Howard M., "Nature of Literary History," *Jour. Hist. Ideas,* 28 (1967), 147.
Jones, Joseph, et al., comps., *American Literary Manuscripts: Checklist of Holdings* (1960).
Kurtz, S. Kenneth, *Literature of the Southwest: Selected Bibliography* (1956).
Leary, Lewis, ed., *Articles on American Literature 1900–1950* (1954).

Marshall, Thomas F., comp., *Analytical Index to American Literature, 1929–1949* (20 vols., 1954).
Patten, Nathan Van, *Index to Work of American and British Authors, 1923–1932* (1934).
Rubin, Louis D., Jr., ed., *Bibliographical Guide to the Study of Southern Literature* (1969).
Spiller, Robert E., et al., *Literary History of the United States.* Vol. II. (3d ed. rev., 1963).
Welch, D'Alté A., *Bibliography of American Children's Books Printed Prior to 1821* (1972).
Woodress, James, *Dissertations in American Literature, 1891–1961* (2nd ed., 1962).
Wright, Lyle H., *American Fiction. 1774–1875: A Contribution toward a Bibliography* (2nd rev. ed., 1969).

See also 10.3 for biographies/writings of:

AUTHORS

Aiken, Conrad, 1889–
Alcott, Louisa May, 1832–1888
Aldrich, Thomas Bailey, 1836–1907
Alger, Horatio, 1834–1899
Allen, James Lane, 1849–1925
Alsop, Richard, 1761–1815
Anderson, Sherwood, 1876–1941
Arp, Bill, See Charles H. Smith, 1826–1903
Austin, Mary, 1868–1934
Bacon, Delia S., 1811–1859
Barlow, Joel, 1754–1812
Bellow, Saul, 1915–
Benchley, Robert, 1889–1945
Benet, Stephen Vincent, 1898–1943
Bierce, Ambrose, 1842–1914
Bodenheim, Maxwell, 1893–1954
Boker, George H., 1823–1890
Brackenridge, Hugh H., 1748–1816
Bromfield, Louis, 1896–1956
Brown, Charles Brockden, 1771–1810
Bryant, William Cullen, 1794–1878
Buck, Pearl, 1892–
Buntline, Ned. See Edward Zane Carroll Judson, 1823–1886
Cabell, James Branch, 1879–1958
Cable, George W., 1844–1925
Cain, James M., 1892–
Caldwell, Erskine, 1903–
Cather, Willa, 1873–1947
Chapman, John Jay, 1862–1933
Chase, Mary Ellen, 1887–
Child, Lydia M., 1802–1880
Churchill, Winston, 1871–1947
Coffin, Robert Peter Tristram, 1892–1955
Cooper, James Fenimore, 1789–1851
Craddock, Charles E., See Mary N. Murfree, 1850–1922
Crane, [Harold] Hart, 1899–1932
Crane, Stephen, 1871–1900
Crawford, Francis M., 1854–1909
Cummings, E. E., 1894–1962
Dana, Richard Henry, Jr., 1815–1882
De Forest, John W., 1826–1906
Derby, George H., 1823–1861
Dickinson, Emily, 1830–1886

Dixon, Thomas, 1864–1946
Dos Passos, John, 1896–1970
Dreiser, Theodore, 1871–1945
Dunne, Finley Peter, 1867–1936
Eggleston, Edward, 1837–1902
Eliot, T. S., 1888–1965
Emerson, Ralph Waldo, 1803–1882
Faulkner, William, 1897–1962
Fessenden, Thomas G., 1771–1837
Fitzgerald, F. Scott, 1896–1940
Frank, Waldo D., 1889–1967
Frederic, Harold, 1856–1898
Freeman, Mary Wilkins, 1852–1930
Freneau, Philip, 1752–1832
Frost, Robert, 1874–1963
Gale, Zona, 1874–1938
Garland, Hamlin, 1860–1940
Gilder, Richard W., 1844–1909
Ginsberg, Allen, 1926–
Glasgow, Ellen, 1874–1945
Goodrich, Samuel G., 1793–1860
Hale, Edward Everett, 1822–1909
Harris, George Washington, 1814–1869
Harris, Joel Chandler, 1848–1908
Harrison, Constance Cary, 1843–1920
Harte, Francis Brett, 1836–1902
Hawthorne, Nathaniel, 1804–1864
Hearn, Lafcadio, 1850–1904
Hemingway, Ernest, 1899–1961
Henry, O., See William S. Porter, 1862–1910
Herrick, Robert, 1868–1938
Hersey, John, 1914–
Heyward, Dubose, 1885–1940
Holmes, Oliver Wendell, 1809–1894
Howells, William Dean, 1837–1920
Hubbard, Elbert G., 1856–1915
Humphreys, David, 1752–1818
Irving, Washington, 1783–1859
Jackson, Helen Hunt, 1830–1885
James, Henry, 1843–1916
Jarrell, Randall, 1914–1965
Jeffers, Robinson, 1887–1962
Jewett, Sarah Orne, 1849–1909
Johnson, Robert U., 1853–1937
Kennedy, John Pendleton, 1795–1870
Kilmer, Alfred Joyce, 1886–1918
King, Grace E., 1852–1932
Lanier, Sidney, 1842–1881
Larcom, Lucy, 1824–1893
Lardner, Ring, 1885–1933
Leland, Charles G., 1824–1903
Lewis, Sinclair, 1885–1951
Lindsay, N. Vachel, 1879–1931
Lodge, George Cabot, 1873–1909
London, Jack, 1876–1916
Longfellow, Henry Wadsworth, 1807–1882
Longstreet, Augustus B., 1790–1870
Lowell, Amy, 1874–1925
Lowell, James Russell, 1819–1891
McCarthy, Mary, 1912–
McCullers, Carson S., 1917–1967
McHenry, James, 1753–1816

MacLeish, Archibald, 1892–
Malamud, Bernard, 1914–
Marquand, John P., 1893–1960
Melville, Herman, 1819–1891
Michener, James A., 1907–
Millay, Edna St. Vincent, 1892–1950
Miller, Joaquin, See C. H. Miller, 1839–1913
Miller, Henry, 1891–
Mitchell, Silas W., 1829–1914
Monroe, Harriet, 1860–1936
Moody, William V., 1869–1910
Moore, Marianne, 1887–1972
More, Paul Elmer, 1864–1937
Morris, Wright, 1910–
Nathan, Robert, 1894–
Norris, Frank, 1870–1902
Nye, Edgar W., "Bill", 1850–1896
O'Hara, John, 1905–
O'Reilly, John Boyle, 1844–1890
Page, Thomas Nelson, 1853–1922
Paulding, James K., 1778–1860
Peabody, Josephine P., 1874–1922
Phillips, David Graham, 1867–1911
Pinkney, Edward C., 1802–1828
Poe, Edgar Allan, 1809–1849
Porter, Katherine Anne, 1894–
Porter, William T., 1809–1858
Ransom, John Crowe, 1888–
Rascoe, Burton, 1892–1957
Read, Opie, 1852–1939
Richter, Conrad, 1890–1971
Riley, James Whitcomb, 1849–1916
Roberts, Elizabeth Madox, 1886–1941
Robinson, Edwin Arlington, 1869–1935
Roethke, Theodore, 1908–1963
Rowson, Susanna H., 1762–1824
Salinger, J. D., 1919–
Saltus, Edgar, 1855–1920
Sandburg, Carl, 1878–1967
Saroyan, William, 1908–
Sigourney, Lydia Howard, 1791–1865
Sill, Edward R., 1841–1887
Simms, William Gilmore, 1806–1870
Sinclair, Upton, 1878–1971
Smith, Margaret B., 1778–1844
Spalding, Henry H., 1803–1874
Standish, Burt L., See Gilbert Patten, 1866–1945
Stedman, Edmund C., 1833–1908
Stein, Gertrude, 1874–1946
Steinbeck, John E., 1902–1968
Stevens, Wallace, 1879–1955
Stockton, Francis Richard, 1834–1902
Stoddard, Richard H., 1825–1903
Stowe, Harriet Beecher, 1811–1896
Stuart, Jesse, 1907–
Suckow, Ruth, 1892–1960
Tate, Allen, 1899–
Thaxter, Celia, 1835–1894
Thurber, James, 1894–1961
Timrod, Henry, 1828–1867
Tourgée, Albion W., 1838–1905
Trumbull, John, 1750–1831

Twain, Mark. See Samuel L. Clemens 1835–1910
Tyler, Royall, 1757–1826
Van Vechten, Carl, 1880–1964
Very, Jones, 1813–1880
Viereck, Peter, 1916–
Wallace, Lew, 1827–1905
Ward, Artemus, See Charles Farrar Browne, 1834–1867
Warner, Charles Dudley, 1829–1900
Warren, Robert Penn, 1905–
Welty, Eudora, 1909–
Wescott, Glenway, 1901–
West, Nathanael, 1902–1940
Wharton, Edith, 1862–1937
Whitman, Walt, 1819–1892
Whittier, John Greenleaf, 1807–1892
Wilder, Thornton, 1897–
Williams, William Carlos, 1883–1963
Wilson, Edmund, 1895–1972
Wister, Owen, 1860–1938
Wolfe, Thomas, 1900–1938
Woolson, Constance F., 1840–1894
Wylie, Elinor, 1885–1928

LITERARY CRITICS

Brooks, Van Wyck, 1886–1963
Eastman, Max, 1883–
Lewisohn, Ludwig, 1883–1955
Matthews, James Brander, 1852–1929
Mencken, H. L., 1880–1956
Sherman, Stuart P., 1881–1926
Wilson, Edmund, 1895–1972

26.2 NINETEENTH CENTURY

Howard, Leon, *Connecticut Wits* (1942).
Knight, Grant C., *Critical Period in American Literature* (1951). The 1890's.
Levin, Harry, *Power of Blackness* (1960). Melville, Poe, and Hawthorne.
Lewis, Richard W. B., *The American Adam: Innocence, Tragedy and Tradition in Nineteenth Century* (1955).
Matthiessen, Francis O., *American Renaissance* (1941).
Miller, Perry, *The Raven and the Whale: The Era of Poe and Melville* (1956).
Mumford, Lewis, *The Golden Day: Study in American Literature and Culture* (1926).
Rusk, Ralph L., *Literature of Middle Western Frontier* (1925).
Spiller, Robert E., *The American Literary Revolution, 1783–1837* (1967).
Walker, Franklin D., *San Francisco's Literary Frontier* (1939). Covers the period, 1848–1875
Walker, Robert H., "Poet and Robert Baron," *Am. Quar.*, 13 (1961), 447. Social justice in poetry.
Wilson, Edmund, *Patriotic Gore: Literature of American Civil War* (1962).
Ziff, Larzer, *The American 1890's: Life and Times of a Lost Generation* (1966).

26.3 TWENTIETH CENTURY

Aldridge, John W., *After Lost Generation: Writers of Two Wars* (1951).
Allen, Walter Ernest, *The Modern Novel in Britain and the United States* (1964).
Beach, J. W., *American Fiction, 1920–1940* (1941).
Blake, Nelson Manfred, *Novelists' America: Fiction as History, 1910–1940* (1969).

Bogan, Louise, *Achievement in American Poetry, 1900–1950* (1951).
Bradbury, John M., *Renaissance in the South: History of Literature, 1920–1960* (1963).
Brodbeck, May, et al., *American Non-Fiction, 1900–1950* (1952).
Brooks, Cleanth, *Modern Poetry* (1939).
Cowley, Malcolm, ed., *After the Genteel Tradition* (1937).
Cowley, Malcolm, *Exile's Return* (1934).
Hoffman, Frederick J., *The Modern Novel in America, 1900–1950* (1951).
―――― *The Twenties: American Writing* (1962).
Kazin, Alfred, *On Native Grounds* (1942).
Knight, Grant C., *Strenuous Age in American Literature, 1900–1910* (1954).
Matthiessen, F. O., "American Poetry, 1920–1940," *Sewanee Review*, 55 (1947), 24.
O'Connor, William V., *Age of Criticism, 1900–1950* (1952).
Ransom, John C., *New Criticism* (1941).
Rosenthal, Macha L., ed., *New Modern Poetry: British and American Poetry since World War II* (1967).
Rubin, Louis D., Jr., *Faraway Country: Writers of Modern South* (1963).
―――― and Robert D. Jacobs, eds., *South: Modern Literature* (1961).
―――― eds., *Southern Renascence: Literature of the Modern South* (1953).
Schneider, Robert W., *Five Novelists of the Progressive Era* (1965).
Stepanchev, Stephen, *American Poetry since 1945* (1965).
Stewart, John L., *Burden of Time: Fugitives and Agrarians* (1965). Southern writers.
Straumann, Heinrich, *American Literature in the Twentieth Century* (1951).
Tate, Allen, *Recent American Poetry and Criticism* (1943).
Thorp, W. Willard, *American Writing in the Twentieth Century* (1960).
West, Ray B., *The Short Story in America, 1900–1950* (1952).
Wilson, Edmund, *Axel's Castle* (1931).
―――― *Classics and Commercials* (1950).
―――― *Shores of Light* (1952).

26.4 GENRE AND THEMES

Aaron, Daniel, *Writers on the Left* (1961).
Blotner, Joseph L., *The Modern American Political Novel, 1900–1960* (1966).
Bretnor, Reginald, ed., *Modern Science Fiction* (1953).
Davis, David B., *Homicide in American Fiction, 1798–1860* (1957).
Feidelson, Charles N., Jr., *Symbolism and American Literature* (1953).
Fiedler, Leslie A., *Love and Death in the American Novel* (1966).
―――― *Return of the Vanishing American* (1968). The Indian.
Frohock, William M., *The Novel of Violence, 1920–1950* (1950).
Fussell, Edwin, *Frontier: American Literature and the West* (1965).
Gilbert, James B., *Writers and Partisans: Literary Radicalism* (1968).
Haycraft, Howard, *Murder for Pleasure: The Detective Story* (1941).
Hazard, Lucy L., *The Frontier in American Literature* (1927).
Herron, Ima H., *Small Town in Literature* (1939).
Hicks, Granville, et al., eds., *Proletarian Literature* (1935).
Hoffman, Frederick J., *Freudianism and Literary Mind* (1945).
Jones, Howard M., *Belief and Disbelief in American Literature* (1967).
―――― *The Frontier in American Fiction* (1956).
Karolides, Nicholas J., *The Pioneer in the American Novel, 1900–1950* (1967).
Lukacs, Georg, *The Historical Novel* (1962).
Madden, David, ed., *Proletarian Writers of the Thirties* (1968).
Malin, Irving, *Psychoanalysis and American Fiction* (1965).
Meyer, Roy W., *The Middle Western Farm Novel in Twentieth Century* (1965).
Milne, Gordon, *The American Political Novel* (1966).
Parrington, Vernon L., Jr., *American Dreams: Study of American Utopias* (1947).
Rideout, Walter B., *The Radical Novel in the United States, 1900–1954: Some Interpretations of Literature and Society* (1956).

Rourke, Constance M., *American Humor* (1931).

Trilling, Lionel, *Liberal Imagination* (1950).

Van Nostrand, Albert D., *Everyman His Own Poet: Romantic Gospels in American Literature* (1968).

West, Thomas R., *Flesh of Steel: Literature and Machine in American Culture* (1967).

Yates, Norris W., *The American Humorist: Conscience of the Twentieth Century* (1964).

26.5 POPULAR LITERATURE

Curti, Merle E., "Dime Novels," *Yale Rev.*, 26 (1937), 761.

Cutler, John L., *Patten and His Merriwell Saga* (1934).

Hackett, A. P., *Seventy Years of Best Sellers, 1895–1965* (1968).

Hart, James D., *The Popular Book: History of America's Literary Taste* (1950).

Mott, Frank L., *Golden Multitudes* (1947).

Pearson, Edmund L., *Dime Novels* (1929).

Waples, Douglas, *Reading Habits in the Depression* (1937).

See also 28.7, Popular Culture.

26.6 AMERICAN LANGUAGE

Bartlett, John, *Familiar Quotations* (14th ed., 1968).

Bohle, Bruce, *Home Book of American Quotations* (1967).

Craigie, William A., and J. R. Hulbert, *Dictionary of American English on Historical Principles* (4 vols., 1938–1944).

Evans, Bergen, and Cornelia Evans, *Dictionary of Contemporary American Usage* (1957).

Fishman, Joshua A., et al., *Language Loyalty: Maintenance of Non-English Mother Tongues* (1966).

Krapp, George P., *English Language in America* (2 vols., 1925).

Kurath, Hans, et al., *Handbook of Linguistic Geography of New England* (1939).

Marckwardt, Albert H., *American English* (1958).

Mathews, Mitford M., ed., *Dictionary of Americanisms on Historical Principles* (2 vols., 1951).

Mencken, Henry L., *American Language* (4th ed., 1936). Supplements 1-2 published 1945–1948. Abridged by Raven I. McDavid, Jr. (1963).

Partridge, Eric, *Dictionary of Cliches* (4th ed., 1950).

—— *Dictionary of Slang and Unconventional English* (1967).

—— *Dictionary of the Underworld: British and American* (rev. ed., 1961).

Pei, Mario A., *Words in Sheep's Clothing* (1969).

Safire, William L., *New Language of Politics: Anecdotal Dictionary* (1968).

Sperber, Hans, and Travis Trittschuh, *American Political Terms: Historical Dictionary* (1962).

Taylor, Archer, and Bartlett J. Whiting, *Dictionary of American Proverbs and Proverbial Phrases, 1820–1880* (1958).

Wentworth, Harold, and Stuart B. Flexner, *Dictionary of American Slang* (1960).

26.7 FOLKLORE

26.7.1 General

Beck, Earl C., *Lore of the Lumber Camps* (rev. ed., 1948).

Blair, Walter, and Franklin J. Meine, eds., *Half Horse, Half Alligator: Mike Fink Legend* (1956).

Botkin, Benjamin A., ed., *Sidewalks of America: Folklore of City Folk* (1954).
—— *Treasury of American Folklore* (1944).
—— and Alvin F. Harlow, eds., *Treasury of Railroad Folklore* (1953).
Brewer, J. Mason, ed., *American Negro Folklore* (1968).
Brunvand, Jan H., *Study of American Folklore* (1968).
Chappell, Louis W., *John Henry: A Folk-lore Study* (1933).
Clough, Benjamin C., ed., *American Imagination: Tall Tales and Folk Tales* (1947).
Coffin, Tristram P., *Analytical Index to Journal of American Folklore* (1958). Covers the period 1888–1957.
—— ed., *Our Living Tradition: Introduction to American Folklore* (1968).
Dobie, J. Frank, et al., *In the Shadow of History* (1966).
Dorson, Richard M., *American Folklore* (1959).
—— *Buying the Wind: Regional Folklore* (1964).
Glanz, Rudolph, *The Jew in Old American Folklore* (1961).
Hoffman, Daniel G., *Form and Fable in American Fiction* (1961).
Thompson, Stith, *Motif-Index of Folk Literature* (rev. ed., 6 vols., 1955–1958).
Vogt, Evon Z., and Ray Hyman, *Water Witching, U.S.A.* (1959).

* * * * * * *

Beckwith, Martha W., *Folklore in America: Its Scope and Method* (1931).
Davidson, Levette J., *Guide to American Folklore* (1951).
Dorson, Richard M., "Oral Tradition and Written History: The Case for the United States," *Jour. of Folklore Inst.* 1 (1965),220.
Haywood, Charles, *Bibliography of North American Folklore and Folk Song* (2 vols., 2nd ed., 1961).

See also 28.9.4, Ballads and Folk Music.

26.7.2 Northeast

Beck, Horace, *Folklore of Maine* (1957).
Botkin, Benjamin A., ed., *New York City Folklore* (1956).
—— *Treasury of New England Folklore* (1947).
Dorson, Richard M., *Jonathan Draws the Long Bow* (1946).
Gardner, Emelyn E., *Folklore from Schoharie Hills, New York* (1937).
Korson, George, *Black Rock: Mining Folklore of the Pennsylvania Dutch* (1960).
—— ed., *Pennsylvania Songs and Legends* (1949).
Thompson, Harold W., *Body, Boots & Britches: Folktales from New York* (1939).

26.7.3 South

Botkin, Benjamin A., ed., *Treasury of Southern Folklore* (1949).
Chase, Richard, ed., *The Jack Tales* (1943). North Carolina and Virginia.
Johnson, Guy B., *Folk Culture on St. Helena Island, South Carolina* (1930).
Masterson, James R., *Tall Tales of Arkansas* (1943).
Puckett, Newbell N., *Folk Beliefs of the Southern Negro* (1926).
Randolph, Vance, *Ozark Superstitions* (1947).
—— *We Always Lie to Strangers: Tall Tales from the Ozarks* (1951).
Roberts, Leonard W., ed., *South from Hell-fer-Sartin: Kentucky Mountain Folk Tales* (2nd ed., 1964).
White, Newman I., ed., *Frank C. Brown Collection of North Carolina Folklore* (4 vols., 1952–1957).

26.7.4 Midwest

Botkin, Benjamin A., ed., *Treasury of Mississippi River Foklore* (1955).
Carriere, Joseph M., ed., *Tales from French Folklore of Missouri* (1937).

Dorson, Richard M., *Bloodstoppers & Bearwalkers: Folk Traditions of the Upper Peninsula* (1952).
————— ed., *Negro Folktales in Michigan* (1956).
Gard, Robert E., and L. G. Sorden, eds., *Wisconsin Lore* (1962).
Hoffman, Daniel G., *Paul Bunyan* (1952).
Kramer, Frank R., *Voices in the Valley: Mythmaking in Middle West* (1964).
Pound, Louise, *Nebraska Folklore* (1959).
Sackett, Samuel J., and William E. Koch, eds., *Kansas Folklore* (1961).
Welsch, Roger L., ed., *Treasury of Nebraska Pioneer Folklore* (1966).

26.7.5 West

Boatright, Mody C., et al., eds., *Texas Folk and Folklore* (1954).
Botkin, Benjamin A., ed., *Treasury of Western Folklore* (1951).
Davidson, Levette J., and Forrester Blake, eds., *Rocky Mountain Tales* (1947).
De Pillis, Mario S., "Folklore and American West," *Ariz. and West,* 5 (1963), 291.
Dobie, J. Frank, *Coronado's Children* (1934).
————— *The Mustangs* (1952).
————— ed., *Tales of Old-Time Texas* (1955).
Espinosa, José M., *Spanish Folk-Tales from New Mexico* (1937).
Fife, Austin, and Alta Fife, *Saints of Sage and Saddle: Folklore among the Mormons* (1956).
Meine, Franklin J., *Tall Tales of the Southwest* (1930).

*   *   *   *   *   *   *

Tully, Marjorie F., and Juan B. Rael, *Annotated Bibliography of Spanish Folklore in New Mexico and Southern Colorado* (1950).

26.8 HUMOR

Bier, Jesse, *Rise and Fall of American Humor* (1968).
Blair, Walter, *Native American Humor, 1800–1900* (1937).
Boatright, Mody C., *Folk Laughter on American Frontier* (1949).
Lynn, Kenneth S., ed., *Comic Tradition in America* (1968).
Murrell, William, *History of American Graphic Humor* (2 vols., 1933–1938).
Rourke, Constance M., *American Humor* (1931).
Tandy, Jeannette R., *Crackerbox Philosophers in American Humor and Satire* (1925).
Yates, Norris W., *American Humorist: Conscience of the Twentieth Century* (1964).

27 Communication

27.1 NEWSPAPERS

27.1.1 General

Bagdikian, Ben H., "Grass-Roots Press," *Harpers Mag.*, 229 (1964), 102.
Chambers, Lenoir, et al., *Salt Water and Printer's Ink: Norfolk Newspapers, 1865–1965* (1967).
Clark, Thomas D., *The Southern Country Editor* (1948).
Ellison, Rhoda C., comp., *History and Bibliography of Alabama Newspapers in the Nineteenth Century* (1954).
Emery, Edwin, *History of the American Newspaper Association* (1950).
—————— *The Press and America: An Interpretive History of Journalism* (2nd ed., 1962).
Gramling, Oliver, *AP, the Story of News* (1940).
Griffith, Louis T., and John E. Talmadge, *Georgia Journalism, 1763–1950* (1951).
Hachten, William A., "Sunday Newspaper," *Journalism Quar.*, 38 (1961) 281. The period 1939–1959.
Hooper, Osman C., *History of Ohio Journalism, 1793–1933* (1933).
Johnson, Walter C., and Arthur T. Robb, *The South and Its Newspapers, 1903–1953* (1954).
Jones, Robert W., *Journalism in the United States* (1947).
Keller, Morton, *Art and Politics of Thomas Nast* (1968).
Kobre, Sidney J., *Development of American Journalism* (1969).
—————— *Modern American Journalism* (1959).
Lee, Alfred M., *The Daily Newspaper in America* (1937).
Mott, Frank L., *American Journalism: A History, 1690–1960* (3d ed., 1962).
—————— *The News in America* (1952).
Nevins, Allan, and Frank Weitenkampf, *A Century of Political Cartoons, 1800 to 1900* (1944).
Pollard, James E., *Presidents and Press* (1947).
Rosewater, Victor, *History of Cooperative News-Gathering in the United States* (1930).
Sim, John Cameron, *The Grass Roots Press: America's Community Newspapers* (1969).
Smith, David C., "Wood Pulp and Newspapers, 1867–1900," *Bus. Hist. Rev.*, 38 (1964), 328.
Tebbel, John, *Compact History of the American Newspaper* (rev. ed., 1969).
Turnbull, George S., *History of Oregon Newspapers* (1939).
Villard, Oswald G., *Disappearing Daily* (1944).
Vinson, John Chalmers, *Thomas Nast, Political Cartoonist* (1967).
Watson, Elmo S., *History of Newspaper Syndicates in the United States, 1865–1935* (1936).
Waugh, Coulton, *The Comics* (1947).
Weitenkampf, Frank, comp., *Political Caricature in United States in Cartoons* (1953).

*   *   *   *   *   *   *

Brigham, Clarence S., *History and Bibliography of American Newspapers, 1690–1820* (2 vols., 1947).

Ford, Edwin H., *Bibliography of Books and Annotated Articles on History of Journalism in the United States* (1939).

Gregory, Winifred, comp., *American Newspapers, 1821–1936* (1937).

McCoy, Ralph E., *Freedom of the Press: Annotated Bibliography* (1968).

Nevins, Allan, "American Journalism and Historical Treatment," *Journalism Quar.*, 36 (1959), 411.

Price, Warren C., *Literature of Journalism: Annotated Bibliography* (1959).

Wolseley, Roland E., *Journalist's Bookshelf: Annotated Bibliography of United States Journalism* (6th ed., 1955).

27.1.2 Individual Histories

Acheson, Sam, *35,000 Days in Texas: A History of the Dallas News and its Forbears* (1938).

Ames, William E., "Samuel H. Smith Founds 'National Intelligencer'," *Journalism Quar.*, 42 (1965), 389.

Andrews, J. C., *Pittsburgh's Post-Gazette* (1936). Founded as the *Pittsburgh Gazette*.

Ashton, Wendell, J., *Voice in the West: Biography of a Pioneer Newspaper* (1950). Salt Lake City's *Deseret News*.

Baehr, H. W., Jr., *The New York Tribune since the Civil War* (1936).

Bell, Earl L., and Kenneth C. Crabbe, *Augusta Chronicle: Voice of Dixie, 1785–1960* (1960).

Berger, Meyer, *The Story of the New York Times* (1951).

Chamberlin, Joseph E., *The Boston Transcript* (1930).

Christian, C. M., ed., *Two Hundred Years with the Maryland Gazette, 1727–1927* (1927).

Conrad, William C., Kathleen F. Wilson, and Dale Wilson, *Milwaukee Journal: Eighty Years* (1964).

Cortissoz, Royal, *The New York Tribune* (1923).

Dabney, T. E., *One Hundred Great Years* (1944). The *New Orleans Times-Picayune*.

Elliott, Robert N., Jr., *Raleigh Register, 1799–1863* (1955).

Fowler, Gene, *Timber Line: Story of Bonfils and Tammen* (1951). *Denver Post*.

Hooker, Richard, *The Story of an Independent Newspaper* (1924). The *Springfield Republican*.

Johnson, Gerald W., et al., *The Sunpapers of Baltimore* (1937).

Juergens, George, *Joseph Pulitzer and the New York World* (1966).

Kinsley, Philip, *The Chicago Tribune, Its First Hundred Years* (3 vols., 1943–1946).

Laney, Al, *Paris "Herald": The Incredible Newspaper* (1947).

Lyons, Louis M., *Newspaper Story: One Hundred Years of the Boston Globe* (1971).

Nevins, Allan, *The New York Evening Post* (1922).

O'Brien, Frank M., *The Story of the New York Sun* (rev. ed., 1928).

Perkin, Robert L., *First Hundred Years: History of Denver and Rocky Mountain News* (1959).

Rammelkamp, Julian S., *Pulitzer's Post Dispatch, 1878–1883* (1967). St. Louis Newspaper.

Ross, Margaret, *Arkansas Gazette, 1819–1866* (1969).

Sass, Herbert R., *Outspoken: 150 Years of the "News and Courier"* (1953). Charleston, S. C. newspaper.

Shaw, Archer H., *The Plain Dealer, One Hundred Years in Cleveland* (1942).

Smith, James Eugene, *One Hundred Years of Hartford's Courant* (1949). Covers the period to 1865.

Talese, Gay, *The Kingdom and the Power* (1969). The *New York Times*.

Tebbel, John W., *An American Dynasty* (1947). The *Chicago Tribune, New York Daily News*, and *Washington Times-Herald*.

27.1.3 Newspaper Profession

Daniels, Jonathan, *They Will Be Heard: America's Crusading Newspaper Editors* (1965).
Liebling, A. J., *Wayward Pressman* (1947).
Lyon, William H., *The Pioneer Editor in Missouri* (1965).
Ogilvie, William E., *Pioneer Agricultural Journalists* (1927).
Rosten, Leo C., *Washington Correspondents* (1937).
Stewart, Kenneth, and John Tebbel, *Makers of Modern Journalism* (1952).
Sutton, Albert A., *Education for Journalism in the United States to 1940* (1945).
Weisberger, Bernard A., *American Newspaperman* (1961).

See also 10.3 for biographies/writings of:

Abbott, Robert S., 1868–1940
Baker, Ray Stannard, 1870–1946
Ball, William W., 1868–1952
Bennett, James Gordon, 1795–1872
Bennett, James Gordon, Jr., 1841–1918
Bigelow, John, 1817–1911
Brown, Charles Brockden, 1771–1810
Bryant, William Cullen, 1794–1878
Brownlow, Louis, 1879–1963
Cash, Wilbur J., 1901–1941
Charles, Joseph, 1772–1834
Church, William C., 1836–1917
Collins, Isaac, 1746–1817
Cox, James M., 1870–1957
Creel, George, 1876–1953
Daggett, Rollin M., 1831–1901
Dana, Charles A., 1819–1897
Daniels, Josephus, 1862–1948
Davis, Elmer H., 1890–1958
Davis, Richard Harding, 1864–1916
Fessenden, Thomas G., 1771–1837
Frederic, Harold, 1856–1898
Freneau, Philip M., 1752–1832
Goddard, William, 1740–1817
Godkin, Edwin L., 1831–1902
Grady, Henry W., 1851–1889
Greeley, Horace, 1811–1872
Gurowski, Adam, 1805–1866
Hall, A. Oakey, 1826–1898
Hay, John M., 1838–1905
Hearst, William Randolph, 1863–1951
Heinzen, Karl, 1809–1880
Helper, Hinton R., 1829–1909
Holland, Josiah G., 1819–1881
Holt, Hamilton, 1872–1951
Hopkins, Stephen, 1707–1785
Hudson, William C., 1843–1915
Kendall, Amos, 1789–1869
Kendall, George W., 1809–1867
Leslie, Miriam F., ca. 1836–1914
List, George F., 1789–1846
Lovejoy, Elijah P., 1802–1837
McIntyre, O. O., 1884–1938
Mansfield, Edward D., 1801–1880
Marble, Manton M., 1834–1917
Mencken, H. L., 1880–1956

Mitchell, Edward Page, 1852–1927
Moley, Raymond, 1886–
Murrow, Edward R., 1908–1965
Nicolay, John G., 1832–1901
Noah, Mordecai M., 1785–1851
Older, Fremont, 1856–1935
O'Reilly, John Boyle, 1844–1890
Pearson, Drew, 1897–1969
Phillips, David Graham, 1867–1911
Pike, James S., 1811–1882
Poe, Clarence H., 1881–1964
Pulitzer, Joseph, 1847–1911
Ray, Charles H., 1821–1870
Raymond, Henry J., 1820–1869
Reed, John, 1887–1920
Reid, Whitelaw, 1837–1912
Riis, Jacob A., 1849–1914
Ritchie, Thomas, 1778–1854
Robinson, William S., 1818–1876
Ruthenberg, Charles E., 1882–1927
Scripps, Edward W., 1854–1926
Seward, Frederick W., 1830–1915
Shirer, William L., 1904–
Stanley, Henry M., 1841–1904
Steffens, Lincoln, 1866–1936
Stokes, Thomas L., Jr., 1898–1958
Stone, Melville E., 1848–1929
Storey, Wilbur F., 1819–1884
Sulzberger, Cyrus L., 1912–
Thomas, Isaiah, 1750–1831
Trotter, William M., 1872–1934
Tyler, Robert, 1816–1877
Villard, Henry, 1835–1900
Villard, Oswald Garrison, 1872–1949
Warner, Charles Dudley, 1829–1900
Watterson, Henry, 1840–1921
Weed, Thurlow, 1797–1882
White, William Allen, 1868–1944
Willis, Nathaniel P., 1806–1867

27.2 SPECIAL INTEREST PRESS

Anderson, Arlow W., *Emigrant Takes His Stand: Norwegian-American Press, 1847–1872* (1953).
Backlund, Jonas O., *Century of Swedish American Press* (1952).
Baumgarten, Apollinaris W., *Catholic Journalism. 1789–1930* (1931).
Capps, Finis H., *From Isolationism to Involvement: Swedish Immigrant Press, 1914–1945* (1966).
Demaree, A. L., *American Agricultural Press* (1941).
Forsyth, David P., *Business Press, 1750–1865* (1964).
Kolehmainen, John I., *Sow the Golden Seed* (1955). A Finnish language newspaper.
Noel, Mary, *Villains Galore: Popular Story Weekly* (1954).
Ogilvie, William E., *Pioneer Agricultural Journalists* (1927).
Park, Robert E., *Immigrant Press and Its Control* (1922).
Schlebecker, John T., and Andrew W. Hopkins, *History of Dairy Journalism in United States, 1810–1950* (1957).
Soltes, Mordecai, *The Yiddish Press, an Americanizing Agency* (1950).
Stewart, Donald, *Opposition Press of the Federalist Period* (1969).

Wallace, Wesley H., "North Carolina's Agricultural Journals, 1838–1861," *No. Car. Hist. Rev.,* 36 (1959), 275.
Wittke, Carl F., *The German Language Press in America* (1957).

See also 18.11.9, Agricultural Press.

27.3 MAGAZINES

Austin, James C., *Fields of the Atlantic Monthly: Letters to an Editor, 1861–1870* (1953).
Bainbridge, John, *Little Wonder: Reader's Digest* (1946).
Carver, Charles, *Brann and The Iconoclast* (1957).
Cline, H. F., "B. O. Flower and The Arena," *Journalism Quar.,* 17 (1940), 139.
Entrikin, Isabelle W., *Sarah Hale and Godey's Lady's Book* (1946).
Fairfield, R. P., "Flower," *Am. Lit.,* 22 (1950), 272.
Free, William J., *The* Columbian Magazine *and American Literary Nationalism* (1968).
Grimes, Allen P., *Political Liberalism of the New York* Nation, *1865–1932* (1953).
Hill, Ralph N., "Mr. Godey's Lady," *Am. Heritage,* 9 (1958), 20.
Hoffman, Frederick J., et al., *Little Magazine* (1946).
Howe, Mark A. De W., *Atlantic Monthly* (1919).
Joost, Nicholas, *Years of Transition,* The Dial, *1912–1920* (1967).
Lewis, Benjamin M., *Introduction to American Magazines, 1800–1810* (1961).
Luxon, Norval N., *Niles' Weekly Register* (1947).
Mott, Frank L., *A History of American Magazines* (5 vols., 1930–1968).
——— "Magazine Revolution and Popular Ideas in the Nineties," Am. Antiq. Soc., *Proc.,* 64 (1954), 195.
O'Neill, William L., ed., *Echoes of Revolt: The Masses, 1911–1917* (1966).
Peterson, Theodore, *Magazines in the Twentieth Century* (2nd ed., 1964).
Semonche, John E., "The *American Magazine* of 1906–15: Principles vs. Profit," *Journalism Quar.,* 40 (1963), 36.
Singleton, Marvin K., *H. L. Mencken and "American Mercury" Adventure* (1962).
Smith, James Steel, "America's Magazine Missionaries of Culture," *Journalism Quar.,* 43 (1966), 449.
Stewart, Paul R., *"The Prairie Schooner" Story: Magazine's First 25 Years* (1955).

See also 10.3 for biographies/writings of:

Abbott, Lyman, 1835–1922
Barnard, Henry, 1811–1900
Barron, Clarence W., 1855–1928
Bok, Edward W., 1863–1930
Butler, Burridge D., 1868–1948
Capper, Arthur, 1865–1951
Carey, Mathew, 1760–1839
Cousins, Norman, 1912–
De Bow, J. D. B., 1820–1867
De Voto, Bernard A., 1897–1955
Fields, James T., 1817–1881
Godkin, Edward L., 1831–1902
Hale, Sarah, 1788–1879
Holland, Josiah G., 1819–1881
Howells, William Dean, 1837–1920
Johnson, Robert U., 1853–1937
La Farge, John, Jr., 1880–1963
Luce, Henry R., 1898–1967
McClure, Samuel Sidney, 1857–1949
MacFadden, Bernarr, 1868–1955
Mencken, Henry L., 1880–1956
Monroe, Harriet, 1860–1936

Munsey, Frank A., 1854–1925
Page, Walter Hines, 1855–1918
Poor, Henry Varnum, 1812–1905?
Straight, Willard D., 1880–1918
Tooker, Lewis F., 1855–1925
Villard, Oswald Garrison, 1872–1949
Wallace, Henry, 1836–1916
Wallace, Henry A., 1888–1965
Wallace, Henry C., 1866–1924
Youmans, Edward L., 1821–1887

27.4 BOOK PUBLISHING

"The American Reading Public," *Daedalus,* 92 (1963), 3.
Ballou, Ellen B., *The Building of the House: Houghton Mifflin's Formative Years* (1970).
Berger, Abraham, et al., eds., *Joshua Bloch Memorial Volume: Booklore* (1960).
Boynton, Henry W., *Annals of American Bookselling, 1638–1850* (1932).
Burlingame, Roger, *Of Making Many Books: A Hundred Years* (1946). Charles Scribner's Sons.
Charvat, William, *Literary Publishing, 1790–1850* (1959).
Doran, G. H., *Chronicles of Barabbas* (1935).
Dozer, D. M., "Tariff on Books," *MVHR,* 36 (1949), 73.
Exman, Eugene, *House of Harper* (1967).
Greenslet, Ferris, *Under the Bridge* (1943).
Guinzburg, Harold K., et al., *Books and the Mass Market* (1953).
Hackett, Alice P., *Seventy Years of Best Sellers* (rev. ed., 1968).
Hamilton, Sinclair, *Early American Book Illustrators and Wood Engravers, 1670–1870: Catalogue* (2 vols., 1958–1968).
Harper, Joseph H., *House of Harper* (1912).
Hawes, Gene R., *To Advance Knowledge: University Publishing* (1967).
Kaser, David, ed., *Books in America's Past: Essays Honoring Rudolph H. Gjelsness* (1966).
Kaser, David, *Messrs. Carey & Lea of Philadelphia: History of the Booktrade* (1957).
Lehmann-Haupt, Hellmut, *The Book in America* (rev. ed., 1951).
—— ed., *Bookbinding in America: Three Essays* (1941).
Lewis, Freeman, *Paper-Bound Books in America* (1952).
Madison, Charles A., *Book Publishing in America* (1966).
Miller, William, *Book Industry* (1949).
Randall, David A., *Dukedom Large Enough* (1969).
Schmeckebier, Lawrence F., *The Government Printing Office: Its History* (1925).
Sheehan, Donald, *This Was Publishing: Book Trade in Gilded Age* (1952).
Shove, R. H., *Cheap Book Production* (1937).
Stern, Madeleine B., *Imprints on History: Book Publishers and American Frontiers* (1956).
Stokes, Frederick A., *Publisher's Random Notes* (1935).
Sutton, Walter, *Western Book Trade: Cincinnati, 1796–1880* (1961).
Wiley and Sons Inc., *The First One Hundred and Fifty Years, 1807–1957* (1957).

See also 10.3 for biographies/writings of:

Fields, James T., 1817–1881
Holt, Henry, 1840–1926
Lea, Henry C., 1825–1909
Putnam, George H., 1844–1930
Putnam, George P., 1814–1872

See also 26.5, Popular Literature.

27.5 COPYRIGHT

Bugbee, Bruce W., *Genesis of American Patent and Copyright Law* (1967).
Clark, Aubert J., *Movement for International Copyright in Nineteenth-Century America* (1960).
Goldstein, Paul, "Copyright and the First Amendment," *Columbia Law Rev.*, 70 (1970), 983.
Ladas, Stephen P., *International Protection of Literary Artistic Property* (1938).
Patterson, Lyman R., *Copyright in Historical Perspective* (1968).
Shaw, Ralph R., *Literary Property* (1950).
"Symposium on Copyright and Patent Law in Honor of Walter Julius Derenberg," *N.Y.U. Law Rev.*, 44 (1969), 447.

* * * * * * *

Derenberg, Walter J., "Recent Publications in the Field of Copyright, Trademarks and Unfair Competition," *Am. Jour. Comparative Law*, 17 (1969), 297.

27.6 PRINTING

Gress, Edmund G., *Fashions in American Typography, 1780 to 1830* (1931).
Hamilton, Milton W., *Country Printer* (1936).
Kainen, Jacob, *George Clymer and Columbian Press* (1950).
McMurtrie, Douglas C., *History of Printing in the United States* (4 vols., 1936).
Oswald, J. C., *Printing in the Americas* (1937).
Seidensticker, Oswald, *First Century of German Printing in America, 1728–1830* (1893).
Silver, Rollo G., *American Printer, 1787–1825* (1967).
——— *Typefounding in America, 1787–1825* (1965).
Winship, George P., *Daniel Berkeley Updike and the Merrymount Press of Boston* (1947).
Wroth, Lawrence C., *Typographic Heritage: Essays* (1949).

27.7 LIBRARIES

Abbot, George M., *A Short History of the Library Company of Philadelphia* (1913).
American Library Association, *American Library Pioneers* (8 vols., 1924–1953).
Angle, Paul M., *Library of Congress: An Account Historical and Descriptive* (1958).
Barker, T. D., *Libraries of the South: A Report on Developments, 1900–1935* (1936).
Berelson, Bernard, *The Library's Public* (1949).
Brodman, Estelle, "The Special Library: Mirror of its Society," *Jour. Lib. Hist.*, 1 (1966), 108.
Clemons, Harry, *The University of Virginia Library, 1825–1950* (1954).
Compton, Charles H., *Twenty-five Crucial Years of the St. Louis Public Library, 1927–1952* (1953).
Ditzion, Sidney Herbert, *Arsenals of a Democratic Culture; A Social History of the American Public Library Movement in New England and Middle States* (1947). Covers the period 1850–1900.
Gray, Austin K., *Benjamin Franklins's Library: A Short Account of the Library Company of Philadelphia, 1731–1931* (1937).
Green, S. S., *Public Library Movement in the United States, 1853–1893* (1913).
John Crerar Library, *The John Crerar Library 1895–1944: An Historical Report* (1945).
Lee, Robert E., *Continuing Education for Adults through the American Public Library, 1833–1964* (1966).

Leigh, Robert D., *The Public Library* (1950).

McMullen, Haynes, "Use of Books in the Ohio Valley Before 1850," *Jour. Lib. Hist.*, 1 (1966), 43.

Marshall, John D., *American Library History Reader* (1961).

Mearns, David C., *The Story up to Now: The Library of Congress, 1800–1946* (1947).

Potter, Alfred C., *The Library of Harvard University* (1934).

Robinson, Charles F., and Robin Robinson, "Three Early Massachusetts Libraries," Col. Soc. Mass., *Trans.*, 28 (1930), 107.

Shera, Jesse H., *Foundations of the Public Library: Origins of the Public Library Movement in New England 1629–1855* (1949).

Shores, Louis, *Origins of the American College Library 1638–1800* (1934).

Spencer, Gwladys, *The Chicago Public Library* (1943).

Thompson, C. Seymour, *Evolution of American Public Library, 1653–1876* (1952).

Whitehill, Walter M., *The Boston Public Library: A Centennial History* (1956).

Williamson, William L., *William Frederick Poole and the Modern Library Movement* (1963).

Wroth, Lawrence C., *First Century of the John Carter Brown Library: A History with a Guide to Its Collections* (1946).

*   *   *   *   *   *   *

Harris, Michael H., *Guide to Research in American Library History* (1968).

27.8 RADIO AND TELEVISION

27.8.1 General

Archer, G. L., *Big Business and Radio* (1939).

Barnouw, Erik, *History of Broadcasting in the United States* (3 vols., 1966–1971).

Bluem, A. William, et al., *Television in the Public Interest* (1961).

Bogart, Leo, *Age of Television* (1958).

Cantril, Hadley, and Gordon W. Allport, *Psychology of Radio* (1935).

Friendly, Fred, *Due to Circumstances beyond Our Control* (1967). Television news policy.

Head, Sydney, *Broadcasting in America* (1956).

Lazarsfeld, P. F., *People Look at Radio* (1946).

—— *Radio and the Printed Page* (1940).

—— and Frank N. Stanton, eds., *Radio Research* (1941).

MacNeil, Robert, *People Machine: Influence of Television on American Politics* (1958).

Minow, Newton N., *Equal Time: Private Broadcasters and Public Interest*, L. Laurent, ed. (1964).

Parker, Everett C., et al., *Television-Radio Audience and Religion* (1955).

Schiller, Herbert I., *Mass Communications and American Empire* (1969).

Settel, Irving, *Pictorial History of Radio* (1967).

Siepmann, Charles A., *Radio, Television and Society* (1950).

Skornia, Harry J., *Television and Society* (1965).

Summers, Robert E., and H. B. Summers, *Broadcasting and the Public* (1966).

27.8.2 Government Regulation

Edelman, Jacob M., *Licensing of Radio Services in the United States* (1950).

Emery, Walter B., *Broadcasting and Government: Responsibilities and Regulation* (1961).

Friedenthal, Jack H., and Richard J. Medalie, "Impact of Federal Regulation on Political Broadcasting," *Harv. Law Rev.*, 72 (1959), 445.

Herring, James M., and Gerald C. Gross, *Telecommunications: Economics and Regulation* (1936).

Robinson, Thomas P., *Radio Networks and Federal Government* (1943).

Schmeckebier, Lawrence F., *Federal Radio Commission* (1932).

Stern, Robert H., "Regulatory Influences upon Television's Development," *Am. Jour. Econ. Sociol.*, 22 (1963), 347.

U.S. Federal Communications Commission, *Public Service Responsibility of Broadcast Licensees* (1946).

28 The Arts

28.1 GENERAL

Berman, Eleanor D., *Jefferson among the Arts* (1947).
Boas, George, "Rediscovery of America," *Am. Quar.,* 7 (1955), 142.
Cowdrey, Mary B., ed., *American Academy of Fine Arts and American Art-Union, 1816–1852* (2 vols., 1953).
Dickson, Harold E., *Arts of the Young Republic: The Age of William Dunlap* (1968).
Jackman, Rilla E., *American Arts* (1928).
Garrett, Wendell D., et al., *Arts in America: The Nineteenth Century* (1969).
Keppel, F. P., and R. L. Duffus, *Arts in American Life* (1933).
Kostelanetz, Richard, ed., *New American Arts* (1965).
Kouwenhoven, John A., *The Arts in Modern American Civilization* (1948).
Larkin, Oliver W., *Art and Life in America* (rev. ed., 1960).
McLanathan, Richard, *American Tradition in the Arts* (1968).
Miller, James E., Jr., and Paul D. Herring, eds., *Arts and the Public* (1967).
Mumford, Lewis, *Brown Decades: Arts in America, 1865–1895* (2nd ed., 1955).
O'Connor, William V., ed., *History of the Arts in Minnesota* (1958).
Seldes, Gilbert, *The Seven Lively Arts* (1924).
Stein, Roger B., *John Ruskin and Aesthetic Thought in America, 1840–1900* (1967).

* * * * * * *

Garrett, Wendell D., and Jane Garrett, "Bibliography," in Walter M. Whitehill et al., *Arts in Early American History: Opportunities for Study* (1965).

28.2 PAINTING AND SCULPTURE

28.2.1 General

Adams, Adeline, *Spirit of American Sculpture* (1923).
Art in America, *The Artist in America* (1967).
Barker, Virgil, *American Painting* (1950).
Bizardel, Yvon, *American Painters in Paris,* Richard Howard, trans. (1960).
Born, Wolfgang, *American Landscape Painting* (1948).
—— *Still-life Painting in America* (1947).
Brewington, Marion V., and Dorothy Brewington, *Marine Paintings and Drawings in the Peabody Museum* (1968).
Burroughs, Alan, *Limners and Likenesses* (1936).
Cahill, Holger, and A. H. Barr, Jr., *Art in America* (1935).
Clark, Eliot, *History of National Academy of Design, 1825–1953* (1954).
Craven, Wayne, *Sculpture in America* (1968).
Eliot, Alexander, *Three Hundred Years of America Painting* (1957).

Gardner, Albert T., *American Sculpture* (1964).
Gerdts, William H., *Painting and Sculpture in New Jersey* (1964).
Goodrich, Lloyd, *Three Centuries of American Art* (1967).
Green, Samuel M., *American Art* (1966).
Hartman, Sadakichi, *History of American Art* (rev. ed., 2 vols., 1932).
Isham, Samuel, *American Painting* (rev. ed., 1968).
Klitgaard, Kaj, *Through the American Landscape* (1941).
LaFollette, Suzanne, *Art in America* (1929).
Larkin, Oliver W., *Art and Life in America* (rev. ed., 1960).
McCoubrey, John W., *American Tradition in Painting* (1963).
McSpadden, J. W., *Famous Sculptors* (1927).
Mather, F. J., et al., *The American Spirit in Art* (1927).
Mendelowitz, Daniel M., *History of American Art* (1960).
Monro, Isabel S., and Kate M. Monro, *Index to Reproductions of American Paintings* (1948). *First Supplement* (1964).
Myron, Robert, and Abner Sundell, *Art in America from Colonial Days through the Nineteenth Century* (1969).
Neuhaus, Eugen, *History and Ideals of American Art* (1931).
Pearce, John, *American Painting: 1560–1913* (1964).
Richardson, Edgar P., *Painting in America: From 1502 to the Present* (1965).
Rutledge, Anna W., *Artists in Life of Charleston* (1949).
Saint-Gaudens, Homer, *The American Artist and His Times* (1941).
Taft, Lorado, *The History of American Sculpture* (new ed., 1930).
Tillim, Sidney, "Culture in a Democracy: Painting," *Arts Mag.,* 39, no. 7 (1965), 36.
Ulanov, Barry, *Two Worlds of American Art: Private and Public* (1965).
Walker, John, and Macgill James, eds., *Great American Paintings from Smibert to Bellows, 1729–1924* (1943).
Wilmerding, John, *History of American Marine Painting* (1963).

* * * * * * *

Chamberlin, Mary W., *Guide to Art Reference Books* (1959).
Lancour, Harold, comp., *American Art Auction Catalogues, 1785–1942* (1944).
McCoubrey, John W., *American Art, 1700–1960: Sources* (1965).

28.2.2 Collective Biography

Cirker, Hayward, and Blanche Cirker et al., eds., *Dictionary of American Portraits* (1967).
Cortissoz, Royal, *American Artists* (1923).
Cummings, Paul, *Dictionary of Contemporary Artists* (1966).
Fielding, Mantle, *Dictionary of American Painters, Sculptors, and Engravers* (1965).
New York Historical Society, *Dictionary of Artists in America, 1564–1860,* George C. Groce and David H. Wallace, eds. (1957).
Peat, Wilbur D., *Pioneer Painters of Indiana* (1954).
Smith, Ralph C., *Biographical Index of American Artists* (1930).
Stauffer, David M., *American Engravers on Copper and Steel* (1907).
Taft, Robert, *Artists and Illustrators of Old West, 1850–1900* (1953).
Thorp, Margaret F., *Literary Sculptors* (1965).

See also 10.3 for biographies/writings of:

PAINTERS

Allston, Washington, 1779–1843
Ames, Ezra, 1768–1836
Bellows, George W., 1882–1925
Benton, Thomas Hart, 1889–
Biddle, George, 1885–

Bingham, George Caleb, 1811–1879
Cassatt, Mary, 1845–1926
Catlin, George, 1796–1872
Cole, Thomas, 1801–1848
Copley, John Singleton, 1738–1815
Curry, John Steuart, 1897–1946
De Kooning, Willem, 1904–
Duveneck, Frank, 1848–1919
Eakins, Thomas, 1844–1916
Earle, Ralph, 1751–1801
Eastman, Seth, 1808–1875
Feke, Robert, ca. 1705–ca. 1750
Fisher, Jonathan, 1768–1847
Glackens, William, 1870–1938
Healy, George P., 1813–1894
Henri, Robert, 1865–1929
Hicks, Edward, 1780–1849
Homer, Winslow, 1836–1910
Hopper, Edward, 1882–1967
Hunt, William Morris, 1824–1879
Inness, George, 1825–1894
Jackson, John B., 1701–1780?
Jarvis, John W., 1781–1839
Jennys, Richard, fl. 1760–1790
Johnson, Eastman, 1824–1906
Keith, William, 1839–1911
Kern, Edward M., 1823–1863
La Farge, John, 1835–1910
Lane, Fitz Hugh, 1804–1865
Levine, Jack, 1915–
Louis, Morris, 1912–1962
Luks, George, 1867–1933
Malbone, Edward G., 1777–1807
Moran, Thomas, 1837–1926
Morse, Samuel F. B., 1791–1872
Mount, William S., 1807–1868
Page, William, 1811–1885
Peale, Charles Willson , 1741–1827
Peale, Titian R., 1799–1885
Pollock, Jackson, 1912–1956
Porter, Rufus, 1792–1884
Remington, Frederick, 1861–1909
Ryder, Albert Pinkham, 1847–1917
Sargent, John Singer, 1856–1925
Shahn, Ben, 1898–
Sheeler, Charles, 1883–
Sloan, John, 1871–1951
Smibert, John, 1688–1751
Stella, Frank, 1936–
Stella, Joseph, 1880–1946
Strother, David H., 1816–1888
Stuart, Gilbert, 1755–1828
Sully, Thomas, 1783–1872
Tanner, Henry O., 1859–1937
Thayer, Abbot H., 1849–1921
Theus, Jeremiah, 1719–1774
Thorpe, Thomas B., 1815–1878
Tiffany, Louis C., 1848–1933
Trumbull, John, 1756–1843
Vanderlyn, John, 1775–1852
Waugh, Frederick J., 1861–1940
Weir, Julian A., 1852–1919

West, Benjamin, 1738–1820
Whistler, James McNeill, 1834–1903
Wood, Grant, 1892–1942
Wyeth, Andrew, 1917–

SCULPTORS

Calder, Alexander, 1898–
Crawford, Thomas, 1813–1857
French, Daniel Chester, 1850–1931
Greenough, Horatio, 1805–1852
Milles, Carl, 1875–1955
Noguchi, Isamu, 1904–
Rinehart, William H., 1825–1874
Rogers, John, 1829–1904
Saint-Gaudens, Augustus, 1848–1907
Story, William W., 1819–1895
Taft, Lorado, 1860–1936

28.2.3 Nineteenth Century

Callow, James T., *Kindred Spirits: Knickerbocker Writers and Artists, 1807–1855* (1967).

Demos, John, "George Caleb Bingham: Artist as Social Historian," *Am. Quar.,* 17 (1965), 218.

Dickason, David H., *Daring Young Men: American Pre-Raphaelites* (1953).

Dodd, Loring H., *Golden Moments of American Sculpture* (1936).

Flexner, James T., *American Painting: Light of Distant Skies, 1760–1835* (1954).

―――― *That Wilder Image: Painting of America's Native School from Thomas Cole to Winslow Homer* (1962).

Frankenstein, Alfred V., *After the Hunt: William Harnett and Other Still Life Painters, 1870–1900* (rev. ed., 1969).

Gardner, Albert T. E., *Yankee Stone-cutters: American Sculpture, 1800–1850* (1945).

Greenough, Horatio, *Travels, Observations, and Experience of a Yankee Stonecutter* (1852).

Harris, Neil, *Artist in American Society, 1790–1860* (1966).

Miller, Lillian B., "Paintings, Sculpture, and the National Character, 1815–1860," *JAH,* 53 (1967), 696.

New York Metropolitan Museum of Art, *Nineteenth Century America: Paintings and Sculpture* (1970).

Novak, Barbara, *American Painting of the Nineteenth Century* (1969).

Pinckney, Pauline A., *Painting in Texas: Nineteenth Century* (1967).

Prown, Jules D., *American Painting: From Its Beginnings to the Armory Show* (1969).

Sears, Clara E., *Highlights among Hudson River Artists* (1947).

Thorp, Margaret F., *Literary Sculptors* (1965).

―――― "White, Marmorean Flock," *NEQ,* 32 (1959), 147.

Weyle, Harry B., and Theodore Bolton, *American Miniatures, 1730–1850* (1927).

Wyckoff, Alexander, *Art and Artists in America, 1735–1835* (1966).

28.2.4 Twentieth Century

"The Armory Show, 1913" *Art in America,* 51, no. 1 (1963), 30.

Art Criticism in the Sixties (1967). Symposium at Brandeis University.

Battock, Gregory, ed., *Minimal Art* (1968).

Baur, John I. H., et al., eds., *New Art in America* (1957).

Baur, John I. H., *Revolution and Tradition in Modern American Art* (1951).

Blesh, Rudi, *Modern Art U.S.A., 1900–1956* (1956).

Boswell, Peyton, Jr., *Modern American Painting* (1940).

Breeskin, Adelyn, *Roots of Abstract Art in America, 1910–1930* (1965).

Brown, Milton W., *American Painting from the Armory Show to the Depression* (1955).

Brummé, C. Ludwig, *Contemporary American Sculpture* (1948).

Cheney, Martha, *Modern Art* (1939).

Finch, Christopher, *Pop Art* (1968).

Fite, Gilbert C., *Mount Rushmore* (1952).

Geldzahler, Henry, *American Painting in the Twentieth Century* (1965).

Goldwater, Robert, "Reflections on New York School," *Quadrum*, 8 (1960) 17.

Goodrich, Lloyd, and John I. H. Baur, *American Art of Our Century* (1961).

Goodrich, Lloyd, *Pioneers of Modern Art in America, 1910–1920* (1963).

Hess, Thomas B., *Abstract Painting* (1951).

Hunter, Sam, *Modern American Painting and Sculpture* (1959).

Kampf, Avram, *Contemporary Synagogue Art, 1945–1965* (1966).

Kepes, Gyorgy, ed., *The Visual Arts Today* (1960).

Kibel, Alvin C., "'Tradition' and New Art," *Am. Scholar*, 34 (1965), 413.

Kootz, Samuel M., *Modern American Painters* (1930).

—— *New Frontiers of American Painting* (1943).

Kwiat, Joseph J., "John Sloan: American Artist as Social Critic, 1900–17," *Ariz. Quar.*, 10 (1954), 52.

Mellquist, Jerome, *Emergence of American Art* (1942).

O'Conner, Francis, "New Deal Murals in New York," *Art Forum*, 7 (1968), 41.

Pearson, Ralph M., *Modern Renaissance in American Art* (1954).

Pousette-Dart, Nathaniel, ed., *American Painting Today* (1956).

Reed, Walt, ed., *Illustrator in America, 1900–1960's* (1966).

Ritchie, Andrew C., *Abstract Painting and Sculpture in America* (1951).

Rose, Barbara, *American Art since 1900* (1967).

—— *American Painting: Twentieth Century* (1969).

—— comp., *Readings in American Art since 1900* (1968).

Rosenberg, Bernard, and Norris E. Fliegel, "Vanguard Artist in New York," *Social Research*, 32 (1965), 141.

Rublowsky, John, *Pop Art* (1965).

Russell, John, and Suzi Gablik, *Pop Art Redefined* (1969).

Schnier, Jacques P., *Sculpture in Modern America* (1948).

Schroeder, Fred, "Andrew Wyeth and Transcendental Tradition," *Am. Quar.*, 17 (1965), 559.

Sloan, John, *Gist of Art* (1939).

Three American Painters: Noland, Olitski, Stella (1965). Harvard's Fogg Art Museum exhibition catalog.

Tuchman, Maurice, *American Sculpture in the Sixties* (1967).

Weller, Allen S., *Joys and Sorrows of Recent American Art* (1968).

Wheeler, Monroe, ed., *Painters and Sculptors of Modern America* (1942).

28.3 PRINTMAKING AND GRAPHICS

Goodrich, Lloyd, *Graphic Art of Winslow Homer* (1969).

Hamilton, Sinclair, *Early American Book Illustrators and Wood Engravers, 1670–1870: Catalogue of Collection of American Books in Princeton University Library* (2 vols., 1958–1968).

Lewis, Benjamin M., *Guide to Engravings in American Magazines, 1741–1810* (1959).

Museum of Graphic Art, *American Printmaking: The First 150 Years* (1969).

Peters, Harry T., *America on Stone* (1931). Lithography.

—— *Currier and Ives: Printmakers to the American People* (2 vols., 1925–1931).

Pitz, Henry C., "N. C. Wyeth," *Am. Heritage*, 16 (1965), 36.

Zigrosser, Carl, *Artist in America: Contemporary Printmakers* (1942).

See also 10.3 for biographies/writings of:

Abbey, Edwin Austin, 1852–1911

Buell, Abel, 1741/42–1822

Currier, Nathaniel, 1813–1888
Durand, Asher B., 1796–1886
Duveneck, Frank, 1848–1919
Ives, James M., 1824–1895
Jackson, John B., 1701–1780?
Pennell, Joseph, 1857–1926
Pyle, Howard, 1853–1911
Revere, Paul, 1735–1818
Sartain, John, 1808–1897

28.4 DECORATIVE ARTS AND HOME FURNISHINGS

28.4.1 General

American Heritage, *American Heritage History of Colonial Antiques,* Marshall B. Davidson, ed. (1967).
Brazer, Esther S., *Early American Decoration* (2nd ed., 1947).
Butler, Joseph T., *American Antiques, 1800–1900* (1965).
Chapman, Suzanne E., *Early American Design Motifs* (1952).
Christensen, Erwin O., *Index of American Design* (1950).
Comstock, Helen, ed., *Concise Encyclopedia of American Antiques* (2 vols., 1958).
Fleming, E. McClung, "Early American Decorative Arts as Social Documents," *MVHR* 45 (1958), 276.
Gould, Mary E., *Early American Wooden Ware and Kitchen Utensils* (1962).
Gowans, Alan, *Images of American Living: Four Centuries of Architecture and Furniture as Cultural Expression* (1964).
Hayward, Arthur H., *Colonial Lighting* (rev. ed., 1927).
Hornung, Clarence P., *Source Book of Antiques and Jewelry Designs* (1968).
Kauffman, Henry J., *Pennsylvania Dutch American Folk Art* (1946).
Langdon, William C., *Everyday Things in American Life.* 2 vols., (1937–1941).
Lipman, Jean, and Mary C. Black, *American Folk Decoration* (1967).
Lipman, Jean, "Rufus Porter, Yankee Wall Painter," *Art in America,* 38 (1950), 135.
Little, Nina F., *American Decorative Wall Painting, 1700–1850* (1952).
Lord, Priscilla, S., and Daniel J. Foley, *Folk Arts and Crafts of New England* (1965).
McClelland, Nancy V., *Furnishing the Colonial and Federal House* (1947).
McClintock, Inez, and Marshall McClintock, *Toys in America* (1961).
McClinton, Catherine (Morrison), *The Complete Book of American Country Antiques* (1967).
Montgomery, Charles F., ed., *America's Arts and Skills* (1957).
New York Metropolitan Museum of Art, *Nineteenth Century America: Furniture and Other Decorative Arts* (1970).
Ramsey, Natalie A., ed., *Decorator Digest: Early American Decoration* (1964).
Rogers, Meyric R., *American Interior Design: Colonial Times to the Present* (1947).
Van Wagenen, Jared, Jr., *Golden Age of Homespun* (1953).
Waring, Janet, *Early American Stencils on Walls and Furniture* (1937).
Yates, Raymond F., and Marguerite W. Yates, *Guide to Victorian Antiques* (1949).

28.4.2 Ceramics and Glassware

Barber, Edwin A., *Pottery and Porcelain of the United States* (2nd ed., 1901).
Clement, Arthur W., *Notes on American Ceramics, 1607–1943* (1944).
Comstock, Helen, *Looking Glass in America, 1700–1825* (1968).
Knittle, Rhea M., *Early American Glass* (1927).
Lee, Ruth W., *Sandwich Glass* (rev. ed., 1966).
McKearin, George S., and Helen McKearin, *American Glass* (1948).

McKearin, Helen, "American Glass—Stiegel to Steuben," *Art in America,* 44 (Spring 1956), 46.

McKearin, Helen, and George S. McKearin, *Two Hundred Years of American Blown Glass* (1950).

Mudge, Jean M., *Chinese Export Porcelain for American Trade, 1785–1835* (1963).

Ramsay, John, *American Potters and Pottery* (1939).

Revi, Albert C., *American Pressed Glass and Figure Bottles* (1964).

Spargo, John, *Early American Pottery and China* (1926).

Stiles, Helen E., *Pottery in United States* (1941).

Thistlethwaite, Frank, "Atlantic Migration of the Pottery Industry," *Econ. Hist. Rev.,* 11 (1958), 264.

Tiffany, Louis C., *Art Work* (1914).

Watkins, Lura W., *American Glass and Glassmaking* (1950).

——— *Early New England Potters* (1950).

Wilson, Kenneth M., *Glass in New England* (1959).

28.4.3 Furniture and Clocks

Andrews, Edward D., and Faith Andrews, *Shaker Furniture* (1937).

Bjerkoe, Ethel Hall, *The Cabinetmakers of America* (1957).

Bulkeley, Houghton, *Contributions to Connecticut Cabinet Making* (1967).

Comstock, Helen, *American Furniture, Seventeenth, Eighteenth, and Nineteenth Century Styles* (1962).

Cornelius, Charles O., *Early American Furniture* (1926).

Downs, Joseph, *American Furniture: Queen Anne and Chippendale Periods* (1952).

Drepperd, Carl W., *American Clocks and Clockmakers* (2nd ed., 1958).

——— *Handbook of Antique Chairs* (1948).

Eckhardt, George H., *Pennsylvania Clocks and Clockmakers* (1955).

Gamon, Albert T., *Pennsylvania Country Antiques* (1968).

Kovel, Ralph M., *American Country Furniture 1780–1875* (1965).

Lea, Zella Rider, ed., *Ornamental Chair, 1700–1890* (1960).

Margon, Lester, *Masterpieces of American Furniture* (1964).

Miller, Edgar G., *American Antique Furniture* (2 vols., 1937).

Montgomery, Charles F., *American Furniture: Federal Period in the Winterthur Museum* (1966).

Nagel, Charles, *American Furniture, 1650–1850* (1949).

Ormsbee, Thomas H., *Early American Furniture Makers* (1930).

——— *Field Guide to American Victorian Furniture* (1952).

Palmer, Brooks, *Book of American Clocks* (1950).

28.4.4 METALWARE

Avery, Clara L., *Early American Silver* (1930). *Supplement* (1968).

Buhler, Kathryn C., *American Silver* (1950).

Cutten, George B., *Silversmiths of Virginia from 1694–1850* (1952).

De Voe, Shirley S., *Tinsmiths of Connecticut* (1968).

Goyne, Nancy A., "Britannia in America: The Introduction of a New Alloy and a New Industry," *Winterthur Portfolio,* 2 (1965), 160.

Kauffman, Henry, *Early American Copper, Tin, and Brass* (1950).

——— *Early American Ironware* (1966).

Laughlin, Ledlie I., *Pewter in America* (2 vols., 1940).

Phillips, John M., *American Silver* (1949).

Powers, Beatrice F., and Olive Floyd, *Early American Decorated Tinware* (1957).

Sonn, Albert H., *Early American Wrought Iron* (3 vols., 1928).

28.4.5 Textiles

Bendure, Zelma, and Gladys Pfeiffer, *America's Fabrics* (1946).

Bolton, Ethel S., and Eva J. Coe, *American Samplers* (1921).

Fennelly, Catherine, *Textiles in New England, 1790–1840* (1961).
Harbeson, Georgiana B., *American Needlework: From the Late 16th to the 20th Century* (1939).
Little, Frances, *Early American Textiles* (1931).
Parslow, Virginia D., *Weaving and Dyeing in Early New York* (1949).
Reath, Nancy A., *Weaves of Hand-Loom Fabrics* (1927).
Vanderpoel, Emily N., *American Lace & Lace-Makers,* Elizabeth C. B. Buel, ed. (1924).

28.5 FOLK ART

Andrews, Edward D., and Faith Andrews, *Visions of the Heavenly Sphere: Shaker Religious Art* (1969).
Black, Mary, and Jean Lipman, *American Folk Painting* (1966).
Brewington, Marion V., *Shipcarvers of North America* (1962).
Cahill, Holger, ed., *American Folk Art, 1790–1900* (1932).
Carrick, Alice V., *A History of American Silhouettes, 1790–1840* (1968). First published in 1928 as *Shades of Our Ancestors.*
Christensen, Erwin O., *Early American Wood Carving* (1952).
Janis, Sidney, *They Taught Themselves: American Primitive Painters of the Twentieth Century* (1942).
Kauffman, Henry J., *Pennsylvania Dutch American Folk Art* (1946).
Lipman, Jean, *American Folk Art in Wood, Metal and Stone* (1948).
———— *American Primitive Painting* (1942).
———— and Alice Winchester, *Primitive Painters in America 1750–1950: An Anthology* (1950).
Ludwig, Allan I., *Graven Images: New England Stonecarving, 1650–1815* (1966).
Miller, Lewis, *Sketches and Chronicles,* Robert P. Turner, ed. (1968). Pennsylvania primitive painter, covering years 1799–1870.
Pinckney, Pauline A., *American Figureheads and Their Carvers* (1940).
Polley, Robert L., ed., *America's Folk Art* (1968).
Sears, Clara E., *Some American Primitives: New England Portraits* (1941).

28.6 ART PATRONAGE AND COLLECTIONS

Art in Federal Buildings (1936).
Behrman, Samuel N., *Duveen* (1952).
Billington, Ray A., "W.P.A. Experience," *Am. Quar.,* 13 (1961), 466.
Cahill, Holger, *Art as a Function of Government* (1937).
Constable, W. G., *Art Collecting in the United States* (1964).
Eells, Richard, *The Corporation and the Arts* (1967).
Fox, Daniel M., *Engines of Culture: Philanthropy and Art Museums* (1963).
Jarves, James J., *The Art-Idea* (1864); Benjamin Rowland, Jr., ed. (1960).
Katz, Herbert and Marjorie Katz, *Museums, U.S.A.* (1965).
La Follette, Suzanne, "American Art: Economic Aspects," *Am. Mag. Art,* 28 (1935), 337.
Lerman, Leo, *The Museum: One Hundred Years and the Metropolitan Museum of Art* (1969).
McDonald, William F., *Federal Relief Administration and the Arts* (1969).
Miller, Lillian B., *Patrons and Patriotism: Fine Arts in the United States, 1790–1860* (1966).
Official Museum Directory: United States, Canada (1970).
Overmyer, Grace, *Government and Arts* (1939).
Purcell, Ralph, *Government and Art* (1956).
Reid, Benjamin L., *Man from New York: John Quinn* (1968).
Reitlinger, Gerald, *Economics of Taste, 1750–1960* (1964).
Saarinen, Aline B., *Proud Possessors: American Art Collectors* (1958).
Tomkins, Calvin, *Merchants and Masterpieces: Metropolitan Museum of Art* (1970).

Towner, Wesley, and Stephen Varble, *Elegant Auctioneers* (1970).
Whitehill, Walter M., *Museum of Fine Arts, Boston: A Centennial History* (2 vols., 1970).
Wittke, Carl, *First Fifty Years: Cleveland Museum of Art, 1916–1966* (1966).

28.7 POPULAR CULTURE

Bode, Carl, *Anatomy of American Popular Culture, 1840–1861* (1959).
Denny, Reuel, *Astonished Muse* (1957).
Ehrlich, George, "Chautauqua 1880–1900: Education in Art History and Appreciation," *Art Bull.*, 38 (1956), 175.
Harrison, Harry P., and Karl Detzer, *Culture under Canvas: Tent Chautauqua* (1958).
Jacobs, Norman, et al., "Mass Culture and Mass Media," *Daedalus, 89* (1960), 273.
Lynes, Russell, *Art-Makers of Nineteenth Century America* (1970).
——— *The Tastemakers* (1954).
Macdonald, Dwight, *Against the American Grain: Essays on the Effects of Mass Culture* (1962).
McLuhan, Marshall, *Understanding Media* (1964).
Mendelsohn, Harold, *Mass Entertainment* (1966).
Nye, Russel B., *Unembarrassed Muse: Popular Arts in America* (1970).
Rosenberg, Bernard, and David M. White, eds., *Mass Culture: Popular Arts in America* (1957).
Ross, Ishbel, *Taste in America: An Illustrated History* (1967).
Seldes, Gilbert, *Public Arts* (1956).
Toffler, Alvin, *Culture Consumers: Art and Affluence in America* (1964).
Wallace, David H., *John Rogers: People's Sculptor* (1967).

See also 26.5, Popular Literature; 28.5, Folk Art; 28.9.4, Ballads and Folk Music; 28.9.5, Popular Music; 28.9.6, Jazz and Blues; 28.10.4, Musical Theater.

28.8 ARCHITECTURE

28.8.1 General

Andrews, Wayne, *Architecture, Ambition and Americans* (1955).
Avery Memorial Architectural Library [Columbia], *Index to Architectural Periodicals* (12 vols., 1963). Supp. (1967).
Burchard, John, and Albert Bush-Brown, *Architecture of America* (1961).
Coles, William A., and Henry H. Reed, Jr., eds., *Architecture in America* (1961).
Dorsey, Stephen P., *Early English Churches in America, 1607–1807* (1952).
Dunlap, William, *History of the Arts of Design* (1834); F. W. Bayley and C. E. Goodspeed, eds. (3 vols., 1918).
Gowans, Alan, *Images of American Living: Four Centuries of Architecture and Furniture* (1964).
Hamlin, Talbot F., *The American Spirit in Architecture* (1926).
Hitchcock, Henry-Russell, *Architecture* (1958).
Kaufman, Edgar, Jr., ed., *Rise of an American Architecture* (1970).
Kelly, J. Frederick, *Early Connecticut Meetinghouses* (2 vols., 1948).
Kervick, Francis W., *Architects in America of Catholic Tradition* (1962).
Kimball, Sidney Fiske, *American Architecture* (1928).
Klauder, Charles, *College Architecture in America* (1929).
Lancaster, Clay, *Architectural Follies in America* (1960).
McCallum, Ian, *Architecture U.S.A.,* (1959).
Meeks, Carroll L. V., *The Railroad Station: Architectural History* (1956).
Mumford, Lewis, *Sticks and Stones* (2nd ed., 1955).
Rogers, Meyric R., *American Interior Design: Colonial Times to the Present* (1947).

Saylor, Henry H., *A.I.A.'s First Hundred Years* (1957).
Shoemaker, Alfred L., ed., *Pennsylvania Barn* (1955).
Sinnott, Edmund W., *Meetinghouse and Church in Early New England* (1963).
Sloane, Eric: *American Barns and Covered Bridges* (1954).
Tallmadge, T. E., *The Story of Architecture in America* (rev. ed., 1936).
Weslager, C. A., *Log Cabin in America* (1969).
Whiffen, Marcus, *Architecture since 1780: Styles* (1969).
Wischnitzer, Rahel, *Synagogue Architecture in the United States* (1955).

*   *   *   *   *   *   *

American Association of Architectural Bibliographers, *Index of Drawings before 1900* (1957).
Harvard Graduate School of Design, *Catalog* (44 vols., 1968). *Supplement* (2 vols., 1970).
Historic American Buildings Survey, *Catalog of the Measured Drawings and Photographs of the Survey in the Library of Congress* (1941). *Supplement* (1959).
Hitchcock, Henry R., *Architectural Books* (1946).
O'Neal, William B., ed., *Papers of American Association of Architectural Bibliographers* (6 vols., 1965–1969).
Roos, Frank J., Jr., *Bibliography of Early American Architecture* (rev. ed., 1968).
⸺ *Writings on Early American Architecture, before 1860* (1943).
Wall, Alexander J., *Books on Architecture Printed in America, 1775–1830* (1925).
Wood, Charles B., III, "A Survey and Bibliography of Writings on English and American Architectural Books Published Before 1895," in *Winterthur Portfolio* II, 1965, 127.

28.8.2 Nineteenth Century

Downing, Andrew J., *Cottage Residences, Rural Architecture and Landscape Gardening* (4th ed., 1852).
Early, James, *Romanticism and American Architecture* (1965).
Gifford, Don, ed., *Literature of Architecture* (1966).
Hamlin, Talbot F., *Greek Revival Architecture* (1944).
Hersey, George L., "Godey's Choice," *Jour. Society Archit. Historians,* 18 (1959), 104.
Kimball, Sidney Fiske, *Domestic Architecture of the American Colonies and Early Republic* (1922).
Major, Howard, *Domestic Architecture of Early American Republic: The Greek Revival* (1926).
Meeks, Carroll L. V., "Picturesque Eclecticism," *Art Bull.,* 32 (1950), 226.
⸺ "Romanesque before Richardson in United States," *Art Bull.,* 35 (1953), 17.
Myers, Denys P., "Architectural Development of Western Floating Palace," *Jour. Society Archit. Historians,* 11 (1952), 25.
Newcomb, Rexford, *Spanish-Colonial Architecture in the United States* (1937).
Omoto, Sadayoshi, "Queen Anne Style," *Jour. Society Architectural Historians,* 23 (1964), 29.
Resseguie, Harry E., "A. T. Stewart's Marble Palace: Department Store," *N. Y. Hist. Soc. Quar.,* 48 (1964), 131.
Schmidt, Carl F., *Cobblestone Architecture* (1944).
⸺ *Greek Revival Architecture in Rochester Area* (1946).
⸺ "Octagon Fad," *Jour. Am. Instit. Archit.,* 33, no. 3 (1960), 42.
Scully, Vincent J., Jr., "Romantic Rationalism and Expression of Structure in Wood, 1840–1876," *Art Bull.,* 35 (1953), 121.
⸺ *Shingle Style: Architectural Theory and Design from Richardson to Wright* (1955).
Sexton, Randolph W., *Spanish Influence on American Architecture and Decoration* (1927).
Stanton, Phoebe B., *Gothic Revival & American Church Architecture, 1840–1856* (1968).

Tselos, Dimitri, "Chicago Fair and Myth of 'Lost Cause'," *Jour. Society Archit. Historians,* 26 (1967), 259.

28.8.3 Twentieth Century

Architectural Forum, *Building U.S.A.: Architecture* (1957).
Casteels, Maurice, *The New Style: Its First Phase in Europe and America* (1931).
Cheney, Sheldon, *New World Architecture* (1930).
Collins, George R., and Adolf K. Placzek, eds., "Modern Architecture, 1929–1939," *Jour. Soc. Archit. Historians,* 24 (1965), 1.
Condit, Carl W., *Rise of Skyscraper* (1952).
Ford, James, and K. M. Ford, *Modern House in America* (1940).
Hitchcock, Henry-Russell, and Philip Johnson, *Inter-International Style: Architecture since 1922* (1932).
Holland, Laurence B., ed., *Who Designs America?* (1966).
Kampf, Avram, *Contemporary Synagogue Art, 1945–1965* (1966).
Lancaster, Clay, "American Bungalow," *Art. Bull.,* 40 (1958), 239.
Mock, Elizabeth, ed., *Built in USA, 1932–1944* (1944).
Robsjohn-Gibbings, Terence H., *Homes of the Brave* (1954).
Scully, Vincent J., Jr., *American Architecture and Urbanism* (1969).
—— *Modern Architecture* (1961).
Tunnard, Christopher, and Boris Pushkarev, *Man-Made America* (1963).

28.8.4 Regional Histories

28.8.4.1 New England
Boston Society of Architects, *Boston Architecture* (1970).
Bunting, Bainbridge, *Houses of Boston's Back Bay, 1840–1917* (1967).
Cady, John H., *Civic and Architectural Development of Providence, 1636–1950* (1957).
Cambridge Historical Commission, *Survey of Architectural History in Cambridge* (2 vols., 1965–1968).
Connally, Ernest A., "Cape Cod House," *Jour. Society Archit. Historians,* 19 (1960), 47.
Downing, Antoinette F., and Vincent J. Scully Jr., *Architectural Heritage of Newport, Rhode Island, 1640–1915* (2nd ed., 1967).
Goody, Marvin E., and Robert P. Walsh, eds., *Boston Society of Architects, 1867–1967* (1967).
Halsey, Richart T. H., and Elizabeth Tower, *Homes of our Ancestors* (1935).
Kilham, Walter H., *Boston after Bulfinch: Architecture, 1800–1900* (1946).
Kirker, Harold, and James Kirker, *Bulfinch's Boston, 1787–1817* (1964).

28.8.4.2 Middle Atlantic States
Ames, Kenneth, "Robert Mills and Philadelphia Row House," *Jour. Society Archit. Historians,* 27 (1968), 140.
Andrews, Wayne, *Architecture in New York: A Photographic History* (1969).
Burnham, Alan, *New York Landmarks* (1963).
Dickson, Harold E., *A Hundred Pennsylvania Buildings* (1954).
Gowans, Alan, *Architecture in New Jersey* (1964).
Huxtable, Ada L., *Classic New York* (1964).
Jackson, Huson, *New York Architecture, 1650–1952* (1952).
Massey, James C., ed., *Two Centuries of Philadelphia Architectural Drawings,* (1964).
Stotz, Charles M., *Architectural Heritage of Early Western Pennsylvania, before 1860* (2nd ed., 1966).
Tatum, George B., *Penn's Great Town, 250 Years of Philadelphia Architecture Illustrated in Prints and Drawings* (1961).
Weisman, Winston, "Commercial Palaces of New York, 1845–1875," *Art Bull.,* 36 (1954), 285.

White, Theophilus B., ed., *Philadelphia Architecture in the Nineteenth Century* (1953).

28.8.4.3 South

Alexander, Drury B., and Todd Webb, *Texas Homes of the 19th Century* (1966).

American Institute of Architects, *Guide to Architecture in New Orleans, 1699–1959* (1959).

Eberlein, Harold D., and C. V. D. Hubbard, *Historic Houses of Georgetown and Washington City* (1958).

Forman, Henry C., *Architecture of the Old South: 1585–1850* (1948).

—— *Maryland Architecture: 1634 through the Civil War* (1968).

Hammond, Ralph, *Ante-Bellum Manions of Alabama* (1951).

Howland, Richard H., and Eleanor P. Spencer, *Architecture of Baltimore* (1953).

Lewis, Hunter, "Capitol Hill's Ugliness Club," *Atlantic,* 219 (1967), 60.

Manucy, Albert, *Houses of St. Augustine (Architecture from 1565 to 1821)* (1962).

Newcomb, Rexford, *Architecture in Old Kentucky* (1953).

Overdyke, W. Darrell, *Louisiana Planatation Homes: Colonial and Ante Bellum* (1965).

Radoff, Morris L., *Buildings of State of Maryland at Annapolis* (1954).

Ravenel, Beatrice St. J., *Architects of Charleston* (1945).

Reps, John W., *Monumental Washington* (1967).

Smith, Joseph F., *White Pillars: Life and Architecture of Lower Mississippi Valley Country* (1941).

Waugh, Edward, and Elizabeth Waugh, *South Builds, New Architecture in Old South* (1960).

28.8.4.4 Middle West

Andrews, Wayne, *Architecture in Chicago and Mid-America: Photographic History* (1968).

—— *Architecture in Michigan: Photographic Survey* (1967).

Drury, John, *Historic Midwest Houses* (1947).

Hoffmann, Donald, "John Root's Monadnock Building," *Jour. Society Archit, Historians,* 26 (1967), 269.

Kennedy, Roger, "Some Distant Vision, Harvey Ellis and the Flowering of Midwestern Architecture," *Am. West,* 5 (1968), 16.

Koeper, Frederick, *Illinois Architecture; from Territorial Times to the Present* (1968).

Newcomb, Rexford, *Architecture of Old Northwest Territory* (1950).

Peat, Wilbur D., *Indiana Houses of the Nineteenth Century* (1962).

Perrin, Richard W. E., *Architecture of Wisconsin* (1967).

Siegel, Arthur, *Chicago's Famous Buildings: Photographic Guide* (2nd ed., 1965).

Tallmadge, Thomas E., *Architecture in Old Chicago* (1940).

Torbert, Donald R., *Century of Minnesota Architecture* (1958).

28.8.4.5 West

Baer, Kurt, *Architecture of the California Missions* (1958).

Baird, Joseph A., Jr., *Time's Wondrous Changes: San Francisco Architecture, 1776–1915* (1962).

Bangs, Edward G., *Portals West: Folio of Late Nineteenth Century Architecture in California* (1960).

Gebhard, David, and Robert Winter, *Guide to Architecture in Southern California* (1965).

Gebhard, David, "Spanish Colonial Revival in Southern California (1895–1930)," *Jour. Society Archit. Historians,* 26 (1967), 131.

Kirker, Harold, *California's Architectural Frontier in the Nineteenth Century* (1960).

Kubler, George, *Religious Architecture of New Mexico* (1940).

Sanford, Trent E., *Architecture of the Southwest* (1950).

Steinbrueck, Victor, *Seattle Cityscape* (1962).

Stubblebine, Jo, ed., *Northwest Architecture of Pietro Belluschi* (1953).

28.8.5 Architects and Schools of Architecture

Bastlund, Knud, *Jose Luis Sert* (1967).
Bayer, Herbert, and Walter and Ise Gropius, eds., *Bauhaus 1919–1928* (1938).
Blake, Peter, *Master Builders: Le Corbusier, Mies van der Rohe, Frank Lloyd Wright* (1960).
Condit, Carl W., *Chicago School of Architecture, 1875–1925* (1964).
Cram, Ralph A., *Work of Cram and Ferguson, Architects* (1929).
Eaton, Leonard K., *Two Chicago Architects and Their Clients; Frank Lloyd Wright and Howard Van Doren Shaw* (1969).
Elstein, Rochelle S., "Architecture of Dankmar Adler," *Jour. Society Archit. Historians*, 26 (1967), 242.
Fitch, James Marston, "Architects of Democracy: Jefferson and Wright," in *Architecture and the Esthetics of Plenty* (1961).
Frary, Ihna T., *Thomas Jefferson, Architect* (1931).
Gropius, Walter, *Scope of Total Architecture* (1955).
Hines, Thomas S., Jr., "Frank Lloyd Wright—Madison Years," *Jour. Society Archit. Historians,* 26 (1967), 227.
Jordy, William H., "Aftermath of Bauhaus in America," in Donald Fleming and Bernard Bailyn, eds., *The Intellectual Migration: Europe and America, 1930–1960* (1968).
Kennedy, Roger G., "Daniel H. Burnham: Tycoon of Western Architecture," *Am. West,* 5 (1968), 4.
Kervick, Francis W., *Architects in America of Catholic Tradition* (1962).
Kirker, Harold, *Architecture of Charles Bulfinch* (1969).
Landy, Jacob, *The Architecture of Minard Lafever* (1970).
Newton, Roger H., *Town and Davis, Architects* (1942).
Nichols, Frederick D., comp., *Thomas Jefferson's Architectural Drawings* (2nd ed., 1961).
Peisch, Mark L., *Chicago School of Architecture* (1965).
Root, John Wellborn, *Meaning of Architecture: Buildings and Writings,* Donald Hoffmann, ed. (1970).
Saarinen, Eero, *Buildings dating from 1947 to 1964,* Aline B. Saarinen, ed. (1962).
Schuyler, Montgomery, *American Architecture and Other Writings,* William H. Jordy and Ralph Coe, eds. (2 vols., 1961).
Schwab, Gerhard, *Architecture of Paul Rudolph* (1970).
Van Brunt, Henry, *Architecture and Society: Selected Essays,* William A. Coles, ed. (1969).
Venturi, Robert, *Complexity and Contradiction in Architecture* (1966).
Withey, Henry F. and Elsie R. Withey, *Biographical Dictionary of American Architects* (1956).
Wright, Frank Lloyd, *Genius and Mobocracy* (1949).
―――― *Modern Architecture* (1931).
―――― *On Architecture, 1894–1910,* Frederick Gutheim, ed. (1941).
―――― *When Democracy Builds* (1945).

See also 10.3 for biographies/writings of:

Buckland, William 1734–1774
Bulfinch, Charles, 1763–1844
Burnham, Daniel H., 1846–1912
Cram, Ralph A., 1863–1942
Fuller, Richard Buckminster, 1895–
Goodhue, Bertram G., 1869–1924
Gropius, Walter, 1883–1969
Harrison, Peter, 1716–1775
Johnson, Philip C., 1906–
Kahn, Louis I., 1901–
Latrobe, Benjamin H., 1764–1820
McIntire, Samuel, 1757–1811
McKim, Charles F., 1847–1909
McMurtry, John, 1812–1890

Mendelsohn, Eric, 1887–1953
Mies Van Der Rohe, Ludwig, 1886–1969
Mills, Robert, 1781–1855
Neutra, Richard, 1892–1970
Richardson, Henry H., 1838–1886
Root, John W., 1850–1891
Saarinen, Eero, 1910–1961
Saarinen, Eliel, 1873–1950
Starrett, Paul, 1866–1957
Strickland, William, 1787–1854
Sullivan, Louis H., 1856–1924
Tinsley, William, 1804–1885
Upjohn, Richard, 1802–1878
Van Brunt, Henry, 1832–1903
White, Stanford, 1853–1906
Wright, Frank Lloyd, 1869–1959

28.8.6 Landscape Architecture

Cleveland, Horace W., *Landscape Architecture as Applied to Wants of West* (1873); Roy Lubove, ed. (1965).
Dober, Richard P., *Campus Planning* (1964).
Olmsted, Frederick L., *Forty Years of Landscape Architecture: Professional Papers,* Frederick L. Olmsted, Jr., and Theodora Kimball, eds. (1928).
Simonds, John O., *Landscape Architecture* (1961).

See also 10.3 for biographies/writings of:

Eliot, Charles, 1859–1897
Jensen, Jens, 1860–1951
Olmsted, Frederick Law, 1822–1903

See also 19.3.6, Urban History–City Planning.

28.8.7 Construction

Bannister, Turpin C., "Iron Fronts," *Jour. Society Archit. Historians,* 15 (1956), 12.
———— "Iron Towers," *Jour. Society Archit. Historians,* 16 (1957), 11.
Behrendt, W. C., *Modern Building* (1937).
Collins, George R., "Transfer of Thin Masonry Vaulting from Spain to America," *Jour. Society Archit. Historians,* 27 (1968), 176.
Condit, Carl W., *American Building: Materials and Techniques* (1968).
———— *American Building Art: Nineteenth Century* (1960).
Dadger, D. D., and James Bogardus, *Origins of Iron Architecture in America* (2nd ed., 1968).
Edwards, Llewellyn N., *Record of History and Evolution of Early American Bridges* (1959).
Fitch, James M., *American Building* (2nd ed., 1966).
Hitchcock, Henry-Russell, *In Nature of Materials: Buildings of Frank Lloyd Wright* (1942).
Kniffen, Fred, "Building in Wood in Eastern United States," *Geog. Rev.,* 56 (1966), 40.
Peterson, Charles E., "Early American Prefabrication," *Gazette des Beaux-Arts,* 6 ser., 33 (1948), 37.
Raafat, Aly A., *Reinforced Concrete* (1958).
Steinman, David B., and Sara R. Watson, *Bridges and Their Builders* (1941).
Trachtenberg, Alan, *Brooklyn Bridge* (1965).
Tyrrell, H. G., *History of Bridge Engineering* (1911).

Wachsmann, Konrad, *Turning Point of Building* (1961).
Webster, J. Carson, "Skyscraper," *Jour. Society Archit. Historians,* 18 (1959), 126.
Weisman, Winston, "New York and First Skyscraper," *Jour. Society Archit. Historians,* 12 (1953), 13.

See also 10.3 for biographies/writings of:

BRIDGE BUILDERS

Eads, James B., 1820–1887
Roebling, John A., 1806–1869
Roebling, Washington A., 1837–1926

28.9 MUSIC

28.9.1 General

Ayars, Christine M., *Contributions to the Art of Music in America by Music Industries of Boston, 1640–1936* (1937).
Barzun, Jacques, *Music in American Life* (1956).
Carpenter, Paul S., *Music: Art and Business* (1950).
Chase, Gilbert, ed., *The American Composer Speaks: Historical Anthology, 1770–1965* (1966).
—— *America's Music* (2nd rev. ed., 1966).
Copland, Aaron, *Our New Music* (1941).
Cowell, Henry, ed., *American Composers on American Music* (1933).
Downes, Olin, *Olin Downes on Music: A Selection from Writings, 1906–1955* (1957).
Franko, Richard, *The Wind Band* (1961).
Howard, John T., *Our American Music from 1620 to the Present* (4th ed., 1965).
Lang, Paul H., ed., *One Hundred Years of Music in America* (1961).
Leiter, Robert D., *Musicians and Petrillo* (1953).
Lowens, Irving, *Music and Musicians in Early America* (1964).
Marrocco, W. Thomas, and Harold Gleason, *Music in America: 1620–1865* (1964).
Mattfeld, Julius, *Variety Music Cavalcade, 1620–1961* (1962).
Mellers, Wilfred, *Music in a New Found Land* (1965).
Miller, Thomas W., "Influence of Progressivism on Music Education, 1917–1947," *Jour. Research in Music Educ.,* 14 (1966), 3.
Reis, Claire R., *Composers, Conductors and Critics* (1955).
Sablosky, Irving L., *American Music* (1969).
Schickel, Richard, *World of Carnegie Hall* (1960).
Swan, Howard, *Music in the Southwest, 1825–1950* (1952).
Thomson, Virgil, "America's Musical Maturity," *Yale Rev.,* 51 (1961), 66.
—— "Music in the 1950's," *Harpers Mag.,* 221 (1960), 59.
Woodworth, G. Wallace, *World of Music* (1964).
Zanzig, Augustus D., *Music in American Life, Present and Future* (1932).

*   *   *   *   *   *   *

Duckles, Vincent H., *Music Reference and Research Materials: Bibliography* (2nd ed. 1967).
Historical Records Survey. District of Columbia, *Bio-Bibliographical Index of Musicians in the United States since Colonial Times* (2nd ed., 1956).
Sonneck, Oscar G., *Bibliography of American Secular Music,* William T. Upton, ed. (1945).
Philadelphia Library Company, *American Song Sheets, Slip Ballads, and Poetical Broadsides, 1850–1870: Collection of Library Company of Philadelphia,* by Edwin Wolf II, (1963).

28.9.2 Composers

Ewen, David, *American Composers Today: Biographical and Critical Guide* (1949).
Howard, John T., *Our Contemporary Composers* (1941).
Hughes, Rupert, *Contemporary American Composers* (1900).
Leonard, Neil, "Edward MacDowell and the Realists," *Am. Quar.*, 18 (1966), 175.

*   *   *   *   *   *   *

Edmunds, John, and Gordon Boelzner, *Some Twentieth Century American Composers: Selective Bibliography* (2 vols., 1959–1960).

See also 10.3 for biographies/writings of:

Barber, Samuel, 1910–
Berlin, Irving, 1888–
Copland, Aaron, 1900–
Foster, Stephen, 1826–1864
Fry, William H., 1815–1864
Gershwin, George, 1898–1937
Guthrie, Woodrow W., 1912–1967
Herbert, Victor, 1859–1924
Hopkinson, Joseph, 1770–1842
Ives, Charles, 1874–1954
MacDowell, Edward, 1861–1908
Nevin, Ethelbert, 1862–1901
Parker, Horatio, 1863-1919
Schuman, William H., 1910–
Thompson, Virgil, 1896–

28.9.3 Symphony Orchestras

Erskine, John, *Philharmonic-Symphony Society of New York: First Hundred Years* (1943).
Howe, Mark A. DeW., *Boston Symphony Orchestra* (1931).
Johnson, H. Earle, *Symphony Hall, Boston* (1950).
Kupferberg, Herbert, *Those Fabulous Philadelphians: Life and Times of a Great Orchestra* (1969).
Mueller, John H., *The American Symphony Orchestra* (1951).
Otis, P. A., *Chicago Symphony Orchestra* (1925).
Russell, Charles E., *American Orchestra and Theodore Thomas* (1927).
Sherman, John K., *Music and Maestros: Minneapolis Symphony Orchestra* (1952).
Wister, F. A., *Twenty-Five Years of the Philadelphia Orchestra* (1925).

See also 10.3 for biographies/writings of:

Damrosch, Walter, 1862–1950
Fiedler, Arthur, 1894–
Koussevitzky, Sergei, 1874–1951
Thomas, Christian Friedrich Theodore, 1835–1905
Toscanini, Arturo, 1867–1957
Walter, Bruno, 1877–1962

28.9.4 Ballads and Folk Music

Abrahams, Roger D., and George Foss, *Anglo-American Folksong Style* (1968).
Ames, Russell, *Story of American Folk Song* (1955).
Arnold, Byron, comp., *Folksongs of Alabama* (1950).
Barry, Phillips, et al., *British Ballads from Maine* (1929).

Barry, Phillips, *Folk Music in America,* George Herzog and Herbert Halpert, eds. (1939).

Belden, Henry M., ed., *Ballads and Songs Collected by the Missouri Folklore Society* (2nd ed., 1955).

Botkin, Benjamin A., *American Play-Party Song* (1937).

Brewster, Paul G., ed., *Ballads and Songs of Indiana* (1940).

Bronson, Bertrand H., *Ballad as Song* (1969).

Child, Francis J., *English and Scottish Popular Ballads* (5 vols., 1883–1898).

Coffin, Tristram P., *British Traditional Ballads in North America* (rev. ed., 1963).

Cox, John H., ed., *Folk-Songs of the South* (1925).

Doerflinger, William M., comp., *Shantymen and Shantyboys: Songs of Sailor and Lumberman* (1951).

Eddy, Mary O., comp., *Ballads and Songs from Ohio* (1939).

Flanders, Helen H., and Marguerite Olney, comps., *Ballads Migrant in New England* (1953).

Fowler, David C., *Literary History of the Popular Ballad* (1968).

Friedman, Albert B., *Viking Book of Folk Ballads of the English-Speaking World* (1956).

Gardner, Emelyn E., and Geraldine J. Chickering, eds., *Ballads and Songs of Southern Michigan* (1939).

Greenway, John, *American Folksongs of Protest* (1953).

—— "Country-Western: The Music of America," *Am. West,* 5 (1968), 32.

Guthrie, Woodie, *Bound for Glory* (1943).

Hudson, Arthur P., *Folksongs of Mississippi* (1936).

Jackson, George P., *White Spirituals in the Southern Uplands: Fasola Folk* (1933).

Korson, George G., ed., *Pennsylvania Songs and Legends* (1949).

Lawless, Ray M., *Folksingers and Folksongs in America* (rev. ed., 1965).

Leach, MacEdward, ed., *Ballad Book* (1955).

Linscott, Eloise H., ed., *Folk Songs of Old New England* (1939).

Lomax, John A., *Adventures of a Ballad Hunter* (1947).

Malone, Bill C., *Country Music U.S.A.* (1969).

Morris, Alton C., ed., *Folksongs of Florida* (1950).

Randolph, Vance, ed., *Ozark Folksongs* (4 vols., 1946–1950).

Scarborough, Dorothy, *A Song Catcher in Southern Mountains: Songs of British Ancestry* (1937).

Sharp, Cecil J., comp., *English Folk Songs from the Southern Appalachians,* Maud Karpeles, ed. (2 vols., 1932).

Thomas, Jeanette B., *Ballad Makin' in Mountains of Kentucky* (1939).

Walker, William, comp., *Southern Harmony Songbook* (1854).

Wells, Evelyn K., *Ballad Tree* (1950).

Wolford, Leah J., *Play-Party in Indiana,* W. E. Richmond and M. W. Tillson, eds. (rev. ed., 1959).

*   *   *   *   *   *   *

Haywood, Charles, *Bibliography of North American Folklore and Folksong* (2 vols., 2nd ed., 1961).

Laws, G. Malcolm, Jr., *Native American Balladry: Descriptive Study and Bibliographical Syllabus* (rev. ed., 1964).

Wilgus, Donald K., *Anglo-American Folksong Scholarship since 1898* (1959).

8.9.5 Popular Music

Blesh, Rudi, and Harriet Janis, *They All Played Ragtime* (1950).

Browne, Ray B., "Poets in Nineteenth-Century 'Popular' Songbooks," *Am. Lit.,* 30 (1959), 503.

Condon, Eddie, *We Called It Music* (1947).

Dichter, Harry, and Elliot Shapiro, *Early American Sheet Music, 1768–1889* (1941).

Eisen, Jonathan, ed., *Age of Rock* (1969).

Ewen, David, ed., *American Popular Songs from the Revolutionary War to the Present* (1966).

—— *Panorama of American Popular Music* (1957).

Gilbert, Douglas, *Lost Chords* (1942).

Gillett, Charlie, *Sound of the City: Rock and Roll* (1970).

Goldberg, Isaac, *Tin Pan Alley* (1930).

Goodman, Benny, and Irving Kolodin, *Kingdom of Swing,* (1939).

Levy, Lester S., *Grace Notes in American History: Popular Sheet Music from 1820–1900* (1967).

Marks, E. B., and A. J. Liebling, *They All Sang* (1934).

Mooney, Hughson F., "Songs, Singers, and Society, 1890–1954," *Am. Quar.*, 6 (1954), 221.

Spaeth, Sigmund, *History of Popular Music* (1948).

28.9.6 Jazz and Blues

Blesh, Rudi, *Shining Trumpets: A History of Jazz* (rev. ed., 1958).

Charters, Samuel B., *Country Blues* (1959).

Feather, Leonard G., *Encyclopedia of Jazz in the Sixties* (1968).

Goffin, Robert, *Jazz* (1946).

Handy, W. C., *Father of the Blues* (1941).

Hansen, Chadwick, "Social Influences on Jazz: Chicago, 1920–30," *Am. Quar.*, 12 (1960), 493.

Hentoff, Nat, *The Jazz Life* (1961).

—— and Albert J. McCarthy, eds., *Jazz: New Perspectives* (1959).

Hobson, Wilder, *American Jazz* (1939).

Keil, Charles, *Urban Blues* (1966).

Kmen, Henry A., *Music in New Orleans: The Formative Years, 1791–1841* (1966).

Leonard, Neil, *Jazz and White Americans* (1962).

Newton, Francis, *Jazz Scene* (1960).

Oliver, Paul, *Blues Fell This Morning: Meaning of the Blues* (1960).

—— *The Story of the Blues* (1969).

Pleasants, Henry, *Serious Music—and All That Jazz* (1969).

Rose, Al, and Edmond Souchon, *New Orleans Jazz: A Family Album* (1967).

Sargeant, Winthrop, *Jazz: A History* (1964). Originally published under the title, *Jazz Hot and Hybrid* (1946).

Schuller, Gunther, *Early Jazz* (1968).

Shapiro, Nat, and Nat Hentoff, eds., *Hear Me Talkin' to Ya: Jazz* (1955).

—— *Jazz Makers* (1957).

Stearns, Marshall W., *The Story of Jazz* (1956).

Ulanov, Barry, *History of Jazz in America* (1952).

See also 20.12.22, Negroes–Music.

28.9.7 Religious Music

Barbour, James M., *Church Music of William Billings* (1960).

Daniel, Ralph T., *The Anthem in New England before 1800* (1966).

Davison, Archibald T., *Protestant Church Music in America* (1933).

Ellinwood, Leonard W., *English Influences in American Church Music* (1954).

—— *History of American Church Music* (1953).

Foote, Henry W., *Three Centuries of American Hymnody* (1940).

Hooper, William L., *Church Music in Transition* (1963).

Jackson, George P., ed., *Spiritual Folksongs of Early America* (2nd ed., 1953).

—— *White and Negro Spirituals* (1944).

Metcalf, Frank J., *American Writers and Compilers of Sacred Music* (1967).

Nininger, Ruth, *Church Music Comes of Age* (1957).

Osbeck, Kenneth W., *The Ministry of Music* (1961).

Stevenson, Robert M., *Protestant Church Music in America, from 1564 to the Present* (1966).

Wyeth, John, *Repository of Sacred Music* (1820).

Yoder, Don, *Pennsylvania Spirituals* (1961).

28.9.8 Opera

Bloomfield, Arthur J., *San Francisco Opera, 1923–1961* (1961).
Blum, Daniel, *Pictorial Treasury of Opera* (1954).
Davis, Ronald L., *Opera in Chicago* (1966).
—— *Opera in the West* (1965).
Eaton, Quintance, *Miracle of the Met: History of Metropolitan Opera 1883–1967* (1968).
—— *Opera Caravan: Metropolitan on Tour, 1883–1956* (1956).
Glackens, Ira, *Yankee Diva: Lillian Nordica and the Golden Days of Opera* (1963).
Graf, Herbert, *Opera for the People* (1951).
Hipsher, E. E., *American Opera and Its Composers* (1934).
Johnson, H. Earle, *Operas on American Subjects* (1964).
Kolodin, Irving, *Metropolitan Opera, 1883–1966* (1966).
Krehbiel, H. E., *Chapters of Opera* (1911).
Lahee, H. C., *Grand Opera in America* (1902).

28.10 THEATER

28.10.1 General

Anderson, John, *American Theatre* (1938).
Bernheim, Alfred L., et al., *Business of the Theatre* (1932).
Blum, Daniel, *Pictorial History of the American Theatre, 1860–1960* (1960).
Bond, Frederick W., *Negro and Drama* (1940).
Coad, O. S., and Edwin Mims, Jr., *The American Stage* (1929).
Hartman, John G., *Development of the American Social Comedy from 1787 to 1936* (1939).
Herron, Ima H., *The Small Town in American Drama* (1968).
Hewitt, Barnard, *Theatre U.S.A., 1668 to 1957* (1959).
Hornblow, Arthur, *A History of the Theatre in America* (2 vols., 1919).
Hughes, Glenn, *History of the American Theatre, 1700–1950* (1951).
Isaacs, Edith J. R., *The Negro in American Theatre* (1947).
—— ed., *Theatre: Essays on the Arts* (1927).
Mayorga, M. G., *A Short History of American Drama* (1932).
Morris, Lloyd, *Curtain Time: American Theatre* (1953). On actors since the 1820's.
Moses, M. J., and J. M. Brown, *American Theatre* (1934).
Nannes, Caspar H., *Politics in American Drama* (1968).
Odell, G. C. D., *Annals of the New York Stage* (15 vols., 1927–1949).
Poggi, Jack, *Theater in America: Impact of Economic Forces, 1870–1967* (1968).
Quinn, A. H., *History of American Drama from the Beginning to the Present* (rev. ed., 1936).
Taubman, Howard, *The Making of American Theatre* (rev. ed., 1967).

* * * * * * *

Angotti, Vincent L., *Source Materials in Theatre: Annotated Bibliography and Subject Index to Microfilm Collection* (1967). University of Michigan (Ann Arbor) Collection.
Baker, Blanche M., *Dramatic Bibliography* (1933).
—— *Theatre and Allied Arts: Guide to Books* (1952).
Gohdes, Clarence, comp., *Literature and Theatre of the States and Regions of the U.S.A.: Bibliography* (1967).

See also 10.3 for biographies/writings of:

PLAYWRIGHTS

Ade, George, 1866–1944
Albee, Edward, 1928–

Belasco, David, 1854–1931
Boucicault, Dion, 1820–1890
Daly, John A., 1838–1899
Dunlap, William, 1776–1839
Eliot, T. S., 1888–1965
Fitch, William C., 1865–1909
Glaspell, Susan, 1882–1948
Hart, Moss, 1904–1961
Hellman, Lillian, 1905–
Inge, William, 1913–
MacKaye, J. M. Steele, 1842–1894
Miller, Arthur, 1915–
Moody, William V., 1869–1910
Noah, Mordecai M., 1785–1851
Odets, Clifford, 1906–
O'Neill, Eugene, 1888–1953
Peabody, Josephine P., 1874–1922
Rice, Elmer, 1892–1967
Sherwood, Robert E., 1896–1955
Wallack, Lester, 1820–1888
Wilder, Thornton, 1897–
Williams, Tennessee, 1914–

ACTORS

Aldridge, Ira F., ca. 1805–1867
Barrymore Family, 20th century
Barrymore, John, 1882–1942
Belasco, David, 1854–1931
Boucicault, Dion, 1820–1890
Cohan, George M., 1878–1942
Cornell, Katharine, 1898–
Crabtree, Lotta, 1847–1924
Cushman, Charlotte S., 1816–1876
Dickinson, Anna E., 1842–1932
Drew, John, 1853–1927
Durang, John, fl. 1785–1816
Forrest, Edwin, 1806–1872
Hull, Josephine, 1886–1957
Jefferson, Joseph, 1829–1905
Keaton, Buster, 1896–1966
Kemble, Fanny, 1809–1893
Lahr, Bert, 1895–1967
Mansfield, Richard, 1854–1907
Marx Brothers, 20th century
Mowatt, Anna C., 1819–1870
Payne, John Howard, 1791–1852
Skinner, Otis, 1858–1942
Tyler, Priscilla, 1816–1889
Warren, William, 1812–1888

28.10.2 Nineteenth Century

Bowen, Elbert R., *Theatrical Entertainments in Rural Missouri before the Civil War* (1959).
Brown, Thomas Allston, *History of the American Stage* (1870).
────── *History of the New York Stage* (3 vols., 1903).
Carson, William G. B., *Theatre on the Frontier: St. Louis Stage* (2nd ed., 1965). Covers the period 1815–1845.
Clapp, J. B., and E. F. Edgett, *Players of Present* (3 vols., 1899–1901).
Dormon, James H., Jr., *Theater in the South, 1815–1861* (1967).
Dunlap, William, *History of American Theatre* (1832).
Ernst, Alice H., *Trouping in the Oregon Country: Frontier Theatre* (1961).

Felheim, Marvin, *The Theater of Augustin Daly: An Account of the Late Nine-teenth Century American Stage* (1956).
Firkins, Ina Ten Eyck, *Index to Plays* (1927).
Grimsted, David, *Melodrama Unveiled: American Theatre and Culture, 1800–1850* (1968).
Hapgood, Norman, *The Stage in America* (1901).
Hodge, Francis, *Yankee Theatre: The Image of America on Stage, 1825–1850* (1964).
Hoole, William S., *Ante-bellum Charleston Theatre* (1946).
Kendall, John S., *Golden Age of New Orleans Theatre* (1952).
Leavitt, M. G., *Fifty Years in Theatrical Management* (1912).
Le Gardeur, René J., Jr., *First New Orleans Theatre, 1792–1803* (1963).
McKay, Frederic E., and C. E. L. Wingate, eds., *Famous American Actors* (1896).
Moody, Richard, *America Takes the Stage: Romanticism in Drama and Theatre, 1750–1900* (1955).
Patrick, J. Max, *Savannah's Pioneer Theatre, 1778–1838* (1953).
Rourke, Constance M., *Troupers of Gold Coast* (1928).
Watson, Margaret G., *Silver Theatre: Amusements of the Mining Frontier in Nevada, 1850–1864* (1964).
Wemyss, Francis C., *Chronology of American Stage, from 1752 to 1852* (1852).
Strang, L. C., *Famous Actors of the Day* (1899).
———— *Famous Actresses of the Day* (1901).
———— *Players and Plays of the Last Quarter Century* (1902).
Wilson, Garff B., *History of American Acting* (1966).

28.10.3 Twentieth Century

Blau, Herbert, *Impossible Theatre* (1964).
Blum, Daniel, ed., *A Pictorial History of the American Theater* (1951). From 1900.
Burleigh, Louis, *Community Theatre* (1917).
Churchill, Allen, *The Great White Way: Broadway's Golden Age* (1962). Covers the period 1900–1919.
Clurman, Harold, *Fervent Years: Group Theatre* (1945).
Davis, Hallie Flanagan, *Arena: Federal Theatre* (1940).
Downer, Alan S., *Fifty Years of American Drama, 1900–1950* (1951).
———— *Recent American Drama* (1961).
Federal Theatre Project, *Federal Theatre Plays* (2 vols., 1938).
Flexner, Eleanor, *American Playwrights: 1918–1938* (1938).
Gagey, E. M., *Revolution in American Drama* (1947).
Guthrie, Tyrone, *New Theatre* (1964).
Hayes, Helen, and Sandford Dody, *On Reflection* (1968).
Henderson, Archibald, *Changing Drama* (1914).
Himelstein, Morgan Y., *Drama Was a Weapon: Left Wing Theater in New York, 1929–1941* (1963).
Houghton, Norris, *Advance from Broadway* (1941).
Krutch, J. W., *American Drama Since 1918* (1939).
Lewis, Allan, *American Plays and Playwrights of the Contemporary Theatre* (1965).
Mackay, Constance D'A., *Little Theatre* (1917).
Mathews, Jane D., *The Federal Theatre, 1935–1939* (1967).
Morehouse, Ward, *Matinee Tomorrow: Fifty Years of Our Theatre* (1949).
Moses, Montrose J., *American Dramatist* (1925).
Nannes, Caspar H., *Politics in American Drama* (1960). Covers the period 1890–1959.
Phelps, William L., *Twentieth Century Theatre* (1918).
Porter, Thomas E., *Myth and Modern American Drama* (1969).
Theatre: Annual of Repertory Theatre of Lincoln Center, 1961–
Theatre Arts Anthology, Rosamond Gilder et al., eds. (1950). Covers the period, 1916–1948.
Villard, Leonie, *Le Théâtre Américain* (1929).
Weales, Gerald C., *Jumping-Off Place: American Drama in the 1960's* (1969).

28.10.4 Musical Theater

Coffin, Caroline, *Vaudeville* (1914).
Cone, John F., *Oscar Hammerstein's Manhattan Opera House* (1966).
Elliott, Eugene C., *History of Variety-Vaudeville in Seattle to 1914* (1944).
Engel, Lehman, *American Musical Theatre* (1967).
Ewen, David, *Complete Book of the American Musical Theatre: A Guide, from 1866 to the Present* (1958).
———— *Story of America's Musical Theater* (rev. ed., 1968).
Gilbert, Douglas, *American Vaudeville* (1940).
Green, Stanley, *The World of Musical Comedy* (1960).
McLean, Albert F., Jr., *American Vaudeville as Ritual* (1965).
Nathan, Hans, *Dan Emmett and the Rise of Early Negro Minstrelsy* (1962).
Paskman, Dailey, and Sigmund Spaeth, *Gentlemen, Be Seated!* (1928).
Smith, Cecil M., *Musical Comedy in America* (1950).
Sobel, Bernard, *Burleycue* (1931).
———— *Pictorial History of Vaudeville* (1961).
Strang, L. C., *Celebrated Comedians of Light Opera* (1900).
———— *Prima Donnas and Soubrettes of Light Opera* (1900).
Wittke, Carl, *Tambo and Bones: A History of the American Minstrel Stage* (1930).

See also 10.3 for biographies/writings of:

Brice, Fanny, 1891–1951
Cohan, George M., 1878–1942
Hammerstein, Oscar, 1895–1960
Herbert, Victor, 1859–1924
Kern, Jerome, 1885–1945
Rodgers, Richard, 1902–

28.11 DANCE

Amberg, George, *Ballet in America* (1949).
Chujoy, Anatole, and P. W. Manchester, eds., *Dance Encyclopedia* (rev. ed., 1967).
Chujoy, Anatole, *New York City Ballet* (1953).
Damon, S. Foster, "Square Dancing," Am. Antiq. Soc., *Proc.,* 62 (1953), 63.
Horst, Louis, and Carroll Russell, *Modern Dance Forms in Relation to Other Modern Arts* (2nd ed., 1963).
Kirstein, Lincoln, *Dance: Short History of Classic Theatrical Dancing* (1969).
———— *Three Pamphlets: Ballet* (1967).
Maynard, Olga, *American Ballet* (1959).
Sorell, Walter, "Isadora Duncan," Univ. Kan. City Rev., 21 (1954), 95.
Stearns, Marshall, and Jean Stearns, *Jazz Dance: Story of American Vernacular Dance* (1968).
Terry, Walter, *Dance in America* (1956).

See also 10.3 for biographies/writings of:

Duncan, Isadora, 1878–1927
Graham, Martha, 1895–

28.12 MOTION PICTURES

Barry, Iris, *D. W. Griffith* (1966).
Blum, Daniel, *Pictorial History of the Silent Screen* (1953).
Brownlow, Kevin, *Parade's Gone By* (1968).
Cahn, William, *Harold Lloyd's World of Comedy* (1964).
Conant, Michael, *Anti-Trust in the Motion Picture Industry* (1960).
Cowie, Peter, *Seventy Years of Cinema* (1969).

Crowther, Bosley, *Great Films* (1967).

Gish, Lillian, *Movies, Mr. Griffith and Me* (1969).

Griffith, Linda A., *When Movies Were Young* (1925).

Guback, Thomas H., *The International Film Industry: Western Europe and America since 1945* (1969).

Haettig, Mae D., *Economic Control of the Motion Picture Industry* (1944).

Hampton, Benjamin B., *History of Movies* (1931).

Jacobs, Lewis, *Rise of the American Film: A Critical History* (2nd ed., 1968).

Lahue, Kalton C., *Continued Next Week: History of the Moving Picture Serial* (1964).

———— *World of Laughter: Motion Picture Comedy Short, 1910–1930* (1966).

Leonard, Harold, ed., *Film as Art* (1941).

Macgowan, Kenneth, *Behind the Screen: History of the Motion Picture* (1965).

Mayer, Arthur, *Merely Colossal* (1953).

Mayer, Michael F., *Foreign Films on American Screens* (1965).

Moley, Raymond, *Hays Office* (1945).

Niver, Kemp R., *Motion Pictures from the Library of Congress Paper Print Collection, 1894–1912,* Bebe Bergsten, ed. (1967).

Powdermaker, Hortense, *Hollywood Dream Factory* (1950).

Ramsaye, Terry, *Million and One Nights* (2 vols., 1926).

Randall, Richard S., *Censorship of the Movies* (1968).

Renan, Sheldon, *Introduction to American Underground Film* (1967).

Robinson, William R., ed., *Man and the Movies: Essays on the Art of Our Time* (1967).

Rosten, L. C., *Hollywood* (1941).

Rotha, Paul, *Film till Now* (1930).

Sadoul, Georges, *Histoire générale du cinema* (1946).

Sarris, Andrew, *American Cinema, 1929–1968* (1968).

Schickel, Richard, *Movies: Art and Institution* (1964).

Sharp, Dennis, *Picture Palace and Other Buildings for Movies* (1968).

Sinclair, Upton, *Upton Sinclair Presents William Fox* (1933).

Taylor, Deems et al., *Pictorial History of Movies* (1950).

Thorp, Margaret, *America at the Movies* (1939).

Tyler, Parker, *Magic and Myth of Movies* (1947).

Wagenknecht, Edward, *Movies in the Age of Innocence* (1962).

Wolfenstein, Martha, and Nathan Leites, *Movies* (1950).

*   *   *   *   *   *   *

Film Index: Bibliography. Vol I: *Film as Art* (1968).

For listings of copyrighted American films see the volumes of the Library of Congress, National Union Catalog, *Motion Pictures and Filmstrips.*

See also 10.3 for biographies/writings of:

Belasco, David, 1854–1931
Chaplin, Charles, 1889–
Disney, Walter E., 1901–1968
Fairbanks, Douglas, 1883–1939
Fields, W. C., 1880–1946
Frohman, Charles, 1860–1915
Hart, William S., 1872–1946
Laemmle, Carl, 1867–1939
Marx Brothers, 20th century
Thalberg, Irving, 1889–1936

28.13 PHOTOGRAPHY

Gernsheim, Helmut, *Creative Photography: Aesthetic Trends, 1839–1960* (1962).

Newhall, Beaumont, *Daguerreotype in America* (rev. ed., 1968).

———— *History of Photography, 1830 to the Present Day* (1964).
———— and Nancy Newhall, eds., *Masters of Photography* (1958).
Taft, Robert, *Photography and the American Scene* (1938).

See also 10.3 for biographies/writings of:

Brady, Mathew, 1823–1896
Eastman, George, 1854–1932
Jackson, William H., 1843–1942
Steichen, Edward, 1879–
Stieglitz, Alfred, 1864–1946

29 Pure and Applied Sciences

29.1 SCIENCE

29.1.1 General

Barber, Bernard, and Walter Hirsch, eds., *The Sociology of Science* (1962).
Bush, G. P., and L. H. Hattery, eds., *Scientific Research* (1950).
"Science in the American Context," *Cahiers d'Histoire Mondiale,* 8 (1965), No. 4. Entire issue devoted to this topic.
Cohen, I. Bernard, "Science in America during Nineteenth Century," Natl. Acad. of Sciences, *Proc.,* 45 (1959), 666.
—— *Some Early Tools of American Science* (1950). Harvard, 1764–1825.
Conant, James B., "Knowledge in the Nineteenth Century," *Colo. Quar.,* 11 (1963), 229.
Dana, E. S., *Century of Science in America* (1918).
Daniels, George H., *American Science in the Age of Jackson* (1968).
Don, H. M., ed., "Social Implications of Modern Science," Am. Acad. Pol. Soc. Sci., *Annals,* 249 (1947).
Dupree, A. Hunter, ed., *Science and the Emergence of Modern America, 1865–1916* (1963).
Fleming, Donald, *Science and Technology in Providence, 1760–1914: An Essay in the History of Brown University in the Metropolitan Community* (1952).
—— "Science in Australia, Canada and the United States: Some Comparative Remarks," 10th Internatl. Cong. Hist. Sci., *Proc.,* 1 (1964), 179.
Greene, John C., "American Science Comes of Age, 1780–1820," *JAH,* 55 (1968), 22.
—— "Science and the Public in Age of Jefferson," *Isis,* 49 (1958), 13.
Hagstrom, Warren O., *Scientific Community* (1965).
Handlin, Oscar, "Science and Technology in Popular Culture," *Daedalus,* 94 (1965), 156.
Holton, Gerald, ed., *Science and Culture: Study of Cohesive and Disjunctive Forces* (1965).
Johnson, Thomas C., Jr., *Scientific Interests in the Old South* (1936).
Kuhn, Thomas, *Structure of Scientific Revolutions* (1962).
Meacham, Standish, "Priestley in America," *Hist. Today,* 12 (1962), 568.
Miller, Howard S., *Dollars for Research: Science and Patrons in Nineteenth-Century America* (1970).
Reingold, Nathan, ed., *Science in Nineteenth-Century America: Documentary* (1964).
Shryock, Richard H., "American Indifference to Basic Science during Nineteenth Century," *Archives Internationales d'Histoire des Sciences,* 5 (1948), 50.
Struik, Dirk J., *Yankee Science in Making* (rev. ed., 1962).
Van Tassel, David D., and Michael G. Hall, eds., *Science and Society in United States* (1966).
Wilson, Mitchell, *American Science and Invention* (1954).

*   *   *   *   *   *   *

Bell, Whitfield J., Jr., *Early American Science: Needs and Opportunities for Study* (1955).
Clagett, Marshall, ed., *Critical Problems in the History of Science* (1959).
"Conference on Science Manuscripts," *ISIS*, 53 (Mar. 1962) Entire issue.
Dupree, A. Hunter, "History of American Science: A Field Finds Itself," *AHR*, 71 (1966), 863.
Fulton, John F., "Impact of Science on American History," *Isis*, 42 (1951), 176.
Hindle, Brooke, "Historiography of Science in the Middle Colonies," Am. Philos. Soc., *Proc.*, 108 (1964), 158.
Reingold, Nathan, "Manuscript Resources for the History of Science and Technology in the Library of Congress," *Quar. Jour. of Current Acquisitions*, 17 (1960), 161.
———— "National Archives and the History of Science in America," *Isis*, 46 (1955), 22.
Rosenberg, Charles E., "Writing the History of American Science," in Herbert J. Bass, ed., *State of American History* (1970).

See also 25.13, Impact of Science and Technology.

29.1.2 Scientific Profession

American Men of Science: Biographical Directory, Jacques Cattell, ed. (2 vols., 12th ed., 1971–1973).
Blank, David M., and George J. Stigler, *Demand and Supply of Scientific Personnel* (1957). Covers the period 1870–1955.
Fermi, Laura, *Illustrious Immigrants: Intellectual Migration from Europe, 1930–1941* (1968).
Fleming, Donald, and Bernard Bailyn, eds., *Intellectual Migration: Europe and America, 1930–1960* (1969).
Hill, Karl, ed., *Management of Scientists* (1964).
Jaffe, Bernard, *Men of Science in America* (rev. ed., 1958).
Jordan, D. S., ed., *Leading American Men of Science* (1910).
Knapp, R. H., and H. B. Goodrich, *Origins of American Scientists* (1952).
Kornhauser, William, *Scientists in Industry: Conflict and Accommodation* (1962).
Lasby, Clarence G., *Project Paperclip: German Scientists and the Cold War*, (1971).
Mattfeld, Jacquelyn A., and Carol G. Van Aken, eds., *Women and the Scientific Professions* (1965).
National Academy of Sciences, *Biographical Memoirs* (40 vols., 1877–1969).
Price, Don K., *The Scientific Estate* (1965).

See also 10.3 for biographies/writings of:

Cooper, Thomas, 1759–1839
Davis, Charles H., 1807–1877
Draper, John W., 1811–1882
Hewitt, Peter Cooper, 1861–1921
Hitchcock, Ethan A., 1798–1870
Mitchill, Samuel L., 1764–1831

See also 29.1.8–29.1.13, for biographical lists of scientists in specific areas.

29.1.3 Societies and Institutions

American Physiological Society, *History of the American Physiological Society, Semicentennial, 1887–1937* (1938).
Bates, Ralph S., *Scientific Societies in the United States* (3d. ed., 1965).
Bell, Whitfield J., Jr., "American Philosophical Society as a National Academy of Sciences," 10th Internatl. Cong. Hist. Sci., *Proc.*, 1 (1964), 165.

Brewington, Marion V., *Peabody Museum Collection of Navigating Instruments* (1963).

Browne, Charles A., and Mary E. Weeks, *History of the American Chemical Society* (1952).

Chittenden, Russell H., *History of the Sheffield Scientific School of Yale University, 1846–1922* (1928).

Conklin, Edwin G., "History of the American Philosophical Society," Am. Philos. Soc., *Yearbook* (1966), 37.

Dupree, A. Hunter, "Founding of the National Academy of Sciences," Am. Philos. Soc., *Proc.,* 101 (1957), 434.

Fairchild, Herman L., *Geological Society of America* (1932).

—— *History of New York Academy of Sciences, formerly the Lyceum of Natural History* (1887).

Fenn, Wallace O., *History of American Physiological Society, 1937–1962* (1963).

Goode, G. B., ed., *Smithsonian Institution* (1897).

History of the American Physiological Society, Semicentennial, 1887–1937 (1938).

Multhauf, Robert P., comp., *Catalogue of Instruments and Models in Possession of the American Philosophical Society* (1961).

Oehser, Paul H., *Sons of Science: Story of the Smithsonian Institution and Its Leaders* (1949).

Rhees, W. J., ed., *Smithsonian Institution: Documents, 1835–1889* (1901).

"Museums of Science and Technology," *Tech. and Cult.,* 4 (1963), 130.

True, Frederick W., *History of the First Half-Century of the National Academy of Sciences, 1863–1913* (1913).

Wright, John K., *Geography in the Making: American Geographical Society, 1851–1951* (1952).

*   *   *   *   *   *   *

Skallerup, Harry R., "Bibliography of the Histories of American Academies of Science," Kansas Acad. Sci., *Trans.,* 66 (1963), 274.

29.1.4 Science in Industry

Birr, Kendall A., "Science in American Industry," in David D. Van Tassel and M. G. Hall, eds., *Science and Society in the United States* (1966).

—— *Pioneering in Industrial Research: General Electric* (1957).

Flinn, A. D., and Ruth Cobb, *Research Laboratories in Industrial Establishments* (1921).

Hall, Courtney R., *History of American Industrial Science* (1954).

White, Frederick A., *American Industrial Research Laboratories* (1961).

29.1.5 Science and the Federal Government

Auerbach, Lewis E., "Scientists in the New Deal," *Minerva,* 3 (1965), 457.

Baxter, James P., III, *Scientists against Time* (1946). World War II.

Burchard, John E., *QED: MIT in World War II* (1948).

—— *Rockets, Guns, and Targets* (1948). The Office of Scientific Research and Development.

Bush, Vannevar, *Science, the Endless Frontier: A Program for Postwar Scientific Research* (1945).

Bushnell, David, and Nick A. Komons, *History of the Office of Research Analyses* (1963). The Office of Aerospace Research.

Cox, Donald W., *America's New Policy Makers: The Scientists' Rise to Power* (1964).

Dupré, Joseph S., and Sanford A. Lakoff, *Science and the Nation: Policy and Politics* (1962).

Dupree, A. Hunter, "Central Scientific Organisation," *Minerva,* 1 (1963), 453.

—— *Science in the Federal Government: A History of Policies and Activities to 1940* (1957).

Fleming, Donald, "Big Money and High Politics of Science," *Atlantic,* 216 (1965), 41.

Friedman, Saul, "Rand Corporation and Our Policy Makers," *Atlantic,* 212 (1963), 61.

Gilpin, Robert, and Christopher Wright, eds., *Scientists and National Policy-Making* (1964).

Holley, Irving B., Jr., *Ideas and Weapons: The Aerial Weapon during World War I* (1953).

Jahns, Patricia, *Matthew Fontaine Maury and Joseph Henry: Scientists of the Civil War* (1961).

Lapp, Ralph E., *The New Priesthood: Scientific Elite* (1965).

Leiserson, Avery, "Scientists and Policy Process," *Am. Pol. Sci. Rev.,* 59 (1965), 408.

National Academy of Sciences, *Basic Research and National Goals: Science and Astronautics* (1965).

Nieburg, Harold L., *In the Name of Science* (1966).

Orlans, Harold, ed., *Science Policy and the University* (1968).

Penick, James L., Jr. et al., eds., *Politics of American Science, 1939 to Present* (1965).

Price, Don K., "Escape to Endless Frontier," *Science,* 148 (1965), 743.

—— *Government and Science* (1954).

Pursell, Carroll W., Jr., "Administration of Science in the Department of Agriculture, 1933–1940," *Agric. Hist.,* 42 (1968), 231.

—— "Science Advisory Board, 1933–1935," *Am. Philos. Soc., Proc.,* 109 (1965), 342.

Reingold, Nathan, "Science in Civil War," *ISIS,* 49 (1958), 307.

Rosenberg, Charles E., "Adams Act [1906]: Politics and Scientific Research," *Agric. Hist.,* 38 (1964), 3.

Skolnikoff, Eugene B., *Science, Technology, and American Foreign Policy* (1967).

Smith, Alice K., *Peril and Hope: Scientists' Movement, 1945–47* (1965).

Stewart, Irvin, *Organizing Scientific Research for War: Office of Scientific Research and Development* (1948).

U.S. President's Scientific Research Board, *Science and Public Policy* (5 vols., 1947).

Weiss, Paul, "Science in the University," *Daedalus,* 93 (1964), 1184.

Wengert, Norman, "Perspectives on Government and Science," *Am. Acad. Pol. and Soc. Sci., Annals,* 327 (1960), 1.

Wiesner, Jerome B., *Where Science and Politics Meet* (1965).

Wolfle, Dael L., *Science and Public Policy* (1959).

—— "Support of Science in U.S.," *Scient. Am.,* 213 (1965), 19.

Yerkes, Robert M., *New World of Science: Its Development during the War* (1920). World War I.

*   *   *   *   *   *   *

Caldwell, Lynton K., et al., *Science, Technology and Public Policy: Annotated Bibliography, 1945–1965* (rev. ed., 1968).

See also 29.1.10, Atomic Energy and Atomic Weapons.

29.1.6 Exploration Outside the United States

See 13.2, Westward Expansion and the Frontier–Exploration, for reference to exploration in the United States.

Anderson, William R., and Clay Blair, Jr., *Nautilus 90 North* (1959).

Bingham, Hiram, *Lost City of the Incas* (1948).

Byrd, Richard E., *Discovery: The Story of the Second Byrd Antarctic Expedition* (1935).

—— *Little America: Flight to the South Pole* (1930).

Calvert, James, *Surface at the Pole: USS Skate* (1960).

Caswell, John E., *Arctic Frontiers: Explorations in Far North* (1956).

Debenham, Frank, *Antartica* (1961).

Dufek, George J., *Operation Deepfreeze* (1957).
Kemp, Norman, *Conquest of the Antarctic* (1957).
Ledyard, John, *Journey through Russia and Siberia, 1787–1788; Journal and Letters,* Stephen D. Watrous, ed. (1966).
MacMillan, D. B., *How Peary Reached the Pole: The Personal Story of His Assistant* (1934).
Mitterling, Philip I., *America in Antarctic to 1840* (1959).
National Archives, *United States Scientific Geographical Exploration of Pacific Basin, 1783–1899* (1961).
Nichols, Roy F., *Advance Agents of American Destiny* (1956).
Poesch, Jessie, *Titian Ramsay Peale and His Journals of the Wilkes Expedition* (1961).
Stackpole, E. A., *The Voyage of Huron and the Huntress: American Sealers and the Discovery of Antarctica* (1955).
Tyler, David B., *Wilkes Expedition, 1838–1842* (1968).
Von Hagen, Victor W., *Maya Explorer: John Lloyd Stephens* (1947).
Wilkes, Charles, *A Narrative of the United States Exploring Expedition* (18 vols., 1845).

See also 10.3 for biographies/writings of:

Kane, Elisha K., 1820–1857
Peary, Robert E., 1856–1920
Stephens, John L., 1805–1852
Wilkes, Charles, 1798–1877

29.1.7 Darwinism and American Science

Gray, Asa, *Darwiniana* (1876); A. Hunter Dupree, ed. (1963).
Loewenberg, B. J., "Reaction of American Scientists to Darwinism," *AHR,* 38 (1933), 687.
——— "Darwinism Comes to America," *MVHR,* 28 (1940), 339.
Pfeifer, Edward J., "Genesis of American Neo-Lamarckism," *Isis,* 56 (1965), 156.
Ratner, Sidney, "Evolution and Rise of Scientific Spirit," *Philos. of Science,* 3 (1936), 104.

See also 24.4, Darwinism and Religion.

29.1.8 Natural History

Beidleman, Richard G., "Thomas Nuttall," Am. Philos. Soc., *Proc.,* 104 (1960), 86.
Burroughs, Raymond D., ed., *Natural History of Lewis and Clark Expedition* (1961).
Goode, George B., *A Memorial, together with a Selection of His Papers on Museums and History of Science in America* (1901).
Matthiesen, Peter, *Wildlife in America* (1959).
Smallwood, W. M., and Mabel Smallwood, *Natural History and the American Mind* (1941).
Wiley, Farida A., ed., *John Burrough's America* (1951).

*   *   *   *   *   *   *

Meisel, Max, ed., *Bibliography of American Natural History . . . 1769–1865* (3 vols., 1924–1929).

See also 10.3 for biographies/writings of:

Agassiz, J. Louis, 1807–1873
Audubon, John J., 1785–1851
Bartram, William, 1739–1823

Burroughs, John, 1837–1921
Muir, John, 1838–1914
Nuttall, Thomas, 1786–1859
Peale, Titian R., 1799–1885
Rafinesque, Constantine S., 1783–1840
Romans, Bernard, 1720–1784
Wilson, Alexander, 1766–1813

29.1.9 Astronomy, Mathematics, and Physics

Bailey, Solon Irving, *The History and Work of Harvard Observatory, 1839 to 1927* (1931).
Barnett, Lincoln K., *The Universe and Dr. Einstein* (1948).
Bell, Whitfield J., Jr., "Astronomical Observatories of American Philosophical Society, 1769–1843," Am. Philos. Soc. *Proc.,* 108 (1964), 7.
Billings, Cecil M., *History of Rittenhouse Astronomical Society, 1888–1960* (1961).
Greene, John C., "American Astronomy 1750–1815," *Isis,* 45 (1954), 339.
Jaffe, Bernard, *Michelson and Speed of Light* (1960).
Joncich, Geraldine, "Scientists and Schools of Nineteenth Century: Physicists," *Am. Quar.,* 18 (1966), 667.
Jones, Bessie Z., *Lighthouse of the Skies: Smithsonian Astrophysical Observatory* (1965).
King, W. James, "The Project on the History of Recent Physics in the United States," *Am. Archivist,* 27 (1964), 237.
Oppenheimer, J. Robert, *The Flying Trapeze: Three Crises for Physicists* (1964).
Smith, David E., and Jekuthiel Ginsburg, *History of Mathematics before 1900* (1934).
Weiner, Charles, "New Site for the Seminar: Refugees and American Physics in the Thirties," *Perspectives in Am. Hist.,* 2 (1968), 190.
Wright, Helen, *Palomar, the World's Greatest Telescope* (1953).

See also 10.3 for biographies/writings of:

ASTRONOMERS

Bowditch, Nathaniel, 1773–1838
Davidson, George, 1825–1911
Hale, George E., 1868–1938
Lowell, Percival, 1855–1916
Mitchell, Maria, 1818–1889
Newcomb, Simon, 1835–1909
Peirce, Benjamin, 1809–1880
Rittenhouse, David, 1732–1796

MATHEMATICIANS

Ellicott, Andrew, 1754–1820
Gibbs, Josiah W., 1790–1861
Peirce, Benjamin, 1809–1880
Peirce, Charles S., 1839–1914
Wiener, Norbert, 1894–1964
Wright, Chauncey, 1830–1875

PHYSICISTS

Bache, Alexander D., 1806–1867
Bohr, Niels H., 1885–1962
Bridgman, Percy Williams, 1882–1961
Einstein, Albert, 1879–1955
Fermi, Enrico, 1901–1954
Gibbs, Josiah W., 1790–1861
Goddard, Robert H., 1882–1945
Henry, Joseph, 1797–1878

Langmuir, Irving, 1881–1957
Lawrence, Ernest O., 1901–1958
Oppenheimer, J. Robert, 1904–1967
Pupin, Michael I., 1858–1935

29.1.10 Atomic Energy and Atomic Weapons

Allardice, Corbin, and Edward R. Trapnell, *First Pile* (1955).
Bishop, Amasa S., *Project Sherwood: U.S. Program in Controlled Fusion* (1958).
Compton, Arthur H., *Atomic Quest* (1956).
Dahl, R. A., and R. S. Brown, *Domestic Control of Atomic Energy* (1951).
Gilpin, Robert, *American Scientists and Nuclear Weapons Policy* (1962).
Glasstone, Samuel, *Sourcebook on Atomic Energy* (3d ed., 1967).
Groves, Leslie R., *Now It Can Be Told* (1962).
Hewlett, Richard G., and Oscar E. Anderson, Jr., *The New World, 1939–1946: Atomic Energy Commission* (1962).
Hewlett, Richard G., and Francis Duncan, *Atomic Shield, 1947/1952* (1969).
Hiebert, Erwin N., *Impact of Atomic Energy* (1961).
Jacobson, Harold K., and Eric Stein, *Diplomats, Scientists, and Politicians: United States and Nuclear Test Ban Negotiations* (1966).
Lang, Daniel, *Early Tales of the Atomic Age* (1959).
Laurence, William L., *Men and Atoms* (1959).
Oppenheimer, J. Robert, *Open Mind* (1955).
Orlans, Harold, *Contracting for Atoms: Atomic Energy Commission* (1967).
Smith, Alice K., *Peril and Hope: Scientists' Movement, 1945–47* (1965).
Strauss, Lewis L., *Men and Decisions* (1962).
Strickland, Donald A., *Scientists in Politics: Atomic Scientists Movement, 1945–46* (1968).
Thomas, Morgan, *Atomic Energy and Congress* (1956).

29.1.11 Chemistry

Beardsley, Edward H., *Rise of the American Chemistry Profession, 1850–1900* (1964).
Chittenden, Russell Henry, *The Development of Physiological Chemistry in the United States* (1930).
Duveen, Denis I., and Herbert S. Klickstein, "Introduction of Lavoisier's Chemical Nomenclature," *Isis,* 45 (1954), 278, 368.
Miles, Wyndham, "Benjamin Rush, Chemist," *Chymia,* 4 (1953), 37.
Robbins, Caroline, "Joseph Priestley in America, 1794–1804," *Am. Philos. Soc., Proc.,* 106 (1962), 60.
Strauss, Anselm L., et al., *The Professional Scientist: Chemists* (1962).
Taylor, Frank S., *History of Industrial Chemistry* (1957).

See also 10.3 for biographies/writings of:

Conant, James B., 1893–
Coolidge, William D., 1873–1949
Cottrell, Frederick G., 1877–1948
Fieser, Louis Frederick, 1899–
Hare, Robert, 1781–1858
Loeb, Morris, 1863–1912
Priestley, Joseph, 1733–1804
Silliman, Benjamin, 1779–1864
Whitney, Josiah D., 1819–1896
Wiley, Harvey W., 1844–1930

29.1.12 Earth Sciences

Ahnert, Frank, "Some Reflections on the Place and Nature of Physical Geography in America," *The Professional Geographer,* 14 (1962), 1.

Bascom, Willard, *A Hole in the Bottom of the Sea: The Story of the Mohole Project* (1961).

Halacy, Daniel S., Jr., *Weather Changers* (1968).

Hawes, Joseph M., "Signal Corps and Its Weather Service," *Mil. Affairs,* 30 (1966), 68.

Henrickson, Walter B., "Nineteenth Century State Geological Surveys," *Isis,* 52 (1961), 357.

James, Preston E., and Clarence E. Jones, eds., *American Geography, Inventory and Prospect* (1954).

Kiersch, George A., *Engineering Geology: Historical Development* (1955).

Manning, Thomas G., *Government in Science: Geological Survey, 1867–1894* (1967).

Maury, Matthew F., *The Physical Geography of the Sea, and Its Meteorology* (1863); John Leighly, ed., (1963).

Merrill, George Perkins, *The First One Hundred Years of American Geology* (1924).

Nash, Gerald D., "California State Geological Survey, 1860–1874," *Isis,* 54 (1963), 217.

Paul, Rodman W., "Colorado as Pioneer of Science in Mining West," *MVHR,* 47 (1960), 34.

Smith, H. N., "King, Powell, and Establishment of Geological Survey," *MVHR,* 34 (1947), 37.

Whitnah, Donald R., *History of the United States Weather Bureau* (1961).

See also 10.3 for biographies/writings of:

GEOGRAPHERS

Davidson, George, 1825–1911
Erskine, Robert, 1735–1780
Evans, Lewis, 1700–1756
Hassler, Ferdinand R., 1770–1843
Morse, Jedidiah, 1761–1826
Smith, Joseph Russell, 1874–1966.

GEOLOGISTS

Agassiz, J. Louis, 1807–1873
Dana, James D., 1813–1895
Eaton, Amos, 1776–1842
Hall, James, 1811–1898
Houghton, Douglass, 1809–1845
King, Clarence, 1842–1901
Le Conte, Joseph, 1823–1901
Powell, John Wesley, 1834–1902
Pumpelly, Raphael, 1837–1923
Shaler, Nathaniel S., 1841–1906
Van Hise, Charles R., 1857–1918
Whitney, Josiah D., 1819–1896

OCEANOGRAPHER

Maury, Matthew Fontaine, 1806–1873

29.1.13 Life Sciences

Allen, Elsa G., *History of American Ornithology before Audubon* (1951).

Brock, Thomas, *Milestones in Microbiology* (1961).

Cairns, John, Gunther S. Stent, James D. Watson, eds., *Phage and the Origins of Molecular Biology* (1966).

Centre National de la Recherche Scientifique, *Les botanistes français en Amérique du Nord avant 1850* (Paris, 1957).

Clark, Paul F., *Pioneer Microbiologists of America* (1961).

Doetsch, Raymond N., ed., *Microbiology: Historical Contributions from 1776 to 1908* (1960).
Dunn, Leslie C., *Short History of Genetics* (1966).
Ewan, Joseph A., ed., *Short History of Botany in the United States* (1969).
Ewan, Joseph A., "Frederick Pursh, 1774–1820, and His Botanical Associates," Am. Philos. Soc., *Proc.,* 96 (1952), 599.
Fairchild, D. G., *Exploring for Plants* (1930).
Fleming, Donald, "Emigré Physicists and the Biological Revolution," *Perspectives in Am. Hist.,* 2 (1968), 152.
Harshberger, John W., *Botanists of Philadelphia* (1899).
Hayes, Herbert K., *Professor's Story of Hybrid Corn* (1963).
Hedrick, Ulysses P., *History of Horticulture in America* (1950).
Holton, Charles S., et al., eds., *Plant Pathology, 1908–1958* (1959). Historical development since 1664.
Howard, L. O., *A History of Applied Entomology* (1930).
Humphrey, Harry B., *Makers of North American Botany* (1961).
Loeb, Jacques, *Mechanistic Conception of Life* (1912), Donald Fleming, ed., (1964).
Lyon, John, *Journal, 1799–1814,* Joseph and Nesta Ewan, eds. (1963).
McKelvey, Susan Delano, *Botanical Exploration of the Trans-Mississippi West 1759–1850* (1955).
Oppenheimer, Jane M., *Essays in the History of Embryology and Biology* (1967).
Rodgers, Andrew D., III, *American Botany 1873–1892* (1944).
Rosenberg, Charles E., "Development of Genetics in the United States," *Jour. Hist. Med.,* 22 (1967), 27.
Sturtevant, Alfred H., *History of Genetics* (1965).
Waksman, Selman A., *Scientific Contributions,* H. Boyd Woodruff, ed. (1968).
Welker, Robert H., *Birds and Men, 1800–1900* (1955).
Zirkle, Conway, *Beginnings of Plant Hybridization* (1935).

See also 10.3 for biographies/writings of:

BOTANISTS

Beal, William J., 1833–1924
Gray, Asa, 1810–1888
Mazzei, Philip, 1730–1816
Palmer, Edward, 1831–1911
Ravenel, Henry W., 1814–1887

See also 18.11.8, Scientific Agriculture.

BIOLOGISTS AND ZOOLOGISTS

Agassiz, Alexander, 1835–1910
Baird, Spencer F., 1823–1887
Barbour, Thomas, 1884–1946
Cannon, Walter Bradford, 1871–1945
Carson, Rachel L., 1907–1964
Cope, Edward D., 1840–1897
Goldschmidt, Richard B., 1878–1958
Jordan, David Starr, 1851–1931
Loeb, Jacques, 1859–1924
Loewi, Otto, 1873–1961
Smith, Homer W., 1895–1962
Waksman, Selman A., 1888–

ORNITHOLOGISTS

Audubon, John J., 1785–1851
Chapman, Frank M., 1864–1945
Thoreau, Henry David, 1817–1862

PALEONTOLOGISTS

Cope, Edward D., 1840–1897
Hall, James, 1811–1898
Marsh, Othniel C., 1831–1899

29.2 TECHNOLOGY

29.2.1 General

Bennett, Edward M., James Degan and Joseph Spiegel, eds., *Human Factors in Technology* (1963).
Chase, Stuart, *Men and Machines* (1929).
Derry, T. Kingston, and Trevor I. Williams, *Short History of Technology to 1900* (1961).
Ferguson, Eugene S., "Origin and Development of American Mechanical Know-How," *Midcontinent Am. Studies Jour.*, 3 (1962), 3.
Gould, Jay M., *Technical Elite* (1966).
Habakkuk, H. J., *American and British Technology in the Nineteenth Century* (1962).
Harvey, Bartlett, "World Impact of American Technology," Am. Acad. Pol. Soc. Sci. *Annals*, 366 (1966), 41.
Marx, Leo, *Machine in the Garden: Technology and Pastoral Ideal* (1964).
Meier, Hugo A., "Technology and Democracy, 1800–1860," *MVHR*, 43 (1957), 618.
——— "Technology and Nineteenth Century World," *Am. Quar.*, 10 (1958), 116.
Morison, Elting E., *Men, Machines, and Modern Times* (1966).
Mumford, Lewis, *Technics and Civilization* (1934).
Oliver, John W., *History of American Technology* (1956).
Singer, Charles J., et al., eds., *History of Technology: From the Renaissance to the Industrial Revolution, c.1500 to c.1750* (1957).
Singer, Charles J., et al., eds., *History of Technology: Industrial Revolution, c.1750 to c.1850* (1958).

*   *   *   *   *   *   *

Daniels, George H., "Questions in History of American Technology," in Herbert J. Bass, ed., *State of American History* (1970).
Ferguson, Eugene S., *Bibliography of History of Technology* (1968).
Hindle, Brooke, *Technology in Early America: Needs and Opportunities for Study* (1966).

29.2.2 Invention and Innovation

29.2.2.1 General

Anderson, Oscar E., Jr., *Refrigeration in America* (1953).
Burlingame, Roger, *Engines of Democracy* (1940).
——— *March of the Iron Men* (1938).
Casson, H. N., *History of the Telephone* (1910).
Cooper, Grace R., *The Invention of the Sewing Machine* (1968).
Current, Richard N., *The Typewriter and the Men Who Made It* (1954).
De Camp, L. Sprague, *Heroic Age of American Invention* (1961).
Eckhardt, George H., *United States Clock and Watch Patents, 1790–1890* (1960).
Flexner, James T., *Steamboats Come True: American Inventors in Action* (1944).
Gelatt, Roland, *Fabulous Phonograph* (1955).
Harlow, Alvin F., *Old Wires and New Waves* (1936).
Hunter, Dard, *Papermaking: History and Technique* (rev. ed., 1947).
Iles, George, *Flame, Electricity and Camera* (1900).
——— *Leading American Inventors* (1912).
Jewkes, John, David Sawers, and Richard Stillerman, *Sources of Invention* (1958).

Kaempffert, W. B., ed., *Popular History of American Invention* (2 vols., 1924).

Kirby, Richard S., ed., *Inventors and Engineers of Old New Haven* (1939).

McCallum, Henry D., and Frances T. McCallum, *The Wire that Fenced the West* (1965).

MacLaren, Malcolm, *Rise of Electrical Industry during the Nineteenth Century* (1943).

McLaurin, W. R., *Invention and Innovation in the Radio Industry* (1949).

Rogers, Everett, *Diffusion of Innovations* (1962).

Schmookler, Jacob, *Invention and Economic Growth* (1966).

—— *Patents, Invention, and Economic Change* (1972).

Schroeder, Henry, *Electric Light* (1923).

Smart, Charles E., *Makers of Surveying Instruments since 1700* (1962).

Usher, Abbott P., *A History of Mechanical Inventions* (rev. ed., 1954).

Welsh, Peter C., *Tanning in the United States to 1850* (1964).

See also 10.3 for biographies/writings of:

Bell, Alexander Graham, 1847–1922
Browning, John M., 1855–1926
Colt, Samuel, 1814–1862
Cooper, Peter, 1791–1883
Eastman, George, 1854–1932
Edison, Thomas A., 1847–1931
Ericsson, John, 1803–1889
Evans, Oliver, 1755–1819
Field, Cyrus W., 1819–1892
Fitch, John, 1743–1798
Franklin, Benjamin, 1706–1790
Fulton, Robert, 1765–1815
Goodyear, Charles, 1800–1860
Green, Andrew H., 1820–1903
Hewitt, Peter Cooper, 1861–1921
Holland, John P., 1840–1914
Hussey, Obed, 1792–1860
Latrobe, John H. B., 1803–1891
Lowe, Thaddeus S. C., 1832–1913
McCormick, Cyrus H., 1809–1884
Maxim, Hiram S., 1840–1916
Miller, Lewis, 1829–1899
Morse, Samuel F. B., 1791–1872
Nott, Eliphalet, 1773–1866
Perkins, Jacob, 1766–1849
Porter, Rufus, 1792–1884
Stevens, John, 1749–1838
Warren, Josiah, 1798–1874
Westinghouse, George, 1846–1914
Whitney, Eli, 1765–1825

29.2.2.2 Patents

Berle, Alf K., and L. Sprague de Camp, *Inventions, Patents, and Their Management* (1959).

Bugbee, Bruce W., *Genesis of American Patent and Copyright Law* (1967).

Deller, Anthony W., "Social and Economic Impact of Patents," Patent Off. Soc., *Jour.,* 46 (1964), 424.

Federico, P. J., ed., "Outline of History of the United States Patent Office," Patent Off Soc., *Jour.,* 18 (1936), 1.

Reingold, Nathan, "U. S. Patent Office Records as Sources for the History of Invention and Technological Property," *Tech. and Cult.,* 2 (1960), 156.

Schmookler, Jacob, *Patents, Invention, and Economic Change* (1972).

Vaughan, Floyd L., *Economics of Our Patent System* (rev. ed., 1956).

—— *The United States Patent System* (1956).

Weber, Gustavus A., *The Patent Office* (1924).

29.2.3 Engineering

Armytage, Walter H., *Social History of Engineering* (1961).
Bathe, Greville, *Engineer's Miscellany* (1938).
Bjork, Kenneth, *Saga in Steel and Concrete: Norwegian Engineers* (1947).
Calhoun, Daniel H., *The American Civil Engineer* (1960).
Calvert, Monte A., *Mechanical Engineer in America, 1830–1910* (1967).
Finch, James K., *Story of Engineering* (1960).
Kiersch, George A., *Engineering Geology: Historical Development* (1955).
Kirby, Richard S. et al., *Engineering in History* (1956).
Lincoln, Samuel P., *Lockwood Greene: History of an Engineering Business, 1832–1958* (1960).
Merritt, Raymond H., *Engineering in American Society, 1850–1875* (1969).
Sellers, George E., *Early Engineering Reminiscences, 1815–1840,* Eugene S. Ferguson, ed. (1965).
Shaw, Ralph R., comp., *Engineering Books in America prior to 1830* (1933).
Stuart, Charles B., *Lives and Works of Civil and Military Engineers of America* (1871).
Terman, Frederick E., "Herbert Hoover, Engineer," *Science,* 147 (1965), 125.

See also 10.3 for biographies/writings of:

Baldwin, Loammi, Jr., 1780–1838
Crozet, Claudius, 1790–1864
Ellet, Charles, Jr., 1810–1862
Ellicott, Andrew, 1754–1820
Ericsson, John, 1803–1889
Erskine, Robert, 1735–1780
Geary, John W., 1819–1873
Goethals, George W., 1858–1928
Hammond, John H., 1855–1936
Hoover, Herbert, 1874–1964
Isherwood, Benjamin F., 1822–1915
Latrobe, Benjamin H., 1764–1820
Livermore, Robert, 1876–1959
Stevens, John, 1749–1838
Warren, Gouverneur K., 1830–1882

29.2.4 Tools, Mechanization, and Automation

Battison, Edwin A., "Eli Whitney and the Milling Machine," *Smithsonian Jour. Hist.,* 1 (1966), 9.
Brady, Robert A., *Industrial Standardization* (1929).
———— *Organization, Automation and Society: Scientific Revolution in Industry* (1961).
Broehl, Wayne G., Jr., *Precision Valley: Machine Tool Companies of Springfield, Vermont* (1959).
Dickinson, H. W., *Short History of the Steam Engine* (2nd ed., 1963).
Dunsheath, Percy, *History of Electrical Power Engineering* (1969).
Elsner, Henry, Jr., *Technocrats* (1967).
Fabricant, Solomon, *Labor Savings in American Industry, 1899–1939* (1945).
Francois, William, *Automation: Industrialization Comes of Age* (1964).
Gibo, George S., *The Saco-Lowell Shops: Textile Machinery Building in New England, 1813–1949* (1950).
Giedion, Sigfried, *Mechanization Takes Command* (1948).
Green, Constance M., *Eli Whitney and the Birth of American Technology* (1956).
Jaffe, Abram J., and Joseph Froomkin, *Technology and Jobs: Automation in Perspective* (1968).
Jerome, Harry, *Mechanization in Industry* (1934).
Lytle, Richard H., "Introduction of Diesel Power in the United States, 1897–1912," *Bus. Hist. Rev.,* 42 (1968), 115.

National Commission on Technology, Automation and Economic Progress, *Technology and American Economy* (1966).

Richards, John, *Treatise on Construction and Operation of Wood-Working Machines* (1872).

Roe, Joseph W., *English and American Tool Builders* (1916).
—— "Interchangeable Manufacture," Newcomen Soc., *Trans.*, 17 (1937), 165.
—— "Machine Tools in America," Franklin Inst., *Jour.*, 225 (1938), 499.

Rolt, L. T. C., *Short History of Machine Tools* (1965).

Rosenberg, Nathan, "Technological Change in the Machine Tool Industry, 1840–1910," *Jour. Econ. Hist.*, 23 (1963), 414.

Rosenbloom, Richard S., "19th-Century Analyses of Mechanization," *Tech. and Cult.*, 5 (1964), 489.

Sawyer, John E., "The Social Basis of the American System of Manufacturing," *Journal of Economic History*, 14 (1954), 361. Discusses interchangeable parts.

Shelton, F. H., "Windmills: Motors of the Past," Franklin Instit., *Jour.* 187 (1919), 171.

Simon, Herbert Alexander, *Shape of Automation for Men and Management* (1966).

Sloane, Eric, *Museum of Early American Tools* (1964).

Strassmann, W. Paul, *Risk and Technological Innovation: Manufacturing Methods during the Nineteenth Century* (1959).

Temin, Peter, "Steam and Waterpower in the Early Nineteenth Century," *Jour. Econ. Hist.*, 26 (1966), 187.

Thurston, Robert H., *History of Growth of the Steam Engine* (1878).

Wagoner, Harless D., *U.S. Machine Tool Industry, 1900–1950* (1968).

Wik, Reynold M., *Steam Power on the American Farm* (1953).

Woodbury, Robert S., "The Legend of Eli Whitney and Interchangeable Parts," *Tech. and Cult.*, 1 (1960), 235.

Woodworth, J. V., *American Tool Making and Interchangeable Manufacturing* (1911).

29.2.5 Transit of European Technology

Hummel, Charles F., "English Tools in America: Evidence of the Dominys," *Winterthur Portfolio*, 2 (1965), 27.

Pursell, Carroll W., Jr., *Early Stationary Steam Engines in America: A Study in Migration of Technology* (1969).
—— "An Example of Transit of Technology," *WMQ*, 3 ser., 21 (1964), 551.

Thistlethwaite, Frank, "British Influence on American Technology," *Progress*, 46 (1958), 71.

Wilkinson, Norman B., "Brandywine Borrowings from European Technology," *Tech. and Cult.*, 4 (1963), 1.

See also 10.3 for biographies/writings of:

Slater, Samuel, 1768–1835

29.2.6 Metallurgy

Aitchison, Leslie, *History of Metals* (2 vols., 1960).

Boyer, Charles S., *Early Forges and Furnaces in New Jersey* (1963).

Crout, George C., and Wilfred D. Vorhis, "John Butler Tytus: Inventor of Continuous Steel Mill," *Ohio Hist.*, 76 (1967), 132.

Smith, Cyril S., *History of Metallography, before 1890* (1960).

Wertime, Theodore A., *The Coming of Age of Steel* (1962).

29.2.7 Aeronautics and Astronautics

American Heritage, *American Heritage History of Flight*, Alvin M. Josephy, Jr., ed. (1962).

Carpenter, M. Scott, et al., *We Seven: By the Astronauts Themselves* (1962).

Emme, Eugene M., *Aeronautics and Astronautics: Chronology, 1915–1960* (1961).
——— "Early History of the Space Age, Part I," *Aerospace Hist.*, 13 (1966), 74.
——— "History of Rocket Technology," *Tech. and Cult.*, 4 (1963), 377.
——— *History of Space Flight* (1965).
Frutkin, Arnold W., *International Cooperation in Space* (1965).
Grimwood, James M., *Project Mercury* (1963).
Grissom, Virgil I., *Gemini: Personal Account of Venture into Space* (1968).
Levy, Lillian, *Space: Impact on Man and Society* (1965).
Lewis, Richard S., *Appointment on the Moon: America's Space Venture* (1968).
Ley, Willy, *Rockets, Missiles and Men in Space* (4th ed., 1968).
Means, James H., *James Means and the Problem of Man-Flight, 1882–1920* (1964).
National Aeronautics and Space Administration, *Astronautics and Aeronautics, 1966* (1967).
Pomerantz, Sidney I., "Washington and Inception of Aeronautics in Young Republic," Am. Philos. Soc., *Proc.*, 98 (1954), 131.
Rosholt, Robert L., *Administrative History of NASA, 1958–1963* (1966).
Swenson, Lloyd S., Jr., et al., *This New Ocean: Project Mercury* (1966).
Wilbank, Jeremiah, Jr., *First Century of Flight in America* (1943).

See also 10.3 for biographies/writings of:

Goddard, Robert H., 1882–1945
Langley, Samuel P., 1834–1906
Lowe, Thaddeus S. C., 1832–1913
Means, James, 1853–1920
Moffett, William A., 1869–1933
Von Karman, Theodore, 1881–1963
Wright Brothers

29.3 MEDICINE

29.3.1 General

Anderson, Fannie, *Doctors Under Three Flags* (1951). Detroit.
Arrington, George E., *History of Opthalmology* (1959).
Ashburn, Percy M., *Ranks of Death: Medical History of Conquest of America*, Frank D. Ashburn, ed. (1947).
Blake, John B., "Women and Medicine in Ante-Bellum America," *Bull. Hist. Med.*, 39 (1965), 99.
Bonner, Thomas N., *The Kansas Doctor* (1959).
——— *Medicine in Chicago, 1850–1950* (1957).
Brecher, Ruth, and Edward Brecher, *The Rays: History of Radiology in the United States* (1969).
Castiglioni, Arturo, *History of Medicine,* E. B. Krumbhaar, trans. and ed. (2nd ed., 1947).
Clausen, John A., and Robert Straus, eds., "Medicine and Society," Am. Acad. Pol. Soc. Sci., *Annals*, 346 (1963) 1.
Cowen, David L., *Medicine and Health in New Jersey: A History* (1964).
Davison, M. H. Armstrong, *The Evolution of Anaesthesia* (1965).
Duffy, John, "Medical Practice in Ante Bellum South," *JSH*, 25 (1959), 53.
Earle, A. Scott, ed., *Surgery in America from the Colonial Era to the Twentieth Century* (1965).
Eaton, Leonard K., "Medicine in Philadelphia and Boston, 1805–1830," *Penn. Mag. Hist. Biog.*, 75 (1951), 66.
Faulconer, Albert, Jr., and Thomas E. Keys, *Foundations of Anesthesiology* (1965).
Flexner, James T., *Doctors on Horseback: Pioneers of American Medicine* (1937).
Galdston, Iago, *Medicine in Transition* (1965).
Garrison, Fielding H., *Introduction to the History of Medicine* (3rd ed., 1924).
Heaton, Claude E., "Three Hundred Years of Medicine in New York City," *Bull. Hist. Med.*, 32 (1958), 517.

Lasagna, Louis, *Life, Death and the Doctor* (1968).
Marti-Ibañez, Felix, ed., *History of American Medicine* (1958).
Matas, Rudolph, *History of Medicine in Louisiana,* John Duffy, ed. (2 vols., 1958–1962).
Packard, F. R., *History of Medicine in the United States* (2 vols., 1931).
Pickard, Madge, and R. Carlyle Buley, *The Midwest Pioneer: His Ills, Cures, and Doctors* (1945).
Riznik, Barnes, "Early Nineteenth Century New England Doctors," *Jour. Hist. Med.,* 19 (1964), 1.
Rosenberg, Charles E., "Medicine in New York a Century Ago," *Bull. Hist. Med.,* 41 (1967), 223.
Shryock, Richard H., *Development of Modern Medicine* (1947).
—— *Medicine and Society in America, 1660–1860* (1960).
—— *Medicine in America: Essays* (1966).
—— "Significance of Medicine in American History," *AHR,* 62 (1956), 81.
Sigerist, H. E., *American Medicine,* Hildegard Nagel, trans. (1934).
Stieglitz, Julius, ed., *Chemistry in Medicine* (1928).
Thoms, Herbert, *Chapters in American Obstetrics* (2nd ed., 1961).
Viets, H. R., *Brief History of Medicine in Massachusetts* (1930).
Waring, Joseph I., *History of Medicine in South Carolina, 1670–1900* (2 vols., 1964–1967).
Whipple, Allen O., *Evolution of Surgery in the United States* (1963).

*   *   *   *   *   *   *

Blake, John B., and Charles Roos, eds., *Medical Reference Works, 1679–1966: Selected Bibliography* (1967).
Gilbert, Judson B., *Bibliography of Articles on History of American Medicine, 1902–1937* (1951).
U.S. National Library of Medicine, *Early American Imprints: A Guide to Works Printed in the United States 1668–1820,* by Robert B. Austin (1961).

See also 10.3 for biographies/writings of:

Beaumont, William, 1785–1853
Biggs, Hermann M., 1859–1923
Billings, John Shaw, 1838–1913
Blackwell, Elizabeth, 1821–1910
Bowditch, Henry I., 1808–1892
Cullen, Thomas S., 1868–1953
Cushing, Harvey, 1869–1939
Drake, Daniel, 1785–1852
Edsall, David Linn, 1869–1945
Floyd, John, 1783–1837
Garden, Alexander, 1730–1791
Gorgas, William C., 1854–1920
Gregg, Alan, 1890–1957
Grubbe, Emil H., 1875–1960
Halsted, William S., 1852–1922
Hamilton, Alice, 1869–1970
Holmes, Oliver Wendell, 1809–1894
Howe, Samuel Gridley, 1801–1876
Jacobi, Mary P., 1842–1906
Kelly, Howard A., 1858–1943
Larison, Cornelius W., 1837–1910
Lewis, Henry C., 1825–1850
Lincecum, Gideon, 1793–1874
Long, Crawford W., 1815–1878
McHenry, James, 1753–1816
Mayo, Charles William, 1898–1968
Mayo Family, 20th century
Mazzei, Philip, 1730–1816
Minot, George Richards, 1885–1950

Mitchell, S. Weir, 1829–1914
Mitchill, Samuel L., 1764–1831
Nichols, Thomas L., 1815–1901
Osler, William, 1849–1919
Reed, Walter, 1851–1902
Rush, Benjamin, 1745–1813
Shaw, Anna H., 1847–1919
Sims, James Marion, 1813–1883
Swain, Clara A., 1834–1910
Trudeau, Edward L., 1848–1915
Walker, Mary E., 1832–1919
Warren, John C., 1778–1856
Warren, Joseph, 1741–1775
Welch, William H., 1850–1934
Whitman, Marcus, 1802–1847
Wilbur, Ray Lyman, 1875–1949
Williams, Daniel H., 1858–1931
Williamson, Charles S., 1872–1933
Wood, Leonard, 1860–1927
Woodhouse, James, 1770–1809

29.3.2 Medical Profession

Burrage, Walter L., *History of the Massachusetts Medical Society* (1923).
Burrow, James G., *AMA: Voice of American Medicine* (1963).
Fishbein, Morris, *American Medical Association* (1947).
Garceau, Oliver, "Organized Medicine Enforces its 'Party Line'," *Pub. Opinion Quar.,* 4 (1940), 408.
———— *The Political Life of the American Medical Association* (1941).
Glaser, William A., "Doctors and Politics," *Am. Jour. Sociol.,* (1960), 230.
Horine, Emmet F., "Daniel Drake and the Origin of Medical Journalism West of the Allegheny Mountains," *Bull. Hist. Med.,* 27 (1953), 217.
Kett, Joseph F., *Formation of American Medical Profession, 1780–1860* (1968).
Konold, Donald E., *History of American Medical Ethics, 1847–1912* (1962).
Losacco, Charles L., "Philadelphia Journal of Medical and Physical Sciences, 1820–1827," *Bull. Hist. Med.,* 34 (1960), 75.
Pizer, Irwin H., and Harriet Steuernagel, "Medical Journals in St. Louis before 1900," Mo. Hist. Soc., *Bull.,* 20 (1964), 221.
Shafer, Henry B., *American Medical Profession* (1936).
Shryock, Richard H., *Medical Licensing in America, 1650–1965* (1967).
Stern, Bernhard J., *American Medical Practice* (1945).

29.3.3 Education and Research

Arey, Leslie B., *Northwestern University Medical School, 1859–1959: Pioneer in Educational Reform* (1959).
Becker, Howard, et. al., *Boys in White: Student Culture in Medical School* (1961).
Ben-David, Joseph, "Scientific Productivity and Academic Organization in Nineteenth Century Medicine, *Am. Sociol. Rev.,* 25 (1960), 828.
Blake, John B., ed., *Education in the History of Medicine* (1968).
Bonner, Thomas N., *American Doctors and German Universities, 1870–1914* (1963).
Chesney, Alan M., *Johns Hopkins Hospital and the University School of Medicine* (3 vols., 1943–1963).
Corner, George W., *History of the Rockefeller Institute* (1964).
———— *Two Centuries of Medicine: School of Medicine, University of Pennsylvania* (1965).
Cowen, David L., *Medical Education: Queen's-Rutgers Experience, 1792–1830* (1966).
Cunningham, E. R., "Medical Education," *Ann. Med. Hist.,* 7 (1935), 228.

Davis, Nathan S., *Contributions to the History of Medical Education* (1877).
De Kruif, Paul, *Microbe Hunters* (1926).
Flexner, Abraham, *Medical Education in the United States and Canada* (1910).
Knowles, John H., ed., *The Teaching Hospital: Evolution and Contemporary Issues* (1966).
—— *Views of Medical Education and Medical Care* (1968).
Means, James H., *Ward 4: The Mallinckrodt Research Ward of the Massachusetts General Hospital* (1958).
Merton, Robert K., et al., eds., *The Student-Physician: Introductory Studies in the Sociology of Medical Education* (1957).
Moore, Thomas E., Jr., "Early Years of Harvard Medical School, 1782–1810," *Bull. Hist. Med.*, 27 (1953), 530.
Mumford, Emily, *Interns: From Students to Physicians* (1970).
Norwood, William F., *Medical Education before the Civil War* (1944).
Robinson, G. Canby, *Adventures in Medical Education* (1957).
Rosenberg, Charles E., "On the Study of American Biology and Medicine," *Bull. Hist. Med.*, 38 (1964), 364.
Shryock, Richard H., *American Medical Research Past and Present* (1947).
—— *Unique Influence of Johns Hopkins University on American Medicine* (1953).
Stookey, Byron, *History of Colonial Medical Education: New York, 1767–1830* (1962).
Thayer, William S., *Osler and Other Papers* (1931).
Waite, Frederick C., *First Medical College in Vermont: Castleton, 1818–1862* (1949).
—— *History of New England Female Medical College, 1848–1874* (1950).
Ward, Harold, ed., *New Worlds in Medicine* (1946).
Williams, Greer, *Virus Hunters* (1959).

See also 10.3 for biographies/writings of:

Beaumont, William, 1785–1853
Caldwell, Charles, 1772–1853
Corner, George Washington, 1889–
Drake, Daniel, 1785–1852
Dunglison, Robley, 1798–1869
Goldberger, Joseph, 1874–1929
Gregg, Alan, 1890–1957
Hosack, David, 1769–1835
Larison, Cornelius W., 1837–1910
Long, Crawford W., 1815–1878
McCollum, Elmer Verner, 1879–1967
Mall, Franklin P., 1862–1917
Mitchell, Silas W., 1829–1914
Morgan, John, 1735–1789
Noguchi, Hideyo, 1876–1928
Reed, Walter, 1851–1902
Rivers, Thomas M., 1888–1962
Shippen, William, 1736–1808
Sternberg, George M., 1838–1915
Trudeau, Edward L., 1848–1915
Welch, William H., 1850–1934

29.3.4 Hospitals and Nursing

Bullough, Bonnie, and Vern L. Bullough, *Emergence of Modern Nursing* (1964).
Cannon, Ida M., *On the Social Frontier of Medicine: Pioneering in Medical Social Service* (1952). Massachusetts General Hospital.
Corwin, Edward H. L., *The American Hospital* (1946).
Dock, L. L., *History of Nursing* (4 vols., 1912).
Eaton, Leonard K., *New England Hospitals, 1790–1833* (1957).

Faxon, Nathaniel W., *The Massachusetts General Hospital, 1935–1955* (1959).
Hawkins, Hugh, *Pioneer: Johns Hopkins University, 1874–1889* (1960).
Morton, Thomas G., *History of Pennsylvania Hospital, 1751–1895* (1895).
Roberts, Mary M., *American Nursing: History and Interpretation* (1954).
Washburn, Frederic A., *Massachusetts General Hospital: Its Development, 1900–1935* (1939).
Woodford, Frank B., and Philip P. Mason, *Harper of Detroit: Metropolitan Hospital* (1964).
Yost, Edna, *American Women in Nursing* (rev. ed., 1955).

29.3.5 Diseases and Epidemics

Ackerknecht, Erwin H., *Malaria in Upper Mississippi Valley 1760–1900* (1945).
Blake, John B., *Benjamin Waterhouse and Vaccination: Reappraisal* (1957).
Carter, Richard, *Breakthrough: Saga of Jonas Salk* (1966).
Chambers, John S., *Conquest of Cholera* (1938).
Cohn, Alfred E., and Claire Lingg, *The Burden of Diseases in the United States* (1950). Primarily 1900–1940.
DeKruif, Paul, *Microbe Hunters* (1926).
Drake, Daniel, *Systematic Treatise on Principal Diseases of the Interior Valley of North America* (2 vols., 1850–1854). Selections published as *Malaria in the Interior Valley of North America,* Norman D. Levine, ed. (1964).
Duffy, John, "Epidemic Fevers in the City of New York 1791–1822," *N.-Y. Hist. Soc. Quar.,* 50 (1966). 333.
────── *Sword of Pestilence: New Orleans Yellow Fever Epidemic of 1853* (1966).
Goldberger, Joseph, *Pellagra,* Milton Terris, ed. (1964).
Henry, Robert S., *Armed Forces Institute of Pathology, 1862–1962* (1964).
Holmes, Chris, "Benjamin Rush and Yellow Fever," *Bull. Hist. Med.,* 40 (1966), 246.
Landis, H. R. M., "Reception of Koch's Discovery in United States," *Ann. Med. Hist.,* 4 (1932), 531.
Long, Esmond R., *History of American Pathology* (1962).
Powell, John H., *Bring Out Your Dead: Yellow Fever in Philadelphia in 1793* (1949).
Rosenberg, Charles E., *The Cholera Years: 1832, 1849, and 1866* (1962).
Rosenblatt, Milton B., "Lung Cancer in the Nineteenth Century," *Bull. Hist. Med.,* 38 (1964), 395.
Smith, Ashbel, *Yellow Fever in Galveston, Republic of Texas, 1839* (1951).
Steiner, Paul E., *Disease in the Civil War: Natural Biological Warfare in 1861–1865* (1968).
Stiles, C. W., *Report upon Prevalence and Distribution of Hookworm Disease* (1903).
Top, Franklin H., ed., *History of American Epidemiology* (1952).
Williams, Greer, *Virus Hunters* (1959).
Wilson, John R., *Margin of Safety* (1963). Polio vaccine.
Winslow, Charles-Edward, et al., *History of Epidemiology* (1952).

See also 10.3 for biographies/writings of:

Biggs, Hermann M., 1859–1923
Gorgas, William C., 1854–1920
Reed, Walter, 1851–1902

29.3.6 Psychiatry and Mental Health

Brown, James A. C., *Freud and the Post-Freudians* (1961).
Burnham, John C., *Psychoanalysis and American Medicine: 1894–1918* (1967).
Caplan, Ruth B., *Psychiatry and the Community in Nineteenth Century America* (1969).
Carlson, Eric T., "Charles Poyen Brings Mesmerism to America," *Jour. Hist. Med.,* 15 (1960), 121.

Dain, Norman, *Concepts of Insanity, 1789–1865* (1964).

Deutsch, Albert, *The Mentally Ill in America: A History of Their Care and Treatment from Colonial Times* (1937).

Ebaugh, Franklin G., and Charles A. Rymer, *Psychiatry in Medical Education* (1942). Surveys the period 1932–1940.

Galdston, Iago, *Historic Derivations of Modern Psychiatry* (1967).

Gauld, Alan, *The Founders of Psychical Research* (1968).

Greenblatt, Milton, et al., *From Custodial to Therapeutic Patient Care in Mental Hospitals* (1955).

Grob, Gerald N., *The State and the Mentally Ill: Worcester State Hospital in Massachusetts, 1830–1920* (1966).

Hale, Nathan G., Jr., *Freud and the Americans: The Beginnings of Psychoanalysis in the United States, 1876–1917* (1971).

Hurd, Henry M., et al., *Institutional Care of the Insane* (4 vols., 1916–1917).

Kanner, Leo, *History of Care and Study of the Mentally Retarded* (1964).

Kornhauser, Arthur, *Mental Health of the Industrial Worker: Detroit* (1965).

Lidz, Theodore, "Adolph Meyer and the Development of American Psychiatry," *Am. Jour. Psychiatry*, 123 (1966), 320.

Massachusetts Commission on Lunacy, *Insanity and Idiocy in Massachusetts: Report of the Commission on Lunacy, 1855,* by Edward Jarvis (1856); Gerald N. Grob, ed. (1971).

Matthews, Fred H., "The Americanization of Sigmund Freud: Adaptations of Psychoanalysis before 1917," *Jour. Am. Studies,* 1 (1967), 39.

Oberndorf, Clarence P., *History of Psychoanalysis in America* (1953).

Putnam, James Jackson, et al., *James Jackson Putnam and Psychoanalysis: Letters between Putnam and Sigmund Freud, Ernest Jones, William James, Sandor Ferenczi and Morton Prince, 1877–1917,* Nathan G. Hale, Jr., ed., Judith B. Heller, trans. (1971).

Ridenour, Nina, *Mental Health in the United States: A Fifty-Year History* (1961).

Rosen, George, *Madness in Society: Chapters in the Historical Sociology of Mental Illness* (1968).

Rosenberg, Charles E., *The Trial of the Assassin Guiteau: Psychiatry and Law in the Gilded Age* (1968).

Ross, Bertrand, and Helen Ross, *Psychoanalytic Education in the United States* (1960).

Russell, William L., *The New York Hospital: History of the Psychiatric Service, 1771–1936* (1945).

Selling, Lowell S., *Men Against Madness* (1940).

Spingarn, Natalie D., "St. Elizabeth's: Pacesetter for Mental Hospitals," *Harpers Mag.,* 212 (1956), 58. Washington, D.C. hospital.

Zilboorg, Gregory, and J. K. Hall, *One Hundred Years of American Psychiatry* (1944).

Zinberg, Norman E., "Psychoanalysis and the American Scene: A Reappraisal," *Diogenes* [France] 50 (1965), 73.

See also 10.3 for biographies/writings of:

Erikson, Erik H., 1902–
Menninger, Karl, 1893–
Menninger, William Clair, 1899–1966.
White, William Alanson, 1870–1937

29.3.7 Public Health

Abbott, Samuel W., *Condition of Public Hygiene* (1900).

Anderson, Odin W., *Uneasy Equilibrium: Financing of Health Services in United States, 1875–1965* (1968).

Anderson, Oscar E., Jr., *Health of a Nation: Harvey W. Wiley and Fight for Pure Food* (1958).

Bachman, G. W., and Lewis Meriam, *Issue of Compulsory Health Insurance* (1948).

Blake, John B., *Public Health in the Town of Boston, 1630–1822* (1959).

Bowditch, H. I., *Public Hygiene* (1877).

Brieger, Gert H., "Sanitary Reform in New York City," *Bull. Hist. Med.*, 40 (1966), 407.

Cannon, Ida M., *On the Social Frontier of Medicine: Pioneering in Medical Social Service* (1952).

Carter, Richard, *Gentle Legions* (1961). Voluntary health organizations.

Cassedy, James H., *Charles V. Chapin and the Public Health Movement* (1962).

—— "Muckraking and Medicine: Samuel Hopkins Adams," *Am. Quar.*, 16 (1964), 85.

Cavins, Harold M., *National Health Agencies: Survey with Especial Reference to Voluntary Association* (1945).

Duffy, John, *History of Public Health in New York City, 1625–1866* (1968).

—— "Public Health in Early Pittsburgh," *Penn. Mag. Hist. Biog.*, 87 (1963), 294.

Ewing, Oscar R., *Nation's Health* (1948).

Fremont-Smith, Marion R., *Foundations and Government* (1965).

Harris, Seymour E., *Economics of American Medicine* (1964).

—— *National Health Insurance* (1953).

Hazlett, T. Lyle, and William W. Hummel, *Industrial Medicine in Western Pennsylvania, 1850–1950* (1958).

Hirshfield, Daniel S., *The Lost Reform: The Campaign for Compulsory Health Insurance in the United States from 1932 to 1943* (1970).

Horder, T. J., ed., *Health and Social Welfare, 1945–1946* (1946).

Huntington, E. H., *Cost of Medical Care* (1951).

Jordan, Philip D., *People's Health: Public Health in Minnesota to 1948* (1953).

Kagan, Morris, "Federal Public Health," *Jour. Hist. Med.*, 16 (1961), 256.

Leigh, R. D., *Federal Health Administration* (1927).

Lerner, Monroe, and Odin W. Anderson, *Health Progress in the United States, 1900–1960* (1963).

Means, Richard K., *History of Health Education in the United States* (1962).

Moore, H. H., *Public Health in United States* (1923).

Rosen, George, *History of Public Health* (1958).

Rothenberg, R. E., and Karl Pickard, *Group Medicine in Action* (1949).

Shryock, Richard H., *National Tuberculosis Association, 1904–1954* (1957).

—— "Origins and Significance of the Public Health Movement," *Ann. Med. Hist.*, 1 (1929), 645.

Sills, David L., *Volunteers: Means and Ends in a National Organization* (1957).

Smillie, Wilson G., *Public Health: Development in United States, 1607–1914* (1955).

Tobey, J. A., *National Government and Public Health* (1926).

U.S. President's Commission on Health Needs of Nation, *Building America's Health* (5 vols., 1952–1953).

Viseltear, Arthur J., "Compulsory Health Insurance in California, 1915–18," *Jour. Hist. Med.*, 24 (1969), 151.

Williams, Ralph C., *The United States Public Health Service, 1798–1950* (1951).

29.3.8 Pharmacy and the Drug Industry

Ballard, Charles W., *History of the College of Pharmacy, Columbia University* (1954).

Bender, George A., "Rough and Ready Research—1887 Style," *Jour. Hist. Med.* 23 (1968), 159.

Blake, John B., ed., *Safeguarding the Public: Historical Aspects of Medicinal Drug Control* (1970).

Cowen, David L., *America's Pre-Pharmacopoeial Literature* (1961).

Harris, Richard, *The Real Voice* (1964). Kefauver hearings on the drug industry.

Jackson, Charles O., *Food and Drug Legislation in the New Deal* (1970).

Kremers, Edward, and George Urdang, *History of American Pharmacy*, Glenn Sonnedecker, ed. (3d ed., 1963).

Mahoney, John T., *Merchants of Life: American Pharmaceutical Industry* (1959).

Young, James H., *Toadstool Millionaires: Patent Medicines before Federal Regulation* (1961).

29.3.9 Dentistry

Carr, Malcolm W., *Dentistry: An Agency of Health Service* (1946).
Crain, Robert L., Elihu Katz, and Donald B. Rosenthal, *Politics of Community Conflict: Fluoridation* (1969).
Lufkin, Arthur W., *History of Dentistry* (1938).
McCluggage, Robert W., *History of the American Dental Association* (1959).
McNeil, Donald R., *Fight for Fluoridation* (1957).
Taylor, James A., *History of Dentistry* (1922).
Warner, Robert M., *Profile of a Profession: Michigan State Dental Association* (1964).

29.3.10 Health Quackery

Baur, John E., *Health Seekers of Southern California 1870–1900* (1959).
Bryan, Leon S., Jr., "Blood-Letting in American Medicine, 1830–1892," *Bull. Hist. Med.,* 38 (1964), 516.
Davies, John D., *Phrenology, Fad and Science* (1955).
Fishbein, Morris, *Fads and Quackery in Healing* (1932).
Young, James H., "American Medical Quackery in the Age of Common Man," *MVHR,* 47 (1961), 579.
———— *Medical Messiahs: Quackery in Twentieth-Century America* (1967).

Harvard Guide to American History Volume II

VOLUME II

Harvard Guide to American History

REVISED EDITION

Frank Freidel, Editor
With the assistance of Richard K. Showman

The Belknap Press of Harvard University Press

Cambridge, Massachusetts
and London, England

Contents

Part Seven   Civil War and Reconstruction

Serial Abbreviations

AAUP *Bull.*	American Association of University Professors, *Bulletin*
Aerospace Hist.	*Aerospace History*
Agric. Hist.	*Agricultural History*
AHA Newsletter	*American Historical Association Newsletter*
AHR	*American Historical Review*
Ala. Rev.	*Alabama Review*
Am. Acad. Pol. Soc. Sci., *Annals*	American Academy of Political and Social Science, *Annals*
Am. Anthropol.	*American Anthropologist*
Am. Antiq. Soc., *Proc.*	American Antiquarian Society, *Proceedings*
Am. Archivist	*American Archivist*
Am. Assoc. State Local Hist., *Bull.*	American Association for State and Local History, *Bulletins*
Am. Bar Assoc. *Jour.*	*American Bar Association Journal*
Am. Cath. Hist. Soc., *Records*	American Catholic Historical Society, *Records*
Am. Eccles. Rev.	*American Ecclesiastical Review*
Am. Econ. Assoc., *Publ.*	American Economic Association, *Publications*
Am. Econ. Rev.	*American Economic Review*
Am. For. Serv. *Jour.*	*American Foreign Service Journal*
Am. Geneal.	*American Genealogist*
Am. Geog. Soc. *Jour.*	*American Geographical Society Journal*
Am. Heritage	*American Heritage*
Am. Hist. Assoc., *Papers*	American Historical Association, *Papers*
Am. Hist. Assoc., *Report*	American Historical Association, *Report*
Am. Instit. Crim. Law and Criminol., *Jour.*	American Institute of Criminal Law and Criminology, *Journal*
Am. Jew. Archives	American Jewish Archives

Am. Jew. Hist. Quar.	*American Jewish Historical Quarterly*
Am. Jew. Hist. Soc., Publ.	American Jewish Historical Society, *Publications*
Am. Jew. Yr. Bk.	*American Jewish Yearbook*
Am. Jour. Econ. Sociol.	*American Journal of Economics and Sociology*
Am. Jour. Internatl. Law	*American Journal of International Law*
Am. Jour. Legal Hist.	*American Journal of Legal History*
Am. Jour. Phys. Anthropol.	*American Journal of Physical Anthropology*
Am. Jour. Psychiatry	*American Journal of Psychiatry*
Am. Jour. Sociol.	*American Journal of Sociology*
Am. Lit.	*American Literature*
Am. Mag. Art	*American Magazine of Art*
Am. Neptune	*American Neptune*
Am. Philos. Soc., Lib. Bull.	American Philosophical Society, *Library Bulletin*
Am. Philos. Soc., Proc.	American Philosophical Society, *Proceedings*
Am. Philos. Soc., Yearbook	American Philosophical Society, *Yearbook*
Am. Pol. Sci. Rev.	*American Political Science Review*
Am. Quar.	*American Quarterly*
Am. Rev.	*American Review*
Am. Scholar	*American Scholar*
Am. Soc. Church Hist., *Papers*	American Society of Church History, *Papers*
Am. Soc. Civil Engineers, Trans.	American Society of Civil Engineers, *Transactions*
Am. Sociol. Rev.	*American Sociological Review*
Am. Speech	*American Speech*
Am. Stat. Assoc., Jour.	American Statistical Association, *Journal*
Am. Stat. Assoc., Quar. Publ.	American Statistical Association, *Quarterly Publications*
Am. Studies	*American Studies*
Am. Univ. Law Rev.	*American University Law Review*
Am. West	*American West*
Anchor Rev.	*Anchor Review*
Ann. Iowa	*Annals of Iowa*
Ann. Med. Hist.	*Annals of Medical History*
Antioch Rev.	*Antioch Review*
Ariz. and West	*Arizona and the West*
Ariz. Hist. Rev.	*Arizona Historical Review*

Arizona Law Rev.   Arizona Law Review
Ariz. Quar.   Arizona Quarterly
Ark. Hist. As-   Arkansas Historical Association, *Publications*
soc., *Publ.*
Ark. Hist. Quar.   Arkansas Historical Quarterly
Art Bull.   Art Bulletin
Art in Am.   Art in America
Art Jour.   Art Journal
Arts Mag.   Arts Magazine
Asiatic Soc.   Asiatic Society of Japan, *Transactions*
Japan, *Trans.*
Assoc. Am. Ge-   Association of American Geographers, *Annals*
ographers, *An-*
nals
Atl. Community   Atlantic Community Quarterly
Quar.
Atlantic   Atlantic Magazine
Bapt. Hist. and   Baptist History and Heritage
Heritage
Baylor Law Rev.   Baylor Law Review
Bibliog. Soc.   Bibliographical Society of America, *Papers*
Am., *Papers*
Birmingham   Birmingham University Historical Journal
Univ. Hist.
Jour.
Boston Pub. Lib.,   Boston Public Library, *Quarterly*
Quar.
Boston Univ. Law   Boston University Law Review
Rev.
Brit. Assoc. Am.   British Association for American Studies, *Bulletin*
Studies, *Bull.*
Brit. Jour. Sociol.   British Journal of Sociology
Buffalo Hist.   Buffalo Historical Society, *Publications*
Soc., *Publ.*
Buffalo Law Rev.   Buffalo Law Review
Bull. Atomic Sci-   Bulletin of Atomic Scientists
entists
Bull. Hist. Med.   Bulletin of the History of Medicine
Bur. Am.   Bureau of American Ethnology, *Annual Report*
Ethnol., *An-*
nual Report
Bur. Amer. Eth-   Bureau of American Ethnology, *Bulletin*
nol., *Bull.*
Bus. Hist. Rev.   Business History Review
Bus. Hist. Soc.,   Business Historical Society, *Bulletin*
Bull.
CAAS, *Bull.*   Canadian Association for American Studies, *Bulletin*
Calif. Hist. Soc.,   California Historical Society, *Quarterly*
Quar.
Calif. Law Rev.   California Law Review
Can. Hist. As-   Canadian Historical Association, *Annual Report*
soc., *Ann.*
Rep.

Can. Hist. Rev.	Canadian Historical Review
Can. Jour. Hist.	Canadian Journal of History
Cath. Hist. Rev.	Catholic Historical Review
Cath. Univ. Law Rev.	Catholic University of America Law Review
Centennial Rev.	Centennial Review of Arts and Science
Chicago Hist.	Chicago History
Chicago Rev.	Chicago Review
Chronicles Okla.	Chronicles of Oklahoma
Church Hist.	Church History
Civil War Hist.	Civil War History
Classical Jour.	Classical Journal
Col. Hist. Soc., Rec.	Columbia Historical Society, *Records*
Col. Soc. Mass., Publ.	Colonial Society of Massachusetts, *Publications*
Col. Soc. Mass., Trans.	Colonial Society of Massachusetts, *Transactions*
Colo. Mag.	Colorado Magazine
Colo. Quar.	Colorado Quarterly
Columbia Law Rev.	Columbia Law Review
Columbia Univ. Forum	Columbia University Forum
Comp. Studies in Society and Hist.	Comparative Studies in Society and History
Conn. Acad. Arts & Sci., Trans.	Connecticut Academy of Arts and Sciences, *Transactions*
Conn. Hist. Soc., Bull.	Connecticut Historical Society, *Bulletin*
Conn. Hist. Soc., Coll.	Connecticut Historical Society, *Collections*
Cornell Law Rev.	Cornell Law Review
Dakota Law Rev.	Dakota Law Review
Dalhousie Rev.	Dalhousie Review
Del. Hist.	Delaware History
Del . Notes	Delaware Notes
Delaware Hist. Soc., *Papers*	Delaware Historical Society, *Papers*
Duke Univ., Trinity Coll. Hist. Soc., Papers	Duke University, Trinity College Historical Society, *Historical Papers*
Duquesne Hisp. Rev.	Duquesne Hispanic Review
Duquesne Rev.	Duquesne Review
Early Am. Lit.	Early American Literature
East Tenn. Hist. Soc., Publ.	East Tennessee Historical Society, *Publications*
Econ. Hist. Rev.	Economic History Review
Econ. Jour.	Economic Journal

Educ. Forum	*Educational Forum*
Educ. Rev.	*Education Review*
Eng. Hist. Rev.	*English Historical Review*
Essex Inst., Hist. Coll.	Essex Institute, *Historical Collections*
Explorations in Entrepren. Hist.	*Explorations in Entrepreneurial History*
Filson Club Hist. Quar.	*Filson Club History Quarterly*
Fla. Hist. Quar.	*Florida Historical Quarterly*
For. Affairs	*Foreign Affairs*
Forest Hist.	*Forest History*
Franklin Inst., Jour.	Franklin Institute, *Journal*
French Am. Rev.	*French American Review*
Friends' Hist. Assoc., Bull.	Friends' Historical Association, *Bulletin*
Ga. Bar Jour.	*Georgia Bar Journal*
Ga. Hist. Quar.	*Georgia Historical Quarterly*
Ga. Hist. Soc., Coll.	Georgia Historical Society, *Collections*
Geog. Rev.	*Geographical Review*
George Washington Law Rev.	*George Washington Law Review*
Georgetown Law Jour.	*Georgetown Law Journal*
Gt. Plains Jour.	*Great Plains Journal*
Harpers Mag.	*Harper's Magazine*
Harv. Bus. Rev.	*Harvard Business Review*
Harv. Educ. Rev.	*Harvard Educational Review*
Harv. Law Rev.	*Harvard Law Review*
Harv. Lib. Bull.	*Harvard Library Bulletin*
Harv. Theol. Rev.	*Harvard Theological Review*
Hastings Law Jour.	*Hastings Law Journal*
Hisp. Am. Hist. Rev.	*Hispanic-American Historical Review*
Hist. and Phil. Soc. of Ohio, Trans.	Historical and Philosophical Society of Ohio, *Transactions*
Hist. and Theory	*History and Theory*
Hist. Educ. Jour.	*History of Education Journal*
Hist. Educ. Quar.	*History of Education Quarterly*
Hist. Jour.	*Historical Journal*
Hist. Mag. Prot. Episc. Church	*Historical Magazine of the Protestant Episcopal Church*
Hist. Mexicana	*Historical Mexicana*
Hist. N.H.	*Historical New Hampshire*
Hist. Soc. of Montana, Contributions	Historical Society of Montana, *Contributions*

Hist. Soc. Penn, Publ.	Historical Society of Pennsylvania, *Publications*
Hist. Today	*History Today*
Howard Law Jour.	*Howard Law Journal*
Huntington Lib. Quar.	Henry E. Huntington Library, *Quarterly*
Ill. Hist. Coll.	Illinois State Historical Library, *Collections*
Ill. Law Rev.	*Illinois Law Review*
Ill. State Hist. Soc., Jour.	*Journal of the Illinois State Historical Society*
Ill. State Univ. Jour.	*Illinois State University Journal*
Ind. Hist. Soc., Publ.	Indiana Historical Society, *Publications*
Ind. Law Jour.	*Indiana Law Journal*
Ind. Mag. Hist.	*Indiana Magazine of History*
Ind. Univ. Extension Division, Bull.	Indiana University Extension Division, *Bulletin*
India Quar.	*India Quarterly*
Indust. and Labor Rel. Rev.	*Industrial and Labor Relations Review*
Infantry Jour.	*Infantry Journal*
Internatl. Affairs	*International Affairs*
Internatl. Cong. Hist. Sci., Proc.	International Congress of Historical Sciences, *Proceedings*
Internatl. Jour.	*International Journal*
Internatl. Organ.	*International Organization*
Internatl. Studies	*International Studies; Quarterly Journal of the Indian School of International Studies*
Iowa Jour. Hist.	*Iowa Journal of History*
Iowa Jour. Hist. and Pol.	*Iowa Journal of History and Politics*
JAH	*Journal of American History*
James Sprunt Hist. Publ.	*James Sprunt Historical Publications*
Jew. Quar. Rev.	*Jewish Quarterly Review*
Jour. Aesthetics and Art Crit.	*Journal of Aesthetics and Art Criticism*
Jour. Am. Folklore	*Journal of American Folklore*
Jour. Am. Inst. Archit.	*Journal of the American Institute of Architecture*
Jour. Am. Studies	*Journal of American Studies*
Jour. Brit. Studies	*Journal of British Studies*
Jour. Church and State	*Journal of Church and State*
Jour. Conflict Resolution	*Journal of Conflict Resolution*
Jour. Contemp. Hist.	*Journal of Contemporary History*

Jour. Crim. Law	Journal of Criminal Law, Criminology and Police Science
Jour. Devel. Areas	Journal of Developmental Areas
Jour. Eccl. Hist.	Journal of Ecclesiastical History
Jour. Econ. and Bus. Hist.	Journal of Economic and Business History
Jour. Econ. Hist.	Journal of Economic History
Jour. Farm Hist.	Journal of Farm History
Jour. Folklore Inst.	Journal of the Folklore Institute
Jour. Hist. Behavioral Sci.	Journal of the History of the Behavioral Sciences
Jour. Hist. Ideas	Journal of the History of Ideas
Jour. Hist. Med.	Journal of the History of Medicine
Jour. Hist. Phil.	Journal of the History of Philosophy
Jour. Human Rel.	Journal of Human Relations
Jour. Inter-Am. Studies	Journal of Inter-American Studies and World Affairs
Jour. Land Public Utility Econ.	Journal of Land and Public Utility Economics
Jour. Law and Econ.	Journal of Law and Economic Development
Jour. Legal Ed.	Journal of Legal Education
Jour. Lib. Hist.	Journal of Library History
Jour. Miss. Hist.	Journal of Mississippi History
Jour. Mod. Hist.	Journal of Modern History
Jour. Negro Educ.	Journal of Negro Education
Jour. Negro Hist.	Journal of Negro History
Jour. of Abnormal and Soc. Psych.	Journal of Abnormal and Social Psychology
Jour. of Business	Journal of Business
Jour. of Folklore Inst.	Folklore Institute Journal
Jour. of Int. Affairs	Journal of International Affairs
Jour. of Relig.	Journal of Religion
Jour. of Soc. Issues	Journal of Social Issues
Jour. of West	Journal of the West
Jour. of World Hist.	Journal of World History
Jour. Pac. Hist.	Journal of Pacific History
Jour. Philos.	Journal of Philosophy
Jour. Pol. Econ.	Journal of Political Economy
Jour. Politics	Journal of Politics
Jour. Presby. Hist.	Journal of Presbyterian History
Jour. Pub. Law	Journal of Public Law
Jour. Relig. Hist.	Journal of Religious History
Jour. Research in Music Educ.	Journal of Research in Music Education
Jour. Soc. Hist.	Journal of Social History
Jour. Soc. Philos.	Journal of Social Philosophy

Jour. Soc. Sci.	*Journal of Social Sciences*
Jour. Society Archit. Historians	*Journal of the Society of Architectural Historians*
Jour. Urban Law	*Journal of Urban Law*
Journalism Quar.	*Journalism Quarterly*
JSH	*Journal of Southern History*
Kan. Acad. Sci., Trans.	*Transactions of the Kansas Academy of Science*
Kan. Hist. Quar.	*Kansas Historical Quarterly*
Kan. Law Rev.	*Kansas Law Review*
Kan. State Hist. Soc., Coll.	Kansas State Historical Society, *Collections*
Kenyon Rev.	*Kenyon Review*
Ky. Hist. Soc., Reg.	Kentucky Historical Society, *Register*
Ky. Law Jour.	*Kentucky Law Journal*
L.I. Hist. Soc., Memoirs	Long Island Historical Society, *Memoirs*
La. Hist.	*Louisiana History*
La. Hist. Quar.	*Louisiana Historical Quarterly*
La. Law Rev.	*Louisiana Law Review*
Labor Hist.	*Labor History*
Lancaster County Hist. Soc., *Papers*	Lancaster County Historical Society, *Papers*
Law and Contemp. Problems	*Law and Contemporary Problems*
Law Lib. Jour.	*Law Library Journal*
Law Quar. Rev.	*Law Quarterly Review*
Lib. Quar.	*Library Quarterly*
Lib. Trends	*Library Trends*
Mag. of Art	*Magazine of Art*
Mag. of Hist.	*Magazine of History*
Maine Hist. Soc., Coll.	Maine Historical Society, *Collections*
Marquette Law Rev.	*Marquette Law Review*
Marxist Quar.	*Marxist Quarterly*
Mass. Hist. Soc., Coll.	Massachusetts Historical Society, *Collections*
Mass. Hist. Soc., Proc.	Massachusetts Historical Society, *Proceedings*
Md. Hist. Mag.	*Maryland Historical Magazine*
Md. Hist. Soc., Fund-Publ.	Maryland Historical Society, *Fund-Publications*
Md. Law Rev.	*Maryland Law Review*
Mennonite Quar. Rev.	*Mennonite Quarterly Review*
Mich. Acad. Sci., Papers	Michigan Academy of, Arts, and Letters, *Papers*
Mich. Alumni Quar. Rev.	*Michigan Alumni Quarterly Review*

Mich. Hist.	*Michigan History*
Mich. Law Rev.	*Michigan Law Review*
Midcontinent Am Studies Jour.	*Midcontinent American Studies Journal*
Midw. Jour. Pol. Sci.	*Midwest Journal of Political Science*
Midw. Quar.	*Midwest Quarterly*
Mil. Affairs	*Military Affairs*
Mil. Rev.	*Military Review*
Minn. Hist.	*Minnesota History*
Minn. Hist. Bull.	*Minnesota History Bulletin*
Minn. Law Rev.	*Minnesota Law Review*
Miss. Hist. Soc., Publ.	Mississippi Historical Society, *Publications*
Miss. Law Jour.	*Mississippi Law Journal*
Miss. Quar. \	*Mississippi Quarterly*
Miss. Valley Hist. Assoc., *Proc.*	Mississippi Valley Historical Association, *Proceedings*
Mo. Hist. Rev.	*Missouri Historical Review*
Mo. Hist. Soc., Bull.	Missouri Historical Society, *Bulletin*
Mont. Mag. Hist.	*Montana, the Magazine of Western History*
Monthly Lab. Rev.	*Monthly Labor Review*
MVHR	*Mississippi Valley Historical Review*
Narragansett Club, *Publ.*	Narragansett Club, *Publications*
Natl. Acad. of Sciences, *Proc.*	National Academy of Sciences, *Proceedings*
Natl. Geographic	*National Geographic Magazine*
Navy Rec. Soc., *Publ.*	Navy Records Society, *Publications*
Neb. Hist.	*Nebraska History*
Negro Hist. Bull.	*Negro History Bulletin*
NEQ	*New England Quarterly*
New Eng. Hist. Geneal. Reg.	*New England Historical and Genealogical Register*
New Engl. Mag.	*New England Magazine*
New Haven Colony Hist. Soc., *Papers*	New Haven Colony Historical Society, *Papers*
New Mex. Hist. Rev.	*New Mexico Historical Review*
New Princeton Rev.	*New Princeton Review*
Newcomen Soc., *Trans.*	Newcomen Society, *Transactions*
N.J. Hist.	*New Jersey History*
N.J. Hist. Soc., *Proc.*	New Jersey Historical Society, *Proceedings*
No. Am. Rev.	*North American Review*
No. Car. Hist. Rev.	*North Carolina Historical Review*

No. Car. Law Rev.	North Carolina Law Review
No. Dak. Hist.	North Dakota History
No. Dak. Hist. Quar.	North Dakota Historical Quarterly
No. Dak. Quar.	North Dakota Quarterly
Northw. Ohio Quar.	Northwest Ohio Quarterly
Northw. Univ. Law Rev.	Northwestern University Law Review
Norwegian-Am. Stud. and Rec.	Norwegian-American Studies and Records
N.Y. Hist.	New York History
N.Y. Hist. Soc., Coll.	New York Historical Society, Collections
N.Y. Hist. Soc. Quar.	New York Historical Society Quarterly
N.Y. Law Forum	New York Law Forum
N.Y. Law Rev.	New York Law Review
N.Y. Pub. Lib., Bull.	New York Public Library, Bulletin
N.Y. State Hist. Assoc., Quar. Jour.	New York State Historical Association, Quarterly Journal
N.Y. Times Bk. Rev.	New York Times Book Review
N.Y.U. Law Rev.	New York University Law Review
Ohio Hist.	Ohio History
Ohio Hist. Quar.	Ohio Historical Quarterly
Ohio State Archaeol. and Hist. Quar.	Ohio State Archaeological and Historical Quarterly
Ontario Hist.	Ontario History
Ontario Hist. Soc., Papers	Ontario Historical Society, Papers and Records
Ore. Hist. Quar.	Oregon Historical Quarterly
Ore. Hist. Soc., Quar.	Oregon Historical Society, Quarterly
Ore. Law Rev.	Oregon Law Review
Pac. Affairs	Pacific Affairs
Pac. Hist. Rev.	Pacific Historical Review
Pac. Northw. Quar.	Pacific Northwest Quarterly
Pac. Northwesterner	Pacific Northwesterner
Partisan Rev.	Partisan Review
Patent Off. Soc., Jour.	Journal of the Patent Office Society
Penn. German Soc., Proc.	Pennsylvania German Society, Proceedings
Penn. Hist.	Pennsylvania History
Penn. Mag. Hist. Biog.	Pennsylvania Magazine of History and Biography

Perspectives in Am. Hist.	Perspectives in American History
Philos. of Science	Philosophy of Science
Pol. Quar.	Political Quarterly
Pol. Sci. Quar.	Political Science Quarterly
Princeton Rev.	Princeton Review
Psych. Bull.	Psychological Bulletin
Pub. Archives Can., Report	Public Archives of Canada, Report
Pub. Admin. Rev.	Public Administration Review
Pub. Opinion Quar.	Public Opinion Quarterly
Pub. Policy	Public Policy
Quaker Hist.	Quaker History
Quar. Jour. Econ.	Quarterly Journal of Economics
Quar. Jour. Lib. of Congress	Quarterly Journal of the Library of Congress
Quar. Jour. of Current Acquisitions	Quarterly Journal of Current Acquisitions
Quar. Jour. Speech	Quarterly Journal of Speech
Quar. Rev.	Quarterly Review
Quartermaster Rev.	Quartermaster Review
Queen's Quar.	Queen's Quarterly
Queen's Univ., Bull	Queen's University, Department of History and of Political and Economic Science, Bulletin
Register of Kentucky Hist. Soc.	Register of the Kentucky Historical Society
Relig. Educ.	Religious Education Association, Proc.
Rev. and Expositor	Review and Expositor
Rev. Econ. Stat.	Review of Economic Statistics
Rev. Hist. Am. Fr.	Revue d'histoire de l'Amérique française
Rev. Politics	Review of Politics
R.I. Hist.	Rhode Island History
R.I. Hist. Soc., Coll.	Rhode Island Historical Society, Collections
R.I. Jewish Historical Notes	Rhode Island Jewish Historical Notes
Rochester Hist. Soc., Publ. Fund Ser.	Rochester Historical Society, Publication Fund Series
Rochester Hist.	Rochester History
Rocky Mtn. Law Rev.	Rocky Mountain Law Review
Rocky Mtn. Soc. Sci. Jour.	Rocky Mountain Social Science Journal
Royal Hist. Soc., Trans.	Royal Historical Society, Transactions

Royal Soc. Cana- da, *Proc.*	Royal Society of Canada, *Proceedings*
Rural Sociol.	*Rural Sociology*
Scandinavian *Econ. Hist.* *Rev.*	*Scandinavian Economic and Historical Review*
School Rev.	*School Review*
Scient. Am.	*Scientific American*
Scient. Monthly	*Scientific Monthly*
Slavonic & East *Eur. Rev.*	*Slavonic and East European Review*
Smithsonian Jour. *Hist.*	*Smithsonian Journal of History*
So. Atl. Quar.	*South Atlantic Quarterly*
So. Calif. Quar.	*Southern California Quarterly*
So. Car. Hist. As- soc., *Proc.*	South Carolina Historical Association, *Proceedings*
So. Car. Hist. *Geneal. Mag.*	*South Carolina Historical and Genealogical Magazine*
So. Car. Hist. *Mag.*	*South Carolina Historical and Genealogical Magazine*
So. Dak. Hist.	*South Dakota History*
So. Dak. Hist. *Coll.*	*South Dakota Historical Collections*
Soc. Army Hist. Research, *Jour.*	Society for Army Historical Research, *Journal*
Soc. Sci. Res. Council, *Bull.*	Social Science Research Council, *Bulletin*
Social Sci. Quar.	*Social Science Quarterly*
South. Econ. Jour.	*Southern Economic Journal*
South. Folklore *Quar.*	*Southern Folklore Quarterly*
South. Hist. As- soc., *Publ.*	Southern Historical Association, *Publications*
South. Hist. Soc., *Papers*	Southern Historical Society, *Papers*
South. Quar.	*Southern Quarterly Review*
Southw. Hist. *Quar.*	*Southwestern Historical Quarterly*
Southw. Pol. Sci. *Quar.*	*Southwest Political Science Quarterly*
Southw. Rev.	*Southwest Review*
Southw. Soc. Sci. *Quar.*	*Southwestern Social Science Quarterly*
Soviet Rev.	*Soviet Review*
Stanford Law *Rev.*	*Stanford Law Review*
State Dept. of Archives and Hist., *Report*	State Department of Archives and History, *Report* [West Virginia]
Supreme Ct. Rev.	*Supreme Court Review*
Swedish Hist. Soc., *Yearbook*	Swedish Historical Society, *Yearbook*

Teachers College Rec.	*Teachers College Record*
Tech. and Cult.	*Technology and Culture*
Tenn. Hist. Mag.	*Tennessee Magazine of History*
Tenn. Hist. Quar.	*Tennessee Historical Quarterly*
Tex. Law Rev.	*Texas Law Review*
Tex. Quar.	*Texas Quarterly*
Tex. State Hist. Assoc., *Quar.*	Texas State Historical Association, *Quarterly*
Tri-Quar.	*Tri-Quarterly*
Tulane Law Rev.	*Tulane Law Review*
Tyler's Quar.	*Tyler's Quarterly*
UCLA Law Rev.	*University of California, Los Angeles, Law Review*
Univ. of Chi. Law Rev.	*University of Chicago Law Review*
Univ. of Cinc. Law Rev.	*University of Cincinnati Law Review*
Univ. of Colo., *Studies*	University of Colorado, *Studies*
Univ. Kan. City Rev.	*University of Kansas City Review*
Univ. of Maine, *Studies*	University of Maine, *Studies*
Univ. of Mo., *Studies*	University of Missouri, *Studies*
Univ. Penn. Law Rev.	*University of Pennsylvania Law Review*
Univ. of Wyoming Publ.	*University of Wyoming Publications*
U.S. Natl. Museum, *Bull.*	United States National Museum, *Bulletin*
U.S. Naval Inst., *Proc.*	United States Naval Institute, *Proceedings*
U.S. News & World Rep.	*U.S. News & World Report*
Utah Hist. Quar.	*Utah Historical Quarterly*
Va. Hist. Soc., *Coll.*	Virginia Historical Society, *Collections*
Va. Law Rev.	*Virginia Law Review*
Va. Mag. Hist. Biog.	*Virginia Magazine of History and Biography*
Va. Quar. Rev.	*Virginia Quarterly Review*
Va. State Lib. *Bull.*	Virginia State Library *Bulletin*
Vanderbilt Law Rev.	Vanderbilt Law Review
Vt. Hist.	*Vermont History*
W. Va. Hist.	*West Virginia History*
Wash. and Lee Law Rev.	*Washington and Lee Law Review*
Wash. Hist. Quar.	*Washington Historical Quarterly*

Wash. Law Rev.	*Washington Law Review*
Wash. Univ. Law Rev.	*Washington University Law Review*
West. Econ. Jour.	*Western Economic Journal*
West. Humanities Rev.	*Western Humanities Review*
West. Penn. Hist. Mag.	*Western Pennsylvania History Magazine*
West. Pol. Quar.	*Western Political Quarterly*
West. Reserve Law Rev.	*Western Reserve Law Review*
Westchester Co. Hist. Soc., *Publ.*	Westchester County Historical Society, *Publications*
Western Reserve Hist. Soc., *Tracts*	Western Reserve Historical Society, *Tracts*
Wis. Acad. Sciences, Trans.	Wisconsin Academy of Sciences, Arts and Letters, *Transactions*
Wis. Hist. Soc., Proc.	State Historical Society of Wisconsin, *Proceedings*
Wis. Law Rev.	*Wisconsin Law Review*
Wis. Mag. Hist.	*Wisconsin Magazine of History*
WMQ	*William and Mary Quarterly*
Women's Bur., *Bull.*	Women's Bureau, *Bulletin*
Yale Law Jour.	*Yale Law Journal*
Yale Jour. Biol. and Med.	*Yale Journal of Biology and Medicine*
Yale Rev.	*Yale Review*
YIVO	*YIVO Annual of Jewish Social Science*

Part Five   America to 1789

Alden, John R., *Rise of the American Republic* (1963).

American Heritage, *American Heritage History of the Thirteen Colonies*, Michael Blow, ed. (1967).

Andrews, Charles M., *The Colonial Period of American History* (4 vols., 1934–1938).

Barck, Oscar T., Jr., and Hugh T. Lefler, *Colonial America* (2nd ed., 1968).

Boorstin, Daniel J., *The Americans: Colonial Experience* (1958).

Channing, Edward, *A History of the United States* (6 vols., 1905–1925).

Chitwood, Oliver P., *History of Colonial America* (1961).

Craven, Wesley Frank, *The Colonies in Transition, 1660–1761* (1968).

Davenport, Frances G., ed., *European Treaties Bearing on the History of the United States and Its Dependencies*, vols. I–II (1917).

Demos, John, ed., *Remarkable Providences: 1600–1760* (1971).

Force, Peter, ed., *Tracts and Other Papers Relating Principally to the Colonies in North America* (4 vols., 1836–1846).

Gipson, Lawrence H., *The British Empire before the American Revolution* (15 vols., 1936–1970).

Grant, William L., and James Munro, eds., *Acts of the Privy Council of England, Colonial Series* (6 vols., 1908–1912).

Greene, Jack P., ed., *Great Britain and the American Colonies, 1606–1763* (1970).

——— ed., *Settlements to Society, 1584–1763* (1966).

Hart, Albert B., ed., *American History Told by Contemporaries*, vols. I–II (1897).

Hawke, David, *Colonial Experience* (1966).

Jameson, J. Franklin, *Original Narratives of Early American History* (19 vols., 1906–1917).

Jensen, Merrill, ed., *English Historical Documents: American Colonial Documents, 1607–1776* (1955).

Katz, Stanley M., ed., *Colonial America: Essays in Politics and Social Development* (1971).

Labaree, Benjamin W., *America's Nation-Time 1607–1789* (1972).

Labaree, Leonard W., ed., *Royal Instructions to British Colonial Governors* (2 vols., 1935).

Leder, Lawrence H., *America—1603–1789: Prelude to a Nation* (1972).

——— ed., *Dimensions of Change: Problems and Issues of American Colonial History* (1972).

MacDonald, William, ed., *Select Charters and Other Documents Illustrative of American History, 1606–1775* (1899).

Malone, Dumas, and Basil Rauch, *American Origins to 1789* (1969).

Miller, John C., *Rise of the American Colonies* (1972).

Nettels, Curtis P., *Roots of American Civilization* (2nd ed., 1963).

Osgood, Herbert L., *American Colonies in the Seventeenth Century* (3 vols., 1904–1907).

——— *American Colonies in the Eighteenth Century* (4 vols., 1924–1925).

Savelle, Max, and Robert Middlekauff, *History of Colonial America* (rev. ed., 1964).

——— *Seeds of Liberty* (1948).

Stock, Leo F., ed., *Proceedings and Debates of the British Parliaments Respecting North America* (3 vols., 1924–1930).

Thorpe, Francis N., ed., *The Federal and State Constitutions: Colonial Charters and Other Organic Laws* (7 vols., 1909).

Ubbelohde, Carl, *American Colonies and British Empire, 1607–1763* (1968).

Ver Steeg, Clarence L., *Formative Years, 1607–1763* (1964).

Walsh, Richard, ed., *The Mind and Spirit of Early America: Sources in American History, 1607–1789* (1969).

*   *   *   *   *   *   *

Billington, Ray A., ed., *Reinterpretation of Early American History: Essays in Honor of John E. Pomfret* (1966).

Gipson, Lawrence H., *The British Empire before the American Revolution,* vol. XV (1970).

Greene, Jack P., *The American Colonies in the Eighteenth Century, 1689–1763* (1969).

31 Age of Discovery

31.1 GENERAL

Beaglehole, John C., *Exploration of the Pacific* (1934).
Boland, Charles M., *They All Discovered America* (1961).
Bolton, Herbert E., and Thomas M. Marshall, *Colonization of North America, 1492–1783* (1920).
Brebner, John B., *The Explorers of North America, 1492–1806* (1933).
Crone, Gerald R., *Discovery of America* (1969).
Crouse, Nellis M., *In Quest of the Western Ocean* (1928).
Gillespie, James E., *A History of Geographical Discovery, 1400–1800* (1933).
Harisse, Henry, *Discovery of North America* (1892).
Harlow, Vincent T., ed., *Voyages of the Great Pioneers* (1929).
Heawood, Edward, *A History of Geographical Discovery in the Seventeenth and Eighteenth Centuries* (1912).
Herrmann, Paul, *Great Age of Discovery* (1958).
Mauro, Frédéric, *L'expansion européenne, 1600–1870* (1964).
Morison, Samuel E., *The European Discovery of America: Northern Voyages, A.D. 500–1600* (1971).
Newton, Arthur P., ed., *The Great Age of Discovery* (1932).
Norman, Charles, *Discoverers of America* (1968).
Nowell, Charles E., *Great Discoveries and the First Colonial Empires* (1954).
Olson, Julius E., and Edward G. Bourne, eds., *Northmen, Columbus, and Cabot, 985–1503* (1906).
Parker, John, ed., *Merchants and Scholars: Essays in History of Exploration and Trade* (1965).
Parry, John Horace, *Age of Reconnaissance: Discovery, Exploration and Settlement 1450 to 1650* (1963).
—— *Europe and a Wider World, 1415–1715* (1950).
Penrose, Boies, *Travel and Discovery in the Renaissance, 1420–1620* (1955).
Sykes, Percy, *History of Exploration* (3d ed., 2 vols., 1950).
Washburn, Wilcomb E., "The Meaning of 'Discovery' in the Fifteenth and Sixteenth Centuries," *AHR*, 68 (1962), 1.
Woodbury, Charles L., *Relation of Fisheries to Discovery and Settlement of North America* (1880).

31.2 PRE-COLUMBIAN VOYAGES

Best, George, *A True Discourse of Late Voyages of Discovery of Martin Frobisher* (1578).
—— *Three Voyages of Martin Frobisher*, Vilhjalmur Stefansson, ed. (1938).
Bjørnbo, A. A., "Cartographia Groenlandica," *Meddelelser om Grønland*, 48 (1912).
Brögger, A. W., *Vinlandsferdene* (1937).

Gathorne–Hardy, Geoffrey M., *The Norse Discoverers* (1921).
Haugen, Einar, *Voyages to Vinland* (1942).
Hermannsson, Halldór, "Northmen in America," *Islandica*, 2 (1909), 1.
Hovgaard, William, *Voyages of Norsemen to America* (1914).
Ingstad, Helge M., *Land under Pole Star: Voyage to the Norse Settlements of Greenland and Saga of People That Vanished* (1959). Naomi Walford, trans. (1966).
———— *Westward to Vinland: Discovery to Pre-Columbian Norse House Sites in North America* (1969).
Jones, Gwyn, *Norse Atlantic Saga* (1964).
Mowat, Farley, *Westviking: Ancient Norse in Greenland and North America* (1965).
Nansen, Fridtjof, *In Northern Mists* (2 vols., 1911); Arthur Chater, trans. (2 vols., 1969).
Oleson, Tryggvi J., *Early Voyages, 1000–1632* (1964).
Oxenstierna, Eric, *Norsemen*, Catherine Hutter, trans. (1965).
Pohl, Frederick J., *Atlantic Crossings before Columbus* (1961).
Reeves, Arthur M., *Finding of Wineland the Good* (1890).
Scisco, Louis D., "Pre-Colombian Discovery by Basques," Royal Soc. Can., *Proc.*, 3 ser., 18, sec. 2 (1924), 51.
Skelton, Raleigh A., et al., *The Vinland Map and the Tartar Relation* (1965).
Slafter, Edmund F., ed., *Voyages of Norsemen to America in the Tenth and Eleventh Centuries* (1966).
Stefansson, Vilhjalmur, *Ultima Thule* (1940).
———— *Unsolved Mysteries of the Arctic* (1939).
Tornøe, Johannes Kristoffer, *Early American History: Norsemen before Columbus* (1964).
Vinland Sagas: Norse Discovery of America, Magnus Magnusson and Hermann Palsson, ed. and trans. (1966).
Zechlin, Egmont, "Das Problem der vorkolumbischen Entdeckung Amerikas u. die Kolumbusforschung," *Historische Zeitschrift*, 152 (1935), 1.

*   *   *   *   *   *   *

Collier, Christopher, "Who Discovered America? Review of Recent Historiography," *So. Atl. Quar.*, 66 (1967), 31.
Hermannsson, Halldór, "Problem of Wineland," *Islandica*, 25 (1936). Entire issue.
Wahlgren, Erik, "Review Article: Norse Discovery of America," *Scandinavian Studies*, 37 (1965), 377.

31.2.1 Legendary Voyages

Babcock, William H., *Legendary Islands of the Atlantic* (1922).
Blegen, Theodore C., *Kensington Rune Stone* (1968).
Dunn, Joseph, "Brendan Problem," *Cath. Hist. Rev.*, 6 (1921), 395.
Elliott, O. C., and C. T. Currelly, "Case of Beardmore Relics," *Can. Hist. Rev.*, 22 (1941), 254.
Gaffarel, Paul, *LesIrlandais en Amérique avant Colomb* (1890).
Godfrey, William S., Jr., "Newport Puzzle," *Archaeology*, 2 (1949), 146.
Hencken, Hugh, "Irish Monastery at New Salem, N.H.," *NEQ*, 12 (1939), 492.
Hennig, Richard, "Atlantische Fabelinseln u. Entdeckung Amerikas," *Historische Zeitschrift*, 153 (1936), 461.
Hobbs, W. H., "Zeno and Cartography of Greenland," *Imago Mundi*, 6 (1949), 15.
Larsen, Sofus, *Discovery of America Twenty Years before Columbus* (1925).
Means, Philip A., *Newport Tower* (1942).
Pohl, Frederick S., "The Newport Tower: An Answer to Mr. Godfrey," *Archaeology*, 3 (1950), 183.
Wahlgren, Eric, *Kensington Stone* (1958).

31.3 EUROPEAN BACKGROUND TO EXPANSION

31.3.1 General

Abbott, Wilbur C., *Expansion of Europe* (1938).

Beard, Miriam, *A History of the Business Man* (1938).

Cambridge Economic History of Europe. Vol. IV: *Economy of Expanding Europe in the Sixteenth and Seventeenth Centuries,* E. E. Rich and C. H. Wilson, eds. (1967).

Cheyney, Edward P., *Dawn of New Era, 1250–1453* (1936).

—— *European Background of American History* (1904).

Ehrenberg, Richard, *Capital and Finance in the Age of the Renaissance: A Study of the Fuggers and their Connections,* H. M. Lucas, trans. (1928).

Friedrich, Carl J., *The Age of the Baroque, 1610–1660* (1952).

Hauser, Henri, *Les débuts du capitalisme* (1927).

Heckscher, Eli F., *Mercantilism,* Mendel Shapiro, trans. and E. F. Soderlund, ed. (rev. ed., 2 vols., 1955).

Mattingly, Garrett, *Renaissance Diplomacy* (1955).

Nussbaum, F. L., *History of Economic Institutions of Modern Europe* (1933).

Packard, Laurence B., *Commercial Revolution, 1400–1776* (1927).

Pike, Ruth, *Enterprise and Adventure: Genoese in Seville and New World* (1966).

Pirenne, Henri, *Economic and Social History of Medieval Europe* (1936).

Potter, George R., ed., *The Renaissance, 1493–1520* (1957).

von Schmoller, G. F., *Mercantile System* (1931).

Sée, Henri, *Modern Capitalism* (1928).

Tawney, R. H., *Religion and the Rise of Capitalism* (1926).

Zavala, Silvio, *The Political Philosophy of the Conquest of America,* Teener Hall, trans. (1953).

31.3.2 Geographic Knowledge

Baker, John N. L., *History of Geographical Discovery and Exploration* (1931).

Beazley, C. R., *Dawn of Modern Geography* (3 vols., 1897–1906).

de Ispizúa, Segundo, *Historia de la geografía y de la cosmografía en las edades antigua y media* (2 vols., 1922–1926).

Harisse, Henry, *Discovery of North America* (1892).

Haugen, Einar, "Sources of the Vinland Map," *Arctic,* 19 (1966), 287.

Kimble, George H. T., *Geography in the Middle Ages* (1938).

Nunn, G. E., *Geographical Conceptions of Columbus* (1924).

Ravenstein, E. G., *Martin Behaim, His Life and Globe* (1908).

Skelton, Raleigh A., *Explorers' Maps: Cartographic Record of Geographical Discovery* (1958).

Stevenson, Edward L., *Atlas of Portolan Charts* (1911).

Tillinghast, W. H., "Geographical Knowledge of Ancients," in Justin Winsor, ed., *Narrative and Critical History,* vol. I (1884).

Washburn, Wilcomb E., "Japan on Early European Maps," *Pac. Hist. Rev.,* 21 (1952), 221.

Wright, John K., *Geographical Lore of Time of Crusades: Medieval Science and Tradition in Western Europe* (rev. ed., 1965).

31.3.3 Medieval and Early Renaissance Travel

Blake, J. W., *European Beginnings in West Africa* (1937).

Dawson, Christopher, ed., *Mongol Mission: Narratives of Franciscan Missionaries in Mongolia and China in the Thirteenth and Fourteenth Centuries* (1959).

Hourani, George F., *Arab Seafaring in Indian Ocean in Ancient and Early Medieval Times* (1951).

La Roncière, Charles G. M. B. de, *La découverte de l 'Afrique au moyen âge* (3 vols., 1924–1927).

Lybyer, A. H., "Influence of Turks upon Routes of Oriental Trade," Am. Hist. Assoc., *Report*, 1 (1914), 125.

Olschki, Leonardo, *Marco Polo's Precursors* (1943).

Polo, Marco, *Book of Ser Marco Polo*, Colonel Sir Herny Yule, trans. and ed. (3d ed., 2 vols., 1903).

—— *The Most Noble and Famous Travels of Marco Polo*, N. M. Penzer, ed. (2nd ed., 1937).

31.3.4 Navigation and Ships

de Artiñano y de Galdacano, Gervasio, *Arquitectura naval española* (1920).

Bensuade, Joaquim, *Histoire de la science nautique portugaise, résumé* (1917).

Cipolla, Carlo M., *Guns, Sails and Empires: Technological Innovation of European Expansion, 1400–1700* (1965).

Fontoura da Costa, Abel, *Science nautique des Portugais à l'époque des découvertes* (1935). A résumé of his *Marinharia dos descobrimentos* (1933).

Hewson, J. B., *History of Practice of Navigation* (1951).

Lane, Frederic C., "Economic Meaning of Invention of Compass," *AHR*, 68 (1963), 605.

—— *Venetian Ships and Shipbuilders of the Renaissance* (1934).

Nordenskiold, A. E., *Periplus: An Essay on the Early History of Charts and Sailing–Directions* (1897).

Parry, John Horace, *Age of Reconnaissance: Discovery, Exploration and Settlement, 1450 to 1650* (1963).

Quirino da Fonseca, Henrique, *Caravela portuguesa* (1934).

Stevenson, Edward L., *Atlas of Portolan Charts* (1911).

Taylor, Eva G. R., *The Haven–Finding Art: History of Navigation to Captain Cook* (1956).

Winter, Heinrich, "Late Portolan Charts," *Imago Mundi*, 7 (1950), 37.

—— "Who Invented the Compass?," *Mariner's Mirror*, 23 (1937), 95.

Wroth, Lawrence C., *Way of a Ship* (1937).

31.3.5 Portuguese Voyages

Boxer, C. R., *Portuguese Seaborne Empire, 1415–1825* (1969).

Braz, Henrique, and José Agostinho, "Fernandez-Barcellos and Diego de Tieve Voyages," Instituto Historico de Ilha Terceira, *Boletim*, 1 (1943), 7; 2 (1944), 1; 3 (1945), 259; 9 (1951), 211.

Cortesão, Armando, *Cartografia e cartógrafos portugueses dos seculos XV e XVI* (2 vols., 1935).

Diffie, Bailey W., *Prelude to Empire: Portugal Overseas before Henry the Navigator* (1960).

Eannes de Azurara, Gomes, *Conquests and Discoveries of Henry the Navigator*, Virginia de Castro e Almeida, ed. and Bernard Miall, trans. (1936).

Hart, Henry H., *Sea Road to the Indies: The Voyages and Exploits of Portuguese Navigators* (1950).

Morison, Samuel E., *Portuguese Voyages to America in the Fifteenth Century* (1940).

Oliveira Martins, J. P., *Golden Age of Prince Henry the Navigator*, J. J. Abraham and W. E. Reynolds, trans. (1914).

—— *Historia da colonização portuguesa do Brasil* (1921).

Prestage, Edgar, *Portuguese Pioneers* (1933).

Rogers, Francis M., *Quest for Eastern Christians: Travels and Rumor in Age of Discovery* (1962).

—— *The Travels of the Infante Dom Pedro of Portugal* (1961).

31.4 CHRISTOPHER COLUMBUS

Alvárez Pedroso, Armando, *Cristóbal Colón* (1944).

Carbia, R. D., *La nueva historia del descubrimiento de América* (1936).

Charcot, J. B., *Christophe Colomb vu par un marin* (1928).

Colón, Fernando, *Histoire della vita e dei fatti di Christoforo Colombo* (1569); Partly translated in John R. Pinkerton, comp., *Collection of Voyages*, vol. XII [1812]. Best modern ed., *The Life of Admiral Christopher Columbus, by his son, Ferdinand*, Benjamin Keen, trans. and ed. (1960).

Columbus, Christopher, *Journal*, Cecil Jane, trans., and L. S. Vigneras, ed. (1960).

—— *Journals and Other Documents*, Samuel E. Morison, ed. and trans. (1963).

Cronau, Rudolf, *Discovery of America: Landfall and Last Resting Place of Columbus* (1921).

Gould, R. T., "Landfall of Columbus," *Geog. Jour.*, 69 (1927), 403.

Harrisse, Henry, *Christophe Colomb* (2 vols., 1884–1885).

Hobbs, W. H., "Track of Columbus Caravels," *Mich. Alumni Quar. Rev.*, 56 (1950), 118.

McElroy, J. W., "Ocean Navigation of Columbus on his First Voyage," *Am. Neptune*, 1 (1940), 209.

Martinez-Hidalgo, Jose Maria, *Columbus' Ships*, Howard I. Chapelle, ed. and trans. (1966).

Morison, Samuel E., *Admiral of the Ocean Sea* (2 vols., 1942).

—— and Maurice Obregón, *The Caribbean as Columbus Saw It* (1964).

Nowell, Charles E., "Toscanelli Letters," *Hisp.-Am. Hist. Rev.*, 17 (1937), 346.

Nunn, G. E., *Geographical Conceptions of Columbus* (1924).

Revelli, Paolo, *Il Genovese* (1951).

Schoenrich, Otto, ed., *Legacy of Columbus* (2 vols., 1949–1950).

Thacher, J. B., *Christopher Columbus* (3 vols., 1903–1904).

Toscanelli, Paolo del Pozzo, *Correspondence de Toscanelli avec Christophe Colomb*, N. Sumien, ed. (1927).

Vignaud, Henry, *Histoire critique de la grande enterprise de Christophe Colomb* (2 vols., 1911). Summarized in his *Columbian Tradition* (1920).

—— *Toscanelli and Columbus* (1902).

Winter, Heinrich, *Die Kolumbusschiffe* (1944).

*   *   *   *   *   *   *

Biggar, H. P., "Recent Books on Columbus," *Can. Hist. Rev.*, 12 (1931), 59.

Mugridge, Donald H., *Christopher Columbus: Selected List of Books and Articles by American Authors, 1892–1950* (1950).

Nowell, Charles E., "Columbus Question: A Survey of Recent Literature," *AHR*, 44 (1939), 802.

31.5 AMERIGO VESPUCCI AND NAMING OF AMERICA

Almagìa, Roberto, *Gli Italiani, primi esploratori dell'America* (1937).

Arciniegas, Germán, *Amerigo and the New World* (1955).

Fischer, Joseph, and Franz von Wieser, eds., *Oldest Map with Name America* (1903).

Levillier, Roberto, *América la bien llamada* (2 vols., 1949).

Magnaghi, Alberto, *Amerigo Vespucci: studio critico* (1926).

Northrup, G. T., ed., *Vespucci Reprints* (7 vols., 1916).

Pohl, F. J., *Amerigo Vespucci: Pilot Major* (1944).

31.6 LATER EXPLORERS

Cook, James, *Journals of Captain James Cook on His Voyages of Discovery*, John C. Beaglehole, ed. (3 vols., 1955–1967).

Parr, Charles M., *Ferdinand Magellan, Circumnavigator: His Life and Explorations* (1964).

Pigafetta, Antonio, *Magellan's Voyage: Narrative Account of the First Circumnavigation*, R. A. Skelton, trans. and ed. (2 vols., 1969).
Powys, Llewelyn, *Henry Hudson* (1928).
Whitebrook, Robert B., *Coastal Exploration of Washington* (1959).

See also 33.1.5, Voyages of Discovery and Privateering.

32 Non-English Settlements in America

32.1 SPANISH SETTLEMENT

32.1.1 General

Bourne, Edward G., *Spain in America, 1450–1580* (1904).
Brazão, Eduardo, "Corte-Reals et le nouveau monde," *Revue d'histoire de l'Amérique française,"* 19 (1965), 163.
De Voto, Bernard, *Course of Empire* (1952).
Diffie, Bailey W., *Latin American Civilization: Colonial Period* (1945).
Elliott, J. H., *Imperial Spain, 1469–1716* (1963).
Frederici, George, *Charakter der Entdeckung u. Eroberung Amerikas durch die Europaer* (3 vols., 1925–1936).
Gibson, Charles, *Spain in America* (1966).
Hanke, Lewis, *Spanish Struggle for Justice in the Conquest of America* (1949).
Haring, Clarence H., *Spanish Empire in America* (1952).
Horgan, Paul, *Conquistadors in North American History* (1963).
Kirkpatrick, Frederick A., *Spanish Conquistadores* (1934).
Leon-Portilla, Miguel, ed., *Broken Spears: Aztec Account of the Conquest of Mexico* (1962).
Lynch, John, *Spain under the Hapsburgs: Empire and Absolutism, 1516–1598* (1964).
MacNutt, F. A., *Hernando Cortés and the Conquest of Mexico* (1909).
Madariaga, Salvador de, *Rise of the Spanish American Empire* (1947).
Means, Philip A., *Spanish Main: 1492–1700* (1935).
Merriman, Roger B., *Rise of the Spanish Empire* (4 vols., 1918–1934).
Neasham, V. Aubrey, "Spain's Emigrants to the New World," *Hisp. Am. Hist. Rev.,* 19 (1939), 147.
Parry, John Horace, *Spanish Seaborne Empire* (1966).
——— *Spanish Theory of Empire in the Sixteenth Century* (1940).
Petrie, Charles, *Philip II of Spain* (1963).
Prescott, William H., *Conquest of Mexico* (1843).
Sauer, Carl O., *The Early Spanish Main* (1966).
Wright, Irene A., ed., "Documents on Spanish Policy," *AHR,* 25 (1920), 448.
——— "Documents on Spanish Policy," Mass. Hist. Soc., *Proc.,* 54 (1922), 61.
Zavala, Silvio, *New Viewpoints on Spanish Colonization of America* (1943).

32.1.2 Social, Economic, and Cultural Studies

Anderson, Lawrence, *Art of the Silversmith in Mexico 1519–1936* (2 vols., 1941).
Bayle, Constantino, *España y la educación popular en América* (1934).
Bolton, Herbert E., "The Mission as a Foreign Institution in Spanish-American Colonies," *AHR,* 23 (1917), 42.
Braden, Charles S., *Religious Aspects of Conquest of Mexico* (1930).

Coester, Alfred, *Literary History of Spanish America* (1928).
Conway, G. R. G., *An Englishman and the Mexican Inquisition 1556–1560* (1927).
Cossío del Pomar, Filipe, *Pintura colonial* (1928).
Fisher, Lillian E., *Intendant System in Spanish America* (1929).
—— *Viceregal Administration in the Spanish-American Colonies* (1926).
Hamilton, Earl J., *American Treasure and the Price Revolution in Spain, 1501–1650* (1934).
Hanke, Lewis, *The First Social Experiments in America: A Study in the Development of Spanish Indian Policy in the Sixteenth Century* (1935).
Haring, Clarence H., *Trade and Navigation between Spain and the Indies in the Time of the Hapsburgs* (1918).
Henríquez Ureña, Pedro, *Literary Currents in Hispanic America* (1945).
Kelemen, Pál, *Baroque and Rococo in Latin America* (1951).
Kubler, George, and Martin Soria, *Art and Architecture in Spain and Portugal and Their American Dominions, 1500 to 1800* (1959).
Lanning, John T., *Academic Culture in the Spanish Colonies* (1940).
Lea, Henry C., *Inquisition in the Spanish Dependencies* (1922).
Leonard, Irving A., *Books of the Brave* (1949).
—— *Don Carlos de Sigüenza y Góngora* (1939).
McAlister, Lyle N., "Social Structure and Social Change in New Spain," *Hisp. Am. Hist. Rev.*, 43 (1963), 349.
Mecham, John L., *Church and State in Latin America* (1934).
de la Plaza y Jaén, C. B., *Crónica de la Universidad de México* (2 vols., 1931).
Ricard, Robert, *La conquête spirituelle du Méxique 1523 à 1572* (1933).
Rubio, J. P., *El piloto mayor de la casa contratación* (1923).
Simpson, Leslie B., *Emancipation of Indian Slaves* (1940).
—— *Encomienda in New Spain* (1950).
—— *Repartimiento System* (1938).
Torre Revello, José, *El libro, la imprenta y el periodismo en América* (1940).
Toussaint, Manuel, *Arte colonial en México* (1948).

32.1.3 Exploration and Settlement within Present U.S. Boundaries

32.1.3.1 General

Bannon, John F., *The Spanish Borderlands Frontier* (1970).
Bobb, Bernard E., *Viceregency of Antoni Bucareli in New Spain, 1771–1779* (1962).
Bolton, Herbert E., and T. M. Marshall, *Colonization of North America* (1936).
—— *Spanish Borderlands* (1921).
Hanke, Lewis, *Handbook of Latin American Studies: The Colonial Experience* (1967).
Hodge, Frederick W., and T. H. Lewis, eds., *Spanish Explorers in the Southern United States* (1907).
Lowery, Woodbury, *Spanish Settlements within Present Limits of the United States, 1513–1561* (1901).

*   *   *   *   *   *   *

Clemence, S. R., ed., *Calendar of Documents, Harkness Collection, Library of Congress* (2 vols., 1932–1936).
Wilgus, A. C. *Histories and Historians of Hispanic America* (1936).

32.1.3.2 Southeast

Arnade, Charles W., *The Siege of St. Augustine in 1702* (1959).
de Barcia, A. G., *Ensayo cronológico de la Florida* (1723); Anthony Kerrigan, trans. (1951).
Barrientos, Bartolomé, *Pedro Menéndez de Avilés* (1567); Anthony Kerrigan, trans., (1965).
Bayle, Constantino, *Pedro Menéndez de Avilés* (1928).
Bolton, Herbert E., *Spain's Title to Georgia* (1925).
—— "Spanish Resistance to Carolina Traders," *Ga. Hist. Quar.*, 9 (1925), 115.

Boyd, M. F., "Mission Sites in Florida," *Fla. Hist. Quar.*, 17 (1939), 225.

Chatelain, Verne E., *Defenses of Spanish Florida 1565–1763* (1941).

Connor, Jeannette T., ed., *Colonial Records of Spanish Florida, 1570–1580* (2 vols., 1925–1930).

Coulter, E. M., *Georgia's Disputed Ruins* (1937).

Crane, Verner W., *Southern Frontier, 1670–1732* (1928).

Geiger, Maynard J., *Franciscan Conquest of Florida, 1573–1618* (1937).

Hallenbeck, Cleve, *Alvar Nuñez Cabeza de Vaca* (1940).

Jackson, William R., Jr., *Early Florida through Spanish Eyes* (1954).

Johnson, J. G., "Spanish Colonies in Georgia and South Carolina," *Ga. Hist. Quar.*, 15 (1931), 301.

—— "Spanish Southeast in the Seventeenth Century," *Ga. Hist. Quar.*, 16 (1932), 17.

Lanning, John T., *Spanish Missions of Georgia* (1935).

Leonard, Irving A., ed., *Spanish Approach to Pensacola, 1689–1693* (1939).

Lewis, Clifford M., and Albert J. Loomie, *Spanish Mission in Virginia, 1570–1572* (1953).

Lowery, Woodbury, *Spanish Settlements in Florida, 1562–74* (1905).

Manucy, A. C., "Florida History in Spanish Records of North Carolina State Archives," *Fla. Hist. Quar.*, 25 (1947), 319; 26 (1947), 77.

Priestley, Herbert I., ed., *Luna Papers* (2 vols., 1928).

Quattlebaum, Paul, *Land Called Chicora: Carolinas under Spanish Rule* (1956).

Romans, Bernard, *Concise Natural History of East and West Florida* (1775).

Ruidíaz y Caravia, Eugenio, ed., *La Florida* (2 vols., 1893).

Salley, Alexander S., "Spanish Settlement at Port Royal," *So. Car. Hist. Mag.*, 26 (1925), 31.

Scisco, Louis D., "Track of Ponce de Leon in 1513," *Am. Geog. Soc., Bull.*, 45 (1913), 721.

Vigneras, L. A., "A Spanish Discovery of North Carolina in 1566," *No. Car. Hist. Rev.*, 46 (1969), 398.

Wright, Irene A., "Spanish Policy toward Virginia, 1606–1612," *AHR*, 25 (1920), 448.

Wright, J. Leitch, "Spanish Reaction to Carolina," *No. Car. Hist. Rev.*, 41 (1964), 464.

*   *   *   *   *   *   *

Arnade, Charles W., "Spanish Florida Source Material," *Fla. Hist. Quar.*, 35 (1957), 320.

Mowat, Charles L., "Material Relating to British East Florida in the Clements Library," *Fla. Hist. Quar.*, 18 (1939), 46.

Robertson, James A., "Archival Distribution of Florida Manuscripts," *Fla. Hist. Quar.*, 10 (1931), 35.

—— "Spanish MSS. of the Florida State Historical Society," *Am. Antiq. Soc., Proc.*, new ser., 39 (1929), 16.

Serrano y Sanz, Manuel, ed., *Documentos históricos de la Florida y la Luisiana* (1912).

Whitaker, Arthur P., ed., *Documents Relating to Commercial Policy of Spain in Floridas*, Fla. State Hist. Soc., *Publ.*, 10 (1931). Entire issue.

Wroth, Lawrence C., "Source Materials of Florida History in the John Carter Brown Library," *Fla. Hist. Quar.*, 20 (1941), 3.

See also 33.2.4, Carolinas.

32.1.3.3 Louisiana and Mississippi Valley

Alvord, Clarence W., "Conquest of St. Joseph, Michigan, by Spaniards in 1781," *Mich. Hist.*, 14 (1930), 398.

Bolton, Herbert E., *Athanase de Mezières and the Louisiana-Texas Frontier, 1768–1780* (2 vols., 1914).

Caughey, John W., *Bernardo de Gálvez in Louisiana, 1776–1783* (1934).

Deiler, J. H., *German Coast of Louisiana* (1909).

Dunn, William E., *Spanish and French Rivalry* (1917).

Fortier, Alcée, *History of Louisiana*, vols. 1 and 2 (1904).

Gayarré, Charles, *History of Louisiana*, vol. 1 (1903).

Holmes, Jack D. L., *Gayoso: Spanish Governor in the Mississippi Valley, 1789–1799* (1965).

Houck, Louis, *Spanish Regime in Missouri* (2 vols., 1909).

James, James A., "Spanish Influence in West during the Revolution," *MVHR*, 4 (1918), 193.

Kinnaird, Lawrence, "Spanish Expedition against Fort St. Joseph," *MVHR*, 19 (1933), 173.

Nasatir, Abraham P., "Anglo-Spanish Frontier in Illinois, 1779–1783," Ill. State Hist. Soc., *Jour.*, 21 (1928), 291.

Priestley, Herbert I., *José de Gálvez* (1916).

Robertson, James A., *Louisiana* (2 vols., 1911).

Serrano y Sanz, Manuel, ed., *Documentos históricos de la Florida y la Luisiana* (1912).

Teggart, F. J., "Capture of St. Joseph, Michigan, by Spaniards in 1781," *Mo. Hist. Rev.*, 5 (1911), 214.

Winston, J. E., "Revolution of 1768 in Louisiana," *La. Hist. Quar.*, 15 (1932), 181.

32.1.3.4 Southwest

Bancroft, Hubert H., *North Mexican States and Texas* (2 vols., 1883–1889).

Bloom, L. B., ed., "Campaign against the Moqui Pueblos," *New Mex. Hist. Rev.*, 6 (1931), 158.

Bolton, Herbert E., ed., *Anza's California Expeditions* (5 vols., 1930).

Bolton, Herbert E., *Coronado* (1949).

———— "Mission as a Frontier Institution," *AHR*, 23 (1917), 42.

Bolton, Herbert E., ed., *Spanish Exploration in the Southwest* (1963).

Bolton, Herbert E., "Spanish Occupation of Texas, 1519–1690," *Southw. Hist. Quar.*, 16 (1912), 1.

———— *Texas in the Middle Eighteenth Century* (1915).

Bourne, Edward G., ed., *Narratives of the Career of Hernando de Soto* (2 vols., 1903–1905).

Burrus, Ernest J., *Kino and Cartography of Northwestern New Spain* (1965).

Castañeda, C. E., *Catholic Heritage in Texas* (2 vols., 1936).

Chapman, Charles E., *Founding of Spanish California* (1916).

Chavez, Angelico, *Coronado's Friars* (1968).

Cunninghame Graham, R. B., *Hernando de Soto* (1903).

Day, A. Grove, *Coronado's Quest: The Discovery of the Southwestern States* (1940).

Dominguez, Francisco A., *Missions of New Mexico, 1776*, Eleanor B. Adams and Fray Angelico Chavez, trans. and eds. (1956).

Espinosa, J. M., *Crusaders of Rio Grande: D. Diego de Vargas* (1942).

———— ed., *First Expedition of Vargas into New Mexico, 1692* (1940).

Hackett, C. W., ed., *Historical Documents Relating to New Mexico* (2 vols., 1923–1937).

Hammond, George P., *Don Juan de Oñate and the Founding of New Mexico* (1927).

———— and Agapito Rey, eds. and trans., *Don Juan de Oñate, Colonizer of New Mexico, 1595–1628* (2 vols., 1953).

Hammond, George P., ed. and trans., *Narratives of the Coronado Expedition, 1540–1542* (1940).

Hammond, George P., and Agapito Rey, *Rediscovery of New Mexico, 1580–1594* (1966).

Hittell, Theodore H., *History of California* (1885–1898).

Hutchinson, C. Alan, *Frontier Settlement in Mexican California: Hijar-Padrés Colony, 1769–1835* (1969).

Jones, Oakah L., Jr., *Pueblo Warriors and the Spanish Conquest* (1966).

Kino, Eusebio F., *Historical Memoir of Pimería Alta*, Herbert E. Bolton, ed. (2 vols., 1919).

Moorhead, Max L., *Apache Frontier: Jacobo Ugarte and Spanish-Indian Relations in Northern New Spain, 1769–1791* (1968).
Palóu, Francisco, *Life of Fray Junípero Serra* (1787); Maynard J. Geiger, trans. and ed. (1955).
Powell, Philip W., *Soldiers, Indians, and Silver: Advance of New Spain, 1550–1600* (1952).
Sedelmayr, Jacobo, *Explorer in Arizona: Narratives, 1744–1751*, Peter M. Dunne, trans. and ed. (1955).
Sigüenza y Góngora, Carlos de, *Mercurio Volante: Expedition of Diego de Vargas into New Mexico, 1692*, Irving A. Leonard, trans. (1932).
Simmons, Marc, *Spanish Government in New Mexico* (1968).
Smith, Fay J., John L. Kessell, and Francis J. Fox, *Father Kino in Arizona* (1966).
Wagner, Henry R., *Cartography of the Northwest Coast* (1937).
────── *Spanish Voyages to the Northwest Coast* (1929).
Whitaker, Arthur P., *Spanish American Frontier, 1783–1795* (1927).

*   *   *   *   *   *   *

Cowan, R. E., *Bibliography of California* (3 vols., 1933).
Wagner, Henry R., *Spanish Southwest 1542–1794: An Annotated Bibliography* (rev. ed., 2 vols., 1937).

32.2 FRENCH SETTLEMENT

32.2.1 General

Goldstein, Robert, *French-Iroquois Diplomatic and Military Relations: 1609–1701* (1969).
Hanotaux, Gabriel, and Alfred Martineau, *Histoire des colonies françaises* (1929).
La Roncière, Charles G. M. B. de, *Histoire de la marine française* (4 vols., 1906–1910).
Margry, Pierre, *Découvertes et établissements des français, 1614–1754: Mémoires et documents originaux* (6 vols., 1876–1886).
Priestly, Herbert I., *France Overseas through the Old Regime: Study of European Expansion* (1939).
Thwaites, Reuben G., *France in America, 1497–1763* (1905).
Wroth, Lawrence C., and G. L. Annan, eds., *Acts of French Royal Administration Concerning Canada, Guiana, West Indies and Louisiana to 1791* (1930).

*   ,   *   *   *   *   *   *

Beers, Henry P., *French in North America: Bibliographical Guide to French Archives, Reproductions, and Research Missions* (1957).
O'Neil, James E., "French Manuscripts for American History in the Library of Congress," *JAH*, 51 (1965), 674.
Wrong, George M., et al., eds., *Review of Historical Publications Relating to Canada* (22 vols., 1896–1918).

32.2.2 Exploration and Fur Trade

Baxter, James P., *Jacques Cartier* (1906).
Bennett, Charles E., *Laudonnière and Fort Caroline: History and Documents* (1964).
Biggar, H. P., *Early Trading Companies of New France* (1901).
────── ed., "Collection of Documents relating to Cartier and Roberval," Pub. Archives Can. *Publ.*, no. 14 (1930).
────── ed., *Precursors of Cartier, 1497–1535: Documents Relating to the Early History of Canada* (1911).
────── ed., "Voyages of Jacques Cartier," Pub. Archives Can. *Publ.*, no. 11 (1924).

Bishop, Morris, *Champlain* (1948).
Bourne, Edward G., *Voyages of Champlain* (2 vols., 1922).
Champagne, Antoine, *Les La Vérendyre et le poste de l'Ouest* (1968).
Champlain, Samuel de, *Works*, H. P. Biggar, ed. (6 vols., and portfolio of plates and maps, 1922–1936).
Crouse, Nellis M., *Lemoyne d'Iberville: Soldier of New France* (1954).
———— *La Vérendyre, Fur Trader and Explorer* (1956).
Diamond, Sigmund, "Norumbega," *Am. Neptune*, 11 (1951), 95.
Donnelly, Joseph P., *Jacques Marquette, 1637–1675* (1968).
Frémont, Donatien, *Pierre Radisson, voi des coureurs de bois* (1933).
Grant, W. L., ed., *Voyages of Samuel de Champlain* (1907).
Hoffman, Bernard G., *Cabot to Cartier: Sources for Historical Ethnography of Northeastern North America, 1497–1550* (1961).
Innis, Harold A., *Fur Trade in Canada* (rev. ed., 1956).
La Roncière, Charles G. M. B. de, *Jacques Cartier* (1931).
Laut, Agnes C., *Cadillac* (1931).
Martin, Gaston, *Jacques Cartier et la découverte de l'Amérique du Nord* (1939).
Munro, William B., "The coureurs de bois," Mass. Hist. Soc., *Proc.*, 57 (1924), 192.
Nute, Grace L., *Caesars of the Wilderness* (1943).
Parkman, Francis, *La Salle and the Discovery of the Great West* (1869).
Preston, Richard A., "Laconia Company of 1629: English Attempt to Intercept Fur Trade," *Can. Hist. Rev.*, 31 (1950), 125.
Ribaut, Jean, *Whole and True Discoverye of Terra Florida* (1563). Also in facsimile in Fla. State Hist. Soc., *Publ.*, 7 (1927).
Thevet, André, *Les singularitez de la France antarctique* (1558); Paul Gaffarel, ed. (1878).

32.2.3 Development of New France

Boucher, Pierre, *Histoire véritable et naturelle des moeurs et productions du pays de la Nouvelle France* (1664).
Charlevoix, Pierre de, *Histoire et description générale de la Nouvelle France* (1744), J. G. Shea, trans. (1880).
Colby, Charles W., *Founder of New France* (1915).
Delalande, J., *Le conseil souverain de la Nouvelle-France* (1927).
Diamond, Sigmund, "French Canada in the Seventeenth Century," *WMQ*, 3 ser., 18 (1961), 3.
Eccles, William J., *Canada under Louis XIV* (1964).
———— *Canadian Frontier, 1534–1760* (1969).
———— *Frontenac, the Courtier Governor* (1959).
Ford, Worthington C., "French Royal Edicts on America," Mass. Hist. Soc., *Proc.*, 60 (1927), 250.
Ganong, William F., "Crucial Maps in Early Cartography of Canada," Royal Soc. Can. *Proc.*, 3 ser., 25 (1931), 169; 27 (1933), 149; 28 (1934), 149; 29 (1935), 101.
Heneker, Dorothy A., *Seignorial Regime in Canada* (1927).
Kennedy, John Hopkins, *Jesuit and Savage in New France* (1950).
King, J. E., "Glorious Kingdom of Saguenay," *Can. Hist. Rev.*, 31 (1950), 390.
Lanctot, Gustave, *A History of Canada*, Margaret M. Cameron and Josephine Hambleton, trans., (3 vols., 1963–1965).
Lescarbot, Marc, *Histoire de la Nouvelle France* (1609); H. P. Biggar, ed. (3 vols., 1907–1914).
———— *Nova Francia* (1609); H. P. Biggar, ed. (1928).
———— *Les muses de la Nouvelle France* (1609). Published as *Theatre of Neptune*, H. T. Richardson, trans. (1927).
L'Incarnation, Mére Marie de, *Ecrits spirituels et historiques publiés par dom Claude* [Martin], Albert Jamet, ed. (3 vols., 1929).
Marion, Seraphin, *Un pionnier canadien: Pierre Boucher* (1927).
Munro, William B., ed., *Documents Relating to Seignorial Tenure in Canada 1598–1854* (1908).
Munro, William B., *Seigneurs of Old Canada* (1915).

—— *Seignorial System in Canada* (1907).

Parkman, Francis, *Count Frontenac and New France under Louis XIV* (1892).

—— *Jesuits in North America* (1867).

—— *Old Regime in Canada* (1874).

—— *Pioneers of France in New World* (rev. ed., 1885).

Rochemonteix, Camille de, *Les Jésuites et la Nouvelle-France aux XVII ème siècle* (3 vols., 1895–1896).

Saintoyant, Jules F., *La colonisation française sous l'ancien regime* (1929).

Salone, Émile, *La colonisation de la Nouvelle-France* (1905).

Thwaites, Reuben G., *Jesuit Relations* (73 vols., 1896–1901).

Wrong, George M., *Rise and Fall of New France* (2 vols., 1928).

*   *   *   *   *   *   *

Staton, F. M., and Marie Tremaine, *Bibliography of Canadiana* (1934).

Wrong, George M., et al. eds., *Review of History Publications Relating to Canada* (22 vols., 1896–1918).

32.2.4 Acadia

Couillard Després, Azarie, *Charles de la Tour, gouverneur en Acadie 1593–1666* (1932).

Mores, William I., ed., *Acadiensia Nova* (2 vols., 1935).

Richard, Edouard, *Acadie*, Henri d'Arles, ed. (3 vols., 1916–1921).

Winzerling, Oscar W., *Acadian Odyssey* (1955).

32.2.5 Midwest and Gulf Region

Alvord, Clarence W., *Illinois Country 1673–1818* (1920).

Belting, Natalie M., *Kaskaskia under French Regime* (1948).

Bolton, Herbert E., "Location of La Salle's Colony on the Gulf," *Southw. Hist. Quar.*, 27 (1924), 171.

Bovey, Wilfrid, "Notes on Arkansas Post and St. Philippe," *Royal Soc. Can., Proc.*, 3 ser., 33 (1939), 29.

Dart, H. P. "Legal Institutions of Louisiana," *La. Hist. Quar.*, 2 (1919), 72.

Delanglez, Jean, *French Jesuits in Louisiana, 1700–1763* (1935).

Dunn, William E., *Spanish and French Rivalry in Gulf Region* (1917).

Finley, John, *The French in the Heart of America* (1915).

Giraud, Marcel, *Histoire de la Louisiane française* (3 vols., 1953–1966).

Goodrich, Calvin, *First Michigan Frontier* (1940).

Hamilton, Peter J., *Colonial Mobile* (1910).

Heinrich, Pierre, *Louisiane sous la compagnie des Indes* (1908).

Hennepin, Louis, *Description de la Louisiana* (1683); J. G. Shea, ed. (1880).

Kellogg, Louise P., ed., *Early Narratives of the Northwest, 1634–1699* (1917).

Kellogg, Louise P., "France and the Mississippi Valley," *MVHR*, 18 (1931), 3.

—— *French Regime in Wisconsin and the Northwest* (1925).

King, Grace, *Le Moyne de Bienville* (1892).

Lauvrière, Émile, *Histoire de la Louisiane française 1673–1939* (1940).

Lyon, Elijah W., *Louisiana in French Diplomacy 1759–1804* (1934).

McDermott, John F., ed., *French in the Mississippi Valley* (1965).

Parkman, Francis, II, "French Policy in the Lower Mississippi Valley, 1697–1712," *Col. Soc. Mass., Publ.*, 28 (1932), 225.

Pease, Theodore C., and Ernestine Jenison, eds., *Illinois on Eve of Seven Years' War 1747–55* (1940).

Riddell, W. R., "When Detroit Was French," *Mich. Hist. Mag.*, 23 (1939), 37.

Selden, G. B., "Expedition of Denonville against the Senecas, 1687," *Rochester Hist. Soc., Publ. Fund Ser.* 4 (1925), 1.

Severance, Frank H., *An Old Frontier of France: Niagara Region under French Control* (2 vols., 1917).

Shea, J. G., *Discovery and Exploration of the Mississippi Valley* (1852).

Surrey, Nancy Marie (Miller), *Commerce of Louisiana during the French Regime* (1916).
────── "Development of Industries in Louisiana during the French Regime," *MVHR*, 9 (1923), 227.
Thwaites, Reuben G., ed., *French Regime in Wisconsin, 1634–1760* (3 vols., 1902–1908).
Vogel, Claude L., *Capuchins in French Louisiana, 1722–1766* (1928).

32.2.6 West Indies

Banbuck, Cabuzel A., *Histoire de la Martinique* (1935).
Crouse, Nellis M., *French Pioneers in West Indies, 1624–64* (1940).
────── *French Struggle for the West Indies, 1665–1713* (1943).
Gould, Clarence P., "Trade between the Windward Isles and the French Continental Colonies," *MVHR*, 25 (1939), 473.
Labat, Jean B., *Voyage aux isles d'Amérique* (6 vols., 1722–1742; abridged ed., 2 vols., 1931).
Mims, Stewart L., *Colbert's West India Policy* (1912).
Moreau, Médéric L. E. de Saint-Méry, *Description de la partie française de l'isle Saint Dominique* (2 vols., 1787).
Newton, Arthur P., *European Nations in the West Indies* (1914).
Parry, John Horace, and P. M. Sherlock, *Short History of the West Indies* (2nd ed., 1963).
Roberts, W. A., *The French in the West Indies* (1942).
Satineau, M., *Histoire de la Guadeloúpe sous l'ancien régime* (1928).

32.3 DUTCH SETTLEMENT

32.3.1 General

Ballard, G. A., *Rulers of the Indian Ocean* (1927).
Boxer, C. R., *Dutch Seaborne Empire, 1600–1800* (1965).
van Brakel, S., *De Hollandsche handelscompagieën de XVII eeuw* (1908).
Bromley, John S., and E. H. Kossman, eds., *Britain and Netherlands in Europe and Asia* (1968).
Edmundson, George, *Anglo-Dutch Rivalry during the First Half of the Seventeenth Century* (1911).
Geyl, Pieter, *Netherlands in the 17th Century* (rev. ed., 2 vols., 1961–1964).
Jameson, J. Franklin, "Willem Usselinx," Am. Hist. Assoc., *Papers*, 2 (1887), 161.
van Klaveren, J. J., *Dutch Colonial System* (1953).
Parr, Charles M., *Jan van Linschoten: Dutch Marco Polo* (1964).
Wertenbaker, Thomas J., *Founding of American Civilization: The Middle Colonies* (1938).
Weslager, C. A., *Dutch Explorers, Traders and Settlers* (1961).

*   *   *   *   *   *   *

Brown, Robert B., *Netherlands and America* (1947).

32.3.2 New Netherland

Bachman, Van Cleaf, *Peltries or Plantations: Economic Policies of the Dutch West India Company in New Netherland, 1623–1639* (1970,.
Beverwyck, N.Y. Kleine Banck van Justitie, *Court Minutes of Fort Orange and Beverwyck, 1652–1660*, A. J. F. Van Laer, ed. (2 vols. 1920–1923).
Brodhead, J. R., *History of New York*, (2 vols., 1853–1871).
Burpee, L. J., "Fate of Henry Hudson," *Can. Hist. Rev.*, 21 (1940), 401.

Condon, Thomas J., *New York Beginnings: Commercial Origins of the New Netherland* (1968).

De Forest, Emily J., *A Walloon Family in America* (2 vols., 1914).

Flick, Alexander C., ed., *History of the State of New York*, vol. I (1933).

Goodwin, Maud W., *The Dutch and English on the Hudson* (1919).

Hart, Simon, *Prehistory of the New Netherland Company* (1959).

Jameson, J. Franklin, ed., *Narrative of New Netherland, 1609–1664* (1909).

Kessler, Henry H., and Eugene Rachlis, *Peter Stuyvesant and His New York* (1959).

Kilpatrick, William H., *Dutch Schools of New Netherland* (1912).

Van Laer, A. J. F., ed., *Documents Relating to New Netherland in the Huntington Library* (1924).

Leiby, Adrian C., *Early Dutch and Swedish Settlers of New Jersey* (1964).

McKinley, Albert E., "English and Dutch Towns of New Netherlands," *AHR*, 6 (1900), 1.

———— "Transition from Dutch to English Rule in New York," *AHR*, 6 (1900), 693.

New York. State Library, Albany, *Van Rensselaer Bowier MSS.*, A. J. F. Van Laer, ed. (1908).

Nissenson, Samuel G., *Patroon's Domain* (1937).

Nordholt, J. W. Schulte, "Nederlanders in Nieuw Nederland," *Bijdragen en Mededelingen van het Historisch Genootschap*, 80 (1966), 38.

O'Callaghan, E. B., *History of New Netherlands* (2 vols., 1846–1848).

Paltsits, Victor H., "Founding of New Amsterdam in 1626," Am. Antiq. Soc., *Proc.*, new ser., 34 (1924), 39.

Powys, Llewelyn, *Henry Hudson* (1928).

Raesly, Ellis L., *New Netherland* (1945).

Van Rensselaer, Jeremias, *Correspondence, 1651–1674*, A. J. F. Van Laer, ed. (1935).

Van Rensselaer, M. G., *History of the City of New York in the Seventeenth Century* (2 vols., 1909).

Van Rensselaer, Maria, *Correspondence, 1669–1689*, A. J. F. Van Laer, ed. (1935).

Rensselaerwyck, N.Y. Court, *Minutes of the Court of Rensselaerwyck, 1648–1652*, A. J. F. Van Laer, ed. (1922).

Sherwood, Warren G., "Patroons of New Netherland," N.Y. State Hist. Assoc., *Quar. Jour.*, 12 (1931), 271.

Singleton, Esther, *Dutch New York* (1909).

Stokes, Isaac N., *Iconography of Manhattan* (6 vols., 1895–1928).

Tuckerman, Bayard, *Peter Stuyvesant* (1898).

Ward, Christopher, *Dutch and Swedes on the Delaware, 1609–1664* (1930).

*　*　*　*　*　*　*

Asher, G. M., *Essay on the Dutch Books and Pamphlets: New Netherland and the Dutch West India Company* (1960).

32.4 NEW SWEDEN

Acrelius, Israel, *History of New Sweden* (1759); W. M. Reynolds, trans. (1874).

Benson, Adolph B., and Naboth Hedin, eds., *Swedes in America, 1638–1938* (1938).

Jameson, J. Franklin, "Willem Usselinx," Am. Hist. Assoc., *Papers*, 2 (1887), 161.

Johnson, Amandus K., *Instruction of Johan Printz for Governor of New Sweden* (1932).

———— *Swedish Settlements on the Delaware 1638–1644* (2 vols., 1911).

Köhlin, Harold, "First Maps of Delaware," *Imago Mundi*, 5 (1948), 78.

Leiby, Adrian C., *Early Dutch and Swedish Settlers of New Jersey* (1964).

Louhi, Evert A., *Delaware Finns* (1925).
Myers, Albert C., ed., *Narratives of Early Pennsylvania, West New Jersey, and Delaware* (1912).
Shurtleff, H. R., *Log Cabin Myth* (1939). On Swedish origins.
Ward, Christopher, *Dutch and Swedes on the Delaware, 1609–64* (1930).
Wuorinen, John H., *The Finns of the Delaware, 1638–1655* (1938).

33 Rise of Anglo-America

33.1 ENGLISH BACKGROUND

33.1.1 General

Allen, John W., *English Political Thought, 1603–1660* (1938).

Ashley, Maurice, *England in the Seventeenth Century* (3d ed., 1961).

—— *Great Britain to 1688* (1961).

—— *The Greatness of Oliver Cromwell* (1957).

Aylmer, G. E., *The Struggle for the Constitution, 1603–1689: England in the Seventeenth Century* (2nd ed., 1968).

Beer, George L., *Origins of British Colonial System* (1908).

Bindoff, S. T., *Tudor England* (1950).

Black, J. B., *The Reign of Elizabeth, 1558-1603* (2nd ed., 1959).

Bushman, Richard L., "English Franchise Reform in the Seventeenth Century," *Jour. Brit. Studies,* 3 (1963), 36.

Cambridge History of the British Empire, vol. VIII (rev. ed., 1963).

Campbell, Mildred, "The Conflict of Opinion on Population in Its Relation to Emigration," in William A. Aiken and B. D. Hening, eds., *Conflict in Stuart England: Essays in Honour of Wallace Notestein* (1960).

Cheyney, Edward P., *History of England* (2 vols., 1913–1926).

Clark, George N., *Three Aspects of Stuart England* (1960).

Davies, Godfrey, *The Early Stuarts, 1603–1660* (rev. ed., 1959).

Eggleston, Edward, *Transit of Civilization from England in the Seventeenth Century* (1901).

Elton, Geoffrey R., *England under the Tudors* (1955).

Firth, Charles H., *Oliver Cromwell and the Puritans in England* (1953).

Gooch, George P., *English Democratic Ideas,* H. J. Laski, ed. (1927).

Graham, Gerald S., *Empire of the North Atlantic* (1950).

Hexter, Jack H., *Reappraisals in History* (1961).

—— *Reign of King Pym* (1941).

Hill, Christopher, *Century of Revolution, 1603–1714* (1961).

—— *God's Englishman: Oliver Cromwell and the English Revolution* (1970).

—— *Intellectual Origins of the English Revolution* (1965).

Jenkins, Elizabeth, *Elizabeth the Great* (1958).

Judson, Margaret A., *The Crisis of the Constitution: An Essay in Constitutional and Political Thought in England, 1603–1645* (1949).

Koebner, Richard, *Empire* (1961).

Lockyer, Roger, *Tudor and Stuart Britain, 1471–1714* (1964).

Lucas, Charles P., *Historical Geography of the British Colonies* (1911).

Mackie, J. D., *Earlier Tudors, 1485–1558* (1952).

Mattingly, Garrett, *The Armada* (1959).

Neale, J. E., *Elizabeth I and Her Parliaments* (2 vols., 1953–1957).

—— *The Elizabethan House of Commons* (1949).

Newton, Arthur P., "Great Migration, 1618–1648," in *Cambridge History of British Empire,* vol. I (1929).

Pocock, J. G. A., *The Ancient Constitution and the Feudal Law: English Historical Thought in the Seventeenth Century* (1957).

Quinn, David B., "Sir Thomas Smith (1513–1577) and Beginnings of English Colonial Theory," Am. Philos. Soc., *Proc.,* 89 (1945), 543.

Roberts, Clayton, *Growth of Responsible Government in Stuart England* (1966).

Rowse, A. L., *The England of Elizabeth* (1950).

Tanner, Joseph R., *English Constitutional Conflicts of the Seventeenth Century* (1928).

Wedgewood, Cecily V., *Coffin for Charles: Trial and Execution* (1964).

―――― *The King's Peace, 1637–1641* (1959).

―――― *The King's War, 1641–1647* (1959).

Wernham, R. B., *Before the Armada: English Nation, 1485–1588* (1966).

Willey, Basil, *Seventeenth Century Background* (1934).

Williams, C. H., ed., *English Historical Documents, 1485–1558* (1967).

Williamson, James A., *Short History of British Expansion* (4th ed., 2 vols., 1955).

―――― *Tudor Age* (2nd ed., 1958).

Willson, David H., *King James VI and I* (1956).

Wormald, B. H. G., *Clarendon: Politics, History, and Religion, 1640–1660* (1951).

Zagorin, Perez, *The Court and the Country: Beginning of the English Revolution* (1970).

*　　*　　*　　*　　*　　*　　*

Davies, Godfrey, *Bibliography of British History, Stuart Period* (1928).

Read, Conyers, *Bibliography of British History: Tudor Period, 1485–1603* (2nd ed., 1959).

Zagorin, Perez, "English History, 1558–1640: Bibliographical Survey," *AHR,* 68 (1963), 364.

See also 5.8, Colonial and Federation Records.

33.1.2 Economic History

Albion, Robert G., *Forests and Sea Power: The Timber Problem of the Royal Navy, 1652–1862* (1926).

Clapham, John, *Concise Economic History of Britain to 1750* (1963).

Clark, George N., *The Wealth of England, 1496–1760* (1946).

Davies, Kenneth G., *The Royal African Company* (1957).

Davis, Ralph, *A Commercial Revolution: English Overseas Trade in the Seventeenth and Eighteenth Centuries* (1967).

―――― "English Foreign Trade, 1660–1700," *Econ. Hist. Rev.,* 7 (1954), 150.

―――― *The Rise of the English Shipping Industry in the Seventeenth and Eighteenth Centuries* (1962).

Foster, William, *England's Quest of Eastern Trade* (1933).

Hannay, David, *Great Chartered Companies* (1926).

Heckscher, Eli F., *Mercantilism* (2 vols., 1935).

Hinton, Raymond W. K., *The Eastland Trade and the Common Weal in the Seventeenth Century* (1959).

Jackson, Luther P., "Elizabethan Seamen and the African Slave Trade," *Jour. Negro Hist.,* 9 (1924), 1.

Judah, Charles B., *North American Fisheries and British Policy to 1713* (1933).

Lingelbach, W. E., *Merchant Adventurers of England* (1902).

Liubimenko, Inna, *Relations commerciales et politiques de l'Angleterre avec la Russie avant Pierre le Grand* (1933).

MacInnes, Clarke M., *The Early English Tobacco Trade* (1926).

Nef, John U., *Industry and Government in France and England, 1540–1640* (1940).

Power, Eileen, and M. M. Postan, eds., *Studies in English Trade in the Fifteenth Century* (1933).

Rabb, Theodore K., *Enterprise & Empire: Merchant and Gentry Investment in Expansion of England, 1575–1630* (1967).

Ramsay, George D., *English Overseas Trade during Centuries of Emergence* (1957).

Rich, E. E., and C. H. Wilson, eds., *Cambridge Economic History of Europe*. Vol. IV: *Economy of Expanding Europe in the Sixteenth and Seventeenth Centuries* (1967).

Richards, Richard D., *Early History of Banking in England* (1929).

Robertson, Hector M., *Aspects of Rise of Economic Individualism* (1933).

Salter, Frank R., *Sir Thomas Gresham* (1925).

Scott, William R., *Constitution and Finance of Joint Stock Companies* (2 vols., 1910–1912).

Seebohm, M. E., *The Evolution of the English Farm* (1927).

Smith, H. F. Russell, *Harrington and His Oceana* (1914).

Supple, B. E., *Commercial Crisis and Change in England, 1600–1642* (1959).

Tawney, R. H., *Agrarian Problem in the Sixteenth Century* (1912).

————— *Religion and the Rise of Capitalism* (1926).

————— "Rise of the Gentry, 1558–1640," *Econ. Hist. Rev.*, 11 (1941), 1.

————— and Eileen Power, *Tudor Economic Documents* (3 vols., 1924).

Thirsk, Joan, ed., *Agrarian History of England and Wales, 1500–1640* (1967).

Unwin, George, *Industrial Organization in the Sixteenth and Seventeenth Centuries* (1904).

————— *Studies in Economic History* (1927).

Usher, Abbott P., *Introduction to Industrial History of England* (1920).

Weber, Max, *The Protestant Ethic* (1930).

Willan, T. S., *Studies in Elizabethan Foreign Trade* (1959).

Wright, Louis B., *Religion and Empire: Piety and Commerce in English Expansion, 1558–1625* (1943).

Zook, George F., "The Company of Royal Adventurers of England Trading in Africa 1660–1672," *Jour. Negro Hist.*, 4 (1919), 134.

33.1.3 Social and Cultural History

Ashley, Maurice, *Life in Stuart England* (1964).

Bridenbaugh, Carl, *Vexed and Troubled Englishmen, 1590–1642* (1967).

Campbell, Mildred, *English Yeoman under Elizabeth and the Early Stuarts* (1942).

Carr, Cecil T., ed., *Select Charters of Trading Companies* (1913).

Clark, George Kitson, *English Inheritance* (1950).

Gillespie, James E., *Influence of Overseas Expansion on England to 1700* (1920).

Hoskins, W. G., *Provincial England* (1963).

Jordan, Wilbur K., *Philanthropy in England, 1480–1660* (1959).

Kearney, Hugh, *Scholars and Gentlemen: Universities and Society in Pre-Industrial Britain, 1500–1700* (1970).

Laslett, Peter, *World We Have Lost* (1966).

Morpurgo, J. E., ed., *Life under the Stuarts* (1950).

Notestein, Wallace, *English People on the Eve of Colonization, 1603–1630* (1954).

Quinn, David B., "Sir Thomas Smith (1513–1577) and Beginnings of English Colonial Theory," *Am. Philos. Soc. Proc.*, 89 (1945), 543.

Simon, Joan, *Education and Society in Tudor England* (1966).

Stone, Lawrence, *Crisis of the Aristocracy, 1558–1641* (1965).

Whinney, Margaret D., and Oliver Miller, *English Art, 1625–1714* (1957).

Wright, Louis B., *Middle-Class Culture in Elizabethan England* (1935).

33.1.4 Religious History

Collinson, Patrick, *The Elizabethan Puritan Movement* (1967).

Cragg, Gerald R., *From Puritanism to the Age of Reason: A Study of Changes in Religious Thought within the Church of England, 1660–1700* (1950).

Dickens, A. G., *The English Reformation* (1964).

Emerson, Everett H., ed., *English Puritanism from John Hooper to John Milton* (1968).

George, Charles, and Katherine George, *Protestant Mind of English Reformation* (1961).

Greaves, Richard L., "John Bunyan and Covenant Thought in the Seventeenth Century," *Church Hist.*, 36 (1967), 151.

Haller, William, *Liberty and Reformation in the Puritan Revolution* (1955).

—— *Rise of Puritanism, 1570–1643* (1938).

Hill, Christopher, *Puritanism and Revolution* (1958).

—— *Society and Puritanism in Pre-Revolutionary England* (2nd ed., 1967).

Jones, Rufus M., *George Fox, Seeker and Friend* (1930).

Jordan, W. K., *Development of Religious Toleration in England* (4 vols., 1932–1940).

Knappen, Marshall, *Tudor Puritanism* (1939).

Kocher, Paul H., *Science and Religion in Elizabethan England* (1953).

Little, David, *Religion, Order and Law* (1969).

Mosse, George L., *The Holy Pretense: A Study in Christianity and Reason of State from William Perkins to John Winthrop* (1957).

Nuttall, Geoffrey, *Holy Spirit in Puritan Faith and Experience* (1946).

Trevor-Roper, H. R., *Archbishop Laud, 1573–1645* (2nd ed., 1962).

Walzer, Michael, *The Revolution of the Saints* (1965).

Westfall, Richard S., *Science and Religion in Seventeenth-Century England* (1958).

33.1.5 Voyages of Discovery and Privateering

Andrews, Kenneth R., ed., *English Privateering Voyages to the West Indies, 1588–95* (1959).

Andrews, Kenneth R., *Drake's Voyages* (1968).

—— *Elizabethan Privateering* (1964).

Aydelotte, Frank, "Elizabeth Seamen in Mexico and Ports of the Spanish Main," *AHR*, 48 (1942), 1.

Best, George, *A True Discourse of Late Voyages of Discovery of Martin Frobisher* (1578).

—— *Three Voyages of Martin Frobisher,* Vilhjalmur Stefansson, ed. (1938).

Biggar, H. P., *Voyages of Cabots and Corte-Reals* (1903).

Burrage, H. S., ed., *Early English and French Voyages* (1906).

Chatterton, E. K., *Seed of Liberty* (1929). Also published under the title, *English Seamen and Colonization of America* (1930).

Connell-Smith, Gordon, *Forerunners of Drake* (1954).

Corbet, Julien S., *Drake and the Tudor Navy* (2 vols., 1917).

Davis, John, *Voyages and Works*, A. H. Markham, ed. (1880).

Dawson, S. E., "Voyages of the Cabots; Latest Phases," Royal Soc. Can., *Proc.*, 2 ser., 3 (1897), 139.

Fletcher, Francis, *World Encompassed by Sir Francis Drake* (1628); Sir R. C. Temple, ed., (1926).

Francis, W. Nelson, "Hakluyt's Voyages: An Epic of Discovery," *WMQ*, 3 ser., 12 (1955), 447.

Gosling, W. G., *Sir Humphrey Gilbert* (1911).

Hakluyt, Richard, *Principall Navigations, Voiages, Traffiques and Discoveries of English Nation* (1589); John Masefield, ed. (8 vols., 1927).

Harisse, Henry, *Les Corte-Real* (1883).

—— *Découverte et évolution cartographique de Terre Neuve* (1900).

—— *Discovery of North America* (1892).

—— *John Cabot and Sebastian, His Son* (1896).

Hawkins, Richard, *Observations in His Voyage into the South Sea, 1593*, J. A. Williamson, ed. (1933).

Juricek, John T., "John Cabot's First Voyage," *Smithsonian Jour. Hist.*, 2, no. 4 (1968), 1.

Levermore, Charles H., ed., *Forerunners and Competitors of Pilgrims and Puritans* (2 vols., 1912).

Lloyd, Christopher, *Sir Francis Drake* (1957).

Lyman, Edward, ed., *Richard Hakluyt and His Successors* (1946).

McCann, F. T., *English Discovery of America to 1585* (1952).

McIntyre, Ruth A., "William Sanderson: Elizabethan Financier of Discovery," *WMQ*, 3 ser., 13 (1956), 184.

Oppenheim, Michael, *Administration of the Royal Navy* (1896).

Parks, George B., *Richard Hakluyt and English Voyages* (1959).

Penrose, Boies, *Tudor and Early Stuart Voyaging* (1962).

Powys, Llewelyn, *Henry Hudson* (1928).

Purchas, Samuel, *Hakluytus Posthumus or Purchas His Pilgrimes* (1625; 20 vols., 1905–1907).

Quinn, David B., *The New Found Land: The English Contribution to the Discovery of North America* (1965).

Rowse, A. L., *The Elizabethans and America* (1959).

—— *The Expansion of Elizabethan England* (1955).

—— *Sir Richard Grenville* (1937).

Taylor, Eva G. R., *Late Tudor and Early Stuart Geography* (1934).

—— *Tudor Geography 1485–1583* (1930).

—— ed., *Writings of Two Hakluyts* (1935).

Wagner, Henry R., *Sir Francis Drake's Voyage around the World* (1926).

Wallace, Willard M., *Sir Walter Raleigh* (1959).

Waters, David W., *Art of Navigation in England in Elizabethan and Early Stuart Times* (1958).

Williamson, James A., *Age of Drake* (1938).

—— *Cabot Voyages and Bristol Discovery under Henry VII* (1962).

—— "England and the Opening of the Atlantic," *Cambridge History of the British Empire*, vol. I (1929).

—— *Sir Francis Drake* (1951).

—— *Sir John Hawkins* (1927).

Wright, Irene A., ed. and trans., *Further English Voyages to Spanish America, 1583–1594* (1951).

Wright, Louis B., *Gold, Glory and the Gospel* (1971).

33.1.6 Colonizing Efforts before 1607

Adams, Randolph G., *Brief Account of Raleigh's Roanoke Colony* (1935).

Adamson, J. H., and H. F. Folland, *The Shepheard of the Ocean: An Account of Sir Walter Raleigh and his Times* (1969).

Cell, Gillian T., "The Newfoundland Company: A Study of Subscribers to a Colonizing Venture," *WMQ*, 3 ser., 22 (1965), 611.

Connor, Robert D. W., *Raleigh's Settlements on Roanoke* (1907).

Davis, Richard Beale, *George Sandys, Poet-Adventurer* (1955).

Gookin, W. F., "Who Was Bartholomew Gosnold?" *WMQ*, 3 ser., 6 (1949), 398.

Hariot, Thomas, *Briefe and True Report of New Found Land of Virginia* (1588). The De Bry edition of 1590 includes engravings of John White's drawings.

Hulton, Paul H., and David B. Quinn, eds., *American Drawings of John White, 1577–1590* (2 vols., 1964).

Powell, William S., "Roanoke Colonists and Explorers: An Attempt at Identification," *No. Car. Hist. Rev.*, 34 (1957), 202.

Preston, Richard A., *Gorges of Plymouth Fort: A Life of Sir Ferdinando Gorges* (1953).

—— "Laconia Company of 1629: English Attempt to Intercept Fur Trade," *Can. Hist. Rev.*, 31 (1950), 125.

Quinn, David B., "Preparations for the 1585 Virginia Voyages," *WMQ*, 3 ser., 6 (1949), 208.

—— *Raleigh and the British Empire* (1949).

—— ed., *Roanoke Voyages, 1584–1590* (2 vols., 1955).

—— "Thomas Hariot and Virginia Voyages of 1602," *WMQ*, 3 ser., 27 (1970), 268.

Strathmann, Ernest A., *Sir Walter Raleigh* (1951).

33.2 AMERICAN COLONIES IN THE SEVENTEENTH CENTURY

33.2.1 General

Adams, James T., *Founding of New England* (1921).
Andrews, Charles M., *The Colonial Period* (4 vols., 1934–1938).
Bailyn, Bernard, *The New England Merchants in the Seventeenth Century* (1955).
Barnes, Viola F., *Dominion of New England* (1923).
Beer, George L., *Origins of the Colonial System* (1908).
Brown, Alexander, *Genesis of United States* (2 vols., 1890).
Craven, Wesley F., *Colonies in Transition 1660–1713* (1968).
—— *The Southern Colonies in the Seventeenth Century* (1949).
Dunn, Richard S., *Puritans and Yankees: Winthrop Dynasty of New England, 1630–1717* (1962).
Fiske, John, *Beginnings of New England* (1889).
Graham, Gerald S., *Empire of North Atlantic* (1950).
Great Britain. Public Record Office, *Calendar of State Papers, Colonial America and West Indies* (44 vols., 1860-1969). Covers the period, 1574-1738.
—— *Calendar of State Papers, Spain* (23 vols., 1485–1603). Covers the period, 1485–1603.
Greene, Jack P., "Publication of Official Records of Southern Colonies," *WMQ*, 3 ser., 14 (1957), 268.
—— *The Quest for Power: The Lower Houses of Assembly in the Southern Royal Colonies, 1689–1763* (1963).
Howe, Henry F., *Prologue to New England* (1943).
Innes, Arthur D., *The Maritime and Colonial Expansion of England under the Stuarts (1603–1714)* (1932).
Kammen, Michael, *Deputyes and Libertyes: Origins of Representative Government in Colonial America* (1969).
Leach, Douglas E., *Flintlock and Tomahawk: New England in King Philip's War* (1958).
Lefler, Hugh T., "Promotional Literature of Southern Colonies," *JSH*, 33 (1967), 3.
Osgood, Herbert L., *American Colonies in the Seventeenth Century* (3 vols., 1904–1907).
Palfrey, John G., *History of New England*, vol. I (1858).
Pomfret, John E., and Floyd M. Shumway, *Founding the American Colonies, 1583–1660* (1970).
Preston, R. A., "Fishing and Plantation, New England in the Parliament of 1621," *AHR*, 45 (1939), 29.
Smith, James Morton, ed., *Seventeenth-Century America: Essays* (1959).
Vaughn, Alden T., "Societies Apart: American Colonies in the Seventeenth Century," in Stanley Coben and Lorman Ratner, eds., *The Development of an American Culture* (1970).
Ward, Harry M., *United Colonies of New England, 1643–90* (1961).
Weis, Frederick L., "New England Company of 1649 and Its Missionary Enterprises," Col. Soc. Mass., *Publ.*, 38 (1948), 134.
Wertenbaker, Thomas J., *The Founding of American Civilization: The Middle Colonies* (1938).
—— *The Old South: The Founding of American Civilization* (1942).
—— *Puritan Oligarchy* (1947).
Wright, Louis B., *The Colonial Search for a Southern Eden* (1953).
—— ed., *The Elizabethans' America: A Collection of Reports by Englishmen on the New World* (1965).

*   *   *   *   *   *   *

"Annual Bibliography of New England History," *NEQ*, 2-40 (1929–1967).
Morse, Jarvis M., *American Beginnings: Highlights of Birth of the New World* (1952).
Vaughn, Alden T., comp., *The American Colonies in the Seventeenth Century* (1971).

33.2.2 Virginia

33.2.2.1 General

Ames, Susie M., *Virginia Eastern Shore in the Seventeenth Century* (1940).
Andrews, Matthew Page, *Virginia, the Old Dominion* (1937).
Beverley, Robert, *History of Virginia, in Four Parts* (2nd ed., 1722); Louis B. Wright, ed. (1947). Covers the period, 1584–1720.
Campbell, Thomas E., *Colonial Caroline County, Virginia* (1954).
Jones, Hugh, *The Present State of Virginia* (1724); Richard L. Morton, ed. (1956).
Mapp, Alf. J., *Virginia Experiment, 1607–1781* (1957).
Morton, Richard L., *Colonial Virginia* (2 vols., 1960).
Sams, C. W., *The Conquest of Virginia* (4 vols., 1916–1939).
Swem, Earl G., *Maps Relating to Virginia* (1914).
Tyler, Lyon G., *Cradle of the Republic* (1906).
Wertenbaker, Thomas J., *Patrician and Plebian in Virginia* (1910).
—————— *Planters of Colonial Virginia* (1922).
—————— *Virginia under the Stuarts, 1607–1688* (1914). The Wertenbaker works listed above were published in a single volume under the title, *Shaping of Colonial Virginia* (1958).
Willison, George F., *Behold Virginia* (1951).

*   *   *   *   *   *   *

Swem, Earl G., "A Bibliography of Virginia," *Va. State Lib. Bull.*, 8, nos. 2-4; 10, nos. 1-4; 12, nos. 1-2; 17, no. 2 (1915–1932).

See also 10.3 for biographies/writings of:

Strachey, William, 1572–1621

33.2.2.2 Settlement

Barbour, Philip L., ed., *Jamestown Voyages under First Charter* (1969).
Barbour, Philip L., *Pocahontas and Her World: A Chronicle of Americas First Settlement . . .* (1970).
—————— *Three Worlds of Captain John Smith* (1964).
Cotter, John L., and J. Paul Hudson, *New Discoveries at Jamestown* (1957).
Craven, Wesley F., *Dissolution of the Virginia Company* (1932).
—————— *Virginia Company of London* (1957).
Culliford, S. G., *William Strachey* (1965).
Davis, Richard B., *George Sandys, Poet-Adventurer* (1955).
Diamond, Sigmund, "From Organization to Society: Virginia in the Seventeenth Century," *Am. Jour. Sociol.*, 63 (1958), 457.
Emerson, Everett H., "Captain John Smith as Editor, 'Generall Historie'," *Va. Mag. Hist. Biog.*, 75 (1967), 143.
Hamor, Ralph, *True Discourse of Present State of Virginia* (1615); A. L. Rowse, ed. (1957).
Hatch, Charles E., Jr., *First Seventeen Years: Virginia, 1607–1624* (1957).
Johnson, Robert C., "Lotteries of Virginia Company, 1612–1621," *Va. Mag. Hist. Biog.*, 74 (1966), 259.
Kingsbury, Susan M., ed., *Records of the Virginia Company of London* (4 vols., 1906–1935).
McCary, Ben C., *Smith's Map of Virginia* (1957).
Morgan, Edmund S., "The Labor Problem at Jamestown, 1607–1618," *AHR*, 76 (1971), 595.
Neill, Edward D., *History of Virginia Company of London, with Letters* (1869).
O'Brien, Terence H., "London Livery Companies and Virginia Company," *Va. Mag. Hist. Biog.*, 68 (1960), 137.
Parker, John, *Van Meteren's Virginia, 1607–1612* (1961).
Porter, Henry C., "Alexander Whitaker: Cambridge Apostle to Virginia," *WMQ*, 3 ser., 14 (1957), 317.
Quinn, David B., "Advice for Investors in Virginia, Bermuda, and Newfoundland, 1611," *WMQ*, 3 ser., 23 (1966), 136.

Rolfe, John, *True Relation of the State of Virginia Lefte by Sir Thomas Dale, Knight, in May Last 1616* (1971).

Rutman, Darrett B., "Virginia Company and Its Military Regime," in *The Old Dominion: Essays for Thomas P. Abernethy* (1964).

Smith, Bradford, *Captain John Smith* (1953).

Smith, John, *Travels and Works*, Edward Arber, ed., (2 vols., 1884); A. G. Bradley, ed. (1910).

———— *True Travels, Adventures, and Observations* (1630); John G. Fletcher, ed. (1930).

Smith, William, *History of First Discovery and Settlement of Virginia* (1747).

Strachey, William, *Historie of Travell into Virginia Britania* (1612); Louis B. Wright and Virginia Freund, eds. (1953).

Swem, Earl G., ed., *Jamestown 350th Anniversary Historical Booklets* (1957).

Tyler, Lyon G., ed., *Narratives of Early Virginia, 1606–1626* (1907).

Wright, Louis B., ed., *Voyage to Virginia in 1609: Strachey's "True Reportory" and Jourdain's "Discovery of the Bermudas"* (1965).

*　　*　　*　　*　　*　　*　　*

Phillips, Philip L., *Virginia Cartography: A Bibliographical Description* (1896).

See also 10.3 for biographies/writings of:

Gosnold, Bartholomew, 1572–1607
Pocahontas, 1595–1617
Smith, John, 1579/80–1631

33.2.2.3 Government and Politics

Adams, O. Burton, "Virginia Reaction to Glorious Revolution, 1688–1692," *West Va. Hist.*, 29 (1967), 6.

Andrews, Charles M., ed., *Narratives of the Insurrections, 1675–1690* (1915).

Bailyn, Bernard, "Politics and Social Structure in Virginia," in James Morton Smith, ed., *Seventeenth Century America: Essays in Colonial History* (1959).

Brown, Alexander, *English Politics in Virginia* (1901).

———— *First Republic* (1898).

———— *Genesis of the United States* (2 vols., 1890).

Bruce, Philip A., *Institutional History of Virginia in the Seventeenth Century* (2 vols., 1910).

Chandler, Julian A. C., *The History of Suffrage in Virginia* (1901).

———— *Representation in Virginia* (1896).

Flippin, Percy S., *Financial Administration in Virginia* (1915).

———— *Royal Government in Virginia* (1919).

Frantz, John B., ed., *Bacon's Rebellion: Prologue to Revolution?* (1969).

Kammen, Michael G., ed., "Virginia at Close of the Seventeenth Century: Appraisal by James Blair and John Locke," *Va. Mag. Hist. Biog.*, 74 (1966), 141.

Leamon, James S., "Governor Fletcher's Recall," *WMQ*, 3 ser., 20 (1963), 527.

Leonard, Sister Joan de Lourdes, "Operation Checkmate: Birth and Death of a Virginia Blueprint for Progress, 1660–1676," *WMQ*, 3 ser., 24 (1967), 44.

Miller, Elmer, *Legislature of Province of Virginia* (1907).

Morgan, Edmund S., "The First American Boom: Virginia 1618 to 1630," *WMQ*, 3 ser., 28 (1971), 169.

Morton, Richard L., *Struggle against Tyranny, 1677–1699* (1957).

Pargellis, Stanley M., "The Procedure of the Virginia House of Burgesses," *WMQ*, 2 ser., 7 (1927), 73.

Porter, Albert O., *County Government in Virginia: A Legislative History, 1607–1904* (1947).

Rainbolt, John C., "Stuart 'Tyranny': The Crown's Attack on the Virginia Assembly, 1676–1689," *Va. Mag. Hist. Biog.*, 75 (1967), 387.

Rankin, Hugh F., "General Court of Colonial Virginia," *Va. Mag. Hist. Biog.*, 70 (1962), 142.

Thornton, J. Mills, III, "Thrusting out of Governor Harvey," *Va. Mag. Hist. Biog.*, 76 (1968), 11.

Voorhis, Manning C., "Crown versus Council in Virginia Land Policy," *WMQ*, 3 ser., 3 (1946), 499.

Washburn, Wilcomb E., "The Effect of Bacon's Rebellion on Government in England and Virginia," *U.S. Natl. Museum Bull.*, 225 (1962), 135.

—— *Governor and Rebel: Bacon's Rebellion* (1957).

—— *Virginia under Charles I and Cromwell, 1624–1660* (1957).

Wertenbaker, Thomas J., *Bacon's Rebellion, 1676* (1957).

—— *Government of Virginia in the Seventeenth Century* (1957).

Wright, Louis B., "William Byrd's Defense of Sir Edmund Andros," *WMQ*, 3 ser., 2 (1945), 47.

See also 10.3 for biographies/writings of:

Bacon, Nathaniel, 1647–1676
Sandys, George, 1577/78–1643/44

33.2.3 Maryland

Alsop, George, *Character of Province of Maryland* (1666); Newton D. Mereness, ed. (1902).

Andrews, Charles M., *Narratives of the Insurrections 1675–1690* (1915).

Andrews, Matthew P., *Founding of Maryland* (1933).

Bernard, L. Leon, "Some New Light on the Early Years of the Baltimore Plantation," *Md. Hist. Mag.*, 44 (1949), 93.

Browne, William Hand, *George and Cecilius Calvert* (1890).

Browne, William P., *Maryland: The History of a Palatinate* (rev. ed., 1912).

"Calvert Papers," Md. Hist. Soc., *Fund Publ.*, 28 (1889); 34 (1894); 35 (1899).

Gleissner, Richard H., "Religious Causes of Glorious Revolution in Maryland," *Md. Hist. Mag.*, 64 (1969), 327.

Hall, Clayton Coleman, *The Lords Baltimore and the Maryland Palatinate* (2nd ed., 1904).

——, ed., *Narratives of Early Maryland 1633–84* (1910).

Hall, Michael G., Lawrence H. Leder, and Michael G. Kammen, *Glorious Revolution in America: Documents on Colonial Crisis of 1689* (1964).

Hanley, Thomas, *Their Rights and Liberties: Beginning of Religious and Political Freedom in Maryland* (1939).

High, James, "The Proprietary Governor and Maryland Charter," *Md. Hist. Mag.*, 55 (1960), 67.

James, Bartlett B., *Labadist Colony in Maryland* (1899).

Johnson, Gerald, ed., *Maryland Act of Religious Toleration* (1949).

Kammen, Michael G., "Causes of the Maryland Revolution of 1689," *Md. Hist. Mag.*, 55 (1960), 293.

Lapsley, G. T., *County Palatine of Durham* (1900).

Latané, J. H., *Early Relations between Maryland and Virginia* (1895).

McAnear, Beverly, ed., "Mariland's Grevances Wiy They Have Taken Op Arms" [1689], *JSH*, 8 (1942), 392.

Mereness, Newton D., *Maryland as Proprietary Province* (1901).

Randall, Daniel R., *Puritan Colony in Maryland* (1886).

Rohr, C. J., *Governor of Maryland* (1932).

Sommes, Raphael, *Captains and Mariners of Early Maryland* (1937).

Steiner, Bernard C. *Beginnings of Maryland* (1903).

—— *Citizenship and Suffrage in Maryland* (1895).

—— *Maryland during the English Civil Wars* (1906).

—— *Maryland under the Commonwealth* (1911).

—— "Protestant Revolution in Maryland," Am. Hist. Assoc., *Report* (1897), 279.

—— "Religious Freedom in Provincial Maryland," *AHR*, 28 (1923), 258.

Stratemeier, G. B., *Thomas Cornwaleys, Commissioner of Maryland* (1922).

*   *   *   *   *   *   *

Baer, Elizabeth, *Seventeenth Century Maryland: Bibliography* (1949).

Mathews, Edward B., *Maps and Map-Makers of Maryland* (1898).
Wroth, Lawrence C., "Maryland Colonization Tracts," in *Essays Offered to Herbert Putnam* (1929).

See also 10.3 for biographies/writings of:

Sandys, George, 1577/78-1643/44

33.2.4　Carolinas

Ashe, Samuel A., *History of North Carolina* (2 vols., 1908).
Baldwin, Agnes L., *First Settlers of South Carolina, 1670–1680* (1969).
Bassett, John S., *Constitutional Beginnings of North Carolina* (1894).
Cheves, Langdon, ed., "Shaftesbury Papers," So. Car. Hist. Soc., *Coll.*, 5 (1897), 3.
Childs, St. Julien R., "Cavaliers and Burghers of Carolina Low Country," in Eric F. Goldman, ed., *Historiography and Urbanization* (1941).
——— *Malaria and Colonization in Carolina Low Country* (1940).
Connor, Robert D. W., *North Carolina: Colonial and Revolutionary Periods, 1584–1783* (1919).
——— *Studies in the History of North Carolina* (1923).
Courtenay, W. A., *Genesis of South Carolina, 1562–1670* (1907).
Ford, Worthington C., "Early Maps of Carolina," *Geog. Rev.*, 16 (1926), 264.
von Graffenried, Christopher, *Account of Founding of New Bern*, V. H. Todd, ed. (1920).
Guess, William C., "County Government in Colonial North Carolina," *James Sprunt Historical Studies*, 11 (1911), 5.
Hilton, William, *Brief Description* (1666).
——— *Relation* (1664).
Hirsch, Arthur H., *Huguenots of South Carolina* (1928).
Karpinsky, Louis, *Early Maps of Carolina* (1930).
Lee, E. Lawrence, *Lower Cape Fear in Colonial Days* (1965).
McCain, Paul M., *The County Court in North Carolina before 1750* (1954).
McCrady, Edward, *History of South Carolina under Proprietary Government* (1897).
Powell, William S., *The Proprietors of Carolina* (1963).
Ravenel, H. H., *Charleston* (1906).
Rivers, W. J., *History of South Carolina to 1719* (1856).
Salley, Alexander S., *The Early English Settlers of South Carolina* (1946).
Sirmans, M. Eugene, *Colonial South Carolina: Political History, 1663–1763* (1966).
Smith, Henry A. M., "Baronies of South Carolina," *So. Car. Hist. Mag.*, 11 (1910), 75; 12 (1911), 5; 13 (1912), 3; 14 (1913), 61; 15 (1914), 1; 18 (1917), 3.
——— "Town of Dorchester," *So. Car. Hist. Mag.*, 6 (1905), 62.
Thomas, J. P., "Barbadians in Early South Carolina," *So. Car. Hist. Mag.*, 31 (1930), 75.
Wallace, David D., *South Carolina*, vol. I (1934).

*　*　*　*　*　*　*

Easterby, J. H., *South Carolina Bibliographies* (1950).

33.2.5　Massachusetts

33.2.5.1　General

Adams, Charles Francis, Jr., *Three Episodes of Massachusetts History* (2 vols., 1892).
Banks, Charles E., *The Planters of the Commonwealth* (1930).
Bolton, Charles K., *Real Founders of New England* (1929).
Deane, Charles, ed., "Records of Council for New England," Am. Antiq. Soc., *Proc.*, (1867) 51.

Hart, Albert B., *Commonwealth History of Massachusetts* (5 vols., 1927–1930).
Hutchinson, Thomas, *History of the Colony and Province of Massachusetts Bay* (3 vols., 1764–1828); Lawrence Shaw Mayo, ed. (3 vols., 1936).
Johnson, Edgar A. J., "Mercantilism in Massachusetts Bay," *NEQ*, 1 (1928), 371.
Morison, Samuel E., *Builders of the Bay Colony* (1930).
Young, Alexander, ed., *Chronicles of Massachusetts Bay* (1846).

*   *   *   *   *   *   *

Morgan, Edmund S., ed., *Founding of Massachusetts: Historians and Sources* (1964).

See also 10.3 for biographies/writings of:

Conant, Roger, 1592–1679
Cotton, John, 1584–1652
Endecott, John, 1589–1665
Mather, Increase, 1639–1723
Winthrop, John, 1587/88 o.s.–1649

33.2.5.2 Plymouth

Banks, Charles E., *English Ancestry and Homes of Pilgrims* (1929).
Bradford, William, *Of Plymouth Plantation, 1620–1647*, Samuel E. Morison, ed. (1952).
"Bradford's Letter-Book," Mass. Hist. Soc., *Coll.*, 3 (1794), 27; repr. 1 ser., 3 (1968), 27.
Burrage, Champlin, ed., *John Pory's Lost Description of Plymouth Colony* (1918).
Demos, John, *Little Commonwealth: Family Life in Plymouth Colony* (1970).
Dexter, Henry M. and Morton, *England and Holland of Pilgrims* (1905).
Haskins, George L., "The Legacy of Plymouth," *Social Education*, 26 (1962), 7.
Heath, Dwight B., ed., *Journal of the Pilgrims* (1963).
Langdon, George D., Jr., "Franchise and Democracy in Plymouth Colony," *WMQ*, 3 ser., 20 (1963), 513.
────── *Pilgrim Colony: New Plymouth, 1620–1691* (1966).
Leach, D. E., "Military System of Plymouth," *NEQ*, 24 (1951), 342.
Moody, Robert E., ed., "Versions of Mayflower Compact," *Old South Leaflet* no. 225 (1951).
Morison, Samuel E., "The Pilgrim Fathers' Significance in History," in *By Land and By Sea* (1953).
Morton, George, "Mourt's Relation" in Alexander Young, *Chronicles of Pilgrim Fathers* (1844). Also published in Dwight B. Heath, ed. *Journal of Pilgrims at Plymouth* (1963).
Perry, Thomas W., "New Plymouth and Old England," *WMQ*, 3 ser., 18 (1961), 251.
Plooij, Daniel, *Pilgrim Fathers from a Dutch Point of View (1932)*.
Pory, John, et al., *Three Visitors to Early Plymouth: Letters*, Sydney V. James, Jr., ed. (1963).
Shurtleff, Nathaniel B., et al., eds., *Records of New Plymouth (1620–1692)* (12 vols., 1855–1861).
Smith, Bradford, *Bradford of Plymouth* (1951).
Stearns, Raymond P., "New England Way in Holland," *NEQ*, 6 (1933), 747.
Usher, Roland G., *Pilgrims and Their History* (1918).
Willison, George F., *Saints and Strangers: Pilgrim Fathers* (1945).
Young, Alexander, *Chronicles of Pilgrim Fathers* (1844).

See also 10.3 for biographies/writings of:

Bradford, William, 1589/90–1657
Morton, Thomas, ca. 1590–ca. 1647
Peter, Hugh, 1598–1660

33.2.5.3 Puritan Migration and Massachusetts Bay

Banks, Charles E., and Samuel E. Morison, "Persecution as a Factor in Emigration," Mass. Hist. Soc., *Proc.*, 63 (1930), 136.

Banks, Charles E., *Winthrop Fleet* (1930).

Crouse, Nellis M., "Causes of Great Migration," *NEQ*, 5 (1932), 3.

Hansen, Ann N., "Ships of Puritan Migration to Massachusetts Bay," *Am. Neptune,* 23 (1963), 62.

Lapham, A. G., *Old Planters of Beverly* (1930).

Mayo, Lawrence S., *John Endecott* (1936).

Morton, Thomas, *New English Canaan* (1637); Charles F. Adams, ed. (1883).

Newton, Arthur, *Colonizing Activities of English Puritans* (1914).

Rose-Troup, Frances, *John White, Founder of Massachusetts* (1930).

────── *Massachusetts Bay Company and Its Predecessors* (1930).

Rutman, Darrett B., *Winthrop's Boston: Portrait of a Puritan Town, 1630–1649* (1965).

Sachse, William L., "The Migration of New Englanders to England, 1640–1660," *AHR*, 53 (1948), 251.

Shepard, Thomas, "Autobiography," Col. Soc. Mass., *Publ.*, 27 (1932), 345.

Sprunger, Keith L., "William Ames and Settlement of Massachusetts Bay," *NEQ*, 39 (1966), 66.

Winship, G. P., ed., *New England Company of 1649 and John Eliot* (1920).

Winthrop, John, *Journal, History of New England, 1630–1649*, James K. Hosmer, ed. (2 vols., 1908).

────── *Papers*, A. B. Forbes, ed. (5 vols, 1929–1947).

Wood, William, *New England's Prospect* (1634; repr. 1865).

See also 10.3 for biographies/writings of:

White, John, 1575–1648

33.2.5.4 Government and Politics

Adams, Charles Francis, Jr., "The Genesis of the Massachusetts Town, and the Development of Town-meeting Government," Mass. Hist. Soc., *Proc.*, 2 ser., 7 (1892), 172.

Akagi, Roy H., *The Town Proprietors of the New England Colonies: A Study of Their Development, Organization, Activities and Controversies, 1620–1770* (1924).

Breen, Timothy H., "Town Franchise in Seventeenth-Century Massachusetts," *WMQ*, 3 ser., 27 (1970), 460.

Brennan, Eileen E., "Massachusetts Council of Magistrates," *NEQ*, 4 (1931), 54.

Brown, B. Katherine, "Freemanship in Puritan Massachusetts," *AHR*, 59 (1954), 865.

────── "Puritan Concept of Aristocracy," *MVHR*, 41 (1954), 105.

────── "Puritan Democracy: A Case Study (Cambridge)," *MVHR*, 50 (1963), 377.

────── "Puritan Democracy in Dedham, Massachusetts," *WMQ*, 3 ser., 24 (1967), 378.

Buffington, A. H., "Isolationist Policy of Colonial Massachusetts," *NEQ*, 1 (1928), 158.

Bumsted, J. M., "Church and State in Plymouth Colony," *Jour. Church and State*, 10 (1968), 265.

Colegrove, Kenneth, "New England Town Mandates," Col. Soc. Mass., *Publ.*, 21 (1919), 411.

Foster, Stephen, "Massachusetts Franchise in the Seventeenth Century," *WMQ*, 3 ser., 24 (1967), 613.

Jones, Matt B., *Thomas Maule and Free Speech* (1936).

Kittredge, G. L., "Dr. Robert Child the Remonstrant," Col. Soc. Mass., *Publ.*, 21 (1919), 1.

Koch, Donald W., "Income Distribution and Political Structure in Seventeenth Century Salem, Massachusetts," Essex Inst., *Hist. Coll.*, 105 (1969), 50.

Labaree, Benjamin W., "New England Town Meeting," *Am. Archivist*, 25 (1962), 165.

Laws and Liberties of Massachusetts (1648); Max Farrand, ed., (1929).

Lockridge, Kenneth A., *New England Town: Dedham, Massachusetts, 1636–1736* (1970).

Lucas, Paul R., "Colony or Commonwealth: Massachusetts Bay, 1661–1666," *WMQ*, 3 ser., 24 (1967), 88.

Massachusetts (Colony) Laws, Statutes, *Colonial Laws of Massachusetts* (1890).

Morison, Samuel E., "William Pynchon, Founder of Springfield," Mass. Hist. Soc., *Proc.*, 64 (1930), 67.

Nelson, Anne K., "King Philip's War and Hubbard-Mather Rivalry," *WMQ*, 3 ser., 27 (1970), 615.

Powell, Sumner C., *Puritan Village: The Formation of a New England Town* (1963).

Records of the Governor and Company of the Massachusetts Bay in New England (1628–86), Nathaniel B. Shurtleff, ed. (5 vols., 1853–1854).

Seidman, A. B., "Church and State in the Early Years of Bay Colony," *NEQ*, 18 (1945), 211.

Simmons, Richard C., "Early Massachusetts," *Hist. Today*, 18 (1968), 259.

—— "Freemanship in Early Massachusetts: Some Suggestions and a Case Study," *WMQ*, 3 ser., 19 (1962), 422.

—— "Godliness, Property and Franchise in Puritan Massachusetts," *JAH*, 55 (1968), 495.

—— "Massachusetts Revolution of 1689: Three Broadsides," *Jour. Am. Studies*, 2 (1968), 1.

Sly, John F., *Town Government in Massachusetts* (1930).

Toppan, R. N., ed., "Andros Records," Am. Antiq. Soc., *Proc.*, n.s., 13 (1899–1900), 237.

—— "Dudley Records," Mass. Hist. Soc., *Proc.*, 2 ser., 13 (1899), 222.

Tuttle, J. H., ed., "Land Warrants under Andros," Col. Soc. Mass., *Publ.*, 21 (1919), 292.

Wall, Robert E., Jr., "Massachusetts Bay Colony Franchise, 1647," *WMQ*, 3 ser., 27 (1970), 136.

—— "New Look at Cambridge," *JAH*, 52 (1965), 599.

Whitmore, William H., ed., *Andros Tracts* (3 vols., 1868–1874).

Zimmerman, Joseph F., "Genesis of the Massachusetts Town," *Social Science*, 41 (1966), 76.

*   *   *   *   *   *   *

Whitmore, William H., ed., *Bibliographical Sketch of the Laws of Massachusetts Colony from 1630–1686* (1890).

See also 10.3 for biographies/writings of:

Dudley, Joseph, 1647–1720
Eliot, John, 1604–1690
Gookin, Daniel, 1612–1686/87
Hutchinson, Anne, 1591–1643
Randolph, Edward, 1632–1703

33.2.6 Connecticut

Ahlstrom, Sydney E., "Thomas Hooker-Puritanism and Democratic Citizenship," *Church Hist.*, 32 (1963), 415.

Andrews, Charles M., *Beginnings of Connecticut, 1632–1662* (1934).

—— *Connecticut and the British Government* (1933).

—— *Connecticut Intestacy Law* (1933).

—— *River Towns of Connecticut: Wethersfield, Hartford, and Windsor* (1889).

Bates, Albert C., ed., "Wyllys Papers," Conn. Hist. Soc., *Coll.*, 21 (1924).

Bradstreet, Howard, *War with the Pequots* (1933).

Calder, Isabel M., "Earl of Stirling and Colonization of Long Island," in *Essays in Colonial History Presented to Charles M. Andrews* (1931).

———— *New Haven Colony* (1934).
Coleman, Roy V., *Fundamental Orders* (1934).
———— *Old Patent* (1936).
———— *Roger Ludlow* (1934).
Connecticut (Colony) Charters, *The Charter of Connecticut, 1662* (1933).
Connecticut (Colony) Constitution, *The Fundamental Orders of Connecticut* (1934).
Deming, Dorothy, *Settlement of Connecticut Towns* (1933).
Drake, Samuel G., *Old Indian Chronicle* (1867).
Dunn, Richard, *Puritans and Yankees: Winthrop Dynasty of New England, 1630–1713* (1962).
Dutcher, George M., ed., *Fundamental Orders of Connecticut* (1934).
Fowler, David H., "Connecticut's Freemen: First Forty Years," *WMQ,* 3 ser., 15 (1958), 312.
Jones, Mary J. A., *Congregational Commonwealth: Connecticut, 1636–1662* (1968).
Labaree, Leonard W., *Milford* (1933).
Levermore, Charles H., *Republic of New Haven* (1886).
Love, W. deL., *Colonial History of Hartford* (1914).
Mason, John, "Brief History of Pequot War (1736)," Mass. Hist. Soc., *Coll.,* 2 ser., 8 (1819), 120.
Mead, Nelson P., *Connecticut as a Corporate Colony* (1906).
Miller, Perry, "Hooker and Democracy of Early Connecticut," *NEQ,* 4 (1931), 663.
Steiner, Bernard C., *History of Guilford* (1897).
Trumbull, Benjamin, *History of Connecticut* (2 vols., 1815).

*   *   *   *   *   *   *

Crofut, Florence S. M., *Guide to History and Historic Sites of Connecticut* (2 vols., 1937).

See also 10.3 for biographies/writings of:

Hooker, Thomas, 1586–1647
Winthrop, John, 1605/06–1676

33.2.7 Rhode Island

Bicknell, T. W., *History of Rhode Island and Providence Plantations* (4 vols., 1920).
Channing, Edward, *Narragansett Planters* (1886).
Chapin, Howard M., *Documentary History of Rhode Island* (2 vols., 1916–1919).
Conley, Patrick T., "Rhode Island Constitutional Development, 1636–1775," *R.I. Hist.,* 27 (1968), 55.
Harris, William, *A Rhode Islander Reports on King Philip's War,* Douglas E. Leach, ed. (1963).
Miller, William D., "The Narrangansett Planters," Am. Antiq. Soc., *Proc.,* 43 (1933), 49.
Moore, LeRoy, Jr., "Roger Williams and Historians," *Church Hist.,* 32 (1963), 432.
Rhode Island (Colony), *Records of the Colony of Rhode Island and Providence Plantations* (10 vols., 1856–1865).
Simpson, Alan, "How Democratic Was Roger Williams?" *WMQ,* 3 ser., 13 (1956), 53.
Weeden, W. B., *Early Rhode Island: A Social History* (1910).

*   *   *   *   *   *   *

Bartlett, J. R., *Bibliography of Rhode Island* (1864).
Brigham, C. S., "List of Books upon Rhode Island History," *Rhode Island Educational Circular,* Historical Series, 2 (1908).

See also 10.3 for biographies/writings of:

Coddington, William, 1601–1678
Gorton, Samuel, ca. 1592–1677
Hutchinson, Anne, 1591–1643
Smith, Richard, 1596–1666
Williams, Roger, 1603–1682/83

33.2.8 New Hampshire

Bell, Charles H., *John Wheelwright* (1876).
Clark, Charles E., *The Eastern Frontier: The Settlement of Northern New England, 1610–1763* (1970).
Fry, William Henry, *New Hampshire as a Royal Province* (1908).
Hammond, Otis G., "Mason Title," Am. Antiq. Soc., *Proc.,* n.s., 26 (1916), 245.
Moyer, P. E., "Settlement of New Hampshire," *Granite Monthly*, 54 (1922), 153.
Page, E. L., "A.D. 1623," *Granite Monthly*, 54 (1922), 205.
Pope, Charles H., *Pioneers of Maine and New Hampshire, 1623–1660: A Descriptive List* (1908).
Sanborn, Franklin B., *New Hampshire* (1904).
Scales, John, "First Permanent Settlement," *Granite Monthly*, 54 (1922), 269.
Tuttle, C. W., *Captain John Mason, Founder of New Hampshire* (1887).

33.2.9 Maine

Baldwin, J. F., "Feudalism in Maine," *NEQ*, 5 (1932), 352.
Banks, Charles E., ed., "Popham Expedition Documents," Am. Antiq. Soc., *Proc.,* n.s., 39 (1929), 307.
Baxter, James P., *George Cleeve of Casco Bay 1630–67* (1885).
———— *Sir Ferdinando Gorges and His Province of Maine* (3 vols., 1890).
Burrage, Henry, *Beginnings of Colonial Maine* (1914).
———— *Gorges and Grant of Province of Maine* (1923).
"Documentary History of Maine," Maine Hist. Soc., *Coll.*, 2 ser. 3–9 (1884–1907).
Gardiner, Henry, *New England's Vindication* (1660); Charles E. Banks, ed. (1884).
Levett, Christopher, "Voyage of 1622–23," Maine Hist. Soc., *Coll.*, 2 (1847), 74.
Libby, C. T., ed., *Province and Court Records of Maine* (2 vols., 1928–1931).
Preston, Richard A., *Gorges of Plymouth Fort: Sir Ferdinando Gorges* (1953).
Spencer, Wilbur D., *Pioneers on Maine Rivers* (1930).
Thayer, Henry O., *The Sagadahoc Colony* (1892).

*   *   *   *   *   *   *

O'Brien, Francis M., "Suggested Reading in Maine History," Maine Hist. Soc., *News-Letter*, 5 (1966), 5.
Williamson, Joseph, *Bibliography of Maine* (2 vols., 1896).

See also 10.3 for biographies/writings of:

Gosnold, Bartholomew, 1572–1607

33.2.10 Newfoundland

Berkley, H. J., "Lord Baltimore's Contest with Sir David Kirke," *Md. Hist. Mag.*, 12 (1917), 107.
Cell, Gillian T., "Newfoundland Company," *WMQ*, 3 ser., 22 (1965), 611.
Insh, G. P., *Scottish Colonial Schemes, 1620–1686* (1922).
Lounsbury, R. G., "British Fishery at Newfoundland 1634–1763 (1934).

——— "Yankee Trade at Newfoundland," *NEQ*, 3 (1930), 607.

Moore-Smith, G. C., "Robert Hayman and Newfoundland," *Eng. Hist. Rev.*, 33 (1918), 21.

Prowse, Daniel W., *History of Newfoundland* (1895).

Scisco, Louis D., "Kirke's Memorial on Newfoundland," *Can. Hist. Rev.*, 7 (1926), 46.

Slafter, E. F., *Sir William Alexander and American Colonization* (1873).

33.2.11 Pennsylvania and Delaware

Beatty, E. C. O., *William Penn as Social Philosopher* (1939).

Bolles, Albert Sydney, *Pennsylvania: Province and State: A History from 1609 to 1790* (2 vols., 1898).

Brailsford, M. R., *Making of William Penn* (1930).

Bronner, Edwin S., "William Penn's "Holy Experiment": Founding of Pennsylvania (1962).

Carlson, H. L., "Genesis of Charter of Pennsylvania," *Penn. Mag. Hist.*, 43 (1919), 289.

deValinger, Leon, Jr., ed., *Court Records of Kent County, Delaware, 1680–1705.* Vol. VIII of *American Legal Records* (1959).

Dobree, Bonamy, *William Penn: Quaker and Pioneer* (1932).

Dunaway, Wayland Fuller, *A History of Pennsylvania* (1948).

Dunn, Mary Maples, *William Penn: Politics and Conscience* (1967).

Fisher, Sydney George, *The Making of Pennsylvania* (1896).

Hough, Oliver, "Captain Thomas Holme," *Penn. Mag. Hist.*, 19 (1895), 413; 20 (1896), 128.

Hull, W. I., *Penn and Dutch Quaker Migration* (1935).

——— *William Penn* (1937).

Illick, Joseph E., "The Pennsylvania Grant: A Re-Evaluation," *Penn. Mag. Hist. Biog.*, 86 (1962), 375.

——— *William Penn the Politician* (1965).

Kane, F. H., "Early Pennsylvania Promotion Literature," *Penn. Mag. Hist.*, 63 (1939), 144.

Konkle, B. A., "A Grant Yet Not a Grant," *Penn. Mag. Hist.*, 54 (1930), 241.

Myers, Albert C., ed., *Narratives of Early Pennsylvania, West Jersey and Delaware* (1912).

Nash, Gary B., *Quakers and Politics: Pennsylvania, 1681–1726* (1968).

Pastorius, Francis D., *Description of Pennsylvania, 1700* (1898).

Peare, Catherine Owens, *William Penn: A Biography* (1959).

Penn, William, and James Logan, "Correspondence," Deborah Logan and Edward Armstrong, eds., Hist. Soc. of Penn., *Publ.*, 9–10 (1870–1872).

Penn, William, *Witness of William Penn*, Frederick B. Tolles and E. Gordon Alderfer, eds. (1957).

Pomfret, John E., "First Purchasers of Pennsylvania, 1681–1700," *Penn. Mag. Hist. Biog.*, 80 (1956), 137.

Pound, Arthur, *Penns of Pennsylvania and England* (1932).

Roach, Hannah B., "Planting of Philadelphia: Seventeenth Century Real Estate Development," *Penn. Mag. Hist. Biog.*, 92 (1968), 3.

Rodney, R. S., "Early Relations of Delaware and Pennsylvania," *Penn. Mag. Hist. Biog.*, 54 (1930), 209.

Scharf, John T., *History of Delaware, 1609–1888* (2 vols., 1888).

Vulliamy, Colwyn E., *William Penn* (1934).

Wainwright, N. B., "Mystery of Pennsylvania's Royal Charter," *Penn. Mag. Hist. Biog.*, 73 (1949), 415.

Weslager, C. A., *English on the Delaware, 1610–1682* (1967).

*   *   *   *   *   *   *

Illick, Joseph E., "Writing of Colonial Pennsylvania History," *Penn. Mag. Hist. Biog.*, 94 (1970), 3.

33.2.12 New Jersey

Budd, Thomas, *Good Order Established in Pennsylvania and New Jersey* (1685; repr. 1902).
Claypoole, James, *Letter Book: London and Philadelphia, 1681–1684*, Marion Balderston, ed. (1967).
Craven, Wesley F., *New Jersey and the English Colonization of North America* (1964).
Johnson, R. G., "John Fenwicke," N.J. Hist. Soc., *Proc.*, 4 (1849), 53.
Leiby, Adrian C., *Early Dutch and Swedish Settlers of New Jersey* (1964).
McCormick, Richard P., *History of Voting in New Jersey: Development of Election Machinery, 1664–1911* (1953).
———— *New Jersey from Colony to State, 1609–1789* (1964).
Nelson, William, *Discovery and Early History of New Jersey* (1912).
Pomfret, John E., *New Jersey Proprietors and Their Lands, 1664–1776* (1964).
———— ed., "Edward Byllynge's Proposed Gift of Land," *Penn. Mag. Hist. Biog.*, 61 (1937), 88.
Pomfret, John E., *Province of East New Jersey, 1609–1702* (1962).
———— *Province of West New Jersey, 1609–1702* (1956).
"Scots East Jersey Proprietors' Letters, 1683–84," N.J. Hist. Soc., *Proc.*, n.s., 7 (1922), 4.

See also 10.3 for biographies/writings of:

Fenwick, John, 1618–1683

33.2.13 New York

Abbott, Wilbur C., "Colonel John Scott of Long Island," *Conflicts with Oblivion* (1924).
Bonomi, Patricia U., *A Factious People: Politics and Society in Colonial New York* (1971).
Brodhead, J. R., *History of New York* (2 vols., 1853–1871).
Ellis, David M., et al., *A History of New York State* (rev. ed., 1967).
Flick, Alexander C., ed., *History of the State of New York* (10 vols., 1933–1937).
Kennedy, John Hopkins, *Thomas Dongan* (1930).
Lovejoy, David S., "New York Charter of Libertyes, 1683," *WMQ*, 3 ser., 21 (1964), 493.
McKinley, Albert E., "Transition from Dutch to English Rule," *AHR*, 6 (1900), 693.
Melick, Harry C. W., *Manor of Fordham and Its Founder* (1950).
O'Callaghan, E. B., *Origin of Legislative Assemblies in New York* (1861).
Pennypacker, Morton, *Duke's Laws: Their Antecedents, Implications and Importance* (1944).
Reich, Jerome R., *Jacob Leisler's Rebellion: Democracy in New York, 1664–1720* (1953).
Van Rensselaer, M. G., *History of City of New York in Seventeenth Century* (2 vols., 1909).
Smith, William, Jr., *History of the Late Province of New York, from Its Discovery to 1762*, New York Hist. Soc., *Coll.*, 4 (1829); 5 (1830).
———— *History of the Province of New York*, Michael Kammen, ed. (2 vols., 1972).
Still, Bayrd, "New York's Mayoralty," *N.Y. Hist. Quar.*, 47 (1963), 239.
Stokes, Isaac N. P., *Iconography of Manhattan, 1498–1909* (6 vols., 1915–1928).
Varga, Nicholas, "Election Procedures and Practices in Colonial New York," *N.Y. Hist.*, 41 (1960), 249.

34 Development of the Colonies, 1688–1763

34.1 GENERAL

Adams, James T., *Provincial Society, 1690–1763* (1927).
—— *Revolutionary New England, 1691–1776* (1923).
Andrews, Charles M., *Colonial Period of American History* (4 vols., 1934–1938).
Channing, Edward, *History of the United States.* Vol. II: *A Century of Colonial History, 1660–1760* (1908).
Crane, Verner W., "Projects for Colonization in the South, 1684–1732," *MVHR*, 12 (1925), 23.
Craven, Wesley F., *Colonies in Transition 1660–1713* (1968).
Gipson, Lawrence H., *The British Empire Before the American Revolution* (14 vols., 1936–1969).
Greene, Evarts B., *Provincial America* (1905).
Hall, Michael G., Lawrence H. Leder, and Michael G. Kammen, eds., *Glorious Revolution in America: Documents on Colonial Crisis of 1689* (1964).
Osgood, Herbert L., *The American Colonies in the Eighteenth Century* (4 vols., 1924).
Rankin, Hugh F., "Colonial South," in Arthur S. Link and Rembert W. Patrick, eds., *Writing Southern History: Essays in Honor of Fletcher M. Green* (1965).
Shipton, Clifford K., "Shaping of Revolutionary New England, 1680–1740," *Pol. Sci. Quar.*, 50 (1935), 584.
Winsor, Justin, ed., *Narrative and Critical History of America.* Vol. V: *The English and French in North America, 1689–1763* (1887).

* * * * * * *

Greene, Jack P., *The American Colonies in the Eighteenth Century* (1968).

See also 37.1 Government and Politics.

34.2 SOUTH

34.2.1 Georgia

Abbot, William W., *Royal Governors of Georgia, 1754–1775* (1959).
Church, Leslie F., *Oglethorpe: A Study of Philanthropy in England and Georgia* (1932).
Coulter, E. Merton, *Short History of Georgia* (1933).
Crane, Verner W., "Dr. Thomas Bray and the Charitable Colony Project, 1730," *WMQ*, 3 ser., 19 (1962), 49.
—— "Origins of Georgia," *Ga. Hist. Quar.*, 14 (1930), 93.
—— "Philanthropists and Genesis of Georgia," *AHR*, 26 (1921), 63.
—— *Promotion Literature of Georgia* (1925).
Dunn, Richard S., "Trustees of Georgia and House of Commons, 1732–1752," *WMQ*, 3 ser., 11 (1954), 551.
Egmont, John P., *Journal, 1732–1738*, Robert G. McPherson, ed. (1962).
Ettinger, Amos A., *James Edward Oglethorpe, Imperial Idealist* (1936).
Fant, H. B., "Indian Trade Policy of Trustees," *Ga. Hist. Quar.*, 15 (1931), 207.
—— "Labor Policy of Trustees," *Ga. Hist. Quar.*, 16 (1932), 1.
—— "Thomas Coram," *Ga. Hist. Quar.*, 32 (1948), 77.
Flippin, Percy S., "Royal Government in Georgia, 1752–1776," *Ga. Hist. Quar.*, 8 (1924), 1; 9 (1925), 186; 10 (1926), 1; 12 (1928) 326; 13 (1929), 128.
Gordon, Peter, *Journal, 1732–1735*, E. Merton Coulter, ed. (1963).
Jones, Charles C., *History of Georgia* (2 vols. 1883).

Klingberg, Frank J., "Humanitarian Spirit in Eighteenth-Century England," *Penn. Mag. Hist. Biog.*, 66 (1942), 260.

McCain, James R., *Georgia as a Proprietary Province: Execution of a Trust* (1917).

Meroney, Geraldine, "London Entrepot Merchants and Georgia Colony," *WMQ*, 3 ser., 25 (1968), 230.

Newman, Henry, *Salzburger Letterbooks*, George F. Jones, ed., (1966).

Pennington, Edgar L., "John Wesley's Georgia Ministry," *Church Hist.*, 8 (1939), 231.

Reese, Trevor R., *Colonial Georgia: British Imperial Policy in the Eighteenth Century* (1963).

—— "Religious Factors in Settlement of Georgia," *Jour. Relig. Hist.*, 1 (1961), 206.

Saye, Albert B., *Constitutional History of Georgia, 1732–1845* (1948).

—— "Genesis of Georgia Reviewed," *Ga. Hist. Quar.*, 50 (1966), 153.

—— *New Viewpoints* (1943).

Stephens, William, *Journal, 1741–1745*, E. Merton Coulter, ed. (2 vols., 1958–1959).

Strickland, Reba C., *Religion and State in Georgia* (1939).

Strobel, P. A., *Salzburgers and Their Descendants* (1855).

Taylor, Paul, "Colonizing Georgia, 1732–1752: Statistical Note," *WMQ*, 3 ser., 22 (1965), 119.

Tailfer, Patrick, et al., *A True and Historical Narrative of the Colony of Georgia* (1741); Clarence L. Ver Steeg, ed. (1960).

Temple, Sarah B. G., and Kenneth Coleman, *Georgia Journeys: Original Settlers, 1732–1754* (1961).

Urlsperger, Samuel, ed., *Detailed Reports on Salzburger Emigrants Who Settled in America* (1735); George F. Jones and Herman J. Lacher, eds. and trans. (1968).

Wesley, John, *Journal*, Nehemiah Curnock and John Telford, eds., vol. I (1909).

*   *   *   *   *   *   *

Coleman, Kenneth, "Colonial Georgia: Needs and Opportunities," *Ga. Hist. Quar.*, 53 (1969), 184.

See also 10.3 for biographies/writings of:

Oglethorpe, James E., 1696–1785
Whitefield, George, 1714–1770

34.2.2 Maryland

Edgar, Matilda R., *A Colonial Governor in Maryland: Horatio Sharpe and His Times, 1753–1773* (1912).

High, James, "Maryland's Middle Class in Colonial Aristocratic Pattern," *Md. Hist. Mag.*, 57 (1962), 334.

—— "Proprietary Governor and Maryland Charter," *Md. Hist. Mag.*, 55 (1960), 67.

Kammen, Michael G., "Causes of the Maryland Revolution of 1689," *Md. Hist. Mag.*, 55 (1960), 293.

Land, Aubrey C., "Eighteenth Century Chesapeake," *JSH*, 33 (1967), 469.

Mereness, Newton D., *Maryland as a Proprietary Province* (1901).

Nash, Gary B., "Maryland's Economic War with Pennsylvania," *Md. Hist. Mag.*, 60 (1965), 231.

Owings, Donnell M., *His Lordship's Patronage: Offices of Profit in Colonial Maryland* (1953).

Powell, Walter A., "Fight of a Century between the Penns and Calverts," *Md. Hist. Mag.*, 29 (1934), 83.

Riley, Elihu S., *History of the General Assembly of Maryland, 1635–1904* (1905).

Scharf, John T., *History of Maryland, from the Earliest Period to the Present Day* (3 vols., 1879).

Sioussat, St. George L., *Economics and Politics in Maryland, 1720–1750* (1903).
Steiner, Bernard C., *Citizenship and Suffrage in Maryland* (1895).

See also 10.3 for biographies/writings of:

Dulany Family

34.2.3 North Carolina

Ashe, Thomas, *History of North Carolina*, vol. 1 (1908).
Bassett, John S., *Constitutional Beginnings of North Carolina* (1894).
Boyd, Julian P., "Sheriff in Colonial North Carolina," *No. Car. Hist. Rev.*, 5 (1928), 151.
Boyd, William K., ed., *Some Eighteenth-Century Tracts Concerning North Carolina* (1927).
Connor, Robert D. W., *North Carolina: Colonial and Revolutionary Periods, 1584–1783* (1919).
Cook, Florence, "Procedure in the North Carolina Assembly, 1731–1770," *No. Car. Hist. Rev.*, 8 (1931), 258.
Crittenden, Charles C., "Surrender of the Charter of Carolina," *No. Car. Hist. Rev.*, 1 (1924), 383.
Greene, Jack P., "North Carolina Lower House, 1711–1775," *No. Car. Hist. Rev.*, 40 (1963), 37.
Guess, William C., "County Government in Colonial North Carolina," *James Sprunt Studies in History and Political Science*, 11 (1911), 5.
Johnston, Gideon, *Carolina Chronicle: Papers of Commissary Gideon Johnston, 1707–1716*, Frank J. Klingberg, ed. (1946).
Kay, Marvin L., "Payment of Provincial and Local Taxes in North Carolina, 1748–1771," *WMQ*, 3 ser., 26 (1969), 218.
―――― "Provincial Taxes in North Carolina during the Administration of Dobbs and Tryon," *No. Car. Hist. Rev.*, 42 (1965), 440.
Lawson, John, *History of Carolina* (1718).
―――― *New Voyage to Carolina* (1709); Hugh T. Lefler, ed. (1967).
Le Jau, Francis, *Carolina Chronicle: Papers of Commissary Francis Le Jau, 1706–1717*, Frank J. Klingberg, ed. (1956).
Lee, E. Lawrence, *Lower Cape Fear in Colonial Days* (1965).
Lefler, Hugh T., and Albert R. Newsome, *North Carolina: History of a Southern State* (1954).
London, Lawrence F., "Representation Controversy in Colonial North Carolina," *No. Car. Hist. Rev.*, 11 (1934), 255.
McCain, Paul M., *County Court in North Carolina before 1750* (1954).
Merrens, H. Roy, *Colonial North Carolina in the Eighteenth Century: Study in Historical Geography* (1964).
Parker, Coralie, *History of Taxation in North Carolina during the Colonial Period, 1663–1776* (1928).
Powell, William S., "Eighteenth-Century North Carolina Imprints: Supplement to McMurtrie," *No. Car. Hist. Rev.*, 35 (1958), 50.
Raper, Charles L., *North Carolina: Study in English Colonial Government* (1904).
Skaggs, Marvin L., "Progress in North Carolina-South Carolina Boundary Dispute," *No. Car. Hist. Rev.*, 15 (1938), 341.
Ubbelohde, Carl W., "Vice-Admiralty Court of Royal North Carolina, 1729–1759," *No. Car. Hist. Rev.*, 31 (1954), 517.
Watson, Alan D., "Regulation and Administration of Roads and Bridges in Colonial Eastern North Carolina," *No. Car. Hist. Rev.*, 45 (1968), 399.

34.2.4 South Carolina

Cole, David, "South Carolina Colonial Militia System," *So. Car. Hist. Assoc. Proc.*, 3 (1954), 14.

Greene, Jack P., "South Carolina Quartering Dispute 1757–1758," *So. Car. Hist. Mag.*, 60 (1959), 193.

Johnston, Gideon, *Carolina Chronicle: Papers of Commissary Gideon Johnston, 1707–1716,* Frank J. Klingberg, ed. (1946).

Lawson, John, *History of Carolina* (1718).

────── *New Voyage to Carolina* (1709); Hugh T. Lefler, ed. (1967).

Le Jau, Francis, *Carolina Chronicle: Papers of Commissary Francis Le Jau, 1706–1717,* Frank J. Klingberg, ed. (1956).

McCrady, Edward, *History of South Carolina under the Proprietary Government, 1670–1719* (1897).

────── *History of South Carolina under the Royal Government, 1719–1776* (1899).

McDowell, W. L., ed., *Colonial Records of South Carolina: Series 2, Journals of the Commissioners of the Indian Trade, Sept. 20, 1710 to Aug. 29, 1718* (1955).

Milling, Chapman J., ed., *Colonial South Carolina: Two Contemporary Descriptions* (1951).

Sherman, Richard P., *Robert Johnson: Royal Governor of South Carolina* (1966).

Sirmans, M. Eugene, *Colonial South Carolina: A Political History, 1663–1763* (1966).

────── "South Carolina Royal Council, 1720–1763," *WMQ*, 3 ser., 18 (1961), 373.

Skaggs, Marvin L., "Progress in the North Carolina-South Carolina Boundary Dispute," *No. Car. Hist. Rev.*, 15 (1938), 341.

Tennent, William, "Writings, 1740–1777," Newton B. Jones, ed., *So. Car. Hist. Mag.*, 61 (1960), 129, 189.

Smith, William Roy, *South Carolina as a Royal Province* (1903).

Wallace, David D., *Constitutional History of South Carolina from 1725 to 1775* (1906).

────── *History of South Carolina*, vol. I (1934).

Weir, Robert M., "Interpretation of Pre-Revolutionary South Carolina Politics," *WMQ*, 3 ser., 26 (1969), 473.

Whitney, Edson L., *Government of Colony of South Carolina* (1895).

*   *   *   *   *   *   *

Lee, Charles E., and Ruth Green, "Guide to Commons House Journals of the South Carolina General Assembly, 1721–1775," *So. Car. Hist. Mag.*, 68 (1967), 165.

────── "Guide to Upper House Journals of the South Carolina General Assembly, 1721–1775," *So. Car. Hist. Mag.*, 67 (1966), 187.

Whitney, Edson L., "Bibliography of the Colonial History of South Carolina," *Am. Hist. Assoc., Report,* (1895), 563.

See also 10.3 for biographies/writings of:

Johnson, Robert, 1676–1735

34.2.5 Virginia

Abernethy, Thomas P., *Three Virginia Frontiers* (1940).

Brown, Robert E. and Katherine, *Virginia, 1705–1786: Democracy or Aristocracy* (1964).

Byrd, William, *Histories of Dividing Line,* W. K. Boyd, ed. (1929).

Ernst, Joseph A., "Robinson Scandal Redivivus: Money, Debts, and Politics in Revolutionary Virginia," *Va. Mag. Hist. Biog.,* 77 (1969), 146.

Ferguson, Isabel, "County Court in Virginia, 1700–1830," *No. Car. Hist. Rev.,* 8 (1931), 14.

Flippin, Percy S., *Financial Administration of the Colony of Virginia* (1915).

────── *Royal Government in Virginia* (1919).

────── "William Gooch, Governor of Virginia," *WMQ*, 2 ser., 5 (1925), 225; 6 (1926), 1.

Greene, Jack P., "Opposition to Lieutenant Governor Alexander Spotswood, 1718," *Va. Mag. Hist. Biog.*, 70 (1962), 35.

––––– ed., "Pistole Fee Dispute," *Va. Mag. Hist. Biog.*, 66 (1958), 399.

Greene, Jack P., "Political Power in Virginia House of Burgesses, 1720–1776," *WMQ*, 3 ser., 16 (1959), 485.

––––– "Speaker and Treasurer in Virginia, 1758–1766," *Va. Mag. Hist. Biog.*, 71 (1963), 11.

Griffith, Lucille, *Virginia House of Burgesses, 1750–1774* (1963).

Harrison, Fairfax, "Western Explorations in Virginia," *Va. Mag. Hist. Biog.*, 30 (1922), 323.

Jones, Hugh, *Present State of Virginia* (1724); Richard L. Morton, ed. (1956).

McAnear, Beverly, "Income of Royal Governors of Virginia," *JSH*, 16 (1950), 196.

Mapp, Alf J., *Virginia Experiment, 1607–1781* (1957).

Miller, Elmer I., *Legislature of the Province of Virginia, Its Internal Development* (1907).

Morton, Richard L., *Colonial Virginia* (2 vols., 1960).

Ripley, William Z., *Financial History of Virginia, 1609–1776* (1893).

Smith, G. C., "Pistole Fee" *Va. Mag. Hist. Biog.*, 48 (1940), 209.

Sydnor, Charles S., *Gentlemen Freeholders: Political Practices in Washington's Virginia* (1952).

––––– *Political Leadership in Eighteenth-Century Virginia* (1951).

Wertenbaker, Thomas J., *Give Me Liberty: Self-Government in Virginia* (1958).

––––– *Planters of Colonial Virginia* (1922).

Wright, Louis B., "William Byrd's Opposition to Governor Francis Nicholson," *JSH*, 11 (1945), 68.

Young, Chester R., "Stress of War upon Civilian Population of Virginia, 1739–1760," *W. Va. Hist.*, 27 (1966), 251.

Zornow, William F., "Tariff Policies of Virginia, 1755–1789," *Va. Mag. Hist. Biog.*, 62 (1954), 306.

See also 10.3 for biographies/writings of:

Byrd, William, 1674–1744
Carter, Landon, 1710–1778
Carter, Robert, 1663–1732
Fairfax, Lord Thomas, 1693–1781
Spotswood, Alexander, 1676–1740
Washington, George, 1732–1799

34.3 MIDDLE COLONIES

34.3.1 Delaware

Daugherty, Martin M., *Early Colonial Taxation in Delaware* (1938).

Gipson, Lawrence H., "Anomalous American Colony," *Penn. Hist.*, 27 (1960), 144.

Johannsen, Robert W., "Conflict between the Three Lower Counties on the Delaware and the Province of Pennsylvania, 1682–1704," *Del. Hist.*, 5 (1952), 96.

Rodney, Richard S., *Colonial Finances in Delaware* (1928).

––––– "Delaware Under Governor Keith 1717–1726," *Del. Hist.*, 3 (1948), 1.

––––– "Early Relations of Delaware and Pennsylvania," *Penn. Mag. Hist. Biog.*, 54 (1930), 209.

Scharf, John T., *History of Delaware, 1609–1888* (2 vols., 1888).

34.3.2 New Jersey

Fisher, Edgar J., *New Jersey as a Royal Province* (1911).

Johannsen, Robert W., "The Conflict Between the Three Lower Counties on the

Delaware and the Province of Pennsylvania, 1682–1704," *Del. Hist.*, 5 (1952), 96.

Kemmerer, Donald L., "Judges' Good Behavior Tenure in Colonial New Jersey," N.J. Hist. Soc., *Proc.*, 56 (1938), 18.

—— *Path to Freedom* (1940).

McCormick, Richard P., *History of Voting in New Jersey: Development of Election Machinery, 1664–1911* (1953).

—— *New Jersey from Colony to State, 1609–1789* (1964).

"Papers of Lewis Morris, Governor of New Jersey 1738–1746," N.J. Hist. Soc., *Coll.*, 4 (1852).

Parker, Charles W., "Lewis Morris, First Colonial Governor of New Jersey," N.J. Hist. Soc., *Proc.*, 13 (1928), 273.

Pomfret, John E., *The Province of East New Jersey, 1609–1702: The Rebellious Proprietary* (1962).

—— *The Province of West New Jersey, 1609–1702: Origins of an American Colony* (1956).

Rich, Robert H., "Election Machinery in New Jersey, 1702–1775," N. J. Hist. Soc., *Proc.*, 67 (1949), 198.

Shy, John, "Quartering His Majesty's Forces in New Jersey," N.J. Hist. Soc., *Proc.*, 78 (1960), 82.

Smith, Samuel, *History of the Colony of Nova-Caesaria or New Jersey to the Year 1721* (1765).

Tanner, Edwin P., *The Province of New Jersey* (1908).

See also 10.3 for biographies/writings of:

Penn, William, 1644–1718
Read, Charles, 1713–1774

34.3.3 New York

Alexander, James, *Brief Narrative of the Case and Trial of John Peter Zenger*, Stanley N. Katz, ed. (2nd ed., 1972).

Bailyn, Bernard, "Beekmans of New York," *WMQ*, 3 ser., 14 (1957), 598.

Bloch, Julius M., et al., eds., *An Account of Her Majesty's Revenue in the Province of New York, 1701–1709: Customs Records of Early Colonial New York* (1966).

Buranelli, Vincent, "Governor Cosby and His Enemies (1732–1736)," *N.Y. Hist.*, 37 (1956), 365.

Champagne, Roger J., "Family Politics versus Constitutional Principles: New York Assembly Elections of 1768 and 1769," *WMQ*, 3 ser., 20 (1963), 57.

Davis, Alice, "Administration of Benjamin Fletcher in New York," *N.Y. Hist. Soc. Quar.*, 2 (1921), 213.

Dillon, Dorothy R., *New York Triumvirate: Study of Legal and Political Careers of William Livingston, John Morin Scott, William Smith, Jr.* (1949).

Hamlin, Paul M., and Charles E. Baker, *Supreme Court of Province of New York, 1691–1704* (3 vols., 1959).

Katz, Stanley N., *Newcastle's New York: Anglo-American Politics, 1732–1753* (1968).

Klein, Milton M., "Democracy and Politics in Colonial New York," *N.Y. Hist.*, 40 (1959), 221.

—— "Politics and Personalities in Colonial New York," *N.Y. Hist.*, 47 (1966), 3.

Leder, Lawrence H., Politics of Upheaval in New York, 1689–1709," *N.Y. Hist. Soc. Quar.*, 44 (1960), 413.

—— "Robert Livingston: New View of New York Politics," *N.Y. Hist.*, 40 (1959), 358.

Livingston, William, et al., *The Independent Reflector*, Milton M. Klein, ed. (1963).

McAnear, Beverly, "Mr. Robert R. Livingston's Reasons Against a Land Tax," *Jour. Pol. Econ.*, 48 (1940), 63.

MacCracken, Henry N., *Prologue to Independence: Trials of James Alexander* (1964).

Mark, Irving, *Agrarian Conflicts in Colonial New York, 1711–1775* (1940).

Runcie, John D., "Anglo-American Politics in Bellomont's New York," *WMQ*, 3 ser., 26 (1969), 191.

Varga, Nicholas, "Election Procedures in Colonial New York," *N.Y. Hist.*, 41 (1960), 249.

Waller, G. M., "New York's Role in Queen Anne's War, 1702–1713," *N.Y. Hist.*, 33 (1952), 40.

See also 10.3 for biographies/writings of:

Alexander, James, 1691–1756
Colden, Cadwallader, 1688–1776
Hamilton, Andrew, 1676–1741
Livingston, William, 1723–1790
Smith, William, 1728–1793

34.3.4 Pennsylvania

Bolles, Albert S., *Pennsylvania: A History from 1609 to 1790* (2 vols., 1898).

Brewster, William, *Pennsylvania and New York Frontier: From 1720 to the Close of the Revolution* (1954).

Bridenbaugh, Carl and Jessica, *Rebels and Gentlemen: Philadelphia in the Age of Franklin* (1942).

Bronner, Edwin B., "Disgrace of John Kinsey, Quaker Politician, 1739–1750," *Penn. Mag. Hist. Biog.*, 75 (1951), 400.

Cohen, Norman S., "Philadelphia Election Riot of 1742," *Penn. Mag. Hist. Biog.*, 92 (1968), 306.

Connor, Paul W., *Poor Richard's Politics: Benjamin Franklin and His New American Order* (1965).

Davidson, Robert L. D., *War Comes to Quaker Pennsylvania, 1682–1756* (1957).

Fisher, Sydney G., *Making of Pennsylvania* (1896).

—— *Pennsylvania, Colony and Commonwealth* (1897).

—— *Quaker Colonies* (1919).

Gleason, Philip, "Colonial Election and Franklin's Reputation," *WMQ*, 3 ser., 18 (1961), 68.

Hannah, William S., *Benjamin Franklin and Pennsylvania Politics* (1964).

Hershberger, Guy F., "Pacifism and the State in Colonial Pennsylvania," *Church Hist.*, 8 (1939), 54.

Hutson, James H., "Benjamin Franklin and Pennsylvania Politics, 1751–1755: Reappraisal," *Penn. Mag. Hist. Biog.*, 93 (1969), 303.

—— "Franklin and Parliamentary Grant for 1758," *WMQ*, 3 ser., 23 (1966), 575.

Johannsen, Robert W., "Conflict Between the Three Lower Counties on the Delaware and the Province of Pennsylvania, 1683–1704," *Del. Hist.*, 5 (1952), 96.

Keith, Charles P., *Chronicles of Pennsylvania*, vol. I (1917).

—— *Provincial Councillors of Pennsylvania* (1883).

Ketcham, Ralph L., "Benjamin Franklin and William Smith: An Old Philadelphia Quarrel," *Penn. Mag. Hist. Biog.*, 88 (1964), 142.

—— "Conscience, War, and Politics in Pennsylvania, 1755–1757," *WMQ*, 3 ser., 20 (1963), 416.

Leonard, Joan de Lourdes, "Elections in Colonial Pennsylvania," *WMQ*, 3 ser., 11 (1954), 385.

—— "Organization and Procedure of the Pennsylvania Assembly 1682–1776," *Penn. Mag. Hist. Biog.*, 71 (1948), 215.

Logan, James, "State of the British Plantations [1732]," J. E. Johnson, ed., *Penn. Mag. Hist. Biog.*, 60 (1936), 97.

Lokken, Roy N., *David Lloyd, Colonial Lawmaker* (1959).

Nash, Gary B., "Maryland's Economic War with Pennsylvania," *Md. Hist. Mag.*, 60 (1965), 231.

———— *Quakers and Politics: Pennsylvania, 1681–1726* (1968).

Olson, Alison G., "William Penn," *WMQ*, 3 ser., 18 (1961), 176.

Powell, Walter A., "Fight of a Century between the Penns and Calverts," *Md. Hist. Mag.*, 29 (1934), 83.

Root, Winfred T., *Relations of Pennsylvania with the British Government 1696–1765* (1912).

Rothermund, Dietmar, *Layman's Progress: Colonial Pennsylvania, 1740–1770* (1962).

———— "Political Factions and the Great Awakening," *Penn. Hist.*, 26 (1959), 317.

Sharpless, Isaac, *History of Quaker Government in Pennsylvania* (2 vols., 1898).

———— *Political Leaders of Provincial Pennsylvania* (1919).

Shepherd, William R., *Proprietary Government in Pennsylvania* (1896).

Thayer, Theodore, *Pennsylvania Politics and Growth of Democracy, 1740–1776* (1954).

Trask, Roger R., "Pennsylvania and Albany Congress, 1754," *Penn. Hist.*, 27 (1960), 273.

Wainwright, Nicholas B., "Governor William Denny in Pennsylvania," *Penn. Mag. Hist. Biog.*, 81 (1957), 170.

Warden, G. B. "Proprietary Group in Pennsylvania, 1754–1764," *WMQ*, 3 ser., 21 (1964), 367.

Weaver, Glenn, "Benjamin Franklin and Pennsylvania Germans," *WMQ*, 3 ser., 14 (1957), 536.

Wendel, Thomas, "Keith–Lloyd Alliance: Politics in Colonial Pennsylvania," *Penn. Mag. Hist. Biog.*, 92 (1968), 289.

Young, Chester R., "Evolution of Pennsylvania Assembly, 1682–1748," *Penn. Hist.*, 35 (1968), 147.

Zimmerman, Albright G., "James Logan, Proprietary Agent," *Penn. Mag. Hist. Biog.*, 78 (1954), 143.

Zimmerman, John J., "Benjamin Franklin and 'Heads of Complaints,'" *Penn. Mag. Hist. Biog.*, 85 (1961), 75.

———— "Benjamin Franklin and the Quaker Party, 1755–1756," *WMQ*, 3 ser., 17 (1960), 291.

———— "Governor Denny and Quartering Act of 1756," *Penn. Mag. Hist. Biog.*, 91 (1967), 266.

See also 10.3 for biographies/writings of:

Alexander, James, 1691–1756
Chew, Benjamin, 1722–1810
Franklin, Benjamin, 1706–1790
Lloyd, David, 1656–1731
Logan, James, 1674–1751
Pastorius, Francis D., 1651–1719/1720
Penn, Hannah, 1671–1726
Penn, William, 1644–1718

34.4 NEW ENGLAND

34.4.1 Connecticut

Bushman, Richard L., *From Puritan to Yankee: Character and the Social Order in Connecticut, 1690–1765* (1967).

Fitch, Thomas, "Correspondence and Documents during Thomas Fitch's Governorship of Colony of Connecticut, 1754–1766," Albert C. Bates, ed., Conn. Hist. Soc., *Coll.*, 17 (1918); 18 (1920).

Grant, Charles S., *Democracy in the Connecticut Frontier Town of Kent* (1961).

Law, Jonathan, *Papers during Governorship of the Colony of Connecticut, 1741–1750*, Albert C. Bates, ed. (3 vols., 1907–1914).

Mead, Nelson P., *Connecticut as a Corporate Colony* (1906).

Sklar, Robert, "Great Awakening and Colonial Politics: Connecticut's Revolution in the Minds of Men," Conn. Hist. Soc., *Bull.*, 28 (1963), 81.

Zeichner, Oscar, *Connecticut's Years of Controversy, 1750–1776* (1949).

See also 10.3 for biographies/writings of:

Trumbull, Jonathan, 1710–1785

34.4.2 Massachusetts

Allen, Neal W., Jr., ed., *Province and Court Records of Maine* (5 vols. 1964).

Billias, George A., *Massachusetts Land Bankers of 1740* (1959).

Boyer, Paul S., "Massachusetts Excise Controversy of 1754," *WMQ*, 3 ser., 21 (1964), 328.

Buchanan, John G., "Natural Law in Colonial Election Sermons of Massachusetts," *Am. Jour. Legal Hist.*, 12 (1968), 232.

Freiberg, Malcolm, "Thomas Hutchinson and Province Currency," *NEQ*, 30 (1957), 190.

Gummere, Richard M., "Thomas Hutchinson and Samuel Adams: Controversy in Classical Tradition," Boston Pub. Lib., *Quart.*, 10 (1958), 119.

Hart, Albert B., ed., *Commonwealth History of Massachusetts* (Vol. II, 1928).

Hutchinson, Thomas, *History of the Colony and Province of Massachusetts Bay* (3 vols., 1936).

Radabaugh, Jack S., "Militia of Colonial Massachusetts," *Mil. Affairs*, 18 (1954), 1.

Reed, Susan M., *Church and State in Massachusetts, 1691–1740* (1914).

Schutz, John A., "Succession Politics in Massachusetts, 1730–1741," *WMQ*, 3 ser., 15 (1958), 508.

Simmons, Richard C., "Massachusetts Revolution of 1689," *Jour. Am. Studies*, 2 (1968), 1.

Smith, Jonathan, "Massachusetts and New Hampshire Boundary Line Controversy, 1693–1740," Mass. Hist. Soc., *Proc.*, 43 (1910), 77.

Stearns, Raymond P., "John Wise of Ipswich," Essex Inst., *Hist. Coll.*, 97 (1961), 2.

Walett, Francis G., "Governor Bernard's Undoing: Earlier Hutchinson Letters Affair," *NEQ*, 38 (1965), 217.

Warden, G. B., "Caucus and Democracy in Colonial Boston," *NEQ*, 43 (1970), 19.

Zemsky, Robert M., "Leadership Patterns in Massachusetts Assembly, 1740–1755," *WMQ*, 3 ser., 26 (1969), 502.

Zuckerman, Michael, "Social Context of Democracy in Massachusetts," *WMQ*, 3 ser., 25 (1968), 523.

See also 10.3 for biographies/writings of:

Dudley, Joseph, 1647–1720
Hutchinson, Thomas, 1711–1780
Mather, Cotton, 1662/63–1727/28.
Pepperrell Family
Pownall, Thomas, 1722–1805
Shirley, William, 1694–1771
Wise, John, 1652–1725

34.4.3 New Hampshire

Belknap, Jeremy, *History of New Hampshire* (2nd ed., 3 vols., 1813).

Clark, Charles E., *Eastern Frontier: Settlement of Northern New England, 1610–1763* (1970).

Daniell, Jere R., *Experiment in Republicanism: New Hampshire Politics and The American Revolution, 1741–1794* (1970).

Fry, William Henry, *New Hampshire as a Royal Province* (1908).
Robinson, Maurice H., *History of Taxation in New Hampshire* (1903).
Smith, Jonathan, "Massachusetts and New Hampshire Boundary Line Controversy, 1693–1740," Mass. Hist. Soc., *Proc.*, 43 (1910), 77.
Stackpole, E. S., *History of New Hampshire* (4 vols., 1916).

*   *   *   *   *   *   *

Kaplan, Sidney, "History of New Hampshire: Jeremy Belknap as a Literary Craftsman," *WMQ*, 3 ser. 21 (1964), 18.

34.4.4 Rhode Island

Arnold, Samuel G., *History of the State of Rhode Island and Providence Plantations* (2 vols., 1859–1860).
Bicknell, Thomas W., *History of the State of Rhode Island and Providence Plantations* (4 vols., 1920).
Chapin, Howard M., *Documentary History of Rhode Island* (2 vols., 1916–1919).
Conley, Patrick T., "Rhode Island Constitutional Development, 1636–1775," *R.I. Hist.*, 27 (1968), 55.
Richman, Irving B., *Rhode Island, Its Making and Its Meaning* (2 vols., 1902).
Thompson, Mack E., "Ward-Hopkins Controversy and the American Revolution in Rhode Island," *WMQ*, 3 ser., 16 (1959), 363.
Weeden, William B., *Early Rhode Island* (1909).

See also 10.3 for biographies/writings of:

Hopkins, Stephen, 1707–1785
Ward, Samuel, 1725–1776

34.5 RELATIONS AMONG THE COLONIES

34.5.1 General

Carse, Robert, *Ports of Call* (1967).
Lokken, Roy N., "Sir William Keith's Theory of British Empire," *Historian*, 25 (1963), 403.
Merritt, Richard L., "American Nationalism: Quantitative Approach," *Am. Quar.*, 17 (1965), 319.
Roberts, Penfield, *Quest for Security, 1715–1740* (1947).
Usher, John, "Report on the Northern Colonies 1698," *WMQ*, 3 ser., 7 (1950), 95.

34.5.2 Albany Plan

Alden, J. R., "Albany Congress and Indian Superintendencies," *MVHR*, 27 (1940), 193.
Crane, Verner W., "Letter on the Albany Congress Plan," *Penn. Mag. Hist. Biog.*, 75 (1951), 350.
Gipson, Lawrence H., "Drafting of the Albany Plan of Union," *Penn. Hist.*, 26 (1959), 291.
———— "Massachusetts Bay and American Colonial Union, 1754," Am. Antiq. Soc., *Proc.*, 71 (1961), 63.
———— "Thomas Hutchinson and the Framing of the Albany Plan of Union, 1754," *Penn. Mag. Hist. Biog.*, 74 (1959), 5.
Morris, Richard B., "Benjamin Franklin's Grand Design: Albany Plan of Union," *Am. Heritage*, 7 (1956), 4.
Newbold, Robert C., *Albany Congress and Plan of Union of 1754* (1955).

Olson, Alison G., "British Government and Colonial Union, 1754," *WMQ*, 3 ser., 17 (1960), 22.
Priestley, Herbert I., *France Overseas through the Old Regime* (1939).

See also 10.3 for biographies/writings of:

Franklin, Benjamin, 1706–1790

34.6 BRITISH WEST INDIES

34.6.1 General

Ayearst, Morley, *British West Indies* (1960).
Bourne, Ruth, *Queen Anne's Navy in the West Indies* (1939).
Burn, William L., *British West Indies* (1951).
Burns, Alan C., *History of the British West Indies* (1954).
Carrión, A. Morales, *Puerto Rico and the Non-Hispanic Caribbean* (1952).
Cutteridge, J. O., *Geography of the West Indies* (1956).
Dampier, William, *New Voyage Round the World* (1697). Reissued with an introduction by Sir Albert Gray (1937).
Edwards, Bryan, *History of British West Indies* (3d ed., 1801).
Esquemeling, A. O., *History of Bucaniers of America* (1684).
Haring, C. H., *Buccaneers in the West Indies in the Seventeenth Century* (1910).
Harlow, Vincent T., ed., *Colonizing Expeditions to the West Indies and Guiana* (1925).
Hart, Francis R., *Admirals of the Caribbean* (1922).
Insh, G. P., *Company of Scotland Trading to Africa and Indies* (1932).
Lucas, Charles P., *Historical Geography of the British Colonies* (1905).
MacPherson, John, *Caribbean Lands: Geography of the West Indies* (2nd ed., 1967).
Newton, A. P., *European Nations in the West Indies* (1933).
Pares, Richard, *Merchants and Planters* (1960).
——— *War and Trade in the West Indies, 1739–1763* (1936).
——— *West-India Fortune* (1950).
Parry, John Horace, and P. M. Sherlock, *Short History of the West Indies* (2nd ed., 1963).
Penson, L. M., "London West Indies Interest in the Eighteenth Century," *Eng. Hist. Rev.*, 36 (1921), 373.
Pitman, F. W., *Development of the British West Indies 1700–1763* (1917).
Ragatz, Lowell J., *Fall of the Planter Class in the Caribbean, 1763–1833* (1928).
——— *The Old Plantation System in the British Caribbean* (1925).
Southey, Thomas, *Chronological History of the West Indies* (3 vols., 1827).
Thomas, Dalby, *Rise and Growth of West India Collonies* (1690).
Venables, General Robert, *Narrative of the Expedition to the West Indies*, C. H. Firth, ed. (1900).
Waugh, Alec, *Family of Islands: West Indies from 1492 to 1898* (1964).
Wilgus, A. Curtis, ed., *Caribbean: British, Dutch, French, United States* (1958).
Wright, Irene A., "Coymans Asiente, 1685–1689," *Bijdragen voor Vaderlansche Geschiednis*, 6 (1924), 23.

* * * * * * *

Cundall, Frank, *Bibliography of the West Indies (Excluding Jamaica)* (1909).
Goveia, Elsa V., *A Study on the Historiography of the British West Indies to the End of the Nineteenth Century* (1956).
Great Britain. Public Record Office, *Calendar of State Papers: Colonial America and the West Indies, Preserved in Public Record Office* (38 vols., 1880–1969).
"List of Works Relating to the West Indies," N.Y. Pub. Lib., *Bull.*, 16 (1912).
Ragatz, Lowell J., *Guide for Study of British Caribbean History, 1743–1834, Including Abolition and Emancipation Movements* (1932).

34.6.2 Barbados and Lesser Antilles

Dunn, Richard S., "Barbados Census of 1680: Profile of the Richest Colony in English America," *WMQ*, 3 ser., 26 (1969), 3.
Harlow, Vincent T., *History of Barbados 1625–1685* (1926).
Higham, C. S. S., *Development of the Leeward Islands under Restoration* (1921).
Klingberg, Frank J., ed., *Codrington Chronicle: Anglican Altruism on Barbados Plantation, 1710–1834* (1949).
Makinson, David H., *Barbados: North-American West-Indian Relations, 1739–1789* (1964).
Schomburck, R. H., *History of Barbados* (1847).
Spurdle, Frederick G., *Early West Indian Government: Barbados, Jamaica and the Leeward Islands, 1660–1783* (1962).
Williams, Eric E., *History of the People of Trinidad and Tobago* (1962).
Williamson, James A., *Caribbee Islands under Proprietary Patents* (1936).

34.6.3 Bermuda and Bahamas

Craven, Wesley F., *Introduction to a History of Bermuda* (1938).
Dunn, Richard S., "Downfall of the Bermuda Company," *WMQ*, 3 ser., 20 (1963), 487.
Hughes, Lewis, "Goodness of God towards the Sommer Islands," W. F. Craven, ed., *WMQ*, 2 ser., 17 (1937), 56.
Lefroy, John H., *Memorials of the Discovery and Early Settlement of the Bermudas* (2 vols., 1877–1879).
Mood, Fulmer, "Henry Robinson and the Bahama Articles of 1647," Col. Soc. Mass., *Publ.*, 32 (1934), 155.
Wilkinson, Henry, *Adventurers of Bermuda* (1923).
——— *Bermuda in Old Empire 1684–1784* (1950).

34.6.4 Jamaica

Cundall, Frank, *Governors of Jamaica in the First Half of the Eighteenth Century* (1937).
——— *Governors of Jamaica in the Seventeenth Century* (1936).
——— *Historic Jamaica* (1915).
Long, Edward, *History of Jamaica* (3 vols., 1774).
Metcalf, George, *Royal Government and Political Conflict in Jamaica, 1729–1783* (1965).
Spurdle, Frederick G., *Early West Indian Government: Barbados, Jamaica and Leeward Islands, 1660–1783* (1962).
Whitson, A. M., *Constitutional Development of Jamaica 1660–1729* (1929).

*   *   *   *   *   *   *

Cundall, Frank, *Bibliographia Jamaicensis* (1902). *Supplement* (1908).

35 British Empire and Colonial Policy, 1660–1763

35.1 GENERAL

Clark, George, *Later Stuarts, 1660–1714* (2nd ed., 1961).
English Historical Documents. Vol. X: *1714–1783* (1957).
Marshall, Dorothy, *Eighteenth-Century England* (1962).
Ogg, David, *England in the Reign of Charles II* (2 vols., 1934).
────── *England in the Reigns of James II and William III* (1955).
Plumb, J. H., *England in the Eighteenth Century* (1950).
────── *First Four Georges* (1957).
Wiener, Frederick B., *Civilians under Military Justice: British Practice since 1689* (1967).

*   *   *   *   *   *   *

Pargellis, S. M., and D. J. Medley, *Bibliography of British History: Eighteenth Century 1714–1789* (1951).
Royal Historical Society, *Writings on British History, 1901–1933.* Vol. III: *Tudor and Stuart Periods, 1485–1714* (1968). Vol. IV: *The Eighteenth Century* (1969).

35.2 POLITICS AND GOVERNMENT

35.2.1 1660–1714

Ashley, Maurice, *Glorious Revolution of 1688* (1967).
Baxter, Stephen B., *Development of the Treasury, 1660–1702* (1957).
────── *William III and Defense of European Liberty, 1650–1702* (1966).
Brown, L. F., *First Earl of Shaftesbury* (1933).
Bryant, Arthur, *King Charles II* (2nd ed., 1955).
Davies, Godfrey, *Restoration of Charles II, 1659–1660* (1955).
Feiling, Keith, *History of Tory Party 1640–1714* (1924).
Fryer, W. R., "Study of British Politics between the Revolution and the Reform Act," *Renaissance and Modern Studies,* 1 (1957), 91.
Gibbons, Philip A., *Ideas of Political Representation in Parliament, 1651–1832* (1914).
Hanson, Laurence W., *Government and the Press, 1695–1763* (1936).
Hart, Jeffrey, *Viscount Bolingbroke* (1965).
Holmes, Geoffrey S., *British Politics in the Age of Anne* (1967).
Horn, D. B., *British Diplomatic Service, 1689–1789* (1961).
Horwitz, Henry, "Parties, Connection, and Parliamentary Politics, 1689–1714," *Jour. Brit. Studies,* 6 (1966), 45.

Jones, George H., *Main Stream of Jacobitism* (1954).

Jones, J. R., *The First Whigs* (1961).

Kemp, Betty, *King and Commons* (1955).

Kenyon, John P., ed., *Stuart Constitution, 1603–1688: Documents* (1966).

Kramnick, Isaac, *Bolingbroke and His Circle: The Politics of Nostalgia in the Age of Walpole* (1968).

La Prade, William T., *Public Opinion and Politics in Eighteenth-Century England to the Fall of Walpole* (1936).

Merriman, R. D., *Queen Anne's Navy, 1702–1714* (1961).

Plumb, J. H., *Origins of Political Stability: England, 1675–1725* (1967).

Rubini, Dennis, *Court and Country, 1688–1702* (1967).

Trevelyan, George M., *The English Revolution, 1688–1689* (1938).

Walcott, Robert, *English Politics in the Early Eighteenth Century* (1956).

Witcombe, D. T., *Charles II and Cavalier House of Commons, 1663–1674* (1966).

*   *   *   *   *   *   *

Walcott, Robert, "Later Stuarts (1660–1714): Significant Work of Last Twenty Years," *AHR*, 67 (1962), 352.

35.2.2 1714–1763

Beattie, John M., *English Court in the Reign of George I* (1967).

Beer, Samuel H., "Representation of Interests in British Government," *Am. Pol. Sci. Rev.*, 51 (1957), 613.

Burns, J. H., "Bolingbroke and the Concept of Constitutional Government," *Political Studies*, 10 (1962), 264.

Ellis, Kenneth, *The Post Office in the Eighteenth Century* (1958).

Foord, Archibald S., *His Majesty's Opposition, 1714–1830* (1964).

Hunt, Norman C., *Two Early Political Associations: Quakers and Dissenting Deputies in the Age of Sir Robert Walpole* (1961).

Judd, Gerrit P., IV, *Members of Parliament, 1734–1832* (1955).

Mansfield, Harvey C., *Statesmanship and Party Government: Burke and Bolingbroke* (1965).

Namier, Lewis, *Crossroads of Power: Essays on England in the Eighteenth Century* (1962).

—— *England in the Age of the American Revolution* (2nd ed., 1961).

—— and John Brooke, *History of Parliament: House of Commons, 1754–1790* (3 vols., 1964).

—— *Monarchy and Party System* (1952).

—— *Structure of Politics at Accession of George III* (2nd ed., 1957).

Owen, John B., *Rise of the Pelhams* (1957).

Perry, Thomas W., *Public Opinion, Propaganda, and Politics in Eighteenth-Century England* (1962).

Plumb, J. H., *Sir Robert Walpole* (2 vols., 1956–1960).

Pole, J. R., *Political Representation in England and Origins of the American Republic* (1966).

Robertson, Charles G., *Chatham and the British Empire* (1946).

Sherrard, Owen A., *Lord Chatham: Pitt and the Seven Years' War* (1955).

—— *Lord Chatham and America* (1958).

Sutherland, Lucy S., *The East India Company in Eighteenth-Century Politics* (1952).

Thomson, Mark A., *Constitutional History of England, 1642 to 1801* (1938).

Western, J. R., *English Militia in the Eighteenth Century* (1965).

Wiggin, Lewis M., *Faction of Cousins: Grenvilles, 1733–1763* (1958).

Wilkes, John W., *Whig in Power: Henry Pelham* (1964).

Williams, Basil, *Carteret and Newcastle* (1943).

—— *Whig Supremacy, 1714–1760* (1939); Charles H. Stuart, ed. (1962).

Williams, E. Neville, ed., *Eighteenth-Century Constitution, 1688–1815: Documents* (1960).

35.3 ECONOMY AND TRADE

Ashton, Thomas S., *Economic Fluctuations in England, 1700–1800* (1959).
———— *Economic History of England: 18th Century* (1955).
Bryant, Samuel W., *Sea and States: Maritime History* (1967).
Carswell, John, *South Sea Bubble* (1960).
Clapham, John, *The Bank of England, 1694–1914* (2 vols., 1944).
———— *Concise Economic History of Britain to 1750* (1963).
Cole, W. A., "Trends in Eighteenth-Century Smuggling," *Econ. Hist. Rev.*, 10 (1958), 395.
Court, William H. B., *Rise of Midland Industries, 1600–1828* (1953).
Davies, K. G., *Royal African Company* (1957).
Davis, Ralph, *A Commercial Revolution: English Overseas Trade in Seventeenth and Eighteenth Centuries* (1967).
———— *Rise of English Shipping Industry in the Seventeenth and Eighteenth Centuries* (1962).
Deane, Phyllis, and W. A. Cole, *British Economic Growth, 1688–1959* (1967).
Dickson, Peter M. G., *Financial Revolution in England, 1688–1756* (1967).
Donnan, Elizabeth, "Eighteenth-Century English Merchants: Micajah Perry," *Jour. Econ. and Bus. Hist.*, 4 (1931), 70.
Hill, Christopher, *Reformation to Industrial Revolution, 1530–1780* (1967).
Innis, Harold A., *The Cod Fisheries* (1940).
John, A. H., "Agricultural Productivity and Economic Growth in England, 1700–1760," *Jour. Econ. Hist.*, 25 (1965), 19.
———— "War and the English Economy, 1700–1763," *Econ. Hist. Rev.*, 7 (1955), 329.
Jones, E. L., ed., *Agriculture and Economic Growth in England 1650–1815* (1967).
Keith, Theodora, "Scottish Trade with Plantations before 1707," *Scottish Hist. Rev.*, 6 (1908), 32.
Lipson, Ephraim, *Economic History of England* (3 vols., 1931).
Mantoux, Paul, *The Industrial Revolution in the Eighteenth Century* (rev. ed., 1928).
Minchinton, Walter E., comp., *Growth of English Overseas Trade in the Seventeenth and Eighteenth Centuries* (1969).
Pares, Richard, *Yankees and Creoles: The Trade between North America and the West Indies before the American Revolution* (1956).
Price, Jacob M., *Tobacco Adventure to Russia, 1676–1722* (1961).
Ramsay, George D., *English Overseas Trade during Centuries of Emergence* (1957).
Rich, Edwin E., *Hudson's Bay Company, 1670–1870* (1958).
Schumpeter, Elizabeth B., *English Overseas Trade Statistics, 1697–1808* (1960).
Thomas, Robert P., "Sugar Colonies of Old Empire," *Econ. Hist. Rev.*, 2 ser., 21 (1968), 30.
Walton, Gary M., "Colonial Commerce," *Jour. Econ. Hist.*, 2 ser., 28 (1968), 363.
———— "Sources of Productivity Change in American Colonial Shipping, 1675–1775," *Econ. Hist. Rev.*, 20 (1967), 67.
Westerfield, Ray B., *Middlemen in English Business, 1660–1760* (1915).
Williams, Glyndwr, *British Search for the Northwest Passage in the Eighteenth Century* (1962).
Wilson, Charles H., *England's Apprenticeship, 1603–1763* (1965).

35.4 SOCIETY, CULTURE, AND RELIGION

Bahlman, Dudley W. R., *Moral Revolution of 1688* (1957).
Butt, John E., *The Augustan Age* (1950).
Cragg, Gerald R., *From Puritanism to the Age of Reason: Changes in Religious Thought within the Church of England, 1660 to 1700* (1950).
———— *Puritanism in the Period of Great Persecution, 1660–1688* (1957).
———— *Reason and Authority in the Eighteenth Century* (1964).
George, Mary D., ed., *England in Johnson's Day* (1928).
George, Mary D., *English Social Life in the Eighteenth Century* (1923).

—— *London Life in the XVIIIth Century* (1925).

Hecht, J. Jean, *Continental and Colonial Servants in Eighteenth-Century England* (1954).

Loftis, John, *Politics of Drama in Augustan England* (1963).

Mingay, G. E., *English Landed Society in the Eighteenth Century* (1963).

Paulson, Ronald, *Satire and the Novel in Eighteenth Century England* (1967).

Robson, Robert, *The Attorney in Eighteenth Century England* (1959).

Schlatter, Richard B., *Social Ideas of Religious Leaders, 1660–1668* (1940).

Stephen, Leslie, *History of English Thought in the Eighteenth Century* (2 vols., 1927).

Stone, Lawrence, "Social Mobility in England, 1500–1700," *Past and Present,* 33 (1966), 16.

Stromberg, Ronald N., *Religious Liberalism in Eighteenth-Century England* (1954).

Summerson, John N., *Architecture in Britain, 1530–1830* (1953).

Sykes, Norman, *Church and State in England in the Eighteenth Century* (1934).

—— *From Sheldon to Secker: Aspects of English Church History, 1660–1768* (1959).

Waterhouse, Ellis K., *Painting in Britain, 1530–1790* (1953).

Whinney, Margaret D., and Oliver Miller, *The Oxford History of English Art.* Vol. VIII: *English Art: 1625–1714* (1957).

Willey, Basil, *Eighteenth-Century Background: Studies on the Idea of Nature in Thought of the Period* (1940).

—— *Seventeenth-Century Background: Studies in the Thought of the Age in Relation to Poetry and Religion* (1935).

Wrigley, E. A., *Introduction to English Historical Demography from the Sixteenth to Nineteenth Century* (1966).

*   *   *   *   *   *   *

Williams, Judith B., *Guide to Printed Materials for English Social and Economic History, 1750–1850* (2 vols., 1926).

35.5 COLONIAL SYSTEM

35.5.1 General

Andrews, Charles M., *Colonial Background of the American Revolution: Four Essays in American Colonial History* (rev. ed., 1931).

—— *Colonial Period of American History,* vol. IV (1938).

Beer, George L., *British Colonial Policy 1754–1765* (1907).

Crane, Verner W., ed., "Hints Relative to Division and Government of America," *MVHR,* 8 (1922), 367.

Egerton, H. E., and A. P. Newton, *Short History of British Colonial Policy, 1606–1909* (12th ed., 1950).

Gipson, Lawrence H., *The British Empire Before the American Revolution* (14 vols., 1936–1969).

Kammen, Michael, *Empire and Interest: American Colonies and the Politics of Mercantilism* (1970).

Keith, A. Berriedale, *Constitutional History of the First British Empire* (1930).

Knorr, Klaus E., *British Colonial Theories, 1570–1850* (1944).

Koebner, Richard, *Empire* (1961).

Labaree, Leonard W., *Royal Government in America* (1930).

Savelle, Max, and Margaret Anne Fisher, *Origins of American Diplomacy: Angloamerica, 1492–1763* (1967).

Ubbelohde, Carl, *American Colonies and British Empire 1607–1763* (1968).

*   *   *   *   *   *   *

Craven, Wesley F., "Historical Study of the British Empire," *Jour. Mod. Hist.,* 6 (1934), 40.

Middlekauff, Robert L., "American Continental Colonies in the Empire," in Robin Winks, ed., *Historiography of the British Empire and Commonwealth* (1964).

Morris, Richard B., "Spacious Empire of Lawrence Henry Gipson," *WMQ*, 3 ser., 24 (1967), 169.

Savelle, Max, "International Approach to Early Anglo-American History, 1492–1763," in Ray A. Billington, ed., *Reinterpretation of Early American History: Essays in Honor of John Edwin Pomfret* (1966).

35.5.2 Institutional Structure

Andrews, Charles M., *British Committees of Trade, 1622–75* (1908).

—— "The Royal Disallowance," Am. Antiq. Soc., *Proc.*, new ser., 24 (1914), 342.

Appleton, Marguerite, "Richard Partridge: Colonial Agent," *NEQ*, 5 (1932), 293. Covers the period, 1715–1759.

Armytage, Frances, *The Free Port System in the British West Indies: Study in Commercial Policy, 1766–1822* (1953).

Barrow, Thomas C., *Trade and Empire: The British Customs Service in Colonial America, 1660–1775* (1967).

Basye, Arthur H., *The Lords Commissioners of Trade and Plantations, Commonly Known as the Board of Trade, 1748–1782* (1925).

Baugh, Daniel A., *British Naval Administration* (1965).

Bieber, R. P., *Lords of Trade, 1675–1696* (1919).

Burns, James J., *Colonial Agent of New England* (1935).

Clark, Dora Mae, "American Board of Customs, 1767–1783," *AHR*, 45 (1940), 777.

—— *Rise of British Treasury: Colonial Administration in the Eighteenth Century* (1960).

Cross, Arthur L., *The Anglican Episcopate and American Colonies* (1902).

Davies, K. G., "Origins of the Commission System," Royal Hist. Soc., *Trans.*, 5 ser., 2 (1952), 89.

Dickerson, Oliver M., *American Colonial Government 1696–1765: Study of the British Board of Trade* (1912).

Doty, Joseph D., *British Admiralty Board as a Factor in Colonial Administration, 1689–1763* (1932).

Freiberg, Malcolm, "William Bollan: Agent of Massachusetts," *More Books*, 23 (1949), 43.

Greene, Evarts B., *Provincial Governor in the English Colonies* (1898).

Haffenden, Philip S., "Colonial Appointments and Patronage under the Duke of Newcastle, 1724–1739," *Eng. Hist. Rev.*, 78 (1963), 417.

—— "Crown and Colonial Charters, 1675–1688," *WMQ*, 3 ser., 15 (1958), 297.

Hall, Michael G., *Edward Randolph and American Colonies, 1676–1703* (1969).

Hoon, Elizabeth E., *Organization of the English Customs System, 1696–1786* (1938).

Hutson, James H., "Benjamin Franklin and Parliamentary Grant for 1758," *WMQ*, 3 ser., 23 (1966), 575.

Jacobsen, Gertrude A., *William Blathwayt, a Late Seventeenth Century English Administrator* (1932).

Kammen, Michael G., *Rope of Sand: Colonial Agents, British Politics and the American Revolution* (1968).

Kellogg, Louise P., *American Colonial Charter: Study of English Administration in Relation Thereto, Chiefly after 1688* (1904).

Laslett, Peter, "John Locke, The Great Recoinage, and Origins of Board of Trade, 1695–1698," *WMQ*, 3 ser., 14 (1957), 370.

Lily, Edward P., *Colonial Agents of New York and New Jersey* (1936).

Lonn, Ella, *The Colonial Agents of the Southern Colonies* (1945).

McAnear, Beverly, *Income of Colonial Governors of British North America* (1967).

Namier, Lewis B., "Charles Garth and His Connections," *Eng. Hist. Rev.*, 54 (1939), 443.

Penson, Lillian M., *Colonial Agencies of the British West Indies: A Study in Colonial Administration, Mainly in the Eighteenth Century* (1924).

Pool, Bernard, *Navy Board Contracts, 1660–1832* (1966).

Reitan, E. A., "Civil List in Eighteenth-Century British Politics," *Hist. Jour.*, 9 (1966), 318.

Root, Winfred T., "Lords of Trade and Plantations, 1675–1696," *AHR*, 23 (1917), 20.

Russell, Elmer B., *Review of American Colonial Legislation by the King in Council* (1915).

Schlesinger, Arthur M., "Colonial Appeals to Privy Council," *Pol. Sci. Quar.*, 28 (1913), 279.

Schuyler, R. L., *Parliament and the British Empire* (1929).

Sellers, Charles G., Jr., "Private Profits and British Colonial Policy: Speculations of Henry McCulloh," *WMQ*, 3 ser., 9 (1951), 535.

Smith, Joseph H., *Appeals to the Privy Council from American Plantations* (1950).

Steel, I. K., *Politics of Colonial Policy: Board of Trade, 1696–1720* (1968).

Thomason, M. A., *Secretaries of State, 1681–1782* (1932).

Turner, Edward R., *Privy Council of England in the Seventeenth and Eighteenth Centuries, 1603–1784* (2 vols., 1927–1928).

Varga, Nicholas, "Robert Charles, New York Agent, 1748–1770," *WMQ*, 3 ser., 18 (1961), 211.

Washburn, George A., *Imperial Control of Administration of Justice 1684–1776* (1923).

Webb, Stephen S., "Strange Career of Francis Nicholson," *WMQ*, 3 ser., 23 (1966), 513.

—— "William Blathwayt," *WMQ*, 3 ser., 25 (1968), 3; 26 (1969), 373.

Wolff, Mabel P., *Colonial Agency of Pennsylvania 1712–1757* (1933).

See also 10.3 for biographies/writings of:

Newman, Henry, 1670–1743
Randolph, Edward, 1632–1703

35.5.3 Policies and Programs

Albion, Robert G., *Forests and Sea Power: The Timber Problem of the Royal Navy, 1652–1862* (1926).

Barrow, Thomas C., "Background to the Grenville Program, 1757–1763," *WMQ*, 3 ser., 22 (1965), 93.

—— "Project for Imperial Reform," *WMQ*, 3 ser., 24 (1967), 108.

Beer, G. L., *Commercial Policy of England toward American Colonies* (1893).

Bining, Arthur C., *British Regulation of the Colonial Iron Industry* (1933).

Bond, Beverly W., *Quit-Rent System in American Colonies* (1919).

Clark, Dora Mae, "Impressment of Seamen," in *Essays in Colonial History Presented to Charles M. Andrews* (1931).

Clark, George N., "Navigation Act of 1651," *History*, new ser., 7 (1923), 282.

Dickerson, Oliver M., *Navigation Acts and the American Revolution* (1951).

Grant, William L., *The Colonial Policy of Chatham* (1911).

Greene, Jack P., ed., "Martin Bladen's Blueprint for a Colonial Union," *WMQ*, 3 ser., 17 (1960), 516.

Guttridge, George H., *Colonial Policy of William III* (1922).

Harper, Lawrence A., *English Navigation Laws* (1939).

Hotblack, Kate, *Chatham's Colonial Policy* (1917).

Judah, Charles B., *North American Fisheries and British Policy to 1713* (1933).

Knittle, Walter A., *Early Eighteenth-Century Palatine Emigration: British Government Redemptioner Project to Manufacture Naval Stores* (1936).

Lawson, Murray G., *Fur: Study in English Mercantilism, 1700–1775* (1943).

Leder, Lawrence H., "Glorious Revolution and Pattern of Imperial Relationships," *N.Y. Hist.*, 46 (1965), 203.

Lokken, Roy N., "Sir William Keith's Theory of the British Empire," *Historian*, 25 (1963), 403.

Malone, Joseph J., *Pine Trees and Politics: Naval Stores and Forest Policy in Colonial New England, 1691–1775* (1964).

Nettels, Curtis P., "British Mercantilism and Economic Development of the Thirteen Colonies," *Jour. Econ. Hist.*, 12 (1952), 105.
—— "Menace of Colonial Manufacturing, 1690–1720," *NEQ*, 4 (1931), 230.
Olson, Alison G., "British Government and Colonial Union, 1754," *WMQ*, 3 ser., 17 (1960), 22.
Ransom, Roger L., "British Policy and Colonial Growth: Some Implications of the Burden from Navigation Acts," *Jour. Econ. Hist.*, 28 (1968), 427.
Robbins, Caroline, "'When It Is That Colonies May Turn Independent' Analysis of Francis Hutcheson (1694–1746)," *WMQ*, 3 ser., 11 (1954), 214.
Southwick, Albert B., "The Molasses Act—Source of Precedents," *WMQ*, 3 ser., 8 (1951), 389.
Thomas, Robert P., "Quantitative Approach to Study the Effects of Imperial Policy upon Colonial Welfare," *Jour. Econ. Hist.*, 18 (1965), 615.
Thornton, A. P., *West-India Policy under the Restoration* (1956).
Walton, Gary M., "New Economic History and Burdens of the Navigation Acts," *Econ. Hist. Rev.*, 24 (1971), 533.
Williams, Justin, "English Mercantilism and Carolina Naval Stores," *JSH*, 1 (1935), 169.

See also 10.3 for biographies/writings of:

Oglethorpe, James E., 1696–1785

35.6 COMPETITION FOR EMPIRE, 1689–1763

35.6.1 General

Dorn, Walter L., *Competition for Empire, 1740–1763* (1940).
Ford, Lawrence C., *Triangular Struggle for Spanish Pensacola 1689–1739* (1939).
Gilbert, Felix, "English Background of American Isolationism in the Eighteenth Century," *WMQ*, 3 ser., 1 (1944), 138.
Pares, Richard, "American Versus Continental Warfare, 1739–63," *Eng. Hist. Rev.*, 51 (1936), 429.
—— *Colonial Blockade and Neutral Rights, 1739–1763* (1938).
—— *War and Trade in the West Indies* (1936).
Peckham, Howard H., *Colonial Wars 1689–1762* (1964).
Savelle, Max, "American Balance of Power and European Diplomacy, 1713–78," in R. B. Morris, ed., *Era of the American Revolution* (1939).
—— *The Origins of American Diplomacy: The International History of Anglo-America, 1492–1763* (1967).
Williams, Glyndwr, *Expansion of Europe in the Eighteenth Century: Overseas Rivalry* (1966).

35.6.2 Rivalry with Spain

Arnade, Charles W., *Siege of St. Augustine, 1702* (1959).
Bolton, Herbert E., and Mary Ross, *Debatable Land: Anglo-Spanish Contest for Georgia Country* (1925).
Bolton, Herbert E., *Rim of Christendom* (1936).
—— *Spain's Title to Georgia* (1925).
—— "Spanish Resistance to Carolina Traders," *Ga. Hist. Quar.*, 9 (1925), 115.
Boyd, M. F., "Mission Sites in Florida," *Fla. Hist. Quar.*, 17 (1939), 255.
Brown, V. L., "Anglo-Spanish Relations in America," *Hisp. Am. Hist. Rev.*, 5 (1922), 329.
Chatelain, V. E., *Defenses of Spanish Florida 1565–1763* (1941).
Harkness, Albert, "Americanism and Jenkins' Ear," *MVHR*, 37 (1950), 61.
Howard, Clinton N., "Colonial Pensacola," *Fla. Hist. Quar.*, 19 (1940–1941), 109.
—— "Governor Johnstone," *Fla. Hist. Quar.*, 17 (1939), 281.
—— "Military Government in West Florida," *La. Hist. Quar.*, 22 (1939), 18.

—— "Military Occupation of West Florida," *Fla. Hist. Quar.*, 17 (1939), 181.
Johnson, James G., "Spanish Colonies in Georgia and South Carolina," *Ga. Hist. Quar.*, 15 (1931), 301.
—— "Spanish Southeast in the Seventeenth Century," *Ga. Hist. Quar.*, 16 (1932), 17.
Lanning, John T., *Diplomatic History of Georgia: Epoch of Jenkins' Ear* (1936).
—— *Spanish Missions of Georgia* (1935).
Leonard, I. A., ed., *Spanish Approach to Pensacola, 1689–1693* (1939).
Lockey, Joseph B., *East Florida, 1783–1785*, John W. Caughey, ed. (1949).
McLachlan, Jean O., *Trade and Peace with Old Spain, 1667–1750* (1940).
Nasatir, Abraham P., *Spanish War Vessels on the Mississippi, 1792–1796* (1968).
Reese, Trevor R., "Georgia in Anglo-Spanish Diplomacy 1736–1739," *WMQ*, 3 ser., 15 (1958), 168.
TePaske, John J., *Governorship of Spanish Florida, 1700–1763* (1964).
Wright, J. Leitch, Jr., *Anglo-Spanish Rivalry in North America* (1971).

35.6.3 Rivalry with France

35.6.3.1 General

Edmonds, Walter D., *Musket and Cross: Struggle of France and England for North America* (1968).
Morgan, W. T., "English Fear of 'Encirclement,'" *Can. Hist. Rev.*, 10 (1929), 4.
Mulkearn, Lois, "English Eye the French in North America," *Penn. Hist.*, 21 (1954), 316.
Pargellis, Stanley M., *Military Affairs in North America: Documents from Cumberland Papers in Windsor Castle* (1936).
Parkman, Francis, *France and England in North America* (9 vols., 1865–1892).
Pease, Theodore C., ed., *Anglo-French Boundary Disputes in the West, 1749–1763* (1936).
Rich, Edwin E., *Hudson's Bay Company, 1670–1870* (3 vols., 1961).
Rutledge, Joseph L., *Century of Conflict: French and British in Colonial America* (1956).
Savelle, Max, *Diplomatic History of the Canadian Boundary 1749–1763* (1940).

35.6.3.2 Conflict, 1689–1754

Barnes, V. F., "Rise of William Phips," *NEQ*, 1 (1928), 271.
Biggar, H. P., "Frontenac's Projected Attempt on New York in 1689," N.Y. State Hist. Assoc., *Quar. Jour.*, 5 (1924), 139.
Buffington, A. H., "Canadian Expedition of 1746," *AHR*, 45 (1940), 552.
Caldwell, Norman W., "Southern Frontier in King George's War," *JSH*, 7 (1941), 37.
Chapin, Howard M., *Privateering in King George's War* (1928).
Clark, George N., *Dutch Alliance and War against French Trade 1688–97* (1923).
De Forest, L. E., ed., *Louisbourg Journals, 1745* (1932).
Dièreville, Sieur de, *Voyage du Port Royal* (1686); J. C. Webster, ed. (1933).
Eaton, A. W. H., "Settling of Colchester County," Royal Soc. Can., *Trans.*, 3 ser., 6 (1912), 221.
Eccles, W. J., *Frontenac the Courtier Governor* (1959).
Ehrman, John, *The Navy in the War of William III, 1689–1697* (1953).
Frégault, Guy, "L'Empire Britannique et la Conquête du Canada 1700–1713," *Rev. Hist. Am. Fr.*, 10 (1956), 153.
Graham, Gerald S., ed., *Walker Expedition to Quebec, 1711* (1953).
Henderson, Archibald, "Dr. Thomas Walker and the Loyal Company," Am. Antiq. Soc., *Proc.*, new ser., 61 (1931), 77.
Lacour-Gayet, Georges, *La marine militaire sous le règne de Louis XV* (1910).
"Letters Relating to the Expedition against Cape Breton," Mass. Hist. Soc., *Coll.*, 1 ser., 1 (1792), 5.
McLennan, J. S., *Louisbourg from Its Foundation to Its Fall* (1918).
Morgan, W. T., "Attempts at Imperial Cooperation during the Reign of Queen Anne," Royal Hist. Soc., *Trans.*, 4 ser., 10 (1927), 171.

———— "Economic Aspects of Ryswick Negotiations," Royal Hist. Soc., Trans., 4 ser., 14 (1931), 225.

———— "Five Nations and Queen Anne," MVHR, 13 (1927), 169.

———— "Origins of the South Sea Company," Pol. Sci. Quar., 44 (1929), 16.

———— "Queen Anne's Canadian Expedition of 1711," Queen's Univ., Bull., no. 56 (1928).

———— "South Sea Company and Canadian Expedition," Hisp. Am. Hist. Rev., 8 (1928), 143.

Nant, Fr. Candide de, Pages glorieuses de l'épopée canadienne: Une mission capucine en Acadie (1927).

Rawlyk, George A., Yankees at Louisbourg (1967).

Richmond, Herbert W., The Navy in the War of 1739–48 (3 vols., 1920).

Sosin, Jack M., "Louisbourg and the Peace of Aix-la-Chapelle, 1748," WMQ, 3 ser., 14 (1957), 516.

Wall, Robert E., Jr., "Louisbourg, 1745," NEQ, 37 (1964), 64.

Waller, G. M., "New York's Role in Queen Anne's War, 1702–1713," N.Y. Hist., 33 (1952), 40.

Webster, John C., Samuel Vetch (1929).

———— Forts of Chignecto (1930).

Wilson, Arthur Mc Candless, French Foreign Policy during the Administration of Cardinal Fleury, 1726–1743: Study in Diplomacy and Commercial Development (1936).

See also 10.3 for biographies/writings of:

Shirley, William, 1694–1771
Vetch, Samuel, 1668–1732

35.6.3.3 Acadia under English Rule

Akins, T. B., Public Documents of Nova Scotia (1869).

Brebner, John B., Neutral Yankees of Nova Scotia (1937).

———— New England's Outpost: Acadia before the Conquest of Canada (1927).

Casgrain, H. R., Les Sulpiciens en Acadie (1897).

Doughty, A. G., Acadian Exiles (1916).

Lauvrière, Emilie, Deux traitres d'Acadie et leur victime (1932).

———— La tragedie d'un peuple: histoire du peuple acadien, vol. I (1922).

Macmechan, A. M., ed., Minutes of H. M. Council at Annapolis Royal, 1720–1739 (1908).

Martell, J. S., "Second Expulsion of Acadians," Dalhousie Rev., 13 (1934), 359.

Raymond, W. O., "Alexander McNutt and Pre-Loyalist Settlements of Nova Scotia," Royal Soc. Can., Trans., 3 ser., 5 (1911), 23; 6 (1912), 201.

———— "Nova Scotia under English Rule, 1710–1760," Royal Soc. Can., Trans., 3 ser., 4 (1910), 55.

Sawtelle, W. O., "Acadia: Pre-Loyalist Migration and Philadelphia Plantation," Penn. Mag. Hist. Biog., 51 (1927), 244.

Shortt, Adam, and V. K. Johnston, eds., Documents Relating to Nova Scotia 1675–1758 (1933).

Winzerling, Oscar W., Acadian Odyssey (1955).

See also 32.2.4, French Settlement–Acadia.

35.6.3.4 French and Indian War

Amherst, Jeffrey, Journal in America, 1758–1763, J. Clarence Webster, ed. (1931).

Baker-Crothers, Hayes, Virginia and the French and Indian War (1928).

Cuneo, John R., Robert Rogers of the Rangers (1959).

Frégault, Guy, La guerre de la conquête (1955).

Grenier, Fernand, ed., Papiers contrecoeur et autres documents concernant le conflict Anglo-Français sur l'Ohio (1952).

Hamilton, Charles, ed., Braddock's Defeat (1959). Journals and orderly book.

Hamilton, Edward P., *French and Indian Wars: Battles and Forts in Wilderness* (1962).

Hamilton, Milton W., "General William Johnson's Letter to Governors, Lake George, September 9–10, 1755," Am. Antiq. Soc., *Proc.*, 74 (1964), 19.

Hart, Francis R., *Siege of Havana, 1762* (1931).

Hibbert, Christopher, *Wolfe at Quebec* (1959).

Higonnet, Patrice L. R., "Origins of the Seven Years War," *Jour. Mod. Hist.*, 40 (1968), 57.

Kennett, Lee, *French Armies in the Seven Years War* (1967).

Ketcham, Ralph L., "Conscience, War, and Politics in Pennsylvania, 1755–1757," *WMQ*, 3 ser., 20 (1963), 416.

Labaree, Leonard W., "Benjamin Franklin and the Defense of Pennsylvania, 1754–1757," *Penn. Hist.*, 29 (1962), 7.

Lloyd, Christopher, *Capture of Quebec* (1959).

Loescher, Burt G., *History of Rogers Rangers* (3 vols., 1946).

McCardell, Lee, *Ill-Starred General: Braddock* (1958).

McCormac, E. I., *Colonial Opposition to Imperial Authority during French and Indian War* (1911).

Montcalm, L. J., Marquis de, "Correspondence," Public Archives of Canada, *Report* (1929), 31.

—— *Journal*, H. R. Casgrain, ed. (1895).

Nichols, Francis T., "Organization of Braddock's Army," *WMQ*, 3 ser., 4 (1947), 127.

Norkus, Nellie, "Virginia's Role in Capture of Fort Duquesne, 1758," *West Penn. Hist. Mag.*, 45 (1962), 291.

Pargellis, Stanley M., "Braddock's Defeat," *AHR*, 41 (1936), 253.

—— *Loudoun in North America* (1933).

Parkman, Francis, *Montcalm and Wolfe* (2 vols., 1884).

Pitt, William, *Correspondence of William Pitt with Colonial Governors*, Gertrude S. Kimball, ed. (2 vols., 1906).

Rashed, Z. E., *Peace of Paris, 1763* (1952).

Root, William T., *Relations of Pennsylvania with the British Government 1696–1765* (1912).

Samuel, Sigmund, *Seven Years' War in Canada: Records and Illustrations* (1934).

Smelser, Marshall, *Campaign for the Sugar Islands, 1759* (1955).

Stacey, Charles P., *Quebec, 1759: Seige and Battle* (1959).

Thayer, Theodore, "Army Contractors for Niagara Campaign, 1755–1756," *WMQ*, 3 ser., 14 (1957), 31.

Vitzthum, Richard C., "Francis Parkman's Reconstruction of Sources in Montcalm and Wolfe," *JAH*, 53 (1966), 471.

Wrong, George M., *Conquest of New France* (1918).

—— *Fall of Canada 1759–60* (1914).

Zimmerman, John J., "Governor Denny and Quartering Act of 1756," *Penn. Mag. Hist. Biog.*, 91 (1967), 266.

See also 10.3 for biographies/writings of:

36.1 GENERAL

American Archives . . . A Documentary History of . . . the North American Colonies, Peter Force, ed., 4 ser. (6 vols.), 1837–1846); 5 ser. (3 vols., 1848–1853). Covers the periods, March 7, 1774–August 21, 1776, and July 4, 1776–September 3, 1783.

American Heritage Book of the Revolution (1958).

Aptheker, Herbert, *American Revolution* (1960).

Arendt, Hannah, *On Revolution* (1963).

Bailyn, Bernard, *The Ideological Origins of the American Revolution* (1967).

Barrow, Thomas C., "The American Revolution as a Colonial War for Independence," *WMQ*, 3 ser., 25 (1968), 452.

Billias, George A., ed., *The American Revolution, How Revolutionary Was It?* (1965).

Billington, Ray A., ed., *The Reinterpretation of Early American History: Essays in Honor of John Edwin Pomfret* (1968).

Buel, Richard, Jr., "Democracy and American Revolution," *WMQ*, 3 ser., 21 (1964), 165.

Craven, Wesley F., *Legend of Founding Fathers* (1956).

——— "The Revolutionary Era," in John Higham, ed., *The Reconstruction of American History* (1962).

Douglass, Elisha P., *Rebels and Democrats: Struggle for Political Rights and Majority Rule during the Revolution* (1955).

Egnal, Marc, and Joseph A. Ernst, "An Economic Interpretation of the American Revolution," *WMQ*, 3 ser., 29 (1972), 3.

English Historical Documents, vol. X (1957).

Goodwin, A., ed., *New Cambridge Modern History*, vol. VIII (1965).

Greene, Evarts B., *Revolutionary Generation, 1763–1790* (1943).

Greene, Jack P., comp., *The Ambiguity of the American Revolution, 1763–1789* (1968).

Guthorn, Peter J., *American Maps and Map Makers of the Revolution* (1966).

Hooker, Richard J., ed., *The American Revolution: The Search for Meaning* (1970).

Howe, John R., comp., *The Role of Ideology in the American Revolution* (1970).

Jacobson, David L., ed., *Essays on the American Revolution* (1970).

Jameson, J. Franklin, *The American Revolution as Social Movement* (1926).

Jensen, Merrill, "Democracy and the American Revolution," *Huntington Lib. Quar.*, 20 (1957), 321.

——— ed., *Tracts of the American Revolution* (1967).

Lacy, Dan, *Meaning of the American Revolution* (1964).

Latham, Earl, ed., *Declaration of Independence and Constitution* (1949).

Leder, Lawrence H., ed., *Meaning of the American Revolution* (1969).

MacDonald, William, ed., *Select Charters and Other Documents Illustrative of American History, 1606–1775* (1899).
—— *Select Documents Illustrative of the History of the United States, 1776–1861* (rev. ed., 1905).
McIlwain, Charles H., *American Revolution: A Constitutional Interpretation* (1923).
Merritt, Richard L., *Symbols of American Community, 1735–1775* (1966).
Miller, John C., *Origins of the American Revolution* (1943).
—— *Triumph of Freedom* (1948).
Morgan, Edmund S., ed., *American Revolution* (1965).
—— *Birth of the Republic, 1763–1789* (1956).
Morison, Samuel E., ed., *Sources and Documents Illustrating the American Revolution, 1764–1788* (2nd ed., 1965).
Morris, Richard B., *The American Revolution Reconsidered* (1967).
—— *The American Revolution: A Short History* (1955).
—— "Class Struggle and the American Revolution," *WMQ*, 3 ser., 19 (1962), 3.
—— ed., *Era of the American Revolution* (1939).
Palmer, Robert R., *Age of Democratic Revolution: Europe and America, 1760–1800* (2 vols., 1959–1964).
Robson, Eric, *The American Revolution* (1955).
Savelle, Max, "Nationalism and Other Loyalties in the American Revolution," *AHR*, 67 (1962), 901.
Schlesinger, Arthur M., Jr., *Birth of the Nation* (1968).
Stark, Werner, *America: Ideal and Reality: United States of 1776 in Contemporary European Philosophy* (1947).
Trevelyan, George O., *American Revolution* (4 vols., 1909–1912).
Ver Steeg, Clarence L., "The American Revolution as an Economic Movement," *Huntington Lib. Quar.*, 20 (1957), 361.
Winsor, Justin, *Narrative and Critical History of America* (8 vols., 1884–1889).
Wood, Gordon S., *Creation of the American Republic* (1969).
Wright, Esmond, ed., *Causes and Consequences of the American Revolution* (1966).
Wright, Esmond, *Fabric of Freedom, 1763–1800* (1961).

*   *   *   *   *   *   *

Brun, Christopher, ed., *Guide to Manuscript Maps in the William L. Clements Library* (1959).
Butler, Ruth L., ed., *Check List of Revolutionary War Pamphlets in the Newberry Library* (1922).
Clark, David S., *Index to Maps of the American Revolution in Books and Periodicals Illustrating the Revolutionary War and Other Events of the Period, 1763–1789* (1969).
Gephart, Ronald M., comp., *Periodical Literature on the American Revolution: Historical Research and Changing Interpretations, 1895–1970* (1971).
Greene, Jack P., *Reappraisal of the American Revolution in Recent Historical Literature* (1967).
—— ed., *Reinterpretation of the American Revolution, 1763–1789* (1968).
Morgan, Edmund S., "American Revolution: Revisions in Need of Revising," *WMQ*, 3 ser., 14 (1957), 3.
Pole, J. R., "Historians and the Problem of Early American Democracy," *AHR*, 67 (1962), 626.
Smith, Page, "David Ramsay and Causes of the Revolution," *WMQ*, 3 ser., 17 (1960), 51.
Smith, William R., *History as Argument: Three Patriot Historians of the American Revolution* (1966).
Streirer, William F., Jr., "Recent Trends in Historiography of the Revolution," *So. Car. Hist. Assoc.*, *Proc.* (1967), 32.
Tolles, Frederick B., "American Revolution Considered as Social Movement: A Re-evaluation," *AHR*, 60 (1954), 1.

36.2 SOUTH

36.2.1 General

Alden, John R., *The First South* (1961).
—— *South in the Revolution* (1957).
Blassingame, John W., "Nationalism and Other Loyalties in Southern Colonies, 1763–1775," *JSH*, 34 (1968), 50.
Cummings, Hubertis M., *Mason-Dixon Line* (1962).
Dodd, Walter F., "The First State Constitutional Conventions," *Am. Pol. Sci. Rev.*, 2 (1908), 545.
Green, Fletcher M., *Constitutional Development in the South Atlantic States 1776–1860* (1930).
Sellers, Charles G., Jr., "The American Revolution: Southern Founders of National Tradition," in Arthur S. Link and Rembert W. Patrick, eds., *Writing Southern History* (1965).

36.2.2 Georgia

Abbot, William W., *Royal Governors of Georgia, 1754–1775* (1959).
—— "Structure of Politics in Georgia: 1782–1789," *WMQ*, 3 ser., 14 (1957), 47.
Coleman, Kenneth, *American Revolution in Georgia, 1763–1789* (1958).
Daniel, Marjorie L., *Revolutionary Movement in Georgia, 1763–1777* (1937).
Greene, Jack P., "Georgia Commons House of Assembly, 1765–1775," *Ga. Hist. Quar.*, 46 (1962), 151.
Roberts, Lucien E., "Sectional Problems in Georgia, 1776–1789," *Ga. Hist. Quar.*, 18 (1934), 207.

36.2.3 Maryland

Barker, Charles A., *Background of the Revolution in Maryland* (1940).
—— "Revolutionary Impulse in Maryland," *Md. Hist. Mag.*, 36 (1941), 125.
Bond, Beverley W., *State Government in Maryland, 1777–1781* (1905).
Cometti, Elizabeth, "Inflation in Revolutionary Maryland," *WMQ*, 3 ser., 8 (1951), 228.
Crowl, Philip A., *Maryland during and after the Revolution* (1943).
Giddens, Paul H., "Governor Horatio Sharpe," *Md. Hist. Mag.*, 32 (1937), 156.
Hazard, Ebenezer, "Travels through Maryland in 1777," Fred Shelley, ed., *Md. Hist. Mag.*, 46 (1951), 44.
Klingelhofer, Herbert E., "Maryland and Independence, 1774–1776," *Md. Hist. Mag.*, 60 (1965), 261.
Main, Jackson T., "Political Parties in Revolutionary Maryland, 1780–1787," *Md. Hist. Mag.*, 62 (1967), 1.
Maryland (Colony), Convention, *Proceedings of the Conventions of the Province of Maryland Held at the City of Annapolis, in 1774–1776* (1936).
Pole, J. R., "Suffrage and Representation in Maryland, from 1776 to 1810," *JSH*, 24 (1958), 218.
Silver, John Archer, *Provisional Government of Maryland, 1774–1777* (1895).
Sioussat, St. George L., "Luzerne and Ratification of Articles by Maryland," *Penn. Mag. Hist. Biog.*, 60 (1936), 391.
Skaggs, David C., "Maryland's Impulse Toward Social Revolution, 1750–1776," *JAH*, 54 (1968), 771.
Strawser, Neil, "Samuel Chase and the Annapolis Paper War," *Md. Hist. Mag.*, 57 (1962), 177.

See also 10.3 for biographies/writings of:

Carroll, Charles, 1737–1832
Johnson, Thomas, 1732–1819
Martin, Luther, 1748–1826

36.2.4 North Carolina

Alexander, C. B., "Richard Caswell: Leader of the Revolution," *No. Car. Hist. Rev.*, 23 (1946), 119.

Bailyn, Bernard, "Blount Papers: Notes on the Merchant 'Class' in Revolutionary Period," *WMQ*, 3 ser., 11 (1954), 98.

Douglass, Elisha P., "Thomas Burke," *No. Car. Hist. Rev.*, 26 (1949), 150.

Gaynard, Robert L., "Radicals and Conservatives in Revolutionary North Carolina," *WMQ*, 3 ser., 24 (1967), 568.

Henderson, Archibald, *Cradle of Liberty: Essays Concerning Mecklenburg Declaration of Independence, May 20, 1775* (1955).

Keith, Alice B., "William Blount," in J. Carlyle Sitterson, ed., *Studies in Southern History* (1957).

Morrill, James R., *Practice and Politics of Fiat Finance: North Carolina in the Confederation 1783–1789* (1969).

Nash, Frank, "North Carolina Constitution of 1776 and Its Makers," *James Sprunt Hist. Publ.*, 11 (1912), 9.

North Carolina (Colony) Provincial Congress, *Journal of the Proceedings of the Provincial Congress of North Carolina, 1775–1776* (1831).

Sellers, Charles G., Jr., "Making a Revolution: North Carolina Whigs, 1765–1775," in J. Carlyle Sitterson, ed., *Studies in Southern History* (1957).

Weir, Robert M., "North Carolina's Reaction to the Currency Act of 1764," *No. Car. Hist. Rev.*, 31 (1963), 183.

Whitaker, B. L., *Provincial Council and Committee of Safety in North Carolina* (1908).

See also 10.3 for biographies/writings of:

Blount, John G., 1752–1833
Blount, William, 1749–1800
Harnett, Cornelius, 1723–1781
Iredell, James, 1751–1799

36.2.5 South Carolina

Calhoon, Robert M., and Robert M. Weir, "The Scandalous History of Sir Egerton Leigh," *WMQ*, 3 ser., 26 (1969), 47.

Gibbes, Robert W., ed., *Documentary History of the American Revolution, South Carolina* (3 vols., 1855–1857).

Greene, Jack P., "Gadsden Election Controversy in South Carolina," *MVHR*, 46 (1959), 469.

———— "Wilkes Fund Controversy in South Carolina, 1769–1775," *JSH*, 29 (1963), 19.

McCowen, George S., "The Charles Town Board of Police, 1780–1782," So. Car. Hist. Assoc., *Proc.* (1964), 25.

Maier, Pauline, "Charleston Mobs and Popular Politics in Revolutionary South Carolina, 1765–1784," *Perspectives in Am. Hist.*, 4 (1970), 173.

Powell, William S., et al., eds., *The Regulator Papers* (1971).

Ryan, Frank W., Jr., "South Carolina in the First Continental Congress," *So. Car. Hist. Mag.*, 60 (1959), 147.

Singer, Charles G., *South Carolina in Confederation* (1941).

South Carolina (Colony), Provincial Congress, *Journals of the Provincial Congresses of South Carolina, 1775–1776*, William E. Hemphill and Wylma A. Wates, eds. (1960).

Walsh, Richard, *Charleston's Sons of Liberty: The Artisans, 1763–1789* (1959).

*   *   *   *   *   *   *

Lee, Charles E., and Ruth S. Green, "Guide to South Carolina Council Journals, 1671–1775," *So. Car. Hist. Mag.*, 68 (1967), 1.

See also 10.3 for biographies/writings of:

Gadsden, Christopher, 1724–1805
Laurens, Henry, 1724–1792
Pinckney, Charles Cotesworth, 1746–1825
Pinckney, Thomas, 1750–1828
Ramsay, David, 1749–1815
Rutledge, John, 1739–1800

36.2.6 Virginia

Bridenbaugh, Carl, "Violence and Virtue in Virginia, 1766," Mass. Hist. Soc., *Proc.*, 76 (1964), 3.

Brydon, G. MacLaren, "Antiecclesiastical Laws of Virginia," *Va. Mag. Hist. Biog.*, 64 (1956), 259.

Dodd, Walter F., "Effect of Adoption of the Constitution on Finances of Virginia," *Va. Mag. Hist. Biog.*, 10 (1903), 360.

Dodd, William E., "Virginia Takes Road to Revolution," in Carl Becker et al., *Spirit of '76 and Other Essays* (1927).

Eckenrode, H. J., *Revolution in Virginia* (1916).

—— *Separation of Church and State in Virginia* (1910).

Evans, Emory G., "Planter Indebtedness and the Coming of Revolution in Virginia," *WMQ*, 3 ser., 19 (1962), 511.

Gipson, Lawrence H., "Virginia Planter Debts before the Revolution," *Va. Mag. Hist. Biog.*, 69 (1961), 259.

Grigsby, Hugh B., *Virginia Convention of 1776* (1855).

Henderson, Patrick, "Norfolk Riots, 1768–1769," *Va. Mag. Hist. Biog.*, 73 (1965), 413.

Main, Jackson T., "Sections and Politics in Virginia, 1781–1787," *WMQ*, 3 ser., 12 (1955), 96.

Pilcher, George W., "Pamphlet War on Proposed Virginia Anglican Episcopate, 1767–1775," *Hist. Mag. Prot. Episc. Church*, 30 (1961), 266.

Pole, J. R., "Representation and Authority in Virginia from Revolution to Reform," *JSH*, 24 (1958), 16.

Rutman, Darrett B., ed., *Old Dominion: Essays for Thomas Perkins Abernethy* (1964).

Summers, Lewis P., *Annals of Southwest Virginia, 1769–1800* (1929).

Sydnor, Charles S., *Gentlemen Freeholders: Political Practices in Washington's Virginia* (1952).

Tate, Thad W., "Coming of Revolution in Virginia: Britain's Challenge to the Ruling Class, 1763–1776," *WMQ*, 3 ser., 19 (1962), 323.

See also 10.3 for biographies/writings of:

Carter, Landon, 1710–1778
Henry, Patrick, 1736–1799
Jefferson, Thomas, 1743–1826
Lee, Richard Henry, 1732–1794
Madison, James, 1750/51–1836
Mason, George, 1725–1792
Monroe, James, 1758–1831
Pendleton, Edmund, 1721–1803
Randolph, Edmund, 1753–1813
Washington, George, 1732–1799

36.3 MIDDLE STATES

36.3.1 Delaware

Delaware (Colony) General Assembly, *Votes and Proceedings of the House of Representatives of . . . Delaware . . . 1765–1770* (1770).

Munroe, John A., *Federalist Delaware, 1775–1815* (1954).
Reed, H. Clay, "Delaware Constitution of 1776," *Del. Notes*, 6 ser. (1930), 7.
Tilton, James, *Timoleon's Biographical History of Dionysius, Tyrant of Delaware* (1788); John A. Munroe, ed. (1958).

See also 10.3 for biographies/writings of:

Boudinot, Elias, 1740–1821
Dickinson, John, 1732–1808
Read, George, 1733–1798
Rodney, Caesar, 1728–1784

36.3.2 New Jersey

Bill, Alfred H., *New Jersey and the Revolutionary War* (1964).
Cowen, David L., "Revolutionary New Jersey, 1763–1787," N.J. Hist. Soc., *Proc.,* 71 (1953), 1.
Erdman, Charles R., Jr., *New Jersey Constitution of 1776* (1929).
Fennelly, Catherine, "William Franklin of New Jersey," *WMQ*, 3 ser., 6 (1949), 361.
Haskett, Richard C., "William Paterson, Attorney General," *WMQ*, 3 ser., 7 (1950), 26.
Leiby, Adrian C., *Revolutionary War in Hackensack Valley: Jersey Dutch and Neutral Ground* (1962).
Lundin, Leonard, *Cockpit of Revolution: War for Independence in New Jersey* (1940).
McCormick, Richard P., *Experiment in Independence: New Jersey in the Critical Period 1781–1789* (1950).
Pole, J. R., "Suffrage Reform and the Revolution in New Jersey," N. J. Hist. Soc., *Proc.,* 74 (1956), 173.
Rosenberg, Leonard B., "William Paterson: New Jersey's Nation-Maker," N. J. Hist. Soc., *Proc.,* new ser., 85 (1967), 7.
Shy, John, "Quartering His Majesty's Forces in New Jersey," N.J. Hist. Soc., *Proc.,* 78 (1960), 82.
Taylor, Robert J., "Trial at Trenton," *WMQ*, 3 ser., 26 (1969), 521.

See also 10.3 for biographies/writings of:

Livingston, William, 1723–1790
Witherspoon, John, 1723–1794

36.3.3 New York

Abbott, Wilbur C., *New York in Revolution* (1929).
Becker, Carl, *Political Parties in New York, 1760–1766* (1909).
Bonomi, Patricia U., "Political Patterns in Colonial New York City: The General Assembly Election of 1768," *Pol. Sci. Quar.,* 81 (1966), 432.
Burke, Edmund, *Edmund Burke, New York Agent, with His Letters to the New York Assembly and Correspondence with Charles O'Hara, 1761–1776,* Ross J. S. Hoffman, ed. (1956).
Champagne, Roger J., "Liberty Boys and New York City, 1764–1774," *Labor Hist.,* 8 (1967), 115.
——— "New York and Intolerable Acts, 1774," *N. Y. Hist. Soc. Quar.,* 45 (1961), 195.
——— "New York Politics and Independence, 1776," *N.Y. Hist. Soc. Quar.,* 46 (1962), 281.
——— "New York's Radicals and Coming of Independence," *JAH*, 51 (1964), 21.
Cochran, Thomas C., *New York in Confederation* (1932).
Dillon, Dorothy R., *New York Triumvirate* (1949).
Friedman, Bernard, "New York Assembly Elections of 1768 and 1769," *N. Y. Hist.,* 46 (1965), 3.

—— "Shaping of Radical Consciousness in Provincial New York," *JAH*, 56 (1970), 781.

Fox, Dixon R., *Yankees and Yorkers* (1940).

Harrington, Virginia D., *New York Merchant on the Eve of Revolution* (1935).

Jones, Thomas, *History of New York during the Revolutionary War*, E. F. de Lancey, ed. (2 vols., 1879).

Klein, Milton M., "Prelude to Revolution in New York: Jury Trials and Judicial Tenure," *WMQ*, 3 ser., 17 (1960), 439.

Leder, Lawrence H., "New York Elections of 1769," *MVHR*, 49 (1963), 675.

—— "Robert Livingston: New View of New York Politics," *N.Y. Hist.*, 40 (1959), 358.

Lemisch, L. Jesse, "New York's Petitions and Resolves of December 1765," *N.Y. Hist. Soc. Quar.*, 49 (1965), 313.

Lincoln, Charles Z., *Constitutional History of New York*, vol. I (1906).

Lynd, Staughton, and Alfred Young, "After Carl Becker: Mechanics and New York City Politics, 1774–1801," *Labor Hist.*, 5 (1964), 215.

Lynd, Staughton, "Tenant Rising at Livingston Manor, 1777," *N.Y. Hist. Soc. Quar.*, 48 (1964), 163.

—— "Who Should Rule at Home? Dutchess County, New York, in the Revolution," *WMQ*, 18 (1961), 330.

Mark, Irving, *Agrarian Conflicts in Colonial New York, 1711–1775* (1940).

Mason, Bernard, *Road to Independence: Revolutionary Movement in New York, 1773–1777* (1966).

New York (Colony) General Assembly, *Journal of the Votes and Proceedings of the General Assembly of the Colony of New York . . . [1691–1765]* (2 vols., 1746–1766).

Smith, William, *Historical Memoirs from 1763–1776*, William H. W. Sabine, ed. (1956).

Spaulding, E. W., *New York in the Critical Period 1783–1789* (1932).

Wertenbaker, Thomas J., *Father Knickerbocker Rebels* (1948).

Young, Alfred F., *Democratic Republicans of New York, 1763–1797* (1967).

*   *   *   *   *   *   *

Breuer, Ernest H., comp., *Constitutional Developments in New York, 1777–1958: Bibliography* (1958).

See also 10.3 for biographies/writings of:

Clinton, George, 1739–1812
Duane, James, 1733–1797
Hamilton, Alexander, 1755–1804
Jay, John, 1745–1829
Livingston, Robert R., 1746–1813
Morris, Gouverneur, 1752–1816
Schuyler, Philip J., 1733–1804
Willett, Marinus, 1740–1830

36.3.4 Pennsylvania

Anderson, James L., "The Impact of the Revolution on the Governor's Councillors," *Penn. Hist.*, 34 (1967), 131.

Brunhouse, Robert L., *Counter-Revolution in Pennsylvania, 1776–1790* (1942).

Cummings, Hubertis M., "Robert Morris and the Episode of the Polacre 'Victorious'," *Penn. Mag. Hist. Biog.*, 70 (1946), 239.

Gerson, Noel B., *Franklin, America's "Lost State"* (1968).

Gibson, James E., "The Pennsylvania Provincial Conference of 1776," *Penn. Mag. Hist. Biog.*, 58 (1934), 312.

Hanna, William S., *Benjamin Franklin and Pennsylvania Politics* (1964).

Hawke, David, *In the Midst of a Revolution* (1961).

Hindle, Brooke, "March of Paxton Boys," *WMQ*, 3 ser., 3 (1946), 461.

Hutson, James H., "An Investigation of the Inarticulate: Philadelphia's White Oaks," *WMQ*, 3 ser., 28 (1971), 3.

Jacobson, David L., *John Dickinson and Revolution in Pennsylvania* (1965).

Lemisch, Jesse, and John K. Alexander, "The White Oaks, Jack Tar, and the Concept of the 'Inarticulate'," *WMQ*, 3 ser., 29 (1972), 109.

Lincoln, Charles H., *Revolutionary Movement in Pennsylvania 1760–1776* (1901).

Newcomb, Benjamin H., "Stamp Act and Pennsylvania Politics," *WMQ*, 3 ser., 23 (1966), 257.

Pennsylvania (Colony), General Assembly, *Debates and Proceedings of the Assembly of Pennsylvania Anulling Charter of Bank*, Mathew Carey, ed. (1786).

Powell, John H., "John Dickinson as President of Pennsylvania," *Penn. Hist.*, 28 (1961), 254.

Rasmusson, Ethel E., "Democratic Environment—Aristocratic Aspiration," *Penn. Mag. Hist. Biog.*, 90 (1966), 155.

Roche, John F., "Was Joseph Reed Disloyal?" *WMQ*, 3 ser., 8 (1951), 406.

Root, William T., *Relations of Pennsylvania with the British Government, 1696–1765* (1912).

Rossman, Kenneth R., *Thomas Mifflin and Politics of the American Revolution* (1952).

Selsam, John P., and J. G. Rayback, "French Comment on the Pennsylvania Constitution of 1776," *Penn. Mag. Hist. Biog.*, 76 (1952), 311.

Selsam, John P., *Pennsylvania Constitution of 1776* (1936).

Smith, Charles Page, "The Attack on Fort Wilson," *Penn. Mag. Hist. Biog.*, 78 (1954), 177.

Smith, W. Roy, "Sectionalism in Pennsylvania," *Pol. Sci. Quar.*, 24 (1909), 208.

Thayer, Theodore, *Pennsylvania Politics and Growth of Democracy, 1740–1776* (1954).

Warden, G. B., "The Proprietary Group in Pennsylvania," *WMQ*, 3 ser., 21 (1964), 367.

Wilson, Janet, "The Bank of North America and Pennsylvania Politics," *Penn. Mag. Hist. Biog.*, 66 (1942), 3.

Young, Henry J., "Treason and Its Punishment in Revolutionary Pennsylvania," *Penn. Mag. Hist. Biog.*, 90 (1966), 287.

Zimmerman, John J., "Charles Thomson, The Sam Adams of Philadelphia," *MVHR*, 45 (1958), 464.

See also 10.3 for biographies/writings of:

Bingham, William, 1752–1804
Chew, Benjamin, 1722–1810
Dickinson, John, 1732–1808
Franklin, Benjamin, 1706–1790
Hopkinson, Francis, 1737–1791
Maclay, William, 1734–1804
Mifflin, Thomas, 1744–1800
Morris, Gouverneur, 1752–1816
Paine, Thomas, 1737–1809
Reed, Joseph, 1741–1785
Willing, Thomas, 1731–1821
Wilson, James, 1742–1798

36.4 NEW ENGLAND

36.4.1 General

Adams, James T., *New England in the Republic, 1766–1850* (1926).
—— *Revolutionary New England 1691–1776* (1923).
Baldwin, Alice M., *New England Clergy and the American Revolution* (1928).
—— "Sowers of Sedition, Presbyterian Clergy," *WMQ*, 3 ser., 5 (1948), 53.

Breen, Timothy H., "John Adams' Fight against Innovation in the New England Constitution, 1776," *NEQ*, 40 (1967), 501.

Davies, Wallace E., "The Society of the Cincinnati in New England," *WMQ*, 3 ser., 5 (1948), 3.

Scott, Kenneth, "Price Control in New England during the Revolution," *NEQ*, 19 (1946), 453.

36.4.2 Connecticut

Gipson, Lawrence H., "Connecticut Taxation and Parliamentary Aid," *AHR*, 36 (1931), 721.

Johnson, William S., "Letters of William Samuel Johnson to Governors of Connecticut [1766–1771]," Mass Hist. Soc., *Coll.*, 5 ser., 9 (1885), 211.

Purcell, Richard J., *Connecticut in Transition* (rev. ed., 1963).

Zeichner, Oscar, *Connecticut's Years of Controversy* (1950).

See also 10.3 for biographies/writings of:

Hawley, Joseph, 1723–1788
Johnson, William Samuel, 1727–1819
Sherman, Roger, 1721–1793
Trumbull, Jonathan, 1710–1785

36.4.3 Massachusetts

Brennan, Ellen E., *Plural Office-Holding in Massachusetts 1760–1780* (1945).

Brown, Ernest F., ed., "Shays's Rebellion," *AHR*, 36 (1931), 776.

Brown, Robert E., *Middle-Class Democracy and Revolution in Massachusetts, 1691–1780* (1955).

Cary, John, "Statistical Method and Brown Thesis on Colonial Democracy," *WMQ*, 3 ser., 20 (1963), 251.

Dickerson, Oliver M., "John Hancock," *MVHR*, 32 (1946), 517.

Dyer, W. A., "Embattled Farmers," *NEQ*, 4 (1931), 460.

East, Robert A., "The Massachusetts Conservatives," in Richard B. Morris, ed., *Era of the American Revolution* (1939).

Fiore, Jordan D., "Temple-Bernard Affair," Essex Inst., *Hist. Coll.*, 90 (1954), 58.

Freiberg, Malcolm, "Thomas Hutchinson of Massachusetts," *Rev. Politics*, 21 (1959), 646.

Gummere, Richard M., "Thomas Hutchinson and Samuel Adams: Controversy in Classical Tradition," Boston Pub. Lib., *Quar.*, 10 (1958), 119.

Handlin, Oscar, and Mary F. Handlin, *Commonwealth: Massachusetts 1774–1861* (rev. ed., 1969).

———— eds., *The Popular Sources of Political Authority: Documents on the Massachusetts Convention of 1780* (1966).

Handlin, Oscar, and Mary F. Handlin, "Radicals and Conservatives in Massachusetts," *NEQ*, 17 (1944), 343.

———— "Revolutionary Economic Policy in Massachusetts," *WMQ*, 3 ser., 4 (1947), 3.

Holland, Josiah G., *History of Western Massachusetts*, vol. I (1855).

Hutchinson, Thomas, *History of Massachusetts Bay* (new ed., 3 vols., 1936).

Kaplan, Sidney, "Veteran Officers and Politics in Massachusetts, 1783–1787," *WMQ*, 3 ser., 9 (1952), 29.

King, Joseph E., "Judicial Flotsam in Massachusetts Bay, 1760–1765," *NEQ*, 27 (1954), 366.

Labaree, Benjamin W., *Patriots and Partisans: The Merchants of Newburyport, 1764–1815* (1962).

Lord, Donald C., and Robert M. Calhoon, "Removal of Massachusetts General Court from Boston, 1769–1772," *JAH*, 55 (1969), 735.

Massachusetts (Colony), Superior Court of Judicature, *Reports of Cases Argued and Adjudged in the Superior Court of Judicature of the Province of Mas-*

sachusetts Bay, between 1761 and 1772, Josiah Quincy, Jr. and Samuel M. Quincy, eds. (1865).

Moody, Robert E., "Samuel Ely: Forerunner of Shays," *NEQ*, 5 (1932), 105.

Morison, Samuel E., "Struggle over Adoption of Constitution of Massachusetts, 1780," Mass. Hist. Soc., *Proc.*, 50 (1917), 353.

Nash, George H., III, "The Political Career of Josiah Quincy, Jr.," Am. Antiq. Soc., *Proc.*, 79 (1969), 253.

Newcomer, Lee N., *Embattled Farmers: Massachusetts Countryside in American Revolution* (1953).

Norton, W. B., "Paper Currency in Massachusetts during Revolution," *NEQ*, 7 (1934), 43.

Riley, Stephen T., "Dr. William Whiting and Shays' Rebellion," Am. Antiq. Soc., *Proc.*, 66 (1956), 119.

Smith, Jonathan, *Some Features of Shays' Rebellion* (1903). Reprinted in *WMQ*, 3 ser., 5 (1948), 77.

Sosin, Jack M., "Massachusetts Act of 1774," *Huntington Lib. Quar.*, 26 (1962–1963), 235.

Starkey, Marion L., *Little Rebellion* (1955).

Syrett, David, "Town-Meeting Politics in Massachusetts, 1776–1786," *WMQ*, 3 ser., 21 (1964), 352.

Taylor, Robert J., ed., *Massachusetts: Documents on Formation of Its Constitution, 1775–1780* (1961).

———— *Western Massachusetts in the Revolution* (1954).

Walett, Francis G., "Governor Bernard's Undoing," *NEQ*, 38 (1965), 217.

———— "Massachusetts Council, 1766–1774," *WMQ*, 3 ser., 6 (1949), 605.

Warren, Joseph P., ed., "Documents Relating to the Shays' Rebellion," *AHR*, 2 (1897), 693.

Waters, John J., and John A. Schutz, "Patterns of Massachusetts Colonial Politics: The Writs of Assistance and the Rivalry between the Otis and Hutchinson Families," *WMQ*, 3 ser., 24 (1967), 543.

See also 10.3 for biographies/writings of:

Adams, John, 1735–1826
Adams, Samuel, 1722–1803
Edwards, Jonathan, 1703–1758
Gerry, Elbridge, 1744–1814
Hancock, John, 1736–1793
Hutchinson, Thomas, 1711–1780
Parsons, Theophilus, 1750–1813
Pickering, Timothy, 1745–1829
Quincy, Josiah, Jr., 1744–1775
Revere, Paul, 1735–1818
Sedgwick, Theodore, 1746–1813
Sullivan, James, 1744–1808
Sullivan, William, 1774–1839
Warren, James, 1726–1808
Warren, Joseph, 1741–1775

36.4.4 New Hampshire and Vermont

Daniell, Jere R., *Experiment in Republicanism: New Hampshire Politics and the American Revolution, 1741–1794* (1970).

Gemmill, John K., "The Problems of Power: New Hampshire Government during the Revolution," *Hist. N. H.*, 22 (1967), 27.

Jones, Matt B., *Vermont in the Making, 1750–1777* (1939).

Kaplan, Sidney, "The History of New Hampshire: Jeremy Belknap as Literary Craftsman," *WMQ*, 3 ser., 21 (1964), 18.

Rife, Clarence, "Ethan Allen," *NEQ*, 2 (1929), 561.

Thompson, Charles M., *Independent Vermont* (1942).

Williamson, Chilton, *Vermont in Quandary, 1763–1825* (1949).

See also 10.3 for biographies/writings of:

Allen, Ethan, 1737/8–1789
Allen, Ira, 1751–1814
Plumer, William, 1759–1850
Sullivan, John, 1740–1795

36.4.5 Rhode Island

Bates, Frank G., *Rhode Island and Formation of the Union* (1899).
Field, Edward, *State of Rhode Island, And Providence Plantations at the End of the Century* (3 vols., 1902).
Lovejoy, David S., *Rhode Island Politics and the American Revolution, 1760–1776* (1958).
Polishook, Irwin H., *Rhode Island and Union 1774–1795* (1969).
Potter, Elisha R., and S. S. Rider, *Paper Money of Rhode Island* (1880).
Staples, William R., *Rhode Island and the Continental Congress, 1765–1790* (1870).
Thompson, Mack E., "Ward-Hopkins Controversy and the Revolution in Rhode Island," *WMQ,* 3 ser., 16 (1959), 363.
Ward, Governor Samuel, *Correspondence,* Bernhard Knollenberg, ed. (1952).

See also 10.3 for biographies/writings of:

Hopkins, Stephen, 1707–1785
Ward, Samuel, 1725–1776

36.5 FRONTIER

36.5.1 General

Abernethy, Thomas P., *Western Lands and the American Revolution* (1937).
Alvord, Clarence W., *Mississippi Valley in British Politics* (1916).
Henderson, Archibald, "Pre-Revolutionary Revolt in the Old Southwest," *MVHR,* 17 (1930), 191.
Sosin, Jack M., *Revolutionary Frontier, 1763–1783* (1967).
—— *Whitehall and the Wilderness: The Middle West in British Colonial Policy, 1760–1775* (1961).

See also 10.3 for biographies/writings of:

Ellicott, Andrew, 1754–1820
Franklin, Benjamin, 1706–1790
Harrod, James, 1742–1793
Kenton, Simon, 1755–1836

36.5.2 South

Abernethy, Thomas P., *From Frontier to Plantation in Tennessee* (1932).
Alden, John R., *John Stuart and the Southern Colonial Frontier, 1754–1775* (1944).
Bassett, J. S., "Regulators in North Carolina," Am. Hist. Assoc., *Report* (1894), 141.
Boyd, William K., *Eighteenth Century Tracts Concerning North Carolina* (1927).
Brown, Richard M., *The South Carolina Regulators* (1963).
Carter, Clarence E., "British Policy toward Indians in the South, 1763–1768," *Eng. Hist. Rev.,* 33 (1918), 37.
Davidson, Philip, "Southern Backcountry on the Eve of Revolution," in Avery O. Craven, ed., *Essays in Honor of William E. Dodd* (1935).
Filson, John, *Discovery, Settlement, and Present State of Kentucky* (1784).

Hanna, Charles A., *Wilderness Trail* (2 vols., 1911).

Hart, Freeman H., *Valley of Virginia in American Revolution* (1942).

Henderson, Archibald, "Origin of Regulation in North Carolina," *AHR*, 21 (1916), 320.

Hulbert, Archer B., *Boone's Wilderness Road* (1903).

Kincaid, Robert L., *Wilderness Road* (1955).

Lefler, Hugh T., and Paul Wagner, eds., *Orange County—1752–1952* (1953). Regulator movement.

Lockey, Joseph B., *East Florida, 1783–1785*, John W. Caughey, ed. (1949).

McCrady, Edward, *South Carolina* (4 vols., 1897–1902).

Mowat, Charles L., *East Florida as a British Province, 1763–1784* (1943).

Stuart, John, "Observations," *AHR*, 20 (1915), 815.

Walker, Thomas, "Journal (1750)," in J. S. Johnston, ed., *First Explorations of Kentucky* (1898).

Williams, Samuel C., *Dawn of Tennessee Valley and Tennessee History* (1937).

———— *History of Lost State of Franklin* (1933).

———— *Tennessee during the Revolutionary War* (1944).

Woodmason, Charles, *Carolina Backcountry on Eve of the Revolution: Journal and Other Writings*, Richard J. Hooker, ed. (1953).

Young, Carol F., "A Study of Some Developing Interpretations of History of Revolutionary Tennessee (1776–1781)," East Tenn. Hist. Soc., *Publ.*, 25 (1953), 24.

See also 10.3 for biographies/writings of:

Boone, Daniel, 1734–1820
Logan, Benjamin, 1743–1802
Morgan, George, 1734–1810
Sevier, John, 1745–1815
Stuart, John, 1700–1779
Wilkinson, James, 1757–1825

36.5.3 North

Alvord, Clarence W., ed., "Cahokia Records," *Ill. Hist. Coll.*, 2 (1907).

———— "Kaskaskia Records," *Ill. Hist. Coll.*, 5 (1909).

———— and Clarence E. Carter, eds., *New Regime, 1765–1767* (1916).

Bailey, Kenneth, *Ohio Company of Virginia and Westward Movement* (1939).

Barnhart, John D., *Valley of Democracy: Frontier in the Ohio Valley, 1775–1818* (1953).

Boyd, Julian P., *Susquehannah Company* (1935).

———— and Robert J. Taylor, eds., *Susquehannah Company Papers* (11 vols., 1930–1971).

Brown, Lloyd A., *Early Maps of Ohio Valley: From 1673 to 1783* (1959).

Carter, Clarence E., *Great Britain and Illinois Country, 1763–1774* (1910).

Clark, George Rogers, "Papers, 1771–1781," J. A. James, ed., *Ill. Hist. Coll.*, 8 (1912).

Higgins, Ruth, *Expansion in New York* (1931).

Hurt, N. Franklin, "Growth of Local Action during British Military Rule at Detroit, 1760–1774," *Mich. Hist.*, 40 (1956), 451.

Huston, John W., "The British Evacuation of Fort Pitt, 1772," *West. Penn. Hist. Mag.*, 48 (1965), 317.

James, Alfred P., "George Mercer, of the Ohio Company," *West. Penn. Hist. Mag.*, 46 (1963), 1, 141.

———— *Ohio Company* (1959).

Kellogg, Louise P., *British Regime in Wisconsin and Northwest* (1935).

Lester, William S., *Transylvania Company* (1935).

Lewis, George E., *Indiana Company 1763–1798* (1941).

Leyland, Herbert T., *Ohio Company: Colonial Corporation* (1921).

Matthews, Lois K., *Expansion of New England* (1936).

Metzger, C. H., *Quebec Act* (1936).

Shimmell, L. S., *Border Warfare in Pennsylvania during the Revolution* (1901).
Thwaites, Reuben G., *Frontier Defense on the Upper Ohio, 1777–1778* (1912).
────── and Louise P. Kellogg, *Revolution on the Upper Ohio* (1908).
Wrong, George M., *Canada and the American Revolution, 1760–1776* (1935).

See also 10.3 for biographies/writings of:

Barlow, Joel, 1754–1812
Brackenridge, Hugh Henry, 1748–1816
Burd, James, 1726–1793
Croghan, George, d. 1782
Cutler, Manasseh, 1742–1823
Franklin, Benjamin, 1706–1790
Mercer, George, 1733–1784
Pontiac, d. 1769
Putnam, Rufus, 1738–1824
Symmes, John Cleves, 1742–1814
Trent, William, 1715–1787

36.5.4 Indian Relations

Atkin, Edmund, *Indians of Southern Colonial Frontier: Atkin Report and Plan of 1775*, Wilbur R. Jacobs, ed. (1954).
Berry, Jane M., "The Indian Policy of Spain in the Southwest, 1783–1795," *MVHR*, 3 (1917), 462.
Billington, Ray A., "The Fort Stanwix Treaty of 1768," *N.Y. Hist.*, 25 (1944), 182.
Bouquet, Henry, "The Orderly Book of Colonel Henry Bouquet's Expedition against Ohio Indians, 1764," Edward G. Williams, ed., *West. Penn. Hist. Mag.*, 42 (1959), 9.
Carter, Clarence E., "British Policy towards the American Indians in the South," *Eng. Hist. Rev.*, 33 (1918), 37.
Coleman, Kenneth, "Federal Indian Relations in the South, 1781–1789," *Chronicles Okla.*, 35 (1957–1958), 435.
Cummings, Hubertis M., "Paxton Killings [1763]," *Jour. Presby. Hist.* 44 (1966), 219.
De Vorsey, Louis, Jr., *Indian Boundary in Southern Colonies, 1763–1775* (1966).
Downes, Randolph C., *Council Fires on the Upper Ohio* (1940).
────── "Creek-American Relations, 1782–1790," *Ga. Hist. Quar.*, 21 (1937), 142.
────── "Dunmore's War," *MVHR*, 21 (1934), 311.
Dunbar, John R., ed., *Paxton Papers* (1957).
Farrand, Max, "Indian Boundary Line," *AHR*, 10 (1905), 782.
Grant, Charles S., "Pontiac's Rebellion and the British Troop Moves of 1763," *MVHR*, 40 (1953), 75.
Hamer, Philip M., "John Stuart's Indian Policy during the Early Months of the Revolution," *MVHR*, 17 (1930), 351.
Jacobs, Wilbur R., "The Indian Frontier of 1763," *West. Penn. Hist. Mag.*, 34 (1951), 185.
James, James Alton, "Indian Diplomacy and Opening of Revolution in West," *Wis. Hist. Soc.*, *Proc.* (1909), 125.
────── "Problems of Northwest in 1779," in Guy S. Ford, ed., *Essays in American History Dedicated to F. J. Turner* (1910).
Mohr, Walter H., *Federal Indian Relations 1774–1788* (1933).
Osborn, George C., "Relations with the Indians in West Florida, 1770–1781," *Fla. Hist. Quar.*, 16 (1907), 269.
Parkman, Francis, *Conspiracy of Pontiac* (2 vols., 1851).
Peckham, Howard H., *Pontiac and Indian Uprising* (1947).
Sosin, Jack M., "British Indian Department and Dunmore's War," *Va. Mag. Hist. Biog.*, 74 (1966), 34.
────── "Use of Indians in War of the American Revolution," *Can. Hist. Rev.*, 46 (1965), 101.

Stanley, George F., "The Six Nations and the American Revolution," *Ontario Hist.*, 56 (1964), 217.
Sullivan, John, *Journals of Expedition against Six Nations* (1887).
—— *Letters and Papers of Major General John Sullivan, Continental Army*, Otis G. Hammond, ed. (1930–1931).
Thwaites, Reuben G., and Louise P. Kellogg, eds., *Dunmore's War* (1905).
Vivian, James F. and Jean H., "Congressional Indian Policy during the Revolution," *Md. Hist. Mag.*, 63 (1968), 241.

See also 10.3 for biographies/writings of:

Bowles, William Augustus, 1763–1805
Brant, Joseph, 1742–1807
Cresap, Thomas, ca. 1702–1790
Elliott, Matthew, fl. 1776–1812
Hawkins, Benjamin, 1754–1816
Sullivan, John, 1740–1795

36.6 BRITAIN AND THE AMERICAN REVOLUTION

36.6.1 General

Boulton, James T., *Language of Politics in the Age of Wilkes and Burke* (1963).
Christie, Ian R., *End of Lord North's Ministry, 1780–1782* (1958).
Coupland, Reginald, *American Revolution and British Empire* (1930).
Currey, Cecil B., *Road to Revolution: Franklin in England, 1765–1775* (1968).
Donoughue, Bernard, *British Politics and American Revolution, 1773–1775* (1964).
Gipson, Lawrence H., *The British Empire before the American Revolution* (14 vols., 1936–1969).
Gruber, Ira D., "American Revolution as a Conspiracy: The British View," *WMQ*, 3 ser., 26 (1969), 360.
Harlow, Vincent T., *Founding of the Second British Empire, 1763–1793* (2 vols., 1952–1964).
Hinkhouse, Fred J., *Preliminaries of the American Revolution as Seen in the English Press* (1926).
Kallich, Martin, and Andrew MacLeish, eds., *The American Revolution through British Eyes* (1962).
Kammen, Michael G., *Rope of Sand: Colonial Agents, British Politics and the American Revolution* (1968).
Lutnick, Solomon, *American Revolution and the British Press* (1967).
Marshall, Peter, "British Empire and the American Revolution," *Huntington Lib. Quar.*, 27 (1964), 135.
Namier, Lewis B., *England in the Age of the American Revolution* (2nd ed., 1961).
Squire, Marjorie J., *British Views of the American Revolution* (1965).
Van Alstyne, Richard W., "Europe, Rockingham Whigs and War for American Independence: Documents," *Huntington Lib. Quar.*, 25 (1961), 1.
Watson, J. Steven, *Reign of George III, 1760–1815* (1960).

*   *   *   *   *   *   *

Greene, Jack P., "Plunge of Lemmings: Consideration of Recent Writings on British Politics and the American Revolution," *So. Atl. Quar.*, 67 (1968), 141.

36.6.2 British Politics

Bargar, Bradley D., "Lord Dartmouth's Patronage, 1772–1775," *WMQ*, 3 ser., 15 (1958), 191.
Black, Eugene C., *The Association: British Extraparliamentary Political Organization 1769–1793* (1963).

Brooke, John, *Chatham Administration, 1766–1768* (1956).
Butterfield, Herbert, *George III and the Historians* (1957).
—— *George III, Lord North and the People, 1779–1780* (1949).
Christie, Ian R., *End of Lord North's Ministry, 1780–1782* (1958).
—— *Wilkes, Wyvill and Reform: Parliamentary Reform, 1760–1785* (1962).
George III, *Correspondence from 1760 to 1783, Printed from Original Papers in Royal Archives,* John Fortescue, ed. (6 vols., 1967).
Mansfield, Harvey C., *Statesmanship and Party Government: Burke and Bolingbroke* (1965).
Namier, Lewis B., and John Brooke, *History of Parliament: House of Commons, 1754–1790* (3 vols., 1964).
Namier, Lewis B., "King George III: A Study in Personality," in *Personalities and Powers* (1955).
Norris, John, *Shelburne and Reform* (1963).
Pares, Richard, *King George III and Politicians* (1953).
Rea, Robert R., *English Press in Politics, 1760–1774* (1963).
Reitan, Earl A., ed., *George III, Tyrant or Constitutional Monarch?* (1964).
Ritcheson, Charles R., *British Politics and the American Revolution* (1954).
Rudé, George, *Wilkes and Liberty* (1962).
Schuyler, Robert L., *Parliament and the British Empire* (1929).
Sherrard, Owen A., *Lord Chatham* (3 vols., 1952–1958).
Trevelyan, George O., *Early History of Charles James Fox* (1901).
—— *George III and Charles Fox* (2 vols., 1912–1914).
Valentine, Alan C., *British Establishment, 1760–1784: Biographical Dictionary* (2 vols., 1970).
—— *Lord North* (1967).
Winstanley, Denys A., *Lord Chatham and Whig Opposition* (1912).

*   *   *   *   *   *   *

Thomas, Peter D. G., *Sources for Debates of the House of Commons, 1768–1774* (1959).

36.6.3 Colonial Institutions and Policies

Bargar, Bradley D., *Lord Dartmouth and the American Revolution* (1965).
Barrow, Thomas C., "Project for Imperial Reform," *WMQ,* 3 ser., 24 (1967), 108.
Basye, Arthur H., "Secretary of State for Colonies," *AHR,* 28 (1922), 13.
Brown, Gerald S., *American Secretary: Colonial Policy of Lord George Germain, 1775–1778* (1963).
Burke, Edmund, *Edmund Burke, New York Agent, with His Letters to the New York Assembly and Correspondence with Charles O'Hara, 1761–1766,* Ross S. J. Hoffman, ed. (1956).
—— *Speeches and Letters on American Affairs* (1908).
Clark, Dora M., "American Board of Customs, 1767–1783," *AHR,* 45 (1940), 777.
Cone, Carl B., *Burke and the Nature of Politics: American Revolution* (1957).
Dickerson, Oliver M., "*Use Made of Revenue from Tax on Tea,*" *NEQ,* 31 (1958), 232.
Ericson, F. J., "British Opposition to Stamp Act," *Mich. Acad. Sci., Papers,* 29 (1943), 489.
Ernst, Joseph A., "Currency Act Repeal Movement, 1764–1767," *WMQ,* 3 ser., 25 (1968), 177.
—— "Genesis of the Currency Act of 1764," *WMQ,* 3 ser., 22 (1965), 33.
Gage, Thomas, *Correspondence with Secretaries of State and War Office and Treasury, 1763–1775,* Clarence E. Carter, ed. (2 vols., 1931–1933).
Gipson, Lawrence H., "Great Debate on the Stamp Act, 1766, as Reported by Nathaniel Ryder," *Penn. Mag. Hist. Biog.,* 86 (1962), 10.
Grant, William L., *Colonial Policy of Chatham* (1911).
Greene, Jack P., and Richard M. Jellison, "Currency Act of 1764 in Imperial-Colonial Relations, 1764–1776," *WMQ,* 3 ser., 18 (1961), 485.

Hickman, Emily, "Colonial Writs of Assistance," *NEQ*, 5 (1932), 83.

Hughes, Edward, "The English Stamp Duties, 1664–1764," *Eng. Hist. Rev.*, 56 (1941), 234.

Hull, C. H., and H. W. V. Temperley, eds., "Debates on Repeal of the Stamp Act," *AHR*, 17 (1912), 563.

Humphreys, Robert A., "British Colonial Policy and the American Revolution, 1763–1776," *History*, 19 (1934), 42.

—— "Lord Shelburne and British Colonial Policy, 1776–1768," *Eng. Hist. Rev.*, 50 (1935), 257.

Johnson, Allen S., "British Politics and Repeal of Stamp Act," *So. Atl. Quar.*, 62 (1963), 169.

—— "Passage of Sugar Act," *WMQ*, 3 ser., 16 (1959), 507.

Kammen, Michael G., *Rope of Sand: Colonial Agents, British Politics and the American Revolution* (1968).

Laprade, W. T., "Stamp Act in British Politics," *AHR*, 35 (1930), 735.

Lilly, Edward P., *Colonial Agents of New York and New Jersey* (1936).

McClelland, Peter D., "The Cost to America of British Imperial Policy," *Am. Econ. Rev.*, 59 (1969), 370.

Metzger, Charles H., *Quebec Act* (1936).

—— "Shelburne's Western Policy," *Mid-America*, 8 (1937), 169.

Mullett, Charles F., "English Imperial Thinking, 1764–1783," *Pol. Sci. Quar.*, 45 (1930), 548.

Murray, James, *Letters from America, 1773–1780*, Eric Robson, ed. (1951).

Namier, Lewis B., and John Brooke, *Charles Townshend* (1964).

Pownall, Thomas, *Administration of the Colonies* (4th ed., 1768).

Quincy, Josiah, Jr., "London Journal and Correspondence, 1774–1775," Mass. Hist. Soc., *Proc.*, 50 (1917), 433.

Ransom, Roger L., "British Policy and Colonial Growth," *Jour. Econ. Hist.*, 28 (1968), 427.

Rashed, Z. E., *Peace of Paris, 1763* (1951).

Ritcheson, Charles R., "The Preparation of the Stamp Act," *WMQ*, 3 ser., 10 (1953), 543.

Schutz, John A., *Thomas Pownall, British Defender of American Liberty* (1951).

Sheridan, Richard B., "The British Credit Crisis of 1772 and the American Colonies," *Jour. Econ. Hist.*, 20 (1960), 161.

Sosin, Jack M., *Agents and Merchants: British Colonial Policy and Origins of American Revolution, 1763–1775* (1965).

—— "George Grenville's Revenue Measures: Drain on Colonial Specie?" *AHR*, 63 (1958), 918.

—— "Imperial Regulation of Colonial Paper Money, 1764–1773," *Penn. Mag. Hist. Biog.*, 88 (1964), 174.

—— "The Massachusetts Acts of 1774," *Huntington Lib. Quar.*, 26 (1963), 235.

—— *Whitehall and the Wilderness: The Middle West in British Colonial Policy, 1760–1775* (1961).

Spector, Margaret M. M., *American Department of British Government, 1768–1782* (1940).

Stout, Neil R., "Goals and Enforcement of British Colonial Policy," *Am. Neptune*, 27 (1967), 211.

Thomas, Peter D. G., *Sources for Debates of House of the Commons, 1768–1774* (1959).

Thomas, Robert P., "Imperial Policy and Economic Interpretation of the Revolution," *Jour. Econ. Hist.*, 28 (1968), 436.

—— "A Quantitative Approach to the Study of the Effects of British Imperial Policy upon Colonial Welfare: Some Preliminary Findings," *Jour. Econ. Hist.*, 25 (1965), 639.

Ubbelohde, Carl, *Vice-Admiralty Courts and the American Revolution* (1960).

Valentine, Alan, *Lord George Germain* (1962).

Van Alstyne, Richard W., "Parliamentary Supremacy vs. Independence: Notes and Documents," *Huntington Lib. Quar.*, 26 (1963), 201.

Varga, Nicholas, "Robert Charles: New York Agent, 1748–1770," *WMQ*, 3 ser., 18 (1961), 211.

Virtue, George O., *British Land Policy and the American Revolution* (1955).
Warren, Winslow, "Colonial Customs Service in Massachusetts," *Mass. Hist. Soc., Proc.*, 46 (1913), 440.
Watson, Derek H., "The Rockingham Whigs and the Townshend Duties," *Eng. Hist. Rev.*, 84 (1969), 561.
—— "William Baker's Account of Debate on Repeal of the Stamp Act," *WMQ*, 3 ser., 26 (1969), 259.
Wickwire, Franklin B., *British Subministers and Colonial America, 1763–1783* (1966).

See also 10.3 for biographies/writings of:

Franklin, Benjamin, 1706–1790
Pownall, Thomas, 1722–1805

36.7 RESISTANCE AND MOVEMENT FOR INDEPENDENCE

36.7.1 General

Almon, John, comp., *Collection of Tracts on Taxing the British Colonies* (4 vols., 1773).
Andrews, Charles M., *Colonial Background of the American Revolution* (rev. ed., 1931).
Bailyn, Bernard, *The Ideological Origins of the American Revolution* (1967).
Barrow, Thomas C., "The American Revolution as a Colonial War for Independence," *WMQ*, 3 ser., 25 (1968), 452.
Becker, Carl, *Eve of the Revolution* (1911).
Cecil, Robert, "Oligarchy and Mob-Rule in American Revolution," *Hist. Today*, 13 (1963), 197.
Cobbett, William, *Parliamentary History of England*, vol. XVIII (1814).
Dickerson, Oliver M., *Navigation Acts and American Revolution* (1951).
Gipson, Lawrence H., "The American Revolution as Aftermath of Great War for Empire 1754–1763," *Pol. Sci. Quar.*, 65 (1950), 86.
—— *Coming of the Revolution, 1763–1775* (1954).
Jensen, Merrill, *Founding of a Nation: American Revolution* (1968).
Lemisch, Jesse, "Jack Tar in the Streets: Merchant Seamen in the Politics of Revolutionary America," *WMQ*, 3 ser., 25 (1968), 371.
Maier, Pauline, *From Resistance to Revolution, 1765–1776* (1972).
—— "Popular Uprisings and Civil Authority in Eighteenth-Century America," *WMQ*, 3 ser., 27 (1970), 3.
Miller, John C., *Origins of the American Revolution* (rev. ed., 1959).
Morison, Samuel E., ed., *Sources and Documents Illustrating the American Revolution, 1764–1788* (2nd ed., 1951).
Mullett, Charles F., *Colonial Claims to Home Rule 1764–1775* (1927).
Rossiter, Clinton, *Seedtime of the Republic: Origin of American Tradition of Political Liberty* (1953).
Schlesinger, Arthur M., *Colonial Merchants and the American Revolution* (1918).
Varg, Paul A., "Advent of Nationalism, 1758–1776," *Am. Quar.*, 16 (1964), 169.
Wahlke, John C., ed., *The Causes of the American Revolution* (1962).
Wood, Gordon S., "Note on Mobs in the American Revolution," *WMQ*, 3 ser., 23 (1966), 635.

* * * * * * *

Colbourn, H. Trevor, *Lamp of Experience: Whig History and Intellectual Origins of the American Revolution* (1965).
Greene, Jack P., "Flight From Determinism: Review of Recent Literature on the Coming of the American Revolution," *So. Atl. Quar.*, 61 (1962), 235.

See also 10.3 for biographies/writings of:

Adams, John, 1735–1826
Adams, Samuel, 1722–1803
Carroll, Charles, 1737–1832
Franklin, Benjamin, 1706–1790
Hancock, John, 1736–1793
Henry, Patrick, 1736–1799
Jefferson, Thomas, 1743–1826
Johnson, Thomas, 1732–1819
Laurens, Henry, 1724–1792
Lee, Richard Henry, 1732–1794
Livingston, William, 1723–1790
Madison, James, 1750/51–1836
Mason, George, 1725–1792
Mifflin, Thomas, 1744–1800
Otis, James, 1725–1783
Revere, Paul, 1735–1818
Rodney, Caesar, 1728–1784
Rush, Benjamin, 1745–1813
Sherman, Roger, 1721–1793

36.7.2 Ideological Movement

36.7.2.1 Intellectual Contexts

Bailyn, Bernard, "Political Experience and Enlightenment Ideas in Eighteenth-Century America," *AHR*, 67 (1962), 339.

Becker, Carl L., *Heavenly City of Eighteenth-Century Philosophers* (1932).

Dunn, John, *Political Thought of John Locke* (1969).

—— "Politics of Locke in England and America in the Eighteenth Century," in John W. Yolton, ed., *John Locke: Problems and Perspectives* (1969).

Gay, Peter, *The Enlightenment* (2 vols., 1966–1969).

—— *Party of Humanity: Essays in the French Enlightenment* (1963).

Greenleaf, W. H., *Order, Empiricism and Politics: Two Traditions of English Political Thought, 1500–1700* (1964).

Guttridge, George H., *English Whiggism and the American Revolution* (1942).

Heimert, Alan E., *Religion and the American Mind: From the Great Awakening to the Revolution* (1966).

Hudson, Winthrop S., "John Locke—Preparing the Way for Revolution," *Jour. Presby. Hist.*, 42 (1964), 19.

Koch, Adrienne, ed., *The American Enlightenment* (1965).

Koch, Adrienne, "Pragmatic Wisdom and the American Enlightenment," *WMQ*, 3 ser., 18 (1961), 313.

Kramnick, Isaac, *Bolingbroke and His Circle: The Politics of Nostalgia in the Age of Walpole* (1968).

Leder, Lawrence H., "Constitutionalism in American Thought, 1689–1763," *Penn. Hist.*, 36 (1969), 411.

Locke, John, *Two Treatises on Government*, Peter Laslett, ed. (1960).

Lokken, Roy N., "The Concept of Democracy in Colonial Political Thought," *WMQ*, 3 ser., 16 (1959), 568.

Morgan, Edmund S., "American Revolution Considered as an Intellectual Movement," in Arthur M. Schlesinger, Jr., and Morton White, eds., *Paths of American Thought* (1963).

—— "Puritan Ethic and the American Revolution," *WMQ*, 3 ser., 24 (1967), 3.

Robbins, Caroline H., *The Eighteenth-Century Commonwealthman: Studies in the Transmission, Development, and Circumstances of English Liberal Thought from the Restoration of Charles II until the War with the Thirteen Colonies* (1959).

—— "Library of Liberty—Assembled for Harvard College by Thomas Hollis," *Harv. Lib. Bull.*, 5 (1951), 5, 181.

—— "Sidney's Discourses on Government," *WMQ*, 3 ser., 4 (1947), 267.

Smith, Hugh Russell, *Harrington and His Oceana* (1914).
Spurlin, Paul M., *Montesquieu in America 1760–1801* (1940).
—— *Rousseau in America, 1760–1809* (1969).
Windolph, F. L., *Leviathan and Natural Law* (1951).
Wishy, Bernard, "John Locke and Spirit of '76," *Pol. Sci. Quar.*, 73 (1958), 413.

* * * * * * *

Gay, Peter, "Carl Becker's Heavenly City," *Pol. Sci. Quar.*, 72 (1957), 182.

36.7.2.2 Political Thought

Adams, John, *Novanglus and Massachusettensis: Or Political Essays Published in Years 1774 and 1775* (1819).
Adams, Randolph G., *Political Ideas of the American Revolution* (1922; new ed., 1958).
Adams, W. Paul, "Republicanism in Political Rhetoric Before 1776," *Pol. Sci. Quar.*, 85 (1970), 397.
Almon, John, comp., *Collection of Tracts on Taxing the British Colonies* (4 vols., 1773).
Bailyn, Bernard, *The Ideological Origins of American Revolution* (1967).
—— ed., *Pamphlets of American Revolution, 1750–1776* (1965–).
Bailyn, Bernard, "Religion and Revolution: Three Biographical Studies," *Perspectives in Am. Hist.*, 4 (1970), 85. Andrew Eliot, Jonathan Mayhew, and Stephen Johnson.
Baldwin, Alice, *New England Clergy and the Revolution* (1928).
Barrington, William Wildman, 2nd Viscount Barrington, *Barrington-Bernard Correspondence*, Edward Channing and A. C. Coolidge, eds. (1912).
Beloff, Max, ed., *Debate on American Revolution* (2nd ed., 1963).
Benton, William A., *Whig-Loyalism: Political Ideology in the American Revolutionary Era* (1969).
Berger, Carl, *Broadsides and Bayonets: Propaganda of the Revolution* (1961).
"Bowdoin–Temple Papers," *Mass. Hist. Soc., Coll.*, 6 ser., 9 (1897); 7 ser., 6 (1907).
Bumsted, John M., and Charles E. Clark, "New England's Tom Paine: John Allen and the Spirit of Liberty," *WMQ*, 3 ser., 21 (1964), 561.
Champion, Richard, *American Correspondence of a Bristol Merchant, 1766–1776*, G. H. Guttridge, ed. (1934).
Colbourne, H. Trevor, "Jefferson's Use of the Past," *WMQ*, 3 ser., 15 (1958), 56.
—— "John Dickinson," *Penn. Mag. Hist. Biog.*, 83 (1959), 271.
Davidson, Philip, *Propaganda and the American Revolution 1763–83* (1941).
De Berdt, Dennys, "Letters," *Col. Soc. Mass., Publ.*, 13 (1911), 293.
D'Elia, Donald J., "Republican Theology of Benjamin Rush," *Penn. Hist.*, 33 (1966), 187.
Duff, Stella, "The Case Against the King: The *Virginia Gazettes* Indict George III," *WMQ*, 3 ser., 6 (1949), 383.
Ellsworth, John W., "John Adams: American Revolution as a Change of Heart?" *Huntington Lib. Quar.*, 28 (1965), 293.
Fink, Z. S., *Classical Republicans* (1945).
Franklin, Benjamin, *Franklin's Letters to the Press, 1758–1775*, Verner W. Crane, ed. (1950).
Granger, Bruce I., *Political Satire in American Revolution* (1960).
—— "Stamp Act in Satire," *Am. Quar.*, 8 (1956), 368.
Greene, Jack P., ed., "Not to Be Governed or Taxed but by Our Representatives: Four Essays in Opposition to the Stamp Act by Landon Carter," *Va. Mag. Hist. Biog.*, 76 (1968), 259.
Handler, Edward, *America and Europe in the Political Thought of John Adams* (1964).
Handlin, Oscar, and Mary F. Handlin, "James Burgh and American Revolutionary Theory," *Mass. Hist. Soc., Proc.*, 73 (1961), 38.
Hartz, Louis, "American Political Thought and the Revolution," *Am. Pol. Sci. Rev.*, 46 (1952), 321.

Howell, Wilbur S., "The Declaration of Independence and Eighteenth-Century Logic," *WMQ*, 3 ser., 18 (1961), 463.

Humphreys, R. A., "Rule of Law and American Revolution," *Law Quar. Rev.*, 53 (1937), 80.

Jacobson, Norman, "Class and Ideology in the American Revolution," in Seymour M. Lipset, ed., *Class, Status and Power* (1953).

Kaestle, Carl F., "Public Reaction to John Dickinson's 'Farmer's Letters'," Am. Antiq. Soc., *Proc.*, 78 (1968), 323.

Kenyon, Cecelia M., "Republicanism and Radicalism in American Revolution," *WMQ*, 3 ser., 19 (1962), 153.

—— "Where Paine Went Wrong," *Am. Pol. Sci. Rev.*, 45 (1951), 1086.

Kerr, Harry P., "Politics and Religion in Colonial Fast and Thanksgiving Sermons," *Quar. Jour. Speech*, 46 (1960), 372.

Knollenberg, Bernhard, "John Dickinson vs. John Adams, 1774–1776," Am. Philos. Soc., *Proc.*, 107 (1963), 138.

Lovejoy, David S., "Rights Imply Equality: The Case against Admiralty Jurisdiction in America, 1764–1776," *WMQ*, 3 ser., 16 (1959), 459.

Maier, Pauline, "John Wilkes and American Disillusionment with Britain," *WMQ*, 3 ser., 20 (1963), 373.

Metzger, Charles H., "Propaganda in the American Revolution," *Mid-America*, 22 (1940), 243.

Morgan, Edmund S., "Colonial Ideas of Parliamentary Power, 1764–1766," *WMQ*, 3 ser., 5 (1948), 311.

—— ed., "New York Declarations of 1764," *Old South Leaflet*, no. 224 (1948).

—— "Stamp Act Congress Declarations and Petitions," *Old South Leaflet*, no. 223 (1948).

Morris, Richard B., "Legalism *versus* Revolutionary Doctrine," *NEQ*, 4 (1931), 195.

Mullett, Charles F., "Coke and the American Revolution," *Economica*, 12 (1932), 457.

—— *Fundamental Law and the American Revolution* (1933).

Otis, James, *Some Political Writings*, Charles F. Mullett, ed., Univ. of Missouri, *Studies*, 4 (1929), Nos. 3, 4.

Penniman, Howard R., "Thomas Paine—Democrat," *Am. Pol. Sci. Rev.*, 37 (1943), 244.

Ripley, Randall B., "Adams, Burke and Eighteenth-Century Conservatism," *Pol. Sci. Quar.*, 80 (1965), 216.

Rossiter, Clinton, "Richard Bland: The Whig in America," *WMQ*, 3 ser., 10 (1953), 33.

—— *Seedtime of the Republic: Origin of American Tradition of Political Liberty* (1953).

Sanders, Jennings B., "'The Crisis' of London and American Revolutionary Propaganda," *Social Studies*, 58 (1967), 7.

Schlesinger, Arthur M., "Politics, Propaganda, and Philadelphia Press," *Penn. Mag. Hist. Biog.*, 60 (1936), 309.

—— *Prelude to Independence: Newspaper War on Britain, 1764–1776* (1958).

—— "Propaganda and Boston Press," *Col. Soc. Mass., Publ.*, 32 (1937), 396.

Scott, Arthur P., "Constitutional Aspects of the 'Parson's Cause'," *Pol. Sci. Quar.*, 31 (1916), 558.

Shapiro, Darline, "Ethan Allen: Philosopher-Theologian to a Generation of Revolutionaries," *WMQ*, 3 ser., 21 (1964), 236.

Shoemaker, Robert W., "'Democracy' and 'Republic' as Understood in Late Eighteenth-Century America," *Am. Speech*, 41 (1966), 83.

Stoudt, John J., "German Press in Pennsylvania and the American Revolution," *Penn. Mag. Hist. Biog.*, 59 (1935), 74.

Stourzh, Gerald, "Reason and Power in Benjamin Franklin's Political Thought," *Am. Pol. Sci. Rev.*, 47 (1953), 1092.

Tate, Thad, "Social Contract in America, 1774–1787," *WMQ*, 3 ser., 22 (1965), 375.

Varg, Paul A., "The Advent of Nationalism, 1758–1776," *Am. Quar.*, 16 (1964), 169.

Walett, Francis G., "James Bowdoin, Patriot Propagandist," *NEQ*, 23 (1950), 320.
Wright, Benjamin F., *American Interpretations of Natural Law* (1931).

* * * * * * *

Adams, Thomas R., ed., *American Independence: Bibliographical Study of American Political Pamphlets Printed between 1764 and 1776* (1965).
Shalhope, Robert E., "Toward a Republican Synthesis: Emergence of an Understanding of Republicanism in American Historiography," *WMQ*, 3 ser., 29 (1972), 49.
Wood, Gordon S., "Rhetoric and Reality in the American Revolution," *WMQ*, 3 ser., 23 (1966), 3.

See also 10.3 for biographies/writings of:

Adams, John, 1735–1826
Adams, Samuel, 1722–1803
Backus, Isaac, 1724–1806
Dickinson, John, 1732–1808
Franklin, Benjamin, 1706–1790
Hamilton, Alexander, 1755–1804
Hopkins, Stephen, 1707–1785
Jefferson, Thomas, 1743–1826
Paine, Thomas, 1737–1809
Quincy, Josiah, Jr., 1744–1775
Warren, Mercy, 1728–1814
Wilson, James, 1742–1798

36.7.3 Growth of Political Resistance

36.7.3.1 Developing Tensions and Stamp Act Controversy, 1760–1766

Alvord, Clarence W., and Clarence E. Carter, eds., *Critical Period, 1763–1765* (1915).
Chroust, Anton-Hermann, "Lawyers of New Jersey and the Stamp Act," *Am. Jour. Legal Hist.*, 6 (1962), 286.
Crane, Verner W., "Franklin and the Stamp Act," Col. Soc. Mass., *Publ.*, 32 (1937), 56.
D'Innocenzo, Michael, and John J. Turner, Jr., "New York Newspapers in the Stamp Act Crisis, 1764–1766," *N.Y. Hist. Soc. Quar.*, 51 (1967), 215.
Ellefson, C. Ashley, "Stamp Act in Georgia," *Ga. Hist. Quar.*, 46 (1962), 1.
Engelman, F. L., "Cadwallader Colden and the New York Stamp Riots," *WMQ*, 3 ser., 10 (1953), 560.
Ernst, Joseph A., "The Currency Act Repeal Movement, 1764–1767," *WMQ*, 3 ser., 25 (1968), 177.
Giddens, Paul H., "Maryland and the Stamp Act Controversy," *Md. Hist. Mag.*, 27 (1932), 79.
Greene, Jack P., and Richard M. Jellison, "The Currency Act of 1764," *WMQ*, 3 ser., 18 (1961), 485.
Haywood, C. Robert, "North Carolina Opponents of the Stamp Act," *No. Car. Hist. Rev.*, 29 (1952), 317.
Johnson, Herbert A., and David Syrett, " 'New York' Affair, 1763–1767," *WMQ*, 3 ser., 25 (1968), 432.
Kerr, Wilfred B., "The Stamp Act and the Floridas, 1765–1766," *MVHR*, 21 (1935), 463.
———. "The Stamp Act in Nova Scotia," *NEQ*, 6 (1933), 552.
Knollenberg, Bernhard, *Origin of the American Revolution: 1759–1766* (1960).
Lee, E. Lawrence, "Resistance to the Stamp Act in Lower Cape Fear," *No. Car. Hist. Rev.*, 43 (1966), 186.
Lemisch, L. Jesse, "New York's Petitions and Resolves of December 1765," *N.Y. Hist. Soc. Quar.*, 49 (1965), 313.

McAnear, Beverly, "Albany Stamp Act Riots," *WMQ*, 3 ser., 4 (1947), 486.

Morgan, Edmund S., ed., *Prologue: Sources on Stamp Act Crisis, 1764–1766* (1959).

Morgan, Edmund S. and Helen M., *Stamp Act Crisis* (rev. ed., 1963).

Newcomb, Benjamin H., "The Stamp Act and Pennsylvania Politics," *WMQ*, 3 ser., 23 (1966), 257.

Reichenbach, Karl H., "Connecticut Clergy and the Stamp Act," in Arthur E. Boak, ed., *University of Michigan Historical Essays* (1937).

Schlesinger, Arthur M., "Colonial Newspapers and the Stamp Act," *NEQ*, 8 (1935), 63.

Smith, Glen C., " 'Parsons Cause'," *Tyler's Quar.*, 21 (1940), 140.

Stout, Neil R., "Captain Kennedy and the Stamp Act," *N.Y. Hist.*, 45 (1964), 44.

Warren, Winslow, "Colonial Customs Service in Massachusetts," Mass. Hist. Soc., *Proc.*, 46 (1913), 440.

Waters, John J., and John A. Schutz, "Writs of Assistance and Rivalry between the Otis and Hutchinson Families," *WMQ*, 3 ser., 24 (1967), 543.

Young, Henry J., "Agrarian Reactions to the Stamp Act in Pennsylvania," *Penn. Hist.*, 34 (1967), 25.

See also 10.3 for biographies/writings of:

Dulany Family
Ingersoll, Jared, 1722–1781
Jay, John, 1745–1829
Johnson, Thomas, 1732–1819
Morris, Robert, 1734–1806
Otis, James, 1725–1783
Washington, George, 1732–1799

36.7.3.2 Worsening Crisis, 1767–1774

Almon, John, comp., *Collection of Tracts on Taxing the British Colonies* (4 vols., 1773).

Alvord, Clarence W., and Clarence E. Carter, eds., *Trade and Politics, 1767–1769* (1921).

Andrews, Charles M., "Boston Merchants and Non-Importation," Col. Soc. Mass., *Publ.*, 19 (1917), 159.

Bartlett, John R., *History of the Destruction of His Britannic Majesty's Schooner Gaspee in Naragansett Bay* (1861).

Brown, Richard D., *Revolutionary Politics in Massachusetts: The Boston Committee of Correspondence and the Towns, 1772–1774* (1970).

Bryant, Samuel W., ed., "HMS Gaspee": Courtmartial," *R.I. Hist.*, 25 (1966), 65.

Burnett, Edmund C., ed., *Letters of Members of the Continental Congress* (8 vols., 1921–1936).

Chaffin, Robert J., "Townshend Acts, 1767," *WMQ*, 3 ser., 27 (1970), 90.

Champagne, Roger J., "New York and the Intolerable Acts, 1774," *N.Y. Hist. Soc. Quar.*, 45 (1961), 195.

Dickerson, Oliver M., comp., *Boston under Military Rule* (1936).

Dickerson, Oliver M., "British Control of American Newspapers on the Eve of the Revolution," *NEQ*, 24 (1951), 453.

———— "Commissioners of Customs and the 'Boston Massacre'," *NEQ*, 27 (1954), 307.

Drake, Francis, S., ed., *Tea Leaves: Documents Relating to Shipment of Tea to American Colonies in 1773* (1884).

Gerlach, Don R., "Note on the Quartering Act of 1774," *NEQ*, 39 (1966), 80.

Henderson, Patrick, "Norfolk Riots, 1768–1769," *Va. Mag. Hist. Biog.*, 73 (1965), 413.

King, Joseph E., "The Real Quebec Act," *Mid-America*, 34 (1952), 14.

Knollenberg, Bernhard, "Did Samuel Adams Provoke the Boston Tea Party?" Am. Antiq. Soc., *Proc.*, 70 (1960), 493.

Labaree, Benjamin W., *The Boston Tea Party* (1964).

Leslie, William R., "Gaspee Affair: Constitutional Significance," *MVHR*, 39 (1952), 233.

Massachusetts (Colony) General Court, House of Representatives, *Glorious Ninety-Two: Selections from Journals of the House, Massachusetts-Bay, 1767–1768* (1949).

Morris, Richard B., "Insurrection in Massachusetts," in Daniel Aaron, ed., *America in Crisis* (1952).

Schlesinger, Arthur M., "Political Mobs and the American Revolution, 1765–1776," Am. Philos. Soc., *Proc.*, 99 (1955), 244.

Smith, Glenn C., "Era of Non-Importation Associations, 1768–1773," *WMQ*, 2 ser., 20 (1940), 84.

Sosin, Jack M., "Massachusetts Acts of 1774," *Huntington Lib. Quar.*, 26 (1962–1963), 235.

Staples, William R., comp., *Documentary History of Destruction of the Gaspee* (1845).

Upton, Leslie F. S., ed., "Proceedings of Ye Body Respecting the Tea," *WMQ*, 3 ser., 22 (1965), 287.

Varga, Nicholas, "New York Restraining Act," *N.Y. Hist.*, 37 (1956), 233.

Watson, Derek H., ed., "Joseph Harrison and the *Liberty* Incident," *WMQ*, 3 ser., 20 (1963), 585.

Wuslin, Eugene, "Political Consequences of the Burning of the *Gaspee*," *R.I. Hist.*, 3 (1944), 1, 55.

Zobel, Hiller B., *The Boston Massacre* (1970).

36.7.3.3 Intercolonial Cooperation and Continental Congress to 1776

Becker, Carl L., "Election of Delegates from New York to the Second Continental Congress," *AHR*, 9 (1903), 66.

Burnett, Edmund C., *The Continental Congress* (1941).

——— ed., *Letters of Members of Continental Congress*, vol. I (1921).

Collins, E. D., "Committees of Correspondence," Am. Hist. Assoc., *Report* (1901), 1.

Garver, Frank H., "Attendance at the First Continental Congress," Am. Hist. Assoc. (Pacific Coast Branch), *Proc.*, 25 (1929), 21.

Knollenberg, Bernhard, "John Dickinson vs. John Adams, 1774–1776," Am. Philos. Soc., *Proc.*, 107 (1963), 138.

Mullett, Charles F., "Imperial Ideas at the First Continental Congress," *Southw. Soc. Sci. Quar.*, 12 (1931), 238.

Ryan, Frank W., "The Role of South Carolina in the First Continental Congress," *So. Car. Hist. Mag.*, 60 (1959), 147.

Staples, William R., *Rhode Island and the Continental Congress, 1765–1790* (1870).

U.S. Continental Congress, *Journals 1774–1789*, Worthington C. Ford et al., eds. (34 vols. 1904–1937).

36.7.3.4 Attempts at Reconciliation, 1767–1774

Boyd, Julian P., *Anglo-American Union: Joseph Galloway's Plans* (1941).

Brown, William A., *Empire or Independence: A Study in Failure of Reconciliation, 1774–1783* (1941).

Calhoon, Robert M., "Joseph Galloway's Concept of His Role, 1774–1775," *Penn. Hist.*, 35 (1968), 356.

Duff, Stella F., "Case against the King," *WMQ*, 3 ser., 6 (1949), 383.

Wickersham, Cornelius W., and Gilbert H. Montague, eds., *Olive Branch: Petition to George III, 1775, and Letters of Envoys* (1954).

Wolf, Edwin, II, "Authorship of 1774 Address to the King Restudied," *WMQ*, 3 ser., 22 (1965), 189.

See also 10.3 for biographies/writings of:

Dickinson, John, 1732–1808

36.7.3.5 To the Declaration of Independence, 1775–1776

Barker, John, *The British in Boston: Diary from November 15, 1774 to May 31, 1776* (1924).

Becker, Carl, *Declaration of Independence* (1922).

Boyd, Julian P., *Anglo-American Union* (1941).

——— "Authorship of the Declaration of Causes," *Penn. Mag. Hist. Biog.*, 74 (1950), 51.

——— *Declaration of Independence, Evolution of Text* (1945).

Donovan, Frank R., *Mr. Jefferson's Declaration* (1968).

Dumbauld, Edward, *Declaration of Independence and What It Means Today* (1950).

Evelyn, W. Glanville, *Memoir and Letters . . . from North America, 1774–1776*, G. D. Scull, ed. (1879).

Gage, Thomas, *Correspondence*, C. E. Carter, ed. (2 vols., 1931–1933).

Hawke, David, *Transaction of Free Men: Declaration of Independence* (1964).

Head, John M., *Time to Rend: Essay on Decision for American Independence* (1968).

Howell, Wilbur S., "Declaration of Independence and Eighteenth-Century Logic," *WMQ*, 3 ser., 18 (1961), 463.

Hoyt, William H., *Mecklenburg Declaration* (1907).

Hunt, Gaillard, "Cardinal Bellarmine and the Virginia Bill of Rights," *Cath. Hist. Rev.*, 3 (1917), 276.

Malone, Dumas, *Story of Declaration of Independence* (1954).

Meigs, Cornelia L., *Violent Men: Human Relations in the First American Congress* (1949).

Morison, Samuel E., "Virginia Resolutions of May 15, 1776," *WMQ*, 3 ser., 8 (1951), 483.

Salley, Alexander S., Jr., "Mecklenburg Declaration," *AHR*, 13 (1908), 16.

Schaff, David S., "Bellarmine-Jefferson Legend," Am. Soc. Church Hist., *Papers*, 2 ser., 8 (1928), 239.

Westmoreland County, Virginia Committee of Safety, *Committees of Safety of Westmoreland and Fincastle*, Richard B. Harwell, ed. (1956).

Willard, M. W., ed., *Letters on the American Revolution, 1774–76* (1925). In English newspapers.

36.8 WAR FOR INDEPENDENCE, MILITARY ASPECTS

36.8.1 General

Alden, John R., *American Revolution, 1775–1783* (1954).

——— *History of the American Revolution* (1969).

Almon, John, comp., *Collection of Papers Relative to the Dispute between Great Britain and America, 1764–1775* (1777).

——— *Remembrancer* (17 vols., 1775–1784).

Augur, Helen, *Secret War of Independence* (1956).

Bakeless, John C., *Turncoats, Traitors and Heroes* (1959).

Blumenthal, Walter H., *Women Camp Followers of the Revolution* (1952).

Boatner, Mark M., III, *Encyclopedia of American Revolution* (1966).

Brown, Wallace, "Negroes and American Revolution," *Hist. Today,* 14 (1964), 556.

Carrington, H. B., *Battles of American Revolution* (1876).

Clark, William B., ed., *Naval Documents of American Revolution* (4 vols., 1964–1969).

Clinton, Henry, *American Rebellion: Narrative of Campaigns, 1775–1782,* William B. Willcox, ed. (1954).

Dearborn, Henry, *Revolutionary War Journals*, L. A. Brown and Howard H. Peckham, eds. (1939).

Greene, Francis V., *Revolutionary War* (1911).

Higginbotham, Don, *The War of American Independence* (1971).

Lancaster, Bruce, *Lexington to Liberty: American Revolution* (1955).

Lossing, Benson J., *Pictorial Field-Book of the Revolution* (2 vols., 1851).

Mackesy, Piers G., *The War for America, 1775–1783* (1964).
Macmillan, M. B., *War Governors in the American Revolution* (1943).
Murray, James, *Letters from America, 1773–80*, Eric Robson, ed. (1951).
de Noailles, A. M. R. A., *Marins et soldats français en Amérique* (1903).
Peckham, Howard H., *War for Independence: Military History* (1958).
Quarles, Benjamin, *The Negro in the American Revolution* (1961).
Rankin, Hugh F., *The American Revolution* (1964).
Richmond, Herbert, *Statesmen and Sea Power* (1946).
Robertson, Eileen A., *Spanish Town Papers: Sidelights on the American War of Independence* (1959).
Rochambeau, J. B. D. de V., Comte de, *Mémoires*, vol. I (1809).
Scheer, George F., and Hugh F. Rankin, *Rebels and Redcoats* (1957).
Sosin, Jack M., "Use of Indians in the War of the American Revolution," *Can. Hist. Rev.*, 46 (1965), 101.
Uhlendorf, Bernhard A., *Revolution in America* (1957).
Wallace, Willard M., *Appeal to Arms: A Military History of the Revolution* (1951).
Ward, Christopher, *War of the Revolution*, J. R. Alden, ed. (2 vols., 1952).

*   *   *   *   *   *   *

Great Britain, Historical Manuscripts Commission, *Calendar of American Manuscripts in the Royal Institute* (4 vols., 1904–1909).
Higginbotham, Don, "Military History of the American Revolution," *AHR*, 70 (1964), 18.
Newmeyer, R. Kent, "Charles Stedman's 'History of the American War'," *AHR*, 63 (1958), 924.

36.8.2 American Army

Alexander, Arthur J., "Desertion and Its Punishment in Virginia," *WMQ*, 3 ser., 3 (1946), 383.
——— "Pennsylvania's Militia," *Penn. Mag. Hist. Biog.*, 69 (1945), 15.
Anderson, John R., "Militia Law in Colonial New Jersey: 1775–1776," N.J. Hist. Soc., *Proc.*, 76 (1958), 280.
Applegate, Howard L., "Medical Administrators of the American Army," *Mil. Affairs*, 25 (1961), 1.
Baurmeister, Carl L., *Letters and Journals, 1776–1784*, Bernhard A. Uhlendorf, trans. (1957).
Bernath, Stuart L., "George Washington and Genesis of American Military Discipline," *Mid-America*, 49 (1967), 83.
Billias, George A., ed., *George Washington's Generals* (1964).
Boller, Paul F., "Washington and Civilian Supremacy," *Southw. Rev.*, 39 (1954), 9.
Bolton, Charles K., *Private Soldier under Washington* (1902).
Bowman, Allen, *Morale of American Revolutionary Army* (1943).
Bradford, S. Sydney, "Hunger Menaces the Revolution," *Md. Hist. Mag.*, 61 (1966), 1.
Champagne, Roger J., "Military Association of the Sons of Liberty," *N.Y. Hist. Soc. Quar.*, 41 (1957), 338.
Dillin, J. G. W., *Kentucky Rifle* (1924).
Echeverria, Durand, and Orville T. Murphy, "The American Revolutionary Army: A French Estimate in 1777," *Mil. Affairs*, 27 (1963), 1, 153.
Gottschalk, Louis, *LaFayette and the Close of the American Revolution* (1942).
——— *LaFayette between the American and the French Revolution* (1950).
——— *LaFayette Comes to America* (1935).
——— *LaFayette Joins the American Army* (1937).
Greene, Lorenzo, "The Black Regiment of Rhode Island," *Jour. Negro Hist.*, 37 (1952), 142.
Haiman, Miecislaus, *Kosciuszko in the American Revolution* (1943).
——— *Kosciuszko, Leader and Exile* (1946).
Hatch, Louis C., *Administration of the American Revolutionary Army* (1904).
Kaplan, Sidney, "Rank and Status among Massachusetts Continental Officers," *AHR*, 56 (1951), 318.

LaFayette, Marquis de, and Thomas Jefferson, *Letters*, Gilbert Chinard, ed.(1929).
LaFayette, Marquis de, *Letters . . . to Washington, 1777–1799*, Louis Gottschalk, ed. (1944).
—— *Mémoires* (6 vols., 1837–1838).
LaFuye, Maurice de, and Emile Babeau, *Apostle of Liberty: LaFayette*, Edward Huams, trans. (1956).
Lutz, Paul V., "How North Carolina Provided for Her Troops," *No. Car. Hist. Rev.*, 42 (1965), 315.
—— "Land Grants for Service in the Revolution," *N.Y. Hist. Soc. Quar.*, 48 (1964), 221.
Luzader, John F., "The Arnold-Gates Controversy," *W. Va. Hist.*, 27 (1966), 75.
Martin, Joseph P., *Private Yankee Doodle*, George E. Scheer, ed. (1962).
Montross, Lynn, *Rag, Tag and Bobtail: Continental Army, 1775–1783* (1952).
Nell, William C., *Colored Patriots of the Revolution* (1855).
Neumann, George C., *History of Weapons of the American Revolution* (1967).
O'Callaghan, Jerry, "The War Veteran and the Public Lands," *Agric. Hist.*, 28 (1954), 163.
Palmer, John M., *General von Steuben* (1937).
Peterson, Harold L., *Book of the Continental Soldier* (1968).
Pugh, Robert C., "The Revolutionary Militia in the Southern Campaign," *WMQ*, 3 ser., 14 (1957), 154.
Reichmann, Felix, "Pennsylvania Rifle," *Penn. Mag. Hist. Biog.*, 69 (1945), 3.
Robson, Eric, "Expedition to the Southern Colonies, 1775–1776," *Eng. Hist. Rev.*, 66 (1951), 535.
Stoesen, Alexander R., "The British Occupation of Charleston, 1780–1782," *So. Car. Hist. Mag.*, 63 (1962), 71.
Van Doren, Carl, *Mutiny in January* (1943).
—— *Secret History of American Revolution* (1941).
Vivian, Jean H., "Military Land Bounties," *Md. Hist. Mag.*, 61 (1966), 231.
Von Closen, Baron Ludwig, *Revolutionary Journal, 1780–1783*, Evelyn M. Acomb, trans. and ed. (1958).
Wade, Herbert T., and Robert A. Lively, *This Glorious Cause: Two Company Officers in Washington's Army* (1958).
Wells, Thomas L., "An Inquiry into the Resignation of Quartermaster General Nathanael Greene in 1780," *R.I. Hist.*, 24 (1965), 41.
Whitlock, Brand, *LaFayette* (2 vols., 1929).
Whitridge, Arnold, *Rochambeau* (1965).
Wright, J. W., "Corps of Light Infantry," *AHR*, 31 (1926), 454.
—— "Notes on the Continental Army," *WMQ*, 2 ser., 11 (1931), 81, 185.
Wrong, George M., *Washington and Comrade at Arms* (1921).
Zucker, Adolf Eduard, *General de Kalb: LaFayette's Mentor* (1966).

*   *   *   *   *   *   *

U.S. National Archives, *Preliminary Inventory of War Department Collection of Revolutionary War Records*, Mabel E. Deutrich, comp. (1962).

See also 10.3 for biographies/writings of:

Lee, Charles, 1731–1782
Lee, Henry "Light-Horse Harry," 1756–1818
Marion, Francis, 1732–1795
Mifflin, Thomas, 1744–1800
Morgan, Daniel, 1736–1802
Morris, Robert, 1734–1806
Muhlenberg, John Peter, 1746–1807
Pickens, Andrew, 1739–1817
Pickering, Timothy, 1745–1829
Pollock, Oliver, 1737–1823
Reed, Joseph, 1741–1785
Schuyler, Philip J., 1733–1804
Sullivan, John, 1740–1795
Sumter, Thomas, 1734–1832
Tallmadge, Benjamin, 1754–1835
von Steuben, Frederick William, 1730–1794
Wayne, Anthony, 1745–1796
Wilkinson, James, 1757–1825
Willett, Marinus, 1740–1830

36.8.3 American and French Navies

Allen, Gardner W., "Captain Hector McNeill," Mass. Hist. Soc., *Proc.*, 55 (1922), 46.
———— *Naval History of the American Revolution* (2 vols., 1913).
Antier, Jean Jacques, *L'Amiral de Grasse* (1965).
Barnes, John S., ed., *Logs of Serapis–Alliance–Ariel under Jones' Command* (1911).
Clark, William B., *Ben Franklin's Privateers (1956).*
———— *George Washington's Navy: In New England Waters* (1960).
Corbett, Julien S., "Signals and Instructions, 1776–1794," Navy Rec. Soc., *Publ.*, 35 (1908).
Davies, W. E., "Privateering around Long Island during the Revolution," *N.Y. Hist.*, 20 (1939), 283.
Howe, O. T., "Beverly Privateers," Col. Soc. Mass., *Publ.*, 24 (1922), 318.
Kaminkow, Marion J. and Jack, comps., *Mariners of the American Revolution* (1967).
Knox, Dudley W., *Naval Genius of Washington* (1932).
Lewis, Charles L., *Admiral de Grasse and American Independence* (1945).
Maclay, Edgar S., *History of American Privateers* (1899).
Morgan, William J., *Captains to Northward: New England Captains in the Continental Navy* (1959).
Morse, S. G., "State or Continental Privateers?" *AHR*, 52 (1947), 68.
———— "Yankee Privateersman of 1776," *NEQ*, 17 (1944), 71.
Paullin, Charles O., *Navy of the American Revolution* (1906).
———— ed., *Out-Letters of Continental Marine Committee and Board of Admiralty* (2 vols., 1914).
Phillips, James D., "Salem Revolutionary Privateers Condemned at Jamaica," Essex Inst., *Hist. Coll.*, 76 (1940), 46.
Stewart, R. H., *Virginia's Navy* (1933).
Tornquist, K. J., *Naval Campaigns of Count de Grasse* (1787); Amandus Johnson, trans. (1942).

*   *   *   *   *   *   *

Allen, Gardner W., *Naval History* (2 vols., 1913).
"H. H.," "Naval History, Admiral Mahan and his Successors," *Military Historian and Economist*, 3 (1918), 7.
U.S. Library of Congress, Division of Manuscripts, *Naval Records of the American Revolution*, Charles H. Lincoln, comp. (1906).
U.S. Naval History Division, *Naval Documents of the American Revolution*, William B. Clark, ed. (4 vols., 1964–1969).

See also 10.3 for biographies/writings of:

Dobbs, Arthur, 1689–1765
Thorndike, Israel, 1755–1832

36.8.4 British Army

Adams, Randolph G., *British Headquarters Maps and Sketches: A Descriptive List* (1928).
Alden, John R., *General Gage in America* (1948).
Alexander, John K., "Case Study of British Prisoner of War Policy," Essex Inst., *Hist. Coll.*, 103 (1967), 365.
Amerman, Richard H., "Treatment of American Prisoners," N.J. Hist. Soc., *Proc.*, new ser., 78 (1960), 257.
Anderson, Troyer S., *Command of Howe Brothers* (1936).
Atkinson, C. T., "British Forces in North America, 1774–1781," *Jour. Soc. Army Hist. Research*, 16 (1937), 3; 19 (1940), 163.
Billias, George A., ed., *George Washington's Opponents: British Generals and Admirals* (1969).
Bowie, Lucy L., "German Prisoners," *Md. Hist. Mag.*, 11 (1945), 185.
Burt, Alfred L., "The Quarrel between Germain and Carleton," *Can. Hist. Rev.*, 11 (1930), 202.
Curtis, Edward E., *Organization of the British Army in the American Revolution* (1936).
Dabney, William M., *After Saratoga: The Convention Army* (1954).
Eelking, Max von, *German Allied Troops in the War of Independence*, J. G. Rosengarten, trans. (1893).
Flexner, James T., *Traitor and Spy: Arnold and André* (1953).
Fortescue, John W., *History of the British Army*, vol. III (1902).
Gage, Thomas, *Correspondence*, C. E. Carter, ed. (2 vols., 1931–1933).
Gradish, Stephen F., "German Mercenaries," *Can. Jour. Hist.*, 4 (1969), 23.
Gruber, Ira D., "Lord Howe and Lord Germain: British Politics and American Independence," *WMQ*, 3 ser., 22 (1965), 225.
Guttridge, George H., "Lord George Germain in Office," *AHR*, 33 (1928), 23.
Lowell, Edward J., *Hessians in Revolution* (1884).
Mackesy, Piers G., "British Strategy in the War of American Independence," *Yale Rev.*, 52 (1963), 539.
Mowat, Charles L., "Southern Brigade: British Military in America, 1763–1775," *JSH*, 10 (1944), 59.
Pettengill, Ray W., ed., *Letters from America of Brunswick, Hessian and Waldeck Officers* (1924).
Quarles, Benjamin, "Lord Dunmore as Liberator," *WMQ*, 3 ser., 15 (1958), 494.
Shy, John, "Quartering His Majesty's Forces in New Jersey," N.J. Hist. Soc., *Proc.*, 78 (1960), 82.
—— *Toward Lexington: British Army in the Coming of American Revolution* (1965).
Simcoe, John G., *Queen's Rangers* (1787).
Usher, Roland G., "Royal Navy Impressment," *MVHR*, 37 (1951), 673.
von Riedesel, F. C. L., Baroness, *Letters and Memoirs* (1827).
Willcox, William B., "British Planning before Saratoga," *Jour. Brit. Studies*, 2 (1962), 56.
—— "British Strategy in America, 1778," *Jour. Mod. Hist.*, 19 (1947), 97.
—— *Portrait of a General: Sir Henry Clinton in the War of Independence* (1964).
Wyatt, Frederick, and William B. Willcox, "Sir Henry Clinton," *WMQ*, 3 ser., 16 (1959), 3.

36.8.5 British Navy

Billias, George A., ed., *George Washington's Opponents: British Generals and Admirals* (1969).

Clinton, Henry, *American Rebellion: Narrative of Campaigns, 1775–1782*, William B. Willcox, ed. (1954).
Clowes, William L., *Royal Navy*, vol. III (1898).
James, William M., *British Navy in Adversity: A Study of the War of Independence* (1926).
Stout, Neil R., "Manning the Royal Navy in North America, 1763–1775," *Am. Neptune*, 23 (1963), 174.
Usher, R. G., "Royal Navy Impressment during the American Revolution," *MVHR*, 37 (1951), 673.

* * * * * * *

Manwaring, G. E., *Bibliography of British Naval History* (1929).

36.8.6 From Lexington through 1778

Anburey, Thomas, *With Burgoyne from Quebec: Battle of Saratoga* (1789); Sydney W. Jackman, ed. (1964).
Baurmeister, Carl, *Letters during the Philadelphia Campaign*, Bernhard A. Uhlendorf and Edna Vosper, eds. (1937).
Bill, A. H., *Campaign of Princeton* (1948).
—— *Valley Forge* (1952).
Bird, Harrison, *Attack on Quebec: American Invasion of Canada, 1775* (1968).
—— *March to Saratoga: General Burgoyne* (1963).
Bliven, Bruce, Jr., *Battle for Manhattan* (1956).
Butterfield, Lyman H., "Psychological Warfare in 1776," Am. Philos. Soc., *Proc.*, 94 (1950), 233.
Chidsey, Donald B., *Valley Forge* (1959).
Clark, Jane, "Responsibility for Failure of the Burgoyne Campaign," *AHR*, 35 (1930), 542.
Coburn, F. W., *Battle of April 19, 1775* (1922).
Cohen, Joel A., "Lexington and Concord: Rhode Island Reacts," *R.I. Hist.*, 26 (1967), 97.
Fleming, Thomas J., *Now We Are Enemies: Bunker Hill* (1960).
French, Allen, *The Day of Lexington and Concord* (1925).
—— *First Year of the American Revolution* (1934).
Frothingham, Richard, *Siege of Boston* (1849).
Huston, James A., "The Logistics of Arnold's March to Quebec," *Mil. Affairs*, 32 (1968), 110.
Johnston, Henry P., "Campaign of 1776 around New York and Brooklyn," L.I. Hist. Soc., *Memoirs*, 3 (1878).
Ketchum, Richard M., *Battle for Bunker Hill* (1962).
Leiby, Adrian C., *Revolutionary War in Hackensack Valley: Jersey Dutch and Neutral Ground* (1962).
Leonard, E. A., "Paper as Critical Commodity," *Penn. Mag. Hist. Biog.*, 74 (1950), 488.
Merritt, Elizabeth, "Lexington Alarm, Messages Sent to Southward," *Md.Hist. Mag.*, 41 (1946), 89.
Moomaw, William H., "Denouement of Howe's Campaign," *Eng. Hist. Rev.*, 79 (1964), 498.
Murdock, Harold, *The 19th of April 1775* (1923).
Naisawald, L. V. L., "Howe's Activities in South Carolina and Georgia," *Ga. Hist. Quar.*, 35 (1951), 23.
Nickerson, Hoffman, *Turning Point of the Revolution* (1928).
Robson, Eric, "Expedition to the Southern Colonies, 1775–1776," *Eng. Hist. Rev.*, 66 (1951), 535.
Shipton, Nathaniel N., "General Joseph Palmer: Scapegoat for the Rhode Island Fiasco of October, 1777," *NEQ*, 39 (1966), 498.
Smith, Justin H., *Arnold's March to Quebec* (1903).
—— *Struggle for the Fourteenth Colony* (2 vols., 1907).
Stephenson, O. W., "Supply of Gunpowder in 1776," *AHR*, 30 (1925), 271.
Stoudt, John J., *Ordeal at Valley Forge* (1963).

Stryker, W. S., *Battle of Monmouth* (1927).
—— *Trenton and Princeton* (1898).
Tourtellot, Arthur B., *William Diamond's Drum, Beginning of the American Revolution* (1959).
Tyler, J. E., "Account of Lexington in Rockingham Mss. at Sheffield," *WMQ*, 3 ser., 10 (1953), 99.

*   *   *   *   *   *   *

Tourtellot, Arthur B., *Bibliography of Battles of Concord and Lexington* (1959).

See also 10.3 for biographies/writings of:

Allen, Ethan, 1737/38–1789
Arnold, Benedict, 1741–1801
Gates, Horatio, 1728/29–1806
Glover, John, 1732–1797
Hale, Nathan, fl. 1775–1776
Schuyler, Philip J., 1733–1804

36.8.7 From French Alliance through Yorktown

Adams, Randolph G., "View of Cornwallis' Surrender," *AHR*, 37 (1932), 25.
Britt, Albert S., Jr., "Battle of Cowpens," *Mil. Rev.*, 30 (1950), 47.
Callender, Geoffrey A. R., "With Grand Fleet in 1780," *Mariner's Mirror*, 9 (1923), 258, 290.
Cometti, Elizabeth, "Depredations in Virginia," in Darrett B. Rutman, ed., *The Old Dominion: Essays for Thomas Perkins Abernethy* (1964).
Davis, Burke, *The Campaign that Won America: Yorktown* (1970).
—— *Cowpens-Guilford Courthouse Campaign* (1962).
Fleming, Thomas J., *Beat the Last Drum: Yorktown, 1781* (1963).
Haarman, Albert W., "Spanish Conquest of British West Florida," *Fla. Hist. Quar.*, 39 (1960), 107.
Hassler, Warren W., "Washington and the Revolution's Crucial Campaign," *West. Penn. Hist. Mag.*, 48 (1965), 249.
Keim, DeB. R., *Rochambeau* (1907).
Kyte, George W., "Appraisal of General Greene's Strategy in the Carolinas," *No. Car. Hist. Rev.*, 31 (1954), 336.
—— "British Invasion of South Carolina in 1780," *Historian*, 14 (1952), 149.
—— "General Greene's Plans for the Capture of Charleston," *So. Car. Hist. Mag.*, 62 (1961), 96.
Landers, H. F., *Virginia Campaign and the Blockade and Siege of Yorktown* (1931).
Larrabee, Harold A., "Claude-Anne, Marquis de Saint-Simon," *Journal des Américanistes*, 24 (1932), 245.
—— *Decision at the Chesapeake* (1964).
Lawrence, Alexander A., "General Robert Howe and the Capture of Savannah," *Ga. Hist. Quar.*, 36 (1952), 303.
Lee, Henry, *Campaign of 1781 in the Carolinas* (1824).
Lee, Henry, *Memoirs of War in the Southern Department*, R. E. Lee, ed. (1869).
Moomaw, William, "The British Leave Colonial Virginia," *Va. Mag. Hist. Biog.*, 66 (1958), 147.
Oswald, Richard, *Memorandum on the Folly of Invading Virginia* (1781); W. Stitt Robinson, Jr., ed. (1953).
Rankin, Hugh F., "Cowpens: Prelude to Yorktown," *No. Car. Hist. Rev.*, 31 (1954), 336.
Smith, Paul H., "Sir Guy Carleton, Peace Negotiations, and the Evacuation of New York," *Can. Hist. Rev.*, 50 (1969), 245.
Tarleton, Banastre, *History of the Campaigns of 1780 and 1781 in the Southern Provinces of North America* (1787).
Thayer, Theodore G., "The War in New Jersey," N.J. Hist. Soc., *Proc.*, 71 (1953), 83.
Thwaites, Reuben G., *How George Rogers Clark Won the Northwest* (1903).

Treacy, M. F., *Prelude to Yorktown: Nathanael Greene, 1780–1781* (1963).
Uhlendorf, Bernhard A., ed. and trans., *Siege of Charleston: Diaries and Letters of Hessian Officers* (1938).
Willcox, William B., "The Road to Yorktown," *AHR*, 52 (1946), 1.

36.8.8 Naval Engagements

Ainslie, Thomas, *Journal*, Sheldon S. Cohen, ed. (1969).
Bass, Robert D., *Green Dragoon: Banastre Tarleton and Mary Robinson* (1957).
Bradford, Gershom, "Nelson in Boston Bay," *Am. Neptune*, 11 (1951), 239.
Brewington, M. V., "Battle of Delaware Bay, 1782," *U.S. Naval Inst., Proc.*, 65, no. 2 (1939), 231.
Chadwick, F. E., ed., *Graves Papers and Other Documents relating to Naval Operations of the Yorktown Campaign* (1916).
Clark, William B., *First Saratoga: John Young and His Sloop-of-War* (1953).
Cummings, Hubertis, "Robert Morris and Polacre *Victorious*," *Penn. Mag. Hist. Biog.*, 70 (1946), 239.
Fleming, Thomas J., *Now We Are Enemies: Bunker Hill* (1960).
Jameson, John F., "St. Eustatius in Revolution," *AHR*, 8 (1903), 638.
Koke, Richard J., "The Struggle for the Hudson, 1776," *N.Y. Hist. Quar.*, 40 (1956), 114.
Larrabee, Harold A., *Decision at the Chesapeake* (1964).
Lawrence, Alexander A., *Storm over Savannah: Count D'Estaing and Siege of 1779* (1951).
Lloyd, Malcolm, Jr., "Taking of the Bahamas in 1776," *Penn. Mag. Hist. Biog.*, 49 (1925), 349.
Mahan, Alfred T., *Major Operations of Navies in the War of American Independence* (1913).
Middlebrook, Lewis F., *History of Maritime Connecticut during the Revolution* (2 vols., 1925).
Rush, N. Orwin, *Battle of Pensacola, March 9 to May 8, 1781: Spain's Triumph over Great Britain in the Gulf of Mexico* (1966).
Scott, James B., *De Grasse à Yorktown* (1931).
Stevens, Benjamin F., *Campaign in Virginia, 1781* (1888).
Willcox, William B., "Rhode Island in British Strategy, 1780–1781," *Jour. Mod. Hist.*, 17 (1945), 304.

*　　*　　*　　*　　*　　*　　*

Bibliography of the Virginia Campaign and the Siege of Yorktown, 1781 (1941).

See also 10.3 for biographies/writings of:

Barney, Joshua, 1759–1818
Barry, John, 1745–1803
Biddle, Nicholas, 1750–1778
Fiske, John, 1744–1797
Harding, Seth, 1734–1814
Jones, John Paul, 1747–1792
Wickes, Lambert, 1735?–1777

36.9 DIPLOMACY AND INTERNATIONAL RELATIONS

36.9.1 General

Bemis, Samuel F., *Diplomacy of the American Revolution* (1935).
Boyd, Julian P., "Silas Deane, Death by a Kindly Teacher of Treason?" *WMQ*, 3 ser., 16 (1959), 165.
Brown, William A., *Empire or Independence* (1941).

Burnett, Edmund C., ed., *Letters of Members of the Continental Congress* (8 vols., 1921–1936).

Darling, A. B., *Our Rising Empire, 1763–1803* (1940).

Deane, Silas, "Papers," Charles Isham, ed., N.Y. Hist. Soc., *Coll.*, 19 (1887); 20 (1887); 21 (1888); 22 (1889); 23 (1890). Entire issues.

—— "Papers," Conn. Hist. Soc., *Coll.*, 23 (1930). Entire issue.

Looze, Helene Johnson, *Alexander Hamilton and American Foreign Policy, 1783–1803* (1968).

Morris, Richard B., *Peacemakers: Great Powers and American Independence* (1965).

Peterson, Merrill D., "Jefferson and Commercial Policy, 1783–1793," *WMQ*, 3 ser., 22 (1965), 584.

Stevens, Benjamin F., ed., *Facsimiles of Manuscripts in European Archives Relating to America 1773–1783* (25 vols., 1889–1895).

Stourzh, Gerald, *Benjamin Franklin and American Foreign Policy* (1954).

U.S. Department of State, *Diplomatic Correspondence of the United States, 1783–1789* (7 vols., 1829–1830).

Van Alstyne, Richard W., *Empire and Independence: American Revolution* (1965).

Varg, Paul A., *Foreign Policies of the Founding Fathers* (1963).

Wharton, Francis, *Revolutionary Diplomatic Correspondence* (6 vols, 1889).

Winsor, Justin, *Narrative and Critical History* (8 vols., 1884–1889).

See also 10.3 for biographies/writings of:

Adams, John, 1735–1826
Deane, Silas, 1737–1789
Franklin, Benjamin, 1706–1790
Jay, John, 1745–1829
Jefferson, Thomas, 1743–1826
Laurens, Henry, 1724–1792
Lee, Arthur, 1740–1792
Lee, William, 1739–1795
Mazzei, Philip, 1730–1816

36.9.2 Britain and Its Colonies

Augur, Helen, *Secret War of Independence* (1955).

Barnes, Viola F., "Governor Francis Legge of Nova Scotia," *NEQ*, 4 (1931), 420.

Barrs, Burton, *East Florida in the American Revolution* (1932).

Beirne, Francis F., "Mission to Canada, 1776," *Md. Hist. Mag.*, 60 (1965), 404.

Bemis, Samuel F., "British Secret Service and the French-American Alliance," *AHR*, 14 (1933), 265.

Brebner, J. B., *Neutral Yankees of Nova Scotia* (1937).

Brown, Gerald S., "The Anglo-French Naval Crisis, 1778," *WMQ*, 3 ser., 13 (1956), 3.

Burt, A. L., *United States, Great Britain, and British North America* (1940).

"Calendar of Correspondence Politique, États-Unis," Pub. Arch. Can., *Report* (1912), 162; (1913), 152.

"Carlisle Peace Mission Documents, Calendar," Historical Manuscripts Commission, *Fifteenth Report*, Appendix, pt. 6 (1899).

Coupland, Reginald, *American Revolution and British Empire* (1930).

Einhorn, N. R., "Reception of the British Peace Offer of 1778," *Penn. Hist.*, 16 (1949), 191.

Fitzmaurice, Edmond G.P., *Life of William, earl of Shelburne*, vol. III (1876).

George III, *Correspondence, 1760–1783*, J. W. Fortescue, ed., vols. IV–VI (1928).

Graham, Gerald S., *British Policy and Canada 1774–1791* (1930).

Guttridge, George H., *David Hartley* (1926).

Harris, James, Lord Malmesbury, *Diaries and Correspondence* (1845).

Kerr, Wilfred B., *Bermuda and American Revolution* (1936).

—— *Maritime Provinces and the American Revolution* (1941).

Lanctot, Gustave, *Canada and the American Revolution, 1774–1783,* Margaret M. Cameron, trans. (1967).

"Landsdowne Manuscripts Calendar," Historical Manuscripts Commission, *Fifth Report* (1876), 215.

Rawly, George A., "American Revolution and Nova Scotia Reconsidered," *Dalhousie Rev.*, 43 (1963), 378.

Ritcheson, Charles R., *Aftermath of Revolution: British Policy toward the United States 1783–1795* (1969).

"Strachey Manuscripts Calendar," Historical Manuscripts Commission, *Sixth Report* (1877), 399.

Van Alstyne, Richard W., "Great Britain, War for Independence, and the Gathering Storm in Europe, 1775–1778," *Huntington Lib. Quar.*, 27 (1964), 311.

Verrill, Addison E., "Relations between Bermuda and the American Colonies during the Revolutionary War," Conn. Acad. Arts and Sci., *Trans.*, 13 (1907), 47.

Weaver, E. P., "Nova Scotia and New England during the Revolution," *AHR*, 10 (1904), 52.

Williamson, Chilton, *Vermont in Quandary: 1763–1825* (1949).

Wrong, George M., *Canada and the American Revolution* (1935).

36.9.3 France

Boyd, Julian P., "Two Diplomats Between Revolutions: John Jay and Thomas Jefferson," *Va. Mag. Hist. Biog.*, 66 (1958), 131.

Buron, Edmond, "Statistics on Franco-American Trade," *Jour. Econ. and Bus. Hist.*, 4 (1932), 571.

Corwin, Edward S., *French Policy and the American Alliance* (1916).

Deane, Silas, "Papers," Charles Isham, ed., N.Y. Hist. Soc., *Coll.*, 19(1887); 20(1887); 21(1888); 22(1889); 23(1890). Entire issues.

———— "Papers," Conn. Hist. Soc., *Coll.*, 23 (1930). Entire issue.

Doniol, Henri, *Histoire de la participation de la France à l'établissement des États-Unis d'Amérique* (5 vols., 1886–1892).

———— "Le ministère des affaires étrangères sous le Comte de Vergennes," *Revue d'Histoire Diplomatique*, 7 (1893), 528.

d'Ormesson, Wladimir, *La première mission officielle de la France aux États-Unis, C. A. Gérard* (1924).

Fay, Bernard, *Revolutionary Spirit in France and America* (1927).

Godechot, Jacques, *France and the Atlantic Revolution, 1770–1799* (1965).

Hale, Edward E., *Franklin in France* (2 vols., 1887).

Hamon, Joseph, *Le Chevalier de Bonvouloir, premier émissaire secret de la France auprès du Congrès de Philadelphie avant l'indépendance américaine* (1953).

Henderson, H. James, "Congressional Factionalism and Attempt to Recall Benjamin Franklin," *WMQ*, 3 ser., 27 (1970), 246.

Irvine, Dallas, "The Newfoundland Fishery: A French Objective," *Can. Hist. Rev.*, 13 (1932), 268.

Ketcham, Ralph L., "France and American Politics, 1763–1793," *Pol. Sci. Quar.*, 78 (1963), 198.

Kite, Elizabeth S., "French 'Secret Aid', 1776–1777," *French Am. Rev.*, 1 (1948), 143.

Leland, Waldo G., and E. C. Burnett, eds., "Letters from Lafayette to Luzerne," *AHR*, 20 (1915), 341, 576.

Lopez, Claude A., "Franklin, Lafayette, and the *Lafayette*," Am. Philos. Soc., *Proc.*, 108 (1964), 181.

Marraro, H. R., *Philip Mazzei, Virginia's Agent in France* (1935).

Martin, Gaston, "Commercial Relations between Nantes and the Colonies," *Jour. Econ. and Bus. Hist.*, 4 (1932), 812.

Meng, John J., *Comte de Vergennes, European Phases of His American Diplomacy* (1932).

———— "French Diplomacy in Philadelphia, 1778–1779," *Cath. Hist. Rev.*, 24 (1938), 39.

Nussbaum, F. L., "French Colonial Arrêt of 1784," *So. Atl. Quar.*, 27 (1928), 62.

Perkins, James B., *France in the American Revolution* (1911).

Sée, Henri, "Commerce between France and the United States," *AHR*, 31 (1926), 732.

Stinchcombe, William C., *American Revolution and French Alliance* (1969).

Sullivan, Kathryn, *Maryland and France, 1774–89* (1936).

Van Tyne, Claude H., "French Aid before the Alliance of 1778," *AHR*, 31 (1925), 20.

———— "Influences which Determined the French Government to Make the Treaty with America, 1778," *AHR*, 21 (1916), 528.

Warren, James and Mercy, *Warren-Adams Letters*, Worthington C. Ford, ed., Mass. Hist. Soc., *Coll.*, 72 (1917); 73 (1925).

See also 10.3 for biographies/writings of:

Adams, John, 1735–1826
Deane, Silas, 1737–1789
Franklin, Benjamin, 1706–1790
Izard, Ralph, 1741/42–1804

36.9.4 Spain

Padrón, Francisco Morales, *Spanish Help in American Independence* (1952).

Phillips, Paul C., *West in Diplomacy of American Revolution* (1913).

Sánchez Mantero, Rafael, "Misión de John Jay en España (1770–1782)," *Anuario de estudios americanos*, 24 (1967), 1389.

Urtasun, Valentin, *Historia Diplomática de América* (2 vols., 1920–1924).

Whitaker, Arthur P., *Spanish-American Frontier, 1783–1795* (1927).

Yela Utrilla, J. F., *España* (2 vols., 1925).

36.9.5 Other Countries

Barton, H. A., "Sweden and the War of American Independence," *WMQ*, 3 ser., 23 (1966), 408.

Benson, A. B., *Sweden and the American Revolution* (1926).

Brown, Marvin L., ed. and trans., *American Independence: Selections from the Prussian Diplomatic Correspondence* (1959).

Burnett, Edmund C., "Negotiations with Austria," *AHR*, 16 (1911), 567.

de Madariaga, Isabel, *Britain, Russia, and Armed Neutrality of 1780* (1962).

Edler, Friedrich, *Dutch Republic and the American Revolution* (1911).

Fauchille, Paul, *La diplomatie française et la ligue des neutres de 1780* (1893).

Griffiths, David M., "American Commercial Diplomacy in Russia, 1780–1783," *WMQ*, 3 ser., 27 (1970), 379.

Haiman, Miecislaus, *Poland and American Revolutionary War* (1932).

Irwin, Ray W., *Diplomatic Relations of United States with the Barbary Powers, 1776–1816* (1931).

Reeves, Jesse S., "Prussian-American Treaties," *Am. Jour. Internatl. Law*, 11 (1917), 475.

Scott, James B., ed., *Armed Neutralities of 1780 and 1800* (1918).

Vossler, Otto, *Die amerikanischen Revolutionsideale in ihrem Verhältnis zu den Europäischen* (1929).

Winter, Pieter J. van, *Het Aandell van den Amsterdamschen Handel aan den Opbouw van het Amerikaansche Gemeenebest* (2 vols., 1927–1933).

See also 10.3 for biographies/writings of:

Humphreys, David, 1752–1818

36.9.6 Peace Negotiations

Bemis, Samuel F., "Canada and the Peace Settlement of 1782–1783," *Can. Hist. Rev.*, 14 (1933), 265.

Brown, Alan S., "The British Peace Offer of 1778," Mich. Acad. Sci., *Papers*, 40 (1954), 259.

Gee, Olive, "The British War Office in the Later Years of the War of Independence," *Jour. Mod. Hist.*, 26 (1954), 123.

Murphy, Orville T., "The Comte de Vergennes, the Newfoundland Fisheries, and the Peace Negotiation of 1783," *Can. Hist. Rev.*, 46 (1965), 32.

Woodburn, James A., "Benjamin Franklin and the Peace Treaty of 1783," *Ind. Mag. Hist.*, 30 (1934), 223.

36.10 LOYALISTS IN THE REVOLUTION

36.10.1 General

Bakeless, John E., *Turncoats, Traitors and Heroes* (1959).

Barnes, Viola F., "Francis Legge, Loyalist Governor of Nova Scotia, 1773–1776," *NEQ*, 4 (1931), 420.

Belcher, Henry, *First American Civil War, 1775–1778* (2 vols., 1911).

Benton, William A., *Whig-Loyalism: Political Ideology in the American Revolutionary Era* (1969).

Brown, Wallace, *Good Americans: Loyalists in the American Revolution* (1969).

—— *The King's Friends: American Loyalist Claimants* (1965).

—— "Loyalists of the American Revolution," Am. Antiq. Soc., *Proc.*, 80 (1970), 25.

Callahan, North, *Tories of the Revolution* (1963).

Coke, D. P., *Notes on Royal Commission on Losses and Services of American Loyalists*, H. E. Egerton, ed. (1915).

Ellis, George E., "The Loyalists and their Fortunes," in Justin Winsor, ed., *Narrative and Critical History of America*, vol. VII (1888).

Haskett, Richard C., "Prosecuting the Revolution," *AHR*, 59 (1954), 578.

Labaree, Leonard W., "Nature of American Loyalism," Am. Antiq. Soc., *Proc.*, 54 (1944), 15.

Metzger, Charles H., "Some Catholic Tories in the Revolution," *Cath. Hist. Rev.*, 35 (1949–1950), 276.

Mullett, Charles F., "Tory Imperialism on the Eve of the Declaration of Independence," *Can. Hist. Rev.*, 12 (1931), 262.

Nelson, William H., *American Tory* (1961).

Oliver, Peter, *Origin and Progress of American Rebellion: Tory View*, Douglass Adair and John A. Shutz, eds. (1961).

Roth, Cecil, "Some Jewish Loyalists," Am. Jew. Hist. Soc., *Publ.*, 38 (1948), 81.

Sabine, Lorenzo, *Biographical Sketches of Loyalists* (2 vols., 1864); Ralph A. Brown, ed. (1966).

Sargent, Winthrop, ed., *Loyalist Poetry of the Revolution* (1857).

—— *Loyal Verses of Joseph Stansbury and Dr. Jonathan Odell* (1860).

Smith, Paul H., "American Loyalists: Notes on Their Organizaton and Numerical Strength," *WMQ*, 3 ser., 24 (1968), 259.

—— *Loyalists and Redcoats: British Revolutionary Policy* (1964).

Thompson, James W., "Anti-Loyalist Legislation during the Revolution," *Ill. Law Rev.*, 3 (1908), 81.

Upton, Leslie F. S., ed., *Revolutionary Versus Loyalist: First American Civil War, 1774–1784* (1968).

Van Tyne, C. H., *Loyalists in the American Revolution* (1929).

36.10.2 South

Andreano, Ralph L., and Herbert D. Werner, "Charleston Loyalists: A Statistical Note," *So. Car. Hist. Mag.*, 60 (1959), 164.

Beirne, R. R., "Governor Robert Eden," *Md. Hist. Mag.*, 45 (1950), 153.

Boucher, Jonathan, "Letters of Reverend Jonathan Boucher," *Md. Hist. Mag.*, 7 (1912), 2; 8(1913), 34.

—— *Reminiscences of an American Loyalist, 1738–1789*, Jonathan Boucher, ed. (1925).

—— *View of Causes and Consequences of the American Revolution* (1797).

DeMond, R. O., *Loyalists in North Carolina* (1940).

Eckenrode, Hamilton J., *The Revolution in Virginia* (1916).

Ellefson, C. Ashley, "Loyalists and Patriots in Georgia," *Historian*, 24 (1962), 347.

Evanson, Philip, "Jonathan Boucher: The Mind of an American Loyalist," *Md. Hist. Mag.*, 58 (1963), 123.

Fall, Ralph E., "Rev. Jonathan Boucher, Turbulent Tory," *Hist. Mag. Prot. Episc. Church*, 36 (1967), 323.

Fanning, David, *Narrative of Exploits as a Loyalist of North Carolina* (1865).

Frech, Laura P., "Wilmington Committee of Public Safety and Loyalist Rising of February, 1776," *No. Car. Hist. Rev.*, 41 (1964), 21.

Harrell, I. S., *Loyalism in Virginia* (1926).

Johnston, Elizabeth L., *Recollections of a Georgia Loyalist* (1901).

Lambert, Robert S., "Confiscation of Loyalist Property in Georgia, 1782–1786," *WMQ*, 3 ser., 20 (1963), 80.

Levett, Ella P., "Loyalism in Charleston, 1761–1789," So. Car. Hist. Assoc., *Proc.*, (1936), 3.

See also 10.3 for biographies/writings of:

Fairfax, Thomas, 6th Lord, 1693–1781
Stuart, John, 1700–1779

36.10.3 Middle States

Baldwin, E. H., "Joseph Galloway," *Penn. Mag. Hist. Biog.*, 26 (1902), 161.

Barck, Oscar T., *New York City during the War for Independence* (1931).

Brown, Ralph A., "The *Philadelphia Ledger*," *Penn. Hist.*, 9 (1942), 161.

Calhoon, Robert M., "William Smith Jr.'s Alternative to the Revolution," *WMQ*, 3 ser., 22 (1965), 105.

Colden, Cadwallader, "Papers," N.Y. Hist. Soc., *Coll.*, 50–56 (1917–1923); 67–68 (1934–1935).

Crary, Catherine S., "Forfeited Loyalist Lands in the Western District of New York, Albany and Tryon Counties," *N.Y. Hist.*, 35 (1954), 239.

Fennelly, Catherine, "Governor William Franklin of New Jersey," *WMQ*, 3 ser., 6 (1949), 361.

Flick, Alexander C., *Loyalism in New York* (1901).

Frech, Laura P., "Wilmington Committee of Public Safety and the Loyalist Rising of February, 1776," *No. Car. Hist. Rev.*, 41 (1964), 21.

Galloway, Joseph, *Candid Examination of Mutual Claims of Great Britain and Colonies* (1775).

—— *Claim of American Loyalists* (1788).

—— *Historical and Political Reflections on Rise and Progress of American Rebellion* (1780).

Hancock, Harold, *Delaware Loyalists* (1940).

—— "Kent County Loyalists," *Del. Hist.*, 6 (1954), 3.

—— "Newcastle County Loyalists," *Del. Hist.*, 4 (1951), 315.

—— "Thomas Robinson: Delaware's Loyalist," *Del. Hist.*, 4 (1950), 1.

Jones, Edward A., *The Loyalists of New Jersey* (1927).

Keesey, Ruth M., "Loyalism in Bergen County, New Jersey," *WMQ*, 3 ser., 18 (1961), 558.

Kenney, Alice P., "The Albany Dutch," *N.Y. Hist.*, 42 (1961), 331.

Kyte, G. W., "Plans for Loyalist Stronghold in Middle Colonies," *Penn. Hist.*, 16 (1949), 177.

"Minutes of Committee for Detecting Conspiracies," N.Y. Hist. Soc., *Coll.* (2 vols., 1924–1925).

Morison, Samuel E., "Property of Harrison Gray," Col. Soc. Mass., *Publ.*, 14 (1913), 320.

Riccards, Michael P., "Confiscation of Loyalists' Lands in New Jersey," *N.J. Hist.*, 86 (1968), 14.

Seabury, Samuel, *Letters of a Westchester Farmer (1774–1775)*, C. H. Vance, ed., Westchester Co. Hist. Soc., *Publ.*, 8 (1930). Entire issue.

Shammas, Carole, "Cadwallader Colden and the Role of the King's Prerogative," *N.Y. Hist. Soc. Quar.*, 53 (1969), 103.

Smith, Paul H., "New Jersey Loyalists and British 'Provincial' Corps in War for Independence," *N.J. Hist.*, 87 (1969), 69.

Smith, William, *Diary and Selected Papers, 1784–1793*, Leslie F. S. Upton, ed. (2 vols., 1963–1965).

—— *Historical Memoirs, 1763–1776*, William H. W. Sabine, ed. (1956).

Swiggett, Howard, *War out of Niagara: Butler and the Tory Rangers* (1933).

Upton, Leslie F. S., *Loyal Whig: William Smith of New York and Quebec* (1969).

Yoshpe, H. B., *Disposition of Loyalist Estates in the Southern District of New York* (1939).

Zeichner, Oscar, "Loyalist Problem in New York after the Revolution," *N.Y. Hist.*, 21 (1940), 284.

See also 10.3 for biographies/writings of:

Colden, Cadwallader, 1688–1776
Pemberton, Israel, 1715–1779
Seabury, Samuel, 1729–1796
Smith, William, 1728–1793

36.10.4 New England

Bowles, F. T., "Loyalty of Barnstable," Col. Soc. Mass., *Publ.*, 25 (1924), 265.

Bradford, Alden, ed., *Speeches of Governors of Massachusetts from 1765 to 1775* (1818).

Brown, Richard D., "Confiscation and Disposition of Loyalists' Estates in Suffolk County, Massachusetts," *WMQ*, 3 ser., 21 (1964), 534.

Browne, William, "Letters, American Loyalist," Sydney W. Jackman, ed., Essex Inst., *Hist. Coll.*, 96 (1960), 1.

Cohen, Joel A., "Rhode Island Loyalism and the American Revolution," *R.I. Hist.*, 27 (1968), 97.

Davis, Andrew M., *Confiscation of John Chandler's Estate* (1903).

Gilbert, George A., "Connecticut Loyalists," *AHR*, 4 (1899), 273.

Hammond, Otis G., *Tories of New Hampshire* (1917).

Jones, Edward A., *Loyalists of Massachusetts, Memorials, Petitions and Claims* (1930).

Peck, Epaphroditus, *Loyalists of Connecticut* (1934).

Siebert, W. H., "Exodus of Loyalists from Penobscot to Passamaquoddy," Ohio State Univ. *Bull.*, 18, no. 26 (1914).

—— "Loyalist Refugees of New Hampshire," Ohio State Univ. *Bull.*, 21, no. 2 (1916).

—— "Loyalist Troops of New England," *NEQ*, 4 (1931), 108.

—— "Refugee Loyalists in Connecticut," Royal Soc. Can., *Trans.*, 3 ser., 10, sec. 2 (1916), 75.

Smith, Jonathan, "Toryism in Worcester County," Mass. Hist. Soc., *Proc.*, 48 (1915), 15.

Stark, J. H., *Loyalists of Massachusetts* (1910).

Zeichner, Oscar, "Rehabilitation of Loyalists in Connecticut," *NEQ*, 11 (1938), 308.

See also 10.3 for biographies/writings of:

Byles, Mather, 1706/07–1788
Copley, John Singleton, 1738–1815
Hutchinson, Thomas, 1711–1780
Ingersoll, Jared, 1722–1781
Thompson, Benjamin, 1753–1814

36.10.5 Exiles

Bradley, Arthur G., *Colonial Americans in Exile* (1932).
—— *United Empire Loyalists* (1932).
Brown, Wallace, "American Loyalists in Britain," *Hist. Today*, 19 (1969), 672.
Callahan, North, *Flight from Republic: Tories of the American Revolution* (1967).
Cruikshank, E. A., "King's Royal Regiment," Ontario Hist. Soc., *Papers*, 27 (1931), 193.
Eardley, John W., *Historical View of Commission for Enquiring into Losses, Services and Claims of American Loyalists* (1815).
Einstein, Lewis, *Divided Loyalties* (1933).
Ells, Margaret, "Clearing Decks for Loyalists," Can. Hist. Assoc., *Reports* (1933), 43.
—— "Settling Loyalists in Nova Scotia," Can. Hist. Assoc., *Reports* (1934), 105.
Mathews, Hazel C., *Mark of Honor* (1965).
Mekeel, Arthur J., "The Quaker-Loyalist Migration to New Brunswick and Nova Scotia in 1783," Friends' Hist. Assoc., *Bull.*, 32 (1943), 65.
Nelson, William H., "Last Hopes of American Loyalists," *Can. Hist. Rev.*, 32 (1951), 22.
Peters, Thelma, "The American Loyalists in the Bahama Islands," *Fla. Hist. Quar.*, 40 (1962), 226.
"Proceedings of Commissioners on Loyalist Claims," Ontario Bureau of Archives, *Second Report* (2 vols., 1905).
Shelton, W. G., "United Empire Loyalists," *Dalhousie Rev.*, 45 (1965), 5.
Siebert, Wilbur H., "American Loyalists in Eastern Quebec," Royal Soc. Can., *Trans.*, 3 ser., 7 (1913), section II, 1.
—— "Dispersion of American Tories," *MVHR*, 1 (1914), 185.
—— *Flight of American Loyalists to British Isles* (1911).
—— "Kentucky's Struggle," *MVHR*, 7 (1920), 113.
—— "Legacy of American Revolution to British West Indies," Ohio State Univ., *Bull.*, 17, no. 27 (1913).
—— "Loyalist Settlements on Gaspé," Royal Soc. Can., *Trans.*, 3 ser., 8 (1914), section II, 399.
—— *Loyalists in East Florida* (2 vols., 1929).
—— "Loyalists in Niagara Peninsula," Royal Soc. Can., *Trans.*, 3 ser., 9 (1915), section II, 79.
—— "Loyalists in Prince Edward's Island," Royal Soc. Can., *Trans.*, 3 ser., 4 (1910), section II, 109.
—— "Loyalists in West Florida," *MVHR*, 2 (1916), 465.
Talman, J. J., ed., *Loyalist Narratives from Upper Canada* (1946).
Trueman, A. W., *Story of United Empire Loyalists* (1946).
Upton, Leslie F. S., ed., *United Empire Loyalists* (1967).
Wallace, William S., *United Empire Loyalists* (1914).
Wright, Esther C., *Loyalists of New Brunswick* (1955).

36.11 NEW NATION

36.11.1 General

Beard, Charles A., *An Economic Interpretation of the Constitution* (1913).
Burnett, Edmund C., ed., *Letters of Members of the Continental Congress* (8 vols., 1921–1936).
Corwin, Edward S., "Constitutional Theory between Declaration of Independence and Philadelphia Convention," *AHR*, 30 (1925), 511.
Dunbar, L. B., *Study of "Monarchical" Tendencies in United States 1776–1801* (1923).
Dutcher, George M., "Rise of Republican Government in the United States," *Pol. Sci. Quar.*, 55 (1940), 199.
East, R. A., *Business Enterprise in the American Revolutionary Era* (1938).
Ferguson, E. James, *Power of the Purse* (1961).

Fiske, John, *Critical Period in American History* (1888).

Hawke, David, *In the Midst of a Revolution* (1961).

Jensen, Merrill, *The New Nation: A History of the United States during the Confederation* (1959).

Johnson, Herbert A., "Toward Reappraisal of the 'Federal' Government, 1783–1789," *Am. Jour. Legal Hist.*, 8 (1964), 314.

McDonald, Forrest, *E Pluribus Unum: The American Republic, 1776–1790* (1965).

McLaughlin, Andrew C., *Confederation and Constitution* (1905).

Miller, John C., *Triumph of Freedom, 1775–1783* (1948).

Morgan, Edmund S., ed., "Political Establishments of the United States, 1784," *WMQ*, 3 ser., 23 (1966), 286.

Morison, Samuel E., ed., *Sources and Documents Illustrating the American Revolution, 1764–1788* (1923).

Nettels, Curtis P., *Emergence of National Economy, 1775–1815* (1962).

Nevins, Allan, *American States during and after the Revolution* (1924).

U.S. Continental Congress, *Journals, 1774–1789*, Worthington C. Ford et al., eds. (34 vols., 1904–1937).

Warren, Joseph P., "The Confederation and the Shays Rebellion," *AHR*, 11 (1905), 42.

Wood, Gordon S., *Creation of the American Republic, 1776–1787* (1969).

Wright, Benjamin F., *Consensus and Continuity, 1776–1787* (1958).

* * * * * * *

Lander, Ernest M., Jr., "'Critical Period', Constitution and New Nation," in Arthur S. Link and Rembert W. Patrick, eds., *Writing Southern History* (1965).

Morris, Richard B., "Confederation Period and American Historians," *WMQ*, 3 ser., 13 (1956), 139.

See also 10.3 for biographies/writings of:

Jefferson, Thomas, 1743–1826
King, Rufus, 1755–1827
Lee, Richard Henry, 1732–1794
Livingston, Robert R., 1746–1813
Madison, James, 1750/51–1836
Morris, Robert, 1734–1806
Washington, George, 1732–1799

36.11.2 Organization and Government

Bevan, Edith R., "The Continental Congress in Baltimore, December 20, 1776–February 27, 1777," *Md. Hist. Mag.*, 42 (1947), 21.

Burnett, Edmund C., "Committee of States," Am. Hist. Assoc., *Report*, (1913), 139.

Cometti, Elizabeth, "Civil Servants of the Revolutionary Period," *Penn. Mag. Hist. Biog.*, 75 (1951), 159.

Ferguson, E. James, "Business, Government, and Congressional Investigation in the Revolution," *WMQ*, 3 ser., 16 (1959), 293.

——— "State Assumption of Federal Debt during the Confederation," *MVHR*, 38 (1951), 403.

Harlow, V., "Aspects of Revolutionary Finance," *AHR*, 35 (1929), 46.

Harmon, George D., "The Proposed Amendments to the Articles of Confederation," *So. Atl. Quar.*, 24 (1925), 298.

Henderson, H. James, "Constitutionalists and Republicans in the Continental Congress, 1778–1786," *Penn. Hist.*, 36 (1969), 119.

Jensen, Merrill, *Articles of Confederation: Interpretation of the Social-Constitutional History of the American Revolution* (1940).

Kohn, Richard H., "The Inside History of the Newburgh Conspiracy," *WMQ*, 3 ser., 27 (1970), 187.

Main, Jackson T., "American Revolution and Democratization of Legislatures," *WMQ*, 3 ser., 23 (1966), 391.
——— *The Upper House in Revolutionary America* (1967).
Montross, Lynn, *Reluctant Rebels: The Continental Congress* (1950).
Morey, W. C., "First State Constitutions," Am. Acad. Pol. Soc. Sci., *Annals*, 4 (1893), 201.
Nichols, Marie A., "Evolution of Articles of Confederation, 1775–1781," *South. Quar.*, 2 (1964), 307.
Sanders, Jennings B., *Evolution of Executive Departments of the Continental Congress, 1774–1789* (1935).
——— *Presidency of the Continental Congress 1774–1789* (1930).
Sumner, William G., *The Financier and the Finances of the American Revolution* (2 vols., 1891). Robert Morris.
Ward, Harry M., *The Department of War, 1781–1795* (1962).

See also 10.3 for biographies/writings of:

Boudinot, Elias, 1740–1821
Gerry, Elbridge, 1744–1814
Monroe, James, 1758–1831
Morris, Gouverneur, 1752–1816
Salomon, Haym, 1740–1785
Willing, Thomas, 1731–1821

36.11.3 Constitutional and Political Thought

Cattelain, Fernand, *L'influence de Montesquieu dans les constitutions américaines* (1927).
Corwin, Edward S., "The Progress of Constitutional Theory Between the Declaration of Independence and the Philadelphia Convention," *AHR*, 30 (1925), 511.
Handler, Edward, *America and Europe in the Political Thought of John Adams* (1964).
Kurtz, Stephen G., "Political Science of John Adams," *WMQ*, 3 ser., 25 (1968), 605.
McLoughlin, William G., "Isaac Backus and the Separation of Church and State in America," *AHR*, 73 (1968), 1392.
Morgan, Edmund S., ed., "The Political Establishments of the United States, 1784," *WMQ*, 3 ser., 23 (1966), 286.
Palmer, Robert R., "Thomas Jefferson in Bourbon France," *Pol. Sci. Quar.*, 72 (1957), 388.
Ranney, John C., "Bases of American Federalism," *WMQ*, 3 ser., 3 (1946), 1.
Tate, Thad, "Social Contract in America, 1774–1787," *WMQ*, 3 ser., 22 (1965), 375.
Warren, James, and Mercy Warren, "Warren-Adams Letters," Worthington C. Ford, ed., Mass. Hist. Soc., *Coll.*, 72 (1917); 73 (1925).
Wood, Gordon, *Creation of the American Republic* (1969).

See also 10.3 for biographies/writings of:

Adams, John, 1735–1826

36.11.4 Territorial Policy

Adams, Herbert Baxter, *Maryland's Influence upon Land Cessions* (1885).
Barrett, J. A., *Evolution of the Ordinance of 1787* (1891).
Berkhofer, Robert F., Jr., "Jefferson, the Ordinance of 1784, and the Origins of the American Territorial System," *WMQ*, 3 ser., 29 (1972), 231.
Eblen, Jack E., "Origins of United States Colonial System: Ordinance of 1787," *Wis. Mag. Hist.*, 51 (1968), 294.

Galbreath, Charles B., "The Ordinance of 1787: Its Origin and Authorship," *Ohio State Archaeol. and Hist. Quar.*, 33 (1924), 111.

Gerlach, Larry R., "Connecticut, the Continental Congress, and the National Domain, 1776–1786," Conn. Hist. Soc., *Bull.*, 31 (1966), 65.

Howay, Frederick W., "Voyages of 'Columbia' to Northwest Coast 1787–1790 and 1790–1793," Mass. Hist. Soc., *Coll.*, 79 (1941). Entire issue.

Illinois (Territory) Laws, Statutes, *Laws of Illinois Territory*, Francis S. Philbrick, ed. (1950).

Jensen, Merrill, "Cession of Old Northwest," *MVHR*, 23 (1936), 27.

––––– "Creation of National Domain, 1781–1784," *MVHR*, 26 (1939), 323.

Pease, Theodore C., "The Ordinance of 1787," *MVHR*, 25 (1938), 167.

Smith, Jonathan, "The Depression of 1785 and Shays' Rebellion," *WMQ*, 3 ser., 5 (1948), 77.

Tatter, Henry, "State and Federal Land Policy during the Confederation Period," *Agric. Hist.*, 9 (1935), 176.

Treat, P. J., *National Land System* (1910).

Turner, Frederick J., "Western State-Making in the American Revolution," *AHR*, 1 (1895–1896), 70.

36.11.5 European Views of America

Appleby, Joyce, "America as a Model for the Radical French Reformers of 1789," *WMQ*, 3 ser., 28 (1971), 267.

Clark, Dora M., "British Opinion of Franco-American Relations, 1775–1795," *WMQ*, 3 ser., 4 (1947), 305.

Douglass, Elisha P., "German Intellectuals and the American Revolution," *WMQ*, 3 ser., 17 (1960), 200.

Echeverria, Durand, "Condorcet's 'The Influence of the American Revolution on Europe'," *WMQ*, 3 ser., 25 (1968), 85.

––––– "French Publications of the Declaration of Independence and the American Constitutions, 1776–1783," Bibliog. Soc. Am., *Papers*, 47 (1953), 313.

––––– ed. and trans., "A Frenchman Views the New Republic from Philadelphia, 1779," *WMQ*, 3 ser., 16 (1959), 376.

Fagerstrom, Dalphy I., "Scottish Opinion and the Revolution," *WMQ*, 3 ser., 11 (1954), 252.

Gottschalk, Louis R., "The Place of the American Revolution in the Causal Pattern of the French Revolution," American Friends of LaFayette, *Publications*, 2 (1948). Entire issue.

Kraus, Michael, "America and the Irish Revolutionary Movement in the Eighteenth Century," in Richard B. Morris, ed., *The Era of the American Revolution* (1939).

Price, Richard, *Observations on Importance of the American Revolution* (1784).

Selsam, John Paul, and Joseph G. Rayback, "French Comment on the Pennsylvania Constitution of 1776," *Penn. Mag. Hist. Biog.*, 76 (1952), 311.

Weed, Eunice, "British Public Opinion of the Peace with America," *AHR*, 34 (1929), 513.

36.12 CREATION AND ADOPTION OF THE CONSTITUTION

36.12.1 General

Bancroft, George, *History of the Formation of Constitution*, vol. II (1882).

Beard, Charles A., *An Economic Interpretation of the Constitution* (1913).

Brant, Irving, *James Madison: Father of the Constitution* (1950).

Burns, Edward M., *James Madison: Philosopher of the Constitution* (rev. ed., 1968).

Chaffee, Zechariah, Jr., *Three Human Rights in the Constitution of 1787* (1956).

Coleman, John M., "Thomas McKean and the Origin of an Independent Judiciary," *Penn. Hist.*, 34 (1967), 111.

Commager, Henry S., "The Constitution," *Am. Heritage*, 10 (1958), 58.
Crosskey, William W., *Politics and Constitution* (2 vols., 1953).
Elkins, Stanley M., and Eric McKitrick, "Founding Fathers: Young Men of the Revolution," *Pol. Sci. Quar.*, 76 (1961), 181.
Farrand, Max, *Fathers of the Constitution* (1921).
—— *Framing of the Constitution* (1913).
Ford, Paul L., ed., *Essays on the Constitution of the United States, Published during Its Discussion by the People, 1787–1788* (1892).
—— *Pamphlets on the Constitution of the United States* (1888).
Gerlach, Larry R., "Toward 'a More Perfect Union': Connecticut, the Continental Congress, and the Constitutional Convention," *Conn. Hist. Soc., Bull.*, 34 (1969), 65.
Gwyn, William B., *Meaning of the Separation of Powers* (1965).
Hamilton, Walton, and Douglass Adair, *Power to Govern* (1937).
Henderson, Gordon D., "Courts-Martial and the Constitution," *Harv. Law Rev.*, 71 (1957), 293.
Jensen, Merrill, *Making of the American Constitution* (1964).
Kenyon, Cecelia M., "Alexander Hamilton, Rousseau of the Right," *Pol. Sci. Quar.*, 73 (1958), 161.
Ketcham, Ralph L., "James Madison and Nature of Man," *Jour. Hist. Ideas*, 19 (1958), 62.
Koch, Adrienne, *Power, Morals, and the Founding Fathers* (1961).
Levy, Leonard W., ed., *Essays on the Making of the Constitution* (1969).
Lovejoy, Arthur O., *Reflections on Human Nature* (1961).
McDonald, Forrest, *We the People: Economic Origins of the Constitution* (1958).
McLaughlin, Andrew C., *Confederation and Constitution* (1905).
—— *Foundations of American Constitutionalism* (1932).
Miller, Ralph N., "American Nationalism as a Theory of Nature," *WMQ*, 12 (1955), 74.
Mitchell, Broadus, and Louise P. Mitchell, *Biography of the Constitution* (1964).
Pargellis, Stanley, "Theory of Balanced Government," in Conyers Read, ed., *Constitution Reconsidered* (1938).
Riemer, Neal, "The Republicanism of James Madison," *Pol. Sci. Quar.*, 69 (1954), 45.
Roche, John P., "The Founding Fathers: A Reform Caucus in Action," *Am. Pol. Sci. Rev.*, 55 (1961), 799.
Rossiter, Clinton, *Alexander Hamilton and the Constitution* (1964).
Schachner, Nathan, *Founding Fathers* (1954).
Schuyler, R. L., *Constitution of the United States* (1923).
Seed, Geoffrey, "The Democratic Ideas of James Wilson," Brit. Assoc. Am. Studies, *Bull.*, 10 (1965), 3.
Thayer, J. B., "Origin and Scope of the American Doctrine of Constitutional Law," in *Legal Essays* (1908).
U.S. Library of Congress, Legislative Reference Service, *Documents Illustrative of the Formation of the Union* (1927).
Vile, Maurice J. C., *Constitutionalism and Separation of Powers* (1967).
Warren, Charles, *Making of Constitution* (1928).

*   *   *   *   *   *   *

Barker, E. C., "Economic Interpretation of Constitution," *Tex. Law Rev.*, 22 (1944), 373.
Brogan, Denis W., "Quarrel over Beard and the American Constitution," *Econ. Hist. Rev.*, 18 (1965), 199.
Brown, Robert E., *Charles Beard and the Constitution* (1956).
—— *Reinterpretation of the Formation of the American Constitution* (1963).
Ferguson, E. James, "Nationalists of 1781–1783 and Economic Interpretation of Constitution," *JAH*, 56 (1969), 241.
Hofstadter, Richard, "Beard and the Constitution: History of an Idea," *Am. Quar.*, 2 (1950), 195.
Katz, Stanley N., "Origins of American Constitutional Thought," *Perspectives in Am. Hist.*, 3 (1969), 474.

Kenyon, Cecelia M., " 'Economic Interpretation of the Constitution' after Fifty Years," *Centennial Rev.*, 7 (1963), 327.

Lynd, Staughton, "Abraham Yates's History of the Movement for the United States Constitution," *WMQ*, 3 ser., 20 (1963), 223.

See also 10.3 for biographies/writings of:

Adams, John, 1735–1826
Gerry, Elbridge, 1744–1814
Hamilton, Alexander, 1755–1804
Jefferson, Thomas, 1743–1826
Johnson, William Samuel, 1727–1819
King, Rufus, 1755–1827
Livingston, William, 1723–1790
Madison, James, 1750/51–1836
Mason, George, 1725–1792
Morris, Robert, 1734–1806
Randolph, Edmund, 1753–1813
Sherman, Roger, 1721–1793
Washington, George, 1732–1799

36.12.2 Philadelphia Convention

Banks, Margaret A., "Drafting the American Constitution: Attitudes in the Philadelphia Convention towards the British System of Government," *Am. Jour. Legal Hist.*, 10 (1966), 15.

Bowen, Catherine D., *Miracle at Philadelphia: Constitutional Convention* (1966).

Farrand, Max, *Framing of the Constitution* (1913).

———— *Records of the Federal Convention* (4 vols., 1911–1937).

Gwyn, William B., *Meaning of the Separation of Powers* (1965).

Lansing, John, Jr., *Delegate from New York*, Joseph R. Strayer, ed. (1939).

Lynd, Staughton, *Class Conflict, Slavery and the United States Constitution* (1967).

O'Brien, F. William, "Executive and Separation Principle at the Constitutional Convention," *Md. Hist. Mag.*, 55 (1960), 201.

Ohline, Howard A., "Origins of the Three-Fifths Clause," *WMQ*, 3 ser., 28 (1971), 563.

Padover, Saul K., *To Secure These Blessings: Great Debates of the Convention* (1962).

Prescott, A. T., *Drafting the Federal Constitution* (1941).

Rodell, Fred, *Fifty-Five Men* (1936).

Rogow, Arnold A., "Federal Convention: Madison and Yates," *AHR*, 60 (1954), 323.

Rossiter, Clinton, *1787: Grand Convention* (1966).

Ulmer, S. Sidney, "Sub-Group Formation in the Constitutional Convention," *Midw. Jour. Pol. Sci.*, 10 (1966), 288.

U.S. Constitutional Convention, 1787, *Notes of Debates in the Federal Convention of 1787, reported by James Madison* (1893).

Van Doren, Carl, *Great Rehearsal* (1948).

See also 10.3 for biographies/writings of:

Ellsworth, Oliver, 1745–1807
Pinckney, Charles Cotesworth, 1746–1825
Rutledge, John, 1739–1800

36.12.3 Struggle for Ratification

36.12.3.1 Anti-Federalists

Borden, Morton, ed., *Antifederalist Papers* (1965).

Crowl, Philip A., "Anti-Federalism in Maryland," *WMQ*, 3 ser., 4 (1947), 446.

Kenyon, Cecelia M., ed., *Antifederalists* (1966).

Kenyon, Cecelia M., "Men of Little Faith: Anti-Federalists on Nature of Representative Government," *WMQ*, 3 ser., 12 (1955), 3.

Lee, Richard H., *Letters from a Federal Farmer to the Republican* (1788; repr. 1962).

Lewis, John D., ed., *Anti-Federalists versus Federalists: Documents* (1967).

Lynd, Staughton, *Anti-Federalism in Dutchess County, New York* (1962).

McDonald, Forrest, "Anti-Federalists, 1781–1789," *Wis. Mag. Hist.*, 46 (1963), 206.

Main, Jackson T., *Anti-Federalists, 1781–1788* (1961).

Mason, Alpheus T., *States Rights Debate: Antifederalism and the Constitution* (1964).

Rutland, Robert A., *Ordeal of the Constitution: Antifederalist and Ratification Struggle of 1787–1788* (1966).

See also 10.3 for biographies/writings of:

Clinton, George, 1739–1812
Franklin, Benjamin, 1706–1790
Lee, Richard Henry, 1732–1794
Macon, Nathaniel, 1758–1837
Martin, Luther, 1748–1826

36.12.3.2 Federalists

Adair, Douglass, "Authorship of the Disputed Federalist Papers," *WMQ*, 3 ser., 1 (1944), 97.

———— "Politics Reduced to Science: Hume, Madison, and Tenth *Federalist*," *Huntington Lib. Quar.*, 20 (1957), 343.

———— "The Tenth *Federalist* Revisited," *WMQ*, 3 ser., 8 (1951), 48.

Beard, Charles A., *Enduring Federalist* (1948).

Brant, Irving, "Madison: On the Separation of Church and State," *WMQ*, 3 ser., 8 (1951), 3.

Diamond, Martin, "Democracy and the *Federalist*," *Am. Pol. Sci. Rev.*, 53 (1959), 52.

Dietze, Gottfried, *The Federalist* (1960).

The Federalist, Benjamin F. Wright, ed. (1961).

Mason, Alpheus T., "The Federalist—A Split Personality," *AHR*, 57 (1952), 625.

Mosteller, Frederick, and David L. Wallace, *Inference and Disputed Authorship: The Federalist* (1964).

Scanlan, James P., "The *Federalist* and Human Nature," *Rev. Politics* 21 (1959), 657.

36.12.4 Ratification

Ambler, Charles H., *Sectionalism in Virginia* (1910).

Bates, Frank G., *Rhode Island and Formation of the Union* (1899).

Bishop, Hillman Metcalf, "Why Rhode Island Opposed Federal Constitution," *R.I. Hist.*, 8 (1949), 1.

Brooks, Robin, "Alexander Hamilton, Melancton Smith and Ratification of the Constitution in New York," *WMQ*, 3 ser., 24 (1967), 339.

Delaware. Constitutional Convention, 1776, *Proceedings of the Convention* (1776).

De Pauw, Linda G., *Eleventh Pillar: New York and Federal Constitution* (1966).

Elliot, Jonathan, ed., *Debates in the Several State Conventions on the Adoption of the Federal Constitution . . . Together with the Journal of Federal Convention . . .* (2nd ed., 5 vols., 1861–1863).

Foster, Theodore, *Minutes of the Convention at South Kingstown, Rhode Island, 1790*, Robert C. Cotner, ed. (1929).

Harding, Samuel B., *Contest over Ratification in Massachusetts* (1896).

Hart, Freeman H., *Valley of Virginia* (1942).

Hollister, Gideon H., *History of Connecticut*, vol. II (2nd ed., 1857).

Libby, Orin G., *Geographical Distribution of the Vote* (1894).

Lycan, Gilbert L., "Hamilton and the North Carolina Federalists," *No. Car. Hist. Rev.*, 25 (1948), 442.

McMaster, John B., and F. D. Stone, *Pennsylvania and the Federal Constitution* (1888).

Miner, Clarence E., *Ratification of the Federal Constitution in New York* (1921).

Newsome, Albert R., "North Carolina's Ratification of the Federal Constitution," *No. Car. Hist. Rev.*, 17 (1940), 287.

Roll, Charles W., Jr., "Apportionment in Thirteen State Conventions Ratifying the Constitution," *JAH*, 56 (1969), 21.

Steiner, B. C., "Maryland's Adoption of the Federal Constitution," *AHR*, 5 (1900), 22.

Thomas, Robert E., "Virginia Convention of 1788: Criticism of Beard's *An Economic Interpretation of the Constitution*," *JSH*, 19 (1953), 63.

Trenholme, L. I., *Ratification of the Federal Constitution in North Carolina* (1932).

Virginia (Colony) Convention, March 20, 1775, *Proceedings of the Convention of Delegates for the Counties and Corporations in the Colony of Virginia* (1775).

Walker, Joseph B., *New Hampshire Convention 1788* (1888).

See also 10.3 for biographies/writings of:

McHenry, James, 1753–1816
Marshall, John, 1755–1835
Pendleton, Edmund, 1721–1803
Read, George, 1733–1798
Rush, Benjamin, 1745–1813

36.12.5 Bill of Rights

Bowers, Claude G., "Jefferson and the Bill of Rights," *Va. Law Rev.*, 41 (1955), 709.

Brant, Irving, *The Bill of Rights* (1966).

Chaffee, Zechariah, Jr., *How Human Rights Got into the Constitution* (1952).

Dumbauld, Edward, "State Precedents for the Bill of Rights," *Jour. Pub. Law*, 7 (1958), 323.

Dunbar, Leslie W., "Madison and the Ninth Amendment," *Va. Law Rev.*, 42 (1956), 627.

Hand, Learned, *The Bill of Rights* (1958).

Levy, Leonard, *Origins of the Fifth Amendment* (1968).

Perry, Richard L., ed., *Sources of Our Liberties: Documentary Origins of Individual Liberties in the Constitution and Bill of Rights* (1959).

Rutland, Robert A., *Birth of the Bill of Rights, 1776–1791* (1955).

See also 10.3 for biographies/writings of:

Warren, James, 1726–1808

37 Histories of Special Subjects, 1607–1789

37.1 GOVERNMENT AND POLITICS

37.1.1 General

This section is limited to general surveys and institutional histories. Most of the works on the development of government and politics in the colonial period will be found in the preceding four chapters.

Bailyn, Bernard, *Origins of American Politics* (1968).
Bellot, H. Hale, "Council and Cabinet in the Mainland Colonies," Royal Hist. Soc., *Trans.*, 5 ser., 5 (1955), 161.
Bishop, Courtland, *History of Elections in the American Colonies* (1893).
Breen, Timothy H., *The Character of the Good Ruler: Puritan Political Ideas in New England, 1630–1730* (1970).
Burns, John F., *Controversies between Royal Governors and Their Assemblies in Northern American Colonies* (1923).
Chute, Marchette, *The First Liberty: History of the Right to Vote in America, 1619–1850* (1969).
Clarke, Mary P., *Parliamentary Privilege in the American Colonies* (1943).
Dickerson, Oliver M., *American Colonial Government, 1696–1765* (1912).
Franklin, W. Neil, "Some Aspects of Representation in the American Colonies," *No. Car. Hist. Rev.*, 6 (1929), 38.
Greene, Evarts B., *The Provincial Governor in the English Colonies of North America* (1898).
Greene, Jack P., *The Quest for Power: Lower Houses of Assembly in the Southern Royal Colonies, 1689–1763* (1963).
Henige, David P., *Colonial Governors from the Fifteenth Century to the Present: A Comprehensive List* (1970).
Kammen, Michael, *Deputyes and Libertyes: Origins of Representative Government in Colonial America* (1969).
Karraker, Cyrus H., *The Seventeenth Century Sheriff: Comparative Study of the Sheriff in England and the Chesapeake Colonies, 1607–1689* (1930).
Labaree, Leonard W., *Royal Government in America* (1930).
Leder, Lawrence H., *Liberty and Authority: Early American Political Ideology, 1689–1763* (1968).
Lokken, Roy N., "Concept of Democracy in Colonial Political Thought," *WMQ*, 3 ser., 16 (1959), 568.
Lynd, Staughton, *Intellectual Origins of American Radicalism* (1968).
McAnear, Beverly, *Income of the Colonial Governors of British North America* (1967).
McKinley, Albert E., *Suffrage Franchise in the Thirteen English Colonies in America* (1905).
McLaughlin, Andrew C., *The Foundations of American Constitutionalism* (1932).

Moran, Thomas F., *Rise and Development of the Bicameral System in America* (1895).

Murrin, John M., "Myths of Colonial Democracy and Royal Decline in Eighteenth-Century America: A Review Essay," *Cithara*, 5 (1965), 53.

Phillips, Hubert, *Development of a Residential Qualification for Representatives in Colonial Legislatures* (1921).

Rossiter, Clinton, *Seedtime of the Republic: Origin of American Tradition of Political Liberty* (1953).

Varg, Paul A., "Advent of Nationalism, 1758–1776," *Am. Quar.*, 16 (1964), 169.

*   *   *   *   *   *   *

Greene, Jack P. "Changing Interpretations of Early American Politics," in Ray A. Billington, ed., *Reinterpretation of Early American History* (1967).

—— "Publication of Official Records of Southern Colonies," *WMQ*, 3 ser., 14 (1957), 268.

37.1.2 Civil Rights

Alexander, James, *Brief Narrative of the Case and Trial of John Peter Zenger*, Stanley N. Katz, ed. (2nd ed., 1972).

Hanley, Thomas O., *Their Rights and Liberties: Beginnings of Religious and Political Freedom in Maryland* (1959).

Levy, Leonard W., and Lawrence H. Leder, "Right against Compulsory Self-Incrimination in Colonial New York," *WMQ*, 3 ser., 20 (1963), 3.

MacCracken, Henry N., *Prologue to Independence: Trials of James Alexander* (1964).

Nelson, Harold, "Seditious Libel in Colonial America," *Am. Jour. Legal Hist.*, 3 (1959), 160.

Pittman, R. Carter, "Colonial and Constitutional History of Privilege against Self-Incrimination in America," *Va. Law Rev.*, 21 (1935), 763.

Rackow, Felix, "The Right to Counsel: English and American Precedents," *WMQ*, 3 ser., 11 (1954), 3.

See also 10.3 for biographies/writings of:

Hamilton, Andrew, 1676–1741

37.2 LAW

37.2.1 General

Andrews, Charles M., *The Connecticut Intestacy Law* (1933).

Billias, George A., ed., *Law and Authority in Colonial America: Essays* (1965).

Brown, Elizabeth G., in consultation with William W. Blume, *British Statutes in American Law, 1776–1836* (1964).

Carpenter, A. H., "Habeas Corpus in the Colonies," *AHR*, 8 (1902), 18.

Chafee, Zechariah, Jr., "Colonial Courts and the Common Law," Mass. Hist. Soc., *Proc.*, 68 (1952), 132.

Chapin, Bradley, *American Law of Treason: Revolutionary and Early National Origins* (1964).

Chitwood, Oliver P., *Justice in Colonial Virginia* (1905).

Chumbley, George L., *Colonial Justice in Virginia* (1938).

Dalzell, George W., *Benefit of Clergy in America and Related Matters* (1955).

Flaherty, David H., ed., *Essays in the History of Early American Law* (1969).

Flaherty, David H., "Law and the Enforcement of Morals in Early America," *Perspectives in Am. Hist.*, 5 (1971), 203.

Goebel, Julius, "King's Law and Local Custom in Seventeenth Century New England," *Col. Law Rev.*, 31 (1931), 416.

Hall, Ford W., "The Common Law: Its Reception in the United States," *Vanderbilt Law Rev.*, 4 (1951), 33.

Hamilton, William B., *Anglo-American Law on Frontier: Thomas Rodney and Territorial Cases* (1953).

Hamlin, Paul M., and Charles E. Baker, *Supreme Court of Province of New York, 1691–1704* (3 vols., 1959).

Haskins, George L., "Beginnings of the Recording System in Massachusetts," *Boston Univ. Law Rev.*, 21 (1941), 281.

- —— *Law and Authority in Early Massachusetts* (1960).

Hilkey, Charles J., *Legal Development in Massachusetts, 1630–1686* (1910).

Johnson, Herbert A., *Law Merchant and Negotiable Instruments in Colonial New York, 1664–1730* (1963).

Katz, Stanley N., "Politics of Law: Controversies over Chancery Courts and Equity Law in the Eighteenth Century," *Perspectives in Am. Hist.*, 5 (1971), 257.

Morris, Richard B., "Massachusetts and Common Law: The Declaration of 1646," *AHR*, 31 (1926), 443.

—— *Studies in the History of American Law, with Special Reference to the Seventeenth and Eighteenth Centuries* (1930).

Pound, Roscoe, *The Formative Era of American Law* (1938).

Reinsch, Paul S., *English Common Law in Early American Colonies* (1899).

Sioussat, St. George L., "Extension of English Statutes to Plantations," *Select Essays in Anglo-American Legal History*, vol. I (1907).

Smith, Joseph Henry, *Appeals to the Privy Council from the American Plantations* (1950).

Surrency, Erwin C., "Revision of Colonial Laws," *Am. Jour. Legal Hist.*, 9 (1965), 189.

Wolford, T. L., "Laws and Liberties of 1648," *Boston Univ. Law Rev.*, 28 (1948), 426.

Wright, Benjamin F., *American Interpretation of Natural Law* (rev. ed., 1962).

*   *   *   *   *   *   *

Brown, C. R., et. al., comps., *Legal Bibliography of British Commonwealth of Nations.* Vol. III, *Canadian and British-American Colonial Law from Earliest Times* (1957).

Kammen, Michael G., "Colonial Court Records and the Study of Early American History: A Bibliographical Review," *AHR*, 70 (1965), 732.

37.2.2 Legal Profession

Bedwell, C. E. A., "American Middle Templars," *AHR*, 25 (1920), 680.

Boorstin, Daniel J., *Mysterious Science of the Law* (1941).

Chroust, Anton-Hermann, *Rise of the Legal Profession in America* (2 vols., 1965).

Fisher, Samuel H., *Litchfield Law School: Biographical Catalogue of Students, 1774–1833* (1946).

Hamilton, J. G. de Roulhac, "Southern Members of the Inns of Court," *No. Car. Hist. Rev.*, 10 (1933), 273.

Hamlin, Paul M., *Legal Education in Colonial New York* (1939).

Jones, E. Alfred, *American Members of the Inns of Court* (1924).

Klein, Milton M., "Rise of New York Bar: William Livingston," *WMQ*, 3 ser., 15 (1958), 334.

Reed, Alfred Z., *Training for the Public Profession of the Law* (1921).

Warren, Charles, *History of the American Bar* (1912).

37.3 JUDICIARY

Albany. Court of Albany, Colony of Rensselaerswyck and Schaenhechtede, *Minutes of the Court of Albany, Rensselaerswyck and Schaenhechtede, 1668–1685*, A. J. F. Van Laer, ed. (3 vols., 1926–1932).

Chafee, Zechariah, Jr., "Colonial Courts and Common Law," Mass. Hist. Soc. Proc., 68 (1952), 132.

——— Introduction to Records of Suffolk County Court 1671–80, Col. Soc. Mass., Publ., 29 (1933), xvii–xl.

Dimond, Alan J., Superior Court of Massachusetts (1960).

Farrell, John T., "The Early History of Rhode Island's Court System," R.I. Hist., 9 (1950), 65; 10 (1951), 14.

Ferguson, Isabel, "County Court in Virginia, 1700–1830," No. Car. Hist. Rev., 8 (1931), 14.

Goodman, Leonard S., "Mandamus in the Colonies—Rise of Superintending Power in American Courts," Amer. Jour. Legal Hist., 1 (1957), 308; 2 (1958), 1.

Grinnell, Frank W., "Bench and Bar in Colony and Province," in Albert B. Hart, ed., Commonwealth History of Massachusetts, vol. II (1928).

Hamlin, Paul M., and Charles E. Baker, Supreme Court of Province of New York, 1691–1704 (3 vols., 1959).

Howe, Mark A. DeW., and Louis F. Eaton, Jr., "The Supreme Judicial Power in the Colony of Massachusetts Bay," NEQ, 20 (1947), 291.

Johnson, William Samuel, Superior Court Diary, 1772–1773, of The Colony of Connecticut, John T. Farrell, ed. (1942).

Jonas, Manfred, "Wills of Early Settlers of Essex County, Massachusetts," Essex Inst., Hist. Coll., 96 (1960), 228.

Karraker, Cyrus H., The Seventeenth Century Sheriff: Comparative Study of the Sheriff in England and in the Chesapeake Colonies (1930).

Lloyd, William H., The Early Courts of Pennsylvania (1910).

McCain, Paul M., County Court in North Carolina before 1750 (1954).

Maryland (Colony). County Court, Court Records of Prince Georges County, Maryland, 1696–1699, Joseph H. Smith and Philip A. Crowl, eds. (1964).

Maryland (Colony). Court of Appeals, Proceedings of the Maryland Court of Appeals 1695–1729, Carroll T. Bond, ed. (1933).

Massachusetts (Colony). County Court, Records of the Suffolk County Court, 1671–1680 (2 vols., 1933).

Massachusetts (Colony). Quarterly Courts, Records and Files of the Quarterly Courts of Essex County, 1636–1683, George F. Dow, ed. (8 vols., 1911–1921).

Massachusetts (Colony). Superior Court of Judicature, Reports of Cases Argued and Adjudged in Superior Court of Judicature of the Province of Massachusetts Bay, between 1761 and 1772, Josiah Quincy, Jr., and Samuel M. Quincy, eds. (1865).

Murrin, John M., "Bench and Bar of Eighteenth-Century Massachusetts," in Stanley N. Katz, ed., Colonial America: Essays in Political and Social Development (1971).

New Jersey (Colony). Courts, The Burlington Court Book: Record of Quaker Jurisprudence in West New Jersey, 1680–1709, H. Clay Reed and George J. Miller, eds. (1944).

New York (Colony). Court of Vice-admiralty, Reports of Cases in Vice-admiralty of New York, 1715–1788, Charles M. Hough, ed. (1925).

Page, Elwin L., Judicial Beginnings in New Hampshire, 1640–1700 (1959).

Pittman, R. Carter, "Judicial Supremacy in America: Its Colonial and Constitutional History," Ga. Bar Jour., 16 (1953), 148.

Pynchon, William, Colonial Justice in Western Massachusetts (1639–1702): An Original Judges' Diary, Joseph H. Smith, ed. (1961).

Rankin, Hugh F., Criminal Trial Proceedings in the General Court of Colonial Virginia (1965).

Reed, H. Clay, "Early New Castle Court," Del. Hist., 4 (1951), 227.

Smith, Joseph H., "Administrative Control of Courts of American Plantations," Col. Law Rev., 61 (1961), 1210.

Surrency, Erwin C., "Courts in the American Colonies," Am. Jour. Legal Hist., 11 (1967), 253.

——— "Directions for Holding Court in Colonial Georgia," Am. Jour. Legal Hist., 2 (1958), 321.

——— "Report on Court Procedures in the Colonies—1700," Am. Jour. Legal Hist., 9 (1965), 69.

Ubbelohde, Carl, "Vice-Admiralty Court of Royal North Carolina, 1729–1759," No. Car. Hist. Rev., 31 (1954), 517.

—— *Vice-Admiralty Courts and the American Revolution* (1960).
Virginia (Colony). County Court, *County Court Records of Accomack-Northampton, Virginia, 1632–1640,* Susie M. Ames, ed. (1954).
Wroth, L. Kinvin, "Massachusetts Vice Admiralty Court and Federal Admiralty Jurisdiction," *Am. Jour. Legal Hist.,* 6 (1962), 250.
York County, Maine, *Court Records of York County, Maine, 1692–1711,* Neal W. Allen, ed. Vol IV of *Province and Court Records of Maine* (1958).

*   *   *   *   *   *   *

Prager, Herta, and William W. Price, "Bibliography on History of Courts of Thirteen Original States, Maine, Ohio and Vermont," *Amer. Jour. Legal Hist.,* 1 (1957), 336; 2 (1958), 35.

See also 10.3 for biographies/writings of:

Chew, Benjamin, 1722–1810
Parsons, Theophilus, 1750–1813
Sewall, Samuel, 1652–1730
Smith, William, 1728–1793

37.4 MILITARY

Bernardo, C. Joseph, and Eugene H. Bacon, *American Military Policy since 1775* (2nd ed., 1961).
Bird, Harrison, *Navies in the Mountains: Battles on Lake Champlain and Lake George, 1609–1814* (1962).
Cole, David, "South Carolina Colonial Militia System," So. Car. Hist. Assoc., *Proc.,* 1954 (1955), 14.
Dupuy, Richard E. and Trevor, *Military Heritage of Americans* (1968).
Ekirch, Arthur A., Jr., *The Civilian and the Military* (1956).
Graham, Gerald S., "Naval Defense of British North America, 1739–1763," Royal Hist. Soc., *Trans.,* 4 ser., 8 (1948), 95.
Hamilton, Edward Pierce, "Colonial Warfare in North America," Mass. Hist. Soc., *Proc.,* 80 (1968), 3.
Israel, Fred L., "New York's Citizen Soldiers: Militia and Their Armories," *N.Y. Hist.,* 42 (1961), 145.
Leach, Douglas E., "The Military System of Plymouth Colony," *NEQ,* 34 (1951), 342.
Mahon, John K., "Anglo-American Methods of Indian Warfare, 1676–1794," *MVHR,* 45 (1958), 254.
Matloff, Maurice, ed., *American Military History* (1969).
Morton, Louis, "Origins of American Military Policy," *Mil. Affairs,* 22 (1958), 75.
Mugridge, Donald H., comp., *Album of American Battle Art, 1755–1918* (1947).
Pares, Richard, "American Versus Continental Warfare, 1739–1763," *Eng. Hist. Rev.,* 51 (1936), 429.
Pargellis, Stanley, "The Four Independent Companies of New York," in *Essays in Colonial History Presented to Charles McLean Andrews* (1931).
Peckham, Howard H., *The Colonial Wars, 1689–1762* (1964).
Peterson, Harold L., *Arms and Armor in Colonial America* (1956).
Quarles, Benjamin, "Colonial Militia and Negro Manpower," *MVHR,* 45 (1959), 643.
Radabaugh, Jack S., "Militia of Colonial Massachusetts," *Mil. Affairs,* 18 (1954), 1.
Scisco, Louis D., "Evolution of the Colonial Militia in Maryland," *Md. Hist. Mag.,* 35 (1940), 166.
Sharp, Morison, " Leadership and Democracy in Early New England System of Defense," *AHR,* 50 (1945), 244.
Shy, John W., "New Look at Colonial Militia," *WMQ,* 3 ser., 20 (1963), 175.

de Valinger, Leon, Jr., *Colonial Military Organization in Delaware, 1638–1776* (1938).

Wheeler, E. Milton, "North Carolina Militia," *No. Car. Hist. Rev.*, 41 (1964), 307.

Williams, T. Harry, *Americans at War: Military System* (1960).

See also 36.8, War for Independence, Military Aspects.

37.5 ECONOMY

37.5.1 General

Bjork, Gordon C., "Weaning of American Economy," *Jour. Econ. Hist.*, 24 (1964), 541.

Bruce, Philip A., *Economic History of Virginia in the Seventeenth Century* (2 vols., 1896).

Bruchey, Stuart, *The Roots of American Economic Growth, 1607–1861* (1965).

Diamond, Sigmund, "Values as Obstacle to Economic Growth: The American Colonies," *Jour. Econ. Hist.*, 27 (1967), 561.

Dorfman, Joseph, *Economic Mind in American Civilization*, vol. I (1946).

Gould, C. P., "Economic Causes of the Rise of Baltimore," in *Essays in Colonial History Presented to Charles McLean Andrews* (1931).

Henretta, James A., "Economic Development and Social Structure in Colonial Boston," *WMQ*, 3 ser., 22 (1965), 75.

Hitchens, Harold L., "Sir William Berkeley, Virginian Economist," *WMQ*, 2 ser., 18 (1938), 158.

Labaree, Leonard W., *Conservatism in Early American History* (1948).

McKee, Samuel, Jr., "Economic Pattern of Colonial New York," in Alexander C. Flick, ed., *History of the State of New York*, vol. II (1933).

Moody, Robert E., "Massachusetts Trade with Carolina, 1686–1709," *No. Car. Hist. Rev.*, 20 (1943), 43.

Nash, Gary B., "Maryland's Economic War with Pennsylvania," *Md. Hist. Mag.*, 60 (1965), 231.

Nettels, Curtis P., "Economic Relations of Boston, Philadelphia, and New York, 1680–1715," *Jour. Econ. and Bus. Hist.*, 3 (1931), 185.

Sioussat, St. George L., *Economics and Politics in Maryland, 1720–1750* (1903).

Soltow, James H., *Economic Role of Williamsburg* (1965).

Syrett, Harold C., "Private Enterprise in New Amsterdam," *WMQ*, 3 ser., 11 (1954), 536.

Taylor, George R., "American Economic Growth before 1840," *Jour. Econ. Hist.*, 24 (1964), 427.

Weeden, W. B., *Economic and Social History of New England, 1620–1789*, vol. II (1891).

Wright, Louis B., *The Dream of Prosperity of Colonial America* (1965).

See also 10.3 for biographies/writings of:

Coxe, Tench, 1755–1824

37.5.2 Government and Economy

Baird, E. G., "Business Regulation in Colonial Massachusetts (1620–1780)," *Dakota Law Rev.*, 3 (1931), 227.

Giesecke, Albert A., *American Commercial Legislation before 1789* (1910).

Handlin, Oscar, and Mary F. Handlin, *Commonwealth: Role of Government in the American Economy: Massachusetts, 1774–1861* (rev. ed., 1969).

Hartz, Louis, *Economic Policy and Democratic Thought: Pennsylvania, 1776–1860* (1948).

Jensen, Arthur L., "Inspection of Exports in Colonial Pennsylvania," *Penn. Mag. Hist. Biog.*, 78 (1954), 275.

Jones, Newton B., "Weights, Measures, and Mercantilism: The Inspection of Exports in Virginia, 1742–1820," in Darrett B. Rutman, ed., *The Old Dominion: Essays for Thomas Perkins Abernethy* (1964).

Morris, Richard B., *Government and Labor in Early America* (1946).

—— and Jonathan Grossman, "The Regulation of Wages in Early Massachusetts," *NEQ*, 11 (1938), 470.

Setser, Vernon G., *The Commercial Reciprocity Policy of the United States, 1774–1829* (1937).

Williams, William A., "The Age of Mercantilism: An Interpretation of the American Political Economy, 1763–1828," *WMQ*, 3 ser., 15 (1958), 419.

Wyckoff, Vertrees J., *Tobacco Regulation in Colonial Maryland* (1936).

Zornow, William F., "Tariff Policies of Virginia, 1755–1789," *Va. Mag. Hist. Biog.*, 62 (1954), 306.

37.5.3 Land

Akagi, R. H., *Town Proprietors of New England Colonies* (1924).

Barker, C. A., "Property Rights in Provincial System of Maryland," *JSH*, 2 (1936), 211.

Barnes, Viola F., "Land Tenure in English Colonial Charters of the Seventeenth Century," in *Essays in Colonial History Presented to Charles McLean Andrews* (1931).

Beale, Joseph N., Jr., "Origin of System of Recording Deeds in America," *The Green Bag*, 3 (1907), 335.

Bond, Beverley W., *Quit-Rent System in the American Colonies* (1919).

Ford, Amelia C., *Colonial Precedents of our National Land System* (1910).

Fox, Edith M., *Land Speculation in Mohawk Country* (1949).

Giddens, Paul H., "Land Policies and Administration in Colonial Maryland, 1753–1769," *Md. Mag. Hist.*, 28 (1933), 142.

Gould, Clarence P., *Land System in Maryland, 1720–1765* (1913).

Grant, Charles S., "Land Speculation and Settlement of Kent, 1738–1760," *NEQ*, 25 (1955), 51.

Greven, Philip J., "Distribution of Land in 17th Century Andover," *Essex Inst., Hist. Coll.*, 101 (1965), 133.

Harley, R. Bruce, "Dr. Charles Carroll—Land Speculator, 1730–1755," *Md. Hist. Mag.*, 46 (1951), 93.

Harris, Marshall D., *Origin of Land Tenure System in United States* (1953).

Harrison, Fairfax, *Landmarks of Old Prince William*, vol. I (1924).

—— *Virginia Land Grants* (1925).

Kim, Sung Bok, "New Look at the Great Landlords of Eighteenth-Century New York," *WMQ*, 3 ser., 27 (1970), 581.

Livermore, Shaw, *Early American Land Companies: Their Influence on Corporate Development* (1939).

Liversage, Vincent, *Land Tenure in the Colonies* (1945).

Miller, W. D., "Narragansett Planters," *Am. Antiq. Soc., Proc.*, new ser., 43 (1933), 49.

Newman, Harry W., *Seignory in Early Maryland with a List of Manors and Manor Lords* (1949).

Nye, Mary G., ed., *New York Land Patents, 1688–1786* (1947).

Perzel, Edward S., "Landholding in Ipswich," *Essex Inst., Hist. Coll.*, 104 (1968), 303.

Pomfret, John E., *The New Jersey Proprietors and Their Lands, 1664–1776* (1964).

Robinson, W. Stitt, Jr., *Mother Earth: Land Grants in Virginia, 1607–1699* (1957).

Seiler, William H., "Land Processioning in Colonial Virginia," *WMQ*, 3 ser., 6 (1949), 416.

Sioussat, St. George L., "Breakdown of Royal Management of Lands in Southern Provinces, 1773–1775," *Agric. Hist.*, 3 (1929), 67.

Voorhis, Manning C., "Crown versus Council in Virginia Land Policy," *WMQ*, 3 ser., 3 (1946), 499.

Wyckoff, Vertrees J., "The Sizes of Plantations in Seventeenth-Century Maryland," *Md. Mag. Hist.*, 32 (1937), 331.

See also 10.3 for biographies/writings of:

Croghan, George, ? –1782
Morgan, George, 1743–1810
Trent, William, 1715–1787

37.5.4 Agriculture

Arents, George, "Seed from which Virginia Grew," *WMQ*, 2 ser., 19 (1939), 123.
Bidwell, Percy W., and John I. Falconer, *History of Agriculture in the Northern United States, 1620–1860* (1925).
Bressler, Leo A., "Agriculture among the Germans in Pennsylvania during the Eighteenth Century," *Penn. Hist.*, 22 (1955), 102.
Carrier, Lyman, *Beginnings of Agriculture in America* (1923).
"Colonial Agriculture," *Agric. Hist.*, 43 (1969). Entire issue.
Coxe, Tench, *Observations on Agriculture, Manufactures and Commerce of the United States* (1789).
Craven, Avery O., *Soil Exhaustion as a Factor in the Agricultural History of Virginia and Maryland, 1606–1860* (1926).
Doar, David, *Rice and Rice Planting in the South Carolina Low Country* (1936).
Eliot, Jared, *Essays upon Field Husbandry in New England and Other Papers, 1748–1762*, Harry J. Carman and Rexford G. Tugwell, eds. (1934).
Franklin, W. Neil, "Agriculture in Colonial North Carolina," *No. Car. Hist. Rev.*, 3 (1926), 539.
Gagliardo, John G., "Germans and Agriculture in Colonial Pennsylvania," *Penn. Mag. Hist. Biog.*, 83 (1959), 192.
Gray, Lewis C., *History of Agriculture in the Southern United States to 1860* (2 vols., 1933).
———— "Market Surplus Problems of Colonial Tobacco," *Agric. Hist.*, 2 (1928), 1.
Haywood, C. Robert, "Mercantilism and South Carolina Agriculture, 1700–1763," *So. Car. Hist. Mag.*, 60 (1959), 15.
Hemphill, John M., II, "Freight Rates in Maryland Tobacco Trade, 1705–1762," *Md. Hist. Mag.*, 54 (1959), 36.
Herndon, G. Melvin, "Hemp in Colonial Virginia," *Agric. Hist.*, 37 (1963), 86.
———— "Indian Agriculture in the Southern Colonies," *No. Car. Hist. Rev.*, 44 (1967), 283.
Laing, Wesley N., "Cattle in Seventeenth Century Virginia," *Va. Mag. Hist. Biog.*, 67 (1959), 143.
Lemon, James T., "Agricultural Practices of National Groups in Eighteenth-Century Southeastern Pennsylvania," *Geog. Rev.*, 56 (1966), 467.
Low, W. A., "Farmer in Virginia, 1783–1789," *Agric. Hist.*, 25 (1951), 122.
Mairs, Thomas I., *Some Pennsylvania Pioneers in Agricultural Science* (1928).
Mark, Irving, *Agrarian Conflicts in the Colony of New York* (1940).
Miller, W. D., "Narragansett Planters," *Am. Antiq. Soc., Proc.*, new ser., 43 (1933), 49.
Mingay, G. E., "The Agricultural Depression, 1730–1750," *Econ. Hist. Rev.*, 2 ser., 8 (1956), 323.
Olson, Albert L., *Agricultural Economy and the Population in Eighteenth-Century Connecticut* (1935).
Phillips, Ulrich B., ed., *Plantation and Frontier Documents, 1649–1863* (2 vols., 1909).
Rutman, Darrett B., "Agriculture in Early Commerce of Massachusetts Bay," *WMQ*, 3 ser., 20 (1963), 396.
———— *Husbandmen of Plymouth, 1620–1692* (1967).
Sachs, W. S., "Agricultural Conditions in the Northern Colonies before the Revolution," *Jour. Econ. Hist.*, 13 (1953), 274.
Salley, A. S., *Introduction of Rice Culture into South Carolina* (1919).
Saloutos, Theodore, "Efforts at Crop Control in Seventeenth Century America," *JSH*, 12 (1946), 45.

Scoville, Warren C., "Did Colonial Farmers 'Waste' Our Land?" *South. Econ. Jour.*, 20 (1953), 178.

Shryock, Richard H., "British versus German Traditions in Colonial Agriculture," *MVHR*, 26 (1939), 39.

Walcott, R. R., "Husbandry in Colonial New England," *NEQ*, 9 (1936), 218.

Weiss, Roger W., "Mr. Scoville on Colonial Land Wastage," *South. Econ. Jour.*, 21 (1954), 87.

Wertenbaker, Thomas J., *The Planters of Colonial Virginia* (1922).

Wilson, Mary T., "Americans Learn to Grow the Irish Potato," *NEQ*, 32 (1959), 333.

Woodward, Carl R., *Ploughs and Politicks: Charles Read of New Jersey and His Notes on Agriculture, 1715–1774* (1941).

* * * * * * *

Edwards, Everett E., *References on American Colonial Agriculture* (1938).

37.5.5 Commerce

Andrews, John H., "Anglo-American Trade in the Early Eighteenth Century," *Geog. Rev.*, 45 (1955), 99.

Bailyn, Bernard, "Communications and Trade: The Atlantic in The Seventeenth Century," *Jour. Econ. Hist.*, 13 (1953), 378.

—— and Lotte Bailyn, *Massachusetts Shipping 1697–1714: A Statistical Study* (1959).

Bailyn, Bernard, *New England Merchants in the Seventeenth Century* (1955).

Baxter, W. T., "Accounting in Colonial America," in A. C. Littleton and B. S. Yamey, eds., *Studies in the History of Accounting* (1956).

Berg, Harry D., "Organization of Business in Colonial Philadelphia," *Penn. Hist.*, 10 (1943), 157.

Bruchey, Stuart, "Success and Failure Factors: American Merchants in Foreign Trade in the Eighteenth and Early Nineteenth Century," *Bus. Hist. Rev.*, 32 (1958), 272.

Cole, Arthur H., "Tempo of Mercantile Life in Colonial America," *Bus. Hist. Rev.*, 33 (1959), 277.

"Commerce of Rhode Island, 1726–1800," Mass. Hist. Soc., *Coll.*, 7 ser., 9, 10 (1914–1915).

Coulter, Calvin B., Jr., "Import Trade of Colonial Virginia," *WMQ*, 3 ser., 2 (1945), 296.

Crittenden, C. C., *The Commerce of North Carolina, 1763–1789* (1936).

Dolan, J. R., *Yankee Peddlers of Early America* (1964).

Dow, George F., "Shipping and Trade in Early New England," Mass. Hist. Soc., *Proc.*, 64 (1930), 185.

East, Robert A., "The Business Entrepreneurs in a Changing Colonial Economy, 1763–1795," *Jour. Econ. Hist.*, 6 (1946), 16.

Farnie, D. A., "The Commercial Empire of the Atlantic, 1607–1783," *Econ. Hist. Rev.*, 15 (1962), 205.

Gabert, Glen, "New York Tobacco Trade, 1716–1742," Essex Inst., *Hist. Coll.*, 105 (1969), 103.

Giddens, P. H., "Trade and Industry in Colonial Maryland, 1753–69," *Jour. Econ. and Bus. Hist.*, 4 (1932), 512.

Gillingham, Harold E., *Marine Insurance in Philadelphia, 1721–1800* (1933).

Goebel, Dorothy B., " 'New England Trade' and the French West Indies, 1763–1774," *WMQ*, 3 ser., 20 (1963), 331.

Hanna, Mary A., *Trade of Delaware District before the Revolution* (1917).

Hemphill, John M., II, "Freight Rates in Maryland Tobacco Trade, 1705–1762," *Md. Hist. Mag.*, 54 (1959), 36.

Hooker, Roland M., *Colonial Trade of Connecticut* (1936).

Huntley, Francis C., "The Seaborne Trade of Virginia in Mid-Eighteenth Century: Port Hampton," *Va. Mag. Hist. Biog.*, 59 (1951), 297.

Innis, Harold A., *Fur Trade in Canada* (rev. ed., 1956).

Jacobs, Wilbur R., "Unsavory Sidelights on the Colonial Fur Trade," *N.Y. Hist.*, 34 (1953), 125.

James, Francis G., "Irish Colonial Trade in the Eighteenth Century," *WMQ*, 3 ser., 20 (1963), 574.

Jensen, Arthur L., *Maritime Commerce of Colonial Philadelphia* (1963).

Johnson, Keach, "Baltimore Company: Anglo-American Iron Trade 1731–1755," *WMQ*, 3 ser., 16 (1959), 37.

Klingaman, David C., "Coastwise Trade of Virginia in the Late Colonial Period," *Va. Mag. Hist. Biog.*, 77 (1969), 26.

Lydon, James G., "Fish and Flour for Gold: Southern Europe and the Colonial American Balance of Payments," *Bus. Hist. Rev.*, 39 (1965), 171.

—— "Philadelphia's Commercial Expansion, 1720–1739," *Penn. Mag. Hist. Biog.*, 91 (1967), 401.

Makinson, David H., *Barbados: A Study of North American–West Indian Relations, 1739–1789* (1964).

Martin, Margaret E., *Merchants and Trade of the Connecticut River Valley, 1750–1820* (1939).

Meroney, Geraldine, "London Entrepot Merchants and Georgia Colony," *WMQ*, 3 ser., 25 (1968), 230.

Middleton, A. Pierce, *Tobacco Coast: Maritime History of Chesapeake Bay in Colonial Era* (1953).

Moloney, F. X., *Fur Trade in New England, 1620–76* (1931).

Morison, Samuel E., "The Commerce of Boston on the Eve of the American Revolution," *Am. Antiq. Soc., Proc.*, 32 (1922), 24.

Morriss, Margaret S., *Colonial Trade of Maryland, 1689–1715* (1914).

Nash, Gary B., "Quest for the Susquehanna Valley: New York, Pennsylvania, and the Seventeenth-Century Fur Trade," *N.Y. Hist.*, 48 (1967), 3.

Nettels, Curtis P., "England's Trade with New England and New York, 1685–1720," *Col. Soc. Mass., Publ.*, 28 (1935), 322.

Ostrander, Gilman M., "Colonial Molasses Trade," *Agric. Hist.*, 30 (1956), 77.

Pares, Richard, *Yankees and Creoles: Trade between North America and the West Indies before the American Revolution* (1956).

Phillips, Paul, *The Fur Trade* (1961).

Price, Jacob M., "Economic Growth of Chesapeake and European Market, 1697–1775," *Jour. Econ. Hist.*, 24 (1964), 496.

—— *Tobacco Adventure to Russia, 1676–1722* (1961).

Rosenblatt, Samuel M., "Credit in Tobacco Consignment Trade: John Norton and Sons, 1768–1775," *WMQ*, 3 ser., 19 (1962), 383.

—— "Merchant-Planter Relations in the Tobacco Consignment Trade: John Norton and Robert C. Nicholas," *Va. Mag. Hist. Biog.*, 72 (1964), 454.

Saltonstall, William G., *Ports of Piscataqua* (1941).

Schlesinger, Arthur M., *The Colonial Merchants and the American Revolution, 1763–1776* (1918).

Sellers, Leila, *Charleston Business on the Eve of the American Revolution* (1934).

Sioussat, St. George L., "Virginia and English Commercial System," *Am. Hist. Assoc., Report*, I (1905), 71.

Soltow, J. H., "Scottish Traders in Virginia, 1750–1775," *Econ. Hist. Rev.*, 2 ser., 12 (1959), 83.

"State of the Trade, 1763," *Col. Soc. Mass., Publ.*, 19 (1918), 379.

Surrey, M. M., *The Commerce of Louisiana during the French Regime, 1699–1763* (1916).

Sutherland, Stella H., "Colonial Statistics," *Explorations in Entrepren. Hist.*, 5 (1967), 58.

Tapley, Harriet S., ed., *Early Coastwise and Foreign Shipping of Salem* (1934).

Thomson, Robert P., "The Tobacco Export of the Upper James River Naval District, 1733–1775," *WMQ*, 3 ser., 18 (1961), 393.

Walton, Gary M., "A Measure of Productivity Change in American Colonial Shipping," *Econ. Hist. Rev.*, 2 ser., 21 (1968), 268.

—— "Quantitative Study of American Colonial Shipping," *Jour. Econ. Hist.*, 26 (1966), 595.

Weslager, C. A., and A. R. Dunlap, *Dutch Explorers, Traders and Settlers in Delaware Valley, 1609–1664* (1961).

Witthoft, John, "Archaeology as a Key to the Colonial Fur Trade," *Minn. Hist.*, 40 (1966), 203.

* * * * * * *

Donnolly, Joseph P., *Tentative Bibliography for Colonial Fur Trade in the American Colonies, 1608–1800* (1947).

37.5.6 Merchants

Ames, S. M., "Virginia Business Man N. L. Savage," *Jour. Econ. and Bus. Hist.*, 3 (1931), 407.

Bailyn, Bernard, "Blount Papers: Notes on Merchant 'Class' in the Revolutionary Period," *WMQ*, 3 ser., 11 (1954), 98.

Bassett, J. S., "Virginia Planter and London Merchant," *Am. Hist. Assoc., Report*, I (1901), 551.

Baxter, W. T., *The House of Hancock: Business in Boston, 1724–1775* (1945).

Bigelow, B. M., "Aaron Lopez, Colonial Merchant of Newport," *NEQ*, 4 (1931), 757.

Browne, James, *Letter-Book of James Browne of Providence, Merchant, 1735–1738* (1929).

Bruchey, Stuart, comp., *Colonial Merchant: Sources and Readings* (1966).

Buffinton, A. H., "Sir Thomas Temple in Boston," *Col. Soc. Mass., Publ.*, 27 (1929), 308.

Carroll, Charles, "Accounts and Letter Books, 1735–1755," *Md. Hist. Mag.*, 20-27 (1925–1932).

Davison, Robert A., *Isaac Hicks: New York Merchant and Quaker, 1767–1820* (1964).

Edelman, Edward, "Thomas Hancock," *Jour. Econ. and Bus. Hist.*, 1 (1928–1929), 77.

Fitzhugh, William, "Letters, 1679–99," *Va. Mag. Hist. Biog.* 1–6 (1893–1899).

Freund, Miriam K., *Jewish Merchants in Colonial America* (1939).

Harrington, V. D., *New York Merchant on Eve of the Revolution* (1935).

Labaree, Benjamin W., *Patriots and Partisans: The Merchants of Newburyport, 1764–1815* (1962).

Leder, Lawrence H., and Vincent P. Carosso, "Robert Livingston (1654–1728): Businessman of Colonial New York," *Bus. Hist. Rev.*, 30 (1956), 18.

MacMaster, Richard K., and David C. Skaggs, eds., "The Letterbooks of Alexander Hamilton, Piscataway Factor," *Md. Hist. Mag.*, 61 (1966), 146.

Minchinton, Walter E., "Richard Champion, Nicholas Pocock, and Carolina Trade," *So. Car. Hist. Mag.*, 65 (1964), 87.

Norton, John, *John Norton and Sons, Merchants of London and Virginia: Papers, 1750–1795*, Frances N. Mason, ed. (1937).

Peabody, Robert E., *Merchant Venturers of Old Salem* (1912).

Sanford, Peleg, *Letter Book of Newport Merchant, 1666–1668*, Howard W. Preston et al., eds. (1928).

Tapley, Harriet S., "Richard Skinner, an Early Eighteenth-Century Merchant of Marblehead," *Essex. Inst., Hist. Coll.*, 68 (1942), 5.

Tolles, Frederick B., *Meeting House and Counting House: Quaker Merchants of Colonial Philadelphia* (1948).

Watts, John, "Letter-Book of John Watts, Merchant and Councillor of New York," *N. Y. Hist. Soc., Coll.*, 61 (1928).

Weaver, Glenn, *Jonathan Trumbull: Connecticut's Merchant Magistrate* (1952).

—— "Some Aspects of Early Eighteenth-Century Connecticut Trade," *Conn. Hist. Soc., Bull.*, 22 (1957), 23.

See also 10.3 for biographies/writings of:

Beekman Family
Brown Family
Cabot, George, 1752–1823

Fitzhugh, William, 1651–1701
Gadsden, Christopher, 1724–1805
Girard, Stephen, 1750–1831
Hancock, John, 1736–1793
Hull, John, 1624–1683
Hutchinson, Thomas, 1711–1780
Lee, William, 1739–1795
Livingston, Robert, 1654–1728
Lopez, Aaron, 1731–1782
Morris, Robert, 1734–1806
Oliver, Robert, ca. 1757–1819
Peabody, Joseph, 1757–1844
Pemberton, Israel, 1715–1779
Pepperrell Family
Pynchon, William, 1590–1662
Salomon, Haym, 1740–1785
Sewall, Samuel, 1652–1730
Thorndike, Israel, 1755–1832
Watson, Elkanah, 1758–1842

37.5.7 Pricing

Bezanson, Anne, *Prices and Inflation during the Revolution: Pennsylvania, 1770–1790* (1951).
—— et al., *Prices in Colonial Pennsylvania* (1935).
Crandall, Ruth, "Wholesale Commodity Prices in Boston during the Eighteenth Century," *Rev. Econ. Stat.*, 16 (1934), 117.
Davisson, William I., "Essex County Price Trends: Money and Markets in Seventeenth-Century Massachusetts," Essex Inst., *Hist. Coll.*, 103 (1967), 144.
Taylor, George R., "Wholesale Commodity Prices at Charleston, 1732–1791," *Jour. Econ. and Bus. Hist.*, 4 (1932), 356.
Wyckoff, Vertrees J., "Seventeenth Century Maryland Prices," *Agric. Hist.*, 12 (1938), 299.

37.5.8 Smuggling, Privateering, and Piracy

Barker, T. C., "Smuggling in the Eighteenth Century: The Evidence of the Scottish Tobacco Trade," *Va. Mag. Hist. Biog.*, 62 (1954), 387.
Chapin, Howard M., *Privateer Ships and Sailors: The First Century of American Colonial Privateering, 1625–1725* (1926).
—— *Privateering in King George's War, 1739–1748* (1928).
Cole, W. A., "Trends in Eighteenth-Century Smuggling," *Econ. Hist. Rev.*, 2 ser., 10 (1958), 395.
Dow, George F., and John H. Edmonds, *The Pirates of New England Coast, 1630–1730* (1923).
Harman, Joyce E., *Trade and Privateering in Spanish Florida, 1732–1763* (1969).
Hughson, Shirley C., "Carolina Pirates and Colonial Commerce, 1670–1740," *Johns Hopkins Studies*, 12 (1894), 241.
Jameson, John F., ed., *Privateering and Piracy in the Colonial Period* (1923).
Johnson, Victor L., "Fair Traders and Smugglers in Philadelphia, 1754–1763," *Penn. Mag. Hist. Biog.*, 83 (1959), 125.
Karraker, Cyrus H., *Piracy Was a Business* (1953).
Williams, Lloyd H., *Pirates of Colonial Virginia* (1937).
Winston, Alexander, *No Man Knows My Grave: The Great Age of Pirates, 1665–1715* (1969).

37.5.9 Money, Banking, and Finance

Behrens, Kathryn L., *Paper Money in Maryland, 1727–1789* (1923).
Belz, Herman, "Paper Money in Colonial Massachusetts, 1749–1750," Essex Inst., *Hist. Coll.*, 101 (1965), 149.

Billias, George A., *The Massachusetts Land Bankers of 1740* (1959).

Burstein, M. L., "Colonial Currency and Contemporary Monetary Theory," *Explorations in Entrepren. Hist.*, 2 ser., 3 (1966), 220.

Cole, Arthur H., "Evolution of the Foreign Exchange Markets of the United States," *Jour. Econ. and Bus. Hist.*, 1 (1929), 386.

Davis, Andrew M., ed., *Colonial Currency Reprints, 1682–1751* (4 vols., 1910).

Davis, Andrew M., *Currency and Banking in the Province of Massachusetts Bay* (2 vols., 1901).

——— "Provincial Banks: Land and Silver," Col. Soc. Mass., *Publ.*, 3 (1900), 2.

Ernst, Joseph A., "Colonial Currency," *Explorations in Entrepren. Hist.*, 6 (1969), 187.

——— "Currency Act of 1764, Virginia Paper Money and Protection of British Investments," *WMQ*, 3 ser., 22 (1965), 33.

Ezell, John S., *Fortune's Merry Wheel: Lottery in America* (1960).

Ferguson, E. James, "Currency Finance: Colonial Monetary Practices," *WMQ*, 3 ser., 10 (1953), 153.

Freiberg, Malcolm, "Thomas Hutchinson and the Province Currency," *NEQ*, 30 (1957), 190.

Gould, Clarence P., *Money and Transportation in Maryland* (1915).

Greene, Jack P., and Richard M. Jellison, "The Currency Act of 1764 in Imperial-Colonial Relations, 1764–1776." *WMQ*, 3 ser., 18 (1961), 485.

Heath, William E., "Colonial Money System of Georgia," *Ga. Hist. Quar.*, 19 (1935), 145.

Horsefield, J. Keith, *British Monetary Experiments, 1650–1710* (1960).

——— "Origins of Blackwell's Model of a Bank," *WMQ*, 3 ser., 23 (1966), 121.

Jellison, Richard M., "Antecedents of South Carolina Currency Acts of 1736 and 1746," *WMQ*, 3 ser., 16 (1959), 556.

——— "Paper Currency in Colonial South Carolina: A Reappraisal," *So. Car. Hist. Mag.*, 62 (1961), 134.

Kemmerer, Donald L., "Paper Money in New Jersey, 1668–1775," N.J. Hist. Soc., *Proc.*, 74 (1956), 107.

Lester, Richard A., "Currency Issues to Overcome Depressions," *Jour. Pol. Econ.*, 45 (1938), 324; 47 (1939), 182.

——— *Monetary Experiments: Early American and Recent Scandinavian* (1939).

Lydon, James G., "Southern Europe and Colonial American Balance of Payments," *Bus. Hist. Rev.*, 39 (1965), 171.

Nettels, Curtis P., *Money Supply of the American Colonies before 1720* (1934).

——— "The Origins of Paper Money in the English Colonies," *Econ. Hist.*, 3 (1934), 35.

Newman, Eric P., *Coinage for Colonial Virginia* (1956).

——— *Early Paper Money of America* (1967).

Norton, William B., "Paper Currency in Massachusetts during the Revolution," *NEQ*, 7 (1934), 43.

Peckham, Howard H., "Speculations on the Colonial Wars," *WMQ*, 3 ser., 17 (1960), 463.

Ripley, William Z., *Financial History of Virginia, 1609–1776* (1893).

Scott, Kenneth, *Counterfeiting in Colonial America* (1957).

Sheridan, Richard B., "The British Credit Crises of 1772 and the American Colonies," *Jour. Econ. Hist.*, 20 (1960), 161.

Thayer, Theodore, "Land Bank System in American Colonies," *Jour. Econ. Hist.*, 13 (1953), 145.

Vickers, Douglas, *Studies in Theory of Money, 1690–1776* (1959).

Wainwright, Nicholas B., *A Philadelphia Story: The Philadelphia Contributionship for the Insurance of Houses from Loss by Fire* (1952).

See also 10.3 for biographies/writings of:

Bingham, William, 1752–1804
Girard, Stephen, 1750–1831
Hull, John, 1624–1683
Morris, Robert, 1734–1806

37.5.10 Industry

Abbott, Collamer M., "Colonial Copper Mines," *WMQ*, 3 ser., 27 (1970), 295.
Bining, Arthur C., "Early Ironmasters of Pennsylvania," *Penn. Hist.*, 18 (1951), 93.
────── *Pennsylvania Iron Manufacture in the Eighteenth Century* (1938).
Bishop, James L., *History of American Manufactures, 1608–1860* (3 vols., 1867).
Boyer, Charles S., *Early Forges and Furnaces in New Jersey* (1931).
Bridenbaugh, Carl, *The Colonial Craftsman* (1950).
Brydon, G. M., "Bristol Iron Works," *Va. Mag. Hist. Biog.*, 42 (1934), 97.
Bruce, Kathleen, *Virginia Iron Manufacture* (1930).
Coyne, F. E., *Development of the Cooperage Industry in the United States, 1620–1940* (1940).
Hartley, Edward N., *Ironworks on the Saugus* (1957).
Haywood, C. Robert, "Use of the Threat of Manufacturing by Southern Colonies," *JSH*, 25 (1959), 207.
Hecht, Arthur, "Lead Production in Virginia during the Seventeenth and Eighteenth Centuries," *W. Va. Hist.*, 25 (1964), 173.
Hohman, Elmo P., *The American Whaleman* (1928).
Hunter, Dard, *Papermaking in Pioneer America* (1952).
Innis, Harold A., *The Cod Fisheries: The History of an International Economy* (1940).
Johnson, Keach, "Baltimore Company Seeks English Subsidies for Colonial Iron Industry," *Md. Hist. Mag.*, 46 (1951), 27.
────── "Genesis of Baltimore Ironworks," *JSH*, 19 (1953), 157.
Keith, Herbert C., and Charles R. Harte, *Early Iron Industry of Connecticut* (1935).
Lord, Eleanor L., *Industrial Experiments in British Colonies of North America* (1898).
Nettels, Curtis P., "Menace of Colonial Manufacturing, 1690–1720," *NEQ*, 4 (1931), 230.
Neu, Irene D., "Iron Plantations of Colonial New York," *N.Y. Hist.*, 33 (1952), 3.
Pearson, John C., "The Fish and Fisheries of Colonial Virginia," *WMQ*, 2 ser., 22 (1942), 213; 2 ser., 23 (1943), 1; 3 ser., 1 (1944), 179.
Pease, George B., "Timothy Palmer, Bridge-Builder of the Eighteenth Century," *Essex Inst., Hist. Coll.*, 83 (1947), 97.
Price, Jacob M., "The Beginnings of Tobacco Manufacture in Virginia," *Va. Mag. Hist. Biog.*, 64 (1956), 3.
Snow, Sinclair, "Naval Stores in Colonial Virginia," *Va. Mag. Hist. Biog.*, 72 (1964), 75.
Stephens, Pauline T., "Silk Industry in Georgia," *Ga. Rev.*, 7 (1953), 39.
Tunis, Edwin R., *Colonial Craftsmen and the Beginnings of American Industry* (1965).
Tustin, E. B., Jr., "Story of Salt in New England," *Essex Inst., Hist. Coll.*, 85 (1949), 259.
Van Wagenen, Jared, *Golden Age of Homespun* (1953).
Weaver, Glenn, "Industry in an Agrarian Economy: Early Eighteenth Century Connecticut," *Conn. Hist. Soc., Bull.*, 19 (1954), 82.
Weiss, Harry B., and Grace M. Ziegler, *Early Fulling Mills of New Jersey* (1957).
Weiss, Harry B., and Grace M. Weiss, *Forgotten Mills of Early New Jersey* (1960).
────── *Revolutionary Saltworks of New Jersey Coast* (1959).
Welsh, Peter C., "Brandywine Mills: Chronicle of Industry, 1762–1816," *Del. Hist.*, 7 (1956), 17.

37.5.11 Transportation

Baker, William A., *Colonial Vessels: Some Seventeenth Century Sailing Craft* (1962).
Chandler, Charles L., *Early Shipbuilding in Pennsylvania, 1683–1812* (1932).
Colles, Christopher, *A Survey of the Roads of the United States of America, 1789*, Walter W. Ristow, ed. (1961).

Crittenden, C. C., "Overland Travel and Transportation in North Carolina, 1763–1789," *No. Car. Hist. Rev.*, 8 (1931), 239.

Gould, Clarence P., *Money and Transportation in Maryland, 1720–1765* (1915).

Gray, Ralph D., *National Waterway: Chesapeake and Delaware Canal, 1769–1965* (1967).

Jones, Herbert G., *The King's Highway from Portland to Kittery* (1953).

Kincaid, Robert L., *The Wilderness Road* (1947).

Lane, Wheaton J., *From Indian Trail to Iron Horse: Travel and Transportation in New Jersey, 1620–1860* (1939).

McElroy, John W., "Seafaring in Seventeenth-Century New England," *NEQ*, 8 (1935), 331.

Meyer, Balthasar H., et al., *History of Transportation before 1860* (1917).

Middleton, Arthur P., "The Chesapeake Convoy System, 1662–1763," *WMQ*, 3 ser., 3 (1946), 182.

Mitchell, Isabel S., *Roads and Road-Making in Colonial Connecticut* (1933).

Morison, Samuel E., *Maritime History of Massachusetts, 1783–1860* (1921).

Paine, Ralph D., *Ships and Sailors of Old Salem* (rev. ed., 1923).

Robinson, John, and George F. Dow, *The Sailing Ships of New England, 1607–1907* (1953).

Semmes, Raphael, *Captains and Mariners of Early Maryland* (1937).

Wallace, Paul A., *Indian Paths of Pennsylvania* (1965).

Wroth, Lawrence C., "Some American Contributions to the Art of Navigation, 1519–1802," Mass. Hist. Soc., *Proc.*, 68 (1944–1947), 72.

Wyckoff, Vertrees J., "Ships and Sailing of Seventeenth-Century Maryland," *Md. Hist. Mag.*, 33 (1938), 334; 34 (1939), 46.

37.5.12 Labor

Ballagh, James C., *White Servitude in Virginia* (1895).

Geiser, Karl F., *Redemptioners and Indentured Servants in Pennsylvania* (1901).

Harrower, John, *Journal, 1773–1776*, Edward M. Riley, ed. (1963).

Handlin, Oscar, and Mary F. Handlin, "Origins of the Southern Labor System," *WMQ*, 3 ser., 7 (1950), 199.

Herrick, C. A., *White Servitude in Pennsylvania* (1926).

Jernegan, Marcus W., *Laboring and Dependent Classes in Colonial America* (1931).

Jonas, Manfred, "Wages in Early Colonial Maryland," *Md. Hist. Mag.*, 51 (1956), 27.

McCormac, E. I., *White Servitude in Maryland* (1904).

McKee, Samuel, Jr., *Labor in Colonial New York, 1664–1776* (1935).

Morris, Richard B., *Government and Labor in Early America* (1946).

Phillips, George L., *American Chimney Sweeps* (1957).

Phillips, Ulrich B., *Life and Labor in the Old South* (1929).

Sears, William P., Jr., "Indentured Servants in Colonial America," *Dalhousie Rev.*, 37 (1957), 121.

Seybolt, Robert F., *Apprenticeship and Apprenticeship Education in Colonial New England and New York* (1917).

Smith, Abbot E., *Colonists in Bondage: White Servitude and Convict Labor in America, 1607–1776* (1947).

Smith, Warren B., *White Servitude in Colonial South Carolina* (1961).

U.S. Department of Labor, Bureau of Labor Statistics, *Wages in the Colonial Period* (1929).

37.6 SLAVERY

37.6.1 General

Aptheker, Herbert, *American Negro Slave Revolts* (1943).

———— "The Quakers and Negro Slavery," *Jour. Negro Hist.*, 25 (1940), 331.

Bennett, J. Harry, Jr., *Bondsmen and Bishops: Slavery and Apprenticeship on Codrington Plantation of Barbados, 1710–1838* (1958).

Ballagh, James C., *History of Slavery in Virginia* (1902).

Bassett, J. S., *Slavery and Servitude in the Colony of North Carolina* (1896).

Carroll, Kenneth L., "Maryland Quakers and Slavery," *Md. Hist. Mag.*, 45 (1950), 215.

Clark, Ernest J., Jr., "Aspects of the North Carolina Slave Code, 1715–1860," *No. Car. Hist. Rev.*, 39 (1962), 148.

Clarke, T. Wood, "The Negro Plot of 1741," *N.Y. Hist.*, 25 (1944), 167.

Clifton, Denzil T., "Anglicanism and Negro Slavery in Colonial America," *Hist. Mag. Prot. Episc. Church*, 39 (1970), 29.

Davis, David Brion, *The Problem of Slavery in Western Culture* (1964).

Degler, Carl N., "Slavery in Brazil and the United States," *AHR*, 75 (1970), 1004.

Elkins, Stanley M., and Eric McKitrick, "Institutions and Law of Slavery: Dynamics of Unopposed Capitalism," *Am. Quar.*, 9 (1957), 3.

—— "Institutions and Law of Slavery: Slavery in Capitalist and Non-Capitalist Cultures," *Am. Quar.*, 9 (1957), 159.

Flanders, R. B., *Plantation Slavery in Georgia* (1933).

Goveia, Elsa V., *Slave Society in British Leeward Islands at the End of the Eighteenth Century* (1965).

Grant, Douglas, *The Fortunate Slave: An Illustration of African Slavery in the Early Eighteenth Century* (1968).

Handlin, Oscar, and Mary F. Handlin, "Origins of the Southern Labor System," *WMQ*, 3 ser., 7 (1950), 199.

Haywood, C. Robert, "Mercantilism and Colonial Slave Labor, 1700–1763," *JSH*, 23 (1957), 454.

Jernegan, Marcus W., "Slavery and Beginnings of Industrialism in the American Colonies," *AHR*, 25 (1920), 220.

Jordan, Winthrop D., "The Influence of the West Indies on the Origins of New England Slavery," *WMQ*, 3 ser., 18 (1961), 243.

—— "Modern Tensions and the Origins of American Slavery," *JSH*, 27 (1962), 18.

Klein, Herbert S., *Slavery in the Americas: Comparative Study of Cuba and Virginia* (1967).

Lauber, A. W., *Indian Slavery in Colonial Times* (1913).

McManus, Edgar J., *History of Negro Slavery in New York* (1966).

Mitchell, Mary H., "Slavery in Connecticut and Especially in New Haven," New Haven Colony Hist. Soc., *Papers*, 10 (1951), 286.

Moore, G. H., *Notes on Slavery in Massachusetts* (1866).

Moss, Simeon F., "The Persistence of Slavery and Involuntary Servitude in a Free State (1685–1866)," *Jour. Negro Hist.*, 25 (1950), 289.

Nadelhaft, Jerome, "Somerset Case and Slavery: Myth, Reality, and Repercussions," *Jour. Negro Hist.*, 51 (1966), 193.

Padgett, James A., "The Status of Slaves in Colonial North Carolina," *Jour. Negro Hist.*, 14 (1929), 300.

Palmer, Paul C., "Servant into Slave: The Evolution of the Legal Status of Negro Laborer in Colonial Virginia," *So. Atl. Quar.*, 65 (1966), 355.

Phillips, Ulrich B., *American Negro Slavery* (1918).

Pitman, F. W., "Slavery on British West Indies Plantations," *Jour. Negro Hist.*, 11 (1926), 584.

Postell, William D., *Health of Slaves on Southern Plantations* (1951).

Scott, Kenneth, "The Slave Insurrection in New York in 1712," *N.Y. Hist. Soc. Quar.*, 45 (1961), 43.

Sirmans, M. Eugene, "Legal Status of the Slave in South Carolina, 1670–1740," *JSH*, 28 (1962), 462.

Starobin, Robert, "Disciplining Industrial Slaves in the Old South," *Jour. Negro Hist.*, 53 (1968), 111.

Steiner, Bernard C., *History of Slavery in Connecticut* (1893).

Szasz, Ferenc M., "The New York Slave Revolt of 1741: A Re-examination," *N.Y. Hist.*, 48 (1967), 215.

Taylor, Rosser H., *Slaveholding in North Carolina: An Economic View* (1926).

Turner, Edward R., "Slavery in Colonial Pennsylvania," *Penn. Mag. Hist. Biog.*, 25 (1911), 141.

Wax, Darold D., "Demand for Slave Labor in Colonial Pennsylvania," *Penn. Hist.*, 34 (1967), 331.

Winston, Sanford, "Indian Slavery in the Carolina Region," *Jour. Negro Hist.*, 19 (1934), 431.

37.6.2 Slave Trade

Curtin, Philip D., ed., *Africa Remembered: Narratives by West Africans from the Era of the Slave Trade* (1967).

Curtin, Philip D., *The Atlantic Slave Trade: A Census* (1969).

Davies, Kenneth G., *Royal African Company* (1957).

Donnan, Elizabeth, ed., *Documents Illustrative of the History of the Slave Trade to America,* vol. I (1930).

Du Bois, W. E. B., *Suppression of the African Slave Trade to the United States, 1638–1870* (1896).

Duignan, Peter, and Clarence Clendenen, *The United States and the African Slave Trade, 1619–1862* (1963).

Mannix, Daniel, *Black Cargoes: History of the Atlantic Slave Trade, 1518–1865* (1962).

Platt, Virginia B., "East India Company and the Madagascar Slave Trade," *WMQ*, 3 ser., 26 (1969), 548.

Pope-Hennessey, James, *Sins of the Fathers: Atlantic Slave Traders, 1441–1807* (1968).

Wax, Darold D., "Negro Imports into Pennsylvania, 1720–1766," *Penn. Hist.*, 32 (1965), 254.

———— "Quaker Merchants and Slave Trade in Colonial Pennsylvania," *Penn. Mag. Hist. Biog.*, 86 (1962), 143.

37.6.3 Antislavery Sentiment

Brooks, G. S., *Friend Anthony Benezet* (1937).

Carroll, Kenneth L., "Maryland Quakers and Slavery," *Md. Hist. Mag.*, 45 (1950), 215.

———— "Religious Influences on the Manumission of Slaves in Caroline, Dorchester, and Talbot Counties," *Md. Hist. Mag.*, 56 (1961), 176.

———— "William Southeby, Early Quaker Antislavery Writer," *Penn. Mag. Hist. Biog.*, 89 (1965), 416.

Drake, Thomas E., *Quakers and Slavery in America* (1950).

Duberman, Martin, ed., *The Antislavery Vanguard: New Essays on the Abolitionists* (1965).

Edwards, Jonathan, *The Injustice and Impolicy of the Slave-trade and of the Slavery of the Africans* (1792).

Hopkins, Samuel, *A Dialogue concerning the Slavery of the Africans* (1776).

Klingberg, Frank J., *Anglican Humanitarianism in Colonial New York* (1940).

Kraus, Michael, "Slavery Reform in the Eighteenth Century: Transatlantic Intellectual Cooperation," *Penn. Mag. Hist. Biog.*, 60 (1936), 53.

Locke, Mary S., *Anti-Slavery Sentiment in America, 1619–1808* (1901).

Lovejoy, David S., "Samuel Hopkins: Religion, Slavery and the Revolution," *NEQ*, 40 (1967), 227.

Moulton, Phillips, "John Woolman's Approach to Social Action, as Exemplified in Relation to Slavery," *Church Hist.*, 35 (1966), 399.

O'Brien, F. William, "Did the Jennison Case Outlaw Slavery in Massachusetts?" *WMQ*, 3 ser., 17 (1960), 219.

Rice, David, *Slavery Inconsistent with Justice and Good Policy, Proved in a Speech Delivered at Danville, Kentucky* (1792).

Sewall, Samuel, *The Selling of Joseph* (1700).

Spector, Robert M., "Quock Walker Cases (1781-83)," *Jour. Negro Hist.*, 53 (1968), 12.

Towner, Lawrence W., "The Sewall-Saffin Dialogue on Slavery," *WMQ*, 3 ser., 21 (1964), 40.

Weeks, Stephen B., *Southern Quakers and Slavery* (1896).

Zilversmit, Arthur, *The First Emancipation: The Abolition of Slavery in the North* (1967).

———— "Quock Walker, Mumbet, and the Abolition of Slavery in Massachusetts," *WMQ*, 3 ser., 25 (1968), 4.

See also 10.3 for biographies/writings of:

Benezet, Anthony, 1713–1784
Pastorius, Francis D., 1651–1719/20
Woolman, John, 1720–1772

37.7 DEMOGRAPHY

Aldridge, Alfred O., "Franklin as Demographer," *Jour. Econ. Hist.*, 9 (1949), 25.

Bartlett, John R., ed., *Census of Inhabitants of the Colony of Rhode Island in 1774* (1858).

Blake, John B., "Early History of Vital Statistics in Massachusetts," *Bull. Hist. Med.*, 29 (1956), 46.

Brush, John E., *Population of New Jersey* (1956).

Cassedy, James H., *Demography in Early America: Beginnings of the Statistical Mind, 1600–1800* (1969).

Chickering, Jesse, *Statistical View of Population of Massachusetts, 1765–1840* (1846).

Demos, John, "Families in Colonial Bristol, Rhode Island: Exercise in Historical Demography," *WMQ*, 3 ser., 25 (1968), 40.

Dethlefsen, Edwin S., "Colonial Gravestones and Demography," *Am. Jour. Phys. Anthropol.*, 31 (1969), 321.

Dunaway, Wayland F., "Pennsylvania as an Early Distributing Center of Population," *Penn. Mag. Hist. Biog.*, 55 (1931), 134.

Fales, Martha G., "The Early American Way of Death," Essex Inst., *Hist. Coll.*, 100 (1964), 75.

Friis, Herman R., "A Series of Population Maps of the Colonies and the United States, 1625–1790," *Geog. Rev.*, 30 (1940), 463.

Greene, Evarts B., and Virginia D. Harrington, *American Population before the Federal Census of 1790* (1932).

Greven, Philip J., Jr., *Four Generations: Population, Land, and Family in Colonial Andover, Massachusetts* (1970).

———— "Historical Demography and Colonial America," *WMQ*, 3 ser., 24 (1967), 438.

Higgs, Robert, and H. Louis Stettler III, "Colonial New England Demography: Sampling Approach," *WMQ*, 3 ser., 27 (1970), 282.

Jacobus, Donald L., "Age of Girls at Marriage in Colonial New England," *Am. Geneal.*, 27 (1951), 116.

Karinen, Arthur E., "Maryland Population: 1631–1730," *Md. Hist. Mag.*, 54 (1959), 365.

———— "Maryland Population, 1631–1840," *Md. Hist. Mag.*, 60 (1965), 139.

Lockridge, Kenneth A., "Land, Population, and the Evolution of New England Society, 1630–1790," *Past and Present*, 39 (1968), 62.

———— "Population of Dedham, Massachusetts, 1636–1736," *Econ. Hist. Rev.*, 19 (1966), 318.

Mood, Fulmer, "Studies in the History of American Settled Areas and Frontier Lines, 1625–1790," *Agric. Hist.*, 26 (1952), 16.

Moller, Herbert, "Sex Composition and Correlated Culture Patterns of Colonial America," *WMQ*, 3 ser., 2 (1945), 113.

Olson, Albert L., *Agricultural Economy and the Population in Eighteenth-Century Connecticut* (1935).

Petty, Julian J., *The Growth and Distribution of Population in South Carolina* (1943).

Potter, J., "The Growth of Population in America, 1700–1860," in David Glass and D. E. C. Eversley, eds., *Population in History: Essays in Historical Demography* (1965).

Sutherland, Stella H., *Population Distribution in Colonial America* (1936).

Whitney, Herbert A., "Estimating Precensus Populations: A Method Suggested and Applied to the Towns of Rhode Island and Plymouth Colonies in 1689," Assoc. Am. Geographers, *Annals*, 55 (1965), 179.

37.8 SOCIAL AND ECONOMIC CLASSES

Bailyn, Bernard, "The Beekmans of New York: Trade, Politics, and Families," *WMQ*, 3 ser., 14 (1957), 601.

—— "Politics and Social Structure in Virginia," in James Morton Smith, ed., *Seventeenth Century America* (1959).

Bridenbaugh, Carl, *Myths and Realities: Societies of the Colonial South* (1963).

Brown, B. Katherine, "Puritan Concept of Aristocracy," *MVHR*, 41 (1954), 105.

Bruce, Philip A., *Social Life of Virginia* (1927).

Cady, Edwin H., *The Gentleman in America* (1949).

Campbell, Mildred, "Social Origins of Some Early Americans," in James Morton Smith, ed., *Seventeenth Century America* (1959).

Crary, Catherine Snell, "The American Dream: John Tabor Kempe's Rise from Poverty to Riches," *WMQ*, 3 ser., 14 (1957), 176.

Dawes, Norman H., "Titles as Symbols of Prestige," *WMQ*, 3 ser., 6 (1949), 69.

Diamond, Sigmund, "From Organization to Society: Virginia in the Seventeenth Century," *Am. Jour. Sociol.*, 63 (1958), 457.

Evans, Emory G., "The Rise and Decline of the Virginia Aristocracy in the Eighteenth Century: The Nelsons," in Darrett B. Rutman, ed., *The Old Dominion: Essays for Thomas Perkins Abernethy* (1964).

Hemphill, John M., ed., "John Wayles Rates His Neighbors," *Va. Mag. Hist. Biog.*, 66 (1958), 302.

Henretta, James A., "Social Structure in Colonial Boston," *WMQ*, 3 ser., 22 (1965), 75.

High, James, "Maryland's Middle Class in Colonial Aristocratic Pattern," *Md. Hist. Mag.*, 57 (1962), 334.

Keim, C. Ray, "Primogeniture and Entail in Colonial Virginia," *WMQ*, 3 ser., 25 (1968), 545.

Kenney, Alice P., "Dutch Patricians in Colonial Albany," *N.Y. Hist.*, 49 (1968), 249.

Krout, John A. "Behind the Coat of Arms: A Phase of Prestige in Colonial New York," *N. Y. Hist.*, 16 (1935), 45.

Land, Aubrey C., "Economic Base and Social Structure: Northern Chesapeake in Eighteenth Century," *Jour. Econ. Hist.*, 25 (1965), 639.

Lemon, James T., and Gary B. Nash, "Distribution of Wealth in Eighteenth-Century America: Chester County, Pennsylvania, 1693-1802," *Jour. Soc. Hist.*, 2 (1968), 1.

Lockridge, Kenneth A., "Evolution of New England Society, 1630–1790," *Past and Present*, 39 (1968), 62.

Main, Jackson T., "The One Hundred," *WMQ*, 3 ser., 11 (1954), 354.

—— *Social Structure of Revolutionary America* (1965).

Morison, Samuel E., "Precedence at Harvard College in the Seventeenth Century," Am. Antiq. Soc., *Proc.*, 42 (1933), 371.

Nash, Gary B., *Class and Society in Early America* (1970).

Rasmusson, Ethel E., "Democratic Environment--Aristocratic Aspiration," *Penn. Mag. Hist. Biog.*, 90 (1966), 155.

Reavis, William A., "Maryland Gentry and Social Mobility, 1637–1676," *WMQ*, 3 ser., 14 (1957), 418.

Schlesinger, Arthur M., "Aristocracy in Colonial America," Mass. Hist. Soc., *Proc.*, 74 (1962), 3.

Schonfeld, Albert G., and Spencer Wilson, "Value of Personal Estates in Maryland, 1700–1710," *Md. Hist. Mag.*, 58 (1963), 333.

Weeden, W. B., *Economic and Social History of New England, 1620–1789*, vol. II (1890).
Wertenbaker, Thomas J., *Patrician and Plebian in Virginia* (1910).
Winslow, Ola E., *Meetinghouse Hill, 1630–1783* (1952).
Wright, Louis B., *First Gentlemen of Virginia* (1940).

37.9 DEVELOPMENT OF TOWNS AND CITIES

Akagi, R. H., *Town Proprietors of New England Colonies* (1924).
American Philosophical Society, *Historic Philadelphia from Founding to the Early Nineteenth Century* (1953).
Bridenbaugh, Carl, *Cities in Revolt: Urban Life in America, 1743–1776* (1955).
——— *Cities in the Wilderness* (1938).
——— "The New England Town: A Way of Life," Am. Antiq. Soc., *Proc.*, 56 (1947), 19.
———and Jessica Bridenbaugh, *Rebels and Gentlemen: Philadelphia in the Age of Franklin* (1942).
Eberlein, Harold D., and C. V. D. Hubbard, *Portrait of a Colonial City: Philadelphia, 1670–1838* (1939).
Edwards, George W., *New York as an Eighteenth Century Municipality, 1731–1766* (1917).
Grant, Charles S., *Democracy in Connecticut Frontier Town of Kent* (1961).
Griffith, Ernest S., *History of American City Government: The Colonial Period* (1938).
Haller, William, Jr., *Puritan Frontier: Town Planning in New England, 1630–1660* (1951).
Innes, J. H., *New Amsterdam and Its People* (1902).
Kimball, Gertrude S., *Providence in Colonial Times* (1912).
Koch, Donald W., "Income Distribution and Political Structure in Seventeenth-Century Salem, Massachusetts," Essex Inst., *Hist. Coll.*, 105 (1969), 50.
Labaree, Benjamin W., "New England Town Meeting," *Am. Archivist*, 25 (1962), 165.
Labaree, Leonard W., *Milford, Connecticut: Early Development of a Town as Shown in Its Land Records* (1933).
Lemon, James T., "Urbanization and Development of Eighteenth-Century Southeastern Pennsylvania and Adjacent Delaware," *WMQ*, 3 ser., 24 (1967), 501.
Lockridge, Kenneth A., *New England Town: Dedham, Massachusetts, 1636–1736* (1970).
MacLear, Anne B., *Early New England Towns: A Comparative Study of Their Development* (1908).
Nash, Gary B., "City Planning and Political Tension in the Seventeenth Century: Philadelphia," Am. Philos. Soc., *Proc.*, 112 (1968), 54.
Parker, Joel, "Origin, Organization, and Influence of Towns of New England," Mass. Hist. Soc., *Proc.*, 9 (1866), 14.
Phillips, James D., *Salem in the Seventeenth Century* (1933).
Powell, Sumner C., *Puritan Village: The Formation of a New England Town* (1963).
Rainbolt, John C., "Absence of Towns in Seventeenth-Century Virginia," *JSH*, 35 (1969), 343.
Reps, John W., *Town Planning in Frontier America* (1969).
Rutman, Darrett B., *Husbandmen of Plymouth, 1620–1692* (1967).
——— *Winthrop's Boston: A Puritan Town, 1630–1649* (1965).
Seybolt, Robert F., *Colonial Citizen of New York City* (1918).
Sly, John F., *Town Government in Massachusetts* (1930).
Warden, Gerald B., *Boston, 1689–1776* (1970).
Waters, John J., "Hingham, Massachusetts, 1631–1661," *Jour. Soc. Hist.*, 1 (1968), 351.
Zimmerman, Joseph F., "Genesis of Massachusetts Town," *Social Sci. Quar.*, 41 (1966), 76.

Zuckerman, Michael, *Peaceable Kingdoms: New England Towns in Eighteenth Century* (1970).

37.10 FRONTIER

Abernethy, Thomas P., *From Frontier to Plantation in Tennessee* (1932).
—— *Three Virginia Frontiers* (1940).
Alden, John R., *John Stuart and the Southern Colonial Frontier, 1754–75* (1944).
Alvord, Clarence W., ed., "Cahokia Records," Ill. Hist., *Coll.*, 2 (1907).
Alvord, Clarence W., and Lee Bidgood, *The First Exploration of the Trans-Allegheny Region by Virginians, 1650–1674* (1912).
—— "Kaskaskia Records," Ill. Hist., *Coll.*, 5 (1909).
Alvord, Clarence W., *Mississippi Valley in British Politics* (1916).
—— and Clarence E. Carter, eds., *New Regime, 1765–1767* (1916).
Billington, Ray A., *Westward Expansion: History of the American Frontier* (2nd ed., 1960).
Boyd, Julian P., *Susquehannah Company* (1935).
—— and Robert J. Taylor, eds., *Susquehannah Company Papers* (11 vols., 1930–1971).
Boyd, M. F., "Remote Frontier," *Fla. Hist. Quar.*, 19 (1941), 179; 20 (1941), 82; 21 (1942), 44.
Boyd, William K., *Eighteenth Century Tracts Concerning North Carolina* (1927).
Brock, R. A., ed., "Official Letters of Lieutenant Governor Spotswood," Va. Hist. Soc., *Coll.*, new ser., 1-2 (1882–1885).
Broshar, Helen, "First Push Westward of the Albany Traders," *MVHR*, 7 (1921), 228.
Buffinton, Arthur H., "Policy of Albany and English Westward Expansion," *MVHR*, 8 (1922), 327.
Carroll, Peter N., *Puritanism and the Wilderness: The Intellectual Significance of the New England Frontier, 1629–1700* (1969).
Caruso, John A., *The Appalachian Frontier: America's First Surge Westward* (1959).
—— *Southern Frontier* (1963).
Clark, Charles E., *Eastern Frontier: Settlement of Northern New England, 1610–1763* (1970).
Crane, Verner W., *Southern Frontier, 1670–1732* (1928).
Davidson, Philip, "Southern Backcountry on the Eve of the Revolution," in Avery Craven, ed., *Essays in Honor of William E. Dodd* (1935).
Dunn, Richard S., "John Winthrop, Jr., and the Narragansett Country," *WMQ*, 3 ser., 13 (1956), 68.
East, Robert A., "Puritanism and New Settlement," *NEQ*, 17 (1944), 255.
Edwards, C. R., *Frontier Policy of the Colony of Virginia* (1915).
Haller, William, Jr., *The Puritan Frontier: Town Planning in New England Colonial Development, 1630–1660* (1951).
Halsey, Francis W., *The Old New York Frontier* (1901).
Hanna, Charles A., *Wilderness Trail* (2 vols., 1911).
Heimert, Alan, "Puritanism, the Wilderness, and the Frontier," *NEQ*, 26 (1953), 361.
Henderson, Archibald, *Conquest of the Old Southwest, 1740–1790* (1920).
—— "Pre-Revolutionary Revolt in Old Southwest," *MVHR*, 17 (1930), 191.
Higgins, Ruth L., *Expansion in New York* (1931).
Hunter, William A., *Forts on the Pennsylvania Frontier, 1735–1758* (1960).
Jacobs, Wilbur R., *Wilderness Politics: Northern Colonial Frontier, 1748–1763* (1966).
James, Alfred P., "George Mercer, of the Ohio Company," *West. Penn. Hist. Mag.*, 46 (1963), 1.
—— *Ohio Company* (1959).
Johnson, J. G., "Colonial Southeast, 1732–63," Univ. of Colo., *Studies*, 19 (1932), 163.

Kenny, James, "Journal to Ye Westward, 1758–59," John W. Jordan, ed., *Penn. Mag. Hist. Biog.*, 37 (1913), 395.

Koontz, L. K., *Virginia Frontier, 1754–63* (1925).

Leach, Douglas E., *Northern Colonial Frontier, 1607–1763* (1966).

Lederer, John, *Discoveries with Unpublished Letters*, Douglas L. Rights and William P. Cummings, eds. (1958).

LeJau, Francis, *Carolina Chronicle, 1706–1717*, Frank J. Klingberg, ed. (1956).

Mathews, Lois K., *The Expansion of New England* (1909).

Mercer, George, *Papers Relating to the Ohio Company of Virginia*, Lois Mulkearn, ed. (1954).

Meriwether, Robert L., *Expansion of South Carolina, 1729–1765* (1940).

Morris, F. G., "Rural Settlement of New England in Colonial Times," in Laurence D. Stamp, ed., *London Essays in Geography* (1951).

Nixon, Lilly L., *James Burd: Frontier Defender, 1726–1793* (1941).

Philbrick, Francis S., *Rise of the West, 1754–1830* (1965).

Ramsey, Robert W., *Carolina Cradle: Northwest Carolina Frontier, 1747–1762* (1964).

Scott, W. W., "Knights of Horseshoe," *WMQ*, 2 ser., 3 (1923), 145.

Seymour, Flora W., *Lords of the Valley: Sir William Johnson* (1930).

Shannon, James P., *Catholic Colonization on the Western Frontier* (1957).

Shipton, Clifford K., "New England Frontier," *NEQ*, 10 (1937), 25.

Sosin, Jack M., *Whitehall and the Wilderness: Middle West in British Colonial Policy, 1760–1775* (1961).

Trewartha, Glenn T., "Rural Settlement in Colonial America," *Geog. Rev.*, 36 (1946), 568.

Turner, Frederick J., *The Frontier in American History* (1920).

Vail, R. W. G., *The Voice of the Old Frontier* (1949).

Volwiler, A. T., *George Croghan and Westward Movement* (1926).

Wilson, Samuel M., *Ohio Company of Virginia, 1748–1798* (1926).

Woodmason, Charles, *Carolina Backcountry on the Eve of the Revolution: Journal and Other Writings*, Richard J. Hooker, ed. (1953).

Wright, Louis B., *Culture on the Moving Frontier* (1955).

* * * * * * *

Mood, Fulmer, "Studies in History of American Settled Areas and Frontier Lines, 1625–1790," *Agric. Hist.*, 26 (1952), 16.

See also, 13.7.2, Turner Thesis.

See also 10.3 for biographies/writings of:

Brackenridge, Hugh Henry, 1748–1816
Burd, James, 1726–1793
Cresap, Thomas, ca. 1702–1790
Lederer, John, fl. 1668–1671

37.11 WOMEN

Benson, Mary S., *Women in Eighteenth-Century America* (1935).

Bishop, Isabella L. Bird, *Englishwoman in America* (1856).

Cobbledick, M. R., "Property Rights of Women in Puritan New England," in George P. Murdock, ed., *Studies in Science of Society*, (1937).

Cometti, Elizabeth, "Women in Revolution," *NEQ*, 20 (1947), 329.

Dexter, Elizabeth A., *Colonial Women of Affairs* (2nd ed., 1931).

Douglas, James, *Status of Women in New England and New France* (1912).

Drinker, Sophie H., "Women Attorneys of Colonial Times," *Md. Hist. Mag.*, 56 (1961), 335.

Earle, Alice M., *Colonial Dames* (1896).

Holliday, Carl, *Woman's Life in Colonial Days* (1922).

Leonard, Eugenie A., et al., *American Woman in Colonial and Revolutionary Times* (1962).

Moller, Herbert, "Sex Composition and Correlated Culture Patterns of Colonial America," *WMQ*, 3 ser., 2 (1945), 113.

Notable American Women, 1607–1950, Edward T. James, Janet Wilson James, and Paul S. Boyer, eds. (3 vols., 1971).

Spruill, Julia C., *Women's Life and Work in the Southern Colonies* (1938).

37.12 MARRIAGE AND FAMILY

Bremner, Robert H., et al., eds., *Children and Youth in America: Documentary History, 1600–1832* (2 vols., 1970).

Caley, Percy B., "Child Life in Colonial Western Pennsylvania," *West. Penn. Hist. Mag.*, 9 (1926), 188.

Calhoun, Arthur W., *Social History of the American Family from Colonial Times to the Present*, vol. I (1917).

Clemens, William M., ed., *American Marriage Records before 1690* (1927).

Demos, John, "Families in Colonial Bristol, Rhode Island: An Exercise in Historical Demography," *WMQ*, 3 ser., 25 (1968), 40.

—— *Little Commonwealth: Family Life in Plymouth Colony* (1970).

Doten, Dana, *Art of Bundling* (1938).

Dow, George F., *Domestic Life in New England in the Seventeenth Century* (1925).

Earle, Alice M., *Child Life in Colonial Days* (1899).

—— *Home Life in Colonial Days* (1907).

Fleming, Sandford, *Children and Puritanism: Place of Children in Life and Thought of New England Churches, 1620–1847* (1933).

Gemming, Elizabeth, *Huckleberry Hill: Child Life in Old New England* (1968).

Greven, Philip J., Jr., "Family Structure in Seventeenth-Century Andover, Massachusetts," *WMQ*, 3 ser., 23 (1966), 234.

Howard, George E., *History of Matrimonial Institutions, Chiefly in England and the United States* (2 vols., 1904).

Jacobus, Donald L., "Age of Girls at Marriage in Colonial New England," *Am. Geneal.*, 27 (1951), 116.

Kiefer, Monica M., *American Children Through Their Books, 1700–1835* (1948).

Lemon, James T., "Household Consumption in Eighteenth-Century America: Farmers in Southeastern Pennsylvania," *Agric. Hist.*, 41 (1967), 59.

Monahan, Thomas P., *Pattern of Age at Marriage in the United States* (2 vols., 1951).

Morgan, Edmund S., *Puritan Family: Religion and Domestic Relations in Seventeenth-Century New England* (rev. ed., 1966).

—— *Virginians at Home: Family Life in the Eighteenth Century* (1952).

O'Brien, Edward J., *Child Welfare Legislation in Maryland, 1634–1936* (1937).

Powell, Chilton L., "Marriage in Early New England," *NEQ*, 1 (1928), 323.

Rothenberg, Charles, "Marriage, Morals and the Law in Colonial America," *N.Y. Law Rev.*, 74 (1940), 393.

Rothman, David J., "Note on a Study of the Colonial Family," *WMQ*, 3 ser., 23 (1966), 627.

Schlesinger, Elizabeth B., "Cotton Mather and His Children," *WMQ*, 3 ser., 10 (1953), 181.

Stevenson, Noel C., "Marital Rights in the Colonial Period," *New Eng. Hist. Geneal. Reg.*, 109 (1955), 84.

Stiles, Henry R., *Bundling* (1869).

37.13 IMMIGRATION AND ETHNICITY

37.13.1 General

Banks, Charles E., and Samuel E. Morison, "Persecution as a Factor in Emigration," *Mass. Hist. Soc.*, *Proc.*, 63 (1930), 136.

Bolton, Ethel S., comp., *Immigrants to New England, 1700–1775* (1931).
Butterfield, Roy L., "American Migrations," *N.Y. Hist.*, 38 (1957), 368.
Corry, John P., "Racial Elements in Colonial Georgia," *Ga. Hist. Quar.*, 20 (1936), 30.
Crary, Catherine S., "Humble Immigrant and the American Dream: Case Histories, 1746–1776," *MVHR*, 46 (1959), 46.
Crouse, Nellis M., "Causes of the Great Migration," *NEQ*, 5 (1932), 3.
Diamond, Sigmund, "Values as an Obstacle to Economic Growth: The American Colonies," *Jour. Econ. Hist.*, 27 (1967), 561.
Duffy, John, "The Passage to the Colonies," *MVHR*, 38 (1951), 21.
Dunaway, W. F., "Pennsylvania as an Early Distributing Center of Population," *Penn. Mag. Hist. Biog.*, 55 (1931), 134.
French, Allen, *Charles I and the Puritan Upheaval: A Study of the Causes of the Great Migration* (1955).
Hansen, Marcus L., *The Atlantic Migration, 1607–1860* (1940).
Hoyt, Edward A., "Naturalization under the American Colonies," *Pol. Sci. Quar.*, 67 (1952), 248.
Lefler, Hugh T., "Promotional Literature of the Southern Colonies," *JSH*, 33 (1967), 3.
Newton, Arthur, *Colonizing Activities of English Puritans* (1914).
Proper, Emberson E., *Colonial Immigration Laws* (1900).
Risch, Erna, "Encouragement of Immigration as Revealed in Colonial Legislation," *Va. Mag. Hist. Biog.*, 45 (1937), 1.
Shipton, Clifford K., "Immigration to New England, 1680–1740," *Jour. Pol. Econ.*, 44 (1936), 225.
Smith, Abbot E., "Transportation of Convicts to the American Colonies in the Seventeenth Century," *AHR*, 39 (1934), 232.

37.13.2 English and Welsh

Browning, Charles H., *Welsh Settlement of Pennsylvania* (1912).
Campbell, Mildred, "English Emigration on the Eve of Revolution," *AHR*, 61 (1955), 1.
Kaminkow, Jack and Marion, *List of Emigrants from England to America, 1718–1759* (1964).
Mellor, George R., "Emigration from British Isles to New World, 1765–1775," *History*, 40 (1955), 68.
Rees, T. Hardy, *History of the Quakers in Wales and Their Emigration to North America* (1925).
Thomas, John P., Jr., "The Barbadians in Early South Carolina," *So. Car. Hist. Mag.*, 31 (1930), 75.

37.13.3 Scots

Bolton, Charles K., *Scotch Irish Pioneers in Ulster and America* (1910).
Dickson, R. J., *Ulster Emigration to Colonial America, 1718–1775* (1966).
Dunaway, Wayland F., *Scotch Irish of Colonial Pennsylvania* (1944).
Ford, Henry J., *Scotch-Irish in America* (1915).
Glasgow, Maude, *Scotch-Irish in Northern Ireland and American Colonies* (1936).
Graham, Ian C. C., *Colonists from Scotland: Emigration to North America, 1707–1783* (1956).
Green, Edward R. R., "Queensborough Township: Scotch-Irish Emigration and Expansion of Georgia, 1763–1776," *WMQ*, 3 ser., 17 (1960), 183.
——— "The 'Strange Humors' that Drove the Scotch-Irish to America, 1729," *WMQ*, 3 ser., 12 (1955), 113.
Hanna, C. A., *The Scotch-Irish* (2 vols., 1902).
Leyburn, James G., *The Scotch-Irish* (1962).
MacDonell, Alexander R., "The Settlement of the Scotch Highlanders at Darien," *Ga. Hist. Quar.*, 20 (1936), 250.
Meyer, Duane G., *Highland Scots of North Carolina, 1732–1776* (1961).

Pryde, George S., "Scottish Colonization in the Province of New York," *N.Y. Hist.*, 16 (1935), 138.

37.13.4 Irish

Cook, Albert C., *Immigration of the Irish Quakers into Pennsylvania, 1682–1750* (1902).
Donovan, G. F., *Pre-Revolutionary Irish in Massachusetts, 1620–1775* (1932).
Purcell, Richard J., "Irish Builders of Colonial Rhode Island," *Studies: An Irish Quarterly Review*, 24 (1935), 289.
—— "Irish Colonists in Colonial Maryland," *Studies: An Irish Quarterly Review*, 23 (1934), 279.
—— "Irish Contributions to Colonial New York," *Studies: An Irish Quarterly Review*, 29 (1940), 591.

37.13.5 Dutch

Eckman, Jeannette, "Life Among the Early Dutch at New Castle," *Del. Hist.*, 4 (1951), 246.
Hull, William I., *William Penn and the Dutch Quaker Migration to Pennsylvania* (1935).
Leiby, Adrian C., *Early Dutch and Swedish Settlers of New Jersey* (1964).
Wabeke, Bertus H., *Dutch Emigration to North America, 1625–1860* (1944).
Ward, Christopher, *The Dutch and Swedes on the Delaware, 1609–1664* (1930).
Weslager, C. A., and A. R. Dunlap, *Dutch Explorers, Traders and Settlers in the Delaware Valley, 1609–1664* (1961).

37.13.6 French Huguenots

Baird, Charles W., *History of Huguenot Emigration to America* (2 vols., 1885).
Brydon, G. M., "Huguenots of Manakin Town," *Va. Mag. Hist. Biog.*, 42 (1934), 325.
Carpenter, Esther B., "Huguenot Influence in Rhode Island," in *South County Studies* (1924).
—— "John Saffin His Book," in *South County Studies* (1924).
Chinard, Gilbert, *Les Réfugiés Huguenots en Amérique* (1925).
Douglas, Donald, *The Huguenot: Emigrations, Particularly to New England* (1954).
Harrison, Fairfax, ed. and trans., *Frenchman in Virginia, Being the Memoirs of a Huguenot Refugee in 1686* (1923).
Hirsch, Arthur H., *The Huguenots of Colonial South Carolina* (1928).
Laux, J. B., *The Huguenot Element in Pennsylvania* (1896).
Maury, Anne, *Memoirs of a Huguenot Family* (1872). Fontaine family.
Reaman, G. Elmore, *Trail of the Huguenots* (1964).
Weiss, Charles, *History of the French Protestant Refugees* (2 vols., 1854).

37.13.7 Germans

Beauchamp, William M., ed., *Moravian Journals Relating to Central New York, 1745–66* (1916).
Bernheim, G. D., *German Settlements in North and South Carolina* (1872).
Bittinger, Lucy F., *Germans in Colonial Times* (1900).
Cunz, Dieter, *Maryland Germans* (1948).
"Diary of a Journey of Moravians from Bethlehem, Pennsylvania to Bethabara in Wachovia, North Carolina, 1753," in Newton D. Mereness, ed., *Travels in the American Colonies* (1916).
Diffenderffer, F. R., *German Immigration into Pennsylvania through Philadelphia, 1700–1775* (1900).
Dorpalen, Andreas, "Political Influence of the German Element in Colonial America," *Penn. Hist.*, 6 (1939), 147.

Fries, Adelaide L., "The Moravian Contribution to Colonial North Carolina," *No. Car. Hist. Rev.*, 11 (1934), 167.

———— *Moravians in Georgia* (1905).

Johnson, William T., "Relations of the Government and German Settlers in Colonial Pennsylvania, 1683–1754," *Penn. Hist.*, 11 (1944), 81.

Knittle, W. A., *Early Eighteenth-Century Palatine Emigration* (1936).

Krebs, Frederick, *Emigrants from the Palatinate in the 18th Century* (1953).

Kuhns, Levi O., *The German and Swiss Settlements of Colonial Pennsylvania* (1901).

Newton, Hester W., "Industrial and Social Influences of Salzburgers in Colonial Georgia," *Ga. Hist. Quar.*, 18 (1934), 35.

Rothermund, Dietmar, "German Problem of Colonial Pennsylvania," *Penn. Mag. Hist. Biog.*, 84 (1960), 3.

Schantz, F. J. F., *Domestic Life of Pennsylvania German Pioneers* (1900).

Schultz, Selina G., "Schwenkfelders of Pennsylvania," *Penn. Hist.*, 24 (1957), 293.

Smith, C. Henry, *Mennonite Immigration to Pennsylvania in the Eighteenth Century* (1929).

Strassburger, R. B., and W. J. Hinke, "Pennsylvania German Pioneers," Penn. German Soc., *Proc.*, 42–44 (1934).

Urlsperger, Samuel, ed., *Detailed Reports on the Salzburger Emigrants Who Settled in America* (1735); George F. Jones and Herman J. Lacher, trans. and eds. (1968).

Weaver, Glenn, "Germans of British North America during the French and Indian War," *Social Studies*, 48 (1957), 227.

37.13.8 Other West Europeans

Barbour, Philip L., "The Identity of the First Poles in America," *WMQ*, 3 ser., 21 (1964), 77.

Beeson, Kenneth H., Jr., "Janas in British East Florida," *Fla. Hist. Quar.*, 44 (1965), 121.

Faust, Albert B., "Swiss Emigration in Eighteenth Century," *AHR*, 22 (1916), 98.

Louhi, Evert A., *The Delaware Finns* (1925).

Marraro, Howard R., "Italo-Americans in Eighteenth-Century New York," *N.Y. Hist.*, 21 (1940), 316.

———— "Italo-Americans in Pennsylvania in the Eighteenth Century," *Penn. Hist.*, 7 (1940), 159.

Panagopoulos, E. P., *New Smyrna: Eighteenth Century Greek Odyssey* (1966).

Wuorinen, John H., *The Finns on the Delaware, 1638–1655* (1938).

37.13.9 Jews

Adelman, David C., "Civil Rights of Jews in the Colony of Rhode Island," *R.I. Jewish Historical Notes*, 1 (1954), 104.

Broches, Samuel, *Jews in New England* (2 vols., 1942).

Freund, Miriam K., *Jewish Merchants in Colonial America* (1939).

Friedman, Lee M., *Early American Jews* (1934).

Goodman, Abram V., *American Overture: Jewish Rights in Colonial Times* (1947).

Grinstein, Hyman B., *Rise of the Jewish Community of New York, 1654–1860* (1945).

Karp, Abraham J., ed., *The Jewish Experience in America: Selected Studies from Publications of the American Jewish Historical Society*. Vol. I: *The Colonial Period* (1969).

Korn, Bertram W., *Early Jews of New Orleans* (1969).

Lebeson, Anita L., *Jewish Pioneers in America, 1492–1848* (1931).

Marcus, Jacob R., ed., *American Jewry: Documents, Eighteenth Century* (1959).

Marcus, Jacob R., *Early American Jewry* (2 vols., 1951–1953).

Pool, David deSola, *Portraits Etched in Stone: Early Jewish Settlers, 1682–1831* (1952).

Rosenbloom, Joseph R., *Biographical Dictionary of Early American Jews through 1800* (1960).

Sandler, Philip, "Earliest Jewish Settlers in New York," *N.Y. Hist.*, 36 (1955), 39.

Stern, Malcolm H., "Jewish Settlement of Savannah," *Am. Jew. Hist. Quar.*, 52 (1963), 169.

Wolf, Edwin, II, and Maxwell Whiteman, *History of Jews of Philadelphia from Colonial Times to the Age of Jackson* (1957).

37.13.10 Indians

37.13.10.1 General

Adair, James, *History of American Indians* (1755; repr., 1930).

Alden, John R., "The Albany Congress and the Creation of Indian Super-intendencies," *MVHR*, 27 (1940), 193.

Bailey, Alfred G., *Conflict of European and Eastern Algonkin Cultures, 1504–1700* (1937).

Beaver, R. Pierce, *Church, State, and the American Indians* (1966).

Flannery, Regina, *An Analysis of Coastal Algonquian Culture* (1939).

Huddleston, Lee E., *Origins of the American Indians: European Concepts, 1492–1729* (1967).

Hyde, George E., *Indians of the Woodlands to 1725* (1962).

Jacobs, Wilbur R., "The Protocol of Indian Diplomacy," *WMQ*, 3 ser., 6 (1949), 596.

Knowles, Nathaniel, "The Torture of Captives by the Indians of Eastern North America," Am. Philos. Soc., *Proc.*, 82 (1940), 151.

Lauber, Almon W., *Indian Slavery in Colonial Times within the Present Limits of the United States* (1913).

Lurie, Nancie O., "Indian Cultural Adjustment to European Civilization," in James M. Smith, ed., *Seventeenth-Century America: Essays on Colonial History* (1959).

MacLeod, William C., *The American Indian Frontier* (1928).

Mahon, John K., "Anglo-American Methods of Indian Warfare, 1676–1794," *MVHR*, 45 (1958), 254.

Pearce, Roy H., *Savages of America: The Indian and the Idea of Civilization* (rev. ed., 1965).

Peckham, Howard, and Charles Gibson, *Attitudes of Colonial Powers toward the American Indian* (1970).

Peckham, Howard H., *Captured by Indians: Tales of Pioneer Survivors* (1954).

Priestley, Herbert J., *The Coming of the White Man, 1492–1848* (1927).

Saum, Lewis O., *The Fur Trader and the Indian* (1965).

Smoyer, Stanley C., "Indians as Allies in the Intercolonial Wars," *N. Y. Hist.*, 17 (1936), 411.

Washburn, Wilcomb E., "The Moral and Legal Justifications for Dispossessing the Indians," in James Morton Smith, ed., *Seventeenth Century America: Essays in Colonial History* (1959).

Wraxall, Peter, *Abridgment of Indian Affairs*, C. H. McIlwain, ed. (1915).

*   *   *   *   *   *   *

Fenton, William N., *American Indian and White Relations to 1830: Needs and Opportunities for Study* (1957).

—— "Collecting Materials for a Political History of the Six Nations," Am. Philos. Soc., *Proc.*, 93 (1949), 233.

Sheehan, Bernard W., "Indian-White Relations: Review Essay," *WMQ*, 3 ser., 26 (1969), 267.

Washburn, Wilcomb E., "A Moral History of Indian-White Relations: Needs and Opportunities for Study," *Ethnohistory*, 4 (1957), 47.

See also 10.3 for biographies/writings of:

Croghan, George, ? –1782

37.13.10.2 South

Alden, John R., *John Stuart and the Southern Colonial Frontier: Indian Relations, War, Trade, and Land Problems in the Southern Wilderness, 1754–1775* (1944).

Atkin, Edmond, *Indians of the Southern Colonial Frontier: Atkin Report and the Plan of 1755,* Wilbur R. Jacobs, ed. (1954).

Brown, John P., *Old Frontiers: Story of the Cherokee Indians from Earliest Times to the Date of Their Removal, 1838* (1938).

Corkran, David H., *The Cherokee Frontier: Conflict and Survival, 1740–62* (1962).
——— *Creek Frontier, 1540–1783* (1967).

Corry, J. P., *Indian Affairs in Georgia, 1732–1756* (1936).

Cotterill, R. S., *The Southern Indians: Story of the Civilized Tribes before Removal* (1954).

Covington, James W., comp., *The British Meet the Seminoles: Negotiations between British Authorities in East Florida and the Indians, 1763–68* (1961).

Craven, Wesley F., "Indian Policy in East Virginia," *WMQ,* 3 ser., 1 (1944), 65.

Feest, Christian F., "The Virginia Indian in Pictures, 1612–1624," *Smithsonian Jour. Hist.,* 1 (1966), 1.

Glenn, Keith, "Captain John Smith and the Indians," *Va. Mag. Hist. Biog.,* 52 (1944), 228.

Herndon, G. Melvin, "Indian Agriculture in the Southern Colonies," *No. Car. Hist. Rev.,* 44 (1967), 283.

Lofton, John M., Jr., "White, Indian, and Negro Contacts in Colonial South Carolina," *Southern Indian Studies,* 1 (1949), 3.

McCary, Ben C., *Indians in Seventeenth-Century Virginia* (1957).

McDowell, William L., Jr., ed., *The Colonial Records of South Carolina.* Series Two: *Documents Relating to Indian Affairs, May 21, 1750–August 7, 1754* (1958).

Milling, Chapman J., *Red Carolinians* (1940).

Phelps, Dawson A., "The Chickasaw, English, and French, 1699–1744," *Tenn. Hist. Quar.,* 16 (1957), 117.

Randel, William, "Captain John Smith's Attitude toward Indians," *Va. Mag. Hist. Biog.,* 67 (1939), 21.

Rights, D. L., *American Indian in North Carolina* (2nd ed., 1957).

Robinson, W. Stitt, Jr., "The Legal Status of the Indian in Colonial Virginia," *Va. Mag. Hist. Biog.,* 61 (1953), 249.

Semmes, Raphael, "Aboriginal Maryland, 1608–1689," *Md. Hist. Mag.,* 24 (1929), 157, 195.

Shaw, Helen L., *British Administration of the Southern Indians* (1931).

Smith, Hale G., *European-Indian Contacts in Georgia and Florida* (1956).

Tolles, Frederick B., "Quakers and Indians," *Am. Philos. Soc., Proc.,* 107 (1964), 93.

Willis, William S., "Red, White, and Black in the Southeast," *Jour. Negro Hist.,* 48 (1963), 157.

Winston, Sanford, "Indian Slavery in the Carolina Region," *Jour. Negro Hist.,* 19 (1934), 431.

Woodward, Grace S., *Pocahontas* (1969).

See also 10.3 for biographies/writings of:

Bowles, William Augustus, 1763–1805
Lederer, John, fl. 1668–1671
Stuart, John, 1700–1779

37.13.10.3 Middle Colonies

Colden, Cadwallader, *History of the Five Indian Nations* (1747).

Davidson, Robert L. D., *War Comes to Quaker Pennsylvania, 1682–1756* (1957).

Eshleman, H. Frank, *Lancaster County Indians: Annals of the Susquehannocks and Other Indian Tribes of the Susquehanna Territory from About the Year 1500 to 1763* (1909).

Everett, Edward G., "Pennsylvania's Indian Diplomacy, 1747–1753," *West. Penn. Hist. Mag.,* 44 (1961), 241.

Flexner, James T., *Mohawk Baronet: Sir William Johnson* (1959).

Gray, Elma E., and Leslie R. Gray, *Wilderness Christians: Moravian Mission to the Delaware Indians* (1956).

Hamilton, Milton W., "Sir William Johnson: Interpreter of the Iroquois," *Ethnohistory*, 10 (1963), 270.

Henry, Thomas R., *Wilderness Messiah: Hiawatha and the Iroquois* (1955).

Hunt, George T., *The Wars of the Iroquois: Study in Intertribal Relations* (1940).

Jacobs, Wilbur R., ed., *Paxton Riots and Frontier Theory* (1967).

Jennings, Francis, "Glory, Death, Transfiguration: The Susquehannock Indians in the Seventeenth Century," Am. Philos. Soc., *Proc.*, 112 (1968), 15.

―――― "The Indian Trade of the Susquehanna Valley," Am. Philos. Soc., *Proc.*, 110 (1966), 406.

Leder, Lawrence H., ed., *Livingston Indian Records, 1666–1723* (1956).

Lydekker, John W., *The Faithful Mohawks* (1938).

Ruttenber, Edward M., *History of the Indian Tribes of Hudson's River* (1872).

Shaw, Helen L., *British Administration of the Southern Indians* (1931).

Speck, Frank G., "The Wampanachi Delawares and the English," *Penn. Mag. Hist. Biog.*, 57 (1943), 319.

Stone, William L., *Life of Joseph Brant* (2 vols., 1838).

Trelease, Allen W., *Indian Affairs in Colonial New York: Seventeenth Century* (1960).

―――― "Iroquois and Western Fur Trade," *MVHR*, 49 (1962), 32.

Wallace, Anthony F. C., et al., *Death and Rebirth of the Seneca* (1970).

Wallace, Anthony F. C., *King of the Delawares: Teedyuscung, 1700–1763* (1949).

―――― "Origins of Iroquois Neutrality: Grand Settlement of 1701," *Penn. Hist.*, 24 (1957), 223.

Wallace, Paul A. W., *Indians in Pennsylvania* (1961).

―――― "The Iroquois: A Brief Outline of their History," *Penn. Hist.*, 23 (1956), 15.

Weslager, C. A., "The Nanticoke Indians in Early Pennsylvania," *Penn. Mag. Hist. Biog.*, 67 (1943), 345.

See also 10.3 for biographies/writings of:

Brant, Joseph, 1742–1807
Burd, James, 1726–1793
Johnson, Sir William, 1715–1774
Pemberton, Israel, 1715–1779
Red Jacket, ca. 1758–1830
Teedyuscung, ca. 1700–1763
Trent, William, 1715–1787

37.13.10.4 New England

Bond, Richmond P., *Queen Anne's American Kings* (1952).

Bradshaw, Harold C., *The Indians of Connecticut: Effect of English Colonization and of Missionary Activity on Indian Life in Connecticut* (1935).

Bradstreet, Howard, *The Story of the War with the Pequots, Re-Told* (1933).

Bushnell, David, "Treatment of the Indians in Plymouth Colony," *NEQ*, 26 (1953), 193.

Chapin, H. M., *Sachems of Narragansetts* (1931).

Church, Benjamin, *Entertaining History of King Philip's War* (1716).

DeForest, John W., *History of the Indians of Connecticut* (1952).

Eisinger, Chester E., "The Puritans' Justification for Taking the Land," Essex Inst., *Hist. Coll.*, 84 (1948), 131.

Ellis, George W., and John E. Morris, *King Philip's War* (1906).

Harris, William, *A Rhode Islander Reports on King Philip's War*, Douglas E. Leach, ed. (1963).

Huden, John C., comp., *Indian Place Names of New England* (1962).

Kawashima, Yasu, "Jurisdiction of Colonial Courts over Indians in Massachusetts, 1689–1763," *NEQ*, 42 (1969), 532.

———— "Legal Origins of the Indian Reservation in Colonial Massachusetts," *Am. Jour. Legal Hist.*, 13 (1969), 42.

Kellaway, William, *The New England Company, 1649–1776: Missionary Society to the American Indians* (1961).

Leach, Douglas E., *Flintlock and Tomahawk: New England in King Philip's War* (1958).

Lincoln, Charles H., ed., *Narratives of the Indian Wars, 1675–1699* (1913). Contains John Easton, *Relacion* (1675); Nathaniel Saltonstall, *Present State of New England* (1675) and *New and Further Narrative* (1676); Mary Rowlandson, *Captivity* (1682); Cotton Mather, *Decennium Luctuosum* (1699).

Moloney, Francis Xavier, *The Fur Trade in New England, 1620–1676* (1931).

Nammack, Georgianna C., *Fraud, Politics and Dispossession of Indians: Iroquois Land Frontier in Colonial Period* (1969).

Pearce, Roy H., "The 'Ruines of Mankind': The Indian and the Puritan Mind," *Jour. Hist. Ideas*, 13 (1952), 200.

Sheldon, George, *History of Deerfield, Massachusetts, with a Special Study of the Indian Wars in the Connecticut Valley* (2 vols., 1895–1896).

Spiess, Mathias, *The Indians of Connecticut* (1933).

Sylvester, Herbert M., *Indian Wars of New England* (3 vols., 1910).

Vaughan, Alden T., *New England Frontier: Puritans and Indians, 1620–1675* (1965).

———— "Test of Puritan Justice," *NEQ*, 38 (1965), 331.

Washburn, Wilcomb E., "Governor Berkeley and King Philip's War," *NEQ*, 30 (1957), 363.

Weis, Frederick L., "The New England Company of 1649 and Its Missionary Enterprises," Col. Soc. Mass., *Publ.*, 38 (1959), 134.

Willoughby, Charles C., *Antiquities of the New England Indians* (1935).

Winship, G. P., ed., *New England Company of 1649 and John Eliot* (1920).

See also 10.3 for biographies/writings of:

Gookin, Daniel, 1612–1686/87

37.13.11 Negroes

Brewer, James H., "Negro Property Owners in Seventeenth-Century Virginia," *WMQ*, 3 ser., 12 (1955), 575.

Cantor, Milton, "The Image of the Negro in Colonial Literature," *NEQ*, 36 (1963), 452.

Evans, Emory G., ed., "Documents Concerning the Negro and Franchise in Eighteenth-Century Virginia," *Va. Mag. Hist. Biog.*, 71 (1963), 411.

Franklin, John Hope, *From Slavery to Freedom* (3d ed., 1967).

Greene, Lorenzo J., *The Negro in Colonial New England* (1942).

Hast, Adele, "The Legal Status of the Negro in Virginia, 1705–1765," *Jour. Negro Hist.*, 54 (1969), 217.

Haynes, Leonard L., Jr., *The Negro Community within American Protestantism, 1619–1844* (1954).

Jones, Jerome W., "The Established Virginia Church and the Conversion of Negroes and Indians, 1620–1760," *Jour. Negro Hist.*, 46 (1961), 12.

Klingberg, Frank J., "The African Immigrant to Colonial Pennsylvania and Delaware," *Hist. Mag. Prot. Episc. Church*, 11 (1942), 126.

———— *The Negro in Colonial South Carolina* (1941).

Munroe, John A., "The Negro in Delaware," *So. Atl. Quar.*, 56 (1957), 428.

Pennington, E. L., "Thomas Bray's Associates' Work among Negroes," Am. Antiq. Soc., *Proc.*, new ser., 48 (1938), 311.

Pilcher, George W., "Samuel Davies and the Instruction of Negroes in Virginia," *Va. Mag. Hist. Biog.*, 74 (1966), 293.

Pinchbeck, Raymond B., *The Virginia Negro Artisan and Tradesman* (1926).

Porter, Kenneth W., "Negroes on the Southern Frontier, 1670–1763," *Jour. Negro Hist.*, 33 (1948), 53.

———— "Relations between Negroes and Indians within the Present Limits of the United States," *Jour. Negro Hist.*, 17 (1932), 287.

Quarles, Benjamin, "Colonial Militia and Negro Manpower," *MVHR*, 45 (1959), 643.

—— *The Negro in the American Revolution* (1961).

Russell, John H., *The Free Negro in Virginia, 1619–1865* (1913).

Tate, Thad W., Jr., *The Negro in Eighteenth-Century Williamsburg* (1965).

Turner, Edward R., *The Negro in Pennsylvania* (1910).

Twombly, Robert C., and Robert H. Moore, "The Negro in Seventeenth-Century Massachusetts," *WMQ*, 3 ser., 24 (1967), 224.

Wax, Darold D., "Georgia and the Negro before the American Revolution," *Ga. Hist. Quar.*, 51 (1967), 63.

—— "Negro Imports into Pennsylvania, 1720–1766," *Penn. Hist.*, 32 (1965), 254.

Willis, William S., "Red, White, and Black in the Southeast," *Jour. Negro Hist.*, 48 (1963), 157.

Wright, James M., *The Free Negro in Maryland, 1634–1860* (1921).

Wright, Marian T., "New Jersey Laws and the Negro," *Jour. Negro Hist.*, 28 (1943), 156.

See also 37.6, Slavery.

37.14 POVERTY AND WELFARE

Deutsch, Albert, "The Sick Poor in Colonial Times," *AHR*, 46 (1941), 560.

Heffner, William C., *History of Poor Relief Legislation in Pennsylvania* (1913).

Hunter, Robert J., "Franklin and Free Treatment of the Poor by the Medical Profession of Philadelphia," *Bull. Hist. Med.*, 31 (1957), 137.

James, Sydney V., Jr., *People among Peoples: Quaker Benevolence in Eighteenth-Century America* (1963).

Jernegan, Marcus W., "Development of Poor Relief in Colonial Virginia," *Social Service Review*, 3 (1929), 1.

Kelso, R. W., *History of Public Poor Relief in Massachusetts* (1922).

Klebaner, Benjamin J., "Some Aspects of North Carolina Public Poor Relief, 1700–1860," *No. Car. Hist. Rev.*, 31 (1954), 479.

Mackey, Howard, "The Operation of the English Old Poor Law in Colonial Virginia," *Va. Mag. Hist. Biog.*, 73 (1965), 29.

—— "Social Welfare in Colonial Virginia: The Importance of the English Old Poor Law," *Hist. Mag. Prot. Episc. Church*, 36 (1967), 357.

Schneider, David M., *History of Public Welfare in New York State, 1609–1866* (1938).

See also 10.3 for biographies/writings of:

Brown, Moses, 1738–1836
Girard, Stephen, 1750–1831

37.15 CRIME AND PUNISHMENT

Coleman, Peter J., "Insolvent Debtor in Rhode Island, 1745–1828," *WMQ*, 3 ser., 22 (1965), 413.

Feer, Robert A., "Imprisonment for Debt in Massachusetts before 1800," *MVHR*, 48 (1961), 252.

Fitzroy, Herbert K., "Punishment of Crime in Provincial Pennsylvania," *Penn. Mag. Hist. Biog.*, 60 (1936), 242.

Flaherty, David H., "Law and the Enforcement of Morals in Early America," *Perspectives in Am. Hist.*, 5 (1971), 203.

Gipson, Lawrence H., *Crime and Punishment in Provincial Pennsylvania* (1935).

——"Criminal Codes of Connecticut," Am. Instit. Crim. Law and Criminol., *Jour.*, 6 (1915), 177.

Goebel, Julius, Jr., and T. Raymond Naughton, *Law Enforcement in Colonial New York: A Study in Criminal Procedure (1664–1776)* (1944).

Haskins, George L., "Ecclesiastical Antecedents of Criminal Punishment in Early Massachusetts," Mass. Hist. Soc., *Proc.,* 72 (1963), 21.

——— "Precedents in English Ecclesiastical Practices for Criminal Punishments in Early Massachusetts," in Morris D. Forkosch, ed., *Essays in Honor of Felix Frankfurter* (1966).

Mason, P. C., "Jayle Birds in Colonial Virginia," *Va. Mag. Hist. Biog.,* 53 (1945), 37.

Parkes, H. B., "Morals and Law Enforcement in Colonial New England," *NEQ,* 5 (1932), 431.

Powers, Edwin, *Crime and Punishment in Early Massachusetts, 1620–1692* (1966).

Randall, Edwin T., "Imprisonment for Debt in America: Fact and Fiction," *MVHR,* 39 (1952), 89.

Rankin, Hugh F., *Criminal Trial Proceedings in the General Court of Colonial Virginia* (1965).

Riddell, William R., "Judicial Execution by Burning at the Stake in New York," *Am. Bar Assoc. Jour.,* 15 (1929), 373.

Ryan, Edward, "Imprisonment for Debt: Its Origin and Repeal," *Va. Mag. Hist. Biog.,* 42 (1934), 53.

Scott, Arthur P., *Criminal Law in Colonial Virginia* (1930).

Semmes, Raphael, *Crime and Punishment in Early Maryland* (1938).

Steers, Don, *The Counsellors: Courts and Crimes of Colonial New York* (1968).

Weiss, Harry B., and Grace M. Weiss, *An Introduction to Crime and Punishment in Colonial New Jersey* (1960).

Zanger, Jules, "Crime and Punishment in Early Massachusetts," *WMQ,* 3 ser., 22 (1965), 471.

37.16 WITCHCRAFT

Burr, George L., "Literature of Witchcraft," Am. Hist. Assoc., *Papers,* 4 (1890), 237.

——— ed., *Narratives of Witchcraft Cases, 1648–1706* (1914). Includes Robert Calef, *More Wonders of Invisible World* (1700); Richard Chamberlain, *Lithobolia* (1698); Deodat Lawson, *Brief and True Narrative of Witchcraft at Salem Village* (1692).

Burr, George L., "New England's Place in Witchcraft," Am. Antiq. Soc., *Proc.,* new ser., 21 (1911), 185.

Davis, Richard B., "The Devil in Virginia in the Seventeenth Century," *Va. Mag. Hist. Biog.,* 65 (1957), 131.

Demos, John, "Underlying Themes in Witchcraft in Seventeenth-Century New England," *AHR,* 75 (1970), 1311.

Drake, Frederick C., "Witchcraft in the Colonies, 1647–62," *Am. Quar.,* 20 (1968), 694.

Drake, Samuel G., *Witchcraft Delusion in New England* (1866).

Fitzroy, Herbert W., "Punishment of Crime in Provincial Pennsylvania," *Penn. Mag. Hist. Biog.,* 60 (1936), 242.

Fox, Sanford J., *Science and Justice: Massachusetts Witchcraft Trials* (1969).

Fuess, Claude M., "Witches at Andover," Mass. Hist. Soc., *Proc.,* 70 (1950–1953), 8.

Hansen, Chadwick, *Witchcraft at Salem* (1969).

Haraszti, Zoltán, "Cotton Mather and Witchcraft Trials," *More Books,* 15 (1940), 179.

Kittredge, George Lyman, *Witchcraft in Old and New England* (1928).

Levermore, Charles H., "Witchcraft in Connecticut," *New Eng. Mag.,* 6 (1892), 636.

Levin, David, ed., *What Happened in Salem?* (1952).

Nevins, Winfield S., *Witchcraft in Salem Village in 1692* (1916).

Notestein, Wallace, *History of Witchcraft in England, 1558–1718* (1911).

Parke, Francis N., *Witchcraft in Early Maryland* (1937).

Proper, David R., "Salem Witchcraft," Essex Inst., *Hist. Coll.*, 102 (1966), 213.
Riddell, William R., "William Penn and Witchcraft," *Jour. Crim. Law*, 18 (1927), 11.
—— "Witchcraft in Old New York," *Jour. Crim. Law*, 19 (1928), 252.
Robbins, Fred G., "Witchcraft," Essex Inst., *Hist. Coll.*, 65 (1929), 209.
Starkey, Marion L., *The Devil in Massachusetts: A Modern Inquiry into Salem Witch Trials* (1949).
Taylor, E. W., "Some Medical Aspects of Witchcraft," in C. M. Campbell et al., eds., *Problems of Personality* (1925).
—— "Witchcraft Episode," in Albert B. Hart, ed., *Commonwealth History of Massachusetts*, vol. II (1928).
Upham, Charles W., *Salem Witchcraft* (2 vols., 1867).
Woodward, W. E., ed., *Records of Salem Witchcraft* (2 vols., 1864).

See also 10.3 for biographies/writings of:

Mather, Cotton, 1662/63–1727/28
Mather, Increase, 1639–1723
Sewall, Samuel, 1652–1730

37.17 SOCIAL HISTORY

37.17.1 General

Adams, James T., *Provincial Society* (1928).
Bushman, Richard L., *From Puritan to Yankee: Character and Social Order in Connecticut, 1690–1765* (1967).
Bruce, Philip A., *Social Life of Virginia* (1927).
Bridenbaugh, Carl, *Myths and Realities: Societies of the Colonial South* (1952).
Noel-Hume, Ivor, *Here Lies Virginia: An Archaeologist's View of Colonial Life and History* (1963).
Kraus, Michael, *Inter-colonial Aspects of American Culture on the Eve of the Revolution* (1928).
Lockridge, Kenneth A., "Evolution of New England Society, 1630–1790," *Past and Present*, 39 (1968), 62.
Shipton, Clifford K., *New England Life in the Eighteenth Century: Representative Biographies from "Sibley's Harvard Graduates"* (1963).
Wertenbaker, Thomas J., *Patrician and Plebian in Virginia* (1910).
—— *Planters of Colonial Virginia* (1922).
Weeden, W. W., *Economic and Social History of New England, 1620–1789* (1890).

37.17.2 Social Manners and Customs

Albertson, Dean, "Puritan Liquor in the Planting of New England," *NEQ*, 23 (1950), 477.
Andrews, Charles M., *Colonial Folkways: American Life in the Reign of the Georges* (1919).
Bridenbaugh, Carl, "Colonial Newport as a Summer Resort," R. I. Hist. Soc., *Coll.*, 26 (1933), 1.
—— "The High Cost of Living in Boston, 1728," *NEQ*, 5 (1932), 800.
—— "Watering Places of Colonial America," *WMQ*, 3 ser., 3 (1946), 151.
Brown, John Hull, *Early American Beverages* (1966).
Cady, Edwin H., *The Gentleman in America* (1949).
Carson, Jane, *Colonial Virginia Cookery* (1968).
—— *Colonial Virginians at Play* (1965).
Carter, Landon, *Diary*, Jack P. Greene, ed. (2 vols., 1965).
Dow, George F., *Domestic Life in New England in the Seventeenth Century* (1925).
—— *Every Day Life in the Massachusetts Bay Colony* (1935).
Earle, Alice Morse, *Costume of Colonial Times* (1894).

—— *Customs and Fashions in Old New England* (1894).
—— *Home Life in Colonial Days* (1898).
—— *The Sabbath in Puritan New England* (1891).
Fales, Martha G., "The Early American Way of Death," Essex Inst., *Hist. Coll.*, 100 (1964), 75.
Field, Edward, *The Colonial Tavern* (1897).
Fisher, Sidney G., *Men, Women and Manners in Colonial Times* (2 vols., 1898).
Greene, Evarts B., "Code of Honor in Colonial and Revolutionary Times, with Special Reference to New England," Col. Soc. Mass., *Publ.*, 26 (1927), 367.
Hartdagen, Gerald E., "Vestries and Morals in Colonial Maryland," *Md. Hist. Mag.*, 63 (1968), 360.
Langdon, William C., *Everyday Things in American Life, 1607–1776* (1937).
Lathrop, Elise, *Early American Inns and Taverns* (1926).
Leighton, Ann, *Early American Gardens* (1970).
Love, W. de L., *Fast and Thanksgiving Days in New England* (1895).
McClellan, Elisabeth, *History of American Costume, 1607–1870* (1937).
Mather, Increase, *Testimony against Prophane Customs* (1687); William Peden, ed. (1953).
Mussey, Jane Barrows, ed., *Yankee Life as Told by Those Who Lived It* (rev. ed., 1947).
Noble, John, *A Glance at Suicide as Dealt with in the Colony and Province of the Massachusetts Bay* (1903).
Roth, Rodris, *Tea Drinking in Eighteenth-Century America* (1961).
Ryan, Frank W., Jr., "Travelers in South Carolina in the Eighteenth Century," *Charleston South Carolina Yearbook, 1945* (1948), 184.
Schantz, F. J. F., *Domestic Life and Characteristics of the Pennsylvania-German Pioneer* (1900).
Singleton, Esther, *Social New York under the Georges, 1714–1776: Houses, Streets, and Country Homes, with Chapters on Fashions, Furniture, China, Plate, and Manners* (1902).
Stanard, Mary Newton, *Colonial Virginia: Its People and Customs* (1917).
Tattershall, Edward S., *The Wigmaker in Eighteenth-Century Williamsburg* (1959).
Thomas, Gertrude I., *Foods of Our Forefathers* (1941).
Thomas, Gertrude Z., *Richer than Spices: How a Royal Bride's Dowry Revolutionized Both England and America* (1965).
Tyler, Alice F., *Freedom's Ferment: Social History from the Colonial Period to the Civil War* (1944).
Warwick, Edward, Henry C. Pitz, and Alexander Wyckoff, *Early American Dress: Colonial and Revolutionary Periods* (1965).
Watson, Alan D., "Ordinaries in Colonial Eastern North Carolina," *No. Car. Hist. Rev.*, 45 (1968), 67.
Wright, Louis B., *The First Gentlemen of Virginia* (1940).
Yoder, Paton, "Private Hospitality in the South, 1774–1850," *MVHR*, 47 (1960), 419.

See also 10.3 for biographies/writings of:

Byrd, William, 1674–1744

37.18 EDUCATION

37.18.1 General

Bailyn, Bernard, *Education in the Forming of American Society* (1960).
Cremin, Lawrence A., *American Education: Colonial Experience, 1607–1783* (1970).
Gegenheimer, A. F., *William Smith, Educator and Churchman* (1943).
Hansen, Allen O., *Liberalism and American Education in the Eighteenth Century* (1926).
Livingood, Frederick G., *Eighteenth-Century Reformed Church Schools* (1930).

Meriwether, Colyer, *Our Colonial Curriculum, 1607–1776* (1907).

Monroe, Paul, *Founding of the American Public School System* (1940).

Nash, Ray, *American Writing Masters and Copybooks, History and Bibliography through Colonial Times* (1959).

Parsons, Elsie W. C., *Educational Legislation and Administration of Colonial Governments* (1899).

Pears, Thomas C., Jr., "Colonial Education among Presbyterians," *Jour. Presby. Hist.*, 30 (1952), 115, 165.

Seybolt, Robert F., *Evening School in Colonial America* (1925).

—— *Source Studies in American Colonial Education: Private School* (1925).

Sloane, William, *Children's Books in England and America in the Seventeenth Century* (1955).

Stander, Golder G., "Jesuit Educational Institutions in the City of New York (1683–1860)," *Cath. Hist. Soc. Rec.*, 24 (1934), 209.

Tyack, David B., "Benjamin Franklin and Instruction of 'A Rising People'," *Hist. Educ. Quar.*, 6 (1966), 3.

Woody, Thomas, ed., *Educational Views of Benjamin Franklin* (1931).

*   *   *   *   *   *   *

Nash, Ray, *American Writing Masters and Copybooks, History and Bibliography through Colonial Times* (1959).

37.18.2 South

Ames, Susie M., *Reading, Writing and Arithmetic in Virginia, 1607–1699* (1957).

Corry, J. P., "Education in Colonial Georgia," *Ga. Hist. Quar.*, 16 (1932), 136.

Easterby, J. H., ed., "The South Carolina Education Bill of 1770," *So. Car. Hist. Geneal. Mag.*, 48 (1947), 95.

Fithian, Philip Vickers, *Journal and Letters, 1773–1774: A Plantation Tutor of the Old Dominion*, Hunter D. Farish, ed. (1943).

Griffith, Lucille, "English Education for Virginia Youth," *Va. Mag. Hist. Biog.*, 79 (1961), 7.

Jernegan, Marcus W., "Educational Development of the Southern Colonies," *School Rev.*, 27 (1919), 360.

McCaul, Robert L., "Education in Georgia during the Period of Royal Government, 1752–1776," *Ga. Hist. Quar.*, 40 (1956), 103.

Wells, Guy F., *Parish Education in Colonial Virginia* (1923).

37.18.3 Middle Colonies

Bell, Whitfield J., Jr., "Benjamin Franklin and German Charity Schools," *Am. Philos. Soc., Proc.*, 99 (1955), 381.

Burr, Nelson R., *Education in New Jersey, 1630–1871* (1942).

Kemp, W. W., *Support of Schools in Colonial New York* (1913).

Kilpatrick, William H., *The Dutch Schools of New Netherland and Colonial New York* (1912).

Klein, Milton M., "Church, State and Education: Colonial New York," *N.Y. Hist.*, 45 (1964), 291.

McAnear, Beverly, "Charter of the Academy of Newark," *Del. Hist.*, 4 (1950), 149.

Seybolt, Robert F., *Apprenticeship and Apprenticeship Education in Colonial New England and New York* (1917).

—— "Schoolmasters of Colonial Philadelphia," *Penn. Mag. Hist. Biog.*, 52 (1928), 361.

Straub, Jean S., "Quaker School Life in Pennsylvania before 1800," *Penn. Mag. Hist. Biog.*, 89 (1965), 447.

—— "Teaching in the Friends' Latin School of Philadelphia in the Eighteenth Century," *Penn. Mag. Hist. Biog.*, 91 (1967), 436.

Weaver, Glenn, "Benjamin Franklin and the Pennsylvania Germans," *WMQ*, 3 ser., 14 (1957), 536.

Weber, Samuel E., *Charity School Movement in Colonial Pennsylvania* (1905).
Woody, Thomas, *Early Quaker Education in Pennsylvania* (1920).
——— ed., *Quaker Education in New Jersey* (1923).

See also 10.3 for biographies/writings of:

Dock, Christopher, ca. 1698–1771

37.18.4 New England

Ford, Paul L., ed., *The New England Primer* (1897).
Hale, Richard W., *Tercentenary History of Roxbury Latin School* (1946).
Jackson, George L., *Development of School Support in Colonial Massachusetts* (1909).
Littlefield, George E., *Early Schools and School-Books of New England* (1904).
Marr, Harriet W., *Old New England Academies Founded before 1826* (1959).
Middlekauff, Robert, *Ancients and Axioms: Secondary Education in Eighteenth-Century New England* (1963).
Seybolt, Robert F., *Apprenticeship and Apprenticeship Education in Colonial New England* (1917).
——— *The Private Schools of Colonial Boston* (1935).
——— *The Public Schoolmasters of Colonial Boston* (1939).
——— *The Public Schools of Colonial Boston, 1635–1775* (1935).
Shipton, Clifford K., "Puritan Influence in Education," *Penn. Hist.*, 25 (1958), 223.
——— "Secondary Education in the Puritan Colonies," *NEQ*, 7 (1934), 646.
Small, Walter H., *Early New England Schools*, William H. Eddy, ed. (1914).
Suzzallo, Henry, *Rise of Local School Supervision in Massachusetts* (1906).
Updegraff, Harlan, *Origin of Moving School in Massachusetts* (1907).

See also 10.3 for biographies/writings of:

Mather, Cotton, 1662/63–1727/28

37.18.5 Higher Education

Bainton, Roland H., *Yale and the Ministry* (1955).
Brinton, Howard H., "Quaker Contribution to Higher Education in Colonial America," *Penn. Hist.*, 25 (1958), 234.
Broderick, Francis L., "Curriculum of the College of New Jersey, 1746–94," *WMQ*, 3 ser., 6 (1949), 42.
Carson, Jane, *James Innes and His Brothers of the F. H. C.* (1965).
Cohen, I. Bernard, "The Beginning of Chemical Instruction in America: Teaching of Chemistry at Harvard Prior to 1800," *Chymia*, 3 (1950), 17.
Come, Donald R., "The Influence of Princeton on Higher Education in the South before 1825," *WMQ*, 3 ser., 2 (1945), 352.
Connor, R. D. W., "Higher Education in North Carolina," *No. Car. Hist. Rev.*, 28 (1951), 1.
Cowie, Alexander, *Educational Problems at Yale College in the Eighteenth Century* (1936).
Dexter, Franklin B., ed., *Documentary History of Yale, 1701–1745* (1916).
Eells, Walter C., *Baccalaureate Degrees Conferred in the Seventeenth and Eighteenth Centuries* (1958).
Foster, Margery S., "Out of Smalle Beginings . . . ": An Economic History of Harvard College in the Puritan Period, 1636 to 1712 (1962).
Haller, Mabel, "Moravian Influences on Higher Education in Colonial America," *Penn. Hist.*, 25 (1958), 205.
Hofstadter, Richard, and Walter P. Metzger, *Development of Academic Freedom* (1955).
Hudson, Winthrop S., "Morison Myth concerning the Founding of Harvard College," *Church Hist.*, 8 (1939), 148.

Land, Robert H., "Henrico and Its College," *WMQ*, 2 ser., 18 (1938), 453.
Lane, William C., "Early Harvard Broadsides," Am. Antiq. Soc., *Proc.*, 24 (1914), 264.
McAnear, Beverly, "College Founding in the Colonies, 1745–1775," *MVHR*, 42 (1955), 24.
────── "Raising Funds by Colonial Colleges," *MVHR*, 38 (1952), 591.
────── "Selection of an Alma Mater by Pre-Revolutionary Students," *Penn. Mag. Hist. Biog.*, 73 (1949), 429.
McCaul, Robert L., "Whitefield's Bethesda College Projects and Other Major Attempts to Found Colonial Colleges," *Ga. Hist. Quar.*, 44 (1960), 263.
McKeehan, Louis W., *Yale Science: First Hundred Years* (1947).
Middleton, A. Pierce, "Anglican Contributions to Higher Education in Colonial America," *Penn. Hist.*, 25 (1958), 251.
Morison, Samuel E., *The Founding of Harvard College* (1935).
────── *Harvard College in the Seventeenth Century* (2 vols., 1936).
Norton, Arthur O., "Harvard Textbooks and Reference Books of the Seventeenth Century," Col. Soc. Mass., *Publ.*, 28 (1935), 361.
Olson, Alison B., "Founding of Princeton University: Religion and Politics in Eighteenth-Century New Jersey," *N. J. Hist.*, 87 (1969), 133.
Oviatt, Edwin, *Beginnings of Yale (1701–1726)* (1916).
"Papers Relating to Governor Nicholson and the Founding of William and Mary," *Va. Mag. Hist. Biog.*, 7 (1899/1900), 153; 8 (1900/1901), 46; 9 (1901/1902), 18.
Pfeiffer, Robert H., "Teaching of Hebrew in Colonial America," *Jew. Quar. Rev.*, 45 (1955), 363.
Potter, Alfred C., "Harvard College Library, 1723–1735," Col. Soc. Mass., *Publ.*, 25 (1924), 1.
Potter, David, *Debating in Colonial Chartered Colleges, 1642 to 1900* (1944).
Rand, Edward K., "Liberal Education in Seventeenth-Century Harvard," *NEQ*, 6 (1933), 525.
Robbins, Caroline, "Library of Liberty—Assembled for Harvard College by Thomas Hollis of Lincoln's Inn," *Harv. Lib. Bull.*, 5 (1951), 5, 181.
Schmidt, George P., *Princeton and Rutgers: The Two Colonial Colleges of New Jersey* (1964).
Walsh, James J., *Education of the Founding Fathers: Scholasticism in Colonial Colleges* (1935).
Wertenbaker, Thomas J., *Princeton, 1746–1896* (1946).

See also 10.3 for biographies/writings of:

Blair, James, 1655–1743
Clap, Thomas, 1703–1767
Johnson, Samuel, 1696–1772
Mather, Increase, 1639–1723
Smith, William, 1727–1803
Stiles, Ezra, 1727–1795
Wheelock, Eleazar, 1711–1779
Witherspoon, John, 1723–1794

37.19 RELIGION

37.19.1 General

Baldwin, Alice M., *The Clergy in Connecticut in Revolutionary Days* (1936).
Brock, Henry I., *Colonial Churches in Virginia* (1930).
Brydon, George M., *Religious Life of Virginia in the Seventeenth Century* (1957).
────── ed., "Virginia Clergy: Governor Gooch's Letters to Bishop of London, 1727–49," *Va. Mag. Hist. Biog.*, 32 (1924), 209; 33 (1925), 51.
Gambrell, Mary L., *Ministerial Training in Eighteenth Century New England* (1937).

Goodwin, Edward L., *The Colonial Church in Virginia* (1927).

Heimert, Alan E., *Religion and the American Mind: From the Great Awakening to the Revolution* (1966).

Mead, Sidney E., "American Protestantism during the Revolutionary Epoch," *Church Hist.*, 22 (1953), 279.

—— *Lively Experiment: Christianity in America* (1963).

—— "The Rise of the Evangelical Conception of the Ministry in America: 1607–1850," in H. Richard Niebuhr and Daniel D. Williams, eds., *The Ministry in Historical Perspective* (1956).

Newlin, Claude M., *Philosophy and Religion in Colonial America* (1962).

Shewmaker, William O., "Training of the Protestant Ministry before the Establishment of Theological Seminaries," Am. Soc. Church Hist., *Papers*, 2 ser., 6 (1921), 71.

Shipton, Clifford K., "New England Clergy in the Glacial Age," Col. Soc. Mass., *Publ.*, 32 (1933), 24.

Smith, H. Shelton, Robert T. Handy, and Lefferts A. Loetscher, *American Christianity, 1607–1820* (1960).

Smith, James W., and A. Leland Jamison, *Religion in American Life*, vol. I (1961).

Smith, Timothy L., "Forming of American Religious Structure," *WMQ*, 3 ser., 25 (1968), 155.

Sweet, William W., *Religion in Colonial America* (1942).

—— *Religion in the Development of American Culture, 1765–1840* (1952).

Weis, Frederick L., *Colonial Churches and Colonial Clergy in the Middle and Southern Colonies* (1938).

—— *Colonial Clergy and Colonial Churches of New England* (1936).

—— *Colonial Clergy of Maryland, Delaware, and Georgia* (1950).

—— "Colonial Clergy of the Middle Colonies, 1628–1776," Am. Antiq. Soc., *Proc.*, 66 (1956), 167.

—— *Colonial Clergy of Virginia, North Carolina, and South Carolina* (1955).

See also 10.3 for biographies/writings of:

Billings, William, 1764–1800
Bradford, William, 1589/90–1657
Edwards, Jonathan, 1703–1758

37.19.2 Puritanism

37.19.2.1 General

Ahlstrom, Sydney E., "Thomas Hooker—Puritanism and Democratic Citizenship," *Church Hist.*, 32 (1963), 415.

Burg, R. Richard, "Ideology of Richard Mather and Its Relationship to English Puritanism Prior to 1660," *Jour. Church and State,* 9 (1967), 364.

Carroll, Peter N., *Puritanism and the Wilderness: Intellectual Significance of New England Frontier, 1629–1700* (1969).

Davis, Thomas M., "Edward Taylor and the Traditions of Puritan Typology," *Early Am. Lit.*, 4 (1969), 27.

—— "The Exegetical Traditions of Puritan Typology," *Early Am. Lit.*, 5 (1970), 11.

Emerson, Everett H., "Calvin and Covenant Theology," *Church Hist.*, 25 (1956), 136.

Erikson, Kai T., *Wayward Puritans: The Sociology of Deviance* (1966).

Feinstein, Howard M., "The Prepared Heart: Comparative Study of Puritan Theology and Psychoanalysis," *Am. Quar.*, 22 (1970), 166.

Fingerhut, Eugene R., "Were the Massachusetts Puritans Hebraic?" *NEQ*, 40 (1967), 521.

Grant, Leonard T., "Puritan Catechizing," *Jour. Presby. Hist.*, 46 (1968), 107.

Hall, David D., ed., *Puritanism in Seventeenth-Century Massachusetts* (1968).

Haraszti, Zoltán, *Enigma of the Bay Psalm Book* (1956).

James, Sydney V., ed., *New England Puritans* (1968).

Levy, Babette M., "Early Puritanism in the Southern and Island Colonies," Am. Antiq. Soc., *Proc.*, 70 (1960), 69.

McGiffert, Michael, ed., *Puritanism and American Experience* (1969).

MacLear, James F., "The Heart of New England Rent: The Mystical Element in Early Puritan History," *MVHR*, 42 (1956), 621.

Mather, Cotton, *Bonifacius: An Essay upon the Good* (1710); David Levin, ed. (1966).

———— *Magnalia Christi* (1702).

Middlekauff, Robert, "Piety and Intellect in Puritanism," *WMQ*, 3 ser., 22 (1965), 457.

Miller, Perry, "Declension in a Bible Commonwealth," Am. Antiq. Soc., *Proc.*, 51 (1941), 37.

———— *Errand into the Wilderness* (1956).

———— *The New England Mind: From Colony to Province* (1953).

———— *The New England Mind: The Seventeenth Century* (1939).

———— *Orthodoxy in Massachusetts* (1933).

———— "'Preparation for Salvation' in Seventeenth-Century New England," *Jour. Hist. Ideas*, 4 (1943), 253.

Møller, Jens G., "Puritan Covenant Theology," *Jour. Eccl. Hist.*, 14 (1963), 46.

Morgan, Edmund S., *Visible Saints: History of a Puritan Idea* (1963).

Niebuhr, H. Richard, "Idea of Covenant and American Democracy," *Church Hist.*, 23 (1954), 126.

Nuttall, Geoffrey, *The Holy Spirit in Puritan Faith and Experience* (1946).

Park, Charles E., "Puritans and Quakers," *NEQ*, 27 (1954), 320.

Pettit, Norman, *Heart Prepared: Grace and Conversion in Puritan Spiritual Life* (1966).

Pope, Robert G., "New England Versus the New England Mind: The Myth of Declension," *Jour. Soc. Hist.*, 3 (1969–1970), 301.

Rutman, Darrett B., *American Puritanism: Faith and Practice* (1970).

Schneider, Herbert W., *The Puritan Mind* (1930).

Simpson, Alan, *Puritanism in Old and New England* (1955).

Stearns, Raymond P., "Assessing the New England Mind," *Church Hist.*, 10 (1941), 3.

———— and David H. Brawner, "New England Church 'Relations' and Continuity in Early Congregational History," Am. Antiq. Soc., *Proc.*, 75 (1965), 13.

Taylor, Edward, *Christographia* [*1701–1703*], Norman S. Grabo, ed. (1962).

Trinterud, Leonard J., "Origins of Puritanism," *Church Hist.*, 20 (1951), 37.

Van de Wetering, John E., "God, Science, and Puritan Dilemma," *NEQ*, 38 (1965), 494.

Waller, George M., ed., *Puritanism in Early America* (1950).

Ziff, Larzer, "Salem Puritans in Free Aire of New World," *Huntington Lib. Quar.*, 20 (1957), 373.

*　　*　　*　　*　　*　　*　　*

Hall, David D., "Understanding the Puritans," in Herbert J. Bass, ed., *State of American History* (1970).

McGiffert, Michael, "American Puritan Studies, 1960's," *WMQ*, 3 ser., 27 (1970), 36.

Morgan, Edmund S., "New England Puritanism; Another Approach," *WMQ*, 3 ser., 18 (1961), 236.

Rutman, Darrett B., "'Another Approach' to New England Puritanism Assayed," *WMQ*, 3 ser., 19 (1962), 408.

Vail, R. W. G., "Checklist of New England Election Sermons," Am. Antiq. Soc., *Proc.*, 45 (1935), 233.

See also 10.3 for biographies/writings of:

Byles, Mather, 1706/07–1788
Cotton, John, 1584–1652
Eliot, Jared, 1685–1763

Hooker, Thomas, 1586–1647
Mather, Cotton, 1662/63–1727/28
Mather, Increase, 1639–1723
Mayhew, Jonathan, 1720–1766
Peter, Hugh, 1598–1660
Stiles, Ezra, 1727–1795
Wigglesworth, Michael, 1631–1705
Wise, John, 1652–1725

37.19.2.2 Controversy and Dissent

Adams, Charles F., "The Antinomian Controversy," in *Three Episodes of Massachusetts History* (2 vols., 1892).

Battis, Emery, *Saints and Sectaries: Anne Hutchinson and Antinomian Controversy* (1962).

Bercovitch, Sacvan, "Typology in Puritan New England: Williams-Cotton Controversy," *Am. Quar.*, 19 (1967), 166.

Calamandrei, Mauro, "Neglected Aspects of Roger Williams' Thought," *Church Hist.*, 21 (1952), 239.

Cotton, John, "Answer to Master Roger Williams," Jeremiah L. Diman, ed., Narragansett Club, *Publ.*, 1 ser., 2 (1867).

Goodwin, Gerald J., "The Myth of 'Arminian Calvinism,'" *NEQ*, 41 (1968), 213.

Hall, David D., comp., *Antinomian Controversy, 1636–1638: Documentary History* (1968).

Parkes, Henry B., "Cotton and Williams Debate Toleration," *NEQ*, 4 (1931), 735.

Polishook, Irwin H., *Roger Williams, John Cotton, and Religious Freedom* (1967).

Rosenmeier, Jesper, "John Cotton and Roger Williams," *WMQ*, 3 ser., 25 (1968), 408.

───── "New England's Perfection: The Image of Adam and the Image of Christ in the Antinomian Crisis, 1634 to 1638," *WMQ*, 3 ser., 27 (1970), 435.

Simpson, Alan, "How Democratic was Roger Williams?" *WMQ*, 3 ser., 13 (1956), 53.

Stead, G. A., "Williams and Massachusetts," *NEQ*, 7 (1934), 235.

*   *   *   *   *   *   *

Moore, LeRoy, Jr., "Roger Williams and the Historians," *Church Hist.*, 32 (1963), 432.

Morgan, Edmund S., "Miller's Williams," *NEQ*, 38 (1965), 513.

See also 10.3 for biographies/writings of:

Cotton, John, 1584–1652
Gorton, Samuel, ca. 1592–1677
Hutchinson, Anne, 1591–1643
Williams, Roger, 1603–1682/83

37.19.2.3 Puritan Church

Boston, First Church, *Records of the First Church in Boston, 1630–1868*, Richard D. Pierce, ed. (3 vols., 1961).

Buchanan, John G., "Natural Law in Colonial Election Sermons of Massachusetts," *Am. Jour. Legal Hist.*, 12 (1968), 232.

Cotton, John, *On the Churches of New England,* Larzer Ziff, ed. (1968). Three sermons delivered, 1636–1648.

Foote, Henry W., ed., *The Cambridge Platform of 1648* (1949).

Hall, David D., *The Faithful Shepherd: History of the New England Ministry in the Seventeenth Century* (1971).

Kobrin, David, "Expansion of the Visible Church in New England: 1629–1650," *Church Hist.*, 36 (1967), 189.

Levy, Babette M., *Preaching in the First Half Century of New England History* (1945).

Lockridge, Kenneth A., "History of a Puritan Church, 1637–1736," *NEQ*, 40 (1967), 399.

Miller, Perry, "Solomon Stoddard, 1643–1729," *Harv. Theol. Rev.*, 34 (1941), 277.

Oberholzer, Emil, Jr., "The Church in New England Society," in James Morton Smith, ed., *Seventeenth Century America: Essays in Colonial History* (1959).

—— *Delinquent Saints: Disciplinary Action in Early Congregational Churches of Massachusetts* (1956).

Plumstead, A. W., ed., *Wall and Garden: Massachusetts Sermons, 1670–1775* (1968).

Pope, Robert G., *The Half-Way Covenant: Church Membership in Puritan New England* (1969).

Simmons, Richard C., "Founding of the Third Church in Boston," *WMQ*, 3 ser., 26 (1969), 241.

Stearns, Raymond P., and David H. Brawner, "New England Church 'Relations' and Continuity in Early Congregational History," Am. Antiq. Soc., *Proc.*, 75 (1965), 13.

Taylor, Edward, *Treatise concerning the Lord's Supper* (1694); Norman S. Grabo, ed. (1966).

Walsh, James P., "Solomon Stoddard's Open Communion: A Re-examination," *NEQ*, 43 (1970), 97.

Winslow, Ola, *Meetinghouse Hill, 1630–1783* (1952).

Wise, John, *A Vindication of Government of New-England Churches* (1717).

Ziff, Larzer, "Social Bond of Church Covenant," *Am. Quar.*, 10 (1958), 454.

37.19.3 Great Awakening

37.19.3.1 General

Belden, Albert D., *George Whitefield, the Awakener: A Modern Study of the Evangelical Revival* (1953).

Brynestad, Lawrence E., "The Great Awakening in the New England and Middle Colonies," *Jour. Presby. Hist.*, 14 (1930), 80, 104.

Bushman, Richard L., ed., *The Great Awakening: Documents, 1740–1745* (1969).

Gaustad, Edwin S., *The Great Awakening in New England* (1957).

Gewehr, W. M., *The Great Awakening in Virginia, 1740–90* (1930).

Goen, C. C., *Revivalism and Separatism in New England, 1740–1800: Strict Congregationalists and Separate Baptists in the Great Awakening* (1962).

Goodwin, Gerald J., "Anglican Reaction to the Great Awakening," *Hist. Mag. Prot. Episc. Church*, 35 (1966), 343.

Hardy, Edwin N., *George Whitefield: The Matchless Soul Winner* (1938).

Heimert, Alan, and Perry Miller, eds., *The Great Awakening: Documents* (1967).

Heimert, Alan, *Religion and the American Mind: From the Great Awakening to the Revolution* (1966).

Kenney, William H., III, "Alexander Garden and George Whitefield: Revivalism in South Carolina, 1738–1741," *So. Car. Hist. Mag.*, 71 (1970), 1.

Labaree, Leonard W., "Conservative Attitude toward the Great Awakening," *WMQ*, 3 ser., 1 (1944), 331.

Maxson, Charles H., *The Great Awakening in the Middle Colonies* (1920).

Mitchell, Mary H., *The Great Awakening and Other Revivals in Connecticut* (1934).

Morgan, David T., Jr., "The Great Awakening in North Carolina, 1740–1775," *No. Car. Hist. Rev.*, 45 (1968), 264.

Rothermund, Dietmar, "Political Factions and the Great Awakening," *Penn. Hist.*, 26 (1959), 317.

Sklar, Robert, "The Great Awakening and Colonial Politics: Connecticut's Revolution in the Minds of Men," Conn. Hist. Soc., *Bull.*, 28 (1963), 81.

Tolles, Frederick B., "Quietism versus Enthusiasm: The Philadelphia Quakers and the Great Awakening," *Penn. Mag. Hist. Biog.*, 69 (1945), 26.

White, Eugene E., "Decline of the Great Awakening in New England: 1741 to 1746," *NEQ*, 24 (1951), 35.

Wright, Conrad, *Beginnings of Unitarianism in America* (1955).

See also 10.3 for biographies/writings of:

Chauncy, Charles, 1705–1787
Clap, Thomas, 1703–1767
Frelinghuysen, Theodorus J., 1691–ca. 1748
Wheelock, Eleazar, 1711–1779
Whitefield, George, 1714–1770

37.19.3.2 Jonathan Edwards

Carse, James, *Jonathan Edwards and the Visibility of God* (1967).

Cherry, C. Conrad, "Puritan Notion of Covenant in Jonathan Edwards' Doctrine of Faith," *Church Hist.*, 34 (1965), 328.

—————— *Theology of Jonathan Edwards* (1966).

—————— *Treatise Concerning Religious Affections*, John E. Smith, ed. (1959).

Elwood, Douglas J., *Philosophical Theology of Jonathan Edwards* (1960).

Illick, Joseph E., "Jonathan Edwards and the Historians," *Jour. Presby. Hist.*, 39 (1961), 230.

Parker, Gail T., "Jonathan Edwards and Melancholy," *NEQ*, 41 (1968), 193.

Pierce, David C., "Jonathan Edwards and the 'New Sense of Glory,'" *NEQ*, 41 (1968), 82.

Schaefer, Thomas A., "Jonathan Edwards and Justification by Faith," *Church Hist.*, 21 (1952), 55.

Thomas, Vincent, "Modernity of Jonathan Edwards," *NEQ*, 25 (1952), 60.

See also 10.3 for biographies/writings of:

Edwards, Jonathan, 1703–1758

37.19.4 Church, State, and Religious Liberty

Adelman, David C., "Strangers: Civil Rights of Jews in the Colony of Rhode Island," *R.I. Jewish Historical Notes*, 1 (1954), 104.

Beth, Loren P., *American Theory of Church and State* (1958).

Brydon, G. MacLaren, "Antiecclesiastical Laws of Virginia," *Va. Mag. Hist. Biog.*, 64 (1956), 259.

Cobb, Sanford H., *Rise of Religious Liberty in America* (1902).

Cushing, John D., "Disestablishment in Massachusetts, 1780–1833," *WMQ*, 3 ser., 26 (1969), 169.

Greene, M. Louise, *Development of Religious Liberty in Connecticut* (1905).

Hanley, Thomas O., "Church and State in the Maryland Ordinance of 1639," *Church Hist.*, 26 (1957), 325.

Holifield, E. Brooks, "On Toleration in Massachusetts," *Church Hist.*, 38 (1969), 188.

James, Charles F., *Documentary History of the Struggle for Religious Liberty in Virginia* (1900).

Kinney, Charles B., Jr., *Church and State: Separation in New Hampshire, 1630–1900* (1955).

Klein, Milton M., "Church, State, and Education: Colonial New York," *N. Y. Hist.*, 45 (1964), 291.

McIlwaine, Henry R., "Struggle of Protestant Dissenters for Religious Toleration in Virginia," *Johns Hopkins Studies*, 12 (1894), 171.

McLoughlin, William G., *New England Dissent, 1630–1833: The Baptists and the Separation of Church and State* (2 vols., 1971).

Mead, Sidney, "Rise of Religious Liberty and Emergence of Denominationalism," *Church Hist.*, 25 (1956), 317.

Meyer, Jacob C., *Church and State in Massachusetts from 1740 to 1833* (1930).

Miller, Perry, "The Contribution of the Protestant Churches to Religious Liberty in Colonial America," *Church Hist.*, 4 (1935), 57.

Monroe, Haskell, "Religious Toleration and Politics in Early North Carolina," *No. Car. Hist. Rev.*, 24 (1962), 267.

Perry, William S., "Foundations of Church and State in Virginia," *Hist. Mag. Prot. Episc. Church*, 26 (1957), 34.

Pilcher, George W., "Samuel Davies and Religious Toleration in Virginia," *Historian*, 28 (1965), 48.

Reed, Susan M., *Church and State in Massachusetts, 1691–1740* (1914).

Slafter, Edmund P., *John Checkley: or Evolution of Religious Tolerance in Massachusetts Bay* (2 vols., 1897).

Steiner, B. C., ed., "Religious Freedom in Provincial Maryland," *AHR*, 28 (1923), 258.

Stokes, Anson P., *Church and State in the United States*, vol. I (1950).

Strickland, Reba C., *Religion and the State in Georgia in the Eighteenth Century* (1939).

Sweet, William W., "American Colonial Experiment and Religious Liberty," *Church Hist.*, 4 (1935), 43.

Tucker, Louis L., "The Church of England and Religious Liberty at Pre-Revolutionary Yale," *WMQ*, 3 ser., 17 (1960), 314.

Werline, Albert W., *Problems of Church and State in Maryland during the Seventeenth and Eighteenth Centuries* (1948).

See also 10.3 for biographies/writings of:

Davies, Samuel, 1723–1761
Leland, John, 1757–1841
Murray, John, 1741–1815

37.19.5 Missions to the Indians

Gray, Elma E. and Leslie R., *Wilderness Christians: Moravian Mission to the Delaware Indians* (1956).

Huddleston, Lee E., *Origins of the American Indians: European Concepts, 1492–1729* (1967).

Kellaway, William, *The New England Company, 1649–1776: Missionary Society to the American Indians* (1961).

Thompson, H. P., *Into All Lands: Society for the Propagation of Gospel in Foreign Parts, 1701–1950* (1951).

Vaughan, Alden T., *New England Frontier: Puritans and Indians, 1620–1675* (1965).

Weis, Frederick L., "The New England Company of 1649 and its Missionary Enterprises," Col. Soc. Mass., *Publ.*, 38 (1959), 134.

Winship, G. P., ed., *The New England Company of 1649 and John Eliot* (1920).

See also 10.3 for biographies/writings of:

Brainerd, David, 1718–1747
Eliot, John, 1604–1690
Heckewelder, John, 1743–1823
Jogues, Isaac, 1607–1646
Weiser, (Johann) Conrad, 1696–1760

37.19.6 Anglicanism

Baldwin, Simeon E., "American Jurisdiction of the Bishop of London in Colonial Times," Am. Antiq. Soc., *Proc.*, 13 (1901), 179.

Beardsley, E. Edward, *The History of the Episcopal Church in Connecticut* (2 vols., 1869).

Bridenbaugh, Carl, *Mitre and Sceptre: Transatlantic Faiths, Ideas, Personalities and Politics, 1689–1775* (1962).

Brydon, George M., *Virginia's Mother Church* (2 vols., 1947).

Burr, Nelson R., *The Anglican Church in New Jersey* (1954).

Clement, John, "Anglican Clergymen Licensed to the American Colonies, 1710–1744," *Hist. Mag. Prot. Episc. Church*, 17 (1948), 207.

Conkin, Paul, "Church Establishment in North Carolina, 1765–1776," *No. Car. Hist. Rev.*, 32 (1955), 1.

Cross, Arthur L., *The Anglican Episcopate and American Colonies* (1902).

Dalcho, Frederick, *Historical Account of the Protestant Episcopal Church in South Carolina* (1820).

Davidson, Elizabeth, *Establishment of the English Church in the Continental American Colonies* (1936).

Ervin, Spencer, "The Anglican Church in North Carolina," *Hist. Mag. Prot. Episc. Church*, 25 (1956), 102.

—— "The Church in Colonial Virginia," *Hist. Mag. Prot. Episc. Church*, 26 (1957), 65.

—— "The Established Church of Colonial Maryland," *Hist. Mag. Prot. Episc. Church*, 24 (1955), 232.

Goodwin, Edward L., *The Colonial Church in Virginia* (1927).

Greene, Evarts B., "The Anglican Outlook on the American Colonies," *AHR*, 20 (1914), 64.

Hartdagen, Gerald E., "Vestries and Morals in Colonial Maryland," *Md. Hist. Mag.*, 63 (1968), 360.

Hawkins, Ernest, ed., *Historical Notices of Missions of the Church of England* (1845).

Jarratt, Devereux, "Autobiography, 1732–1763," Douglass Adair, ed., *WMQ*, 3 ser., 9 (1952), 346.

Johnston, Gideon, *Carolina Chronicle: Papers of Commissary Gideon Johnston, 1707–1716*, Frank J. Klingberg, ed. (1946).

Klingberg, Frank J., *Anglican Humanitarianism in Colonial New York* (1940).

—— "Sir William Johnson and S. P. G." *Hist. Mag. Prot. Episc. Church*, 8 (1939), 4.

Le Jau, Francis, *Carolina Chronicle of Dr. Francis Le Jau, 1706–1717*, Frank J. Klingberg, ed. (1956).

Loveland, Clara O., *Critical Years: Reconstitution of Anglican Church, 1780–1789* (1956).

Manross, William W., "Catalog of Articles," *Hist. Mag. Prot. Episc. Church*, 23 (1954), 367.

Oliver, D. D., "Society for the Propagation of the Gospel in North Carolina," *James Sprunt Hist. Publ.*, 9 (1910).

Pilcher, George W., "Pamphlet War on Proposed Virginia Anglican Episcopate, 1767–1775," *Hist. Mag. Prot. Episc. Church*, 30 (1961), 266.

Porter, Henry C., "Alexander Whitaker: Cambridge Apostle to Virginia," *WMQ*, 3 ser., 14 (1957), 317.

Posey, Walter B., "The Protestant Episcopal Church: An American Adaptation," *JSH*, 25 (1959), 3.

Reeves, Thomas C., "John Checkley and Episcopal Church in New England," *Hist. Mag. Prot. Episc. Church*, 34 (1965), 349.

Rightmyer, Nelson W., *The Anglican Church in Delaware* (1947).

—— *Maryland's Established Church* (1956).

Seiler, William H., "The Anglican Parish in Virginia," in James M. Smith, ed., *Seventeenth-Century America: Essays in Colonial History* (1959).

—— "Church of England as the Established Church in Seventeenth-Century Virginia," *JSH*, 15 (1949), 478.

Sosin, Jack M., "Proposal for Establishing Anglican Bishops in the Colonies," *Jour. Eccl. Hist.*, 13 (1962), 76.

Steiner, Bruce E., "New England Anglicanism: A Genteel Faith?" *WMQ*, 3 ser., 27 (1970), 122.

Tucker, Louis L., "Church of England and Religious Liberty at Pre-Revolutionary Yale," *WMQ*, 3 ser., 17 (1960), 314.

Weaver, Glenn, "Anglican-Congregationalist Tensions in Pre-Revolutionary Connecticut," *Hist. Mag. Prot. Episc. Church,* 26 (1957), 269.

*   *   *   *   *   *   *

Nelson, William, *Controversy Over a Proposition for an American Episcopate, 1767–1774: Bibliography* (1909).

See also 10.3 for biographies/writings of:

Bray, Thomas, 1656–1729/30
Johnson, Samuel, 1696–1772
Keith, George, 1638–1716
Seabury, Samuel, 1729–1796
Smith, William, 1727–1803
Talbot, John, 1645–1727

37.19.7 Baptists

Backus, Isaac, *History of New England with Particular Reference to Baptists* (3 vols., 1777–1796).
—— *On Church, State, and Calvinism: Pamphlets, 1754–1789,* William G. McLoughlin, ed. (1968).
"Baptist Debate of April 14–15, 1668," William G. McLoughlin and Martha W. Davidson, eds. and trans., Mass. Hist. Soc., *Proc.,* 76 (1964), 91.
Goen, C. C., *Revivalism and Separatism in New England, 1740–1800: Strict Congregationalists and Separate Baptists in the Great Awakening* (1962).
Hudson, Winthrop S., "Ecumenical Spirit of Early Baptists," *Rev. and Expositor,* 55 (1958), 182.
Lumpkin, William L., *Baptist Foundations in the South, 1754–1787* (1961).
McLoughlin, William G., *Isaac Backus and the American Pietistic Tradition* (1967).
—— *New England Dissent, 1630–1833: The Baptists and the Separation of Church and State* (2 vols., 1971).
Paschal, George W., *History of North Carolina Baptists, 1663–1805* (1930).
Semple, R. B., *Rise and Progress of Baptists in Virginia* (1810).
Townsend, Leah, *South Carolina Baptists, 1670–1805* (1935).

See also 10.3 for biographies/writings of:

Colman, Benjamin, 1673–1747
Kinnersley, Ebenezer, 1711–1778
Leland, John, 1757–1841
Williams, Roger, 1603–1682/83

37.19.8 Catholicism

Beitzell, Edwin W., *Jesuit Missions of St. Mary's County Maryland* (1960).
Ellis, John T., *Catholics in Colonial America* (1965).
Kennedy, William H. J., "Catholics in Massachusetts before 1750," *Cath. Hist. Rev.,* 17 (1931), 10.
Madden, Richard C., "Catholics in Colonial South Carolina," Am. Cath. Hist. Soc., *Records,* 73 (1962), 10.
Metzger, Charles H., *Catholics and the American Revolution* (1962).
Mulvey, Mary D., *French Catholic Missionaries in the Present United States, 1604–1791* (1936).
Nuesse, Celestine J., *Social Thought of American Catholics, 1634–1829* (1945).
Phelan, Thomas P., *Catholics in Colonial Days* (1935).
Ray, M. A., *American Opinion of Roman Catholicism* (1936).
Riley, Arthur J., *Catholicism in New England to 1788* (1936).
Shea, John D. G., *The Catholic Church in Colonial Days* (1886).

See also 10.3 for biographies/writings of:

Carroll, John, 1735–1815

37.19.9 Dutch Reformed Church

DeJong, Gerald F., "Dominie Johannes Megapolensis: Minister to New Netherland," *N.Y. Hist. Soc. Quar.*, 52 (1968), 7.
Eekhof, A., *Jonas Michaelus: Founder of the Church of New Netherland* (1926).
Harder, Leland and Marvin, *Plockhoy from Zurik-zee: Story of a Dutch Reformer in Puritan England and Colonial America* (1952).
Zwierlein, Frederick J., *Religion in New Netherland, 1623–1664* (1910).

See also 10.3 for biographies/writings of:

Frelinghuysen, Theodorus J., 1691–ca. 1748

37.19.10 German Churches

Bender, H. S., "Founding of the Mennonite Church at Germantown," *Mennonite Quar. Rev.* 7 (1933), 227.
Bittinger, Lucy F., *German Religious Life in Colonial Times* (1906).
"Diary of a Journey of Moravians from Bethlehem, Pennsylvania to Bethabara in Wachovia, North Carolina, 1753," in Newton D. Mereness, ed., *Travels in the American Colonies* (1916).
Durnbaugh, Donald F., comp., *The Brethren in Colonial America: A Source Book* (1967).
Eisenberg, William E., *The Lutheran Church in Virginia, 1717–1962* (1967).
Fries, Adelaide L., et al., eds., *Records of Moravians in North Carolina* (11 vols., 1922–1969).
Gollin, Gillian L., *Moravians in Two Worlds: Study of Changing Communities* (1967).
Kreider, Harry J., *Lutheranism in Colonial New York* (1942).
Qualben, Lars P., *The Lutheran Church in Colonial America* (1940).
Sachse, Julius F., *German Pietists of Provincial Pennsylvania, 1694–1708* (1895).
―――― *German Sectarians of Pennsylvania, 1708–1742* (2 vols., 1899–1900).
Schmauk, Theodore E., *History of the Lutheran Church in Pennsylvania, 1638–1820* (1903).
Sessler, J. J., *Communal Pietism among Early American Moravians* (1933).
Smith, Charles H., *Mennonite Immigration to Pennsylvania* (1929).
Stoeffler, E. Ernest, *Mysticism in German Devotional Literature of Colonial Pennsylvania* (1950).
Weinlick, John R., "Colonial Moravians: Their Status among the Churches," *Penn. Hist.*, 26 (1959), 213.
Wust, Klaus G., "German Mystics and Sabbatarians in Virginia, 1700–1764," *Va. Mag. Hist. Biog.*, 72 (1964), 330.

See also 10.3 for biographies/writings of:

Beissel, Johann C., 1690–1768
Dock, Christopher, ca. 1698–1771
Heckwelder, John, 1743–1823
Muhlenberg, Henry M., 1711–1787
Muhlenberg, John P. G., 1746–1807
Weiser, (Johann) Conrad, 1696–1760
Zinzendorf, Count Nicolaus Ludwig, 1700–1760

37.19.11 Methodism

Barclay, Wade C., *Early American Methodism, 1769–1844* (1949).
Maser, Frederick E., *Dramatic Story of Early American Methodism* (1965).
Sweet, William W., *Men of Zeal: Methodist Beginnings* (1935).

See also 10.3 for biographies/writings of: •

Asbury, Francis, 1745–1816
Whitefield, George, 1714–1770

37.19.12 Presbyterianism

Christensen, Merton A., "Franklin on Hemphill Trial," *WMQ*, 3 ser., 10 (1953), 422.
Drury, Clifford M., "Presbyterian Beginnings in New England and the Middle Colonies (1640–1714)," *Jour. Presby. Hist.*, 34 (1956), 19.
Funk, Henry D., "Influence of Presbyterian Church in Early American History," *Jour. Presby. Hist.*, 12 (1924), 26; 13 (1925), 152: 14 (1926), 281.
Klett, Guy S., *Presbyterians in Colonial Pennsylvania* (1937).
Presbyterian Church in the U.S.A., *Records of the Presbyterian Church, 1706–1788* (1904).
Scott, Robert F., "Colonial Presbyterianism in Virginia, 1727–1775," *Jour. Presby. Hist.*, 34 (1957), 71.
Thompson, Ernest T., *Presbyterians in the South, 1607–1861* (1963).
Trinterud, Leonard J., *Forming of an American Tradition: Colonial Presbyterianism* (1949).

*   *   *   *   *   *   *

Trinterud, Leonard, comp., *Bibliography of American Presbyterianism during the Colonial Period* (1968).

See also 10.3 for biographies/writings of:

Davies, Samuel, 1723–1761
McMillan, John, 1752–1833
Witherspoon, John, 1723–1794

37.19.13 Society of Friends

Braithwaite, William C., *Beginnings of Quakerism*, Henry J. Cadbury, ed. (2nd ed., 1955).
———— *Second Period of Quakerism*, Henry J. Cadbury, ed. (2nd ed., 1961).
Brodin, Pierre, *Les Quakers en Amérique au XVIIe siècle* (1935).
Carroll, Kenneth L., "Persecution of Quakers in Maryland (1658–1661), *Quaker Hist.*, 53 (1964), 67.
———— "Quakerism on the Eastern Shore of Virginia," *Va. Mag. Hist. Biog.*, 74 (1966), 170.
"Correspondence of James Logan and Thomas Story, 1724–41," Friends Hist. Assoc., *Bull.*, 15, no. 1 (1926).
Fox, R. H., *Dr. John Fothergill and His Friends* (1919).
Hallowell, R. P., *Quaker Invasion of Massachusetts* (1883).
James, Sydney V., *A People among Peoples: Quaker Benevolence in Eighteenth-Century America* (1963).
———— "Quaker Meetings and Education in the Eighteenth Century," *Quaker Hist.*, 51 (1962), 87.
Jones, Rufus M., *Quakers in American Colonies* (1911).
Lloyd, Arnold, *Quaker Social History, 1669–1738* (1950).
Lowenherz, Robert J., "Roger Williams and the Great Quaker Debate," *Am. Quar.*, 11 (1959), 157.
Nash, Gary B., *Quakers and Politics: Pennsylvania, 1681–1726* (1968).
Park, Charles E., "Puritans and Quakers," *NEQ*, 27 (1954), 320.
Philips, Edith, *Good Quaker in French Legend* (1932).
Pomfret, John E., "West New Jersey, a Quaker Society," *WMQ*, 3 ser., 8 (1951), 493.
Thomas, Allen C., *History of the Friends in America* (1930).

Tolles, Frederick B., *The Atlantic Community of the Early Friends* (1952).
—— *Meeting House and Counting House: The Quaker Merchants of Colonial Philadelphia* (1963).
—— *Quakers and Atlantic Culture* (1960).

See also 10.3 for biographies/writings of:

Hicks, Elias, 1748–1830
Keith, George, 1638–1716
Pastorius, Francis D., 1651–1719/20
Pemberton, Israel, 1715–1779
Woolman, John, 1720–1772

37.20 INTELLECTUAL AND CULTURAL HISTORY

37.20.1 General

Boorstin, Daniel J., *The Americans: The Colonial Experience* (1958).
Bowes, Frederick P., *Culture of Early Charleston* (1942).
Breen, Timothy H., *The Character of the Good Ruler: Puritan Political Ideas in New England, 1630–1730* (1970).
Bridenbaugh, Carl, *Myths and Realities: Societies of the Colonial South* (1963).
Buranelli, Vincent, "Colonial Philosophy," *WMQ*, 3 ser., 16 (1959), 343.
Cady, Edwin H., *The Gentleman in America: Literary Study in American Culture* (1949).
Carlson, C. Lennart, "Samuel Keimer, Study in Transit of English Culture to Colonial Pennsylvania," *Penn. Mag. Hist. Biog.*, 61 (1937), 357.
Clive, John, and Bernard Bailyn, "England's Cultural Provinces: Scotland and America," *WMQ*, 3 ser., 11 (1954), 200.
Connor, Paul W., *Poor Richard's Politicks: Benjamin Franklin and His New American Order* (1965).
Davidson, Edward J., "Locke to Edwards," *Jour. Hist. Ideas*, 24 (1963), 355.
Davis, Richard B., *George Sandys, Poet-Adventurer: Anglo-American Culture in the Seventeenth Century* (1955).
—— "Intellectual Golden Age in Colonial Chesapeake Bay Country," *Va. Mag. Hist. Biog.*, 78 (1970), 131.
Gay, Peter, *A Loss of Mastery: Puritan Historians in Colonial America* (1966).
Gibbons, Philip A., *Ideas of Political Representation in Parliament, 1651–1832* (1914).
Grabo, Norman S., "The Veiled Vision: Role of Aesthetics in Early American Intellectual History," *WMQ*, 3 ser., 19 (1962), 493.
Gummere, Richard M., *The American Colonial Mind and the Classical Tradition: Essays in Comparative Culture* (1963).
—— "John Wise, Classical Controversialist," Essex Inst., *Hist. Coll.*, 92 (1956), 265.
Hall, Thomas C., *Religious Background of American Culture* (1930).
Jones, Howard M., *O Strange New World: American Culture, The Formative Years* (1964).
Labaree, Leonard W., *Conservatism in Early American History* (1948).
Leder, Lawrence H., *Liberty and Authority: Early American Political Ideology, 1689–1763* (1968).
Lokken, Roy N., "Concept of Democracy in Colonial Political Thought," *WMQ*, 3 ser., 16 (1959), 570.
—— "Social Thought of James Logan," *WMQ*, 3 ser., 27 (1970), 68.
Lynd, Staughton, *Intellectual Origins of American Radicalism* (1968).
Merritt, Richard L., *Symbols of American Community, 1735–1775* (1966).
Miller, John C., ed., *Colonial Image: Origins of American Culture* (1961).
Morgan, Edmund S., *Puritan Political Ideas, 1558–1794* (1965).
Morison, Samuel E., *Puritan Pronaos* (1936). Reissued under title, *Intellectual Life of Colonial New England* (1960).

Palmer, Robert R., *Great Inversion: America and Europe in the Eighteenth-Century Revolution* (1965).

Persons, Stow, "The Cyclical Theory of History in Eighteenth-Century America," *Am. Quar.*, 6 (1954), 147.

Sachse, William L., *The Colonial American in Britain* (1956).

Savelle, Max, *Seeds of Liberty: The Genesis of the American Mind* (1948).

Tolles, Frederick B., "The Culture of Early Pennsylvania," *Penn. Mag. Hist. Biog.*, 81 (1957), 119.

—— *James Logan and the Culture of Provincial America* (1957).

Wertenbaker, Thomas J., *The Founding of American Civilization: The Middle Colonies* (1938).

—— *The Golden Age of Colonial Culture* (1942).

—— *The Old South: The Founding of American Civilization* (1942).

Wright, Louis B., *Atlantic Frontier* (1947).

—— *Cultural Life of the American Colonies, 1607–1763* (1957).

—— *Dream of Prosperity in Colonial America* (1965).

—— *The First Gentlemen of Virginia* (1940).

—— "Intellectual History and Colonial South," *WMQ*, 3 ser., 16 (1959), 214.

37.20.2 Racial Thought

Degler, Carl N., "Slavery and the Genesis of American Race Prejudice," *Comp. Studies in Society and Hist.*, 2 (1959), 49.

Greene, John C., "Negro's Place in Nature, 1780–1815," *Jour. Hist. Ideas*, 15 (1954), 384.

Harris, Marvin, *Patterns of Race in the Americas* (1964).

Jordan, Winthrop D., *White over Black: American Attitudes toward the Negro, 1550–1812* (1968).

Livermore, George, *Historical Research Respecting Opinions of Founders on Negroes as Slaves, Citizens, and Soldiers* (1862).

Nash, Gary B., "Red, White, and Black: Origins of Racism in Colonial America," in Gary B. Nash and Richard Weiss, eds., *The Great Fear: Race in the Mind of America* (1970).

Ruchames, Louis, "Sources of Racial Thought in Colonial America," *Jour. Negro Hist.*, 52 (1967), 251.

Woodson, Carter G., "Beginnings of Miscegenation of Whites and Blacks," *Jour. Negro. Hist.*, 3 (1918), 335.

37.21 LITERATURE

Adams, Charles F., "Milton's Impress on the Provincial Literature of New England," *Mass. Hist. Soc., Proc.*, 42 (1909), 154.

Bailyn, Bernard, "The Apologia of Robert Keayne," *WMQ*, 3 ser., 7 (1950), 568.

Bercovitch, Sacvan, "New England Epic: Cotton Mather's *Magnalia Christi Americana*," *ELH: A Journal of English Literary History*, 33 (1966), 337.

Bradford, E. F., "Conscious Art in Bradford's History of Plymouth Plantation," *NEQ*, 1 (1928), 133.

Davis, Richard B., ed., *Colonial Virginia Satirist* (1967).

Davis, Richard Beale, "The Gentlest Art in Seventeenth-Century Virginia," *Tennessee Studies in Literature*, 2 (1957), 51.

Ford, Paul L., ed., *The New England Primer* (1897).

Fussell, Edwin S., "Benjamin Tompson, Public Poet," *NEQ*, 26 (1953), 494.

Gummere, Richard M., *Seven Wise Men of Colonial America* (1967).

Hall, Max, *Benjamin Franklin and Polly Baker* (1960).

Haraszti, Zoltán, *Enigma of the Bay Psalm Book* (1956).

Hubbell, Jay B., *The South in American Literature, 1607–1900* (1954).

Jackson, M. Katherine, *Outlines of the Literary History of Colonial Pennsylvania* (1906).

Jantz, Harold S., *First Century of New England Verse* (1949).

Jones, Howard M., "American Prose Style: 1700–1770," *Huntington Lib. Bull.*, no. 6 (1934), 115.

—— "The Colonial Impulse: An Analysis of the 'Promotion' Literature of Colonization," Am. Antiq. Soc., *Proc.*, 90 (1946), 131.

—— *Literature of Virginia in the Seventeenth Century* (1946).

Kane, Hope F., "Notes of Early Pennsylvania Promotion Literature," *Penn. Mag. Hist. Biog.*, 63 (1939), 144.

Kaplan, Sidney, "History of New Hampshire: Jeremy Belknap as a Literary Craftsman," *WMQ*, 3 ser., 21 (1964), 18.

Leffler, Hugh T., "Promotional Literature of the Southern Colonies," *JSH*, 33 (1967), 3.

Lemay, J. A. Leo, *Ebenezer Kinnersley: Franklin's Friend* (1964).

Mathiessen, F. O., "Michael Wigglesworth, a Puritan Artist," *NEQ*, 1 (1928), 491.

Miller, Perry, "Religion and Society in the Early Literature of Virginia," *WMQ*, 3 ser., 5 (1948), 492; 6 (1949), 24.

Murdock, Kenneth B., "Clio in the Wilderness: History and Biography in Puritan New England," *Church Hist.*, 24 (1955), 221.

—— *Literature and Theology in Colonial New England* (1949).

Otis, William B., *American Verse, 1625–1807* (1909).

Parrington, Vernon L., *Main Currents in American Thought*. Vol. I: *The Colonial Mind* (1927).

Piercy, Josephine K., *Studies in Literary Types in Seventeenth-Century America, 1607–1710* (1939).

Seigel, Jules P., "Puritan Light Reading," *NEQ*, 37 (1964), 185.

Sensabaugh, George F., *Milton in Early America* (1964).

Shea, Daniel B., Jr., *Spiritual Autobiography in Early America* (1968).

Shipton, Clifford K., "Literary Leaven in Provincial New England," *NEQ*, 9 (1936), 203.

Sibley, Agnes M., *Alexander Pope's Prestige in America, 1725–1835* (1949).

Spiller, Robert E., ed., *American Literary Revolution, 1783–1837* (1967).

Spiller, Robert E., et al., *Literary History of the United States*, vol. I (3d ed., 1963).

Stoudt, John J., ed., *Pennsylvania German Poetry, 1685–1830* (1956).

Trent, William P., et al., eds., *Cambridge History of American Literature*, vol. I (1917).

Wheeler, Joseph T., "Literary Culture and Eighteenth-Century Maryland," *Md. Hist. Mag.*, 38 (1943), 273.

Winslow, Ola E., ed., *American Broadside Verse from Imprints of 17th & 18th Centuries* (1930).

Winslow, Ola E., "Seventeenth-Century Prologue," in Clarence Gohdes, ed., *Essays on American Literature in Honor of Jay B. Hubbell* (1967).

Wright, Louis B., "Literature in the Colonial South," *Huntington Lib. Quar.*, 10 (1947), 297.

Wright, Luella M., *The Literary Life of the Early Friends, 1650–1725* (1932).

Wright, Thomas G., *Literary Culture in Early New England* (1920).

See also 10.3 for biographies/writings of:

Mayhew, Jonathan, 1720–1766
Ramsay, David, 1749–1815
Sandys, George, 1577/78–1643/44
Strachey, William, 1572–1621
Taylor, Edward, 1645–1729
Tompson, Benjamin, 1642–1714
Trumbull, John, 1750–1831
Warren, Mercy, 1728–1814
Wigglesworth, Michael, 1631–1705

37.22 NEWSPAPERS AND MAGAZINES

37.22.1 General

Brigham, Clarence, *Journals and Journeymen* (1950).
Cappon, Lester J., and Stella Duff, *Virginia Gazette Index* (2 vols., 1950).
Cohen, Hennig, *South Carolina Gazette, 1732–1775* (1953).
Cook, Elizabeth C., *Literary Influences in Colonial Newspapers, 1704–1750* (1912).
Crittenden, C. C., *North Carolina Newspapers before 1790* (1928).
Davidson, Philip, *Propaganda and the American Revolution* (1941).
DeArmond, Anna J., *Andrew Bradford, Colonial Journalist* (1949).
Franklin, Benjamin, *Letters to the Press, 1758–1775*, Verner W. Crane, ed. (1950).
Kobre, Sidney, *Development of the Colonial Newspaper* (1944).
Leder, Lawrence H., "Role of Newspapers in Early America," *Huntington Lib. Quar.*, 30 (1966), 1.
LeMay, J. A. Leo, "Hamilton's Literary History of the *Maryland Gazette*," *WMQ*, 3 ser., 23 (1966), 273.
Littlefield, George E., *Early Massachusetts Press 1638–1711* (2 vols., 1907).
Merritt, Richard L., "Colonists Discover America: Colonial Press, 1735–1775," *WMQ*, 3 ser., 21 (1964), 270.
—— "Public Opinion in Colonial America," *Pub. Opinion Quar.*, 27 (1963), 356.
Morse, Jarvis M., *Connecticut Newspapers in the Eighteenth Century* (1935).
Mott, Frank L., *A History of American Magazines.* Vol. I: *1741–1850* (1930).
Paltsits, Victor H., "New Light on *Public Occurrences*: America's First Newspaper," Am. Antiq. Soc., *Proc.*, 59 (1949), 75.
Richardson, L. N., *History of Early American Magazines* (1931).
Schlesinger, Arthur M., "Colonial Newspapers and the Stamp Act," *NEQ*, 8 (1935), 63.
—— "Politics, Propaganda, and the Philadelphia Press," *Penn. Mag. Hist. Biog.*, 60 (1936), 309
—— "Propaganda and the Boston Press," Col. Soc. Mass., *Publ.*, 32 (1937), 396.
Wroth, Lawrence C., William Parks, *Printer and Journalist of England and Colonial America* (1926).

*   *   *   *   *   *   *

Brigham, Clarence, *History and Bibliography of American Newspapers, 1690–1820* (2 vols., 1947).

See also 10.3 for biographies/writings of:

Gaine, Hugh, 1726/27–1807
Goddard, William, 1740–1817
Parks, William, 1698–1750
Thomas, Isaiah, 1750–1831
Zenger, John Peter, 1697–1746

37.22.2 Freedom of the Press

Alexander, James, *Brief Narrative of Case and Trial of John Peter Zenger* (1736); Stanley N. Katz, ed. (2nd ed., 1972).

Buranelli, Vincent, *Trial of Peter Zenger* (1957).

Duniway, C. A., *Development of Freedom of the Press in Massachusetts* (1906).

Hanson, Laurence W., *Government and the Press, 1695–1763* (1936).

Levy, Leonard W., "Did the Zenger Case Really Matter?" *WMQ*, 3 ser., 17 (1960), 35.

———— ed., *Freedom of the Press from Zenger to Jefferson* (1966).

Levy, Leonard W., *Legacy of Suppression: Freedom of Speech and Press in Early American History* (1960).

Schuyler, Livingston R., *Liberty of the Press in Colonies before the Revolutionary War* (1905).

Terwilliger, W. Bird, "William Goddard's Victory for Freedom of the Press," *Md. Hist. Mag.*, 36 (1941), 139.

See also 10.3 for biographies/writings of:

Alexander, James, 1691–1756
Bradford, Andrew, 1686–1742
Hamilton, Andrew, 1676–1741
Zenger, John Peter, 1697–1746

37.23 PRINTING AND BOOK PUBLISHING

Boynton, Henry W., *Annals of American Bookselling, 1638–1850* (1932).

Bridenbaugh, Carl, "The Press and the Book in Eighteenth Century Philadelphia," *Penn. Mag. Hist. Biog.*, 65 (1941), 1.

Eames, Wilberforce, *First Year of Printing in New York* (1928).

Ford, Worthington C., *Boston Book Market, 1679–1700* (1917).

Green, Samuel A., "Early History of Printing in New England," *Mass. Hist. Soc., Proc.*, 2 ser., 11 (1897), 240.

Harlan, Robert D., "William Strahan's American Book Market, 1744–1776," *Lib. Quar.*, 31 (1961), 235.

Herrick, C. A., *The Early New-Englanders: What Did They Read?* (1918).

Hildeburn, Charles R., *Century of Printing: Pennsylvania, 1685–1784* (2 vols., 1885–1886).

———— *Printers and Printing in New York* (1895).

———— *Sketches of Printers and Printing in Colonial New York* (1895).

Hixson, Richard F., *Isaac Collins: Quaker Printer in 18th Century America* (1968).

Littlefield, George E., *Early Boston Booksellers, 1642–1711* (1900).

———— *Early Massachusetts Press 1638–1711* (2 vols., 1907).

McCullock, William, "William McCullock's Additions to Thomas' History of Printing," *Am. Antiq. Soc., Proc.*, 31 (1921), 89.

Parker, Peter J., "Philadelphia Printer: Study of an Eighteenth-Century Businessman," *Bus. Hist. Rev.*, 40 (1966), 24.

Roden, Robert, *The Cambridge Press, 1638–1692* (1905).

Salley, A. S., "First Presses of South Carolina," Bibliog. Soc. Am., *Papers*, 2 (1907), 28.

Samford, C. Clement, and John M. Hemphill II, *Bookbinding in Colonial Virginia* (1966).

Seidensticker, Oswald, *First Century of German Printing in America, 1728–1830* (1893).

Sloane, William, *Children's Books in England and America in the Seventeenth Century* (1955).

Thomas, Isaiah, *History of Printing in America* (2 vols., 1810).

Wall, Alexander J., Jr., "William Bradford, Colonial Printer," *Am. Antiq. Soc., Proc.*, 73 (1963), 361.

Wheeler, Joseph T., *The Maryland Press, 1777–1790* (1938).

Winship, G. P., *The Cambridge Press, 1638–92* (1945).
Wroth, Lawrence C., *An American Bookshelf, 1755* (1934).
—— *Colonial Printer* (1938).
—— *History of Printing in Maryland, 1686–1776* (1922).
—— "Maryland Muse, by Ebenezer Cooke," Am. Antiq. Soc., *Proc.*, new ser., 44 (1934), 267.
—— *Typographic Heritage: Essays* (1949).

*   *   *   *   *   *   *

Bristol, Roger P., *Index of Printers, Publishers, and Booksellers Indicated by Charles Evans in American Bibliography* (1961).
Reichmann, Felix, comp., *Christopher Sower Sr., 1694–1758, Printer in Germantown: Annotated Bibliography* (1943).

See also 10.3 for biographies/writings of:

Bradford, Andrew, 1686–1742
Bradford, William, 1663–1752
Buell, Abel, 1741/42–1822
Collins, Isaac, 1746–1817
Franklin, Benjamin, 1706–1790
Gaine, Hugh, 1726/27–1807
Parks, William, 1698–1750
Thomas, Isaiah, 1750–1831

37.24 LIBRARIES

Abbot, George M., *Short History of the Library Company of Philadelphia* (1913).
Dexter, Franklin B., "Early Private Libraries in New England," Am. Antiq. Soc., *Proc.*, 18 (1907), 135.
Jennings, John M., *Library of the College of William and Mary, 1693–1763* (1968).
Keep, Austin B., *The Library in Colonial New York* (1909).
Lamberton, E. V., "Colonial Libraries of Pennsylvania," *Penn. Mag. Hist. Biog.*, 42 (1918), 193.
Potter, Alfred C., "Catalogue of John Harvard's Library," Col. Soc. Mass., *Publ.*, 21 (1919), 190.
Powell, William S., "Books in the Virginia Colony before 1624," *WMQ*, 3 ser., 5 (1948), 177.
Pratt, Anne S., *Isaac Watts and His Gifts of Books to Yale College* (1938).
Robinson, Charles F., and Robin Robinson, "Three Early Massachusetts Libraries," Col. Soc. Mass., *Trans.*, 28 (1930), 107.
Shera, Jesse H., *Foundations of the Public Library in New England, 1629–1855* (1949).
Shores, Louis, *Origins of the American College Library, 1638–1800* (1934).
Smart, George K., "Private Libraries in Colonial Virginia," *Am. Lit.*, 10 (1938), 24.
Thompson, C. Seymour, *Evolution of American Public Library, 1653–1876* (1952).
"A Virginian Minister's Library, 1635," *AHR*, 11 (1905–06), 328.
Weeks, Stephen B., "Libraries and Literature in North Carolina in the Eighteenth Century," Am. Hist. Assoc., *Report*, 1895 (1896), 171.
Wheeler, Joseph T., "Books Owned by Marylanders, 1700–1776," *Md. Hist. Mag.*, 35 (1940), 337.
—— "Booksellers and Circulating Libraries in Colonial Maryland," *Md. Hist. Mag.*, 34 (1939), 111.
—— "Reading Interests of the Professional Classes in Colonial Maryland, 1700–1776," *Md. Hist. Mag.*, 36 (1941), 184, 281; 37 (1942), 26, 291; 38 (1943), 37, 167.
Wolf, Edwin, II, "Library of William Byrd of Westover," Am. Antiq. Soc., *Proc.*, 68 (1958), 19.

Wright, Louis B., "The 'Gentleman's Library' in Early Virginia: Literary Interests of the First Carters," *Huntington Lib. Quar.*, 1 (1937), 3.

See also 10.3 for biographies/writings of:

Bray, Thomas, 1656–1729/30

37.25 THE ARTS

37.25.1 General

Wright, Louis B., et al., *Arts in America: Colonial Period* (1966).

* * * * * * *

Whitehill, Walter M., Wendell D. Garrett, and Jane Garrett, *Arts in Early American History: Needs and Opportunities* (1965).

37.25.2 Painting and Graphic Arts

Allen, Edward B., *Early American Wall Paintings, 1710–1850* (1926).
Belknap, Waldron P., Jr., *American Colonial Paintings: Materials for a History,* Charles Coleman Sellers, ed. (1959).
Boston. Museum of Fine Arts, *Eighteenth-Century American Arts: The M. and M. Karolik Collection* (1941).
Brigham, Clarence S., *Paul Revere's Engravings* (1954).
Burroughs, Alan, *John Greenwood in America, 1745–1752* (1943).
Dresser, Louisa, "Background of Colonial American Portraiture," Am. Antiq. Soc., *Proc.*, 76 (1966), 19.
—— *Seventeenth Century Painting in New England* (1935).
Dunlap, William, *History of the Arts of Design* (1834); F. W. Bayley and C. E. Goodspeed, eds. (3 vols., 1918).
Flexner, James T., *American Painting: Light of Distant Skies, 1760–1835* (1954).
—— *First Flowers of Our Wilderness* (1947).
Flournoy, Mary H., "Art in the Early South," *So. Atl. Quar.*, 24 (1930), 402.
Foote, Henry W., "Charles Bridges: Sergeant-Painter of Virginia," *Va. Mag. Hist. Biog.*, 50 (1952), 3.
Gloag, John, *Georgian Grace: Social History of Design, 1660–1830* (1956).
Hagen, Oskar, *Birth of the American Tradition in Art* (1940).
Hamilton, Sinclair, *Early American Book Illustrators and Wood Engravers, 1670–1870: Catalogue* (2 vols., 1958–1968).
Howland, Garth A., "John Valentine Haidt, A Little Known Eighteenth Century Painter," *Penn. Mag. Hist. Biog.*, 7 (1941), 304.
Kainen, Jacob, *John Baptist Jackson: 18th-Century Master of Color Woodcut* (1962).
Lee, Cuthbert, *Early American Portrait Painters* (1929).
Lewis, Benjamin M., *Guide to Engravings in American Magazines, 1741–1810* (1959).
Little, Nina F., *American Decorative Wall Painting, 1700–1850* (1952).
Morse, John D., ed., *Prints in and of America to 1850* (1970).
Museum of Graphic Art, *American Printmaking: The First 150 Years* (1969).
New York Historical Society, *Dictionary of Artists in America, 1564–1860*, George C. Groce and David H. Wallace, eds. (1957).
Park, Lawrence, *Joseph Blackburn: Colonial Portrait Painter* (1923).
Pleasants, Jacob H., "Justus Engelhardt Kuhn, Early Eighteenth Century Maryland Portrait Painter," Am. Antiq. Soc., *Proc.*, 46 (1937), 243.
—— "William Dering: A Mid-Eighteenth Century Williamsburg Portrait Painter," *Va. Mag. Hist. Biog.*, 60 (1952), 56.
Richardson, Edgar P., "Gustavus Hesselius," *Art Quarterly*, 12 (1949), 220.

Sears, Clara E., *Some American Primitives: New England* (1941).
Waterhouse, Ellis K., *Painting in Britain, 1530–1790* (1953).
Wheeler, Robert G., "Use of Symbolism in Hudson Valley Painting of Early 18th Century," *N. Y. Hist.*, 36 (1955), 357.
Wyckoff, Alexander, *Art and Artists in America, 1735–1835* (1966).

See also 10.3 for biographies/writings of:

Catesby, Mark, 1679–1749
Copley, John Singleton, 1738–1815
Earl(e), Ralph, 1751–1801
Feke, Robert, ca. 1705–ca. 1750
Jackson, John Baptist, 1701–1780?
Jennys, Richard, fl. 1760–1790
Johnston, Henrietta, fl. 1720
Peale, Charles Willson, 1741–1827
Revere, Paul, 1735–1818
Smibert, John, 1688–1751
Stuart, Gilbert, 1755–1828
Theus, Jeremiah, 1719–1774
Trumbull, John "Colonel," 1756–1843
West, Benjamin, 1738–1820

37.25.3 Decorative Arts and Crafts

American Heritage, *American Heritage History of Colonial Antiques*, Marshall B. Davidson, ed. (1967).
Avery, Clara L., *Early American Silver* (1930).
Bigelow, Francis H., *Historic Silver of the Colonies and its Makers* (1917).
Boston Museum of Fine Arts, *Colonial Silversmiths, Masters and Apprentices* (1956).
Brazer, Esther S., *Early American Decoration* (2nd ed., 1947).
Bridenbaugh, Carl, *The Colonial Craftsman* (1950).
Chapman, Suzanne E., *Early American Design Motifs* (1952).
Christensen, Erwin O., *Early American Wood Carving* (1952).
Clarke, Hermann F., *John Coney, Silversmith, 1655–1722* (1932).
Comstock, Helen, *American Furniture: Seventeenth, Eighteenth, and Nineteenth Century Styles* (1962).
——— *The Looking Glass in America, 1700–1825* (1968).
Cornelius, Charles O., *Early American Furniture* (1926).
Cutten, George B., *Silversmiths of Virginia from 1694–1850* (1952).
De Matteo, William, *The Silversmith in Eighteenth-Century Williamsburg* (1956).
Dow, G. F., *Arts and Crafts in New England, 1704–75* (1927).
Downs, Joseph, *American Furniture: Queen Anne and Chippendale Periods* (1952).
Eckhardt, John H., *Pennsylvania Clocks and Clockmakers* (1955).
Fleming, E. McClung, "Early American Decorative Arts as Social Documents," *MVHR*, 44 (1958), 276.
Forbes, Harriette M., *Gravestones of Early New England* (1927).
Kauffman, Henry, *Early American Copper, Tin, and Brass* (1950).
——— *Early American Ironware* (1966).
Gardner, Albert T., *Yankee Stonecutters* (1945).
Gottesman, Rita S., comp., *Arts and Crafts in New York from 1726* (3 vols., 1936–1954).
Gould, Mary E., *Early American Wooden Ware and Kitchen Utensils* (1962).
Halsey, Richard T. H., and Elizabeth Tower, *Homes of Our Ancestors* (1935).
Harrington, Jean C., *Glassmaking at Jamestown* (1952).
Hayward, Arthur H., *Colonial Lighting* (rev. ed., 1927).
Hill, H. W., *Maryland's Colonial Charm Portrayed in Silver* (1938).
Hume, Ivor Noël, *Guide to Artifacts of Colonial America* (1970).

Jones, Edward Alfred, *Old Silver of American Churches* (1913).
Kettell, Russell H., ed., *Early American Rooms* (1936).
Knittle, Rhea M., *Early American Glass* (1927).
Laughlin, Ledlie I., *Pewter in America* (2 vols., 1940).
Little, Frances, *Early American Textiles* (1931).
Lockwood, Luke V., *Colonial Furniture in America* (1926).
Ludwig, Allan I., *Graven Images: New England Stonecarving, 1650–1815*
   (1966).
McClelland, Nancy V., *Furnishing the Colonial and Federal House* (1947).
McLanathan, B. K., ed., *Colonial Silversmiths* (1956).
Mercer, Henry C., *Ancient Carpenters' Tools in the Eighteenth Century* (1929).
Nagel, Charles, *American Furniture, 1650–1850* (1949).
Nutting, Wallace, *Furniture of the Pilgrim Century* (1921).
Ormsbee, Thomas H., *Early American Furniture Makers* (1930).
Parslow, Virginia D., *Weaving and Dyeing in Early New York* (1949).
Prime, A. C., *Arts and Crafts in Philadelphia, Maryland and North Carolina
   1721–85* (2 vols., 1929).
Ramsey, Natalie A., ed., *Decorator Digest: Early American Decoration* (1964).
Rosenbaum, Jeanette W., *Myer Myers, Goldsmith* (1954).
Sonn, Albert H., *Early American Wrought Iron* (3 vols., 1928).
Spargo, John, *Early American Pottery and China* (1926).
Van Wagenen, Jared, Jr., *Golden Age of Homespun* (1953).
Waring, Janet, *Early American Stencils on Walls and Furniture* (1937).
Watkins, Lura W., *Early New England Potters and Their Wares* (1950).
White, Margaret E., *The Decorative Arts of Early New Jersey* (1964).
Wilkinson, O. N., *Old Glass* (1968).

See also 10.3 for biographies/writings of:

Buell, Abel, 1741/42–1822
Myers, Myer, 1723–1795
Revere, Paul, 1735–1818

37.25.4 Architecture

37.25.4.1 General

Bottomley, William L., *Great Georgian Houses of America* (2 vols., 1970).
Dorsey, Stephen P., *Early English Churches in America, 1607–1807* (1952).
Eberlein, Harold D., *Architecture of Colonial America* (1915).
——— and Cortland V. Hubbard, *American Georgian Architecture* (1952).
Egbert, Donald Drew, "Religious Expression in American Architecture," in
   James W. Smith and A. Leland Jameson, eds., *Religion in American Life*, vol. II
   (1961).
Halsey, Richard T. H., and Elizabeth Tower, *Homes of Our Ancestors* (1935).
Howells, John M., *Lost Examples of Colonial Architecture* (1931).
Kettell, Russell H., ed., *Early American Rooms* (1936).
Kimball, Sidney Fiske, "Architecture in the History of the Colonies and of the
   Republic," *AHR*, 27 (1921), 47.
——— *Domestic Architecture of the American Colonies* (1927).
Millar, John F., *Architects of the American Colonies* (1968).
Morrison, Hugh, *Early American Architecture* (1952).
Murtagh, William J., *Moravian Architecture and Town Planning: Eighteenth Cen-
   tury* (1967).
Omoto, Sadayoshi, "Queen Anne Style," *Jour. Society Archit. Historians*, 23
   (1964), 29.
Pratt, Dorothy and Richard, *Guide to Early American Homes* (2 vols., 1956).
   Pictorial.
Rines, Edward F., *Old Historic Churches of America* (1936).
Roach, Hannah B., "Thomas Nevel (1721–1797)," *Jour. Society Archit. Histori-
   ans*, 24 (1965), 153.

Rose, Harold W., *Colonial Houses of Worship in America, 1607–1789* (1964).
Schmidt, Carl F., *Cobblestone Architecture* (1944).
Senn, T. L., "Landscape Architecture and Horticulture in Eighteenth-Century America," *Agric. Hist.*, 43 (1969), 149.
Shurtleff, Harold R., *The Log Cabin Myth: A Study of the Early Dwellings of the English Colonists in North America*, Samuel E. Morison, ed. (1939).
Waterman, Thomas T., *Dwellings of Colonial America* (1950).
Weslager, C. A., *The Log Cabin in America* (1969).

*   *   *   *   *   *   *

Park, Helen, "Architectural Books Available in America before the Revolution," *Jour. Society Archit. Historians*, 20 (1961), 115.
Roos, Frank J., Jr., *Bibliography of Early American Architecture* (rev. ed., 1968).
Wall, Alexander J., *Books on Architecture Printed in America, 1775–1830* (1925).

See also 10.3 for biographies/writings of:

Buckland, William, 1734–1774
Bulfinch, Charles, 1763–1844
Harrison, Peter, 1716–1775
Jefferson, Thomas, 1743–1826
McIntire, Samuel, 1757–1811

37.25.4.2 South

Bannister, Turpin C., "Oglethorpe's Sources for Savannah Plan," *Jour. Society Archit. Historians*, 20 (1961), 47.
Brock, Henry I., *Colonial Churches in Virginia* (1930).
Claiborne, Herbert A., *Comments on Virginia Brickwork before 1800* (1957).
Forman, Henry Chandlee, *Architecture of the Old South: The Medieval Style, 1585–1850* (1948).
———— *Early Manor and Plantation Houses of Maryland* (1934).
———— *Maryland Architecture: 1634 through the Civil War* (1968).
———— *Old Buildings, Gardens, and Furniture in Tidewater Maryland* (1967).
———— *Tidewater Maryland Architecture and Gardens* (1957).
Johnston, Frances B., and Thomas T. Waterman, *Early Architecture of North Carolina* (1941).
Kocher, A. Lawrence, and Howard Dearstyne, *Colonial Williamsburg, Its Buildings and Gardens* (rev. ed., 1961).
Mason, George C., *Colonial Churches of Tidewater Virginia* (1945).
Moorehead, S. P., "The Castle," *Va. Mag. Hist. Biog.*, 42 (1934), 298.
Nichols, Frederick D., and Frances B. Johnston, *Early Architecture of Georgia* (1957).
Patton, Glenn, "The College of William and Mary, Williamsburg, and the Enlightenment," *Jour. Society Archit. Historians*, 29 (1970), 24.
Ravenel, Beatrice St. J., *Architects of Charleston* (1945).
Waterman, Thomas T., and John A. Barrows, *Domestic Colonial Architecture of Tidewater Virginia* (1932).
Waterman, Thomas T., and F. B. Johnston, *The Early Architecture of North Carolina* (1941).
Waterman, Thomas T., *Mansions of Virginia, 1706–1776* (1945).
Whiffen, Marcus, "County Courthouses of Virginia," *Jour. Society Archit. Historians*, 18 (1959), 2.
———— *Eighteenth-Century Houses of Williamsburg* (1960).
———— *Public Buildings of Williamsburg* (1958).

*   *   *   *   *   *   *

Nichols, Frederick D., comp., "Early Architecture of Virginia: Original Sources and Books," in *Papers of American Association of Architectural Bibliographers*, vol. I (1965).

37.25.4.3 Middle Colonies

Bailey, Rosalie F., *Pre-Revolutionary Dutch Houses and Families in Northern New Jersey and Southern New York* (1936).
Brumbaugh, G. Edwin, *Colonial Architecture of the Pennsylvania Germans* (1933).
Cousins, Frank, and Philip M. Riley, *Colonial Architecture of Philadelphia* (1920).
Eberlein, Harold D., and Cortlandt Hubbard, *Portrait of a Colonial City: Philadelphia, 1670–1838* (1939).
Huxtable, Ada Louise, *Classic New York: Georgian Gentility to Greek Elegance* (1964).
Reynolds, Helen W., *Dutch Houses in the Hudson Valley before 1776* (1929).
Shoemaker, Alfred L., ed., *The Pennsylvania Barn* (1959).
Wallace, Philip B., and William A. Dunn, *Colonial Churches and Meeting Houses: Pennsylvania, New Jersey and Delaware* (1931).

37.25.4.4 New England

Briggs, Martin S., *Homes of Pilgrim Fathers in England and America* (1932).
Cady, John H., *Civic and Architectural Development of Providence, 1636–1950* (1957).
Coolidge, John, "Hingham Builds a Meetinghouse," *NEQ*, 34 (1961), 435.
Cousins, Frank, and Philip M. Riley, *Colonial Architecture of Salem* (1919).
Donnelly, Marian C., *New England Meeting Houses of the Seventeenth Century* (1968).
Downing, Antoinette F., and Vincent J. Scully, Jr., *The Architectural Heritage of Newport, Rhode Island 1640–1915* (1952).
Garrett, Wendell D., *Apthorp House, 1760–1960* (1960).
Garvan, Anthony N. B., *Architecture and Town Planning in Colonial Connecticut* (1951).
Isham, Norman M., and Albert F. Brown, *Early Connecticut Houses* (1900).
Kelly, J. Frederick, *Early Connecticut Meetinghouses* (2 vols., 1948).
——— *Early Domestic Architecture of Connecticut* (1927).
Poor, Alfred E., *Colonial Architecture of Cape Cod, Nantucket, and Martha's Vineyard* (1970).
Powell, Sumner C., "Seventeenth-Century Sudbury, Massachusetts," *Jour. Society Archit. Historians*, 11 (1952), 3.
Sinnott, Edmund W., *Meetinghouse & Church in Early New England* (1963).

37.25.4.5 Spanish Borderlands

Baer, Kurt, *Architecture of the California Missions* (1958).
Kubler, George, and Martin Soria, *Art and Architecture in Spain and Portugal and Their American Dominions, 1500 to 1800* (1959).
Kubler, George, *Religious Architecture of New Mexico* (1940).
Manucy, Albert, *Houses of St. Augustine* (1962). Architecture from 1565 to 1821.
Newcomb, Rexford, *Spanish-Colonial Architecture in the United States* (1937).

37.25.5 Music

Barbour, James M., *Church Music of William Billings* (1960).
Covey, Cyclone, "Puritanism and Music in Colonial America," *WMQ*, 3 ser., 8 (1951), 378.
Daniel, Ralph T., *The Anthem in New England before 1800* (1966).
David, H. T., "Ephrata and Bethlehem: A Comparison," International College of Musicology of 1939, *Papers* (1944), 97.
Davis, Arthur K., Jr., *Traditional Ballads of Virginia* (1929).
Ewen, David, *Music Comes to America* (1947).
Flexner, Beatrice H., "Music of the Puritans," *Am. Heritage*, 8 (1956), 65.
Foote, Henry W., "Musical Life in Boston in the Eighteenth Century," *Am. Antiq. Soc., Proc.,* 49 (1940), 293.
Gilborn, Craig, "Samuel Davies' Sacred Muse," *Jour. Presby. Hist.,* 41 (1963), 63.
Jackson, George P., ed., *Spiritual Folksongs of Early America* (2nd ed., 1953).
McCorkle, Donald M., "Moravian Contribution to American Music (1740–1840)," *Notes*, 13 (1956), 597.

Macdougall, Hamilton C., *Early New England Psalmody* (1940).
Moore, Frank, *Songs and Ballads of the American Revolution* (1856).
Pennsylvania Society of Colonial Dames, *Church Music and Musical Life in Pennsylvania* (3 vols., 1926–1947).
Pichierri, Louis, *Music in New Hampshire, 1623–1800* (1960).
Pratt, Waldo S., *Music of the Pilgrims* (1921).
Scholes, Percy A., *Puritans and Music in England and New England* (1934).
Sonneck, Oscar G., *Early Concert-Life in America, 1731–1800* (1907).
Upton, W. T., "Secular Music in the United States One Hundred and Fifty Years Ago," International College of Musicology of 1939, *Papers* (1944), 105.
Wilcox, Glenn C., "Jacob Kimball, Pioneer Musician," Essex Inst., *Hist. Coll.*, 94 (1958), 356.

*   *   *   *   *   *   *

Ford, Worthington C., comp., *Broadsides, Ballads, etc. Printed in Massachusetts, 1639–1800* (1922).

See also 10.3 for biographies/writings of:

Billings, William, 1764–1800
Hopkinson, Francis, 1737–1791
Law, Andrew, 1749–1821

37.25.6 Theater

Baine, Rodney M., *Robert Munford: First Comic Dramatist* (1967).
Brown, Thomas Allston, *History of the American Stage* (1870).
Cole, Arthur C., "The Puritans and Fair Terpsichore," *MVHR*, 29 (1942), 3.
Clapp, William W., Jr., *A Record of the Boston Stage* (1953).
Land, Robert H., "First Williamsburg Theatre," *WMQ*, 3 ser., 5 (1948), 359.
McNamara, Brooks, *The American Playhouse in the Eighteenth Century* (1969).
Mates, Julian, *The American Musical Stage before 1800* (1962).
Morgan, Edmund S., "Puritan Hostility to the Theatre," Am. Philos. Soc., *Proc.*, 110 (1966), 340.
Pollock, Thomas C., *The Philadelphia Theatre in the Eighteenth Century* (1933).
Quinn, Arthur H., *History of the American Drama, from the Beginnings to the Civil War* (2nd ed., 1943).
Rankin, Hugh F., *Theater in Colonial America* (1965).
Seilhamer, George O., *History of the American Theatre before the Revolution* (1888).
Willis, Eola, *Charleston Stage in the Eighteenth Century* (1924).

See also 10.3 for biographies/writings of:

Munford, Robert, ca. 1730–1784
Tyler, Royall, 1757–1826

37.26 SCIENCE

37.26.1 General

Allen, Elsa G., *History of American Ornithology before Audubon* (1951).
Bedini, Silvio A., *Early American Scientific Instruments and Their Makers* (1964).
Cohen, I. Bernard, *Some Early Tools of American Science: An Account of the Early Scientific Instruments and Mineralogical and Biological Collections in Harvard University* (1950).
Denny, Margaret, "The Royal Society and American Scholars," *Scientific Monthly*, 45 (1947), 415.

Duveen, Denis I., and Herbert S. Klickstein, "Introduction of Lavoisier's Chemical Nomenclature," *Isis,* 45 (1954), 278.
Fleming, Donald, "The Judgment upon Copernicus in Puritan New England," in *Mélanges Alexandre Koyré,* vol. II (1964).
Greene, John C., "American Astronomy, 1750–1815," *Isis,* 45 (1954) 339.
——— "American Science Comes of Age, 1780–1820," *JAH,* 55 (1968), 22.
Hindle, Brooke, *Pursuit of Science in Revolutionary America, 1735–1789* (1956).
——— "Quaker Background and Science in Colonial Philadelphia," *Isis,* 46 (1955), 243.
"History of Science," *WMQ,* 3 ser., 13 (1956), 459.
Hornberger, Theodore, *Science and the New World* (1937).
——— *Scientific Thought in the American College, 1638–1800* (1945).
Humphrey, Harry B., *Makers of North American Botany* (1961).
Jellison, Richard M., "Scientific Enquiry in Eighteenth Century Virginia," *Historian,* 25 (1963), 292.
Kilgour, F. G., "Rise of Scientific Activity in Colonial New England," *Yale Jour. Biol. and Med.,* 22 (1949), 123.
McKeehan, Louis W., *Yale Science, 1701–1801* (1947).
Stahlman, William D., "Astrology in Colonial America," *WMQ,* 3 ser., 13 (1956), 551.
Stearns, Raymond P., "Colonial Fellows of the Royal Society of London, 1661–1788," *Notes and Records of Royal Society,* 8 (1951), 178.
——— *Science in the British Colonies of America* (1970).
Struik, Dirk J., *Yankee Science in the Making* (rev. ed., 1962).
Tilton, E. M., "Lightning-Rods and the Earthquake of 1755," *NEQ,* 13 (1940), 86.
White, George W., "Early American Geology," *Scient. Monthly,* 76 (1953), 134.
Woolf, Harry, *Transit of Venus: Eighteenth-Century Science* (1959).
Wroth, Lawrence C., "American Contributions to the Art of Navigation, 1519–1802," Mass. Hist. Soc., *Proc.,* 68 (1952), 72.

* * * * * * *

Bell, Whitfield J., Jr., *Early American Science: Needs and Opportunities* (1955).
Hindle, Brooke, "Historiography of Science in the Middle Colonies," Am. Philos. Soc., *Proc.,* 108 (1964), 158.

See also 10.3 for biographies/writings of:

Banister, John, 1650–1692

37.26.2 Individual Scientists

Babb, Maurice J., "David Rittenhouse," *Penn. Mag. Hist. Biog.,* 56 (1932), 193.
Bartram, John, *Observations on Soil, Rivers* (1751).
Bell, Whitfield J., Jr., ed., "Nicholas Collin's Appeal to Scientists," *WMQ,* 3 ser., 13 (1956), 519.
Catesby, Mark, *Natural History of Carolina, Florida, and Bahama Islands* (2 vols., 3d ed., 1771).
Cohen, I. Bernard, "Anguetil-Duperron, Franklin, and Ezra Stiles," *Isis,* 33 (1941), 17.
——— "Franklin and Transit of Mercury," Am. Philos. Soc. *Proc.,* 94 (1950), 222.
Collinson, Peter, and John Custis, *Correspondence, 1734–1746,* Earl G. Swem, ed. (1957).
Cope, Thomas D., "David Rittenhouse—Physicist," Franklin Inst., *Jour.,* 215 (1933), 287.
Denny, Margaret, "Linnaeus and his Disciple in Carolina: Alexander Garden," *Isis,* 38 (1948), 161.
Ganter, Herbert L., "William Small, Jefferson's Beloved Teacher," *WMQ,* 3 ser., 4 (1947) 505.
Hindle, Brooke, "Cadwallader Colden's Extension of Newtonian Principles," *WMQ,* 3 ser., 13 (1956), 459.

Hornberger, Theodore, "Science of Thomas Prince," *NEQ*, 9 (1936), 26.

Kilgour, Frederick G., "Thomas Robie (1689–1729) Colonial Scientist and Physician," *Isis*, 30 (1939), 473.

Lingelbach, William E., "B. Franklin and the Scientific Societies," Franklin Inst., *Jour.*, 261 (1956), 9.

Meacham, Standish, "Priestly in America," *Hist. Today*, 12 (1962), 568.

Miles, Wyndham, "Benjamin Rush, Chemist," *Chymia*, 4 (1953), 37.

Rice, Howard C., Jr., *Rittenhouse Orrery* (1954).

Stearns, Raymond P., "James Petiver: Promoter of Natural Science, c. 1663–1718," Am. Antiq. Soc., *Proc.*, 62 (1952), 243.

—— "John Winthrop and His Gifts to the Royal Society," Col. Soc. Mass., *Publ.*, 42 (1952–1956), 206.

Wilkinson, Ronald S., "Alchemical Library of John Winthrop, Jr., in Colonial America," *Ambix*, 11 (1963), 33; 13 (1966), 139.

See also 10.3 for biographies/writings of:

Bartram, John, 1699–1777
Bartram, William, 1739–1823
Catesby, Mark, 1679–1749
Clayton, John, 1685–1733
Eliot, Jared, 1685–1763
Erskine, Robert, 1735–1780
Evans, Lewis, ca. 1700–1756
Evans, Oliver, 1755–1819
Franklin, Benjamin, 1706–1790
Garden, Alexander, 1730–1791
Kinnersley, Ebenezer, 1711–1778
Read, Charles, 1713–1774
Rittenhouse, David, 1732–1796
Romans, Bernard, 1720–1784
Thompson, Benjamin, 1753–1814

37.27 TECHNOLOGY

Berkebile, Don H., *Conestoga Wagons in Braddock's Campaign, 1755* (1959).

Hummel, Charles F., "English Tools in America: Evidence of the Dominys," *Winterthur Portfolio*, 2 (1965), 27.

——*With Hammer in Hand: The Dominy Craftsmen of East Hampton* (1968).

See also 10.3 for biographies/writings of:

Erskine, Robert, 1735–1780
Evans, Oliver, 1755–1819
Fitch, John, 1743–1798
Franklin, Benjamin, 1706–1790
Romans, Bernard, 1720–1784
Stevens, John, 1749–1838

37.28 MEDICINE

Ashburn, Percy M., *Ranks of Death: Medical History of the Conquest of America* Frank D. Ashburn, ed. (1947).

Beall, Otho T., Jr., "*Aristotle's Master Piece* in America: Landmark in Folklore of Medicine," *WMQ*, 3 ser., 20 (1963), 207.

—— and Richard H. Shryock, *Cotton Mather: First Significant Figure in American Medicine* (1954).

Beck, John B., *Medicine in American Colonies* (1850).

Bell, Whitfield J., Jr., ed., "Nicholas Collin's Appeal to Scientists," *WMQ*, 3 ser., 13 (1956), 519.

Billias, George A., "Pox and Politics in Marblehead, 1773—," Essex Inst., *Hist. Coll.*, 92 (1956), 43.

Binger, Carl, *Revolutionary Doctor: Benjamin Rush* (1966).

Blake, John B., *Public Health in the Town of Boston, 1630–1822* (1959).

Blanton, Wyndham B., "Epidemics Real and Imaginary, and Other Factors Influencing Seventeenth-Century Virginia's Population," *Bull. Hist. Med.*, 31 (1957), 454.

—— *Medicine in Virginia in the Eighteenth Century* (1931).

Caulfield, Ernest, "The Pursuit of a Pestilence," Am. Antiq. Soc., *Proc.*, 60 (1950), 21.

—— "Some Common Diseases of Colonial Children," Col. Soc. Mass., *Publ.*, 35 (1951), 4.

—— *True History of the Epidemic Called Throat Distemper* (1939).

Childs, St. Julien R., *Malaria and Colonization in the Carolina Low Country, 1526–1696* (1940).

Corner, George W., *Two Centuries of Medicine: School of Medicine, University of Pennsylvania* (1965).

Cowen, David L., *America's Pre-Pharmacopoeial Literature* (1961).

Deutsch, Albert, *The Mentally Ill in America: History of Their Care and Treatment in Colonial Times* (1949).

Duffy, John, "Eighteenth-Century Carolina Health Conditions," *JSH*, 18 (1952), 289.

—— *Epidemics in Colonial America* (1953).

—— *History of Public Health in New York City, 1625–1866* (1968).

Heaton, Claude E., "Medicine in New York, 1664–1775," *Bull. Hist. Med.*, 17 (1945), 9.

Holmes, Chris, "Benjamin Rush and Yellow Fever," *Bull. Hist. Med.*, 40 (1966), 246.

Hunter, Robert J., *Origin of Philadelphia General Hospital, Blockley Division* (1955).

Jarcho, Saul, "Cadwallader Colden as Student of Infectious Disease," *Bull. Hist. Med.*, 29 (1955), 99.

—— "Correspondence of Cadwallader Colden and Hugh Graham on Infectious Fevers (1716–1719)," *Bull. Hist. Med.*, 30 (1956), 195.

King, Lester S., *Medical World of the Eighteenth Century* (1958).

Miller, Genevieve, "European Influences on Colonial Medicine," *Ciba*, 7 (1947), 511.

—— "Medical Apprenticeship in the American Colonies," *Ciba*, 7 (1947), 502.

—— "Smallpox Inoculation in England and America," *WMQ*, 3 ser., 13 (1956), 476.

Morton, Charles, "Compendium Physicae," Col. Soc. Mass., *Publ.*, 33 (1940). Reprint of a 1685 textbook.

Scriven, George B., "Doctors, Drugs and Apothecaries of Seventeenth-Century Maryland," *Bull. Hist. Med.*, 37 (1963), 516.

—— "Maryland Medicine in the Seventeenth Century," *Md. Hist. Mag.*, 57 (1962), 29.

Shryock, Richard H., *Medicine and Society in America, 1660–1860* (1960).

Stookey, Byron, *History of Colonial Medical Education: New York, 1767–1830* (1962).

Thoms, Herbert, *Beginning of Medical Practice in the New Haven Colony* (1924).

—— *Doctors of Yale College, 1702–1815* (1960).

Viets, H. R., *Brief History of Medicine in Massachusetts* (1930).

—— "Features of Medicine in Massachusetts," *Isis*, 23 (1935), 391.

Walsh, J. L., *History of Medicine in New York*, vol. I (1919).

Waring, Joseph I., *History of Medicine in South Carolina, 1670–1825* (1964).

*   *   *   *   *   *   *

Austin, Robert B., *Early American Medical Imprints: Guide to Works Printed in the United States, 1668–1820* (1961).

Guerra, Francisco, *American Medical Bibliography, 1639–1783* (1962).
—— "Bibliographers of Early Medical Americana," *Jour. Hist. Med.*, 17 (1962),
  94.

See also 10.3 for biographies/writings of:

Eliot, Jared, 1685–1763
Garden, Alexander, 1730–1791
McHenry, James, 1753–1816
Mather, Cotton, 1662/63–1727/28
Morgan, John, 1735–1789
Rush, Benjamin, 1745–1813
Shippen, William, 1736–1808
Warren, Joseph, 1741–1775

Part Six   United States, 1789–1860

38   United States, 1789–1860

38.1 POLITICAL HISTORY

38.1.1 General

Adams, Henry, *History of the United States* (9 vols., 1889–1891). Covers the period, 1800–1817.
Channing, Edward, *History of the United States* (6 vols., 1905–1925). Covers the period to 1865.
Cunliffe, Marcus, *The Nation Takes Shape, 1789–1837* (1959).
McMaster, John B., *A History of the People of the United States from the Revolution to the Civil War* (8 vols., 1883–1913). Covers the period, 1783–1861.
Wiltse, Charles M., *New Nation, 1800–1845* (1961).
Wright, Esmond, *Fabric of Freedom, 1763–1800* (1961).

38.1.2 Special Topics

Aronson, Sidney, *Status and Kinship in Higher Civil Service: Standards of Selection in the Administration of John Adams, Thomas Jefferson and Andrew Jackson* (1964).
Hofstadter, Richard, *Idea of a Party System: 1780–1840* (1969).
Koch, Gustav A., *Republican Religion: A Study of Nationalism as Type of American Religious Thought from the Revolution to 1810* (1933).
McCormick, Richard P., "Suffrage, Classes and Party Alignments: Voter Behavior," *MVHR,* 46 (1959), 397.
Nichols, Roy F., *Invention of American Politics* (1967).
Williamson, Chilton, *American Suffrage: From Property to Democracy, 1760–1860* (1960).

38.1.3 Regions, States and Cities

Alexander, De Alva S., *A Political History of the State of New York, 1774–1882* (3 vols., 1906–1909).
Ambler, Charles H., *Sectionalism in Virginia, 1776–1861* (1910).
Buley, R. C., *The Old Northwest: Pioneer Period, 1815–1840* (2 vols., 1950).
Fee, Walter R., *The Transition from Aristocracy to Democracy in New Jersey, 1789–1829* (1933).
Ferguson, R. J., *Early Western Pennsylvania Politics* (1938).
Fox, Dixon Ryan, *Decline of Aristocracy in the Politics of New York* (1919).
Green, Constance M., *Washington: Village and Capital, 1800–1878* (1962).
Handlin, Oscar, and Mary Handlin, *Commonwealth: Massachusetts, 1774–1861* (1947).
Kass, Alvin, *Politics in New York, 1800–1830* (1965).
Ludlum, David M., *Social Ferment in Vermont, 1791–1850* (1939).

Pole, J. R., "Election Statistics in Pennsylvania, 1790–1840," *Penn. Mag. Hist. Biog.*, 82 (1958), 217.
Riker, Dorothy, and Gayle Thornbrough, comps., *Indiana Election Returns, 1816–1851* (1960).
Wade, Richard C., *The Urban Frontier: Rise of Western Cities, 1790–1830* (1959).

38.2 ECONOMIC HISTORY

Albion, Robert G., *Square Riggers on Schedule: New York Sailing Packets* (1938).
Berry, Thomas S., *Western Prices before 1861: A Study of the Cincinnati Market* (1943).
Bidwell, P. W., and J. I. Falconer, *History of Agriculture in the Northern United States, 1620–1860* (1925).
Buck, Norman S., *Development of Organization of Anglo-American Trade, 1800–1850* (1925).
Gray, Lewis C., *History of Agriculture in the Southern United States to 1860* (2 vols., 1933).
Martin, Robert F., *National Income of the United States, 1799–1938* (1939).
Meyer, B. H., et al., *History of Transportation in the United States before 1860* (1917).
Morison, Samuel E., *Maritime History of Massachusetts, 1783–1860* (1921).
North, Douglass C., *Economic Growth of United States, 1790–1860* (1961).
Smith, Walter B., and Arthur H. Cole, *Fluctuations in American Business, 1790–1860* (1935).
Taylor, George R., *Transportation Revolution, 1815–1860* (1951).

38.3 SOCIAL AND CULTURAL HISTORY

Billington, Ray A., *Protestant Crusade, 1800–1860* (1938).
Hansen, Marcus L., *Atlantic Migration, 1670–1860* (1940).
Harris, Neil, *Artist in American Society, 1790–1860* (1966).
Litwack, Leon F., *North of Slavery: Negro in the Free States, 1790–1860* (1961).
Matthiessen, Francis O., *American Renaissance* (1941).
Rothman, David J., *Discovery of Asylum: Social Order and Disorder in the New Republic* (1971).
Tyler, Alice Felt, *Freedom's Ferment: Phases of American Social History to 1860* (1944).

39   Federalist Era, 1789–1801

39.1 GENERAL

Abernethy, Thomas P., *The South in the New Nation, 1789–1819* (1961).
Bassett, John Spencer, *Federalist System, 1789–1801* (1906).
Krout, John A., and Dixon Ryan Fox, *Completion of Independence, 1790–1830* (1944).
Miller, John C., *The Federalist Era, 1789–1801* (1960).
—— *The Young Republic, 1789–1815* (1970).
Nettels, Curtis P., *Emergence of a National Economy, 1775–1815* (1962).
Smelser, Marshall, "Federalist Period as an Age of Passion," *Am. Quar.*, 10 (1958), 391.

See also 10.3 for biographies/writings of:

Adams, John, 1735–1826
Ames, Fisher, 1758–1808
Burr, Aaron, 1756–1836
Ellsworth, Oliver, 1745–1807
Giles, William Branch, 1762–1830
Hamilton, Alexander, 1755–1804
Henry, Patrick, 1736–1799
Jay, John, 1745–1829
Jefferson, Thomas, 1743–1826
King, Rufus, 1755–1827
McHenry, James, 1753–1816
Maclay, William, 1734–1804
Madison, James, 1750/51–1836
Monroe, James, 1758–1831
Read, George, 1733–1798
Schuyler, Philip J., 1733–1804
Washington, George, 1732–1799

39.2 ORGANIZATION OF FEDERAL GOVERNMENT

39.2.1 Executive Branch

Hunt, Gaillard, "Office Seeking," *AHR*, 1 (1896), 270; 2 (1897), 241.
Jacobs, James R., *The Beginning of the United States Army, 1783–1812* (1947).
Monaghan, Frank, and Marvin Lowenthal, *This Was New York, the Nation's Capital in 1789* (1943).
Rich, Wesley Everett, *The History of the United States Post Office to the Year 1829* (1924).
Smelser, Marshall, *Congress Founds the Navy, 1787–1798* (1959).

Stephens, Frank F., *Transitional Period, 1788–1789* (1909).
Thach, Charles C., Jr., *The Creation of the Presidency, 1775–1789* (1922).
Ward, Harry M., *Department of War, 1781–1795* (1962).
White, Leonard D., *The Federalists* (1948).

See also 10.3 for biographies/writings of:

Adams, John, 1735–1826
Hamilton, Alexander, 1755–1804
Jefferson, Thomas, 1743–1826
Knox, Henry, 1750–1806
McHenry, James, 1753–1816
Pickering, Timothy, 1745–1829
Randolph, Edmund, 1753–1813
Washington, George, 1732–1799

39.2.2 Legislative Branch

Furlong, Patrick J., "Origins of the House Committee of Ways and Means,"
   WMQ, 3 ser., 25 (1968), 587.
Goodman, Paul, "Social Status of Party Leadership: House of Representatives,
   1797–1804," *WMQ*, 3 ser., 25 (1968), 465.
Harlow, Ralph V., *History of Legislative Methods before 1825* (1917).
Hayden, Joseph R., *Senate and Treaties 1789–1817* (1920).
MacLay, William, *Journal, 1789–1791*, Edward MacLay, ed. (1969).
Swanstrom, Roy, *The United States Senate, 1787–1801* (1962).

39.2.3 Judicial Branch

Farrand, Max, "The Judiciary Act," *AHR*, 5 (1900), 682.
Jacobs, Clyde E., "Prelude to Amendment: The States Before the Court," *Am.
   Jour. Legal Hist.*, 12 (1968), 19.
Morris, Richard B., *John Jay, the Nation and the Court* (1967).
Surrency, Erwin C., "Judiciary Act of 1801," *Am. Jour. Legal Hist.*, 2 (1958), 53.
Turner, Kathryn, "Federalist Policy and the Judiciary Act of 1801," *WMQ*, 3 ser.,
   22 (1965), 3.
Warren, Charles, "The Judiciary Act of 1789," *Harvard Law Rev.*, 37 (1923), 49.

See also 10.3 for biographies/writings of:

Ellsworth, Oliver, 1745–1807
Iredell, James, 1751–1799
Jay, John, 1745–1829

39.3 RISE OF POLITICAL PARTIES

39.3.1 General

Beard, Charles A., *Economic Origins of Jeffersonian Democracy* (1915).
Borden, Morton, *Parties and Politics in the Early Republic, 1789–1815* (1967).
Chambers, William N., *Political Parties in a New Nation, 1776–1809* (1963).
Charles, Joseph E., *Origins of American Party System* (1956).
Cunliffe, Marcus, "Elections of 1789 and 1792," in Arthur M. Schlesinger, Jr.,
   and Fred L. Israel, eds., *History of American Presidential Elections, 1789–1968*
   Vol. I (1971).
Cunningham, Noble E., Jr., ed., *Making of the American Party System, 1789 to
   1809* (1965).
Daniels, Jonathan, *Ordeal of Ambition: Jefferson, Hamilton, Burr* (1970).

Hockett, Homer C., *Western Influences on Political Parties* (1917).
Hofstadter, Richard, *The Idea of a Party System, 1780–1840* (1969).
Libby, Orin G., "Political Factions in Washington's Administrations," *Quar. Jour.*, 3 (1913), 293.
Ostrogorskii, Moisei I., *Democracy and Organization of Political Parties* (1908).

39.3.2 Federalists

Adams, Henry, ed., *Documents Relating to New England Federalism, 1800–1815* (1877).
Banner, James M., *To the Hartford Convention: Federalists and Origins of Party Politics in Massachusetts, 1789–1815* (1970).
Clark, Malcolm C., "Election of 1796 in Maryland," *Md. Hist. Mag.*, 61 (1966), 210.
Dunbar, Louise B., *Study of "Monarchical" Tendencies in the United States, 1776–1801* (1922).
Farrand, Max, "The Judiciary Act," *AHR*, 5 (1900), 682.
Ferguson, R. J., *Early Western Pennsylvania Politics* (1938).
Hockett, Homer C., *Western Influences on Political Parties* (1917).
Lycan, Gilbert L., "Hamilton and North Carolina Federalists," *No. Car. Hist. Rev.*, 25 (1948), 442.
Phillips, Ulrich B., "South Carolina Federalists," *AHR*, 14 (1909), 529.
Purcell, Richard J., *Connecticut in Transition, 1775–1818* (1963).
Risjord, Norman K., "Virginia Federalists," *JSH*, 33 (1967), 486.
Rose, Lisle A., *Prologue to Democracy: Federalists in South, 1789–1800* (1968).
Stauffer, Vernon, *New England and the Bavarian Illuminati* (1918).
Tinkcom, H. M., *Republicans and Federalists in Pennsylvania, 1790–1801* (1950).

*   *   *   *   *   *   *

Rozwenc, Edwin C., "Henry Adams and the Federalists," in H. Stuart Hughes, ed., *Teachers of History* (1954).

See also 10.3 for biographies/writings of:

Adams, John, 1735–1826
Ames, Fisher, 1758–1808
Bayard, James A., 1767–1815
Bingham, William, 1752–1804
Cabot, George, 1752–1823
Coit, Joshua, 1758–1798
Coxe, Tench, 1755–1824
Ellsworth, Oliver, 1745–1807
Hamilton, Alexander, 1755–1804
Henry, Patrick, 1736–1799
Humphreys, David, 1752–1818
Jay, John, 1745–1829
King, Rufus, 1755–1827
Knox, Henry, 1750–1806
Marshall, John, 1755–1835
Morris, Gouverneur, 1752–1816
Otis, Harrison Gray, 1765–1848
Pickering, Timothy, 1745–1829
Plumer, William, 1759–1850
Rutledge, John, 1739–1800
Smith, William L., 1758–1812
Tallmadge, Benjamin, 1754–1835

39.3.3 Republicans

Ammon, Harry, "Republican Party in Virginia, 1789–1796," *JSH*, 19 (1953), 283.
Brown, Stuart Gerry, *First Republicans: Jefferson and Madison* (1954).

Cunningham, Noble E., Jr., *Jeffersonian Republicans, 1789–1801* (1957).
—— "John Beckley: An Early American Party Manager," *WMQ*, 3 ser., 13 (1956), 40.
Forman, Samuel E., *Political Activities of Freneau* (1902).
Gilpatrick, Delbert H., *Jeffersonian Democracy in North Carolina* (1931).
Goodman, Paul, *Democratic-Republicans of Massachusetts: Politics in a Young Republic* (1964).
Howe, John R., Jr., "Republican Thought and Political Violence of 1790's," *Am. Quar.*, 19 (1967), 147.
Jahoda, Gloria, "John Beckley: Jefferson's Campaign Manager," N.Y. Pub. Lib., *Bull.*, 64 (1960), 247.
Link, Eugene P., *Democratic-Republican Societies, 1790–1800* (1942).
Robinson, William Alexander, *Jeffersonian Democracy in New England* (1916).
Stewart, Donald, *The Opposition Press of the Federalist Period* (1969).
Tinkcom, H. M., *Republicans and Federalists in Pennsylvania, 1790–1801* (1950).
Van Der Linden, Frank, *Turning Point: Jefferson's Battle for Presidency* (1962).
Wolfe, John Harold, *Jeffersonian Democracy in South Carolina* (1940).

See also 10.3 for biographies/writings of:

Dallas, Alexander James, 1759–1817
Freneau, Philip Morin, 1752–1832
Gerry, Elbridge, 1744–1814
Jefferson, Thomas, 1743–1826
Livingston, Edward, 1764–1836
Maclay, William, 1734–1804
Macon, Nathaniel, 1758–1837
Madison, James, 1750/51–1836
Monroe, James, 1758–1831
Randolph, John, 1773–1833
Taylor, John, 1753–1824

39.4 HAMILTONIAN PROGRAM

39.4.1 General

Bates, Whitney K., "Northern Speculators and Southern State Debts, 1790," *WMQ*, 3 ser., 19 (1962), 30.
Moramarco, Fred, "Hamilton and the Historians: The Economic Program in Retrospect," *Midcontinent Am. Studies Jour.*, 8 (1967), 34.
Rose, Stanley D., "Alexander Hamilton and Historians," *Vanderbilt Law Rev.*, 11 (1958), 853.
Stourzh, Gerald, *Alexander Hamilton and Idea of Republican Government* (1970).

39.4.2 First Bank of the United States

Elazar, Daniel J., "Banking and Federalism in the Early American Republic," *Huntington Lib. Quar.*, 28 (1965), 301.
Hammond, Bray, *Banks and Politics in America from Revolution to Civil War* (1957).
Holdsworth, John T., *First Bank of United States* (1910).
Wettereau, J. O., "Branches of First Bank," *Jour. Econ. Hist.*, 2 (1942), 66.
—— "New Light on First Bank," *Penn. Mag. Hist. Biog.*, 61 (1937), 263.

*   *   *   *   *   *   *

Griffin, Appleton P. C., *List of Works Relating to First and Second Banks* (1908).

See also 10.3 for biographies/writings of:

Coxe, Tench, 1755–1824
Dallas, Alexander James, 1759–1817
Gallatin, Albert, 1761–1849
Hamilton, Alexander, 1755–1804

39.5 FRONTIER AND WEST

Baldwin, Leland D., *Whiskey Rebels* (1939).
Biddle, Nicholas, *History of the Expedition under the Command of Captains Lewis and Clark to the Sources of the Missouri, across the Rocky Mountains and down the Columbia to the Pacific*, Paul Allen, ed. (2 vols., 1814). Covers the period 1804–1806.
Cooke, Jacob E., "Whiskey Insurrection," *Penn. Hist.*, 30 (1963), 316.
Darling, Arthur B., *Our Rising Empire, 1763–1803* (1940).
Horsman, Reginald, *The Frontier in the Formative Years, 1783–1815* (1970).
Ludlum, David M., *Social Ferment in Vermont, 1791–1850* (1939).
Miller, William, "Democratic Societies and the Whiskey Insurrection," *Penn. Mag. Hist. Biog.*, 62 (1938), 325.
Prucha, Francis P., *Sword of the Republic: Army on Frontier, 1783–1846* (1969).
Whitaker, Arthur P., *Mississippi Question* (1934).
Williamson, Chilton, *Vermont in Quandary: 1763–1825* (1949).

See also 10.3 for biographies/writings of:

Blount, William, 1749–1800
Clark, George Rogers, 1752–1818
Sevier, John, 1745–1815
Symmes, John Cleves, 1742–1814
Wayne, Anthony, 1745–1796
Wilkinson, James, 1757–1825

39.6 FOREIGN RELATIONS

39.6.1 General

Bowman, Albert H., "Jefferson, Hamilton and American Foreign Policy," *Pol. Sci. Quar.*, 71 (1956), 18.
Clarfield, Gerald H., *Timothy Pickering and American Diplomacy, 1795–1800* (1969).
Hyneman, Charles S., *First American Neutrality: Neutral Obligations during the Years 1792–1815* (1934).
Lycan, Gilbert L., *Alexander Hamilton and American Foreign Policy: A Design for Greatness* (1970).
Peterson, Merrill D., "Thomas Jefferson and Commercial Policy," *WMQ*, 3 ser., 22 (1965), 584.
Varg, Paul A., *Foreign Policies of the Founding Fathers* (1963).

39.6.2 Diplomacy under Washington

Boyce, Myrna, "The Diplomatic Career of William Short," *Jour. Mod. Hist.*, 15 (1943), 97.
Boyd, Julian P., *Number 7: Alexander Hamilton's Secret Attempts to Control Foreign Policy* (1964).
DeConde, Alexander, *Entangling Alliance: Politics and Diplomacy under Washington* (1958).

Gilbert, Felix, *To the Farewell Address: Early American Foreign Policy* (1961).

Looze, Helene J., *Alexander Hamilton and British Orientation of American Foreign Policy, 1783–1803* (1969).

Thomas, Charles M., *American Neutrality in 1793* (1931).

39.6.3 France and French Revolution

Ammon, Harry, "The Genet Mission and the Development of American Political Parties," *JAH*, 52 (1966), 725.

Bond, Beverly W., Jr., *Monroe Mission to France, 1794–1796* (1907).

Childs, Frances S., *French Refugee Life in the United States, 1790–1800* (1940).

Godechot, Jacques, *France and the Atlantic Revolution, 1770–1799* (1965).

Hazen, Charles D., *Contemporary American Opinion of the French Revolution* (1897).

Hyslop, Beatrice F., "The American Press and the French Revolution of 1789," *Amer. Philos. Soc., Proc.*, 104 (1960), 54.

Kaplan, Lawrence S., *Jefferson and France* (1967).

Nussbaum, Frederick L., *Commercial Policy in the French Revolution: G. J. A. Ducher* (1923).

Palmer, Robert R., "The Great Inversion: America and Europe in the Eighteenth-Century Revolution," in Richard Herr and Harold T. Parker, eds., *Ideas in History Presented to Louis Gottschalk by His Former Students* (1965).

Rain, Pierre, *La diplomatie française: De Mirabeau à Bonaparte* (1950).

Sears, Louis M., *George Washington and the French Revolution* (1960).

Smelser, Marshall, "Jacobin Phrenzy," *Rev. Politics*, 13 (1951), 457.

Stoddard, Theodore L., *French Revolution in San Domingo* (1914).

See also 10.3 for biographies/writings of:

Genet, Edmond Charles, 1763–1834

39.6.4 Great Britain and Jay's Treaty

Bemis, Samuel F., *Jay's Treaty: A Study in Commerce and Diplomacy* (rev. ed., 1962).

Burt, A. L., *United States, Great Britain, and British North America* (1940).

Clarfield, Gerald, "Timothy Pickering and Anglo-American Relations, 1795–1797," *WMQ*, 3 ser., 23 (1966), 106.

Combs, Jerald A., *The Jay Treaty: Political Battleground of the Founding Fathers* (1970).

Cross, Jack Lee, *London Mission: The First Critical Years* (1969).

Neel, Joanne L., *Phineas Bond: Anglo-American Relations, 1786–1812* (1968).

Perkins, Bradford, *First Rapprochement: England and the United States, 1795–1805* (1955).

39.6.5 Spain and Pinckney's Treaty

Bemis, Samuel F., *Pinckney's Treaty* (rev. ed., 1960).

Clarfield, Gerald H., "Victory in the West: A Study of the Role of Timothy Pickering in the Successful Consummation of Pinckney's Treaty," *Essex Inst., Hist. Coll.*, 101 (1965), 333.

Holmes, Jack D. L., *Gayoso: Spanish Governor in Mississippi Valley, 1789–1799* (1965).

Nasatir, Abraham P., *Spanish War Vessels on the Mississippi, 1792–1796* (1968).

Whitaker, Arthur P., "Godoy's Knowledge," *AHR*, 35 (1930), 804.

—— *Spanish-American Frontier* (1934).

—— "Treaty of San Lorenzo," *MVHR*, 15 (1929), 435.

Young, Raymond A., "Pinckney's Treaty," *Hisp. Am. Hist. Rev.*, 43 (1963), 526.

39.6.6 Russia

Bolkhovitinov, Nikolai N., *Stanovlenie Russko-Amerikanskikh Othoshenii, 1775–1815* (1966).
Hildt, John C., *Early Diplomatic Negotiations of the United States with Russia* (1906).

39.7 WASHINGTON'S FAREWELL ADDRESS AND ELECTION OF 1796

Bemis, Samuel F., "Washington's Farewell Address," *AHR*, 39 (1934), 263.
DeConde, Alexander, "Washington's Farewell, the French Alliance, and Election of 1796," *MVHR*, 43 (1957), 641.
Paltsits, Victor H., ed., *Washington's Farewell Address* (1935).
Smith, Page, "Election of 1796," in Arthur M. Schlesinger, Jr., and Fred L. Israel, eds., *History of American Presidential Elections, 1789–1968*, vol. I (1971).

39.8 JOHN ADAMS ADMINISTRATION, 1797–1801

39.8.1 General

Aronson, Sidney H., *Status and Kinship in the Higher Civil Service: Standards of Selection in the Administrations of John Adams, Thomas Jefferson, and Andrew Jackson* (1964).
Dauer, Manning J., *Adams Federalists* (1953).
Koch, Adrienne, "Hamilton, Adams and Pursuit of Power," *Rev. Politics*, 16 (1954), 37.
Kurtz, Stephen G., *Presidency of John Adams: The Collapse of Federalism, 1795–1800* (1957).

See 10.3 for biographies/writings of:

Adams, Abigail, 1744–1818
Adams, John, 1735–1826
Coxe, Tench, 1755–1824
McHenry, James, 1735–1816
Pickering, Timothy, 1745–1829

39.8.2 Diplomatic Relations and Quasi-War with France

39.8.2.1 General

Bonnel, Ulane, *La France, Les États-Unis et la guerre de course, 1797–1815* (1961).
DeConde, Alexander, *Quasi-War: Undeclared War with France, 1797–1801* (1966).
James, James A., "French Opinion Preventing War," *AHR*, 30 (1924), 44.
Kramer, Eugene F., "Adams, Gerry, and the Origins of the XYZ Affair," Essex Inst., *Hist. Coll.*, 94 (1958), 57.
Kurtz, Stephen G., "The French Mission of 1799–1800: Concluding Chapter in the Statecraft of John Adams," *Pol. Sci. Quar.*, 80 (1965), 543.
Lyon, Elijah W., "The Directory and United States," *AHR*, 43 (1938), 514.
——— "The Franco-American Convention of 1800," *Jour. Mod. Hist.*, 12 (1940), 305.
Madelin, Louis, *Talleyrand* (1948).

Morison, Samuel E., ed., "DuPont, Talleyrand, and French Spoliations," Mass. Hist. Soc., *Proc.*, 49 (1915), 63.

Tolles, Frederick B., "George Logan's Mission to France, 1798," *WMQ*, 3 ser., 7 (1950), 3.

U.S. 64th Congress, 1st sess., *French Spoliation Claims*, prepared by G. A. King, Sen. Doc. no. 451.

See also 10.3 for biographies/writings of:

Gerry, Elbridge, 1744–1814
Logan, George, 1753–1821

39.8.2.2 Military and Naval Operations

Allen, Gardner W., *Our Naval War with France* (1909).

Collot, General, "General Collot's Plan for a Reconnaissance of the Ohio and Mississippi Valleys," Durand Eccheverria, trans., *WMQ*, 3 ser., 9 (1952), 512.

Jones, Robert F., "Naval Thought and Policy of Benjamin Stoddert, First Secretary of the Navy: 1798–1801," *Am. Neptune*, 24 (1964), 61.

Knox, Dudley W., ed., *Naval Documents Related to the Quasi War between the United States and France* (7 vols., 1935–1938).

Kyte, George W., "Military Intelligence Mission of General Collot in 1796," *MVHR*, 34 (1947), 427.

Phillips, James Duncan, "Salem's Part in the Naval War with France," *NEQ*, 16 (1943), 543.

Smelser, Marshall, *The Congress Founds the Navy, 1787–1798* (1957).

Turner, Harriet Stoddert, "Memoirs of Benjamin Stoddert, First Secretary of the United States Navy," Col. Hist. Soc., *Rec.*, 20 (1917), 141.

See also 10.3 for biographies/writings of:

Barlow, Joel, 1754–1812
Ellsworth, Oliver, 1745–1807
Gerry, Elbridge, 1744–1814
Logan, George, 1753–1821
Marshall, John, 1755–1835
Pickering, Timothy, 1745–1829
Truxtun, Thomas, 1755–1822

39.8.3 Alien and Sedition Acts, Virginia and Kentucky Resolutions

Anderson, Frank M., "Contemporary Opinion of Resolutions," *AHR*, 5 (1900), 225.

——— "Enforcement of Alien and Sedition Laws," Am. Hist. Assoc., *Report*, (1912), 115.

Carroll, Thomas F., "Freedom of Press in the Federalist Period," *Mich. Law Rev.*, 18 (1920), 615.

Howe, Mark DeW., "Freedom's Fetters: The Alien and Sedition Laws and American Civil Liberties," *WMQ*, 3 ser., 13 (1956), 573.

Koch, Adrienne, and Harry Ammon, "Virginia and Kentucky Resolutions: Defense of Civil Liberties," *WMQ*, 3 ser., 5 (1948), 145.

Levy, Leonard W., *Jefferson and Civil Liberties: The Darker Side* (1963).

——— *Legacy of Suppression: Freedom of Speech and Press in Early American History* (1960).

McLaughlin, Andrew C., "Social Compact and Constitutional Construction," *AHR*, 5 (1900), 467.

Miller, John C., *Crisis in Freedom* (1951).

Smelser, Marshall T., "George Washington and Alien and Sedition Acts," *AHR*, 59 (1954), 322.

Smith, James Morton, *Freedom's Fetters: Alien and Sedition Laws* (1956).

——— "Grass Roots Origins of Kentucky Resolutions," *WMQ*, 3 ser., 27 (1970), 221.

Stevens, John D., "Congressional History of 1798 Sedition Law," *Journalism Quar.*, 43 (1966), 247.

*   *   *   *   *   *   *

U.S. Library of Congress. Division of Bibliography, *List of References on Alien and Sedition Laws, 1798* (1925).

See also 10.3 for biographies/writings of:

Cooper, Thomas, 1759–1839
Hamilton, Alexander, 1755–1804
Jefferson, Thomas, 1743–1826
Madison, James, 1750/51–1836
Paine, Thomas, 1737–1809

39.9 ELECTION OF 1800

Cunningham, Noble E., Jr., "Election of 1800," in Arthur M. Schlesinger, Jr., and Fred L. Israel, eds., *History of American Presidential Elections, 1789–1968*, vol. I (1971).
Lerche, Charles O., "Jefferson and the Election of 1800, A Case Study of the Political Smear," *WMQ*, 3 ser., 5 (1948), 467.
Pancake, John S., "Aaron Burr: Would-Be Usurper," *WMQ*, 3 ser., 8 (1951), 204.

See also 10.3 for biographies/writings of:

Bayard, James A., 1767–1815
Burr, Aaron, 1756–1836

40 Republican Supremacy, 1801–1817

40.1 GENERAL

Abernethy, Thomas P., *The South in the New Nation, 1789–1819* (1961).
Adams, Henry, *History of the United States during the Administrations of Jefferson and Madison* (9 vols., 1889–1891).
Beard, Charles A., *The Economic Origins of Jeffersonian Democracy* (1915).
Brant, Irving, *James Madison and American Nationalism* (1968).
Channing, Edward, *A History of the United States* (6 vols., 1905–1925).
——— *Jeffersonian System* (1906).
Johnson, Allen, *Jefferson and His Colleagues* (1921).
Krout, John A., and Dixon Ryan Fox, *Completion of Independence, 1790–1830* (1944).
McMaster, John B., *A History of the People of the United States from the Revolution to the Civil War* (8 vols., 1883–1913).
Nettels, Curtis P., *Emergence of a National Economy, 1775–1815* (1963).
Parrington, Vernon L., *Main Currents in American Thought* (3 vols., 1927–1930).
Smelser, Marshall T., *Democratic Republic, 1801–1815* (1968).
Wiltse, Charles, *New Nation: 1800–1845* (1961).

*　　*　　*　　*　　*　　*　　*

Bellot, H. Hale, "Thomas Jefferson in Historiography," Royal Hist. Soc., *Trans.*, 5 ser., 4 (1954), 135.
McMillan, Malcolm C., "Jeffersonian Democracy and the Origins of Sectionalism," in Arthur S. Link and Rembert W. Patrick, eds., *Writing Southern History: Essays in Historiography in Honor of Fletcher M. Green* (1965).
Peterson, Merrill D., "Henry Adams on Jefferson the President," *Va. Quar. Rev.*, 39 (1963), 187.
——— *The Jefferson Image in the American Mind* (1960).
Shaw, Peter, "Henry Adams' *History*," *NEQ*, 40 (1967), 163.
Vitzthum, Richard C., "Henry Adams' Paraphrase of Sources in the *History of the United States*," *Am. Quar.*, 17 (1965), 81.

40.2 JEFFERSONIAN DEMOCRACY

Beard, Charles A., *Economic Origins of Jeffersonian Democracy* (1915).
Boorstin, Daniel J., *Lost World of Jefferson* (1948).
Griswold, A. Whitney, "The Agrarian Democracy of Thomas Jefferson," *Am. Pol. Sci. Rev.*, 40 (1964), 657.
Jones, Howard M., *Pursuit of Happiness* (1953).
Levy, Leonard W., *Jefferson and Civil Liberties: The Darker Side* (1963).
Mott, Frank L., *Jefferson and the Press* (1943).

Patterson, Caleb P., *Constitutional Principles of Thomas Jefferson* (1953).
Peterson, Merrill D., *Jefferson Image in American Mind* (1960).
Robinson, William Alexander, *Jeffersonian Democracy in New England* (1916).
Wiltse, Charles M., *The Jeffersonian Tradition in American Democracy* (1935).

See also 10.3 for biographies/writings of:

Burr, Aaron, 1756–1836
Clinton, George, 1739–1812
Jefferson, Thomas, 1743–1826
Madison, James, 1750/51–1836
Monroe, James, 1758–1831

40.3 POLITICS

40.3.1 General

Aronson, Sidney H., *Status and Kinship in Higher Civil Service: Standards of Selection in the Administrations of John Adams, Thomas Jefferson, and Andrew Jackson* (1964).
Borden, Morton, *Parties and Politics in the Early Republic, 1789–1815* (1967).
Brant, Irving, "Election of 1808," in Arthur M. Schlesinger, Jr., and Fred L. Israel, eds., *History of American Presidential Elections, 1789–1968*, vol. I (1971).
Dauer, Manning, "Election of 1804," in Arthur M. Schlesinger Jr., and Fred L. Israel, eds., *History of American Presidential Elections, 1789–1968*, vol. I (1971).
Goodman, Paul, ed., *Federalists vs. Jeffersonian Republicans* (1967).
Higginbotham, Sanford W., *Keystone in the Democratic Arch: Pennsylvania Politics, 1800–1816* (1952).
Hunt, Gaillard, "Office Seeking," *AHR*, 1 (1896), 270; 2 (1897), 241.
Merriam, J. M., "Jefferson's Use of Executive Patronage," Am. Hist. Assoc., *Papers*, 2 (1887), 47.

40.3.2 Federalists

Banner, James M., *To the Hartford Convention: Federalists and Origins of Party Politics in Massachusetts, 1789–1815* (1970).
Brown, Charles R., *Northern Confederacy* (1915).
Fischer, David H., *Revolution of American Conservatism: Federalist Party in Jeffersonian Democracy* (1965).
Kerber, Linda K., *Federalists in Dissent: Imagery and Ideology in Jeffersonian America* (1970).
Livermore, Shaw, Jr., *Twilight of Federalism: Federalist Party, 1815–1830* (1962).
Munroe, John A., *Federalist Delaware, 1775–1815* (1954).

See also 10.3 for biographies/writings of:

Bayard, James A., 1767–1815
Dwight, Timothy, 1752–1817
Kent, James, 1763–1847

40.3.3 Republicans

Ammon, Harry, "James Monroe and Election of 1808 in Virginia," *WMQ*, 3 ser., 20 (1963), 33.
——— "Jeffersonian Republicans in Virginia," *Va. Mag. Hist. and Biog.*, 71 (1963), 153.
Brown, Stuart G., *First Republicans: Jefferson and Madison* (1954).
Cunningham, Noble E., Jr., *Jeffersonian Republicans in Power: Party Operations, 1801–1809* (1963).
——— "Who Were the Quids?" *MVHR*, 50 (1963), 252.

Douglass, Elisha P., "Fisher Ames, Spokesman for New England Federalism," Am. Philos. Soc., *Proc.*, 103 (1959), 693.

Goodman, Paul, *The Democratic-Republicans of Massachusetts: Politics in a Young Republic* (1964).

McLoughlin, William G., "Bench, Church and Republican Party in New Hampshire, 1790–1820," *Hist. N.H.*, 20 (1965), 3.

MacPhee, Donald A., "The Yazoo Controversy: The Beginning of the 'Quid' Revolt," *Ga. Hist. Quar.*, 49 (1965), 23.

Prince, Carl E., *New Jersey's Jeffersonian Republicans, 1789–1817* (1967).

Risjord, Norman K., *Old Republicans: Southern Conservatism in Age of Jefferson* (1965).

Wolfe, John H., *Jeffersonian Democracy in South Carolina* (1940).

See also 10.3 for biographies/writings of:

Ames, Nathaniel, Jr., fl. 1758–1822
Breckinridge, John, 1760–1806
Burk, John D., 1775–1808
Macon, Nathaniel, 1758–1837
Mitchill, Samuel Latham, 1764–1831
Worthington, Thomas, 1773–1827

40.4 JEFFERSON AND MADISON ADMINISTRATIONS, 1801–1817

40.4.1 General

Foster, Augustus John, *Jeffersonian America: Notes, 1805–12*, Richard B. Davis, ed. (1954).

Green, Constance M., *Washington, Village and Capital, 1800–1950* (2 vols., 1962–1963).

Harrison, Lowell H., "Attorney General John Breckinridge," *Filson Club Hist. Quar.*, 36 (1962), 319.

Padover, Saul K., ed., *Thomas Jefferson and National Capital* (1946).

Plumer, William, *Memorandum of Proceedings in the Senate, 1803–1807* (1923).

Smith, Margaret B., *The First Forty Years of Washington Society*, Gaillard Hunt, ed. (1906).

White, Leonard D., *The Jeffersonians: Administrative History, 1801–1829* (1951).

Young, James S., *Washington Community, 1800–1828* (1966).

See also 10.3 for biographies/writings of:

Campbell, George Washington, 1769–1848
Clinton, George, 1739–1812
Crawford, William Harris, 1772–1834
Dallas, Alexander James, 1759–1817
Gallatin, Albert, 1761–1849
Gerry, Elbridge, 1744–1814
Jefferson, Thomas, 1743–1826
Madison, Dolly, 1768–1849
Madison, James, 1750/51–1836
Monroe, James, 1758–1831
Pinkney, William, 1764–1822
Rush, Richard, 1780–1859

40.4.2 Financial Policies

Grampp, William D., "A Re-examination of Jeffersonian Economics," *South. Econ. Jour.*, 12 (1946), 263.

Mai, Chien Tseng, *Fiscal Policies of Gallatin* (1930).
Nielson, Peter R., *Financial History, 1811–1816* (1926).

See also 10.3 for biographies/writings of:

Campbell, George W., 1769–1848
Dallas, Alexander J., 1759–1817
Gallatin, Albert, 1761–1849

40.4.3 Supreme Court and Politics

Boyd, Julian P., "The Chasm that Separated Thomas Jefferson and John Marshall," in Gottfried Dietze, ed., *Essays on the American Constitution: A Commemorative Volume in Honor of Alpheus T. Mason* (1964).
Ellis, Richard E., *The Jeffersonian Crisis: Courts and Politics in the Young Nation* (1971).
Faulkner, Robert K., *Jurisprudence of John Marshall* (1968).
Haar, Charles, *Golden Age of American Law* (1965).
Johnson, Herbert A., "Impeachment and Politics," *So. Atl. Quar.*, 63 (1964), 552.
"Judge Spencer Roane of Virginia—Champion of States' Rights—Foe of John Marshall," *Harvard Law Rev.*, 66 (1953), 1242.
Lillich, Richard B., "The Chase Impeachment," *Am. Jour. Legal Hist.*, 4 (1960), 49.
Magrath, C. Peter, *Yazoo: Law and Politics in the New Republic, Case of Fletcher v. Peck* (1967).
Mathis, Doyle, "'Chisholm v. Georgia': Background and Settlement," *JAH*, 54 (1967), 19.
Morgan, Donald G., "The Origin of Supreme Court Dissent," *WMQ*, 3 ser., 10 (1953), 353.
Newmyer, R. Kent, *The Supreme Court under Marshall and Taney* (1969).
Roper, Donald M., "Judicial Unanimity and the Marshall Court—A Road to Reappraisal," *Am. Jour. Legal Hist.*, 9 (1965), 118.
Treacy, Kenneth, "The Olmstead Case, 1778–1809," *West. Pol. Quar.*, 10 (1957), 675.

See also 10.3 for biographies/writings of:

Marshall, John, 1755–1835
Story, Joseph, 1779–1845

40.4.4 Burr Conspiracy

Abernethy, Thomas P., *Burr Conspiracy* (1954).
Beirne, Francis F., *Shout Treason: Trial of Aaron Burr* (1959).
Carpenter, T., *Trial of Colonel Aaron Burr on an Indictment for Treason before the Circuit Court of the United States, 1807* (2 vols., 1807).
Cox, Isaac J., "General Wilkinson and His Later Intrigues," *AHR*, 19 (1914), 794.
Faulkner, Robert K., "John Marshall and Burr Trial," *JAH*, 53 (1966), 247.
McCaleb, Walter F., *The Aaron Burr Conspiracy* (1936).
Robertson, David, *Reports of Trials of Aaron Burr in Circuit Court, 1807* (2 vols., 1808),
Syrett, Harold C., and Jean G. Cooke, eds., *Interview in Weehawken: Burr-Hamilton Duel* (1960).
Wright, Louis B., and Julia H. Macleod, "William Eaton's Relations with Aaron Burr," *MVHR*, 31 (1945), 523.

*   *   *   *   *   *   *

Pratt, Julius W., "Aaron Burr and the Historians," *N.Y. Hist.*, 26 (1945), 447.

See also 10.3 for biographies/writings of:

Blennerhassett, Harman, 1756–1831
Burr, Aaron, 1756–1836
Marshall, John, 1755–1835
Martin, Luther, 1748–1826
Wilkinson, James, 1757–1825

40.5 FOREIGN AND MILITARY POLICIES

40.5.1 Great Britain

Briggs, Herbert W., *Doctrine of Continuous Voyage* (1926).
Burt, A. L., *United States, Great Britain, and British North America* (1940).
Crouzet, Francois, *L'Economie britannique et le blocus continental, 1806–1813* (2 vols., 1958).
Emmerson, John C., Jr., *Chesapeake Affair of 1807* (1954).
Graham, Gerald S., *Sea Power and British North America* (1941).
Hyneman, Charles S., *First American Neutrality: Neutral Obligations during the Years 1792–1815* (1934).
Lingelbach, William E., "England and Neutral Trade," *Military Historian and Economist*, 2 (1927), 153.
Neel, Joanne L., *Phineas Bond: A Study in Anglo-American Relations, 1786–1812* (1968).
Perkins, Bradford, *Prologue to War: England and United States, 1805–1812* (1961).
Zimmerman, J. F., *Impressment of American Seamen* (1925).

40.5.2 Barbary War

Allen, Gardner W., *Navy and Barbary Corsairs* (1905).
Barnby, Henry G., *Prisoners of Algiers: American-Algerian War, 1785–1797* (1966).
Carr, James A., "John Adams and Barbary Problem," *Am. Neptune*, 26 (1966), 231.
Cathcart, James L., "Diplomatic Journal and Letter Book, 1788–1796," Am. Antiq. Soc., *Proc.*, 64 (1954), 303.
Dupuy, Émile, *Américains et Barbaresques* (1910).
Fisher, Godfrey, *Barbary Legend, 1415–1830* (1957).
Irwin, Ray W., *Diplomatic Relations of United States with Barbary Powers, 1776–1816* (1931).
Paullin, Charles O., *Diplomatic Negotiations of American Naval Officers* (1912).
Pratt, Fletcher, *Preble's Boys: Commodore Preble and the Birth of American Sea Power* (1950).
Tucker, Glenn, *Dawn Like Thunder: Barbary Wars and Birth of the U.S. Navy* (1963).
Wright, Louis B., and J. H. Macleod, *First Americans in North Africa* (1945).

See also 10.3 for biographies/writings of:

Eaton, William, 1764–1811

40.5.3 France

Kaplan, Lawrence S., "Jefferson's Foreign Policy and Napoleon's Ideologues," *WMQ*, 3 ser., 19 (1962), 344.
Lokke, Carl Ludwig, *France and the Colonial Question* (1932).
Shulim, Joseph I., *Old Dominion and Napoleon Bonaparte: American Opinion* (1952).

40.5.4 Louisiana Purchase

40.5.4.1 General

Adams, Mary P., "Jefferson's Reaction to the Treaty of San Ildefonso," *Jour. Southern Hist.*, 21 (1955), 173.

Bailey, Hugh C., and Bernard C. Weber, "A British Reaction to the Treaty of San Ildefonso," *WMQ*, 3 ser., 17 (1960), 242.

Darling, A. B., *Our Rising Empire, 1763–1803* (1940).

Clark, Daniel, "Despatches from United States Consulate in New Orleans," Arthur Whitaker, ed., *AHR*, 32 (1927), 801; 33 (1928), 331; 38 (1933), 291.

Dunbar, William, *Documents Relating to the Purchase and Exploration of Louisiana* (1904).

Hosmer, James K., *History of the Louisiana Purchase* (1902).

Lokke, Carl Ludwig, "Jefferson and the Leclerc Expedition," *AHR*, 33 (1928), 322.

Lyon, E. Wilson, *Louisiana in French Diplomacy, 1759–1804* (1934).

——— *TheMan Who Sold Louisiana: François Barbe-Marbois* (1942).

Renaut, François P., *La question de la Louisiane, 1796–1806* (1918).

Whitaker, Arthur P., *Mississippi Question, 1795–1803* (1934).

40.5.4.2 Domestic Aspects

Brown, Everett S., *Constitutional History of the Louisiana Purchase* (1920).

Farnham, Thomas J., "Federal-State Issue and the Louisiana Purchase," *La. Hist.*, 6 (1965), 5.

Pelzer, Louis, "Economic Factors in the Acquisition of Louisiana," Miss. Valley Hist. Assoc., *Proc.*, 6 (1912), 109.

40.5.4.3 Administration of Louisiana Territory

Brown, Elizabeth G., "Law and Government in the 'Louisiana Purchase,' 1803–1804," *Wayne Law Rev.*, 2 (1956), 169.

——— "Legal Systems in Conflict: Orleans Territory, 1804–1812," *Am. Jour. Legal Hist.*, 1 (1957), 35.

Claiborne, William C. C., *Official Letter Books . . . 1801–1816* (1917).

Coles, Harry L., Jr., "Public Lands System, Louisiana," *MVHR*, 43 (1956), 39.

40.5.5 West Florida Controversy

Cox, Isaac J., *West Florida Controversy* (1918).

Fuller, H. B., *Purchase of Florida* (1906).

40.5.6 Exploration and Lewis and Clark Expedition

Bakeless, John E., *Lewis and Clark, Partners in Discovery* (1947).

Burroughs, Raymond D., ed., *Natural History of the Lewis and Clark Expedition* (1961).

Cox, Isaac J., *Early Explorations of Louisiana* (1906).

——— "Explorer of the Louisiana Purchase," Am. Philos. Soc., *Lib. Bull.*, 1946, 73.

Cutright, Paul R., *Lewis and Clark: Pioneering Naturalists* (1969).

Guinness, R. B., "Purpose of Lewis and Clark Expedition," *MVHR*, 20 (1933), 90.

Jackson, Donald, ed., *Letters of the Lewis and Clark Expedition with Related Documents, 1783–1854* (1962).

Lewis, Meriwether, and William Clark, *History of the Expedition to the Sources of the Missouri, across the Rocky Mountains and down the Columbia to the Pacific* (1804–1806).

Marshall, Thomas M., *History of the Western Boundary of Louisiana Purchase* (1914).

See also 10.3 for biographies/writings of:

Clark, William, 1770–1838
Lewis, Meriwether, 1774–1809
Pike, Zebulon, 1779–1813

40.5.7 Effect of Napoleonic Wars on Neutral Trade

40.5.7.1 General

Albion, R. G., and J. B. Pope, *Sea Lanes in Wartime* (1942).
Clauder, A. C., *American Commerce as Affected by the Wars of the French Revolution* (1932).
Galpin, William F., "American Grain Trade," *Jour. Econ. and Bus. Hist.*, 2 (1929), 71.
——— *Grain Supply of England* (1925).
Heckscher, Eli F., *Continental System* (1922).
Kaplan, Lawrence S., "Jefferson, Napoleonic Wars, and the Balance of Power," *WMQ*, 3 ser., 14 (1957), 196.
Labaree, Benjamin W., *Patriots and Partisans: The Merchants of Newburyport, 1764–1815* (1962).
Melvin, Frank E., *Napoleon's Navigation System* (1919).
Morison, Samuel E., *Maritime History of Massachusetts, 1783–1860* (1921).

40.5.7.2 Russia and the Baltic

Bolkhovitinov, Nikolai N., *Stanovlenie Russko-Amerikanskikh Othoshenii, 1775–1815* (1966).
Crosby, Alfred W., Jr., *America, Russia, Hemp, and Napoleon: American Trade with Russia and the Baltic, 1783–1812* (1965).
Hildt, John C., *Early Diplomatic Negotiations of the United States with Russia* (1906).
Rasch, Aage, "American Trade in the Baltic, 1783–1807," *Scandinavian Econ. Hist. Rev.*, 13 (1965), 31.
Shulim, Joseph I., "The United States Views Russia in the Napoleonic Age," *Am. Philos. Soc., Proc.*, 102 (1958), 148.

40.5.7.3 Embargo and Non-Intercourse, 1807–1811

Brown, Dorothy M., "Embargo Politics in Maryland," *Md. Hist. Mag.*, 58 (1963), 193.
Daitsman, George, "Labor and the 'Welfare State' in Early New York," *Labor Hist.*, 4 (1963), 248.
Daniels, G. W., "American Cotton Trade with Liverpool under the Embargo and Non-Intercourse Acts," *AHR*, 21 (1916), 276.
Heaton, Herbert, "Non-Importation, 1806–1812," *Jour. Econ. Hist.*, 1 (1941), 178.
Jennings, Walter W., *American Embargo* (1921).
Sears, Louis M., *Jefferson and the Embargo* (1967).

40.6 WAR OF 1812

40.6.1 General

Coles, Harry Lewis, *The War of 1812* (1965).
Horsman, Reginald, *The War of 1812* (1969).
Sapio, Victor A., *Pennsylvania and the War of 1812* (1970).
Tucker, Glenn, *Poltroons and Patriots: War of 1812* (2 vols., 1954).
White, Patrick C. T., *Nation on Trial: America and War of 1812* (1965).

40.6.2 Causes

Brown, Roger H., *Republic in Peril: 1812* (1964).
Carr, Albert H. Z., *Coming of War of 1812* (1960).
Goodman, W. H., "Origins of the War of 1812," *MVHR*, 28 (1942), 171.
Haynes, Robert V., "Southwest and the War of 1812," *La. Hist.*, 5 (1964), 41.
Horsman, Reginald, *Causes of War of 1812* (1962).
—— "Who Were the Warhawks?" *Ind. Mag. Hist.*, 60 (1964), 121.
Latimer, Margaret K., "South Carolina—War of 1812," *AHR*, 61 (1956), 914.
Perkins, Bradford, ed., *Causes of the War of 1812: National Honor or National Interest* (1961).
Perkins, Bradford, *Prologue to War, 1802–1812* (1961).
Pratt, Julius W., *Expansionists of 1812* (1949).
Risjord, Norman K., "1812: Conservatives, War Hawks, and the Nation's Honor," *WMQ*, 3 ser., 18 (1962), 196.
—— "Election of 1812," in Arthur M. Schlesinger, Jr. and Fred L. Israel, eds., *History of American Presidential Elections, 1789–1968*, vol. I (1971).
Smith, Theodore C., "War Guilt in 1812," Mass. Hist. Soc., *Proc.*, 64 (1932), 319.
Taylor, George R., "Agrarian Discontent in Mississippi Valley Preceding the War of 1812," *Jour. Pol. Econ.*, 39 (1931), 471.
—— ed., *The War of 1812: Past Justifications and Present Interpretations* (1963).

See also 10.3 for biographies/writings of:

Calhoun, John C., 1782–1850
Clay, Henry, 1777–1852
Grundy, Felix, 1777–1840
Macon, Nathaniel, 1758–1837
Webster, Daniel, 1782–1852

40.6.3 France

Bonnel, Ulane, *La France, les États-Unis, et la guerre de course, 1797–1815* (1961).
Brant, Irving, "Joel Barlow, Madison's Stubborn Minister," *WMQ*, 3 ser., 15 (1958), 438.
Glover, Richard, "The French Fleet, 1807–1814: Britain's Problem and Madison's Opportunity," *Jour. Modern Hist.*, 39 (1967), 233.
Kaplan, Lawrence S., "France and Madison's Decision for War, 1812," *MVHR*, 50 (1964), 652.

40.6.4 Opposition

Anderson, Frank M., "Opposition to the War of 1812," Miss.Valley Hist. Assoc., *Proc.*, 6 (1912–1913), 176.
Dwight, Theodore, *History of the Hartford Convention: With a Review of the Policy of the United States Government Which Led to the War of 1812* (1833).
Fischer, David H., "Myth of Essex Junto," *WMQ*, 3 ser., 21 (1964), 191.
Morison, Samuel E., Frederick Merk, and Frank Freidel, *Dissent in Three American Wars* (1970).

See also 10.3 for biographies/writings of:

Cabot, George, 1752–1823
Giles, William B., 1762–1830

40.6.5 Naval Operations

Forester, C. S., *The Age of Fighting Sail: Naval War of 1812* (1956).
Mahan, Alfred T., *Sea Power in the War of 1812* (2 vols., 1905).

Mindte, R. W., "Another Navy Rodgers," *Am. Neptune*, 19 (1959), 213.
Roosevelt, Theodore, *Naval War of 1812* (1882).

See also 10.3 for biographies/writings of:

Bainbridge, William, 1774–1833
Hull, Isaac, 1773–1843
Perry, Oliver Hazard, 1785–1819
Porter, David, 1780–1843
Truxtun, Thomas, 1755–1822

40.6.6 Privateers

Cranwell, John P., and William B. Crane, *Men of Marque: Private Armed Vessels out of Baltimore during War of 1812* (1940).
Maclay, Edward S., *American Privateers* (1899).
Williams, Gomer, *History of the Liverpool Privateers* (1897).

40.6.7 War along Northern Borders

40.6.7.1 General

Babcock, Louis L., *War of 1812 on the Niagara Frontier* (1927).
Doyle, James T., *The Organizational and Operational Administration of the Ohio Militia in the War of 1812* (1958).
Edgar, Matilda, *General Brock* (1926).
Hallaman, Emmanuel, *British Invasions of Ohio—1813* (1958).
Hitsman, J. Mackay, *Incredible War of 1812* (1965).
Kellogg, Louise P., *The British Regime in Wisconsin and the Northwest* (1935).
Knopf, Richard C., ed., "Return Jonathan Meigs Jr. and the War of 1812," in Ohio Historical Society, *Document Transcriptions of the War of 1812 in the Northwest*, vol. 2 (1957).
LeRoy, Perry, *The Weakness of Discipline and Its Consequent Results in the Northwest during the War of 1812* (1958).
Lucas, Charles P., *Canadian War of 1812* (1906).
Zaslow, Morris, and Wesley B. Turner, eds., *Defended Border: Upper Canada and War of 1812* (1964).

See also 10.3 for biographies/writings of:

Harrison, William Henry, 1773–1841
Scott, Winfield, 1786–1866
Tecumseh, 1768–1813
Wilkinson, James, 1757–1825

40.6.7.2 Harrison and Tippecanoe

Hoffnagle, Warren, M., *The Road to Fame: William H. Harrison and the Northwest* (1959).
Knopf, Richard C., *William Henry Harrison and the War of 1812* (1957).
Mason, Philip P., ed., *After Tippecanoe: Aspects of War of 1812* (1963).

40.6.8 War along Southern Borders

40.6.8.1 General

Brown, Wilburt S., *The Amphibious Campaign for West Florida and Louisiana, 1814–1815: A Critical Review of Strategy and Tactics at New Orleans* (1969).
Halbert, H. S., and T. H. Ball, *Creek War of 1813 and 1814* (1970).
Owsley, Frank L., Jr., "British and Indian Activities in Spanish West Florida during the War of 1812," *Fla. Hist. Quar.*, 46 (1967), 111.

Patrick, Rembert W., *Florida Fiasco, 1810–1815* (1954).
Rowland, Eron O. M., *Mississippi Territory in the War of 1812* (1968).

40.6.8.2 Jackson and New Orleans

Brooks, Charles B., *Siege of New Orleans* (1961).
Forrest, Charles R., *Battle of New Orleans—A British View: Journal of Major C. R. Forrest*, Hugh F. Rankin, ed. (1961).
Grummond, Jane L. de, *Baratarians and the Battle of New Orleans* (1961).
LeBreton, Dagmar R., "Man Who Won the Battle of New Orleans," *La. Hist. Quar.*, 38, no. 3 (1955), 20. Jean-Claude Hudry.
Mahon, John K., "British Command Decisions Relative to Battle of New Orleans," *La. Hist.*, 6 (1965), 53.
Rowland, Eron O. M., *Andrew Jackson's Campaign against the British* (1926).

See also 10.3 for biographies/writings of:

Claiborne, William C., 1775–1817
Jackson, Andrew, 1767–1845

40.6.9 Peace Negotiations and Aftermath

Burt, A. L., *United States, Great Britain and British North America* (1940).
Engelman, F. L., *Peace of Christmas Eve* (1962).
Jones, Wilbur D., "A British View of the War of 1812 and the Peace Negotiations," *MVHR*, 65 (1958), 481.
Merk, Frederick, "Negotiations of 1818," *AHR*, 55 (1950), 530.
Perkins, Bradford, *Castlereagh and Adams: England and United States, 1812–1823* (1964).
Updyke, F. A., *Diplomacy of the War of 1812* (1915).
Webster, Charles K., *Foreign Policy of Castlereagh 1815–1822* (1925).

See also 10.3 for biographies/writings of:

Adams, John Quincy, 1767–1848
Bayard, James A., 1767–1815
Clay, Henry, 1777–1852
Gallatin, Albert, 1761–1849
Monroe, James, 1758–1831
Randolph, John, 1773–1833

41 New Nationalism, 1815–1829

41.1 GENERAL

Adams, Henry, *History of the United States* (9 vols., 1889–1891).
Barnhart, John D., *Valley of Democracy: Frontier in the Ohio Valley, 1775–1818* (1953).
Channing, Edward, *History of the United States* (6 vols., 1912–1925).
Dangerfield, George, *Awakening of American Nationalism, 1815–1828* (1965).
———— *Era of Good Feelings* (1963).
Gates, Paul W., *Farmer's Age, 1815–1860: Economic History of the United States* (1960).
Krout, John A., and Dixon Ryan Fox, *Completion of Independence* (1944).
Livermore, Shaw, *Twilight of Federalism: The Disintegration of the Federalist Party, 1815–1830* (1962).
McMaster, John B., *History of the People of the United States from the Revolution to the Civil War* (8 vols., 1883–1913).
Sydnor, Charles S., *Development of Southern Sectionalism* (1948).
Taylor, George R., *Transportation Revolution: 1815–1860* (1951).
Turner, Frederick Jackson, *Rise of the New West* (1906).
Young, James S., *Washington Community, 1800–1828* (1966).

See also 10.3 for biographies/writings of:

Adams, John Quincy, 1767–1848
Calhoun, John C., 1782–1850
Clay, Henry, 1777–1852
Jackson, Andrew, 1767–1845
Madison, James, 1750/51–1836
Monroe, James, 1758–1831
Webster, Daniel, 1782–1852

41.2 MONROE AND ADAMS ADMINISTRATIONS, 1817–1829

Ammon, Harry, "James Monroe," *Va. Mag. Hist. Biog.*, 66 (1958), 387.
Harlow, Ralph V., *History of Legislative Methods before 1825* (1915).
Sydnor, Charles S., "One-Party Period of American History," *AHR*, 51 (1946), 439.
Thompson, Charles S., *Rise and Fall of the Congressional Caucus* (1902).
Turner, Lynn W., "Elections of 1816 and 1820," in Arthur M. Schlesinger, Jr., and Fred L. Israel, eds., *History of American Presidential Elections, 1789–1968* (vol. I, 1971).
———— "Electoral Vote against Monroe in 1820," *MVHR*, 42 (1955), 250.

See also 10.3 for biographies/writings of:

Adams, John Quincy, 1767–1848
Calhoun, John C., 1782–1850
Clay, Henry, 1777–1852
Crawford, William H., 1772–1834
MacLean, John, 1785–1861
Monroe, James, 1758–1831
Rush, Richard, 1780–1859
Tompkins, Daniel D., 1774–1825
Wirt, William, 1772–1834

41.3 PANIC OF 1819

Kehl, James A., *Ill Feeling in the Era of Good Feeling* (1956).
Rezneck, Samuel, "Depression of 1819–1822," *AHR*, 39 (1933), 28.
Rothbard, Murray N., *The Panic of 1819* (1962).
Smith, Walter B., and Arthur H. Cole, *Fluctuations in American Business, 1790–1860* (1935).

41.4 MISSOURI COMPROMISE

Banks, Ronald P., *Maine Becomes a State: Movement to Separate Maine from Massachusetts, 1785–1820* (1970).
Brown, Everett S., *Missouri Compromises and Presidential Politics from the Letters of William Plumer, Jr.* (1926).
Dunne, Gerald T., "Joseph Story: The Salem Years," Essex Inst. *Hist. Coll.*, 101 (1965), 307.
Ernst, Robert, "Rufus King, Slavery, and the Missouri Crisis," *N.Y. Hist. Soc. Quar.*, 46 (1962), 337.
Hodder, Frank H., "Sidelights on the Missouri Compromise," Am. Hist. Assoc., *Report* (1909), 151.
Johnson, William R., "Prelude to the Missouri Compromise," *N.Y. Hist. Soc. Quar.*, 48 (1964), 31.
Moore, Glover, *Missouri Controversy* (1953).
Shoemaker, F. C., *Missouri's Struggle for Statehood* (1916).
Trexler, H. A., *Slavery in Missouri* (1914).

41.5 SECOND BANK OF THE UNITED STATES

Bogart, E. L., "Taxation of Second Bank," *AHR*, 17 (1912), 312.
Brown, Kenneth L., "Stephen Girard, Promoter of Second Bank of the United States," *Jour. Econ. Hist.*, 2 (1942), 125.
Gleick, Harry S., "Banking in Early Missouri," *Mo. Hist. Rev.*, 61 (1967), 427; 62 (1967), 30.
Hammond, Bray, *Banks and Politics in America from the Revolution to the Civil War* (1967).
Huntington, C. C., "Banking and Currency in Ohio," *Ohio State Archaeol. and Hist. Quar.*, 24 (1915), 235.
Schur, Leon, "The Second Bank of the United States and Inflation After the War of 1812," *Jour. Pol. Econ.*, 68 (1960), 118.
Sellers, Charles G., Jr., "Banking and Politics in Jackson's Tennessee, 1817–1827," *MVHR*, 41 (1954), 61.
Smith, Walter B., *Economic Aspects of the Second Bank of the United States* (1953).
Walters, Raymond, Jr., "The Origins of the Second Bank of the United States," *Jour. Pol. Econ.*, 53 (1945), 115.

41.6 MARSHALL COURT

Baxter, Maurice G., *Daniel Webster and the Supreme Court* (1966).
Faulkner, Robert K., *The Jurisprudence of John Marshall* (1966).
Frankfurter, Felix, *The Commerce Clause under Marshall, Taney, and Waite* (1937).
Gates, Paul W., "Tenants of the Log Cabin," *MVHR*, 49 (1962), 3.
Haar, Charles, ed., *The Golden Age of American Law* (1965).
Nettels, Curtis P., "The Mississippi Valley and the Constitution," *MVHR*, 11 (1924), 332.
Newmyer, R. Kent, "Daniel Webster as Tocqueville's Lawyer: The 'Dartmouth College' Case Again," *Am. Jour. Legal Hist.*, 11 (1967), 127.
Plous, H. J., and Gordon Baker, "McCulloch vs. Maryland, Right Principle, Wrong Case," *Stanford Law Rev.*, 9 (1957), 710.
Stickles, Arndt M., *Critical Court Struggle in Kentucky, 1819–1829* (1929).

See also 10.3 for biographies/writings of:

Jefferson, Thomas, 1743–1826
Johnson, William, 1771–1834
Marshall, John, 1755–1835
Story, Joseph, 1779–1845
John Taylor of Caroline, 1753–1824
Webster, Daniel, 1782–1852

41.7 STATE AND LOCAL POLITICS

Adams, James Truslow, *New England in the Republic, 1776–1850* (1926).
Alexander, De Alva S., *A Political History of the State of New York, 1774–1882* (3 vols., 1906–1909).
Buck, Solon J., *Illinois in 1818* (1917).
Davis, Harold E., "The Economic Basis of Ohio Politics, 1820–1840," *Ohio State Archaeol. and Hist. Quar.*, 47 (1938), 288.
Eiselen, M. R., *The Rise of Pennsylvania Protectionism* (1932).
Flanagan, Sue, *Sam Houston's Texas* (1964).
Haller, Mark H., "The Rise of the Jacksonian Party in Maryland, 1820–1829," *JSH*, 28 (1962), 307.
Handlin, Oscar, and Mary F. Handlin, *Commonwealth, Government in Economy: Massachusetts, 1774–1861* (rev. ed., 1969).
Hartz, Louis, *Economic Policy and Democratic Thought: Pennsylvania, 1776–1860* (1948).
Klein, Philip S., *Pennsylvania Politics, 1817–1832: A Game without Rules* (1940).
McCandless, Perry, "The Rise of Thomas H. Benton in Missouri Politics," *Mo. Hist. Rev.*, 50 (1955), 16.
Pease, Theodore C., *Illinois, Frontier State, 1818–1840* (1919).
Phillips, Ulrich B., "Georgia and State Rights," Am. Hist. Assoc., *Report*, 2 (1901), 24.
Stevens, Harry R., *Early Jackson Party in Ohio* (1957).
Thomas, Benjamin P., *Lincoln's New Salem* (rev. ed., 1966).
Wade, Richard C., *Urban Frontier: Pioneer Life in Early Pittsburgh, Cincinnati, Lexington, Louisville, and St. Louis* (1964).

41.8 DEMOCRATIZATION IN THE STATES

Coleman, Peter J., *Transformation of Rhode Island, 1790–1860* (1963).
Darling, A. B., *Political Changes in Massachusetts, 1824–1848* (1925).
Fell, W. R., *Transition from Aristocracy to Democracy* (1933).
Fox, Dixon Ryan, *Decline of Aristocracy in the Politics of New York* (1919).

Gilpatrick, Delbert H., *Jeffersonian Democracy in North Carolina* (1931).
Green, Fletcher M., *Constitutional Development in the South Atlantic States, 1776–1860* (1930).
McCormick, Richard P., *History of Voting in New Jersey: A Study of the Development of Election Machinery, 1664–1911* (1953).
Marshall, Lynn L., "Grass Roots Democracy in Kentucky," *Mid-America*, 47 (1965), 269.
Peterson, Merrill D., ed., *Democracy, Liberty and Property: State Constitutional Conventions of the 1820's* (1966).
Pole, J. R., "Suffrage and Representation in Massachusetts: A Statistical Note," *WMQ*, 3 ser., 14 (1957), 560.
Williamson, Chilton, *American Suffrage from Property to Democracy, 1760–1860* (1960).

See also 10.3 for biographies/writings of:

Kent, James, 1763–1847
Marcy, William L., 1786–1857
Polk, James K., 1795–1849
Van Buren, Martin, 1782–1862

41.9 ELECTIONS OF 1824 AND 1828

Ames, William E., and S. Dean Olson, "Washington's Political Press and Election of 1824," *Journalism Quar.*, 40 (1963), 343.
Curry, Leonard P., "Election Year—Kentucky, 1828," Ky. Hist. Soc., *Reg.*, 55 (1957), 196.
Hopkins, James F., "Election of 1824," in Arthur M. Schlesinger, Jr. and Fred L. Israel, eds., *History of American Presidential Elections, 1789–1968*, vol. 1 (1971).
McCormick, Richard P., "New Perspectives on Jacksonian Politics," *AHR*, 65 (1960), 288.
Morgan, William G., "John Quincy Adams versus Andrew Jackson: Their Biographers and 'Corrupt Bargain' Charge," *Tenn. Hist. Quar.*, 26 (1967), 43.
Newsome, Albert R., *Presidential Election of 1824 in North Carolina* (1939).
Remini, Robert V., *Election of Andrew Jackson* (1963).
——— "Election of 1828," in Arthur M. Schlesinger, Jr. and Fred L. Israel, eds., *History of American Presidential Elections, 1789–1968*, vol. 1 (1971).
——— *Martin Van Buren and the Making of the Democratic Party* (1959).
Weston, Florence, *Presidential Election of 1828* (1938).

41.10 FOREIGN RELATIONS

41.10.1 Latin America

Bernstein, Harry, *Origins of Inter-American Interest* (1945).
Evans, Henry C., *Chile and Its Relations with the United States* (1927).
Griffin, Charles C., *United States and the Disruption of the Spanish Empire* (1937).
Hill, Lawrence F., *Diplomatic Relations between the United States and Brazil* (1932).
Kaufmann, William W., *British Policy and the Independence of Latin America, 1804–1828* (1951).
Logan, Rayford W., *Diplomatic Relations of United States with Haiti* (1941).
Mack, Gerstle, *Land Divided* (1944).
Manning, William R., *Early Diplomatic Relations between the United States and Mexico* (1916).
Perkins, Bradford, *Castlereagh and Adams: England and the United States, 1812–1823* (1964).

Rippy, J. F., *Rivalry of the United States and Great Britain over Latin America* (1929).
Robertson, William S., *France and Latin American Independence* (1939).
Rydjord, John, *Foreign Interest in the Independence of New Spain* (1935).
Scroggs, William O., *Filibusters and Financiers* (1916).
Tansill, C. C., *United States and Santo Domingo* (1938).
Tatum, Edward L., *United States and Europe, 1815–1823* (1936).
Temperley, Harold W. V., *Foreign Policy of Canning, 1822–1827* (1925).
Webster, Charles K., *Foreign Policy of Castlereagh 1815–1822* (1925).
Whitaker, Arthur P., *The United States and the Independence of Latin America, 1800–1830* (1941).

41.10.2 Acquisition of Florida

Brooks, Phillip C., *Diplomacy and Borderlands* (1939).
Fuller, Hubert B., *Purchase of Florida* (1906).

41.10.3 Monroe Doctrine

Bolkhovitinov, Nikolai N., *Doktrina Monro* (1959).
Logan, John A., Jr., *No Transfer: An American Security Principle* (1961).
McGee, Gale W., "Monroe Doctrine–Stopgap Measure," *MVHR*, 38 (1951), 233.
Nichols, Irby C., Jr., "The Russian Ukase and Monroe Doctrine: A Reevaluation," *Pac. Hist. Rev.*, 36 (1967), 13.
Perkins, Dexter, *A History of the Monroe Doctrine* (rev. ed., 1963).
Rappaport, Armin, ed., *Monroe Doctrine* (1964).

41.10.4 British Interest in the Northwest and West Indies

Allen, Gardner W., *Our Navy and West Indian Pirates* (1929).
Ambler, Charles H., "The Oregon Country, 1810–1830: A Chapter in Territorial Expansion," *MVHR*, 30 (1943), 3.
Benns, F. Lee, *American Struggle for British West India Carrying Trade, 1815–1830* (1923).
Bradlee, F. B. C., "Suppression of Piracy," Essex Inst., *Hist. Coll.*, 58 (1922), 297; 59 (1923), 33.
Merk, Frederick, *Albert Gallatin and the Oregon Problem: A Study in Anglo-American Diplomacy* (1950).
—— *The Oregon Question: Essays in Anglo-American Diplomacy and Politics* (1967).

41.10.5 East Asia

Danton, George H., *Culture Contacts of the United States and China* (1931).
Dermigny, Louis, *La Chine et l'Occident: Le commerce à Canton au XVIIIe siècle, 1719–1833* (3 vols. plus "Album," vol. 4, 1964).
Downs, Jacques M., "American Merchants and the China Opium Trade, 1800–1840," *Bus. Hist. Rev.*, 42 (1968), 418.
Dulles, Foster Rhea, *Old China Trade*, (1930).
Latourette, Kenneth S., "Early Relations between the United States and China," Conn. Acad. Arts Sci., *Trans.*, 22 (1917), 1.
Livermore, Seward W., "Early Relations with East Indies," *Pacific Hist. Rev.*, 15 (1946), 31.
Phillips, Clifton J., *Protestant America and the Pagan World: The First Half Century of the American Board of Commissioners for Foreign Missions, 1810–1860* (1969).
Porter, Kenneth W., *The Jacksons and the Lees: Two Generations of Massachusetts Merchants, 1765–1844* (2 vols., 1937).

Stelle, Charles C., "American Trade in Opium to China, Prior to 1820," *Pac. Hist. Rev.*, 9 (1940), 425.

See also 10.3 for biographies/writings of:

Astor, John Jacob, 1763–1848

41.10.6 Hawaii

Bradley, Harold W., "Hawaiian Islands and Pacific Fur Trade," *Pac. Northw. Quar.*, 30 (1939), 275.
Pierce, Richard A., *Russia's Hawaiian Adventure, 1815–1817* (1965).
Rolle, Andrew F., "California Filibustering and Hawaiian Kingdom," *Pac. Hist. Rev.*, 19 (1950), 251.
Tate, Merze, "Great Britain and Sovereignty of Hawaii," *Pac. Hist. Rev.*, 31 (1962), 327.

41.10.7 Other Areas

Bennett, Norman R., and George E. Brooks, Jr., eds., *New England Merchants in Africa: 1802–1865* (1966).
Dakin, Douglas, *British and American Philhellenes, 1821–1833* (1955).

See also 10.3 for biographies/writings of:

Howe, Samuel Gridley, 1801–1876

42.1 GENERAL

Bode, Carl, ed., *American Life in the 1840's* (1967).
Buley, R. Carlyle, *Old Northwest: Pioneer Period, 1815–1840* (2 vols., 1951).
Channing, Edward, *History of the United States* (6 vols., 1912–1925).
Fish, Carl Russell, *Rise of the Common Man, 1830–1850* (1927).
Gatell, Frank O., ed., *Essays on Jacksonian America* (1970).
McMaster, John B., *History of the People of the United States from the Revolution to the Civil War* (8 vols., 1883–1913).
Schlesinger, Arthur M., Jr., *The Age of Jackson* (1945).
Sellers, Charles G., Jr., *Jacksonian Democracy* (1958).
Sydnor, Charles S., *Development of Southern Sectionalism 1819–1848* (1948).
Taylor, George Rogers, *Transportation Revolution, 1815–1860* (1951).
Turner, Frederick J., *The United States, 1830–1850* (1935).
Van Deusen, Glyndon G., *Jacksonian Era, 1828–1848* (1959).
White, Leonard D., *Jacksonians: Administrative History, 1829–1861* (1954).
Wiltse, Charles M., *New Nation, 1800–1845* (1961).

See also 9.4 for travel accounts of:

Buckingham, James S.
Chevalier, Michel
Dickens, Charles
Grund, Francis J.
Hall, Basil
Lieber, Francis
Marryat, Frederick
Martineau, Harriet
Trollope, Frances
Wright, Frances

See also 10.3 for biographies/writings of:

Adams, John Quincy, 1767–1848
Benton, Thomas Hart, 1782–1858
Biddle, Nicholas, 1786–1844
Calhoun, John C., 1782–1850
Cass, Lewis, 1782–1866
Clay, Henry, 1777–1852
Harrison, William Henry, 1773–1841
Hayne, Robert Y., 1791–1839
Kendall, Amos, 1789–1869
Livingston, Edward, 1764–1836
Monroe, James, 1758–1831
Polk, James, 1795–1849

Randolph, John, 1773–1833
Story, Joseph, 1779–1845
Taney, Roger, 1777–1864
Webster, Daniel, 1782–1852
Wirt, William, 1772–1834

42.2 ESSAYS AND SOURCES

Eaton, Clement, ed., *Leaven of Democracy: Time of Jackson* (1963).
Probst, George E., ed., *Happy Republic: A Reader in Tocqueville's America* (1962).
Rozwenc, Edwin C., ed., *Ideology and Power in Age of Jackson* (1964).
—— *Meaning of Jacksonian Democracy* (1963).

*   *   *   *   *   *   *

Cave, Alfred A., *Jacksonian Democracy and Historians* (1964).
Miles, Edwin A., "The Jacksonian Era," in Arthur Link and Rembert W. Patrick, eds., *Writing Southern History: Essays in Historiography in Honor of Fletcher M. Green* (1965).
Sellers, Charles G., Jr., "Andrew Jackson versus the Historians," *MVHR*, 44 (1958), 615.
Stevens, Harry, "Jacksonian Democracy, 1825–1849," in W. H. Cartwright and R. L. Watson, Jr., eds., *Interpreting and Teaching American History* (1961).
Ward, John William, "Age of Common Man," in John Higham, ed., *Reconstruction of American History* (1962).

42.3 ECONOMIC POLICIES

Dorfman, Joseph, *The Economic Mind in American Civilization*, (3 vols., 1946–1949).
Gates, Paul W., *Farmer's Age: Agriculture, 1815–1860* (1968).
Goodrich, Carter, *Government Promotion of Canals and Railroads,1800–1900* (1960).
—— "The Virginia System of Mixed Enterprise," *Pol. Sci. Quar.*, 64 (1949), 355.
Handlin, Oscar, and Mary F. Handlin, *Commonwealth: A Study of the Role of Government in the American Economy—Massachusetts, 1774–1861* (rev. ed., 1969).
Handlin, Oscar, Louis Hartz, and Milton Heath, "Laissez-Faire Thought in Massachusetts, 1790–1880," *Tasks of Economic History*, 3 (1943), 55.
Hartz, Louis, *Economic Policy and Democratic Thought* (rev. ed., 1968).
Kirkland, Edward C., *Men, Cities, and Transportation: A Study in New England History, 1820–1900* (2 vols., 1948).
North, Douglass C., *Economic Growth of the United States, 1790–1860* (1966).
Taylor, George R., *Transportation Revolution, 1815–1860* (1951).
Temin, Peter, *Jacksonian Economy* (1969).
Wellington, R. G., *Political and National Influence of Public Lands 1826–1842* (1914).

42.4 REFORM MOVEMENTS

Cole, Charles C., Jr., *Social Ideas of Northern Evangelists, 1826–1860* (1954).
Griffin, Clifford S., *Their Brothers' Keepers: Moral Stewardship in the United States, 1800–1865* (1960).
Riegel, Robert E., *Young America, 1830–1840* (1949).

Schlesinger, Arthur M., *The American as Reformer* (1950). With a new preface by Arthur M. Schlesinger, Jr. (1968).
Tyler, Alice Felt, *Freedom's Ferment* (1944).

42.5 POLITICAL THOUGHT

Blau, Joseph L., ed., *Social Theories of Jacksonian Democracy* (1947).
Goetzmann, William H., "Mountain Man as Jacksonian Man," *Am. Quar.*, 15 (1963), 402.
Hartz, Louis, *Liberal Tradition in America* (1955).
Hofstadter, Richard, *American Political Tradition* (1948).
Meyers, Marvin, *Jacksonian Persuasion* (1957).
Parrington, Vernon L., *Main Currents in American Thought* (3 vols., 1927–1930).
Rozwenc, Edwin C., ed., *Ideology and Power in Age of Jackson* (1964).
Schlesinger, Arthur M., Jr., *The Age of Jackson* (1945).
Tocqueville, Alexis de, *Democracy in America*, Phillips Bradley, ed. (2 vols., 1948).
Van Deusen, Glyndon G., "Aspects of Whig Thought in the Jacksonian Period," *AHR*, 64 (1959), 305.
Ward, John William, *Andrew Jackson, Symbol for an Age* (1955).
Wright, Benjamin F., "Political Institutions and the Frontier," in Dixon Ryan Fox, ed., *Sources of Culture in the Middle West* (1934).

See also 10.3 for biographies/writings of:

Bancroft, George, 1800–1891
Brownson, Orestes A., 1803–1876

42.6 POLITICS

42.6.1 General

Cobun, Frank E., "The Educational Level of the Jacksonians," *Hist. Educ. Quar.*, 7 (1967), 515.
Degler, Carl N., "Locofocos: Urban 'Agrarians'," *Jour. Econ. Hist.*, 16 (1956), 322.
Eriksson, Erik M., "Official Newspaper Organs," *Tenn. Hist. Mag.*, 8 (1925), 231; 9 (1926), 37.
Ford, Henry J., *Rise and Growth of American Politics* (1898).
McBain, Howard L., *DeWitt Clinton and the Spoils System* (1907).
McCarthy, Charles, "Anti-Masonic Party," Am. Hist. Assoc., *Report*, I (1902), 365.
McCormick, Richard P., "New Perspectives on Jacksonian Politics," *AHR*, 65 (1960), 288.
—— *Second American Party System: Jacksonian Era* (1966).
Ostrogorskii, Moisei I., *Democracy and the Party System in the United States* (1910).
Trimble, William, "Social Philosophy of Loco-Foco Democracy," *Am. Jour. Sociol.*, 26 (1921), 705.

See also 10.3 for biographies/writings of:

Brownson, Orestes A., 1803–1876
Cobb, Howell, 1815–1868
Crawford, William H., 1772–1834
Eaton, Margaret L. O'Neale, 1796–1879
Everett, Edward, 1794–1865
Floyd, John, 1783–1837

Hayne, Robert Y., 1791–1839
Hone, Philip, 1780–1851
Legaré, Hugh S., 1797–1843
Poinsett, Joel R., 1779–1851
Ritchie, Thomas, 1778–1854
Wise, Henry A., 1806–1876

42.6.2 Elections of 1832, 1836, and 1840

Alexander, Thomas B., "Presidential Campaign of 1840 in Tennessee," *Tenn. Hist. Quar.*, 1 (1942), 21.
Brown, Norman D., *Daniel Webster and the Politics of Availability* (1969). The 1836 election.
Chambers, William Nisbet, "Election of 1840," in Arthur M. Schlesinger, Jr., and Fred L. Israel, eds., *History of American Presidential Elections, 1789–1968.* Vol. I (1971).
Cole, Donald B., "Presidential Election of 1832 in New Hampshire," *Hist. N.H.*, 21 (1966), 32.
Gammon, Samuel R., *Presidential Campaign of 1832* (1922).
Gunderson, Robert G., *Log-Cabin Campaign* (1957). The 1840 Election.
Remini, Robert V., "Election of 1832," in Arthur M. Schlesinger, Jr. and Fred L. Israel, eds., *History of American Presidential Elections, 1789–1968.* Vol. I (1971).
Silbey, Joel H., "Election of 1836," in Arthur M. Schlesinger, Jr. et al., eds., *History of American Presidential Elections, 1789–1968.* Vol. I (1971).

42.6.3 State and Local Politics

41.6.3.1 New York City and Tammany

Chalmers, Leonard, "Fernando Wood and Tammany Hall: The First Phase," *N.Y. Hist. Soc. Quar.*, 52 (1968), 379.
Gatell, Frank O., "Money and Party in Jacksonian America: Quantitative Look at New York City's Men of Quality," *Pol. Sci. Quar.*, 82 (1967), 235.
Myers, Gustavus, *History of Tammany Hall* (1917).
Pratt, John W., "Governor Seward and New York City School Controversy, 1840–1842," *N.Y. Hist.*, 42 (1961), 351.
——— "Religious Conflict in Development of New York City Public School System," *Hist. Educ. Quar.*, 5 (1965), 110.

See also 10.3 for biographies/writings of:

Seward, William H., 1801–1872
Weed, Thurlow, 1797–1882
Wood, Fernando, 1812–1881

42.6.3.2 Anti-Rent War and Dorr Rebellion

Cheyney, E. P., *Anti-Rent Agitation in New York* (1887).
Christman, Henry, *Tin Horns and Calico* (1945).
Coleman, Peter J., *Transformation of Rhode Island, 1790–1860* (1963).
Ellis, David M., *Landlords and Farmers in Hudson-Mohawk Region* (1946).
Mowry, Arthur M., *Dorr War* (1901).

See also biographies/writings of:

Dorr, Thomas W., 1805–1854

42.6.3.3 Other Studies

Abernethy, Thomas P., *Frontier to Plantation in Tennessee* (1932).
Alexander, Thomas B., et al., "Alabama's Ante-Bellum Two-Party System," *Ala. Rev.*, 19 (1966), 243.

Ambler, Charles H., *Sectionalism in Virginia* (1910).

Benson, Lee, *Concept of Jacksonian Democracy: New York* (1961).

Bullock, C. J., "Finances and Financial Policy of Massachusetts, 1780–1905," Am. Econ. Assoc., *Publ.*, 8 (1907), 269.

Donovan, H. D. A., *The Barnburners: Study of Internal Movements in the Political History of New York State, 1830–1852* (1925).

Hailperin, Herman, "Pro-Jackson Sentiment in Pennsylvania," *Penn. Mag. Hist. Biog.*, 50 (1926), 193.

Hamilton, J. G. de Roulhac, *Party Politics in North Carolina, 1835–1860* (1916).

Hoffman, William S., *Andrew Jackson and North Carolina Politics* (1958).

Holt, Edgar Allan, *Party Politics in Ohio, 1840–1850* (1931).

Jack, Theodore H., *Sectionalism and Party Politics in Alabama, 1819–1842* (1919).

Klein, Philip S., *Pennsylvania Politics, 1817–1832* (1940).

Ludlum, David M., *Social Ferment in Vermont, 1791–1850* (1948).

Miles, Edwin A., *Jacksonian Democracy in Mississippi* (1960).

Miller, Douglas T., *Jacksonian Aristocracy: Class and Democracy in New York, 1830–1860* (1967).

Moore, Powell, "Polk: Tennessee Politician," *JSH*, 17 (1951), 493.

Morse, Jarvis M., *A Neglected Period of Connecticut's History, 1818–1850* (1933).

Norton, Clarence C., *Democratic Party in Ante-Bellum North Carolina, 1835–1861* (1930).

Pease, Theodore C., *The Frontier State, 1818–1848* (1918). Illinois.

Pierce, Bessie L., *Chicago* (2 vols., 1937–1940).

Pole, J. R., "Election Statistics in North Carolina to 1861," *JSH*, 24 (1958), 225.

Shugg, Roger W., *Origins of Class Struggle in Louisiana, 1840–1875* (1939).

Snyder, Charles M., *Jacksonian Heritage: Pennsylvania Politics, 1833–1848* (1958).

Stevens, Harry R., *Early Jackson Party in Ohio* (1957).

Sutton, Robert M., "Illinois' Year of Decision, 1837," Ill. State Hist. Soc., *Jour.*, 58 (1965), 34.

Thompson, Arthur W., *Jacksonian Democracy on the Florida Frontier* (1961).

Webster, Homer J., "History of Democratic Party Organization in the Northwest, 1820–1840," *Ohio State Archaeol. and Hist. Quar.*, 24 (1915), 1.

Williamson, Chilton, *Vermont in Quandary* (1949).

42.6.4 Workingmen's Parties and Movements

Arky, Louis H., "Mechanics' Union of Trade Associations and Foundation of Philadelphia Workingmen's Movement," *Penn. Mag. Hist. Biog.*, 76 (1952), 142.

Commons, John R., et al., *History of Labour in the United States* (4 vols., 1918–1935).

Dorfman, Joseph, "Jackson Wage-Earner Thesis," *AHR*, 54 (1949), 296.

Fox, Dixon Ryan, *Decline of Aristocracy in Politics of New York* (1919).

Hofstadter, Richard, "William Leggett, Spokesman of Jacksonian Democracy," *Pol. Sci. Quar.*, 58 (1943), 581.

Hugins, Walter E., *Jacksonian Democracy and the Working Class: The New York Workingmen's Movement, 1829–1837* (1960).

Pessen, Edward, "Did Labor Support Jackson?: The Boston Story," *Pol. Sci. Quar.*, 64 (1949), 262.

—— "Thomas Skidmore, Agrarian Reformer in Early American Labor Movement," *N.Y. Hist.*, 35 (1954), 280.

—— "Working Men's Party Revisited," *Labor Hist.*, 4 (1963), 203.

—— "Workingmen's Movement of the Jacksonian Era," *MVHR*, 43 (1956), 428.

Sullivan, William A., *The Industrial Worker in Pennsylvania, 1800–1840* (1955).

Zahler, H. S., *Eastern Workingmen and Land Policy, 1829–1862* (1941).

42.6.5 Rise of Whig Party

Carroll, Eber M., *Origins of the Whig Party* (1925).

Cole, Arthur C., *Whig Party in the South* (1914).

Hoffmann, William S., "Willie P. Mangum and the Whig Revival of the Doctrine of Instructions," *JSH*, 22 (1956), 338.

McWhiney, Grady, "Were the Whigs a Class Party in Alabama?" *JSH*, 23 (1957), 510.

Marshall, Lynn L., "Whig Party," *AHR*, 72 (1967), 445.

Mering, John V., *Whig Party in Missouri* (1967).

Moore, Powell, "Revolt Against Jackson in Tennessee, 1835–1836," *JSH*, 2 (1936), 335.

Mueller, H. R., *Whig Party in Pennsylvania* (1922).

Murray, Paul, *The Whig Party in Georgia, 1825–1853* (1948).

Poage, G. R., *Clay and the Whig Party* (1936).

Sellers, Charles G., Jr., "Who Were the Southern Whigs?" *AHR*, 59 (1954), 335.

Simms, H. H., *Rise of Whigs in Virginia, 1824–1840* (1929).

See also 10.3 for biographies/writings of:

Calhoun, John C., 1782–1850
Clay, Henry, 1777–1852
Palfrey, John G., 1796–1881
Thompson, Richard W., 1809–1900
Webster, Daniel, 1782–1852
Weed, Thurlow, 1797–1882
Wise, Henry A., 1806–1876

42.7 TANEY COURT

Frankfurter, Felix, *Commerce Clause under Marshall, Taney, and Waite* (1937).

Garvey, Gerald, "Constitutional Revolution of 1837 and Myth of Marshall's Monolity," *West. Pol. Quar.*, 18 (1965), 27.

Harris, Robert J., "Chief Justic Taney: Prophet of Reform and Reaction," *Vanderbilt Law Rev.*, 10 (1957), 227.

Longaker, Richard, "Andrew Jackson and the Judiciary," *Pol. Sci. Quar.*, 71 (1956), 341.

Newmyer, R. Kent, *The Supreme Court under Marshall and Taney* (1968).

Schmidhauser, John R., "Judicial Behavior and the Sectional Crisis of 1837–1860," *Jour. of Pol.*, 23 (1961), 615.

See also 10.3 for biographies/writings of:

Campbell, John Archibald, 1811–1889
Curtis, Benjamin Robbins, 1809–1874
Daniel, Peter V., 1784–1860
McLean, John, 1785–1861
Story, Joseph, 1779–1845
Taney, Roger B., 1777–1864

42.8 JACKSON ADMINISTRATION, 1829–1837

42.8.1 General

Eriksson, Erik M., "Official Newspaper Organs," *Tenn. Hist. Mag.*, 8 (1925), 231; 9 (1926), 37.

Govan, Thomas P., "John M. Berrien and the Administration of Andrew Jackson," *JSH*, 5 (1939), 447.

Longaker, Richard P., "Was Jackson's Kitchen Cabinet a Cabinet?" *MVHR*, 64 (1957), 94.

Morris, Richard B., "Andrew Jackson, Strikebreaker," *AHR*, 55 (1949), 54.

Smith, William Ernest, *Francis Preston Blair Family in Politics* (1933).
Somit, Albert, "New Papers: Sidelights upon the Jacksonian Administration," *MVHR*, 35 (1948), 91.

See also 10.3 for biographies/writings of:

Calhoun, John C., 1782–1850
Cass, Lewis, 1782–1866
Forsyth, John, 1780–1841
Jackson, Andrew, 1767–1845
Kendall, Amos, 1789–1869
Livingston, Edward, 1764–1836
Taney, Roger B., 1777–1864
Van Buren, Martin, 1782–1862
Woodbury, Levi, 1789–1851

42.8.2 Patronage

Aronson, Sidney H., *Status and Kinship in the Higher Civil Service: Standards of Selection in the Administrations of John Adams, Thomas Jefferson, and Andrew Jackson* (1964).
Eriksson, Erik M., "Federal Civil Service under Jackson," *MVHR*, 13 (1927), 517.
Fish, Carl R., *Civil Service and Patronage* (1904).
Smith, William Ernest, *Francis Preston Blair Family in Politics* (1933).

See also 10.3 for biographies/writings of:

Kendall, Amos, 1789–1869
Marcy, William L., 1786–1857

42.8.3 Second Bank of the United States and Bank War

Catterall, R. C. H., *Second Bank of the United States* (1903).
Gatell, Frank O., comp., *Jacksonians and Money Power, 1829–1840* (1967).
Gouge, William M., *Paper Money and Banking* (2 vols., 1833).
Hammond, Bray, *Banks and Politics in America from the Revolution to the Civil War* (1957).
Hoogenboom, Ari, and Herbert Ershkowitz, "Levi Woodbury's 'Intimate Memoranda' of the Jackson Administration," *Penn. Mag. Hist. Biog.*, 92 (1968), 507.
Macesich, George, "Sources of Monetary Disturbances, 1834–1845," *Jour. Econ. Hist.*, 20 (1960), 407.
Madeleine, M. G., *Monetary and Banking Theories of Jacksonian Democracy* (1942).
Marshall, Lynn L., "Authorship of Jackson's Bank Veto Message," *MVHR*, 50 (1963), 466.
Meerman, Jacob P., "Climax of Bank War: Biddle's Contraction, 1833–34," *Jour. Pol. Econ.*, 71 (1963), 378.
Miller, Harry E., *Banking Theories before 1860* (1927).
Redlich, Fritz L., *Molding of American Banking: Men and Ideals* (2 vols., 1947–1951).
Remini, Robert V., *Andrew Jackson and the Bank War* (1967).
Smith, Walter B., *Economic Aspects of the Second Bank of the United States* (1953).
Taylor, George R., ed., *Jackson Versus Biddle* (1949).
Wilburn, Jean A., *Biddle's Bank* (1967).

* * * * * * *

Griffin, A. P. C., *List of Works Relating to the First and Second Banks* (1908).

See also 10.3 for biographies/writings of:

Benton, Thomas Hart, 1782–1858
Biddle, Nicholas, 1786–1844
Taney, Roger B., 1777–1864

42.8.4 State Banking and "Pet Banks"

Gatell, Frank O., "Secretary Taney and Baltimore Pets," *Bus. Hist. Rev.*, 39 (1965), 205.
——— "Sober Second Thoughts on Van Buren, the Albany Regency, and the Wall Street Conspiracy," *JAH*, 53 (1966), 19.
——— "Spoils of Bank War: Political Bias in the Selection of Pet Banks," *AHR*, 70 (1964), 35.
Lebowitz, Michael A., "In Absence of Free Banks, What?," *CAAS Bull.*, 2 (1967), 73.
Scheiber, Harry N., "Pet Banks in Jacksonian Politics and Finance, 1833–1841," 23 (1963), 196.
Sharp, James Roger, *Jacksonians Versus Banks: Politics in the States after the Panic of 1837* (1970).

42.8.5 Tariff and Nullification

Bancroft, Frederic, *Calhoun and the South Carolina Nullification Movement* (1928).
Boucher, C. S., *Nullification Controversy in South Carolina* (1916).
Brown, Norman D., "Movement for Constitution and Union Party in 1833," *Mid-America*, 46 (1964), 147.
Eiselen, M. R., *Pennsylvania Protectionism* (1932).
Freehling, William W., ed., *Nullification Era: Documentary Record* (1967).
Freehling, William W., *Prelude to Civil War: Nullification Controversy in South Carolina, 1816–1836* (1966).
Houston, David F., *Critical Study of Nullification in South Carolina* (1896).
Miller, W. T., "Nullification in Georgia and South Carolina," *Ga. Hist. Quar.*, 14 (1930), 286.
Phillips, Ulrich B., *Georgia and State Rights* (1902).
Rogers, George C., Jr., "South Carolina Federalists and Nullification," *So. Car. Hist. Mag.*, 71 (1970), 17.
Russel, Robert R., *Economic Aspects of Southern Sectionalism* (1924).
Schaper, William A., *Sectionalism and Representation in South Carolina* (1901).
Sydnor, Charles S., *Development of Southern Sectionalism, 1819–1848* (1948).
Van Deusen, J. G., *Economic Bases of Disunion in South Carolina* (1928).
Wellington, R. G., "Tariff and Public Lands," Am. Hist. Assoc., *Report*, 1 (1911), 177.
White, Laura A., "Fate of Calhoun's Convention," *AHR*, 34 (1929), 757.
Wilson, Major L., "Three Concepts Involved in the Nullification Controversy," *JSH*, 33 (1967), 331.

*   *   *   *   *   *   *

U. S. Library of Congress, *Tariff in Its Relation to the South* (1929).

See also 10.3 for biographies/writings of:

Calhoun, John C., 1782–1850
Clay, Henry, 1777–1852
Hayne, Robert Y., 1791–1839
Jackson, Andrew, 1767–1845
Livingston, Edward, 1764–1836
Petigru, James L., 1789–1863
Poinsett, Joel R., 1779–1851
Quitman, John A., 1798–1858

Van Buren, Martin, 1782–1862
Webster, Daniel, 1782–1852
Wright, Silas, 1795–1847

42.8.6 Indian Removal

Abel, A. H., "History of Events Resulting in Indian Consolidation West of the Mississippi," Am. Hist. Assoc., *Report*, 1 (1906), 233.
Foreman, Grant, *Indian Removal: Emigration of the Five Civilized Tribes* (1932).
Malone, H. T., *Cherokees of the Old South* (1956).
Phillips, Ulrich B., *Georgia and State Rights* (1902).

See also 10.3 for biographies/writings of:

Black Hawk, 1767–1838

42.9 PANIC OF 1837 AND STATE DEBTS

Bogart, E. L., *Financial History of Ohio* (1912).
———— *Internal Improvements and State Debt in Ohio* (1924).
Bourne, E. G., *Surplus Revenue of 1837* (1885).
McGrane, R. C., *Panic of 1837* (1924).
Rezneck, Samuel, "Social History of an American Depression, 1837–1843," *AHR*, 40 (1935), 662.
Scott, W. A., *Repudiation of State Debts* (1893).
Smith, Walter B., and Arthur H. Cole, *Fluctuations in American Business, 1790–1860* (1935).
Timberlake, Richard H., Jr., "Species Circular and Distribution of Surplus," *Jour. Pol. Econ.*, 68 (1960), 109.
Warren, Charles, *Bankruptcy in United States History* (1935).

See also 10.3 for biographies/writings of:

Mason, Stevens T., 1811–1843

42.10 VAN BUREN ADMINISTRATION, 1837–1841

Curtis, James C., *Fox at Bay: Van Buren and the Presidency, 1837–1841* (1970).
Kinley, David, *Independent Treasury* (1910).
Taus, Esther R., *Central Banking Functions of the United States Treasury, 1789–1941* (1943).

See also 10.3 for biographies/writings of:

Forsyth, John, 1780–1841
Grundy, Felix, 1777–1840
Johnson, Richard Mentor, 1780–1850
Kendall, Amos, 1789–1869
Paulding, James K., 1778–1860
Poinsett, Joel R., 1779–1851
Van Buren, Martin, 1782–1862
Woodbury, Levi, 1789–1851
Wright, Silas, 1795–1847

43 Manifest Destiny

43.1 GENERAL

Billington, Ray A., *Far Western Frontier, 1830–1860* (1956).
De Voto, Bernard, *Year of Decision* (1943).
Goetzmann, William H., *When the Eagle Screamed* (1966).
Graebner, Norman A., *Empire on Pacific* (1955).
——— comp., *Manifest Destiny* (1968).
Horsman, Reginald, "American Indian Policy and Origins of Manifest Destiny," *Birmingham Univ. Hist. Jour.*, 11 (1968), 128.
Merk, Frederick and Lois B., *Manifest Destiny and Mission in American History* (1963).
——— *The Monroe Doctrine and American Expansionism, 1843–1849* (1966).
Perkins, Dexter, *Monroe Doctrine, 1826–1867* (1933).
Silbey, Joel H., *Shrine of Party: Congressional Voting Behavior, 1841–1852* (1967).
——— ed., *Transformation of American Politics, 1840–1860* (1967).
Weinberg, Albert K., *Manifest Destiny* (1935).

See also 10.3 for biographies/writings of:

Adams, Charles Francis, 1807–1886
Adams, John Quincy, 1767–1848
Bancroft, George, 1800–1891
Benton, Thomas Hart, 1782–1858
Buchanan, James, 1791–1868
Calhoun, John C., 1782–1850
Clay, Henry, 1777–1852
Crittenden, John J., 1787–1863
Davis, Jefferson, 1808–1889
Frémont, John C., 1813–1890
Grant, Ulysses S., 1822–1885
Lee, Robert E., 1807–1870
Lincoln, Abraham, 1809–1865
Pierce, Franklin, 1804–1869
Polk, James K., 1795–1849
Rhett, Robert B., 1800–1876
Scott, Winfield, 1786–1866
Sherman, William T., 1820–1891
Stevens, Thaddeus, 1792–1868
Sumner, Charles, 1811–1874
Taylor, Zachary, 1784–1850
Toombs, Robert, 1810–1885
Webster, Daniel, 1782–1852
Winthrop, Robert C., 1809–1894

43.2 HARRISON AND TYLER ADMINISTRATIONS, 1841–1845

Lambert, Oscar D., *Presidential Politics in the United States, 1841–1844* (1936).
McPherson, James M., "Joshua Leavitt and Antislavery Insurgency in the Whig Party, 1839–1942," *Jour. Negro Hist.*, 48 (1963), 177.
Morgan, Robert J., *A Whig Embattled: Presidency under John Tyler* (1954).

See also 10.3 for biographies/writings of:

Bell, John, 1797–1869
Calhoun, John C., 1782–1850
Crittenden, John J., 1787–1863
Harrison, William Henry, 1773–1841
Legaré, Hugh S., 1797–1843
McLean, John, 1785–1861
Tyler, John, 1790–1862
Upshur, Abel P., 1791–1844
Webster, Daniel, 1782–1852

43.3 ELECTION OF 1844

Miles, Edwin A., " 'Fifty-Four Forty or Fight,' " *MVHR*, 44 (1957), 291.
Sellers, Charles G., Jr., "Election of 1844," in Arthur M. Schlesinger, Jr. and Fred L. Israel, eds., *History of American Presidential Elections, 1789–1968.* Vol. I (1971).

See also 10.3 for biographies/writings of:

Birney, James G., 1792–1857
Clay, Henry, 1777–1852
King, Thomas B., 1800–1864
Polk, James K., 1795–1849
Walker, Robert J., 1801–1869

43.4 POLK ADMINISTRATION, 1845–1849

Graebner, Norman A., "James Polk," in Morton Borden, ed., *America's Ten Greatest Presidents* (1961).
———— "James K. Polk: Federal Patronage," *MVHR*, 38 (1952), 613.
McCoy, Charles A., *Polk and the Presidency* (1960).

*   *   *   *   *   *   *

Horn, James J., "Historical Interpretations: James K. Polk," *No. Car. Hist. Rev.*, 42 (1965), 454.
Merk, Frederick, "Presidential Fevers," *MVHR*, 47 (1960), 3.

See also 10.3 for biographies/writings of:

Bancroft, George, 1800–1891
Buchanan, James, 1791–1868
Larkin, Thomas O., 1802–1858
Marcy, William L., 1786–1857
Polk, James K., 1795–1849
Walker, Robert J., 1801–1869

43.5 OREGON QUESTION

Howay, Frederick W., et al., *British Columbia and the United States* (1942).
McCabe, James O., *San Juan Water Boundary Question* (1964).
Merk, Frederick, *Albert Gallatin and the Oregon Problem: A Study in Anglo-American Diplomacy* (1950).
—— *The Oregon Question: Essays in Anglo-American Diplomacy and Politics* (1967).
Pratt, Julius W., "James K. Polk and John Bull," *Can. Hist. Rev.*, 24 (1943), 341.
Van Alstyne, R. W., "International Rivalries in the Pacific Northwest," *Ore. Hist. Quar.*, 46 (1945), 185.
Winther, Oscar O., "British in Oregon Country," *Pac. Northw. Quar.*, 58 (1967), 179.

43.6 PREWAR RELATIONS WITH MEXICO

Cox, Isaac J., "Louisiana-Texas Frontier," Tex. State Hist. Assoc., *Quar.*, 10 (1907), 1.
Manning, William R., *Early Diplomatic Relations between the United States and Mexico* (1916).
Rives, George L., *United States and Mexico* (2 vols., 1913).

43.7 TEXAS QUESTION

43.7.1 Colonization

Anderson, John Q., ed., *Tales of Frontier Texas, 1830–1860* (1966).
Bancroft, Hubert H., *North Mexican States and Texas* (2 vols.). Vols. 10 and 11 of *History of the Pacific States of North America* (34 vols., 1883–1889).
Barker, Eugene C., *Mexico and Texas, 1821–35* (1928).
Biesele, R. L., *German Settlements in Texas* (1930).
Bugbee, L. G., "Difficulties of a Texas Empresario," So. Hist. Assoc., *Publ.*, 3 (1899), 95.
Dewees, William B., *Letters from an Early Settler of Texas* (1854).
Lathrop, B. F., *Migration into East Texas* (1949).
Rather, E. Z., "Influence of Slavery in Colonization of Texas," *MVHR*, 11 (1924), 3.
Ross, Alexander, *Red River Settlement* (1856).

43.7.2 Revolution

Ashford, Gerald, "Jacksonian Liberalism and Spanish Law in Early Texas," *Southw. Hist. Quar.*, 57 (1953), 1.
Barker, Eugene C., "Land Speculation as Cause of Texas Revolution," Tex. State Hist. Assoc., *Quar.*, 10 (1906), 76.
—— "President Jackson and the Texas Revolution," *AHR*, 12 (1907), 788.
Binkley, William C., *Expansionist Movement in Texas* (1925).
—— ed., *Official Correspondence of Texas Revolution, 1835–36* (1936).
Binkley, William C., *Texas Revolution* (1925).
Callcott, Wilfrid H., *Santa Anna* (1936).
Castañeda, C. E., ed., *Mexican Side of Texas Revolution* (1928).
Dixon, Sam H., and Louis W. Kemp, *Heroes of San Jacinto* (1932).
Leclerc, Frédéric, *Texas and Its Revolution* (1840).
Lowrie, Samuel H., *Culture Conflict in Texas, 1821–1835* (1932).
Morton, Ohland, *Terán and Texas: Texas-Mexican Relations* (1948).
Nance, Joseph M., *After San Jacinto: Texas-Mexican Frontier, 1836–1841* (1963).

———— *Attack and Counter-Attack: Texas-Mexican Frontier, 1842* (1964).
Pierce, Gerald S., *Texas under Arms, 1836–1846* (1969).
Rather, E. Z., *Recognition of Republic of Texas* (1911).
Stephenson, Nathaniel W., *Texas and the Mexican War* (1921).
Warren, Harris G., *Sword Was Their Passport: Filibustering in the Mexican Revolution* (1943).
Williams, Elgin, *Animating Pursuits of Speculation: Land Traffic in Annexation of Texas* (1949).

43.7.3 Republic of Texas

43.7.3.1 General

Hill, Jim D., *Texas Navy* (1937).
Hogan, William R., *Texas Republic* (1946).
Muir, Andrew F., ed., *Texas in 1837: Contemporary Narrative* (1958).
Schmitz, J. W., *Texas Statecraft* (1941).
Siegel, Stanley, *Political History of Texas Republic, 1836–1845* (1956).

See also 10.3 for biographies/writings of:

Austin, Stephen F., 1793–1836
Burnet, David G., 1788–1870
Houston, Sam, 1793–1863
Lamar, Mirabeau B., 1798–1859

43.7.3.2 Foreign Influences

Adams, Ephraim Douglass, *British Correspondence Concerning Texas, 1838–1846* (1918).
———— *British Interests in Texas* (1910).
Chase, M. K., *Négociations de la république du Texas en Europe* (1932).
Garrison, George P., ed., *Texas Diplomatic Correspondence* (3 vols., 1908–1911).
Taylor, Virginia H., *Franco-Texan Land Company* (1969).

43.7.4 Annexation

Barker, Eugene C., "Annexation of Texas," *Southw. Hist. Quar.*, 50 (1946), 49.
Brauer, Kinley J., *Cotton versus Conscience: Massachusetts Whig Politics and Southwestern Expansion, 1843–1848* (1967).
Hamilton, Holman, "Texas Bonds and Northern Profits," *MVHR*, 43 (1957), 579.
Phillips, Ulrich B., ed., "Correspondence of Toombs, Stephens, and Cobb," Am. Hist. Assoc., *Report*, 2 (1911). Entire issue.
Smith, Justin H., *Annexation of Texas* (1911).
Winston, J. E., "Annexation of Texas and Mississippi Democrats," *Southw. Hist. Quar.*, 25 (1921), 1.

See also 10.3 for biographies/writings of:

Adams, John Quincy, 1767–1848
Austin, Stephen F., 1793–1836
Benton, Thomas Hart, 1782–1858
Buchanan, James, 1791–1868
Calhoun, John C., 1782–1850
Cass, Lewis, 1782–1866
Clay, Henry, 1777–1852
Giddings, Joshua R., 1795–1864
Houston, Sam, 1793–1863
Jackson, Andrew, 1767–1845

Poore, Benjamin P., 1820–1887
Rhett, Robert B., 1800–1876
Tyler, John, 1790–1862
Van Buren, Martin, 1782–1862
Webster, Daniel, 1782–1852
Woodbury, Levi, 1789–1851

43.8 WAR WITH MEXICO

43.8.1 General

Bill, A. H., *Rehearsal for Conflict* (1947).
Callcott, Wilfrid H., *Santa Anna* (1936).
Chidsey, Donald B., *War with Mexico* (1968).
Dufour, Charles L., *The Mexican War: A Compact History* (1968).
Henry, Robert S., *Story of the Mexican War* (1950).
Nichols, Edward J., *Zach Taylor's Little Army* (1963).
Rives, George L., *The United States and Mexico* (2 vols., 1913).
Ruiz, Ramón Eduardo, ed., *Mexican War: Was It Manifest Destiny?* (1963).
Singletary, Otis A., *Mexican War* (1960).
Smith, Justin H., *War with Mexico* (2 vols., 1919).

See also 10.3 for biographies/writings of:

Frémont, John Charles, 1813–1890
Kearney, Stephen Watts, 1794–1848
Marcy, William L., 1786–1857
Scott, Winfield, 1786–1866
Taylor, Zachary, 1784–1850
Walker, Robert J., 1801–1869
Wilmot, David, 1814–1868
Worth, William J., 1794–1849

43.8.2 Personal Accounts

Alessio Robles, Vito, *Coahuila y Texas desde la independencia hasta Guadalupe Hidalgo* (2 vols., 1945–1946).
Beauregard, Pierre G. T., *With Beauregard in Mexico: Mexican War Reminiscences*, T. Harry Williams, ed., (1956).
Calderón de la Barca, Frances, *Life in Mexico* (1843).
McClellan, George B., *Mexican War Diary*, W. S. Myers, ed. (1917).
Phillips, Ulrich B., ed., "Correspondence of Toombs, Stephens and Cobb," Am. Hist. Assoc., *Report*, 2 (1911). Entire issue.
Roa Bárcena, J. M., *Recuerdos de la invasion norteamericana* (3 vols., 1947).
Santa Anna, A. L. de, "Letters Relating to War," J. H. Smith, ed., Am. Hist. Assoc., *Report*, (1917), 355.
Sedgwick, John, *Correspondence* (2 vols., 1902–1903).
Smith, Ephraim K., *To Mexico with Scott: Letters of Captain E. Kirby Smith to His Wife* (1917).
Smith, George W., and Charles Judah, eds., *Chronicles of Gringos: U.S. Army in the Mexican War, 1846–1848* (1968).

43.8.3 Special Topics

Bauer, K. Jack, "Veracruz Expedition of 1847," *Mil. Affairs*, 20 (1956), 162.
Ellsworth, C. S., "American Churches and the Mexican War," *AHR*, 45 (1940), 301.
Golder, Frank A., et al., eds., *March of the Mormon Battalion* (1928).

Merk, Frederick, "Dissent in the Mexican War," in Samuel E. Morison,
    Frederick Merk, and Frank Freidel, *Dissent in Three American Wars* (1970).
Price, Glenn W., *Origins of War with Mexico: Polk-Stockton Intrigue* (1967).
Stenberg, R. R., "Failure of Polk's Mexican War Intrigue," *Pac. Hist. Rev.*, 4
    (1935), 39.
Webb, Walter P., *Texas Rangers* (2nd ed., 1965).

43.8.4 Treaty of Guadalupe Hidalgo and Gadsden Purchase

Fuller, John D. P., *Movement for Acquisition of All Mexico* (1936).
Garber, Paul N., *Gadsden Treaty* (1923).
Sears, Louis M., "Nicholas P. Trist," *MVHR*, 11 (1924), 85.

* * * * * * *

Esquenazi-Mayo, Roberto, "Historiografía de la guerra entre Mexico y los Es-
    tados Unidos," *Dusquesne Hisp. Rev.*, 1 (Fall 1962), 33; 1 (Winter 1962), 7.
Harstad, Peter T., and Richard W. Resh, "Causes of the Mexican War," *Ariz.
    and West*, 6 (1964), 289.

43.9 CALIFORNIA

Adams, Ephraim Douglass, "English Interest in California," *AHR*, 14 (1909),
    744.
Cutts, James M., *Conquest of California and New Mexico in the Years 1846 & 1847*
    (1847).
Downey, Joseph T., *Cruise of the Portsmouth, 1845–1847: Sailor's View of the
    Naval Conquest of California* (1958).
Gates, Paul W., "California's Embattled Settlers," *Calif. Hist. Soc., Quar.*, 41
    (1962), 99.
Grivas, Theodore, *Military Governments in California, 1846–1850* (1963).
Hawgood, John A., "John C. Frémont and Bear Flag Revolution: Reappraisal,"
    So. Calif. Quar., 44 (1962), 67.
Jones, Oakah L., Jr., "Pacific Squadron and Conquest of California, 1846–1847,"
    Jour. of West, 5 (1966), 187.
Nasatir, Abraham P., *French Activities in California* (1945).
——— "Rivalry for California and the Establishment of British Consulate," *Calif.
    Hist. Soc., Quar.*, 46 (1967), 53.
Stenberg, R. R., "Polk and Frémont," *Pac. Hist. Rev.*, 7 (1938), 211.
Tays, George, "Frémont Had No Secret Instructions," *Pac. Hist. Rev.*, 9 (1940),
    157.

See also 10.3 for biographies/writings of:

Frémont, John C., 1813–1890
Halleck, Henry W., 1815–1872
Larkin, Thomas O., 1802–1858
Sutter, John A., 1803–1880

43.10 EXPANSION OF SLAVERY INTO TERRITORIES

43.10.1 General

Auer, John J., ed., *Antislavery and Disunion, 1858–1861* (1963).
Berwanger, Eugene H., *Frontier against Slavery: Western Anti-Negro Prejudice*
    (1967).
Cole, Arthur C., *Whig Party in the South* (1913).

Ganaway, L. M., *New Mexico and Sectional Controversy, 1846–1861* (1944).
Lynch, William O., "Anti-Slavery Tendencies of the Democratic Party," *MVHR*, 11 (1924), 319.
Ramsdell, C. W., "Natural Limits of Slavery Expansion," *MVHR*, 16 (1929), 151.
Smith, Theodore C., *Liberty and Free Soil Parties* (1897).
—— *Parties and Slavery* (1906).

43.10.2 Wilmot Proviso

Morrison, Chaplain W., *Democratic Politics and Sectionalism: Wilmot Proviso Controversy* (1967).
Persinger, C. E., "Bargain of 1844 and Wilmot Proviso," Am. Hist. Assoc., *Report*, 1 (1911), 189.
Silbey, Joel H., "Slavery-Extension Controversy and Illinois Congressmen, 1846–50," Ill. State Hist. Soc., *Jour.*, 58 (1965), 378.
Stenberg, R. R., "Motivation of the Wilmot Proviso," *MVHR*, 18 (1932), 535.

See also 10.3 for biographies/writings of:

Wilmot, David, 1814–1868

43.11 ELECTION OF 1848

Hamilton, Holman, "Election of 1848," in Arthur M. Schlesinger, Jr. and Fred L. Israel, eds., *History of American Presidential Elections, 1789–1968*. Vol. II (1971).
Rayback, Joseph G., *Free Soil: Election of 1848* (1971).
Stevens, Walter W., "Lewis Cass and the Presidency," *Mich. Hist.*, 49 (1965), 123.

See also 10.3 for biographies/writings of:

Cass, Lewis, 1782–1866
Cobb, Howell, 1815–1868
Crittenden, John J., 1787–1863
Everett, Edward, 1794–1865
Fillmore, Millard, 1800–1874
Johnson, Reverdy, 1796–1876
Kennedy, John P., 1795–1870
Taylor, Zachary, 1784–1850
Van Buren, Martin, 1782–1862
Webster, Daniel, 1782–1852
Winthrop, Robert C., 1809–1894

43.12 FOREIGN RELATIONS

43.12.1 General

Blumenthal, Henry, *Reappraisal of Franco-American Relations, 1830–1871* (1959).
Cline, M. A., *American Attitude toward the Greek War of Independence* (1930).
Curti, Merle E., "Young America," *AHR*, 32 (1926), 34.
Finnie, David H., *Pioneers East: The Early American Experience in the Middle East* (1967).
Goetzmann, William H., *When the Eagle Screamed* (1966).
Larrabee, Stephen A., *Hellas Observed: American Experience of Greece, 1775–1865* (1957).

Lerski, Jerzy J., *Polish Chapter in Jacksonian America* (1958).

McLemore, Richard A., *Franco-American Diplomatic Relations: 1816–1836* (1941).

Perkins, Dexter, *Monroe Doctrine, 1826–1867* (1933).

Rémond, René, *Les États-Unis devant l'opinion française, 1815–1852* (2 vols., 1962).

Rodriguez, Mario, "'Prometheus' and the Clayton-Bulwer Treaty," *Jour. Mod. Hist.*, 36 (1964), 260.

Sioussat, St. George L., "James Buchanan," in Samuel F. Bemis, ed., *American Secretaries of State and Their Diplomacy*, vol. V (1928).

Somkin, Fred, *Unquiet Eagle* (1967).

White, Elizabeth B., *American Opinion of France* (1927).

Williams, M. W., "John Middleton Clayton," in Samuel F. Bemis, ed., *American Secretaries of State and Their Diplomacy*, vol. VI (1928).

43.12.2 Canada and Northeast Boundary Dispute

Arthur, George, *Papers*, Charles Sanderson, ed. (1947).

Brebner, John B., *North Atlantic Triangle* (1945).

Burrage, Henry S., *Maine in the Northeastern Boundary Controversy* (1919).

Callahan, J. M., *American Foreign Policy in Canadian Relations* (1937).

———— *Neutrality of American Lakes* (1898).

Corey, A. B., *Crisis of 1830–1842 in Canadian-American Relations* (1941).

Craig, Gerald M., *Upper Canada, 1784–1841* (1963).

Ganong, W. F., *Boundaries of New Brunswick* (1901).

Jones, Wilbur D., *Lord Aberdeen and the Americas* (1958).

Keenleyside, H. L., and G. S. Brown, *Canada and the United States* (1952).

LeDuc, Thomas, "Maine Frontier," *AHR*, 53 (1947), 30.

Masters, Donald C., *Reciprocity Treaty of 1854* (1937).

Officer, Lawrence H., and Lawrence B. Smith, "Canadian-American Reciprocity Treaty of 1855 to 1866," *Jour. Econ. Hist.*, 28 (1968), 598.

Shippee, L. B., *Canadian-American Relations, 1849–1874* (1939).

Shortridge, Wilson P., "Canadian American Frontier," *Can. Hist. Rev.*, 7 (1926), 16.

Warner, Donald F., *The Idea of Continental Union: Annexation of Canada to United States, 1849–1893* (1960).

Wise, Sydney F., "Through the Lace Curtain: Canadian Views of American Democracy in Pre-Civil War Period," *CAAS Bull.*, 2 (1968), 46.

43.12.3 Webster-Ashburton Treaty

Baldwin, J. R., "Ashburton-Webster Settlement," Can. Hist. Assoc., *Ann. Rep.*, (1938), 121.

Current, Richard N., "Webster's Propaganda and the Ashburton Treaty," *MVHR*, 34 (1947), 187.

Le Duc, Thomas, "Webster-Ashburton Treaty and Minnesota Iron Ranges," *JAH*, 51 (1964), 476.

Watt, Alastair, "Alexander McLeod," *Can. Hist. Rev.*, 12 (1931), 145.

43.12.4 East Asia

43.12.4.1 General

Griffin, Eldon, *Clippers and Consuls: American Consular and Commercial Relations with Eastern Asia, 1845–1860* (1938).

Phillips, Clifton J., *Protestant America and the Pagan World: The First Half Century of the American Board of Commissioners for Foreign Missions, 1810–1860* (1969).

43.12.4.2 China

Curti, Merle E., and John Stalker, "American Image in China, 1840–1900," Am. Philos. Soc., *Proc.*, 96 (1952), 663.

Dulles, Foster R., *Old China Trade* (1930).
Fairbank, John K., *Trade and Diplomacy on the China Coast: The Opening of the Treaty Ports, 1842–1854* (2 vols., 1953).
Lockwood, Stephen C., *Augustine Heard and Company, 1858–1862: American Merchants in China on the Eve of the Opening of the Yangtze* (1971).
Swisher, Earl, *China's Management of American Barbarians: Sino-American Relations, 1841–1861, with Documents* (1952).
Tong, Te-kong, *United States Diplomacy in China, 1844–1860* (1964).

See also 10.3 for biographies/writings of:

Cushing, Caleb, 1800–1879

43.12.4.3 Japan and Perry Expedition

Barr, Pat, *The Coming of the Barbarians: The Opening of Japan to the West, 1853–1870* (1967).
Cole, Allen B., ed., *Scientist with Perry* (1947).
Hawks, F. L., *Narrative of the Expedition to China Seas and Japan* (1850; repr., 1967).
Heusken, Henry C., *Japan Journal, 1855–1861*, Jeanette C. van der Corput and Robert A. Wilson, eds. (1964).
Neumann, William L., "Religion, Morality, and Freedom: Perry Expedition," *Pac. Hist. Rev.*, 23 (1954), 247.
Perry, Matthew C., *Japan Expedition, 1852–1854*, Roger Pineau, ed. (1969).
——— *Narrative of Expedition of an American Squadron to China Seas and Japan, 1852–1854* (3 vols., 1856).
Preble, George H., *Opening of Japan: Diary, 1853–1856*, Boleslaw Szczshiak, ed. (1962).
Sakamaki, Shunzo, "Japan and the United States, 1790–1853," Asiatic Soc. of Japan, *Trans.*, 18, 2 ser. (1939).
Statler, Oliver, *The Shimoda Story* (1969).
Walworth, Arthur, *Black Ships off Japan* (1946).

See also 10.3 for biographies/writings of:

Harris, Townsend, 1804–1878
Perry, Matthew C., 1794–1858

43.12.5 Europe

Curti, Merle E., *Austria and the United States* (1926).
Hildt, J. C., *Early Diplomatic Negotiations with Russia* (1906).
Szilassy, Sandor, "America and the Hungarian Revolution of 1848–1849," *Slavonic and East Eur. Rev.*, 44 (1966), 180.
Thomas, Benjamin P., *Russo-American Relations, 1815–1867* (1930).
Van Alstyne, Richard W., ed., "Anglo-American Relations, 1853–1857," *AHR*, 42 (1937), 491.

43.12.6 Cuba

Broussard, Ray F., "John Quitman and Lopez Expeditions of 1851–52," *Jour. Miss. Hist.*, 28 (1966), 103.
Caldwell, R. G., *Lopez Expeditions* (1915).
Ettinger, A. A., *Mission to Spain of Pierre Soulé* (1932).
Henderson, G. B., "Southern Designs on Cuba," *JSH*, 3 (1939), 371.
Rauch, Basil, *American Interests in Cuba* (1948).

See also 10.3 for biographies/writings of:

Quitman, John A., 1798–1858

44   Old South, Slavery, and Abolitionism

44.1 GENERAL

Abernethy, Thomas P., *South in the New Nation, 1789–1815* (1961).
Cotterill, R. S., *Old South* (1939).
Craven, Avery O., *Growth of Southern Nationalism, 1848–1861* (1953).
Dodd, William E., *Cotton Kingdom* (1921).
—— *Old South* (1937).
Eaton, Clement, *Growth of Southern Civilization, 1790–1860* (1961).
—— *History of the Old South* (2nd ed., 1966).
Sydnor, Charles S., *Development of Southern Sectionalism 1819–1848* (1948).

*   *   *   *   *   *   *

Link, Arthur S., and Rembert W. Patrick, eds., *Writing Southern History: Essays in Historiography in Honor of Fletcher M. Green* (1965).
Stephenson, W. H., *South Lives in History* (1955).

44.2 SPECIAL TOPICS

Bertelson, David, *Lazy South* (1967).
Carpenter, Jesse T., *The South as a Conscious Minority* (1930).
Cash, Wilbur J., *The Mind of the South* (1941).
Eaton, Clement, *Freedom-of-Thought Struggle in the Old South* (rev. ed., 1964).
—— *The Mind of the Old South* (rev. ed., 1967).
—— "Mob Violence in the Old South," *MVHR*, 29 (1942), 351.
Franklin, John Hope, *The Militant South, 1800–1861* (1956).
Fredrickson, George M., "Introduction," in Hinton Rowan Helper, *The Impending Crisis of the South: How to Meet It* (1968).
Genovese, Eugene D., *The World the Slaveholders Made: Two Essays in Interpretation* (1969).
Govan, Thomas P., "Was the Old South Different?" *JSH*, 21 (1955), 447.
Green, Fletcher M., "Democracy in the Old South," *JSH*, 12 (1946), 3.
Harris, George W., *High Times and Hard Times*, M. Thomas Inge, ed. (1967).
Johnson, Thomas C., *Scientific Interests in the Old South* (1936).
Kendrick, Benjamin B., and A. M. Arnett, *The South Looks at Its Past* (1935).
Osterweis, R. G., *Romanticism and Nationalism in the Old South* (1949).
Phillips, Ulrich B., "The Central Theme of Southern History," *AHR*, 34 (1928), 30.
Potter, David M., *The South and Sectional Conflict* (1968).
Sellers, Charles G., ed., *The Southerner as American* (1960).
Simkins, Francis B., *The Everlasting South* (1963).
Strother, David H., *Old South Illustrated*, Cecil D. Eby, ed. (1959).

Taylor, William R., *Cavalier and Yankee: Old South and American National Character* (1961).
Thorpe, Earl E., *Eros and Freedom in Southern Life and Thought* (1967).
Vandiver, Frank E., ed., *The Idea of the South: Pursuit of a Central Theme* (1964).
Williams, T. Harry, *Romance and Realism in Southern Politics* (1961).

44.3 STATE AND LOCAL STUDIES

Baldwin, J. G., *Flush Times of Alabama* (1853).
Boyd, Minnie C., *Alabama in the Fifties* (1931).
James, D. Clayton, *Antebellum Natchez* (1968).
Johnson, Guion G., *Ante-Bellum North Carolina* (1937).
Page, Thomas N., *Social Life in Old Virginia before War* (1897).
Ripley, E. M., *Social Life in Old New Orleans* (1912).

44.4 SOUTHERN POLITICS

44.4.1 Growth of Southern Nationalism

Carpenter, J. T., *South as Conscious Minority* (1930).
Cole, Arthur C., *Whig Party in South* (1913).
Graebner, Norman A., "1848: Southern Politics," *Historian*, 25 (1962), 14.
Green, Fletcher M., *Constitutional Development in the South Atlantic States, 1776–1860* (1930).
Sellers, Charles G., Jr., "Who Were the Southern Whigs?," *AHR*, 59 (1954), 335.
Wooster, Ralph A., *People in Power: Courthouse and Statehouse in the Lower South, 1850–1860* (1969).

See also 10.3 for biographies/writings of:

Adams, Charles F., 1807–1886
Bates, Edward, 1793–1869
Bigelow, John, 1817–1911
Birney, James G., 1792–1857
Browning, Orville H., 1806–1881
Buchanan, James, 1791–1868
Call, Richard K., 1791–1862
Chase, Salmon P., 1808–1873
Crittenden, John J., 1787–1863
Cushing, Caleb, 1800–1879
Douglas, Stephen A., 1813–1861
Frémont, John C., 1813–1890
Graham, William A., 1804–1875
Greeley, Horace, 1811–1872
Hammond, James H., 1807–1864
Hunter, Robert M. T., 1809–1887
Johnson, Herschel V., 1812–1880
Lincoln, Abraham, 1809–1865
Mangum, Willie P., 1792–1861
Parker, Theodore, 1810–1860
Pierce, Franklin, 1804–1869
Poore, Benjamin P., 1820–1887
Quitman, John A., 1798–1858
Schurz, Carl, 1829–1906
Seward, William H., 1801–1872
Sherman, John, 1823–1900
Stephens, Alexander H., 1812–1883
Stevens, Thaddeus, 1792–1868

Toombs, Robert, 1810–1885
Weed, Thurlow, 1797–1882
Wilmot, David, 1814–1868
Winthrop, Robert C., 1809–1894
Zollicoffer, Felix K., 1812–1862

44.4.2 State Studies

Alexander, Thomas B., et al., "Alabama Whigs," *Ala. Rev.*, 16 (1963), 5.
—— "Basis of Alabama's Ante-Bellum Two-Party System," *Ala. Rev.*, 19 (1966), 243.
Ambler, Charles H., *Sectionalism in Virginia, 1776–1861* (1910).
Campbell, Mary E. R., *Attitude of Tennesseans toward the Union, 1847–1861* (1961).
Lacy, Eric R., *Vanquished Volunteers: East Tennessee Sectionalism from Statehood to Secession* (1965).
McMillan, Malcolm C., *Constitutional Development in Alabama, 1798–1901* (1955).
McWhiney, Grady, "Were the Whigs a Class Party in Alabama?," *JSH*, 23 (1957), 510.
Mering, John V., *Whig Party in Missouri* (1967).
Montgomery, Horace, *Cracker Parties* (1950).
Murray, Paul, *Whig Party in Georgia, 1825–1853* (1948).
Norton, Clarence C., *The Democratic Party in Ante-Bellum North Carolina, 1835–1861* (1930).
Porter, Albert O., *County Government in Virginia, 1607–1904* (1947).
Rainwater, Percy L., *Mississippi: Storm Center of Secession, 1856–1861* (1938).
Schaper, William A., *Sectionalism and Representation in South Carolina* (1901).
Schultz, Harold S., *Nationalism and Sectionalism in South Carolina, 1852–1860* (1950).
Shanks, Henry T., *Secession Movement in Virginia, 1847–1861* (1934).
Shugg, Roger W., *Origins of Class Struggle in Louisiana: A Social History of White Farmers and Laborers during Slavery and After, 1840–1875* (1939).
Skelton, Lynda W., "States Rights Movement in Georgia, 1825–1850," *Ga. Hist. Quar.*, 50 (1966), 391.

44.5 SOUTHERN ECONOMY

44.5.1 General

Jordan, Weymouth T., *Rebels in the Making: Planters' Conventions and Southern Propaganda* (1958).
Kettell, Thomas P., *Southern Wealth and Northern Profits* (1860); Fletcher M. Green, ed. (1965).
Russel, Robert R., *Economic Aspects of Southern Sectionalism, 1840–1861* (1924).

See also 44.6.8, Economics of Slavery.

44.5.2 Manufacturing and Commerce

Bruce, Kathleen, *Virginia Iron Manufacture in the Slave Era* (1930).
Clark, John G., "Antebellum Grain Trade of New Orleans," *Agric. Hist.*, 38 (1964), 131.
Collins, Herbert, "Southern Industrial Gospel before 1860," *JSH*, 12 (1964), 386.
Cotterill, R. S., "Early Agitation for a Pacific Railroad," *MVHR*, 5 (1919), 396.
—— "Memphis Railroad Convention," *Tenn. Hist. Mag.*, 4 (1918), 83.
Griffin, Richard W., and Diffee W. Standard, "Cotton Textile Industry in Ante-Bellum North Carolina, 1830–1860," *No. Car. Hist. Rev.*, 34 (1957), 131.

Griffin, Richard W., "Manufacturing Interests of Mississippi Planters, 1810–1832," *Jour. Miss. Hist.*, 22 (1960), 110.

Lander, Ernest M., Jr., "Charleston: Manufacturing Center of Old South," *JSH*, 26 (1960), 330.

Moore, John H., "Mississippi's Ante-Bellum Textile Industry," *Jour. Miss. Hist.*, 16 (1954), 81.

Phillips, Ulrich B., *Transportation in the Eastern Cotton Belt* (1908).

Van Deusen, J. G., *Ante-Bellum Southern Commercial Conventions* (1926).

Wender, Herbert, *Southern Commercial Conventions, 1837–1859* (1930).

See also 10.3 for biographies/writings of:

Gregg, William, 1800–1867

44.5.3 Agriculture

Bagley, William C., Jr., *Soil Exhaustion and the Civil War* (1942).

Bonner, James C., *History of Georgia Agriculture, 1732–1860* (1964).

Boyle, J. E., *Cotton and New Orleans Cotton Exchange* (1934).

Bruchey, Stuart W., ed., *Cotton and Growth of American Industry, 1790–1860: Sources and Readings* (1967).

Cathey, Cornelius O., *Agricultural Developments in North Carolina, 1783–1860* (1956).

Craven, Avery O., "Agricultural Reformers," *AHR*, 33 (1928), 302.

—— *Soil Exhaustion as a Factor in the Agricultural History of Virginia and Maryland, 1606–1860* (1925).

Davis, Charles S., *Cotton Kingdom in Alabama* (1939).

Gray, Lewis C., *History of Agriculture in the Southern United States to 1860* (2 vols., 1933).

Kemmerer, Donald L., "Pre-Civil War South's Leading Crop, Corn," *Agric. Hist.*, 23 (1949), 236.

Marmor, Theodore R., "Anti-Industrialism and the Old South: Agrarian Perspective of J. C. Calhoun," *Comp. Studies in Society and Hist.*, 9 (1967), 377.

Moore, John H., *Agriculture in Ante-Bellum Mississippi* (1958).

Smith, Alfred G., Jr., *Economic Readjustment of an Old Cotton State: South Carolina, 1820–1860* (1958).

44.5.4 Yeoman Farmers and Poor Whites

Bonner, James C., "Profile of a Late Ante-Bellum Community," *AHR*, 49 (1944), 663.

Buck, P. H., "Poor Whites of the Ante-Bellum South," *AHR*, 31 (1925), 41.

Clark, Blanche H., *Tennessee Yeoman, 1840–1860* (1942).

Craven, Avery O., "Poor Whites and Negroes," *Jour. Negro Hist.*, 15 (1930), 14.

Griffin, Richard W., "Poor White Laborers in Southern Cotton Factories, 1789–1865," *So. Car. Hist. Mag.*, 61 (1960), 26.

Linden, Fabian, "Economic Democracy in Slave South," *Jour. Negro Hist.*, 31 (1946), 140.

McIlwaine, Shields, *Southern Poor-White from Lubberland to Tobacco Road* (1939).

Owsley, Frank L., and H. C. Owsley, "Economic Structure of Rural Tennessee," *JSH*, 8 (1942), 162.

Owsley, Frank L., *Plain Folk of the Old South* (1949).

Shugg, Roger W., *Origins of Class Struggle in Louisiana: A Social History of White Farmers and Laborers during Slavery and After, 1840–1875* (1939).

Weaver, Herbert, *Mississippi Farmers, 1850–1860* (1945).

See also 10.3 for biographies/writings of:

Brownlow, William G., 1805–1877

44.5.5 Plantation System

Barrow, Bennet H., *Plantation Life in the Florida Parishes of Louisiana: Diary*, Edwin A. Davis, ed. (1943).

Bassett, J. S., *Southern Plantation Overseer* (1925).

Easterby, J. H., ed., *South Carolina Rice Plantation* (1945).

Gaines, F. P., *Southern Plantation* (1924).

Granger, Mary, ed., *Savannah River Plantations* (1947).

Grant, Hugh F., *Planter Management in Ante-Bellum Georgia: Journal*, Albert V. House, ed. (1954).

Green, Fletcher M., ed., *Ferry Hill Plantation Journal, 1838–1839* (1961).

House, Albert V., "Labor Management Problems on Georgia Rice Plantations, 1840–1860," *Agric. Hist.*, 28 (1954), 149.

Jones, Katharine M., ed., *Plantation South* (1957).

Marshall, Martin, *Daybook of a Planter*, Weymouth T. Jordan, ed. (1960).

Nuermberger, Ruth K., *The Clays of Alabama* (1958).

Pennington, Patience, *A Woman Rice Planter* (1913); Cornelius O. Cathey, ed. (1961).

Phillips, Ulrich B., and J. D. Glunt, *Florida Plantation Records* (1927).

Phillips, Ulrich B., *Life and Labor in Old South* (1929).

——— ed., *Plantation and Frontier, 1649–1863* (1910).

Potter, David M., Jr., "Rise of the Plantation System in Georgia," *Ga. Hist. Quar.*, 16 (1932), 114.

Riley, Franklin L., ed., "Diary of a Mississippi Planter," *Miss. Hist. Soc., Pub.*, 10 (1909), 305.

Ruffin, Edmund, *Essay on Calcareous Manures* (1832); J. Carlyle Sitterson, ed., (1961).

Scarborough, William K., *The Overseer: Plantation Management in the Old South* (1966).

Sitterson, J. Carlyle, ed., "Magnolia Plantation," *MVHR*, 25 (1938), 197.

44.6 SLAVERY

44.6.1 General

Davis, David B., *The Problem of Slavery in Western Culture* (1966).

Elkins, Stanley M., *Slavery: A Problem in American Institutional and Intellectual Life* (2nd ed., 1968).

Liston, Robert A., *Slavery in America* (1970).

Phillips, Ulrich B., *American Negro Slavery* (1918).

——— *Slave Economy of the Old South: Essays*, Eugene D. Genovese, ed. (1968).

Stampp, Kenneth M., *The Peculiar Institution: Slavery in the Ante-Bellum South* (1956).

Weinstein, Allen, and Frank O. Gatell, eds., *American Negro Slavery: A Modern Reader* (1968).

*　　*　　*　　*　　*　　*　　*

Genovese, Eugene D., "Rebelliousness and Docility in the Negro Slave: Critique of Elkins Thesis," *Civil War Hist.*, 13 (1967), 293.

——— "Recent Contributions to Economic Historiography of the Slave South," *Science and Society*, 24 (1960), 53.

Kugler, John F., "U. B. Phillips' Use of Sources," *Jour. Negro Hist.*, 47 (1962), 153.

Lynd, Staughton, "On Turner, Beard and Slavery," *Jour. Negro Hist.*, 48 (1963), 235.

Miller, Elizabeth W., and Mary L. Fisher, "History," in *The Negro in America: A Bibliography* (2nd ed., 1970).

Porter, Dorothy, "Slavery," in *The Negro in the United States: A Bibliography* (1970).

Preyer, Norris W., "Historian, Slave, and Ante-Bellum Textile Industry," *Jour. Negro Hist.*, 46 (1961), 67.

Salem, Sam E., "U. B. Phillips and Scientific Tradition," *Ga. Hist. Quar.*, 44 (1960), 172.

Stampp, Kenneth M., "Historian and Southern Negro Slavery," *AHR*, 57 (1952), 613.

Stephenson, Wendell H., "Ulrich B. Phillips," *Ga. Hist. Quar.*, 41 (1957), 103.

Wall, Bennett H., "African Slavery," in Arthur S. Link and Rembert W. Patrick, eds., *Writing Southern History: Essays in Honor of Fletcher M. Green* (1965).

44.6.2 Special Topics

Berwanger, Eugene H., *Frontier against Slavery: Western and Anti-Negro Prejudice* (1967).

Davis, David B., *Slave Power Conspiracy and Paranoid Style* (1969).

Degler, Carl N., "Slavery and the Genesis of American Race Prejudice," *Comp. Studies in Society and Hist.*, 2 (1959), 49.

Eaton, Clement, "Slave-Hiring in the Upper South," *MVHR*, 46 (1960), 663.

Fisher, Miles M., *Negro Slave Songs* (1953).

Franklin, John Hope, "Slavery and the Martial South," *Jour. Negro Hist.*, 37 (1952), 36.

Greene, John C., "Negro's Place in Nature, 1780–1815," *Jour. Hist. Ideas*, 15 (1954), 384.

Handlin, Oscar, *Race and Nationality in American Life* (1957).

Jackson, James C., "Religious Education of the Negro in South Carolina Prior to 1850," *Hist. Mag. Prot. Episc. Church*, 36 (1967), 35.

Lewis, Mary Agnes, "Slavery and Personality: Further Comment," *Am. Quar.*, 19 (1967), 114.

Linden, Fabian, "Economic Democracy in the Slave South," *Jour. Negro Hist.*, 31 (1946), 140.

Mathews, Donald G., *Slavery and Methodism: A Chapter in American Morality, 1780–1845* (1965).

Morris, Richard B., "Bondage in the Slave States," *MVHR*, 41 (1954), 219.

Sellers, Charles G., Jr., "Travail of Slavery," in *The Southerner as American* (1960).

Starobin, Robert, *Industrial Slavery in the Old South* (1970).

Taylor, Paul S., "Plantation Laborer before the Civil War," *Agric. Hist.*, 28 (1954), 1.

Wade, Richard C., *Slavery in Cities: South, 1820–1860* (1964).

Weeks, Stephen B., *Southern Quakers and Slavery* (1896).

44.6.3 Comparative Studies

Davis, David B., *The Problem of Slavery in Western Culture* (1966).

Degler, Carl N., *Neither Black nor White: Slavery and Race Relations in Brazil and the United States* (1971).

Klein, Herbert S., *Slavery in the Americas: A Comparative Study of Virginia and Cuba* (1967).

Sio, Arnold A., "Slave Status in the Americas," *Comp. Studies in Society and Hist.*, 7 (1965), 289.

Tannenbaum, Frank, *Slave and Citizen: The Negro in the Americas* (1946).

Williams, Eric Eustace, *Capitalism and Slavery* (1944). West Indies.

44.6.4 Area Studies

44.6.4.1 South

Ballagh, J. C., *Slavery in Virginia* (1902).

Bassett, John S., *Slavery in North Carolina* (1896).

Brackett, J. R., *The Negro in Maryland* (1889).

Bradford, S. Sydney, "Negro Ironworker in Ante-Bellum Virginia," *JSH*, 25 (1959), 194.

Coleman, John W., *Slave Times in Kentucky* (1940).

Flanders, Ralph B., *Plantation Slavery in Georgia* (1933).

Green, Constance M., *Secret City: Race Relations in the Nation's Capital* (1967).

Holt, Bryce R., *Supreme Court of North Carolina and Slavery* (1927).

Johnston, James H., *Race Relations in Virginia and Miscegenation in the South, 1776–1860* (1970).

McColley, Robert, *Slavery and Jeffersonian Virginia* (1964).

McCrady, Edward, "Slavery in South Carolina," Am. Hist. Assoc., *Report* (1895), 629.

Menn, Joseph D., *Large Slaveholders of Louisiana, 1860* (1964).

Moody, Vernie A., *Slavery on Louisiana Sugar Plantations* (1924).

Mooney, Chase C., *Slavery in Tennessee* (1957).

Pilcher, George William, "Samuel Davies and the Instruction of Negroes in Virginia," *Va. Mag. Hist. Biog.*, 74 (1966), 293.

Sellers, James B., *Slavery in Alabama* (1950).

Sydnor, Charles S., *Slavery in Mississippi* (1933).

Taylor, Joe G., *Negro Slavery in Louisiana* (1963).

Taylor, Orville W., *Negro Slavery in Arkansas* (1958).

Taylor, Rosser H., *Slaveholding in North Carolina* (1926).

Tremaine, Mary, *Slavery in the District of Columbia* (1892).

Trexler, H. A., *Slavery in Missouri* (1914).

Woolfolk, George R., "Cotton Capitalism and Slave Labor in Texas," *Southw. Soc. Sci. Quar.*, 37 (1956), 43.

44.6.4.2 North

Harris, N. D., *History of Negro Servitude in Illinois* (1904).

McManus, Edgar J., *A History of Negro Slavery in New York* (1966).

44.6.5 Memoirs of Slaves

Botkin, Benjamin A., ed., *Lay My Burden Down: A Folk History of Slavery* (1945).

Curtin, Philip D., ed., *Africa Remembered: Narratives by West Africans from Era of the Slave Trade* (1967).

Jefferson, Isaac, *Memoirs of a Monticello Slave as Dictated to Charles Campbell*, Rayford W. Logan, ed. (1951).

Nichols, Charles H., *Many Thousand Gone: Ex-Slaves' Account of Their Bondage and Freedom* (1963).

Northrup, Solomon, *Twelve Years a Slave* (1853); Sue Eakin and Joseph Logsdon, eds. (1968).

Payne, Daniel A., *Recollections of Seventy Years* (1888).

Said, Omar ibn, "Autobiography," J. F. Jameson, ed., *AHR*, 30 (1925), 787.

Wish, Harvey, ed., *Slavery in the South: First-Hand Accounts of the Ante-Bellum American Southland from Northern and Southern Whites, Negroes, and Foreign Observers* (1964).

Woodson, Carter G., *The Mind of Negro as Reflected in Letters Written during the Crisis, 1800–1860* (1926).

Yetman, Norman R., "Background of the Slave Narrative Collection," *Am. Quar.*, 19 (1967), 534.

44.6.6 Resistance and Revolts

Addington, Wendell G., "Slave Insurrections in Texas," *Jour. Negro Hist.*, 35 (1950), 408.

Aptheker, Herbert, *American Negro Slave Revolts* (1943).

—— *Nat Turner's Slave Rebellion* (1966).

Bauer, Raymond A. and Alice H., "Day to Day Resistance to Slavery," *Jour. Negro Hist.*, 27 (1942), 388.

Drewry, W. S., *Slave Insurrections in Virginia* (1900).

Fredrickson, George M., and Christopher Lasch, "Resistance to Slavery," *Civil War Hist.*, 13 (1967), 315.

Freehling, William, *Prelude to Civil War: Nullification Controversy in South Carolina, 1816–1836* (1966).

Holmes, Jack D. L., "Abortive Slave Revolt at Pointe Coupée, Louisiana, 1795," *La. Hist.*, 11 (1970), 341.

Kilson, Marion D. de B., "Slave Revolts in the United States," *Phylon*, 25 (1964), 175.

Lofton, John, *Insurrection in South Carolina: The Turbulent World of Denmark Vesey* (1964).

McKibben, Davidson B., "Negro Slave Insurrections in Mississippi, 1800–1865," *Jour. Negro Hist.*, 34 (1949), 73.

Porter, Kenneth W., "Negroes and Indians on Texas Frontier, 1831–1876," *Jour. Negro Hist.*, 41 (1956), 185.

———— "Negroes and the Seminole War, 1835–1842," *JSH*, 30 (1964), 427.

Russell, Marion J., "American Slave Discontent in Records of High Courts," *Jour. Negro Hist.*, 31 (1946), 411.

Wade, Richard C., "The Vesey Plot: A Reconsideration," *JSH*, 30 (1964), 143.

Wish, Harvey, "Slave Insurrection Panic of 1856," *JSH*, 5 (1939), 206.

44.6.7 Fugitive Slaves and Underground Railroad

Breyfogle, William, *Make-Free: Story of Underground Railroad* (1958).

Buckmaster, Henrietta, pseud., *Let My People Go: The Story of the Underground Railroad and the Growth of the Abolition Movement* (1941).

Gara, Larry, *The Liberty Line: The Legend of Under-Ground Railroad* (1961).

———— "The Professional Fugitive in the Abolition Movement," *Wis. Mag. Hist.*, 48 (1965), 196.

Hensel, W. U., *Christiana Riots* (1911).

Landon, Fred, "Negro Migration to Canada," *Jour. Negro Hist.*, 5 (1920), 22.

McDougall, Marion G., *Fugitive Slaves* (1891).

Siebert, Wilbur H., *The Underground Railroad from Slavery to Freedom* (1898).

Still, William, *The Underground Railroad* (1872).

44.6.8 Economics of Slavery

Conrad, Alfred H., and John R. Meyer, *Economics of Slavery and Other Studies in Econometric History* (1965).

Conrad, Alfred H., et al., "Slavery as an Obstacle to Economic Growth in the United States," *Jour. Econ. Hist.*, 27 (1967), 518.

Elkins, Stanley, and Eric L. McKitrick, "Institutions and the Law of Slavery: Dynamics of Unopposed Capitalism," *Am. Quar.*, 9 (1957), 3.

Evans, Robert, Jr., "Economics of American Negro Slavery," in National Bureau of Economic Research, *Aspects of Labor Economics* (1962).

Genovese, Eugene D., "Medical and Insurance Costs of Slaveholding in the Cotton Belt," *Jour. Negro Hist.*, 45 (1960), 141.

———— *Political Economy of Slavery* (1965).

———— "Ulrich Bonnell Phillips and His Critics," foreword to Phillips' *American Negro Slavery* (1966).

Govan, Thomas P., "Plantation Slavery," *JSH*, 8 (1942), 513.

Owsley, Frank L., and H. C. Owsley, "Economic Basis of Society," *JSH*, 6 (1940), 24.

Saraydar, Edward, "Note on Profitability of Ante-Bellum Slavery," *South. Econ. Jour.*, 30 (1964), 325.

Smith, Robert W., "Was Slavery Unprofitable in Ante-Bellum South?" *Agric. Hist.*, 20 (1946), 62.

Starobin, Robert S., "Economics of Industrial Slavery in the Old South," *Bus. Hist. Rev.*, 44 (1970), 131.

Woodman, Harold D., "Profitability of Slavery," *JSH*, 29 (1963), 303.

—— ed., *Slavery and the Southern Economy* (1966).

Woolfolk, George R., "Planter Capitalism and Slavery," *Jour. Negro Hist.*, 41 (1956), 103.

—— "Taxes and Slavery in the Ante-Bellum South," *JSH*, 26 (1960), 180.

Yarbrough, W. H., *Economic Aspects of Slavery* (1932).

44.6.9 Slave Trade

44.6.9.1 International

Bandinel, James, *Some Account of Trade in Slaves from Africa as Connected with Europe and America* (1968).

Bernstein, Barton J., "Southern Politics and Attempts to Reopen the African Slave Trade," *Jour. Negro Hist.*, 51 (1966), 16.

Carnathan, W. J., "Proposal to Reopen the African Slave Trade," *So. Atl. Quar.*, 25 (1926), 410.

Dow, G. F., *Slave Ships and Slaving* (1927).

Du Bois, W. E. B., *The Suppression of the African Slave-Trade to the United States of America, 1638–1870* (1896).

Duignan, Peter, and Clarence Clendenon, *United States and the African Slave Trade, 1619–1862* (1963).

Duram, James C., "Britain, U.S.A. and African Slave Trade, 1815–1870," *Social Sci.*, 40 (1965), 220.

Hill, Lawrence F., *United States and Brazil* (1932).

Howard, Warren S., *American Slavers and the Federal Law, 1837–1862* (1963).

Mannix, Daniel P., *Black Cargoes: Atlantic Slave Trade, 1518–1865* (1962).

Mathieson, William L., *Great Britain and the Slave Trade* (1929).

Mayer, Brantz, ed., *Captain Canot, or 20 Years of an African Slaver* (1854).

Platt, Virginia B., "East India Company and Madagascar Slave Trade," *WMQ*, 3 ser., 26 (1969).

Pope-Hennessy, James, *Sins of Fathers: The Atlantic Slave Traders, 1441–1807* (1968).

Soulsby, H. G., *Right of Search and Slave Trade in Anglo-American Relations, 1814–1862* (1933).

Spears, John R., *American Slave Trade* (1900).

Takaki, Ronald, "Movement to Reopen the African Slave Trade in South Carolina," *So. Car. Hist. Mag.*, 66 (1965), 38.

Van Alstyne, Richard W., "British Right of Search and the African Slave Trade," *Jour. Mod. Hist.*, 2 (1930), 39.

Ward, W. E. F., *The Royal Navy and the Slavers: Suppression of the Atlantic Slave Trade* (1969).

Wells, Tom H., *Slave Ship "Wanderer"* (1967).

44.6.9.2 Domestic

Bancroft, Frederic, *Slave Trading in the Old South* (1931).

Collins, Winfield H., *Domestic Slave Trade* (1904).

Miller, William L., "Interstate Slave Trade of the Ante-Bellum South," *Jour. Pol. Econ.*, 73 (1965), 181.

44.6.10 Proslavery Thought

Bailor, Keith M., "John Taylor of Caroline, 1790–1820," *Va. Mag. Hist. Biog.*, 75 (1967), 290.

Bestor, Arthur, "Proslavery Constitutional Doctrine, 1846–1860," Ill. State Hist. Soc., *Jour.*, 54 (1961), 117.

Carsel, Wilfred, "Slaveholders' Indictment of Northern Wage Slavery," *JSH*, 6 (1940), 504.

Dowty, Alan, "Urban Slavery in Pro-Southern Fiction of the 1850's," *JSH*, 32 (1966), 25.

Fitzhugh, George, *Cannibals All! Or, Slaves without Masters* (1857); C. Vann Woodward, ed. (1960).

Gardner, Robert, "A Tenth-Hour Apology for Slavery," *JSH*, 26 (1960), 352.

Genovese, Eugene D., "A Georgia Slaveholder Looks at Africa," *Ga. Hist. Quar.*, 51 (1967), 186.

Jenkins, William S., *Pro-Slavery Thought* (1935).

McKitrick, Eric L., ed., *Slavery Defended: Views of Old South* (1963).

Morrow, Ralph E., "Pro-Slavery Argument," *MVHR*, 48 (1961), 79.

Purifoy, Lewis M., "The Southern Methodist Church and the Proslavery Argument," *JSH*, 32 (1966), 325.

Stampp, Kenneth, "An Analysis of T. R. Dew's *Review of Debates in Virginia Legislature*," *Jour. Negro Hist.*, 27 (1942), 380.

Stanton, William R., *The Leopard's Spots: Scientific Attitudes toward Race in America, 1815–1859* (1960).

44.7 FREE NEGROES TO 1860

44.7.1 North and West

Berwanger, Eugene H., *The Frontier against Slavery: Western and Anti-Negro Prejudice* (1967).

Fishel, Leslie H., Jr., "Wisconsin and Negro Suffrage," *Wis. Mag. Hist.*, 46 (1963), 180.

Hirsch, L. H., "Negro and New York," *Jour. Negro Hist.*, 16 (1931), 382.

Langley, Harold D., "The Negro in the Navy and Merchant Service, 1789–1860," *Jour. Negro Hist.*, 52 (1967), 273.

Lapp, Rudolph M., "The Negro in Gold Rush California," *Jour. Negro Hist.*, 49 (1964), 81.

Litwack, Leon F., *North of Slavery: The Negro in the Free States, 1790–1860* (1961).

Pease, William H. and Jane H., *Black Utopia: Negro Communal Experiments in America* (1963).

Rox, Dixon R., "Negro Vote in Old New York," *Pol. Sci. Quar.*, 32 (1917), 252.

Thornbrough, Emma L., *The Negro in Indiana* (1957).

Turner, Edward R., *The Negro in Pennsylvania* (1910).

Watkins, Sylvestre C., Sr., "Some of Early Illinois' Free Negroes," Ill. State Hist. Soc., *Jour.*, 56 (1963), 495.

44.7.2 South

England, J. M., "The Free Negro in Ante-Bellum Tennessee," *JSH*, 9 (1943), 47.

Fitchett, E. Horace, "Free Negro Population of Charleston," *Jour. Negro Hist.*, 36 (1941), 421.

Flanders, Ralph B., "The Free Negro in Georgia," *No. Car. Hist. Rev.*, 9 (1932), 250.

Franklin, John Hope, *The Free Negro in North Carolina* (1943).

Jackson, Luther P., *The Free Negro in Virginia* (1942).

Johnson, William, *Natchez: Ante-Bellum Diary of a Free Negro*, William R. Hogan and Edwin Adams Davis, eds. (1951).

Johnston, James H., *Race Relations in Virginia and Miscegenation in the South, 1776–1860* (1970).

McConnell, Roland C., *Negro Troops of Antebellum Louisiana: A History of the Battalion of Free Men of Color* (1968).

Reinders, Robert C., "The Free Negro in the New Orleans Economy," *La. Hist.*, 6 (1965), 273.

Russell, John H., *The Free Negro in Virginia* (1913).

Senese, Donald J., "The Free Negro and the South Carolina Courts, 1790–1860," *So. Car. Hist. Mag.*, 68 (1967), 140.

Stahl, Annie L. W., "The Free Negro in Ante-Bellum Louisiana," *La. Hist. Quar.*, 25 (1942), 300.

Winston, James E., "The Free Negro in New Orleans, 1803–1860," *La. Hist. Quar.*, 21 (1938), 1075.

Woodson, Carter G., ed., "Negro Owners of Slaves," *Jour. Negro Hist.*, 9 (1924), 41.

Wright, James M., *The Free Negro in Maryland* (1921).

44.7.3 Anti-Black Laws and Negro Protest

Angle, Paul M., "Illinois Black Laws," *Chicago Hist.*, 8 (1967), 65.

Bell, Howard H., "Expressions of Negro Militancy in the North, 1840–1860," *Jour. Negro Hist.*, 45 (1960), 11.

Berwanger, Eugene H., " 'Black Law' Question in Ante-Bellum California," *Jour. of West*, 6 (1967), 205.

Calligaro, Lee, "Negro's Legal Status in Pre-Civil War New Jersey," *N.J. Hist.*, 85 (1967), 167.

Gertz, Elmer, "Black Laws of Illinois," *Ill. Hist. Soc., Jour.*, 56 (1963), 454.

Ruchames, Louis, "Jim Crow Railroads in Massachusetts," *Am. Quar.*, 8 (1956), 61.

44.8 ABOLITION MOVEMENT, 1789–1850

44.8.1 General

Auer, John Jeffrey, ed., *Antislavery and Disunion, 1858–1861* (1963).

Barnes, Gilbert H., *Anti-Slavery Impulse* (1933).

Dumond, Dwight L., *Antislavery: The Crusade for Freedom in America* (1961).

—— *Antislavery Origins of the Civil War in the United States* (1939).

Filler, Louis, *The Crusade against Slavery, 1830–1860* (1960).

Lloyd, Arthur Y., *The Slavery Controversy, 1831–1860* (1939).

Simms, Henry H., *Emotion at High Tide: Abolition, 1830–1845* (1960).

Sorin, Gerald, *New York Abolitionists: Case Study of Political Radicalism* (1971).

Turner, Lorenzo D., *Antislavery Sentiment in American Literature Prior to 1865* (1926).

Zilversmit, Arthur, *The First Emancipation: The Abolition of Slavery in the North* (1967).

*   *   *   *   *   *   *

Dillon, Merton L., "Abolitionists: Decade of Historiography, 1959–1969," *JSH*, 35 (1969), 500.

Dumond, Dwight L., *A Bibliography of Antislavery in America* (1961).

Kraditor, Aileen S., "Elkins and Abolitionists," *Civil War Hist.*, 13 (1967), 330.

Skotheim, Robert A., "David Donald's 'Toward a Reconsideration of Abolitionists'," *JSH*, 25 (1959), 356.

Williams, David A., "William Lloyd Garrison," Essex Hist., *Hist. Coll.*, 98 (1962), 84.

44.8.2 Early Antislavery Thought and Colonization

Adams, Alice Dana, *Neglected Period of Anti-Slavery in America, 1808–1831* (1908).

Binder, Frederick M., *The Color Problem in Early National America as Viewed by John Adams, Jefferson and Jackson* (1968).
Kates, Don B., "Attitudes toward Slavery in the Early Republic," *Jour. Negro Hist.*, 53 (1968), 33.
Staudenraus, P. J., *The African Colonization Movement, 1816–1865* (1961).

44.8.3 Abolitionist Thought

Curry, Richard O., ed., *Abolitionists* (1965).
Demos, John, "Antislavery Movement and the Problem of Violent 'Means'," *NEQ*, 37 (1964), 501.
Dillon, Merton L., "Failure of American Abolitionists," *JSH*, 25 (1959), 159.
Donald, David, *Lincoln Reconsidered* (1956).
Duberman, Martin B., "Abolitionists and Psychology," *Jour. Negro Hist.*, 47 (1962), 183.
———— ed., *The Antislavery Vanguard: New Essays on the Abolitionists* (1965).
Fladeland, Betty, "Who Were the Abolitionists?" *Jour. Negro Hist.*, 49 (1964), 99.
Hawkins, Hugh, ed., *Abolitionists* (1964).
Lutz, Alma, *Crusade for Freedom: Women of Antislavery Movement* (1968).
Lynd, Staughton, *Intellectual Origins of American Radicalism* (1968).
Mathews, Donald G., "Abolitionists on Slavery," *JSH*, 33 (1967), 163.
Nuermberger, R. K., *Free Produce Movement* (1942).
Pease, William H. and Jane H., "Antislavery Ambivalence," *Am. Quar.*, 17 (1965), 682.
Quarles, Benjamin, *Black Abolitionists* (1969).
———— "Sources of Abolitionist Income," *MVHR*, 32 (1945), 63.
Savage, William S., *Controversy over Distribution of Abolition Literature* (1938).
Skotheim, Robert A., "David Donald's 'Toward a Reconsideration of Abolitionists'," *JSH*, 25 (1959), 356.
Tyler, Alice F., *Freedom's Ferment* (1944).
Walker, David, *Appeal in Four Articles: With Preamble to Coloured Citizens of World* (1829); Charles M. Wiltse, ed. (1965).
Wolf, Hazel C., *On Freedom's Altar: Martyr Complex in the Abolition Movement* (1952).
Zorn, Roman J., "New England Anti-Slavery Society: Pioneer Abolition Organization," *Jour. Negro Hist.*, 42 (1957), 157.

44.8.4 Specific Abolitionists

Bartlett, Irving H., "Wendell Phillips and Eloquence of Abuse," *Am. Quar.*, 11 (1959), 509.
Geffen, Elizabeth M., "William Henry Furness, Philadelphia Anti-slavery Preacher," *Penn. Mag. Hist. Biog.*, 82 (1958), 259.
Kearns, Francis E., "Margaret Fuller and Abolition Movement," *Jour. Hist. Ideas*, 25 (1964), 120.
Kraditor, Aileen S., *Means and Ends in American Abolitionism: Garrison and his Critics, 1834–1850* (1969).
Miller, Perry, "Theodore Parker," *Harv. Theol. Rev.*, 54 (1961), 275.
Pease, William H. and Jane H., "Boston Garrisonians and Problem of Frederick Douglass," *Can. Jour. Hist.*, 2 (1967), 29.
Wyatt-Brown, Bertram, "William Lloyd Garrison and Antislavery Unity," *Civil War Hist.*, 1 (1967), 5.

See also 10.3 for biographies/writings of:

Allen, Richard, 1760–1831
Andrew, John A., 1818–1867
Beecher, Catherine E., 1800–1878
Beecher, Edward, 1803–1895
Birney, James G., 1792–1857

Brown, John, 1800–1859
Child, Lydia M., 1802–1880
Clarke, James F., 1810–1888
Clay, Cassius M., 1810–1903
Coffin, Levi, 1789–1877
Dana, Richard H., Jr., 1815–1882
Douglass, Frederick, 1817–1895
Follen, Charles, 1796–1840
Garrison, William Lloyd, 1805–1879
Giddings, Joshua R., 1795–1864
Grimké Sisters
Hale, John P., 1806–1873
Higginson, Thomas W., 1823–1911
Julian, George W., 1817–1899
Lovejoy, Elijah P., 1802–1837
Lundy, Benjamin, 1789–1839
May, Samuel J., 1797–1871
Mott, Lucretia, 1793–1880
Palfrey, John Gorham, 1796–1881
Parker, Theodore, 1810–1860
Phillips, Wendell, 1811–1884
Robinson, William S., 1818–1876
Sanborn, Franklin B., 1831–1917
Smith, Gerrit, 1797–1874
Tappan, Arthur, 1786–1865
Tappan, Lewis, 1788–1873
Ward, Samuel R., 1817–1866
Weld, Theodore, 1803–1895
Whittier, John Greenleaf, 1807–1892

44.8.5 Abolitionist Writings

Aptheker, Herbert, *One Continual Cry: David Walker's Appeal to Colored Citizens, 1829–30* (1965).
Beecher, Edward, *Narrative of Riots at Alton* (1838).
Child, Lydia M., *Appeal in Favor of Americans Called Africans* (1836).
Garrison, William Lloyd, *Documents of Upheaval: Selections from "The Liberator", 1831–1865*, Truman Nelson, ed. (1966).
——— *Thoughts on African Colonization* (1832; repr., 1968).
Pease, William H., and Jane H. Pease, eds., *Antislavery Argument* (1965).
Ruchames, Louis, ed., *Abolitionists* (1963).
Stowe, Harriet Beecher, *Uncle Tom's Cabin* (1852); Kenneth S. Lynn, ed. (1962).
Thomas, John L., ed., *Slavery Attacked: Abolitionist Crusade* (1965).
Ward, John W., "*Uncle Tom's Cabin*, As Matter of Historical Fact," *Columbia Univ. Forum*, 9 (1966), 42.
Weld, Theodore D., *American Slavery: A Thousand Witnesses* (1839).

44.8.6 Antislavery Politics

Adams, Charles F., "John Quincy Adams and Emancipation through Martial Law," *Mass. Hist. Soc., Proc.*, 2nd ser., 15 (1902), 436.
Bretz, J. P., "Economic Background of the Liberty Party," *AHR*, 34 (1929), 250.
Nye, Russel B., *Fettered Freedom* (rev. ed., 1963).
Smith, Theodore C., *Liberty and the Free Soil Parties* (1897).

See also 10.3 for biographies/writings of:

Hale, John P., 1806–1873
Palfrey, John G., 1796–1881
Sumner, Charles, 1811–1874

44.8.7 Religion and Abolitionism

Bodo, John R., *Protestant Clergy and Public Issues, 1812–1848* (1954).
Cole, Charles C., Jr., *Social Ideas of Northern Evangelists, 1826–1860* (1954).
Cross, Whitney R., *Burned-Over District* (1950).
Drake, T. E., *Quakers and Slavery* (1950).
Loveland, Anne C., "Evangelicalism and 'Immediate Emancipation' in Anti-
    slavery Thought," *JSH*, 32 (1966), 172.
Mathews, Donald G., *Slavery and Methodism: A Chapter in American Morality,
    1780–1845* (1965).
Rice, Madeleine H., *American Catholic Opinion in the Slavery Controversy* (1944).

44.8.8 Northern Opposition

Floan, Howard R., *South in Northern Eyes, 1831 to 1861* (1958).
Foner, Phillip S., *Business and Slavery* (1941).
Gibson, Florence E., *Attitudes of New York Irish* (1951).
Kerber, Linda K., "Abolitionists and Amalgamators: New York City Race Riots
    of July 1834," *N.Y. Hist.*, 48 (1967), 28.
Levy, Ronald, "Bishop Hopkins and the Dilemma of Slavery," *Penn. Mag. Hist.
    Biog.*, 91 (1967), 56.
Lofton, W. H., "Abolition and Labor," *Jour. Negro Hist.*, 33 (1948), 249.
Mandel, Bernard, *Labor, Free and Slave: Workingmen and Anti-Slavery* (1955).
Ratner, Lorman, "Northern Concern for Social Order as Cause for Rejecting
    Anti-Slavery, 1831–1840," *Historian*, 28 (1965), 1.
——— *Powder Keg: Northern Opposition to the Antislavery Movement, 1831–1840*
    (1968).
Richards, Leonard L., *"Gentlemen of Property and Standing": Anti-Abolition
    Mobs in Jacksonian America* (1970).

44.8.9 Southern Antislavery Thought

Martin, Asa E., *Antislavery Movement in Kentucky* (1918). .
Robert, Joseph C., *Road from Monticello* (1941).
Stampp, Kenneth M., "Fate of Southern Anti-Slavery Sentiment," *Jour. Negro
    Hist.*, 28 (1943), 10.

45 Making of the Civil War

45.1 GENERAL

Alexander, Thomas B., *Sectional Stress and Party Strength* (1967).
Cole, Arthur C., *Irrepressible Conflict* (1934).
Craven, Avery O., *Civil War in the Making, 1815–1860* (1959).
—— *The Coming of the Civil War* (rev. ed., 1957).
—— *Growth of Southern Nationalism, 1848–1861* (1953).
Fehrenbacher, Donald, *Prelude to Greatness: Lincoln in the Fifties* (1962).
Nevins, Allan, *Emergence of Lincoln* (2 vols., 1950).
—— *Ordeal of the Union* (2 vols., 1947).
Nichols, Roy F., *Disruption of American Democracy* (1948).
—— *Stakes of Power, 1845–1877* (1961).
O'Connor, Thomas H., *Lords of the Loom: Cotton Whigs and the Coming of War* (1968).
Randall, James G., "Blundering Generation," *MVHR*, 27 (1940), 3.
—— and David Donald, *Civil War and Reconstruction* (2nd ed., 1969).
Silbey, Joel H., *Transformation of American Politics, 1840–1860* (1967).
Simms, Henry H., *Decade of Sectional Controversy, 1851–1861* (1942).
Smith, Elbert B., *Death of Slavery, 1837–65* (1967).

See also 43.10, Expansion of Slavery into Territories.

45.2 COMPROMISE OF 1850

Ames, Herbert V., "Calhoun and Secession 1850," Am. Antiq. Soc., *Proc.*, 28 (1918), 19.
Doherty, Herbert J., Jr., "Florida and the Crisis of 1850," *JSH*, 19 (1953), 32.
Hamilton, Holman, *Prologue to Conflict: Compromise of 1850* (1964).
Harmon, G. D., "Douglas and the Compromise of 1850," Ill. State Hist. Soc., *Jour.*, 21 (1929), 453.
Parks, Joseph H., "John Bell and Compromise of 1850," *JSH*, 9 (1943), 328.
Rosenberg, Morton M., "Iowa Politics and the Compromise of 1850," *Iowa Jour. Hist.*, 56 (1958), 193.
Russel, Robert R., "Compromise of 1850," *JSH*, 22 (1956), 292.
Shryock, R. H., *Georgia and Union in 1850* (1926).
Sioussat, St. George L., "Tennessee, Compromise of 1850, and Nashville Convention," *MVHR*, 2 (1915), 313.
Smith, William E., *Francis Preston Blair Family in Politics* (2 vols., 1933).
Stephenson, N. W., "Southern Nationalism in South Carolina, in 1851," *AHR*, 36 (1931), 314.

See also 10.3 for biographies/writings of:

Calhoun, John C., 1782–1850
Cass, Lewis, 1782–1866
Clay, Henry, 1777–1852
Davis, Jefferson, 1808–1889
Douglas, Stephen A., 1813–1861
Fillmore, Millard, 1800–1874
Johnson, Herschel V., 1812–1880
Lincoln, Abraham, 1809–1865
Pierce, Franklin, 1804–1869
Seward, William H., 1801–1872
Stephens, Alexander H., 1812–1883
Sumner, Charles, 1811–1874
Taylor, Zachary, 1784–1850
Toombs, Robert, 1810–1885
Webster, Daniel, 1782–1852
Wilmot, David, 1814–1868
Winthrop, Robert C., 1809–1894

45.3 ELECTION OF 1852 AND PIERCE ADMINISTRATION, 1853–1857

Nichols, Roy F., *Democratic Machine 1850–1854* (1923).
———— and Jeannette Nichols, "Election of 1852," in Arthur M. Schlesinger, Jr. and Fred L. Israel, eds., *History of American Presidential Elections, 1789–1968*, vol. II (1971).

See also 10.3 for biographies/writings of:

Cushing, Caleb, 1800–1879
Davis, Jefferson, 1808–1889
Everett, Edward, 1794–1865
Marcy, William L., 1786–1857
Pierce, Franklin, 1804–1869
Scott, Winfield, 1786–1866

45.4 FUGITIVE SLAVE CONTROVERSY

Campbell, Stanley W., *Slave Catchers: Enforcement of the Fugitive Slave Law, 1850–1860* (1970).
Johnson, Allen, "Constitutionality of Fugitive Slave Acts," *Yale Law Jour.*, 31 (1921), 161.
Nadelhaft, Jerome, "Somersett Case and Slavery," *Jour. Negro Hist.*, 51 (1966), 193.
Russel, Robert R., "Constitutional Doctrines with Regard to Slavery in the Territories," *JSH*, 32 (1966), 466.

45.5 KANSAS-NEBRASKA ACT

Hodder, Frank H., "Genesis of the Kansas-Nebraska Act," Wis. Hist. Soc., *Proc.* (1912), 69.
———— "Railroad Background of the Kansas-Nebraska Act," *MVHR*, 12 (1925), 3.
Johannsen, Robert W., "Kansas-Nebraska Act and Pacific Northwest Frontier," *Pac. Hist. Rev.*, 22 (1953), 129.

Malin, James C., "Motives of Douglas in the Organization of Nebraska Territory," *Kan. Hist. Quar.*, 19 (1951), 321.
—— *Nebraska Question, 1852–1854* (1953).
Parks, Joseph H., "Tennessee Whigs and Kansas-Nebraska Bill," *JSH*, 10 (1944), 308.
Ray, P. O., *Repeal of the Missouri Compromise* (1909).
Russel, Robert R., "Kansas-Nebraska Bill, 1854," *JSH*, 29 (1963), 187.
—— "Pacific Railway Issue," *MVHR*, 12 (1925), 187.
Smith, William E., *Francis Preston Blair Family and Politics* (2 vols., 1933).

*   *   *   *   *   *   *

Nichols, Roy F., "Kansas-Nebraska Act," *MVHR*, 43 (1956), 187.

See also 10.3 for biographies/writings of:

Cass, Lewis, 1782–1866
Douglass, Frederick, 1817–1895
Johnson, Reverdy, 1796–1876
Mason, James M., 1798–1871
Pierce, Franklin, 1804–1869
Seward, William H., 1801–1872
Weed, Thurlow, 1797–1882

45.6 KANSAS STRUGGLE, 1854–1861

Andrews, Horace, Jr., "Kansas Crusade: Eli Thayer and the New England Emigrant Aid Company," *NEQ*, 35 (1962), 497.
Baltimore, Lester B., "Benjamin F. Stringfellow: Fight for Slavery on the Missouri Border," *Mo. Hist. Rev.*, 62 (1967), 14.
Fleming, W. L., "Buford Expedition to Kansas," *AHR*, 6 (1900), 38.
Gaeddert, G. R., *Birth of Kansas* (1940).
Gates, Paul W., *Fifty Million Acres: Conflicts over Kansas Land Policy, 1845–1890* (1954).
Harlow, Ralph V., "Rise and Fall of the Kansas Aid Movement," *AHR*, 41 (1935), 1.
Hodder, Frank H., "English Bill," Am. Hist. Assoc., *Report*, 1 (1906), 201.
Isely, W. H., "Sharps Rifle Episode," *AHR*, 12 (1907), 546.
Johannsen, Robert W., "Lecompton Constitutional Convention: Analysis of Its Membership," *Kan. Hist. Quar.*, 23 (1957), 225.
Johnson, Samuel A., *Battle Cry of Freedom: New England Emigrant Aid Company in the Kansas Crusade* (1954).
Malin, James C., *John Brown and the Legend of Fifty-Six* (1942).
—— "Proslavery Background of Kansas Struggle," *MVHR*, 10 (1923), 285.
Moody, Robert E., "First Year of the Emigrant Aid Company," *NEQ*, 4 (1931), 148.
Nichols, Alice, *Bleeding Kansas* (1954).
Shoemaker, Floyd C., "Missouri's Proslavery Fight for Kansas, 1854–1855," *Mo. Hist. Rev.*, 48 (1954), 41.
Weisberger, Bernard A., "Newspaper Reporter and Kansas Embroglio," *MVHR*, 36 (1950), 633.

See also 10.3 for biographies/writings of:

Atchison, David R., 1807–1886
Brown, John, 1800–1859
Buchanan, James, 1791–1868
Higginson, Thomas W., 1823–1911
Pierce, Franklin, 1804–1869

Robinson, Charles, 1818–1894
Seward, William H., 1801–1872
Sumner, Charles, 1811–1874
Toombs, Robert, 1810–1885
Walker, Robert J., 1801–1869

45.7 RISE OF REPUBLICAN PARTY

Crandall, Andrew W., *Early History of the Republican Party* (1930).
Foner, Eric, *Free Soil, Free Labor, Free Men: Ideology of the Republican Party before the Civil War* (1970).
Harrington, F. H., "Frémont and North Americans," *AHR*, 44 (1939), 842.
Isely, Jeter A., *Greeley and Republican Party* (1947).
Mayer, George H., *Republican Party, 1854–1964* (1964).
Sparks, David S., "Birth of the Republican Party in Iowa, 1854–1856," *Iowa Jour. Hist.*, 54 (1956), 1.
Van Bolt, Roger H., "Rise of the Republican Party in Indiana, 1855–1856," *Ind. Mag. Hist.*, 51 (1955), 185.

See also 10.3 for biographies/writings of:

Banks, Nathaniel P., 1816–1894
Cameron, Simon, 1799–1889
Chase, Salmon P., 1808–1873
Davis, David, 1815–1886
Frémont, John C., 1813–1890
Greeley, Horace, 1811–1872
Grimes, James Wilson, 1816–1872
Grow, Galusha A., 1822–1907
Hamilton, James A., 1788–1878
Hoar, George F., 1826–1904
Lincoln, Abraham, 1809–1865
McLean, John, 1785–1861
Morgan, Edwin D., 1811–1883
Raymond, Henry J., 1820–1869
Stevens, Thaddeus, 1792–1868
Sumner, Charles, 1811–1874
Trumbull, Lyman, 1813–1896
Wade, Benjamin F., 1800–1878
Weed, Thurlow, 1797–1882
Wentworth, John, 1815–1888
Wilmot, David, 1814–1868

45.8 ELECTION OF 1856 AND BUCHANAN ADMINISTRATION, 1857–1861

Auchampaugh, P. G., *James Buchanan and His Cabinet* (1926).
Crenshaw, Ollinger, "Speakership Contest of 1859–1860," *MVHR*, 29 (1942), 323.
Halstead, Murat, *Trimmers, Trucklers, and Temporizers: Notes from Political Conventions of 1856*, William B. Hesseltine and Rex G. Fisher, eds. (1961).
Luthin, Reinhard H., "Democratic Split During Buchanan's Administration," *Penn. Hist.*, 11 (1944), 13.
Nichols, Roy F., and Philip S. Klein, "Election of 1856," in Arthur M. Schlesinger, Jr. and Fred L. Israel, eds., *History of American Presidential Elections, 1789–1968*, vol. II (1971).

Sears, L. M., "Slidell and Buchanan," *AHR*, 27 (1922), 709.

See also 10.3 for biographies/writings of:

Banks, Nathaniel P., 1816–1894
Black, Jeremiah S., 1810–1883
Buchanan, James, 1791–1868
Cass, Lewis, 1782–1866
Cobb, Howell, 1815–1868
Frémont, John C., 1813–1890
Stanton, Edwin M., 1814–1869

45.9 LEGALITY OF SLAVERY IN TERRITORIES

45.9.1 General

Bestor, Arthur E., Jr., "State Sovereignty and Slavery," Ill. State Hist. Soc., *Jour.*, 54 (1961), 117.
Howe, Mark DeW., "Federalism and Civil Rights," Mass. Hist. Soc., *Proc.*, 77 (1966), 15.
Nevins, Allan, "Constitution, Slavery, and Territories," in *Gaspar Bacon Lectures on the Constitution of United States, 1940–1950* (1953).
Russel, Robert R., "Constitutional Doctrines with Regard to Slavery in the Territories," *JSH*, 32 (1966), 466.

45.9.2 Dred Scott Decision

Alexander, Thomas B., "Dred Scott Case," So. Car. Hist. Assoc., *Proc.* (1953), 37.
Allis, Frederick S., "Dred Scott Labyrinth," in Stuart Hughes, ed., *Teachers of History: Essays in Honor of Laurence Bradford Packard* (1954).
Auchampaugh, Philip, "James Buchanan, the Court, and the Dred Scott Case," *Tenn. Hist. Mag.*, 9 (1924), 56.
Catterall, H. T., "Some Antecedents of the Dred Scott Case," *AHR*, 30 (1924), 56.
Corwin, Edward S., "Dred Scott Decision," *AHR*, 17 (1911), 52.
Ehrlich, Walter, "Was the Dred Scott Case Valid?" *JAH*, 55 (1968), 256.
Hagan, H. H., "Dred Scott Decision," *Georgetown Law Jour.*, 15 (1927), 95.
Hodder, Frank H., "Dred Scott Case," *MVHR*, 16 (1929), 3.
Hopkins, Vincent C., *Dred Scott's Case* (1951).
Hurd, John C., *Law of Freedom and Bondage* (2 vols., 1858–1862).
Kutler, Stanley I., *Dred Scott Decision* (1967).
McCormac, Eugene I., "Justice Campbell and the Dred Scott Decision," *MVHR*, 19 (1933), 565.
Mendelson, Wallace, "Dred Scott's Case," *Minn. Law Rev.*, 38 (1953), 16.
Stenberg, R. R., "Political Aspects of the Dred Scott Case," *MVHR*, 19 (1933), 571.
Swisher, Carl B., "Dred Scott One Hundred Years After," *Jour. Politics*, 19 (1957), 167.

See also 10.3 for biographies/writings of:

Campbell, John A., 1811–1889
Curtis, Benjamin R., 1809–1874
Johnson, Reverdy, 1796–1876
McLean, John, 1785–1861
Taney, Roger B., 1777–1864

45.10 JOHN BROWN AND HARPER'S FERRY

Furnas, J. C., *The Road to Harper's Ferry* (1959).
Harlow, Ralph V., "Gerrit Smith and Brown Raid," *AHR*, 38 (1932), 32.
Hinton, Richard J., *John Brown and His Men* (1894).
Keller, Allan, *Thunder at Harper's Ferry* (1958).
Landon, Fred, "Canadian Negroes and John Brown Raid," *Jour. Negro Hist.*, 6 (1921), 174.

See also 10.3 for biographies/writings of:

Brown, John, 1800–1859
Douglass, Frederick, 1817–1895
Higginson, Thomas W., 1823–1911
Howe, Samuel G., 1801–1876
Memminger, Christopher G., 1803–1888
Wise, Henry A., 1806–1876

45.11 NATIVISM AND KNOW-NOTHING PARTY

Bean, W. G., "Puritan and Celt," *NEQ*, 7 (1934), 70.
Berger, Max, "Irish Emigrant and American Nativism, *Penn. Mag. Hist. Biog.*, 70 (1946], 146.
Billington, Ray A., *Protestant Crusade 1800–1860* (1938).
Brand, Carl, "The Know Nothing Party in Indiana," *Ind. Mag. Hist.*, 18 (1922), 47.
Broussard, James H., "Some Determinants of Know-Nothing Electoral Strength in the South, 1856," *La. Hist.*, 7 (1966), 5.
Curran, Thomas J., "Seward and the Know Nothings," *N.Y. Hist. Soc. Quar.*, 51 (1967), 141.
Davis, David B., "Some Ideological Functions of Prejudice in Ante-Bellum America," *Am. Quar.*, 15 (1963), 115.
Gibson, Florence E., *Attitudes of New York Irish* (1951).
Handlin, Oscar, *Boston's Immigrants: A Study in Acculturation* (rev. ed., 1959).
Leonard, Ira M., "Rise and Fall of the American Republican Party in New York City, 1843–45," *N.Y. Hist. Soc. Quar.*, 50 (1966), 151.
McGann, Agnes G., *Nativism in Kentucky* (1944).
McGrath, Sister Paul-of-the-Cross, *Political Nativism in Texas* (1930).
McKay, Ernest A., "Henry Wilson: Unprincipled Know Nothing," *Mid-America*, 46 (1964), 29.
Overdyke, W. D., *Know-Nothing Party in the South* (1950).
Rand, Larry A., "Know-Nothing Party in Rhode Island," *R.I. Hist.*, 23 (1964), 102.
Rice, Philip M., "Know-Nothing Party in Virginia, 1854–1856," *Va. Mag. Hist. Biog.*, 55 (1947), 61.
Schmeckebier, Laurence F., *Know-Nothing Party in Maryland* (1899).
Scisco, Louis D., *Political Nativism in New York* (1901).
Soulé, Leon C., *Know Nothing Party in New Orleans* (1962).
Stephenson, George M., "Nativism in Forties and Fifties," *MVHR*, 9 (1922), 185.
Stickney, Charles, *Know-Nothingism in Rhode Island* (1894).
Thompson, Arthur W., "Political Nativism in Florida," *JSH*, 15 (1949), 39.
Wooster, Ralph A., "Analysis of Texas Know Nothings," *Southw. Hist. Quar.*, 70 (1967), 414.

45.12 NORTHERN POLITICS IN 1850's

Hendrickson, James E., *Joe Lane of Oregon: Machine Politics and the Sectional Crisis, 1849–1861* (1967).

Pendergraft, Daryl, "Thomas Corwin and Conservative Republican Reaction, 1858–1861," *Ohio State Archaeol. and Hist. Quar.*, 57 (1948), 1.

Shapiro, Samuel, "Massachusetts Constitutional Convention of 1853," *NEQ*, 33 (1960), 207.

Van Bolt, Roger H., "Indiana in Political Transition, 1851–1853," *Ind. Mag. Hist.*, 49 (1953), 131.

45.13 LINCOLN-DOUGLAS DEBATES

Angle, Paul M., ed., *Created Equal? Lincoln-Douglas Debates* (1958).

Fehrenbacher, Don E., *Prelude to Greatness: Lincoln in the 1850's* (1962).

Heckman, Richard A., *Lincoln vs. Douglas* (1967).

Jaffa, Harry V., *Crisis of House Divided: Lincoln-Douglas Debates* (1959).

—— "Expediency and Morality in Lincoln-Douglas Debates," *Anchor Rev.*, no. 2 (1957), 179.

Johannsen, Robert W., ed., *The Lincoln-Douglas Debates of 1858* (1965).

King, Willard L., and Allan Nevins, "The Constitution and the Declaration of Independence as Issues in the Lincoln-Douglas Debates," Ill. State Hist. Soc., *Jour.*, 52 (1959), 7.

See also 10.3 for biographies/writings of:

Douglas, Stephen A., 1813–1861
Lincoln, Abraham, 1809–1865

45.14 PANIC OF 1857

Eiselen, M. R., *Rise of Pennsylvania Protectionism* (1932).

Kinley, David, *Independent Treasury* (1910).

Rosenberg, Hans, *Die Weltwirtschaftskrisis von 1857–1859* (1934).

Taylor, George R., *Transportation Revolution* (1951).

Van Vleck, George W., *Panic of 1857* (1943).

45.15 ELECTION OF 1860

Crenshaw, Ollinger, *Slave States in the Presidential Election of 1860* (1945).

Fite, Emerson D., *Presidential Campaign of 1860* (1911).

Graebner, Norman A., ed., *Politics and Crisis of 1860* (1961).

Halstead, Murat, *Three against Lincoln: Caucuses of 1860*, William B. Hesseltine, ed. (1960).

Kleppner, Paul J., "Lincoln and Immigrant Vote: Religious Polarization," *Mid-America*, 48 (1966), 176.

Luthin, Reinhard H., *First Lincoln Campaign* (1944).

Meerse, David E., "Buchanan and Election of 1860," *Civil War Hist.*, 12 (1966), 116.

Milton, George F., *Eve of Conflict: Stephen A. Douglas and the Needless War* (1934).

Monaghan, Jay, *Man Who Elected Lincoln* (1956).

Morison, Elting, "Election of 1860," in Arthur M. Schlesinger, Jr. and Fred L. Israel, eds., *History of American Presidential Elections, 1789–1968*. Vol. II (1971).

Odle, Thomas D., "Commercial Interests of the Great Lakes and Campaign Issues of 1860," *Mich. Hist.*, 40 (1956), 1.

Pitkin, T. M., "Western Republicans and Tariff in 1860," *MVHR*, 27 (1940), 401.

Smith, Donnal V., "Chase and Election of 1860," *Ohio State Archaeol. and Hist. Quar.*, 39 (1930), 515.

Swierenga, Robert P., "Ethnic Voter and the First Lincoln Election," *Civil War Hist.*, 11 (1965), 27.
Thomas, David Y., "Southern Non-Slaveholders in the Election of 1860," *Pol. Sci. Quar.*, 26 (1911), 222.

See also 10.3 for biographies/writings of:

Bates, Edward, 1793–1869
Bell, John, 1797–1869
Cameron, Simon, 1799–1889
Chase, Salmon P., 1808–1873
Davis, David, 1815–1886
Douglass, Frederick, 1817–1895
Kasson, John A., 1822–1910
Lane, Joseph, 1801–1881
Seward, William H., 1801–1872
Yancey, William L., 1814–1863

Part Seven Civil War and Reconstruction

46 Civil War, 1860–1865

46.1 GENERAL

Boatner, Mark M., III, *Civil War Dictionary* (1959).
"Civil War—Russian Version (I)," Ada Stoflet, trans., *Civil War Hist.*, 8 (1962), 357. From the *Soviet Encyclopedia*.
Nevins, Allan, *Ordeal of the Union* (8 vols., 1947–1971).
Randall, James G., and David Donald, *Civil War and Reconstruction* (2nd rev. ed., 1969).
Rhodes, J. F., *History of the United States from the Compromise of 1850* (7 vols., 1893–1906).

46.2 INTERPRETATIVE STUDIES

Catton, Bruce, *America Goes to War* (1958).
Holmes, William F., and Harold M. Hollingsworth, eds., *Essays on the American Civil War* (1968).
McWhiney, Grady, *Grant, Lee, Lincoln and the Radicals: Essays on Civil War Leadership* (1964).
Marx, Karl, and Frederick Engels, *Civil War in the United States*, R. Enmale, ed. (1937).
Miers, Earl S., *Great Rebellion: Emergence of the American Conscience* (1958).
Nichols, Roy F., "Operation of American Democracy, 1861–1865," *JSH*, 25 (1959), 31.
Shryock, R. H., "Nationalistic Tradition of the Civil War," *So. Atl. Quar.*, 22 (1933), 294.

*   *   *   *   *   *   *

"A Bibliography of Civil War Articles," *Civil War Hist.*, 6 (1960–   ).
Brogan, Dennis W., "A Fresh Appraisal of the Civil War," *Harper's*, 220 (1960), 121.
Craven, Avery O., *An Historian and the Civil War* (1964).
Curry, Richard O., "Recent Interpretations of 'Copperheads'," *Civil War Hist.*, 13 (1967), 25.
Harper, Alan D., "William A. Dunning: Historian as Nemesis," *Civil War Hist.*, 10 (1964), 54.
Logsdon, Joseph A., "Civil War—Russian Version (II): Soviet Historians," *Civil War Hist.*, 8 (1962), 365.
Newman, Ralph G., ed., "For Collectors Only [Personal Narratives]," *Civil War Hist.*, 1 (1955), 71.
———— "For Collectors Only [Notable Biographies, Military and Political]," *Civil War Hist.*, 1 (1955), 175.
Pressly, Thomas J., *Americans Interpret Their Civil War* (1954).

Ramsdell, Charles W., "Changing Interpretation of Civil War," *JSH*, 3 (1937), 3.
Randall, James G., "Civil War Restudied," *JSH*, 6 (1940), 439.
Williams, T. Harry, "Freeman, Historian of the Civil War," *JSH*, 21 (1955), 91.

46.3 CAUSES

Bagley, W. C., *Soil Exhaustion and Civil War* (1942).
Bestor, Arthur, "Civil War as a Constitutional Crisis," *AHR*, 69 (1964), 327.
Campbell, Alexander E., "Isolationism and Civil War," *JSH*, 29 (1963), 161.
Cole, A. C., *Irrepressible Conflict* (1934).
Craven, Avery O., *Coming of the Civil War* (2nd rev. ed., 1957).
——— *Repressible Conflict* (1939).
Davidson, P. G., "Industrialism in the South," *So. Atl. Quar.*, 27 (1928), 405.
Dumond, Dwight L., *Anti-Slavery Origins of the Civil War* (1939).
Govan, Thomas P., "Slavery and the Civil War," *Sewanee Rev.*, 48 (1940), 533.
Owsley, Frank L., "Fundamental Cause of the Civil War," *JSH*, 7 (1941), 3.
Rozwenc, Edwin C., *Slavery as a Cause of the Civil War* (1949).
Schlesinger, Arthur M., Jr., "Causes of the Civil War," *Partisan Rev.*, 16 (1949), 969.
Stampp, Kenneth M., ed., *Causes of the Civil War* (1959).

*   *   *   *   *   *   *

Beale, Howard K., "What Historians Said about the Causes of the Civil War," Soc. Sci. Res. Council, *Bull.*, No. 54 (1946), 53.
Benson, Lee, and T. J. Pressly, *Can Differences in Interpretation of American Civil War be Resolved Objectively?* (1956).
Benson, Lee, and Cushing Strout, "Causation and the American Civil War," *Hist. and Theory*, 1 (1961), 163.
Bonner, Thomas N., "Civil War Historians and the Needless War Doctrine," *Jour. Hist. Ideas*, 17 (1956), 193.
Cauthen, C. E., and Lewis P. Jones, "Coming of the Civil War," in Arthur S. Link and Rembert W. Patrick, eds., *Writing Southern History: Essays in Honor of Fletcher M. Green* (1965).
Donald, David, "American Historians and Causes of the Civil War," *So. Atl. Quar.*, 59 (1960), 351.
Dray, William, "Some Causal Accounts of the American Civil War," *Daedalus*, 91 (1962), 578.
Garver, Newton, "Comments on Dray's 'Some Causal Accounts of American Civil War'," *Daedalus*, 91 (1962), 592.
Geyl, Pieter, "American Civil War and the Problem of Inevitability," *NEQ*, 24 (1951), 147.
Newman, Ralph G., ed., "For Collectors Only [Causes of the Civil War]," *Civ. War Hist.*, 1 (1955), 305.

46.4 SECESSION CRISIS, 1860–1861

46.4.1 General

Catton, Bruce, *Centennial History of the Civil War* (3 vols., 1961–1965).
Catton, William B., and Bruce Catton, *Two Roads to Sumter* (1963).
Dumond, Dwight L., *Secession Movement, 1860–1861* (1931).
——— ed., *Southern Editorials on Secession* (1931).
Hamilton, J. G. de Roulhac, "Lincoln's Election as Menace to Slavery?" *AHR*, 37 (1932), 700.
Knoles, George H., ed., *Crisis of Union* (1965).
Smiley, David L., "Revolutionary Origins of South's Constitutional Defenses," *No. Car. Hist. Rev.*, 44 (1967), 256.

Stern, Philip V., ed., *Prologue to Sumter* (1961).
White, Melvin J., *Secession Movement, 1847–1852* (1910).
Wooster, Ralph A., *Secession Conventions of the South* (1962).

*   *   *   *   *   *   *

Donnelly, William J., "Historiography of Support for Secession," *No. Car. Hist. Rev.*, 42 (1965), 70.

See also 10.3 for biographies/writings of:

Adams, Charles F., 1807–1886
Adams, Henry B., 1838–1918
Andrew, John A., 1818–1867
Bates, Edward, 1793–1869
Bell, John, 1797–1869
Benjamin, Judah P., 1811–1884
Brown, Joseph E., 1821–1894
Browning, Orville H., 1806–1881
Buchanan, James, 1791–1868
Campbell, John A., 1811–1889
Chandler, William E., 1835–1917
Chandler, Zachariah, 1813–1879
Chase, Salmon P., 1808–1873
Cobb, Howell, 1815–1868
Cox, Samuel S. "Sunset", 1824–1889
Crittenden, John J., 1787–1863
Cushing, Caleb, 1800–1879
Davis, Jefferson, 1808–1889
Dix, John A., 1798–1879
Douglas, Stephen A., 1813–1861
Ellis, John W., fl. 1841–1861
Fitzhugh, George, 1806–1881
Greeley, Horace, 1811–1872
Hammond, James H., 1807–1864
Houston, Sam, 1793–1863
Jay, William, 1789–1858
Johnson, Herschel V., 1812–1880
Kendall, Amos, 1789–1869
Lincoln, Abraham, 1809–1865
Memminger, Christopher G., 1803–1888
Rhett, Robert B., 1800–1876
Ruffin, Thomas, 1787–1870
Scott, Winfield, 1786–1866
Seward, William H., 1801–1872
Sherman, John, 1823–1900
Slidell, John, 1793–1871
Stephens, Alexander H., 1812–1883
Stevens, Thaddeus, 1792–1868
Toombs, Robert, 1810–1885
Tyler, Robert, 1816–1877
Wade, Benjamin F., 1800–1878
Weed, Thurlow, 1797–1882
Welles, Gideon, 1802–1878
Wilmot, David, 1814–1868
Yancey, William L., 1814–1863

46.4.2 Northern Reaction

Baringer, William E., *A House Dividing: Lincoln as President Elect* (1945).
Bonner, Thomas N., "Horace Greeley and the Secession Movement," *MVHR*, 38 (1951), 425.

Johannsen, Robert W., "Douglas Democracy and the Crisis of Disunion," *Civil War Hist.*, 9 (1963), 1963.

Perkins, Howard C., ed., *Northern Editorials on Secession* (2 vols., 1942).

Potter, David M., "Horace Greeley and Peaceable Secession," *JSH*, 7 (1941), 145.

——— *Lincoln and His Party in the Secession Crisis* (1942).

Stampp, Kenneth M., *And the War Came* (1950).

Van Deusen, Glyndon G., "Seward and the Secession Winter of 1860–1861," Can. Hist. Assoc., *Ann. Rep.* (1966), 84.

White, Laura A., "Sumner and Crisis of 1861," in Avery O. Craven, ed., *Essays in Honor of William E. Dodd* (1935).

46.4.3 Peace Convention and Efforts at Compromise

Glover, G. G., *Immediate Pre-Civil War Compromise Efforts* (1934).

Gunderson, Robert G., *Old Gentlemen's Convention: Washington Peace Conference of 1861* (1961).

Keene, Jesse L., *Peace Convention of 1861* (1961).

Knox, C. E., "Possibilities of Compromise in Senate Committee of Thirteen," *Jour. Negro Hist.*, 17 (1932), 437.

Lee, R. Alton, "Corwin Amendment in the Secession Crisis," *Ohio Hist. Quar.*, 70 (1961), 1.

Morison, Samuel E., "Peace Convention of February, 1861," Mass. Hist. Soc., *Proc.*, 73 (1961), 58.

Simms, Henry H., *Ohio Politics on the Eve of Conflict* (1961).

46.4.4 State Studies

46.4.4.1 Alabama

Brantley, William H., Jr., "Alabama Secedes," *Ala. Rev.*, 7 (1954), 165.

Denman, C. P., *Secession Movement in Alabama* (1933).

Long, Durward, "Unanimity and Disloyalty in Secessionist Alabama," *Civil War Hist.*, 11 (1965), 257.

46.4.4.2 Georgia

Bryan, T. Conn, "Secession of Georgia," *Ga. Hist. Quar.*, 31 (1947), 89.

Johnson, Herschel V., "From the Autobiography [of a Georgia Governor]," *AHR*, 30 (1925), 311.

46.4.4.3 Louisiana

Caskey, Willie M., *Secession and Restoration of Louisiana* (1938).

46.4.4.4 Mississippi

Rainwater, P. L., *Mississippi, Storm-Center of Secession, 1856–1861* (1938).

46.4.4.5 Missouri

Ryle, W. W., *Missouri, Union or Secession* (1931).

46.4.4.6 North Carolina

Sitterson, J. Carlyle, *Secession Movement in North Carolina* (1939).

46.4.4.7 South Carolina

Boucher, C. S., *South Carolina and the South* (1919).

Channing, Steven A., *Crisis of Fear: Secession in South Carolina* (1970).

Hamer, Philip M., *Secession Movement in South Carolina, 1847–1852* (1918).

Kibler, L. A., "Unionist Sentiment in South Carolina in 1860," *JSH*, 4 (1938), 346.
May, John A., and Joan R. Faunt, *South Carolina Secedes* (1960).

46.4.4.8 Tennessee

Henry, J. Milton, "Revolution in Tennessee, February, 1861, to June, 1861," *Tenn. Hist. Quar.*, 18 (1959), 99.

46.4.4.9 Texas

Winkler, E. W., ed., *Journal of the Secession Convention of Texas, 1861* (1912).

46.4.4.10 Virginia

Arnold, Dean A., "Ultimatum of Virginia Unionists: 'Security for Slavery or Disunion'," *Jour. Negro Hist.*, 48 (1963), 115.
Shanks, H. T., *Secession Movement in Virginia* (1934).
Walmsley, J. E., ed., "Change of Secession Sentiment in Virginia," *AHR*, 31 (1925), 82.

46.4.5 Fort Sumter and Outbreak of War

Current, Richard N., "Confederates and the First Shot," *Civil War Hist.*, 7 (1961), 357.
——— *Lincoln and the First Shot* (1963).
Hoogenboom, Ari A., "Gustavus Fox and Relief of Fort Sumter," *Civil War Hist.*, 9 (1963), 383.
McWhiney, Grady, "Confederacy's First Shot," *Civil War Hist.*, 14 (1968), 5.
Ramsdell, Charles W., "Lincoln and Fort Sumter," *JSH*, 3 (1937), 259.
Smith, William E., *Francis Preston Blair Family in Politics* (2 vols., 1933).
Swanberg, William A., *First Blood: Fort Sumter* (1957).

See also 10.3 for biographies/writings of:

Bates, Edward, 1793–1869
Browning, Orville H., 1806–1881
Cameron, Simon, 1799–1889
Chandler, William E., 1835–1917
Chase, Salmon P., 1808–1873
Davis, David, 1815–1886
Everett, Edward, 1794–1865
Fessenden, William P., 1806–1869
Field, Stephen J., 1816–1899
Frémont, John C., 1813–1890
Gurowski, Adam, 1805–1866
Hamlin, Hannibal, 1809–1881
Hay, John M., 1838–1905
Lieber, Francis, 1800–1872
Lincoln, Abraham, 1809–1865
McClellan, George B., 1826–1885
McCulloch, Hugh, 1808–1895
Miller, Samuel F., 1816–1890
Morgan, Edwin D., 1811–1883
Seward, William H., 1801–1872
Strong, George T., 1820–1875
Sumner, Charles, 1811–1874
Taney, Roger B., 1777–1864
Usher, John P., 1816–1889
Weed, Thurlow, 1797–1882

Welles, Gideon, 1802–1878
Wood, Fernando, 1812–1881

46.5 LINCOLN ADMINISTRATION, 1861–1865

46.5.1 General

Bruce, Robert V., *Lincoln and Tools of War* (1956).
Carman, H. J., and R. H. Luthin, *Lincoln and Patronage* (1943).
Donald, David, *Lincoln Reconsidered: Essays on the Civil War Era* (2nd ed., 1962).
Dorris, Jonathan T., *Pardon and Amnesty under Lincoln and Johnson* (1953).
Leech, Margaret, *Reveille in Washington, 1860–1865* (1941).
Randall, James G., *Lincoln and the South* (1946).
Van Riper, Paul P., and Keith A. Sutherland, "Northern Civil Service: 1861–1865," *Civil War Hist.*, 11 (1965), 351.
Wheare, Kenneth C., *Abraham Lincoln and the United States* (1948).

See also 47.4, Reconstruction during the Civil War.

46.5.2 Cabinet

Frank, John P., "Edward Bates, Lincoln's Attorney-General," *Am. Jour. Legal Hist.*, 10 (1966), 34.
Hendrick, B. J., *Lincoln's War Cabinet* (1946).
Pratt, Fletcher, *Stanton: Lincoln's Secretary of War* (1953).
Smith, Donnal V., *Chase and Civil War Politics* (1931).

See also 10.3 for biographies/writings of:

Bates, Edward, 1793–1869
Cameron, Simon, 1799–1889
Chase, Salmon P., 1808–1873
McCulloch, Hugh, 1808–1895
Nicolay, John G., 1832–1901
Seward, William H., 1801–1872
Stanton, Edwin M., 1814–1869
Usher, John P., 1816–1889
Welles, Gideon, 1802–1878

46.5.3 Lincoln as Politician

Harper, Robert S., *Lincoln and the Press* (1951).
Hesseltine, William B., "Lincoln and the Politicians," *Civil War Hist.*, 6 (1960), 43.
——— *Lincoln and the War Governors* (1948).
——— *Lincoln's Plan of Reconstruction* (1960).
Monaghan, Jay, *Diplomat in Carpet Slippers* (1945).
Williams, T. Harry, "Abraham Lincoln," *MVHR*, 40 (1953), 89.
——— *Lincoln and Radicals* (1941).
Zornow, William F., *Lincoln and the Party Divided* (1954).

46.5.4 Assassination

Moore, Guy W., *Case of Mrs. Surratt: Conspiracy in the Lincoln Assassination* (1954).
Stewart, Charles J., "Lincoln's Assassination and Protestant Clergy of the North," *Ill. State Hist. Soc., Jour.*, 54 (1961), 268.

46.6 CONSTITUTIONAL QUESTIONS AND SUPREME COURT

Hyman, Harold M., *Era of the Oath: Northern Loyalty Tests* (1954).
—— "Law and Impact of Civil War: Review Essay," *Civil War Hist.*, 14 (1968), 51.
Klaus, Samuel, ed., *Milligan Case* (1929).
Randall, James G., *Constitutional Problems under Lincoln* (rev. ed., 1951).
Silver, David M., *Lincoln's Supreme Court* (1956).
Sprague, Dean, *Freedom under Lincoln* (1965).

46.7 CONGRESS

Bogue, Allan G., "Bloc and Party in the Senate, 1861–1863," *Civil War Hist.*, 13 (1967), 221.
Brichford, Maynard J., "Congress at the Outbreak of War," *Civil War Hist.*, 3 (1957), 153.
Curry, Leonard P., *Blueprint for Modern America: Non-Military Legislation of the First Civil War Congress* (1968).
Donald, David, "Devils Facing Zionwards," in Grady McWhiney, ed., *Grant, Lee, Lincoln and the Radicals: Essays in Civil War Leadership* (1964).
Gambill, Edwin L., "Who Were the Senate Radicals?" *Civil War Hist.*, 11 (1965), 237.
Linden, Glenn M., "'Radicals' and Economic Policies: House of Representatives, 1861–1873," *Civil War Hist.*, 13 (1967), 51.
—— "'Radicals' and Economic Policies: Senate, 1861–1873," *JSH*, 32 (1966), 189.
Mallam, William D., "Lincoln and Conservatives," *JSH*, 28 (1962), 31.
Simon, John Y., "From Galena to Appomattox: Grant and Washburne," Ill. State Hist. Soc., *Jour.*, 58 (1965), 165.
Trefousse, Hans L., "Joint Committee on Conduct of War: A Reassessment," *Civil War Hist.*, 10 (1964), 5.
Williams, T. Harry, *Lincoln and the Radicals* (1941).

*   *   *   *   *   *   *

Williams, T. Harry, "Lincoln and the Radicals: Civil War History and Historiography," in Grady McWhiney, ed., *Grant, Lee, Lincoln and the Radicals: Essays in Civil War Leadership* (1964).

See also 10.3 for biographies/writings of:

Blaine, James G., 1830–1893
Chandler, Zachariah, 1813–1879
Conkling, Roscoe, 1829–1888
Cox, Samuel S. "Sunset", 1824–1889
Davis, Henry W., 1817–1865
Greeley, Horace, 1811–1872
Grimes, James W., 1816–1872
Grow, Galusha A., 1822–1907
Hale, John P., 1806–1873
Johnson, Andrew, 1808–1875
Johnson, Reverdy, 1796–1876
Julian, George W., 1817–1899
Lovejoy, Owen, 1811–1864
Morgan, Edwin D., 1811–1883
Stevens, Thaddeus, 1792–1868
Trumbull, Lyman, 1813–1896
Tweed, William, 1823–1878
Wade, Benjamin F., 1800–1878

46.8 ELECTION OF 1864

Hyman, Harold M., "Election of 1864," in Arthur M. Schlesinger, Jr. and Fred L. Israel, eds., *History of American Presidential Elections, 1789–1968*, vol. II (1971).
Kirkland, Edward C., *Peacemakers of 1864* (1927).
Zornow, William F., *Lincoln and the Party Divided* (1954).

See also 10.3 for biographies/writings of:

Johnson, Andrew, 1808–1875
Lincoln, Abraham, 1809–1865
McClellan, George B., 1826–1885

46.9 UNION

46.9.1 General

Harwell, Richard B., ed., *Union Reader* (1958).
Smith, George W., and Charles Judah, eds., *Life in the North during the Civil War: Source History* (1966).

46.9.2 Politics

Benton, Josiah H., *Voting in the Field: Civil War* (1915).
Freidel, Frank, ed., *Union Pamphlets of the Civil War, 1861–1865* (2 vols., 1967).
Kleppner, Paul J., "Lincoln and the Immigrant Vote: Religious Polarization," *Mid-America*, 48 (1966), 176.
McPherson, James M., *Struggle for Equality: Abolitionists and the Negro in Civil War and Reconstruction* (1964).

46.9.3 Economy

46.9.3.1 General

Andreano, Ralph L., ed., *Economic Impact of the Civil War* (1962).
Clark, Victor S., "Manufacturing Development during the Civil War," *Military Historian and Economist*, 3 (1918), 92.
Cochran, Thomas C., "Did the Civil War Retard Industrialization?" *MVHR*, 48 (1961), 197.
Fish, Carl R., "Social Relief in the Northwest," *AHR*, 22 (1917), 309.
Fite, Emerson D., *Social and Industrial Conditions in the North* (1910).
Gilchrist, David T., and W. David Lewis, eds., *Economic Change in the Civil War Era* (1965).
Lerner, Eugene M., "Investment Uncertainty during Civil War: McCormick Brothers," *Jour. Econ. Hist.*, 16 (1956), 34.
Merk, Frederick, *Economic History of Wisconsin during the Civil War Decade* (1916).
Scheiber, Harry N., "Economic Change in the Civil War Era: Analysis of Recent Studies," *Civil War Hist.*, 11 (1965), 396.
Shapiro, Henry D., *Confiscation of Confederate Property in the North* (1962).
Vartanian, Pershing, "Cochran Thesis: Critique in Statistical Analysis," *JAH*, 51 (1964), 77.

46.9.3.2 Fiscal Policies

Barrett, D. C., *Greenbacks and Resumption* (1931).
Davis, Andrew M., *Origin of the National Banking System* (1910).

Hammond, Bray, *Sovereignty and an Empty Purse: Banks and Politics in the Civil War* (1970).

Rein, Bert W., *Analysis and Critique of Union Financing of the Civil War* (1962).

Sellers, J. L., "Interpretation of Civil War Finance," *AHR*, 30 (1925), 282.

Trescott, Paul B., "Federal Government Receipts and Expenditures,1861–1875," *Jour. Econ. Hist.*, 26 (1966), 206.

See also 10.3 for biographies/writings of:

Belmont, August, 1816–1890
Chase, Salmon P., 1808–1873
Cooke, Jay, 1821–1905
Fessenden, William P., 1806–1869
Morrill, Justin S., 1810–1898

46.9.3.3 Railroads

"Civil War Railroads," *Civil War Hist.*, 7 (1961). Entire issue.

Farnham, Wallace D., "Weakened Spring of Government," *AHR*, 68 (1963). Union Pacific.

Fogel, Robert W., *Union Pacific Railroad: Case in Premature Enterprise* (1960).

Lord, Francis A., *Lincoln's Railroad Man: Herman Haupt* (1969).

Summers, Festus P., *Baltimore and Ohio in the Civil War* (1939).

Sutton, Robert M., "Illinois Central: Thoroughfare for Freedom," *Civil War Hist.*, 7 (1961), 273.

Turner, George E., *Victory Rode the Rails: Railroads in the Civil War* (1953).

Weber, Thomas, *Northern Railroads in the Civil War* (1952).

46.9.3.4 Agriculture and Land Grant Policies

Gates, Paul W., *Agriculture and the Civil War* (1965).

—— "Homestead Law in an Incongruous Land System," *AHR*, 41 (1936), 652.

James, Edmund J., *Origins of the Land Grant Act of 1862* (1910).

Merk, Frederick, "Eastern Antecedents of Grangers," *Agric. Hist.*, 23 (1949), 1.

Rasmussen, Wayne D., "Civil War: Catalyst of the Agricultural Revolution," *Agric. Hist.*, 39 (1965), 187.

Simon, John Y., "Politics of the Morrill Act," *Agric. Hist.*, 37 (1963), 103.

46.9.3.5 Commerce

Belcher, W. W., *Economic Rivalry St. Louis and Chicago* (1947).

Coulter, E. Merton, "Effects of Secession upon the Mississippi Valley," *MVHR*, 3 (1916), 275.

Johnson, Ludwell H., "Commerce Between Northeastern Ports and the Confederacy, 1861–1865," *JAH*, 54 (1967), 30.

—— "Contraband Trade during the Last Year of the Civil War," *MVHR*, 49 (1963), 635.

46.9.3.6 Labor

Baxter, Maurice G., "Encouragement of Immigration to the Middle West during Civil War," *Ind. Mag. Hist.*, 46 (1950), 25.

Man, Albon P., Jr., "Labor Competition and the New York Draft Riots of 1863," *Jour. Negro Hist.*, 36 (1951), 375.

Ware, Norman J., *Labor Movement in the United States, 1860–1895* (1929).

46.9.4 Religion and Ethnicity

"Civil War Religion," *Civil War Hist.*, 6 (1960). Entire issue.

Dunham, Chester F., *Attitude of the Northern Clergy toward the South, 1860–1865* (1942).

Gibson, Florence E., *Attitudes of the New York Irish* (1951).
Korn, B. W., *American Jewry and Civil War* (1951).
Meyer, Isidore S., ed., "American Jew in the Civil War," *Am. Jew. Hist. Quar.*, 50 (1961), 263.
Wilson, Edmund, "Abraham Lincoln: Union as Religious Mysticism," in Edmund Wilson, *Eight Essays* (1954).

46.9.5 Women

Greenbie, Marjorie B., *Lincoln's Daughters of Mercy* (1944).
Massey, Mary E., *Bonnet Brigades: Women and the Civil War* (1966).

46.9.6 Opposition to War

Clark, Charles B., "Suppression and Control of Maryland, 1861–1865; Study of Federal-State Relations," *Md. Hist. Mag.*, 54 (1959), 241.
Curry, Richard O., "The Union as It Was: Recent Interpretations of Copperheads," *Civil War Hist.*, 13 (1967), 25.
Fesler, Mayo, "Secret Political Societies," *Ind. Mag. Hist.*, 14 (1918), 183.
Freidel, Frank, ed., *Union Pamphlets of the Civil War, 1861–1865* (2 vols., 1967).
Gibson, Florence E., *Attitudes of New York Irish* (1951).
Gray, Wood, *Hidden Civil War* (1942).
Kirkland, Edward C., *Peacemakers of 1864* (1927).
Klement, Frank L., "Clement L. Vallandigham's Exile in the Confederacy, 1863," *JSH*, 31 (1965), 149.
—— *Copperheads in the Middle West* (1960).
Talmadge, John E., "Peace Movement in Civil War Connecticut," *NEQ*, 27 (1964), 306.
Wainwright, Nicholas B., "Loyal Opposition in Civil War Philadelphia," *Penn. Mag. Hist. Biog.*, 88 (1964), 294.
Wright, Edward N., *Conscientious Objectors in the Civil War* (1931).

See also 10.3 for biographies/writings of:

Vallandigham, Clement L., 1820–1871

See also 46.12.3, Military History–Recruiting, Conscription, Draft Riots, and Desertion.

46.9.7 State and Local Studies

46.9.7.1 General
U.S. War Department, *Bibliography of State Participation in the Civil War* (1913).

46.9.7.2 Connecticut
Lane, Jarlath R., *Political History of Connecticut during the Civil War* (1941).
Niven, John, *Connecticut: Role in the Civil War* (1965).

46.9.7.2 Delaware
Hancock, Harold B., *Delaware during the Civil War* (1961).

46.9.7.4 District of Columbia
Green, Constance M., *Washington* (2 vols., 1962–1963).
Leech, Margaret, *Reveille in Washington, 1860–1865* (1941).
Mitchell, Mary A., *Divided Town* (1968).

46.9.7.5 Illinois

Cole, A. C., *Era of the Civil War*, Vol. III of Clarence W. Alvord, ed., *Centennial History of the Civil War* (1919).
Hicken, Victor, *Illinois in the Civil War* (1966).

46.9.7.6 Indiana

Stampp, Kenneth M., *Indiana Politics during the Civil War* (1949).

46.9.7.7 Kansas

Castel, Albert E., *Frontier State at War: Kansas, 1861–1865* (1958).

46.9.7.8 Kentucky

Smith, Edward C., *Borderland in the Civil War* (1927).
Townsend, William H., *Lincoln and the Bluegrass: Slavery and the Civil War in Kentucky* (1955).

46.9.7.9 Maryland

Manakee, Harold R., *Maryland in the Civil War* (1961).
Radcliffe, George L. P., *Governor Thomas H. Hicks of Maryland and the Civil War* (1901).

46.9.7.10 Massachusetts

Ware, Edith E., *Political Opinion in Massachusetts during the Civil War and Reconstruction* (1916).

46.9.7.11 Michigan

Woodford, Frank B., *Father Abraham's Children: Michigan Episodes in the Civil War* (1961).

*   *   *   *   *   *   *

May, George S., et al., eds., *Michigan Civil War History: Annotated Bibliography* (1961).

46.9.7.12 Missouri

Parrish, William E., *Turbulent Partnership: Missouri and the Union, 1861–1865* (1963).
Potter, Marguerite, "Hamilton R. Gamble, Missouri's War Governor," *Mo. Hist. Rev.*, 35 (1940), 25.
Smith, Edward C., *Borderland in the Civil War* (1927).

46.9.7.13 New Jersey

Knapp, Charles M., *New Jersey Politics during the Civil War* (1924).
Miers, Earl S., ed., *New Jersey and the Civil War* (1964).

46.9.7.14 New York

Brummer, Sidney D., *Political History of New York State during the Civil War* (1911).
Gibson, Florence E., *Attitudes of New York Irish* (1951).
Rayback, Robert J., "New York State in the Civil War," *N.Y. Hist.*, 42 (1961), 56.

46.9.7.15 Ohio

Porter, George H., *Ohio Politics during the Civil War* (1911).
Roseboom, Eugene H., *The Civil War Years*, vol. IV of Carl Wittke, ed., *History of the State of Ohio* (1944).

Tucker, Louis L., *Cincinnati During the Civil War* (1962).
Wheeler, Kenneth W., ed., *For the Union: Ohio Leaders in the Civil War* (1968).

46.9.7.16 Pennsylvania

Bradley, Erwin S., *Triumph of Militant Republicanism: Pennsylvania and Presidential Politics, 1860–1872* (1964).
Davis, Stanton L., *Pennsylvania Politics, 1860–1863* (1935).
Dusinberre, William, *Civil War Issues in Philadelphia, 1856–1865* (1965).
Wilkinson, Norman B., *Brandywine Home Front During the Civil War, 1861–1865* (1966).

46.9.7.17 West Virginia

Curry, Richard O., *House Divided: Statehood Politics and the Copperhead Movement in West Virginia* (1964).
Smith, Edward C., *Borderland in the Civil War* (1927).
Stutler, Boyd B., *West Virginia in the Civil War* (1963).
Taylor, A. A., "Making West Virginia Free," *Jour. Negro Hist.*, 6 (1921), 131.

46.9.7.18 Wisconsin

Klement, Frank L., *Wisconsin and the Civil War* (1963).
Merk, Frederick, *Economic History of Wisconsin during the Civil War Decade* (1916).

46.10 NEGROES

46.10.1 General

Castel, Albert, "Civil War Kansas and the Negro," *Jour. Negro Hist.*, 51 (1966), 125.
Du Bois, W. E. B., "The Negro and the Civil War," *Science and Society*, 25 (1961), 347.
Johnson, Ludwell J., "Lincoln's Solution to the Problem of Peace Terms, 1864–1865," *JSH*, 34 (1968), 576.
Lofton, Williston H., "Northern Labor and the Negro during the Civil War," *Jour. Negro Hist.*, 34 (1949), 251.
McPherson, James M., *Marching toward Freedom: The Negro in the Civil War* (1968).
—— *The Negro's Civil War* (1965).
Quarles, Benjamin, *Lincoln and the Negro* (1962).
—— *The Negro in the Civil War* (1953).
Voegeli, V. Jacques, *Free But Not Equal: The Midwest and the Negro during the Civil War* (1967).
—— "Northwest and the Race Issue, 1861–1862," *MVHR*, 50 (1963), 235.

46.10.2 Emancipation

Franklin, John Hope, *Emancipation Proclamation* (1963).
Klement, Frank L., "Midwestern Opposition to Lincoln's Emancipation Policy," *Jour. Negro Hist.*, 49 (1964), 169.
Krug, Mark M., "Republican Party and the Emancipation Proclamation," *Jour. Negro Hist.*, 48 (1963), 98.
McPherson, James, *The Struggle for Equality: Abolitionists and the Negro* (1964).
Moser, Harold D., "Reaction in North Carolina to the Emancipation Proclamation," *No. Car. Hist. Rev.*, 44 (1967), 53.
Wagandt, Charles L., *Mighty Revolution: Negro Emancipation in Maryland, 1862–1864* (1964).
Williams, Lorraine A., "Northern Intellectual Reaction to Emancipation," *Jour. Negro Hist.*, 46 (1961), 174.

Wood, Forrest G., *Black Scare: The Racist Response to Emancipation and Recon-struction* (1968).

See also 10.3 for biographies/writings of:

Andrew, John A., 1818–1867
Douglass, Frederick, 1817–1895
Garrison, William Lloyd, 1805–1879
Phillips, Wendell, 1811–1884
Stevens, Thaddeus, 1792–1868

46.10.3 Union Army

Burchard, Peter, *One Gallant Rush: Robert Shaw and the Brave Black Regiment* (1965).
Cornish, Dudley T., *The Sable Arm: Negro Troops in the Union Army, 1861–1865* (1956).
Higginson, T. W., *Army Life in a Black Regiment* (1869).
Williams, George W., *History of Negro Troops in the War* (1888).
Wilson, Joseph T., *Black Phalanx* (1888).

46.10.4 South

Brewer, James H., *The Confederate Negro: Virginia's Craftsmen and Military Laborers, 1861–1865* (1969).
Hay, Thomas R., "South and Arming Slaves," *MVHR*, 6 (1920), 34.
Spraggins, T. L., "Mobilization of Negro Labor," *No. Car. Hist. Rev.*, 24 (1947), 160.
Wesley, Charles H., "Employment of Negroes as Soldiers in the Confederate Army," *Jour. Negro Hist.*, 4 (1919), 239.
Wiley, Bell I., *Southern Negroes, 1861–1865* (2nd ed., 1953).

46.11 CONFEDERACY

46.11.1 General

Bradford, Gamaliel, *Confederate Portraits* (1912).
Carpenter, Jessie T., *The South as a Conscious Minority* (1930).
Coddington, Edwin B., "Soldiers' Relief in Seaboard States of Confederacy," *MVHR*, 37 (1950), 17.
Coulter, E. Merton, *Confederate States of America* (1950).
Eaton, Clement, *History of the Southern Confederacy* (1954).
Harwell, Richard B., ed., *Confederate Reader* (1957).
Kirwan, Albert D., ed., *The Confederacy* (1959).
Lonn, Ella, *Foreigners in the Confederacy* (1940).
Massey, Mary E., *Ersatz in the Confederacy* (1952).
———— *Refugee Life in the Confederacy* (1964).
Ramsdell, Charles W., *Behind the Lines in the Southern Confederacy* (1944).
Roland, Charles P., *The Confederacy* (1960).
Stephenson, Nathaniel W., *Day of Confederacy* (1919).
Vandiver, Frank E., *Basic History of the Confederacy* (1962).
Wiley, Bell I., *Plain People of the Confederacy* (1943).

*   *   *   *   *   *   *

Freeman, Douglas S., *South to Posterity: An Introduction to the Writing of Confederate History* (1939).
Harwell, Richard B., *Confederate Hundred: Selection of Books* (1964).

Massey, Mary E., "Confederate States of America, Homefront," in Arthur S. Link and R. W. Patrick, eds., *Writing Southern History: Essays in Honor of Fletcher M. Green* (1965).

Stephenson, Wendell H., "Charles W. Ramsdell: Historian of the Confederacy," *JSH*, 26 (1960), 501.

46.11.2 Contemporary Accounts

DeLeon, T. C., *Four Years in Rebel Capitals* (1890).

Eggleston, G. C., *Rebel's Recollections* (1875; 5th ed. 1959).

Fremantle, James A. L., *Three Months in the Southern States, April–June, 1863* (1864); Walter Lord, ed., (1954).

Jones, John Beauchamp, *Rebel War Clerk's Diary* (2 vols., 1866); Howard Swiggert, ed. (rev. ed., 2 vols., 1935).

Smith, Mason, *Family Letters, 1860–1868*, Daniel E. H. Smith, ed. (1950).

von Borcke, Heros, *Memoirs of Confederate War for Independence* (2 vols., 1866; 2nd ed., 1938).

46.11.3 Politics and Government

46.11.3.1 General

Alexander, Thomas B., "Persistent Whiggery in the Confederate South, 1860–1877," *JSH*, 27 (1961), 305.

Amlund, Curtis A., *Federalism in the Southern Confederacy* (1966).

Dietz, August, *Postal Service of the Confederate States* (1929).

Hendrick, Burton J., *Statesmen of Lost Cause* (1939).

Hill, Louise B., *Joseph E. Brown and the Confederacy* (1939).

Lee, Charles R., Jr., *Confederate Constitutions* (1963).

Monroe, Haskell, "Early Confederate Political Patronage," *Ala. Rev.*, 20 (1967), 45.

Owsley, Frank L., *States Rights in Confederacy* (1925).

Parks, Joseph H., "Governor Joseph Brown versus Jefferson Davis," *JSH*, 32 (1966), 3.

Patrick, Rembert W., *Jefferson Davis and His Cabinet* (1944).

Richardson, Ralph, "Choice of Jefferson Davis as Confederate President," *Jour. Miss. Hist.*, 17 (1955), 161.

Ringold, May S., *Role of State Legislatures in the Confederacy* (1966).

Robinson, William M., *Justice in Grey* (1941).

Van Riper, Paul P., and Harry N. Scheiber, "Confederate Civil Service," *JSH*, 25 (1959), 448.

See also 10.3 for biographies/writings of:

Petigru, James L., 1789–1863
Reagan, John H., 1818–1905
Rhett, Robert B., 1800–1876
Ruffin, Thomas, 1787–1870
Stephens, Alexander H., 1812–1883
Toombs, Robert, 1810–1885
Walker, Leroy P., 1817–1884
Yancey, William L., 1814–1863

46.11.3.2 Congress

Akin, Warren, *Letters of a Confederate Congressman*, Bell I. Wiley, ed. (1960).
Beringer, Richard E., "A Profile of Members of Confederate Congress," *JSH*, 33 (1967), 518.
Confederate States of America. Provisional Congress, *Statutes at Large* (1862–1864).
Ramsdell, Charles M., ed., *Laws and Joint Resolutions of Last Session of the Confederate Congress* (1941).
Richardson, James David, comp., *Messages and Papers of Confederacy* (2 vols., 1905).
U.S. Congress. Senate, *Journal of the Confederate States* (8 vols., 1904–1905, 58th Cong., 2nd sess., Sen. Doc. no. 234.
Vandiver, Frank E., ed., "Proceedings of the Confederate Congress," So. Hist. Soc., *Papers*, vols. 44–52 (1923–1959).
Yearns, Wilfred B., *Confederate Congress* (1960).

46.11.4 Economy

46.11.4.1 General

Cappon, Lester J., "Government and Private Industry in Confederacy," in *Humanistic Studies in Honor of John C. Metcalf* (1941).
Dew, Charles B., *Ironmaker to Confederacy: Joseph R. Anderson and the Tredegar Iron Works* (1966).
Gilchrist, David T., and W. David Lewis, eds., *Economic Change in Civil War Era* (1965).
Lerner, Eugene M., "Money, Prices, and Wages in the Confederacy," *Jour. Pol. Econ.*, 63 (1955), 20.
Lonn, Ella, *Salt in the Confederacy* (1933).
Roberts, A. S., "Federal Government and Confederate Cotton," *AHR*, 32 (1927), 262.
Roland, Charles P., *Louisiana Sugar Plantations during the American Civil War* (1957).
Sellers, J. L., "Economic Incidence of War in the South," *MVHR*, 14 (1927), 179.
Vandiver, Frank E., ed., *Confederate Blockade Running through Bermuda* (1947).
Vandiver, Frank E., "Shelby Iron Company in Civil War," *Ala. Rev.*, 1 (1948), 203.
Wright, Gordon, "Economic Conditions in the Confederacy as Seen by French Consuls," *JSH*, 7 (1941), 195.

See also 46.15.5, Blockade and Blockade Running.

46.11.4.2 Fiscal Policies

Andreano, Ralph L., "Confederate Finance," *Civil War Hist.*, 2 (1956), 21.
Hammond, Bray, *Sovereignty and an Empty Purse: Banks and Politics in the Civil War* (1970).
Lerner, Eugene M., "Inflation in the Confederacy, 1861–1865," in Milton Friedman, ed., *Studies in Quantity Theory of Money* (1956).
——— "Monetary and Fiscal Programs of Confederate Government, 1861–65," *Jour. Pol. Econ.*, 62 (1954), 506.
Todd, Richard C., *Confederate Finance* (1954).

46.11.4.3 Railroads

Black, Robert C., III, *Railroads of the Confederacy* (1952).
Johnston, Angus J., II, *Virginia Railroads in the Civil War* (1961).
Price, Charles L., "North Carolina Railroads during the Civil War," *Civil War Hist.*, 7 (1961), 298.
Riegel, Robert E., "Federal Operation of Southern Railroads during the Civil War," *MVHR*, 9 (1922), 126.

46.11.5 Religion and Ethnicity

"Civil War Religion," *Civil War Hist.*, 6 (1960). Entire issue.
Daniel, W. Harrison, "Southern Protestantism and Army Missions in the Confederacy," *Miss. Quar.*, 17 (1964), 179.
—— "Southern Protestantism–1861 and After," *Civil War Hist.*, 5 (1959), 276.
Horst, Samuel, *Mennonites in the Confederacy: Civil War Pacifism* (1967).
Korn, Bertram W., *American Jewry and the Civil War* (1951).
—— "Jews of the Confederacy," *Am. Jew. Archives*, 13 (1961), 3.
Meyer, Isidore S., ed., "American Jew in the Civil War," *Am. Jew. Hist. Quar.*, 50 (1961), 263.
Silver, James W., *Confederate Morale and Church Propaganda* (1957).

46.11.6 Women

Andrews, Eliza F., *War Time Journal of a Georgia Girl* (1908).
Chesnut, Mary B., *Diary from Dixie*, J. D. Martin and M. L. Avary, eds. (1905); Ben A. Williams, ed. (1949).
Dawson, Sarah M., *Confederate Girl's Diary*, James I. Robertson, Jr., ed. (1960).
Habersham, Josephine C., *Diary, 1863*, Spencer B. King, Jr., ed. (1958).
Holmes, Sarah K. [Stone], *Journal, 1861–1868*, John Q. Anderson, ed. (1955).
Jones, Katharine M., ed., *Heroines of Dixie* (1955).
—— *Ladies of Richmond* (1962).
—— *When Sherman Came: Southern Women* (1964).
Le Conte, Emma, *Diary*, Earl S. Miers, ed. (1957).
McDonald, Cornelia P., *Diary, 1860–1865*, Hunter McDonald, ed. (1934).
Massey, Mary E., *Bonnet Brigades: Women and the Civil War* (1966).
Pember, Phoebe Y., *Life in Confederate Richmond*, Bell I. Wiley, ed. (1959).
Simkins, F. B., and J. W. Patton, *Women of the Confederacy* (1940).
Waitz, Julia LeGrand, *Journal, 1862–1863*, Kate M. Rowland and Mrs. Morris L. Croxall, eds. (1911).

See also 10.3 for biographies/writings of:

Blackford, Mary B., 1802–1896

46.11.7 Discontent

Ambrose, Stephen E., "Yeoman Discontent in the Confederacy," *Civil War Hist.*, 8 (1962), 259.
Bailey, Hugh C., "Disloyalty in Early Confederate Alabama," *JSH*, 23 (1957), 522.
Hoole, William S., *Alabama Tories: First Alabama Cavalry, 1862–1865* (1960).
Horst, Samuel, *Mennonites in the Confederacy: Civil War Pacifism* (1967).
Hyman, Harold M., "Deceit in Dixie," *Civil War Hist.*, 3 (1957), 65.
Klingberg, Frank W., *Southern Claims Commission* (1955).
Long, Durward, "Unanimity and Disloyalty in Secessionist Alabama," *Civil War Hist.*, 11 (1965), 257.
Owsley, Frank L., *States Rights in the Confederacy* (1925).
Tatum, Georgia L., *Disloyalty in Confederacy* (1934).
Wright, Edward N., *Conscientious Objectors in the Civil War* (1931).

46.11.8 State and Local Studies

46.11.8.1 Alabama

Fleming, Walter L., *Civil War and Reconstruction in Alabama* (1905).
McMillan, Malcolm C., ed., *Alabama Confederate Reader* (1963).

46.11.8.2 Florida

Johns, John E., *Florida during the Civil War* (1963).

46.11.8.3 Georgia

Bryan, Thomas C., *Confederate Georgia* (1953).
Coleman, Kenneth, *Confederate Athens* (1967).
Lawrence, Alexander A., *Present for Mr. Lincoln: Story of Savannah* (1961).

46.11.8.4 Louisiana

Bragg, Jefferson D., *Louisiana in the Confederacy* (1941).
Capers, Gerald M., *Occupied City: New Orleans* (1965).
Caskey, W. M., *Secession and Restoration in Louisiana* (1938).
Shugg, Roger W., *Origins of Class Struggle in Louisiana: A Social History of White Farmers and Laborers during Slavery and After, 1840–1875* (1939).
Winters, John D., *Civil War in Louisiana* (1963).

46.11.8.5 Mississippi

Bearss, Edward C., *Decision in Mississippi* (1962).
Bettersworth, John K., *Confederate Mississippi* (1943).
——— and James W. Silver, eds., *Mississippi in the Confederacy* (2 vols., 1961).

46.11.8.6 North Carolina

Barrett, John G., *Civil War in North Carolina* (1963).
Roberts, A. S., "Peace Movement in North Carolina," *MVHR*, 11 (1924), 190.

See also 10.3 for biographies/writings of:

Ellis, John W., fl. 1841–1861
Holden, William W., 1818–1892
Vance, Zebulon B., 1830–1894

46.11.8.7 South Carolina

Cauthen, Charles E., *South Carolina Goes to War* (1950).

46.11.8.8 Tennessee

Parks, Joseph H., "Memphis under Military Rule, 1862–1865," East Tenn. Hist. Soc., *Publ.*, 14 (1942), 31.
Patton, James W., *Unionism and Reconstruction in Tennessee* (1934).

46.11.8.9 Texas

Elliott, Claude, "Union Sentiment in Texas," *Southw. Hist. Quar.*, 50 (1947), 449.
Oates, Stephen B., "Texas under Secessionists," *Southw. Hist. Quar.*, 67 (1963), 167.

46.11.8.10 Virginia

Bill, Alfred H., *Beleaguered City: Richmond, 1861–1865* (1946).
Fleet, Benjamin R., *Green Mount: Virginia Plantation Family during the Civil War: Journal and Letters,* Betsy Fleet and John D. P. Fuller, eds. (1962).
Manarin, Louis H., ed., *Richmond at War, 1861–1865* (1966).

46.12 MILITARY HISTORY

46.12.1 General

Angle, Paul M., and Earl S. Miers, eds., *Tragic Years, 1860–1865* (2 vols., 1960).
Burne, Alfred H., *Lee, Grant and Sherman* (1938).
Catton, Bruce, *Centennial History of the Civil War* (3 vols., 1961–1965).
—— *This Hallowed Ground: Union Side of Civil War* (1956).
Commager, Henry Steele, *Blue and Gray* (2 vols., 1951).
Dupuy, Richard E., and Trevor N. Dupuy, *Compact History of the Civil War* (1960).
Dyer, Frederick H., *Compendium of the War of the Rebellion* (1908; new ed., 3 vols., 1960).
Eisenschiml, Otto, and Ralph Newman, eds., *American 'Iliad'* (1947).
Falls, Cyril, *A Hundred Years of War* (1954).
Foote, Shelby, *The Civil War* (2 vols., 1958–1963).
Freidel, Frank, "General Orders 100 and Military Government," *MVHR*, 32 (1946), 541.
Fuller, John F. C., *Grant and Lee* (1933).
Hagerman, Edward, "From Jomini to Dennis Hart Mahan: Evolution of Trench Warfare and the American Civil War," *Civil War Hist.*, 13 (1967), 197.
Johnson, R. V., and C. C. Buel, eds., *Battles and Leaders of the Civil War* (4 vols., 1887); Ned Bradford, ed. (1956).
Livermore, Thomas L., *Numbers and Losses in the Civil War* (1901).
Lord, Francis A., *They Fought for the Union* (1960).
Luraghi, Raimondo, *Storia Della Guerra Civile Americana* (1966).
Luvaas, Jay, *Military Legacy of the Civil War: European Inheritance* (1959).
Mahon, John K., "Civil War Infantry Assault Tactics," *Mil. Affairs*, 25 (1961), 57.
Maurice, Frederick, *Statesmen and Soldiers of the Civil War* (1926).
Mitchell, Joseph Brady, *Decisive Battles of the Civil War* (1955).
Moore, John G., "Mobility and Strategy in the Civil War," *Mil. Affairs*, 24 (1960), 66.
Peterson, Harold L., *Notes on Ordnance of the Civil War* (1959).
Rawley, James A., *Turning Points of the Civil War* (1966).
Ross, Fitzgerald, *Cities and Camps of Confederate States* (1865); Richard B. Harwell, ed. (1958).
Steiner, Paul E., *Medical-Military Portraits of Union and Confederate Generals* (1968).
Stern, Philip V., *Secret Missions of the Civil War* (1959).
—— ed., *Soldier Life in the Union and Confederate Armies* (1961).
Turner, George E., *Victory Rode the Rails: Railroads in the Civil War* (1953).
U.S. War Department, *War of the Rebellion . . . Official Records of the Union and Confederate Armies*, Robert N. Scott, et al., eds. (70 vols., 1880–1901).

46.12.2 Science and Technology

Haydon, Frederick S., *Aeronautics in the Union and Confederate Armies* (1941).
Jahns, Patricia, *Matthew Fontaine Maury and Joseph Henry: Scientists of the Civil War* (1961).
Reingold, Nathan, "Science in the Civil War," *Isis*, 49 (1958), 307.

46.12.3 Recruiting, Conscription, Draft Riots, and Desertion

Dorris, Jonathan T., *Pardon and Amnesty under Lincoln and Johnson* (1953).
Fish, Carl R., "Conscription," *AHR*, 21 (1915), 100.
Leach, Jack F., *Conscription in the United States* (1952).
Lonn, Ella, *Desertion during the Civil War* (1928).
McCague, James, *Second Rebellion: New York City Draft Riots of 1863* (1968).
Martin, Bessie, *Desertion of Alabama Troops* (1932).

Mitchell, Memory F., *Legal Aspects of Conscription and Exemption in North Carolina, 1861–1865* (1965).
Moore, Albert B., *Conscription and Conflict in the Confederary* (1924).
Murdock, Eugene C., "Horatio Seymour and 1863 Draft," *Civil War Hist.*, 11 (1965), 117.
—— *Ohio's Bounty System in the Civil War* (1963).
—— *Patriotism Limited, 1862–1865: Draft and Bounty System* (1967).
—— "Was It a Poor Man's Fight?" *Civil War Hist.*, 10 (1964), 241.
Raney, W. F., "Recruiting in Canada," *MVHR*, 10 (1923), 21.
Wright, Edward N., *Conscientious Objectors in the Civil War* (1931).

46.12.4 Prisons

"Civil War Prisons," *Civil War Hist.*, 8 (1962), 117.
Futch, Ovid L., *History of Andersonville Prison* (1968).
Hesseltine, W. B., *Civil War Prisons* (1930).
Lawrence, F. Lee, and Robert W. Glover, *Camp Ford, C.S.A.: Union Prisoners in Texas* (1964).

46.12.5 Medicine

Adams, George Worthington, "Confederate Medicine," *JSH*, 6 (1939), 151.
—— *Doctors in Blue* (1952).
Barnes, Joseph K., et al., *Medical and Surgical History of the War of Rebellion* (6 vols., 1870–1878).
Baxter, J. H., *Statistics, Medical and Anthropological, of Provost-Marshal-General's Bureau* (2 vols., 1875).
Cunningham, Horace H., *Doctors in Gray* (1958).
—— *Field Medical Services at Battles of Manassas (Bull Run)* (1968).
Maxwell, William Q., *Lincoln's Fifth Wheel: Sanitary Commission* (1956).
Smith, George W., *Medicines for the Union Army: Army Laboratories during the Civil War* (1962).
Steiner, Paul E., *Disease in the Civil War: Natural Biological Warfare in 1861–1865* (1968).

46.12.6 Journalists and the War

Andrews, J. Cutler, *The North Reports the Civil War* (1955).
—— *The South Reports the Civil War* (1970).
Cadwallader, Sylvanus, *Three Years with Grant*, Benjamin P. Thomas, ed. (1955).
Crozier, Emmet, *Yankee Reporters, 1861–65* (1956).
Fahrney, R. R., *Horace Greeley and the Tribune in the Civil War* (1936).
Hoole, William S., *Lawley Covers the Confederacy* (1964).
—— *Viztelly Covers the Confederacy* (1957).
Horner, Harlan H., *Lincoln and Greeley* (1953).
Nasby, Petroleum V., *Civil War Letters*, Harvey S. Ford, comp. (1962).
Randall, James G., "The Newspaper Problem in Its Bearing upon Military Secrecy during the Civil War," *AHR*, 23 (1918), 303.
Starr, Louis M., *Bohemian Brigade: Civil War Newsmen* (1954).
Townsend, George A., *Rustics in Rebellion: Yankee Reporter on the Road to Richmond, 1861–65*, Linda Mayo, ed. (1950).
Weisberger, Bernard A., *Reporters for the Union* (1953).

46.12.7 Pictorial History

American Heritage, *American Heritage Picture History of the Civil War* (1960).
Angle, Paul M., *Pictorial History of the Civil War* (1967).
Battles of Civil War: Pictorial (1960).

Brentano's, *American Caricatures Pertaining to the Civil War* (1918).
Buchanan, Lamont, ed., *Pictorial History of the Confederacy* (1951).
Donald, David, et al., eds., *Divided We Fought* (1953).
Fishwick, Marshall, *General Lee's Photographer: Michael Miley* (1954).
Horan, James D., *Mathew Brady: Historian with a Camera* (1955).
Meredith, Roy, *Lincoln's Camera Man Brady* (1946).
───── ed., *Mr. Lincoln's Contemporaries* (1951).
Miers, Earl S., *The American Civil War: An Illustrated History* (1961).
Milhollen, Hirst D., and James R. Johnson, *Best Photos of the Civil War* (1961).
Miller, F. T., ed., *Photographic History of the Civil War* (10vols., 1911–1912).
Morgan, M. S., ed., *American Civil War Cartoons of Matt Morgan and Other English Artists* (1874).
Pratt, Fletcher, *The Civil War in Pictures* (1955).
Volck, A. J., *Confederate War Etchings* (1863).
Wiley, Bell I., *Embattled Confederates: Illustrated History* (1964).
───── and Hirst D. Milhollen, *They Who Fought Here* (1959).
Williams, Hermann W., Jr., *Civil War: Artist's Record* (1961).

46.13   UNION ARMY

46.13.1   General

Meneely, Alexander H., *War Department: 1861* (1928).
Naisawald, L. Van Loan, *Grape and Canister: Field Artillery of the Army of the Potomac, 1861–1865* (1960).
Shannon, Fred A., *Organization and Administration of the Union Army* (2 vols., 1928).
Wiley, Bell I., *Life of Billy Yank* (1952).

See also 46.10.3, Negroes–Union Army.

46.13.2   Contemporary Accounts

Calvert, Henry M., *Reminiscences of a Boy in Blue* (1920).
Connolly, James A., *Letters and Diary*, Paul M. Angle, ed. (1959).
Cox, Jacob D., *Military Reminiscences* (1900).
De Forest, John W., *Volunteer's Adventures: Union Captain's Record of the Civil War*, James H. Croushore, ed. (1946).
Dunham, Alburtus, and Laforest Dunham, *Through the South with a Union Soldier*, Arthur H. DeRosier, Jr., ed. (1969).
Henderson, George F. R., *The Civil War: A Soldier's View*, Jay Luvaas, ed. (1958).
Hitchcock, Henry, *Marching with Sherman*, Mark A. DeW. Howe, ed. (1927).
Jackson, Isaac, *Civil War Letters*, Joseph O. Jackson, ed. (1960).
Lyman, Theodore, *Meade's Headquarters, 1863–1865*, G. R. Agassiz, ed. (1922).
McAllister, Robert, *Civil War Letters*, James I. Robertson, Jr., ed. (1965).
McClellan, George B., *McClellan's Own Story* (1887).
Miers, Earl S., *New Jersey and the Civil War: Contemporary Accounts* (1964).
Mitchell, Joseph B., *Badge of Gallantry: Recollections of Civil War Congressional Medal of Honor Winners* (1968).
Patrick, Marsena R., *Inside Lincoln's Army: Diary*, David S. Sparks, ed. (1964).
Porter, Horace, *Campaigning with Grant* (1897); Wayne C. Temple, ed. (1961).
Reid, Harvey, *Civil War Letters*, Frank L. Byrne, ed. (1965).
Ripley, Edward H., *War Experiences, 1862–1865*, Otto Eisenschiml, ed. (1960).
Small, Abner R., *Road to Richmond: Civil War Memoirs*, Harold A. Small, ed. (1939).

de Trobriand, P. R., *Four Years with the Army of the Potomac* (1889).
Wainwright, Charles S., *Personal Journals, 1861–1865*, Allan Nevins, ed.
  (1962).

See also 10.3 for biographies/writings of:

Canby, Edward R., 1817–1873
Chamberlain, Joshua L., 1828–1914
Fox, Gustavus V., 1821–1883
Higginson, Thomas W., 1823–1911
Howard, Oliver Otis, 1830–1909
Keyes, Erasmus D., 1810–1895

46.13.3 Special Groups

Anderson, Charles C., *Fighting by Southern Federals* (1912).
Brown, Dee A., *Galvanized Yankees* (1963).
Conway, Alan, "Welshmen in Union Armies," *Civil War Hist.*, 4 (1958), 143.
Lonn, Ella, *Foreigners in the Union Army and Navy* (1951).
Nolan, Alan T., *Iron Brigade: Military History* (1961).
Pullen, John J., *The Twentieth Maine* (1957).

46.13.4 Leadership

Ballard, C. R., *Military Genius of Lincoln* (1926).
Catton, Bruce, *Glory Road* (1952).
—————— *Grant Moves South* (1960).
—————— *Mr. Lincoln's Army* (1951).
—————— *Ulysses Simpson Grant and American Military Tradition* (1954).
Fuller, John F. C., *Generalship of Ulysses S. Grant* (1958).
Hassler, Warren W., Jr., *Commanders of the Army of the Potomac* (1962).
Macartney, Clarence E., *Lincoln and His Generals* (1925).
Parrish, William E., "General Nathaniel Lyon," *Mo. Hist. Rev.*, 49 (1954), 1.
Smith, Louis, *American Democracy and Military Power* (1951).
Warner, Ezra J., *Generals in Blue: Union Commanders* (1964).
Williams, Kenneth P., *Lincoln Finds a General: Military Study of the Civil War* (5
  vols., 1949–1959).
Williams, T. Harry, *Lincoln and His Generals* (1952).

See also 10.3 for biographies/writings of:

Anderson, Robert, 1805–1871
Banks, Nathaniel P., 1816–1894
Burnside, Ambrose E., 1824–1881
Butler, Benjamin F., 1818–1893
Chamberlain, Joshua L., 1828–1914
De Forest, John W., 1826–1906
Ellsworth, Elmer E., 1837–1861
Frémont, John C., 1813–1890
Grant, Ulysses S., 1822–1885
Halleck, Henry W., 1815–1872
Hancock, Winfield S., 1824–1886
Hitchcock, Ethan A., 1798–1870
Hooker, Joseph, 1814–1879
Kearney, Philip, 1814–1862
Logan, John A., 1826–1886
McClellan, George B., 1826–1885
MacKenzie, Ranald S., 1840–1889
McPherson, James B., 1828–1864
Marcy, Randolph B., 1812–1887
Meade, George G., 1815–1872

Meigs, Montgomery C., 1816–1892
Rawlins, John A., 1831–1869
Rosecrants, William S., 1819–1898
Scott, Winfield, 1786–1866
Sheridan, Philip H., 1831–1888
Sherman, William T., 1820–1891
Sickles, Daniel E., 1825–1914
Thomas, George Henry, 1816–1870
Upton, Emory, 1839–1881
Warren, Gouverneur K., 1830–1882

46.13.5 Military Campaigns

46.13.5.1 Virginia

Brice, Marshall M., *Conquest of a Valley* (1965).
Patrick, Rembert W., *Fall of Richmond* (1960).
Steere, Edward, *Wilderness Campaign* (1960).
Whan, Vorin E., Jr., *Fiasco at Fredericksburg* (1961).

46.13.5.2 Gettysburg

Coddington, Edward B., *Gettysburg Campaign* (1968).
Dowdey, Clifford, *Death of a Nation: Lee and His Men at Gettysburg* (1958).
Montgomery, James S., *Shaping of a Battle: Gettysburg* (1959).
Nye, Wilbur S., *Here Come the Rebels!* (1965).
Stackpole, Edward J., *They Met at Gettysburg* (1956).
Stewart, George R., *Pickett's Charge* (1959).
Tucker, Glenn, *High Tide at Gettysburg* (1958).
——— *Lee and Longstreet at Gettysburg* (1968).

46.13.5.3 Western Campaigns

Hough, Alfred L., *Civil War Letters*, Robert G. Athearn, ed. (1957).
Hunt, Aurora, *Army of the Pacific, 1860–1866* (1951).
Jones, Robert H., *Civil War in the Northwest* (1960).
Kibby, Leo P., "California's Military Problems during the Civil War," *Civil War Hist.*, 5 (1959), 251.
Monaghan, Jay, *Civil War on the Western Border, 1854–1865* (1955).
Pratt, Fletcher, *Civil War on Western Waters* (1956).
Ware, Eugene F., *Indian War of 1864* (1911); Clyde C. Walton, ed. (1960).

46.13.5.4 Tennessee and Mississippi

Cunningham, Edward, *Port Hudson Campaign, 1862–1863* (1963).
Downey, Fairfax, *Storming of Gateway: Chattanooga, 1863* (1960).
Hay, Thomas R., *Hood's Tennessee Campaign* (1929).
Horn, Stanley F., *Decisive Battle of Nashville* (1956).
Miers, Earl S., *Web of Victory: Grant at Vicksburg* (1955).
Tucker, Glenn, *Chickamauga* (1961).

46.13.5.5 Sherman's March

Barrett, John G., *Sherman's March through the Carolinas* (1956).
Gibson, John M., *Those 163 Days: Sherman's March* (1961).

46.13.5.6 Other Campaigns

Barrett, John G., *Civil War in North Carolina* (1963).
Britton, Wiley, *Civil War on the Border* (2 vols., 1891–1899).
Brown, Dee A., *Grierson's Raid* (1954).
Hamilton, James J., *Battle of Fort Donelson* (1968).
Johnson, Ludwell H., *Red River Campaign: Politics and Cotton in the Civil War* (1958).

McWhiney, Grady, "Controversy in Kentucky: Braxton Bragg's Campaign of 1862," *Civil War Hist.*, 6 (1960), 5.

46.13.5.7 Appomattox

Adams, Francis R., Jr., "Robert E. Lee," *Am. Quar.*, 12 (1960), 367.
Catton, Bruce, *Stillness at Appomattox* (1953).

46.14 CONFEDERATE ARMY

46.14.1 General

Goff, Richard D., *Confederate Supply* (1969).
Nichols, James L., *Confederate Engineers* (1957).
Vandiver, Frank E., *Ploughshares into Swords: Josiah Gorgas and the Confederate Ordnance* (1952).
———— *Rebel Brass: Confederate Command System* (1956).
Wiley, Bell I., *Life of Johnny Reb* (1943).

*   *   *   *   *   *   *

Barrett, John G., "Confederate States of America at War on Land and Sea," in Arthur S. Link and Rembert W. Patrick, eds., *Writing Southern History: Essays in Honor of Fletcher M. Green* (1965).

46.14.2 Contemporary Accounts

Dooley, John E., *War Journal*, Joseph T. Durkin, ed. (1945).
Fay, Edwin H., *Confederate Letters*, Bell I. Wiley and Lucy E. Fay, eds. (1958).
Green, John W., *Journal of a Confederate Soldier*, Albert D. Kirwan, ed. (1956).
Marshall, Charles, *Papers, 1862–1865*, Frederick Maurice, ed. (1927).
Scheibert, Justus, *Seven Months in the Rebel States during the North American War, 1863*, Joseph C. Hayes, trans. and William S. Hoole, ed. (1958).
Sorrel, G. Moxley, *Recollections of a Confederate Staff Officer* (1905); Bell I. Wiley, ed. (1958).

See also 10.3 for biographies/writings of:

Mosby, John S., 1833–1916
Quantrill, William C., 1837–1865
Wheat, Roberdeau, 1826–1862

46.14.3 Leadership

Bean, William G., *Stonewall's Man: Sandie Pendleton* (1959).
Freeman, Douglas S., *Lee's Lieutenants* (3 vols., 1942–1944).
Henderson, George F. R., *Stonewall Jackson and the American Civil War* (2 vols., 1898).
Hughes, Nathaniel C., Jr., *General William Hardee* (1965).
Milham, Charles G., *Gallant Pelham* (1959).
Montgomery, Horace, *Howell Cobb's Confederate Career* (1959).
Warner, Ezra J., *Generals in Gray: Confederate Commanders* (1959).

See also 10.3 for biographies/writings of:

Beauregard, P. G. T., 1818–1893
Bragg, Braxton, 1817–1876
Browne, William M., 1823–1883
Buckner, Simon B., 1823–1914

Early, Jubal A., 1816–1894
Forrest, Nathan B., 1821–1877
Gordon, John B., 1832–1904
Hampton, Wade, III, 1818–1902
Hill, Ambrose P., 1825–1865
Hill, Daniel H., 1821–1889
Hood, John B., 1831–1879
Jackson, "Stonewall," 1824–1863
Johnston, Albert S., 1803–1862
Johnston, Joseph E., 1807–1891
Kirby-Smith, Edmund, 1824–1893
Lee, Robert E., 1807–1870
Longstreet, James, 1821–1904
Pemberton, John C. 1814–1881
Pickett, George E., 1825–1875
Pike, Albert, 1809–1891
Polk, Leonidas, 1806–1864
Stuart, J. E. B. "Jeb," 1833–1864
Van Dorn, Earl, 1820–1863
Wheeler, Joseph, 1836–1906
Young, Pierce M. B., 1836–1896

46.14.4 Military Campaigns

46.14.4.1 General

Brown, Dee A., *Bold Cavaliers: Morgan's 2nd Kentucky Cavalry Raiders* (1959).
Connelly, Thomas L., *Army of the Heartland: Army of Tennessee, 1861–1862* (1967).
Dowdey, Clifford, *Lee's Last Campaign* (1960).
―――― *The Seven Days: Emergence of Lee* (1964).
Duke, Basil W., *History of Morgan's Cavalry* (1867).
Evans, Clement A., ed., *Confederate Military History* (12 vols., 1899).
Horn, Stanley F., *Army of Tennessee* (2nd ed., 1953).
Jones, Archer, *Confederate Strategy from Shiloh to Vicksburg* (1961).
Jones, Virgil C., *Gray Ghosts and Rebel Raiders* (1956).
Robertson, James I., Jr., *Stonewall Brigade* (1963).
Stackpole, Edward J., *Chancellorsville: Lee's Greatest Battle* (1958).
Vandiver, Frank E., *Jubal's Raid: General Early's Famous Attack on Washington in 1864* (1960).
Wise, Jennings C., *Long Arm of Lee: Army of Northern Virginia* (2nd ed., 1959).

46.14.4.2 Western Campaigns

Brownlee, Richard S., *Gray Ghosts of the Confederacy: Guerrilla Warfare in the West* (1958).
Castel, Albert E., *General Sterling Price and Civil War in West* (1968).
Colton, Ray C., *Civil War in Western Territories* (1959).
Cunningham, Frank, *General Stand Watie's Confederate Indians* (1959).
Hall, Martin H., *Sibley's New Mexico Campaign* (1960).
Nichols, James L., *Confederate Quartermaster in the Trans-Mississippi* (1964).
Oates, Stephen B., *Confederate Cavalry West of the River* (1961).

46.15 NAVAL WARFARE

46.15.1 General

Anderson, Bern, *By Sea and By River: Naval History of the Civil War* (1962).
Gosnell, H. Allen, *Guns on the Western Waters: River Gunboats in the Civil War* (1949).

Hill, Jim D., *Sea Dogs of Sixties* (1935).
Jones, Virgil C., *Civil War at Sea* (3 vols., 1960–1962).
Official Records of Union and Confederate Navies in the War of Rebellion (30 vols., 1894–1922).
Stick, David, *Outer Banks of North Carolina, 1584–1958* (1958).
U.S. Department of Navy, *Civil War Naval Chronology* (3 vols., 1961–1966).

46.15.2 Union Navy

Dufour, Charles L., *Night the War Was Lost* (1960).
Macartney, Clarence E., *Mr. Lincoln's Admirals* (1956).
Merrill, James M., *Rebel Shore: Union Sea Power in the Civil War* (1957).
Milligan, John D., *Gunboats Down the Mississippi* (1965).
Paullin, Charles O., "President Lincoln and the Navy," *AHR*, 14 (1909), 284.
West, Richard S., Jr., *Mr. Lincoln's Navy* (1957).

See also 10.3 for biographies/writings of:

Du Pont, Samuel F., 1803–1865
Farragut, David G., 1801–1870
Porter, David D., 1813–1891
Rodgers, John, 1812–1882
Winslow, John A., 1811–1873

46.15.3 Confederate Navy

46.15.3.1 General

Dalzell, George W., *Flight from Flag: The Continuing Effect of the Civil War upon American Carrying Trade* (1940).
Hoole, William S., *Four Years in the Confederate Navy: Captain John Low* (1964).
Horn, Stanley F., *Gallant Rebel: Cruise of the Shenandoah* (1947).
Perry, Milton F., *Infernal Machines: Confederate Submarine and Mine Warfare* (1965).
Robinson, William M., *Confederate Privateers* (1928).
Scharf, John T., *History of Confederate Navy* (1894).
Still, William N., Jr., "Facilities for Construction of War Vessels in the Confederacy," *JSH*, 31 (1965), 285.

See also 10.3 for biographies/writings of:

Maury, Matthew F., 1806–1873
Semmes, Raphael, 1809–1877

46.15.3.2 Alabama

Boykin, Edward C., *Ghost Ship of the Confederacy: The "Alabama" and Raphael Semmes* (1957).
Maynard, Douglas H., "Escape of the 'Alabama'," *JSH*, 20 (1954), 197.
Robinson, William M., "Alabama-Kearsarge Battle," Essex Inst., *Hist. Coll.*, 60 (1924), 97.
Semmes, Raphael, *Confederate Raider "Alabama"* (1869); Philip V. Stern, ed. (1962).

46.15.4 Ironclads

Baxter, James P., 3d, *Introduction of the Iron-clad Warship* (1933).
Daly, Robert W., *How the "Merrimac" Won* (1957).
Nash, Howard P., Jr., "Civil War Legend," *Am. Neptune*, 23 (1963), 197.

Still, William N., Jr., "Confederate Naval Policy and the Ironclad," *Civil War Hist.*, 9 (1963), 145.
White, William C. and Ruth, *Tin Can on a Shingle* (1957).

46.15.5 Blockade and Blockade Running

Carse, Robert, *Blockade: Civil War at Sea* (1958).
Cochran, Hamilton, *Blockade Runners of the Confederacy* (1958).
Vandiver, Frank E., ed., *Confederate Blockade Running through Bermuda* (1947).

46.16 UNION VICTORY

Commager, Henry S., *Defeat of the Confederacy: Documentary Survey* (1964).
Donald, David, ed., *Why the North Won the Civil War* (1960).
Gipson, Lawrence H., "Collapse of Confederacy," *MVHR*, 4 (1918), 437.
McWhiney, Grady, "Confederate Defeat Reexamined," *Civil War Hist.*, 11 (1965), 5.
Stern, Philip V., *An End to Valor: The Civil War* (1958).
Wesley, C. H., *Collapse of the Confederacy* (1937).
Wiley, Bell I., *The Road to Appomattox* (1956).

46.17 CULTURAL HISTORY

Baxter, Charles N., and J. M. Dearborn, *Confederate Literature* (1917).
"Civil War Humor," *Civil War Hist.*, 2 (1956). Entire issue.
"Civil War Music," *Civil War Hist.*, 4 (1958). Entire issue.
Fredrickson, George M., *Inner Civil War: Northern Intellectuals* (1965).
Harwell, Richard B., *Confederate Music* (1950).
Heaps, Willard A. and Porter W., *Singing Sixties: Civil War Days* (1960).
Steinmetz, Lee, ed., *Poetry of the American Civil War* (1960).
Wilson, Edmund, *Patriotic Gore: Literature of the American Civil War* (1962).

*   *   *   *   *   *   *

Newman, Ralph G., ed., "For Collectors Only [Great Civil War Novels]," *Civ. War Hist.*, 1 (1955), 415.

46.18 CIVIL WAR AND INTERNATIONAL RELATIONS

46.18.1 General

Graebner, Norman A., "Northern Diplomacy and European Neutrality," in David Donald, ed., *Why the North Won the Civil War* (1960).
Hyman, Harold M., ed., *Heard Round the World: Impact of the Civil War* (1968).
Jordan, [Henry] Donaldson, and Edwin J. Pratt, *Europe and the American Civil War* (1931).
Luvaas, Jay, *Military Legacy of the Civil War: European Inheritance* (1959).
Monaghan, Jay, *Diplomat in Carpet Slippers* (1945). Lincoln.
Sideman, Belle B., and Lillian Friedman, eds., *Europe Looks at the Civil War* (1960).
Stern, Philip Van Doren, *When the Guns Roared: World Aspects of Civil War* (1965).

See also 10.3 for biographies/writings of

Adams, Charles F., 1807–1886
Adams, Henry B., 1838–1918
Bigelow, John, 1817–1911
Clay, Cassius M., 1810–1903
Evarts, William M., 1818–1901
Forbes, John M., 1813–1898
Körner, Gustav P., 1809–1896
Lincoln, Abraham, 1809–1865
Marsh, George P., 1801–1882
Motley, John L., 1814–1877
Schurz, Carl, 1829–1906
Seward, William H., 1801–1872
Sickles, Daniel E., 1825–1914
Sumner, Charles, 1811–1874

46.18.2 Confederate Diplomacy

Blumenthal, Henry, "Confederate Diplomacy: Popular Notions and International Realities," *JSH*, 32 (1966), 151.
Callahan, J. M., *Diplomatic History of the Southern Confederacy* (1901).
Cullop, Charles P., *Confederate Propaganda in Europe, 1861–1865* (1969).
Headley, John W., *Confederate Operations in Canada* (1906).
Owsley, Frank L., and H. C. Owsley, *King Cotton Diplomacy: Foreign Relations of the Confederate States* (2nd ed., 1959).

See also 10.3 for biographies/writings of:

Benjamin, Judah P., 1811–1884
King, Thomas B., 1800–1864
Lamar, Lucius Q. C., 1825–1893
Mason, James M., 1798–1871
Slidell, John, 1793–1871

46.18.3 Great Britain

46.18.3.1 General

Adams, Brooks, "Seizure of the Laird Rams," Mass. Hist. Soc., *Proc.*, 45 (1911), 243.
Adams, Charles F., "Crisis in Downing Street," Mass. Hist. Soc., *Proc.*, 47 (1914), 372.
—— "Negotiation of 1861," Mass. Hist. Soc., *Proc.*, 46 (1912), 23.
—— *Seward and Declaration of Paris* (1912).
Adams, Ephraim D., *Great Britain and the American Civil War* (2 vols., 1925).
Albion, R. G., and J. B. Pope, *Sea Lanes in Wartime* (1942).
Baxter, James P., "British Government and Neutral Rights," *AHR*, 34 (1928), 9, 77.
Beloff, Max, "Great Britain and the Civil War," *Civil War Hist.*, 37 (1952), 40.
Bonham, M. L., *British Consuls in the Confederacy* (1911).
Clausen, M. P., "Peace Factors in Anglo-American Relations," *MVHR*, 26 (1940), 511.
Ginzberg, Eli, "Economics of British Neutrality," *Agric. Hist.*, 10 (1936), 147.
Hernon, Joseph M., Jr., "British Sympathies in the American Civil War," *JSH*, 33 (1967), 356.
Jones, Robert H., "The American Civil War in British Sessional Papers: Catalogue and Commentary," Am. Philos. Soc., *Proc.*, 107 (1963), 415.
—— "Long Live the King?" *Agric. Hist.*, 37 (1963), 166.
Jones, Wilbur D., "British Conservatives and the Civil War," *AHR*, 58 (1953), 527.

———— *Confederate Rams at Birkenhead* (1961).

Khasigian, Amos, "Economic Factors and British Neutrality," *Historian*, 25 (1963), 451.

Maynard, Douglas H., "Forbes-Aspinwall Mission," *MVHR*, 45 (1958), 67.

———— "Plotting Escape of *Alabama*," *JSH*, 20 (1954), 197.

Moran, Benjamin, *Journal, 1857–1865*, Sarah A. Wallace and Frances E. Gillespie, eds. (2 vols., 1948–1949).

Newton, Thomas W. L., *Lord Lyons* (1913).

Owsley, Frank L., "America and Freedom of Seas," in Avery O. Craven, ed., *Essays in Honor of William E. Dodd* (1935).

Pole, J. R., *Abraham Lincoln and the Working Classes of Britain* (1959).

Villiers, Brougham, and W. H. Chesson, *Anglo-American Relations, 1861–65* (1919).

See also 10.3 for biographies/writings of:

Adams, Charles F., 1807–1886
Semmes, Raphael, 1809–1877
Stowe, Harriet Beecher, 1811–1896

46.18.3.2 Trent Affair

Adams, Charles F., "Trent Affair," Mass. Hist. Soc., *Proc.*, 45 (1911), 35.

Cohen, Victor H., "Charles Sumner and the 'Trent' Affair," *JSH*, 22 (1956), 205.

Ferris, Norman B., "The Prince Consort, 'The Times', and the Trent Affair," *Civil War Hist.*, 6 (1960), 152.

John, Evan, *Atlantic Impact, 1861* (1952).

46.18.4 France

Case, Lynn M., ed., *French Opinion on the United States and Mexico* (1936).

———— "La secession aux États-Unis, problème diplomatique français en 1861," *Revue d'Histoire Diplomatique*, 77 (1963), 290.

Case, Lynn M., and Warren F. Spencer, *United States and France: Civil War Diplomacy* (1970).

Casper, H. W., *American Attitudes toward Napoleon III* (1947).

Galle, Hubert, *La 'Famine du coton,' 1861–1865* (1967).

Gavronsky, Serge, *French Liberal Opposition and the American Civil War* (1968).

Pecquet du Bellet, Paul, *Diplomacy of the Confederate Cabinet*, William S. Hoole, ed. (1963).

Sears, Louis M., "Confederate Diplomat at the Court of Napoleon III," *AHR*, 26 (1921), 255.

West, Warren R., *Contemporary French Opinion on the American Civil War* (1924).

Willson, Beckles, *Slidell in Paris* (1932).

46.18.5 Russia

Adamov, E. A., "Russia and United States at Time of Civil War," *Jour. Mod. Hist.*, 2 (1930), 586.

Bailey, Thomas A., "Russian Fleet Myth Re-Examined," *MVHR*, 38 (1951), 81.

Golder, F. A., ed., "American Civil War through Eyes of a Russian Diplomat," *AHR*, 26 (1921), 454.

Pomeroy, Earl S., "Myth after the Russian Fleet, 1863," *N.Y. Hist.*, 31 (1950), 169.

Thomas, Benjamin P., *Russo-American Relations, 1815–1867* (1930).

46.18.6 Other European Nations

Hernon, Joseph M., Jr., *Celts, Catholics, and Copperheads: Ireland Views the American Civil War* (1968).

Lombardo, Agostino, et al., *Italia e Stati Uniti Nell'Eta' del Risorgimento e della guerra civile* (1969).

Tyrner-Tyrnauer, A. R., *Lincoln and Emperors* (1962).

Wieczerzak, Joseph W., *Polish Chapter in the Civil War: Effects of the January Insurrection on American Opinion and Diplomacy* (1967).

46.18.7 Western Hemisphere

46.18.7.1 General

DeRosier, Arthur H., Jr., "Confederates in Canada: A Survey," *South. Quar.*, 3 (1965), 312.

Ferris, Nathan L., "Relations of United States with South America during Civil War," *Hisp. Am. Hist. Rev.*, 20 (1941), 51.

Macdonald, Helen G., *Canadian Public Opinion on the Civil War* (1926).

Winks, Robin W., *Canada and the United States: Civil War Years* (1960).

46.18.7.2 Mexico and French Intervention

Auer, John J., "Lincoln's Minister to Mexico," *Ohio State Archaeol. and Hist. Quar.*, 59 (1950), 115.

Callahan, J. B., *American Foreign Policy in Mexican Relations* (1932).

Carreño, A. M., *La diplomacía extraordinaria entre México y los Estados Unidos* (2 vols., 1951).

Corti, E. C., *Maximilian* (2 vols., 1928).

Crenshaw, Ollinger, "Knights of the Golden Circle," *AHR*, 47 (1941), 23.

Frias y Soto, Hilarión, *México y los Estados Unidos durante la Intervención Francesa* (1901).

Hoskins, Herbert L., "French View of the Monroe Doctrine and Mexican Expedition," *Hisp. Am. Hist. Rev.*, 4 (1921), 677.

Hyde, Harford M., *Mexican Empire* (1946).

Lally, F. E., *French Opposition to Mexican Policy* (1931).

MacCorkle, S. A., *American Policy of Recognition towards Mexico* (1933).

Mares, José Fuentes, "Washington, Paris y el imperio Mexicano," *Hist. Mexicana*, 13 (1963), 244.

Martin, Percy F., *Maximilian in Mexico* (1914).

Perkins, Dexter, *The Monroe Doctrine, 1826–1867* (1933).

47   Era of Reconstruction, 1865–1877

47.1 GENERAL

Coulter, E. Merton, *The South during Reconstruction* (1947).
Craven, Avery O., *Reconstruction: Ending of the Civil War* (1969).
Current, Richard N., ed., *Reconstruction* (1965).
Dunning, W. A., *Reconstruction* (1907).
Fleming, Walter L., ed., *Documentary History of Reconstruction* (2 vols., 1906).
Fleming, Walter L., *Sequel of Appomattox* (1919).
Franklin, John Hope, *Reconstruction* (1961).
Henry, Robert S., *Reconstruction* (1938).
Lynd, Staughton, ed., *Reconstruction* (1967).
Nevins, Allan, *Emergence of Modern America* (1927).
Patrick, Rembert W., *Reconstruction of the Nation* (1967).
Randall, James G., and David Donald, *Civil War and Reconstruction* (2nd ed., 1969).
Shenton, James P., *Reconstruction: Documentary History* (1963).
Stampp, Kenneth M., *Era of Reconstruction* (1965).
White, Leonard D., *Republican Era, 1869–1901* (1958).
Wish, Harvey, ed., *Reconstruction in the South: First-Hand Accounts* (1965).

*   *   *   *   *   *   *

Beale, Howard K., "On Rewriting Reconstruction History," *AHR*, 44 (1939–1940), 807.
Clark, John G., "Historians and Reconstruction," *Historian*, 23 (1961), 348.
Curry, Richard O., "Abolitionists and Reconstruction: Critical Appraisal," *JSH*, 34 (1968), 527.
Franklin, John Hope, "Whither Reconstruction Historiography?" *Jour. Negro Educ.*, 17 (1948), 446.
Green, Fletcher M., "Reconstruction Historiography," in William Watson Davis, ed., *The Civil War and Reconstruction in Florida* (1964).
Lynd, Staughton, "Rethinking Slavery and Reconstruction," *Jour. Negro Hist.*, 50 (1965), 198.
Pressly, Thomas J., "Racial Attitudes, Scholarship, and Reconstruction," *JSH*, 32 (1966), 88.
Randall, James G., and David Donald, *Civil War and Reconstruction* (2nd ed., 1969).
Taylor, A. A., "Historians of the Reconstruction," *Jour. Negro Hist.*, 23 (1938), 16.
Weisberger, Bernard A., "Reconstruction Historiography," *JSH*, 25 (1959), 427.
Wharton, Vernon L., "Reconstruction," in Arthur S. Link and Rembert W. Patrick, eds., *Writing Southern History: Essays in Honor of Fletcher M. Green* (1965).

Wood, Forrest G., "On Revising Reconstruction History: Negro Suffrage, White Disfranchisement, and Common Sense," *Jour. Negro Hist.*, 51 (1966), 98.

See also 10.3 for biographies/writings of:

Allen, William, 1803–1879
Blaine, James G., 1830–1893
Brown, Joseph E., 1821–1894
Brownlow, William G., 1805–1877
Butler, Benjamin F., 1818–1893
Chandler, Zachariah, 1813–1879
Chase, Salmon P., 1808–1873
Conkling, Roscoe, 1829–1888
Cox, Samuel S. "Sunset," 1824–1889
Cullom, Shelby M., 1829–1914
Dabney, Thomas S., 1789–1885
Davis, Henry W., 1817–1865
Davis, Jefferson, 1808–1889
Evarts, William M., 1818–1901
Fessenden, William P., 1806–1869
Forrest, Nathan B., 1821–1877
Garfield, James A., 1831–1881
Grant, Ulysses S., 1822–1885
Greeley, Horace, 1811–1872
Hampton, Wade, III, 1818–1902
Johnson, Andrew, 1808–1875
Johnson, Herschel V., 1812–1880
Julian, George W., 1817–1899
Kasson, John A., 1822–1910
Kirkwood, Samuel J., 1813–1894
Körner, Gustav P., 1809–1896
Lamar, Lucius Q. C., 1825–1893
Lee, Robert E., 1807–1870
McCulloch, Hugh, 1808–1895
Morrill, Justin S., 1810–1898
Morton, Oliver P., 1823–1877
Schurz, Carl, 1829–1906
Seward, William H., 1801–1872
Seymour, Horatio, 1810–1886
Sheridan, Philip H., 1831–1888
Sherman, John, 1823–1900
Sherman, William T., 1820–1891
Stanton, Edwin M., 1814–1869
Stephens, Alexander H., 1812–1883
Stevens, Thaddeus, 1792–1868
Sumner, Charles, 1811–1874
Toombs, Robert, 1810–1885
Tourgée, Albion W., 1838–1905
Wade, Benjamin F., 1800–1878
Washburn Family
Welles, Gideon, 1802–1878

47.2 INTERPRETATIVE STUDIES

Allen, James A., *Reconstruction* (1937).
Bennett, Lerone, Jr., *Black Power, U.S.A.: The Human Side of Reconstruction* (1967).
Clemenceau, Georges, *American Reconstruction, 1865–1870* (1928).
Du Bois, W. E. B., *Black Reconstruction* (1935).
Dunning, W. A., *Essays on the Civil War and Reconstruction* (1904).

Hyman, Harold M., ed., *New Frontiers of American Reconstruction* (1966).
Williams, T. Harry, "Reconstruction Attitudes," *JSH*, 12 (1946), 470.

*   *   *   *   *   *   *

Stampp, Kenneth M., and Leon F. Litwack, eds., *Reconstruction: Anthology of Revisionist Writings* (1969).

47.3 SPECIAL TOPICS

Buck, Paul H., *Road to Reunion* (1937).
Dennett, John R., *The South as It Is: 1865–1866*, Henry M. Christman, ed. (1965).
Donald, David, *Politics of Reconstruction, 1863–1867* (1965).
Hyman, Harold M., *Era of the Oath* (1954).
Payne, J. A., "Reconstruction on the Lower Mississippi," *MVHR*, 21 (1934–1935), 387.
Persons, W. M., et al., "Business and Financial Conditions Following the Civil War," *Rev. Econ. Stat.*, 2 (1920), supplement 2.
Reid, Whitelaw, *After the War: Tour of Southern States, 1865–1866*, C. Vann Woodward, ed. (1965).
Roach, H. G., "Sectionalism in Congress, 1870 to 1890," *Am. Pol. Sci. Rev.*, 19 (1925), 500.
Scarborough, L. P., "So It Was When Life Began," *La. Hist. Rev.*, 13 (1930), 428.
Sefton, James E., *United States Army and Reconstruction* (1967).
Sharkey, Robert P., *Money, Class and Party: Economic Study of the Civil War and Reconstruction* (1959).
Trowbridge, John T., *Desolate South, 1865–1866*, Gordon Carroll, ed. (1966).
Wecter, Dixon, *When Johnny Comes Marching Home* (1944).
Yearley, C. K., *The Money Machines: The Breakdown and Reform of Governmental and Party Finance in the North, 1860–1920* (1970).

47.4 RECONSTRUCTION DURING THE CIVIL WAR

Belz, Herman, *Reconstructing the Union: Theory and Policy during the Civil War* (1969).
Hesseltine, William B., *Lincoln's Plan of Reconstruction* (1960).
Roper, Laura W., "Frederick Law Olmsted and the Port Royal Experiment," *JSH*, 31 (1965), 272.
Rose, Willie L., *Rehearsal for Reconstruction: The Port Royal Experiment* (1964).

47.5 ANDREW JOHNSON AND PRESIDENTIAL RECONSTRUCTION

47.5.1 General

Beale, Howard K., *The Critical Year: Andrew Johnson* (rev. ed., 1958).
Brigance, W. N., "Jeremiah Black and Johnson," *MVHR*, 19 (1932), 205.
Brock, William R., *American Crisis: Congress and Reconstruction, 1865–1867* (1963).
Cox, LaWanda, and John H. Cox, *Politics, Principle, and Prejudice, 1865–1866* (1963).
Dorris, Jonathan T., *Pardon and Amnesty under Lincoln and Johnson* (1953).
McKitrick, Eric L., *Andrew Johnson and Reconstruction* (1960).

Schell, Herbert S., "Hugh McCulloch and the Treasury Department, 1865–69," *MVHR*, 17 (1930), 404.

47.5.2 Impeachment

Donald, David, "Why They Impeached Andrew Johnson," *Am. Heritage*, 8 (1956), 20.
Hyman, Harold M., "Johnson, Stanton, and Grant: The Army's Role and Events Leading to Impeachment," *AHR*, 66 (1960), 85.
Jellison, Charles A., "Ross Impeachment Vote: A Need for Reappraisal," *Southw. Soc. Sci. Quar.*, 41 (1960), 150.
Roske, Ralph J., "Seven Martyrs?" *AHR*, 64 (1959), 323.
Trefousse, Hans L., "Acquittal of Andrew Johnson and the Decline of Radicals," *Civil War Hist.*, 14 (1968), 148.

*   *   *   *   *   *   *

Castel, Albert E., "Andrew Johnson: Historiographical Rise and Fall," *Mid-America*, 45 (1963), 175.
Hays, Willard, "Andrew Johnson's Reputation," East Tenn. Hist. Soc., *Publ.*, 31 (1959), 1.
Notaro, Carmen Anthony, "History of the Biographic Treatment of Andrew Johnson in the Twentieth Century," *Tenn. Hist. Quar.*, 24 (1965), 143.
Sefton, James E., "Impeachment of Andrew Johnson: A Century of Writing," *Civil War Hist.*, 14 (1968), 120.

See also 10.3 for biographies/writings of:

Butler, Benjamin F., 1818–1893
Grimes, James W., 1816–1872
Logan, John A., 1826–1886
Stevens, Thaddeus, 1792–1868
Worth, Jonathan, 1802–1869

47.6 RADICAL RECONSTRUCTION

47.6.1 General

Donald, David, *Politics of Reconstruction, 1863–1867* (1965).
Gambill, Edward L., "Who Were the Senate Radicals?" *Civil War Hist.*, 11 (1965), 237.
House, Albert V., "Northern Congressional Democrats as Defenders of South during Reconstruction," *JSH*, 6 (1940), 46.
Hyman, Harold M., ed., *Radical Republicans and Reconstruction, 1861–1870* (1967).
Lerche, Charles O., "Congressional Interpretations of the Guarantee of a Republican Form of Government during Reconstruction," *JSH*, 15 (1949), 192.
McPherson, James, *Struggle for Equality: Abolitionists and the Negro in Civil War and Reconstruction* (1964).
Riddleberger, Patrick W., "Radicals' Abandonment of the Negro during Reconstruction," *Jour. Negro Hist.*, 45 (1960), 88.
Ruchames, Louis, "William Lloyd Garrison and the Negro Franchise," *Jour. Negro Hist.*, 50 (1965), 37.
Scroggs, Jack B., "Southern Reconstruction," *JSH*, 24 (1958), 407.
Thompson, Charles M., "Carpetbaggers in the United States Senate," in *Studies in Southern History and Politics* (1920).
Trefousse, Hans L., "Ben Wade and the Negro," *Ohio Hist. Quar.*, 68 (1959), 161.
——— *Radical Republicans: Lincoln's Vanguard for Racial Justice* (1969).

Williams, T. Harry, *Lincoln and the Radicals* (1941).
Woodward, C. Vann, "Seeds of Failure in Radical Race Policy," Am. Philos. Soc., *Proc.*, 110 (1966), 1.

* * * * * * *

Cox, LaWanda, and John H. Cox, "Negro Suffrage and Republican Politics: The Problem of Motivation in Reconstruction Historiography," *JSH*, 33 (1967), 303.

47.6.2 Economic Aspects

Coben, Stanley, "Northeastern Business and Radical Reconstruction," *MVHR*, 46 (1959), 67.
Linden, Glenn M., " 'Radicals' and Economic Policies: House of Representatives, 1861–1873," *Civil War Hist.*, 13 (1967), 51.
———— " 'Radicals' and Economic Policies: Senate, 1861–1873," *JSH*, 32 (1966), 189.
Montgomery, David, *Beyond Equality: Labor and Radical Republicans, 1862–1872* (1967).

47.7 COURTS AND CONSTITUTIONAL AMENDMENTS

47.7.1 General

Fairman, Charles, *Mr. Justice Miller and the Supreme Court, 1864–1890* (1939).
Hughes, David F., "Salmon P. Chase: Chief Justice," *Vanderbilt Law Rev.*, 18 (1965), 569.
Kutler, Stanley I., *Judicial Power and Reconstruction Politics* (1968).
Mayers, Lewis, "Habeas Corpus Act of 1867," *Univ. of Chi. Law Rev.*, 33 (1965), 31.

47.7.2 Fourteenth Amendment

Beth, Loren P., "Slaughter-House Cases," *La. Law Rev.*, 23 (1963), 487.
Bickel, Alexander M., "Original Understanding and the Segregation Decision," *Harv. Law Rev.*, 69 (1955), 1.
Graham, Howard J., "Antislavery Backgrounds of Fourteenth Amendment," *Wis. Law Rev.*, 30 (1950), 479.
———— " 'Conspiracy Theory' of Fourteenth Amendment," *Yale Law Jour.*, 47 (1938), 371.
———— "Fourteenth Amendment and School Segregation," *Buffalo Law Rev.*, 3 (1953), 1.
James, Joseph B., *Framing of the Fourteenth Amendment* (1956).
Kelly, Alfred H., "Fourteenth Amendment," *Mich. Law Rev.*, 54 (1956), 1049.
Kendrick, Benjamin B., ed., *Journal of the Joint Committee on Reconstruction* (1914).
McLoughlin, Andrew C., "Court, Corporation, and Conkling," *AHR*, 46 (1940), 45.
Randolph, Bessie C., "Foreign Bondholders and Repudiated Debts of Southern States," *Am. Jour. Internatl. Law*, 25 (1931), 63.
Russell, James F., "Railroads in 'Conspiracy Theory' of Fourteenth Amendment," *MVHR*, 41 (1955), 601.
TenBroek, Jacobus, *Antislavery Origins of the Fourteenth Amendment* (1951).

47.7.3 Fifteenth Amendment

Gillette, William, *The Right to Vote: Politics and the Passage of the Fifteenth Amendment* (1969).
Swinney, Everette, "Enforcing the Fifteenth Amendment, 1870–1877," *JSH*, 28 (1962), 202.

47.7.4 Civil Rights Act of 1875

Avins, Alfred, "The Civil Rights Act of 1875: Some Reflected Light on the Fourteenth Amendment and Public Accommodations," *Columbia Law Rev.*, 66 (1966), 873.

Davis, William Watson, "Enforcement Acts," in *Studies in Southern History and Politics* (1920).

McPherson, James M., "Abolitionists and the Civil Rights Act of 1875," *JAH*, 52 (1965), 493.

Russ, William A., Jr., "Negro and White Disfranchisement," *Jour. Negro Hist.*, 19 (1934), 171.

———— "Registration and Disfranchisement under Radical Reconstruction," *MVHR*, 21 (1934), 163.

Vaughn, William P., "Separate and Unequal: The Civil Rights Act of 1875 and Defeat of the School Integration Clause," *Southw. Soc. Sci. Quar.*, 48 (1967), 146.

Wyatt-Brown, Bertram, "Civil Rights Act of 1875," *West. Pol. Quar.*, 18 (1965), 763.

47.8 RELIGIOUS AND EDUCATIONAL RESPONSE

Bond, Horace M., *Negro Education in Alabama* (1969). First submitted as doctoral dissertation at the University of Chicago in 1939 under the title, "Social and Economic Influences on the Public Education of Negroes in Alabama, 1865–1900."

Drake, Richard B., "Freedmen's Aid Societies and Sectional Compromise," *JSH*, 29 (1963), 175.

Heckman, O. S., "Presbyterian Church in the U.S.A. in Reconstruction," *No. Car. Hist. Rev.*, 20 (1943), 219.

Knight, Edgar W., *Influence of Reconstruction on Education in South* (1913).

Mohler, Mark, "Episcopal Church and Conciliation," *Pol. Sci. Quar.*, 41 (1926), 567.

Morrow, Ralph E., *Northern Methodism and Reconstruction* (1956).

Russ, William A., Jr., "Anti-Catholic Agitation during Reconstruction," *Am. Cath. Hist. Soc., Records*, 45 (1934), 312.

Swint, Henry L., *Northern Teacher in the South* (1941).

See also 47.11.4, Freedmen's Bureau.

47.9 NORTHERN AND BORDER STATE STUDIES

47.9.1 District of Columbia

Whyte, James H., *Uncivil War: Washington during Reconstruction, 1865–1878* (1958).

47.9.2 Illinois

Dante, Harris L., "Western Attitudes and Reconstruction Politics in Illinois, 1865–1872," Ill. State Hist. Soc., *Jour.*, 49 (1956), 149.

47.9.3 Indiana

Carleton, William G., "Money Question in Indiana Politics, 1865–1890," *Ind. Mag. Hist.*, 42 (1946), 107.

———— "Why Was the Democratic Party in Indiana a Radical Party, 1865–1890?" *Ind. Mag. Hist.*, 42 (1946), 207.

Thornbrough, Emma Lou, *Indiana, 1850–80* (1965).

Van Deusen, J. G., "Did Republicans 'Colonize' Indiana in 1879?" *Ind. Mag. Hist.*, 30 (1934), 335.

47.9.4 Kentucky

Coulter, E. Merton, *The Civil War and Readjustment in Kentucky* (1933).

47.9.5 Maryland

Myers, W. S., *Self-Reconstruction of Maryland* (1909).

47.9.6 Massachusetts

Shapiro, Samuel, "Butler-Dana Campaign in Essex County in 1868," *NEQ*, 31 (1958), 340.

Ware, Edith E., *Political Opinion in Massachusetts during the Civil War and Reconstruction* (1916).

47.9.7 Michigan

Dilla, Harriette M., *Politics of Michigan, 1865–1878* (1912).

47.9.8 Missouri

Barclay, T. S., *Liberal Republican Movement in Missouri* (1926).
Parrish, William E., *Missouri, 1865–1870* (1965).

47.9.9 Minnesota

Heck, Frank H., *Civil War Veteran in Minnesota Life and Politics* (1941).

47.9.10 New Jersey

Knapp, Charles M., *New Jersey Politics during the Civil War* (1924).

47.9.11 New Mexico

Murphy, Lawrence R., "Reconstruction in New Mexico," *New Mex. Hist. Rev.*, 43 (1968), 99.

47.9.12 New York

Stebbins, H. A., *Political History of New York, 1865–1869* (1913).

47.9.13 Ohio

Bonadio, Felice A., *North of Reconstruction: Ohio Politics, 1865–1870* (1970).
Moore, C. H., "Ohio in National Politics," *Ohio State Archaeol. and Hist. Quar.*, 37 (1928), 220.
Unger, Irwin, "Business and Currency in the Ohio Gubernatorial Campaign of 1875," *Mid-America*, 41 (1959), 27.

47.9.14 Pennsylvania

Bradley, Erwin S., *Triumph of Militant Republicanism: Pennsylvania, 1860–1872* (1964).

Evans, Frank B., *Pennsylvania Politics, 1872–1877* (1966).
House, Albert V., "Men, Morals, and Manipulation in the Pennsylvania Democracy of 1875," *Penn. Hist.*, 23 (1956), 248.
Montgomery, David, "Radical Republicanism in Pennsylvania, 1866–1873," *Penn. Mag. Hist. Biog.*, 85 (1961), 439.

47.9.15 Wisconsin

Cosmas, Graham A., "Democracy in Search of Issues: Wisconsin Reform Party, 1873–1877," *Wis. Mag. Hist.*, 46 (1962–1963), 93.
Williams, Helen J., and T. Harry Williams, "Wisconsin Republicans and Reconstruction, 1865–70," *Wis. Mag. Hist.*, 23 (1939), 17.

47.10 EX-CONFEDERATE STATES

47.10.1 Economy

47.10.1.1 General

Anderson, George L., "South and Post-Civil War Finance," *JSH*, 9 (1943), 181.
Berthoff, R. T., "Southern Attitudes toward Immigration," *JSH*, 17 (1951), 328.
Brandfon, Robert L., *Cotton Kingdom of the New South: Yazoo Mississippi Delta from Reconstruction to the Twentieth Century* (1967).
Carleton, Mark T., "Politics of Convict Lease System in Louisiana, 1868–1901," *La. Hist.*, 8 (1967), 5.
Durden, Robert F., *Reconstruction Bonds and Twentieth-Century Politics: South Dakota* v. *North Carolina* (1904).
Eckert, Edward K., "Contract Labor in Florida during Reconstruction," *Fla. Hist. Quar.*, 47 (1968), 34.
Goodrich, Carter, "Public Aid to Railroads in the Reconstruction South," *Pol. Sci. Quar.*, 71 (1956), 407.
Green, Fletcher M., "Some Aspects of Convict Lease System in the Southern States," in *Essays in Southern History* (1949).
Kolchin, Peter, "Business Press and Reconstruction, 1865–1868," *JSH*, 33 (1967), 183.
Loewenberg, B. J., "Efforts of the South to Encourage Immigration," *So. Atl. Quar.*, 33 (1934), 363.
Osborn, George C., "Life of a Southern Plantation Owner during Reconstruction Revealed in Clay-Sharkey Papers," *Jour. Miss. Hist.*, 6 (1944), 103.
Riegel, R. E., "Federal Operation of Southern Railroads," *MVHR*, 9 (1922), 126.
Woolfolk, George R., *Cotton Regency: Northern Merchants and Reconstruction, 1865–1880* (1958).
Zeichner, Oscar, "Transition from Slave to Free Labor," *Agric. Hist.*, 13 (1939), 22.

See also 47.6.2, Radical Reconstruction–Economic Aspects.

47.10.1.2 Land Policy

Cox, LaWanda, "Land for the Freedman," *MVHR*, 45 (1958), 413.
Gates, Paul W., "Federal Land Policy in the South, 1866–1888," *JSH*, 6 (1940), 303.
——— "Private Land Claims in the South," *JSH*, 22 (1956), 183.
Klingberg, Frank W., *Southern Claims Commission* (1955).

47.10.2 Politics

47.10.2.1 General

Alexander, Thomas B., "Persistent Whiggery in the Confederate South, 1860–1877," *JSH*, 27 (1961), 305.

Lewinson, Paul, *Race, Class, and Party: History of Negro Suffrage and White Politics in the South* (1932).

See also 10.3 for biographies/writings of:

Davis, Henry W., 1817–1865
Davis, Jefferson, 1808–1889
Fessenden, William P., 1806–1869
Julian, George W., 1817–1899
Stanton, Edwin M., 1814–1869
Stephens, Alexander H., 1812–1883
Stevens, Thaddeus, 1792–1868
Wade, Benjamin F., 1800–1878

47.10.2.2 Carpetbaggers

Current, Richard N., "Carpetbaggers Reconsidered," in David H. Pinkney and Theodore Ropp, eds., *A Festschrift for Frederick B. Artz* (1964).
—— *Three Carpetbag Governors* (1967).
Daniels, Jonathan, *Prince of Carpetbaggers* (1958).
Gross, Theodore L., "The Fool's Errand of Albion W. Tourgée," *Phylon*, 24 (1963), 240.
Overy, David H., Jr., *Wisconsin Carpetbaggers in Dixie* (1961).
Pomeroy, Earl S., "Carpetbaggers in the Territories, 1861 to 1890." *Historian*, 2 (1939), 53.
Scroggs, Jack B., "Carpetbagger Constitutional Reform in the South Atlantic States, 1867–1868," *JSH*, 27 (1961), 475.
Thompson, Charles M., "Carpetbaggers in the United States Senate," in *Studies in Southern History and Politics* (1920).
Walker, S. A., "Carpetbaggers," *Jour. Negro Hist.*, 14 (1929), 44.
Weissbuch, Ted N., "Albion W. Tourgée: Critic of Reconstruction," *Ohio Hist. Quar.*, 70 (1961), 27.

See also 10.3 for biographies/writings of:

Littlefield, Milton S., 1830–1899

47.10.2.3 Scalawags

Donald, David, "Scalawag in Mississippi Reconstruction," *JSH*, 10 (1944), 447.
Olsen, Otto H., "Scalawags," *Civil War Hist.*, 12 (1966), 304.
Trelease, Allen W., "Who Were the Scalawags?" *JSH*, 29 (1963), 445.

47.10.3 Ex-Confederates

Burger, Nash K., and John K. Bettersworth, *South of Appomattox* (1959).
Dorris, Jonathan T., *Pardon and Amnesty under Lincoln and Johnson* (1953).
—— "Pardon Seekers and Brokers," *JSH*, (1928), 276.
—— "Pardoning Leaders of Confederacy," *MVHR*, 15 (1928), 3.
Grantham, Dewey W., Jr., "Southern Bourbons Revisited," *So. Atl. Quar.*, 60 (1961), 286.
Hesseltine, William B., *Confederate Leaders in the New South* (1950).
McClendon, R. E., "Status of Ex-Confederate States as Seen in Readmission of Senators," *AHR*, 41 (1936), 703.

47.10.4 Confederate Exiles

Hanna, Alfred J., and Kathryn A. Hanna, *Confederate Exiles in Venezuela* (1960).
Hesseltine, William B., and Hazel C. Wolf, *The Blue and Gray on the Nile* (1961).
Hill, Lawrence F., "Confederate Exodus to Latin America," *Southw. Hist. Quar.*, 39 (1935), 100.
Rolle, Andrew F., *Lost Cause: Confederate Exodus to Mexico* (1965).

47.10.5 State Studies

47.10.5.1 Alabama

Alexander, Thomas B., "Persistent Whiggery in Alabama and the Lower South, 1860–1867," *Ala. Rev.*, 12 (1959), 35.

Bond, Horace M., "Alabama Reconstruction," *Jour. Negro Hist.*, 23 (1938), 290.

Fleming, Walter L., *Civil War and Reconstruction in Alabama* (1905).

Moore, Albert B., "Railroad Building in Alabama during Reconstruction," *JSH*, 1 (1935), 421.

Williamson, Edward C., "Alabama Election of 1874," *Ala. Rev.*, 17 (1964), 210.

47.10.5.2 Arkansas

Staples, T. S., *Reconstruction in Arkansas* (1923).

Thomas, David Y., *Arkansas in War and Reconstruction* (1926).

47.10.5.3 Florida

Cox, Merlin G., "Military Reconstruction in Florida," *Fla. Hist. Quar.*, 46 (1968), 219.

Davis, William Watson, *Civil War and Reconstruction in Florida* (1913).

Peek, Ralph L., "Curbing Voter Intimidation in Florida, 1871," *Fla. Hist. Quar.*, 43 (1965), 333.

——— "Election of 1870 and the End of Reconstruction in Florida," *Fla. Hist. Quar.*, 45 (1967), 352.

Roberts, Derrell, "Social Legislation in Reconstruction Florida," *Fla. Hist. Quar.*, 43 (1965), 349.

Shofner, Jerrell H., "Constitution of 1868," *Fla. Hist. Quar.*, 41 (1963), 356.

Smith, George W., "Carpetbag Imperialism in Florida, 1862–1868," *Fla. Hist. Quar.*, 27 (1948–1949), 99.

Wallace, John, *Carpetbag Rule in Florida* (1888).

47.10.5.4 Georgia

Conway, Alan, *Reconstruction of Georgia* (1966).

Nathans, Elizabeth S., *Losing the Peace: Georgia Republicans and Reconstruction, 1865–1871* (1968).

Shadgett, Olive H., *Republican Party in Georgia: Reconstruction through 1900* (1964).

Thompson, C. Mildred, *Reconstruction in Georgia* (1915).

See also 10.3 for biographies/writings of:

Brown, Joseph E., 1821–1894
Gordon, John B., 1832–1904
Stephens, Alexander H., 1812–1883
Toombs, Robert, 1810–1885
Watson, Thomas E., 1856–1922

47.10.5.5 Louisiana

Caskey, Willie M., *Secession and Restoration in Louisiana* (1938).

Ficklen, John R., *History of Reconstruction in Louisiana* (1910).

Gonzales, John E., "William Pitt Kellogg, Reconstruction Governor of Louisiana, 1873–1877," *La. Hist. Quar.*, 29 (1946), 394.

Grosz, Agnes S., "Political Career of Pinckney Benton Stewart Pinchback," *La. Hist. Quar.*, 27 (1944), 527.

Landry, Stuart O., *Battle of Liberty Place: Overthrow of Carpetbag Rule in New Orleans* (1955).

Lonn, Ella, *Reconstruction in Louisiana after 1868* (1918).

McGinty, Garnie W., *Louisiana Redeemed* (1941).

Pitre, Althea D., "Collapse of the Warmoth Regime, 1870–72," *La. Hist.*, 6 (1965), 161.

Shugg, Roger W., *Origins of Class Struggle in Louisiana: Social History of White Farmers and Laborers during Slavery and After, 1840–1875* (1939).

Warmoth, Henry C., *War, Politics and Reconstruction: Louisiana* (1930).

Williams, T. Harry, "Louisiana Unification Movement of 1873," *JSH*, 11 (1945), 349.

See also 10.3 for biographies/writings of:

Banks, Nathaniel P., 1816–1894
Warmoth, Henry C., 1842–1931

47.10.5.6 Mississippi

Brandfon, Robert L., *Cotton Kingdom of the New South: A History of the Yazoo Mississippi Delta from Reconstruction to the Twentieth Century* (1967).

Garner, James W., *Reconstruction in Mississippi* (1901).

Hall, L. Marshall, "William L. Sharkey and Reconstruction," *Jour. Miss. Hist.*, 27 (1965), 1.

Harris, William C., "Black Code of 1865," *Jour. Miss. Hist.*, 29 (1967), 181.

―――― *Presidential Reconstruction in Mississippi* (1967).

Lynch, John R., *Facts of Reconstruction* (1913).

Ringold, May S., "James Lusk Alcorn," *Jour. Miss. Hist.*, 25 (1963), 1.

Urofsky, Melvin I., "Blanche K. Bruce: United States Senator, 1875–1881," *Jour. Miss. Hist.*, 29 (1967), 118.

See also 10.3 for biographies/writings of:

Alcorn, James L., 1816–1894
Ames, Adelbert, 1847–1939
Lamar, Lucius Q. C., 1825–1893

47.10.5.7 North Carolina

Connor, R. D. W., "Rehabilitation of a Rural Commonwealth," *AHR*, 36 (1930), 44.

Evans, W. McKee, *Ballots and Fence Rails: Reconstruction on Lower Cape Fear* (1967).

Hamilton, J. G. deR., *Reconstruction in North Carolina* (1914).

Ratchford, B. U., "North Carolina Public Debt, 1870–1878," *No. Car. Hist. Rev.*, 10 (1933), 1.

See also 10.3 for biographies/writings of:

Holden, William W., 1818–1892
Jarvis, Thomas J., 1836–1915
Littlefield, Milton S., 1830–1899
Tourgée, Albion W., 1838–1905
Vance, Zebulon B., 1830–1894

47.10.5.8 South Carolina

Ball, William W., *State That Forgot* (1932).

Bleser, Carol K. R., *The Promised Land: History of South Carolina Land Commission, 1869–1890* (1969).

Lander, Ernest M., *History of South Carolina, 1865–1900* (1960).

Pike, James S., *Prostrate State* (1874).

Post, Langdon F., "A 'Carpetbagger' in South Carolina," *Jour. Negro Hist.*, 10 (1925), 10.

Rose, Willie Lee, *Rehearsal for Reconstruction: Port Royal Experiment* (1964).

Sheppard, William A., *Red Shirts Remembered: Southern Brigadiers of the Reconstruction Period* (1940).

Simkins, F. B., and R. H. Woody, *South Carolina during Reconstruction* (1932).
Thompson, Henry T., *Ousting Carpetbagger from South Carolina* (1926).

*   *   *   *   *   *   *

Macaulay, Neill W., Jr., "South Carolina Reconstruction Historiography," *So. Car. Hist. Mag.*, 65 (1964), 20.

See also 10.3 for biographies/writings of:

Hampton, Wade, III, 1818–1902
Pike, James S., 1811–1882

47.10.5.9 Tennessee

Alexander, Thomas B., *Political Reconstruction in Tennessee* (1950).
Patton, James W., *Unionism and Reconstruction in Tennessee* (1934).
Queener, Verton M., "Decade of East Tennessee Republicanism, 1867–1876," East Tenn. Hist. Soc., *Publ.*, 14 (1942), 59.

See also 10.3 for biographies/writings of:

Brownlow, William G., 1805–1877
Nelson, Thomas A. R., 1812–1873
Washburn Family

47.10.5.10 Texas

Casdorph, Paul C., *History of the Républican Party in Texas, 1865–1965* (1965).
Nunn, W. C., *Texas Under Carpetbaggers* (1962).
Ramsdell, C. W., *Reconstruction in Texas* (1910).

See also 10.3 for biographies/writings of:

Hamilton, Andrew J., 1815–1875
Reagan, John H., 1818–1905

47.10.5.11 Virginia

Eckenrode, H. J., *Political History of Virginia during Reconstruction* (1904).

See also 10.3 for biographies/writings of:

Mahone, William, 1826–1895

47.11 NEGROES

47.11.1 General

Child, Lydia M., *Freedmen's Book* (1865).
Cruden, Robert, *The Negro in Reconstruction* (1969).
Donald, Henderson H., *Negro Freedman* (1952).
Du Bois, W. E. B., *Black Reconstruction* (1935).
Hoffman, Edwin D., "From Slavery to Self-Reliance," *Jour. Negro Hist.*, 41 (1956), 8.
McPherson, James M., *Struggle for Equality: Abolitionists and the Negro in the Civil War and Reconstruction* (1964).
Riddleberger, Patrick W., "Radicals' Abandonment of the Negro during Reconstruction," *Jour. Negro Hist.*, 45 (1960), 88.

Seifman, Eli, "Schism Within the African Colonization Movement, 1865–1875," *Hist. Educ. Quar.*, 7 (1967), 36.
Singletary, Otis A., *Negro Militia and Reconstruction* (1957).
Smith, Samuel D., *The Negro in Congress, 1870–1901* (1940).

47.11.2 State Studies

47.11.2.1 Alabama

Bond, Horace M., *Negro Education in Alabama* (1969). First submitted as doctoral dissertation at the University of Chicago in 1939 under the title, "Social and Economic Influences on the Public Education of Negroes in Alabama, 1865–1900."

47.11.2.2 Kentucky

Montell, William L., *Saga of Coe Ridge: A Study in Oral History* (1970).

47.11.2.3 Florida

Richardson, Joe M., *Negro in Reconstruction of Florida, 1865–1877* (1965).

47.11.2.4 Mississippi

Harris, William C., "Black Code of 1865," *Jour. Miss. Hist.*, 29 (1967), 181.
Wharton, Vernon L., *The Negro in Mississippi, 1865–1900* (1947).

47.11.2.5 North Carolina

Bell, John L., Jr., "The Presbyterian Church and the Negro in North Carolina during Reconstruction," *No. Car. Hist. Rev.*, 40 (1963), 15.
Bernstein, Leonard, "Participation of Negro Delegates in the Constitutional Convention of 1868 in North Carolina," *Jour. Negro Hist.*, 34 (1949), 391.

47.11.2.6 South Carolina

Taylor, A. A., *The Negro in South Carolina during Reconstruction* (1924).
Williamson, Joel, *After Slavery: The Negro in South Carolina during Reconstruction, 1861–1877* (1965).

47.11.2.7 Tennessee

Taylor, Alrutheus A., *The Negro in Tennessee* (1941).

47.11.2.8 Virginia

Jackson, Luther P., *Negro Office Holders in Virginia, 1865–1895* (1945).
Morton, Richard L., *The Negro in Virginia Politics, 1865–1902* (1919).
Taylor, Alrutheus A., *The Negro in Reconstruction of Virginia* (1926).

47.11.3 Racial Conflict and Segregation

Harlan, Louis R., "Desegregation in New Orleans Public Schools during Reconstruction," *AHR*, 67 (1962), 663.
Kaplan, Sidney, "Albion W. Tourgée: Attorney for the Segregated," *Jour. Negro Hist.*, 49 (1964), 128.
Kelly, Alfred H., "Congressional Controversy over School Segregation, 1867–1875," *AHR*, 64 (1959), 537.
Norris, Marjorie M., "Nonviolence: Louisville Demonstrations of 1870–71," *JSH*, 32 (1965), 488.
Richardson, Joe M., ed., "Memphis Race Riot and Aftermath," *Tenn. Hist. Quar.*, 24 (1965), 63.
Johnson, Guion G., "Southern Paternalism toward Negroes after Emancipation," *JSH*, 23 (1957), 483.
Tebeau, C. W., "Aspects of Planter-Freedman Relations," *Jour. Negro Hist.*, 21 (1936), 130.

47.11.4 Freedmen's Bureau

47.11.4.1 General

Bentley, George R., *History of the Freedmen's Bureau* (1955).
Cox, John H., and LaWanda Cox, "General O. O. Howard and the 'Misrepresented Bureau'," *JSH*, 19 (1953), 427.
Fleming, Walter L., *Freedmen's Savings Bank* (1927).
Peirce, Paul S., *Freedmen's Bureau* (1904).
Sproat, John G., "Blueprint for Radical Reconstruction," *JSH*, 23 (1957), 25. Land reform.

See also 10.3 for biographies/writings of:

Howard, Oliver O., 1830–1909

47.11.4.2 State Studies

ALABAMA

Bethel, Elizabeth, "The Freedmen's Bureau in Alabama," *JSH*, 14 (1948), 49.

FLORIDA

Richardson, Joe M., "The Freedmen's Bureau and Negro Labor in Florida," *Fla. Hist. Quar.*, 39 (1960), 167.

LOUISIANA

Engelsman, John C., "The Freedmen's Bureau in Louisiana," *La. Hist. Quar.*, 32 (1949), 145.
May, J. Thomas, "Freedmen's Bureau at the Local Level: Study of a Louisiana Agent," *La. Hist.*, 9 (1968), 5.
White, Howard A., *The Freedmen's Bureau in Louisiana* (1970).

SOUTH CAROLINA

Abbott, Martin, *The Freedmen's Bureau in South Carolina* (1967).
De Forest, John W., *Union Officer in Reconstruction,* James H. Croushore and David M. Potter, eds. (1948).

TENNESSEE

Jordan, Weymouth T., "The Freedmen's Bureau in Tennessee," East Tenn. Hist. Soc., *Publ.*, 11 (1939), 47.
Phillips, Paul D., "White Reaction to the Freedmen's Bureau in Tennessee," *Tenn. Hist. Quar.*, 25 (1966), 50.

TEXAS

Elliott, Claude, "The Freedmen's Bureau in Texas," *Southw. Hist. Quar.*, 56 (1952), 1.

VIRGINIA

Alderson, William T., Jr., "The Freedmen's Bureau and Negro Education in Virginia," *No. Car. Hist. Rev.*, 29 (1952), 64.

47.11.5 White Supremacists

47.11.5.1 General

Burns, F. P., "White Supremacy in the South," *La. Hist. Quar.*, 18 (1935), 581.
Dew, Lee A., "Reluctant Radicals of 1866," *Midw. Quar.*, 8 (1967), 261.

Wood, Forrest G., *Black Scare: The Racist Response to Emancipation and Recon-struction* (1968).
Woodward, C. Vann, "Seeds of Failure in Radical Race Policy," Am. Philos. Soc., *Proc.*, 110 (1966), 1.

47.11.5.2 Ku Klux Klan

Horn, Stanley F., *Invisible Empire* (2nd ed., 1969).
Lestage, H. O., Jr., "White League in Louisiana," *La. Hist. Quar.*, 18 (1935), 617.
Randel, William P., *The Ku Klux Klan: Century of Infamy* (1965).
Shapiro, Herbert, "The Ku Klux Klan During Reconstruction: North Carolina," *Jour. Negro Hist.*, 49 (1964), 34.
Trelease, Allen W., *White Terror: The Ku Klux Klan Conspiracy and Southern Reconstruction* (1971).

47.12 GREENBACK MOVEMENT

Destler, C. M., "Influence of Edward Kellogg," *Jour. Pol. Econ.*, 40 (1932), 338.
McGrane, R. C., "Ohio and the Greenback Movement," *MVHR*, 11 (1925), 526.
Martin, R. C., "The Greenback Party in Texas," *Southw. Hist. Quar.*, 30 (1927), 161.
Nugent, Walter T. K., *Money and American Society, 1865–1880* (1968).
—— *Money Question during Reconstruction* (1967).
Ridge, Martin, "Ignatius Donnelly and the Greenback Movement," *Mid-America*, 39 (1957), 156.
Ruggles, C. O., "The Greenback Movement in Iowa and Wisconsin," Miss. Valley Hist. Assoc., *Proc.* (1912), 142.
Shipley, M. L., "Background of the Pendleton Plan," *MVHR*, 24 (1938), 329.
Unger, Irwin, *The Greenback Era, 1865–1879* (1964).
—— "Northern Calvinist Churches and the Reconstruction Financial Issue," *Jour. Presby. Hist.*, 40 (1962), 38.
Usher, Ellis B., *The Greenback Movement* (1911).

47.13 FEDERAL FINANCE

Beale, Howard K., "Tariff and Reconstruction," *AHR*, 35 (1930), 276.
Patterson, Robert T., *Federal Debt-Management Policies, 1865–1879* (1954).
Redlich, Fritz, "'Translating' Economic Policy into Business Policy: Specie Pay-ments in 1879," Bus. Hist. Soc., *Bull.*, 20 (1946), 190.
Smith, Harry Edwin, *United States Internal Tax History from 1861 to 1871* (1914).
Treascott, Paul B., "Federal Government Receipts and Expenditures, 1861–1875," *Jour. Econ. Hist.*, 26 (1966), 206.

47.14 ELECTION OF 1868 AND GRANT ADMINISTRATION, 1869–1877

47.14.1 General

Coleman, Charles H., *Election of 1868* (1933).
Fairman, Charles, "Bradley's Appointment to the Supreme Court and the Legal Tender Cases," *Harvard Law Rev.*, 54 (1941), 977.
Franklin, John Hope, "Election of 1868," in Arthur M. Schlesinger, Jr. and Fred L. Israel, eds., *History of American Presidential Elections, 1789–1968*, vol. II (1971).
Hoogenboom, Ari A., *Outlawing Spoils: Civil Service Reform Movement, 1865–1883* (1961).
Isaacs, Joakin, "Candidate Grant and the Jews," *Am. Jew. Archives*, 17 (1965), 3.

Ratner, Sidney, "Was the Supreme Court Packed by Grant?" *Pol. Sci. Quar.*, 50 (1935), 343.
White, Leonard D., *Republican Era, 1869–1901: Administrative History* (1958).

See also 10.3 for biographies/writings of:

Blaine, James G., 1830–1893
Brinkerhoff, Roeliff, 1828–1911
Chandler, Zachariah, 1813–1879
Colfax, Schuyler, 1823–1885
Curtis, George W., 1824–1892
Dana, Charles A., 1819–1897
Fish, Hamilton, 1808–1893
Garfield, James A., 1831–1881
Grant, Julia T., 1826–1902
Grant, Ulysses S., 1822–1885
Greeley, Horace, 1811–1872
Hoar, Ebenezer R., 1816–1895
Julian, George W., 1817–1899
Morton, Oliver P., 1823–1877
Rawlins, John A., 1831–1869
Schurz, Carl, 1829–1906
Seymour, Horatio, 1810–1886
Sherman, William T., 1820–1891
Sumner, Charles, 1811–1874
Tilden, Samuel J., 1814–1886
Trumbull, Lyman, 1813–1896
Ward, Samuel, 1814–1884
White, Andrew D., 1832–1918

See also 47.20.4, Great Britain and *Alabama* Claims.

47.14.2 Corruption

47.14.2.1 General

Carpenter, John A., "Washington, Pennsylvania, and the Gold Conspiracy of 1869," *West. Penn. Hist. Mag.*, 48 (1965), 345.
Green, Fletcher M., "Origins of Credit Mobilier," *MVHR*, 46 (1959), 238.
Guese, Lucius E., "St. Louis and the Great Whiskey Ring," *Mo. Hist. Rev.*, 36 (1942), 160.
Klotsche, J. Martin, "Star Route Cases," *MVHR*, 22 (1935), 406.
Loth, D. G., *Public Plunder* (1938).
Prickett, R. C., "Malfeasance of Belknap," *No. Dak. Hist.*, 17 (1950), 5.
Resseguie, Harry E., "Federal Conflict of Interest: The A. T. Stewart Case," *N.Y. Hist.*, 47 (1966), 271.
Spence, Clark C., "Schenck and Emma Mine Affair," *Ohio Hist. Quar.*, 68 (1959), 141.
Trottman, Nelson, *Union Pacific* (1923).

47.14.2.2 New York State

Adams, Charles F., Jr., and Henry Adams, *Chapters of Erie* (1866).
Callow, Alexander B., Jr., *Tweed Ring* (1966).
Hirsch, M. D., "More Light on Boss Tweed," *Pol. Sci. Quar.*, 60 (1945), 267.
Lynch, Denis T., *Tweed* (1927).
Mandelbaum, Seymour, *Boss Tweed's New York* (1965).
Myers, Gustavus, *Tammany Hall* (1917).
Pratt, John W., "Boss Tweed's Public Welfare Program," *N.Y. Hist. Soc. Quar.*, 45 (1961), 396.

Stoddard, Theodore L., *Master of Manhattan* (1931). Croker.
Werner, M. R., *Tammany Hall* (1928).

See also 10.3 for biographies/writings of:

Choate, Joseph H., 1832–1917
Fisk, James, 1834–1872
Gould, Jay, 1836–1892
Green, Andrew H., 1820–1903
Hall, A. Oakey, 1826–1898
Nast, Thomas, 1840–1902
Seymour, Horatio, 1810–1886
Tilden, Samuel J., 1814–1886
Tweed, William, 1823–1878

47.15 ELECTION OF 1872 AND LIBERAL REPUBLICAN MOVEMENT

Barclay, Thomas S., *The Liberal Republican Movement in Missouri* (1926).
Downey, Matthew T., "Horace Greeley and Politicians: Liberal Republican Convention in 1872," *JAH*, 53 (1967), 727.
Gillette, William, "Election of 1872," in Arthur M. Schlesinger, Jr. and Fred L. Israel, eds., *History of American Presidential Elections, 1789–1978*, vol. II (1971).
McPherson, James M., "Abolitionists Dilemma in the Election of 1872," *AHR*, 71 (1965), 43.
Riddleberger, Patrick W., "Liberals vs. Stalwarts in the Election of 1872," *Jour. Negro Hist.*, 44 (1959), 136.
Ross, Earl D., *The Liberal Republican Movement* (1919).
Smart, James G., "Whitelaw Reid and the Nomination of Greeley," *Mid-America*, 49 (1967), 227.
Sproat, John G., *"The Best Men": Liberal Reformers in the Gilded Age* (1968).

See also 10.3 for biographies/writings of:

Adams, Charles F., Jr., 1835–1915
Adams, Henry B., 1838–1918
Brown, B. Gratz, 1826–1885
Curtis, George W., 1824–1892
Davis, David, 1815–1886
Greeley, Horace, 1811–1872
Julian, George W., 1817–1899
Reid, Whitelaw, 1837–1912
Schurz, Carl, 1829–1906
Sumner, Charles, 1811–1874
Trumbull, Lyman, 1813–1896
Watterson, Henry, 1840–1921

47.16 SPECIE RESUMPTION AND DEMONETIZATION OF SILVER

Nugent, Walter T. K., *Money and American Society, 1865–1880* (1968).
O'Leary, Paul M., "Crime of 1873," *Jour. Pol. Econ.*, 68 (1960), 388.
Unger, Irwin, "Business Community and 1875 Resumption Act," *Bus. Hist. Rev.*, 35 (1961), 247.
—— "Business Men and Specie Resumption," *Pol. Sci. Quar.*, 74 (1959).
Weinstein, Allen, "Bonanza King Myth: Western Mine Owners and the Remonetization of Silver," *Bus. Hist. Rev.*, 42 (1968), 195.
—— *Prelude to Populism: Origins of the Silver Issue, 1867–1878* (1970).
—— "Was There a 'Crime of 1873'?: Case of Demonetized Dollar," *JAH*, 54 (1967), 307.

47.17 DEPRESSION OF 1873–1879

Fels, Rendigs, "American Business Cycles, 1865–79," *Am. Econ. Rev.*, 41 (1951), 325.

Gutman, Herbert G., "Failure of Movement by the Unemployed for Public Works in 1873," *Pol. Sci. Quar.*, 80 (1965), 254.

McCartney, Ernest R., *Crisis of 1873* (1935).

Rezneck, Samuel, "Distress, Relief, and Discontent during the Depression of 1873–78," *Jour. Pol. Econ.*, 58 (1950), 494.

Wells, O. V., "Depression of 1873–1879," *Agric. Hist.*, 11 (1937), 237.

47.18 END OF RECONSTRUCTION

Hesseltine, William B., "Economic Factors in the Abandonment of Reconstruction," *MVHR*, 22 (1935), 191.

House, Albert V., "Speakership Contest of 1875," *JAH*, 52 (1965), 252.

Riddleberger, Patrick W., "Radicals' Abandonment of the Negro during Reconstruction," *Jour. Negro Hist.*, 45 (1960), 88.

47.19 ELECTION OF 1876 AND THE COMPROMISE OF 1877

Bone, F. Z. L., "Louisiana in Disputed Election," *La. Hist. Quar.*, 14 (1931), 408; 15 (1932), 93, 234.

Bruce, Robert V., *1877: Year of Violence* (1959).

Dippre, Harold, "Corruption and Disputed Vote of Oregon in 1876 Election," *Ore. Hist. Quar.*, 67 (1966), 257.

Haworth, Paul L., *Hayes-Tilden Disputed Election of 1876* (1906).

Kelley, Robert L., "Samuel J. Tilden," *Historian*, 26 (1964), 176.

Pomerantz, Sidney, "Election of 1876," in Arthur M. Schlesinger, Jr. and Fred L. Israel, eds., *History of American Presidential Elections, 1789–1968*, vol. II (1971).

Shofner, Jerrell H., "Fraud and Intimidation in the Florida Election of 1876," *Fla. Hist. Quar.*, 42 (1964), 321.

Tunnell, T. B., Jr., "The Negro, the Republican Party, and the Election of 1876 in Louisiana," *La. Hist.*, 7 (1966), 101.

Woodward, C. Vann, *Origins of the New South* (1951).

——— *Reunion and Reaction* (1951).

47.20 FOREIGN RELATIONS

47.20.1 General

Armstrong, William M., *Godkin and American Foreign Policy, 1865–1900* (1957).

Dozer, D. M., "Anti-Expansionism during the Johnson Administration," *Pac. Hist. Rev.*, 12 (1943), 253.

Dyer, Brainerd, "R. J. Walker on Acquiring Greenland and Iceland," *MVHR*, 27 (1940), 263.

Koht, Halvdan, "Origins of Seward's Plan to Purchase the Danish West Indies," *AHR*, 50 (1945), 762.

May, A. J., "Crete and United States, 1866–69," *Jour. Mod. Hist.*, 16 (1944), 286.

Perkins, Dexter, *The Monroe Doctrine, 1867–1907* (1937).

Smith, Joe Patterson, *Republican Expansionists of the Early Reconstruction Era* (1933).

Tansill, Charles C., *United States and Santo Domingo, 1798–1873* (1938).

Trauth, Sister Mary P., *Italo-American Diplomatic Relations, 1861–1882* (1958).

Xydis, Stephen G., "Diplomatic Relations between the United States and Greece, 1868–1878," *Balkan Studies*, 5 (1964), 47.

See also 10.3 for biographies/writings of:

Fish, Hamilton, 1808–1893
Johnson, Reverdy, 1796–1876
Marsh, George P., 1801–1882
Motley, John Lothrop, 1814–1877
Seward, William H., 1801–1872
Sumner, Charles, 1811–1874

See also 46.18.7.2, Civil War and International Relations–Mexico and French Intervention.

47.20.2 Alaska Purchase

Bailey, Thomas A., "Why the United States Purchased Alaska," *Pac. Hist. Rev.*, 3 (1934), 39.
Belov, Mikhail, "Sale of Alaska," *Mankind*, 1 (1967), 74.
Callahan, J. M., *Alaska Purchase and Americo-Canadian Relations* (1908).
Chevigny, Hector, *Russian America: Alaskan Venture, 1741–1867* (1965).
Farrar, Victor, *Annexation of Russian America to the United States* (1937).
Gilbert, Benjamin F., "Alaska Purchase," *Jour. of West*, 3 (1964), 163.
Reid, Virginia H., *Purchase of Alaska: Contemporary Opinion* (1939).
Sherwood, Morgan B., *Exploration of Alaska, 1865–1900* (1965).
Shiels, Archie W., *Purchase of Alaska* (1967).

47.20.3 Canada and Fenianism

Morrow, R. L., "The Anglo-American Treaty of 1870," *AHR*, 39 (1934), 663.
Tansill, Charles C., *America and the Fight for Irish Freedom, 1866–1922* (1957).
Shippee, Lester B., *Canadian-American Relations, 1849–1874* (1939).
Warner, Donald F., *Idea of Continental Union: Agitation for Annexation of Canada, 1849–1893* (1960).

47.20.4 Great Britain and *Alabama* Claims

Baxter, James P., "British High Commissioners at Washington, 1871," *Mass. Hist. Soc., Proc.*, 65 (1940), 334.
Bernath, Stuart L., *Squall across the Atlantic: Civil War Prize Cases and Diplomacy* (1970).
Chamberlain, Daniel H., *Charles Sumner and the Treaty of Washington* (1902).
McIntyre, W. D., "British Annexation of the Fiji Islands in 1874," *Pac. Hist. Rev.*, 29 (1960), 361.
Reale, Egidio, *L'Arbitrage international. Le Réglement judiciare du conflit de l'Alabama* (1929).
Robson, Maureen M., "The *Alabama* Claims and the Anglo-American Reconciliation, 1865–71," *Can. Hist. Rev.*, 42 (1961), 1.
Smith, Goldwin A., *Treaty of Washington* (1941).

47.20.5 East Asia

Biggerstaff, Knight, "Official Chinese Attitude Toward the Burlingame Mission," *AHR*, 41 (1936), 682.
Clyde, Paul H., "China Policy of J. Ross Browne, American Minister to Peking, 1868–1869," *Pac. Hist. Rev.*, 1 (1932), 312.
——— "Frederick F. Low and the Tientsin Massacre," *Pac. Hist. Rev.*, 2 (1933), 100.

Cohen, Paul A., *China and Christianity: Missionary Movement and Growth of Chinese Antiforeignism, 1860–1870* (1963).

Griffin, Eldon, *Clippers and Consuls: American Consular and Commercial Relations with Eastern Asia* (1938).

Kamikawa, Hikomatsu, ed., *Japan-American Diplomatic Relations in the Meiji-Taisho Era* (1958).

King, Frank H. H., *Money and Monetary Policy in China, 1845–1895* (1965).

Liu, Kwang-ching, *Anglo-American Steamship Rivalry in China, 1862–1874* (1962).

Tate, E. Mowbray, "U.S. Gunboats on the Yangtze, 1842–1922," *Studies on Asia*, 7 (1966), 121.

Treat, Payson J., *Diplomatic Relations between the United States and Japan, 1853–1895* (2 vols., 1932).

Part Eight　Rise of Industry and Empire

48 The Gilded Age, 1877–1900

48.1 GENERAL

Diamond, Sigmund, ed., *Nation Transformed* (1963).
Faulkner, Harold U., *Politics, Reform and Expansion, 1890–1900* (1959).
Garraty, John, *The New Commonwealth, 1877–1890* (1968).
———— ed., *Transformation of American Society, 1870–1890* (1969).
Ginger, Ray, *Age of Excess: United States from 1877 to 1914* (1965).
———— *Altgeld's America* (1958).
———— ed., *Nationalizing of American Life, 1877–1900* (1965).
Harris, Neil, ed., *Land of Contrasts: 1880–1901* (1970).
Hays, Samuel P., *Response to Industrialization, 1885–1914* (1957).
Hoogenboom, Ari A., and Olive H. Hoogenboom, eds., *The Gilded Age* (1967).
Morgan, H. Wayne, ed., *The Gilded Age* (2nd ed., 1970).
Shannon, Fred A., *Centennial Years: America from the Late 1870's to the Early 1890's*, Robert H. Jones, ed. (1967).
Weisberger, Bernard A., *New Industrial Society, 1848–1900* (1969).
White, Leonard D., *Republican Era, 1869–1901: Administrative History* (1958).
Wiebe, Robert H., *Search for Order, 1877–1920* (1967).

48.2 URBAN GROWTH

48.2.1 General

Blake, N. M., *Water for the Cities: History of the Urban Water Supply Problem in the United States* (1956).
Cassedy, James H., *Charles V. Chapin and the Public Health Movement* (1962).
Dykstra, Robert R., *Cattle Towns* (1968).
McKelvey, Blake, *Urbanization of America, 1860–1915* (1963).
Schlesinger, Arthur M., *Rise of the City, 1878–1898* (1933).
Smith, Duane A., *Rocky Mountain Mining Camps: Urban Frontier* (1967).
Warner, Sam B., Jr., *Streetcar Suburbs: Process of Growth in Boston, 1870–1900* (1962).

48.2.2 Poverty

Atkins, Gordon, *Health, Housing and Poverty in New York City: 1865–1898* (1947).
Bremner, Robert H., *From the Depths: Discovery of Poverty* (1956).
Riis, Jacob A., *How the Other Half Lives* (1890); Sam Bass Warner, ed. (1970).

48.2.3 Reform

Mann, Arthur, *Yankee Reformers in the Urban Age* (1954).
Merk, Lois B., "Boston's Historic Public School Crisis," *NEQ*, 21 (1958),
172.
Patton, Clifford W., *Battle for Municipal Reform, 1875–1900* (1940).

48.2.4 Social Mobility

Sennett, Richard, *Families Against the City: Middle Class Homes of Industrial
Chicago, 1872–1890* (1970).
Thernstrom, Stephan, *Poverty and Progress: Social Mobility in a Nineteenth-
Century City* (1964).

48.2.5 Immigrants and Nativism

Brown, Thomas N., *Irish-American Nationalism, 1870–1890* (1966).
Erickson, Charlotte, *American Industry and the European Immigrant, 1860–1885*
(1957).
Handlin, Oscar, *Boston's Immigrants* (rev. ed., 1959).
——— *Uprooted* (1951).
Higham, John, *Strangers in the Land: American Nativism, 1860–1925* (1955).
Rischin, Moses, *Promised City: New York's Jews, 1870–1914* (1962).
Solomon, Barbara M., *Ancestors and Immigrants: A Changing New England
Tradition* (1956).

48.3 INTELLECTUAL AND RELIGIOUS CURRENTS

Berthoff, Warner, *Ferment of Realism: American Literature, 1884–1919*
(1965).
Hofstadter, Richard, *Social Darwinism in American Thought* (rev. ed., 1955).
McCloskey, Robert G., *American Conservatism in the Age of Enterprise: A Study
of William Graham Sumner, Stephen J. Field, and Andrew Carnegie*
(1951).
Tully, Andrew, *Era of Elegance* (1947).
Warren, Sidney, *American Freethought, 1860–1914* (1943).
White, Edward A., *Science and Religion in American Thought* (1952).
White, Morton G., *Social Thought in America* (rev. ed., 1957).
Ziff, Larzer, *American 1890's: Life and Times of a Lost Generation* (1966).

See also 10.3 for biographies/writings of:

Adams, Brooks, 1848–1927
Anthony, Susan B., 1820–1906
Bellamy, Edward, 1850–1898
Donnelly, Ignatius, 1831–1901
Ely, Richard T., 1854–1943
George, Henry, 1839–1897
Godkin, Edwin L., 1831–1902
Holmes, Oliver Wendell, Jr., 1841–1935
James, William, 1842–1910
Lloyd, Henry Demarest, 1847–1903
Patten, Simon N., 1852–1922
Schurz, Carl, 1829–1906
Sumner, William G., 1840–1910
Veblen, Thorstein, 1857–1929
Ward, Lester F., 1841–1913
Wilson, Woodrow, 1856–1924

48.4 REFORM

48.4.1 General

Blodgett, Geoffrey T., *Gentle Reformers: Massachusetts Democrats in the Cleveland Era* (1966).

Destler, Chester McA., *American Radicalism, 1865–1901* (1946).

Godkin, Edwin L., *Problems of Modern Democracy: Political and Economic Essays* (1896); Morton Keller, ed. (1966).

Gronlund, Laurence, *Cooperative Commonwealth* (1884); Stow Persons, ed. (1965).

Malin, James C., "At What Age Did Men Become Reformers?" *Kan. Hist. Quar.*, 29 (1963), 250.

Quint, H. H., *Forging American Socialism* (1953).

Sproat, John G., *Best Men: Liberal Reformers in the Gilded Age* (1968).

48.4.2 Religion and Reform

Abell, Aaron I., *American Catholicism and Social Action, 1865–1950* (1960).

—— *Urban Impact on American Protestantism, 1865–1900* (1943).

Cross, Robert D., ed., *Church and City: 1865–1910* (1967).

Hopkins, Charles Howard, *Rise of the Social Gospel in American Protestantism, 1865–1915* (1940).

May, Henry F., *Protestant Churches and Industrial America* (1949).

48.5 BUSINESS AND ECONOMY

48.5.1 General

Barnett, Paul, *Business Cycle Theory in the United States, 1860–1900* (1941).

Cochran, Thomas C., and William Miller, *The Age of Enterprise* (1942).

Emmet, Boris, and J. E. Jeuck, *Catalogues and Counters: History of Sears, Roebuck and Company* (1950).

Evans, George H., Jr., *Business Incorporations in the United States: 1800–1943* (1948).

Fels, Rendigs, *American Business Cycles: 1865–1897* (1959).

Fine, Sidney, *Laissez Faire and General-Welfare State, 1865–1901* (1956).

Friedman, Milton, and A. J. Schwartz, *Monetary History of the United States, 1867–1960* (1963).

Habbakuk, H. J., *American and British Technology in the Nineteenth Century* (1962).

Kirkland, Edward C., *Industry Comes of Age, 1860–1897* (1961).

Strassmann, W. P., *Risk and Technological Innovation: American Manufacturing Methods during the Nineteenth Century* (1959).

Tarbell, Ida M., *Nationalizing of Business, 1878–1898* (1936).

48.5.2 Business Leaders and Ideology

Carnegie, Andrew, *The Gospel of Wealth, and Other Timely Essays* (1900), Edward C. Kirkland, ed. (1962).

Cochran, Thomas C., *Railroad Leaders, 1845–1890: The Business Mind in Action* (1953).

Diamond, Sigmund, *The Reputation of the American Businessman* (1955).

Josephson, Matthew, *Robber Barons: Great American Capitalists, 1861–1901* (1934).

Kirkland, Edward C., *Dream and Thought in a Business Community, 1860–1900* (1956).

Miller, William, ed., *Men in Business* (1952).
Tebbel, John W., *From Rags to Riches: Horatio Alger, Jr. and the American Dream* (1963).
Wyllie, Irvin G., *Self-Made Man in America* (1954).

See also 10.3 for biographies/writings of:

Carnegie, Andrew, 1835–1919
Poor, Henry Varnum, 1812–1905
Rockefeller, John D., 1839–1937
Taylor, Frederick W., 1856–1915

See also 18.12.3.1, "Robber Barons."

48.5.3 Tariff Issue

Stanwood, Edward, *American Tariff Controversies* (2 vols., 1903).
Taussig, Frank W., *Tariff History of the United States* (8th ed., 1931).

48.5.4 Anti-Trust Movement and Sherman Act of 1890

Bork, Robert H., "Legislative Intent and Policy of Sherman Act," *Jour. Law and Econ.*, 9 (1966), 7.
Dudden, Arthur P., "Men Against Monopoly: Prelude to Trust-Busting," *Jour. Hist. Ideas*, 18 (1957), 587.
Gordon, Sanford D., "Attitudes towards Trusts Prior to the Sherman Act," *South. Econ. Jour.*, 30 (1963), 156.
Letwin, William L., "First Decade of the Sherman Act," *Yale Law Jour.*, 68 (1959), 464, 900.
———— *Law and Economic Policy in America: Evolution of the Sherman Antitrust Act* (1965).
Lloyd, Henry Demarest, *Wealth Against Commonwealth* (1894).
Thorelli, Hans B., *Federal Antitrust Policy* (1955).

48.5.5 Railroads

Campbell, Edward G., *Reorganization of the American Railroad System, 1893–1900* (1938).
Chandler, Alfred D., ed., *Railroads: Nation's First Big Business* (1965).
Decker, Leslie E., *Railroads, Lands, and Politics: Taxation of Railroad Land Grants, 1864–1897* (1964).
Fogel, Robert W., *Railroads and Economic Growth* (1964).
Grodinsky, Julius, *Iowa Pool: Study in Railroad Competition, 1870–84* (1950).
———— *Transcontinental Railway Strategy, 1869–1893* (1962).
Kirkland, Edward C., *Men, Cities, and Transportation: A Study in New England History, 1820–1900* (1948).
Lewis, Oscar, *Big Four* (1938).
Stover, John F., *Railroads of the South, 1865–1900: Finance and Control* (1955).
Taylor, George R., and Irene D. Neu, *The American Railroad Network, 1861–1890* (1956).

See also 10.3 for biographies/writings of:

Adams, Charles F., Jr., 1835–1915
Brown, Joseph E., 1821–1894
Dodge, Grenville M., 1831–1916
Gould, Jay, 1836–1892
Hill, James J., 1838–1916
Hogg, James S., 1851–1906

Vanderbilt, Cornelius, 1794–1877
Villard, Henry, 1835–1900

48.5.6 Railroad Regulation

48.5.6.1 General

Beard, Earl S., "Background of State Railroad Regulation in Iowa," *Iowa Jour. Hist.*, 51 (1963), 1.

Benson, Lee, *Merchants, Farmers, and Railroads: Railroad Regulation and New York Politics, 1850–1887* (1955).

Daland, Robert T., "Enactment of Potter Law," *Wis. Mag. Hist.*, 33 (1949), 45.

Goodrich, Carter, *Government Promotion of Canals and Railroads: 1800–1890* (1960).

Haney, L. H., *Congressional History of Railways: 1850–1887* (1910).

Kolko, Gabriel, *Railroads and Regulation: 1877–1916* (1965).

Miller, George H., "Origins of the Iowa Granger Law," *MVHR*, 40 (1954), 657.

Ripley, W. Z., *Railroads, Rates and Regulations* (1912).

Throne, Mildred, "Repeal of the Iowa Granger Law, 1878," *Iowa Jour. Hist.*, 51 (1953), 97.

See also 10.3 for biographies/writings of:

Adams, Charles F., Jr., 1835–1915
Cullom, Shelby M., 1829–1914
Reagan, John H., 1818–1905

48.5.6.2 Interstate Commerce Act of 1887

Jones, Alan, "Thomas M. Cooley and 'Laissez Faire Constitutionalism': A Reconsideration," *JAH*, 53 (1967), 751.

—— "Thomas M. Cooley and the Interstate Commerce Commission," *Pol. Sci. Quar.*, 81 (1966), 602.

Nash, Gerald D., "The Interstate Commerce Act of 1887," *Penn. Hist.*, 24 (1957), 181.

Sharfman, I. L., *The Interstate Commerce Commission* (4 vols., 1931–1937).

48.5.7 Labor

48.5.7.1 General

Garraty, John A., ed., *Labor and Capital in the Gilded Age* (1968).

Leiby, James, *Carroll Wright and Labor Reform: The Origin of Labor Statistics* (1960).

Long, Clarence D., *Wages and Earnings in the United States, 1860–1890* (1960).

Ware, Norman J., *The Labor Movement in United States, 1860–1865* (1929).

48.5.7.2 Unions and Strikes

Bruce, R. V., *1877: Year of Violence* (1959).

Buder, Stanley, *Pullman: Experiment in the Industrial Order and Community Planning, 1880–1930* (1967).

David, Henry, *The Haymarket Affair* (1936).

Eggert, G. G., *Railroad Labor Disputes: Beginnings of Federal Strike Policy* (1967).

Gutman, Herbert, "Trouble on Railroads in 1873–74: Prelude to 1877 Crisis?" *Labor Hist.*, 2 (1961), 215.

Lindsey, Almont, *Pullman Strike* (1942).

McMurry, Donald L., *The Great Burlington Strike of 1888: A History in Labor Relations* (1956).

Taft, Philip, *The A.F. of L. in the Time of Gompers* (2 vols., 1957–1959).

Warne, Colston, ed., *Pullman Boycott of 1894: Problem of Federal Intervention* (1955).

Wolff, Leon J., *Lockout: Story of the Homestead Strike of 1892* (1965).

See also 10.3 for biographies/writings of:

Debs, Eugene V., 1855–1926
DeLeon, Daniel, 1852–1914
Gompers, Samuel, 1850–1924
Powderly, Terence V., 1849–1924

48.6 AGRICULTURE AND AGRARIAN PROTEST

48.6.1 General

Benedict, M. R., *Farm Policies of the United States* (1953).

Buck, Solon J., *Agrarian Crusade* (1920).

Hayter, Earl W., *The Troubled Farmer, 1850–1900* (1968).

Saloutos, Theodore, *Farmer Movements in the South, 1865–1933* (1960).

Shannon, Fred A., *American Farmers' Movements* (1957).

——— *Farmer's Last Frontier, 1860–1897* (1945).

See also 10.3 for biographies/writings of:

Bryan, William Jennings, 1860–1925
Donnelly, Ignatius, 1831–1901
Garland, Hamlin, 1860–1940
Lloyd, Henry Demarest, 1847–1903
Morton, J. Sterling, 1832–1902
Sandoz, Jules Ami, 1857?–1928
Simpson, Jerry, 1842–1905
Teller, Henry M., 1830–1914
Tillman, "Pitchfork" Ben, 1847–1918
Vardaman, James K., 1861–1930
Watson, Thomas E., 1856–1922
White, William Allen, 1868–1844

48.6.2 Special Topics

Bogue, Allan G., *From Prairie to Corn Belt: Farming on Illinois and Iowa Prairies in the Nineteenth Century* (1963).

——— *Money at Interest: Farm Mortgage on the Middle Border* (1955).

Curti, Merle, *The Making of an American Community: Democracy in a Frontier County* (1959).

Destler, Chester M., "Agrarian Unrest in Illinois, 1880–1896," *Agric. Hist.*, 21 (1947), 104.

Dick, Everett N., *Sod House Frontier: 1854–1890* (1937).

Fite, Gilbert C., *Farmers' Frontier, 1865–1900* (1966).

Galambos, Louis, "Agrarian Image of a Large Corporation," 1879–1920: A Study in Social Accommodation," *Jour. Econ. Hist.*, 28 (1968), 341.

Ross, Earle D., "Department of Agriculture during the Commissionership," *Agric. Hist.*, 20 (1946), 129.

Scott, Roy V., *The Agrarian Movement in Illinois: 1880–1896* (1962).

Tryon, W. S., "Agriculture and Politics in South Dakota," *So. Dak. Hist. Coll.*, 13 (1926), 284.

48.6.3 Granger Movement

48.6.3.1 General

Ander, O. F., "The Immigrant Church and Patrons of Husbandry," *Agric. Hist.*, 8 (1934), 155.

Barns, William D., "Oliver H. Kelley and the Grange," *Agric. Hist.*, 41 (1967), 229.

Buck, Solon J., *The Granger Movement* (1913).

Finneran, Helen T., "Records of the National Grange in Washington Office," *Am. Archivist*, 27 (1964), 27.

Gardner, Charles M., *The Grange: Friend of the Farmer* (1949).

Merk, Frederick, "Eastern Antecedents of Grangers," *Agric. Hist.*, 23 (1949), 1.

48.6.3.2 Midwest

Anderson, Oscar E., "The Granger Movement in the Middle West," *Iowa Jour. Hist. and Pol.*, 22 (1924), 3.

Cerny, George, "Cooperation in the Midwest in the Granger Era, 1869–1875," *Agric. Hist.*, 37 (1963), 187.

Hirsch, Arthur H., "Grange Efforts in the Middle West to Control Price of Farm Machinery," *MVHR*, 15 (1929), 473.

Klement, Frank L., "Middle Western Copperheadism and the Granger Movement," *MVHR*, 38 (1952), 679.

48.6.3.3 State Studies

Easterby, J. H., "Granger Movement in South Carolina," *So. Car. Hist. Assoc., Proc.*, 1 (1931), 21.

Ferguson, J. S., "The Grange and Farmer Education in Mississippi," *JSH*, 8 (1942), 497.

Gilman, Rhoda R., and Patricia Smith, "Oliver Hudson Kelley: Minnesota Pioneer, 1849–1868," *Minn. Hist.*, 40 (1967), 330.

Miller, George H., "Iowa Granger Law," *MVHR*, 40 (1954), 657.

Paine, A. E., *The Granger Movement in Illinois* (1904).

Paul, Rodman W., "The Great California Grain War," *Pac. Hist. Rev.*, 27 (1958), 331.

Schell, Herbert S., "Grange and Credit Problem in Dakota," *Agric. Hist.*, 10 (1936), 59.

Smith, Ralph A., "Grange Movement in Texas, 1873–1900," *Southw. Hist. Quar.*, 42 (1939), 297.

48.6.4 Farmers' Alliances

Clevenger, Homer, "Farmers' Alliance in Missouri," *Mo. Hist. Rev.*, 39 (1944), 24.

Hayter, E. W., "Patent System and Agrarian Discontent," *MVHR*, 34 (1947), 59.

Knauss, J. O., "Farmers' Alliance in Florida," *So. Atl. Quar.*, 25 (1926), 300.

Nixon, H. C., "Cleavage within the Alliance Movement," *MVHR*, 15 (1928), 22.

Proctor, Samuel, "The National Farmers' Alliance Convention of 1890," *Fla. Hist. Quar.*, 28 (1950), 161.

48.6.5 Populism

48.6.5.1 General

Donnelly, Ignatius, *Caesar's Column* (1890); Walter B. Rideout, ed. (1960).

Destler, Chester M., *American Radicalism* (1946).

Hicks, John D., *Populist Revolt* (1931).

Hofstadter, Richard, *The Age of Reform: From Bryan to FDR* (1955).

Pearson, Charles Chilton, *Readjuster Movement in Virginia* (1935).

Pollack, Norman, ed., *The Populist Mind* (1967).
Pollack, Norman, *The Populist Response to Industrial America* ((1962).
Tindall, George B., ed., *Populist Reader* (1966).

* * * * * * *

Going, Allen J., "Agrarian Revolt," in Arthur S. Link and Rembert W. Patrick, eds., *Writing Southern History: Essays in Honor of Fletcher M. Green* (1965).
Handlin, Oscar, "Reconsidering the Populists," *Agric. Hist.*, 39 (1965), 68.
Pollack, Norman, "Hofstadter on Populism: Critique of 'The Age of Reform,'" *JSH*, 26 (1960), 478.
Saloutos, Theodore, "Professors and Populists," *Agric. Hist.*, 40 (1966), 235.
Unger, Irwin, "Critique of Norman Pollack's 'Fear of Man,'" *Agric. Hist.*, 39 (1965), 75.

48.6.5.2 Special Topics

Clanton, O. Gene, "Intolerant Populist? Disaffection of Mary Elizabeth Lease," *Kan. Hist. Quar.*, 34 (1968), 189.
Kane, R. James, "Populism, Progressivism, and Pure Food," *Agric. Hist.*, 38 (1964), 161.
Klotsche, J. M., "'United Front' Populists," *Wis. Mag. Hist.*, 20 (1937), 375.
Nichols, Jeannette P., "Sherman and Silver Drive of 1877–78," *Ohio State Archaeol. and Hist. Quar.*, 46 (1937), 148.
Pollack, Norman, "Myth of Populist Anti-Semitism," *AHR*, 68 (1962), 76.
Trask, David F., "Politics of Populism," *Neb. Hist.*, 46 (1965), 157.

48.6.5.3 South

Arnett, A. M., *Populist Movement in Georgia* (1922).
Clark, John B., *Populism in Alabama* (1927).
Daniel, L. E., "The Louisiana People's Party," *La. Hist. Quar.*, 26 (1943), 1055.
Delap, S. A., "The Populist Party in North Carolina," Duke Univ., Trinity Coll. Hist. Soc., *Papers*, 14 (1922), 40.
Kirwan, Albert D., *Revolt of the Rednecks: Mississippi Politics, 1876–1925* (1951).
Martin, R. C., *People's Party in Texas* (1933).
Robison, D. M., *Bob Taylor and the Agrarian Revolt in Tennessee* (1935).
Sheldon, William D., *Populism in the Old Dominion* (1935).
Simkins, F. B., *The Tillman Movement in South Carolina* (1926).

See also 10.3 for biographies/writings of:

Tillman, "Pitchfork" Ben, 1847–1918
Watson, Thomas E., 1856–1922

48.6.5.4 Midwest and Great Plains

Barnhart, J. D., "Rainfall and Populist Party in Nebraska," *Am. Pol. Sci. Rev.*, 19 (1925), 527.
Bicha, Karel D., "Jerry Simpson: Populist without Principles," *JAH*, 54 (1967), 291.
Clanton, O. Gene, *Kansas Populism: Ideas and Men* (1969).
Destler, Chester M., *American Radicalism* (1946).
Farmer, Hallie, "Economic Background of Frontier Populism," *MVHR*, 10 (1924), 406.
——— "Railroads and Frontier Populism," *MVHR*, 13 (1926), 387.
Harrington, W. P., "Populist Party in Kansas," Kan. State Hist. Soc., *Coll.*, 16 (1923–1925), 403.
Nixon, H. C., "Populist Movement in Iowa," *Iowa Jour. Hist.*, 24 (1926), 3.
Nugent, Walter T. K., "Some Parameters of Populism," *Agric. Hist.*, 40 (1966), 255.
——— *Tolerant Populists: Kansas* (1963).
Parsons, Stanley B., "Who Were Nebraska Populists?" *Neb. Hist.*, 44 (1963), 83.
Scott, Roy V., *Agrarian Movement in Illinois, 1880–1896* (1962).

Stewart, E. D., "The Populist Party in Indiana," *Ind. Mag. Hist.*, 14 (1918), 332; 15 (1919), 53.

48.6.5.5 West

Clinch, Thomas A., *Urban Populism and Free Silver in Montana* (1970).
Fuller, L. W., "Colorado's Revolt against Capitalism," *MVHR*, 21 (1934), 343.
Glass, Mary Ellen, *Silver and Politics in Nevada: 1892–1902* (1969).
Harrington, Marion, *The Populist Movement in Oregon* (1940).
Johnson, Claudius O., "Silver Politics in Idaho," *Pac. Northw. Quar.*, 33 (1942), 283.
Taggart, H. F., "California and the Silver Question," *Pac. Hist. Rev.*, 6 (1937), 249.
Wooddy, C. H., "Populism in Washington," *Wash. Hist. Quar.*, 21 (1930), 103.

48.7 NEW SOUTH

48.7.1 General

Clark, Thomas D., and Albert D. Kirwan, *The South since Appomattox* (1967).
Woodward, C. Vann, *Origins of the New South* (1951).

48.7.2 Special Topics

Buck, Paul, *The Road to Reunion, 1865–1900* (1937).
Clark, T. D., *Pills, Petticoats, and Plows: The Southern Country Store* (1944).
Davenport, F. Garvin, Jr., "Thomas Dixon's Mythology of Southern History," *JSH*, 36 (1970), 350.
Doherty, Herbert J., Jr., "Voices of Protest from the New South, 1875–1910," *MVHR*, 42 (1955), 45.
Eaton, Clement, *Waning of the Old South Civilization, 1860–1880's* (1968).
Gaston, Paul, *The New South Creed* (1970).
Grantham, Dewey W., Jr., ed., *The South and the Sectional Image* (1967).
Jones, Virgil C., *The Hatfields and McCoys* (1948).
Lonn, Ella, "Reconciliation between North and South," *JSH*, 13 (1947), 3.
Mitchell, George Sinclair, *Textile Revolution and the South* (1931).
Woodman, Harold D., *King Cotton and His Retainers, 1800–1925* (1968).

*   *   *   *   *   *   *

Gaston, Paul M., "The 'New South'" in Arthur S. Link and Rembert W. Patrick, eds., *Writing Southern History: Essays in Honor of Fletcher M. Green* (1965).

See also 10.3 for biographies/writings of:

Bailey, Joe, 1863–1929
Beauregard, P. G. T., 1818–1893
Brown, Joseph E., 1821–1894
Duke, James B., 1856–1925
Grady, Henry W., 1851–1889
Lamar, Lucius Q. C., 1825–1893
Mahone, William, 1826–1895
Page, Thomas Nelson, 1853–1922
Page, Walter Hines, 1855–1918
Tompkins, Daniel A., 1851–1914
Washington, Booker T., 1856–1915
Watson, Thomas E., 1856–1922
Watterson, Henry, 1840–1921
Wilson, Woodrow, 1856–1924

48.7.3 Politics

48.7.3.1 General

Cooper, William J., Jr., *Conservative Regime: South Carolina, 1877–1890* (1968).
Grantham, Dewey, Jr., *The Democratic South* (1963).
Hair, William I., *Bourbonism and Agrarian Protest: Louisiana Politics, 1877–1900* (1969).
Williams, Frank B., Jr., "Poll Tax as Suffrage Requirement in the South, 1870–1901," *JSH*, 18 (1952), 469.

See also 48.6.5.3, Populism–South.

48.7.3.2 Republicans and the South

DeSantis, Vincent P., *Republicans Face the Southern Question, 1877–1897* (1959).
Hirshon, Stanley P., *Farewell to Bloody Shirt: Northern Republicans and the Southern Negro, 1877–1893* (1953).
Welch, Richard E., Jr., "Federal Elections Bill of 1890," *JAH*, 52 (1965), 511.

48.7.4 Race Relations and Segregation

Calista, Donald J., "Booker T. Washington: Another Look," *Jour. Negro Hist.*, 49 (1964), 240.
Edmonds, Helen G., *The Negro and Fusion Politics in North Carolina, 1894–1901* (1951).
Woodward, C. Vann, *The Strange Career of Jim Crow* (2nd rev. ed., 1966).
Wynes, Charles E., *Race Relations in Virginia, 1870–1902* (1961).

48.8 GOVERNMENT AND POLITICS

48.8.1 General

Bailey, Thomas A., "Party Irregularity in Senate, 1869–1901," *Southw. Soc. Sci. Quar.*, 11 (1931), 355.
———— "West and Radical Legislation, 1890–1930," *Am. Jour. Sociol.*, 38 (1933), 603.
Bryce, James, *American Commonwealth* (2 vols., 1888).
Goldman, Eric, *Rendezvous with Destiny* (1952).
Hofstadter, Richard, *The Age of Reform: Bryan to F. D. R.* (1955).
Josephson, Matthew, *Politicos: 1865–1896* (1938).
Marcus, Robert D., *Grand Old Party: Political Structure in the Gilded Age, 1880–1896* (1971).
Merrill, Horace S., *Bourbon Democracy of the Middle West, 1865–1896* (1953).
Morgan, H. Wayne, *From Hayes to McKinley: National Party Politics, 1877–1896* (1969).
Nye, Russell B., *Midwestern Progressive Politics* (1951).
Pomeroy, Earl S., *Territories and United States, 1861–1890* (1949).
Rothman, David J., *Politics and Power: The Senate, 1869–1901* (1966).
White, Leonard D., *Republican Era, 1869–1901: Administrative History* (1958).

See also 10.3 for biographies/writings of:

Adams, Henry B., 1838–1918
Aldrich, Nelson W., 1841–1915
Allison, William B., 1829–1908
Altgeld, John P., 1847–1902
Arthur, Chester A., 1830–1886
Belmont, August, 1816–1890
Beveridge, Albert J., 1862–1927
Bigelow, John, 1817–1911

Blaine, James G., 1830–1893
Carlisle, John G., 1835–1910
Chandler, William E., 1835–1917
Cleveland, Grover, 1837–1908
Conkling, Roscoe, 1829–1888
Depew, Chauncey M., 1834–1928
Evarts, William M., 1818–1901
Foraker, Joseph B., 1846–1917
Garfield, James A., 1831–1881
Gresham, Walter Q., 1832–1895
Hanna, Marcus A., 1837–1904
Harrison, Benjamin, 1833–1901
Hay, John M., 1838–1905
Hayes, Rutherford B., 1822–1893
Hoar, George F., 1826–1904
Holmes, Oliver Wendell, Jr., 1841–1935
Ingalls, John J., 1833–1900
Lodge, Henry Cabot, 1850–1924
McKinley, William, 1843–1901
Morgan, J. Pierpoint, 1837–1913
Morton, Oliver P., 1823–1877
Nast, Thomas, 1840–1902
Olney, Richard, 1835–1917
Platt, Orville H., 1827–1905
Platt, Thomas C., 1833–1910
Poore, Benjamin P., 1820–1887
Reed, Thomas B., 1839–1902
Roosevelt, Theodore, 1858–1919
Sawyer, Philetus, 1816–1900
Schurz, Carl, 1829–1906
Sherman, John, 1823–1900
Wanamaker, John, 1838–1922
White, Stephen M., 1853–1901
Whitney, William C., 1841–1904

48.8.2 Civil Service Reform

Foulke, William D., *Fighting the Spoilsmen* (1919).
———— *Lucius B. Swift* (1930).
Hoogenboom, Ari A., *Outlawing the Spoils: The Civil Service Reform Movement,
1865–1883* (1961).
McFarland, Gerald W., "Partisanship of Non-Partisan Dorman B. Eaton and the
Genteel Reform Tradition," *JAH*, 54 (1968), 806.
Sageser, Adelbert B., *Two Decades of the Pendleton Act* (1935).
Stewart, Frank M., *The National Civil Service Reform League* (1929).

48.8.3 Supreme Court

Paul, A. M., *Conservative Crisis and the Rule of Law: Attitudes of Bar and Bench,
1887–1895* (1960).

See also 10.3 for biographies/writings of:

Field, Stephen, J., 1816–1899
Miller, Samuel F., 1816–1890
Waite, Morrison R., 1816–1888

48.8.4 Veterans and Patriotic Organizations

Davies, Wallace E., *Patriotism on Parade: Story of Veterans' and Hereditary
Organizations in America, 1783–1900* (1955).
Dearing, Mary R., *Veterans in Politics* (1952).

48.9 HAYES ADMINISTRATION, 1877–1881

Burgess, John W., *Administration of Hayes* (1916).
Newcomer, Lee, "Arthur's Removal from the Custom House," *N.Y. Hist.*, 18 (1937), 401.
Richardson, Lyon N., and Curtis W. Garrison, eds., "George William Curtis, Rutherford B. Hayes, and Civil Service Reform," *MVHR*, 32 (1945), 235.
Shores, V. L., *The Hayes-Conkling Controversy* (1919).

See also 10.3 for biographies/writings of:

Evarts, William M., 1818–1901
Goff, Nathan, Jr., 1843–1920
Hayes, Rutherford B., 1822–1893
Key, David M., 1824–1900
McCulloch, Hugh, 1808–1895
Schurz, Carl, 1829–1906
Sherman, John, 1823–1900
Thompson, Richard W., 1809–1900

See also 48.5.3, Tariff Issue; 48.5.6, Railroad Regulation; 48.5.7.2, Unions and Strikes.

48.10 ELECTION OF 1880

Clancy, Herbert J., *The Presidential Election of 1880* (1958).
Dinnerstein, Leonard, "Election of 1880," in Arthur M. Schlesinger, Jr. and Fred L. Israel, eds., *History of American Presidential Elections, 1789–1968*, vol. II (1971).

See also 10.3 for biographies/writings of:

Arthur, Chester A., 1830–1886
Blaine, James G., 1830–1893
Carlisle, John G., 1835–1910
Chandler, William E., 1835–1917
Evarts, William M., 1818–1901
Garfield, James A., 1831–1881
Gresham, Walter Q., 1832–1895
Hancock, Winfield S., 1824–1886
Hayes, Rutherford B., 1822–1893
Key, David M., 1824–1900
McCulloch, Hugh, 1808–1895
Schurz, Carl, 1829–1906
Sherman, John, 1823–1900
Teller, Henry M., 1830–1914

48.11 GARFIELD AND ARTHUR ADMINISTRATIONS, 1881–1885

Aaron, Daniel, *Men of Good Hope: Story of American Progressives* (1951).
Bellamy, Edward, *Looking Backward, 2000–1887* (1888); John L. Thomas, ed. (1967).
Dorfman, Joseph, *The Economic Mind in American Civilization* (3 vols., 1946–1949).
George, Henry, *Progress and Poverty* (1880).
Glasson, William H., *Federal Military Pensions* (1918).
Klotsche, J. M., "Star Route Cases," *MVHR*, 22 (1935), 407.
Miller, Clarence L., *The Old Northwest and the Tariff* (1929).
Mitchell, Stewart, "The Man Who Murdered Garfield," *Mass. Hist. Soc., Proc.*, 67 (1944), 452.

Oliver, John W., *Civil War Military Pensions* (1917).
Rezneck, Samuel, "Thought and Action in American Depression, 1882–1886,"
  AHR, 61 (1956), 284.
Rosenberg, Charles E., *Trial of the Assassin Guiteau: Psychiatry and Law in the
  Gilded Age* (1968).

See also 10.3 for biographies/writings of:

Arthur, Chester A., 1830–1886
Blaine, James G., 1830–1893
Carlisle, John G., 1835–1910
Conkling, Roscoe, 1829–1888
Cullom, Shelby M., 1829–1914
Curtis, George W., 1824–1892
Depew, Chauncey M., 1834–1928
Garfield, James A., 1831–1881
Grant, Ulysses S., 1822–1885
Hoar, George F., 1826–1904
Lowell, James Russell, 1819–1891
McClure, Alexander K., 1828–1909
McCulloch, Hugh, 1808–1895
Platt, Thomas C., 1833–1910
Sherman, John, 1823–1900
White, Andrew D., 1832–1918

See also 48.5.3, Tariff Issue; 48.5.7.2, Unions and Strikes; 48.8.2, Civil Service
Reform.

48.12 ELECTION OF 1884

Chase, P. P., "Protestant Clergy in Massachusetts," Mass. Hist. Soc., *Proc.*, 64
  (1930–1932), 467.
Fuess, Claude M., "Schurz, Lodge and Campaign of 1884," *NEQ*, 5 (1932), 453.
Hirsch, Mark D., "Election of 1884," in Arthur M. Schlesinger, Jr. and Fred L.
  Israel, eds., *History of American Presidential Elections, 1789–1968*, vol. II
  (1971).
McFarland, Gerald W., "New York Mugwumps of 1884," *Pol. Sci. Quar.*, 78
  (1963), 40.
Malin, James C., "Roosevelt and Elections of 1884 and 1888," *MVHR*, 14 (1927),
  25.
Wood, Gordon S., "Massachusetts Mugwumps," *NEQ*, 33 (1960), 435.

See also 10.3 for biographies/writings of:

Blaine, James G., 1830–1893
Cleveland, Grover, 1837–1908
Elkins, Stephen B., 1841–1911
Gorman, Arthur P., 1839–1906

48.13 CLEVELAND'S FIRST ADMINISTRATION, 1885–1889

Dana, R. H., "Sir William Harcourt and Australian Ballot Law," Mass. Hist.
  Soc., *Proc.*, 58 (1925), 401.
Evans, Eldon C., *Australian Ballot System* (1917).
Glasson, William H., *Federal Military Pensions* (1918).
Hollingsworth, J. Rogers, *Whirligig of Politics: Democracy of Cleveland and Bryan*
  (1963).
Kelly, Robert, "Presbyterianism, Jacksonianism and Grover Cleveland," *Am.
  Quar.*, 18 (1966), 615.

Kraines, Oscar, *Congress and the Challenge of Big Government* (1958).
McMurry, Donald L., "The Pension Question," *MVHR,* 9 (1922), 19.
Volwiler, A. T., ed., "Tariff Strategy and Propaganda, 1887–88," *AHR,* 36 (1930), 76.

See also 10.3 for biographies/writings of:

Lamar, Lucius Q. C., 1825–1893
Schurz, Carl, 1829–1906
Vilas, William F., 1840–1908
Whitney, William C., 1841–1904

See also 48.5.3, Tariff Issue; 48.5.6, Railroad Regulation; 48.5.7.2, Unions and Strikes.

48.14 ELECTIONS OF 1888 AND 1892

Buley, R. C., "Campaign of 1888 in Indiana," *Ind. Mag. Hist.,* 10, no. 2, (1914), 30.
Dozer, D. M., "Harrison and Campaign of 1892," *AHR,* 54 (1948), 49.
Knoles, George H., *Presidential Campaign and Election of 1892* (1942).
Morgan, H. Wayne, "Election of 1892," in Arthur M. Schlesinger, Jr. and Fred L. Israel, eds., *History of American Presidential Elections, 1789–1968,* vol. II (1971).
Wesser, Robert F., "Election of 1888," in Arthur M. Schlesinger, Jr. and Fred L. Israel, eds., *History of American Presidential Elections, 1789–1968,* vol. II (1971).

See also 10.3 for biographies/writings of:

Cleveland, Grover, 1837–1908
Harrison, Benjamin, 1833–1901
Whitney, William C., 1841–1904

48.15 HARRISON ADMINISTRATION AND CLEVELAND'S SECOND ADMINISTRATION, 1889–1897

48.15.1 General

Barnes, J. A., "Gold-Standard Democrats and Party Conflict," *MVHR,* 17 (1930), 422.
Nichols, J. P., "Silver Diplomacy," *Pol. Sci. Quar.,* 48 (1933), 565.
——— "Silver Repeal in the Senate," *AHR,* 41 (1935), 26.
Wellborn, Fred, "Silver Republican Senators, 1889–1891," *MVHR,* 14 (1928), 462.

See also 10.3 for biographies/writings of:

Blaine, James G., 1830–1893
Carlisle, John G., 1835–1910
Elkins, Stephen B., 1841–1911
Foster, John W., 1836–1917
Gresham, Walter Q., 1832–1895
Morton, J. Sterling, 1832–1902
Morton, Levi P., 1824–1920
Olney, Richard, 1835–1917
Voorhees, Daniel, 1827–1897
Wanamaker, John, 1838–1922
Wilson, William L., 1843–1900

See also 48.5.3, Tariff Issue; 48.5.4, Anti-Trust Movement and Sherman Act of 1890; 48.17.5.5, Annexation of Hawaii; 48.17.6.3, Venezuelan Crisis of 1896.

48.15.2 Economic Unrest and Panic of 1893

Hoffman, Charles, "Depression of the Nineties," *Jour. Econ. Hist.*, 16 (1956), 137.
McMurry, Donald L., *Coxey's Army* (1929).
Simon, Matthew, "Morgan-Belmont Syndicate of 1895 and the Intervention in the Foreign-Exchange Market," *Bus. Hist. Rev.*, 62 (1968), 385.
Steeples, Douglas W., "Panic of 1893," *Mid-America*, 47 (1965), 155.
Weberg, F. P., *Background of Panic of 1893* (1929).

See also 48.5.7.2, Unions and Strikes.

48.16 ELECTION OF 1896

Barnes, J. A., "Myths of the Bryan Campaign," *MVHR*, 34 (1947), 367.
Diamond, William, "Urban and Rural Voting in 1896," *AHR*, 46 (1941), 281.
Durden, Robert F., *Climax of Populism: Election of 1896* (1965).
Ellis, Elmer, "Silver Republicans in 1896," *MVHR*, 18 (1932), 519.
Fite, Gilbert C., "Election of 1896," in Arthur M. Schlesinger, Jr. and Fred L. Israel, eds., *History of American Presidential Elections, 1789–1968*, vol. II (1971).
——— "Republican Strategy and the Farm Vote in the Campaign of 1896," *AHR*, 65 (1960), 787.
Glad, Paul W., *McKinley, Bryan, and the People* (1964).
Harvey, William Hope, *Coin's Financial School* (1893); Richard Hofstadter, ed. (1963).
Hollingsworth, J. Rogers, *Whirligig of Politics: Cleveland and Bryan* (1963).
Jones, Stanley L., *Presidential Election of 1896* (1964).
Nichols, Jeannette P., "Bryan's Benefactor: Coin Harvey," *Ohio Hist. Quar.*, 67 (1958), 299.
——— "Monetary Problems of William McKinley," *Ohio Hist. Quar.*, 72 (1963), 263.
Schruben, Francis W., "William Jennings Bryan," *Social Studies*, 55 (1964), 12.
Wish, Harvey, "Altgeld and the Election of 1896," *MVHR*, 24 (1938), 503.

See also 10.3 for biographies/writings of:

Bryan, William Jennings, 1860–1925
Hanna, Marcus A., 1837–1904
Herrick, Myron T., 1854–1929
Hill, David B., 1843–1910
McKinley, William, 1843–1901

48.17 FOREIGN RELATIONS

48.17.1 General

Dulebohn, G. R., *Principles of Foreign Policy under the Cleveland Administrations* (1941).
Dulles, Foster R., *Imperial Years* (1956).
——— *Prelude to World Power: Diplomatic History, 1860–1900* (1965).
Grenville, John A. S., and George B. Young, *Politics, Strategy, and American Diplomacy, 1873–1917* (1966).
Knoles, George H., "Cleveland on Imperialism," *MVHR*, 37 (1950), 303.
Plesur, Milton, "Across the Wide Pacific," *Pac. Hist. Rev.*, 28 (1959), 73.

—— "America Looking Outward: Hayes to Harrison," *Historian,* 22 (1960), 280.

Pletcher, David M., *Awkward Years: American Foreign Relations under Garfield and Arthur* (1962).

Tyler, Alice Felt, *Foreign Policy of Blaine* (1927).

See also 10.3 for biographies/writings of:

Adams, Charles F., 1807–1886
Arthur, Chester A., 1830–1886
Blaine, James G., 1830–1893
Day, William R., 1849–1923
Evarts, William M., 1818–1901
Fairchild, Lucius, 1831–1896
Foster, John W., 1836–1917
Garfield, James A., 1831–1881
Gresham, Walter Q., 1832–1895
Harrison, Benjamin, 1833–1901
Hay, John M., 1838–1905
Hayes, Rutherford B., 1822–1893
Langston, John M., 1829–1897
McKinley, William, 1843–1901
Mahan, Alfred T., 1840–1914
Olney, Richard, 1835–1917
Rockhill, William W., 1854–1914
Schurz, Carl, 1829–1906
Sherman, John, 1823–1900
Straus, Oscar S., 1850–1926
White, Henry, 1850–1927

48.17.2 Expansionism and Imperialism

Healy, David, *U.S. Expansionism: Imperalist Urge in the 1890's* (1970).
Hollingsworth, J. Rogers, comp., *American Expansion in the Late Nineteenth Century* (1968).
LaFeber, Walter, *New Empire: American Expansion, 1860–1898* (1963).
Langer, William L., *Diplomacy of Imperialism, 1890–1902* (2 vols., 1935).
Livezey, William E., *Mahan on Sea Power* (1947).
May, Ernest R., *American Imperialism* (1968).
—— *Imperial Democracy: Emergence of America* (1961).
Merk, Frederick, *Manifest Destiny and Mission* (1963).
Nichols, Jeannette P., "Congress and Imperialism, 1861–1897," *Jour. Econ. Hist.,* 21 (1961), 526.
Weinberg, A. K., *Manifest Destiny* (1935).

See also 10.3 for biographies/writings of:

Beveridge, Albert J., 1862–1927
Hoar, George F., 1826–1904
Lodge, Henry Cabot, 1850–1924
Mahan, Alfred T., 1840–1914
Roosevelt, Theodore, 1858–1919
Schurz, Carl, 1829–1906

48.17.3 Canada

48.17.3.1 General

Brown, Robert C., *Canada's National Policy, 1883–1900* (1964).
Clark, R. C., "Diplomatic Mission of Sir John Rose," *Pac. Northw. Quar.,* 27 (1936), 227.

Gluek, Alvin C., Jr., "Riel Rebellion and Canadian-American Relations," *Can. Hist. Rev.*, 36 (1955), 199.

Grimm, Ferdinand, *Northwest Water Boundary*, Hunter Miller, ed. (1942).

Sandborn, R. E., "United States and British Northwest," *No. Dak. Hist. Quar.*, 6 (1931), 5.

Tansill, Charles C., *Canadian-American Relations, 1875–1911* (1943).

Warner, Donald F., "Drang nach Norden: United States and the Riel Rebellion," *MVHR*, 39 (1953), 693.

48.17.3.2 Fisheries and Seal Trade

Bailey, Thomas A., "North Pacific Sealing Convention, 1911," *Pac. Hist. Rev.*, 4 (1935), 1.

Campbell, Charles S., Jr., "The Anglo-American Crisis in Bering Sea, 1890–1891," *MVHR*, 48 (1961), 393.

Shapiro, Samuel, "The Halifax Fisheries Commission of 1877," Essex Inst., *Hist. Coll.*, 95 (1959), 21.

See also 10.3 for biographies/writings of:

Blaine, James G., 1830–1893
Foster, John W., 1836–1917

48.17.4 Europe

48.17.4.1 General

Dulles, Foster R., *The American Red Cross* (1950).

Gazley, John G., *American Opinion of German Unification* (1926).

Keim, Jeannette, *German-American Political Relations* (1919).

Marraro, H. R., "Closing of Diplomatic Mission to the Vatican," *Cath. Hist. Rev.*, 33 (1948), 423.

Perkins, Bradford, *Great Rapprochement: England and United States, 1895–1914* (1968).

Sly, J. F., "Genesis of the Postal Union," *International Conciliation*, no. 233 (1927), 395.

Snyder, L. L., "Pork Dispute," *Jour. Mod. Hist.*, 17 (1945), 16.

Trauth, Mary P., *Italo-American Diplomatic Relations, 1861–1882* (1958).

48.17.4.2 New Orleans Lynchings and Italy

Coxe, J. E., "New Orleans Mafia Incident," *La. Hist. Quar.*, 20 (1937), 1067.

Karlin, J. A., "Indemnification of Aliens," *Southw. Soc. Sci. Quar.*, 25 (1945), 235.

―――― "New Orleans Lynchings of 1891 and American Press," *La. Hist. Quar.*, 24 (1941), 187.

―――― "Some Repercussions of New Orleans Mafia Incident of 1891," Wash. State Coll., *Research Studies*, 11 (1943), 267.

48.17.5 East Asia and Pacific

48.17.5.1 General

Battistini, Lawrence H., *Rise of American Influence in Asia and the Pacific* (1960).

Dennett, Tyler, *Americans in Eastern Asia* (1922).

Dulles, Foster R., *America in the Pacific* (1932).

Griswold, A. Whitney, *Far Eastern Policy of the United States* (1938).

Malozemoff, Andrew, *Russian Far Eastern Policy, 1881–1904* (1958).

Plesur, Milton, "Across the Wide Pacific," *Pac. Hist. Rev.*, 28 (1959), 73.

48.17.5.2 China

GENERAL

Clyde, Paul H., "Attitudes and Policies of George F. Seward, American Minister at Peking, 1876–1880," *Pac. Hist. Rev.*, 2 (1933), 387.

Dulles, Foster R., *China and America: Relations since 1784* (1946).

King, Frank H. H., *Money and Monetary Policy in China, 1845–1895* (1965).

McClellan, Robert, *Heathen Chinee: American Attitudes toward China, 1890–1905* (1970).

McCormick, Thomas J., *China Market, 1893–1901* (1967).

May, Ernest R., "Benjamin Parke Avery," Calif Hist. Soc., *Quar.*, 30 (1951), 125.

Varg, Paul A., *Making of a Myth: United States and China, 1879–1912* (1968).

Young, Marilyn B., *The Rhetoric of Empire: American China Policy, 1895–1901* (1968).

BOXER REBELLION AND OPEN DOOR POLICY

Campbell, Charles S., Jr., *Special Business Interests and Open Door Policy* (1951).

Esthus, Raymond A., "Changing Concept of Open Door, 1899–1910," *MVHR*, 46 (1959), 435.

Pao, Ming-ch'ien, *Open Door Policy in Relation to China* (1923).

Tan, Chester C., *Boxer Catastrophe* (1955).

48.17.5.3 Japan

Bailey, Thomas A., "Japan's Protest against Annexation," *Jour. Mod. Hist.*, 3 (1931), 46.

Jones, Francis C., *Extraterritoriality in Japan* (1931).

Kamikawa, Hikomatsu, ed., *Japan-American Diplomatic Relations in the Meiji-Taisho Era* (1958).

Treat, Payson J., *Diplomatic Relations between the United States and Japan, 1853–1905* (3 vols., 1932–1938).

See also 10.3 for biographies/writings of:

Foster, John W., 1836–1917

Hearn, Lafcadio, 1850–1904

48.17.5.4 Korea

Cable, E. M., *United States-Korean Relations, 1866–71* (1939).

Harrington, Fred H., *God, Mammon, and the Japanese* (1944).

Noble, Harold J., "United States and Sino-Korean Relations, 1885–87," *Pac. Hist. Rev.*, 2 (1933), 292.

48.17.5.5 Annexation of Hawaii

Adler, Jacob, "Claus Spreckles and the Hawaiian Revolution of 1893," *Jour. of West*, 5 (1966), 71.

Appel, John C., "American Labor and the Annexation of Hawaii," *Pac. Hist. Rev.*, 23 (1954), 1.

Dole, S. B., *Memoirs of Hawaiian Revolution* (1936).

Dozer, D. M., "Opposition to Hawaiian Reciprocity," *Pac. Hist. Rev.*, 14 (1945), 157.

Kuykendall, R. S., *Hawaiian Kingdom* (2 vols., 1938–1953).

Rolle, Andrew F., "California Filibustering and the Hawaiian Kingdom," *Pac. Hist. Rev.*, 19 (1950), 251.

Rowland, Donald, "Establishment of the Republic of Hawaii," *Pac. Hist. Rev.*, 4 (1935), 201.

Russ, William A., Jr., *Hawaiian Republic and Annexation* (1961).

—— *Hawaiian Revolution, 1893–1894* (1959).

Spitz, Allan, "Transplantation of American Democratic Institutions: Hawaii,"
  Pol. Sci. Quar., 82 (1967), 386.
Stevens, Sylvester K., *American Expansion in Hawaii, 1842–1898* (1945).
Tate, Merze, "Canada's Interest in Trade and Sovereignty of Hawaii," *Can. Hist.
  Rev.*, 44 (1963), 20.
—— *United States and the Hawaiian Kingdom* (1965).
Thurston, L. A., *Memoirs of the Hawaiian Revolution* (1936).

See also 10.3 for biographies/writings of:

Dole, Sanford B., 1844–1926
Judd, Gerrit P., 1803–1873

48.17.5.6 Samoa

Ellison, J. W., "Partition of Samoa," *Pac. Hist. Rev.*, 8 (1939), 259.
Masterman, Sylvia, *International Rivalry in Samoa* (1934).
Otto, Graf zu Stolberg-Wernigerode, *Germany and the United States* (1937).
Ryden, George H., *Foreign Policy in Relation to Samoa* (1933).
Vagts, Alfred, *Deutschland und Vereinigten Staaten in der Weltpolitik* (2 vols.,
  1935).

48.17.6 Latin America

48.17.6.1 General

Bastert, Russell H., "Frelinghuysen's Opposition to Blaine's Pan-American Pol-
  icy in 1882," *MVHR*, 42 (1956), 653.
—— "New Approach to Origins of Blaine's Pan American Policy," *Hisp. Am.
  Hist. Rev.*, 39 (1959), 375.
Callcott, Wilfrid H., *Caribbean Policy of the United States, 1890–1920* (1942).
Casey, C. B., "Pan American Union," *Hisp. Am. Hist. Rev.*, 13 (1933), 437.
Gantenbein, J. W., *Latin-American Policy* (1950).
Mecham, John L., *United States and Inter-American Security, 1889–1960*
  (1961).
Millington, Herbert, *American Diplomacy and the War of the Pacific* (1948).
Perkins, Dexter, *The Monroe Doctrine, 1867–1907* (1937).
—— *The United States and the Caribbean* (1947).
Robertson, William S., *Hispanic-American Relations with the United States*
  (1923).
Scott, James B., *International Conferences of American States* (1931).
Tyler, Alice F., *Foreign Policy of Blaine* (1927).
Volwiler, A. T., "Harrison, Blaine, and Foreign Policy," Am. Philos. Soc., *Proc.*,
  79 (1938), 637.
Wilgus, A. Curtis, "Blaine and the Pan American Movement," *Hisp. Am. Hist.
  Rev.*, 5 (1922), 662.
—— "Official Manifest Destiny Sentiment Concerning Hispanic America," *La.
  Hist. Quar.*, 15 (1932), 486.

48.17.6.2 Argentina, Brazil, and Chile

Eister, A. W., *United States and A.B.C. Powers* (1950).
Evans, Henry C., *Chile and Its Relations with the United States* (1927).
Hardy, Osgood, "Itata Incident," *Hispanic Am. Hist. Rev.*, 5 (1922), 195.
—— "Was Egan a 'Blundering Minister'?" *Hisp. Am. Hist. Rev.*, 8 (1928), 65.
Hill, Lawrence F., *Diplomatic Relations between the United States and Brazil*
  (1932).
McGann, Thomas F., *Argentina, the United States and the Inter-America System,
  1880–1914* (1957).
Rippy, J. Fred, "The United States and the Establishment of Republic of Brazil,"
  Southw. Pol. Sci. Quar., 3 (1922), 39.
Sherman, William R., *Diplomatic Relations of the United States and Chile* (1927).

Timm, C. A., "United States and Brazil during the Naval Revolt of 1893," *Southw. Pol. Sci. Quar.*, 5 (1924), 119.

48.17.6.3 Venezuelan Crisis of 1896

Blake, N. M., "Background of Cleveland's Venezuelan Policy," *AHR*, 47 (1942), 259.
———— "Olney-Pauncefote Treaty," *AHR*, 50 (1945), 228.
Child, C. J., "Venezuela-British Guiana Boundary Arbitration of 1889," *Am. Jour. Internatl. Law*, 44 (1950), 682.
Clark, Thomas C., "Olney's Real Credit in the Venezuela Affair," Mass. Hist. Soc., *Proc.*, 65 (1940), 112.
Fossum, Paul R., "Anglo-Venezuelan Controversy," *Hisp. Am. Hist. Rev.*, 8 (1928), 299.
LaFeber, Walter, "Background of Cleveland's Venezuelan Policy: A Reinterpretation," *AHR*, 66 (1961), 947.
Mathews, Joseph J., "The Venezuelan Crisis of 1896," *MVHR*, 50 (1963), 195.
Mowat, Robert B., *Life of Lord Pauncefote* (1929).
Rippy, J. Fred, "Mexican Reactions to Cleveland's Message," *Pol. Sci. Quar.*, 39 (1924), 280.
Sloan, Jennie A., "Anglo-American Relations and the Venezuelan Boundary Dispute," *Hisp. Am. Hist. Rev.*, 18 (1938), 495.
Young, G. B., "Intervention under the Monroe Doctrine," *Pol. Sci. Quar.*, 57 (1942), 247.

See also 10.3 for biographies/writings of:

Cleveland, Grover, 1837–1908
Olney, Richard, 1835–1917

48.17.6.4 Mexico and Díaz

Hackett, Charles W., "Recognition of Díaz by the United States," *Southw. Hist. Quar.*, 28 (1924), 34.
Relyea, P. S., *Relations between the United States and Mexico under Díaz* (1924).
Villegas, Daniel Cosio, *U. S. vs. Porfirio Díaz*, Nettie Lee Benson, trans. (1963).

49 American Empire, 1898–1933

49.1 GENERAL

Adams, Brooks, *America's Economic Supremacy* (1900); M. W. Childs, ed. (1947).
—— *New Empire* (1902).
Bailey, Thomas A., "America's Emergence as a World Power," *Pac. Hist. Rev.*, 30 (1961), 1.
Braeman, John, "Seven Progressives," *Bus. Hist. Rev*, 35 (1961), 581.
Coletta, Paolo E., ed., *Threshold to American Internationalism: Essays on Foreign Policies of McKinley* (1970).
Giddings, Franklin H., *Democracy and Empire* (1900).
Grenville, John A. S., "Diplomacy and War Plans in the United States, 1890–1917," *Royal Hist. Soc., Trans.*, 5 ser., 11 (1961), 1.
Kennedy, Padraic C., "LaFollette's Imperialist Flirtation," *Pac. Hist. Rev.*, 29 (1960), 131.
Leuchtenburg, William E., "Progressive Movement and American Foreign Policy, 1898–1916," *MVHR*, 39 (1952), 483.
May, Ernest R., *American Imperialism* (1968).
—— *Imperial Democracy: Emergence of America as a Great Power* (1961).
Muller, Dorothea R., "Josiah Strong and American Nationalism," *JAH*, 53 (1966), 487.
Rozwenc, Edwin C., and Kenneth Lindfors, *United States and New Imperialism, 1898–1912* (1968).
Seed, Geoffrey, "British Reactions to American Imperialism Reflected in Journals of Opinion, 1898–1900," *Pol. Sci. Quar.*, 73 (1958), 254.
Strong, Josiah, *Expansion under New World Conditions* (1900).
Welch, Richard E., Jr., "G. F. Hoar and H. C. Lodge," *NEQ*, 39 (1966), 182.

49.2 SPANISH-AMERICAN WAR

49.2.1 General

Azacárate y Flórez, Pablo de, *La Guerra del 98* (1960).
Chadwick, F. E., *Relations of the United States and Spain: Spanish-American War* (2 vols., 1911).
Ferrara, Orestes, *The Last Spanish War* (1937).
Freidel, Frank, *Splendid Little War* (1958). Pictorial.
May, Ernest R., *Imperial Democracy: Emergence of America as a Great Power* (1961).
Millis, Walter, *Martial Spirit* (1931).
Morgan, H. Wayne, *America's Road to Empire: War with Spain* (1965).
Pratt, Julius W., *Expansionists of 1898: Acquisition of Hawaii and the Spanish Islands* (1936).

49.2.2 Journalism and Public Opinion

Auxier, S. S., "Middle Western Newspapers and the Spanish-American War," *MVHR*, 26 (1940), 523.

—— "Propaganda Activities of the Cuban Junta," *Hisp. Am. Hist. Rev.*, 19 (1939), 286.

Brown, Charles H., *Correspondents' War: Journalists in the Spanish-American War* (1967).

Wilkerson, M. M., *Public Opinion and Spanish-American War* (1932).

Wisan, J. E., *Cuban Crisis in the New York Press* (1934).

49.2.3 Cuban Campaign

Azoy, Anastasio C. M., *Charge! Story of the Battle of San Juan Hill* (1961).

Dickman, J. T., ed., *Santiago Campaign* (1927).

Vilá, Herminio Portell, *Historia de Cuba en sus relaciones con los Estados Unidos y España* (4 vols., 1938–1941).

Roosevelt, Theodore, *Rough Riders* (1899).

See also 10.3 for biographies/writings of:

Evans, Robley D., 1846–1912
Schley, Winfield S., 1839–1909
Wainwright, Richard, 1849–1926
Wood, Leonard, 1860–1927

49.2.4 Philippine Campaign

Bailey, Thomas A., "Dewey and the Germans at Manila," *AHR*, 45 (1939), 59.

Braisted, William R., *The United States Navy in Pacific, 1897–1909* (1958).

LeRoy, James A., *Americans in the Philippines* (2 vols., 1914).

Sargent, Nathan, comp., *Dewey and the Manila Campaign* (1947).

Walker, L. W., "Guam's Seizure," *Pac. Hist. Rev.*, 14 (1945), 1.

Williams, Dion, "Battle of Manila Bay," United States Naval Institute, *Proceedings*, 54 (1928), 345.

See also 10.3 for biographies/writings of:

Dewey, George, 1837–1917

49.2.5 Diplomacy

Bailey, Thomas A., "United States and Hawaii during the Spanish-American War," *AHR*, 36 (1931), 552.

Benton, Elbert J., *International Law and Diplomacy of the Spanish-American War* (1908).

Chadwick, French E., *Relations of the United States and Spain: Diplomacy* (1909).

Einstein, Lewis, "British Diplomacy in the Spanish American War," Mass. Hist. Soc., *Proc.*, 76 (1964), 30.

Grenville, John A. S., *Lord Salisbury and Foreign Relations* (1964).

Holbo, Paul S., "William McKinley and the Turpie-Foraker Amendment," *AHR*, 72 (1967), 1321.

Morgan, H. Wayne, "DeLome Letter," *Historian*, 26 (1963), 36.

Neale, Robert G., *Great Britain and United States Expansion, 1898–1900* (1966).

Perkins, Bradford, *Great Rapprochement: England and the United States, 1895–1914* (1968).

Quinn, P. E., "Diplomatic Struggle for the Carolines, 1898," *Pac. Hist. Rev.*, 14 (1945), 290.

Reuter, B. A., *Anglo-American Relations during the Spanish-American War* (1924).

Rippy, J. F., "European Powers and Spanish-American War," *James Sprunt Historical Studies*, 19 (1927), 22.

Sears, Louis M., "French Opinion of the Spanish-American War," *Hisp. Am. Hist. Rev.*, 7 (1927), 25.

Shippee, L. B., "Germany and the Spanish-American War," *AHR*, 30 (1925), 754.

49.2.6 Treaty of Paris

Chadwick, French E., *Relations of United States and Spain: Diplomacy* (1909).

Coletta, Paolo E., "Bryan, McKinley, and Treaty of Paris," *Pac. Hist. Rev.*, 26 (1957), 131.

—— "McKinley, Peace Negotiations, and Acquisition of the Philippines," *Pac. Hist. Rev.*, 30 (1961), 341.

Holt, W. Stull, *Treaties Defeated by the Senate* (1933).

Reid, Whitelaw, *Making Peace with Spain: Diary, September–December, 1898*, H. Wayne Morgan, ed. (1965).

49.3 ANTI-IMPERIALISM

Baron, Harold, "Anti-Imperialism and Democrats," *Science and Society*, 21 (1957), 222.

Beisner, Robert L., *Twelve against Empire: Anti-Imperialists, 1898–1900* (1968).

Coletta, Paolo E., "Bryan, Anti-Imperialism and Missionary Diplomacy," *Neb. Hist.*, 44 (1963), 167.

Harrington, Fred H., "Anti-Imperialist Movement," *MVHR*, 22 (1935), 211.

—— "Literary Aspects of Anti-Imperialism," *NEQ*, 10 (1937), 650.

Lasch, Christopher, "Anti-Imperialists, the Philippines, and Inequality of Man," *JSH*, 24 (1958), 319.

Rollins, John W., "Anti-Imperialists and Twentieth Century American Foreign Policy," *Studies on the Left*, 3 (1962), 9.

Welch, Richard E., Jr., "Senator George Frisbie Hoar and the Defeat of Anti-Imperialism, 1898–1900," *Historian*, 26 (1964), 362.

See also 10.3 for biographies/writings of:

Adams, Charles F., Jr., 1835–1915
Bryan, William Jennings, 1860–1925
Carnegie, Andrew, 1835–1919
Clemens, Samuel L., 1835–1910
Godkin, Edwin L., 1831–1902
Hoar, George F., 1826–1904
Jordan, David Starr, 1851–1931
Lloyd, Henry Demarest, 1847–1903
Olney, Richard, 1835–1917
Reed, Thomas B., 1839–1902
Schurz, Carl, 1829–1906

49.4 ELECTION OF 1900

Bailey, Thomas A., "Was the Election of 1900 a Mandate on Imperialism?" *MVHR*, 24 (1937), 43.

Beisner, Robert L., *Twelve Against Empire: Anti-Imperialists, 1898–1900* (1968).

LeFeber, Walter, "Election of 1900," in Arthur M. Schlesinger, Jr. and Fred L. Israel, eds., *History of American Presidential Elections, 1789–1968*, vol. III (1971).

Tompkins, E. Berkeley, "The Anti-Imperialist Dilemma in the Election of 1900," *Pac. Hist. Rev.*, 36 (1967), 143.

See also 10.3 for biographies/writings of:

Bryan, William Jennings, 1860–1925
Carlisle, John G., 1835–1910
Day, William R., 1849–1923
Debs, Eugene V., 1855–1926
Foraker, Joseph B., 1846–1917
Hanna, Marcus A., 1837–1904
Long, John D., 1838–1915
McKinley, William, 1843–1901
Roosevelt, Theodore, 1858–1919
Root, Elihu, 1845–1937
Sherman, John, 1823–1900

49.5 CUBA AND PLATT AMENDMENT

Chapman, Charles E., *Cuban Republic* (1927).
Cummins, Lejeune, "Formulation of 'Platt' Amendment," *Americas*, 23 (1967), 370.
Fitzgibbon, Russell, *Cuba and the United States* (1935).
Guggenheim, Harry F., *United States and Cuba* (1934).
Healy, David F., *The United States in Cuba, 1898–1902* (1963).
Lockmiller, David A., *Magoon in Cuba* (1938).
Millett, Allan R., *Politics of Intervention: Military Occupation of Cuba, 1906–1909* (1968).

* * * * * * *

Hitchman, James H., "Platt Amendment Revisited: Bibliographical Survey," *Americas*, 23 (1967), 343.

49.6 PHILIPPINES AND FILIPINO INSURRECTION

Blount, J. H., *American Occupation* (1912).
Elliott, Charles Burke, *Philippines* (1917).
Forbes, William C., *The Philippine Islands* (rev. ed., 1945).
Forbes-Lindsay, C. H., *The Philippines under Spanish and American Rules* (1906).
Graff, Henry F., ed., *American Imperialism and the Philippine Insurrection: Testimony before the Senate Committee on the Philippines, 1902* (1969).
Hayden, Joseph R., *Philippines* (1942).
Minger, Ralph E., "Taft, MacArthur, and Civil Government in the Philippines," *Ohio Hist. Quar.*, 70 (1961), 308.
Reuter, Frank T., *Catholic Influence on American Colonial Policies, 1898–1904* (1967).
Reyes, J. S., *Legislative History of American Economic Policy toward the Philippines* (1923).
Salamanca, Bonifacio S., *Filipino Reaction to American Rule, 1901–1913* (1968).
Schott, Joseph L., *Ordeal of Samar* (1964).
Storey, Moorfield, and M. P. Lichanco, *Conquest of Philippines, 1898–1925* (1926).
Wolff, Leon, *Little Brown Brother: Philippine Islands* (1961).

49.7 PUERTO RICO

Berbusse, Edward J., *United States in Puerto Rico, 1898–1900* (1966).
Diffie, Bailey and Justine W., *Porto Rico* (1931).
Lewis, G. K., *Puerto Rico: Freedom and Power in the Caribbean* (1967).

See also 10.3 for biographies/writings of:

Anderson, Larz, 1866–1937
Foraker, Joseph B., 1846–1917
Newlands, Francis G., 1848–1917

49.8 OVERSEAS TERRITORIES AND PROTECTORATES

Gray, J. A. C., *Amerika Samoa* (1960).
Haas, William H., ed., *American Empire* (1940).
Leff, David N., *Uncle Sam's Pacific Islets* (1940).
Nearing, Scott, and Joseph Freeman, *Dollar Diplomacy* (1925).
Pratt, Julius W., *America's Colonial Experiment* (1950).

Part Nine   Twentieth Century

50.1 GENERAL

Adams, David K., *America in the Twentieth Century* (1967).
Allen, Frederick L., *Big Change: America Transforms Itself, 1900–1950* (1952).
Barck, Oscar T., Jr., and N. M. Blake, *Since 1900* (4th ed., 1965).
Bonner, Thomas N., *Our Recent Past* (1963).
Cronon, E. David, ed., *Twentieth Century America: Selected Readings, 1909 to the Present* (2 vols., 1965–1966).
Freidel, Frank, *America in the Twentieth Century* (3d ed., 1970).
———— and Norman Pollack, eds., *American Issues in the Twentieth Century* (1966).
Garraty, John A., and Robert A. Divine, eds., *Twentieth-Century America: Contemporary Documents and Opinions* (1968).
Goldman, Eric F., *Rendezvous with Destiny: Modern American Reform* (1952).
Handlin, Oscar, *The American People in the Twentieth Century* (2nd ed., 1966).
Huthmacher, J. Joseph, *Twentieth Century America* (1966).
Knoles, George H., *The New United States* (1959).
Lasch, Christopher, *New Radicalism in America, 1889–1963* (1965).
Link, Arthur S., William B. Catton, and William M. Leary, Jr., *American Epoch: The United States since the 1890's* (3d ed., 1967).
Luthin, Reinhard H., *American Demagogues: Twentieth Century* (1954).
McCoy, Donald R., and Raymond G. O'Connor, eds., *Readings in Twentieth Century American History* (1963).
McKelvey, Blake, *Emergence of Metropolitan America, 1915–1966* (1968).
Madison, Charles A., *Leaders and Liberals in 20th Century America* (1961).
Maurois, André, *From New Freedom to New Frontier* (1963).
Mayer, George H., and Walter O. Forster, *United States and the Twentieth Century* (1958).
Ostrander, Gilman M., *American Civilization in the First Machine Age: 1890–1940* (1970).
Parkes, Henry B., and Vincent P. Carosso, *Recent America* (2 vols., 1963).
Shannon, David A., *Twentieth Century America: United States since the 1890's* (1963).
Spiller, Robert E., et al., *American Perspectives: The National Self-Image in the Twentieth Century* (1961).

50.2 INTERPRETATIVE STUDIES

Bernstein, Barton J., and Allen J. Matusow, *Twentieth-Century America: Recent Interpretations* (1969).
Beaver, Daniel R., ed., *Some Pathways in Twentieth-Century History: Essays in Honor of Reginald Charles McGrane* (1969).

Braeman, John, et al., eds., *Change and Continuity in Twentieth-Century America* (2nd ed., 1967).
Hays, Samuel P., "Social Analysis of American Political History, 1880–1920," *Pol. Sci. Quar.*, 80 (1965), 373.

50.3 SOUTH

Brandfon, Robert L., comp., *The American South in Twentieth Century* (1967).
Davis, Allison, B. B. Gardner and M. R. Gardner, *Deep South* (1941).
Dollard, John, *Caste and Class in a Southern Town* (1937).
Dykeman, Wilma, "Southern Demagogue," *Va. Quar. Rev.*, 33 (1957), 558.
Ewing, Cortez A. M., *Primary Elections in the South: Uniparty Politics* (1953). Covers the period, 1911–1948.
Key, V. O., Jr., *Southern Politics* (1949).
Rubin, Morton, *Plantation County* (1951).
Sherrill, Robert, *Gothic Politics in the Deep South* (1968).
Tindall, George B., "Benighted South," *Va. Quar. Rev.*, 40 (1964), 281.
Tindall, George B., *Emergence of the New South, 1913–1945* (1967).
Woodward, C. Vann, *Origins of the New South, 1877–1913* (1951).

*   *   *   *   *   *   *

Grantham, Dewey W., Jr., "Twentieth-Century South," in Arthur S. Link and Rembert W. Patrick, eds. *Writing Southern History: Essays in Honor of Fletcher M. Green* (1965).

50.4 FOREIGN RELATIONS

50.4.1 General

Adler, Selig, *Uncertain Giant: American Foreign Policy 1921–1941* (1965).
Davids, Jules, *America and the World: Diplomacy in the Twentieth Century* (1960).
Dulles, Foster R., *America's Rise to World Power, 1898–1954* (1955).
Duroselle, Jean Baptiste, *From Wilson to Roosevelt: Foreign Policy*, Nancy L. Roelker, trans. (1963).
Grenville, John A. S., "Diplomacy and War Plans in the United States, 1890–1917," *Royal Hist. Soc., Trans.*, 5 ser., 11 (1961), 1.
Jonas, Manfred, comp., *American Foreign Relations in the Twentieth Century: Documents* (1967).
Kennan, George F., *American Diplomacy, 1900–1930* (1951).
Leopold, Richard W., *Growth of American Foreign Policy* (1962). Covers the period, 1889–1961.
Schapsmeier, Frederick H. and Edward L., "Walter Lippmann, Critic of American Foreign Policy," *Midw. Quar.*, 7 (1966), 123.
Trask, David F., *Victory without Peace: American Foreign Relations in the Twentieth Century* (1968).
Van Alstyne, Richard W., *American Crisis Diplomacy: Collective Security, 1918–1952* (1952).

50.4.2 Interpretative Studies

Adler, Selig, *Isolationist Impulse: Twentieth Century Reaction* (1957).
Anderson, George L., ed., *Issues and Conflicts: 20th Century American Diplomacy* (1959).
Coudert, Frederic R., *Half Century of International Problems: A Lawyer's Views*, Allan Nevins, ed. (1954).

De Conde, Alexander, ed., *Isolation and Security: Twentieth-Century American Foreign Policy* (1957).

Foreign Policy Association, *Cartoon History of United States Foreign Policy since World War I* (1967).

Graebner, Norman A., ed., *An Uncertain Tradition: American Secretaries of State in the Twentieth Century* (1961).

Meecham, J. L., *United States and Inter-American Security, 1889–1960* (1961).

Osgood, Robert E., *Ideals and Self Interest in America's Foreign Relations* (1953).

Riencourt, Amaury de, *American Empire* (1968).

Warren, Sidney, *The President as World Leader* (1964).

50.5 DEFENSE POLICIES

Ambrose, Stephen E., *Upton and the Army* (1964).

Reinhardt, George C., and William R. Kintner, *Haphazard Years: How America Has Gone to War* (1960).

Tate, Merze, *United States and Armaments* (1948).

51 Progressive Era

51.1 GENERAL

Chamberlain, John, *Farewell to Reform* (1932).
Hayes, Samuel P., *Response to Industrialization, 1885–1914* (1957).
Hofstadter, Richard, *The Age of Reform: From Bryan to F.D.R.* (1955).
———— ed., *Progressive Movement* (1963).
Josephson, Matthew, *The President Makers* (1940).
Nye, Russel B., *Midwestern Progressive Politics, 1870–1958* (rev. ed., 1959).
Pease, Otis, ed., *Progressive Years* (1962).
Riis, Jacob A., *How the Other Half Lives* (1890); Sam Bass Warner, Jr., ed. (1970).
Shannon, David A., ed., *Progressivism and Postwar Disillusionment, 1898–1928* (1966).

*　*　*　*　*　*　*

Link, Arthur S., and William M. Leary, Jr., comps., *The Progressive Era and the Great War, 1896–1920* (1969).
Watson, Richard L., Jr., "American Political History, 1900–1920," *So. Atl. Quar.,* 54 (1955), 107.

51.2 INTERPRETATIVE STUDIES

Fuller, Wayne E., "The Rural Roots of Progressive Leaders," *Agric. Hist.,* 42 (1968), 1.
Huthmacher, J. Joseph, "Urban Liberalism and the Age of Reform," *MVHR,* 49 (1962), 231.
McNaught, Kenneth, "Progressives and the Great Society," *JAH,* 53 (1966), 504.
Margulies, Herbert F., "Decline of the Progressive Movement," *Mid-America,* 45 (1963), 250.
Scott, Andrew M., "Progressive Era," *Jour. Politics,* 21 (1959), 685.
Tager, Jack, "Progressives, Conservatives and the Theory of the Status Revolution," *Mid-America,* 48 (1966), 162.

51.3 SOCIETY

Busbey, K. G., *Home Life in America* (1910).
Morris, Lloyd R., *Postscript to Yesterday* (1947).
Sullivan, Mark, *Our Times* (6 vols., 1926–1935).

51.4 PROGRESSIVE THOUGHT

51.4.1 General

Aaron, Daniel, *Men of Good Hope: American Progressives* (1951).

Filler, Louis, *Crusaders for American Liberalism* (1950).

Flower, Benjamin O., *Progressive Men, Women, and Events* (1914).

Forcey, Charles, *Crossroads of Liberalism: Croly, Weyl, Lippmann and the Progressive Era* (1961).

Hofstadter, Richard, *Progressive Historians: Turner, Beard, Parrington* (1968).

Lasch, Christopher, *New Radicalism in America, 1889–1963: The Intellectual as a Social Type* (1965).

Levine, Daniel, *Varieties of Reform Thought* (1964).

McGovern, James R., "David Graham Phillips and the Virility Impulse of Progressives," *NEQ*, 39 (1966), 334.

Madison, C. A., *Leaders and Liberals in Twentieth Century America* (1961).

Mann, Arthur, *Yankee Reformers in the Urban Age* (1954).

May, Henry F., *End of American Innocence, 1912–1917* (1959).

Noble, David W., *Paradox of Progressive Thought* (1958).

Paulson, Ross E., *Radicalism and Reform: Vrooman Family* (1968).

Pickens, Donald K., *Eugenics and Progressives* (1968).

Quandt, Jean B., *From the Small Town to the Great Community: Social Thought of Progressive Intellectuals* (1970).

White, Morton, ed., *Age of Analysis: Twentieth Century Philosophers* (1955).

White, Morton, *Social Thought in America: The Revolt Against Formalism* (1949).

See also 10.3 for biographies/writings of:

Beard, Charles A., 1874–1948

Brandeis, Louis D., 1856–1941

Croly, Herbert D., 1869–1930

Dewey, John, 1859–1952

Holmes, Oliver Wendell, Jr., 1841–1935

James, William, 1842–1910

Lippmann, Walter, 1889–

Patten, Simon N., 1852–1922

Turner, Frederick Jackson, 1861–1932

Veblen, Thorstein, 1857–1929

51.4.2 Contemporary Works

Bentley, Arthur F., *Process of Government* (1908); Peter H. Odegard, ed. (1967).

Croly, Herbert, *Promise of American Life* (1909); Arthur M. Schlesinger, Jr., ed. (1965).

Gilman, Charlotte Perkins, *Women and Economics* (1898); Carl N. Degler, ed. (1966).

Patten, Simon N., *New Basis of Civilization* (1907); Daniel M. Fox, ed. (1968).

51.5 SOCIAL GOSPEL AND RELIGION

Abell, Aaron I., *American Catholicism and Social Action, 1865–1950* (1960).

Hopkins, Charles Howard, *Rise of Social Gospel, 1865–1915* (1940).

Meyer, Donald, *Positive Thinkers: Study of American Quest for Health, Wealth and Personal Power from Mary Baker Eddy to Norman Vincent Peale* (1965).

Wisbey, H. A., *Soldiers without Swords: Salvation Army* (1955).

See also 10.3 for biographies/writings of:

Eddy, Mary Baker, 1821–1910
Gladden, Washington, 1836–1918
Rauschenbusch, Walter, 1861–1918

51.6 SOCIAL JUSTICE AND REFORM

Anderson, Oscar Edward, *Health of a Nation: Harvey W. Wiley and Fight for Pure Food* (1958).
Bremner, Robert H., *From the Depths: Discovery of Poverty* (1956).
Bruno, Frank J., and Louis Towley, *Trends in Social Work, 1874–1956* (2nd ed., 1957).
Davis, Allen Freeman, *Spearheads for Reform: Social Settlements and the Progressive Movement* (1967).
Faulkner, Harold U., *Quest for Social Justice* (1931).
Gusfield, Joseph, *Symbolic Crusade: Status Politics and the Temperance Movement* (1963).
Hays, Samuel P., *Conservation and the Gospel of Efficiency: The Progressive Conservation Movement, 1890–1920* (1959).
Kraditor, A. S., *Ideas of the Woman Suffrage Movement, 1890–1920* (1965).
Lubove, Roy, *Progressives and Slums: Tenement House Reform in New York City, 1890–1917* (1962).
———— *The Struggle for Social Security, 1900–1935* (1968).
National Consumers' League, *National Consumers' League, 1899–1924* (1925).
O'Neill, William L., *Divorce in the Progressive Era* (1967).
Richardson, Elmo R., *Politics of Conservation, 1897–1913* (1962).
Shryock, R. H., *National Tuberculosis Association, 1904–1954* (1957).
Timberlake, James H., *Prohibition and the Progressive Movement, 1900–1920* (1963).
Wood, S. B., *Constitutional Politics in Progressive Era: Child Labor and the Law* (1968).

See also 10.3 for biographies/writings of:

Addams, Jane, 1860–1935
Anthony, Susan B., 1820–1906
Folks, Homer, 1867–1963
Marshall, Louis, 1856–1929
Pinchot, Gifford, 1865–1946
Riis, Jacob A., 1849–1914
Stanton, Elizabeth Cady, 1815–1902
Wiley, Harvey W., 1844–1930

51.7 SOCIALISM

Bedford, Henry F., *Socialism and Workers in Massachusetts, 1886–1912* (1966).
Kipnis, Ira, *The American Socialist Movement, 1897–1912* (1952).
Quint, Howard H., *Forging of American Socialism* (1953).
Shannon, David, *Socialist Party of America* (1955).

See also biographies/writings of:

Debs, Eugene V., 1855–1926
London, Meyer, 1871–1926

51.8 MUCKRAKING AND JOURNALISM

Cassedy, James H., "Muckraking and Medicine: Samuel Hopkins Adams," *Am.
    Quar.*, 16 (1964), 85.
Chalmers, David M., *Social and Political Ideas of Muckrakers* (1964).
Filler, Louis, *Crusaders for American Liberalism* (1939).
Glanz, Rudolph, "Jewish Social Conditions as Seen by the Muckrakers," *YIVO*,
    9 (1954), 308.
Regier, Cornelius C., *Era of Muckrakers* (1932).
Wilson, Harold S., *McClure's Magazine and the Muckrakers* (1970).

See also 10.3 for biographies/writings of:

Baker, Ray Stannard, 1870–1946
McClure, S. S., 1857–1949
Phillips, David Graham, 1867–1911
Steffens, Lincoln, 1866–1936
Whitlock, Brand, 1869–1934

51.9 NEGROES

Baker, Ray Stannard, *Following the Color Line* (1908).
Kellogg, Charles F., *History of the National Association for the Advancement of
    Colored People, 1909–1920* (1967).
Meier, August, *Negro Thought in America, 1880–1915* (1963).
Newby, Idus A., *Jim Crow's Defense, Anti-Negro Thought, 1900–1930* (1965).
Osofsky, Gilbert, *Harlem, 1890–1930* (1966).
Redkey, Edwin S., *Black Exodus: Black Nationalist and Back-to-Africa Move-
    ments, 1890–1910* (1970).
Spear, Allan H., *Black Chicago, 1890–1920* (1967).

See also 10.3 for biographies/writings of:

Du Bois, W. E. B., 1868–1963
Trotter, William M., 1872–1934
Washington, Booker T., 1856–1915

51.10 REGIONAL, STATE, AND LOCAL STUDIES

51.10.1 South

Kennedy, Stetson, *Southern Exposure* (1946).
Link, Arthur S., "Progressive Movement in the South, 1870–1914," *No. Car.
    Hist. Rev.*, 23 (1946), 172.
Scott, Anne Firor, "Progressive Wind from the South, 1906–1913," *JSH*, 29
    (1963), 53.

51.10.2 Alabama

Hackney, Sheldon, *Populism to Progressivism in Alabama* (1969).

51.10.3 California

Bean, Walton E., *Boss Ruef's San Francisco* (1952).
Hichborn, Franklin, *"The System" as Uncovered by San Francisco Graft Prosecu-
    tion* (1915).

Mowry, G. E., *California Progressives* (1951).
Older, Fremont, *My Own Story* (1919). San Francisco.
Olin, Spencer C., Jr., *California's Prodigal Sons: Hiram Johnson and the Progressives, 1911–1917* (1968).

See also 10.3 for biographies/writings of:

Johnson, Hiram W., 1866–1945
Lane, Franklin K., 1864–1921

51.10.4 Colorado

Costigan, E. P., *Papers Relating to the Progressive Movement in Colorado*, C. B. Goodykoontz, ed. (1941).

51.10.5 Illinois

Tarr, Joel A., "President Theodore Roosevelt and Illinois Politics, 1901–1904," Ill. State Hist. Soc., *Jour.*, 58 (1965), 245.

51.10.6 Kansas

Malin, James C., *Concern about Humanity: Reform, 1872–1912, at National and Kansas Levels* (1964).

51.10.7 Maryland

Crooks, James B., *Politics & Progress: Urban Progressivism in Baltimore, 1895 to 1911* (1968).

51.10.8 Massachusetts

Abrams, Richard M., *Conservatism in a Progressive Era: Massachusetts Politics, 1900–1912* (1964).
Cole, Donald B., *Immigrant City: Lawrence, Massachusetts, 1845–1921* (1963).
Hart, Albert B., *Commonwealth History of Massachusetts*, vol. V (1930).
Loring, A. P., "Short Account of Massachusetts Constitutional Convention," *NEQ*, 6 (1933), supplement.
Sherman, Richard B., "Status Revolution and Massachusetts Progressive Leadership," *Pol. Sci. Quar.*, 78 (1963), 59.

See also 10.3 for biographies/writings of:

Brandeis, Louis D., 1856–1941
Coolidge, Calvin, 1872–1933

51.10.9 Minnesota

Chrislock, Carl H., "Minnesota Republicanism," *Minn. Hist.*, 39 (1964), 93.

See also 10.3 for biographies/writings of:

Johnson, John A., 1861–1909
Lind, John, 1854–1930

51.10.10 Mississippi

Bigelow, Martha, "Mississippi Progressivism," *Jour. Miss. Hist.*, 29 (1967), 202.
Kirwan, A. D., *Revolt of Rednecks* (1951).

51.10.11 Missouri

Dorset, L. W., *Pendergast Machine* (1968).
Thurman, A. L., Jr., "Joseph Wingate Folk," *Mo. Hist. Rev.*, 59 (1965), 173.

51.10.12 New Jersey

Mahoney, Joseph F., "Backsliding Convert: Woodrow Wilson and the 'Seven Sisters,'" *Am. Quar.*, 18 (1966), 71.
Noble, Ransom E., Jr., *New Jersey Progressivism before Wilson* (1946).

See also 10.3 for biographies/writings of:

Tumulty, Joseph P., 1879–1954
Wilson, Woodrow, 1856–1924

51.10.13 New York

Arent, Leonora, *Electric Franchise in New York City* (1919).
Dubofsky, Melvyn, *When Workers Organize: New York City in Progressive Era* (1968).
Huthmacher, J. Joseph, "Charles Evans Hughes and Charles F. Murphy: Metamorphosis of Progressivism," *N.Y. Hist.*, 46 (1965), 25.
Lubove, Roy, *Progressives and the Slums: Tenement House Reform in New York City, 1890–1917* (1962).
McKelvey, Blake, *Rochester, 1812–1961* (4 vols., 1945–1961).
Riordan, William L., *Plunkitt of Tammany Hall* (1963).
Wesser, Robert F., "Charles Evans Hughes and Urban Sources of Political Progressivism," *N.Y. Hist. Soc. Quar.*, 50 (1966), 365.
—— "Theodore Roosevelt: Republican Party in New York, 1901–1906," *N.Y. Hist.*, 46 (1965), 230.
Yellowitz, Irwin, *Labor and Progressive Movement in New York* (1965).

See also 10.3 for biographies/writings of:

Gaynor, William J., 1849–1913
Hughes, Charles Evans, 1889–1950
McClellan, George B., Jr., 1865–1940
Murphy, Charles F., 1858–1924
Platt, Thomas C., 1833–1910
Roosevelt, Theodore, 1858–1919

51.10.14 Ohio

Anderson, Elaine S., "Ohio Election of 1910," *Northw. Ohio Quar.*, 38 (1966), 50.
Johnson, Tom Loftin, *My Story* (1911). Cleveland.
Miller, Zane L., *Boss Cox's Cincinnati* (1968).
Warner, Hoyt L., *Progressivism in Ohio, 1897–1917* (1964).

See also 10.3 for biographies/writings of:

Baker, Newton D., 1871–1937
Whitlock, Brand, 1869–1934

51.10.15 Oklahoma

Jones, Stephen, "Captain Frank Frantz, Rough Rider Governor of Oklahoma Territory," *Chronicles Okla.*, 43 (1965), 374.

51.10.16 Oregon

Barnett, James Duff, *Operation of the Initiative, Referendum and Recall in Oregon* (1915).
McClintock, Thomas C., "Seth Lewelling, William S. U'Ren and Birth of Oregon Progressive Movement," *Ore. Hist. Quar.*, 68 (1963), 197.

51.10.17 Pennsylvania

Abernethy, Lloyd M., "Insurgency in Pennsylvania, 1905," *Penn. Mag. Hist. Biog.*, 87 (1963), 3.
McCullough, David G., *Johnstown Flood* (1968).

See also 10.3 for biographies/writings of:

Pennypacker, Samuel W., 1843–1916
Penrose, Boies, 1860–1921

51.10.18 Tennessee

Miller, William D., *Memphis during the Progressive Era* (1957).

51.10.19 Vermont

Flint, Winston A., *Progressive Movement in Vermont* (1941).

51.10.20 Washington

Kerr, William T., Jr., "Progressives of Washington, 1910–12," *Pac. Northw. Quar.*, 55 (1964), 16.

51.10.21 Wisconsin

Howe, Frederic C., *Wisconsin* (1912).
Kennedy, Padraic C., "Lenroot, La Follette and Campaign of 1906," *Wis. Mag. Hist.*, 42 (1959), 163.
Korman, Gerd, "Wisconsin German-American Press and Progressivism, 1904–1912," *Wis. Mag. Hist.*, 40 (1957), 161.
McCarthy, Charles, *Wisconsin Idea* (1912).
Maxwell, Robert S., *La Follette and the Rise of Progressives in Wisconsin* (1956).

See also 10.3 for biographies/writings of:

La Follette, Robert M., 1855–1925
Philipp, Emanuel L., 1861–1925

51.11 GOVERNMENTAL REFORM

51.11.1 General

Beard, Charles A., and B. E. Shultz, *Documents on Initiative, Referendum and Recall* (1912).
Brooks, Robert C., *Corruption in American Politics* (1910).
Commons, J. R., *Proportional Representation* (1907).
Fredman, L. E., *Australian Ballot* (1968).
Munro, William B., *Initiative, Referendum, and Recall* (1912).
Oberholtzer, E. P., *Referendum in America* (1912).

51.11.2 Municipal

Bartlett, Dana W., *Better City* (1907).
Beard, M. R., *Women's Work in Municipalities* (1915).
Bradford, Ernest S., *Commission Government in American Cities* (1911).
Bruere, Henry, *New City Government* (1912).
Chang, Tso-shuen, *History and Analysis of Commission and City Manager Plans* (1918).
Hamilton, John J., *Dethronement of the City Boss* (1910).
Hichborn, Franklin, *"The System" as Uncovered by San Francisco Graft Prosecution* (1915).
Howe, Frederic C., *City the Hope of Democracy* (1905); Otis Pease, ed. (1967).
Huthmacher, J. Joseph, "Urban Liberalism and Age of Reform," *MVHR*, 49 (1962), 231.
King, Clyde L., *Regulation of Municipal Utilities* (1912).
MacGregor, F. H., *City Government by Commission* (1911).
Steffens, Lincoln, *Shame of Cities* (1904).
——— *Upbuilders* (1909).
Thompson, Carl D., *Public Ownership* (1925).
Whitlock, Brand, *Forty Years of It* (1925).
Wilcox, Delos Franklin, *Municipal Franchises* (2 vols., 1910).
Zink, Harold, *City Bosses in the United States* (1930).

See also biographies/writings of:

Baker, Ray Stannard, 1870–1946
Brownlow, Louis, 1879–1963
Steffens, Lincoln, 1866–1936

51.12 BUSINESS AND ECONOMY

51.12.1 General

Allen, Frederick Lewis, *Lords of Creation* (1935).
Caine, Stanley P., *Myth of a Progressive Reform: Railroad Regulation in Wisconsin, 1903–1910* (1970).
Cowing, Cedric B., "Market Speculation in the Muckraker Era," *Bus. Hist. Rev.*, 31 (1957), 403.
Faulkner, Harold U., *Decline of Laissez-Faire* (1951).
Keller, Morton, *Life Insurance Enterprise, 1885–1910: Study of Limits of Corporate Power* (1963).
Kolko, Gabriel, *Railroads and Regulation, 1877–1916* (1965).
——— *Triumph of Conservatism, 1900–1916* (1963).
Mitchell, Wesley C., et al., *Income in the United States, 1909–1919* (2 vols., 1921–1922).
Newcomer, Mabel, *Big Business Executive: Factors That Made Him, 1900–1950* (1955).
Weinstein, James, *Corporate Ideal in Liberal State, 1900–1913* (1968).
Wiebe, Robert H., *Businessmen and Reform: A Study of the Progressive Movement* (1962).

See also 10.3 for biographies/writings of:

Duke, James B., 1856–1925
Edison, Thomas A., 1847–1931
Ford, Henry, 1863–1947
Gary, Elbert H., 1846–1927
Harriman, Edward H., 1848–1909
Morgan, J. Pierpont, 1837–1913
Perkins, George W., 1862–1920

Rockefeller, John D., 1839–1937
Young, Owen D., 1874–1962

51.12.2 Scientific Management

Aitken, Hugh G. J., *Taylorism at the Watertown Arsenal* (1960).
Haber, Samuel, *Efficiency and Uplift: Scientific Management in Progressive Era, 1890–1920* (1964).
Nadworny, M. J., *Scientific Management and Unions, 1900–1932* (1955).

51.12.3 Labor

Brody, David, *Steelworkers in America: The Nonunion Era* (1960).
Dubofsky, Melvin, *We Shall Be All: History of Industrial Workers of the World* (1969).
Green, Marguerite, *National Civic Federation and Labor Movement, 1900–1925* (1956).
Karson, Marc, *American Labor Unions and Politics, 1900–1918* (1958).
Leiby, James, *Carroll Wright and Labor Reform: The Origin of Labor Statistics* (1960).
Rees, Albert, *Real Wages in Manufacturing, 1890–1914* (1961).
Taft, Philip, *The A.F. of L. in the Time of Gompers* (1957).

See also 10.3 for biographies/writings of:

Debs, Eugene V., 1855–1926
Gompers, Samuel, 1850–1924
Haywood, William D., 1869–1928
Mitchell, John, 1870–1919

51.13 THEODORE ROOSEVELT ADMINISTRATION, 1901–1909

Bates, J. Leonard, "Conservation Movement, 1907 to 1921," *MVHR*, 44 (1957), 29.
Braeman, John, "Square Deal in Action: Case Study in Growth of 'National Police Power'," in John Braeman et al., eds., *Change and Continuity in Twentieth Century America* (1964).
Cross, Whitney R., "Ideas in Politics: Conservation Policies of Two Roosevelts," *Jour. Hist. Ideas*, 14 (1953), 421.
Ellsworth, Clayton S., "Theodore Roosevelt's Country Life Commission," *Agric. Hist.*, 34 (1960), 155.
Hansen, Alvin H., *Cycle of Prosperity and Depression, 1902–1908* (1921).
Harbaugh, William H., "Election of 1904," in Arthur M. Schlesinger, Jr. and Fred L. Israel, eds., *History of American Presidential Elections, 1789–1968*, vol. III (1971).
Heffron, Paul T., "Theodore Roosevelt and Mr. Justice Moody," *Vanderbilt Law Rev.*, 18 (1965), 545.
Johnson, Arthur M., "Antitrust Policy in Transition, 1908: Ideal and Reality," *MVHR*, 48 (1961), 415.
—— "Roosevelt and the Bureau of Corporations," *MVHR*, 45 (1959), 571.
Meyer, Balthasar H., *History of the Northern Securities Case* (1906).
Mowry, George E., *Era of Theodore Roosevelt* (1958).
O'Callaghan, Jerry A., "Senator Mitchell and the Oregon Land Frauds, 1905," *Pac. Hist. Rev.*, 21 (1952), 255.
Pinkett, Harold T., "The Keep Commission, 1905–1909: Rooseveltian Effort for Administrative Reform," *JAH*, 52 (1965), 297.
Rozwenc, Edwin C., *Roosevelt, Wilson and Trusts* (1950).
Scheinberg, Stephen J., "Theodore Roosevelt and the A.F. of L.'s Entry into Politics, 1906–1908," *Labor Hist.*, 3 (1962), 131.

Semonche, John E., "Theodore Roosevelt's 'Muck-Rake Speech': A Reassessment," *Mid-America*, 46 (1964), 114.

Straus, Oscar S., *Under Four Administrations from Cleveland to Taft* (1922).

Thornbrough, Emma Lou, "Brownsville Episode and the Negro Vote," *MVHR*, 44 (1957), 469.

Tinsley, James A., "Roosevelt, Foraker, and the Brownsville Affair," *Jour. Negro Hist.*, 41 (1956), 43.

*   *   *   *   *   *

Grantham, Dewey W., Jr., "Theodore Roosevelt in Historical Writings, 1945–1960," *Mid-America*, 43 (1961), 3.

See also 10.3 for biographies/writings of:

Aldrich, Nelson W., 1841–1915
Allison, William Boyd, 1829–1908
Aycock, Charles B., 1859–1912
Bailey, Joe, 1863–1929
Beveridge, Albert J., 1862–1927
Bonaparte, Charles J., 1851–1921
Bryan, William Jennings, 1860–1925
Cannon, Joseph G., 1836–1926
Hanna, Marcus A., 1837–1904
Hay, John M., 1838–1905
Holmes, Oliver Wendell, Jr., 1841–1935
La Follette, Robert M., 1855–1925
Lodge, Henry Cabot, 1850–1924
Long, John D., 1838–1915
Meyer, George von Lengerke, 1858–1918
Morgan, J. Pierpont, 1837–1913
Norris, George W., 1861–1944
Pinchot, Gifford, 1865–1946
Platt, Orville A., 1827–1905
Platt, Thomas C., 1833–1910
Roosevelt, Theodore, 1858–1919
Root, Elihu, 1845–1937
Steffens, Lincoln, 1866–1936
Stimson, Henry L., 1867–1950
Straus, Oscar S., 1850–1926
Taft, William H., 1857–1930
Tillman, "Pitchfork" Ben, 1847–1918
Watson, Thomas E., 1856–1922
White, William A., 1868–1944

See also 51.18.2, Naval Policy; 51.18.3, Theodore Roosevelt's Diplomacy; 51.18.5, Panama and Canal Projects; 51.18.6, Foreign Relations and Defense–Caribbean; 51.18.7.2, Venezuelan Crises of 1902–1903, 1907; 51.18.9, Foreign Relations and Defense–East Asia; 51.18.10, Europe and Quest for Peace.

51.14 ELECTION OF 1908 AND TAFT ADMINISTRATION, 1909–1913

51.14.1 General

Brandeis, Louis D., *Other People's Money and How Bankers Use It* (1913); Richard M. Abrams, ed. (1968).

Coletta, Paolo E., "Election of 1908," in Arthur M. Schlesinger, Jr. and Fred L. Israel, eds., *History of American Presidential Elections, 1789–1968*. Vol. III (1971).

Dix, George E., "Commerce Court," *Am. Jour. Legal Hist.*, 8 (1964), 238.

Hahn, Harlan, "Taft and Discipline of Patronage," *Jour. Politics*, 28 (1966), 368.

Hechler, Kenneth W., *Insurgency* (1940).

Holt, L. James, *Congressional Insurgents and the Party System, 1909–1916* (1967).

Kelley, Florence, *Some Ethical Gains through Legislation* (1910).

Kemmerer, Edwin W., *Postal Savings* (1917).

Manners, William, *TR and Will: Friendship That Split the Republican Party* (1970).

Mowry, George E., *Theodore Roosevelt and the Progressive Movement* (1946).

National Monetary Commission, *Report* (1912).

Solvick, Stanley D., "The Conservative as Progressive: William Howard Taft and the Politics of the Square Deal," *Northw. Ohio Quar.*, 39 (1967), 38.

—— "William H. Taft and the Payne-Aldrich Tariff," *MVHR*, 50 (1963), 424.

Tweton, D. Jerome, "Border Farmer and Canadian Reciprocity Issue, 1911–1912," *Agric. Hist.*, 37 (1963), 235.

U.S. Congress, 62d Congress, 3d sess., House, Committee to Investigate the Concentration of Control of Money and Credit, *Report* (1913). Pujo Committee.

See also 10.3 for biographies/writings of:

See also 51.18.4, Foreign Relations and Defense–Mexico; 51.18.11, Foreign Relations and Defense–Arbitration.

51.14.2 Conservation and Ballinger-Pinchot Controversy

Havemeyer, Loomis, et al., eds., *Conservation of Our Natural Resources* (1936).

Hays, Samuel P., *Conservation and the Gospel of Efficiency: The Progressive Conservation Movement 1890–1920* (1959).

Ickes, Harold L., "Not Guilty! Richard A. Ballinger," *Saturday Evening Post*, 212 (May 25, 1940), 9.

Mason, Alpheus T., *Bureaucracy Convicts Itself* (1941).

Penick, James L., Jr., "Postscript to the Ballinger–Pinchot Controversy," *Pac. Northw. Quar.*, 55 (1964), 67.

—— *Progressive Politics and Conservation: Ballinger-Pinchot Affair* (1968).

Richardson, Elmo R., *Politics of Conservation, 1897–1913* (1962).

See also 10.3 for biographies/writings of:

1.15 ELECTION OF 1912 AND PROGRESSIVE PARTY

Chandler, Alfred D., Jr., "Origins of Progressive Leadership," in Elting E. Morison, ed., *Letters of Theodore Roosevelt*, vol., 8, appendix III (1954).

Davis, Allen F., "Social Workers and the Progressive Party, 1912–1916," *AHR*, 69 (1964), 671.

Ickes, Harold L., "Who Killed the Progressive Party?" *AHR*, 46 (1941), 306.

Lincoln, A., "Theodore Roosevelt, Hiram Johnson and Vice-Presidential Nomination of 1912," *Pac. Hist. Rev.*, 28 (1959), 267.

Mowry, George E., "Election of 1912," in Arthur M. Schlesinger, Jr. and Fred L. Israel, eds., *History of American Presidential Elections, 1789–1968*, vol. III (1971).

—— *Theodore Roosevelt and Progressive Movement* (1946).

Olin, Spencer C., Jr., *California's Prodigal Sons: Hiram Johnson and the Progressives, 1911–1917* (1968).

Pinchot, Amos R. E., *History of the Progressive Party, 1912–1916*, Helene M. Hooker, ed. (1958).

Roosevelt, Theodore, *New Nationalism* (1910).

Warner, Robert M., "Chase S. Osborn and Presidential Campaign of 1912," *MVHR*, 46 (1959), 19.

White, Hollis L., "Champ Clark, 'Leather-Bound Orator,'" *Mo. Hist. Rev.*, 56 (1961), 26.

Wilensky, Norman M., *Conservatives in the Progressive Era: Taft Republicans of 1912* (1965).

Wilson, Woodrow, *Crossroads of Freedom: 1912 Campaign Speeches*, John W. Davidson, ed. (1956).

—— *New Freedom* (1913).

See also 10.3 for biographies/writings of:

Debs, Eugene V., 1855–1926
La Follette, Robert M., 1855–1925
Perkins, George W., 1862–1920
Roosevelt, Theodore, 1858–1919
Taft, William H., 1857–1930
White, William Allen, 1868–1944
Wilson, Woodrow, 1856–1924

1.16 WILSON'S FIRST ADMINISTRATION, 1913–1917

Blumenthal, Henry, "Wilson and the Race Question," *Jour. Negro Hist.*, 48 (1963), 1.

Braeman, John, "Albert J. Beveridge and Child Labor Bill," *Ind. Mag. Hist.*, 60 (1964), 1.

Canfield, Leon H., *Presidency of Woodrow Wilson* (1966).

Corwin, Edward S., "Woodrow Wilson," *Va. Law Rev.*, 42 (1956), 761.

Daniels, Jonathan, *End of Innocence* (1954).

Davis, Allen F., "Industrial Relations Commission, 1911–1913," *Mid-America*, 45 (1963), 211.

Garrison, Elisha E., *Roosevelt, Wilson and the Federal Reserve Law* (1931).

Glass, Carter, *Adventures in Constructive Finance* (1927).

Haynes, Frederick E., *Social Politics* (1924).

Holt, L. James, *Congressional Insurgents and Party System, 1909–1916* (1967).

Holt, W. Stull, *Bureau of Public Roads* (1923).

Howe, Frederic C., *Confessions of a Reformer* (1925).

Link, Arthur S., *Woodrow Wilson and the Progressive Era, 1910–1917* (1954).

Morlan, Robert L., *Political Prairie Fire: Nonpartisan League, 1915–1922* (1955).

Shapiro, Yonathan, "Jews in Politics: Louis D. Brandeis," *Am. Jew. Hist. Quar.*, 55 (1965), 199.

Smith, John S., "Organized Labor and Government in the Wilson Era, 1913–1921," *Labor Hist.*, 3 (1962), 265.

Sprague, Oliver M. W., "Crisis of 1914," *Am. Econ. Rev.*, 5 (1915), 499.

Tindall, George B., *Emergence of New South, 1913–1945* (1967).

Torodash, Martin, "Underwood and the Tariff," *Ala. Rev.*, 20 (1967), 115.

Urofsky, Melvin I., "Wilson, Brandeis and the Trust Issue, 1912–1914," *Mid-America*, 49 (1967), 3.

Watson, Richard L., Jr., "Furnifold M. Simmons," *No. Car. Hist. Rev.*, 44 (1967), 166.

Weiss, Nancy J., "The Negro and the New Freedom: Fighting Wilsonian Segregation," *Pol. Sci. Quar.*, 84 (1969), 61.

Wolgemuth, Kathleen L., "Woodrow Wilson and Federal Segregation," *Jour. Negro Hist.*, 44 (1959), 158.

See also 10.3 for biographies/writings of:

Anthony, Susan B., 1820–1906
Bailey, Joe, 1863–1929
Baker, Newton D., 1871–1937
Baker, Ray Stannard, 1870–1946
Brandeis, Louis D., 1856–1941
Bryan, William Jennings, 1860–1925
Clark, Champ, 1850–1921
Creel, George, 1876–1953
Daniels, Josephus, 1862–1948
Glass, Carter, 1858–1946
Gompers, Samuel, 1850–1924
Holmes, Oliver Wendell, Jr., 1841–1935
House, Edward M., 1858–1938
Houston, David F., 1866–1940
Hull, Cordell, 1871–1955
Kitchin, Claude, 1869–1923
La Follette, Robert M., 1855–1925
Lane, Franklin K., 1864–1921
McAdoo, William G., 1863–1941
Montague, Andrew J., 1862–1937
Morgenthau, Henry, 1856–1946
Norris, George, 1861–1944
Palmer, A. Mitchell, 1872–1936
Roosevelt, Franklin D., 1882–1945
Tillman, "Pitchfork" Ben, 1847–1918
Tumulty, Joseph P., 1879–1954
Underwood, Oscar W., 1862–1929
White, William Allen, 1863–1944
Williams, John S., 1854–1923
Wilson, Woodrow, 1856–1924

See also 51.19, Wilsonian Diplomacy; 51.20, Background of World War I.

51.17 ELECTION OF 1916

Leary, William M., Jr., "Woodrow Wilson, Irish Americans, and Election of 1916," *JAH*, 54 (1967), 57.

Link, Arthur S., and William M. Leary, Jr., "Election of 1916," in Arthur M. Schlesinger, Jr. and Fred L. Israel, eds., *History of American Presidential Elections, 1789–1968*, vol. III (1971).

See also 10.3 for biographies/writings of:

Hughes, Charles Evans, 1889–1950
Wilson, Woodrow, 1856–1924

See also 51.20.6, Entry into War; 51.22, Home Front; 51.24.4, Domestic Politics.

51.18 FOREIGN RELATIONS AND DEFENSE, 1901–1917

51.18.1 General

Leuchtenburg, William E., "Progressive Movement and American Foreign Policy, 1898–1916," *MVHR*, 39 (1952), 483.
Pratt, Julius W., *Challenge and Rejection: United States and World Leadership, 1900–1921* (1967).

51.18.2 Naval Policy

Duncan, Francis, "Mahan—Historian with a Purpose," U.S. Naval Inst., *Proc.*, 83 (1957), 498.
LaFeber, Walter, " 'Mercantilistic Imperialism' of Alfred Thayer Mahan," *MVHR*, 48 (1962), 674.
Livermore, Seward W., "American Naval-Base Policy in the Far East, 1850–1914," *Pac. Hist. Rev.*, 13 (1944), 113.
———— "The Navy as a Factor in World Politics, 1903–1913," *AHR*, 63 (1958), 863.
Mahan, Alfred T., *Interest of America in Sea Power* (1897).
Moll, Kenneth L., "A. T. Mahan, American Historian," *Mil. Affairs*, 27 (1963), 131.
Snowbarger, Willis E., "Pearl Harbor in Pacific Strategy, 1898–1908," *Historian*, 19 (1957), 361.

See also 10.3 for biographies/writings of:

Evans, Robley D., 1846–1912
Sims, William S., 1858–1936

51.18.3 Theodore Roosevelt's Diplomacy

Beale, Howard K., *Theodore Roosevelt and Rise of America to World Power* (1956).
Blake, Nelson M., "Ambassadors at the Court of Theodore Roosevelt," *MVHR*, 42 (1955), 179.
Burton, David H., *Theodore Roosevelt: Confident Imperialist* (1969).
Esthus, Raymond A., *Theodore Roosevelt and International Rivalries* (1970).

51.18.4 Mexico

Callahan, J. M., *American Foreign Policy in Mexican Relations* (1932).
Gregg, Robert D., *Influence of Border Troubles on Relations Between the United States and Mexico, 1876–1910* (1937).
Pletcher, David M., *Rails, Mines, and Progress: Seven American Promoters in Mexico, 1867–1911* (1959).
Rippy, J. Fred, *The United States and Mexico* (1931).
Turner, Frederick C., "Anti-Americanism in Mexico, 1910–1913," *Hisp. Am. Hist. Rev.*, 47 (1967), 502.
Ulloa, Berta, "Las Relaciones Mexico-Norteamericanas, 1910–1911," *Historia Mexicana*, 15 (1965), 25.

51.18.5 Panama and Canal Projects

Ameringer, Charles D., "Philippe Bunau-Varilla: New Light on Panama Canal Treaty," *Hisp. Am. Hist. Rev.,* 46 (1966), 28.

Bunau-Varilla, Philippe, *Panama* (1914).

DuVal, Miles P., Jr., *And the Mountains Will Move: Building the Panama Canal* (1947).

—— *Cadiz to Cathay: Panama Canal* (2nd ed., 1968).

Friedlander, Robert A., "Reassessment of Roosevelt's Role in the Panamanian Revolution of 1903," *West. Pol. Quar.,* 14 (1961), 535.

Gatell, Frank O., "Canal in Retrospect—Some Panamanian and Colombian Views," *Americas,* 15 (1958), 23.

Grenville, John A. S., "Great Britain and Isthmian Canal, 1898–1901," *AHR,* 61 (1955), 48.

Keasbey, Lindley M., *Nicaragua Canal* (1896).

Kemble, John H., *Panama Route* (1943).

Liss, Sheldon B., *The Canal: Aspects of United States–Panamanian Relations* (1967).

McCain, William D., *The United States and Panama* (1937).

Mack, Gerstle, *Land Divided: Panama Canal and Other Isthmian Canal Projects* (1944).

Miller, Hugh G., *Isthmian Highway* (1929).

Miner, Dwight C., *Fight for Panama Route* (1940).

Padelford, Norman J., *The Panama Canal in Peace and War* (1942).

Pennell, Joseph, *Pictures of the Panama Canal* (5th ed., 1913).

Rodriquez, Mario, "The 'Prometheus' and the Clayton-Bulwer Treaty," *Jour. Mod. Hist.,* 36 (1964), 260.

See also 10.3 for biographies/writings of:

Goethals, George W., 1858–1928
Gorgas, William C., 1854–1920

51.18.6 Caribbean

Callcott, Wilfrid H., *The Caribbean Policy of United States, 1890–1920* (1942).

Cox, Isaac J., *Nicaragua and the United States* (1927).

Denny, H. N., *Dollars for Bullets* (1929). Nicaragua.

Hill, Howard C., *Roosevelt and the Caribbean* (1927).

Jones, Chester L., *The Caribbean since 1900* (1936).

Kepner, Charles D., and J. H. Soothill, *Banana Empire* (1935).

Knight, Melvin M., *Americans in Santo Domingo* (1928).

Logan, Rayford W., *Relations of the United States with Haiti* (1941).

Montague, Ludwell L., *Haiti and the United States* (1940).

Munro, Dana G., *Intervention and Dollar Diplomacy in the Caribbean, 1900–1921* (1964).

Perkins, Dexter, *History of the Monroe Doctrine* (rev. ed., 1963).

—— *The United States and the Caribbean* (rev. ed., 1966).

Rippy, J. Fred, "Antecedents of the Roosevelt Corollary of the Monroe Doctrine," *Pac. Hist. Rev.,* 9 (1940), 267.

—— "British Bondholders and Roosevelt Corollary of the Monroe Doctrine," *Pol. Sci. Quar.,* 49 (1934), 198.

Tansill, Charles C., *The United States and Santo Domingo* (1938).

Welles, Sumner, *Naboth's Vineyard: Dominican Republic* (2 vols., 1928).

51.18.7 South America

51.18.7.1 General

Burns, E. Bradford, *The Unwritten Alliance: Rio-Branco and Brazilian–American Relations* (1966).

Livermore, S. W., "Battleship Diplomacy in South America: 1905–1925," *Jour. Mod. Hist.*, 16 (1944), 31.
McGann, Thomas F., *Argentina, the United States and the Inter-America System, 1880–1914* (1957).
Marsh, Margaret A., *Bankers in Bolivia* (1928).
Parks, E. Taylor, *Colombia and the United States* (1935).
Rippy, J. Fred, *Capitalists and Colombia* (1931).
Scholes, Walter V. and Marie V., "United States and Ecuador, 1909–1913," *Americas*, 19 (1963), 276.

51.18.7.2 Venezuelan Crises of 1902–1903, 1907

Hendrickson, Embert J., "Root's Watchful Waiting and the Venezuelan Controversy," *Americas*, 23 (1966), 115.
Livermore, S. W., "Theodore Roosevelt, the American Navy, and the Venezuelan Crisis of 1902–1903," *AHR*, 51 (1946), 452.

51.18.8 Canada

Bailey, Thomas A., "Theodore Roosevelt and the Alaska Boundary Settlement," *Can. Hist. Rev.*, 18 (1937), 123.
Ellis, Lewis E., *Reciprocity 1911* (1939).
Swartz, W. G., "Proposed Canadian-American Reciprocity Agreement of 1911," *Jour. Econ. and Bus. Hist.*, 3 (1930), 118.

51.18.9 East Asia

51.18.9.1 General

Braisted, William R., *The United States Navy in the Pacific, 1909–1922* (1970).
Grenville, John A. S., and George B. Young, *Politics, Strategy, and American Diplomacy, 1873–1917* (1966).
Griswold, A. Whitney, *Far Eastern Policy of the United States* (1938).
Reed, Peter Mellish, "Standard Oil in Indonesia, 1898–1928," *Bus. Hist. Rev.*, 32 (1958), 311.

51.18.9.2 Japan

Bailey, Thomas A., "Root-Takahira Agreement of 1908," *Pac. Hist. Rev.*, 9 (1940), 19.
—— *Theodore Roosevelt and Japanese-American Crises* (1934).
Chamberlin, Eugene K., "Japanese Scare at Magdalena Bay," *Pac. Hist. Rev.*, 24 (1955), 345.
Clinard, O. J., *Japan's Influence on American Naval Power* (1947).
Curry, Roy W., *Woodrow Wilson and Far Eastern Policy* (1957).
Daniels, Roger, *Politics of Prejudice: Anti-Japanese Movement in California* (1962).
Dulles, Foster R., *Forty Years of American-Japanese Relations* (1937).
Esthus, Raymond A., "Taft Katsura Agreement—Reality or Myth," *Jour. Mod. Hist.*, 31 (1959), 46.
—— *Theodore Roosevelt and Japan* (1966).
Gordon, Donald C., "Roosevelt's 'Smart Yankee Trick'," *Pac. Hist. Rev.*, 30 (1961), 351.
Minger, Ralph E., "Taft's Missions to Japan," *Pac. Hist. Rev.*, 30 (1961), 279.
Neu, Charles E., *An Uncertain Friendship: Theodore Roosevelt and Japan, 1906–1909* (1967).
Treat, P. J., *Diplomatic Relations between the United States and Japan, 1853–1905*, vol. III (1938).
—— *Japan and the United States, 1853–1921* (1921).
Tupper, Eleanor, and G. E. McReynolds, *Japan in American Opinion* (1937).

51.18.9.3 Russo-Japanese War

Dennett, Tyler, *Roosevelt and the Russo-Japanese War* (1925).
Godwin, Robert K., "Russia and Portsmouth Peace Conference," *American Slavic and East European Review*, 9 (1950), 279.
May, Ernest R., "Far Eastern Policy of the United States in the Period of the Russo-Japanese War: Russian View," *AHR*, 62 (1956–1957), 345.
Okamoto, Shumpei, *Japanese Oligarchy and the Russo-Japanese War* (1970).
Thorson, W. B., "American Opinion and the Portsmouth Conference," *AHR*, 53 (1948), 439.
——— "Pacific Northwest Opinion on the Russo–Japanese War of 1904–1905," *Pac. Northw. Quar.*, 35 (1944), 305.
Trani, Eugene P., *Treaty of Portsmouth: Adventure in American Diplomacy* (1969).
White, John A., *Diplomacy of the Russo–Japanese War* (1964).

51.18.9.4 China

Braisted, William R., "China, the United States Navy and Bethlehem Steel Company, 1909–1929," *Bus. Hist. Rev.*, 42 (1968), 50.
——— "United States and American China Development Company," *Far Eastern Quar.*, 11 (1951), 147.
Cameron, Meribeth E., *Reform Movement in China, 1898–1912* (1931).
Clyde, P. H., ed., *United States Policy toward China, 1838–1939* (1940).
Field, Frederick V., *American Participation in China Consortiums* (1931).
Finch, G. A., "American Diplomacy and Financing China," *Am. Jour. Internatl. Law*, 16 (1922), 25.
Israel, Jerry, *Progressivism and the Open Door: America and China, 1905–1921* (1971).
Langer, William L., *Diplomacy of Imperialism* (1951).
McCormick, Thomas J., *China Market, 1893–1901* (1967).
Pan, Shü-Lun, *Trade with China* (1924).
Pan, Stephen C. Y., *American Diplomacy Concerning Manchuria* (1938).
Remer, C. F., *Foreign Investments in China* (1933).
——— *Foreign Trade of China* (1926).
Ride, John G., *Manchu Abdication and the Powers* (1935).
Varg, Paul, *Making of a Myth: The United States and China, 1879–1912* (1968).
——— *Missionaries, Chinese, and Diplomats: The American Protestant Missionary Movement in China, 1890–1952* (1958).
Vevier, Charles, *United States and China, 1906–1913: Finance and Diplomacy* (1955).

51.18.10 Europe and Quest for Peace

Anderson, Eugene N., *First Moroccan Crisis, 1904–1906* (1930).
Askew, William C., and J. Fred Rippy, "United States and Europe's Strife, 1908–1913," *Jour. of Politics*, 4 (1942), 68.
Davis, Calvin D., *United States and the First Hague Conference* (1962).
Ford, T. K., "Genesis of the First Hague Conference," *Pol. Sci. Quar.*, 51 (1936), 354.
Holls, Frederick W., *Peace Conference at the Hague* (1900).
Mahan, Alfred T., *Lessons of War with Spain* (1899).
Scott, James B., *Hague Peace Conferences*, vol. I (1909).
Tate, Merze, *Disarmament Illusion* (1942).

See also 10.3 for biographies/writings of:

Bryan, William Jennings, 1860–1925
Carnegie, Andrew, 1835–1919
Holt, Hamilton, 1872–1951
Reid, Whitelaw, 1837–1912
Roosevelt, Theodore, 1858–1919
Taft, William H., 1857–1930

Tower, Charlemagne, 1848–1923
White, Henry, 1850–1927
Wilson, Woodrow, 1856–1924

51.18.11 Arbitration

Campbell, John P., "Taft, Roosevelt, and the Arbitration Treaties of 1911," *JAH*,
53 (1966), 279.
Foster, John W., *Arbitration and the Hague Court* (1904).
World Peace Foundation, *Arbitration and the United States* (1926).

51.18.12 Great Britain

Campbell, A. E., *Great Britain and the United States, 1895–1903* (1960).
Campbell, Charles S., Jr., *Anglo-American Understanding, 1898–1903* (1957).
Ferguson, John H., *American Diplomacy and the Boer War* (1939).
Gelber, Lionel M., *Rise of Anglo-American Friendship, 1898–1906* (1938).
Heindel, Richard H., *American Impact on Great Britain* (1940).
Perkins, Bradford, *Great Rapprochement: England and the United States, 1895–
1914* (1968).
Russett, Bruce M., *Community and Contention: Britain and America in the Twen-
tieth Century* (1963).
Watt, D. C., "America and British Foreign Policy-Making Elite, 1895–1956," *Rev.
Politics*, 25 (1963), 3.

51.18.13 Russia

Lebedev, Viacheslav Vladimirovich, *Russko-Amerikanskie Ekonomicheskie Otno-
sheniia, 1900–1917 gg.* (1964).
Lincoln, A., "Theodore Roosevelt and the First Russian-American Crisis," *So.
Calif. Quar.*, 45 (1963), 323.
Zabriskie, E. H., *American-Russian Rivalry in the Far East* (1946).

See also 51.18.9.3, Russo-Japanese War.

51.18.14 Middle East

DeNovo, John A., *American Interests and Policies in the Middle East, 1900–1939*
(1963).
——— "Oil Policy Abroad, 1918–1920," *AHR*, 61 (1956), 854.
Goldblatt, Charles I., "Impact of Balfour Declaration in America," *Am. Jew.
Hist. Quar.*, 57 (1968), 455.
Yeselson, Abraham, *United States-Persian Diplomatic Relations, 1883–1921*
(1956).

51.19 WILSONIAN DIPLOMACY

51.19.1 General

Buehrig, Edward H., ed., *Wilson's Foreign Policy in Perspective* (1957).
Buehrig, Edward H., *Woodrow Wilson and Balance of Power* (1955).
Dudden, Arthur P., ed., *Woodrow Wilson and the World of Today: Essays* (1957).
George, Alexander L., and Juliette L. George, *Woodrow Wilson and Colonel
House* (1956).
Hoover, Herbert, *The Ordeal of Woodrow Wilson* (1958).
Levin, N. Gordon, Jr., *Woodrow Wilson and World Politics* (1968).
Link, Arthur S., *Wilson the Diplomatist* (1957).
Notter, Harley, *The Foreign Policy of Wilson* (1937).

Osgood, Robert E., "Woodrow Wilson, Collective Security, and the Lessons of History," *Confluence,* 5 (1957), 341.

Parrini, Carl, *Heir to Empire: United States Economic Diplomacy, 1916–1923* (1969).

Smith, Daniel M., *Aftermath of War: Bainbridge Colby and Wilsonian Diplomacy, 1920–1921* (1970).

*   *   *   *   *   *   *

Turnbull, L. S., comp., *Woodrow Wilson, a Selected Bibliography* (1948).

Watson, Richard L., Jr., "Woodrow Wilson and His Interpreters, 1947–1957," *MVHR,* 44 (1957), 207.

51.19.2 Latin America

Baker, George W., Jr., "Wilson Administration and Nicaragua," *Americas,* 22 (1966), 339.

—— "Wilson Administration and Panama," *Jour. Inter-Am. Studies,* 8 (1966), 279.

—— "Wilson Administration's Relations with Honduras," *Americas,* 21 (1965), 3.

Goodell, Stephen, "Woodrow Wilson in Latin America," *Historian,* 28 (1965), 96.

Smith, Daniel M., "Bainbridge Colby and Good Neighbor Policy," *MVHR,* 50 (1963), 55.

51.19.3 Mexico

Clendenen, Clarence C., *United States and Pancho Villa* (1961).

Guerrero Yoacham, Christián, *Las conferencias del Niagara Falls* (1966).

Meyer, Michael C., "Mexican-German Conspiracy of 1915," *Americas,* 23 (1966), 76.

Quirk, Robert E., *Affair of Honor: Woodrow Wilson and Occupation of Veracruz* (1962).

See also 51.18.4, Foreign Relations and Defense–Mexico.

51.19.4 Caribbean

51.19.4.1 General

Adler, Selig, "Bryan and Wilsonian Caribbean Penetration," *Hisp. Am. Hist. Rev.,* 20 (1940), 198.

Baker, George W., Jr., "Wilson Administration and Cuba," *Mid-America,* 46 (1964), 48.

Tansill, Charles C., *Purchase of Danish West Indies* (1932).

See also 51.18.6, Foreign Relations and Defense–Caribbean.

51.19.4.2 Haitian Intervention

Chapman, Charles E., "Development of Intervention in Haiti," *Hisp. Am. Hist. Rev.,* 7 (1927), 299.

Kelsey, Carl, "American Intervention in Haiti," Am. Acad. Pol. Soc. Sci., *Annals,* 100 (1922), 109.

McCrocklin, J. H., *Garde d'Haiti, 1915–1934: Twenty Years of Organization and Training by the Marine Corps* (1957).

51.19.5 East Asia

Beers, Burton F., *Vain Endeavor: Robert Lansing's Attempts to End American-Japanese Rivalry* (1962).

Bose, Nemai Sadhan, *American Attitude and Policy to the Nationalist Movement in China, 1911–1921* (1970).

Chi, Madeleine, *China Diplomacy, 1914–1918* (1970).

Cohen, Warren I., "America and the May Fourth Movement: Response to Chinese Nationalism, 1917–1921," *Pac. Hist. Rev.*, 35 (1966), 83.

Coletta, Paolo E., " 'Most Thankless Task': Bryan and the California Alien Land Legislation," *Pac. Hist. Rev.*, 36 (1967), 163.

Curry, Roy W., *Woodrow Wilson and Far Eastern Policy, 1913* (1957).

Daniels, Roger, *Politics of Prejudice: Anti-Japanese Movement in California* (1962).

Field, Frederick V., *American Participation in Chinese Consortiums* (1931).

Fifield, Russell, *Woodrow Wilson and the Far East: Shantung Question* (1952).

Hosack, Robert E., "Shantung Question and the Senate," *So. Atl. Quar.*, 43 (1944), 181.

Israel, Jerry, " 'For God, for China, and for Yale'–Open Door in Action," *AHR*, 75 (1970), 796.

LaFargue, Thomas Edward, *China and the World War* (1937).

Li, T'ien-yi, *Woodrow Wilson's China Policy, 1913–1917* (1952).

Olin, Spencer C., Jr., "European Immigrant and Oriental Alien: Acceptance and Rejection by California Legislature of 1913," *Pac. Hist. Rev.*, 25 (1966), 303.

Pugach, Noel, "Making the Open Door Work: Paul S. Reinsch in China, 1913–1919," *Pac. Hist. Rev.*, 38 (1969), 157.

Scheiber, Harry N., "World War I as Entrepreneurial Opportunity: Willard Straight and American International Corporation," *Pol. Sci. Quar.*, 84 (1969), 486.

See also 10.3 for biographies/writings of:

Rockhill, William W., 1854–1914

Straight, Willard D., 1880–1918

See also 51.18.9, Foreign Relations and Defense–East Asia.

51.19.6 Europe

Brooks, Sidney, *America and Germany, 1918–1925* (1927).

Evans, Laurence, *United States Policy and the Partition of Turkey, 1914–1924* (1965).

Fowler, W. B., *British American Relations, 1917–1918: Role of Sir William Wiseman* (1969).

Gerson, Louis L., *Woodrow Wilson and Rebirth of Poland, 1914–1920: Influence of Minority Groups of Foreign Origin* (1953).

Mamatey, Victor S., *United States and East Central Europe, 1914–1918* (1957).

Martin, Laurence W., *Peace without Victory: Wilson and British Liberals* (1958).

Tarulis, Albert N., *American-Baltic Relations, 1918–1922* (1965).

Willert, Arthur, *Road to Safety: Anglo-American Relations* (1953).

Yates, Louis A. R., *United States and French Security, 1917–1921* (1957).

51.20 BACKGROUND OF WORLD WAR I

51.20.1 General

Albertini, Luigi, *Origins of War of 1914*, Isabella M. Massey, trans. (3 vols., 1952–1957).

Fay, Sidney B., *The Origins of the World War* (2 vols., 1931).

Hallgarten, G. W. F., *Imperialismus vor 1914* (2 vols., 1951).

Paxson, Frederick L., *American Democracy and the World War* (3 vols., 1936–1948).

Schmitt, Bernadotte E., *Coming of War, 1914* (2 vols., 1930).
Smith, Daniel M., *Great Departure: United States and World War I* (1965).

* * * * * * *

Cohen, Warren I., *American Revisionists: Intervention in World War I* (1967).
Smith, Daniel M., "National Interest and American Intervention, 1917: Historiographical Appraisal," *JAH*, 52 (1965), 5.

51.20.2 Problems of Neutrality

51.20.2.1 General

Borchard, Edwin, and W. P. Lage, *Neutrality for the United States* (1940).
Grattan, C. Harley, *Why We Fought* (1929).
May, Ernest R., *World War and American Isolation, 1914–1917* (1959).
Millis, Walter, *Road to War* (1935).
Morrissey, Alice M., *American Defense of Neutral Rights* (1939).
Schmitt, B. E., "American Neutrality," *Jour. Mod. Hist.*, 8 (1936), 200.
Seymour, Charles, *American Neutrality* (1935).
Smith, Daniel M., *Robert Lansing and American Neutrality, 1914–1917* (1958).
Tansill, Charles C., *America Goes to War* (1938).
Van Alstyne, R. W., "Policy of United States Regarding the Declaration of London," *Jour. Mod. Hist.*, 7 (1935), 435.

See also 10.3 for biographies/writings of:

Bryan, William Jennings, 1860–1925
Daniels, Josephus, 1862–1948
Davison, Henry P., 1867–1922
House, Edward M., 1858–1938
Houston, David F., 1866–1940
Kitchin, Claude, 1869–1923
Lansing, Robert, 1864–1928
McAdoo, William G., 1863–1941
Morrow, Dwight, 1873–1931
Page, Walter H., 1855–1918
Reed, John, 1887–1920
Roosevelt, Theodore, 1858–1919
Taft, William H., 1857–1930
Tumulty, Joseph P., 1879–1954
Villard, Oswald G., 1872–1949
White, Henry, 1850–1927
White, William Allen, 1868–1944
Whitlock, Brand, 1869–1934
Wilson, Woodrow, 1856–1924

51.20.2.2 Politics

Allen, Howard W., "Republican Reformers and Foreign Policy, 1913–1917," *Mid-America*, 44 (1962), 222.
Buchanan, Russell, "Theodore Roosevelt and American Neutrality," *AHR*, 43 (1938), 7.
Dubin, Martin D., "Elihu Root and Advocacy of League of Nations, 1914–1917," *West. Pol. Quar.*, 19 (1966), 439.
Kennedy, Padraic C., "LaFollette's Foreign Policy," *Wis. Mag. Hist.*, 46 (1963), 287.

51.20.2.3 Economic Pressures

Birdsall, Paul, "Neutrality and Economic Pressures," *Science and Society*, 3 (1939), 217.

Fuller, J. V., "Munitions Traffic," *Jour. Mod. Hist.*, 6 (1934), 280.
Phillips, E. C., "American Participation in Belligerent Commercial Controls," *Am. Jour. Internatl. Law*, 27 (1933), 675.
Van Alstyne, R. W., "Private American Loans to the Allies," *Pac. Hist. Rev.*, 2 (1933), 180.

51.20.2.4 Blockade and Effects on American Shipping

Bailey, Thomas A., "German Documents Lusitania," *Jour. Mod. Hist.*, 8 (1936), 320.
———— "Sinking of the Lusitania," *AHR*, 41 (1935), 54.
Borchard, Edwin, "Neutrality Claims against Great Britain," *Am. Jour. Internatl. Law*, 21 (1927), 764.
von Rintelen, Franz, *Dark Invader* (1933).
Siney, Marion C., *Allied Blockade of Germany, 1914–1916* (1957).
Smith, Gaddis, *Britain's Clandestine Submarines, 1914–1915* (1964).

See also 10.3 for biographies/writings of:

Daniels, Josephus, 1862–1948
Lane, Franklin K., 1864–1921
Roosevelt, Franklin D., 1882–1945

51.20.3 Opponents of War and Pacifists, 1914–1918

Bourne, Randolph S., *War and the Intellectuals: Collected Essays, 1915–1919*, Carl Resek, ed. (1964).
Brock, Peter, *Pacifism in the United States: Colonial Era to First World War* (1968).
Child, C. J., *German-Americans in Politics* (1939).
Cuddy, Edward, "Pro-Germanism and American Catholicism, 1914–1917," *Cath. Hist. Rev.*, 54 (1968), 427.
Curti, Merle E., *Peace or War: American Struggle, 1636–1936* (1936).
Degen, M. L., *History of the Woman's Peace Party* (1939).
Grubbs, Frank L., Jr., *Struggle for Labor Loyalty: Gompers, A.F. of L., and Pacifists, 1917–1920* (1968).
Guthrie, M. B., "Anti-War Minority in Congress," *Historian*, 2 (1940), 85.
Herman, Sondra R., *Eleven against War: American Internationalist Thought, 1898–1921* (1969).
Hershey, Burnet, *Odyssey of Henry Ford and the Great Peace Ship* (1967).
Nearing, Scott, *Great Madness* (1917).
Peterson, Horace C., and Gilbert C. Fite, *Opponents of War, 1917–1918* (1957).
Schieber, Clara E., *American Sentiment toward Germany* (1923).
Stephenson, George M., "Attitude of Swedish-Americans toward the World War," *Miss. Valley Hist. Assoc., Proc.*, 10 (1918), 79.
Syrett, H. C., "Business Press and American Neutrality," *MVHR*, 32 (1945), 215.
Thomas, Norman, *Conscientious Objector* (1923).
Wittke, Carl, *German-Americans and the World War* (1936).

See also 10.3 for biographies/writings of:

Addams, Jane, 1860–1935
Bourne, Randolph S., 1886–1919
Debs, Eugene V., 1855–1926
Ford, Henry, 1863–1947
Kitchin, Claude, 1869–1923
La Follette, Robert M., 1855–1925
London, Meyer, 1871–1926
Norris, George W., 1861–1944
Young, Art, 1866–1943

51.20.4 Press and Propaganda

Peterson, Horace C., *Propaganda for War* (1939).
Rappaport, Armin, *British Press and Wilsonian Neutrality* (1951).
Read, J. M., *Atrocity Propaganda* (1941).
Squires, J. D., *British Propaganda* (1935).

51.20.5 Preparedness Campaign

Perry, Ralph B., *Plattsburg Movement* (1942).
Swisher, C. B., "Control of War Preparations," *Am. Pol. Sci. Rev.*, 34 (1940),
1085.

See also 10.3 for biographies/writings of:

Lodge, Henry Cabot, 1850–1924
Roosevelt, Theodore, 1858–1919
Wood, Leonard, 1860–1927

51.20.6 Entry into War

Birnbaum, Karl E., *Peace Moves and U-Boat Warfare: Germany's Policy toward
the United States, April 18, 1916–January 9, 1917* (1958).
Dupuy, Richard E., *Five Days to War, April 2–6, 1917* (1967).
Gerard, James W., *My Four Years in Germany* (1917).
Spencer, Samuel R., Jr., *Decision for War, 1917: Laconia Sinking and Zimmerman
Telegram* (1953).
Tuchman, Barbara, *Zimmerman Telegram* (1958).
von Bernstorff, Johann, *Memoirs* (1936).
von Bernstorff, Johann, *My Three Years in America* (1920).
von Papen, Franz, *Memoirs* (1952).

51.21 AMERICAN PARTICIPATION IN WORLD WAR I

51.21.1 General Military History

American Heritage, *American Heritage History of World War I*, Samuel L. A.
Marshall, ed. (1964).
Baldwin, Hanson W., *World War I: Outline History* (1962).
Esposito, Vincent J., ed., *Concise History of World War I* (1964).
Falls, Cyril, *The Great War* (1959).
Terraine, John, *Western Front, 1914–1918* (1964).

51.21.2 American Military History

51.21.2.1 General

Coffman, Edward M., *War to End All Wars: Military in World War I* (1968).
Crozier, Emmet, *American Reporters on the Western Front, 1914–1918* (1959).
De Weerd, Harvey A., *President Wilson Fights His War* (1968).
Frothingham, Thomas G., *American Reinforcement in World War* (1927).
Official Record of the United States in the Great War (1923).

51.21.2.2 Army

Barnett, Corelli, *The Swordbearers: Supreme Command in First World War*
(1964).
Dickinson, John, *Building of an Army* (1922).

Harbord, James G., *American Army in France* (1936).
────── *Leaves from War Diary* (1925).
Trask, David F., *United States in Supreme War Council, 1917–1918* (1961).
U.S. Army War College, Historical Section, *Order of Battle of Land Forces in the World War* (1931).

See also 10.3 for biographies/writings of:

Baker, Newton D., 1871–1937
Eisenhower, Dwight D., 1890–1969
Liggett, Hunter, 1857–1935
MacArthur, Douglas, 1880–1964
March, Peyton C., 1864–1955
Marshall, George C., 1880–1959
Mitchell, William "Billy," 1879–1936
Pershing, John J., 1860–1948

51.21.2.3 Navy

Frothingham, Thomas G., *Naval History of World War* (3 vols., 1926).
Guichard, Louis, *Naval Blockade, 1914–1918* (1930).
Mitchell, Donald William, *History of Modern American Navy* (1946).
Sims, William S., and B. J. Hendrick, *Victory at Sea* (1920).
Sprout, H. H., and Margaret Sprout, *Rise of American Naval Power* (1939).
Westcott, Allan, ed., *American Sea Power* (1947).

See also 10.3 for biographies/writings of:

Daniels, Josephus, 1862–1948
Mahan, Alfred Thayer, 1840–1914
Roosevelt, Franklin D., 1882–1945
Sims, William S., 1858–1936

51.21.2.4 Air Service

Holley, Irving B., Jr., *Ideas and Weapons: The Aerial Weapon during World War I* (1953).
Hudson, James J., *Hostile Skies: American Air Service in World War I* (1968).
Parsons, Edwin C., *Great Adventure: Lafayette Escadrille* (1937).

See also 10.3 for biographies/writings of:

Mitchell, William "Billy," 1879–1936
Rickenbacker, Edward V., 1890–1973

51.21.3 Food and Relief

Gay, G. I., *Statistical Review of Relief Operations* (1925).
Hoover, Herbert, *An American Epic* (4 vols., 1959–1964). European famine.
Surface, F. M., and R. L. Bland, *American Food in World War* (1931).
Szajkowski, Zosa, "Private and Organized American Jewish Overseas Relief," *Am. Jew. Hist. Quar.*, 57 (1967), 52.

51.21.4 Allied Diplomacy

Bailey, Thomas A., *Policy of United States toward Neutrals* (1942).
Fowler, W. B., *British-American Relations, 1917–1918: Role of Sir William Wiseman* (1969).
Mayer, Arno J., *Political Origins of New Diplomacy, 1917–1918* (1959).

O'Grady, Joseph P., ed., *Immigrants' Influence on Wilson's Peace Policies* (1967).
Seymour, Charles, *American Diplomacy during the World War* (1934).

51.21.5 Armistice

Rudin, H. R., *Armistice, 1918* (1944).

51.21.6 Pictorial History

American Heritage, *American Heritage History of World War I*, Samuel L. A. Marshall, ed. (1964).
Freidel, Frank, *Over There* (1964).
Hecht, George J., ed., *The War in Cartoons* (1919).
Mackey, Frank J., and M. W. Jernegan, eds., *Forward—March: Photographic Record of America in the World War and Post War Social Upheaval* (2 vols., 1935).
Robinson, Boardman, *Cartoons of the War* (1915).

51.22 AMERICA AND THE SOVIET UNION

51.22.1 General

Anderson, Paul H., *Attitude of American Leftist Leaders Toward Russian Revolution* (1942).
Filene, Peter G., *Americans and Soviet Experiment, 1917–1933* (1967).
Gankin, Olga H., and H. H. Fisher, *Bolsheviks and World War* (1940).
Kennan, George F., *Russia and the West under Lenin and Stalin* (1961).
—— *Soviet-American Relations, 1917–1920* (2 vols., 1956–1958).
Lasch, Christopher, *American Liberals and the Russian Revolution* (1962).
Schuman, Frederick L., *American Policy toward Russia since 1917* (1928).
Strakhovsky, Leonid Ivan, *American Opinion about Russia, 1917–1920* (1961).
Thompson, John M., *Russia, Bolshevism, and Versailles Peace* (1966).
Ullman, Richard H., *Anglo-Soviet Relations, 1917–1921* (2 vols., 1961).
Warth, Robert D., *Allies and Russian Revolution* (1954).

51.22.2 Armed Intervention in Soviet Union

Bradley, John, *Allied Intervention in Russia, 1917–1920* (1968).
Graves, William S., *America's Siberian Adventure* (1931).
Lasch, Christopher, "American Intervention in Siberia," *Pol. Sci. Quar.*, 77 (1962), 205.
Maddox, Robert James, "Woodrow Wilson, the Russian Embassy, and Siberian Intervention," *Pac. Hist. Rev.*, 36 (1967), 435.
Morley, James W., *The Japanese Thrust into Siberia, 1918* (1957).
Unterberger, Betty M., comp., *American Intervention in Russian Civil War* (1969).
Unterberger, Betty M., *America's Siberian Expedition, 1918–1920* (1956).
White, John A., *Siberian Intervention* (1950).
Williams, William A., "American Intervention in Russia, 1917–1920," *Studies on the Left*, 3, no. 4 (1963), 24; 4, no. 4 (1964), 39.

51.23 HOME FRONT

51.23.1 General

Churchill, Allen, *Over Here! Informal Re-creation of Home Front in World War I* (1968).

Leuchtenburg, William E., *Perils of Prosperity, 1914–1932* (1958).
Paxson, Frederick L., *American Democracy and World War* (3 vols., 1936–1948).
Soule, George, *Prosperity Decade, 1917–1929* (1947).
Tindall, George B., *Emergence of the New South, 1913–1945* (1967).

*   *   *   *   *   *   *

Drewry, E. R., "Historical Units of Agencies of the First World War," National Archives, *Bulletin*, no. 4 (1942), 1.
Holbrook, F. F., "Collection of State War Service Records," *AHR*, 25 (1919), 72.
Leland, Waldo G., and Newton D. Mereness, comps., *Introduction to American Official Sources for the Economic and Social History of the World War* (1926).
Mereness, Newton D., ed., "American Historical Activities during the World War.," Am. Hist. Assoc., *Report,* 1 (1919), 204.
Wright, A. R., "Food and Society: War-Time Archives," *Am. Scholar,* 7 (1938), 243.

See also 10.3 for biographies/writings of:

Baker, Newton D., 1871–1937
Baker, Ray Stannard, 1879–1946
Beck, James M., 1861–1936
Creel, George, 1876–1953
Daniels, Josephus, 1862–1948
Debs, Eugene V., 1855–1926
Du Pont Family
Gompers, Samuel, 1850–1924
Holmes, Oliver Wendell, Jr., 1841–1935
Hoover, Herbert, 1874–1964
House, Edward M., 1858–1938
Houston, David F., 1866–1940
Kellogg, Frank B., 1856–1937
Lane, Franklin K., 1864–1921
Lansing, Robert, 1864–1928
McAdoo, William G., 1863–1941
Morrow, Dwight, 1873–1931
Norris, George W., 1861–1944
Page, Walter H., 1855–1918
Roosevelt, Franklin D., 1882–1945
Root, Elihu, 1845–1937
Tumulty, Joseph P., 1879–1954
Wilson, Woodrow, 1856–1924

51.23.2 Wartime Politics and Congress

Hirschfeld, Charles, "Progressivism and World War I," *Mid-America,* 45 (1963), 139.
Livermore, Seward W., *Politics Is Adjourned: Wilson and the War Congress* (1966).
Newby, Idus A., "States' Rights and Southern Congressmen during World War I," *Phylon,* 24 (1963), 34.

51.23.3 War Administration

51.23.3.1 General
Beaver, Daniel R., *Newton D. Baker and the American War Effort, 1917–1919* (1966).
Crowder, E. H., *Spirit of Selective Service* (1920).

Crowell, Benedict, and R. F. Wilson, *How America Went to War* (6 vols., 1921).
Willoughby, William F., *Government Organization in War Time* (1919).

51.23.3.2 Food Production

Mullendore, William C., *History of United States Food Administration* (1941).
Surface, F. M., *American Pork Production in the World War* (1926).

51.23.3.3 Finance and Inflation

Clark, John M., *Costs of World War* (1931).
Mitchell, Wesley C., *History of Prices during War* (1919).
Noyes, Alexander D., *War Period of American Finance* (1926).
Stein, Herbert, *Government Price Policy during the World War* (1939).

51.23.3.4 Industry

Baruch, Bernard M., *American Industry in War*, R. H. Hippelheuser, ed. (1941).
Clarkson, G. B., *Industrial America in World War* (1923).
Himmelberg, Robert R., "The War Industries Board," *JAH*, 52 (1965), 43.
Kester, R. B., "War Industries Board," *Am. Pol. Sci. Rev.*, 34 (1940), 655.
Urofsky, Melvin I., *Big Steel and Wilson Administration* (1969).

51.23.3.5 Transportation

Crowell, Benedict, and R. F. Wilson, *Road to France* (2 vols., 1921).
Cunningham, William J., "Railroads under Government Operation," *Quar. Jour. Econ.*, 35 (1921), 228; 36 (1921), 30.
Elderton, W. P., *Shipping Problems* (1927).
Hines, Walker D., *War History of American Railroads* (1928).
Kerr, K. Austin, "Decision for Federal Control: Wilson, McAdoo, and the Railroads, 1917," *JAH*, 54 (1967), 550.
Salter, James A., *Allied Shipping Control* (1921).
Smith, Darrell H., and P. V. Betters, *United States Shipping Board* (1931).

51.23.3.6 Labor

Bernhardt, Joshua, *Railroad Labor Board: History, Activities and Organization* (1923).
Bing, Alexander, *War-Time Strikes* (1921).
"National War Labor Board History," U.S. Bureau of Labor Statistics, *Bulletin*, no. 287 (1922). Entire issue.
Gompers, Samuel, *American Labor and the War* (1919).
Grubbs, Frank L., Jr., *Struggle for Labor Loyalty: Gompers, A.F. of L., and Pacifists, 1917–1920* (1968).
Watkins, Gordon S., *Labor Problems and Labor Administration during World War* (2 vols., 1920).

51.23.4 Civil Liberties

Chafee, Zechariah, Jr., *Free Speech in the United States* (1941).
Jensen, J. M., *Price of Vigilance* (1968). American Protective League.
Johnson, Donald, *Challenge to American Freedoms: World War I and Rise of ACLU* (1963).
Mock, James R., *Censorship, 1917* (1941).
Peterson, Horace Cornelius, and G. C. Fite, *Opponents of War, 1917–1918* (1957).
Preston, William, Jr., *Aliens and Dissenters: Federal Suppression of Radicals, 1903–1933* (1963).
Scheiber, Harry N., *Wilson Administration and Civil Liberties, 1917–1921* (1960).

See also 51.20.3, Opponents of War and Pacifists, 1914–1918.

51.23.5 Press and Propaganda

Bruntz, George G., *Allied Propaganda and Collapse of German Empire* (1938).
Buchanan, Russell, "American Editors Examine War Aims," *Pac. Hist. Rev.,* 9
(1940), 253.
Creel, George, *How We Advertised America* (1920).
Gathings, J. A., *International Law and American Treatment of Alien Enemy
Property* (1940).
Lasswell, Harold D., *Propaganda Technique in the World War* (1927).
Mock, James R., *Censorship, 1917* (1941).
—— and Cedric Larson, *Words That Won the War* (rev. ed., 1968).

51.23.6 Education and Religion

Abrams, Ray H., *Preachers Present Arms* (1933).
Kolbe, P. R., *Colleges in War Time and After* (1919).
Seabrook, John H., "Bishop Manning and World War I," *Hist. Mag. Prot. Episc.
Church,* 36 (1967), 301.
Todd, Lewis P., *Wartime Relations of Federal Government and Public Schools,
1917–1918* (1945).

51.23.7 Negroes

Kellogg, Charles F., *History of the National Association for the Advancement of
Colored People, 1909–1920* (1967).
Leavell, R. H., et al., *Negro Migration in 1916–1917* (1919).
Reid, Ira DeA., *Negro Immigrant* (1939).
Scott, Emmett J., *Negro Migration during War* (1920).

*   *   *   *   *   *   *

Ross, Frank A., and Louise V. Kennedy, *Bibliography of Negro Migration* (1934).

51.23.8 State Studies

Costrell, Edwin, *How Maine Viewed War* (1940).
Crichton, J. C., *Missouri and World War* (1947).
Cummins, C. C., *Indiana Public Opinion and World War* (1945).
Holbrook, Franklin, and Livia Appel, *Minnesota in the War* (2 vols., 1928–1932).

51.24 VERSAILLES CONFERENCE AND LEAGUE OF NATIONS

51.24.1 General

Bailey, Thomas A., *Woodrow Wilson and Lost Peace* (1944).
Baker, Ray Stannard, *Woodrow Wilson and World Settlement* (3 vols., 1922).
Birdsall, Paul, *Versailles Twenty Years After* (1941).
Levin, Norman G., *Wilson and World Politics* (1968).
Marston, Frank S., *Peace Conference of 1919* (1944).
Mayer, Arno J., *Politics of Peacemaking: Versailles, 1918–1919* (1967).
Temperley, H. W. V., et al., *History of Peace Conference* (6 vols., 1920–1924).

*   *   *   *   *   *   *

Binkley, R. C., "Ten Years of Peace Conference History," *Jour. Mod. Hist.,* 1
(1929), 607.
Birdsall, Paul, "Second Decade of Peace Conference History," *Jour. Mod. Hist.,*
11 (1939), 362.

51.24.2 Special Topics

Bartlett, Ruhl J., *League to Enforce Peace* (1944).
Briggs, Mitchell P., *Herron and European Settlement* (1932).
Burnett, Philip M., *Reparation at Paris Peace Conference* (2 vols., 1940).
Degen, M. L., *History of Woman's Peace Party* (1939).
Gelfand, Lawrence E., *The Inquiry: American Preparations for Peace, 1917–1919* (1963).
Martin, Laurence W., *Peace Without Victory: Wilson and British Liberals* (1958).
Miller, Hunter, *Drafting the Covenant* (1928).
Shotwell, James T., ed., *Origins of International Labor Organization* (2 vols., 1934).
Tillman, Seth P., *Anglo-American Relations at Paris Peace Conference of 1919* (1961).

51.24.3 Contemporary Accounts and Reminiscences

Bandholtz, H. H., *Undiplomatic Diary* (1933).
Baruch, Bernard M., *Making of the Reparation and Economic Sections of the Treaty* (1920).
Bonsal, Stephen, *Unfinished Business* (1944).
Haskins, Charles H., and Robert H. Lord, *Some Problems of the Peace Conference* (1920).
Hoover, Herbert, *Ordeal of Wilson* (1958).
House, Edward M., and Charles Seymour, eds., *What Really Happened at Paris* (1921).
Keynes, John M., *Economic Consequences of Peace* (1919).
Lansing, Robert, *The Big Four and Others of the Peace Conference* (1921).
Lloyd-George, David, *Memoirs of Peace Conference* (1939).
────── *War Memoirs* (6 vols., 1933–1937).
Miller, Hunter, *My Diary at Peace Conference* (21 vols., 1928).
Nicolson, Harold, *Peacemaking, 1919* (1933).
Noble, George B., *Policies and Opinions at Paris* (1935).
Poincaré, Raymond, *Memoirs* (1931).
Seymour, Charles, *Letters from Paris Peace Conference*, Harold B. Whiteman, Jr., ed. (1965).
Shotwell, James T., *At the Paris Peace Conference* (1937).
Thompson, Charles T., *Peace Conference Day by Day* (1920).

See also 10.3 for biographies/writings of:

Baruch, Bernard M., 1870–1965
Beveridge, Albert J., 1862–1927
Bliss, Tasker H., 1853–1930
Gibbons, James, 1834–1921
Gompers, Samuel, 1850–1924
Hoover, Herbert, 1874–1964
House, Edward M., 1858–1938
Houston, David F., 1866–1940
Lansing, Robert, 1864–1928
Lodge, Henry C., 1850–1924
Moore, John Bassett, 1860–1947
Norris, George W., 1861–1944
Reed, John, 1887–1920
Roosevelt, Franklin D., 1882–1945
Root, Elihu, 1845–1937
Taft, William H., 1857–1930
Tumulty, Joseph P., 1879–1954
Villard, Oswald G., 1872–1949
White, Henry, 1850–1927

Whitlock, Brand, 1869–1934
Wilson, Woodrow, 1856–1924

51.24.4 Domestic Politics

Adler, Selig, "Congressional Election of 1918," *So. Atl. Quar.*, 36 (1937), 4.
Bailey, Thomas A., *Woodrow Wilson and Great Betrayal* (1945).
Berdahl, C. A., *Policy of United States with Respect to League* (1932).
Fleming, Denna F., *United States and League of Nations* (1932).
Grantham, D. W., "Southern Senators and League," *No. Car. Hist. Rev.*, 26 (1949), 187.
Lancaster, James L., "The Protestant Churches and the Fight for Ratification of the Versailles Treaty," *Pub. Opinion Quar.*, 31 (1967/1968), 597.
Livermore, S. W., "Sectional Issue in 1918 Elections," *MVHR*, 35 (1948), 29.
Lodge, Henry C., *Senate and League* (1925).
Logan, Rayford W., *Senate and Versailles Mandate System* (1945).
Stone, Ralph, *The Irreconcilables: The Fight Against the League of Nations* (1970).
Vinson, J. Chalmers, *Referendum for Isolation: Defeat of Article Ten of League of Nations Covenant* (1961).

52   The Twenties

52.1 GENERAL

Braeman, John, et al., eds., *Change and Continuity in Twentieth-Century America: The 1920's* (1968).
Carter, Paul A., *Twenties in America* (1968).
Faulkner, Harold U., *From Versailles to New Deal* (1950).
Hicks, John D., *Republican Ascendancy, 1921–1933* (1960).
Leuchtenburg, William E., *Perils of Prosperity, 1914–32* (1958).
Litt, Edgar, *Political Cultures of Massachusetts* (1965).
May, Henry F., "Shifting Perspectives on the 1920's," *MVHR*, 43 (1956), 405.
Mowry, George E., *Urban Nation, 1920–1960* (1965).
Newby, Idus A., "Southern Agrarians," *Agric. Hist.*, 37 (1963), 143.
Patterson, Robert T., *Great Boom and Panic, 1921–1929* (1965).
Schlesinger, Arthur M., Jr., *The Age of Roosevelt: Crisis of the Old Order, 1919–1933* (1957).
Shannon, David A., *Between the Wars, 1919–1941* (1965).
Shover, John L., ed., *Politics of the Nineteen Twenties* (1970).
Slosson, P. W., *Great Crusade and After* (1930).
Soule, George, *Prosperity Decade, 1917–1929* (1947).
Tindall, George B., *Emergence of New South, 1913–1945* (1967).

*　　*　　*　　*　　*　　*　　*

Kirschner, Don S., "Conflicts and Politics in the 1920's: Historiography," *Mid-America*, 48 (1966), 219.
Noggle, Burl, "The Twenties: Historiographical Frontier," *JAH*, 53 (1966), 299.

See also 21.8, Temperance and Prohibition.

52.2 POPULAR ACCOUNTS

Allen, Frederick L., *Only Yesterday* (1931).
Daniels, Jonathan, *Time between Wars: Armistice to Pearl Harbor* (1966).
Leighton, Isabel, ed., *Aspirin Age* (1949).
Morris, Lloyd, *Not So Long Ago* (1949).
Sann, Paul, *Lawless Decade* (1957).
Schriftgiesser, Karl, *This Was Normalcy* (1948).
Sullivan, Mark, *Our Times*, vols. 5–6 (1933–1935).

52.3 BUSINESS AND ECONOMY

52.3.1 Income and Production

Barger, Harold, *Outlay and Income in United States, 1921–1938* (1942).
Kuznets, Simon, Lillian Epstein, and Elizabeth Jenks, *National Income and Its Composition, 1919–1938* (1941).
Leven, Maurice, et al., *America's Capacity to Consume* (1934).
Mills, Frederick C., *Economic Tendencies in the United States* (1932).
Nourse, Edwin G., et al., *America's Capacity to Produce* (1934).
Schumpeter, Joseph A., *Business Cycles* (rev. ed., 1964).

52.3.2 Business and Economic Thought

Dorfman, Joseph, *The Economic Mind in American Civilization* (3 vols., 1946–1949).
Giedion, Sigfried, *Mechanization Takes Command* (1948).
Heald, Morrell, "Business Thought in the Twenties," *Am. Quar.*, 13 (1961), 126.
Prothro, James W., *Dollar Decade: Business Ideas in the 1920's* (1954).

52.3.3 Government Regulation of Business

Fabricant, Solomon, and R. E. Lipsey, *Trend of Government Activity since 1900* (1952).
Fainsod, Merle, and Lincoln Gordon, *Government and the American Economy* (1941).
Gayer, Arthur D., *Public Works in Prosperity and Depression* (1938).
Goodykoontz, Colin P., "Edward P. Costigan and the Tariff Commission, 1917–1928," *Pac. Hist. Rev.*, 16 (1947), 410.
Hawley, Ellis W., "Secretary Hoover and the Bituminous Coal Problem, 1921–1928," *Bus. Hist. Rev.*, 42 (1968), 247.
Howenstine, E. Jay, Jr., "Public Works Policy in the Twenties," *Social Research*, 13 (1946), 500.
—— "Public Works after World War I," *Jour. Pol. Econ.*, 51 (1943), 523.
Hubbard, Preston J., *Origins of TVA: Muscle Shoals Controversy, 1920–1932* (1961).
Keezer, Dexter M., and Stacy May, *Public Control of Business* (1930).
Lyon, L. S., et al., *Government and Economic Life* (2 vols., 1939–1940).
Wooddy, C. H., *Growth of Federal Government, 1915–1932* (1934).

52.3.4 Monetary and Fiscal Policy

Goldenweiser, Emanuel A., *American Monetary Policy* (1951).
Hendricks, Henry G., *Federal Debt, 1919–1930* (1933).
Ingle, H. Larry, "Dangers of Reaction: Repeal of Revenue Act of 1918," *No. Car. Hist. Rev.*, 44 (1967), 72.
Wicker, Elmus R., *Federal Reserve Monetary Policy, 1917–1933* (1966).
Willoughby, William F., *Financial Operations of the National Government, 1921–1930* (1931).

52.3.5 Money, Banking, and Securities

Clarke, Stephen V. O., *Central Bank Cooperation, 1924–1931* (1967).
Jolliffe, M. F., *United States as Financial Centre, 1919–1933* (1935).
Noyes, C. R., "Gold Inflation, 1921–1929," *Am. Econ. Rev.*, 20 (1938), 181.
Pecora, Ferdinand, *Wall Street Under Oath* (1936).

52.3.6 Speculation

Brooks, John, *Once in Golconda: Wall Street, 1820–1938* (1969).
Cowing, Cedric B., *Populists, Plungers, and Progressives: Social History of Stock and Commodity Speculation, 1890–1936* (1965).
Flynn, John T., *Security Speculation* (1934).
Galbraith, John K., *The Great Crash, 1929* (1955).
Pontecorvo, Giulio, "Investment Banking and Security Speculation in Late 1920's," *Bus. Hist. Rev.*, 32 (1958), 166.
Sakolski, Aaron M., *Great American Land Bubble* (1932).
Sobel, Robert, *Great Bull Market: Wall Street in the 1920's* (1968).
Vanderblue, H. B., "Florida Land Boom," *Jour. Land Public Utility Econ.*, 3 (1927), 113.

52.3.7 Labor

Berman, Edward, *Labor Disputes and the President* (1924).
Bernstein, Irving, *Lean Years: American Worker, 1920–1933* (1960).
Brody, David, *Labor in Crisis: The Steel Strike of 1919* (1965).
Saposs, D. J., "The American Labor Movement Since the War," *Quar. Jour. Econ.*, 49 (1935), 236.
Taft, Philip, *The A. F. of L. from Death of Gompers to Merger* (1959).

52.4 AGRICULTURE

52.4.1 General

Anderson, Clifford B., "Agrarian Idealism in the 1920's and 1930's," *Agric. Hist.*, 35 (1961), 182.
Capper, Arthur, *Agricultural Block* (1922).
Christensen, A. M., "Agricultural Pressure and Governmental Response, 1919–1929," *Agric. Hist.*, 11 (1937), 33.
Davis, Chester, "Development of Agricultural Policy since the World War," in *Yearbook of Agriculture* (1940).
Enfield, R. R., *Agricultural Crisis, 1920–1923* (1924).
McConnell, Grant, *Decline of Agrarian Democracy* (1953).
Neprash, Jerry A., *Brookhart Campaigns in Iowa, 1920–1926* (1932).
Nye, Russel B., *Midwestern Progressive Politics* (1951).
Saloutos, Theodore, and J. D. Hicks, *Agricultural Discontent in the Middle West, 1900–1939* (1951).
Shideler, James H., *Farm Crisis, 1919–1923* (1957).
Tucker, Ray, and F. R. Barkley, *Sons of the Wild Jackass* (1932).
Winters, Donald L., "Harry Cantwell Wallace and the Movement for Agricultural Economics," *Agric. Hist.*, 41 (1967), 109.

See also 10.3 for biographies/writings of:

Capper, Arthur, 1865–1951
Wallace Family

52.4.2 Federal Programs

52.4.2.1 General

Baker, Gladys, *County Agent* (1939).
Blaisdell, D. C., *Government and Agriculture* (1940).
Link, Arthur S., "Federal Reserve Policy and Agricultural Depression," *Agric. Hist.*, 20 (1946), 166.
Powell, Fred W., *Bureau of Animal Industry* (1927).

Schapsmeier, Edward L., and Frederick H. Schapsmeier, "Disharmony in the Harding Cabinet: Hoover-Wallace Conflict," *Ohio Hist.*, 75 (1966), 126.

Seligman, Edwin R. A., *Economics of Farm Relief* (1929).

Winters, Donald L., *Henry Cantwell Wallace as Secretary of Agriculture, 1921–1924* (1970).

52.4.2.2 McNary-Haugenism and Farm Relief

"Agricultural Situation," Am. Acad. Pol. Soc. Sci., *Annals*, 117 (1925). Entire issue.

Black, John D., *Agricultural Reform in the United States* (1929).

Davis, Joseph S., *Farm Export Debenture Plan* (1929).

Kelley, D. N., "McNary-Haugen Bills, 1924–1928," *Agric. Hist.*, 14 (1940), 170.

Peek, George N., and H. S. Johnson, *Equality for Agriculture* (1922).

Tugwell, Rexford G., "Reflections on Farm Relief," *Pol. Sci. Quar.*, 43 (1928), 481.

Wallace, Henry C., *Our Debt and Duty to Farmer* (1925).

52.4.2.3 Rural Credits

Baird, Frieda, and C. L. Benner, *Ten Years of Federal Intermediate Credits* (1933).

Benner, C. L., *Federal Intermediate Credit System* (1926).

Eliot, Clara, *Farmer's Campaign for Credit* (1927).

Norman, J. B., *Farm Credits* (1924).

52.4.3 Agrarian Discontent

52.4.3.1 General

Capper, Arthur, *Agricultural Bloc* (1922).

Eliot, Clara, *Farmer's Campaign for Credit* (1927).

Fite, Gilbert C., *George N. Peek and the Fight for Farm Parity* (1954).

Kramer, Dale, *Wild Jackasses: The American Farmer in Revolt* (1956).

Shideler, James H., *Farm Crisis, 1919–1923* (1957).

52.4.3.2 Non-Partisan League

Gaston, H. E., *Non-Partisan League* (1920).

Huntington, S. P., "Election Tactics of Non-Partisan League," *MVHR*, 36 (1950), 613.

Morlan, Robert L., *Political Prairie Fire: Nonpartisan League, 1915–1922* (1955).

Saloutos, Theodore, "The Expansion and Decline of the Non-Partisan League," *Agric. Hist.*, 20 (1946), 235.

——— "Rise of the Non-Partisan League in North Dakota," *Agric. Hist.*, 20 (1946), 43.

Tostlebe, A. S., *Bank of North Dakota* (1924).

52.4.3.3 Farm Co-op Movement

Bergengren, R. F., *Cooperative Banking* (1923).

Comish, N. H., *Co-operative Marketing of Agricultural Products* (1929).

Elsworth, R. H., *Development of Farmers' Cooperative Organizations* (1924).

Filley, Horace C., *Cooperation in Agriculture* (1929).

Nourse, Edwin G., and J. G. Knapp, *Co-operative Marketing of Livestock* (1931).

Warbasse, J. P., *Co-operative Democracy* (1927).

52.4.3.4 Farmers' Associations

Chambers, Clarke A., *California Farm Organizations, 1929–1941* (1952).

Crampton, John A., *National Farmers Union* (1965).

Kile, Orville M., *Farm Bureau Movement* (1921).

——— *Farm Bureau through Three Decades* (1948).

McConnell, Grant, *Decline of Agrarian Democracy* (1953).

52.4.3.5 Emigration to Canadian Plains

Bicha, Karel D., "American Farmer and Canadian West, 1896–1914," *Agric. Hist.*, 38 (1964), 43.
———— "The Plains Farmer and the Prairie Province Frontier, 1897–1914," Am. Philos. Soc., *Proc.*, 109 (1965), 398.
Sharp, Paul F., *Agrarian Revolt in Western Canada: American Parallels* (1948).

52.5 RED SCARE AND POSTWAR REPRESSION

52.5.1 General

Brody, David, *Labor in Crisis: The Steel Strike of 1919* (1965).
Chafee, Zechariah, Jr., *Free Speech in the United States* (1941).
Coben, Stanley, "The American Red Scare of 1919–1920," *Pol. Sci. Quar.*, 79 (1964), 52.
Gutfeld, Arnon, "The Ves Hall Case, Judge Bourquin and the Sedition Act of 1918," *Pac. Hist. Rev.*, 37 (1968), 163.
Hays, Arthur G., *Let Freedom Ring* (1928).
Johnson, Donald D., *Challenge to American Freedoms: Civil Liberties Union* (1963).
Labor Research Association, *Palmer Raids* (1948).
Lusk Committee, *Revolutionary Radicalism* (1920).
Murphy, Paul L., "Normalcy, Intolerance, and American Character," *Va. Quar. Rev.*, 40 (1964), 445.
Murray, Robert K., *Red Scare, 1919–1920* (1955).
Preston, William, Jr., *Aliens and Dissenters: Federal Suppression of Radicals, 1903–1933* (1963).
Scheiber, Harry N., *Wilson Administration and Civil Liberties, 1917–1921* (1960).
Urofsky, Melvin I., "Note on the Expulsion of Five Socialists," *N.Y. Hist.*, 47 (1966), 41.
U.S. Department of Justice, *Red Radicalism as Described by Its Own Leaders* (1920).
Vadney, Thomas E., "Politics of Repression: Case Study of Red Scare in New York," *N.Y. Hist.*, 49 (1968), 56.
Warth, R. D., "Palmer Raids," *So. Atl. Quar.*, 48 (1949), 1.

See also 10.3 for biographies/writings of:

Holmes, Oliver Wendell, Jr., 1841–1935
Palmer, A. Mitchell, 1872–1936

52.5.2 Left-Wing Parties

Ameringer, Oscar, *If You Don't Weaken* (1940).
Bittelman, Alexander, *Fifteen Years of the Communist Party* (1934).
Cannon, James P., *History of American Trotskyism* (1944).
Draper, Theodore, *American Communism and Soviet Russia: Formative Period* (1960).
———— *Roots of American Communism* (1957).
Egbert, D. D., and Stow Persons, *Socialism and American Life* (2 vols., 1952).
Foster, William Z., *History of the Communist Party of the United States* (1952).
Gitlow, Benjamin, *I Confess* (1940).
Hillquit, Morris, *Loose Leaves from a Busy Life* (1934).
Howe, Irving, and Lewis Coser, *The American Communist Party* (1962).
Lovestone, Jay, *Pages from Party History* (1929).
Petersen, Arnold, *Revolutionary Milestones* (1931).
Russell, Charles E., *Bare Hands and Stone Walls* (1933).
Ruthenberg, Charles E., *Speeches and Writings*, Jay Lovestone, ed. (1928).

52.5.3 Sacco-Vanzetti Case

Bush, Martin H., *Ben Shahn: Passion of Sacco and Vanzetti* (1968).
Ehrmann, Herbert B., *The Case That Will Not Die: Sacco and Vanzetti* (1969).
Felix, David, *Protest: Sacco-Vanzetti and the Intellectuals* (1965).
Frankfurter, Felix, *Case of Sacco and Vanzetti* (1927).
Joughin, G. L., and E. M. Morgan, *Legacy of Sacco and Vanzetti* (1948).
Russell, Francis, *Tragedy in Dedham: Sacco-Vanzetti Case* (1962).

52.5.4 Ku Klux Klan

Alexander, Charles C., *The Ku Klux Klan in the Southwest* (1965).
Jackson, Kenneth T., *The Ku Klux Klan in the City, 1915–1930* (1967).
Rice, Arnold S., *The Ku Klux Klan in American Politics* (1962).

52.5.5 Race Riots

Essien-Udom, Essien Udosen, *Black Nationalism: Search for Identity in America* (1962).
Illinois, Chicago Commission on Race Relations, *The Negro in Chicago: Study of Race Relations and a Race Riot* (1922).
Sherman, Richard B., "Republicans and Negroes: Lessons of Normalcy," *Phylon*, 27 (1966), 63.
Tuttle, William M., Jr., *Race Riot: Chicago in the Red Summer of 1919* (1970).
Waskow, Arthur I., *From Race Riot to Sit-In, 1919 and the 1960's: Study in Connections between Conflict and Violence* (1966).

See also 10.3 for biographies/writings of:

Du Bois, W. E. B., 1868–1963
Trotter, William M., 1872–1934
White, Walter Francis, 1893–1955

52.6 POLITICS

52.6.1 General

Burner, David, *Politics of Provincialism: Democratic Party, 1918–1932* (1967).
Burnham, Walter D., "American Political Universe," *Am. Pol. Sci. Rev.*, 59 (1965), 7.
Cranston, Pat, "Political Convention Broadcasts," *Journalism Quar.*, 37 (1960), 186.
Huthmacher, J. Joseph, *Massachusetts People and Politics, 1919–1933* (1959).
Lippmann, Walter, *Men of Destiny* (1927).
Mitchell, Franklin D., *Embattled Democracy: Missouri Democratic Politics, 1919–1932* (1968).
Morrison, Joseph L., *Governor O. Max Gardner* (1971). North Carolina.
O'Brien, Patrick G., "Reanalysis of Republican Insurgency in Nineteen-Twenties," *Rocky Mtn. Soc. Sci. Jour.*, 5 (1968), 93.
Ruetten, Richard T., "Senator Burton K. Wheeler and the Insurgency in the 1920's," *Univ. of Wyoming Publ.*, 32 (1966), 111, 164.

See also 10.3 for biographies/writings of:

Borah, William E., 1865–1940
Cox, James M., 1870–1957
Davis, John W., 1873–1955
Garner, John Nance, 1868–1967

Harding, Warren G., 1865–1923
Hughes, Charles Evans, 1889–1950
Hull, Cordell, 1871–1955
La Follette, Robert M., 1855–1925
La Guardia, Fiorello H., 1882–1947
Longworth, Nicholas, 1869–1931
Mellon, Andrew, 1855–1937
Norris, George W., 1861–1944
Pinchot, Gifford, 1865–1946
Smith, Alfred E., 1873–1944
Villard, Oswald G., 1872–1949
White, William Allen, 1868–1944

52.6.2 Progressivism and Reform

Chambers, Clarke A., *Seedtime of Reform: Social Service and Social Action, 1918–1933* (1963).
Glad, Paul W., "Progressives and Business Culture of the 1920's," *JAH*, 53 (1966), 75.
Link, Arthur S., "What Happened to the Progressive Movement in 1920's?" *AHR*, 64 (1959), 833.
Maxwell, Robert S., "Reform Sentiment between New Freedom and New Deal," *Ind. Mag. Hist.*, 63 (1967), 83.
Tindall, George B., "Business Progressivism: Southern Politics in the Twenties," *So. Atl. Quar.*, 62 (1963), 92.
Weinstein, James, "Radicalism in the Midst of Normalcy," *JAH*, 52 (1966), 773.

52.7 DEMOBILIZATION

Crowell, Benedict, and R. F. Wilson, *Demobilization* (1921).
Howenstine, E. Jay, Jr., "Demobilization," *Quar. Jour. Econ.*, 58 (1943), 91.
Mock, James R., and Evangeline Thurber, *Report on Demobilization* (1944).
National Housing Agency, *Housing After World War I* (1945).
Paxson, Frederic L., *Great Demobilization and Other Essays* (1941).
Samuelson, Paul A., and E. E. Hagen, *After the War* (1943).
Wecter, Dixon, *When Johnny Comes Marching Home* (1944).

52.8 DEPRESSION, 1919–1921

Howenstine, E. Jay, Jr., "Public Works after World War I," *Jour. Pol. Econ.*, 51 (1943), 523.
Payne, W. F., *Business Behavior, 1919–22* (1942).
Persons, W. M., "Crisis of 1920," *Am. Econ. Rev.*, 12 (1922), 5.
U.S. President's Conference on Unemployment, *Report* (1921).

52.9 ELECTION OF 1920

Bagby, Wesley M., *Road to Normalcy: Campaign of 1920* (1962).
———— "Woodrow Wilson, a Third Term, and the Solemn Referendum," *AHR*, 60 (1955), 567.
McCoy, Donald R., "Election of 1920," in Arthur M. Schlesinger, Jr. and Fred L. Israel, eds., *History of American Presidential Elections, 1789–1968*, vol. III (1971).
Merritt, Richard L., "Woodrow Wilson and 'Great and Solemn Referendum,' 1920," *Rev. Politics*, 27 (1965), 78.
Pollock, J. K., *Party Campaign Funds* (1926).

See also 10.3 for biographies/writings of:

Borah, William E., 1865–1940
Coolidge, Calvin, 1872–1933
Cox, James M., 1870–1957
Harding, Warren G., 1865–1923
Hoover, Herbert, 1874–1964
Lodge, Henry Cabot, 1850–1924
Lowden, Frank O., 1861–1943
Roosevelt, Franklin D., 1882–1945
Wilson, Woodrow, 1856–1924
Wood, Leonard, 1860–1927

52.10 HARDING ADMINISTRATION, 1921–1923

52.10.1 General

Dawes, Charles G., *First Year of Budget of the United States* (1923).
Downes, Randolph C., "The Harding Muckfest: Warren G. Harding—Chief Victim of the Muck-For-Muck's-Sake Writers and Readers," *Northw. Ohio Quar.*, 39 (1967), 5.
Murray, Robert K., *The Harding Era: Harding and His Administration* (1969).
Paxson, Frederic L., *Postwar Years, 1918–1923* (1948).
Price, Don K., "General Dawes and Executive Staff Work," *Pub. Admin. Rev.*, 11 (1951), 167.
White, William Allen, *Masks in a Pageant* (1928).

See also 10.3 for biographies/writings of:

Davis, James J., 1873–1947
Dawes, Charles G., 1865–1951
Harding, Warren G., 1865–1923
Hoover, Herbert, 1874–1964
Hughes, Charles Evans, 1889–1950
Mellon, Andrew, 1855–1937
Wallace, Henry C., 1866–1924
Walsh, Thomas J., 1859–1933
Wilbur, Ray Lyman, 1875–1949

52.10.2 Teapot Dome and Harding Scandals

Adams, Samuel Hopkins, *Incredible Era* (1939).
Bates, J. Leonard, *Origins of the Teapot Dome* (1963).
Daugherty, H. M., and Thomas Dixon, *Inside Story of the Harding Tragedy* (1932).
Ise, John, *Oil Policy* (1926).
Noggle, Burl, *Teapot Dome: Oil and Politics in the 1920's* (1962).
Swain, Donald C., *Federal Conservation Policy, 1921–1933* (1963).
Werner, Morris R., and John Starr, *Teapot Dome* (1959).
Wooddy, C. H., *Case of Frank L. Smith* (1931).

52.11 COOLIDGE ADMINISTRATION, 1923–1929

Clemens, Cyril, and A. P. Daggett, "Coolidge's 'I Do Not Choose to Run,'" *NEQ*, 18 (1945), 147.
Coolidge, Calvin, *Mind of a President: President Coolidge's Views on Public Questions*, C. B. Slemp, ed. (1926).

——— *Talkative President: Press Conferences,* Robert H. Ferrell and Howard H. Quint, eds. (1964).
Maddox, Robert J., "Keeping Cool with Coolidge," *JAH,* 53 (1967), 772.

See also 10.3 for biographies/writings of:

Coolidge, Calvin, 1872–1933
Dawes, Charles G., 1865–1951
Hoover, Herbert, 1874–1964
Hughes, Charles Evans, 1889–1950
Kellogg, Frank B., 1856–1937
Mellon, Andrew, 1855–1937
Stone, Harlan F., 1872–1946

52.12 ELECTION OF 1924

Allen, Lee N., "McAdoo Campaign, 1924," *JSH,* 29 (1963), 211.
Bates, J. Leonard, "Teapot Dome Scandal and Election of 1924," *AHR,* 60 (1955), 303.
Burner, David, "Election of 1924," in Arthur M. Schlesinger, Jr. and Fred L. Israel, eds., *History of American Presidential Elections, 1789–1968,* vol. III (1971).
MacKay, Kenneth Campbell, *Progressive Movement of 1924* (1947).
Shideler, James H., "La Follette Campaign," *Wis. Mag. Hist.,* 33 (1950), 444.

See also 10.3 for biographies/writings of:

Bryan, William Jennings, 1860–1925
Coolidge, Calvin, 1872–1933
Davis, John W., 1873–1955
Dawes, Charles G., 1865–1951
La Follette, Robert M., 1855–1925
McAdoo, William G., 1863–1941
Roosevelt, Franklin D., 1882–1945
Smith, Alfred E., 1873–1944

52.13 ELECTION OF 1928

Bornet, Vaughn D., *Labor Politics in a Democratic Republic: Presidential Election of 1928* (1964).
Burner, David J., *Politics of Provincialism: Democratic Party, 1918–1932* (1967).
Carlson, Earland I., "Franklin D. Roosevelt's Post-Mortem of 1928 Election," *Midw. Jour. Pol. Sci.,* 8 (1964), 298.
Carter, Paul A., "Campaign of 1928 Re-Examined," *Wis. Mag. Hist.,* 46 (1963), 263.
——— "1928 Presidential Bid of Thomas J. Walsh," *Pac. Northw. Quar.,* 55 (1964), 1.
Eldersveld, S. J., "Influence of Metropolitan Party Pluralities in Presidential Elections since 1920," *Am. Pol. Sci. Rev.,* 43 (1949), 1189.
Fite, Gilbert C., "Agricultural Issue in Campaign of 1928," *MVHR,* 37 (1951), 653.
Fuchs, Lawrence H., "Election of 1928," in Arthur M. Schlesinger, Jr. and Fred L. Israel, eds., *History of American Presidential Elections, 1789–1968,* vol. III (1971).
Hoover, Herbert, *New Day* (1928).
Lubell, Samuel, *Future of American Politics* (1952).
Moore, Edmund A., *A Catholic Runs for President, 1928* (1956).
Neal, Nevin E., "Smith-Robinson Arkansas Campaign of 1928," *Ark. Hist. Quar.,* 19 (1960), 3.

Peel, Roy V., and T. C. Donnelly, *Campaign of 1928* (1931).
Pollock, J. K., "Campaign Funds in 1928," *Am. Pol. Sci. Rev.*, 29 (1929), 59.
Silva, Ruth C., *Rum, Religion, and Votes: 1928 Re-Examined* (1962).
Smith, Alfred E., *Campaign Speeches* (1929).
Smylie, James H., "Roman Catholic Church, the State, and Al Smith," *Church Hist.*, 29 (1960), 321.
Tompkins, C. David, "Arthur Vandenberg Goes to the Senate," *Mich. Hist.*, 51 (1967), 19.
Watson, Richard L., Jr., "F. M. Simmons in the Presidential Election of 1928," *No. Car. Hist. Rev.*, 37 (1960), 516.
—— "Religion and Politics in Mid-America: Presidential Voting in Missouri, 1928 and 1960," *Midcontinent Am. Studies Jour.*, 5 (1964), 33.

See also 10.3 for biographies/writings of:

Cannon, James, Jr., 1864–1944
Curtis, Charles, 1860–1936
Hoover, Herbert, 1874–1964
Roosevelt, Franklin D., 1882–1945
Smith, Alfred E., 1873–1944

52.14 FOREIGN RELATIONS

52.14.1 General

Council on Foreign Relations, *United States in World Affairs* (1931–   ). Supersedes *Survey of American Foreign Relations* (1928–1931).
Ellis, Lewis Ethan, *Frank B. Kellogg and American Foreign Relations, 1925–1929* (1961).
—— *Republican Foreign Policy, 1921–1933* (1968).
Ferrell, Robert H., *American Diplomacy in the Great Depression, 1929–1933* (1957).
Moffat, Jay P., *Selections from Diplomatic Journals, 1919–1943*, Nancy H. Hooker, ed. (1956).
Van Alstyne, Richard W., *American Crisis Diplomacy* (1952).

*   *   *   *   *   *   *

Carnegie Endowment for International Peace, *Disarmament and Security* (1931).
—— *Hoover-Stimson Doctrine* (1934).
Kelchner, Warren H., *Inter-American Conferences, 1926–1933* (1933).
Langer, William L., and H. F. Armstrong, eds., *Foreign Affairs Bibliography, 1919–32* (1933).
League of Nations, *Annotated Bibliography on Disarmament and Military Questions* (1931).
Pan-American Union, *Selected List on Inter-American Relations* (1932).
U.S. Library of Congress, *Disarmament* (1929). Supplement (1934).
—— *Inter-Allied Debt* (1931). Supplements (1933, 1934, 1936).
—— *List of References on Washington Conference* (1925). Supplements (1927, 1929).
—— *List on Reparations* (1932). Supplement (1933).
—— *London Naval Conference* (1930).
—— *Selected List on Relations with Union of Soviet Socialist Republics, 1919–1935* (1935).
—— *United States Relations with Mexico and Central America* (1928).

See also 10.3 for biographies/writings of:

Borah, William E., 1865–1940
Grew, Joseph C., 1880–1965

Harding, Warren G., 1865–1923
Herrick, Myron T., 1854–1929
Hoover, Herbert, 1874–1964
Hughes, Charles Evans, 1889–1950
Kellogg, Frank B., 1856–1937
Morrow, Dwight, 1873–1931
Phillips, William, 1878–1968
Stimson, Henry L., 1867–1950

52.14.2 Hoover's Foreign Policy

Bennett, Edward W., *Germany and the Diplomacy of the Financial Crisis, 1931* (1962).
Ferrell, Robert H., *American Diplomacy in the Great Depression* (1957).
Myers, William Starr, *Foreign Policies of Herbert Hoover* (1940).
Stimson, Henry L., "Bases of American Foreign Policy," *For. Affairs*, 11 (1933), 383.
Stuart, Graham Henry, *Department of State* (1949).

52.14.3 Manchurian Crisis and Stimson Doctrine

Bassett, Reginald, *Democracy and Foreign Policy, Sino-Japanese Dispute, 1931–33* (1952).
Clyde, P. H., "Diplomacy of Secretary Stimson and Manchuria, 1931," *MVHR*, 35 (1948), 187.
Crowley, James B., *Japan's Quest for Autonomy: National Security and Foreign Policy, 1930–1938* (1966).
Langer, Robert, *Seizure of Territory: Stimson Doctrine* (1947).
Perkins, E. R., "Non-application of Sanctions against Japan, 1931–1932," in D. E. Lee and G. E. McReynolds, eds., *Essays in History and International Relations in Honor of George Hubbard Blakeslee* (1949).
Rappaport, Armin, *Henry L. Stimson and Japan* (1963).
Smith, Sara R., *Manchurian Crisis, 1931–1932* (1948).
Stimson, Henry L., *Far Eastern Crisis* (1936).
Wallace, B. J., "How the United States 'Led the League' in 1931," *Am. Pol. Sci. Rev.*, 39 (1945), 101.

52.14.4 Organization of Foreign Service

Moffat, Jay P., *Selections from Diplomatic Journals, 1919–1943*, Nancy H. Hooker, ed. (1956).
"Ten Years under Rogers Act," *Am. For. Serv. Jour.*, 11 (1934), 341.

See also 10.3 for biographies/writings of:

Grew, Joseph C., 1880–1965

52.14.5 Congress and Foreign Policy

Dennison, E. E., *Senate Foreign Relations Committee* (1942).
Grassmuck, G. L., *Sectional Biases in Congress on Foreign Policy* (1951).
Westphal, A. C. F., *House Committee on Foreign Affairs* (1942).

52.14.6 Isolationism

Watt, D. C., "American 'Isolationism' in 1920's," Brit. Assoc. Am. Studies, *Bull.*, 6 (1963), 3.
Williams, William A., "Legend of Isolationism in 1920's," *Science and Society*, 18 (1954), 1.

52.14.7 Economic Aspects

52.14.7.1 General

Angell, James Waterhouse, *Financial Foreign Policy* (1933).
Bloomfield, Arthur I., "Mechanism of Adjustment of Balance of Payments: 1919–1929," *Quar. Jour. Econ.*, 57 (1943), 333.
Brandes, Joseph, *Herbert Hoover and Economic Diplomacy, 1921–1928* (1962).
Brown, William A., Jr., *International Gold Standard, 1914–1934* (1940).
Feis, Herbert, *Diplomacy of Dollar, 1919–1932* (1950).
Lewis, Cleona, *America's Stake in International Investments* (1938).
Noyes, Alexander D., *War Period of American Finance, 1908–1925* (1926).
Southard, F. A., *American Industry in Europe* (1931).
Wilson, J. H., *American Business and Foreign Policy, 1920–1933* (1968).

52.14.7.2 Debts, Reparations, and War Guilt

Adler, Selig, "War-Guilt Question, 1918–1928," *Jour. Mod. Hist.*, 22 (1951), 1.
Auld, G. P., *Dawes Plan and New Economics* (1927).
────── "Dawes and Young Loans," *For. Affairs*, 13 (1934), 6.
Bergmann, Carl, *History of Reparations* (1927).
Dawes, Charles G., *Journal of Reparations* (1939).
Dawes, Rufus C., *Dawes Plan in the Making* (1925).
Moulton, Harold G., and Leo Pasvolsky, *War Debts and World Prosperity* (1932).
────── *World War Debt Settlements* (1926).
Myers, Denys P., *Reparation Settlement* (1930).
Wheeler-Bennett, John W., *Wreck of Reparations* (1933).

52.14.8 United States and International Organizations

Berdahl, C. A., "Relations of the United States with the Assembly of the League," *Am. Pol. Sci. Rev.*, 26 (1932), 99.
────── "Relations of the United States with the Council of the League," *Am. Pol. Sci. Rev.*, 26 (1932), 497.
Clark, Keith, *International Communications: American Attitude* (1931).
Cooper, Russell M., *American Consultation in World Affairs* (1934).
Coudert, F. R., "The United States and the Court of International Justice," *Am. Bar Assoc. Jour.*, 18 (1932), 415.
Fleming, Denna F., *United States and the World Court* (1945).
────── *United States and World Organization, 1920–1933* (1938).
Hubbard, Ursula P., *Cooperation with the League of Nations, 1931–1936* (1937).
Hudson, Manley O., *The Permanent Court of International Justice and American Participation* (1925).
Jessup, Philip C., comp., *United States and the Court of International Justice* (1931).
Myers, James, "American Relations with the International Labor Office, 1919–1932," *Am. Acad. Pol. Soc. Sci., Annals*, 146 (1933), 135.
Schmeckebier, Laurence F., *International Organizations in which United States Participates* (1935).
Wriston, H. M., "American Participation in International Conferences," *Am. Jour. Internatl. Law*, 20 (1926), 33.

52.14.9 Recognition Policies

Cole, Taylor, *Recognition Policy since 1901* (1928).
Hill, Chesney, *Recent Policies of Non-Recognition* (1933).
Jaffe, L. L., *Judicial Aspects of Foreign Relations* (1933).
McMahon, John L., *Recent Changes in Recognition Policy* (1933).

52.14.10 Disarmament and Security

52.14.10.1 General

Buckley, Thomas H., *The United States and Washington Conference: 1921–1922* (1970).
Bywater, H. C., *Sea-Power in the Pacific* (1921).
Davis, George T., *Navy Second to None* (1940).
Ferrell, Robert H., *Peace in Their Time* (1952).
Hoag, Charles L., *Preface to Preparedness* (1941).
Kintner, William R., *Haphazard Years* (1960).
Morrison, Charles C., *Outlawry of War* (1927).
Morton, Louis, "War Plan ORANGE: Evolution of a Strategy," *World Politics*, 11 (1959), 221.
Myers, Denys P., *Origin of Paris Pact* (1929).
—— *World Disarmament* (1932).
O'Connor, Raymond G., *Perilous Equilibrium: The United States and the London Naval Conference of 1930* (1962).
—— "The 'Yardstick' and Naval Disarmament in the 1920's," *MVHR*, 45 (1958), 441.
Rappaport, Armin, *The Navy League of the United States* (1962).
Roskill, Stephen Wentworth, *Naval Policy between the Wars: Period of Anglo-American Antagonism, 1919–1929* (1968). British naval policy.
Shotwell, James T., *War as an Instrument of Policy* (1929).
Sprout, H. H., and Margaret Sprout, *Toward a New Order of Sea Power* (1940).
Vinson, John Chalmers, *William E. Borah and Outlawry of War* (1957).
Wheeler, Gerald E., *Prelude to Pearl Harbor: U.S. Navy and the Far East, 1921–1931* (1963).
Wheeler-Bennett, John, *Disarmament and Security* (1932).
Williams, Benjamin H., *United States and Disarmament* (1931).
Winkler, Fred H., "War Department and Disarmament, 1926–1935," *Historian*, 28 (1966), 426.

52.14.10.2 Washington Naval Conference and Four-Power Pact

Asada, Sadao, "Japan's 'Special Interests' and the Washington Conference, 1921–1922," *AHR*, 67 (1962), 62.
Buckley, Thomas H., *United States and the Washington Conference, 1921–1922* (1970).
Buell, R. L., *Washington Conference* (1922).
Fifield, Russell H., "Secretary Hughes and Shantung Question," *Pac. Hist. Rev.*, 23 (1954), 373.
Hoag, Charles Leonard, *Preface to Preparedness: Washington Disarmament Conference and Public Opinion* (1941).
Ichihashi, Yamato, *Washington Conference and After* (1928).
Kane, Albert E., *China and Washington Conference* (1937).
King, Wunsz, *China at the Washington Conference, 1921–1922* (1963).
Sullivan, Mark, *Great Adventure at Washington* (1922).
Vinson, John Chalmers, *Parchment Peace: United States Senate and Washington Conference, 1921–1922* (1955).

52.14.10.3 Kellogg-Briand Pact

Miller, David Hunter, *Peace Pact of Paris* (1928).
Stimson, Henry L., *Pact of Paris* (1932).
Stoner, J. E., *S. O. Levinson and Pact of Paris* (1943).

52.14.11 Europe

Cassels, Alan, "Fascism for Export: Italy and the United States in the Twenties," *AHR*, 69 (1964), 707.

Fisher, Harold H., and Sidney Brooks, *America and New Poland* (1928).
Gottwald, Robert, *Deutsch-Amerikanischen Beziehungen in Ara Stresemann* (1965).
Lochner, Louis P., *Hoover and Germany* (1960).
Roosevelt, Nicholas, *America and England* (1930).
Tardieu, André, *France and America* (1927).

52.14.12 Soviet Union

Filene, Peter G., ed., *American Views of Soviet Russia, 1917–1965* (1968).
—— *Americans and the Soviet Experiment, 1917–1933* (1967).
Hodgson, James Goodwin, comp., *Recognition of Soviet Russia* (1925).
Kennan, George F., *Russia and the West under Lenin and Stalin* (1961).
Lovenstein, Meno, *American Opinion of Soviet Russia* (1941).

52.14.13 East Asia

Borg, Dorothy, *American Policy and the Chinese Revolution, 1925–28* (1947).
Buhite, Russell D., *Nelson T. Johnson and American Policy toward China, 1925–1941* (1968).
Burns, Richard D., "Inspection of Mandates, 1919–1941," *Pac. Hist. Rev.*, 37 (1968), 445.
Griswold, A. Whitney, *Far Eastern Policy of the United States* (1938).
Kirwin, Harry W., "Federal Telegraph Company: Testing of the Open Door," *Pac. Hist. Rev.*, 22 (1953), 271.
Ma, Wen-Haun, *American Policy toward China in Debates of Congress* (1934).
Pollard, Robert T., *China's Foreign Relations, 1917–1931* (1933).
Popova, Evgeniia I., *Politiki Ssha Na Dal'men Vostoke, 1918–1922* (1967). Politics of the United States in the Far East.

52.14.14 Latin America

52.14.14.1 General

Bemis, Samuel, *Latin American Policy of the United States* (1943).
De Conde, Alexander, *Herbert Hoover's Latin American Policy* (1951).
Haring, Clarence H., *South America Looks at the United States* (1928).
Hughes, Charles Evans, *Our Relations to the Nations of the Western Hemisphere* (1928).
Murdock, James O., "Arbitration and Conciliation in Pan America," *Am. Jour. Internatl. Law*, 23 (1929), 273.
Perkins, Dexter, *United States and the Caribbean* (1947).
Stimson, Henry L., *United States and Other American Republics* (1931).
Welles, Sumner, *Naboth's Vineyard: Dominican Republic* (2 vols., 1928).
Winkler, Max, *Investments of United States Capital in Latin America* (1929).

52.14.14.2 Mexico

Dunn, Frederick S., *Diplomatic Protection of Americans in Mexico* (1933).
Feller, Abraham H., *Mexico Claims Commission, 1923–1934* (1935).
Gruening, Ernest H., *Mexico and Its Heritage* (1928).
Meyer, Lorenzo, *México y Estados Unidos en el conflicto petrolero, 1917–1942* (1968).
Ross, S. R., "Dwight Morrow and the Mexican Revolution," *Hisp. Am. Hist. Rev.*, 38 (1958), 506.

52.14.14.3 Nicaragua

Cox, Isaac J., *Nicaragua and the United States* (1927).
Kamman, William, *Search for Stability: Nicaragua, 1925–1933* (1968).
Stimson, Henry L., *American Policy in Nicaragua* (1927).

52.14.14.4 Cuba

Fitzgibbon, Russell H., *Cuba and the United States* (1935).
Guggenheim, Harry F., *United States and Cuba* (1934).
Jenks, Leland H., *Our Cuban Colony* (1928).
Wright, Philip G., *The Cuban Situation* (1931).

52.14.14.5 Haiti and Santo Domingo

Cotts, G. W., *United States and Haiti* (1931).
Knight, Melvin M., *Americans in Santo Domingo* (1928).
McCain, William D., *United States and Panama* (1937).
Millspaugh, Arthur C., *Haiti, 1915–1930* (1931).
Montague, Ludwell L., *Haiti and the United States* (1940).
Rotberg, Robert I., *Haiti: Politics of Squalor* (1971).
Spector, Robert M., "W. Cameron Forbes in Haiti: Additional Light on the Genesis of the 'Good Neighbor' Policy," *Caribbean Studies*, 6 (1966), 28.

52.14.15 Middle East and Africa

Daniel, Robert L., "The Armenian Question and American Turkish Relations, 1914–1927," *MVHR*, 46 (1959), 252.
Evans, Laurence, *United States Policy and Partition of Turkey, 1914–1924* (1965).
Manheim, F. J., "United States and Ethiopia," *Jour. Negro Hist.*, 17 (1932), 141.

53 Depression, Hoover Administration, and New Deal

53.1 DEPRESSION

53.1.1 General

Beard, Charles A., *America in Midpassage* (1939).
—— and George H. E. Smith, *The Old Deal and the New* (1940).
Bernstein, Irving, *Turbulent Years: The American Worker, 1933–1941* (1970).
Himmelberg, Robert F., comp., *Great Depression and American Capitalism* (1968).
Johnson, Walter, *1600 Pennsylvania Avenue: Presidents and the People, 1929–1959* (1960).
Mitchell, Broadus, *Depression Decade* (1947). Economic history.
Schlesinger, Arthur M., Jr., *The Age of Roosevelt* (3 vols., 1957–1960).
Wecter, Dixon, *Age of Great Depression* (1948). Social history.

*　*　*　*　*　*　*

Brooks, Eugene C., and L. M. Brooks, "Decade of 'Planning' Literature," *Social Forces*, 12 (1934), 427.
Shirley, W. W., "World Depression," N. Y. Pub Lib., *Bull.*, 37 (1933), 970, 1040.
U.S. Bureau of Agricultural Economics, *Farmers' Response to Price* (1932).
—— *Farmers' Strikes, 1932–1933* (1933).
—— *State Measures for Relief of Agricultural Indebtedness* (1933).
U.S. Library of Congress, *Economic Councils and Economic Planning* (1932).
—— *Federal Farm Board* (1931).
—— *List on Economic Planning* (1933).
—— *List on Technocracy* (1933).

53.1.2 Contemporary Accounts

Angly, Edward, comp., *Oh Yeah?* (1931).
Hallgren, Mauritz A., *Seeds of Revolt* (1933).
Seldes, Gilbert, *Years of Locust* (1933).
Waters, Walter W., and W. C. White, *B.E.F.* (1933).
Wilson, Edmund, *American Jitters* (1932).

53.1.3 Causes

Fisher, Irving, *Stock Market Crash—And After* (1930).
Galbraith, John K., *The Great Crash, 1929* (1955).

Hansen, Alvin H., *Business Cycles and National Income* (1951).
—— *Fiscal Policy and Business Cycles* (1941).
—— *Full Recovery or Stagnation?* (1938).
Leven, Maurice, et al., *America's Capacity to Consume* (1934).
Lowenthal, Max, *Investor Pays* (1936).
Nourse, Edwin G., et al., *America's Capacity to Produce* (1934).
Pecora, Ferdinand, *Wall Street under Oath* (1936).
Pontecorvo, Guilio, "Investment Banking and Security Speculation in the Late
1920's," *Bus. Hist. Rev.*, 32 (1958), 166.
Rothbard, Murray N., *America's Great Depression* (1963).
Schumpeter, Joseph A., *Business Cycles* (1939).
—— "Decade of the Twenties," *Am. Econ. Rev.*, 36 (1946, supplement), 1.
Wilson, Thomas, *Fluctuations in Income and Employment* (1948).

53.1.4 Popular Histories

Allen, Frederick L., *Since Yesterday* (1940).
Bird, Caroline B., *Invisible Scar: The Great Depression* (1966).
Phillips, Cabell, *From the Crash to the Blitz: 1929–1939* (1969).
Terkel, Studs, *Hard Times: Oral History of the Great Depression in America*
(1970).

53.1.5 Social Impact

Agee, James, *Let Us Now Praise Famous Men* (1941).
Baigell, Matthew, "Beginnings of the 'American Wave' and the Depression," *Art
Jour.*, 27 (1968), 387, 398.
Caldwell, O. W., et al., *Depression, Recovery and Higher Education* (1937).
Daniels, Jonathan, *Washington Quadrille* (1968).
Draper, Hal, "The Student Movement of the Thirties: A Political History," in
Rita J. Simon, ed., *As We Saw the Thirties* (1967).
Enzler, C. J., *Some Social Aspects of Depression* (1939).
Evans, Walker, *American Photographs* (1938).
Kincheloe, Samuel C., *Religion in the Depression* (1937).
Leonard, Jonathan N., *Three Years Down* (1939).
National Education Association, *Education in the Depression* (1937).
Ogburn, W. F., ed., *Social Change and the New Deal* (1934).
Ogburn, W. F., *Social Changes during the Depression and Recovery* (1935).
Ridley, E. C., and O. F. Nolting, eds., *What Depression Has Done to Cities*
(1935).
Severin, Werner J., "Photojournalists of F. S. A.," *Journalism Quar.*, 41 (1964),
191.
Shannon, David A., ed., *The Great Depression* (1960).
Social Science Research Council, *Research Bulletins on Social Aspects of Depres-
sion* (1937).
U.S. Bureau of Labor Statistics, "Differences in Living Costs in Northern and
Southern Cities," *Monthly Lab. Rev.*, 49 (1939), 22.
U.S. Department of Agriculture, *Family Expenditures for Medical Care* (1941).
—— *Family Food Consumption* (1941).
—— *Family Housing and Facilities* (1940).
—— *Family Income and Expenditures* (7 pts., 1933–1940).
U.S. National Resources Committee, *Consumer Incomes, 1935–1936* (1938).
Vaile, R. S., *Social Aspects of Consumption in the Depression* (1937).

53.1.6 Negroes

Carter, Dan T., *Scottsboro: A Tragedy of the American South* (1969).
Myrdal, Gunnar, *An American Dilemma* (2 vols., 1944).

Nolan, W. A., *Communism Versus Negro* (1951).
Record, Wilson, *The Negro and the Communist Party* (1951).
Sternsher, Bernard, *The Negro in Depression and War* (1969).

See also 10.3 for biographies/writings of:

Bethune, Mary McLeod, 1875–1955
Du Bois, W. E. B., 1868–1963
Robeson, Paul, 1898–1972
White, Walter Francis, 1893–1955

53.1.7 Proposals for Planning

Beard, Charles A., ed., *America Faces Future* (1932).
Bicha, Karel D., "League for Independent Political Action, 1928–1933," *Mid-America,* 48 (1966), 19.
Laidler, Harry W., *Socialist Planning and a Socialist Program* (1932).
Scott, Howard, et al., *Introduction to Technocracy* (1933).
Thomas, Norman, *America's Way Out* (1931).

See also 52.4.2.2, McNary-Haugenism and Farm Relief; 52.4.3, Agrarian Discontent.

53.2 HOOVER ADMINISTRATION, 1929–1933

53.2.1 General

Degler, Carl N., "Herbert Hoover," *Yale Rev.,* 52 (1963), 563.
Joslin, Theodore G., *Hoover Off the Record* (1934).
Myers, William S., and W. H. Newton, *The Hoover Administration* (1936).
Romasco, Albert U., *Poverty of Abundance: Hoover, the Nation, the Depression* (1965).
Schwarz, Jordan A., *Interregnum of Despair: Hoover, Congress, and the Depression* (1970).
Warren, Harris G., *Herbert Hoover and the Great Depression* (1959).
Wilbur, R. L., and A. M. Hyde, *Hoover Policies* (1937).

See also 10.3 for biographies/writings of:

Curtis, Charles, 1860–1936
Hoover, Herbert, 1874–1964
Stimson, Henry L., 1867–1950
Wilbur, Ray L., 1875–1949

See also 53.9, Interregnum and Launching of New Deal.

53.2.2 Hoover Programs

Berglund, Abraham, "Tariff Act of 1930," *Am. Econ. Rev.,* 20 (1930), 467.
Brown, Josephine C., *Public Relief, 1929–1939* (1940).
Colcord, J. C., et al., *Emergency Work Relief* (1932).
Jones, Jesse H., and Edward Angly, *Fifty Billion Dollars* (1951).
Kellogg, Ruth M., *United States Employment Service* (1933).
Nash, Gerald D., "Herbert Hoover and the Reconstruction Finance Corporation," *MVHR,* 46 (1959), 455.

Schattschneider, Elmer E., *Politics, Pressures and Tariff* (1935).
Stokdyk, E. A., and C. H. West, *The Farm Board* (1930).
Taussig, Frank W., "Tariff, 1929–1930," *Quar. Jour. Econ.*, 44 (1930), 175.

See also 10.3 for biographies/writings of:

Dawes, Charles G., 1865–1951
Jones, Jesse H., 1874–1956
Legge, Alexander, 1866–1933
Wilbur, Ray L., 1875–1949

53.3 ELECTION OF 1932

Davies, Richard O., "Politics of Desperation: William A. Hirth and the Presidential Election of 1932," *Agric. Hist.*, 38 (1964), 226.
Freidel, Frank, "Election of 1932," in Arthur M. Schlesinger, Jr. and Fred L. Israel, eds., *History of American Presidential Elections, 1789–1968*, vol. III (1971).
Lindley, Ernest K., *Roosevelt Revolution* (1933).
Mencken, Henry Louis, *Making a President* (1932).
Myers, William S., and W. H. Newton, *Hoover Administration* (1936).
Overacker, Louise, "Campaign Funds in the Depression," *Am. Pol. Sci. Rev.*, 27 (1933), 769.
Peel, Roy V., and T. C. Donnelly, *1932 Campaign* (1935).
Sussman, Leila A., *Dear FDR: Political Letter-Writing* (1963).
Tugwell, Rexford G., *The Brains Trust* (1968).

See also 10.3 for biographies/writings of:

Baker, Newton D., 1871–1937
Baruch, Bernard M., 1870–1965
Farley, James A., 1888–
Flynn, Edward J., 1891–1953
Garner, John Nance, 1868–1967
Hoover, Herbert, 1874–1964
Howe, Louis M., 1871–1936
Hull, Cordell, 1871–1955
Moley, Raymond, 1886–
Murray, "Alfalfa Bill," 1869–1956
Roosevelt, Franklin D., 1882–1945
Smith, Alfred E., 1873–1944

53.4 NEW DEAL

53.4.1 General

Artaud, Denise, *Le New Deal* (1969).
Brogan, Denis W., *The Era of Franklin D. Roosevelt* (1950).
Chambers, Clarke A., ed., *New Deal at Home and Abroad, 1929–1945* (1965).
Freidel, Frank, *The New Deal and American People* (1964).
Hamby, Alonzo L., comp., *The New Deal* (1969).
Keller, Morton, ed., *The New Deal: What Was It?* (1967).
Leuchtenburg, William E., *Franklin D. Roosevelt and the New Deal, 1932–1940* (1963).
———— ed., *New Deal: Documentary History* (1968).
Major, John, *New Deal* (1967).
Perkins, Dexter, *New Age of Franklin Roosevelt, 1932–45* (1957).
Rauch, Basil, *History of the New Deal* (1944).

Schlesinger, Arthur M., Jr., *The Age of Roosevelt* (3 vols., 1957–1960).
Warren, Frank A., and Michael Wreszin, comps., *The New Deal: An Anthology* (1968).
Woods, John A., *Roosevelt and Modern America* (1959).

*   *   *   *   *   *   *

Chambers, Clarke A., "FDR, Pragmatist–Idealist: Essay in Historiography," *Pac. Northw. Quar.*, 52 (1961), 50.
Freidel, Frank, *New Deal in Historical Perspective* (1959).
Graham, Otis L., Jr., "Historians and New Deals," *Social Studies*, 54 (1963), 133.
Kirkendall, Richard S., "New Deal as Watershed: Recent Literature," *JAH*, 54 (1968), 839.
Stewart, William J., comp., *Era of Franklin D. Roosevelt: A Selected Bibliography of Periodical and Dissertation Literature* (1967).
Watson, Richard L., Jr., "Franklin D. Roosevelt in Historical Writing, 1950–1957," *So. Atl. Quar.*, 57 (1958), 104.
U.S. Library of Congress, *Selected List on the New Deal* (1940).

53.4.2 Interpretative Studies

Conkin, Paul K., *FDR and Origins of the Welfare State* (1967).
Einaudi, Mario, *Roosevelt Revolution* (1959).
Frisch, Morton J., and Martin Diamond, eds., *The Thirties* (1968).
Hollingsworth, Harold M., and William F. Holmes, eds., *Essays on the New Deal* (1969).
Robinson, Edgar E., *Roosevelt Leadership* (1955).
Simon, Rita J., ed., *As We Saw the Thirties* (1967).

53.4.3 Foreign Commentary

Brogan, Denis W., *American Character* (1944).
Halasz, Nicholas, *Roosevelt through Foreign Eyes* (1961).
Laski, Harold J., *American Democracy* (1948).
Maurois, André, *En Amérique* (1933).
—— *États-Unis 39* (1939).
Wells, H..G., *New America—New World* (1935).

53.4.4 New Deal Thought

Alexander, Charles C., *Nationalism in American Thought, 1930–1945* (1969).
Ekirch, Arthur A., Jr., *Ideologies and Utopias: Impact of New Deal on American Thought* (1969).
Flynn, George Q., *American Catholics & Roosevelt Presidency, 1932–1936* (1968).
Fusfeld, Daniel R., *Economic Thought of Franklin D. Roosevelt* (1956).
Greer, Thomas H., *What Roosevelt Thought: Social and Political Ideas of Franklin D. Roosevelt* (1958).
O'Brien, David J., *American Catholics and Social Reform: New Deal* (1968).
Shachtman, Max, "Radicalism in the Thirties: The Trotskyist View," in Rita J. Simon, ed. *As We Saw the Thirties* (1967).
Thomas, Norman J., "The Thirties in America as a Socialist Recalls Them," in Rita J. Simon, ed., *As We Saw the Thirties* (1967).
Trilling, Lionel, "Young in the Thirties," *Commentary*, 41 (1966), 43.
Zinn, Howard, ed., *New Deal Thought* (1966).

53.4.5 Contemporary Views

Berle, Adolf A., et al., *America's Recovery Program* (1934).
Berle, Adolf A., *New Directions in New World* (1940).

Bingham, Alfred M., and Selden Rodman, eds., *Challenge to the New Deal* (1934).

Coyle, D. C., *Roads to a New America* (1938).

Eccles, Marriner S., *Economic Balance and a Balanced Budget* (1940).

Ezekiel, Mordecai, *Jobs for All* (1939).

———— *$2,500 a Year* (1936).

Ickes, Harold L., *New Democracy* (1934).

Roosevelt, Franklin D., *Looking Forward* (1933).

———— *On Our Way* (1934).

Rozwenc, Edwin C., ed., *The New Deal, Revolution or Evolution* (rev. ed., 1959).

Tugwell, Rexford G., *Battle for Democracy* (1935).

———— *Industrial Discipline and Governmental Arts* (1933).

Wallace, Henry A., *Democracy Reborn* (1945).

———— *New Frontiers* (1934).

53.5 POLITICS IN AGE OF ROOSEVELT, 1933–1945

53.5.1 General

Childs, Marquis, *I Write from Washington* (1942).

Graham, Otis L., Jr., *Encore for Reform: Old Progressives and the New Deal* (1967).

Herring, Pendleton, *Politics of Democracy* (1940).

Holcombe, Arthur N., *Middle Classes in American Politics* (1940).

Krock, Arthur, *In the Nation, 1932–1966* (1966).

Perkins, Frances, *The Roosevelt I Knew* (1946).

Roper, Elmo B., *You and Your Leaders, 1936–1956* (1957).

Salter, John T., ed., *Public Men In and Out of Office* (1946).

See also 10.3 for biographies/writings of:

DEMOCRATS

Acheson, Dean G., 1893–1971
Ashurst, Henry Fountain, 1874–1962
Bailey, Josiah W., 1873–1946
Baker, Newton D., 1871–1937
Barkley, Alben W., 1877–1956
Baruch, Bernard M., 1870–1965
Bilbo, Theodore G., 1877–1947
Black, Hugo, 1886–1971
Bloom, Sol, 1870–1949
Bowles, Chester, 1901–
Byrnes, James F., 1879–1972
Connally, Thomas T., 1877–1963
Farley, James A., 1888–
Flynn, Edward J., 1891–1953
Frankfurter, Felix, 1882–1965
Garner, John Nance, 1868–1967
Green, Theodore F., 1867–1966
Harriman, W. Averell, 1891–
Hopkins, Harry, 1890–1946
Hull, Cordell, 1871–1955
Ickes, Harold L., 1874–1952
Jackson, Robert H., 1892–1954
Johnston, Olin D., 1896–
Kennedy, Joseph P., 1888–1969

Lehman, Herbert H., 1878–1963
Long, Huey P., 1893–1935
McAdoo, William G., 1863–1941
Moley, Raymond, 1886–
Morgenthau, Henry, Jr., 1891–1967
Murphy, Frank, 1890–1949
Pittman, Key, 1872–1940
Roosevelt, Eleanor, 1884–1962
Roosevelt, Franklin D., 1882–1945
Truman, Harry S., 1884–1972
Wagner, Robert F., 1877–1953
Wallace, Henry A., 1888–1965
Wheeler, Burton K., 1882–

REPUBLICANS

Borah, William E., 1865–1940
Dewey, Thomas E., 1902–1971
Hoover, Herbert, 1874–1964
Johnson, Hiram W., 1866–1945
La Follette, Robert M., Jr., 1895–1953
La Guardia, Fiorello H., 1882–1947
Landon, Alf, 1887–
Lodge, Henry Cabot, II, 1902–
Norris, George W., 1861–1944
Nye, Gerald P., 1892–
Taft, Robert A., 1889–1953
Vandenberg, Arthur H., 1884–1951
White, William Allen, 1868–1944
Willkie, Wendell, 1892–1944

53.5.2 Presidential Politics

Clark, Wesley C., *Economic Aspects of President's Popularity* (1943).
Gosnell, Harold F., *Champion Campaigner: Franklin D. Roosevelt* (1952).
Hand, Samuel B., "Rosenman, Thucydides, and the New Deal," *JAH*, 55 (1968), 334.
Key, V. O., Jr., *The Responsible Electorate: Rationality in Presidential Voting, 1936–1960* (1966).
Overacker, Louise, *Presidential Campaign Funds* (1946).

*   *   *   *   *   *   *

Stewart, William J., comp., *Era of Franklin D. Roosevelt: A Selected Bibliography of Periodical and Disseration Literature* (1967).

53.5.3 Congress

Coker, William S., "Pat Harrison," *Jour. Miss. Hist.*, 28 (1966), 267.
Patterson, James T., *Congressional Conservatism and the New Deal* (1967).
Zeigler, Luther H., Jr., "Senator Walter George's 1938 Campaign," *Ga. Hist. Quar.*, 43 (1959), 333.

53.5.4 Lobbies

Crawford, Kenneth G., *Pressure Boys* (1939).
Key, V. O., Jr., *Politics, Parties and Pressure Groups* (1948).
Schriftgiesser, Karl, *Lobbyists* (1951).

53.5.5 Campaign of 1936

Gosnell, Harold F., *Champion Campaigner: Franklin D. Roosevelt* (1952).
Landon, Alfred M., *America at Crossroads* (1936).
Leuchtenburg, William E., "Election of 1936," in Arthur M. Schlesinger, Jr. and Fred L. Israel, eds., *History of American Presidential Elections, 1789–1968*, vol. III (1971).
Lunt, Richard D., "Frank Murphy's Decision to Enter the 1936 Gubernatorial Race," *Mich. Hist.*, 47 (1963), 327.
Mayer, George H., "Alf M. Landon, Leader of the Republican Opposition, 1937–1940," *Kan. Hist. Quar.*, 32 (1966), 325.
Ogburn, W. F., and L. C. Coombs, "Economic Factor in Roosevelt Elections," *Am. Pol. Sci. Rev.*, 34 (1940), 719.
White, William Allen, *What It's All About: Campaign of 1936* (1936).

See also 10.3 for biographies/writings of:

Hoover, Herbert, 1874–1964
Landon, Alf, 1887–
Roosevelt, Franklin D., 1882–1945

53.5.6 Supreme Court Controversy

Alsop, Joseph, and Turner Catledge, *168 Days* (1938).
Barnes, W. R., and A. W. Littlefield, eds., *The Supreme Court Issue and the Constitution* (1937).
Corwin, Edward S., *Constitutional Revolution, Ltd.* (rev. ed., 1946).
——— *Court Over Constitution* (1939).
Crouch, Barry A., "Dennis Chavez and Roosevelt's 'Court Packing' Plan," *New Mex. Hist. Rev.*, 42 (1967), 261.
Cummings, Homer S., *Selected Papers*, Carl Brent Swisher, ed. (1939).
Curtis, Charles P., Jr., *Lions Under Throne* (1947).
Eriksson, E. McK., *The Supreme Court and New Deal* (1941).
Frank, Jerome, *If Men Were Angels* (1942).
Jackson, Robert H., *The Struggle for Judicial Supremacy* (1941).
Lerner, Max, "Great Constitutional War," *Va. Quar. Rev.*, 18 (1942), 530.
Pearson, Drew, and Robert Allen, *Nine Old Men* (1936).
Pritchett, Charles H., *The Roosevelt Court* (1948).
Pusey, M. J., *The Supreme Court Crisis* (1937).
Stone, Isidor F., *Court Disposes* (1937).

* * * * * * *

U.S. Library of Congress, *The Supreme Court Issue* (1938).

See also 10.3 for biographies/writings of:

Brandeis, Louis D., 1856–1941
Cardozo, Benjamin N., 1870–1938
Hughes, Charles Evans, 1889–1950
Stone, Harlan F., 1872–1946
Sutherland, George, 1862–1942

53.5.7 Campaign of 1940

Appleby, P. H., "Roosevelt's Third-Term Decision," *Am. Pol. Sci. Rev.*, 46 (1952), 754.
Barnes, Joseph, *Willkie* (1952).
Burke, Robert E., "Election of 1940," in Arthur M. Schlesinger, Jr. and Fred L. Israel, eds., *History of American Presidential Elections, 1789–1968*. Vol. IV (1971).

Donahoe, Bernard F., *Private Plans: FDR's Third Nomination* (1965).
———— "Willkie Campaign," *Jour. Politics*, 14 (1952), 241.
Johnson, Donald B., *The Republican Party and Wendell Willkie* (1960).
Moscow, Warren, *Roosevelt and Willkie* (1968).
Parmet, Herbert S., and Marie B. Hecht, *Never Again: A President Runs for a Third Term* (1968).
Rodell, Fred, *Democracy and Third Term* (1940).
"This Man Willkie," *New Republic*, 103 (1940), 315. Special section by the editors.

See also 10.3 for biographies/writings of:

Dewey, Thomas E., 1902–1971
Farley, James A., 1888–
Flynn, Edward J., 1891–1953
Garner, John Nance, 1868–1967
Hopkins, Harry L., 1890–1946
Hull, Cordell, 1871–1955
Roosevelt, Franklin D., 1882–1945
Vandenberg, Arthur H., 1884–1951
Wallace, Henry A., 1888–1965
Willkie, Wendell, 1892–1944

53.5.8 South

Cole, Taylor, and John H. Hallowell, eds., *Southern Political Scene, 1938–1948* (1948).
Freidel, Frank, *F.D.R. and the South* (1965).
Key, V. O., Jr., *Southern Politics in State and Nation* (1949).

See also 10.3 for biographies/writings of:

Bilbo, Theodore G., 1877–1947
Byrd, Harry F., 1887–1966
Byrnes, James F., 1879–1972
Daniels, Josephus, 1862–1948
Johnston, Olin D., 1896–
Long, Huey P., 1893–1935
Rayburn, Sam, 1882–1961

53.5.9 New Deal and the States

Burke, Robert E., *Olson's New Deal for California* (1953).
Cox, Merlin G., "David Sholtz: New Deal Governor of Florida," *Fla. Hist. Quar.*, 43 (1964), 142.
Johnson, Roger T., *Robert M. La Follette, Jr. and the Decline of the Progressive Party in Wisconsin* (1964).
Kane, Harnett T., *Louisiana Hayride* (1941).
Kehl, James A., and Samuel J. Astorino, "A Bull Moose Responds To the New Deal: Pennsylvania's Gifford Pinchot," *Penn. Mag. Hist. Biog.*, 88 (1964), 37.
McSeveney, Samuel T., "The Michigan Gubernatorial Campaign of 1938," *Mich. Hist.*, 45 (1961), 97.
Malone, Michael P., *C. Ben Ross and the New Deal in Idaho* (1970).
Patterson, James Tyler, *The New Deal and the States: Federalism in Transition* (1969).
Puryear, Elmer L., *Democratic Party Dissension in North Carolina, 1928–1936* (1962).
Sindler, Allan P., *Huey Long's Louisiana: State Politics, 1920–1952* (1956).

See also 10.3 for biographies/writings of:

Landon, Alf, 1887–
Lehman, Herbert H., 1878–1963
Long, Huey P., 1893–1935
Olson, Floyd B., 1891–1936
Pinchot, Gifford, 1865–1946
Ross, C. Ben, 1876–1946

53.5.10 Urban Politics

McKean, Dayton D., *Boss: Hague Machine* (1940).
Reddig, W. M., *Tom's Town, Kansas City* (1947).
Stave, Bruce M., *The New Deal and the Last Hurrah: Pittsburgh Machine Politics* (1970).
Van Devander, C. W., *Big Bosses* (1944).

See also 10.3 for biographies/writings of:

Brownlow, Louis, 1879–1963
Crump, Edward H., ?–1954
Curley, James Michael, 1874–1958
Farley, James A., 1888–
Flynn, Edward J., 1891–1953
La Guardia, Fiorello H., 1882–1947

53.6 OPPOSITION TO ROOSEVELT AND NEW DEAL

53.6.1 General

Wolfskill, George, and John A. Hudson, *All But the People: Franklin D. Roosevelt and His Critics, 1933–1939* (1969).

53.6.2 Conservatives

Boskin, Joseph, comp., *Opposition Politics: Anti-New Deal Tradition* (1968).
Cleveland, A. S., "NAM: Spokesman for Industry?" *Harv. Bus Rev.*, 26 (1948), 353.
Douglas, Lewis W., *Liberal Tradition* (1935).
Hand, Samuel B., "Al Smith, Franklin D. Roosevelt, and the New Deal," *Historian*, 27 (1965), 366.
Hoover, Herbert, *Addresses upon the American Road* (1938).
———— *Challenge to Liberty* (1934).
Mills, Ogden L., *What of Tomorrow?* (1935).
Polenberg, Richard, "National Committee to Uphold Constitutional Government, 1937–1941," *JAH*, 52 (1965), 582.
Rudolph, Frederick, "American Liberty League," *AHR*, 56 (1950), 19.
Schwarz, Jordan A., "Al Smith in the Thirties," *N.Y. Hist.*, 45 (1964), 316.
Wolfskill, George, *Revolt of Conservatives: American Liberty League, 1934–1940* (1962).

53.6.3 Left Wing Movements

53.6.3.1 General

Bingham, A. M., *Insurgent America* (1935).
———— and Selden Rodman, eds., *Challenge to the New Deal* (1934).
Carter, John Franklin, *American Messiahs* (1935).

McCoy, Donald R., *Angry Voices: Left-of-Center Politics in the New Deal Era* (1958).
Sinclair, Upton, *I, Candidate for Governor* (1935).
———— *I, Governor of California* (1933).

53.6.3.2 The Aged and Townsend Movement

Holtzman, Abraham, *Townsend Movement* (1963).
Neuberger, Richard L., and Kelly Loe, *Army of the Aged* (1936).
Putnam, Jackson K., *Old-Age Politics in California: From Richardson to Reagan* (1970).
Townsend, Francis Everett, *New Horizons* (1943).
Twentieth Century Fund, *Townsend Crusade* (1936).

53.6.3.3 Father Coughlin

Coughlin, Charles E., *Lectures on Social Justice* (1935).
Kernan, William C., *Ghost of Royal Oak* (1940).
Shenton, James P., "The Coughlin Movement and the New Deal," *Pol. Sci. Quar.*, 73 (1958), 352.
———— "Fascism and Father Coughlin," *Wis. Mag. Hist.*, 44 (1960), 6.
Soderbergh, Peter A., "Rise of Father Coughlin, 1891–1930," *Social Science*, 42 (1967), 10.
Tull, Charles J., *Father Coughlin and the New Deal* (1965).

53.6.3.4 Huey Long

Kane, Harnett T., *Louisiana Hayride* (1941).
Long, Huey P., *Every Man a King* (1933).
———— *My First Days in the White House* (1935).

See also 10.3 for biographies/writings of:

Long, Huey P., 1893–1935

53.6.3.5 Union Party

Bennett, David H., *Demagogues in the Depression: American Radicals and the Union Party, 1932–1936* (1969).
Powell, David O., "Union Party of 1936," *Mid-America*, 46 (1964), 126.

See also 10.3 for biographies/writings of:

Lemke, William, 1878–1950

53.7 SOCIALIST PARTY

Egbert, Donald Drew, and Stow Persons, *Socialism and American Life* (2 vols., 1952).
Laidler, Harry W., *American Socialism* (1937).
Thomas, Norman, *After the New Deal What?* (1936).
———— *America's Way Out* (1936).

53.8 COMMUNIST PARTY

Beal, F. E., *Proletarian Journey* (1937).
Browder, Earl, "The American Communist Party in the Thirties," in Rita J. Simon, ed., *As We Saw the Thirties* (1967).
———— *Communism in the United States* (1935).

—— *People's Front* (1938).
—— *Second Imperialist War* (1940).
Chambers, Whittaker, *Witness* (1952).
Cooke, Alistair, *Generation on Trial* (1950).
Crossman, Richard, ed., *The God That Failed* (1949).
Dies, Martin, *Trojan Horse in America* (1940).
Gellerman, William, *Martin Dies* (1944).
Gitlow, Benjamin, *I Confess* (1940).
Goodman, Walter, *The Committee: Extraordinary Career of the House Committee on Un-American Activities* (1968).
Hicks, Granville, "How Red Was the 'Red Decade'?" *Harper's*, 207 (1953), 53.
Kampelman, Max M., *The Communist Party vs. the C.I.O.: A Study in Power Politics* (1957).
Lasswell, Harold D., and Dorothy Blumenstock, *World Revolutionary Propaganda* (1939).
Latham, Earl, *The Communist Controversy in Washington: From the New Deal to McCarthy* (1966).
Lyons, Eugene, *Red Decade* (1941).
Nolan, W. A., *Communism Versus Negro* (1951).
Ogden, A. R., *Dies Committee* (1943).
Record, Wilson, *The Negro and the Communist Party* (1951).
Toledano, Ralph de, and Victor Lasky, *Seeds of Treason* (1952).
Warren, Frank A., III, *Liberals and Communism: The "Red Decade" Revisited* (1966).
Wechsler, James A., *The Age of Suspicion* (1953).

53.9 INTERREGNUM AND LAUNCHING OF NEW DEAL

Feis, Herbert, *1933: Characters in Crisis* (1966).
Lindley, Ernest K., *Roosevelt Revolution* (1933).
Moley, Raymond, *First New Deal* (1966).
Rosen, Elliot A., "Intranationalism vs. Internationalism: New Deal," *Pol. Sci. Quar.*, 81 (1966), 274.
Schlesinger, Arthur M., Jr., *The Age of Roosevelt: Coming of the New Deal* (1959).
Seligman, Lester G., and Elmer E. Cornwell, Jr., eds., *New Deal Mosaic: Roosevelt Confers with National Emergency Council, 1933–1936* (1965).
Tugwell, Rexford G., *The Brains Trust* (1968).

See also 10.3 for biographies/writings of:

Hoover, Herbert, 1874–1964
Moley, Raymond, 1886–
Roosevelt, Franklin D., 1882–1945
Stimson, Henry L., 1867–1950

53.10 ADMINISTRATION AND EXECUTIVE REORGANIZATION

Emmerich, Herbert, *Essays on Federal Reorganization* (1950).
Karl, Barry D., *Executive Reorganization and Reform in the New Deal: Administrative Management, 1900–1939* (1963).
Polenberg, Richard, *Reorganizing Roosevelt's Government: The Controversy over Executive Reorganization, 1936–1939* (1966).
U.S. President's Committee on Administrative Management, *Administrative Management* (1937).
Wann, A. J., *President as Chief Administrator: A Study of Franklin Delano Roosevelt* (1968).

53.11 RELIEF AND SOCIAL SECURITY PROGRAMS

53.11.1 Unemployed and Their Families

Armstrong, Louise V., *We Too Are People* (1938).
Bakke, E. W., *Citizens without Work* (1940).
―――― *Unemployed Worker* (1940).
Cavan, Ruth, and K. H. Ranck, *Family and Depression* (1938).
Feder, Leah H., *Unemployment Relief* (1936).
Ginzberg, Eli, et al., *Unemployed* (1943).
Komarovsky, Mirra, *Unemployed Man and His Family* (1940).
Morgan, Winona L., *Family Meets Depression* (1939).
Stouffer, S. A., et al., *Family in Depression* (1937).
Webbink, Paul, "Unemployment, 1930–1940," *Am. Econ. Rev.*, 30 (1941), 248.

53.11.2 Relief

53.11.2.1 General

Abbott, Edith, *Public Assistance* (1940).
Abbott, Grace, *From Relief to Social Security* (1941).
Adams, Grace, *Workers on Relief* (1939).
Atkinson, Raymond C., et al., *Public Employment Service* (1938).
Baird, Enid, and H. B. Brinton, *Average General Relief Benefits, 1933–1938* (1940).
Brown, Josephine C., *Public Relief, 1929–1939* (1940).
Chapin, Francis S., and S. A. Queen, *Social Work in the Depression* (1937).
Charles, Searle F., *Minister of Relief: Harry Hopkins* (1963).
Colcord, J. C., *Cash Relief* (1936).
Coppock, J. D., *Food Stamp Plan* (1947).
Davis, Maxine, *They Shall Not Want* (1937).
Lane, Marie D., and Francis Steegmuller, *America on Relief* (1938).
Palmer, Gladys L., and K. D. Wood, *Urban Workers on Relief* (1936).
Radowski, A. L., *Work Relief in New York State, 1931–1935* (1947).
Riesenfeld, Stefan A., "American Public Assistance Law," *Calif. Law Rev.*, 43 (1955), 175.
Sherwood, Robert E., *Roosevelt and Hopkins* (1950).
U.S. National Resources Planning Board, *Security, Work and Relief Policies* (1942).
White, Reuel C. and M. K., *Social Aspects of Relief Policies in the Depression* (1937).
Whiting, T. E., and T. J. Woofter, Jr., *Summary of Relief and Federal Work Program Statistics* (1941).
Williams, Edward A., *Federal Aid for Relief* (1939).
Wynne, Waller, Jr., *Five Years of Rural Relief* (1938).
Zimmerman, C. C., and N. L. Whetten, *Rural Families on Relief* (1938).

53.11.2.2 Federal Work Relief

Alsberg, H. G., ed., *America Fights Depression, A Photographic Record of the CWA* (1934).
Burns, Arthur E., and Peyton Kerr, "Recent Changes in Work-Relief Wage Policy," *Am. Econ. Rev.*, 31 (1941), 56.
―――― "Survey of Work–Relief Wage Policies," *Am. Econ. Rev.*, 27 (1937), 711.
Gilboy, Elizabeth W., *Applicants for Work Relief* (1940).
Gill, Corrington, *Wasted Manpower* (1939).
Hopkins, Harry L., *Spending to Save* (1936).
Macmahon, Arthur W., et al., *Administration of Federal Work Relief* (1941).
Walter, Forrest A., "Graft and Civil Works Administration," *Southw. Soc. Sci. Quar.*, 46 (1965), 164.

*   *   *   *   *   *   *

Chicago University Library, *Unemployment and Relief Documents* (1934).
U.S. Federal Emergency Relief Administration, *Subject Index of Research Bulletins Issued by the FERA and WPA, Division of Social Research* (1937).
Wilcox, Jerome K., *Unemployment Relief Documents* (1936).

53.11.2.3 Works Progress Administration

Baker, Jacob, *Government Aid to Professional Service Workers* (1936).
Campbell, Doak S., et al., *Educational Activities of the Works Progress Administration* (1939).
Howard, Donald S., *WPA and Federal Relief Policy* (1943).
Whatley, Larry, "Works Progress Administration in Mississippi," *Jour. Miss. Hist.*, 30 (1968), 35.
Works Progress Administration, *Inventory: Appraisal of Results* (1938).

53.11.2.4 Federal Arts and Cultural Programs

Billington, Ray A., "Government and the Arts: The WPA Experience," *Am. Quar.*, 13 (1961), 466.
Binkley, R. C., "Cultural Program of WPA," *Harv. Educ. Rev.*, 9 (1939), 156.
De Rohan, Pierre, ed., *Federal Theatre Plays* (1938).
Flanagan, Hallie, *Arena: The History of the Federal Theatre* (1940).
Fox, Daniel M., "Achievement of Federal Writers' Project," *Am. Quar.*, 13 (1961), 3.
Kellock, Katharine, "WPA Writers," *Am. Scholar*, 9 (1940), 743.
McDonald, William F., *Federal Relief Administration and the Arts* (1969).
Mathews, Jane D., *The Federal Theatre, 1935–1939* (1967).
New York. Museum of Modern Art, *New Horizons in American Art*, Holger Cahill, introduction (1936).
O'Conner, Francis V., "New Deal Murals in New York," *Art Forum*, 7 (1968), 41.
Whitman, Willson, *Bread and Circuses* (1937).
"Work of the Federal Writers' Project of WPA," *Publishers' Weekly*, 135 (1939), 1130.

See also 10.3 for biographies/writings of:

Biddle, George, 1885–
Wright, Richard, 1908–1960

53.11.2.5 Civilian Conservation Corps and National Youth Administration

Holland, Kenneth, and F. E. Hill, *Youth in CCC* (1942).
Johnson, Palmer O., and O. L. Harvey, *National Youth Administration* (1938).
Lindley, Betty, and Ernest K. Lindley, *New Deal for Youth* (1938).
Lorwin, Lewis L., *Youth Work Programs* (1941).
Salmond, John A., "A Civilian Conservation Corps and the Negro," *Jour. Am. Hist.*, 52 (1965), 75.
—— *The Civilian Conservation Corps, 1933–1942* (1967).

*   *   *   *   *   *   *

Civilian Conservation Corps, *Civilian Conservation Corps Bibliography* (1939).
Menefee, Louis A., and M. M. Chambers, comps., *American Youth* (1938).

53.11.3 Social Security

Abbott, Grace, *From Relief to Social Security* (1941).
Altmeyer, Arthur J., *Formative Years of Social Security* (1966).
Baker, Helen, *Social Security* (1939).
Burns, Eveline M., *American Social Security* (1949).
Douglas, Paul H., *Social Security* (1939).

Epstein, Abraham, *Insecurity, A Challenge to America* (2nd rev. ed., 1967).
Haber, William, and W. J. Cohen, *Readings in Social Security* (1948).
Harris, Seymour E., *Economics of Social Security* (1941).
Lubove, Roy, *Struggle for Social Security, 1900–1935* (1968).
Perkins, Frances, *The Roosevelt I Knew* (1946).
U.S. President's Committee on Economic Security, *Report* (1935).
Witte, Edwin E., *Development of Social Security Act* (1962).
—— *Social Security Perspectives: Essays*, Robert J. Lampman, ed. (1962).

*   *   *   *   *   *   *

U.S. Social Security Board, *Brief Reading List on Social Security Act* (1941).

53.11.4 Health and Welfare

"American Medical Association," *Fortune*, 18 (1938), 89.
Cabot, Hugh, *Doctor's Bill* (1935).
Collins. S. D., and Clark Tibbitts, *Social Aspects of Health in Depression* (1937).
Falk, Isidore S., et al., *Costs of Medical Care* (1933).
Falk, Isidore S., *Security Against Sickness* (1936).
Garceau, Oliver, *The Political Life of the American Medical Association* (1941).
Hirschfield, Daniel S., *Lost Reform: Campaign for Compulsory Health Insurance from 1932–1943* (1970).
Jackson, Charles O., *Food and Drug Legislation in the New Deal* (1970).
Rorty, James, *American Medicine Mobilizes* (1939).
Warbasse, J. P., *Cooperative Medicine* (1936).

*   *   *   *   *   *   *

U.S. Library of Congress, *Health Insurance* (1938).

53.11.5 Public Works Administration

Galbraith, John K., and Gove Griffith Johnson, Jr., *Economic Effects of the Federal Public Works Expenditures, 1933–1938* (1940).
Gayer, Arthur D., *Public Works in Prosperity and Depression* (1935).
Ickes, Harold L., *Accomplishments of the Federal Emergency Administration* (1936).
—— *Back to Work* (1935).
—— *Secret Diary* (3 vols., 1953).
Isakoff, Jack F., *Public Works Administration* (1938).
Williams, J. Kerwin, *Grants in Aid under the Public Works Administration* (1939).

53.11.6 Housing Loans and Public Housing

Harriss, C. L., *History and Policies of Home Owners' Loan Corporation* (1952).
McDonnell, Timothy L., *Wagner Housing Act* (1957).
Post, Langdon W., *Challenge of Housing* (1938).
Schoenfeld, M. H., "Progress of Public Housing," *Monthly Lab. Rev.*, 51 (1940), 267.
Straus, M. W., and Talbott Wegg, *Housing Comes of Age* (1938).
Straus, Nathan, *Four Years of Public Housing* (1941).
—— *Seven Myths of Housing* (1944).
U.S. National Resources Planning Board, *Housing: Continuing Problem* (1940).

*   *   *   *   *   *   *

U.S. Library of Congress, *References on Housing* (1934). *Supplement* (1935).

See also 10.3 for biographies/writings of:

Wagner, Robert F., 1877–1953

53.12 ECONOMY AND RECOVERY PROGRAMS

53.12.1 General

Brookings Institution, *The Recovery Program in the United States* (1936).
Hawley, Ellis W., *New Deal and the Problem of Monopoly* (1966).
Lindley, Ernest K., *Halfway with Roosevelt* (1936).
Mitchell, Broadus, *Depression Decade* (1947).
Smithies, Arthur, "American Economy in the Thirties," *Am. Econ. Rev.*, 36 (1946, supplement), 11.
U.S. National Resources Committee, *Structure of the American Economy* (2 vols., 1939–1940).

See also 10.3 for biographies/writings of:

Hoover, Herbert, 1874–1964
Ickes, Harold L., 1874–1952
Jones, Jesse H., 1874–1956
Moley, Raymond, 1886–
Morgenthau, Henry, Jr., 1891–1967
Roosevelt, Franklin D., 1882–1945

53.12.2 Special Topics

Bell, Spurgeon, *Productivity, Wages, and National Income* (1940).
Bloomfield, Arthur I., *Capital Imports and American Balance of Payments, 1934–1939* (1950).
Epstein, R. C., *Industrial Profits* (1934).
Klein, Lawrence R., "National Income and Product, 1929–1950," *Am. Econ. Rev.*, 43 (1953), 117.
Mendershausen, Horst, *Changes in Income Distribution during the Great Depression* (1946).
Stigler, G. J., *Trends in Output and Employment* (1947).
Twentieth Century Fund, *Debts and Recovery, 1929–1937* (1938).

53.12.3 Industrial and Financial Recovery

53.12.3.1 Banking Crisis and Deposit Insurance
Ballantine, A. A., "When All Banks Closed," *Harv. Bus. Rev.*, 26 (1948), 129.
Bogen, J. I., and Marcus Nadler, *Banking Crisis* (1933).
Bremer, C. D., *American Bank Failures* (1935).
Emerson, Guy, "Guaranty of Deposits," *Quar. Jour. Econ.*, 48 (1934), 229.
Moley, Raymond, *First New Deal* (1966).
O'Connor, James F. T., *Banking Crisis* (1938).
Upham, C. B., and Edwin Lamke, *Closed and Distressed Banks* (1934).

See also 10.3 for biographies/writings of:

Couzens, James, 1872–1936
Ford, Henry, 1863–1947

53.12.3.2 Banking Act of 1935
Bradford, F. A., "Banking Act of 1935," *Am. Econ. Rev.*, 25 (1935), 661.
Eccles, Marriner S., *Beckoning Frontiers* (1951).

——— *Economic Balance and a Balanced Budget* (1940).
Gayer, Arthur D., "Banking Act of 1935," *Quar. Jour. Econ.*, 50 (1935), 97.
Viner, Jacob, "Recent Legislation and Banking Situation," *Am. Econ. Rev.*, 26
   (1936, supplement), 96.

53.12.3.3 Monetary Policy

Blum, John M., *From the Morgenthau Diaries: Years of Crisis, 1928–1938* (3 vols.,
   1959–1967).
Brennan, John A., *Silver and the First New Deal* (1969).
Crawford, Arthur W., *Monetary Management under the New Deal* (1940).
Everest, A. S., *Morgenthau, New Deal and Silver* (1950).
Friedman, Milton, and Anna J. Schwartz, *Monetary History of the United States,
   1867–1960* (1963).
Hardy, Charles O., *Warren-Pearson Price Theory* (1935).
Johnson, Gove Griffith, Jr., *Treasury and Monetary Policy, 1933–1938*
   (1939).
Nichols, Jeannette P., "Roosevelt's Monetary Diplomacy in 1933," *AHR*, 56
   (1951), 295.
Paris, James D., *Monetary Policies, 1932–1938* (1938).
Pasvolsky, Leo, *Current Monetary Issues* (1933).
Reeve, J. R., *Monetary Reform Movements* (1943).

53.12.3.4 Security Regulation

Atkins, W. E., et al., *Regulation of Security Markets* (1946).
Cherrington, H. V., *Investor and Securities Act* (1942).
De Bedts, Ralph F., "First Chairmen of Securities and Exchange Commission,"
   Am. Jour. Econ. Sociol., 23 (1964), 165.
——— *New Deal's SEC: Formative Years* (1964).
Douglas, William O., *Democracy and Finance* (1940).
Flynn, John T., *Security Speculation* (1934).
Haven, T. Kenneth, *Investment Banking under the Securities and Exchange Com-
   mission* (1940).
Kennedy, Edward D., *Dividends to Pay* (1939).
Landis, James M., "Legislative History of the Securities Act of 1933," *George
   Washington Law Rev.*, 28 (1959), 29.
Parrish, Michael E., *Securities Regulation and the New Deal* (1970).
Stein, Emanuel, *Government and Investor* (1941).
Twentieth Century Fund, *Security Markets* (1935).
Vernon, Raymond, *Regulation of Stock Exchange Members* (1941).
Weissman, R. L., *New Wall Street* (1939).

*   *   *   *   *   *   *

U.S. Library of Congress, *List on Securities Act of 1933* (1935).
——— *List on Securities and Exchange Act of 1934* (1935).

53.12.3.5 Reconstruction Finance Corporation

Glover, J. D., "Industrial Loan Policy of RFC," *Harv. Bus. Rev.*, 17 (1939), 465.
Jones, Jesse H., and Edward Angly, *Fifty Billion Dollars* (1951).
Reconstruction Finance Corporation, *Seven-Year Report* (1939).
Spero, Herbert, *Reconstruction Finance Corporation Loans to Railroads, 1932–1937*
   (1939).

53.12.3.6 Tax Policy

Blakey, R. G., *Federal Income Tax* (1940).
Blough, Roy, *Federal Taxing Process* (1952).
Colm, Gerhard, and Fritz Lehman, *Economic Consequences of Recent Tax Policy*
   (1938).
Kendrick, Myron S., *Undistributed Profits Tax* (1937).

Lent, G. E., *Impact of Undistributed Profits Tax, 1936–1937* (1948).
Ratner, Sidney, *American Taxation* (1942).

53.12.3.7 National Recovery Administration and Fair Trade Policy

Campbell, P. C., *Consumer Representation in New Deal* (1940).
Connery, R. H., *Administration of an NRA Code* (1938).
Corwin, Edward S., "Schechter Case—Landmark, or What?" *N.Y.U. Law Rev.*, 12 (1936), 151.
Fine, Sidney, *Automobile under the Blue Eagle* (1963).
Hawley, Ellis W., *New Deal and the Problem of Monopoly* (1966).
Johnson, Hugh S., *Blue Eagle* (1935).
Lyon, Leverett S., et al., *National Recovery Administration* (1935).
Nash, Gerald D., "Experiments in Industrial Mobilization: WIB and NRA," *Mid-America*, 45 (1963), 157.
Nourse, Edwin G., *Marketing Agreements under NRA* (1935).
Patman, Wright, *Robinson-Patman Act* (1938).
Pearce, Charles A., *NRA Trade Practice Programs* (1939).
Richberg, D. R., *Rainbow* (1936).
Roos, C. F., *NRA Economic Planning* (1937).
Rowe, Frederick M., "Robinson–Patman Act," *Columbia Law Rev.*, 57 (1957), 1059.
Stern, Robert L., "Commerce Clause and the National Economy, 1933–1946," *Harv. Law Rev.*, 59 (1946), 645.
U.S. Congress, House, *National Recovery Administration: Report of President's Committee of Analysis* (75 Cong., 1st sess., H. Doc. no. 158).
Werne, Benjamin, ed., *Business and the Robinson-Patman Law* (1938).

53.12.3.8 Compensatory Fiscal Policy

Alsop, Joseph, and Robert Kintner, *Men around the President* (1939).
Brown, E. Cary, "Fiscal Policy in the Thirties," *Am. Econ. Rev.*, 46 (1956), 857.
Burns, Arthur E., and D. S. Watson, *Government Spending and Economic Expansion* (1941).
Galbraith, John K., and Gove Griffith Johnson, Jr., *Economic Effects of Federal Works Expenditures, 1933–1938* (1940).
Galbraith, John K., "How Keynes Came to America," in John K. Galbraith, *Contemporary Guide to Economics, Peace, and Laughter*, Andrea D. Williams, ed. (1971).
Gilbert, Richard V., et al., *Economic Program for American Democracy* (1938).
Hansen, Alvin H., *Business Cycles and National Income* (1951).
——— *Full Recovery or Stagnation?* (1938).
——— *Guide to Keynes* (1953).
Harris, Seymour E., ed., *New Economics* (1947).
Klein, Lawrence R., *Keynesian Revolution* (1947).
Lindholm, R. W., *Public Finance and Fiscal Policy* (1950).
Stein, Herbert, *The Fiscal Revolution in America* (1969).
Terborgh, George, *Bogey of Economic Maturity* (1945).
Villard, H. H., *Deficit Spending and National Income* (1941).

53.12.3.9 Recession of 1937–1938

Roose, Kenneth D., *Economics of Recession and Revival, 1937–1938* (1954).

53.12.3.10 Price Rigidity and Anti-Monopoly

GENERAL

Arnold, Thurman W., *Bottlenecks of Business* (1940).
——— *Democracy and Free Enterprise* (1942).
Edwards, Corwin D., "Thurman Arnold and Antitrust Laws," *Pol. Sci. Quar.*, 58 (1943), 338.
Hamilton, Walton H., *Antitrust in Action* (1940).

SPECIFIC INDUSTRIES

Baker, Ralph H., *National Bituminous Coal Commission* (1941).
Daugherty, C. R., et al., *Economics of Iron and Steel* (1937).
Freudenthal, Elsbeth E., *Aviation Business* (1940).
Rostow, E. V., *National Policy for Oil* (1948).
Wallace, Donald H., *Market Control in Aluminum* (1937).
Watkins, Myron W., *Oil: Stabilization or Conservation* (1937).

TEMPORARY NATIONAL ECONOMIC POWER

Lynch, David, *Concentration of Economic Power* (1946).
"Papers Relating to Temporary National Economic Committee," *Am. Econ. Rev.,* 32 (1942, supplement), 129.
"Publications of the Temporary National Economic Committee," *Am. Econ. Rev.,* 31 (1941), 347.
U.S. Temporary National Economic Committee, *Investigation of Concentration of Economic Power. Description of Hearings and Monographs* (77 Cong., 1st sess., Sen. Comm. Pr., 1941).
―――― *Investigation of Concentration of Economic Power. Final Report and Recommendations* (77 Cong., 1st sess., Sen. Doc. no. 35, 1941).
―――― *Investigation of Concentration of Economic Power. Final Report of Executive Secretary* (77 Cong., 1st sess., Sen. Comm. Pr., 1941).
―――― *Investigation of Concentration of Economic Power. Hearings* (1939–1941).
―――― *Investigation of Concentration of Economic Power. Monographs* (Nos. 1–43, 1940–1941).

53.12.3.11 Transportation Policy

Fuess, Claude M., *Joseph B. Eastman* (1952).
Latham, Earl, *The Politics of Railroad Coordination, 1933–1936* (1959).
Moulton, Harold G., *American Transportation Problem* (1933).
U.S. National Resources Planning Board, *Transportation and National Policy* (1942).

53.13 LABOR

53.13.1 General

Bernstein, Irving, *Turbulent Years: The American Worker, 1933–1941* (1970).
Harris, Herbert, *American Labor* (1938).
Young, Edwin, and Milton Derber, eds., *Labor and the New Deal* (1957).

See also 10.3 for biographies/writings of:

Hillman, Sidney, 1887–1946
Lewis, John L., 1880–1969

53.13.2 Special Topics

Auerbach, Jerold S., *Labor and Liberty: The La Follette Committee* (1966).
Brooks, Robert R. R., *As Steel Goes* (1940).
―――― *Unions of Their Own Choosing* (1939).
―――― *When Labor Organizes* (1937).
Christenson, Carroll L., and R. A. Myren, *Wage Policy under the Walsh–Healey Public Contracts Act* (1966).
Higgins, George G., *Voluntarism in Organized Labor, 1930–1940* (1944).
Levinson, Edward, *Labor on March* (1938).

McFarland, Charles K., *Roosevelt, Lewis and the New Deal, 1933–1940* (1970).

Muste, A. J., "My Experience in the Labor and Radical Struggles of the Thirties," in Rita J. Simon, ed., *As We Saw the Thirties* (1967).

Overacker, Louise, "Labor's Political Contribution," *Pol. Sci. Quar.*, 54 (1939), 56.

Parrish, J. B., "Changes in Labor Supply, 1930–1937," *Am. Econ. Rev.*, 29 (1939), 325.

53.13.3 Early Legislation

Bernstein, Irving, *New Deal Collective Bargaining Policy* (1950).

Daugherty, C. R., *Labor Under NRA* (1934).

Fine, Sidney, *The Automobile under the Blue Eagle* (1963).

Lorwin, Lewis L., and Arthur Wubnig, *Labor Relations Boards* (1935).

McCabe, D. A., "Effects of the Recovery Act upon Labor Organizations," *Quar. Jour. Econ.*, 49 (1934), 52.

MacDonald, Lois, et al., *Labor and the NRA* (1934).

Marshall, Leon C., *Hours and Wages in NRA Codes* (1935).

Schoenfeld, M. H., "Analysis of Labor Provisions of NRA Codes," *Monthly Lab. Rev.*, 40 (1935), 574.

53.13.4 Wagner Act and National Labor Relations Board

Aiken, Charles, ed., *National Labor Relations Board Cases* (1939).

Cortner, Richard C., *Wagner Act Cases* (1964).

Eby, H. O., *Labor Relations Act in Courts* (1943).

Gregory, C. O., and H. A. Katz, *Policy Development under the National Labor Relations Act* (1947).

Kaltenborn, Howard S., *Governmental Adjustment of Labor Disputes* (1943).

McNaughton, Wayne L., *Development of Labor Relations Law* (1941).

Metz, Harold, *Labor Policy of the Federal Government* (1945).

Millis, Harry A., and E. C. Brown, *From the Wagner Act to the Taft-Hartley* (1950).

Rosenfarb, Joseph, *National Labor Policy* (1946).

Salny, S. M., *Independent Unions under the Wagner Act* (1944).

Silverberg, L. G., *Wagner Act* (1945).

Taylor, George W., *Government Regulation of Industrial Relations* (1948).

53.13.5 Fair Labor Standards Act of 1938

Douglas, Paul H., and Joseph Hackman, "Fair Labor Standards Act of 1938," *Pol. Sci. Quar.*, 53 (1938), 491; 54 (1939), 29.

Phelps, Orme W., *Legislative Background of Fair Labor Standards Act* (1939).

Richter, Irving, "Four Years of Fair Labor Standards Act," *Jour. Pol. Econ.*, 51 (1943), 95.

53.14 AGRICULTURE

53.14.1 General

Baker, Oliver E., et al., *Agriculture in Modern Life* (1939).

Hardin, C. M., *Politics of Agriculture* (1952).

Saloutos, Theodore, and J. D. Hicks, *Agricultural Discontent in the Middle West, 1900–1939* (1951).

U.S. Department of Agriculture, *Farmers in a Changing World* (1940).

53.14.2 Policies and Proposals

Albertson, Dean, *Roosevelt's Farmer: Claude R. Wickard in the New Deal* (1961).
Black, John D., *Parity, Parity, Parity* (1942).
Kirkendall, Richard S., *Social Scientists and Farm Politics in the Age of Roosevelt* (1966).
Rosenof, Theodore, "Economic Ideas of Henry A. Wallace, 1933–1948," *Agric. Hist.*, 41 (1967), 143.
Rowley, William D., *M. L. Wilson and the Campaign for the Domestic Allotment* (1970).
Shover, John L., "Communist Party and Midwest Farm Crisis of 1933," *JAH*, 51 (1964), 248.
Wallace, Henry A., *New Frontiers* (1934).
Wilson, Milburn L., *Farm Relief and Domestic Allotment Plan* (1933).

See also 10.3 for biographies/writings of:

Wallace, Henry A., 1888–1965

53.14.3 Farmers' Associations

Auerbach, Jerold S., "Southern Tenant Farmers: Socialist Critics of the New Deal," *Lab. Hist.*, 7 (1966), 3.
Campbell, Christiana M., *Farm Bureau and New Deal* (1962).
Carey, James C., "Farmers' Independence Council, 1935–1938," *Agric. Hist.*, 35 (1961), 70.
Chambers, Clarke A., *California Farm Organizations, 1929–1941* (1952).
Grubbs, Donald H., "Gardner Jackson, That 'Socialist' Tenant Farmers' Union, and the New Deal," *Agric. Hist.*, 42 (1968), 125.
Johnson, William R., "National Farm Organizations and Reshaping Agricultural Policy in 1932," *Agric. Hist.*, 37 (1963), 35.
Kile, Orville M., *Farm Bureau through Three Decades* (1948).
McConnell, Grant, *Decline of Agrarian Democracy* (1953).
McCune, Wesley, *Farm Bloc* (1943).
Noblin, Stuart L., *The Grange in North Carolina, 1929–1954* (1954).
Shover, John L., "Communist Party and Midwest Farm Crisis of 1933," *JAH*, 51 (1964), 248.
────── *Cornbelt Rebellion: Farmers' Holiday Association* (1965).
Tucker, W. P., "Populism Up-to-date," *Agric. Hist.*, 21 (1947), 198.

53.14.4 Agricultural Programs

53.14.4.1 General

Gaus, John M., and L. O. Wolcott, *Public Administration and Department of Agriculture* (1940).
Nourse, Edwin G., *Government in Relation to Agriculture* (1940).
Pursell, Carroll W., Jr., "Administration of Science in the Department of Agriculture, 1933–1940," *Agric. Hist.*, 42 (1968), 231.

53.14.4.2 Agricultural Adjustment Administration

Black, John D., *Dairy Industry and the AAA* (1935).
Dalton, John E., *Sugar* (1937).
Davis, Joseph S., *Wheat and the AAA* (1935).
Ezekiel, Mordecai, and L. H. Bean, *Economic Bases for the Agricultural Adjustment Act* (1933).
Fite, Gilbert C., *George N. Peek and the Fight for Farm Parity* (1954).
Fitzgerald, Dennis A., *Livestock under the AAA* (1935).
Martin, R. E., "Referendum Process in Agricultural Adjustment Programs," *Agric. Hist.*, 25 (1951), 34.

Nourse, Edwin G., *Marketing under the AAA* (1935).
———— et al., *Three Years of Agricultural Adjustment Administration* (1937).
Peek, George N., and Samuel Crowther, *Why Quit Our Own?* (1936).
Perkins, Van L., *Crisis in Agriculture: Agricultural Adjustment and the New Deal, 1933* (1969).
Richards, Henry I., *Cotton and the AAA* (1936).
Rowe, Harold B., *Tobacco under the AAA* (1935).
Shover, John L., "Populism in 1930's: Battle for AAA," *Agric. Hist.*, 39 (1965), 17.

See also 10.3 for biographies/writings of:

Wallace, Henry A., 1888–1965

53.14.4.3 Rural Electrification

Childs, Marquis, *Farmer Takes a Hand* (1952).
Cooke, M. L., "Early Days of Rural Electrification," *Am. Pol. Sci. Rev.*, 42 (1948), 431.
Muller, F. W., *Public Rural Electrification* (1944).
Person, Harlow S., "Rural Electrification Administration," *Agric. Hist.*, 24 (1950), 70.

53.14.4.4 Farm Security Administration

Baldwin, Sidney, *Poverty and Politics: Farm Security Administration* (1968).
Severin, Werner J., "Cameras with a Purpose: The Photojournalists of F.S.A.," *Journalism Quar.*, 41 (1964), 191.

See also 10.3 for biographies/writings of:

Alexander, Will, 1884–1956

53.14.4.5 Community Programs

Conkin, Paul K., "Pine Mountain Valley," *Ga. Hist. Rev.*, 47 (1963), 1.
———— *Tomorrow a New World: New Deal Community Program* (1959).

53.14.5 Rural Life

53.14.5.1 Sharecroppers and Tenancy

Black, John D., and R. H. Allen, "Growth of Farm Tenancy," *Quar. Jour. Econ.*, 51 (1937), 393.
Caldwell, Erskine, and Margaret Bourke-White, *You Have Seen Their Faces* (1937).
Cantor, Louis, *Prologue to the Protest Movement: Missouri Sharecropper Roadside Demonstration of 1939* (1969).
Conrad, David E., *Forgotten Farmers: Sharecroppers in the New Deal* (1965).
Frey, F. C., and T. L. Smith, "Influence of AAA Cotton Program upon Tenant, Cropper and Laborer," *Rural Sociol.*, 1 (1936), 483.
Hoffsommer, Harold, "AAA and Cropper," *Social Forces*, 13 (1935), 494.
Johnson, Charles S., et al., *Collapse of Cotton Tenancy* (1935).
Kester, Howard, *Revolt Among Sharecroppers* (1936).
Kroll, Harry H., *I Was a Sharecropper* (1937).
Maris, P. V., *Land Is Mine* (1950).
Raper, A. F., *Preface to Peasantry* (1936).
———— and I. DeA. Reid, *Sharecroppers All* (1941).
Southern Tenant Farmers' Union, *Disinherited Speak* (1936).
Thomas, Norman, *Plight of the Sharecropper* (1934).
U.S. Congress. House Agricultural Committee, *Farm Tenancy* (75 Cong., 1st sess., Hearings, 1937).
U.S. National Resources Committee, *Farm Tenancy* (1937).

Venkataramani, M. S., "Norman Thomas, Arkansas Sharecroppers, and Roosevelt Agricultural Policies, 1933–1937," *MVHR*, 47 (1960), 225.

*   *   *   *   *   *   *

Bercaw, L. O., *Southern Sharecropper* (1935).

53.14.5.2 Migratory Labor

Hendrickson, Kent, "The Sugar-Beet Laborer and the Federal Government: Episode in History of Great Plains in 1930's," *Gt. Plains Jour.*, 3 (1964), 44.
Lange, Dorothea, and Paul S. Taylor, *American Exodus: Human Erosion in the Thirties* (1969).
Lively, Charles E., and Conrad Taeuber, *Rural Migration* (1939).
McWilliams, Carey, *Factories in Field* (1939).
—— *Ill Fares the Land* (1942).
Steinbeck, John, *The Grapes of Wrath* (1939).
Thompson, Warren S., *Internal Migration in the Depression* (1937).
U.S. Department of Labor, *Migration of Workers* (2 vols., 1938).
Webb, John N., and Malcolm Brown, *Migrant Families* (1939).
Webb, John N., *Migratory-Casual Worker* (1937).

53.14.5.3 Changes in Rural Life

Brunner, E. deS., and J. H. Kolb, *Rural Social Trends* (1933).
Brunner, E. deS., and Irving Lorge, *Rural Trends in the Depression* (1937).
Melvin, B. L., and E. N. Smith, *Rural Youth* (1938).
Sanderson, Dwight, *Rural Life in the Depression* (1937).
Sufrin, S. C., "Labor Organization in Agricultural America, 1930–1935," *Am. Jour. Sociol.*, 43 (1938), 544.
U.S. Department of Agriculture, *Technology on the Farm* (1940).

53.14.5.4 Poverty

Taylor, Carl C., et al., *Disadvantaged Classes in Agriculture* (1938).
Wilson, Charles M., *Landscape of Rural Poverty* (1940).
Wilson, Milburn L., "Problem of Poverty in Agriculture," *Jour. Farm Econ.*, 22 (1940), 10.
Wynne, Waller, Jr., *Five Years of Rural Relief* (1938).
Zimmerman, C. C., and N. L. Whetten, *Rural Families on Relief* (1938).

53.15 CONSERVATION

53.15.1 General

Gustafson, A. F., et al., *Conservation* (1939).
Parkins, A. E., and J. R. Whitaker, eds., *Our National Resources* (1936).
U.S. National Resources Committee, *Patterns of Resource Use* (1939).
U.S. National Resources Planning Board, *National Resources Development* (1943).

53.15.2 Forest Policies

Gulick, Luther H., *American Forest Policy* (1951).
Lilliard, Richard G., *Great Forest* (1947).

53.15.3 Soil Erosion and Conservation

Brink, Wellington, *Big Hugh* (1951).
California. University. Bureau of Public Administration, *Land Utilization* (1935).

Chase, Stuart, *Rich Land, Poor Land* (1936).
Clawson, Marion, *Uncle Sam's Acres* (1951).
Lord, Russell, *Behold Our Land* (1938).
Sears, Paul B., *Deserts on March* (1935).

*   *   *   *   *   *   *

Soil Conservation Service, *Bibliography on Soil Conservation* (1936).
U.S. Bureau of Agricultural Economics, *Land Utilization* (1936).
———— *Soil Erosion* (1935).

53.15.4 Flood Control

Bennett, Hugh H., *Conservation Practices and Flood Control* (1936).
Leuchtenburg, William E., *Flood Control Politics* (1953).
Maass, Arthur, *Muddy Waters: The Army Engineers and the Nation's Rivers* (1951).
Person, Harlow S., et al., *Little Waters* (1936).

53.15.5 Electric Power

Bauer, John, and Peter Costello, *Public Organization of Electric Power* (1949).
Bauer, John, and Nathaniel Gold, *Electric Power Industry* (1939).
Baum, R. D., *Federal Power Commission and State Regulation* (1942).
Bonbright, J. C., *Public Utilities and National Power Policies* (1940).
Twentieth Century Fund, *Power Industry and Public Interest* (1944).

*   *   *   *   *   *   *

Leininger, G. C., "Bibliography on Utility Holding Companies," *Jour. Land Public Utility Econ.*, 11 (1935), 419.

53.16 TENNESSEE VALLEY AUTHORITY

Clapp, Gordon R., *TVA: Approach to Development of a Region* (1955).
Droze, Wilmon H., *High Dams and Slack Waters: TVA* (1965).
Finer, Herman, *TVA* (1944).
Hodge, Clarence L., *Tennessee Valley Authority* (1938).
Hubbard, Preston J., *Origins of the TVA: Muscle Shoals Controversy, 1920–1932* (1961).
Kyle, John H., *Building of TVA* (1958).
Lilienthal, David E., *TVA* (rev. ed., 1953).
———— and R. H. Marquis, "Conduct of Business by the Federal Government," *Harv. Law. Rev.*, 54 (1941), 545.
Pritchett, Charles H., *Tennessee Valley Authority* (1943).
Ransmeier, J. S., *Tennessee Valley Authority* (1942).
Selznick, Philip, *TVA and Grass Roots* (1949).
Wengert, N. I., *Valley of Tomorrow: TVA and Agriculture* (1952).

*   *   *   *   *   *   *

Foy, B. L., comp., *Bibliography of Tennessee Valley Authority* (1949).
Norwood, A. M., comp., *Congressional Hearings, Reports and Documents Relating to TVA, 1933–1946* (1946).

See also 10.3 for biographies/writings of:

Lilienthal, David E., 1899–

Norris, George W., 1861–1944
Willkie, Wendell, 1892–1944

53.17 REGIONALISM AND REGIONAL PLANNING

53.17.1 General

Leuchtenburg, William E., "Roosevelt, Norris and the 'Seven Little TVAs'," *Jour. Politics*, 14 (1952), 418.
Lohmann, Karl B., *Regional Planning* (1936).
Mangus, Arthur R., *Rural Regions* (1940).
Odum, Howard W., and H. E. Moore, *American Regionalism* (1938).
Odum, Howard W., and Katherine Jocher, eds., *In Search of Regional Balance* (1945).
"Symposium on Regional Planning," *Iowa Law Rev.*, 32 (1947), 193.
U.S. National Resources Committee, *Regional Factors in National Planning* (1935).
────── *Twenty-Two Drainage Basin Committee Reports* (1937).
U.S. National Resources Planning Board, *Regional Planning Reports* (13 vols., 1936–1943).

53.17.2 National Resources Planning Board

Gruchy, Allen G., "Economics of National Resources Committee," *Am. Econ. Rev.*, 29 (1939), 60.
Merriam, Charles E., "National Resources Planning Board," *Am. Pol. Sci. Rev.*, 38 (1944), 1075.
Millett, John, *Process of Government Planning* (1947).
Tugwell, Rexford G., "Utility of the Future in the Present," *Pub. Admin. Rev.*, 8 (1947), 49.
U.S. National Resources Committee, *City and County Planning* (1937).

53.17.3 South

Arnall, Ellis G., *The Shore Dimly Seen* (1946).
Berge, Wendell, "Monopoly and South," *South. Econ. Jour.*, 13 (1947), 360.
Cash, Wilbur J., *The Mind of the South* (1941).
Cason, Clarence, *90° in the Shade* (1935).
Daniels, Jonathan, *A Southerner Discovers the South* (1938).
Federal Writers' Project, *These Are Our Lives* (1939).
Herring, Harriet L., *Passing of the Mill Village* (1949).
────── *Southern Industry and Regional Development* (1940).
Holley, William C., et al., *Plantation South, 1934–1937* (1940).
Krueger, Thomas A., *And Promises to Keep: The Southern Conference for Human Welfare, 1938–1948* (1967).
Livesey, R. A., *South in Action* (1949).
Lumpkin, Katherine D., *Making of a Southerner* (1947).
────── *The South in Progress* (1940).
Nixon, Herman C., *Possum Trot* (1941).
Odum, Howard W., *Southern Regions* (1936).
────── *Way of South* (1947).
Percy, William A., *Lanterns on the Levee: Recollections of a Planter's Son* (1941).
U.S. National Emergency Council, *Report on Economic Conditions of South* (1938).
Vance, R. B., *Human Geography of South* (1935).
────── and Nadia Danilevsky, *All These People* (1945).
Van Sickle, J. V., *Planning for the South* (1943).
Webb, Walter P., *Divided We Stand* (1937).

See also 10.3 for biographies/writings of:

Alexander, Will, 1884–1956

See also 53.5.8, Politics in Age of Roosevelt, 1933–1945–South.

53.17.4 West

Baumhoff, R. G., *Damned Missouri Valley* (1951).
De Voto, Bernard, "West: Plundered Province," *Harper's*, 169 (1934), 355.
Howard, Joseph K., *Montana: High, Wide and Handsome* (1943).
Lilliard, Richard G., *Desert Challenge: An Interpretation of Nevada* (1942).
McKinley, Charles, *Uncle Sam in the Pacific Northwest* (1952).
Neuberger, Richard L., *Our Promised Land* (1938).
Terral, Rufus, *Missouri Valley* (1947).
U.S. Forest Service, *Western Range* (1936).

53.18 DEPENDENCIES

53.18.1 Puerto Rico

Gayer, Arthur D., et al., *Sugar Economy of Puerto Rico* (1938).
Goodsell, Charles T., Jr., *Administration of a Revolution: Executive Reform in Puerto Rico under Governor Tugwell, 1941–1946* (1965).
Mathews, Thomas, *Puerto Rican Politics and the New Deal* (1960).
Tugwell, Rexford G., *Stricken Land: Puerto Rico* (1947).

53.18.2 Philippines

Bernstein, David, *Philippine Story* (1947).
Friend, Theodore, *Between Two Empires: Ordeal of the Philippines, 1929–1946* (1965).
Grunder, G. A., and W. E. Livezey, *Philippines and the United States* (1951).
Kirk, Grayson L., *Philippine Independence* (1936).
Woodford, Howard, "Frank Murphy and the Philippine Commonwealth," *Pac. Hist. Rev.*, 33 (1964), 45.

*   *   *   *   *   *   *

Carnegie Endowment for International Peace, *Philippine Independence* (1939).

53.18.3 Other Dependencies

Evans, Luther H., *Virgin Islands* (1945).
Pomeroy, Earl S., "American Policy Respecting the Marshalls, Carolines, and Marianas, 1898–1941," *Pac. Hist. Rev.*, 17 (1948), 43.
———— *Pacific Outpost: American Strategy in Guam and Micronesia* (1953).

53.19 FOREIGN RELATIONS

53.19.1 General

Adler, Selig, *Uncertain Giant: American Foreign Policy, 1921–1941* (1965).
Council on Foreign Relations, *United States in World Affairs* (1931–).
Dahl, R. A., *Congress and Foreign Policy* (1950).

Divine, Robert A., *Roosevelt and World War II* (1969).
Landecker, Manfred, *The President and Public Opinion: Leadership in Foreign Affairs* (1968).
Nevins, Allan, *The New Deal and World Affairs* (1950).
Perkins, Dexter, "The Department of State and American Public Opinion," in Gordon A. Craig and Felix Gilbert, eds., *The Diplomats, 1919–1939* (1953).
Range, Willard, *Franklin D. Roosevelt's World Order* (1959).
Roosevelt, Franklin D., *Franklin D. Roosevelt and Foreign Affairs*, Edgar B. Nixon, ed. (3 vols., 1969). Covers the period through January 1937.
Welles, Sumner, *Time for Decision* (1944).
Wiltz, John E., *From Isolation to War, 1931–1941* (1968).

*   *   *   *   *   *   *

Cam, G. A., "United States Neutrality Resolutions," N.Y. Pub. Lib., *Bull.*, 41 (1937), 417.
Carnegie Endowment for International Peace, *Intellectual Relations United States and Latin America* (1935).
———— *Neutrality* (1938).
———— *Peace Movement* (1940).
Foreign Affairs Bibliography, 1932–1942, R. G. Woolbert, comp. (1945).
U.S. Library of Congress, *Nationalism* (1934).
———— *Recent References on Neutrality* (1941).
———— *References on American National Defense* (1936).
———— *References on Traffic in Arms* (1934).
U.S. Tariff Commission, *Reciprocal Trade* (1936).

See also 10.3 for biographies/writings of:

Hopkins, Harry L., 1890–1946
Hull, Cordell, 1871–1955
Phillips, William, 1878–1968
Pittman, Key, 1872–1940
Roosevelt, Franklin D., 1882–1945

53.19.2 Recognition of Russia

Bishop, Donald G., *Roosevelt–Litvinov Agreements* (1965).
Bowers, Robert E., "American Diplomacy, the 1933 Wheat Conference, and Recognition of the Soviet Union," *Agric. Hist.*, 40 (1966), 39.
Browder, Robert P., *Origins of Soviet–American Diplomacy* (1953).

53.19.3 Economic Aspects

53.19.3.1 General

Feis, Herbert, *Changing Pattern of International Economic Affairs* (1940).
Gardner, Lloyd C., *Economic Aspects of New Deal Diplomacy* (1964).
Gayer, Arthur D., and C. T. Schmidt, *American Economic Foreign Policy* (1939).

53.19.3.2 London Economic Conference and Monetary Diplomacy

Bowers, Robert E., "William Bullitt's Secret Mission to Europe," *Ind. Mag. Hist.*, 61 (1965), 189.
Feis, Herbert, *1933: Characters in Crisis* (1966).
Nichols, Jeannette P., "Roosevelt's Monetary Diplomacy in 1933," *AHR*, 56 (1951), 295.

See also 10.3 for biographies/writings of:

Cox, James M., 1870–1957

Hull, Cordell, 1871–1955
Moley, Raymond, 1886–
Morgenthau, Henry, Jr., 1891–1967
Pittman, Key, 1872–1940

53.19.3.3 Foreign Trade and Reciprocal Agreements

Adler, J. H., *Pattern of Import Trade* (1952).
Allen, W. R., "International Trade Philosophy of Cordell Hull," *Am. Econ. Rev.*, 43 (1953), 101.
Beard, Charles A., and George H. Smith, *Open Door at Home* (1934).
Buell, R. L., *Hull Trade Program* (1939).
Dulles, Eleanor L., *Export-Import Bank* (1944).
Kottman, Richard N., *Reciprocity and North Atlantic Triangle, 1932–1938* (1968).
Kreider, Carl, *Anglo-American Trade Agreement* (1943).
—— "Effect of American Trade Agreements on Third Countries," *Am. Econ. Rev.*, 31 (1941), 780.
Larkin, John D., *Trade Agreements* (1940).
Letiche, J. M., *Reciprocal Trade Agreements in the World Economy* (1948).
Molyneux, Peter, *Cotton South and American Trade Policy* (1936).
Peek, George N., and Samuel Crowther, *Why Quit Our Own?* (1936).
Rau, Allan, *Agricultural Policy and Trade Liberalization, 1934–1956* (1957).
Sayre, Francis B., *The Way Forward: American Trade Agreements Program* (1939).
Snyder, R. C., "Commercial Policy in Treaties 1931 to 1939," *Am. Econ. Rev.*, 30 (1940), 787.
Tasca, H. J., *Reciprocal Trade Policy* (1938).
Taylor, Alonzo E., *New Deal and Foreign Trade* (1935).
Wallace, Henry A., *America Must Choose* (1934).

53.19.3.4 International Investments

Lewis, Cleona, *America's Stake in International Investment* (1938).
Madden, John T., *America's Experience as Creditor* (1937).
Singh, Baljit, "The Survival of the Weakest: A Case History of the Liberian Crisis of the 1930's," *Jour. Human Rel.*, 14 (1966), 242.

53.19.4 Good Neighbor Policy

53.19.4.1 General

Bemis, Samuel F., *Latin American Policy of the United States* (1943).
Bushnell, David, *Eduardo Santos and the Good Neighbor, 1938–1942* (1967).
Cooper, Donald B., "Withdrawal of the United States from Haiti, 1928–1934," *Jour. Inter-Am. Studies*, 5 (1963), 83.
Cronon, E. David, "Good Neighbor Policy: Cuban Crisis of 1933," *Hisp. Am. Hist. Rev.*, 39 (1959), 538.
Cuevas Cancino, Francisco M., *Roosevelt y la Buena Vecindad* (1954).
Duggan, Lawrence, *Americas: Search for Hemispheric Security* (1949).
Fenwick, Charles G., *Inter-American Regional System* (1949).
Feuerlein, Willy, and Elizabeth Hannan, *Dollars in Latin America* (1941).
Guerrant, E. O., *Roosevelt's Good Neighbor Policy* (1950).
Smith, Oscar E., Jr., *Yankee Diplomacy: Argentina* (1953).
Wood, Bryce, *Making of Good Neighbor Policy* (1961).
—— *The United States and Latin American Wars, 1932–1942* (1966).

53.19.4.2 Mexico

Cline, Howard F., *The United States and Mexico* (rev. ed., 1963).
Cronon, E. David, *Josephus Daniels in Mexico* (1960).
—— "American Catholics and Mexican Anticlericalism, 1933–1936," *MVHR*, 45 (1958), 201.

Gordon, Wendell C., *Expropriation of Foreign-Owned Property in Mexico* (1941).
Meyer, Lorenzo, *Mexico y Estados Unidos en el Conflicto Petrolero, 1917–1942* (1968).

See also 10.3 for biographies/writings of:

Daniels, Josephus, 1862–1948

53.19.5 Canada

Granatstein, J. L., "Conservative Party and the Ogdensburg Agreement," *Internatl. Jour.*, 22 (1967), 73.
Keenleyside, Hugh L., and G. S. Brown, *Canada and the United States* (rev. ed., 1952).
Kottman, Richard N., *Reciprocity and the North Atlantic Triangle, 1932–1938* (1968).
Riddell, Walter, ed., *Documents on Canadian Foreign Policy, 1917–1939* (1962).

53.19.6 Neutrality and Interventionism

53.19.6.1 General

Barnes, Harry E., *Perpetual War for Perpetual Peace: Foreign Policy of Franklin Delano Roosevelt* (1953).
Beard, Charles A., *American Foreign Policy, 1932–1940* (1946).
Divine, Robert A., *Illusion of Neutrality* (1962).
Drummond, Donald F., *Passing of American Neutrality, 1937–1941* (1955).
Stromberg, Roland, "American Business and the Approach to War, 1935–1941," *Jour. Econ. Hist.*, 13 (1953), 58.
Tansill, Charles C., *Back Door to War: Roosevelt Foreign Policy, 1933–1941* (1952).

53.19.6.2 Contemporary Writings

Borchard, Edwin, and W. P. Lage, *Neutrality for the United States* (1940).
Browder, Earl, *Second Imperialist War* (1940).
Buell, R. L., *Isolated America* (1940).
Dulles, Allen W., and H. F. Armstrong, *Can America Stay Neutral?* (1939).
Dulles, John Foster, *War, Peace and Change* (1939).
Fenwick, Charles G., *American Neutrality* (1940).
Grattan, Clinton H., *Deadly Parallel* (1939).
Hoover, Herbert, *Shall We Send Our Youth to War?* (1939).
Lavine, Harold, and James Wechsler, *War Propaganda* (1940).
Lindbergh, Anne M., *Wave of the Future* (1940).
Johnson, H. S., *Hell-bent for War* (1941).
Thomas, Norman, and B. D. Wolfe, *Keep America Out of War* (1939).

53.19.6.3 Legislation

Crecraft, E. W., *Freedom of the Seas* (1935).
Jessup, Phillip C., *International Security* (1935).
Seavey, James M., *Neutrality Legislation* (1939).
Wright, Quincy, *Neutrality and Collective Security* (1936).

53.19.6.4 Isolationism

Adler, Selig, *Isolationist Impulse: Its Twentieth Century Reaction* (1957).
Burns, Richard D., and W. Addams Dixon, "Foreign Policy and the 'Democratic Myth': The Debate on the Ludlow Amendment," *Mid-America*, 47 (1965), 288.
Cole, Wayne S., *America First: Battle against Intervention, 1940–1941* (1953).
De Conde, Alexander, ed., *Isolation and Security: Ideas and Interests in Twentieth-Century American Foreign Policy* (1957).

Donovan, J. C., "Congressional Isolationists and the Roosevelt Foreign Policy," *World Politics*, 2 (1951), 299.

Jonas, Manfred, *Isolationism in America, 1935–1941* (1966).

Leopold, Richard W., "Mississippi Valley and Foreign Policy, 1890–1941," *MVHR*, 37 (1951), 625.

Nelson, John K., *The Peace Prophets: American Pacifist Thought, 1919–1941* (1967).

Smuckler, R. H., "Region of Isolationism," *Am. Pol. Sci. Rev.*, 47 (1953), 386.

Wilkins, Robert P., "Non-Ethnic Roots of North Dakota Isolationism," *Neb. Hist.*, 44 (1963), 205.

See also 10.3 for biographies/writings of:

Borah, William E., 1865–1940
Lindbergh, Charles A., 1902–
Nye, Gerald P., 1892–
Wheeler, Burton K., 1882–

53.19.6.5 Nye Committee and International Arms Traffic

"Arms and the Men," *Fortune*, 9 (1934), 53.

Atwater, Elton, *American Regulation of Arms Exports* (1941).

Cole, Wayne S., *Senator Gerald P. Nye and American Foreign Relations* (1962).

Engelbrecht, H. C., and F. C. Hanighen, *Merchants of Death* (1934).

Stedman, M. S., *Exporting Arms, 1935–1945* (1947).

Wiltz, John E., *In Search of Peace: Senate Munitions Inquiry, 1934–1936* (1963).

See also 10.3 for biographies/writings of:

Nye, Gerald P., 1892–

53.19.7 World Crisis, 1937–1941

53.19.7.1 General

Anglin, Douglas G., *St. Pierre and Miquelon Affaire of 1941: A Study in Diplomacy in the North Atlantic Quadrangle* (1966).

Beard, Charles A., *President Roosevelt and the Coming of War, 1941* (1948).

Churchill, Winston L. S., *Grand Alliance* (1950).

——— *Their Finest Hour* (1949).

Craig, Gordon A., and Felix Gilbert, eds., *The Diplomats, 1919–1939* (1953).

Divine, Robert A., *Reluctant Belligerent: American Entry into World War II* (1965).

Esthus, Raymond A., *From Enmity to Alliance: United States–Australian Relations, 1931–1941* (1964).

Friedländer, Saul, *Prelude to Downfall: Hitler and United States, 1939–1941* (1967).

Harriman, Florence J., *Mission to North* (1941).

Harris, Brice, Jr., *United States and the Italo-Ethiopian Crisis* (1964).

Holborn, Louise W., ed., *War and Peace Aims of the United Nations* (1943).

Langer, William L., and S. E. Gleason, *Challenge to Isolation, 1937–1940* (1952).

——— *Undeclared War* (1953).

Rauch, Basil, *Roosevelt from Munich to Pearl Harbor* (1950).

Tansill, Charles C., *Back Door to War* (1952).

See also 10.3 for biographies/writings of:

Bullitt, William C., 1891–1967
Hull, Cordell, 1871–1955
Jones, Jesse H., 1874–1956

Morgenthau, Henry, Jr., 1891–1967
Roosevelt, Franklin D., 1882–1945

53.19.7.2 Fascist and Nazi Activities

Carlson, J. R., *Undercover* (1943).
Dennis, Lawrence, *Dynamics of War and Revolution* (1940).
"Fascists in the United States," *Fortune*, 22 (1940), 85.
Lavine, Harold, *Fifth Column* (1940).
Norman, John, "Influence of Pro-Fascist Propaganda on Neutrality," in Dwight
E. Lee and George E. McReynolds, eds., *Essays in History and International
Relations in Honor of George Hubbard Blakeslee* (1951).
Turrou, L. G., *Nazi Spies* (1939).

53.19.7.3 Collective Security and Intervention

Borg, Dorothy, "Roosevelt's 'Quarantine' Speech," *Pol. Sci. Quar.*, 72 (1957),
405.
Chadwin, Mark L., *The Hawks of World War II: Interventionist Movement in the
U.S. Prior to Pearl Harbor* (1968).
Friedman, Donald J., *The Road from Isolation; The Campaign of the American
Committee for Non-Participation in Japanese Aggression, 1938–1941* (1968).
Johnson, Walter, *Battle Against Isolationism* (1944).
Sobel, Robert, *Origins of Interventionism: United States and the Russo–Finnish
War* (1960).

53.19.7.4 East Asian Diplomacy

GENERAL

Bisson, T. A., *American Policy in Far East, 1931–1941* (1941).
Browder, R. P., "Soviet Far Eastern Policy and American Recognition, 1932–
1934," *Pac. Hist. Rev.*, 21 (1952), 263.
Buhite, Russell D., *Nelson T. Johnson and American Policy towards China, 1925–
1941* (1968).
Esthus, Raymond A., *From Enmity to Alliance: United States–Australian Rela-
tions, 1931–1941* (1964).
Griswold, A. Whitney, *The Far Eastern Policy of the United States* (1938).
Hornbeck, Stanley K., *The United States and the Far East* (1942).
Thomson, James C., Jr., *While China Faced West: American Reformers in Nation-
alist China, 1928–1937* (1969).

JAPAN

Borg, Dorothy, *The United States and the Far Eastern Crisis of 1933–1938: From
the Manchurian Incident through the Initial Stages of the Undeclared Sino-
Japanese War* (1964).
Koginos, Manny T., *The "Panay" Incident: Prelude to War* (1967).
Maxon, Yale C., *Control of Japanese Foreign Policy, 1930–1945* (1957).
Perry, Hamilton D., *"Panay" Incident: Prelude to Pearl Harbor* (1969).

See also 10.3 for biographies/writings of:

Grew, Joseph C., 1880–1965

53.19.7.5 Spanish Civil War

Bowers, Claude G., *My Mission to Spain: Rehearsal for World War II* (1954).
Brenan, Gerald, *Spanish Labyrinth* (2nd ed., 1950).
Cattell, David T., *Communism and the Spanish Civil War* (1955).
—— *Soviet Diplomacy and the Spanish Civil War* (1957).
Eby, Cecil, *Between the Bullet and the Lie: American Volunteers in the Spanish
Civil War* (1969).

Feis, Herbert, *The Spanish Story* (1948).

Guttmann, Allen, ed., *American Neutrality and the Spanish Civil War* (1963).

—— *Wound in the Heart: America and the Spanish Civil War* (1962).

Landis, Arthur H., *Abraham Lincoln Brigade* (1967).

Rosenstone, Robert A., *Crusade on the Left: Lincoln Battalion in the Spanish Civil War* (1969).

Taylor, F. Jay, *United States and the Spanish Civil War, 1936–1939* (1956).

Traina, Richard P., *American Diplomacy and the Spanish Civil War* (1968).

Valaik, J. David, "American Catholic Dissenters and the Spanish Civil War," *Cath. Hist. Rev.*, 53 (1968), 537.

—— "Catholic Neutrality and the Spanish Embargo, 1937–1939," *JAH*, 54 (1967), 73.

*   *   *   *   *   *   *

Duràn, Juan García, *Bibliography of the Spanish Civil War, 1936–1939* (1964).

53.19.7.6 Germany

Compton, James V., *The Swastika and the Eagle* (1967).

Friedländer, Saul, *Prelude to Downfall: Hitler and the United States, 1939–1941* (1963); Aline B. and Alexander Werth, trans. (1967).

Frye, Alton, *Nazi Germany and the American Hemisphere, 1933–1941* (1967).

Jonas, Manfred, "Hans Dieckhoff's Reports from Washington," *Mid-America*, 47 (1965), 222.

Kennan, George F., *From Prague after Munich: Papers, 1938–1940* (1968).

Moltmann, Günter, "Roosevelts Friedensappell vom 14. April 1939," *Jahrbuch für Amerikastudien*, 9 (1964), 91.

Offner, Arnold A., *American Appeasement: United States Foreign Policy and Germany, 1933–1938* (1969).

Seabury, Paul, *Wilhelmstrasse: German Diplomats under the Nazi Regime* (1954).

Trefousse, H. L., *Germany and American Neutrality* (1951).

Weinberg, Gerhard L., "Hitler's Image of the United States," *AHR*, 69 (1964), 1006.

—— "Schachts Besuch in den U.S.A. im Jahre 1933," *Vierteljahrshefte für Zeitgeschichte*, 11 (1963), 166.

See also 10.3 for biographies/writings of:

Dodd, William E., 1869–1940

53.19.7.7 Refugees from Nazism

Feingold, Henry L., *The Politics of Rescue: The Roosevelt Administration and the Holocaust, 1938–1945* (1970).

Long, Breckinridge, *War Diary, 1939–1944*, Fred L. Israel, ed. (1966).

Spear, Sheldon, "The United States and the Persecution of the Jews in Germany, 1933–1939," *Jew. Soc. Stud.*, 30 (1968), 215.

Wyman, David S., *Paper Walls: Refugee Crisis, 1938–1941* (1968).

53.19.7.8 Intellectual Migration from Europe

Fermi, Laura, *Illustrious Immigrants: Intellectual Migration from Europe, 1930–1941* (1968).

Fleming, Donald, and Bernard Bailyn, eds., *Intellectual Migration: Europe and America, 1930–1960* (1969).

53.19.8 Origins of World War II

53.19.8.1 General

Lafore, Laurence, *The End of Glory: An Interpretation of Origins of World War II* (1969).

Renouvin, Pierre, *World War II and Its Origins: International Relations, 1929–1945* (1969).
Sontag, Raymond J., "Origins of Second World War," *Rev. Politics*, 25 (1963), 497.

See also 54.6.5, German Diplomacy and Military Actions.

53.19.8.2 Aid to Britain and Allies

GENERAL

Brown, William A., and Redvers Opie, *American Foreign Assistance* (1953).
Feis, Herbert, *Seen from E.A.* (1947).
Goodhart, Philip, *Fifty Ships that Saved the World: Anglo-American Alliance* (1965).
Haight, John McVickar, *American Aid to France, 1938–1940* (1970).
Wilson, Theodore A., *The First Summit: Roosevelt and Churchill at Placentia Bay, 1941* (1969).

LEND–LEASE

Dawson, Raymond H., *Decision to Aid Russia, 1941* (1959).
Jones, Robert H., *Roads to Russia: Lend–Lease* (1969).
Kimball, Warren F., *The Most Unsordid Act: Lend–Lease, 1939–1941* (1969).
Stettinius, Edward R., Jr., *Lend–Lease* (1944).

See also 10.3 for biographies/writings of:

Hopkins, Harry L., 1890–1946
Morgenthau, Henry, Jr., 1891–1967

53.19.8.3 Crisis with Japan

Butow, Robert J. C., *Tojo and Coming of War* (1961).
Esthus, Raymond A., "Roosevelt's Commitment to Britain to Intervene in the Pacific War," *MVHR*, 50 (1963), 28.
Feis, Herbert, *Road to Pearl Harbor* (1950).
Hsu, I. C. Y., "Kurusu's Mission," *Jour. Mod. Hist.*, 24 (1952), 301.
Morton, Louis, "Japan's Decision for War 1941," in Kent R. Greenfield, ed., *Command Decisions* (1960).
Schroeder, Paul W., *Axis Alliance and Japanese–American Relations, 1941* (1958).

*   *   *   *   *   *   *

Cole, Wayne S., "American Entry into World War II," *MVHR*, 43 (1957), 595.

See also 10.3 for biographies/writings of:

Grew, Joseph C., 1880–1965
Hull, Cordell, 1871–1955
Kimmel, Husband E., 1882–1968
Roosevelt, Franklin D., 1882–1945
Stimson, Henry L., 1867–1950

54 World War II, 1941–1945

54.1 GENERAL

Buchanan, Albert Russell, *The United States and World War II* (2 vols., 1964).
Churchill, Winston L. S., *The Second World War* (6 vols., 1948–1953).
Divine, Robert A., *Roosevelt and World War II* (1969).
Morison, Samuel E., *Strategy and Compromise* (1958).

54.2 WARTIME DIPLOMACY

54.2.1 General

Feis, Herbert, *Churchill, Roosevelt, Stalin: The War They Waged and the Peace They Sought* (1957).
Gardner, Lloyd C., *Architects of Illusion: Men and Ideas in American Foreign Policy, 1941–1949* (1970).
Kolko, Gabriel, *Politics of War: Foreign Policy, 1943–1945* (1968).
McNeill, William H., *America, Britain and Russia, 1941–1946* (1953).
Neumann, William L., *After Victory: Churchill, Roosevelt, Stalin* (1967).
Rozek, Edward J., *Allied Wartime Diplomacy: Poland* (1958).
Smith, Gaddis, *American Diplomacy during the Second World War, 1941–1945* (1965).
Snell, John L., *Illusion and Necessity: Global War, 1939–1945* (1963).
U.S.S.R. Ministry of Foreign Affairs, *Correspondence between the Chairman of the Council of Ministers of the U.S.S.R. and the Presidents of the U.S.A. and the Prime Ministers of Great Britain, 1941–1945* (2 vols., 1957).
Westerfield, H. Bradford, *Foreign Policy and Party Politics: Pearl Harbor to Korea* (1955).

54.2.2 Special Topics

Armstrong, Anne, *Unconditional Surrender: Casablanca Policy and World War II* (1961).
Brown, William A., Jr., and Redvers Opie, *American Foreign Assistance* (1953).
Feis, Herbert, *Petroleum and American Foreign Policy* (1944).
Gordon, David L., and Royden Dangerfield, *Hidden Weapon: Economic Warfare* (1947).
Kecskemeti, Paul, *Strategic Surrender: Politics of Victory and Defeat* (1958).
Moltmann, Günter, *Amerikas Deutschlandpolitik im zweiten Weltkrieg, 1941–1945* (1958).
Welles, Sumner, *Seven Decisions That Shaped History* (1950).

54.2.3 Yalta and Potsdam

Byrnes, James F., *Speaking Frankly* (1947).
Clemens, Diane Shaver, *Yalta* (1970).
Feis, Herbert, *Between War and Peace: Potsdam Conference* (1960).
—— *Churchill, Roosevelt, Stalin: The War They Waged and the Peace They Sought* (1957).
Fenno, Richard F., ed., *Yalta Conference* (1955).
Snell, John L., ed., *Meaning of Yalta* (1956).
Stettinius, Edward R., Jr., *Roosevelt and the Russians* (1949).
Theoharis, Athan G., *Yalta Myths: An Issue in U.S. Politics, 1945–1955* (1970).
U.S. Department of State, *Participation in International Conferences, July 1, 1947 . . . June 30, 1950* (3 vols., 1949–1951).

See also 10.3 for biographies/writings of:

Byrnes, James F., 1879–1972
Cutler, Robert, 1895–
Leahy, William D., 1875–1959
Stettinius, Edward R., Jr., 1900–1949
Stimson, Henry L., 1867–1950
Truman, Harry S., 1884–1972

54.3 FOREIGN RELATIONS

54.3.1 Great Britain

Brogan, Denis W., "America and Britain, 1939–1946," *Yale Rev.*, 35 (1946), 193.
Feis, Herbert, *Churchill, Roosevelt, Stalin: The War They Waged and the Peace They Sought* (1957).
Higgins, Trumbull, *Winston Churchill and the Second Front, 1940–1943* (1957).
Macmillan, Harold, *Blast of War, 1939–1945* (1968).
Nicholas, Herbert, *Britain and U.S.A.* (1963).
Winant, John G., *Letter from Grosvenor Square* (1947).
Woodward, Ernest L., *British Foreign Policy in the Second World War* (1962).

See also 10.3 for biographies/writings of:

Roosevelt, Franklin D., 1882–1945
Winant, John G., 1889–1947

54.3.2 Soviet Union

Carr, Albert H. Z., *Truman, Stalin and Peace* (1950).
Davies, Joseph E., *Mission to Moscow* (1941).
Deane, J. R., *Strange Alliance* (1947).
Dennett, Raymond, and J. E. Johnson, eds., *Negotiating with the Russians* (1951).
Feis, Herbert, *Churchill, Roosevelt, Stalin: The War They Waged and the Peace They Sought* (1957).
Fischer, George, "Genesis of Soviet Relations in World War II," *Rev. Politics*, 12 (1950), 363.
Gardner, Lloyd C., Arthur M. Schlesinger, Jr., and Hans J. Morgenthau, *The Origins of the Cold War* (1970).
May, Ernest R., "United States, Soviet Union, and Far Eastern War, 1941–1945," *Pac. Hist. Rev.*, 24 (1955), 153.

Motter, T. H. Vail, *Persian Corridor and Aid to Russia* (1952).
Tompkins, Pauline, *American-Russian Relations in the Far East* (1949).

See also 10.3 for biographies/writings of:

Hull, Cordell, 1871–1955
Leahy, William D., 1875–1959
Roosevelt, Franklin D., 1882–1945
Stettinius, Edward R., Jr., 1900–1949
Wallace, Henry A., 1888–1965
Willkie, Wendell, 1892–1944

54.3.3 France

de Gaulle, Charles, *War Memoirs* (3 vols., 1955–1960).
d'Ornano, H. F., *L'action gaulliste aux États-Unis, 1940–1945* (1948).
Langer, William L., *Our Vichy Gamble* (1947).
McKay, Donald Cope, *The United States and France* (1951).
Murphy, Robert Daniel, *Diplomat Among Warriors* (1964).
Pendar, Kenneth, *Adventure in Diplomacy* (1945).
Pierre-Gosset, R. R., *Conspiracy in Algiers* (1945).
Soustelle, Jacques, *Envers et contre tout* (2 vols., 1947–1950).
Viorst, Milton, *Hostile Allies: FDR and Charles de Gaulle* (1965).
Weygand, Maxime, *Recalled to Service* (1952).
White, Dorothy S., *Seeds of Discord: De Gaulle, Free France and the Allies* (1964).

See also 10.3 for biographies/writings of:

Bullitt, William C., 1891–1967
Leahy, William D., 1875–1959

54.3.4 Far East

Drachman, Edward R., *United States Policy toward Vietnam, 1940–1945* (1970).
Fairbank, John K., *The United States and China* (rev. ed., 1971).
Feis, Herbert, *China Tangle* (1953).
Jones, Francis C., et al., *Far East, 1942–1946* (1955).
Tsou, Tang, *America's Failure in China, 1941–1950* (2 vols., 1963–1967).
Young, Arthur N., *China and the Helping Hand, 1937–1945* (1963).

54.3.5 European Neutral Nations and the Vatican

Beaulac, W. L., *Career Ambassador* (1951).
Hayes, Carlton J. H., *Wartime Mission in Spain* (1945).
Hughes, Emmet J., *Report from Spain* (1947).
Roosevelt, Franklin D., *Wartime Correspondence between Roosevelt and Pope Pius XII*, Myron C. Taylor, ed. (1947).

54.3.6 Latin America

Duggan, Lawrence, *Americas: Search for Hemispheric Security* (1949).
Furniss, E. S., Jr., "American Wartime Objectives in Latin America," *World Politics*, 2 (1950), 373.
Guerrant, E. O., *Roosevelt's Good Neighbor Policy* (1950).
U.S. Office of Inter-American Affairs, *History of Office of Coordinator of Inter-American Affairs* (1947).
Whitaker, Arthur P. ed., *Inter-American Affairs* (1941–1945). Annual.

54.4 POSTWAR PLANNING AND ESTABLISHMENT OF UNITED NATIONS

Divine, Robert A., *Second Chance: Triumph of Internationalism during World War II* (1967).
Goodrich, Leland M., and Edvard Hambro, *Charter of the United Nations* (1949).
Kirk, Grayson, and L. H. Chamberlain, "Organization of San Francisco Conference," *Pol. Sci. Quar.*, 60 (1945), 321.
Lorwin, Lewis L., *Postwar Plans of United Nations* (1943).
Penrose, E. F., *Economic Planning for Peace* (1953).
Russell, Ruth B., *History of the United Nations Charter: Role of the United States, 1940–1945* (1958).
U.S. Department of State, *Postwar Foreign Policy Preparation, 1939–1945* (1950).

54.5 WAR AIMS: CONTEMPORARY VIEWS

Holborn, Louise W., *War and Peace Aims of the United Nations* (1943).
Hoover, Herbert, and Hugh Gibson, *Problems of Lasting Peace* (1942).
Lippmann, Walter, *U.S. Foreign Policy* (1943).
———— *U.S. War Aims* (1944).
Luce, Henry R., *American Century* (1941).
Spykman, N. J., *America's Strategy* (1942).
Wallace, Henry A., *Century of Common Man* (1943).
Welles, Sumner, *Time for Decision* (1944).
Willkie, Wendell L., *One World* (1943).

54.6 MILITARY HISTORY

54.6.1 General

Churchill, Winston L. S., *The Second World War* (6 vols., 1948–1953).
Fuller, John F. C., *Second World War, 1939–1945* (1948).
Hart, B. H. Liddell, *History of the Second World War* (1971).

*   *   *   *   *   *   *

Dornbusch, C. E., ed., *Unit Histories of World War II* (1950). Supplement (1952).
Morton, Louis, "Sources for History of World War II," *World Politics*, 13 (1961), 435.
"Papers Presented at the Joint Session, AMI–AHA, San Francisco, California, 29 December 1965," *Mil. Affairs*, 30 (1966), 1.
U.S. National Archives, *Federal Records of World War II* (2 vols., 1951–1952).

54.6.2 Interpretative Studies

Baldwin, Hanson W., *Battles Lost and Won: World War II* (1966).
———— *Great Mistakes of the War* (1950).
Greenfield, Kent R., *American Strategy in World War II: A Reconsideration* (1963).
Wilmot, Chester, *Struggle for Europe* (1952).

54.6.3 Pictorial History

Mauldin, Bill, *Up Front* (1945).
Sulzberger, Cyrus L., *American Heritage Picture History of World War II* (1960).

Tourtellot, A. B., et al., eds., *Life's Picture History of World War II* (1950).
U.S. Department of the Army, Office of Chief of Military History, *Pictorial Record* (3 vols., 1951–1952).

54.6.4 American Participation

54.6.4.1 General

Buchanan, A. Russell, *United States and World War II* (2 vols., 1964).
Butcher, Harry E., *Three Years with Eisenhower* (1946).
Karig, Walter, et al., *Battle Reports* (6 vols., 1944–1952).
Marshall, George C., *Biennial Reports of Chief of Staff of Army, 1941–1945* (1945).
Morison, Samuel E., *History of United States Naval Operations in World War II* (14 vols., 1947–1960).
Pratt, Fletcher, *War for the World: Our Fighting Forces in World War II* (1950).
Williams, Mary H., comp., *Chronology: 1941–1945* (1960).
U.S. Department of the Army, Office of Chief of Military History, *United States in World War II* (1947–).

*　　*　　*　　*　　*　　*　　*

U.S. Department of the Army, Office of the Chief of Military History, *United States in World War II: Master Index Reader's Guide II* (1960).

See also 10.3 for biographies/writings of:

Bradley, Omar Nelson, 1893–
Eisenhower, Dwight D., 1890–1969
Forrestal, James, 1892–1949
Hopkins, Harry L., 1890–1946
Leahy, William D., 1875–1959
MacArthur, Douglas, 1880–1964
Marshall, George C., 1880–1959
Roosevelt, Franklin D., 1882–1945

54.6.4.2 Strategy

Baldwin, Hanson W., *Great Mistakes of the War* (1950).
Brune, A. H., *Strategy in World War II* (1947).
Coakley, Robert W., and Richard M. Leighton, *Global Logistics and Strategy: 1940–1945* (2 vols., 1955–1968).
Ehrman, John, *Grand Strategy, August 1943–September 1944* (1956).
Emerson, William, "Franklin D. Roosevelt as Commander-in-Chief in World War II," *Mil. Affairs*, 22 (1958), 181.
Greenfield, Kent R., *American Strategy in World War II* (1963).
Matloff, Maurice, and Edwin M. Snell, *Strategic Planning for Coalition Warfare, 1941–1942* (1953).
Matloff, Maurice, *Strategic Planning for Coalition Warfare, 1943–1944* (1959).
Morton, Louis, *Strategy and Command: The First Two Years* (1962).
——— "War Plan ORANGE: Evolution of a Strategy," *World Politics*, 11 (1959), 221.

54.6.4.3 Attack on Pearl Harbor

Farago, Ladislas, *Broken Seal: "Operation Magic" and Pearl Harbor* (1967).
Feis, Herbert, *Road to Pearl Harbor* (1950).
Ferrell, Robert H., "Pearl Harbor and Revisionists," *Historian*, 17 (1955), 215.
Lord, Walter, *Day of Infamy* (1957).
Millis, Walter, *This is Pearl!* (1947).
Trefousse, Hans L., ed., *What Happened at Pearl Harbor* (1958).
Wohlstetter, Roberta, *Pearl Harbor: Warning and Decision* (1962).

See also 10.3 for biographies/writings of:

Kimmel, Husband Edward, 1882–1968

54.6.4.4 Hemisphere Defense

Conn, Stetson, and Byron Fairchild, *Framework of Hemisphere Defense* (1960).
Conn, Stetson, et al., *Guarding the United States and Its Outposts* (2 vols., 1964).
Fenwick, Charles G., "Inter-American Neutrality Committee," *Am. Jour. Internatl. Law*, 35 (1941), 12.
Rippy, J. F., *Caribbean Danger Zone* (1940).
Stowell, E. C., "Havana Conference," *Am. Jour. Internatl. Law*, 35 (1941), 123.

54.6.4.5 Military Relations with Allies

Brereton, Lewis H., *The Brereton Diaries: The War in the Air in the Pacific, Middle East and Europe, 3 October 1941–8 May 1945* (1946).
Bryant, Arthur, *Triumph in the West: History of the War Years Based on Diaries of Field-Marshall Lord Alanbrooke, Chief of Imperial General Staff* (1959).
—— *Turn of the Tide: History of the War Based on Diaries of Field-Marshal Lord Alanbrooke, Chief of Imperial General Staff* (1957).
Donnison, Frank S. V., *Civil Affairs and Military Government: Central Organization and Planning* (1966).
Dziuban, Stanley W., *Military Relations between the United States and Canada, 1939–1945* (1959).
Hall, H. Duncan, *North American Supply* (1955).
Motter, T. H. Vail, *Persian Corridor and Aid to Russia* (1952).
Vigneras, Marcel, *Rearming the French* (1957).

54.6.5 German Diplomacy and Military Actions

Bullock, A. L. C., *Hitler* (1952).
Dulles, Allen W., *Germany's Underground* (1947).
Gilbert, Felix, ed., *Hitler Directs His War* (1950).
Gisevius, Hans B., *To the Bitter End*, Richard and Clara Winston, trans. (1947).
Goebbels, Joseph, *Diaries, 1942–1943* (1948).
Guderian, Heinz, *Panzer Leader* (1952).
Hart, B. H. Liddell, *German Generals Talk* (1948).
Hinsley, F. H., *Hitler's Strategy* (1951).
Hitler, Adolf, *Hitler's Secret Conversations* (1953).
Jacobsen, Hans A., and Jürgen Rohwer, *Decisive Battles of World War II: German View*, Edward Fitzgerald, trans. (1965).
Martjenssen, A. K., *Hitler and His Admirals* (1949).
Rothfels, Hans, *German Opposition to Hitler* (1948).
Schmidt, Paul, *Hitler's Interpreter* (1951).
Trevor-Roper, Hugh R., *Last Days of Hitler* (1947).
von Hassell, Ulrich, *Von Hassell Diaries* (1947).
Wheeler-Bennett, John W., *Munich* (1948).
Wiskemann, Elizabeth, *Rome–Berlin Axis* (1949).
Ziemke, Earl F., *Stalingrad to Berlin: German Defeat in the East* (1968).

54.7 EUROPEAN THEATER

54.7.1 General

Eisenhower, Dwight D., *Crusade in Europe* (1948).
—— *Report on Operations in Europe* (1946).
Harris, Arthur T., *Bomber Offensive* (1947).
Howard, Michael E., *Mediterranean Strategy in Second World War* (1968).

MacDonald, Charles Brown, *Mighty Endeavor: American Forces in the European Theater in World War II* (1969).
Patton, George S., *War As I Knew It* (1947).
U.S. Strategic Bombing Survey, *Summary Report (European War)* (1945).

See also 10.3 for biographies/writings of:

Bradley, Omar Nelson, 1893–
Eisenhower, Dwight D., 1890–1969
Marshall, George C., 1880–1959

54.7.2 African Campaign

Clark, Mark W., *Calculated Risk* (1950).
Howe, George F., *Northwest Africa: Seizing the Initiative in the West* (1957).
Langer, William L., *Our Vichy Gamble* (1947).
Murphy, Robert Daniel, *Diplomat among Warriors* (1964).

54.7.3 Sicilian and Italian Campaigns

Badoglio, Pietro, *Italy in Second World War* (1948).
Ciano, Galeazzo, *Ciano Diaries, 1939–1943* (1946).
Clark, Mark W., *Calculated Risk* (1950).
Garland, Albert N., and Howard M. Smyth, *Sicily and the Surrender of Italy* (1965).
Higgins, Trumbull, *Soft Underbelly: Anglo-American Controversy over Italian Campaign, 1939–1945* (1968).
Jackson, William G. F., *Battle for Italy* (1967).
Mussolini, Benito, *Fall of Mussolini* (1948).
—— *Memoirs, 1942–1943* (1948).
Sheehan, Fred, *Anzio: Epic of Bravery* (1964).
Shepperd, G. A., *Italian Campaign, 1943–1945* (1968).
Starr, C. G., ed., *Salerno to the Alps* (1948).

54.7.4 Allied Invasion

Leighton, Richard M., "OVERLORD Revisited: An Interpretation of American Strategy in the European War, 1942–1944," *AHR*, 68 (1963), 919.
Marshall, Samuel L. A., *Night Drop: American Airborne Invasion of Normandy* (1962).
Morgan, Frederick, *Overture to Overlord* (1950).
Norman, Albert, *Operation Overlord: Allied Invasion of Western Europe* (1952).
Ryan, Cornelius, *Longest Day, June 6, 1944* (1959).
Speidel, Hans, *Invasion 1944* (1950).
Stanford, Alfred, *Force Mulberry* (1951).
U.S. War Department, Historical Division, *Omaha Beachhead* (1946).

54.7.5 Battle of the Bulge

Cole, Hugh M., *Ardennes: Battle of the Bulge* (1965).
Eisenhower, John S. D., *Bitter Woods* (1969).
Marshall, Samuel L. A., et al., *Bastogne* (1946).
Merriam, Robert E., *Dark December: Battle of the Bulge* (1947).
Nobécourt, Jacques, *Hitler's Last Gamble: Battle of the Bulge*, R. H. Barry, trans. (1967).

4.7.6 Allied Victory

Allen, Robert S., *Lucky Forward Patton's Third Army* (1947).
Ambrose, Stephen E., *Eisenhower and Berlin, 1945: Decision to Halt at the Elbe* (1967).
Blumenson, Martin, *Breakout and Pursuit* (1961).
Cole, Hugh M., *The Lorraine Campaign* (1950).
DeGuingaud, F. W., *Operation Victory* (1947).
Dulles, Allen W., *Secret Surrender* (1966).
MacDonald, Charles Brown, *Siegfried Line Campaign* (1963).

54.8 PACIFIC THEATER

54.8.1 General

Bateson, Charles, *The War with Japan: A Concise History* (1969).
Collier, Basil, *War in Far East 1941–1945: Military History* (1969).
Halsey, William F., and J. Bryan, *Admiral Halsey's Story* (1947).
Eyre, J. K., *Roosevelt–MacArthur Conflict* (1950).
MacArthur, Douglas, *Reports of General MacArthur* (2 vols., 1966).

*   *   *   *   *   *   *

Knoles, George H., "Pacific War: Survey of Its Literature," *Pac. Hist. Rev.*, 16 (1947), 420.

See also 10.3 for biographies/writings of:

Forrestal, James, 1892–1949
Kimmel, Husband Edward, 1882–1968
Leahy, William D., 1875–1959
Lindbergh, Charles A., 1902–
MacArthur, Douglas, 1880–1964
Nimitz, Chester William, 1885–1966
Spruance, Raymond Ames, 1886–
Standley, William Harrison, 1872–1963
Vandegrift, Alexander, 1887–

54.8.2 Japanese Diplomacy and Military Actions

Butow, Robert J. C., *Tojo and Coming of War* (1961).
Hashimoto, Mochitsura, *Sunk: Japanese Fleet, 1941–1945*, E. H. M. Colegrave, trans. (1954).
Inoguchi, Rikihei, et al., *Divine Wind: Kamikaze Force in World War II* (1958).
Jones, Francis C., *Japan's New Order in East Asia, 1937–1945* (1954).
Kase, Toshidazu, *Journey to the Missouri* (1950).
Morton, Louis, "Japan's Decision for War," in Kent R. Greenfield, ed., *Command Decisions* (1960).

54.8.3 Fall of Philippines

Falk, Stanley L., *Bataan: March of Death* (1962).
Morton, Louis, *The Fall of the Philippines* (1953).
Romulo, Carlos P., *I Saw the Fall of the Philippines* (1942).
Steinberg, David J., *Philippine Collaboration in World War II* (1967).
Wainwright, Jonathan M., *General Wainwright's Story* (1946).

54.8.4 Alaska and Aleutians

Garfield, Brian, *Thousand-Mile War: World War II in Alaska and the Aleutians* (1969).

54.8.5 Midway

Fuchida, Mitsuo, and Masatake Okumiya, *Midway: The Battle that Doomed Japan* (1955).
Lord, Walter, *Incredible Victory* (1967).
Smith, William W., *Midway: Turning Point of the Pacific* (1966).
Tuleja, Thaddeus V., *Climax at Midway* (1960).

54.8.6 Guadalcanal

Cook, Charles, *Battle of Cape Esperance: Guadalcanal* (1968).
Griffith, Samuel B., *Battle for Guadalcanal* (1963).
Leckie, Robert H., *Challenge for the Pacific: Guadalcanal* (1965).
Miller, John, Jr., *Guadalcanal* (1949).
Zimmerman, J. L., *Guadalcanal* (1949).

54.8.7 South and Central Pacific

54.8.7.1 General

Barbey, Daniel, *MacArthur's Amphibious Navy: Seventh Amphibious Force Operations, 1943–1945* (1969).
Crowl, Philip A., *Campaign in the Marianas* (1960).
—— and Edmund G. Love, *Seizure of the Gilberts and Marshalls* (1955).
Eichelberger, R. L., and Milton Mackaye, *Our Jungle Road to Tokyo* (1950).
Hoffman, Carl W., *Saipan* (1950).
Hough, F. O., and J. A. Crown, *Campaign on New Britain* (1952).
Krueger, Walter, *From Down Under to Nippon* (1953).
Miller, John, Jr., *Cartwheel: The Reduction of Rabaul* (1959).
Milner, Samuel, *Victory in Papua* (1957).
Rentz, J. N., *Bougainville and Northern Solomons* (1948).
Shaw, Henry I., Jr., et al., *Central Pacific Drive* (1966).
Shaw, Henry I., Jr., and Douglas T. Kane, *Isolation of Rabaul* (1963).
Sherrod, R. L., *Tarawa* (1944).
Smith, Robert R., *Approach to the Philippines* (1953).
Stockman, J. R., *Battle for Tarawa* (1947).
Tolley, Kemp, "Divided We Fell," U.S. Naval Inst., *Proc.*, 92 (1966), 36.
Wolfert, Ira, *Battle for the Solomons* (1943).

54.8.7.2 Liberation of Philippines

Boggs, C. W., Jr., *Marine Aviation in the Philippines* (1951).
Cannon, M. Hamlin, *Leyte: The Return to the Philippines* (1954).
Falk, Stanley L., *Decision at Leyte* (1966).
Field, James A., Jr., *Japanese at Leyte Gulf* (1947).
Friend, Theodore, *Between Two Empires: Ordeal of the Philippines, 1929–1946* (1965).
Quezon, M. L., *The Good Fight* (1946).
Smith, Robert R., *Triumph in the Philippines* (1963).
Woodward, C. Vann, *Battle for Leyte Gulf* (1947).

54.8.8 Burma and China

Anders, Leslie, *Ledo Road: Stilwell's Highway to China* (1965).
Belden, Jack, *Retreat With Stilwell* (1943).

Chennault, Claire L., *Way of a Fighter* (1949).
Romanus, Charles F., and Riley Sunderland, *Stilwell's Command Problems* (1956).
———— *Stilwell's Mission to China* (1953).
———— *Time Runs Out in CBI* (1959).
Stilwell, Joseph W., *Stilwell Papers* (1948).
Tuchman, Barbara, *Stilwell and the American Experience in China, 1911–1945*
   (1970).
White, Theodore H., and Annalee Jacoby, *Thunder out of China* (1946).

See also 10.3 for biographies/writings of:

Stilwell, Joseph Warren, 1883–1946

54.8.9 Fall of Japan

54.8.9.1 General

Appleman, R. E., et al., *Okinawa* (1948).
Brooks, Lester, *Behind Japan's Surrender* (1968).
Butow, Robert J. C., *Japan's Decision to Surrender* (1954).
Craig, William, *Fall of Japan* (1967).
Feis, Herbert, *The Atomic Bomb and the End of World War II* (1966).
Morton, Louis, "Soviet Intervention in War with Japan," *For. Affairs*, 40 (1962),
   653.
U.S. Strategic Bombing Survey, *Effects of Strategic Bombing on Japan's War
   Economy* (1946).
———— *Effects of Strategic Bombing on Japanese Morale* (1946).
———— *Interrogation of Japanese Officials* (2 vols., 1946).
———— *Summary Report (Pacific War)* (1946).
Zacharias, E. M., *Secret Missions* (1946).

See also 54.11.3, Decision to Drop the Bomb.

54.8.9.2 Hiroshima

Hersey, John R., *Hiroshima* (1946).
Lifton, Robert J., *Death in Life: Hiroshima* (1968).
Osada, Arata, *Children of the A-Bomb* (1959).
U.S. Strategic Bombing Survey, *Effects of Atomic Bombs on Hiroshima and
   Nagasaki* (1946).

54.9 ARMED FORCES

54.9.2 Organization

Alsop, Stewart, and Thomas Braden, *Sub Rosa: O.S.S. and American Espionage*
   (1946).
Cline, Ray S., *Washington Command Post: Operations Division* (1951).
Huzar, Elias, *Purse and Sword* (1950).
Leighton, Richard M., "Allied Unity of Command," *Pol. Sci. Quar.*, 67 (1952),
   399.
Pogue, Forrest C., *The Supreme Command* (1954).
Rosen, S. McK., *Combined Boards of Second World War* (1951).
Watson, Mark S., *Chief of Staff: Pre-War Plans and Preparations* (1950).
Helfers, M. C., "The United States Army's History of World War II," *Mil.
   Affairs*, 19 (1955), 32.

See also 10.3 for biographies/writings of:

Donovan, "Wild Bill," 1883–1959

54.9.2 Army

54.9.2.1 Army and American Industry

Fairchild, Byron, and Jonathan Grossman, *The Army and Industrial Manpower* (1960).
Smith, Ralph Elberton, *The Army and Economic Mobilization* (1959).

54.9.2.2 Weapons Development

Barnes, Gladeon M., *Weapons of World War II* (1947).
Baxter, James P., III, *Scientists against Time* (1946).
Boyce, J. C., ed., *New Weapons for Air Warfare* (1947).
Burchard, John Ely, ed., *Rockets, Guns and Targets* (1948).
Stewart, Irvin, *Organizing Scientific Research for War* (1948).
Thiesmeyer, L. R., and John Ely Burchard, *Combat Scientists* (1947).

54.9.2.3 Chemical Warfare

Brown, Frederic J., *Chemical Warfare: A Study in Restraints* (1968).
Kleber, Brooks E., and Dale Birdsell, *Chemical Warfare Service: Chemicals in Combat* (1966).

54.9.2.4 Ordnance

Green, Constance M., et al., *The Ordnance Department: Planning Munitions for War* (1955).
Mayo, Lida, *The Ordnance Department: On Beachhead and Battlefront* (1968).
Thomson, Harry C., and Lida Mayo, *The Ordnance Department: Procurement and Supply* (1960).

54.9.2.5 Medicine

Andrus, E. C., et al., eds., *Advances in Military Medicine* (2 vols., 1948).
Smith, Clarence M., *Medical Department: Hospitalization and Evacuation, Zone of Interior* (1956).
U.S. Army Medical Service, *Medical Department of U.S. Army in World War II: Administrative Series* (1963–   ).
────── *Medical Department of U.S. Army in World War II: Clinical Series* (1952–   ). Titles of subseries: Internal Medicine in World War II, Miscellaneous, Neuropsychiatry in World War II, Preventive Medicine in World War II, and Surgery in World War II.
Wiltse, Charles M., *The Medical Department: Medical Service in the Mediterranean and Minor Theaters* (1965).

54.9.2.6 Service Forces, Quartermaster Corps, and Logistics

Millet, John D., *The Organization and Role of the Army Service Forces* (1954).
Risch, Erna, and Chester L. Kieffer, *The Quartermaster Corps: Organization, Supply, and Services* (2 vols., 1953–1955).
Ross, William F., and Charles F. Romanus, *The Quartermaster Corps: Operations in the War against Germany* (1965).
Ruppenthal, Roland G., *Logistical Support of the Armies* (2 vols., 1953–1959).
Stauffer, Alvin P., *The Quartermaster Corps: Operations in the War against Japan* (1956).

54.9.2.7 Transport

Bykofsky, Joseph, and Harold Larson, *Transportation Corps: Overseas* (1957).
Lafarge, Oliver, *Eagle in Egg: Military Air Transport* (1949).
Wardlow, Chester, *Transportation Corps: Movements, Training, and Supply* (1956).
────── *Transportation Corps: Responsibilities, Organization, and Operations* (1951).

4.9.2.8 Corps of Engineers

Coll, Blanche D., Jean E. Keith, and Herbert H. Rosenthal, *Corps of Engineers: Troops and Equipment* (1958).

Dod, Karl C., *The Corps of Engineers: The War against Japan* (1966).

54.9.2.9 Signal Corps

Terrett, Dulaney, *The Signal Corps: The Emergency to December 1941* (1956).

Thompson, George R., and Dixie R. Harris, *The Signal Corps: The Outcome (Mid-1943 through 1945)* (1966).

Thompson, George R., et al., *The Signal Corps: The Test (December 1941 to July 1943)* (1957).

54.9.2.10 Armored Force

Gillie, Mildred H., *Forging the Thunderbolt: Development of Armored Force* (1947).

Hall, Walter P., *Iron Out of Calvary* (1946).

54.9.2.11 Landing Operations

Vagts, Alfred, *Landing Operations* (1946).

54.9.2.12 Ground Forces

Greenfield, Kent R., et al., *The Organization of Ground Combat Troops* (1947).

Palmer, Robert R., et al., *Procurement and Training of Ground Combat Troops* (1948).

54.9.2.13 Women's Army Corps

Treadwell, Mattie E., *The Women's Army Corps* (1954).

54.9.2.14 American Soldier

Biddle, George, *Artist at War* (1944).

Bray, C. W., *Psychology and Military Proficiency* (1948).

Greenfield, Kent R., et al., *The Organization of Ground Combat Troops* (1947).

Martin, Ralph G., *The GI War, 1941–1945* (1967).

Mauldin, Bill, *Bill Mauldin's Army* (1951).

—— *Up Front* (1945).

Myers, Debs, et al., *Yank: G.I. Story of War* (1947).

New Yorker Book of War Pieces (1947).

Pyle, Ernie, *Brave Men* (1945).

—— *G.I. Joe* (1944).

—— *Here is Your War* (1943).

Stouffer, S. A., *American Soldier* (2 vols., 1949).

Yank, *Best from "Yank, the Army Weekly,"* (1945).

54.9.3 Air Force

Arnold, Henry H., *Global Mission* (1949).

Craven, Wesley F., and J. L. Cate, eds., *Army Air Forces in World War II* (5 vols., 1948–1953).

Holley, Irving B., Jr., *Buying Aircraft: Materiel Procurement for the Army Air Forces* (1964).

Verrier, Anthony, *Bomber Offensive* (1969).

See also 10.3 for biographies/writings of:

Lemay, Curtis E., 1906–

54.9.4 Navy

54.9.4.1 General

Connery, R. H., *Navy and Industrial Mobilization in World War II* (1951).
Furer, Julius A., *Administration of Navy in World War II* (1959).
Halsey, William F., and J. Bryan, *Admiral Halsey's Story* (1947).
King, Ernest J., and Walter M. Whitehill, *Fleet Admiral King* (1952).
King, Ernest J., *United States Navy at War, 1941–1945, Official Reports to the Secretary of the Navy* (1946).
Morison, Samuel E., *History of United States Naval Operations in World War II* (14 vols., 1947–1960).
────── *Two-Ocean War: Navy in the Second World War* (1963).
Roskill, Stephen W., *The War at Sea, 1939–1945* (3 vols., 1954–1961).

See also 10.3 for biographies/writings of:

Forrestal, James, 1892–1949
Kimmel, Husband Edward, 1882–1968
Leahy, William D., 1875–1959
Nimitz, Chester W., 1885–1966
Spruance, Raymond A., 1886–
Standley, William H., 1872–1963

54.9.4.2 Special Topics

Brodie, Bernard, *Guide to Naval Strategy* (1944).
Bulkley, Robert J., Jr., *At Close Quarters: PT Boats* (1962).
Howeth, L. S., *History of Communications: Electronics in the Navy* (1963).
Puleston, W. D., *Influence of Sea Power in World War II* (1947).
Reynolds, Clark G., *Fast Carriers: Forging of an Air Navy* (1968).
Roscoe, Theodore, *United States Destroyer Operations in World War II* (1953).

54.9.4.3 Logistics

Ballantine, Duncan S., *U.S. Naval Logistics in the Second World War* (1947).
Carter, Worrall R., *Beans, Bullets and Black Oil; The Story of Fleet Logistics Afloat in the Pacific during World War II* (1953).
────── and Elmer E. Duvall, *Ships, Salvage, and Sinews of War: The Story of Fleet Logistics Afloat in Atlantic and Mediterranean Waters during World War II* (1954).

54.9.4.4 Submarines

Casey, R. J., *Battle Below: War of Submarines* (1945).
Cope, Harley F., and Walter Karig, *Battle Submerged: Submarine Fighters of World War II* (1951).
Roscoe, Theodore, *United States Submarine Operations in World War II* (1949).

54.9.5 Marine Corps

Isely, J. A., and Philip A. Crowl, *U.S. Marines and Amphibious War* (1951).
Sherrod, R. L., *History of Marine Corps Aviation* (1952).
U.S. Marine Corps, *History of U.S. Marine Corps Operations in World War II* (1958–).

See also 10.3 for biographies/writings of:

Vandegrift, Alexander A., 1887–

54.9.6 Minorities in Armed Forces

Dalfiume, Richard M., *Desegregation of the U.S. Armed Forces: Fighting on Two Fronts, 1939–1953* (1969).
Davis, P. C., "Negro in Armed Services," *Va. Quar. Rev.*, 24 (1948), 499.
Lee, Ulysses G., *Employment of Negro Troops* (1966).
Murphy, Thomas D., *Ambassadors in Arms: Hawaii's 100th Batallion* (1954).
Nelson, Dennis D., *Integration of the Negro into the Navy* (1951).

54.10 HOME FRONT

54.10.1 General

Catton, Bruce, *War Lords of Washington* (1948).
Craf, J. R., *Survey of American Economy, 1940–1946* (1947).
Hart, Scott, *Washington at War, 1941–1945* (1970).
Janeway, Eliot, *Struggle for Survival* (rev. ed., 1968).
Nelson, Donald M., *Arsenal of Democracy* (1946).
Polenberg, Richard, comp., *America at War: Home Front, 1941–1945* (1968).
U.S. Bureau of the Budget, *United States at War* (1946).

*   *   *   *   *   *   *

Cappon, Lester J., "War Records Projects in States," Am. Assoc. State and Local Hist., *Bull.*, 1 (1944), 189.
Rodabaugh, J. H., "War Records Projects in States," Am. Assoc. State and Local Hist., *Bull.*, 2 (1947), 1.
U.S. National Archives, *Materials Relating to Historical Programs of Civilian Agencies during World War II* (1952).
U.S. National Historical Publications Commission, *List of World War II Historical Studies by Civilian Agencies* (1951).

54.10.2 Congress and Politics

Daniels, Jonathan, *Frontier on the Potomac* (1946).
Drury, Allen, *Senate Journal, 1943–1945* (1963).
Harding, John, "The 1942 Congressional Elections," *Am. Pol. Sci. Rev.*, 38 (1944), 41.
Hassett, William D., *Off the Record with F.D.R.* (1958).
Larsen, Laurence H., "William Langer: A Maverick in the Senate," *Wis. Mag. Hist.*, 44 (1961), 189.
Moore, John R., "The Conservative Coalition in the United States Senate, 1942–1945," *JSH*, 33 (1967), 368.
Riddle, Donald H., *The Truman Committee* (1964).
Toulmin, Aubrey, Jr., *Diary of Democracy: Senate War Investigating Committee* (1947).
Young, Roland A., *Congressional Politics in the Second World War* (1956).

54.10.3 Election of 1944

Friedman, Leon, "Election of 1944," in Arthur M. Schlesinger, Jr., and Fred L. Israel, eds., *History of American Presidential Elections, 1789–1968*, vol. IV (1971).
Overacker, Louise, "Presidential Campaign Funds, 1944," *Am. Pol. Sci. Rev.*, 39 (1945), 899.

See also 10.3 for biographies/writings of:

Byrnes, James F., 1879–1972
Dewey, Thomas E., 1902–1971
Roosevelt, Franklin D., 1882–1945
Truman, Harry S., 1884–1972
Wallace, Henry A., 1888–1965

54.10.4 Industrial Mobilization

54.10.4.1 General

Allen, Ethan P., *Policies Governing Private Financing of Emergency Facilities* (1946).
Beasley, Norman, *Knudsen* (1947).
Civilian Production Administration, *Industrial Mobilization for War* (1947).
Committee on Public Administration Cases, *Feasibility Dispute* (1950).
Connery, R. H., *Navy and Industrial Mobilization in World War II* (1951).
Gulick, Luther H., *Administrative Reflections from World War II* (1948).
Harris, Seymour E., *Economics of Defense* (1941).
Jones, Drummond, *Role of Office of Civilian Requirements* (1946).
Kuznets, Simon, *National Product in Wartime* (1945).
Nelson, Donald M., *Arsenal of Democracy* (1946).
Novik, David, and G. A. Steiner, *Wartime Industrial Statistics* (1949).
Novik, David, et al., *Wartime Production Controls* (1949).
O'Brian, J. L., and Manly Fleischmann, "War Production Board Administrative Policies," *George Washington Law Rev.*, 13 (1944), 1.
Somers, H. M., *Presidential Agency, OWMR* (1950).
Stein, Harold, ed., *Public Administration and Policy Development* (1952).
Stone, Isidore F., *Business as Usual* (1941).
Toulmin, Aubrey, Jr., *Diary of Democracy: Senate War Investigating Committee* (1947).

See also 10.3 for biographies/writings of:

Byrnes, James F., 1879–1972
Hillman, Sidney, 1887–1946
Ickes, Harold L., 1874–1952
Jones, Jesse H., 1874–1956
Morgenthau, Henry, Jr., 1891–1967
Truman, Harry S., 1884–1972
Wallace, Henry A., 1888–1965

54.10.4.2 Specific Industries

Bernstein, Barton J., "Automobile Industry and Second World War," *Southw. Soc. Sci. Quar.*, 47 (1966), 22.
Frey, J. W., and H. C. Ide, eds., *History of Petroleum Administration* (1946).
Howard, Frank A., *Buna Rubber* (1947).
Ickes, Harold L., *Fightin' Oil* (1943).
Lilley, Tom, et al., *Problems of Accelerating Aircraft Production* (1947).
Moore, Geoffrey H., *Production of Industrial Materials* (1944).
Morgan, John D., *Domestic Mining Industry* (1949).
Sill, Van Rensselaer, *American Miracle: War Construction* (1947).
Stoughton, Bradley, *History of Tools Division, War Production Board* (1949).

54.10.5 Shipping and Shipbuilding

Land, Emory S., *Winning the War with Ships* (1958).
Lane, Frederic C., et al., *Ships for Victory* (1951).

4.10.6 Transportation

Dearing, Charles L., and Wilfred Owen, *National Transportation Policy* (1949).
Rose, Joseph R., *American Wartime Transportation* (1953).
U.S. Office of Defense Transportation, *Civilian Transport* (1948).

See also 10.3 for biographies/writings of:

Eastman, Joseph B., 1882–1944

4.10.7 Agriculture

Arant, W. D., "Wartime Meat Policies," *Jour. Farm Econ.*, 28 (1946), 903.
Baker, Benjamin, *Wartime Food Procurement and Production* (1951).
Benedict, M. R., *Farm Policies of the United States* (1953).
Black, John D., and C. A. Gibbons, "War and American Agriculture," *Rev. Econ. Stat.*, 26 (1944), 1.
Blum, Albert A., "Farmer, Army and Draft," *Agric. Hist.*, 38 (1964), 34.
Butz, E. L., *Production Credit System* (1944).
Gold, Bela, *Wartime Economic Planning in Agriculture* (1949).
Schmidt, Carl T., *American Farmers in World Crisis* (1941).
Tostlebe, A. S., *Impact of War on Financial Structure of Agriculture* (1945).
Wilcox, Walter W., *The Farmer in the Second World War* (1947).

See also 10.3 for biographies/writings of:

Wickard, Claude R., 1893–

4.10.8 Economic Policy

4.10.8.1 Stabilization

Chandler, Lester V., and D. H. Wallace, eds., *Economic Mobilization and Stabilization* (1951).
Worsley, T. B., *Wartime Economic Stabilization and Government Procurement* (1949).

4.10.8.2 Manpower and Personnel

Adams, Leonard P., *Wartime Manpower Mobilization* (1951).
Blum, Albert A., "Sailor or Worker: Manpower Dilemma during Second World War," *Labor Hist.*, 6 (1965), 232.
Kammerer, G. M., *Impact of War on Federal Personnel Administration* (1951).
Long, Clarence D., *Labor Force in War and Transition* (1952).
White, Leonard D., ed., *Civil Service in Wartime* (1945).

4.10.8.3 Labor and Wages

Afros, J. L., "Labor Participation in Office of Price Administration," *Am. Pol. Sci. Rev.*, 40 (1946), 458.
Blackman, John L., Jr., *Presidential Seizure in Labor Disputes* (1967).
Duffy, Doris, *Role of Government in Labor–Management Production Committees* (1947).
Dunlop, John T., and Arthur D. Hill, *The Wage Adjustment Board: Wartime Stabilization in the Building and Construction Industry* (1950).
Feldman, Herman, ed., "Labor Relations and War," *Am. Acad. Pol. Soc. Sci., Annals*, 224 (1942). Entire issue.
Gaer, Joseph, *First Round: CIO Political Action Committee* (1944).
International Labour Office, *Labour Management Co-operation in United States War Production* (1948).

Keezer, Dexter M., "Observations on War Labor Board," *Am. Econ. Rev.*, 36 (1946), 233.

Morse, Wayne, "National War Labor Board," *Ore. Law Rev.*, 22 (1942), 1.

Purcell, R. J., *Labor Policies of National Defense Advisory Commission and Office of Production Management, May 1940–April 1942* (1946).

Riegelman, Carol, *Labour-Management Co-operation in United States War Production* (1948).

Seidman, Joel, *American Labor from Defense to Reconversion* (1953).

Shister, Joseph, "National War Labor Board," *Jour. Pol. Econ.*, 53 (1945), 37.

Stein, Bruno, "Labor's Role in Government Agencies during World War II," *Jour. Econ. Hist.*, 17 (1957), 389.

U.S. National War Labor Board, *Termination Report* (3 vols., 1947–1949).

Warne, Colston E., et al., eds., *War Labor Policies.* Vol. I of *Yearbook of American Labor* (1945).

Witney, Fred, *Wartime Experiences of the National Labor Relations Board* (1949).

54.10.8.4 Inflation and Price Control

Adams, George P., Jr., *Wartime Price Control* (1942).

Armstrong, Robert B., et al., *Problems in Price Control* (1947).

Benes, R. J., et al., *Problems in Price Control* (1947).

Benes, R. J., *Studies in Industrial Price Control* (1947).

Bliss, J. A., *OPA and Public Utility Commissions* (1947).

Brown, Arthur J., *The Great Inflation, 1939–1951* (1955).

Campbell, Robert F. *History of Basic Metals: Price Controls in World War II* (1948).

Carsel, Wilfred, *Wartime Apparel Price Control* (1947).

Cavers, David F., et al., *Problems in Price Control* (1947).

Chandler, Lester V., *Inflation, 1940–1948* (1951).

Friedman, Milton, "Price, Income and Monetary Changes in Three Wartime Periods," *Am. Econ. Rev.*, 42 (1952), 612.

Galbraith, John K., *Theory of Price Control* (1952).

Harris, Seymour E., *Inflation and the American Economy* (1945).

Mansfield, H. C., et al., *Short History of OPA* (1949).

Nathanson, N. L. and Harold Leventhal, *Problems in Price Control* (1947).

Pranck, P. G., ed., *Problems in Price Control* (1948).

Putnam, Imogene H., *Volunteers in OPA* (1947).

Shepherd, G. S., *Agricultural Price Control* (1945).

Thompson, Victor A., *Regulatory Process in OPA Rationing* (1950).

U.S. Office of Temporary Controls, *Historical Reports on War Administration: Office of Price Administration* (1947).

Wilson, William J., et al., *Beginnings of OPA* (1947).

Zimmerman, V. B., *Problems in Price Control* (1947).

*   *   *   *   *   *   *

Wilson, William J., et al., *OPA Bibliography* (1948).

54.10.8.5 Rationing

Kershaw, Joseph A., *History of Ration Banking* (1947).

Maxwell, J. A., "Gasoline Rationing, United States," *Quar. Jour. Econ.*, 60 (1946), 561; 61 (1946), 125.

Nielander, W. A., *Wartime Food Rationing in the United States* (1947).

O'Leary, P. M., "Wartime Rationing," *Am. Pol. Sci. Rev.*, 39 (1945), 1089.

Redford, E. S., *Field Administration of Wartime Rationing* (1947).

Russell, Judith, and Renee Fantin, *Studies in Food Rationing* (1947).

54.10.8.6 Taxation and Bond Drives

Allen, E. D., "Treasury Tax Policies in 1943," *Am. Econ. Rev.*, 34 (1944), 707.

Blakey, R. G. and G. C., "Federal Revenue Act of 1942," *Am. Pol. Sci. Rev.*, 36 (1942), 1069.

Lent, G. E., "Excess-Profits Taxation," *Jour. Pol. Econ.,* 59 (1951), 481.
Merton, Robert K., *Mass Persuasion of a War Bond Drive* (1946).
Newcomer, Mabel, "Congressional Tax Policies in 1943," *Am. Econ. Rev.,* 34 (1944), 734.
Paul, Randolph E., *Taxation for Prosperity* (1947).

4.10.9 Selective Service

Dawson, R. M., *Conscription Crisis of 1944* (1961).

54.10.10 War Information and Censorship

Carroll, Wallace, *Persuade or Perish* (1948).
Koop, Theodore F., *Weapons of Silence* (1946).
Price, Byron, "Governmental Censorship in Wartime," *Am. Pol. Sci. Rev.,* 36 (1942), 837.
Steele, Richard W., "Preparing the Public for War: Efforts to Establish a National Propaganda Agency, 1940–1941," *AHR,* 75 (1970), 1640.
Weinberg, Sydney, "What to Tell America; Writers Quarrel in the Office of War Information," *JAH,* 53 (1968), 73.

54.10.11 Civil Liberties and Conscientious Objectors

Biddle, Francis, *Democratic Thinking and War* (1944).
Corwin, Edward S., *Total War and Constitution* (1947).
Sibley, M. Q., and P. E. Jacob, *Conscription of Conscience: Conscientious Objector, 1940–1947* (1952).
Wittner, Lawrence S., *Rebels against War: The American Peace Movement, 1941–1960* (1969).

54.10.12 Wartime Society

54.10.12.1 General

Bruner, J. S., *Mandate from People* (1944). Opinion polls.
Carr, Lowell J., and J. E. Stermer, *Willow Run: Industrialization and Cultural Inadequacy* (1952).
Clinard, M. B., *Black Market* (1952).
Havighurst, Richard J., and H. G. Morgan, *Social History of a War Boom Community* (1951).
Hill, Reuben, *Families Under Stress* (1949).
Lever, Harry, and Joseph Young, *Wartime Racketeers* (1945).
Miller, Joseph Hillis, and Dorothy V. N. Brooks, *Role of Higher Education in the War and After* (1944).
Odum, Howard W., *Race and Rumors of Race* (1943).
Ogburn, W. F., *American Society in Wartime* (1943).
Stevens, Alden, *Arms and the People* (1942).
U.S. Displaced Persons Commission, *Memo to America: Final Report* (1952).
Watson, Goodwin B., ed., *Civilian Morale* (1942).

54.10.12.2 Contemporary Accounts

Childs, Marquis, *I Write from Washington* (1942).
Dos Passos, John, *State of the Nation* (1944).
Goodman, Jack, ed., *While You Were Gone* (1946).
Grafton, Samuel, *American Diary* (1943).
Graves, John T., II, *The Fighting South* (1943).
Lerner, Max, *Public Journal* (1945).
Menefee, Selden, *Assignment: U.S.A.* (1943).

Meyer, Agnes E., *Journey through Chaos* (1944).
Pyle, Ernie, *Home Country* (1947).

54.10.12.3 Negroes

Brown, Earl L., *Why Race Riots?* (1944).
Northrup, H. R., "Organized Labor and Negro Workers," *Jour. Pol. Econ.*, 51 (1943), 206.
Ottley, Roi, *New World A-Coming* (1943).
Wright, Richard, *Twelve Million Black Voices* (1943).

See also 10.3 for biographies/writings of:

White, Walter Francis, 1893–1955

54.10.12.4 Japanese Americans

Barnhart, Edward N., "Exclusion of Japanese Americans in World War II," *Pac. Hist. Rev.*, 29 (1960), 111.
Girdner, Audrie, and Anne Loftis, *Great Betrayal: The Evacuation of Japanese-Americans during World War II* (1969).
Grodzins, Morton, *Americans Betrayed* (1949).
—— "Making Unamericans," *Am. Jour. Sociol.*, 60 (1955), 57.
Hosokawa, Bill, *Nisei: The Quiet Americans* (1969).
Leighton, Alexander H., *Governing of Men* (1945).
McWilliams, Carey, *Prejudice* (1944).
Rostow, E. V., "Japanese-American Cases--Disaster," *Yale Law Jour.* , 54 (1945), 489.
Ten Broek, Jacobus, Edward Barnhart and Floyd W. Matson, *Prejudice, War and the Constitution* (1958).
Thomas, Dorothy S., et al., *Japanese–American Evacuation and Resettlement* (3 vols., 1946–1958).
U.S. Army. Western Defense Command and Fourth Army, *Final Report, Japanese Evacuation* (1943).
U.S. War Relocation Authority, *WRA* (1946).

54.11 DEVELOPMENT OF ATOMIC WEAPONS AND ENERGY

54.11.1 Atomic Bomb

Blackett, P. M. S., *Fear, War, and the Bomb* (1948).
Bradley, David V., *No Place to Hide* (1948).
Brodie, Bernard, ed., *Absolute Weapon* (1946).
Delmas, Claude, *Histoire politique de la bombe atomique* (1967).
Irving, David J. C., *German Atomic Bomb* (1967).
Kissinger, Henry A., *Nuclear Weapons and Foreign Policy* (1957).
Lapp, R. E., *Must We Hide?* (1949).
—— *New Force* (1953).
Osborn, Frederick, *Atomic Impasse* (1948).
Smyth, Henry D., *Atomic Energy for Military Purposes* (1945).
U.S. Atomic Energy Commission, *Effects of Atomic Weapons* (1950).

See also 54.8.9, Fall of Japan; 54.9.2.2, Army–Weapons Development; 55.17.13.6, Atomic Espionage.

54.11.2 Manhattan Project and Early Atomic Technology

Clark, Ronald W., *Birth of the Bomb: Britain's Part* (1961).
Compton, Arthur H., *Atomic Quest* (1956).

Groueff, Stephane, *Manhattan Project: Atomic Bomb* (1967).
Groves, Leslie R., *Now It Can Be Told* (1962).
Hewlett, Richard G., and Oscar E. Anderson, Jr., *The New World, 1939–1946* (1962).

4.11.3 Decision to Drop the Bomb

Alperovitz, Gar, *Atomic Diplomacy: The Use of the Atomic Bomb and the American Confrontation with Soviet Power* (1967).
Baker, Paul R., ed., *Atomic Bomb* (1968).
Giovanitti, Len, and Fred Freed, *Decision to Drop the Bomb* (1965).
Goldwin, Robert A., Gerald Stourzh and Ralph Lerner, eds., *The Case of the Impenetrable Cloud: Decision to Drop Atomic Bomb* (1957).
Morton, Louis, "The Decision to Use the Atomic Bomb," in Kent R. Greenfield, ed., *Command Decisions* (1960).

See also 10.3 for biographies/writings of:

Stimson, Henry L., 1867–1950
Truman, Harry S., 1884–1972

4.11.4 Control of Atomic Energy

Anderson, Oscar E., Jr., "International Control of the Atom: Roots of a Policy," in David H. Pinkney and Theodore Ropp, eds., *A Festschrift for Frederick B. Artz* (1964).
Gilpin, Robert, *American Scientists and Nuclear Weapons Policy* (1962).
Hewlett, Richard G., and Francis Duncan, *Atomic Shield, 1947/1952* (1969).
Hiebert, Erwin N., *Impact of Atomic Energy* (1961).
Newman, J. R., and B. S. Miller, *Control of Atomic Energy* (1948).
Piccard, Paul J., "Scientists and Public Policy: Los Alamos, August–November, 1945," *West. Pol. Quar.*, 18 (1965), 251.
U.S. Department of State, *International Control of Atomic Energy: Growth of a Policy* (1946).
——— *Report on International Control of Atomic Energy* (1946).

See also 10.3 for biographies/writings of:

Lilienthal, David, 1899–
Oppenheimer, J. Robert, 1904–1967

4.11.5 Public Opinion

Erskine, Hazel G., "The Polls: Atomic Weapons and Nuclear Energy," *Pub. Opinion Quar.*, 27 (1963), 155.
Rosi, Eugene J., "Mass and Attentive Opinion on Nuclear Weapons Tests and Fallout, 1954–1963," *Pub. Opinion Quar.*, 29 (1965), 280.

55 Domestic Issues since 1945

55.1 GENERAL

Agar, Herbert, *Price of Power: America since 1945* (1957).
Goldman, Eric F., *Crucial Decade: America 1945–1955* (1956).
Leuchtenburg, William E., et al., *The Life History of the United States*. Vol. XII: *The Great Age of Change* (1964).
Lubell, Samuel, *Revolt of the Moderates* (1956).
Siegfried, André, *America at Mid-Century*, Margaret Ledesert, trans. (1955).
Zornow, William F., *America at Mid-Century: Truman, Eisenhower* (1959).

55.2 SPECIAL TOPICS

Ambrose, Stephen E., ed., *Institutions in Modern America* (1967).
Brzezinski, Zbigniew K., and Samuel P. Huntington, *Political Power: USA/USSR* (1964).
Truman, David B., *Governmental Process: Political Interests and Public Opinion* (1951).

55.3 CONTEMPORARY ACCOUNTS

Alsop, Stewart J. O., *The Center: People and Power in Political Washington* (1968).
Krock, Arthur, *In the Nation, 1932–1966* (1966).
Putt, Samuel G., ed., *Cousins and Strangers: Comments on America by Commonwealth Fund Fellows from Britain, 1946–1952* (1956).

55.4 EXECUTIVE BRANCH

Bell, Jack L., *Splendid Misery: Presidency and Power Politics* (1960).
Warner, W. Lloyd, et al., *American Federal Executive* (1963).

55.5 LEGISLATIVE BRANCH

Barth, Alan, *Government by Investigation* (1955).
Bendiner, Robert, *Obstacle Course on Capitol Hill* (1964).

Bolling, Richard W., *House out of Order* (1965).

Boyd, James P., *Above the Law* (1968).

Boynton, George R., "Southern Conservatism: Constituency Opinion and Congressional Voting," *Pub. Opinion Quar.*, 29 (1965), 259.

Clapp, Charles L., ed., *The Congressman: His Work as He Sees It* (1963).

Clark, Joseph S., *Congress: The Sapless Branch* (rev. ed., 1965).

Congressional Quarterly Service, *Congress and the Nation* (2 vols., 1965–1968).

Deakin, James, *The Lobbyists* (1966).

Farris, Charles D., "Method of Determining Ideological Groupings in Congress," *Jour. Politics*, 20 (1958), 308.

Froman, Lewis A., Jr., and Randall B. Ripley, "Conditions for Party Leadership: The Case of the House Democrats," *Am. Pol. Sci. Rev.*, 59 (1965), 52.

Griffith, Ernest E., *Congress: Its Contemporary Role* (4th ed., 1967).

Grundy, Kenneth W., "J. William Fulbright," *Va. Quar. Rev.*, 43 (1967), 382.

Hacker, Andrew, *Congressional Districting, Issue of Equal Representation* (rev. ed., 1964).

Jones, Charles O., *Party and Policy-Making: The House Republican Policy Committee* (1964).

McKay, Robert B., "Congressional Investigations and the Supreme Court," *Calif. Law Rev.*, 51 (1963), 267.

Mayhew, David R., *Party Loyalty among Congressmen: The Difference between Democrats and Republicans, 1947–1962* (1966).

Pearson, Drew, and Jack Anderson, *Case against Congress: Corruption on Capitol Hill* (1968).

Ripley, Randall B., *Majority Party Leadership in Congress* (1969).

Rusher, William A., *Special Counsel* (1968).

Sundquist, James L., *Politics and Policy: Eisenhower, Kennedy, and Johnson Years* (1968).

Surrey, Stanley S., "Congress and Tax Lobbyist—How Special Tax Provisions Get Enacted," *Harv. Law Rev.*, 70 (1957), 1145.

Wolfinger, Raymond E., "Safe Seats, Seniority, and Power in Congress," *Am. Pol. Sci. Rev.*, 59 (1965), 337.

55.6 FEDERAL ECONOMIC POLICY AND ADMINISTRATION

Baratz, Morton S., *Economics of the Postal Services* (1962).

Congressional Quarterly Service, *Federal Economic Policy, 1945–1967* (2nd ed., 1967).

Cox, Edward F., Robert C. Fellmeth, and John E. Schultz, *'The Nader Report' on the Federal Trade Commission* (1969).

Federal Reserve System, *Postwar Economic Studies* (8 vols., 1945–1947).

Fisher, Robert M., *20 Years of Public Housing* (1959).

Flash, Edward S., *Economic Advice and Presidential Leadership: The Council of Economic Advisors* (1965).

Holmans, Alan E., *United States Fiscal Policy, 1945–1959* (1961).

Knipe, James L., *Federal Reserve and American Dollar: Problems and Policies, 1946–1964* (1965).

Lewis, Wilfred, *Federal Fiscal Policy in Postwar Recessions* (1962).

Parris, Addison W., *Small Business Administration* (1968).

Schrifftgeisser, Karl, *Business Comes of Age: Story of Committee for Economic Development, 1942–1960* (1960).

Slesinger, Reuben E., *National Economic Policy: Presidential Reports* (1968).

Smith, Bruce L. R., *The Rand Corporation: Case Study of a Nonprofit Advisory Corporation* (1966).

U.S. President, *Economic Report of the President* (1947–   ).

See also 55.16, Agricultural Politics.

55.7 POLITICS AND POLITICAL PARTIES

Burns, James MacGregor, *Four-Party Politics in America* (1963).
Cater, Douglass, *Power in Washington: A Critical Look at Today's Struggle to Govern in the Nation's Capitol* (1964).
Hacker, Andrew, "Elected and Anointed: Two American Elites," *Am. Pol. Sci. Rev.*, 55 (1961), 539.
Harris, Seymour E., *Economics of Political Parties* (1962).
Lubell, Samuel, *Future of American Politics* (rev. ed., 1965).
Morgenthau, Hans J., *The Purpose of American Politics* (1960).
Pinner, Frank A., et al., *Old Age and Political Behavior* (1959).
Zeigler, Harmon, *Interest Groups in American Society* (1964).

See also 10.3 for biographies/writings of:

Byrd, Harry F., 1887–1966
Kefauver, Estes, 1903–1963
Louchheim, Katie S., 1903–
Roosevelt, Eleanor, 1884–1962
Stevenson, Adlai E., 1900–1965
Taft, Robert A., 1889–1953

55.8 VOTING BEHAVIOR

Andrews, William G., "Voting Participation," *West. Pol. Quar.*, 19 (1966), 639.
Berelson, Bernard R., P. F. Lazarsfeld, and W. N. McPhee, *Voting: A Study of Opinion Formation in a Presidential Campaign* (1954).
Key, V. O., Jr., *Responsible Electorate: Rationality in Presidential Voting, 1936–1960* (1966).
MacNeil, Robert, *People Machine: Influence of Television on American Politics* (1958).
Scammon, Richard M., ed., *America Votes: A Handbook* (8 vols., 1956–1970).
Zikmund, Joseph, II, "Suburban Voting in Presidential Elections, 1948–1964," *Midw. Jour. Pol. Sci.*, 12 (1968), 239.

55.9 CAMPAIGNS AND CONVENTIONS

Bain, Richard C., *Convention Decisions and Voting Records* (1960).
Epstein, Edwin M., *Corporations, Contributions and Political Campaigns: Federal Regulation* (1968).
Heard, Alexander, *Costs of Democracy: Financing Political Campaigns* (1960).

55.10 SOUTH

Grantham, Dewey W., Jr., "South and Reconstruction of American Politics," *JAH*, 53 (1966), 227.
Shannon, Jasper B., *Toward a New Politics in the South* (1949).

55.11 STATES

55.11.1 General

Brooks, Glenn E., *When Governors Convene* (1961).
Derthick, Martha A., *The National Guard in Politics* (1965).
Reichley, James, et al., *States in Crisis, 1950–1962* (1964).

55.11.2 Specific States

Belvin, William L., Jr., "Georgia Gubernatorial Primary of 1946," *Ga. Hist. Quar.*, 50 (1966), 36.

Boyarsky, Bill, *Rise of Ronald Reagan* (1968). California.

Harvey, Richard B., "Governor Earl Warren of California," *Calif. Hist. Soc., Quar.*, 46 (1967), 33.

Hill, Gladwin, *Dancing Bear: An Inside Look at California Politics* (1968).

Jewell, Malcolm E., and Everett W. Cunningham, *Kentucky Politics* (1968).

Moynihan, Daniel P., and James Q. Wilson, "Patronage in New York State, 1955–1959," *Am. Pol. Sci. Rev.*, 58 (1964), 286.

Williams, Murat W., "Virginia Politics," *Va. Quar. Rev.*, 42 (1966), 177.

55.12 PUERTO RICO

Anderson, Robert W., *Party Politics in Puerto Rico* (1965).

55.13 URBAN AND SUBURBAN POLITICS

Costikyan, Edward N., *Behind Closed Doors: Politics in Public Interests* (1966).

Milligan, Maurice M., *Missouri Waltz: Pendergast Machine* (1948).

Ruchelman, Leonard I., ed., *Big City Mayors: Crisis in Urban Politics* (1970).

Wood, Robert C., *Suburbia: Its People and Their Politics* (1959).

55.14 CONSERVATIVES AND RADICAL RIGHT

Auerbach, M. Morton, *The Conservative Illusion* (1959).

Bell, Daniel, ed., *The Radical Right* (1964).

Broyles, J. Allen, *The John Birch Society: Anatomy of a Protest* (1964).

Forster, Arnold, and Benjamin R. Epstein, *Danger on the Right* (1964).

Hart, Jeffrey P., *American Dissent: A Decade of Modern Conservatism* (1966).

Hillbrunner, Anthony, "Failure of Neo-Conservatism," *Ariz. Quar.*, 15 (1959), 113.

Hofstadter, Richard, *Anti-Intellectualism in American Life* (1963).

—— *The Paranoid Style in American Politics and Other Essays* (1965).

Jones, J. Harry, Jr., *The Minutemen* (1968).

Lens, Sidney, *The Futile Crusade: Anti-Communism as American Credo* (1964).

Lipset, Seymour M., and Earl Raab, *The Politics of Unreason: Right-Wing Extremism, 1790–1970* (1970).

Mahoney, J. Daniel, *Actions Speak Louder* (1968).

Redekop, John H., *American Far Right: Billy James Hargis and Christian Crusade* (1968).

Rosenstone, Robert A., comp., *Protest from the Right* (1968).

Thayer, George, *Farther Shores of Politics: The American Political Fringe Today* (1967).

See also 10.3 for biographies/writings of:

Goldwater, Barry, 1909–
McCarthy, Joseph, 1908–1957

55.15 LIBERALS AND RADICAL LEFT

Brock, Clifton, *Americans for Democratic Action: Its Role in National Politics* (1962).

Howe, Irving, ed., *Radical Papers* (1966).

Jacobs, Paul, and Saul Landau, *New Radicals* (1966).
Kaufman, Arnold S., *Radical Liberal: New Man in American Politics* (1968).
Kennan, George F., et al., *Democracy and the Student Left* (1968).
Lasch, Christopher, *Agony of the American Left* (1969).
Lens, Sidney, *Radicalism in America* (1966).
Newfield, Jack, *Prophetic Minority* (1966).
Newman, William J., *Liberalism and Retreat from Politics* (1964).
Savelle, Max, *Is Liberalism Dead? And Other Essays* (1967).

See also 55.23.7, Johnson Administration–Student Unrest.

55.16 AGRICULTURAL POLITICS

Block, William J., *The Separation of the Farm Bureau and the Extension Service: Political Issue in a Federal System* (1960).
Gilpatrick, Thomas V., "Price Support Policy and the Midwest Farm Vote," *Midw. Jour. Pol. Sci.*, 3 (1959), 319.
Hathaway, Dale E., *Government and Agriculture* (1963).

See also 55.17.8, Truman Administration–Agriculture.

55.17 TRUMAN ADMINISTRATION, 1945–1953

55.17.1 General

Bernstein, Barton J., ed., *Politics and Policies of the Truman Administration* (1970).
———— and Allen J. Matusow, eds., *The Truman Administration: A Documentary History* (1966).
Koenig, Louis W., ed., *The Truman Administration: Its Principles and Practice* (1956).
Phillips, Cabell, *The Truman Presidency: The History of a Triumphant Succession* (1966).

*   *   *   *   *   *   *

Kirkendall, Richard S., ed., *The Truman Period as a Research Field* (1967).

See also 10.3 for biographies/writings of:

Acheson, Dean G., 1893–1971
Barkley, Alben W., 1877–1956
Marshall, George C., 1880–1959
Martin, Joseph W., 1884–1968
Sawyer, Charles, 1887–
Truman, Harry S., 1884–1972

55.17.2 Special Topics

Lorenz, A. L., Jr., "Truman and the Press Conference," *Journalism Quar.*, 43 (1966), 671.
"Truman and the Pendergast Machine," *Midcontinent Am. Studies Jour.*, 7 (1966), 3.

55.17.3 Contemporary Political Thought

Block, Herbert, *Herblock Book* (1952). Cartoons.
Coffin, Tristram, *Missouri Compromise* (1947).
Fortune and Russell W. Davenport, *U.S.A. Permanent Revolution* (1951).
Moley, Raymond, *How to Keep Our Liberty* (1952).
Schlesinger, Arthur M., Jr., *Vital Center* (1949).

55.17.4 Congress

Lee, R. Alton, "The Turnip Session of the Do-Nothing Congress: Presidential
   Campaign Strategy," *Southw. Soc. Sci. Quar.*, 44 (1963), 256.
Riddick, F. M., "Eighty-First Congress," *West. Pol. Quar.*, 4 (1951), 48.
———— "Eighty-Second Congress," *West. Pol. Quar.*, 5 (1952), 94.
Truman, David B., *The Congressional Party* (1959).

55.17.5 Economy

55.17.5.1 General

Hamberg, Daniel, "Recession of 1948–1949," *Econ. Jour.*, 62 (1952), 1.
Harris, Seymour E., *Economics of Mobilization and Inflation* (1951).
Kuznets, Simon, et al., *Population Redistribution and Economic Growth, United
   States, 1870–1950* (1960).
U.S. National Bureau of Economic Research, *Appraisal of 1950 Census Income
   Data* (1958).

55.17.5.2 Government and Economy

Abels, Jules, *Welfare State* (1951).
Bernstein, Barton J., "The Postwar Famine and Price Control, 1946," *Agric.
   Hist.*, 38 (1964), 235.
Director, Aaron, ed., *Defense, Controls, and Inflation* (1952).
Glueck, Sheldon, ed., *Welfare State* (1952).
Kaysen, Carl, *United States v. United Shoe Machinery Corporation* (1956).
Steiner, G. A., *Government's Role In Economic Life* (1953).

55.17.5.3 Monetary and Fiscal Policy

Bernstein, Barton J., "Charting a Course between Inflation and Depression:
   Secretary of the Treasury Fred Vinson and the Truman Administration's Tax
   Bill," *Ky. Hist. Soc., Reg.*, 66 (1968), 53.
Harris, Seymour E., ed., "How to Manage National Debt," *Rev. Econ. Stat.*, 31
   (1949), 15.
Murphy, Henry C., *National Debt* (1950).
Tobin, James, "Monetary Policy and Management of Public Debt," *Rev. Econ.
   Stat.*, 35 (1953), 118.

55.17.5.4 Employment Act of 1946 and Council of Economic Advisors

Bailey, Stephen K., *Congress Makes a Law: Employment Act of 1946* (1950).
Colm, Gerhard, ed., *The Employment Act: Past and Future* (1956).
Flash, Edward S., *Economic Advice and Presidential Leadership: The Council of
   Economic Advisors* (1965).
Nourse, Edwin G., "Early Flowering of the Employment Act," *Va. Quar. Rev.*, 43
   (1967), 233.
———— *Economics in Public Service* (1953).
U.S. Council of Economic Advisors, *Reports and Reviews* (1946–1950).

55.17.5.5 Regional Studies

Berge, Wendell, *Economic Freedom for West* (1946).
Harris, Seymour E., *Economics of New England* (1952).

Hoover, Calvin B., and B. U. Ratchford, *Economic Resources and Policies of the South* (1951).

55.17.6 Reconversion and Veterans' Programs

Baruch, Bernard M., and J. M. Hancock, *Report on War and Post-War Adjustment* (1944).

Bernstein, Barton J., "The Debate on Industrial Reconversion: The Protection of Oligopoly and Military Control of the Economy," *Am. Jour. Econ. Sociol.*, 26 (1967), 159.

———— "Reluctance and Resistance: Wilson Wyatt and Veterans' Housing in the Truman Administration," *Ky. Hist. Soc., Reg.*, 65 (1967), 47.

———— "The Removal of War Production Board Controls on Business, 1944–1946," *Bus. Hist. Rev.*, 39 (1965), 243.

———— "The Truman Administration and Its Reconversion Wage Policy," *Labor Hist.*, 6 (1965), 214.

Brown, Francis J., ed., *National Defense and Higher Education* (1951).

Clark, John M., *Demobilization of Wartime Economic Controls* (1944).

Deming, Frederick L., and Weldon A. Stein, *Disposal of Southern War Plants* (1949).

Harris, Seymour E., ed., *Economic Reconstruction* (1945).

Havighurst, R. J., et al., *American Veteran Back Home: A Study of Veteran Readjustment* (1951).

Kaplan, Abraham D. H., *Liquidation of War Production* (1944).

Martin, Ralph G., *Best is None too Good* (1948).

Mauldin, Bill, *Back Home* (1947).

Nathan, R. R., *Mobilizing for Abundance* (1944).

Ross, Davis R. B., *Preparing for Ulysses: Politics and Veterans during World War II* (1969).

Sitterson, J. Carlyle, *Development of Reconversion Policies* (1946).

Small, J. D., *From War to Peace* (1946).

U.S. Congress. Senate, Military Affairs Committee, *War Mobilization and Post-War Adjustment* (78 Cong., 2d sess., Sen. Report, no. 1036.)

U.S. National Resources Planning Board, *Report* (1943).

U.S. Office of Contract Settlement, *History of War Contract Terminations* (1947).

55.17.7 Labor

55.17.7.1 General

Bernstein, Barton J., "The Truman Administration and Its Reconversion Wage Policy," *Labor Hist.*, 6 (1965), 214.

———— "The Truman Administration and the Steel Strike of 1946," *JAH*, 52 (1966), 791.

Broude, Henry W., *Steel Decisions and National Economy* (1963).

Calkins, Fay, *CIO and the Democratic Party* (1952).

Gregory, Charles O., *Labor and the Law* (1949).

McConnell, Grant, *President Seizes the Steel Mills* (1960).

Millis, Harry A., and Emily C. Brown, *From Wagner Act to Taft-Hartley* (1950).

Mills, C. Wright, *Men of Power* (1948).

Stein, Bruno, "Wage Stabilization in Korean War Period: Role of Subsidiary Wage Boards," *Labor Hist.*, 4 (1963), 161.

Warne, Colston E., et al., eds., *Labor in Postwar America* (1949).

See also 10.3 for biographies/writings of:

Lewis, John L., 1880–1969
Sawyer, Charles, 1887–
Taft, Robert A., 1889–1953

55.17.7.2 Taft-Hartley Act

Aaron, Benjamin, "Amending the Taft-Hartley Act: A Decade of Frustration," *Indust. and Labor Rel. Rev.*, 11 (1958), 327.

Bell, Daniel, "Taft-Hartley, Five Years Old," *Fortune*, 46 (1952), 69.

Bernstein, Irving, et al., eds., *Emergency Disputes and National Policy* (1955).

Lee, R. Alton, *Truman and Taft-Hartley: A Question of Mandate* (1966).

Pomper, George, "Labor and Congress: The Repeal of Taft-Hartley," *Labor Hist.*, 2 (1961), 323.

Slichter, S. H., "Taft-Hartley Act," *Quar. Jour. Econ.*, 63 (1949), 1.

—— "Revision of the Taft-Hartley Act," *Quar. Jour. Econ.*, 67 (1953), 149.

U.S. Department of Labor, *Problems and Policies of Dispute Settlement* (1950).

55.17.8 Agriculture

Bernstein, Barton J., "Postwar Battle between the Office of Price Administration and Agriculture," *Agric. Hist.*, 41 (1967), 45.

Christenson, Reo M., *Brannan Plan: Farm Politics and Policy* (1959).

Matusow, Allen J., *Farm Policies and Politics in the Truman Years* (1967).

55.17.9 Government Reorganization

Burns, James MacGregor, *Congress on Trial* (1949).

Carpenter, William S., *Unfinished Business of Civil Service Reform* (1952).

Douglas, Paul H., *Economy in National Government* (1952).

Fesler, James W., "Administrative Literature and the Second Hoover Commission Reports, *Am. Pol. Sci. Rev.*, 51 (1957), 135.

Finer, Herman, "Hoover Commission Reports," *Pol. Sci. Quar.*, 64 (1949), 404.

Gervasi, F. H., *Big Government* (1949).

Griffith, Ernest S., *Congress* (1951).

Gross, B. M., *Legislative Struggle* (1953).

Koenig, L. W., ed., "Hoover Commission," *Am. Pol. Sci. Rev.*, 43 (1949), 933.

Nash, Bradley, and Cornelius Lynde, *Hook in Leviathan* (1950).

U.S. Commission on the Organization of Executive Branch of the Government, *Reports, Task Reports, Digests, Indexes* (1949).

55.17.10 Election of 1948

Abels, Jules, *Out of the Jaws of Victory* (1959).

Americans for Democratic Action, *Henry Wallace, the First Three Months* (1948).

—— *Henry A. Wallace, the Last Seven Months of His Presidential Campaign* (1948).

Berelson, Bernard R., et al., *Voting: Opinion Formation in a Presidential Campaign* (1954).

Calkins, Fay, *CIO and the Democratic Party* (1952).

Carleton, W. G., "Fate of the Dixiecrat Movement," *Yale Rev.*, 37 (1949), 449.

Kirkendall, Richard S., "Election of 1948," in Arthur M. Schlesinger, Jr. and Fred L. Israel, eds., *History of American Presidential Elections, 1789–1968*. vol. IV (1971).

Leeds, Morton, "AFL in 1948 Elections," *Social Research*, 17 (1950), 207.

Lemmon, S. M., "Ideology of the 'Dixiecrat' Movement," *Social Forces*, 30 (1951), 162.

MacDougall, Curtis D., *Gideon's Army* (3 vols., 1965).

Martin, B. A., and J. E. Holmes, "1948 Elections in Eleven Western States," *West. Pol. Quar.*, 2 (1949), 89.

Mosteller, Frank, *Pre-election Polls of 1948* (1949).

Redding, John M., *Inside the Democratic Party* (1958).

Ross, Irwin, *Loneliest Campaign: Truman Victory of 1948* (1968).

Schmidt, Karl M., *Henry A. Wallace: Quixotic Crusader* (1948).

Van Auken, Cecelia, "Negro Press in the 1948 Presidential Election," *Journalism Quar.*, 26 (1949), 431.
Wallace, Henry A., *Toward World Peace* (1948).
Wechsler, J. A., "My Ten Months With Wallace," *Progressive*, 12 (1948), 4.

See also 10.3 for biographies/writings of:

Truman, Harry S., 1884–1972
Wallace, Henry A., 1888–1965

55.17.11 Housing

Bernstein, Barton J., "Reluctance and Resistance: Wilson Wyatt and Veterans' Housing in the Truman Administration," Ky. Hist. Soc., *Reg.*, 65 (1967), 47.
Davies, Richard O., *Housing Reform during the Truman Administration* (1966).

55.17.12 Negroes and Civil Rights

Berman, William C., *Politics of Civil Rights in the Truman Administration* (1970).
Dalfiume, Richard M., *Desegregation of the U.S. Armed Forces: Fighting on Two Fronts, 1939–1953* (1969).
Norgren, Paul H., and Samuel E. Hill, *Toward Fair Employment* (1964).
Rose, A. M., *The Negro in Postwar America* (1950).
Stillman, Richard J., *Integration of the Negro in U.S. Armed Forces* (1968).
U.S. President. Committee on Civil Rights, *To Secure These Rights* (1947).

55.17.13 Loyalty Procedures and Controversies

55.17.13.1 General

Barth, Alan, *Loyalty of Free Men* (1951).
Biddle, Francis, *Fear of Freedom* (1951).
Bontecou, Eleanor, *Federal Loyalty-Security* (1953).
Brown, Ralph S., Jr., *Loyalty and Security: Employment Tests* (1960).
Caughey, John W., *In Clear and Present Danger* (1958).
Countryman, Vern, *Un-American Activities in the State of Washington: Canwell Committee* (1951).
Gellhorn, Walter, *Security, Loyalty, and Science* (1950).
——— *States and Subversion* (1952).
Harper, Alan D., *Politics of Loyalty: White House and the Communist Issue, 1946–1952* (1969).
Jowitt, William A., *Strange Case of Alger Hiss* (1953).
Lasswell, Harold D., *National Security and Individual Freedom* (1950).
Lowenthal, Max, *Federal Bureau of Investigation* (1950).
Morgenthau, Hans J., "Impact of Loyalty-Security Measures on the State Department," *Bull. Atomic Scientists*, 11 (1955), 134.
Nixon, Richard M., *Six Crises* (1962).
Shattuck, Henry L., "Loyalty Review Board of the U.S. Civil Service Commission, 1947–1953," Mass. Hist. Soc., *Proc.*, 78 (1966), 63.
Stewart, George R., *Year of Oath* (1950).

*   *   *   *   *   *   *

Westin, Alan F., "Loyalty Controversy," *Commentary*, 28 (1959), 528.

55.17.13.2 Contemporary Accounts

Calomiris, Angela, *Red Masquerade* (1950).
Chambers, Whittaker, *Witness* (1952).
Lasky, Victor, and Ralph de Toledano, *Seeds of Treason* (1950).

Lattimore, Owen, *Ordeal by Slander* (1950).
Philbrick, Herbert A., *I Led Three Lives* (1952).
Weyl, Nathaniel, *Battle Against Disloyalty* (1951).

55.17.13.3 Communist Party and Prosecutions

Allen, R. B., et al., "Communism and Academic Freedom," *Am. Scholar*, 18 (1949), 323.
American Civil Liberties Union, *Trial of Elizabeth Gurley Flynn*, Corliss Lamont, ed. (1968).
Budenz, Louis F., *Men without Faces: Communist Conspiracy* (1950).
Cooke, Alistair, *Generation on Trial* (1950).
Ernst, Morris L., and David Loth, *Report on the American Communist* (1952).
Howe, Irving, and Lewis Coser, *The American Communist Party: A Critical History* (1957).
Latham, Earl, *The Communist Controversy in Washington: From the New Deal to McCarthy* (1966).
Nathanson, Nathaniel L., "Communist Trial and Clear-and-Present Danger Test," *Harv. Law Rev.*, 64 (1950), 1167.
Packer, Herbert L., *Ex-Communist Witnesses* (1962).
Palmer, E. E., ed., *Communist Problem* (1951).
Shannon, David A., *Decline of American Communism: The Communist Party since 1945* (1959).
Stouffer, Samuel A., *Communism, Conformity, and Civil Liberties* (1955).

55.17.13.4 House Un-American Activities Committee

Beck, Carl, *Contempt of Congress: Prosecutions Initiated by the Committee on Un-American Activities, 1951–1957* (1958).
Carr, Robert K., *House Committee on Un-American Activities* (1952).
Goodman, Walter, *Committee: House Committee on Un-American Activities* (1968).

55.17.13.5 McCarthyism

de Antonio, Emile, and Daniel Talbot, producers, *Point of Order! A Documentary of the Army–McCarthy Hearings* (1964). Transcript of the film.
DeSantis, Vincent P., "American Catholics and McCarthyism," *Cath. Hist. Rev.*, 51 (1965), 1.
Hofstadter, Richard, *Anti-Intellectualism in American Life* (1963).
——— *The Paranoid Style in American Politics* (1965).
Latham, Earl, ed., *The Meaning of McCarthyism* (1965).
McCarthy, Joseph R., *McCarthyism* (1952).
Polsby, Nelson W., "Towards an Explanation of McCarthyism," *Pol. Studies*, 8 (1960), 250.
Potter, Charles E., *Days of Shame* (1965).
Rogin, Michael P., *Intellectuals and McCarthy* (1967).
Shannon, David A., "Was McCarthy a Political Heir of LaFollette?" *Wis. Mag. Hist.*, 45 (1961), 3.
Sokol, Robert, "Power Orientation and McCarthyism," *Am. Jour. Sociol.*, 73 (1968), 443.
U.S. Congress. Senate, Committee on Rules and Administration, *Investigation of Senators Joseph R. McCarthy and William Benton* (82 Cong., 2d Sess., 1952).
Wiebe, G. D., "The Army-McCarthy Hearings and the Public Conscience," *Pub. Opinion Quar.*, 22 (1959), 490.
Wisconsin Citizens' Committee, *McCarthy Record* (1952).

See also 10.3 for biographies/writings of:

Hennings, Thomas, 1903–1960
Marcantonio, Vito, 1902–1954

55.17.13.6 Atomic Espionage

GENERAL

[Canada]. *Royal Commission Report on Information Leakage on Atomic Research to Soviet Agents* (1946).
Pilat, O. R., *Atom Spies* (1952).
Schneir, Walter and Miriam, *Invitation to an Inquest: Rosenberg–Sobell Case* (1968).
U.S. Congress. Joint Committee on Atomic Energy, *Soviet Atomic Espionage* (82 Cong., 1st sess., 1951).

OPPENHEIMER CASE

Alsop, Joseph and Stewart, *We Accuse: J. Robert Oppenheimer* (1954).
Stern, Philip M., *The Oppenheimer Case: Security on Trial* (1969).
Strout, Cushing, "The Oppenheimer Case: Melodrama, Tragedy, and Irony," *Va. Quar. Rev.*, 40 (1964), 268.

See also 10.3 for biographies/writings of:

Lilienthal, David E., 1899–
Oppenheimer, J. Robert, 1904–1967

55.17.14 Corruption Issue

Bolles, Blair, *How to Get Rich in Washington* (1952).
Douglas, Paul H., *Ethics in Government* (1952).
Schriftgiesser, Karl, *Lobbyists* (1951).
Wilson, Harper H., *Congress: Corruption and Compromise* (1951).

55.18 ELECTION OF 1952

Bernstein, Barton J., "Election of 1952," in Arthur M. Schlesinger, Jr., and Fred L. Israel, eds., *History of American Presidential Elections, 1789–1968*, vol. IV (1971).
Brown, Stuart G., *Conscience in Politics: Adlai E. Stevenson* (1961).
Campbell, Angus, et al., "Political Issues and the Vote: November, 1952," *Am. Pol. Sci. Rev.*, 47 (1953), 359.
———— *The Voter Decides* (1954).
David, Paul T., Malcolm Moos, and Ralph M. Goldman, eds., *Presidential Nominating Politics in 1952* (5 vols., 1954).
Davies, James C., "Charisma in the 1952 Campaign," *Am. Pol. Sci. Rev.*, 48 (1954), 1083.
DeSantis, Vincent P., "Presidential Election of 1952," *Rev. Pol.*, 15 (1953), 131.
Eulau, Heinz, *Class and Party in the Eisenhower Years* (1962).
Lane, Robert E., "Politics of Consensus in Age of Affluence," *Am. Pol. Sci. Rev.*, 59 (1965), 874.
Lubell, Samuel, *Revolt of Moderates* (1956).
Stevenson, Adlai E., *Major Campaign Speeches* (1953).

See also 10.3 for biographies/writings of:

Eisenhower, Dwight D., 1890–1969
Nixon, Richard M., 1913–
Stevenson, Adlai E., 1900–1965
Taft, Robert A., 1889–1953

55.19 EISENHOWER ADMINISTRATION, 1953–1961

55.19.1 General

Adams, Sherman, *Firsthand Report: Eisenhower Administration* (1961).
Benson, Ezra T., *Cross Fire: Eight Years with Eisenhower* (1962).
Donovan, Robert J., *Eisenhower: Inside Story* (1956).
Hughes, Emmet J., *Ordeal of Power: Eisenhower Years* (1963).
Pusey, Merlo J., *Eisenhower, the President* (1956).
Rovere, Richard H., *Eisenhower Years* (1956).

See also 10.3 for biographies/writings of:

Dirksen, Everett M., 1896–1969
Dulles, John Foster, 1888–1959
Eisenhower, Dwight D., 1890–1969
Humphrey, George M., 1890–1970
Martin, Joseph W., 1884–1968
Nixon, Richard M., 1913–
Warren, Earl, 1891–

55.19.2 Politics

Acheson, Dean, *A Democrat Looks at His Party* (1955).
Gruening, Ernest, *The Battle for Alaska Statehood* (1967).
Kornhauser, Arthur, et al., *When Labor Votes* (1956).
Larson, Arthur, *A Republican Looks at His Party* (1956).
Lubell, Samuel, *Revolt of the Moderates* (1956).
Wildavsky, Aaron, *Dixon-Yates: A Study in Power Politics* (1962).
Wilson, James Q., *Amateur Democrat: Club Politics in Three Cities* (1962).

55.19.3 Economy

55.19.3.1 General

Berle, Adolf A., *Power Without Property* (1959).
Galbraith, John K., *The Affluent Society* (rev. ed., 1969).
Kolko, Gabriel, *Wealth and Power in America* (1962).
Lekachman, Robert, *Age of Keynes* (1966).
Peterson, William H., *Great Farm Problem* (1959).
Vatter, Harold G., *U.S. Economy in 1950's: An Economic History* (1963).

55.19.3.2 Government and Economy

Bartley, Ernest R., *Tidelands Oil Controversy* (1953).
Benedict, M. B., and O. C. Stine, *Agricultural Commodity Programs: Two Decades of Experience* (1956).
Dale, Edwin L., Jr., *Conservatives in Power* (1960). Fiscal and monetary policy.
Landis, James M., *Report on Regulatory Agencies to the President-Elect* (1960).
Miller, Glenn W., and Stephen B. Ware, "Right-To-Work Campaign in Ohio," *Labor Hist.*, 4 (1963), 51.
Triffin, Robert, *Gold and Dollar Crisis* (1960).

55.19.3.3 Federal Policy in Recessions

Holmans, A. E., "Eisenhower Administration and Recession," *Oxford Economic Papers*, 10 (1958), 34.
Lee, R. Alton, "Federal Assistance to Depressed Areas in Postwar Recessions," *West. Econ. Jour.*, 2 (1963), 1.
Lewis, Wilfred, Jr., *Federal Fiscal Policy in Postwar Recessions* (1962).

55.19.4 Supreme Court, Civil Liberties, and Civil Rights

Abrams, Charles, *Forbidden Neighbors: Prejudice in Housing* (1955).

Anderson, John W., *Eisenhower, Brownell, and Congress: Civil Rights Bill of 1956–57* (1964).

Berman, Daniel M., *A Bill Becomes a Law: Civil Rights Act of 1960* (1962).

Carter, Hodding, *The South Strikes Back* (1959). Citizens Councils.

Cox, Archibald, *The Warren Court: Constitutional Decision as an Instrument of Reform* (1968).

Harris, Robert, *Quest for Equality: Constitution, Congress and Supreme Court* (1960).

Hyman, H. M., *To Try Men's Souls: Loyalty Tests in American History* (1959).

Lewis, Anthony, and New York Times, *Portrait of a Decade: Second American Revolution* (1964).

Lytle, Clifford M., *Warren Court and Its Critics* (1968).

Mason, Alpheus, *Supreme Court from Taft to Warren* (1958).

Miller, Loren, *The Petitioners: Supreme Court and the Negro* (1966).

Murphy, Walter F., *Congress and the Court* (1962).

Peltason, Jack W., *Fifty-Eight Lonely Men: Southern Federal Judges and School Desegregation* (1961).

Quint, Howard H., *Profile in Black and White: South Carolina* (1958).

Weaver, J. D., *Warren: The Man, the Court, the Era* (1967).

55.20 ELECTION OF 1956

Eulau, Heinz, *Class and Party in Eisenhower Years: Class Roles and Perspectives in 1952 and 1956 Elections* (1962).

Moos, Malcolm, "Election of 1956," in Arthur M. Schlesinger, Jr. and Fred L. Israel, eds., *History of American Presidential Elections, 1789–1968* (Vol. 4, 1971).

Stevenson, Adlai E., *New America*, S. E. Harris et al., eds. (1957).

Thomson, Charles A. H., and Frances M. Shattuck, *1956 Presidential Campaign* (1960).

See also 10.3 for biographies/writings of:

Eisenhower, Dwight D., 1890–1969
Kefauver, Estes, 1903–1963
Nixon, Richard M., 1913–
Stevenson, Adlai E., 1900–1965

55.21 ELECTION OF 1960

Barrett, Patricia, *Religious Liberty and the American Presidency* (1963).

Dawidowicz, Lucy S., and Leon J. Goldstein, *Politics in Pluralist Democracy: Voting in 1960 Election* (1963).

Scoble, Harry M., and Leon D. Epstein, "Religion and Wisconsin Voting in 1960," *Jour. Politics*, 26 (1964), 381.

Sorensen, Theodore C., "Election of 1960," in Arthur M. Schlesinger, Jr. and Fred L. Israel, eds., *History of American Presidential Elections, 1789–1968*. Vol. IV (1971).

Tillett, Paul, ed., *Inside Politics: National Conventions, 1960* (1962).

Watson, Richard A., "Religion and Politics in Mid-America: Presidential Voting in Missouri, 1928 and 1960," *Midcontinent Am. Studies Jour.*, 5 (1964), 33.

White, Theodore H., *The Making of the President, 1960* (1961).

See also 10.3 for biographies/writings of:

Kennedy, John F., 1917–1963
Johnson, Lyndon B., 1908–1973
Nixon, Richard M., 1913–

55.22 KENNEDY ADMINISTRATION, 1961–1963

55.22.1 General

Donald, Aida DiPace, ed., *Kennedy and the New Frontier* (1966).
Kraft, Joseph, *Profiles of Power* (1966).
Lincoln, Evelyn, *My Twelve Years with John F. Kennedy* (1965).

See also 10.3 for biographies/writings of:

Dirksen, Everett M., 1896–1969
Goldberg, Arthur J., 1908–
Johnson, Lyndon B., 1908–1973
Kennedy, John F., 1917–1963

35.22.2 Special Topics

Baker, Leonard, *Johnson Eclipse: President's Vice Presidency* (1966).
Burns, James MacGregor, *Deadlock of Democracy: Four Party Politics in America* (1963).
Chase, Harold W., and Allen H. Lerman, eds., *Kennedy and the Press: News Conferences* (1965).
Fuchs, Lawrence H., *John F. Kennedy and American Catholicism* (1967).
Gilbert, Charles E., "Policy-Making in Public Welfare: 1962 Amendments," *Pol. Sci. Quar.*, 81 (1966), 196.
Golden, James L., "John F. Kennedy and the 'Ghosts'," *Quar. Jour. Speech*, 52 (1966), 348.
Heckscher, August, *Public Happiness* (1962).
Ions, Edmund S., *Politics of John F. Kennedy* (1967).
Levine, Gene N., and John Modell, "American Public Opinion and the Fallout-Shelter Issue," *Pub. Opinion Quar.*, 29 (1965), 270.
Schlesinger, Arthur M., Jr., *Politics of Hope* (1963).

55.22.3 Government and Economy

Harris, Seymour E., *Economics of the Kennedy Years* (1964).
Heath, Jim F., *John F. Kennedy and the Business Community* (1969).
Mangum, Garth L., *MDTA: Federal Manpower Policy* (1968).
Steele, Henry, "Fortunes of Economic Reform Legislation: Drug Amendments Act of 1962," *Am. Jour. Econ. Sociol.*, 25 (1966), 39.

55.22.4 Space Programs

Odishaw, Hugh, ed., *Challenges of Space* (1962).
Rosholt, R. L., *Administrative History of NASA, 1958–1963* (1966).
Swenson, L. S., et al., *This New Ocean: History of Project Mercury* (1966).

55.22.5 Assassination

Bickel, Alexander M., "Failure of the Warren Report," *Commentary*, 42 (1966), 31.
Bishop, Jim, *The Day Kennedy Was Shot* (1968).

Greenberg, Bradley S., and Edwin B. Parker, eds., *Kennedy Assassination and the American Public* (1965).

Manchester, William, *Death of a President* (1967).

Newman, Albert H., *Assassination of Kennedy* (1970).

U.S. President. Commission on Assassination of President Kennedy, *Report* (1964).

White, Stephen, *Should We Now Believe the Warren Report?* (1968).

55.23 JOHNSON ADMINISTRATION, 1963–1969

55.23.1 General

Bell, Jack, *Johnson Treatment* (1965).

Roberts, Charles W., *LBJ's Inner Circle* (1965).

Shannon, William V., *Heir Apparent: Robert Kennedy and the Struggle for Power* (1967).

Sherril, Robert, *Accidental President* (1967).

See also 10.3 for biographies/writings of:

Dirksen, Everett M., 1896–1969
Humphrey, Hubert H., 1911–
Johnson, "Lady Bird," 1912–
Johnson, Lyndon B., 1908–1973
Kennedy, Robert F., 1925–1968

55.23.2 Special Topics

Bayh, Birch, *One Heartbeat Away* (1968). The twenty-fifth amendment.

Gettleman, Marvin E., and David Mermelstein, eds., *Great Society Reader: Failure of American Liberalism* (1967).

55.23.3 Government and Economy

Boote, M. J., "Area and Regional Development in the United States, 1955–1965," *CAAS Bull.*, 1 (1966), 45.

Cochrance, Willard W., *City Man's Guide to the Farm Problem* (1965).

Kahn, Alfred E., "Depletion Allowance in Context of Cartelization," *Am. Econ. Rev.*, 54 (1964), 286.

"Labor-Management in Great Society," *Current Hist.*, 49 (1965), 65.

Minsky, Hyman, "Crunch of 1966-Model for New Financial Crises?" *Transaction*, 5 (1968), 44.

Rolfe, Sidney E., and Robert G. Hawkins, *Gold and World Power: The Dollar, the Pound, and Plans for Reform* (1966).

Ruttan, Vernon W., et al., eds., *Agricultural Policy in an Affluent Society* (1969).

Schlebecker, John T., "The Great Holding Action: The NFO in September, 1962," *Agric. Hist.*, 39 (1965), 204.

Sheahan, John, *Wage-Price Guideposts* (1967).

55.23.4 Reapportionment

de Grazia, Alfred, *Apportionment and Representative Government* (1963).

McKay, Robert B., *Re-Apportionment: Law and Politics of Equal Representation* (1965).

55.23.5 Civil Rights and Black Revolution

Bell, Inge P., *CORE and Strategy of Non-violence* (1968).
Carmichael, Stokely, and C. V. Hamilton, *Black Power: Politics of Liberation* (1967).
Coles, Robert, *Children of Crisis: Study of Courage and Fear* (1967).
Conot, R. E., *Rivers of Blood, Years of Darkness: Watts Riot* (1967).
Daedalus, *The Negro American*, Talcott Parsons and Kenneth B. Clark, eds., (1966).
Farmer, James, *Freedom—When?* (1966).
Goldston, Robert C., *Negro Revolution* (1968).
Grier, William H., and Price M. Cobbs, *Black Rage* (1968).
Hersey, John R., *Algiers Motel Incident* (1968).
Isaacs, Harold R., *New World of Negro Americans* (1963).
Jacobson, Julius, ed., *Negro and American Labor Movement* (1968).
King, Martin Luther, Jr., *Stride Toward Freedom (1958).*
—— *Where Do We Go From Here: Chaos or Community?* (1967).
Konvitz, Milton R., *Expanding Liberties: Freedom's Gains in Postwar America* (1966).
Lomax, Louis E., *When the Word is Given: Elijah Muhammad, Malcolm X, and Black Muslim World* (1963).
Marx, Gary T., *Protest and Prejudice: Belief in Black Community* (1968).
Matthews, Donald R., and James W. Prothro, *Negroes and New Southern Politics* (1966).
Metcalf, George R., *Black Profiles* (1968).
Moynihan, Daniel P., *Negro Family: Case for National Action* (1965).
—— "President and the Negro," *Commentary*, 43 (1967), 31.
Muse, Benjamin, *American Negro Revolution: From Nonviolence to Black Power, 1963–1967* (1968).
Newby, Idus A., *Challenge to the Court: Social Scientists and Defense of Segregation, 1954–1966* (1968).
Pettigrew, Thomas F., *Profile of Negro American* (1964).
Rainwater, Lee, and William L. Yancey, *Moynihan Report and Politics of Controversy* (1967).
Schwartz, Mildred A., *Trends in White Attitudes toward Negroes* (1967).
U.S. National Advisory Commission on Civil Disorders, *Report* (1968).
Warren, Robert Penn, *Who Speaks for the Negro?* (1965).
Waskow, Arthur I., *From Race Riot to Sit-In, 1919 and 1960's: Study in Connections between Conflict and Violence* (1966).

See also 10.3 for biographies/writings of:

King, Martin Luther, Jr., 1929–1968
Little, "Malcolm X," 1925–1965

55.23.6 War on Poverty

Caudill, Harry M., *Night Comes to the Cumberlands: Biography of a Depressed Area* (1963).
Clark, Kenneth, ed., *Relevant War against Poverty: Study of Community Action Programs and Observable Social Change* (1969).
Donovan, John C., *Politics of Poverty* (1967).
Gallaway, Lowell E., "Foundations of 'War on Poverty'," *Am. Econ. Rev.*, 55 (1965), 122.
Harrington, Michael, *The Other America* (1962).
Hunter, David R., *The Slums: Challenge and Response* (1968).
Larner, Jeremy, and Irving Howe, eds., *Poverty: Views from the Left* (1969).
Levitan, Sar A., *Great Society's Poor Law: New Approach to Poverty* (1969).
Lewis, Oscar, *La Vida: Puerto Rican Family: Life in Culture of Poverty—San Juan and New York* (1966).

Moynihan, Daniel P., *Maximum Feasible Misunderstanding: Community Action in the War on Poverty* (1969).
Seligman, Ben B., *Permanent Poverty: American Syndrome* (1968).

55.23.7 Student Unrest

Avorn, Jerry L., et al., *Up Against the Ivy Wall: Columbia Crisis* (1969).
Bell, Daniel, and Irving Kristol, eds., *Confrontation: Student Rebellion and the Universities* (1969).
Keniston, Kenneth, "Youth, Change, and Violence," *Am. Scholar*, 37 (1968), 227.
Kennan, George F., et al., *Democracy and the Student Left* (1968).
Kunen, James S., *Strawberry Statement* (1969).

55.24 ELECTION OF 1964

Alexander, Herbert E., *Financing the 1964 Election* (1966).
Converse, Philip E., Aage R. Clausen, and Warren E. Miller, "1964 Election," *Am. Pol. Sci. Rev.*, 59 (1965), 321.
Cosman, Bernard, and R. J. Huckshorn, *Republican Politics: 1964 Campaign and Aftermath* (1968).
Crespi, Irving, "Goldwater Case," *Pub. Opinion Quar.*, 29 (1966), 523.
Cummings, Milton C., Jr., ed., *National Election of 1964* (1966).
De Toledano, Ralph, *Case for Goldwater Republicanism* (1963).
Goldwater, Barry, *Conscience of a Conservative* (1961).
Huebner, Lee W., and Thomas E. Petri, eds., *Ripon Papers, 1963–1968* (1969).
Kessel, John H., *Goldwater Coalition: Republican Strategies in 1964* (1968).
Lipset, Seymour M., and Earl Raab, *Politics of Unreason: Right Wing Extremism, 1790–1970* (1970).
McKenna, William J., "Negro Vote in Philadelphia Elections," *Penn. Hist.*, 32 (1965), 406.
MacNeil, Robert, *People Machine: Influence of Television on American Politics* (1968).
Martin, John Bartlow, "Election of 1964," in Arthur M. Schlesinger, Jr. and Fred L. Israel, eds., *History of American Presidential Elections, 1789–1968* (Vol. 4, 1971).
New York Times, Road to the White House: 1964 Election, Harold Faber, ed. (1965).
Rice, Ross R., "1964 Elections in the West," *West. Pol. Quar.*, 18 (1965), 431.
Waltzer, Herbert, "Television Coverage of 1964 National Convention," *Pub. Opinion Quar.*, 30 (1966), 33.
White, Theodore H., *The Making of the President 1964* (1965).

See also 10.3 for biographies/writings of:

Goldwater, Barry, 1909–
Johnson, Lyndon B., 1908–1973

55.25 ELECTION OF 1968

Boyarsky, William, *Rise of Ronald Reagan* (1968).
Broder, David S., "Election of 1968," in Arthur M. Schlesinger, Jr. and Fred L. Israel, eds., *History of American Presidential Elections, 1789–1968* (Vol. 4, 1971).
Chester, Lewis, Godfrey Hodgson, and Bruce Page, *American Melodrama: Presidential Campaign of 1968* (1969).
Frady, Marshall, *Wallace* (1968).

Halberstam, David, *Unfinished Odyssey of Robert Kennedy* (1969).
Herzog, Arthur, *McCarthy for President* (1969).
Larner, Jeremy, *Nobody Knows: Reflections on McCarthy Campaign of 1968*
    (1970).
McCarthy, Eugene J., *Year of the People* (1969).
Mailer, Norman, *Miami and the Siege of Chicago: Informal History of the Repub-*
    lican and Democratic Conventions of 1968 (1968).
Ripon Society, *Lessons of Victory* (1969).
Rovere, Richard H., *Waist Deep in the Big Muddy: Personal Reflections on 1968*
    (1968).
Stavis, Ben, *We Were the Campaign: New Hampshire to Chicago for McCarthy*
    (1969).
White, Theodore H., *The Making of the President 1968* (1969).

See also 10.3 for biographies/writings of:

Humphrey, Hubert H., 1911–
Johnson, Lyndon B., 1908–1973
Kennedy, Robert F., 1925–1968
Nixon, Richard M., 1913–

55.26 NIXON ADMINISTRATION, 1969–

Dutton, Frederick G., *Changing Sources of Power: American Politics in the 1970's*
    (1971).
Evans, Rowland, Jr., and Richard D. Novak, *Nixon in the White House* (1971).
Gordon, Kermit, *Agenda for the Nation* (1969).
Hickel, Walter J., *Who Owns America?* (1971).
Marsh, Robert, *Agnew the Unexamined Man* (1971).

See also 10.3 for biographies/writings of:

Nixon, Richard M., 1913–

56 Foreign Relations since 1945

56.1 GENERAL

Bell, Coral, *Negotiation from Strength: Study in Politics of Power* (1963).
Bohlen, Charles E., *The Transformation of American Foreign Policy* (1969).
Brown, Seyom, *The Faces of Power: Foreign Policy from Truman to Johnson* (1968).
Carleton, William G., *Revolution in American Foreign Policy* (1964).
Kennan, George F., *American Diplomacy, 1900–1950* (1951).
Osgood, Robert E., et al., *America and the World: Truman Doctrine to Vietnam* (1970).
Perkins, Dexter, *Diplomacy of a New Age: Major Issues in U.S. Policy since 1945* (1967).
Reitzel, William, et al., *United States Foreign Policy, 1945–1955* (1956).
Rostow, Walt W., *The United States in the World Arena* (1960).
Spanier, John W., *American Foreign Policy since World War II* (4th rev. ed., 1971).
Watson, Richard L., Jr., ed., *United States in the Contemporary World, 1945–1962* (1965).

56.2 ANNUAL SURVEYS AND DOCUMENT COLLECTIONS

Brookings Institution, *Major Problems of United States Foreign Policy* (1947–1954).
Documents on American Foreign Relations (vol. 7– , 1947–).
Royal Institute of International Affairs, *Documents on International Affairs* (1928–1971).
——— *Survey of International Affairs* (1920/1923–1970).
United States in World Affairs (1931–).

56.3 COLD WAR

Aptheker, Herbert, *American Foreign Policy and the Cold War* (1962).
Barraclough, Geoffrey, *Introduction to Contemporary History* (1964).
Campbell, John C., *American Policy toward Communist Eastern Europe* (1965).
Crabb, Cecil V., Jr., "United States and Neutralists," Am. Acad. Pol. Sci., *Annals*, 362 (1965), 92.
Donnelly, Desmond, *Struggle for the World: Cold War, 1917–1965* (1965).
Feis, Herbert, *From Trust to Terror: Onset of the Cold War, 1945–1950* (1970).
Fleming, Denna F., *Cold War and Its Origins, 1917–1960* (2 vols., 1961).
Graebner, Norman A., *Cold War Diplomacy, 1945–1960* (1962).
Halle, Louis J., *Cold War as History* (1967).

Herz, Martin F., *Beginnings of the Cold War* (1966).
Kennan, George F., *Russia, the Atom, and the West* (1958).
Kissinger, Henry A., "American Strategic Doctrine and Diplomacy," in Michael
     E. Howard, ed., *Theory and Practice of War: Essays Presented to Captain B. H.
     Liddell Hart* (1965).
LaFeber, Walter, *America, Russia, and the Cold War, 1945–1966* (1967).
Lincoln, G. A., "Military and Strategic Aspects of American Foreign Policy," in
     Alfred H. Kelly, ed., *American Foreign Policy and American Democracy* (1954).
Lukacs, John A., *Great Powers and Eastern Europe* (1953).
—— *New History of the Cold War* (3d ed., 1966).
Maier, Charles S., "Revisionism and Interpretation of Cold War Origins," *Per-
     spectives in Am. Hist.*, 4 (1970), 313.
Seabury, Paul, and Brian Thomas, "Cold War Origins, I and II," *Jour. Contemp.
     Hist.*, 3 (1968), 169.
Venkataramani, M. S., *Undercurrents in American Foreign Relations: Four Studies*
     (1965).
Viskov, S. I., "Amerikanskie Istoriki i Publitsisty o Kholodnoi Voine," *Novaia i
     Noveishaia Istoriia* [USSR], 11 (1967), 114.

See also 54.3.2, World War II–Foreign Relations–Soviet Union; 56.4.9, Berlin
     Problem; 56.6.2, Cuban Missile Crisis; 56.10, Soviet Union.

56.4 TRUMAN ADMINISTRATION, 1945–1953

56.4.1 General

Almond, Gabriel A., *American People and Foreign Policy* (1950).
Byrnes, James F., "Byrnes Answers Truman," *Collier's*, 129 (1952), 15.
Cheever, Daniel S., and H. Field Haviland, Jr., *American Foreign Policy and
     Separation of Powers* (1952).
Czemoiel, Ernst-Otto, *Das Amerikanische Sicherheitssystem, 1945–1949* (1966).
Elliott, William Y., et al., *United States Foreign Policy* (1952).
Westerfield, H. Bradford, *Foreign Policy and Party Politics: Pearl Harbor to Korea*
     (1955).

See also 10.3 for biographies/writings of:

Acheson, Dean G., 1893–1971
Byrnes, James F., 1879–1972
Marshall, George C., 1880–1959
Truman, Harry S., 1884–1972

56.4.2 Contemporary Discussion

Acheson, Dean G., *Pattern of Responsibility*, McGeorge Bundy, ed. (1952).
Churchill, Winston L. S., *Sinews of Peace* (1949).
Dulles, John Foster, *War or Peace* (1950).
Finer, Herman, *America's Destiny* (1947).
Hoffman, P. G., *Peace Can Be Won* (1951).
Lippmann, Walter, *Cold War* (1947).
Morgenthau, Hans J., *In Defense of National Interest* (1951).
Taft, Robert A., *Foreign Policy for Americans* (1951).
Welles, Sumner, *Where Are We Heading?* (1946).

56.4.3 United Nations Relief and Rehabilitation Administration

Klemmé, Marvin, *Inside Story of UNRRA* (1949).
Woodbridge, George, comp., *UNRRA* (3 vols., 1950).

See also 10.3 for biographies/writings of:

Lehman, Herbert H., 1878–1963

56.4.4 Truman Doctrine and Postwar Greece

Kousoulas, D. George, "The Success of the Truman Doctrine Was Not Accidental," *Mil. Affairs*, 29 (1965), 88.
McNeill, William H., *Greece: American Aid in Action, 1947–1956* (1957).
Munkman, C. A., *American Aid to Greece* (1958).

56.4.5 Peace Negotiations, 1941–1947

Neumann, William L., *Making the Peace, 1941–1945* (1950).
U.S. Department of State, *Making Peace Treaties, 1941–1947* (1947).

56.4.6 Occupation Policy

Coles, Harry L., and Albert K. Weinberg, *Civil Affairs: Soldiers Become Governors* (1964).
Friedrich, Carl J., et al., *American Experiences in Military Government* (1948).
Holborn, Hajo, *American Military Government* (1947).
Rundell, Walter, Jr., *Black Market Money: Collapse of U.S. Military Currency Control in World War II* (1964).
U.S. Department of State, *Cartels and Combines in Occupied Areas* (1947).

56.4.7 German Occupation

Bach, Julian, Jr., *America's Germany* (1946).
Clay, Lucius D., *Decision in Germany* (1950).
Davidson, Eugene, *Death and Life of Germany: American Occupation* (1959).
DuBois, Josiah E., Jr., *Devil's Chemists* (1952).
Friedmann, Wolfgang, *Allied Military Government of Germany* (1947).
Friedrich, Carl J., "Rebuilding the German Constitution," *Am. Pol. Sci. Rev.*, 43 (1949), 461.
Gimbel, John, *American Occupation of Germany, 1945–1949* (1968).
—— *A German Community under American Occupation: Marburg, 1945–1952* (1961).
Hill, Russell, *Struggle for Germany* (1947).
Knappen, Marshall M., *And Call It Peace* (1947).
Martin, Joseph S., *All Honorable Men* (1950).
Middleton, Drew, *Struggle for Germany* (1949).
Morgenthau, Henry, Jr., *Germany Is Our Business* (1945).
Mosely, Philip E., "Dismemberment of Germany," *For. Affairs*, 28 (1950), 487.
—— "Occupation of Germany," *For. Affairs*, 28 (1950), 580.
Padover, S. K., *Experiment in Germany* (1946).
Plischke, Elmer, *History of Allied High Commission for Germany* (1951).
Pollock, J. K., and J. H. Meisel, *Germany under Occupation* (1947).
Ratchford, B. U., and W. D. Ross, *Berlin Reparations Assignment* (1947).
Snell, John L., *Wartime Origins of East–West Dilemma over Germany* (1959).
U.S. Department of State, *Germany, 1947–1949* (1950).
—— *Occupation of Germany* (1947).
—— *United States Economic Policy toward Germany* (1946).
Zink, Harold, *American Military Government in Germany* (1947).
—— *United States in Germany, 1944–1945* (1957).

See also 10.3 for biographies/writings of:

Byrnes, James F., 1879–1972

Conant, James Bryant, 1893–
Eisenhower, Dwight D., 1890–1969
Hull, Cordell, 1871–1955
Stimson, Henry L., 1867–1950

55.4.8 Nuremberg Trials

Bosch, William J., *Judgement on Nuremburg: American Attitudes* (1970).
Davidson, Eugene, *Trial of the Germans* (1966).
Glueck, Sheldon, *Nuremberg Trial and Aggressive War* (1946).
International Military Tribunal, *Trials of War Criminals, 1946–1949* (15 vols., 1949–1953).
────── *Trial of Major War Criminals, 1945–1946* (42 vols., 1947–1949).
Jackson, Robert H., *Case Against Nazi War Criminals* (1946).
────── *Nürnberg Case* (1947).
Storey, Robert G., *Final Judgement? Pearl Harbor to Nuremberg* (1968).
U.S. Chief Counsel for the Prosecution of Axis Criminality, *Nazi Conspiracy and Aggression* (10 vols., 1946–1948).

56.4.9 Berlin Problem

Ambrose, Stephen E., *Eisenhower and Berlin, 1945* (1967).
Davison, W. Phillips, *Berlin Blockade* (1958).
Gottlieb, Manuel, *German Peace Settlement and the Berlin Crisis* (1960).
Howley, F. L., *Berlin Command* (1950).
Smith, Jean E., *Defense of Berlin* (1963).

56.4.10 Occupation of Italy

Hughes, H. Stuart, *The United States and Italy* (rev. ed., 1965).
Kogan, Norman, *Italy and the Allies* (1956).
U.S. Department of State, *United States and Italy, 1936–1946* (1946).

56.4.11 Former Lesser Axis States

Mosely, Philip E., "Peace-Making, 1946," *Internatl. Organ.*, 1 (1947), 22.
Neumann, Robert G., "United States and Soviet Satellites," *Rev. Politics*, 11 (1949), 220.
Welles, Sumner, *Where Are We Heading?* (1946).

56.4.12 Japanese Occupation and Peace Settlement

Brines, Russell, *MacArthur's Japan* (1948).
Cohen, Bernard C., *Political Process and Foreign Policy: Japanese Peace Settlement* (1957).
Cohen, Jerome B., *Japan's Economy in War and Reconstruction* (1949).
Dunn, Frederick S., et al., *Peace-Making and the Settlement with Japan* (1963).
Edwards, Corwin D., "Dissolution of Japanese Combines," *Pac. Affairs*, 19 (1946), 227.
Fearey, R. A., *Occupation of Japan* (1950).
Feis, Herbert, *Contest over Japan* (1967).
Fishel, Wesley R., "Japan under MacArthur," *West. Pol. Quar.*, 4 (1951), 210.
Gunther, John, *Riddle of MacArthur* (1951).
Ike, Nobutaka, *Beginnings of Democracy in Japan* (1950).
Keenan, Joseph B., and Brendan F. Brown, *Crimes Against International Law* (1950).
Martin, Edwin M., *Allied Occupation of Japan* (1948).
Reel, Adolf F., *Case of General Yamashita* (1949).

Reischauer, Edwin O., *The United States and Japan* (3d ed., 1965).
Sebald, William J., and Russell Brines, *With MacArthur in Japan: Personal History* (1965).
Sheldon, Walt, *Honorable Conquerors: Japan, 1945–1952* (1965).
Supreme Commander Allied Powers, *Japanese Land Reform Program* (1950).
——— *Political Reorientation of Japan, 1945 to 1948* (2 vols., 1949).
U.S. Department of State, *Occupation of Japan* (1946).
Wildes, Harry E., *Typhoon in Tokyo: Occupation* (1954).
Yoshida, Shigeru, *Memoirs: Japan in Crisis*, Kenichi Yoshida, trans. (1962).

56.4.13 Korean War

56.4.13.1 General

Berger, Carl, *Korea Knot: A Military-Political History* (rev. ed., 1964).
Fehrenbach, T. R., *This Kind of War: Unpreparedness* (1963).
U.S. Department of State, *Conflict in Korea* (1951).

See also 10.3 for biographies/writings of:

Acheson, Dean G., 1893–1971
Dulles, John Foster, 1888–1959
MacArthur, Douglas, 1880–1964
Taft, Robert A., 1889–1953
Truman, Harry S., 1884–1972

56.4.13.2 Special Topics

Caridi, Ronald J., *The Korean War and American Politics: The Republican Party as a Case Study* (1969).
Goodrich, Leland M., *Korea: U.S. Policy in the United Nations* (1956).
——— "United Nations and Korea," *Jour. Internatl. Affairs*, 6 (1952) 115.
Grey, Arthur L., Jr., "Thirty-Eighth Parallel," *For. Affairs*, 29 (1951), 482.
Halperin, Morton H., "Limiting Process in the Korean War," *Pol. Sci. Quar.*, 78 (1963), 13.
Mitchell, C. Clyde, Jr., *Korea, Second Failure in Asia* (1951).
Padelford, Norman J., "United Nations and Korea," *Internatl. Organ.*, 5 (1951), 685.
Rovere, Richard H., and Arthur M. Schlesinger, Jr., *General and President* (1951).
Stevenson, Adlai E., "Korea in Perspective," *For. Affairs*, 30 (1952), 349.

56.4.13.3 Antecedents of War

McCune, George M., and Arthur L. Grey, Jr., *Korea Today* (1950).
Meade, Edward G., *American Military Government in Korea* (1951).
Soon Sung Cho, *Korea, 1940–1950: An Evaluation of American Responsibility* (1967).
U.S. Department of State, *Korea, 1945 to 1948* (1948).

56.4.13.4 Decision to Intervene

Paige, Glenn D., *Korean Decision, June 24–30, 1950* (1968).
U.S. Department of State, *U.S. Policy in Korean Crisis* (1950).

56.4.13.5 Military and Naval Operations

Appleman, Roy E., *South to the Naktong, North to the Yalu, 1950* (1961).
——— *The United States Army in the Korean War* (1961).
Cagle, Malcolm W., and Frank A. Manson, *Sea War in Korea* (1957).
Duncan, David D., *This is War!* (1967). Photo-narrative.
Field, James A., Jr., *History of Naval Operations: Korea* (1962).

Futrell, Robert F., *United States Air Force in Korea, 1950–1953* (1961).
Heinl, Robert D., Jr., *Victory at High Tide: The Inchon-Seoul Campaign* (1968).
Higgins, Trumbull, *Korea and the Fall of MacArthur: Précis in Limited War* (1960).
Karig, Walter, et al., *Battle Report.* Vol. VI: *War in Korea* (1952).
Leckie, Robert, *Conflict: Korean War* (1962).
Marshall, Samuel L. A., *River and Gauntlet* (1953).
Montross, Lynn, and Nicholas A. Canzona, *Chosin Reservoir Campaign* (1957).
Montross, Lynn, et al., *East-Central Front* (1962).
Montross, Lynn, and Nicholas A. Canzona, *Inchon-Seoul Operation* (1955).
———— *Pusan Perimeter* (1954).
Rees, David, *Korea: The Limited War* (1964).
Ridgway, Matthew B., *Korean War* (1967).
Ruetten, Richard T., "Douglas MacArthur's 'Reconnaissance in Force': Defeat in Korea," *Pac. Hist. Rev.*, 36 (1967), 79.
Sawyer, Robert K., *Military Advisors in Korea: KMAG in Peace and War*, Walter G. Hermes, ed. (1962).

56.4.13.6 Truman–MacArthur Controversy

MacArthur, Douglas, *Revitalizing a Nation* (1952).
Rovere, Richard H., and Arthur M. Schlesinger, Jr., *General and President* (1951).
Spanier, John W., *Truman-MacArthur Controversy and the Korean War* (2nd ed., 1965).
Sheldon, Walter J., *Hell or High Water: MacArthur's Landing at Inchon* (1968).
U.S. Department of the Army, *Korea—1950* (1952).
White, William L., *Back Down the Ridge* (1953).
Whiting, Allen, *China Crosses the Yalu* (1960).

56.4.13.7 Negotiations with North Korea

Hermes, Walter G., *Truce Tent and Fighting Front* (1966).
Joy, Charles T., *How Communists Negotiate* (1955).

56.5 EISENHOWER ADMINISTRATION, 1953–1961

56.5.1 General

Barber, Hollis W., *Foreign Policies of the United States* (1953).
Berding, Andrew H., *Dulles on Diplomacy* (1965).
Drummond, Roscoe, and Gaston Coblentz, *Duel at the Brink: John F. Dulles* (1960).
Dulles, Eleanor L., *John Foster Dulles: Last Year* (1963).

See also 10.3 for biographies/writings of:

Dulles, John Foster, 1888–1959
Eisenhower, Dwight D., 1890–1969

56.5.2 Contemporary Discussion

Brandt-Peltier, Louis, *Conceptions Américaines: Kennan et Dulles* (1953).
Brogan, Denis W., *America in the Modern World* (1960).
Cook, Thomas I., and Malcolm Moos, *Power through Purpose* (1954).
Kennan, George F., *Realities of American Foreign Policy* (1954).
Lederer, William J., *Nation of Sheep* (1961).
Morison, Elting E., ed., *The American Style: Essays, Dedham Conference, May 23–27, 1957* (1958).

56.6 KENNEDY ADMINISTRATION, 1961–1963

56.6.1 General

Bundy, McGeorge, "Presidency and the Peace," in Aida Di Pace Donald, ed., *John F. Kennedy and the New Frontier* (1966).
Galbraith, John Kenneth, *Ambassador's Journal: A Personal Account of the Kennedy Years* (1969).
Hilsman, Roger, *To Move a Nation: Foreign Policy of John F. Kennedy* (1967).
Mel'nikov, Iu. M., *Vneshnepoliticheskie Doktriny SSHA* (1970).

See also 10.3 for biographies/writings of:

Bowles, Chester, 1901–
Fulbright, J. William, 1905–
Kennedy, John F., 1917–1963

56.6.2 Cuban Missile Crisis

Crane, Robert D., "Cuban Crisis: A Strategic Analysis of American and Soviet Policy," *Orbis*, 6 (1963), 528.
Kennedy, Robert F., *Thirteen Days: Cuban Missile Crisis* (1969).
Larson, David L., ed., *The "Cuban Crisis" of 1962: Selected Documents and Chronology* (1963).
Pachter, Henry, *Collision Course: Cuban Missile Crisis and Coexistence* (1963).
Pedersen, John C., "Soviet Reporting of the Cuban Crisis," U.S. Naval Inst., *Proc.*, 91, no. 10 (1965), 54.
Wohlstetter, Roberta, "Cuba and Pearl Harbor: Hindsight and Foresight," *For. Affairs*, 43 (1965), 691.

56.7 JOHNSON ADMINISTRATION, 1963–1969

Ball, George W., *Discipline of Power: Essentials of a Modern World Structure* (1968).
Bowie, Robert R., *Shaping the Future: Foreign Policy* (1964).
Chomsky, Noam, *American Power and the New Mandarins* (1969).
Cleveland, Harlan, *Obligations of Power: American Diplomacy in Search for Peace* (1966).
Fulbright, J. William, *Arrogance of Power* (1967).
—— *Old Myths and New Realities* (1964).
Heren, Louis, *New American Commonwealth* (1968).
Hoffman, Stanley, *Gulliver's Troubles; Or American Foreign Policy* (1969).
Howe, Irving, ed., *Dissenter's Guide to Foreign Policy* (1968).
Kaplan, Lawrence, *Recent American Foreign Policy: Conflicting Interpretations* (1968).
Kennan, George F., *On Dealing with the Communist World* (1964).
Kissinger, Henry A., *American Foreign Policy: Three Essays* (1969).
—— *The Necessity for Choice* (1961).
McNamara, Robert S., *Essence of Security: Reflections* (1968).
May, Ernest R., "The Nature of Foreign Policy: The Calculated versus the Axiomatic," *Daedalus*, 91 (1962), 653.
Mendel, Douglas H., *American Foreign Policy in a Polycentric World* (1968).
Osgood, Robert E., *Alliances and American Foreign Policy* (1968).
Rostow, Walt W., *View from the Seventh Floor* (1964).
Stillman, Edmund, and William Pfaff, *New Politics: America and the End of the Postwar World* (1961).
—— *Power and Impotence: Failure of Foreign Policy* (1966).
Tucker, Robert W., *Nation or Empire? Debate over American Foreign Policy* (1968).

Waltz, Kenneth N., "The Stability of a Bipolar World," *Daedalus*, 93 (1964), 881.

See also 10.3 for biographies/writings of:

Johnson, Lyndon B., 1908–1973

56.8 VIETNAM WAR

56.8.1 General

Boettinger, John R., ed., *Vietnam and American Foreign Policy* (1968).
Buttinger, Joseph, *The Smaller Dragon: Political History of Vietnam* (1958).
———— *Vietnam: A Dragon Embattled* (1967).
Corson, William R., *The Betrayal* (1968).
Draper, Theodore, *Abuse of Power* (1967).
Fishel, Wesley R., ed., *Vietnam* (1968).
Goodwin, Richard N., *Triumph or Tragedy: Vietnam* (1966).
Hammer, Ellen, *Vietnam: Yesterday and Today* (1966).
Kahin, George, and John W. Lewis, *United States in Vietnam* (1967).
McCarthy, Mary, *Hanoi* (1968).
Mailer, Norman, *The Armies of the Night: History as a Novel, The Novel as History* (1968).
Schlesinger, Arthur M., Jr., *The Bitter Heritage: Vietnam and Democracy, 1941–1968* (rev. ed., 1968).
Shaplen, Robert, *The Lost Revolution: Vietnam, 1946–1966* (rev. ed., 1966).
Washburn, A. Michael, and Willard H. Mitchell, *Walt Rostow, Vietnam and Future Tasks of American Foreign Policy* (1967).

56.8.2 Vietnam before 1964

Bátor, Viktor, *Vietnam: Origins of United States Involvement* (1965).
Bodard, Lucien, *The Quicksand War: Prelude to Vietnam*, Patrick O'Brien, trans. (1967). Covers the period to 1950.
Drachman, Edward R., *United States Policy toward Vietnam, 1940–1945* (1970).
Gurtov, Melvin, *The First Vietnam Crisis, 1953–1954* (1967).
Halberstam, David, *Making of a Quagmire* (1965).
Murti, Bhaskaria S. N., *Vietnam Divided: The Unfinished Struggle* (1964).

56.8.3 Policy Making and Diplomacy

Goulden, Joseph C., *Truth is the First Casualty: The Gulf of Tonkin Affair— Illusion and Reality* (1969).
Hoopes, Townsend, *Limits of Intervention: Inside Account of How the Johnson Policy of Escalation In Vietnam Was Reversed* (1969).
Kraslow, David, and Stuart H. Loory, *Secret Search for Peace in Vietnam* (1968).
Sheehan, Neil, et al., *Pentagon Papers: As Published by New York Times* (1971).
Thomson, James C., Jr., "How Could Vietnam Happen?" *Atlantic*, 221 (1968), 47.
White, Ralph K., *Nobody Wanted War: Misperception in Vietnam and Other Wars* (1968).

56.8.4 Legality of War

Falk, Richard A., ed., *The Vietnam War and International Law* (2 vols., 1968–1969).
"Legality of United States Participation in Viet Nam Conflict: A Symposium," *Yale Law Jour.*, 75 (1966), 1084.

56.8.5 Military Aspects

Fall, Bernard B., *Last Reflections on a War* (1967).
—— *Vietnam Witness, 1953–1966* (1966).
Johnson, Raymond W., *Postmark: Mekong Delta* (1968).
Marshall, Samuel L. A., *Battles in the Monsoon: South Vietnam, 1966* (1966).
Schell, Jonathan, *Military Half: Quang Ngai and Quang Tin* (1968).
—— *The Village of Ben Suc* (1967).
Vito, A. H., Jr., "Carrier Air and Vietnam . . . An Assessment," U.S. Naval Inst., *Proc.*, 93, no. 10 (1967), 66.

56.8.6 United States and Economic Aid

Lindholm, R. W., *Economic Development Policy with Emphasis on Viet Nam* (1964).
Tanham, George K., et al., *War without Guns: American Civilians in Rural Vietnam* (1966).

56.8.7 North Vietnam and Vietcong

Gerassi, John, *North Vietnam: A Documentary* (1968).
O'Neill, Robert J., *General Giap: Politician and Strategist* (1969).
Pike, Douglas, *Viet Cong: National Liberation Front of South Vietnam* (1966).
—— *War, Peace, and the Viet Cong* (1969).
Salisbury, Harrison E., *Behind the Lines—Hanoi: December 23, 1966–January 7, 1967* (1967).

56.9 EUROPE

56.9.1 General

Chester, Edward W., *Europe Views America: A Critical Evaluation* (1962).
Kleiman, Robert, *Atlantic Crisis: American Diplomacy Confronts a Resurgent Europe* (1964).

56.9.2 France

Arnavon, Cyrille, *L'Américanisme et nous* (1958).
Brinton, C. Crane, *The Americans and the French* (1968).
Carduner, Jean R. and Sylvie, eds., *L'Amérique d'aujourd'hui vue par les Français* (1968).
de Gaulle, Charles, *Memoirs of Hope: Renewal and Endeavor* (1971).
—— *War Memoirs* (3 vols., 1955–1960).
Hoffman, Stanley, "Franco-American Conflict," *Jour. Internatl. Affairs*, 21 (1967), 57.
Monnet, Jean, *Europe-Amérique: Relations de partenaires nécessaires à la paix* (1963).
Servan-Schreiber, Jean Jacques, *The American Challenge*, Ronald Steel, trans. (1968).

56.9.3 Great Britain

Bell, Coral, *Debatable Alliance: An Essay in Anglo-American Relations* (1964).
Gelber, Lionel, *America in Britain's Place* (1961).
Neustadt, Richard E., *Alliance Politics* (1970). Suez, Skybolt Crises.
Williams, Raymond C., "Skybolt and American Foreign Policy," *Mil. Affairs*, 30 (1966), 153.

6.9.4 Austria

Bader, William B., *Austria between East and West, 1945–1955* (1966).

6.10 SOVIET UNION

Barghoorn, Frederick C., *Soviet Image of United States* (1950).
Clabaugh, Samuel F., and Edwin J. Feulner, Jr., *Trading with Communists: Research Manual* (1968).
Dalrymple, Dana G., "American Tractor Comes to Soviet Agriculture," *Tech. and Cult.*, 5 (1964), 191.
Dennett, Raymond, and Joseph E. Johnson, eds., *Negotiating with the Russians* (1951).
Deutscher, Isaac, *Great Contest: Russia and the West* (1960).
———— *Stalin* (1949).
Dulles, Eleanor L., and Robert D. Crane, *Détente* (1965).
Finletter, Thomas K., *Power and Policy: Foreign Policy and Military Power in the Hydrogen Age* (1954).
Foster, William Z., *Marxism-Leninism vs. Revisionism* (1946).
Georgetown University. Center for Strategic Studies, *The Soviet Military Technological Challenge* (1967).
Horelick, Arnold L., and Myron Rush, *Strategic Power and Soviet Foreign Policy* (1966).
Lane, Arthur B., *I Saw Poland Betrayed* (1948).
Smith, Walter B., *My Three Years in Moscow* (1950).
Tompkins, Pauline, *American-Russian Relations in the Far East* (1949).
Wise, David, and Thomas B. Ross, *U–2 Affair* (1962).

See also 10.3 for biographies/writings of:

Byrnes, James F., 1879–1972
Eisenhower, Dwight D., 1890–1969
Johnson, Lyndon B., 1908–1973
Kennan, George F., 1904–
Kennedy, John F., 1917–1963
Nixon, Richard M., 1913–
Standley, William H., 1872–1963
Truman, Harry S., 1884–1972

56.11 AFRICA

Atwood, William, *The Reds and the Blacks* (1967).
Baker, William G., *United States and Africa in the United Nations: A Case Study in American Foreign Relations* (1968).
Emerson, Rupert, *Africa and United States Policy* (1967).
Kaplan, Lawrence S., "United States, Belgium, and the Congo Crisis of 1960," *Rev. Politics*, 29 (1967), 239.

56.12 MIDDLE EAST AND NORTH AFRICA

56.12.1 General

Agwani, Mohammed S., *United States and the Arab World, 1945–1952* (1955).
Badeau, John S., *American Approach to the Arab World* (1968).
Campbell, John C., *Defense of the Middle East: American Policy* (rev. ed., 1960).
Gallagher, Charles F., *United States and North Africa: Morocco, Algeria, and Tunisia* (1963).

Hoskins, Halford L., *Middle East Oil* (1950).
Hurewitz, Jacob C., ed., *Soviet-American Rivalry in the Middle East* (1969).
Kerr, Malcolm, "Coming to Terms with Nasser," *Internatl. Affairs*, 43 (1967), 65.
Mikesell, Raymond F., and H. B. Chenery, *Arabian Oil* (1949).
Millspaugh, Arthur C., *Americans in Persia* (1946).
Polk, William R., *United States and the Arab World* (rev. ed., 1969).
Roosevelt, Kermit, *Arabs, Oil and History* (1949).
Speiser, Ephraim A., *United States and Near East* (rev. ed., 1949).
Stevens, Georgiana, ed., *United States and the Middle East* (1964).
Thomas, Lewis V., and Richard N. Frye, *The United States and Turkey and Iran* (rev. ed., 1971).
Thornburg, Max W., *People and Policy in the Middle East* (1964).

56.12.2 Israel

Crossman, Richard, *Palestine Mission* (1947).
McDonald, James G., *My Mission in Israel, 1948–1951* (1951).
Manuel, Frank E., *The Realities of American–Palestine Relations* (1949).
Safran, Nadav, *The United States and Israel* (1963).

56.12.3 Suez Crisis

Finer, Herman, *Dulles over Suez* (1964).
Fitzsimmons, M. A., "Suez Crisis and Containment Policy," *Rev. Politics*, 19 (1957), 419.

56.12.4 Lebanon Crisis

Agwani, Mohammed S., ed., *The Lebanese Crisis, 1958* (1965).
McClintlock, Robert, "American Landing in Lebanon," *U.S. Naval Inst., Proc.*, 88, no. 10 (1962), 65.

56.13 INDIA AND PAKISTAN

Brown, William Norman, *The United States and India, Pakistan, and Bangladesh* (1972). An enlargement and revision of *The United States and India and Pakistan*, published first in 1953 and revised in 1963.
Hope, A. Guy, *America and the Swaraj: U.S. Role in Indian Independence* (1968).
Venkataramani, M. S., and Harish Chandra Arya, "America's Military Alliance with Pakistan," *Internatl. Studies* [India], 8 (1966), 73.
Venkataramani, M. S., and B. K. Shrivastava, "The United States and the Cripps Mission," *India Quar.*, 19 (1963), 214.
——— "The United States and the 'Quit India' Demand," *India Quar.*, 20 (1964), 101.

56.14 EAST ASIA

56.14.1 General

Fairbank, John K., et al., *Next Step in Asia* (1949).
Greene, Fred, *U.S. Policy and the Security of Asia* (1968).
Iriye, Akira, *Across the Pacific: Inner History of American-East Asian Relations* (1967).
Isaacs, Harold R., *No Peace for Asia* (1947).

Latourette, Kenneth S., *American Record in Far East, 1945–1951* (1952).
Lederer, William J., and Eugene Burdick, *The Ugly American* (1958).
May, Ernest R., and James C. Thomson, eds., *American–East Asian Relations: A Survey* (1972).
Rostow, Walt W., *American Policy in Asia* (1955).
Vinacke, H. M., *United States and the Far East* (1952).
Vincent, John Carter, et al., *America's Future in the Pacific* (1947).

See also 56.4.13, Korean War.

56.14.2 Southeast Asia

56.14.2.1 General

Barry, Jean, *Thai Students in the United States* (1967).
Clubb, Oliver E., *United States and the Sino-Soviet Bloc in Southeast Asia* (1962).
Fifield, Russell, *Southeast Asia in United States Policy* (1963).
Gould, James W., *The United States and Malaysia* (1969).

See also 56.8, Vietnam War.

56.14.2.2 Laos

Dommen, Arthur J., *Conflict in Laos: The Politics of Neutralization* (1965).
Fall, Bernard B., *Anatomy of the Laotian Crisis of 1960–1961*, Roger M. Smith, ed. (1969).

56.14.2.3 Philippines

Kim, Sung Yong, *United States–Philippine Relations, 1946–1956* (1968).
Ornorato, Michael P., *A Brief Review of American Interest in Philippine Development* (1968).
Smith, Robert A., *Philippine Freedom, 1946–1958* (1958).
Wheeler, Gerald E., "Movement to Reverse Philippine Independence," *Pac. Hist. Rev.*, 33 (1964), 167.

56.14.3 Japan

Cary, James, *Japan Today: Reluctant Ally* (1962).
Conroy, Hilary, "Japan's Anti-Americanism," *Am. Quar.*, 7 (1955), 247.
Packard, George R., III, *Protest in Tokyo: The Security Treaty Crisis of 1960* (1966).
Reischauer, Edwin O., "Our Dialogue with Japan," *For. Affairs*, 45 (1967), 215.
—— *The United States and Japan* (3d ed., 1965).

See also 56.4.12, Japanese Occupation and Peace Settlement.

56.14.4 China

Ballantine, Joseph W., *Formosa* (1952).
Chang, Carsun, *Third Force in China* (1952).
Congressional Quarterly Service, *China and U.S. Far East Policy, 1945–1967* (1967).
Fairbank, John K., *China: The People's Middle Kingdom and the U.S.A.* (1967).
—— *The United States and China* (3d ed., 1971).
Feis, Herbert, *China Tangle* (1953).
Fishel, Wesley R., *End of Extraterritoriality in China* (1952).

Iriye, Akira, comp., *U.S. Policy toward China: Testimony from the Senate Foreign Relations Committee Hearings, 1966* (1968).

Lall, Arthur, *How Communist China Negotiates* (1968).

Pye, Lucian W., "China in Contest," *For. Affairs*, 45 (1967), 229.

Rankin, Karl L., *China Assignment* (1964).

Steele, Archibald T., *American People and China* (1966).

Tsou, Tang, "American Image of Chinese Communism," *Pol. Sci. Quar.*, 77 (1962), 570.

––––– *America's Failure in China, 1941–1950* (2 vols., 1963–1967).

––––– ed., *China in Crisis* (2 vols., 1968).

U.S. Department of State, *The China White Paper* (1967). Covers the period, 1944–1949.

Wedemeyer, Albert C., *Wedemeyer Reports!* (1958).

Wertenbaker, Charles, et al., "China Lobby," *Reporter*, April 15, 1952, 2; April 29, 1952, 5.

Young, Kenneth T., "American Dealings with Peking," *For. Affairs*, 45 (1966), 77.

––––– *Negotiating with the Chinese Communists, 1953–1967* (1968).

56.15 LATIN AMERICA

56.15.1 General

Berle, Adolf A., *Latin America—Diplomacy and Reality* (1962).

Connell-Smith, Gordon, *Inter-American System* (1966).

Dozer, Donald M., *Are We Good Neighbors? Inter-American Relations, 1930–1960* (1959).

Eisenhower, Milton S., *Wine is Bitter: United States and Latin America* (1963).

Lieuwen, Edwin, *Arms and Politics in Latin America* (rev. ed., 1961).

––––– *Generals vs. Presidents: Neomilitarism in Latin America* (1964).

Perkins, Dexter, *The United States and Latin America* (1961).

Rippy, J. Fred, *Globe and Hemisphere: Latin America in Post-War Relations* (1958).

Rockefeller, Nelson A., *The Rockefeller Report on the Americas* (1969).

Wagner, R. Harrison, *United States Policy toward Latin America* (1970).

See also 56.30.3, Latin American Aid and Alliance for Progress.

56.15.2 Organization of American States

Ball, M. Margaret, *The OAS in Transition* (1969).

Dreier, John C., *Organization of American States and the Hemisphere Crisis* (1962).

––––– "Organization of American States and United States Policy," *Internatl. Organ.*, 17 (1963), 36.

Morrison, DeLesseps S., *Latin American Mission* (1965).

Slater, Jerome, *OAS and United States Foreign Policy* (1967).

Thomas, Ann V. and A. J., Jr., *Organization of American States* (1963).

56.15.3 Specific Countries

Cline, Howard, *The United States and Mexico* (1953).

Schneider, Ronald M., *Communism in Guatemala, 1944–1954* (1959).

U.S. Department of State, *Blue Book on Argentina* (1946).

Whitaker, Arthur P., *Inter-American Affairs* (annual, 1941–1945).

––––– *The United States and Argentina* (1954).

56.16 CARIBBEAN

56.16.1 General

Fox, A. B., *Freedom and Welfare in Caribbean* (1949).
Perkins, Dexter, *The United States and the Caribbean* (rev. ed., 1966).
Plank, John N., "Caribbean: Intervention," *For. Affairs*, 44 (1965), 37.

56.16.2 Cuba

56.16.2.1 General

Bonsal, Philip W., "Cuba, Castro and the United States," *For. Affairs*, 45 (1967), 260.
Draper, Theodore, *Castroism* (1965).
———— *Castro's Revolution* (1962).
Mills, C. Wright, *Listen, Yankee: Revolution in Cuba* (1960).
Ruiz, Ramon E., *Cuba: Making of a Revolution* (1968).
Smith, Earl E. T., *Fourth Floor: Castro Communist Revolution* (1962).
Smith, Robert F., *United States and Cuba. Business and Diplomacy 1917–1960* (1960).
———— *What Happened in Cuba?* (1963).
"U.S. Quarantine of Cuba, Oct., 1962," *Am. Jour. Internatl. Law*, 57 (1963), 515.
Williams, William A., *United States, Cuba and Castro* (1962).
Wilson, Larman C., "Cuba and the Dominican Republic," *Jour. Politics*, 28 (1966), 322.
Wohlstetter, Roberta, "Cuba and Pearl Harbor: Hindsight and Foresight," *For. Affairs*, 43 (1965), 691.

See also 56.6.2, Cuban Missile Crisis.

56.16.2.2 Invasion of Cuba

Houghton, Neal D., "Cuban Invasion of 1961 and the U.S. Press," *Journalism Quar.*, 42 (1965), 422.
Johnson, Haynes B., et al., *Bay of Pigs: Brigade 2506* (1964).
Meyer, Karl E., and Tad Szulc, *Cuban Invasion* (1962).

56.16.3 Dominican Republic and Crisis of 1965

Bosch, Juan, *The Unfinished Experiment: Dominican Republic* (1965).
Dare, James A., "Dominican Diary," *U.S. Naval Inst. Proc.*, 91, no. 12 (1965), 36.
Draper, Theodore, *The Dominican Revolt: A Case Study in American Policy* (1968).
Kurzman, Dan, *Santo Domingo: Revolt of the Damned* (1965).
Martin, John B., *Overtaken by Events: The Dominican Crisis from the Fall of Trujillo to the Civil War* (1966).
Niedergang, Marcel, *La Révolution de Saint-Dominique* (1966).
Szulc, Tad, *Dominican Diary* (1965).

56.17 CANADA

Clark, Gerald, *Canada: Uneasy Neighbor* (1965).
Keenleyside, Hugh L., and G. S. Brown, *Canada and the United States* (rev. ed., 1952).

Mitchell, J. R., *United States and Canada* (1968).
Roussin, Marcel, *Le Canada et le Système Interaméricain* (1959).
Soward, F. H., "Changing Relations of Canada and United States," *Pac. Hist. Rev.*, 22 (1953), 155.
Willoughby, William R., *St. Lawrence Waterway: Politics and Diplomacy* (1961).

56.18 AUSTRALIA

Brash, Donald T., *American Investment in Australian Industry* (1966).
Gelber, Harry G., *Australian–American Alliance* (1968).

56.19 PACIFIC TRUST TERRITORIES

Emerson, Rupert, et al., *America's Pacific Dependencies* (1949).
Price, Willard, *America's Paradise Lost* (1966).
Richard, Dorothy E., *United States Naval Administration of Trust Territory of the Pacific Islands* (3 vols., 1957).
U.S. Department of State, *United States and Non-Self-Governing Territories* (1947).

56.20 DEFENSE ESTABLISHMENT SINCE 1945

56.20.1 General

Borklund, Carl W., *Department of Defense* (1968).
———— *Men of the Pentagon: From Forrestal to McNamara* (1966).
Caraley, Demetrios, *Politics of Military Unification* (1966).
Herzog, Arthur, *War-Peace Establishment* (1965).
Huntington, Samuel P., ed., *Changing Patterns of Military Politics* (1962).
Mollenhoff, Clark R., *The Pentagon* (1967).
Yarmolinsky, Adam, *The Military Establishment: Its Impact on American Society* (1971).

56.20.2 National Security Council

Clark, Keith C., and Laurence J. Legere, eds., *The President and the Management of National Security: A Report by the Institute for Defense Analysis* (1969).
Jackson, Henry M., ed., *National Security Council: Jackson Subcommittee Papers on Policy-Making at Presidential Level* (1965).

56.20.3 Civilian Control

Coles, Harry L., ed., *Total War and Cold War: Civilian Control of the Military* (1962).
Huntington, Samuel P., *The Soldier and the State: The Theory and Politics of Civil-Military Relations* (1957).

56.20.4 Congress

Kolodziej, Edward A., *Uncommon Defense and Congress, 1945–1963* (1966).
Ries, John C., "Congressman Vinson and the 'Deputy' to the JCS Chairman," *Mil. Affairs*, 30 (1966), 16.

56.20.5 Economics of Defense

Hitch, Charles J., and Roland N. McKean, *The Economics of Defense in the Nuclear Age* (1967).
Schelling, Thomas C., *Arms and Influence* (1966).
Tobin, James, "Defense, Dollars, and Doctrines," *Yale Rev.*, 47 (1958), 321.
Williams, Benjamin H., "Search for National Security," Am. Acad. Pol. Soc. Sci., *Annals*, 278 (1951), 1.

56.20.6 Defense Policy

Davis, Vincent, *Postwar Defense Policy and U.S. Navy, 1943–1946* (1966).
Deitchman, Seymour J., *Limited War and American Defense Policy* (rev. ed., 1969).
Huntington, Samuel P., *Common Defense: Strategic Programs in National Politics* (1961).
Kaufmann, William W., *The McNamara Strategy* (1964).
Kissinger, Henry A., "American Strategic Doctrine and Diplomacy," in Michael E. Howard, ed., *Theory and Practice of War: Essays Presented to Captain B. H. Liddell Hart* (1965).
———— ed., *Problems of National Strategy* (1965).
Laird, Melvin, *A House Divided—America's Strategy Gap* (1962).
Levine, Robert A., *The Arms Debate* (1963).
Posvar, Wesley W., et al., *American Defense Policy* (1965).
Reinhardt, George C., *American Strategy in Atomic Age* (1955).
Schwarz, Urs, *American Strategy: Politico-Military Thinking* (1966).
Smith, Mark E., III, and Claude J. Johns, Jr., eds., *American Defense Policy* (2nd ed., 1968).
Taylor, Maxwell D., *Uncertain Trumpet* (1960).
Williams, Benjamin H., ed., "Search for National Security," Am. Acad. Pol. Soc. Sci., *Annals*, 278 (1951). Entire issue.
U.S. President's Advisory Commission on Universal Training, *Program for National Security* (1947).
"Counterinsurgency," *World Affairs*, 126, no. 3 (1963), 159. Entire issue.

56.20.7 North Atlantic Treaty Organization

Amme, Carl H., Jr., *NATO without France: A Strategic Appraisal* (1967).
Barnet, Richard J., and Marcus G. Raskin, *After 10 Years* (1965).
Geiger, Theodore, and H. van B. Cleveland, *Making Western Europe Defensible* (1951).
Heindel, Richard H., et al., "North Atlantic Treaty in Senate," *Am. Jour. Internatl. Law*, 43 (1949), 633.
Hoskins, Halford L., *Atlantic Pact* (1949).
Kissinger, Henry A., *Troubled Partnership: Atlantic Alliance* (1965).
McCloy, John J., *Atlantic Alliance: Origin and Future* (1969).
Middleton, Drew, *Defense of Western Europe* (1952).
Osgood, Robert E., *NATO* (1962).
Stambuk, George, *American Military Forces Abroad* (1963).

56.20.8 Intelligence and CIA

Dulles, Allen, *The Craft of Intelligence* (1963).
Kent, Sherman, *Strategic Intelligence* (1949).
Kirkpatrick, Lyman B., Jr., *The Real CIA* (1968).
Ransom, Harry H., *The Intelligence Establishment* (1970). A revision of *Central Intelligence and National Security* (1958).

56.20.9 Weapons Policy

56.20.9.1 General

Art, Robert J., *TFX Decision: McNamara and Military* (1968).
Bush, Vannevar, *Modern Arms and Free Men* (1949).
Hayward, John T., and Paul J. Keaney, "Command and Control in Nuclear Age," U.S. Naval Inst., *Proc.*, 89, no. 11 (1963), 38.
Hersh, Seymour M., *Chemical and Biological Warfare* (1968).
Lapp, Ralph E., *Weapons Culture* (1968).
Peck, Merton J., and Frederic M. Scherer, *Weapons Acquisition Process* (1962).
Skolnikoff, Eugene B., *Science, Technology, and American Foreign Policy* (1967).
U.S. President's Air Policy Commission, *Survival in Air Age* (1948).

56.10.9.2 Nuclear Weapons and Ballistic Missiles

Chayes, Abram, and Jerome B. Wiesner, eds., *ABM: Evaluation of the Decision to Deploy an Anti-Ballistic Missile System* (1969).
Holst, Johan J., and William Schneider, Jr., eds., *Why ABM?* (1969).
Larus, Joel, *Nuclear Weapons Safety and the Common Defense* (1967).
McClelland, Charles A., *Nuclear Weapons, Missiles, and Future War* (1960).
Morris, Christopher, *The Day They Lost the H-Bomb* (1966).
Morton, Louis, "Anti-Ballistic Missile," *Va. Quar. Rev.*, 42 (1966), 28.
Parson, Nels A., Jr., *Missiles and the Revolution in Warfare* (1962).
Schwiebert, Ernest G., *History of U.S. Air Force Ballistic Missiles* (1965).

56.20.9.3 Navy and Polaris Submarines

Anderson, William R., and Clay Blair, Jr., *Nautilus 90 North* (1959).
Baar, James, and William E. Howard, *Polaris* (1960).
Baldwin, Hanson W., *New Navy* (1964).
Beach, Edward L., "Nuclear-Powered Submarines," U.S. Naval Inst., *Proc.*, 93, no. 8 (1967), 87.
Blair, Clay, *Atomic Submarine and Admiral Rickover* (1954).
Calvert, James, *Surface at the Pole: USS Skate* (1960).
Freund, James C., "Revolt of the Admirals," *Airpower Historian*, 10 (1963), 1.
Stambler, Irwin, *Battle for Inner Space—Undersea Warfare and Weapons* (1962).

56.20.9.4 Arms Race and Control

Abel, Elie, *Missile Crisis* (1966).
Batchelder, Robert C., *The Irreversible Decision, 1939–1950* (1961).
Bechhoeffer, Bernhard G., *Postwar Negotiations for Arms Control* (1961).
Dean, Arthur H., *Test Ban and Disarmament* (1966).
Henkin, Louis, ed., *Arms Control* (1961).
Jacobson, Harold K., and Eric Stein, *Diplomatists, Scientists and Politicians: Nuclear Test Ban Negotiations* (1966).
McGuire, Martin C., *Secrecy and the Arms Race: A Theory of the Accumulation of Strategic Weapons and How Secrecy Affects It* (1965).
McNamara, Robert S., *Essence of Security: Reflections* (1968).
Nieburg, Harold L., *Nuclear Secrecy and Foreign Policy* (1964).
Singer, J. David, ed., "Weapons Management in World Politics: Proceedings of International Arms Control Symposium, December, 1962," *Jour. Conflict Resolution*, 7(1963), 185, and *Jour. Arms Control*, 1 (1963), 286.
Thayer, George, *War Business: International Trade in Armaments* (1969).
Willrich, Mason, "The Treaty on Non-Proliferation of Nuclear Weapons: Nuclear Technology Confronts World Politics," *Yale Law Jour.*, 77 (1968), 1447.

56.21 MAKING OF DIPLOMACY

Cardozo, Michael H., *Diplomats in International Cooperation* (1962).
Jackson, Henry M., ed., *The Secretary of State and the Ambassador* (1964).

McCamy, James L., *Conduct of New Diplomacy* (1964).
Price, Don K., ed., *Secretary of State* (1960).
Robinson, Edgar E., et al., *Powers of the President in Foreign Affairs, 1945–1965* (1966).
Sorensen, Theodore C., *Decision-Making in the White House* (1963).
Villard, Henry S., *Affairs at State* (1965).
Wriston, Henry M., *Diplomacy in a Democracy* (1956).

56.22 ORGANIZATION AND ADMINISTRATION OF FOREIGN RELATIONS

Childs, James R., *American Foreign Service* (1948).
McCamy, James L., *Administration of Foreign Affairs* (1950).
Parks, Wallace J., *United States Administration of International Economic Affairs* (1951).
Stein, Harold, *Public Administration and Policy Development* (1952).

56.23 OVERSEAS INFORMATION AND UNITED STATES INFORMATION AGENCY

Barrett, Edward W., *Truth Is Our Weapon* (1953).
Dizard, Wilson P., *Strategy of Truth: U.S. Information Service* (1961).
Henderson, John W., *United States Information Agency* (1969).
Rubin, Ronald I., *Objectives of U.S. Information Agency: Controversies and Analysis* (1968).
Stephens, Oren, *Facts to a Candid World: Overseas Information Program* (1955).
Thomson, Charles A. H., *Overseas Information Service* (1948).
Whitton, John B., ed., *Propaganda and the Cold War* (1963).

56.24 AMERICANS ABROAD

56.24.1 General

Cleveland, Harlan, et al., *Overseas Americans* (1960).
Garraty, John A., and Walter Adams, *From Main Street to Left Bank: Students and Scholars Abroad* (1959).

56.24.2 Fulbright Program

Johnson, Walter, and F. J. Colligan, *The Fulbright Program: A History* (1965).
Spiller, Robert E., "American Studies Abroad," Am. Acad. Pol. Soc. Sci., *Annals*, 366 (1966), 1.

56.25 DOMESTIC INFLUENCES

56.25.1 General

Almond, Gabriel A., *American People and Foreign Policy* (2nd ed., 1960).
Baker, Roscoe, *The American Legion and American Foreign Policy* (1955).

Belknap, George M., and Angus Campbell, "Political Party Identification and Foreign Policy," *Pub. Opinion Quar.*, 15 (1952), 601.

Gerson, Louis L., *The Hyphenate in Recent Politics and Diplomacy* (1964).

Gustafson, Merlin, "Church, State and the Cold War, 1945–1952," *Jour. Church and State*, 8 (1966), 49.

Hero, Alfred O., Jr., *The Southerner and World Affairs* (1965).

Kristol, Irving, "American Intellectuals and Foreign Policy," *For. Affairs*, 45 (1967), 594.

Lerche, Charles O., Jr., *Uncertain South: Politics in Foreign Policy* (1964).

McLellan, David S., and Charles E. Woodhouse, "Business Elite and Foreign Policy," *West. Pol. Quar.*, 13 (1960), 172.

Perkins, Dexter, *American Approach to Foreign Policy* (1962).

——— "American Foreign Policy and its Critics," in Alfred H. Kelly, ed., *American Foreign Policy and American Democracy* (1954).

Rappaport, Armin, *The Navy League of the United States* (1962).

Roper, Elmo, "How Isolationist is America Today?" *Atl. Community Quar.*, 1 (1963), 486.

Schapsmeier, Frederick H., and Edward L. Schapsmeier, "Walter Lippmann, Critic of American Foreign Policy," *Midw. Quar.*, 7 (1966), 123.

Westerfield, H. Bradford, *Foreign Policy and Party Politics: Pearl Harbor to Korea* (1955).

56.25.2 Congress

Carroll, Holbert N., *House of Representatives and Foreign Affairs* (1958).

Czempiel, Ernst-Otto, *Das Amerikanische Sicherheitssystem, 1945–1949* (1966).

Farnsworth, David N., *The Senate Committee on Foreign Relations* (1961).

Jewell, Malcolm E., "Senate Republican Policy Committee and Foreign Policy," *West. Pol. Quar.*, 12 (1959), 966.

——— *Senatorial Politics and Foreign Policy* (1962).

Kolodziej, Edward A., "Congress and Foreign Policy," *Va. Quar. Rev.*, 42 (1966), 12.

Rieselbach, Leroy N., *Roots of Isolationism: Congressional Voting and Presidential Leadership in Foreign Policy* (1966).

Robinson, James A., *Congress and Foreign Policy-Making* (rev. ed., 1967).

56.26 UNITED NATIONS

Annual Review of United Nations Affairs (8 vols., 1949–1957/1958).

Beichman, Arnold, *Other State Department: United States Mission to United Nations* (1968).

Bloomfield, Lincoln P., *Evolution or Revolution: The United Nations and the Problem of Peaceful Territorial Change* (1957).

Dallin, Alexander, *The Soviet Union at the United Nations* (1962).

Feller, A. H., *United Nations and World Community* (1952).

Gross, Franz B., ed., *The United States and the United Nations* (1964).

Haviland, H. Field, Jr., *Political Role of General Assembly* (1951).

Hero, Alfred O., Jr., "American Public and UN, 1954–1966," *Jour. Conflict Resolution*, 10 (1966), 436.

Levi, Werner, *Fundamentals of World Organization* (1950).

Lie, Trygve, *Public Papers, 1946–1953* (1969).

Russell, Ruth B., *United Nations and United States Security Policy* (1968).

Scott, William A., and Stephen B. Withey, *United States and United Nations: The Public View, 1945–1955* (1958).

Weiler, Lawrence D., and Anne P. Simons, *United States and United Nations: The Search for International Peace and Security* (1967).

Wilcox, Francis O., and H. Field Haviland, Jr., eds., *United States and United Nations* (1961).

56.27 INTERNATIONAL MONETARY AGREEMENTS

Behrman, J. N., "Political Factors in International Financial Cooperation, 1945–1950," *Am. Pol. Sci. Rev.*, 47 (1953), 431.
Bloch, Ernest, "United States Foreign Investment and Dollar Shortage", *Rev. Econ. Stat.*, 35 (1953), 154.
Ferguson, John H., "Anglo-American Financial Agreement," *Yale Law Jour.*, 55 (1946), 1140.
Kindleberger, Charles R., *Dollar Shortage* (1950).
Machlup, Fritz, *Remaking the International Monetary System: Rio Agreement* (1968).
Matecki, Bronislaw E., *Establishment of International Finance Corporation and United States Policy* (1957).
Morgenthau, Henry, Jr., "Bretton Woods," *For. Affairs*, 23 (1945), 82.
Tew, Brian, *International Monetary Cooperation 1945–1952* (1952).

56.28 FOREIGN TRADE

Adler, John H., et al., *Pattern of Import Trade since 1923* (1952).
Bauer, Raymond A., et al., *American Business and Public Policy: Foreign Trade* (1963).
Berge, Wendell, *Cartels: Challenge to a Free World* (1944).
Berman, Harold J., and John R. Garson, "Export Controls," *Columbia Law Rev.*, 67 (1967), 791.
Gardner, Richard N., *Sterling-Dollar Diplomacy: Anglo-American Collaboration in Reconstruction of Multilateral Trade* (1956).
Hinshaw, Randall, *European Community and American Trade* (1964).
Humphrey, Don D., *United States and the Common Market* (rev. ed., 1964).
Johnson, Harry G., "The Kennedy Round," *World Today*, 23 (1967), 326.
Kingsley, Robert E., "Public Diplomacy of U.S. Business Abroad: Latin America," *Jour. Inter-Am. Studies*, 9 (1967), 413.
Letiche, J. M., *Reciprocal Trade Agreements in World Economy* (1948).
Mason, Edward S., *Controlling World Trade* (1946).
Meade, James E., *Theory of International Economic Policy* (1951).
Rau, Allan, *Agriculture Policy and Trade Liberalization, 1934–1956* (1957).
Smithies, Arthur, "Effect Abroad of American Private Enterprise," *Am. Acad. Pol. Soc. Sci.*, Annals, 366 (1966), 51.
Wilcox, Clair, *Charter for World Trade* (1949).

56.29 FOREIGN AID AND ECONOMIC RECONSTRUCTION, 1945–1953

56.29.1 General

Brown, William A., Jr., and Redvers Opie, *American Foreign Assistance* (1953).
Council of Economic Advisers, *Impact of Foreign Aid upon Domestic Economy* (1948).
Ellis, Howard S., *Economics of Freedom* (1950).
Hansen, Alvin H., *America's Role in World Economy* (1945).
Harris, Seymour E., ed., *Foreign Economic Policy* (1948).
Krug, Julius A., *Report on National Resources and Foreign Aid* (1947).
Mikesell, Raymond F., *United States Economic Policy and International Relations* (1952).
Penrose, Ernest F., *Economic Planning for Peace* (1953).
Public Affairs Institute, *Bold New Program Series* (8 vols., 1950).
U.S. Department of State, *Land Reform* (1952).

56.29.2 European Recovery Program (Marshall Plan)

Galantière, Lewis, *America and Mind of Europe* (1952).
Gordon, Lincoln, "ERP in Operation," *Harv. Bus. Rev.*, 27 (1949), 129.
Hickman, W. L., *Genesis of European Recovery Program* (1949).
Jones, Joseph M., *Fifteen Weeks (February 21–June 5, 1947)* (1955).
Mallalieu, William C., *British Reconstruction and American Policy, 1945–1955* (1956).
—— "The Origin of the Marshall Plan: A Study in Policy Formation and National Leadership," *Pol. Sci. Quar.*, 73 (1958), 481.
Price, Harry B., *Marshall Plan* (1955).
van der Beugel, Ernst H., *From Marshall Aid to Atlantic Partnership* (1966).

*   *   *   *   *   *   *

U.S. Library of Congress, *United States and Postwar Europe* (1948).

56.29.3 Point Four: Aid to Underdeveloped Countries

Bingham, Jonathan B., *Shirt-Sleeve Diplomacy: Point 4* (1954).
Hoskins, H. L., ed., "Aiding Underdeveloped Areas Abroad," *Am. Acad. Pol. Soc. Sci., Annals*, 268 (1950).
U.S. Department of State, *Point Four* (1950).
—— *Point Four Pioneers* (1951).
—— *Technical Assistance in Action* (1951).

56.30 FOREIGN AID, 1953–

56.30.1 General

Baldwin, David A., *Economic Development and American Foreign Policy* (1966).
Bell, David E., "Quality of Aid," *For. Affairs.*, 44 (1966), 601.
Black, Eugene R., *The Diplomacy of Economic Development* (1960).
Black, Lloyd D., *The Strategy of Foreign Aid* (1968).
Feis, Herbert, *Foreign Aid and Foreign Policy* (1964).
Haviland, H. Field, Jr., "Foreign Aid and Policy Process, 1957," *Am. Pol. Sci. Rev.*, 52 (1958), 689.
Kauffman, Kenneth M., and Helena Stalson, "U.S. Assistance to Less Developed Countries, 1956–1965," *For. Affairs, 45* (1967), 715.
Kramish, Arnold, *Peaceful Atom in Foreign Policy* (1963).
Mahajani, Usha, "Kennedy and Strategy of Aid: Clay Report," *West. Pol. Quar.*, 18 (1965), 656.
Mason, Edward S., *Foreign Aid and Foreign Policy* (1964).
Mikesell, Raymond F., *Economics of Foreign Aid* (1968).
Morgner, Aurelius, "American Foreign Aid Program," *Rev. Politics*, 29 (1967), 65.
O'Leary, Michael K., *Politics of American Foreign Aid* (1967).
Packenham, Robert A., "Foreign Aid and National Interest," *Midw. Jour. Pol. Sci.*, 10 (1966), 214.
Paddock, William and Paul, *Hungry Nations* (1964).
Perkins, James A., "Foreign Aid and the Brain Drain," *For. Affairs*, 44 (1966), 608.
Rubin, Jacob A., *Your Hundred Billion Dollars: Foreign Aid* (1964).
Terry, Luther L., "Appeal Abroad of American Medicine and Public Health," *Am. Acad. Pol. Soc. Sci., Annals*, 366 (1966), 78.
"U.S. Foreign Aid: Overview," *Current Hist.*, 50 (1966), 321.
Walters, Robert S., *American and Soviet Aid: A Comparative Analysis* (1970).
Weaver, James H., *International Development Association* (1965).

56.30.2 Asia

Chandrasekhar, Sripati, *American Aid and India's Economic Development* (1965).
Jacoby, Neil H., *U.S. Aid to Taiwan* (1966).
Jordan, Amos A., Jr., *Foreign Aid and the Defense of Southeast Asia* (1962).
Lewis, John P., *Quiet Crisis in India: Economic Development and American Policy* (1962).
Nichols, Jeannette P., "United States Aid to south and Southeast Asia, 1950–1960," *Pac. Hist. Rev.*, 32 (1963), 171.
"United States Aid in Asia," *Current Hist.*, 49 (1965), 257.
Wolf, Charles, Jr., *Foreign Aid: Southern Asia* (1960).

56.30.3 Latin American Aid and Alliance for Progress

Glick, Philip M., *Administration of Technical Assistance: Growth in the Americas* (1957).
McCamant, John F., *Development Assistance in Central America* (1968).
May, Ernest R., "Alliance for Progress in Historical Perspective," *For. Affairs*, 41 (1963), 757.
May, Herbert K., *Problems and Prospects of the Alliance for Progress* (1968).
Perloff, Harvey S., *Alliance for Progress: A Social Invention in the Making* (1969).
Rogers, William D., *Twilight Struggle: Alliance for Progress in Latin America* (1967).

56.30.4 Peace Corps

Carey, Robert G., *The Peace Corps* (1970).
Hapgood, David, and Meridan Bennett, *Agents of Change: Close Look at Peace Corps* (1968).
Textor, Robert B. ed., *Cultural Frontiers of Peace Corps* (1966).

Index of Names

Raskin, Marcus G., (joint au.) *After 10 Years* (NATO), 1061
Rasmussen, Wayne D., "Forty Years of Agric. History," 389; ". . . Tech. Change on American Agriculture," 395; (joint au.) *Bibliog. on Agriculture of Indians,* 467; "Civil War: Catalyst of Agric. Rev.," 855
Rasmussen, Ethel E., "Democratic Environment," 673, 729
Ratchford, B. U., *American State Debts,* 355; (joint au.) *Economic Resources and Policies of South,* 383, 1034; "North Carolina Public Debt," 886; *Berlin Reparations Assignment,* 1048
Rath, Frederick L., Jr., *Historic Preservation,* 56
Rathburn, J. W., "George Bancroft," 284
Rather, E. Z., ". . . Slavery in Colonization of Texas," 815; . . . *Republic of Texas,* 816
Ratner, Leonard G., "Congressional Power over Appellate Jurisdiction of Sup. Court," 372
Ratner, Lorman, *Pre-Civil War Reform,* 483; (joint au.) *Develop. of Am. Culture,* 632; "Northern Concern . . . Anti-Slavery," 835; . . . *Northern Opposition to Antislavery Mvemt.,* 835
Ratner, Sidney, *Taxation and Democracy in America,* 356; "Evolution and Rise of Scientific Spirit," 589; "Was Supreme Court Packed by Grant?," 891; *American Taxation,* 992
Rau, Allan, *Agriculture Policy and Trade Liberalization,* 393, 1002, 1065
Rauch, Basil: (joint au.) *Empire for Liberty,* 279; (joint au.) *Am. Origins to 1789,* 609; *American Interests in Cuba,* 821; *Hist. of New Deal,* 978; *Roosevelt from Munich to Pearl Harbor,* 1004
Raucher, Alan R., *Public Relations and Business,* 404
Rauschenbusch, Walter, *Christianity and Social Crisis,* 515; *Rauschenbusch Reader,* 515
Ravenel, Beatrice St. J., *Architects of Charleston,* 572, 767
Ravenel, Henry W., *Private Journal,* 243
Ravenel, H. H., . . . *William Lowndes,* 223; *Eliza Pinckney,* 240; *Charleston,* 317, 636
Ravenstein, E. G., *Martin Behaim,* 613
Ravitz, Abe C., *Clarence Darrow,* 182; *David Graham Phillips,* 239
Rawley, James A., *Edwin D. Morgan,* 231; *Turning Points of Civil War,* 864
Rawling, Gerald, *Pathfinders,* 326
Rawlings, Marjorie K., *Cross Creek,* 297
Rawlyk, George A., *Yankees at Louisbourg,* 664; "Am. Revolution and Nova Scotia," 698
Rawson, M. N., *New Hampshire Borns a Town,* 309
Ray, M. A., *American Opinion of Rom. Catholicism,* 755
Ray, P. O., *Repeal of Missouri Compromise,* 838
Rayback, Joseph G., *History of Am. Labor,* 427; (joint au.) "French Comment on Pa. Constitution," 673, 706; *Free Soil,* 819
Rayback, Robert J., *Millard Fillmore,* 190; "New York State in Civil War," 857
Raymer, R. G., *Montana,* 308
Raymond, Allen, (joint au.) *Gang Rule in New York,* 493
Raymond, E. T., *Tecumseh,* 259
Raymond, W. O., "Alexander McNutt and Nova Scotia," 664; "Nova Scotia under English Rule," 664
Rayner, K., "Am. Episcopal Church and Anglican Communion," 522
Raywid, Mary Anne, *Ax-Grinders: Critics of Our Pub. Schools,* 502
Rea, Robert R., *English Press in Politics,* 680
Read, Allen W., "Spread of German Linguistic Learning in N.E.," 542
Read, Conyers, *Bibliog. of Br. History,* 628; (ed.) *Constitution Reconsidered,* 707
Read, George W., *Pioneer of 1850,* 148; (ed.) *Gold Rush,* 340
Read, J. M., *Atrocity Propaganda,* 952
Read, T. T., *Labor Standards and Metal Mining,* 432

Read, William T., . . . *George Read,* 243
Readers' Guide to Periodical Literature, 63
Reale, Egidio, *L'Arbitrage international,* 894
Reaman, G. Elmore, *Trail of the Huguenots,* 735
Reath, Nancy A., *Weaves of Hand-Loom Fabrics,* 568
Reavis, William A., "Maryland Gentry," 729
Reber, J. Benjamin, *History of St. Joseph,* 306
Reck, Franklin M., *4-H Club Story,* 394
Reconstruction Finance Corporation, *Seven-Year Report,* 991
Record, Wilson, "Negro Intellectuals and Negro Movement," 477; *Race and Radicalism,* 478; *Little Rock, U.S.A.,* 481; *Negro and Communist Party,* 977, 986
Rector, William G., *Log Transportation in Lake States Lumber Industry,* 413
Redden, Carolyn L., (joint au.) *Black Muslims in U.S.,* 479
Reddig, W. M., . . . *Kansas City,* 984
Redding, J. Saunders, "Black Revolution in Am. Studies," 472; *No Day of Triumph,* 472; *The Lonesome Road,* 473
Redding, John M., *Inside Democratic Party,* 1035
Redekop, John H., *American Far Right,* 1031
Redford, E. S., . . . *Admin. of Wartime Rationing,* 1024
Redgrave, G. R., (joint au.), *Catalogue of English Books,* 62
Redkey, Edwin S., *Black Exodus,* 479, 933
Redlich, Fritz L., *Hist. of Am. Business Leaders,* 398; *Molding of Am. Banking,* 406, 810; ". . . Specie Payments in 1879," 890
Redmond, C. F., (joint au.) *Treaties, Conventions, International Acts,* 75
Reed, Alfred Z., *Training for . . . the Law,* 713
Reed, Anna Y., *Occupational Placement,* 424
Reed, Benjamin F., . . . *Kossuth County, Iowa,* 300
Reed, Charles B., *First Great Canadian,* 208
Reed, E. B., *Comm. Fund Fellows' Impressions of America,* 151
Reed, Germaine A., "Race Legislation in Louisiana," 472
Reed, Henry Clay, *Delaware,* 79, 296; (ed.) *Burlington Court Book,* 83, 714; *Bibliog. of Delaware,* 296; "Delaware Constitution of 1776," 671; "Early New Castle Court," 714
Reed, Henry H., Jr.: (joint au.) *American Skyline,* 440; (ed.) *Architecture in America,* 569
Reed, John, *Hudson River Valley,* 312
Reed, Louis, . . . *Wirt County, West Virginia,* 322
Reed, Louis S., *Labor Philosophy of Gompers,* 197
Reed, Marion B., (joint au.) *Bibliog. of Delaware,* 296
Reed, Merl E., *New Orleans and the Railroads,* 422
Reed, Peter Mellish, "Standard Oil in Indonesia," 945
Reed, Susan M., *Church and State in Massachusetts,* 652, 753
Reed, Walt, *Illustrator in America,* 565
Reed, William Bradford, . . . *Joseph Reed,* 243
Reel, Adolf F., . . . *General Yamashita,* 1049
Rees, Albert, *Real Wages in Manufacturing,* 425, 938; "Wage-Price Relations in Basic Steel Industry," 432
Rees, David, *Korea,* 1051
Rees, T. Hardy, . . . *Quakers in Wales and Their Emigration to N. America,* 734
Reese, Jim E., (joint au.) *Economic History of U.S.,* 381
Reese, Trevor R., *Colonial Georgia,* 645; "Religious Factors in Settlement of Ga.," 645; "Georgia in Anglo-Spanish Diplomacy," 663
Reeve, J. R., *Monetary Reform Movements,* 991
Reeves, Arthur M., *Finding of Wineland the Good,* 612
Reeves, Jesse S., "Prussian-American Treaties," 699
Reeves, Thomas C., "John Checkley," 754

Stackpole, Edward J., *They Met at Gettysburg*, 868; *Chancellorsville*, 870

Stadtman, Verne A., *Univ. of California*, 510

Stagg, A. A., *Touchdown*, 500

Stahl, Annie L. W., "Free Negro in Ante-bellum Louisiana," 832

Stahl, Jasper J., . . . *Old Broad Bay and Walda-boro* (Maine), 303

Stahlman, William D., "Astrology in Colonial America," 770

Stalker, John, (joint au.) "American Image in China," 364, 820

Stallman, R. W.: (ed.) Crane *Letters*, 179; *Stephen Crane*, 179

Stalson, Helena, (joint au.) "U.S. Assistance to Less Devel. Countries," 1066

Stalson, J. Owen, *Marketing Life Insurance*, 410

Stambler, Irwin, . . . *Undersea Warfare*, 367, 1062

Stambuk, George, *Am. Military Forces Abroad*, 1061

Stamp, Laurence D., (ed.) *London Essays in Geography*, 732

Stampp, Kenneth M., . . . *Slavery in Ante-bellum South*, 826; "Historian and Southern Negro Slavery," 827; ". . . Dew's *Review of Debates in Va. Legislature*," 831; ". . . Southern Anti-Slavery Sentiment," 835; (ed.) *Causes of Civil War*, 848; *And the War Came*, 850; *Indiana Politics during Civil War*, 857; *Era of Reconstruction*, 876; (ed.) *Reconstruction: Anthology*, 878

Stanard, Mary Newton, *Colonial Virginia*, 744

Standard, Diffee W., (joint au.) "Cotton Textile Ind. in . . . N.C.," 824

Stander, Golder G., "Jesuit Ed. Institutions in . . . N.Y.," 745

Standing Bear, Luther, *My People the Sioux*, 464

Standley, William H., *Admiral Ambassador to Russia*, 254

Stands in Timber, John, *Cheyenne Memories*, 463

Stanford, Alfred, *Force Mulberry* (Allied invasion), 1014

Stanford University, *Western Politica*, 118

Stanhope, Robert E., ". . . Understanding of Republicanism in Am. Historiography," 686

Stanley, Dorothy, (ed.) H.M. Stanley *Autobiography*, 254

Stanley, George F. G., "Indians in War of 1812," 468; "Six Nations and Am. Rev.," 679

Stanley, Henry M., *Autobiography*, 254

Stanton, Elizabeth, . . . *Reminiscences*, 254; . . . *Letters, Diary and Reminiscences*, 254; *History of Woman Suffrage*, 445

Stanton, Frank N., (joint au.) *Radio Research*, 559

Stanton, Pheobe B., *Gothic Revival and Am. Church Arch.*, 570

Stanton, Theodore, (ed.) *Elizabeth Cady Stanton*, 254

Stanton, William, *Leopard's Spots*, 538, 831; ". . . Study of Man in America," 540

Stanwood, Edward, *History of Presidency*, 358; *Am. Tariff Controversies*, 387, 902

Staples, H. L., *Fall of a Railroad Empire*, 422

Staples, T. S., *Reconstruction in Alabama*, 885

Staples, William R., *Annals . . . of Providence*, 317; *R. I. and Continental Congress*, 676, 688; . . . *Destruction of the Gaspee*, 688

Stark, George W., *City of Destiny*, 306; (joint au.) *Made in Detroit*, 411

Stark, J. H., *Loyalists of Massachusetts*, 702

Stark, John D., . . . *William Watts Ball*, 161

Stark, Werner, . . . *U.S. of 1776 in Contemporary European Philosophy*, 667

Starke, Aubrey H., *Sidney Lanier*, 216

Starkey, Lycurgus M., Jr., *Money, Mania and Morals*, 515

Starkey, Marion L., *Cherokee Nation*, 462; *Congregational Way*, 522; *Little Rebellion*, 675; . . . *Salem Witch Trials*, 743

Starobin, Robert, "The Negro," 726; ". . . Industrial Slaves in Old South," 726; *Industrial Slavery in Old South*, 827; "Economics of Ind. Slavery," 830

Starr, C. G., (ed.) *Salerno to Alps*, 1014

Starr, Edward C., *History of Cornwall*, 296; *Baptist Bibliography*, 521

Starr, H. E., *William G. Sumner*, 257

Starr, Isidore, (joint au.) *Negro in 20th-Century America*, 478

Starr, John, (joint au.) *Teapot Dome*, 967

Starr, Louis M., *Oral History*, 107; . . . *Civil War Newsmen*, 865

Starr, Mark, (joint au.) *Labor in America*, 427

Starrett, Paul, . . . *Autobiography*, 254

State Historical Society of Colorado, *Colorado Magazine*, 122

State Historical Society of Iowa, *Annals*, 123; *Iowa Historical Record*, 123; *Iowa Jour. of History and Politics*, 123; *Studies in Iowa History*, 123; *Iowa Applied History Series*, 123; *Iowa Biographical Series*, 123; *Iowa Economic History Series*, 123; *Iowa Social History Series*, 123; *Palimpset*, 123

State Historical Soc. of Missouri, *Documentary Publications*, 124; *Mo. Historical Review*, 124

State Historical Soc. of North Dakota, *Quarterly*, 125; *Collections*, 125; *N. D. History*, 125

State Historical Soc. of South Dakota, *Collections*, 126; *Review*, 126

State Historical Society of Wisconsin, *Reports and Collections*, 127; *Proceedings*, 127; *Calendar Series*, 127; *Doomsday Book*, 127; *History Series*, 127; *Biography Series*, 127; *Magazine*, 127

State Law Index, 78

Statistical Abstract of the United States, 42

Statler, Oliver, *The Shimoda Story*, 821

Staton, F. M., *Bibliography of Canadiana*, 623

Statutes at Large, 71, 72

Staudenraus, P. J., *African Colonization Movement*, 833

Stauffer, Alvin P., *Quartermaster Corps . . . Japan*, 1018

Stauffer, David M., *Am. Engravers on Copper and Steel*, 562

Stauffer, Vernon, *New England and Bavarian Illuminati*, 492, 781

Staupers, Mabel K., *No Time for Prejudice*, 475

Stave, Bruce M., . . . *Pittsburgh Machine Politics*, 984

Stavis, Ben, . . . *New Hampshire to Chicago for McCarthy*, 1045

Stead, G. A., "Williams and Massachusetts," 750

Steamer, Robert J., *Supreme Court in Crisis*, 369

Stearns, Ezra, *History of Rindge*, 309

Stearns, Jean, (joint au.) *Jazz Dance*, 582

Stearns, Marshall W., *The Story of Jazz*, 578; *Jazz Dance*, 582

Stearns, Raymond P.: (joint au.) *Mark Catesby*, 173; . . . *Hugh Peter*, 239; "N.E. Way in Holland," 637; "John Wise of Ipswich," 652; "Assessing New England Mind," 749; "New England Church 'Relations,'" 749, 751; "Colonial Fellows of Royal Society," 770; "Science in British Colonies of America," 770; "James Petiver," 771; "John Winthrop," 771

Stebbins, Emma, *Charlotte Cushman*, 181

Stebbins, H. A., *Political History of New York*, 882

Steckmesser, L., *Western Hero in History and Legend*, 338

Stedman, Laura, . . . *Edmund Clarence Stedman*, 254

Stedman, Murray S., Jr., *Discontent at the Polls*, 379; *Religion and Politics in America*, 515; *Exporting Arms*, 1004

Stedman, Susan W., (joint au.) *Discontent at the Polls*, 379

Steegmuller, Francis, . . . *James Jackson Jarves*, 210; (joint au.) *America on Relief*, 987

Steel, I. K., *Politics of Colonial Policy*, 661

Steel, Ronald, (trans.) *American Challenge*, 542, 1054

Subject Index